DATE DUE

GROVES DICTIONARY OF
MUSIC AND MUSICIANS

P-SON
MacMillan

| DATE DUE | BORROWER'S NAME | |
|----------|-----------------|--|
|  |  |  |
|  |  |  |
|  |  |  |

GROVES DICTIONARY OF MUSIC AND
MUSICIANS

P-SON

MacMillan

# A DICTIONARY

OF

# MUSIC AND MUSICIANS

THE MACMILLAN COMPANY
NEW YORK · BOSTON · CHICAGO · DALLAS
ATLANTA · SAN FRANCISCO

MACMILLAN AND CO., Limited
LONDON · BOMBAY · CALCUTTA · MADRAS
MELBOURNE

THE MACMILLAN COMPANY
OF CANADA, Limited
TORONTO

MUSICAL INSTRUMENTS — FRANCE, 1411

(British Museum, 19 D. iii)

1. Buzine (*Buisine*).   2. Lutina (*Mandore*).   3. Recorder (*Flûte douce*).   4. Kettledrums (*Nacaires*).
5. Psaltery (*Psaltérion*).   6. Lute (*Luth*).   7. Rebec (*Gigue*).   8. Trumpet (*Clairon*).   9. Shawm (*Chalemie*).
Centre: left, Harp; right, Vielle.

# GROVE'S
# DICTIONARY OF MUSIC
# AND MUSICIANS

THIRD EDITION

EDITED BY

## H. C. COLLES, M.A. (Oxon.)

IN FIVE VOLUMES

VOL. IV

NEW YORK
THE MACMILLAN COMPANY
1947

Published with new material, January, 1928.
Reissued, 1935. Reprinted July, 1936;
August, 1937; June, 1938; November,
1939; May, 1941; December, 1942;
March, 1944; April, 1945; February,
1946; March, 1947.

SET UP AND ELECTROTYPED BY J. S. CUSHING CO.
PRINTED IN THE UNITED STATES OF AMERICA
BY BERWICK & SMITH CO.

# CONTRIBUTORS

H. E. ADKINS, Lieutenant, Director of Music, Royal Military School of
Music, Kneller Hall . . . . . . . H. E. A.
W. A. AIKIN, Esq., M.D. . . . . . . . W. A. A.
RICHARD ALDRICH, Esq., New York . . . . . R. A.
E. HERON-ALLEN, Esq. . . . . . . E. H.-A.
HERBERT ANTCLIFFE, Esq. . . . . . . H. A.
G. E. P. ARKWRIGHT, Esq. . . . . . . G. E. P. A.
*CARL ARMBRUSTER, Esq.* . . . . . . C. A.
F. J. ARNOLD, Esq. . . . . . . . F. J. A.

*DAVID BAPTIE, Esq.* . . . . . . . D. B.
Dr. JOSEF BARTOŠ, Prague . . . . . . J. B.
J. R. STERNDALE-BENNETT, Esq. . . . . . J. R. S.-B.
Mrs. EDITH OLDHAM BEST (formerly Miss Oldham) . . E. O. B.
D. J. BLAIKLEY, Esq. . . . . . . . D. J. B.
ERIC BLOM, Esq. . . . . . . . E. B.
F. BONAVIA, Esq. . . . . . . . F. B.
Mons. E. BORREL, Paris . . . . . . E. B<sup>L</sup>.
*LEONARD BORWICK, Esq.* . . . . . . L. B.
*R. H. M. BOSANQUET, Esq.* . . . . . R. H. M. B.
ADRIAN C. BOULT, Esq., Mus.D. (Oxon.) . . . . A. C. B.
Mons. CHARLES BOUVET, Administrateur de la Bibliothèque des Archives
et du Musée de l'Opéra, Paris . . . . . C. B.
J. C. BRIDGE, Esq., Mus.D., Trinity College, London . . J. C. B.
*HORATIO ROBERT FORBES BROWN, Esq.* . . . . H. F. B.
PERCY C. BUCK, Esq., Mus.D. (Oxon.), Professor of Music in London
University . . . . . . . P. C. B.
Dr. HERMANN BUDY . . . . . . . H. B<sup>Y</sup>.
*The Hon. Mrs. M. BURRELL* . . . . . . M. B.
HUGH BUTLER, Esq. . . . . . . . H. B.
*G. S. KAYE-BUTTERWORTH, Esq.* . . . . . G. S. K.-B.

M. D. CALVOCORESSI, Esq. . . . . . . M. D. C.
J. W. CAPSTICK, Esq., Trinity College, Cambridge . . J. W. C.
Mrs. WALTER CARR . . . . . . . M. C. C.
*EDWARD CHADFIELD, Esq.* . . . . . . E. C.
*WILLIAM CHAPPELL, Esq., F.S.A.* . . . . . W. C.

v

W. B. CHASE, Esq., New York . . . . . W. B. C.
ALEXIS CHITTY, Esq. . . . . . . A. C.
*Mons. GUSTAVE CHOUQUET* . . . . . G. C.
Mons. ERNEST CLOSSON, Professor at Brussels Conservatoire . . E. C^N.
W. W. COBBETT, Esq. . . . . . . W. W. C.
*A. D. COLERIDGE, Esq.* . . . . . . A. D. C.
FREDERICK CORDER, Esq. . . . . . . F. C.
*GEORGE ARTHUR CRAWFORD, Major* . . . . G. A. C.
WALTER R. CREIGHTON, Esq. . . . . . W. R. C.
*W. H. CUMMINGS, Esq., Mus.D., F.S.A.* . . . . W. H. C.
*Sir WILLIAM GEORGE CUSINS* . . . . . W. G. C.

WILLIAM H. DALY, Esq., Edinburgh . . . . W. H. D.
H. G. DANIELS, Esq., Berlin . . . . . H. G. D.
*EDWARD DANNREUTHER, Esq.* . . . . . E. D.
*PAUL DAVID, Esq.* . . . . . . . P. D.
J. H. DAVIE, Esq. . . . . . . . J. H. D.
Sir H. WALFORD DAVIES, Mus.D., Gresham Professor of Music, etc. . H. W. D.
*J. W. DAVISON, Esq.* . . . . . . J. W. D.
*H. C. DEACON, Esq.* . . . . . . . H. C. D.
EDWARD J. DENT, Esq., Professor of Music in Cambridge University . E. J. D.
L. M^CL. L. DIX, Esq. . . . . . . L. M^CL. L. D.
Miss JANET DODGE . . . . . . . J. D.
*Herr ALFRED DÖRFFEL* . . . . . . A. D.
*EDWARD H. DONKIN, Esq.* . . . . . E. H. D.
GEORGE DYSON, Esq., Mus.D., Director of Music in Winchester College G. D.

CLARENCE EDDY, Esq. . . . . . . C. E.
*F. G. EDWARDS, Esq.* . . . . . . F. G. E.
*H. SUTHERLAND EDWARDS, Esq.* . . . . H. S. E.
Dr. ALFRED EINSTEIN, Editor of Riemann's *Lexikon*, 1922 . . A. E.
THOMAS ELLISTON, Esq. . . . . . . T. E.
CARL ENGEL, Esq., Librarian of Music, Library of Congress, Washington C. E^L.
EDWIN EVANS, Esq. . . . . . . . E. E.

The Rev. E. H. FELLOWES, Mus.D. . . . . E. H. F.
GUSTAVE FERRARI, Esq. . . . . . . G. F.
SHELLEY FISHER, Esq. . . . . . . S. F.
Chevalier WM. HY. GRATTAN FLOOD, Hon. Mus.D., N.U.I., K.S.G. . W. H. G. F.
WALTER FORD, Esq. . . . . . . . W. F.
The Rt. Rev. WALTER H. FRERE, D.D., C.R., Lord Bishop of Truro . W. H. F.
ARTHUR M. FRIEDLANDER, Esq. . . . . A. M. F.
Dr. MAX FRIEDLÄNDER . . . . . . M. F.
*H. FREDERICK FROST, Esq.* . . . . . H. F. F.
JOHN T. FYFE, Esq. . . . . . . . J. T. F.
*CHARLES ALAN FYFFE, Esq.* . . . . . C. A. F.

The Rev. Canon F. W. GALPIN . . . . . F. W. G.
Signor GUIDO M. GATTI . . . . . . G. M. G.
NICHOLAS COMYN GATTY, Esq., Mus.B. . . . N. C. G.
*Dr. FRANZ GEHRING, Vienna.* . . . . . F. G.
SCOTT GODDARD, Esq. . . . . . . S. G.
M. VAN SOMEREN GODFERY, Major . . . . M. V. S. G.
HARVEY GRACE, Esq. . . . . . . H. G.
CHARLES L. GRAVES, Esq. . . . . . . C. L. G.

| | |
|---|---|
| J. C. GRIFFITH, Esq. | J. C. G. |
| *Sir GEORGE GROVE, C.B., D.C.L., Editor of the First Edition* | G. |
| | |
| Sir W. HENRY HADOW, Mus.D., Vice-Chancellor of Sheffield University | W. H. H$^{\text{w}}$. |
| H. V. HAMILTON, Esq. | H. V. H. |
| Mrs. ROBERT HARRISON | B. H. |
| Herr KARL HASSE | K. H$^{\text{z}}$. |
| L. W. HAWARD, Esq., Curator of the Manchester Art Gallery | L. W. H. |
| *The Rev. T. HELMORE* | T. H. |
| *WILLIAM HENDERSON, Esq.* | W. H. |
| W. J. HENDERSON, Esq., New York | W. J. H. |
| *GEORGE HERBERT, Esq.* | G. H. |
| ARTHUR F. HILL, Esq. | A. F. H. |
| *Dr. FERDINAND HILLER* | F. H$^{\text{R}}$. |
| *A. J. HIPKINS, Esq., F.S.A.* | A. J. H. |
| Miss EDITH J. HIPKINS | E. J. H$^{\text{s}}$. |
| CLAUDE HOBDAY, Esq. | C. H. |
| *EDWARD JOHN HOPKINS, Esq., Mus.D.* | E. J. H. |
| *The Rev. Canon T. PERCY HUDSON (Canon Pemberton)* | T. P. H. |
| *FRANCIS HUEFFER, Esq.* | F. H. |
| The Rev. Dom ANSELM HUGHES, O.S.B. | A. H. |
| A. HUGHES-HUGHES, Esq. | A. H.-H. |
| A. EAGLEFIELD HULL, Esq., Mus.D. | A. E. H. |
| *JOHN HULLAH, Esq.* | J. H. |
| *DUNCAN HUME, Esq.* | D. H. |
| W. HUME, Esq. | W. H$^{\text{z}}$. |
| HUBERT W. HUNT, Esq., Mus.D. | H. W. H. |
| Miss KATHLEEN D. HURST | K. D. H. |
| *WILLIAM H. HUSK, Esq.* | W. H. H. |
| | |
| IVOR JAMES, Esq. | I. J. |
| *F. H. JENKS, Esq.* | F. H. J. |
| *Mons. ADOLPHE JULLIEN* | A. J. |
| | |
| H. J. KALCSIK, Esq. | H. J. K. |
| A. KALISCH, Esq. | A. K. |
| *J. A. KAPPEY, Esq.* | J. A. K. |
| CUTHBERT KELLY, Esq. | C. K. |
| *FRANK KIDSON, Esq.* | F. K. |
| HERMAN KLEIN, Esq. | H. K. |
| The Rev. Dr. ALOIS KOLIČEK | A. K$^{\text{K}}$. |
| E. KRALL, Esq. | E. K. |
| *H. E. KREHBIEL, Esq.* | H. E. K. |
| *Mons. MAURICE KUFFERATH, Brussels* | M. K. |
| | |
| Herr ROBERT LACHMANN | R. L. |
| *MORTON LATHAM, Esq.* | M. L. |
| JAMES LECKY, Esq. | J. L. |
| ROBIN H. LEGGE, Esq. | R. H. L. |
| J. MEWBURN LEVIEN, Esq. | J. M. L. |
| CECIL LEWIS, Esq. | C. L. |
| *H. J. LINCOLN, Esq.* | H. J. L. |
| *R. B. LITCHFIELD, Esq.* | R. B. L. |
| R. E. LONSDALE, Esq. | R. E. L. |
| *STANLEY LUCAS, Esq.* | S. L. |

| | |
|---|---|
| R. F. McEwen, Esq. | R. F. McE. |
| Sir G. A. Macfarren, Mus.D. | G. A. M. |
| The Rev. Charles Mackeson, F.R.S. | C. M. |
| Charles Maclean, Esq., Mus.D. | C. Mᴺ. |
| H. S. Macran, Esq. | H. S. M. |
| Herr A. Maczewsky | A. M. |
| J. A. Fuller Maitland, Esq., F.S.A., Editor of the Second Edition | M. |
| Jeffery Mark, Esq. | J. Mᴷ. |
| Mrs. Julian Marshall | F. A. M. |
| Julian Marshall, Esq. | J. M. |
| Russell Martineau, Esq. | R. M. |
| H. J. L. J. Massé, Esq. | H. J. L. M. |
| Signor Giannandrea Mazzucato | G. M. |
| The Rev. J. H. Mee | J. H. M. |
| Senhor Carlos de Mello | C. de M. |
| Herr Rudolf Mengelberg | R. Mᴳ. |
| Miss Louisa Middleton | L. M. M. |
| The Rev. J. R. Milne | J. R. M. |
| R. O. Morris, Esq. | R. O. M. |
| D. L. Murray, Esq. | D. L. M. |
| | |
| V. E. Negus, Esq., F.R.C.S. | V. E. N. |
| Mrs. Rosa Newmarch | R. N. |
| | |
| E. M. Oakeley, Esq. | E. M. O. |
| Sir Herbert S. Oakeley, Mus.D. | H. S. O. |
| C. B. Oldman, Esq., British Museum | C. B. O. |
| The Rev. Sir F. A. Gore Ouseley, Bt., Mus.D. | F. A. G. O. |
| | |
| Sidney H. Pardon, Esq. | S. H. P. |
| Henry Parr, Esq. | H. P. |
| Sir Walter Parratt, Mus.D., M.V.O. | W. Pᴬ. |
| Sir C. Hubert H. Parry, Bt., C.V.O., Mus.D. | C. Ч. H. P. |
| Mons. K. Paucitis, Riga | K. F. |
| Edward John Payne, Esq. | E. J. P. |
| The Rev. Hugh Pearson | H. Pᴺ. |
| Edward H. Pember, Esq., K.C. | E. H. P. |
| The Rev. Canon T. P. Pemberton (formerly Hudson) | T. P. P. |
| Mlle. Marie Louise Pereyra | M. L. P. |
| Miss Phillimore | C. M. P. |
| F. Piggott, Esq. | F. P. |
| Mons. Marc Pincherle | M. P. |
| Herr C. Ferdinand Pohl | C. F. P. |
| William Pole, Esq., F.R.S., Mus.D. | W. P. |
| E. Polonaski, Esq. | E. Pᴵ. |
| Victor de Pontigny, Esq. | V. de P. |
| Reginald Lane Poole, Esq. | R. L. P. |
| Mons. J. G. Prod'homme | J. G. P. |
| Ebenezer Prout, Esq., Mus.D. | E. P. |
| The Rev. W. Pulling | W. Pᴳ. |
| Charles H. Purday, Esq. | C. H. P. |
| | |
| Miss Olga Racster | O. R. |
| Mons. Félix Raugel, Paris | F. Rᴸ. |

WILLIAM HENRY REED, Esq. . . . . W. H. R.
*LUIGI RICCI, Esq.* . . . . . . L. R.
*EDWARD F. RIMBAULT, Esq., LL.D.* . . . . E. F. R.
Signor F. RIZZELLI . . . . . . F. R<sup>z</sup>.
*W. S. ROCKSTRO, Esq.* . . . . . . W. S. R.
Dr. KURT ROGER, Vienna . . . . . K. R.
*DESMOND LUMLEY RYAN, Esq.* . . . . . D. L. R.


Mons. GUSTAVE SAMAZEUILH, Paris . . . . G. S.
H. A. SCOTT, Esq. . . . . . . H. A. S.
*J. S. SHEDLOCK, Esq.* . . . . . J. S. S.
A. J. SHELDON, Esq. . . . . . A. J. S.
CARL SIEWERS, Esq. . . . . . . C. S<sup>s</sup>.
The Hon. Mrs. SINCLAIR . . . . . G. A. S.
WARREN STOREY SMITH, Esq., Boston . . . W. S. S.
Miss BARBARA SMYTHE . . . . . B. S.
O. G. SONNECK, Esq., New York . . . . O. G. S.
Dr. Ing. OTTOKAR SOUREK, Prague . . . . O. S.
*T. L. SOUTHGATE, Esq.* . . . . . T. L. S.
WALTER R. SPALDING, Esq., Professor of Music in Harvard Univer-
  sity, Cambridge, Mass. . . . . . W. R. S.
*Dr. PHILIPP SPITTA* . . . . . . P. S.
S. J. SPURLING, Esq. . . . . . S. J. S.
*WILLIAM BARCLAY SQUIRE, Esq., M.V.O.* . . . W. B. S.
Miss C. STAINER . . . . . . C. S.
*Sir JOHN STAINER, Mus.D.* . . . . . J. S.
J. F. R. STAINER, Esq. . . . . . J. F. R. S.
W. W. STARMER, Esq. . . . . . W. W. S.
E. IRENAEUS PRIME STEVENSON, Esq. . . . E. I. P. S.
*Sir ROBERT P. STEWART, Mus.D.* . . . . R. P. S.
*T. L. STILLIE, Esq.* . . . . . . T. L. S<sup>E</sup>.
*WILLIAM H. STONE, Esq., M.D.* . . . . W. H. S.
E. VAN DER STRAETEN, Esq. . . . . E. v. d. S.
A. H. FOX-STRANGWAYS, Esq. . . . . A. H. F.-S.
*R. A. STREATFEILD, Esq.* . . . . . R. A. S.
The Rt. Rev. THOMAS B. STRONG, D.D., Lord Bishop of Oxford . T. B. S.
J. STUTTERFORD, Esq. . . . . . J. S<sup>D</sup>.
*Sir ARTHUR SEYMOUR SULLIVAN, Mus.D.* . . . A. S. S.


*FRANKLIN TAYLOR, Esq.* . . . . . F. T.
CHARLES SANFORD TERRY, Esq., Litt. D. (Cantab.), Hon. Mus. D. (Edin.),
  Hon. LL.D. (Glasgow) . . . . . C. S. T.
Mons. ANDRÉ TESSIER, Paris . . . . A. T.
*ALEXANDER W. THAYER, Esq.* . . . . A. W. T.
Miss BERTHA THOMAS . . . . . B. T.
HERBERT THOMPSON, Esq., D.Litt., Leeds . . . H. T.
G. H. THRING, Esq., Incorporated Society of Authors, Playwrights and
  Composers . . . . . . . G. H. T.
H. JULIUS W. TILLYARD, Esq., Professor in Birmingham University . H. J. W. T.
FRANCIS TOYE, Esq. . . . . . . F. T<sup>ye</sup>.
J. B. TREND, Esq. . . . . . . J. B. T.


Mons. RICHARD VEŠELÝ, Prague . . . . R. V.
Dr. BOLESLAV VOMAČKA . . . . . B. V.

ERNEST WALKER, Esq., Mus.D., Fellow of Balliol College, Oxford    .    E. W.
WILLIAM WALLACE, Esq.      .         .         .         .         .    W. W.
S. H. WALROND, Esq.         .         .         .         .         .    S. H. W.
Miss SYLVIA TOWNSEND WARNER    .         .         .         .    S. T. W.
EDWARD WATSON, Esq., National Institute for the Blind       .       .    E. W^N.
P. G. L. WEBB, Esq.         .         .         .         .         .    P. G. L. W.
C. WELCH, Esq.         .         .         .         .         .    C. W.
FREDERICK WESTLAKE, Esq. .         .         .         .         .    F. W.
H. A. WHITEHEAD, Esq.         .         .         .         .    H. A. W.
W. E. WHITEHOUSE, Esq.      .         .         .         .         .    W. E. W.
C. F. ABDY WILLIAMS, Esq.         .         .         .         .    C. F. A. W
R. VAUGHAN WILLIAMS, Esq., Mus.D.         .         .         .    R. V. W.
C. W. WILSON, Esq., Dublin         .         .         .         .    C. W. W.
Mrs. EDMOND WODEHOUSE         .         .         .         .    A. H. W.
J. MUIR WOOD, Esq.         .         .         .         .         .    J. M. W.
H. E. WOOLDRIDGE, Esq.      .         .         .         .         .    H. E. W.
H. SAXE-WYNDHAM, Esq., Secretary of the Guildhall School of Music  .    H. S.-W.

THE EDITOR         .         .         .         .         .         .    C.

# CONTRIBUTORS

LIST II. ARRANGED IN ALPHABETICAL ORDER OF THE INITIALS BY WHICH ARTICLES
ARE SIGNED

*The names of deceased writers are printed in italics*

| | |
|---|---|
| A. C. | Alexis Chitty, Esq. |
| A. C. B. | Adrian C. Boult, Esq., Mus.D. |
| A. D. | *Herr Alfred Dörffel.* |
| A. D. C. | *A. D. Coleridge, Esq.* |
| A. E. | Dr. Alfred Einstein. |
| A. E. H. | A. Eaglefield Hull, Esq., Mus.D |
| A. F. H. | Arthur F. Hill, Esq. |
| A. H. | Rev. Dom Anselm Hughes, O.S.B |
| A. H. F.-S. | A. H. Fox-Strangways, Esq. |
| A. H.-H. | A. Hughes-Hughes, Esq. |
| A. H. W. | *Mrs. Edmond Wodehouse.* |
| A. J. | *Mons. Adolphe Jullien.* |
| A. J. H. | *A. J. Hipkins, Esq., F.S.A.* |
| A. J. S. | A. J. Sheldon, Esq. |
| A. K. | A. Kalisch, Esq. |
| A. Kᴷ. | Rev. Dr. Alois Količek. |
| A. M. | *Herr A. Maczewsky.* |
| A. M. F. | Arthur M. Friedlander, Esq. |
| A. S. S. | *Sir Arthur S. Sullivan, Mus.D.* |
| A. T. | Mons. André Tessier. |
| A. W. T. | *Alexander W. Thayer, Esq.* |
| | |
| B. H. | Mrs. Robert Harrison. |
| B. S. | Miss Barbara Smythe. |
| B. T. | Miss Bertha Thomas. |
| B. V. | Dr. Boleslav Vomačka. |
| | |
| C. | The Editor. |
| C. A. | *Carl Armbruster, Esq.* |
| C. A. F. | *Charles Alan Fyffe, Esq.* |
| C. B. | Mons. Charles Bouvet. |
| C. B. O. | C. B. Oldman, Esq. |
| C. E. | Clarence Eddy, Esq. |
| C. Eᴸ. | Carl Engel, Esq. |
| C. F. A. W. | *C. F. Abdy Williams, Esq.* |
| C. F. P. | *Herr C. Ferdinand Pohl.* |

| | | |
|---|---|---|
| C. H. | . . . . | CLAUDE HOBDAY, Esq. |
| C. H. P. | . . . . | *CHARLES H. PURDAY, Esq.* |
| C. H. H. P. | . . . | *Sir C. HUBERT H. PARRY, Mus.D., C.V.O.* |
| C. K. | . . . | *CUTHBERT KELLY, Esq.* |
| C. L. | . . . | *CECIL LEWIS, Esq.* |
| C. L. G. | . . . | *CHARLES L. GRAVES, Esq.* |
| C. M. | . . . . | *Rev. CHARLES MACKESON, F.R.S.* |
| C. M$^N$. | . . . | *CHARLES MACLEAN, Esq., Mus.D.* |
| C. de M. | . . . | *Senhor CARLOS DE MELLO.* |
| C. M. P. | . . . | Miss PHILLIMORE. |
| C. S. | . . . | Miss C. STAINER. |
| C. S$^S$. | . . . | CARL SIEWERS, Esq. |
| C. S. T. | . . . | CHARLES SANFORD TERRY, Esq., Mus.D. |
| C. W. | . . . | *C. WELCH, Esq.* |
| C. W. W. | . . . | C. W. WILSON, Esq. |
| | | |
| D. B. | . . . | *DAVID BAPTIE, Esq.* |
| D. H. | . . . | *DUNCAN HUME, Esq.* |
| D. J. B. | . . . | D. J. BLAIKLEY, Esq. |
| D. L. M. | . . . | D. L. MURRAY, Esq. |
| D. L. R. | . . . | *DESMOND LUMLEY RYAN, Esq.* |
| | | |
| E. B. | . . . | ERIC BLOM, Esq. |
| E. B$^L$. | . . . | Mons. E. BORREL. |
| E. C. | . . . | *E. C. CHADFIELD, Esq.* |
| E. C$^N$. | . . . | Mons. ERNEST CLOSSON. |
| E. D. | . . . | *EDWARD DANNREUTHER, Esq.* |
| E. E. | . . . | EDWIN EVANS, Esq. |
| E. F. R. | . . . | *EDWARD F. RIMBAULT, Esq., LL.D.* |
| E. H.-A. | . . . | E. HERON-ALLEN, Esq. |
| E. H. D. | . . . | *EDWARD H. DONKIN, Esq.* |
| E. H. F. | . . . | Rev. E. H. FELLOWES, Mus.D. |
| E. H. P. | . . . | *EDWARD H. PEMBER, Esq., K.C.* |
| E. I. P. S. | . . . | E. IRENAEUS PRIME STEVENSON, Esq. |
| E. J. D. | . . . | EDWARD J. DENT, Esq. |
| E. J. H. | . . . | *EDWARD JOHN HOPKINS, Esq., Mus.D.* |
| E. J. H$^S$. | . . . | Miss EDITH J. HIPKINS. |
| E. J. P. | . . . | *EDWARD JOHN PAYNE, Esq.* |
| E. K. | . . . | E. KRALL, Esq. |
| E. M. O. | . . . | E. M. OAKELEY, Esq. |
| E. O. B. | . . . | Mrs. EDITH OLDHAM BEST (Miss Oldham). |
| E. P. | . . . | *EBENEZER PROUT, Esq., Mus.D.* |
| E. P$^I$. | . . . | E. POLONASKI, Esq. |
| E. v. d. S. | . . . | E. VAN DER STRAETEN, Esq. |
| E. W. | . . . | ERNEST WALKER, Esq., Mus.D. |
| E. W$^N$. | . . . | EDWARD WATSON, Esq. |
| | | |
| F. A. G. O. | . . | *Rev. Sir F. A. GORE OUSELEY, Bt., Mus.D.* |
| F. A. M. | . . . | *Mrs. JULIAN MARSHALL.* |
| F. B. | . . . | F. BONAVIA, Esq. |
| F. C. | . . . | FREDERICK CORDER, Esq. |
| F. G. | . . . | *Dr. FRANZ GEHRING.* |
| F. G. E. | . . . | *F. G. EDWARDS, Esq.* |
| F. H. | . . . | *FRANCIS HUEFFER, Esq.* |
| F. H$^R$. | . . . | *Dr. FERDINAND HILLER* |

| | | | | | |
|---|---|---|---|---|---|
| F. H. J. | . | . | . | . | . *F. H. JENKS, Esq.* |
| F. J. A. | . | . | . | . | . F. J. ARNOLD, Esq. |
| F. K. | . | . | . | . | . *FRANK KIDSON, Esq.* |
| F. P. | . | . | . | . | . F. PIGGOTT, Esq. |
| F. R<sup>z</sup>. | . | . | . | . | . Signor F. RIZZELLI. |
| F. R<sup>L</sup>. | . | . | . | . | . Mons. FÉLIX RAUGEL. |
| F. T. | . | . | . | . | . *FRANKLIN TAYLOR, Esq.* |
| F. T<sup>YE</sup>. | . | . | . | . | . FRANCIS TOYE, Esq. |
| F. W. | . | . | . | . | . *FREDERICK WESTLAKE, Esq.* |
| F. W. G. | . | . | . | . | . Rev. Canon F. W. GALPIN. |
| | | | | | |
| G. | . | . | . | . | . *Sir GEORGE GROVE, C.B., D.C.L.* |
| G. A. C. | . | . | . | . | . *Major GEORGE ARTHUR CRAWFORD.* |
| G. A. M. | . | . | . | . | . *Sir G. A. MACFARREN, Mus.D.* |
| G. A. S. | . | . | . | . | . The Hon. Mrs. SINCLAIR. |
| G. C. | . | . | . | . | . *Mons. GUSTAVE CHOUQUET.* |
| G. D. | . | . | . | . | . GEORGE DYSON, Esq., Mus.D. |
| G. E. P. A. | . | . | . | . | . G. E. P. ARKWRIGHT, Esq. |
| G. F. | . | . | . | . | . GUSTAVE FERRARI, Esq. |
| G. H. | . | . | . | . | . *GEORGE HERBERT, Esq.* |
| G. H. T. | . | . | . | . | . G. H. THRING, Esq. |
| G. M. | . | . | . | . | . *Signor GIANNANDREA MAZZUCATO.* |
| G. M. G. | . | . | . | . | . Signor GUIDO M. GATTI. |
| G. S. | . | . | . | . | . Mons. GUSTAVE SAMAZEUILH. |
| G. S. K.-B. | . | . | . | . | . *G. S. KAYE-BUTTERWORTH, Esq.* |
| | | | | | |
| H. A. | . | . | . | . | . HERBERT ANTCLIFFE, Esq. |
| H. A. S. | . | . | . | . | . H. A. SCOTT, Esq. |
| H. A. W. | . | . | . | . | . H. A. WHITEHEAD, Esq. |
| H. B. | . | . | . | . | . HUGH BUTLER, Esq. |
| H. B<sup>Y</sup>. | . | . | . | . | . Dr. HERMANN BUDY. |
| H. C. D. | . | . | . | . | . *H. C. DEACON, Esq.* |
| H. E. A. | . | . | . | . | . Lieut. H. E. ADKINS. |
| H. E. K. | . | . | . | . | . *H. E. KREHBIEL, Esq.* |
| H. E. W. | . | . | . | . | . *H. E. WOOLDRIDGE, Esq.* |
| H. F. B. | . | . | . | . | . *HORATIO ROBT. FORBES BROWN, Esq.* |
| H. F. F. | . | . | . | . | . *H. FREDERICK FROST, Esq.* |
| H. G. | . | . | . | . | . HARVEY GRACE, Esq. |
| H. G. D. | . | . | . | . | . H. G. DANIELS, Esq. |
| H. J. K. | . | . | . | . | . H. J. KALCSIK, Esq. |
| H. J. L. | . | . | . | . | . *H. J. LINCOLN, Esq.* |
| H. J. L. M. | . | . | . | . | . H. J. L. J. MASSÉ, Esq. |
| H. J. W. T. | . | . | . | . | . Professor H. JULIUS W. TILLYARD. |
| H. K. | . | . | . | . | . HERMANN KLEIN, Esq. |
| H. P. | . | . | . | . | . *HENRY PARR, Esq.* |
| H. P<sup>N</sup>. | . | . | . | . | . *Rev. HUGH PEARSON.* |
| H. S. E. | . | . | . | . | . *H. SUTHERLAND EDWARDS, Esq.* |
| H. S. M. | . | . | . | . | . H. S. MACRAN, Esq. |
| H. S. O. | . | . | . | . | . *Sir HERBERT S. OAKELEY, Mus.D.* |
| H. S.-W. | . | . | . | . | . H. SAXE-WYNDHAM, Esq. |
| H. T. | . | . | . | . | . HERBERT THOMPSON, Esq., D.Litt. |
| H. V. H. | . | . | . | . | . H. V. HAMILTON, Esq. |
| H. W. D. | . | . | . | . | . Sir H. WALFORD DAVIES, Mus.D. |
| H. W. H. | . | . | . | . | . HUBERT W. HUNT, Esq., Mus.D. |

I. J. . . . . . . Ivor James, Esq.

J. A. K. . . . . . *J. A. Kappey, Esq.*
J. B. . . . . . Dr. Josef Bartoš.
J. B. T. . . . . . J. B. Trend, Esq.
J. C. B. . . . . . J. C. Bridge, Esq., Mus.D.
J. C. G. . . . . . J. C. Griffith, Esq.
J. D. . . . . . Miss Janet Dodge.
J. F. R. S. . . . . . J. F. R. Stainer, Esq.
J. G. P. . . . . . Mons. J. G. Prod'homme.
J. H. . . . . . *John Hullah, Esq.*
J. H. D. . . . . . J. H. Davie, Esq.
J. H. M. . . . . . *Rev. J. H. Mee.*
J. L. . . . . . James Lecky, Esq.
J. M. . . . . . *Julian Marshall, Esq.*
J. M<sup>K</sup>. . . . . . Jeffery Mark, Esq.
J. M. L. . . . . . John Mewburn Levien, Esq.
J. M. W. . . . . . *J. Muir Wood, Esq.*
J. R. M. . . . . . Rev. J. R. Milne.
J. R. S.-B. . . . . . J. R. Sterndale-Bennett, Esq.
J. S. . . . . . *Sir John Stainer, Mus.D.*
J. S<sup>D</sup>. . . . . . J. Stutterford, Esq.
J. S. S. . . . . . *J. S. Shedlock, Esq.*
J. T. F. . . . . . John T. Fyfe, Esq.
J. W. C. . . . . . J. W. Capstick, Esq.
J. W. D. . . . . . *J. W. Davison, Esq.*

K. D. H. . . . . . Miss Kathleen D. Hurst.
K. H<sup>E</sup>. . . . . . Herr Karl Hasse.
K. P. . . . . . Mons. K. Paucitis.
K. R. . . . . . Dr. Kurt Roger.

L. B. . . . . . *Leonard Borwick, Esq.*
L. M<sup>C</sup>. L. D. . . . . . L. M<sup>C</sup>. L. Dix, Esq.
L. M. M. . . . . . Miss Louisa Middleton.
L. R. . . . . . *Luigi Ricci, Esq.*
L. W. H. . . . . . L. W. Haward, Esq.

M. . . . . . J. A. Fuller Maitland, Esq.
M. B. . . . . . *The Hon. Mrs. M. Burrell.*
M. C. C. . . . . . Mrs. Walter Carr.
M. D. C. . . . . . M. D. Calvocoressi, Esq.
M. F. . . . . . Dr. Max Friedländer.
M. K. . . . . . *Mons. Maurice Kufferath.*
M. L. . . . . . *Morton Latham, Esq.*
M. L. P. . . . . . Mlle. M. L. Pereyra.
M. P. . . . . . Mons. Marc Pincherle.
M. V. S. G. . . . . . Major M. van Someren Godfery.

N. C. G. . . . . . Nicholas C. Gatty, Esq.

O. G. S. . . . . . O. G. Sonneck, Esq.
O. R. . . . . . Miss Olga Racster.
O. S. . . . . . Dr. Ing. Ottokar Šourek.

| | | | |
|---|---|---|---|
| P. C. B. | | | Percy C. Buck, Esq., Mus.D. |
| P. D. | | | *Paul David, Esq.* |
| P. G. L. W. | | | P. G. L. Webb, Esq. |
| P. S. | | | *Dr. Philipp Spitta.* |
| | | | |
| R. A. | | | Richard Aldrich, Esq. |
| R. A. S. | | | *R. A. Streatfeild, Esq.* |
| R. B. L. | | | *R. B. Litchfield, Esq.* |
| R. E. L. | | | R. E. Lonsdale, Esq. |
| R. F. M'E. | | | *R. F. M'Ewen, Esq.* |
| R. H. L. | | | Robin H. Legge, Esq. |
| R. H. M. B. | | | *R. H. M. Bosanquet, Esq.* |
| R. L. | | | Herr Robert Lachmann. |
| R. L. P. | | | Reginald Lane Poole, Esq. |
| R. M. | | | *Russell Martineau, Esq.* |
| R. M<sup>G</sup>. | | | Herr Rudolf Mengelberg. |
| R. N. | | | Mrs. Rosa Newmarch. |
| R. O. M. | | | R. O. Morris, Esq. |
| R. P. S. | | | *Sir Robert P. Stewart, Mus.D.* |
| R. V. | | | M. Richard Vešelý. |
| R. V. W. | | | R. Vaughan Williams, Esq., Mus.D. |
| | | | |
| S. F. | | | Shelley Fisher, Esq. |
| S. G. | | | Scott Goddard, Esq. |
| S. H. P. | | | *Sidney H. Pardon, Esq.* |
| S. H. W. | | | S. H. Walrond, Esq. |
| S. J. S. | | | S. J. Spurling, Esq. |
| S. L. | | | *Stanley Lucas, Esq.* |
| S. T. W. | | | Miss Sylvia Townsend Warner. |
| | | | |
| T. B. S. | | | The Rt. Rev. Thomas B. Strong, D.D., Lord Bishop of Oxford. |
| T. E. | | | Thomas Elliston, Esq. |
| T. H. | | | *Rev. Thomas Helmore.* |
| T. L. S. | | | *T. L. Southgate, Esq.* |
| T. L. S<sup>E</sup>. | | | *T. L. Stillie, Esq.* |
| T. P. H. | | | *Rev. Canon T. Percy Hudson (Canon Pemberton).* |
| T. P. P. | | | *Rev. Canon T. P. Pemberton (formerly Hudson).* |
| | | | |
| V. E. N. | | | V. E. Negus, Esq., F.R.C.S. |
| v. de P. | | | *Victor de Pontigny, Esq.* |
| | | | |
| W. A. A. | | | W. A. Aikin, Esq., M.D. |
| W. B. C. | | | W. B. Chase, Esq. |
| W. B. S. | | | *William Barclay Squire, Esq.* |
| W. C. | | | *William Chappell, Esq., F.S.A.* |
| W. E. W. | | | W. E. Whitehouse, Esq. |
| W. F. | | | Walter Ford, Esq. |
| W. G. C. | | | *Sir William George Cusins.* |
| W. H. | | | *William Henderson, Esq.* |
| W. H<sup>E</sup>. | | | W. Hume, Esq. |
| W. H. C. | | | *W. H. Cummings, Esq., Mus.D.* |
| W. H. D. | | | William H. Daly, Esq. |
| W. H. F. | | | The Rt. Rev. W. H. Frere, D.D., C.R., Lord Bishop of Truro. |
| W. H. G. F. | | | W. H. Grattan Flood, Esq., Mus.D. |

| | | | | |
|---|---|---|---|---|
| W. H. H. | . | . | . | . *WILLIAM H. HUSK, Esq.* |
| W. H. H^W. | . | . | . | . Sir W. HENRY HADOW, Mus.D. |
| W. H. R. | . | . | . | . WILLIAM HENRY REED, Esq. |
| W. H. S. | . | . | . | . *WILLIAM H. STONE, Esq., M.D.* |
| W. J. H. | . | . | . | . W. J. HENDERSON, Esq. |
| W. P. . | . | . | . | . *WILLIAM POLE, Esq., F.R.S., Mus.D.* |
| W. P^A. | . | . | . | . *Sir WALTER PARRATT, Mus.D., M.V.O.* |
| W. P^G. | . | . | . | . *Rev. W. PULLING.* |
| W. R. C. | . | . | . | . WALTER R. CREIGHTON, Esq. |
| W. R. S. | . | . | . | . WALTER R. SPALDING, Esq. |
| W. S. R. | . | . | . | . *W. S. ROCKSTRO, Esq.* |
| W. S. S. | . | . | . | . WARREN STOREY SMITH, Esq. |
| W. W. | . | . | . | . WILLIAM WALLACE, Esq. |
| W. W C. | . | . | . | . W. W. COBBETT, Esq. |
| W. W. S. | . | . | . | . W. W. STARMER, Esq. |

# LIST OF PLATES

## VOLUME I

# VOLUME III

# VOLUME IV

## VOLUME V

# ABBREVIATIONS

## PERIODICALS AND WORKS OF REFERENCE, ETC.

| | |
|---|---|
| *Allgemeine Musikalische Zeitung* | *A.M.Z.* |
| *American Supplement of Grove's Dictionary* | *Amer. Supp.* |
| *Bach-Gesellschaft* (complete critical edition of J. S. Bach's works) | *B.-G.* |
| *Bach Jahrbuch* | *B. J.-B.* |
| *Baker's Biographical Dictionary* | *Baker.* |
| *British Musical Biography* | *Brit. Mus. Biog.* |
| *British Musical Society's Annual*, 1920 | *B.M.S. Ann.*, 1920. |
| *Davey's History of English Music* | *Hist. Eng. Mus.* |
| *Denkmäler deutsche Tonkunst* | *D.D.T.* |
| *Denkmäler der deutsche Tonkunst in Österreich* | *D.T.Ö.* |
| *Dictionary of National Biography* | *D.N.B.* |
| *Eitner's Quellen-Lexicon* | *Q.-L.* |
| *Fétis's Biographie universelle* (with Supplement) | *Fétis.* |
| *Imperial Dictionary of Universal Biography* | *Imp. Dict. Univ. Biog.* |
| *Mendel's Lexicon* | *Mendel.* |
| *Monatshefte für Musikgeschichte*, Leipzig | *M.f.M.* |
| *Musical Antiquary* | *Mus. Ant.* |
| *Musical Association's Proceedings* | *Mus. Ass. Proc.* |
| *Musical Times* | *Mus. T.* |
| *Music and Letters* | *M. and L.* |
| *Oxford History of Music* | *Oxf. Hist. Mus.* |
| *Quarterly Musical Review* | *Q. Mus. Rev.* |
| *Revista de Filogia española*, Madrid | *R.F.E.* |
| *Revista musical Catalona*, Barcelona | *R.M.C.* |
| *Revista musical de Bilbao* | *R.M.B.* |
| *Revista musicale italiana*, Turin | *R.M.I.* |
| *Revue musicale*, Paris | *R.M.* |
| *Riemann's Musik Lexikon*, 1922 | *Riemann.* |
| *Sammelbände der Internationalen Musikgesellschaft*, Leipzig | *S.I.M.*, also *I.M.G.* |
| *Studien zu Musikwissenschaft* | *S.z.M.W.* |
| *Walker's History of Music in England* | *Hist. Mus. Eng.* |
| *Zeitschrift für Musikwissenschaft*, Leipzig | *Z.M.W.* |

## ENGLISH LIBRARIES AND COLLECTIONS

| | |
|---|---|
| Batten Organ Book at St. Michael's College, Tenbury | Tenb. O.B. |
| Bodleian Library, Oxford | Bodl. Lib. |
| British Museum | B.M. |
| Buckingham Palace Library (now in the British Museum) | Roy. Lib. B.M. |
| Caius College, Cambridge | Caius. |
| Christ Church, Oxford | Ch. Ch. |
| Commonplace Book of John Baldwin | Baldwin. |
| Durham Cathedral | Durh. |
| Ely Cathedral | Ely. |
| First Book of Selected Church Music, edited by John Barnard, 1641 | Barnard. |
| Fitzwilliam Library, Cambridge | Fitzw. |

| | |
|---|---|
| Harleian MSS., British Museum . . . . . . . | Harl. |
| Lambeth Palace . . . . . . . . . | Lambeth. |
| Organ Book at Christ Church . . . . . . | Ch. Ch. O.B. |
| Organ Book at Durham Cathedral . . . .. . . | Durham O.B. |
| Oxford Music School Collection (now in the Bodleian Library) . . | Bodl. Mus. Sch. |
| Peterhouse, Cambridge . . . . . . . . | PH. |
| Royal Collection Appendix MSS., British Museum . . . . | Roy. MSS. |
| Royal College of Music . . . . . . . . | R.C.M. |
| Sadler Partbooks (now in the Bodleian Library) . . . . | Sadler. |
| St. George's Chapel, Windsor . . . . . . | St. G. Ch. |
| St. Michael's College, Tenbury . . . . . . | Tenb. |
| Wimborne Minster . . . . . . . . | Wimb. |
| Worcester Cathedral . . . . . . . . | Worc. |
| York Minster . . . . . . . . . | Yk. |

## CHURCH MUSIC

| | | | | | |
|---|---|---|---|---|---|
| Benedicite . . . | (Bcte.) | Litany . . . | (L.) |
| Benedictus . . | (B.) | Magnificat . . | (M.) |
| Creed . . . | (C.) | Nunc Dimittis . | (N.D.) |
| Gloria . . . | (G.) | Sanctus . . | (S.) |
| Jubilate . . . | (J.) | Te Deum . . | (T.D.) |
| Kyrie . . . | (K.) | Venite . . | (V.) |

## INSTITUTIONS, Etc.

| | |
|---|---|
| Bibliothèque National, Paris . . . . . . | Bibl. Nat. Paris. |
| Breitkopf & Härtel . . . . . . . . | B. &. H. |
| Guildhall School of Music, London . . . . . | G.S.M. |
| Incorporated Society of Musicians . . . . . | I.S.M. |
| International Musik Gesellschaft . . . . . . | Int. Mus. Ges. |
| Musical Antiquarian Society . . . . . . | Mus. Ant. Soc. |
| Musical Association . . . . . . . | Mus. Ass. |
| Real Conservatorio di Musica, Naples . . . . . | R.C.M. Naples. |
| Royal Academy of Music, London . . . . . | R.A.M. |
| Royal College of Music, London . . . . . . | R.C.M. |
| Royal College of Organists, London . . . . . | R.C.O. |

# DICTIONARY

## OF

## MUSIC AND MUSICIANS

### VOL. IV

## P—SONATINA

# P

**P,** (1) abbreviation of *piano* = soft, generally in the form of the small letter italicised.

(2) Abbreviation for *Pedale*, indicating the use of the damper pedal in pianoforte music, generally in the form of the capital letter italicised.

**PABST,** (1) AUGUST (*b*. Elberfeld, May 30, 1811 ; *d*. Riga, July 21, 1885), was cantor and organist at Königsberg and afterwards director of a music school at Riga. He composed several operas produced at Königsberg and Dresden. His two sons were esteemed musicians, viz. :

(2) LOUIS (*b*. Königsberg, July 18, 1846) appeared in 1862 as a pianist with the Königsberg Philharmonic and toured in Germany. In 1867 he came to England and was at Liverpool for two years, whence he went to Riga, where he founded a music school. He also visited Australia and established a school at Melbourne (1887), and afterwards he went to Russia and held a professorship at Moscow (1903). He composed piano-music, songs and melodramas.

(3) PAUL (*b*. Königsberg, May 27, 1854 ; *d*. Moscow, June 9, 1897), a pupil of Liszt, settled at Moscow as a teacher in the Conservatoire. A prolific composer, he is remembered chiefly for his brilliant ' paraphrases ' for the pianoforte of operatic music, especially that on Tchaikovsky's ' Eugene Oniegen.' (*Riemann*.)

**PACCHIEROTTI** (PACCHIAROTTI), GASPARO (*b*. Fabriano, near Ancona, 1744 ; *d*. Oct. 28, 1821 [1]), a famous singer (*evirato*).

His ancestors came from Siena, where one of them, Jacopo dal Pecchia, called Pacchierotto, studied the works of Perugino and Raffaelle to such good effect that his own pictures have been sometimes taken by connoisseurs to be by the hand of the latter great master.[2] Driven from Siena by political troubles, the family of Pacchierotto in 1575 took refuge in Pianca-stagnaio ; from whence a branch settled in Fabriano.

About 1757 Gasparo Pacchierotti was admitted into the choir of S. Mark's at Venice, where the great Bertoni was his master, according to the memoir written by the singer's adopted son, Giuseppe Cecchini Pacchierotti.[3] This, however, is contradicted by Fétis, who states that it was in the choir of the cathedral at Forlì that the young singer received his first instruction, and that it was impossible that he could have sung under Bertoni, since boys were never employed at S. Mark's, where Bertoni did not become maestro di cappella till 1785, having been up to that date (from 1752) only organist. However this may be, it is certain

that the young Pacchierotti, having been prepared for the career of a sopranist, studied long and carefully before he began, at the age of 16, to sing secondary parts at Venice, Vienna and Milan.

Milan was the last place in which he sang a secondary rôle. Returning to Venice in 1769, he took the place of Guarducci, *primo musico* at the S. Benedetto, then the chief theatre in that city. Successful here, he was immediately invited by the impresario of the Opera at Palermo for the season of 1771. H. E. the Procuratore Tron, his good and generous patron, furnished Pacchierotti with recommendations, and the latter set out, taking Naples in his way. Arrived there, he was informed that the celebrated *prima donna*, De Amicis, had protested against the proposition that she should sing with him, ' a player of second parts.' The Venetian minister, to whom he was recommended, comforted him in this juncture, but only with the humiliating permission accorded to him to show his powers by singing two pieces, with full orchestra, at the San Carlo, before Lacillo, Piccinni and Caffarelli as judges. Here he was brilliantly successful, and was immediately offered his choice between the theatres of Palermo and Naples. He proudly chose the former, where even De Amicis herself was surprised into sincere and kindly admiration.

This set the seal on Pacchierotti's reputation, which never faded for twenty-five years. He remained for a time in Italy, singing at Parma, Milan, Florence and Forlì, and at Venice in 1777. After this, he sang at Milan in the carnival of 1778, then at Genoa, Lucca and Turin ; but in the autumn of that year he came to London with Bertoni, and made his first appearance here with Bernasconi in the pasticcio ' Demofoönte.' Great expectations had been formed of him, not only from his continental reputation, but from the account given by Captain Brydone in his *Travels*, and from some airs sung ' in his manner ' by Piozzi, ' in a style that excited great ideas of his pathetic powers.' These expectations were not disappointed ; and Dr. Burney's warm but intelligent praise must be read by those who would form an idea of the truly great singer that Pacchierotti was.

After a second visit to London, where he was engaged for the season of 1782–83 at a salary of £1150, with a benefit, Pacchierotti again returned to Italy. He sang at the Tuileries in Paris on his way back again to England from Venice, where Bertoni had written fresh operas for him. Galuppi had died there in 1784, and at his funeral Pacchierotti took part in a Requiem. ' I sang very devoutly indeed,' he

---

[1] Cecchini.   [2] Lanzi, tom. i. p. 305.
[3] Published at Padua, 1844, 8vo.

wrote to Burney, ' to obtain a quiet to his soul.'
Pacchierotti arrived here, on his third visit, in
1790, sang at the Pantheon, and at the Festival
in Westminster Abbey in 1791. At the opening
of the Fenice at Venice in 1792 he took his
leave of the stage, after which he settled in
Padua. In 1796, however, he was compelled
to appear once more to sing before General
Buonaparte, who was passing through the city.

At Padua he enjoyed the society and the
esteem of all the literati of the city, among
whom he spent the rest of his life in a peaceful
and happy manner, only interrupted by one
unfortunate incident. Having imprudently
lamented ' le splendide miserie della vittoria,'
in a letter to Catalani, which he had entrusted
to Dragonetti, who was on the point of escaping
from Italy, both fugitive and letter were inter-
cepted ; and the unlucky Pacchierotti was
thrown into prison, where he was detained for
a month. He published, in collaboration with
A. Calegari, a method entitled *Modi generali del
canto premessi alle maniere parziali onde ador-
nare o rifiorire le nude o semplici melodie o
cantilene giusta il metodo di Gasp. Pacchiarotti
opera di Ant. Calegari*. (*Q.-L.*) Not long
before his death he was visited by Rossini, to
whom he deplored the depraved modern taste
in singing, and the growth of a noisy and *rococo*
style, for which, doubtless, the old singer
thought the Pesarese in a great degree to
blame : ' Give me another Pacchierotti,' the
latter replied, ' and I shall know how to write
for him ! '                                J. M.

PACCHIONI, ANTONIO MARIA (*b.* Modena,
July 5, 1654 ; *d.* July 16, 1738), received his
musical instruction from Marzio Erculeo,
soprano singer at the Modena Cathedral. In
composition he endeavoured to form himself
on the principles of the Palestrina school.
Taking priest's orders he became chaplain to
the court of Modena, and afterwards vice-
choirmaster. His compositions, including
oratorios and other church music, remain in
MS. at Modena and Bologna with the exception of two pieces received by Martini in his
*Esemplare*, and one in Paolucci's *L' arte pratica
di contrappunto*. In 1733 Pacchioni's name
occurs in connexion with a dispute [1] which took
place between Martini, then a young man, and
the older Tommaso Redi of Siena as to the
proper solution of a Canon of Animuccia's,
which required the use of two clefs in one part
to avoid leger - lines. Martini appealed to
Pacchioni and Pitoni, who both decided in his
favour.                                J. R. M.

PACE, ANTONIO, CAVALIERE (*b. circa* 1544 ;
*d.* Florence, 1579), composed 2 books of madrigals *a* 6 v. ; his first printed compositions published 1577. (See *Q.-L.*)

PACE (PACIUS), PIETRO, described as of
Loreto, was, about 1597, organist at Pesaro,

and afterwards, about 1613, organist at the
Santa Casa of Loreto. His works belong to the
period of transition from the polyphonic vocal
style to the solo and dialogue style with instrumental accompaniment inaugurated by VIA-
DANA. As enumerated in *Q.-L.*, they consist of
nine books of motets (some books missing and
others imperfectly preserved), for one to six
voices, all provided with Bassus Generalis for
organ, and several books of madrigals and ' Arie
spirituali ' for one to seven voices, partly with
and partly without accompaniment. Commer
reprinted two Magnificats by Pacius *a* 4 (tom.
i. and viii.) from Kaufmann's collection of
1600.                                J. R. M.

PACELLI, ASPRILIO (*b.* Varciano, near Narni,
Umbria, *c.* 1570 ; *d.* Warsaw, May 4, 1623),
was at first choirmaster to the German College
at Rome, and afterwards for a time at the Vatican Basilica. In 1603 he accepted an invitation from the music-loving King of Poland,
Sigismund III., to preside over the Royal
Chapel at Warsaw, where he remained till his
death. The Royal Chapel at Warsaw was then
one of the best appointed in Europe, as Sigismund, fanatically anxious to re-establish the
strictest Romanism in his dominions even at
the cost of civil war, spared neither trouble nor
expense in the engagement of the best Italian
singers and musicians to restore the Roman form
of worship to its former splendour. He had
previously engaged Luca Marenzio [2] as his choirmaster at what was then the magnificent salary
of 1000 ducats. To Pacelli Sigismund showed
the special distinction of erecting to him a
monument with bust and laudatory epitaph [3] in
one of the chapels of the cathedral of Warsaw.
Pacelli's publications are one book of psalms
and motets, *a* 8 (Rome, 1597) ; one book, ditto,
*a* 4 (1599) ; Sacrae cantiones, *a* 5-20 (Venice,
1608) ; one book of madrigals, *a* 4 (Venice,
1601). The volume of 1608 no doubt shows the
brilliant style of polychoric music that was then
so much in favour at Warsaw as elsewhere.
The ' Promptuarium ' of Schadaeus, 1611, contains ten motets of Pacelli *a* 6-8, and Bodenschatz's ' Florilegium,' 1621, 3 *a* 8. Ambros
gives high praise to a motet for eight voices,
' Factum est silentium,' in Constantini's collection, 1614.                                J. R. M.

PACHELBEL, (1) JOHANN (*b.* Nuremberg,
1653 [4] ; *d.* there, Mar. 3, [5] 1706), received
his first instruction in music from Heinrich
Schwemmer, and subsequently at the university of Altdorf for one year, undertaking duties
as organist at the same time. In 1668 or 1669
he went to Ratisbon to the ' Gymnasium poeti-

---

[1] See Baini, *Palestrina*, tom. i. note 195 on p. 120.

[2] Eitner throws doubt on Marenzio ever having accepted the
post, on account of the difficulty, arising from bibliographical considerations, of fixing the period of his residence in Poland. But
see Haberl, *Kirchenmusikalisches Jahrbuch*, 1900, pp. 94-6.
[3] For the terms of this epitaph see *Kirchenmusik. Jahrb.*, 1890,
p. 76.
[4] Baptized in the Lorenzkirche at Nuremberg, Sept. 1, 1653.
[5] Or Mar. 6 or 7. Compare the statements of Sandberger with
those of Eitner on this point.

cum,' and in 1671 or 1672 to Vienna, where, from 1673 onwards, he was a pupil of J. Kaspar Kerl, and apparently acted as his deputy as organist for him in the Imperial chapel. (See *Q.-L.*) In 1677 he was appointed court organist at Eisenach, and in May of the following year went to Erfurt to be organist of the Prediger-kirche. In 1690–92 he was court organist at Stuttgart (in the latter year he was offered an organist's place at Oxford) and in 1692–95 at Gotha, after which period he was appointed to the Sebalduskirche in Nuremberg. Pachelbel's importance in the history of music is due to the fact that he was one of the spiritual an-cestors of Sebastian Bach.[1] His special line of composition was in the highly elaborate varying of chorales, four of which were comprised in his 'Musikalische Sterbens-Gedancken' (1683); the 'Erster Theil etlicher *Chorale* welche bey währenden Gottes Dienst zum präambuliren gebraucht werden können,' etc., appeared in 1693, 'Musikalische Ergötzen,' six suites for two violins, in 1691 ; and his most notable work, the 'Hexachordum Apollinis,' six sets of variations on different kinds of airs, in 1699. Many suites and other works were preserved in MS., and some were reprinted in German collections before 1901, when the *D.T.Ö.* contained a volume (VIII. ii.) of ninety-four fugues on the Magnificat, edited by H. Botstiber and Max Seiffert, and shortly after-wards the 'Hexachordum Apollinis ' and many other things were edited by A. Sandberger in the *D.T.B.* II. i. This latter contained also specimens of the work of W. H. Pacheibel (2), and the two composers were associated again in Max Seiffert's edition of their organ works (*D.T.B.* IV. i.). The editor last mentioned contributed an interesting article, with some additional chorales, to the *Sammelbände* of the Int. Mus. Ges. vol. v. p. 476. Mattheson's *Ehrenpforte* contains the earliest notice of Pachelbel's life and career, and in the preface to the volume of the *D.T.B.* containing the 'Hexachordum' is an elaborate critical bio-graphy by Sandberger. His son,

(2) WILHELM HIERONYMUS (*b.* Erfurt c. 1685; *d.* ? 1764 [2]), was almost an exact contemporary of Sebastian Bach. He was his father's pupil, became organist at Wöhrd, near Nuremberg, and in 1706 was appointed to one of the churches at Nuremberg. Mattheson gives it as the S. Jakobi-kirche, but in the title of Pachelbel's single publication it is called the Sebalduskirche, and it is probable that he succeeded to his father's post there. The book is called 'Musicalisches Vergnügen bestehend in einem Preludio, Fuga und Fan-tasia,' etc. (for organ or harpsichord), and ap-peared in 1725. Besides MS. compositions in various libraries, there are, in accessible edi-

1 See Spitta, *J. S. Bach* (Engl. transl.), i. 107-25, etc.
2 The date of death is stated in *Q.-L.* to be unknown, but Seiffert (*D.T.B.* IV. i.) gives it as 1764.

tions, a few pieces for organ or harpsichord included in the *D.T.B.* volumes above re-ferred to. A prelude in B minor, formerly attri-buted to W. H. Pachelbel, is now considered to be by J. S. Bach, and was published in the B.-G. vol. xlii. p. 211. It is discussed by Spitta, *J. S. Bach* (orig. edn. i. 797).     M.

PACHMANN, VLADIMIR DE (*b.* Odessa, July 27, 1848), celebrated pianist and outstanding exponent of Chopin's works.

His father was a professor in the university there, and an amateur violinist of considerable celebrity. Before taking up his residence in Russia, he had lived in Vienna, where he came in contact frequently with Beethoven, Weber and other great musicians of the time. He was his son's teacher, and ultimately sent him, at the age of 18, to the Conservatorium of Vienna, where he remained two years under Dachs. He obtained the gold medal, and re-turned to Russia in 1869, when he made his first appearance as a pianist, giving a series of concerts which were very successful, although the young artist was not contented with his own performances. He refused to appear again for eight years, during which time he engaged in hard study. At the end of this long period of probation he played at Leipzig, Berlin and elsewhere, but again he was his own severest critic, and after a time he once more retired for two years. Being at last satisfied with his own achievements, he gave three concerts in Vienna, and subsequently three in Paris, and was uni-formly successful. On May 20, 1882, he ap-peared in London at one of Ganz's orchestral concerts, playing the E♭ concerto of Beethoven, and achieving a brilliant success. Since this time he has occupied a very high position in the estimation of musicians and the public. He has played in all the principal cities of Europe and America, and when in Copenhagen received the rank of Chevalier of the illustrious order of Dannebrog. Although his individuality is too strong and too little under control to allow of his being considered a perfect player of con-certed music, and in spite of many eccentricities of manner which do not diminish as time goes on, yet as a solo player, more especially of the works of Chopin, he is justly admired.     M.

PACINI, GIOVANNI (*b.* Catania, Feb. 17, 1796; *d.* Pescia, Dec. 6, 1867). Being the son of a celebrated tenor, he was trained to the musical profession from his childhood. He studied under Marchesi in Bologna, and afterwards, from 1808–12, was a pupil of Furlanetto in Venice.

In 1813, when only 16 years old, he wrote his first opera, 'Annetta e Lucinda,' for the theatre S. Redegonda, in Milan ; and from that year until 1834 he produced at the principal theatres of Italy forty-two operas with various success. Those which met the warmest approval were 'La Sacerdotessa d' Irminsul ' (Trieste,

1817); 'Cesare in Egitto' (Rome, 1822);
'L' ultimo giorno di Pompei' (1825); 'Niobe'
(S. Carlo, Naples, 1826); and 'Gli Arabi
nelle Gallie' (Scala, Milan, 1827). In 1834,
on the failure of his 'Carlo di Borgogna'
at the Fenice in Venice, he went to live at
Viareggio, where he opened a school of music.
He had already been appointed Kapellmeister to
the Empress Marie Louise, widow of Napoleon I.,
and had married in 1825 Adelaide Castelli, of
Naples. His school, for which he also built a
theatre seating 800 spectators, met with great
success, and pupils flocked there from all parts
of Italy. For these he wrote a *Corso teoretico-
prattico di lezioni di armonia, Cenni storici sulla
musica e trattato di contrappunto* (publ. 1864); a
*Memoria sul migliore indirizzo degli studi musi-
cali* had appeared in 1863, and his autobiography, *Memorie artistiche*, in 1865 (finished by
Cicconetti and publ. 1872). He afterwards
transferred his school to the town of Lucca.

In 1840 he produced in Naples his best opera,
'Saffo,' which met with a great and well-deserved success, notwithstanding it had been
written in the short period of four weeks. In
1843 his 'Medea' was enthusiastically received
in Palermo, and the Sicilians there and then
went so far as to erect a statue to him by the
side of that of Bellini in the Royal Villa. 'La
Regina di Cipro,' given in 1846 at Turin, and
'Niccolò de' Lapi,' a posthumous opera given in
Florence in 1873, are also amongst his best.

Pacini was thrice married, and by each of his
wives had three children, five of whom survived
him. His son, EMILIO (*b. circa* 1810; *d.* Neu-
illy, Dec. 2, 1898), was the librettist of 'Il
Trovatore.' Giovanni was musical director
of the musical school of Florence, and was a
knight of half-a-dozen continental orders. In
1854 he went to Paris to superintend the representations of his 'Arabi nelle Gallie,' under the
new title of 'L' ultimo de' Clodovei,' and there
wrote a cantata for Napoleon III., who had
applauded that same opera twenty-seven years
previously in Rome.

Pacini wrote altogether ninety operas, of
which several are still unpublished, and more
than seventy other compositions, such as
masses, oratorios and cantatas, which do not
call for particular mention, if we except a beautiful quartet in C and the cantata for a Dante
Centenary.

Pacini, though a successful imitator of Rossi-
ini, was still an imitator; and for that reason
he can rank only among the minor masters of
Italy. He tried in 'Saffo' to free himself from
the yoke, but it was too late, nor was he altogether successful. He was called *il maestro
delle cabalette* by his contemporaries; and the
immense number of cabalettas which he wrote,
their beauty and endless variety, show plainly
how well he deserved that appellation. He
made even his recitatives melodic, and was

accustomed to use his accompaniments for
strengthening the voices, by merely making
them sustain the upper part. His instrumentation is consequently very weak. All his
operas were written hastily; and, as he himself avows in his letters, without much study or
reflection. One of Pacini's great merits was
that he devoted himself to his vocal parts; he
always suited them to the capabilities of his
executants, and thus ensured at least the temporary success of his works.          L. R.

PACIOTTI, PIETRO PAOLO, a Roman musi-
cian of the 16th century, of whose life all that is
known is that he was in 1591 choirmaster of
the Seminario Romano. Of his works there
was published in 1591 a Book of Masses (which,
however, on the title-page is described as a republication 'nunc denuo in lucem editus'), containing three masses and two separate Credos *a*
4 and two masses *a* 5. One of the masses *a* 5
entitled 'Si bona suscepimus' was republished
by Proske with some prefatory words of high
commendation in his 'Selectus novus missarum,' 1861. It may be remarked that the
leading theme of this Mass, which recurs in all
the movements, is identical with the opening
theme of a motet *a* 5 by Orlando Lassus, on the
text 'Si bona suscepimus,' first published in
1571, but the resemblance does not extend
further. Paciotti's other publications are a
book of motets *a* 5 (Rome, 1601) containing
thirty-four numbers, and a book of madrigals
*a* 6 (Venice, 1582) incompletely preserved.
                                       J. R. M.

PACIUS, see PACE, PIETRO.

PACK, CAPTAIN HENRY, a late 17th-century
English song composer. Some of his songs are
in Playford's 'Choice Ayres' (1675, 1679), 'The
Theatre of Music' (1685) (probably the only
instance where his Christian name is given).
Two of his songs are in B.M. Add. MS. 19,759,
one in Add. MSS. 29,397. The song, 'Tell me,
Thyrsis,' printed at the end of Dryden and
Lee's 'Duke of Guise,' was very popular, and
was several times reprinted.          E. V. D. S.

PACKE, SIR THOMAS, an English composer of
church music of the 15th or early 16th century,
some of whose work is in the British Museum
(Add. MSS. 5665). This is a MS. of Henry
VIII.'s time, which once belonged to Joseph
Ritson; examples from it are given in his
'Ancient Songs' (1790), and some others in
J. Stafford Smith's 'Musica antiqua' (1812).
Packe's setting of the Te Deum (one of the very
earliest on record in England) is peculiar. The
words 'Te deum laudamus' are first sung by a
solo voice and are immediately followed by a
5-part chorus singing the 'Te Dominum confitemur.' When the Te Deum proper begins
(set to the English text but with Latin words
occasionally introduced), the verses are sung
by three solo voices, with the refrain 'Te
Dominum confitemur' repeated by the chorus

after each verse. For the verses in the latter half, an alternative setting for solo voice is given.

Missa *a* 3, ' Gaudete.'  B.M. Add. MSS. 5665/84*b*.
Missa *a* 3, ' Rex summe.'  B.M. Add. MSS. 5665/73*b*.
T.D.  B.M. Add. MSS. 5665/95*b*-106.

MOTETS
Gaude sancta Magdalena *a* 3.  B.M. Add. MSS. 5665/112*b*.
Lumen ad revelacionem *a* 5, ' from the Nunc Dimittis.'  B.M. Add. MSS. 5665/62*b*-63*b*.
Secundum verbum tuum *a* 5, ' from the Nunc Dimittis.'  B.M. Add. MSS. 5665/62*b*-63*b*.

J. M<sup>K</sup>.

PADBRUÉ, CORNELIS THYMONS (THYMONS-SON), (mid-17th cent.), singing master, etc. of Harlem, composed ' Kusjes ' (Little Kisses), songs *a* 3, 4 and 5 v. 2nd edition, 1641 ; ' 'I Sof van Jubal ' (the prayse of Jubal), put into Latin verse by various poets, *a* 4, 5 and 6 v. with basso continuo, 1643 ; second book, op. 4, 3-6 v. 1645 ; also various occasional ' symphonias,' etc. (See *Q.-L.*)

PADEREWSKI, IGNAZ JAN (*b.* Kurylówka, Podolia, Poland, Nov. 6, 1860), eminent pianist and composer, was at first a pupil of Raguski at the Warsaw Conservatorium. He went on his first concert-tour in 1876–77, and was in 1879–1881 teacher of the pianoforte at the Warsaw Conservatorium. He went next to Berlin, where he studied under Urban and Wüerst, and finally to Leschetizky at Vienna in 1884. After a short time as professor in the Conservatorium of Strassburg, he went again to Leschetizky, and from 1887 onwards, from the time of his débuts in Vienna and Paris, his career has been one continued triumph.

In May 1890 he visited London and gave a series of pianoforte recitals in St. James's Hall, being previously known in England only as the composer of the popular Minuet in G. In 1891 he toured in America, gave his first concert there in Carnegie Hall, New York, on Nov. 17, undertook in all 117 concerts, and repeated his visits in 1892–93, 1895–96, 1900–01, 1901–02, 1907–08, 1913–14, 1915–16. After the tour of 1895–96 he founded the PADEREWSKI FUND (*q.v.*). In Europe he continued to play always with the utmost success, and paid periodic visits to England up to 1914. Meantime his position as a composer was established by his opera ' Manru ' (3 acts), given with great success at Dresden (May 29, 1901) and at the Metropolitan Opera House, New York (Feb. 14, 1902). His symphony in B minor, played by the Boston Symphony Orchestra under Max Fiedler (Feb. 12, 1909), and in London under Richter (Nov. 9, 1909), was another important landmark in his career. It, like the earlier piano concerto, as well as several minor works, showed the strength of the composer's national enthusiasm in the handling of Polish themes and his welding of them into symphonic design.

His style of pianoforte technique was something quite new at the time of his first appearance ; his tone in loud passages was often forced, but his position was secured by the gentler qualities in his art, by exquisite gradation of tone in the softer parts, by the glittering brilliance of his execution, by the wonderful originality of his readings and the ardour of his temperament. The estimate of him as a pianist of outstanding ability who appealed to the imagination of the crowd as much by his romantic bearing and appearance (particularly the aureole of red-gold hair) as by his purely musical gifts was proved to be inadequate by the events of later years. Paderewski's patriotism was of a tougher texture than that of the artist who idealises his country in song or symphonic poem or who in a time of stress is ready to devote his gifts to raising funds for charitable purposes. He had done both. Early in the war (1914–18) he raised large sums for the Polish Victims Relief Fund by his performances in America ; but as soon as the time was ripe he abandoned his artistic career, returned to Poland, headed the national party and was elected first President of the Polish Republic (1919). His personal qualities enabled him to unify contending political parties under his inspiring leadership and in a short time he accomplished an unique work in the founding of the Republic. Nothing showed his greatness of vision more completely than the fact that here too he was ready to sink personal considerations, and he relinquished office as soon as his work was done. He retired in 1920, returned to his music, and in 1923 gave recitals first in America and then in England. His renewed performance has been the subject of some criticism on the ground of his freedom of *tempo* and disregard of interpretative tradition, but it is that of a commanding personality and a great mind. His generosity in devoting the proceeds of his work to post-war charities has been conspicuous, and after a series of recitals given for the British Legion (1925) he was created Knight Commander of the British Empire.

Paderewski's compositions include the following :

Op.
1. Deux Morceaux, Prelude and Minuet.
4. Élégie.
5. 3 Danses polonaises.
6. Introduction et Toccata.
7. Four Songs.
8. Chants du voyageur.
9. 6 Danses polonaises.
10. Album de Mai, scènes romantiques (5).
11. Variations et Fugue.
12. Tatra-Album, Polish dances and songs, for pf. 4-hands.
13. Sonata for pf. and violin.
14. 6 Humoresques de Concert (Menuet en Sol, Sarabande, Caprice genre Scarlatti, Burlesque, Intermezzo Pollaco, Cracovienne fantastique), pf.
15. Dans le désert, toccata, pf.
16. 4 Morceaux (Légende, Mélodie, Thème varié (in A), and Nocturne (in B flat), pf.
17. Concerto for piano and orchestra in A minor.
18. Songs to words by Mickiewicz.
19. Fantaisie polonaise, for piano and orchestra.
20. Légende, No. 2, pf.
21. Sonata for pf. in E flat minor.
22.
23. Variations and Fugue for pf.
24. Symphony in B minor.

Minuet in A.
Opera in three acts, libretto by Alfred Nossig. ' Manru.'
Opera, libretto by Catulle Mendès, ' Sakuntala.'

The beautiful drawing of him by Burne Jones has been photographed and otherwise reproduced. H.R.H. Princess Louise, Duchess of Argyll, and Sir L. Alma-Tadema, R.A., painted remarkable portraits of him. M.; addns. C.

BIBL.—ALFRED NOSSIG, *Paderewski*; E. A. BAUGHAN, *Paderewski*; H. FINCK, *Paderewski and his Art.*

PADEREWSKI FUND, THE, was established by I. J. Paderewski by a deed of trust, dated May 15, 1900, transferring to Henry L. Higginson and William P. Blake, of Boston, as trustees, a sum of $10,000 to be held as a permanent trust fund for the purpose of aiding musical education in the United States of America, and especially for the encouragement and support of American composers. The terms of the trust provide that once in three years the trustees shall offer prizes from the income in hand for the best compositions submitted by native-born American composers, the awards to be made by a board of judges, three or more, selected by Paderewski or the trustees. The first competition was held in 1902, when three prizes of $500 each were awarded as follows: (1) to Henry K. Hadley for a symphony ('The Seasons'); (2) to Horatio W. Parker for a composition for chorus, solos and orchestra ('A Star Song'); (3) to Arthur Bird for a sextet for wind instruments. H. E. K.

PADILLA-Y-RAMOS, MARIANO (*b.* Murcia, 1842; *d.* Nov. 1906), a Spanish baritone singer who married Desirée ARTÔT (*q.v.*).

He studied under Mabellini in Florence and sang in Italian opera in most European countries. His appearances in England were comparatively few. His first was on Oct. 1, 1881, when he sang the part of Hoel in 'Dinorah' with success. He played in 1886 in the short season at Her Majesty's and in the autumn with Mapleson's company in the provinces. In 1887 he was at Covent Garden. In the same year he sang at Prague in the centenary performance of 'Don Giovanni.'

PADLOCK, THE, a notable English opera, produced at Covent Garden in 1768. The libretto was written by Isaac Bickerstaffe, the author of other successful pieces of a similar kind, who founded it upon Cervantes's 'Jealous Husband.' Charles Dibdin wrote the whole of the music, and it was his first important work. He also took the character of Mungo, the black servant. Bannister, Vernon, Mrs. Dorman and Mrs. Arne were the other principals. Its original run was fifty-three nights, and the music was issued in oblong folio, with a dedication to Mrs. Garrick. In this dedication, Dibdin alludes to the rumours, then current, that the music was the work of an Italian master, which he indignantly refutes.

For a great number of years 'The Padlock' held the boards of country theatres, and Mungo's philosophic sayings were general stock quotations. F. K.

PADUA. The first musical academy at Padua was that of the 'Costanti,' founded in 1566 by the nobles of the city. It embraced, besides music, natural philosophy, ethics, oratory, poetry and languages. The first president was Francesco Portenari. But that the science of music must have been studied far earlier in the ancient Paduan university appears from the writings of Marchetto di Padova, which date between the years 1274 and 1309. Prosdocimus de Beldemandis, the musical theorist, was also a native of Padua. He was Professor of Astrology there in 1422, with a stipend of forty silver ducats annually. His works on music are still preserved in the library at Padua (see Burney, *Hist.* ii. 350). Padua probably gave its name to the ancient dance Paduan, or PAVAN (*q.v.*). C. M. P.

BIBL.—BRUNO BRUNELLI: *I teatri di Padova dalle origini alla fine del secolo XIX.* (Padua, 1921.)

PAËR, FERDINANDO (*b.* Parma, June 1, 1771; *d.* Paris, May 3, 1839), Italian opera composer, studied under Gasparo Ghiretti at Parma.

At 20 he became maestro di cappella at Venice, and there composed industriously, though leading a gay and dissolute life. His operas were not all equally successful, but they made his name known beyond Italy, and in 1798 he received an invitation to Vienna, whither he went with his wife, a singer named Riccardi, who was engaged at the Italian Opera. The most celebrated of the operas which he composed for the national theatre, and indeed his best work, was 'Camilla, ossia il Sotteraneo' (1801). In 1803 he went to Dresden as Kapellmeister, remaining, except for occasional tours and visits to Vienna and Italy, till 1806. Here he composed 'Sargino, ossia l' Allievo dell' amore' (1803), and 'Eleonora, ossia l' Amore conjugale' (1804), the same subject which Beethoven has immortalised in 'Fidelio.' In 1806 Paër accompanied Napoleon to Warsaw and Posen, and in 1807 was formally installed as his maître de chapelle, and took up his abode in Paris. He composed the Bridal March for the Wedding of Napoleon with Josephine (Apr. 2, 1810). In 1812 he succeeded Spontini at the Italian Opera, to which he remained attached until 1827, in spite of many changes and disputes and of the pecuniary embarrassments which beset the theatre. He and Rossini were temporarily associated from 1824–26. During this period he produced but eight operas, including 'Agnese' (1811), and 'Le Maître de Chapelle' (1821), none of which were marked successes. In 1831 he became a member of the Académie, and in 1832 director of the king's chamber-music, as then reconstituted.

As a man Paër was not beloved; self-interest and egotism, servility to his superiors, and petty intrigues against his professional brethren, being faults commonly attributed to him. But as a composer he is one of the most important representatives of the Italian operatic school at the close of the 18th century. His invention is

flowing, his melody suave and pleasing, his form
correct, and in simple compositions finished,
although not developed to the fullest extent.
Like all the other Italian composers of his time
he had the gift of true comedy. In lyric expression he was also successful, as here his
Italian love of sweet sounds stood him in good
stead; but he was completely wanting in the
force and depth necessary for passionate, pathetic, or heroic music, and when such was required
he fell back upon common opera phrases
and stock passages. This is perhaps most
apparent in the operas composed after he left
Italy, when his acquaintance with German
music, especially that of Mozart, may have
influenced his style. His treatment of the
orchestra was original and remarkable, and his
instrumentation very effective. The partial
success only of the operas composed during his
stay in Paris is easily explained; he had not
sufficient means of expression to attempt French
opera, and in Italian opera he could not contend
with Rossini, whose genius, with its indifference
to the trammels of form, and its exuberant
melody, fairly captivated the public. Forty
operas are enumerated in Q.-L. Paër also composed much for church and chamber—oratorios
('Il santo sepolcro,' and 'La Passione'), masses,
motets, cantatas for one and more voices; also
instrumental music, a Bacchanalian symphony,
etc., now of historical interest only.    A. M.

PAESIELLO, GIOV., see PAISIELLO.

PAGANINI, NICCOLO (b. Genoa, Oct. 27,
1782; d. Nice, May 27, 1840), violinist, first
of virtuosi.

Paganini's father, Antonio, was connected
in a humble capacity with the large export
shipping interests of Genoa. He was a
musical enthusiast, played the mandoline with
skill, and gave his son rudimentary instruction
in violin-playing. The undue severity which
characterised the child's earliest training undoubtedly undermined his fragile constitution.
Had the future prince of violinists been endowed with less fervour for his art, the incidents of his home life might have cut short
his artistic career; but, fortunately, he was
imbued with a firm determination to become
an artist, and his mother nourished the resolve
by her frequent recital of a dream, wherein an
angel had promised her that her son should
become the greatest violinist in the world.
Paganini swiftly exhausted the slender paternal
musical knowledge, and was handed over to
Servetto, a violinist in the theatre orchestra,
and two years later became a pupil of Giacomo
Costa, maestro di cappella of the Cathedral of
St. Lorenzo. In 1793, at the age of 9, Paganini
made his début at a concert given by the
great singer Luigi Marchesi and the cantatrice
Madame Albertinotti at the principal theatre
of Genoa. He followed up this first appearance with a benefit concert, at which he was

assisted in return by the same two artists. On
both occasions he played his own variations
upon the French patriotic air, 'La Carmagnole,'
and roused his audience to a great degree of
enthusiasm. These early successes served to
strengthen his father's crafty zeal on his behalf,
and caused him to accept Costa's proposition
that the child should play a solo in church
every Sunday. In after life Paganini attached
much importance to the rigour of these weekly
performances, which enforced the constant
study of new works. While under Costa's
tuition the boy made the acquaintance of
Francesco Gnecco, a distinguished operatic
composer of the day, to whom he was indebted
for much valuable advice.

At length the time arrived when, in turn,
Costa's teaching became inadequate, and
Paganini's father decided to take his son to
Alessandro Rolla, a celebrated violinist, conductor and composer then residing at Parma.
The following advertisement, printed and circulated together with the play-bills of coming
performances, gives a clue to the manner in
which the funds were raised for the journey:

'July 25, 1795, Niccolo Paganini of Genoa, a boy
already known to his country for his skill in handling
the violin, having determined to study at Parma to
improve his talents under the direction of the renowned Signor Rolla, but lacking the means to do
so, has adopted this plan, and has taken courage to
beg his compatriots to contribute towards this object,
inviting them to come to this entertainment for his
benefit.'

The concert proving remunerative, Antonio
Paganini and his son accordingly travelled to
Parma, and, upon their arrival, presented
themselves at Rolla's residence. They found
him ill in bed, and pending his wife's inquiry
as to whether he would see them they were
ushered into an adjoining room. On a table
lay a violin and the composer's latest concerto.
At a command from his father Niccolo took
up the instrument and played the music at
sight with such wonderful precision that Rolla
forgot his indisposition, and, raising himself
in bed, eagerly demanded the name of the
professor he had just heard. ''Tis a child,'
was the reply. But he would not believe this
until Paganini was brought to him. 'I can
teach you nothing,' he is reported to have said,
and advised the father to take his son to Paër,
for instruction in composition. However, Rolla
did teach Paganini for several months; and
Paër being then in Germany the boy went to
Paër's master, Ghiretti, and during six months
received three lessons a week from him. He
composed twenty-four fugues, unaided by any
musical instrument, and devoted much labour
to the study of instrumentation. This excellent knowledge of various instruments stood
him in good stead some years later, when a
wealthy Swedish amateur relieved Paganini's
poverty by rewarding him handsomely for a
set of compositions for his favourite instrument,

the bassoon. He had complained that he could find nothing difficult enough for his ambitious talent, and the great virtuoso at once cleverly supplied the need.

At the beginning of the year 1797 Paganini quitted Parma, and, accompanied by his father, made his first professional tour. He visited all the principal towns in Lombardy, and at each successive appearance enhanced his growing reputation. On his return to Genoa, he wrote his first compositions for the violin (this is not counting the lost work, which he composed at the age of 9), and filled his music with such novel technical difficulties that he was himself compelled to study certain passages with assiduity. He was now almost 14, and, looking back on a childhood of ceaseless labour, he resolved to strike for freedom. The opportunity arrived with the annual musical fête celebrated on St. Martin's day at Lucca. He entreated his father to allow him to go thither with his elder brother. The consent was at first withheld, but in the end he prevailed, and set forth upon his journey. Lucca hailed the young artist's efforts with such unanimous applause that he extended his travels to Pisa and the neighbouring towns.

At last, released from home restraint, and with but small knowledge of the world, Paganini's nature became prone to welcome every form of licence, and to mistake licence for independence. On one occasion his losses at cards reduced him to the extremity of pawning his violin. In this condition he arrived at Leghorn to fulfil an engagement, and was at his wits' end how to procure an instrument, when the kindness of a French merchant— Livron—relieved him of his difficulty, by lending him a fine Joseph Guarnerius. After the concert Paganini essayed to return the instrument to its owner, but nothing would induce the amateur to accept it. ' No,' he said ; ' my hands shall never profane the violin which your fingers have touched ; the instrument belongs to you.' Paganini, on a later occasion, gained another violin—a Stradivarius—from Pasini the painter for his easy accomplishment of the artist's challenge to play a certain difficult concerto at sight, but the Guarnerius was ever his most cherished possession.

At this time Paganini's career was chequered by many adventures. Art — love affairs — gambling—interrupted by long intervals of utter exhaustion, filled his life and put a severe strain upon his fragile constitution. At length an event happened which effectually cured him of his gambling propensities. A certain Prince had for some time coveted Paganini's Guarnerius violin, and, coming upon the virtuoso in great poverty, offered him 2000 francs for it. Paganini was sorely tempted to accept the offer, being inconveniently pressed by a debt of honour, but, as a last resource, resolved to risk

his only available funds—thirty francs—at the gaming-table. After reducing the original sum to the perilous amount of three francs, fortune turned in his favour, and he won 160 francs. From that day he ceased to gamble, being convinced, as he said, ' that a gamester is an object of contempt to all well-regulated minds.'

From 1801–04 Paganini resided at the Château of a lady of rank in Tuscany. During the absorption of this love affair he ceased to play in public, and devoted himself to the study of the guitar, for which he composed two sets of duets (opp. 2, 3), with violin. In after years the period of this amorous adventure was selected to give credence to sensational stories of his supposed imprisonment. Not until his arrival in Vienna in 1828 did he publicly challenge the calumny by issuing a manifesto, which was inserted in the leading Viennese journals, in Italian and German, on Apr. 10. In spite of this, his detractors continued to circulate rumours concerning his league with the devil, and similar fancies ; these followed him, and were repeated about him wherever he went. In Paris in 1830 he was greatly mortified by the sight of a picture of himself which depicted him in prison. Again he wrote a full statement, which was published in the *Revue musicale*, in which he proved that the mistake was caused by the confusion of his name with a violinist called Durawoski, who had been arrested for conspiring to murder a wealthy priest.

In 1804 Paganini's love for the violin was reawakened by an acquaintance with Locatelli's studies for the violin, and his ' Arte di nuova modulazione.' He returned to Genoa, applied himself to assiduous study, and composed his two sets (opp. 4, 5) of three quartets, for violin, viola, guitar and violoncello, as well as a set of bravura variations for violin, with guitar accompaniment. In 1805 Paganini resumed his public appearances in Italy, everywhere creating a *furore*. In March of this year Napoleon's sister—Elisa Bacecocchi, Princess of Lucca and Piombo—invited him to her court, and, in spite of his vow that he would ever remain unfettered by any regular post, induced him to accept that of director of her private music. She also conferred the rank of Captain of the Royal Bodyguard upon him, so that he might be admitted to all the court functions, and made him conductor of the Opera orchestra. The emoluments granted him at the court were so scanty that inference suggests sentimental reasons for his temporary resignation of the roving life he delighted in. While at the Piombo Court an ' affair ' with a lady of rank whom he dared not approach publicly induced him to write his ' Scène amoureuse,' for two strings only. The lady was excessively touched with his performance, and ' the Princess,' says Paganini,

TARTINI

From an engraving by C. Calcinoto

PAGANINI

From a water-colour by D. Maclise, R.A., in the Victoria and Albert Museum

lauded me up to the skies; and then said in her most gracious manner: " You have just performed impossibilities on two strings; would not a single string suffice for your talent ? " I promised to make the attempt. The idea delighted me, and some weeks after I composed my military Sonata for the G string entitled " Napoleon," which I performed on Aug. 25, before a numerous and brilliant court audience.'

Such a successful first attempt led to further developments of the original idea, until, by unremitting study, and the employment of the harmonic tones, Paganini succeeded in extending the compass of the fourth string to three octaves. In 1808 Paganini obtained his Royal mistress's permission to travel again, and, after seven years' absence, revisited Leghorn, the scene of his former triumphs. For some unaccountable reason he was at first received with coldness. He himself has humorously related how, at the first concert, owing to his having run a nail into his heel, he came limping on to the stage, at which the audience laughed. At the moment he began to play both the candles fell out of his music desk—another laugh. A string breaking after the first few bars of his solo caused more hilarity. But, when he was seen to continue steadily, and play the piece upon *three* strings, the sarcastic ridicule of the audience was quickly transformed into wild applause. Paganini has often been accused of purposely using frayed strings, so that their effective snapping might show up his extraordinary powers in a more sensational manner. The strong vein of charlatanism which pervaded his mighty genius probably induced him to resort to this trick. ' Paganini,' says Sir Thomas Moore in his *Memories*,

' abuses his powers; he *could* play divinely, and *does* so sometimes for a minute or two; but then come his tricks and surprises, his bow in convulsions, and his enharmonics like the mewlings of an expiring cat.'

About the beginning of the year 1813 Paganini severed the ties which bound him to the service of the Princess Elisa. The court had been transferred to Florence in 1809—the Princess assuming the title of Grand Duchess of Tuscany; and it was in that year that Bartollino executed his famous bust of the virtuoso. At Bologna, in October of the same year, he made the acquaintance of Rossini, then on his way to Milan to write his opera ' Il Turco in Italia '; and on the 29th of the same month Paganini's marvellous achievements at a concert in Milan first made him renowned beyond Italy. He grew much attached to Milan, and gave no less than thirty-seven concerts there; eleven took place alternately at La Scala and at the Teatro Caraccino; and the rest, in the beginning of the year 1814, at the Teatro Rè. In 1814, after returning to Romagna and giving some concerts there, he was prostrated for several months at Ancona by the internal malady which had first attacked

him at Turin in 1808. While in Venice in 1815 he first met Antonia Bianchi, the dancer, whose career was afterwards destined to be so closely allied with his. Writing to his friend, L. G. Germi, the lawyer, who managed the violinist's financial affairs for him, he says,

' I was not a little enamoured of the Signora at Venice, but letters reached me with such reports about her conduct that I can no longer think of speaking to her.'

However, Paganini soon overcame his scruples, and Antonia Bianchi kept jealous guard over him for many years. Two years later (1816) he revisited Milan, anxious to hear the French violinist Lafont, who was giving concerts in that city. A certain measure of artistic rivalry sprang up between the two, and Lafont persuaded Paganini to give a concert at La Scala in conjunction with himself. Paganini placed the arrangement of the programme in the French violinist's hands. In recounting the event, Paganini has modestly remarked,

' Lafont probably surpassed me in tone, but the applause which followed my efforts convinced me that I did not suffer by comparison.'

A similar rivalry existed at a later date between the Polish violinist Lipinski and himself.

FROM VIENNA TO PARIS.—While at Rome in 1817 Paganini met the Austrian Ambassador, Count Metternich, who invited him to come to Vienna. The weak state of his health, however, proved an obstacle to his plans, and the wished-for journey to the north was deferred from time to time. In 1823 a more than usually severe attack of his malady nearly killed him. In 1826 Paganini's son, Achillino, was born at Palermo, and two years later he separated from Antonia Bianchi, the mother of his child. After many years of devotion, this lady's jealous temper had become so violent that this step became necessary. He paid the Bianchi 2000 Milanese *scudi* for renouncing all rights to the child, and on Aug. 1, 1828, Bianchi left him for ever. On Mar. 29, Paganini gave his first concert in Vienna with prodigious success. All the Vienna newspapers teemed with unstinted praise of the virtuoso for two months. The public became absolutely intoxicated, a fever of admiration seized all classes of society. Hats, dresses, shawls, boots, perfumes, gloves, etc., appeared in the shop windows ' à la Paganini.' His portrait was displayed everywhere; his bust adorned the sticks of the Vienna dandies, and even dainty dishes were named after him. The Emperor conferred upon him the title of ' Virtuoso of the Court,' and the town presented him with the Gold Medal of St. Salvator. After his triumphs in the Austrian capital, Paganini started upon a tour in Germany, everywhere creating a sensation. At Cassel he gave two concerts at the theatre, which were attended with great interest by Spohr. The pure intonation sustained by Paganini throughout his entire performance astonished the German violinist, but he was not altogether satisfied, being alternately charmed by his genius and disappointed by the mixture of power and childish tastelessness which he displayed. The two virtuosi dined together, and Paganini's extravagant hilarity is said to have somewhat surprised the pedantic Spohr. Three years' journeyings in Austria, Bohemia, Saxony, Poland, Bavaria, Prussia, and the Rhenish provinces, terminated in Paris, 1831, where he gave his first concert at the Opera-House on Mar. 9. Here, again, wild enthusiasm greeted him, and he remained until May.

VISIT TO ENGLAND.—In that month he travelled to England, and made his début in London at the Opera-House on Friday, June 3. His appearance in London had been looked forward to on May 21, but owing to the newspapers severely censuring the high prices demanded for admission the concert was put off until the artist yielded to the voice of the public, and definitely announced his intention of charging the accustomed prices.[1] His English reception was full of warmth,[2] and even more curiosity was aroused by his personality in England than in other countries. He was annoyed by the 'excessive and noisy admiration' to which he was subjected. People followed him and mobbed him, and frequently got in front of him in such a manner as to prevent his going either way. They addressed him in English, of which he knew not a single word, and even felt him to see if he were really flesh and blood. The sensation he produced in London was fully sustained during his subsequent tour in the provinces, Scotland and Ireland. Speaking of the high fees demanded by the virtuoso, *The Constitution or Cork Advertiser* (Aug. 25, 1831) remarks :

'He h is been engaged by Sir George Smart at the Coronation, for which he is to receive 1000 guineas. The proprietors of Vauxhall Gardens offered him £1000 for three nights; the offer was refused, and when desired to name his terms his demand was £5000 for twelve nights.'

Paganini remained in England until June 1832. He gave a farewell [3] concert at the Victoria Theatre on the 17th of that month, and returned to his native country after an absence of six years, having made net profits which, in England alone, amounted to £16,000 or £17,000. The writer well remembers an old amateur who assisted at these concerts, concerning which the following punning rhyme was current :

'Who are these who pay five guineas,
To hear this tune of Paganini's ?
—Echo answers—"Pack o' ninnies." '

LAST YEARS. — He invested part of his

[1] See *The Times*, June 1, 1831.
[2] See accounts in the *Athenœum*, 1831.
[3] His last concert in England was at Portsmouth, Sept. 11, 1832.
W. H. G. F.

fortune in landed estates, purchasing, among other properties, the 'Villa Gajona' near Parma, where he decided to reside. Here he occupied himself with projects for the publication of his compositions. Unfortunately he set such a high price on his manuscripts that even the publisher Troupenas—who was accustomed to pay large sums to Rossini, Auber and other celebrated composers—could not come to terms with him. The winter of 1833 was passed in Paris, and it was early in Jan. 1834 that he invited Berlioz to write him a solo for his Stradivarius viola. From this request the symphony 'Harold en Italie' originated. It was performed for the first time at the Paris Conservatoire on Nov. 23, 1834, with Paganini as soloist. The following December the great artist was again in Italy, and on the 12th of that month played at the court of the Duchess of Parma, from whom he received the Imperial Order of St. George. Paganini now began to enjoy the fruits of his fortune and world-wide fame. In 1834–35 he played at rare intervals at charity concerts and for the relief of indigent artists. In 1836 he became involved in the finances of the 'Casino Paganini,' a gambling-house which was opened in Paris bearing his name. The Government refusing to grant an opening licence, the speculators were reduced to giving concerts to defray the expenses of the undertaking. The disastrous failure of the Casino cost Paganini 50,000 francs and such health as was left him. At the beginning of the year 1839 Paganini was in a dying state. Medical men advised him to remove to Marseilles, to which town he accordingly went. His wonderful energies struggled with his failing strength ; he seemed to revive, and one day performed his favourite Beethoven quartet with all his old energy. The renewed vigour was, however, but fleeting ; a restless yearning to return to his native town seized upon him, and he travelled thither, anticipating favourable results from the sea voyage. From Genoa he fled to Nice, where he intended to pass the winter in recruiting his health. But his hopes were vain, Nice was destined to be his last abode. His malady progressed rapidly, the voice became almost extinct, and a shocking cough racked his frail body. On the last night of his life he was unusually tranquil, and his final effort was to stretch forth his hands for the violin which had been the faithful companion of his travels. Listeners have declared that his improvisation during these last hours was the most remarkable feat of his whole life. He was 56 years of age when he died, the immediate cause of his death being a disease of the larynx. By his will, made on Apr. 27, 1837, and opened on June 1, 1840, he left his son Achillino—legitimised by process of law—a fortune estimated at two millions (£80,000 sterling). Out of this sum two legacies of fifty and sixty thousand francs were to be paid to Paganini's two sisters, and an annuity of 1200 francs to Antonia Bianchi. He requested that his burial should be without pomp. ' I desire that no musicians play a Requiem for me ; and I bequeath my violin [1] to the city of Genoa where it may be perpetually kept.' Independently of his wealth Paganini possessed some valuable instruments—a Stradivarius, a Guarnerius of the smaller pattern, an excellent Amati, a Stradivarius viola, and a bass of the same maker.

By reason of certain superstitious rumours concerning him, and of the fact that he died without receiving the last rites of the Church, permission to inter his body in consecrated ground was withheld until five years after his death. An inquiry having then been concluded with regard to Paganini's orthodoxy, his son, the Baron Achillino, defrayed the expenses of a solemn service to the memory of his father as ' Chevalier de St. George,' in the church of Steccata, belonging to that order of chivalry, in Parma. The body was finally laid in its last resting-place in the month of May 1845, in the village church adjoining Paganini's property, the Villa Gajona, near Parma.

PERSONAL CHARACTERISTICS.—The extraordinary dexterity of his playing was sustained by his concert appearances entirely. George Harrys—an *attaché* at the Hanoverian court, who acted as the virtuoso's secretary for a year—asserts that Paganini never touched his violin in private save to test or tune it. ' I have laboured enough to acquire my talent,' was the violinist's remark when questioned ; ' it is time I should rest myself.' Sleep was a never-failing source of delight to him, but in eating and drinking he was extremely frugal. The state of his health required the strictest diet, and if he started on a journey early in the morning he frequently fasted nearly the whole day. Ordinarily a basin of soup or a cup of chocolate constituted his breakfast, and a cup of camomile tea his supper.

For his son Achillino he cherished a tender affection, and many anecdotes of his wonderful patience and touching devotion to the child have been preserved. To his inferiors he was contemptuous and disdainful, and he was by no means subservient to people of rank and wealth. His tall skeleton figure, waxen narrow face, enshrined in long dark hair, usually provoked some ridicule, when he first appeared upon the platform, but a few bars of his sensational playing quickly won him the profound admiration of his audience. Sir Charles Hallé, who was introduced to Paganini in Paris, describes him as ' a striking, awe-inspiring figure,' most difficult to converse with. When he wished the young pianist to

play he indicated his desire by a movement of his long hand, but otherwise sat rigid and taciturn.

Few artists have ever aroused such a fund of gossiping scandal as did Paganini. His supposed present of 20,000 francs to his friend Berlioz on Dec. 18, 1838, astonished the world, for not the least of the accusations levelled against him was that of sordid avarice. As a matter of fact, the real donor was Armand Bertin, the wealthy proprietor of the *Journal des Débats*. Berlioz was a member of his staff ; he had a high regard for his talents, and was anxious to lighten his troubles. A certain delicacy of feeling suggested that such a gift would be more acceptable if offered as a tribute of admiration from one artist to another. He therefore persuaded Paganini to appear as the donor of this munificent gift. Only one or two of Bertin's friends were admitted into the secret, and Berlioz was always kept in ignorance of the true state of the matter.[2]

ARTISTIC ACHIEVEMENTS.—As an executant Paganini created the difficulties he performed. The disciple of no school, his concentration and perseverance alone produced the daring flights and brilliant technicalities which were destined to inaugurate the epoch of virtuosity. Before Paganini artists had not discovered the utility of harmonics. Viotti, Rode, Kreutzer, employed natural harmonics for isolated effects, but the advantages of the stopped harmonic of every tone and half-tone on the violin remained unknown. It was these sounds that Paganini developed to such a remarkable degree. He alone estimated their varied functions : (1) in extending the compass of the violin ; (2) in adding charm and brilliance; (3) in the execution of high passages in double notes formerly reckoned to be impossible. The novelty of these effects, the facility with which he executed them, the sensational, though often exaggerated, expression he put into them, combined with his varied staccato and pizzicato passages, were the qualities which threw the whole of musical Europe into a paroxysm of wonder and admiration. His inventive talent also augmented his art. For instance, his diverse modes of tuning his violin had been employed in the early part of the 17th century by Biber (see BIBER ; SCORDATURA), and the familiar custom of playing a melody on one string and an accompaniment upon another was developed by him into a variety of left-hand pizzicato accompaniments. But the combined pizzicato and arco runs, the chromatic slides with one finger, and the guitar effects, employed by later violinists, especially by Sarasate, were originated by Paganini. The quality of tone which he produced, even in the swiftest passages, was true and pure, but it lacked the richness so characteristic of Spohr or Baillot, and was wanting in tenderness. His excellences

[1] The Guarnerius, preserved in the Sala Rossa of the Municipal Palace at Genoa.

[2] See *Life and Letters of Ch. Hallé* (1896).

in fact consisted in a combination of mechanical perfection, daring originality, and striking individuality. Outside his own particular *genre* he was unsuccessful. His performance of a concerto by Kreutzer in Paris scarcely rose above mediocrity, but in his own 'Witches' Dance ' (' Le Streghe '), the prayer from 'Mosé' on the G string, or the variations on ' Di tanti palpiti,' etc., which were in accordance with his own peculiar style, he never failed to arouse the enthusiasm of his audience. Paganini's care in guarding the secrets of his discoveries made him withhold the publication of his compositions, and to be excessively wary of imparting his art to others. But sometimes caprice led him to interest himself in encouraging genius, as in the cases of Camillo Sivori, to whom, at the age of six, he gave some lessons, and Catarina Calcagno, a little girl whom he instructed for a few months while in Genoa in 1804. The mantle of Paganini's greatness fell easily upon the shoulders of SIVORI (*q.v.*), whose execution of Paganini's B minor Concerto never failed to arouse fervent applause, but Catarina Calcagno, after astonishing Italy with the boldness of her style at the age of 15, is lost trace of after the year 1816. While it has been admitted that Paganini's compositions and effects savoured of charlatanism, yet the revolution which he caused in the art of violin-playing, and its lasting results, entitle him to rank amongst the greatest geniuses of his age. Notwithstanding his triumphant successes in Germany (a curious testimony to this is in the fact that Schumann, Liszt and Brahms all founded remarkable pianoforte works on themes from Paganini) Spohr's example held most sway in that country, but the French and Belgian schools reveal his influence at every point.

LIST OF COMPOSITIONS PUBLISHED IN PAGANINI'S LIFETIME

Ventiquattro Capricci per violino solo dedicati agli artisti, op. 1.
Sei Sonati per violino e chitarra, op. 2.
Sei Sonati per violino e chitarra, op. 3.
Tre gran Quartetti a violino, viola, chitarra, e violoncello, opp. 4 and 5.

POSTHUMOUS PUBLISHED COMPOSITIONS

Concerto in E, op. 6 (posthumous op. 1). The first movement was frequently performed by Wilhelmj, with orchestral accompaniment.
Concerto in B minor, op. 7 (posthumous op. 2), with the celebrated Rondo à la Clochette. Orchestral accompaniment.
' Le Streghe ' (Witches' Dance, on an air by Simone Mayr), op. 8 (posthumous op. 3). Set of variations upon a theme taken from Süssmayer's ballet ' Il noce di Benevento,' with orchestral accompaniment. Variations on ' God save the King,' with orchestral accompaniment, op. 9 (posthumous op. 4).
' Le Carnaval de Venise.' Burlesque variations upon the popular Italian air, without accompaniment, op. 10 (posthumous op. 5).
' Moto perpetuo.' Allegro de Concert, op. 11 (posthumous op. 6). With orchestra.
Variations upon Rossini's air, ' Non più mesta ' from ' La Cenerentola,' op. 12 (posthumous op. 7). Variations upon the air ' Di tanti palpiti,' with orchestral part, op. 13 (posthumous op. 8).
Sixty variations in all keys upon the popular Genoese air ' Barucaba,' with piano or guitar accompaniment. Written in Genoa in Feb. 1835, and dedicated to his friend M. L. G. Germi, op. 14 (posthumous op. 9).
Schumann and Liszt have each transcribed Paganini's ' Twenty-four Caprices ' for the piano, and Brahms has written twenty-eight variations upon a theme of Paganini's. The ' Witches' Dance' was arranged for piano by J. B. Cramer in 1832 ; for violoncello by R. E. Backmund in 1877, and for concertina and piano by R. Blagrove. Paganini's last waltz, written at Nice, May 1840, was transcribed for the piano by H. Herz, London, 1840. David edited the two concertos, and Alard included excerpts from Paganini in his ' Maîtres classiques,' 1862. Other transcriptions have been made by W. V. Wallace, Henri Léonard, M. Hambourg, L. Auer Pauer, etc.

BIBLIOGRAPHY

CONESTABILE : *N. Paganini*, with picture, Perugia, 1851. FÉTIS : *N. Paganini*, Paris, 1851 ; Translation by W. E. Guernsey, London, 1876, with pictures. SCHOTTKY : *Paganinis Leben und Treiben*, Prague, 1830, with picture. SCHUTZ : *Leben, Charakter, und Kunst*, Leipzig, 1830, with picture. DE LAPHALEQUE : *Notice sur le célèbre violiniste, N. Paganini*, Paris, 1830 with picture. ANDERS : *Paganini, his Life*, etc., Paris, 1831. DU RIVAGE : *Reflections sur le talent de N. Paganini*, Paris, 1830. HARRYS : *Paganini in seinem Reisewagon* etc., Brunswick, 1830. NIGGLI : *N. Paganini*, Leipzig, 1882. VINETA : *Paganinis Leben und Charakter*, Hamburg, 1830, with picture. JULES JANIN : *La Mort de Paganini*, MS. in the possession of the writer. BRUNI : *N. Paganini*, Florence, 1873. POLKO : *Racconto storico di Oreste Bruni*, Leipzig, 1876, with picture. GUHR : *Über Paganinis Kunst*, Mainz, 1829. ESCUDIER : *Aus dem Leben Paganini*, Leipzig. Anon., *Biographie von N. Paganini*, Zürich, 1846. Anon., *Memoir of Paganini*, Liverpool, 1832, with picture. *Paganini*, a Genoese periodical published 1887 and onward. *The Athenœum*, 1831 ; *New Monthly Magazine*, 1831 ; *The Literary Gazette and Journal of the Belles Lettres*, 1831 ; *The Examiner*, 1831 ; *Chambers's Edinburgh Journal*, 1832 ; *Fraser's Magazine*, Apr. 1832 ; for the ' Correspondence of Niccolo Paganini' ; J. THEODORE BENT : ' Nicolo Paganini,' *Lady's Magazine*, 1831 (also reprinted separately). EDGAR ISTEL : *Nicolo Paganini*, Leipzig, 1919. PROD'HOMME : *Paganini* (Musiciens célèbres), 1907. S. STRATTON and J. KAPP : *Nicolo Paganini*, 1913.

O. R. and E. H.-A.

PAGE, JOHN (*d*. London, Aug. 1812), a tenor singer, was elected a lay-clerk of St. George's Chapel, Windsor, Dec. 3, 1790. He resigned the appointment Nov. 9, 1795, having for some time previously officiated as deputy at the Chapel Royal and St. Paul's. In 1800 he edited and published ' Harmonia sacra ; a collection of anthems in score, selected from the most eminent masters of the 16th, 17th and 18th centuries,' [1] 3 vols. fol. ; an excellent work supplementary to the collections of Boyce and Arnold. On Jan. 10, 1801, upon the resignation of Richard Bellamy, he was appointed a vicarchoral of St. Paul's. In 1804 he issued ' A Collection of Hymns by various composers, with 12 Psalm tunes and an Ode composed by Jonathan Battishill.' Also ' Festive Harmony ; a collection of the most favourite Madrigals, Elegies, and Glees, selected from the works of the most eminent composers.' In 1806 he published ' The Burial Service, Chant, Evening Service, Dirge and Anthems appointed to be performed at the funeral of Lord Nelson Jan. 9, 1806, composed by Dr. Croft, Purcell, Dr. Greene, Attwood and Handel.' In 1808 he joined William Sexton, organist of St. George's Chapel, Windsor, in the publication of a selection from Handel's Chandos Anthems, in a mutilated form.

W. H. H.

PAGIN, ANDRÉ NOEL (*b*. Paris 1721), violinist, favourably mentioned by Dr. Burney,[2] was a pupil of Tartini, having travelled to Italy in his youth with the object of studying under the great Italian. In 1750 he returned to Paris and performed at the Concert Spirituel, with a success which unfortunately was not enduring. He accepted an appointment—bearing an annual stipend of £250 a year—in the Duc de Clermont's household, and frequently took part in soirées given by musical amateurs.

Compositions.—Six Sonatas with bass (Paris, 1748), dedicated to Prince de Grünberghem. The same, with harpsichord accompaniment, London, 1770. The adagio of the Sixth Sonata appears under No. 139 in Cartier's ' École de violon,' and Sonata No. 5 is included in Alard's ' Les Maîtres classiques.'

E. H.-A.

[1] The collection consisted almost entirely of late 17th and 18th century works. A full list of contents was published in previous editions of this Dictionary.　　　　　　　　　　　　　　　c.
[2] *Present State of Music in France and Italy*, p. 42.

PAGLIACCI, opera in 2 acts (said to be founded on an actual incident),words and music by Ruggiero Leoncavallo. Produced Teatro del Verme, Milan, May 21, 1892 ; Covent Garden, May 19, 1893 ; New York, Grand Opera House, June 15, 1893 ; in English, Rouseby Opera Co., Leicester, 1893. Known in Germany as ' Bajazzi,' and in France as ' Paillasse.'

PAGLIARDI, GIOVANNI MARIA (b. Florence, mid - 17th cent.), maestro di cappella to the Duke of Tuscany, 2nd half of 17th cent.; to the church of Gesù di Genova, Rome, c. 1663 ; to S. Apollinare, Rome, 1665. He composed operas, melodramas, motets, sacred songs, vocal duets, etc. (Q.-L.).

PAHISSA, JAIME (b. Barcelona, Oct. 7, 1880), Spanish composer, a pupil of MORERA, who has written operas, symphonic works and numerous pieces for PF. His opera ' La presó de Lleida ' (1906), founded on a Catalan ballad, brought him fame. He followed it with ' Canigó ' (1910), also on a ballad subject, ' Gala Placidia ' (1913), ' La Morisca ' (1919) and ' Marianela ' (1922).

J. B. T.

PAINE, JOHN KNOWLES (b. Portland, Maine, U.S.A., Jan. 9, 1839 ; d. Cambridge, Mass., Apr. 25, 1906), American organist and composer, and for twenty years professor of music at Harvard University, received his earliest musical instruction from Hermann Kretschmar in the city of his birth.

In 1858 he went to Berlin, where for three years he studied in the Hochschule für Musik under Haupt, Wieprecht and Teschner. He had chosen the organ to be his solo instrument, and became so proficient that he gave organ concerts in several German cities before returning to his native land in 1861. Going back to the United States he gave organ concerts and taught. There was at the time no chair of music in any American university (see DEGREES IN MUSIC: AMERICAN UNIVERSITIES). On Mar. 29, 1862, Paine was appointed instructor in music at Harvard University to serve for the remainder of the year, and on June 2, 1873, assistant professor of music to serve from Sept. 1 of that year. After two years, during which time he laboured zealously to win recognition for his art in scholastic circles by giving lessons in harmony and counterpoint (music having been raised to the dignity of an elective study at Harvard in 1870–71), he was appointed full professor (Aug. 30, 1875), being the first incumbent of a chair of music in an American university. From 1862–82 he also served as college organist. He received the honorary degree of M.A. from Harvard in 1869, and that of D.Mus. from Yale in 1890. He resigned his professorship in May 1905, to take effect the following September, and died after a very brief illness. A minute on his life and services which appeared in the Harvard University Gazette, on June 1, 1906, mentioned his services in the following words :

' From the beginning of his career as a teacher, he regarded it as a sacred duty to justify the recognition of music as an academic study, and to familiarise the College public with the best music. For years it was his practice to supplement his regular instruction by a series of pianoforte recitals of the works of the great masters, prefacing each work with a few well-chosen remarks about the personality of the composer and the significance of his music. These recitals, given in the evening in the lecture-room of Boylston Hall, were always well attended by students, to many of whom they furnished the first opportunity to hear classical music.'

Paine was neither a rapid nor a voluminous composer, and his significant works are all in the larger forms. A Mass in D was performed by the Singakademie in Berlin under his direction in Feb. 1867. In 1873 he attracted attention by producing, first in Portland and then in Boston (Handel and Haydn Society), an oratorio entitled ' St Peter.' A symphony in C minor followed, which Theodore THOMAS (q.v.) took into his repertory in 1876 as he did later another symphony in A entitled ' Spring,' op. 23 (1880), and a symphonic poem entitled ' An Island Fantasy ' (1882). It was also due to the interest of Thomas that Paine composed a cantata entitled ' A Song of Promise ' for the Cincinnati Festival of 1888. During the first two decades of his creative career Paine was an uncompromising exemplar of conservatism in musical composition, but liberal notions found expressions in the music to ' Oedipus Tyrannus,' especially the truly noble introduction written for a performance of Sophocles's tragedy under the auspices of Harvard University's Department of the Classics in May 1881. After the first performances at the Sanders Theatre the tragedy was given in English with Paine's music at public theatres in Boston and New York. For the Harvard Classical Club's performance of the ' Birds ' of Aristophanes in 1901, Paine also wrote incidental music. For the Centennial Exposition held in Philadelphia in 1876 he made a setting of a hymn written by the poet Whittier, for the World's Columbian Exposition of 1893 a ' Columbus March and Hymn,' and for the Exposition held in St. Louis in 1904 to celebrate the Louisiana Purchase a ' Hymn of the West,' the words by Edmund Clarence Stedman. Of his other works in the larger forms mention may be made of an overture, ' As You Like It ' ; a symphonic poem ' The Tempest'; three cantatas, ' Phoebus Arise ' (1882), ' The Realm of Fancy,' words by Keats (1882), and ' The Nativity,' words by Milton, composed for the Festival of the Handel and Haydn Society of Boston in 1883. H. E. K.

PAISIBLE (b. Paris, 1745 ; d. St. Petersburg, 1781), violinist, was a pupil of Gaviniès, through whose influence he became a member of the orchestra of the Concert Spirituel, and one of the musicians attached to the household of the Duchesse de Bourbon Conti. Imbued with an enthusiastic and hopeful disposition, Paisible's youthful ambition led him to throw up these posts and travel. After visiting the principal French towns, he rambled through the Netherlands and Germany as far as St. Petersburg, where his previous triumphant successes led him to hope for an appearance before the Empress Catherine. Owing, however, to the intrigues of Antonio Lolli, who was then attached to the Imperial court, his endeavours to be heard were frustrated. Two public concerts which he gave failed to attract attention. Much disheartened he entered the service of a Russian Count, with whom he travelled to Moscow. This resource lasted but for a short time. He gave further concerts, but with discouraging results, and at length, distracted by misfortune and crippled with debts, he shot himself at St. Petersburg. His touching farewell letter left instructions that his valuable violin should be sold towards defraying his debts. Published compositions :

Two violin concertos, op. 1, Paris ; six string quartets, op. 2, London ; six ditto, op. 3, Paris.

E. H.-A.

PAISIBLE (PEASABLE), JAMES (d. London, 1721), resident in London in the latter part of the 17th and beginning of the 18th century, was a member of the King's Band of Music. He composed overtures and act tunes for the following pieces—' King Edward the Third,' 1691; ' Oroonoko ' and ' The Spanish Wives,' 1696 ; ' The Humours of Sir John Falstaff,' Henry IV., Part i., 1700 ; ' She would and she would not,' 1703 ; and ' Love's Stratagem.' Some of these were ' performed before Her Majesty and the new King of Spain.' He also wrote Duets for flutes, published in ' Thesaurus musicus,' 1693–1696 ; and Sonatas and other pieces for flutes published at Amsterdam. (See Q.-L.) He assisted St. Evremond in composing music for the Duchess of Mazarine's concerts at Chelsea.

Various information, including Paisible's will, has been collected by W. J. Lawrence and published in Mus. Ant. ii. 57 and 241 ; iii. 117, iv. 191.                                              W. H. H.

PAISIELLO (PAESIELLO), GIOVANNI (b. Taranto, May 9, 1741 ; d. Naples, June 5, 1816), eminent composer of the Italian school was the son of a veterinary surgeon at Taranto. At 5 years old he entered the Jesuit school at Taranto, where he attracted notice by the beauty of his voice. The elements of music were taught him by one Carlo Presta, a priest and tenor singer, and he showed such talent that his father, who had intended to educate him for the legal profession, abandoned this idea, and succeeded in obtaining admission for him in 1754 to San Onofrio, at Naples, where he received instruction from the veteran Durante, and afterwards from Cotumacci and Abos.

During his nine years of studentship, Paisiello's powers were exercised on church music, but in 1765 he indulged in the composition of a

dramatic intermezzo, which, performed at the little theatre of the Conservatorio, revealed where his real talent lay. The piece pleased so much that its composer was summoned to Bologna to write two comic operas, ' La Pupilla' and ' Il mondo a Rovescio ' ; which inaugurated a long series of successes in all the chief Italian towns. At Naples, where Paisiello finally took up his abode, he found a formidable rival in Piccinni, and later, when Piccinni had departed to Paris, in Cimarosa. The enthusiastic reception met with by his own operas, and by ' L' idolo cinese ' (1767) in particular, was insufficient to set him at ease while his own supremacy was at all in danger. He seems all his life to have regarded every possible rival with jealous dislike, and on more than one occasion to have stooped to intrigue, not only to ensure his own success, but to defeat that of others.

In 1776, on the invitation of the Empress Catherine, who offered him a splendid salary, Paisiello left Naples for St. Petersburg. Among a number of operas written there must be mentioned ' Il barbiere di Siviglia ' (c. 1780), one of his best works, and to which a special interest attaches from its effect on the first representation of Rossini's opera of the same name. Coldly received when performed at Rome (after Paisiello's return from Russia), it ended by obtaining so firm a hold on the affections of the Roman public that the attempt of another composer to write a new ' Barber ' was regarded as sacrilege, nor would this audience at first give even a hearing to the famous work which finally consigned its predecessor to oblivion.

After eight years in St. Petersburg, Paisiello returned to Italy, stopping at Vienna on his way back, where he wrote twelve ' symphonies ' for Joseph II., and an opera ' Il rè Teodoro,' (1784) containing some of his best music. ' Il Marchese di Tulipano,' written for Rome, was played in London, Jan. 21, 1786 (under Cherubini, who added six airs of his own) and enjoyed for years a European popularity. He was named, about 1784, maestro di cappella to Ferdinand IV. of Naples, and during the next thirteen years produced several of the works by which he became most widely known, notably ' I zingari in fiera ' (1789), ' Nina, o la Pazza d'Amore ' (1789), and ' La molinara.' In 1797, on the death of General Hoche, Paisiello wrote a Funeral March, to order, for Napoleon, then General Buonaparte, who always showed a marked predilection for this composer's music, and now gave preference to his work over one by Cherubini.

When, in 1799, the Republican government was declared at Naples, Paisiello accommodated himself to the new state of things, and was rewarded by the post of ' Director of the National Music.' At the Restoration he naturally found himself out of favour with his old patrons, and lost his former appointment. After two years he succeeded in getting it back again, but this had hardly come about when the First Consul demanded the loan of his favourite musician from the King of Naples to organise and direct the music of his chapel. Paisiello was accordingly despatched to Paris, where Buonoparte treated him with a magnificence rivalling that of Catherine of Russia, and an amount of favour that excited frantic jealousy in the resident musicians, especially Méhul and Cherubini, who did not care for Paisiello's music, and whom he punished by bestowing on their enemies all the patronage at his disposal.

He was occupied chiefly in writing sacred compositions for the First Consul's chapel, but in 1803 he gave an opera, ' Proserpine,' which was not a success. This probably determined him next year to beg for permission to return to Naples, on the plea of his wife's ill-health. It was granted, although unwillingly, by Napoleon, who desired him before leaving to name his successor, when he surprised every one by designating L'esueur, who was then almost unknown and in destitute circumstances.

On Paisiello's return to Italy he was endowed with a considerable pension, was re-established in his old place at Naples, and was maintained in it by Joseph Buonaparte, and after him by Murat. But the favour he enjoyed under Napoleonic dynasties inevitably brought him once more into trouble when the Bourbons returned. He then lost all the pensions settled on him by the various crowned heads he had served. He retained, it is true, his salary at the Royal Chapel, but this, after the luxury he had known, was poverty. Anxiety had undermined his health, and he suffered a fresh blow in the loss of his wife, in 1815. He did not long survive her.

Paisiello composed about a hundred operas, and at least as many other works, of different kinds. Expression, within certain restricted limits, was Paisiello's strong point. All his airs are remarkable for simplicity and grace, and some have considerable charm, such as ' Nel cor più non mi sento ' in the ' Molinara,' long known in England as ' Hope told a flattering tale,' and destined to survive still longer owing to the variations on it written by Beethoven. Some of his music is tinged with mild melancholy, as in ' Nina ' (a favourite part of Pasta's), but it is never tragic ; or with equally mild *bonhomie*, as in the ' Zingari in fiera,' but it is never genuinely comic. It has great purity of style. No *bravura* songs for *prime donne* do we find in these operas. No doubt his simple airs received embellishment at the hands of singers ; we know that the custom prevailed, at that time, to such an extent as to determine Rossini to write down all his own *fioriture* for himself. This may account for the degree of repetition to

be found in Paisiello's pieces. Trios, quartets, etc. enter largely into his works, and he was among the first, if not *the* first, to introduce concerted finales into serious opera. In his orchestration he arrives at charming effects through very simple means ; it is distinguished by clearness and good taste, and by the independent parts given to the instruments.

For a complete list of Paisiello's compositions the reader is referred to *Q.-L.* Besides the operas, there are eight masses and other church pieces ; fifty-one instrumental pieces. F. A. M.

BIBL.—HERMANN ABERT, *Paisiellos Buffokunst und ihre Beziehunger zu Mozart*. *A.M.* 1³, 1919 ; FRANCESCO BARBERIO, *I primi dieci anni di vita artistica di Paisiello*. *R.M.I.* 1922, fasc. 2, pp. 264-76 ; ANDREA DELLA CORTE, *Settecento italiano. Paisiello. L' estetica musicale di P. Metastasio*, pp. 372 (Turin, 1922).

PAIX, JACOB (*b.* Augsburg, 1556 ; *d.* there, *c.* 1590), son of Peter Paix, organist of St. Anne's. The family are supposed to have come originally from the French Netherlands. Jacob Paix became organist at Lauingen, where in 1583 he published an Organ Book with the title,

' Ein schön Nutz und gebräuchlich Orgel-Tabulatur. Darinnen etlich der berümbten Komponisten beste Moteten mit 12, 8, 7, 6, 5, und 4 Stimmen auserlesen, dieselben auf all fürnemen Festa des ganzen Jahrs und zu dem Chormas gesetzt. Zuletzt auch allerhand der schönsten Lieder Pass' e' mezzo und däntz, alle mit grossem Fleiss coloriert . . .'

In this work Paix shows himself as one of the school of German colourists in organ-writing, who busied themselves in transcribing vocal pieces for the organ in a purely mechanical fashion, breaking up the melody throughout into the same monotonous figure of four notes without the slightest attempt at any variety of movement. A specimen of his manner of ' colouring ' Palestrina's motet, ' O beata et gloriosa Trinitas,' may be seen in Schlecht, *Geschichte der Kirchenmusik*, Ex. 63. But the work also contains two fantasias and two French canzonas, which being free from this purely mechanical ' colouring,' have greater artistic value. One of them is given in Schlecht, Ex. 64. (See also Ritter, *Geschichte der Orgelmusik*, pp. 106-7, etc.) In his preface Paix gives some useful hints on fingering, recommending the freer use of the thumb, etc. Other works of Paix are mentioned in *Q.-L.*, among them two Missae Parodiae on motets by Mouton and Crecquillon, *a* 4 and 6 respectively. Paix would seem to have been the first to adopt the designation Missa Parodia for this class of work. In 1583 Paix is also mentioned as being organist at Augsburg. J. R. M.

PALADILHE, ÉMILE (*b.* Montpellier, Hérault, June 3, 1844 ; *d.* Paris, Jan. 8, 1926) entered the Conservatoire at the age of 9, under the protection of Halévy, and studied hard, carrying off the first piano prize in 1857, and the organ-prize and Prix de Rome in 1860. The cantata which won him the latter distinction, ' Le Czar Ivan IV,' he neither printed nor sent to the library of the Conservatoire, doubtless from the consciousness that it was an immature work. The specimens of his

composition received by the Institut during his
stay in Italy gave a favourable idea of his
powers, but on his return to Paris he had great
difficulty in obtaining a libretto.  At length
attention was drawn to his merits, and he
obtained Coppée's one-act piece, 'Le Passant,'
which was produced at the Opéra-Comique,
Apr. 24, 1872, and the taking song, 'La Man-
dolinata,' from it obtained a wide popularity.
Notwithstanding the favourable reception of
the music, sung by Mme. Galli - Marié and
Marguérite Priola,[1] three years passed before
the appearance of 'L'Amour africain' (Opéra-
Comique, May 8, 1875), in two acts.  The libretto
of this, by Legouvé, was not approved, and the
music was condemned as laboured.  Nevertheless many of the numbers bear traces not
only of solid musicianship, but of spontaneous
and original melody.

Paladilhe's first important work was ' Suzanne ' (Dec. 30, 1878), an opéra-comique in
three acts.  Here we find something beyond
mere ingenuity in devising effects ;  the
melodies are graceful and refined, and show an
unconventionality of treatment which is both
charming and piquant.  It had, however, but
a moderate success in spite of the merit of its
first act, a delicately treated idyll, and the
young composer turned his attention to the
concert-room, and produced a work entitled
'Fragments symphoniques ' at the Concerts
Populaires, Mar. 5, 1882.  It is a composition
of no extraordinary merit, but some of the songs
which he wrote at the time are exceedingly
graceful.  On Feb. 23, 1885, his ' Diana ' was
brought out at the Opéra-Comique, but only
played four times.  The libretto was considered dull and childish, and the music heavy
and crude.  Undismayed by this failure,
Paladilhe set to work on a grand opera
on Sardou's drama 'Patrie.'  Legouvé, who
always showed an almost paternal affection
for Paladilhe, and who was anxious to make
amends for the failure into which he had
led the composer by his libretto of 'L'Amour
africain,' obtained for him from Sardou the
exclusive right of composing the music.  The
work was given at the Opéra, Dec. 20, 1886,
and at the time was successful.  It was given
at Hamburg as ' Vaterland ' in 1889, and at La
Scala, Milan, as ' Patria,' in 1895.  In Jan.
1881 he was decorated with the Légion
d'Honneur.  In 1892 his ' Saintes Maries de
la mer,' a lyric drama, was produced at Montpellier, and he was made a member of the
Institut (Académie des Beaux-Arts in 1892),
in succession to Guiraud.  Two masses and
a symphony are among his non-dramatic
compositions.                          A. J.

PALADINI, GIOVANNI PAOLO, of Milan
(early and mid - 16th cent.), a lutenist who
appears to have lived in France.  He wrote a

[1] A promising singer who died young.

book of ' chansons, fantaisies, pavanes, gail-
lardes et la bataille ' for lute tablature, published by Jacques Moderne at Lyons ;  and 1.
' livre de tablature de luth, conten. fantaisies, motetz,' etc., with instructions for the
tablature of the lute, Lyons, 1560.

PALAZZOTTO - TAGLIAVIA, GIOSEPPE
(16th-17th cent.) ;  D.D. and Archdeacon of
Cefalu in Sicily.  He composed 2 books of
madrigals 5 v. (1617, 1620), also a Ricercare in
B. Cali's Ricercare of 1605 (Q.-L.).

PALESTRINA, GIOVANNI PIERLUIGI DA
(b. 1525/26 ;  d. Rome, Feb. 2, 1594), takes the
name by which he is generally known from the
place of his birth, the small cathedral town of
Palestrina in the Roman Campagna, one of the
seven suffragan episcopal sees of the Diocese
of Rome.  In Latin dedications and letters the
composer usually signed his name Joannes
Petraloysius (or Petrus Aloysius) Praenestinus,
Praeneste being the ancient classical name of
the modern Palestrina.  Many of his early
secular compositions appeared in collections
under the diminutive pet name of Giannetto.
Formerly there was the greatest uncertainty
as to the year of his birth, various dates being
given, ranging from 1514–29.  Haberl first
discovered an inscription which pointed to
1526 approximately as year of birth, and late
writers [2] have produced evidence which points
to 1525.

The old tradition that Palestrina was of very
humble origin is now refuted by the discovery
that his parents, Sante Pierluigi and Maria
Gismondi,[3] occupied a fairly good social position
in Palestrina as owners of houses and lands.
The other tradition of his early association
with the great Church of Santa Maria Maggiore
in Rome is so far confirmed by the appearance
of the name 'Joannes de Pelestrina' in the
church archives as one of six choir boys in
1537 under the care of a chaplain and choirmaster.  It further appears that a certain
Firmin Le Bel was appointed choirmaster in
1540, which induces Casimiri to surmise that
Firmin Le Bel is the real Gaudio Mel of later
Roman tradition, Palestrina's master in the art
of musical composition.[4]  But though Le Bel
may have instilled into the youthful chorister
some of the elements of musical science, it may
seriously be doubted whether Palestrina continued under his tuition afterwards for instruction in composition.  Another solution of the
mystery surrounding the name of Gaudio Mel
is possible.  Firmin Le Bel hardly corresponds
to the description of Palestrina's teacher given
by Antimo Liberati, who, writing in the year
1685, is the only source for the name Gaudio

[2] See K. Weinmann, Palestrinas Geburtstag, 1915.  Casimiri
believed that he had succeeded in establishing the precise date as
May 9, 1525, and published the discovery in his periodical, Note
d' Archivio, but frankly admitted in a subsequent number that he
had been deceived.  See Note d' Archivio, June 1924.
[3] From A. Cametti's Palestrina (1925) it appears that Maria
Gismondi was stepmother to the composer;  Sante's first wife,
Palma, dying in 1536.
[4] Casimiri, Nuovi documenti, etc., p. 17.

Mel. This teacher is described as being a Flemish musician of great talent and master of a very graceful and polished style, who opened a school of music in Rome from which proceeded many excellent musicians, and chief among them Palestrina. This description points to Arcadelt more than to any one else, and Arcadelt was a prominent member of the Sistine Chapel Choir from 1540–49. We may account for the substitution of the name Gaudio Mel by the fact that Goudimel, though never in Rome, was afterwards the editor of a volume of compositions by Arcadelt, and may thus have been confused with him by Liberati, and the transformation of the name Goudimel into Gaudio Mel is easier to be explained than that of Firmin Le Bel. We might therefore hazard the conjecture that when, as an old record says, Palestrina returned to Rome in 1540 for the study of music, it was to place himself under the tuition of a real master of musical composition like Arcadelt between that date and 1544. However this may be, there can be little doubt of the fact that the Fleming Arcadelt and the Spaniard Morales, who was also in the Sistine Chapel Choir to 1545, were Palestrina's first models in the development of his own particular style, Arcadelt standing to him in somewhat of the same relation as Perugino to Raphael, and Morales as Signorelli, or some other of that school.

On October 28, 1544, the Cathedral Chapter of his native town engaged Palestrina as organist and choirmaster, assigning him the revenues of a canonry. His duties were to play the organ on festivals, to sing daily in the choir at Mass, Vespers and Compline, and to instruct the canons as well as the boys in singing and the musical art generally. In 1547 he married Lucretia de Goris, who brought him some considerable accession of worldly means. What music Palestrina may have written at this time we have no means of knowing. Before the middle of the 16th century composers had hardly begun to publish works on their own account. Morales was one of the first to do so by his books of masses published at Rome in 1544. But musical works usually circulated in manuscript for some time before the music-printers obtained copies for publication with or without the sanction of the composers. A work which there seems good reason for taking to be one of Palestrina's earliest works is a Mass a 5, which only appeared in print as late as 1592 in a collection of 'Missae dominicales' published at Milan under the editorship of a Carmelite friar Giulio Pellini, who seems to have been an early acquaintance of the composer. This Mass is partly based on themes from the plain-song Mass 'Orbis Factor,' and in the Gloria and Credo there is the peculiarity of the alternation of Palestrina's music with passages sung in simple plain-song, an early style of Mass composition.

On Feb. 7, 1550, the Bishop of Palestrina, Cardinal Gian Maria del Monte, was elected Pope, and assumed the name of Julius III. in memory of his former patron Julius II. At his instance Palestrina was recalled to Rome in September 1551 to become choirmaster of the Cappella Giulia, the choir in connexion with St. Peter's founded by Julius II. to be a nursery of native singers for the Sistine Chapel in the Vatican, where foreign singers had hitherto predominated. In token of gratitude for his appointment Palestrina in 1544 published his 'First Book of Masses' with a dedication to the Pope, in which with flattering allusions to the Pope's encouragement of music, he also refers to the care he himself had bestowed on the composition of these masses ('exquisitioribus rhythmis') to make them worthy of the occasion. This book contains 4 masses a 4 and one a 5. The first Mass in it is a further flattering tribute to the Pope, not only by its title, 'Ecce sacerdos magnus,' but by the use which the composer makes of the whole text as well as of the musical theme of the plain-song Antiphon, which begins with these words. Thus while in the greater part of the Mass one or other voice sings in long sustained notes of plain-song the words, 'Ecce sacerdos magnus qui in diebus suis placuit Deo et inventus est justus,' the other voices sing the ordinary words of the Mass in free, quicker counterpoint. Another feature of this Mass is the use of the devices of proportional notation in the Hosanna and Agnus. The other masses a 4 in this book are 'O regem coeli,' 'Virtute magna,' these two based on themes taken from motets beginning with these words by Andreas de Silva, a former composer to the Papal Chapel, and 'Gabriel Archangelus,' similarly based on a motet by Verdelot. This seems to show the interest Palestrina took in the works of his Flemish predecessors. The Mass a 5 is entitled 'Ad coenam agni providi,' and is based on a later Roman form of plain-song tune to the Easter Hymn beginning with these words. The tune in this form is not in accordance with older manuscripts of plain-song, and has therefore been rejected from the revised Vatican edition of the Antiphonal, but it suited Palestrina's purpose for polyphonic setting. It is given complete, note by note, in the soprano part of the Christe Eleison and the Benedictus. In the rest of the Mass two of the voices sing in canon diapente or subdiapente. It is interesting to note in the first Agnus of this Mass the first appearance of the phrase in the soprano with which the Missa Papae Marcelli begins the Kyrie, and there are other general resemblances of musical phrase between the two masses.

On Jan. 13, 1555, by express command of the Pope, Palestrina was admitted a member of the college of singers of the Papal Chapel. This appointment seems to have given umbrage to the other singers of the chapel, as being a contravention of a recent regulation issued by Julius himself, limiting the future number of singers to 24 and requiring that no one should be admitted without examination and approval by the whole college. But in this very regulation there was a clause reserving the right of the Pope to appoint by a Motu Proprio signed with his own hand. To accept this appointment Palestrina was obliged to resign his office as choirmaster of the Cappella Giulia, in which he was succeeded by the Florentine Animuccia. Meantime he was busy with the preparation for publication of his First Book of Madrigals a 4, which he intended to dedicate once more to his Papal patron. This intention was frustrated by the unexpected death of Pope Julius on Mar. 23, 1555. The book was published later in the year without any dedication, but on the title-page the composer was still able to designate himself as a singer of the Papal Chapel. There were 22 numbers, in later editions increased to 23. In these early madrigals we may notice a certain subordination of the technique of imitation to that of simple harmony in note for note counterpoint. A large number of them begin with these bursts of four-part harmony with only slight points of imitation afterwards. In this respect Palestrina follows the lines of madrigal composition laid down by Verdelot and Arcadelt. It is interesting to note in No. 11, towards the end on the words ' l' anima vi consacro,' exactly the same succession of chords as give so unearthly an impression to the opening of the famous Stabat Mater. Mention may also be made of one number with verses written by Palestrina himself in praise of Francesco Rosselli, one of his predecessors, as choirmaster of the Cappella Giulia from 1548–50. Baini observes that what he has been able to see of Rosselli's compositions does not merit the high eulogium which Palestrina gives to them, but it is remarkable that of two settings of the words ' Adoramus te,' [1] by Rosselli, one has been persistently attributed to Palestrina's authorship, and seems good enough to warrant this attribution.

On Apr. 9, 1555, Cardinal Marcello Cervini was elected Pope and took the title of Marcellus II. He was a devout and exemplary prelate, who announced his intention of reforming various practical abuses in church worship and discipline, and was also interested in the question of a proper church music. His death, however, only 3 weeks after his accession prevented the carrying out of any plans he may have formed. The Missa Papae Marcelli is Palestrina's great

[1] See Proske, *Mus. div.* tom. iv. pp. 307–10.

tribute to his memory, and it is just possible that Palestrina may have begun the composition of this work during his reign and at his instigation, although it was not published or known by this name till 12 years afterwards. Marcellus was succeeded in the Papal Chair by Cardinal Pietro Caraffa, who took the title of Paul IV. In the passionate zeal of the new Pope for what he conceived to be a necessary disciplinary reform in the Papal establishment he issued a Motu Proprio on July 30, 1555, dismissing from the service of the Sistine Chapel the three members who happened to be married men, including Palestrina, assigning them a small pension as compensation. The two others were Leonard Barré, who had served in the chapel with great distinction for 18 years, and Domenico Ferrabosco, usually considered to be the father of Alfonso Ferrabosco, who afterwards settled in England, and gave the original impetus to the cultivation of madrigal music here. The humiliation of this dismissal seems to have affected Palestrina's health for a time, and he may have felt it as a great blow, not so much perhaps from the merely financial point of view, as from its possible injury to his reputation and the loss of the distinguished patronage he may have hoped to secure in the Papal Court and its entourage for the further publication of his works.

St. John Lateran.—From Oct. 1, 1555, he became choirmaster of the church of St. John Lateran. Although this church proudly proclaims itself the ' Mother and Head of all the churches of the city and the world,' and is the proper Cathedral church of the Bishop of Rome, it has, ever since the removal of the Papal residence to the Vatican in 1377, taken a very secondary place to the great church of St. Peter. Its choir service was not so well endowed, and it does not appear that the dignitaries connected with it gave Palestrina the least encouragement to publish his works. During the reign of Pope Paul IV., 1555–59, Palestrina published nothing on his own account; but contributions from him were sought by the editors and publishers of madrigal collections, in which his authorship was for some time concealed under the name of Giannetto. To a collection of madrigals a 4 by Cyprian da Rore, first published in 1557, there is appended ' una canzon di Gianetto ' which, however, consists of 14 stanzas, paraphrasing at undue length a single sonnet of Petrarch. The whole work is in consequence somewhat heavy and monotonous, both in melody and harmony. In one of three contributed to a collection of 1558, a setting a 4 of all the stanzas of Petrarch's canzona ' Chiare fresch' e dolci acque ' we find on the words ' alle dolenti mie parole ' another example of the same sequence of chords as in the opening of the Stabat Mater. In the Secondo Libro delle Muse a 5, published at

Venice in 1559, under the fuller name, Giannetto da Palestrina, there is a very expressive number ' Ogni loco mi porge dolor e 'l pianto,' in which much more use is made throughout of imitation and less of mere blocks of chords as in earlier works of the kind. In the Terzo Libro delle Muse of 1561 there are 8 madrigals by Palestrina which have a greater variety of interest and expression. Among them is ' Io son ferito,' which seems to have become a favourite number, with its themes used afterwards by other composers for masses and organ ricercari. Meantime, among works for the church written in those years, but not published during his lifetime, or indeed, till long afterwards, we may mention a beautiful book of the ' Lamentations ' a 4 to 8, mostly for low voices, now published by F. X. Haberl as Book 2 in the complete edition of works Bd. 25. The ' Lamentations ' are the Lessons for the First Nocturns of the last 3 days of Holy Week, two or three verses only of each Lesson being composed, but with the refrain at the end ' Jerusalem convertere,' etc. Another work probably of this time is a book of Magnificats a 4-6, composed on the eight tones, the alternate verses only being composed, some of them very elaborately, with various canonic devices after the old Flemish manner. This is numbered as Book 3 in the volume of Magnificats in the complete edition Bd. 27. But the work of this time by which Palestrina leapt at once into sudden fame, and began to be hailed as the first church composer of the day, is the very simple but touching setting for 2 responsive choirs of the Improperia or Reproaches in the service for Good Friday. This work secured for him the favour of the new Pope, Pius IV., who requested a copy for the use of the Sistine Chapel, where afterwards it always formed a striking feature of the Good Friday service, creating a deep impression. It was the first work of the composer copied into the great MS. choir-books of the chapel.

In 1558 Palestrina somewhat suddenly resigned his post at St. John Lateran, apparently being dissatisfied with certain conditions which the Chapter sought to impose on him. Evidently the Chapter did not appreciate their choirmaster at his true worth. On March 1, 1561, he was appointed choirmaster to the better-endowed church of Santa Maria Maggiore, otherwise known as the Basilica Liberiana. Encouraged by the request of his Improperia for the Papal Chapel, also perhaps anxious to retain and deserve his pension in connexion with it, he presented to the college of singers two motets and a Mass. The motets were Beatus Laurentius a 5, composed after the old manner with the plain-song antiphon as cantus firmus on long notes in the quintus part, with the other voices in free imitative counterpoint on the same theme ; ' Estote fortes

in bello' a 6, composed differently, with free use of the plain-song antiphon as a canon between two of the voices. The Mass is that which is known as the Hexachord Mass a 6, based on the syllables ' Ut, re, mi, fa, sol, la,' and is one of the finest works of the master, in which the whole beauty of his later style is definitely manifested. Ingenuity and beauty are wonderfully blended in it. The second soprano sings nothing else throughout but the scale of six notes on varying time values, sometimes ascending, sometimes descending. The Gloria and Credo are almost entirely in note for note counterpoint, making the words to stand out with peculiar distinctness. Ambros comments on the seraphic beauty of the Crucifixus and Pleni sung by the 4 high voices. In the Sanctus advantage is taken of the opportunity which the word Sanctus affords for flowing ornamental scale passages. The Hosanna and Benedictus show other features in the treatment of the scale appropriate to the words which the music is intended to illustrate. The Second Agnus is a 7 with a close canon in subdiapente at one bar's distance between two of the voices on the ascending and descending scale. The whole work might thus be thought as a commentary in music on the ladder set between heaven and earth with angels ascending and descending. These works were copied into the great choir-books of the Sistine Chapel, and contributed to extend the composer's growing reputation. The success thus attained may have induced Palestrina in 1563 to publish his First Book of Motets a 4 dedicated to the Cardinal Bishop of Ostia, Ridolfo Pio Carpi. Its proper title is ' Motecta festorum totius anni cum communi Sanctorum quaternis vocibus.' It contains 36 numbers on texts taken from the Gradual and Antiphonal for all the chief feasts of the Church Year in order beginning with Christmas. In his dedication the composer declares the function of music in church to be the seasoning of devotion by the added delight of sweetness of song and variety of harmony, and expresses his own desire to commend religion to the ears of men by the utmost beauty of musical art. And, indeed, all or nearly all of the pieces of this book are gems of the first water.

THE COUNCIL OF TRENT.—Meanwhile, in 1562 the Council of Trent had been reassembled, and the question of church music came up for consideration, specially in connexion with the service of the Mass. Much exaggerated language has been used with regard to the state of church music before this time. One chief ground of complaint against elaborate contrapuntal music in the Mass was that the words could not be properly heard and understood. ' There was a considerable party of bishops in the Council who desired to banish polyphonic music altogether from the service of the Church, retaining only the unison plain-song; but others, and especially the Spanish bishops, were eager in defence of polyphony, urging in its favour the Scriptural text 'non impedias musicam' (Ecclus. xxxii. 5, Vulg.). It was at the same time forgotten that the complaint was quite as much directed against the florid plain-song of Introits, Graduals and Offertories, and its bad execution as against the florid counterpoint on single words of the older polyphonic music; while ever since the time of Josquin composers themselves had been reforming their style of composition by simplifying their counterpoint to give greater prominence to the words, and the increased attention to expression in the motet and madrigal had encouraged this tendency. Another ground of complaint was the use of secular tunes for the designation and in the composition of masses, whereby it came about, as was alleged, that singers often indulged in the irreverent practice of singing the original unedifying words of the tunes along with the sacred words of the Mass. It may be doubted whether this latter practice was at all common, but, strange to say, it was not altogether unknown in the Papal Chapel.[1] The reason for the choice of these tunes as themes for Mass composition was no doubt their more melodious character, and the opportunity they afforded for greater freedom and variety of treatment than the plain-song. Apart from the use of secular tunes the combination of other sacred or quasi-sacred words with the proper words of the Mass was also objected to. This practice was more frequently indulged in by early composers, and might be considered as only carrying further the earlier mediæval practice of the insertion of texts known as Tropes and Sequences into the more florid pieces of plain-song, a practice which was only afterwards liturgically disallowed. Palestrina may be open to some blame for adopting it in his Mass 'Ecce sacerdos magnus' as a mere compliment to a Pope, but it was less reprehensible when adopted with some degree of appropriateness to special occasions, as when on a Saint's Day a motet in honour of the Saint was interwined with the Mass, or when Palestrina in an Ave Maria Mass written for his own church of St. Mary makes a tenor voice sing the plain-song Ave Maria. The practice was more common in the motet than in the mass, and often adds some element of significance or beauty to the composition. To all these complaints of abuses in church music, the answer of the Council of Trent in its 22nd Session, Sept. 17, 1562, was couched in very general terms, namely, that from the church all music in which there was any mingling of the impure and profane should be excluded, everything that was inconsistent with the reverence due to churches as houses of prayer. In a later session of 1563,

further consideration of the subject was adjourned by the resolution to commit the carrying out in detail of this and other measures of reform to Provincial Synods, and meanwhile until such assemblies could be held, bishops with the assistance of their chapters were to take steps in the same direction in their own dioceses.

THE PAPAL COMMISSION.— In accordance with this resolution, Pius IV., in 1564, instituted a commission of eight cardinals to provide for the execution and observance of the Tridentine decrees in his own diocese of Rome, and two of their number, Cardinals Vitelozzo Vitelli and Carlo Borromeo, were specially delegated to regulate the affairs of the Papal Chapel. It is in connexion with this commission, and by the free exercise of his own imagination in bold but mistaken conjectures, that the Abbé Baini[2] built up the romantic tale, which has so long found acceptance in musical and other histories, of Palestrina's salvation of the cause of artistic church music by his composition of the Missa Papae Marcelli. Various legends had long been current of the origin and purpose of this Mass. Baini took particular pains to demonstrate the unhistorical character of previous legends, but unfortunately substituted an equally unhistorical legend of his own invention. By research in the Roman Archives F. X. Haberl[3] has shown the facts to be quite otherwise than as Baini represents them. Music occupied but a small part of the attention and reforming labours of the Commission. Its main object was disciplinary. The number of the singers was reduced from 37 to 24 in accordance with the older Constitutions, a pension being awarded to those dismissed. On the other hand, the pensions previously granted to Palestrina and Domenico Ferrabosco were augmented to the same amount as the pay of the actual singers ; to Palestrina specially on the ground of compositions which he had already provided and would continue to provide for the use of the chapel. This is the only direct connexion of Palestrina with the Commission, so far as any records go. Baini wrongly infers that he was then created Composer to the Papal Chapel. On April 28, 1565, the diary of the chapel records that some masses were sung by the Papal singers before the two cardinals privately, in order to enable them to judge whether the words could be properly heard and understood. No mention is made of what these masses were, or what was the result, nor is there any record of consultations between the singers and the cardinals about other requirements of a proper church music, such as Baini professes to be able to report at length. But finding three masses of Palestrina associated together in a MS. Codex of the Sistine archives, one, the Marcellus Mass

---

[1] Cf. Haberl, *Katalog der Musikwerke im päptlichen Archiv* (Leipzig, 1887), under the names Obrecht and Silva.

[2] Baini, *Memorie storico-critiche della vita e delle opere di Giovanni Pierluigi da Palestrina* (Rome, 1828), pp. 214-34.
[3] Cf. Haberl. *Kirchenmusikalisches Jahrbuch* (1892), pp. 82-7.

without any title, and another with the date inscribed 1565, Baini proceeds to make the bold conjecture that Cardinal Borromeo had made a special appeal to Palestrina to compose a Mass which would save church music by satisfying the requirements of devotion as well as of art, and that Palestrina, to ensure success, had written three, the third bearing the title ' Illumina oculos meos ' as if implying a special prayer of the composer for the divine assistance in his task. Examination of this Codex proves that there is no real foundation for the imaginative story of Baini. The three masses had no original association with each other, but have only been brought together by a later rebinding of the MSS. It is proved that the Mass in which the date 1565 is inscribed, is one based on Josquin's motet ' Benedicta,' and an earlier copy of it is found in Munich. The date 1565 is only that of its transcription into the Sistine choir - books, and Baini mistakenly supposes it to belong to the Marcellus Mass. But of the Marcellus Mass an older copy, too, is found in the archives of S. Maria Maggiore, in which church it may therefore be presumed to have had its first performance. The other Mass a 6 happens to have the title ' Illumina oculos meos,' merely because its themes are taken from a motet of Andreas de Silva beginning with these words. It is also very unlikely that three masses by the same composer would have been chosen for so important a trial, on which, according to Baini, so much depended. As likely as not, one of the masses sung before the cardinals may have been by Animuccia, choirmaster of St. Peter's, who also professedly made it his aim to secure the clear enunciation of the liturgical text, and even adopted a stricter attitude than Palestrina in the avoidance of everything but plain-song themes for the composition of masses. Without producing any further shred of evidence in favour of his assertion, Baini goes on to relate that from the three masses he mentions, the cardinals singled out the Marcellus as that which fully satisfied all their requirements as a model for future Mass composition, and that it was afterwards first publicly performed in the presence of the Pope in the Sistine Chapel on a great occasion of public thanksgiving, June 19, 1565, when it met with universal approval and laudation. But neither the chapel diary nor the other authority which Baini quotes at length with regard to this Papal function give the least hint as to what Mass was sung on the occasion, so that it remains a pure conjecture on his part that it was the Marcellus Mass. His whole story must thus be dismissed into the realm of fable, and can only be regarded as a laboured attempt to account for the celebrity which the Mass afterwards obtained, a celebrity due to its merits and not to any official recognition. In any case all that the decision of the Papal

Commission could possibly amount to was a reform in the repertory of the chapel itself by the exclusion of the older works in the polyphonic style which did not correspond with the new demand for the clear enunciation of the liturgical text. It is also worth while to notice that Cardinal Borromeo in his own diocese of Milan seems to have interpreted this demand as requiring a more drastic reform in the style of church music than Palestrina or the Roman School ever adopted. At Borromeo's instigation and under his patronage Vincenzo Ruffo, choirmaster at Milan, published a book of masses claiming to be ' composte secondo la forma del Concilio Tridentino,' in which the text is set in simple note for note counterpoint with simultaneous utterance by all the voices, a style similar to that adopted in certain early English services (see SERVICE) of the Reformation period by Tallis and others.[1]

MASSES AND MADRIGALS.—In 1567 Palestrina published his Second Book of Masses, and, if Baini's story were true, it might be matter for surprise that he should dedicate it to Philip II. of Spain, and not to one or other of the dignitaries of the Papal court, and specially to the saintly Cardinal Borromeo, who according to Baini had incited him to the composition of the work which had saved church music. In his dedication Palestrina simply says that, following the counsel of grave and religious men, he had applied his utmost zeal and industry to adorn the holy sacrifice of the Mass by a new style of musical art (*novo modorum genere*). The language is hardly strong enough to warrant a supposed reference to any official approval of this new style by a Papal Commission. It is very much the same language as in the dedication of his First Book. The masses of the Second Book are indeed more concise, and comply better with all requirements of the clear enunciation of the liturgical text. There are four a 4 : ' De Beata Virgine,' ' Inviolata,' ' Sine Nomine,' ' Ad Fugam '; two a 5 : 'Aspice Domine,' 'Salvum me fac,' and one a 6 : ' Missa Papae Marcelli.' The ' De Beata Virgine ' is based throughout on themes from the plain-song Mass ' De Beata,' and thus has the peculiarity of its different parts being based on different Church modes. The ' Inviolata ' is based on the melody of a Prose used in Advent processions. The 'Sine Nomine' has very beautiful themes which might be taken from a French chanson, which the composer has preferred not to name. Its second Agnus is a 7 by means of a canon having three resolutions by different clefs on the same stave. ' Ad Fugam ' is only written on two staves with a close canon between each pair of voices. In the Benedictus and second Agnus the canon has the device ' Trinitas in unitate.' ' Aspice Domine ' takes its leading theme from a Motet

1 Cf. Torchi, *L' arte musicale in Italia*, vol. i. pp. 193-204.

by Jachet of Mantua.[1] ' Salvum me fac ' is
based on a Motet which in the complete edition
of Palestrina's works Haberl includes among
Opera dubia in vol. xxxi., but the close resemblance between the Mass and the Motet
hardly leaves room for doubt as to the authenticity of the latter. The ' Dona nobis pacem '
at the end of the Mass is almost note for note
the same as the conclusion of the Motet. The
Marcellus Mass entirely differs from these and
others by being freely composed throughout
without being based on any recurring set
themes taken from some other source. As
originally published it was without its second
Agnus *a* 7 which has a canon with two resolutions. Baini thinks to explain the omission by
supposing that the composer was afterwards
conscious of having temporarily lost the flow of
divine inspiration by too great a desire to display his mastery of contrapuntal art. A reduced
edition of the Mass *a* 4 was published at Milan
in 1590, which is included in vol. xxx. of the
complete edition among the Opera dubia. In
1609 Soriano arranged an edition *a* 8, and in
1619 Francesco Anerio another edition *a* 4,
which was frequently reprinted.

To a collection of madrigals *a* 5 entitled ' Il
desiderio,' published at Venice in 1566, Palestrina contributed ' Vestiva i colli,' one of the
most delightful of his secular pieces, which from
its frequent republication in other collections
seems to have acquired great popularity. With
an adaptation to English words it is included in
Yonge's ' Musica transalpina,' 1588. On its
themes Palestrina himself composed an important Mass, and in the Sistine Archives are
two similar masses, one *a* 5 by Nanino, and
another *a* 8 by Giovanelli. In 1605 it reappears
as a motet, with the words ' Surge propera,
amica mea.' It was also arranged in lute
tablature, and for the cantus part to be sung
by a solo voice with florid ornamental passages
termed diminutions.

According to Baini, Palestrina remained
quietly in the service of the Liberian Basilica up
to the year 1571, but Casimiri[2] has recently
produced documentary evidence which seems to
show that he had resigned his position there
some time before Apr. 1567, and in August of the
same year had entered the service of Cardinal
Ippolito d' Este. Baini had thought that the
two positions had been all along held conjointly,
but this does not seem to have been the case.
In token of gratitude for benefits received from
his new patron, Palestrina dedicates to him his
First Book of Motets *a* 5-7. In the dedication he
speaks of himself as now in his mature years
verging on old age, and therefore all the more
desirous to use what talent he has in the service
of religion. The book contains a very large

[1] P. Wagner in his *Geschichte der Messe*, Bd. 1, p. 448, by an
oversight attributes the ' Salvum me fac ' to Jachet instead of
the ' Aspice Domine.'
[2] Casimiri, *Nuovi documenti biografici*, pp. 98 ff.

number of his finest and best known motets, as
' O admirabile commercium,' ' O beata e.
gloriosa Trinitas,' ' O Domine Jesu Christe
adoro te,' ' Viri Galilaei,' ' Dum complerentur,'
' Vidi turbam magnam,' etc., in which we find
the characteristic combination of beautiful
passages of expressive homophonic harmony
with others of flowing melody in imitative
counterpoint. It is the madrigal style in its
perfection applied to the expression of devotional feeling. There are 24 numbers *a* 5,
7 *a* 6, and 2 *a* 7. The two last are wonderful
pieces of musical architecture.

Palestrina was now in the full tide of pub-
lication. In 1570 appeared his Third Book of
Masses, dedicated like the second to Philip II.
of Spain. It contains four *a* 4, ' Spem in alium,'
' Primi toni,' ' Brevis,' ' De Feria,' two *a* 5,
' L'homme armé,' ' Repleatur os meum,' two *a* 6,
' De Beata Virgine,' ' Ut, re, mi, fa, sol, la.'
' Spem in alium ' and ' Repleatur os meum '
are said to be written on motets by Jachet
of Mantua, but the latter is also a study in
canons, being written throughout (except in the
Crucifixus and Benedictus) in canons at all
the intervals beginning with the octave and descending to the unison, and concluding with a
double canon at the octave and fourth. It is
as if he wished by the employment of canons to
show how he could ' untwist all the chains that
tie the hidden soul of harmony.' The Mass
' Primi toni ' is in a later edition denominated
' Io mi son giovanetta,' and is probably based
on a madrigal by Domenico Ferrabosco. Among
the previously unpublished masses now included
in vol. xxxii. of the complete edition, there is
one *a* 6, which might also have the same title,
as being based on very much the same themes,
though differently worked out in detail. The
Missa Brevis takes its themes from Goudimel's
Mass ' Audi filia,' and has been one of the most
frequently performed on account of its general
simplicity and clearness. The ' De Feria ' has
also much simple beauty, but as its name
implies, omits the Gloria and Credo. With the
works of his Flemish predecessors Palestrina
had evidently a wide acquaintance, and in the
Mass ' L'homme armé,' shows his desire to rival
with the older musicians on their own ground.
It has always been hailed as a brilliant masterpiece in which musical learning in the application of the various devices of proportional
notation is most happily blended with great
beauty of melody and harmony. The quintus
part has nothing else but the old tune as cantus
firmus in its mixolydian or major form, mostly
in long sustained notes, round which the other
parts play in free or imitative counterpoint,
and sometimes in homophonic harmony as the
text may require. The Benedictus *a* 4 has the
peculiarity of the opening phrase of the tune
used in the soprano part as cantus firmus.
The whole Mass may be said to be a wonderful

combination of the old style of cantus firmus Mass with the new style of the Marcellus. There is also this little point of connexion between the two Masses that we find something like the opening phrase of the ' L'homme armé ' in the Bassus I. of the Kyrie of the Marcellus Mass, and as the beginning of the canon in the second Agnus. It is also the same succession of notes with which Bach opens his Magnificat, so that it might seem as if it had specially struck the fancy of composers as appropriate to the theme of divine praise. The ' De Beata Virgine ' a 6 is, like the earlier one a 4, based on the themes of the plain-song Mass of the same title, but is composed on a larger scale and with greater freedom of development. The Gloria has the interpolations in the text which were formerly used on Feasts of the Blessed Virgin, and were only struck out from the Roman Missal in the revision of 1570. In the later editions of the Mass, repetitions of the proper text were substituted.

REAPPOINTMENT AT ST. PETERS.—On the death of Giovanni Animuccia in March 1571, Palestrina was reappointed choirmaster of St. Peter's, apparently under better conditions than on his first appointment. In the same year he presented two masses to the Papal Chapel, one a 5, on his own splendid Christmas Motet, ' O magnum mysterium,' the other a 6, which has as cantus firmus in the first soprano part throughout (except in the Crucifixus) the plain-song melody of the hymn ' Veni Creator Spiritus,' in various rhythms and with occasional sharpening of the note before the final of the mode for the sake of the harmony. This latter Mass was only first published by Haberl in the modern complete edition. In 1572 Palestrina published his Second Book of Motets, a 5, 6 and 8, dedicated to William, Duke of Mantua. This prince, who was a generous patron of music and musicians, and even attempted composition himself, had already from 1568 begun a correspondence with Palestrina by commissioning from him a Mass and other works, for which he rewarded him handsomely. He sent compositions of his own for criticism and correction, and at a later time made overtures to Palestrina to enter his service, and, although this invitation was declined, friendly communications through his agents at Rome were not interrupted till his death in 1587. This Second Book of Motets contains 17 a 5, 8 a 6 and 4 a 8. By including two works by his brother Sylla and one each by his sons Angelo and Ridolfo, it would appear as if Palestrina wished to commend these members of his family to the notice of the Duke. Two motets in honour of St. Barbara were evidently meant for the ducal chapel at Mantua dedicated to that saint. The most striking numbers in this book are two of a penitential character, and very ex-

pressive. ' Peccantem me quotidie,' a 5, with modulations on the words ' conturbat me,' unusual in Palestrina, and ' Tribularer si nescirem,' a 6, in which he adopts from Josquin's Miserere the device of a ' pes ascendens and descendens ' with the same theme and text as Josquin, ' Miserere mei Deus.' By way of contrast two specially bright numbers may be mentioned, ' Ascendo ad Patrem,' a 5, and ' Tu es Petrus,' a 6, on both of which Palestrina has also composed important masses.

On Oct. 7, 1571, was fought the Battle of Lepanto, in which Don John of Austria as commander-in-chief of the combined Papal, Spanish and Venetian forces, by inflicting a decisive defeat of the Turkish navy, turned back the tide of Turkish conquest in Europe. This was naturally hailed as a decisive victory of the Cross over the Crescent, and in celebration of the event Palestrina composed two madrigals a 5, one ' Saggio e Santo Pastor,' in honour of Pope Pius V., whose zeal had inspired this new crusade, the other, ' Le selv' avea,' in honour of Don John, the hero of the occasion. These with two others of a different character, first appeared in ' Il IV. Libro delle Muse à 5,' published at Venice in 1574. Of the two latter, ' Se di pianti e di stridi ' has been edited with an English translation in L. Benson's ' Oriana ' series. In 1575 Palestrina published his Third Book of Motets a 5, 6 and 8, dedicated to Alfonso II. of Este, Duke of Ferrara. Baini strangely infers from the modest language of Palestrina in this dedication that he was aware of the inferior merits of the book in comparison with the two previous, but there is little justification for his disparaging estimate. There are 18 numbers a 5, 9 a 6 and 6 a 8. The crown of the book for brilliant effect is no doubt those a 8 written in the Venetian manner for 2 responsive choirs a 4, especially ' Surge illuminare,' 'Hodie Christus natus ' and ' Jubilate Deo.' In the Sistine Archives ' Surge illuminare ' has a second part, ' Et ambulabunt,' which was printed for the first time in the 6th volume of the complete edition. Of the numbers a 6 may be specially mentioned ' O bone Jesu ' and ' Haec dies quam fecit.' Of the numbers a 5 we might judge ' Congrega, Domine ' and ' Domine qui conteris bella ' as having been specially written for some occasion of prayers for the success of the expedition of 1571 against the Turks. ' Quid habes, Hester,' is remarkable for the semi-dramatic effect at the end of the first part on the words, ' Cur mihi non loqueris.' In 1576, in a collection entitled ' Musica XIII. autori illustri,' published by Gardano at Venice and dedicated by him to Duke Albert of Bavaria, there appeared two very remarkable madrigals by Palestrina, ' Placide l' acque ' and ' Soave fia il morir,' both a 5, remarkable not only for their general expressiveness, but for unusual modulations such as Palestrina nowhere else makes use of, in the one case on the words, ' ma poi cangiossi l' onda,' in the other, ' dolce il cangiar,' and evidently suggested by the words ' cangiar ' and ' dolce.'

THE LITURGICAL CHANT.—We have now to touch upon a matter which has been the subject of much heated discussion, and on which there still hangs a good deal of uncertainty, namely, Palestrina's share in the revision of the liturgical chant. After the revision of the Breviary and Missal under Pius V. in 1568 and 1570, there naturally came up for consideration the question of the revision of the plain-song in the Gradual and Antiphonarium. On Oct. 25, 1577, Gregory XIII., who in 1572 had succeeded to the Papal chair on the death of Pius V., issued a Breve, entrusting the revision of the liturgical chant to Palestrina and Annibale Zoilo as members of the Papal Chapel. Their task was defined as that of ' purifying, correcting and reforming ' the chant on the same principles as had been applied to the text by removing ' barbarisms, superfluities and obscurities.' The general effect was to secure the same degree of clear enunciation of the text as had come to be insisted on in figured music. The comprehensiveness of the instructions was sufficient to justify considerable alteration of the old plainsong by the suppression of the florid neumes on single syllables, and by the correction of what were considered to be faults of prosody and accent. Palestrina undertook the revision of that part of the gradual known as the ' Proprium de tempore,' while to Zoilo was allotted the ' De Sanctis.' This work occupied Palestrina's attention during the year 1578, and was well advanced towards completion, when it was suddenly abandoned, mainly it appears in consequence of strong representations made to the Pope by a Spanish musician, Don Fernando de las Infantas, in favour of the unmutilated plainsong, backed up by the personal influence of Philip II. of Spain.[1] But another account alleges as the only reason of this abandonment some disputes with regard to the printing, and the disappointment of the expectations of Palestrina and Zoilo for some reward of their labours.[2] However the case may be, the manuscript remained and became the subject of further dispute afterwards. A certain amount of revision was left to private enterprise, without any formal official recognition, as by Guidetti's publication of the Directorium Chori in 1582 with a recommendation from Palestrina.

Meantime the composer had suffered severe losses in his own household. His son Angelo had died in 1576, leaving to his care two young children, who also died a few years later. There is no record of Ridolfo's death, which, however, appears to have taken place between

1576 and 1580. In the Register of St. Peter's there is the record of the death and burial of Lucretia, Palestrina's wife, July 23, 1580. There was one son remaining, of whom we hear more later. In 1581 Palestrina married again, probably for the sake of his household, taking for his second wife Virginia Dormuli, a widow possessed of some private means, which enabled him to proceed with the further publication of important works.

SPIRITUAL MADRIGALS, ETC.—Early in 1581 he had published a First Book of Spiritual Madrigals a 5, dedicated to Giacomo Buoncompagno, created Duke of Sora, being a son born to Gregory XIII., before he had taken holy orders. This book contains 26 numbers beginning with elaborate settings of the first eight stanzas of Petrarch's celebrated ' Vergini,' invocations of the Blessed Virgin under various titles, appended by Petrarch to his sonnets on the death of Madonna Laura, which Palestrina may also have thought appropriate for the expression of his own sentiments after the death of his wife. These are followed by 18 pieces on a smaller scale, but equally beautiful in their way, consisting of invocations to the Holy Spirit and the Divine Redeemer, which were probably composed for performance at the popular devotions of the Oratory of Philip Neri. Also in 1581 he dedicates to the same patron his Second Book of Motets a 4, containing 21 numbers of the finest quality, beginning with some of a penitential character as if expressive of the composer's personal desire to find in renewed penitence and devotion some consolation for the loss he had sustained, and concluding with eleven pieces for equal voices, including such miniature gems as ' Adoramus,' ' Pueri Hebraeorum,' ' Surrexit pastor bonus,' etc. In 1582 he dedicates his Fourth Book of Masses to Pope Gregory XIII. In the dedication he mentions his early determination to consecrate his whole talent to the praises of God, language which he could fairly use, even though he still continued to contribute secular madrigals to various collections at the solicitation of publishers. This dedication is one of his best, being written with the full consciousness of his own merits as a composer, and without any undue flattery of his patron. In this book the masses have originally no titles, but are simply numbered, but the thematic sources of all but two can be specified. There are four a 4 and 3 a 5. The first is based on the well-known Sequence of St. Thomas Aquinas's 'Lauda Sion,' the third on the plain-song Ascension Hymn, ' Jesu nostra redemptio,' the fourth is a ' L'homme armé' Mass with the old melody in its Doric or minor form. The four masses a 4 are all very concise and practical, with clear homophonic declamation of the text in the Gloria and Credo, but with more display of polyphonic art in the Sanctus and Agnus. The

---

[1] Cf. Respighi, *Nuovo studio su Giovanni Pierluigi da Palestrina e l' emendazione del graduale Romano.*
[2] Cf. Haberl, *Kirchenmusikalisches Jahrbuch* (1902), p. 140 ff.

three masses *a* 5 are on a larger scale, one with the title in another MS. ' Eripe me de inimicis,' another the ' O magnum mysterium,' differing a little in its printed form from the earlier copy presented to the Papal Chapel.

It was in 1583 that Duke William of Mantua entered into the negotiations to which we have previously alluded, to induce Palestrina to enter his service, an invitation which the composer prudently declined. It would appear from the correspondence that Palestrina was more anxious to secure a good position for his son Iginio than desirous on his own account to leave Rome, and therefore asked for higher terms than the Duke was willing to meet. But there was no interruption of their friendly correspondence.

THE SONG OF SONGS.—In 1584 appeared the work which has always roused the highest admiration of musicians, the Fourth Book of Motets *a* 5, containing 29 numbers on texts from the Song of Songs. In his dedication to Pope Gregory XIII., Palestrina expresses his regret that like others he had devoted so much of his time and talent to the composition of secular songs glorifying human earthly love, and declares his desire to atone for this mistake by now endeavouring to glorify the higher divine love, the spiritual love of Christ and the human soul as allegorically represented in the Book of Canticles. He has also thought it to be more appropriate to this subject to use a somewhat more animated style (usus sum genere aliquanto alacriore) than in other church compositions. By this more animated style he evidently means one more suffused with the expression of intimate personal feeling. And indeed attention has often been drawn to the glow of inward passionate feeling that pervades the work, the wonderful expression of intense spiritual longing in some numbers in the musical setting of such words as ' langueo ' and ' amore,' and of the rapture of satisfied delight in others. The whole work shows throughout the transfiguration of the madrigal style into a higher grace and beauty by religious idealism.

MOTETS, MADRIGALS, ETC.—In the same year Palestrina published his Fifth Book of Motets *a* 5, containing numbers of great value. This book was dedicated to Andrea Bathory, nephew of Stephen Bathory, Prince of Transylvania, and from 1575 elected King of Poland. Andrea had come to Rome in 1583 on an embassy from Poland, and in the following year was created a Cardinal of the Roman Church. From the dedication it would appear that he had sought Palestrina's acquaintance, and had several colloquies with him on the subject of music. The first number in the book is a setting of some verses which may have been written by the composer himself, laudatory of the merits of the two Bathorys

and felicitating Andrea on his elevation to the Cardinalate. The book might seem to have been put together rather hastily for presentation to the Cardinal, as its contents are in no proper order. Near the beginning but not together are three deeply impressive numbers on texts taken from the Office of the Dead, ' Paucitas dierum meorum,' ' Domine secundum actum ' and ' Parce mihi Domine,' and with them may be found another penitential piece, 'Tribulationes civitatum.' Other fine numbers are of a joyful character, as ' Exultate Deo ' and ' Tempus est ut revertar.' The Marian motets are as usual very fine, and the last number in the book is perhaps the most beautiful setting of the Salve Regina ever written. Early in 1585 Palestrina presented to the Papal Chapel three very fine masses *a* 6, ' Dum complerentur,' ' Viri Galilaei ' and ' Te Deum laudamus,' the two former based on his own bright and joyous motets, the last of a more severe character corresponding with the antique severity of the plain-song themes of the hymn on which it is founded. In the same year a copy of a Mass *a* 8, written for St. Peter's, ' Confitebor tibi Domine,' based on one of his own motets, came into the hands of Giovanni Becci, a canon of Fiesole, who on his own account had it printed at Venice, dedicating it to a noble lady in a convent at Florence with a remark implying that it might usefully be partly played by instruments when there were not sufficient voices for all the parts. This would seem indeed to have been a common practice of the time.

On Apr. 10, 1585, Gregory XIII. died, and on the 24th of same month Felice Peretti was elected in his place, assuming the name of Sixtus V. To the new Pope Palestrina presented a Motet and Mass, ' Tu es Pastor ovium,' *a* 5, as suitable for the use of the Papal Chapel on the occasion of his enthronisation, with which, however, on its performance Sixtus was dissatisfied, remarking that the composer had forgotten his Marcellus Mass and the motets of the Canticles. There is no reason, however, for considering this Mass to be so inferior a work as Baini represents. He goes on to relate how Palestrina made up for this mishap and recovered the favour of Sixtus by the composition of the Mass ' Assumpta est Maria ' *a* 6, which he got printed in a great hurry in time for performance on the following Feast of the Assumption on Aug. 15 at the church of S. Maria Maggiore, when it gave the utmost satisfaction. The printed copy, however, to which Baini refers bears no date, and according to Haberl cannot have been printed before 1612. But there is a MS. copy of the Mass in the Sistine archives, which is dated as the first year of the Pontificate of Sixtus, and it is from this that Baini builds up his somewhat imaginative story. The Mass indeed based on the corresponding motet *a* 6, is, next to the Marcellus Mass, the most celebrated of all Palestrina's works of the kind. Yet it was not just the spur of worldly ambition to secure the favour of a new Pope that incited Palestrina to its composition. We might rather say, it was the ideal of heavenly grace and beauty suggested by the Feast of the Assumption which made a special appeal to the artistic nature of Palestrina, and inspired him to clothe the words of the Mass as of the motet with a corresponding grace and beauty in the form of music. As Proske has said, ' In this Mass his genius soars to the highest regions of the purest ether, and there is in it a majesty, a grace and an inspiration for which our only fitting object of comparison is Raphael's ' Sistine Madonna.' Meantime, even before the performance of these masses, we are told that Sixtus desired to appoint Palestrina as actual choirmaster of the Papal Chapel, and only desisted from his proposal in consequence of the opposition of the members of the choir. It is hardly worth while to enter into the details of this part of the story as Baini recounts them. It is difficult to understand the independent attitude which the choir were able to maintain against an absolute Pope, and the intrigues that had to be resorted to in order to gain their consent to the Pope's wishes, and at the same time why the Pope could only revenge himself by dismissing some of the members. On other occasions Baini has no difficulty in admitting that where the Pope commanded it was necessary for the choir to obey.[1] It is sufficient for us to relate that in the end the Pope contented himself with formally bestowing on Palestrina the official title of ' Composer to the Papal Chapel.' This invident, however, caused a temporary coldness on the part of the members of the choir towards Palestrina, for even when in the same year he presented to the chapel three new and very fine masses, ' Salve Regina ' and ' O Sacrum convivium ' *a* 5, and ' Ecce ego Joannes ' *a* 6, they remained forgotten and unused until they were transcribed into the choir-books in 1594 after the composer's death. The ' Ecce ego Joannes,' a Mass for All Saints' Day, as its name implies, has since been recognised worthy to be bracketed with the Marcellus and the ' Assumpta est Maria ' as representing the high-water mark of the Palestrina style in the composition of masses. Haberl would assign it the highest place of the three.

In 1586 appeared at Venice the Second Book of Madrigals *a* 4, dedicated to Giulio Cesare Colonna, who in 1571 had been created Prince of Palestrina. This prince is known to have been a man of learning and culture, and also as a benefactor to the town from which he

derives his title. In the dedication the composer describes himself as his ' fidelissimo vassallo,' and opens the work itself with a madrigal in his honour. As the prince is known to have died in 1581, it has been rightly surmised that this publication can only have been a reprint of a lost earlier edition. Of this book it is sufficient to say that all the madrigals contained in it are written in a much freer and more graceful style than those of the early book of 1555. Several of them afterwards appeared with English words in Yonge's ' Musica Transalpina ' of 1588. Other fine madrigals of Palestrina continued to appear and reappear in such collections as ' Dolci Affetti ' and ' Li amorosi ardori,' etc., notwithstanding his professed renunciation of all such work in 1584. One in 1586, ' Dido chi giace entro quest' urna ' *a* 5, is remarkable for the use of an echo effect in one of the voice-parts. Another, ' O felici ore,' was contributed to a collection, ' Corona di dodici sonetti,' in celebration of a somewhat discreditable marriage of Francesco de' Medici and the beautiful Venetian Bianca Capello ! Owing to the circumstances of this marriage, Palestrina might have had more reason to ' blush and grieve ' for any association with it than for any other works of the kind. But the music itself is not so unworthy of its composer as Baini represents it to be. Better work published in 1586 are his contributions to a collection, ' Diletto spirituale,' consisting of three short and simple but very beautiful settings, two *a* 3 and one *a* 4 of verses from the hymn ' Jesu dulcis memoria,' which are also provided with an arrangement for cembalo and lute, either as accompaniment or for separate performance. This arrangement may have been the work of Verovio the printer, who published other works in the same way.

LAMENTATIONS OF JEREMIAH. — In 1588 Palestrina published his ' Lamentationum Hieremiae prophetae liber primus,' dedicated to Pope Sixtus V. According to Baini, this work was undertaken at the instigation of Pope Sixtus. This makes it all the more strange that in the dedication the composer should have such occasion to make his own pitiful lament of want of means to enable him to bring out his works in the splendid large folio form which he thinks would have been more befitting for church compositions, and to excuse the appearance of this work in its smaller and less attractive form (minutiore hac forma). He was no doubt thinking of the splendid folio editions in which just at this time the Spanish musician Victoria was enabled to bring out similar works under the patronage of the King of Spain, and was indirectly appealing for more substantial patronage in order to further publication. This set of Lamentations *a* 4 - 5 is quite distinct from the earlier set *a* 4-8 composed for St. John Lateran, and also from another set *a* 5-6, more elaborate, composed for S. Maria Maggiore. The Liber Primus was thus really the third book in order of composition, and there was a fourth set *a* 5-6 probably composed later for the chapel of the Duke of Altaemps. Besides these complete books several separate Lamentations have now been published from the Sistine and other Roman archives. With the nine Lamentations Liber Primus also included a setting of the Canticle Benedictus *a* 4 to be sung in alternate verses with the plain-song, and a Fauxbourdon setting of the Psalm Miserere. Palestrina's Lamentations have always been a subject of admiration for the deep religious pathos which pervades them.[1]

HYMMS OF THE WHOLE YEAR. — Another magnificent liturgical work of the master followed in 1589, ' Hymni totius anni secundum sanctae Romanae ecclesiae consuetudinem quatuor vocibus concinendi necnon hymni religionum.' This work, dedicated like the preceding to Sixtus V., appeared first in a splendid large folio edition, from which it would seem that the appeal for more substantial patronage had met with some response. It consists of polyphonic settings of the plain-song melodies of all the Vesper Hymns of the Church year, together with some hymns peculiar to certain religious Orders. Only the odd verses are treated in this way, the even verses being sung to the unison plain-song. There are some exceptions, as when in the Vexilla Regis the composer could not forbear to add his splendid setting of the sixth verse, ' O crux ave, spes unica.' This hymn had been sung three years before, under the composer's direction, on the occasion of the erection by Sixtus V. of the Obelisk in the Piazza of St. Peter's. The last verses of the more important hymns are set *a* 5 and 6, with the occasional use of canonic devices. Baini is eloquent in praise of Palestrina's Hymns, and rightly says that they reunite what is most beautiful and most sublime in all his other works. Incidentally it may be re-

[1] There may be reason for doubting the strict accuracy of some of Baini's statements with respect to the earlier use of the Lamentations in the Papal Chapel. He says that up to 1586 only those of Elzéar Genet of Carpentras, a former choirmaster of the chapel, had been in use. But from the list of choir-books in the archives, it would seem that some by Morales and Festa had also been in use. On the alleged authority of ' Memorie a penna,' of which no trace has ever been found, he goes on to tell us that for 1587 Sixtus V. ordained that only the first Lamentation of each of the three days in Holy Week should be sung *in concerto*, with music better adapted to the occasion than that of Genet (of which, indeed, Baini speaks too contemptuously), and that the other two lessons of each day should always be in the plain-song. Accordingly, Palestrina, he says, was induced to compose one Lamentation for 1587, which gave such satisfaction as encouraged him to publish his Liber Primus in 1588. It is strange, however, that the one Lamentation which gave such satisfaction in 1587 does not appear in the printed book, and that Palestrina should have substituted another. Also, though Palestrina composed all the nine lessons, it would appear from Baini's account that only three, the first of each day, were ever sung, the other six being always sung by a solo voice in plain-song. This usage, indeed, became part of the later routine of the Papal Chapel, but it may be doubted whether it dates from Sixtus V. There is this further consideration. Baini makes no mention of Victoria's Lamentations as ever having been used. But apart from Victoria's publication of his ' Officium hebdomadae sanctae ' in 1585, an earlier copy of all his nine Lamentations is found in the choir-books of the Chapel.

marked that the forms of plain-song melody which Palestrina employs are such as were current in Rome in his time, and are not always the best or most correct, though they may have appealed more to his personal taste, and suited his purpose better, as in the case of the Ad coenam agni providi, the melody of which he has also employed for other hymns. In the revised Roman Breviary of 1631, a serious alteration of the text of the old hymns was carried out under the personal direction of Pope Urban VIII., whose fastidious classical taste was offended by what was supposed to be their faulty Latinity and incorrect prosody.[2] The result is now regarded as a senseless and unwarrantable ' deformation of the work of Christian antiquity,' destroying the noble simplicity and poetic beauty of the hymns. A rearrangement of Palestrina's music to the new text was entrusted to four singers of the Papal Chapel, and in 1644 this new edition was published at the Pope's expense by the Plantin-Morctus house at Antwerp. Naturally, no value whatever can be attached to it. Ten hymns (the ' hymni religionum,' Nos. 36 to 45) were omitted and two others substituted, one with text composed by Pope Urban himself.

In 1590 Palestrina published his Fifth Book of Masses, dedicated to Duke William of Bavaria, the patron of Orlando Lassus. It contains four masses *a* 4: ' Aeterna Christi munera,' ' Jam Christus astra ascenderat,' ' Panis quem ego dabo,' ' Iste Confessor ' ; two *a* 5 : ' Nigra sum,' ' Sicut lilium inter spinas ' ; two *a* 6 : ' Nasce la gioia mia ' and ' Sine nomine.' Of these the ' Aeterna Christi munera ' and ' Iste Confessor ' have been the most frequently performed by reason of their brevity and comparative simplicity, also their general brightness of character. On the Mass, ' Panis quem ego dabo,' founded on themes from a motet by Lupus Hellinck, Baini makes some very strange remarks. Professing to defend it against certain objections, he considers it, because included in a volume dedicated to the Duke of Bavaria, and not to the Pope or the Papal Chapel, as having been deliberately written by Palestrina more in an instrumental style than in the vocal style proper to church music, and represents Palestrina as himself admitting that he had sometimes been constrained by poverty to lower his standard of writing to this extent. If what Baini alleges were true, his defence would be more damaging than any criticism. But, first of all, he misconstrues the phrase which he quotes from the dedication of the ' Book of Hymns.'[3] Palestrina says not a word of having been constrained by poverty to lower his standard of writing church music, but only refers to having been obliged by others to devote his talents occasionally to lighter subjects,

[2] Cf. Batiffol, *Histoire du Breviaire Romain* (1893), pp. 262-4, also Baumer, *Geschichte des Breviers* (1895), pp. 507-10.

[3] Cogor praestantissimam facultatem demittere ad res levissimas.

that is, to secular composition. Further, there is not the least foundation for the assertion that this Mass is composed in an instrumental style, and not in a proper vocal style. The occasional runs on consecutive notes that occur in it are not more frequent than in so many of his other first-rate masses. The Mass, indeed, is of a very devotional character throughout, the themes being such as lend themselves in Palestrina's hands to the expression of devotional feeling. With regard to the Mass, ' Nigra sum,' though it is said in some books to be based on the Motet beginning with these words in Palestrina's ' Book of the Canticles,' it has very little in common with that Motet, and the themes are evidently taken from some other source. So also the ' Sicut lilium ' does not take its themes from the book of Canticles, but from the Motet in the book of 1569. While in ' Nasce la gioia mia ' the composer plainly avows the source of his themes, he has declined to do so with the ' Sine nomine.' From the nature of the themes in the latter, we might conjecture them to be taken from a French chanson, or from some popular song other than a madrigal, which on this account he might have more hesitation in naming. But whatever be the source of the themes the Mass is a very distinguished one, noble and earnest throughout in its treatment of them. It was reprinted in 1591 as the last in a new edition of the ' First Book of Masses.'

Sixtus V. died Aug. 27, 1590, and Palestrina's Missa pro defunctis a 5 may have been first sung as his Requiem. It has no setting of the Introit or of the Dies Irae. While its themes are suggested by the plain-song, one may notice the free use of the chromatic note in the Sanctus and Agnus. It was first printed in the reprint of the ' First Book of Masses,' 1591. In the Sistine MS. copy there is joined with it the Responsorium ' Libera,' to which Baini gives the highest praise. On Dec. 5, 1590, Niccolo Sfondrato was elected Pope, assuming the title of Gregory XIV. One of his early acts was to augment the pay of the members of the Papal Chapel, by which Palestrina also benefited. About this time he presented to the Chapel a series of important works, not, however, as Baini represents, a separate collection specially dedicated to the Pope. Among them is the justly celebrated Stabat Mater a 8, the exquisitely pathetic beauty of which there is no need to dilate upon; also a splendid Magnificat a 8 with all the verses composed. Other works are four motets a 6, one of which, ' Tradent enim vos,' Baini specially falls foul of, representing it as an early work still tainted with what he describes as the ' fiammingo squalore,' simply because it has a cantus firmus on the plain-song Antiphon, with close canon in diapente between two of the voices. It is really a scholarly work, though it has not the same brilliant character

as its companion pieces a 6, which are written with more of homophonic harmony. There are four other brilliant pieces a 8, written antiphonally for two choirs. With the exception of the Stabat Mater all these pieces remained unpublished until they were included in vol. 6 of the Breitkopf & Härtel Complete Edition. The Stabat was first published by Dr. Burney in ' La musica della settimana santa,' 1771, from a MS. copy presented to him by Santarelli, one of the singers of the Papal Chapel. Partly in token of gratitude for the increase of his stipend, Palestrina in 1591 dedicated to Pope Gregory XIV. his ' Magnificat Octotonum liber primus.' This work consists of two sets of Magnificats a 4 on each of the eight psalm tones in order, one set with the odd verses composed, the other with the even, the intermediate verses being sung in unison to the respective tones. The Magnificats are remarkable for the art by which by fugal imitation and otherwise Palestrina contrives to invest the same tone in the different verses with new and surprisingly beautiful turns of melody and harmony. This book, though designated by him the first, is really the third in order of composition. An earlier book composed for St. John Lateran, now numbered as the third in the Complete Edition, consists of eight Magnificats a 5 and 6 of a much more elaborate character, the verses being composed at greater length, and with occasional use of Canons. Another book, numbered as the second, was composed for St. Peter's, and consists of eight a 4 and 5, of a slightly less elaborate character. The lengthy treatment of the verses is partly accounted for by the ceremony of incensation which accompanied the use of the Magnificat on occasions of greater solemnity. Besides these books there are two separate Magnificats of some value included in the Complete Edition. But those of 1591 are more concise and more adapted for practical use by their general clearness and simple beauty.

LAST WORKS.—Going back a little, it may be necessary to mention that in 1584 a Society of Roman Musicians had been formed, apparently for the purpose of raising the standard of qualification for choirmasters in the various churches of the city. At first the members of the Papal Choir took up an attitude of opposition to the Society, but afterwards a reconciliation was effected, and as if to attest this happy result, Felice Anerio, who had been appointed choirmaster to the Society, published in 1589 a collection of madrigals a 5, entitled ' Le Gioie ' (Jewels), with contributions from the members of the Society, among whom were now included prominent members of the Papal Chapel.[1] To this collection Palestrina contributed one interesting number, ' Dunque perfido amante,'

[1] Cf. Haberl, *Kirchenmusikalisches Jahrbuch* (1891), pp. 86, 87.

which has something of a dramatic character. About this time, beside the stately form of the madrigal, there began to be cultivated by Italian musicians the slighter form of the canzonet *a* 3 or 4, with several verses to the same music, and sometimes with cembalo or lute accompaniment. In publications by the Roman printer, Simon Verovio, 1589 and 1591, Palestrina shows that he did not disdain to encourage this new style of composition.[1] A more important secular work was the Madrigal *a* 6, ' Quando del terzo cielo,' [2] contributed to the collection, ' Il trionfo di Dori,' 1592. A testimony to the commanding position which Palestrina had now attained in the world of music is afforded by the dedication to him in 1592 of a Collection of Vesper Psalms composed by the best musicians of Northern Italy, Matteo Asola, Costanzo Porta, Giovanni Croce, Leone Leoni and others. The dedication, written by Asola, is couched in terms of the highest respect and admiration. He says, ' As rivers are naturally borne to the sea as their common parent and lord, and rest in its bosom as the attainment of their own perfection, so all who profess the art of music desire to approach thee as the ocean of musical knowledge to testify their homage and veneration.' Asola was unwilling to approach the master all by himself, and therefore enlisted the aid and companionship of friends and fellow musicians that they might all as a body, not altogether to be despised, acknowledge him as the common father of all musicians.

On Jan. 30, 1592, Ippolito Aldobrandini became Pope, assuming the title of Clement VIII. During 1592 no new publication by Palestrina appeared, but about this time he found a new and generous patron in a certain Abbé Anton Baume, belonging to a wealthy family of Franche-Comté, who must have come to Rome on a visit, and made the composer's acquaintance. To him in 1593 he dedicates, as an expression of gratitude for many benefits received, his ' Offertoria totius anni,' *a* 5. This very comprehensive work was published in two parts, and consists of settings of the offertory texts of the Roman Missal for all the Sundays and chief festivals of the year in order, mostly verses from the Psalms, 68 Nos. in all, written in the master's most refined mature style, with perhaps a touch of austerity from the nature of some of the texts. A smaller publication of the same year is a Book of Litanies *a* 4 for private chapels in which Rosary devotions were sung, but no copy of the original edition is known. It was reprinted in 1600, and consists of two Litanies in 5 parts each, corresponding to the five divisions of the Rosary, composed in simple homophonic harmony. Mention may

suitably here be made of eight other Litanies on a larger scale *a* 5, 6 and 8, which have now been published from MS. sources in Vol. 26 of the Complete Edition. Towards the end of 1593 Palestrina had ready for the press his Sixth Book of Masses, dedicated to Cardinal Pietro Aldobrandini, the Pope's nephew, a pupil of the Oratory of Philip Neri, who had taken the composer into his service for domestic chamber music. Perhaps the easy book of Litanies above mentioned may have been composed for the Cardinal's household or for oratory services. The Book of Masses contains four *a* 4: ' Dies Sanctificatus,' ' In te Domine speravi,' ' Sine nomine,' ' Quam pulchra es,' and one *a* 5, ' Dilexi quoniam.' The Mass ' Sine nomine' takes its themes from a chanson, ' Je suis désheritée,' and we may point out that the soprano part in the three Kyries put together is almost note for note identical with the soprano part of the chanson as set by Pierre Cadéac,[3] and there is also a certain resemblance in the opening counterpoint. It is probable, therefore, that Palestrina took the themes direct from the chanson, rather than, as has been alleged, from a Mass with the same title by Maillard or Meolas de Marle. Palestrina's Mass is very concise after the French manner, but it is remarkable what devotional feeling he imparts to the themes by his harmonic and contrapuntal treatment of them. It is as if he gave to the love-longing of the French song a spiritual meaning. The Mass ' Dies Sanctificatus ' is a brilliant work based on his own Christmas Motet ; the others probably take their themes from unknown motets by other composers. The ' Dilexi quoniam' is a specially lovely work. To the second edition of this book in 1596 there was added an earlier Mass *a* 6, Ave Maria, in which one of the voices interpolates as an occasional cantus firmus the text ' Ave Maria gratia plena.'

On Jan. 1, 1594, Palestrina signed his dedication to Christina of Lorraine, Grand Duchess of Tuscany, of the last work published by himself, his ' Second Book of Madrigali Spirituali' *a* 5, sometimes acclaimed as the perfect flower of his art, remarkable alike for exquisite grace and intense spirituality. It consists of 30 settings of a series of Italian stanzas forming one long Litany, addressed with the exception of the opening and closing numbers to the Blessed Virgin. It is a sort of counterpart to the motets on the Canticles, only of a graver cast, being pitched in a more meditative and penitential key. A Seventh Book of Masses was being prepared for the press when death overtook the master on Feb. 2, 1594, in the 69th year of his age. Baini's account of the last hours of his life is pure invention as what might seem to be its fitting conclusion,

---

1 The Canzonette of 1591 with cembalo and lute is now republished complete in *Chansons italiennes de la fin du XVIe siècle,* A. Wotquenne Plateel.

2 This has been edited with English words in L. Benson's Oriana series.

3 Cf. text and music of the chanson in Eitner *Publikation,* Bd. 23 p. 20.

but rests on no authority. We know, however, that Palestrina was buried in one of the side chapels of the old Basilica of St. Peter's, but in the erection of the gorgeous new building his remains, with those of others, were transferred to some other part of the building, and his actual resting-place is not now known. On the plate of his coffin was simply inscribed :

JOANNES PETRUS ALOYSIUS PRAENESTINUS
MUSICAE PRINCEPS.

At his funeral his own ' Libera me Domine ' was probably sung, and on Feb. 14 a solemn Requiem for him was sung in St. Peter's, probably his own Missa pro defunctis.

POSTHUMOUS PUBLICATIONS. — From the diary of the Papal Chapel Baini quotes a notice to the effect that Pope Clement VIII. on Feb. 9, 1594, the anniversary of his coronation, declared his intention to order the publication of a complete edition of the works of Palestrina. Meantime Iginio, his only surviving son, had brought out the Seventh Book of Masses with a dedication to Pope Clement, dated Mar. 1, in which he states that his father had charged him to proceed with the publication of his remaining works, and expresses the hope that the benevolence of the Pope would enable him to carry out his father's wishes. Baini professes to know that owing to the generosity of his patrons of the previous year Palestrina had also left sufficient means to Iginio for further publication, and represents that by concealing this fact Iginio lost the favour of Pope Clement, who took no further interest in the matter ; but all this is pure conjecture on Baini's part, for which he gives no authority, and it is a very poor reason to give for the Pope's cessation of interest, considering the numerous MSS. of Palestrina in the various Roman archives, over which Iginio had no control whatever. But Iginio was also implicated in another matter in which he may have incurred greater disfavour. Under the patronage of the Medici a printing press had been established at Rome, which had recently been provided with a set of new large types for the printing of plain-song, and negotiations had been entered into either with Palestrina himself before his death, or with his son Iginio afterwards, for the printing of his MS. of the Gradual. A contract was made with Iginio according to which he was to receive the exorbitant sum he had asked for on condition that the MS. obtained the official approval of the Sacred Congregation of Rites. No absolute approval was ever obtained, objection being taken that part of the work was not by Palestrina, and was full of errors. A prolonged lawsuit followed which gave satisfaction to neither party, and the MS. was set aside till after Iginio's death in 1610. In 1611 the printing project was resumed, and the work of

revision was entrusted to Felice Anerio and Soriano. It has always been a moot point whether this revision was based on the previous work of Palestrina, or was quite independent.[1] In any case it was conducted on principles of musical reform adopted by all the leading musicians of the time, which, however, were at variance with the general tradition of plain-song. As thus revised, the work was published in 1614 with some appearance of official approval, though its use was not made obligatory. It is known as the 'Editio medicaea,' but has now been officially rejected in favour of a return to earlier and purer tradition.

Leaving this embittered controversy, we may now return to the further publication of Palestrina's own works. The Seventh Book of Masses, published in 1594, contained three a 4, ' Ave Maria,' ' Sanctorum Meritis,' ' Emendemus,' and two a 5, ' Sacerdos et Pontifex,' ' Tu es pastor ovium,' all works of distinction, and with the exception of the ' Emendemus,' based on plain-song themes. The opening theme of ' Emendemus ' is strikingly similar to the first phrase of ' Je suis désheritée.' Iginio, disappointed in his expectations of support from the Vatican, took no further steps in the publication of his father's works, but in 1598 two Venetian admirers of Palestrina's music seem to have acquired from him the MSS. of masses remaining on his hands, and from 1599 to 1601 six further books of masses were published at Venice, numbered as Books 8 to 13. The eighth book contains two a 4, ' Quem dicunt homines,' ' Dum esset summus Pontifex,' two a 5, ' O admirabile commercium,' ' Memor esto,' and two a 6, ' Dum complerentur,' ' Sacerdotes Domini.' Of these, ' O admirabile commercium ' and ' Dum complerentur,' based on his own beautiful motets, have been universally admired. ' Sacerdotes Domini ' is remarkable for its combination of great beauty with extraordinary mastery of canonic device. The canon has the motto ' Trinitas in unitate,' and, beginning in the lowest tenor is resolved by the two other tenors at the second and third respectively. It runs throughout the Mass with the usual exception of the Crucifixus and Benedictus. The Pleni of the Sanctus is only for the three voices in canon. The whole Mass is, as Baini says, an exquisite product of consummate art. The ninth book has two masses a 4, ' Ave Regina coelorum,' ' Veni sponsa Christi,' two a 5, ' Vestiva i colli,' ' Sine nomine,' two a 6, ' In te Domine speravi,' ' Te Deum laudamus.' The ' Sine nomine ' is another specimen of an elaborate canonic mass, but not otherwise very interesting than for its conquest of difficulties. It has canons on all degrees of the scale and at various time-intervals. Baini and Haberl extol very highly ' In te Domine speravi,' but we might

[1] Cf. Haberl, *Kirchenmusikalisches Jahrbuch* (1902), pp. 138 ff., also Respighi, *Nuovo studio su G. P. L. da Palestrina e l' emendazioni del Graduale Romano, con Appendice di documenti*.

conjecture its themes to be taken from some unknown motet rather than, as Haberl says, from the plain-song of the Ambrosian hymn. The Tenth Book of Masses was published in 1600 and contains two *a* 4, ' In illo tempore,' ' Gia fu chi m' ebbe cara,' this latter based on one of the composer's own early madrigals, two *a* 5, ' Petra sancta,' ' O Virgo simul et mater,' two *a* 6, ' Quinti toni,' ' Illumina oculos meos,' the two last particularly fine. The eleventh book has one Mass *a* 4, ' Descendit Angelus,' two *a* 5, ' Regina coeli,' ' Quando laeta sperai,' two *a* 6, ' Octavi Toni,' ' Alma Redemptoris.' The ' Octavi Toni ' has in the second soprano part a Cantus Firmus of the eighth mode, which, however, might seem to be the melody of some popular song, treated freely by the introduction of occasional F and C sharp and B flat. ' Alma Redemptoris ' is no doubt the finest of this set. The twelfth book appeared in 1601, and contains two *a* 4, ' Regina coeli,' ' O rex gloriae,' two *a* 5, ' Ascendo ad Patrem,' ' Qual e il più grand' amor,' two *a* 6, ' Tu es Petrus,' ' Viri Galilaei.' Of these the third, fifth and sixth, based on his own very bright motets, are the finest. The thirteenth book has the four masses *a* 8, all splendid works based on the composer's own motets, ' Laudate Dominum omnes gentes,' ' Hodie Christus natus est,' ' Fratres enim ego accepi,' ' Confitebor tibi.'

With the exception of the Mass ' Assumpta ' in 1612 and four motets in collections of 1609 and 1614, and the Stabat Mater by Dr. Burney in 1771, there was no further publication of other works by Palestrina during the 17th and 18th centuries. Repeated editions of already published works appeared for a time until towards the middle of the 17th century. From 1650 the musical world, occupied with new problems, ceased to take further interest in the old vocal style *alla Palestrina*, although the tradition was still kept up in the Sistine Chapel and other churches of Rome by a succession of minor masters. Towards the end of the 18th century a certain amount of interest in the older music, and specially that of Palestrina, was awakened by the writings of Padre Martini, Dr. Burney, and Hawkins, but it was not till well on into the 19th century that any practical steps were taken towards further publication and performance. The romantic literary movement in France and Germany stimulated the growing interest in the older Italian church music, and much was done in the MS. copying of old works by amateur collectors. Alexandre Choron in 1815 appealed for the provision of MS. copies of Palestrina's works for public libraries in France. In a collection which he published he unfortunately included as an early work of Palestrina a series of 27 Responsoria for Holy Week, which have only recently been discovered to be the work of another composer at a later date (see INGEGNERI). In Germany, in opposition to the prevailing shallowness of the church music of the time, Anton Thibaut in his book *Über Reinheit der Tonkunst*, published 1825–26, eloquently pleaded for the study and performance of the works of Palestrina, Victoria, and others of the older school. Greater influence was exercised in the same direction by the appearance of the Abbé Baini's enthusiastic biography of Palestrina, published in 1828 (*Memorie storico-critiche*, etc.), which though inaccurate in detail, and gravely misleading on certain points, and too one-sided, yet led the way to a fuller appreciation of the special merits of Palestrina, and also later on to further critical investigation. Baini had also issued a prospectus intimating his intention to issue a complete edition of the works of the master, and in 1835 negotiations were entered into and a contract signed with the house of Breitkopf & Härtel in Leipzig, but the death of Baini in 1844, before anything had really been done by him, led to the temporary abandonment of this enterprise. Meantime in 1841–43 Alfieri in Rome had published, though very uncritically, a large collection of the works of Palestrina in seven volumes. Better work was done by Canon Proske of Ratisbon, who after laborious copying of MSS. from various Roman and other Italian libraries, published from 1853–61 his very comprehensive collection entitled ' Musica divina,' containing for practical use a large selection of the finest works of Palestrina and other composers of his epoch, many of them previously unknown.

The complete edition of Breitkopf & Härtel was begun in a tentative way by the publication in 1862–63 of the first three volumes containing the motets of 1569, 1572 and 1575, which had been prepared for the press by Theodore De Witt seven years before. The work was resumed by the publication, under the editorship of Franz Espagne of the Berlin Royal Library, in 1874 of vol. iv. containing the two books of motets *a* 5 of 1584; in 1875 vol. v., containing the motets *a* 4 of 1563 and 1581. Vols. vi. and vii. appeared in 1876, containing a large collection of previously unpublished motets gathered by Espagne from the various Roman libraries. Vol. viii., containing the ' Hymni totius anni ' of 1589, was published in 1880. After Espagne's death Franz Commer edited vol. ix., containing the ' Offertoria ' of 1593. From 1881 the editorship of the remaining works was entrusted to F. X. Haberl of Ratisbon. Vols. x.-xxii. contain the thirteen Books of Masses in order; vols. xxiii. and xxiv. 12 additional masses edited from MSS. in the Sistine and other Roman archives. Vol. xxv. consists of the ' Four Books of Lamentations.' Vol. xxvi. contains 10 litanies and 6 motets *a* 12, or for 3 choirs *a* 4, the third choir having to be filled up by M. Haller of Ratisbon, the original being lost. Vol. xxvii. consists of three books of Magnificats and three separate, making 35 in all. Vol. xxviii. contains the two published Books of Madrigals of 1555 and 1586, with a third book of 30 numbers gathered from various collections. Vol. xxix. consists of the two Books of Spiritual Madrigals of 1581 and 1594. Vols. xxx. to xxxiii. are supplementary, and contain a large number of other works, sacred and secular, gleaned from various printed and MS. sources, including a good many doubtful or unauthenticated, among which may be mentioned 8 textless Ricercari on the eight tones, which may be regarded as instrumental works, and ' xi. Exercizi sopra la scala ' for choir practice. A biography with full documents was promised as a concluding volume, but has never appeared. On the basis of this edition the genuine works of Palestrina may be classified as follows : 94 Masses, about 350 Motets without reckoning separately their second parts, 35 Magnificats, 64 Hymns, 42 Lamentation-Lessons, 10 Litanies, the Improperia and some Fauxbourdon and other settings of Benedictus and Miserere ; 140 Madrigals, without reckoning separate parts. Numerous editions of single masses and motets with Latin and English words have appeared in recent years. A useful English monograph on the life and works of Palestrina by Zoë Kendrick Pyne was published in 1922 (see MODERN BIBLIOGRAPHY below).

### GENERAL LIST OF PALESTRINA'S WORKS

#### I. Original Editions in Chronological Order

**1554.** *Missarum Liber I.*, dedicated to Pope Julius III., containing originally five masses : 4 *a* 4, ' Ecce Sacerdos Magnus,' ' O regem coeli,' ' Virtute magna,' ' Gabriel Archangelus ' ; 1 *a* 5, ' Ad coenam agni.' A later edition of 1591 contains two more : 1 *a* 5, ' Pro defunctis ' ; 1 *a* 6, ' Sine nomine.'

**1555.** *Il primo libro di Madrigali*, without dedication, containing originally 22 n. *a* 4, the last being a sestina in six parts. A later edition in 1594 added one more, making 23 n.

**1563.** *Motetta Festorum totius anni cum communi Sanctorum*, Liber I., dedicated to Ridolfo Pio di Carpi, Cardinal Bishop of Ostia, containing 36 n. *a* 4.

**1567.** *Missarum Liber II.*, dedicated to Philip II. of Spain, containing seven masses : 4 *a* 4, ' De Beata Virgine,' ' Inviolata,' ' Sine nomine,' ' Ad fugam ' ; 2 *a* 5, Aspice Domine,' ' Salvum me fac ' ; 1 *a* 6, ' Papae Marcelli.'

**1569.** *Motettorum, quae partim 5, partim 6, partim 7 vocibus concinuntur*, Liber I., dedicated to the Cardinal of Ferrara, Hippolito d' Este, contains 24 n. *a* 5, 7 *a* 6, 2 *a* 7.

**1570.** *Missarum Liber III.*, dedicated to Philip II. of Spain, containing eight masses : 4 *a* 4, ' Spem in alium,' ' Primi toni,' ' Brevis,' ' De Feria ' ; 2 *a* 5, ' L'homme armé,' ' Repleatur os meum ' ; 2 *a* 6, ' De Beata Virgine,' ' Ut re mi fa sol la.'

**1572.** *Motettorum quae partim 5, partim 6, partim 8 vocibus concinuntur*, Liber II., dedicated to Duke William of Mantua, containing 17 n. *a* 5, of which three are by two sons and a brother of Palestrina ; 8 n. *a* 6, of which one by the brother of Palestrina ; and 4 n. *a* 8.

**1575.** *Motettorum quae partim 5, partim 6, partim 8 voc. concinuntur*, Liber III., dedicated to Alfonso II. Duke of Ferrara, containing 18 n. *a* 5, 9 *a* 6, 6 *a* 8.

**1581.** *Il primo libro di Madrigali a cinque voci*, dedicated to Jacomo Buoncompagni, Duke of Sora, contains twenty-six spiritual madrigals, beginning with seven of the ' Vergini ' of Petrarch, all *a* 5.

**1581.** *Motettorum quatuor vocibus partim plena voce et partim paribus vocibus*, also dedicated to Jacomo Buoncompagni, contains 21 n., of which 11 are for equal voices.

**1582.** *Missarum Lib. IV.*, dedicated to Pope Gregory XIII., contains 4 *a* 4, ' Lauda Sion,' ' Primi toni,' ' Jesu nostra redemptio,' ' L'homme armé ' (Dorian mode) ; 3 *a* 5, ' Eripe me,' ' Secunda,' ' O magnum mysterium.'

**1584.** *Motettorum quinque voc.* Liber IV. ex Canticis Canticorum, dedicated to Pope Gregory XIII., contains 29 n. *a* 5.

**1584.** *Motettorum 5 voc.* Liber V., dedicated to Cardinal Bathory, nephew of the King of Poland, contains 20 n., the first of which is a setting of some laudatory verses on the Bathory family.

**1586.** *Il secondo libro di Madrigali a quatro voci*, dedicated to Giulio Cesare Colonna, Prince of Palestrina, contains 25 n. *a* 4.

**1588.** *Lamentationum* Lib. I., 4 voc., dedicated to Pope Sixtus V.

**1589.** *Hymni totius anni* . . . . 4 voc., also dedicated to Pope Sixtus V., contains 45 n. *a* 4-6.

(In 1644 a new edition of this book was published at Antwerp by order and at the expense of Pope Urban VIII., with the texts altered in accordance with the Breviary of 1631. The last ten hymns were left out and two others substituted. The new texts were an alteration for the worse, and also caused alteration of Palestrina's music.)

**1590.** *Missarum Lib. V.*, dedicated to Duke William of Bavaria, Count Palatine of the Rhine, contains four masses *a* 4, ' Aeterna Christi Munera,' ' Jam Christus astra ascenderat,' ' Panis quem ego dabo,' ' Iste Confessor ' ; 2 *a* 5, ' Nigra sum,' ' Sicut lilium inter spinas ' ; 1 *a* 6, ' Nasce la gioia mia.'

**1591.** *Magnificat Octotonum* Lib. I., dedicated to Pope Gregory XIV. contains two sets of eight Magnificats *a* 4 on the eight church tones, the first set being a setting of the odd verses, the second of the even verses.

**1593.** *Offertoria totius anni secundum sanctae Romanae ecclesiae consuetudinem 5 voc. concinenda*, dedicated to the Abbé Antoine de Baume, appeared in two parts, containing together 68 n. *a* 5.

**1593.** *Litaniae Deiparae Virginis quae in sacellis societatis S. Rosarii ubique dicatis concinuntur*, contains ten litanies, or rather two litanies in five parts each *a* 4, with an Ave Maria *a* 4 in each.

**1593–94.** *Missarum Lib. VI.*, dedicated to Cardinal Aldobrandini, contains 4 *a* 4, ' Dies Sanctificatus,' ' In te Domine speravi,' ' Sine nomine ' (or ' Je suis déshéritée '), ' Quam pulchra ' ; 1 *a* 5, ' Dilexi quoniam ' 1 *a* 6, Ave Maria (this last Mass was not in the first edition of Book VI. as arranged by Palestrina himself before his death, but appears in the second edition published at Venice in 1596).

**1594.** *Delli Madrigali Spirituali a cinque voci* Lib. II., dedicated to the Grand Duchess of Tuscany, Christina of Lorraine, married to Ferdinand de' Medici, contains 30 n. *a* 5.

**1594.** *Missarum Lib. VII.*, dedicated after Palestrina's death to Pope Clement VIII., contains 3 *a* 4, Ave Maria, ' Sanctorum Meritis,' ' Emendemus ' ; 2 *a* 5, ' Sacerdos et Pontifex,' ' Tu es pastor ovium.'

**1599.** *Missarum Lib. VIII.*, contains 2 *a* 4, ' Quem dicunt hommes,' ' Dum esset summus pontifex ' ; 2 *a* 5, ' O admirabile commercium,' ' Memor esto ' ; 2 *a* 6, ' Dum complerentur,' ' Sacerdotes Domini.'

**1599.** *Missarum Lib. IX.*, contains 2 *a* 4, ' Ave Regina coelorum,' ' Veni sponsa Christi ' ; 2 *a* 5, ' Vestiva i colli,' ' Sine nomine ' ; 2 *a* 6, ' In te Domine speravi, Te Deum laudamus.'

**1600.** *Missarum Lib. X.*, contains 2 *a* 4. ' In illo tempore,' ' Giz fu chi m' ebbe cara ' ; 2 *a* 5, ' Petra sancta,' ' O Virgo simul et mater ' ; 2 *a* 6, ' Quinti toni,' ' Illumina oculos meos.'

**1600.** *Missarum Lib. XI.*, contains 1 *a* 4, ' Descendit Angelus ' ; 2 *a* 5, ' Regina coeli,' ' Quando laeta speral ' ; 2 *a* 6, ' Octavi Toni,' ' Alma Redemptoris.'

**1601.** *Missarum Lib. XII.*, contains 2 *a* 4, ' Regina coeli,' ' O rex gloriae ' ; 2 *a* 5, ' Ascendo ad Patrem,' ' Qual è il più grand' amor ' ; 2 *a* 6, ' Tu es Petrus,' ' Viri Galilaei.'

**1601.** *Missarum Lib. XIII.*, contains 4 *a* 8, ' Laudate Dominum,' ' Hodie Christus natus,' ' Fratres enim ego accepi,' ' Confitebor tibi.' The Mass ' Confitebor ' had been previously published separately by Scotto in Venice in 1585.

**1612.** The celebrated Mass *a* 6, ' Assumpta est Maria,' composed and presented to the Papal Chapel in 1585, was not then printed, as Baini says, but was only printed some time after 1611 (according to Haberl).

Other works of Palestrina which appeared in his lifetime or shortly after his death are :

1. Over forty madrigals which appeared in various collections from 1554–92, of which thirty-five have been recovered complete with all their parts, and are now republished in the complete edition of Breitkopf & Härtel. Among them may be mentioned a canzor *a* 4 in fourteen parts, appended originally to the Second Book of Madrigals of Cyprian de Rore, 1557 ; two *a* 5, composed to commemorate the victory of Lepanto, 1571 ; one *a* 6, contributed to the *Trionfo di Dori*, 1592.

2. Two motets *a* 4 and 8 in collections 1563 and 1592.

3. Three contributions to ' Verovio Diletto Spirituale,' 1586, 2 *a* 3, 1 *a* 4 provided with lute or cembalo accompaniment.

4. Three motets and a litany *a* 8 published in F. Constantini's collections 1614 and 1620, including the famous ' Fratres ego enim ' sung in the services of Maundy Thursday.

The famous Stabat Mater *a* 8, with the ' Improperia,' was first published by Dr. Burney in 1771 from a MS. copy presented to him by Santarelli, a singer in the Papal Chapel. Dr. Burney's publication was entitled *La musica della Settimana Santa*.

**II.** PREVIOUSLY UNPUBLISHED WORKS from the MS. choir-books of the Sistine Chapel and other Roman archives. now for the first time printed in the complete edition of Breitkopf & Härtel, edited by Th. de Witt, F. Espagne, and from Vol. X. by Dr. F. X. Haberl.

1. Twelve masses as follows : (1) (dated 1565) ' Sine titulo ' *a* 6 (which may, however, bear the title ' Benedicta,' as being based on Josquin's motet *a* 6, ' Benedicta es coelorum regina ') ; (2) two presented to the Papal Chapel in 1571, ' Beatus Laurentius ' *a* 5, ' Veni Creator Spiritus ' *a* 6 ; (3) three presented to the Papal Chapel, 1585–86, Salve Regina *a* 5, ' O sacrum convivium ' *a* 5, ' Ecce ego Joannes ' *a* 6 ; (4) two others about 1590, ' Pater Noster ' *a* 4, ' Panem nostrum ' *a* 5 ; (5) three masses composed for the chapel of the Duke of Altaemps, ' Tu es Petrus ' *a* 6, ' In majoribus duplicibus ' *a* 4, ' In minoribus duplicibus ' *a* 4 ; (6) a ' Sine titulo ' *a* 6, which is based on the same themes as ' Missa Primi toni,' 1570.

2. Over sixty undoubtedly genuine motets *a* 4-8, besides a large number doubtful or unauthenticated. There are also 6 *a* 12, or for three choirs *a* 4, of which, however, the parts for the third choir have been lost, but have been filled up by M. Haller. A Stabat Mater *a* 12, attributed to Palestrina, is believed by Proske and Ambros to be the composition of Felice Anerio.

3. Three further books of Lamentations *a* 5-8, besides a few single Lamentations and Fragments.

4. Two further books of Magnificats *a* 5-6, earlier and more elaborate compositions than those published in 1591. Also two single Magnificats *a* 4, one for equal voices, and one *a* 8 for two choirs with all the verses composed.

5. Eight Litanies *a* 5-8 (' De B. V. M.' and ' Sacrosanctae Eucharistiae,' etc.).

6. Twenty hymns a 4-5, and various settings of the ' Miserere ' and ' Benedictus,' and the Responsorium ' Libera ' (the Responsoria for Holy Week are now known to be by Ingegneri).

7. Two sets of textless ' Ricercari ' a 4 (attributed to Palestrina), one entitled ' XI Exercizi sopra la scala ' ; the other, ' VIII sopra ii toni.'

### MODERN BIBLIOGRAPHY

ALBERTO CAMETTI : (1) Le case di Giovanni Perluigi da Palestrina in Roma. R.M.I., 1921, pp. 419-32.

(2) G. P. da Palestrina e il suo commercio di pelliccerie. (Rome, 1922.)

(3) Rubino Mallanert, maestro di Giovanni Perluigi da Palestrina. R.M.I. Anno 29, 1922, pp. 335-47.

(4) Giovanni Pierluigi da Palestrina e le sue alleanze matrimoniali. R.M.I., 1923, pp. 489-510.

RAFFAELLO CASIMIRI : (1) Giovanni Pierluigi da Palestrina. Nuovi documenti biografici, pp. 36. (Rome, 1918.) See review by P. Wagner in Z.M.W., Dec. 1918, pp. 198-200.

(2) Il codice 59 dell' archivio musicale lateranense, autografo di Giov. Pierluigi da Palestrina. Con appendice di composizioni inedite a dieci tavole fotolipiche, pp. x. 138, 28. (Rome, 1919.) See review by P. Wagner in Z.M.W., Sept. 1919, pp. 722-25.

(3) Fasc. 2 of Raffaele Casimiri's Nuovi documenti biografici, appeared at Rome, 1922.

A. GUZZO : Il Gregoriano e Palestrina. R.M.I., 1921, pp. 1-52.

ZOE KENDRICK PYNE : Giovanni Perluigi da Palestrina : his Life and Times. (London, 1922.)

EUGEN SCHMITZ : Giovanni Perluigi Palestrina. (Leipzig, 1914.)

KARL WEINMANN : (1) Palestrinas Geburtsjahr. Eine historisch-kritische Untersuchung, pp. 20. (Regensburg and Rome, 1915.) See notice in Z.M.W., Oct. 1918, p. 76.

(2) Zur Geschichte von Palestrinas Missa Papae Marcelli. J.M.P., 1916.

(3) Das Konzil von Trient und die Kirchenmusik. Eine historisch-kritische Untersuchung, pp. ix. 155. (Leipzig, 1919.) See review in Z.M.W., Feb. 1920, pp. 312-15.     J. R. M.

**PALLAVICINI** (PALLAVICINO), CARLO (b. Brescia[1] ; d. Dresden Jan. 29, 1688), composed no fewer than twenty-one operas or ' dramme per musica,' which were performed at Venice between 1666 and 1687. He lived first at Salò, and was married to Giulia Rossi, of Padua. At Padua, Mar. 21, 1672, his son Stefano Benedetto was born, who later furnished the text of more than one opera, and also wrote a Discorso della musica.[2]

Carlo Pallavicini went for a while to Venice, but from 1667-73 he was at Dresden, first as vice-Kapellmeister, then as Kapellmeister to Johann Georg II. of Saxony. Lindau[3] mentions the Kapellmeister Pallavicini being one of the company at a private celebration of Mass at the French Embassy in Dresden on Apr. 6, 1673. But he appears to have returned to Venice shortly afterwards, for in the autumn of 1674 his operas, which had ceased since 1667, re-started at the theatres there. Early in 1685 Johann Georg III., the son of his former patron, invited him to return to Dresden in order to place the Italian opera on a satisfactory footing ; presumably he made but flying visits there, but on Jan. 1, 1687, he was formally appointed ' Camerae ac theatralis musicae Praefectum.'[4] He received leave to visit Venice in September of the same year, but died very shortly after his return to Dresden, and was buried on Feb. 4, 1688, in the Kloster Marienstern.

Although there seems to be no record of Pallavicini's earlier works being performed at Dresden, two of his later operas were certainly first produced there, in 1687 and 1689. Fürstenau, comparing his music with that of Bontempi, his fellow-worker, thinks that he shows more facility in his treatment of melody

---

1 Riemann gives 1630 at Salò.
2 Algarotti, Delle opere del S.B.P., 1744.
3 Gesch. Dresden, 1862.
4 Fürstenau, Zur Gesch. der Musik, 1861, p. 291.

and rhythm and in his use of the limited instrumental resources at his command. As a rule only string instruments, trumpets and drums formed the orchestra for the ritornelli or short symphonies interspersed between the songs ; often, as in the case of ' L' Amazzone corsara,' no mention is made in the score of the instruments required for the performance. The following list of the operas performed at Venice is taken from Bonlini's Glorie della poesia, Venice, c. 1732, and Galvani's I teatri musicali di Venezia, Milan, 1878 :

1666. ' Il Demetrio,' also ' L' Aureliano,' text by Giacomo dall' Angelo, at the Teatro S. Moisé. MS. score of the former in the library of S. Marco, Venice, No. 408 (Wiel, I codici musicali, Venezia, 1888).

1667. ' Il tiranno umiliato dall' amore, overo il Meraspe,' text by Gio. Faustini, at the Teatro Grimano de' SS. Gio. e. Paolo.

1675. ' Il Dioclezlano,' by Matteo Noris, at SS. Gio. e. Paolo. MS. scores at S. Marco, Venice, No. 409 ; and at Modena.

1675. ' Enea in Italia,' by G. F. Bussani, at SS. Gio. e. Paolo. MS. scores at S. Marco, Venice, Nos. 412 and 414.

1676. ' Il Galieno,' by M. Noris, at SS. Gio. e Paolo. An autograph score at the Vienna Imperial Library, No. 16,491 (Mantuani's Cat.). MS. score at S. Marco, Venice, No. 424 ; part of the score in MS. at Dresden, No. 1074.

1678. ' Il Vespasiano,' by G. C. Corradi, was performed at the opening of the new Teatro Grimano di S. Gio. Grisostomo, and again in 1680. MS. scores at Modena and at Venice, No. 462.

1679. ' Il Nerone,' by G. C. Corradi, at S. Gio. Grisostomo. On Oct. 3, 1693, it was performed at the Italian Opera House in Leipzig, under the direction of N. A. Strungk. ' Le Amazoni nell' Isole Fortunate,' prologue and three acts by Piccioli. A copy of the libretto, published at Padua, is in the library of the Brussels Conservatoire, the title - page states ' da rappresentarsi in Piazzola, nel nobilissimo Teatro del Ill. et Eccel. Sig. Marco Contarini. Proc. di S. Marco, l' anno 1679 ' (Wotquenne, Cat.). The MS. score is at S. Marco, Venice, No. 384. Act II., Scene IX., a solo with ritornelli for ' trombe e timpano ' will be found in H. Goldschmidt's Studien zur Gesch. der ital. Oper, Leipzig, 1901. Beilage, p. 403.

1680. ' Messalina,' by Piccioli, at the Teatro Vendramino di San Salvatore. MS. score at S. Marco, Venice, No. 437.

1682. ' Bassiano, overo il maggior impossibile,' by M. Noris, at SS. Gio. e Paolo. MS. score at Modena.

1683. ' Carlo, re d' Italia ' ; 1683, ' Il re infante ' ; 1684, ' Licinio Imperatore,' and ' Il Ricimero, re de' Vandali ' ; 1685, ' Penelope la casta ' ; were all by M. Noris, and performed at S. Gio. Grisostomo.

1685. ' Massimo Puppieno,' by Aurelio Aureli, at SS. Gio. e Paolo.

1686. ' Amore innamorato,' by M. Noris, at S. Gio. Grisostomo. ' La Didone delirante,' by Ant. Franceschi, at SS. Gio. e Paolo. ' L' Amazzone corsara, overo l' Alvilda, regina de' Gotti,' by G. C. Corradi, at SS. Gio. e Paolo, and again in 1688. In the preface to the libretto (Venice, 1686), Corradi draws attention to ' la musica del Sig. Carlo Pallavicini ; il quale si fin hora feci miracolo ne' Teatri ' (Wotquenne, Cat.). The MS. score is in the Munich State Library, No. 235. The first movement of the symphony was published by A. Heuss Die venetianische Opern-Sinfonien, 1902-3.

1687. ' Elmiro, re di Corinto,' text probably by Vinc. Grimani, at S. Gio. Grisostomo. Many of the airs are in MS. Mus. Sch. c. 103, in the Bodleian Library.

' La Gerusalemme liberata,' by G. C. Corradi, at SS. Gio. e Paolo. It was performed at Dresden on Feb. 2, 1687 ; and at Hamburg in 1693, where also a German version by Fiedler, under the title of ' Armida,' was given in 1695 (Mattheson, Der musicalische Patriot, 1728, pp. 181-2). MS. scores at the Library of the Brussels Conservatoire, and at Dresden, B 595a.

1689. ' Antiope,' dramma per musica, by Steffano B. Pallavicini, only partly composed by Carlo Pallavicini before his death, was completed by Nic. Adam Strungk and performed four times at Dresden in Feb. 1689. The MS. score at Dresden.

There are various compositions in manuscript ; at Modena, some arie e canzoni with two violins and basso continuo from ' L' Adalinda,' Florence, 1679 ; three cantatas and one aria ; and ' Il trionfo della castità,' an oratorio for seven voices with instruments, Modena, 1688. Burney[5] writes :

' If Carlo Pallavicini ever had any genius, it was exhausted when he set this oratorio, which has neither invention nor learning to recommend it.'

At Munich, MS. 233, a cantata for soprano with basso continuo ; at Ch. Ch., Oxford, three Fantasias a 4 e 5 voci, by ' Pallavicino ' ; at

---

5 Hist. of Music, iv. pp. 113-14.

Dresden, a Mass for five voices with two violins and basso continuo ; Kyrie, Gloria, Dixit, Confitebor, for four voices ; Laetatus sum, for bass voice with instruments (*Q.-L.*).

In Marco Silvani's *Canzonette per camera a voce sola*, Bologna, 1670, is ' La speranza ' in three movements by Carlo Pallavicini, and in Silvani's *Raccolta di motetti*, ' Ecce filii,' a voce sola col basso continuo.                C. S.

PALLAVICINI, VINCENZO (*b.* Brescia), was maestro di cappella at the Conservatorio degl' In curabili at Venice. The name of 'Pallavicini, Vincenzo, bresciano, del 1743,' appears among the composers of some pieces of manuscript music in the Bologna Liceo Musicale, which were the trial compositions for election to the Accademia dei Filarmonici of Bologna.[1] He composed the music to the first act of an opera buffa, ' Lo speziale ' (The Apothecary), written by Goldoni, the two remaining acts oeing set to music by Domenico Fischietti, a Neapolitan ; a manuscript score is in the library of the Brussels Conservatoire.[2] The opera was performed at the Teatro San Samuele, Venice, in 1755. Among the manuscript sinfonie given in the Breitkopf list for 1767 (Supplemento ii. p. 30), is one ' di Pallavicini. Accommodate per il cembalo solo.' ·

Succi's catalogue of the International Musical Exhibition at Bologna in 1888 includes among the autographs a letter from Pallavicini to Padre Martini, which deplores the recent death of G. A. Perti ; it is dated from Venice, Apr. 21, 1756. The eighteenth volume of Martini's correspondence, preserved in the Bologna Liceo Musicale, consists of letters from Pallavicini, to whom Martini was evidently a counsellor and friend.                C. S.

PALLAVICINO, BENEDETTO (*b.* Cremona ; *d.* 1612/13). His first musical work was published at Venice in 1579. A few years later he was at Mantua, and his name is found in documents in the Gonzaga Archives ; in one, dated May 11, 1582, Cardinal Annibale Ippolito promises to send a sonnet to the Duke ' come prima sarà posto in musico dal Pallavicino ' ; in another, dated Dec. 18, 1584, Pallavicino signs himself ' musico di sua Altezza ' ; and in 1587 his name appears in the list of cantori.[3] Giaches de Wert, maestro di cappella to the Duke of Mantua, died on May 23, 1596 ; Pallavicino was appointed in his place, and uses the title for the first time in the 1596 edition of his fourth book of madrigals. He must have resigned the post in 1601, and Monteverdi, his successor, in a letter dated Nov. 28, 1601, mistakenly writes of him as if he were dead.[4] This probably led Pietro Phalesio, in reprinting the first book of madrigals for six voices in 1606, to write in the dedication of ' Benedetto

Pallavicino di felice memoria.' [5] But Pallavicino had joined the monks of Camaldoli in Tuscany ; the dedication of his seventh book of madrigals, 1604, to Francesco Gonzaga of Mantua, is signed B. P. ' monaco Camaldolese.' It is here that he mentions his twenty-two years of faithful service to the house of Gonzaga. There is some doubt as to the exact date of his death ; he wrote the dedication in his eighth book of madrigals, 1611–12, but he probably died soon after, either in 1612 or 1613.

A great many books of madrigals composed by Pallavicino were published at Venice, and also at Antwerp. Burney [6] states that the music lacks variety, both of melody and harmony, and shows no spirit of invention. A contemporary Italian [7] verdict is not so uncompromising—

' Che non basta, che siano fatte al proposito degl' instromenti, e delle voci, ma che siano uscite da valente pratico come quella di Benedetto Palauicino, etc.

The following works were first published at the dates given, but were constantly reprinted :

' Di B. P. Cremonese, Il primo libro de madrigali a quattro voci.' Venetia, 1579, obl. 4to. ' Il primo libro de madrigali a cinque voci.' Venetia, 1581, obl. 4to. ' Il secondo libro,' (?) 1583 and 1606. ' Il terzo libro,' 1585, B. P. writes the dedication from Mantua, Aug. 8, 1585. ' Il quarto libro,' 1588 ; reprinted in 1596 with ' Di B. F. maestro di cappella del serenissimo Sig. Duca di Mantua,' which title is used until the change to ' B. P. monaco Camaldolese ' in the 1604 and later works. ' Il quinto libro,' 1593. ' Il sesto libro, 1600. ' Il settimo libro,' 1604. ' L' ottav› libro,' 1911–12. ' Madrigali a cinque voci.' Anversa, Phalesio, 1604 was a reprint of the fourth and fifth books. ' Di B. P. servitore del serenisss. Sig. Duca di Mantova e di Monferato, Il primo libro de madrigali a sei voci.' Venetia, 1587. Of his church music little is known ; two volumes passed from the church of S. Barbara, Mantua, into the library of the Milan Conservatorio musicale: ' Libro primo di messe a 4, 5 e 6 voci,' Venetia, and ' Salmi delle Laudi a 8 voci,' Venetia. There is also: ' Sacrae Dei Laudes octo et una duodecim duae vero sexdecim vocibus concinendae. Ac omnium instrumentorum genere accomodatae. Additae etiam infimae partes pro Organo continuato.' Benedicto Palauicino Cremon. Auctore. Venetia R. Amadino, 1605, 4to. It contains fifteen motets ; the preface is signed ' Ravennae XI cal. Septembris, 1605. Di Ben. P. monaco camaldolese.' (Müller, *Cat.* Königsberg Bibl.) Fétis mentions an earlier edition, 1595–96, in four books. The popularity of Pallavicino's madrigals is shown by the way in which they appear in collections of that time. ' Quando benigna stella,' for four voices, is in Andrea Pevernage's *Harmonia celeste*, Antwerp, 1583, and from then on to 1624 there was hardly a single important collection, whether published at Venice, Nuremberg, Copenhagen, Munich, Leipzig, or at Utrecht, where Joachim van den Hove's *Florida sive cantiones*, with voice parts and lute accompaniment, was printed in 1601, that did not include some of his madrigals. In London, Nicolas Yonge's *Musica Transalpina*, 1597, had two of the madrigals for six voices.
*MSS.* In the British Museum, in the Add. MSS. 11,585, f. 22, a melody and a fugue from books 7 and 8 of madrigals ; 12,532, f. 199, ' Quando benigna stella ' from the 1579 madrigals ; 18,936-39, f. 39b, ' La Bella, Palevicyno ' for four voices ; 29,366-68, f. 12b, Cantus, Bassus, and Quintus only ' Cruell unkynd adieu ' for five voices ; 29,372-77 (date 1616), ' Love quench this heate ' and ' Cruell why dost thou flie me ' for six voices.
In the New York Library : twenty-seven madrigals for six voices in a 17th-century MS. entitled ' Francis Sambrook his book.' (H. Botstiber.)
In the Berlin Staat Bibliothek : MS. Z27, dated 1624, the score of ' Canite tuba ' for eight voices. (Eitner.)
In Bologna Liceo Musicale : in a 17th-century MS. score, for eight voices—' Dixit,' ' Confitebor,' ' Beatus vir,' ' Laudate pueri ' ; for four voices—' Miserere mei Deus.' A MS. copy by Santini of ' Canite tuba ' for eight voices, from Pallavicino's *Laudes*, 1605. (Parisini, ii. 169. etc.)
In the Breslau Stadtbibliothek : ' Jubilate Deo ' in MS. 19, and ' Canite tuba ' and ' Dum complerentur ' scored in MS. 20, and in partbooks MS. 23, all for eight voices. (Bohn's *Cat.*)
In the Liegnitz Ritter-Akademie Bibliothek : MS. 98, four motets for eight voices ; MS. 99, madrigal for six voices. (Pfudel's *Cat.*)
In the Munich Hofbibliothek : MS. 218, ' Qui super thronum ' (= ' Tutt' eri fuoco ') for five voices, and ' Omnes morti vicini ' (= ' Tirsi morir volea ') for six voices. (Maier's *Cat.*)
Two examples of Pallavicino's madrigals were included by L. Torchi in his publication of old music *L' arte musicale*, 1897, vol. ii., ' Dolcemente dormiva ' (1593), and ' Dolce, grave e acute' (1600), taken from the fifth book of madrigals for five voices.                C. S.

---

1 Parisini, *Catalogo*, iv. 181.
2 Wotquenne, *Catalogue*, No. 2276.
3 Canal, *Della musica in Mantova*, 1881, p. 69.
4 Vogel, *Vierteljahrsschrift*, 1887. iii. p. 323 ; vii. p. 282.

5 Vogel, *Weltl. Vocalmusik Italiens*, ii. p. 44.
6 *Hist. of Music*, iv. p. 113.
7 *L' Artusi overo delle imperfettioni della moderna musica*, Ven. 1600 p. 3.

PALMA, Silvestro (*b.* Ischia, 1762; *d.* Naples, Aug. 8, 1834), studied at the conservatoire of the Madonna di Loreto at Naples, and under Paisiello. He composed a considerable number of operas for Rome, Venice and Naples, where his last opera, ' Il geloso di se stesso,' was given in 1814. The autographs of a number of church compositions are preserved at the Milan Conservatoire (*Q.-L.*).

PALMER, Elizabeth Annie (known as Bessie) (*b.* 9 Fountain Court, Strand, Aug. 9, 1831 ; *d.* Oct. 1910), studied from 1851 to Jan. 1853 at the R.A.M. pianoforte from Jewson, harmony and counterpoint from Bannister, and singing from Cox and Crivelli. She then received private lessons from Garcia, and on Mar. 13, 1854, made her début at a concert of Alexandre Billet at the smaller St. Martin's Hall. On Dec. 20, at the larger hall, she sang in the ' Messiah ' under Hullah with great success. She became a favourite contralto singer at such institutions as the Sacred Harmonic ; the National Choral Society ; the Popular Concerts ; the Leeds Festival, 1858, where she sang at the opening of the New Town Hall in ' Elijah '; Worcester, Birmingham, and Norwich Festivals ; at a State Concert, Buckingham Palace, etc. From 1870 for some years she sang in various English opera enterprises, some of whose work was included in prises in the provinces, at the Crystal Palace, 1878, Her Majesty's Theatre, etc. From 1877–1886 she was in great request as a teacher of singing at Newcastle and elsewhere. In 1904 she published her *Musical Recollections*.

A. C.

PALMER, G. Molyneux (*b.* Staines, Oct. 8, 1882), of Irish parents, graduated Mus.B. at Oxford, in 1901. He studied under Stanford at the R.C.M. (1906–09), and came to Ireland in 1910, acting as organist of various churches. After winning two Feis Ceoil prizes with cantatas and songs, he produced an Irish opera, ' Sruth na maoile ' (Gaiety Theatre, Dublin, 1923), which was successfully revived at the Tailteann Games in August 1924. W. H. G. F.

PALMER, Henry, an English Church composer, probably of the first half of the 17th century, some of whose work was included in the Durham choir-books made in 1664, when John Cosin was Bishop there. In the British Museum (Add. MSS. 30,478-9), are the tenor cantoris parts of these books.

SERVICES

K. and C. PH.　　　　　　Preces and B. PH.

ANTHEMS

Almighty and everlasting God. Collect for the Feast of the Purification. Durh.; B.M. Add. MSS. 30,478-9.
Almighty and everlasting God. Collect for Ash Wednesday. Durh. B.M. Add. MSS. 30,478-9.
Almighty and everlasting God. Collect for Sunday before Easter. Durh.; B.M. Add. MSS. 30,478-9.
Almightie God, who out. B.M. Add. MSS. 30,478-9.
Heare my prayer. Durh.; O.B. A 5/33 ; Durh. C 16/58.
Lord what is man. P.H.
O Almighty God. Durh.
O goe not from me, *a* 5. B.M. Add. MSS. 17,792-6 (attributed to M. Pierson in Add. MSS. 29,372).
O God whose nature. Durh.; B.M. Add. MSS. 30,478-9.
The end of all things. Durh.; O.B. A 5/280.

One, Robert Palmer, contributed some settings to the second edition of Ravenscroft's Psalter (1633).　　　　　　　　　　J. M<sup>K</sup>.

PALMGREN, Selim (*b.* Björneborg, Finland, Feb. 16, 1878), pianist, conductor and composer, was educated at the Helsingfors Conservatorium from 1895–99, studying harmony and counterpoint with Martin Wegelius, and the pianoforte with Walter Petzet. He afterwards visited Germany and Italy, continuing his studies under Konrad Ansorge, Wilhelm Beyer and Ferruccio Busoni. On his return to his native country he had grown into a brilliant pianist and a composer of considerable promise. His first appointment was that of conductor to the Finnish Students' Choral Society, which proved an excellent opportunity to gain practical experience, and a fruitful incentive to compose a number of choral works. From 1909–12 he was conductor of the Musical Society of Åbo.

Palmgren's first opera, ' Daniel Hjort,' was produced at Helsingfors and Åbo in 1910, while his second work for the stage, the libretto of which is based on Chamisso's ' Peter Schlemihl,' has not yet been performed. In 1912 he threw up his official appointments, devoting himself exclusively to the career of composer and pianist. He undertook several extensive European tours, on some of which he was accompanied by his wife, the well-known Finnish singer, Maikki Järnefelt. During the European War Palmgren lived in Copenhagen. In 1920–1921 he toured the U.S.A. In 1923 he became teacher of composition at the Eastman School of Music, Rochester, N.Y.

Apart from the operas, some choral works and a number of songs, Palmgren has written almost exclusively for the piano. There are two concertos for that instrument, entitled ' Metamorphoses ' and ' The River,' but the bulk of his music consists of small pieces, some published singly, others in sets (' Finnish Lyric Pieces,' ' Light and Shade,' etc.).

The work of Selim Palmgren is distinguished by technical mastery of pianistic writing, a remarkable faculty for suggesting definite and widely contrasting moods, and an agreeably proportionate mixture of melodic, harmonic and rhythmic invention. The construction of ample forms is not a strong point with him, and his essentially pictorial art is at its best in short characteristic or lyrical pieces. In some ways Palmgren resembles Grieg, more especially in his power to infuse into his music a strong national flavour, on which, however, he is by no means compelled to rely altogether in order to create a work of distinction. He is frequently fanciful and individual where his nationality does not betray itself.

Palmgren is related by marriage to Armas Järnefelt and Jean Sibelius.　　　　E. B.

PALOTTA Matteo (*b.* Palermo *c.* 1689;

*d.* Vienna, Mar. 28, 1758), called Il Panormitano, from his birthplace Palermo, studied in the Conservatorio San Onofrio a., Naples. On his return to Palermo he passed the necessary examinations, and was ordained priest. He then devoted himself with great ardour to studies in part-writing and counterpoint, and produced a valuable work *Gregoriani cantus enucleata praxis et cognitio*, being a treatise on Guido d' Arezzo's Solmisation, and an instruction-book in the church-tones. It has been supposed that the Emperor Charles VI. invited Palotta to Vienna as Kapellmeister, but Palotta himself applied to the Emperor in 1733, asking for the post of composer of *a cappella* music. The then court-Kapellmeister warmly recommended him, and he was appointed one of the court-composers with a salary of 400 florins, on Feb. 25, 1733, was dismissed in 1741, and reinstated in 1749. The libraries of the court-chapel and the Gesellschaft der Musikfreunde possess a number of his masses in four to eight parts, motets, etc. (see *Q.-L.*), all written in a pure and elevated church style, the parts moving easily and naturally in spite of their elaborate counterpoint. In many points they recall Caldara. One special feature in Palotta's music is the free development of the chief subject, and the skilful way in which he combines it with the counter-subjects.　　　　C. F. P.

PAMINGER (PÄMINGER), LEONHARD (*b.* Aschau or Aschach, Bavaria, Mar. 29, 1495; *d.* May 3, 1567). According to Gerber he received his earlier instruction at the Convent of St. Nicolas at Passau. He afterwards studied at Vienna, but in 1516 returned to Passau to hold some scholastic post at St. Nicolas, where he is last mentioned as having been secretary. He became an adherent of the Lutheran reformation, and is known as the author of a few German hymns and controversial tracts. But in spite of this his chief musical work consists of a vast collection of Latin motets for four to six and more voices, providing for the requirements of the whole ecclesiastical year. The first volume of this work gives his portrait with the date of his death. The work itself was published by his sons, the first two parts in 1573 (Gerlach, Nuremberg), the third in 1576, and the fourth in 1580. The fourth part contains psalms both with simple falsobordone harmonies of the plain-song tones, and also more elaborately treated, along with some additional motets. In all the parts there are some contributions by his three sons Balthasar, Sophonias and Sigismund. In this work Proske says :

'The liturgy of the whole Church year is most exhaustively treated, and the harmonisation of the Psalms carried out with a completeness not to be found in any similar work.'

He also gives Paminger the credit of being one of the greatest contrapuntists of his time, and says that all his works show the fervently pious

master who was thoroughly penetrated by the devotional spirit of the words which he set to music.[1] Proske has reprinted from this work a comparatively simple and somewhat sombre setting of the Pater Noster, based on the plain-song melody. Compositions by Paminger also appear in the Collections of Ott, 1537–44, and Montanus, 1553–59. The ' Tricinia ' of Montanus, 1559, contain twelve settings *a* 3 of German hymns. Ott's Liederbuch, 1544 (reprinted by Eitner & Kade), has a very expressive setting of ' Ach Gott straf mich nicht im Zorn dein' *a* 4, the tenor melody of which seems also to be of Paminger's own invention, since it is nowhere else to be found, and it is also reckoned as one of the best of the time. Forster concludes his great Lieder collection, 1556, with a remarkable piece by Paminger, ' Ach Gott wem soll ich's klagen,' which, without pauses, is to be sung *a* 5, but with pauses *a* 10. A curious epitaph on Paminger in German verse, which was set to music for four voices by his son Sophonias, is given in Wackernagel's *Das deutsche Kirchenlied*, Bd. iv. No. 154.

　　　　　　　　　　　　　　　J. R. M.

PAMMELIA, the first collection of Canons, Rounds and Catches published in this country. It was issued in 1609, under the editorship of Thomas Ravenscroft, with the title of :

'Pammelia. Mvsicks Miscellanie, Or, Mixed Varietie of Pleasant Roundelayes, and delightfull Catches, of 3. 4. 5. 6. 7. 8. 9. 10. Parts in one. Never so ordinarie as musicall, none so musical, as not to all very pleasing and acceptable.'

It contains 100 compositions, many of considerable antiquity, several of which are still well known and have been reprinted in modern publications, amongst them ' Heyhoe to the green wood,' ' All in to service,' ' Now kiss the cup, cousin,' ' Joan, come kiss me now,' ' There lies a pudding,' ' Jack boy, ho boy ' (alluded to in Shakespeare's ' Taming of the Shrew '), ' Banbury Ale,' ' Now Robin lend to me thy bow' and ' Let's have a peal for John Cook's soul.' A second edition appeared in 1618. A second part was issued, also in 1609, under the title of :

'Deuteromelia. or, The Second part of Musicks melodie, or melodius Musicke of Pleasant Roundelaies ; K. H. mirth, or Freemens Songs and such delightfull Catches. Qui Canere potest canat. Catch that catch can. Vt Mel Os, sic Cof melos afficit & reficit.'

This contains thirty-one compositions, viz. seven Freemen's Songs for three, and seven for four voices, and eight rounds or catches for three, and nine for four voices. Of the Freemen's Songs the following are still well known : ' As it fell on a holy day ' (John Dory), ' We be soldiers three,' ' We be three poor mariners,' ' Of all the birds ' and ' Who liveth so merry in all this land ' ; and of the catches, ' Hold thy peace, thou knave ' (directed to be sung in Shakespeare's ' Twelfth Night ') and ' Mault's come down.' No composers' names are given in either part.　　　　　　　W. H. H.

PANDEAN PIPE (Fr. *flûte de Pan*; Ger. *Syrinx, Panflöte*), a simple instrument, of many

1 See the prefaces to ' Musica divina,' tom. i. iv.

forms and materials, which is probably the oldest and the most widely disseminated of any. It is thought to be identical with the ' Ugab,' the first wind instrument mentioned in the Bible (Gen. iv. 21, and Psalm cl.), in the former of these passages translated ' organ,' in the latter, ' pipe.' (See ORGAN.) It was well known to the Greeks under the name of ' syrinx,' being made with from three to nine tubes,[1] but usually with seven, a number which is also mentioned by Virgil.[2] It is depicted in a MS. of the 11th century preserved in the National Library of Paris, and is probably the ' frestele,' ' frêtel ' or ' frêtiau,' of the Ménétriers in the 12th and 13th centuries. It is known in China as ' Koan-tfee,' with twelve tubes of bamboo ; was used by the Peruvians under the name of ' huayra-puhura,' being made of cane, and also of a greenish steatite or soapstone. Of the former material is a fine specimen now in the South Kensington Museum,[3] consisting of fourteen reed pipes of a brownish colour tied together with thread in two rows, so as to form a double set of seven reeds. Both sets are of almost exactly the same dimensions, and are placed side by side, the shortest measuring 3, the longest 6½ inches. One set is open at the bottom, the other closed, in consequence of which arrangement octaves are produced. The scale is pentatonic.

The soapstone instrument is even more remarkable. It measures 5⅝ inches high by 6¼ wide, and contains eight pipes bored from the solid block, and quaintly ornamented. Four of the tubes have small lateral finger-holes, which, when closed, lower the pitch a semitone. Thus twelve notes in all can be produced. The scale is peculiar and perhaps arbitrary ; or the holes may have served for certain modes, of the use of which by the Peruvians there is evidence in Garcilasso de la Vega and other historians.

A modern Roumanian specimen, containing twenty-five tubes arranged in a curve, is in the Victoria and Albert Museum ; the longest pipes are over 12 inches in length.

There is an excellent and well-preserved example in a bas-relief from the Abbey of St. George de Boscherville, Normandy, of 11th century date, which is figured in Engel's excellent work above quoted.

The Pandean Pipe is theoretically a series of stopped tubes blown from the edge of the upper, and, in this case, the only orifice, as already described under FLUTE (see also PIPES, EVOLUTION AND DISTRIBUTION OF MUSICAL). One note and occasional harmonics are usually produced from each tube, the scale being diatonic, and of variable extent according to the skill and convenience of the performer. At the present day it is rarely heard except as an

accompaniment to the drama of Punch and Judy. It is enclosed in a leather or paper case which is pushed into the open waistcoat of the player, the different parts of the scale being reached by rotation of the head. The quality of the tone is reedy and peculiar, somewhat veiled from the absence of harmonics of even numbers, it being a stopped pipe, of which, however, the first harmonic on the twelfth, and not the fundamental tone, is habitually sounded. In this respect and in its quality it closely resembles the ' Harmonic flute ' stop of the organ.

It had a temporary popularity in this country at the beginning of the 19th century, when itinerant parties of musicians, terming themselves Pandeans, went about the country, and gave performances. ' The lowest set of reeds (the ' septem discrimina vocum ' of Virgil),' says a writer in 1821,

' is called the *contra basso* or double base ; the next *fagotto*, or bassoon ; the third septenary is the tenor or second treble ; and the fourth or highest range of pipes, the first treble ; so that in the aggregate there is a complete scale of four octaves, and they can play in three or four parts. The reeds or pipes are fastened under the chin of the performer, and the lip runs from one to the other with seeming facility, without moving the instrument by manual assistance.[4]

' A company of them was introduced at Vauxhall Gardens a few years ago, and since that they are common enough in the streets of London. It is to be observed that some of the performers, particularly the first treble, have more than seven pipes, which enables them to extend the melody beyond the septenary.' (*Encyclop. Londinensis*, 1821.)

A Tutor for this instrument was published in 1807, entitled *The Complete Preceptor for Davies's new invented Syrrynx* (sic) *or patent Pandean Harmonica, containing tunes and military pieces in one, two, three, and four parts.* The writer states that ' by making his instrument of glass he gains many advantages over the common reed, the tone being inconceivably more brilliant and sonorous.' The scale given begins on A below the treble stave, rising by fifteen intervals to the A above the same stave. The C is indicated as the keynote, which is marked as such. The instrument appears to have been susceptible of double-tonguing like the flute.

w. h. s.

**PANDORA.** The Greek πανδοῦρα ; Arabic *tanbur*, now rendered tamboura, is of great antiquity ; and the long, straight - necked, stringed instrument with comparatively small body contrasted with the pear-shaped lute, has been handed down from the distant civilisations of Egypt and Babylon to the pandoura and COLASCIONE (*q.v.*) of Southern Europe (see *PLATE XXIII.* No. 4), the various tambouras of Bulgaria, Turkey and India, the Chinese ' san-hsien ' or ' sientzē ' and the Japanese ' samisen ' and other Eastern descendants and representatives.

The Egyptian instrument is depicted on

---

[1] Theocritus. *Idyll* ix.
[2] ' Est mihi disparibus septem compacta cicutis Fistula.'
[3] See *Catalogue of Instruments in South Kensington Museum,* by C. Engel, p. 65, for a woodcut of this specimen.

[4] ' " Et supra calamos unco percurrere labro."—Lucretius. This line clearly indicates the identity of the instrument.'

monuments of a great age, and in the early wall paintings (c. 1580 B.C.) there are indications of a fretted finger-board. For the supposed name of this instrument see NEFER. The ancient Greeks were acquainted with an instrument of the kind which they called πανδοῦρα; there is good reason to suppose it preceded the lyre, but for open-air music the latter had the better chance, and became ultimately the national Hellenic stringed instrument of the classic and Graeco-Roman periods. Julius Pollux (iv. 60), and Athenaeus (iv. 183), quote Pythagoras for the ascription of the πανδοῦρα to the Troglodytes of the Persian Gulf, who made it of laurel, which grew near the sea-shore. With reference to the Asiatic 'tanbur,' Al Fārābi, the greatest Arabic writer on music (d. A.D. 950), has preserved for us, in his description of the tanbur of Bagdad, an echo of the past, the characteristic note and accordance of the old 'pagan' scale, which preceded the Persian and Arabic invasions. This note, the septimal whole tone and 7-8 ratio (the equal temperament semitone 2·31), must have been the original Arabic 'wosta' or middle finger-note on the finger-board, equivalent to the index finger or Lichanos on the lyre which was the characteristic tone of the old Greek soft diatonic genus (μαλακός). Dr. Land (Recherches sur l'histoire de la gamme arabe, Leyden, 1884) saw in this scale a distortion, from the constant practice of instruments, of a natural scale, an intuition with which he credits the ancient Persians, but this mental recognition of harmonious intervals implies the conception of modern harmony in which we are educated, but in which the musicians of the ancient world, Persians, Indians or Greeks, certainly were not. Instead of this the more mechanical adaptation of the finger-board to the hand accounts for that conception of the tetrachord we find with the ancient Greeks, and can now trace to the still older civilisation of Babylon and Nineveh. Al Fārābi sees music, theoretical and practical, through Greek spectacles of that later age in which he wrote, and his tanbur of Khorassan, like his lute, is the music of Islam translated into Greek. The arithmetical reasonings of philosophers who sought to explain the musical scale could never have been, excepting in the larger intervals, the practical art of musicians; limmas and commas were evolved from a simpler diatonic system enriched to suit the finer ears of the time with small intervals; of which we have within the last hundred years the quarter tone analysis of Mechāga, a mathematician and musician of Damascus, and the third tone (Pythag. O. 680) insisted upon as the unit by Villoteau (Description de l'Égypte, tomes xiii et xiv, 8vo, Paris, 1823), who was one of the scientific expedition sent by Napoleon I. to Egypt, and who brought back a collection of instruments now, unhappily for the settlement of a much-debated question, no longer to be found. The intention of Dr. Land's admirable and essential book is in the main polemic, to upset the dictum of Villoteau, since reproduced by musical historians such as Fétis, Ambros and Kiesewetter in collaboration with Hammer-Purgstall, but the battle remains undecided, as the great Arabic authorities, Al Fārābi, Caxio'ddin, Abdo'lgadir and others were as obviously making their native musical material Greek, as the Japanese are trying to Europeanise their own to-day. To find the real Arabic music we must take the advice of the traveller Dr. Landberg, and penetrate among the Bedouin inhabitants of the interior.

We find in Mechāga a diatonic framework, but with neuter, not minor or major thirds; the latter, when they occur, are subordinate. The hypo or plagal mode with the minor seventh called 'Ochag, c, d, e, f, g, a, b♭, c, is advanced to the first place before Rāst, f, g, a, b♭, c, d, e, f, but that the latter was once regarded as the original is proved by the names of the notes which follow Rāst, thus 'Dou-kah,' the second, 'Sik-hah,' the third, and 'Tchār-kah,' the fourth. As in India, in the present day, it is possible that small intervals were in use for a refined expression or for grace. (See INDIAN MUSIC.) But in the pandoura or tamboura we find a diatonic scale which has much in common with the flutes or auloi of antiquity, and of Eastern music to-day. Villoteau has given magnificent engravings of tambouras after the very precise drawings of Auguste Herbin, which form part of the atlas of La Description de l'Égypte. Their accuracy suggested to Dr. Land the desirability of minutely measuring the finger-boards, in the absence of the instruments themselves, to compare with the results with Villoteau's text. He has given the results in millimètres sometimes carried to two places of decimals for the Bulgarian tanbur; the large Turkish, the small and large Persian, and one simply called 'd'orient.' With these he has compared calculated intervals against Villoteau's naming and the nearest Pythagorean or harmonic intervals, the result of which is, however, impaired by the influence of tension when the intervals are stopped upon the finger-board, unavoidable in producing the note, and tending always to sharpen the vibration number. This will be more perceptible as the sounds ascend from the diminished length of the string. In Dr. Land's tables no exact gradation is noticeable, although the diatonic intervals including the neuter thirds and sixths and minor seventh are not remote. But with thirds of the whole tone, to which Dr. Land has not given attention, the results very frequently come as near.

The modern Egyptian or Arabian, and the various Indo-Chinese varieties of the tamboura have no frets, but there are marks on the finger-board of the Japanese samisen that are guides to the intervals required. The small Turkish tamboura called Ehaz, a very beautiful-looking instrument, has twenty-three frets. (See FRET.)

The first syllable of many of these names points to a common derivation from a root perhaps expressive of tension.

A. J. H. ; rev. F. W. G.

PANDORE (BANDORA) (Ital. Neapolitan dialect, *pandura* ; Arabic, *tanbur*; Indian languages *tambura*). The English pandore is a variety of the cither with ribs shaped in incurvations and an oblique bridge. According to Praetorius (*Syntagma*) the smallest size was called Orpharion (see ORPHEOREON), the name a combination, according to Dr. Murray, of Orpheus with Arion ; the medium size, Penorcon ; and the largest, Pandore. Praetorius spells this Pandorra or Bandoer. The forms orpharion and pandora occur in *The School of Musicke*, by Thomas Robinson, London, 1603. Queen Elizabeth's Lute preserved at Helmingham in Suffolk is an instrument of this genus. It was made by John Rose in Bridewell, London, 1580 ; the name he gavè it, 'Cymbalum Decachordum,' shows that it was intended for ten strings, which, according to Praetorius, would be tuned five notes in pairs. lute fashion. Such an instrument would be used for accompaniment only. It is called an English instrument by Praetorius in the *Syntagma* (1618), who says it had a flat back, and was like a cither strung with six and sometimes seven twisted metal strings, which were plucked with the finger. William Barley (1596), in his *New Booke of Tabliture*, has instructions for the bandora [1] in the third part. The instrument there is described and depicted as having six pairs of strings tuned in unison. (See *PLATE I.* No. 2.) Music for the bandora was always written in tablature, but, as in the case of the lute, there is a good deal of variety in the *accordatura* employed. The bandora was often used to maintain the bass part in consort, as in Morley's 'Consort Lessons' (1599 and 1611), Rosseter's 'Consort Lessons' (1609), and Leighton's 'Teares' (1614), but only in the last of these three has the bandora part survived. It is for a seven-stringed instrument, *Bandurrias*. (See MANDOLINE.)     A. J. H

PANDORINA, a small lute. (*PLATE XLV.* Nos. 1, 2 ; see MANDORE.)

PANE, DOMENICO DEL (*b.* Rome), describes himself as having been a pupil of Antonio Maria Abbatini. In 1650 he became soprano singer in the Imperial Chapel at Vienna under Ferdinand III., but in 1654 was received into the Papal Chapel at Rome, where also in 1669 he became choirmaster. When he had completed his jubilee of service in the Papal Chapel, and his voice began to fail, not wishing, as he says, to

[1] In the Hengrave Inventory, 1603, is one item ' one bandore and a sithern with a double case.'

be idle, he composed and published in 1687 a volume of masses for four to eight voices, based on favourite motets of Palestrina : 2 *a* 4, ' O doctor bonus,' ' Domine quando veneris ' ; 3 *a* 5, 'Stella quam viderant,' ' O beatum virum,' ' Jubilate Deo ' ; 1 *a* 6, ' Canite tuba ' ; 1 *a* 8, ' Frates ego enim.' This was his op. 5. Previous works published were Motetti *a* 2-5, op. 2 (Rome, 1675) ; Sagri Concerti *a* 2-6, op. 3 (1675) ; two Books of Madrigals *a* 5. In 1677 he edited Abbatini's Antiphons for twelve bass and twelve tenor voices. A few other works remain in MS. in the archives of the Sistine Chapel.     J. R. M.

PANIZZA, ETTORE (*b.* Buenos Ayres, Aug. 12, 1875), operatic conductor and composer. He studied at Milan Conservatoire, won the 1st prize for piano and composition, and made his début in Rome in 1899. He gained his experience as an orchestral conductor in Italy, and introduced there several works by Elgar. He was engaged for some years at various opera-houses in Italy and South America, during which period he composed and brought out three operas : ' Il fidanzato del mare ' (Buenos Ayres, 1897) ; ' Medio, Eno, Latino' (a trilogy, Genoa, 1900) ; and 'Aurora' (Buenos Ayres, 1908). He first appeared at Covent Garden in June 1907, and conducted there for several seasons, invariably earning admiration for his musicianship and firm rhythmical beat. He directed the first performances in England of Baron F. d'Erlanger's 'Tess' in 1909, of Zandonai's ' Conchita ' in 1912, of Camussi's ' La du Barry ' in 1913, and Zandonai's ' Francesca da Rimini ' in 1914. He also returned in 1924 and conducted some of the Italian revivals of that year. He brought out (Milan, 1913) a new edition in 3 vols. of Berlioz's *Traité de l'instrumentation*.

BIBL.—*International Who's Who in Music* ; NORTHCOTT, *Covent Garden and the Royal Opera.*     H. K.

PANNY, JOSEPH (*b.* Kohlmitzberg, Austria, Oct. 23, 1794 ; *d.* Sept. 7, 1838), violinist and composer.

After some early education from his father, who was director of the local school of music, and his maternal grandfather, Joseph Bremberger, an esteemed organist, Panny, at the age of 19, while occupying a tutor's post at Greinburg, attracted the keen interest of von Eybler, Kapellmeister to the Emperor Francis II. In 1815 Panny went to Vienna, and studied composition with Eybler. In 1824 he gave his first concert of his own compositions in Vienna, gaining a warm reception for his ' Kriegerchor.' In 1825 he met Paganini in Venice, and two years later renewed the acquaintance in Vienna, where he composed a ' scène dramatique ' for the fourth string, which was performed by Paganini at his farewell concert in the Austrian capital. During 1829 and 1830 Panny toured in Germany. In 1831 he travelled to Norway and conducted concerts at Bergen, and on his return to Germany in 1834 founded a school of music at Weisserling (Alsace), for the education of the children of the wealthy manufacturers of the town, who financed it. He visited Paris and London in 1835, married, and settled in Mainz in 1836, where he founded another College of Music. R. L. de Pearsall was his pupil. His death, from spinal meningitis, occurred two years later, at the age of 48. He left a widow and one child. His published compositions include : string quartets ; trios ; solos for violin, violoncello and clarinet ; three masses ; Requiem ; male choruses ; songs, etc. ; a MS. opera ' Das Mädchen von Rügen,' and a hymn to the New Year, which was performed at Bergen, Dec. 18, 1831. Panny also left some literary MS., dealing with the history of music in Italy, Germany, France and England.

BIBL.—*Baker*; CLARKE, *Dict. of Fiddlers*; *Fétis*; article in Supplement to the *Gazette de Mayence*, 1838.        E. H.-A.

PANOFKA, HEINRICH (b. Breslau, Oct. 2, 1807 ; d. Florence, Nov. 18, 1887), violinist. At the age of 17 he quitted the College of Breslau and put himself under Mayseder for the violin, and Hoffmann for composition, both at Vienna. In 1827 he gave his first concert. In 1829 he left Vienna for Munich, and thence went to Berlin. In 1831 his father died, and Panofka came into his patrimony. After some lengthened travelling he settled at Paris in 1834 as a violin-player. After a time he turned his attention to singing, and in conjunction with Bordogni founded in 1842 an Académie de Chant. In 1844 he came to London, and in 1847 (Jenny Lind's year) was engaged by Lumley as one of his assistants at Her Majesty's Theatre. The Revolution of 1848 fixed him here ; he published a ' Practical Singing Tutor,' and was widely known as a teacher. In 1852 he returned to Paris, and in 1866 settled in Florence. His principal works are ' L'Art de chanter ' (op. 81) ; ' L'École de chant,' twenty-four Vocalises progressives (op. 85) ; Abécédaire vocal (2nd ed.) ; twelve Vocalises d'artiste (op. 86)—all published by Brandus. He translated Baillot's *Nouvelle Méthode* for the violin into German. He also published many works for violin and piano, and for violin and orchestra, but they are of slight importance.

BIBL.—*Baker*; BROWN, *Biog. Dict. Mus.*; CLARKE, *Dict. of Fiddlers*; *Fétis*.        E. H.-A.

PANORMO (1) VINCENZO TRUSAINO (b. Monreale, near Palermo, Nov. 30, 1734 ; d. London, 1813[1]). The career of this excellent violin-maker has been much obscured by the placing of false labels in his instruments, and only conjecture locates and dates his birth and death. It is presumed that he acquired a knowledge of his craft, both at Cremona and Turin, and that he went to Paris in 1750, but, failing to find a field for his efforts, returned

[1] These places and dates are conjectural only.

south as far as Marseilles. In 1772 Panormo visited England, and from 1783-89 alternated betwixt London and Paris, establishing in the latter town a business at No. 70 Rue de Chartres, with a workshop in the Rue de l'Arbre Sec. His favourite model was the large pattern Stradivarius, which he copied to perfection. The workmanship throughout his instruments is neat and well executed, the scrolls and f holes being particularly well cut. Some of his best fiddles were made out of an old maple billiard-table, which Panormo purchased whilst in Dublin. He employed several forms of printed label ; the earliest bear the arms of Palermo at the right-hand side of the ticket. He was a fairly prolific maker. Panormo's eldest son (2) JOSEPH (b. London, 1773 ; d. circa 1825), carried on a fiddle-making business, first at New Compton Street, and later in King Street, Soho, and excelled as a violoncello-maker. His brother (3) GEORGE LEWIS (b. London, 1774 ; d. circa 1842), was principally a guitar-maker, but made also violins, following the Strad model, first in Oxford Street, and later in High Street, St. Giles. He is mostly esteemed as a bow-maker, in the mastery of which art he resembles Duke, whom he closely followed. Joseph Panormo's son (4) EDWARD FERDINAND, was also a violin-maker, but of little importance.

BIBL.—VON LÜTGENDORFF, *Die Geigen und Lautenmacher* ; HERON-ALLEN, *Violin-making as it was and is* ; VIDAL, *Les Instruments a archet*, vol. i. ; *Fétis* ; HART, *The Violin*.
        E. H.-A.

PANSERON, AUGUSTE MATHIEU (b. Paris, Apr. 26, 1796; d. there, July 29, 1859), received his first instruction in music from his father, a musician, who scored many of Grétry's operas for him. He entered the Conservatoire as a child, passed successfully through the course, and after studying harmony and composition with Berton and Gossec, ended by carrying off the Grand Prix de Rome (1813). He made good use of his time in Italy, took lessons in counterpoint and fugue from the Abbé Mattei, at Bologna, and studied especially the art of singing, and the style of the old Italian masters. After travelling in Austria and Germany, and even reaching St. Petersburg, he returned to Paris and became a teacher. Shortly afterwards he was appointed ' accompagnateur ' to the Opéra-Comique, a position which enabled him to produce two small one-act pieces long since forgotten. He does not appear to have possessed the necessary qualities for success on the stage, but he had a real gift of tune, and this secured great popularity for a number of French romances composed between 1825 and 1840, melodious, well written for the voice, easily remembered, and often pleasing or even more ; but marred by too much pretension. His wide experience during his professorships at the Conservatoire—solfège, 1826 ; vocalisation, Sept. 1831 ; and singing, Jan. 1836—taught him the requirements of pupils, and how those requirements can best be met. His works are thus of value from an educational point of view, and we give a complete list, classified under the various heads.

| | |
|---|---|
| 1. Progressive solfèges for single voice—' A, B, C musical ' ; with continuation. | Method for soprano and tenor, in 2 parts ; with appendix. |
| 2. Progressive solfèges for several voices—Primary manual for 2 and 3 voices. | 5. On the art of composition— A Practical Treatise on harmony and modulation; with 60 exercises on figured and 70 on unfigured basses, and a course of lectures on writing a bass to a given melody. The art of modulating on the Violin. |
| 3. Do. for instrumental performers—Do. for Pianists ; Do. for Violin players. | |
| 4. On the art of singing— | |

Panseron also composed two masses for three treble voices, and a ' Mois de Marie,' containing motets and cantiques for one, two and three voices.        G. C.

PANTALEON (PANTALON), a very large DULCIMER (q.v.) invented and played upon in the early part of the 18th century by Pantaleon Hebenstreit, whose name was transferred to the instrument by Louis XIV. HEBENSTREIT (q.v.) quadrupled the size of the dulcimer and had it constructed as a double hackbrett with two sound-boards, each with its scale of strings—on the one side overspun catgut, on the other, wire. There were 185 strings in all, costing 100 thalers a year to keep in order. Kuhnau [1] praises this powerful chromatic instrument and its prerogative over harpsichords and clavichords in the properties it possesses of *piano* and *forte*.

The name was also given in Germany to horizontal pianofortes with the hammers striking downwards.        A. J. H.

PANTHEON, a building in Oxford Street, erected in 1770–71 from the designs of James Wyatt, at a cost of £60,000, for masquerades, concerts, balls, etc., and as ' a Winter Ranelagh.' It occupied a large space of ground, and besides the principal entrance in Oxford Street there were entrances in Poland Street and Great Marlborough Street. The interior contained a large rotunda and fourteen other rooms splendidly decorated ; the niches in the rotunda being filled with white porphyry statues. The building was opened on Jan. 26, 1772. For some years it proved a formidable rival to the Italian Opera, as the proprietors always provided the best performers. In 1775 the famous Agujari was engaged, who was succeeded, a few years later, by the equally famed Giorgi, afterwards Banti. The second concert of the Commemoration of Handel was given here, May 27, 1784, the place being specially fitted up for the occasion. Later in the same year the balloon in which Lunardi had made his first successful ascent from the Artillery Ground was exhibited. The King's Theatre having been burnt down in 1788, the Pantheon was fitted up as a theatre and opened for the performance of Italian operas, Feb. 17, 1791. On Jan. 14, 1792, the theatre was destroyed by fire. In 1795 the interior of the building was reconstructed for its original purpose, and opened in April with a masquerade, but it met with little success, and

[1] Mattheson's *Critica Musica*, Dec. 8, 1717.

in 1812 was again converted into a theatre, and opened Feb. 17, with a strong company, principally composed of seceders from the King's Theatre, for the performance of Italian operas. The speculation, however, failed, and the theatre closed on Mar. 19. In the following year (July 23, 1813) an attempt was made to open it as an English opera-house, but information being laid against the manager and performers, at the instance of the Lord Chamberlain, for performing in an unlicensed building, and heavy penalties inflicted (although not exacted), the speculation was abandoned. Subsequent efforts to obtain a license failed, and in Oct. 1814 the whole of the scenery, dresses, properties and internal fittings were sold under a distress for rent, and the building remained dismantled and deserted for nearly twenty years. In 1834 the interior was reconstructed by Sydney Smirke, at a cost of between £30,000 and £40,000, and opened as a bazaar ; part being devoted to the sale of paintings, and the back part, entered from Great Marlborough Street, fitted up as a conservatory for the sale of flowers and foreign birds. The bazaar in its turn gave way, and early in 1867 the premises were transferred to Messrs. Gilbey, the well-known wine merchants, by whom they are still occupied. During all the vicissitudes of the building Wyatt's original front in Oxford Street has remained unaltered.        W. H. H.

PANTOMIME (Gr.), ' an imitation of everything,' (1) a kind of dramatic entertainment in which the performers express themselves by gestures to the accompaniment of music, and which may be called a prose ballet. It has been in use among Oriental nations from very ancient times. The Greeks introduced pantomime into their choruses, some of the performers gesticulating, accompanied by music, whilst others sang. The Romans had entire dramatic representations consisting of dancing and gesticulation only, and some of their performers attained high excellence in the art. The wordless play with music has made only sporadic appearances in recent times ; a typical example is ' L'Enfant prodigue.' (See WORMSER.) A mixture of pantomime and dancing constitutes the modern *ballet d'action*. (See BALLET-DANCING.)

(2) The first occurrence of an English equivalent to the Italian ' Commedia dell' Arte '— the ultimate origin of which is exceedingly obscure—seems to have been at Drury Lane in 1702, when ' Tavern Bilkers,' by John Weaver (the friend of Addison and Steele), was produced. It was not successful, but in 1716–17, at Lincoln's Inn Theatre, John Rich, under the name of Lun, performed the character of Harlequin in a style which extorted the admiration of those who most disapproved of the class of piece. His pantomimes were originally musical masques, usually upon some classical

mythological subject, between the scenes of which harlequinade scenes were introduced, the two parts having no connexion. The music for the majority of them was composed by J. E. Galliard. Their popularity compelled the managers of Drury Lane to adopt pantomimes in order to compete successfully with their rival, and they were then soon produced at other theatres also. After a time the original form was changed, and in lieu of the mythological masque, a short drama, of three or four scenes, was constructed, the invariable characters in which, under different shapes, were an old man, his pretty daughter, or ward—whom he was desirous of uniting to a wealthy but foolish suitor, but who had a poorer and favoured lover—and the old man's knavish serving-man. The girl and her lover were protected by a benevolent fairy, whilst the old man and his favourite had the assistance of a malevolent spirit. To counteract the machinations of the evil being, the fairy determined that her protégés should undergo a term of probation under different shapes, and accordingly transformed them into Harlequin and Columbine, giving to the former a magic bat to assist him in his progress. The evil spirit then transformed the old man and his servant into Pantaloon and Clown, and the wealthy suitor into the Dandy Lover, and the harlequinade began, the two lovers being pursued by the others through a variety of scenes, but always foiling them by the aid of the bat.[1] At length the fairy reappeared and declared the success of the lovers, and the piece terminated. Vocal music was largely introduced, not only in the opening, but also in the harlequinade, and the best English composers did not disdain to employ their talents in producing it. The two Arnes, Dibdin, Battishill, Linley, Shield, Attwood and others, all composed music for this class of entertainment. About 1830 the length of the opening was greatly extended, more spectacular effects introduced, and the ' transformation scene ' became by degrees the climax of the whole. Original music was still composed for the pantomime, but the task of producing it was entrusted to inferior composers. Gradually the harlequinade scenes were reduced in number, the opening assumed the character of an extravaganza upon the subject of some nursery tale, and the music became a selection of the popular tunes of the day. In the early pantomimes Harlequin was the principal character, and continued so until the genius of Grimaldi placed the Clown in the most prominent position.

In pantomimes of the middle period the pantomimists who sustained the principal parts in the harlequinade invariably performed in the

opening the characters who were transformed. A consideration of the difference between the Italian Arlecchino and the English Harlequin is beyond the scope of our present purpose.

w. h. h.

(3) The entertainment now generally described as pantomime is historically descended from the above, but bears few traces of its descent. The harlequinade has vanished. The fairy-tale is retained merely as an indication that the entertainment is intended for children. The hero, called ' principal boy,' is acted by a woman ; the comic character, generally principal boy's mother, is acted by a man. Beyond these conventions the pantomime is practically a revue, the attraction being the number of ' turns ' from the variety stage incorporated into it. The music matches the ' turns.' c.

PAOLO, ARETINO (b. Arezzo, 1544), musician to the Duke of Ferrara ; maestro di cappella of Arezzo Cathedral, 1558. He composed a book of ' Madrigali cromati ' (1549) ; a book of madrigals a 5-8 v. (1558) ; a Passion according to St. John ; a Te Deum, Magnificats and other church music ; the last dated composition, Milan, 1565 (Q.-L.).

PAOLUCCI, GIUSEPPE (b. Siena, May 25, 1726 ; d. Apr. 26, 1776), pursued his musical studies under Padre Martini at Bologna, and like him became a Franciscan friar. After holding the position of choirmaster at a church in Venice and at Sinigaglia, he returned in 1771 to Assisi to be choirmaster of the Franciscan church there. He is chiefly known as the author of Arte pratica di contrappunto dimostrata con esempi di varj autori e con osservazioni . . . Venice, 1765, a work of the same nature as Martini's treatise.          J. R. M.

PAPE, JEAN-HENRI (b. Sarsted near Hanover, July 1, 1789 ; d. Asnières, near Paris, Feb. 2, 1875), pianoforte-maker. He went to Paris in 1811, and after visiting England his services were secured by Ignace Pleyel to organise the works of the piano factory which he had just founded. About 1818 he appears to have set up on his own account ; and thenceforward, for nearly half a century, there was perhaps no year in which he did not produce something new. His active mind never rested from attempts to alter the shape, diminish the size, and radically change the framing, bellying and action of the pianoforte ; yet, in the result, with small influence upon the progress of its manufacture. In shape he produced table pianos, rounded and hexagonal : he made an oval piano, a piano console (very like a chiffonier), and novel oblique, vertical and horizontal forms. Like Wornum in London and Streicher in Vienna, to do away with the break of continuity between wrest-plank and sound-board in the grand piano, he repeated the old idea that had suggested itself to Marius and Schroeter, of an overstriking action—that is, the hammers de-

---

[1] The names Harlequin, Columbine and Pantaloon are derived from the Italian—Arlecchino, Colombina and Pantalone. Clown is known in Italy as Pagliaccio ; in France as Pierrot, Paillasse, or Pitre ; in German as Bajas, or Hanswurst (Jack-pudding)

scending upon the strings. This is said to have been in 1826. In this action he worked the hammers from the front ends of the keys, and thus saved a foot in the length of the case, which he strengthened up to due resistance of the tension without iron barring. He lowered the sound-board, glueing the belly-bars to the upper instead of the under surface, and attached the belly-bridge by a series of sound-posts. His constant endeavour was to keep down the tension or drawing power of the strings, and to reduce the length and weight of the instrument; for, as he says (*Notice de M. H. Pape*, Benard, Paris, 1862), 'it is not progress in art to make little with much; the aim should be to make much with little.' Yet he extended compass to eight octaves, maintaining that the perception of the extremes was a question of ear-education only. He reduced the structure of his actions to the simplest mechanism possible, preferring for under-striking grand pianos the simple crank escape-ment of Petzold, and for upright pianos that of Wornum, which he adopted in 1815, as stated in the *Notice* already referred to. His inventions of clothed key-mortices and of felt for hammers are the only important bequests makers have accepted from him, unless the cross or overstringing on different planes, devised by Pape for his table instruments, and already existing in some old clavichords, was first introduced into pianos by him. He claimed to have invented it, and in 1840 gave Tomkinson, a London maker, special permis-sion to use it. (See PIANOFORTE.) He made a piano with springs instead of strings, thus doing away with tension altogether; added reed attachments, and invented a transposing piano, moving by his plan the whole instru-ment by means of a key while the clavier remained stationary. He also invented an ingenious saw for veneers of wood and ivory; in 1839 he veneered a piano for St. James's Palace, entirely with the latter substance. Pape received many distinctions in France, including the decoration of the Legion of Honour.      A. J. H.

PAPILLON DE LA FERTÉ, DENIS-PIERRE-JEAN (*b.* Châlons-sur-Marne, Feb. 18, 1727 [1]), became in 1777 by purchase Intendant des Menus Plaisirs to Louis XVI. and as such had the direction of the École Royale de Chant, founded by the Baron de Breteuil and of the Opéra (from 1780–90) after the Paris munici-pality had given up the administration of it. In 1790 he published a reply to a pamphlet by the artists of the opéra—' Mémoire justificatif des sujets de l'Académie royale de musique ' —in which they demanded a reform of the administration. A learned man of high artistic disposition, he left anonymous works on mathe-matics, astronomy and architecture. He was

guillotined in Paris, July 7, 1794.[2] His son occupied the same post after the Restoration.
                 M. C. C. ; addns. M. L. P.

BIBL.—A. JULLIEN, *Un Potentat musical, Papillon de la Ferté: son règne à l'Opéra de 1780 à 1790* (Paris, 1876).

PAPINI, GUIDO (*b.* Camagiore near Florence, Aug. 1, 1847 ; *d.* London, Oct. 3, 1912), a dis-tinguished violinist, was a pupil of the Italian violin professor Giorgetti, and made his début at 13 years of age in Florence, in Spohr's third concerto. He was for some years leader of the Società del Quartetto in that city. In 1874 he appeared at the Musical Union, which was his principal *locale* during his annual visits to London, though he was also heard at the Crystal Palace, the Old and New Philharmonic Societies, etc. In 1876 he appeared in Paris with success at the Pasdeloup Concerts, also at the Bordeaux Philharmonic Concerts, which were then much in vogue. In 1893 he accepted the post of principal violin professor in Dublin at the Royal Irish Academy of Music: he instituted the Classical Concerts of the Royal Society of Music while in that city, but ill-heath compelled him to resign his professorship in 1896. He returned to London, dividing his time between composition and occasional private tuition. His published compositions, besides arrangements, transcriptions, etc., comprise two concertos for violin and violoncello respectively; an excellent Violin School; ' Exercices de mécanisme pour le violon seul,' and smaller pieces, such as the ' Feuillets d'album,' Romances, Nocturnes, etc., for violin and violoncello. He published songs, trios for two violins and piano, quartet for three violins and piano, and edited the twenty-four ' Caprices de Paganini,' and other classical works.

BIBL.—LEGGE, *Celebrated Violinists*, 'Strad' Library, No. IV.; T. L. PHIPSON, *Guido Papini*; Dict. of Fiddlers; CLARKE, *Cyclopedia of Music and Musicians*; MENDEL, *Musik Lex.*; BROWN, *Biog. Dict. Mus.*          E. H.-A.

PAQUE, (1) GUILLAUME (*b.* Brussels, July 24, 1825 ; *d.* Mar. 2, 1876), a well-known violon-cellist. He entered the Conservatoire of his native city at an early age as De Munck's pupil, and at 15 gained the first prize. He then went to Paris and was solo violoncello at Musard's Concerts. Thence he went to Madrid as violoncellist to the Queen of Spain. In 1851 he was employed by Jullien for his English Concerts, and thenceforward London became his home. He played in the Royal Italian Opera orchestra, occasionally replaced Piatti at the Monday Popular Concerts, led the violon-cellos at the new Philharmonic, and was a mem-ber of the Queen's Private Band. He played at the Philharmonic, June 18, 1860. He was buried in Brompton Cemetery. He left numerous works.

His brother, (2) PHILIPPE J., was trumpeter to the Queen from 1864, and was a member of Her Majesty's Private Band.      G.

---

[1] Parish Register of Notre Dame, Châlons-sur-Mer.
    [2] Date verified from copy of death act.

PARADIES (PARADISI), PIETRO DOMENICO (b. Naples, 1710 ; d. Venice, 1792), a pupil of Porpora, and an esteemed teacher and composer, lived for many years in London. He wrote ' Alessandro in Persia ' for Lucca in 1738, and ' Il decreto del fato ' (serenata) for Venice in 1740. In 1747 he produced at the King's Theatre ' Fetonte,' six airs from which were published by Walsh, and frequently sung at concerts by Signora Galli. He also printed twelve ' Sonate di gravicembalo,' dedicated to the Princess Augusta (Johnson ; 2nd ed. Amsterdam, 1770). Such players as Clementi and Cramer studied his works conscientiously, and he was in great request as a teacher. When Gertrude Schmeling (afterwards Mme. Mara) made her first appearance in London as a violinist of 11 Paradies was engaged as her singing-master, but her father soon found it necessary to withdraw her from his influence. An earlier pupil, and one of his best, was Cassandra Frederick,[1] who at the age of five and a half gave a concert in the Little Haymarket Theatre (1749), playing compositions by Scarlatti and Handel. The last we hear in England of this eccentric Italian is his connexion with the elder Thomas Linley, to whom he gave instruction in harmony and thorough-bass. He returned to Italy. Ten sonatas are in the *Trésor des pianistes*, one in D is printed by Pauer in his ' Alte Meister,' and another, in A, in his ' Alte Klaviermusik ' ; and a Toccata is given in Breitkopf's ' Perles musicales.' The Fitzwilliam Collection at Cambridge contains much MS. music by him (including the scores of the operas 'Antioco,' ' Fetonte,' ' La forza d' amore ' and ' Il decreto del fato '), apparently in his autograph.                                            C. F. P.

PARADIS, MARIE THERESE VON (b. Vienna, May 15, 1759 ; d. Feb. 1, 1824), daughter of Joseph Anton, an Imperial Councillor. She was a highly esteemed pianist, and Mozart wrote a concerto for her (in B♭, Köchel, 456). She also attained to considerable skill on the organ, in singing, and in composition, and this in spite of her being blind from early childhood. The piano she studied with Richter (of Holland), and afterwards with Kozeluch, whose concertos were her favourite pieces ; singing with Salieri and Righini ; and composition with Friberth, and the Abbé Vogler. The Empress, her godmother, took a great interest in her, and made her a yearly allowance of 200 gulden. In 1784 she went to Paris, where she remained six months, playing before the court, and at the Concert Spirituel, with great applause. In November she went to London. Here she stayed five months, played before the King, Queen and Prince of Wales, whom she accompanied in a violoncello sonata, at the then recently founded

Professional Concerts (Hanover Square Rooms, Feb. 16, 1785), and finally at a concert of her own, conducted by Salomon, in Willis's Rooms on Mar. 8. A notice of her appeared in the *St. James's Chronicle* for Feb. 19. She next visited Brussels and the more important courts of Germany, attracting all hearers by her playing and her intellectual accomplishments. After her return to Vienna she played twice at the concerts of the Tonkünstler-Societät, and took up composition with great ardour, using a system of notation[2] invented for her by a friend of the family named Riedinger. Of her works, the following were produced : ' Ariadne und Bacchus,' a melodrama, played first at Laxenburg, before the Emperor Leopold (1791), and then at the national court-theatre ; ' Der Schulcandidat,' a pastoral Singspiel (Leopoldstadt Theatre, 1792) ; ' Deutsches Monument,' a Trauer-cantate for the anniversary of the death of Louis XVI. (small Redoutensaal, Jan. 21, 1794, repeated in the Kärnthnerthor Theatre) ; and ' Rinaldo und Algina,' a magic opera (Prague). She also printed a Clavier-trio, sonatas, variations (dedicated to Vogler) ; 12 Lieder ; Bürger's ' Lenore,' etc. After her father's death she founded a music school for girls, and towards the close of her life she devoted herself exclusively to teaching singing and the pianoforte, and with great success.
                                            C. F. P.

PARADISE AND THE PERI, the second of the four poems which form Moore's *Lalla Rookh*, has been several times set to music.

(1) ' Das Paradies und die Peri,' by Robert Schumann, for solos, chorus and orchestra (op. 50). The words were compiled by Schumann himself from the translations of Flechsig and Oelkers, with large alterations of his own ; produced Leipzig, Dec. 2, 1843 ; in England, Philharmonic Society, June 23, 1856, having previously been heard in Dublin, Feb. 10, 1854.[3]

(2) A fantasia-overture, ' Paradise and the Peri ' (op. 42), composed by Sterndale Bennett for the Jubilee Concert of the Philharmonic Society, July 14, 1862, and produced then.

(3) A cantata, for solos, chorus, orchestra and organ, by J. F. Barnett ; the words selected from Moore. Produced Birmingham Festival, Aug. 31, 1870.                                            G.

(4) ' La Peri,' ' poème dansé ' by Paul Dukas, Paris (Châlelet) 1912.

PARAVICINI, SIGNORA (b. Turin, 1769), daughter of Isabella Gandini the singer. Viotti was her master, and her full pure tone, graceful bowing, and scholarly style gained her considerable fame as a violinist. During the Milanese festivities which celebrated the battle of Lodi, she felicitously attracted the attention of the Empress Josephine, who engaged her to teach her son Eugène Beauharnais, and took

---

[1] Miss Frederica, a favourite of Handel, also played the organ in public in 1760, and sang in Handel's oratorios. She married Thomas Wynne, a land-owner in South Wales, and exercised considerable influence over the musical education of her nephew Mazzinghi.

[2] Described in detail in the Leipzig *A.M.Z.*, 1810, No. 57.
[3] See *Musical World*, Mar. 9, 1878, p. 174. See also ' Lalla Rookh ' and ' Veiled Prophet.'

her to Paris in 1797. Paravicini was most successful in the French capital, and became a leading soloist at the concerts given in the Salle de la Rue des Victoires Nationales. Unfortunately, the royal favour became less marked after a time, and finally ceased. The violinist sank into abject poverty, and, reduced to the utmost indigence, applied to the Italian residents in Paris, who eventually assisted her to return to her native country. Once arrived at Milan, her ability soon regained for her both competence and repute. Her performances of some concertos at the Italian Theatre at Lisbon in 1799 created a sensation, as did also her appearances at Leipzig, in the same year, and Dresden in 1800. She returned to Paris in 1801, and was received with enthusiasm at the Fridzeri concerts. She was at Berlin in 1802, Ludwigslust in 1805, and gave notable concerts at Munich and Vienna in 1827, but all trace of her is lost after her performance at Bologna in 1830.

BIBL.—LAHEE, *Famous Violinists*; CLARKE, *Dict. Fiddlers*; DUBOURG, *The Violin*; FÉTIS; Q.L.; MENDEL, *Musik Lexikon.*

E. H.-A.

PARAY, PAUL M. A. CHARLES (*b.* Tréport, May 24, 1886), composer and conductor. He was precociously gifted, and the influence of Dallier enabled him to overcome his family's objections to a musical career for him.

He entered the Paris Conservatoire in 1905, becoming a pupil of Caussade and Xavier Leroux, won the first prize for harmony in 1908, and the Prix de Rome in 1911. He was taken prisoner during the war, returning in 1918. He owed it to a happy concourse of circumstances that he was asked to conduct, as a test, the orchestra of the Concerts Lamoureux (Feb. 1920). His success was such that he was made second conductor to Chevillard, whom he succeeded soon afterwards. He has proved himself a true master, particularly in classic repertory, to which he is particularly attached.

As a composer, his personality is less pronounced. His works, already numerous, are sincere, finely written, occasionally a little academic. The best known are the sonata for PF. and vln.; the oratorio 'Jeanne d'Arc' (Rouen, 1921); and the symphonic poem 'Adonis troublé' (1921), given at the Opéra in 1922 under the title 'Artemis troublée.'

BIBL.—D. SORDET, *Douze chefs d'orchestre* (Paris, 1924).

M. P.

PARDON DE PLOËRMEL, LE, see DINORAH.

PAREPA - ROSA, EUPHROSYNE (*b.* Edinburgh, May 7, 1836; *d.* Jan. 21, 1874), the daughter of Demetrius Parepa, Baron de Boyescu, a Wallachian boyard, by his marriage with the singer Elizabeth SEGUIN (*d.* 1870), sister to Edward SEGUIN, a well-known bass singer. On her father's death, the child, having shown great aptitude for music, was educated by her mother and eminent masters for an artistic career. At the age of 16 Miss Parepa made a successful début on the stage as Amina, at Malta, and afterwards played at Naples, Genoa, Rome, Florence, Madrid and Lisbon. In this country she made her first appearance May 21, 1857, as Elvira in 'I Puritani' at the Royal Italian Opera, Lyceum, and played, Aug. 5, 1858, as Camilla on the revival of 'Zampa' at Covent Garden, on each occasion with fair success. During some of the seasons between 1859 and 1865 she played in English opera at Covent Garden and Her Majesty's, and created the parts of Victorine in Mellon's opera of that name (Dec. 19, 1859); the title-part of 'La Reine Topaze' of Massé, on its production in England (Dec. 26, 1860); that of Mabel in Macfarren's 'Helvellyn' (Nov. 3, 1864); playing also Arline, Satanella, and the two Zerlinas. In 1863 she was married to Captain H. de Wolfe Carvell (*d.* Lima, Peru, Apr. 26, 1865).

Her fine voice combined power and sweetness, good execution and extensive compass (of two octaves and a half, extending to *d'''* in alt); but she obtained but moderate success in opera. On the other hand, she won almost from the first a great reputation in oratorios and in the concert-room, and was frequently engaged at the various Societies and Festivals, including the Handel Festivals of 1862 and 1865. She also sang abroad in Germany and elsewhere. At the close of 1865 she went to America for a concert tour with Carl Rosa (whom she afterwards married there in Feb. 1867) and Levy the cornet-player, returning to England the following year. After their marriage Madame Parepa-Rosa and her husband remained in America for four years, and established their famous Opera Company, in which she was principal singer, achieving great success in English and Italian opera, oratorio and concerts. On her return to England, 1871, she was prevented by illness from fulfilling an engagement at the Royal Italian Opera, Covent Garden, but played for the winter season in Italian opera at Cairo, and the next year was heard with pleasure at Covent Garden as Donna Anna and Norma, and sang at the Philharmonic 'Ah Perfido' of Beethoven. In the autumn of 1871, Madame Parepa and her husband made a third visit to America with their company. In 1872 she sang at the Niederrheinische Festival at Düsseldorf, and later at Covent Garden, as Norma and Donna Anna. In 1873 she sang in Italian at Cairo with great success; her health prevented her singing in the provincial company that had been established by her husband, but she intended to sing the part of Elsa at the projected production of an English version of 'Lohengrin' at Drury Lane in Mar. 1874. Before the scheme could be realised Madame

Parepa was seized with a severe illness, from which she died. Carl Rosa abandoned his Drury Lane season, and founded the Parepa-Rosa scholarship at the R.A.M. in his wife's memory. (See ROSA, CARL.)          A. C.

PARIS. The musical life of Paris is here summarised with reference to opera, concerts and educational institutions. Special accounts of the two most famous Parisian institutions, the Opéra and the Conservatoire, appear elsewhere under the headings ACADÉMIE DE MUSIQUE and CONSERVATOIRE DE MUSIQUE (q.v.).

MUSICAL THEATRES. — From the definite establishment of the Comédie-Italienne at Paris in 1660, up to 1800, there existed successively about 22 theatres or theatrical enterprises for the production of musical works, including the Opéra, Opéra-Comique and their transformations (see ACADÉMIE DE MUSIQUE); some particulars of the Opéra-Comique, the theatres Lyrique, Ventadour and Italien are given below. Bare mention must suffice of the Colysée (1771), Menus-Plaisirs (1780), Théâtre de Monsieur (1789), Odéon (1797), (Théâtre-Italien), etc. From 1801 up to the first quarter of the 20th century about 30 such theatres can be counted, including: Société Olympique (Opera Buffa) (1801), Théâtre des Italiens, Théâtre-Lyrique, Bouffes-Parisiens (1855), Athénée Musical, Lyrique-Dramatique, Eden, Nouveau-Théâtre, Moncey, Marigny, Trianon-Lyrique, Théâtre des Champs-Élysées, etc., La Petite Scène (revives old works).

THE OPÉRA-COMIQUE, a theatre for French pieces with spoken dialogue, originated in the 'spectacles de la Foire,' which were a parody of the lyrical 'tragédie.' The title of 'Opéra-Comique' dates from the execution of an agreement between the comedians and the directors of the Académie Royale de Musique in 1715. The new enterprise, thus recognised, succeeded so well as to excite the jealousy of the large theatres, and in 1745 to cause the closing of the Opéra-Comique. In 1752, however, Monet received permission to re-establish it at the Fair of St. Germain, and under his skillful management it progressed so rapidly that in 1762 the Opéra-Comique joined the Comédie-Italienne, and took possession of the room in the Rue Mauconseil, whence in 1783 it migrated to the theatre in the Rue Favart.

In 1791 a second Opéra-Comique Company established itself in the Rue Feydeau, and a fierce competition ensued, which ended in the ruin and closing of both houses in 1801. After this the two companies were amalgamated and settled at the Théâtre-Feydeau, leaving the Salle Favart to the Italian troupe. At the Feydeau this company remained till April 1829.

The following play-houses were occupied afterwards by the Opéra-Comique:

Théâtre-Ventadour, 1829–32.
Théâtre des Nouveautés, Place de la Bourse (no longer existing), 1832.
Salle Favart, 1840, its present abode.

The Salle Favart restored by Crépinet (1879), was burnt down, May 25, 1887, after which the company was transferred to the Théâtre-Sarah Bernhardt. On Dec. 7, 1898, the theatre was opened on the old site.

In competition with the 'Théâtre-Lyrique' during the 19th century, the influence of the Opéra-Comique became gradually more important, with Carvalho as director, 1876–87, 1891–97. His successors were: Paravey, Carré, Carré-Gheusi, Isola-Carré; and from Oct. 1925, Masson-Ricou-Albert Carré.

THÉÂTRE-LYRIQUE, in a general way the name given in France to a theatre intended for performances of musical dramatic works. As a special enterprise, it was inaugurated at Paris, Sept. 21, 1851, by Edmond Souveste, followed by his brother Jules (1852–54), E. Perrin (1854–55), Pellegrin, and above all, Carvalho (1856–60, 1862–68), under whose influence the theatre attained an artistic level.[1]

From 1868 the principal endeavours to revise the institution were:

Pasdeloup (1868), successor of Carvalho (at the Théâtre - Sarah Bernhardt); Théâtre de la Gaîté, Vizentini, 1876–77; Théâtre - Ventadour, Escudier, 1878; Théâtre du Château d'Eau,1879: performances of 'Étienne Marcel' (Saint-Saëns), 'Jocelyn' (Godard). Théâtre de l'Éden, Lamoureux, 1887, 'Lohengrin,' 'Samson et Dalila,' 1890, Porel-Colonne, 1893; Nouveau Théâtre, Lamoureux, 1899, 'Tristan et Isolde'; Théâtre de la Renaissance, 1899–1900, ' Obéron '; Théâtre du Château d'Eau, Cortot, 1902, ' Crépuscule des Dieux,' ' Tristan ' ; Théâtre du Trianon Lyrique, since Dec. 1902 onwards.

More recently must be mentioned the following seasons:

Théâtre du Châtelet, 1907–12, 'Salomé' (Richard Strauss), 1908 ; Théâtre des Champs-Élysées, 1913, both under the direction of G. Astruc ; Théâtre de la Gaîté, Isola, 1903–4, 1907–14 ; Théâtre des Arts (Théâtre des Batignolles), J. Rouché, 1912, revival of old works, Monteverdi's ' Incoronazione di Poppea,' etc. ; Théâtre du Vaudeville, Gheusi, 1919–20.

THÉÂTRE-VENTADOUR [2] has had a long and chequered musical history. The theatre was built to replace the Salle Feydeau, and a new street being planned to run from the Rue des Petits Champs to the Rue Neuve St. Augustin, and to be called the Rue Neuve Ventadour, it was decided to place the theatre in the middle of the street and call it by the same name. The street in which the principal façade stands is now called Rue Méhul, and that at the back, Rue Monsigny. The building was erected by the architect Huvé, superintended by M. de Guerchy, and cost, including site, 4,620,000 francs (£184,800), which was paid out of the Civil List. The theatre was sold to a company

---

[1] See A. Soubies, *Histoire du Théâtre-Lyrique, 1851–70* (1899).
[2] Ventadour, which has given its name to a street and a lyric theatre in Paris, is a village in the Limousin, created a duchy in 1568 in behalf of Gilbert de Levis, whose descendants have since borne the name of Levis de Ventadour. The Rue Ventadour, opened in 1640 as the Rue St. Victor, took the name it still bears in 1672. It begins at No. 26 in the Avenue de l'Opéra, and ends at No. 57 in the Rue des Petits Champs.

of speculators for 2,000,000 francs (£80,000), a disastrous transaction, in keeping with much of the financial history of the Théâtre-Ventadour.

The following theatrical companies occupied the theatre :

Apr. 20, 1829–32, Opéra-Comique.
June 10, 1834–35, Théâtre-Nautique (not musical).
Jan. 30, 1838, Italian Company with Rubini, Zamboni, Lablache, etc.
Autumn 1838–41, Théâtre de la Renaissance; director, Anténor Joly.
1841–71, Théâtre des Italiens.
1871–Jan. 11, 1879, several attempts to resuscitate the Italian repertory, e.g. 'Aïda' (Apr. 22), Verdi's 'Requiem,' (May 30, 1876), at the Théâtre-Lyrique until 1878.
Jan. 19, 1874, the Opéra Company after the burning of Salle Le Peletier.
In 1879 the theatre was sold to a financial company and became the ' Banque d'escompte de Paris.' It is actually an auxiliary branch of the ' Banque de France.'

THÉÂTRE-ITALIEN. — The foundation of the so-called 'Théâtre-Italien' or 'Théâtre des Italiens' for the permanent performance of the Italian repertory in France can be traced back to 1570, when Italian comedians played in Paris, in the reign of Charles IX. They were followed by others, Gelosi, Comici Confidenti, Fedeli, until 1660, definite establishment of an Italian troupe with 'Scaramouche' (Dominique), who performed with Molière's company at the Palais Royal up to 1673. From then the important dates in its evolution are the following : 1723, the Italian comedians take the name of 'Comédiens du roi' and join the Opéra-Comique, Feb. 3, 1762 (see BOUFFONS) ; Jan. 21, 1789, the Théâtre de Monsieur opens at the Tuileries ; May 31, 1801, the 'Opera Buffa' at the Salle Olympique, Salle Favart, Théâtre-Louvois until 1808 (Théâtre de l'Impératrice) ; 1808–15, performances at the Odéon of the above company ; 1815–41, performances of the 'Théâtre Royal Italien' in different playhouses, Salles Favart, Louvois, Odéon, etc. ; Oct. 2, 1841–76, the Italian troupe is located at the Théâtre-Ventadour. From then the Théâtre-Italien loses its permanent character ; Italian performances take place in different theatres ; 1881, 17 performances by A. Patti ; 1883, performances with V. Maurel, etc. In the 20th century, from 1905–1922, Italian seasons have followed one another under different directions (Sonzogno, Gunsbourg, etc.).

BIBLIOGRAPHY

OPÉRA-COMIQUE

Encyclopédie de la musique et dictionnaire du Conservatoire (France, 17e 18e siècles, L. de La Laurencie), with an extensive general bibliography.
A. POUGIN : L'Opéra-Comique pendant la Révolution de 1788 à 1801. (1891.)
A. SOUBIES and CH. MALHERBE : Histoire de l'Opéra-Comique (1892–1893.)
JEAN RAPHAEL : Histoire au jour le jour de l'Opéra-Comique. (1898.)
MAURICE ALBERT : Les Théâtres de la Foire (1660–1789). (1900.)
G. CUCUEL : Les Créateurs de l'Opéra-Comique. (1914.)

THÉÂTRE VENTADOUR

FOUQUE : Histoire du Théâtre-Ventadour (1881). Fuller particulars in former editions of this Dictionary.

THÉÂTRE LYRIQUE AND ITALIEN

LASSALLE (DE) : Mémorial du Théâtre-lyrique. (1877.)

G. SERVIÈRES : Le Théâtre-lyrique à Paris de 1870 à 1920 (Revue musicale, Mar.-Apr. 1921).
A. SOUBIES : Le Théâtre-italien. (1913.)

GENERAL

L. H. LECOMTE : Histoire des théâtres de Paris (1402–1904). Notice préliminaire. (1905.)
Almanach Duchesne, 1874–1914. (Soubies). See SOUBIES.
Almanach des théâtres (1922), ed. by A. Aynard.

CONCERT SPIRITUEL (1725–91), a great musical institution of France, dating from the reign of Louis XV. The Académie Royale de Musique (the Opera House) being closed on the great religious festivals, it occurred to Anne Danican Philidor (see PHILIDOR, 5) to give concerts on these occasions in place of the prohibited performances. Having obtained the necessary permission, Philidor entered into an agreement with Francine, the impresario of the Opéra, by which he pledged himself to pay 1000 francs a year, and to perform neither French nor opera music. The first Concert Spirituel accordingly took place between 6 and 8 P.M. on Sunday in Passion Week, March 18, 1725. The programme included a suite for violin and a capriccio by Lalande, Corelli's 'Nuit de Noël' (Concerto 8, op. 6), and a 'Confitebor' and 'Cantate Domino' of Lalande, and the concert was most successful. The number of concerts in the year never exceeded twenty-four. They were held in the Salle des Suisses of the Tuileries, on the Feast of the Purification, Feb. 2 ; Lady Day, March 25 ; on certain days between Palm Sunday and Low Sunday (first Sunday after Easter) ; Whitsunday ; Corpus Christi Sunday ; on Aug. 15, Sept. 8, Nov. 1, 8 ; Dec. 24, 25 — those being the days on which the Opéra was closed.

In 1728 Philidor, having previously acquired the right of introducing French and opera music into the programmes, transferred his privilege to Simard, on an annual payment of 3000 francs, and the musical direction of the concerts was confided to Mouret. His followers were : Dec. 25, 1734, Thuret, with Rebel as conductor ; 1741, Royer ; 1749, Royer and Caperan ; 1755–1762, Mondonville ; 1762–71, Dauvergne, Joliveau, Caperan ; 1771, Dauvergne, Berton ; 1773, Gaviniés, Le Duc, Gossec ; 1777, Le Gros with Berthaume (1789). Political events gave a fatal blow to the undertaking, and in 1791 the Concert Spirituel ceased to exist.[1]

Mouret, Rebel, Dauvergne and Berton are among the best composers and leaders of the orchestra that the Académie Royale can show in the 18th century ; Gaviniés, Simon Leduc, Lahoussaye, Guénin and Berthaume, who conducted the concerts during the last eighteen years of their existence, were all violin-players of very great merit.

Among the celebrated artists who appeared, it will be sufficient to mention the famous brothers Besozzi, whose duets for oboe and bassoon made a furore in 1735 ; the violinists

[1] The Concert Spirituel was revived in 1805, however, by the impresario of the Italian Opera House, and the sacred concerts given during Holy Week at the Opéra, the Conservatoire and elsewhere, are still known by that name,

Traversa, Jarnowick, François Lamotte, Viotti and Frederic Eck ; the horn players Punto and Rodolphe ; Jérome Besozzi and Louis Lebrun (oboe) ; Etienne Ozi (bassoon) ; Michel Yost (clarinet), and many others of less repute. Among many illustrious singers we must content ourselves with mentioning Farinelli, Raff, Caffarelli, Davide, Mmes. Agujari, Danzi, Todi and Mara.

In 1770 the important enterprise of the CONCERT DES AMATEURS was founded by d'Ogni and Delahaye at the Hôtel Soubise. It was conducted by Gossec, and its solo violin was the famous Chevalier de St. Georges. At these concerts the symphonies of J. B. Toeschi, Van Maldere, Vanhall, Stamitz and Gossec, for wind instruments, were first produced. When the association removed to the Galerie du Henri III., in the Rue Coq Héron, they adopted the title of Concert de la Loge Olympique, and their orchestra contained the best players of the day. The change took place in 1780, a year after the introduction of Haydn's symphonies into France by the violinist Fonteski. So great was the success of these compositions as to induce the directors to engage Haydn to write six symphonies specially for the society. They date from 1784–89 ; are in C, G minor, E♭, B♭, D and A ; and were afterwards published in Paris as op. 51, under the special title of 'Répertoire de la Loge Olympique.' (See HAYDN, List of Symphonies.)

Two similar institutions, the CONCERT DE LA RUE DE CLÉRY (1789), and the CONCERT FEYDEAU (1794), may be considered as feeble imitations of the Loge Olympique. They had, however, their periods of success — according to Fétis in 1796 and 1802. Among the artists who chiefly contributed to the éclat of the performances were the violinists R. Kreutzer and Rode, Fred. Duvernoy the horn-player, and the singers Garat and Mme. Barbier-Valbonne.

THE CONCERTS FRANÇAIS, the first of which took place in 1786, had their origin in the public exercises of the pupils of the École Royale de Musique et de Déclamation ; the 'exercises' were in danger of suppression, when the old pupils of the Conservatoire formed themselves into a society quite independent of the school. The first concert took place in the foyer of the Théâtre Olympique, Nov. 21, 1801, and from 1802 the series was continued in the small theatre of the Conservatoire, rue Bergère, which theatre existed until 1911. The concerts were directed successively by Marcel Duret, F. Habeneck (then aged 22 years, but already a conductor of remarkable ability), and by Gasse, all of whom had been violin pupils. Besides songs and instrumental solos a symphony of Haydn, Mozart, or Méhul, etc., was always played, as well as an overture. Some of the symphonies of Beethoven (which the professional orchestras had not then attempted) were heard there for the first time in Paris (the C major symphony on Feb. 22, 1807). This orchestra of students won general admiration by the excellence of its performances.[1]

THE CONCERTS DU CONSERVATOIRE.—The creation of the celebrated Société des Concerts du Conservatoire was due to Habeneck, and its first 'Matinée dominicale' took place on Sunday, March 9, 1828, at 2 P.M., in the theatre of the Conservatoire. This programme, which produced a very deep impression, was as follows :

(1) Eroica Symphony, Beethoven.
(2) Duet from ' Semiramide,' Rossini, sung by Nélia and Caroline Maillard.
(3) Horn Solo, composed and executed by Meifred.
(4) Concerto for violin, Rode, performed by Eugène Sauzay.
(5) Air by Rossini, sung by Nélia Maillard.
(6) Chorus from ' Blanche de Provence,' Cherubini.
(7) Overture, ' Les Abencérages,' Cherubini.
(8) Kyrie and Gloria from the 'Coronation Mass,' Cherubini.

The following table shows the direction of these famous concerts from their inception to the present day :

| Conductor. | Sub-Conductor. | Date. |
|---|---|---|
| Habeneck . | Tilmant aîné | Mar. 9, 1828–Apr. 10, 1848 |
| Narcisse Girard | ,, | Jan. 14, 1849–Jan. 1860 |
| Tilmant . . | Deldevez | 1860–63 |
| G. Hainl . . | ,, | 1864–Mar. 17, 1872 |
| Deldevez . . | Lamoureux | May 25, 1872–77 |
| ,, | E. Altès | 1877–85 |
| Jules Garcin . | Jules Danbé | June 2, 1885–92 |
| Paul Taffanel . | D. Thibault | Nov. 27, 1892–1901 |
| Georges Marty { | Gasser Ed. Nadaud } | June 12, 1901–8 |
| A. Messager . | Gaubert | 1908–18 |
| Phil. Gaubert . | Tracol | 1919 (onwards) |

During 1897–98 the Société des Concerts du Conservatoire gave its concerts provisionally at the Opéra, as the Commission supérieure des Théâtres ordered the hall in the rue Bergère to be shut after the disastrous fire at the Charity bazaar. Fourteen concerts were given at the Opéra, for which the orchestra was augmented to ninety-eight performers. From the date of the resumption of the concerts in the original building (Nov. 27, 1898) the former number of performers (84) was restored ; and the Commission des Théâtres ordered a certain number of seats to be removed, so that the number of concerts had to be increased to make up for the diminution in the receipts.

Minor institutions of some historic importance may be summarised as follows :

ORCHESTRAL CONCERTS

L'ATHÉNÉE MUSICALE, founded by Chelard in 1829 at the Hôtel de Ville, directed by Barbereau, Vidal, Gérard, 60th to 66th concert in 1837. President, Onslow.

CONCERTS HISTORIQUES, founded by Fétis (4 concerts) ; 1st concert, Apr. 8, 1832 ; 4th, Apr. 2, 1833. From 1832 onwards : CONCERTS MUSARD (rue

---

[1] Constant Pierre, Le Conservatoire National de Musique et de Déclamation (Paris, 1900).

Vivienne); CONCERTS BESSELIÈVRE; GYMNASE MUSI-
CAL, opened May 23, 1835, conductor, Tilmant aîné;
performances of Berlioz's Harold (June); CONCERTS
A. JULLIEN (dance music), 1836–38; CONCERTS VALEN-
TINO, 1837–1841; 1st concert, Oct. 15, 1837, and the
first popular concerts in France; CASINO PAGANINI;
1st concert, Dec. 3, 1837.

L'UNION MUSICALE, founded by Manera, pupil of
Habeneck; conductors, F. David, H. Berlioz.

SOCIÉTÉ SAINTE-CÉCILE, 1849–54: conductor,
Seghers. Performances of Gounod, Saint-Saëns,
Reber, Mendelssohn, Schumann, etc.

SOCIÉTÉ PHILHARMONIQUE, founded by Berlioz,
1850–51.

The SOCIÉTÉ DES JEUNES ARTISTES DU CON-
SERVATOIRE, founded by PASDELOUP (q.v.), 1851,
transformed into Concerts Populaires de Musique
Classique (Oct. 27, 1861), had a successful career until
1884, and exerted a great influence on the musical
development of France.

The SOCIÉTÉ DES CONCERTS DE CHANT CLASSIQUE,
founded by D. Beaulieu in 1860, is still active.

SOCIÉTÉ DES COMPOSITEURS DE MUSIQUE founded
by Weckerlin, 1862 (concerts of historical tendencies).

NOUVELLE SOCIÉTÉ STE. CÉCILE, by the same, 1865.

With the CONCERTS DU GRAND HOTEL
founded by J. Danbé (1871–74), the modern
history of orchestral concerts in Paris begins.
The institutions set on foot in the later part
of the 19th century may be summarised as
follows:

L'HARMONIE SACRÉE, founded by Lamoureux, 1873;
CONCERT NATIONAL, founded by Colonne and G.
Hartmann, 1873, at the Odéon. This was transformed, Oct. 1874, to L'Association Artistique and
later on to CONCERTS COLONNE (both at the Châtelet).
Since 1910 the conductor has been G. Pierné. In
1897 a temporary new series of concerts was organised
(see COLONNE).

NOUVEAUX CONCERTS, founded by Lamoureux in
1881, were afterwards known as CONCERTS LAMOUREUX
(see CHEVILLARD, LAMOUREUX). These concerts were
successively housed at: Château d'Eau, 1881–85,
1899–1900; Eden, 1885–87; Cirque des Champs-
Élysées, 1887–98; Nouveau Théâtre, 1900–6; Théâtre
Sarah Bernhardt, 1906–7; 1907 onwards, at Salle
Gaveau.

Others were:

CONCERTS ÉCLECTIQUES POPULAIRES, founded by
Eug. d'Harcourt, 1892–95, resumed in 1900 as LES
GRANDS ORATORIOS À L'ÉGLISE ST. EUSTACHE.

CONCERTS DE L'OPÉRA, founded by G. Marty and
P. Vidal, 1895–97. Concerts de la Schola Cantorum
(see SCHOLA, below).

CONCERTS SPIRITUELS DE LA SORBONNE, founded
by P. de Saunières, 1898 (still active).

ASSOCIATION DES GRANDS CONCERTS CHARPENTIER
(Victor), 1905 onwards.

ASSOCIATION DES CONCERTS PASDELOUP, as a
continuation of the work which Pasdeloup had
achieved at an earlier date as mentioned above, was
founded in 1918 by Rhené-Baton (also its conductor),
and O. Sandberg. The first named with Albert Wolf
was conducting this Society from 1925 onwards.

BIBLIOGRAPHY

MICHEL BRENET: Les Concerts en France sous l'ancien régime.
    (1900.)
CONSTANT PIERRE: Le Concert spirituel, 1725–90, précédé d'un
    historique des concerts publics à Paris. (1900.)
ELWART: Histoire de la Société des Concerts du Conservatoire (1860),
    continued as:
DELDEVEZ: La Société des Concerts de 1860 à 1885.
A. DANDELOT: (1) La Société des Concerts du Conservatoire de
    1828 à 1897 (1897); (2) La Société des Concerts du Conservatoire
    de 1828 à 1923 (1923).
H. DE CURZON: Histoire et gloire de l'ancienne salle du Conservatoire
    de Paris, 1811–1911. (1917.)

### CHAMBER MUSIC AND CHORAL SOCIETIES

The first institution for the cultivation of
stringed chamber music in Paris was the
quartet founded by BAILLOT (q.v.), Dec. 12,
1814. It was not until the middle of the

century that societies of the kind began to be
formed. The earliest were:

SOCIÉTÉ ALARD-FRANCHOMME, 1848.

SOCIÉTÉ DES DERNIERS QUATUORS DE BEETHOVEN
(Maurin-Chevillard), 1851.

SOCIÉTÉ DE MUSIQUE DE CHAMBRE ARMAINGAUD
(E. Lalo, 2nd violin), 1856.

SÉANCES POPULAIRES DE MUSIQUE DE CHAMBRE
(Lamoureux), 1859.

SOCIETIES: ARMINGAUD-JACQUARD; MAURIN-
CHEVILLARD, 1861.

SOCIÉTÉ DES BEAUX ARTS, 1863–64, transformed
into SOCIÉTÉ DE MUSIQUE DE CHAMBRE JACOBY-
VUILLAUME, 1864.

Institutions which have survived to later
times include:

SOCIÉTÉ DANCLA, 'LA TROMPETTE,' founded in 1860
by Émile Lemoine; present director, A. Bloch.

SOCIÉTÉ-HAYDN-MOZART-BEETHOVEN, 1895 onwards.

SOCIÉTÉ PHILHARMONIQUE DE PARIS, 1902 onwards;
present director, E. Rey.

QUARTETS: Geloso, Loeb, Touche, Hayot, Parent,
Capet, Chailley, Poulet, etc.

CONCERTS ROUGE, 1889 onwards; present conductor, L. Loicq. CONCERTS TOUCHE, conductor F.
Touche, both of popular character.

The development of trio-societies was parallel
to the preceding movement. It began (1827–
1830) with the brothers Bohrer: Beethoven's
trios. In Jan.-Feb. 1837 were given four performances of the same by Liszt, Urhan, Batta;
1840, by the brothers Franco Mendez, etc. In
1865, Société des Trios Anciens et Modernes,
V. de la Nux (pianist), was started, and the
Société Saint-Saëns-Sarasate gave one concert
(Feb. 7).

From the last quarter of the 19th century up
to the present time, the number of these
societies has increased with the extension of
the practice of chamber music; the Cortot,
Casadesus trios are noteworthy.

Music for wind instruments has been cultivated by the

SOCIÉTÉ DES INSTRUMENTS À VENT, founded
1879 by P. Taffanel (flute); original members
were: Boullard (oboe); Grisez, Turban
(clarinet); Espaignet, Bourdeau (bassoon);
Garigue, Bremond (horn); Louis Diémer (piano).
Members in 1927 are Gaubert, Le Roy; L. Bas,
Morel; Périer, Gras; Letellier, Henon; Vialet,
Pénable; L. Wurmser (piano).

SOCIÉTÉ MODERNE D'INSTRUMENTS À VENT,
founded 1895, by G. Barrère (flute); L. Aubert
(piano), Foucault (oboe), Vionne (clarinet),
Bulteau (bassoon), Servat (horn); from 1905
directed by L. Fleury till his death. Members
in 1926: the preceding, Beauduin; Garès,
Gaudard, Lamorlette; Cahuzac, Delacroix;
Hermans, Dherin; Entraigue, Levasseur.

Similar associations are: Dixtuor à vent de
la Société des Concerts du Conservatoire,
Double quintette de Paris, Quintette instrumental de Paris.

The cult of ancient instruments and their
music is furthered by the

SOCIÉTÉ DES INSTRUMENTS ANCIENS, founded
1895 by L. Diémer with VAN WAEFELGHEM
(q.v.), L. Grillet, Bleuzet (not active);

SOCIÉTÉ DES INSTRUMENTS ANCIENS, founded 1901 (onwards) by H. CASADESUS (q.v.); and SOCIÉTÉ 'VIOLES ET CLAVECINS,' founded by E. Macon (active).

**BIBLIOGRAPHY**
(for Chamber Music and Concerts in general)
EYMIEU ET COMETTANT: *La Musique de chambre à Paris* (1893-99, 7 vol.)
A. DE LASSUS: *Un Demi-siècle de musique de chambre. La Trompette* (1911).
J. COMBARIEU: *Histoire de la musique.* (Deals also with concerts in the French Provinces.)

The following associations of artists for professional purposes, etc., deserve mention :

SOCIÉTÉ DES AUTEURS ET COMPOSITEURS DE MUSIQUE, founded 1829.
ASSOCIATION DES ARTISTES MUSICIENS, founded by Baron Taylor, 1843.
SOCIÉTÉ DES AUTEURS, COMPOSITEURS ET ÉDITEURS DE MUSIQUE, founded 1851.
SOCIÉTÉ DES COMPOSITEURS DE MUSIQUE.
SOCIÉTÉ DE L'HISTOIRE DU THÉÂTRE.
SOCIÉTÉ DE L'HISTOIRE DE L'ART, etc.

For full list of professional and syndical associations, see *Annuaire des artistes*.

Choral music, apart from the stage and the Church, held a comparatively subordinate position in Paris until the middle of the 19th century. It was furthered by the work of CHORON (q.v.) and his follower NIEDERMEYER (q.v.) and the 'Société des Concerts de Chant Classique,' founded by BEAULIEU (q.v.). The 'Société de Musique Vocale Religieuse et Classique,' which the Prince de la Moskowa founded in 1843, marked a revival of interest in the older choral art, and the important ORPHÉON (q.v.) movement of the mid century brought a great popular extension of interest in choral (male-voiced) singing. The principal choral societies, most of which are now active, are here summarised.

SOCIÉTÉ CHORALE D'AMATEURS GUILLOT-SAINBRIS (now Griset-Sainbris), founded 1865, by A. Guillot de Sainbris, singing professor at the Paris Conservatoire. Conductors after him were Maton, Griset, E. Millot.
SOCIÉTÉ BOURGAULT-DUCOUDRAY, 1869-74 (?). L'Harmonie Sacrée (q.v.)
CHANTEURS DE SAINT-GERVAIS, founded 1892 by Charles Bordes (conductor), followed by L. Saint Requier, afterwards P. Le Flem.
SOCIÉTÉ J. S. BACH, 1904-14, founded by G. Bret, followed by LES CONCERTS SPIRITUELS DE L'ÉGLISE DE L'ÉTOILE; has now resumed its original name (same conductor).
SOCIÉTÉ HÄNDEL, 1909-14, founded by E. Borrel, and F. Raugel.
LA MANÉCANTERIE DES PETITS CHANTEURS À LA CROIX DE BOIS, founded 1907 by Abbé Rebuffat (Church and Gregorian music), is still active. Similar societies are: La Cantoria (not active), conductor J. Meunier; Les Chanteurs de la Sainte Chapelle.
CHORALE UNIVERSITAIRE, founded 1918 by Mlle. Bonnet (University students); conductor, H. Expert, now E. Borrel.
CHŒUR MIXTE DE PARIS, founded 1921 by M. de Ranse, also conductor.
CHORALE FRANÇAISE (not active), founded 1922 by Mme. Danner; conductors, F. Raugel and R. Siohan.
L'ART CHORAL, founded and conducted by the last named.

Musical societies specially concerned with modern works are :

SOCIÉTÉ NATIONALE DE MUSIQUE, a permanent institution, founded Feb. 1871, by Romain Bussine, singing professor at the Conservatoire (1830-99), and

C. Saint-Saëns; it gives performances of works, chamber and orchestral, of modern and specially of living French composers. Its first concert was given on Nov. 25, 1871. On Jan. 22, 1927, it reached its 487th concert ; 8 or 9 concerts are given annually.
SOCIÉTÉ MUSICALE INDÉPENDANTE (S.M.I.), founded 1910 (onwards), under presidency of G. Fauré, with an original committee : Ravel, Caplet, Schmitt, Roger-Ducasse, etc. It has the same aims as the preceding, but more performances of foreign composers.
L'ŒUVRE INÉDITE, founded 1920, has similar aims.
CERCLE MUSICAL UNIVERSITAIRE, founded 1919 (onwards) by Chabé, president Ch. Guignebert, aims at developing the taste for music amongst university students.
SOCIÉTÉ FRANÇAISE DE MUSICOLOGIE, founded 1917 (onwards), by L. de La Laurencie, took the place of the French section of the INTERNATIONAL MUSICAL SOCIETY (q.v.) (1904-14). It published the *Bulletin de la Société Française de Musicologie* (10 numbers), followed by the *Revue de Musicologie* and an annex publication of rare musical works (*Publications de la Société Française de Musicologie*). (See PERIODICALS.)

### EDUCATIONAL

The CONSERVATOIRE DE MUSIQUE (q.v.) stands at the head of specialist education in the art. Before the establishment of official musical teaching in France at the end of the 18th century, education was disseminated from the organists and the 'maîtrises' (precentorships) in the Cathedrals and Collegiate churches. A special singing school existed at the Opéra from 1672-1807.[1] In 1784 the 'École Royale de Chant et de Déclamation' was formed, and proved to be the ancestor of the Conservatoire (founded 1795).

Choron founded the 'Institution Royale de Musique Classique et Religieuse' (1817-30), and L. Niedermeyer followed this with the 'École de Musique Religieuse et Classique' in 1853, on similar lines. The latter is now known as ÉCOLE NIEDERMEYER. It trains singers, organists, composers and church musicians, basing the system primarily on the study of the older masters (16th, 17th, 18th centuries). It has had as directors : Niedermeyer, G. Lefèvre and H. Büsser (at the present time). Amongst its students have been Gabriel Fauré, A. Messager, E. Gigout, Claude Terrasse, A. Georges, etc.

Of far wider importance, however, is the SCHOLA CANTORUM, founded in 1894 by Ch. Bordes, Al. Guilmant and V. d'Indy. It had as its original purpose the study of the Gregorian tradition of plain-song, and the revival of music of the Palestrina era with the object of raising the standard of music in French churches. Transformed into an 'École de Chant Liturgique et de Musique Religieuse' (Oct. 1896), it was transferred from the original premises (rue Stanislas) to its present dwelling, the convent of the 'Bénédictins Anglais'[2] (rue St. Jacques 269), as an 'École Supérieure de Musique' (1900). Under its director, Vincent d'Indy, its aim has always been to produce artists and not merely

[1] See Constant Pierre, *L'École de chant à l'Opéra* (1896). Two early provincial schools of music deserve mention, that of Lille (1733) and one at Dijon (1793-96).
[2] The remains of James II, of England were deposited in this convent.

virtuosi. The educational staff (three degrees), is as follows:

*Superior degree:* V. d'Indy, director of studies, composition from the beginning, orchestra playing; L. de Serres, general inspector of studies, entrusted with the choral, chamber-music, lyric declamation classes; Vierne (organ), Gastoué (plain-song), Lejeune (violin), G. de Lioncourt and P. Le Flem (counterpoint), etc.

Former professors there were: Guilmant, until his death, Bordes, M. Labey, Blanche Selva, A. Sérieyx, etc.

The concerts (monthly up to 1914; 2 or 3 a year at the present time), on historical lines, have had a certain influence on public taste, and increased its interest for old music. Programmes consisted of: J. S. Bach, Rameau, Gluck, Monteverdi, also Gregorian and polyphonic music, French school, of the 17th and 18th centuries; Haydn, Beethoven, Weber; modern French works (C. Franck, V. d'Indy (Chant de la Cloche), Chausson, P. de Bréville, Fauré, Debussy, etc.).

The affiliated provincial societies have greatly helped the cause of good music; the 'Bureau d'édition' connected with the school (founded 1896) has a large catalogue of organ and sacred music (ancient and modern), Bordes's 'Anthologie des maîtres religieux primitifs' (not the 'Archives de l'orgue'), collections including plain-song and popular songs (Le Chant populaire) (Concerts spirituels anciens), polyphonic music XII.–XV. centuries, dramatic music, etc., pedagogic works, musical literature, etc. The 'Édition mutuelle' is concerned with the production of contemporary composers, and the 'Tablettes de la Schola' act as a regular chronicle for the institution; associations of its professors and of the Schola's older pupils have been formed in recent years.

The INSTITUT GRÉGORIEN at the Institut Catholique is directed by J. Bonnet.

BIBL.—R. DE CASTERA, *Dix années d'action musicale religieuse;* V. D'INDY, *Une École de musique répondant aux besoins modernes* (extracts of the *Tribune de St. Gervais* (Bureau d'édition) existing separately).

Of the many existing schools in private hands the following are the chief:

ÉCOLE NORMALE DE MUSIQUE DE PARIS, founded 1919; director, A. Mangeot. President of the administrative committee, Alfred Cortot. Committee: Widor, Charpentier, H. Rabaud, Hüe.
CONSERVATOIRE RAMEAU; director, F. Delgrange.
ÉCOLE SUPÉRIEURE DE MUSIQUE ET DE DÉCLAMATION; president, Widor.
CONSERVATOIRE MUSICA (foundation, X. Leroux); directors, Mme. Héglon, G. de Lausnay.
ÉCOLE DE PIANO LOUIS DIÉMER; director, Armand Ferté.
ÉCOLE DE CHANT CHORAL, director, H. Radiguer, mainspring of the 'Association pour le Développement du Chant Choral,' founded by J. d'Estournelle de Constant.
CONSERVATOIRE AMÉRICAIN ('École des hautes Études Musicales'), founded 1921, by M. Fragnaud and Francis Casadesus, at the Palace of Fontainebleau. Director general of studies, Ch. M. Widor. Directors: Casadesus, Max d'Ollone, Decreus. Summer courses only are held.

Concourses and prizes of the Institut de France (Académie des Beaux Arts—6 members for musical section) are as follows:

*Prix de Rome* (see article).
*Prix Chartier* (1861): chamber music.
*Prix Crescent:* comic opera, opera.
*Prix Monbinne:* comic opera.
*Prix de Saussay:* opera-libretto.
*Prix Rossini:* (1) lyrical or sacred composition; (2) poetry intended for music-setting.
*Prix Nicolo:* vocal composition.
*Prix: Clamageran-Hérold, Fondation Pinette:* to winner of the second Grand Prix de Rome and pupils of French Academy, Rome (Villa Medicis).
*Prix: Jean Reynaud, Estrade-Delcros.*
*Prix: Bordin, Kastner - Boursault, Houllevigue, Charles Blanc, J. J. Weiss:* (musical history and criticism).

Other prizes are:

*Prix de là Ville de Paris* (since 1877): symphonic or choral music. Principal awarders: Th. Dubois, V. d'Indy (Le Chant de la Cloche), J. Cras.
*Concours de la Société des Compositeurs de Musique:* symphonic, chamber music.
*Prix: de la Société des Auteurs et Compositeurs Dramatiques; de la Société de l'Histoire du Théâtre, etc.*
*Concours Rubinstein* (International). Specially bequeathed to the Conservatoire: 41 prizes and endowments: Georges Hainl, Henri Herz, Jules Garcin, Louis Diémer, A. Guilmant, etc.
Recent prizes (1920), composition: *Prix Verley, Blumenthal.*
(See M. Daubresse, *Le Musicien dans la société moderne* (Paris, 1914).)

The courses of the University of Paris are:

(1) History of Music: Lionel Dauriac, 1896–1903; Romain Rolland, 1903–1911 (replaced 1906–7 by L. Laloy); A. Pirro, 1911 (onwards). From 1920 a special course for 'musicology' is held by the last-named (Bibliothèque Pierre Aubry).

(2) Institut Phonétique de la Sorbonne: Dr. Marage, course on physiology of word and song.

LIBRARIES.—Exclusively musical and theatrical are the Bibliothèque du Conservatoire, de l'Opéra, de l'Opéra-Comique.

There are musical sections in the Bibliothèques Nationale, Ste Geneviève, de l'Arsénal, Mazarine, de l'Institut.

Paris University (Sorbonne) contains the Bibliothèque Pierre Aubry bequeathed by its possessor, occupying a special room; also the musical library of A. Guilmant, bequeathed to the University Library. (See LIBRARIES.)

M. L. P. and J. G. P., incorporating material from G. C.

PARIS, AIMÉ, see CHEVÉ.

PARISH-ALVARS, ELIAS (*b.* Teignmouth, Feb. 28, 1808; *d.* Vienna, Jan. 25, 1849), was of Hebrew descent. He studied the harp under Dizi, Labarre and Bochsa, and became one of the most distinguished performers on that instrument. He was also an excellent pianist. In 1831 he visited Germany, and performed at Bremen, Hamburg and other places, with great success. In 1834 he went to Upper Italy and gave concerts at Milan. In 1836 he went to Vienna, where he remained for two years, occasionally visiting London. The years 1838–1842 were occupied by a journey to the East, where he collected many Eastern melodies; the *Voyage d'un harpiste en Orient* contains numerous specimens. He returned to Europe and gave concerts at Leipzig in 1842, and at Berlin, Frankfort, Dresden and Prague in 1843. In 1844 he went to Naples, where he was received with enthusiasm. In 1846 he stayed some time at Leipzig, where his association with Mendelssohn produced a sensible improvement in his style of composition. In 1847 he settled at Vienna, where he was appointed chamber musician to the Emperor. His compositions consist of concertos for harp and orchestra, and numerous fantasias for harp and piano-forte, and harp alone. He was remarkable for his assiduity in seeking for new effects from his instrument, in some of which he anticipated Thalberg's most characteristic treatment.

w. h. h.

PARISINA. (1) opera in 3 acts; libretto (founded on Byron's poem) by Romani; music by Donizetti. Produced Pergola Theatre, Florence, Mar. 18, 1833; Théâtre des Italiens, Paris, Feb. 24, 1838; Her Majesty's Theatre, June 1, 1838.

(2) 'Overture to Lord Byron's Poem of Parisina,' for orchestra, by Sterndale Bennett (op. 3), in F♯ minor; composed in 1835, while Bennett was a student; performed Philharmonic, June 8, 1840.　　　　　　g.

PARKE (1) JOHN (b. London, 1745; d. there, Aug. 2, 1829), studied the oboe under Simpson, and the theory of music under Baumgarten. In 1768 he was engaged as principal oboist at the Opera, and in 1771 succeeded the celebrated Fischer as concerto-player at Vauxhall, and became principal oboist at Drury Lane. In 1776 he appeared in the same capacity in the Lenten oratorios conducted by J. C. Smith and John Stanley, and soon afterwards at Ranelagh and Marylebone Gardens. He was appointed one of the King's band of music, and in 1783 chamber musician to the Prince of Wales. He was engaged at the Concert of Antient Music, and other principal concerts, and at all the provincial festivals, until his retirement in 1815. He composed many oboe concertos for his own performance, but never published them.

(2) MARIA HESTER, his daughter (b. London, 1775; d. Aug. 15, 1822), was instructed by him in singing and pianoforte-playing, and made her first appearance as a singer at the Gloucester Festival in 1790, and for about seven years afterwards sang at the principal London concerts and oratorios and the provincial festivals. She afterwards became Mrs. Beardmore, and retired from the musical profession, but distinguished herself by her attainments in science, languages and literature. Her husband survived her only four months. She composed several sets of pianoforte sonatas, some songs and a set of glees.

(3) WILLIAM THOMAS, younger brother of John (1) (b. London, 1762; d. there, Aug. 26, 1847), began the study of music under his brother in 1770. He subsequently studied under Dance, Burney (nephew of Dr. Burney), and Baumgarten. In 1775 he was a soprano chorister at Drury Lane, and in 1776 was engaged as viola-player at Vauxhall. In 1779 he appeared at Vauxhall as an oboist, and in 1783 was employed as principal oboist at Covent Garden. He was afterwards engaged at the Ladies' and the Professional Concerts, and in 1800 was appointed principal oboist and concerto player at Vauxhall, where he continued until 1821. He extended the compass of the oboe upwards to G in alt, a third higher than former players had reached. He composed several concertos for his instrument, the overtures to 'Netley Abbey' (1794), and 'Lock and Key' (1796), and numerous songs, glees, etc., for the theatre and Vauxhall. He retired in 1825, and in 1830 published *Musical Memoirs; comprising an Account of the General State of Music in England from 1784 to 1830*, 2 vols. 8vo, an amusing work, but of very little authority.　　　　　w. h. h.

PARKER, HORATIO WILLIAM, Mus.D. Cantab. (b. Auburndale, Mass., near Boston, Sept. 15, 1863; d. Cedarhurst, N.Y., Dec. 18, 1919), American church musician and composer.

His parents were Charles Edward Parker, an architect, and Isabella G. Jennings, daughter of a clergyman, a lady of both musical and literary gifts, which made her the teacher of her son and also in later years collaborator with him in some of his most important compositions. The ancestry of both parents was English, the American branches having emigrated to the American colonies before the middle of the 17th century. Love for music did not awaken in the future composer until his fourteenth year. The first lessons on the pianoforte and organ were imparted by his mother, but at 15 years he began composition of his own volition, in two days setting to music the fifty poems of Kate Greenaway's 'Under the Window.' At 16 he modestly began those labours on behalf of church music which he never suspended, though called to larger duties and dignities in other fields. His early activities were spent near Boston, and thither he now went for more advanced study. Stephen A. Emery became his master in harmony, John Orth in pianoforte-playing, and George W. Chadwick in composition.

In 1881 he went to Munich and entered the Hochschule für Musik, where he soon won the affectionate interest of Rheinberger, who perfected him in organ technique and laid the foundations for the broad and fluent counterpoint which characterises his compositions. After three years of study in Munich he returned to the United States and took up his residence in New York, where, for eight years, after a brief term of service as musical instructor in the schools of St. Paul and St. Mary in Garden City, L.I., he performed the duties of organist and choirmaster, and during a part of the time taught counterpoint in the National Conservatory of Music, which was then under the direction of Antonin Dvořák, the stimulating influence of whose presence and example was keenly felt by the industrious young musician. In 1893, when this period was drawing to a close, he won one of a series of prizes offered by the Conservatory to stimulate composition in America, with a cantata entitled ' The Dream King and his Love' ; but he was already spreading his pinions for a higher and wider flight. An invitation came to him from Boston to become organist and director of the music in Trinity Church. He accepted it, but before severing his connexions with New York put into the hands of his publishers the manuscript score of a work which was destined to carry his fame far beyond his native land. This was ' Hora Novissima,' an oratorio, the words chosen from Bernard de Morlaix's *Rhythm of the Celestial Country,* for which the composer's mother provided an English translation. ' Hora Novissima ' was first performed on May 3, 1893, by the Church Choral Society (see NEW YORK), under the direction of the composer. It made its way to Boston, was given at the festivals in Cincinnati and Worcester, Mass., and in 1899 was the principal novelty at the Three Choirs Festival at Worcester (England), this being the first time that an American composition had been admitted to the schemes of these historical meetings. Dr. Parker conducted many of the rehearsals as well as the performance of his work, and established personally quite as amiable relations with the choristers as his music did with the critics and public. The choir presented him with a vase of Worcester ware on his birthday, and on the following Christmas sent to his home in New Haven, Conn., U.S.A., a pedestal to support it and a suitably inscribed plate. In 1900 ' Hora Novissima ' was performed at the Chester Festival under his direction, and he conducted a new work, ' A Wanderer's Psalm,' at the Hereford Festival. On June 10, 1902, being again in Europe, he went to Cambridge to receive the degree of Mus.D. from the University. In September he conducted the third part of his ' Legend of St. Christopher ' at the Worcester Festival, and the entire work at the Bristol Festival in October. Almost simultaneously a cantata entitled ' A Star Song,' for which he had received the award of the PADEREWSKI FUND (*q.v.*) in 1901, was performed at the Norwich Festival, but the composer had to hurry home to his duties at Yale University, and could not stay to conduct the new work.

In the spring of 1894 Parker was appointed professor of music in Yale University (see DEGREES IN MUSIC: AMERICAN UNIVERSITIES), which conferred the degree of M.A. upon him in token of affiliation. He retained this post until his death. He was the second incumbent of the Chair of music which had been founded by Robbins Battell, a Yale alumnus. With the appointment of Parker the chair was lifted high in dignity, and the new incumbent at once began a series of movements which soon centred the musical activities of New Haven in the University. Orchestral concerts were given under its auspices, under the direction of the professor its protection was thrown around a reorganised choral society also conducted by him, and interest in music so greatly stimulated that before the end of the first decade of Dr. Parker's professorship the city could boast of Woolsey Hall, a superb concert building with a seating capacity of over 2000, to build which a gift of $500,000 was received by the University on the occasion of its bi-centenary in 1901. For the bi-centennial celebration of the University Parker composed a Greek Ode for chorus and orchestra, to conduct which he came home from Germany where he was spending his first Sabbatical year. A portion of the summer of 1901 was spent in the composition of a ' Concerto for Organ and Orchestra with Harp,' which in the next musical season figured on the programmes of the Boston, Chicago and New Haven symphony concerts with the composer at the organ. In the same year Parker resigned his position at Trinity Church, Boston, and accepted a similar appointment in New York, which entailed less fatiguing travel, as being nearer the scene of his week-day labours. In later years his compositions included two excursions in the field of opera. Both won valuable prizes ($10,000) ; the first, ' Mona,' won that offered by the Metropolitan Opera House, New York, and was produced there, Mar. 14, 1912 ; the second, ' Fairyland,' won the prize offered by the National Federation of Women's Clubs and was performed at Los Angeles, July 1, 1915. Following is a list of Parker's compositions with the dates of publication. There are but few of his writings remaining in manuscript, most of them the products of his study years in Munich, where they had performance at the students' concerts in the Hochschule. As a rule the date of publication indicates the order of composition, though there are exceptions.

Op.
1. ' The Shepherd Boy ' ; ch. for men's voices. 1882.
2. Five Partsongs for mixed voices. (MS.) 1882.
3. Psalm XXIII., for women's voices, org and harp. (MS.) 1883.
4. Concert Overture, in E flat. (MS.) 1883.
5. Overture, in A major. (MS.) 1884.
6. ' The Ballad of a Knight and his Daughter.' Produced in Munich in 1884, published in 1891.
7. Symphony in C minor. Performed in Munich in 1885. (MS.)
8. ' King Trojan ' ; for ch., soli, orch. and harp. First performance in Munich in 1885 ; published in 1886.
9. Five pieces for PF. 1887.

Op.
10. Three Love Songs·for Tenor. 1887.
11. Quartet for Strings, in F major. Performed in Buffalo, Detroit, Cleveland, Boston, and elsewhere. (MS.)
12. 'Venetian' Overture, in B flat. Performed in Munich in 1884. (MS.)
13. Scherzo for orch. in G. Performed in Munich and New York, 1884 and 1886. (MS.)
14. 'Blow, thou Winter Wind,' male ch. 1890.
15. Idylle (Goethe) ; performed in Providence. 1891.
16. 'Normannenzug' (The Ballad of the Normans) ; for ch.
17. Four Pieces for the org. 1890.
18. The Morning and Evening Service, together with the office for the Holy Communion, in E major. 1892.
19. Four Pieces for the PF. 1890.
20. Four Pieces for the org. 1891.
21. 'The Kobolds'; for ch. and orch. Performed at Springfield, and published in 1891.
22. Three Sacred Songs. 1891.
23. Six Lyric. for the PF. 1891.
24. Six Songs. 1891.
25. Two Love Songs. 1891.
26. 'Harold Harfagar'; for ch. and orch. Performed in 1891 in New York and published the same year.
27. Two Choruses for Women's Voices. 1891.
28. Four Pieces for the organ. 1891.
29. Six Songs. 1892.
30. 'Hora Novissima'; an oratorio. (See above.) 1893.
31. 'The Dream King and his Love' ; a cantata. (See above.) 1893.
32. Five Pieces for the organ. 1893.
33. Six Choruses for men's voices. 1893.
34. Three Songs. 1893.
35. Suite for vln. PF., and v'cl. (MS.)
36. Four Pieces for the org. 1893.
37. 'The Holy Child'; a cantata, for Christmas. 1893.
38. Quintet in D minor, for strings. (MS.)
39. Four Choruses for Male Voices. 1893.
40. 'Cáhal Mór of the Wine-red Hand'; for baritone and orch.
41. Suite for vln. and PF. (MS.)
42. Ode for Commencement. 1895.
43. 'The Legend of St. Christopher'; an oratorio. (See above.) 1898.
45. 'Adstant Angelorum Chori'; motet for mixed voices *a cappella*. Prize Composition of the Musical Art Society, New York, 1899.
46. 'A Northern Ballad'; for orch. Performed in Boston, Chicago and New York. (MS.)
47. Six Old English Songs. 1899.
48. Choruses for Male Voices. 1899.
49. Three Pieces for the PF. 1899.
50. 'A Wanderer's Psalm.' (See above.) 1900.
52. Three Songs. 1900.
53. 'Hymnos andron'; Greek Ode for the Celebration of the Bi-centenary of Yale University. 1901.
54. 'A Star Song'; for ch., soli and orch. (See above.) 1901.
55. Concerto for org. and orch. 1902.
56. Symphonic Poem ; for orch. (MS.)
57. Communion Service, in B flat. 1904.
58. Three Settings of Mediæval Hymns ; for solo voice. 1905.
59. Four Songs.
60. 'Union and Liberty'; patriotic song with orch. Sung at the Inauguration of President Roosevelt. 1905.
61. Ode for the Dedication of the Albright Art Gallery in Buffalo. 1905.
62. 'Crépuscule,' mezzo sop. and orch.
63. 'The Shepherd's Vision.'
64. Ballad, 'King Gorm the Grim,' ch. and orch.
65. Sonata in E flat for org.
66. Songs for high-schools.
67-68. Nine organ pieces.
69. The Norsemen's Raid. Male ch. and orch.
70. Swan Songs.
71. Opera, 'Mona,' libretto by Brian Hooker.
72. 'Collegiate' Overture.
73. Cantata, 'A Song of the Times.'
74. Seven 'Greek Pastoral Scenes,' women's voices, harp, oboe and strings.
75. Ballad, The Leap of 'Roushan Beg,' male voices and orch.
76. Songs.
77. Opera, 'Fairyland,' libretto by Brian Hooker.
78. Books of public school music.
79. Oratorio, 'Morven and the Grail.'
80. Masque, 'Cupid and Psyche' (for 50th anniversary Yale Art School, 1916).
81. Music for Yale pageant (Oct. 1916).
82. Cantata, 'The Dream of Mary,' soli, ch. and orch. (Norfolk Test, 1918).
83. Red Cross Hymn, contralto and orch.
84. 'A.D. 1919,' sop. and ch.

H. E. K.

**PARLANDO, PARLANTE,** 'speaking': (1) a direction in instrumental music allowing greater freedom in rendering than *cantando* or *cantabile*, and yet referring to the same kind of expression. It is generally used in the case of a few notes or bars only, and is often expressed by the signs — - placed over single notes, and by a slur together with staccato dots over a group of notes. Sometimes, however, it is used of an entire movement, as in the 6th Bagatelle from Beethoven's op. 33, which is headed 'Allegretto quasi Andante. Con una certa

espressione parlante,' and in the second of Schumann's variations on the name 'Abegg,' op. 1, where the direction 'Basso parlando' stands at the beginning and refers to the whole variation. M.

(2) A direction in vocal music to indicate that the tone of the voice must approximate to speech.

**PARMA, NICOLA** (*b*. Mantua, latter part of 16th cent.), was at Pavia, 1592 ; maestro di cappella of Novara Cathedral, 1611. He composed 2 books of madrigals, and 3 books of motets (1580, 1586, 1606), the 3rd book, 8-12 v., only known to Eitner (*Q.-L.*; *Fétis*).

**PARRATT, SIR WALTER** (*b*. Huddersfield, Feb. 10, 1841 ; *d*. Windsor, Mar. 27, 1924), organist. His father, Thomas Parratt (1793–1862), was organist of the parish church of Huddersfield from 1812 to his death, and at the head of his profession. The boy displayed much precocity, and was thoroughly grounded by his father at an early age. At 7 years old he took the service in church, and at the age of 10 he played on one occasion the whole of the forty-eight preludes and fugues of Bach by heart, without notice. He thus laid the foundation of that affectionate and intimate knowledge of Bach's music which afterwards distinguished him. His predilection for the organ was no doubt grounded on his father's example and on his familiarity with Conacher's organ factory, which he haunted when very young. At any rate he was an organist from the beginning. At 11 years of age he held his first appointment at Armitage Bridge Church. After a few months he was sent to the choir school of St. Peter's Chapel, Pimlico, where he officiated as organist, and became a pupil of George Cooper; but the school was unsatisfactory, and he was recalled to Huddersfield, and was organist of St. Paul's Church there, from 1854–61. In that year he received the appointment of organist to Lord Dudley, at Witley Court, Worcestershire. Here he had time and opportunity for study, of which he availed himself. His next step was to the parish church, Wigan, in 1868 ; in 1872, when Stainer was appointed to St. Paul's Cathedral, Parratt succeeded him at Magdalen College, Oxford, and while there he held the organistship of St. Giles's, was choirmaster of Jesus and Trinity College chapels, conductor of the Exeter College Musical Society, the Trinity College Glee Club, and college societies at Jesus and Pembroke. He also conducted the Oxford Choral Society, and was a prominent member of the University Musical Club. In 1882 he was appointed to St. George's Chapel, Windsor, *vice* Sir G. Elvey, a post which he held till his death. In 1873 he had taken the degree of Mus.B. at Oxford, and in 1883 was chosen professor of the organ in the R.C.M., as well as conductor of the choral class. He was conductor of the Madrigal Society of Windsor and of other choral organisations there, and ' Past Grand Organist ' of the Freemasons. In 1892 he received the honour of knighthood, and in 1893 was appointed ' Master of the Queen's Musick ' and private organist to Her Majesty. He was also a Commander of the Victorian Order, and received the honorary degree of Mus.D. at Oxford in 1894 and at Cambridge in 1910. He succeeded Parry as Professor of Music at Oxford in 1908, resigning the office in 1918. G., with addns.

Parratt's compositions were few and inconsiderable. They comprised music to the 'Agamemnon,' for performance at Oxford (1880) (see GREEK PLAYS, MUSIC TO), and for ' The Story of Orestes,' Prince's Hall, London, 1886, a contribution to ' Choral Songs . . . in honour of H.M. Queen Victoria ' (1899), a series edited by him in imitation of the 'Triumphes of Oriana,' and a few church and organ pieces written for occasions. A man of fastidious tastes, quick wit and a caustic tongue, strong sympathies and antipathies, he made many lasting friendships and aroused some temporary enmities. He was a first-rate chess-player, and it was commonly said that he could play a fugue and direct the moves of more than one game of chess at the same time. His brain readily ' thought in parts,' a fact which made anything like smudginess or untidiness in organ playing abhorrent to him. He became the champion of a style founded on accurate part-playing, clean phrasing and simple registration, and by his own example and forty years of teaching at the R.C.M. he revolutionised the performance of church organists throughout England and English-speaking countries. His devotion to Bach and to the contrapuntal interests of organ music earned him the reputation of a purist, and at one time he was regarded as the opponent of W. T. BEST (q.v.), who was popularising the organ by his brilliant playing of arrangements from orchestral and other scores. The contrapuntal interests of Reger's music attracted Parratt when Reger's name was little known in England, and his inherent classicism never blinded him to new interests in the development of the art. His personal culture gained much from intimacy with Sir George Grove, with whom he travelled abroad on certain of his research expeditions. He was a valued contributor to this Dictionary and also wrote the chapter on music in Humphrey Ward's *Reign of Queen Victoria* (1887). Grove wrote of him here, ' He is a very hard worker, and the delight of his colleagues, friends and pupils,' words which remained true to the end. c.

PARRY, SIR CHARLES HUBERT HASTINGS, Bart. (b. Bournemouth, Feb. 27, 1848; d. Knight's Croft, Rustington, Oct. 7, 1918), was the second son of Thomas Gambier Parry, of Highnam Court, near Gloucester, a highly skilled amateur painter and patron of the arts, the inventor of a process of ' spirit fresco,' in which his own decorations of Highnam Church and parts of Ely and Worcester Cathedrals are preserved.

Hubert Parry was educated successively at Malvern, Twyford (near Winchester), Eton, and Exeter College, Oxford. We hear of his composing chants and hymn-tunes when he was about 8, but his first deep musical impression seems to have been received from Samuel Sebastian Wesley, while he was at school at Twyford. In 1861, when he went to Eton, his musical proclivities made themselves felt at once, and he became famous in the school as a baritone singer, a pianist and a composer of songs, etc. In 1867, just before leaving Eton for Oxford, he took the Mus.B. degree at the latter university, and his exercise, a setting of ' O Lord, Thou hast cast us out,' was performed at Eton, and published. At Oxford studies and sports took the first place, and music was rather neglected for a time, excepting in occasional performances, and in the founding of the Oxford University Musical Club (see LLOYD, C. H.; OXFORD). He took the B.A. degree in 1870, but before this he had taken composition lessons from Sterndale Bennett and G. A. Macfarren, besides going to Stuttgart for one long vacation to study with Henry Hugo Pierson. After leaving Oxford he was in Lloyd's for about three years, but at the end of that time music was too strong for him, and thenceforward he devoted himself exclusively to the art.

In these early years in London the friendship, counsel and instruction of Edward Dannreuther were of the utmost benefit to him, and it was at the semi-private music-meetings at Dannreuther's house in Orme Square that all Parry's chamber music was played almost as soon as it was written. The fortunate subscribers to these concerts little knew how unique was the privilege they enjoyed, for in many cases Parry's MS. works were mislaid, and, in some instances, inadvertently destroyed, in the following years. In 1877 Parry, while on a visit to Cannes, gave a series of chamber concerts there with Edoardo Guerini the violinist, and among other things his suite for the two instruments (probably the ' Partita ') was played. In 1879 a private concert of Parry's works was given at the house of the Right Hon. A. J. Balfour, when in addition to some of the works already performed at Dannreuther's house, we hear of a fantasia-sonata in one movement for piano and violin, and a set of pianoforte variations on a theme of Bach ; and in the same year an overture, ' Guillem de Cabestanh,' was played at the Crystal Palace. As long before as 1868 an ' Intermezzo religioso ' for strings had been produced at the Gloucester Festival.

It was in 1880 that Parry's name first came before the world at large. Dannreuther played his pianoforte concerto in F sharp minor at the Crystal Palace, and in the autumn his first important choral work, the 'Scenes from Prometheus Unbound,' was given at the Gloucester Festival. It was not a success, but it is not the less interesting on that account; it undoubtedly marks an epoch in the history of English music, and the type of composition of which it was the first specimen has had great consequences in the development of our national art. The dramatic monologue of Prometheus had a new note of sincerity in it; besides the wonderful faithfulness of accentuation, in which Parry has always been unrivalled among modern composers, there is a wealth of noble melodic ideas, such as the theme of Jupiter's song, 'Pour forth heaven's wine,' and the lovely passage for unaccompanied quartet, 'Our feet now, every palm,' while the final climax, 'To an ocean of splendour,' is now realised as a prophecy of that power of culminating effect which has been so finely shown over and over again by the composer. For the following Gloucester Festival Shirley's ode, 'The Glories of our Blood and State,' was set for chorus and orchestra, and the conviction that a new composer had arisen to revive the art of choral writing gradually grew, until the fullest confirmation was given in the famous 'Blest Pair of Sirens,' first performed by the Bach Choir in 1887. After that time Parry's choral works succeeded one another at the great festivals with most welcome regularity.

His instrumental compositions, meanwhile, were a good deal longer in gaining wide recognition; the orchestral works were considered obscure, a circumstance due to their extreme conciseness and the elaborate development of the themes. The first symphony was given in 1882, the second, in F, in the following year, the third and fourth in 1889, and the fifth in B minor in 1912. As in his orchestral writing Parry always laid more stress on the substance of the ideas and development than on the manner of their presentment, it was sometimes considered that he did not excel in orchestration; but such things as the third and fourth symphonies, or the 'Characteristic Variations' (1897), must always appeal strongly to the cultivated musician.

In the choral works, from 'Blest Pair of Sirens' onwards, there is apparent the same mastery of accentuation that was noticed in his songs; besides this, the composer shows a wonderful power of handling large masses with the utmost breadth and simplicity of effect, and of using the voices of the choir in obtaining climax after climax, until an overwhelming impression is created. This is the secret of Parry's power over the musical people of his

time, and it is a power that is felt not only by the educated hearer, but even by the untrained listener. Without the smallest trace of the actual influence of Handel, there is a grandeur which is commonly called 'Handelian' about many of Parry's choruses, and in one work after another he touches a point which can only be called sublime. The more delicate side of his choral writing is beautifully shown in the various partsongs which came out in 1897, and several of these are among the most expressive and tender things in music. 'Since thou, O fondest and truest,' 'There rolls the deep,' and 'Music, when soft voices die,' have never been surpassed in pathetic quality, and in perfect command of simple resources the whole series is most remarkable. The strong vein of humour which his friends knew so well has appeared in his music on many occasions; in the music to the comedies of Aristophanes (see GREEK PLAYS, MUSIC TO), both wit and humour are strongly apparent throughout, and his way of weaving in themes from well-known works, and of imitating various styles, makes these works unique in music. In 'The Pied Piper,' too, his music fits the humorous parts of Browning's poem no less perfectly than the picturesque or narrative passages.

A large number of unison songs for children appeared from time to time during the composer's life, and one such unison song, set to words from Blake's *Milton*, obtained a great popular and even national success during and after the war under the title of 'Jerusalem.' [1] Like some other of the greatest masters of music, Parry was at his best at the end of his life. Nearly all the music of his latest years is suggested by words of a lofty seriousness, and a large proportion of his last works are religious in character. Whether or no this represents a process of spiritual development, it is certain that none of his earlier music exceeds the motets in pregnant beauty of choral writing or in sublimity of musical ideas, while his hymn-tune preludes have a deep spiritual beauty that looks straight back to Bach, though they are strongly individual and most characteristic.

In 1883 Parry was appointed Choragus of the University of Oxford, and in 1900 succeeded Sir John Stainer as Professor of Music, a post he resigned in 1908; in 1894 he was appointed Director of the Royal College of Music, in succession to Sir George Grove, a post to which he devoted his best energies right up to the time of his death (see ROYAL COLLEGE OF MUSIC). In 1898 he received the honour of knighthood; at the Coronation of King Edward VII. in 1903 he was created a baronet. In 1883 he was given the honorary degree of Mus.D. at Cambridge, and in 1884,

[1] This was sung at the Leeds Festival, 1922, with the accompaniment orchestrated for the occasion by Elgar.

*Photo, E. O. Hoppé*

HUBERT PARRY

*Photo, Herbert Lambert*

C. V. STANFORD

the same degree at Oxford. A similar degree followed at Dublin in 1891, in which year he was appointed Examiner of Music in the London University. He received the honorary degree of D.C.L. from the University of Durham in 1894. It would be impossible to give a list of all the musical societies of which Parry was president; his geniality of disposition, remarkable powers of organisation, strong common sense, and the purity of his artistic ideals made him the most powerful influence in English music, even apart from his own creations, which mark him as the most important figure in English art since the time of Purcell.

In literary [1] work he did much that is memorable; besides some early poems in *Macmillan's Magazine* for May 1875, he wrote and arranged the words for his own 'Judith,' 'War and Peace' and 'A Vision of Life' (1907); his contributions to this Dictionary are among the most valuable things in the first edition; his *Studies of the Great Composers* (1886) is full of useful information conveyed in a terse style very different from that of the average writer on music at the time of its publication; his best work as an historian of the art is undoubtedly contained in *The Art of Music* (1893), enlarged and republished in 1896 as *The Evolution of the Art of Music, The Seventeenth Century*, vol. iii. of *The Oxford History of*

[1] An extensive manuscript with the title *Instinct and Character* was left unpublished by Parry at his death. It has not been published, but typescript copies have been deposited by the executors in the British Museum, the Bodleian and the R.C.M.

*Music*, and *Johann Sebastian Bach, the study of a great personality* (1909). In these the established facts of history are put in a suggestive new light, and the conclusions based on research of all kinds are full of value. His *Summary of Musical History*, a valuable textbook for students, is among Novello's music primers. His masterly *Style in Musical Art* was published in 1911, and after his death a small volume of the addresses to students with which he was accustomed to begin each term at the R.C.M. was published (Macmillan), with the title *College Addresses*.

Parry died at Knight's Croft, Rustington, Oct. 7, 1918, was cremated, and his ashes placed in the crypt of St. Paul's Cathedral after a memorable service at which his motet ' There is an old belief ' (one of the ' Six Songs of Farewell,' 1916) and some of his chorale preludes for organ were performed. A memorial tablet was placed by public subscription at the west end of Gloucester Cathedral ·(1922). It contains verses written for the purpose by the Poet Laureate, Robert Bridges.     M.

BIBLIOGRAPHY

C. L. GRAVES: *Hubert Parry*. 2 vols. (1926). The official Life, based on full examination of documents, diaries, etc.
ERNEST WALKER: *History of Music in England* (2nd edition). Parry's place in the history of his time carefully considered.
W. H. HADOW: *Sir Hubert Parry*. Proc. Mus. Assn. 45th session, 1918-19, pp. 135-47.
R. O. MORRIS: *Hubert Parry*. Music and Letters, Apr. 1920, pp. 92-103. Both are valuable critical estimates.
H. C. COLLES: Short memoir in *College Addresses* (see above). Parry as a Song - Writer. *Mus. T.*, 1921, Feb., pp. 82-7; Mar., pp. 155-8; Apr., pp. 235-8. Article in *D.N.B.* supplementary volumes. (In preparation.)

---

The following complete catalogue of Parry's published and unpublished works is taken from that compiled by Miss Emily Daymond, Mus.D., and published here complete for the first time through her kindness.

| No. | Description. | Written. | First Performance. | Publisher.* |
|---|---|---|---|---|
| | 1858-62.—Many chants, hymn tunes, a Kyrie for 4 v. and canons. | | | |
| 1 | Little PF. piece. | 1862 | | |
| 2 | Three movements for vln. and PF. | 1863 | | |
| 3 | Anthem: ' In my distress.' | 1863 ? | | |
| 4 | Four-part fugue in G for organ, ' Grand Fugue with 3 subjects.' | 1864 | Sir George Elvey, Windsor, Feb. 22, 1865. | |
| 5 | Anthem: ' Fear thou not.' | Oct.-Nov. 1864 | | |
| 6 | Song: ' Fair is my Love' (Ed. Spenser). | 1864-65 | | |
| 7 | Choral: ' Praise God from Whom all blessings flow.' | 1864-65 | | |
| 8 | Four - part songs: ' Tell me where is fancy bred ' (Shakespeare). | 1864 | | |
| 9 | Magnificat and Nunc Dimittis in A. | 1864 | | |
| 10 | Chorus of an anthem: ' O sing unto the Lord a new song.' | June 1864 | | |
| 11 | Anthem: ' Blessed is He.' | Begun Apr. 19, 1864 | St. George's Chapel, Windsor. | Novello, 1865. |
| 12 | Anthem: ' Prevent us, O Lord.' | 1865 | Eton College Musical Soc., Dec. 9, 1865. | |
| 13 | Five-part anthem: ' Why boastest thou thyself ' (with solo quartet in latter part). | 1865 | | |
| 14 | PF. piece in G minor. | 1865 | | |
| 15 | Song: ' When stars are in the quiet sky.' | 1865 | | |
| 16 | Four-part song, ' Take, O take those lips away.' (T.T.B.B.) (Shakespeare.) | 1865 | Eton College Mus. Soc., Dec. 9, 1865. | |
| 17 | Fugue in E minor for PF. | 1865 | | |
| 18 | Overture in B minor for PF. duet. | 1865 | ? Eton College Mus. Soc., Dec. 9, 1865. | |
| 19 | Song: ' Why does azure deck the sky ? ' (Moore). | 1865-66 | Eton Coll Mus. Soc. Concert, Mar. 22, 1866. Sung by F.C. Ricardo. | Lamborn Cook, 1866. |
| 20 | Sonata in F minor for PF. duet. | Oct. 20-30, 1865 | | |
| 21 | Setting of Horace's ode, *Persicos odi* (S.A.T.B.). | Feb. 1865 | | |

* Where no publisher is given it may be understood that the work has not been published. The majority of the first performances at festivals, etc., other than those for which a conductor's name is given, were directed by the composer.

| No. | Description | Written. | First Performance. | Publisher. |
|---|---|---|---|---|
| 22 | Song : ' Love not me.' | 1865 | | |
| 23 | Exercise for Mus.B. at Oxford : oratorio, ' O Lord Thou hast cast us out.' | 1865–66 | Eton Coll. Mus. Soc., Dec. 8, 1867. | Lamborn Cock, 1876 |
| 24 | Madrigal in five parts : ' Fair Daffodils ' (Herrick). | 1866 | Roy. Glee and Madrigal Union, Feb. 12 1866.  Eton Coll. Mus. Soc., Mar. 22, 1866. | Lamborn Cock, 1866. |
| 25 | Four-part song : ' Oft in the stilly night ' (Moore). | 1866 | Eton Coll. Mus. Soc., Dec. 11, 1867. | |
| 26 | Song : ' Autumn ' (Thomas Hood). | ? 1866 | .. | Lamborn Cock, 1867. |
| 27 | Song : ' When the grey skies are flushed with rosy streaks.' | | | |
| 28 | Song : ' Angel hosts, sweet love, befriend thee ' (Lord Francis Hervey). | | .. | Lamborn Cock, 1867. |
| 29 | Allegretto scherzando in E flat for orchestra. | 1867 | | |
| 30 | 1st string quartet in G minor. | 1867 | | |
| 31 | Song : ' Sleep, my love.' | 1867 | | |
| 32 | Eight-part fugue : ' Kyrie eleison.' | ? 1867 | (Nos. 32 and 33 are preserved among Parry's MSS., but are not in his autograph.) | |
| 33 | Five-part chorus : ' Lobet den Herren.' | ? 1867 | | |
| 34 | Andante in C for PF. | 1867 | | |
| 35 | Two duettinos for PF. and vcl.  1. In F.  2. In G. | 1868 | | |
| 36 | Romance in D for violin. | | | |
| 37 | Te Deum and Benedictus in D. | 1866–68 | .. | Novello. 1868. |
| | Remainder of Morning and Evening Service and Communion Service. | ? 1868 | .. | Novello, 1869. |
| 38 | Sonnets and Songs without Words, set 1 :  1. A Pastoral  2. Owlet.  3. Gnome.  4. Lied. | | .. | Lamborn Cock, 1869. |
| 39 | Intermezzo religioso for orch. | 1868 | Gloucester Fest., 1868. | |
| 40 | Short trios in F for PF., vln. and viola. | 1868 | | |
| 41 | 2nd string quartet in C minor. | 1868 | | |
| 42 | Song : ' Dainty Form.' | 1868 | | |
| 43 | Four-part song (A.T.B.B.) :  Battle of the Baltic ' (words incomplete). | ? 1868 | | |
| 44 | Song : ' O world, O life, O time ' (Shelley).  (See No. 221.) | 1868 | .. | Novello, 1920. |
| 45 | Partsong (T.T.B.B.) : ' There lived a sage.' | May 1869 | | |
| 46 | Song : ' Ah, woe is me, poor silver-wing.' | 1869 | | |
| 47 | 1. Three miniatures for PF.  2. Berceuse.  3. Romance.  4. Study, etc. | Sketched 1868 | | |
| 48 | Sonnets and Songs without Words, set 2 :  1. Resignation.  2. L'Allegro.  3. Il Penseroso. | 1867 and onwards | .. | Lamborn Cock, 1875. |
| 49 | Song : ' The River of Life ' (Lord Pembroke). | .. | .. | Lamborn Cock, 1870. |
| 50 | ' Fairest dreams may be forgotten.' | 1870 | | |
| 51 | Anthem : ' Blessed are they who dwell in Thy house.' | 1870 | | |
| 52 | Anthem : ' Lord, I have loved the habitation of Thy house.' | 1870 | | |
| 53 | Allegretto pastorale in G for vln. and PF. | 1870 | | |
| 54 | Six pieces (Freundschaftslieder) for PF. and violin :  1. ' The Confidence of Love.'  Andante E major.  2. Allegro in C major.  3. Nocturne in G minor.  4. Ballade in D minor.  5. Andante in F.  6. Allegro in C minor. | 1872 | | |
| 55 | Seven ' Charakterbilder ' for PF. :  1. Dreaming.  2. Con energia.  3. Passion.  4. Allegro.  5. Espressivo.  6. Allegro energetico.  7. Adagio con sentimento. | 1872 | .. | Augener, ? 1872. |
| 56 | Song : ' Not unavailing.' | ? 1872 | | |
| 57 | Three songs :  1. ' The Poet's Song ' (Tennyson).  2. ' More fond than Cushat Dove ' (Barham).  3 ' Music ' (Shelley). | ? 1873 | .. | Lamborn Cock, 1873. |
| 58 | Songs :  1. ' An Evening Cloud.'    2. ' A Shadow.' | 1873 | | |
| 59 | Two short pieces for PF. '  1. In C.    2. In F. | | | |
| 60 | Te Deum in E flat. | 1873 | | |
| 61 | Overture : ' Vivien.' | 1873 | Seems to have been played (? rehearsed) Crystal Palace, Nov. 21, 1873 (Manns).  No trace left of the work. | |
| 62 | Song : ' Twilight ' (Lord Pembroke). | 1874 | .. | Lamborn Cock, 1875. |
| 63 | A Garland of Old-fashioned Songs :  1. ' On a day, alack the day ' (Shakespeare).  2. ' A Spring Song ' (Shakespeare).  3. ' A Contrast ' (Anon.).  4. ' Concerning Love ' (S. Daniel).  5. ' A Sea Dirge ' (Shakespeare).  6. ' Merry Margaret ' (Skelton). | 1873 to 1881  1873 | .. | Lamborn Cock, 1874.  Boosey, 1880–81. |
| 64 | Christmas carol : ' He is coming ' (Mrs. H. Gladstone). | .. | .. | Novello, 1874. |
| 65 | Four sonnets with English and German words (all Shakespeare) :  1. ' When in disgrace.'  2. ' Farewell, thou art too dear.'  3. ' Shall I compare thee to a summer's day ? '  4. ' When to the sessions of sweet silent thought.' | 1873 to 1882  (1874–75)  (1882) | ..  .. | Stanley Lucas 1887.  Augener, 1904. |
| 66 | Song : ' If thou survive my well-contented day ' (Shakespeare). | 1874 | | |
| 67 | Three trios for female voices :  1 ' To Night ' (Hamilton Aide). | .. | .. | Lamborn Cock, 1875. |

| No. | Description. | Written | First Performance. | Publisher |
|---|---|---|---|---|
| 68 | 2. 'To Diana' (Ben Jonson). 3. 'Take, O take those lips away' (Shakespeare). Variations for PF. on an air by Bach. | 1873–75 | 4 Carlton Gardens, Apr 1, 1879. (Probably the variations referred to as having been played at a concert in Cannes, 1876.) | |
| 69 | Grosses Duo in E minor for 2 PF.s. | 1875 and 1876 | 12 Orme Square, Apr. 11, 1878. | B. & H., 1877 |
| 70 | Nonet for wind instruments in B flat (fl., ob., cor. angl., 2 clar., 2 fag., 2 horns). | 1877 | | |
| 71 | Sonata No. 1 in F for PF. (dedicated to G. Grove). | 1877 | .. | Lamborn Cock 1877. |
| 72 | Three odes of Anacreon (translated by Moore) : 1. 'Away, away, you men of rules.' 2. Fill me, boy, as deep a draught.' 3. 'Golden hues of life are fled.' | 1869–78 | .. | Augener, 1880. |
| 73 | Sonnets and Songs without Words, set 3 : 1. Prelude. 2. Interlude. 3. Reminiscence. | 1877 (and onwards) | .. | Lamborn Cock. |
| 74 | Trio in E minor, for PF., vln. and vcl. | 1878 | 12 Orme Square, Jan. 30, 1878 ; R.A.M., May 14, 1878 (Dannreuther, Franke and Hausmann). | Breitkopf, 1879. |
| 75 | Fantasie-sonata in B minor for PF. and vln., in 1 movement. | 1878 | 12 Orme Square, Jan. 30, 1879 (Dannreuther and Holmes). | |
| 76 | Overture for orchestra : 'Guillem de Cabestanh.' | 1878–79 | Crystal Palace, Mar. 15, 1879 (Manns). | |
| 77 | Quartet in A flat for PF. and strings. | 1879 | 12 Orme Square, Feb. 1879. (Dannreuther, Gompertz, Gibson and R. Mendelssohn) ; Monday Pop., Dec. 3, 1883. | Novello, 1884 |
| 78 | 3rd quartet for strings in G major. | Feb. 1878–80 | 12 Orme Square, Feb. 26, 1880. | |
| 79 | Sonata No. 2 in A for PF. | .. | .. | Stanley Lucas, 1878. Augener, 1903. |
| 80 | Concerto in F sharp for PF. and orch. | 1878–79 | Crystal Palace, Apr. 3. Richter Concert, Apr. 10, 1880 (Richter). Pianist both times, Dannreuther. | |
| 81 | Song : 'Absence, hear my protestation.' | 1881 | | |
| 82 | Song : 'And wilt thou leave me thus ?' | 1881 | 12 Orme Square, Dec. 1881 (Anna Williams). | |
| 83 | Song : 'My passion you regard with scorn.' | .. | Gloucester Fest., 1880. London, Bach Choir, Feb. 1885 (O. Goldschmidt). | Novello, 1880. |
| 84 | Scenes from Shelley's Prometheus Unbound, A.T.B. soli, chorus and orch. | | | |
| 85 | Sonata in A major for PF. and vcl. | .. | 12 Orme Square, Feb. 12, 1880 (Dannreuther and J. Lasserre). | Novello, 1883. |
| 86 | Symphony No. 1 in G major. | 1878–82 | Birmingham Fest., Aug. 31, 1882. Crystal Palace, Apr. 1883. | |
| 87 | Evening Service in D. | .. | Trinity Coll. Chapel, Camb. | |
| 88 | Music to The Birds of Aristophanes. | .. | Cambridge A.D.C., Nov. 1883 (Stanford). Played as 'Incidental music,' Dec. 11 1888 (Stanford). | Stanley Lucas, 1885 ; Univ. Press, Camb., 1903. |
| 89 | Symphony No. 2 in F major (the Cambridge). | 1883 | Camb. C.U.M.S., June 12, 1883 (Stanford). Revised for Richter Concert, 1887. Last movement at Antwerp, Oct 1885. | Novello, 1906 |
| 90 | Song : 'I arise from dreams of thee' (Shelley). | 1883 | | |
| 91 | Ode from The Contention of Ajax and Ulysses : 'The Glories of our Blood and State' (Shirley), for chorus and orch. | 1883 | Gloucester Fest., 1883. | Novello, 1885. |
| 92 | Quintet for strings in E flat. | 1884 | 12 Orme Square, Mar. 18, 1884 (MS.) | Novello, 1909. |
| 93 | Trio in B minor for PF., vln. and vcl. | .. | 12 Orme Square, Nov. 25, 1884 (MS.). Dresden, July 1894. | Novello, 1884. 1903 ? |
| 94 | Theme and 19 variations in D minor. | 1878–85 | 12 Orme Square, Feb. 10, 1885 | Stanley Lucas, 1885. |
| 95 | English Lyrics, 1st set : 1. 'My true love hath my heart' (Sir Philip Sidney). 2. 'Good-night' (Shelley). | 1881 1883 | 12 Orme Square, Dec. 1, 1881 (Anna Williams). .. | Stanley Lucas. 8vo. Pub. in folio later by Novello. |
| 96 | 3. 'Where shall the lover rest ?' (Sir Walter Scott). 4. 'Willow, willow, willow' (Shakespeare). Suite moderne for orch. : 1. Ballade. 2. Idyll. 3. Romance. 4. Rhapsody. | Jan. 16, 1885. Begun Aug. 1, 1886 | Gloucester Fest., Sept. 1886. London (Henschel Concert), Dec. 1886. | |
| 97 | Partita in D minor for PF. and vln. : 1. Maestoso. 2. Allemande. 3. Presto. 4 Sarabande. 5. Bourrées fantastiques. 6. Passepied en rondo. | 1877–86 | An early form (called 'Suite' played by C. H. H. P. and Guerini at one of their concerts in Cannes, Jan. 1877 Later in its present form. 12 Orme Square, Dec. 2, 1886 (Dannreuther and Henry Holmes). | Czery ; later by Chanot, 1890. |
| 98 | English Lyrics, 2nd set : 1. 'O Mistress mine' (Shakespeare). 2. 'Take, O take those lips away' (Shakespeare). 3. 'No longer mourn for me' (Shakespeare). 4. 'Blow, blow, thou winter wind' (Shakespeare). 5. 'When icicles hang by the wall' (Shakespeare) | .. 1881 Jan. 16, 1885 | .. 12 Orme Square, Dec. 1, 1881 (Anna Williams). | Stanley Lucas ; Weber & Co., 1886 ; later Novello. |
| 99 | Characteristic Popular Tunes of the British Isles, for PF. duet. 2 books : Book I. English and Welsh Book II. Scotch and Irish. | 1885 | .. | Stanley Lucas, 1887 ; Augener, 1901. |
| 100 | Opera : 'Guinevere.' Libretto, Una Taylor : trans. German by Althaus. | 1885–86 | | |

| No. | Description. | First Performance. | Publisher. |
|---|---|---|---|
| 101 | Ode at a Solemn Music : ' Blest Pair of Sirens ' (trans. German by Josephson, Italian by Visetti) (Milton), for chorus and orch. | Bach Choir, May 17, 1887 (Stanford). Full score now at Trinity Coll., Cambridge. | Novello, 1887. |
| 102 | Oratorio : ' Judith ' (Apocrypha and C. H. H. P.). S.A.T.B. soli, chorus and orch. | Birmingham Fest., 1888 (Richter). London, Bach Choir, May 1889 (Stanford) ; also Novello Choir, 1888 (Mackenzie). | Novello, 1888. |
| 103 | Sonata in D major for PF. and violin. | 12 Orme Square, Feb. 14, 1889 (Dannreuther and ? Gibson). | |
| 104 | Symphony No. 3 in C (' the English '). | Philharmonic, June 1889. Dresden, July 1894 (last movement). | Novello 1907. |
| 105 | Symphony No. 4 in E minor. | Richter Concert, St. James's Hall, July 1, 1889 (Richter). Largely rewritten for Philharmonic, Feb. 10, 1910 (L. Ronald). | Novello, 1921. |
| 106 | ' Ode on St. Cecilia's Day ' (Pope). S. and B. soli, chorus and orch. | Leeds Fest., 1889. | Novello, 1889. |
| 107 | Trio in G major for PF., vln. and vcl. Begun May 1884. | 12 Orme Square, Feb. 12, 1890. | |
| 108 | ' L' Allegro ed il Pensieroso ' (Milton). S. and B. soli, chorus and orch. | Norwich Fest., 1890. London, Crystal Palace, Dec. 1890. | Novello, 1890. |
| 109 | ' Eton '—Ode for chorus and orch. (Swinburne). | Eton Celebration, June 28, 1891. | Novello, 1891. |
| 110 | ' De Profundis ' for sop. solo, twelve-part chorus and orch. | Hereford Fest., 1891. | Novello, 1891. |
| 111 | Song : ' The Maid of Elsinore ' (Harold Boulton). | .. | Leadenhall Press, 1891 ; later, Novello. |
| 112 | Music to The Frogs of Aristophanes. | Oxford O.U.D.S., Feb. 24, 1892. | B. & H., 1892. |
| 113 | Arrangement of suite in E minor by Boyce. for str. | Lady Radnor's String Orchestra, June 29, 1894. | Joseph Williams, 1892. |
| 114 | Choric song from Tennyson's Lotos Eaters, for sop. solo, chorus and orch. | Camb., June 1892 (Stanford). | Novello, 1892. |
| 115 | ' Cosy ' Piece for PF. (included in 224). | .. | Girls' Own Paper, 1892. |
| 116 | Oratorio : ' Job ' (Bible and C. H. H. P.). S.T.B.B. soli, chorus and orch. | Gloucester Fest., 1892. | Novello, 1892. |
| 117 | Incidental music to Hypatia (Jas. Ogilvy) : 1. Overture. 2. Entr'acte. 3. Street Scene. 4. Second Entr'acte. 5. Orestes' March. | Produced by Beerbohm Tree, Haymarket Theatre, Jan. 1893 (C. Armbruster). | |
| 118 | Overture to an Unwritten Tragedy. Allegro energico in A minor. | Worcester Fest., 1893. London, Philharmonic (Mackenzie). | Novello, 1893. |
| 119 | Song : ' Rock-a-bye ' (song for children). | Written for the Columbian Exposition, Chicago, 1893. | Novello, 1893. ' Children's Souvenir Song Book.' |
| 120 | ' Lady Radnor's Suite ' for str. orch. : 1. Prelude. 2. Allemande. 3. Sarabande. 4. Slow Minuet. 5. Bourree. 6. Gigue. | Lady Radnor's String Orchestra, June 29, 1894. | Novello, 1902. |
| 121 | Anthem for chorus and orch. : ' Hear my words, ye people.' | Fest. of Salisbury Diocesan Choral Assoc., Salisbury, May 10, 1894. | Novello, 1894 ? |
| 122 | Oratorio : ' King Saul ' (Bible and C. H. H. P.). S.A.T.B. soli, chorus and orch. | Birmingham Fest., 1894. | Novello, 1894 ? |
| 123 | English Lyrics, 3rd set : 1. ' To Lucasta ' (Lovelace). 2. ' If thou would'st ease thine heart ' (Beddoes). 3. ' To Anthea ' (Lovelace). 4. ' Why so pale and wan ? ' (Suckling). 5. ' Through the Ivory Gate ' (Julian Sturgis). 6. ' Of all the torments ' (A. Walsh). | .. | Novello, 1895. |
| 124 | Invocation to Music (Bridges). S.T.B. soli, chorus and orch. | Leeds Fest. 1895. London, Roy. Chor. Soc., Nov. 1895. | Novello, 1895. |
| 125 | Unison song : ' Land to the Leeward Ho ! ' (Margaret Preston). | .. | Novello, 1895. |
| 126 | Twelve Short Pieces for vln. and PF. Bk. I. 1. Idyll. 2. Romance. 3. Capriccio. 4. Lullaby. | .. | Novello, 1895. |
| 127 | Bk. II. 1. Prelude. 2. Romance. 3. Capriccio. 4. Envoi. | | |
| 128 | Bk. III. 1. Preamble. 2. Romance. 3. Capriccio. 4. Envoi. | | |
| 129 | Piece in G for vln. and PF. | | |
| 130 | Romance in F for vln. and PF. | .. | R. Maver, Glasgow, in a musical album, 1896 ? |
| 131 | English Lyrics, 4th set : 1. ' Thine eyes still shined for me ' (Emerson). 2. ' When lovers meet again ' (L. E. Mitchell). 3. ' When we two parted ' (Byron). 4. ' Weep you no more ' (Anon.). 5. ' There be none of beauty's daughters ' (Byron). 6. ' Bright Star ' (Keats). | .. | Novello, 1897. |
| 132 | Elegy in A minor for Brahms (Apr. 1897). | R.C.M., Parry Memorial Concert, Nov. 1918 (Stanford). | |
| 133 | Partsongs (four parts except where noted) : (a) Six Lyrics from an Elizabethan Song Book : 1. ' Follow your Saint ' (Campian). 2. ' Love is a sickness ' (S. Daniel). 3. ' Turn all thy thoughts to eyes ' (Campian). 4. ' Whether men do laugh or weep.' 5. ' The sea hath a thousand sands.' 6. ' Tell me, O love ' (6 parts). | .. Magpie Madrigal Soc., May 19, 1898. Magpie Madr. Soc., St. James's Hall, June 3, 1897. Magpie Madr. Soc., St. James's Hall, June 3, 1897. | Novello, 1897. |
| 134 | (b) Six Modern Lyrics : 1. ' How sweet the answer ' (Moore). 2. ' Since thou, O fondest ' (Bridges). 3. ' If I had but two little wings ' (S. T. Coleridge). 4. ' There rolls the deep ' (Tennyson). 5. ' What voice of gladness ' (Bridges). 6. ' Music, when soft voices die ' (Shelley). | Magpie Madr. Soc. (Lionel Benson). May 17, 1892. Do. June 3, 1897. Do. June 3, 1897. Do. May 15, 1897. Do. May 19, 1898. Do. May 25, 1897. | Novello, 1897. |

| No. | Description. | First Performance. | Publisher. |
|---|---|---|---|
| 135 | Four-part Grace before Meat. | Dinner of a City Company, 1897. | |
| 136 | 3 Kyrie and a chant, 1897. | | |
| 137 | Symphonic variations for orch. | Philharmonic Concert, June 3, 1897. Naples, 1906 (Martucci). Gürzenich Concert, Cologne, Feb. 1912. Bologna, 1898 (Martucci). | Novello, 1897. |
| 138 | Magnificat in F. Sop. solo, chorus and orch. | Hereford Fest., Sept. 1897. | Novello, 1897. |
| 139 | Eight four-part songs : 1. ' Phillis.' 2. ' O Love, they wrong thee much.' 3. ' At her fair hands ' (Robt. Jones). 4. ' Home of my heart ' (Arthur Benson). 5. ' You gentle nymphs.' 6. ' Come, pretty wag ' (M. Pierson). 7. ' Ye thrilled me once ' (Bridges). 8. ' Better music ne'er was known ' (Beaumont and Fletcher). | Windsor and Eton Amateur Madr. Society's concert, Albert Institute, Windsor, Dec. 1898. (Walter Parratt.) | Novello, 1898. |
| 140 | ' A Song of Darkness and Light ' (Bridges). Sop. solo, chorus and orch. | Gloucester Fest., 1898. | Novello, 1898. |
| 141 | Song for bass voice and orch. : ' The North Wind.' | New Brighton Concert of C. H. H. P.'s works, July 9, 1899 (Ivor Foster). | |
| 142 | Incidental music to A Repentance (Mrs. Teresa Craigie). | St. James's Theatre, Feb. 1899 (Norman O'Neill). | |
| 143 | Five-part song : ' Who can dwell with greatness ' (Austin Dobson). | Windsor Madr. Soc., May 29, 1900. | Macmillan Co. Novello (limited edition), 1900. ' Choral Songs ' for Queen Victoria. |
| 144 | Te Deum in F (Latin words). S. and B. soli, chorus and orch. (See No. 191). | Hereford Fest., 1900. | Novello, 1900. |
| 145 | Scena for baritone voice and orch. : ' The Soldier's Tent.' | Birmingham Fest., 1900 (H. P. Greene). | Novello, 1900. |
| 146 | ' Von edler Art ' (Nuremberg Song-book of 1549) (trans. Paul England). | Magpie Madr. Soc., May 30, 1900 (H. P. Greene). | Boosey, 1906. |
| 147 | Music to the Agamemnon of Aeschylus. | Cambridge A.D.C., 1900, Feb. 16 (C. H. H. P. and C. Wood). | Novello, 1900. |
| 148 | Setting of one verse of Adeste Fideles (pro nobis egenum). | | Novello, 1901. |
| 149 | Ode to Music (A. C. Benson). S.T.B. soli, chorus and orch. | R.C.M. Opening of the new Concert Hall, June 13, 1901. | Novello, 1901. |
| 150 | Hymn : ' God of all created things.' | .. | Novello, 1902. |
| 151 | English Lyrics, 5th set : 1. ' A Stray Nymph of Dian ' (J. Sturgis). 2. ' Proud Maisie ' (Scott). 3. ' Crabbed Age and Youth ' (Shakespeare). 4. ' Lay a Garland ' (Beaumont and Fletcher). 5. ' Love and Laughter ' (Arthur Butler). 6. ' A Girl to her Glass ' (J. Sturgis). 7. ' A Welsh Lullaby ' (C. O. Jones). | .. | Novello, 1902. |
| 152 | English Lyrics, 6th set : 1. ' When comes my Gwen ' (E. O. Jones). 2. ' And yet I love her till I die ' (Anon.). 3. ' Love is a bable ' (Anon.). 4. ' A Lover's Garland ' (A. Perceval Graves). 5. ' At the hour the long day ends ' (A. P. Graves). 6. ' Under the greenwood tree ' (Shakespeare). | .. H. P. Greene, June 1, 1904 (Magpie Madr. Soc.) Do.        do. Do.        do. | Novello, 1902. |
| 153 | Symphonic ode : ' War and Peace ' (A. C. Benson and C. H. H. P.). S.A.T.B. soli, chorus and orch. | Roy. Chor. Soc., Albert Hall, Apr. 30, 1903. | Novello, 1903. |
| 154 | Anthem : ' I was glad ' ; and the Processional Music for Edward VII.'s coronation. | Westminster Abbey, Aug. 9, 1902, at the coronation (J. F. Bridge). | Novello, 1903. |
| 155 | Motet : ' Voces clamantium ' (Bible and C. H. H. P.). S. and B. soli, chorus and orch. | Hereford Fest., 1903. | Novello, 1903. |
| 156 | Hymn : ' Crossing the Bar ' (Tennyson). | .. | Novello, 1903. |
| 157 | Sinfonia sacra : ' The Love that casteth out fear ' (Bible and, largely, C. H. H. P.). | Gloucester Fest., 1904. London, Bach Choir, Feb. 8, 1907 (Walford Davies). | Novello, 1904. |
| 158 | Song : ' Newfoundland ' (Sir Cavendish Boyle). | .. | Novello, 1904. |
| 159 | Hymn tune : ' Through the night of doubt and sorrow.' | | Novello, 1904. |
| 160 | Four-part and eight-part song : ' In Praise of Song ' (C. H. H. P.). | Berks., Bucks. and Oxon. Competitive Mus. Fest., Oxford, 1904. | Novello, 1904. |
| 161 | Music to The Clouds of Aristophanes. | Oxford O.U.D.S., Mar. 1905. | B. & H., 1905. |
| 162 | Song : ' Fear no more the heat of the sun ' (Shakespeare). | .. | Ditson Co., U.S.A., 1905. |
| 163 | ' The Pied Piper of Hamelin ' (Browning). T. and B. soli, chorus and orch. | Norwich Fest., 1905. | Novello, 1905. |
| 164 | Song : ' Praise God in His Holiness.' | Hurstbourne, May 19, 1906 (H. P. Greene). | |
| 165 | Sinfonia sacra : ' The Soul's Ransom ' (a psalm of the poor) (Ezekiel and C. H. H. P.). S. and B. soli, chorus and orch. | Hereford Fest., 1906. | Novello, 1906. |
| 166 | Symphonic poem : ' A Vision of Life ' (1st version) (C. H. H. P.). S. and B. soli, chorus and orch. (See No. 193.) | Cardiff Fest., 1907. | Novello, 1907. |
| 167 | Suite in D for vln. and PF. : 1. Prelude. 2. Capriccioso. 3. Scherzo. 4. Dialogue. 5. Finale. | .. | Novello, 1907. |
| 168 | Suite in F for vln. and PF. : 1. Prelude. 2. Intermezzo. 3. Capriccioso. 4. Retrospective. 5. Finale. | .. | Novello, 1907. |
| 169 | English Lyrics, 7th set : 1. ' On a time the amorous Silvy ' (Anon.). 2. ' Follow a shadow ' (Ben Jonson). 3. ' Ye little birds that sit and sing ' (Heywood). 4. ' O never say that I was false of heart ' (Shakespeare). 5. ' Julia ' (Herrick). 6. ' Sleep ' (J. Sturgis). | .. | Novello, 1907. |
| 170 | English Lyrics, 8th set : 1. ' Whence ' (J. Sturgis). 2. ' Nightfall in Winter ' (L. E. Mitchell). 3. ' Marian ' (Meredith). 4 ' Dirge in the Woods ' (Meredith). 5. ' Looking backward ' (J. Sturgis). 6. ' Grapes ' (J. Sturgis). | H. P. Greene, June 1, 1904. M.M. Soc. | Novello, 1907. |
| 171 | Baritone song : ' The Laird of Cockpen ' (Lady Nairn). | H. P. Greene at his Recital, Nov. 30, 1906. | Novello, 1907. |
| 172 | Motet : ' Beyond these voices there is peace ' (Ecclesiasticus and C. H. H. P.). S. and B. soli, chorus and orch. | Worcester Fest., 1908. | Novello, 1908. |

| No. | Description. | First Performance. | Publisher. |
|---|---|---|---|
| 173 | Eton Memorial Ode (Bridges). Chorus and orch. | Eton Coll., Nov. 18, 1908. | Novello, 1908. |
| 174 | Song for Clifton College : ' The best school of all ' (Henry Newbolt). | Clifton College, Dec. 21, 1908 (H. P. Greene). | Year Book Press, 1916. |
| 175 | Six partsongs : | | Novello, 1909. |
|  | 1. ' In a harbour grene ' (R. Weber) (4 parts). | | |
|  | 2. ' Sweet day, so cool ' (G. Herbert) (4 parts). | | |
|  | 3. ' Sorrow and Pain ' (Lady C. Elliott) (6 parts). | Magpie Madr. Soc. (Lionel Benson), May 12, 1909. | |
|  | 4. ' Wrong not, sweet Empress ' (Sir W. Raleigh) (4 parts). | Do.            May 30, 1910. | |
|  | 5. ' Prithee, why ? ' (Sir J. Suckling) (4 parts). | Do.            May 12, 1909. | |
|  | 6. ' My delight and thy delight ' (Bridges) (4 parts). | Do.            May 30, 1910. | |
| 176 | English Lyrics, 9th set : | .. | Novello, 1909. |
|  | 1. ' Three Aspects.' | | |
|  | 2. ' A Fairy Town.' | | |
|  | 3. ' The Witches' Wood.' | | |
|  | 4. ' Whether I live or whether I die.' | | |
|  | 5. ' Armida's Garden.' | | |
|  | 6. ' The Maiden.' | | |
|  | 7. ' There.'   (All by Mary Coleridge.) | | |
| 177 | Four unison songs : | .. | Year Book Press, 1909. |
|  | 1. ' The Owl ' (Tennyson). | | |
|  | 2. ' A Contented Mind ' (Sylvester). | | |
|  | 3. ' Sorrow and Song ' (Hedderwick). | | |
|  | 4. ' The Mistletoe ' (' Father Prout'). | | |
| 178 | Seven partsongs for male voice choir : | Gloucester Orpheus Society. | |
|  | 1. ' Hang fear, cast away care ' (C. H. H. P.). | Feb. 5, 1906. | 1910. |
|  | 2. ' Love wakes and weeps ' (Walter Scott). | Feb. 5, 1906. | 1910. |
|  | 3. ' The Mad Dog ' (Goldsmith). | Jan. 1, 1907. | 1910. |
|  | 4. ' That very wise man, old Aesop ' (Dickens). | Feb. 8, 1912 (A. H. Brewer). | |
|  | 5. ' Orpheus ' (C. H. H. P.). | Jan. 27, 1904 (A. H. Brewer). | Novello, 1903. |
|  | 6. ' Out upon it ! ' (Suckling). | | |
|  | 7. ' An Analogy ' (C. H. H. P.). | Feb. 9, 1911. | Novello, 1910. |
| 179 | Te Deum in D for chorus and orch. | Westminster Abbey, June 11, 1911. Coronation of George V. | Novello, 1911. |
| 180 | School songs : | | Year Book Press, 1911. |
|  | 1. ' The way to succeed ' (2 parts) (N. Macleod). | | |
|  | 2. ' Hie away ' (3 parts) (Sir Walter Scott). | | |
|  | 3. ' Dreams ' (3 parts) (C. F. Alexander). | | |
| 181 | Hymn tune : ' O Sylvan Prophet ' (Dryden). | .. | Sands & Co., Edinburgh, Glasgow and London, 1910. |
| 182 | ' An Ode on the Nativity ' (William Dunbar). Sop. solo, chorus and orch. | Hereford Fest., 1912. | Novello, 1912. |
| 183 | Soliloquy from Browning's Saul : ' I believe it,' for bass voice and organ accompaniment. | Browning Centenary, Westminster Abbey, May 7, 1912 (Bertram Mills). | |
| 184 | Incidental music to Proserpine (Keats) : | Keats-Shelley Fest., St. James's Theatre, 1912. | |
|  | 1. Prelude. | | |
|  | 2. Intermezzo. | | |
|  | 3. Conclusion. | | |
| 185 | Symphonic fantasia in B minor : ' 1912 ' (symphony in four linked movements). Stress—Love—Play—Now. | Philharmonic Soc. Concert, Dec. 5, 1912. | Goodwin & Tabb, 1922. (Full score; and miniature full score.) |
| 186 | 1st set of Seven Chorale Preludes for Organ : | .. | Novello, 1912. |
|  | 1. Dundee. | | |
|  | 2. Rockingham. | | |
|  | 3. Hampton. | | |
|  | 4. Old 104th. | | |
|  | 5. Melcombe. | | |
|  | 6. Christe Redemptor. | | |
|  | 7. St. Ann. | | |
| 187 | Psalm 46 : ' God is our Hope.' B. solo, double chorus and orch. | Fest. of Sons of Clergy, St. Paul's Cathedral, Apr. 1913. | Novello, 1913. |
| 188 | Fantasia and fugue in G major for organ. | .. | Novello, 1913. |
| 189 | Three unison songs : | .. | Year Book Press, 1913. |
|  | 1. ' You'll get there ' (' The Trent Otter '). | | |
|  | 2. ' Good-night ' (A. M. Champneys). | | |
|  | 3. ' Ripple on ' (A. M. Champneys). | | |
| 190 | Elegy in A flat for organ. | Funeral of Lord Pembroke, Apr. 7, 1913, at Wilton. | Privately by Novello, 1913. For general use, 1922. |
| 191 | Te Deum in F (to English words). (See No. 144.) | Gloucester Fest., 1913. | Novello, 1913. |
| 192 | Music to Acharnians of Aristophanes. | Oxford O.U.D.S., 1914 (H. P. Allen and C. H. H. P.). | B. & H., 1914. |
| 193 | ' A Vision of Life ' (revised).  (See No. 166.) | Revised for the postponed Norwich Fest., 1914. Leeds Choral Union (Bairstow), Oct. 31, 1924. London, St. Michael's, Cornhill, Nov. 17, 1926 (Harold Darke). | Novello, 1914. |
| 194 | School songs : | .. | Year Book Press, 1914. |
|  | 1. ' The Fairies ' (2 parts in places ' optional ') (A. M. Champneys). | | |
|  | 2. ' The Brown Burns of the Border ' (3 parts) (W. H. Ogilvie). | | |
| 195 | Symphonic poem in two connected movements (first called ' From Death to Life ') : | Brighton Fest., Nov. 12, 1914. London Philharmonic Concert, Mar. 18, 1915. | |
|  | 1. Via Mortis.            2. Via Vitae. | | |
| 196 | Revised version of ' The Glories of our Blood and State.' (See No. 91.) | Bach Choir, Dec. 11, 1914 (H. P. Allen). | |
| 197 | Shulbrede tunes for PF. : | .. | Augener, 1914. |
|  | 1. Shulbrede. | | |
|  | 2. Elizabeth. | | |
|  | 3. Dolly (No. 1). | | |
|  | 4. Bogies and Sprites. | | |
|  | 5. Matthew. | | |
|  | 6. Prior's Chamber by Firelight. | | |
|  | 7. Children's Pranks. | | |
|  | 8. Dolly (No. 2). | | |
|  | 9. In the Garden with the Dew on the Grass. | | |
|  | 10. Father Playmate. | | |
| 198 | Three Choral Fantasies for organ : | .. | Novello, Composer's property, 1915. |
|  | 1. Old 100th. | | |
|  | 2. An old English tune to ' When I survey.' | | |
|  | 3. St. Ann. | | |
| 199 | West Downs School song, reprinted : ' Come, join the merry chorus ' (Horace Smith). | .. | Year Book Press, 1915. |
| 200 | Five-part madrigal : ' La Belle Dame Sans Merci ' (Keats). | Bristol, Jan. 1915 (D. G. Rootham). | Lithographed only. |
| 201 | Song : ' A Hymn for Aviators ' (Mary C. D. Hamilton). | Clara Butt's Red Cross Concert, Albert Hall, May 13, 1915. | Boosey, 1915. |

| No. | Description. | First Performance. | Publisher. |
|---|---|---|---|
| 202 | Carol : ' When Christ was born ' (Harleian MS.). | Roy. Chor. Soc., Albert Hall, Dec. 1915 (Bridge). | Novello, 1915. |
| 203 | Hymn : ' O praise ye the Lord ' (Sir W. H. Baker). | | |
| 204 | Naval ode : ' The Chivalry of the Sea ' (Bridges), for chorus and orch. | Bach Choir, Albert Hall Concert, Dec. 12, 1916 (H. P. Allen). | Novello, 1916. |
| 205 | 2nd set of Seven Chorale Preludes for Organ (all English tunes) : <br> 1. ' Ye boundless realms of joy.' <br> 2. ' Martyrdom.' <br> 3. ' St. Thomas.' <br> 4. ' St. Mary.' <br> 5. ' Eventide.' <br> 6. ' St. Cross.' <br> 7. ' Hanover.' | .. | Novello, 1916. |
| 206 | Four motets for ' Songs of Farewell ' (see Nos. 211, 214) : <br> 1. ' My soul, there is a country ' (4 parts).  (Vaughan.) <br> 2. ' I know my soul hath power ' (4 parts) (J. Davies). <br> 3. ' Never weatherbeaten sail ' (5 parts) (Campian). <br> 4. ' There is an old belief ' (6 parts) (Lockhart). | Bach Choir Concert, R.C.M., May 22, 1916 (H. P. Allen), together with No. 211. <br> The six ' Songs of Farewell ' first heard together in Exeter Coll. Chapel, Oxford, Feb. 28, 1919 (H. P. Allen). | Year Book Press, 1916. |
| 207 | Three songs for ' Kookoorookoo Songs ' : <br> 1. ' Brown and furry.' <br> 2. ' The Peacock.' <br> 3. ' The wind has such a rainy sound ' (all by Christina Rossetti). | .. | Year Book Press, 1916. |
| 208 | Choral song : ' Jerusalem ' (Blake). | ' Fight for Right ' Meeting, Queen's Hall, Mar. 28, 1916. | Curwen, 1916. |
| 209 | Partsong (S.A.T.B.) : ' I know an Irish Lass.' | | |
| 210 | A unison song : ' For all we have and are ' (Kipling). | | |
| 211 | Motet for ' Songs of Farewell ' : ' At the round earth's imagined corners ' (7 parts) (Donne). | See No. 206. | Year Book Press, 1917. |
| 212 | Two carols : <br> 1. ' I sing the Birth.' <br> 2. ' Welcome, Yule.'  (15th century carol.) | Roy. Chor. Soc. Albert Hall, Dec. 1917 (J. F. Bridge). | Novello, 1917. |
| 213 | PF. piece : ' Sleepy.' | | |
| 214 | Motet (8 parts) for ' Songs of Farewell ' : ' Lord, let me know mine end.' | New College, Oxford, June 17, 1918 (H. P. Allen). | Year Book Press, 1918. |
| 215 | Hymn : ' Hush, for amid our tears.' | .. | Novello, 1918. |
| 216 | English Lyrics, 10th set : <br> 1. ' A Birthday ' (Christina Rossetti). <br> 2. ' Gone were but the winter cold ' (Allan Cuningham). <br> 3. ' A moment of farewell ' (J. Sturgis). <br> 4. ' The Child and the Twilight ' (L. E. Mitchell). <br> 5. ' From a City Window ' (L. E. Mitchell). <br> 6. ' One Silent Night of late ' (Herrick). | Bechstein (Wigmore) Hall, Nov. 16, 1909 (Agnes Nicholls). | Novello, 1918. |
| 217 | Suite for PF. : ' Hands Across the Centuries ' : <br> 1. Prelude.            5. Gavotte and Musette. <br> 2. The Passionate Allemande.  6. Quasi Minuetto. <br> 3. The Wistful Courante.     7. The Whirling Jig. <br> 4. Quasi Sarabande. | .. | Augener, 1918. |
| 218 | Three school songs : <br> 1. ' Neptune's Empire ' (unison) (Campian). <br> 2. ' The Wind and the Leaves ' (2 parts) (Cooper). <br> 3. ' Song of the Nights ' (2 parts) (Barry Cornwall). | | Edward Arnold, 1918. |
| 219 | Unison song : ' England.' | Oxford, July 1918 (H. P. Allen). | Year Book Press, 1919. |
| 220 | English Lyrics, 11th set : <br> 1. ' One golden link, unbroken ' (J. Chatterton). <br> 2. ' What part of dread eternity ' (? C. H. H. P.). <br> 3. ' The Spirit of the Spring ' (A. P. Graves). <br> 4. ' The Blackbird ' (A. P. Graves). <br> 5. ' The Faithful Lover ' (A. P. Graves). <br> 6. ' If I might ride on puissant wing ' (J. Sturgis). <br> 7. ' Why art thou slow ' (Massinger). <br> 8. ' She is my love ' (A. P. Graves). | The 11th and 12th sets of English lyrics were selected and edited by E. Daymond. | Novello, 1920. |
| 221 | English Lyrics, 12th set : <br> 1. ' When the dew is falling ' (J. Chatterton). <br> 2. ' To Blossoms ' (Herrick). <br> 3. ' Rosaline ' (Lodge). <br> 4. ' When the sun's great orb ' (Warner). <br> 5. ' Dream Pedlary ' (Beddoes). <br> 6. ' O World, O Life, O Time ' (Shelley, 1st version, 1868). <br> 7. ' The sound of hidden music ' (Julia Chatterton, MS. signed Feb. 27, 1918—on his last birthday). | .. | Novello, 1920. |
| 222 | Toccata and fugue in G major and E minor for organ : ' Wanderer.'  Toccata begins and ends in G.  Fugue begins in E minor and ends in G. | Westminster Abbey (G. Thalben Ball). | Novello, 1921. |
| 223 | An English suite for string orchestra : <br> 1. Prelude.        5. Pastoral. <br> 2. In Minuet Style.   6. Air. <br> 3. Saraband.       7. Frolic. <br> 4. Caprice. | Semi-privately at a R.C.M. orchestral concert, and at the Parry (Bach Choir) Concert (R.C.M.), May 10, 1921, both times (H. P. Allen).  Publicly, Promenade Concerts, Oct. 20, 1922 (Henry Wood).  (Edited by E. Daymond.) | Novello, 1921. A PF. version, Novello, 1923. |
| 224 | Five miniatures for PF. : <br> 1. Sleepy.            4. Pause. <br> 2. Little Christmas Piece (see 115).  5. Envoi. <br> 3. Capriccio. | .. | Curwen, 1926. |

PARRY, JOHN (d. Ruabon, North Wales, Oct. 7, 1782), was domestic harper to Sir Watkin Williams Wynne, of Wynnstay. One of his earliest public performances was in Dublin, where he gave a concert on Dec. 21, 1736.[1]  He came and played in 1746 in London, where his playing is said to have been admired by Handel, and he also played at Cambridge before Gray, thereby inciting him to the completion of his poem, ' The Bard.'  In 1742 he put forth the earliest published collection (only one part published) of Welsh melodies, under the title of ' Antient British Music of the Cambro-Britons.'  He afterwards published (undated) ' A Collection of Welsh, English and Scotch Airs ; also Lessons for the Harpsichord ' : and, in 1781, ' Cambrian Harmony ; a Collection of Antient Welsh Airs, the traditional remains of those sung by the Bards of

[1] Information from W. H. G. F.

Wales.' Though totally blind, he is reported to have been an excellent draught-player. (See WELSH MUSIC.) w. h. h.

PARRY, (1) JOHN (b. Denbigh, North Wales, Feb. 18, 1776 ; d. Apr. 8, 1851), received his earliest musical instruction from a dancing-master, who taught him also to play the clarinet. In 1795 he joined the band of the Denbighshire militia, and in 1797 became master of it. In 1807 he resigned his appointment, and settled in London as a teacher of the flageolet, then greatly in vogue. In 1809 he was engaged to compose songs, etc., for Vauxhall Gardens, which he continued to do for several years afterwards, and also adapted English words to a selection of Welsh melodies. He composed the music for T. Dibdin's extravaganza, 'Harlequin Hoax ; or, A Pantomime proposed,' 1814 ; 'Oberon's Oath,' 1816 ; 'High Notions, or A Trip to Exmouth,' 1817 ; and adapted the music for 'Ivanhoe,' 1820 ; and 'Caswallon,' a tragedy, 1829. He was author as well as composer of the musical pieces, 'Fair Cheating,' 1814 ; 'Helpless Animals,' 1818 ; 'Two Wives, or, A Hint to Husbands,' 1821 ; and 'The Sham Prince,' 1836. He conducted the Cymmro-dorion and Eisteddfodau, or Congresses of Welsh Bards, at Wrexham in 1820 and at Brecon in 1822, and in 1821 he received the degree of 'Bardd Alaw,' or Master of Song. He was one of the promoters of the Cambrian Society. He was author of *An Account of the Rise and Progress of the Harp* ; *An Account of the Royal Musical Festival held in Westminster Abbey in 1834* (of which he had been secretary) ; and *Il Puntello, or, The Supporter*, containing the first rudiments of music. In June 1837 he gave a farewell concert, at which he sang his own ballad of 'Jenny Jones' (made popular by Charles Mathews the year before), accompanied on the harp by his son. From 1834–48 he was concert music critic to the *Morning Post*. He published several collections of Welsh Melodies, the most important embodying the greater part of Jones's 'Relics of the Welsh Bards,' under the title of 'The Welsh Harper' (1839–48). From 1831 to Aug. 5, 1849, he was treasurer of the Royal Society of Musicians.

His son, (2) JOHN ORLANDO (b. London, Jan. 3, 1810 ; d. East Molesey, Feb. 20, 1879), studied the harp under Bochsa, and in May 1825 appeared (as Master Parry) as a performer on that instrument. He also became an excellent pianist. In 1830 he sang 'Arm, Arm, ye brave,' at Franz Cramer's concert, and subsequently had much success as a baritone singer, chiefly of ballads accompanied by himself on the harp. Neukomm's once famous song, 'Napoleon's Midnight Review,' was written for him ; and in 1833 he went to Italy, living for some time at Naples, and learning from Lablache, with whom he appeared as Desdemona in a burlesque of 'Othello.' At his benefit con-

cert in June 1836 he gave the first public indication in England of the possession of that extraordinary *vis comica* by which he was afterwards so remarkably distinguished, by joining Madame Malibran in Mazzinghi's duet, 'When a little farm we keep,' and introducing an admirable imitation of Harley. Later in the same year he appeared upon the stage at the St. James's Theatre in his father's 'Sham Prince,' in Hullah's 'Village Coquettes' and other pieces. In the following year he gave his 'Buffo Trio Italiano' (accompanied by himself on the pianoforte), in which he successfully imitated Grisi, Ivanoff and Lablache. In 1840 he introduced 'Wanted, a Governess' (words by George Dubourg), the success of which induced him to abandon serious, and devote himself wholly to comic, singing. The songs he selected differed materially from those of the immediately preceding generation in the absence of coarseness or vulgarity, and were consequently most favourably received. They comprised, among others, 'Wanted, a Wife,' 'Berlin Wool,' 'Blue Beard,' 'Matrimony,' 'Fayre Rosamonde' and 'The London Season' ; the words being mostly by Albert Smith and the music arranged by Parry himself. Many of his songs, glees, etc., were published. (See *D.N.B.*) In 1849 he gave up concert-singing and produced an entertainment, 'Notes, Vocal and Instrumental,' written by Albert Smith, in which he exhibited a number of large water-colour paintings executed by himself, and which was very successful. He gave similar entertainments in 1850 and 1852. In 1853 ill health compelled him to retire from public performance, and he became organist of St. Jude's, Southsea, and practised as a teacher. In 1860 he again appeared in public at the German Reed's entertainments, but in 1869 ill health again necessitated his retirement. He took final leave of the public at a performance for his benefit at the Gaiety Theatre, Feb. 7, 1877. w. h. h.

PARRY, (1) JOSEPH, Mus.D. (b. Merthyr Tydvil, May 21, 1841 ; d. Penarth, Feb. 17, 1903), composer, who enriched Welsh hymnody with a number of fine tunes,[1] came of poor Welsh parents, the mother a superior woman with much music in her nature. There is a great deal of singing and brass-band-playing among the Welsh workmen, and at chapel and elsewhere the boy soon picked up enough to show that he had a real talent. At 10, however, he was forced to go to the puddling furnaces and to stop all education of any kind. In 1853 his father emigrated to the United States, and in 1854 the family followed him. After a few years Joseph returned from America, and then received some instruction in music from John Abel Jones of Merthyr and John Price of Rhymney. In 1862 he won prizes at the Llandudno Eisteddfod. He then went again to

[1] See 'Aberystwyth' *English Hymnal*, No. 87.

America, and during his absence there a prize was adjudged to him at the Swansea Eisteddfod of 1863, for a harmonised hymn tune.

Its excellence roused the attention of Brinley Richards, one of the musical adjudicators of the meeting, and at his instance a fund was raised for enabling Parry to return to England and enter the R.A.M. The appeal was well responded to by Welshmen here and in the States, and in Sept. 1868 he entered the Academy and studied under Sterndale Bennett, Garcia and Steggall. He took a bronze medal in 1870 and a silver one in 1871, and an overture of his to ' The Prodigal Son ' (Mab Afradlon) was played at the Academy in 1871. He was appointed professor of music at the University College, Aberystwyth, and soon after took his Mus.B. degree at Cambridge, proceeding, in May 1878, to that of Mus.D. at the same university. In 1888 he was appointed to the musical lectureship of the University College of South Wales, Cardiff ; and in 1896 at the Llandudno Eisteddfod was presented with a cheque for £600 for services rendered to Welsh music. His works include :

The oratorios, ' Emmanuel ' (London, 1880) ; ' Saul of Tarsus ' (Rhyl and Cardiff, 1892) ; ' The Prodigal Son ' and ' Nebuchadnezzar.' ' Cambria,' a cantata performed at Llandudno in 1896. His operas are ' Blodwen,' produced at Aberdare in 1878, and at the Alexandra Palace ; ' Virginia,' 1883 ; ' Arianwen ' (Cardiff, 1890) ; ' Sylvia ' (Cardiff, 1895) ; ' King Arthur,' completed 1897. Many choral works, an orchestral ballad (Cardiff, 1892), overtures, a string quartet, etc., are among his compositions, and he edited six vols. of Cambrian Minstrelsy.

G. ; addns. *Brit. Mus. Biog.*

His son, (2) JOSEPH HAYDN (*b.* Pennsylvania, U.S.A., May 1864; *d.* Hampstead, Mar. 29, 1894), studied mainly under the parental guidance. In 1884 he gained a prize for a pianoforte sonata. In 1890 he was appointed a professor at the G.S.M. ; he wrote a successful cantata for female voices, ' Gwen ' ; a comic opera, ' Cigarette,' was produced at Cardiff in 1892 ; ' Miami,' a more ambitious work, set to an adaptation of ' The Green Bushes,' came out at the Princess's Theatre, London, Oct. 16, 1893 ; and a third, ' Marigold Farm,' was finished but never produced. M.

PARSIFAL, a ' Bühnenweihfestspiel ' (or ' dedicatory stage-play.') in 3 acts ; words and music by Wagner. The poem was published in 1877, and the music completed in 1879. The first performance, for subscribers, took place at Bayreuth, July 26, 1882, and the first public performance, July 30. For twenty-one years the stage representation of the work took place only at Bayreuth, but the bulk of the music was heard under Barnby at the Albert Hall, London, Nov. 10, 1884. On Dec. 24, 1903, the first complete performance outside the original theatre took place in the Metropolitan Opera House, New York; and in English, Tremont Theatre, Boston, Oct. 17, 1904. On June 20, 1905, the Wagner-Verein of Amsterdam gave a performance in that city. It was first heard on the stage in England at Covent Garden, Feb. 2, 1914; Paris, Opéra, Jan. 1, 1914; and in English, Covent Garden (Beecham), Nov. 17, 1919. M.

PARSLEY (PARSELEY, PERSLEYE, PARCELE, etc.), OSBERT (*b.* 1511; *d.* 1585), singing-man of Norwich Cathedral and composer of church music. He is referred to and quoted in Morley's *Plaine and Easie Introduction* (1597). The extracts below, taken from an inscription on his monument in the north aisle of Norwich Cathedral, give all that is known of Parsley's biography :

OSBERTO PARSLEY
Musicae Scientissimo
Ei quondam Consociati
Musici posuerunt. Anno 1585.

Here lies the man whose Name in spight of Death,
Renowned lives by Blast of Golden Fame,
Whose Harmony survives his vital Breath,
Whose Skill no Pride did spot, whose Life no Blame.
: . : . : . :
Whose Life in Seventy and Four Years entwin'd.
: . : . : . :
Who here a Singing-man did spend his Days,
Full Fifty Years, in our Church melody.
His Memory shines bright whom thus we praise.

The British Museum contains the following arrangements of motets by Parsley : ' Spease noster' [*sic*], arranged for 5 viols (B.M. Add. MSS. 31,390/120) ; arrangements, in Italian tablature, of 3 others, ' Conserva me,' ' Multiplicati,' ' Benedicam Domino' (B.M. Add. MSS. 29,246-7). B.M. Add. MSS. 30,480-4 also contains a composition for 5 voices called ' Perslis clocke.'

SERVICES, ETC.
Short Service (T.D. ; B.). PH.
T.D. in F. B.M. Add. MSS. 30,480-3.
B. B.M. Add. MSS 30,480-3.

MOTETS
Benedicam Domino, *a* 3. R.C.M. 2035.
Conserva me, *a* 3. Bodl. Mus. Sch. e 1-5 ; B.M. Add. MSS. 34,726/17. Score ; R.C.M. 2035.
Cui comparabote. Bodl. Mus. Sch. e 1-5.
Multiplicati, *a* 3. R.C.M. 2035.        J. Mᴷ.

PARSONS, (1) ROBERT (*d.* Newark, Jan. 25, 1569/70), a native of Exeter, was on Oct. 17, 1563, sworn a gentleman of the Chapel Royal. He is said, but erroneously, to have been organist of Westminster Abbey. He composed some church music. A Morning, Communion and Evening Service is printed in Barnard's ' Selected Church Musick,' and a Burial Service in Low's ' Directions,' 1664. An anthem, ' Deliver me,' is contained in the Tudway Collection (Harl. MS. 7339), and an ' In Nomine ' and a madrigal, ' Enforced by love and feare,' are in B.M. Add. MSS. 11,586. Various ' In Nomines,' etc., are in Add. MSS. 22,597, 29,246, 31,390, 32,377 and 30,380/84 ; one in the Fitzwilliam Museum at Cambridge (published in the ' Fitzwilliam Virginal Book,' ii. 135) is probably by him. Three services (the third printed in Barnard), an anthem, ' Ah, helpless wretch,' a motet, ' Anima Christi,' and pieces for viols are in Barnard's MS. collections in the R.C.M. Many of his compositions, including partbooks of ' Pandolpho,' a song from a stage play, are in the library of Christ Church, Oxford. He was drowned in the Trent at Newark. His scientific skill and feeling for curious effects of harmony make him an important figure in English music.

(2) JOHN (d. 1623), probably his son, was in 1616 appointed one of the parish clerks and also organist of St. Margaret's, Westminster. On Dec. 7, 1621, he was appointed organist and master of the choristers of Westminster Abbey. A score of his Burial Service, in the hand of Henry Purcell, is in the library of St. Michael's College, Tenbury (MS. 787). It is bound in black covers, and was probably the copy used by Purcell at the funeral of Charles II. at Westminster Abbey, when Parsons's service was certainly performed. The irregular barring is a noteworthy feature of this score. A MS. of this service is also at the R.C.M. Parsons was buried, Aug. 3, in the cloisters of Westminster. A quaint epitaph on him, preserved in Camden's *Remains*, is reprinted in the *D.N.B.* See also *Mus. ant.* i. 38.

w. h. h. ; addns. e. h. f. and *D.N.B.*

PART. (1) The single line of music from which the instrumental or vocal performer reads, and also the music itself ; so that ' he reads his part from a part ' is a phrase readily understood by musicians, as indicating that nothing in the shape of a score is used by the individual referred to. (2) This sense of the word is transferred to music for keyboard instruments written in contrapuntal style. Hence a fugue for piano or organ may be described as written in 2, 3, 4 or more parts or voices. (See PART-PLAYING.)

(3) The division of large works, the equivalent of ' act ' in theatrical music ; oratorios, cantatas, etc., are divided into so many ' parts ' or great sections, after any of which a pause might appropriately be made. M. ; addns. c.

PARTBOOKS. The polyphonic composers of the 15th and 16th centuries usually issued their works in separate parts, and generally in separate volumes.

Of these partbooks the greater number may be divided into three distinct classes.

In the first class—that of the true representative partbook—each vocal part was transcribed or printed in a separate volume.

In the second class, the parts were indeed transcribed or printed separately—but in the form called in early times *cantus lateralis, i.e.* side by side and one above the other, in such a manner that the whole number of parts could be seen at one view on the double pages of the open book, and that all the performers could sing at once from a single copy of the work.

In the third class, the plan employed was that known in Germany as Tafel-Musik ; the parts being arranged side-ways and upside-down so that four performers, seated at the four sides of the little table on which the open book was placed, could each read his own part the right way upwards.

The most famous, and, with one exception only, by far the most perfect and beautiful specimens of the first class are those published,

at Venice and Fossombrone, at the beginning of the 16th century, by Ottaviano dei Petrucci, the inventor of the art of printing music from movable types. Of these now exceedingly rare and costly partbooks, more than fifty volumes have been catalogued, since the time of Conrad Gesner, who, however, in his ' Pandecta ' mentions some few which cannot now be identified. The perfection of their typography would have rendered them precious to collectors, even without reference to the value of the compositions, which, but for them, would have been utterly lost to us.[1] Each part is printed in a separate volume, oblong 4to, without a title-page at the beginning, but with a colophon on the last page of the bassus, recording the date and place of publication. In one instance only has the brilliance and clearness of the typography been surpassed. The British Museum possesses the unique bassus part of a collection of songs, printed by Wynkyn de Worde in 1530, which exceeds in beauty everything that has ever been produced, in the form of music-printing from movable types, from the time of its invention by Petrucci until now. The volume [2] is an oblong 4to, corresponding very nearly in size with those of Petrucci ; but the staves are much broader, and the type larger, the perfection of both being such as could only be rivalled at the present day by the finest steel engraving. The volume contains nine songs $a$ 4, and eleven $a$ 3, by Fayrfax, Taverner, Cornyshe, Pygott, Ashwell, Cowper, Gwynneth and Jones ; and at the end of the book is the first leaf of the Triplex, containing the title and index only. This, unhappily, is all that has hitherto been discovered of the work.

Petrucci's successors were as far as those of Wynkyn de Worde from approaching the excellence of the leader—and even farther. The separate parts of Palestrina's masses and the madrigals of Luca Marenzio, printed at Venice in the closing years of the 16th century, though artistic in design, and in bold and legible type, are greatly inferior in execution to the early examples ; and the motets of Giovanni Croce published by Giacomo Vincenti (Venice, 1605) are very rough indeed. The nearest approach to the style of Petrucci is to be found in the earlier works printed in London by John Day ; the ' Cantiones sacrae ' of Tallis and Byrd, printed by Thomas Vautrollier (London, 1575); and the earlier works published by Thomas East, under the patent of William Byrd, such as Byrd's ' Psalmes, Sonets and Songes of Sadnes and Pietie ' (1588) and his ' Songs of sundrie natures ' (1589). But East's later productions, including the second book of Yonge's ' Musica Transalpina ' (1597), and the works of the

---

[1] Facsimiles will be found in *Ottaviano dei Petrucci da Fossombrone* by Anton Schmid (Vienna, 1845), and *Ottaviano dei Petrucci da Fossombrone*, by Augusto Vernarecci (2nd edit. Bologna, 1882). The student may also consult Catelani, *Bibliogr. di due stampi ignoti da Ottav. dei Petrucci* (Milan), and the Catalogue of Eitner.
[2] K. l. e. l.

later madrigalists, are far from equalling these, and little, if at all, superior to the later Italian partbooks.

The finest partbooks of the second class, presented in *cantus lateralis*, are the magnificent MS. volumes in the archives of the Sistine Chapel ; huge folios, transcribed in notes of such gigantic size that the whole choir can read from a single copy, and adorned with illuminated borders and initial letters of exquisite beauty. In these, the upper half of the left-hand page is occupied by the cantus, and the lower half by the tenor ; the upper half of the right-hand page by the altus, and the lower half by the bassus. When a quintus is needed half of it is written on the left-hand page below the tenor, and the remainder (*reliquium*) below the bassus, on the right-hand page. When six parts are needed, the quintus is written below the tenor, and the sextus below the bassus. Books of this kind seem to have been less frequently used in England than in Italy ; unless, indeed, the MSS. were destroyed during the Civil War.[1]

The finest printed examples of this class are the large folio edition of Palestrina's 'First Book of Masses' (Roma, apud heredes Aloysii Dorici, 1572) and the still finer edition of ' Hymni totius anni ' (Roma, apud Jacobum Tornerium et Bernardinum Donangelum, 1589). A very beautiful example of this kind of partbook, on a small scale, will be found in Tallis's ' Eight Tunes,' printed by John Day at the end of Archbishop Parker's metrical translation of the Psalms (London, 1567) ; and one not very much inferior is Thomas East's ' Whole Booke of Psalmes ' (London, 1592). Ravenscroft's ' Briefe Discourse ' (1614), is a very rough example ; and the ' Dodecachordon ' of Glareanus (Basle, 1547), though so much earlier, is scarcely more satisfactory in point of typography.

The third class of partbooks, designed to be read from the four sides of a table, was more common in England than in any other country. One of the best-known examples is that given in the closing pages of Morley's *Plaine and Easie Introduction* (London, 1597 and 1606), in which the parts are presented in a rectangular arrangement, each part facing

outwards as the book is placed open on the table.

[1] A large folio MS. of this kind, containing a Mass by Philippus de Monte, was lent to the Inventions Exhibition of 1885 by Miss Elvington, and another exceedingly fine specimen, containing a Gloria *a* 5, written by Fayrfax for his degree of Mus.D., was lent to the same exhibition from the Lambeth Palace Library.

In Dowland's ' First Booke of Songs or Ayres,' a still more complicated arrangement is dictated by the necessity for accommodating a lutenist by the side of the cantus, the part for these two performers appearing on two parallel staves on the left-hand page, while the other three voices share the right-hand page.

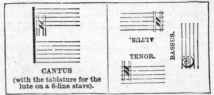

W. S. R.

Much of the English church music of the 16th century has only survived in MS. partbooks, for scarcely any church music of that period was printed. Large numbers of these books perished in the 17th century, partly at the hands of religious fanatics, and partly because they began to be replaced by printed books and scores. Of the sets that survive only a very small proportion are complete ; isolated and incomplete voice-parts are scattered about in various libraries throughout England, while some are in private hands. The most important collections of these books apart from those in such libraries as the B.M., the Bodleian and Cambridge Univ. Lib., are at the cathedrals of Durham, York and Ely, and in the libraries of St. Michael's, Tenbury, Ch. Ch., Oxford, and Peterhouse, Cambridge.                    E. H. F.

PARTE, see COLLA PARTE.

PARTHENIA. The first music for the virginals printed from engraved plates in England. The title is

' Parthenia or The Maydenhead of the first musicke that euer was printed for the Virginalls Composed By three famous Masters William Byrd, Dr. John Bull and Orlando Gibbons Gentilmen of his Ma^ties most Illustrious Chappell. Ingrauen by William Hole.'

The work consists of the following twenty-one pieces, all upon six-line staves, and engraved upon copper - plates, being the first musical work so produced.

| W. Byrd. | Galiardo ; St. Thos. Wake. |
|---|---|
| Preludium. | Pavana. |
| Pavana ; Sir W. Petre. | Galiardo. |
| Galiardo. | Galiardo. |
| Preludium. | Galiardo. |
| Galiardo ; Mrs. Mary Brownlo. | |
| Pavana ; The Earl of Salisbury. | O. Gibbons. |
| Galiardo. | Galiardo. |
| Galiardo. 2 do. ; Mrs. Mary Brownlo. | Fantazia of foure parts. |
| | The Lord of Salisbury his Pavin. |
| Dr. Bull. | Galiardo. |
| Preludium. | The Queene's command. |
| Pavana ; St. Thos. Wake. | Preludium. |

It first appeared in 1611. On the title is a three-quarter-length representation of a lady playing upon the virginals. Commendatory verses by Hugh Holland and George Chapman are prefixed. It was reprinted in 1613 with a dedication to the Elector Palatine and Princess Elizabeth. Other impressions appeared in 1635, 1650, 1655, 1659 and probably 1689, the

1659 edition with a letterpress title bearing the imprint of John Playford. All these impressions were from the same plates. The work was reprinted by the Musical Antiquarian Society in 1847, under the editorship of Rimbault, with facsimiles of the title-page and a page of the music.    w. h. h.

PARTHENIA INVIOLATA. A companion work to that described above ; the full title is

'Parthenia Inviolata or Mayden-Musicke for the Virginalls and Bass-Viol Selected out of the Compositions of the most famous in that Arte By Robert Hole And Consecrated to all true Louers & Practicers thereof.'

Eight lines of verse and a cut follow, and the imprint is :

'Printed at London for John Pyper, and are to be sold at his shopp at Pauls gate next vnto Cheapside at the Crosse Keies. Cum priuilegio.'

It is an oblong small quarto, engraved throughout on copper-plate. Collation : Title, verso blank ; 'The Kinges Morisck,' 2 pp. ; 'The Lordes Mask,' 1 p. ; 'The Irish Dance,' 1 p. ; 'New Noddie,' 2 pp. ; 'Old Noddie,' 2 pp. ; 'Ages youth,' 1 p. ; 'The first part of the old yeere,' 2 pp. ; 'The last part of the olde yeere,' 1 p. ; 'Miserere,' 2 pp. ; 'Almaine,' 1 p. ; Tune XI., 2 pp. ; Tune XII., 1 p. ; Tune XIII., 2 pp. ; Tune XIIII., 1 p. ; 'Almaine,' 1 p. ; 'Almaine,' 1 p. ; Tune XVII., 1 p. ; Tune XVIII., w. 2 pp. ; Tune XIX., 1 p. ; Tune XX., 1 p. The only known copy was bought at Dr. E. F. Rimbault's sale by Mr. Drexel, and is now in the New York Public Library. It was described in some detail in *Notes and Queries*, Dec. 11, 1869.    m.

PARTIALS (Fr. *sons partiels* ; Ger. *Partialtöne, Aliquottöne*). The members of the harmonic series (see Acoustics) which form the constituents of a musical note are called the partials of the note. The constituents above the fundamental are often called the upper partials. The terms partials and harmonics are generally treated as having the same meaning, when referring to the separate tones which make up a complex note.    j. w. c.

PARTICIPANT (from the Lat. *participare*, 'to share in '). One of the 'Regular Modulations' of the Ecclesiastical Modes. (See Modes, Ecclesiastical, Vol. III. p. 482 ; Modulations. Regular and Conceded.)

PARTIMENTI, 'divisions'; exercises in florid counterpoint, written generally, but not always, on a figured bass, for the purpose of cultivating the art of accompanying or of playing at sight from a figured bass.    m.

PARTITA (Ger. *Partie*). Though the Italian form of the name is the one in common use, it is said to have originated about the beginning of the 17th century with the Kunst- or Stadt-Pfeifers, or town musicians, and given by them to the collections of dance tunes which were played consecutively, and which afterwards were taken to form suites. Bach uses the name in two senses ; first, as the equivalent of 'Suite' in the Six Partitas for Clavier ; and

second, for three sets of Variations on Chorales for Organ, viz. those on 'Christ, der du bist der helle Tag' (7 Partitas, including the theme itself), on 'O Gott, du frommer Gott' (9 Partitas including the theme), and on 'Sey gegrüsset Jesu gütig' (11 Partitas or variations, exclusive of the theme itself). He also wrote three Partitas (in Suite-form) for the lute. The name has very seldom been used since Bach ; the chief instance of its occurrence in the original title of Beethoven's Octuor, 'Parthia in Es.' (See Octet.) Parry's 'Partita' for violin and piano in D minor is a modern instance of the name.    m.

PARTITION (Fr.), (Ger. *Partitur*), see Score.

PART-PLAYING is the art of playing polyphonic music on a keyboard instrument in such a way as to preserve the identities and characters of the several parts (see Part) by attention not only to the exact values of the notes but by phrasing in accordance with melodic contours.    c.

PARTSONG (Fr. *chanson à parties* ; Ger. *mehrstimmiges Lied*) is a term properly applied to any song for two or more voices in harmony with or without instrumental accompaniment. In common use, however, Partsong has acquired a more restricted connotation in the English language, since it is distinguished from the Madrigal (*q.v.*) and its attendant forms by its harmonic style, and from the Glee (*q.v.*) by the fact that it implies choral performance, *i.e.* more than one voice to a part, rather than a solo ensemble. It is applicable therefore to any choral piece which has the character of a harmonised song-melody. The harmonised versions of Dowland's 'First Book of Songs to the Lute' (1597) may be taken as the starting-point of the English Partsong, as a distinct style, but the special application of the term did not become prevalent until the 19th century, when such composers as J. L. Hatton and R. L. de Pearsall specialised in the type. The growth of small choral societies and male voice choirs created a demand to which Sullivan and Barnby ministered with such popular specimens as 'The long day closes' and 'Sweet and low.' A later generation— Parry, Stanford, Elgar—has enriched the type with many works of greater artistic distinction, and the increased choral technique stimulated largely by the competitive festival movement (see Competitive Festivals), has now almost obliterated the restrictions of style which formerly separated the English Partsong from the larger choral piece.    c.

PART-WRITING (Ger. *Stimmführung*), a term of criticism usually applied to the general disposition of the parts in a composition (see Part (1) and (2) and Part-playing), having regard to their individual melodic characters as well as to their resultant effect in harmony.

Thus the part-writing may be awkward even to the verge of impossibility or dull to the point of monotony, although the resultant harmony is unimpeachable. On the other hand, perfectly written parts may be produced and multiplied at the expense of harmonic clarity and the beauty of the passage as a whole.

For educational purposes part-writing has generally been considered as a department of the study of harmony, though the cultivation of a good style of part-writing is the special purpose of contrapuntal training. (See COUNTERPOINT.)        C.

PASCAL BRUNO, opera in 3 acts; music by J. L. Hatton. Produced Kärnthnerthor Theatre, Vienna, as 'Pasqual Bruno,' Mar. 2, 1844.        G.

PASCHE (PASHE, PAYSHE), W., English church music composer, probably of the 15th century (what remains of his music is preserved in MSS. of the early 16th). He is mentioned by Morley among his list of 'Practicioners' of music in his *Plaine and Easie Introduction* (1597). A Mass by Pasche, 'Christus resurgens,' is in the library at Caius College, Cambridge; the tenor part of this is also at St. John's. In the Peterhouse partbooks there are two Magnificats, and a motet, 'Sancta Maria, Mater Dei,' by him.        J. Mᴷ.

PASDELOUP, JULES ETIENNE (b. Paris, Sept. 15, 1819; d. Fontainebleau, Aug. 13, 1887), gained the first prize of the Conservatoire for solfège in 1832, and the first for the piano in 1834. He then took lessons in harmony from Dourlen, and in composition from Carafa. Though active and ambitious he might have had to wait long for an opportunity of making his powers known, had not a post in the Administration des Domaines fallen to his lot during the political changes of 1848 and enabled him to provide for his family. As Governor of the Château de St. Cloud he was not only thrown into contact with persons of influence, but had leisure at command for composition.

The general refusal of the societies in Paris to perform his orchestral works had, doubtless, much to do with his resolve to found the 'Société des Jeunes Artistes du Conservatoire,' the first concert of which he conducted on Feb. 20, 1851. Pasdeloup now found his vocation, which was neither that of a Government official nor a composer, but of an able conductor bringing forward the works of other masters, native and foreign. At the concerts of the 'Société des Jeunes Artistes' in the Salle Herz, Rue de la Victoire, he produced the symphonies of Gounod, Lefébure-Wély, Saint-Saëns, Gouvy, Demersseman and other French composers, and there Parisians heard for the first time Mozart's 'Entführung,' Meyerbeer's 'Struensee' and several of Schumann's

standard works. After two years spent in forming his young band,[1] and struggling against the indifference of the paying portion of the public, Pasdeloup resolved on a bold stroke and moved his quarters to the Cirque d'Hiver, then the Cirque Napoléon, where, on Oct. 27, 1861, he opened his Concerts Populaires, given every Sunday at the same hour as the Concerts du Conservatoire. The striking and well-deserved success of these entertainments roused universal attention and procured their conductor honours of various kinds. Baron Haussmann had already requested him to organise and conduct the concerts at the Hôtel de Ville; the Prefect of the Seine appointed him one of the two directors of the ORPHÉON (q.v.); and de Nieuwerkerke, Surintendant des Beaux-Arts, frequently called upon him to select and conduct the concerts which formed the main attraction of the soirées given by the director of the Museum of the Louvre. He also received the Legion of Honour.

An ardent admirer of Wagner, Pasdeloup made use of his short managership of the Théâtre-Lyrique (1868–70) to produce 'Rienzi' (Apr. 6, 1869). He undertook this office on disadvantageous terms and lost heavily by it. The Franco-German war gave a serious check to his career, but when it was over he resumed the Concerts Populaires with the aid of a Government subsidy of 25,000 francs. Elwart compiled a history of the concerts, but he does not go beyond their first start.        G. C.

After a popularity of many years' duration, during which the Concerts Populaires acquired an almost universal celebrity and did much to develop musical taste in France, and to cultivate the symphonic school of music, the enterprise rapidly declined. The Sunday matinées at the theatres were formidable rivals to Pasdeloup's concerts, besides which the public taste which he had done so much to train was turning altogether in the direction of the concerts given by Colonne and Lamoureux, whose standard of performance was more careful and who succeeded better in gauging the requirements of the audience. Under these circumstances Pasdeloup, after vain efforts to reinstate himself in public favour, decided to resign, and closed the Concerts Populaires in Apr. 1884, the 23rd year of their existence. On May 31, 1884, a grand festival benefit was organised in Pasdeloup's honour at the Trocadéro, by which a sum of nearly 100,000 francs was raised; all French artists, whether composers, singers or instrumentalists, joined to contribute towards assuring a competence for the excellent man who had done so much to make the fortunes of many artists without furthering his own interests. In the winter of 1885 Pasdeloup organised concerts at Monte

---

[1] Recruited from the pupils of the Conservatoire.

Carlo, and afterwards founded pianoforte classes in Paris. At the conclusion of the educational course he gave paying concerts of chamber music. In Oct. 1886, after Godard had failed (in 1884) in his attempt to reconstruct the Concerts Populaires, Pasdeloup began a new series with the old title, giving one concert a month from Oct. 1886 to Mar. 1887, with a sacred concert on Good Friday.  A. J.

PASINO, detto Ghizzolo Stefano, of Brescia ; in 1642 town organist of Lonato ; in 1651 maestro di cappella of Salo. He wrote masses *a* 4 v., op. 4 (1642) ; motets *a* 2, 3 and 4 concerted parts, op. 6 (1651) ; XII. sonatas for 2, 3 and 4 instruments, in one of which are imitated the cries of sundry wild animals, op. 8. It is curious to see this childish trick, which had been shown by Carlo Farina *c.* 1628, and later on by Paganini, treated in all seriousness. A collection of Ricercari for instruments appeared as op. 7 (*Q.-L.* ; *Fétis*).          E. v. d. s.

PASQUALI (Paschali, Pascale), Francesco (*b.* Cosenza, late 16th cent.), studied and lived mostly in Rome ; composed three books of madrigals and several books of sacred and secular songs in 1-5 parts, between 1615–1633 (*Q.-L.*).

PASQUALI, Nicolò (*d.* Edinburgh, Oct. 13, 1757), a violinist and composer who settled in Edinburgh about 1740 until his death, with the exception of the years 1748–51, during which he lived in Dublin, producing his oratorio ' Noah ' at Fishamble Street Music Hall. He was in London in 1752, and then returned to Edinburgh. He published numerous compositions, an opera called ' L' ingratitudine punita,' songs in ' The Tempest,' ' Apollo and Daphne ' and ' The Triumph of Hibernia,' as well as the ' Solemn Dirge in Romeo and Juliet.' Most of these are printed in the ' XII English Songs in Score,' dated 1750, and published in London. Two sets of sonatas, one for violin and bass, and one for two violins, tenor and thorough-bass, were also published in London. ' XII Overtures for French horns ' were printed in Edinburgh, ' for Rob. Bremner, the assigney of Signor Pasquali ' ; and the book by which his name is best known, *Thoroughbass made Easy*, was published in Edinburgh in the year of his death. About three years after his death his *Art of Fingering the Harpsichord* was published in Edinburgh.          M.

PASQUINI, Bernardo (*b.* Massa di Valnevola, Tuscany, Dec. 8, 1637 ; *d.* Nov. 22, 1710[1]), an important musician of the latter half of the 17th century. His masters were Loreto Vittori and Antonio Cesti, but the study of Palestrina's works did more for him than any instruction. While still young he came to Rome, and was appointed organist of Sta. Maria Maggiore.

Among his numerous pupils were Durante **and** Gasparini ; the Emperor Leopold also sent young musicians to benefit by his instruction. Special mention is made of an opera, ' Dov' è amore e pietà,' produced at the Teatro Capranica in 1679, and of another in 1686, in honour of Queen Christina of Sweden. Mattheson, on visiting the opera-house in Rome, was much struck at finding Corelli playing the violin, Pasquini the harpsichord and Gattani the lute, all in the orchestra. Pasquini's music is terse, vigorous and at the same time graceful ; in fact he had much in common with Handel, and exercised a certain amount of influence upon German musicians. A ' favola pastorale,' or small opera in three parts, called ' La forza d' amore ' (libretto by Apolloni, a gentleman in Prince Chigi's household), is fine, and elevated in style. Copies are in the Fitzwilliam Museum at Cambridge, the Brussels Conservatoire and the Istituto Musicale at Florence. Five oratorios are mentioned in *Q.-L.*, as well as six more operas. His contributions to various collections of harpsichord music are more important ; one such collection was printed at Amsterdam in 1704, and another by Walsh, probably later. Selected sonatas were published by Novello in an album of music by Pasquini and Grieco, edited by J. S. Shedlock, whose *Pianoforte Sonata* contains an interesting chapter on Pasquini.          F. G., with addns.

BIBL.—Ch. van den Borren, *Note sur Bernardo Pasquini et ses œuvres. Bulletin de la Société de Musicologie*, 1921.
Reprints —Farrenc, *Trésor des pianistes III* ; J. S. Shedlock, *Pieces by Pasquini* ; F. Boghen, (1) *Dieciarie per cembalo or organo* (Casa editua musicale Italiana, Florence), (2) *Deux Sonates pour 2 clavecins* (Paris) ; Torchi, *Arte musicale in Italia III.* contains three pieces.

PASSACAGLIA, Passacaglio, Passecaille, an early Italian or Spanish dance, similar in character to a Chaconne (*q.v.*).

The name (according to Littré) is derived from the Spanish *pasar*, ' to walk,' and *calle*, ' a street,' in which case a passacaglia may mean a tune played in the streets by itinerant musicians. This derivation is confirmed by Walther's *Lexicon*, where the name is translated by ' Gassenhauer.' Other authorities have attempted to connect the word passacaglia with *gallo*, ' a cock ' ; thus Mendel translates it ' Hahnentrapp.' The original dance was performed by one or two dancers ; it survived in France until the 18th century, and directions for dancing it may be found in Feuillet's *Chorégraphie*. But the feature which, in common with the chaconne, has elevated the passacaglia above the majority of dance forms, is the construction of the music on a Ground Bass (*q.v.*), generally consisting of a short theme of two, four or eight bars.

This form attracted the attention of the organ and harpsichord composers of the 17th and 18th centuries, with whom the construction of elaborate passacaglias and chaconnes became a favourite exercise for contrapuntal skill. It is somewhat difficult to ascertain in what the difference between these two dance forms consists. Mattheson,[1] a contemporary authority, distinguishes four points : the chaconne was slower and more stately than the passacaglia ; the former was always in a major key, the latter in a minor ; passacaglias were never sung ; and chaconnes were always on a ground bass. The above distinction of keys is not borne out by the specimens that have come down to us, and the passacaglia is, if anything, generally of a more solemn character than the chaconne. The only material difference between the two seems to be that in the chaconne the theme is kept invariably in the bass, while in the passacaglia it was used in any part, often so disguised and embroidered amid ever-varying contrapuntal devices as to become hardly recognisable. Among the most celebrated passacaglias may be mentioned those by Buxtehude, Bach (B.-G. vol. xv.), Couperin, Frescobaldi (*Toccate d' intavolatura*, vol. i.) and Handel (Suite VII. and the fourth sonata of ' VII Sonatas or Trios ').

There are also in existence some curious ' Passagagli flebili,' by Salvatore Mazzella, in his ' Balli, Correnti, Gighe, Gavotte, Brande, e Gagliarde, con la misura giusta per ballare al stile Inglese ' (Rome, 1689).    **W. B. S.**

PASSAGE. The word ' passage ' is used of music in the same general sense that it is used of literature, without any special implication of its position or relations in the formal construction of a work, but merely as a portion which can be identified through some characteristic trait or conterminous idea.

Thus in modern writings on music such expressions as ' passage in first violins,' ' passage in strict counterpoint,' 'passage where the basses go gradually down through two octaves,' show that the amount or extent of music embraced by the term is purely arbitrary, and may amount to two bars or to two pages at the will of the person using the term, so long as the definition, epithet or description given with it sufficiently covers the space so as to make its identification easy and certain ; short of this the word by itself conveys no meaning.

It is, however, sometimes used in a special and not altogether commendatory sense, of runs and such portions of music as are meaningless except as opportunities for display of dexterity on the part of executants, which are therefore in fact and by implication nothing more than ' passages.' In this respect literature and language are fortunate in having long ago arrived at such a pitch of development that it is hardly possible to find a counterpart except in the byways of gushing sentimental poetry or after-dinner oratory. It is possible that the musical use of the term originated in the amount of attention and labour which executants have

had, especially in former days, to apply to such portions of the works they undertook, and the common habit of speaking of practising ' passages,' growing by insensible degrees to imply practising what it is hardly worth the while of an intelligent audience to listen to, except for the sake of the technique. It is probable that this use of the word in its special sense, except for mere exercises, will become less frequent in proportion to the growth of public musical intelligence.    **C. H. H. P.**

PASSAGGIO, ' passage.' This word is used in two senses : (1) of the passing from one key to another—hence used for all modulations ; (2) of bravura ornaments introduced, either in vocal or instrumental music, whether indicated by the composer or not, in order to show off the skill of the performer. Bach uses Passaggio for a ' flourish ' at the beginning of the Prelude to the Suite in E minor (B.-G. xlv. p. 149). **M.**

PASSAMEZZO (PASSEMEZZO), an old Italian dance which was probably a variety of the PAVAN. In England, where it was popular in Queen Elizabeth's time, it was sometimes known as the ' Passing Measures Pavan.'[2] Tabourot in his *Orchésographie* says that when the pavan was played less solemnly and more quickly, it was called a ' Passemezzo.' Hawkins says that the name is derived from ' *passer*, to walk, and *mezzo*, middle or half,' and that the dance was a diminutive of the galliard ; but both these statements are probably incorrect. Praetorius (*Syntagma*, iii. 24) says that as a galliard has five steps, and is therefore called a ' Cinquepas,' so a ' Passamezzo ' has scarcely half as many steps as the latter, and is therefore called ' mezzo passo.' These derivations seem somewhat far-fetched, and it is probable that the name ' Passemezzo ' (in which form it is found in the earliest authorities) is simply an abbreviation of ' Passo e mezzo,' *i.e.* a step and a half, which may have formed a distinctive feature of the old dance. Reismann (*Geschichte der Musik*, ii. 22) quotes a ' Pass e mezzo antico,' from Jacob Paix's ' Ein Schön Nutz Lautentabulaturbuch,' in which periods of eight bars can be distinguished. It is written with five variations and a ' ripresa.'

Full directions for dancing the passamezzo may be found in Caroso da Sermoneta's curious works *Il Ballarino* (Venice, 1581) and *Nobiltà di dame* (*ib.* 1600), from which the following example is taken :

[2] In a MS. volume of airs and dances by Strogers, Dowland and Reade, preserved in the Cambridge University Library, it is called ' Passmezures Pavan.' See *Twelfth Night*, Act v. Sc. 1.

At page 102 of the 'Fitzwilliam Virginal Book' there is a 'Passamezzo Pavana' by William Byrd, and at page 142 another (dated 1592) by Peter Philips; both are written in an elaborate style, and followed by a 'Galiarda Passamezzo.' See published edition, vol. i. pp. 203, 209, 299, 306.

W. B. S.

PASSARINI, FRA FRANCESCO (b. Bologna, first half of 17th cent.; d. there, 1698), Franciscan monk, maestro di cappella of S. Francesco, Bologna, 1671; and in 1672 in his own monastery. He composed oratorios, masses, psalms, motets and other church music (*Fétis*; *Q.-L.*).

PASSEPIED (English PASPY), a dance which originated amongst the sailors of Basse Bretagne, and is said to have been first danced in Paris by street-dancers in the year 1587. It was introduced into the ballet in the time of Louis XIV., and was often included in instrumental suites and partitas; it was placed among the 'intermezzi,' or dances which strictly form no part of the SUITE (*q.v.*), but were sometimes introduced into it between the saraband and the final gigue. Bach, however, does not adhere to this rule, but in his partita in B minor places the passepied before the saraband. In character the passepied somewhat resembles the minuet, but it is played much faster, and should always begin on the last beat of the bar, although in some examples, chiefly by English composers, it begins on the first beat. It is written in 3-4 or 3-8 time, and generally consists of two, three or four parts of eight or sixteen bars each, played with two or more repeats.

In the suite the first part (or first two parts, if the passepied consists of three or four divisions) is generally in a major key, and the last part (or last two parts, if it consists of four divisions) forms a sort of trio or second passepied, and is in the minor, in which key the dance concludes. Couperin develops this still further, and has a passepied with variations. The dance became popular in England towards the beginning of the 18th century, and many examples by English composers are extant. Directions for dancing it,[1] as it was performed in the ballet by one or two dancers, will be found in Feuillet's *Chorégraphie*. (See ARBEAU.)

W. B. S.

PASSING NOTES are in essential discordant notes which are interposed between the essential

---

[1] The proper expression seems to be ' to run a Passepied.' Thus Noverre, *Lettres sur la danse*, p. 164, has the following : ' Ils font des *Passepieds* parce que Mademoiselle Prévôt les *couroit* avec élégance.'

factors of the harmonic structure of music on melodic principles. See HARMONY.

PASSION MUSIC (Lat. *cantus passionis Domini nostri Jesu Christi*; Ger. *Passionsmusik*). A musical presentation of the Gospel story of the Passion of Jesus Christ, five varieties of which can be distinguished : (1) Choral Passion ; (2) Motet Passion ; (3) Scenic Passion ; (4) Oratorio Passion ; (5) Passion Oratorio.

THE CHORAL PASSION.—Recitation of the Gospel narratives of the Passion in Holy Week is of very ancient usage. As early as the 4th century St. Matthew's (chaps. xxvi. xxvii.) was prescribed on Palm Sunday (*Dominica Passionis*); St. Luke's (chaps. xxii. xxiii.) on the following Wednesday. In addition, by the 8th and 9th century, St. Mark's (chaps. xiv. xv.) was enjoined for Tuesday in Holy Week; St. John's (chaps. xviii. xix.) for Good Friday (*dies parasceve*). It was customary then for the Deacon of the Mass, wearing the alb, to recite the prescribed Gospel at the altar, distinguishing the words of Christ from the general narrative by using the Gospel tone, *i.e.* inflexions and cadences. In the 12th century this simple ritual was superseded by one more complex and dramatic, in which the narrative was recited by three ' Deacons of the Passion,' of whom the Deacon intoned the narrative text, the Subdeacon represented the people (*turba*) and individual characters other than Christ, while the Priest intoned the Saviour's utterances. Since the intention was vividly to impress the Passion story upon a congregation ignorant of Latin, the voices of the three clergy were contrasted, the Deacon a tenor (*media vox*), the Priest a bass (*bassa vox*), the Sub-deacon an alto (*suprema vox*). The reciting-note (*tonus currens*, *Hauptton*) of each was the highest in the plain-song formula allotted to it.

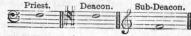

The complete compass of the three *voces* was three tetrachords, an octave and a half :

The plain-song formulas were of the following character :

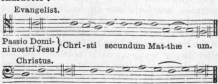

Turba.

*Non in di-e, etc., fie-ret in po-pu-lo,*

The cadences used by the Evangelist (Deacon)
differed according to the *vox* that followed him,
moving *up* to the *suprema vox* and *down* to the
*bassa vox*. The persistence of these traditional
cadences permits their illustration from Thomas
Mencken's (Mancinus) Passion (1610), whose
harmonised Turba, however, is not characteristic of early use :

Evangelist.

*Und* {*es begab sich, da Jesus* / *alle diese Rede vollendet*} *hatte, sprach*
Christus.

*er zu seinen Jung-ern.* {*Ihr wisset, dass* / *nach zweien Tagen*}

*O-stern wird, und* {*des Menschen Sohn wird* / *überantwortet wer-*}

*den, dass er ge-kreu-zi-get · · wer-de.*

Evangelist.

*Da* {*versammelten sich die* / *Hohenpriester, etc.,*} *und hiel-ten*

*Rath, etc. Sie spra - - chen a-ber.*

Turba (4 parts).

*Ja, nicht auf · · das Fest,    auff dass nicht*

*· · · ein Auf-ruhr wer-de im Volck.*

The Saviour's cry, **Eli, Eli, lama asabthani,**
invariably was sung to a more expressive formula than the severer plain-song otherwise
prescribed. The early Lutheran composers
adopted it; it appears alike in the Passions of
Johann Walther (*c.* 1530) and Thomas Mencken
(1610):

E · · · · · · · · · li,

E · · · · · · · · li.

*la-ma · a-sab-tha-ni.*

Sung exclusively to plain-song or liturgical
melody (hence *Choralpassion*) this type of
Passion prevailed throughout the Middle Ages.
But a ritual of such solemnity naturally reacted
to the progressive musical apparatus. Discovering in it a high theme for musical illustration,
16th century composers either (1) harmonised
the whole Gospel text as *a cappella* music
(*Motettepassion*), or (2), retaining the solo plain-
song for the utterances of Christ and the Evangelist, harmonised the Turba sentences (*forma
scenica in certas personas distributa*).

THE MOTET PASSION.—The earliest example
of this species was composed by the Dutchman
Jakob Obrecht (Hobrecht) (*d.* 1505) for the
Duke of Ferrara. Written for four voices
(D.A.T.B.), it begins with the traditional *Introitus, Exordium,* or *Praefatio,* 'Passio Domini
nostri Jesu Christi secundum Matthaeum,' and
ends with the customary *Conclusio,* 'Qui
passus es pro nobis miserere nobis. Amen.'
Its text actually is a mosaic of the four Gospels
from which subsidiary episodes are excluded,
*e.g.* Christ's anointing, and the Institution of
the Holy Supper. The work is divided into
three Parts; the first ends with Christ's 'Tu
dixisti' to Pilate, the second records His condemnation, the third His crucifixion and death.
As was usual, the music is in the transposed Ionian mode. The following example
illustrates Obrecht's treatment of the traditional plain-song as a *canto fermo* :

*In il-lo tem - - po -*

*In il - - lo tem-po-re*

Evangelist (*canto fermo*).

*In il-lo tem - po-re*

*il - - · · lo tem - - po-*

*-re di-xit Je-sus di-sci-pu-lis*

*di-xit Je-sus di-sci - pu-lis*

*di-xit Je-sus di-sci - pu-lis · ·*

*-re di-xit Je-sus di-sci-pu-lis*

Obrecht writes his Turba passages in four-part harmony. Christ, Judas and Pilate usually speak in two parts, one of them, in the case of the Saviour, a bass. In this respect, and in his retention of the conventional formulas, Obrecht was essentially conservative. Printed by Georg Rhau at Wittenberg in 1538, his Passion had wide vogue and influence. Johannes Galliculus (c. 1520–50), the first German composer of a Latin Passion, Ludwig Daser (d. 1589), Vincenzo Ruffo (b. 1554), Jakob Handl (Gallus) (1550–91), Jakob Regnart (1540–1600), Bartholomäus Gesius (1555 ?– 1613 or 1614), writing for a varying number of parts (4, 6 or 8), and with an increasing disposition to disregard the old formulas, all wrote Latin Passions of the Motet form and generally followed Obrecht's method.

It will be shown in a subsequent paragraph that Passion music found its way immediately into the Lutheran service. Here it must be remarked that in 1568 Joachim von Burgk (Möller or Müller) (d. 1616) composed the earliest Motet Passion in the German vernacular, 'Die deutsche Passion, das ist, die Historia des Leidens unsers Herrn Jhesu Christi, nach dem Evangelisten S. Johanne in Figural Gesang.' In a Preface he acknowledges his debt to 'der berümbte Musicus' Obrecht; but his model was Orlando di Lasso—'Orlandum quantum possem imitarer.' The old Passion formulas are faintly reproduced and he writes his *Conclusio* to the words, 'Wir glauben, lieber Herr, mehre unsern Glauben. Amen.' In one text his Passion is followed by Gallus's Motet: 'Ecce quomodo moritur justus,' an association which survived at Leipzig into Bach's cantorate. German Motet Passions were also written by Johannes Steurlin (1576), Johann Machold (1593), and Christoph Demantius (1631).

The Scenic Passion.—While Luther advocated the observance of Holy Week—'die Marterwoche lassen wir bleiben '—he preferred a single recitation of the Passion narrative by the minister, 'auf dem Predigtstuhl,' either on Palm Sunday or Good Friday, 'solches ist dem Volk mehr nütz, denn da man die Passion laut sang und die Priester giengen davon, die Laien aber verstunden es nicht.' But the tradition of the musical Passion prevailed, and before 1530 Johann Walther, Luther's coadjutor, composed

the earliest Lutheran Passion, eight years at least before Galliculus produced the first vernacular example of the Motet type.

Johann Walther's (1496–1570) setting of St. Matthew's text was probably composed 1522–1527, certainly before 1530, the date of a MS. Tenor part in the Luther Codex. It represents the earliest association of the ancient plain-song formulas with Luther's vernacular New Testament (1522), from which occasionally it differs, anticipating the reformer's subsequent revision. The Gospel text proceeds uninterruptedly between the traditional *Exordium*, 'Das Leiden unsers Herrn Jhesu Christi,' etc., and a new *Conclusio* or *Gratiarum actio*, 'Danck sey unserm Herren Jhesu Christo, der uns erlöset hat durch sein Leiden von der Helle.' The Evangelist is a tenor, in whose plain-song melody the most signal departure from tradition is the adoption of a uniform cadence to introduce the utterances of Christ (bass) and the Turba (D.A.T.B.) :

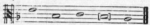

The minor individual characters are allotted to an alto voice, their several utterances generally being introduced by the Evangelist's cadence :

Walther's Turba passages are in the simplest four-part *faux bourdon* harmony, of which the following example is typical :

Walther's Passion had a remarkable vogue and was widely printed and used. It appears anonymously in Gottfried Vopelius's Leipzig hymn-book (1682), and was in use there until 1721. At Nürnberg it was sung in 1806. The text is not divided into Parts. But in general use the Sermon followed the Saviour's desertion by the disciples (St. Matth. xxvi. 56; St. John xviii. 27), leaving His trial and crucifixion for Part II.; while a pause for a silent Lord's Prayer followed the words, 'Jesus yielded up the ghost' (St. Matth. xxvii. 50; St. John xix. 30). In Leipzig use Walther's setting of the St. Matthew Passion was sung at Vespers on Palm Sunday. A similar setting of St. John's narrative (also in Vopelius) was sung at the corresponding service on Good Friday.

A generation after Walther, Antonio Scandelli (1517–80) wrote (*ante* 1561) a St. John Passion for the Dresden court chapel, which unites the characteristics of the Motet and Scenic types. The Evangelist (tenor) employs the conventional plain-song. Otherwise the music is in two-part to five-part vocal harmony. Pilate's words are usually sung by three, occasionally by two, parts; Peter's, by three; the high priest's officer's (chap. xviii. 22), by two; the maid's, by three; Christ's and the high priest's servant's (chap. xviii. 26), by four. Christ's utterances alone have the richer harmony of D.A.T.B., a distinction anticipatory of the instrumental accompaniment to the Saviour's words in Bach's St. Matthew Passion. The Turba sentences throughout are in five parts (D1, D2, A.T.B.), and in dramatic force show a marked advance upon Walther's *faux bourdons*:

Walther's and Scandelli's Passions may be accepted as types of the Scenic Passion produced by Protestant and Roman Catholic musicians in the 16th and early 17th centuries.

Notable among the composers of German texts are: Jakob Meiland (1542–77) (St. John, 1568; St. Matthew, 1570), Bartholomäus Gesius (1555?–1613 or 1614) (St. John, 1588), Thomas Mencken (1550–1620) (St. Matthew and St. John, 1610), Samuel Besler (1574–1625) (all four Evangelists, 1612), Melchior Vulpius (*d.* 1615) (St. Matthew, 1613), Otto Siegfried Harnisch (*d.* 1630) (St. John, 1621). Among the composers of Latin texts: Claude de Sermisy (*d.* 1562) (St. Matthew, 1534), Orlando di Lasso (*d.* 1594) (all four Evangelists, 1575–94), Jakob Reiner (*d.* 1606) (St. John, St. Matthew and St. Mark, *post* 1579), Giovanni Matteo Asola (*d.* 1609) (St. Matthew, St. Mark, St. Luke), Tomás Luis Victoria (*d. circa* 1613) (St. Matthew and St. John, 1585), Francisco Guerrero (1528–99) (St. Matthew and St. John), and William Byrd (1543–1623) (St. John, 1607), whose three-part Turba choruses anticipate Schütz in concise dramatic intention, *e.g.*:

THE ORATORIO PASSION.—With Heinrich Schütz (1585–1672) the Italian style entered Germany to influence Passion music. Four Passions are attributed to him, of which only those according to St. Matthew (1661), St. Luke and St. John are authentic. So far as relates to their text they do not differ materially from those of Walther and Scandelli. They begin with the conventional *Exordium*; the Bible narrative is followed without interruption; and a *Gratiarum actio* closes the work. Excepting the Turba choruses and the Duet of the false witnesses the Passions are written for a solo voice. There are no arias and no reflective Chorals, though stanza viii. of 'Christus der uns selig macht' (with its melody) concludes the St. John. The Evangelist's (tenor) recitative is written in a sort of Gregorian notation, and, though it lacks the sensitiveness of Bach's text, is flexible and moves easily with the words; *e.g.* from the St. Matthew Passion:

Christ's recitative (bass) is arioso in character. Departing from tradition, Schütz breaks the text in order to obtain dramatic effect; *e.g.* from the St. Matthew Passion:

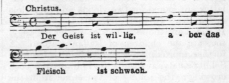

The four-part choruses, vivid and dramatic, are the ancestors of Bach's; *e.g.* from the St. John Passion:

heaven is marked by a fall from a high note. The disciples' 'Lord, is it I?' is treated in Bach's manner:

Probably Schütz proposed an organ accompaniment for the Passions, in none of which is one provided. In his Christmas and Easter oratorios the recitatives are accompanied by figured *continuo*, while the choruses of the latter are scored for two violins and four viole da gamba. In their dramatic force Schütz's Passions are the ancestors of Bach's, as they, too, are the children of Italian oratorio. A further approximation to Bach's art is found in Schütz's naïve realism. He imitates the cock crowing; the rolling of the stone from the sepulchre invites a passage of descending quavers, each group of which carries an accent to suggest propulsion; an angel's descent from

Schütz approached the Passion in a new spirit, exhibiting an emotion no longer repressed and employing an idiom no longer formal. But he made no innovation in the libretto. The Gospel narrative proceeds uninterruptedly, without pauses for reflective or devotional comment. The *Exordium* and *Gratiarum actio* constitute the only prose additions to the Bible text; and, with the single exception already noticed, hymn stanzas, so appropriate as a vehicle of devotion, are excluded. Having regard to the ends which the performance was designed to serve, these omissions were a defect. But before the close of the 17th century considerable progress was made. Lyrical stanzas suitable for aria treatment were admitted; the introduction of Chorals engaged the congregation in a solemn ritual of remembrance; a figured *continuo* supported the recitatives, orchestral accompaniments the arias and choruses; the recitatives, shaking loose the formulas of an earlier school, became increasingly plastic and expressive; the choruses increased in dramatic significance; and the music generally adjusted itself to the new standards of the period. Thus, the Oratorio Passion came into being, a composition in which the traditions of the Passion remained uppermost—the Bible narrative, the Gospel characters, hymns of the Passion. Not until the 18th century were these characteristics disturbed.

The earliest examples of the new Passion are discovered in Hamburg, an active centre of musical experiment. Thomas Selle (1599–1663), one of C. P. E. Bach's predecessors as cantor there, left in MS. a St. John Passion ' à 6 cum Capella à 5,' a St. Matthew Passion ' in dialogo à 10 ' (1642), and a second setting of St. John's narrative, ' mit 6 Vocal- und 6 Instrumentalstimmen sampt einer vocal-capella à 5 einfaltigst pro choro remoto und dem Choro pro organo à 4 gesetzt in stylo recitativo ' (*i.e.* oratorio) (1643). The last is remarkable especially for an elaborate orchestral scheme which distinguishes the characters by particular accompanying instruments ; the Evangelist (tenor) by two fagotti (or viole da gamba) and two ' Pandoren ' (an instrument of the lute family) ; Christ (bass) by two violins and two lutes. Into each of his three Parts also, borrowing a term used by Schütz in his *Weihnachts-Oratorium*, Selle introduces an ' Intermedium ' (Intermezzo). The first, in nine parts, is a setting of Isaiah liii. 4 ff. and follows Christ's question, 'Wherefore smitest thou me?' The second, also in nine parts, on Psalm xxii. 1, follows ' We have a law, and by our law he ought to die.' The third, a Choral concerto on the melody ' O Lamm Gottes unschuldig,' for chorus and organ, concludes the work.

In the year following Selle's death, Thomas Strutius, organist in Danzig, produced (1664) a setting of St. Matthew's text, the MS. of which has not survived. Scored for strings and in four ' Acts,' the work included eight Chorals, four of which were set as arias, three as five-part choruses, and one (' Erbarm dich mein, O Herre Gott ') for solo, chorus, organ and viole. They began and ended the work and followed Christ's institution of the Holy Supper, Peter's denial, the death of Judas, and other incidents, the last-named being accompanied by a ' vierstimmig - bebenden (tremolo) Saitenspiel.' In some of these innovations Strutius anticipated Johann Sebastiani (1622–83), who introduced (1672) into his St. Matthew Passion a number of Chorals as descant solos with strings and *continuo* accompaniment deliberately 'zur Erweckung mehrer Devotion' in the congregation. The *continuo* accompanies the Evangelist, and Christ's utterances are supported by strings, as in Bach's St. Matthew Passion. The conventional *Conclusio* is preceded by a short (17 bars) Interlude for 4 viole and *continuo* :

Sebastiani's work marks the transition of the Passion into its oratorio form. Its characteristics were repeated in the Passions of Johann Theile (1646–1724) and Johann Valentin Meder (1649–1719) ; and in 1721 Johann Kuhnau (1660–1722), Bach's immediate predecessor at St. Thomas's, brought the oratorio form to Leipzig with his St. Mark Passion, superseding Walther's version, which for so many generations had been sung there.

THE PASSION ORATORIO.—Meanwhile, the influence of Italian art deflected Passion music from the traditions which so long had governed it. Early in the 18th century a new libretto found favour which rejected the literal Bible text, substituted a rhymed paraphrase, and insinuated lyrical stanzas of reflective commentary. Erdmann Neumeister's first cycle of cantata texts (1700) led the way. He defined a cantata as ' a fragment of Opera,' and Johann Adolf Scheibe, in the *Kritischer Musikus* of 1737, distinguished the cantata from the oratorio only in the more dramatic purpose of the latter ; the oratorio from the opera only in the surroundings in which it was performed. In their Italian development, in fact, the two differed only in the topics that inspired them. The Hamburg critic, Johann Mattheson, insisted (1739) that ' An oratorio is merely a sacred opera.' Therefore, if it was inevitable that the Passion story should be treated as an oratorio of the Italian type, circumstances ordained that the experiment should be made at Hamburg, where, in 1678, Johann Adam Reinken and others established an opera-house to produce the new art form. In view of the imminent appearance of the operatic Passion, it is significant that the Hamburg Opera opened with a Biblical subject, Theile's ' Adam and Eva ' whose production required the services of a *maître de ballet*! It was followed by ' Michal und David ' (1679), ' Esther ' (1680), ' Kain und Abel ' (1689), and others.

In 1704 the Passion succumbed to the popular inclination to dramatise Biblical stories, in a setting by Reinhard Keiser (1674–1739) of Christian Friedrich Hunold-Menantes's *Der blutige und sterbende Jesus*, an ' Oratorio musicalisch gesetzt.' The libretto, rhymed throughout, contained no Chorals, and dispensed with the Biblical narrative. The author cast the work in the form of three cantatas or ' Soliloquia ' : the Lamentations of Mary Magdalene ; the Tears of Peter ; the Love-song of Zion's Daughter, a character adopted later by Brockes, Picander and Bach. Its theatrical music and the elimination of the Bible narrative invited grave displeasure and even public condemnation by one of the Hamburg clergy. It found imitators, however, in Johann Ulrich König's *Tränen unter dem Kreuze Jesu*, to which Keiser put music in 1711 ; Johann Georg Seebach's *Der leidende und sterbende Jesus*, published at

Gotha in 1714; Joachim Beccau's *Heilige Fastenlust, oder das Leyden und Sterben unseres Heilandes Jesu Christ* (1719); Johann Philipp Kafer's *Der leidende und sterbende Jesus* (1719); and Benjamin Neukirch's *Der weinende Petrus* (1721), in the libretto of which actually stage directions were printed to assist the listener mentally to dramatise its episodes.

BACH.—The flippant tone of these operatic texts stirred a reaction, which declared itself first in Postel's St. John Passion, set to music by Handel in 1704. It reinstated the Evangelist and the Bible text, though the libretto otherwise was not without blemish. In 1712 Barthold Hinrich Brockes, a member of the Hamburg Council, wrote a Passion text which avoided the more glaring indecencies of Hunold-Menantes's, and obtained remarkable popularity among composers. Brockes's Passion, *Der für die Sünden der Welt gemarterte und sterbende Jesus*, is rhymed throughout. After an opening chorus, the text begins with a versified rendering of the institution of the Holy Supper as narrated by St. Matthew xxvi. 26 :

*Recit.*
'Als Jesus nun zu Tische sasse,
Und Er das Osterlamm, das Bild von seinem Tod,
Mit seinen Jüngern asse,
Nahm Er das Brod ;
Und wie Er es dem Höchsten dankend brach,
Gab Er es ihnen hin und sprach :

JESUS
Das ist mein Leib : kommt, nehmet, esset,
Damit ihr meiner nicht vergesset.'

Christ's agony on the Mount of Olives follows, and is freely treated by the librettist; the Saviour's ' Thy will be done ' is parodied in a four-line stanza as an aria. The Evangelist interpolates a picture of the Saviour's distress :

'Das bange Herz fing an so stark zu klopfen,
Dass blutge Schweiss in ungezahlten Tropfen
Aus seinen Adern drang.'

Judas's act of betrayal follows :

JUDAS
'Nimm, Rabbi, diesen Kuss von mir.

JESUS
Mein Freund, sag ! warum kommst du hier ? '

Peter denounces the betrayer in a vigorous aria and, after the Saviour's rebuke, proclaims his resolution to follow his Master :

'Hier ist Petrus ohne Schwert.
Lasst, was Jesus widerfährt,
Mir auch widerfahren.'

The scene of Peter's cowardly denial, Christ's appearance before Caiaphas, His trial by Pilate, condemnation, crucifixion and burial are told with severe compression of the Bible text, but with a wealth of lyrical commentary and pictorial detail in recitative and aria. The ' Daughter of Zion ' and ' The Faithful ' are prominent throughout, as in Picander's later texts, and five hymn-stanzas voice the emotion of the ' Christian Church.' If turgid and lacking in taste, the libretto, as a whole, is vivid and

pictorial. Keiser, Telemann, Mattheson, Handel, and more than twenty other composers set it within fifteen years of its appearance ; Bach himself borrowed some of its lyrics for his St. John Passion.

Thus when, on the eve of his settlement at Leipzig, Bach turned to the composition of Passion music, he found it divorced from its traditions, a compound of old and new forms, ideas, materials : sacred and secular in juxtaposition, the apparatus of Italian oratorio, operatic, non-ecclesiastical, and the Bible text with congregational Chorals. It was his individual achievement to assimilate these incongruities. Accepting the Neumeister libretto for the Passion, as for the cantata, he reinstated the Bible narrative ; infused a spiritual intention into the secular forms—aria and recitative—which the Passion had borrowed from the oratorio ; and reconciled the Choral with its context, to knit together and elevate the whole. In a task that was beyond Handel's ability, Bach triumphed as much by the simple piety of his character as by the splendour of his technique. Simultaneously with the appearance of his St. John Passion (1723) the Hamburg operatic Passion receded to the background, disappeared from North Germany during his lifetime, and survived elsewhere only where Italian influence prevailed.

The earliest catalogue of Bach's compositions, published in 1754, four years after his death, enumerates among his unprinted works, ' Fünf Passionem, worunter eine zweychörige befindlich ist.' Forkel repeated the statement half a century later (1802). It is probable, however, that Bach composed no more than four, of which the scores of two and portions of the music of a third alone are extant. The earliest of them, the St. John Passion, was written at Cöthen and produced at Leipzig on Good Friday 1723, shortly before Bach's induction as cantor. The significance of its libretto, whose construction may be attributed to Bach himself, is in its deliberate restoration of the Bible text, the comparative lack of lyrical material, and the prominence of Choral stanzas. Of its twelve lyrical numbers only three are original, and eight of the remainder are more or less borrowed from Brockes's text. Two years later (1725) Bach's literary collaborator, Christian Friedrich Henrici (Picander), published a Passion, *Über den leidenden Jesus*, rhymed and otherwise closely modelled upon Brockes's text. The Bible narrative is stated in the same meagre outline, Chorals are almost entirely excluded, and the personality of the Saviour is but faintly sketched. It cannot have satisfied Bach ; but, at the outset of his Leipzig career, he may have been willing to please his constituents with a Passion of the popular type. Four years later (1729) he produced the St. Matthew Passion, whose libretto, by Picander, clearly had been prepared under Bach's direction. It combines the characteristics of the Oratorio Passion and Passion Oratorio : the Bible text, Chorals, and ecclesiastical atmosphere of the one, the lyrical apparatus, textual and musical, of the other, harmonised by a mind intensely alert to the dramatic significance of the story but controlled by a religious sentiment deep but critical. The work is unapproachable, a masterpiece, dramatic but essentially devotional. Two years later (1731) Picander published a St. Mark Passion which was performed on Good Friday in that year. Inferior to its predecessor, it is upon the same literary design, and Bach put it to music, part of which survives in the ' Trauer-Ode ' (cf. BACH). A few years after Bach's death, Breitkopf's 1761 Catalogue attributed to him a St. Luke Passion, published as his in B.-G. Jhrg. xlv. (2), in 1898. But, like the score of Handel's setting of Brockes's text, the MS. is only partly Bach's autograph. The work is probably of North German origin.

Bach's Passions were performed on Good Fridays at Vespers, alternately in St. Thomas' and St. Nicholas' Churches, Leipzig. Such performances dated from 1721, when for the first time a Passion of the Oratorio type—Johann Kuhnau's St. Mark Passion—was produced. Bach's St. John Passion (1723) was the second or third [1] of the series, and was sung at St. Thomas'. The prescribed ceremonial was as follows : The bells were rung at 1.15 P.M. At 1.45 Johann Böschenstein's hymn, ' Da Jesus an dem Kreuze stund,' was sung. The first part of the Passion followed, and concluded with the hymn ' O Lamm Gottes unschuldig.' After the sermon, preceded by the hymn ' Herr Jesu Christ, dich zu uns wend,' the second part of the Passion was performed, followed by Jakobus Gallus's Motet, ' Ecce quomodo moritur justus.' The Passion Collect was intoned, Martin Rinkart's hymn ' Nun danket alle Gott ' was sung, and the service concluded with the Blessing.

LATER PASSIONS.—Since Bach's death (1750) the Passion has been treated by composers either in cantata or oratorio form, using the latter word in its modern meaning ; none has adventured to meet Bach upon his own ground. His son, C. P. E. Bach, wrote two Passions for Hamburg use (1787, 1788) (cf. BACH, C. P. E.), and his kinsman, Johann Ernst Bach (1722–77), composed a ' Passionsoratorium ' (published in D.D.T. Bd. 48). Graun's ' Der Tod Jesu ' (1755) alone has challenged the popularity of Bach's Passions in Germany. The other most important works inspired by the Passion are Haydn's ' Die

---

sieben Worte am Kreuze ' (1785), Beethoven's ' Christus am Ölberg ' (1803), Spohr's ' Des Heilands letzte Stunden ' (1835), and Lorenzo Perosi's ' La Passione di Jesu Cristo, secondo San Marco ' (1897). Their popularity in England requires mention of Stainer's ' Crucifixion ' (1887), Lee Williams's ' Gethsemane ' (1892), and Arthur Somervell's ' The Passion of Christ ' (1914).

### BIBLIOGRAPHY

GUIDO ADLER : Handbuch der Musikgeschichte. (Frankfurt a./M., 1924.)
JOH. SEB. BACH : Matthäuspassion and Johannespassion. Ed. Julius Rietz and Wilhelm Rust (B.-G. Jhrg. iv. u. xii. (1)).
CARL H. BITTER : Beiträge zur Geschichte des Oratoriums. (1872.)
PAUL GRAFF : Geschichte der Auflösung der alten gottesdienstlichen Formen in der evangelischen Kirche Deutschlands. (Göttingen, 1921 )
OTTO KADE : Die ältere Passionskomposition bis zum Jahre 1631. (Gütersloh, 1893.)
HERMANN KRETZSCHMAR : Führer durch den Konzertsaal, II. Abteilung, Bd I. (Leipzig, 1916.)
WALTER LOTT : Zur Geschichte der Passionskomposition von 1650–1800, Bückeburg Archiv für Musikwissenschaft, Jhrg. III. Pt. 3. (Bückeburg and Leipzig, n.d.)
JOACHIM MOSER : Aus der Frühgeschichte der deutschen Generalbasspassion, Jahrbuch Peters 1920. (Leipzig, 1921.)
RICHARD MÜNNICH : Geschichte der Passion, ' Kleine Handbücher der Musikgeschichte,' Breitkopf u. Härtel. (Leipzig, in the press.)
GUIDO PASQUETTI : L' oratorio musicale in Italia. (Florence, 1906 (1912).)
ANDRÉ PIRRO : L'Esthétique de J. S. Bach (Paris, 1907) ; Heinrich Schütz (Paris, 1913).
ARNOLD SCHERING : Geschichte des Oratoriums. (Leipzig, 1911.)
LUDWIG SCHOEBERLEIN : Schatz des liturgischen Chor- und Gemeindegesangs, Bd. II. 348 f. (Göttingen, 1868.)
HEINRICH SCHÜTZ : Werke : eine kritische Gesamtausgabe, in 16 Bdn., redigiert von Ph. Spitta. (Leipzig, 1885–94.)
RUDOLF SCHWARTZ : Das erste deutsche Oratorium, Jahrbuch Peters 1898. (Leipzig, 1899.)
ALBERT SCHWEITZER : J. S. Bach, vol. i. ch. 6. (London, 1911.)
JOHANN SEBASTIANI : Passionsmusik. Ed. Fr. Spitta. (D.D.T. Bd. XVII.)
FRIEDRICH SPITTA : Die Passionen von Heinrich Schütz. (Leipzig, 1886.)
PHILIPP SPITTA : Die Passionsmusiken von Sebastian Bach und Heinrich Schütz (Hamburg, 1893) ; Johann Sebastian Bach, vol. ii. Bk V. Sec. 7 (London, 1899).
C. S. TERRY. Joh. Seb. Bach : Cantata Texts (London, 1925) ; Bach : The Passions (Oxford, 1925).
JOHANN THEILE : Passionsmusik. Ed. Fr. Spitta (D.D.T. Bd. XVII.)
CARL VON WINTERFELD : Der evangelische Kirchengesang, Bd. III. Buch I. (Leipzig, 1847.)

C. S. T.

PASTA, GIUDITTA (b. Como, near Milan, 1798 ; d. there, Apr. 1, 1865), came of a Jewish family named Negri. She is said to have received her first instruction from the maestro di cappella at Como, Bartolomeo Lotti ; but, at the age of 15, she was admitted into the Conservatoire at Milan, under Asiolo. Her voice was then heavy and strong, but unequal and very hard to manage ; she never, in fact, succeeded in producing certain notes without some difficulty ; and, even in the zenith of her powers, there still remained a slight veil which was not dissipated until she had sung through a few scenes of an opera.

In 1815 she left the Conservatorio ; and, after trying her first theatrical steps on an amateur stage, she made her début in the theatres of Brescia, Parma and Leghorn, and later in Paris. A year later, 1816, she and her husband, Pasta, a tenor, were engaged by Ayrton, at a salary of £400 (together) for the season, for the King's Theatre. She appeared Jan. 11, 1817, in Cimarosa's ' Penelope ' and other rôles without obtaining success.

The young singer, however, did not despair. Though her voice was rebellious and her style

---

[1] The Custos Rost does not mention a performance in 1722, and states specifically that the first performance in St. Nicholas'—whose turn it was in 1722—took place in 1724. Bach very reluctantly bowed to authority in holding the service there in that year ; he complained that the accommodation was inadequate. The evidence points to his own Passions having been always performed in St. Thomas'.

as yet quite unfinished, she had many advantages even then which promised future excellence as the reward of unremitting and laborious study. Below the middle height, her figure was, nevertheless, very well proportioned ; she had a noble head with fine features, a high forehead, dark and expressive eyes, and a beautiful mouth. The dignity of her face, form and natural gestures fitted her eminently for tragedy, for which she was not wanting in the necessary fire and energy.

Having returned to Italy, she meditated seriously on the causes of her ill success, and studied for some time with Scappa. In 1819 she appeared at Venice, with marked effect ; and this first success was repeated at Rome and Milan, in that year and the next. In the autumn of 1821 she first attracted the attention of the Parisian public at the ' Italiens ' ; but it was after singing at Verona, during the congress of 1822, that she returned to Paris, where she at length became suddenly famous, and excited the wildest enthusiasm. Her voice, a splendid soprano, extending from the low A to the highest D, even then was not absolutely free from imperfection ; but the individuality of her impersonations, and the peculiar and penetrating expression of her singing, made the severest critics forget any faults of production in the sympathy and emotion she irresistibly created. She continued, however, to work, to study and to triumph over her harsh and rebellious organ by these means. ' Though but a moderate musician,' says Fétis, 'she instinctively understood that the kind of ornaments which had been introduced by Rossini could only rest a claim for novelty on their supporting harmony ' ; and she therefore invented the embellishments in arpeggio which were afterwards carried to a still higher pitch of excellence by Malibran. On Apr. 24, 1824, Pasta reappeared in London in ' Otello,' and had another enthusiastic success, which she followed up with ' Tancredi,' ' Romeo ' and ' Semiramide.' In Aug. 1827 she sang at the Theatre Royal, Dublin, appearing nine times at 100 guineas for each performance.

She then went to Italy and played at Trieste, and at Naples, where Pacini wrote ' Niobe ' for her. The Neapolitans failed to recognise her full merits, but she was better appreciated at Bologna, Milan, Vienna and Verona. At Milan, Bellini wrote for her the ' Sonnambula ' (1831) and ' Norma ' (1832).

From June to Sept. 1833, Pasta and Bellini were together in London, and in 1833 and 1834 she was once more at Paris, singing in ' Sonnambula ' and ' Anna Bolena.' Now, for the first time, her voice seemed to have lost something of its beauty and truth ; her intonation had become very uncertain, and she sang flat sometimes through the whole of an

opera. But her dramatic talent, far from being impaired, was even more remarkable than ever.

Once more in Italy, Pasta reappeared in a few of her famous rôles at some of the chief theatres, spending every summer at the beautiful villa which she had bought in 1829 near the Lake of Como, where she gave herself up to the delights of cultivating a magnificent garden.

Pasta sang again in England in 1837 ; but her voice was nearly gone. In 1840, though so long retired from the stage, she accepted an offer of 200,000 frs. to sing at St. Petersburg ; but it would have been better for her reputation as a singer had she refused it. The same may be said of her last visit to London, in 1850, when she only appeared twice in public.

Madame Pasta was said to have had only one child, a daughter ; but she had a son also, whom she mentions in a letter [1] to the Princess Belgiojoso, her ' Carissima Teresa.' She had some pupils, of whom Parodi was the most distinguished. This great singer died at her villa on the Lake of Como.

J. M. ; addn. W. H. G. F.

PASTERWITZ, GEORG (b. Bierhütten, Diocese of Passau, June 7, 1730 ; d. Kremsmünster, Jan. 26, 1803), received his education chiefly in the Benedictine Abbey of Kremsmünster, in Upper Austria, where music was zealously cultivated. He afterwards studied at Salzburg, and had lessons in counterpoint from Johann Ernst Eberlin, Kapellmeister to the Archbishop of Salzburg. He took the monastic vows in Kremsmünster, and was ordained priest in 1755, devoting himself for a while almost exclusively to music. His chief models were Fux, Caldara and Eberlin. From 1767–82 he was Kapellmeister to the Abbey, and was also largely employed in other educational work. From 1785–95 he lived chiefly at Vienna as Agent for the Abbey, and enjoyed friendly intercourse with Haydn, Mozart, Salieri and Albrechtsberger. Several of his masses were performed at St. Stephen's and the Imperial Chapel. His works, published by himself, were all instrumental, and consist of eight Fugues, according to the order of the Church Tones, described as being either for the organ or the clavicembalo, op. 1, dedicated to the Abbé Stadler ; eight Fugues, op. 2, dedicated to Salieri ; eight Fugues, op. 3, dedicated to the Baron van Swieten ; ' 300 Themata und Versetten zum präambuliren und fugiren mit orgel oder clavier,' op. 4. A Requiem Mass of his was afterwards printed at Munich, but an enormous quantity of his church music remains in MS. at Kremsmünster; also various works for the theatre. His fugues are of the light and pleasing order, rather than suited for the organ. E. von Werra has edited three in his organ book. 　　　J. R. M.

PASTICCIO, literally ' a pie,' a species of

---

[1] Formerly in the possession of the writer.

lyric drama composed of airs, duets and other movements, selected from different operas and grouped together, not in accordance with their original intention, but in such a manner as to provide a mixed audience with the greatest possible number of favourite airs in succession.

It is not at all necessary that the movements contained in a pasticcio should all be by the same composer.[1] During the greater part of the 18th century, when the pasticcio enjoyed its highest degree of popularity, some of the greatest masters then living patronised it openly, and apparently without any feeling of reluctance.

In early times it was a very common custom to mention the name of the librettist of an opera upon the public announcement of its performance, without that of the composer; and it seems exceedingly probable that when this was done, more than one composer was concerned, and the work was, in reality, a pasticcio. We know that Caccini contributed some of the music to Peri's ' Euridice ' in the year 1600, though his name does not appear upon the title-page; and that as early as 1646 a genuine pasticcio was performed, at Naples, under the title of ' Amor non a legge,' with music by several different composers, of whose names not one has been recorded. Such cases, however, are much rarer in the 17th century than in that which followed, and serve only to show how the practice of writing these compound operas originated.

Perhaps the most notable pasticcio on record is ' Muzio Scevola,' of which, in the year 1721, Filippo Mattei composed the first act, Giovanni Maria Bononcini the second, and Handel the third. Each composer prepared a complete overture to his own share of the work; and each, of course, did his best to outshine the efforts of his rivals; yet the opera survived very few representations, notwithstanding the éclat which attended its production; and it was never afterwards revived.

In the year 1746 Gluck produced at the King's Theatre, in the Haymarket, a pasticcio, called ' Piramo e Tisbe,' in which he introduced all his own most successful airs. (See OPERA.)

The leading principle of the Pasticcio has been frequently introduced into English operas, more especially those of the older school. The ' Beggar's Opera ' will occur to the reader as a notable instance of its application. But it must be remembered that in operas of this class the music is often only of an incidental character, and the objection to the system is, therefore, far less serious than in the case of Italian operas of the same, or even earlier, date. The ephemeral ' musical comedies' of our own day are generally the work of several composers or compilers, and so bear a certain analogy to the pasticcio above described.      W. S. R., rev.

[1] In 1789 a Pasticcio called ' L'Ape ' was produced at Vienna, in which no less than twelve composers were represented. (Pohl, *Mozart in London.* p. 75, note.)

PASTON, EDWARD, a 16th-century English musician, music-master of Princess (afterwards Queen) Mary, daughter of Henry VIII.; collected and (?) wrote in Italian lute tablature, several books of lute pieces, including some of his own composition (*Q.-L.*).

PASTORALE. (1) A dramatic composition or opera, the subject of which is generally of a legendary and pastoral character. Pastorales had their origin in Italy, where, at the time of the Renaissance, the study of the Eclogues of Theocritus and Virgil led to the stage representation of pastoral dramas such as Politian's 'Favola di Orfeo,' which was played at Mantua in 1472. The popularity of these dramatic pastorales spread from Italy to France and Spain, and eventually to Germany; but it is principally in France that they were set to music, and became of importance as precursors of the opera. In Apr. 1659 ' La Pastorale en musique,' the words by the Abbé Perrin, the music by Cambert, was performed at Issy, at the house of M. de Lahaye, and proved so successful that the same authors wrote another similar work, ' Pomone,' which was played in public with great success, Mar. 19, 1671. These two pastorales are generally considered as the earliest French operas. The pastorale, owing to the weakness of its plot, was peculiarly suited for the displays of ballet and spectacle which were so much in vogue at the French court, and examples of this type of composition exist by nearly all the French composers before the Great Revolution. Lully's ' Acis et Galathée ' (' Pastorale héroïque mise en musique ') is perhaps one of his finest compositions. Mattheson (*Vollkommener Kapellmeister*), with his passion for classifying, divides pastorales into the very obvious categories of comic and tragic, and gives some quaint directions for treating subjects in a pastoral manner. The pastorale must not be confounded with the pastourelle, which was an irregular form of poetry popular in France in the 12th and 13th centuries.

(2) Any instrumental or vocal composition in 6-8, 9-8 or 12-8 time (whether on a drone bass or not), which assumes a pastoral character by its imitation of the simple sounds and melody of a shepherd's pipe. The Musette and the Siciliana are both ' pastoral' forms; the former is of a slower tempo, and the latter contains fewer dotted quavers. ' He shall feed his flock' and the 'Pastoral Symphony ' in the ' Messiah ' are both in 12-8, and so is the Pastoral Sinfonia which begins the second part of Bach's Christmas Oratorio. Other examples of this class of composition are the first movement of Bach's Pastorale for organ (B.-G. xxxviii. p. 135), and the air ' Pour Bertha moi je soupire' in Meyerbeer's ' Le Prophète.' The ' Sonnambula' was originally entitled 'dramma pastorale.'      W. B. S.

PASTORAL OBOE, see SHEPHERD'S PIPE.

**PASTORAL SYMPHONY.** ' Sinfonia Pastorale, No. 6,' is the title of the published score of Beethoven's sixth symphony, in F, op. 68 (Breitkopf & Härtel, May 1826).

The autograph, in possession of the Baron van Kattendyke, of Arnheim, bears the following inscription in Beethoven's own writing :

' Sinf<sup>ia</sup> 6 ta. Da Luigi van Beethoven. Angenehme heitre Empfindungen welche bey der Ankunft auf dem Lande im Menschen erwa—Allo ma non troppo—Nicht ganz geschwind—N.B. die deutschen Überschriften schreiben sie alle in die erste Violini—Sinfonie von Ludwig van Beethoven ' ;

or, in English :

' 6th Symphony, by Luigi van Beethoven. The pleasant, cheerful feelings, which arise in man on arriving in the country—Allo ma non troppo—not too fast—N.B. [this is to the copyist] the German titles are all to be written in the first-violin part—Symphony by Ludwig van Beethoven.'

Besides the ' titles ' referred to in this inscription, which are engraved in the first violin part, on the back of the title-page, Beethoven has given two indications of his intentions—(1) on the programme of the first performance, Dec. 22, 1808, and (2) on the printed score. We give the three in parallel columns :

| First Violin Part. | Programme of Concert, Dec. 22, 1808. | Printed Score. |
|---|---|---|
| Pastoral Sinfonie oder Erinnerungen an das Landleben (mehr Ausdruck der Empfindung als Mahlerey). | Pastoral Symphonie (No. 5) mehr Ausdruck der Empfindung als Mahlerey. | Sinfonia Pastorale, No. 6. Erwachen heiterer Empfindungen bey der Ankunft auf dem Lande. Allo ma non troppo. |
| 1. Allegro ma non molto. Erwachen heiterer Empfindun en bey der Ankunft auf dem Lande. | 1stes Stück. Angenehme Empfindungen, welche bey der Ankunft auf dem Lande im Menschen erwachen. | Scene am Bach. Andante molto moto. Lustiges Zusammenseyn der Landleute. Allegro. |
| 2. Andante con moto. Scene am Bach. | 2tes Stück. Scene am Bach. | Gewitter. Sturm. Allegro. |
| 3. Allegro. Lustiges, Zusammenseyn der Landleute. | 3tes Stück. Lustiges Beysammenseyn der Landleute ; fällt ein | Hirtengesang. Frohe und dankbare Gefühle nach dem Sturm. Allegretto. |
| 4. Allegro. Gewitter. Sturm. | 4tes Stück. Donner und Sturm; in welches einfällt | |
| 5. Allegretto. Hirtengesang. Frohe und dankbare Gefühle nach dem Sturm. | 5tes Stück. Wohlthätige, mit Dank an die Gottheit verbundene Gefühle nach dem Sturm. | |
| Pastoral Symphony or Recol ections of country life. (More expression of fee.ing than painting.) | Pastoral Symphony (No. 5) more expression of feeling than painting. | Sinfonia Pastorale, No. 6. The awakening of cheerful feelings on arriving in the country. Allo ma non troppo. |
| 1. Allegro ma non molto. The awakening of cheerful feelings on arriving in the country | 1st piece. The pleasant feelings aroused in the heart on arriving in the country. | Scene at the brook. Andante molto moto. |
| 2. Andante con moto. Scene at the brook. | 2nd piece. Scene at the brook. | Merry meeting of country folk. Allegro. |
| 3. Allegro. Merry me:ting of country folk. | 3rd piece. Jovial assemblage of country folk, interrupted by | Thunderstorm, tempest. Allegro. |
| 4. Allegro. Thunderstorm, tempest. | 4th piece. Thunderstorm, interrupted by | Song of the shepherds. Glad and thankful feelings after the storm. Allegretto. |
| 5. Allegretto. Song of the shepherds. Glad and thankful feelings after the storm. | 5th piece. Pleasurable feelings after the storm, mixed with gratitude to God. | |

A book of sketches for the first movement, now in the British Museum, is inscribed ' Sinfonie caracteristica. Die Erinnerungen von dem Landleben ' ; with a note to the effect that ' the hearer is to be allowed to find out the situations for himself '—' Man überlässt dem Zuhörer sich selbst die Situationen auszufinden.'

The work was composed in the neighbourhood of Vienna, in the wooded meadows between Heiligenstadt and Grinzing, in the summer of 1808, at the same time with the Symphony in C minor. The two were each dedicated to the same two persons, Prince Lobkowitz and the Count Rasoumowsky; their opus numbers follow one another, and so closely were the two connected that at the first performance—in the Theater an der Wien, Dec. 22, 1808—their numbers were interchanged, the Pastoral being called ' No. 5 ' and the C minor ' No. 6.' This confusion lasted as late as 1820, as is shown by the list of performances of th<sup>e</sup> Concert

Spirituel at Vienna, given by Hanslick (Concertwesen in Wien, p. 189).

The titles of the movements were curiously anticipated by KNECHT (q.v.), more than twenty years earlier, in a ' Portrait musical de la Nature.'

The symphony was first played in London at a concert given for the benefit of Mrs. Vaughan, at Hanover Square Rooms, May 27, 1811. On Apr. 14, 1817, it first appears in the programmes of the Philharmonic Society.[1] On three occasions attempts were made to turn the symphony into a stage-piece. At Bochsa's benefit at the Haymarket (June 22, 1829) ; at Düsseldorf, in Feb. 1863, by the Artists' Club, ' Der Malkasten ' ; and at Drury Lane, Jan. 30, 1864, it was given with scenery, and in the two English performances, with action also.

G.

**PATERSON & SONS,** one of the most important among the Scottish music-publishers. The business was started in 1819 by Robert Paterson, Mortimer & Co., at 18 North Bridge, Edinburgh, who in the following year removed to No. 51 in the same street. In 1826 the firm went to 43 Hanover Street, when by the advent of Peter Walker Roy it became Paterson & Roy. Under this last name it existed until the death of Roy in 1850, when Paterson's sons took share in the business, and the house traded under the name Paterson & Sons. Before 1837 the firm had removed to 27 George Street ; later a depôt was opened in Castle Street, Berners Street, London. Branches were at different times started in other parts of Scotland, at Glasgow, 1857 ; Perth, 1864 ; Ayr, 1868 ; Dundee, 1882 ; Dumfries, 1886 ; Paisley, 1887 ; Kilmarnock, 1892, and later, at Aberdeen, Oban, and other places.

The original Robert Paterson died in 1859, when his second son, Robert Roy Paterson (b. 1830 ; d. Dec. 3, 1903), became senior partner. The latter was a skilful performer on several instruments and did much to advance

---

[1] But see *Beethoven and his Nine Symphonies*, by Sir G. Grove, p. 225, note.

music in Scotland (see sketch of life and portrait in *Mus. T.*, Jan. 1904).

Robert E. Stirling Paterson, grandson of the founder, succeeded to his father's position.

The firm is distinguished for its great issue of Scottish music of all kinds, which includes reprints of standard editions of Scottish songs, etc.        F. K.

PATEY, JANET MONACH, *née* WHYTOCK (*b.* London, May 1, 1842; *d.* Feb. 28, 1894). Her father was a native of Glasgow. She received instruction in singing from John Wass, and made her first appearance in public at a very early age, at the Town Hall, Birmingham. She became a member of Henry Leslie's Choir, and afterwards received further instruction from Mrs. Sims Reeves and Pinsuti. In 1865 she was engaged by Lemmens for a provincial concert tour. In 1866 she was married to J. G. PATEY (2), and sang at the Worcester Festival of that year. From that time her reputation continued to increase, until in 1870, on the retirement of Madame Sainton-Dolby, she succeeded to her position as leading contralto concert-singer, and as such sang in all the principal new works. In the part of Blanche of Devan, in Macfarren's 'Lady of the Lake,' she developed an amount of dramatic power for which her admirers had not given her credit.

In 1871 she started on a concert tour in America with Edith Wynne, Cummings, Santley, and her husband, and enjoyed great success. In 1875 she sang with her usual success at the Cirque des Champs Elysées, Paris, in French, in four performances of the 'Messiah,' on the invitation of Lamoureux, and under his direction. Also on Jan. 31 of the same year she sang in English 'O rest in the Lord,' at the concert of the Conservatoire, with such effect that she was re-engaged for the next concert, Feb. 7, when she more than confirmed the previous impression. In commemoration of this the directors presented her with a medal bearing the dates of the concerts, a compliment rarely accorded by that body to any singer. On Mar. 15, 1881, when Lamoureux gave his first concert in England at St. James's Hall, she sang Godard's scena 'Aurore,' and in Berlioz's Duo Nocturne from 'Béatrice et Bénédict' with Mme. Brunet-Lafleur, who had sung with her previously in the 'Messiah' at Paris. In 1890 and 1891 she sang on tour in Australia, and on her return appeared, Oct. 11, 1891, at the Crystal Palace. Intending to retire, she undertook a farewell tour, but it was brought to a tragic close by her sudden death. She had sung at the Albert Hall, Sheffield, the previous evening, and after singing 'The Banks of Allan Water,' in response to an encore, fainted as she left the platform, dying at her hotel next morning, without regaining consciousness. Mme. Patey possessed

'a magnificent contralto . . . produced with marvellous art . . . the real contralto, such as one admired formerly in Mesdames Pisaroni, Brambilla, and Alboni' (*L'Art Musical*).        A. C.

(2) JOHN GEORGE (*b.* Stonehouse, Devonshire, 1835; *d.* Falmouth, Dec. 4, 1901), husband of the above, son of a clergyman, was educated for medicine, but abandoned it for music. His voice was a baritone; he studied at Paris and Milan, made his first appearance, Oct. 11, 1858, at Drury Lane, as Plunkett, in an English version of 'Martha,' and sang for several seasons in English opera at Covent Garden and Her Majesty's, creating parts in 'Robin Hood' (Oct. 10, 1860), 'La Reine Topaze' (Dec. 26, 1860), 'Puritan's Daughter' (Nov. 30, 1861), 'Lily of Killarney' (Feb. 8, 1862), etc. He also sang in Italian opera at the Lyceum in 1861, and was frequently heard in oratorio and concerts. He accompanied his wife on her American and Australian tours. He retired in 1888, and entered into partnership with Willis as a music-publisher.        A. C.

PATIÑO, CARLOS (17th cent.), Spanish composer, first heard of in 1632, when he received a sum of money from John IV. of Portugal. In the following year (in which another grant was made to him by John IV.) he was appointed to the Chapel Royal, as assistant director under Matias Romero. He is said to have died about 1683; but this is improbable, seeing that the Benedictus for the funeral of Philip II. (1599) is attributed to him. His works include incidental music to plays and church compositions. MSS. exist at Madrid (Bibl. Municipal, Benedictus; Bibl. Nac., 4 choruses from plays (?), 4 v.; also in Pizarro MS., M. 1262; Saragossa, Catedral de N.S. del Pilar (villancicos for Christmas and Epiphany); Seville (Letania, 8 v.); Berlin (villancico, 3 v.). Eslava printed a Mass for 8 v. in two choirs.        J. B. T.

PATON, MARY ANNE (*b.* Edinburgh, Oct. 1802; *d.* Bulcliffe Hall, Chapelthorpe, July 21, 1864), daughter of George Paton, writingmaster in the High School of Edinburgh. From a very early age she manifested a capacity for music, and when little more than 4 years old learned to play the harp, pianoforte and violin. She came, indeed, of a musical family; her father was a violinist, and a great-uncle, Walter Nicoll, was instrumental in founding the Aberdeen Musical Society in 1748. In 1810 Miss Paton appeared at concerts in Edinburgh, singing, reciting and playing—among other pieces, Viotti's Concerto in G. She also published several compositions. In 1811 the family removed to London, and during the next three seasons she sang at private concerts, and annually at a public concert of her own. In 1814 she was withdrawn from public life for the purpose of completing her education. In 1820 she reappeared and sang at the Bath concerts with success, and in 1821 at various other places. On Aug. 3, 1822, she made her first appearance on the stage at the Haymarket Theatre as Susanna in 'The Marriage of Figaro,' with decided success. On Oct. 19, 1822, she appeared at Covent Garden as Polly, and on Dec. 7 fully established herself by her impersonation of Mandane in Arne's 'Artaxerxes.' On July 23, 1824, she achieved a great success in the part of the heroine in Weber's 'Der Freischütz,' then first produced in England. In the same year she was married in Scotland to Lord William Pitt Lennox, a younger son of the 4th Duke of Richmond, but continued her professional appearances under her maiden name. On Apr. 12, 1826, on the production of Weber's 'Oberon,' she took the part of Reiza. Weber had previously written to his wife, 'Miss Paton is a singer of the very first rank, and will play Reiza divinely.' From that time she was at the head of her profession, alike in the theatre, the concert-room, and the oratorio orchestra. In June 1830 she separated from her husband, and on Feb. 26, 1831, obtained a decree of the Court of Session in Scotland dissolving the marriage. Shortly afterwards she was married to Joseph Wood, the tenor singer, and in the same year reappeared at Covent Garden and afterwards at the King's Theatre in 'La Cenerentola.' She was next engaged at Drury Lane, and appeared as Alice in an English version of Meyerbeer's 'Robert le Diable,' produced Feb. 20, 1832. In 1833 Mr. and Mrs. Wood began to reside at Woolley Moor, Yorkshire. In 1834 they paid a visit to the United States, and repeated it twice within the next few years. In Apr. 1837 Mrs. Wood reappeared in London, and continued to perform until Feb. 1843, when she became a Roman Catholic, and took up her residence in the convent by Micklegate Bar, York. The change, however, was of short duration, and in July she quitted the convent. In 1844 she was engaged at the Princess's Theatre. She soon afterwards retired from her profession, and settled with her husband at Woolley Moor. Here she took a warm interest in the Anglican service at Chapelthorpe. She composed for it, formed and trained a choir, in which she herself took the leading part. In 1854 they left Yorkshire and went abroad. In 1863 they returned to Bulcliffe Hall, in the neighbourhood of Chapelthorpe, and there Mrs. Wood died, leaving a son (b. Woolley Moor, 1838) as the only representative of her family. Mrs. Wood's voice was a pure soprano, of extensive compass (A below the staff to D or E above), powerful, sweet-toned, and brilliant. She was mistress of the florid style, and had great powers of expression. She was renowned for her beauty, both of feature and expression, inherited from her mother, Miss Crawford of Cameron Bank; and the portraits of her are numerous, including those by Sir Thos. Lawrence, Sir W. Newton, Wageman

and others. Her younger sisters were both singers; ISABELLA appeared at Drury Lane about 1825, and ELIZA at the Haymarket as Mandane in 1833.         W. H. H.

PATROCINIUM MUSICES, see BERG, Adam.

PATRON'S FUND OF THE R.C.M. This fund (£27,000) was given in 1903 by Sir S. Ernest Palmer to the R.C.M. for the encouragement of young British musicians. It is primarily for the benefit of past and present pupils of the R.C.M., but it can be, and is, extended to any other British subject, whether educated at any of the music schools or privately. Composers and performers are given a hearing at concerts and public rehearsals, or they may receive grants towards the costs of public recitals, study abroad or musical publication. In recent years the public rehearsals have replaced the concerts. They are usually held in the concert-hall of the R.C.M., a professional orchestra being engaged—the London Symphony, New Queen's Hall and Royal Albert Hall in turn—under the general direction of Adrian Boult. Composers may be asked to conduct their own works, if they show sufficient ability. Many leading musicians of the day, especially composers, owe something to the activities of the fund, either from the actual production of a work which has become well known, or from the valuable experience of hearing their music played, an experience otherwise unobtainable.        N. C. G.

PATTA, DOM SERAFINO, a 16th-17th-century Benedictine monk of Monte Cassino, near Naples; organist at various churches, probably belonging to that monastery; composer of at least 6 books of masses, sacred songs, etc., published between 1606 and 1619 (Q.-L.).

PATTERSON, ANNIE WILSON (b. Lurgan, Oct. 27, 1868), was educated at Alexandra College, Dublin, and R.I.A.M.; graduated Mus.B. and B.A., 1887, and Mus.D., 1889, Royal University of Ireland (the first woman to obtain the degree); examiner in music, R.U.I. from 1892–95. She originated the FEIS CEOIL (q.v.) in 1897. She has been a lecturer on Irish Music for 30 years, and in 1924 was appointed to the chair of Irish Music at University College, Cork. After holding several organ appointments she accepted her present post of organist of Shandon Church, Cork, in 1904. Beginning with a cantata, 'Finola,' in 1888, she has essayed most forms of composition with considerable success. She is best known as the author of numerous musical books, including the Story of Oratorio, Schumann (Master Musician Series), Chats with Music Lovers. She is indefatigable in disseminating Irish folk-music, of which she has made a life-long study.        W. H. G. F.

PATTER-SONG. 'Patter' is the technical —or rather slang—name for the kind of gabbling speech with which a cheap-jack extols his wares, or a conjuror distracts the attention of the audience while performing his tricks. It is used in music to denote a kind of song, the humour of which consists in getting the greatest number of words uttered in the shortest possible time. Instances of this form of composition are Quaver's song in Samuel Arnold's ' Enraged Musician ' (1788) ; Haydn's ' Durch Italien, Frankreich, Preussen,' from ' Der Ritter Roland ' ; Grétry's syllabic duet in ' La Fausse Magie ' ; Dulcamara's song in Donizetti's ' L' elisir d' amore,' etc. Mozart and many other composers often introduce bits of ' patter ' into buffo solos, as, for instance, the middle of ' Madamina ' in ' Don Juan,' etc. This form of song has for long been popular with ' entertainers ' from Albert Smith to Corney Grain, and probably owes its technical name to a song sung by Charles Mathews in ' Patter versus Clatter.' Patter-songs fill an important place in the comic operas of Sullivan. ' My Aged Employer' in Burnand's libretto to ' Cox and Box ' was followed by ' My name is John Wellington Wells ' in Gilbert's ' The Sorcerer,' the first of a whole series.          M.

PATTI, (1) ADELINA (ADELA JUANA MARIA) (b. Madrid, Feb. 10, 1843 ; d. Craig-y-Nos Castle, Wales, Sept. 27, 1919), the most famous soprano singer of her day, was the youngest daughter of Salvatore Patti, an Italian singer (1800–69), by his marriage with Caterina Barili or Barilli, née Chiesa, also well known as a singer in Italy. The family went to America, the father being for a time manager of Italian opera at New York. Having shown great aptitude as a singer, Patti received some instruction from her half-brother, Ettore Barili. She sang at a concert in 1850 under the direction of Max Maretzek. From 8 to 12 years of age she sang at concerts under the direction of Maurice Strakosch, who had married her elder sister Amalia, but in 1855 was wisely withdrawn for some years for the purpose of further study.[1] She went on a short concert tour with Gottschalk in the West Indies, then reappeared Nov. 24, 1859, at New York, making her début on the operatic stage as Lucia, and sang other parts, in all of which she was highly successful. Patti made her début in England, May 14, 1861, at the Royal Italian Opera, as Amina in ' La Sonnambula,' and from that time became famous, confirming an extraordinary success by her performances of Lucia, Violetta, Zerlina, Martha and Rosina. She sang that autumn at the Birmingham Festival, in opera at Liverpool, Manchester, etc., and afterwards was engaged at Berlin, Brussels and Paris. From 1861 until 1884 she sang every season at Covent Garden, and in 1885 and 1887 at Her Majesty's during Mapleson's last

1 See a letter from Maurice Strakosch in The Times, Sept. 25, 1884.

seasons of opera, in a repertory of about thirty parts in the operas of Mozart, Rossini, Bellini, Donizetti, Verdi, Meyerbeer and Gounod. She was more closely identified with Rosina in ' Il Barbiere ' than with any other character, and Rossini rearranged a good deal of the music for her voice. Patti made an operatic tour in the provinces in 1862 ; sang at the Birmingham Festivals of 1861 and 1864, notably as Adah on the production of Costa's ' Naaman ' ; at the Handel Festivals of 1865, 1877 and 1880 ; at the Liverpool Festival of 1874, as well as in several brilliant provincial concert tours. She enjoyed the same unparalleled popularity on the Continent, having fulfilled engagements at Paris, Vienna, St. Petersburg, Moscow, etc., in various cities of Germany, Italy, Spain, and later in North and South America.

The new parts which she created in England are Annetta (' Crispino e la Comare '), July 14, 1866 ; Campana's Esmeralda, June 14, 1870 ; Poniatowski's Gelmina, June 4, 1872 ; Juliet, July 11, 1867 ; La Catarina (' Diamans de la couronne'), July 3, 1873 ; Aïda, June 22, 1876; Estella (' Les Bluets ') of Jules Cohen (Covent Garden, under the title of ' Estella,' July 3, 1880), and Lenepveu's Velléda, July 4, 1882. In 1888 she sang Juliette in French in Paris, and in 1895 reappeared at Covent Garden at six special performances, at which she sang Rosina, Violetta, and Zerlina, the only Mozart character she played. Her perfect method and finished singing of familiar songs attracted large audiences to the Albert Hall, until the end of 1906, when she gave a farewell concert on Dec. 1, and afterwards undertook a final tour in the provinces.

She married (1) July 29, 1868, Henri, Marquis de Caux, equerry to Napoleon III., from whom she was separated in 1877 and divorced in 1885 ; (2) in 1886, the singer Ernest Nicolas (NICOLINI), who died in 1898 ; and (3) in 1899, Baron Cederström.

The professional retirement of the great singer was followed by an occasional public appearance on behalf of some charity in which she was interested ; as, for example, at the Albert Hall in Nov. 1907, at the benefit concert given by her concert impresario, Percy Harrison ; and again, a year later, at a concert organised by Father Vaughan in aid of East End children. She also took part in the ' farewells ' of her old colleagues Mme. Albani and Wilhelm Ganz : her last appearance in public being on Oct. 20, 1914 (that is, in her 72nd year), at a concert given at the Albert Hall in aid of the Red Cross War Fund. Even then her voice retained a marvellous degree of freshness, and its timbre was still beautiful as it faded to silence for the last time in ' Home, sweet Home.' In 1918 her health began to give way, and she died after a short illness at the age of 75 at her Welsh home

Craig-y-Nos Castle. The remains were temporarily deposited in London at the Kensal Green (R.C.) cemetery, and afterwards removed to a grave in the principal avenue at Père Lachaise, Paris.

The career of Adelina Patti as a public singer was the longest on record : reckoned from her first appearance in 1850 at New York, as a child of seven, to her farewell in London, it extended over a period of fifty-six years. It was, in many other respects as well, a career without parallel ; for she stood alone among the operatic *prime donne* of her time, the sole inheritor of the title ' diva ' which descended to her from Giulia Grisi, and in the general opinion the last of the illustrious line of great coloratura sopranos that included Catalani and Pasta. At the same time, such was her genius, such the extraordinary nature of her vocal gifts, apart from the flexibility and the haunting beauty of her organ, that among the forty-two operas in which she sang there were comprised works of every calibre and every style and, with but few exceptions, she triumphed in them all. A complete list of these forty-two operas is given below. From her girlhood in America to the time when she created the rôle of Aïda at Covent Garden (1876) she had been accustomed to sing heavy as well as light parts ; but it was during the years that followed the latter event that her surprising dramatic development occurred ; while the irresistible fascination of her singing remained unimpaired and incomparable to the end.

MOZART.—' Don Giovanni.'
ROSSINI.—' Il Barbiere di Siviglia,' ' Mosè in Egitto,' ' La gazza ladra,' ' Otello,' ' Semiramide.'
BELLINI.—' La Sonnambula,' ' I Puritani.'
DONIZETTI.—' Lucia di Lammermoor,' ' Linda di Chamouni,' ' Don Pasquale,' ' L' elisir d' amore,' ' La figlia del reggimento '
VERDI.—' Il Trovatore,' ' Giovanna d' Arco,' ' La Traviata,' ' Luisa Miller,' ' Ernani,' ' Rigoletto,' ' Aïda.'
MEYERBEER.—' Dinorah,' ' Les Huguenots,' ' L'Étoile du nord,' ' L'Africaine.'
FLOTOW.—' Martha.'
GOUNOD.—' Faust,' ' Mireille,' ' Roméo et Juliette.'
AUBER.—' Les Diamans de la couronne,' ' Fra Diavolo.'
THOMAS.— Hamlet.'
BIZET.— ' Carmen.'
DELIBES.—' Lakmé.'
GOMEZ.—' Il Guarany.'
D'IVRY.—' Les Amants de Vérone.'
CAMPANA.—' Esmeralda.'
LENEPVEU.—' Velleda.'
RICCI.—' Crispino e la Comare.'
PONIATOWSKI.—' Gelmina.'
COHEN.—' Estella ' (' Les Bluets ').
PIZZI.—' Gabriella.'
POLLONNAIS.—' Dolores.'

BIBL.—HERMAN KLEIN, *The Reign of Patti,* authorised biography.
H. K.

(2) CARLOTTA (*b.* Florence, 1840 ; *d.* Paris, June 27, 1889), elder sister of Adelina, was educated as a pianist under Herz, but abandoned the piano in favour of singing. She made her début in 1861 at New York as a concert-singer, and afterwards fulfilled an engagement there in Italian opera, and was successful ; but soon after abandoned the stage on account of her lameness. She made her début in England, Apr. 16, 1863, at a concert at Covent Garden Theatre, attracted attention on account of her remarkable facility of execution and a compass extending to *f'''*. She obtained a position here in concerts

as an accomplished soprano leggiero, and was for several seasons a great attraction at promenade and other concerts. In 1872 she sang at the Philharmonic Society Mozart's florid aria, ' Nò, che sei non capace,' with great success. She made several tours in the provinces, on the Continent, and in North and South America. She married, Sept. 3, 1879, Ernst de Munck, the Belgian violoncellist. She finally settled in Paris as a teacher, and lived there till her death.

(3) CARLO, their brother (*b.* Madrid, 1842 ; *d.* St. Louis, U.S.A., Mar. 17, 1873), was taken to America, like his sisters, when a child, studied the violin, and at the age of 20 became leader at the New Orleans Opera-House, afterwards at New York and the Wakefield Opera-House, St. Louis, Missouri.       A. C.

PATTRICK, NATHANIEL (*d.* Worcester, Mar. 1594/95), organist and composer. It seems likely that he was the son of Dr. Gyles Pattrick, who for many years was the cathedral physician and lived in the parish of St. Michael's, Worcester, where Nathaniel was buried. Nathaniel was Master of the Choristers at Worcester Cathedral from about 1590 until his death. He married, on Sept. 23, 1593, Alice (or Eleanor) Hassard. Their only child died as an infant. Pattrick's will was proved at Worcester on May 25, 1595 ; it is printed in full, together with an interesting inventory of his goods, in Sir 'Ivor Atkins's *The Early Occupants of the office of Organist . . . of the Cathedral Church of . . . Worcester.* Pattrick's widow married Thomas TOMKINS (*q.v.*), who succeeded him as organist of Worcester Cathedral.

Text of his Service in G is to be found among the early MS. partbooks in Worcester, Durham, Ely and elsewhere. It was printed in Arnold's *Cathedral Music,* but wrongly ascribed there to Richard Pattrick, a lay-clerk at Westminster Abbey, *c.* 1616–26. It has more recently been printed under the editorship of J. E. West.

In 1597 licence was granted at the Stationers' Hall to print a work entitled :

' Songes of Sundrye Natures whereof some ar Divine, some are Madrigalles and the rest Psalmes and Hymnes in Latin composed for 5. and 6. voyces and one for 8. voyces by Nathanaell Pattrick sometyme Master of the children of the Cathedrall Churche o. Worcester and organist of the same.'

Pattrick died two years before this, and it is pretty certain that the book was never printed. Three madrigals by this composer are in B.M. Add. MSS. 17,786-91, and another fragment is in B.M. Add. MSS. 18,936-39.       E. H. F.

PAUER, (1) ERNST (*b.* Vienna, Dec. 21, 1826 ; *d.* May 9, 1905), pianist and eminent teacher. His father was first minister of the Lutheran church, director of the theological seminary in Vienna, and superintendent-general of the Lutheran churches of the Austrian Empire ; his mother was a Streicher, of the great pianoforte-making family. He studied the pianoforte, first under Theodor Dirzka, and then under Mozart's son, Wolfgang Amadeus, and harmony and counterpoint under Sechter. He appeared first in public in 1842 ; one of his compositions was published in that year. In 1845 he went to Munich to study instrumentation and dramatic composition under Franz Lachner. In Apr. 1847 he competed for and obtained the appointment of director of the musical societies at Mainz, and was employed by the publishing firm of Schott to compose operas, ' Don Riego ' (1849), ' Die rothe Maske ' (1850) and ' Die Braut ' (1861), which were performed in Mainz and Mannheim ; also some important vocal works, and overtures and entr'actes for the use of the local theatre. This appointment, in which he gained great experience, he resigned in Apr. 1851, and proceeded to London, where his performances at the Philharmonic (June 23, Hummel's A minor concerto) and the Musical Union were received with much favour. After this success he resolved to pursue his career in England, though returning for a time to Germany.

In 1852 he married Miss Andreae, of Frankfort, a good contralto singer.

In 1861 Pauer gave a series of six performances with a view of illustrating the foundation and development of pianoforte composition and playing, in chronological series from about 1600 to modern times, elucidated and assisted by programmes containing critical and biographical notices. Similar performances, but with different programmes, were given in 1862 and 1863, and again in 1867, in Willis's and the Hanover Square Rooms. In 1862 he was selected by Austria and the Zollverein for the Musical Jury of the London International Exhibition. He was at the same time the official reporter for the Prussian Government, and his report was reproduced by some of the chief industrial journals, and was translated into various languages. For these services he received the Imperial Austrian Order of Francis Joseph, and the Prussian Order of the Crown. During the next few years Pauer played in Holland, Leipzig, Munich and Vienna, in fulfilment of special engagements, and was appointed pianist to the imperial Austrian court in 1866.

In 1870 he began a new phase of his active career, that of lecturing upon the composers for the harpsichord and pianoforte ; the form and spirit of the varieties of modern music, as the Italian, French and German ; the history of the oratorio ; the practice of teaching ; and many cognate subjects. These lectures were given at the Royal Institution, the South Kensington Museum, and in many other important places in Great Britain and Ireland. When Cipriani Potter retired from the R.A.M., Pauer took his class, and retained it for five years. In 1876, on the foundation of the National Training School for Music at Kensington Gore, he became the principal pianoforte professor of that institution, and in 1878 was made a member of the Board for Musical Studies at Cambridge University, and the following year an examiner. He edited many of the works of the classical and romantic composers, among them ' Alte Klavier-Musik ' (Senff, Leipzig), twelve books ; ' Alte Meister ' (Breitkopf & Härtel, Leipzig), 40 Nos. Also ' Old English Composers for the Virginals and Harpsichord ' (Augener, London) ; and, under the auspices of the last-named publisher, an edition of the classical composers in a cheap form, embracing and including all the great masters from Bach and Handel to Schumann, and extending, up to July 1880, to nearly thirty volumes, of admirable clearness and convenience. Besides this are arrangements for children, and educational works, including the ' New Gradus ad Parnassum,' 100 studies, some of them by himself ; *Primer of the Pianoforte* (Novello & Co., 1876) ; *Elements of the Beautiful in Music* (ditto, 1876) ; *Primer of Musical Forms* (ditto, 1878) ; and *The Pianist's Dictionary* (1895). Also some interesting arrangements of Schumann's symphonies for four hands, and of Mendelssohn's PF. concerto for two pianos. As a pianist his style was distinguished by breadth and nobility of tone, and by a sentiment in which seriousness of thought was blended with profound respect for the intention of the composer. He retired to Germany in 1896.                    A. J. H.

His son, (2) MAX (b. London, Oct. 31, 1866), pianist, was a pupil of his father till 1881, when he went to Carlsruhe and studied theory with Vincenz Lachner till 1885. In that year he made a successful appearance as a pianist in London, where, except for concert tours, he remained till 1887, when he settled in Cologne as piano teacher at the Conservatorium. In 1897 he migrated to a similar post at Stuttgart, and in 1908 succeeded De Lange as director of the Stuttgart Conservatorium. He held this position till 1924, when, on Stephan Krehl's death, he was appointed director of the Leipzig Conservatorium, where his energetic personality has already made itself felt in salutary reforms for widening the basis of musical education, and in the encouragement of ear-training.

As a pianist he ranks very highly indeed. His powers of interpretation are remarkable, and his sense of style enables him to do justice to music of all kinds and dates, except perhaps that of the modern extremists, with which he is not often in sympathy. His repertory is an exceptionally large one, and his memory is so amazing that it is scarcely an exaggeration to say that he never forgets anything that he has once learned. One can play to him any bar, and often less than a bar, taken at random out of the whole range of piano literature from Scarlatti to Brahms, and, provided he has at some time in his life learned the piece (and there is exceedingly little that he has not learned), he can without any hesitation give the exact context and play as many of the preceding or succeeding bars as one cares to ask for.

He is a most stimulating teacher and employs many ingenious devices for quickening the interest and intelligence of his pupils. One of his methods is to have two pupils sitting at different pianos, and to ask one of them to start some piece (which both must know by heart) and to break off at any bar or note of a bar, as though he were playing for 'musical chairs,' whereupon the other pupil has to take up the thread and respond in like fashion— and so on till the end of the piece. Sometimes, again, he will tell a pupil to play (by heart) the first three or four or five bars of a movement and then, with hands away from the keyboard, to play *mentally* an equal number of the following bars, and to continue these alternations till the movement is ended. It needs a very short trial to discover how precise and thorough the knowledge of a piece must be before either of these tests can be successfully surmounted. Finally, mention should be made of Pauer's admirable teaching of ensemble-playing, where he makes generous and enthusiastic use of his consummate musicianship.        H. B.

PAUKEN. The German name for Kettle-drums. See DRUM.        v. de P.

PAUL, OSCAR (*b.* Freiwaldau, Silesia, Apr. 8, 1836; *d.* Leipzig, Apr. 18, 1898), writer on music, was educated at Görlitz, where he first learned music from Klingenberg, and at the University of Leipzig. Here he studied music with Plaidy, Richter and Hauptmann, of whose system of harmony he became a warm partisan. In 1860 he graduated Ph.D., and after spending some time in various towns of Germany, especially Cologne, settled in Leipzig in 1866. Becoming known by his private lessons in the science of music, and by his treatise on *Die absolute Harmonik der Griechen* (1866), he was made teacher of musical history, pianoforte, composition, etc., at the Conservatorium in 1869, and Professor Extraordinarius at the University in 1872. His best and most important work is his translation (the first in Germany) and elucidation of Boethius (Leipzig, Leuckart, 1872). His important *Lehrbuch der Harmonik*, first published in 1880, went into a second edition in 1894. He also edited Hauptmann's *Lehre von der Harmonik* (1868), the *Geschichte des Claviers* (1869), the *Handlexicon der Tonkunst* (1871–73) and two musical periodicals, the *Tonhalle*, and its successor, the *Musikalisches Wochenblatt*. He was for many years musical critic of the *Leipziger Tagblatt*.        F. G.

PAUMANN, CONRAD (*b. circa* 1410 ; *d.* Munich, Jan. 24, 1473), was a native of Nuremberg. Although heavily handicapped (he was born blind), he eventually attained an honoured position as a musician and as a fine organ-player. He was adopted by Ulrich Grundherr, burgher of Nuremberg, who, recognising the child's musical gifts, had them carefully cultivated. Ulrich died in 1423, but his son Paul also took Paumann under his protection. There is a reference in Hirsch's *Lebensbeschreibungen*, Nuremberg, 1756, p. 19, to the large organ made and erected in the church of S. Sebald, Nuremberg, by Heinrich Traxdorf in 1444, at the cost of 1150 gulden : possibly Paumann was at once appointed organist; he was certainly occupying the post in 1446. He was married the same year according to a document he issued in 1446, in which he and his wife Margaret Weichserin promised never to leave Nuremberg, where they had been treated with so much kindness, without first obtaining the permission of the burghers.[1] That Paumann was a person of some mark at that time is shown by Hans Rosenplüt's poem, *Spruchgedichte auf die Stadt Nürnberg*, published in 1447, in which he is eulogised as organist and as contrapuntist.

In 1450 Paumann visited various towns ; some time later, in 1467, he took up his residence in Munich, as organist to Duke Albrecht III., receiving a yearly salary of eighty gulden. A visit of his to Ratisbon in 1471 is recorded, when his playing of the organ in the Benedictine monastery, on St. Jacob's Day, drew a large crowd to listen, including the Emperor Friedrich III. and many notable persons in his suite.[2] A manuscript volume chiefly treating of events in Ratisbon fell into the hands of A. F. Oefele,[3] who quotes a long passage from it stating that Paumann excelled his contemporaries in knowledge of the organ, lute, flute and other instruments, that his fame spread over Europe, and he received many presents from the Emperor Friedrich III., the Duke of Ferrara and others. It must be remembered that practically the only contemporary organist of note was the Florentine Antonio Squarcialupi, who died in 1475.

Paumann was buried in the Frauenkirche, where a tablet was erected with the inscription :

'Anno 1473 an Sanct Pauli Bekerungs Abent ist gestorben und hie begraben, der Kunstreichist aller Instrument und der Musica Meister, Conrad Paumann Ritter, bürtig von Nürnberg, und blinter geboren, dem Gott Gnad.'

An Italian decoration, received from the Pope, entitled Paumann to be called 'Ritter' or knight. Virdung, in his *Musica getutscht*, 1511, attributes the invention of the lute tablature to Paumann :

'Ich höre das ayn Blind zu Nürenberg geborn und zu München begraben sei gewesen hatt meister

1 *Jahrbücher der Mus. Wissenschaft*, ii. p. 75.
2 *Mettenleiter*, i. 202.
3 *Rerum Boicarum scriptores*, 1763, i. p. 539.

Conrat von Nürenberg gehaissen, der zu seyner zeytt vor ander instrumentisten gelopt und gerumptt sey worden. Der hatt auf den kragen der fünff kore, und uff siben bünde das gantz alphabet haissen schreiben, und als das ayn mall auss ist gewesen, hatt er wider von vornen an dem alphabet angefangen, und die selben buchstaben alle des andern alphabets dupliert,' etc.

Martin Agricola, a few years later in his *Musica instrumentalis*, 1532, xxix., alludes scoffingly to this alphabetical notation :

> ' Weiter hab ich mich manchmal bekümmert
> Vnd heymlich bey mir selber verwundert,
> Der Alphabetischen Tabulathur
> Wie sie doch erstmals sey komen herfur.
>
> ' Das ihre Tabelthur erfunden sey
> Ists war, so las ichs auch bleiben dabey,
> Von eim Lautenschlager blind geborn
> So han sie den rechten meister erkorn.'

And makes merry at the expense of the blind man trying to lead the blind [1] :

> ' Dieweil ein blinder den andern füret
> So werden sie beide narrn gespüret.'

A few of Paumann's compositions are still in existence. A three-part song, to the text ' Wiplich figur,' is in the Munich State Library, Mus. MS. 3232, date about 1461 ; it was published by Eitner in *Das deutsche Lied*, 1880, ii. p. 161. In the same library the 15th-century manuscript known as the Buxheimer Orgelbuch, Mus. MS. 3725, contains three organ pieces by Paumann, printed by Eitner in *Monatshefte*, 1886, p. 82, and again in 1888, *Beilage*, pp. 67-8 and 78. The most important work, the ' Fundamentum organisandi magistri Conradi Paumanns ceci de Nurenberga anno 1452,' acquired by the Wernigerode gräfl. Bibliothek in 1858, is written in the German organ-tablature by a Nuremberg scribe, and bound in one volume with the manuscript called the Locheimer Liederbuch. The occurrence of the organ alphabetical TABLATURE (*q.v.*) in this manuscript is of even earlier date than its first appearance in print, in Arnold Schlick's 'Tabulaturen etlicher lobgesang,' published at Mainz in 1512. The twenty-four pieces of simple organ music in two-part writing by Paumann are obviously only preliminary exercises for those learning to play the organ ; they are followed by a short Latin treatise on mensural music signed ' W. de Sa ' (Walter de Salice) ; compositions by G. v. Putenheim; a three-part song by Wilh. Legrant, one by Paumgartner, and three Preludes added to the manuscript in 1455. The music, transcribed by F. W. Arnold shortly before his death, was published with his scholarly account of the whole manuscript in Chrysander's *Jahrbücher*, 1867, ii., revised and edited by H. Bellermann.                    C. S.

PAUR, EMIL (*b.* Czernowitz, Bukovina, Aug. 29, 1855), was at first a pupil of his father, the director of a musical society ; when 8 years old he played the violin and piano in public, and in 1866 entered the Vienna Conservatorium under Dessoff for composition, and Hellmesberger for

violin. He became a member of the court orchestra as violinist in 1870. His career as a conductor began at Cassel in 1876 ; he was next at Königsberg, and in 1880 was appointed first court Kapellmeister and conductor of the subscription concerts at Mannheim ; in 1891 he was made conductor at the Leipzig Stadt-theater, and in 1893 went to America, succeeding Nikisch as conductor of the Boston Symphony Orchestra.

In 1898 he was elected conductor of the New York Philharmonic Concerts in succession to Anton Seidl, and in 1899 became director of the National Conservatory in New York. In 1903 he returned to Europe, and has conducted concerts in Madrid as well as in Berlin. In 1900 he visited England, conducting German opera at Covent Garden, and he conducted one of the Queen's Hall Symphony Concerts in Nov. 1902. From 1904–10 he was conductor of the Pittsburgh Symphony Orchestra, where his symphony ' In der Natur ' was played (1909). His compositions also include a violin concerto and some chamber music. Returning to Europe he directed the Berlin Opera (1912–13). (*Riemann and Baker.*)            M., with addns.

PAUSE (Fr. *point d'orgue* ; Ital. *fermata* ; which has an equivocal meaning, as it also signifies what we call ' pedal point '), a temporary cessation of the time of the movement, expressed by the sign ⌢ placed over a note or a rest. If the pause is over a note, it signifies that the note is to be prolonged at the pleasure of the performer, or conductor ; if over a rest, the sound, as well as the time, must stop. The initials G.P. (*General Pause*) are often found in German scores as a warning that the whole orchestra is silent. One special use of the pause, no doubt, had its origin in the practical difficulty of getting a congregation to finish each line of a chorale-tune together ; the organist must make a pause at the end of every line, and in order to fill up the space, interludes were inserted between the lines, which interludes became gradually more and more important, until, as in many of Bach's cantatas, the embroidery upon the chorale-tune reaches the very height of sublimity. Pauses at the end of a movement, over a rest, or even over a silent bar are intended to give a short breathing-space before going on to the next movement. They are then exactly the reverse of the direction ' attacca ' (*q.v.*).            M.

PAVAN (PAVANE, PAVIN), a slow and solemn dance, very popular in the 16th and 17th centuries. The name, derived from ' Padovana,' [2] points to an Italian origin, although it is generally said to have come from Spain, owing to its popularity in that country. The Spanish pavan, however, was a variation of the original dance. According to some authorities, the name is derived from the Latin *pavo*, owing

---

[1] See also Wasielewski, *Gesch. der Instrumentalmusik im XVI. Iahrh.*, 1878, p. 37.

[2] In the Cambridge University Library is a MS. volume of airs and dances (in Lute Tablature) by Dowland and Holborne, in which there occurs a ' Padovana de la Milanessa.'

to the fancied resemblance to a peacock's tail, caused by the robes and cloaks worn by the dancers, as they swept out in the stately figures of the dance. Several good descriptions of the pavan have come down to us. Rabelais [1] tells us that it was one of the 180 dances performed at the court of the Queen of Lanternois on the visit of Pantagruel and his companions ; Tabourot, in his *Orchésographie*, says that in his time pavans were still popular, although not as much danced as formerly.[2] At state balls the dancers wore their long robes, caps and swords, and the music was performed by sackbuts and oboes. In masquerades, pavans were played as processional music, and were similarly used at weddings and religious ceremonies. Like all early dances, the pavan was originally sung as well as danced, and Tabourot gives the following example for four voices, accompanied throughout by the drum on one note.

*Pauane à quatre parties.*

Bel - le qui tiens ma vi - e cap - ti - ue

dans tes yeulx, Qui m'as l'a - me ra - ui - e D'un

soubz-riz gra - ci - eux, Viens tost me se-cou-

rir Ou me. fauld - ra mou - rir Viens tost me

se - cou - rir ou me fauld - ra mou - rir.

\* The treble sings D, the alto F.

[1] *Pantagruel*, Bk. v., published 1562.
[2] Besard, in the Preface to his *Thesaurus harmonicus Divini Laurencini Romani* (Cologne, 1603) after praising the sweetness and elegance of the English music of his day, makes particular mention of the Pavans, adding that the word ' Pavan ' is nothing else than the Italian ' Paduana.' He also mentions that the French often call their Passomezzos, Pavans.

Sir John Davies in his *Orchestra* (1596) has the following curious verses, in which the motions of the sun and the moon are compared to dancers of pavans and galliards :

' For that braue Sunne the Father of the Day,
Doth loue this Earth, the Mother of the Night ;
And like a reuellour in rich array,
Doth daunce his galliard in his lemman's sight,
Both back, and forth, and sidewaies, passing light.

' Who doth not see the measures of the Moone,
Which thirteene times she daunceth euery yeare ?
And ends her pauine thirteene times as soone
As doth her brother.'

There are numerous specimens extant of pavans by instrumental composers of the 16th and 17th centuries, and in almost every case the pavan is followed by a galliard, the two thus anticipating the saraband and gigue of the later suite. Thus Morley (*Introduction*, Part 3), after speaking of Fantasies, says :

' The next in grauity and goodnes vnto this is called a pauane, a kind of staide musicke, ordained for graue dauncing, and most commonlie made of three straines, whereof euerie straine is plaid or sung twice, a straine they make to containe 8, 12 or 16 semibreues as they list, yet fewer then eight I haue not seene in any pauan. . . . After euery pauan we vsually set a galliard.'

And Butler (*Principles of Music*, 1636), speaking of the Doric mode, has the following :

' Of this sort are Pavins, invented for a slow and soft kind of Dancing, altogether in duple Proportion. Unto which are framed Galliards for more quick and nimble motion, always in triple proportion, and therefore the triple is oft called Galliard-time or the duple, Pavin-time.'

Amongst the best known of these forerunners of the Suite, we may mention John Dowland's ' Lachrymae or Seauen Teares, figured in seauen passionate Pauans with diuers other Pauans, Galliards and Almands ' (1605) ; and Johann Ghro's 30 pavans and galliards ' nach teutscher art gesetzet ' (1604). For another description of the dance see Bishop Earle's *Microcosmographie*, ed. by Bliss (Nares's *Glossary*).

The Spanish pavan, a variety of the original dance which came from Spain (where it was called the ' Grand Dance,') was of a more elaborate character than the original. Judging from the frequent occurrence of its air in the early English Lute and Virginal Books, it must have become very popular in England.[3] The following is the tune which Tabourot gives for it : it is not the same as that which is found in the English books.

W. B. S.

[3] In Starter's *Friesche Lust Hof* (1634) it is called ' Engelsche Indraeyende Dans Londesteyn.'

PAVESI, Steffano (b. Casaletto Vaprio, near Crema, Jan. 22, 1779 ; d. Crema, July 28, 1850), studied at the Conservatoire dei Turchini, Naples, 1795–99 ; prolific composer of operas. The first, ' Avvertimento ai gelosi,' was given at the Theatre S. Moïse, Venice, in 1803 (list of works in Q.-L.).

PAXTON, (1) Stephen (b. London, 1735 ; d. Aug. 18, 1787), a composer of vocal music, was a pupil of W. Savage, produced several graceful and elegant glees, nine of which, with two catches, are printed in Warren's Collections. The Catch Club awarded him prizes for the following glees : ' How sweet, how fresh,' 1779 ; ' Round the hapless Andre's urn,' 1781 ; ' Blest Power,' 1784 ; and ' Come, O come,' 1785 ; and for a catch, ' Ye Muses, inspire me,' 1783. He published ' A Collection of two Songs, Glees and two Catches,' and ' A Collection of Glees.' Two masses by him are printed in Webbe's Collection. He was buried in St. Pancras old churchyard.

His brother, (2) William (b. 1737 ; d. 1781), was a violoncellist, who composed several sets of solos and duets for his instrument. He gained prizes from the Catch Club for two canons, ' O Lord in Thee,' 1779, and ' O Israel, trust in the Lord,' 1780. His glee, ' Breathe soft, ye winds,' was for long a favourite.

                                       W. H. H.

PAYNE, Edward John (b. 1844 ; d. Wendover, Dec. 1904), a talented amateur musician and writer upon musical subjects, and historian, known to readers of this Dictionary by his initials E. J. P. By profession a barrister-at-law, he became in 1883 Recorder of High Wycombe, his native town. Educated at High Wycombe Grammar School and Magdalen College, Oxford (1867), he took a first class in 1871 and was elected Fellow of University College in 1872. He contributed the opening chapters to the Cambridge Modern History. His best-known works were (1) A History of European Colonies ; (2) The Voyages of Elizabethan Seamen to America ; (3) History of the New World called America. He was one of the leaders of the movement which reintroduced the study of the old viols, and was an accomplished performer on the viola da gamba, and viole d'amour. He was first President of the Cremona Society (1889), and contributed an erudite paper on ' The Viol da Gamba ' to the Proceedings of the Musical Association (Mar. 4, 1889). In his later years he suffered much from ill-health, and was found drowned in the Canal at Wendover, Dec. 24, 1904. (See The Times, Dec. 28, 1904.)      E. H.-A.

PEABODY (1) Concerts, given under the auspices of the Conservatory of Music of the Peabody Institute, Baltimore, Maryland. Beginning in 1865, eight concerts were given every season, each being preceded by a public rehearsal, the director of the Conservatory officiating as conductor. The programmes have been made up of symphonies, suites, overtures, concertos and vocal solos, nearly everything presented being classic in style. Many important compositions have been performed for the first time in America in the course of these concerts. Under Asger Hamerik's direction (since 1871) especial attention has been given to the production of works by American, English and Scandinavian composers. The orchestra has generally included fifty musicians. The institution elicited the warm approbation of von Bülow (1875–76) for its exceptionally fine performances.      F. H. J.

(2) Conservatory.—The Peabody Conservatory is a department of the Institute founded by George Peabody in 1857. It provides a complete musical education to some 1700 students annually, including orchestra and opera classes. (See Amer. Supp.)

PEACE, Albert Lister, Mus.D. (b. Huddersfield, Jan. 26, 1844 ; d. Liverpool, Mar. 14, 1912), exhibited in his childhood precocity hardly exceeded by that of Crotch ; naming with unerring accuracy individual notes and combinations of notes when sounded, before attaining his fifth year. At the age of 9 he was appointed organist of the parish church of Holmfirth, and subsequently of other churches in that neighbourhood. In 1865, at the age of 21, he removed to Glasgow, to fill the office of organist to Trinity Congregational church, and soon afterwards, along with other posts, that of organist to the University. In 1870 he graduated as Bachelor, and in 1875 as Doctor of Music in the University of Oxford. In 1879 he was appointed to Glasgow Cathedral. He became organist of St. George's Hall, Liverpool, in succession to W. T. Best, in Jan. 1897, where his brilliant executive abilities enabled him to continue the work of his predecessor of popularising music of many kinds by means of organ performance. (See Best, W. T.) His published compositions include anthems, services and organ works, a setting of Psalm 138 for soli, chorus and orchestra ; and a cantata, ' St. John the Baptist.'      J. H., rev.

PEAL, (1) a set of bells tuned to the notes of the major scale and hung (so that they can be swung) for the particular requirements of Change-ringing (q.v.).

(2) A succession of changes rung on such a set of bells.      W. W. S.

PEARCE (Piers, Piarse), Edward, sworn in as gentleman of the Chapel Royal, London, Mar. 16, 1588 ; retired in 1600 and became organist and choirmaster (Rimbault says also treasurer) of St. Paul's Cathedral. Three madrigals of his are in Ravenscroft's ' A Brief Discourse, etc.,' one song ' Heytrola' in a MS. in the R.C.M., and a song from the above madrigals in Jos. Gwilt's collection of 1815.      E. v. d. s.

PEARCE, Joseph, jun., ostensible author of

a useful little handbook entitled *Violins and Violin Makers* (London, 1866), traditionally supposed to have been written by Charles Reade. It contains an alphabetical list of violin-makers, short chapters on bow makers, also on the ' Amati family ' ; ' Stradivarius,' ' Guarnerius,' the ' Tyrolese makers,' ' Jacobus Stainer ' ; and an excellent little essay on ' Why are certain violins of more value than others ? '

BIBL.—HERON-ALLEN, *De fidiculis bibliographia* ; MATTHEW, *The Literature of Music* ; VIDAL, *Les Instruments à archet*.

E. H.-A.

PEARSALL, ROBERT LUCAS (*b.* Clifton, Mar. 14, 1795 ; *d.* Wartensee, Aug. 5, 1856), composer, came of an old family, originally of Halesowen, Worcestershire, and then of Horsley, Staffordshire. He was privately educated for the bar, and was called in 1821, going on the western circuit for four years. At the age of 13 he wrote a cantata, ' Saul and the Witch of Endor,' which was privately printed ; and in 1817 he married Miss Hobday. In 1825, being abroad for the benefit of his health, he settled at Mainz and studied music under Josef Panny, remaining there until 1829, when he returned for a year to England, staying at Willsbridge in Gloucestershire, which his mother had purchased in 1816, and which he inherited on her death in 1836.

He removed once more to Germany, where he lived at Carlsruhe for a time, diligently composing. There he wrote a little ' ballet opera ' which was never performed ; some choruses from it were published by Weekes & Co. His op. 1, ' Miserere mei, Domine,' was published by Schott of Mainz about 1830 ; the fact that it is a ' canon perpetuus a 3 vocibus in hypodiatessaron et hypodiapason ' shows that even in these early days the ingenuities of the older music had a special attraction for him. The compositions between this and an overture to *Macbeth*, with the witches' chorus, the parts of which appeared as op. 25 in 1839, do not seem to have been published (with the exception of op. 7, a Graduale *a* 5, 1835, and op. 8, an Ave Verum *a* 4, 1835), and the system of numbering his compositions seems to have been given up after this. In 1835 he published at Carlsruhe *Stray Leaves from an Idler's Commonplace-book*.[1] He moved from place to place on the Continent, studying successively at Munich with Caspar Ett, and at Vienna. In 1836 he was in England, and he made a more intimate acquaintance with the music of the English madrigal school. The BRISTOL MADRIGAL SOCIETY (*q.v.*), founded in 1837, contributed thereto. To this style he became so attached for the remainder of his life that he wrote all his works in madrigal style within two or three years of this time, with two exceptions. He wrote several settings of psalms (68th, 77th

[1] A copy is in the possession of the Bristol Madrigal Society.

and 57th), a Requiem Mass, a Pange Lingua for three female voices (published 1857) ; the office of Tenebrae (in the library of the Gesellschaft für Musikforschung, Berlin), two settings of Salve Regina, and other compositions for the Roman Catholic Church, which he joined at the end of his life. He also took a deep interest in Anglican Church music, and wrote a number of works for its service. A collection of his sacred compositions, edited by W. F. Trimnell, was published about 1880. In 1837 he sold his property in England, and in 1842 bought the castle of Wartensee on the Lake of Constance. Here he appended the ' de ' to his name, and enjoyed intercourse with many distinguished people. He died of apoplexy, and was buried in a vault at Wartensee.

His published partsongs and madrigals number about sixty, and include a remarkable number of works which will remain as long as unaccompanied singing is practised. He understood the madrigal form thoroughly, but did not confine himself to the strict rules practised in the Elizabethan period ; his works are no mere curiosities of a bastard archæology, but living creations of art, full of fire, nobility of thought, high imagination, and splendid vocal sonority. Such things as ' Great God of Love,' ' Lay a Garland ' and ' Light of my Soul ' are masterpieces in a form that has seldom been successfully employed in modern times ; his partsongs, ' The Hardy Norseman ' and ' O who will o'er the downs so free,' are known and delighted in by every choral society in the country ; and the noble choral ballad ' Sir Patrick Spens,' in ten parts, is a triumphantly successful adaptation of the partsong form to the requirements of a narrative in which eager intensity and hurry have to be depicted.

Pearsall edited a 6-part Magnificat by Lasso about 1833, and was part-editor of the old hymn-book of St. Gall, published in 1863 under the title of ' Katholisches Gesangbuch zum Gebrauch bei dem öffentlichen Gottesdienste.' He was a skilful draughtsman and had considerable literary facility ; he contributed in early days to magazines in England, and made translations of *Faust* and *Wilhelm Tell*, the latter being published in 1829. He wrote many of his own words for madrigals. A great number of interesting treatises and compositions of different kinds are still in MS. at Einsiedeln, Vienna, Bristol, the R.C.M. and the British Museum.

BIBL.—*D.N.B., Musical Herald*, Aug. 1906, the *Sammelbände* of the Int. Mus. Ges. for 1907, etc.

M.; addns. H. W. H. and W. B. S.

PEARSON, HENRY HUGO, see PIERSON.

PEARSON, WILLIAM, a notable printer, who made many improvements in musical typography, and carried further Heptinstall's improvements. (See HEPTINSTALL.) Several works of his are dated 1699, one

being 'Twelve New Songs' by Dr. Blow and
Dr. Turner, as the title-page informs us, issued
'chiefly to encourage William Pearson's New
London Character,' 1699, folio. In 1700 followed the important and excellently printed
work, Blow's 'Amphion Anglicus.' Pearson's
printing-office was at first in Aldersgate Street,
'next the Hare and Feathers'; but in 1700
his imprint changes to Red Cross Alley, Jewin
Street. In 1724 it is 'over against Wright's
Coffee House, in Aldersgate Street.' As these
addresses are in close proximity, one may
indicate Pearson's house and the other his
printing-office. Shortly after the death of
Henry Playford, c. 1706, he, with John Young,
succeeded to the copyright (probably after
Cullen) of such of the Playford publications as
were continued. These include 'The Dancing-
Master,' and Playford's 'Introduction to the
Skill of Music,' Simpson's 'Compendium of
Practicall Musick,' 'Orpheus Britannicus,' 'Harmonia sacra,' and Playford's 'Whole Book of
Psalms,' 'The Divine Companion,' and others.
He also published, in folio, Bassani's 'Harmonia
festiva,' op. 8 and op. 13, the first English
publication of the book, which Hawkins dates
about 1726. Pearson was the principal printer
and publisher of the many octavo psalm-books
which were issued at this time. So far as the
present writer is aware no engraved work bears
his imprint. In 1736 he was succeeded by
A. Pearson, who may be presumed to be either
his widow or his son.

A. Pearson continued the business only for
a short time, printing and publishing such
works as : Tans'ur's 'Complete Melody or the
Harmony of Sion,' 1736 ; 'Heaven upon the
Earth,' 1738, by the same author ; Green's
'Book of Psalmody,' 1738, etc. The first
Wesleyan tune book, 'A Collection of Tunes
as they are commonly sung at the Foundry,'
1742, also was printed by A. Pearson, and this
is the latest date the present writer can find
for his work.　　　　　　　　　　　　F. K.

PECCATE, DOMINIQUE (b. Mirecourt, July
15, 1810 ; d. there, Jan. 13, 1874), an excellent
bow-maker who maintained the qualities and
excellence traditional in the work of François
Tourte. Son of a barber, he early forsook the
paternal profession, and adopted the vocation
of fiddle-maker. In 1826 François Vuillaume
sent him to Paris, to his brother Jean Baptiste,
under whose guidance he developed his superior
gift as a maker of bows. After the death of
François Lupot in 1837, Peccate left Vuillaume,
and set up an independent business at Lupot's
vacated workshop, 18 Rue d'Angivilliers. In
1847 he returned to Mirecourt, where he continued working until his death. He occasionally
stamped his bows, but more frequently left
them unmarked ; a habit which has caused his
bows to be confused with those of a modern
French maker of the same name but spelt

'Peccatte.' Peccate's brother, called 'Peccate
jeune,' also worked with J. B. Vuillaume, but
his productions were much inferior to those of his
brother Dominique. He died in Paris in 1856.

BIBL.—VIDAL, Les Instruments à archet, vol. i. ; SAINT GEORGE,
The Bow, Strad Library, No. iii.　　　　　　E. H.-A.

PECCI, (1) TOMASO (b. Siena, 1576 ; d. there,
(?) 1606), composed, under the name of L' In-
vaghito, given to him as member of the Aca-
demia dei Filomeli, 2 books of madrigals a 5 v.,
3 books of canzonets a 3 v., 1 book of church
music. A MS. volume of sacred and secular
compositions by him is in the Berlin Library ;
the MS. of 16 madrigals is at Christ Church ;
single numbers are in various collective
volumes (Q.-L.).

(2) DESIDERIO, a 16th-17th-century composer of Siena, probably a younger brother
of Tomaso, wrote 1 book of arias, op. 2, 1-3 v.
(1626), 1 book of madrigals (1617) and some
madrigals and sacred music in printed collective volumes and MS. (Q.-L.)

PECHAČEK, FRANZ (b. Vienna, July 4,
1793 ; d. Carlsruhe, Sept. 15, 1840), violinist
and composer, son of Franz Pechaček, a
Viennese conductor who wrote several operas
and some thirty ballets, and who, as a composer of dance music, was the Strauss of his
epoch. The precocious musical aptitude of
Franz the younger was cultivated by his father
at the tender age of 4, when the child began to
learn the violin. At the age of 8 he played
before the imperial court, and a year later,
1803, won great success at two concerts at
Prague, by his performance of a concerto by
Fodor, an adagio by Rode and some variations of his own composition. On his return
to Vienna he resumed his studies with increased
ardour, and became a pupil of Förster in composition. In 1818 he was appointed leader of
the orchestra at the court of Hanover, and
in 1824 and 1825 was heard, gaining success at
many concerts in different German towns. In
1827 he became director of the music at the
court of the Grand Duke of Baden, and
appeared at a concert in Paris in 1832, but
was eclipsed by the extraordinary talent of
Paganini, who had taken the Parisians by
storm. He still occupied his post at the Baden
court in 1837. His published compositions
include a concerto for violin and orchestra,
some polonaises for violin and orchestra,
thèmes variés, rondos, two string quartets,
and duos concertants for two violins. E. H.-A.

PÊCHEURS DE PERLES, LES, opera in
3 acts, libretto by Cormon and Carré, music
by Bizet. Produced Théâtre-Lyrique, Paris,
Sept. 29, 1863 ; Covent Garden, as 'Leïla,'
Apr. 22, 1887, and as 'I pescatori di perle,'
May 18, 1889 ; New York, Metropolitan Opera
House, Jan. 11, 1896.　　　　　　　　　M.

PECK, JAMES, a London music engraver and
publisher, principally of sacred music. He was

at Westmorland Buildings, in Aldersgate Street, c. 1800, and at 47 Lombard Street in 1802–03, and here he remained for over twenty years. From this last - named address most of his publications were issued. In Dec. 1824 he had recently removed to 52 Paternoster Row. He engraved and published, both on his own behalf and on that of individual composers, great numbers of Psalmodies, and books of hymn tunes for the Wesleyan body, besides sheet-music of a secular nature. In 1850 the business had come into the hands of John Peck, at 44 Newgate Street.　　　　　　　F. K.

PEDAL (from *pes*, 'a foot'), certain appliances in the organ, pianoforte and harp, worked by the feet.

(1) In the organ there are keys, sounding notes, and played by the feet instead of the hands ; and the PEDAL-BOARD is the whole *breadth* or range of such keys. According to R. Schlechte, pedals were invented by Ludwig van Vaelboke of Brabant, about 1306. In England pedals seem not to have been introduced until 1772, when Snetzler employed them in the German Lutheran Chapel, London. (For the evolution of the pedal-board see under ORGAN, Vol. III. p. 753.)

The compass almost universally adopted in England for the pedal-board extends from CCC up to tenor F, thirty notes — $2\frac{1}{2}$ octaves. Occasionally they are carried up even to G. Bach wrote twice up to F—in his Toccata in that key—once up to F♯, and two or three times to E. Once he wrote down to BB, for the sake of preserving a certain figure unaltered.

COMPOSITION PEDALS.—Pedals placed above the pedal-board throw out or draw in the stops in groups. When they act upon the wind and not upon the stops, they are sometimes called Combination pedals, and are practically the same as the 'Ventils' of the old German organs, and the ' pédales des Combinaisons ' of the modern French builders.

SWELL PEDAL.—The treadle, usually placed to the extreme right, by which the swell shutters are opened or closed. A balanced swell pedal placed directly in front of the player is now largely adopted in new organs, the vertical shutters remaining in any position.

Other pedals, horseshoe-shaped as well as of other forms, are sometimes introduced to act upon the manual and pedal-couplers. E. J. H.

(2) In the pianoforte, the pedals are levers, usually two,[1] which are pressed either to diminish or to increase and prolong the tone of a pianoforte. That for the left foot, the *piano* pedal, acts by reducing the number of strings struck by the hammers, or softens their impact either by interposing a strip of felt, or by diminishing their length of blow. That for the right foot, the *forte* pedal, takes the dampers

[1] Piano or Soft Pedal (Fr. *petite pédale*; Ger. *Verschiebung, Pianozug*) ; Forte or Damper or Sustaining Pedal (Fr. *grande pédale*; Ger. *grosses Pedal, Fortezug*).

out of use altogether, or allows the player, by judicious management with the foot, so as to avoid confusing the sound, to augment and prolong it by increasing what are called sympathetic vibrations, an invaluable help to the beauty of tone of the instrument. Pedals were first adapted to the harpsichord, the right to move the swell, and the left to relieve the hands from the interruption of moving stops. This ' beautiful invention,' as C. P. E. Bach calls it (*Versuch*, etc., 1762, 2ter Theil, p. 245), was attributed by him to ' our celebrated Herr Holefeld,' but Mace, in *Musick's Monument*, enables us to claim the invention for the English harpsichord-maker, John Hayward.[2] The pedals were attached on either side of the stand upon which the harpsichord rested, as they were in the grand pianoforte until 1806, or even later. The name of the inventor of the lyre-shaped frame for the pedals is not forthcoming. Zumpe's square piano (1766 and later) had stops next to the left hand of the player, to raise the dampers in two divisions.[3] Stein's and other German pianos had a lever to be pressed by the knee. (See MUTE.)

Real *Piano* and *Forte* pedals first occur in John Broadwood's patent of Nov. 1783. The first he effected by damping the strings near the belly - bridge with a strip of soft material which he called a 'sordin' or mute; the second by taking away the dampers from the strings. Sebastian Erard, whose first English patent is dated 1794, and includes a soft-pedal effect obtained by means of a shifting beam, or rail, to support the hammers, and so lessening the striking distance, apparently adopted a principle in use in the German pianos of the 18th century, and placed the strip of cloth between the hammers and the strings, an invention which Adolphe Adam, in his Tutor for the Paris Conservatoire, called *céleste*. The Germans call it *flauto pedal*, and BÖSENDORFER of Vienna re-introduced it in grand pianofortes as a third pedal, which may be fixed by a notch when an almost dumb instrument is required for practising. The 'céleste pedal' cannot, however, rival the Æolian charm of the shifting pedal, first introduced by Stein in his ' Saitenharmonica,' the beauty of which arises from the vibrations of the unused strings which are excited from the sound-board; and as they have not been jerked by a hammer-blow, they sound with another and more ethereal timbre than those which have been struck.[4] The piano pedal used to be controlled in its shifting by a small stop or wedge in the right-hand key-block, so that the shift could be made to either two strings or one at the discretion of the player. The latter was Stein's ' Spinetchen,' the *una corda* or *eine Saite* of Beethoven, who expressed the return to the

[2] See footnote to article HARPSICHORD describing an early instrument by Haywood.
[3] The division of the dampers in grand pianos was retained until as late as 1830, by division of the right pedal-foot.
[4] See Hipkins's *History of the Pianoforte*, p. 42.

three strings by *Nach und nach mehrere Saiten, Tutte le corde*, or *Tutto il cembalo* (op. 101). The one-string shift in grand pianofortes has been for many years discarded, sharing the fate of the extra pedals that produced an imitation of a bassoon, or added a drum, a bell, etc. The use of the céleste pedal was indicated by Hummel with a special sign, thus △.[1]

The effect of the *forte* or damper pedal is to increase the tone of the note struck by calling out the partial tones of lower notes which are equivalent to its full vibrating length or prime; the strings of higher registers becoming primes to the partials composing the note struck ; in both cases by relation of measurement and by excitement from the sound-board.[2] The Pedal thus adds a wonderful enrichment to the tone. The modern signs for its use and disuse are respectively ' Ped.' and ⊕, or a star.

A pedal (*pédale de prolongement ou tonale* ; Ger. *Kunstpedal*) was introduced by Montal of Paris, a blind man, and exhibited by him in 1862 in London (see PIANOFORTE), to allow selected notes to vibrate while the rest are immediately damped. It has been again brought forward by Steinway and others, and its value much insisted upon. Hitherto it has not proved to be of much use in the concert-room. The Kunstpedal of Zachariae of Stuttgart divides the row of dampers by four cleft pedal feet into eight sections, and thus facilitates the use of the staccato.

(3) In the harp the pedals alter the pitch in two gradations of a semitone each. The mechanical contrivance for this is described in the article HARP. The invention of these chromatic pedals is attributed to a Bavarian, named Hochbrucker, about 1720. The gradual improvement and extended use of them culminated in 1810, in the double-action harp at that date perfected by Sebastian Erard.

                            A. J. H.

**PEDAL-BOARD**, the pedal-clavier of an organ.

**PEDAL CLARINET**, see CLARINET (5).

**PEDALIER.** (1) A pedal keyboard attached to a pianoforte, and acting by connexion with its mechanism upon the hammers and strings proper to it.

(2) An independent bass pianoforte so called by its inventors, Pleyel, Wolff & Cie of Paris, to be played by pedals only, and used with an ordinary pianoforte.

J. S. Bach had a harpsichord with two rows of keys and pedals, although it would be difficult to point with any degree of certainty to works written for this, rather than for the organ. In some few pieces (the Sonata in D, B.-G. xxxvi. p. 19, and the two fugues in A, *ib.* pp. 169 and 173) single notes near the end are clearly intended to be played on the pedal. Since Bach many clavecinists and pianists have had their instruments fitted with two rows of pedals, and compositions have been specially written—as, for instance, by Schumann, who wrote several ' Studien ' and ' Skizzen ' (opp. 56 and 58) for the Pedal-Flügel or Pedalier Grand Pianoforte. C. V. Alkan also wrote some noble works for this instrument, which, together with some adaptations from Bach, were brought forward in 1871 by E. M. Delaborde of Paris, in his performance at the Hanover Square Rooms, upon a Pedalier Grand Piano specially constructed for him by Broadwood. Gounod wrote a concertante for pedal piano with orchestra, and a fantasia on the Russian National Hymn, for Mme. Lucie Palicot, by whom they were played at the Philharmonic Concert on Apr. 21, 1887.

                            A. J. H.

**PEDAL NOTES.** On trombones and the majority of brass wind instruments the easy practical compass begins with the second note of the harmonic series. The extension of the slide of the trombone, or a similar lengthening of the tube by means of the valves on a valve instrument, lowers the general pitch, as from *c* to B, A or G, but the *relative* pitch of each note compared with its new prime remains the same. The descending chromatic scale on the trombone, or on a three-valved instrument, in *c*, ends with F♯, leaving a gap between this note and C, the prime or fundamental note of the instrument. This C, however, and the notes below it to F♯, although rarely used, should not be regarded as forced or ' made ' notes, as they are part of the natural compass of the instrument, requiring, it must be admitted, a specially slack lip. It is these prime notes, the lowest proper tones of the instrument, as obtained either from its normal length, or its length as varied by shifting slide or valves, which are known as pedal notes. In other words, a pedal note always stands for the first note or No. 1 in the harmonic series.

On trumpets and some other instruments the pedal notes are practically impossible. D. J. B.

**PEDAL ORGAN**, the organ belonging exclusively to the Pedal-board.

**PEDAL PIANO**, see PEDALIER.

**PEDAL POINT** (Fr. *point d'orgue*), is a term used to describe the sustaining of a note in one part while the other parts pass through harmonies which may or may not be normally related to the sustained note itself. The term is of great historical importance, and it is usual to reserve it for those cases in which the idiom involved is of substantial length or significance. The incidental occurrence of a

---

[1] This arrangement of the shifting soft pedal exists in an unaltered grand piano of John Broadwood's, dated 1793. It is thus possible that in this form it may have been an invention of that maker, or, if not his, an English invention simultaneously with Stein's.

[2] The partials above the prime also excite their equivalents in vibrating length, but will probably not be audible above the third or fourth. Owing to equal-temperament tuning the fifth partial could only be very feebly excited. At the seventh and eighth we arrive about the striking-place of the hammer by which those partials are obliterated.

sustained note which is common to a few consecutive chords is not necessarily sufficient to establish an accepted pedal point.

The pedal point is undoubtedly derived from the various kinds of drone found frequently in early or primitive music. Where such drones have a fixed pitch their musical function is important, if only to the extent that they sustain the chosen relations of pitch. When harmonic inferences are also involved, the drone assumes a more or less definite harmonic relation towards the various ideas that may be combined with it. This latter is the true function of a pedal point, and it is for this reason that the notes most commonly used as pedal points are those which infer most clearly a particular harmonic meaning or direction.

The evolution of instrumental music found the organ especially adapted for effects of this kind, and as the harmonic sense had by this time learnt to classify its impressions with reference to roots which were generally either stated or implied in the bass, the traditional view of a pedal point became primarily associated with the sustaining of an important bass note, after the manner of an organ pedal. Hence the alternative title : *point d'orgue.*

Harmonic logic, however, could with equal propriety accept sustained points in parts other than the lowest, and there are therefore numerous examples of both inverted and internal pedal points which have the same harmonic significance as the more common pedal points in the bass.

The most important notes in a chosen scale are by definition the tonic and dominant, and these are the notes commonly selected for the purposes of a drone. In similar fashion the harmony which finds its ultimate argument in the logic of tonality, makes the tonic and dominant its chief pivots of thought. Thus the pedal points of classical music are almost exclusively confined to the tonic and dominant of the key of the particular movement or section. That the tonic is common to chords of tonic, subdominant and relative minor, and that the dominant is common to chords of tonic, dominant and mediant, are circumstances which have naturally assisted the traditional handling of the device. And though the more fluid harmonic intuitions of later times have permitted composers to use other degrees of the scale in like fashion, the function of preserving a particular harmonic atmosphere or relation, through a sequence of incidental changes, is common to all the idioms which properly belong to the category of pedal points. It is therefore more or less axiomatic that however extreme may be the possible clashes of harmonic inference involved in the bold use of a pedal point, yet the beginning of it must be strictly connected with the harmonies which precede it, and the end of it must

similarly be consistently related to those which follow. This means, in classical terminology, that pedal points must begin and end on concords, or on chords which have an unequivocal context.

Some of the harmonic consequences of the

DOMINANT PEDAL.        BACH. *Chromatic Fantasia.*
1.

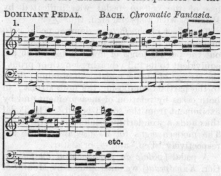

TONIC PEDAL.    BACH. *Das Wohltemperirte Klavier.*
2.                    Prelude : Book I, No. 22.

INVERTED TONIC PEDAL.
3.                    BACH. *Das Wohltemperirte Klavier.*
                     Prelude - Book I, No.18.

INTERNAL TONIC PEDAL.  BACH. *Choralvorspiel.*
4.                    "Am Wasserflüssen Babylon."

use of the pedal point have been discussed in the article on HARMONY. The preceding examples will sufficiently define the normal applications of the term.

PEDRELL, (1) FELIPE (b. Tortosa, Feb. 19, 1841 ; d. Barcelona, Aug. 19, 1922), Spanish composer and historian. Though the most learned musician in Spain, he was almost entirely self-taught ; but the direction of his subsequent development was given him by his first master, Juan Antonio Nin y Serra, who advised him to take the themes for his exercises from the songs sung by his mother. As a choir-boy in the cathedral of his native town, Pedrell gained an intimate working knowledge of old Spanish church music ; and in after life he spoke of the terror inspired in him by one of the primitive chants (with words in the vernacular) which he had to sing in a procession on Good Friday. Pedrell's earliest compositions were published in 1871, before anything of Granados or Albéniz. His first opera, ' El último Abencerraje,' dates from 1874. Soon after that, he was teacher of musical history and æsthetics at the Madrid Conservatoire, a post which he held until 1894, when bad health drove him back to Barcelona. In that year his 3-act opera ' Los Pirineos ' was published (performed Barcelona, 1892 ; Buenos Aires, 1910) ; and this, and his pamphlet Por nuestra musica (translated into French), brought him to the notice of European musicians as a Spaniard who was preaching reform on the lines of Wagner. This was a mistaken idea of what Pedrell was doing. He had taken to heart the saying of EXIMENO (q.v.) in the 18th century, that every country should build its music on the foundation of native song ; and the revival of music in Spain (as in England, Hungary and elsewhere) has depended on the discovery of the genuine folk-songs of the country, as opposed to those which had falsely passed as such. To this Pedrell added that the characteristics of all music which is truly national are to be found, not only in folk-song and the instinctive music of primitive times, but also in the masterpieces of the centuries of great artistic development—a generalisation which modern research has shown to be as true of England as it is of Spain. Pedrell's compositions, though based on native traditions, are written in too serious a style for them to have been a success with the public. They interested neither the Wagnerites nor the others, and their proper understanding demanded a knowledge of musical history which few members of an audience possess. The opera ' La Celestina,' however, contains much fine music and intensely dramatic situations. ' El Comte Arnau,' though adaptable to the theatre or the concert-room, is really intended for performance in the open air, under the conditions of a Greek theatre. Besides the

chorus on the stage there is also a chorus in the orchestra ; while the subject (a fine poem on a character from an old Catalan ballad) is one which readily lends itself to music, since Comte Arnau (Count Arnold), having lost his soul through carrying off Adelaisa from her convent, finds it again in a song.

As a musical archæologist Pedrell's great achievement was the publication of a reliable text of the complete works of VICTORIA. His researches threw a flood of light on the composer's last years in Madrid and only ended, during the war, with the discovery of the death-certificate, proving that the greatest of Spanish musicians lived several years longer than is generally supposed, dying on Aug. 7 or 27, 1611. His ' Hispaniae scholae musica sacra,' an edition of selected works of Morales, Guerrero, Victoria, G.nés Pérez and Diego Ortiz, with the complete keyboard pieces of Antonio Cabezón, is (with the exception of the vols. devoted to Cabezón) hardly as satisfactory as the edition of Victoria, though it made much fine Spanish church music available for performance. A greater achievement was the splendid catalogue of the music in the municipal library at Barcelona (the Biblioteca de la Diputació or Bibl. Catalana). Pedrell also published valuable collections of old Spanish theatre music and organ music ; and contributed striking articles (e.g. on the Mystery of ELCHE) to the Sammelbände of the I.M.G. His folk-lore studies culminated in the ' Cancionero musical popular español,' though he was inclined to distort his texts (e.g. Salinas and the lutenists) to fit his theories. By this time he was an old and in some ways a disappointed man, with the reputation of being difficult to deal with ; his printers were not as careful as they might have been. His last editorial work was concerned with an accurate and scholarly edition of the madrigals of BRUDIEU (q.v.), his collaborator being Mn. Higini Anglés, chief of the music section of the Bibl. de la Diputació.

Spanish composers of the 20th century certainly owe a great debt to Pedrell, and they have not hesitated to declare themselves his pupils. This, however, s only true of FALLA, who has inherited the master's attitude to folk-lore, although his music sounds totally different. Pedrell (like Morales in the 16th century' raised the status of Spanish musicians in the opinion of the rest of Europe. By the Spanish public, however, he was unknown, and by the official world unrecognised ; and he was unable to perform a task still waiting to be done—that of raising the status of music in the opinion of educated Spanish men and women. In Barcelona that status is certainly high, fostered as it has been by Pablo CASALS and the Orfeó Català, while to the majority in Spain the only serious music is folk-song. No one has recognised the importance of folk-song more clearly than Pedrell; yet he knew that there was more in music than that. To him music also meant Victoria, an art which, independent of folk-lore or even the Church, went straight to the human consciousness as an experience of beauty, and an experience in which every one might share.

The most important compositions of Pedrell are the operas 'Los Pirineos' (1894), 'La Celestina' (1903) and 'El Comte Arnau' (published 1921). For his other works, in music and criticism, see P. G. Morales, in *A Dictionary of Modern Music*, 1924; E. Istel, in the *Musical Quarterly*, Apr. 1924; A. Reiff, *Z.M.W.* iii. 304, Feb. 1921. His place in modern Spanish music is best described in the *Revue musicale*, Feb. 1923 (reprinted Barcelona, 1923), by Manuel de Falla.

J. B. T.

(2) CARLOS (b. Minas, Uruguay, Oct. 16, 1878), nephew of the above, studied with his uncle (1898–1900) and afterward at the Schola Cantorum in Paris. He settled in Buenos Aires as inspector of music in schools, lecturer, etc. He has composed much, including an opera, 'Ardid de Amor,' given at Buenos Aires in 1917, symphonic works and songs.

PEDROTTI, CARLO (b. Verona, Nov. 12, 1817; d. there, Oct. 16, 1893), studied music in his native town under Domenico Foroni, and produced his first opera, 'Lina,' at the Teatro Filodrammatico, Verona, in 1840. To its success he owed his appointment as conductor of the Italian opera at Amsterdam, where he remained until 1845. While at Amsterdam he wrote and produced the operas 'Matilde' (1841) and 'La figlia dell' arciere' (1844). He returned to Italy in 1845 and undertook the direction of the Nuovo and Filarmonico Theatres at Verona, which he retained until 1868. During this period he produced the operas 'Romea di Montfort' (Verona, 1845); 'Fiorina' (Verona, 1851); 'Il parrucchiere della reggenza' (Verona, 1852); 'Gelmina' (Milan, 1853); 'Genoveffa del Brabante' (Milan, 1854); 'Tutti in maschera' (Verona, 1856), which was unquestionably his masterpiece, and was performed in a French translation at the Athénée Theatre, Paris, in 1869; 'Isabella d' Aragona' (Turin, 1859); 'Mazeppa' (Bologna, 1861); 'Guerra in quattro' (Milan, 1861); and 'Marion Delorme' (Trieste, 1865). In 1868 Pedrotti migrated to Turin, where he had been appointed director of the Liceo Musicale and conductor at the Teatro Regio. Here he founded the 'Concerti sinfonici popolari,' which took place every week in the Teatro Vittorio Emmanuele, and were the means of introducing the works of Beethoven, Wagner, and other German composers to Italian audiences. Pedrotti's latest operas were 'Il favorito' (Turin, 1870) and 'Olema la schiava' (Modena, 1872), but he found that

his vogue was past, and that the younger generation cared little for his music. The closing years of his life were devoted almost exclusively to teaching. He committed suicide by throwing himself into the Adige. At his best Pedrotti was a master of light *opera buffa*. His music was invariably bright and tuneful, and the rhythmic swing and unforced gaiety of 'Tutti in maschera' were irresistible; but he was unable to keep pace with the changing fashions of his time, and fell unavoidably into the background.                    R. A. S.

PEEBLES, DAVID (d. St. Andrews, Scotland, Dec. 1579), a 16th-century musician of St. Andrews, whom Thomas Wood describes as a 'notable cunning man.' He wrote a book of psalms in parts, and, about 1530, a 5-part motet, 'si quis diliget me,' which he presented to James V.[1]

PEERSON, MARTIN (b. circa 1580; d. between Dec. 26, 1650, and Jan. 17, 1650/51). By his will he bequeathed a legacy to the poor of the parish of Dunnington in the Isle of Ely, and it seems likely that this was his birthplace. He was probably born about 1580, because in the year 1604 he set Ben Jonson's words 'See O see who comes here a maying' for 'the King and Queenes entertaynment at Highgate on May Day.' This composition was published in 1620 as the last number in his

'Private Musicke, or the First Booke of Ayres and Dialogues, Contayning Songs of 4, 5 and 6 parts, of severall sorts, and being verse and Chorus is fit for Voyces and Viols. And for the want of Viols, they may be performed to either the Virginall or Lute, where the proficient can play upon the Ground, or for a shift to the Base viol alone. All made and composed according to the rules of art.'

As the title indicates, the character of the music differs in many respects from the strict madrigalian style. Most of the pieces are for solo or duet and chorus, and none should properly be sung without accompaniment. 'Upon my lap my Sovereign sits' is a song of the Blessed Virgin and is for two voices and chorus; the words are those of Robert Verstegan. 'Sing, Love is blind' is much more modern in design than a madrigal. Peerson's second volume was published in 1630 under the title of :

'Mottects or Grave Chamber Musique. Containing Songs of five parts of severall sorts, some ful, and some Verse and Chorus. But all fit for Voyces and Vials, with an Organ Part; which for want of Organs, may be performed on Virginals, Base-Lute, Bandora, or Irish Harpe. Also, a Mourning Song of sixe parts for the Death of the late Right Honorable Sir Fulke Grevil, Knight of the Honourable order of the Bath, Lord Brooke, Baron Brooke of Beauchamp-Court in the Countie of Warwicke, and of his Maiesties most honourable privie Councell, etc. Composed according to the Rules of Art.'

The whole of the poems of this set, with the necessary exception of the Elegy, are taken from Fulke Greville's *Caelica* sonnets. There is a 5-part setting of the Elegy as well as the 6 part one mentioned on the title-page. Greville died in 1628. In his secular vocal music Peerson stands in an intermediate position between the madrigalists and the Restoration composers.

Peerson's instrumental music is of a very interesting character; the fantasies in B.M. Add. MSS. 17,786-92 are among the most attractive

[1] G. Davey, *Hist. Eng. Mus.*

of all the string pieces of this period. There are 6 fantasies and 7 almains in this collection and some more are at Christ Church, Oxford (see Arkwright, *Cat.*). Four pieces by this composer are in the ' Fitzwilliam Virginal Book.' Among these ' The Primerose ' has a special charm.

The merits of his church music are little known, for excepting his 3 contributions to Leighton's ' Teares or Lamentacions,' none of it was printed, and none of it has been published in modern editions.

Peerson took the degree of B.Mus. at Oxford on July 8, 1613, and shortly after this date he became master of the choristers and organist of St. Paul's Cathedral. He was buried in the chapel of St. Faith in the Cathedral.

E. H. F.

LIST OF CHURCH MUSIC

All laude and praise, *a* 5. B.M. Add. MSS. 29427/26*b*, Altus part only.
Blow out the trumpet. Durh.; Bodl. Mus. Sch., D. 212-6; B.M. Add. MSS. 29372-7.
Bow down thine ear. PH.
By Euphrates flowrie side, *a* 5. B.M. Add. MSS. 29427/20*b*, altus part only.
Fly ravisht soule, *a* 3. B.M. Add. MSS. 29372-7.
I am brought into so great trouble, *a* 2. B.M. Add. MSS. 29372-7.
I will magnify. Durh.
Lord ever bridle my desires. B.M. Add. MSS. 31418/47. Score. (B.M.) R. Ac. 63/26. Cantus part only; attributed to Henry Palmer; B.M. Add. MSS. 17792-6.
(?) O goe not from me, *a* 5. B.M. Add. MSS. 29372-7.
O God that no tyrne doot despise. B.M. Add. MSS. 31418/15. Score. (B.M.) R. Ac. 63/14*b*, cantus part only.
O lett me at thy footstoole fall. B.M. Add. MSS. 29372-7.
O Lord in Thee. Ch. Ch. 56-60. Bass part wanting.
O Lord, Thou hast searched me out, *a* 4. B.M. Add. MSS. 29372-7.
O that my wayes (2nd part). I will thanke thee } B.M. Add. MSS. 29372-7.
Plead thou my cause. B.M. Add. MSS. 29372-7.
Raine, eyes. B.M. Add. MSS. 29372-7.
Who will rise up. B.M. Add. MSS. 29372-7.
(2nd part) But when I said. B.M Add. MSS. 29372-7.

J. Mᴷ.

**PÈLERINS DE LA MECQUE, LES**, see Rencontre imprévue, La.

**PELLÉAS ET MÉLISANDE**, opera in 5 acts, set to Maeterlinck's play by Debussy. Produced Opéra-Comique, Paris, Apr. 30, 1902; New York, Feb. 19, 1908; Covent Garden, May 21, 1909; in English, Denhof Opera Co., Prince of Wales's Theatre, Birmingham, Sept. 19, 1913.

Schönberg has written a symphonic poem, op. 5, on this subject, produced Berlin, 1911.

**PELLEGRINI**, Vincenzo (*b.* Pesaro, late 16th cent.), a canon at Pesaro, *c.* 1603; maestro di cappella at Milan Cathedral, 1611–31. He composed 2 books of masses, other church music and secular canzonets in collective volumes, also a book of canzonets in organ tablature, in the French style (Venice, 1599); and instrumental pieces in 3 and 4 parts in Lucino e Fil. Lomazzo's ' Seconda aggiunta alli Concerti,' 1617 (*Q.-L.*).

**PEÑALOSA**, Francisco (15th-16th cent.), Spanish composer. He is said to have been choirmaster to Ferdinand the Catholic after 1504, and then to have been in the choir of the Cappella Giulia under Leo X., but is not mentioned by Haberl or Celani. Barbieri printed 10 compositions in his edition of the ' Cancionero de los siglos XV. y XVI.' (Madrid, 1890), including a quodlibet, in which 5 voices sing different folk-songs, while the bass remarks *Loquebantur variis linguis.* . . . Church music by him exists in several MSS. at Barcelona (Bibl. de la Diputació; Orfeó Catelà), Tarazona (Cathedral) and elsewhere. A complete edition is in preparation by Mn. Higini Anglés.

J. B. T.

**PEÑALOSA**, Juan (mid-16th cent.), Spanish church-composer, elected organist of Toledo Cathedral in 1549. The motets preserved in MS. at Toledo,[1] are probably by him, and not by Francisco, judging by the style and by the fact that one of them (' Memorare piissima oprobria ') is dated 1549. Eight of these were printed by Eslava, attributed to Francisco Peñalosa. The cathedral archives at Granada contain a ' Missa pro defunctis ' by ' Peñalosa,' probably also Juan.

J. B. T.

**PÉNÉLOPE**, lyric poem in 3 acts; words of R. Fauchois, music by Gabriel Fauré. First performed Monte Carlo, Mar. 4, 1913; Paris, Théâtre des Champs Élysées, May 10, 1913; Opéra-Comique, Apr. 11, 1922.

M. L. P.

**PENET**, Hilaire, described as a clerk of the Diocese of Poitiers (clericus Pictavensis), was admitted in 1514 as a singer in the Papal Chapel, and was also appointed one of the *cantores secreti* or chamber musicians to Pope Leo X.[2] His compositions which are preserved are not numerous, a Mass *a* 4 in the choir-books of the Papal Chapel, and a few motets and other works in the collections of the time. Ambros commends his motets as good, tasteful work.

J. R. M.

**PENNA**, Lorenzo (*b.* Bologna, 1613; *d.* Oct. 20, 1693), maestro di cappella of S. Ilario, Casalo Monferrato, 1656. Shortly before 1669 he entered the Carmelite Order at Mantua, and after that he became maestro of the Carmelite church at Parma. At the same time he was Master of Theology and Doctor of the College of the Academy ' dei Filaschisi e Resoluti,' and held a similar position at Imola Cathedral. He composed masses and other church music, French Correntes in 4 parts (1673); also 2 theoretical works, one, on counterpoint and figured bass, having appeared in 5 editions as well as in a piracy by Phalèse of Antwerp (1690).

E. V. D. S.

**PENTATONIC SCALE.** A pentatone is a scale of five notes, *i.e.* in which the octave is reached on the sixth note. This involves some of the notes being more than a tone apart. Similarly six-note scales are hexatones and seven-note may be called, for distinction, heptatones. No instances are found of a scale with less than five notes to the octave, and those with more than seven are rare or doubtful.

A tetrachord is the interval of a fourth with one or two, seldom more, interior notes. The

1 Bibl Provincial and Cathedral.
2 See Haberl, *Bausteine*, iii. p. 69.

remainder of the octave (another tetrachord and a tone) is a pentachord. The additional tone is called the disjunctive tone. A tone is obtained by ascending a fifth and descending a fourth, or *vice versa*; but the ear is cognisant of the interval long before it makes this analysis.

TONAL PENTATONIC.—The study of present-day primitive music (the only and the sufficient substitute for antiquity of record) shows certain tendencies in scale-making. The vocal scale, the first stage, proceeds downward; the instrumental, later and more precise, upward. After some first tentative efforts the tetrachord is taken as the basis. The tetrachord is filled first with one note, later with two. As this becomes familiar the compass is gradually enlarged to two tetrachords, the central note being usually the tonic. From these tendencies, which are supported by copious evidence, we may argue to an early form of scale such as

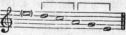

As instruments came in, with diverse pitch and compass, fragments or extensions of this came into use, and eventually the five pentatones

became familiar, though locally one or two of them were preferred to the others.

SEMITONAL PENTATONIC.—So far we have considered pentatones as based only on the octave and fifth and their derivatives, fourth and tone. But in some parts of the world—China, Japan and India, for instance—the major third also became audible, and this, when placed inside the fourth, gave the semitone.

Hence the tetrachord, 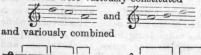 giving another set of five pentatones.

HEXATONES, ETC.—As the pentatones, either tonal or semitonal, became familiar, their tetrachords were variously constituted

 and

and variously combined

and

and when, in addition to this, tonal and semitonal met in one country—in India and China, and to a less degree Japan, which borrowed from China—a very great number of pentatones were produced. A good musician would know not far short of a hundred.

Comparing the last three notes of the two scales just given we see that together they produce the tetrachord ♪ . This combination gives us the hexatone

;

and we can easily devise many others—

—for instance, which is so common in modern Greek folk-song, formed from two semitonal tetrachords. The step from hexatone to heptatone is only a matter of time.

The octave very rarely exceeds eight notes (inclusive) or the tetrachord four; and from the way in which the latter was formed we see why.

'GAPPED' SCALES.—These pentatones and hexatones are sometimes called 'gapped' or 'transilient,' implying that a note has been left out. But it was never there. The five notes of the scale were felt as adjacent. There is no more of a gap between D and F for an ear that has never heard it filled than there is between F and G for us who are for the moment ignoring the F♯. But if we continue, as we conveniently may, to call them gaps, we may notice that they always occur at the interval of a fourth (or fifth); and that is the distinguishing mark of the true pentatonic

Such a scale as ♪ would be a mongrel—a τόνος μικτός, as the Greeks said.

The Scotch pentatones are mostly tonal, the Irish and English also occasionally semitonal. The Arabian scales have divided the 'gap' mechanically, and obtained a three-quarter tone, and the result is there also to this day in the bagpipe, however it may have been arrived at. The theory that gapped scales were formed by taking the 5th, 6th, 7th and other harmonics needs more substantiation than it has at present received, and such scales are not pentatonic in the accepted sense of the word.      A. H. F. S.

PENTATONON (πεντάτονον), the Greek term for the interval known in modern music as the Augmented Sixth, which consists, in the aggregate, of five Tones; *i.e.* two Greater and two Lesser Tones, and one Diatonic and one Chromatic Semitone.      W. S. R.

PEOPLE'S CHORAL UNION AND SINGING CLASSES, see NEW YORK.

PEOPLE'S CHORUS OF NEW YORK, see NEW YORK.

PEOPLE'S CONCERT SOCIETY. This Society, which exists for the purpose of popularising good music in the poorer parts of London, was founded in June 1878 by a number of enthusiastic musical amateurs. A small charge for admission is an essential feature of the plan,

The concerts are given in various centres, sometimes in co-operation with local settlements, etc. (see SOUTH PLACE SUNDAY CONCERTS), and in late years in H.M. Prisons. At the end of the 45th season, 1923–24, over 1600 concerts, orchestral and chamber, had been given. The 47th season, 1925–26, included an extension of the work through co-operation with the British Broadcasting Company. The funds of the Society are derived from the receipts from the concert and from annual subscriptions and donations. Sir Henry Hadow is chairman of the Society.                                    N. C. G.

PEOPLE'S SYMPHONY CONCERTS, see NEW YORK.

PEOPLE'S SYMPHONY ORCHESTRA, see BOSTON.

PEPUSCH, JOHN CHRISTOPHER, Mus.D. (b. Berlin, 1667; d. London, July 20, 1752), son of the minister of a Protestant congregation in Berlin, studied the theory of music under Gottlieb Klingenberg, organist at Stettin, and the practice of it under Grosse, a Saxon organist. At 14 years of age he obtained an appointment at the Prussian court. Devoting himself to the study of the ancient Greek writers, he became a deeply skilled theorist. He retained his appointment until he was thirty years old, when, being an eye-witness (according to Hawkins) of an act of savage ferocity on the part of the King (the decapitation, without trial, of an officer who had uttered some words at which the barbarous despot took offence), he determined on quitting his native land for some country where human life was not in danger of destruction by the unbridled will of an individual. He first went to Holland, where he remained for upwards of a year.

He came to England about 1700 and was engaged in the orchestra at Drury Lane. In 1707 he adapted the music of the opera 'Thomyris, Queen of Scythia,' besides composing the recitatives and some additional songs, and probably did the same for others of the Anglo-Italian operas produced about that period. And at the same time, with the assistance of Abraham de Moivre, the celebrated mathematician, he zealously pursued his study of the music of the ancients. In 1710 he took an active part in the establishment of the ACADEMY OF ANCIENT MUSIC, in which he took a deep interest throughout his life. In 1712 he was engaged by the Duke of Chandos as organist and composer to his chapel at Cannons, for which he produced several services and anthems. About 1716 he published 'Six Cantatas' (in English and Italian) and 'Six English Cantatas,' the words by John Hughes, which were received with great favour, and one of which, 'Alexis,' with violoncello obbligato, continued to be sung in public until the first half of the 19th century had nearly passed away. On July 9, 1713, he took the degree of Mus.D. at Oxford, his exer-

cise (performed July 13) being a dramatic ode on the Peace of Utrecht : the words were printed on both sides of a folio leaf. About the same time he revived the practice of solmisation by hexachords, which had been abandoned for upwards of a century. Soon afterwards he became music director at Lincoln's Inn Fields Theatre, and continued so for many years. During his engagement there he composed the music for 'Venus and Adonis,' masque, 1715; Colley Cibber's 'Myrtillo,' 1715; 'Apollo and Daphne' and 'The Death of Dido,' masques, 1716; and 'The Union of the Three Sister Arts,' masque for St. Cecilia's Day, 1723; 'The Squire of Alsatia,' 1726; besides arranging the tunes and composing overtures for 'The Beggar's Opera,' 1728, and 'The Wedding,' another ballad opera, 1729.[1] He also arranged the tunes for Gay's interdicted opera 'Polly,' 1729. (See BALLAD OPERA.)

In 1724 he was induced to join in Dr. Berkeley's scheme of a college in the Bermudas, and actually embarked, but the ship being wrecked, the undertaking was abandoned, and he returned to England. In 1718 he had married Margarita de l'Épine (see ÉPINE), the eminent singer, who brought him a fortune of £10,000. In 1730 there was published anonymously *A Treatise on Harmony, containing the chief Rules for composing in two, three and four parts*. As the rules contained in the book were those which Pepusch was in the habit of imparting to his pupils, and as they were published without the necessary musical examples, he felt compelled to adopt the work, and accordingly in 1731 published a second edition with the requisite additions, but still without his name. It was conjectured that the first edition was put forth by Viscount Paisley, afterwards Earl of Abercorn, who had been a pupil of Pepusch's; but on this point nothing is known. Corroboration of this theory is given in a copy in the British Museum containing a transcript of many of the examples in the second edition, in a hand closely resembling Lord Paisley's, and with the inscription 'aet. 44' corresponding to Lord Paisley's age in 1730. In 1737 he obtained the appointment of organist of the Charter House, where he passed the remainder of his days, devoting himself to his studies, the care of the Academy of Ancient Music, and the instruction of a few favourite pupils. His wife died early in Aug. 1746. Cooke writes under date 'Sunday, Aug. 10, 1746':

'I was at the [Surrey] Chapel in the morning, but in the afternoon went to Vauxhall with the Doctor, Mrs. Pepusch being dead.'

Pepusch lost his only child, a son, a youth of great promise, some short time before. He wrote a paper on the ancient Genera, which was read before the Royal Society, and published in the *Philosophical Transactions* for 1746, and for

[1] He arranged the music for 'Perseus and Andromeda' (Apr. 2, 1717) and 'Dioclesian' (Dec. 1724).                    W. H. C. F.

which he was elected F.R.S.   He was buried in
the chapel of the Charter House, where a tablet
was placed to his memory in 1757.   Besides the
compositions before named he produced odes to
the memory of the Duke of Devonshire, 1707
(sung by Margarita de l'Épine and Mrs. Tofts),
and for the Princess of Wales's birthday, Mar.
1, 1715–16 ; airs, sonatas, and concertos for
various combinations of string and wind instruments, and some Latin motets.   He also edited
Corelli's sonatas in score.   (See *Q.-L.*)   In
1751 he dictated *A Short Account of the Twelve
Modes of Composition and their Progression in
every Octave*, never published.   He bequeathed
his library to John Travers and Ephraim
Kelner, on whose deaths it was dispersed.   A
portrait of him is in the New Schools, Oxford.
Another portrait, by Hudson, has been engraved.   Although Pepusch was somewhat
pedantic, he was profoundly skilled in musical
science, and the musicians he formed (of whom
it is only necessary to mention Travers, Boyce
and Cooke) sufficiently attest his skill as a
teacher.　　　　　　w. h. h. ; addn. a. h. h.

PERABO, Ernst (*b.* Wiesbaden, Nov. 14,
1845 ; *d.* Oct. 29, 1920), one of ten children, all
followers of music.   His talent showed itself
very early, and at 12 years old he played
Bach's ' Wohltemperirtes Clavier ' by heart.   In
1852 his parents took him to New York, and
after a time arrangements were made through
the interest of William Schaufenberg, himself a
pupil of Hummel, to send him back to Germany
for education.   He left the United States
Sept. 1, 1858, and after nearly four years with
Joh. Andersen, at Eimsbüttel, near Hamburg,
he entered the Leipzig Conservatorium, Oct.
22, 1862.   After going successfully through
the course there under Moscheles, Richter,
Reinecke, etc., he returned to New York in
Nov. 1865, and after some hesitation settled at
Boston, where he made his first appearance at
the symphony concert of the Harvard Musical
Association, Apr. 19, 1866, and where he was
well known and much esteemed as a teacher, a
pianoforte-player, and a composer and arranger
of music for that instrument.   Amongst other
things he played the whole of Schubert's PF.
sonatas in public.   His compositions embrace a
scherzo, op. 2 ; three studies, op. 9 ; ' Pensées,'
op. 11, containing a musical setting of Hamlet's
Soliloquy (Augener & Co., London) ; ' Circumstance ' (Tennyson's Song, op. 13) ;  Prelude,
Romance and Toccatina, op. 19 ; and his
arrangements, ten transcriptions from Arthur
Sullivan's ' Iolanthe,' op. 14, Concert-Fantasies
from Beethoven's ' Fidelio,' opp. 16 and 17.   He
also published six sets of selections from various
composers, fingered and adapted for the piano.
　　　　　　g. ; additional information from
　　　　　　　　　E. P. Warren.

PERCUSSION.   The treatment of a large
proportion of discords is divided into three

stages — preparation, percussion and resolution.   The Preparation is the sounding of a discordant note in a previous chord, percussion
is the actual sounding of the discord, and
resolution the particular mode of its release,
or passage into concordance.   In the following
example, where E in the treble of the second
chord is the discordant note, (*a*) is the preparation, (*b*) the percussion, and (*c*) the resolution.
(See Preparation and Resolution.)

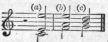

　　　　　　　　　　　　　　c. h. h. p.

PERCUSSION INSTRUMENTS.   Orchestral instruments are usually grouped under
the headings — string, wind and percussion.
The percussion group includes in one section
strained membranes such as drums and tambourines, and in another section plates and bars,
whether of wood or other hard material, appearing as cymbals, triangles, steel chimes, the
glockenspiel, castanets, xylophone and tubular
bells.　　　　　　　　　　　　　d. j. b.

PERCY, John (*b.* 1749 ; *d.* Jan. 24, 1797),
was a composer of ballads which were in favour
in the latter part of the 18th century, but which
have now passed out of remembrance, with the
single exception of ' Wapping Old Stairs.'   He
composed *Select Songs* (26) in 1795–97, which
included ' Gaffer Grey ' (No. 10) and ' I know a
bank ' (No. 17).   He published eight songs, op.
1, in 1781 ;  the Garden Scene from *Romeo and
Juliet* as a duet, Apr. 2, 1785 ;  and six ariettas,
op. 5, in 1786.   He was an organist and a tenor
vocalist.　　　　w. h. h. ; addn. w. h. g. f.

PERDENDOSI, PERDENDO LE FORZE,
' losing strength,' a direction like ' morendo,'
nearly always used at the end of a movement or
section of a movement.   It denotes a gradual
diminuendo, and in the later modern writers, a
slight rallentando as well.　　　　　　　　m.

PEREZ, Davide (David Peres) (*b.* Naples,
1711 ; *d.* ? Lisbon, after 1780), son of
Spaniard, was admitted in 1718 to the Conservatorio di Sta. Maria di Loreto, where he
studied the violin under Antonio Gallo, and
counterpoint under Francesco Mancini.   His
first opera, ' Siroë,'[1] was composed for San
Carlo in 1740.   At the invitation of Prince
Naselli he went to Palermo, and became master
of the Real Cappella Palatina.   Here he remained till 1748, and produced ' Li travesti-
menti amorosi' (1740), 'L'eroismo di Scipione'
(1741), ' Astartea,' ' Medea ' and ' L' isola disabitata.'   After ' La clemenza di Tito ' (1749),
given at San Carlo in Naples, and ' Semiramide'
(1750) at the Teatro delle Dame in Rome, he
composed operas for all the principal towns in
Italy.   In 1752 he accepted an invitation to
Lisbon, where he composed ' Demofoönte ' for
Gizziello and the tenor Raaff (Mozart's Munich

[1] The score, dated 1740, is in the Real Collegio of Naples.

friend), the success of which was so great that the King bestowed on him the Order of Christ, and the post of maestro at the Real Cappella, with a salary of 30,000 francs. The new theatre in Lisbon was opened in 1755 with Perez's opera 'Alessandro nelle Indie,' in which a corps of cavalry and a Macedonian phalanx appeared on the stage. Perez procured the best Italian singers for the opera during his managership. Other operas are mentioned in *Q.-L.* In 1755 he came to London, and produced 'Ezio' with great success. Here also was published in 1774 a fine edition, with portrait, of his 'Mattutino de' Morti,' his best sacred work, though he also composed, when in Lisbon, a 'Credo' for two choirs, and other church music. An oratorio, 'Il martirio di San Bartolomeo,' was performed at Padua in 1779. His compositions can scarcely be called remarkable, and Fétis ranks him below Jommelli. In person he resembled Handel, and like him he lost his sight in old age, but worked on up to his death. Specimens of Perez's work will be found in Vincent Novello's various publications.

In 1780 the composer resolved to return to Naples. On June 2 he embarked with his family on a Swedish ship, which was soon afterwards attacked by pirates. Perez and his son escaped the general massacre by hiding in the hold amongst the cargo; the ship was scuttled, and ran ashore at Albufeira. The composer lost all his possessions, which were considerable.      F. G.; addns. J. B. T.

**PÉREZ, JUAN GINEZ,** see GINES PÉREZ, Juan.

**PEREZ CASAS, BARTHOLOMÉ** (*b.* Lorca, Jan. 24, 1873), Spanish conductor and composer. Originally 1st clarinet, and then a military bandmaster, he became a teacher at the Madrid Conservatoire, and founded a wind-instrument society. In 1914–15 he was enabled to found the Madrid Philharmonic Orchestra, which, with the Symphony Orchestra (conducted by Fernández Arbós), provides Madrid and many other Spanish towns with symphonic music. He has produced many new works, including Vaughan Williams's 'London Symphony.' His own works include a 'Suite Murciana' for orch. and a string quartet.      J. B. T.

**PERFECT,** used principally of INTERVALS and CADENCES; see those headings, also HARMONY and TEMPERAMENT.

**PERFECT FOOL, THE,** opera in one act, written and composed by Gustav Holst; produced (B.N.O.C.) Covent Garden, May 14, 1923.

**PERGETTI.** Probably the last castrato who ever sang in England. He made his first appearance at the Società Armonica, May 6, 1844, in an aria from 'Ciglio,' an opera of his own, and is described as 'a brilliant and expressive singer, who won a deserved encore' (*Mus. Examiner*).      G.

**PERGOLA, LA,** see FLORENCE.

**PERGOLESI (PERGOLESE), GIOVANNI BATTISTA** (*b.* Jesi, near Ancona, Jan. 3, 1710[1]; *d.* Pozzuoli, Mar. 17, 1736), composer.

The original name of the family appears to have been Draghi, but in accordance with local custom those members of it who settled at Jesi were known as Pergolese or Pergolesi from Pergola, a town in the Marche, of which they were natives. This partly accounts for the error of Saverio Mattei, who maintained that the composer's surname was Jesi, and that he was given the name of Pergolese from his birthplace. He himself signed his name both as Pergolese and as Pergolesi; the form Pergolesi (*i.e.* dei Pergolesi) is more generally preferred in Italy, and the form Pergolese (Pergolèse) appears to have become popularised by French writers. Villarosa supposed the family of Pergolesi to have belonged to the nobility; but it is evident from a work entitled *Picenorum mathematicorum elogia* by Giuseppe Santini di Staffolo, professor at the University of Macerata (Macerata, 1779), that his father was a surveyor, and his grandfather a shoemaker. He appears to have been an only child.

Pergolesi studied music at Jesi with a local master, Francesco Santini, and had lessons on the violin from one Francesco Mondini until his 16th year (1725, when he was sent to Naples and admitted to the Conservatorio dei Poveri di Gesù Cristo, through the influence of Count Cardolo Maria Pianetti Mannelli, a nobleman of Jesi, whose services to the Austrians during the war of the Spanish Succession had earned him the protection of Charles VI. At Naples Pergolesi was placed first under Gaetano Greco and later (probably after Greco's death) under Durante. It has also been stated that he studied with Francesco Feo when Durante was summoned to Vienna. There is, however, no foundation for the story (given by Villarosa and reproduced by H. M. Schletterer) of Durante's visit to the Austrian capital. Between 1725 and 1728 he became master at the Conservatorio della Madonna di Loreto, and it was doubtless for this reason that Pergolesi became a pupil of Feo. His teacher of the violin was Domenico de Matteis. It has been stated that he showed a remarkable facility for extemporising chromatic passages on this instrument, and that his powers of composition were first made known to his teachers in this manner. The story, however, given by Villarosa with some detail and reproduced by some later writers, does not appear to have been believed by Florimo, in spite of his love of picturesque anecdote.

Pergolesi made his first public appearance as a composer with a sacred drama entitled 'La

---

[1] The date and place of his birth were given wrongly by many historians until the Marquis de Villarosa finally settled the question by reference to the register of his baptism, a facsimile of which is given by E. Faustini-Fasini in his life of Pergolesi (*Gazzetta musicale di Milano*, Aug. 31, 1899, etc.; published in book form by Ricordi, 1900).

Conversione di San Guglielmo d' Aquitania,' performed in 1731, probably by his fellow-pupils, at the monastery of S. Agnello Maggiore. Between the acts of this was performed the comic intermezzo 'Il maestro di musica.' The success of the performance gained Pergolesi the protection of the Prince of Stigliano, a distinguished amateur, for whose marriage in 1723 Alessandro Scarlatti had composed a serenata. Through the influence of this nobleman, who was equerry to the Viceroy of Naples, aided by the patronage of the Prince of Avellino and the Duke of Maddaloni, Pergolesi was commissioned to write an opera for the court theatre, and produced ' La Sallustia ' with the comic intermezzo ' Nerino e Nibbia ' (sometimes known as ' Amor fa l' uomo cieco ') for the winter season of 1731. The opera was successful, but the intermezzo did not please. ' Ricimero,' produced in 1732 with the intermezzo ' Il geloso schernito,' was a failure, which may perhaps be accounted for by the fact that Pergolesi composed it just after the death of his father. Discouraged by its reception, he devoted himself to other forms, and it was at this time, according to Florimo, that he wrote thirty sonatas for two violins and bass at the request of the Prince of Stigliano ; twenty-four of these were printed in London. He was also commissioned by the municipality of Naples to write a Mass on the occasion of the earthquake of March 20, 1731. The Mass, which was for double choir and orchestra, was much admired, and was followed by a second of the same scale, which is said to have won the public praises of Leonardo Leo, who was present at the performance. Florimo further states that Pergolesi afterwards added a third and fourth choir to this work ; but there is no trace remaining of any Mass by him for more than two choirs.

In spite of the failure of ' Ricimero ' it was not long before Pergolesi returned to dramatic composition, and in Sept. 1732, he produced at the Teatro dei Fiorentini a comic opera in Neapolitan dialect, ' Lo frate nnammorato,' which, according to a contemporary (Chracas, *Diario ordinario*, 1732), met with considerable success. The following year he returned to serious opera with ' Il prigionier ' (so called in the libretto, but generally known as ' Il prigionier superbo ' to distinguish it from the ' Prigioniero fortunato ' of A. Scarlatti), to which ' La serva padrona ' furnished the intermezzi (Aug. 28, 1733). There seems no reason to suppose that the success of ' La serva padrona ' was in any way extraordinary, especially as Pergolesi was already known as a composer of comic opera.

It was about this time (1733–34) that Pergolesi entered the service of the Duke of Maddaloni. After he left Jesi his father had become involved in financial difficulties. His mother died in 1727, and her dowry should

have been paid to her son, but her husband was unable to find the money, and even after the father's death in 1732 Giovanni Battista still had to negotiate with the executors until 1734. On his appointment to the service of the Duke, Pergolesi appears to have considered his affairs more settled, as he sent for his aunt, Donna Cecilia Giorgi, to keep house for him. In the spring of 1734 the Duke took him to Rome, and Ghezzi the caricaturist gives an amusing account of the performance at S. Lorenzo in Lucina of a Mass by him (that in F for five voices).

' L' Ill. Duca di Matalona e Duchessa fecero fare una Musica spaventosa in S. Lorenzo in Lucina con tutti Musici e Violini di Roma, la qual Musica fù fatta dal Mastro di Cappella chiamato Pergolese il quale stà al servizio del Principe di Stigliano et è stato fatto venire da Napoli à posta e fu fatta da festa ad onore di S. Giovanni Pomuceno [*i.e.* St. John Nepomuk]. La qual Compositione è stata spi.itosa e fuori dell' ordinario '

Chracas records the departure of the Duke of Maddaloni and his suite from Rome for Naples in June 1734, and Pergolesi probably returned with his patron. It is not clear whether he was in the service of both the Duke and the Prince at the same time ; perhaps he left the Prince later. On Oct. 25, 1734, his opera ' Adriano in Siria ' was performed at the Teatro di S. Bartolomeo, with ' Livietta e Tracollo ' as intermezzi. The intermezzi were well received, but the opera did not please. It has generally been stated that Pergolesi became maestro di cappella at the Casa Santa at Loreto in this year, but this has no foundation. The archives of the ' Holy House ' do not mention Pergolesi, and other musicians held the post without any kind of interruption during his lifetime. It is possible that the tradition may have arisen from some connection of Pergolesi either with the convent of Loreto near Avellino, some sixty miles distant from Naples, or with the Conservatorio della Madonna di Loreto at Naples itself. The libretto of ' Il Flaminio,' a comic opera produced at Naples in the autumn of 1735, tells us that he was organist of the royal chapel at Naples.

On Jan. 31, 1735, the famous opera ' L' Olimpiade ' was produced under Pergolesi's own direction at the Tordinona Theatre in Rome. It was badly received, and Grétry tells us that an orange was thrown at the composer's head. It is related that Egidio Romualdo Duni, whose opera ' Nerone ' was produced at the same theatre on May 21, assured Pergolesi that his opera was far too good to succeed, and after the result which he had foreseen did his best to console him. It is also related that the failure of ' L' Olimpiade ' hastened the death of the composer, who returned to Naples and devoted himself to sacred music. His devotion to sacred music, however, can only have been partial, as he produced the comic opera ' Il Flaminio ' in the autumn at Naples (Teatro Nuovo), where it was thoroughly successful.

It is not known when he first showed symptoms of consumption. He went to Pozzuoli for his health in February 1736, as the guest of the Duke of Maddaloni, leaving his aunt in Naples, and verbally handing over to her all that he did not take to Pozzuoli; we may thus infer that he did not expect to live much longer. There is no reason to suppose that he stayed f⁻st at Torre del Greco. At Pozzuoli he is commonly supposed to have written the celebrated Stabat Mater, commissioned by the Confraternity of S. Luigi di Palazzo at Naples as a substitute for the setting by A. Scarlatti, which had hitherto been sung there annually on Good Friday. According to Paisiello, however, the work was written very soon after he left the Conservatorio, which he did in 1729, if Florimo is to be trusted. He was lodged in the Capuchin monastery at Pozzuoli, founded by the ancestors of the Duke of Maddaloni; and even under these circumstances his comic spirit did not desert him, as we see from the well-known ' Scherzo fatto ai Cappuccini di Pozzuoli,' a musical jest for tenor and bass voices, the humour of which is too coarse for explanation here. During his illness he was visited several times by Feo, his former teacher, to whom he is said to have expressed himself with great diffidence with regard to the value of his Stabat Mater. He was supposed to have been promised ten ducats for this, but whether it was paid is doubtful, as his possessions had to be sold to pay the expenses of his funeral, which amounted to eleven ducats. He was buried in the cathedral of Pozzuoli.

After his death Cecilia Giorgi returned to Jesi, and the details given above of his financial relations with her and his other relatives are made evident from a notarial act dated Jesi, Oct. 4, 1736, by which the claims of Cecilia Giorgi and her nephew's paternal uncle, Giuseppe Maria Pergolesi, to his estate were finally settled.[1] Some biographers supposed that Pergolesi died of poison, but this is doubtless due to confusion with his contemporary Leonardo Vinci, who met his death by this means in 1732. More credence may be given to the tradition that his death was hastened by the profligacy for which he was apparently notorious. A number of legends have grown up relating to his love affairs, two of which deserve mention. Florimo printed a story which he professed to have reproduced verbatim from a contemporary chronicle found among the papers of the Prince of Colobrano, by whose permission he published it. According to this document a certain Maria Spinelli, of the princely house of Cariati, was told by her three brothers that unless she chose within three days a husband who was her equal by birth, they would kill the composer Pergolesi, with whom she was in love, and who returned her affection. After

1 G. Annibaldi, *Il Pergolesi in Pozzuoli, vita intima.* Jesi, 1890.

three days the lady decided to enter a nunnery instead, stipulating that Pergolesi was to conduct the Mass on the occasion of her taking the veil. She entered the convent of S. Chiara, and, dying a year later, was buried on Mar. 11, 1735, Pergolesi again conducting the Requiem for her. His own death took place little more than a year after this, and Florimo suggested that the tragic anniversary was one of the causes of it. Unfortunately for the romantic admirers of Pergolesi, the story has been shown to be devoid of foundation. Benedetto Croce pointed out (1) that no biographer previous to Florimo had made any allusion to it; (2) that the papers of the Prince of Colobrano, now in possession of the Duke of Maddaloni, contain nothing of the kind; (3) that the archives of the nunnery of S. Chiara showed that no Maria Spinelli had been a member of that community during the 18th century; and finally that, according to the statement of the Duke of Maddaloni, the story was the invention of one Carlo Coda, and had appeared in some periodical of Florimo's time.

The other legend was put forward by a certain A. Piazza, who professed to have discovered from contemporary memoirs that Pergolesi was in love with the daughter of ' Lord Bulwer, British Ambassador Extraordinary to the Court of Naples,' and that the lady's name was ' Betzi.' This story hardly requires formal refutation. Pergolesi's romantic history has formed the subjects of two operas bearing his name, one by Paolo Serrao (Naples, 1857), and the other by Stefano Ronchetti Monteviti (Milan, 1857).

An oil-painting, supposed to represent Pergolesi, is in the library of the Naples Conservatoire, to which it was presented by Florimo. There are also several lithographed and engraved portraits of him, some of which are reproduced in *Musica e musicisti*, Dec. 1905. The difficulty of finding any two which might conceivably represent the same person, makes it impossible to decide which is the most authentic. The most interesting portrait is certainly the caricature by Ghezzi in the Vatican Library (Cod. Ottob. No. 3116, p. 139), which is reproduced in the *Gazzetta musicale di Milano* for Dec. 14, 1899. The revolting hideousness of this drawing may have been due to personal animosity—Ghezzi's criticism on Pergolesi's Mass in 1734 was not that of a friend—but the artist is hardly likely to have wilfully invented a deformity of the left leg, to which he draws particular attention, and which caused the composer to walk lame. This characteristic had not been noticed by any biographer until it was pointed out by E. Faustini-Fasini.

The importance of Pergolesi as a composer has been exaggerated since his death to an extent so extraordinary that it is worth while attempting to account for the development of the tradition. Paisiello[1] very sensibly remarked that he would not have been so much esteemed if he had lived longer. His death of consumption at the age of 26, just after a conspicuous failure at Rome, caused the undoubted success of his comic operas (that is, his three-act comic operas in dialect, not his little intermezzi) to be overlooked, and lent a fictitious interest to the revival of works which are in no way above the average merit of the Italian music of that period. The celebrity of Pergolesi in later times depended almost entirely on 'La serva padrona' and the Stabat Mater, to which may be added the air 'Tre giorni son che Nina,' which recent research has shown to be wrongly attributed to him. (See Ciampi.) As far as can be traced, this enthusiasm for the two former works originated not in Italy but in Paris. 'La serva padrona' first appeared in Paris at the Hôtel de Bourgogne in 1746, obtaining a mere *succès d'estime*. 'La musique en a été trouvée excellente; elle est d'un auteur ultramontain, mort fort jeune' (*Mercure de France*). On its reappearance in 1752, in the repertory of the 'Bouffons Italiens,' it was received with enthusiasm, and for some reason regarded as the type of all Italian music. It is sufficient to cite the words of an anonymous satirist of the time (quoted in Geoffroy's *Cours de la littérature dramatique*):

> 'Lulli n'est plus à l'Opéra
> Le favori de Polymnie;
> Rameau bientôt s'éclipsera
> Malgré sa profonde harmonie;
> Géliot n'a rien d'étonnant,
> Il faut des bouffons d'Italie:
> Aujourd'hui tout Français galant
> Ne se montre qu'en fredonnant
> E si e no, e piou et giou,
> C'est à qui sera le plus fou.'

The allusion is to the words 'e si e no, e sú e giù' from the air 'Sempre in contrasti' ('Serva padrona,' Act I.). While the other operas remained in manuscript and so forgotten, the not too discriminating enthusiasm of Rousseau was perpetuated by Fétis and later historians. The Stabat Mater was also printed in Paris not long after the composer's death, and was even printed at Leipzig with German words by Klopstock as early as 1782. In Italy it has always been regarded with exaggerated veneration, and no doubt this has been enhanced by the fact that Bellini (who also died young) called it 'divino poema del dolore.' De Brosses' opinion of Pergolesi will serve as an example of contemporary criticism:

'Parmi tous ces musiciens, mon auteur d'affection est Pergolèse. Ah! le joli génie, simple et naturel. On ne peut pas écrire avec plus de facilitié, de grâces et de goût. . . . Ses petits intermèdes sont charmants, si gais, si réjouissants.'

We must, however, be on our guard against

accepting blindly the criticism of any contemporary, and the value of De Brosses' appreciation of Pergolesi must be measured by his opinion on Handel—'Sur ce que j'ai vu de sa musique vocale, je le croirais inférieur à tous ceux que je vous ai nommés [*i.e.* Pergolesi, Vinci, Porpora, Sarri, etc.].' Paisiello and Padre Martini, however, were less enthusiastic, and pointed out that the Stabat Mater was written in the style of a comic opera. Paisiello is not far wrong in saying that

'His "Olimpiade," the intermezzo "La serva padrona," a Mass, and other compositions of his that remain to us, differ in no way from the Stabat Mater, in which, moreover, there are incoherent passages; that is to say, certain verses set without sense of expression, such as the theme of the "Eia mater," which suggests the comic style.'

As a composer of sacred music, Pergolesi is no more than a clever imitator of his master Durante. His masses for double choir are effective and well written, but commonplace in their material. It should be noted that his two choirs are used separately only for antiphonal or cumulative effects on single chords, there being no attempt at polyphonic writing in more than five parts at most. The chief merit of the Stabat Mater is the sentimental charm of its melodies. Sentimental charm is indeed the chief merit of all Pergolesi's work, sacred or secular. It reaches its highest in the beautiful duet 'Se cerca, se dice' in 'L' Olimpiade,' and we can see that it was an inborn gift and not the result of long development, from the fact that the other duet in 'L' Olimpiade'—'Nei giorni tuoi felici,' which is hardly inferior to the first, was transferred unaltered from Pergolesi's first dramatic composition, 'La conversione di S. Guglielmo.' The comic opera 'Lo frate nnammorato' contains several pleasing airs, including the well-known 'Ogne pena cchiù spiatata,' as well as some genuinely humorous numbers, the best of which is an absurd parody of an *aria di bravura*, sung by a baritone, but demanding a compass from F below the bass stave to C in the treble, which was no doubt intended to be produced in a grotesque falsetto. There are also interesting types of popular Neapolitan songs, and a bright quintet at the end of Act II. On the whole, however, Pergolesi is inferior to Leo and Logroscino in comic opera, and indeed could only be considered a great composer in any department by critics who were entirely ignorant of the work of his predecessors and contemporaries.

CATALOGUE[2] OF THE EXTANT WORKS OF PERGOLESI

I. Operas and Oratorios

1. S. Guglielmo d' Aquitania (Naples, 1731). Score—Brit. Mus., Berlin, Naples R.C.M.
2. Il maestro di musica (Naples, 1731. Score (MS.)—Berlin. Le Maître de musique (Paris, 1752). Score (MS.)—Dresden, Paris, Bibl. Nat. The engraved score, published by Boivin at Paris, is in most important libraries. This opera was also performed at Venice in 1743 as 'L' Orazio,' and at Florence in 1760 as 'La scolara alla moda.'

---

[1] Paisiello's opinions are quoted from the *Osservazioni musicali intorno a' compositori napoletani, ricavate dalla conversazione col Signor Paisiello,* compiled by Agostino Gervasio. The MS. in the Bibl. de' Gerolamini at Naples was printed in *Musica e musicisti,* Dec. 1905.

[2] The writer was indebted to Alfred Wotquenne for kind assistance in the preparation of this catalogue.

3. **La Sallustia** (Naples, 1731). Libretto—Rome, Bibl. Vitt. Em. Score—Naples R.C.M.
4. **Nerino e Nibbia** (Naples, 1731). Libretto—Rome, Bibl. Vitt. Em.
5. **Ricimero** (Naples, 1732).
6. **Il geloso schernito** (Naples, 1732). Score—Berlin, Brussels Cons.
7. **Lo frate nnammorato** (Naples, 1732). Score—Brit. Mus., Brussels Cons., Naples R.C.M.
8. **Il prigioniero superbo** (Naples, 1733). Libretto—Rome, Bibl. Vitt. Em. Score—Naples R.C.M.
9. **La serva padrona** (Naples, 1733). Libretto—Rome, Bibl. Vitt. Em. Score in all important libraries. There are many printed editions, both Italian and French (La Servante maîtresse).
10. **Adriano in Siria** (Naples, 1734). Score—Brit. Mus., Naples R.C.M.
11. **Tracollo** (Naples, 1734). Score in all important libraries. Performances under other titles : Livietta e Tracollo (reprint by G. Radiciotti, Paris) ; La finta Polacca (Rome, 1748) ; La contadina astuta (Venice, 1744) ; Il ladro convertito per amore (Venice, 1750) ; Il finto pazzo, etc.
12. **L' Olimpiade** (Rome, 1735). Score—Brit. Mus., London R.C.M., Dresden, Milan Cons., Münster, Paris Cons., Vienna Hofbibl.
13. **Il Flaminio** (Naples, 1735). Libretto—Rome, Bibl. Vitt. Em. Score—London R.C.M., Brussels Cons., Naples R.C.M.
14. **Il transito di San Giuseppe** (?). London R.C.M., Einsiedeln, Vienna Musikfreunde.
15. **Il Temistocle** (ascribed to Pergolesi). Score—Bologna.

H. M. Schletterer's biography in the *Sammlung musikalischer Vorträge* edited by Count P. von Waldersee, gives a very full account of later performances of the operas in Italy and in other countries, but is otherwise inaccurate and uncritical.

### II CANTATAS

1. **Chi non ode e chi non vede.** Brit. Mus., London R.C.M., Berlin, Brussels Cons.
2. **Clori, se mai rivolgi.** London R.C.M.
3. **Della città vicina di Mergellina.** Münster.
4. **Dalsigre, ahi l mia Dalsigre.** Brit. Mus., Berlin, Brussels Cons. Münster.
5. **Ecco, Tirsi, quel mirto.** London R.C.M.
6. **In queste piagge amene.** London R.C.M.
7 **Luce degli occhi miei.** Brit. Mus., London R.C.M., Berlin, Brussels Cons., Münster.
8. **Nel chiuso centro** (L' Orfeo). Brit. Mus., Berlin, Brussels Cons., Cambridge Fitzw., Vienna Hofbibl.
9. **Quest' è amor, quest' è fede.** Münster.
10. **Quest' è il piano e quest' è il rio.** Brit. Mus. (autograph ?).
11. **Rinfacciar son costretto.** London R.C.M.
12. **Io mi rido : Serenata for two voices.** London R.C.M.

### PRINTED EDITIONS

**Quattro cantate da camera** . . . raccolté da G. Bruno. (Napoli, 1750 (?)), four cantatas ; London, Preston & Son (1790 ?)

### III. SACRED MUSIC

**Mass** (Kyrie and Gloria) for ten voices (two choirs) and two orchestras, in F. Brit. Mus., Milan, Münster.
**Mass** (Kyrie and Gloria) for five voices and orchestra in C. Published at Vienna, *Contojo d' arti e d' industria.*
**Mass** (Kyrie and Gloria) for five voices and orchestra in D. Brit. Mus. (2 copies), Brussels Cons., Milan, Münster, etc.
**Mass** for four voices in D minor. Brit. Mus.
**Aure sacratis amoris,** motet for S. and orchestra. Brussels, Ste. Gudule.
**Confitebor,** psalm for S.S.A.T.B. and orchestra (in most libraries).
**De placido torrente,** motet for S. and orchestra. Brussels, Ste. Gudule.
**Dies irae,** motet for S.A. and orchestra. Münster.
**Dixit Dominus** (in D), psalm for ten voices (two choirs) and orchestra. Naples R.C.M. (autograph).
**Dixit Dominus** (in B flat), psalm for S.A.T.B. and orchestra. Münster.
**Domine ad adjuvandum** (in D), motet for S.A.T.B. and orchestra. Münster.
**Domine ad adjuvandum** (in G), motet for S.S.A.T.B. and orchestra. Brit. Mus., Milan, Münster.
**Domine ad adjuvandum** (in D), motet for A.T.B. and orchestra. Brit. Mus.
**Ecce pietatis signa,** motet for S. and orchestra. Milan.
**Ecce superbos hostes,** motet for S. and orchestra. Brussels, Ste. Gudule.
**In coelestibus regnis,** motet for S. and orchestra. Milan.
**In hac die tam decora,** motet for S.S.A.T.B. and orchestra. Brit. Mus., Milan.
**Laetatus sum,** psalm for S.A.T.B. and orchestra. Münster.
**Laetatus sum,** psalm for S. and orchestra. Brussels Cons.
**Laudate pueri,** psalm for S.A.T.B. and orchestra. Brussels Cons.
**Laudate pueri,** for canto solo, vocal quartet, strings and wind, the MS. of which is in the Santini Library
**Miserere mei Deus** (in C minor), psalm for S.A.T.B. and orchestra. London R.C.M.
**Miserere mei Deus** (in C minor), psalm for S.A.T.B. and orchestra. Brit. Mus., Milan, Münster.
**Miserere mei Deus** (in G minor), psalm for S.A.T.B., unaccompanied. Brussels Cons.
**Miserere mei Deus** (in A minor) for nine voices and organ. Schwerin.
**Quis sicut Deus noster,** motet for B. and orchestra. Brussels, Bibl. Roy.
**Salve regina** (in F minor) for S.S. and orchestra. Brussels Cons.
**Salve regina** (in A minor) for S. and orchestra. Milan.
**Salve regina** (in A minor) for S. and orchestra. Brit. Mus., London R.C.M., Brussels Cons., Milan, Schwerin, etc.
**Salve regina** (in F minor) for S. and harpsichord. Milan.
**Salve regina** (in C minor) for S.B. and orchestra. Münster.
**Stabat Mater** for S.A. and orchestra. Montecassino (autograph). MS. copies in most libraries ; several printed editions.
**Tuba et timpano,** motet for S. and orchestra. Brussels, Ste. Gudule. A De Profundis, mentioned by De Brosses, is no longer extant.
**Venerabilis barba capucinorum,** for T.B. (Scherzo fatto al Cappucini di Pozzuoli). Milan, Münster, Munich, Naples R.C.M.

### IV. INSTRUMENTAL MUSIC

**Sonata** for violoncello and continuo. Milan, Naples R.C.M.
**Concerto** for violin and strings. Milan, Naples R.C.M.
**Symphony** in G for orchestra. Münster.
**Concerto** for flute in G. (Breitkopf's thematic catalogue, 1765.)
**Fourteen sonatas** for two violins and bass. (12mo, London, 1780 ?)
**Twelve sonatas** for two violins and bass. (London.)
**Eight lessons** for the harpsichord. (London, c. 1780 ?)
A second set of eight lessons for the harpsichord.
There are in addition many fragments of unidentified operas, including fifteen airs in Breitkopf's thematic catalogue (1765), and the incomplete autograph parts of a trio, 'Parla, che dirmi vuoi,' at Milan.

E. J. D.

Apart from the Stabat Mater, 'La serva padrona,' the spurious 'Tre giorni' and a certain Gloria in excelsis, all of which exist in numerous modern editions of more or less value (the first was re-instrumented by Lvov, and the last was mainly popular in an arrangement for organ solo), there are not many of Pergolesi's works accessible in modern reprints. The series of songs called 'Gemme d' antichità' contains the motet 'Sanctum et terribile,' three airs from 'La conversione di San Guglielmo,' a 'Salve Regina,' the airs 'Euridice, dove sei' and 'Ogni pena' (the latter in many other editions) ; Gevaert's 'Gloires d'Italie' has airs from 'Il maestro di musica' and 'Olimpiade' ; and the air 'Tremende oscura' from 'Meraspe' is in the *Oxf. Hist. Mus.* vol. iv. p. 221. Banck's 'Duetten alter Meister' contains a duet, and his 'Arien und Gesänge älterer Tonmeister' contains an air by Pergolesi, 'Se cerca, se dice' ; a sonata for two violins and violoncello was published by Joseph Williams ; the harpsichord suites were edited by J. Pittman, and a solo sonata in D by J. A. Fuller Maitland.                                                     M.

**PERI, JACOPO** (*b.* Florence,[1] Aug. 20, 1561 ; *d.* Florence, Aug. 12, 1633), Florentine composer, called by his contemporaries 'Il Zazzerino' in allusion to his long hair ; a pupil of Cristoforo Malvezzi.

Malvezzi, a native of Lucca, became a canon of San Lorenzo in Florence, maestro di cappella to the Medician Grand Dukes Francesco and Fernando I. and died in Florence, 1597. Little is known of the facts of Peri's life. He became attached to the grand-ducal court of Florence and seems to have had some part in Medician diplomacy. He was appointed maestro di cappella (*Principale direttore della musica e dei musici*), a post which he held under Francesco, Fernando I. and Cosmo II. In 1618 he was created a 'Camerlengo generale.' His name is closely connected with that group of futuristic poets and musicians who centred first around Giovanni Bardi dei Conti Vernio, and later around Jacopo Corsi. In this way he will have come into contact with and been influenced by much of the finest Florentine culture of his day. The intensive forces of the Renaissance, liberating men's minds, rendering acute their intellects, opening up immeasurable vistas of art and philosophy, found in the Bardi-Corsi

[1] *Riemann* has Rome of Florentine parents.

gatherings a notable opportunity for comparison and synthetic reasoning. As far as the art of music is concerned one of the chief results of these meetings, and one with which the name of Peri is most nearly associated, is the memorable attempt that was made to restore the mode of declamation peculiar to Hellenic tragedy, an attempt which resulted at last in the discovery of modern recitative. After the declamatory foreshadowings of the madrigalists culminating in Orazio Vecchi's 'Amfiparnasso,' Vincenzo Galilei and Caccini produced the first monodic cantatas in which the new style was attempted ; but their efforts were confessedly tentative, and their productions conceived upon a very small scale, fitted only for use as chamber music. Peri took a higher flight. At the instigation of Jacopo Corsi and the poet Rinuccini he attempted a regular musical drama called 'Dafne.' The libretto for this was supplied by Rinuccini, and Peri composed the music (now lost) entirely in the style which was then believed to be identical with that cultivated by the ancient Greek tragedians. Count Bardi having been summoned to Rome in 1592 to act as maestro di camera to Clement VIII., the work was privately performed in the Palazzo Corsi in the year 1597, Peri himself playing the part of Apollo. This performance was witnessed only by a select circle of Corsi's personal friends. But in the year 1600 Peri was commissioned to produce an opera for public performance on the occasion of the marriage of Henry IV. of France with Maria de' Medici. The subject chosen for this was 'Euridice.' Rinuccini again supplied the libretto, and Peri wrote the music in the same style as that he had already adopted in 'Dafne,' though, it is to be supposed, with greater freedom and vigour. The first performance took place on Feb. 9, 1600. The success of the work was all that could possibly be desired. It proved that the ideal conceived by the little band of enthusiasts was capable of satisfactory embodiment in a practical form ; and that form was at once adopted as the normal type of the long-desired lyric-drama. It is true that, in the same month as the production of 'Euridice,' Emilio de Cavalieri's oratorio, 'La rappresentazione di anima e di corpo' was publicly performed in Rome with scenery, dresses and action, and that the music of this work is written in exactly the same kind of recitative as 'Euridice.' But Peri's claim to be regarded as the composer of the first opera rests not on 'Euridice' but on 'Dafne,' though that work was never produced in public ; and the only ground on which that claim can be disputed is the fact that Cavalieri is known to have composed two secular pieces, called 'Il satiro' and 'La disperazione di Fileno,' both privately performed in 1590, and a third work, entitled 'Il giuoco della cieca,' performed

before the Grand Duke Ferdinand in 1595. Not a trace of either of these three works now remains to us. They are described as 'pastorals,' and may or may not have been of sufficiently large dimensions to entitle them to rank as dramas. Moreover, we cannot be quite certain that they were written in the same style as the oratorio. As the case now stands, therefore, and until we are furnished with more decisive evidence than that we now possess, Jacopo Peri stands before us as the acknowledged father of a form of art which is very nearly the greatest that it has ever entered into the mind of man even to conceive, or to bring through so many difficulties to a successful issue.

Strange to say, Peri made no attempt to follow up his wonderful success. Probably no opportunity for the production of another public performance on so extensive a scale occurred during his lifetime. But whatever may have been the cause of his retirement Peri produced no more operas. In 1608 he wrote the recitatives for Rinuccini's 'Arianna,' Monteverdi composing the arias. An opera 'Tetide,' to a libretto by Cini, was sent to Mantua in 1608, but did not appear. Peri wrote part of the opera 'La guerra d' amore,' with Grazie, Signorini and del Turco. This work saw light at Florence in 1615. Another opera, 'Adone,' written in 1620 for Mantua, was probably never performed. In 1625 Peri wrote 'La precedenza delle dame' for the Florentine court. In 1628 he wrote the part of *Clori* in Gagliano's 'Flora.'

It does not appear that 'Dafne' was ever published, though some numbers were discovered at Brussels. 'Euridice' was printed in complete form in the year of its production, under the title of 'Le musiche di Jacopo Peri, nobil fiorentino, sopra l' Euridice del Sig. Ottavio Rinuccini' etc., Fiorenza, 1600 ; and reprinted in Venice in 1608, and again at Florence in 1863, in small 8vo. Both the early editions are exceedingly rare. (See *Q.-L.*) This interesting work and the 'Varie musiche,' are believed to be the only specimens of Peri's compositions now in existence, with the exception of a 'Lamento d' Iole' for soprano solo, at Bologna. Kiesewetter reprinted three madrigals for four voices in his *Schicksale und Beschaffenheit des weltlichen Gesanges* (Leipzig, 1841).                          w. s. r. ; rev. and addns. s. g.

BIBLIOGRAPHY
ROLLAND : *Histoire de l'opéra en Europe avant Lulli et Scarlatti.* (Paris, 1895.)
GOLDSCHMIDT : *Studien zur Geschichte der italienischen Oper im 17, Jahrhundert.* (Leipzig, 1901.)
PARRY : *Oxford History of Music,* iii. (Oxford, 1902.)
KRETSCHMAR : *Geschichte der Oper.* (Leipzig, 1919.)
ADLER : *Handbuch der Musikgeschichte.* (Frankfort, 1924.)
VOGEL : *Vierteljahrsschrift,* v. 404.

**PÉRI, LA,** a danced poem, in one tableau ; music by Paul Dukas. Produced Paris, Théâtre du Châtelet, Apr. 22, 1912 ; Opéra, Dec. 5, 1921.                          M. L. P.

PÉRIER, Jean Alexis (b. Paris, Feb. 2, 1869), a singer of Belgian origin, first a baritone, then a tenor, was the son of Émile Périer, a violinist at the Opéra. Périer was a pupil of Bussine and Taskin at the Conservatoire; won the first prize for singing and opéra-comique (1892); made his début at the Opéra-Comique in ' La Flûte enchantée ' (Monostatos, 1892) and created the principal part in ' Phryné ' (Saint-Saëns, 1893). He left this theatre after 1900, having there created the chief parts in ' Pelléas et Mélisande ' (Debussy, 1902), ' L'Enfant-roi ' (Bruneau, 1905), ' Miarka ' (Alexandre Georges, 1905), ' Mme. Butterfly ' (Puccini, 1906), ' Fortunio ' Messager), ' Le Chemineau ' (X. Leroux, 1907), ' L'Heure espagnole ' (Ravel, 1911), ' Le Roi Candaule ' (Bruneau, 1920), etc.

During his absences from the Opéra-Comique, Périer has belonged to various Paris theatres: the Menus-plaisirs (1894); the Folies-dramatiques (1895–96), in productions of ' François-les-bas-bleus ' and ' La Fiancée en loterie ' (Messager); the Bouffes-parisiens (1898–1900) in Messager's ' Véronique ' and Lecocq's ' La Belle au bois dormant '; the Châtelet (1903) in ' Les Aventures du Capitaine Corcoran '; the Gaîté (1910) in A. Mariotte's ' Salomé '; the Nouveautés (1923) in Reynaldo Hahn's ' Ciboulette.' A notable comedian, Périer has sung since then on various comedy stages. He has published, in collaboration with Mlle. Marguerite Babaïan, *Mes exercices, tirés des chansons populaires de France.* He is a chevalier of the Légion d'Honneur (1922).

Bibl.—H. de Curzon, *Croquis d'artistes, Jean Périer* (*Nouvelle Revue,* Feb. 15, 1922).

J. G. P.

PERIGOURDINE (Perijourdine), a country dance which takes its name from Perigord, where it is chiefly danced. It is sometimes accompanied by singing. The following example is from the *Essai sur la musique* (Paris, 1780) of De la Borde and Roussier:

Gai.

W. B. S.

PERINELLO, Carlo (b. Trieste, Feb. 13, 1877), Italian writer and composer, studied composition at first in Trieste with Wieselberger, then with Jadassohn at the Leipzig Conservatoire. Appointed teacher of composition at the Trieste Conservatoire in 1904, he resigned ten years later to hold a similar appointment at the Milan Conservatoire. He has composed a good deal of chamber music and orchestral works, but is best known for his work in connexion with the Istituto Editoriale Italiano, of which he is the ' technical director.'

Of its publications, Perinello has prepared the volumes of Caccini, Monteverdi, Peri, Paisiello, Palestrina, Porpora, Sammartini and Orazio Vecchi. A quartet in C major and a quintet for pianoforte and strings (published Schmidl, Trieste) have been favourably received in Italy and in Germany.

F. B.

PERIOD. A period is a group of bars. Simple melodies, often actually set to verse, are usually thought in terms of line and stanza, and their sections, if with accompanying words, are called ' strains,' if without, ' phrases ' or ' periods,' according to their length. This may sometimes be a useful nomenclature, but in composed music the distinction becomes blurred or disappears. On the other hand, in all music just as there is a normal bar so there is a normal group of bars. This has sometimes been called a rhythm; but as another and a broader meaning has here been given to that word, it will be better to use for this group the word ' period.'

The period is usually of four bars, less often of six or three, and seldom for long together of five (Brahms, 3rd Intermezzo, op. 117). Sometimes the composer puts the dots on the i's, as Haydn did with his fermatas and G.P.'s, or Beethoven with that dramatic ' bridge ' in op. 110, bar 38. The bar's rest in the first movement of the C minor symphony (114 from the end) is usually ignored; and as it stands it certainly does not make sense. Yet it is difficult to believe that it found its way into the score without the composer's intention. Is it possible that he omitted to write a similar rest eight bars later, and that the two were meant to recall the fermatas at the opening? The minim rest in the 16th bar of Mozart's second (C minor) Fantasia is a blemish, and he seems to have found it so, since he has done away with it in the reprise. It seems certain that Mozart and Franz, by filling up the 33rd bar of ' He was rejected,' defeated Handel's intention of an eloquent silence. In the first prelude of the ' Wohltemperirtes Clavier ' many editors have interpolated a bar between bars 22 and 23. The MS. authority is decidedly against this; but the interpolation would also spoil the symmetry of the periods, as may be seen if the bass is written out with a different barring:

Without the extra bar the periods are of 4, 6, 8, 4, 8, 4 bars.

The less any one grouping is maintained the more rhythmically flexible the music is. Thus in Mozart's G minor quintet the minuet is in four-bar and the trio in three-bar grouping, mainly; but the actual grouping is:

Minuet :

4 2 4 3 || 4 4 4, 4 2 2 4 3 3 ||

Trio :

3 3, 3 4, 3 3 || 3 3, 2 2 2, 3 3 4, 3 3 ||

Haydn is fond of veiling the squareness of a four-bar period at any rate at the beginning of a movement, although he drops back into strict periods later on where irregularity would tend to become confusing. The first eight bars of the PF. sonata in D (No. 20) are taken as $3+2+3$; and of the adagio of the sonata in F (No. 3) as $5\frac{1}{2}+2\frac{1}{2}$. In the symphony in D (No. 3) he presents the four-bar theme of the presto under the guise of a five-bar, and in the 'clock' movement the drowsy feeling is partly due to an eight-bar theme being begun a bar too soon and dragged on a bar beyond its time into ten bars. Chopin's music, on the other hand, has so much variation of figure that he feels the necessity of keeping, as a rule, steadily to his four-bar period; the G minor Nocturne (op. 15, No. 3) is a rare exception : he has marked it *languido e rubato* as opposed to the *a tempo religioso* in strict periods which comes later.

METHODS OF RELIEF.—Thus relief from the monotony of the period is as important as the period itself. This relief is afforded mainly in three ways.

(1) Inside the phrase by interpolation and stretto. Thus, in the opening of Mozart's G minor symphony the action is delayed by an interpolation at the 13th bar and the balance restored by a stretto at the 28th.

(2) Between one phrase and another by overlap and hiatus. Hiatus is used to prolong four bars into five (Brahms, Rhapsodie No. 4, op. 119). A good instance is Mozart's D minor quartet, andante (K 421),

whereby six bars become eight. Overlap of one phrase with the next is too common to be worth an instance.

(3) In the phrase considered as a complete structure, by multiplication and division. The first seven bars of the overture to 'Figaro' may be described as a (geometrical) progression $-1+1\cdot2+1\cdot4$—and so, in the opposite sense $-\frac{8}{1}+\frac{8}{2}+\frac{8}{4}+\frac{8}{8}$—may the last fifteen bars of the

great G pedal in the finale of Schubert's symphony in C. Both of them create an illusion of great speed.        A. H. F. S.

PERIODICALS, MUSICAL. The following summary is concerned primarily with periodicals exclusively devoted to music and published in the English, French, German or Italian languages.

### ENGLAND

Musical journalism began in England with *The Quarterly Musical Magazine and Review* (1818–28), edited by R. M. Bacon, of Norwich. It was intended to contain articles of the following kind : 1. Original correspondence upon all the branches of the science, theoretical and practical; 2. Critical and impartial accounts of musical performers; 3. Reviews of musical publications; 4. Anecdotes of music and musical men; 5. Poetry, original or selected, that might appear calculated for musical adaptation; 6. A register or chronicle of musical transactions. Among the most interesting articles which appeared were—a review of Forkel's life of Bach in vol. ii. ; an account of the performance at the Philharmonic of Beethoven's Eighth Symphony (vol. vii. 1825), and an extremely depreciatory criticism of Beethoven and his works (vol. ix., 1827). In vol. iii. began the publication of music in each number, which was continued till the end of the magazine in 1828.

In the meantime [1] a monthly journal, *The Harmonicon* (1823–33), had begun to appear, under the editorship of W. Ayrton. It contained ably written memoirs of eminent musicians (some of the earlier being accompanied by engraved portraits), essays, reviews of new music, correspondence, criticisms of musical performances of all kinds, foreign musical news, information on all subjects interesting to musicians, and original and selected vocal and instrumental music. *The Musical Magazine* (1835–36), a monthly, edited by C. H. Purday, met with little success.

*The Musical World* (1836–91) began on a new footing : its policy was not entirely to confine itself to musical matters, but to combine general interests with those of music. It was edited by Cowden Clarke, with the co-operation of an able staff of writers, amongst them Samuel Wesley, the elder, who contributed the first paper, 'A Sketch of the State of Music in England from 1778'; Dr. Gauntlett; Dr. Hodges ; Egerton Webbe ; Carl Klingemann ; W. J. Thoms ; John Parry, the elder ; C. H. Purday ; A. H. H. Strumpff ; Lowell Mason, of Boston, U.S.A. ; Collet Dobson ; John Ella ; and Joseph Warren. It was originally published by J. A. Novello, in small 8vo weekly, from Mar. 18, 1836, to Dec. 29, 1837, which date completed its seventh

---

[1] The *English Musical Gazette or Monthly Intelligencer*, published by Arding & Merrett, only survived from Jan.–July 1819. It contained, however, a substantial memoir of Haydn that is still of interest.

quarterly volume. A new series began on Jan 5, 1838, in large 8vo, published by Henry Hooper. With its third series (Jan. 1842) it became 4to, a form it retained to the end of its career. It changed hands frequently till the beginning of 1854, when it was acquired by Boosey & Co., who published it till 1863, when it went to Duncan Davison & Co. *The Musical World* was edited by J. W. Davison from 1844 until his death in 1885, and few periodicals have embraced a more varied and curious mass of literature more or less directly connected with music, and in a great measure of a humorous, often Rabelaisian cast. Among the contributors after 1840 may be mentioned G. A. Macfarren—Analytical essays on Beethoven's works; on Mendelssohn's ʻAntigone,ʼ ʻŒdipus,ʼ ʻAthalie,ʼ etc.; on the ʻMessiahʼ; on Mozart; on Day's *Theory of Harmony*; on the Leipzig Bach Society's publications, etc. Dr. Kenealy—Translations from the Italian, Danish and Icelandic, and original papers. John Oxenford—Original poetry (171 sonnets); translations from the Greek Anthology, Goethe's Venetian Epigrams, Goethe's Affinities, Aristotle, Lessing, Winkelmann, etc. J. V. Bridgeman—Translations of Oulibicheff on History of Music, and on ʻDon Giovanniʼ; Hiller's Conversations with Rossini; Lenz's *Beethoven*; Lobe's *Mendelssohn*; Wagner's *Oper und Drama*, and ʻLohengrinʼ; Lampadius's *Mendelssohn*; Hanslick on Wagner, etc. Other contributors were E. F. Rimbault, W. Chappell, H. S. Edwards, Shirley Brooks, Joseph Bennett, and many other well-known members of the press. During its later years clever humorous caricatures by Lyall were added. In 1886 Francis Hueffer became editor, the paper at that time being published by Messrs. Mallett, of Wardour Street. In 1888 it was bought by E. F. Jacques, by whom it was edited until its demise in 1891. During the last two years of its existence it was published by Messrs. Biddlecombe, of the Strand

In 1842 appeared two new weekly musical journals, *The Dramatic and Musical Review* (1842–52), edited and owned by the brothers Eames, one a violinist and the other organist of St. Paul's, Covent Garden; and *The Musical Examiner* (1842–44), edited by J. W. Davison, among the contributors to which were Henry Smart, G. A. Macfarren, E. J. Loder, Dion Boucicault and Albert Smith.

*The Musical Times* (1844– )[1] was founded by J. A. Novello in continuation of a periodical of the same name published by Mainzer. It was issued monthly and besides printed matter contained sheets of part music. The interest of the paper dates from about 1846, when Edward Holmes began writing for it. From this time

till his death in 1859 he was a constant contributor. Among his most interesting series of articles are the following —ʻLife of Henry Purcellʼ (1847), ʻCuriosities of Musical Historyʼ and ʻCathedral Music and Composersʼ (1850), ʻEnglish Glee and Madrigal Composersʼ (1851), ʻMozart's Masses,ʼ ʻHaydn's Massesʼ (1852, etc.), ʻAddenda to the life of Mozartʼ and ʻBeethoven's Mass in Cʼ (1858). In 1855–56 appeared translations by Sabilla Novello of Berlioz's *Soirées de l'orchestre*, and his treatise on orchestration, and a series of papers translated by her called ʻTruth about Music and Musiciansʼ (1856–57). From Dec. 1853 to Sept. 1854 several essays were contributed by Leigh Hunt. In Sept. 1863, Henry C. Lunn undertook the office of editor, contributing constantly interesting articles and criticisms on current musical topics. Among the most frequent contributors during the 19th century were G. A. Macfarren, E. F. Rimbault, W. H. Cummings, Carl Engel, E. Prout, W. A. Barrett, H. H. Statham and Joseph Bennett. From time to time series of articles of special interest have appeared, as for example, Dr. Wm. Pole's ʻStory of Mozart's Requiemʼ (1869), Dr. Chrysander's ʻSketch of the History of Music Printing from the 15th to the 19th centuriesʼ (1877). In 1887, on the retirement of Lunn, W. A. Barrett assumed the editorship, which he retained until his death in 1891. He was followed by E. F. Jacques, who in his turn was succeeded in 1897 by F. G. Edwards. Under Edwards's régime *The Musical Times* was much enlarged and its scope considerably widened, special attention being devoted to the illustrations, among which were published many interesting portraits of musicians and facsimiles of valuable historical documents. On his death in 1909 W. G. M'Naught took over the editorship. He was succeeded in 1918 by the present editor, Harvey Grace. *The Musical Times* is to-day the most widely read of all English musical journals.

*The Tonic Sol-fa Reporter* (1853–1920) was founded by John Curwen, whose lectures at Newcastle on the Tonic Sol-fa Notation were the origin of the publication. A tentative double number had already been issued in 1851. Each monthly issue contained criticisms, reports of the progress of the Sol-fa movement in different parts of England, and a series of anthems, glees, rounds, hymn tunes, etc., in the Sol-fa notation. In 1881 J. Curwen resigned the post of editor to his son, J. S Curwen, who retained it until his death in 1916. In Jan. 1889 a new monthly issue of *The Reporter* was begun, under the title *The Musical Herald and Tonic Sol-fa Reporter*, a change intended to indicate that the paper was conducted upon catholic rather than controversial lines. Under that name it appeared until 1920,

[1] A blank space following the date of a journal's foundation indicates that it is still in progress.

when it was amalgamated with *The Musical News*.

A short-lived journal devoted to similar aims was *The Tonic Sol-fa Record* (1904–06), the official organ of the Tonic Sol-fa College.

*The Musical Standard* (1862–   ) was projected by an amateur, A. W. Hammond, who was at first both proprietor and editor. It was issued fortnightly, and professed to be unfettered by clique, and not devoted to the behests of houses in the trade. It paid special attention to the interests of church music and organists. Its earlier numbers contained, besides leading articles on topics of current interest, notices of concerts, specifications of old and new organs, extracts from ancient church registers relating to musical matters, biographical notices of the lesser masters and public performers, and reprints of old and curious works bearing on the subject of music. Among the contributors to the early numbers were W. J. Westbrook, Dr. Gauntlett, Joseph Bennett and J. Crowdy. In an early number proposals were made to establish a Musical College. This was the origin of the College of Organists. (See ROYAL COLLEGE OF ORGANISTS.) In vol. v. the paper began a weekly issue. The old series of the journal ended with vol. xiii., when Hammond sold the copyright to George Carr, and T. L. Southgate became editor. The scope of the journal was now considerably widened, and letters and notices from France, Germany, Italy and America were included. Vocal music as well as instrumental was now given weekly in the paper, among which were compositions by Sir W. Sterndale Bennett, Sir J. Goss, H. Gadsby, E. J. Hopkins, Berthold Tours, etc. In Feb. 1872 Reeves & Turner purchased the paper. Southgate retired in 1873, and was succeeded by J. Crowdy. In 1875 Bowden became the proprietor. With vol. viii. the weekly issue of music was discontinued. In May 1876 Broadhouse became editor. Among the most prominent articles that appeared under his regime may be mentioned a remarkable series, entitled ' Beethoven's Symphonies critically and sympathetically discussed,' by A. Teetgen. Turpin edited *The Musical Standard* from 1880 to 1886. He was succeeded again by Broadhouse, and in 1888 by Ernest Bergholt. In recent years it has been edited successively by E. A. Baughan and J. H. G. Baughan. It now appears fortnightly, and is published by W. Reeves.

The year 1863 brought two new weekly musical periodicals, *The Orchestra* (1863–87), and *The Choir* (1863–78). The first, published originally by Cramer, Wood & Co., and subsequently by Swift & Co., contained, besides criticisms of music in London and the provinces, correspondence from the principal musical centres of the Continent, serial ' feuilletons,' etc.

*The Choir and Musical Record*, published weekly by Thomas Wright, ' Choir ' Office, 188 Strand, was intended to ' promote the art of church music by the publication of essays and papers advocating sound principles and directing taste.' Among the contributors were E. F. Rimbault, G. A. Macfarren, and E. J. Hopkins. Four pages of music were issued weekly. In 1879 it was incorporated in the short-lived *Saturday Musical Review* (1879, 42 nos.).

*The Monthly Musical Record* (1871–   ) was founded by Augener & Co., and first edited by Prof. E. Prout. Among the principal contributors to the earlier numbers were : W. G. Cusins, E. Dannreuther, S. Jadassohn, L. Nohl, F. Niecks, E. Pauer, C. F. Pohl and X. Scharwenka. Historical and analytical notices in a serial form have been given from time to time by Pauer, Niecks and others. In vol. ii. appeared Dannreuther's articles on ' Wagner : his Tendencies, Life and Writings.' From 1874–76 the editor was C. A. Barry ; from that time until 1887 the post was held by W. A. Barrett. Admirable analyses of Schubert's masses, Schumann's symphonies, Weber's cantatas, etc., and descriptions of Urio's Te Deum and Stradella's Serenata, with reference to Handel's plagiarisms from them, all by Professor Prout, appeared in the earlier volumes. In recent years one of the most notable series of papers has been Prof. Niecks's ' Notes supplementary and corrective to the biography of Robert Schumann ' (1921–23). The issue of four sheets of music with the publication began in the number for Feb. 1880. The present editor is A. Eaglefield-Hull.

' *Concordia* (1875–76), a journal of music and the sister arts,' was published by Novello, Ewer & Co., under the editorship of Joseph Bennett. The paper consisted of articles, reviews, criticisms, and London, provincial and foreign intelligence on music, poetry, the drama and the fine arts, and was published weekly. The principal contributors were Dr. W. H. Stone, Dr. Gauntlett, Rev. Maurice Davies, W. Chappell, W. H. Cummings, J. Knight, Walter Thornbury, H. H. Statham, C. K. Salaman, Clement Scott, E Prout, H. Sutherland Edwards, H. Howe, H. C. Lunn and Joseph Bennett. The following articles of special interest appeared in this paper : Recollections of Catalani, Czerny, Mozart's son, Mozart's widow, Charles Neate, Schumann, Thalberg, the Philharmonic Society, the Lent Oratorios, the Shakespeare Jubilee of 1830, by C. K. Salaman ; A comparison of the original and revised scores of ' Elijah,' by Joseph Bennett ; Witty French Songs of the last century, by W. Chappell ; Helmholtz's New Musical Theories, by W. Chappell ; London Choirs, by Rev. Maurice Davies ; ' Don Juan ' and ' Faust,' by H Sutherland Edwards ; Purcell's works, by Dr. Rimbault ; Purcell's ' Yorkshire Feast '

and Theatre Music, by W. H. Cummings; and
a series of interesting facsimiles, letters and a
song by Handel, a caricature of Handel, an
autograph of J. S. Bach, and MSS. and letters
of C. P. E. Bach. A weekly list of services
in London churches, and a Shakespearean
calendar, were also included. The publication
was withdrawn in 1876, after fifty-two numbers
had been published.

*The Quaver* (1876–85) was chiefly devoted to
the exposition of the 'letter-note method' of
sight-reading.

*The London and Provincial Music Trades Re-
view*, now *The Music Trades Review* (1877–  )
appears on the 15th of each month. Besides
much trade information connected with music
patents, bankruptcies, etc., it has notices of
concerts and other musical events, and reviews
of both books and music, lists of new inventions and publications, and much miscellaneous
intelligence.

*Musical Opinion and Music Trade Review*
(1877–  ) is, as its name implies, an organ of
the music trade. Of late years its scope has
been much enlarged, and it now contains reviews and critical articles of high quality, many
of which are subsequently republished in book
form. A special section in each issue is devoted to the interests of the organist.

A paper more exclusively devoted to the interests of the trade is *The Piano, Organ and
Music Trades Journal*, first issued as *The Pianoforte Dealers' Guide* (1882–  ).

*The Musical Review* (1883) was started by
Novello & Co. with aims of a loftier kind than
have often been associated with English musical
periodicals. The *Review* was addressed mainly
to serious musicians and to students of musical
history. It contained a series of admirable
articles by leading writers on music, and was
conducted upon scholarly and independent
lines. Unfortunately it received inadequate
support from the public, and after a career of a
few months ceased to appear.

*The Lute* (1883–99) published by Patey &
Willis, made its first appearance under the
editorship of Joseph Bennett. Besides the usual
reviews, criticisms and miscellaneous articles it
contained a musical supplement, and was the
means of introducing to the world many partsongs and anthems by contemporary composers.
In 1888 Bennett was succeeded in the office of
editor by Lewis Thomas.

*The Magazine of Music* (1884–97) was founded
by the Musical Reform Association, primarily
for the purpose of introducing a new system of
musical notation to the English public. Portraits and musical supplements were a special
feature.

*The British Bandsman* (1887–  ) has appeared under various names, but in 1899 reverted to its original title. It is devoted to the
interests of brass, reed and string bandsmen,

and of the musical trade generally. It appeared
monthly until Mar. 1902, when it became a
weekly.

*The Meister* (1888–95), the quarterly journal
of the London branch of the Wagner Society,
was founded and edited by W. Ashton Ellis.
It did excellent work in spreading the knowledge of Wagner and his music at a time when
there was still much prejudice to be overcome,
containing as it did articles upon Wagner's
works and translations from his prose writings,
as well as miscellaneous information with regard
to the progress of the Wagnerian movement in
different parts of the world.

*The Nonconformist Musical Journal* (1888–
1910), known from 1906–10 as *The Musical
Journal*, was devoted, as its title implies, to
the musical activities of the Nonconformist
Churches. In 1910 it was incorporated in *The
Choir*.

*The Strad* (1890–  ) is concerned almost entirely with violins and violinists. Somewhat
similar in scope were: *The Fiddler* (1884–87);
*The Violin Monthly Magazine* (1890–94),
edited by J. M. Fleming; *The Violin Times*
(1893–1907), edited by E. Polonaski and E.
Heron-Allen; *Strings*, edited by J. Broadhouse (1894–95); and *The Cremona* (1906–11).

*Musical News* (1891–  ), founded under the
direction of E. H. Turpin and T. L. Southgate,
was designed to fill the place of the recently
defunct *Musical World*. According to its prospectus it was intended to be 'the chosen
expositor of academical intelligence,' and proposed to deal with 'all subjects connected with
examinations and other departments of musical
studentship.' In 1920 it was acquired by
Curwen & Sons, and to mark its absorption of
the *Musical Herald*, took the title *Musical News
and Herald*. It was then edited by Edwin
Evans and later for a short time by Sir R. R.
Terry. It appeared weekly till 1927; since
then monthly.

*The Early English Musical Magazine*, of
which a few numbers were published in 1891,
aimed at fostering a taste for antiquarian
music, but unfortunately received little support,
and soon expired. It contained many excellent articles, and some interesting reprints of
Elizabethan music.

The scope of *The School Music Review*
(1892–  ) is sufficiently indicated by its title.
It appears monthly, and is published by Novello.

*The New Quarterly Musical Review* (1893–96)
was founded in 1893 under the editorship of
Granville Bantock. Its aims were high, and
during its too brief existence it occupied a
unique position in the world of culture. It represented the views of the younger school of
English musicians, and the reviews and articles
which appeared in it were, as a rule, of great
interest, and often contained criticism of a
high order of merit.

*The Organist and Choirmaster* (1894–1920) was, as its name implies, concerned chiefly with ecclesiastical music and the organist's profession. It was edited by Dr. E. J. Hopkins, Dr. C. W. Pearce and Dr. C. Vincent. After Apr. 1920 it was incorporated with *The Sackbut*. The last three numbers appeared under the title of *The Organist*.

*The Musician*, which appeared first in May 1897, and was discontinued in the following November, had a brief but not inglorious career. It was edited by Robin Grey, and employed the services of almost every writer of note connected with the profession of music in England, and of many distinguished foreign authors. Reviews, criticisms, and articles upon musical æsthetics were included in the scheme of the paper, which also presented its subscribers with several excellent illustrated supplements. A selection of the articles which had appeared in *The Musician* was published in book form, as *Studies in Music*, in 1903.

*The Chord* (1899–1900, 5 nos.), was a prettily-got-up quarterly, which was intended to occupy in the world of music the position that *The Dome* occupied in the world of art and literature. It had some able writers on its staff, but its tone was unnecessarily polemical, and it failed to enlist the sympathies of the public.

Other periodicals published during the 19th century [1] were : *The Gregorian Quarterly Magazine* (1879, 4 nos.); *Musical Society* (1886–87), a monthly issued by W. Morley & Co.; *The Church Musician* (1891–95), the monthly journal of the Church Choir Guild ; *The Keyboard* (1892–94); *The Minim* (1893–1902); *The Strand Musical Magazine* (1895–99); *The Amateur Orchestra* (1899, 6 nos.); *The Musical Gazette* (1899–1902), published by Joseph Williams and edited by Ernest Walker; and *The Music Student* (1899–1902), published by W. Reeves and edited successively by Pascal Needham and H. Saint George.

The first quarter of the 20th century saw the birth of a whole host of short-lived journals, including: *The Precentor* (1901–07, 29 nos.); *The Vocalist* (1902–05); *The Bass Drum* (1903, 6 nos.); *The Weekly Musical Review* (1903, 10 nos.); *The Music Students' Magazine* (1903–1906, monthly, incorporated with ' The Minstrel '); *The Musician* (1905–06), published by the Vincent Music Co. and edited by T. Tapper; *The Musical Home Journal* (1905–08); *The Musical Era* (1905–10), which took the place of the old *Magazine of Music* as the official gazette of the Musical Reform Association; *Euterpe* (1909–10, 4 nos.); *The Literary and Musical Review* (1909–12, 17 nos.); *The Musical Antiquary* (1909–13), published quarterly under the editorship of G. E. P. Arkwright; *The Young Musician and the School Orchestra*

(1909–16, 43 nos.); *The Musical Observer* (1910–13, monthly); *The Musical Press* (1912–1913, 5 nos.); *The Music Review* (1912–13, 4 quarterly nos.); *The Musician* (1919–21), incorporated with ' The Music Student ' after Aug. 1921; and *Fanfare* (1921), a monthly edited by Leigh Henry and devoted exclusively to contemporary music, of which 6 nos. only appeared.

Of these *The Musical Antiquary* (1909–13) was easily the most important ; indeed, as a repository for the results of historical research on musical subjects it has found no successor. Among the scholars who contributed to it were G. E. P. Arkwright (its founder and editor), E. J. Dent, W. H. Grattan Flood, W. J Lawrence, E. W. Naylor, W. Barclay Squire, R. A. Streatfeild, R. R. Terry, Ernest Walker and H. E. Wooldridge.

Of the London periodicals founded since 1900 which are still in progress the following (arranged in chronological order) are the most noteworthy :

(1) *The Music Teacher* (1908–   ), originally entitled *The Music Student* and issued as the organ of the Home Music Study Union under the editorship of P. A. Scholes. In 1921 it absorbed *The Musician* (1919–21). With its change of title in 1922 it became the organ of the Music Teachers' Association. It is issued monthly, and is at present edited by W. R. Anderson. An important supplement, *Chamber Music*, was issued from 1913–16 under the editorship of W. W. Cobbett. A supplement for young people, *Music and Youth*, first issued in 1915 as *Youth and Music*, is still in progress.

(2) *The Choir* (1910–   ), which appears monthly under the editorship of J. T. Lightwood and deals chiefly, though not exclusively, with church music.

(3) *The Chesterian* (1915–   ), the house organ of J. & W. Chester, Ltd., edited by G. Jean-Aubry and appearing eight times yearly. It devotes special attention to contemporary music.

(4) *The Music Bulletin* (1919–   , monthly), the official journal of the British Music Society, founded (as *The British Music Bulletin*), and originally edited, by A. Eaglefield-Hull.

(5) *Music and Letters* (1920–   ), a quarterly publication which, under the editorship of A. H. Fox-Strangways, enjoys a high reputation on account of the literary quality and authoritative character of its articles. A list of recent books on music, English and foreign, is an important feature.

(6) *The Sackbut* (1920–   ), which, like *The Chesterian*, deals mainly with modern music and contains frequent contributions from foreign writers. Originally edited by Philip Heseltine, it was acquired in 1921 by Curwen & Sons, and is at present edited by Ursula Greville. It appears monthly.

(7) *The Organ* (1921– ), a quarterly journal issued by the proprietors of *Musical Opinion.*

(8) *The Gramophone* (1923– ), a monthly edited by Compton Mackenzie, which, in addition to its technical articles, publishes a number of contributions of general musical interest.

A complete list of provincial musical periodicals would not be very extensive, but the most important only can be mentioned here. Of those no longer current the most ambitious was *The Quarterly Musical Review* (1885–88), published at Manchester under the editorship of Henry Hiles. It contained many valuable articles on musical history and educational questions. *The Yorkshire Musician* (Leeds, 1887–89) and *The Irish Musical Monthly* (1902–1903), both met with little support. Of those still in progress the most important are *The British Musician*[1] (1926– ), edited by Sidney Grew, a monthly founded by A. C. Boult to help the work of the Birmingham Orchestra, *Y Cerddor Newydd* or *The Welsh Musical Magazine*, formerly *Y Cerddor* (1899– ), and *The Scottish Musical Magazine* (1919– ).

### FRANCE AND BELGIUM

**FRANCE.**—The earliest musical periodical published in the French language[2] appears to have been *Sentiments d' un harmonophile sur différents ouvrages de musique* (Mar.-Apr. 1756), edited by Morambert. It was followed by the *Journal de musique française et italienne* (1764–68), the *Journal de musique historique théorique et pratique* (1770–71), and the *Journal de musique par une Société d'amateurs* (1773–78). About this time there also appeared a number of publications such as the 'Journal de clavecin,' 'Journal de violin,' 'Journal d'ariettes,' which do not strictly come within the scope of this article, as they consisted entirely of music. Of 19th century periodicals the earliest were *La Correspondance des amateurs musiciens*, afterwards *Correspondance des professeurs et des amateurs de musique* (1802–05), edited by Cocatrix, and *Les Tablettes de Polymnie* (1810–1811), edited by Garaudé and Cambini. The first journal of real importance, however, was *La Revue musicale* (1827–80), founded by Fétis. In 1835 it joined forces with the *Gazette musicale de Paris* (itself the continuation of *La Dilettante*, 1833–35), which had been started the year before, and appeared under the title of *Revue et Gazette musicale* until 1880. Amongst its contributors were J. Janin, Berlioz, Liszt, R. Wagner, Balzac and Stephen Heller. *Le Ménestrel* (1833– ), founded by Heugel, still

enjoys wide popularity. It gives a valuable summary of musical events throughout the world, and its longer articles are extremely able and scholarly. F. Clément, E. David, A. Jullien, V. Wilder, A. Pougin, and J. Tiersot may be mentioned among its contributors. *La France musicale* (1833–70) was a weekly journal, edited by Marie and Léon Escudier, which contained musical biographies and many other articles of interest. Among its contributors at different times were Castil-Blaze, G. Maurel, Farrenc, Méry, Philarète Chasles and V. Schoelcher. Next in order came the *Revue de musique religieuse populaire et classique* (1845–48, 1854), edited by Danjou, and containing many important articles by him and by Fétis, Laurens, Morelot and other contributors, and *La Critique musicale* (1846–1847), edited by Azevedo and continued under the title of *L'Univers musicale* (1847-64). The second half of the 19th century saw the birth of a large number of musical journals of which the chief were : *La Chronique musicale* (1850–1865), edited by P. Villeblanche ; *L'Orphéon* (1855– ) ; *La Réforme musicale* (1856–70), devoted to the exposition of the Galin-Paris-Chevé system ; *La Maîtrise* (1857–60, edited by J. d'Ortigue and L. Niedermeyer, and dealing exclusively with religious music ; *Le Moniteur musical* (1858– ), devoted to military band music ; *La Paroisse* (1860–61), subsequently incorporated, together with *Le Plain Chant* (1860–61) in the *Revue de musique sacrée ancienne et moderne* (1861–70) ; *L'Art musical* (1860–94), which as the organ of the publishing house of Escudier took an important place in the musical world, its staff including many eminent writers, among them Scudo, Chouquet, Neukomm, Lacome and Vizentini ; *Le Monde artiste illustré* (1860–1914), which, under the editorship of Jules Ruelle, was for long the recognised authority upon dramatic and musical events in the French provinces and in Algeria ; *La France chorale* (1861–67) and *L'Écho des Orphéons* (1861– ), two journals devoted to choral music, the latter of which is still in progress ; the *Bulletin de la Société des compositeurs de musique* (1863–70), edited by Weckerlin, and containing much antiquarian and historical matter ; *L'Avenir musical* (1865– ), like the earlier 'La Réforme musicale' an organ of the Méthode Galin-Paris-Chevé ; *L'Instrumental* (1867 – 1914), a fortnightly periodical intended chiefly as a practical guide to musical societies ; *La Chronique musicale* (1873–76), edited by A. Heulard, and to be distinguished from the journal of the same name which has already been mentioned ; *La Renaissance musicale* (1881–83), edited by E. Hippeau ; *Le Monde orphéonique* (1882– ), a weekly devoted to male-voice part-singing ; *La Revue wagnérienne* (1885–88), edited by E. Dujardin ; the *Revue d'art dramatique et*

---

[1] Originally *The Midland Musician.*
[2] See J. G. Prod'homme, *Essai de bibliographie des périodiques musicaux en langue française* ('Bulletin de la Soc. Française de Musicologie,' 1918, No. 2). The present article is greatly indebted to M. Prod'homme's paper. For the period before 1750, the *Mercure de France* is of great value. See E. Deville, *Index du 'Mercure de France,'* 1672–1832, donnant l'indication, par ordre alphabétique, de toutes les notices, mentions, annonces, planches, etc. concernant les beaux-arts et l'archéologie (Paris, 1910).

*musical* (1886–1914) ; *L'Indépendance musicale et dramatique* (1887–88) ; *Le Monde musical* (1889–   ), edited by A. Mangeot; *La Quinzaine musicale* (1894) ; *La Tribune de St. Gervais* (1895–1922), the official organ of the Schola Cantorum ; the *Revue internationale de musique* (1898–99), edited by H. Gauthier-Villars ; and *Le Courrier musical* (1899–   ), with its weekly supplement *La Semaine musicale*.

The list of periodicals founded in the 20th century is headed by the *Revue musicale d'histoire et de critique* (1901–   ), edited by J. Combarieu and L. Laloy, a paper of serious and scholarly aim, which numbered among its contributors P. Aubry, M. Emmanuel and R. Rolland. In the following year appeared *Musica* (1902–14) and *Le Courrier de l'orchestre* (1902–17). *Le Mercure musical* (1905–06), after two years of independent existence under the editorship of J. Marnold and L. Laloy, was converted into the *Bulletin français de la Section française de la Société internationale de Musique* (1906–15) and edited by J. Ecorcheville. *Le Guide de concert* (1910–   ) gives particulars of concert programmes and descriptions of the music performed. *L'Année musicale* (1911–13), edited by M. Brenet, J. Chantavoine, L. Laloy and L. de La Laurencie, met with little support, but it contains some full-length articles of considerable importance, in particular a comprehensive 'bibliography of musical bibliographies' by M. Brenet. *L'Écho musical* (1912–20), edited by A. Doily and P. Brunold, was amalgamated in 1920 with *La Revue musicale* (1920–   ). This latter periodical, which is edited by H. Prunières, is one of the most interesting of present-day musical journals. Special numbers devoted to individual composers or to particular subjects are issued from time to time. The *Revue de musicologie*, originally entitled *Bulletin de la Société Française de Musicologie* (1917–   ), though slight in bulk, contains many important contributions. Other recently founded periodicals are *Lyrica* (1922–   ), *La Revue Pleyel* (1924–   ), and *L'Orgue et les organistes* (1924–   ), edited by J. Huré.

Among French provincial periodicals may be mentioned : *Bulletin polymathique des musiciens de Bordeaux* (1802–13) ; the *Revue de musique ancienne et moderne* (1865), published by Nisard at Rennes ; the *Angers-Revue* (1878–1890 ?) ; *La Semaine musicale de Lille et du département du Nord* (Lille, 1881–95) ; *L'Ouest artiste* (Nantes, 1885–1914) ; *Caecilia* (Strasbourg, 1887–   ) ; *La Revue du chant grégorien* (Grenoble, 1892–   ) ; *Saint-Cécile* (Reims, 1893–189 ?) ; the *Nouvelle Revue musicale de Lyon*, formerly *La Revue musicale de Lyon* (1902–   ) ; and *Angers-musical* (1910–14).

BELGIUM.—The earliest musical periodical to be published in Belgium was the *Gazette musicale de la Belgique* (1833–34), published by

Fétis.[1] Next in order came *Le Franc Jug* (1834–39). *La Revue musicale belge* (1840–42) was the first of a succession of journals which culminated in the foundation of *Le Guide musical*. Its immediate successor was *La Belgique musicale* (1842–50). This in turn was succeeded by *Le Diapason* (1850–52), which shortly before its demise took the title of *La Chronique musicale*. This was the progenitor of *Le Guide musical* (1855–1914, 1917–18), which soon took rank as one of the most interesting and valuable musical periodicals published in the French language. It was edited successively by F. Delhasse, M. Kufferath, H. Imbert and H. de Curzon. For the last two years of its existence it was issued from Paris. All the above periodicals were published in Brussels. Belgium now once more possesses a musical journal of its own in *La Revue musicale belge*, founded in 1926 under the editorship of Paul Gilson. The provincial journals include *Caecilia* (Bruges, 1847–50 ?), edited by R. J. van Maldeghem; *Musica sacra* (Ghent, 1881–   ) ; and *La Revue grégorienne* (Tournai, 1911–   ).

### GERMANY AND AUSTRIA

The parent of German musical periodicals, though it can hardly be called a periodical in the modern sense, was Mattheson's *Musica critica* (Hamburg, 1722). It was issued in numbers, and contained musical news as well as critical essays. It was followed by Scheibe's *Critischer Musikus* (1737–40),[2] Mitzler's *Musikalische Bibliothek* (1736–54), and *Musikalischer Staarstecher* (1740), Henke's *Der musikalische Patriot* (1741–42), and Marpurg's numerous publications (1750–78). Hiller's *Wöchentliche Nachrichten* was perhaps the first musical periodical in the stricter sense of the word. It was published once a week at Leipzig from 1766–70. During the closing years of the 18th and the opening of the 19th century the musical activity in Germany was very remarkable, and the number of musical periodicals, most of which enjoyed but a brief period of activity, was truly extraordinary. For a complete list of these the reader is referred to *Riemann*. Only the most important can be discussed here. At the head of them stands the *Allgemeine musikalische Zeitung* (Oct. 1798–Dec. 28, 1848), published at Leipzig by Breitkopf & Härtel, and edited successively by Rochlitz and G. W. Finck. The importance of this periodical for information on all musical matters during the first half of the 19th century will be best estimated from the concluding remarks of the publishers in the last number.

'This journal was founded when musical production was at its richest and best. Mozart was not long dead, Haydn was near the end, and Beethoven

---

[1] *L'Écho ou Journal de musique française et italienne* (Liège 1758–66 ?) consisted entirely of music.
[2] An enlarged edition of the whole was published in 1745.

at the beginning of his career. To bring the works of such a period as this before the notice of connoisseurs and amateurs, to elucidate and explain them, to educate the public up to understanding them—such were the objects of the *Musikalische Zeitung*; and these objects were attained in a degree which entitles it without hesitation to a high place in the history of music. But with the lapse of time the conditions of the musical world have materially changed. There is no longer a centre either for musical production or appreciation, both being now disseminated far and wide. Under these circumstances, a general musical journal is an anachronism ; local papers are better fitted to supply the various necessities of the musical world.'

Nevertheless, after an interval of 15 years an attempt was made to revive the journal, under the editorship of S. Bagge, who from 1860–62 had directed a *Deutsche Musikzeitung* from Vienna, but the new series only lasted for 3 years (1863–65). The *Leipziger allgemeine musikalische Zeitung*, afterwards known simply as *Allgemeine musikalische Zeitung* (1866–82) may, however, be considered as its direct successor, although it was issued by a different firm of publishers (Rieter-Biedermann). The first numbers of the new series, which was also edited by Bagge, were interesting, on the one hand from the support given to the rising talent of Brahms, and on the other to the revival of the old classical school and the cult of Bach and Handel. Bagge was succeeded by Eitner, and he again by Chrysander. He attracted a brilliant staff, and many of the articles, such as Nottebohm's ' Beethoveniana,' would do credit to any periodical. Chrysander was succeeded in 1871 by Joseph Müller but resumed the editorship in 1875.

The Viennese *Allgemeine musikalische Zeitung* (1817–24), important for special information on music in Vienna, was edited successively by J. von Mosel (1817–18), by von Seyfried (1819–1820), and by Kanne (1821–24). It contained portraits of celebrated musicians, including Beethoven, and was notable as the first independent effort of Viennese journalism.

The *Berliner allgemeine musikalische Zeitung*, 1824–30 (Schlesinger), founded by A. B. Marx, did important service to the rapid spread of Beethoven's works in North Germany even during his lifetime, and in promoting the revival of the taste for Bach's and Handel's music in Berlin. In his farewell address Marx says :

' The usual habit of critics is to give way to the fluctuating inclinations of the public, in order to insinuate a little, a very little, of the truth. This has never been *my* way ; I have never been carried away by the fashion of the day, for I have neither formed my opinions by it, nor succumbed to its attractions, and thus I have been preserved from inconsistency. For instance, with regard to Spontini, I neither lauded his " Vestale " as the work of a great artist, nor depreciated his later compositions as the productions of a mere academical pupil, or an imbecile, like so many musicians of our day. Nor again was I so far dazzled by the novelty of Rossini's and Auber's operas, as to endorse the popular verdict upon them.'

*Caecilia* (1824–48) was conducted by an association of scholars, art critics and artists,

under the editorship of Gottfried Weber, and was published by Schott. It appeared at irregular intervals and forms a series of twenty-seven volumes of four numbers each. Weber conducted it till his death in 1839, and was succeeded by Dehn, who continued editor till its discontinuance in consequence of the political troubles of 1848. Its opening prospectus declared that it was intended to be not so much a regular periodical as a collection of original articles of permanent interest, and a medium for the exchange of views and opinions on art. It contained papers on the theory of music and acoustics, on history and æsthetics, reviews and notices of music and treatises on the art, and its contributors included G. Weber himself, Kiesewetter, Krieger, A. Schmid, A. Fuchs, S. W. Dehn, Chladni, Fink, von Drieberg and Rochlitz. The whole formed a valuable record of the progress of the historical and theoretical departments of music during a quarter of a century. The practical portion of the art was not so well represented. In fact, the romantic movement carried on by Schumann, Chopin and others, not only received no recognition but was treated with a certain covert hostility.

The *Neue Zeitschrift für Musik* (1834–  ) was founded by Robert Schumann, who relates in his *Gesammelte Schriften* how a number of musicians, who had met in Leipzig in the end of 1833 to compare ideas on the new lights Mendelssohn and Chopin, were roused to do something more for the cause of art than merely carrying on their calling as musicians. Thus arose the *Neue Zeitschrift* (Apr. 3, 1834) ; Hartmann the publisher was the first editor, but from 1835–44 Schumann conducted it himself. After him Oswald Lorenz took it for a short time, and was succeeded by Franz Brendel (1845–68), under whom it espoused the cause of the so-called new German school. From 1903–1906, when it was incorporated with the *Musikalisches Wochenblatt*, it was edited by A. Schering and W. Niemann. In 1910 it reappeared under its old title and under the editorship of F. Brandes, who was succeeded in 1919 by Max Unger. In May 1920 it was acquired by the Steingräber Verlag and renamed *Zeitschrift für Musik*. Its present editor is A. Heuss.

The *Allgemeine Wiener musikalische Zeitung* (1841–48), edited until 1847 by Dr. Aug. Schmidt (joint-founder of the Viennese Männergesangverein), contained a series of articles (beginning with No. 28, 1846) by Eduard Hanslick, highly laudatory of Wagner's ' Tannhäuser ' ! Luib was editor in 1847–48, the last twelve months of its existence. It was replaced by the *Wiener Musikzeitung* (1852–60) edited by Glöggl, jun., almost the only reliable source of information on musical affairs for that period.

The *Signale für die musikalische Welt* (1842–  ), a well-known musical periodical, founded by Bartholf Senff of Leipzig, is more strictly a record of news than of criticism, though it occasionally contains original articles of great interest, letters of musicians and other documents. Its list of contributors has included F. Hiller, von Bülow, Bernsdorf, C. F. Pohl, Richard Pohl, Stockhausen, Szarvady, Marchesi, and many other of the most eminent musical writers. Though not strictly a weekly publication, 52 numbers are published yearly. It is at present edited by M. Chop.

The *Berliner musikalische Zeitung* (1844–47), the first periodical to praise Wagner's works on their production in Dresden, was started by Gaillard, and continued as the *Neue Berliner Musikzeitung* (Bote & Bock) until 1896  It contains amongst others well-known articles by von Lenz.

The *Rheinische Musikzeitung* (1850–53) and the *Niederrheinische Musikzeitung* (1853–67), both edited by Prof. L. Bischoff (inventor of the expression 'music of the future'), are important for the history of music in the Rhenish Provinces. The latter journal, in particular, gained a reputation as one of the best conducted of all the German musical papers. The Shakespearean scholar Gervinus was one of its contributors. The Rhine district is at present served by the *Rheinische Musik- und Theaterzeitung* (1900–  ), published at Cologne and edited successively by R. Wolff, W. Thomas San Galli and G. Tischer.

The *Echo* (1851–79), published by Schlesinger of Berlin, was conducted in 1851 and 1852 by Kossak the well-known feuilletonist, then by the publisher. In 1866 it passed into the hands of Robert Lienau (with Men lel as editor), in 1873 into those of Oppenheim (editor, Dr. Langhans), in 1874 it returned to Lienau, and finally ceased Dec. 1879. It had at one time a certain importance as an opposition paper to Wagner.

*Fliegende Blätter für Musik* (3 vols., 1855–57) was hardly a periodical in the strict sense, as it appeared irregularly and was written entirely by one man. The author, J. C. Lobe, the writer of the interesting ' Musikalische Briefe eines Unbekannten,' was one of the most capable critics of his day, and his paper contains many excellent full-length essays, often of a polemical character, copiously illustrated with musical examples.

The *Monatsschrift für Theater und Musik* (1855–61), edited by Joseph Klemm, went less into detail, but like its successor, the *Recensionen und Mittheilungen für Theater, Musik und bildende Kunst* (1862–65), contained valuable articles by Sonnleithner on Mozart, and on music in Vienna at that date.

*Tonhalle* (Payne, Leipzig) was edited by Oscar Paul from Mar. 23, 1868, to the end of 1869, when it was merged in the *Musikalische Wochenblatt* (the first illustrated paper of the kind) (Fritzsch), which soon became a demonstrative organ of the Wagner party, and at the same time a champion of Brahms. It also published Nottebohm's ' Neue Beethoveniana,' and may thus fairly be called eclectic in its views. The first ten numbers were edited by Paul, but it was then managed entirely by the publisher until 1902, when K. Kipke became the editor. From 1902–06 the ' Neue Zeitschrift für Musik ' was incorporated in it. It is now published by Siegel under the editorship of L. Frankenstein. It has a very large circulation in Germany, and is distinguished for its notices of foreign music.

*Monatshefte für Musikgeschichte* (1869–1905), founded and edited by R. Eitner as the organ of the ' Gesellschaft für Musikforschung,' was predominantly antiquarian in character. It contained lists and bibliographies of the works of ancient composers, Hucbald, Lasso, Okeghem, Crüger, etc., and many valuable articles. An index to the first ten years was published in 1879. Several important monographs were issued as supplementary volumes.

The *Allgemeine Musikzeitung*, originally entitled *Allgemeine deutsche Musikzeitung* (1874–  ) must not be confused with the *Allgemeine deutsche Musikzeitung* published by F. Nedl at Türmitz since 1923 or with the two journals entitled *Allgemeine musikalische Zeitung* (Leipzig, 1798–1882; Vienna, 1817–24) or the *Berliner allgemeine musikalische Zeitung* (1824–1830), which have been already discussed. Originally founded by F. Luckhardt in Cassel but now published in Berlin, it is a weekly whose aim, according to its subtitle, is ' the reform of present-day musical activities.' It is edited by P. Schwers.

*Bayreuther Blätter* (1878–  ) has published numerous articles of extreme interest to the musical historian, dealing chiefly with the progress of the Wagnerian movement. Many of Wagner's letters have here been published for the first time.

The *Vierteljahrsschrift für Musikwissenschaft* (1885–95) dealt with musical history in an able and scholarly manner. It was edited by F. Chrysander and P. Spitta.

The *Jahrbuch der Musikbibliothek Peters* (1895–  ), besides reporting on recent additions to the Library, provides each year a valuable bibliography of recent musical literature and prints a few important articles of a general character. It is at present edited by R Schwartz.

In 1899 the Internationale Musik-Gesellschaft was founded (see INTERNATIONAL MUSICAL SOCIETY). From that date until 1914, when the war brought about its dissolution, the Society published two periodicals, the monthly *Zeitschrift* and the quarterly *Sammelbände*, the former devoted principally to current topics of interest, the latter to long articles on special points of musical history, technique or æsthetics. A special series of monographs was also issued as a supplement. An English edition of the two periodicals was published, with a summary in English of the articles written in German.

*Die Musik* (1901-15, 1922- ) was founded by Schuster & Loeffler of Berlin and was at first issued fortnightly. It ceased publication shortly after the outbreak of the war, but was revived as a monthly in 1922 by the Deutsche Verlags-Anstalt of Stuttgart. It contains excellent articles on musical history, æsthetics, etc., and makes a special feature of illustrations. From time to time special numbers are devoted to the lives and work of individual musicians. It has been edited from the commencement by B. Schuster.

Two of the most important German musical periodicals, the *Archiv für Musikwissenschaft* and the *Zeitschrift für Musikwissenschaft*, are of recent date, both having been founded in 1919. The *Archiv*, published quarterly by Kistner & Siegel of Leipzig and edited by J. Wolf, is the organ of the ' Fürstliches Institut für musikwissenschaftliche Forschung ' at Bückeburg. The *Zeitschrift*, published monthly by Breitkopf & Härtel and edited by A. Einstein, is the organ of the ' Deutsche Musikgesellschaft,' a body formed to take the place of the German branch of the defunct International Musical Society. Both are predominantly journals for original musical research, and contain little in the way of comment on current events. The *Zeitschrift*, however, provides a very comprehensive list of recently published books on music.

Of the other general periodicals founded in the course of the present century the most notable are: *Der Merker* (1909- ), a fortnightly magazine dealing with music and the theatre, published at Vienna, and at present edited by J. Bittner and D. J. Bach ; *Musikblätter des Anbruch* (1919- ), published by the Universal-Edition in Vienna and edited by P. Stefan, a monthly periodical dealing exclusively with modern music ; and *Melos* (1920- ), another monthly journal of modernist tendencies, now published by Schott of Mainz under the editorship of H. Mersmann.

Most of the above periodicals cover the whole field of music. Of the specialist journals we can only mention here a few of the numerous papers which deal exclusively with church music. They include : *Cäcilienkalender* (1876-1885), continued as *Kirchenmusikalisches Jahrbuch* (Ratisbon, 1886-1911) ; *Der Chorwächter* (1875- ), now published at Lucerne under the editorship of F. Frey ; *Der Kirchenchor* (Bregenz, 1871- ), *Der katholische Kirchensänger* (Freiburg, 1887- ), *Cäcilia* (Treves, 1862- ), *Cäcilia* (Strassburg, 1894- ), *Cäcilia* (Breslau, 1893- ), *Musica sacra* (Regensburg, 1866- ), *Fliegende*

*Blätter für katholische Kirchenmusik*, now known as *Cäcilienvereins-Organ* (1866- ) and published at Paderborn, *Gregoriusblatt* (Aachen, 1876- ), *Gregoriusbote* (Düsseldorf, 1884- ), *Literarischer Handweiser* (Regensburg, 1893- ), *Musica divina* (1913- ), the organ of the ' Schola Austriaca,' *Der katholische Organist* (Düsseldorf, 1913- ). The above are Catholic. The principal periodicals dealing with music in the Lutheran Church are : *Fliegende Blätter des Schlesischen Vereins zur Hebung der evangelischen Kirchenmusik* (Brieg, 1867- ), *Siona* (Gütersloh, 1876- ), *Halleluja* (Quedlinburg, 1879- ), *Korrespondenzblatt des Evangelischen Kirchengesangvereins* (Leipzig, 1886- ), *Der Kirchenchor* (Leipzig, 1890- ), *Monatsschrift für Gottesdienst und kirchliche Kunst* (Göttingen, 1896), and *Kirchenmusikalische Blätter* (Nuremberg, 1920- ).

### ITALY

The leading Italian musical periodical, from the point of view of the student and historian, is the *Rivista musicale* (Turin), a quarterly magazine first published in 1894, edited originally by L. Torchi and at present by L. Torrefranca. It contains articles of the utmost value and interest, and is conducted throughout with singular ability and brilliant scholarship. One of the best-known periodicals dealing with more ephemeral matters is the *Gazzetta musicale* (Milan), the official organ of the house of Ricordi, first published in 1845, which for many years gave a useful conspectus of the progress of Italian opera in all parts of the world. In 1903 its *format* was changed from folio to octavo, its title was altered to *Musica e musicisti*, and it became little more than a trade circular. In 1906 the title was further changed to *Ars et labor*, *Musica e musicisti* being retained as a subtitle. It ceased publication in 1912. The present journal of the firm is *Musica d'oggi* (1919- ), which is chiefly of value for its annotated analyses of the contents of the chief musical periodicals. Among other Italian musical periodicals still in progress may be mentioned : *Il trovatore* (Milan, 1863), *Il mondo artistico* (Milan, 1866), *Gazzetta musicale di Firenze* (1877), *Palestra musicale* (Rome, 1878), *Napoli musicale* (Naples, 1878), *L' osservatore musicale* (Naples, 1879), *Archivio musicale* (Naples, 1882), *Gazzetta musicale di Torino* (1879), *Roma musicale* (1885), *La cronaca musicale* (Pesaro, 1897), *Il pianoforte* (Turin, 1920) the monthly journal of the ' Fabbrica Italiana di Pianoforte,' of special importance for modern music, *Musica italiana* (Turin, 1921), *Il pensiero musicale* (Bologna, 1921) and *La cultura musicale* (Bologna, 1922). The following are devoted to church music : *Musica sacra* (Milan, 1878), *S. Cecilia* (Turin, 1899), *Rassegna Gregoriana* (Rome, 1902), *Guido Aretinus*, the quarterly organ of the Guido d' Arezzo Society (Milan, 1885) and *La scuola Veneta di musica sacra* (1892).

## OTHER EUROPEAN COUNTRIES

Of the musical periodicals published in other countries the following are likely to prove most useful to English readers : The *Bulletin de la Société ' Union Musicologique '* (The Hague, 1921– ), an international review somewhat similar in scope to the journal of the old International Musical Society ; the *Tijdschrift der Vereeniging voor Noordnederlands Musikgeschiedenis* (Amsterdam, 1886– ); *De Musiek* (1926– ), edited by Paul F. Sanders and Willem Pijper, and published by Seyffardt of Amsterdam ; the *Svensk Tidskrift för Musikforskning* (Stockholm, 1919– ); *Ur Nutidens Musikliv* (Stockholm, 1920– ); and *Der Auftakt* (Prague, 1920– ), a monthly magazine edited by E. Steinhard which is cosmopolitan in character and deals almost exclusively with contemporary music.

## UNITED STATES

There are published in the United States about sixty weekly, fortnightly and monthly journals ostensibly devoted to music. The majority of them are little else than advertising mediums for music-publishing houses, their few pages of letterpress serving to carry through the mails as second-class matter the remaining pages, which are filled with music for choirs, brass bands, banjo and mandoline clubs, small dance orchestras and the like ; or they are trade journals whose business it is to exploit the wares of their advertisers who manufacture musical instruments in whole or in part. Few are devoted to the art in its higher phases, and the best of these pursue pedagogical purposes. The publication of musical periodicals in America began before the expiration of the 18th century, but the first, if Andrew Law's *Musical Magazine* may be looked upon as such (it was a collection of psalm tunes which began in 1792), already exemplified the description given of the majority of latter-day publications, though without the ulterior purpose ascribed to them. The earliest American reprints of European compositions were thus accomplished. It seems probable that within the period which has elapsed since the publication of Law's magazine not less than 400 periodicals of various kinds have appeared in the United States and disappeared within an extremely short time after their birth. In 1906 there were about 250 musical magazines of all kinds on file in the library of Congress, most of them dead. The most important of these earlier publications was Dwight's *Journal of Music*, which was published in Boston under the editorship of John S. DWIGHT (*q.v.*) from 1852–81. In the first edition of this Dictionary, the journal being still in existence, Col. H. Ware, librarian of the public library of Boston, said of it :

' Mr. Dwight, though not an educated musician, was musical editor of the *Harbinger*, a periodical published at Brook Farm, and a frequent contributor of musical critiques to the daily papers of Boston, where he did good service in directing attention to what was noblest and best in music. For six years he was editor, publisher and proprietor of the journal, the publication of which was then assumed by Oliver Ditson & Co. [1858–78]. During the war it was changed from a weekly to a fortnightly paper. Its object was to advocate music and musical culture in the highest sense, and to give honest and impartial criticisms, a purpose to which it has been always steadily devoted. . . . Mr. Dwight has been sole editor up to this day, although the volumes contain valuable contributions from other pens. Among the most noticeable of these are those from A. W. Thayer, the biographer of Beethoven, who has written for it many valuable biographical and historical articles, as well as musical tales. Especially noteworthy are his articles on some of the contemporaries of Beethoven, Salieri, Gyrowetz, Gelinek, Hummel and others. Prof. Ritter and his wife, . . . W. S. B. Mathews of Chicago and C. C. Perkins of Boston have also contributed frequent and valuable articles to its columns.'

From 1879–81 the journal was published by Houghton, Mifflin & Co. Ten years after it had suspended publication, W. S. B. Mathews, mentioned by Colonel Ware as one of its contributors, made an ambitious essay in Chicago by beginning the publication of a monthly magazine called *Music*. The first number appeared in Nov. 1891, the last in Dec. 1902. In this magazine comparatively little attention was paid to current events or local criticism, but much to critical studies of a special character and to pedagogical subjects. *The American Art Journal*, which was founded by Henry C. Watson in January 1863 as *Watson's Art Journal*, for many years devoted much space to musical subjects.

A publication of the highest character, though pursuing a special aim, was *Church Music* (1905–1909), a quarterly of 144 pages, with music supplement of eight pages, founded for the purpose of forwarding the reform in music in the Roman Catholic Church as prescribed in the ' Motu Proprio ' of Pope Pius X. issued on the Feast of St. Cecilia, 1903. Its principal contributors were the Benedictines of Solesmes. Amongst American contributors were the Rev. Ludwig Bonvin, S.J., of Buffalo ; Harold B. Gibbs, of Covington, Ky.; the Rev. W. J. Finn, C.S.P., Catholic University at Washington ; the Rev. Norman Holly, Dunwiddie Seminary, New York ; George Herbert Wells, Georgetown, D.C. ; the Rev. Dom. Waedenschwiler, Mt. Angel, Oregon; and the editor, the Rev. H. T. Henry, Litt.D., Overbrook Seminary, Philadelphia. It was published by the *American Ecclesiastical Review* at Philadelphia.

*The Étude* (1883– ), also published at Philadelphia by Theodore Presser, devoted chiefly to musical pedagogics, the publication of aids to teachers, and the betterment of standards of instruction and music, was established by Presser at Lynchburg, Va. In 1884 the place of publication was changed to Philadelphia. It has been edited successively by T. Presser (till 1888), E. E. Ayres (1888–93), A. L. Manchester (1893–96), W. J. Baltzell (1897–1907) and J. F. Cooke (since 1907). It is published monthly and its average circulation is 200,000 copies.

Similar in purpose and scope is *The Musician* (1896– ) founded by the Hatch Music Co. of Philadelphia; its first issue appeared on Jan. 1, 1896, A. L. Manchester being the editor. It remained the property of the Hatch Co. until Nov. 1904, when it was purchased by the Ditson Co. In 1918 it passed for a short time into the hands of the Henderson Publications, New York, and was then acquired by its present editor, P. Kempf. Its distinctive purpose under its first editor, T. Tapper, and his successors, has been to present in each issue some material from writers of the highest authority, and to specialise community music in two ways—in suggesting means for the encouragement of music in small communities, and means by which school and church music may become more distinct community factors than they are at present. From Nov. 1905–Sept. 1906 *The Musician* published an English edition through the Vincent Music Co., Berners Street, London. Among frequent contributors to *The Musician* have been Dr. Percy Goetschius, Henry T. Finck, Lawrence Gilman, H. E. Krehbiel of New York; Julien Tiersot, Paris; William Shakespeare, London; Arthur Bird, Berlin; Ernest Newman, London; and Isidor Philipp, Paris.

But by far the most important of the American periodicals from the point of view of musical scholarship is *The Musical Quarterly* (1915– ), published by G. Schirmer of New York and edited by O. G. Sonneck. It is a serious review, cosmopolitan in character, and has published valuable contributions from most of the leading writers on music in Europe and America.

*Modern Music* (1923– ) is a 'Quarterly Review' published by the League of Composers—managing editor, Minna Lederman. It contains short, and generally slight, essays on aspects of modern music from a great variety of contributors, both American and European.

*The Choir and Choral Magazine*, published by the Ditson Co. and edited by T. Tapper, is devoted to the music of schools, churches and choral societies.

*The New Music Review* (1904– ), published by the H. W. Gray Co., New York, grew out of *The Church Music Review*, founded in Dec. 1901 by Novello, Ewer & Co., and edited by H. W. Gray and Mallinson Randall. The change was made on Nov. 1, 1904, and simultaneously its scope was enlarged to include all the interests of organists, choirmasters, choirs and choral societies. The *Review*, which is the official journal of the American Guild of Organists, enjoys a high reputation for its able editorials and the excellence of its contributed articles.

*The Choir Journal* (1899– ), published by the B. F. Wood Music Co., Boston, is a monthly chiefly devoted to the dissemination of the church music publications of its proprietors.

*School Music*, originally entitled *The School Music Monthly* (1900– ), edited and published by P. C. Hayden in Keokuk, Iowa, is the only periodical in the United States devoted exclusively to the interests of music teachers in the public schools. There are now only five issues each year.

*The Musical Leader and Concert Goer* (1895– ) is published weekly by the Musical Leader Publishing Co. in Chicago. It divides its attention chiefly between Chicago and New York.

At the head of the weekly journals which purvey current musical news is *The Musical Courier* (1880– ), published by The Musical Courier Co. in New York.

*Musical America* (1904– ), edited by John C. Freund, is published by the Musical American Co., New York.

*The Musical Digest* (1921– ), published weekly in New York under the editorship of Pierre V. R. Key, provides a useful summary of the chief musical events throughout the world and preserves an independent character.

Amongst the larger trade publications are *The Music Trade Review*, New York (1879– ); *The Musical Age* (New York, 1896– ); *Presto* (Chicago, 1884– ); and *The Music Trades* (New York, 1890– ).

The above article, revised, with addns. by C. B. O., incorporates material from M., F. G., A. M., R A. S. and H. E. K.

**PERLE DU BRÉSIL, LA**, lyrical drama in 3 acts; words by MM. St. Etienne, music by Félicien David. Produced Théâtre Lyrique, Paris, Nov. 22, 1851. David afterwards added recitatives.      G.

**PERNE**, FRANÇOIS LOUIS (*b.* Paris, Oct. 4, 1772; *d.* there, May 26, 1832), was educated in a maîtrise, and during the Revolution became a chorus-singer at the Opéra. In 1799 he exchanged into the band, where he played the double-bass. A Mass for St. Cecilia's day, performed in 1800 at St. Gervais, secured him the esteem of musicians; and in the following year he published a fugue in four parts with three subjects, which placed him amongst the foremost masters of harmony of the day. It is not, however, by his compositions that Perne's name will be preserved, but by his laborious and erudite works on some of the most obscure points in the history of music. His expenditure of time, patience and learning, in hunting up, cataloguing, copying and annotating the most important sources of information, printed and MS., on the music of the Greeks and the

Middle Ages, was almost superhuman. One instance of his devotion will suffice. After publishing his *Exposition de la Séméiographie, ou Notation musicale des Grecs* (Paris, 1815), Perne actually transcribed the complete score of Gluck's ' Iphigénie en Tauride ' in Greek notation. In 1813 he was chosen to succeed Catel as professor of harmony at the Conservatoire, but his *Cours d'harmonie et d'accompagnement* was not so clear as that of his predecessor. In 1816 he became Inspector-general of the Conservatoire, and in 1819 librarian, but in 1822 retired to the country, and resided near Laon. In 1830 he removed to Laon itself, but the air was too keen for him, and he returned to Paris only to die. His last published work was the ' Chansons du Châtelain de Coucy ' (Paris, 1830) ; but the *Revue musicale* contains many of his articles, such as *Les Manuscrits relatifs à la musique de l'Église Grecque, Josquin Deprés, Jérôme de Moravie* and *La Musique ancienne.* Perne left most of his notes and MSS. to the library of the Institut ; and his books and annotated catalogues, bought in 1834 by Fétis, are now in the Royal Library at Brussels. His unpublished sacred works also passed into the hands of Fétis, but the library of the Conservatoire possesses the autographs of his choruses for ' Esther,' performed in 1821 by the pupils of the École Royale de Musique (Conservatoire), his ' Messe de Ste. Cécile ' (1800), his Mass ' Vivat Rex ' for four voices (1816), a ' Veni Creator ' for three voices, and the ' Offices,' arranged in three parts with the plain-song.            G. C. ; rev. M. L. P.

PEROSI, Dom Lorenzo (*b.* Tortona, Dec. 20,[1] 1872), son of the director of the music in the cathedral at Tortona, was early destined to the priesthood. He studied music at the Milan Conservatorio in 1892–93, and then proceeded to Ratisbon to prosecute his studies in church music under Haberl. He became maestro di cappella at Imola, but after a very short tenure of the post was given the more important position of choirmaster at St. Mark's, Venice (Apr. 1894). He was organist at Monte Cassino in 1890 and was ordained priest in 1896. Late in 1898 he was appointed musical director of the Sistine Chapel in Rome, and it is an open secret that the great improvement in the style of Italian church music, which culminated in the decree of Pope Pius X., was largely due to Perosi's influence. It was not as an influence in church music, but as a composer, that Perosi reached the ear of the general public. A trilogy of oratorios, ' The Transfiguration,' ' The Raising of Lazarus ' and ' The Resurrection of Christ,' was given in Italy in 1897–99 with remarkable success, and all three were given at the London Musical Festival of May 1899. There is in them very little originality of musical

conception, but the idea of combining the austere melodic forms of the past and many of the idioms of Palestrina and Bach with the trappings of modern orchestration was regarded as a new one. The result is a singular mixture of styles. Two more oratorios, ' Moses ' in 1901, and ' Leo the Great ' in 1902, bring us to the most ambitious of his works, ' The Last Judgment ' (' Il Giudizio Universale '), which was conducted by the composer, together with a setting of the Stabat Mater, at the Costanzi Theatre in Rome on the occasion of the Gregorian celebrations of Apr. 1904. Among earlier works of the composer are 25 masses, a Requiem Mass, a Christmas Oratorio, psalms, a Te Deum, etc., besides much organ music. A set of orchestral variations came out in 1904, and from time to time rumours were circulated concerning the production of an opera on the subject of *Romeo and Juliet.* A cantata for mezzo-soprano, chorus and orchestra, entitled ' Anima,' was announced for the winter of 1907–08, and later still the composer's attention has been given to the realisation of a grand scheme of ten symphonies, each to be dedicated to and named after one of the cities of Italy. ' Florence,' ' Rome,' ' Venice ' and ' Bologna ' have been finished, and the final work, ' Italy,' is to be furnished with parts for chorus. In 1909 there was performed a funeral Mass for the sixth anniversary of the death of Pope Leo XIII. A cantata, ' Dies iste,' and a new oratorio, ' In Patris memoriam,' were announced to be given during the spring of 1910, at Naples and Paris. ' Vespertina oratio ' (Rome 1912) and smaller works followed.            M.

In 1917 he developed symptoms of mental breakdown, and, in Apr. 1922, had to go to a mental hospital. However, in 1923, he recuperated, and produced a revised version of his ' Resurrection of Christ,' under Molinari at the Augusteum, Rome. By the *regolamento* of Pope Pius X., on June 20, 1905, Perosi was constituted ' Perpetual Master of the Pontifical Chapel.'            W. H. G. F.

PEROTINUS (surnamed Magnus) (early 12th cent.), maître de chapelle of ' Beatae Mariae virginis ' (afterwards rebuilt as ' Notre Dame '), Paris. He did much towards the improvement of musical notation. He was one of the chief representatives of the 12th century Parisian Ars Antiqua, and revised and re-edited the ' Liber organi de graduali,' etc. of Leoninus. His compositions were used at Notre Dame down to the time of Robert de Sabilon. Some have been reproduced by Coussemaker in *L'Art harmonique*, etc., and by Wooldridge in *Oxf. Hist. Mus.*, vol. i. (*Riemann*; *Q.-L.*).

PEROTTI, (1) Giovanni Agostino (*b.* Vercelli *c.* 1774 ; *d.* Venice, June 28, 1855), studied under his brother Giov. Domenico and under Mattei. He went as composer to the Viennese

---

[1] Thus *Riemann. Amer. Supp.*, gives Dec. 23, and W. H. G. F. Dec. 27.

court in 1795, and to London in 1798 to write operas. About 1800-01 he settled at Venice, where, in 1812, he became deputy maestro di cappella of St. Mark's and was definitely appointed successor of Furlanetto in 1817. He composed operas, ballets, oratorios, a considerable amount of church music and some sonatas and other pieces for pianoforte.

His brother, (2) GIOVANNI DOMENICO (b. Vercelli, late 18th cent.), a pupil of Padre Martini, was maestro di cappella of Vercelli Cathedral until after 1820. He composed operas and a large number of church music works, of which but little has been preserved.　　E. v. d. s.

PERRIN, ÉMILE CÉSAR VICTOR (b. Rouen, Jan. 19, 1814 ; d. Paris, Oct. 8, 1885), was a successful manager of several of the subventioned theatres in Paris. He was first at the Opéra-Comique from 1848–57, and in 1854–55 ran that theatre jointly with the Théâtre Lyrique. In 1862 he was for a short time again manager at the same theatre, and in the same year was appointed manager of the Opéra, a post he retained until 1870. He was subsequently manager of the Théâtre Français until his death. During his management of the Opéra - Comique ' L'Étoile du nord ' was brought out, and Faure, Ugalde, Galli-Marié and Carvalho made their débuts. While he was at the Opéra, ' L'Africaine,' ' Don Carlos,' ' Hamlet ' and ' Faust,' were produced, as well as Delibes's ballets, ' La Source ' and ' Coppélia.' Nilsson's first appearance at the Opéra took place at this time. At the Français Perrin's chief work as connected with music was the revival of ' Le Roi s'amuse ' with Delibes's incidental music.　　A. C.

PERRIN, PIERRE (b. Lyons c. 1616; d. Paris, Apr. 25, 1675), called ' l'Abbé Perrin,' though he was neither ordained nor held a benefice. He succeeded Voiture as ' introducteur des Ambassadeurs ' to Gaston, Duke of Orleans, a post which brought him into relations with several great personages, including Mazarin, who became his patron, and the musician Cambert, for whom he wrote the words of ' La Pastorale,' in five acts, produced first at Issy (1659), and then at Vincennes before the king. After the deaths of Gaston d'Orléans and Mazarin, Perrin was reduced to living upon his wits ; and fancied himself on the sure road to fortune when he obtained from Louis XIV. the privilege of founding an Académie de Musique (Nov. 10, 1668), and letters patent securing him the management of the theatre (June 28, 1669). (See ACADÉMIE DE MUSIQUE.) Unfortunately, the management of an opera requires capital, and the Abbé Perrin was a poor poet in all senses of the word. His partners quarrelled among themselves, and in spite of the success of Cambert's ' Pomone ' (Mar. 19, 1671) he was compelled to resign his privilege just as his

' Ariane ' was about to be produced. The patent, revoked on Mar. 30, 1672, was transferred to Lully. Perrin's Œuvres de poésie (Paris, 1661, 3 vols.) contain, besides his operas, translations—of the Æneid amongst others—and ' Jeux de poésie sur divers insectes,' the least bad perhaps of all his verses, which even in that licentious day drew forth the rebukes of Boileau and Saint-Évremond.
　　　　　　　　　　　　　　　G. C.

PERRINE, a French lutenist of the 17th century, who published a ' Livre de musique pour le lut ' in 1680 and a collection of ' Pièces de luth en musique, avec des règles pour le toucher parfaitement ' (1682), of which none bears his name.

BIBL.—Fétis,; Q.-L.; MICHEL BRENET, R.M.I., 1898-99.
　　　　　　　　　　　　　　　J. G. P.

PERRY, GEORGE FREDERICK (b. Norwich, 1793 ; d. London, Mar. 4, 1862), was a chorister of Norwich Cathedral under Dr. Beckwith. On leaving the choir he learned to play on the violin, and in a few years became leader of the band at the theatre. Whilst resident in Norwich he produced his oratorio, ' The Death of Abel.' In 1817 he composed an overture for ' The Persian Hunters,' produced at the English Opera-House, and in 1818 a short oratorio, ' Elijah and the Priests of Baal.' In 1822 he settled in London and was appointed director of the music at the Haymarket Theatre, for which he composed the opera of ' Morning, Noon and Night ' (1822), and numerous songs for introduction into various pieces. He also held the post of organist of Quebec Chapel. In 1830 he produced his oratorio, ' The Fall of Jerusalem.' On the establishment of the Sacred Harmonic Society in 1832, Perry became leader of the band, an office which he retained until the end of 1847. On the removal of Surman from the conductorship of the Society early in 1848, Perry assumed the baton until the end of the season, but not being elected conductor, he shortly afterwards resigned his leadership, and quitted the Society. On Feb. 10, 1836, he produced a sacred cantata, ' Belshazzar's Feast,' and in 1847 a short oratorio, ' Hezekiah.' In 1846 he resigned his appointment at Quebec Chapel and became organist of Trinity Church, Gray's Inn Road. He composed some anthems, including two with orchestra on the accession of Queen Victoria (1837) and the birth of the Princess Royal (1840), and additional accompaniments to several of Handel's oratorios and other pieces. He was buried in Kensal Green Cemetery. His ' Death of Abel ' and ' Fall of Jerusalem ' were performed by the Sacred Harmonic Society. Perry was a man of considerable ability. He was in the constant habit of doing that which in the case of Mozart is usually spoken of as a remarkable effort of memory—namely, writing out the separate

parts of a large work without first making a
score. One, at least, of his oratorios was
committed to paper in this way.     w. h. h.

PERS, Dirk Pieterszon (b. Amsterdam
c. 1615; still living there in 1655), collector
and editor of several books of secular and sacred
songs. The latter are partly provided with
popular melodies in general use at the time,
lending a special interest to the works which
appeared in several editions (Q.-L.).

PERSIA, see Muhammedan Music.

PERSIANI, Fanny (b. Rome, Oct. 4, 1812;
d. Passy, May 3, 1867), one of the most accomplished singers of the 19th century. She was
the second daughter of Nicolo Tacchinardi,
who had fitted up a little theatre for the use of
his pupils at his country house, near Florence,
and here, at 11 years of age, Fanny played a
principal part.

In 1830 she married the composer Giuseppe
Persiani (1804–69), and in 1832 made her début
at Leghorn, in ' Francesca da Rimini,' an opera
by Fournier, where she replaced Madame
Caradori. Her success was sufficient to lead
to her subsequent engagement at Milan and
Florence, then at Vienna, where she made a
great impression, afterwards at Padua and
at Venice. Here she played in ' Romeo e
Giulietta,' ' Il pirata,' ' La gazza ladra,'
' L' elisir d' amore ' and ' Tancredi,' in the
last two of which she performed with Pasta.
Her success was complete. In 1834, at Naples,
Donizetti wrote for her his ' Lucia di Lammermoor,' which always remained a favourite part
with her.

When she first appeared at the Opéra in
Paris (in Lucia, Dec. 12, 1837) she was much
admired by connoisseurs, but her talents hardly
met with the recognition they deserved until
after her excellent performance of the part of
Carolina in the ' Matrimonio segreto.'

Her first appearance in London (1838) was
as Amina in the ' Sonnambula,' and, although
she had been preceded in the part by Malibran
and Grisi, she achieved a success which increased at each performance. She was always,
however, a greater favourite with artists and
connoisseurs than with the public at large.
This was partly due to the poverty of her stage-
presence. She was exceedingly refined in
appearance, but small and thin, with a long,
colourless face, not unsightly, like her father,
but, as Chorley puts it, ' pale, plain and
anxious,' with no beauty but her profusion of
fine fair hair, while in her dress she was singularly tasteless. Her voice, too, was against
her rather than in her favour; it was a thin
acute soprano, of great range upwards, clear
and penetrating, but not full or mellow, blending ill with other voices, and always liable to
rise in pitch. But the finish of her singing has
been rarely equalled, probably never surpassed.
As an actress she preserved sensibility, grace

and refinement, but lacked passion and
animation.

From 1838 she sang alternately in London
and Paris for many years. Fétis says that
a sudden hoarseness, which attacked her in
London in 1843, proved the beginning of a
throat-complaint that ultimately forced her to
quit the stage for ever. But she sang in
London, in opera, in 1847, 1848 and 1849, and
at the Italiens, in Paris, in Oct. 1848. In 1850
she went to Holland, and subsequently to
Russia. After performing in almost all the
principal countries of Europe, she, in 1858,
accepted an engagement from E. T. Smith, and
appeared at Drury Lane in several of her old
parts—Linda, Elvira in ' I Puritani,' Zerlina
in 'Don Giovanni,' etc. In December of that
year Madame Persiani took up her residence in
Paris, but afterwards removed to Italy. Her
portrait, by Chalon, in water-colours, was in
the collection of the late Julian Marshall.

                                          F. A. M.

PERSUIS, Luis Luc Loiseau de (b. Metz,
July 4, 1769; d. Paris, Dec. 20, 1819), studied
under his father, one of the musical staff of the
cathedral, composer of two oratorios, ' Le
Passage de la mer rouge ' (1759) and ' La Con-
quête de Jéricho.' The son soon became a good
violinist. Having entered the orchestra of the
theatre, he fell in love with an actress, and
followed her to Avignon. Here he had opportunities of completing his studies, and he also
read a good deal of sacred music. He appeared
at the Concert Spirituel in 1787, and played in
the orchestra of the Théâtre Montansier from
1790, becoming in 1793 a member of the orchestra of the Opéra. Active, ambitious and
self - confident, he managed to produce his
dramatic compositions, and on the foundation
of the Conservatoire in 1795 succeeded in
obtaining the professorship of the violin. This
post he lost in 1802 on the dismissal of his
friend Lesueur; but in 1804 he became chef
du chant at the Opéra, and afterwards, through
Lesueur's interest, was appointed conductor of
the Emperor's court concerts, and (1810–15)
conductor of the orchestra of the Académie.
In 1814 he was appointed Inspecteur Général
de la Musique. He was indeed born to command, and the first lyric stage of Paris was
never better administered than during the
short time (1817–19) of his management. A
fortnight before his death he received the
Order of St. Michel from Louis XVIII., as he
had before received the Legion of Honour from
Napoleon.

The following is a complete list of his
dramatic works :

' La Nuit espagnole,' two acts (1791) ; ' Estelle,' three acts
(1794) ; ' Phanor et Angéla,' three acts ; ' Fanny Morna,' opéra-
comique in three acts, engraved, and ' Léonidas,' three acts, with
Gresnick (1799) ; ' Le Fruit défendu,' one act (1800) ; ' Marcel,'
one act (1801) ; I 'Inauguration du Temple de la Victoire,' inter-
mède, and ' Le Triomphe de Trajan,' three acts, ooth with Lesueur
(1807) ; ' Jérusalem délivrée,' five acts (1812) of which the score
was engraved ; ' Les Dieux rivaux ' (with Spontini, Berton and
Kreutzer), 1816.

Besides these operas he wrote pretty music, sometimes in collaboration with R. Kreutzer, to the following ballets :

'Le Retour d'Ulysse,' three acts (1807) ; 'Nina,' two acts (1813) ; 'L'Epreuve villageoise,' two acts, and 'L'Heureux Retour,' one act (1815) ; 'Le Carnaval de Venise,' two acts (1816).

He also wrote 'La Belle dormante' with Gyrowetz. Persuis also composed several cantates de circonstance, such as the 'Chant de victoire' (1806) and 'Chant français' (1814), and some unpublished church works now in MS. in the library of the Paris Conservatoire.

G. C.

PERTI, GIACOMO ANTONIO (b. Bologna, June 6, 1661 ; d. Apr. 10, 1756), one of the most distinguished church-composers of the 17th century. At 10 began to learn music from his uncle, Lorenzo Perti, a priest of San Petronio. Having finished his education at the Jesuit College and the university, he studied composition with Padre Petronio Franceschini. In 1680 he conducted in San Petronio a Missa Solennis of his own composition for soli, choir and orchestra. His first two operas, 'Atide' (1679) and 'Oreste' (1681), were given in Bologna ; those that followed, 'Marzio Coriolano,' libretto by Frencasco Valsini (anagram of Francesco Silvani) (1683) ; 'La Rosaura' (1689) ; 'Brenno in Efeso' (1690) ; 'L' inganno scoperto' (1690) ; 'Furio Camillo' (1692) ; 'Nerone fatto Cesare' (1693) ; and 'Laodicea e Berenice' (1695), in Venice, at the theatres SS. Giovanni e Paolo and San Salvatore. 'La Flavia' was given at Bologna in 1686, and another, 'Rosinda ed Emirono,' is mentioned. He went to Venice in 1683, and in 1685 to Modena. He became maestro di cappella at San Pietro, Bologna, in 1690, and at San Petronio in 1696. His oratorio on the Passion was produced in 1685, and another, 'Abramo vincitor de' propri affetti,' was printed in Bologna in 1687, and performed under his own direction in the palace of Count Francesco Caprara.[1] Four passions and eight other oratorios are at Bologna (see Q.-L.). Fétis, followed by Mendel, speaks of his relations with the German Emperors Leopold and Carl VI., but the writer of this article has failed to discover any documentary evidence to support the assertion that he was made Kapellmeister by the Emperor Leopold, though he was made Hofrath by Carl VI. In Köchel's Life of Fux, the most trustworthy book on the period, no mention is to be found of Giacomo Perti in connexion with the court ; the only instance of the name being Antonio Perti, a bass singer in the Hofkapelle. It is, moreover, beyond a doubt that Perti was maestro di cappella of San Petronio in Bologna, and retained the post till his death. Gerber states that a Te Deum by Perti was sung under his own direction in Vienna, on the relief of

the Turkish siege in 1683, but this must be a mistake, as Perti had then not made his name, and was scarcely known beyond Bologna. He was elected a member of the Filarmonici on Mar. 13, 1681, and at the time of his death had been 'Principe' six times. Among his friends was Pope Benedict XIV., with whom he kept up a close correspondence. Another friend was Padre Martini, who states in his Saggio di contrappunto (ii. 142) that he held communications on musical subjects with Perti down to 1750. Besides 'Abramo,' he printed in Bologna 'Cantate morali e spirituali' (1688), and 'Messe e Salmi concertati' (1735). Abbate Santini had a fine collection of Perti's church works (four masses, three Confitebors, four Magnificats, etc.), unfortunately now dispersed. (For the list of his church works see Q.-L.) His 'Elogio' was pronounced before the Filarmonici by Dr. Masini in 1812, and printed in Bologna. There is an 'Adoramus Te' by Perti in the Fitzwilliam Museum, Cambridge, and Novello has included two fine choruses by him in his 'Sacred Music' (vol. ii.) and 'Motetts' (bk. xi.). Others are given by Choron, and in the 'Auswahl für vorzüglicher Musikwerke.'

F. G.

PES. A term for the tenor of a MOTET (q.v.), found in the famous Reading Canon 'Sumer is icumen in' (1240) and, at a slightly later date, in the Worcester MSS. The earliest Worcester MSS., however, use the term Tenor, which suggests that the origin of the word Pes is not to be sought in the west.

A. H.

PESANTE, 'heavy.' This direction indicates that the whole passage to which it refers is to be played with great firmness and in a marked manner. It differs from marcato, however, in that it applies to whole passages, which may be quite legato at the same time ; while marcato refers to single notes or isolated groups of notes, which would not as a rule be intended to be played smoothly.

PESCETTI, GIOVANNI BATTISTA (b. Venice, c. 1704 ; d. circa 1766), studied under Lotti, and wrote an opera, 'Nerone detronato,' for the Venetian stage in 1725, collaborating with Galuppi in 'Gli odi delusi dal sangue' in 1728, and in 'Dorinda,' 1729. He came to England probably in 1737,[2] as his 'Demetrio' was given in that year ; in 1738 (according to Burney), his pastoral, 'Angelica and Medoro,' was given in March and April. In the same year came out his 'Diana and Endymion,' the airs from which were printed by Walsh. In 1739 (see Chrysander's Händel, ii. 454) he was appointed director of Covent Garden Theatre, and of the King's Theatre in 1740. His return to Italy would seem to have taken place before 1754, when he wrote an opera with Cocchi, 'Tamerlano,' produced in Venice in that year. Eitner finds it hard to believe Burney's state-

---

[1] Cinelli's Biblioteca volante, Scanzie xiv.

[2] W. H. G. F. gives Nov. 1736.

ment that he contributed to a pasticcio, ' Ezio,'
given in London in 1764–65, but the three songs
which were his share in the work may have
appeared before in some other connexion, or if
they were written specially there was no need
for him to come to England for the production.
He died about 1766, as Domenico Bettoni
succeeded to his post at St. Mark's in April.
An oratorio, ' Gionata,' is in MS. at Padua, a
' Kyrie ' and ' Gloria ' at Dresden, and a set of
harpsichord sonatas was published in London
in 1739, some of which are in the *Trésor des
pianistes* and other collections (*Q.-L.*, etc.).

M.

PESCH (PESCHIN, PESTHIN, PÖSCHIN, PETS-
CHIN, PITSCHNER, etc.), GREGOR (*b.* Bohemia,
mid-15th cent. ; *d.* Salzburg, *c.* 1528). He is
mentioned as organist of Salzburg Cathedral
in 1526 and in 1528, when Hofhaimer was appointed his successor. He composed masses,
motets, etc., and songs, spoken of by Ambros
and others as very beautiful, and heralding
a new era ; a few have appeared in modern
editions (*Q.-L.* ; Ambros).[1]

PESCHKA, MINNA (*née* LEUTNER) (*b.*Vienna,
Oct. 25, 1839 ; *d.* Wiesbaden, Jan. 12, 1890),
received instruction in singing from Heinrich
Proch, and made her début on the stage at
Breslau, in 1856, as Agatha, and afterwards
played Alice, remaining there a year. She next
played at Dessau up to the time of her marriage
with Dr. Peschka of Vienna, in 1861. In Sept.
1863 she appeared at Vienna with great success
as Margaret of Valois, Isabel, etc., and afterwards received further instruction from Mme.
Bockholtz Falconi. She next appeared at Lemberg and Darmstadt, and in 1868–76 at Leipzig,
the most brilliant period of her career, according
to Riemann. She gained great popularity there
both in opera and concerts, being equally successful both in serious and the lighter operatic
parts. Mme. Peschka-Leutner visited England
in 1872, sang (Mar. 20) at the Philharmonic, and
at the Crystal Palace, and was well received at
both concerts. In the autumn of that year she
went to America, and sang at the Boston Festival with very great success. In 1877 she went
to Hamburg, where she was engaged until 1883.
In 1879 she reappeared at the Carola Theatre,
Leipzig, for a short operatic season under
Julius Hoffmann, and played with great success
the title-part of Handel's ' Almira,' on the
revival of that opera. In 1881 she sang again
in the United States, and in 1882 reappeared
at the Crystal Palace, also taking the part of
Eglantine in 'Euryanthe' (Drury Lane, June 13),
but the voice had become worn and destitute
of charm. From 1883 until her retirement in
1887 she was engaged at Cologne, and in the
latter year settled at Wiesbaden. Her voice
was a soprano of great volume and extraordinary compass and agility.          A. C.

[1] Proske calls him Gregor Peschin Boemus.

PESCIOLINI, BIAGIO, of Prato in Tuscany,
canon and maestro di cappella at Volterra,
1563 ; also, 1571–81, at Prato, where in 1599
he is only styled canon. He composed masses,
motets (up to 12 parts), cantatas, etc., and 3
books of madrigals. One book of motets,
masses, and a Magnificat appeared as late as
1605 (*Q.-L.*).

PESENTI, MARTINO (*b.* Venice, *c.* 1600 ;
*d.* there, 1647–48), born blind. He composed
masses, motets, arias and sacred songs, as well
as a large number of madrigals, correntes,
galliards, etc., for the harpsichord and other
instruments. A book of posthumous works
was published Mar. 15, 1648.       E. v. d. S.

PESENTI, MICHELE (*b.* Verona, late 15th
cent.). He is described as a priest in Petrucci's
collection of Frottole (1504–19), where he is
represented by 33 numbers. Riemann looks
upon his fine ' Del lecto me levava ' as probably
a model for the chansons and villanelles of the
16th century (*Riemann*).

PESSARD, ÉMILE LOUIS FORTUNÉ (*b.* Paris,
May 29, 1843 ; *d.* there, Feb. 10, 1917), was a
student of the Conservatoire, where he won the
first prize for harmony in 1862, and the Grand
Prix de Rome in 1866. He filled the offices
of harmony professor at the Conservatoire,
inspector of vocal teaching in the municipal
schools of Paris, director of musical training at
the establishment of the Légion d'honneur
at Saint-Denis. His dramatic works are as
follows :

' La Cruche cassée ' (Opéra-Comique, 1870); ' Le Capitaine
Fracasse,' three acts (Théâtre Lyrique, 1878) ; ' Le Char,' one act
(Opéra-Comique, 1878) ; ' Tabarin,' two acts (Opéra, 1885) ;
' Tartarin sur les Alpes ' (Gaieté, 1888) ; ' Les Folies-Amoureuses '
(Opéra-Comique, 1891); ' Une Nuit de Noël ' (Ambigu) ; ' Mam'zelle
Carabin ' (Bouffes, 1893) ; ' La Dame de Trèfle ' (Bouffes, 1898).

He also wrote many songs, as well as orchestral
and chamber music, and some compositions for
the Church.                          G. F.

PETENERA, see SONG, subsection SPAIN (4).

PETERBOROUGH calls for mention as the
home of one of the less important of the
English cathedral festivals. This originated
in an oratorio service held in Peterborough
Cathedral in 1882. Later the festival was
carried on in collaboration with LINCOLN (*q.v.*).
The meetings were held at Peterborough in
1882, 1885, 1888, 1891, 1894, 1898 and 1901.
They were conducted by Dr. Haydn Keeton,
then organist of the cathedral.

PETERS, CARL FRIEDRICH, bought in 1814
the ' Bureau de Musique ' of Kühnel and Hoffmeister (founded 1800) in Leipzig, and greatly
improved the business. Many important works
by Bach, Haydn, Beethoven, Spohr and Schumann were published by him, besides the first
complete editions of the works of Haydn and
Bach (the latter edited by Dehn, Roitzsch and
Griepenkerl). The later members of the firm,
Dr. Marx Abraham and J. Friedländer, carried
on the old traditions with extraordinary energy
and judgment, and the ' Peters editions ' are

known throughout the world (see AUGENER). In 1894 Dr. Abraham opened a library (Musik-bibliothek Peters), specially intended for the furtherance of musical study, and at his death, in 1900, bequeathed a sum of money to the town of Leipzig in order that the library should be properly maintain d. Dr. Emil Vogel was the first librarian, and was succeeded by Dr. Rudolf Schwarz in 1901. (See LIBRARIES, subsection LEIPZIG.)                                    F. G.

PETERSON - BERGER, OLOF WILHELM (b. Ullånger, Ångermanland, Feb. 27, 1867), a Swedish composer, also distinguished as a poet and musical critic, studied at the Conservatoire in Stockholm, and in Dresden, where he was taught instrumentation by Edm. Kretschmer, and the piano by H. Scholtz. He subsequently became teacher at the Dresdener Musikschule. In composition, Peterson - Berger has endeavoured to create national music, specifically Swedish, based on the folk-melody. His first scenic work, 'Sveagaldrar,' a musical comedy in four tableaux, was written to celebrate the 25-year jubilee of King Oscar II. as regent, and was produced at a gala performance at the Royal Theatre in 1897. Amongst his dramatic productions are 'Lyckan,' a saga-play ; 'Ran,' a musical drama ; 'Arnljot,' which is considered both as regards libretto and music one of his foremost works. Of his orchestral works must be mentioned 'Carneval in Stockholm,' concert-intermezzo; 'Florez and Blanzeflor,' ballad with orchestra ; 'The Banner ' and 'Sunnanfärd,' two symphonies. His songs have gained great popularity in Sweden.

See articles in *Swedish Musical Journal*, 1909, 1910.

G. A. S.

PETER THE SHIPWRIGHT, see CZAAR UND ZIMMERMANN.

PETREIUS, JOHANN (b. Langendorf, Franconia ; d. Nuremberg, Mar. 18, 1550 [1]), printer and publisher of music, graduated 'Magister ' at Nuremberg ; in 1536 began business in that town as a printer. His earliest music publication appears to be :

'Musicae, id est, Artis canendi, libri duo, autor Sebaldus Heyden. Norimbergae apud Joh. Petreium, anno salutis 1537 ';

and his latest,

'Guter, seltsamer, und kunstreicher teutscher Gesang . . . Gedruckt zu Nürnberg, durch Jo. Petreium. 1544.'

Between these two, Eitner (*Bibliographie*) gives six works in nine volumes, including a collection of fifteen masses, a volume of forty-three select motets and two volumes of 158 four-part songs.

G.

PETRELLA, ENRICO (b. Palermo, Dec. 1, 1813 ; d. Genoa, Apr. 7, 1877), learnt music at Naples under Zingarelli, Bellini and Ruggi. He made his first appearance at Majella in 1829, with the opera 'Il Diavolo color di rosa.' It was followed by four others, and then, after an interval, by 'Le precauzioni ' [2] (May 20, 1851,

[1] According to Anton Schmid.
[2] Performed at the Lyceum, London, Mar. 21, 1871.

Naples) and 'Elena di Tolosa' (1852). At La Scala he brought out 'Marco Visconti' (1854) ; 'L' assedio di Leyda' (1856); 'Ione' (1858); 'Il duca di Scilla' (1859); and 'Morosina' (1862). After this nearly every year produced its opera,[3] but we need only mention ' Giovanni II di Napoli ' (Naples, Feb. 27, 1869)—said, in some respects, to surpass ' Ione,' which up to that time was his *chef-d'œuvre*—and 'I promessi sposi ' (Lecco, Oct. 2, 1869). For the latter Petrella was called before the curtain twenty-seven times in the first evening ! In 1873 he produced ' Manfredo ' at Rome ; it was greatly applauded, and a silver crown presented to the composer. His last opera was ' Bianca Orsini,' produced at Naples, Apr. 4, 1874.

PETRI, (1) HENRI WILHELM (b. Zeyst, near Utrecht, Holland, Apr. 5, 1856 ; d. Dresden, Apr. 7, 1914), violinist, came of a musical family, his grandfather having been an excellent organist, and his father an accomplished performer on the oboe. He received primary violin instruction from his father, and in 1866 studied with H. S. Dahmen, a local Konzertmeister, for five years. Wilhelm III., King of Holland, sent him to study with Joachim at the royal expense. In 1876 Joachim brought him to London. Here he played frequently in public with success ; made the acquaintance of Mme. Clara Schumann, who greatly admired his talent, and returned to Germany in 1877 to accept an appointment as Konzertmeister at the Ducal Chapel of Sonderhausen. In 1881 he filled a similar post at the Royal Theatre, Hanover ; in 1883 became Konzertmeister at the Theatre and Gewandhaus, Leipzig ; and in 1889 King Albert of Saxony assigned to him the position of first Konzertmeister to the Royal Chapel at Dresden, in succession to Lauterbach. Petri organised an excellent string quartet which toured in Holland, Switzerland, Belgium, France and Germany, and gave a series of subscription concerts in Dresden during the winter of each year. He published some violin solos and songs, and edited the concertos of Spohr, Bach, Mozart, as well as David's ' Hohe Schule ' and the studies of Rode, Kreutzer and Viotti.

E. H.-A.

(2) EGON (b. Hanover, Mar. 23, 1881), son of the above, is known as a pianist of ability, and especially as a disciple of Busoni, with whom he studied in Dresden, Berlin and Weimar (see *Riemann*).

PETRIE, GEORGE (b. Dublin, 1789; d. there, Jan. 17, 1866), was originally an artist, and afterwards held several public appointments in Ireland. Musically his name is best remembered by his collection of Irish folk-songs. From his earliest youth he devoted himself to noting down the traditional songs of the Irish peasantry, and supplied Thomas Moore with several airs for the ' Irish Melodies,' and assisted

[3] A chronological list is in Pougin's supplement to Fétis.

Edward Bunting. In 1855 he published, under the auspices of the Society for the Preservation and Publication of the Melodies of Ireland (founded in 1851), a large quarto volume of about 140 airs, mostly vocal, taken from the tunes he had noted. The work is full of very thorough notes on the subject of Irish music, and though very scarce is of the utmost value to the student of Irish folk-song.

After his death an attempt towards a second volume of his quarto work was made, but only forty-eight pages were printed. Later the Irish Literary Society of London issued, under the editorship of Sir C. V. Stanford, ' The Complete Petrie Collection ' (Boosey, three parts), which, containing 1582 airs, comprises all the melodies Petrie left behind him in manuscript. It is needless to enlarge on the value of such a collection of airs noted in Ireland, though every one of them cannot be justly claimed as of Irish origin. (See IRISH MUSIC.)      F. K.

PETROBELLI (PIETROBELLI), FRANCESCO (b. Bologna), maestro di cappella of Padua Cathedral (1651–77), composed 4 books of motets, psalms, various church music, 2 books, ' Scherzi amorosi,' a 2 and 3 v., chamber cantatas, etc., published between 1643 and 1693 (Q.-L.; Mendel).

PETRUCCI, OTTAVIANO DEI (b. Fossombrone, near Ancona, June 18, 1466 ; d. May 7, 1539), an illustrious printer (see PRINTING OF MUSIC). In 1491 he was established at Venice ; and on May 25, 1498, he obtained from the Seignory the sole privilege, for twenty years, of printing ' figured music ' (canto figurato) and music in the tablature of the organ and lute— a privilege which he exercised there till about 1511. At that date he left the Venetian business in the hands of Amadeo Scotti and Nicolò da Raphael, and returned to Fossombrone, where, on Oct. 22, 1513, he obtained a patent from Pope Leo X. for the monopoly of music-printing in the Roman States for fifteen years. His latest work, three choral masses, in the Sistine Chapel, Rome, is dated 1523.

Petrucci's process was a double one ; he printed first the lines of the stave, and then, by a second impression, the notes upon them. In fact he discovered a method of doing by the press what the German printers of *Patronendruck*, or pattern-printing, had done by hand. His work is beautifully executed. The ' register,' or fit, of the notes on the lines is perfect ; the ink is a fine black, and the whole effect is admirable. But the process was expensive, and was soon superseded by printing in one impression, which appears to have been first successfully accomplished by Pierre Haultin in 1525.[1]

Petrucci printed no missals, service books,

or other plain-song works ; but masses, motets, lamentations and frottole, all in canto figurato, or measured music, and a few works in lute-tablature. (See MUSICA MENSURATA ; TABLATURE.) His first work was ' Harmonice musices odhecaton A.'—a collection of ninety-six pieces in three and four parts by Isaac, Josquin, Obrecht, Okeghem and other masters of the day, the parts printed opposite one another on the open pages of a small 4to. His activity was very great ; Chrysander [2] gives a list of eighteen works certainly, and two probably, issued between June 12, 1501, and Nov. 28, 1504. The last work cited by Eitner (*Bibliographie*) is the ' Motetti della corona,' a collection of eighty-three motets for four, five and six voices (in separate partbooks) in four portions, the fourth portion of which was published at Fossombrone, Oct. 31, 1519. Fétis, however,[3] mentions three masses, in large folio, printed for the lectern of a church, with the date 1523–25, and knocked down to an unknown buyer at a sale at Rome in 1829. These are now in the Sistine Chapel. His life and works are exhaustively treated by Anton Schmid, *Ottaviano dei Petrucci*, etc., Vienna, 1845.

In the following list of Petrucci's publications, those in the British Museum are indicated by an asterisk, and those at Assisi, Bologna, Munich, Vienna, Rome, Berlin and Paris (Conservatoire) by the letters A., B., M., V., R., Ber. and P. (See also LIBRARIES : SPAIN : Madrid and Seville).

Harmonice musices odhecaton. A.   Venice, 1501,[4] May 14.   (B. P.)
Canti B, numero cinquanta. B.   Venice, 1501, Feb. 5.   (B. P.)
Canti C, numero cento cinquanta.   C.   Venice, 1503, Feb. 10.   (V. P.)
Motetti A, numero trentatre. A.   Venice, 1502, May 9.   (B. unique.)
Motetti B,   „   „   B.   Venice, 1503, May 10.   (* B.)
Motetti C.   Venice, 1504, Sept. 15.   (* imperf. B. M. V.)
Motetti *a* 5.   Lib. I.   Venice, 1505, Nov. 28.   (V. B. M. imperf.)
Missae Josquin.   Venice, 1502, Sept. 27   (Ber. unique.)
Missarum Josquin.   Lib. I.   Venice, 1502, Dec. 57.   (V. unique.)
  „   „   (Reprint.) Fossombrone, 1514, Mar. 1. (B. M. V. R.)
  „   „   (Reprint.) Fossombrone, 1516, May 29. (* unique.)[5]
  „   „   Lib. II.   Venice, 1503, Dec. 27. (V. A.)
  „   „   (Reprint.) Fossombrone, 1515, April 11. (* V. R.)
  „   „   Lib. III.   Venice, 1503, Dec. 27. (V. unique.)
  „   „   (Reprint.) Fossombrone, Mar. 1, 1514 (*).
  „   „   (Reprint.) Fossombrone, 1516, May 29. (V. A.)
Missae Obreth.   Venice, 1503, Mar. 24.   (M. V. Ber.)
Missae Ghiselin.   Venice, 1503, July 15.   (V. A. Ber.)
Missae Brumel.   Venice, 1503, June 17.   (V. Ber.)
Missae Petri de la Rue.   Venice, 1503, Oct. 31.   (* A. B. V. R. Ber.)
Missae Alexandri Agricoli.   Venice, 1504, Mar. 23.   (A. B. V. R. Ber.)   (*imperf.)
Missae de Orto.   Venice, 1505, Mar. 22.   (*imperf. M. V.)
Missae Henrici Izak.   Venice, 1506, Oct. 20.   (* B. V.)
Missae Gaspar.   Venice, 1506, Jan. 7.   (*imperf. V.)
Missae Antonii de Feuin.   Fossombrone, 1515, Nov. 22.   (* V.)
Missarum Joannis Mouton Lib. I. Fossombrone, 1515, Aug. 11. (* V.)
Missarum diversorum Lib. I.   Venice, 1508, Mar. 15.   (* M. B. V.)
Fragmenta Missarum.   Venice, 1505.   (B. V. imperf.)
  „   „   (Reprint.) Venice, 1509. (V. unique.)
Lamentationes Jeremiae. Lib. I.   Venice, 1506, Apr. 8.   (B. Padua, Cap. Ant.)
Lamentationes Jeremiae. Lib. II.   Venice, 1506, May 29. (B. unique.)
Intabulatura de Lauto.   Lib. I.   Venice, 1507. (B. V.)
  „   „   Lib. II.   Venice, 1507.   (Ber. unique.)
  „   „   (Lib. III. caret.)
  „   „   Lib. IV.   Venice, 1508.   (V. unique.)
Tenori e contrebassi intabulati. Lib. I.   Venice, 1509. (V. unique.)[6]
Frottole.   Lib. I.   Venice, 1504, Nov. 28. (Ber. M. V.)
  „   Lib. II.   Venice, 1504, Jan. 8 (*i.e.* 1505). (M. V.)
  „   (Reprint.) Venice, 1507, Jan. 29. (Regensburg.)
  „   Lib. III.   Venice, 1504, Feb. 6 (*i.e.* 1505). (M. V.)
  „   Lib. IV.   Venice, 1505. (M.)
  „   Lib. V.   Venice, 1505, Dec. 23. (M. V.)
  „   Lib. VI.   Venice, 1505, Feb. 5 (*i.e.* 1506). (M. V.)

---

[1] The method of printing by double impression—so as to obtain the stave lines continuous without the breaks inevitable in printing by a single impression—was patented by Scheurmann in 1856. (See SCHEURMANN.)

[2] *Mus. T.*, 1877, p. 325a.      [3] *Biog. univ.* vii. 16a.
[4] But see Vernarecci as to this date.
[5] These two editions are unnoticed by Schmid.
[6] A copy appeared in Marini's Catalogue X. (1909).

**Frottole.** Lib. VII. Venice, 1507, June 6. (M.)
  ,,    Lib. VIII. Venice, 1507, May 21. (M.)
  ,,    Lib. IX. Venice, 1508, Jan. 22. (M. V.)
**Strambotti.** Venice, 1505. (B.) identical with the fourth book of Frottole.
**Missa Choralis.** Fossombrone, 1513. (R. unique.)
**Missarum X.** Libri duo. Fossombrone, 1515. (R. unique.)
III. Missae Choral. Fossombrone, 1520. (R. unique.)
Motetti de la corona. Lib. I. Fossombrone, 1514, Aug. 17. (B. V. (imperf.) M. (imperf.).)
Motetti de la corona. Lib. II   Fossombrone, 1519, June 17. (*V.)
  ,,   ,,    Lib. III. Fossombrone, 1519, Sept. 7. (*V. B.)
  ,,   ,,    Lib. IV. Fossombrone, 1519, Oct. 31. (*V. B.)
Three choral masses, 1523. (R.)

              G.; rev. W. B. S.

PETTIT, WALTER (b. London, Mar. 14, 1835; d. there, Dec. 11, 1882), violoncellist, received his musical education chiefly at the R.A.M. In 1851 he was engaged by Balfe for the orchestra of Her Majesty's Theatre, in which he remained for many years. In 1861 he succeeded Lucas as principal violoncello in the Philharmonic orchestra, and in 1876 took the place of Paque in Her Majesty's private band.     T. P. P.

PETYR (PETRE, PETER), HENRY, an English church composer of the late 15th and early 16th centuries, who, after having studied music for thirty years, took his Mus.B. degree at Oxford in 1516 (C. F. Abdy Williams, *Degrees in Music*). He was a secular chaplain, and a 3-part Mass by him (lacking the Kyrie) is in an early 16th century MS. (B.M. Add. MSS. 5665/113b).   J. Mᴷ.

PETZMAYER, JOHANN (b. Vienna, 1803), the son of an innkeeper. When he was eighteen years old he obtained a common zither, and taught himself to play it with such success that his performances brought a considerable amount of custom to his father. His fame spread in higher quarters, and it was not long before he became the fashion in Vienna. He even played before the Emperor. In later life he took to the bowed zither (Streich - Zither) instead of the ordinary kind he had previously used. In 1833 he made a successful tour in Germany, and in 1837 was made Kammer-virtuos to Duke Maximilian of Bavaria. He was living in Munich in 1870. (Wurzbach's *Biographisches Lexikon*, vol. 22.)     M.

PEUERL (BEURLIN), PAUL, an early 17th-century organist and organ-builder in Styria, creator of the German Variation-Suite, by combining four dance forms into a suite with a free adherence to the subjects. He composed a book of songs, a 5 v. (1613), and 2 books of instrumental pieces 1620, 1625 (Q.-L.; *Riemann*).

PEUT D'ARGENT, see MARTIN PEU D'ARGENT.

PEUTINGER, CONRAD (b. Augsburg, Oct. 14, 1465; d. there, Dec. 24, 1547), a lover and supporter of church music, and a keen devotee for the welfare of literature and art. He was educated in Italy; in 1493 became secretary to the senate of Augsburg (the city of the Fuggers); in 1521, at the Diet of Worms, obtained the confirmation of the ancient privileges of the city, and others in addition. He was a great collector of antiquities, inscriptions, and MSS., and in particular was the owner of the ' Peutinger

Tables,' a map of the military roads of the Lower Roman Empire, probably dating about 225, which is one of the most precious geographical monuments of antiquity, and is now in the State Library at Vienna. His devotion to music is shown by his preface to the ' Liber selectarum Cantionum quas vulgo Mutetas appellant, sex, quinque, et quatuor vocum,' of Grimmius and Wyrsung, Augsburg, 1520, a volume containing twenty-four Latin motets by H. Izac, Josquin des Prés, Obrecht, Pierre de la Rue, Senfl and others.     G.

PEVERNAGE, ANDREAS (b. Courtrai, Flanders, 1543; d. July 30, 1591 [1]). He held an appointment in his native town until his marriage,[2] June 15, 1574, and soon after (about 1577) moved to Antwerp as choirmaster in the cathedral. There he led an active life, composing, editing and giving weekly performances at his house of the best native and foreign music. He died at the age of 48, and was buried in the cathedral. Sweertius [3] describes him as ' vir ad modestiam factus, et totus candidus, quae in Musico mireris, quibus cum leviusculis notis annata levitas videtur.' The same author gives the following epitaph :

    M. Andræ Pevernagio
      Musico excellenti
   Hujus ecclesiæ phonasco
      et Mariæ filiæ
Maria Haecht vidua et FF. M. poss.
Obierunt Hic XXX Julii. Aetat XLVIII.
Illa II Feb.   Aetat XII.   MDLXXXIX.

Four books of chansons were published in 1589–91, and a book of ' Cantiones sacrae ' in 1578; five masses and a book of ' Cantiones sacrae ' were published in 1602. The British Museum contains one book of chansons, and two imperfect copies of the ' Harmonia celeste,' a collection of madrigals edited by Pevernage in 1583, in which seven of his own pieces appear. In addition to these Eitner [4] mentions sixteen detached pieces in various collections of the time. Two pieces have been printed in modern type— an ode to S. Cecilia, ' O virgo generosa,' [5] composed for the inauguration of his house concerts,[6] and a nine-part ' Gloria in excelsis.' [7] (See the *Sammelbände* of the Int. Mus. Ges. for Apr.-June 1902, pp. 466-7.)     J. R. S.-B.

PEYRO, JOSÉ (17th cent.), Spanish composer, author of the music to Calderón's *Jardin de Falerina* (1629), and perhaps also of the music to Lope de Vega's *Selva sin amor.* His

1 ' Master A. Pevernage . . . died July 30, 1591, about half-past four in the afternoon, after five weeks' illness.' (See note discovered by M. de Burbure in Antwerp Cathedral books.) Thus the last two letters of the date in the epitaph have changed places ; it should stand MDLXXXXI. He died at the age of 48, which fixes the date of his birth.
2 Paquot's *Histoire littéraire des Pays-bas*, tom. 9, p. 331 (Louvain, 1767). The author gives a reference, *Franc. Hoemi poemata*, ed. 1578, pp. 239, 240, où il y a deux Epithalames : In nuptias Andreae Pevernage, apud Cortraconses Symphonasci, et Mariae Maeges viduae, 17 cal. julii, anno 1574.
3 *Athenae Belgicae*, Antwerp, 1628 (B.M. 11,901 k). Both the year of death and the name of Pevernage's wife are probably incorrect. See notes 6 and 7.
4 *Bibliographie.*
5 Commer—' Collectio op. musicorum Batav.', vol. viii. (Berlin, Trautwein).
6 Ambros, *Geschichte*, iii. 316.
7 *Caecilia*, von Oberhoffer, Luxemburg, 1863, No. 7.

style shows the transition from the madrigal to the operatic chorus; examples are printed by Pedrell, *Teatro lírico*.　　　　　　　J. B. T.

PEZEL (PEZELIUS), JOHANN, a 17th-century Austrian musician who, in 1672, entered an Augustinian monastery at Prague which he left soon after, and became a Protestant. He went to Bautzen, where he became director of the waits (town musicians). Adelung states that he became afterwards cantor of the school of St. Thomas, Leipzig. He was very influential in the evolution of instrumental forms and the style of orchestral writing. Apart from a large amount of instrumental compositions, including some books of sonatas, etc., for wind instruments, he wrote also sacred vocal music, and 2 books on music (Reissmann, *Allgemeine Geschichte d. Musik*, vol. ii. p. 300; *Q.-L.*; *Mendel*).

PEZZE, ALESSANDRO (b. Milan, Aug. 11, 1835; d. May 27, 1914), an able violoncellist, received his first musical education from his father, an excellent amateur. In 1846 he entered the Milan Conservatorio after competition, receiving instruction from Merighi, also the master of Piatti. After a course of concerts in North Italy he was appointed first violoncello at La Scala. Lumley brought him to Her Majesty's Theatre in 1857, where he remained till the theatre was burnt down. He undertook various tours in the United Kingdom with Tietjens, Santley, and other well-known artists, and in 1870 accepted the post of principal violoncello at Covent Garden and (with Pettit) at the Philharmonic, but resigned three years later in order to devote himself to teaching, on being appointed to fill Piatti's place at the R.A.M. He frequently played at the Popular Concerts either in conjunction with Piatti or replacing him. Pezze formed many excellent pupils. He played upon a fine Ruggieri violoncello and, in latter years, upon the 'Mara' Stradivari.

　　　　　　　　　　　　　　　W. W. C.

PFEIFFER, GEORGES JEAN (b. Versailles, Dec. 12, 1835; d. Paris, Feb. 14, 1908), pianist and composer. His first piano lessons were from his mother, Mme. Clara Pfeiffer, an excellent pianist of the school of Kalkbrenner. Maleden and Damcke first taught him composition. He gained a brilliant success at the Conservatoire concerts in 1862, in which year his operetta 'Capitaine Roche' was performed. His compositions include a symphony, a quintet, trios, sonatas, concertos, of which the third has been repeated several times in Paris. Also an oratorio, 'Agar'; a symphonic poem, 'Jeanne d'Arc'; an overture, 'Le Cid,' and a quantity of piano music, including some well-known studies. An important work is a one-act comic opera, 'L'Enclume,' represented in 1884 and 1885. Pfeiffer succeeded his father, Émile Pfeiffer, as a partner in the piano firm of Pleyel, Wolff et Cie, Paris. His great-uncle,

J. Pfeiffer, was one of the pioneers of piano-making in Paris.　　　　　　　　　A. J. H.

PFITZNER, HANS (b. Moscow, May 5, 1869), the son of German parents, holds in Germany a leading position as the representative of distinctively national ideals in music. He is an eminent composer whose appeal at present is chiefly to his own countrymen.

Pfitzner's father, a violinist, became Musik-director at the Stadttheater of Frankfort and was his son's first teacher. At 17 Pfitzner entered Hoch's Conservatorium at Frankfort where he studied (1886–90) the pianoforte with James Kwart and composition with Ivan Knorr. On completing his course he took a teaching appointment at the Coblenz Conservatorium, and in 1893 gave at Berlin a concert of his own compositions. Minor posts as teacher and conductor occupied him until in 1897 he obtained a more important one at Stern's Conservatorium in Berlin, and in 1903 became first Kapellmeister at the Theater des Westens there. A series of subscription concerts which he conducted in 1907 with the Kaim Orchestra began his association with MUNICH (q.v.), but in the following year a post as Musikdirector at the Opera and Conservatoire of Strassburg claimed him. In 1913 the University of Strassburg presented him with the degree of D.Phil., *honoris causa*, and he continued his labours as conductor of the opera there until 1916. Meantime his compositions had made their mark in Germany, the greater part of them consisting of concerted chamber music, choral pieces and many songs which gave evidence of his affinity with the 'romantic' composers, especially Schumann. Two early music dramas, 'Der arme Heinrich' (Mainz, 1895) and 'Die Rose von Liebesgarten' (Elberfeld, 1901), had shown his quality on the stage, and the latter had been given in some half-dozen German cities as well as at Vienna under Mahler. The production of the dramatic legend, 'Palestrina,' the work of his maturity, at Munich on June 12, 1917, placed him in an altogether different category. He was his own librettist, and following the precedent set by Wagner (and adopted once by Richard Strauss in 'Feuersnot') the composer identified his hero with himself and made Palestrina's inspiration in the composition of the 'Missa Papae Marcelli' a symbol of his own spiritual condition. It is so at any rate that the work has been received, and it has been given with becoming solemnity at Stuttgart, Berlin, Vienna and other strongholds of the German tradition, and regarded by Pfitzner's admirers as a successor to 'Parsifal.' [1]

Pfitzner's philosophy of art, his grounding in Schopenhauer and Wagner, his individual

[1] For a description of 'Palestrina' and a critical estimate of Pfitzner's work as a whole see the article 'Hans Pfitzner,' by E. J. Dent, *Music and Letters*, vol. iv. No. 2.

treatment of the latter's music dramas and his opposition to certain current tendencies in music may be studied in his numerous essays. A volume of them, *Vom musikalisches Drama* (published 1915), is representative. *Futuristengefahr* (1917) appeared as a reply to Busoni's *Ästhetik*, and *Die neue Ästhetik der musikalischen Impotenz* (1919) pursues the controversy with 'modernism.' Among Pfitzner's later musical compositions a 'romantic cantata,' with the title 'Von deutscher Seele' (1922), is outstanding. It is in the nature of a song cycle for solo voices, choir and orchestra, in which poems of Eichendorff are threaded together to illustrate ideas and aspirations which, for the composer, have a profound significance. An elaborate score in which the orchestral writing is peculiarly intricate, its acceptance depends very much on the capacity of an audience to perceive its inner meaning. It was given in New York by the Society of the Friends of Music, under Bodanzky's direction, in the autumn of 1923, and was there received with only partial sympathy. The difficulty to an audience foreign to 'the German Soul' lay in the fact that what appealed as beautiful in the music seemed too obviously reminiscent of the 19th century romantics, and what was unfamiliar seemed overstrained. It still remains to be seen, therefore, how far the high claims put forward for Pfitzner by his immediate circle can be substantiated before a larger public.

The following list of works is based on *Riemann*, from which work many biographical details in the above are taken.

### STAGE WORKS

Incidental Music to Ibsen's *Fest auf Solhang*. (1889.)
' Der arme Heinrich', opera, libretto by J. Grun. (Mainz, 1895.)
' Die Rose vom Liebesgarten', opera, libretto by Grun. (Elberfeld, 1901.)
' Christelflein,' a Christmas play after Stack's *Weihnachtsmärchen*. (Munich, 1906; rev. 1917.)
Music to Kleist's *Käthchen von Heilbronn* (op. 17). (Berlin, 1908.)
' Palestrina,' opera, 3 acts, libretto by composer. (Munich, 1917.)

### ORCHESTRA AND VOICES

Scherzo, orch. (1888.)
' Der Blumen Rache,' alto, women's ch. and orch. (1888.)
Piano concerto in E flat.
Ballades, ' Herr Oluf ' (op. 12), baritone and orch.
   „    ' Die Heinzelmännchen ' (op. 14), bass and orch.
Romantic cantata, ' Von deutscher Seele' (Eichendorff), sch (4), ch., orch. (1922.)
Violin concerto (1923).
Songs with orch. (op. 26), etc.

### CHORAL AND SONGS

' Columbus ' (Schiller), 8 v , unaccompanied.
Songs in the following op. Nos. : 2-7, 9-11, 15, 18, 19, 21, 22, 24, 26, 29, 30.

### CHAMBER MUSIC

Sonata, v'cl. and PF. (op. 1).
Trio, strings and PF. (op. 8).
String quartet in D (op. 13).
Quintet, strings and PF. in C (op. 23)
Sonata, vln. and PF. in E min. (op. 27).

### BIBLIOGRAPHY

A. SEIDL : *Hans Pfitzner*. (1921.)
C. WANDREY : *H. Pfitzner, seine geistlige Persönlichkeit und das ende der Romantik*. (1922.)
Publications of the ' H. Pfitzner Verein für deutsche Tonkunst,' founded Munich, 1918.
                                                                C.

**PHAGOTUS** (Ital. *fagotto, fagoto*), a reed instrument invented or, rather, evolved by Afranio Albonese of Pavia (see AFRANIO). A careful examination of his nephew Teseo's description, together with that of a manuscript

sheet of instructions for the instrument, discovered in 1893 by Count Valdrighi amongst the state archives at Modena [1] makes it quite evident that the phagotus, whatever its name implied, was but an advanced form of bagpipe.

Its history is interesting and romantic. Afranio was residing for a time in Pannonia on the borders of the modern Serbia, and, taking the popular bagpipe of the country called 'piva,' with its double chanter and no drones, as his model, he endeavoured to extend and deepen its compass. His efforts failed, as the instrument would not stay in tune ; so, when he returned to Italy, he left it behind him. In 1521, some years later, Belgrade, the capital of Serbia, was taken by Sultan Soliman and the district ravaged ; but the instrument was rescued and brought as a curiosity to Italy. There it came into the hands of Afranio once more, and he, with the help of a mechanic of Ferrara named Ravilio, at length perfected it. For at a feast given at Mantua by the Duke of Ferrara in 1532 ' il Rev^do Mess: Affranio [*sic*] ' played a solo upon his ' fagotto ' between the fifth and sixth courses.

Apparently more than one instrument of the kind was made, as the MS. Instructions mentioned above (dated 1565) were given by Teseo to a friend to whom he had also presented ' uno de suoi fagoti,' with strict injunctions, however, that he should not divulge the method of playing it to any except his own sons.

Two illustrations of the phagotus, as they appear in Teseo's work of the year 1539, are given on *PLATE LVIII*. It will be seen that the instrument took the form of the letter H, and consisted of two pillars about 22 inches in height joined together by cross-pieces, the shorter central pillar being purely ornamental. Each side pillar was divided into an upper and a lower part : the upper part was bored with two parallel cylindrical tubes united at the top, thus forming one continuous tube, pierced with holes for the fingers and keys. The lower part of each pillar contained the reed similar to that of the piva, viz. a single-beating reed of the clarinet type ; but in this perfected instrument the reeds were made of thin metal like those of the regal. The left-hand pillar or tube, with a reed of silver, provided a diatonic scale of 10 notes from tenor C upwards, while the pillar fingered by the right hand was fitted with a reed of brass and also had a compass of 10 notes, from G below the bass stave to bass B♮. By cross-fingering chromatic notes could be obtained and either pillar silenced or sounded at will by a special key. From the back of the instrument, which was rested on the knees during performance, with a cord round the neck, a flexible pipe passed to a bag held under the left arm ; this formed an air reservoir, being supplied with wind from bellows fastened under

1 *Cf. Musurgiana* Series II., No. 2 ; Modena, 1895.

and actuated by the right arm, as in the Northumbrian and Irish pipes. The bellows and the reservoir are shown in one of the illustrations on the ground on either side of the instrument.

The phagotus was used by the Canon Afranio, not for 'vain and amatory melodies' but for 'divine songs and hymns.' The music could be played either in one or two parts as desired, and Teseo in his Instructions says that he had seen a phagotus with three large pillars or sets of tubes.

As for the name, Teseo in his work on the Chaldaic Language introduces the whole subject from a grammarian's point of view, 'phagotus' suggesting to him a derivation from the Greek word 'phago' (I eat), because the instrument 'devours and fills itself with all musical notes, and having digested them gives them forth again.' Later on he seems a little doubtful as to this derivation, and suggests that the word may come from 'fagus' (a beech tree), or even from 'faunus.' As will have been noticed, however, the manuscript instructions and the programme of the feast give the name as 'fagoto' or 'fagotto.' Probably the Italian form of the word was applied to the instrument as a nickname because it looked so like 'a bundle of sticks': when latinised it became 'phagotus.' From this brief description it will be gathered that neither in shape, reed or bore had the phagotus anything in common with the bassoon; but it is quite possible that Afranio's efforts anticipated and popularised the doubling of the cylindrical tube as found in the sordoni and doppioni of a little later date and in 'the short instruments called Dulceuses' of which Henry VIII. died possessed. At any rate the inventor showed what could be achieved by a more elaborate and perfected use of key mechanism. F. W. G.

PHALÈSE. The firm of music-publishers of this name, which for upwards of a century occupied a leading position in the Netherlands, was founded by PIERRE PHALÈSE (b. Louvain, c. 1510; d. there, 1573 or 74). His family name is supposed to have been Van der Phalesien, but both he and his descendants used either the French form Phalèse or the Latin Phalesius. In the present article the French form is adopted, both for the surname and the Christian names of the various members of his family. About 1545 Pierre Phalèse the elder started publishing musical works. His earlier books were chiefly lute music, and were printed by Servaas Sassen of Diest, Jacob Betius or Bathenius, and Martin Rotarius or Raymakers (Martin Rotaire). In 1553 the imprint first occurs 'Imprimé à Louvain par Pierre Phalèse, pour luy et Martin Rotaire'; in 1554 'Imprimé à Louvain par Pierre Phalèse,' so it seems probable that about this time he started printing as well as publishing. In 1570 he is

associated with Jan Bellern (Jean Bellère) of Antwerp, though he remained at Louvain until his death. His children were (1) Hubert, subprior of the Benedictine Abbey of Afflighem; (2) Antoinette; (3) Robert; (4) Corneille and (5) PIERRE (d. Antwerp, Mar. 13, 1629).

Of these the name of CORNEILLE (or Cornelis) appears in an edition of Lasso's 'Patrocinium Musices,' issued at Louvain in 1574. In 1581 he moved to Antwerp, where he was still living in 1603. His children were (1) Robert, who was a lawyer at Antwerp in 1612; (2) Anne, who married C. van Dale and died at Antwerp in 1612; (3) Marie, married in 1608 to Pierre Willems, and (4) Corneille, baptized at Antwerp, Sept. 27, 1581. Corneille Phalèse seems at an early date to have given up the publishing business to his brother, PIERRE the younger, who at first continued his father's partnership with Bellère. Pierre was inscribed in the Guild of St. Luke at Antwerp in 1581, and on Feb. 17, 1582, was married at the cathedral to Elisabeth Wisschavens, daughter of Jean Wisschavens by Dymphna van Dyck of Malines. In 1582 his books were issued at the sign of the Red Lion in the Cammerstraet; in 1606 the house was sold by its owners. Phalèse's lease lasted for two years longer, but in 1608 he bought the 'Coperen Pot' in the same street and changed its sign to 'De Koning David'; this remained the seat of the business until the firm finally gave up publishing. The younger Pierre Phalèse had five children: (1) Barbara, (b. between 1583 and 1585), married in 1610 to Jean de Vos; (2) Madeleine (bapt. 1586; d. May 30, 1652; (3) Marie (bapt. 1589), married in 1615 to E. de Mayer; (4) Pierre (bapt. 1594; d. 1671) became an Augustinian monk at Antwerp; in 1662 he celebrated the jubilee of his entrance into religion; (5) Anne (bapt. 1603; d. young). Pierre the younger died at Antwerp, and was buried in his son's monastery, in the church of which his children erected a monument to his memory in 1650; his wife had predeceased him, dying in 1619.

After the death of the younger Phalèse the business was carried on by his daughters. Marie and Madeleine were inscribed in the registers of the Guild of St. Luke as 'dochters Phalèse' in 1629, and from 1630-50 the books issued by the firm bear the imprint 'Chez les Héritiers de Pierre Phalèse,' though about 1650 a few works appeared issued 'Apud Magdalenam Phalesium et cohaeredes.' Madeleine Phalèse died at the sign of King David, and was buried in the church of her brother's monastery on June 3. An interesting set of her executor's accounts is printed in Goovaert's Typographie musicale dans les Pay-Bas (Antwerp, 1880); they show how extensive the business was at this time. On the death of Madeleine her sister Marie de Mayer undertook the management of the firm, which she con-

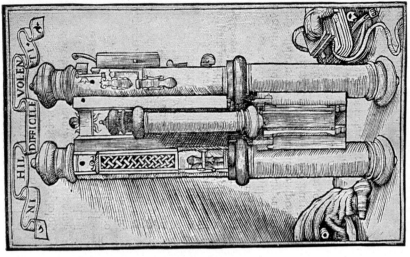

## LVIII

Back View

Front View

THE PHAGOTUS

From the *Introductio in Chaldaicam linguam*, by Teseo Ambrosio, 1539

tinued until 1673 or 1674. The last work issued by the Phalèses is dated in the latter year, so it is possible that Marie de Mayer died about that time, and that with her death the business came to an end.

Six printers' marks are used by the Phalèses : (1) David standing, with a harp; motto, 'Laudate Dominum Psalterio et Cythara.' (2) David kneeling, his harp and sceptre on the ground, an angel with a sword in the sky. (3) St. Peter, a key in his right hand, a book in his left; (4) the B.V. Mary with the child Christ, crowned, in clouds; (5) Melpomene, crowned, holding a ring; (6) The B.V. Mary with the child Christ, seated, an open book in her right hand, a lily on a table to the left.

W. B. S.

PHANTASY, see FANCY (2).

PHILADELPHIA has long been remarkable among the cities of the United States for its vigorous musical life. A large number of societies for the active practice of music exist within its precincts.

The oldest of these, the MUSICAL FUND SOCIETY, was established on Feb. 29, 1820. In 1823 the society built a hall for its meetings, and about seven years later an academy was opened for musical instruction. The first edition of this Dictionary (1880) included a list of over sixty societies then existing in Philadelphia for the performance of music of one kind or another. While many of those societies are still active in 1926, and others have sprung into existence, the musical life of Philadelphia has latterly become concentrated in its orchestra, now one of the finest.

THE PHILADELPHIA ORCHESTRA, whose affairs are administered by the Philadelphia Orchestra Association, aided by committees of ladies from towns and cities contiguous to Philadelphia, was organised in 1900. The history of the Philadelphia Orchestra does not differ essentially from that of a number of the others in the United States; though the desire of the city's society element to have adequate performances of opera as a feature of the social season was largely instrumental in its formation. For a long time in the latter part of the 18th and the first decades of the 19th centuries Philadelphia was a vigorous rival of New York in operatic activity, but in the course of time supremacy went to the latter city. So long as Theodore Thomas was a factor in the orchestral music of the eastern cities, his orchestra gave concerts with greater or less regularity in Philadelphia; but the abandonment of his individual enterprises in 1891 left the music-lovers of the old Federal capital without regular concerts of high-class orchestral music. The Boston Orchestra, on its travels, supplied the want for several years, but could not satisfy the ambitions of a city properly proud of the part which it had played in the political, commercial,

social and artistic history of the country. In the season of 1894–95 there was something like an awakening of the dormant musical interests of the city. In 1895–96 a committee was formed to promote an opera season, and a season of opera in English of forty performances was given under a guarantee with Gustav Hinrichs as director. In the next season Walter Damrosch supplied local operatic needs; in 1897–98 Damrosch and Ellis, and in 1898–1899 Charles Ellis alone with Damrosch as conductor and director. Thereafter, the local committee of opera guarantors made annual arrangements for opera from year to year with Maurice Grau and Heinrich Conried.

During this period of operatic interest orchestral matters were also in a ferment. While Hinrichs was director of the opera he gave orchestral concerts, and tried to develop a symphonic band out of the material which he found at hand. In the same season the Musical Fund Society created conditions which made it possible for a local concert orchestra, the Germania, to increase the number of its members and to give a series of Friday afternoon concerts under the direction of William Stoll, jun., a well-known violinist. The concerts of the Germania continued for two years, whereupon Henry Gordon Thunder, director of the Philadelphia Choral Society, took up the work and out of the same material organised a Philadelphia Orchestra; his concerts, like those of Stoll, however, were tentative in character, and served chiefly to disclose the inadequacy of the players. After five years of these praiseworthy but futile efforts a number of the most prominent men and women in social and musical circles formed the Orchestral Association. Some of the foremost workers in the new enterprise were the cultivated amateurs who had formed a 'Symphony Society of Philadelphia' in 1893, with Dr. W. W. Gilchrist as conductor; this Society gave concerts from time to time until the new orchestra, a brief forerunner of the present organisation, appeared in the field. This new orchestra gave two concerts in the spring of 1900 with Fritz Scheel as conductor. Scheel had been an assistant to von Bülow in Hamburg, and was a man of fine musical parts and splendid energy. The success of the two concerts was such as to induce the Association to send him abroad to recruit the orchestra, and make of it a first-class symphonic organisation. The first regular season of the newly recruited orchestra was given in 1900–01, and from that time till his death in February 1907, Scheel remained conductor of the band; he was succeeded in the season of 1907–08 by Karl Pohlig, who in 1912 was succeeded by Leopold STOKOWSKI (q.v.). The orchestra owes its singularly perfect ensemble to the genius of Stokowski. The subscription, popular, and children's concerts of the orchestra in Philadelphia are held in the ' Academy of Music ' (not a training institution), and besides visiting other neighbouring cities the orchestra gives an annual series of concerts in New York.

H. E. K. ; addns. C.

PHILÉMON ET BAUCIS, opéra-comique in 3 acts (afterwards reduced to 2) ; words by Barbier and Carré ; music by Gounod ; produced Théâtre Lyrique, Feb. 18, 1860 ; Covent Garden, Oct. 24, 1891 ; in English, Guildhall School, Dec. 18, 1893 ; Drury Lane (translated by Joseph Bennett), Apr. 26, 1894.    G.

PHILHARMONIC CHOIR.   This choir of 300 voices was formed in 1919 for the performance of works for chorus and orchestra, and such unaccompanied vocal music as requires a considerable number of singers for its adequate representation.   The honorary conductor is Charles Kennedy SCOTT (q.v.).   The choir made its first appearance at the Royal Philharmonic Society's concert of Feb. 26, 1919, in a Bach motet, Delius's ' The Song of the High Hills ' and Beethoven's ' Choral ' symphony. It gave its first concert at Queen's Hall on June 2, 1920.    N. C. G.

PHILHARMONIC PITCH, see PITCH.

PHILHARMONIC SOCIETY.   This society was founded in London in 1813 for the encouragement of orchestral and instrumental music.   J. B. Cramer, P. A. Corri, and W. Dance invited various professional friends to meet them on Sunday, Jan. 24, 1813, when a plan was formed which resulted in the establishment of a society with thirty members, afterwards increased to forty—seven of whom were made directors for the management of the concerts—and an unlimited number of associates.   The subscription for members was three guineas, and for associates two guineas each. Subscribers were admitted on the introduction of a member on paying four guineas, and resident families of any subscriber two guineas each.

The principal musicians in London readily joined, and gave their gratuitous services in the orchestra.   The first series of eight concerts on Mondays, at irregular intervals, began on Mar. 8, 1813, at the Argyll Rooms, Regent Street— ' Leader, Mr. Salomon ; at the pianoforte ' (in lieu of the conductor as at present), ' Mr. Clementi '—and was both financially and artistically successful.

The following is a list of the members during the first season :

J. B. Cramer, P. A. Corri, W. Dance, M. Clementi, W. Ayrton, W. Shield, J. J. Graeff, H. R. Bishop, W. Blake, J. B. Salomon, C. Neate, R. Potter, Sir Geo. T. Smart, F. Cramer, T. Attwood, J. B. Viotti, Hill, Moralt, G. E. Griffin, J. Bartleman, W. Knyvett, Louis Berger, C. Ashley, R. Cooke, F. Yaniewicz, S. Webbe, jun., V. Novello, W. Horsley, W. Sherrington, A. Ashe.

Among the associates, of whom at the outset there were thirty-eight, are found the names of

Bridgetower, Mori, Naldi, Cipriani Potter, Spagnoletti, Samuel Wesley, and other eminent musicians.

The following have been the Hon. Treasurers of the Society :

W. Ayrton (1813–14); W. Dance (1815); M. Clementi (1816–17) ; R. H. Potter (1818–19) ; T. Attwood (1820) ; W. Dance (1821–32) ; W. Sherrington (1833–1835) ; W. Dance (1836–39) ; G. F. Anderson (1840–1876) ; W. C. Macfarren (1877–80) ; C. E. Stephens (1881–92) ; W. H. Cummings (1892–1915) ; J. Mewburn Levien (1915–18) ; Norman O'Neill (1918– ).   From 1910 onwards it has been usual to appoint also Hon. Co-Treasurers.

The Hon. Secretaries have been :

H. Dance (1813) ; C. J. Ashley (1813–15) ; W. Watts (1815–47) ; G. W. Budd (1847–50) ; G. Hogarth (1850–1864) ; Campbell Clarke (1864–66) ; S. Lucas (1866–1880) ; Henry Heron (1881–84) ; F. Berger (1885–1910) ; W. Wallace (1911–12) ; Stanley Hawley (1913–15) ; Donald Baylis (1916–17) ; J. Mewburn Levien (1918 to the present time).

In the early days of the Society two symphonies, two concertos, two quartets or quintets for string or wind, with two or more vocal concerted pieces, constituted the evening's programme.   A good idea of the popularity of the concerts in 1820 may be formed from Spohr's account in his autobiography.   ' Notwithstanding the high price of admission,' he says, ' the number of subscribers is so great that many hundreds who had inscribed their names could not obtain seats.'

Until Spohr came there was no conductor as we know the term, the responsibilities being divided between the leader of the orchestra and the musician who presided at the piano with the score.   These offices were held by the following :

1813–20. Leaders : Salomon, F. Cramer, Spagnoletti, Viotti, Yaniewicz, Vaccai, Weichsel, Mori, Baillot, J. D. Loder, H. Smart, sen.
Pianists : J. B. Cramer, F. Ries, Griffin, Smart, Crotch, Attwood, Clementi, V. Novello, Bishop, S. Webbe, jun., Kalkbrenner.
1821–43. Conductors : Smart, Ries, Bishop, Potter, Cramer, Clementi, Attwood, Neate, Crotch, T. Cooke Moscheles, C. Lucas, Bennett.
Weber conducted one concert in 1826.
Mendelssohn one in 1833 and one in 1842.
Spohr one in 1843.
1844.  Mendelssohn conducted 5 of the 8 concerts.
1845.  Bishop was appointed for the season but could only conduct 3 concerts owing to ill-health. Moscheles conducted the rest.
1846. Costa.
1855. Wagner.
1856. Bennett.
1867. Cusins.
1884. G. Mount, Stanford, J. F. Barnett, Cowen.
1885. Sullivan.
1888. Cowen.
1893. Mackenzie.
1900. Cowen.
1908. H. J. Wood, Cowen, Ronald, Nikisch.
1908–09. Chevillard, Mancinelli, Nikisch, Wood, Ronald.
1909–10. Ronald, Mancinelli, Nikisch, Elgar, Walter.
1910–11. Chessin, Coates, Safonov, Nikisch, Elgar, Mlynarski, Beecham.
1911–12. Elgar, Ronald, Mackenzie, Nikisch, Pitt, Mengelberg, Stanford, Safonov.
1912–13. Safonov, Ronald, Mengelberg, Pitt, Cowen.
1913–14. Mengelberg, Balfour Gardiner, Safonov.
1914–15. Beecham, Safonov, Pitt.
1915–16. Beecham.
1916–17. Beecham, Ronald.
1917–18. Beecham, Ronald.

1918–19. Ronald, Boult, G. Toye.
1919–20. Coates, Toye, Boult, C. K. Scott, Ronald.
1920–21. Coates, Hamilton Harty.
1921–22. Coates, Boult, Frank Bridge.
1522–23. Coates, Ronald, E. Goossens, jun.
1923–24. Coates, E. Ansermet, Ronald, Furtwängler, Goossens, Weingartner.
1924–25. Furtwängler, Walter, Goossens, Ansermet, Weingartner, P. Klenau, Malcolm Sargent.
1925–26. Coates, Elgar, Sargent, Rhène-Baton, P. Klenau, Ronald.
1926–27. Wood, Walter, Arbos, Monteux, F. Bridge, Allen.

The concerts given by the Society during the earlier years of its existence were the chief means of introducing new music to England, due largely to the policy adopted of commissioning works from composers. As time went on and other organisations appeared, first performances became a less frequent feature of the programmes. The following list gives a summary of the leading events in chronological order; a † signifies 'new to England,' and a * 'composed for the Society.'

1813. Three symphonies of Beethoven (numbers not given in the programmes), 4 of Haydn, 3 of Mozart. Beethoven's septet and other chamber music.
1814. †' Eroica' symphony. Cherubini commissioned to compose a symphony, overture and vocal piece for £200. Début of Catalani.
1815. Cherubini appeared at two concerts; his †' Anacreon' overture and a †*symphony played. 3 overtures bought from Beethoven for £75.
1816. Beethoven's †C minor symphony; Dragonetti played at these concerts for the first time. Début of Baillot.
1817. †' Fidelio' overture and †7th Symphony of Beethoven.
1820. First visit of Spohr, who introduced the use of the baton; from now onwards the musician described as ' at the pianoforte' was styled ' conductor.' Attwood, Smart, Ries, Potter and Welsh were so described this season.
1821. Début of I. Moscheles.
1823. Beethoven's †' Weihe des Hauses' overture.
1824. Beethoven's †C minor concerto. First appearance at these concerts of Pasta and Manuel Garcia.
1825. †*' Choral' symphony; †' Euryanthe' overture. Women associates first elected.
1826. Weber conducted one concert, the programme including the ' Euryanthe' and ' Der Freischütz' overtures and Beethoven's 7th symphony.
1827. £100 sent to Beethoven for his illness. Début of Liszt.
1829. First appearance of Mendelssohn, who conducted his †C minor symphony. Sontag and Malibran sang.

**ARGYLL ROOMS DESTROYED BY FIRE; CONCERTS GIVEN AT KING'S THEATRE:**

1830. Mendelssohn conducted ' Midsummer Night's Dream' overture. Rossini's †' William Tell' overture. De Bériot played and Lablache sang.
1831. Spohr's ' Last Judgment' selection, the first oratorio performed by the Society. Rubini sang and Hummel (first visit to England) played.
1832. Mendelssohn's †' Hebrides' overture; John Field played, Schröder-Devrient and †Tamburini sang. Mendelssohn was offered £105 for a symphony, overture and vocal piece.

**CONCERTS GIVEN IN HANOVER SQUARE ROOMS:**

1833. Mendelssohn's †*' Italian' symphony and †*' Trumpet' overture. Clara Novello sang. Honorary members first elected; they included Auber, Hummel, Mendelssohn and Meyerbeer.
1834. Mendelssohn's †' Melusine' overture. Grisi sang, Vieuxtemps played.
1835. First appearance of Sterndale Bennett.
1836. Mendelssohn's †' Calm Sea' overture. Thalberg and Ole Bull played. Opera directors refused to allow opera singers to appear at the concerts.
1837. Beethoven's ' Choral' symphony revived. Bennett's †' Naiades' overture.

1838. Mendelssohn's †D minor concerto.
1839. Bennett's †' Wood Nymphs' overture. Début of Mario.
1841. Berlioz's †' Benvenuto Cellini' overture.
1842. Mendelssohn conducted his †' Scotch' symphony.
1843. Chopin's †F minor concerto. Staudigl sang, Sivori played, Spohr played and conducted.
1844. Beethoven's †' Leonora,' No. 1, and †' Ruins of Athens' overtures. Ernst, Sainton, Piatti and Joachim (13 years old) played. Mendelssohn conducted 5 concerts.
1845. This year an attempt was made to engage a conductor for the whole season for the first time. See list of conductors.
1846. Costa appointed conductor. Beethoven's †Mass in D; Mendelssohn's violin concerto.
1847. Mendelssohn conducted at the fourth concert (his last visit).
1848. Alboni and Pauline Viardot-Garcia sang.
1849. Début of Mlle. Neruda (9 years old).
1851. Stockhausen sang; Bottesini and Pauer played.
1852. Charles Hallé played.
1853. Berlioz conducted his ' Harold in Italy' symphony; Schumann's †' Overture, Scherzo and Finale' introduced.
1854. Schumann's †symphony in B flat.
1855. Wagner appointed conductor.
1856. Sterndale Bennett appointed conductor. Schumann's †' Paradise and the Peri.' Début of Clara Schumann. Jenny Lind sang.
1857. Rubinstein played.
1859. Joachim introduced his †' Hungarian' violin concerto.
1862. Jubilee season. Commemoration concert at St. James's Hall at which Bennett's †*' Paradise and the Peri' overture was introduced and the soloists included Tietjens, Joachim and Santley.
1863. A Shakespeare tercentenary concert with ' Coriolanus' and ' Merry Wives of Windsor' overtures and all the ' Midsummer Night's Dream' music of Mendelssohn.
1865. Wagner's †' Rienzi' overture.
1867. Cusins appointed conductor. Nilsson sang.
1868. Schumann's †' Concert-stück,' op. 92; Bruch's violin concerto in G minor.

**CONCERTS GIVEN IN ST. JAMES'S HALL:**

1869. Analytical programmes (by G. A. Macfarren) introduced.
1870. All the Beethoven symphonies played and a Beethoven birth centenary concert. †' Preislied' from ' Die Meistersinger.'
1871. Schaller's bust of Beethoven presented by Frau Linzbauer to the Society. Wyon's Beethoven gold medal struck and presented, amongst others to Sterndale Bennett, Nilsson, Joachim and Santley. Gounod conducted his symphony in D.
1873. Brahms's †Requiem. Début of Von Bülow.
1874. Brahms's †Serenade in A. Début of Sarasate and Saint-Saëns.
1875. Concert in memory of Sterndale Bennett. Brahms's †' Haydn' Variations. Wilhelmj played.
1876. Prelude to †' Die Meistersinger.'
1877. Dannreuther played; Henschel sang.
1879. Brahms's violin concerto (Joachim).
1881. Hueffer appointed programme annotator. Berlioz's †' Romeo et Juliette' (complete version); D'Albert and Sophie Menter played; Sembrich and Albani sang.
1882. Guarantee Fund raised in view of losses incurred during the previous six seasons.
1883. Wagner memorial concert. Sarasate introduced Bruch's †' Scottish' concerto. Mackenzie's †*' La Belle Dame sans merci.' Pachmann played.
1884. Several conductors engaged for the season. Dvořák conducted his *' Husitzka' overture, a rhapsody and symphony in D.
1885. Sullivan appointed conductor. Programmes annotated by Hueffer, C. E. Stephens and J. Bennett. Dvořák conducted his *D minor symphony.
1886. Saint-Saëns conducted his *C minor symphony; Fanny Davies played and Ondříček introduced Dvořák's violin concerto.
1888. Cowen appointed conductor. Tchaikovsky conducted his †Serenade for strings and †Tema con variazioni; Grieg played his pianoforte concerto and conducted his ' Two Elegiac Melodies' for

strings ; Svendsen conducted two concerts. These three composers made their first appearance in England.

1889. Joachim played Stanford's †suite for violin and orchestra ; Tchaikovsky conducted his †suite in D and pianoforte concerto in B flat minor ; Parry conducted his †' English ' symphony ; Ysaÿe and Sapellnikoff played.

1890. Dvořák conducted his †symphony in G ; Borwick played.

1891. Paderewski, Jean Gerardy and Lamond played.

1892. Mozart death centenary concert.

1893. Mackenzie appointed conductor.  Tchaikovsky conducted his †symphony in F minor.

CONCERTS GIVEN IN QUEEN'S HALL :

1894. Tchaikovsky's †symphony in B minor and †Fantasie for pianoforte and orchestra ; Saint-Saëns conducted his symphony in C minor.  Cesar Thomson played, Camilla Landi sang.

1895. Stanford conducted his †symphony in D ; Parry conducted his †symphony in F (new version). Sauer played, Bispham sang.

1896. French pitch adopted.  Borodin's †symphony in B minor ; Dvořák conducted his †concerto for violoncello.

1897. This year an autumn season was given for the first time.  Paderewski played Mackenzie's †' Scottish ' concerto ; Parry conducted his †variations in E minor ; Glazounov conducted his †symphony in E flat (his first appearance in England).  Tchaikovsky's †variations for violoncello and orchestra ; Humperdinck conducted excerpts from ' Hänsel und Gretel ' and ' Königskinder.'  Blanche Marchesi sang, Siloti played.

1898. Moskowski played his concerto in E (his début as pianist) ; D'Albert conducted his symphony in F.

1899. Rachmaninov conducted his fantasie in E (his first appearance in England) ; Martucci conducted his symphony in D minor ; Borwick played Stanford's †variations on an English theme.  Dohnanyi and Rosenthal played.

1900. Cowen reappointed conductor.  Elgar conducted his ' Sea-pictures.'  Busoni played.

1901. Elgar conducted his †' Cockaigne ' overture. Kubelik and Godowsky played.

1902. Rachmaninov's †concerto in C minor.

1903. Mackenzie conducted his ' London Day by Day ' ; MacDowell played his 2nd concerto (his first appearance in England) ; Glazounov conducted his 7th symphony and †suite ' Aus dem Mittelalter.'  Kreisler played.

1904. Marie Hall and Raoul Pugno played, Muriel Foster and Maria Gay sang.

1905. First appearance in England of Casals.

1906. Weingartner conducted his †symphony in G ; Coleridge Taylor conducted his †' African ' Variations.  Mischa Elman played.

1907. Programmes annotated by F. G. Webb. Colonne conducted the first concert of the season. Enesco's †symphony in E flat ; Sinding conducted his violin concerto in A (his first appearance in England) ; G. W. Chadwick's ' Cleopatra.'

1908. Various conductors engaged ; see list. Sibelius conducted his symphony in C (his first appearance in England) ; Bantock conducted his prelude and ' Sappho ' songs. Gerhardt sang, Hubay and Lengyel played.

1908–09. The season began in the autumn of 1908. McEwen's †ballad ' Grey Galloway.'  Ethel M. Smyth conducted two songs, the first woman conductor at a Philharmonic.

1909–10. Holbrooke conducted his ' Queen Mab ' ; Rachmaninov's †symphony in E minor ; Elgar's †violin concerto. Programmes annotated by Edwin Evans.

1910–11. Cortot and Katharine Goodson played.

The complete programmes down to this date will be found in M. B. Foster's *History* (see below).  Later programmes are given in more detail.

1911–12. The centenary season.  Rachmaninov played his †concerto in D minor.  Stanford conducted his *D minor symphony, one of the principal British works specially written for the centenary ;

Buhlig, Busoni, Casals and Zimbalist played.  The last concert included a performance of the ' Choral ' symphony under Nikisch.

1912–13. Parry conducted his *B minor symphony, written for the centenary ; Pitt conducted his G minor symphony ; Coleridge Taylor's A minor ballade (in memoriam) ; Brahms's 3rd symphony ; Strauss's ' Also sprach Zarathustra ' (new to Philharmonic), ' Tod und Verklarung ' and ' Don Juan ' ; Walford Davies conducted his ' Wordsworth ' suite ; Schubert's C major symphony ; Rimsky-Korsakov's ' Scheherezade ' ; Norman O'Neill's †' Introduction, Mazurka and Finale ' ; Glazounov's E flat symphony ; Scriabin's †1st symphony ; Beethoven's ' Choral ' ; Bauer played Beethoven's concerto in G ; Sapellnikov played a Chopin concerto ; Busoni played Liszt's E flat concerto ; Katharine Parlow played Saint-Saëns's B minor concerto ; Elwes sang Dunhill's †Song-cycle.

1913–14. This season the Society handed over to the British Museum valuable MS. scores on a permanent loan.  Grainger's ' Mock Morris ' ; Strauss's ' Festliches Praeludium ' and ' Ein Heldenleben ' (new to Philharmonic) ; Beethoven's 3rd, 5th and 7th symphonies ; Bax's ' In the Faery Hills ' ; F. Austin's symphony in E ; Holst conducted his ' In the Street of Ouled Naïls ' ; Vaughan Williams's ' Norfolk Rhapsody,' No. 3 ; Tchaikovsky's 6th symphony ; Rimsky-Korsakov's ' Easter ' overture ; Delius's †' On Hearing the First Cuckoo in Spring ' and †' Summer Night on the River ' ; Stanford's ' Irish Rhapsody,' No. 4 ; Mendelssohn's ' Italian ' symphony ; Frank Bridge conducted his †' Dance Poem ' ; Liszt's ' Les Préludes ' ; Joan Manen played Lalo's ' Symphonie espagnole ' ; Joseph Lhevinne and Lamond played the Tchaikovsky concerto ; Borwick played Schumann's concerto ; Cortot played Franck's ' Les Djinns ' ; Sapellnikov played Rachmaninov's concerto in C minor ; Kirkby Lunn, Muriel Foster and Oriana Madrigal Society sang.

1914–15. Debussy's ' Printemps,' ' Three Nocturnes ' and ' Blessed Damozel ' ; Cyril Scott's †' Passacaglias,' Nos. 1 and 2 ; Saint Saëns's C minor Symphony ; Handel, a concerto grosso ; Delius's ' A Village Romeo and Juliet,' excerpts, ' Paris ' and ' Koanga ' ; Bax's ' Fatherland ' and Berlioz's ' Te Deum ' with the Halle Choir ; Berlioz's ' Symphonie fantastique ' ; Tchaikovsky's 4th Symphony ; Liadov's ' The Enchanted Lake ' ; Vivaldi, a concerto for strings ; Smyth's ' The Wreckers ' overture ; Borodin's B minor symphony ; Wallace's ' Wallace ' symphonic poem ; Vaughan Williams's ' Wasps ' overture ; Elgar's ' Carillons ' melodrama and 2nd symphony ; Parry's ' From Death to Life ' (new to London) ; McEwen's ' Grey Galloway ' ; a Mozart symphony ; Stravinsky's ' L'Oiseau de feu ' ; Sapellnikov played Liszt's A minor concerto ; Goodson played Grieg's concerto ; Isolde Menges played ; Kirkby Lunn, Walter Hyde and Edvina sang.

1915–16. Balakirev's ' Thamar ' ; Borodin's ' Polovtsienne ' dances ; Stravinsky's ' Petrouchka ' and ' L'Oiseau de feu ' ; Balfour Gardiner's †' Fantasy ' ; Rimsky-Korsakov's ' Anton ' and ' Scheherezade ' ; Berlioz's' King Lear ' ; Handel, a concerto for strings ; D'Indy's ' Jour d'été à la montagne ' ; Liszt's ' Tasso ' ; a Mozart symphony and the concertante for violin and viola (Ysaÿe and Tertis) ; Ravel's ' Daphnis et Chloé ' ; Bach's ' Brandenburg ' in G ; Mackenzie conducted his ' La Belle Dame sans merci ' ; Debussy's ' Three Nocturnes ' and ' Ibéria ' (new to London) ; Norman O'Neill's ' Humoresque ' ; Bax's ' In the Faery Hills ' ; Corder's ' Elegy ' for 24 violins and organ ; Frank Bridge conducted his ' Summer ' ; Fanny Davies played a Mozart concerto ; Arthur Rubinstein played a Saint-Saëns concerto ; Sapellnikov and Rumschyisky played Rachmaninov's 2nd Suite for 2 pianofortes ; Pachmann played a Chopin concerto ; Renée Chemet played Lalo's ' Symphonie espagnole ' ; Myra Hess played Schumann's concerto ; Mignon Nevada and Elsa Stralia sang.

1916–17. Delius's ' A Village Romeo and Juliet,' Scene V., ' On hearing the Cuckoo in Spring,' ' A Summer Night on the River ' and march from ' Folkeraadet ' suite ; Debussy's ' Ibéria,' ' Three Nocturnes ' and ' L'Après-midi d'un faun ' ; Tchaikovsky's ' Francesca da Rimini.' ' Romeo and

Juliet' and 5th symphony ; Elgar's 2nd symphony, 'Cockaigne' and 'Variations' ; a Mozart symphony and the 'Impresario' overture ; Glinka's 'A Life for the Tsar' selection, performed by members of the Beecham Opera Co. ; Austin's 'Polsgaard' ; Franck's symphony and 'Le Chasseur maudit' ; Rimsky-Korsakov's 'Anton' ; Smyth's 'The Wreckers' overture ; Ravel's 'Pavane' ; Balakirev's 'Thamar' ; Chabrier's 'Gwendolen' prelude, Act II. ; Ysaÿe played concertos by Vivaldi and Saint-Saens ; Pachmann played a Mendelssohn concerto ; Clara Butt and Kirkby Lunn sang.

1917–18. Borodin's 'Prince Igor' overture ; a Mozart symphony and the violin and viola concertante (Sammons and Tertis) ; Bantock's 'Fifine at the Fair' ; Debussy's 'Clair de lune' (orchestrated by Goossens) and 'Three Nocturnes' ; Schumann's 'Carneval,' Russian ballet version orchestrated by Glazounov, Liadov, Rimsky-Korsakov and Tcherepnin ; Smyth's 'On the Cliffs of Cornwall' prelude ; Paisiello's overture 'Nina o la Pazza d'Amore' ; Tchaïkovsky's 'Francesca da Rimini' and 5th symphony ; Balfour Gardiner's 'Comedy' overture ; Wallace's 'Villon' ; Elgar's 'Variations' and 'Cockaigne' overture ; Bantock's 'Fifine at the Fair' and excerpts from 'Omar Khayyam,' performed by members of the Beecham Opera Co. ; Holbrooke's 'Queen Mab' ; Julius Harrison's 'Rapunzel' (new to London), conducted by the composer ; Beethoven's 'Eroica' symphony ; Delius's 'A Village Romeo and Juliet,' Scene V. ; A. de Greef played Franck's symphonic variations ; Moiseiwitsch played a Rachmaninov concerto ; Beatrice Harrison played the Dvořák violoncello concerto ; Ethel Peake, Edna Thornton and Frank Mullings sang.

1918–19. Elgar's 'Falstaff' and 'Grania and Diarmid' funeral march ; Grieg's Lyric Suite ; Parry's 'The Soldier's Tent,' sung by George Baker ; Delius's †violin concerto (Albert Sammons) and 'In a Summer Garden' ; Bach's 'Brandenburg' concerto in G ; Schumann's symphony in B flat ; Vaughan Williams's 'Wasps' overture ; Bax's 'Festival' overture ; Holst's †'The Planets' ; Ravel's 'Rhapsodie espagnole' ; concert on anniversary of Beethoven's death with 'Leonora' overture No. 3, and symphony in C minor ; German's †'Theme and Six Diversions' ; Tchaïkovsky's 'Romeo and Juliet' ; Stanford's pianoforte concerto No. 2 (new to London), played by Moiseiwitsch ; Dvořák's 4th symphony ; Goossens's 'By the Tarn' and 'Tam o' Shanter,' arranged for orchestra ; Brahms's 'Haydn' Variations ; Rimsky-Korsakov's 'Scheherezade' ; Margaret Fairless played the Mendelssohn concerto ; Myra Hess played Rachmaninov concerto in C minor ; Robert Radford and Olga Haley sang.

1919–20. Rimsky-Korsakov's 'Battle of Kersjenetz' ; Holbrooke's 'Ulalume' ; Debussy's †'Fantasie,' pianoforte and orchestra (Cortot), and 'Fêtes' ; Scriabin's 'Divine Poem' and pianoforte concerto (William Murdoch) ; Meyerbeer's 'Struensee' overture ; Malipiero's †'Le pause del silenzio' ; Holst's 'Beni Mora' and †'Hymn of Jesus' (Philharmonic Choir) ; Delius's violin concerto (Sammons) and †'Song of the High Hills' ; Brahms's 4th symphony ; Beethoven's 'Choral Symphony' ; Rachmaninov's symphony in E minor ; Schubert's symphony in C ; Katherine Eggar's 'Shelley' scena (Carmen Hill) ; Olga Haley and Marguerite Nielka sang ; Suggia played Lalo's concerto.

1920–21. Rimsky - Korsakov's 'Russian Church Themes' overture, 'Cortège des nobles' ; Roussel's 'Le Festin de l'araignée' ; Stanford's †'Travelling Companion' prelude ; Franck's symphony ; Elgar's violin concerto (Heifetz) ; Strauss's 'Till Eulenspiegel' ; Scriabin's 'Poème de l'extase' and 'Prometheus' ; Beethoven's 7th symphony and 'Coriolan' overture ; Hamilton Harty's violin concerto (Murray Lambert) and arrangement of Handel's 'Water Music' ; Bax's †'November Woods' ; Tchaïkovsky's 5th symphony ; Respighi's 'Fountains of Rome' ; W. H. Bell's †'Symphonic Variations,' conducted by the composer ; Debussy's 'La Mer' ; Delius's 'Appalachia' with Philharmonic Choir ; selection of unaccompanied choral music by the choir ; Myra Hess played Mackenzie's pianoforte concerto ; Lamond

played the 'Emperor' ; Siloti played the Tchaïkovsky ; Giorgio Corrado sang.

1921–22. Elgar's variations and transcription of Bach's C minor organ fugue ; Brahms's D minor concerto (Cortot) and 3rd symphony ; Ravel's 'Ma Mère l'Oye' ; Stravinsky's 'Petrouchka' ; Rimsky-Korsakov's 'Cortège' ; Bax's †viola concerto (Tertis) ; Holbrooke's 'Ulalume' ; Delius's 'On hearing the Cuckoo' and †Requiem (Philharmonic Choir) ; De Sabato's †'Juventus' ; Schumann's violoncello concerto (Casals) ; Holst's †'Perfect Fool' ballet (first time in public) ; Tchaïkovsky's 4th symphony ; a Bach 'Brandenburg' concerto ; Vaughan Williams's †'Pastoral' symphony ; Wolf's 'Italian' serenade ; Bainton's concerto fantasia pianoforte (Winifred Christie), conducted by the composer ; Strauss's 'Don Juan' ; Lalo's 'Symphonie espagnole' (Thibaud) ; Butterworth's 'A Shropshire Lad' ; Beethoven's 5th symphony and 'Choral' ; Wagner's 'Die Meistersinger' overture.

1922–23. Mackenzie's 'Youth, Sport and Loyalty' ; Ireland's 'Symphonic Rhapsody' ; Beethoven's G major concerto (Bauer) and 'Eroica' symphony ; Stravinsky's 'The Nightingale' and 'Sacre du printemps' ; Brahms's 1st symphony, 'Song of Destiny' ; Strauss's 'Le Bourgeois Gentilhomme' (new to London) ; Lalo's violoncello concerto (Casals) ; Bax's 'Tintagel' ; Tchaïkovsky's 'Francesca' ; Glazounov's 'Stenka Razin' ; Delius's 'On the High Hills' and pianoforte concerto (Katharine Goodson) ; Scriabin's 'Poème de feu' ; Elgar-Bach's C minor fugue ; Hinton's †'Semele' scena (Marcia van Dresser), conducted by the composer ; a Rachmaninov concerto (Sapellnikov) ; Dvořák's E minor symphony ; Dukas's poème dansé 'Le Péri' ; McEwen's 'Solway' symphony (new to London) ; Bridge's 'The Sea' ; Aubert's 'Habañera.'

1923–24. An appeal made this season for a Trust Fund of £12,000 ; the income derived therefrom to guarantee the future existence of the Society. A centenary performance of Weber's 'Euryanthe' overture ; Moussorgsky's 'A Night on the Lonely Mountain' ; Schumann's pianoforte concerto (Irene Scharrer) ; Bax's 'Garden of Fand' ; Beethoven's 'Pastoral' symphony, 'Emperor' concerto (Cortot) and 'Choral' symphony ; Honegger's †'Chant de joie' ; Ravel's 'Daphnis et Chloé' ; Liszt's 'Hunnenschlacht' ; Brahms's 'Haydn' variations and 1st symphony ; Elgar's 2nd symphony ; a Handel concerto grosso ; Vaughan Williams's 'On Wenlock Edge' (John Booth), first performance of version for orchestra ; Strauss's 'Don Juan' ; Rimsky-Korsakov's sinfonietta or Russian Themes ; Wagner's 'Siegfried' idyll and 'Ring' excerpts ; a Mozart violin concerto (Jelly d'Aranyi) ; Holst's fugal concerto ; Stravinsky's 'L'Oiseau de feu' (new version) ; Dorothy Silk sang.

1924–25. Strauss's 'Tod und Verklarung' and 'Also sprach Zarathustra' ; Brahms's D minor concerto (Goodson) ; Beethoven's 7th and 8th symphonies ; Elgar's 1st symphony ; Schumann's 'Overture, Scherzo and Finale' ; Bach's concerto for violin, flute and pianoforte ; Delius's 'Summer Night' and 'Mass of Life' ; Honegger's †'Pacific No. 231' ; Debussy's 'Ibérla,' 'Three Nocturnes' and 'L'Après-midi d'un faun' ; Monteverdi, a sonata for small orchestra and women's voices ; a Handel concerto grosso ; Prokoviev's †violin concerto (Joska Szigeti) ; Ravel's 'Le Tombeau de Couperin' ; Berlioz's 'King Lear' ; Holst's 'Planets' ; Vaughan Williams's 'Pastoral' symphony ; Howell's pianoforte concerto (Harold Samuel) ; Ireland's symphonic rhapsody ; Bax's 'Garden of Fand' ; Berners's 'Fantaisie espagnole' ; Jeanne Jouve sang.

1925–26. Holst's 'First Choral Symphony' for soprano solo (Dorothy Silk), choir (Leeds Choral Union) and orchestra, given for the first time in London ; with it given Beethoven's 'Choral Symphony' ; a whole programme of Elgar's works included the Enigma variations, the violoncello concerto (Beatrice Harrison), 'Falstaff,' and 'In the South.' At this concert (Nov. 19) the gold medal of the Society was presented to Sir Edward Elgar by Sir Henry Wood in the name of the Society. Elgar's funeral march from 'Grania and Diarmid' (in mem. Queen Alexandra) ; Mozart's concerto in E flat (K. 268) and

Saint-Saëns's 'Fantasia havanaise,' both violin (Thibaud) and orchestra; Falla's 'El amor brujo' suite; Borodin's symphony in B minor; Rimsky-Korsakov's 'La Grande Pâque russe' overture; Roussel's 'Le Festin de l'araignée'; Vuillemin's 'En Kernéo'; D'Indy's 'Sinfonie sur un chant montagnard'; Mozart's concerto in C minor (K. 491) (pianoforte, R. Viñes); Brahms's 'Tragic' overture; Beethoven's violin concerto (Erica Morini); C. von Franckenstein's † 'Rhapsody for Orchestra'; Delius's Eventyr; Bartók's dance suite; Mendelssohn's 'Ruy Blas' overture; Schumann's PF. concerto (Cortot); Mozart's symphony in G minor; Delius's 'Brigg Fair'; Franck's symphonic variations (Cortot); Chabrier's rhapsody 'España.'

1926-27. This season including the centenary of Beethoven's death, the Society secured the co-operation of the ROYAL CHORAL SOCIETY (q.v.) for a performance of the 'Missa Solennis' in D under Allen. This, the sixth concert of the season, was held (Mar. 24, 1927) at the Albert Hall. The others were at Queen's Hall as usual. Weber's 'Oberon' overture marked the centenary of that composer's death. Sibelius's 'En Saga'; Vaughan Williams's 'A London Symphony'; Falla's 'Nights in the Gardens of Spain' (pianoforte, A. Rubinstein); Ravel's 'Rapsodie espagnole'; Schumann's symphony in B flat; Prokofiev's 'Love for three Oranges'; Respighi's 'The Fountains of Rome'; Franck's 'Psyche'; Berlioz's 'Sinfonie fantastique'; Bax's 'In the Fairy Hills'; Brahms's symphony in D. Myra Hess, Pablo Casals, and Albert Sammons were engaged to play concertos and Elisabeth Schumann to sing.

For further details of the Society's transactions, including copies of seven letters from Mendelssohn to Sterndale Bennett, the reader is referred to *The Philharmonic Society of London from its foundation 1813 to its Fiftieth Year, 1862*, by George Hogarth (8vo, London, 1862), and *History of the Philharmonic Society of London, 1813-1912*, by Myles Birket Foster (London, 1912). The Society itself has published the *Documents, Letters, etc., relating to the bust of Beethoven presented to the Society by Frau Fanny Linzbauer*, translated and arranged by Doyne C. Bell (4to, London, 1871); and, in the Programme book of Feb. 5, 1880, five hitherto unprinted letters from Mendelssohn to the Society. (See also LIBRARIES.)

N. C. G., incorporating material by S. L.

PHILHARMONIC SOCIETY OF NEW YORK, see NEW YORK.

PHILIBERT. See JAMBE DE FER.

PHILIDOR, a numerous family of French musicians, whose proper family name was DANICAN. The name by which they are known was (according to B. de La Borde in his *Essai sur la musique ancienne et moderne*) bestowed by Louis XIII. on MICHEL DANICAN, a native of Dauphiné, who died in Paris about 1659, as one of the King's musicians in the Grande Écurie, which he had entered in 1651. He played the oboe, the cromorne,[1] and tromba marina, and his skill on the first-named instrument was such as to procure him the royal compliment above referred to, Filidori having been an eminent oboist of Siena. Michel did not bear the sobriquet as a surname. He left no issue, so that the actual founder of the family was (1) JEAN, probably his brother, from whom all the rest were descended. Jean had

[1] Or Krummhorn.

three sons, (2) ANDRÉ 'l'aîné,' (3) JACQUES 'cadet,' and (4) ALEXANDRE. The two elder sons of Jean each became the father of four musical sons; by his first marriage with Marguérite Mouginot, André 'l'aîné' had sixteen children, the musicians being (5) ANNE, (6) MICHEL, and (7) FRANÇOIS; and by his second, with Elizabeth Le Roy, he had five more children, of whom one was the most celebrated of the family, (8) FRANÇOIS ANDRÉ.

The four musical sons of Jacques, who by his wife, Elizabeth Hanique, had twelve children, were (9) PIERRE, (10) JACQUES, (11) FRANÇOIS and (12) NICOLAS. All these are noticed below in accordance with this numbering.

(1) JEAN (b. circa 1620; d. Paris, Sept. 8, 1679) became in 1659 fifer in the Grande Écurie, and at his death was first player of the cromorne and marine trumpet, as well as an oboist and drummer. He is said to have composed dance-music, preserved in the 25th volume of the collection due to his son André.

(2) ANDRÉ ('Philidor l'aîné') (b. circa 1647[2]; d. Dreux, Aug. 11, 1730), succeeded his uncle Michel as fifth player of the same instruments in the Grande Écurie. Supposing him to have been twelve at that time, he would have been born about 1647. He married young, and the exertions necessary for the support of his numerous family were no hardship to one of his active and laborious disposition. He was a member of the Grande Écurie, the Chambre and the Chapelle, of Louis XIV.; played the bassoon, cromorne (his two best instruments), oboe, marine trumpet and even the drum when required; and after competing, at the King's request, with Lully in writing bugle-calls, fanfares and military marches,[3] composed divertissements for the court. Of these were produced, in presence of the King or the Dauphin, a comic divertissement, 'Le Canal de Versailles' (July 16, 1687), 'Le Mariage de la Couture avec la grosse Cathos' (1688), and 'La Princesse de Crète,' an opéra-ballet, the autograph of which was in his valuable collection of unpublished music. To these three works should be added 'La Mascarade du vaisseau marchand,' produced at Marly before Louis XIV., Thursday, Feb. 18, 1700, and hitherto unnoticed. The splendid collection referred to included all the dance-tunes in favour at court from the reign of Henry III. to the end of the 17th century; all the divertissements and operas of Lully and a few other composers; a selection of old airs, bugle-calls, military marches, and fanfares for the court hunting-parties; and finally all the sacred music in use at the Chapelle. André formed

[2] The date 1652 has also been given.
[3] Ch. Ballard published in 1685 a first book of 'Pièces de trompettes et timballes à 2, 3 et 4 parties.' This curious collection is not mentioned in any of the biographies, although the catalogue in Tholman's study on the Philidors contains the 'Suite de danses' (1699) and the 'Pièces à deux basses de viole, basse de violon et basson' (1700).

it during the time he was Librarian [1] of the King's musical library, from 1684 to his death. It was originally in the library of Versailles, and the greater part of it, fifty-seven vols., in his own hand, was transferred to the library of the Paris Conservatoire, which now, however, possesses only thirty-six, the other twenty-one having disappeared. An article by Fétis in the *Revue musicale* (Aug. 1827) drew attention to the importance of this collection, called *Collection Philidor*, and even mentioned the initials of the delinquent responsible for their loss. The contents of those which still exist are given in the *Vierteljahrsschrift*, vol. i. p. 531. A few other portions are in the Bibliothèque Nationale and the Bibliothèque de Versailles.

André retired on a pension in 1722, and died at Dreux, whither he had removed from Versailles in or about 1724. His brother,

(3) JACQUES, known as 'Philidor le Cadet' (*b.* Paris, May 5, 1657; *d.* Versailles, May 27, 1708), entered the Grande Écurie when a little over twelve as fifer, and was afterwards promoted to the oboe, cromorne and marine trumpet, succeeding his father. In 1683 he was admitted to the Chapelle, and in 1690 to the Musique de la Chambre, in which he played the bassoon. He was a favourite with Louis XIV., who gave him some land at Versailles, where he built a house, and died. He was on the best of terms with his brother, in whose collection his compositions were preserved—marches for drums and kettle-drums, airs for oboe, and dance music. The military music is still in the library at Versailles, but the rest has disappeared.

(4) ALEXANDRE, youngest of the three brothers, is known to have been a player of the favourite family instruments, the bass cromorne and marine trumpet in the royal band, 1679–1683.

(5) ANNE (*b.* Paris, Apr. 11, 1681; *d.* there, Oct. 8, 1728), before he was twenty produced at court, through the patronage of his godfather, Duke Anne de Noailles, three pastorales, 'L'Amour vainqueur' (1697), 'Diane et Endymion' (1698), and 'Danaé' (Marly, 1701), included in one of the lost volumes of the *Collection Philidor*. In 1702 he obtained the succession of his father's posts in the Grande Écurie and the Chambre, and in 1704 became oboist in the Chapelle, often playing before Louis XIV., who had a predilection for the instrument. He also composed [2]; but his real title to a place in the history of music is that he was the founder of the Concert Spirituel, which, however, he conducted for two years only (1725–27). (See PARIS, subsection CONCERT SPIRITUEL.) Laborde says that, after having directed the

[1] He was at first assistant to François Fossard a violinist, whom he soon replaced altogether.
[2] Among his printed works may be specified 'Premier livre de pièces pour la flûte traversière, flûte à bec, violons et hautbois' (Paris, 1712), oblong 4to. There is also a MS. Te Deum for four voices in the Conservatoire. See list in *Fétis: Suppt.*

concerts of the Duchesse du Maine, he became Surintendant de la Musique to the Prince de Conti. (See MOURET.)

(6) MICHEL (*b.* Versailles, Sept. 2, 1683), a godson of Michel de Lalande, played the drums in the king's band.

(7) FRANÇOIS (*b.* Versailles, Mar. 17, 1689; *d.* 1717 or 18) entered the Chapelle in 1708 as player on the bass cromorne and marine trumpet. In 1716 he became oboist in the Chambre, and bass violinist in the Grande Écurie. He seems to have died either in 1717 or the beginning of 1718, leaving some small compositions—amongst others, two books of 'Pièces pour la flûte traversière' (Ballard, 1716 and 1718).

(8) FRANÇOIS ANDRÉ DANICAN (*b.* Dreux, Sept. 7, 1726; *d.* London, Aug. 31, 1795), the most eminent of the family as a composer, and a highly distinguished chess-player. As a child he showed an extraordinary faculty for chess, which he saw played by the musicians of the Chapelle du Roi. Being a page of the Chapelle he had a right to music lessons, and learned the fundamental rules of harmony from André CAMPRA. At the close of his time as page he came to Paris, and supported himself by giving lessons and copying music. Discouraged perhaps by the difficulties of an artist's career, he gave himself up entirely to chess, and, with a natural gift for abstruse calculations, studied it to such purpose that at eighteen he was a match for the best players, and able to make a livelihood out of it. Being, however, hard pressed by his creditors, he started in 1745 on a tour abroad, going first to Amsterdam, where he pitted himself successfully against Stamma, author of *Les Stratagèmes du jeu d'échecs*. Thence he went on to Germany, and spent some time in 1748 at Aix-la-Chapelle, occupied in a work on the principles of the game. He next, on the invitation of Lord Sandwich, visited the English camp between Maestricht and Bois-le-Duc, and was well received by the Duke of Cumberland, who invited him to come to London and publish his *Analyse du jeu des échecs*. The subscriptions of the English officers encouraged him to accept the invitation, and he arrived in England, where he heard Handel's oratorios and where he eventually acquired a profitable celebrity. The first edition of his book appeared in 1749, and met with great and deserved success. It was during this first stay in London that Philidor performed the remarkable feat at the Chess Club of playing and winning three games simultaneously against first-rate players without seeing the boards.

Meantime Diderot, and his other friends, fearing that the continual strain of the pursuit for which he was forsaking his true vocation might prove too severe, recalled him to Paris in 1754. He began at once to compose his 'Motets à grand chœur,' which are influenced by Handel. His motet ' Lauda Jerusalem ' did not procure him the place of a ' Surintendant de la Musique ' to the King, at which it was aimed, but the disappointment turned his attention to dramatic music. His first opéra-comique, ' Blaise le Savetier ' (1759), a brilliant success, was followed by ' L'Huître et les plaideurs ' (1759) ; ' Le Quiproquo,' two acts, and ' Le Soldat Magicien' (1760) ; ' Le Jardinier et son seigneur ' and ' Le Maréchal ferrant ' (1761) ; ' Sancho Panca dans son isle ' (1762) ; ' Le Bûcheron ' and ' Les Fêtes de la Paix,' intermezzo written on the conclusion of peace with England (1763) ; ' Le Diable à quatre ' (1763) ; ' Le Sorcier,' two acts (1764) ; ' Tom Jones,' three acts (1765) ; ' Mélide, ou le Navigateur,' two acts (1766) ; ' Le Jardinier de Sidon,' two acts (1768) ; ' L'Amant déguisé ' (1769) ; ' La Nouvelle École des femmes,' two acts (1770) ; ' Le Bon Fils ' (1773) ; and ' Les Femmes vengées,' one act (1775), all given either at the Théâtre de la Foire, or at the Comédie Italienne. An ' histoire amoureuse de Pierre de Long . . .' was published in London in 1765 ; a copy is in the British Museum. Besides these he composed a Requiem performed in 1766 at the Oratoire, on the anniversary of Rameau's death, and produced the tragedy of ' Ernelinde,' his best work, at the Opéra (Nov. 24, 1767 ; reproduced in 1769 as ' Sandomir '). These successes did not cure him of his passion for chess. In 1777 he returned to London, brought out a second edition of his *Analyse*, and set to music Horace's ' Carmen seculare ' with flattering success (1779).

On his next return to Paris he found Grétry and Gluck at the height of their popularity ; but, nothing daunted, he re-wrote Lully's ' Persée ' (words by Marmontel, after Quinault ; performed at the Académie royale de musique, Oct. 27, 1780), and ' Thémistocle ' (produced Académie Royale de Musique,[1] May 23, 1786), both in three acts, ' L'Amitié au village ' (1785) and ' La Belle Esclave, ou Valcour et Zéïla ' (1787). ' Bélisaire,' three acts, was not given at the Opéra in 1774 as stated by Fétis, but at the Théâtre Favart (Oct. 3, 1796) a year after Philidor's death.

He received a regular pension from the Chess Club in London, and it had been his habit to spend several months of every year in England. In 1792 he obtained permission for the journey from the Comité du Salut Publique, but events prevented his return to Paris, and when his family had succeeded in getting his name erased from the list of émigrés, they learned that he had just died in London.

To estimate Philidor's work rightly, the condition of the French stage at the time he began to write must be taken into consideration ; he will then appear to have possessed not only greater originality, but art of a higher kind than

that of his contemporaries Duni, Monsigny and Grétry. His harmony is more varied, and the form and character of his airs new. He was the first to introduce on the stage the' air descriptif ' (' Le Maréchal '), and the unaccompanied quartet (' Tom Jones '), and to form a duet of two independent and apparently incongruous melodies. Moreover, he understood to a degree then rare the importance of the orchestra and chorus, and undoubtedly surpassed his compatriots in instrumentation. He enjoyed an almost unexampled popularity in his day, being called forward after the representation of his ' Sorcier '—the first instance of the kind in Paris. There is a fine bust of this Philidor by Pajou, and an excellent portrait by Cochin, engraved by St. Aubin in 1772.

BIBL.—H. QUITTARD in *Grande Encyl.* ; L. DE LA LAURENCIE, *France XVIIe-XVIIIe. siècles* (with bibliography) in *Encyl. de la musique* ; LARDIN, *Philidor peint par lui-même* (Paris, 1847), repubd. from *Le Palamède* (1847) ; E. THOINAN, *Les Philidor, généalogie biographique des musiciens de ce nom* (*La France musicale*, Dec. 22, 1867, Feb. 16, 1868) ; A. POUGIN, *André Philidor* (*La Chronique musicale*, 1871) ; GEORGE EDGAR BONNET, *Philidor et l'évolution de la musique française au VIIIe siècle.* (Paris, 1921.)

(9) PIERRE, the eldest son of Jacques ' le cadet ' (*b.* Paris, Aug. 22, 1681 ; *d.* Sept. 1, 1731), produced a pastoral at Versailles in 1697, was in the royal band, became flute-player of the King's private band in 1712, and violist in 1716. He left suites for the flute, issued in 1717, 1718, etc. (see list in *Fétis* : *Suppt.*).

(10) JACQUES (*b.* Sept. 7, 1686 ; *d.* Pampeluna, June 25, 1709[2]), succeeded his father as oboist in 1708. He was the kettle-drummer to the Duke of Orleans.

(11) FRANÇOIS (*b.* Jan. 21, 1695 ; *d.* Oct. 27, 1726[3]), was oboist of the King's chamber.

(12) NICOLAS (*b.* Versailles, Nov. 3, 1699 ; *d.* 1769), was oboist in the Grande Écurie, and violist in the King's private band. In 1747 he played the serpent in the latter.

G. C. ; rev. M. L. P.

PHILIPP, ISIDORE (*b.* Budapest, Sept. 2, 1863), studied at the Paris Conservatoire, where he gained the first prize for piano in 1883, and also received counsel from Stephen Heller, Saint-Saëns and Ritter. He played in different parts of Europe and made his first appearance at the Philharmonic Society in London in Mar. 1890. He took part regularly at the Colonne, Lamoureux and Conservatoire concerts in Paris. In 1890 he founded with Berthelier and Loeb a chamber-music organisation, and in 1896 reorganised the ' Société des instruments à vent,' giving most interesting concerts until the final dissolution of the undertaking in 1901. He published numerous educational works, arrangements (among them a wonderfully clever and effective version of the scherzo from the *Midsummer Night's Dream* music) for two pianos, as well as pianoforte pieces. He became professor of the piano at the Paris Conservatoire in 1893.　　G. F.

_____
[1] Or Opéra.　　　　[2] Bonnet gives 1726　　　[3] Bonnet gives 1766.

PHILIPPE DE VITRY (*b.* between 1285–1295; *d.* 1361), of a noble family of the Champagne. He died as bishop of Meaux. He was one of the foremost musical theoreticians of the 14th century, whose *Ars nova*, *Ars contrapunctus*, *Ars perfecta in musica* and *Liber musicalium* remained standard works for over a century. He simplified the complicated notation of the Italians. Of his compositions nothing has yet been found (*Q.-L.*; *Riemann*).

PHILIPS, PETER (*d.* Brussels ? 1628 [1]), an English composer and organist, who lived in the Netherlands at the end of the 16th and beginning of the 17th centuries.

Very little is known [2] of his biography beyond what can be gathered from the title-pages of his published works, in which his name is given in various Latin, French and Italian forms. Fétis says that he was born in England of Roman Catholic parents, and about 1595 went to Italy, residing for some months in Rome, but these statements cannot be verified, nor does his name occur in the records of the English College at Rome. The ' Fitzwilliam Virginal Book' contains a series of nineteen pieces by Peter Philips, many of which are dated (1580, 1582, 1592, 1593, 1595, 1602, 1603 and 1605). The first (No. lxxxv.—printed edition, i. 343) is a pavana, with the note ' the first one Philips made.' Another of the series is a ' Pavana Dolorosa,' dated 1593, with the abbreviated name ' Treg.,' probably indicating that it is the composition of the elder Tregian, who was at that date imprisoned as a recusant. In a MS. now in the Berlin Library (MS. 191) there is another copy of this pavana, with the name of Philips alone as composer, while the index states that it was ' composta in prigione.' [3] This probably means that Tregian wrote the pavana while he was in prison, and that it was subsequently arranged by Philips.

It is highly improbable that Philips was in England after 1590, for in 1591 there was published at Antwerp his collection of madrigals entitled ' Melodia Olympica di diversi eccellentissimi musici,' dedicated to ' Sig. Giulio Balbani,[4] patrono mio osservantissimo,' and dated Antwerp, Dec. 1, 1590. Other editions of the ' Melodia Olympica ' appeared at Antwerp in 1594 and 1611. This work was followed in 1596 by ' Il primo libro de madrigali a sei voci,' printed at Antwerp by Phalèse, and dedicated (Antwerp, Jan. 8, 1596) to Signor Alessandro di Giunta ; a second edition was issued in 1604. In 1598 he published at Phalèse's press in Antwerp a volume of eight-

part madrigals, on the title-page of which he appears for the first time as organist of the Archduke Albert and Archduchess Isabella This work is dedicated from Antwerp on Sept 24, 1598, to Sir William Stanley (1548–1630) the Catholic adventurer, who is described as ' Collonello d' un Regimento Inglesi & Walloni mio Sig. osseruandiss.' The work was reprinted in 1599, and again in 1615. In 1603 there appeared a second book of madrigals for six voices (Antwerp, Phalèse), dedicated from Antwerp, Nov. 10, 1603, to the Archduke and Archduchess ; a second edition was issued in 1615. On Mar. 9, 1610, Philips was appointed to a canonry in the collegiate church of Saint Vincent, at Soignies, vacant by the death of Claude Carlier. In 1611 he was summoned to Malines, together with several of his colleagues of the archducal chapel, in order to report on a new organ erected in the cathedral. For their services on this occasion Philips and his companions received six pots of Rhine wine, of the value of 24 livres, 15 sous. The entry of this payment in the town accounts seems to imply that Philips and his colleagues took part in the Easter services of 1611.[5] In the same year Philips's name appears as organist at the Chapel Royal at Brussels, in receipt of ' 10 aunes de drap, au prix de six livres l'aune.' On Mar. 12, 1622, at the funeral of the Archduke Albert (ob. July 15, 1621), Philips walked in the procession at the head of the ' Chapellains de la Chapelle de la Cour ' ; his portrait, which is certainly taken from life (as notified in the letterpress) is here reproduced from Jacques Francquart's *Pompa funebris . . . Alberti Pii . . . veris imaginibus expressa* (Brussels, 1623). Two years later (1624) as ' Pietro Filippini ' he is mentioned in a report on the restoration of the organ of the Court Chapel.

After the appearance of his six-part madrigals Philips seems to have devoted himself entirely to sacred music, and it is probable that it was in order to be qualified for the canonry of Soignies that he took holy orders. His first published collection of sacred music, the ' Cantiones sacrae,' for five voices, was published by Phalèse at Antwerp in 1612. It is dedicated to the Blessed Virgin, and in the title-page the composer's name first appears with the prefix ' R.D.' and with the title of Canon of Soignies. The five-part ' Cantiones sacrae ' were followed in 1613 by a similar collection for eight voices, also published by Phalèse, and dedicated to St. Peter. A second edition of this work, with the addition of a ' Bassus Continuus ' for the organ, was brought out by Phalèse in 1625. In 1613 also appeared the first edition of ' Gemmulae Sacrae Binis et Ternis Vocibus cum Basso Continuo ad

1 According to an entry in the notebook of Dr. John Southcote (publ. by Catholic Record Society, vol. i. p. 133). If this is so, publications under Philips's name of 1630 and 1633 are posthumous, but there is nothing to show this on their title-pages. See *Mus. Ant.* ii. 241.
2 Sebastian Westcote's will, which mentions Philips, suggests that he had been brought up as one of the St. Paul's boys. See *Mus. Ant.* iv. 189.
3 It is printed in Fuhrmann's *Testudo Gallo-Germanica* (1615).
4 The Balbanis were a noble family of Lucca, a branch of which was settled at Bruges at the end of the 16th century.

5 See P. Bergmans, *L'Organiste des Archiducs Albert et Isabelle Peter Philips* (Gand, 1903).

Organum' (Antwerp, Phalèse), a second edition of which was issued in 1616 and a third in 1621. In 1616 Jean Veruliet of Valenciennes brought out a little volume of short motets or hymns entitled

'Les Rossignols spirituels. Liguez en duo, dont les meilleurs accords, nommément le Bas, releuent du Seigneur Pierre Philippes, Organiste de leurs Altezes Serenissimes.'

This work, of which a second edition appeared

Pierre Philippe Organiste.

Iacques Daelman

in 1621, a third in 1631, and a fourth (without Philips's name) at Cologne in 1647, is dedicated to Charles de Pas, Abbot of St. Amand. In 1616 Philips also published with Phalèse at Antwerp his 'Deliciae sacrae binis et ternis vocibus, cum basso continuo ad organum,' dedicated to the Archduke and Archduchess; a second edition of this work appeared in 1622. On Jan. 5, 1621, Philips exchanged his canonry

of Soignies with Jerome van der Berghe for a perpetual chaplainship in the church of Saint Germain at Tirlement. The documents relating to this transaction are printed by P. Bergmans. In the title-page of the second edition of the 'Deliciae' (1622) he is still entitled Canon of Soignies, but on that of his next work, a collection of Litanies of Loreto, for from four to nine voices, with Bassus Continuus for the organ (Phalèse, Antwerp, 1623), he appears as Canon of Bethune, a title he also bears in the second edition of the eight-part 'Cantiones sacrae,' issued in 1625. But in 1628, when he issued the first part of his 'Paradisus sacris cantionibus consitus, una, duabus et tribus vocibus decantantis. Cum basso generali ad organum' (Phalèse, Antwerp, dedication dated Brussels, Apr. 1628), he once more appears as Canon of Soignies, a title still accorded him in 1633, when the second and third parts of the 'Paradisus' were printed by Phalèse, though on the title-page of the second (enlarged) edition of the Litanies (1630) his name appears without any title. A volume of masses was published posthumously (see the *Kirchenmusikalisches Jahrbuch*, 1899, p. 89). This is identical with a book entered in a list of the musical library of John IV., King of Portugal (1649), as No. 599 : 'Missas y salmos . . . a 8 & 9 . . . obras postumas.' After this comes a volume of 'Mottetes . . . a 8, 2 partes,' also described as posthumous works, though it seems doubtful whether the eight-part 'Cantiones sacrae ' of 1613 be not intended. Of the masses and psalms no copy is at present known to exist. No record of his death has been found at Soignies, where the present writer has examined the records of the church and the tombstones of the canons without success.

In addition to the works which he himself published, Philips contributed to many collections of the time. Phalèse's 'Madrigali a otto voci de diversi eccellenti et famosi autori ' (Antwerp, 1596) contains two madrigals by him for eight voices ; two more are in the same publisher's 'Paradiso musicale di madrigali et canzoni a cinque voci ' (Antwerp, 1596), and two English madrigals in Thomas Morley's 'Madrigals to five voyces. Celected out of the best approued Italian Authors ' (London, 1598). A Pavan and Galliard are in Morley's 'Consort Lessons ' (1599)—the Pavan is an arrangement of the 1580 Pavan [1] in the 'Fitzwilliam Virginal Book' (No. lxxxv.) ; a six-part madrigal is in the 'Ghirlanda di madrigali ' (Phalèse, Antwerp, 1601), and two more in the 'Nervi d' Orfeo ' (Leyden, 1605). A Pavan and Galliard for five instruments is in the first part of Z. Füllsack's 'Ausserlesene Paduanen und Galliarden' (Hamburg, 1607), and three motets in Books II. and III. of M. Herrerius's 'Hortulus musicalis '

[1] Another arrangement of the 1580 pavan, entitled ' Wy Engelen gret,' is in W. Swart's ' Den Lust-Hof der nieuwe Musycke' (Amsterdam, 1603).

(Munich, 1609), and in the same year the 1580 Pavana ('Fitzwilliam Virginal Book,' No. lxxxv.) was printed in tablature in Thomas Robinson's 'New Citharen Lessons' (London, 1609). Abraham Schadaeus also reprinted two of Philips's eight-part 'Cantiones sacrae' in his 'Promptuarium musicum' (Strassburg, 1611).

From 1605–10 Salomon de Caus was engineer to the Archduke Albert and the Archduchess Isabella at Brussels, where he was succeeded in 1612 by his assistant, Gerard Philippi, who may have been a connexion of the composer. That he was well known to de Caus is proved by the fact that the curious volume of mechanical devices which the celebrated engineer published at Frankfort in 1615, under the title of 'Les Raisons des forces mouvantes' contains part of a Fantasia by Philips (for a barrel-organ turned by water) on Alessandro Striggio's five-part madrigal 'Chi fara fed' al ciel'; the original madrigal appeared at Venice in 1566 in the second book of a collection called 'Il desiderio,' and Philips's complete setting is to be found in the 'Fitzwilliam Virginal Book' (printed edition, 1899, i. p. 312). In the same year (1615) de Caus also printed in his 'Institution harmonique' some instrumental trios by Philips, 'ou les natures de la première, troisiesme, & cinquiesme mode sont tres bien obseruées'; though the composer's name, 'Pietri Filippi,' is only attached to the 'Trio de la première mode,' the context shows that all three are by him. In 1621 Thomas Simpson inserted a short instrumental 'aria à 4' in his 'Taffel Concert,' published at Hamburg, and in 1622 a four-part Paduana from his pen appeared in the anonymous 'Amoenitatum musicalium hortulus,' published at Leipzig. Two motets by Philips for two voices with basso continuo are in the 'Promptuarium musicum' of J. Donfrid (Strassburg, 1622), and two Christmas carols in the 1629 edition of Pevernage's 'Laudes vespertinae B. Mariae Virginis' (Phalèse, Antwerp). For a list of the libraries containing MS. compositions by Philips reference must be made to Q.-L. In many cases the MSS. are only copies of printed works, but at Königsberg (MS. 1645, No. 24) are preserved four parts of a Mass for six voices, unfortunately wanting the tenor and sextus. An account of some instrumental pieces in a MS. formerly in the Library of Count zu Lynar at Lübbenau will be found in Dr. Max Seiffert's introduction to vol. i. of the complete works of Sweelinck (1894, p. 111).

It is often very difficult to distinguish the MS. compositions of Peter Philips from those of an earlier composer—Philip van WILDER (q.v.) —who in English MSS. sometimes appears as 'Mr. Philips.' In the first volume of the new catalogue of the MS. music in the British Museum the two composers are indexed together as 'Philip de Wildroe,' owing to the fact that a metrical motet or anthem, 'Blessed art thou

that fearest God,' occurs in B.M. Add. MSS. 30,480-4 as by 'Philip de Wildroe,' in B.M. Add. MSS. 22,597 as by 'Phillips,' and in Myriell's 'Tristiae Remedium' it is ascribed to Peter Philips. The two first MSS. were clearly written early in the reign of Elizabeth, and Myriell's collection is dated 1616, so it seems probable that Myriell found the composition with the name of 'Phillips' attached and attributed it to Peter Philips, who was well known in his day, while the name of Philip van Wilder was forgotten.

Like his contemporary Bull, who was also a refugee at Antwerp in the early 17th century, Philips seems to have been personally acquainted with Sweelinck; an arrangement of the English composer's early Pavana ('Fitzwilliam Virginal Book,' i. p. 343) by the Dutch organist is printed by Dr. Seiffert in the above-mentioned volume, and the same writer [1] refers to a contemporary record of Philips's opinion that Sweelinck was the cleverest and most talented ('constrijck') organist of his time. That Philips himself was widely appreciated in his day is proved by the number of collections in which works by him appeared. Although his life was spent abroad, he was not forgotten in England, and Peacham, in his *Compleat Gentleman* (London, 1627), says of him:

'Nor must I here forget our rare Countrey-man, *Peter Phillips*, Organist to their *Altezza's* at Bruxels, now one of the greatest Masters of Musicke in Europe. Hee hath sent vs ouer many excellent Songs, as well *Motets* as *Madrigals*: he affecteth altogether the *Italian* veine.'

In Velvet Breughel's picture of the Five Senses (now in the Prado at Madrid) an open music-book on a spinet reproduces the title-page of Philips's six-voice madrigals, and in Ph. Brasseur's *Sydera illustrium Hannoniae scriptorum* (Mons, 1637), the following verses on him appear:

Anglus ubique audit, verum magis Angelus ille est
  Sonegiae Clero, Sonegiaeque choro.
Qui velut eximios semper colit arte canorâ,
  Sic melodis auctum vocibus ille Petrum.
Edidit hic sacris Paradisum cantibus aptum,
  Et modo sacratis servit ubique locis.

Even Burney (who knew so little about Philips as to say that Soignies was in Germany) gives him some stinted praise. Commenting on the 'Fitzwilliam Virginal Book,' the 18th-century historian says (iii. 86):

'The first regular fugue, for the organ, upon one subject that I have seen, was composed by Peter Philips . . . and is inserted in the Virginal Book. . . . This author has manifested considerable abilities in treating a simple subject, which he has introduced no less than thirty-nine times : simple ; in augmentation ; and in diminution. The harmony is very full, but the modulation being chiefly confined to the keynote, and its fifth, is somewhat monotonous, and the divisions, in accompanying the subject, are now become too common and vulgar to afford pleasure, or even to be heard with patience, by fastidious judges of modern melody.'

In estimating Philips's position among English composers it is important to remember that his

1 Geschichte der Klaviermusik (1899), i. pp. 86-8.

whole life was passed abroad. His music exhibits none of the characteristics of his English contemporaries ; as Peacham remarks, it is—at least in his madrigals and instrumental works—entirely in ' the Italian veine.' In his later years he seems to have been more influenced by the later Netherlandish School, and his five-part ' Cantiones sacrae ' often contain passages strongly reminiscent of Sweelinck.[1] After suffering undeserved neglect for three hundred years, attention was drawn to this set of motets by the performances of the choir of Westminster Cathedral under Terry, who had the whole set lithographed for modern use. Their revival has been one of the most interesting features of the Cathedral services, where their admirable combination of melody and dignity has won for them well-merited, if tardy recognition. In his later sacred music Philips seems to a certain extent to have abandoned the polyphonic style of his earlier works and to have adopted a modified kind of homophony, somewhat resembling that of Dering, who, like himself, was a Roman Catholic English organist settled in the Netherlands. It is to be hoped that the attention recently drawn to this very talented composer will cause more of his music to be reprinted. The following is a list of accessible reprints :

### MADRIGALS

1. Voi volete ch' io muoia (4 voc.). Hawkins, *History*, iii. 328.
2. Amor che vuoi.(4 voc.). Ed. W. B. Squire (Stanley Lucas and Weber, 1890).
3. Dispiegate guancie amate (8 voc.). Ed. W. B. Squire (' Ausgewählte Madrigale,' Breitkopf & Härtel, 1906).

### MOTETS

1. O pastor aeterne (8 voc.). (A. H. Jewell's ' Madrigal and Motett Book.' No. 2, 1856.)
2. Hodie Sanctus Benedictus (5 voc.). Ed. W. B. Squire (Novello & Co., 1899).
3. Ego sum panis vivus (5 voc.). Ed. W. B. Squire (J. Williams, 1902).
4. Ave Verum.
5. Ave Regina. 
6. Regina coeli. 
7. Salve Regina.
8. Veni Creator (4 voc.). In C. T. Gatty's ' Arundel Hymns ' (Boosey & Co., 1905).

*5, 6 : (5 voc.). In R. R. Terry's ' Downside Motets ' (Cary & Co., 1904–05).*

### INSTRUMENTAL

1. A shortened version of the Fantasia on Striggio's ' Chi fara fed' al ciel,' as printed by S. de Caus. In E. Van der Straeten's *Musiciens néerlandais en Italie* (1882), p. 506.
2. Another Fantasia on the same subject, from a MS. in the University Library at Liège. In A. E. Ritter's *Zur Geschichte des Orgelspiels* (1884), ii. p. 51.
3-21. Nineteen pieces in the ' Fitzwilliam Virginal Book ' (1899), vol. i.

W. B. S.

PHILIPS (PHELYPPES), SIR THOMAS, a 15th-century English composer. So far only 1 song of his is known, in 6 verses, from the Fayrfax MS. (B.M. Add. MSS. 5465).

PHILLIPPS, ADELAIDE (*b*. Stratford-on-Avon, 1833 ; *d*. Carlsbad, Oct. 3, 1882), a contralto singer who pursued her career chiefly in America. Her father was a chemist and druggist, and her mother, who was of Welsh birth, was a teacher of dancing. The family emigrated to America in 1840, going first to Canada, and then to Boston, Mass. Adelaide was early instructed in dancing by her mother, and on Jan. 12, 1842, made her first appearance

on the stage at the Tremont Theatre, Boston, as an ' infant prodigy.' On Sept. 25, 1843, she began an engagement at the Boston Museum. Her vocal gifts soon attracted the attention of connoisseurs, and in 1850 she was introduced to Jenny Lind, who advised the young actress to give herself up to the study of music. A subscription list was started for the purpose of paying for her training, and she was sent to Manuel Garcia in London. On Dec. 17, 1854, she made a début at the Teatro Carcano, Milan, as Rosina. In Aug. 1855 she returned to Boston, and in October appeared at a concert in the Music Hall. She was then engaged for a series of operas of the English ballad school—' The Duenna,' ' The Devil's Bridge,' and ' The Cabinet '—at the Boston Theatre. Her American début in Italian opera was at the Academy of Music, New York, Mar. 17, 1856, as Azucena in ' Il Trovatore.' Her success secured for her an engagement for five seasons. She went first to Havana, and subsequently to Paris (where she sang Azucena at Les Italiens in Oct. 1861), Madrid, Barcelona and through Hungary and Holland. Her repertory comprised all the contralto parts in the stock Italian operas. In 1879 she became identified with the Boston Ideal Opera Company, devoted to the presentation of operettas. She appeared with this company for the last time in Boston, on the Museum stage, where her early triumphs had been won, on Nov. 30, 1880. Her last appearance on any stage was at Cincinnati in Dec. 1881. In Sept. 1882, the state of her health induced her to go to Carlsbad, where she died. Her remains were carried to Boston, and subsequently buried at Marshfield, Massachusetts, where the family had long lived on a fine estate purchased by Adelaide. She left a sister, Mathilde, also a contralto of excellent reputation in America, and three brothers. F. H. J.

PHILLIPS, ARTHUR, Mus.B. (*b*. 1605 ; *d*. Mar. 27, 1695), became in 1622 a clerk of New College, Oxford, and was appointed organist of Bristol Cathedral, Dec. 1, 1638. On the death of Richard Nicolson in 1639 he succeeded him as organist of Magdalen College, Oxford, and professor of music in the University, and graduated Mus.B., July 9, 1640. Some time afterwards he quitted the English Church for that of Rome, and attended Queen Henrietta Maria to France as her organist. Returning to England he entered the service of a Roman Catholic gentleman of Harting in Sussex, named Caryll, as steward. He composed music in several parts for ' The Requiem, or, Liberty of an imprisoned Royalist,' 1641, and a poem by Dr. Pierce, entitled ' The Resurrection,' 1649. A ' fancy on a ground ' is in the B.M. Add. MSS. 29,996. He describes himself in the subscription book as son of William Phillips of Winchester, gentleman. W. H. H.

PHILLIPS, HENRY (*b*. Bristol, Aug. 13,

---

[1] As to his conjectural influence on Frescobaldi, see Van der Straeten's *Musiciens néerlandais en Italie* (1882), vol. vi.

1801 ; *d.* Dalston, Nov. 8, 1876), was the son of a country actor and manager, and made his first appearance in public as a singing-boy at the Harrogate Theatre about 1807. He afterwards came to London and sang in the chorus at Drury Lane and elsewhere. On the settlement of his voice as a baritone he placed himself under the tuition of Broadhurst, and was engaged in the chorus at the English Opera-House, and to sing in glees at civic dinners. He next had an engagement at Bath, where he sang in ' Messiah ' with success. Returning to London he studied under Sir George Smart and appeared in the Lenten oratorios at the theatres, and at the Liverpool Musical Festival of 1823. In 1824 he was engaged at Covent Garden, and appeared as Artabanes in Arne's 'Artaxerxes,' but made little mark. In the summer of the same year he sang the music of Caspar on the production of 'DerFreischütz,' with great effect. He then made progress, was engaged at the provincial festivals, and in 1825 appointed principal bass at the Concert of Ancient Music, and from that time filled the first place at the theatre and in the concert-room. He was also a member of the choir at the chapel of the Bavarian Embassy. About 1843 he gave up his theatrical engagements and started a series of ' table entertainments,' which, notwithstanding their ill success, he persisted in giving, at intervals, until he quitted public life. In Aug. 1844 he went to America, and remained there, giving his entertainments in various places, for nearly a year. He sang again in London at the first performance of ' Maritana ' (Nov. 15, 1845) and in Balfe's ' Maid of Artois ' (Dec. 1847), and reappeared in opera at Covent Garden in Oct. 1848. On Feb. 25, 1863 (his powers having been for some time on the wane), he gave a farewell concert and retired. He then became a teacher of singing, at first at Birmingham, and afterwards in the vicinity of London. He composed several songs, etc., and was author of *The True Enjoyment of Angling*, 1843, and *Musical and Personal Recollections during half a century*, 1864.    w. h. h.; addns. w. h. g. f.

PHILLIPS, JOHN and SARAH, music engravers, during the middle of the 18th century. Hawkins [1] says of them :

' But the last and greatest improver of the art of stamping music in England was one Phillips, a Welchman, who might be said to have stolen it from one Fortier, a Frenchman and a watchmaker, who stamped some of the parts of Martini's first opera, of concertos, and a few other things. This man Phillips, by repeated essays, arrived at the method of making types (punches) of all the characters used in music ; with these he stamped music on pewter plates, and taught the whole art to his wife and son. In other respects he improved the practice of stamping to so great a degree that music is scarce anywhere so well printed as in England.'

The Phillips pair kept a music shop in St. Martin's Court, St. Martin's Lane, about 1750–1760, and worked much for composers who published their own compositions ; among these were Geminiani (' Art of playing the Violin,' 1751) ; Dr. Arne (' Thomas and Sally,' 1761) ; Dunn (' Six English Songs ') ; Edward Miller (several collections of songs) ; Warren's (' Collection of Catches and Glees,' 1763), etc.

During the lifetime of John Phillips, both his name and that of his wife appear attached to music, but Phillips having died, probably about 1766–68, his wife alone, shortly after this date, is found having a music shop in Bedford Court and still stamping music plates.    F. K.

PHILLIPS, MONTAGUE FAWCETT (*b.* London, Nov. 13, 1885), studied at the R.A.M., and has been a successful composer of songs and slight pieces (for list see *B.M.S. Ann.* 1920). In the theatre Phillips's principal work has been ' The Rebel Maid ' (Empire, 1921), a romantic light opera, the tunefulness of which appealed to a wide public. Most of his larger orchestral works remain in manuscript. A pianoforte concerto in F sharp minor and a symphonic poem ' Boadicea ' were both produced by the Patrons' Fund of the R.C.M. (1908–09), and a symphony in C minor was heard at a concert of his own compositions which Phillips gave in London in 1912. An ' Heroic ' overture was produced by the London Symphony Orchestra in 1915.    C.

PHILLIPS, PETER, see PHILIPS.

PHILLIPS, WILLIAM LOVELL (*b.* Bristol, Dec. 26, 1816 ; *d.* Mar. 19, 1860), at an early age entered the cathedral choir of Bristol, and subsequently proceeded to London, where he sang as Master Phillips, the beauty of his voice attracting the approbation of Miss Stephens, afterwards Countess of Essex. He studied at the R.A.M., where he was a pupil of Cipriani Potter, and class-fellow of Sterndale Bennett, and eventually became professor of composition at that institution. From Robert Lindley he took lessons on the violoncello, and soon became a member of the orchestras of the Philharmonic, Antient Concerts, Her Majesty's, the Sacred Harmonic Society, etc., besides being regularly engaged at all the great Musical Festivals. He was at different times musical director of the Olympic and Princess's Theatres, composing the music for a variety of dramas. For many years he held the post of organist at St. Katherine's Church, Regent's Park, and at one time conducted a series of concerts at St. Martin's Hall. Music to the farce of ' Borrowing a Husband ' was performed in 1844. In addition to numerous songs he composed a Symphony in F minor, performed at the concerts of the R.A.M. and of the Society of British Musicians. Just before his fatal illness he was engaged on an opera founded on a Rosicrucian story, and a cantata on a Welsh subject. He is buried in Highgate cemetery.    G.

PHILP, ELIZABETH (*b.* Falmouth, 1827 ; *d.* London, Nov. 26, 1885), was educated at

Bristol under the care of Mary Carpenter, and taught singing by Manuel Garcia, receiving instruction in harmony and composition from Hiller at Bristol. She afterwards devoted herself to teaching singing and composition. Her first works were published in 1855, and comprised a Ballad, 'Tell me, the summer stars,' words by Edwin Arnold; also six songs from Longfellow, etc. A great number of her ballads became widely popular. Miss Philp was also the author of *How to sing an English Ballad.*

A. C.

PHILTRE, LE, opera in 2 acts; words by Scribe, music by Auber. Produced Opéra, June 20, 1831; in English—'The Love Spell' —Olympic, Oct. 27 the same year. Donizetti's 'L' Elisir d' amore' has the same subject.   G..

PHINOT (FINOT), DOMĬNICUS, a French composer of the 16th century, of whose life absolutely nothing is known, but who has left enough good work behind him to warrant him considerable respect for his attainments as a musician. It is inferred that he was a native of or otherwise connected with Lyons, from the fact that the volumes containing his own works only were first published there. These are two Books of Motets *a* 5-8 (Lyons, 1547–48), and two Books of Chansons *a* 4 (Lyons, 1548). A Mass of his *a* 4, 'Si bona suscepimus,' was published separately at Paris in 1557, and a book of Psalms and Magnificats *a* 4 at Venice, 1555. He is largely represented in the Nuremberg and other important collections of the time from 1538 onward. From the 'Thesaurus musicus' of 1564 Commer has reprinted in his 'Collectio musicorum Batavorum,' tom. viii., ix., the Lamentation 'Incipit Oratio,' also three motets 'Sancta Trinitas,' 'Jam non dicam,' 'Tanto tempore nobiscum,' all *a* 8, excellent works, written in the Venetian fashion for two choirs answering one another.    J. R. M.

PHIPSON, THOMAS LAMB, D.Sc., F.C.S. (*b.* near Birmingham, May 5, 1833; *d.* Putney, Feb. 22, 1908), a prominent amateur violinist and musical littérateur. His father, Samuel Ryland Phipson—who interested himself in the adoption of several scientific innovations— resided for some years in Brussels, and it was at the University there, that Dr. Phipson obtained his Doctor's degree in Science at the age of 22. Although engaged in scientific labour for over forty years, Phipson occupied his leisure in the earnest study of music, and found time to attain a proficiency as a violin virtuoso, unusual among amateurs. His published works (other than scientific treatises) comprise :

*Biographies of celebrated Violinists ; Bellini and the Opera of 'La Sonnambula' ; Confessions of a Violinist ; Voice and Violin,* and two pamphlets entitled *Guido Papini* and *Musical Sounds produced by Carbon.*

BIBL.—C. J. BOUVERIE, *Scientific and Literary works of Dr. Phipson*: *The Strad.* MAY 1903 ; *Biographie et Dictionnaire des littérateurs et savants français contemporains* ; WYMAN, *Biographical Dictionary.*
E. H.-A.

PHRASE is one of the smallest among the divisions which distinguish the form of a musical work. Where there are distinct portions marked off by closes like full stops, and half closes like stops of less emphasis, the complete divisions are generally called periods, and the lesser divisions phrases. The word is not and can hardly be used with much exactness and uniformity, for sometimes a phrase may be all, as it were, contained in one breath, and sometimes subordinate divisions may be very clearly marked. (See PHRASING.)

C. H. H. P.

PHRASING. A musical composition, consists of a series of short sections of various lengths, called phrases, each more or less complete in itself ; and it is upon the interdependence of these phrases, and upon their connexion with each other, that the intelligibility of music depends. The phrases are analogous to the sentences of a literary composition.

The relationship of the different phrases to each other and to the whole work forms no part of our present subject, but may be studied in the article FORM ; what we have at present to do with is the proper rendering of the phrases in performance, that they may be presented to the listener in an intelligible and attractive form. The process by which this is accomplished is called phrasing, and is perhaps the most important of the various elements which go to make a good and artistic rendering of a musical composition. Rousseau [1] says of it, 'The singer who feels what he sings, and duly marks the phrases and accents, is a man of taste.' But he who can only give the values and intervals of the notes without the sense of the phrases, however accurate he may be, is a mere machine.

Just as the intelligent reading of a literary composition depends chiefly upon two things, accentuation and punctuation, so does musical phrasing depend on the relative strength of the sounds, and upon their connexion with or separation from each other. It is this close relationship of language to music which makes their union in vocal music possible and appropriate, and accordingly when music is allied to words it is necessary that the musical accents should coincide with those of the text, while the separation of the various phrases agrees with the division of the text into separate lines or sentences. In instrumental music, although the same principles underlie its construction, there is no such definite guide as that afforded by the sense of the words in a song, and the phrasing must therefore be the result of a just appreciation on the part of the performer of the general sense of the music, and of the observance of certain marks by which phrasing is indicated.

If we now consider more closely the causes

[1] *Dictionnaire de Musique.*

and consequences of a variety in the strength of the notes of a phrase, we notice in the first place the necessity for an accent on the first note of every bar, and, in certain rhythms, on other parts of the bar also. These regularly recurring accents, though an important part of phrasing, need not be dwelt on here, as they have already been fully treated in the article ACCENT ; but there are certain irregular forms of accent occasionally required by the phrasing, which it is necessary to notice.

In rapid passages, when there are many notes in a bar, it is often necessary to introduce more accents than the ordinary rhythm requires, and the number and frequency of the accents will depend upon the number of changes of harmony upon which the passage is founded. Thus in the first bar of the following example, each couple of notes, after the first four, represents a new harmony, and the bar will consequently require seven accents, while the next two bars will receive the ordinary rhythmic accent on the first note of each group ; and in the fourth bar, since the harmony does not change, two accents will suffice. In the example the place of the accents is shown by the asterisks.

1. MÜLLER, Caprice, Op. 29, No. 4.

Sometimes these extra accents have the effect of appearing to alter or add to the harmonies upon which the passage is founded, as in Ex. 2, where the additional accents demanded by the composer's method of writing in groups of two notes instead of four seem to indicate an alternation of the tonic and subdominant harmonies of C minor, whereas if the passage were played as in Ex. 3 the effect would be that of a single C minor harmony.

2. SCHUMANN, ' In der Nacht.'

On the other hand, there are cases in which the phrasing requires the omission of some of the regular accents. This occurs in quick movements, when, owing to the introduction of a

melody written in notes of great length, two or even four of the actual written bars combine and appear to the listener to form a single bar. This is the case in Ex. 4, the effect of which is precisely that of such a bar as Ex. 5, and the whole phrase of four bars will only require two accents, falling upon places corresponding to the first and third beats of Ex. 5. In the movement quoted the effect of the long bars remains in force during no less than forty-four of the actual written bars, the original 3-4 rhythm coming into use again on the entrance of the syncopated subject.

4. BEETHOVEN, Sonata, Op. 28.

5. Moderato.

As a rule, the accent of a passage follows the grouping, the first note of each group receiving the accent; whenever, therefore, the grouping of a passage consisting of notes of equal length varies, the number of accents in the bar must vary also. Thus in Ex. 6 the first bar will contain four accents, while the third requires but two.

6. BEETHOVEN, Sonata, Op. 14, No. 2.

The signs which govern the connexion or disconnexion of the sounds are the dash (ꞌ) or dot (·), and the curved line indicating legato. The ordinary use of these signs has already been described (see DASH ; LEGATO), and the due observance of them constitutes a most essential part of phrasing, but in addition to this the curved line is used to denote an effect of peculiar importance, called the *Slur*.

When two notes of equal length in quick or moderately quick tempo are joined together by a curved line they are said to be *slurred*, and in playing them a considerable stress is laid on the first of the two, while the second is not only weaker, but is made shorter than it is written, as though followed by a rest.

7. HAYDN, Sonata.

The rule that the first of the slurred notes

receives the accent holds good even when it is in an unaccented part of the bar (Ex. 8). In such a case the slur causes a very effective displacement of accent.

**8. BEETHOVEN, Concerto in C minor.**

*Written.*

*Played.*

Groups of two notes of which the second is the shorter may also be slurred in the same way (Ex. 9), but when the second is the longer note it must be but slightly curtailed, though still perceptibly, and there is no displacement of accent (Ex. 10).

**9. HAYDN, Sonata.**

*Written.*        *Played.*

**10. MENDELSSOHN, Presto Agitato.**

*Written.*

*Played.*

The slur is often used in combination with staccato notes in the same group (Ex. 11). When this is the case the second of the two slurred notes must be played both weaker and shorter than the notes marked staccato.

**11. BEETHOVEN, Concerto in G.**

*Written.*

*Played.*

When the curved line is drawn over two notes of considerable length, or in slow tempo, it is not a slur, but merely a sign of legato (Ex. 12), and the same if it covers a group of three or more notes (Ex. 13). In these cases there is no curtailment of the last note.

**12. BEETHOVEN, Horn Sonata, Op. 17.**

**13. MOZART, Rondo in F.**

But if the curved line is so extended as to include and end upon an accented note, then an effect analogous to the slur is intended, and the last of the notes so covered must be shortened (Ex. 14). A similar effect is also sometimes indicated by varying the grouping of the notes, so that the groups do not agree with the rhythmic divisions of the bar (Ex. 15).

**14. SCHUMANN, Humoresken.**

**15. SCHUMANN, Toccata.**

The great value of definite and characteristic phrasing is perhaps nowhere so strikingly manifested as in the performance of music containing imitation. In all such music the leading part must contain some marked and easily recognisable effect, either of variety of force, as in Ex. 16, or of connexion and disconnexion, as in Ex. 17, and it is by means of the repetition of such characteristic effects in the answering part or parts that the imitation is rendered intelligible, or even perceptible, to the ordinary listener.

**16. HAYDN, Sonata.**

**17. MOZART, Gigue.**

F. T.

The foregoing article deals only with the art of phrasing on the pianoforte, and it is in some ways more important to phrase carefully on keyed instruments than on any others. For on keyed instruments alone, with the exception of the harp and instruments of percussion, is it possible to produce a long, meaningless series of sounds without any articulation or division into rationally balanced sections. On the bowed instruments, as on the human voice and on all kinds of instruments blown with the breath, the length of the bow and the capacity of the human lungs necessitate some kind of division into ' phrases'; and the art of phrasing on these is generally spoken of as if a phrase were always synonymous with the number of notes to be played with one bow or sung with one breath. The skill which average performers on the violin attain in the direction of disguising the interval between the up-and-down strokes of the bow leads some performers to disregard phrasing in passages where it is not specially marked, such as this :

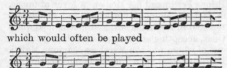

which would often be played

by careless players if their attention were not drawn to the real balance of the phrases by means of slurs, etc. The vocal phrase nearly, but not quite always, is identical with the number of notes to be sung in one breath ; the most pro-minent exception is when in leading back into the opening phrase of a melody the singer chooses to include the first few notes of that opening phrase in the same breath as the pass-age in which the return is made, and then to break the natural phrase in the middle, by breathing in an unusual place. A good ex-ample is the following, from Campra's song ' Charmant Papillon,' as edited by Weckerlin :

que tes bonjours sont courtes! Charmant Pa - pil - lon
etc.

M.

PHRYGIAN MODE (Lat. *modus phrygius* ; *modus mysticus*), the third of the Ecclesiastical Modes. (See MODES, ECCLESIASTICAL.)

PHYSHARMONICA. A little reed organ invented in Vienna in 1818 by Anton Häckel, who intended it to be placed under the key-board of the piano, to sustain the melody. It was increased in size and importance, and by various improvements at length developed into the HARMONIUM (*q.v.*). The name is used in Germany for a free-reed stop in the organ.

A. J. H.

PIACERE, A, ' at pleasure,' is generally prefixed to a cadenza, or cadenza-like passage, in solo music, to indicate that the expressions, and the alterations whether of time or force, are left to the will of the individual performer.

In such cases the accompaniment is generally directed to be played ' colla voce,' ' with the voice,' or ' colla parte,' without regarding the strict time of the composition. ' Ad libitum ' expresses the same thing.

PIACEVOLE, ' agreeable, pleasant.' This word, when used as a musical direction, in-dicates that the piece is to be played in a graceful way, without passion. It has nearly the same meaning as ' grazioso ' or the direction ' con amabilità ' used by Beethoven in the pianoforte sonata, op. 110 (first movement).

M.

PIANETTE ; a very low pianino, or upright pianoforte, introduced in 1857 by Bord, of Paris. The low price and good quality of these instruments soon extended their sale to England, where they received the name ' pianette '—an impossible word in France, ' piano ' being of the masculine gender. The French name, originating in Bord's establish-ment, is ' Bibi,' a workman's corruption of ' Bébé '—' the baby.' Pianettes have been made in London for some years by Broadwood, Cramer and others. Bord's spiral hopper-spring (*ressort à boudin*), used in pianettes, is a useful and very effective contrivance, econo-mical of space. The name is also used, com-monly though incorrectly, of the mechanical pianos of the streets of London.   A. J. H.

PIANGENDO, ' wailingly,' a direction properly only used in vocal music. Its in-strumental equivalent is ' dolente ' or ' con dolore.'   M.

PIANISSIMO, ' very softly.' This direction, which on all ordinary occasions is expressed by *pp*, is sometimes, but not very often, written in full—as a rule, to emphasise the fact of its presence in cases where it would least be ex-pected. Beethoven often uses the full direc-tion simultaneously with the abbreviation, as in the 10th variation of the thirty-three on a valse by Diabelli, op. 120, in which variation may also be found an instance of one of his chief characteristics, the sudden leap from *ff* to *pp* in the 31st bar. Since Beethoven's time, the practice has become very common of using *ppp*, for what Weber in the beginning of the overture to ' Oberon ' calls ' Il tutto pianissimo possibile.' It is equivalent to the direction sometimes met with ' *quasi niente* ' (' as it nothing '). Berlioz goes so far as to use the sign *pppp* ; Verdi, in his Requiem, has gone even farther, and at one point uses *ppppp*. The reticence of Mendelssohn, who says, ' I particularly dislike *ppp*,'[1] was not imitated by Tchaikovsky, whose *pppppp* in the Pathetic Symphony will be recalled.

PIANO, ' soft.' This word, expressed in general by its initial *p*, is used to denote the least degree of strength except *pianissimo*. It is used, as is the case with most other directions,

[1] Letters to Moscheles, p. 96.

in full only when it is necessary to draw particular attention to its presence, or where it is unlikely that it should stand ; for instance, in the finale of Beethoven's PF. sonata, op. 2, No. 1, where the second subject is labelled ' Sempre piano e dolce.' *Mezzo piano* (abbreviated *mp*) denotes a degree of force slightly louder than *piano*. Beethoven was very fond of using a ' sudden *piano* ' directly after a *forte* or *fortissimo*, and the occurrence of the sudden dynamic change is one of his most easily recognised characteristics. (See FORTE.)    M.

PIANOFORTE—or FORTE PIANO, as often written in the 18th century—an instrument of Italian origin. The earliest mention of the name appears in records of the family of Este, in the letters of a musical instrument maker named Paliarino, dated Good Friday, June 27 and Dec. 31, 1598, and addressed to Alfonso II., Duke of Modena (see Table of Dates at end of this article). They were found in 1879 by Count L. F. Valdrighi, custos of the Biblioteca Estense, at Modena ; and the discovery was immediately announced in the Florentine musical paper, *Boccherini*. In August of that year Valdrighi published the text of the letters, with an essay, in a pamphlet entitled *Musurgiana* (Olivari, Modena, 1879). In the first letter Paliarino mentions the recovery of ' the instrument Piano e Forte, with the organ underneath ' [1] ; in the second, ' the recovery from certain priests, with other instruments, of the Piano e Forte above mentioned and another Piano e Forte on which the late Duke Alfonso had played.' [2] Here are two instruments each distinctly named ' Piano e Forte ' (correcting Paliarino's uncertain spelling). In the second letter the same Hippolito Cricca, detto Paliarino, as he there signs himself (or Pagliarini as he spells his name elsewhere), seizes the opportunity of his brother's visit to Venice, to ask for sundry materials to be procured there, as needful for repairs, and for building a new ' Pian e Forte ' ; namely, lime tree, boxwood and ebony for keys, cypress for the belly, brass wire, German glue, etc. etc. In Paliarino's inventory of the Duke's keyed instruments, also given in Count Valdrighi's appendix to his essay, there are, including organs, fifty-two,[3] but only one ' Piano e Forte,' the one with the organ beneath, as specially distinguished ; the other, and perhaps more, being possibly recorded under the simple name ' instrument ' ( ' istromento '), which is used to describe eleven of the fifty-two. The clavicembalo or cembalo (harpsichord) and spinetta (spinet) might also

have been classed under this general designation, yet Paliarino separates them. We can come to no conclusion from these names as to what kind of instrument this Piano e Forte was. It was most likely, as suggested by Sig. Cesare Ponsicchi in the *Boccherini* (1879, No. 6), a harpsichord with a contrivance for dynamic change ; but whether hammers were applied, making it a real pianoforte, we are at present unable to say. The ' gravicembalo col piano e forte ' of Cristofori of Padua, a hundred years later, may not really have been the first attempt to make a hammer - harpsichord ; indeed Cristofori's invention seems almost too completely successful to have been the first conception of this instrument—a dulcimer with keys.[4]

CRISTOFORI'S INVENTION.—We must now transfer our attention from Modena to Florence, and skip from 1598 to 1709, when we find Prince Ferdinand dei Medici,[5] a lover of music, in fact an eminent musician, and deeply interested in mathematical and mechanical questions, accepting at the request of three scholars, one of whom was the Marchese Scipione Maffei, the protection of a quarterly publication intended for learned and cultivated readers, viz. the *Giornale dei letterati d' Italia*. This patronage was the result of a personal visit of Maffei to Florence, where he met with Bartolomeo Cristofori, harpsichord-maker and custodian of the Prince's musical instruments, and was shown by him four specimens of a new harpsichord with piano and forte, the invention and make of Cristofori. Of these, three were of the usual long shape ; the other was different, we know not in what way, but a detailed account of Cristofori's invention, written by Scipione Maffei,[6] appeared in the *Giornale* in 1711, with a diagram, from a rough sketch, of his hammer-action. He calls the inventor Cristofali, which form of the name was generally followed, but an autograph and the inscriptions upon the pianofortes of his make are decisive evidence in favour of the real name being Cristofori.[7] There is no doubt about Cristofori having made these instruments under the patronage of Prince Ferdinand, who had brought him from Padua some time about 1690. (See CRISTOFORI.)

We owe a debt of gratitude to Maffei for his record of the invention, which he reproduced in the collection of his works entitled *Rime e prose*. 1719. The reprint has been the cause of a misconception of the date of the invention,

---

[1] ' Cossi io mi ritrovo l' orghano di carta, et l' istrumento Pian e Forte con l' orgnano di sotto. . . .'

[2] ' L' altezza vostra sappia che mi ritrovo del' suo che lo recuperrato da questi Pretti l' horggano di carta, l' istrumento Piane e Forte con l' horggano disotto, un altro istrumento di dua registri et il Piane e Fortte, quello che adoprava il Ser. Sig. Duca Alfonso buona memoria. . . .'

[3] This large number, as it seems to us, was not then remarkable for a prince to have : a hundred years later Prince Ferdinand dei Medici owned at least forty. See Appendix C, p. 101, to Puliti's *Cenni storici delle vita del Sermo Ferdinando dei Medici* (Florence, 1874).

[4] The small piano of 1610 in the collection of M. René-Savoye of Paris (see Table at end of this article) may be a specimen. A 15th-century drawing of the keyed dulcimer is in the National Library of Paris (No. 7295).

[5] Three of his instruments (two by Cristofori) were included in the Florentine Collection (see COLLECTIONS) of the Signori Kraus and exhibited by them in the Paris Exhibition of 1878.

[6] The complete text of Maffei's article, in the original language, with an indifferent English translation, is to be found in Rimbault's *The Pianoforte* (Cocks, London, 1860)—the faults of translation being most obvious in the technical terms.

[7] This has been adopted in Florence on the memorial stone (See CRISTOFORI, Vol. I. pp. 757 .)

through want of reference to the earlier publication, which was anonymous. An accurate German translation was made at the time by Koenig, and published in Mattheson's *Musikalische Kritik*, vol. iii. p. 340 (Hamburg, 1725). This early translation has been reprinted by Dr. Oscar Paul in his *Geschichte des Klaviers*, p. 105 (Leipzig, 1868), and may be referred to with confidence by those who know German and do not know Italian.

We reproduce the diagram of Cristofori's

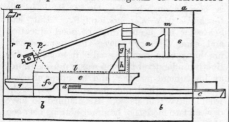

FIG. 1.

*a* is the string; *b* the key-bottom; *c* the first lever, or key. There is a pad, *d*, upon the key, to raise a second lever, *e*, which is pivoted upon *f*. *g* is the hopper—Cristofori's *linguetta mobile*—which, controlled by the springs *i* and *l*, effects the escape, or immediate drop, of the hammer from the strings after a blow has been struck, although the key is still kept down by the finger. The hopper is centred at *h*. *m* is a rack or comb on the beam, *s*, where the butt, *n*, of the hammer, *o*, is centred. In a state of rest the hammer is supported by a cross, or fork, *p*, of silk thread. On the depression of the key, *c*, the tail, *q*, of the second lever, *e*, draws away the damper, *r*, from the strings, leaving them free to vibrate.

action as the kernel of this part of our subject, the action being the equivalent to the violinist's bow; as the instrument itself is the equivalent of the violin, though stopped by a mechanical construction instead of the fingers of the player's left hand. We follow Maffei's lettering of the parts; a lettering which will be adhered to throughout.

The reader will observe the smallness of the

hammer-head and the absence of what is called a 'check,' to arrest the hammer in its rebound; and also of any control but springs over the forward movement, or escapement, of the hopper. To admit of this machinery—so much more complicated than the simple action of the harpsichord—being taken out, Cristofori inverted the tuning-pin block (technically the 'wrestplank'), and attached the wires to the tuningpins ('wrest-pins'), at their lower ends, as in the harp. Being obliged to use heavier strings, which exerted a greater pulling force or tension, to withstand the impact of his hammers, he found it necessary to remove the pins to which the further ends of the strings were attached (the 'hitchpins'), from their old place on the sound-board of the harpsichord, to a stiff rail of wood ('string-block') built round the angle-side and narrow end of the case. Without this alteration his instruments could not have stood in tune and would soon have collapsed.

Two pianofortes of Cristofori's make are fortunately still existing. The earlier one, dated 1720, belonged to Signora Ernesta Mocenni Martelli of Florence (now in the Metropolitan Museum, New York), and is described by Leto Puliti, with illustrations of the action, in the essay referred to above. The second, dated 1726, was in the Kraus collection at Florence; then in the Heyer museum, Cologne; and now (1926) at Leipzig (see *PLATE XL*. No. 2). It happens to be more complete than that of Signora Martelli, because the hammerheads remain in their original condition, as may be seen by comparing Fig. 1 with Fig. 2, which represents the action of the latter.

Both instruments, the 1720 and the 1726,

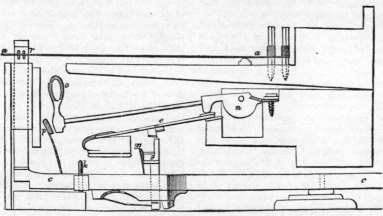

FIG. 2.

On further comparing the two diagrams we observe in No. 2 first the extension of the lever or key, *c*; the transformation of the second lever, *e*, into what is technically an 'underhammer,' removing the hopper, *g*, from direct attack upon the butt, *n*, a change in the wrong direction, but probably necessitated by the want of a regulating button and screw to the hopper. Other modifications will be noticed; one is a pin, *k*, passing through the back part of the key (replacing the piece of whalebone behind the key; see drawing of Zumpe's action, Fig. 5), a step towards the front pin, since used to steady the lateral motion. The damper, *r*, now lies upon the strings, dropping, wedgefashion, between the two unisons. But the great improvement upon the first action is the substitution of the check, *p*—Cristofori's *paramartello*, which graduates the rebound of the hammer according to the blow—for the mere support of the silk threads which formerly received it when it fell.

have the overdampers and check, the latter the mechanical completion of the action. That of 1720 has been restored by Sig. Ponsicchi, a pianoforte-maker, who has himself given, in *Il pianoforte, sua origine e sviluppo (con tavole)*, Florence, 1876, a valuable contribution to the literature of the instrument. Both pianofortes are bichord, and have white natural keys, but the compass differs, the earlier having four and a half octaves, C to F, and the later only four octaves, C to C, the old normal compass equivalent to the human voice.

Cristofori died in 1731, aged 66, and in 1730, the year before his death, his assistant, Giovanni Ferrini, made a pianoforte which has become famous through Burney's reference to it. It was bought by Elisabetta Farnese, Queen of Spain; and by her bequeathed to the singer Farinelli, who inscribed upon it in letters of gold, 'Raffaello d' Urbino,' and esteemed it more highly than any other in his collection of keyed instruments. Burney played upon it in 1771. There were other pupils or followers of Cristofori; we hear of Geronimo of Florence, and Gherardi of Padua, but an end soon came to pianoforte making in Italy; possibly, as suggested by Puliti, from the difficulty felt by clavicembalists of acquiring the touch, and which made them decry the new instrument— or from the imperfection of the means for escapement. Be this as it may, the fruits of the invention were to be gathered and garnered elsewhere; but the invention itself remains with Italy.

OTHER CLAIMANTS.—The idea suggested by the vague character of the Estense 'piano e forte,' that there were perhaps attempts to construct a hammer action before Cristofori, we find strengthened by the known fact that two men in two different countries outside Italy were endeavouring, at the very time of his success, to produce a similar invention to his. The names of Marius and Schroeter,[1] the former a French harpsichord-maker, the latter a German musician, have been put forward to claim the credit of the absolute invention on the strength of certain experiments in that direction. Marius, in February 1716, submitted, perhaps a pianoforte, and certainly four models for actions of 'clavecins à maillets,' or hammer harpsichords, the description and engravings of which were published, nineteen years later, in Nos. 172, 173 and 174 of *Machines et inventions approuvées par l'Académie Royale des Sciences, tome troisième. Depuis 1713 jusqu'en 1719. A Paris MDCCXXXV,* and are to be found *in extenso* in the works of Rimbault and Puliti. Both overstriking and understriking apparatus had occurred to Marius, and his drawings included the alteration of an

upright harpsichord, and the addition of a register of hammers to an horizontal one—rude contrivances of which no subsequent use was or could be made. His object in introducing hammers was an economical one—to save the expense and trouble of constantly requilling the harpsichord. Schroeter must be dismissed less summarily, owing to the frequently repeated statement that he was the actual inventor of the pianoforte; reasserted with a fervid advocacy in which the bias of patriotism is conspicuous, by Dr. Oscar Paul in his *Geschichte des Klaviers*, p. 82. But had Schroeter not been a man of good education and some literary power, his name would not have been remembered; it must be distinctly understood that he was a musician, not an instrument-maker; and he never made a pianoforte or had one made for him, or he would have told us so. He claimed to have devised two models of hammer-actions between 1717 and 1721, which he afterwards neglected, but years afterwards, in 1738, being vexed that his name was not connected with the rising success of the pianoforte, he addressed a letter to Mizler which was printed in the *Neu-eröffnete musikalische Bibliothek* (Leipzig, 1736–54, vol. iii. pp. 474-6). He repeated his claim, with a drawing of one of his actions (then first published), in 1763, in Marpurg's *Kritische Briefe über Tonkunst* (Berlin, 1764, vol. iii. p. 85), showing, although Gottfried Silbermann had been dead ten years, and Cristofori thirty-two, the animus to which we owe these naïve and interesting communications. (See SCHROETER.) In 1715, when Schroeter was only 16 years old, being entrusted with good pupils in Dresden, he found that their study upon the expressive clavichord was thrown away when they came to show off before their friends upon so different an instrument as the inexpressive harpsichord. Shortly after this, there came to Dresden the great dulcimer virtuoso, Pantaleone HEBENSTREIT, whose performances astonished Schroeter, and at the same time convinced him that it was by hammers only that the harpsichord could be made expressive. At this time, like Marius, he could hardly have known that pianofortes had not only been invented, but had for some years been made in Italy, although the intercourse prevailing between that country and Dresden might have brought the knowledge to him. But the inferiority of Schroeter's action to Cristofori's at once exonerates him from plagiarism; and the same applies also to Marius, whose ideas were of even less value mechanically than Schroeter's.

Schroeter gives us no description of his overstriking 'Pantaleon': we may conclude that he suspected the difficulties, not to this day surmounted, of an action in which the hammers are placed above the strings. Of the understriking action, his 'Pianoforte,' he has

[1] It is of interest to note in the set of action models seen in the Kraus exhibit of 1878, how keenly inventors were striving for perfection in the pianoforte. The following dates are indicative: Cristofori (1711), Marius (1716), Schroeter (1721), Stein (1725), Zumpe (1754).

given us full particulars and a drawing here reproduced :

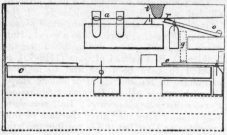

FIG. 3.

*a* is the string ; *c* is the key ; *e*, a second lever ; *g*, a jack to raise the hammer ; *o*, the hammer itself, clothed at the tail, *r*, to serve for a damper. The play, or space, between the jack and the hammer-shank permitted, as in the early square-piano action of Zumpe (which may have been partly derived from Schroeter's idea), the rebound, or escapement, of the hammer.

For his second drawing, a later fancy of no practical value, it is sufficient to refer to Paul or Puliti.

But no sustained tone was possible, owing to the position of the damper, which resumed its place the moment the hammer fell. The rapid repetition of a note, after the old fashion of harps, mandolines and dulcimers, would have been the only expedient to prolong it. Marius's defect was the opposite one ; he had no dampers whatever. But Schroeter had the great merit of perceiving the future use of iron as a resisting power in pianofortes ; he invented a *Widerstandseisen*, or resisting iron, a bar of metal here marked *t*, which was placed transversely over the wrest-plank, rested firmly upon the strings, and formed the straight bridge. We do not know to whose piano this was applied, and it can hardly have been a part of his original conception. It is more likely to have occurred to him from observation of the defects in pianofortes, as did his scheme of stringing by proceeding from one string to a note in the bass, to four strings to a note in the treble ; graduated with two and three unisons of so many notes each, between.

The allusions in Schroeter's letter to an 'ingenious man at Dresden' ('ein anderer sinnreicher Mann') point to Gottfried Sil-BERMANN, who, in the second half of the 18th century, was generally considered to be the inventor of the pianoforte. As late as 1780 De la Borde [1] said that

'The Clavecin Pianoforte was invented about twenty years ago at Freyberg in Saxony by M. Silbermann. From Saxony the invention penetrated to London, whence we obtain nearly all those that are sold in Paris.'

It has been hitherto accepted in Germany and elsewhere that Silbermann adopted Schroeter's idea, and made it practicable ; employing in fact Schroeter's action, with some improvement. Welcker von Gontershausen, *Der*

[1] *Essai sur la musique ancienne et moderne.*

*Clavierbau* (Frankfort, 1870), says, p. 171, 'The Silbermanns always used the action invented by Schroeter.' It is right, however, to warn the inquirer who may meet with Welcker's books, that they are not, either in text or engravings, always to be depended on.

We must now revert to Koenig's translation of Maffei's account of Cristofori's invention, published at Hamburg in 1725, an invention recorded and attributed exclusively to its author in Walther's *Musikalisches Lexicon* (Leipzig, 1732). It was thus early made public in Germany, and we think we shall now be able to show that Gottfried Silbermann followed Cristofori rather than Schroeter when he began to make pianofortes. He is said [2] to have made two as early as 1726 (the year after Mattheson's publication of Koenig's translation), and to have shown them [3] to J. S. Bach, who condemned them for the weakness of their trebles and their heavy touch. This adverse judgment so much annoyed Silbermann that for some years he made, or at least showed, no more ; but ultimately he gained Bach's unlimited praise, though it does not appear that the great composer ever had a pianoforte of his own (Spitta, *Bach*, Engl. tr. ii. 46). Some time after this he seems to have made an instrument for the Prince of Schwarzburg-Rudolstadt, which Schroeter happened to see in 1753 ; but, before that, two had been made, admitted to be copies of it, by Lenker of Rudolstadt, and had met with great praise. We may therefore assume the success of the original. In connexion with this it is not surprising that Frederick the Great (especially when we remember that he had in his service C. P. E. Bach, who owned a most beautiful Silbermann clavichord) should have acquired and placed in the music-room in the Stadtschloss at Potsdam, a pianoforte by that maker. (See SILBERMANN.) He is indeed said to have had more,[4] but no musical anecdote is better known than the visit of J. S. Bach, and his eldest son, to Potsdam in May 1747 ; his warm and almost unceremonious reception by the King, and the extempore performances which took place, in which we may be sure that the pianoforte would not be neglected.

[2] Adlung, *Musica mechanica*, ii. 116 f.
[3] Perhaps in 1733 or 1736, when Bach was in Dresden (see *History of the Pianoforte*, by A. J. Hipkins, p. 102).
[4] We quote from Forkel : 'The King ... urged Bach (then known as the Old Bach) to try his Silbermann Fortepianos then standing in various rooms of the palace.' A footnote adds—'The pianofortes of the Freyberg Silbermann pleased the King so much, that he made up his mind to buy them all. He got fifteen of them together. They must now (1802) be all standing about, of no use, in different corners of the palace.' Recent search has failed to discover these instruments. Fifteen was a large number for Silbermann to have made and had by him, and it must be remembered that Forkel wrote at second hand, and long after the event, although we have the statement of an eye-witness, W. Friedemann, Bach's eldest son. Gerber's *Lexicon*, published 1792, art. 'Silbermann,' states that the King of Prussia had one pianoforte made for him, before Bach's visit, and this pleasing him he ordered others for Berlin. Mooser's *Silbermann der Orgelbauer* (Strasburg, 1857) affirms that they were six in number, and that one more was acquired after Silbermann's death. Burney saw only one at Potsdam, and that not five-and-twenty years after Bach's visit. In 1881 the writer examined the instruments, one of which is in each of the Potsdam palaces associated with Frederick,—the Stadtschloss, Sans Souci and the Neues Palais.

In 1773, Burney (*Tour*, ii. 145) published an account of his own visit to Potsdam. In the Neues Palais there he saw a Silbermann pianoforte ; in other rooms he may have seen the Tschudi harpsichords of 1766. The pianoforte had not yet prevailed over the harpsichord, these London instruments being of later date. But what is of supreme interest is that the same piano which Burney saw was still in Frederick's music-room in 1880. True, the instrument bore no inscription or date, but since everything in the room remained as it was at the time of the King's death, there was no reason to doubt its genuineness ; and it had the whole weight of local tradition in its favour. An examination, made for the writer through the kind permission of Count Seckendorff by Bechstein, the well-known pianoforte-maker of Berlin, revealed the Cristofori action ! Here is Bechstein's drawing,[1] and a comparison of it with that of Cristofori's action (Fig. 2) is at once convincing.

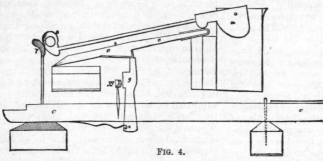

FIG. 4.

It will be observed that Bechstein, as frequently happens in drawing pianoforte actions, has omitted the damper, but that is of no consequence.

The instrument is placed upon an elaborate stand having an extra leg at the angle side, thus reminding us of Mozart's grand piano, by Walter, at Salzburg. (See *PLATE LIX*. No. 1.) The case is of oak ; the strings contain 1½ octave of brass wire, not overspun, in the bass ; the compass is nearly five octaves (F–E), and the keys are covered with ebony for the natural notes, and with ivory for the sharps. Before leaving the only recorded instances of the great J. S. Bach's connexion with the pianoforte, we may remark that the special character of the instrument does not seem to have struck him; there can be no doubt of his having shared the opinion of his son Emanuel, who regarded the pianoforte as only ' fit for rondos,' and always expressed his preference for the clavichord. It was by the youngest brother and pupil of Emanuel, John Christian, known as the ' London Bach,' that a decided preference was first shown

for the pianoforte over the clavichord and harpsichord.

The pianofortes to which we have hitherto alluded were all, like harpsichords, of the ' wing ' or ' tail ' shape (English, *grand piano* ; German, *Flügel* ; French, *piano à queue* ; Ital. *piano a coda*). The distinguished organ-builder, C. E. Frederici of Gera (1712–79), is reputed to have been the first to make a pianoforte in the clavichord or oblong shape (English, *square piano* ; German, *tafelförmiges Piano* ; French, *piano carré* ; Ital. *pianoforte a tavolino*). Fischhof[2] gives the date of this invention as 1760, but this is possibly too late. Frederici named his square piano ' Fortbien,' perhaps a pun upon Forte Biano, in which form he may often have heard the Italian name pronounced by German lips. No writer has described one of these, or appears to have seen one. He may have contrived the action as an improvement on the idea which Schroeter first published in Marpurg in 1764, and Zumpe introduced here in 1765–1766. From comparison of dates and other circumstances, we are, however, inclined to conclude that Zumpe did not imitate Frederici, but that the latter may rather have used that rudimentary German action which Stein in the next decade improved for grand pianos by the addition of a mechanical escapement.[3] This action of a centred hammer with movable axis, the blow caused by contact of the hammer-tail with a back-touch, and without escapement, exists in a drawing of a patent of Sébastien Érard's dating as late as 1801,[4] which shows how general this action had been. Mahillon kindly communicated to the writer that there is still a square piano existing with this action, belonging to M. Gosselin, of Brussels. The style of the furniture of the case and the fragments of painting remaining would make this instrument French, and place the date, according to these authorities, without doubt in the reign of Louis Quinze. It has five stops, to raise the dampers (now unfortunately gone) in two sections, to bring on a ' Pianozug ' in two sections, or, apparently, as a whole. The natural keys are black. Now J. Andreas Stein worked in Paris about 1758, and later J. Heinrich Silbermann of Strassburg made

---

[1] A drawing of the external appearance of the instrument, supplied from the same source, was included in former editions of this Dictionary.                                                          c.

[2] *Versuch einer Geschichte des Clavierbaues*, Vienna, 1853, p. 16.
[3] It must be remarked that Welcker von Gontershausen, whose technical works (published 1856 and 1870, the earlier much the better) on the construction of the Pianoforte are worthy of praise, is not always to be depended upon when the question is historical. He attributes this rudimentary action, of which he gives drawings, to Schroeter and the Silbermanns—apparently without foundation.
[4] Érard's claim to improvement was that the travelling distance of the hammer could be regulated by a springing back-touch, by which the depth of front-touch was made to depend upon the strength expended by the player.

pianos which were sent to Paris and highly thought of. We regret that we have no further historical evidence to offer about this action, so interesting as the foundation of the celebrated ' Deutsche Mechanik ' of the Viennese grand pianos.

THE SQUARE PIANO.—Johannes Zumpe [1] is introduced by Burney, in Rees's *Cyclopædia* (1819, article ' Harpsichord '), as a German who had long worked for the harpsichord-maker Shudi, and was the first to construct small pianos of the shape and size of the virginal. (See *PLATE XL.* No. 1.) He goes on to say that there was such a demand for Zumpe's square pianos that there was scarcely a house in the kingdom where a keyed instrument had ever had admission but was supplied with one of them, and there was nearly as great a call for them in France as in England. Pohlmann, another German, fabricated for those whom Zumpe was unable to supply. There are instruments by

nearly all square piano actions during forty years. The writer of the article ' Pianoforte ' in the fourth edition of the *Encyclopædia Britannica* (1810) claims the invention of Zumpe's action for the Rev. William MASON, composer, poet and writer on church music, and the intimate friend of the poet Gray. Born in 1724, Mason died in 1797, and was therefore, inventor or not, a witness to the introduction of the pianoforte into England, and to its development to a certain grade—that namely of pure wooden construction. The Encyclopædia writer cannot be considered as an authority, although in this case he may have got his information on the point direct from Mason. Apart from such conjecture we have only sure evidence that Mason was one of Zumpe's early patrons.[4]

Zumpe's or Mason's action, drawn from the instrument of 1766, is shown in Fig. 5.

Square pianos were occasionally fitted with

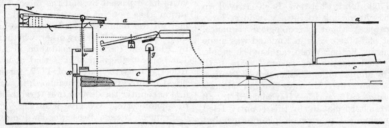

FIG. 5

In the key, *c*, is fixed the jack, *g*, a wire with a leather stud on the top, known by the workmen as the ' old man's head.' This raises the hammer, *o*; the damper, *r*, is lifted by a whalebone jack, *v*, called the ' mopstick,' placed near the end of the key, and is brought back to its place by the whalebone spring, *w*; a third piece of whalebone, *x*, projecting from the end of the key, works in a groove, and serves exactly as in the clavichord to keep the key steady, there being no front key-pin. The two balance-rail key-pins shown in the drawing belong to two keys, the natural and sharp, and indicate the different balancing desiderated in all keyboards by the different lengths of the natural and sharp keys. The dampers were divided into treble and bass sections, raised bodily by two drawstops when not required, there being as yet no pedal.

both these makers still existing; the oldest Zumpe piano known is dated 1766,[2] was formerly Sir George Smart's, and is now owned by Messrs. Broadwood. No number has been found in it; yet it can hardly be the first of Zumpe's make, since he would not have been so bold as to begin with dividing his black notes and thus have eighteen keys in the octave, as he has in this case. The late Mr. Taphouse of Oxford had one with the usual chromatic scale of thirteen in the octave, inscribed ' Johannes Zumpe, Londini, Fecit 1767, Princes Street, Hanover Square,' and with XVIIII stamped on the back of the name-board.[3] The action which Zumpe invented or adopted was simple and facile, having reference to the published model of Schroeter in Marpurg, 1764, in its artless escapement. It became the norm for

drawers for music, and were sometimes made to look like tables : the writer has seen a table piano, in style of furniture about 1780, but which bore on a label the name and date, Zumpe, 1760.[5] This cannot be accepted as authentic, but the action is of so much interest that it must be described, as publication may

[1] It has been suggested that Zumpe may have been an altered name from Zumpt, to suit English habits of pronunciation, as the contemporary Shudi was corrupted from Tschudi, Kirkman from Kirchmann, etc.
[2] Fétis began his musical studies on a Zumpe square piano of 1762.
[3] Mr. Williamson of Guildford had, in 1879, a square piano by Zumpe & Buntebart, dated 1769. In 1776 the firm was Zumpe & Mayer—the instruments remaining the same, almost clavichords, with hammer actions, and nearly five octaves compass, G-F.

[4] Mason appears to have first possessed a pianoforte in 1755. Writing from Hanover to the poet Gray he says : ' Oh, Mr. Gray ! I bought at Hamburg such a pianoforte and so cheap ! It is a harpsichord too of two unisons, and the jacks serve as mutes when the pianoforte stop is played, by the cleverest mechanism imaginable,—won't you buy my Kirkman ? ' (meaning his harpsichord by that maker). Gray, writing to Mason in May 767, after the death of Mrs. Mason, says : ' You will tell me what to do with your Zumpe, which has amused me much here. If you would have it sent down I had better commit it to its maker, who will tune it and pack it up. Dr. Long has bought the fellow to it. The base is not quite of a piece with the treble, and the higher notes are somewhat dry and sticky. The rest discourses very eloquent music.' Mason had married in the autumn of 1765. It is possible that he bought his Zumpe then, or if not, in the course of the ensuing year, 1766. (*The Correspondence of Thomas Gray and William Mason*, London, 1853, pp. 33 and 381.)
[5] Shortly before his death, Mr. A. J. Hipkins, the writer of this article, became possessed of a very remarkable little Viennese piano, not dated or named, but judged by the style of ornamentation to be of about the date 1760. It has single strings from B, to G ; and double strings from A♭ to f‴. It is the ' old man's head ' form of escapement, and a curious underdamping arrangement, with double-forked flannel. There is a knee-lever on the right, which, pressing down those dampers away from the strings, produces exactly the same effect as the modern sustaining pedal, and on the left-hand side is another lever, which applies a bar with flannel from above, and so mutes the tone. There are black naturals, and the arrangement of the strings is almost identical with that of the clavichord. It was left to Mr. Hipkins by Mrs. Rudolf Lehmann.

be the means of ultimately identifying, its origin. The instrument belonged to Mr. Herbert Bowman, and the diagram is from a careful drawing by Mr. Robert Maitland.

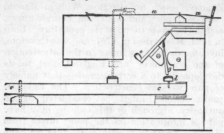

FIG. 6.

Here the pad $d$ upon the key $c$, is regulated in height by a screw, and when raised lifts the jack $g$, which is attached by a leather hinge to the hammer $o$. The damper is conjectural; but Mr. Maitland has probably indicated it correctly. The special feature is the fact of the vicarious space for an escapement being below the jack instead of above it, as in Zumpe's 'old man's head.'

In 1759 John Christian Bach arrived in London. According to Burney, who is, however, careless about chronological sequence, the first pianoforte seen in England was made in Rome by Father Wood, an English monk. It remained unique for several years until copied by an instrument-maker named Plenius. 'After Bach's arrival,' says Burney (Rees's *Cyclopædia*, 1819, article 'Harpsichord'), 'all the harpsichord-makers in this country tried their mechanical powers on pianofortes, but the first attempts were always on the large size.' From a previous sentence we learn that Backers, a harpsichord-maker of the second rank, constructed several pianofortes, 'but the tone, with all the delicacy of Schroeter's touch, lost the spirit of the harpsichord and gained nothing in sweetness.' Now Schroeter the pianist (not he who has been already mentioned) came to London in 1772.

James Shudi Broadwood, writing in the *Gentleman's Magazine* in 1812, attributes the invention of the grand piano in 1772 to a Dutchman, Americus Baccers (accurately Backers [1]); and again, in his *MS. Notes and Observations* (written 1838; printed for private circulation

who got it from Italy. It is so similar in many respects to the action of Stein that it is tempting to believe it to be by him.

E. J. H[S].

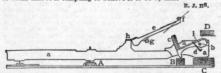

A, Block in the key balance rail; B is the hammer rest; C is the key rest; D is a fixed block which catches the hammer butt, causing the hammer head to strike the string when the key is depressed—a set off; $a$ is the key; $b$ is the hammer butt; $c$ is the hammer head covered with leather; $d$ is a guide to keep the hammer from shifting laterally—made of wire; $e$ is the damper arm; $f$, damper head; $g$, damper rest (along a wire); $h$, hinge of damper; $i$, pivot of the hammer butt. Not shown in the figure is a mute, actuated by a lever moved by the knee. There are only three moving parts—key, hammer, damper.

[1] Burney, in 1773, praised Backers's pianofortes. We have seen a name-board inscribed 'Americus Backers, Inventor et Fecit, ‖ermyn Street, London, 1776.'

1862) he repeats this statement about Backers, but with a later date—about 1776. This probably alludes to the pianoforte of which the name-board is referred to in footnote 1, at that time still existing. The earlier date is nearer the mark, but the 'invention' must be interpreted as meaning a new action, an improvement on that of Cristofori (which may have been transmitted through Silbermann), or rather on Cristofori's first idea, by the contrivance of the regulating button and screw which rendered his direct action certain, and was ultimately known as the 'English action' —as Backers's was always called abroad. Henry Fowler Broadwood (1811–93), in a footnote to his father's statement in the 'MS. notes,' communicates the family tradition that his grandfather, John Broadwood, with his apprentice, Robert Stodart, assisted Backers to bring this action to perfection—a word which he may use unreservedly, as more than a hundred years have passed by and the direct 'English action' has not yet been superseded. It has met all the demands of advanced technique: Chopin preferred it to any other, whether made by Pleyel in Paris or Broadwood in London. The earliest diagram of it is that attached to Robert Stodart's patent of 1777, for a combined pianoforte and harpsichord, in which we first encounter the designation 'grand' applied to a pianoforte. We give it in Fig. 7, with a diagram of Messrs. Broadwood's grand action of 1880—the dampers omitted in both cases.

The earliest public notice of a pianoforte in England is in the year 1767, when a Covent Garden playbill [2] chronicles its first appearance in an orchestra, under date of May 16, as an accompanying instrument. After Act 1 of the 'Beggar's Opera' the bill announces that 'Miss Brickler will sing a favourite song from "Judith," accompanied by Mr. Dibdin, on a new instrument call'd Piano Forte.' As a solo instrument it appears to have been used for the first time in London on June 2, 1768, at the Thatched House, by John Christian Bach.[3] In 1770, Mr. Burney, nephew of Dr. Burney, was appointed 'to the pianoforte' at Drury Lane. We do not know what pianos they were, or of whose make. They may have been by Backers, but to have had his new action we should have to put back Broadwood's earliest date.

During the period ending with 1770, the first division to be observed in the history of the pianoforte, there had been no composition devoted to and proper to the instrument; and there could have been little or no real pianoforte-playing. The new instrument was too unimportant as compared with the harpsichord, and in its then condition presented to the touch differences too essential, and difficulties too obstinate, to permit of the perception of those

[2] In Messrs. Broadwood's possession.
[3] Pohl's *Haydn in London*.

remarkable attributes upon which the highest style in writing and treatment was ultimately to be based. The first real pianoforte music was published in London in 1773.[1] This was the famous op. 2 of Muzio CLEMENTI (three Sonatas), composed three years before, when he was only 18 years old. In these pieces the young composer divined the technique and instrumental treatment to which the pianoforte was responsive, and there founded the true school of pianoforte-playing.

We have dwelt thus long upon London, not

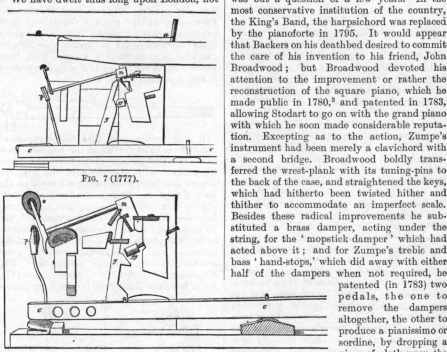

FIG. 7 (1777).

FIG. 8 (1880).

The differences in the two cases are in the proportions and forms of the parts; the principle is the same in both, the only addition in the present action—and that not essential—being a strip of felt beneath the butt of the hammer, to assist the promptness of the checking. The differences of both from that of Cristofori are evident and important. The second lever or underhammer is done away with, and the jack, *g*, now acts directly in a notch of the butt, *n*. The regulating button and screw controlling the escapement are at *gg*. Simplicity and security are combined.

merely because this is an English Dictionary, but because at this epoch London held the first place in harpsichord and pianoforte making. In the decade 1765–75 there can be no doubt about the importance given to the square piano by Zumpe, and the final start given to the grand piano by Backers; soon to be the means of success to BROADWOOD and to STODART, who had helped him in his invention. The great harpsichord-makers, Jacob KIRKMAN and Burkhard SHUDI,[2] had at this time brought their noble instruments to the highest

[1] J. C. Bach published a sonata for the Battle of Rosbach, ' pour le clavecin ou forte-piano,' about 1757–58, not later than the latter year.
[2] Shudi had his name properly written, Tschudi, on the Potsdam harpsichords.

point of development and excellence; and the harpsichord was now endowed with a storehouse of noble compositions, from which the pianoforte, having as yet none of its own, had for a time to borrow. We can understand how little these eminent makers, having realised fortune and done their work in life, would care for the new instrument and its improvement. But with J. C. Bach, Schroeter and Clementi on the one side, and Backers, Stodart and Broadwood on the other, the triumph of the piano was but a question of a few years. In the most conservative institution of the country, the King's Band, the harpsichord was replaced by the pianoforte in 1795. It would appear that Backers on his deathbed desired to commit the care of his invention to his friend, John Broadwood; but Broadwood devoted his attention to the improvement or rather the reconstruction of the square piano, which he made public in 1780,[3] and patented in 1783, allowing Stodart to go on with the grand piano with which he soon made considerable reputation. Excepting as to the action, Zumpe's instrument had been merely a clavichord with a second bridge. Broadwood boldly transferred the wrest-plank with its tuning-pins to the back of the case, and straightened the keys, which had hitherto been twisted hither and thither to accommodate an imperfect scale. Besides these radical improvements he substituted a brass damper, acting under the string, for the ' mopstick damper ' which had acted above it; and for Zumpe's treble and bass ' hand-stops,' which did away with either half of the dampers when not required, he patented (in 1783) two pedals, the one to remove the dampers altogether, the other to produce a pianissimo or sordine, by dropping a piece of cloth upon the strings near the curved bridge on the belly. Last of all in this patent he included a double sound - board and sound-post, which he imagined to be the ' most essential part ' of his improvements (see Patent No. 1379); but neither in his hands nor those of others has this notion of resonance box and cavity, in analogy to the violin and the guitar, been brought to practical value. Having accomplished this, and being stimulated by Stodart's success, and advised by Clementi, who then played on Broadwood's instruments, as to the deficiencies of the grand piano, Broadwood began to consider seriously the charge confided to him by Backers, and resolved to improve the grand instrument. The

[3] Messrs. Broadwood have a Square Piano of John Broadwood's dated with that year.

difficulty in this case being the equalisation of the tension or drawing-power of the strings, he sought the advice of scientific men, and guided by Dr. Gray of the British Museum, and Cavallo, who calculated the tension by a mono-chord (publishing the result in 1788), Broad-wood divided the bridge upon the sound-board, that is, made a separate bridge for the bass strings, an improvement which in the absence of a patent was at once adopted by all makers. As Stodart continued to use the undivided bridge (like a harpsichord) as late as 1788,[1] Broadwood's improvement can hardly have been introduced before that time.

Meantime the Zumpe square action was not to remain unimproved. Broadwood had already in 1780 transformed the instrument, and in 1786 the action met with improvement from John Geib, a workman (probably a German), said to have been in the employ of Longman & Broderip, the predecessors of Clementi & Collard in Cheapside. He took out a patent (London, No. 1571) for a new hopper and underhammer ; both modifications of Cristofori's. He regulated his hopper in two ways, by piercing the blade with the ' set-off ' or regulating screw already invented by Backers, and by turning this screw down upon the key. Both expedients are still in use. Tradition says that Longman & Broderip first used a modification of this patent, known by workmen as the ' grasshopper,' with whom for a long while it was unpopular from its supposed susceptibility to atmospheric changes, and consequent need of constant attention.

Mozart, with all his genius and charm of cantilena, on the importance of which he dwelt by precept no less than by example, was yet not a pianoforte-player in the sense that Clementi was ; his technique, as we know from Beethoven (through Czerny's report), was that of the harpsichord, to which in his early days he had been accustomed. Saust, who heard Mozart play, told the writer that Mozart had no remarkable execution on the instrument, and that he would not have compared, as a virtuoso, with Dussek for instance. And he must have met, at first, with very imperfect instruments, such as those by Spaeth, an organ-builder of Ratisbon, mentioned in his letters. Being at Augsburg in Oct. 1777, he was introduced to the pianos of Stein, also an organ-builder and a good musician. Stein's newly contrived pianoforte escapement appears to have charmed Mozart. In a letter to his father he refers to the evenness of its touch,[2] saying that the action

' never *blocks*, and never fails to sound—as is some-times the case with other pianos. On the other hand, it never sounds too long, and the machine pressed by the knee (to act as a forte pedal) is prompt to raise the dampers, or, on discontinuing the pressure ever so little, is as prompt to let them down upon the strings again.' [3]

C. F. Pohl made inquiries in Vienna as to the existence of any piano by Stein. There is not one, and Streicher, the pianoforte-maker, Stein's descendant, could give no information.[4] In the Library of the Gesellschaft der Musik-freunde, of which Pohl was custodian, there is a small pamphlet entitled *Kurze Bemerkungen über das Spielen, Stimmen und Erhalten des Fortepiano, welcher von den Geschwister Stein in Wien verfertiget werden* (the ' Geschwister Stein ' rectified in ink to ' welche von Nanette Streicher geborne Stein '), Vienna, 1801, from which a small engraving of Stein's escapement is here reproduced (Fig. 9).

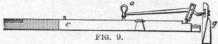

FIG. 9.

It will be observed that this escapement differs from Cristofori's and the English action in the fact that the axis of the hammer changes its position with the rising of the key, the hopper (*auslöser*) *g* becoming a fixture at the back of the key. From this difference a radical change of touch took place ; and an extreme lightness became the characteristic of the Viennese action as developed by Andreas STREICHER, Stein's son-in-law, who, in 1794, improved and finally established the great renown of the Viennese pianofortes.[5] The illustration of Streicher's Viennese action (Fig. 10) is from the *Atlas zum Lehrbuch des Piano-*

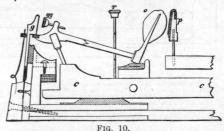

FIG. 10.

*r* is the damper. It must not be overlooked that Stein, who had not himself invented the knee-pedal, did, in 1789, invent a shifting foot pedal, by means of which the keyboard moved, and the three unisons were reduced to a single string—*Spinettchen*, little spinet, he named this ' una corda.' [6]

1 This Grand Piano by Stodart was made for the Prince of Wales, who gave it to Mr. Weltjé, in whose house (at Hammersmith) and family it remained in 1880, a really powerful instrument. The earliest known date of a Broadwood Grand is 1781. No. 40 was made in 1786. But Abraham Kirkman was in the running with a Grand in 1780, and Messrs Broadwood own a Square by Jacobus and Abraham Kirckmann, dated 1772, on the Zumpe model, with three stops, two dampers and a sounding.

2 Much more like the harpsichord in fluency than the English escapement, which Mozart did not know then, if ever.

3 Letter, Oct. 17, 1777.

4 There is a Stein piano at the Brussels Conservatoire, the only one known to exist.                                            E. J. H[s].

5 Stein's son seems to have founded the Vienna business, as shown in the following extracts from a *Musikalische Monatsschrift*, edited by F. X. Glöggl (Linz, Oct. 1803, p. 99) : ' The clavier instruments which have been made by Andreas Stein at Vienna are to be properly understood as Forti Piano, meaning such as respond to every possible degree of strength or softness of tone when played with more or less pressure, or rather stroke of the fingers on the keys ' ; and ' the action in all parts is as simple as possible and at the same time extraordinarily durable. It is original throughout, that is, entirely the invention of the deceased organ-builder and instrument-maker, Stein of Augsburg (father of the present maker), who, with the rarest love of art, has devoted the greatest part of his active life to its completion.' This communication, from C. F. Pohl, is an historical proof of the pedigree of the Viennese action.

6 Walton, a London maker, had shifted the hammers, leaving the keyboard stationary, two years earlier, viz. 1787. (Patent No. 1607.)

*fortebaues* by Blüthner and Gretschel, Leipzig, and shows the damping as well as the escapement.

Returning to Mozart, his Concert Grand in the Mozarteum at Salzburg, shown on *PLATE LIX.*, is a small 5-octave instrument, with black natural keys and white sharps, made by Anton Walter, who became in the end Mozart's favourite maker, as Schanz was Haydn's. According to Schönfeld (*Jahrbuch der Tonkunst von Wien und Prag*, 1796) the pianos of Schanz were weaker and sweeter than those of Walter ; the touch also easier, and the keyfall still less. But both Walter and Schanz were mere copyists of Stein. They made square pianos also in the ' English ' form, most likely imitations of the English instruments, which at that time had a very wide market.

Paris was supplied chiefly with English pianos until Sébastien Erard made, in 1777, the first French one, a square, copied, according to Fétis, from one of English make. For some years he appears to have continued on these lines ; indeed it was not till after he had been driven to London, by the French Revolution, and had gone back again—according to the same authority, in 1796—that he accomplished the making of a grand piano. His London patent for such a piano was, however, dated 1794,[1] and its action is allied to an early German action (not Schroeter's model) improved upon by Stein. Erard appears to have been early bent upon constructing a grand action for himself, but while the perfecting of the Double Action harp remained his chief problem, the century went out with the English and Viennese actions pre-eminent ; the radical differences of which, and the effect of those differences on pianoforte-playing, Hummel, in his Pianoforte School, subsequently explained from his point of view. Extension of compass had now set in. (See KEYBOARD.)

We have referred to the difficulty which presented itself to Cristofori at the outset of the pianoforte, owing to the necessity of stringing with thicker wire than before, to resist the blow of the hammers, and of strengthening the case to bear the greater tension of the thicker strings, which forced him to shift the hitch-pins from the sound-board to a separate strong rail. The gap between the wrest-plank and the sound-board, through which the hammers of the grand piano rose to strike the strings, was the first to be strengthened by metal, as a material at once stronger than wood and very economical of space. This was effected by steel arches, a contrivance which has remained in universal employment, but of the author of which there is no record. There are three in Stodart's grand of 1788 previously referred to ; no doubt earlier examples exist, and to know their date is desirable. Schroeter had suggested a transverse bar across the instrument ; but it is not known if the experiment was made at that time. The first real use of metal longitudinal bracing was suggested in 1799 by Joseph Smith (Patent 2345, London) ; it was to be under the sound-board and to replace the wooden braces, and thus provide space for the introduction of a mechanically-played tambourine ! But for the patent office we might not have known of Joseph Smith's invention, as nothing came of it. The first to use iron or steel in the form of bracing or tension bars placed above the strings—a method now universally adopted—was James Shudi Broadwood, who, in 1804, having carried the compass of the grand piano up to $f''''$, found that the wrest-plank was so much weakened by this extension that the treble sank in pitch more rapidly than the rest of the instrument. Accordingly in 1808, in three grand pianos, he applied steel tension-bars above the strings to remedy the inequality. This experiment is recorded in Messrs. Broadwood's work-books of that date, and the experiment was repeated in 1818, the metal bars being then four in number in place of three. In Messrs. Broadwood's International Exhibition book, 1862, p. 29, we learn that the mode of fixing these bars was at first defective, the wood giving way to the thrust of the bars. It is certain that they did not use tension bars at this time constantly, for the grand piano which was presented to Beethoven by James and Thomas Broadwood in 1817 had no tension bars, and, moreover, only went up to $c''''$ (six octaves C-C).

Sébastien Erard's patent in 1808 (No. 3170) records an ingenious step towards a successful repetition action, viz. the ' double escapement ' : and an improvement which afterwards proved to be of great importance, viz. the upward bearing of the bridge next the tuning-pins by substituting for the pinned wooden bridge, metal studs or agraffes drilled with holes for the passage of the strings, and separately fixed for each note. The same patent includes what is now known as the ' céleste ' piano pedal, in which the hammer strikes a piece of leather (now always felt) interposed between it and the strings. (See PEDAL.)

A very important step in the enlargement and improvement of the square piano appears to have been made in France by Petzold,[2] who in 1806, in the Paris Exhibition of the products of National Industry, exhibited a Square piano with an extended sound-board, an improvement at first not much noticed, though afterwards developed with great success, and probably independently, by the Collards and

---

[1] Erard's factory at Kensington, with trees and orchard, was called the ' tuner's hospital,' being remote from London.

[2] Guillaume Lebrecht Petzold, born, according to Fétis, in 1784, at Lichtenhayn, Saxony, was apprenticed to Wenzky, Dresden, in 1798, and worked for Walther, Vienna, from 1803 to 1805. In 1806 he joined Pfeiffer in Paris, a connexion which lasted till 1814. According to Welcker, Petzold invented the crank lever action since much used by different makers.

Broadwoods of that time. Pape introduced the lever and notch principle of the English Grand action into the square piano action in 1817.

THE UPRIGHT PIANO.—In the very first years of the 19th century an entirely new form of pianoforte was invented, the 'Upright,' with the strings descending below the key-board. There had been upright harpsichords (see CLAVICYTHERIUM and *PLATE XIX.*) and upright grands (the latter patented by John Landreth in 1787), but these were merely horizontal instruments turned up on end, with the necessary modification of the action to adapt it to the position. The oldest upright grand piano is at Brussels. It was made by Frederici of Gera, in Saxony, in 1745. This was the very time when Silbermann was successfully reproducing the Florentine Cristofori's pianofortes at Dresden, which were horizontal grand pianos. Frederici, however, made no use of Cristofori's action. Neither did he avail himself of a model of Schroeter's, said to be at that time known in Saxony. Victor Mahillon, who discovered the Frederici instrument and transferred it to the Museum at Brussels, derived the action from the German striking clocks, and with good reasons. Frederici is also credited with the invention of the square piano, an adaptation of the clavichord, in which Zumpe followed him.

The earliest mention of an upright grand piano in Messrs. Broadwood's books occurs in 1789, when one 'in a cabinett case' was sold. It was, however, by another maker. The first upright grand piano made and sent out by this firm was to the same customer, in 1799. In 1795 William Stodart had patented an upright grand pianoforte with a new mechanism, in the form of a bookcase.[1] He gained a considerable reputation by, and sale for, this instrument. In 1800 Isaac Hawkins patented (No. 2446) a perpendicular pianoforte from 3 to 4 feet in height, descending to within a few inches of the floor, to give the instrument a more 'convenient and elegant shape than any heretofore made.' The bold step of inverting the wrest-plank or tuning-pin block, which in the upright grand was at the bottom near the keys, but in the cabinet was at the top, was due to Isaac Hawkins, as in his specification we find his wrest-plank fixed diagonally in the sides of the case, the bass end near the top, 6 feet 3 inches high, to preserve length for the bass strings, the treble end lower 4 feet 3 inches from the bottom, leaving an angular space above which might be utilised for bookshelves. His patent (taken out for his son, John Isaac Hawkins, the inventor,[2] who was at that time living at Philadelphia, U.S.A.) includes two other important ideas : the use of coiled strings for the

bass, and a *sostinente*, obtained by reiteration of hammers set in motion by a roller. Hawkins's piano, called a 'portable grand,' was played upon in public at the Franklin Institute, Philadelphia, in 1802. In 1802 Thomas Loud (Patent No. 2591) gave a diagonal shape to this upright piano by sloping the strings in an angular direction, portability being the 'leading intention and feature.' James Broadwood claims [3] to have given a sketch for a cabinet piano in 1804 to William Southwell, who in 1807 patented (No. 3029) a damper action to the instrument there called by that name.[4] From this tall instrument the lower upright or 'Cottage' piano followed almost immediately. Robert WORNUM 'the younger' patented (No. 3419) one diagonally strung in 1811, and in 1813 made a vertical one, naming it ' Harmonic.' In the year 1815 Ignace Pleyel, founder of the house of Pleyel, Wolff et Cie, employed Henry PAPE, an ingenious mechanician, to organise the introduction of the construction of these instruments in Paris,[5] from which beginning arose the important manufacture of French cottage pianos. William Frederick COLLARD, who about 1800 had with Muzio Clementi taken up the business of Longman & Broderip, in 1811 essayed an oblique pianoforte (Patent No. 3481) by turning a square one 'upwards on its side.' William Southwell had patented a square thus turned up in 1798. Nearly all improvements in the pianoforte have been of slow and patient elaboration, the introduction of metal in framing, and Erard's special action being prominent examples. Wornum's excellent cottage action was no exception to this general experience, for he did not complete it till 1828 (Patent No. 5678). Camille Pleyel recognised its value, and through his introduction it became generally used in France, so that at last it was known in England as the 'French' action. But Wornum's merit as the inventor of this 'crank' action (the first idea of which is in the 'Upright Grand' of Landreth, patented 1787) needs now no vindication, and Southwell's 'sticker' action, long the favourite in England, gave way before it.

His piccolo piano, a low upright pianoforte, was introduced in 1829. The novelty consisted first in its small size, and then in the application of a new action invented by Robert Wornum and patented three years before. Though the strings were placed vertically, the height of the piccolo piano did not exceed 40 inches. The facile touch gained by the new mechanism soon attracted the attention of the musical public, and with its long-since-proved durability has made it a favourite model of action for manufacturers both here and abroad.

---

[1] William Southwell of Dublin patented an upright piano with six octaves on Oct. 18, 1794.                                    W. H. G. F.
[2] See Hipkins's *History of the Pianoforte* (1896), p. 111.

[3] *Some Notes*, etc., p. 9.
[4] He had patented an 'Irish damper action' in 1794, and made a cabinet piano as early as 1802.                               W. H. G. F.
[5] Pape, *Sur les inventions*, etc. ; Paris, 1845.

The 'piccolo' was finished to stand out in the room away from the wall; its original price was 36 guineas.

THE METAL FRAME.—We may now look back a hundred years, in the first half of which the pianoforte had really no independent existence as a keyed instrument; but between 1770 and 1820 we find the grand piano complete so far as its construction in wood permitted, and a constellation of remarkable players that included Clementi and Dussek, Cramer and Field, Hummel and Ries. Weber in Germany had initiated the Romantic school in pianoforte music; Kalkbrenner in Paris was forwarding technical discipline; and, above all, Beethoven, whose early eminence as a pianist has been to a large extent overshadowed by his sublime genius as a composer, was in the latter years of this epoch engaged in completing that series of masterpieces for the pianoforte that have not only enabled it to rival the orchestra in the wealth of its possessions, but have by their own immortality ensured it an existence as a musical instrument which no change of fashion can affect. The further development of technique, essential to the interpretation of Beethoven, attained perfection between 1820 and 1850, and was based upon conditions rendered possible by the introduction of iron as an essential constituent in the framing of grand pianos, and in a certain degree of that of the other kinds also. Gradation of power was the great desideratum of the player; and the possibilities of this were intimately connected with the freedom of the wrist, which had previously been disallowed, and with the discovery, made almost instinctively, that to give elasticity to the fingers they should be raised in order to descend, and not be drawn inwards as was the case with the Bach touch essential to the clavichord. (See PIANOFORTE-PLAYING.) This change of practice involved a blow by the hammer which the indifferent Berlin wire of that time could not stand. Thicker wire produced greater strain on the framing which the wooden cases were not strong enough to resist. The use also of two metals in the stringing, brass and iron, led to unequal changes in the tuning, and another problem, 'compensation,' received even more attention than 'resistance' had done. To solve this a young Scotch tuner, named Allen, employed at Stodart's, set himself; and soon succeeded in producing a complete and satisfactory upper framing of hollow tubes in combination with plates of iron and brass, bound together by stout wooden crossbars, the whole intended to bear the pull of the strings, and to meet, by give-and-take, the variations in the length of the wires, due to alteration of temperature. The patent (No. 4431) was taken out by William Allen and James Thom (who supplied the necessary technical knowledge of pianoforte-making); it is dated Jan. 15, 1820,

and the exclusive right to use it was acquired by Messrs. Stodart to the great advantage of their business. The accompanying diagram of a Stodart pianoforte with Allen's framing shows the aim and completeness of this remarkable invention, from the inventor's point of view.

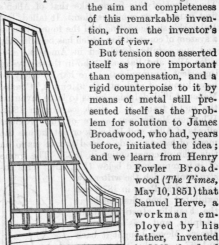

FIG. 11.

But tension soon asserted itself as more important than compensation, and a rigid counterpoise to it by means of metal still presented itself as the problem for solution to James Broadwood, who had, years before, initiated the idea; and we learn from Henry Fowler Broadwood (The Times, May 10, 1851) that Samuel Herve, a workman employed by his father, invented in 1821 the fixed string-plate, in that year first applied to a square piano of Broadwood's. From 1822–27 James Broadwood tried various combinations of the string-plate and iron bars, and in the latter year permanently adopted a system of solid metal bracing (Patent No. 5485). The iron bars, not having been patented, had been adopted by other makers, and in 1825 Pierre Erard had in his turn patented a means of fixing the iron bars to the wooden braces beneath the sound-board by bolts passing through holes cut in the sound-board (Patent No. 5065). He had patented a system of fixed iron bars in Paris in 1822. He could not do so in London, being barred by Stodart's (Thom and Allen's) patent. Stodart refrained [1] from opposing the Broadwoods when James Shudi Broadwood took out his patent for string-plate and bars in 1827. There is no mention of a string-plate in this patent, but a proposition is made to strengthen the case by plating it with sheet iron, which, however, came to nothing.

William Allen, who had invented Stodart's compensating framing, did not rest satisfied with his first success, but invented, and in 1831 patented (No. 6140), a cast-iron frame to combine string-plate, iron bars and wrest-plank in one casting. Wooden bars were let into the wrest-plank to receive the ordinary tuning-pins, which would not conveniently work in metal. This important invention did not find the acceptance which it deserved, and the compound metal and wood framing continued to be preferred in Europe under the idea that it was

[1] The writer had this information from Mr. Joseph Ries, who died in 1882.

beneficial to the tone. But Allen's proposal of one casting had been anticipated in America by Alpheus Babcock of Boston, Mass., who in 1825 patented a cast-iron frame for a square piano. The object of this frame, like that of Allen's first patent, was compensation. It failed, but Babcock's single casting laid the foundation of a system of construction which has been largely and successfully developed in America. Besides Allen and Babcock, who in those days of imperfect communication are hardly likely to have known of each other's attempts,[1] Conrad Meyer of Philadelphia claims to have invented the metal frame in a single casting in 1832. Whether Meyer was aware of the previous efforts of Allen and Babcock or not, he has the merit of having made a good square piano on this plan of construction in 1833. The frame of it is represented below (Fig. 12). This instrument, which the writer saw and tried at Paris in 1878, was exhibited when first made at the Franklin Institute, Philadelphia, and was sold; but Messrs. Meyer bought it back in 1867, and exhibited it in the Centennial Exhibition in 1876, and again, as mentioned, in the Universal Exhibition of Paris in 1878. Jonas CHICKERING of Boston in 1837 improved the single casting by including in it the pin-bridge and damper socket-rail, a construction which he patented in 1840. Chickering subsequently devised a complete frame for grand pianos in one casting, and exhibited two so made at the Great Exhibition of 1851. On

FIG. 12.

the same occasion Lichtenthal of St. Petersburg exhibited two grand pianos 'overstrung,' that is, with the longest bass spun-strings[2] stretched obliquely over the longest unspun ones, a method which is now very well known and extensively adopted, but the advantages of which were formerly impaired by inequality in the scale. The invention of overstringing has had more than one claimant, amongst others the ingenious Henry PAPE. We have found no earlier date for it than 1835, when Theobald BOEHM, well known in connexion with the flute, contrived an overstrung square and an overstrung cottage piano, and had them made in London by Gerock of Cornhill. In the next year, 1836, John Godwin patented (No. 7021) overstrung square and cottage pianos. Whether he acquired Boehm's invention or not, we do not know.

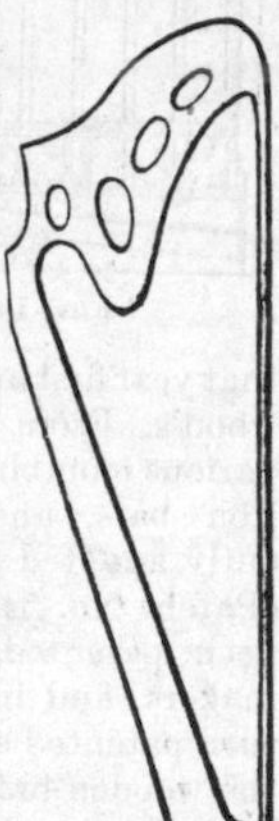

Great use of iron was made by Dr. Steward

of Handsworth, near Birmingham, in a novel upright pianoforte which he called the 'Euphonicon,' and brought out in London in 1844. His patent (No. 9023), which is dated July 1841, includes a complete metal framing, and separate sound-boards, three in number. The instruments were of elegant appearance, and the long strings, in harp-like form, were exposed to view.[3] Though unsuccessful, the Euphonicon should not be forgotten. There is one in the Victoria and Albert Museum, in the musical instrument collection.

To return to America. In 1853 Jonas Chickering combined the overstringing with a metal frame in one casting, in a square piano which he did not live to see completed, but which was finished by his sons. This combination was taken up by Messrs. Steinway & Sons of New York, and further improved in 1859 by the addition of an 'agraffe' (or metal stud) bridge; they then, by dividing the overstringing into two crossings, produced a double overstrung scale. In the same year this firm patented in America a grand piano with fan-shaped overstrung scale in one casting, a diagram of which will show the arrangement of ironwork and bridges (Fig. 13). This system

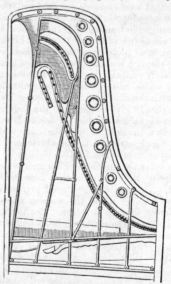

FIG. 13.

was adopted by some of the foremost makers in Germany.

Henry Fowler Broadwood's special concert-grand iron framing, with diagonal tension-bar and transverse suspension-bar (Fig. 14), was invented by him in 1847, and used by the firm until 1895. The barless frame[4] was then

---

[1] See Hipkins's *History of the Pianoforte*, p. 15.
[2] 'Spun, or overspun, strings' are surrounded with an external coil of fine wire, to add to their weight and power of tone.

[3] In the harp shape Dr. Steward had been anticipated by Mussard of Lausanne. We have seen a piano so made by him in 1819.
[4] Invented by Henry John Shudi Broadwood, son of H. F. Broadwood.

dopted by the Broadwood firm. Henry Fowler Broadwood objected to single castings, preferring a combination of cast and wrought iron, wedged up at the points of abutment, into a thoroughly solid structure. His plan gets rid of some of the iron bars, which he believed to be more or less inimical to carrying and equality of tone. The difference between this and his father's or Erard's scale is great; and it only approaches the American—which it preceded in grand pianos—in the fact that the framing is independent of the wooden structure of the instrument. A comparison of the diagram (Fig. 14) with Steinway's (Fig. 13) makes this difference obvious (the diagonal bar is lettered *u*, the suspension-bar *t*).

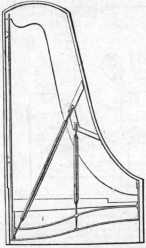

FIG. 14.

The modern pianoforte frame [1] is made of cast iron or steel with or without an arrangement of intermediate struts. Its purpose is to take the major portion of the load due to the tension of the strings which are attached to it by hitch pins. It occupies a position overlaying the sound-board and WREST-PLANK (*q.v.*).

In its present form it developed from a flat string plate which was made of cast or wrought iron attached by screws to the wooden framework of a grand or upright piano. Formerly the string plate and the wrest-plank were the two limits of the string length, the whole of the string tension being taken up by the wooden framework or bracing of the piano, which was therefore made extremely heavy to withstand this load. In modern pianos the metal frame is arranged to bear against the wrest-plank to take the load due to the tension on the wrestpins, whilst the strings are attached to the frame only at one end. The frame is in its

[1] Information from Mr. L. A. Broadwood.

turn bolted round its edge to the wooden bracings of the pianoforte.

The object of the intermediate bars on the

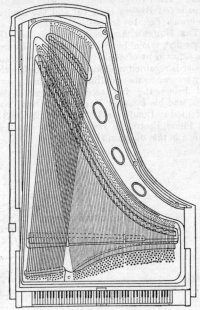

FIG. 15.

frame which run directly over the strings is for extra strength. These intermediate bars

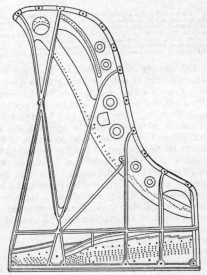

FIG. 16.

may be entirely dispensed with by careful design of the side members of the frame, as has been carried out in the Broadwood Barles

Frame, with the consequent advantage of obtaining an unbroken arrangement of strings and greater equalness of tone throughout the scale. The two preceding diagrams show the Broadwood Barless (Fig. 15) and the modern Steinway (Fig. 16) frames.

THE MODERN ACTION.—We have seen the steps first taken by Sébastien Erard towards the attainment of double escapement, whereby power is regained over the hammer before the key returns to its equilibrium. He had grown old before the full accomplishment of his idea, and his famous 'Repetition action' was patented in London in 1821 (Patent No. 4631) by Pierre Erard, his nephew. The action is shown in this diagram (Fig. 17).

and Kind (under Broadwood's patronage at different times), COLLARD, HOPKINSON and BRINSMEAD in London. Other repetition actions are the simplified copies of Erard's used by HERZ in Paris and by STEINWAY in New York, the latter subsequently adopted by BECHSTEIN of Berlin, in place of Kriegelstein's. The leader in this was John Henry Cary, who in 1853 invented a simple contrivance for repetition on all pianos, which, although neglected for years, was repatented and disputed over by others, and has slowly made its way. It is well known not only in upright pianos but in horizontal grands, where it is used with the old English action and competes successfully with the Erard action proper. Cary's patent (No.

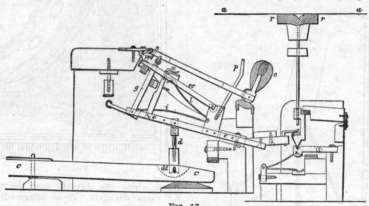

FIG. 17.

*c* is the key; *d* is a pilot, centred at *dd* to give the blow, by means of a carrier, *e*, holding the hopper, *g*, which delivers the blow to the hammer, *o*, by the thrust of the hopper, which escapes by forward movement after contact with a projection from the hammer covered with leather, answering to the notch of the English action. This escapement is controlled at *x*; a double spring, *i l*, pushes up a hinged lever, *ee*, the rise of which is checked at *pp*, and causes the second or double escapement; a little stirrup at the shoulder of the hammer, known as the 'repetition,' pressing down *ee* at the point, and by this depression permitting *g* to go back into its place, and be ready for a second blow, before the key has been materially raised. The check, *p*, is in this action not behind the hammer, but before it, fixed into the carrier, *e*, which also, as the key is put down, brings down the under damper.

Although at once adopted by Hummel and other pianists of note, including Liszt, then a boy, Erard's action was slow to obtain recognition. It did not gain a satisfactory position until Thalberg, after 1830, had identified his admirable playing with its specialities. In 1835 Pierre Erard obtained an extension of his patent on the ground of the loss sustained in working it. Then 'repetition' became the pianoforte-maker's dominant idea in this country and elsewhere, each according to his knowledge and ability contriving a repetition action to call his own, though generally a modification of an existing one. Names that have come prominently forward in connexion with these experiments are BLÜTHNER in Germany, PLEYEL and Kriegelstein in Paris, Southwell the younger, Ramsay

2283) is preserved at the Patent Office. Here simplicity is justified by the result. The following sketch [1] of a modern (1926) grand action (Fig. 18) must serve to complete the account of these developments.

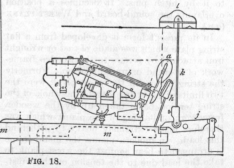

FIG. 18.

*a*, hammer head; *b*, hammer shank and butt; *c*, repetition lever; *d*, jack; *e*, set-off button; *f*, capstan screws; *g*, repetition spring; *h*, check head and wire; *j*, damper body; *k*, damper wire; *l*, damper head; *m*, key

---

[1] Kindly supplied by Messrs. Herrburger Brooks, Ltd.

Further improvement of the square piano, in the application of metal to resist tension, etc., followed closely upon that of the grand; and in America the square outstripped the grand by being first experimented on for the iron framing, the cross stringing, etc., which, through the talent and energy of the Meyers, Chickerings and Steinways, have given a distinctive character to the American manufacture. The Americans brought their squares almost to the size and power of their grands; and with the same tendency as in Europe, to their being superseded entirely by the smaller grands and uprights.

EXPERIMENTS AND MODIFICATIONS.—Beyond the broad summary of inventions in instrument and action which we have sketched, it is impracticable in our space to go further into detail; it would, moreover, be a task of great difficulty, owing to the multiplicity of facts needing to be sifted, and the fact that a writer on this subject must always be influenced by education in taste and use. We may, however, be permitted to refer to the services of James Stewart (particularly in connexion with Messrs. Collard's pianos) and to Henry Pape of Paris, who tried more ingenious experiments in pianofortes than any other maker, although the majority of them are of doubtful utility. It is to him that we owe the use of felt for hammers (much improved, however, by H. F. Broadwood, who first substituted sheep's wool for Pape's rabbit's hair). William Stodart invented a continuous bridge for upward bearing in 1822; and the 'harmonic bar' in the treble, as a bar of alternating pressure has been called, from the peculiar timbre obtained by its use,[1] was the invention of Pierre Erard about 1838, according to Dr. Paul. The main object of this bar was to consolidate the wrest-plank in the treble, a screw tapped into the plank and drawing it upwards alternating with a screw tapped in the bar pressing it downwards. In 1843 A. BORD of Paris invented a different bar independent of the wrest-plank, which served as a bridge of upward bearing and abolished the treble wrest-plank bridge. From its simplicity and cheapness this has found favour, with some modifications, in Germany (where it is known as the Capo tasto, or d' astro, bar) and elsewhere.[2] There was a revival of W. F. Collard's idea, patented in 1821, of utilising the back draught of the wires, between the belly bridge and the hitch-pins, for sympathetic vibration, by means of what he called (Patent No. 4542) a 'bridge of reverberation.' This reappears, in idea, in Steinway's 'Duplex Scale'; but Blüthner of Leipzig has gone further in employing independent sympathetic strings of half length in his 'Aliquot' piano.

By this he adds the octave harmonic throughout three octaves, and thus produces something of the shifting soft pedal timbre; the *forte* or damper pedal in the ordinary pianoforte is, however, an incomparably more efficient floodgate to these sympathetic or, more properly, Æolian reinforcements. In the 20th century we have the Emanuel MOOR Duplex Coupler, a piano with an ingenious double keyboard (the upper keyboard an octave higher than the lower one) and various other contrivances, which, however, change not only the construction but the technique of performance so fundamentally as to place it in a category by itself.

Another invention we have to mention concerns the pedals, and is due to M. Montal, a blind Parisian pianoforte-maker, who, in 1862, exhibited in London (1) a 'pédale d'expression,' diminishing the range of the hammers instead of shifting them, an expedient now employed by American and German makers, and (2) a 'pédale de prolongement,' a third pedal, by using which a note or notes pressed down before the pedal is applied may be prolonged after the fingers have quitted the keys.[3] This pedal has been of late years reintroduced in Paris, Stuttgart and New York. Reference to PEDAL will show the radical change that took place between 1830 and 1850 in 'instrumenting' the pianoforte, giving it what we may call colour of tone, divined by Beethoven, and perfected by Chopin and Liszt. By these parallel advances in technique and instrument the masterpieces composed for the pianoforte by Beethoven have since 1850 found their fullest exposition.

Among structural changes the Gladiator sound-board should be mentioned. It was invented by Albert Schultz (late director of the piano factory of Ritmüller & Sons of Göttingen). Here are two solid slabs of wood, with grain of opposed direction to give the required tension; with a thinning round the edge to facilitate promptness of speech. We are still feeling our way towards an accurate comprehension and statement of reinforcement and resonance.

The great extension of the modern compass acts unfavourably on the instrument and increases the inconvenience of the grand piano as an article of furniture in these days of limited space. From $A_{,,}$ to $c''''$, seven octaves and a minor third, is usual. Bösendorfer of Vienna introduced an extreme compass of eight octaves $(F_{,,}-e''''')$. The classical repertory, including Schumann and Chopin, requires no more than six octaves and a fourth.

Attention, too, has been given to the touch, to make it less tiring for the pianist; especially since Anton Rubinstein (about 1886) went through the feat (for which he travelled without a note

---

[1] In the original application of this invention a third screw pressed upon the bridge.
[2] The Capo tasto bar recalls Schroeter's 'Widerstandseisen,' but was not taken from it.

[3] From the report of M. Fétis on the Paris Exhibition of 1855, it appears that the first idea of this pedal had occurred to Xavier Boisselot of Marseilles, who had shown in the 'Exposition Nationale,' 1844, a piano 'à sons soutenus à volonté.'

of music) of seven historical concerts, played consecutively in the great music centres of Europe, and for which a light touch was indispensable, even to this stupendous player.

In the competition for power the pianoforte makers had been gradually increasing the weight of touch to be overcome by the finger, until to obtain the lightest pianissimo from middle C at the front edge of the key from 3 to 4 ounces was a not uncommon weight. The Broadwood piano used by Chopin in 1848 (for his recitals in London and Manchester), which remains unaltered, shows the resistance he required : the middle C stands at $2\frac{1}{2}$ ounces, and to that weight pianoforte-makers have returned ; regarding $2\frac{3}{4}$ ounces for the front of the key of middle C, for the faintest pianissimo, as permissible : but $2\frac{1}{2}$ is preferable, owing to the difference in the weight of the hammer ; the touch for the bass will always be rather heavier—the treble, rather lighter.

The balance of the black keys is adjusted to the weight of the white ; but as the player attacks the key farther back, the balance is shortened, and the weight proportionally increased.

The calculation of the power expended by a pianist in a performance of what is called a recital, extending over an hour and a half of almost continuous playing, would show an astonishing aggregate.

The increase of tension, which in 1862 had been determined at most as some sixteen tons for a concert grand, has reached a record in recent years of thirty tons. The result is the gain of a *sostinente* unknown to Beethoven or Schumann or Chopin, with an improved standing in tune in well-made instruments due to the intensified elasticity of the wire and in overstrung models the equipoise of stress conditioned by the more favourable position of the bass and treble string departments respectively.

A table of dates, down to the middle of the 19th century, will be found a useful conclusion to this article. The various experiments in detail of more recent date are too numerous for record.

| | |
|---|---|
| 1598 | Piano e Forte.  Name of a keyed instrument at Modena. |
| 1610 | A piano of four octaves, no dampers, small hammers shaped like a dulcimer.   Owned by M. Savoye, Paris, 1920. |
| 1709 | Cristofori had made four pianofortes in Florence. |
| 1716 | Marius submitted models of pianofortes to the Academy in Paris. |
| 1721 | Schroeter submitted two models of pianoforte actions to the court at Dresden. |
| 1726 | Gottfried Silbermann, of Freiberg, showed two pianofortes to John Sebastian Bach. |
| 1731 | Cristofori died. |
| 1738 | Schroeter wrote to Mizler, claiming to have invented the pianoforte. |
| 1739 | An upright grand pianoforte invented and made by Domenico del Mela da Gagliano, with a special action, not copied from Cristofori, though with some similarity in the butt, and not at all like Frederici's, which originated the ' sticker ' principle.[1] |
| 1745 | Christian Ernst Frederici, of Gera, invented upright grand. |
| 1747 | J. S. Bach played on a Silbermann pianoforte before Frederick the Great. |
| 1753 | Gottfried Silbermann died. |
| 1753–80 | Frederici, of Gera, made the first square pianoforte. |

[1] Reported to A. J. Hipkins by Signor Cesare Ponsicchi.

| | |
|---|---|
| 1759 | John Christian Bach came to London. |
| 1762 | Date of oldest Zumpe square piano known.[2] |
| 1764 | Schroeter published in Marpurg's work his claim to have invented the pianoforte. |
| 1767 | A ' new instrument called Piano Forte ' announced at Covent Garden. |
| 1768 | J. C. Bach played a solo on the pianoforte in London. |
| 1770 | Muzio Clementi composed pianoforte music. |
| 1771 | Backers exhibited his invention, ' original Forte Piano,' at the Thatched House in London.[3] |
| 1772 | The pianist J. S. Schroeter (not the organist) came to London. |
| 1772 | Backers about this time invented the English direct action. |
| 1773 | A grand piano, by Americus Backers, was at Pistoia in 1897, where it was wrongly described as dated ' 1713.' |
| 1774 | John Broadwood made a Zumpe model square piano.[4] |
| 1775 | Kirkman's first record of a square piano (see Vol. III. p. 27). |
| 1777 | Mozart played on Stein's pianofortes at Augsburg. |
| 1777 | Stodart adopted the name ' grand ' pianoforte. |
| 1777 | Seb. Erard made the first square piano in France. |
| 1780 | John Broadwood reconstructed the square piano. |
| 1780 | Kirkman's record of a grand piano (see Vol. III. p. 27). |
| 1782 | Mozart and Clementi played upon the pianoforte before the Emperor at Vienna. |
| 1783 | John Broadwood patented loud and soft pedals. |
| 1786 | Geib patented the square ' grasshopper ' action. |
| 1787 | John Landreth patented the ' upright ' grand piano. |
| 1787 | Walton patented a soft pedal with shifting hammers. |
| 1788 | John Broadwood about this time made a new scale grand piano, dividing the curved bridge. |
| 1789 | Stein, of Augsburg, invented a soft pedal with shifting action. |
| 1790 | John Broadwood made the first piano with five and a half octaves. |
| 1794 | William Southwell invented the ' Irish ' damper. |
| 1794 | Andreas Streicher perfected the Viennese grand action. |
| 1794 | John Broadwood made the first piano with six octaves. |
| 1796 | Seb. Erard made his first grand piano in Paris. |
| 1798 | Wm. Southwell patented a square piano turned up. |
| 1800 | Clementi, in partnership with Collard, began about this time to make pianos. |
| 1800 | Isaac Hawkins patented an upright pianoforte for his son Dr. John Isaac Hawkins, of Bordertown, New Jersey, U.S.A. |
| 1802 | Thomas Loud patented a diagonal upright pianoforte. |
| 1807 | William Southwell patented the cabinet pianoforte. |
| 1808 | James Broadwood first applied iron bars to a grand piano. |
| 1808 | Seb. Erard patented the upward bearing and the ' céleste ' pedal. |
| 1811 | Robert Wornum made the first cottage pianoforte. |
| 1820 | William Allen invented and brought out at Stodart's a compensating grand piano with metal tubes and plates. |
| 1821 | Seb. Erard patented his double escapement action. |
| 1821 | S. Herve invented the fixed string-plate (brought out at Broadwood's). |
| 1822 | James Broadwood adapted iron bars to the string-plate. Seven octaves, C-C. |
| 1824 | Liszt came out in Paris on an Erard grand piano. |
| 1825 | P. Erard patented bolts to iron bars. |
| 1825 | Alpheus Babcock patented in America a cast-iron frame square piano. |
| 1826 | R. Wornum patented the crank action, improved 1828. |
| 1827 | James Broadwood patented iron bars and string-plate combined in a grand piano. |
| 1827 | James Stewart patented stringing without ' eyes ' to the strings (in Messrs. Collard's pianos). |
| 1831 | W. Allen patented in London a complete cast-iron frame piano. |
| 1833 | Conrad Meyer patented in America a cast-iron frame square piano. |
| 1835 | Boehm had overstrung pianos made in London. |
| 1838 | P. Erard introduced the ' Harmonic bar.' |
| 1840 | Jonas Chickering patented in America a cast-iron frame with damper socket (square piano). |
| 1843 | A. Bord, of Paris, invented the ' Capo tasto ' bar. |
| 1847 | H. F. Broadwood invented his ' iron ' grand pianoforte. |
| 1851 | Jonas Chickering exhibited in London grand pianos with frames in one casting. |
| 1851 | Lichtenthal, of St. Petersburg, exhibited in London overstrung grand pianos. |
| 1853 | Chickering & Son combined cast frame and over-stringing in a square piano. |
| 1854 | H. Wölfel, of Paris, invented an iron wrest-plank with mechanical screw-pins. |
| 1859 | Steinway & Sons patented in America a cast frame overstrung grand piano, and double overstrung square piano. |
| 1862 | Montal, of Paris, exhibited in London a third pedal for prolonging sounds after the fingers have quitted the keys. |

A. J. H. ; rev. with addns. from the author's notes supplied by E. J. H⁸., information from Mr. L. A. Broadwood and others as mentioned in footnotes.

**PIANOFORTE-PLAYING.** The art of playing the pianoforte, as distinguished from the earlier instruments with keys and strings,

[2] Fétis says that he began his studies on a Zumpe PF. of this date (*Report of the Great Exhibition*, 1851.)
[3] C. F. Pohl, *Mozart und Haydn in London*, p. 128.
[4] In the possession of the firm.

## LIX

1. PIANO (Anton Walter, *c.* 1780): formerly W. A. Mozart's.
2. PIANO (J. Broadwood & Sons, 1817): formerly L. v. Beethoven's.
3. PIANO (J. Broadwood & Sons, 1848): used by F. Chopin.

1. The Mozarteum, Salzburg.   2. National Museum, Budapest.   3. Messrs. Broadwood & Sons, Ltd., London.

consisted largely at first in the task of uniting the special characteristics of the two older instruments. On the clavichord, the notes could be varied in force and emphasis by the pressure of the finger, the parts of a fugue could be clearly differentiated, and deep expression could be conveyed. But the ' disembodied spirit,' to which its tone has often been compared, was incapable of speaking to more than two or three hearers at once, so exceedingly attenuated was the tone of the instrument ; and in very staccato passages there is little of the sparkling brilliance of the harpsichord. On the harpsichord the most perfect staccato was easily obtained, and as the touch was unalterable, there was absolute evenness of tone as long as no mechanical change was made. All dynamic changes must be made, as in playing the organ, by the application of some mechanical device, never by the finger. Harpsichord players, accustomed to use the swell pedal in order to increase the sound, would naturally and readily make use of the far easier resources that were provided in the piano, with its infinitely varying degrees of tone. The possibility of getting increase of tone by pressure of the finger, a pressure that could be applied to any single note or chord, made it no longer necessary to overload the music with those ornaments by which the older composers had obtained a kind of spurious emphasis from the harpsichord. Thus the pattern of the melodies naturally became simpler, and more was left to the player in the way of bringing out the salient features of the melody. C. P. E. Bach led the readers of his *Versuch über die wahre Art das Clavier zu spielen* to aim at the cultivation of a real cantabile style, and seems to have been the first to speak of ' singing ' on the keyed instrument. In his works we find innumerable instances of a melody played simultaneously with its subordinate accompaniment, a musical effect which was only possible on the harpsichord when two manuals were employed. The pianoforte soon began to acquire special ornaments of its own ; in Haydn's famous variations in F minor, the arpeggio figure in the major part of the theme implies gradation of tone as an essential feature, and this is one of the earliest compositions which could not be played with any degree of success on the harpsichord. On the other hand, Mozart's fantasia in C minor includes no effect that cannot be realised on the earlier instrument, and even the earliest sonatas of Beethoven can be performed satisfactorily on the harpsichord.

In the earliest days of technique, when only the three long fingers of the hand were usually employed (see FINGERING, Vol. II. p. 236), a gliding touch was aimed at, and this gentle pressure suited the clavichord perfectly. With the development of the harpsichord it became necessary to acquire a crisper touch, for all notes, even those played with *legato* effect, must be taken up sharply, or the quill would not be in a position to pluck its string again. Sebastian Bach's fingers are said to have ' bent over the keyboard in such a manner that they stood with their points in a downward, vertical line, each finger at every moment ready for action. In taking a finger off a key, he drew it gently inwards, only moving the end joint.' The thumb was, as it were, set at liberty, so that it was now recognised as a practical member of the hand, instead of a useless appendage, which it seems to have been considered in earlier ages. It could be used in the natural position, but it was forbidden to pass it under the other fingers unless it was absolutely necessary. At the same time, great laxity was permitted in part-playing, where the interweaving of the different voices often makes it necessary not only for the thumb, but for the other fingers, to pass over or under the rest.

In the early pianos, the cantabile touch which again seemed desirable was best obtained by a smooth progression, such as was insisted on by Emanuel Bach, who allowed the passage of the second finger over the third. Both Cramer and Clementi devoted their main attention, so far as regarded technique, to the attainment of perfect evenness in all the fingers, substituting, in fact, a living for a mechanical equality of tone. In Clementi's famous ' Gradus ' there is hardly any other point striven after than complete equality of tone, combined with velocity, and the power of giving due importance to the melody as distinguished from the accompaniment. The author's boldness of invention is in structural form rather than technical innovation, and it was enough for him that the player should possess ten exactly evenly balanced fingers, and should be able to give due emphasis to prominent parts. Of course the difficulty of many of the studies is considerable, but a player, perfectly equipped in the school of Clementi, would often find himself at a loss in playing Beethoven, and would have to acquire new powers for an adequate presentation of the music of Schumann or Chopin. It was Clementi who started that system of strengthening the weak fingers of the hand by holding down some of the fingers while playing repeated notes with the others. From Kalkbrenner's merely mechanical plan of keeping down four adjacent notes while one finger is actively exercised, to some of Brahms's 51 ' Übungen,' this system has never failed to commend itself to students of technique ; but there is a danger in its use, for the force necessary to work the weak finger may be got by a kind of muscular reaction from the fingers that are pressing down the held notes, rather than from the weak finger itself ; a far better form of the exercise is to lay the fingers in repose upon the keys, and, while the single finger is playing its repeated notes, to watch that the other fingers never leave their keys, and never depress them.

The divergence of styles between the ' Vienna ' school (that of Mozart) and that of Clementi was in part caused by the difference in the make of the pianos employed. The Viennese action had a remarkably easy mechanism, and was best suited to a rapid style and to the execution of arpeggios. The ' English ' pianos preferred by Clementi—to whom many of the most important improvements in them were due—were more sonorous in tone, the hammer had a deeper fall, and it was altogether better adapted to the larger forms of music and to brilliant execution.

Neither in Cramer nor Clementi is great force required ; the hand is never raised to an excessive height, or brought down upon the keys with any such power as was required in the subsequent period of technique. The use of the sustaining pedal, too, was comparatively rare with them, and they and their contemporaries were fully conscious of the loss of clearness caused by its excessive use. They, like all the older masters, were very particular as to the position of the performer's body. The old German writers, such as C. P. E. Bach, Marpurg, Türk and others, recommended the player to sit exactly in the middle of the keyboard. Dussek inclined a little to the left, because of the difficulty of giving action and power to the left hand ; while Kalkbrenner, having regard to the extension of the instrument in an upward direction, took up his seat a little to the right of the middle. In the matter of the position of the hand there were many different theories, even in the earlier days ; Clementi was of opinion that the upper part of the hand, from the knuckles to the wrist, should present such a surface that a piece of money might be placed there, to prove that the fingers alone were engaged in the execution. Dussek directs that the hands should lean rather towards the thumbs, so that the third and fourth fingers may not be placed too much sideways ; and Hummel says they should lean rather to the outside, so as to give the thumb more liberty on the black keys when required. Kalkbrenner, again, was an advocate of playing octaves or sixths with a loose wrist, whilst Moscheles kept the forearm and wrist quite stiff, in order to gain lightness and facility. Fétis, in his introduction to the *Méthode des méthodes*, points out the danger of a tired wrist becoming so enfeebled as to cause the hand to form an angle with the arm, and thus to clog the articulations of the fingers. Hummel recommended the hand to be placed so that the thumb and little finger formed a line parallel to that of the keyboard, and stated that Mozart held his hands in this way. All these authorities agree as to the general rule that the elbows should be slightly in advance of the body, and that from the elbow to the second joint of the fingers should be a level, horizontal line.

In regard to fingering, the masters of the first period were divided as to whether fingering should or should not be what is called ' symmetrical ' ; that is to say, whether a fingering adopted for a figure ascending on each degree of the scale should be repeated exactly all the way up, regardless of black notes, or whether the rule that the thumb should never be placed on black notes was to hold good. Dussek was a great stickler for this rule, which of course increases the difficulty of making certain of the repetitions, as against the freer way of putting the same fingers on the corresponding notes wherever they occur. Dussek even went so far as to direct that in certain passages where the same figure is repeated in a higher octave than that in which it started, a different fingering should be employed, instead of devising some method which should at least allow the symmetrical use of the same fingers on the same notes.

The Vienna school, with its strong tendency towards superficiality, reached its climax in Hummel, who, deriving his method from Mozart, made all kinds of technical discoveries (see Vol. II. pp. 681-2), some of which were considered hardly legitimate by the more conservative teachers of his time. His method, or ' Pianoforte School,' was in some sort the basis of that of Czerny, whose system was calculated to give the pupil the utmost velocity, smoothness and brilliance ; Moscheles carried on technique to a point slightly more advanced, but both he and Hummel can be disregarded by the student of modern pianoforte-playing.

With the ever-increasing admiration for the music of Beethoven, the aims of the technical experts were turned in the direction of sonority rather than elegance or velocity of execution. He himself, with his splendid equipment as a performer, was said to have given the pianoforte a soul, and ever greater and greater were the demands he made upon the instrument. From the desire on the part of performers to excel in the public interpretation of his works, arose, beyond question, the tendency towards a merely muscular force, and, as a result, a great increase in the resisting power of the pianoforte. With him, and with the best of those that came after him, technique was regarded as means to an end, not as the end in itself. Weber, with his bold treatment of the left hand, his love of widespread chords, and Schubert, whose technique, though occasionally showing the influence of the superficial Viennese school, yet follows Beethoven in his happiest moments, each added something to the resources of the instrument, though neither made any special study of technique nor published any ' method.'

Thalberg's wonderful power of singing on the

pianoforte is historically interesting as having so much impressed Mendelssohn as to incite him to imitate it, and it is at least possible that not only the E minor prelude, where a favourite device of Thalberg's is deliberately imitated, but a great number of the 'Songs without Words' were more or less consciously influenced by Thalberg's ideal cantabile. Concerning Mendelssohn's own technique, see Vol. III. pp. 422, 423.

Before following the main stream of technical development from the requirements of Beethoven's sonatas to the achievements of Liszt and his followers, we must consider in the next place the works of Schumann and Chopin, both of whom realised, as none of their predecessors had done, the artistic value of that evanescent tone of the piano which was at first considered the chief defect of the instrument. Both turned the sustaining pedal to richer account, and got new effects from its use ; and both loved a dreamy, poetical, indefinite form of melody, and a style of ornamentation to which the word ' ethereal ' is suitably applied. Schumann's own experiments, made in order to obtain absolute equality of the fingers, resulted in an injury that prevented his playing in public, so that for his own technique we must depend upon his compositions and upon the playing of his illustrious wife. It is evident that her wonderful sonority of tone, the exquisite gradation of her touch, and the quiet brilliance of her playing in ornamental passages were the practical realisation of Schumann's own ideals ; and if all his little innovations in the way of technique (such as those at the close of the ' Papillons,' the end of the piece called ' Paganini,' in the ' Carnaval,' and other places) have not been accepted as part of the regular repertory of technical devices, yet enough was left to enrich the resources of the instrument very materially. Like the older players, Clara Schumann sat on a comparatively low seat, kept the forearm perfectly horizontal, and got the tone purely by pressure of the finger, not by anything that could be called a ' blow ' on the key.

One peculiarity in the technique of Chopin may be usefully studied by comparing his work with that of John Field, to which in form and style it owes so much. The passages of embroidery in which both delight require, in Field's case, that perfect equality of finger at which, as we have seen, the earlier writers aimed ; in Chopin, the essential weakness of the human hand is turned to beautiful account, for his passages are often devised in such a manner that the weak finger of the hands has to play the note which is to be comparatively unimportant. In the concertos and studies the natural conformation of the hand is kept before the composer's eye, and, as a consequence, his difficulties are always of a kind that is grateful to the player, however intricate they may sound.

Liszt's technique seemed to embrace every merit that was characteristic of all his predecessors, and while he proceeded mainly along the lines laid down by Chopin, he translated, one may almost say, Chopin's technique—which, like his quiet style of playing, was after all only thoroughly effective in a comparatively small room—into a language fit for the largest concert-halls. Schumann and Chopin had the quality that is called ' intimacy ' ; and it sometimes seems as if many of their most individual works could only be properly interpreted to a very small circle of sympathetic hearers ; with Liszt everything was brilliant, showy, surprising and eminently for the public. In point of technique, he used, or allowed his pupils to use, a far higher seat than had been generally used before, so that the forearm, instead of being held horizontally, sloped down towards the hand. This gave, beyond any doubt, a great increase of force to the blow upon the keys ; and in Liszt's own hands tone was never sacrificed to power, nor was it ever possible to say that he went beyond the limits of musical beauty even in the loudest passages. Still he undoubtedly did institute the methods of obtaining great tone, which afterwards were so misused by many of his pupils ; he carried further the principle of turning the inherent weakness of the hand into a beauty, and if it is true of Chopin, it is ten times truer of Liszt, that his passages sound far harder than they are. He exhausted the possibilities of the keyboard in many directions, and carried to an extreme point such devices as that which is sometimes called ' blind octaves,' a device which is hardly a compliment to the musical sense of the average hearer. It can be made less objectionable than it is by nature, if care is taken to make the thumbs more prominent than the outsides of the octaves, but it must always sound rather a makeshift, and to introduce it into the works of the older composers is surely nothing short of blasphemy.

The sustaining pedal, which in the hands of Schumann and Chopin is used very often as if it were a veil enfolding their melodies in a luminous haze, is frequently used by Liszt as a means of setting the hands free for other things ; and a special kind of brilliance was attained by him in rapid ornamental passages in the higher octaves of the piano, by holding the fingers almost stiffly, and not allowing them to move with much independence, and by throwing the hand, as it were, at the passage where it begins. It was Liszt's followers, rather than himself, who formed the habit of exerting undue force in order to get all available volume of tone from the piano. If Rubenstein and Tausig, among the older men of their generation, never produced tones that were not beautiful, others injured their power of playing in a cantabile style by exerting strength in a way that was not scientifically correct. Pianoforte-makers were compelled to provide an increasing amount of resistance[1] in order to stand the attacks of the pianists of the 'seventies. In the present day the resistance of the keys has returned to nearly as small an amount as it was in 1817. This reaction is due to the general recognition of the fact that the most sonorous tone is not produced by uncontrolled violence; the laws of muscular control have been gradually realised even by musicians, and as a consequence a beautifully round tone is nowadays not an unusual possession with modern players, even in their loudest passages.

Down to the last quarter of the 19th century, as far as 1880, if not later, this tendency showed no diminution, and the concertos and show pieces of that time make it clearly manifest that the pianists relied for their effect upon producing a loud tone at any cost of quality. Even the earlier pianoforte works of Brahms, down to the date of the two rhapsodies, op. 79, and the second concerto, op. 83, show traces of this ultra-virile ideal of playing; and his contribution towards the technique of the instrument was mainly in the direction of attaining perfect independence of finger, not merely the physical independence for which the earlier men had striven, but such mental independence that one finger should be able to play three even notes against two even notes in another part of the hand, while two more parts were going on in the other hand, neither of them corresponding with either finger of the first. In his later works, from op. 116 to the end, the peculiar qualities of pianoforte tone are more carefully considered than in his earlier compositions, against which one of the commonest reproaches was that they were not suited to the pianoforte. One of the first examples of this consideration for the characteristics of the pianoforte is the intermezzo in A flat from op. 76, which would lose all its meaning and point if it were played on any other instrument. The 'evanescent' tone of the instrument is definitely required throughout, and in all the later sets of pieces there are passages which show that Brahms demanded from his interpreters something far more than

[1] The following table of resistances is taken from grand pianos of various dates by Broadwood & Sons:

|      | Lowest C. | Middle C. | Highest C. |
|------|-----------|-----------|------------|
| 1817 | 2⅔ oz.    | 2¼ oz.    | 1¼ oz.     |
| 1877 | 4 ,,      | 3¼ ,,     | 2¾ ,,      |
| 1904 | 3 ,,      | 2¼ ,,     | 2 ,,       |

the storm and stress which appealed to him in his earlier life.

Exactly where the reaction against the school of the piano-thumpers began, it would not be easy to say; but while Mme. Schumann was alive, the quiet and truly musical style had never passed away even in Germany, where thumping had its home. The influence of men like Sgambati and Buonamici in Italy, Saint-Saëns in France, and Tchaikovsky in Russia, encouraged the quieter style of playing, and after the enormous vogue of Paderewski's style, pianists began again to devote themselves to the production of tone rather than of noise, and of muscular control rather than of mere force. A lower seat was adopted, the forearm was again held in a horizontal line, instead of slanting downwards towards the keys, and the wrist once again came into play. The technical teaching of Leschetizky, and in an even greater degree that of Deppe, went to encourage an absolute mastery of many gradations of tone, and a scientific system of tone-production.

In most of the modern schools, and in a good many of the later editions of the classics, the pedals were directed to be managed far more carefully than they had been, and in some cases an extra stave of one line was used to indicate the exact treatment of the sustaining pedal. No detail of technique is now regarded as beneath the student's notice, and while the early pieces of Scriabin foreshadowed many of the latest effects of technique, the music of Debussy and Ravel gave the pianoforte a new eloquence. Not only does the passage-writing in these composers lie easily for the hand, but new sonorities are discovered in both which have enormously increased the resources of the instrument. In the 'Cathédrale engloutie' of the former, such use is made of an acoustic phenomenon with which the name of Tartini is associated, that the hearer fancies he hears notes far below the real compass of the pianoforte; and at every turn we meet with treatment so deft that the atmosphere desired by the composer seems to be at the command even of moderately skilful players.

From time to time 'royal roads' to pianoforte-playing have been brought forward in various countries; the detailed analysis of the processes involved in the various kinds of touch, the discovery that useful practice could be contrived away from the keyboard, or with a silent keyboard allowing various touches to be employed, and even modifications of the design of the keyboard, have found their adherents; and it is possible that from each and all some benefit may be derived. The effect of the various mechanical contrivances of the pianola type has been beneficial in one way, for a merely textual accuracy, which can be far more certainly attained by the machine, is no longer an end in itself, but the student knows that much more is required and that a soulless technical proficiency has no longer any appreciable market-value. It is of course impossible to foresee what will be the next stage of development of pianoforte-playing, but it may be taken for granted that no return will be made to the heavy touch of the piano in fashion in the latter part of the 19th century, and that delicacy of tone-gradation will hold an even higher place in the regard of practical musicians.                                          M.

PIANOLA, see MECHANICAL APPLIANCES (5).

PIANO-MÉCANIQUE, see MECHANICAL APPLIANCES (2).

PIANO-ORGAN, see MECHANICAL APPLIANCES (3).

PIANO-VIOLIN, see SOSTINENTE PIANOFORTE.

PIATTI, see CYMBALS.

PIATTI, ALFREDO CARLO (b. Bergamo, Jan. 8, 1822 ; d. Crocetta di Nozzo, July 18, 1901), violoncellist, was the son of Antonio Piatti (b. Bergamo, 1801), a violinist of some repute, who held the post of leader in the orchestra of his native town.

At the age of 5 Piatti began to study the instrument which was destined to make him famous, receiving instruction from his greatuncle, Zanetti, an accomplished violoncellist, and a patient teacher. After two years' study, Zanetti, considering his pupil sufficiently advanced, obtained permission for him to play in the theatre orchestra. Before the beginning of the following season, Zanetti died, and the youthful Alfredo was elected his successor in the orchestra. MAYR (q.v.), who was at that time the maestro di cappella, took a particular fancy to the young artist, and on one occasion, during a festival held by four orchestras in the neighbouring village of Caravaggio, singled Piatti out to play a solo, which by rights should have fallen to Merighi, an experienced artist and professor at the Milan Conservatoire. This episode piqued the elder virtuoso, and when in 1832—at the age of 10—Piatti sought to become a scholar at that institution, Merighi was the only professor who opposed his admittance. Eventually, however, Piatti was granted a five years' scholarship. At the age of 15½ he made his public début as a soloist on Sept. 21, 1837, at a Conservatoire concert. He performed a concerto of his own composition, and received as a prize the instrument upon which he played. Returning to Bergamo, Piatti resumed his post in the orchestra, played nightly at the opera, and accompanied his father to every neighbouring village where a likely opportunity for playing a solo presented itself. After a time he gave a concert at Turin ; played at the Kärnthnerthor Theatre, Vienna, and, his engagement at the Bergamo Theatre coming to an end owing to a misunderstanding, gave concerts in various towns in and about Italy. At Pest he fell ill,

and having no reserve funds, was reduced to selling his violoncello. Fortunately a friend from Bergamo heard of his difficulties, and came and assisted him to return to his native town. The journey necessitated a stoppage at Munich, where Piatti made the acquaintance of Liszt. Liszt encouraged him to go to Paris, where he arrived in 1844. Here he came in contact with Habeneck, received a present of an Amati violoncello from Liszt, and composed his 'Chant religieux,' and ' Sonnambula.'

In the same year occurred Piatti's first visit to England, making his début before an English audience at the Annual Grand Morning Concert given by Mrs. Anderson at Her Majesty's Theatre on May 31, 1844. The critics ranked him at once as an artist of extraordinary excellence. It was at this same concert that (as Piatti was wont to tell the story in after years) a ' little fat boy with ruddy cheeks and a short jacket all over buttons, stepped on the platform and played the violin.' This was Joseph Joachim, whose name in after years was so closely associated with that of Piatti. On June 24 he played at the Philharmonic. After touring in the provinces, Scotland and Ireland in the autumn, with Sivori, Döhler, Lablache and Belletti, he returned to Milan. From the end of 1844 to the latter part of the year 1845 he toured in Russia with Döhler. One outcome of his visit was the composition of his ' Mazurka sentimentale ' (op. 6), the ' Air Baskyr '— suggested to him by a man who occasionally played upon a bagpipe under his window at St. Petersburg—and the ' Fantaisie Russe.'

Piatti's second visit to England took place in 1846, when he made his début as a quartet-player at the benefit concert of the director of the Musical Union at Willis's Rooms ; and on May 4, 1847, played at the private matinée given by the Beethoven Quartet Society on the occasion of Mendelssohn's last visit to England. During the autumn of 1850 Piatti frequently played solos at the National Concerts, which were held at Her Majesty's under the direction of Balfe ; and at the Sacred Harmonic Society's opening concert of the season, Dec. 5, 1851, he replaced Lindley, on his retirement. On the establishment of the Popular Concerts Piatti was engaged, his long association with them beginning on Jan. 3, 1859, and ending with his retirement in 1898. Besides Piatti's active work as a soloist, he developed his powers of composition under Molique ; in his own estimation his most important works were his SIX sonatas for violoncello and piano, which were composed for the Popular Concerts. He also wrote two concertos, and a concertino for violoncello and orchestra played at the Crystal Palace Concerts. Besides his original compositions Piatti collected and edited classical solos of past centuries.

As an artist Piatti gained an unsurpassable reputation (see VIOLONCELLO-PLAYING). His absolute command of technical difficulties, combined with his purity of tone, faultless intonation, exquisite delicacy, and perfect phrasing of cantabile passages, brought him the homage not only of the public, but also of his fellow-artists. The reverential esteem which was felt towards him in England was never more apparent than on the occasion of the 'Joachim-Piatti Jubilee,' on Mar. 22, 1894, at the Grafton Galleries, where a reception was organised by Grove and Mackenzie to celebrate the fiftieth anniversary of the English début of these virtuosi in 1844. In his own country Piatti's appearances were perforce rare owing to his popularity in England, but when—after an absence of eighteen years—he played at a concert given to raise funds to defray the expenses of a monument to Donizetti at Bergamo (Oct. 18, 1893) he was received with wild enthusiasm. The warmth of the reception was enhanced by the presentation of the grade of Commendatore in the Order of the Crown of Italy, which was conferred upon him by King Umberto. Piatti was a keen bibliophile and a remarkable connoisseur of fiddles and violoncellos. For the last twenty years of his life he resided at No. 15 Northwick Terrace, London, but after the purchase of his property—called Villa Piatti—near Cadenabbia on the Lake of Como, he retired to his Italian home after the strenuous labours of the London musical season, returning to Northwick Terrace in the autumn. The last months of his life were passed at Crocetta di Nozzo, about four miles from Bergamo, the residence of his daughter, Countess Lochis, where he died from disease of the heart.

After his death the professors and students of the Bergamo school of music kept solemn watch by the body until it was laid in its last resting-place in the private chapel of the Lochis family. The public funeral took place on July 22, and was attended by the Prefect, the Mayor, members of Parliament and representatives of the leading musical societies. Four professors played the andante from Schubert's quartet in D minor, according to Piatti's express wish, and a week later visited the Lochis chapel again, and made a compact to perform the quartet annually on the anniversary of the master's death.

Piatti's wife, Mary Ann Lucey Welsh, only daughter of Thomas Welsh, a professor of singing, only survived her husband for a few months. The marriage took place at Wolchester, near Stroud, in 1856, but the union was not a happy one and ended in separation. The only surviving daughter of the marriage became the wife of Count Lochis, who died in 1899, leaving the widowed Countess with two children, Marchesita and Alfredo, who was named after his grandfather.

PUBLISHED COMPOSITIONS

Concerto, op. 8, v'cl. and PF., Mainz, 1863 ; Nocturne, op. 2, v'cl. PF., Mainz, 1863 ; Siciliana, v'cl. and PF., Mainz, 1863 ; Dodici capricci per il violoncello, Berlin, 1875 ; Concerto, v'cl. and orchestra, Berlin, 1872 ; Concerto, v'cl. and orchestra, Leipzig, 1877 ; Fantasia romanesca, Berlin, 1885 ; Serenata, for two v'cls. and PF., London, 1890 ; Romanza per violino ; Bergamasca ; Chant religieux ; Souvenir d'Ems ; Mazurka sentimentale, op. 6 ; Air Baskyr, op. 8, Fantaisie russe ; Danza moresca, and numerous songs with violoncello obbligato.

TRANSCRIPTIONS AND ARRANGEMENTS

Sei lezioni per la viola d' amore (d' Attilio Ariosti) ridotti per il violoncello da Piatti ; six Sonatas by Boccherini, also Sonatas of Locatelli ; Veracini, and Porpora ; Kummer's Violoncello Method ; 1st Sonata of Marcello ; Mendelssohn's Lieder ohne Worte ; Three melodies of Schubert ; Variations of Christopher Simpson.

BIBL.—MORTON LATHAM, Alfredo Piatti ; PRATT, People of the Period ; MASON CLARKE, Dictionary of Fiddlers ; Fétis ; Mus. T., Aug. 1901, with portrait ; Athenæum, Mar. 31, 1894, and contemporary dates ; Times, July 20, 1901 ; Graphic, July 27, 1904, with portrait.        O. R. and E. H.-A.

**PIBGORN** (PIB-CORN) (according to Stainer and Barrett's *Dictionary of Musical Terms*, from 'pib' or 'piob,' meaning pipe, and 'corn,' horn), a small instrument of the beating reed type, with cylindrical tube and expanding bell. Its use was mainly among the Welsh and other Celtic peoples. The tube was often of elder or other hollow wood, but sometimes of the shinbone of a sheep or deer, a natural horn being used for the bell. Canon F. W. Galpin gives the following description of one in his possession (see *PLATE LXXV*. No. 4) :

' My pib-corn is in total length 1 foot 8½ inches The tube (of deer bone) is 6½ inches long with a single beating reed (as given in Daines Barrington's description). It has the scale of F major, from $f'$ to $f''$, and it is pierced with six holes in front, and one for the thumb behind.'

(See BARRINGTON, Daines ; HORNPIPE.)
                                        D. J. B.

**PIBROCH** (Gaelic *Piobaireachd,* a 'pipe-tune '), a series of variations for the bagpipe, founded on a theme called the *urlar*. Pibrochs are the highest form of bagpipe music, and are often very difficult to execute properly. The variations, generally three or four in number, increase in difficulty and speed, until the composition concludes with a *creanluidh*, or quick movement. Like all bagpipe music, pibrochs are written in a peculiar scale, and it is impossible to note them down correctly for any other instrument, particularly owing to the presence of an extra note between F and F♮, a peculiarity which is also found in the Alpenhorn. (See BAGPIPE ; RANZ DES VACHES.) Pibrochs are generally of a warlike character, including marches and dirges ; they often bear the names of various historical and legendary events. Thus 'The Raid of Kilchrist' is ascribed to Macdonald of Glengarry's piper, who composed and performed this pibroch in the year 1603, during the burning of a church with its whole congregation ; and the specimen of which a portion is given below—' Failte Phroinsa,' the Prince's Salute—was composed by John MacIntyre, piper to Menzies of Menzies, on the landing of the Pretender in 1715. It must not, however, be supposed that the music is always contemporary with the events which the pibrochs commemorate ; for although many of them are undoubtedly of

considerable antiquity, yet the names of old
pibrochs which have been lost are often transferred to new compositions. There are not
many collections of Highland music, but the
best are those by Patrick Macdonald (of Kil-
more), Donald Macdonald and Mackay. The
last collection, by Angus Mackay, containing
sixty pibrochs, was published in 1838, and was
followed by a collection made by William Ross,
piper to Queen Victoria, issued in 1869, revised
editions in 1876 and 1896. The largest collection is that of Major-General Thomson, published under the title of Ceol Mor, in 1900.
The following is the first part of the *urlar* of a
pibroch, and is interesting, as showing the
' warblers ' or grace-notes in which good pipers
excel. It must be remembered that the note
represented by F is rather sharper in the
bagpipe.

The name Pibroch is used by Mackenzie in
the title of a piece for violin and orchestra.

w. b. s. ; addn. w. h. g. f.

PICCHI, Giovanni, organist, *c.* 1620, at the
church ' Della casa Grande,' Venice. His book
' Intavolatura di balli d'arpicordo ' (1620) is
one of the most interesting monuments of early
Italian harpsichord music ; a toccata of his is
in the ' Fitzwilliam Virginal Book ' (see Virginal Music). A book of ' Canzoni da sonar '
in 2-8 parts with bass contains 16 canzones
and 3 sonatas for violins, cornetti, bassoons,
trombones and flutes. He wrote also some
vocal church music (*Q.-L.*).

PICCINI, Lodovico Alessandra (*b.* Paris,
1779 ; *d.* there, 1850), a natural son of Joseph,
son of Nicolo Piccini ; distinguished himself as
accompanist at first at the Théâtre Feydeau,
and from 1802 at the Opéra, where he became
also chorus-master, but lost his position in 1826,
without a reason being given. He was a prolific composer of comic operas, ballets and
melodramas, of which a long list is given by
Fétis. (See also *Q.-L.*)

PICCINNI, Niccola (*b.* Bari, kingdom of
Naples, Jan. 16, 1728 ; *d.* Passy, May 7, 1800),
was for a considerable time the most popular
of Italian operatic composers.

The son of a musician, he was at first intended by his father for the Church, but at the
instance of the Bishop of Bari he was sent to
the Conservatorio of San Onofrio, then presided

over by Leo. He went there at the age of 14,
and was at first instructed by a *maestrino*, a
kind of pupil-teacher, who by his dry dogmatic
lessons and severity only succeeded in disgust-
ing the gifted boy, who showed on his part a
disposition to throw aside all control. Leo
averted this by taking him for his own pupil,
and Durante (who, at Leo's death, resumed his
previous mastership of San Onofrio) had also
an especial affection for the young student.
' The others are my pupils,' he was wont to say ;
' this one is my son.'

Piccinni quitted the Conservatorio in 1754,
after twelve years of study, and made his début
as a composer with the opera ' Le donne dispet-
tose,' at the Florentine theatre at Naples, in
1755. The success of this piece was remarkable,
as Logroscino's comic operas had so monopolised the stage that it was difficult for any others
to obtain a hearing. Equally fortunate were
' Le gelosie ' and ' Il curioso del proprio danno,'
both in the light comic style, while ' Zenobia '
(San Carlo, 1756) and ' Alessandro nelle Indie '
(Rome, 1758) not only pleased the public, but
showed advance in power, the last-named opera
containing an overture which was greatly
admired. Piccinni married, in 1756, Vincenza
Sibilla, his pupil, who, to great personal charms,
united that of a beautiful and touching voice.
Her husband would not allow her to appear on
the stage. She was, however, an exquisite
singer in private circles, and Piccinni, with a
wide experience of *prime donne,* said he never
heard his own airs so perfectly rendered as by
her.

It was at Rome, in 1760, that he produced
' La Cecchina, ossia la buona figliuola,' perhaps
the most popular *opera buffa* that ever existed,
which for years had a most extraordinary vogue.
It was performed on every stage in Italy, and
on most stages in Europe, and everywhere was
received with the same enthusiasm. At Rome
it was played not only at all the principal
theatres, but at the most insignificant, even
that of the *Burattini*, or marionnettes, and all
classes of people were equally delighted with it.
Fashions were all *alla Cecchina* ; inns, shops,
villas, wines—in fact, all things that could be
named—were called after her. Nor was more
weighty appreciation wanting. ' Sarà qualche
ragazzo o qualche ragazzata ' (' probably some
boy or boy's work '), said Jommelli, impor-
tuned on his return to Italy from Stuttgart
with perpetual praises of ' La Cecchina ' and its
author. He went, however, to hear the work
performed, and his *dictum* to the amateurs who
crowded round him at the end to know his
opinion was ' Ascoltate la sentenza d' Jommelli : questo è inventore ' (' Hear the opinion
of Jommelli : this is an inventor '). It is difficult now to account for the immense preference
given to ' La Cecchina ' over other works of the
time, although the airs it contains are lively, as

well as graceful and pleasing. In the next year another triumph was won by ' L' Olimpiade,' previously set by Leo, Pergolesi, Galuppi and Jommelli, but never so successfully as by Piccinni. Among his other improvements on existing operatic forms must be mentioned his extension of the duet, hitherto treated in a conventional, undramatic way, and the variety and importance he gave to the finale. His fame was equalled by his industry. In the year 1761 alone he wrote six operas, three serious and three comic. In 1773 a rival appeared in the person of Anfossi, sometime Piccinni's pupil, and who owed to him his first theatrical engagement. He was very far inferior to Piccinni, but his ' Incognita perseguitata ' had a popular success, as had two or three weak operas that followed it. The inconstant Roman public forsook its old favourite ; an opera of Piccinni's was hissed by Anfossi's partisans, and withdrawn. This so affected the composer's sensitive nature that, returning to Naples, he fell seriously ill, and was in danger for many months. On his recovery he decided not to return to Rome. In 1774 he had given at Naples a second ' Alessandro nelle Indie,' superior to the first ; he now wrote an *opera buffa*, ' I viaggiatori,' which had at Naples almost the success of ' La Cecchina ' at Rome.

In 1776 he yielded to invitations and powerful inducements held out to him to go to Paris, where, with his family, he arrived in December, on a promised salary of 6000 francs, with travelling expenses. He knew not a word of the French language, but Marmontel undertook to be his instructor, and to make such changes in several operas of Quinault as should adapt them for modern music. For some time he passed every morning with Piccinni, explained a scene to him, taught him to repeat it, marked by signs the quantity of each word and each syllable, and then left him to work. The next morning Piccinni sang over to him what he had composed. His first French opera, ' Roland ' (produced Jan. 27, 1778), was completed after a year's labour of this kind.

He had not long begun it when the famous feud arose between his admirers and those of Gluck. This great man had brought about a revolution in French serious opera, worthy in its way to be compared to the political and social revolution which followed soon after. He had freed the tragic lyrical stage from a mass of uncouth antediluvian conventionality, and had substituted for it a new and living form of Art. Like all innovators, he had enemies, and those who had been disgusted by the uncompromising fury of his partisans ranged themselves under Piccinni's banner. A war of pamphlets and other writings raged unabated for years. It divided society ; the subject was unsafe. Men met each other for the

first time with the question, almost implying a challenge, ' Sir, are you Gluckist or Piccinnist ? '

Poor Piccinni, quiet and peaceable, a stranger to intrigue, kept at a distance from all the turmoil, which was such that, on the night of the first performance of ' Roland,' fears were entertained for his personal safety. To the general surprise, he was brought home in triumph to his family. The opera had had a complete success, especial enthusiasm being elicited by the pretty ballet airs—a curious fact, as Piccinni had no sympathy with dancing, and disliked having to write dance music.

He was in favour with Marie Antoinette, and gave her two singing-lessons a week at Versailles. The satisfaction of teaching so distinguished a pupil was supposed to be its own sufficient reward ; at any rate he received no other payment, not even his travelling expenses.

He as appointed director of a troupe of Italian singers engaged to give performances on alternate nights at the Opéra, and in this capacity produced ' Le finte gemelle ' (June 11, 1778), ' La buona figliuola ' (Dec. 7, 1778), ' La buona figliuola maritata ' (Apr. 15, 1779), ' Il vago disprezzato ' (May 16, 1779). The idea now occurred to the principal director to get two operas on the same subject from the famous rivals, and ' Iphigénie en Tauride ' was fixed on. The poetical version given to Piccinni to set was so bad, that after composing the first two acts he took it to Ginguené, who to a great extent rewrote the book. Meanwhile the manager, violating a promise made to Piccinni to the contrary, had Gluck's ' Iphigénie ' performed first, which met with the brilliant success it deserved. Piccinni in the meantime (Feb. 22, 1780) produced ' Atys,' an opera, superior to ' Roland ' ; some numbers of which, especially the ' Chorus of Dreams,' were for many years very popular at concerts ; and ' Adèle de Ponthieu,' a lyric tragedy (Oct. 27, 1781). His ' Iphigénie ' (produced Jan. 23, 1781) contained many beauties. It had small chance of succeeding after Gluck's, but was fairly well received in spite of the untoward incident which marred its second representation. No sooner had Mlle. Laguerre, the Iphigénie of the evening, appeared on the scene, than it became painfully evident that she was intoxicated. She got through the part without breaking down, but the luckless composer heard Sophie Arnould's *bon mot* going from mouth to mouth, ' C'est Iphigénie en Champagne.' The opera had, however, seventeen consecutive performances.

Gluck had left Paris in 1780, but a new rival now appeared in Sacchini, whose ' Renaud ' (Feb. 28, 1783) had considerable success. ' Didon,' reckoned Piccinni's best French opera, was first produced, by command, before the court at Fontainebleau (Oct. 16, 1783), and afterwards at the Opéra, where it kept the boards till Feb. 8, 1826—its 250th representation. At the same time the smaller works of 'Le Dormeur éveillé' and 'Le Faux Lord' were being performed by the Italian company, and were very popular. About this time a school for singing was established in Paris, of which Piccinni was appointed principal master, and which showed the results of his training in an excellent performance of 'Roland' by the pupils. But the tide of fortune seemed now to turn against him. 'Lucette' and 'Le Mensonge officieux' failed in 1786 and 1787. 'Diane et Endymion' and 'Pénélope' had met with the same fate in 1784 and 1785 respectively. He was not, however, embittered by these reverses. When Sacchini died, of vexation and disappointment, Piccinni pronounced his funeral oration, full of delicate and discriminating praise of all that was best in his works. When Gluck died, in 1787, Piccinni was anxious to found, by subscription, an annual concert in memory of the great man 'to whom,' he wrote, 'the lyrical theatre is as much indebted as is the French stage to the great Corneille.' From lack of support the proposal was not carried out.

'Clytemnestra,' a serious opera, failed to obtain a representation, and when the Revolution broke out in 1789, and he lost his pension, he returned to Naples. Here he was well received by the King, who gave him another pension. Some of his old works were performed, as well as an oratorio, 'Jonathan' (1702), and a new *opera buffa*, 'La serva onorata.' But he got into trouble owing to the marriage of one of his daughters with a young Frenchman of avowed Liberal opinions, was denounced as a Jacobin, disgraced at court, and his next opera purposely hooted down. An engagement to compose two operas at Venice gave him the opportunity of absenting himself, but when, at the end of some months, he was foolish enough to return to Naples, he was immediately placed by the first minister, Acton, in a kind of arrest, and forbidden to leave his house. There he remained, in misery and indigence, for four years. He had previously heard that all the property he had left in France was lost, that a friend for whom he had become security was bankrupt, and that all his scores had been sold to pay this man's debts. He now supported himself and beguiled the time by composing music to several Psalms, translated into Italian by Saverio Mattei. The convents and churches for which these were written became possessors of the original scores, as he was too poor to have them copied.

The treaty of peace with the French Republic brought hope for him. The ambassador, Canclaux, procured for him the means of communicating with his friends in Paris, and David, the famous singer, got him an offer of an engagement at Venice. With some difficulty a passport was procured for him by Garet, successor to Canclaux, and Lachèze, secretary of legation, who also furnished him with the means of going, he being absolutely penniless. At Rome he was fêted by the French Fine Arts Commission, and persuaded to go direct to Paris, where he arrived on Dec. 3, 1798. The annual distribution of prizes in the Conservatoire occurred next day, and Piccinni was invited to be present. He was conducted on to the stage, and presented to the public amid deafening applause. Five thousand francs were granted him for his immediate necessities, as well as a small pension. This was, however, most irregularly paid, and when some months later his family arrived, in utter destitution, from Naples, whence they had had to fly in the wake of the French army, Piccinni found himself again in almost desperate circumstances. His troubles brought on an attack of paralysis, from which he did not recover for some months. Many melancholy MS. letters of his are extant, showing to what a miserable state he was reduced. Some are addressed to Bonaparte, praying that his pension might be paid, for the sake of the many dependent on him. Bonaparte showed him kindness, and paid him twenty-five louis for a military march. A sixth inspector's place was created for him in the Conservatoire, but he was now again prostrated by severe illness, aggravated by the treatment of surgeons who bled him recklessly. He rallied, however, and went to Passy, in the hope of recovering his strength, but fresh domestic anxieties pursued him, and he succumbed on May 7, 1800. He was buried in the common cemetery (which has since been sold), and a stone was placed over him by friends.

His place in the Conservatoire was given to Monsigny, on condition that half the salary attached to it should be paid to Mme. Piccinni during her life, she, in return, instructing four pupils of the Conservatoire in singing.

Piccinni's Paris scores are much more fully orchestrated than those of his earlier Italian works, and show in this the influence both of the French and the German spirit. He was, however, opposed to innovation. It is interesting to read, in Ginguené's life of him, his views on this question.

That he should ever have been opposed, on equal terms, to Gluck, seems now incredible. Yet by numbers of contemporaries—critical and cultivated—he was reckoned Gluck's equal, and his superior by not a few. But his art was of a kind that adapts itself to its age; Gluck's the art to which the age has, in time, to adapt itself.

A complete list of Piccinni's very numerous works is to be found in *R.M.I.* vol. viii. p. 75;

in *Q.-L.* the names of eighty-five operas are given, as well as three oratorios, a mass and some psalms.

Piccinni left two sons, the second of whom, LUDOVICO (*b.* Naples, 1766 ; *d.* Paris, July 31, 1827), learned music from his father and followed it as a career. He followed his father to Paris in 1782, and after a chequered career (he was appointed Kapellmeister at Stockholm in 1796) died in Paris. He wrote many operas, but they are dismissed by Fétis as works of no value. Certainly none of them have survived. The elder son, GIUSEPPE, is known only through his natural son, LOUIS ALEXANDRE (*b.* Paris, Sept. 10, 1779 ; *d.* there, Apr. 24, 1850), a composer of more than 200 pieces for the stage, as well as of twenty-five comic operas, of which a list is given by Fétis.    F. A. M.

BIBLIOGRAPHY

GINGUENÉ : *Notice sur la vie et les ouvrages de Piccinni.* (1800.)
DESNOIRETERRES : *La Musique française au XVIIIe siècle, Gluck et Piccinni, 1774-1800.* (1872.)
A. CAMETTI : *Saggio cronologico delle opere teatrali di N. Piccinni.* (*R.M.I.* viii., 1901.)
HENRI DE CURZON : *Les Dernières Années de Piccinni à Paris.* (Paris, 1890.)
HERMANN ABERT : *Piccinni als Buffokomponist.* (*J.M.P.*, 1913.)
JOSEFINE DAGMAR POPOVICI : *La buona figliuola von Nicola Piccinni.* (Vienna, 1920.)
E. BLOM : *Stepchildren of Music : V. A Misjudged Composer.* London, 1925.)

PICCIONI, GIOVANNI, of Rimini, was, in 1577, maestro di musica in the house of Desiosi of Conegliano, and afterwards, until 1602, organist at Orvieto Cathedral. In 1616 he calls himself organist and maestro di cappella of Monte Fiaschone (province of Rome). He composed masses and other church music, and a large number of madrigals, motets and canzone, a list of which appears in *Q.-L.*

PICCOLELLIS, GIOVANNI DI, author of a scholarly publication entitled *Liutai antichi e moderni. Note critico-biografiche* (Florence, 1885 : Successori le Monnier), and a supplemental volume, *Liutai antichi e moderni. Genealogia degli Amati e dei Guarnieri secondo i documenti ultimamente ritrovati negli atti e stati d' anime delle antiche parrocchie dei SS. Faustino e Giovita e di S. Donato di Cremona. Note aggiunte alla prima edizione sui liutai pubblicata in Firenze nell' anno MDCCLXXXV.* (Florence, 1886 : Successori le Monnier). This work, which is a masterpiece of the finest modern Italian typography, is embellished with twenty-four exquisitely executed photogravure plates of the violins of the greatest masters. The letterpress, which is worthy of the illustrations, gives exhaustive information concerning the bow-instruments of Europe, the Brescian and Cremonese schools, together with laborious analyses and classified biographies of the Italian, French, German and English schools of violin-making. The work is one which forms a valuable addition to the literature of the violin. A discourse which was read by the author before the Florentine Academy of Music on Apr. 29, 1888, and published under title *Della autenticità e pregio di taluni strumenti ad arco*

*appartenti al R. Istituto Musicale di Firenze* (Florence, 1889 : Galleti e Cocci), is an interesting argument on the authorship of several bow-instruments preserved in the museum of the Conservatorio, some of which appear to be hitherto unascribed. The remarks on varnish are interesting and pertinent, and are followed by an interesting discussion on a violin and viola attributed to Stradivarius, and a violoncello assigned to Nicola Amati.

BIBL. — HERON-ALLEN, *De fidiculis bibliographia* ; MATTHEW
*The Literature of Music.*    E. H.-A.

PICCOLO, see FLUTE (2).

PICCOLOMINI, MARIETTA (*b.* Siena, 1834 [1] ; *d.* Florence, Dec. 1899), member of the well-known Tuscan family. Being passionately fond of music she determined to become a public singer, and, in spite of opposition from her family, studied under Signora Mazzarelli and Signor Pietro Romani, both of Florence, and made her début in 1852 at La Pergola as Lucrezia Borgia ; she afterwards played at Rome, Siena, Bologna, etc., and in 1855 at the Carignan Theatre, Turin, as Violetta in ' La Traviata,' on its production there, and was highly successful.

She made her début in London at Her Majesty's Theatre, May 24, 1856, in the same opera, then produced for the first time in England. She immediately became the fashion, partly on account of her charming little figure and clever, realistic acting—especially in the last act, where she introduced a consumptive cough ; and partly perhaps on account of the plot of the opera, which excited much indignation and a warm newspaper controversy.[2] She next played Maria, in the ' Figlia,' and Norma, with fair success. Whatever might be the merits of her acting, of her singing there were many adverse opinions, notably those of Chorley. She afterwards played at the Théâtre des Italiens, Paris. Mlle. Piccolomini reappeared for the seasons of 1857 and 1858 at Her Majesty's, and added to her repertory Adina (' L' Elisir ') (described by Henry Morley [3] as one of her best-acted parts), Zerlina and Susanna of Mozart ; Arline, in the Italian version of ' The Bohemian Girl ' ; Lucia, in ' Luisa Miller,' on the production of that opera, June 8, 1858 ; and ' La serva padrona ' of Paisiello, July 5, 1858.[4] She then went to America, and made a great success. In 1859 she played for a short time at Drury Lane with diminished effect, and for a few nights in 1860 at Her Majesty's, and took farewell of the stage, Apr. 30, as Almina, in the second performance of a new opera of that name by Campana, and in a duet from ' I martiri ' with Giuglini. Soon

[1] Pougin, Paloschi and Mendel give 1836 as the date.
[2] The original play, ' La Dame aux camélias,' was formerly forbidden on the English stage ; but Mme. Modjeska played in a modified version at the Court Theatre in 1880, and later it was frequently given by Sarah Bernhardt, Eleanora Duse and others.
[3] *Recollections of an Old Playgoer.*
[4] Having sung the music previously at Benedict's annual concert June 21, at the same theatre.

after this she married the Marchese Gaetani della Fargia. She nevertheless returned to the stage for four nights in 1863, and generously gave her services in aid of the benefit organised at Drury Lane for her old manager Lumley, having travelled to England for that express purpose. A testimonial was set on foot for her in 1884, when she was reported to be in reduced circumstances (*Daily News*, Mar. 21, 1884).  A. C.

PICCOLO-VIOLINO, see VIOLINO PICCOLO.

PICCO PIPE, a small and unimportant member of the family of *flûtes à bec*. It owes whatever musical significance it may possess to the efforts of a single exceptional player, an Italian peasant, who, under the name of ' Picco, the Sardinian minstrel,' appeared in London in 1856, first on Feb. 21 at Covent Garden. It is stated that this performer was able to produce from it a compass of three octaves.

It consists, as usually made, of a boxwood tube 3½ inches long. Of this 1½ inches are occupied by a mouthpiece, common to it and to the penny whistle, the flageolet, the *flûte à bec* and the diapason pipe of the organ. The remaining 2 inches form all the modulative apparatus required. This consists of three lateral holes ; two in front, one at the back, for the thumb and two first fingers of either hand, and an expanded bell, spreading to ⅞ of an inch in diameter. It is obvious that some additional device is necessary to complete even the simplest and most rudimentary diatonic scale. This is furnished by first using it as a stopped pipe ; the bell being blocked, wholly or partially, by the palm of the hand, twelve semitones being so produced ; then as an open pipe, giving eight consecutive notes ; and lastly, by overblowing on the first harmonic of a stopped pipe (the 12th), obtaining again with a stopped bell six more semitones. Besides these, some intermediate sounds are indicated by half stopping holes, or by forcing the wind, according as the vibrations have to be slackened or accelerated.

The compass is usually twenty-six semitones, and is made to begin with *b*, rising to *c'''*. The lowest note is only to be obtained by covering the bell with the palm of the hand and closing all the holes. At *b'* the open scale begins, and at *g''* the harmonic. It is obvious that this notation is at best only approximative, and at least an octave lower than the real sounds emitted. Probably C is the fundamental note of the instrument, depressed somewhat by the irregular form of the sounding tube. (Compare FLUTE.)  W. H. S.

PICHEL (PICHL), WENZEL (*b.* Bechin, Tabor, Bohemia, Sept. 25, 1741), a good violinist and prolific composer. Having received a good education, general and musical, he went to Prague to study philosophy and theology at the university, and counterpoint under Segert. Here he formed a friendship with Dittersdorf,

who engaged him as first violin in the band of the Bishop of Grosswardein. Having spent two years as Musikdirector to Count Louis von Hartig in Prague, he entered the orchestra of the court theatre at Vienna, and was sent thence, on the recommendation of the Empress, to Milan, as compositore di musica to the Archduke Ferdinand. He now took as much pains in perfecting himself by intercourse with Nardini as he had previously done in the case of Dittersdorf. He visited all the principal cities of Italy, and was elected a member of the Filarmonici, both of Bologna and Mantua. The occupation of Milan by the French in 1796 drove the Archduke back to Vienna, and Pichel not only accompanied him, but remained in his service till his death on Jan. 23, 1805, in spite of an offer twice renewed of the post of Imperial Kapellmeister at St. Petersburg. Pichel's industry was extraordinary, and that his compositions were popular is proved by the fact that a large part of them were published in Paris, London, Amsterdam, Berlin, Offenbach and Vienna. He sent a complete list in 1803 to Dlabacz, the Bohemian lexicographer, who inserted it in his *Allgem. hist. Künstler-Lexicon für Böhmen* (Prague, 1815). An abstract of the extraordinary catalogue is given by Fétis and Gerber. The works—nearly 700 in number— include 88 symphonies ; 13 serenatas ; violin concertos and solos ; duets, trios, quartets and quintets for strings ; concertos for various wind instruments ; sonatas, etc., for PF. ; 14 masses, and many church works of various kinds ; 25 operas to German, Latin, French and Italian librettos ; and ' Sei ariette,' words by Metastasio, op. 42 (Vienna, Eder). For Prince Esterhazy he composed 148 pieces for the baryton in several parts ; and in addition to all wrote a Bohemian translation of Mozart's ' Zauberflöte.'  C. F. P.

BIBL.—ROBERT KOLISKO, *Wenzel Pichls Kammermusik.* (Vienna Dissertation, 1918.)

PICK-MANGIAGALLI, RICCARDO (*b.* Strakonitz, July 10, 1882), composer, studied in Prague, Vienna and Milan. He has produced distinctive work, both in chamber music and opera. A number of compositions for the piano, a string quartet, and a violin sonata were written between 1904 and 1910. His first stage work, ' Salice d' Oro,' a musical fable, was produced at La Scala, Milan, in 1913, and was followed by ' Il carillon magico ' (1918). Other stage works are ' Sumitra,' a monomimic legend (1917), and ' Basi e Bote ' (1919–1920), lyric comedy, the libretto by Boito (see *Mus. T.*, May 1921).

PIECE (Fr. *pièce, morceau* ; Ger. *Stück* ; Ital. *pezzo*). This word, which in the 17th and 18th centuries was used generally for a literary composition (for examples see the criticisms in the *Spectator*, vols. 4 and 5, on ' Paradise Lost,' which is constantly spoken of as ' that sublime piece '), and in later times for a dramatic work, has since the end of the 18th century been applied to instrumental musical compositions as a general and untechnical term. The earliest application of the word in this sense is to the component parts of a suite, which are called pieces (compare the French ' Suite de pièces '). It is not as a rule applied to movements of sonatas or symphonies, unless such movements are isolated from their surroundings, and played alone ; nor is it applied to the symphonies or sonatas taken as a whole. An exception to this rule is found in the direction at the beginning of Beethoven's Sonata, op. 27, No. 2—' S. deve suonare tutto questo pezzo (the first movement) delicatissimamente e senza sordini.' It is not used of vocal music, except in the cases of portions of operas, such as finales, etc., for many voices, to which the name ' Concerted piece,' ' Pezzo concertante,' is not infrequently given.                                    M.

PIELTAIN, Dieudonné Pascal (b. Liège, Mar. 4, 1754 ; d. there, Dec. 10, 1833), pupil of Giornovichi. He appeared from 1778 until 1783 at the Concert Spirituel, Paris ; in the latter year he became 1st violin at the Hanover Square (from 1785 the professional) concerts. In 1791 he became conductor at Vauxhall Gardens. In 1793 he toured in Germany, Russia and Poland, afterwards retiring to Liège. Burney describes his playing as neat and with precision. He composed concertos, sonatas, duets and solos for violin ; also string quartets. His brother was a celebrated horn player in London, who married Miss Chenu, a noted singer (Pohl, Mozart und Haydn in London ; Mendel ; Q.-L.).

PIENO (or Pleno), ' full.' Examples of the use of this direction may be found in Handel's organ concerto, where ' Organo pieno ' denotes that the organ part is to be played with full harmonies, as well as what is now called ' full,' i.e. with the full force of the stops.          M.

PIERNÉ, Henri Constant Gabriel (b. Metz, Aug. 16, 1863), studied at the Paris Conservatoire, winning the first medal for solfège in 1874, the first prize for piano in 1879, for organ in 1882, and for counterpoint and fugue in 1881 ; he gained the Prix de Rome in 1882 with his ' Edith.' He succeeded César Franck as organist of Sainte Clotilde in 1890 and held the post for eight years. In 1903 he became deputy conductor at the Concerts Colonne and replaced E. Colonne at his death in 1910. He is a member of the directing committee of studies at the Conservatoire, and since 1925 has been a member of the Académie des Beaux-Arts at the Institut. He gives regular concerts with the co-operation of the orchestra of which he is conductor.

LIST OF WORKS

Dramatic : ' Les Elfes ' (1884) ; ' Pandore ' (1888) ; ' La Coupe enchantée,' comic opera, two acts (Royan, Casino, Aug. 24, 1895) ; one act (Opéra-Comique, Paris, Dec. 26, 1905) ; ' La Nuit de Noël de 1870 ' (Concerts de l'Opéra, Dec. 8, 1895 ; ' Vendée,' three acts (Lyons, Grand Théâtre, Mar. 11, 1897) ; ' La Fille de Tabarin,' three acts (Opéra-Comique, Paris, Feb. 8, 1901) ; ' Cydalise et le chèvre-pied,' two acts, (Opéra, Paris, Jan. 15, 1923) ; ' On ne badine pas avec l'amour,' three acts (Opéra-Comique, Paris, May 30, 1910).
Amongst his former ballets and pantomimes may be mentioned : Pantomimes : ' Le Collier de saphirs ' (Spa, Paris, 1891) ; ' Le Docteur Blanc ' (Menus-Plaisirs, 1893) ; ' Salomé ' (Comédie Parisienne, 1895).
Ballets : ' Les Joyeuses Commères de Paris ' (1892) ; ' Bouton d'or ' (both at the Nouveau Théâtre, 1893).
He has composed much incidental music to : ' Izeyl,' ' La Princesse lointaine,' ' La Samaritaine ' (Théâtre de la Renaissance, 1894, 1895, 1897) ; ' Yanthis,' ' Ramnatcho ' (Odéon, 1894, 1908) ; ' Françoise de Rimini ' (Théâtre Sarah Bernhardt, 1902), ' Hamlet ' (not published) ; also the following :
' L'An mil,' symphonic poem for orchestra with chorus (1897) ; ' La Croisade des enfants ' (1902), musical legend, which received a prize in the competition of the ville de Paris in 1903 : ' Les Enfants de Bethleem,' a mystery, in two parts (1907), have earned him a well-deserved reputation, not only in France, but in Holland, Germany and in the United States.
He has also written numerous songs since 1879, the most recent of which are ' Six ballades françaises ' (Paul Fort), 1921 ; organ and harp music ; op. 39, ' Concertstück ' for harp and orchestra (Queen's Hall, 1905).
Pianoforte : ' Étude de concert ' ; ' Humoresque ' ; ' Bagatelle ' ; ' Album pour mes petits amis ' (containing the ' Marche des petits soldats de plomb ') ; Variations (1919).
PF. and Orch. : ' Fantaisie-ballet ' ; concerto in C min. (1887) ; ' Scherzo-caprice ' ; ' Poème symphonique (1901), etc.
Orchestral : ' Suites ouverture symphonique ' ; ' Marche solennelle,' etc. ; ' Paysages franciscains ' (1920).
Chamber Music : Separate pieces for various instruments ; sonata (PF. and vln., 1900) ; quintet (PF. and str.) ; trio (PF., vla. and v'cl.) ; sonata for v'cl. and PF. in one part (Société Nationale de Musique, Feb. 22, 1919).
Collections and arrangements of songs : ' Voyez comme on danse ' ; ' Sonnez les matines ' ; ' Gai, gai, marions-nous,' etc. (1903, 1904, 1907).

Bibl.—O. Séré, Musiciens français d'aujourd'hui, 2nd ed. (Paris, Mercure de France, 1922), with list of works and extensive bibliography.

M. L. P.

PIERRE, Constant Victor Désiré, (b. Paris, Aug. 24, 1855 ; d. there, Jan. 1918), first accessit of bassoon at the Paris Conservatoire, played the bassoon in various orchestras, and in 1900 was appointed assistant secretary at the Conservatoire. He became editor of the Monde musical, contributed to the Art musical, Ménestrel, Journal musical, etc., and was author of the following books : Les Noëls populaires (1886) ; La Marseillaise et ses variantes (1887) ; Histoire de l'orchestre de l'Opéra de Paris (1889) ; La Facture instrumentale à l'Exposition de 1889 (1890) ; Les Facteurs d'instruments de musique, les luthiers et la facture instrumentale (1893) ; Le Magasin de décors de l'Opéra 1781–1894 (1894) ; L'École de chant de l'Opéra 1672–1807 (1895) ; B. Sarrette et les origines du Conservatoire, etc. (1895) ; Les Anciennes Écoles de déclamation dramatique (1895) ; Notes inédites sur la musique de la Chapelle royale, 1352–1790 (1899) ; and Le Conservatoire national de musique et de déclamation: documents historiques et administratifs (1900), with a complete list of Pierre's works ; La Musique aux fêtes et cérémonies de la Révolution française ; Musique des fêtes et cérémonies de la Révolution française ; Les Hymnes et chansons de la Révolution française (1901). In the year last mentioned his book on Le Concert spirituel, 1725–1790 (1900), was crowned by the Institut. Many articles by him are in the Parisian reviews.          G. F.

PIERROT AND PIERRETTE, lyrical musical drama in 2 acts ; text by Walter E. Grogan, music by Holbrooke. Produced His Majesty's Theatre, Nov. 11, 1909.

PIERSON (originally Pearson), Henry Hugo (b. Oxford, Apr. 12, 1815 ; d. Leipzig,

Jan. 28, 1873), was the son of the Rev. Dr. Pearson, of St. John's College, afterwards chaplain to George IV., and Dean of Salisbury. He was sent to Harrow School, where he gave proof of the possession of no common abilities, gaining the Governors' prize for Latin hexameters. From Harrow he proceeded to Trinity College, Cambridge, intending, at that time, to take a medical degree. His genius, however, developed so rapidly as to make it evident that music was his destined career. He received his first instruction from Attwood, and was also indebted to Arthur Corfe. His first musical publication was a series of six songs entitled 'Thoughts of Melody'—the words by Byron—written while an undergraduate at Cambridge.

Pearson went to Germany for the first time in 1839, and studied under C. H. Rink, Tomaschek and Reissiger. At Leipzig he had much intercourse with Mendelssohn, and during his residence in Germany also became acquainted with Meyerbeer, Spohr and Schumann. Schumann reviewed the above-mentioned six songs most favourably in the *Neue Zeitschrift für Musik.* In 1844 Pearson was elected to the Reid Professorship of Music in the University of Edinburgh, in succession to Sir Henry Bishop ; but this post he very soon resigned, and returned to Germany, which from that time he virtually adopted as his country, changing his name from Henry Hugh Pearson to that given above. He had married Caroline Leonhardt, a lady distinguished by varied gifts and literary productions ; and the sympathy thenceforward accorded to his genius in continental society was undoubtedly more congenial to his feelings than the slight appreciation he received from English critics.

His first important work, after an early attempt, 'Der Elfensieg' (' The Elves and the Earth King '), given at Brünn in 1845, was the opera ' Leila,' which was brought out at Hamburg with great success in Feb. 1848. From this opera may be instanced a striking song for bass voice, ' Thy heart, O man, is like the sea.' Much of his music at this time was published under the *nom de plume* of ' Edgar Mansfeldt.'

In 1852 appeared the oratorio ' Jerusalem.' [1] This, although not composed expressly for the Norwich Festival, was performed there on Sept. 23 in that year with remarkable effect. The overture, the airs ' Of the rock that begat thee ' and ' O that my head were waters,' the air and chorus ' What are these,' the quintet ' Blessed are the dead,' and the chorus ' The Eternal God is thy refuge,' are some of the most interesting numbers. The success of the work was marred by a foolish attempt to pit Dr. Bexfield's ' Israel Restored ' against it ;

[1] An elaborate criticism of ' Jerusalem,' from the pen of G. A. Macfarren, was published in the *Mus. T.* of Sept. 1, 1852.

the controversy had hardly died down when the oratorio was repeated at Exeter Hall on May 18, 1853, by the Harmonic Union ; it was given again in 1862, at Würzburg.

Pierson's next work was the music to the second part of Goethe's ' Faust,' composed in 1854, which added greatly to his reputation in Germany. It was repeatedly performed at Hamburg, and a selection from it, including the noble chorus ' Sound, immortal harp,' was given at the Norwich Festival of 1857. In acknowledgment of the merit of this composition, the author received the Gold Medal for Art and Science from Leopold I., King of the Belgians, who accepted the dedication of the pianoforte score. It was performed several times at Frankfort and other places on successive anniversaries of Goethe's birthday. Pierson was requested to write for the Norwich Festival of 1869, and offered a selection from a second oratorio, ' Hezekiah.' This work was never completed ; but several numbers were performed on the above-named occasion in Sept. 1869. ' Contarini,' an opera in five acts, produced at Hamburg in Apr. 1872, was Pierson's last work on a large scale ; another opera, ' Fenice,' was given posthumously at Dessau in 1883.

To the works already mentioned, however, must be added a very large number of songs, written at different dates, and bearing, on the whole, more than any other of his works, the stamp of his characteristic style and delicate invention. As good examples may be cited ' Deep in my soul,' ' Thekla's Lament,' and ' All my heart's thine own.' His spirited partsong ' Ye mariners of England ' was constantly performed. He left a vast number of works in manuscript, including several overtures, three of which—those to ' Macbeth,' ' As you Like It' and ' Romeo and Juliet '—were performed at the Crystal Palace Concerts.

He died at Leipzig, and lies buried in the churchyard of Sonning, Berks. His death called forth remarkable tributes from the German musical press, showing the high estimation in which he was held there. A Leipzig journal published on the day after his death, after speaking of him as a ' great artist, whose strivings were ever after the noblest ends,' continues as follows :

' Holding no musical appointment, and consequently without influence ; highly educated, but after the fashion of true genius, somewhat of a recluse, and withal unpractical, he did not know how to make his glorious works valued. He showed himself seldom, though his appearance was poetic and imposing ; and he was such a player on both organ and pianoforte as is rarely met with.'

The above estimate of Pierson's powers, from the pen of the composer's brother, has hardly obtained general acceptance ; for his comparative failure in his native land, the inordinate Mendelssohn-worship of his day has been often assigned as a reason, and Pierson was one of the few who even then discerned that master's weak points. Beside this, however, there is in his more ambitious work a singular lack of continuity of style, which is more than enough to account for the lack of appreciation from which his music has suffered. See the *History of the Norwich Festivals* (1896), p. 135. H. P.

PIERSON, MARTIN, see PEERSON.

PIETEREZ, ADRIAN (*b.* Bruges, early 15th cent.), the earliest known organ-builder in Belgium. He built an instrument in 1455 at Delft, which is still in the new church; but it has been so often restored that nothing remains of his work. V. DE P.

PIÉTON, LOYSET (LOUYS, LOUYSET) (*b.* Bernay, Normandy, last quarter of 15th cent.; *d.* after 1545). There is much confusion between him and the older Loyset Compère which has yet to be cleared up, as their life periods overlap to some extent, and eminent composers of that time were distinguished merely by their Christian names. Where, however, the designation ' de Bernais ' or ' le Normand ' is added it can only refer to Piéton, as Compère was a Fleming who was from his boyhood to his death attached to St. Quentin Cathedral. Although he never attains the height of the older master he occupies a very prominent position among the masters of that period. Lists of his masses, motets, psalms, etc., from collective volumes are given by Fétis, Mendel and in *Q.-L.*, which latter must, however, be modified according to what has been said above.

E. V. D. S.

PIETOSO, ' pitiful ' or ' compassionate.' As a musical direction it indicates that the passage to which it refers is to be performed in a sympathetic style, with much feeling. Although the term appears in Brossard's Dictionary, where it is defined as ' d'une manière capable d'exciter de la pitié ou de la compassion,' composers seem to prefer other terms to indicate the same intention; ' con duolo,' for example, or the more frequent if less definite ' espressivo.'

PIFFERO is really the Italian form of the English word *Fife*, and the German *Pfeife*. In the *Dizionario della musica* it is described as a small flute with six finger-holes and no keys. But the term is also commonly used to denote a rude kind of oboe, or a bagpipe with an inflated sheepskin for reservoir, common in Italy, and formerly to be seen about the streets of London, the players being termed Pifferari. (See PASTORAL SYMPHONY.)

Spohr, in his *Autobiography* (Dec. 5, 1816), quotes a tune which he says was played all over Rome at that season by Neapolitan pipers, one playing the melody on a sort of ' coarse powerful oboe,' the other the accompaniment on a bagpipe sounding like three clarinets at once. We give a few bars as a specimen.

etc.

It is a very different tune from Handel's ' Pastoral Symphony.' W. H. S.

PIGOTT (PIGGOTT), (1) FRANCIS, Mus.B. (*d.* May 15, 1704), appears to have been organist of St. John's College, Oxford, and was appointed, Jan. 18, 1686, organist of Magdalen College, Oxford, which office he resigned in 1687. He was chosen, May 25, 1688, first organist of the Temple Church. On Dec. 11, 1695, he was sworn organist extraordinary of the Chapel Royal, and on Mar. 24, 1697, on the death of Dr. Child, organist in ordinary. He graduated at Cambridge in 1698. He composed some anthems, now forgotten, and contributed to the ' Choice Collection of Ayres for the harpsichord, by Blow, F. Piggott, etc.' 1700. He was succeeded as organist of the Temple by his son, (2) J. PIGOTT (*d.* 1726), who became possessed of a large fortune on the death of his relation, Dr. John Pelling, rector of St. Anne's, Soho. (3) FRANCIS PIGOTT, jun., who held the appointment of organist at St. George's Chapel, Windsor, and Eton College, up to 1756, was probably a grandson of Francis (1). W. H. H.

PIJPER, WILLEM (*b.* Zeist, Sept. 8, 1894), is one of the most gifted of the younger generation of Dutch composers. His works include two symphonies, the first of which was performed by Mengelberg at Amsterdam in 1918; chamber music and songs. One of his sonatas was heard at the Salzburg meeting of the International Society for Contemporary Music in 1922. At first Pijper's compositions showed the influence of both Debussy and Mahler; now he is one of the seekers after ' atonality. R. Mᴳ.

PILGRIME VON MEKKA, DIE, see RENCONTRE IMPRÉVUE, LA.

PILKINGTON, (1) FRANCIS (*d.* 1638), madrigal composer, was probably of the Lancashire family, though his parentage cannot be traced, nor is the date of his birth known.[1] His father and brother were in the service of the Earl of Derby, and Francis no doubt came to Chester through the influence of the same nobleman, as

[1] In a MS. Chester Ordinary of Arms (*c.* 1600), formerly belonging to Dean Cholmondelay of Chester, we find his arms: Ffran Pilkington, artis musicae baccalari's argent a crosspatonce Gules voided of the field: in the fesse point a trefoil sable for difference.

the Stanleys were persons of great consequence in the city. He took his degree of Mus.B. from Lincoln College, Oxford, in 1595, and the Graces for his degree call him 'Pilkington,' and state that he had studied music for sixteen years, and that his exercise was to consist of a 'Choral song in six parts.'

He appears for the first time on the Chester Cathedral Treasurer's books as a singing-man or conduct—or, as Pilkington styles himself, a 'Chaunter'—at Midsummer, 1602.

Bateson was already at Chester, and must have been preparing his first book for publication, which came out in 1604. This was speedily followed, perhaps in friendly emulation, by Pilkington's first compositions;

'The First Booke of Songs or Ayres of 4 parts; with Tableture for the Lute or Orpherian, with the Violl de Gamba. Newly composed by Francis Pilkington, Bachelor of Musicke, and Lutenist: and one of the Cathedrall Church of Christ, in the Citie of Chester. (Folio.) London, printed by T. Este, dwelling in Aldersgate-streete, and are ther to be sould, 1605.'

It is dedicated

'To the Right Honourable William Earl of Derby, Lord Stanley, Lord Strange of Knocking, and of the Isle of Man, and Knight of The Most Noble Order of the Garter';

and in the preface Pilkington says:

'I must confess my selfe many waies obliged to your Lordship's familie, not onely, for that my Father and brother received many Graces of your Honour's noble father whom they followed, but that myself had the like of your most honourable Brother even from the first notice he chanced to take of me.'

The book contains twenty-one vocal pieces and a 'Pavin for the Lute and Bass Viol.' The whole work was reprinted, with a biographical memoir, in the OLD ENGLISH EDITION by G. E. P. Arkwright (Nos. xviii., xix. and xx.); also in ENGLISH SCHOOL OF LUTENIST SONG WRITERS (q.v.). About 1612 Pilkington became a minor canon. His ordination is not in the Bishop's Registry, but his admission to priest's orders is shown by the following extract from the baptismal entries of Holy Trinity Church, Chester: '1614. 23 Decemb. Elizabeth dau. to Rich. Knee Sayler. Baptized by Mr. Francis Pilkington curat of this church beinge made a full minister by Geo. Lloyd bushop of Chester 18 of December beinge the first child he baptized.' In 1614 he issued his second work:

'The First Set of Madrigals and Pastorals of 3, 4 and 5 parts. Newly composed by Francis Pilkington, Batchelor of Musicke, and Lutenist, and one of the Cathedral Church of Christ and blessed Mary the Virgin, in Chester. [4to.] London, Printed for M. L., J. B. and T. S., the assignes of William Barley, 1614.'

It is dedicated

'To the Right Worshipfull Sir Thomas Smith, of Hough, in the County of Chester.'

Pilkington says,

'It is unworthy, yet in regard of the many and manifold favours which I have received at your hands, and your exquisite skill both in theorique and practique of that excellent art, I doe presume to send it to your patronage and protection.'

He dates the preface, with pardonable pride, 'from my own mansion in the monastery, Chester, the 25th day of September 1612.' The contents consist of six pieces for three voices, nine for four voices, and seven for five voices.

The words of No. 11, 'Have I found her?' were afterwards set by Bateson.

On the other hand, No. 21, 'When Oriana walkt to take the ayre,' is a setting of the same words as Bateson's madrigal for the 'Triumphes of Oriana'; the only difference being in the concluding lines, where the couplet—

'Thus sang the Nymphs and Shepherds of Diana:
In Heaven lives fair Oriana,'

shows that Pilkington had written this after the death of Elizabeth. (See Eng. Madr. Sch. vol. xxv.)

In 1614 appeared 'The Teares or Lamentacions of a Sorrowfull Soule,' compiled by 'Sir William Leighton, Knight, one of His Majesty's Honourable Band of Gentleman Pensioners' To this work Pilkington contributed a 'song' or anthem in four parts, 'Hidden O Lorde'; and another in five parts, 'High, Mighty God.' Probably Sir William Leighton was a relative of the Thomas Leighton whom Pilkington had commemorated in an elegy in his first work, 1605.

Pilkington's last work:

'The Second set of Madrigals and Pastorals of 3, 4, 5 and 6 parts; apt for Violls and Voyces: newly composed by Francis Pilkington, Batchelor of Musicke, and Lutenist, and Chaunter of the Cathedrall Church of Christ and blessed Mary the Virgin, in Chester.' [4to.] London, Printed by Thomas Snodham for M. L. and A. B., 1624.

It is dedicated

'To the Right Worshipfull and worthy of much honour Sir Peter Leigh of Lyme, Knight.'

(See Eng. Madr. Sch. vol. xxvi.).

The work consists of six madrigals for three voices, six for four voices, eight for five voices, five for six voices, a 'Fancie for the Violls' only, and 'a Pavin made for the orpharion, by the Right Honourable William, Earle of Darbie, and by him consented to be in my bookes placed.'[1] There are also two laudatory poems by William Webbe and Henry Harper. The latter (who had been a chorister and afterwards became chapter clerk) gives the following remarkable and bold estimate of British musicians, which time has fully justified:

'. . . and must the matchless excellencies
Of Bird, Bull, Dowland, Morley, and the rest
Of our rare artists (who ncw dim the light
Of other lands) be only in Request?'

Although he hoped to 'lagge on one journey more,'[2] Pilkington never, so far as we know, published anything further. He became precentor in 1623, and held this office until his death. It seems probable that he was buried in his native place, for his name does not occur in the old Cathedral (St. Oswald's) register of burials. His will is not entered in the Chester Probate Court.

There is a little lute music by him in the B.M. Add. MSS. 31,392, and in the Cambridge University Library (Dd. ii. 11).

[1] This Pavin has some importance attached to it by a modern French writer who has advanced a theory that the author of the Shakespeare plays was in reality the aforesaid Earl of Derby. As Shakespeare's plays show a decided love and taste for music, Le Franc adduces this Pavin as evidence of the musical skill of his suggested author.
[2] Preface to 'The Second set of Madrigals.'

As he speaks of his ' now aged muse ' [1] in 1624, it is probable that Pilkington came to Chester when fairly old, and he seems to have been married, and to have had a large family, judging from the Treasurer's books, which mention the following members of the family :

(2) ZACHARIAS. A chorister for several years, ending 1612.

(3) THOMAS,[2] chorister from 1612–18. In 1625 he appears again as 6th conduct. In 1627 we find him and Francis still filling their respective positions, and another.

(4) THOMAS as third chorister.

Lastly we find that at his death in 1638 Francis Pilkington's place as minor canon was filled by (5) a JOHN PILKINGTON, who had been previously appointed a conduct.

(Cathedral Treasurer's accounts and other Chester information. Memoir by G. E. P. Arkwright in Old English Edition.)    J. C. B.

Francis Pilkington's book of Ayres is one of those the music of which was designed for performance in two ways ; either by four voices unaccompanied or as solo-song with accompaniment of the lute or bass viol. Several of these songs have considerable charm, notably ' Diaphenia, like the daffdowndilly,' and ' Now peep, bo-peep.' As a madrigal writer Pilkington seldom rises to great heights, although several of his madrigals are well written. By far the finest is ' O softly-singing lute,' a superb madrigal, which challenges comparison with the very best of Wilbye's work. In ' Care for thy Soul ' in the second set of madrigals there are some very remarkable chromatic passages ; but as the set was not published until 1624 chromatic harmonies were already losing something of their novelty.    E. H. F.

PINAFORE, H.M.S., comic opera in 2 acts ; words by W. S. Gilbert, music by Sullivan. Produced Opéra-Comique, London, May 25, 1878.    G.

PINCÉ (Fr.) plucked or pinched. (1) The term is used to describe stringed instruments that are not bowed, such as the lute, mandoline, guitar, zither, as well as the harp ; the *pizzicato* of the instrument of the violin family is also called ' pincé ' by some writers.

(2) The French equivalent for MORDENT (q.v.). See also ORNAMENTS.    M.

PINEL, the name of four French lutenists.

(1) PIERRE, who lived in 1641.

(2) GERMAIN (d. 1664), lutenist of the King's chamber in 1646, lute-master to the King (1649).

He married in 1640. According to de La Laurencie, a great number of pieces attributed to his son, François, are really by him.

(3) FRANÇOIS (d. circa 1709), son of the preceding, appears with his father and his brother, Séraphin, in the 7th entry of the ' Ballet de Psyché ' (Jan. 16, 1656). Elected ' enseigner à Sa Majesté'' (1657), he succeeded Claude Tissu as ' ordinaire de la musique de la chambre du roi pour le théorbe ' (1657). He resigned (Sept. 1, 1771) in favour of Laurent Dupré.

(4) SÉRAPHIN, brother of the preceding, had the ' survivance ' of his father's post in 1659. After 1664 we lose trace of him.

BIBL.—MICHEL BRENET, R.M.I., 1898–99 ; H. PRUNIÈRES, Sammelband der I.M.G., July 1914 ; L. DE LA LAURENCIE, Les Luthistes français (in preparation, 1926).

J. G. P.

PINELLI (PENELLI), ETTORE (b. Rome, Oct. 18, 1843 ; d. there, Sept. 15, 1915), violinist and conductor, was a pupil of Ramaccioti in Rome and of Joachim at Hanover. His professional career was pursued chiefly in Rome, where he furthered the study of concerted chamber music. His co-operation with SGAMBATI (q.v.) in a movement which resulted in the foundation of the Liceo Musicale is described under ROME. He became violin professor at the Liceo, conducted orchestral concerts, gave oratorio performances, and composed a string quartet, an overture and other works.

PINELLO DI GHERARDI, GIOVANNI BATTISTA (b. Genoa, c. 1540 ; d. Prague, June 15, 1587). On the title-page of his first-known publication in 1571 he is described as belonging to a noble Genoese family (nobile Genovese), and as being at that time cantor in the Cathedral Church of Vicenza. In 1577 he was at Innsbruck, a musician in the service of the Archduke of Austria. He is next heard of as a member of the Imperial Chapel at Prague, from which in 1580 he was recommended by the Emperor to the Elector Augustus of Saxony, who appointed him Kapellmeister to the Electoral Chapel at Dresden, in succession to Scandelli. Various causes of friction arose betwixt Pinello and his Dresden colleagues, so that in 1584 the Elector was obliged to dismiss him. Pinello returned to the Imperial Chapel at Prague, where he remained till his death. His first publications consist of four books of Canzoni napolitane a 3, but no traces remain of the first book. The others were published at Venice in 1571, 1572 and 1575. The fourth book is described as containing some pastorals and una battaglia in lode della victoria Christiana, which must refer to the battle of Lepanto, 1571. His other publications consist of works especially composed for the use of the Electoral Chapel at Dresden and the Imperial Chapel at Prague, a volume of German Magnificats on the Church tones a 4 and 5, with some Bene-

1 Preface to ' The Second set of Madrigals.'
2 It seems almost certain that this was the Thomas Pilkington mentioned by Anthony à Wood in his Fasti Oxonienses, vol. i. p. 269. He refers to ' Francis Pilkington, of Lincoln College, Bachelor of Music,' and says : ' Some of his compositions I have seen, and I think some are extant. He was father to, or at least near of kin to, Thomas Pilkington, one of the musicians belonging sometime to Queen Henrietta Maria ; who being a most excellent artist, his memory was celebrated by many persons, particularly by Sir Aston Cockain, Baronet, who hath written [in his Choice Poems of several sorts, etc., London, 1658] his funeral elegy and his epitaph. The said Thomas Pilkington died at Wolverhampton, in Staffordshire, aged thirty-five, and was buried there, in the times of the rebellion or usurpation.'

dicamus (Dresden, 1583), and two books of motets (Dresden, 1584, and Prague, 1588). There is also a book of German songs *a* 5 (Dresden, 1584), after the fashion of Canzoni napolitane. The collection of Bodenschatz contains a motet *a* 8, Pater peccavi. Yonge's 'Musica Transalpina,' 1588, has one of his madrigals with English words.                    J. R. M.

PINI CORSI, ANTONIO (*b.* Zara, June 1859; *d.* Milan, Apr. 21, 1918), Italian baritone. His powerful and flexible voice ripened early, and Pini Corsi was only 19 years old when he made his début in Cremona. He interpreted with equal distinction comic and serious parts, although in the later part of his career he sang mostly comic parts, in which rôles he was unsurpassed by any other Italian singer of his day. Verdi chose him as a member of the first cast of Falstaff.                    F. B.

PINSUTI, CIRO (IL CAVALIERE) (*b.* Sinalunga, Siena, May 9, 1829; *d.* Florence, Mar. 10, 1888), was grounded in music and the piano by his father; at 10 he played in public; at 11, being in Rome, he was made honorary member of the Accademia Filarmonica, and was taken to England by Henry Drummond, M.P., in whose house he resided until 1845, studying the pianoforte and composition under Cipriani Potter, and the violin under H. Blagrove. In 1845 he returned home, and entered the Conservatorio at Bologna, where he became the private pupil of Rossini, taking a degree there in 1847. In 1848 he went back to England and started as a teacher of singing, dividing his time between London and Newcastle. His first opera, 'Il mercante di Venezia,' was brought out at Bologna, Nov. 8, 1873; a second, 'Mattia Corvino,' at La Scala at Milan, Mar. 24, 1877; and a third, 'Margherita,' at Venice in 1882. In 1859 he composed the Te Deum for the annexation of Tuscany to the Italian kingdom, and was decorated with the order of SS. Maurice and Lazarus. In 1878 King Humbert further created him a knight of the Italian crown. In 1871 he represented Italy at the opening festival of the International Exhibition, and contributed a hymn to words by Lord Houghton, beginning, 'O people of this favoured land.'

From 1856 he was professor of singing at the R.A.M. In addition to a large circle of pupils of all ranks, many eminent artists have profited by his counsels, as Grisi, Bosio, Patti, Ronconi, Graziani, Mario, etc. His part-songs were for long great favourites with the singing-societies of England. The list of his published compositions embraces more than 230 songs, English and Italian, 35 duets, 14 trios, 45 part-songs and choruses and 30 PF. pieces, the Te Deum and the opera 'Il mercante di Venezia' already mentioned.                    G.

PINTO, (1) THOMAS (*b.* England, 1714; *d.* 1783), son of a Neapolitan of good family, at 11 years played Corelli's concertos, and led the concerts in St. Cecilia's Hall in Edinburgh. His reading at sight was marvellous; he would even turn the book upside down, and play correctly from it in that position. His great gifts inclined him to carelessness, from which he was fortunately roused by the appearance of Giardini. About 1745 he married Sibilla Gronamann, daughter of a German pastor. After 1750 he played frequently as leader and soloist in benefit concerts, at the Worcester and Hereford Festivals, at Drury Lane Theatre, and, after Giardini, at the King's Theatre. He replaced Giardini in 1757, and after his wife's death he married (in 1766) Miss CHARLOTTE BRENT (*q.v.*), the singer, who died in 1802. A speculation with regard to Marylebone Gardens, into which he had entered with Dr. Arnold, failed, and he took refuge in Scotland, and finally in Ireland. In Sept. 1773, he was appointed leader of the band of the Smock Alley Theatre, Dublin, and remained in that post until 1779; he conducted at a Rotunda Concert in 1780, and he died soon afterwards. A daughter by his first wife married a Londoner named Sanders,[1] and had a son,

(2) GEORGE FREDERIC (*b.* Lambeth, Sept. 25, 1786; *d.* Little Chelsea, Mar. 23, 1806), took his grandfather's name. He early showed a decided talent for music, and the education and progress of the pretty and lively boy were watched over with the greatest interest by his mother's stepmother. His first teachers were soon outstripped, and then Salomon proved a first-rate master and true friend. From 1796 to 1800 the young Pinto frequently appeared at Salomon's concerts, and afterwards under his wing at Bath, Oxford, Cambridge, Winchester, and specially in Scotland. A second and longer tour extended to Paris. Besides playing the violin, he sang with taste, and made considerable progress on the pianoforte, for which he composed, among other music, a sonata dedicated to his friend John Field. In 1805 his health, never strong, suddenly broke down, having been undermined by excesses, and he died at Little Chelsea. His remains lie in St. Margaret's, Westminster, beneath the same monument as those of his grandmother. Pinto's technique was perfect, and his tone full, powerful and touching. Three sets of canzonets were published in 1805, 1807 and 1846 respectively; three duets for two violins appeared as op. 5; three sonatas for pianoforte as op. 4; and three sonatas for PF. and violin were published in 1805.

C. F. P.; addns. W. H. G. F.

PIOCHI, CHRISTOFORO, maestro di cappella in 1623 of Amelia Cathedral, Umbria, from *c.* 1668 until after 1675 of Siena Cathedral. He

[1] One of his first works, the three sonatas for pianoforte, is 'to be had . . . of Mrs. Sanders, No. 15 Bateman's Buildings, Soho Square.'

composed motets, sacred songs, responsoria, ricercari, etc., also a theoretical treatise (*Q.-L.*).

PIOZZI, GABRIEL (*d.* Brynbela, Denbighshire, Mar. 1809), a Florentine of good birth, who, before 1781, had established himself in Bath as a music-master. He numbered among his pupils the daughters of Henry Thrale, the opulent brewer, and whilst engaged in instructing them won the heart of their widowed mother, whom he married in 1784, a proceeding which drew down upon the lady the wrath of Dr. Johnson, who had been for twenty years the cherished guest of Thrale and herself. After his marriage Piozzi visited Italy with his wife, and, returning to England, lived with her in uninterrupted happiness until his death. A canzonet of his composition for a soprano voice, called 'La contradizzione,' is printed in the Musical Library, vol. iv.　　　w. h. h.

PIPE AND TABOR (Fr. *galoubet et tambourin*). The pipe formerly used in this country with the tabor was of the flûte-à-bec or recorder type, but as it was held and played with one hand only (the right hand being used to strike the tabor), the usual six holes of the flute could not be fingered. Three holes only were bored, near the extreme end, two for the first and second fingers and one underneath for the thumb, and these sufficed to give a scale for an octave and five notes, for the available compass of the pipe began with the octave of its fundamental note. The proper tones, or 'harmonics' of a flute are $c'$, $c''$, $g''$, $c'''$, $e'''$, $g'''$, etc., and when the first octave is abandoned, the next interval presenting itself is the fifth from $c''$ to $g''$. Three holes are sufficient to give the intermediate notes, $d''$, $e''$ and $f''$ of the diatonic scale, and with certain cross-fingerings, chromatic notes can be obtained. The tabor was a diminutive drum, without snares, hung by a short string to the waist or left arm, and tapped with a small drumstick (see *PLATE XXV.* No. 2). There is a woodcut of William Kemp the actor playing pipe and tabor in his Morris dance to Norwich, and another of Tarleton, the Elizabethan jester, in the same attitude. The pipe and tabor were known in certain country districts as ' Whittle and Dub.'

In France the Galoubet is still in use in some parts of the country and is accompanied by either the Tambourin, as in Provence, an illustration of which is given under DRUM (5), or by the Tambourin de Béarn, which is not a drum, but a long sound-box having seven strings stretched along it, four being tuned to C and three to G, and struck with a stick.　　　d. j. b.

PIPELARE, MATHIEU (MATHAEUS) (' Pipe-♭ 𝄞,' the notes *la, re*), a 15th-16th century Netherlandish composer of masses, motets, songs, etc., including a Mass on the favourite subject, ' L'homme armé.' He enjoyed a high reputation in his time, and is quoted as an authority by Ornithoparchus (vol. 2, chap. 8). A list of his still extant compositions, between 1505–75, is in *Q.-L.*

PIPES, EVOLUTION AND DISTRIBUTION OF MUSICAL. Whether the drum, the pipe or the vibrating string has the best claim to be considered the first musical instrument must necessarily be an open question ; there is, however, ample evidence to show that very early in the history of mankind the use of the musical pipe was known. Of so vast a subject a summary only can here be given, grouped according to the usual division of wind instruments under the following heads :

1. WHISTLE-PIPES, in which a thin stream of air is forced against a sharp edge, and, 'breaking' upon it, sets the air within a hollow tube or a resonating chamber in vibration. This was undoubtedly the earliest form of musical pipe, as testified by the bone whistles of the prehistoric cave-men and the records of the most ancient nations. At the first the instrument—a simple river reed or a hollow bone—was held vertically, and the breath of the performer, being directed across the open end, impinged on the opposite edge. The Arabian 'Náy' (the successor of the ancient Sebi), the modern 'Aulos' of Greece, the 'Kaval' of Bulgaria, the 'Bansee' of India, the 'Shakuhachi' of Japan, the 'Lena' of the Pueblo Indians, the ivory and reed flutes of Africa, the Maori whistles and the panpipes distributed over every continent are some existing types of this primitive form.

In the next step of its evolution a small notch is found cut on the edge of the pipe, as in the flutes of Uganda and other districts of Central Africa, and also in the Chinese Hsiao, and the Peruvian flute : the lower lip now partially covers the open end of the tube and the breath is sent more directly down the tube than across it. At length the upper end of the tube is almost entirely closed, either by the natural septum or knot of the cane, or by some prepared wax, the little notch only remaining and forming the well-known ' lip ' of the whistle. In a flute used by the Indians of Arizona we can next trace a further development : the cane in this instrument is not cut off immediately above the knot, but allowed to remain as a mouthpiece, the air being directed over the septum and against the lower edge of the notch by a leaf or piece of rag tied tightly over the upper part of the orifice. Thus a primitive whistle-head of the flageolet type is produced, the performer no longer forming the embouchure with his lips, but simply blowing into the upper end of the tube. The flutes of the Kiowa and Dakota Indians are improved forms of the same type, and in the bone whistles from ancient graves in California the same result is obtained by a piece of asphaltum placed within the hollow centre just above the notch-

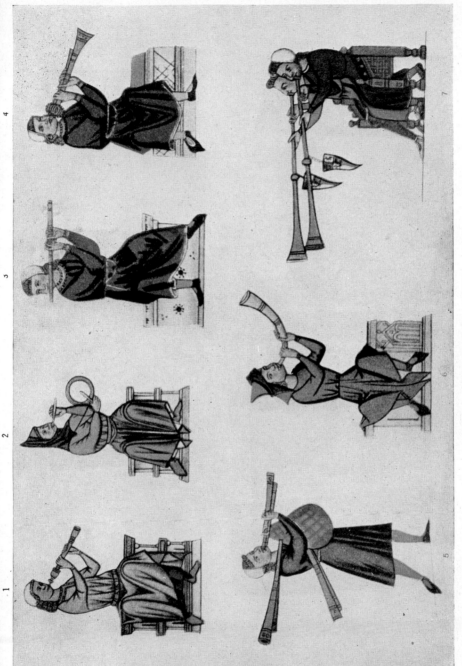

LX

MUSICAL INSTRUMENTS—SPAIN, c. 1270

(Library of the Escorial. Cantigas de S. Maria)

1. Oboe (*Dulzaina*).   2. Pipe and Tabor (*Flautilla y Tamboril*).   3. Flute (*Axabeba*).   4. Bladder Pipe (*Odrecillo*).
5. Bagpipe (*Cornemusa*).   6. Horn (*Buque*).   7. Heralds' Trumpet (*Añafil*).

In the wooden whistles of the American Indians of the N.W. Coast the whistle-head is brought to great perfection, and the 'voicing' is quite equal to that of the European recorders and flageolets. The whistle-head, as seen in the 'flue' pipes of the organ, was certainly known to the Greeks and Romans (see article HY-DRAULUS), and in the Western Hemisphere to the Aztecs and Incas. The resonator of the ocarina, which takes the place of the more usual tube, is prefigured in the ancient Chinese 'Hsuan,' in the grotesque instruments of the Aztec civilisation, and the globular gourd-whistles of Western Africa and Melanesia.

The transverse flute, which in its mouth-piece and embouchure still retains elements of the primitive notch, is distinctly an Asiatic instrument, though occasionally found among certain African tribes in the neighbourhood of the Cameroon and lower Congo districts, where it has been probably introduced by Europeans. An unknown antiquity is attached to the ancient Chinese Chih, which being closed at both ends suggests an affinity with the nose-flutes of Java and Polynesia; in fact, amongst the wild tribes in the Malay Peninsula the transverse flute and the nose-flute are the only forms known. The Indian transverse flute ('Pillagovi') is depicted in sculpture as early as 250 B.C., and is considered the emblem of the god Krishna, its reputed inventor. The earliest illustration of the type in Europe appears on an ivory casket of Italo-Byzantine work of the 10th century, now in the National Museum, Florence. For subsequent history see FLUTE.

2. REED-PIPES, in which the air is set in motion by the pulsations of a tongue of wood, cane, or metal or by the joint vibrations of two thin slips of the same materials, the forms now most generally in use being known as the Double Reed (see OBOE), the Single Reed (see CLARI-NET), and the Free Reed (see HARMONIUM).

Of these the double reed is probably the oldest, as it is also the simplest in construction, requiring only the bringing together by gentle pressure of the open end of a pliant stalk or hollow rush as in Chaucer's 'pipis of grene corn.' Owing to its fragile nature the reed is now usually separate from the body of the pipe, which is made of more durable material, but the American Indians of the N.W. coast construct powerful instruments of this type in one piece with thin wooden reeds. The double reed associated with a conical tube is especially characteristic of the Western Asiatic nations, as seen in the Arabian 'Zamr,' the Persian 'Zourna,' and the Indian 'Nagasara.' It is certainly not indigenous in Eastern Asia, and was probably introduced into Western Europe through the Moorish incursion of the 11th century. Used with a cylindrical tube it is found in the Japanese 'Hitschiriki,' the Chinese 'Kuantzu,' the ancient Greek 'Aulos' and

Roman 'Tibia,' and in the Arabian 'E'ragyeh,' but its use in this way survives in Europe only in certain forms of bagpipe. In Africa the double reed is unknown, except where Muhammedan influence predominates.

The single reed is formed by cutting out a thin slip or tongue in the side of the hollow tube towards the upper end, which in this case must be closed. It appears with a cylindrical tube in the primitive form in the well-known 'Arghool' and 'Zummarah' pipes of Syria and Egypt, the descendants of the 'Mam' of the old Empire. It seems to have been originally confined to the countries bordering on the Eastern Mediterranean, extending to the nations of Western Asia, as in the Indian 'Tubri' and 'Poongi' or snake-charmer's pipe, and the Persian bagpipes. It is found in the islands of the Greek archipelago, and on the northern coast of Africa; it was known also to the Romans. In Britain it appears in the old Celtic pibcorn or hornpipe, and is still used for the drones of the Scottish and Irish bagpipes; while, as the 'Chalumeau,' it proved the parent of the clarinet, and is the characteristic form of the true organ reed. Like the double reed it is not known amongst the African tribes, but it is found amongst the Indians of the N.W. coast of America, where it has been evolved from the double reed by the insertion of a rigid piece of wood to form a 'lay' between the vibrating tongues. In South America it is used with a conical tube, generally of horn, but in this case its presence is evidently due to European settlers. (See SAXOPHONE.)

The home of the free reed, in which the tongue, instead of beating on the body of the tube, vibrates unimpeded through a narrow slit, is Eastern Asia and the Malay Archipelago, being represented there by the 'Engkurai' of Borneo, the 'Phan' of Siam, the 'Heem' of Burmah, the 'Cheng' of China, and the 'Sho' of Japan, all of which take the form of mouth-organs with pipes of hollow cane or bamboo. It is also found associated with a simple cylindrical tube furnished with finger-holes, but its peculiar characteristics render it unsuitable for this purpose. Although it was known in Europe in the 17th century, attention was only drawn to its capabilities at the close of the 18th century in France by Amiot, a Chinese missionary, and in Russia by the organ-builder Kratzenstein. From it have originated the accordion, concertina, harmonium, and other similar instruments.

The ribbon reed, formed by the vibration of a thin piece of vegetable membrane, skin or silk against the sides of a narrow slit, has proved of little practical value, though popularly used in Europe and Asia and by the American Indians.

The retreating-reed is of greater interest; in the primitive form it is made by cutting off the hollow cane at the knot, slitting the knot or the

side of the cane, and blowing through the open end ; the slit edges fly apart and set up a rapid vibration. In many parts of rural England these, as well as the other reed-pipes, are commonly made by children, but the retreating-reed has been observed in Morocco and, in a more elaborate form, amongst the American Indians of the N.W. coast. It has recently found a place in the organ amongst the new methods of tone production. (See ORGAN.)

3. PIPES WITH CUP-MOUTHPIECES, in which the column of air is set in motion by the rapid vibration of the performer's lips. This well-known principle (see HORN, TRUMPET) is in reality closely allied to the last-mentioned form, the retreating-reed ; for although the usual shape of the cup-mouthpiece in Europe is circular, amongst the African tribes it is oval, and in the Chinese metal trumpet, ' Ah-tu,' approximates very nearly to the shape of the double reed, the thin edges of the lips providing the necessary vibration. In this way, too, the mediæval cornetti and clarini were played, the resulting tone closely resembling that of a reed instrument. The distribution of instruments of this type is world-wide, and they are constructed not only of metal, but of the natural horns and tusks of animals, of sea-shells, stems of large plants, branches of trees, hollow gourds, leaves, paper, earthenware, and human bones. By some primitive peoples they have been invested with sacred attributes, as the ' Juruparis ' and ' Botuto.' of the South American Indians, whilst amongst the African tribes they serve not only as incentives to the battle and the dance, but as a recognised system of intercommunal telegraphy. Although the principle was known to the Aztecs, its use among the North American Indians is now practically unrecognised, but in South America horns of gourd, reed and baked clay are found. Throughout the Asiatic continent the trumpet is relegated to religious, civil and ceremonial observances, and remains in a far more primitive state than the reed-pipes, flutes and strings. In Europe, as shown by the fine ' Luren ' of the Bronze age which have been discovered, the principle dates back to prehistoric ages. (Cf. the classification of European forms under WIND INSTRUMENTS.)

In addition to these three great groups of musical pipes there is another peculiar form which deserves notice. In the Indian ' Nyastaranga ' or throat trumpet the column of air is set in vibration by a thin skin or diaphragm placed over the small orifice at the end of the tube and completely closing it ; this end is applied to the vibrating chords of the throat, and the note hummed by the performer is sympathetically reproduced by the diaphragm and transmitted to the trumpet. A vibrating skin is also found in the mediæval ' Onion Flute,' in several forms of African wind instruments, and on many of the Chinese flutes ; but in these and similar cases

the note is formed by the player's voice or breath directed into the open hole of the tube the diaphragm merely adding a reedy timbre to the sound produced.

BIBLIOGRAPHY.

WILSON : *Prehistoric Art* (Smithsonian Instit. Report, 1896).
WEAD : *History of Musical Scales* (Smithsonian Instit. Report, 1900).
BALFOUR: *The Old British Pibcorn* (Anthol. Journal, vol. xx.).
GALPIN : *The Whistles and Reed-Instruments of the N.W. Coast of America* (Trans. Musical Assoc. 1903).
HERMANN SMITH: *The World's Earliest Music*, 1904.
ANKERMANN : *Die afrikanischen Musik-Instrumente*, Berlin, 1897 ; *Annales du Musée du Congo* (Ethnographical), vol. i., Brussels, 1902. See also under HISTORIES OF MUSIC.

F. W. G.

PIPO (PIPPO), see MATTEI, FILIPPO.

PIQUE, LOUIS FRANÇOIS (*b.* Roret, near Mirecourt, France, 1758 ; *d.* Charenton-Saint-Maurice, 1822), an excellent violin-maker. Reputed to have been a pupil of Saunier, a Lorraine violin- and guitar-maker, who settled in Paris in 1770, Pique became one of the best makers of his epoch. The date of his installation in the French capital is unknown, but the label in a theorbo of his fabrication in the Museum of the Paris Conservatoire reveals that he was living at the ' Rue Coquillière, au coin de la Rue Bouloy,' in 1779. Between 1787 and 1789 he made fiddles at the ' Rue Platrière, vis-à-vis l'hôtel de Bullon ' ; in 1791 at the ' Rue Coquillière, vis-à-vis le Roulage de France,' and between 1809 and 1815 at No. 36 Rue de Grenelle-Saint-Honoré. As a copyist of Stradivarius, Pique approached his contemporary Nicolas LUPOT (*q.v.*) more closely than any other French maker of his period. Owing to this fact, it has been said that many of the instruments bearing Pique's name were made by Lupot and only varnished by Pique, but the dissimilarity of their workmanship disproves the suggestion. It is more than likely that the imputation has arisen from an inevitable rivalry which probably existed between the two makers. Pique's work was somewhat unequal, but his best instruments show skilled manipulation of a high order. The qualities of the materials chosen are excellent ; the backs—sometimes whole—are well selected, and the tables are of particularly fine wood. The scroll is well executed, without exaggeration, the sound-holes cut with precision, the varnish red brown. Pique's labels were both autograph and lithograph. His instruments were highly esteemed during his lifetime, and are now valuable. Spohr, in his *Méthode de violo* mentions Lupot and Pique as the best French makers of their time.

BIBL.—LAURENT GRILLET, *Les Ancêtres du violon* ; VIDAL, *Instruments à archet* ; HART, *The Violin* ; GALLAY, *Les Luthiers italiens* ; VON LÜTGENDORFF, *Die Geigen- und Lautenmacher* ; HAWEIS, *Old Violins* ; FLEMING, *The Fiddle Fancier's Guide.*

E. H.-A.

PIQUE DAME (QUEEN OF SPADES), ope. by Tchaikovsky ; libretto (after Poushkin) b Modeste Tchaikovsky ; produced St. Peters burg, Dec. 19, 1890 ; London Opera House (Rosing season), May 29, 1915.

**PIRATA, IL,** opera in 2 acts; text by Romani, music by Bellini. Produced Scala, Milan, Oct. 27, 1827; in Paris, Théâtre Italien, Feb. 1, 1832; in London, King's Theatre, Apr. 17, 1830.       **G.**

**PIRATES OF PENZANCE, THE,** comic opera in 2 acts; words by W. S. Gilbert, music by Sullivan. Produced Fifth Avenue Theatre, New York, Dec. 31, 1879; Opéra-Comique, London, Apr. 3. 1880.     **G.**

**PIROUETTE,** a perforated cap adjusted so as partly to cover the double reed of old instruments of the shawm and pommer classes, corresponding with modern oboes and bassoons. The length of the pirouette was regulated so as to allow of the projection of the proper length of the reed for vibration, and the rim or table afforded some support to the lips of the player, which was probably of value in days when reeds were hard and unmanageable. The pirouette, now unused, indicated a stage of development between the completely enclosed reed of the cromorne and bagpipe and the open reed of modern instruments, which is peculiarly sensitive, and entirely under the control of the lips of the player.       **D. J. B.**

**PIRRO, André** (b. Saint-Dizier, Feb. 12, 1869), organist and writer on music. His father was organist of Saint-Dizier.

He studied law and letters (*Docteur ès lettres*) in 1907, and at the same time pursued a serious study of musical technique. He attended as *auditeur* the organ class of César Franck at the Conservatoire (1890), then that of Widor. When the Schola Cantorum was founded (Oct. 15, 1896) Pirro became a member of the Committee of directors and professor of history of music and organ, second to Guilmant. His musical teaching took a wider range after 1904, when he began his lectures at the École des Hautes Études Sociales, which he continued for about 10 years. In 1912 he succeeded Romain Rolland as professor of history at the Sorbonne. Since 1920, on his advice, this public course has been followed by a final course of practical musical study for students. This instruction shows the same characteristics of culture and learning which early assured favourable notice to his works. They are: *L'Orgue de J. S. Bach,* preface by Widor (1894; appeared in 1897), 'crowned' by the Institut, English ed. by Goodrich (1902); *L'esthétique de J. S. Bach* and *Descartes et la musique* (1907) (the thesis for his doctorate); *J. S. Bach* (1906), German transl. by B. Engelke (1910); *Dietrich Buxtehude* (1913); *Schütz* (1913), German transl. in preparation (1926) by W. Gurlitt; *Les Clavecinistes* (1925). Pirro has moreover contributed extensively to *L'Encyclopédie de la musique* (Delagrave, Paris) (vol. ii. *Musique religieuse allemande, 1619 – 1750, Musique profane allemande, XVII–XVIII*<sup>ième</sup> *siècle*).

He contributed to the *Riemann-Festschrift,*

1909 (*Remarques de quelques voyageurs sur la musique en Allemagne . . . de 1634 à 1700*); the *Archives des maîtres de l'orgue*; the *Revue musicale* (Combarieu); the *Revue musicale* (Prunières); the *Tribune de St. Gervais*; the *Cultura musicale*; the *Revue de musicologie* (Paris); the *Revue Union Musicologique* (La Haye), etc.       **M. P.**

**PISADOR, Diego** (b. Salamanca, 1508–09; d. after 1557), Spanish lutenist, author of a *Libro de musica de vihuela,* Salamanca, 1552.[1] His father was in the household of the archbishop of Santiago (*notario de la audiencia*) and a man of property. The only information concerning his son, the lutenist, is obtained from the records of lawsuits (*vide* N. Alonso Cortés, *Bol. de la Bibl. Menéndez y Pelayo* (Santander, 1921), iii. 331). He took minor orders (1526), but did not pursue an ecclesiastical career any further. He is last heard of in 1557. The *Libro de musica de vihuela* contains settings of several old Spanish ballads (*e.g. Conde Arnaldos*), *villancicos,* madrigals to words by Garci-Lasso (the orig. voice parts in the Bibl. Medinaceli, Madrid), and also 15 transcriptions from the masses of Josquin des Près and 17 of motets by Morales and others. The value of lute transcriptions of polyphonic music, as showing the extent to which chromatic alteration was practised in the 16th century, was pointed out by O. Chilesotti (*I.M.G. Congress Report,* Vienna, 1909, p. 128 ff.).       **J. B. T.**

**PISARI, Pasquale** (b. Rome, 1725; d. there, 1778) (called Pizari in Santini's catalogue), eminent church composer, and, according to Padre Martini, 'the Palestrina of the 18th century,' son of a mason.

A musician named Gasparino, struck by his beautiful voice as a child, urged him to devote himself to music. His voice developed afterwards into a fine bass, but he took less to singing than to composition, which he studied under Giovanni Biordi. In 1752 he was admitted into the Pope's chapel as supernumerary, and remained a member till his death. His poverty was extreme, and many, perhaps apocryphal, stories are told of his writing his compositions with ink made from charcoal and water, etc. His finest work is a 'Dixit' in sixteen real parts, written for the papal jubilee in 1775 and sung by 150 performers. A Kyrie and Gloria in forty-eight parts by Ballabene were performed on the same occasion. Burney was in Rome the same year, and speaks[2] with astonishment of the learning displayed in the 'Dixit.' It was composed for the court of Lisbon, together with a service for every day in the year, but the payment was so long delayed that by the time it arrived Pisari had died, and his nephew, a journeyman mason,

---

[1] B.M.; Bibl. Nat., Paris; Bibl. Nac., Madrid; Bibl. Escurial.
[2] *Present State, France and Italy,* p. 370.

inherited it. The singers of the Pope's chapel, disappointed with Tartini's Miserere, requested Pisari to write one, which he did, in nine parts, but it was a comparative failure. Baini conjectures that the arduous nature of his task for the King of Portugal had exhausted his powers. For the Pope's chapel he composed several masses, psalms, motets in eight parts, two Te Deums in eight parts and one in four, which Baini pronounces a lastingly beautiful work. See *Q.-L.* Santini had twelve large church compositions by Pisari.     F. G.

PISARONI, BENEDETTA ROSAMUNDA (*b.* Piacenza, Feb. 6, 1793 ; *d.* there, Aug. 6, 1872), an excellent contralto singer. Her instructors were Pino, Moschini and Marchesi. Her first public appearances were made at Bergamo in 1811, in the rôles of Griselda, Camilla and others, popular at that period. Her voice was then a high soprano, and her accomplishments as a singer so great that, in spite of a singularly unprepossessing appearance—her features were painfully disfigured by small-pox—she excited great admiration, and her fame spread rapidly all over Italy. A serious illness which she had at Parma, in 1813, resulted in the loss of some of her upper notes, which forced her to abandon her old soprano parts. She then applied herself to cultivating the lower register of her voice, which gained considerably in extent and volume, while the artistic resources she displayed were so great that the career by which she is remembered began in fact at this time. Some few of her notes had always a guttural, unpleasant sound, but in spite of this she was universally admitted to be the first Italian contralto. She appeared at Paris, in 1827, as Arsace in ' Semiramide.'

She herself was so sensible of her physical defects that she never accepted an engagement without first sending her portrait to the manager, that he might be prepared exactly for what he was undertaking.

After singing in ' La donna del lago ' and ' L' Italiana in Algeri,' displaying eminent dramatic as well as vocal qualities, she appeared in London in 1829, but was not appreciated. For two years afterwards she sang at Cadiz, and then returned to Italy. Here she failed to find the favour shown her in past days. She retired accordingly into private life.

F. A. M.

PISCHEK, JOHANN BAPTIST (*b.* Melnick, Bohemia, Oct. 14, 1814 ; *d.* Stuttgart, Feb. 16, 1873), a fine baritone singer, made his début on the boards at the age of 21. In 1844 he was appointed court-singer to the King of Würtemberg at Stuttgart, an appointment which he retained until his retirement, July 1, 1863. He entered on his duties May 1, 1844. At a later date he was also made ' Kammersänger.' Pischek travelled a great deal, and was known

and liked in all the principal towns of North and South Germany, especially at Frankfort, where we find him singing, both on the stage in a variety of parts and in concerts, year after year from 1840–48. In England he was a very great favourite for several years. He made his first appearance here on May 1, 1845, at a concert of Madame Caradori Allan's ; sang at the Philharmonic on the following Monday, and thrice besides during the season there. He reappeared in this country in 1846, 1847 and 1849, and maintained his popularity in the concert-room and in oratorio, singing in 1849 the part of Elijah at the Birmingham Festival with great energy, passion and effect. On the stage of the German opera at Drury Lane during the same year his Don Juan was not so successful, his acting being thought exaggerated. He was heard again in 1853 at the New Philharmonic Concerts.

In voice, enunciation, feeling and style, Pischek was first-rate. His repertory was large, embracing operas and pieces of Gluck, Mozart, Méhul, Beethoven, Spohr, Weber, Donizetti, Hérold, Lachner, Kreutzer, Lindpaintner. In his latter days one of his most favourite parts was Hassan in Benedict's ' Der Alte vom Berge ' (' Crusaders ') ; others were Hans Heiling, Ashton (' Lucia ') and the Jäger in the ' Nachtlager von Granada.'

A. C.

PISENDEL, GEORG JOHANN (*b.* Karlsburg, Franconia, Transylvania, Dec. 26, 1687 ; *d.* Dresden, Nov. 25, 1755), an esteemed violinist. His artistic career began at the age of 9, when he became a choir-boy in the chapel of the Margrave of Ansbach, Bavaria. Corelli, who was at that time leader of the chapel orchestra, taught him the violin, while Antonio Pistocchi instructed him in the rudiments of music and harmony. So rapid was the child's progress that at the age of 15 he was nominated one of the chapel violinists. In 1709 he went to Leipzig, where he pursued his studies at the university. The King of Poland appointed him his Kapellmeister in 1712, and later he became attached to the suite of the hereditary prince of Saxony, whom he accompanied to Paris in 1714, to Berlin in 1715, to Italy during the following two years, and to Vienna in 1718. After the death of Volumier, Pisendel succeeded him as Konzertmeister at the Saxon court in 1730, and in 1731 became leader of the opera orchestra under the baton of Johann Hasse, which post he occupied until his death. As a violinist Pisendel was among the best of the early 18th-century players, and his influence in Dresden, where he established a violin school, was instrumental in raising the art of violin-playing to a high level of efficiency. (See VERACINI.) Pisendel wrote some concertos and solos for the violin, the manuscripts of which are preserved in the State Library at

**Dresden.** A gigue of his composition is included in Telemann's ' Musik-Meister.'

BIBL.—LAHEE, *Famous Violinists*; MASON CLARKE, *Fiddlers Ancient and Modern*; T. LAMB PHIPSON, *Famous Violins, etc.*; DUBOURG, *The Violin*; VIDAL, *Les Instruments à archet*; *Riemann*; *Q.-L.*
E. H.-A.

PISTOCCHI, FRANCESCO ANTONIO MAMILIANO (*b.* Palermo, 1659; *d.* Bologna, May 13, 1726). On the removal of the family to Bologna in 1661, he made such rapid progress in music that he was made a member of the Accademia dei Filarmonici before the publication of his ' Cappricci puerili . . . sopra un basso d' un balletto,' a volume of pieces for harpsichord, harp, violin and other instruments, on the title-page of which it is stated that the composer was 8 years old at the date of issue, 1667. In 1670 he was a chorister at San Petronio, but must have been dismissed shortly afterwards, as his father applies for his re-admission to the choir in 1674. If we may trust the date on a MS. copy of the opera ' Il girello ' at Modena, that work was written as early as 1669; in a printed book this might easily be, as has been suggested, an error for 1696, but hardly in a MS. The opera was performed in Venice in 1682, and Stradella wrote a prologue to it, so that the earlier date of composition may very possibly be correct. In 1675 he began the career of an operatic singer, in which he won considerable renown. In 1679 his opera ' Leandro ' was performed by puppets at Venice, and in 1682 an opera called ' Amori fatali ' at the same place. In 1687–94 he was a singer at the court of Parma. About 1696 he became Kapellmeister to the Margrave of Ansbach; in the following year his opera ' Narciso ' was produced there, and in 1699 his ' Le pazzie d' Amore.' In this period falls the publication of his ' Scherzi musicali,' a set of airs to Italian, French and German words. In 1699 he went to Venice and produced an oratorio, ' Il martirio di San Adriano,' which had apparently been written as early as 1692. In 1700 he produced at Vienna a three-act opera ' Le rise di Democrito.' The date 1698 is given by Riemann for his oratorio ' Maria Vergine addolorata,' from which Burney quotes an aria in his *History*, vol. iv. p. 121. In 1701 he went back to Bologna, and re-entered the choir of San Petronio as a contralto, and a few years afterwards founded the school of singing which made Bologna famous, and was imitated in other Italian cities. The year 1707, when a volume of duets and trios was published as op. 3, at Bologna, seems to have been the date of another opera, ' Bertoldo ' (Eitner gives it as 1787, which is impossible), at Vienna, and 1710 that of ' I rivali generosi ' at Reggio. In 1715 he entered the order of the Oratorians, and in 1717 (according to Riemann) wrote an oratorio ' La fuga di S. Teresia.' Several church compositions mentioned in *Q.-L.* probably date from this last period of his life. The chief authority for his life is Busi's life of G. B. Martini. The list of those few works which are still extant is given in *Q.-L.*, and various others are mentioned in *Riemann*.
M.

PISTON, see VALVE.

PITCH. This word, in its general sense, refers to the position of any sound in the musical scale of acuteness and gravity, this being determined by the corresponding *vibration-number*, *i.e.* the number of double vibrations per second which will produce that sound. Thus when we speak of one sound being ' higher in pitch ' than another, we mean that the vibrations producing the former are more rapid than those producing the latter, so giving what is recognised as a higher sound. The general nature of this relation is dealt with in the article on ACOUSTICS; it is sufficient here to state that, as a matter of practice, when the exact pitch of any musical sound has to be defined, this is most properly done by stating its vibration-number.

STANDARD OF PITCH.—It becomes, then, an important practical question for the musician, what is the exact pitch corresponding with the written notes he is accustomed to use ? or, to put the question in a simpler form, what is the true vibration-number attached to any one given note, say, for example, treble C ? for if this is known, the true pitch of any other note can be calculated from it by well-known rules.

This opens the vexed question of what is called the ' Standard of Pitch.' It is an interesting consideration whether, as a matter of theory, a philosophical standard of pitch can be devised, based on natural facts, like the standards of measure, weight and time. Such a standard is easily deducible. We may assume the existence of a note corresponding with the simplest possible rate of vibration, viz. *one per second*; and the various octaves of this note will be represented by 2, 4, 8, etc. vibrations, being a series of powers of the number 2. This theoretical note is found to agree so nearly with the musician's idea of the note C (the simplest or fundamental note in our modern musical system) that they may be assumed to correspond, and we thus get $c'' = 512$ double vibrations per second, which may be called the ' Philosophical Standard of Pitch,' and which has been adopted, for theoretical purposes, in many books on music. And as it will be seen that this corresponds very fairly with the ' Classical Pitch,' and differs very little from the authorised French pitch and the vocal pitch now followed in England, it would form a reasonably good standard in a practical as well as in a theoretical point of view. According to reason and common sense there ought to be some agreement among the musicians of the world as to what musical note should be

denoted by a certain musical sign ; but unfortunately there is no complete agreement,
though considerable advance has been made
within recent times, as the following account
will show. The question has been much
debated,[1] but it must suffice here to state
some of the more important facts that have
been elicited in the discussion.

HISTORY.—We have no positive data as to
the pitch used in the earliest music of our
present form, but we may arrive at some idea
of it by inference. The two octaves of Pythagoras's Greek scale must have corresponded
with the compass of male voices, and when
Guido added the Gamma (G), one tone below
the Proslambanomenos of the Greeks, we may
fairly assume that it expressed the lowest note
that could be comfortably taken by ordinary
voices of the bass kind. This is a matter of
physiology, and is known to be somewhere
about 90 to 100 vibrations per second ; according to which the note $c''$, two octaves and a
fourth higher (see STAVELESS NOTATION),
would lie between 480 and 532.

At a later period some information of a more
positive kind is obtained by organ pipes, such
as those at Halberstadt (1495)—A$=505\cdot8$—
respecting the dimensions of which evidence
exists ; and it is found that the pitch varied
considerably according to the nature of the
music used, there being very different pitches
for religious and secular purposes severally.[2]
The inconvenience of this, however, seems to
have been found out, and early in the 17th
century an attempt was made to introduce a
*Mean Pitch* which should reconcile the requirements of the church with those of the chamber,
or the ' Chorton ' with the ' Kammerton.' It
was about a whole tone above the flattest, and
a minor third below the highest pitch used.
The effort to introduce this met with some
success, although the tables in the article in
the *Ency. Brit.*, 10th ed., show that from 1495–
1690 the pitch was gradually lowered, from
the pitch above given to that of the Hampton
Court organ (A$=441\cdot7$) ; on the other hand,
from 1713 (Strassburg Minster organ, A$=393\cdot2$)
onwards until 1897 the pitch rose steadily.
Ellis (*History of Musical Pitch*, 1880) gives a
long list of examples taken at various dates
over what is generally called the classical
period, varying for A from 415 to 429, or for C
from 498 to 515 vibrations. This is an extreme
range of only about half a semitone, which,
considering the imperfect nature of the means
then practicable of obtaining identity and

uniformity, is remarkably satisfactory. During
this period lived and wrote Purcell, Bach,
Handel, Haydn, Mozart, Beethoven, Weber,
Schubert, and partly Spohr, Mendelssohn and
Rossini. That is to say, the founders and
perfecters of musical art all thought out their
music and arranged it to be played and sung
in this pitch. This is therefore emphatically
the *Classical Pitch* of music. And, singularly
enough, it agrees with the presumptive determination we have made of the pitch that must
have been used in the earliest times, as well as
with the theoretic standard considered above.

But, unhappily, this satisfactory state of
things was disturbed during the 19th century.
The orchestra began to assume greater importance as regards its wind element, new and
improved wind instruments being introduced,
and the use of them being much extended.
This led to a constant desire for louder and
more exciting effects, and both makers and
users of wind instruments soon perceived that
such effects might be enhanced by raising
slightly the pitch of the sounds. The wind
instruments were of course the standards in an
orchestra, and so a gradual rise crept in, which
both strings and voices were obliged to follow.
The conductors, who ought in the interests of
good music to have checked this, were either
ignorant of, or indifferent to, the mischief that
was being done, until at length it assumed
alarming proportions. In 1878 the opera band
at Covent Garden was playing at about
A$=450$ or C$=540$, being a rise of a semitone
above the ' classical pitch ' used down to Beethoven's day. In 1897 the Strauss band played
at the Imperial Institute, London, at a pitch
of A$=457\cdot5$.

Such a change was attended with many
evils. It altered the character of the best
compositions ; it tended to spoil the performance and ruin the voices of the best singers ;
and it threw the musical world into confusion
from the uncertainty as to the practical meaning of the symbols used ; and all for no object
whatever, as no one could affirm that the new
pitch was on any ground better than the old
one. Accordingly strong remonstrances were
expressed from time to time, and efforts were
made either to restore the original pitch, or at
least to stop its further rise, and to obtain
some general agreement for uniformity.

In 1834 a ' Congress of Physicists ' held at
Stuttgart adopted a proposal by Scheibler to
fix the A at 440 (true C$=528$), but it does not
appear that this had any practical result. In
1858 the French government appointed a commission, consisting partly of musicians [3] and
partly of physicists, to consider the subject.
The instructions stated that

[1] The most thorough investigation of this subject will be found
in two papers read before the Society of Arts, May 12, 1877, and
Mar. 3, 1880, by Dr. A. J. Ellis, F.R.S. See also Ellis's translation
of Helmholtz, 2nd ed. App. p. 493, and an essay by D. J. Blaikley
in the *Descriptive Catalogue of Musical Instruments in the Royal
Military Exhibition, 1890* (1891), p. 235 ; also, by the same writer,
*Memorandum on the Pitch of Army Bands* (Boosey & Co., 1909).
The article ' Pitch ' in the supplementary volume of the *Ency. Brit.*
10th ed., with its valuable tables of pitch, should also be consulted.
[2] In the Elizabethan era in England three pitches seem to have
been generally recognised.

[3] The musicians were Auber, Halévy (who drew the Report),
Berlioz, Meyerbeer, Rossini and Thomas. The other members were
Pelletier, Despretz, Doucet, Lissajous, Monnais and Gen. Mellinet.

the constant and increasing elevation of the pitch presents inconveniences by which the musical art, composers, artists, and musical instrument-makers all equally suffer, and the difference existing between the pitches of different countries, of different musical establishments, and of different manufacturing houses, is a source of embarrassment in musical combinations and of difficulties in commercial relations.'

The Commission reported in Feb. 1859.[1] After substantiating the facts of the rise (which they attributed to the desire for increased sonority and brilliancy on the part of instrument-makers) and the great want of uniformity, they resolved to recommend a fixed standard: A=435 (C true=522; C by equal temperament=517). This was confirmed by a legal decree, and it has been adopted in France generally, to the great advantage of all musical interests in that country.

Soon afterwards an attempt was made to do something in England. A committee was appointed by the Society of Arts, who reported in 1869, recommending the Stuttgart standard of C=528; but the recommendation fell dead, and had no immediate influence. Other agitations and discussions were for a long time without effect, and the state of matters in this country in regard to the standard of pitch was as follows. The principal orchestras continued to play at the elevated pitch; but this was repudiated by the general consensus of vocal performers, and in all cases where an orchestra was not employed, as in churches and at vocal concerts, a much lower pitch was used, corresponding nearly with either the French or the 'classical' one. Hence all idea of uniformity in the practical interpretation of music was out of the question—a state of things most deplorable, and a disgrace to the musical education of the country, and one which complicated immeasurably the business of the piano manufacturers, who had to supply instruments at different pitches. The endeavours of A. J. Hipkins, Dr. A. J. Ellis and Dr. Pole at last bore fruit in the general adoption of what is virtually the French *diapason normal* in 1896, i.e. A=439 double vibrations at a temperature of 68° Fahr., or A=435 double vibrations at 59° Fahr. The difference between A=435 and A=439 represents the rise in pitch between 59° Fahr. and 68° Fahr. in flue organ pipes, due to the change of temperature, and a similar but not so great a rise takes place in orchestral and other wind instruments. For a time, and until the organ in the large concert-hall could be altered to correspond with the change, there was much discrepancy between the 'old' and 'new' Philharmonic pitches, as they were called, but now (1926), except where an organ [2] of the high pitch is still in use, the latter is almost as universal in England as on the Continent, with the exception that the instruments

[1] *Rapport et arrêtés pour l'établissement en France d'un diapason musical uniforme.* Paris, Imprimérie Impériale, 1859.
[2] The organ of the Albert Hall, London, was lowered in 1923.

used in the military bands are still at the high pitch.

w. p. ; rev. with addns. by D. J. B., etc.

ENGLISH MILITARY PITCH.—It is interesting to note that the pitch of drum and fife bands until some time between 1880 and 1890 remained the same as Sir George Smart's pitch of 1828, practically identical with the present low orchestral pitch (Philharmonic, 1896), although from about the middle of last century military bands, in accordance with the Queen's regulations, used the high or 'old' Philharmonic pitch. Drum and fife bands now conform to the military or Kneller Hall pitch, which (in agreement with the 'old Philharmonic' or high pitch) was in 1909 officially defined in the King's Regulations as A=452·4 at 60° Fahr. This is the pitch used not only in the bands of the King's forces, but practically in the vast number of brass bands throughout the country, and at present there seems but little prospect of these military and other wind bands being converted from the 'old' to the 'new' Philharmonic pitch, notwithstanding the desirability and advantage of the change.

D. J. B.

PITCHPIPE, a small stopped diapason pipe with long movable graduated stopper, blown by the mouth, and adjustable approximately to any note of the scale by pushing the stopper inwards or outwards. A pipe of this kind is so much influenced by temperature, moisture, force of blowing, and irregularities of calibre, that it can only be depended on for the pitch of vocal music, and is not to be trusted for more accurate determinations. A small reed pipe of the free species, in which the length of the vibrating portion of metal is controlled by a rotating spiral, is somewhat superior, and far less bulky than the older contrivance. It is known as Eardley's patent chromatic pitchpipe. Sets of single free reeds, each in its own tube, arranged in a box, forming a more or less complete scale, are to be obtained, and form comparatively trustworthy implements; if tuned to equal temperament they may be employed to facilitate pianoforte or organtuning. All pitchpipes are, however, inferior in accuracy to tuning-forks; the only advantage they possess over the latter being their louder, more strident, more coercive tone, and the readiness with which beats are produced. No accurate tuning is practicable except by the principle of beats and interferences.

W. H. S.

PITONI, GIUSEPPE OTTAVIO (b. Rieti, Mar. 18, 1657; d. San Marco, Feb. 1, 1743), eminent musician of the Roman school; from the age of 5 attended the music-school of Pompeo Natale, and was successively chorister at San Giovanni de' Fiorentini, and the SS. Apostoli in Rome. Here he attracted the attention of Foggia, who gave him instruction in counterpoint during several years.  In 1673 he became maestro di cappella at Terra di Rotondo, and afterwards at Assisi, where he began to score Palestrina's works, a practice he afterwards enjoined on his pupils, as the best way of studying style.  In 1676 he removed to Rieti, and in 1677 became maestro di cappella of the Collegio di San Marco in Rome, where his pieces for two and three choirs were first performed. He was also engaged by various other churches, San Apollinare and San Lorenzo in Damaso in 1686, the Lateran in 1708, and St. Peter's in 1719, but he retained his post at San Marco till his death, and was buried there.

Pitoni's ' Dixit.' in sixteen parts is still one of the. finest pieces of music sung at St. Peter's during Holy Week, and his masses, ' Li pastori a maremme,' ' Li pastori a montagna,' and ' Mosca,' founded openly on popular melodies, still sound fresh and new.  His fertility was enormous ; for St. Peter's alone he composed complete services for the entire year.  He also wrote many pieces for six and nine choirs.  He compiled a history of the maestri di cappella of Rome from 1500–1700, the MS. of which is in the Vatican Library, and was used by Baini for his life of Palestrina.  Gaspari drew the attention of Fétis to a work of 108 pages, *Guida armonica di Giuseppe Ottavio Pitoni*, presumably printed in 1689.  The MS. is lost. Among Pitoni's numerous pupils were Durante, Leo and Feo.  The library of the Corsini Palace in Rome contains a biography of him by his friend Geronimo Chiti of Siena.  Proske's ' Musica divina ' contains a Mass and a Requiem, six motets, a psalm, a hymn, and a ' Christus factus est,' by Pitoni.  See *Q.-L.*

F. G.

PITSCH, KAREL FRANT (*b*. Bartošovice-by-Roketnice, Bohemia, 1789[1]; *d*. Prague, June 13, 1858), was organist of St. Nicholas' church, and important as a teacher and the director of the Organ School, where Anton Dvořák was his pupil.  His compositions include a Mass and organ works.

PITT, PERCY (*b*. London, Jan. 4, 1870), composer, organist and pianist, studied music almost entirely abroad, after undergoing a general education in France.  At Leipzig, whither he went from Paris to live, from 1886–1888, he was a pupil of Reinecke and Jadassohn, and for the three following years he worked at Munich under Rheinberger.  On his return to England in 1893 he devoted much time to composition, and, in addition, was appointed in 1895 chorus-master of the Mottl Concerts ; in 1896 official organist of the Queen's Hall ; and in 1902 musical adviser and occasional conductor at Covent Garden.  He became musical director to the Grand Opera Syndicate in 1907, conducted the Beecham Opera Company (1915–1918), and became artistic director of its suc-

cessor, The BRITISH NATIONAL OPERA COM-PANY (*q.v.*), in 1920.  In 1922 he was appointed musical director to the British Broadcasting Company.

His compositions belong mostly to his earlier years.  His symphonic prelude ' Le Sang des crépuscules ' (1900) ; his suite from the incidental music to Stephen Phillips's ' Paola and Francesca ' (1902) ; his overture ' The Taming of the Shrew ' (1898) ; his ballade for violin and orchestra (1900), composed for Ysaÿe, have been played on the Continent and in America, as well as in England.  Pitt has written also a suite for orchestra (1895), and other suites, ' Fêtes galantes ' (after Verlaine, 1896), ' Cinderella ' (1899), ' Dance rhythms ' (1901) ; a concerto for clarinet and orchestra (1897) ; a Coronation march and a march for military band, the last written expressly for the Trooping of the Colour ; an oriental rhapsody ; a ballad for male chorus and orchestra, ' Hohenlinden ' (1899) ; five poems for baritone and orchestra (1902), and others for mezzo-soprano and orchestra (1904) ; incidental music, in addition to that named, to ' Flodden Field ' by Alfred Austin, and to ' King Richard II.,' and a sinfonietta produced at the Birmingham Festival, Oct. 1906, and in the repertory of the Queen's Hall Symphony Concerts in London.            R. H. L., with addns.

PITTMAN, JOSIAH (*b*. Sept. 3, 1816 ; *d*. London, Apr. 23, 1886), the son of a musician.  He began to study both theory and practice at an early age, and became a pupil of Goodman and of S. S. Wesley on the organ, and, at a later date, of Moscheles on the piano.  He held the post of organist at Sydenham (1831), Tooting (1833), and Spitalfields (1835) successively— the last of the three for twelve years.  Feeling the need of fuller instruction in theory, he visited Frankfort in 1836 and 1837, and studied with Schnyder von Wartensee.  In 1852 he was elected organist to Lincoln's Inn ; the service was in a very unsatisfactory condition, but Pittman's zeal, perseverance and judgment improved it greatly, and he remained there for twelve years.  It was in support of this reform that he wrote a little book entitled *The People in Church* (1858), which at the time excited much attention.  He also composed many services and anthems for the Chapel.  Pittman was connected with the opera as maestro al cembalo at Her Majesty's (1865–68) and Covent Garden (1868–80).  His early predilections were for the German organ music, and, like Gauntlett, Jacob and the Wesleys, he worked hard by precept, example and publication to introduce Bach's fugues and pedal organs into England. He edited a series of ' Progressive Studies,' contrapuntal pieces from the works of 18th-century English organists (Stanley, Battishill, James, etc.).  For several years Pittman delivered the annual course of lectures on music at the London Institution. He arranged many operas, etc., for piano.           G.

PIUTTI, CARL (b. Elgersburg, 1846; d. Leipzig, 1902), organist and composer. He studied at Leipzig Conservatoire, becoming a professor there in 1875. In 1880 he succeeded Rust as organist at the Thomaskirche. He wrote much admirable organ music, including three sonatas, some fugues, many choral preludes and short pieces; works for a cappella choir; songs; piano works and a text-book on harmony.
             H. G.

PIXIS, a family of musicians. (1) FRIEDRICH WILHELM, the elder, was a pupil of the Abbé Vogler in Mannheim in 1770, and still lived there in 1805. He published organ music, and sonatas and trios for PF. His eldest son, (2) FRIEDRICH WILHELM (b. Mannheim, 1786; d. Oct. 20, 1842), studied the violin under Ritter, Luigi and Franzel, early made a name, and travelled throughout Germany with his father and brother. At Hamburg he took lessons from Viotti. In 1804 he entered the Elector's chapel at Mannheim, and afterwards went to Prague, where he became professor at the Conservatorium, and Kapellmeister of the theatre. His brother, (3) JOHANN PETER (b. 1788; d. Baden-Baden, Dec. 22, 1874), pianist and composer for the piano, lived with his father and brother till 1809, when he settled in Munich. In 1825 he went to Paris, and became a teacher of great note there. He settled finally in Baden-Baden in 1845, and gave lessons at his well-known villa there almost up to his death. He composed much for the piano—concertos, sonatas and drawing-room pieces, all now forgotten. The fact that he contributed the third variation to the ' Hexameron,' in company with Liszt, Czerny, Thalberg, Herz and Chopin, shows the position which he held in Paris. His works amount in all to more than 150. Though not wholly devoid of originality he was apt to follow too closely in the footsteps of Mozart, Haydn and Beethoven. In 1831 he composed an opera ' Bibiana ' for Mme. Schroeder-Devrient, produced in Paris without success. ' Die Sprache des Herzens ' was composed in 1836 for the Königstadt Theatre in Berlin. His adopted daughter, (4) FRANZILLA GÖHRINGER (b. Lichtenthal, Baden, 1816), developing a good mezzo-soprano voice and real talent, he trained her for a singer, and in 1833 started with her on a tour, which extended to Naples. Here Pacini wrote for her the part of Saffo in his well-known opera of that name. She married an Italian named Minofrio.            F. G.

PIZARRO, DIEGO (17th cent.), Spanish composer, author or compiler of a large and important MS. vol. of secular vocal music in the Bibl. Nac., Madrid (' Libro de tonos humanos,' M. 1262).          J. B. T.

PIZZETTI, ILDEBRANDO (ILDEBRANDO DA PARMA) (b. Parma, Sept. 20, 1880), perhaps the most individual and thoughtful Italian composer of the present time. The chief events of his life are told in the opening chapter of Intermezzi critici, a collection of critical essays dedicated to the memory of an intimate friend and collaborator, Annibale Beggi. He studied at the Parmese Conservatorio with Gallignani and Tebaldini. While still a student his compositions attracted some attention. A first opera, ' Sabina,' on an Alsatian legend, and a second on Shakespeare's ' Romeo and Juliet,' were both written ' between a fugue and a sonata movement ' while Pizzetti was under the discipline of the school. Such labours, if devoid of practical results through lack of experience and technical knowledge, apart from the performance of an Intermezzo at a students' concert, nevertheless produced some fruit in focussing the composer's attention on the problems of opera music, problems which he attempted to solve in various ways until he found the form which finally satisfied him and applied in ' Fedra' and ' Debora e Jaele.' After leaving the Conservatorio (1901) he devoted himself to teaching and conducting, acting as substitute to Cleofonte Campanini at the Parma Opera House. In the following year the competition of the publisher Souzogno resulted in the composition of an opera on the subject of ' The Cid,' which the examiners declined to take into consideration because the last scene was wanting. His notions of opera then inclined towards the accepted canons of Italian composers, and he aimed at carrying on the lyrical tradition of Rossini, Bellini and Verdi, which he was then convinced best suited the Italian temperament. He felt, however, that greater freedom of rhythm and measure was necessary, that new technical means, vocal and instrumental, were needed, and after ' The Cid ' he realised for the first time that lyricism and drama are different things, that the essential point of dramatic expression ' is not in the abandon and exaltation of the singer ; that it was necessary to seek something different and seek elsewhere.'

The years between 1903 and 1907 (when Pizzetti left Parma for Florence) were devoted to the composition of chamber music, of a quartet, a sonata and a symphonic poem. In view of the extraordinary success of his sonatas later, it is interesting to note that he did not, at first, find the symphonic form congenial. ' Unable to create new forms,' he writes, ' I had to accept those which already existed and which I felt were inimical and did violence to my own feelings,' concluding that the only form in which he could express all he wanted to express was the drama. But some time had yet to pass before he could find a solution to all the doubts and questioning of his artistic conscience in respect of opera. Many subjects were considered—Byron's *Sardanapalus*, then Poushkin's *Mazeppa*, were begun and soon set aside. 'Aeneas,' suggested by a reading of Ovid, and 'Lena' were carried further but, in the end, left unfinished. 'Aeneas,' however, showed him that 'drama is not pure epic'; in 'Lena,' on the other hand, he attempted to portray contemporary life and this took him a step further. 'The experience ended in failure, but was useful nevertheless, and perhaps needed.'

The study of the Greek classics turned his thoughts in a new direction. At first Euripides's *Hippolytus* attracted him and he actually began to set it to music; this was discarded for *Phaedra*, of which he wrote part of the text. But after a meeting with D'Annunzio, who was writing a tragedy on the same subject, he decided to wait for the Italian text offered him by the author. The composition of 'Fedra' occupied him three years (1909–12), and the opera was successfully performed at La Scala in Milan some time later, in Mar. 1915. It is the first opera to show his mature dramatic style based on the reforms he had been evolving ever since he had felt the inadequacy of lyricism as a means of expression in musical drama. Long before 'Fedra' Pizzetti's name became known to all Italians through his contribution of choral music to D'Annunzio's drama *La Nave* (1903). Searching study of the old Italian composers had given Pizzetti a masterly grip of the technique of choral writing, which he used with telling effect in the choral sections of the drama. Exceedingly important is also the part he assigned to the chorus in the next opera, 'Debora e Jaele' (1915–21), produced at La Scala in 1923, which may be said to embody all his ideals. What his views are on the subject may be gathered from an article published in *R.M.I.*, where he asserts that the ideal drama for music is that in which not only every word and action can be enhanced and be made more significant by music, but which also gives music the opportunity to reveal 'continuously' the profoundest depths of the human soul and carry their expression beyond the limits set to the words. The poet must eliminate all episodes where music can be only an accompaniment or description.

The chief innovation is in the substitution of a dramatic recitative for the lyricism supreme in all modern Italian operas, a recitative which has often the lyrical beauty of melody but is at once more elastic and more subtle. The chorus becomes more important; but the orchestra, although treated with great skill, has lost the predominance it obtained with Wagner and his successors.

In England Pizzetti is known so far mainly through some songs and the two sonatas for violin and pianoforte (1919); violoncello and pianoforte (1921). The latter was first performed here at a concert in 1923 in which the composer himself played the piano part. Both are excellent examples of an art which is national only in so far as it reflects the intense melancholy of the true Italian folk-song. But lyricism is a new thing in his hands. It appears controlled by a discrimination which at times leaves only a bare skeleton to be clad again in accordance with a strong individual fancy and with considerable resource of technical means. The composer's attitude towards the technique of his art may be briefly defined as an enlightened and liberal conservatism. He admits the claims of modern harmonists, but he expects the idea expressed to be of value, apart from the manner in which it is expressed. Hence his strictures on certain moderns and notably Schönberg, whose complexity Pizzetti maintains to be a cloak for poverty of original invention. In 1924 Pizzetti was appointed director of the Milan Conservatorium.

Besides the works already noted his output includes :

'Ave Maria.'
'Tenebrae factae sunt.'
'Tantum Ergo' for 3 v.
Trio for violin, v'cl. and PF.
'Canzone a Maggio.'
Overture to 'Oedipus et Colon.'
Three Interludes to 'Oedipus Rex.'
Mass for voices and strings.
'Canente,' orchestral poem.
'Épitaphe' on a text of V. Hugo.
'Sera d' inverno,' a lyric.
Three lyrics on a text of Conconi.
'Foglio d' album' for PF.
'I pastori,' a lyric on text of D'Annunzio.
'Poema romantico' for PF.
'La madre al figlio lontano,' a lyric.
Popular Greek Songs.
Three pieces for piano.
Overture for a tragic comedy.
'Due canzoni corali.'
Incidental music to D'Annunzio's 'La Pisanella.'
'Danze antiche' (for a performance of Tasso's 'Aminta').
Poem for violin and orchestra.
Music to D'Annunzio's cinema play 'Cabiria.'
'Terza canzone corale.'
'Passeggiata,' a lyric.
'Angelica.'
'Assunte.' } Neapolitan dramatic lyrics.
Quartet in A.
Mass for voices to the memory of King Humbert.

Critical studies and reviews have appeared in *R.M.I., Giornale dei musicisti, Il Secolo*, etc. Collected essays have been published by Treves (Milan) under the title *Musicisti contemporanei*; also *Intermezzi critici* (Vallecchi, Florence).

BIBL.—LUIGI PAGANO, *Debora e Jaele di Ildebrando Pizzetti, R.M.I.*, anno 30, 1923, pp. 47-108; FILIPPO BRUSA, *Le recenti composizioni di Ildebrando Pizzetti, R.M.I.*, 1923, pp. 586-601.

F. B.

PIZZICATO (Ital. = pinched). On the violin, and other instruments of the violin family, a note or a passage is said to be played pizzicato if the string is set in vibration not by the bow, but by being pinched or plucked with the finger. Early instances of this valuable orchestral effect are to be found in Handel's 'Agrippina,' 'Pastor fido,' 'Terpsichore,' and in an air by Hasse, written for Mingotti in 1748. In solo-playing a distinction is made between the pizzicato executed with the left and that with the right hand. The former one is frequently used, but not so much in classical as in bravura pieces. Paganini made an extensive use of it, either by playing a pizzicato accompaniment to a tune played with the bow (*a*), or in quick passages with arco notes interspersed (*b*) and (*c*).

(The notes marked * to be played pizzicato with the left hand.)

A natural harmonic note, when played pizzicato, produces an effect very similar to that of a note on the harp.

The 'pizzicato tremolando' is an effect devised by Elgar and used by him in his violin concerto, the players 'thrumming' spread chords with the soft part of three or four fingers across the strings.       P. D.

PLAGAL CADENCE is the form in which the final Tonic chord is preceded by Subdominant Harmony. (See CADENCE.)

      C. H. H. P.

PLAICHINGER, THILA (*b.* Vienna, Mar. 13, 1868), operatic soprano. She was a pupil of Gänsbacher at the Vienna Conservatoire, and made her début in that city. Her first real success, however, was achieved at Hamburg in 1893, and it was from there that she secured an engagement for the Municipal Theatre at Strassburg, where she sang from 1894 until 1901. During that period she appeared in most of the dramatic rôles of the Wagnerian and ordinary repertories, her powerful voice and fine acting meanwhile gaining the notice of Bayreuth, where she sang for several summers. From 1901–14 she was one of the principal sopranos of the Berlin Opera, and she made two visits to London, once in 1904 and once during the winter season of 1910, appearing on each occasion as Isolde. She afterwards became a teacher at the Stern Conservatorium in Berlin.

BIBL.—*International Who's Who in Music.*      H. K.

PLAIDY, LOUIS (*b.* Wermsdorf, Saxony, Nov. 28, 1810; *d.* Grimma, Mar. 3, 1874), learnt the pianoforte from Agthe, and the violin from Haase, of Dresden. He was first known as a violinist in the Dresden concerts, and went to Leipzig in 1831; he afterwards turned his attention especially to the pianoforte, and was so successful as to attract the notice of Mendelssohn, who in 1843 induced him to take the post of pianoforte-teacher in the Leipzig Conservatorium. There he attained a great and deserved reputation. His class was always thronged, and his instruction eagerly sought by pupils from all parts of the world. This popularity arose from his remarkable gift (for it was a gift) of imparting technical power. Were a pupil ever so deficient in execution, under Plaidy's care his faults would disappear, his fingers grow strong, his touch become smooth, singing and equal, and slovenliness be replaced by neatness. He devoted his life to technical teaching, and brought all his powers and experience to bear upon his celebrated work *Technische Studien*, which became a standard text-book. Great attention to every detail, unwearying patience, and a genuine enthusiasm for the mechanical part of pianoforte-playing were his most striking characteristics. He was a man of a most simple and kindly nature, and took a warm interest in his pupils. He resigned his post in 1865, and taught privately for the rest of his life.      A. S. S.

PLAIN-SONG (*Cantus Planus*) is the name now given to the style of unisonous ecclesiastical art-music which arose before the development of harmony. In its earliest days it was called by more general names, such as *musica, cantilena* or *cantus*; but when harmony arose and brought with it measured music (*musica mensurata* or *mensurabilis*), with a definite series of time-values, a distinguishing name was required, and *cantus planus* was adopted in order to emphasise the fact that the older music differed from the newer in having no definite time-values. All early unison melody, which is unmeasured, may in the broadest sense of the term be called Plain-song. The melodies to which a Hindu chants his sacred books or the Mahometan the Koran are plain-song. The Synagogue music of the pre-Christian era was probably of the same character, and the traditional music of the Synagogue of to-day is in parts so characteristic of the style that it will be worth while later on to quote some specimens of it for the purposes of comparison. (See HEBREW MUSIC.)

While there is much interest attached to the development of plain-song melody in connexion with other forms of religion than the Christian, the chief interest centres round the plain-song of the Christian Church in the West. The value of the history of the Latin plain-song, apart from its ecclesiastical and liturgical side, lies in the fact that it represents the evolution of melody from the artistic point of view. It is thus a different line of evolution from the rise of harmony on the one side and from the development of folk-song on the other. Plain-song, like sculpture, evolved very rapidly, and reached its climax at an early point in its history, while the art of harmony, like the art of painting, evolved very slowly, and went through many crude stages before reaching its present stage of perfection. The result has been that the masterpieces of melody came into existence at a period when the art of harmony was undeveloped or even non-existent; they had already become old at the time when the new art of music was making its first crude experiments in harmony, just as the art of sculpture was already long past its zenith when the art of painting made its first crude experiments towards perspective. It is only, therefore, by a confusion of thought that the masterpieces of plain-song melody can be compared (to their disadvantage) with the crude attempts of mediæval harmony. Plain-song is archaic only in the sense in which Greek sculpture is archaic; that is to say, it is an art-product which early reached its climax. In consequence its appeal is to a less wide public than the appeal of harmonised music, just as the appeal of sculpture is to a less wide public than the appeal of painting. But there is no justification for treating either the masterpieces of Greek sculpture or the masterpieces of Latin plain-song as being anything less than unsurpassed. To call either of them crude or barbarous reveals a lack of artistic perception.

The relation of plain-song to measured music may again be expressed by another parallel, for plain-song is analogous to prose, while measured music, with its definite subdivisions of time, is analogous to poetry, with its definite subdivisions of metre. The freedom of rhythm which belongs to plain-song is a freedom desirable in itself. It was a sacrifice of freedom when Harmonised Music found itself forced to become also Measured Music, because of the difficulties that beset the performance of music in harmony without strict time. The sacrifice of liberty was well worth making then, in view of what was to be won; but now a reversal is taking place, and the tendency of the present evolution of the musical art is to work back again out of the bondage of strict time towards the recovery of rhythmical freedom. In the future it may well be that even harmonised music may become for certain purposes independent of strict time, and therefore a new form of plain-song.

Meanwhile it is clear that, while measured music can be suitably adapted to a metrical text, plain-song must always be more readily suited to a prose text. The ecclesiastical plain-song, therefore, finds its justification in this, even if in nothing else, since all the early texts to which plain-song is set (apart from the hymns) are prose texts. And it finds its counterpart again in later days in recitative, either of the simpler kind, as used in classical Italian opera, or of the later declamatory kind, as used in the modern German opera.

Plain-song and Measured Music may again be contrasted with regard to tonality. The Modal system which underlies ecclesiastical plain-song has already been described in the article MODES, and the contrast between measured music in the modern scales and plain-song written in the ancient modes has been made clear there.

For the purpose of this article the plain-song of the Eastern Church must be left out of account, and attention must be exclusively directed to the Latin plain-song or the Gregorian music, which has already been described summarily under that heading. It is necessary, however, here to go more fully into the nature and condition of the two collections of music which make up the Gregorian collection. We turn first of all to the collection of music for the Mass comprised in a mediæval or modern Gradual. The chief ancient pieces are the variable items which are inserted into the fixed structure of the service on any given occasion at four special points—the Introit or *Antiphona ad introitum* at the beginning of the service; the Gradual, with *Alleluia* or Tract which precede the Gospel; the Offertory which accompanies the preparation of the oblations; and the Communion or *Antiphona ad communionem* which accompanies the partaking of the Sacrament. There are thus six sorts of composition, and the music written for them belongs almost exclusively to the 5th and 6th centuries. In the parallel collection of music for the Divine Service, embodied in the Antiphonal, we find less variety. The two forms to be considered are, (1) the Responds which belong to the lessons read during the service and form a musical interlude between them, and (2) the Antiphons which form an integral part of the Psalmody. The Hymns stand to a certain extent apart, and must be treated separately.

The same musical principles underlie both these collections. The root-forms of psalmody are described elsewhere under ANTIPHON, PSALMODY and RESPONSORIAL PSALMODY; while the simpler form of music consisting of inflected monotone, which has provided such forms as versicles and responses, the chants for the Lessons, Epistle, Gospel, etc., has been described under INFLEXION.

These simple recitatives are the earliest and most fundamental part of plain-song; they go back, for the most part, to the stage at which there is a clearly defined Dominant which figures as the reciting note, but no clearly defined Final. The most familiar example of this class is the music of the PREFACE (*q.v.*) in the Eucharist; another is the tone of the Lord's Prayer in the same service. This class of recitative stands midway between the mere inflected monotone of the responses or the lectionary tones on one side, and on the other the pieces of plain-song that may be definitely called art-products or compositions.

We come next to investigate the methods and characteristics of plain-song composition in the classical period of the 5th and 6th centuries, starting with the Gradual, rather than with the Antiphonal, as being the more orderly and exclusively classical collection of the two. This great storehouse of plain-song shows many signs of uniformity and order; over against the parallel collection of Ambrosian music it exhibits the character of a well-managed and fertile estate as contrasted with the shapeless luxuriance of primitive forest. Its liturgical orderliness is shown by such things as the sequence of psalms used for the Communions in Lent, or for the Introits, Graduals, etc., in the summer season—points which do not call for discussion here. But its musical orderliness calls for some further exposition. A significant instance of methodical arrangement that has so far escaped notice is connected with the Graduals of the Third and Fourth Modes. These, with one exception, are all confined to the period of penitence between Septuagesima and Easter. The fact is worth noting, for it not only shows arrangement of a careful sort, but it also reveals something of the æsthetic sense of the musicians of the day, inasmuch as they seem to have connected this tonality with a penitential spirit. The one exception is also interesting. The gradual *Benedicite* of Michaelmas is to a large extent modelled on the gradual *Eripe me* of Passion Sunday. Now this festival belongs to the 6th, if not to the 5th, century; the holy day, and perhaps even the Mass itself, came originally from a church dedication. It is probable that, in settling the music of the gradual, such an exception was not made until the reason of the rule and perhaps its very existence had gone out of memory; and if this be so, then this rule of assigning the third and fourth mode graduals to the penitential season carries us back to very early days, and shows systematic arrangement being made early in the 5th century.

While such matters as these point to orderliness, it must be remembered that the classical Gregorian collection is far from being homogeneous in character. It is a stratified collection; and it is not difficult to separate, at any rate roughly, the various strata. The instance just cited suggests the high antiquity of the series of graduals; and on other grounds, too, it is probable that just as the gradual, in some musical form, represents the oldest form of psalmody at the Mass, so the existing graduals in their present form are the most ancient of the extant chants of that service. The Tract—the one instance of 'Direct Psalmody' here—should probably be put next in chronological order and before all the existing Mass music of the antiphonal sort. Among the antiphons those of the Offertory are probably to be assigned to an earlier date than the Introits and Communions. Last in order of time in the true Gregorian collection come the *alleluias*, which are so novel to the collection that their

position there is a much less stable one than that of the rest.

It is important to inquire how far this body of classical plain-song is uniform in its tonality, and presupposes the later modal theory. The answer seems to be that the actual music of the collection is not further removed from the eight-mode theory that prevailed, with slight modifications, through the mediæval period, than theory and practice in music are wont to be. No doubt there are certain features not easily reconcilable, and these have to be accounted for. Those who have supposed that the eight-mode theory was a late Byzantine importation of the 7th or 8th century, have also supposed that there followed upon the new importation a far-reaching transformation process by which the old music was adapted to the new theory; after which process there remained some few irreconcilable items such as these. But there are no signs of such a wholesale transformation visible. The discrepancies, as they at present exist, are to a large extent merely due to the corruption or the ignorant revision of the musical text. Apart from this, some licenses may be detected, which apparently the composers allowed themselves, though contrary to the strict theory. For example, they seem to have used the ♭ for the low B as well as for the high *b*, although the strict theory knew of no such modification. This habit is best shown by a group of Offertories of the second mode, though the same phenomenon is visible also elsewhere. The discrepancy was not a glaring one, for by transposing the melody a fifth higher it was easy to avoid actually writing the low B♭. Such transposition, therefore, in some cases hides the fact; though in others the same Offertory may be found in one MS. transposed and in another kept at its normal pitch, and with the B♭ changed to B♮. (See for example the O. *Meditabor* of the Wednesday in Whitsun-week, which the Sarum Gradual gives untransposed, and therefore with B♮, while the Solesmes Gradual has an F, in the transposed position, equivalent to the B♭ in the normal position.) There are a good many instances of this point to be found, which show that the divergence is not a mere casual mistake. In other cases, too, besides these, the power of transposing, which existed either independently of the B♭ or through it, was utilised so as to allow the introduction of certain notes which were not, strictly speaking, countenanced by the theory, but involved the use of chromatic effects. Thus a sixth-mode melody, which in its natural position used the B♭ uniformly and not the B♮, was transposed a fifth higher, so that by use of the B♭ in the new position the leading note might be avoided, and the effect be obtained of an E♭, which is, properly speaking, alien to the mode. Similarly by transposition the effect of an F♯ could be obtained. Want of space precludes the full discussion of these points with instances, and only the bare statement of the facts can be made here. (Cf. NOTATION; SOLMISATION.)

When these exceptions have been mentioned and allowed for, there remains the general truth that the bulk of the music of the classical Gregorian collection conforms to the mediæval modal theory in its main features. In some smaller points, such as the range of the modes, or the notes on which a melody could begin, the later mediæval theorists, after the 9th century, made certain pedantic rules which were at variance with the practice of previous generations, and even of their own ; but these were of small importance. It is probably true to say that the theory that lies behind the classical plain-song is substantially that which survived as a tradition down to the time of the musical revival of Charlemagne's day, and not true to say that a new Greek theory was introduced then.

From this consideration of theory we turn to consider the art of musical composition in the stricter sense. What were the principles on which such music was written ? There is a radical difference in this respect between the responsorial and the antiphonal music. As these two were confronted with one another in the primitive era we can dimly discern a certain amount of accommodation taking place between them. The responsorial clung to its strong sense of Dominant, but acquired a new definiteness as to Final. This was easily done, because, as we shall see, the method of responsorial composition made it easy to modify, if necessary, the close of a melody. On the other hand, the antiphonal music, that had originally very little sense of dominant, adopted it to a considerable extent. The difference between the Ambrosian and the Gregorian psalm-tones shows the effect of the change. In the former a variety of notes may be employed in each mode for the reciting note, while in the latter the reciting note is regularly the Dominant of the mode. (See PSALMODY.) But even after this mutual borrowing, the two methods of psalmody remained very distinct in their procedure, though to a certain extent they were bound to move along the same lines.

The fundamental lines of all plain-song composition were determined by the circumstances. The parallelism of Hebrew poetry made it necessary that the music which was set to it should be binary in form. The *Cursus*, or law of rhythm that ruled Latin prose, made definite moulds for the musical cadences. The pente-syllabic character of the great cadences is shown in the article RESPONSORIAL PSALMODY, and the shorter cadences of four, three and two accents were similarly determined. Thus though plain-song is not formal in the sense that measured music is formal, with its bar of so many beats

and its rhythm of so many bars, yet it has a very definite form of its own ; and, however much bad execution and want of understanding may have obscured this in time past, and brought plain-song into undeserved bad odour with musicians, the recovery of the true plain-song and the study of its principles and methods are bound to bring it back to their notice not merely as an antiquarian study, but as living and effective artistic music.

Add to the two principles mentioned—the binary form and the rhythmical cadences—the principle of elaboration by vocal adornments, and you have the three root-ideas that are common to plain-song ' form.' This use of melodic enrichment, where elaboration was required, arose also out of the necessities of the case ; for there was as yet no faculty of harmonic enrichment available, and richness was necessarily to be gained only by melodic elaboration. When this is realised, the long *melismata*, which, when ill-executed, are so intolerable in practice and so unjustifiable in theory, become, when properly sung, both artistically defensible and æsthetically ravishing.

The special methods of the responsorial music are exemplified in the graduals. These are very unevenly divided among the modes ; they show less sense than the rest of the distinction between plagal and authentic. While fifty or so belong to the fifth and sixth modes (the old *Tritus*), and some forty to the first and second (the old *Protus*), the third and fourth (the old *Deuterus*) claim only a dozen, properly speaking, and the seventh and eighth (the old *Tetrardus*) only one or two more than that number. The method of composition is a development of inflected monotone. (See RESPONSORIAL PSALMODY.) Many of the cadences are common to many of the graduals of the same mode, but they are not as a rule shared with those belonging to other modes. Thus each mode has its characteristic figures— certain cadences which are used in closing (these may possibly have been modified when it was desired to make more explicit the Final), and others used in the body of the respond or verse. Some of these are combinable with one another, and thus by a skilful use of these figures the plain-song composer gets his effects of melodic richness and beauty just as the master of harmony gets his by the collocation, combination and sequence of familiar chords.

It is one of the chief merits of the new reforms instituted by the Benedictines, and now being carried through under Papal authority, that this music is being recovered from the chaos into which the official music editions current since the 16th century had plunged it : and once again the artistic method of the compositions is being revealed and vindicated. A specimen gradual of the *Tritus* tonality, with some comments, will exemplify this method of composition (it consists of three sections) :

A - ni-ma nos - tra

This opening is found in half-a-dozen other cases ; the closing *melisma* is also occasionally used in the body of the composition as well. The next section stands alone, and is not specially distinctive, but it is made up of common phrases :

Si-cut pas - - ser e - - rep - ta est

The gradual then ends with a characteristic close, which, in combination with various other figures, is the most popular of all the final cadences in this tonality :

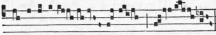

de la-que - o ve - nan - ti-um

There is even more use of common material in the four sections which make up the verse. Its opening section is common to seven gradual verses, while an eighth has the same music but not as its opening section. Its second section is also in whole or in part shared by many of this group, a third section is peculiar to *Anima mea*, and not found elsewhere, while the final section brings in once more the closing cadence with which the gradual has been seen to end.

Even from this single example, and from the specimen given under RESPONSORIAL PSALM-ODY, it is easy to see the way in which the primitive monotone survives, though elaborate cadences have been grafted on to it, and even the monotone itself has become highly ornamented. It is interesting to compare some of the Hebrew cadences which form, with their monotone, the staple bulk of the Jewish ecclesiastical chant. Like the Hebrew writing they are to be read from right to left.

The Great Telisha (written thus ♀ ) :

The Small Pazer (written thus ♩) :

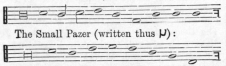

The Zarka is of a minor character (written thus ∾) :

The Shalsheleth is more elaborate still (written thus ξ) :

These forms, given by S. Münster in his *Institutiones Hebraicae* of 1524, are of no great antiquity as it seems, nor do they compare in

interest with the Gregorian *melismata* ; but they exemplify the same method of composition, which is indeed almost universal in early chant music.[1]

It will be well to give here, for purposes of comparison, a few specimens of the cadences as used in the Responds of the Office, which are built up on the same lines. A good set of examples may be drawn from a group of Responds of the eighth mode, used in Holy Week—' In Monte Oliveti ' and others akin to it.

Thus we have this used as a common cadence :

. . . ad pa - trem
volun-tas tu - a
. . . ad mor - - tem

and in many more instances. This, again, is characteristic :

. . . promp-tus est
. . con-ver - sa es

Sometimes a phrase is used with great skill in different positions, thus, on the Final and on the Dominant :

etc.

circunda-bit me, vos fu - - gam capi - e - - - - tis
me - - a
e - lec - - - ta

and the like phrase is also used so as to end on yet another degree of the mode, with a minor effect, thus :—
Thus throughout the whole range of responsorial compositions the same principles prevail.

is - - - - te

The tracts, though they differ from the graduals in their method of performance, do not differ from them in their style of composition. They need not, therefore, be separately treated here. (See TRACT.) It is different, however, with the antiphons. These are all pure melody without any suspicion of a primitive monotone lying behind them. Antiphons in their simplest form are constructed upon certain standard types of melody, and even in the elaborate shape in which they figure in the Mass music they remain true to their history. In the Gregorian antiphon the Dominant figures prominently, but as a reciting note. The Final is equally prominent, and the cadences are so ordered as to produce variety and feeling. Richness is here, too, obtained by the use of *melismata*; they differ in the different modes, and according to the sort of composition.

1 For richer Jewish Plain-song see HEBREW MUSIC, also *Organist and Choirmaster* for 1897; F. Leitner, *Der gottesdienstliche Volksgesang im jüdischen und christlichen Alterthum* (Freiburg, 1906), and *Jewish Encycl.*

The Offertories are the richest sort of chant, and stand on slightly different ground from the antiphons of the Introit and Communion. These two formed a pair, they agreed as to their method of psalmody, each of them being associated with several verses of a psalm sung to a tone, until in the course of the 10th-12th centuries the Communion lost its psalm. The offertory on the contrary was associated with one or more verses set to very elaborate chants, which were assigned to a soloist as if they had been responsorial rather than antiphonal. Similar differences prevail in the musical texture of the two classes. It is not at all uncommon to find the same figures used in introits and communions belonging to the same tonality (authentic and plagal), but it is not so common to find points of contact between them and the offertories of that tonality. When such are found they are usually in the closing phrases, as for example in the stock closing cadence of the fourth mode :—

The figures and phrases found in the antiphons are not unlike some of the simpler *melismata* of responsorial music, though rarely the same. Thus we find constantly in introits and communions of the first mode the phrase :— which is like one cited above. The figure is used also a third higher, so as to end not on D the Final, but on F :— But there is no doubt as to the marked difference between the antiphonal and the responsorial style.

The *Alleluia* differs in character from the preceding. It is essentially a *pneuma* or *jubilus*, that is, a long melody sung merely to a vowel sound. Having thus no liturgical text, it was not specially appropriated to a particular occasion. Even when St. Gregory added a psalm-verse to the *Alleluia* it retained some of its features as a free-lance ; it was the most unstable element in the Gregorian repertory, and the one opening for new compositions for the Mass chants that remained when all other lines of such productivity were closed up in the 7th century. Unhampered by words, the *Alleluia* developed a musical form of its own. There is constant repetition of phrases, so that the same musical idea gains emphasis by reiteration, and also constant repetition with slight differences, so that variety and contrast is obtained as well as reiteration. The *Alleluia* of the fourth Sunday in Advent opens thus :

Al - le - lu - - ia

The verse ' Veni domine ' follows, and in the middle of it comes this long *jubilus* :

fa-ci . . . . . . . . . . . . . . no . ra

At the end of the verse comes a closing *jubilus*, which is not in this case, as is usual, the same as that of the *Alleluia*.

Here also we get the beginnings of musical rhyme clearly established. Signs of it have appeared in the early compositions occasionally —especially in the case of one or two stock phrases already cited ; but it becomes a common procedure in the *Alleluias*. That for Christmas Eve begins its verse thus (Solesmes, not Sarum) :

Cras - ti-na di - e     de - le - bi - - tur in - i - qui-tas

ter-ræ     et reg-na-bit su-per nos    etc.

The tendency will be seen further developed when we come to Sequences.

The same features which have been described as regards the Mass music in the Gradual appear also in the Office music of the Antiphonal. There, too, is to be found the same blending of responsorial and antiphonal psalmody ; but there is not the same clear line drawn between the classical plain-song of the 5th and 6th centuries, and that which (in the case of the Office) was composed subsequently, and added to the Gregorian collection. In some respects both antiphonal and responsorial music are seen in a more primitive stage in the Antiphonal than in the Gradual. The psalm music has not been written for purposes of a choir, and therefore it has not been elaborated as it has in connexion with the Mass. There, it is only in a few cases that that simple music has survived, as for example for one or two communions where the old simple melody has not been superseded. Here it is otherwise. The Responds of the Office, unlike those at Mass, keep as a rule to their stock psalm-tone for the verse ; and, though they indulge in elaborate *melismata*, the structure is on the whole simpler than in the case of the graduals.

So far as antiphons are concerned, they exist in their primitive form in the Psalter of the Office, and are found in a simple shape throughout the whole of it. It is quite exceptional to find in the Office any elaborate form of antiphon at all comparable to the introits in complexity ; though there is some gradation, and the antiphons of the gospel canticles are more florid as a rule than those of the psalms. It is among these antiphons of the Office that it is possible to trace out the way in which a large number are constructed upon the same musical theme. (See ANTIPHON.)

We turn now from the Gregorian collection of classical plain-song to the music which lies outside it. The hymn melodies are not subsequent in date, but they are different in character, and must be treated separately. The rest of the music is subsequent in date, and is to be distinguished on that ground from the classical plain-song. It is not easy to discover what were the primitive melodies to which the hymns were sung at their first introduction to church worship. But it is clear that a hymn melody has always been regarded rather as a piece of folk-music than as an artistic composition; and in this respect it differs from the ordinary plain-song. It differs also inasmuch as it is the setting of metrical words, and therefore takes its character from the metre. It is necessarily, therefore, more closely allied to measured music than any other branch of plain-song; in fact, a simple syllabic melody set to a hymn of pronounced metre is bound to become almost measured in its rhythm. This is less the case with the more elaborate hymn melodies; but even with them there remains the necessity to fit the music to the regular recurrent accents of the words (see HYMN), and this produces a uniformity of rhythm which is not found in plain-song set to prose texts. Hymn melodies, though popular in origin, show, however, clear signs of artistic structure. For example, in the following melody there is considerable skill shown in developing the third line from the second, and making its close rhyme with its central climax.

The music of the ' Ordinary of the Mass ' (see GREGORIAN MUSIC) lies for the most part outside the true Gregorian collection; this music, being essentially congregational in character, was originally simple and unvarying. There is one primitive form of *Kyrie*, one primitive setting of the Creed, *Sanctus* and *Agnus*, and probably also one primitive *Gloria in Excelsis*. These settings are of the simplest sort, and should be classed with the recitatives dealt with above rather than with the Gregorian compositions. It was not till long after the classical period that fresh settings of the Ordinary came into common use. They were for the most part local in character. Some were originally composed for the particular purpose, as, for example, the *Kyrie rex splendens* composed by St. Dunstan while waiting to celebrate. Others were nothing but adapta-

tions; take, for example, the following *Sanctus*, which is an adaptation of the antiphon *O Christi pietas* of the Office of St. Nicholas, in itself a late Office :

Sanc - - tus: Sanctus: Sanc - - tus, Do - - mi-nus     etc.

de-us sa - - - - - ba - oth

O    Christi pi - - - - e - tas om - ni    etc.

pro - se - quen - - - - da lau - de

From the 9th or 10th century onwards these fresh melodies for the Ordinary were being composed or adapted. They have not by any means the merit of the classical compositions. Some began to approximate to the modern tonality, as for example an English *Gloria in Excelsis* which opens thus :

Glo-ri - a in ex-cel - sis De - o    Et in ter - ra pax

ho - min - i - bus bo - nae vo - lun - ta - tis.    etc.

This has a very modern ring, and still more so in the somewhat degraded form in which it has been given in the new Vatican Gradual; and as time went on this tendency exhibited itself more and more fully until it issued in such compositions as the *Missa de Angelis*.

A development of a fresh sort brought about the introduction of tropes, proses and sequences. The influence of the Byzantine singers who came to the West in the early days of the Frankish Empire has probably been over-estimated. No doubt they were responsible for the introduction to the Western Church of certain Greek compositions such as the Lauds antiphons of the octave of the Epiphany. There was no great novelty in a borrowing such as this, for as far back as Latin plain-song can be traced there was going on a continual infiltration of Greek compositions, sometimes appearing singly, sometimes taken over in block, as for example in connexion with Candlemas and other festivals of the Blessed Virgin. It is, however, probably to these Byzantine singers that we must assign the impulse which produced tropes and sequences. The same instinct which had already produced the *Alleluia-jubilus* induced people to go a step further, and interpolate similar musical phrases into the midst of already existing compositions, or to append them at the end. Thus, the *Alleluia* became the starting-point for a new set of *Jubili* ; and even in the body of old-fashioned responds there were inserted long *melismata*, which in process of time were made into proses (see SEQUENTIA). When this had come about, it was not surprising that the same tendency should decorate the music of the Ordinary—the *Kyrie*, etc.—with tropes.

This fresh development marks a further advance in the development of musical form. In these *melismata* we find not only the extension of those same principles of repetition and rhyme which we have already noted in the case of the *Alleluia*, but we find also the first symptoms of key relationship. The fundamental structure of the sequence melody was based upon the principle of repetition, for normally each phrase of the melody was repeated. In many of them the cadences are so framed as to suggest a tonic and dominant relationship. This is remarkable. Hitherto any suggestion of key relationship had been that of tonic and subdominant, and had arisen out of the use of the tetrachord synemmenon and the B♭. But this appearance of tonic and dominant relationship is new. The longer sequence melodies give it in very clear form, and the beginnings of it, at any rate, are observable even in such a short melody as the following, in the sections marked by the change of clef :

The Alleluia melody *Eduxit Dominus*, set later to the Prose *Prome casta concio.*

The tropes and other developments of the sort, because of their liturgical impropriety, disappeared as quickly as they had arisen, surviving mainly in the sequences, which became practically independent compositions, and in the farsed Kyries ; but the fresh principles of form which they had introduced still continued. The new ideas of key relationship naturally formed a league with the folk-song tonality which was invading music ; and since the Church was already provided with a collection of liturgical music, which satisfied for the most part its traditional needs, on the lines of plain-

song composition, further musical experiment, both melodic and harmonic, was restricted to new ecclesiastical forms such as the motet, or was even diverted to a large extent into the secular sphere.

After the 11th century plain-song composition went on, but only to a limited extent. At times it made pathetic attempts to keep the old flavour, just as in later days the Italian composers tried to keep up the polyphonic style even when their thoughts ran more naturally in the operatic style ; but the later writers of plain-song could not fail to be profoundly influenced by the new tendencies out of which modern music was to develop. The true art of plain-song was lost, the best days of plain-song composition were over, and it would have been well for plain-song if the compositions in a degraded style which were put forth in its name, and obtained an unhealthy popularity, had never come into existence. Plain-song, like everything else, must be judged by its classical epoch ; and the decadent compositions of the 15th, 16th and 17th centuries are only worth study as a warning of what plain-song is not.

In conclusion, something must be said about the preservation of the plain-song tradition. The music in the early days was all preserved orally. It is not clear at what time the melodies were written down. Long before that they were probably taught by the teacher to his class from memory, and with the assistance of gestures which indicated the rise and fall of the melodies, and probably also the extent of the intervals. Even when the system of neum notation arose, out of combination of the acute and grave accents (see NOTATION), the practical singing was still a matter of oral tradition, and the noted books were probably few. The change which introduced a staff notation instead of the neumatic notation made it possible to define the intervals accurately, and, in this respect at any rate, to be more secure in the preservation of the tradition. The grouping and phrasing was less well safeguarded by the Guidonian notation ; but the fact that the earliest manuscripts which contain the staff notation agree in the main as regards the tradition, though they are spread over a wide area, shows that on the whole the tradition has been faithfully preserved, and that the mediæval books substantially represent the primitive plain-song.

It is probably true to say that the tradition suffered more at the period subsequent to the invention of printing than it ever suffered in the period of oral tradition. So long as manuscripts continued there was uniformity and faithfulness ; but ill-advised and ignorant reforms were attempted in the 16th century which led up to the Medicean editions at the beginning of the 17th century. These editions were fastened upon the Church, and became official, though they presented a most undesirable and corrupt text of the melodies. Interest in plain-song, however, and knowledge about it were so slight that no rebellion took place against the evil tyranny of the Medicean editions till the 19th century. Simultaneously the tide set against the deformation of the chant by 'Machicotage,' *i.e.* the introduction into the melody of the grace notes and *fioriture* beloved of the 18th century. From 1848 there dates a new interest and a gradual improvement in the tradition. The new Mechlin books of 1848 were no improvement, but they were followed by a better edition issued jointly by the Archbishops of Reims and Cambrai. Good pioneer work was also done by the Jesuit Lambillotte in France, and by Hermesdorff in Germany; but these attempts only provoked suspicion. Official sanction was again given, and in a much more definite and exclusive form, to the corrupt Medicean version of the melodies, and from 1871 onwards the Ratisbon service-books perpetuated the evil. Following on the work of Lambillotte and Hermesdorff came the fuller revival of real plain-song in the hands of the Benedictines of the Congregation of France, led by Guéranger, Pothier and Mocquereau. Their work has been to return to the manuscripts, to show up the unworthiness of the modern printed editions in comparison with the uniform manuscript tradition, and to call for the official adoption of a better set of service-books. The publications issued at Solesmes have led up to this result. The Gradual and other service-books published by the monks showed their superiority and their greater conformity to the true tradition, while the scientific handling of the questions at issue went on in the succeeding volumes of *Paléographie musicale*. Through this patient work and ardent enthusiasm the Vatican itself has been conquered. Plain-song reform has received official sanction, and a new set of books issued from the Vatican press reproduces more faithfully the true Gregorian tradition of plain-song.

In England the plain-song tradition began early, coming straight from Rome with the advent of St. Augustine; and the English plain-song tradition has always been a particularly trustworthy one. When the Latin services were superseded in the 16th century it was only possible to preserve very little of the ancient plain-song. It was retained in the English Litany issued by Cranmer in 1544; and six years later, in 1550, one year after the issue of the First Prayer Book, John Merbecke published his famous *Booke of Common Praier Noted*, in which plain-song melodies, printed in the square-headed Gregorian character, were adapted to the Anglican offices of 'Mattins,' 'Euen Song,' 'The Communion,' 'The

Communion when there is a Burial,' etc., under the serious restriction which was imposed upon him (in rebellion against former elaborateness), namely, that he should only set one note to one syllable. Through these publications and others the Gregorian tones survived in some form even down to the 18th century, but the bulk of the plain-song had passed away out of the English service. (See MERBECKE; CHANT.)

The revived interest in plain-song within the English Church was begun by Dyce, who brought out his *Book of Common Prayer Noted* in 1843. Since then there have been many adaptations of the simpler plain-song of the responses and tones to the English service. The *Hymnal Noted* brought back the hymn melodies in 1851, and these have become increasingly popular. The more genuine and elaborate plain-song compositions have not had the same opportunity, and have not obtained any wide currency, though in some churches plain-song masses are sung at the Holy Communion service, and even Introits also, with the English words adapted to the old melodies. In some of the modern Anglican Communities plain-song has been much studied and is very fully, if not exclusively, used in the community services. The later part of this revival of the plain-song tradition in the English Church has to a large extent focussed round the PLAIN-SONG AND MEDIÆVAL MUSIC SOCIETY, and, apart from rival Plain-song Psalters, its publications represent the greater part of what has been done.

For the study of Plain-song the Benedictine *Paléographie* is indispensable; the most recent and full manual is that of Dr. Wagner, *Einführung in die Greg. Melodien* (Part I., General and Liturgical; Part II., on Notation; Part III., on Theory). An English translation of Part I. is published by the Plain-Song and Mediæval Music Society. A *Grammar of Plain-Song* has been issued by the Benedictines of Stanbrook. Older books are Pothier, *Les Mélodies Grégoriennes*, *The Elements of Plain-Song* (Plain-Song Soc.); Kienle, *Chant Grégorien*. Important scientific points are treated in Gevaert's *Mélopée antique*, and Jacobsthal's *Chromatische Alteration*.

W. H. F.

PLAIN-SONG AND MEDIÆVAL MUSIC SOCIETY, THE. In Nov. 1888 a meeting was held by Somers Clarke, W. J. Birkbeck, H. B. Briggs, Brown, Nottingham, Athelstan Riley and B. Luard Selby, at which was formed the above Society with the following objects:

(1) To be a centre of information in England for students of Plain-song and Mediæval Music, and a means of communication between them and those of other countries.
(2) To publish facsimiles of important MSS., translations of foreign works on the subject, adaptations of the plain-song to the English use, and such other works as may be desirable.
(3) To form a catalogue of all plain-song and

measured music in England, dating not later than the middle of the 16th century.

(4) To form a thoroughly proficient choir of limited numbers, with which to give illustrations of Plain-song and Mediæval Music.

The subscription is £1 per annum, entitling members to all publications gratis. Clergymen and organists are eligible for election as associates, at a subscription of 2s. 6d. per annum, entitling them to the annual publications at a reduced price. H. B. Briggs was honorary secretary from the foundation of the Society till his death in 1901, when he was succeeded by Percy E. Sankey (retired 1925), who also became treasurer. In 1926 Dom Anselm Hughes, O.S.B., became Secretary.

The publications of the Society fall into two branches, one of which, though possibly the more useful of the two, does not need detailed specification in this place. It consists of educational works on the execution of plain-song, and adaptations to the English use. The other branch consists of facsimiles of MSS., and its value from an archæological point of view is very great, even if some of the translations printed in the older issues are here and there open to question. The volumes already published are as follows:

The Musical Notation of the Middle Ages (out of print).
Songs and Madrigals of the 15th century (14 examples).
Gradual Sarisburiense, a facsimile of an English 13th-century Gradual, with an introduction, etc.
The Sarum Gradual, an introduction to the above.
Antiphonale Sarisburiense, a facsimile of an English 13th-century Antiphoner.
Early English Harmony, from the 10th to the 15th century. Vols. i. and ii.
Madrigals of the 15th century (six in modern notation). (Out of print.)
Bibliotheca Musico-Liturgica, a descriptive hand-list of the Musical and Latin Liturgical MSS. of the Middle Ages preserved in English libraries.
Pars antiphonarii, a reproduction of a MS. of the 11th century.
Piæ Cantiones, a collection of church and school songs, A.D. 1582.
Wagner's Introduction to the Gregorian melodies.
The Ordinary of the Mass.
Elements of Plain-song.
Plain-song Hymn melodies and Sequences.
Fauxbourdons to Magnificat.

M.; addns. from P. E. Sankey.

PLAINTE, the name of an ornament of the French school, also called ACCENT or CHUTE. (See ORNAMENTS.)    E. B<sup>L</sup>.

PLANCHÉ, JAMES ROBINSON (b. London, Feb. 27, 1796; d. there, May 30, 1880), of French descent; made Rouge Croix Pursuivant of Arms, 1854, and Somerset Herald, 1866. Planché's many dramas and extravaganzas do not call for notice in these pages; but he requires mention as the author of the librettos of 'Maid Marian, or the Huntress of Harlingford, an Historical Opera,' for Bishop (Covent Garden, Dec. 3, 1822), and 'Oberon, or The Elf-King's Oath, a Romantic and Fairy Opera,' for Weber (Covent Garden, Apr. 12, 1826). He was manager of the musical arrangements at Vauxhall Gardens in 1826-27, and in 1838 he wrote for Chappell a libretto founded on the Siege of Calais by Edward III., with a view to its being set by Mendelssohn. Mendelssohn, however, was not satisfied with the book, and it was ultimately transferred to Henry Smart, by whom a large portion was composed. The correspondence between Mendelssohn and Planché may be read in the Recollections and Reflections of the latter (1872 i. 279-316).    G.

PLANÇON, POL HENRI (b. Fumay, Ardennes, June 12, 1854; d. Paris, Aug. 11, 1914), received instruction in singing at Paris from Duprez, and later from Sbriglia. In 1877 he made his début on the stage at Lyons as St. Bris, and during a two years' engagement there sang, Dec. 1, 1877, as Joseph in Gounod's 'Cinq Mars'; Feb. 8, 1879, as Eustache on the production of Saint-Saëns's 'Étienne Marcel.' On Feb. 11, 1880, he made his début in Paris at the Théâtre de la Gaîté as Colonna in Duprat's 'Pétrarque.' He next sang with great success at the Lamoureux Concerts, and on June 25, 1883, first appeared at the Opéra as Mephistopheles, a part in which he became very popular, and which was sung by him over a hundred times during his ten years' engagement there. His parts included, Apr. 2, 1884, Pittacus on the revival of Gounod's 'Sapho' and in new operas; Nov. 30, 1885, Don Gormas in Massenet's 'Cid'; Mar. 21, 1890, Francis I. in Saint-Saëns's 'Ascanio,' etc. On June 3, 1891, he made his début at Covent Garden as Mephistopheles, with great success. From that time until 1904 inclusive, he sang every season at Covent Garden, and in 1892 for a few nights at Drury Lane, and obtained great popularity in a large number of parts sung in four different languages, notably as both the King and the Priest in 'Aïda'; Capulet and the Friar in 'Roméo'; Oroveso, the bass parts of Meyerbeer and Wagner (Landgrave, Henry the Fowler, Pogner), etc. His later parts included, June 20, 1894, General Garrido in Massenet's 'Navarraise'; July 11, 1898, Ariofarne in Mancinelli's 'Ero e Leandro'; May 30, 1901, in English as the Friar in Stanford's 'Much Ado about Nothing'; July 14, 1902, the King in Bunning's 'Princesse Osra'; July 6, 1904, Phanuel in Massenet's 'Salome,' etc. From 1893 Plançon sang much in America, where he enjoyed the same popularity as in Europe.    A. C.

PLANQUETTE, ROBERT (b. Paris, July 31, 1848; d. there, Jan. 28, 1903), passed rapidly through the Conservatoire, and first appeared as a composer of songs and chansonnettes for the Cafés-concerts. Encouraged by the popularity accorded to these songs, he rose to operettas—'Valet de cour,' 'Le Serment de Mme. Grégoire' and 'Paille d'avoine.' The decided progress evinced by this last piece was confirmed by 'Les Cloches de Corneville,' a three-act operetta, produced with immense success at the Folies Dramatiques on Apr. 19, 1877, adapted to the English stage by Farnie and Reece, and brought out at the Folly Theatre, London, Feb. 23, 1878, with equally extraordinary good fortune. Planquette afterwards composed and published 'Le Chevalier Gaston,' one act (Monte Carlo, Feb. 8, 1879), and 'Les Voltigeurs de la 32me,' three acts (Théâtre de la Renaissance, Jan. 7, 1880). His next piece was 'La Cantinière,' which was followed in 1882 by 'Rip van Winkle' (also given in London with great success), 'Nell Gwynne' in 1884, 'La Crémaillerie' in 1885, and 'Surcouf' in 1887. In the latter year he wrote, especially for England, 'The Old Guard' (Liverpool and London), and in 1889 his 'Paul Jones' was brought out at the Prince of Wales's Theatre in London; his last works were 'La Cocarde tricolore' (1892), 'Le Talisman' (1892), 'Panurge' (1895) and 'Mam'zelle Quat' Sous' (1897).    G., with addns.

PLANTADE, CHARLES HENRI (b. Pontoise, Oct. 14, 1764 ; d. Paris, Dec. 18, 1839), was admitted at the age of 8 to the school of the king's 'Pages de la musique,' where he learned singing and the violoncello. On leaving this he studied composition with Honoré Langlé (b. Monaco, 1741 ; d. Villiers le Bel, 1807), a popular singing-master ; the pianoforte with Hullmandel (b. Strassburg, 1751 ; d. London, 1823) ; and the harp, then a fashionable instrument, from Petrini (b. 1744 ; d. Paris, 1819). Having started as a teacher of singing and the harp, he published a number of romances, and nocturnes for two voices, the success of which procured him admission to the stage. Between 1791 and 1815 Plantade produced a dozen or so dramatic works, three of which, 'Palma, ou le voyage en Grèce,' two acts (1798), 'Zoé, ou la pauvre petite' (1800) and 'Le Mari de circonstance' (1813), one act each, were engraved. The whole of this fluent but insipid music has disappeared. His numerous, sacred compositions are also forgotten ; out of about a dozen masses, the 'Messe de Requiem' alone was published, but the Conservatoire has the MS. of a Te Deum (1807), several motets and five masses. He had a great reputation as a teacher, was a polished man of the world, and a witty and brilliant talker. Queen Hortense, who had learned singing from him, procured his appointment as maître de chapelle to her husband, and also as professor at the Conservatoire (1799). He gave up his class in 1807, but resumed it in 1815 ; was dismissed on Apr. 1, 1816, reinstated Jan. 1, 1818, and finally retired in 1828. He was officially employed in the Opéra in 1812. He was decorated with the Légion d'honneur by Louis XVIII. in 1814. His best pupil was Mme. Cinti-Damoreau. He left two sons, one of whom, CHARLES FRANÇOIS (b. Paris, Apr. 14, 1787 ; d. Mar. 25, 1870), composed numerous chansons and chansonnettes, some of which have been popular.    G. C.

PLANTÉ, FRANÇOIS (b. Orthez, Basses Pyrénées, Mar. 2, 1839), a distinguished pianist, appeared in Paris at a very early age as an infant prodigy, playing the piano with much success. In Dec. 1849 he entered Marmontel's class at the Conservatoire, and in the following year carried off the first prize. He was then before the public again as a performer, for some three years, during which time he played frequently at the chamber concerts given by Alard and Franchomme ; in 1853 he returned to the Conservatoire to study harmony under Bazin. Here he obtained a second prize in 1855. It must be regarded as a fortunate circumstance that at a party at which he was playing the audience persisted in talking to an extent that highly offended Planté ; whereupon he retired in great wrath to the Pyrenees, where he remained for nearly ten years, becoming familiar with the compositions of all schools, and counteracting the evils which necessarily accompany such a career as his had hitherto been. He did not reappear in Paris until 1872, when he devoted himself to playing on behalf of various charitable objects. A series of concerts given with Alard and Franchomme established his position, and thenceforth he held a distinguished place among French pianists. He undertook many successful concert tours on the Continent, and appeared in England in 1878, playing Mendelssohn's second PF. concerto at the Philharmonic Concert of May 1 in that year. His playing, characterised by repose, maturity of style and rare intelligence, was enjoyed in Paris as lately as the war period (1914–18).    M.

BIBL.—POUGIN'S supplement to *Fétis* ; O. COMETTANT, *Francis Planté, portrait musical à la plume* (Paris, 1874); H. SCHIDEN-HELM, *Francis Planté intime (Monde musical)* (1914–19); A. DANDELOT, *Francis Planté. Une belle vie d'artiste.* (Paris, 1921.)

PLATEL, NICOLAS JOSEPH (b. Versailles, c. 1777 ; d. Brussels, Aug. 25, 1835), son of a royal chamber musician, was educated as a page of Louis XVI., and studied music under Richer and Duport (violoncello). In 1796 he was appointed violoncellist at the Théâtre Feydeau, eloped with a singer to Lyons, but returned to Paris in 1801. In 1803 he gave a concert at Brussels, whence he went to England. After touring for some years he went to Antwerp in 1813, became principal violoncello at the Brussels theatre in 1819, and professor at the Conservatoire in 1831. He acquired a great reputation as teacher, and counted Servais, Batta and the elder Demunck (who became his successor) among his pupils. He wrote 5 concertos, sonatas, solos, etc., for violoncello and some duets for violin and violoncello (E. v. d. Straeten : *History of the Violoncello*).

PLAYERA, see SONG, subsection SPAIN (4).

PLAYER PIANO, see MECHANICAL APPLIANCES (5).

PLAYFORD. A family connected with the publication of English music from 1650 to the first decade of the 18th century.

(1) JOHN, the elder (b. 1623 ; d. circa 1686),

was a younger son of John Playford of Norwich.[1] In 1648 his name appears as book-seller in London, and in Nov. 1650 he published his first musical work, 'The English Dancing-Master,' dated 1651. From this time onward his publications included Hilton's 'Catch that Catch can,' 'Select Musicall Ayres and Dialogues' and 'Musick's Recreation on the Lyra Violl.' He was from 1653 clerk to the Temple Church, and held his shop in a dwelling-house connected with the Temple ('in the Inner Temple near the Church door'). As his wife, Hannah, kept a boarding-school for young ladies at Islington, he in due course removed there, still keeping on his place of business in the Temple. His house at Islington was a large one 'near the church,' and after his wife's death in 1679 he advertised it for sale,[2] removing to Arundel Street 'near the Thames side, the lower end and over against the George' (some references give this as 'over against the Blew Ball'). The character of the man appears to have been such as made him liked and respected by all who came into contact with him, and he seems to have well earned his general epithet 'Honest' John Playford. According to the edition of Pepys's Diary edited by Wheatley, Samuel Pepys had very friendly relations with Playford, the latter frequently giving him copies of his publications.

In music-publishing Playford had no rival, and the list of his publications would practically be a list (with the exception perhaps of less than twenty works) of all the music issued in England during the time covered by his business career. Playford was enough of a musician to compose many psalm tunes and one glee which became popular, 'Comely Swain, why sitt'st thou so'; and to write a handbook on the theory of music which, concise, plain and excellent, might well serve for a model to-day. This *Introduction to the Skill of Musick* attained nineteen or twenty editions, and was the standard text-book on the subject for nearly a century; the first edition is dated 1654, and the last 1730. In 1655 Playford published an enlarged edition of it which long passed as the first.[3] It is divided into two books, the first containing the principles of music, with directions for singing and playing the viol; the second the art of composing music in parts, by Dr. Campion, with additions by Christopher Simpson. The book acquired great popularity; in 1730 it reached its nineteenth edition, independent of at least six intermediate unnumbered editions. There are variations both of the text and musical examples, frequently extensive and important, in every edition. In the tenth edition, 1683, Campion's tract was replaced by *A Brief*

1 See researches of Miss L. M. Middleton in *Notes and Queries*; also *D.N.B.*
2 See Smith's *Protestant Magazine*, Apr. 11, 1681.
3 See the *Sammelbände* of the Int. Mus. Ges. vi. 521.

*Introduction to the Art of Descant, or composing Music in parts*, without author's name, which in subsequent editions appeared with considerable additions by Henry Purcell. The seventh edition contained, in addition to the other matter, 'The Order of performing the Cathedral Service,' which was continued, with a few exceptions, in the later editions.

Another of Playford's important works was the 'Dancing-Master,' a collection of airs for the violin used for country dances, the tunes being the popular ballad and other airs of the period. This work ran through a great number of editions from 1650–1728, and is the source of much of our national English melody (see SHARP, Cecil). 'Courtly Masquing Ayres of two parts' (a title-page of the treble part is preserved in the Bagford collection in the British Museum, Harl. MS. 5966) appeared in 1662.

Other valuable works in a series of editions were published by Playford, books of catches, of psalms and songs. Instruction books and 'lessons' for the cithern, viol and flageolet also followed in a number of editions. After Playford's death many of these were continued by his son Henry, and by Wm. Pearson and John Young, who ultimately acquired the rights of publication.

In the early times of his business, Playford was in trade relations, if not in partnership, with others—John Benson, 1652; Zach Walkins, in 1664–65; and later than this with John Carr, who kept a music shop also in the Temple, a few steps from John Playford's.

Many mistaken statements have been made regarding Playford's business. For instance, it is mentioned[4] that he invented the 'new ty'd note' in 1658. This is quite an error. The tied note was not introduced before 1690, some years after Playford's death. Neither is it true that in 1672 he began engraving on copper.

John Playford, senior, was neither a printer nor an engraver, and long before 1672 he had issued musical works printed from engraved copperplates. In 1667 Playford republished Hilton's 'Catch that Catch can,' with extensive additions and the second title of 'The Musical Companion,' and a second part containing 'Dialogues, Glees, Ayres and Ballads, etc.'; and in 1672 issued another edition, with further additions, under the second title only. Some compositions by Playford himself are included in this work. In 1671 he edited 'Psalms and Hymns in solemn musick of four parts on the Common Tunes to the Psalms in Metre: used in Parish Churches'; and in 1677, 'The Whole Book of Psalms, with the . . . Tunes . . . in three parts,' which passed through twenty editions. In 1673 he took part in the Salmon and Locke controversy, by addressing a letter to the former, 'by way of Confutation

4 *D.N.B.*

of his Essay, etc.,' which was printed with Locke's *Present Practice of Musick Vindicated.* The style of writing in this letter contrasts very favourably with the writings of Salmon and Locke. In place of abuse we have quiet argument and clear demonstration of the superiority of the accepted notation (see Locke). Towards the year 1684, Playford, feeling the effects of age and illness, handed over his business to his son Henry; and there is a farewell to the public in the fifth book of 'Choice Ayres and Songs,' 1684. All attempts to settle satisfactorily the date of John Playford's death have hitherto failed. The likeliest date is about Nov. 1686,[1] and this is borne out by his unsigned will, which, dated Nov. 5, 1686, was not proved until 1694, the handwriting being sworn to, on the issue of probate. It may be supposed that the will was written on his death-bed, and that from feebleness or other cause it remained without signature. That he was dead in 1687 is proved by several elegies; one by Nahum Tate, set to music by Henry Purcell, was issued in folio in this year. Cummings suggests[2] that this relates to John Playford the younger, but he has overlooked the fact that an elegy 'on the death of Mr. John Playford, author of these, and several other works' appears in the 1687 and later editions of Playford's *Introduction to the Skill of Musick,* a work incontestably by the elder John Playford.

There are several portraits of the elder Playford extant, taken at different periods of his life, and these are prefixed to various editions of the *Introduction.*

(2) HENRY, son of the above (*b.* May 5, 1657[3]; *d.* after 1706), succeeded to his father's business in 1684. Before this, however, he had published one or two books, notably *An Antidote against Melancholy,* 1682 and 1684. Henry Playford was at first in partnership with Richard Carr, the son of John Carr. The Carrs, father and son, kept a music shop at the Middle Temple Gate, facing St. Dunstan's Church, and the early publications of Henry Playford were sold both at the Inner Temple and here, Henry Playford becoming in due course owner of the shop at the Middle Temple Gate, or at Temple Change as it was otherwise called. Henry Playford republished editions of the works originally issued by his father and a small quantity of his own fresh ventures. In 1698 he advertised a lottery of music-books. He published several important musical works, among which were Purcell's 'Ten Sonatas' and 'Te Deum and Jubilate for St. Cecilia's day,' 1697; 'Orpheus Britannicus,' 1698–1702; Blow's 'Ode on the Death of Purcell,' 1696, and 'Amphion Anglicus,' 1700. It is quite evident that he had not the same business ability as his father, but in 1699 he established a Concert of Music held thrice weekly at a

coffee-room, and in 1701 another series of weekly concerts at Oxford.[4] Later he developed into a dabbler in picture and print dealing, and his music business began in consequence to decline. Walsh had arisen, and Henry Playford must have found in him a very powerful rival in the music trade. The statement[4] that in 1694 he sold his copyright in the 'Dancing-Master' to Heptinstall does not appear to be justified, as long after this date his name as publisher occurs on all copies. About 1706 or 1707 it appears that he had retired from the music business altogether. His stock seems to have been purchased by John CULLEN (*q.v.*), whose address 'at the Buck between the two Temple Gates' appears to be Henry Playford's (formerly John Carr's) shop. His death is variously given as occurring in 1706 and 1710. If his will was proved in 1721, as one authority states, it is likely that his decease must have been much later than either of these dates.

(3) JOHN, the younger (*b.* Stanmore Magna, 1655; *d.* 1685). Miss Middleton has definitely dispelled the error that he was a son of John Playford, the elder; he was his nephew, and son of Matthew Playford, rector of Stanmore Magna. He must have served his apprenticeship to printing in London, and this he no doubt did with William Godbid, a printer of great repute for scientific works and for music, being the one employed in his period by the elder Playford. The printing-office was in Little Britain, and Godbid having died in 1679, young Playford in this year entered into partnership with the widow Anne Godbid. At her death or retirement Playford alone held the business, and printed all the musical works issued by his cousin Henry until 1685.

In this year John Playford, junior, died, and his sister[5] Eleanor advertises the business as for sale.[6]

In regard to the Playford publications it may be mentioned that after the death or retirement of Henry Playford such books as were still saleable, like the 'Dancing-Master,' *The Introduction to the Skill of Musick,* Simpson's 'Compendium of Musick,' Playford's 'Whole Book of Psalms,' etc., were reprinted in fresh editions by William PEARSON (*q.v.*), and were sold by John Young. Cullen certainly acquired Henry Playford's stock (probably he was an assistant with Playford), but never issued any editions. All the Playford publications, with very few exceptions, were from movable music type. The exceptions were some instrumental works, as 'Musick's Handmaid,' etc., and some reprints from earlier copperplates, as Orlando Gibbons's 'Fantazies,' Child's 'Psalms,' etc.; these the

---

1 *D.N.B.*          2 *Life of Purcell,* p. 46.          3 *D.N.B.*

4 *D.N.B.*
5 See her petition to the Privy Council asking to be appointed King's Printer, in which she states that the business in Little Britain was left to her by her brother John. The petition was refused Mar. 18, 1686/7.
6 See *London Gazette* for May 6, 1686.          W. B. S.

elder Playford had got possession of on starting business. Henry Playford also issued a few engraved half-sheet songs. (For list of the Playford publications see the writer's *British Music Publishers.*)          F. K.

PLEASANTS, THOMAS (*b.* 1648 ; *d.* Nov. 20, 1689), became in 1670 organist and master of the choristers of Norwich Cathedral. He was buried on Nov. 23 in the north transept of Norwich Cathedral. (West's *Cath. Org.*)

PLECTRUM, a small piece of horn, wood, ivory, tortoiseshell or other substance used for playing certain stringed instruments, and taking the place of the finger-nails, or fingers in instruments of the lute tribe. From paintings and other evidence it is quite plain that the Greeks generally played the lyre with a plectrum, though this was varied by the use of the fingers. In modern days the instruments of the mandoline family alone are played with the plectrum. Although the wire-strung guitar of the middle of the 18th century appears to have demanded (for the fingers' sake) a plectrum, yet the old instruction books direct it to be played by the unarmed fingers. The touch of the finger on the string produces, of course, a quality of tone which no substitute can effect. The jacks of the spinet and harpsichord are plectra, and though generally these are armed with quill, yet in the later form of harpsichord one set of jacks is supplied with leather tips which produces a more mellow effect.    F. K.

PLEIN JEU, see REGISTRATION.

PLENO, see PIENO.

PLEYEL, (1) IGNAZ JOSEPH (*b.* June 1, 1757 ; *d.* Paris, Nov. 14, 1831), a most prolific instrumental composer, the twenty-fourth child of the village schoolmaster at Ruppersthal in Lower Austria.

His musical talent showed itself early. He learnt to play the clavier and violin in Vienna, the former from Van Hal, or Wanhall, and found a patron in the then Count Erdödy, who put him under Haydn as a pupil in composition in 1774, and appointed him his Kapellmeister in 1777, allowing him, however, leave of absence to continue his studies. After remaining several years with Haydn he went to Italy, where he fully imbibed the taste of the Italian opera, and lived in intercourse with the best singers and composers. In 1783 he was called to Strassburg at first as deputy, and in 1789 as first Kapellmeister to the cathedral. In 1791 he was invited to London to take the control of the Professional Concerts of the following season. He was probably not aware of the fact that his appointment was a blow aimed at Salomon, and that he would be in competition with Haydn. The blow, however, missed its aim. Pleyel conducted his first Professional Concert, Feb. 13, 1792. Haydn was present, and the programme contained three symphonies, by Haydn, Mozart and

Pleyel himself (composed expressly for the concert). On May 14 he took his benefit The visit was a satisfactory one both from an artistic and a pecuniary point of view. On his return to France he found himself denounced as an enemy to the Republic, and was forced to flee. He succeeded in clearing himself from the charge, and at length settled in Paris as a music-seller. In 1800 the musicians of the opera proposed to perform Haydn's ' Creation,' and Pleyel was selected to arrange that Haydn should himself conduct the performance. He got as far as Dresden on the road to Vienna, but all the influence of Haydn and Artaria failed to obtain a pass for him any further, and the direction of the performance came finally into the hands of Steibelt. The evening of the concert—3 Nivôse or Dec. 24, 1800—was a memorable one, since on his road to the operahouse, in the Rue Nicaise, Bonaparte nearly met his death from an infernal machine. Pleyel visited Vienna and obtained great success there in 1805. He was the first to publish the complete collection of Haydn's quartets (except the last three, of which two had not then been printed, and the third was not composed till some time afterwards). The edition, in separate parts only, has a portrait of Haydn by Darcis after Guerin, and is dedicated to the First Consul. It was followed by thirty quartets and five symphonies in score. In 1807 Pleyel founded the pianoforte factory which has since become so widely celebrated. (See PLEYEL & Co.)

Haydn considered Pleyel as his dearest and most efficient pupil. He writes from London :

' Since his arrival [Dec. 23, 1791], Pleyel has been so modest to me that my old affection has revived ; we are often together, and it does him honour to find that he knows the worth of his old father. We shall each take our share of success, and go home satisfied.'

Pleyel dedicated to Haydn his op. 2, six quartets ' in segno di perpetua gratitudine.' When Pleyel's first six string quartets, dedicated to his patron, Count Ladislaus Erdödy, appeared in Vienna, Mozart wrote to his father (Apr. 24, 1784) :

' Some quartets have come out by a certain Pleyel, a scholar of Jos. Haydn's. If you don't already know them, try to get them, it is worth your while. They are very well written, and very agreeable ; you will soon get to know the author. It will be a happy thing for music, if, when the time arrives, Pleyel should replace Haydn for us.'

This wish was not destined to be fulfilled. In his later works Pleyel gave himself up to a vast quantity of mechanical writing, vexing Haydn by copying his style and manner without a trace of his spirit, and misleading the public into neglecting the works of both master and scholar, including many of Pleyel's own earlier compositions, which were written with taste and care, and deserve a better fate than oblivion.

Pleyel was emphatically an instrumental composer, and wrote an enormous number of symphonies, concertos and chamber pieces (list in *Fétis*), comprising twenty-nine symphonies; five books of quintets and seven of quartets, some of them containing as many as twelve compositions each; six flute quartets; four books of trios; eight concertos; five symphonies concertanti; eight books of duets for strings; ten books of sonatas for PF. solo, and twelve sonatas for PF. and violin. When in Italy he wrote an opera, 'Iphigenia in Aulide,' which was performed at Naples in 1785. A hymn or cantata in praise of revolutionary doctrines, called 'La Révolution du 10 août (1792) ou le Tocsin allégorique,' is mentioned by Lobstein, and a 'Hymn to Night' was published by André at Offenbach in 1797. A series of twelve Lieder, op. 47, was published at Hamburg by Günther and Böhme. It has never yet been mentioned that his introduction to the world as a vocal composer was with an opera for the marionette theatre at Esterház in 1776, 'Die Fee Urgele,' containing a quantity of vocal pieces. A portrait of him, painted by H. Hardy and engraved by W. Nutter, was published by Bland during Pleyel's residence in London.            C. F. P.

Pleyel's connexion with Scottish music arose in this way. In 1791 George THOMSON (*q.v.*) of Edinburgh sought Pleyel in London, and applied for assistance in the arrangements of a collection of Scots songs which he was about to issue. He also commissioned him to compose twelve sonatas for the pianoforte, founded upon Scottish airs. Pleyel, after much delay and difficulty, completed six of the sonatas and wrote symphonies and pianoforte arrangements to thirty-two Scots songs, for all of which Thomson, in 1793, paid him £131 : 5s. The sonatas were issued in two sets of three each, and the first twenty-five songs formed the first number of Thomson's collection, the remaining seven being published later. Thomson's relations with Pleyel were by no means satisfactory. He complained that the composer had 'juggled with him' and 'grossly deceived him,' added to which was the delay and uncertainty of communicating with him during the continental war. Thomson, therefore, at a later date obtained the services of Kozeluch and finally Haydn, ultimately rejecting much of Pleyel's work on a republication for new arrangements by Haydn.            F. K.

(2) CAMILLE, eldest son of the foregoing (*b.* Strassburg, Dec. 18, 1788; *d.* Montmorency, near Paris, May 4, 1855), took over the music business in 1824, associating himself with Kalkbrenner for the pianoforte department. He had had a good musical education from his father and Dussek; he lived for some time in London, and published several pieces which evince considerable talent. He died leaving

Auguste WOLFF, his son-in-law, at the head of the firm.

His wife, Marie Felicité Denise Mocke or Mooke, known as (3) MADAME PLEYEL (*b.* Paris, July[1] 4, 1811; *d.* Saint Josseten Noode, near Brussels, Mar. 30, 1875), at an early age developed an extraordinary gift for playing. Herz, Moscheles and Kalkbrenner were successively her masters, and she learnt much from hearing Thalberg; but her own unwearied industry was the secret of her success. Her *tournées* in Russia, Germany, Austria, Belgium, France and England were so many triumphal progresses, in which her fame continually increased. Mendelssohn in Leipzig, and Liszt at Vienna, were equally fascinated by her performances; Liszt led her to the piano, turned over for her, and played with her a duet by Herz. Not less marked was the admiration of Auber and Fétis, the latter pronouncing her the most perfect player he had ever heard. Berlioz[2] was violently in love with her in 1830. In this country she made her first appearance at the Philharmonic, June 27, 1846, in Weber's Concertstück. To Brussels she always felt an attraction, and in 1848 took the post of teacher of the PF. in the Conservatoire there, which she retained till 1872. Her pupils were numerous, and worthy of her remarkable ability.    C. F. P.; rev. M. L. P.

PLEYEL & CO. This distinguished Parisian firm of pianoforte-makers is now styled 'Pleyel, Wolff et Cie.' Its founder was Ignaz Pleyel, the composer, who established it in 1807. The Pleyel firm is remarkable for having always been directed by musicians, such as Camille Pleyel, who became his father's partner in 1821, and Kalkbrenner, who joined them three years later. At starting, the pianoforte-maker, Henry PAPE, lent valuable aid. The influence of Chopin, who made his début in Paris at Pleyel's rooms, in 1831, has remained a tradition in the facile touch and peculiar singing tone of their instruments. Camille Pleyel was succeeded in the control of the business by Auguste WOLFF (*q.v.*), who much improved the Pleyel grand pianos in the direction of power, having made them adequate to the modern requirements of the concert-room, without loss of those refined qualities to which we have referred. The firm has had since 1876 agencies in London.        A. J. H.

Since Wolff's death (1887), the direction has passed to his son-in-law, Gustave Frantz Lyon (*b.* Paris, Nov. 19, 1857), formerly a pupil of the École Polytechnique. Amongst his inventions is the 'harpe éolienne,' adaptable to concert pianos; the 'pédale harmonique,' allowing a struck chord to vibrate at will; various devices for controlling the tone of the piano, etc. He has also made other instru-

[1] September according to Fétis.
[2] See his *Lettres intimes*, xxvii.-xxxiii., and Jullien's *Hector Berlioz*.

ments : ' harpe chromatique,' kettle-drums, etc.                                M. L. P.

BIBL.—H. QUITTARD, in *Grande Encyclopédie*; H. RADIGUER, *France, XIX siècles*, in *Encycl. de la Musique et Dict. du Conservatoire*; CONSTANT PIERRE, *Les Facteurs d'instruments de musique, les luthiers et la facture instrumentale* (Paris, 1893).

PLICA (literally a Fold, or Plait), a character mentioned by Franco of Cologne, Joannes de Muris and other early writers. Franco describes four kinds : (1) the ' Plica longa ascendens,' formed by the addition, to a square note, of two ascending tails, of which that on the right hand is longer than that on the left ; (2) the ' Plica longa descendens,' the tails of which are drawn downwards, that on the right being, as before, longer than that on the left ; (3) the ' Plica brevis ascendens,' in which the longer of the ascending tails is placed on the left side ; and (4) the ' Plica brevis descendens,' in which the same arrangement obtains with the two descending tails :

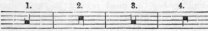

These notes had the ordinary values of longs and breves, but they were sung with some sort of falsetto grace at the end, the art of which has long been lost. The grace occupied one-third of the length of the note when perfect, or one-half when imperfect. Franco tells us that besides longs and breves, semibreves could be plicated when in ligature, but not when standing alone : he defines ' plica ' as ' the division of the same sound into grave and acute ' (Coussemaker's *Scriptores*, i. 123). Pseudo-Aristotle says that the interval taken at the end may be either a semitone, tone, minor or major third, or perfect fourth or fifth : he adds that plication is effected ' per compositionem epiglotti cum repercussione gutturis subtiliter inclusa,' whatever that may mean (Coussemaker, i. 273, ii. 406). Marchettus of Padua tells us that ' to plicate a note is to extend the sound upwards or downwards in a feigned voice, different from that naturally produced,' the interval taken depending on the position of the next note (Gerbert, *Scriptores*, iii. 181).          J. F. R. S.

PLUNKETT, CATHERINE (*b.* Dublin, 1725), almost invariably known as ' Miss Plunkett,' one of the first female violinists of whom there is any record. She was sent as an ' apprentice ' to Dubourg, then Master of the State Music in Ireland, in 1740, made her début as a ' prodigy ' violinist at Crow Street Music Hall on Feb. 27, 1740, and on Dec. 6, 1742, gave a benefit concert in Fishamble Street Music Hall. Having studied sedulously under Dubourg for another year, she determined to try her fortune before a London audience. Accordingly, on Jan. 27, 1743/4, Miss Plunkett, announced as ' a scholar of Mr. Dubourg's lately arrived from Dublin,' gave a concert at the Haymarket Theatre. Apparently this must have been successful, as the young lady again appeared at the same theatre on Feb. 27 following. After the year 1744 no trace of Miss Plunkett is found.                                W. H. G. F.

PNEUMA, from the Greek πνεῦμα, ' a breathing ' ; also written Neuma and Neupma. A melody sung to a vowel sound at the close of a word or sentence. Such decorations, known also as ' Jubili,' have been utilised in church music from very early times. St. Augustine and St. Jerome both speak of the way in which music of this sort, unhampered by words, can be used as an expression of devotional feeling which could not be put into words. While the Pneuma was used to decorate many musical phrases, its chief elaboration was in connexion with the ' Alleluia ' at Mass. Here it is an invariable feature, and the final *a* of the word ' Alleluia ' was always used as a vowel with which to associate an elaborate piece of vocal melody. The following ' Alleluia ' of Easter Sunday will serve as an example :

Al-le-lu - - - - ia

A verse follows, ' Pascha nostrum immolatus est Christus ' ; on the second word there is a long cadence, and others follow on the last two syllables of ' immolatus ' ; the melody of the ' Alleluia ' is then repeated on the word ' Christus.'

A further illustration of the same tendency to ornament melodies with vocal additions led to the evolution of the TROPES and SEQUENCES (*q.v.*).

The ordinary pneums of the psalm-tones are those given at the end of the eight characteristic melodies. (See MODES.)       W. H. F.

PNEUMATIC ACTION, see ORGAN, Vol. III. p. 759.

POCHETTE (Fr. ; Ital. *sordino*), small boat-shaped and diminutive normal-shaped violins, which came into vogue in France about the time of Louis XIII. (See VIOLINO PICCOLO.)

It is difficult to decide accurately the original form of these little instruments, as both types come under the equivocal title of ' Pochette ' ; but judging from Kircher's illustration of a boat-shaped pochette in his ' Musurgia universalis ' (1650), which he calls a *Linterculus* (the name is derived from *linter*, a small boat, wherry or trough), it would appear that the *linter* or boat-shaped form was the earlier. The Padre Bonanni (*Descrizione degli instrumenti armonici*, 1770) also refers to the Latin name, saying : ' This young man is learning to play a little instrument ' (an illustration of a boat-shaped instrument is given) ' which the Latins named *Linterculus*,' and mentions that in Italy it is called *Sordino* and is used for dancing.

Mersenne (*De instrumentis harmonicis*, 1637) gives three different sizes, all boat-shaped, and says they were called *pera* or *poche*, and were carried in the pockets of the professors of dancing ; and de Furetière's *Dictionary* (1690) defines the word ' Poche ' : ' petit violon que les maîtres à danser mettent dans leur poche quand ils vont monter en ville.' In a word, the small tone of the boat-shaped *Linterculus* earned for itself the name of *Sordino* in Italy, and—owing to its convenient dimensions—' Pochette ' in France, and ' Taschengeige ' in Germany ; and the miniature violin known as KIT (*q.v.*) in England was a later development, which crept in and assumed the title of its predecessors.

The boat-shaped ' Pochette ' or ' Sordino ' (see *PLATE LXXXVII.* No. 5) measures from fifteen to twenty inches in length ; there is generally a heart-shaped sound-hole, as well as two *f* holes, and the neck forms part of the instrument —a detail which points to the pochette as a survival of the 'Rebec' of Arabian origin. They are often beautifully embellished, either with inlaying of ivory, tortoise-shell, carving or other ornamentation, and their accompanying cases are usually lined with satin or velvet, and bear conventional designs, mostly of fleurs-de-lys, on the exterior. The bows, which measure from fifteen to seventeen inches in length, are made sometimes entirely of ivory, or partially inlaid to match the accompanying ' Pochette.' The diversity and fancy which was lavished by their makers upon these little instruments has made it almost impossible to determine (as may be done in judging violins) the maker or school to which they belong. The varnish on the boat-shaped pochettes gives place to excessive ornamentation, whereas some of the violin-shaped pochettes have beautiful varnish. At the South Kensington Loan Exhibition in 1874, a sordino by *Matthias Albanus* (1680) was exhibited, and at the Samary Sale two exquisite little pochettes—one by *Matthias Hofmans tot Antwerpen* and the other by *Antonius Medard, Nancy*, were sold. A beautiful pochette of the violin type, made by Stradivarius in 1717, was brought to France by Tarisio on one of his first visits. He sold it to Sylvestre, and it eventually became the property of Clapisson, who was so enchanted with it that he included it in the orchestral score of his opera ' Les Trois Nicolas.' Another exquisite little pochette (violin-shaped), also the property of Clapisson, contained a fan, which opened at will between the belly and the back. Jubinal possessed a pochette which fitted into a walking-stick. At the Donaldson Museum there is a violin-shaped pochette, with very fine varnish, which is thought to be the work of Nicola Amati ; and another, which is exquisitely inlaid with squares of ebony and ivory, has six gut strings and six sympathetic wire strings (17th century,

French). The players of the pochette were mostly dancing-masters. They held the instrument against their left breast and marked the rhythms of the dance, at the same time performing the steps for the instruction of their pupils. Hawkins (*History of Music*) mentions a dancing-master of London named Francis Pemberton who ' was so excellent a master of the " Kit," that he was able to play solos on it, exhibiting in his performance all the graces and elegances of the violin ' ; and the Abbé de Marolles (*Mémoires*, 1745 edition) quotes Constantin and Bocan as ' Fameux joueurs de poche.' The utility of the pochettes has ceased since the accession of the piano, and their occupation being gone, the collector alone cherishes them as handsome curiosities. The South Kensington Museum and the Donaldson Museum in London contain some beautiful specimens, as also do the Musée du Louvre, the Musée Cluny, the Musée du Conservatoire, and that of the Opéra at Paris.

BIBL.—KIRCHER, *Musurgia universalis.* MERSENNE, *De instrumentis harmonicis.* BONANNI, *Descrizioni degli instrumenti armonici.* LA BORDE, *Essai sur la musique.* HAWKINS, *Hist. Music.* ENGEL, *The Violin Family, Musical Instruments in South Kensington Loan Exhib.*, 1874. DE BRICQUEVILLE, *Les Anciens Instruments de musique.* RUHLMANN, *Atlas zur Geschichte der Bogeninstrumente,* Map iv. SANDYS and FORSTER, *History of the Violin.* DANIEL FRYKLUND, *Studien über die Pochette,* pp. 32 (Sundsvall, 1917) ; *En pochette d'amour au Thomas Erlinger,* pp. 10 (Sundsvall, 1918).
E. H.-A.

**POCHON**, ALFRED (*b.* Lausanne, 1878), second violinist in the FLONZALEY QUARTET (*q.v.*), studied at Liège with César Thomson, of whose quartet he became a member, and was also first violin in the Ysaÿe orchestra at Brussels. He started co-operation with the late M. de Coppet in the Flonzaley Quartet in 1902.
W. W. C.

**POCKRICH**, RICHARD (*b.* Derrylusk, Co. Monaghan, Ireland, *c.* 1690 ; *d.* London, 1759), the son of an Irish gentleman of good fortune, settled in Dublin in 1715, having opened a brewery and distillery at Island Bridge. He was an excellent musical amateur, and when his distillery failed he applied in 1742, but unsuccessfully, for the post of master of the choristers of Armagh Cathedral. In 1741 he invented, or rather re-invented, the HARMONICA, and gave concerts exhibiting its powers in Dublin, during the years 1743 and 1744. These concerts were so successful that Pockrich made a tour of England, where the Harmonica was much appreciated. From 1750–56 he had many successful concert tours, but finally met with a tragic death, being burned in a fire at Hamlin's Coffee House, Sweetings Alley, near the Royal Exchange, London. W. H. G. F.

**POCO**, a little ; rather ; as poco adagio, not quite so slow as adagio itself ; poco sostenuto, somewhat sustained. It is the opposite of Assai. POCHETTINO is a diminutive of poco, and implies the same thing but in a smaller degree, as does also the superlative POCHISSIMO. G.

**POELCHAU**, GEORG (*b.* Cremon, Livonia, July 5, 1773 ; *d.* Berlin, Aug. 12, 1836), a distinguished amateur, left Russia during the reign of the Emperor Paul, and settled in Hamburg, where he formed an intimacy with Klopstock. On the death of Emanuel Bach he bought the whole of his music, which contained many autographs of his father. On another occasion he bought the residue of the library of the Hamburg opera, with a set of Reinhard Keiser's works. In 1813 he settled in Berlin, in 1814 became a member of the Singakademie, and assumed the charge of its library in 1833. At the request of the Crown Prince he searched the royal libraries for the compositions of Frederick the Great, and found 120 pieces. His collection of music was bought at his death by the Royal (now State) Library and the Singakademie. In 1855 the Singakademie sold their collection of the autographs of the Bach family to the Royal (now State) Library, which now has a larger number of these treasures than any other institution. There is a bust of Poelchau in one of the rooms.      F. G.

**POGLIETTI**, ALESSANDRO (*d.* 1683), was organist to the Imperial court chapel at Vienna in 1661–83. Of his origin and earlier career nothing has as yet come to light. Walther, in his *Lexicon*, describes him as having been German by birth, but this is highly improbable. He would appear to have been held in high esteem at the Imperial court, since below his portrait and on the title-pages of some of his MS. works there is appended to his name the honorary distinction of Comes Palatinus. He was killed during the siege of Vienna by the Turks in 1683. On the return of the court to Vienna in 1684 his widow was allowed a pension of 18 gulden monthly, until her remarriage.

The works of Poglietti, which are mostly for clavier and organ, circulated chiefly in MS. copies, and none ever appeared in print during his lifetime. His most widely known work, of which a large number of MS. copies exist, is a collection of twelve ricercari for the organ on the church tones, which are comparatively simple and severe in style. Ritter has printed one of them in his *Geschichte des Orgelspiels*, Ex. 25. His most important work for the clavier is a very extended suite entitled ' Rossignolo,' the original autograph MS. of which, magnificently bound, bears a dedication to the Empress Eleonora Magdalena Theresia, the third wife of the Emperor Leopold I. This suite, along with two others, has been printed in *D.T.Ö.*, Jahrg. XIII. ii. ; and the editor (Dr. Hugo Botstiber) takes occasion to correct some mistakes of Max Seiffert in his *Geschichte der Claviermusik* with regard to it. The suite consists of a toccata, canzona, allemande with two doubles, courante, sarabande, gigue with one double each, and following these comes an ' Aria allemagna con alcune variazioni sopra

l' età della Maestà Vostra,' concluding with a ricercar, capriccio and ' Aria bizzara del rossignolo.' To the aria there are thus altogether twenty-three variations ; and Seiffert, understanding its title to refer to the age of the Emperor himself, inferred that the work was written in 1663, when the Emperor was 23 years old. But the chronograms on the title-page of the work prove it to have been written in the year 1677, and since it is dedicated to the Empress, the reference is to her age and not that of the Emperor. The variations are remarkable in other ways. Most of them have special superscriptions, with imitations of various national instruments, meant probably to imply the homage of various nationalities to the Emperor and Empress. So, for instance, the eighth variation is superscribed ' Böhmisch-Dudelsack,' the ninth ' Holländisch-Flageolet,' the fourteenth ' Französische Baiselemens ' (Baiser les mains), the eighteenth ' Ungarische Geigen,' etc. The last two movements consist of an imitation of the song of the nightingale, which gives a title to the whole work. Seiffert thinks the opening of Poglietti's ' Capriccio per lo rossignolo ' must have remained in Handel's memory when he wrote the first movement of his Concerto Grosso, No. 11. The other two suites, now first published, are also extraordinary specimens of early programme music. One is entitled ' Sopra la ribellione di Ungheria,' and the reference is to the rebellion of 1671, when the endeavour was made to separate Hungary from the rule of the House of Hapsburg. This suite opens with a toccatina superscribed ' Galop ' ; the allemande has the title ' La Prisonnie ' ; the courante, ' Le Procès ' ; the sarabande, ' La Sentence ' ; the gigue, ' La Lige,' followed by ' La Décapitation ' and ' Les Cloches,' ' Requiem Aeternam.' The third suite consists of a canzon and ' Capriccio über das Henner und Hannergeschrey,' which may have been in Bach's mind when he wrote his fugue with the ' Thema all' imitatio Gallina cucca.' The only work of Poglietti which was previously published was a Suite for clavier in F, which appeared in the publication of Roger of Amsterdam, entitled 'Toccates et suites pour le clavecin de Messieurs Pasquini, Poglietti et Gaspard Kerle,' 1704. This collection was republished by Walsh in London under the title ' A second collection of toccates voluntarys and fugues made on purpose for the Organ and Harpsichord composed by Pasquini, Poglietti and others, etc.' Another work for clavier, which bears Poglietti's name in several MSS. abroad, is now proved to be the work of Dr. John Bull. It is a fugue upon the hexachord, which appears in the ' Fitzwilliam Virginal Book.' Poglietti may simply have copied it from some source for his own use. Other works of Poglietti remaining in MS. are a few for various combinations of instruments, and some sacred works for voices with instrumental accompaniment. Botstiber also claims for Poglietti the authorship of a theoretical work which Sandberger had previously ascribed to Johann Kaspar Kerl. It is entitled 'Regulae compositionis,' and while two MS. copies ascribe it to Kerl, two others and one very important copy made by the Hamburg organist, Johann Adam Reinken, expressly attest it as Poglietti's.

BIBL.—A. KOCZIRZ, *Zur Lebensgeschichte Alexander de Poglietlis*, S. z. MW. Heft 4, 1916.　　　　　　　J. R. M.

POHL, CARL FERDINAND (*b.* Darmstadt, Sept. 6, 1819 ; *d.* Vienna, Apr. 28, 1887), writer on musical subjects. He came of a musical family, his grandfather having been the first maker of glass harmonicas, his father (*d.* 1869) chamber musician to the Duke of Hesse at Darmstadt, and his mother a daughter of the composer Beczwarzowsky. In 1841 he settled in Vienna, and after studying under Sechter became in 1849 organist of the new Protestant church in the Gumpendorf suburb. At this date he published Variations on an old ' Nachtwachterlied ' (Diabelli), and other pieces. He resigned the post in 1855 on account of his health, and devoted himself exclusively to teaching and literature. In 1862 he published in Vienna an interesting pamphlet, *On the History of the Glass Harmonica.* From 1863–1866 he lived in London, occupied in researches at the British Museum on Haydn and Mozart, the results of which he embodied in his *Mozart und Haydn in London*, two vols. (Vienna, Gerold, 1867), a work full of accurate detail, and indispensable to the student. Through the influence of Jahn and von Köchel, and of his intimate friend the Ritter von Karajan, Pohl was appointed in Jan. 1866 to the important post of archivist and librarian to the Gesellschaft der Musikfreunde in Vienna. His care and conscientiousness brought the immense collections of this great institution into a highly satisfactory condition. In connexion therewith he published two works, which, though of moderate extent, are full of interest, and are marked by that accuracy and sound judgment which distinguish all his works, namely, *Die Gesellschaft der Musikfreunde und ihr Conservatorium in Wien* (Braumüller, 1871), and *Denkschrift aus Anlass des 100jährigen Bestehens der Tonkünstler Societät in Wien* (Gerold, 1871). He was for many years occupied on a biography of Haydn, which he undertook at the instigation of Jahn, and of which vol. i. was published in 1875 (Berlin, Sacco ; since transferred to Breitkopf & Härtel) and vol. ii. in 1882. Pohl left materials at his death in the hands of MANDYCZEWSKY (*q.v.*). The main facts are contained in his article on Haydn in this Dictionary, to the first edition of which he was an extensive contributor. The summaries of the musical events of each year which Pohl furnished to the *Signale für die musikalische Welt*, of which he was the Vienna correspondent, were most careful and correct, and it would be a boon to the student of contemporary music if they could be republished separately. Pohl's courtesy to students desiring to collate MSS., and his readiness to supply information, were well known to the musical visitors to Vienna.

　　　　　　　　　　　　　　　　F. G.

POHL, DR. RICHARD (*b.* Leipzig, Sept. 12, 1826 ; *d.* Baden-Baden, Dec. 17, 1896), a German musical critic, well known for his thoroughgoing advocacy of Wagner. He devoted himself to mathematics, and after concluding his course at Göttingen and Leipzig was elected to a professorial chair at Gratz. This he vacated for political reasons, and then settled at Dresden (1852), and Weimar (1854) as a musical critic. In 1864 he moved to Baden-Baden, where he died. He was one of the editors of the *Neue Zeitschrift für Musik*, in which he strongly championed the cause of Wagner's and other advanced music, and a frequent contributor to the musical periodicals. He began his Autobiography in the *Mus. Wochenblatt* for Dec. 30, 1880. His other works include : *Akustische Briefe* (1853), *Bayreuther Erinnerungen* (1877), *Richard Wagner* (1883), *Franz Liszt* (1883) and *Hector Berlioz* (1884), *Die Hohenzüge der musikalischen Entwickelung* (1888). He also wrote poetry, translated the works of Berlioz into German, made a connecting text for Schumann's 'Manfred' and Liszt's 'Prometheus,' and composed some music of a slight but agreeable kind. G.

POHLENZ, CHRISTIAN AUGUST (*b.* Saalgast, Lower Lusatia, July 3, 1790 ; *d.* Leipzig, Mar. 10, 1843). In 1829 we find him well established in Leipzig as a singing-master, a conductor of concerts, organist of the Thomaskirche, director of the Singakademie and the Musikverein, etc. At the end of 1834 he resigned the post of conductor of the Gewandhaus subscription concerts, which he had held since 1827, and in which he was succeeded by Mendelssohn in the following October. After the death of Weinlig, Mar. 6, 1842, and before the appointment of Hauptmann later in the same year, Pohlenz filled the office of cantor at the St. Thomas's School. Mendelssohn chose him as teacher of singing in the new Leipzig Conservatorium, in the prospectus of which his name appears, in the *A.M.Z.* of Jan. 18, 1843. He died of apoplexy at Leipzig just three weeks before the operations were begun. He published Polonaises for the PF., but his best works are partsongs for equal voices, of which one or two good specimens are given in 'Orpheus.' G.

POILLOT, ÉMILE (*b.* Dijon, Mar. 10, 1886), piano virtuoso and organist, a pupil at the Paris Conservatoire under Philipp, Guilmant and Gigout. He won the first prize for piano in 1907, and for the organ in 1911. He has been organist of Dijon Cathedral since 1911 and professor at the Conservatoire there since 1919. He has composed some pianoforte pieces and motets which are sound and skilful in style.

F. B<sup>L.</sup>

POINT (Lat. *punctus*, vel *punctum*; Fr. *point*; Ger. *Punkt*; Ital. *punto*): (1) See NOTATION.

(2) A term applied to the passages of imitation in vocal music of the madrigalian era to the opening notes of the subject of a fugue or other important theme.

POINT D'ORGUE (Fr.), (1) an organ point or PEDAL (*q.v.*).

(2) The cadenza in a concerto—the flourish interpolated between the chords of the 6–4 and 7–3 of the cadence—the place for which is indicated by a pause ⌢. Rousseau gives a clue to the origin of the term by explaining (under ' Couronne ') that when the above sign, which he denominates 'Couronne,' was placed over the last note of a single part in the score it was then called Point d'orgue, and signified that the sound of the note was to be held on till the other parts had come to the end. Thus the note so held on became a pedal, and is so in theory.

G.

POISE, JEAN ALEXANDRE FERDINAND (*b.* Nîmes, June 3, 1828; *d.* Paris, May 13, 1892), opera composer. He entered the Paris Conservatoire in 1850, and in 1852 gained the second prize for composition, under Adolphe Adam, from whom he derived his taste for easy, flowing melody. ' Bonsoir Voisin,' a pleasing little opera produced at the Théâtre Lyrique, Sept. 18, 1853, was followed at the same theatre by ' Les Charmeurs ' (Mar. 15, 1855), also a success. He next produced ' Polichinelle ' (1856) at the Bouffes Parisiens; and at the Opéra-Comique, ' Le Roi Don Pèdre,' two acts (1857) ; ' Le Jardinier galant,' two acts (Mar. 4, 1861); ' Les Absents,' a charming piece in one act (Oct. 26, 1864); ' Corricolo,' three acts (Nov. 28, 1868) ; ' Les Trois Souhaits' (1873) ; ' La Surprise de l'Amour,' two acts (Oct. 31, 1878); and ' L'Amour médecin ' (Dec. 20, 1880). The last two, arranged by Poise and Monselet from Marivaux and Molière, give a high idea of his powers. He also composed another pretty little opera, ' Les Deux Billets ' (1858), revived at the Athénée in Feb. 1870. Among his later works are ' Joli Gilles ' (1884), ' Le Médecin malgré lui' (1887), ' Carmosine ' and an oratorio, ' Cécilie ' (Dijon, 1888). In their ease and absence of pretension his works resemble those of Adolphe Adam, but there the comparison ends ; the latter had a real vein of comedy, while Poise's merriment has the air of being assumed to conceal his inward melancholy. Nevertheless, his music is flowing and happy ; and being well scored and never

vulgar, it is listened to with pleasure, and is remembered.                                    G. C.

POLACCA (Italian for POLONAISE). Polaccas may be defined as Polonaises treated in an Italian manner, but still retaining much of the rhythm characteristic of their Polish origin. Polaccas are both vocal and instrumental, and are generally of a brilliant and ornate description, gaining in brilliancy what they lose in national character. Thus Chopin, in a letter from Warsaw, dated Nov. 14, 1829 (Karasowski, vol. i.), speaks of an ' Alla Polacca ' with violoncello accompaniment that he had written, as ' nothing more than a brilliant drawing-room piece—suitable for the ladies,' and although this composition is probably the same as the ' Introduction et Polonaise brillante pour piano et violoncelle ' (op. 3) in C major, yet from the above passage it seems as if Chopin did not put it in the same class as his poetical compositions for the pianoforte which bear the same name.                        w. b. s.

POLACCO, GIORGIO (*b.* Venice, Apr. 12, 1875), operatic conductor. The busy career of this excellent *chef-d'orchestre* began when he was in his early ' twenties,' and has embraced no fewer than three continents and some ten capitals. Educated partly in St. Petersburg, partly in Milan, his first experiences with the bâton were gained in Milan, Genoa and Rome ; later, at Brussels, Lisbon, Warsaw and St. Petersburg, where his Wagner productions earned especial eulogy. For seven seasons he was engaged at Rio de Janeiro, and for four at Buenos Ayres ; then at Mexico in 1906, the year in which he made his début in the U.S.A. at San Francisco. In 1911 he directed the first English production of Puccini's ' Girl of the Golden West,' with H. W. Savage's company, and in the following year was engaged for the Metropolitan Opera House, New York, where (replacing Toscanini when his health gave way) he began with ' Manon Lescaut ' on Nov. 11, and remained as principal Italian conductor until 1917. Subsequently he held a similar post at Chicago. Meanwhile, he had been winning popularity at Covent Garden, where he made his début— Destinn singing Tosca—on May 21, 1913. On July 15, 1914, he directed the 300th performance of ' Don Giovanni ' at Covent Garden.

BIBL.—*International Who's Who in Music*; NORTHCOTT: *Covent Garden and the Royal Opera.*                        H. K.

POLAROLI (POLLAROLO), (1) CARLO FRANCESCO (*b.* Brescia, *c.* 1653; *d.* end of 1722), was a pupil of Legrenzi and became a chorister at St. Mark's, Venice, in 1665. In 1690 he became second organist, and in 1692 vice-maestro di cappella in the same church. The statement that he rose to be first maestro lacks authority, but, according to Busi's Life of Marcello, he was maestro at the music school of the Incurabili at Venice about 1706. Three oratorios. ' Jefte,' ' Le Rosinda ' and

'Jesabel,' are in MS. at Vienna and Brussels, and many pieces of church music are mentioned in *Q.-L.* Of his numerous operas (Fétis gives the names of sixty-eight) the following are extant:

'Roderico' (Milan, 1684, performed also at Verona, Naples, Brescia and Rome); 'La forza della virtù' (Venice, 1693); 'Ottone' (Venice, 1693–94); 'Faramondo' (1699); 'Semiramide' (Venice, 1714, nine songs only preserved); 'Marsia deluso' (1714); 'Ariodante' (Venice, 1716); and three without dates, 'Le pazzie degli amanti,' 'Gl' inganni felici' and 'Genuinda' (one act, the other two being provided by G. del Violone and Alessandro Scarlatti).

An organ sonata is in vol. iii. of Torchi's 'L' arte musicale in Italia.' (*Q.-L.*, etc.) M.

(2) ANTONIO, son of Carlo Francesco (*b.* Venice, *c.* 1680; *d.* there, May 4, 1746), was the pupil of his father. In 1723 he became vice-maestro di cappella at St. Mark's, and in 1740 maestro. As early as 1702 he had assisted his father in the duties of the office. His opera 'Aristeo' was performed at Venice in 1700, 'Leucippo e Teonoe' in 1719, 'Cosroë' in 1723 and 'I tre voti,' a serenata, at Vienna in 1724. (See *Q.-L.*) M.

POLE, WILLIAM, MUS.D., F.R.S. (*b.* Birmingham, Apr. 22, 1814; *d.* London, Dec. 30, 1900), an instance of the successful union of science, literature and music. He was bred to the profession of civil engineering, in which he became eminent. He wrote many works and papers on scientific subjects, and was a contributor to the leading reviews, and F.R.S. of London and Edinburgh. He was Professor of Civil Engineering at University College, London, 1859–76. His researches into the question of musical pitch, on which he wrote in this Dictionary (see PITCH), were a valuable contribution to a much-debated subject.

His taste for music developed itself early; he studied hard at both theoretical and practical music, and was organist in St. Mark's Church, North Audley Street, London, in 1836–66. He graduated at Oxford as Mus.B. in 1860, and as Mus.D. in 1867. He was appointed Reporter to the Jury on Musical Instruments at the International Exhibition of 1862, and was one of the examiners for Musical Degrees in the University of London (1878–90), author of a Treatise on the Musical Instruments in the Exhibition of 1851, *The Story of Mozart's Requiem* (1879), *The Philosophy of Music* (1879, reprinted 1895) and various minor critical essays. His only printed musical compositions are a setting of Psalm c. given at Tenbury in 1861, an eight-part motet from which was performed at the Chester Festival of 1882, and some four-handed PF. accompaniments to classical songs. (See *Brit. Mus. Biog.*; *Mus. T.* for Feb. 1901, p. 103, etc.) G., with addns.

POLIPHANT (POLYPHON), a wire-string instrument invented or evolved from the many forms current about the year 1600, by Daniel Farrant, son of the organist of St. George's Chapel, Windsor, and afterwards one of the court musicians to James I. and Charles I. Playford (*Introduction to the Skill of Musick*) says it was an excellent instrument not much unlike a lute, and according to an illustration given by Randle Holme (Academy of Armory, 17th century) it had from 25 to 40 strings and resembled more nearly the later HARP-LUTE (*q.v.*). Queen Elizabeth was particularly partial to the Poliphant and was a proficient performer upon it. Farrant also produced another wire-string instrument of the cittern or pandore class called the 'Stump,' of which, however, no description exists. F. W. G.

POLIUTO, see POLYEUCTE.

POLKA, a well-known round dance, said to be of Bohemian origin. According to Alfred Waldau (*Böhmische Nationaltänze*, Prague, 1859 and 1860) the polka was invented in the year 1830 by a servant girl who lived at Elbeteinitz, the music being written down by a local musician named Neruda. The original name by which the polka was known in its birthplace and in the neighbourhood of Jičin, Kopidlno and Dimokury was the 'Nimra.' This was derived from the song to which it was danced, the first lines of which ran as follows:

> 'Strejček Nimra
> Koupil šimla
> Za půl pāta tolaru.'[1]

In 1835 it was danced in Prague, where it first obtained the name of 'Polka,' which is probably a corruption of the Czech 'pulka' (half), a characteristic feature of the dance being its short half-steps.

According to another account the polka was invented in 1834 by a native of Moksic, near Hitschin in Bohemia, and was from that place introduced into Prague by students. In 1839 it was brought to Vienna by the band of a Bohemian regiment under its conductor, Pergler; in 1840 it was danced at the Odéon in Paris by the Bohemian Raab; and in 1844 it found its way to London. Wherever the polka was introduced, it suddenly attained an extraordinary popularity. Vienna, Paris and London were successively attacked by this curious 'polkamania'; clothes, hats and streets were named after the dance, and in England the absurdity was carried so far that public-houses displayed on their signs the 'Polka Arms.' In the *Illustrated London News* for Mar. 23, 1844, will be found a polka by Offenbach, 'a celebrated French *artiste*,' headed by two rather primitive woodcuts, to which the following description of the dance is appended:

'The Polka is an original Bohemian peasant dance, and was first introduced into the fashionable saloons of Berlin and St. Petersburg about eight years since.[2] Last season it was the favourite at Baden-Baden.

[1] Translation: 'Uncle Nimra bought a white horse for five and a half thalers.'
[2] If this is true, the dates of Waldau's account of the origin of the dance can hardly be correct.

The Polka is written in 2-4 time. The gentleman holds his partner in the manner shown in the engraving; each lift first the right leg, strike twice the left heel with the right heel, and then turn as in the waltz'—

a performance which must have presented a rather curious appearance. On Apr. 13 the same paper, reviewing a polka by Jullien, says:

'It is waste of time to consider this nonsense. The weathercock heads of the Parisians have been delighted always by any innovation, but they never imported anything more ridiculous or ungraceful than this Polka. It is a hybrid confusion of Scotch Lilt, Irish Jig and Bohemian Waltz, and needs only to be seen once to be avoided for ever!'

In spite of this criticism the popularity of the dance went on increasing, and the papers of the day are full of advertisements professing to teach 'the genuine polka.' It was danced at Her Majesty's Opera by Cerito, Carlotta Grisi and Perrot, and the following was published as

'the much celebrated Polka Dance, performed at Her Majesty's Theatre, by Carlotta Grisi and Perrot, composed and arranged for the pianoforte by Alberto Sowinsky.'

Many ways of dancing the polka seem to have been in use, and in order to settle all disputes on the important matter, the *Illustrated London News*, on May 11 (having changed its opinions since April), was

'much gratified in being enabled to lay before its readers an accurate description of the *véritable*, or Drawing-room Polka, as danced at Almack's, and at the balls of the nobility and gentry in this country.'

According to this description, which is accompanied by three very amusing illustrations, the polka began with an introduction (danced *vis-à-vis*), and consisted of five figures. Of these, the 'heel and toe' step, which was the most characteristic feature of the dance, has been quite abandoned, probably owing to the difficulty in executing it properly, which (according to *Punch*, vol. vii. p. 172 [1]) generally caused it to result in the dancers 'stamping their own heels upon other people's toes.' The account of the polka concludes as follows:

'In conclusion we would observe that La Polka is a noiseless dance; there is no stamping of heels, toes or kicking of legs in sharp angles forward. This may do very well at the threshold of a Bohemian *auberge*, but is inadmissible into the *salons* of London or Paris. La Polka, as danced in Paris, and now adopted by us, is elegant, graceful and fascinating in the extreme; it is replete with opportunities of showing care and attention to your partner in assisting her through its performance.'

The music of the polka is written in 2-4 time; according to Cellarius (*La Danse des*

1 See also *Punch*, vol. vi., for an admirable cartoon by Leech, representing Lord Brougham dancing the polka with the woolsack.

*salons*, Paris, 1847) the tempo is that of a military march played rather slowly; Maelzel's metronome, $\downarrow=104$. The rhythm is characterised by the following 2-bar figures:

The music can be divided into the usual 8-bar parts. In all early polkas the figure

is found in the accompaniment of the 4th and 8th bars of these parts, marking a very slight pause in the dance, but in later examples this pause has disappeared, owing to the dance being performed somewhat faster, and more in the spirit of a waltz or galop. The first polka which was published is said to have been composed by Franz Hilmar, a native of Kopidlno in Bohemia. The best national polkas are those by Labitzky, Liebmann, Prochaska, Swoboda and Titl.                    W. B. S.

POLLAROLO, see POLAROLI.

POLLEDRO, GIOVANNI BATTISTA (*b.* Piovà, near Turin, June 10, 1781 [2]; *d.* there, Aug. 15, 1853), an eminent violinist. At 15 he studied for a short time under Pugnani, and soon entered the royal band at Turin. In 1804 he became first violin in the theatre at Bergamo, and after a short stay there began to travel. In Russia he remained for five years, and in 1814 accepted the appointment of leader of the band at Dresden, where he remained till 1824. In that year he accepted a brilliant engagement as director-general of the royal orchestra at Turin.

Polledro was an excellent violinist and sound musician. He had the great tone and dignified style of the classical Italian school. All contemporaneous critics praise his faultless and brilliant execution not less than the deep feeling with which he played. In 1812 he met Beethoven at Carlsbad, and played with him one of Beethoven's violin sonatas (see Thayer's *Life of Beethoven*, iii. 208). His published compositions consist of two concertos, some airs variés, trios and duos for stringed instruments, and a set of exercises for the violin; a Miserere and a Mass for voices and orchestra, and a Sinfonia pastorale for full orchestra.

P. D.

POLLINI, FRANCESCO GIUSEPPE (*b.* Lubiano, Illyria, 1763; *d.* Milan, Sept. 17, 1846),

2 according to one authority, 1776.

was a pupil of Mozart. He became a skilful pianist at an early age, his style having combined some of the distinguishing characteristics of that of his preceptor, of Clementi and of Hummel, each of whom he surpassed in some forms of the mere mechanism of the art. In 1793 he studied with Zingarelli at Milan, where he was appointed professor of the piano on the opening of the Conservatorio in 1809. Pollini indeed may, in this respect, be considered as an inventor, having anticipated Thalberg in the extended grasp of the keyboard by the use of three staves (as in Thalberg's Fantasia on 'God save the Queen' and 'Rule Britannia') —thus enabling the player to sustain a prominent melody in the middle region of the instrument, while each hand is also employed with elaborate passages above and beneath it. This mode of producing by two hands almost the effect of four appears, indeed, to have been originated by Pollini in his 'Trentadue esercizi in forma di toccata,' brought out in 1820. This work was dedicated to Meyerbeer; the original edition containing a preface addressed to that composer by Pollini, which includes the following passage explanatory of the construction of the toccata :

'I propose to offer a simple melody more or less plain, and of varied character, combined with accompaniments of different rhythms, from which it can be clearly distinguished by a particular expression and touch in the cantilena in contrast to the accompaniment.'

Dehn appears to have been the first to draw attention to Pollini's speciality, in his preface to the original edition of Liszt's pianoforte transcriptions of the six great organ preludes and fugues of Bach.

Pollini's productions consist chiefly of pianoforte music, including an elaborate instruction book, many solo pieces, and some for two performers. These works are included in the catalogue of Ricordi, of Milan. Pollini also produced stage music and a Stabat Mater. He was highly esteemed—professionally and personally—by his contemporaries. Bellini dedicated his 'Sonnambula' 'al celebre Francesco Pollini.'          H. J. L.

POLLITZER, ADOLPHE (b. Buda - Pest, July 23, 1832 ; d. London, Nov. 14, 1900), violinist, the youngest of a family numbering nineteen.

He left his native town for Vienna at the age of 10, and there became a pupil of Böhm, at the same time receiving lessons in composition from Preyer. While still a boy he played before the Emperor of Austria, and at the age of 13 performed Mendelssohn's Violin Concerto in the presence of its composer, and was rewarded by his warm congratulations and a lifelong interest in his career. In 1846 Pollitzer gained the first prize for violin-playing at the Vienna Conservatorium, and after a short concert tour in Germany, betook himself to Paris, where he received lessons from Alard. By the advice of Ernst he came to London in 1851. Here his talents gained him speedy recognition. He occupied the post of leader at the Opera, under the baton of Costa, for many years, and held similar positions at the head of the New Philharmonic Orchestra and the Royal Choral Society. In 1861 he was appointed violin professor at the London Academy of Music, and in 1890 succeeded Dr. Henry Wylde as principal of that institution. During the period of his activity as a teacher Pollitzer was responsible for the training of a vast number of professional and amateur violinists, and these, under the presidency of Sir Joseph Barnby, presented him with a signed testimonial and a handsome gold watch at the Hôtel Metropole on Feb. 18, 1888. His published compositions comprise 'Ten Caprices for the Violin' and some short pieces for violin and piano. He revised and edited a prodigious amount of De Bériot's compositions, as well as those of Alard, Léonard, Singelée, Ernst, etc.

BIBL.—Baker ; Riemann ; The Jewish Chronicle, Nov. 23, 1900 ; The Sketch, Nov. 23, 1900, and contemporary publications.

E. H.-A.

POLLY, a ballad opera, written by John Gay as a second part of his 'Beggar's Opera.' When about to be rehearsed a message was received from the Lord Chamberlain that the piece 'was not allowed to be acted, but commanded to be suppressed,' the prohibition being supposed to have been instigated by Sir Robert Walpole, who had been satirised in the 'Beggar's Opera.' Failing to obtain a reversal of the decree, Gay had recourse to the press, and in 1729 published the piece in 4to, with the tunes of the songs, and a numerous list of subscribers, by which he gained at least as much as he would have done by representation. Like most sequels, 'Polly' is far inferior to the first part, and when in 1777 it was produced at the Haymarket Theatre, with alterations by the elder Colman, it was so unsuccessful that it was withdrawn after a few representations. It was revived at the same theatre, June 11, 1782, and again at Drury Lane (for Kelly's benefit), June 16, 1813.          W. H. H.

Following the success of the 'Beggar's Opera' at Hammersmith, a revised version of 'Polly'—the play rewritten by Clifford Bax ; the music arranged by Frederic AUSTIN (q.v.) —was produced at the Kingsway Theatre, London, Dec. 30, 1922.          c.

POLO, see SONG, subsection SPAIN (4).

POLO or OLE, a Spanish dance accompanied by singing, which took its origin in Andalusia. It is said to be identical with the Romalis, which is

'danced to an old religious Eastern tune, low and melancholy, diatonic, not chromatic, and full of sudden pauses, which are strange and startling,' [1]

and is only danced by the Spanish gipsies.

[1] Walter Thornbury, Life in Spain.

It resembles the Oriental dances in being full of wild energy and contortions of the body, while the feet merely glide or shuffle along the ground. The words (' coplas ') of these dances are generally of a jocose character, and differ from those of the Seguidilla in wanting the ' estrevillo,' or refrain ; several examples of them may be found in Preciso's *Coleccion de las Mejores Coplas de Seguidillas, Tiranas y Polos* (Madrid, 1816). They are sung in unison by a chorus, who mark the time by clapping their hands. Some characteristic examples of the music of the Polo will be found in J. Gansino's *La Joya de Andalucia* (Madrid, Romero).

W. B. S.

POLONAISE, a stately dance of Polish origin. According to Sowinski (*Les Musiciens polonais*) the polonaise is derived from the ancient Christmas carols which are still sung in Poland. In support of this theory he quotes a carol, ' W zlobie lezy,' which contains the rhythm and close characteristic of the dance ; but the fact that although in later times they were accompanied by singing, yet the earliest polonaises extant are purely instrumental, renders it more probable that the generally received opinion as to their courtly origin is correct.

According to this latter view, the polonaise originated under the following circumstances. In 1573 Henry III. of Anjou was elected to the Polish throne, and in the following year held a great reception at Cracow, at which the wives of the nobles marched in procession past the throne to the sound of stately music. It is said that after this, whenever a foreign prince was elected to the crown of Poland, the same ceremony was repeated, and that out of it the polonaise was gradually developed as the opening dance at court festivities. If this custom was introduced by Henry III., we may perhaps look upon the polonaise, which is so full of stateliness, as the survival of the dignified pavans and passamezzos which were so much in vogue at the French court in the 15th century. Evidence is not wanting to prove that the dance was not always of so marked a national character as it assumed in later times. Book vii. of Bésard's *Thesaurus harmonicus Divini Laurencini Romani* (Cologne, 1603) consists of ' Selectiores aliquot choreae quas Allemande vocant, germanico saltui maxime accommodatae, una cum Polonicis aliquot et aliis ab hoc saltationis genere haud absimilibus,' and these ' choreae Polonicae ' (which are principally composed by one Diomedes, a naturalised Venetian at the court of Sigismund III.) exhibit very slightly the rhythm and peculiarities of Polish national music. During the 17th century, although it was no doubt during this time that it assumed the form that was afterwards destined to become so popular, the Polonaise left no mark upon musical

history, and it is not until the first half of the 18th century that examples of it begin to occur.[1]

In Walther's *Lexicon* (1732) no mention is made of it, or of any Polish music ; but in Mattheson's *Volkommener Kapellmeister* (1739) we find it (as the author himself tells us) described for the first time. Mattheson notices the spondaic character of the rhythm, and remarks that the music of the polonaise should begin on the first beat of the bar : he gives two examples (one in 3–4, the other in common time) made by himself out of the chorale ' Ich ruf' zu dir, Herr Jesu Christ.' At this time the polonaise seems suddenly to have attained immense popularity, probably owing to the intimate connexion between Saxony and Poland which was caused by the election (1733) of Augustus III. to the Polish throne. In 1742–1743 there was published at Leipzig a curious little collection of songs entitled ' Sperontes Singende Muse,' which contains many adaptations of Polish airs : in the following example (from the second part of the work) some of the peculiarities of the polonaise may be traced.

Deine Blicke Sind die Stricke, All - er - an - ge -
nehmstes Kind, Die die Lie - be so bezwingend nicht
Irgend-wo sonst zugericht. Deiner Anmuth Schein
Nimmt mehr Her - zen ein, Als des Mo - gols Macht
Volk an sich gebracht, Und der gröss-te Feld-herr
und Sol-dat, Noch zur Zeit je-mals be - zwungen hat.

From this time the polonaise has always been a favourite form of composition with instrumental composers, and has not been without influence on vocal music, especially in Italian opera. (See POLACCA.) Bach wrote two polonaises (orchestral partita in B minor, and French suite, No. 6), besides a ' Polacca ' (Brandenburg Concertos, No. 1, Dehn) ; and there are also examples by Handel (Grand Concerto, No. 3, in E minor), Beethoven (op. 89, triple concerto, and serenade trio, op. 8), Mozart (' Rondeau Polonaise,' sonata in D minor), Schubert (polonaises for four hands),

[1] In the State Library at Berlin there is preserved a MS. volume which bears the date 1725, and formerly belonged to Bach's second wife, Anna Magdalena (see B.-G. xliii. 2). In it are five Polonaises written in the owner's autograph ; but it is improbable that they are all of Sebastian Bach's composition.

Weber (op. 21, and the 'Polacca brillante,' op. 72), Wagner (for four hands, op. 2), as well as by the Polish composers Kurpinski and Ogniski, and above all by Chopin, under whose hands it reached what is perhaps the highest development possible for mere dance forms.

Attracted by its striking rhythmical capabilities, and imbued with the deepest national sympathy, Chopin animated the dry form of the old polonaise with a new and intensely living spirit, altering it as (in a lesser degree) he altered the waltz and the mazurka, and changing it from a mere dance into a glowing tone-picture of Poland, her departed glory, her many wrongs, and her hoped-for regeneration. Karasowski (*Chopin*, vol. ii.) divides his polonaises into two classes. The first (which includes those in A major, op. 40, No. 1; F♯ minor, op. 44, and A♭ major, op. 53) is characterised by strong and martial rhythm, and may be taken to represent the feudal court of Poland in the days of its splendour. The second class (including the polonaises in C♯ minor and E♭ minor, op. 26; in C minor, op. 40, No. 2; in D minor, B♭ major and F minor, op. 71) is distinguished by dreamy melancholy, and forms a picture of Poland in her adversity. The 'Fantaisie Polonaise' (A♭ major, op. 61) is different in character from both classes, and is said to represent the national struggles ending with a song of triumph.

As a dance, the polonaise is of little interest: it consists of a procession in which both old and young take part, moving several times round the room in solemn order. It does not depend upon the execution of any particular steps, although it is said to have been formerly danced with different figures, something like the English country dances. It survived in Germany during the Empire, and was danced at the beginning of all court balls. In Mecklenburg a sort of degenerate polonaise is sometimes danced at the end of the evening; it is called 'Der Auskehr' ('The Turn-out'), and consists in a procession of the whole company through the house, each person being armed with some household utensil, and singing in chorus 'Un as de Grotvare de Grotmoder nahm.' (See GROSSVATER-TANZ.)

The tempo of the polonaise is that of a march, played between andante and allegro: it is nearly always written in 3–4 time,[1] and should always begin on the first beat of the bar. It generally consists of two parts, sometimes followed by a trio in a different key; the number of bars in each part is irregular. The chief peculiarity of the polonaise consists in the strong emphasis falling repeatedly on the half-beat of the bar, the first beat generally consisting of a quaver followed by a crotchet (see the polonaise given below). Another peculiarity is that the close takes place on the third beat,

[1] Mattheson says it may be written in common time.

often preceded by a strong accent on the second beat. The last bar should properly consist of four semiquavers, the last of which should fall on the leading note, and be repeated before the concluding chord, thus:

The accompaniment generally consists of quavers and semiquavers in the following rhythm:

The following example, although not conforming entirely with the above rules, is nevertheless interesting as a genuine polonaise danced and sung at weddings in the district of Krzeszowice in Poland:

Poja - lem sobie nieprzepłaconą, Ksiedza plebana siostrę rodgoną. Dał ci mi tyle da tyle wiana, ocipke sloniny i wiąz kę siana. Moji są siedzi osądz cie lepiej, niechze mi choc da zagonek rzepy.[2]

The notes printed in small type are variations of the tune which are performed in some districts.          W. B. S.

POLSKA, a national Swedish dance, popular in West Gothland, something like a Scotch reel in character. Polskas are usually written in minor keys, although they are occasionally found in the major. The example which is given below ('Neckens Polska') is well known,

[2] Translation: I have taken for my wife the reverend Parson's own sister. He gave me as her marriage portion a piece of bacon and a bundle of hay. My neighbours, what do you think? The fellow has refused to give me even a little plot of land sown with turnips.

as Ambroise Thomas has introduced it in Ophelia's mad scene in ' Hamlet.' Other examples will be found in Ahlstrom's ' Walda Svenska Folksånga ' (Stockholm, 1850).

W. B. S.

POLYEUCTE (POLIUTO). (1) Opera in 3 acts ; libretto, after Corneille, conceived by Adolphe Nourrit, and carried out by Cammarano ; music by Donizetti. It was completed in 1838, but the performance was forbidden by the Censure of Naples ; translated into French by Scribe, and as ' Les Martyrs,' produced Opéra (4 acts), Apr. 10, 1840 ; Théâtre Italien, as ' I martiri,' Apr. 14, 1859 ; in London, as ' I martiri,' Royal Italian Opera, Apr. 20, 1852.

(2) Opera in 5 acts ; words by Barbier and Carré, music by Gounod. Produced Opéra, Paris, Oct. 7, 1878.

G.

POLYPHONY. The harmonious combination of two or more melodies, *i.e.* composition considered horizontally as distinct from Homophony, which is vertical in the principle of its structure. Differing from COUNTERPOINT (*q.v.*) rather in the customary use of the term than in its meaning, the name of Polyphony is usually attached to the actual compositions, while that of Counterpoint is applied to the academic or scientific forms.

The history of musical composition up to the year 1500, owing to the overwhelming predominance of the vocal element, is very largely the history of polyphony. It is generally (though not universally) conceded that the only variant from strict monophony or unison singing which was known to the earlier civilisations consisted in a duplication at the octave, which went by the name of *magadising* among the Greeks. For our present purpose the ground of this first section may roughly be mapped out as under :

1. The age of Organum (900–1200).
2. The age of Rhythmic Forms (1200–1400).
3. The birth and development of free composition (1400–1500).

1. The origins of harmony are most obscure, and for that reason have provided fruitful ground for controversy. Scholarship seems to tend, however, more and more to agree that the ultimate source (unless there was more than one) lies outside the Latin civilisation of the early Middle Ages. Ireland, Wales, the Anglo-Saxons, the Danes have each their supporters ; while the earliest Latin texts bifurcate between the Northmen who occupied Northern France in the 10th century, and the group which seems to centre round the monastery of St. Gall in Switzerland. The chief early exception to the list of non-Latin sources is the Abbey of St. Martial at Limoges. The oldest specimen known to exist to-day is from Cornwall, and consists of a two-part setting of four lines from the six-lined hymn of St. Stephen in the Sarum

Breviary, *Sancte dei pretiose* : it is dated about the year 1000.

HARMONY (*q.v.*), considered as a science, has sprung from the mating of the mathematical mind with the musical, and not until the middle of the 15th century does the fledgling leave the nest and bid farewell to the care of the mathematicians. It is significant that music occupies the place immediately next before mathematics in the Quadrivium, or traditional course of higher studies at the universities, and one of the leading musical treatises (Odington, *De speculatione musices*) has its earlier half given over almost entirely to mathematical questions. De Muris and Dunstable also were mathematicians.

The earliest theoretical work of any detail is that of Hucbald (*c.* 880), who describes the practice of singing as it was current in his day, under the name of Organum ; but John Scotus Erigena some 100 years earlier had spoken of the Celtic knowledge of vocal harmony. For fuller information about the various forms taken by the compositions of the earlier centuries, the reader is referred to the separate articles on CONDUCTUS, DESCANT, MOTET, ORGANUM : information will also be found under FAUXBOURDON, GYMEL, HOCKET, ORDINES, PES, and in the earlier part of MASS.

The examples of organum, apart from those in the theoretical treatises, are very scarce, for so simple a form needed no score apart from the plain-song canto fermo ; moreover, the stave had not yet come into use in the 10th century. The harmony of the most extensive collection, the Organa of the Winchester Troper,[1] is practically indecipherable, both voices being provided with neumes *in campo aperto* (see NOTATION). But its historical importance is very great, as showing that the Winchester music before the Norman Conquest was already in advance of the system of parallel fifths and fourths, with occasional oblique motion, described by Hucbald ; for though the actual position of the notes cannot be identified, contrary motion can be discerned.

A later specimen of this early harmony can be seen in the first number of *Revue grégorienne* (Desclée, Tournai, 1911), where a long passage from a Chartres MS. is printed ; here the actual position of the notes is ascertainable. The music appears in the form of two plain-song melodies, harmonising with one another, fifths and thirds being the most frequent intervals. There is much discord, and no trace as yet of any strictly measured rhythm ; both voices are singing plain-song in free time, carefully balanced one against another, a group of two notes in one voice being accompanied by a group of two in the other, and so one. The specimen is dated by Dr. Bannister at about 1100.

[1] For a full account see W. H. Frere, *The Winchester Troper* (Henry Bradshaw Society, 1894).

Meanwhile the theorists were getting busy, and by 1100 two stages of discovery had been reached which gave the necessary material and impetus for real progress in the art of polyphony. The first is the invention of the stave, ascribed to Guido d' Arezzo (*c.* 1050) but in reality a gradual development, which made it no longer necessary for music to depend upon oral tradition (neumes *in campo aperto* being only aids to memory), as compositions could now be written down with accuracy and transmitted by the circulation and copying of MSS. The second invention, more closely bound up with our immediate subject, was that of a notation to express mensurate time-values. These were of course known before, for dance music and march music are absolutely dependent upon a fixed recurring rhythm ; but there was no notation in the modern sense ; and the great advance associated with the name of FRANCO OF COLOGNE (*c.* 1100) was caused by the realisation that music sung in harmony between voices at different pitch and with varying melodic contour is but limited in scope where both (or all) voices are left free to follow plain-song rhythm. So the notation of plain-song was taken over and adapted slightly to express fixed time-values. The earlier ecclesiastical theorists had allowed only the intervals of fifth and fourth, but (probably under the influence of English example) the imperfect concords of third and sixth were now permitted. We already find an abundance of thirds in the Chartres MS. referred to above ; here, as always, theory does not direct practice, but follows and codifies it.

2. We find the first considerable application of the new doctrines of fixed rhythm in the beginning of the 13th century, centred round a flourishing and prolific school of composers at Notre Dame in Paris. A large store of their compositions in two, three and four parts has fortunately come down to us, together with some of the composers' names, Léonin and Pérotin being the leaders. The forms used are Organum (of a newer style in which all but the tenor sang in measured time, the tenor holding long notes as pedals which moved at conventional points), Conductus and Motet.[1] The Notre Dame MSS. and the later collateral remains from Bamberg, Montpelier and Worcester bring us into a second chapter of polyphonic development, that of scientific rhythm. Like many other discoveries it was worked to extremes, and the mathematician tended to predominate over the artist. But the rhythmic relation of voices to one another, in place of the ' double plain-song ' of the older Organum and unmeasured descant, was a genuine and important advance. Probably the advance would have been more rapid had it been recog-

nised that rhythmic *unity* between individual parts is not necessarily a lower stage of art than rhythmic *variety* between the voices. But the fashion was all for complexity in rhythm, and the simpler form of the Conductus seems to have been less popular than the more elaborate Motet.

The early period of Rhythmic Forms is notable for the great landmark of SUMER IS ICUMEN IN (*q.v.*). The apex was reached by Guillaume de MACHAUT (*q.v.*), large quantities of whose work remain in the Bibliothèque Nationale at Paris, and elsewhere, awaiting publication. In Machaut we reach for the first time (with the exception of the Reading Rota) a stage of ' harmoniousness ' according to modern ideas combined with an amazing grasp of technique and high artistic feeling. But the Independent Entry has not yet been discovered, and it is not until the middle of the 15th century that the art, under this new spur, begins to enter upon its Golden Age.

3. It is unsafe to make definite statements as to the age when this or that point of form first makes its appearance, and all we can say is that, so far as present knowledge goes, Independent Entry, of a formal, fugal kind, is not found before 1425. Suspensions, unprepared discords (as distinct from the arbitrary unresolved discords of the 13th century) and the like have to be dated back to an earlier period as some new MS. is discovered and scored. But, broadly speaking, we may say that all the devices of classical counterpoint have their origin in the later part of the 15th century, if not earlier.

The first half of the century is chiefly notable for some good Christmas carols, and for the Agincourt song, in which a duet is followed by a three-part chorus, probably the earliest example of this kind of treatment.

A certain mastery of independent part-writing is reached by the middle of the century, and a strong English school of composers headed by DUNSTABLE and Leonel POWER have left us some of their work in the Old Hall MS. (*c.* 1455). About this time Dunstable and others would seem to have migrated to the Continent, and to have thrown in their lot with their contemporaries and pupils of the ' First Flemish School' (DUFAY; BINCHOIS, etc.), for most of their work is found abroad, notably in some Cambrai choir-books, dated 1459–70, selections from which have been published as ' Sechs Trienter Codices ' (Artaria, Vienna ; the MSS. belong to Italy). In these works we find that three- and four-part writing is the normal form, though occasional five-part items are found, *e.g.* in Mayshuet's ' Arae post libamina ' in the Old Hall MS.

It is with the ' Second Flemish School ' of OKEGHEM (*c.* 1430–1513) and OBRECHT (*c.* 1430–1500) that we find development in the number

---

[1] Many examples are given in *Oxf. Hist. Mus.* vol. i.

of parts, and in looking for advance in the last quarter of the century we shall probably trace progress best by looking in this direction, though the line of Canon followed by most historians is by no means unimportant. Multiple writing was certainly the 'new thing,' and though not always the best work, it had a beneficial influence on the 3- and 4-part composition, giving a greater desire for complete chords and solid cadences, and improving the 'emptiness' conveyed by so much of Dunstable. We note, for instance, in the only existing English collection of this period (Eton MS. 178) that the 9-part Salve Regina and 13-part Apostles' Creed by Wilkinson are monotonous in their repetition of one or two fundamental chords : ingenuity has dominated over art. It is not until modulation is well known and practised that a more complex scheme of voices can be satisfactorily handled, and there is a whole world of difference between these things and Palestrina's 'Stabat Mater.' But excellent 5-part writing of this period may be found in the anonymous Mass 'O quam suavis' at Cambridge, worthy to stand beside the best of Fayrfax. A short extract from the Eton MS. instances the real (though perhaps unrealised) strength of this period in florid 2-part counterpoint.

From a *Magnificat* for four male voices
by Dom William Stratford.
Eton MS. 178 (*c.* 1500).

Time values of the original notes halved.

Ingenuity was expended in another direction in this period by the curious devices of puzzle - canons and enigmas of amazing subtlety. Flemish as well as English excelled in these.

The first quarter of the 16th century brings us to the first peak of the Golden Age—Lassus on the Continent, Taverner in England. In this period of individual composers, an account of whose art will be found under their respective names, we may be relatively brief in dealing with the very important transition of the art from scholastic to expressive composition. Two names stand out in the transitional period, one on either side of the Channel—Robert Fayrfax and Josquin des Prés, the leaders of two vigorous schools.

The art in England now develops in a course somewhat different from that followed by the Netherlanders. The work of the Fayrfax school has not yet been thoroughly explored, very little of their music being in print ; but it is well known to some few who have scored these compositions in MS., and all agree in admiration for Fayrfax's great mastery of technique, his bold sweep of melody, and his massive strength. He wrote chiefly in five and six parts, and some of his music, together with work by his contemporary Ludford, has recently been revived in practical form. By comparison with the Flemings of his day he is said to be conservative ; but in one direction he was progressive, for he seems to have taught English composers to forsake the tiresome habits of enigma, puzzle-canon and the over-elaboration of contrapuntal device.

Josquin des Prés, on the other hand, and his prolific school (known as the 'Third Flemish School'), though freeing their music from the shackles of Okeghem's excessive mathematical subtleties, still make use of 'trick-writing' from time to time. But their great contribution to the development of composition—and here they forged ahead of England for a time—is the alliance of counterpoint and expression. Modal 'flavour' had hitherto been sufficient, but in the hands of the polyphonists the modes have tended to settle more and more into three stereotyped forms—Ionic (Mixo-Lydian) or modern major, Dorian and Aeolian or modern minor. So that from 1500 onwards we find that dramatic effects are produced by the more successful writers with apparent ease ; though analysis often reveals their consummate skill and mastery of technical device. Modal polyphony had its day, a glorious day ; but being a living thing, and one of the most marvellous fruits that the art, devotion and skill of man have ever brought to perfection, it held within itself the seeds of decay : and of rebirth. And by the middle of the 16th century we find musicians writing frankly in the modern major and minor modes, the minor third in the final chord being, of course, always disallowed. A. H.

## PRINCIPLES OF THE 16TH CENTURY

An attempt is made here to state briefly what the principles of composition of the great polyphonic schools really were, so that the reader may see for himself how far they differ from text-book theory. It will be of practical convenience to consider these principles under the separate headings of Scale, Rhythm and Harmony; but no musician will need to be reminded how deeply these three elements interpenetrate and modify one another in practice.

(1) SCALE.—It is not necessary to give here any detailed account of the modal system (see MODES, ECCLESIASTICAL). It has only to be remembered that the two-scale system had not yet completely emerged, although the constant use of accidentals in accordance with the rules of MUSICA FICTA (q.v.) was rapidly transforming the modal system into something very unlike its original self. But in all the accounts of Musica Ficta nothing emerges at all resembling the later idea of modulation. Accidentals are purely local, so to speak, in their action; they are introduced to secure or avoid some particular and momentary effect, and are not at all to be thought of as shifting the harmonic centre of gravity as the later modulation did. In most modern text-books, on the other hand, no attempt is made to preserve this vital element of the older counterpoint; accidentals are used, if at all, for the specific purpose of modulation, and are otherwise banned, except so far as they are required in the ascending form of the melodic minor scale. In this way the historic evolution of the diatonic and chromatic scales, their gradual emergence from the older modal system, is concealed from the student, who is thereby so much the poorer. Scholastic counterpoint would no doubt reply that a student should be trained in the scale-system in which he will ultimately have to work, and that the modes were of historical but not practical interest. To this a modern teacher can only reply that it was so, but is so no longer. What composers seek to-day is freedom from the limits of the major and minor scale-system. That freedom they will attain, but they must have a centre of gravity. They cannot, humanly speaking, do without the point of balance which a scale affords. Atonality tries to dispense with balance altogether; polytonality attempts to balance at more than one point at the same time. Both ventures appear foredoomed. But the resources they are trying to develop are not thereby placed for ever beyond our grasp; they are latent in the music of the 16th century. A composer then, writing for instance in the scale or mode of G, had two thirds at his command, two sixths and two sevenths; he could use B♭ or B♮, E♮ or E♭, F♮ or F♯, according as the natural course of the melody might indicate. He could even use the two forms simultaneously in two different parts: the English composers were constantly doing so. A modern composer has only to develop this method of proceeding to attain the full freedom of a twelve-note scale, with no need of becoming either arbitrary or chaotic. It can thus be realised that music in 1600 did indeed stand at the cross-roads, but saw only one arm. That was right at that time, but now the hour has come to go back and see where the other arm points us. Scholastic counterpoint has little to say on such matters; but it will have to say more if it is to justify itself to the coming generation.

(2) RHYTHM.—The rhythm of the polyphonic period was in every way more complex and more subtle than that of the so-called classical period which succeeded it. One may perhaps best express the nature of this complexity by saying that the rhythm of a piece of music taken as a whole—i.e. harmonically—was quite different from the rhythms of the individual voices of which it was composed, and that these individual rhythms in turn could be, and often were, quite different from one another. That said, it remains to describe the nature of these differences. For the moment, let us put on one side the consideration of the individual voices, and think of the music simply as a sequence of chords, interwoven with suspensions, passing notes, and so on.

Thus viewed, it presents little difficulty. All discords had to be prepared first, and then resolved. The chord of preparation and the resolution invariably occurred on 'weak' beats, the discord itself coming on the intervening 'strong' beat. Which those beats were depended on the time and prolation signatures at the beginning of the movement. If, for example, the sign was ₵, the accentual system was −∪−∪ | −∪−∪, and so on; if the sign was O, the accentuation was ∪−∪ | ∪−∪, and so on (the mark − indicating in each case the 'strong' beats; i.e. the places where discords could occur). It is therefore most misleading to say (as some modern editors seem never tired of saying) that the time-signature was of 'purely arithmetical significance,' when in fact it determined the whole harmonic structure of the composition.

Now let us consider the rhythmical structure of the individual voices. Here one may indeed say that the time-signature is of 'purely arithmetical significance,' for it may exercise no influence whatever on the melodic accentuation. This accentuation is free, plastic and independent, making itself felt by duration rather than by stress (cf. ACCENT). It prefers to follow the natural spoken rhythm of the words, and does not care in the least whether these ' duration accents ' come on a metrically strong or a metrically weak beat. Consider, for example, the two following passages from Palestrina's eight-part Stabat Mater.

Here the ' duration accents ' are most cunningly contrived to fit the natural stress of the words they accompany, yet in both passages they utterly defy the authority of their respective time-signatures. And in this determination to be free at all costs they are an epitome of 16th-century music as a whole, for that music always declined to submit to the bondage of the dance, whose uniformity of rhythmic pattern, though admirable for its own purpose, is more apt to content the body than to refresh the soul. Now this idea of rhythmical freedom, like the idea of metrical regularity, is in itself quite easy to grasp. But the co-existence of the two principles within one and the same piece of music does appear to present a certain difficulty to many modern minds. Scholastic counterpoint does not recognise the existence of the problem; it assures the student that tied notes and dotted notes are ' useful as giving variety to the rhythm ' (or words to that effect), but it makes no attempt to investigate and define the function of the tie, considered from the point of view of the single part in which it occurs. It does not see that the effect of the tie is to hold back the accent, to create a fresh accent, as it were, an accent of duration, whose position is quite independent of the ' strong ' and ' weak ' beats of the measure, although the harmonic stress, as shown by the discords, is determined entirely by these regular beats. This is not theorising: it is a plain fact for any one who will study the English madrigals and observe how free is the position of the stressed syllables in the music, taken as they are quite impartially in ' strong ' or ' weak ' places as the spirit may dictate. Yet it is surely desirable that a student of music should be made familiar

with a rhythmical system so subtle, so complex, and so precise. And it is not only to be desired for the sake of the historical information so acquired. Rhythmical exercise on such lines will give not only knowledge, but power ; it will make the student inwardly mobile, and point him the way to a new rhythmic freedom. There can be no return to the 16th-century system as it stands, for that would imply a return also to the harmonic limitations on which that system depends, which is unthinkable. But a study of that system will show us how to ' think across the bar-line,' to elide an accent or displace a stress, without doing sudden violence to the measure in which we are writing. Measure in itself is good ; the regular periodic rise and fall which measure gives is an element of power for music as for poetry. But freedom must be able to assert itself from time to time within the domain of law, for where there is no freedom the spirit will not enter. The ' free rhythms ' of the present day are unbalanced and self-conscious ; moreover, the constant abrupt changes of time and bar are bewildering to the players and a terror to their conductor. Counterpoint can show us the way to a truer and more spontaneous freedom, working in harmony with metric law, instead of seeking to thrust it aside with violence. But such counterpoint must be taught in the spirit as well as the letter.

(3) HARMONY.—Every one knows that the classic system of harmony, which served mankind from Bach to Brahms, was derived from the counterpoint of the previous age—the age, that is to say, which is here under consideration. Strip that harmony of its trimmings, chromatic passing notes and such like embellishments, and you are left with a handful of simple diatonic chords, which passed into musical currency simply because the sound of them had become familiar. They were originally, so to speak, fortuitous combinations which were so frequently brought about by the normal flow of counterpoint that by constant repetition they acquired independent existence, and were ultimately grouped, classified and labelled as common chords, diatonic sevenths, secondary sevenths and so on. If one wants to press the inquiry farther back, and inquire how these combinations first became possible, one must speak no longer in terms of chords, but of intervals. There is indeed only one harmonic principle underlying the music of the 16th century, and it is this : In every piece of music, no matter how many the parts, every part must make correct two-part harmony with every other part. And to the question, What in their view was correct two-part harmony ? there is a threefold answer : (1) The intervals of the second and the seventh are dissonant,

and require preparation, except when they occur merely as passing notes. (2) The interval of the fourth is also a dissonance when it occurs between one of the upper parts and the bass. But occurring between upper parts it is a consonance, if it is supported by the bass—*i.e.* as we should say, if it constitutes the upper part of a $\frac{5}{3}$ or $\frac{6}{3}$ chord. The same is true of the augmented fourth and the diminished fifth. (3) The other intervals are consonant and require no preparation. But consecutive fifths and octaves are forbidden.

To this question of prohibited consecutives we shall return. For the moment the essential thing to note is that the whole edifice of 16th-century music rests, harmonically speaking, on these three rules. The rest is a matter of detail—how suspensions resolve, where passing notes may occur, and so on. It is superfluous to enter here into these matters of procedure. The prohibited consecutives, however, are worth considering. They can throw light on the problems of the present and the future; but to get our true bearings we must go back still further, and consider summarily the changes that took place in music between the 14th and the 16th centuries. Three of these claim our attention:

(1) At the beginning of this period fourths and fifths are the favoured intervals: seconds and sevenths are quite acceptable: thirds and sixths are curiously infrequent. By the end of it, seconds and sevenths are banned altogether, while octaves and fifths are placed under severe restrictions. Thirds and sixths, on the other hand, are now the only intervals that can be used without let or hindrance.

(2) The number of voices has tended steadily to increase. Two or three parts were usual at first: by the end of the period five- and six-part combinations were normal, and eight- and twelve-part work by no means uncommon.

(3) The centre of interest tends to pass outwards from the tenor. The bass is felt more and more as dominating the harmony (as the interval of the fourth bears witness): the upper parts, on the other hand, claim more and more of the melodic interest. This last feature is perhaps less noticeable in the sacred music than the secular, but of its general existence there is no doubt.

Now these three changes are interconnected. What (2) and (3) together tell us in effect is this:

'In hearing music of many parts, one has not attention to spare for all the parts equally. What one hears is largely, though not entirely, synthetic. So far as one does hear analytically, the outer parts are more prominent than the inner.'

Whereupon (1) says in turn:

'Quite so. And music must recognise the nature and limitations of the faculty by which men apprehend music. Therefore seconds and sevenths must be avoided, for in these is no element of synthesis; they cause the voices to stand sharply apart from one another. Octaves and fifths, on the other hand,

are too synthetic; they blend as though into a single sound. It is in the thirds and the sixths that the analytic and synthetic elements find their true balance and equipoise.'

Now what (2) and (3) said in the 16th century is as true to-day as it was then. To attend to two melodies simultaneously requires intense concentration; to attend to three is beyond even the most expert capacity, so far as the writer, searching carefully, has been able to discover. Therefore one can safely ignore the current theory of 'non-harmonic linear counterpoint,' which seeks to elevate mere simultaneity to the rank of an æsthetic principle. We must admit the need for some real principle of harmonic synthesis, nay more, we must acknowledge, if we are honest, that the burning question for the music of to-day is, Where can such a principle be found? The 16th century, as we have seen, found its own answer to the question, and in that answer we too can find truth if we try, as we should always try, to penetrate beyond the letter into the spirit informing the letter. What the 16th century has really to say on the subject is this: What is called dissonance is not a matter of pleasantness or unpleasantness, nor is it concerned with any theory of beats, or other acoustical abstraction. The fact is simply this —that when two tones are sounded together, one is not conscious of them simply as a single sound. To some extent they tend to remain apart, and that tendency is what we call dissonance. We may also say of the same two tones that one is not conscious of them simply as two sounds. To some extent they tend to merge their separate identities, to fuse into a single sound; and that tendency is what we call consonance. An interval is consonant (or dissonant) in greater or less degree according as one tendency (or the other) is more or less strongly revealed by it. A chord is an assemblage of intervals, and it in turn is more or less concordant according as the more or the less consonant intervals preponderate in its composition. And a composer will therefore choose more concordant or less concordant assemblages from moment to moment according as he wants his different voices to blend or to assert their separate selves. It is not a matter of theory but of plain psychological fact, grounded in the very nature of what we may call our aural consciousness—*i.e.* the way in which we hear music.

Such is the message for our times of 16th-century harmony. The first man to rediscover its true significance was Professor Watt, whose book, *The Foundations of Music*, inquires deeply and exhaustively into the subjects here briefly touched on. Professor Watt, indeed, does not always seem fully aware of the real scope of his inquiries; he seems now and again to shrink, perhaps unconsciously, from the conclusions to which his researches point.

That does not affect the value of the book in the slightest, nor does it absolve the present writer from the necessity of acknowledging, freely and gladly, that without the guidance of that book this article would probably never have been written.    R. O. M.

POLYTONALITY, see TONALITY; HARMONY.

POMMER, see OBOE (5).

POMPOSO, ' pompously,' is used by Schumann in the Humoreske, op. 20, for pianoforte. Handel had employed the term a century before in the first movement of the overture to ' Samson.'    M.

PONCHARD, LOUIS ANTOINE ELEONORE (b. Paris, Aug. 31, 1787; d. there, Jan. 6, 1866), son of ANTOINE PONCHARD, maître de chapelle of St. Eustache, professor at the Conservatoire and composer of church music. Louis Antoine was also a distinguished church composer (masses, etc.), and maître de chapelle in various French towns. An excellent singer, pupil of Garat, he made his début in 1812 at the Opéra-Comique, to which he belonged until 1837. In 1819 he became professor of singing at the Conservatoire, and was the first operatic singer who became a member of the Legion of Honour. His wife, MARIE SOPHIE CALLAULT-PONCHARD (b. Paris, 1792; d. there, 1873), was also a distinguished member of the Opéra-Comique.
    E. v. d. s.

PONCHIELLI, AMILCARE (b. Paderno Fasolaro, Cremona, Sept. 1, 1834; d. Milan, Jan. 16, 1886), opera composer. In Nov. 1843 he entered the Conservatorio of Milan, and remained there till Sept. 1854. Two years afterwards, on Aug. 30, 1856, he was able to produce at the Concordia at Cremona his first opera, ' I promessi Sposi.' His next were ' La Savojarda,' Cremona, Jan. 19, 1861 ; ' Roderico,' Piacenza, 1864 ; ' Bertrand de Born ' (not performed) and ' La stella del monte,' in 1867. Hitherto Ponchielli's reputation had been confined to the provinces ; but in 1872 he was fortunate enough to find an opportunity of coming before the general public at the opening of the new Teatro Dal Verme at Milan, where his ' Promessi sposi ' was performed Dec. 5. He rewrote a considerable portion of the opera for the occasion, and its success was immediate and complete. (The work was given by the Carl Rosa Company at Birmingham in Apr. 1881.) The managers of the theatre of La Scala at Milan at once commissioned him to write a ballet, ' Le due gemelle,' which was produced there Feb. 1873, received with frantic enthusiasm and immediately published. This was followed by a ballet, ' Clarina ' (Dal Verme, Sept. 1873) ; a scherzo or comedy, ' Il parlatore eterno ' (Lecco, Oct. 18, 1873) ; and a piece in three acts, ' I Lituani,' given with immense success at La Scala, Mar. 7, 1874. (It was rearranged and produced as ' Alduna ' at the same theatre in 1884.)

In the following year he wrote a cantata for the reception of the remains of Donizetti and Simone Mayr at Bergamo, a work of some extent and importance, which was performed there Sept. 13, 1875. On Apr. 8, 1876, he produced a new opera at La Scala called ' Gioconda ' (after Victor Hugo's ' Angelo '), with the same success as before (it was given with much success at Covent Garden, May 31, 1883); and on Nov. 17, 1877, he gave at the Dal Verme, the scene of his first triumph, a three-act piece called ' Lina,' which was a réchauffé of his early opera ' La Savojarda,' and does not appear to have pleased. His opera ' Il figliuol prodigo ' was produced at La Scala, Dec. 26, 1880, with astonishing success. In 1881 Ponchielli was appointed maestro di cappella at Bergamo. His last work was a three-act opera, ' Marion Delorme,' produced at La Scala, Mar. 17, 1885. A hymn in memory of Garibaldi was performed in Sept. 1882.

The above notice is indebted to Paloschi's *Annuario*, and Pougin's Supplement to *Fétis*.    G.

PONIATOWSKI, JOSEPH MICHAEL XAVIER FRANCIS JOHN, Prince of Monte Rotondo (b. Rome, Feb. 20, 1816; d. July 3, 1873 [1]), opera composer. He was a nephew of the Prince Poniatowski who was a marshal of the French army and died in the battle of Leipzig, Oct. 19, 1812, and whose portrait was found by Mendelssohn at Wyler inscribed ' Brinz Baniadofsgi.' [2] Poniatowski devoted himself so entirely to music that he can hardly be called an amateur. He regularly attended the musical classes at the Lycée at Florence, and also studied under Ceccherini. He made his début at the Pergola, Florence, as a tenor singer ; produced his first opera, ' Giovanni da Procida '— in which he sang the title-rôle—at Lucca in 1838, and from that time for more than thirty years supplied the theatres of Italy and Paris with a large number of operas. After the Revolution of 1848 he settled in Paris as plenipotentiary of the Grand Duke of Tuscany, and was made Senator under the Empire. After Sedan he followed his friend Napoleon III. to England, produced his opera ' Gelmina ' at Covent Garden, June 4, 1872, his operetta 'Au travers du mur ' at St. George's Hall, June 6, 1873, and selections from his Mass in F at Her Majesty's Theatre, June 27, 1873.

His operas are ' Giovanni da Procida ' (Florence and Lucca, 1838) ; ' Don Desiderio ' (Pisa, 1839 ; Paris, 1858) ; ' Ruy Blas ' (Lucca, 1842); ' Bonifazio ' (Rome, 1844) ; ' I Lambertazzi ' (Florence, 1845) ; ' Malek Adel ' (Genoa, 1846); ' Esmeralda ' (Leghorn, 1847) ; ' La sposa d' Abido ' (Venice, 1847) ; ' Pierre de' Medicis ' (Paris, 1860) ; ' Au travers du mur ' (*ibid.* 1861) ; ' L'Aventurier ' (*ibid.* 1865) ; ' La Contessina ' (*ibid.* 1868).

[1] Buried at Chislehurst, Kent.    [2] Letter, Aug. 9, 1831.

His music evinces much melody and knowledge of the voice, considerable familiarity with stage effect, fluency and power of sustained writing — everything in short but genius and individuality. His popular ballad ' The Yeoman's Wedding Song' is still sometimes heard in England.

G. C.

PONS, José (b. Gerona, Catalonia, 1768 ; d. Valencia, 1818), Spanish musician. He studied under Balins, maestro de capilla at Cordoba. Pons was maestro de capilla of the cathedral of his native town, a post which he left for that at Valencia. He is distinguished for his VILLANCICOS (q.v.) for Christmas, which, in his time, came to resemble oratorios for voices with orchestra or organ. He wrote also Misereres for Holy Week. Eslava (Lira sacro - hispana, iv.) gives a Letrilla of his, ' O madre,' for 8 voices, and characterises him as the typical composer of the Catalan school as opposed to that of Valencia.

G. ; rev. J. B. T.

PONTE, LORENZO DA (b. Ceneda, Republic of Venice, Mar. 10, 1749 ; d. Aug. 17, 1838), Italian poet and author of the libretti of Mozart's ' Nozze di Figaro,' ' Don Giovanni ' and ' Così fan tutte,' was the son of a Jewish leather-merchant named Jeremia Conegliano ; his mother's maiden name was Rachel Pincherle ; his name until his fourteenth year Emmanuel Conegliano.

His precocious talents attracted the attention of the Bishop of Ceneda, Lorenzo da Ponte, who gave him his name when the family, which included two brothers, embraced Christianity and received baptism in the cathedral of Ceneda on Aug. 20, 1763. After five years of study in the seminary of Ceneda (probably with the priesthood as an object), he went to Venice, where he indulged in amorous escapades which compelled his departure from the city. He went to Treviso and taught rhetoric in the University, incidentally took part in political movements, lampooned an opponent in a sonnet, and was ordered out of the Republic. In Dresden, whither he turned his steps, he found no occupation for his talents, and journeyed on to Vienna. There, helped by Salieri, he received from Joseph II. the appointment of poet to the Imperial Theatre and Latin secretary. Good fortune brought him in contact with Mozart, who asked him to make an opera-book of Beaumarchais's ' Mariage de Figaro.' The great success of Mozart's opera on this theme led to further co-operation, and it was on Da Ponte's suggestion that ' Don Giovanni ' was undertaken, the prompting coming largely from the favour enjoyed at the time by Gazzaniga's opera on the same subject, from which Da Ponte made generous draughts—as a comparison of the libretti will show. Having incurred the ill-will of Leopold, Da Ponte was compelled to leave Vienna on

the death of Joseph II. He went to Trieste, where Leopold was sojourning, in the hope of effecting a reconciliation, but failed ; but there he met and married an Englishwoman, who was thenceforth fated to share his chequered fortunes. He obtained a letter recommending him to the interest of Marie Antoinette, but while journeying towards Paris learned of the imprisonment of the Queen and went to London instead. A year was spent in the British metropolis in idleness, and some time in Holland in a futile effort to establish an Italian theatre there. Again he turned his face toward London, and this time secured employment as poet to the Italian Opera and assistant to the manager Taylor. He took a part of Domenico Corri's shop [1] to sell Italian books, but soon ended in difficulties, and to escape his creditors fled to America, arriving in New York on June 4, 1805. His London sojourn had endured eight years, and his wife had preceded him to America carrying with her enough money to enable him to begin business in the New World as vendor of tobacco, drugs and liquors. Discouragement led him to try his fortune in Elizabethtown, N.J., in three months, but in a twelvemonth he failed there also, and came back to New York, where he took up the one form of activity which won him respect and modest emoluments ; he became a teacher of Italian language and literature. After eleven years the mercantile spirit prevailed with him again, and he ventured his savings in a distillery in Sunbury, Penn. Again he failed, and again he returned to New York and a professional career. He wrote his memoirs in three volumes, secured an appointment, which was little more than nominal, as professor of Italian literature in Columbia College, lectured on Italy, sold books to the College library, and enjoyed the friendship of some of New York's most eminent citizens and men of letters until his death, though his last years were spent in comparative poverty. When Manuel Garcia came to New York with the first Italian Opera Company which visited that city, Da Ponte attached himself to the troupe as poet, and was more or less concerned in subsequent operatic ventures during the next decade, but never to his own or anybody else's profit. Dr. J. W. Francis attended him in his last illness, and to him the poet, a day before his death, his leading passion inextinguishable, addressed a sonnet. Allegri's Miserere was sung at his funeral, and, say eyewitnesses, he was buried ' in the Roman Cemetery in Second-Avenue.' The Italians of the city resolved to rear a monument over his grave, but never did so, and the place of his burial is unmarked and unknown, like the grave of Mozart.

BIBL.—H. E. KREHBIEL, Music and Manners in the Classical Period ; Prof. MARCHESAN, University of Treviso, Della vita e delle opere di Lorenzo da Ponte (1900) ; Da Ponte's Letters to Casanova,

[1] 5 Pall Mall.    W. B. S.

*1790–93*, are printed in Pompeo Molmenti's *Carteggi Casanoviani*, Naples, 1918 (Collezione settecentesca) ; JOSEPH LOUIS RUSSO, *Lorenzo da Ponte, Poet and Adventurer*, pp. xviii, 166, New York, 1922 (Columbia University Studies in Romance, Philology and Literature) ; E. J. DENT, *Mozart's Operas*.

H. E. K.

PONTICELLO (Ital. for the bridge of a stringed instrument) is used chiefly in the term *sul ponticello*, indicating that a passage on the violin, viola or violoncello is to be played by crossing the strings with the bow close to the bridge. In this way the vibration of the string is partially stopped, and a sound of a strange, almost uncanny character is produced. It occurs in solo pieces as well as in concerted and orchestral music. See the opening scene, Act II. of ' Tristan und Isolde.'          P. D.

PONTIFICAL CHOIR, see SISTINE CHOIR.

POOLE, ELIZABETH (*b*. London, Apr. 5, 1820 ; *d*. Langley, Bucks, Jan. 14, 1906), a favourite English actress and mezzo-soprano singer. She made her first appearance in a pantomime at the Olympic Theatre in 1827, and continued for some years to play children's parts—Duke of York to Kean's Richard ; Albert to Macready's Tell ; Ariel, etc. In 1834 she came out in opera at Drury Lane as the Page in ' Gustavus ' ; in 1839 visited the United States and sang in ' Sonnambula ' and other operas ; in 1841 was engaged by Bunn for his English operas at Drury Lane. Here she sang many parts, especially Elvira in ' Don Giovanni,' with Malibran in Balfe's ' Maid of Artois,' and as Lazarillo in ' Maritana.' At the same time her ballads and songs were highly popular at concerts both in London and the provinces. Miss Poole appeared at the Philharmonic, June 15, 1846. Balfe wrote for her ' 'Tis gone, the past is all a dream,' which she introduced into ' The Bohemian Girl,' in which she played the Gipsy Queen. She was a leading singer in the operas brought out at the Surrey Theatre by Miss Romer in 1852, where she sang in ' The Daughter of the Regiment,' ' Huguenots,' etc., and was also much engaged by Charles Kean, F. Chatterton and German Reed. Miss Poole (then Mrs. Bacon) retired from public life in 1870. Her portrait is preserved in the collection of the Garrick Club. (See *Musical Herald*, Feb. 1, 1906.)          G.

POOLE, MISS, see DICKONS, MRS.

POPPER, DAVID (*b*. Prague, June 18, 1846 ; *d*. Aug. 7, 1913), violoncellist, received his musical education in the Conservatorium at Prague. He learnt the violoncello under Goltermann, and soon gave evidence of the possession of a remarkable talent.

In 1863 he made his first musical tour in Germany, and quickly rose to very high rank as a player. In the course of the journey he met von Bülow, who was charmed with his playing, performed with him in public, and induced Prince Hohenzollern to make him his Kammervirtuos. Popper afterwards extended his tour to Holland, Switzerland and England. In 1867 he played for the first time in Vienna, where he was made first solo-player at the Hofoper, a post, however, which he resigned after a few years, that he might continue his concert tours on a great scale. His tone was large and full of sentiment, his execution highly finished and his style classical. His compositions were suited to his instrument, and are recognised as such by violoncello-players.          C. F. P.

Early in 1872 Popper married Sophie MENTER ; the marriage was dissolved in 1886. He reappeared in England at a concert at the Crystal Palace on Nov. 10, 1891, and played one movement of his violoncello concerto in C minor with orchestra. He performed at the Popular Concerts, St. James's Hall, for the first time on Nov. 21, 1891. On Nov. 25, 1891, he gave a violoncello recital at St. James's Hall, when he played his ' Requiem ' for three violoncellos, with Delsart and Howell. In 1896 he accepted the post of professor at the Royal Conservatoire in Budapest.          E. H.-A.

POPULAR CONCERTS, THE. This unique institution, more familiarly known as the Monday and Saturday ' Pops,' owed its origin to some miscellaneous concerts given in the early days of the old St. James's Hall, which stood at the back of the Quadrant between Regent Street and Piccadilly. A preliminary series of three concerts, organised by the promoters of the building, with Messrs. Chappell & Co. at their head, took place during the ' Cattle Show Week ' in Dec. 1858, under the direction of Mr. (afterwards Sir) Julius Benedict, and resulted in a loss. It was followed by four more of a similar nature, which were announced as ' Monday Popular Concerts ' ; these proved rather more successful. Then, at the suggestion of James W. Davison, the critic of *The Times*, it was decided to change the character of the concerts and restrict them entirely to ' classical ' music, of which there had been no regular performances in London down to that time such as would bring chamber music within the reach of the general public. The direction of the undertaking was assumed by Arthur CHAPPELL (*q.v.*), and retained by him throughout the 40 years of its existence ; while during the greater part of that period the well-known sixpenny analytical programmes, which formed a conspicuous element in the educative influence of these concerts, were written by Davison—after him by Joseph Bennett. Thus the idea was ' to collect a permanent audience from the lovers of music resident in London and the suburbs,' and, *inter alia*, help to popularise the new hall, which was as yet far from paying its way. With these objects in view it was decided to engage only artists of the highest standing to perform the best music ; and the first six concerts were devoted in turn to a Mendelssohn night, a Mozart night, a Haydn and Weber night, a Beethoven night, a second Mozart night, and a second Beethoven night.

The 'new series of entertainments,' as it was officially described, was started on Feb. 14, 1859, with a programme that included vocal items, sung by Santley, and two organ solos, played by Dr. Edward J. Hopkins. Charles Hallé was the pianist and Benedict the accompanist. The members of the quartet on this occasion were Henri Wieniawski, Louis Ries, C. W. Doyle and Alfredo Piatti; and of these Ries and Piatti retained their respective posts of second violin and violoncello practically for the entire duration of the enterprise—to the great advantage of the ensemble and its unity of artistic spirit. The success of the opening season was in the highest degree encouraging, the audiences becoming more numerous each week; while to the above masters were added compositions by Bach and Handel, including four organ solos played by W. T. Best. There was also one entirely English programme which comprised works by G. A. Macfarren, G. F. Pinto, E. J. Loder and Sterndale Bennett. Altogether fourteen concerts were given between Feb. 14 and June 27, when the season ended. After this excellent beginning there was every justification for lengthening the period of the subscription by starting in the late autumn and concluding at about Easter, which thenceforward became the regular practice. Furthermore, in 1865 the Saturday 'Pops' were started as an occasional supplementary series, and from 1876 they alternated every week with the Monday concerts. The 1000th concert took place on Apr. 4, 1887, while some 400 more concerts were added to this remarkable total during the remaining eleven years that the 'Pops' continued to be given. Their existence was practically coeval with that of the building which gave them birth.

In assessing the just value of these incomparable concerts, as the medium whereby the soul of the English metropolis was awakened to the beauty and meaning of chamber music in its noblest forms, it is essential to recognise above all two things: first, the lofty standard that was maintained throughout in the choice and the interpretation of those works of the great masters, living as well as dead, which had hitherto been as a 'sealed book' to the music-loving community; and, secondly, the unstinted labour and devotion of the distinguished artists who appeared year after year—some with unfailing regularity, others during their brief annual visits to this country—ever associating themselves more conspicuously with their splendid tasks and endearing themselves more closely to an intelligent, grateful and affectionate public. Amid such unprecedented conditions it was no wonder that the warmest personal ties became established

between those who performed and those who listened. And the latter, it should be recalled, included not only the new generation of amateurs who frequented the shilling gallery and three-shilling balcony, but, among the habitués of the five-shilling stalls, some of the most prominent poets, painters and *littérateurs* of the Victorian era.

During the greater part of each season the quartet was led by the illustrious violinist Joseph JOACHIM, the presiding genius of the 'Pops,' whose name was to be associated with their history from the opening year, when he introduced the Rasoumowsky quartets of Beethoven and the Chaconne of Bach. No less worthy of record was the constant co-operation of the great Italian violoncellist Alfredo PIATTI, and of that admirable violinist Wilhelmina Norman-NERUDA (Lady Hallé), to both of whom the public was devotedly attached. With Louis Ries invariably at the second violin desk, the quartet was completed by one of the four excellent viola-players C. W. Doyle, Ludwig Straus, J. B. Zerbini and Benoît Hollander. Foremost among the many gifted pianists who used to appear was Mme. Clara Schumann, the ideal exponent of the works of the romantic school in general and of her husband's in particular; and, when her distinguished career had closed, its inestimable example was worthily carried on by her brilliant pupils, Fanny Davies, Leonard Borwick, N. Janotha and Ilona Eibenschütz, all of whom made their London débuts at these concerts. Invaluable in the same sense were the constant labours of pianists such as Charles Hallé, Ernst Pauer, Agnes Zimmermann and Clotilde Kleeberg, not to mention the occasional appearances of Anton Rubinstein, Hans von Bülow, Edward Grieg and Ignaz Paderewski. So again the vocal music, usually restricted to a couple of items in each programme, was almost invariably of the finest type and contributed by the best concert-singers of the day. The admirable work of the two principal accompanists, Sir Julius Benedict and Henry R. Bird, also deserves mention.

The repertory of the Popular Concerts contained some 1050 works of every calibre. Oddly enough, it did not include a single composition by Purcell, but, on the other hand, comprised chamber works by several contemporary English composers—Sterndale Bennett, Stanford, Hubert Parry and Mackenzie. The following alphabetical list shows the number of works drawn upon from each of the 16 most 'popular' composers: Bach, 66; Beethoven, 99; Brahms, 46; Chopin, 59; Dvořák, 13; Grieg, 13; Handel, 16; Haydn, 58; Mendelssohn, 64; Mozart, 66; Rubinstein, 14; Scarlatti, 22; Schubert, 44; Schumann, 79; Spohr, 44; and Weber, 12. The last of the long series of concerts came with the termination of the season of 1897–98. For some time a few concerts were given annually in the spring by Joachim with the members of his Berlin quartet. An attempt at revival was also made by Johann Kruse in 1903–04; but before the century was much older St. James's Hall, and with it the well-loved 'Pops,' had ceased to be more than a memory.  H. K.

PORDENON, MARCO ANTONIO (b. Padua), was maestro di cappella at S. Marco, Pordenone, Lombardy, in 1578. In 1580 he no longer retained that title. He composed 5 books of madrigals a 5 v. and one book a 4 v., published by Gardano, Venice, between 1564 and 1580.

E. v. d. s.

PORPORA, NICCOLA,[1] or NICCOLO, ANTONIO (b. Naples, Aug. 19, 1686; d. there, 1767), composer and celebrated teacher of singing. His father, a bookseller with a numerous family, obtained admission for him at a very early age to the Conservatorio of S. M. di Loreto, where he received instruction from Padre Gaetano of Perugia (apparently confused with Gaetano Greco by Florimo) and Francesco Mancini, former pupils of the same school. His first opera was 'Basilio, re di Oriente,' written for the theatre 'de' Fiorentini.' On the title-page of this work he styles himself 'maestro di cappella to the Portuguese Ambassador.' The opera of 'Berenice,' written in 1710 for the Capranica theatre at Rome, attracted the notice and elicited the commendation of Handel. It was followed by 'Flavio Anicio Olibrio' (1711); by several masses, motets and other compositions for the Church; by 'Faramondo' (1719) and 'Eumene' (1721), on the title-page of which last work he calls himself 'Virtuoso to the Prince of Hesse Darmstadt.' Having been appointed master of the Conservatorio of San Onofrio, he wrote for it an oratorio, 'La martiria di Santa Eugenia,' which had much success on its first performance there in 1721. In 1723 he wrote for the wedding of Prince Montemiletto a cantata, in which Farinelli sang. He had, before this time, established the school for singing whence issued those wonderful pupils who have made their master's name famous. After 'L' Imeneo' came 'Amare per regnare' and 'Semiramide' (1724) (according to Villarosa); and a MS. in the Conservatoire of Paris gives evidence of another opera, 'Adelaida,' belonging to 1723 and performed at Rome. In 1724 Hasse arrived at Naples with the avowed intention of becoming Porpora's pupil. After a short trial, however, he deserted this master in favour of Alessandro Scarlatti, a slight which Porpora never forgave, and for which, in later years, he had abundant opportunity of revenging himself on HASSE (q.v.).

[1] In his autographs Niccola, but on the title-pages of works published by himself, and in contemporary MS. copies, Niccolo.

Porpora's natural gifts were united to an extremely restless, changeable disposition. He seems never to have remained very long in one place, and the dates of many events in his life are uncertain. It appears that in 1725 he set off for Vienna, but he must have stopped at Venice on his way, as there is evidence to show that he was appointed to the mastership of one of the four great singing-schools for girls there, that of La Pietà. He hoped to get a hearing for some of his music at Vienna, but the Emperor Charles VI. disliked his florid style and profuse employment of vocal ornament, and gave him no encouragement to remain. He therefore returned as far as Venice, where he produced his opera 'Siface' in 1726, and was appointed master to another of the schools above-mentioned, that of the Incurabili. For his pupils at this institution he wrote the vocal cantatas, twelve of which he published in London in 1735, and which are among his best compositions.

In 1728 he set out for Dresden, where the Electoral Princess, Marie Antoinette, was eager to receive instruction from the famous maestro. On the way thither he revisited Vienna, hoping for a chance of effacing the unfavourable impression he had formerly made; but the Emperor's prejudice against him was so strong, and carried so much weight, as to make it seem probable that he would once more find nothing to do. He found a friend, however, in the Venetian ambassador, who not only received him under his own roof but succeeded in obtaining for him an Imperial commission to write an oratorio, accompanied by a hint to be sparing in the use of trills and flourishes. Accordingly, when the Emperor came to hear the work rehearsed, he was charmed at finding it quite simple and unadorned in style. Only at the end a little surprise was reserved for him. The theme of the concluding fugue began by four ascending notes, with a trill on each. The strange effect of this series of trills was increased as each part entered, and in the final stretto became farcical outright. The Emperor's gravity could not stand it; he laughed convulsively, but forgave the audacious composer and paid him well for his work. The name of this oratorio is lost.

Porpora was warmly received at Dresden, where he was specially patronised by his pupil the Electoral Princess, to whom he taught not only singing but composition. So it happened that when Hasse, with his wife Faustina, appeared on the scene in 1730, he found his old master, who had never forgiven his pupil's defection, in possession of the field. A great rivalry ensued, the public being divided between the two maestri, who themselves lost no opportunity of exchanging offices anything but friendly. The erratic Porpora, however, did not by any means spend his whole time in the Saxon capital. Early in 1729 he had produced (or revived) ' Semiramide riconosciuta ' at Venice, and in April of the same year had obtained leave of absence in order to go to London, there to undertake the direction of the opera-house established in opposition to that presided over by HANDEL (*q.v.*). The speculation was a failure, and both houses suffered serious losses. Porpora never was popular in England as a composer, and even the presence of Senesino among his company failed to ensure its success, until, during a sojourn in Dresden, he succeeded in engaging the great Farinelli, who appeared in London in 1734, with Senesino and Signora Cuzzoni, and saved the house. Porpora got his Dresden engagement cancelled in order to remain in London, but that he must have paid several visits to Venice is certain, as ' Mitridate ' was written there in 1730, and ' Annibale ' was produced there in 1731. It seems that he finally quitted England in 1737, at the end of Farinelli's third and last season in that country, and that he established himself again at Venice; for on the title-page of a MS. in the Conservatoire at Paris, dated 1744, he is described as director of the Ospedaletto school of music there. About 1745 he once more went to Vienna, this time in the suite of the Venetian ambassador, Correr. During a sojourn there of some years he published in 1754 a set of twelve sonatas for violin, with figured bass, one of his most esteemed compositions, of which he says in the dedicatory epistle that they are written ' in the diatonic, chromatic and enharmonic styles,' describing himself as now Kapellmeister to the King of Poland. At this time he became acquainted with the young Haydn, whom he helped with instruction and advice.

He returned to Naples, his native town, between 1755 and 1760. Gazzaniga, his pupil, in a biographical notice, says it was in 1759, and that in 1760 he succeeded Abos as maestro di cappella of the cathedral of Naples and of the Conservatorio of San Onofrio. In the same year his last opera, ' Camilla,' was re-presented, with no success. After that he wrote nothing but one or two pieces for the Church. He had outlived his reputation as a composer. His latest years were passed in extreme indigence, a fact hard to reconcile with that of his holding the double appointment named above, but one which is vouched for by contemporary writers and by Villarosa, who says that he died of pleurisy in 1767 : Gazzaniga affirms that his death was the result of an injury to his leg in 1766. Both may be true : it is at least certain that a subscription was raised among the musicians of the town to defray the expenses of the *maestro's* burial.

Besides six oratorios and numerous masses,

thirty-three operas of Porpora's are mentioned by Florimo and twenty-six are in the list of extant works in *Q.-L.* They may have been popular with singers as showing off what was possible in the way of execution, but he was devoid of dramatic genius in composition. Nothing can be more tedious than to read through an opera of his, where one conventional, florid air succeeds another, often with no change of key and with little change of time ; here and there a stray chorus of the most meagre description. When not writing for the stage he achieved better things. His cantatas for a single voice, twelve of which were published in London in 1735, have merit and elevation of style, and the same is asserted of the sonatas, published at Vienna, for violin with bass. The ' six free fugues ' for clavichord (first published by Clementi in his *Practical Harmony*, afterwards by Farrenc in the first number of the *Trésor des pianistes*) will repay attention. Specimens of his violin music will be found in Choron's *Principes*, David's *Hohe Schule* and Alard's *Maîtres classiques* ; and six Latin duets on the Passion (works of remarkable beauty) and some Solfeggi were edited by Nava and published by Breitkopf.

He was the greatest singing-master that ever lived. No singers, before or since, have sung like his pupils. This is made certain by the universal contemporary testimony as to their powers, by the music which was written for them and which they performed, and by the fact that such relics of a grand pure style of vocalisation as remain to us now, have been handed down in direct succession from these artists. He has left us no written account of his manner of teaching, and such *solfeggi* of his as we possess differ only from those of his contemporaries by being perhaps more exclusively directed than others are towards the development of *flexibility* in the vocal organ. In musical interest they are inferior to those of Scarlatti and Leo, and to some of those of Hasse. There is little difference between them and his songs, which are for the most part only so many *solfeggi*. The probability is that he had no peculiar method of his own, but that he was one of those artists whose grand secret lies in their own personality. To a profound knowledge of the human voice in its every peculiarity, and an intuitive sympathy with singers, he must have united that innate capacity of imposing his own will on others which is a form of genius. Powerful indeed must have been the influence that could keep a singer (as he is said to have kept Caffarelli) for five years to one sheet of exercises. And if we are inclined to think that when Caffarelli was dismissed with the words ' You may go, you are the greatest singer in Europe,' there must still have been a good deal for him to learn which that sheet of exercises could not teach him, still, no *mechanical* difficulty then stood between him and the acquisition of these qualities ; the instrument was perfect.

Lists of his works are to be found in *Q.-L.*, in Villarosa's notice of his life, and in those by Farrenc (*Trésor des pianistes*, i.), in *Fétis*, and in Florimo's *Cenno storico sulla scuola di Napoli*, 1869, pp. 376-80.          F. A. M.

PORSILE, GIUSEPPE (*b.* Naples, *c.* 1672 ; *d.* Vienna, May 29, 1750), at first vice-maestro di cappella at Naples, then maestro di cappella to Charles III. at Barcelona until 1711 ; singing-master at the court of the Empress Amalia at Vienna, and composer to the Viennese Imperial court, 1720 to Apr. 1, 1740. He composed 12 oratorios, 6 operas, 13 serenades and festival plays, cantatas, canzonets, 5 partitas for 2 vlns., v'cl. and Bc., Divertimento *a* 3, and solo for flute and bass (*Riemann* ; *Q.-L.*).

PORT, a term formerly in use in Scotland to denominate a 'Lesson,' or more properly a musical composition for an instrument, principally, it appears, the harp. 'Rory Dall's Port' (*i.e.* Blind Rory or Roderick's composition) is the best-known survival. It was a piece associated with the blind harper above-named, in the 17th century, but in more modern times adapted to Burns's song, 'Ae fond kiss and then we sever.' There are several 'Ports' in the Straloch Lute MS., 1627, including 'Jean Lindsay's Port' ; and the 17th-century Skene MS. has 'Port Ballangowne.' Tytler, the writer of a famous 18th-century *Dissertation on Scotish Music*, speaks of it as a particular *type* of composition, and says that 'every great family had its "Port" named after the family.'          F. K.

PORTA, COSTANZO (*b.* Cremona, *c.* 1530 ; *d.* Padua, May 26, 1601), received his musical training under Adrian Willaert at Venice. He became a Minorite friar, when exactly we are not told. From 1552–64 he was choirmaster at Osimo, near Ancona. On Dec. 16, 1564, he was elected choirmaster to the Cappella Antoniana, the church of his Order, at Padua, the same church with which, in later days, Tartini's violin performances were associated. From a Paduan document, 'Arca del Santo,' Proske quotes two entries : one to the effect that at Whitsuntide 1565 Porta was permitted to go to Florence to direct the music at the General Chapter of the Minorite Order, another stating that, on account of his great reputation as a musician and his other virtues, he was assigned a servant. In 1567 he was called to be choirmaster of the cathedral of Ravenna, Proske says at the instance of the vicar-general of his Order, better known afterwards as Pope Sixtus V., and again at his instance in 1575 accepted a similar position at the Casa Santa of Loreto. We learn in 1585 that he had returned to Padua, but it is only in 1595 that he was definitely reappointed choirmaster to the

Basilica of St. Antony, in which position he remained till his death in 1601.

Porta was recognised as one of the most learned musicians of the time, versed in the deepest mysteries of canon and counterpoint. His countryman Francesco Arisio in *Cremona literata* designates him as 'musicorum omnium praeter invidiam princeps.' Padre Martini and Dr. Burney after him quote as an example of Porta's contrapuntal ingenuity his motet *a* 7, 'Diffusa est gratia,' in which four voices are in canon, two *per motum rectum* and two *per motum contrarium*. Leichtentritt [1] considers that this motet unites in a peculiar way the highest learning of the Netherlands with a fine Italian sense of euphony. Hawkins quotes from Artusi (*Delle imperfettioni della modern musica*, 1600) a motet *a* 4, 'Vobis datum est,' which may be equally well sung backwards upside down with change of clefs. Porta's general style Proske characterises as one of great seriousness and solidity. For an Italian he seems to have imbibed from his Flemish master, Willaert, almost too much of Flemish severity, while on the other hand Willaert himself, by his stay in Venice, and especially in his madrigals and villote, gained much of Italian softness and grace. Porta's first publications appeared contemporaneously with those of Lassus and Palestrina : in 1555 a First Book of Motets *a* 5 and a First Book of Madrigals *a* 4 ; in 1559 a First Book of Motets *a* 4 with one of Madrigals *a* 5. It may seem strange that a Minorite friar should occupy himself with madrigals as well as motets, but the madrigal was then the school for the motet, and Porta had also considerable distinction as a madrigalist. From the First Book of Motets *a* 4 Proske has reprinted three in 'Musica divina,' tom. ii. In 1566 Claudio Merulo da Corregio, himself a composer of merit, set up a music-printing press in Venice, and among his first publications in that year was a work by Porta bearing the title 'Quinque vocum Musica in Introitus Missarum quae in diebus Dominicis toto anno celebrantur juxta ritum sanctae Romanae ecclesiae.' Merulo writes of Porta as 'his very dear friend, and one with few equals in his profession,' and apparently published this work for Porta on his own initiative, since it is described as 'nunc primum a Claudio Correggiate in lucem edita.' It was dedicated to the Chapter of St. Antony's Basilica, and consists of 37 contrapuntal settings of the plain-song Introits for the Sundays from the Roman Gradual. It was followed in 1588 by a similar series of Introits for the Saints' Days, 55 in number. In 1571 was published his First Book of Motets *a* 6, and in 1573 a Third Book of Madrigals *a* 5. No mention is made in *Q.-L.* of a Second Book of Madrigals *a* 5, which thus appears to be lost.

[1] *Geschichte der Motette*, p. 144.

While Porta was still at Ravenna in 1575, and before he left for his new appointment at Loreto, he was specially urged by the Archbishop, Cardinal Giulio Feltrio da Rovere, to compose some masses which should both have the merit of brevity and in which the text should be so declaimed as to be easily followed by the hearers. Porta was slow in complying with this request, and it was not till 1578 that he published his 'Missarum liber primus,' containing 7 *a* 4, 2 *a* 5 and 3 *a* 6, which he dedicated to the Archbishop. In the dedication he explains why he hesitated to attempt this task. 'I thought,' he writes, 'it behoved me rather to guard from an unjust oblivion the works which the great composers have left to posterity, so apt as they are to their purpose, so full of beauty, delight and charm.' All this is but the expression of an undue modesty by a Minorite friar, but inferences have been drawn from it which are not warranted by the language itself or by the circumstances of the case. Porta makes no reference to any express prohibition of the older masses by the Council of Trent or other ecclesiastical authority, as there was none such (see PALESTRINA), but there was a general movement of the time, and especially in the north of Italy, with some encouragement from ecclesiastical authority, in favour of the Missa Brevis, with the words clearly declaimed, particularly in the Gloria and Credo. Carlo Borromeo, the famous Archbishop of Milan, seems to have led the way in the encouragement of this movement by his commission to Vincenzo Ruffo sometime before 1570 to compose masses of this kind.[1] These masses of Ruffo were even expressly designated in later editions as 'Missae Borromeae.' Another distinguished composer, Marcantonio Ingegneri of Cremona, followed in the same direction by publishing in 1573 a book of masses 3 *a* 5 and 1 *a* 8,[2] all very short with the text syllabically declaimed. Porta, with his love for imitative polyphony, may have disliked the new style when carried out to an extreme as in Ruffo and Ingegneri, but there was also a middle way to be found, as in masses by Croce and Spontone,[3] and if there had been any prohibition by ecclesiastical authority of the longer very elaborate masses, there was all the more reason for composers like Porta to provide new compositions that would satisfy reasonable requirements.

His next published work in 1580 bears the title ' Liber quinquaginta duorum motettorum 4, 5, 6, 7 et 8 voc. nunc tandem in lucem prodeuntium.' These last words would also lead us to infer that in the opinion of his admirers Porta himself was never too eager in

[1] See extracts from Ruffo's masses in Torchi, *L' arte musicale d' Italia*, vol. i.
[2] One of these masses bears the title ' Susanne un jour,' and another ' Gustate et videte,' and would thus seem to be based on works of Orlando Lasso.
[3] See masses by Croce published by Haberl, and one by Spontone in Torchi, *L' arte musicale d' Italia*, vol. ii.

the publication of his works. In 1583 Leonard Lechner published at Nuremberg a miscellaneous collection of motets (' Harmoniae miscellae '), including three by Porta, one of which, ' Oravi Dominum Deum ' *a* 6, was reprinted by Dehn in his ' Sammlung älterer Musik,' 1837. In 1585 Porta dedicated to Pope Sixtus V. his Third Book of Motets *a* 6, which Proske specially singles out as showing Porta to be a master of real genius over and above his wonderful mastery of contrapuntal technique. One piece from this work, ' Ecce sacerdos magnus,' is given in the continuation of the ' Musica divina.' One might imagine this motet to have been intended as an act of homage to Sixtus V., as Palestrina's Mass with the same title to Julius III. In the same year appeared his Fourth Book of Madrigals *a* 5, but they are described as ' novamente da Marsilio Christoffori raccolti.' Porta's name also appears frequently about this time in the miscellaneous madrigal collections got up by Venetian and other publishers under such titles as ' Li amorosi ardori,' ' I lieti amanti,' ' Sdegnosi ardori,' ' Madrigali pastorali,' etc. The collection entitled ' Sdegnosi ardori ' is peculiar as consisting of 31 settings of the same lines, ' Ardo si, ma non t' amo,' by about as many different composers. Porta's setting is reproduced in Kiesewetter's ' Schicksale des weltlichen Gesanges,' 1844. He was also one of the contributors to the more famous collection ' Il trionfo di Dori,' 1592, and in this year, too, joined with Asola and other North Italian masters in the great tribute of homage to Palestrina as the acknowledged head of their profession by the dedication to him of their collective work, entitled ' Psalmodia vespertina cum cantico B. Virginis.' On its title-page this work bears the inscription, ' ad celeberrimum ac praestantissimum in arte musica Coryphaeum D. Jo. Petrum Aloysium Praenestinum.' Posthumous publications of Porta's works are ' Hymnodia sacra totius per anni circulum ' *a* 4, 44 nos., 1602, and ' Psalmodia vespertina cum 4 canticis B.V.' *a* 8, 1605. From this latter work Torchi, in ' *L' arte musicale d' Italia*,' vol. i., has reprinted ' Lauda Deum tuum ' *a* 8, and from other sources a ' Pater noster ' *a* 6, and two madrigals *a* 4. Other works by Porta are in the older collections of Padre Martini and Paolucci, but mainly as illustrations of contrapuntal technique.                    J. R. M.

PORTA, ERCOLE (*b.* Bologna), organist at the college of S. Giovanni, Persicetto, 1609. He composed between 1609–26 3 books of sacred vocal compositions (*concerti*) with a ' Symphonie ' for 2 instruments, and 3 or more books of secular songs. Neither titles nor number of these, as given by *Riemann, Q.-L.*, Mendel and Fétis, agree, thus making their actual number doubtful. The ' Vagha ghirlanda' contains a sonata for violin, cornetto and 2 trombones. 　　　　　E. v. d. s.

PORTA, FRANCESCO DELLA (b. Monza, c. 1590; d. Milan, Jan. 1666), organist and church composer. The date of his birth is conjectured from his having published in 1619 a collection of 'Villanelle a 1, 2, e 3 voci, accommodate per qualsivoglio stromento' (Rome, Robletti). This fact seems to confute Fétis and Mendel, who place his birth in the beginning of the 17th century. His master was Ripalta, organist of Monza, and he became organist and maestro di cappella of more than one church in Milan. He published Salmi da cappella (1657), motets (1645, 1648, 1651), ricercari, etc., and was one of the first composers to make practical use of the basso continuo. 　　　　　F. G.

PORTA, GIOVANNI (b. Venice, c. 1690; d. Munich, Sept. 1755), was in London from 1720–36, where he produced several operas. Burney, who praises his work, says that he was long in the service of Cardinal Ottoboni. From 1737 to his death he was court Kapellmeister at Munich. He composed 32 operas and a considerable number of masses; also other church music (*Riemann*; *Q.-L.*).

PORTAMENTO (Fr. *port de voix*), a gradual 'carrying' of the sound or voice with extreme smoothness from one note to another,' which can only be really executed by the voice or by a bowed instrument, though the trombone alone among brass instruments can be used in this way to a limited extent. It is of frequent occurrence as a musical direction in vocal music or in that for stringed instruments, and also appears in music for keyed instruments. In old music one of the *agréments* (see ORNAMENTS) was so called. (See SHIFT.) 　　　M.

PORTATIVE ORGAN, see POSITIVE ORGAN.

PORT DE VOIX, an *agrément* of the French school. The term is also sometimes used to denote the Coulé. (See ORNAMENTS.)

PORTER, (1) SAMUEL (b. Norwich, 1733; d. Canterbury, Dec. 11, 1810), was a chorister at St. Paul's Cathedral, and a pupil of Dr. Greene. In 1757 he was elected organist of Canterbury Cathedral. In 1803 he resigned in favour of Highmore Skeats, organist of Salisbury Cathedral. He was buried in the cloisters at Canterbury. A volume of his 'Cathedral Music,' containing two services, five anthems, a Sanctus, Kyrie, suffrages and nine chants, with his portrait on the title, was published by his son, (2) Rev. WILLIAM JAMES PORTER, head master of the College School, Worcester, who also published two anthems and four chants of his own composition, on the title-page of which he is described as 'of the King's School, Canterbury.' 　　　W. H. H.

PORTER, WALTER (b. circa 1595; d. Nov., 1659), 'an English pupil of Monteverdi,'[1] son

[1] So described by Arkwright in an interesting account of Porter in *Mus. Ant.* iv. 236.

of Henry Porter, Mus.B. Oxon. 1600, was sworn gentleman of the Chapel Royal without pay, Jan. 5, 1616, 'for the next place that should fall void by the death of any tenor'; a contingency which happened on Jan. 27, 1617, in the person of Peter Wright, and Porter was sworn in his place on Feb. 1. In 1632 he published

'Madrigales and Ayres of two, three, foure and five voyces, with the continued bass, with Toccatos, Sinfonias and Rittornelles to them after the manner of Consort Musique. To be performed with the Harpsechord, Lutes, Theorbos, Basse-Violl, two Violins or two Viols.'

This book is somewhat similar in character to that of Martin PEERSON (*q.v.*), and like Peerson Porter stands between the madrigalists and the Restoration composers. But he has an individual style of his own, and a special feature of it is the use of rapidly reiterated notes upon a single syllable of the words. This device he undoubtedly borrowed from Monteverdi, whose pupil he was. Porter explains the purpose of it in his 'address to the practicioner' at the beginning of the volume : 'In the Songs which are set forth with Division where you find many Notes in a place after this manner  in rule or space they are set to express the *Trillo*' (see ORNAMENTS, VOCAL). The following is an example of this in Porter's work :

Ye　　that ful - - fil, ful - fil His com-

- mand - ment

The only known copy of this book was formerly in the Christie-Miller collection at Burnham Court and is now in the British Museum.

Both Hawkins and Burney mention a collection bearing the title of

'Ayres and Madrigals for two, three, four and five voices, with a thorough bass for the organ or Theorbo Lute, the Italian way,'

dated 1639, which may probably have been a second edition of the same work. In 1639 Porter was appointed master of the choristers of Westminster Abbey. After losing both his places on the suppression of the choral service in 1644, he found a patron in Sir Edward Spencer. In 1657 he published

'Mottets of Two Voyces for Treble or Tenor and Bass with the Continued Bass or Score. To be performed to an Organ, Harpsycon, Lute or Bass-viol.'

Porter was buried at St. Margaret's Church, Westminster, Nov. 30, 1659. His 'Divine Hymns,' advertised by Playford in 1664, was perhaps identical with 'The Psalms of George Sandys set to Music for two Voyces with a Thorough-bass for the Organ,' which was published about 1671.

　　　　W. H. H. ; with addns. E. H. F.

PORTIMARO, FRANCESCO (b. Padua). In 1560 he was master of the academy at Padua ; in 1568 he was in the service of Cardinal Luigi d' Este. He composed 3 books of motets, and 6 books of madrigals and 'Vergini' (*Q.-L.*).

PORTMAN, RICHARD (*d.* Nov. 1659 [1]), English organist and composer, chiefly of church music. A pupil of Orlando Gibbons, he succeeded Thomas Day as organist of Westminster Abbey in 1633. He was still organist there in 1648 (*Westminster Abbey Records*), and Anthony Wood says he was buried in the Abbey cloisters. When, in 1644, the Protectorate Government suppressed all choral services, Portman became a teacher, and Playford, in a list of the principal London teachers during the Commonwealth, puts Portman first among those 'for Organ or Virginall.' A petition to Cromwell's Council of State, dated Feb. 29, 1656, refers to Portman as 'recently deceased' (Davey, *Hist. Eng. Mus.*). In 1645 Portman published a book of meditations under the title :

'The Soules Life, exercising itself in the sweet Fields of Divine Meditation, collected for the comfort thereof, in these sad days of distraction.'

This was reissued by Playford in 1660, with some alterations and additions. A saraband for harpsichord by Portman is in Ch. Ch. 1177. His anthem, 'How many hired servants,' is from his 'Dialogue of the Prodigal Son,' a miniature cantata with solos by the prodigal, his father and the elder son, and two sections for chorus.

### SERVICES

Whole Service (T.D. : B. ; K. ; C. . M. ; N.D.). Ch. Ch. 1002. Score. Ch. Ch. 1012. Bass part only.
Service in G maj. (V. ; T.D. ; B. ; K. ; C. ; M. ; N.D.) ; PH. ; Yk. ; Harl. 7337/142b. Score.
Evening Service (M. ; N.D.). Ch. Ch. 440. Tenor part only.

### ANTHEMS

Behold, how good and joyful. Durh. ; B.M. Add. MSS. 30,478-9. Tenor cantoris part only.
How many hired servants. Harl. 6346/43. Words only.
I will always give thanks. Durh. ; B.M. Add. MSS. 30,478-9. Tenor cantoris part only.
Lord, who shall dwell. PH. ; R.C.M. 1051. Bassus decani part only.
Most gratious God. Harl. 6346/77. Words only.
O God, my heart is ready. PH.
O God, wherefore art Thou absent. Harl. 6346/85. Words only.
O Lambe of God. Harl. 6346/15. Words only.
O Lord God of my salvation. Harl. 6346/42. Words only.
O sing unto the Lord. Harl. 6346/88. Words only.
Rejoice in the Lord. Tenb. OB/476 ; R.C.M. Ia. 1 ; Ch. Ch. 49. Score.
Save me, O God. Durh. ; B.M. Add. MSS. 30,478-9. Tenor cantoris part only.
The Heavens declare the glory of God. Tenb. OB/477 ; Harl. 6346/71b. Words only.

*Q.-L.* refers to an anthem and a service in Ely Cathedral, and to an anthem in Gloucester Cathedral.        J. M<sup>K</sup>.

PORTUGAL (PORTOGALLO), (1) MARCOS ANTONIO DA FONSECA (*b.* Lisbon, Mar. 24, 1762 ; *d.* Rio de Janeiro, Feb. 7, 1830), Portuguese operatic composer. His real name was MARCOS ANTONIO, son of Manuel Antonio da Ascenção (or Assumpção). He adopted the high-sounding ' da Fonseca Portugal ' in 1785, at the time of his first appointment, taking the name from a Captain José Correia da Fonseca Portugal who had befriended his parents. He was educated at the Seminario Patriarchal at Lisbon, and had music lessons from João de Sousa Carvalho. There is no trace of the teacher ' Orao,' who is said to have taught him

[1] West's *Cath. Org.*

counterpoint ; and the Italian singer Borselli, who is said to have given him singing lessons, may have been BERSELLI (*q.v.*). There is no evidence, either, that he was ever accompanist at the opera in Madrid, or that the Portuguese Ambassador there sent him to Italy in 1787. On his election to the brotherhood of S. Cecilia at Lisbon in 1783, he is described as plain Marcos Antonio, cantor and organist at the Patriarchal Seminary, where he had been to school. The new name first appears in 1785, with his appointment as conductor at the Salitre Theatre ; in July 1787 he was at Lisbon, where he produced a ' Licença pastoril ' (MS. score, Bibl. da Ajuda, Lisbon) for the birthday of the Princess D. Maria Benedicta ; and between 1785 and 1792 he produced five Portuguese comic operas which brought him great popularity, especially ' A Castanheira ' (The Chestnut-seller). He also contributed popular drawing-room airs to the *Journal de Modinhas*, founded in 1790. In 1792 he went to Naples. ' L' Eroe cinese ' was produced at Florence in 1793, and he composed opera after opera with great success at Parma, Rome, Venice and Milan. One of the most successful was ' La confusione nata dalla somiglianza, ossia i Gobbi,' produced in Italian at Dresden in 1793, also performed in German. ' Demofoönte ' was performed in 1794 at Milan, and ' La vedova raggiratrice ' in Florence. In 1796 he went back to Italy, where his ' Zulema ' (Florence), ' L' inganno poco dura ' (Naples) and ' La donna di genio volubile ' (Venice) were played with success. In 1797 his ' Ritorno di Serse ' was given at Florence, and two farces at Venice ; the opera ' Fernando nel Messico,' written for Mrs. Billington and performed at Rome in 1798, was described by Fétis as the composer's *chef-d'œuvre*. Two more operas, ' Alceste ' and ' Le nozze di Figaro,' were played at Venice in 1799. He returned in 1800 to Portugal, where he became director of the San Carlos theatre, and maestro di cappella to the King. In the autumn of 1800 his ' Adrasto ' was played at the San Carlos theatre, and ' La Monte di Semiramide ' in 1801 ; ' Zaira ' and ' Il trionfo di Clelia ' in 1802 ; ' Sofonisba,' at Catalani's benefit, and a revised version of the ' Ritorno di Serse ' in 1803 ; ' L' oro non compra amore ' in 1804, and many others followed until the French invasion in 1807. The court fled to Brazil, but Marcos Portugal remained at Lisbon, directing the San Carlos theatre, rewriting ' Demofoönte,' and composing a new opera, ' La speranza,' the finale of which was adopted as the national hymn until 1834. In 1810 he went with his brother Simão to Brazil, and resumed his court functions. In 1811 he had an apoplectic fit, and a second one in 1817. He was unable to return to Lisbon with the court in 1821, though he lived on until 1830.

In a list of his works, begun in 1809 and afterwards kept up to date, Marcos Portugal enumerates 35 Italian operas, 21 Portuguese comic operas (mainly in one act) and over 100 pieces of church music. Of these 8 operas and the 'Licença pastoril' are preserved in the Ajuda Palace Library, Lisbon, together with 19 MS. scores of sacred music (see Q.-L.). There is a copy of his 'Semiramide' in the Bibl. Nac., Lisbon; also an Italian oratorio on the Immaculate Conception. The library at Mafra possesses folio choir-books with unaccompanied church music for male voices. The most recent authority on the composer is the late Manuel CARVALHAES, whose collection of over 500 libretti shows how widely popular were the operas of Marcos Portugal in all parts of Europe.

Portogallo was not unknown in London. His 'Fernando nel Messico' was played at Mrs. Billington's benefit, Mar. 31, 1803; his 'Argenide e Serse,' Jan. 25, 1806; 'Semiramide,' Dec. 13, 1806; 'La morte di Mitridate' at Catalani's benefit, Apr. 16, 1807; and 'Barseni, Regina di Lidia,' June 3, 1815, 'Il Principe Spazzacamino,' 'Artaserse' and 'L' astuta, ossia La Vedova raggiratrice' were given in Russian at St. Petersburg. His brother, (2) SIMÃO, wrote for the church.

G.; rev. with addns. J. B. T.

POSAUNE, the German name for the TROMBONE (q.v.), also occasionally used for organ reed-stops of a like character. W. H. S.

POSCH, ISAAC (d. in or before 1623), organist at Laibach in 1618. He composed 'Harmonia concertans,' sacred songs 1-4 v. (1623 ed. by Widow); 1 book of instrumental suites in 4 parts and 1 book in 5 parts (3 movements: Gaillard or Courant, Dance, 'Proportio'). In 1626 they appeared combined as 'Musicalische Ehren- und Tafelfreuden' (Q.-L.).

POSITIONS (or SHIFTS). (1) In the case of all instruments of the violin family the term is applied to the places on the finger-board occupied by the left hand, and the spaces which the fingers will cover in each place. Thus in the case of the violin the 1st position covers a perfect 5th on each string, the lowest note being given by the open string, the highest being a 5th above it stopped by the little finger. All other positions comprise normally [1] a 4th, since their lowest note is that stopped by the 1st finger. They ascend according to the position of the 1st finger on the string. Thus on the G string of the violin the 2nd position begins with the 1st finger on B, the 3rd with it on C, the 4th with it on D, and so on. For the technique of the positions see FINGERING (VIOLIN, etc.); for the history see SHIFT. C.

(2) The term is also used to indicate the

[1] Besides the natural compass of a position, notes which really lie beyond it are frequently reached by extension of the fingers, without the hand leaving its position.

various degrees of extension of the trombone slide. When the slide is home or closed it is said to be in the 1st position, and as it is extended to flatten the pitch from one to six semitones, it is described as being in corresponding positions. (See TROMBONE.) D. J. B.

POSITIVE ORGAN (Fr. positif; Ger. Positiv), originally a stationary organ, as opposed to a portative or portable instrument used in processions. Hence the term 'positive' came to signify a 'chamber organ'; and later still, when in a church instrument a separate manual was set aside for the accompaniment of the choir, this also was called a 'positive,' owing, no doubt, to the fact that it generally had much the same delicate voicing as a chamber organ, and contained about the same number and disposition of stops. By old English authors the term is generally applied to a chamber organ, the 'positive' of our church instruments being called from its functions the 'choir organ.' When placed behind the player (Ger. Rückpositiv) it was often styled a 'chair organ,' but it is difficult to say whether this name arose from a play upon the terms 'choir' and 'chair,' or from a misunderstanding as to the origin of its distinctive title. With the French the 'clavier de positif' is our 'Choir manual.' Small portable organs were called REGALS (q.v.). J. S.

In modern days the name has been applied to an organ designed by Thomas Casson to meet the requirements of country and mission churches. The Positive Organ Company, Ltd., was formed to manufacture instruments on the principles of Casson. The earlier and smaller instruments of this Company have a compass from F (6 ft.) to f'''. A pedal effect is obtained in very accurate form by the 'Double Bass' stop on the keyboard, from F to c', by which only the lowest note struck is sounded. The effect of a second manual is obtained by the 'Melodic' stop, which, on the selected stop, sounds only the highest note struck, and if used with a softer stop played in harmony, asserts the melody. A transposing arrangement is also provided. T. E.

POSSENTI, PELLEGRINO, an early 17th-century Italian who composed 2 books of madrigals, canzonets and arie (1st book, 1623, republ. 1628; 2nd book, 1625), Concentus armonici, instrumental sonatas, 7 a 2, 9 a 3, 2 a 4 parts (1628) (Riemann; Q.-L.).

POSTANS, MISS, see SHAW, MRS. ALFRED.

POSTHORN, a small straight brass or copper instrument, varying in length from two to four feet. As now made, the bore usually resembles that of the cornet, but formerly the larger post- or mail-horns were of the bugle type of bore. The mouthpiece for the longer instrument is the same as for the bugle or cornet, but for the short higher-pitched horns the cup requires to be small and shallow. Originally intended as a signal for stage-coaches carrying mails, it has to a limited extent been adopted into light music for the production of occasional effects by exceptional players.

Its pitch varies according to length from the four-foot C to its two-foot octave. The scale consists of the ordinary open notes, beginning with the first harmonic. The fundamental sound cannot easily be obtained with the mouthpiece used. Five, or at most six, sounds, forming a common chord, are available, but no means exist for bridging over the gaps between them. In a four-foot instrument such as was commonly used by mail-guards, the sequence would be as follows—

(Not used.)        (Difficult.)

W. H. S.; addns. D. J. B.

POSTILLON DE LONGJUMEAU, LE, opéra-comique in 3 acts ; words by De Leuven and Brunswick, music by A. Adam. Produced Opéra-Comique, Paris, Oct. 13, 1836; London (Grecian Theatre, City Road), during T. Rouse's opera seasons, 1840 *et seq.*      G.

POSTILLONS. 'Symfonie allegro Postillons' is Handel's autograph inscription to the piece of orchestral music which precedes the entry of the Wise Men in 'Belshazzar,' and begins as follows :

It is written for the strings, with oboes in unison ; no horn is employed ; some of the later passages resemble those which can be played on the ordinary posthorn ; but there is nothing to say whether this was the origin of the indication, or whether it refers to the haste in which the Wise Men may be supposed to have arrived, or contains some allusion now lost.

Bach, in his Capriccio describing the departure of his brother, has introduced an 'Aria di postiglione' and a 'Fuga all' imitazione delle cornetta di Postiglione.'      G.

POSTLUDE, a piece played after service, an outgoing VOLUNTARY (*q.v.*).      G.

POTHIER, DOM JOSEPH, abbot of St. Wandrille (*b.* Bouzemont, near St. Dié, Loire-et-Cher, Dec. 7, 1835 ; *d.* Conques, Belgium, Sept. 8, 1923). In 1859 he entered the Benedictine Order at the abbey of Solesmes, where in 1862 he became sub-prior, and in 1866 professor of theology. In 1893 he was appointed prior of Ligugé (Vienne), in 1895 prior of St. Wandrille (Seine-Inférieure), and

in 1898 abbot of the last-named monastery, subsequently removed temporarily by the expulsion of the religious orders from France to Belgium.

Dom Pothier was one of the pioneers of the movement initiated at Solesmes under Dom Guéranger for the study and reform of plainsong, and his first important work, *Les Mélodies grégoriennes* (Tournai, 1880), became the recognised textbook on the subject. It was reprinted in 1881 and 1890, and has been translated into German by Dom A. Kienle (1881), and into Italian by Dom M. Serafini (1890). This work was followed by a 'Liber Gradualis' (Tournai, 1883 ; Solesmes, 1895) ; 'Hymni de tempore et de Sanctis' (Solesmes, 1885) ; 'Processionale monasticum' (Solesmes, 1888, 1893) ; 'Liber Antiphonarius' (*ib.*, 1891) ; 'Liber Responsorialis' (*ib.*, 1895) ; 'Variae Preces de mysteriis et festis' (*ib.*, 1888, 1889, 1892, 1897, 1901) and 'Cantus Mariales' (Paris, 1903, 1906). In addition to these important works Dom Pothier edited many detached examples of plain-song, and published monthly from 1892, in the *Revue du chant grégorien*, numerous articles on liturgical music. Under his direction was started at Solesmes, in 1889, the valuable series of reproductions, etc., of musical manuscripts of the 9th to the 16th centuries, issued as *Paléographie musicale*, and carried on by his most eminent pupil and successor, Dom André MOCQUEREAU (*q.v.*), prior of Solesmes. In 1904 Dom Pothier was appointed by Pius X. president of the Commission for editing and publishing the musical portions of the Roman liturgy. Further details of the origin of the Solesmes movement for the restoration of plain-song will be found in the *Rassegna Gregoriana* for Apr. 1904, which also contains a portrait of Dom Pothier. (See also SOLESMES.)      W. B. S.

POT-POURRI, a name first given by J. B. Cramer to a kind of drawing-room composition consisting of a string of well-known airs from some particular opera, or even of national or other familiar tunes having no association with each other. These were connected by a few showy passages, or sometimes by short variations on the different themes. The pot-pourri is a less ambitious form of composition than the (modern) fantasia, as there is little or no working-out of the subjects taken, and very little 'fancy' is required in its production. Peters's Catalogue contains thirty-eight by V. Felix and sixty-four by Ollivier, on all the chief operas. Chopin, in a letter, calls his op. 13 a 'Pot-pourri' on Polish airs. The pot-pourri has been invaded by the 'transcription,' which closely resembles it in form although taking only one subject, as a rule, instead of many. 'Olla podrida' was another name for the same sort of production.      M.

POTT, August (b. Nordheim, Hanover, Nov. 7, 1806 ; d. Graz, Aug. 27, 1883). His father was Stadtmusikus of Nordheim. He adopted the violin as his instrument, and shortly after Spohr's appointment to be Hofkapellmeister at Cassel, went there as his pupil, and there made his first public appearance in 1824. He occupied the next few years in travelling through Denmark and Germany. In 1832 he was appointed Konzertmeister to the Duke of Oldenburg, and afterwards advanced to the post of Kapellmeister at the same court. This he resigned in 1861, and went to live at Graz. In 1838 he visited England, and played Lipinski's Concerto in B minor at the Philharmonic on May 21 with great applause. The critic of the *Musical World* speaks with enthusiasm of the extraordinary power of his tone, his great execution and the purity of his style. He published two concertos, and various smaller pieces for the violin with and without orchestra.              G.

POTTER, Philip Cipriani [1] Hambly (Hambley) (b. London, Oct. 2, 1792 ; d. Sept. 23,[2] 1871), composer and pianist, began his musical education at the age of 7, under his father, a teacher of the pianoforte. He afterwards studied counterpoint under Attwood and theory under Callcott and Crotch, and on Woelfl's arrival in England received instruction from him during five years.

In 1816 an overture by Potter was commissioned and performed (Mar. 11) by the Philharmonic Society (q.v.), of which he had been an associate from its foundation in 1813, and a member from the date of his attaining his majority. On Apr. 29 of the same year he made his first public appearance as a performer at the Society's concert, and played the pianoforte part in a sestet of his own composition for pianoforte and stringed instruments. He again performed Mar. 10, 1817. Shortly after this he went to Vienna and studied composition under Aloys Förster, receiving also friendly advice from Beethoven. Writing to Ries in London on Mar. 5, 1818, the great man says : 'Potter has visited me several times : he seems to be a good man and has talent for composition.' After visiting other German towns he made a tour in Italy, and returned to London in 1821, when he performed Mozart's concerto in D minor at the Philharmonic (Mar. 12). In 1822 he was appointed professor of the pianoforte at the R.A.M., and on the resignation of Crotch in June 1832, succeeded him as principal. The latter office he resigned in 1859 in favour of Charles Lucas. He was conductor of the Madrigal Society, 1855–70, and treasurer of the Society of British Musicians, 1858–65.

Potter's published works extend to op. 29, and include 2 sonatas, 9 rondos, 2 toccatas,

6 sets of variations, waltzes, a polonaise, a large number of impromptus, fantasias, romances, amusements, etc., and 2 books of studies [3] composed for the R.A.M.—all for PF. solo. Also a 'Duet Symphony' in D, and 4 other duets, besides arrangements of two of his symphonies and an overture, all for four hands ; a fantasia and fugue for 2 PFs. ; a trio for 3 players on the PF. ; a sestet for PF. and instruments ; a duo for PF. and vln. ; a sonata for PF. and horn ; 3 trios, etc. etc.

His MS. works comprise nine symphonies for full orchestra, of which six are in the Philharmonic Library ; 4 overtures (three ditto) ; 3 concertos, PF. and orch. (ditto) ; a concertante, PF. and violoncello ; a cantata, 'Medora e Corrado' ; an Ode to Harmony ; additional accompaniments to 'Acis and Galatea' (for the production on the stage of the Queen's Theatre in 1831), and many other pieces of more or less importance. These compositions, though well received,[4] and many of them in their time much in vogue, are now forgotten, except the studies. Wagner's favourable opinion deserves record. When Wagner conducted the Philharmonic Society in 1855, the care which he bestowed on one of Potter's works gave great delight to the composer.

As a performer he ranked high, and he had the honour to introduce Beethoven's concertos in C, C minor and G to the English public at the Philharmonic. He played the C minor concerto on Mar. 8, 1824, and the G major in 1825. As a conductor he is most highly spoken of, and it may be worth mentioning that he beat time with his hand and not with a baton. His fresh and genial spirit, and the eagerness with which he welcomed and tried new music from whatever quarter, will not be forgotten by those who had the pleasure and profit of his acquaintance. One of the last occasions on which he was seen in public was assisting in the accompaniment of Brahms's Requiem at its first (private) performance in London, July 10, 1871. He contributed a few papers to periodicals—*Recollections of Beethoven*, to the *Musical World*, Apr. 29, 1836 (reprinted in *Mus. T.*, Dec. 1, 1861) ; *Companion to the Orchestra, or Hints on Instrumentation*, *Musical World*, Oct. 28, Dec. 23, 1836, Mar. 10, May 12, 1837. Potter edited the 'Complete Pianoforte Works of Mozart' for Novello ; and Schumann's 'Album für die Jugend' (op. 68) for Wessel & Co. in 1857.

In 1860 a subscription was raised and an exhibition founded at the R.A.M. in honour of Potter. It is called after him, and entitles the

---

[1] He derived this name from his godmother, a sister of G. B. Cipriani the painter.      [2] *Annual Register.*

[3] Analysed by W. H. Holmes in *Notes upon Notes* (1880). The studies are twenty-four in number, and are arranged for a key and its relative minor—No. 1, C major ; 2, A minor ; 3, D♭ major ; 4, B♭ minor, etc.

[4] The symphonies were played at the Philharmonic as follows : In —, May 29, 1826, June 8, 1835 ; in A, May 27, 1832 ; in G minor, May 19, 1834, May 28, 1855 ; in D, Mar. 21, 1836, Apr. 22, 1850, May 3. 1869.

holder to one year's instruction in the R.A.M. A panegyric on Cipriani Potter was pronounced by Sir G. A. Macfarren at the Musical Association. (See *Proc. of the Mus. Assoc.*, 1883–84, p. 41.) He was buried in Kensal Green Cemetery.       w. h. h., with addns.

POUGIN, Arthur (*b.* Châteauroux, Aug. 6, 1834 ; *d.* Paris, Aug. 8, 1921), registered at Châteauroux as François Auguste Arthur Paroisse-Pougin, eminent writer on musical subjects. As the son of an itinerant actor he had few educational advantages, and his literary attainments were therefore due to his own exertions alone ; his knowledge of music was partly obtained at the Paris Conservatoire, where he passed through the violin class of Alard and studied harmony with Henri Reber. From the age of 13 he played the violin at a theatre, and in 1855 became conductor of the Théâtre Beaumarchais, which, however, he soon quitted for Musard's orchestra. From 1856–59 he was vice-conductor and *répétiteur* (or conductor of rehearsals) at the Folies Nouvelles.

Pougin soon turned his attention to musical literature, beginning with biographical articles on French musicians of the 18th century in the *Revue et Gazette musicale*. At an early period of his career he gave up teaching, and resigned his post among the violins at the Opéra-Comique (1860–63) in order the better to carry out his literary projects. Besides his frequent contributions to *Le Ménestrel, La France musicale, L'Art musical, Le Théâtre, Chronique musicale*, etc., and other periodicals specially devoted to music, he edited the musical articles in the *Dictionnaire universel* of Larousse, and was successively musical feuilletoniste to the *Soir*, the *Tribune, L'Évènement*, and, from 1878, to the *Journal Officiel*, where he succeeded Eugène Gautier. In 1885 he became chief editor of *Le Ménestrel*.

Among his numerous works the following may be specified :

*André Campra* (1861) ; *Gresnick* and *Dezède* (1862) ; *Floquet* (1863) ; *Martini* and *Devienne* (1864) ; the six monographs collected as *Musiciens français du XVIIIe siècle* ; *Meyerbeer, notes biographiques* (1864, 12mo) ; *F. Halévy, écrivain* (1865, 8vo) ; *W. Vincent Wallace, étude biographique et critique* (1866, 8vo) ; *Bellini, sa vie, ses œuvres* (1868, 12mo) ; *Albert Grisar, étude artistique* (1870, 12mo) ; *Rossini, notes, impressions, etc.* (1871, 8vo) ; *Auber* (1872) ; *Boieldieu, sa vie, etc.* (1875, 12mo) ; *Figures d'opéra-comique : Elleviou ; Mme. Dugazon ; La Tribu de Gavaudan* (1875, 8vo) ; *Rameau, sa vie et ses œuvres* (1876, 16mo) ; *Adolphe Adam, sa vie, etc.* (1876, 12mo) ; *Les Vrais Créateurs de l'opéra français: Perrin et Cambert* (1881) ; *Molière et l'Opéra-Comique* (1882) ; *Viotti* (1888) ; *L'Opéra-Comique pendant la Révolution* (1891) ; *Méhul, sa vie, son génie, son caractère* (1889, 1893) ; *Essai historique sur la musique en Russie* (1897, 1904) ; *J.-J. Rousseau, musicien* (1901) ; *La Comédie française et la Révolution* (1902) ; *Monsigny et son temps* (1908) ; *Hérold* (1908) ; *Marie Malibran* (1911) ; *Mme. Favart* (1912) ; *Giuseppina Grassini ; Le Violon, les violonistes et la musique de violon du XVIe au XVIII: siècle* (posthumous) (1920, 1924).

His most important work, the *Life of Verdi*, was published first in Italian (A. Formis) in 1881, and translated by J. E. Matthew, 1887 ; the *Supplément et Complément* to the *Biographie universelle des musiciens* of Fétis, a work of great extent and industry, and containing a mass of new names and information (2 vols. 8vo, Paris), 1878–80 ; and the new edition of

Clément and Larousse's *Dictionnaire lyrique*, 1897. In 1905 he was decorated with the order of the Crown of Italy. On his death his extensive private library was acquired for the University of Rochester, N.Y. (See Libraries.)

        g. c.

POULENC, Francis (*b.* Paris, Jan. 7, 1899), composer, was a member of the group known as the ' Six.' His parents insisting on a classical education, he could devote comparatively little time to music during his youth and student days, but he nevertheless contrived to take piano lessons from Ricardo Viñes and to pick up some technical knowledge of composition here and there. Early in 1918 military service claimed him, and a regular musical training could no longer be thought of. Meanwhile Poulenc had already begun to compose, and from the first his music revealed traces of originality under its raw technique. In 1917 the 'Rhapsodie nègre' for piano, string quartet, flute, clarinet and voice was written, and in 1918 followed the 'Mouvements perpétuels ' for piano, and two sonatas, for piano duet and two clarinets respectively.

Francis Poulenc, who was to some extent influenced by Erik Satie, at once began to show a strong tendency to oppose what seemed to him the excessive sensitiveness and refinement of the French ' impressionist ' school that immediately precedes his generation. The reaction, in which his colleagues of the ' Six ' all shared to a greater or less extent, led to a careful avoidance of anything savouring in the least of romantic sentiment and poetic delicacy. The result was music characterised by a love of plain statement and a frankness of humour sometimes bordering on pretension and vulgarity, but often not without a certain youthful charm. The preference for the circus and the fair to more elevated subjects need not necessarily be regarded as an affectation ; as a protest against romanticism it is perfectly understandable, and attempts to utilise the forms and rhythms of comic songs and popular dance music have been productive of at least a new flavour in the art. In the way of orchestration Poulenc has certainly learnt much from the often fortuitous instrumental combinations found in the ball-rooms and the music-halls frequented by the Parisian populace. The accompaniment of the ' Cocardes ' (songs for two male voices to poems by Jean Cocteau), for instance, is scored for violin, cornet, trombone, bass drum and triangle. This work, like the setting of some poems from *Le Bestiaire* by Guillaume Apollinaire, for voice, string quartet, flute, clarinet and bassoon, dates from 1919.

The years 1920–21 saw the production of four works for piano (Impromptus, Suite, Napoli and Promenades), ' Quatre Poèmes de Max Jacob ' for tenor, flute, oboe, clarinet, bassoon and trumpet, and the *comédie-bouffe* in one act, 'Le Gendarme incompris.' These last two works point to a return to the style of the *opera buffa*.

Poulenc shares the predilection for wind instruments evinced by so many modern composers, and takes an active part in their endeavour to enrich the repertory of chamber music for various wind combinations.   E. B.

LIST OF WORKS

1. 'Rapsodie nègre' for PF., str. quartet, flute, clarinet and voices. 1917.
2. Sonata for PF. 4 hands.  1918.
3. Sonata for 2 clarinets.  1918.
4. 'Mouvements perpétuels' for PF.  1918.
5. 'Le Bestiaire, ou le Cortège d'Orphée (Apollinaire) for voice, str. quartet, flute, clarinet and bassoon.  1919.
6. 'Cocardes' (three poems by Jean Cocteau) for tenor, vla., cornet, trombone, bass drum and triangle.  1919.
7. Suite for PF.  1920.
8. Impromptus for PF.  1920.  (Revised version 1924.)
9. 'Le Gendarme incompris' comédie-bouffe.  1920 (MS.).
10. Promenades for PF.  1921.
11. Sonata for clarinet and bassoon.  1922.
12. Sonata for horn, trumpet and trombone.  1922.
13. 'Chanson à boire ' for male voice choir.  1922.
14. 'Les Biches.'  Ballet with chorus (produced in London as ' The House Party ').  1923.
15. 'Cinq Poèmes de Ronsard,' voice and PF.  1924.
16. Trio for PF., oboe and bassoon.  1924-25 (MS.).
17. Marches militaires (in 3 movements) for PF. and orch.  1925 (MS.).

POUPELINIÈRE (LA POPELINIÈRE), ALEXANDRE JEAN JOSEPH LE RICHE DE LA (*b.* Paris, 1692 ; *d.* there, Dec. 5, 1762), general farmer of taxes ; a great musical enthusiast, and pupil of Rameau, who lived in his house for several years. He was also a patron of Johann Stamitz, and introduced horns, clarinets and the harp into his private orchestra, that being the first time of their appearing in any French orchestra.   E. V. D. S.

POUSSÉ (Fr.). In violin music the word ' Poussé,' or its equivalent sign V, is employed to indicate that the note over which it is placed shall be begun with an upward course of the Bow (*q.v.*).   O. R.

POWELL, JOHN (*b.* Richmond, Virginia, Sept. 6, 1882), American pianist and composer. Following his graduation from the University of Virginia in 1901, he studied in Vienna for some years : piano with Leschetizky and composition with Navrátil. His début as pianist was made in Berlin in Nov. 1907, with the Tonkünstler Orchestra ; for several years he toured widely in Germany, France and England, and since 1913 he has played throughout the United States.

As composer Powell is best known for his effective use of negro themes. His compositions include :

Concerto, B minor, pianoforte and orchestra, op. 13.
Concerto, E, violin and orchestra, op. 23.
' Rapsodie nègre,' pianoforte and orchestra.
String Quartet, op. 19.
' Sonata virginianesque,' violin and pianoforte, op. 27.
Sonata, E, violin and pianoforte, op. 23.
Pianoforte sonatas, smaller pianoforte pieces and songs.
   W. S. S.

POWELL, MAUD (*b.* Peru, Illinois, Aug. 22, 1868 ; *d.* Uniontown, Pa., Jan. 8, 1920), violinist. Four years' study with William Lewis of Chicago, and occasional concert appearances, developed her exceptional gifts as a violinist so rapidly that she was taken to Leipzig, where she became a pupil of Professor Schradieck. At the end of a year (in 1881) she was awarded a diploma at the public examinations held in the Gewandhaus, and then proceeded to Paris, where—out of eighty applicants—she obtained one of the six vacancies in Charles Dancla's class. By the advice of Léonard she came to England in 1883, played at some London concerts and before the Royal Family, and toured in the provinces with Miss José Sherrington. While in London she met Joachim, who invited her to Berlin, where she became his pupil, and made her début in Germany at one of the Philharmonic Concerts in Berlin in 1885, playing Max Bruch's G minor concerto. In the same year she returned to New York and made her début at one of the Philharmonic Society's concerts, under the baton of Theodore Thomas. In 1892 she toured in Germany and Austria with the New York Arion Society, under the conductorship of Van der Stucken, and in 1893 appeared at the World's Exposition in Chicago. In 1894 she organised the Maud Powell String Quartet, with which she toured extensively through the States, and in 1898 again appeared in London, playing at the Philharmonic, the Saturday Popular Concerts and in the provinces. She also toured in Germany, Holland, Belgium, France, Austria, Russia and Denmark. In 1903 she was engaged by Sousa to accompany him on his European tour of thirty weeks, and in the spring of 1905–06 made forty appearances in South Africa with her own concert party, and subsequently undertook annual concert tours in her own country.

Arensky's violin concerto was introduced by her to an American audience, and under the personal supervision and inspiration of Dvořák, his violin concerto was played by her for the first time in America at the New York Philharmonic Society's concert. Other works which she introduced to concert audiences are : Saint - Saëns's concerto in C minor, Lalo's concerto in G major, and compositions by American composers.

BIBL.—LAHEE, *Famous Violinists*, and contemporary journals.
   E. H.-A.

POWELL, SAMUEL (*d.* Nov. 27, 1775), a Dublin printer of some note. At an early date in the history of Irish music-printing he issued some excellently printed musical works for the use of the French Huguenots who were then settled in Dublin. These include an edition of *Les Pseaumes de David mis en vers françois*, 1731, 8vo, and *Cantiques sacrez*, 1748, 12mo, both set up in movable music type. He was working, however, long before this date, as a well-printed edition of Allan Ramsay's poems, dated 1724, testifies. He lived in Crane Lane, but in 1762 removed into Dame Street. Most of his early works were published in conjunction with George Risk, a Dublin bookseller.   F. K.

POWELL, THOMAS (b. London, 1776; d. (?) Edinburgh, after 1863), harpist, violinist and pianist; member of the Royal Society of Music. He married in 1811. He played a violin concerto at the Haymarket Theatre, London; resided as teacher in Dublin, afterwards in Edinburgh, and composed 15 violin concertos, 3 grand sonatas PF. and violin (1825), 3 duets for vln. and v'cl., 3 duets for 2 v'cls., overtures, etc. (Brown and Stratton; Fétis; Q.-L.).

POWELL, WALTER (b. Oxford, 1697; d. Nov. 6, 1744), was on July 1, 1704, admitted a chorister of Magdalen College. In 1714 he was appointed a clerk in the same college. On Apr. 16, 1718, he was elected Yeoman Bedell of Divinity, and on Jan. 26, 1732, Esquire Bedell of the same faculty. He was also a member of the choirs of Christ Church and St. John's Colleges. In July 1733 he sang in the oratorios given by Handel during his visit to Oxford, and later in the year at the meeting of the Three Choirs at Gloucester. He was sworn a gentleman of the Chapel Royal on July 28, 1733, vice Gostling. His voice (counter tenor) and singing were greatly admired. He was buried at St. Peter's-in-the-East, Oxford. W. H. H.; addns. W. H. G. F.

POWER, JAMES (b. Galway, 1766; d. Aug. 26, 1836), a music publisher, first of Dublin and afterwards of London. Being apprenticed to a pewterer, he was by chance called upon to repair the instruments of a regimental band passing through the town where he was working. This incident led him into the musical instrument trade; he set up shop with his brother William at 4 Westmorland Street, Dublin.

A happy idea of the publication of the national music of Ireland, united to words by celebrated poets, caused the brothers to apply to Thomas Moore, and it was ultimately arranged that Moore alone should provide the literary work. The design was to run a similar work to that being issued by George Thomson, of Edinburgh, who was then publishing, in parts, the 'Scottish Melodies,' to which Burns and other writers were supplying verses. The same style of printing, etc., with pictorial engravings was adopted, and the first two numbers were issued in 1808. The success of these parts of the 'Irish Melodies' was beyond expectation. (See MOORE.) Near the end of the year 1807 Power came to London, to 34 Strand, as a military instrument-maker and music-seller, his brother remaining at the Dublin address. After the seventh number of the 'Melodies' a quarrel arose between the brothers, James asserting that he had made an arrangement by which all succeeding numbers should be his own sole copyright, and at the publication of the eighth number, 1821, entered an action against his brother for infringement of copyright. It was decided in the favour of

James, who made an agreement (continued to his widow) that he should have the sole rights in all musical settings of verses by Moore then written and to be written. The ninth (1824) and the tenth (1834) numbers completed the 'Irish Melodies,' and besides these James Power issued Moore's 'Sacred Songs,' 'National Airs,' 'Evenings in Greece,' etc.

Power's other publications include collections of 'Scottish Melodies' by Horace Twiss, 'Indian Airs' arranged by C. E. Horn, 'Welsh Airs' collected by Clifton and Dovaston, and similar works, whose elegance in engraving, paper and binding had to compensate for the lack of other intrinsic qualities. The plates of, and copyright in, the 'Irish Melodies' passed to Addison and Hodson. The friendship of Moore for Power, and his extraordinary dependence on him for help in matters ranging from the purchase of fish to heavy overdrafts and loans, is sufficiently indicated in Moore's own diary, and is more fully set forth in the letters which passed between the two. (See *Letters of Thomas Moore to his Music-publisher James Power*, New York, 1854.) F. K.

POWER, LIONEL, an English musician who flourished in the 15th century, but of whose biography absolutely nothing is known. His name occurs in MSS. as Leonel, Leonell Polbero or Powero, Leonelle, Lyonel, Leonell Leonellus Anglicus and Lyonel Power. In Hothby's *Dialogus in arte musica* (Florence, Magliabecch., Cl. xix. Cod. 36) he is referred to as follows:

'Sic . . . in quamplurimis . . . alijs cantilenis recentissimis quarum conditores plerique adhuc vivunt Dunstable Anglicus ille. Dufay. leonel. plumtri.* frier. Busnoys. Morton. Octinghem. Pelagulfus.* Micheleth.* Bacluin.* Forest. Stane. Fich. Caron,'[1] etc.

From this passage it would seem that he was a contemporary of Dunstable, and the style of the two composers seems to have had so much in common that their compositions are sometimes ascribed indiscriminately to one another in different MSS. Power is best known as the author of an English Treatise[2] preserved in a MS. (dating from about 1450), transcribed by John Wylde, precentor of the abbey of Waltham Cross. The text, which has been partly printed by both Burney and Hawkins, begins:

'This Tretis in contrivd upon ye Gamme for hem yt wil be syngers or makers or techers,'

and is signed 'Q. Lyonel Power.' It is followed by

'A litil tretise acording to ye ferst tretise of ye sight of Descant, and also for ye sight of Counter and for ye syght of the Countertenor and of ffaburdon.'

This second treatise ends abruptly without any author's name, but it is possibly a sequel by Power to the 'Treatise upon the Gamme.'[3]

[1] The passage has been examined by H. P. Horne, and his reading is here followed. Morelot (*De la musique au XVe siècle*, 1856) reads Plumeret, Pelagultus, Bicheleth and Baduin for the names marked above with an asterisk.
[2] Brit. Mus., Lansd. MS. 763.
[3] As to the importance of this little work see Riemann's *Geschichte der Musiktheorie* (1898), cap. 7.

The largest collection of Power's compositions is contained in the Old Hall MS., in which are twenty-one pieces (mostly parts of masses) for three and four voices ; in the Trent MSS. there is a Mass, ' Missa Rex Saeculorum ' (without a Kyrie), and ten other pieces ; at Modena (Cod. vi. H. 15) are eight pieces ; at Bologna four motets (three in Cod. 37 of the Liceo Musicale, and one at the University, MS. 2216) ; the Selden MS. at Oxford (Bodleian, Selden, B. 26) contains an Ave Regina for four voices and the British Museum (Lansd. 462) part of a Kyrie. The following have been printed :

1. Ave Regina (3 voc.). From Old Hall. (I.M.G. *Sammelbände*, 1901.)
2. Ave Regina (4 voc.). From Selden MS. (Stainer's Bodleian Music, 1901.)
3. Salve Regina (3 voc.). At Trent and Modena. (Trienter Codices. I. 1900.)
4. Ave Regina (4 voc.). At Trent and Bologna. (Trienter Codices. I. 1900.)
5. Mater ora filium (3 voc.). At Trent and Modena. (Trienter Codices. I. 1900.)
(Nos. 2 and 4 are the same composition.)

As in the similar case of Dunstable, the almost complete absence of any facts relating to Power's life have caused various fanciful statements to be made about him. Thus he has been said by different writers to have been an ' Anglo-Irish ' cleric, educated at Oxford, to have lived in Italy, to have assumed the name of ' John of Dunstable ' on entering the monastery of Dunstable, to have been a Welshman, to have been ' the inventor of figured bass,' etc. But all these statements are purely imaginary, and at present we know nothing of who Power was, nor of where he lived and died. w. b. s.

POZNANSKI, Barrett Isaac (b. Charleston, Virginia, Dec. 11, 1840 ; d. London, June 24, 1896), violinist and composer for his instrument, son of the Rev. Gustavus Poznanski and his wife Esther G. Barret. He began to study the violin with Pietro Basvecchi at the age of 8, and shortly after made his début at a concert given in aid of the Ladies' Calhoun Monument Association at Charleston. In 1858 he went to Paris and studied with Henri Vieuxtemps for three years, during which period he appeared frequently at concerts given by his master both at Vienna and Paris. After playing in Germany and other continental towns, Poznanski returned to Charleston in 1861 ; but when the Civil War broke out in America he again went to Paris, gave concerts in that city, became leader of the orchestras at the Opéra-Comique and Imperial Theatre, and toured in the south of France with success. In 1866 he was again in his native country. He settled in New York for some time, made an extended concert tour in company with his brother Joseph, and accepted the directorship of the Illinois Conservatoire of music. In 1879 he came to London, where his abilities as a teacher and composer brought him considerable repute. He studied composition with Bagge, who was a

pupil of Sechter, and he was the author of an excellent instruction-book for the violin, *Violine und Bogen*, which aims at instructing the student by a series of illustrations showing correct and faulty positions in violin-playing. He also wrote a vast number of short pieces for violin and piano.

Bibl.—*Magazine of Music*, 1893 ; *The Violin Times* 1894.
E. H.-A.

PRACTICE CLAVIER, see Virgil Practice Clavier.

PRAEGER, Ferdinand Christian Wilhelm (b. Leipzig, Jan. 22, 1815 ; d. London, Sept. 2, 1891), son of Heinrich Aloys Praeger, violinist, composer and Kapellmeister. His musical gifts developed themselves very early ; at 9 he played the violoncello with ability, but was diverted from that instrument to the piano by the advice of Hummel. At 16 he established himself as teacher at The Hague, meanwhile strenuously maintaining his practice of the piano, violin and composition. In 1834 he settled in London, and became esteemed as a teacher. While living in London Praeger acted as correspondent of the *Neue Zeitschrift für Musik*, a post for which he was selected by Schumann himself in 1842. In Jan. 1851 he gave a recital in Paris of his own compositions with success ; in 1852 he played at the Gewandhaus, Leipzig, and at Berlin, Hamburg, etc. ; and later, in 1867, a new PF. trio of his was selected by the United German Musicians and performed at their festival at Meiningen. He was always an enthusiast for Wagner, and it was mainly owing to his endeavours that Wagner was engaged to conduct the Philharmonic Concerts in 1855. A concert of his compositions was organised by his pupils in his honour, on July 10, 1879, in London. An overture from his pen entitled ' Abellino ' was played at the New Philharmonic Concerts of May 24, 1854, and July 4, 1855 (under Lindpaintner and Berlioz) ; and a Symphonic Prelude to Manfred at the Crystal Palace, Apr. 17, 1880. A selection of his best pieces is published in two vols. under the title of the *Präger Album* (Kahnt, Leipzig). The publication of his interesting book, *Wagner as I knew him*, in 1885 drew forth various categorical contradictions and very severe criticisms from the writer of the authorised Life of the composer. (See Ashton Ellis's Life, *passim*.) The book was brought out again in the following year. g., with addns.

PRAENESTINUS, see Palestrina.

PRAETORIUS (Prätorius), the assumed surname of more than one family of distinguished German musicians, whose true patronymic was Schultz.[1]

(1) Bartholomaeus is known as the composer of ' Newe liebliche Paduanen, und Galliarden, mit 5 Stimmen ' (Berlin, 1616).

[1] The word Schultze means the head-man of the village or small town, and may therefore be translated by Praetor.

(2) GODESCALCUS (b. Salzwedel, Mar. 28, 1524; d. July 8, 1573) was for many years professor of philosophy at Wittenberg. He published at Magdeburg, in 1557, a volume entitled 'Melodiae scholasticae,' in the preparation of which he was assisted by Martin Agricola.

(3) HIERONYMUS (b. Hamburg, Aug. 10, 1560; d. there, Jan. 27, 1629) received his first musical instruction from his father, Jacob Schultze or Praetorius, who was organist of the church of St. James, Hamburg. The first appointment of Hieronymus was that of cantor at Erfurt in 1580, but in 1582 he succeeded to his father's post at Hamburg, where he remained till his death. Like Hans Leo Hassler, Hieronymus Praetorius was one of the German followers of the Venetian school of church music. He shows great contrapuntal dexterity in writing for a large number of voices disposed in several choirs. Thus he hardly ever writes for four voices, but from five upwards, and more especially from eight to twenty disposed in two to four choirs. Though a basso continuo part is appended to some of his publications, it is purely *ad libitum*, and he makes no use of an independent instrumental accompaniment. Some of his works, first published independently from 1599–1618, were afterwards republished at his own expense in an enlarged complete edition in five volumes, 1622–25. The titles and contents are as follows : *Opus musicum*, tom. i., 'Cantiones sacrae de praecipuis festis totius anni,' 5-12 voc. This volume was originally dedicated in 1599 to the chief parishioners of St. James's, Hamburg, and contains in its enlarged form forty-six motets or 64 n., reckoning second parts. *Opus musicum*, tom. ii., 'Magnificat octo vocum super octo tonos consuetos cum motetis,' 8-12 voc. This volume contains nine Magnificats, there being a second setting of the fifth tone with Christmas carols appended, also five motets *a* 8-12. It was originally dedicated in 1602 to the Landgraf Moritz of Hesse. *Opus musicum*, tom. iii., 'Liber missarum,' contains six masses *a* 5-8, four of them on themes of his own motets, two on motets by Felis and Meiland (Eitner mistakenly attributes the masses themselves to these composers). This volume was originally dedicated in 1616 to certain Hamburg patricians, the composer's patrons. *Opus musicum*, tom. iv., 'Cantiones variae,' 5, 6, 7, 8, 10, 12, 16, 20 voc., contains twenty-six Latin motets and two settings of German texts, 'Ein Kindelein so löbelich' and 'Herr Gott wir loben dich,' the latter *a* 16 in three parts. *Opus musicum*, tom. v., 'Cantiones novae officiosae,' 5, 6, 7, 8, 10 et 15 voc., dedicated to the Senate of Hamburg, contains twenty-one Latin motets and three German pieces. A representative selection from all these volumes has now been included in *D.D.T.*, Bd. xxiii. Besides these larger works, Hieronymus Praetorius had a considerable share in the *Hamburger Melodeyen-Gesangbuch* of 1604, which contains twenty-one of his settings of chorales in simple counterpoint *a* 4.

(4) JACOB, son of Hieronymus (b. Feb. 8, 1586; d. Oct. 22, 1651), became a pupil of Sweelinck in Amsterdam, and in 1603 organist of the church of St. Peter in Hamburg. Three of his motets were included in the first volume of his father's *Opus musicum*, and he was also one of the contributors to the *Hamburger Melodeyen - Gesangbuch* of 1604. His other works, as enumerated in *Q.-L.*, are chiefly motets for weddings after the fashion of the time. He enjoyed a great reputation as an organ-player and teacher.                          J. R. M.

(5) MICHAEL (b. Kreuzberg, Thuringia, Feb. 15, 1571; d. Wolfenbüttel, Feb. 15, 1621), most celebrated of the name on account of his *Syntagma musicum*, began his artistic career in the character of Kapellmeister at Lüneburg; in 1604 he entered the service of the Duke of Brunswick, first as organist, and then as Kapellmeister and secretary; he was appointed prior of the monastery of Ringelheim, near Gozlar, without necessity of residence.

The compositions of Michael Praetorius are very voluminous. He himself has left us, at the end of his *Syntagma musicum*, a catalogue the most important items of which are : fifteen volumes of 'Polyhymnia,' adapted partly to Latin and partly to German words ; sixteen volumes of 'Musae Sionae,'[1] of which the first five are in Latin and the remainder in German ; nine volumes of a secular work called 'Musa Aonia,' of which the several books are entitled 'Terpsichore' (2 vols.), 'Calliope' (2 vols.), 'Thalia' (2 vols.), 'Erato' (1 vol.), 'Diana Teutonica' (1 vol.) and *Regensburgische Echo* (1 vol.) ; and a long list of other works, 'partly printed, and partly, through God's mercy, to be printed.' The *Syntagma musicum* (Musical Treatise) is a book the excessive rarity and great historical value of which entitle it to a special notice. The full title of this remarkable work is :

'Syntagma Musicum ; ex veterum et recentiorum Ecclesiasticorum autorum lectione, Polyhistorum consignatione, Variarum linguarum notatione, Hodierni seculi usurpatione, ipsius denique Musicae artis observatione: in Cantorum, Organistarum, Organopoeorum, ceterorumque Musicam scientiam amantium & tractantium gratiam collectum ; et Secundum generalem indicem toti Operi praefixum, In Quatuor Tomos distributum, a Michaële Praetorio Creutzbergensi, Coenobii Ringelheimensis Priori, & in aula Brunsvicensi Chori Musici Magistro.'—VVittebergæ (sic), Anno 1615.

Notwithstanding this distinct mention of four volumes, it is morally certain that no more than three were ever printed, and that the much-coveted copy of the fourth, noticed in Forkel's catalogue, was nothing more than the separate set of plates attached to the second.

TOM. I. (Part i., Wolfenbüttel, 1614[2]; Part ii.,

[1] There is rather an extensive collection of separate volumes in the British Museum; but of Part ix. of the 'Musae Sionae,' containing 'Bicinia' and 'Tricinia,' the only copies mentioned in *Q.-L.* are in the State Library at Berlin and at Liegnitz.

[2] In the prefatory pages, which give a conspectus of the contents there is a chronogram which gives the date twice over as 1614:

'IVDICIVM pIos non terreat ; nam
MIHI aDIVtor ChrIstVs.'

Wittenberg, 1615), written chiefly in Latin but with frequent interpolations in German, is arranged in two principal parts, each subdivided into innumerable minor sections. Part i. is entirely devoted to the consideration of Ecclesiastical Music, and its four sections treat, respectively, (1) of Choral Music and Psalmody, as practised in the Jewish, Egyptian, Asiatic,[1] Greek and Latin Churches ; (2) of the Music of the Mass ; (3) of the Music of the Antiphons, Psalms, Tones, Responsoria, Hymns and Canticles, as sung at Matins and Vespers, and the Greater and Lesser Litanies ; and (4) of Instrumental Music, as used in the Jewish and early Christian Churches, including a detailed description of all the musical instruments mentioned either in the Old or the New Testament. Part ii. treats of the Secular Music of the Ancients, including (1) Dissertations on the Invention and Inventors of the Art of Music, its most eminent Teachers, its Modes and Melodies, its connexion with Dancing and the Theatre, its use at Funeral Ceremonies, and many other kindred matters ; and (2) Descriptions of all the Instruments used in ancient Secular Music, on the forms and peculiarities of some of which much light is thrown by copious quotations from the works of classical authors.

Tom. II. (Wolfenbüttel, Part i. in 1619[2]; Part ii. in 1620), written wholly in German, is called *Organographia*, and divided into five principal sections. Section i. treats of the nomenclature and classification of all the musical instruments in use at the beginning of the 17th century. Section ii. contains descriptions of the form, compass, quality of tone and other peculiarities of all these instruments *seriatim*, including, among wind instruments, trombones of four different sizes, the various kinds of trumpet, horns (Jäger Trommetten), flutes, both of the old and the transverse forms, cornetts, hautboys, both treble and bass (here called Pommern, Bombardoni and Schalmeyen), bassoons and dolcians, double bassoons and sordoni, doppioni, racketten and the different kinds of krumhorn (or Lituus), corna-muse, bassanello, schreyerpfeiffe, and sockpfeiffe or bagpipes. These are followed by the stringed instruments, divided into two classes—viole da gamba, or viols, played between the knees, and viole da brazzo, played upon the arm. In the former class are comprised several different kinds of the ordinary viola da gamba, the viola bastarda, and the violone or double-bass ; in the latter, the ordinary viola da braccio, the violino da braccio, the violetta piccola and the tenor viola da braccio. The lyres, lutes, theorbas (*sic*), mandolins, guitars, harps and other instruments in which the strings are plucked by the fingers or by a plectrum, are classed by themselves ; as are

[1] Called, in the German index, the Arabian Church.
[2] But see later, description of the Tenbury copy.

the keyed instruments, including the harpsichord (Clavicymbalum), spinet (Virginall), clavicytherium, claviorganum, arpichordum, the Nürmbergisch Geigenwerck and organs of all kinds, beginning with the ancient regall and positive. Section iii. treats of ancient organs in detail, giving much valuable information concerning their form and construction. Section iv. gives a minute description of modern organs, with details of their construction, the form of their pipes, the number and quality of their stops or registers, and other equally interesting and important matters relating to them. Section v. treats of certain individual organs, celebrated either for their size or the excellence of their tone, with special accounts of more than thirty instruments, including those in the Nicolaikirche and Thomaskirche at Leipzig, the cathedrals of Ulm, Lübeck, Magdeburg and Brunswick, and many other well-known churches.

This part of the work is rendered still more valuable by an Appendix, printed at Wolfenbüttel in 1620, two years after the publication of tom. ii. and iii., under the title of *Theatrum instrumentorum, seu sciagraphia, Michaëlis Praetorii, C.* This consists of forty-two well-executed plates, exhibiting woodcuts of all the more important instruments previously described in the text. Among these there are few more curious than the engraving of the Nürmbergisch Geigenwerck.

Tom. III., also printed at Wolfenbüttel in 1619, is arranged in three main sections. Part i. treats of all the different kinds of secular composition practised during the first half of the 17th century in Italy, France, England and Germany, with separate accounts of the Concerto, Motet, Fauxbourdon, Madrigal, Stanza, Sestina, Sonnet, Dialogue, Canzone, Canzonetta, Aria, Messanza, Quodlibet, Giustiniano, Serenata, Ballo or Balletto, Vinetto, Giardiniero, Villanella, Prélude, Phantasie, Capriccio, Fuga, Ricercare, Symphonia, Sonata, Intrada, Toccata, Padovana, Passamezzo, Galliarda, Bransle, Courante, Volta, Allemanda and Mascherada, the distinctive peculiarities of each of which are described with a clearness which throws much light on certain forms now practically forgotten. Part ii. deals with the technical mysteries of solmisation, notation, ligatures, proportions, sharps, flats, naturals, modes or tones, signs of all kinds, 'Tactus' or rhythm, transposition, the arrangement of voices, the management of double, triple and quadruple choirs, and other like matters. Part iii. is devoted to the explanation of Italian technical terms, the arrangement of a complete 'Cappella,' either vocal or instrumental, the rules of 'General-Bass' (Thorough-bass), and the management of a concert for voices and instruments of all kinds ; the whole concluding with a detailed list of the author's own compositions, both sacred and secular, and a compendium of rules for the training of boys' voices, after the Italian method.

Tom. IV., had it been completed, was to have treated of counterpoint.

There is a copy in the British Museum, one in the Glasgow and West of Scotland Technical College, and one was in Mr. Alfred H. Littleton's possession. For the use of the remarkably fine exemplar which served as the basis of the above description, the writer was indebted to the Rev. Sir F. A. Gore Ouseley, who placed it unreservedly at his disposal. The second volume contains the autograph of J. B. Bach (the B has been altered to E, but the accompanying date, 1739, might refer to either of the Eisenach Bachs, father or son. See Vol. I. p. 148, table, Nos. 11 and 12). The second volume belonged to G. P. Telemann in 1712. The first volume of the edition described by Fétis was printed at Wittenberg in 1615, the second and third at Wolfenbüttel in 1619, and the collection of plates—*Theatrum instrumentorum, seu sciagraphia*—at Wolfenbüttel in 1620. Neither Fétis nor Mendel seems to have been aware of the existence of an older edition. The Rev. Sir F. A. G. Ouseley's copy bears in its first volume the same date as the other editions, 'Wittebergae, 1615,' but the second and third volumes are dated ' Wolfenbüttel, 1618 ' ; and the difference does not merely lie in the statement of the year, but clearly indicates an earlier issue. In the edition of 1618 the title-page of the second volume is printed entirely in black ; in that of 1619 it is in black and red. The Ouseley copy of vol. ii. begins with a summary of contents and an address to organists, instrumentalists, organ- and instrument-makers of Germany and other nations. The other edition has a dedication to the burgomaster and town council of Leipzig. The title-page of the third volume is black in both editions, but in different type ; and, though the contents of the second and third volumes correspond generally in both copies, slight typographical differences may be detected in sufficient numbers to prove the existence of a distinct edition beyond all doubt. The Ouseley copy of vol. iii. begins with a summary of contents, the 1619 edition with a dedication to the burgomaster and town council of Nuremberg, and an ode in praise of the authors. The 1618 edition has another chronogram—

' IesV In te spero, non ConfVnDar In aeternVM,'

pointing again at 1614 as the initial date of the work. The 1618 copy contains at pp. 57-72 musical examples not in the later edition, and pp. 78 and 79 are misplaced. It has long been known that twenty pages of the General Introduction were more than once reprinted ; but these belong to the first volume, and are in no way concerned with the edition of 1618,

of which, so far as we have been able to ascertain, the copy referred to, now at St. Michael's, Tenbury, is a unique exampie.

w. s. r. ; rev. with addns.

PRAGUE (PRAHA), the capital of the ancient kingdom of Bohemia and now the capital of the Republic of Czechoslovakia, has a long musical history dating back to the 10th century. Even before the time of Bedřich SMETANA (1824–84) there was a desire to separate the musical life of the Czechs in Prague from that of the German cohabitants, who, as the ruling race, were better provided with theatres, concert-halls and State emoluments. From the date of the erection of a Provisional Theatre for the performance of operas and plays in the vernacular, in 1862, the two streams of tendency have flowed side by side, each in its own clearly defined course, the Slavonic current gathering an increasing force and volume which culminated with the Declaration of Independence on Feb. 29, 1920. The Ministry of Education and National Culture includes a special department for music, with a Minister-secretary at the head (Dr. Jan Branberger) and an advisory board consisting of leading musical representatives in Bohemia, Moravia and Slovakia. There is an Inspector of Music for Czech Schools, and another for German Schools throughout the Republic. The chief musical institutions in Prague at the present time are as follows :

1. THE NATIONAL THEATRE (*Národní Divadlo*), on the banks of Vltava, built by national subscription, replaced the first building, which was burnt down in 1881 before its actual inauguration. The designs are by the architects Zítek and Schulz ; the decorations by Zeníšek (from drawings by Aleš) and Liebscher ; the curtain by Ad. Hinais ; so that the entire building is a monument to national art. The repertory is not confined to national opera ; Italian, French, German and Russian works are staged from time to time. The chief conductors during its existence have been : Smetana, Ad. Čech (1876–1900), Karel Kovařovic (1900–19), Otokar Ostrčil (since 1920).

2. THE NEW GERMAN THEATRE (*Deutsches Landestheater*) for German, Italian and French opera. Chief conductor, Alexander Zemlinsky.

3. THE CZECH PHILHARMONIC SOCIETY. A series of annual concerts, about 20 in all, in the Smetana Hall of the Národní Dům (National House). Chief conductor, Vaclav Talich.

4. THE ŠAK PHILHARMONIC SOCIETY, conducted by V. V. Šak, L. V. Čelanský, J. Kvapil and others.

5. THE PRAGUE CHORAL UNION (*Hlahol*). Conductor, Jaromír Herle. Four concerts in the year.

6. THE MUSICAL EVENINGS OF THE STATE CONSERVATOIRE. Twice weekly.

7. THE CZECH CHAMBER MUSIC UNION OF

PRAGUE. Sixteen serial concerts yearly, employing the Bohemian (Czech) String Quartet, the Ševčik-Lhotsky Quartet, the Zika and Ondříček Quartets.

8. THE CHORAL UNION OF PRAGUE TEACHERS (*Pěvecké sdruženi pražskych učitelů*). Conductor, Hubert Doležil.

Other- societies on a smaller scale include : the CZECH ASSOCIATION FOR THE ENCOURAGEMENT OF SONG (Lieder); the ASSOCIATION FOR MODERN MUSIC ; the CONCERTS OF THE WORKING MEN'S ACADEMY ; the PEOPLE'S MUSICAL EVENINGS ; the MUSICAL EVENINGS OF THE LEAGUE OF CULTURE (*Svaz Osvětový*).

9. PHILHARMONIC CONCERTS in the NEW GERMAN THEATRE. Conductor, A. Zemlinsky.

10. THE GERMAN CHAMBER MUSIC SOCIETY.

11. *Teaching Institutions.*—(1) THE CZECH UNIVERSITY (Charles IV.). Chair of Music, lecturer in æsthetics, etc., Prof. Dr. Zdeněk Nejedlý ; professor in ordinary and reader in musical theory, Prof. J. B. Foerster ; head of the department of musical books, Prof. Zd. Nejedlý.

(2) THE GERMAN UNIVERSITY. Chair of Music, Dr. Heinrich Rietsch ; history of music, Privatdozent Dr. Paul Nettl ; reader in musical theory, Hans Schneider.

(3) THE STATE CONSERVATOIRE OF MUSIC, established in the Emmaus Monastery since 1920. Founded in 1811, and therefore, with the exception of Paris, the oldest Conservatoire in mid-Europe. Reorganised as a State institution (with recognition of the Czech language) in 1920. It includes a Master-school and a Middle-school under the same direction, and is run upon the lines of other State middle-schools. There are two classes of teachers : professors in ordinary and extraordinary. At the head of all is the Rector, chosen from the ranks of the teachers in the Master-school. This is an annual appointment (1921–22, Vit. Novák ; 1922–23, J. B. Foerster ; 1923–24, Karel Hoffmeister ; 1924–25, Josef Suk). There is also an Administrator in charge of the business side of the institution.

(4) THE GERMAN ACADEMY OF MUSIC (with State subvention). Rector, Prof. Alex. Zemlinsky ; Director, Prof. Romeo Finke.

(5) PRIVATE INSTITUTIONS. Music classes of the Huss School (League of Culture); 'Hudebni Budeč' for the improvement of school singing; Music School of the Choral Society (Lukes); Music School for Blind Children, etc. R. N.

PRALLTRILLER, an ornament of the keyboard instruments not used in the classical French school and possessing no equivalent English name, though it is in fact a short shake and in effect an inverted MORDENT (*q.v.*).

1. *Written.*  *Played.*

The Pralltriller is characterised by C. P. E. Bach as the most agreeable and at the same time the most indispensable of all graces, but also the most difficult. He says that it ought to be made with such extreme rapidity that, even when introduced on a very short note, the listener must not be aware of any loss of value.

The proper, and according to some writers the only, place for the introduction of the Pralltriller is on the first of two notes which descend diatonically, a position which the Mordent cannot properly occupy. This being the case, there can be no doubt that in such instances as the following, where the Mordent is indicated in a false position, the Pralltriller is in reality intended, and the sign is an error either of the pen or of the press.

2. MOZART. Rondo in D.

Nevertheless the Mordent is occasionally, though very rarely, met with on a note followed by a note one degree lower, as in J. S. Bach's fugue in C in Book II. of the '48.' This is, however, the only instance in Bach's works with which the writer is acquainted.

When the Pralltriller is preceded by an appoggiatura, or a slurred note one degree above the principal note, its entrance is slightly delayed (Ex. 3), and the same is the case if the Mordent is preceded by a note one degree below (Ex. 4).

3. W. F. BACH, Sonata in D.

4. J. S. BACH, Sarabande from 'Suite anglaise No. 3.'

C. P. E. Bach says that if this occurs before a pause the appoggiatura is to be held very long, and the remaining three notes to be 'snapped up' very quickly, thus—

5. *Written.*          *Played.*

The earlier writers drew a distinction between the Pralltriller and the so - called Schneller (*schnellen,* ' to fillip '). This grace was in all respects identical with the Pralltriller, but it was held that the latter could only occur on a descending diatonic progression (as in Ex. 1), while the Schneller might appear on detached notes. It was also laid down that the Schneller was always to be written in small notes, thus— , while the sign only indicated the Pralltriller. Türk observes, nevertheless, that the best composers have often made use of the sign in cases where the indispensable diatonic progression is absent, and have thus indicated the Pralltriller where the Schneller was really intended. This is, however, of no consequence, since the two ornaments are essentially the same, and Türk himself ends by saying ' the enormity of this crime may be left for the critics to determine.'

Both Mordent and Pralltriller occur very frequently in the works of Bach and his immediate successors ; perhaps the most striking instance of the lavish use of both occurs in the first movement of Bach's ' Capriccio on the Departure of a Brother,' which though only seventeen bars in length contains no fewer than 17 Mordents and 30 Pralltriller.          F. T.

PRATELLA, FRANCESCO BALILLA (*b.* Lugo, Romagna, Feb. 1, 1880), composer, studied at the Liceo Musicale of Pesaro, where his masters were Antonio Cicognani and Mascagni. He took his degree as a composer in 1903 with the symphonic poem ' La chiesa di Polenta,' based on Carducci's ode of the same name. In 1910 Pratella issued, at Milan, his first pamphlet on futurist music, dealing with æsthetic questions which aroused a considerable amount of controversy among Italian musicians, and he further propagated his views by means of numerous lectures in the principal Italian cities. From 1914–17 he contributed to the futurist review *Gli Avvenimenti,* and subsequently collected all his writing and lectures in the publications entitled *Evoluzione della musica* and *Croniche e critiche.*

Pratella has written the following operas :

' Il regno lontano,' ' Lilia,' ' La Sina d' Vargöun,' ' L' aviatore Dro ' and ' Il dono primaverile.'

Among his orchestral works the most important are :

' Musica futurista per orchestra ' (Inno alla Vita), produced at the Teatro Costanzi in Rome in 1913 ; ' Romagna,' cycle of five symphonic poems ; and three dances, ' La Guerra.'

There are also a number of piano, organ and violin pieces, songs, and a trio for violin, violoncello and piano.          E. B.

PRATI, ALESSIO (*b.* Ferrara, July 19, 1750 ; *d.* there, Jan. 17, 1788), studied at the Conservatorio di Loreto, Naples. He visited Paris, where his opera ' Ifigenia in Aulide ' met with great success. In 1781 he was in St. Petersburg, where he brought out 2 oratorios ; and in 1783 was in Vienna. He returned to Ferrara in 1784 and wrote operas for Venice and Turin ; he also wrote masses and other church music, vocal rondos, arias, romances, concertos for harpsichord and sonatas for harpsichord and for harp, some with violin ; also a duet for 2 violoncellos (*Q.-L.*).

PRATT, JOHN (*b.* Cambridge, 1772 ; *d.* there, Mar. 9, 1855), son of Jonas Pratt, music-seller and teacher. In 1780 he was admitted a chorister of King's College. After quitting the choir he became a pupil of, and deputy for, Dr. Randall, the college organist, and on his death in Mar. 1799 was appointed his successor. In Sept. following he was appointed organist to the University, and in 1813 organist of St. Peter's College. He composed several services and anthems. He published ' A Collection of Anthems, selected from the works of Handel, Haydn, Mozart, Clari, Leo and Carissimi ' (an adaptation to English words of detached movements from the masses, etc., of those composers), and a selection of psalm and hymn tunes first published in 1810, and again in 1820, with the title ' Psalmodia Cantabrigiensis.'
                                        W. H. H.

PRATT, WALDO SELDEN (*b.* Philadelphia, Nov. 10, 1857), writer on musical subjects, edited (1920) a valuable *American Supplement* to this Dictionary (Macmillan Co., New York), giving full accounts of the careers of a great number of American musicians. A *New Encyclopædia of Music and Musicians* followed in 1924 (see DICTIONARIES OF MUSIC). His many publications include works on church music and a *History of Music* (1907). (See *Baker.*)

PRATTEN, (1) ROBERT SIDNEY (*b.* Bristol, Jan. 23, 1824 ; *d.* Ramsgate, Feb. 10, 1868), a distinguished English flute-player. His father was a professor of music in Bristol. The boy was considered a prodigy on the flute, and in his twelfth year was much in request at the concerts at Bath and Bristol. From thence he migrated to Dublin, where he played first flute at the Theatre Royal and musical societies. In 1846 he came to London, and was soon engaged as first flute at the Royal Italian Opera, the Sacred Harmonic and Philharmonic Societies, the Musical Society of London, Alfred Mellon's concerts, etc. Through the kindness of the late Duke of Cambridge, Pratten passed some time in Germany in the study of theory and composition, and became a clever writer for his instrument. His Concertstück and Fantasia on Marie Stuart are among the best of his productions. His widow was a well-known professor of the guitar. His brother, (2) FREDERICK SIDNEY (d. London, Mar. 3, 1873), was an eminent contrabassist, engaged in the principal orchestras.    G.

PREAMBULUM, see PRELUDE.

PRÉ AUX CLERCS, LE, opéra-comique in 3 acts; words by Planard, music by Hérold. Produced Opéra-Comique, Dec. 15, 1832; in London (in French), Princess's, May 2, 1849; in Italian, Covent Garden, June 26, 1880.    G.

PRECENTOR (Fr. *grand chantre*; Ger. *Primicier*; at Cologne, *chorepiscopus*; Span. *chantre, caput scholae* or *capiscol*; Gr. *protopsaltes* and *canonarcha*), the director of the choir in a cathedral, collegiate or monastic church. In the English cathedrals of the old foundation, as well as in the cathedrals of France, Spain and Germany, the Precentor was always a dignitary, and ranked next to the Dean, although in a few instances the Archdeacons preceded him. At Exeter the Precentor installed the Canons : at York he installed the Dean and other dignitaries ; and at Lichfield even the Bishop received visible possession of his office from his hands. At Paris the Precentor of Notre-Dame divided with the Chancellor the supervision of the schools and teachers in the city, and of the respondents in the university. The dignity of Precentor was established at Exeter, Salisbury, York and Lincoln in the 11th century; at Rouen, Amiens, Chichester, Wells, Lichfield and Hereford in the 12th century ; and at St. David's and St. Paul's (London) in the 13th century. In cathedrals of the new foundation (with the exception of Christ Church, Dublin) the Precentor is a minor canon appointed by the Dean and Chapter, and removable at their pleasure. The duties of the Precentor were to conduct the musical portion of the service, to superintend the choir generally, to distribute copes and regulate processions ; on Sundays and great festivals to begin the hymns, responses, etc., and at Mass to give the note to the Bishop and Dean, as the Succentor did to the canons and clerks. In monasteries the Precentor had similar duties, and was in addition generally chief librarian and registrar, as well as superintendent of much of the ecclesiastical discipline of the establishment. In some French cathedrals he carries a silver or white staff as the badge of his dignity. In the Anglican Church his duties are to superintend the musical portions of the service, and he has the general management of the choir. His stall in the cathedral corresponds with that of the Dean. (Walcott, *Sacred Archæology*; Hook, *Church Dictionary*.) See CANTOR.

                    W. B. S.

PRECIOSA, play in 4 acts by P. A. Wolff, with overture and music by Weber; music completed July 15, 1820. Produced Royal Opera House, Berlin, Mar. 14, 1821 ; Paris, in 1825, at the Odéon, adapted and arranged by Sauvage and Cremont ; Apr. 16, 1858, at the Théâtre Lyrique, reduced to 1 act by Nuitter and Beaumont. In London, in English, Covent Garden, Apr. 28, 1825.    G.

PREDIERI, LUC' ANTONIO (b. Bologna, Sept. 13, 1688 ; d. there, 1769 or 1770), became maestro di cappella of the cathedral, was made a member of the Accademia dei Filarmonici in 1706, and its president in 1723. On the recommendation of Fux he was appointed by the Emperor Charles VI. vice-Kapellmeister of the court chapel at Vienna in Feb. 1739. He was promoted to the chief Kapellmeistership in 1746, but dismissed in 1751 with title and full salary, apparently in favour of Reutter. He returned to Bologna, and died there. Among the MSS. of the court library and of the Gesellschaft der Musikfreunde at Vienna are many scores of his operas, oratorios, feste di camera, serenatas, etc., which pleased in their day, and were for the most part produced at court. (See *Q.-L.* for list.)    C. F. P.

PREFACE. One of the most important and familiar of the ecclesiastical recitatives is the dialogue and solo which introduces the *Sanctus* at the Holy Eucharist. After three versicles and responses (or two only in the English rite) the Preface follows, set to a somewhat elaborate melody of the simple recitative type. The two cadences which chiefly distinguish it are as follows :

The whole Preface, including the special additions made to it for special occasions, is based upon these figures.    W. H. F.

PREINDL, JOSEPH (b. Marbach on the Danube, Jan. 30, 1756 ; d. Oct. 26, 1823), a pupil of Albrechtsberger in Vienna, became in 1780 or 1790 choirmaster of the Peterskirche, and in 1809 Kapellmeister of St. Stephen's, in which post he died. He was a solid composer, a skilled pianist and organist, and a valued teacher of singing. His compositions include five masses (printed), a Requiem, a book of choral settings of the 'Lamentationes,' smaller church pieces, and pianoforte and organ music, partly published in Vienna. He also printed a *Gesanglehre* (2nd ed. Steiner) and 'Melodien aller deutschen Kirchenlieder welche in St. Stephansdom in Wien gesungen werden,' with cadences, symphonies and preludes, for organ or pianoforte (Diabelli, 3rd ed. revised and enlarged by Sechter). Seyfried edited his posthumous work, *Wiener Tonschule*, a method of instruction in harmony, counterpoint and fugue (Haslinger, 1827 ; 2nd ed. 1832).

                   C. F. P.

PRELLEUR, PETER, was of French extraction, and in early life a writing-master. About 1728 he was elected organist of St. Alban's,

Wood Street, and shortly afterwards engaged to play the harpsichord at Goodman's Fields Theatre, which he continued to do until the suppression of the theatre under the Licensing Act in 1737, composing also the dances and occasional music. In 1730 he published *The Modern Musick Master, or the Universal Musician*, containing an introduction to singing, instructions for playing the flute, German flute, hautboy, violin and harpsichord, with a brief History of Music and a Musical Dictionary. In 1735 he was elected the first organist of Christ Church, Spitalfields. After the closing of Goodman's Fields Theatre he was engaged at a newly opened place of entertainment in Leman Street close by, called the New Wells, for which he composed some songs, and an interlude entitled ' Baucis and Philemon,' containing a good overture and some pleasing songs and duets, the score of which he published. Fifteen hymn tunes by him were included in a collection of twenty-four published by one Moze, an organist, in 1758, under the title of ' Divine Melody,' in which he is spoken of as dead. W. H. H.

PRELUDE (Fr. *prélude*; Ger. *Vorspiel*; Ital. *preludio*; Lat. *praeludium*), strictly a preliminary movement, an introduction to the main body of a work; also used as the title of a movement of an independent character.

In the sonatas of Corelli and Bach the Prelude developed into a simple movement in the old sonata form (see FORM); in the ' 48 Preludes and Fugues' for clavier, and those for organ, no special form is adhered to, indeed the term may be said to be free from formal restrictions.

In the case of opera the term is used as a synonym for overture to emphasise the fact that the music is very closely related to what follows. Again, however, there is no restriction as regards form. Compare the several Wagner Preludes. (See INTRODUCTION; OVERTURE.)

As a movement apart, the Chopin Preludes set the fashion for a short movement of a suggestive, imaginative nature, often approaching an improvisation. His example was followed by numerous composers of pianoforte music. (See RACHMANINOV and SCRIABIN.) N. C. G.

PRÉLUDES, LES, ' Symphonic Poems' by Liszt for full orchestra; first performed Weimar, Feb. 23, 1854. G.

PRENTICE, THOMAS RIDLEY (*b.* Paslow Hall, Ongar, July 6, 1842; *d.* Hampstead, July 15, 1895), entered the R.A.M. in 1861, studying the piano under Walter Macfarren, and harmony and composition under G. A. Macfarren. In 1863 he obtained the Silver Medal and the Potter Exhibition. In 1869 he started ' monthly popular concerts ' at Brixton, which were carried on for five years, the assistance of first-rate artists being secured, and many new works, both English and foreign,

being performed. For some years he gave an annual concert at the Hanover Square Rooms. At the Crystal Palace he played Beethoven's Rondo in B♭ with orchestra, for the first time in England. In 1872 he was given the post of organist at Christ Church, Lee Park, but ill-health compelled him to resign it after a few years. In 1880 he was appointed professor of the piano at the G.S.M., and in the same year he organised an extremely successful series of ' twopenny concerts ' in Kensington Town Hall, especially intended for the working classes. In 1881 he became professor at the Blackheath Conservatoire of Music. His compositions include a cantata, ' Linda,' for female voices, several anthems, ' Break forth into joy,' ' I love the Lord,' etc., partsongs, trios, etc., besides numerous songs and pianoforte pieces, among the latter of which may be mentioned a ' Gavotte fantastique,' an elegy, a minuet and trio, etc. He edited six cantatas by Carissimi, with accompaniments, and wrote an excellent series of instruction-books for the pianoforte under the collective title of *The Musician* (Swan Sonnenschein & Co.), in which special stress is laid upon the analysis of musical compositions from the beginning of pianoforte study. His *Hand Gymnastics* is No. 36 of Novello's Music Primers. M.

PREPARATION. The possibility of using a very large proportion of the dissonant combinations in music was only discovered at first through the process of ' suspension,' which amounts to the delaying of the progression of a part or voice out of a concordant combination while the other parts move on to a fresh combination; so that until the delayed part moves also to its destination a dissonance is heard. As long as the parts which have moved first wait for the suspended notes to move into their places before moving farther, the group belongs to the order of ordinary suspensions (Ex. 1); but when they move again while the part which was as it were left behind moves into its place, a different class of discords is created (Ex. 2). In both these cases the sounding of the

Ex. 1.   Ex. 2.

discordant note in the previous combination (*i.e.* the upper C in the first chord of both examples) is called the ' preparation ' of the discord, and the latter class are sometimes distinguished especially as prepared discords.
C. H. H. P.

PRÉS, JOSQUIN DES, see JOSQUIN DES PRÉS.

PRESA (literally, ' a taking '), a sign used to indicate the places at which the Guida (or

Subject) of a canon is to be taken up by the several voices.

The following are the forms most frequently adopted :

·S·    :S:    ·Ṡ·    +    ※

In the famous ' Enimme,' or enigmatical canons, of the 15th and 16th centuries an INSCRIPTION (q.v.) is usually substituted for the Presa, though in many cases even this is wanting, and the singer is left without assistance.

W. S. R.

PRESSENDA, JOHANNES FRANCISCUS (b. Lequio-Berria, Alba, Jan. 6, 1777 ; d. Turin, Sept. 11, 1854), a Turin violin-maker of local repute.

When a lad of 12 he begged and fiddled his way to Cremona, where he arrived after an eventful and arduous journey, and in due course became a pupil of Lorenzo Storioni. On the completion of his studies at Cremona he returned to his native town in the same manner in which he came, and in 1814 set up a business of his own at Alba. Meeting with but little encouragement he removed to Carmagnola in 1817, and finally drifted to Turin in 1820. Here success at last attended his efforts, owing to the patronage of Giambattista Polledro. This pupil of Pugnani was appointed conductor of the royal band by King Charles Felix in 1824, and in the reorganisation which ensued, Polledro, together with Ghebart (his successor), adopted the use of Pressenda's violins in the royal band and the orchestras of the theatres. Tarisio bought a considerable number of his violins, predicting an auspicious future for them, and diplomas and silver medals were awarded Pressenda by various Philharmonic Societies. Beyond Italy Pressenda's name is comparatively unknown, but his work was brought before the notice of the musical public in this country in 1882, in connexion with the Hodges v. Chanot case. The violin—a remarkably handsome instrument bearing a Bergonzi label—which was the cause of the suit, brought to light the very doubtful practices of violin-dealers, and their methods of inserting false labels. Von Lütgendorff (Die Geigen- und Lautenmacher) highly commends Pressenda's work, especially praising his varnish, and the individuality displayed in the scrolls.

BIBL.—B.-G. RINALDI, Classica fabricazione di violini in Piemonte (Turin, 1873), followed by a German translation , VON LÜTGENDORFF, Die Geigen- und Lautenmacher; CHANOT, Hodges v. Chanot, Criticisms and Remarks on the great Violin Case ; Times, Standard, Daily Telegraph and contemporary papers between Feb. and June 1882 ; HERON-ALLEN, Hodges against Chanot, being the History of a Celebrated Case (London, 1883).         E. H.-A.

PRESSER, THEODORE (b. Pittsburg, Pennsylvania, July 3, 1848; d. Philadelphia, Nov. 1925), American publisher and musical philanthropist. He was an early student at the New England Conservatory; later he spent two years in Leipzig. In 1883 he founded, at Lynchburg, Virginia, The Étude

(moved a few months later to Philadelphia), a monthly magazine devoted to the interests of music teachers and students, which has a large circulation ; three years later he established a music-publishing business which, as the Theo. Presser Co., is now an important firm. In 1906 he opened, in Philadelphia, the Presser Home for Retired Music Teachers, the only one in America. In 1916 the Presser Foundation was established, with funds of over $1,000,000, which supports, besides the Home, a Department of Scholarships, given directly to institutions and not to individuals, and a Department for the Relief of Deserving Musicians.

W. S. S.

PRESTISSIMO, 'very quickly,' indicates the highest rate of speed used in music.

PRESTO, ' fast,' indicates a rate of speed quicker than allegro, or any other sign except prestissimo. When the time becomes faster in the middle of a movement, ' Più presto ' is used, as for instance in Beethoven's Quartet in E♭ (op. 74), third movement (Presto), where the direction for the part of the movement that serves as the trio is ' Più presto quasi prestissimo.' A curious misuse of this direction is in the pianoforte sonata of Schumann, op. 22, where the first movement is headed ' Il più presto possibile,' and in German below ' So rasch wie möglich.' At forty-one bars from the end of the movement comes ' Più mosso,' translated ' Schneller,' and again, twenty-five bars from the end, ' Ancora più mosso,' ' Noch schneller.'

PRESTON, (1) THOMAS (late 15th or early 16th cent.), English composer of church music. B.M. Add. MSS. 29,996 contains an early 16th-century collection of 91 motets arranged for organ (or possibly virginal), written on two staves of 5, 6 or 8 lines each. Nos. 1-50 are in the hand of John REDFORD (q.v.), who is composer of most, if not all, of these. Preston is similarly the composer of most, if not all, of Nos. 51-69 : the remainder are anonymous. They are mostly composed on plain-songs, and were probably reductions of motets originally written for voices, and used to support the voices. A motet by Preston, ' O Lux,' is in the Commonplace Book of John BALDWIN (q.v.).

(2) THOMAS (b. 1662), English organist and composer. He was organist of Ripon Minster from 1690 to 1730 and was buried in the South Transept (West's Cath. Org.). He is the composer of a piece, ' Tho. Preston's Jig,' which appears in B.M. Add. MSS. 17,853/20b, a miscellaneous collection of tunes for violin (or flute).

(3) THOMAS, son of the above, succeeded his father as organist of Ripon in 1731, and held this post until 1748 (West's Cath. Org.).

J. Mᴷ.

PRESTON & SON, a family of London music publishers during the latter part of the 18th and the early portion of the 19th centuries.

The firm was first started by John Preston, who in 1774 was established at 9 Banbury Court, Long Acre, as a musical instrument-maker. In 1776 he had removed to 105 Strand, near Beaufort Buildings, and was publishing some small and unimportant musical works. Two years later he was at 97 Strand, where the firm remained until 1823. John Preston's business after his removal to the Strand soon became one of the most important in the trade, and he issued a vast quantity of music of all kinds, buying, in 1789, the whole of the plates and stock-in-trade of Robert Bremner, who had then just died. About this time the son, Thomas, came into the business, and towards the end of the century John's name disappears. In 1823 Thomas Preston had left the Strand for 71 Dean Street, Soho, where he remained until about 1835, the business then becoming the property of Coventry & Hollier, who reissued some of the Preston publications. Shortly after 1850 Novello were large purchasers at their sale of effects.

The Preston publications include an interesting series of country dances begun in 1786, and extending for nearly forty years after this date. Others are many of the popular operas of the day ; such works as Bunting's ' Ancient Music of Ireland,' 1796, W. Linley's ' Shakespeare's Dramatic Songs,' J. S. Smith's ' Musica antiqua,' etc. They were also the London publishers of George Thomson's Scottish, Irish and Welsh collections.      F. K.

PRÉVOST, EUGÈNE PROSPER (b. Paris, Aug. 23, 1809 ; d. New Orleans, Aug. 30, 1872), studied harmony and counterpoint at the Conservatoire with Seuriot and Jelensperger, and composition with Lesueur ; took the second Grand Prix de Rome in 1829, and the Prix de Rome in 1831 for his cantata ' Bianca Capello.' Previous to this he had produced ' L'Hôtel des Princes ' and ' Le Grenadier de Wagram '—one-act pieces containing pretty music—both with success, at the Ambigu-Comique. On his return from Italy, ' Cosimo,' an opéra-bouffe in two acts, was well received at the Opéra-Comique, and followed by ' Le bon Garçon,' one act, of no remarkable merit. After his marriage with Eléonore Colon, Prévost left Paris to become conductor of the theatre at Havre. In 1838 he left Havre for New Orleans, where he remained twenty years. He was in great request as a singing-master, conducted the French theatre at New Orleans, and produced with marked success a Mass for full orchestra, and several dramatic works, including ' Esmeralda,' which contained some striking music. None of these was engraved. When the American war broke out he returned to Paris, and became favourably known as a conductor. He directed the concerts of the Champs Elysées, and the fantasias which he arranged for them show great skill in orchestra-

tion. ' L'Illustre Gaspard ' (1 act) was produced at the Opéra-Comique (Feb. 11, 1863), but the fellow-pupil of Berlioz, Reber and A. Thomas had virtually fallen out of the race.

His son LÉON, also a good conductor, recalled him to New Orleans, where he settled finally towards the end of 1867.      G. C.

PREYER, GOTTFRIED (b. Hausbrunn, Lower Austria, Mar. 15, 1807 ; d. Vienna, May 9, 1901), studied at Vienna with Sechter, became in 1835 organist of the Reformed Church, in 1844 supernumerary vice-Kapellmeister to the court, in 1846 court organist, in 1862 vice-Kapell-meister, and retired on a pension in 1876. From 1853 he was Kapellmeister of the cathedral. His connexion with the Conservatorium dates from 1838, when he became professor of harmony and counterpoint, and conductor of the pupils' concerts ; from 1844–48 he directed the institution. The Tonkünstler-Societät performed his oratorio ' Noah ' in 1842, 1845 and 1851. He printed a symphony, op. 16 (Diabelli); several masses and smaller church pieces ; music for pianoforte and organ, choruses, and a large quantity of popular Lieder (chiefly Diabelli) ; ' Hymns for the Orthodox Greek Church,' in three vols., Vienna, 1847 ; a Mass for four male voices with organ, op. 76, etc.

     C. F. P.

PRICE, JOHN, a 16th–17th-century English cornet- and viola bastarda-player. Mersenne in his *Harmonie universelle* calls him an excellent piccolo-player. In 1605 he was appointed at the court at Stuttgart, where in 1625 he had formed an English company together with John and David Morell (his brothers-in-law ?) and John Dixon. On Apr. 23, 1629, he was appointed in the Dresden court chapel, and there formed, with the Elector's permission, the Little Chamber Music (*Kleine Kammer-musik*). The war, however, drove him away, and he received his passport in 1633 ; but in 1634 his wife still wrote to the Elector for support (Q.-L.).

PRICK-SONG, the name given by old English writers upon music to divisions or descant upon a Plain-song or Ground, which were written, or pricked, down, in contradistinction to those which were performed extemporaneously. (See Morley's *Plaine and Easy Introduction*, Second Part.) Shakespeare (*Romeo and Juliet*, Act ii. Sc. 4) makes Mercutio describe Tybalt as one who

'fights as you sing prick-song, keeps time, distance, and proportion ; rests me his minim rest, one, two, and the third in your bosom.'

The term ' pricking of musick bookes ' was formerly employed to express the writing of them. Payments for so doing are frequently found in the accounts of cathedral and college choirs.      W. H. H.

PRIESTNALL, JOHN (b. Saddleworth, near Oldham, Nov. 1819 ; d. Rochdale, Jan. 18,

1899), English violin-maker and repairer. Originally a joiner and pattern-maker, as well as the inventor of several improvements in wood-cutting machines, Priestnall did not devote himself entirely to violin-making until 1870. From that year until his death he made some 300 excellent violins, 30 violas, 6 violoncellos and 8 double-basses. The wood of these instruments is mostly regular in figure, the workmanship finished, the scrolls cut with a free firm hand, the sound-holes pleasing but somewhat quaint, and the gold-amber oil varnish transparent and handsome. The tone of the violins is powerful, but has something of the viola quality on the lower strings. Priestnall's instruments do not bear a conventional label, but his name is stamped upon the wood with a cold punch in several places, and the opus number marked on the button. As a repairer this maker's inventive genius stood him in good stead, and brought him considerable fame, and a vast number of old English and French violins owe their regeneration to his clever manipulation. During his lifetime Priestnall sold his fiddles for £4, but their value has risen considerably since his death.

BIBL.—MEREDITH MORRIS, *British Violin-Makers.*   E. H.-A.

PRIMAVERA, GIOVANNI LEONARDO (*b.* Barletta, kingdom of Naples). All that we know of his career is that about 1573 he was maestro di cappella to the Spanish Governor of Milan. He has sometimes been confused with Giovanni Leonardo di l' Arpa, though the very title of the work in which the two names occur together shows them to belong to two different persons (' Il 1 lib. de Canzone Napolitane a 3 voci di Jo. Leonardo Primavera con alcune Napolitane di Jo. Leonardo di L' Arpa, 1565 '). Primavera's works consist of several Books of Madrigals *a* 5 and 6, some of which are lost, and four Books of Canzone Napolitane or Villotte *a* 3, all published between 1565 and 1584. Palestrina took the themes of a madrigal *a* 6 by Primavera, ' Nasce la gioia mia,' as a subject for richer contrapuntal treatment by himself in a Mass bearing the same title, and having the same distribution of voices. The Mass is No. 7 in his ' Fifth Book of Masses,' dedicated to Duke William of Bavaria and published in 1590.      J. R. M.

PRIME (Lat. *prima* ; *hora prima. Officium* (*vel Oratio*) *ad horam primam*), the first of the ' Lesser Hours ' in the Roman Breviary.

PRIMO, ' first,' is used in two ways in music : (1) In pianoforte duets *Primo* or *1mo* is generally put over the right-hand page, and then means the part taken by the ' treble ' player, while *Secondo* or *2do* is put over that for the ' bass '; while in an orchestral score where, for example, two clarinet parts are written on the same stave, the indications *1mo* or *2do* show which of the pair undertakes

a solo passage. (2) In the repetition of the first section of a movement a few bars are often necessary before the double-bar to lead back to the repetition, which are not required the second time of playing the section. The words *Primo, 1mo, 1ma volta* or *1st time* are then put over all these bars, so that when the repeated portion reaches this direction, the player goes on to the part after the double-bar, leaving out the bars over which ' Primo ' is written. The first few bars after the double-bar are frequently, but not always, labelled *Secondo, 2do* or *2nd time.*

PRINCE FERELON, musical extravaganza in 1 act; text and music by Nicholas Gatty. First performance in public, ' Old Vic,' May 21, 1921.

PRINCE IGOR, opera in a prologue and 4 acts; text and music by Borodin; unfinished, but completed by Rimsky-Korsakov and Glazounov. Produced Imperial Opera, St. Petersburg, Oct. 23 (O.S.), 1890; Drury Lane (in Russian), June 8, 1914; Covent Garden (in English), July 26, 1919.

PRINCESSE D'AUBERGE (Herberg prinses), lyric drama in 3 acts; Flemish text by Nestor de Tière, French translation by Gustave Lagye, music by Jan Blockx. Produced in Flemish at Antwerp in 1896.

PRINCESS IDA ; OR CASTLE ADAMANT, comic opera in a prologue and 3 acts ; written by W. S. Gilbert, music by Sullivan. Produced Savoy Theatre, Jan. 5, 1884.      M.

PRINCESS OF KENSINGTON, A, comic opera in 2 acts ; text by Basil Hood, music by Edward German. Produced Savoy Theatre, Jan. 22, 1903.

PRINCIPAL. (1) An organ stop. In Germany the term is very properly applied to the most important 8-foot stops of open flue-pipes on the manuals, and to open 16-foot stops on the pedals, thus corresponding with our ' open diapasons.' But in this country the Principal is, with very few exceptions, the chief open metal stop of 4-foot pitch, and should more properly be termed an Octave or Principal octave, since it sounds an octave above the diapasons.      J. S.

(2) PRINCIPAL or PRINZIPALE. A term employed in many of Handel's scores for the third trumpet part. This is not usually in unison with the first and second trumpets, which are designated as Tromba *1mo* and *2do*. It is often written for in the old soprano clef with C on the lowest line, and has a range somewhat lower than the trombe. The older works on instrumentation, such as those of Schilling, Koch, Schladebach and Lichtenthal, recognise the difference and draw a distinction between ' Principal-Stimme ' and a ' Clarin-Stimme.' It is obvious that whereas the tromba or clarino represented the old small-bored instrument, now obsolete, for which the

majority of Handel's and Bach's high and difficult solos were composed, the Principal, in tone and compass, more nearly resembled the modern large-bored military trumpet. The contrast can easily be recognised by an examination of the overture to the 'Occasional Oratorio' in Arnold's edition, or that of the Dettingen Te Deum as published by the German Handel Society. In the latter the old soprano, in the former the usual treble clef, is adopted.        w. h. s.

In old trumpet music, in which trumpets with kettle-drums formed the whole band, four and sometimes five trumpet parts occur; in these cases, as in those noted above for three trumpets, the Principal is the name given to the lowest part. (See TRUMPET.)        d. j. b.

(3) Principals, in modern musical language, are the solo singers or players in a concert, and those who lead in the different departments of the orchestra.        w. h. s.

PRING. Three brothers, sons of James Pring, were all choristers of St. Paul's under Robert Hudson, as follows:

(1) JACOB CUBITT (b. Lewisham, 1771; d. 1799) was organist of St. Botolph, Aldersgate Street, London. He graduated as Mus.B. at Oxford in 1797, was the composer of several anthems, glees and other vocal pieces, and one of the founders of the Concentores Sodales. He published two books of glees, canons, etc., a set of eight anthems, and a set of harpsichord sonatinas. Seven glees and a catch by him are included in Warren's Collections.

(2) JOSEPH (b. Kensington, Jan. 15, 1776; d. Bangor, Feb. 13, 1842) was on Apr. 1, 1793, appointed organist of Bangor Cathedral on the resignation of Olive, but not formally elected until Sept. 28, 1810. In 1805 he published 'Twenty Anthems,' and on Jan. 27, 1808, accumulated the degrees of Mus.B. and Mus.D. at Oxford. In June 1813 he and three of the vicars-choral of Bangor Cathedral presented a petition to the Court of Chancery for the proper application of certain tithes which had, by an Act of Parliament passed in 1685, been appropriated for the maintenance of the cathedral choir, but had been diverted by the capitular body to other purposes. The suit lasted until 1819, when Lord Chancellor Eldon, setting at naught the express provisions of the Act, sanctioned a scheme which indeed gave to the organist and choir increased stipends, but yet kept them considerably below the amounts they would have received if the Act had been fully carried out. Dr. Pring, in 1819, printed copies of the proceedings in the suit, and other documents, with annotations, forming a history of the transactions, which has long been a scarce book. He also wrote a pamphlet on the Menai Tubular Bridge. He was buried in the Cathedral Yard at Bangor. His epitaph is given in West's Cath. Org. p. 4.

(3) ISAAC (b. Kensington, 1777; d. Oct. 18, 1799) became in 1794 assistant organist to Dr. Philip Hayes at Oxford, and on his death in 1797 succeeded him as organist of New College. He graduated at Oxford in Mar. 1799, and died of consumption in the same year.

(4) JAMES SHARPE (b. circa 1811; d. Jan. 3, 1868), son of Joseph (2), succeeded his father at Bangor. He was successively chorister, assistant organist and organist from 1842, being appointed from year to year. He was buried in Glenadda Cemetery, Bangor. Some chants by him are in Warren's Collections (West's Cath. Org.).        w. h. h.

PRINTING OF MUSIC. The art of printing music followed quickly upon that of ordinary letterpress typography. Though the printing of music was fairly frequent upon the Continent, yet it was nearly a century after the first continental work that any attempt was made in that direction in England.

The date 1465 is mentioned as that when music was first printed, but this is not confirmed. A more authentic date is 1476, when Ulrich Hahn printed a missal at Rome. Another early musical work is that of Jorg Reyser of Würzburg with the date 1481.

Other music printers of the 15th century were Octavianus Scotus working at Venice, S. Planck (1482), J. Sensenschmidt (1455), Erhard Ratdolt (1487). In the works of these printers the notes were printed in black and the stave lines were red, which, of course, were worked off at a second printing.

It is quite obvious that double printing is a somewhat difficult operation to effect correctly. The registration has to be carefully carried out, so that each note stands upon its particular stave line. It presently occurred to these early printers that as the art of wood engraving was by no means in its infancy, it was quite as easy to cut a page of music in wood as it was to produce a woodcut book illustration, and that this music block could be worked off with the text at one printing. How very clumsily this was done is shown overleaf in the reproduction of a page of Musices opusculum printed by Nicolaus Burtius at Bologna in 1487. Meanwhile Ottaviano dei PETRUCCI (q.v.) effected great improvements in musical typography, and he may be considered the first to print florid song from metal type. He settled at Venice, and his first work was a collection of ninety-six songs, published in 1501; another work of his appeared in 1503.

From this period music printing on the Continent was fairly frequent and more or less good, both from metal type and from wood blocks.

It is perhaps a strain to call the few notes in Higden's Policronicon, printed by Wynkyn de Worde at Westminster in 1495, the first English music printing. It is but eight notes built up from 'quads' and 'rules' to illustrate a passage in the text. In the previous edition, printed by Caxton in 1482, the notes are filled in by hand.

type at this period, and Rastell is credited with four pages set up in movable type in *A New Interlude and Mery of the Nature of iiij Elements*, the date being probably 1539.

Page (Tractatus 2dus, p. 76) from the *Opusculum* of Burtius (Burzio), in the Library of A. H. Littleton, Esq.

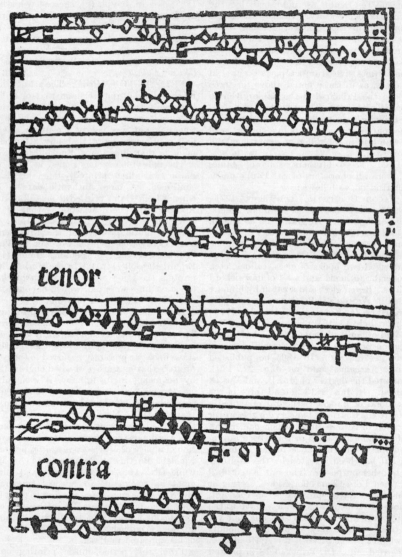

There was little of music printing in England after this first essay of 1495; R. Pynson printed several missals between 1500 and 1520, and Wynkyn de Worde printed the York missal in 1509. Gough, Grafton, Vautroller, Kynston and others were printing off music

One of the finely printed English music books of this time is an oblong quarto work of which only the bass part remains to us. It was printed by Wynkyn de Worde in 1530, the stave lines being printed after the notes had been done. It is a book of songs, and its title runs : *In this boke ar cöteynyd xx söges, ix of iiii ptes and xi of thre ptes*. The book is in the British Museum.

William Seres and John Day were among the early music printers. The editions of Sternhold and Hopkins's metrical Psalter by John Day were very great, and his earliest copy was 1562. (See PSALTER.)

In 1575 Queen Elizabeth granted a patent right over the printing of music and the right of importations from foreign sources. The patent was granted to William Byrd and Thomas Tallis in recognition of services given at the Chapel Royal. Thomas Tallis died in 1585 and Byrd became the sole owner of the right. He allowed, for monetary considerations, sundry printers to print music, and all the imprints during the period of Byrd on the patent state that the book is printed by the assignment of William Byrd. The patent was for twenty-one years. After the expiration of this patent another one in the same terms was granted to Thomas Morley. This was in 1598.

In the madrigal period English music printing began to flourish. Thomas East (Este) was one of the first to print music. He began working in or about 1587–88, and he died in 1609. He was succeeded by Thomas Snodham, who may have married his widow, who was working as late as 1624. Another music printer in the madrigal era was Peter Short, who worked at the 'Star' on Bread Street Hill from 1584–1603, when he was succeeded by Humfrey Lownes. These printed many of the collections of madrigals and similar works from movable type. The other printers of this kind of work were William Barley, John Windet, W. Stansby and Edward Allde. After about 1620 the issue of printed music books in England seemed to languish. The restrictive patents had ceased to be in force, and the printing press was free. It was not until 1651, when John Playford arose, that music found expression in English publications.

John Playford, in the early part of his business career, was practically the only music publisher in England. Thomas Harper printed his first works, and afterwards W. Godbid. John Playford, junior, was apprenticed with Godbid, and when Godbid died, young Playford and the widow, Anne, printed for the elder Playford.

At this time, before the introduction of the 'new tied note,' all quavers and semiquavers were printed separately, and if necessary 'tied' with a semicircular slur. The whole effect of music printing at this period was crudity. The article on Playford in *D.N.B.* is wrong in attributing to him the introduction of the 'new tied note.' Both the Playfords, senior and junior, were dead before any specimen of its use is found. It occurs in the

second book of *Comes Amoris*, dated 1688, which was printed by Thomas Moore. John Heptinstall, another London printer, made some improvements, but William Pearson some years later carried these improvements further. In 1699 he published *Twelve New Songs . . . chiefly to encourage William Pearson's new London character*. The 'tied' note printed the quavers and semiquavers with their tails united, and was generally adopted in place of the earlier form.

In 1767 Henry FOUGT (*q.v.*) obtained a patent for improvements in music type. He issued sheet and other books beautifully printed by the new type at cheap rates. About 1770 Robert Falkener purchased Fougt's plant and continued his business.

Musical typography progressed steadily towards perfection. Certain printers still used woodcut blocks for music printing, notably John Watts, who used wood blocks for his six volumes of *Musical Miscellany*, 1729–31, and for his series of the ballad operas. Most of the magazines which published a page of music used engraved wood blocks, and woodcut blocks were printed from in some psalmbooks published in Wakefield and Leeds.

In 1827 Edward Cowper was granted a patent for his improvements in music printing. The notes, made of copper, were set up separately, and the stave lines printed afterwards. Samuel Chappell, Goulding & Co. and Willis used his patent for a time, but soon reverted to their engraved method.

In Scotland music printing from movable metal type began early. Robert Lekprevick printed at Edinburgh a *Forme of Prayers* in 1565 and T. Bassandine printed psalm tunes in 1575. Henry Chatteris printed an edition of *The Psalmes of David in Metre* in 1595. Another early Edinburgh printer was Andro Hart. In Aberdeen John Forbes printed his *Cantus* in 1662, with two later editions, 1666 and 1682.

Although the art of engraving was well established and practised, nobody appears to have thought of its application to music printing in the 16th century. The first engraved music in England was probably *Parthenia, or the Maydenhead of the First Musicke the euer was printed for the Virginals*. The book is not dated, but it is generally referred to as engraved in 1611. One or two engraved works were printed in the early part of the 16th century, but typographical works were the rule.

Thomas Cross was most active in the production of engraved music. He engraved Henry Purcell's *Sonnates of iii parts*, 1683, the Songs of Leveridge, and many hundred single half-sheet songs which were currently fashionable in the early years of the 18th century. Before his time songs were chiefly in collections, but Cross has the distinction of introducing the single sheet or half-sheet song. The latest date the writer has found for his work is 1732.

After Cross had been working some years the practice of stamping the notes on pewter plates was introduced. Hawkins fixes the date 1710 for this method, and credits John Walsh and John Hare as its authors. The method of punching pewter plates and working off on a copperplate press was continued up to about 1840 or 1850. It is the method used to-day, but the first pull is on a lithograph transfer, and this being placed on a lithographic stone, copies are worked off very rapidly. Cross resented the new method of punching the notes on the plate instead of engraving. At the foot of some of his sheets he makes protest against this practice. One of these is ' Beware of ye nonsensical puncht ones.'

The modern method of music printing from metal type has attained wellnigh to perfection. It is a very complex business to set up, and requires a compositor specially trained for the work. The fount for average use consists of about 400 pieces. The type is too costly to bear the pressure of the printing press, so after the proof the music is worked off from electrotypes or stereotypes.

Double printing is not now in use. For large editions it is found cheapest and best to use music typography, but for ordinary work the stamped pewter plate method with the copies pulled from a lithographic stone is most convenient. The plates can be reserved for a new edition if it be called for.

BIBL.—An important work on the subject is *The Earliest English Music Printing* by ROBERT STEELE, 1903. This gives many reproductions of early music printing. Another work is *The History of Music Engraving and Printing* by WILLIAM GAMBLE, 1923. Two most excellent articles on John Day, the early music printer, appeared in *Mus. T.* for Mar. 1906 and Nov. 1907.

F. K.

PRINTZ, WOLFGANG KASPAR (VON WALD-THURN) (*b.* Waldthurn, Palatinate, Oct. 10, 1641 ; *d.* Sorau, Oct. 13, 1717), was appointed cantor at Sorau in 1665. Printz wrote a considerable number of theoretical and didactic books on music. The only one which is still of historical importance is *Historische Beschreibung der edlen Sing- und Klingkunst* (1690). His compositions have not been preserved (*Riemann*).

PRIORIS, JOHANNES, is mentioned in 1490 as being organist at St. Peter's in Rome, and in 1507 as maître de chapelle to Louis XII. of France. Several of his compositions appear in the choir-books of the Papal Chapel, three masses, five motets and two Magnificats. Only one work of his was ever printed, a Requiem Mass *a* 4 in Attaingnant's collection of 1532, to which Ambros grants considerable merit. Ambros also speaks of his MS. chansons as quite interesting works, but Eitner (*Q.-L.*) points out a serious mistake into which Ambros has

fallen, of attributing other works to Prioris which are not his.         J. R. M.

PRISE DE TROIE, the first part of Berlioz's TROYENS (*q.v.*).

PRIULI (PRIOLI), GIOVANNI (*d.* 1629), a musician in the chapel of the Archduke Ferdinand at Gratz *c.* 1604. From 1619 till his death he was Kapellmeister to the Emperor Ferdinand II. He wrote several books of sacred songs and psalms, as well as 3 books of secular madrigals *a* 5 v. ; also ' Musiche concertate ' *a* 3-9 v. (1622), ' Delicie musicali,' 2-10 v. (1625), and motets and songs in collective volumes (*Q.-L.*).

PROCH, HEINRICH (*b.* Vienna, July 22, 1809 ; *d.* Dec. 18, 1878), well-known composer of Lieder, Kapellmeister and teacher of singing, was destined for the law, but studied the violin with enthusiasm, and in 1833–34 frequently played in public in Vienna. He became in 1837 Kapellmeister of the Josephstadt theatre, Vienna, and in 1840 of the court opera, retiring with a pension in 1870. On the foundation of the short-lived Comic Opera in 1874 he was appointed its Kapellmeister. His popularity is mainly due to his Lieder, among the best-known of which we may cite ' Das Alpenhorn ' and a famous set of florid vocal variations. A three-act comic opera, ' Ring und Maske,' was produced in 1844, and three one-act pieces in the following year. He trained a large number of celebrated singers—among others Dustmann, Csillag and Tietjens. Several good German translations of Italian operas—the ' Trovatore,' for example—are from his pen.     F. G.

PRODANÁ NEVESTÁ (The Bartered Bride), comic opera in 3 acts ; words by K. Sabina, music by Bedřich Smetana. Produced Prague, May 30, 1866 ; London, in German (Die verkaufte Braut), Drury Lane, June 26, 1895, and Covent Garden, Jan. 24, 1907.

PRODIGAL SON, THE, oratorio by Sullivan, composed for the Worcester Festival of 1869. Dr. Samuel Arnold's oratorio on the same subject was performed in 1777. (See ENFANT PRODIGUE for operas, etc., of Auber, Debussy, Gaveaux, Ponchielli and Wormser.)

G.

PROFE (PROFIUS), AMBROSIUS (*b.* Breslau, Feb. 12, 1589 ; *d.* Dec. 27, 1661). After studying theology at Wittenburg, he received the appointment of Lutheran cantor and schoolmaster at Jauer, in Silesia. When in 1629 Lutheranism was suppressed in Jauer, and Catholic worship re-established, Profe was obliged to return to Breslau, where he engaged in mercantile pursuits. In 1633 he was appointed organist to the church of St. Elizabeth, Breslau, not, however, giving up his other business. In consequence of the falling in of part of the church and the destruction of the organ, his organistship came to an end, but he continued his mercantile career, and died as a well-to-do merchant.

It is not specially as a composer, but as a diligent editor and collector that Profe deserves mention. Between 1641 and 1646 he published four considerable collections of 'Geistlicher Concerten und Harmonien a 1, 2, 3, 4, 5, 6, 7, etc., vocibus cum et sine violinis & basso ad organum, aus den berühmsten italianischen und andern Autoribus,' etc. The composers chiefly represented are those of the later Venetian School, with a few of their German followers, as Heinrich Schütz. In 1649 a supplement appeared with the title 'Corollarium geistlicher Collectaneorum.' Prefixed to the first part of this collection, though not in all copies, is a Compendium Musicum, by way of a brief instruction in singing. In this little work Profe attacks the old Solmisation system founded upon the Hexachord, for which he receives the warm commendation of Mattheson. Another collection of Profe bears the title 'Cunis solennibus Jesuli recens-nati sacra genethliaca ' (1646), which, as the title indicates, consists of various songs for Christmas-tide. To this collection Profe contributes two of his own compositions for two to six voices, with instrumental accompaniment. In 1657 Profe put forth a small handy edition of Heinrich Albert's ' Arien.' For a fuller account of Profe see Dr. Reinhold Starke's article in *Monatshefte*, xxxiv. pp. 189-215.           J. R. M.

PROFESSOR is a term which in its application to musicians is used exceedingly loosely in this country. It is often applied to and assumed by private teachers of all grades, and is used commonly of members of the teaching staffs of the various musical colleges.[1]

It is properly applied to the occupant of a chair of music at a university. There is one professorship of music in each of the older universities and in several of the newer ones. The conditions of the appointment and the duties of the professor differ in every case, but while, until late in the 19th century, the holders of musical professorships were generally required only to give occasional public lectures and to preside over examinations for degrees (see DEGREES IN MUSIC), there is a general tendency now to make the professorship of music an active, and in some cases a vigorous, teaching appointment. The following is a list of the principal professorships in the universities of the British Isles, with the names of the holders thereof in 1926 :

Oxford (founded by William Heyther, 1626). Sir Hugh P. Allen, Mus.D.

Cambridge (founded 1684). Edward J. Dent.

Dublin (Trinity College, founded 1764). C. H. Kitson, Mus.D.

Edinburgh (founded by John Reid, 1839). Donald Francis Tovey.

Durham (founded 1897). John C. Bridge, Mus.D.

Birmingham (founded 1903). Granville Bantock.

London (King Edward Professorship, founded 1910) ; Percy C. Buck, Mus.D.

University of Wales (Aberystwyth). Sir H. Walford Davies, Mus.D.

(See also GRESHAM PROFESSOR OF MUSIC.)
                           C.

PROGRAMME (from πρό, ' before,' and γράμμα, ' a writing '), a list of the pieces to be performed at a concert, usually accompanied by the names of the performers. The term seems to have come into use in this connexion in the 19th century, and is now often further applied to the books containing the words and the analytical remarks on the pieces. (See ANALYTICAL NOTES.)

PROGRAMME-MUSIC. Every composition may, theoretically, be described as either Absolute Music or Programme-music, since it will either set out to describe a series of events or it will not. 'There is, however, no hard and fast line of division between the two, and in consequence divergence of opinion is often more than a little acrimonious.

In one sense all music is Programme-music, since it is a panorama of the composer's mood and an index to his character. When a composer, instead of placing the simple word *Allegro* or *Adagio* at the head of his movement, adds *giocoso* or *mesto*, he is telling you beforehand that you are to judge it as the biography of a particular mood. This fact is accentuated when a whole group of movements, in the form of a Sonata or Symphony, is labelled 'Pastorale' or ' Pathétique.'

Since, however, all music that is not deliberately manufactured must be the outcome of feeling, it is agreed to give the name Absolute to music which owes its coherence to structure, even though the development of the emotional basis may be the outstanding feature of the work. If we open Bach's Forty-eight or Beethoven's sonatas and play page one, we are playing Absolute Music ; not because imaginative people find it impossible to invent a ' story ' for the music, but because it is possible to enjoy it to the full without any such help. Indeed, even if music is written on the most definite of programmes, it is still open to us to ignore the fact, and to judge and enjoy the work *qua* Absolute Music.

In its crudest form Programme-music is purely imitative. The songs of birds, the clang of bells, the roll of thunder, the swirl of the wind, or the crackling of fire—all of these are capable of an imitation so exact as to be scarcely distinguishable from the genuine original. No one is so censorious as to say that it is always and essentially derogatory to the Art of Music that it should be put to such purely repre-

---

[1] At the R.C.M. an official distinction is drawn between members of the Board of Professors and of the general teaching staff.

sentative uses, since in opera it is clear that occasions arise where such use is not only justifiable but imperative. But serious musicians do claim, as a fundamental law of Taste, that simple imitation is only justifiable when music has deliberately abdicated its right to be considered the sole end, and is content (as in opera) with being a factor in the end aimed at.

Hence all purely descriptive music—once so popular in the form of ' Battle-pieces,' etc., and still lingering on in the occasional ' Storm '—is put out of court. It may be amusing, as a pun may be ; it may be skilful, as an acrostic may be ; but the one is no more properly Music than the other is properly Literature.

Between these two extremes of Absolute and Imitative there lies an immense uncharted tract. It is the field of Analogy and Suggestion. The real question at issue is not whether the composer may, without losing caste, descend from the Absolute plane to that of Suggestion, since all composers have continually done so. It is merely a question of how far we think they can legitimately stray.

The matter is one so clearly depending on Imagination that our opinions on the limits of the programme are apt to vary as much as our Imaginations do. No one presumably resents Beethoven's hint of ' Fate knocking at the door.' No one thinks it derogatory to Art that Chopin should have tried to suggest the solemn pageantry of a cortège in his 'Marche funèbre.' Both are cases where the suggestion is a help to appreciating the music. But many critics think that when music is definitely founded on facts—as in Debussy's ' La Cathédrale engloutie,' or is definitely illustrating a story—as in Sibelius' ' Valse triste,' its dignity is smirched.

It is not possible, nor desirable, to dogmatise at the present time on the limits that composers should place on their use of the programme. What began as an occasional *jeu d'esprit* has suddenly grown, in modern times, into a serious form of Art. And its growth has possibly been too rapid for its health. There is only one sane test that can be applied, at this moment, to any piece of Programme-music by an unprejudiced person. Is the music, *qua* music, satisfactory to me apart from its programme ; and if not, do I, in my own individual case, think that the deficiency is made good when I apply the programme and review my verdict ? P. C. B.

PROGRESSION is motion from note to note, or from chord to chord. The term is sometimes used to define the general aspect of a more or less extended group of such motions. It is also used of a group of modulations, with reference to the order of their succession. The expression ' progression of parts' is used with special reference to their relative motion in respect of one another, and of the laws to which such relative motion is subject. (See MOTION.) C. H. H. P.

PROKOFIEV, SERGE SERGEIEVITCH (*b.* Solnzevo, Ekaterinoslav, Apr. 11 (23), 1891), composer, received his musical education at the St. Petersburg Conservatoire. His teachers for theory, harmony and composition were Rimsky-Korsakov, Liadov, Wihtol and Nicolas Tcherepnin, and he was one of the most brilliant pupils of the piano class of Anna Nicolaievna Essipova. In 1910 he gained the Rubinstein Prize with his first piano concerto (op. 10), and in 1914 he left the Conservatoire with the highest prize awarded for piano-playing. From that time onward he lived successively in London, Paris, Japan and the U.S.A. In 1921 the Chicago Opera Association produced his opera in 4 acts, ' The Love for three Oranges,' composed to his own libretto based on one of the dramatic fables of Carlo Gozzi, ' L' amore delle tre melarancie.' The same year saw the production of his ballet ' Chout,' by Serge Diaghilev's Russian Ballet Company, in Paris. Prokofiev now lives at Ettal, near Oberammergau in Bavaria, but he frequently appears in the principal European musical centres, chiefly as a brilliant exponent of his own works for the piano.

As a composer Prokofiev does not court popular appreciation. By its deliberate avoidance of all romantic and emotional factors, his music is calculated never to appeal to the hearer's feelings : it is designed to please solely as a kind of decorative pattern and to avoid conveying extra-musical ideas of any kind. Whatever its intrinsic value may be, it has the merit of refusing to force itself on the listener's attention or to capture his affection by any means which are not legitimately and absolutely musical.

No music that refuses to compromise with sentiment and to stimulate sympathy can be expected to strike many hearers as pleasing. The best of Prokofiev's works, nevertheless, produce a kind of physical exhilaration the bracing effect of which few can resist. The third piano concerto, the ' Scythian Suite ' and the fourth piano sonata may be singled out as good and characteristic examples of his art. Elsewhere the composer's invention sometimes loses itself in arid experiments, as in the ' Sarcasmes ' for piano, with their systematic combinations of two distinct tonalities ; or in sheer extravagance of studiedly displeasing sounds, as in the ballet ' Chout,' the scenario of which is based on a folk-tale from the Government of Perm of ' a buffoon who hoodwinked seven other buffoons.'

In his later works, such as the violin concerto and the ' Symphonie classique,' Prokofiev returns to an almost primitive simplicity, and his more recent piano pieces and songs are not always devoid of a certain lyricism, although they never err on the side of sensibility.

Prokofiev might well be described as a cubist

in music. His thematic material is generally square-cut and clearly defined, his idiom hard and dry, his texture free from half-tones and haziness, and his forms are angular and symmetrical. The continuous, unflagging rhythmic motion of many of his movements gives an impression of physical energy and sureness of purpose.

The decision as to whether Prokofiev was successful in his setting of ' The Love for three Oranges ' depends on one's outlook upon the position occupied by Carlo Gozzi in literature. Those who hold the more common view that the 18th-century champion and reviver of the *commedia dell' arte* was an early precursor of the Romantics, are bound to consider that so entirely objective a musician as Prokofiev failed to do him justice ; but those who are aware that Gozzi's fairy-tales are nothing else than biting satires directed against the plays of Goldoni and Chiari, and that he had no feeling for the fantastic beauty they already possessed before he handled them, cannot help agreeing that the grotesque, caustic and wholly unromantic music of Prokofiev is admirably suited to the subject.

### LIST OF PRINCIPAL WORKS
#### PIANO SOLO
5 Sonatas (opp. 1, 14, 28, 29, 38) ; Toccata (op. 11) ; Suite of 10 Pieces (op. 12) ; 'Sarcasmes' (op. 17) ; 'Visions fugitives' (op. 22) ; 'Contes de la vieille grand'mère' (op. 31) ; and several sets of smaller pieces.

#### CHAMBER MUSIC
Ballade, V'cl. and PF. (op. 15) ; Overture on Hebrew Themes, Clar., PF. and Str. quartet (op. 34) ; Quartet for Ob., Clar., Viola and Double Bass ; Scherzo for 4 Bassoons (arr. from one of the PF. pieces).

#### ORCHESTRA
3 PF. Concertos (opp. 10, 16, 26) ; Symphonietta (op. 5) ; Vln. Concerto (op. 19) ; 'Scythian Suite' (Ala and Lolly) (op. 20) ; 'Symphonie classique' (op. 25) ; ' Les Rêves,' Tableau Musical.

#### VOCAL WORKS
2 Songs (op. 9) ; ' The Ugly Duckling ' (after Hans Andersen), Voice and PF. (op. 18) ; 5 Songs (op. 27) ; 5 Songs without Words (op. 35) ; 5 Songs (Balmont) (op. 36) ; ' They are Seven,' Choral Tone Poem.

#### STAGE WORKS
' Chout ' (The Buffoon), ballet (op. 21) ; ' The Love for three Oranges,' opera (after Carlo Gozzi) (op. 33) ; ' Maddalena,' opera (MS.) ; ' The Gambler,' opera (after Dostoievsky) (MS.).

E. B.

**PROLATION** (Lat. *prolatio* ; Ital. *prolazione*), a subdivision of the rhythmic system which in Mediæval Music governed the proportionate duration of the Semibreve and the Minim. (See NOTATION, subsection TIME SIGNATURES.)

**PROMENADE CONCERTS.** Although the concerts given at Vauxhall, Ranelagh, Marylebone and other public gardens might be placed under this head, the class of entertainment now so well known in this country under the name was introduced into London from Paris.

In 1838 some of the leading London instrumentalists gave concerts at the English Opera-House (Lyceum), under the title of ' Promenade Concerts à la Musard.' The pit was boarded over and an orchestra erected upon the stage. The band consisted of sixty performers, including many of the most eminent professors ; J. T. Willy was the leader, and Negri the conductor ; the programmes were composed exclusively of instrumental music, each consisting of four overtures, four quadrilles (principally by Musard), four waltzes (by Strauss and Lanner) and a solo, usually for a wind instrument. The first of the concerts was given on Dec. 12, and they were continued, with great success, during the winter. Early in 1839 the band of Valentino, the rival of Musard, came to London, and gave concerts at the Crown and Anchor Tavern, the programmes being composed of music of a higher class, the first part usually including a symphony ; but they met with little support. In Oct. 1839 the original speculators resumed operations at the Lyceum. On June 8, 1840, ' Concerts d'Été' were begun at Drury Lane under the conductorship of Eliason the violinist, with Jullien as his assistant, and a band of nearly 100, and a small chorus. Some dissensions among the original managers led to concerts of the same class being given by Willy in the autumn and winter at the Princess's Theatre, the majority of the band, however, still performing at the Lyceum. About the same period promenade concerts were given at Drury Lane, and Musard was brought over to conduct them. In Jan. 1841 ' Concerts d'Hiver ' were given in the same house by JULLIEN (*q.v.*), who soon firmly established himself in public favour and continued to give this class of concerts until 1859.

In 1850 promenade concerts conducted by Balfe were given at Her Majesty's Theatre, under the title of ' National Concerts'; a large band and chorus and some eminent principal singers were engaged, but the speculation proved unsuccessful. After Jullien's retirement, promenade concerts were annually given in the autumn at Covent Garden, with Alfred Mellon as conductor until 1866, and afterwards under various conductors, Arditi, Hervé, Sullivan, Riviere, etc.        W. H. H.

The autumnal promenade concerts languished for a good many years, until, in fact, 1895, when Robert Newman, who had been appointed manager of the lately opened QUEEN'S HALL (*q.v.*), and had previously managed such concerts at Covent Garden, started a new series in that hall under the direction of Henry J. Wood. Since then these concerts have been given nightly for ten weeks [1] (Aug. to Oct.) in each year, and have been of the greatest possible benefit to the musical public. They have always had the particular character of a wide catholicity in the selection of the programmes, and it was soon found that the best music could be made attractive, and that gradually the general level of the week's music could be considerably raised. A typical week's programme in the early days differs

---

[1] In 1926 the season lasted only nine weeks, but was followed by some Saturday afternoon concerts, described as Promenade Matinées. In March 1927 Messrs. Chappell announced their intention of abandoning the whole enterprise. The future of the concerts is still in debate.

very little from that obtaining to-day, with its Wagner, classical and 'popular' nights. Later it became the practice to play all the Beethoven symphonies during the season in chronological order, while quite recently special attention has been given to the symphonies of Haydn. Novelties soon began to appear, foreign and native, and it may truly be said that at no period in our musical history has the young British composer been more materially helped. The production of his work and the effect upon so receptive an audience has indeed been a most valuable experience. In more recent years he has received further experience in being invited to conduct his own music. It is interesting to note that the programmes have always been divided into two parts, and that in early days the second part was of the lightest character, fantasias and dance music interspersed with ballads; but Wood did not rest satisfied until he had given the orchestral section of this part the same interest as that of the first. The history of the concerts in certain aspects is that of the orchestra. (See New Queen's Hall Orchestra.)

Among the numerous composers whose works have been given for the first time, actual novelties or new to London, the following names may be mentioned:

American: Chadwick, Converse, Hadley, MacDowell. Belgian: Lekeu, Jules de Swert. Czech: Dvořák (four of the symphonic poems). Finnish: Järnefeldt, Sibelius. French: Bruneau, Debussy ('L'Après-midi d'un faune'), Franck (Variations Symphoniques, pianoforte and orchestra), D'Indy, Lalo, Ravel. German: Bruch, Goetz, Goldmark, Kistler, Korngold, Mahler (two symphonies), Reger, Schönberg, Strauss. Hungarian: Bartók, Dohnányi. Italian: Busoni, Casella, Sinigaglia, Malipiero. Polish: Paderewski. Roumanian: Enesco. Russian: Balakirev, Glazounov, Prokofiev, Rachmaninov, Rimsky-Korsakov (Sheherazade Suite), Stravinsky, Tchaïkovsky (a large number of works, including 'Casse-noisette' suite, the three early symphonies and 'Manfred').

The long British list may be said to contain the names of every composer who has earned distinction.    N. C. G.

PROMETHEUS. (1) Beethoven's only Ballet (op. 43); designed by Salvatore Vigàno; composed in 1800, and produced, for Mlle. Casentini's benefit, Mar. 28, 1801, in the Burgtheater, Vienna, under the title of 'Die Geschöpfe des Prometheus.' It contains an overture, an 'Introduction' and sixteen numbers. The title of the first edition, an arrangement for the piano (Vienna, 1801, numbered in error op. 24), is 'Gli uomini di Prometeo'; English edition, 'The men of Prometheus.'

(2) 'Prometheus Unbound,' a setting for soli, chorus and orchestra of Shelley's poem, by C. H. H. Parry, produced Gloucester Festival, 1880.

(3) 'Prometheus, the poem of fire,' the fifth and last of Scriabin's symphonic works for large orchestra and piano obbligato, originally intended to be accompanied by a 'light' machine, noted in the score as Luce.

PROPHÈTE, LE, opera in 5 acts; words by Scribe, music by Meyerbeer. Produced Opéra, Paris, Apr. 16, 1849; in Italian, in 4 acts, Covent Garden, July 24, 1849; New Orleans, Apr. 2. 1850; New York, Nov. 25, 1853.    G.

PROPORTION (Lat. proportio; Ital. proporzione), a term used in arithmetic to express certain harmonious relations existing between the several elements of a series of numbers; and transferred from the terminology of mathematics to that of theoretical music, in which it plays a very prominent part. In music, however, the word is not always employed in its strict mathematical sense; for a true Proportion can only exist in the presence of three terms; in which point it differs from Ratio, which is naturally expressed by two. Now the so-called 'Proportions' of musical science are almost always expressible by two terms only, and should therefore be more correctly called Ratios; but we shall find it convenient to assume that, in musical phraseology, the two words may be lawfully treated as synonymous —as, in fact, they actually have been treated by almost all who have written on the subject, from Joannes Tinctor, who published the first musical dictionary, in the year 1474,[1] to the Theorists of the 18th and 19th centuries.

Thomas Morley, in his Plaine and easie Introduction to Practicall Musicke (London, 1597), gives a table, reproduced opposite, which exhibits, at one view, all the different kinds of Proportion then in use.

To use this table (1) When the name of the Proportion is known, but not its constituents, find the name in the upper part of the diagram; follow down the lines of the lozenge in which it is enclosed, as far as the first horizontal line of figures; and the two required numbers will be found under the points to which these diagonal lines lead. Thus, Tripla Sesquialtera lies near the left-hand side of the diagram, about midway between the top and bottom; and the diagonal lines leading down from it conduct us to the numbers 2 and 7, which express the required Proportion in its lowest terms. (2) When the constituents of the Proportion are known, but not its name, find the two known numbers in the same horizontal line; follow the lines which enclose them, upwards, into the diagonal portion of the diagram; and, at the apex of the triangle thus formed will be found the required name. Thus, the lines leading from 2 and 8 conduct us to Quadrupla.

The uppermost of the horizontal lines comprises all the Proportions possible, between the series of numbers from 1 to 10 inclusive, reduced to their lowest terms. The subsequent lines give their multiples, as far as 100; and, as

---

[1] 'Proportio est duorum numerorum habitudo' (Joann's Tinctoris, Terminorum musicae diffinitorium. Lit.P.).

these multiples always bear the same names as their lowest representatives, the lines drawn from them lead always to the apex of the same triangle.

By means of the Proportions here indicated the theorist was enabled to define the difference

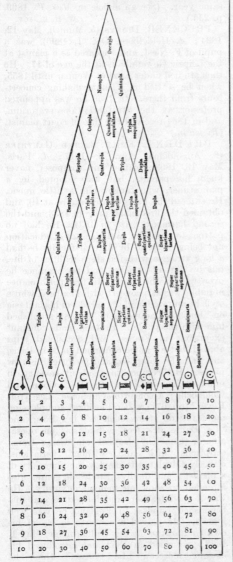

| 1 | 2 | 3 | 4 | 5 | 6 | 7 | 8 | 9 | 10 |
|---|---|---|---|---|---|---|---|---|---|
| 2 | 4 | 6 | 8 | 10 | 12 | 14 | 16 | 18 | 20 |
| 3 | 6 | 9 | 12 | 15 | 18 | 21 | 24 | 27 | 30 |
| 4 | 8 | 12 | 16 | 20 | 24 | 28 | 32 | 36 | 40 |
| 5 | 10 | 15 | 20 | 25 | 30 | 35 | 40 | 45 | 50 |
| 6 | 12 | 18 | 24 | 30 | 36 | 42 | 48 | 54 | 60 |
| 7 | 14 | 21 | 28 | 35 | 42 | 49 | 56 | 63 | 70 |
| 8 | 16 | 24 | 32 | 40 | 48 | 56 | 64 | 72 | 80 |
| 9 | 18 | 27 | 36 | 45 | 54 | 63 | 72 | 81 | 90 |
| 10 | 20 | 30 | 40 | 50 | 60 | 70 | 80 | 90 | 100 |

of pitch between two given sounds with mathematical exactness. Thus the octave, sounded by the half of an open string, is represented by the Proportion called Dupla ; the Perfect Fifth, sounded by 2-3 of the string, by that called Sesquialtera ; the Perfect Fourth, sounded by 3-4, by Sesquitertia. These Ratios are simple enough, and scarcely need a diagram for their

elucidation ; but as we proceed to more complex intervals, and especially to those of a dissonant character, the Proportions grow far more intricate, and Morley's table becomes really valuable.

A certain number of these Proportions are also used for the purpose of defining differences of rhythm ; and, in mediæval music, the latter class of differences involves even greater complications than the former.

The nature of Mood, Time and Prolation are fully explained under NOTATION (q.v.). It was chiefly for the sake of elucidating the mysteries of this style of writing that Morley gave his table ; and, by way of making the matter clearer, he followed it up by a setting of 'Christes Crosse be my speed,' for three voices, containing examples of Dupla, Tripla, Quadrupla, Sesquialtera, Sesquiquarta, Quadrupla-Sesquialtera, Quintupla, Sextupla, Septupla, Nonupla, Decupla and Supertripartiens quartas, giving it to his pupil, Philomathes, with the encouraging direction—' Take this Song, peruse it, and sing it perfectly ; and I doubt not but you may sing any reasonable hard wrote Song that may come to your sight.'

Nevertheless, Morley himself confesses that these curious combinations had fallen quite into disuse long before the close of the 16th century.

w. s. r. abridged.

For the proportions of pitch see MONOCHORD and ACOUSTICS.

PROPOSTA (Lat. dux ; Eng. Subject), a term applied to the leading part in a fugue or point of imitation, in contradistinction to the Risposta, or response (Eng. Answer ; Lat. comes). The leading part of a canon is usually called the Guida, though the term Proposta is sometimes applied to that also.     w. s. r.

PROPRIETAS, propriety (Ger. Eigenheit), a peculiarity attributed by mediæval writers to those ligatures in which the first note was sung as a breve, the breve being always understood to represent a complete measure (Lat. tactus ; Old Eng. Stroke). Franco of Cologne describes ligatures beginning with breves, longs and semibreves as Ligaturæ cum, sine and cum opposita Proprietate, respectively.     w. s. r.

PROSCRITTO, IL., see ERNANI.

PROSE, see SEQUENCE.

PROSKE, KARL (b. Gröbing, Upper Silesia, Feb. 11, 1794 ; d. Dec. 20, 1861), editor of the celebrated collection of ancient church music called MUSICA DIVINA (q.v.). His father was a wealthy land-owner at Gröbing. Having studied medicine he made the campaign of 1813–15 as an army surgeon, but being compelled to retire by his health he took his degree as Doctor of Medicine at Halle, and settled as government physician at Oppeln in Upper Silesia. Here he suddenly became a religious enthusiast, a change to which his devotion to church music doubtless contributed. On Apr. 11, 1826, he was ordained priest by Bishop Sailer at Ratisbon, where he became vicar-choral in 1827, and canon and Kapellmeister of the Cathedral in 1830. From this time, with the aid of his private fortune, he began his celebrated collection of church music, residing for long in Italy exploring the great MS. collections there, and scoring from the voice-parts many very beautiful but hitherto unknown works, and publishing them in a cheap, accurate and legible form as 'Musica divina.' Each volume is preceded by introductory remarks, biographical and bibliographical. Proske died of angina pectoris, bequeathing his collection to the episcopal library of Ratisbon, of which it forms one of the chief ornaments.　　　　　　　　　　　　　　F. G.

BIBL.—*Kirchenmusikalisches Jahrbuch*, 1894 ; Bibliography with diary kept by Proske while in Italy ; K. WEINMANN, *K. Proske, der Restaurator der klassischen Kirchenmusik*, 1909.

PROUT, EBENEZER, Mus.D., B.A. (b. Oundle, Northamptonshire, Mar. 1, 1835 ; d. Hackney, Dec. 5, 1909), earned considerable reputation as teacher, lecturer and theoretician.

He graduated at London, 1854, studied the pianoforte under Charles Salaman, acted as organist at various chapels, and was at Union Chapel, Islington, in 1861–73. From 1861–85 he taught the pianoforte at the Crystal Palace School of Art. In 1862 he gained the first prize of the Society of British Musicians for the best string quartet, and in 1865 their first prize for pianoforte quartet. From 1871–74 he was editor of *The Monthly Musical Record*, and from that time was successively music critic of *The Academy* (1874–79) and *The Athenæum* (1879–89). He conducted the Borough of Hackney Choral Association in 1876–90, and was appointed professor of harmony and composition at the National Training School of Music in 1876. In 1879 he was given a similar post at the R.A.M., and in 1884 at the G.S.M.

His many compositions include cantatas, symphonies, organ concertos and chamber music. Of more importance are his theoretical works which have been received as standard text-books. They include a primer on *Instrumentation* (1876); *Harmony, its Theory and Practice* (1889; twentieth edition, 1903); *Counterpoint, Strict and Free* (1890); *Double Counterpoint and Canon* (1891); *Fugue* (1891); *Fugal Analysis* (1892), *Musical Form* (1893); *Applied Forms* (1895); *The Orchestra* (1897). Most, if not all, of these have gone through several editions. In 1894 Prout was elected Professor of Music in the University of Dublin, and received the honorary degree of Mus.D. from the university in the following year. His work as an editor should also be mentioned ; he provided ADDITIONAL ACCOMPANIMENTS (*q.v.*) for several of Handel's oratorios (such as

'Samson,' for the Leeds Festival of 1880), and in 1902 he brought out a new full score and vocal score of the 'Messiah,' and conducted a performance of the work, according to his own readings, given by the Royal Society of Musicians in the Queen's Hall, Nov. 12, of the same year. (See an article in *Mus. T.*, 1899, p. 255.)　　　　　　　　　　　　W. H. H., rev.

PRUCKNER, DIONYS (b. Munich, May 12, 1834 ; d. Heidelberg, Dec. 1, 1896), was a pupil of F. Niest, and appeared as a pianist at the Leipzig Gewandhaus at the age of 17. He then studied under Liszt at Weimar until 1855, when he settled in Vienna, making concert-tours from there. In 1859 he was appointed professor at the Stuttgart Conservatorium, and in 1864 received the title of court pianist. (*Riemann.*)

PRUDENT, EMILE RACINE GAUTHIER (b. Angoulême, Apr. 3, 1817 ; d. Paris, May 13, 1863), pianist and composer, never knew his parents, but was adopted by a piano-tuner, who taught him a little music. He entered the Paris Conservatoire at 10, and obtained the first piano prize in 1833, and the second harmony prize in 1834. He had no patrons to push him, and his want of education not being supplied by natural facility he had a long struggle with the stern realities of life, but by dint of patience and perseverance he overcame all obstacles. His first performance in public was at a concert with Thalberg, whose style he imitated, and the success of his fantasia on 'Lucia di Lammermoor' (op. 8) established him with the public. He then made constant excursions in France, and occasional trips abroad, but his home continued to be in Paris, and there he composed and produced his new pieces. His compositions, about seventy in number, include a trio for PF., violin and violoncello ; a concerto-symphonie 'Les Trois Rêves' (op. 67) ; several brilliant and pleasing morceaux de genre, such as 'Les Bois,' and 'La Danse des fées' ; fantasias on opera-airs, or themes by classical composers ; transcriptions with and without variations, cleverly calculated to display the virtuosity of a pianist ; and finally 'Études de genre,' also intended to show off manual dexterity. He was a good teacher, and formed several distinguished pupils. In England he was well known. He played a concerto in B♭ of his own composition at the Philharmonic, May 1, 1848 ; returned in 1852 and introduced his elegant morceau 'La Chasse,' which he repeated at the New Philharmonic Concert, June 1, 1853.　　　　　　　　　　　　G. C.

PRUME, FRANÇOIS HUBERT (b. Stavelot near Liège, June 3, 1816 ; d. there, July 14, 1849), violinist. Having received his first instruction at Malmédy, he entered in 1827 the newly opened Conservatoire at Liège, and in 1830 that at Paris, where he studied for two years under Habeneck. Returning to Liège he was appointed professor at the Conservatoire, although only 17 years of age. In 1839 he began to travel, and visited with much success Germany, Russia and the Scandinavian countries. Prume was an elegant virtuoso. He is chiefly remembered as the composer of ' La Mélancolie,' a sentimental *pièce de salon*, which for a time attained an extraordinary popularity.                                P. D.

PRUMIER, (1) ANTOINE (*b.* Paris, July 2, 1794; *d.* there, Jan. 20, 1868), learned the harp from his mother, and afterwards entered the Conservatoire, and obtained the second harmony prize in Catel's class in 1812. After this, however, he was compelled by military law to enter the École polytechnique; but in 1815 he gave up mathematics, re-entered the Conservatoire, and finished his studies in counterpoint under Eler. He then became harpist in the orchestra of the Italiens, and, on the death of Nadermann in 1835, professor of the harp at the Conservatoire. In the same year he migrated to the Opéra-Comique, but resigned his post in 1840 in favour of his son, the best of his pupils. Prumier composed and published about a hundred fantasias, rondeaux and airs with variations for the harp—all well written but now antiquated. He received the Legion of Honour in 1845, and was vice-president of the Association des Artistes Musiciens for seventeen years consecutively. He died from the rupture of an aneurism at a committee meeting of the Conservatoire. He had retired on his pension the year before (1867), and been succeeded by Labarre, at whose death (Apr. 1870) the professorship devolved upon Prumier's son

(2) ANGE CONRAD ANTOINE (*b.* Paris, Jan. 5, 1820; *d.* there, Apr. 3, 1884), lauréat in 1838. He was assistant professor of the harp at the Conservatoire, 1838–51, and professor, 1870–84. Like his father he wrote well for the harp, and was a skilled performer and a musician of taste.                                G. C.

PSALM. (1) For the musical recitation of the prose translation of the Psalms see articles ANTIPHON, GREGORIAN TONES, INFLEXION, PSALMODY, RESPONSORIAL PSALMODY, CHANT and CHANTING.

(2) For the musical settings of metrical versions of the Psalms, see HYMN and PSALTER.

(3) The elaborate settings of entire psalms, whether for chorus alone, for solo voices, or for combinations of voices and instruments, are mentioned under the names of their composers.

PSALMODY. There are three different types of Psalmody which have been in use in the Christian Church, and are broadly distinguished from one another. The two most important classes, the Antiphonal and Responsorial Psalmody, will be found under ANTIPHON and RESPONSORIAL PSALMODY. The third,

which is called Direct Psalmody (*Psalmodia in directum,* or *Psalmus directaneus*), has never had the same vogue, and now only survives in a few positions. The fundamental distinction between the three is as follows: Responsorial Psalmody is the alternation between the soloist and choir, Antiphonal Psalmody the alternation of two choirs, while the Direct Psalmody has no alternation at all, but simply goes straight forward. The last appears in simple shape in the Benedictine services, where still a psalm is sung *in directum,* that is, in unbroken chorus. The method of singing is of the simplest sort, being mere recitation with a slight inflexion, thus:

Do - mi - ne quid multiplicati sunt qui tribulant me:

multi      insurgunt      ad-ver-sum me.

The same type of Psalmody is found in a more elaborate shape in the TRACT sung in the MASS, for, like the antiphonal Responsorial Psalmody, this also varies in degree of ornateness.

The tones employed for the Psalms in conjunction with the Antiphon are simple. They are found in the Ambrosian music in a more primitive form than in the Gregorian, with a less definite tonality, and that absence of methodical arrangement which is characteristic of the Ambrosian music. The Gregorian tones have all been reduced to order. A tone corresponds with each of the eight modes; and its reciting note is the dominant of the mode. Each tone consists of two members corresponding with the two halves of the psalm verse. According to the law already explained in the article INFLEXION it has an intonation leading up to the reciting note, and a cadence called the mediation at the end of the first half, the reciting note is then resumed in the second half and leads to a final cadence called the ending. This is the fixed shape of all Gregorian tones; only in the case of the irregular or ' peregrine' tone it is relinquished and the recitation takes place at a different pitch in the second half from that used in the first half. According to the strict Gregorian system the mediation of the first half of the tone is also fixed. It is only in debased plain-song that the clear distinction between the tones has been obliterated by the introduction of fancy mediations. Variety is secured by the final cadences, technically called the endings. These vary in number according to the different tones. They never have been uniform. The earliest documents show a certain amount of variety of use, and this variety survives. The larger number of mediæval endings, however, were in universal use in the Middle Ages, and there was much more agreement than variety.

A more elaborate form of tone was adopted for the gospel-canticles; the intonation and mediation, and to a certain extent even the reciting note, were decorated, while the ending remained the same as in the case of the ordinary psalms. The forms of tone in use for the antiphons at Mass, namely the Introit and Communion, were of a still more decorated character. Each tone, therefore, exists in three forms, as a psalm tone, as a gospel-canticle tone, and as an introit tone. The Sarum form of the Gregorian tones is here subjoined. It is as good a representative as any of the best mediæval traditions on the subject.

FIRST MODE.
Psalm-tones and endings.
First.

Dixit do-mi-nus do-mi-no me-o:    se - de a dex-tris me-is

Second.    Third.    Fourth.

Fifth.    Sixth.    Seventh.

Eighth.    Ninth.

The Gospel-canticle tone.

Benedictus dominus de-us Is-ra-el:    quia visitavit, etc.

The Introit-tone and endings.
First.

Beati im-ma-cu-la-ti in vi-a:    qui ambulant in lege do-mi-ni

Second.    Third.    Fourth.

SECOND MODE.
Psalm-tone and endings.
First.

Dixit do-mi-nus do-mi-no me-o:    se-de a dex-tris me-is

Second.

The Gospel-canticle tone.

Benedictus dominus de-us Is-ra-el;    quia visitavit, etc.

The Introit-tone and ending.

Quare fremuerunt gentes: et populi . . . sunti - na - ni - a

THIRD MODE.
Psalm-tone and endings.
First.

Dixit do-mi-nus do-mi-no me-o:    se-de a dex-tris me-is

Second.    Third.    Fourth.

Fifth.    Sixth.

The Gospel-canticle tone.

Be - ne - dictus,    etc.

The Introit-tone and endings.

Can-ta - te   do-mi-no  can - ti-cum    no - vum:
First.    Second.

can-ta-te do-mi-no   om-nis ter-ra

FOURTH MODE.
Psalm-tone and endings.
First.

Dixit dominus do-mi-no me-o:    se-de a dex-tris me - is

Second.    Third.    Fourth.

Fifth.    Sixth. Seventh. Eighth. Ninth.

The Gospel-canticle tone.

Be-ne-dic-tus domi-nus de - us Is-ra - el:    quia    visitavit, etc.

The Introit-tone and endings.
First.

Be - a - ti im-ma-cu - la - ti in vi-a:    qui am-bu-lant
Second.

in   le - ge do - mi - ni

FIFTH MODE.
Psalm-tone and endings.
First.

Dixit de-mi-nus do-mi-no me-o:    se-de   a dextris me-is

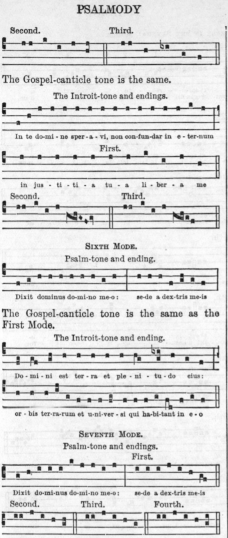

Second.    Third.

The Gospel-canticle tone is the same.

The Introit-tone and endings.

In te do-mi-ne sper-a-vi, non con-fun-dar in e-ter-num

First.

in jus-ti-ti-a tu-a li-ber-a me

Second.    Third.

#### SIXTH MODE.
Psalm-tone and ending.

Dixit dominus do-mi-no me-o:  se-de a dex-tris me-is

The Gospel-canticle tone is the same as the First Mode.

The Introit-tone and ending.

Do-mi-ni est ter-ra et ple-ni-tu-do eius:

or-bis ter-ra-rum et u-ni-ver-si qui ha-bi-tant in e-o

#### SEVENTH MODE.
Psalm-tone and endings.
    First.

Dixit do-mi-nus do-mi-no me-o:  se-de a dex-tris me-is

Second.  Third.  Fourth.

Fifth.  Sixth.  Seventh.

Intonation for Gospel-canticles.

Be-ne-dic-tus, etc.

Introit-tone and endings.
First.

Do-mi-nus . . ., ex-ul-tet ter-ra: le-ten-tur... in-su-lae mul-tae.

Second.    Third.

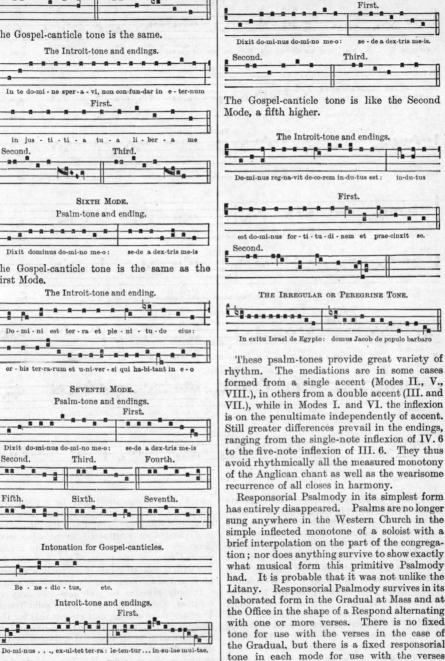

#### EIGHTH MODE.
Psalm-tone and endings.
    First.

Dixit do-mi-nus do-mi-no me-o:  se-de a dex-tris me-is.

Second.    Third.

The Gospel-canticle tone is like the Second Mode, a fifth higher.

The Introit-tone and endings.

Do-mi-nus reg-na-vit de-co-rem in-du-tus est : in-du-tus

First.

est do-mi-nus for-ti-tu-di-nem et prae-cinxit se.

Second.

#### THE IRREGULAR OR PEREGRINE TONE.

In exitu Israel de Egypto: domus Jacob de populo barbaro

These psalm-tones provide great variety of rhythm. The mediations are in some cases formed from a single accent (Modes II., V., VIII.), in others from a double accent (III. and VII.), while in Modes I. and VI. the inflexion is on the penultimate independently of accent. Still greater differences prevail in the endings, ranging from the single-note inflexion of IV. 6 to the five-note inflexion of III. 6. They thus avoid rhythmically all the measured monotony of the Anglican chant as well as the wearisome recurrence of all closes in harmony.

Responsorial Psalmody in its simplest form has entirely disappeared. Psalms are no longer sung anywhere in the Western Church in the simple inflected monotone of a soloist with a brief interpolation on the part of the congregation; nor does anything survive to show exactly what musical form this primitive Psalmody had. It is probable that it was not unlike the Litany. Responsorial Psalmody survives in its elaborated form in the Gradual at Mass and at the Office in the shape of a Respond alternating with one or more verses. There is no fixed tone for use with the verses in the case of the Gradual, but there is a fixed responsorial tone in each mode for use with the verses of the responds of the Office. These eight responsorial verse-tones are here given in outline :

THE TONE OF THE RESPOND-VERSE IN THE SEVERAL MODES.

### First.

Glo-ri - a　　　　pa-tri et fi -li - o　　　　et spi - - ri - - tu - i　　sanct - - o.
Per-fe-cis - ti　　e-is　　qui spe-rant in te　　in con-spectu fili - o - - rum ho - - mi - - num,

### Second.

Glor - - i-a　　pa-tri et fi - li - o　　et spi - - ri - - tu - i　　sanct - - o.
Pec - ca - vimus cum　pat-ri-bus　nos - tris: in-ius - te　　.. ta - tem fe - - ci - - mus.

### Third.

Glo - ri-a　　pa-tri et fi-li - o　　et spi - - ri - - tu - i　　sanct - - o.
Dum er - go　essent ... metum Iu-de - o - rum　so-nus　repente... ve-nit　su - per　e - - - os.

### Fourth.

Glo-ri-a　　pa-tri et fi - li - o　　et spi - - ri - - tu - i　　sanct - - o.
Vi - dens　　vi-di ...　ei - us au - di - vi　et des - cendi li - - be - - ra - re　e - - - um.

### Fifth.

Glo-ri - a　　pa-tri et fi - li - o　　et spi - - ri - - tu - i　　sanct - - o.
In do - mi-no　laudabitur　a - ni-ma　me - a　au-di - ant mansue - ti　et le - - ten - - tur.

### Sixth.

Glo-ri-a　　pa-tri et fi-li - o　　et spi - - ri - - tu - i　　sanct - - o.
Mise-re - re　mei mi - - se-re-re　me - i　quo-ni - am in te ... a - ni - ma　me - - a.

### Seventh.

Glo - ri-a　　pa-tri et fi - li - o　　et spi - - ri - - tu - i　　sanct - - o.
In prin-ci - pi-o　fecit deus　ce - lum et ter - ram　et　cre-avit in　e - - a ho - - mi - - nem.

### Eighth.

Glo - ri-a　　pa - tri et fi - li - o　　et spi - - ri - - tu - i　　sanct - - o.
Con-serva me　domine ...　in te con - fi - do: dix-i　domino De - us　me - us　es　tu.

They will be seen to consist of the same elements as were noted before in the Antiphonal psalm-tone; each of them is double in character, has an intonation leading to the recitation, each in turn is closed by a mediation; then in the second half the recitation is resumed (with or without a second intonation to lead into it), and the whole is closed by a final cadence. Here it is the final cadences that are the most fixed parts of the tone. They are pentesyllabic, that is to say, the last five principal syllables of each half of the verse are set to the five groups of the cadence. If there were small light syllables too unimportant to be counted they were neglected in the reckoning and a small note (represented here with a white centre) was inserted to accommodate them somewhere in the body of the cadence. If the psalm-verse is long the recitation itself may be a good deal decorated. If it is short the reciting note may altogether disappear. Similarly the intonation is expanded or contracted as occasion may demand. The *Gloria Patri* represents a contracted form of the psalm-verse, but side by side with it indications are given to show the employment of the same melody to a longer text.

It only remains to give here, by way of contrast, some of the Ambrosian Psalm Tones. They are more simple, and are notable for the absence of mediation. In the Gregorian system the mediation is an essential inflexion in the first half of the verse, corresponding with the ending in the second half. The archaic Ambrosian tones have no intonation, no mediation, and very simple endings, as the following examples show.

Dixit dominus domino meo:   sede a   dextris meis

Dixit . . . meo:        sede a dextris meis.

Contrast these with the Gregorian forms given above.

The Gregorian tones were adapted to the English Prayer Book by MERBECKE (*q.v.*), and remained in use in some form down at least to the middle of the 18th century. Here, for example, is the First Tone 4th Ending, as given for Venite on Sundays in Playford's *Introduction to the Skill of Musick* (first published 1654), nineteenth edition, 1730 :

O come let us sing, etc.        Let us heartily

rejoice  in the strength, etc.

In harmonised form they were the starting-point of the Anglican chant (see CHANT) which practically superseded the old tones ; and they disappeared until they were revived by the Church movement in the middle of the 19th century (see GREGORIAN TONES).    W. H. F.

For Metrical Psalmody, see PSALTER, THE ENGLISH METRICAL, and BOURGEOIS.

PSALTER, THE ENGLISH METRICAL, or paraphrastic rhyming translation of the Psalms and Evangelical Hymns, intended to be sung, dates from the third year of King Edward the Sixth, the year 1549 ; but if we may believe the accounts usually given of the subject, the practice of singing compositions of this nature in England is far older, having existed among the sympathisers with the new doctrines long before the Reformation ; it may even have had its beginnings among the followers of Wycliffe or Walter Lollard. With regard to this supposition, one thing only is certain : Sternhold's translations—the nucleus of the metrical Psalter which has come down to us—were not by any means the first. Sir Thomas Wyat the elder had already translated the seven penitential Psalms, and the Earl of Surrey three others ; while about the same time Miles Coverdale, an eminent divine—formerly, like Luther, an Augustinian monk, and one of the earliest converts to the reformed doctrines,—brought out thirteen of the most popular Psalms, translated into English (two of them twice) in metrical form, apparently from the rhymed versions contained in the current German hymn-books published between 1524 and 1535. But the scope of the work was not confined to a few of the Psalms of David, as will be seen from the title :

' Goostly psalmes and spirituall songes drawen out of the holy Scripture, for the cōforte and consolacyon of soch as loue to reioyce in God and his worde (Colophon). Imprynted by me Johan Gough. Cum priuilegio Regalj.' No date (? 1539),

the compositions being twenty-six in number. There are, among other hymns, three to the Holy Spirit, two of the Commandments, two of the Creed, two of the Paternoster ; hymns of the Nativity and the Resurrection, the Magnificat and Nunc Dimittis. The rest are for the most part sacred songs of the chorale type ; but there is one office hymn—' Christe qui lux es '—with its proper tune. Of the tunes, which accompany the words throughout—no Psalm or hymn being without a tune—it may be said generally that they were probably taken as they were found in the ' Geistliche Lieder ' referred to above, attached to the hymns or Psalms selected for translation. Many have already been identified, and, judging from the entire similarity of style which is seen throughout the collection, it may be supposed that the rest will eventually reveal their derivation from the same source. They are of course strictly modal. All the modes except the fifth and sixth are represented, both in their original and transposed positions. The first, fourth, twelfth and thirteenth each contribute five tunes ; the rest one or two each. The melodies are often exceedingly fine and striking, but from the nature of the metres employed, metres very different from those adopted for similar purposes in this country, few of them could be thought to have exercised any influence upon the English ideal of metrical music. The only copy of Coverdale's work known to exist is in the Library of Queen's College, Oxford. Its rarity, and also the fact that its methods were not to any apparent extent adopted in England, may be in part due to the circumstance of its suppression in 1539, the year, indeed, of its supposed publication, by order of King Henry VIII.

In 1549, the year in which Sternhold's first small work was published, without tunes, there appeared a metrical translation of the Psalter complete, together with the Evangelical Hymns, and music set in four parts, of which the title is as follows :

' The Psalter of David newely translated into Englysh metre in such sort that it maye the more decently, and wyth more delyte of the mynde, be read and songe of al men. Wherunto is added a note of four partes,[1] with other thynges, as shall appeare in the Epistle to the Readar. Translated and Imprinted by Robert Crowley in the yere of our Lorde MDXLIX the XX daye of September. And are to be sold in Eley rentes in Holbourne. Cum privilegio ad Imprimendum solum.' [2]

In the ' Epistle to the Readar ' the music is described thus :

1 ' Note,' or ' note of song,' was, or rather had been, the usual description of music set to words. At this date it was probably old-fashioned, since it seldom occurs again. In 1544 Cranmer, in his letter to Henry VIII. respecting his Litany, speaks of the whole of the music sometimes as ' the note,' and sometimes as ' the song.'
2 A copy of this book is in the library of Brasenose College, Oxford. Thanks are due to the College for permission to examine it. Another copy—differently set up—is in Christie Miller's library, Britwell, Bucks.

' A note of song of iiii parts, which agreth with the meter of this Psalter in such sort, that it serveth for all the Psalmes thereof, conteyninge so many notes in one part as be syllables in one meter, as appeareth by the dyttie that is printed with the same.'

This book is extremely interesting, not only in itself, but because it points to previous works of which as yet nothing is known. In his preface the author says : ' I have made open and playne that which in other translations is obscure and harde,' a remark which must surely apply to something more than the meagre contributions of Surrey and Wyat ; and indeed the expression of the title, ' the Psalter of David, newly translated,' seems clearly to suggest the existence of at least one other complete version. The metre is the common measure, printed not, as now, in four lines of eight and six alternately, but in two lines of fourteen, making a long rhyming couplet.[1]  The verse, compared with other work of the same kind, is of average merit : the author was not, like Surrey or Wyat, a poet, but a scholar turned puritan preacher and printer, who pretended to nothing more than a translation as faithful as possible, considering the necessities of rhyme.  But the most interesting thing in the book is the music,[2] which here follows :

Mode VII.

That man is happy[3] and blessed, that hath     not gone a-stray ; Counter Tenor.

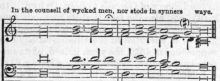

Tenor. Plain Song.

Bass.

In the counsell of wycked men, nor stode in synners     waye.

Its interest is of several kinds.  In the first place it is the earliest music to an English metrical version as yet discovered.  The insertion of the bar also converts it into a double chant, a musical form hitherto supposed unknown till a hundred years later, and thus shows by what a simple transition the passage from chanting the prose Psalter to singing the metrical one might be accomplished.  It would be unwise to argue from this single specimen that it was so accomplished, or that we see here the typical early English metrical Psalm tune ; but certainly the discovery of this little composition, so obviously intermediate in char-

acter, very much diminishes the probability that the chorale form, which soon afterwards prevailed, was known in England at this time.

We now enter upon the history of what afterwards became the authorised version.  In the year 1548 or 1549—it is uncertain which, but possibly early in 1549 — appeared a small volume with the following title :

' Certayne Psalmes chosen out of the Psalter of David and drawen into Englishe Metre by Thomas Sternhold, Grome of yᵉ Kynges Maiesties Robes. London, Edvardus Whitchurche.'

This volume, which is without date, contains nineteen Psalms only, in double common measure, or four lines of fourteen, by Sternhold alone, without music.  Sternhold died in 1549, and on Dec. 14 of that year another edition was published, with a new title :

' All such psalmes of David as Thomas Sternehold late groome of yᵉ Kinges Maiesties Robes didde in his lyfetime draw into English metre.  Newly imprinted by Edward Whitchurche.'

Besides the original nineteen, this edition contains eighteen by Sternhold ; and, printed as a second part, a supplement of seven by J. Hopkins without music.  This is the volume which in previous accounts of the subject [4] has been usually described as the first edition ; and no mention is made of Hopkins's supplement.  It has also been usual to describe the contents as ' fifty-one Psalms ' ; the actual number, it will be seen, is forty-four.  Lowndes mentions a second edition of this work in the following year : ' by the widowe of Jhon Harrington, London, 1550.'  Between 1550 and 1553 six editions of Sternhold were printed.

In this year also William Hunnis, a gentleman of the Chapel Royal, published a small selection of metrical Psalms, in the style of Sternhold, with the following title :

' Certayne Psalmes chosen out of the Psalter of David, and drawen furth into English Meter by William Hunnis, London, by the wydow of John Herforde, 1550.'

A copy of this work is in the public library of Cambridge.  There is no music.  In 1553 appeared a third edition of the volume dated 1549, again published by Whitchurche.  This edition contains a further supplement of seven Psalms by Whittingham, thus raising the number to fifty-one.  There is still no music.  Lowndes mentions another edition of the same year, ' by Thom. Kyngston and Henry Sutton, London.'

To this year also belongs a small volume containing nineteen Psalms in the common measure, which is seldom mentioned in accounts of the subject, but which is nevertheless of great interest, since it contains music in four parts.  The title is as follows :

' Certayne Psalmes select out of the Psalter of David, and drawen into Englyshe Metre, with notes to every Psalme in iiij parts to Synge, by F. S.  Im-

---

[1] This was the usual way of printing the common measure in Crowley's day, and for many years afterwards.
[2] The plain-song of this chant is of course the seventh ecclesiastical tone, with the well-known ending upon the participant A. As this ending, however, is only a modulation which would have been corrected in the Roman service by the subsequent antiphon, the music belongs properly to the mode of the chant.
[3] In the original the reciting note is divided into semibreves, one for each syllable.

[4] Except in that given by Warton, who speaks of *several* editions during Sternhold's lifetime ; it is impossible, however, to corroborate this.

printed at London by Wyllyam Seres, at the Sygne of the Hedge Hogge, 1553.'[1]

In the dedication, to Lord Russell, the author gives his full name, Francys Seagar. The music is so arranged that all the four voices may sing at once from the same book : the parts are separate, each with its own copy of words, the two higher voices upon the left-hand page, the two lower upon the right ; all, of course, turning the leaf together. Though the music continues throughout the book, the actual number of compositions is found to be only two, one being repeated twelve times, the other seven. The first is here given :

MODE II. Transposed.[2]

It will be perceived that we have not yet quite arrived at a tune. The part next above the bass, in descending by one degree upon the final, performs the office of a cantus firmus, but exhibits no other characteristic of a tune that could be sung alone. The composition is in fact a little motet, full of points of imitation, but capable of repetition. It is written in a style which will be easily recognised by those who are acquainted with Dr. Tye's music to his metrical Acts of the Apostles (also published in this year) or with the four-part song ' In going to my naked bed '—a native style, founded upon the secular part-songs of Fayrfax,

Cornysshe, Newark and Banister, which had been growing up during the reign of Henry the Eighth. We see it here, however, in an imperfect shape, and its development into a flowing, consecutive common measure tune is only to be found in Tye's work.[3] It is true that Tye, in the last line of his compositions generally, and occasionally elsewhere, somewhat injured the rhythmical continuity by introducing a point of imitation ; but that was so obviously a concession to scholarship, and could with so little difficulty have been altered, that we may certainly ascribe to him the invention of an English form of Psalm tune, in four parts, suitable for popular use, and far more beautiful than the tunes in chorale form to which it was compelled to give way. The influence of Geneva was at this time exceedingly powerful in England, and the tendency, slight as it is, to florid descant in Tye's work, must have been to the reformers extremely objectionable. To this, no doubt, it is owing that no more tunes were written in this style.

The publications of this year probably took place before July, which was the month of the king's death ; and nothing further was produced in this country during the reactionary reign of his successor. But in 1556 an edition of Sternhold was published in Geneva, for the use of the Protestants who had taken refuge there, which is extremely important in the history of the subject, since it contains the first instalment of those famous ' church tunes,' some at least of which have been sung, Sunday after Sunday, in our English churches, from that day to this. The book appeared with a new title :

' One and fiftie Psalmes of David in English metre, whereof 37 were made by Thomas Sterneholde and the rest by others. Conferred with the hebrewe, and in certeyn places corrected, as the text and sens of the Prophete required.'[4]

The date is gathered from the second part of the book, which contains the Geneva catechism, form of prayer and confession, and is printed ' by John Crespin, Geneva, 1556.' No addition, it will be seen, had been made to the number of translations ; it only remains, therefore, to speak of the tunes. In one respect this edition differs from all others. Here a new tune is given for every Psalm ; in subsequent editions the tunes are repeated, sometimes more than once. They are printed without harmony, in the tenor or alto clef, at the head of the Psalm, the first verse accompanying the notes. The question has often been discussed, what the ' church tunes ' are ; what their origin, and who their author. Burney says they are ' mostly German '; but that is impossible, since the translations in the edition of Sternhold which the emigrants took with them to

---

[1] The copy consulted of this book is in the library of Emmanuel College, Cambridge. Thanks are due to the College for permission to examine it.
[2] The original is without bars.

[3] One of Tye's tunes will be found in the article WINDSOR OR ETON TUNE.
[4] A defective copy of this book is in the Bodleian Library ; a better copy is in the Advocates' Library, Edinburgh.

Geneva were all, except one or two, in double common measure; and there are no foreign tunes of this date which will fit that peculiarly English metre. The true answer is probably to be found in Ravenscroft's classified index of the tunes in his Psalter, published in 1621, where, under the heading of ' English tunes imitating the High Dutch, Italian, French and Netherlandish tunes,' will be found almost all the original ' church tunes ' which remained in use in his day. According to this excellent authority, therefore, the ' church tunes,' as a whole, are English compositions. Furthermore, considering that they appear for the first time in this volume, published at Geneva, three years after the emigration, it becomes exceedingly probable that they are imitations of those which the emigrants found in use at Geneva among the French Protestants, which were chiefly, if not entirely, the tunes composed by Bourgeois for the Psalter of Marot and Bésa. (See BOURGEOIS.) Some of the French tunes evidently at once became great favourites with the English Protestants. Already in this volume we find a most interesting attempt to adapt the famous French tune now known as the Old Hundredth to the double common measure. It is set to the 3rd Psalm. Here the first line is note for note the same as in the French tune : the difference begins with the difference of metre in the second line. We find further that as the translation of the Psalter proceeded towards completion, Keith and Whittingham, residents in Geneva, rendered some of the later Psalms into special metres, and retranslated others—among them the 100th, in order to provide for the adoption of the most admired French tunes intact: these will be mentioned in detail, so far as they have been as yet identified, later on. The question of authorship is of secondary interest. There were at this time, no doubt, many English musicians capable of composing them, among the organists or singing men in the cathedrals and Chapel Royal, who are known to have entered almost as warmly as the clergy into the religious discussions of the time, and of whom many took refuge at Geneva along with the clergy. Immediately upon the death of Mary, in 1558, in which year a second edition appeared,[1] this work found its way to England. The tunes at once became popular, and a strong and general demand was made for liberty to sing them in the churches. In the following year permission was given, in the 49th section of the injunctions for the guidance of the clergy, where, after commanding that the former order of service (Edward's) be preserved, Elizabeth adds :

' And yet nevertheless, for the comforting of such as delight in music, it may be permitted, that in the beginning or in the end of Common Prayer, either at

morning or evening, there may be sung an hymn, or such like song, to the praise of Almighty God, in the best melody and music that may be conveniently devised, having respect that the sentence of the hymn may be understood and perceived.'

This permission, and the immediate advantage that was taken of it, no doubt did much to increase the popular taste for Psalm-singing, and to hasten the completion of the Psalter. For in the course of the next year, 1560, a new edition appeared, in which the number of Psalms is raised to 64, with the following title :

' Psalmes of David in Englishe Metre, by Thomas Sterneholde and others : conferred with the Ebrue, and in certeine places corrected, as the sense of the Prophete required : and the Note joyned withall. Very mete to be used of all sorts of people privately for their godly solace & comfort, laying aparte all ungodly songes & ballades, which tende only to the nourishing of vice, and corrupting of youth. Newly set foarth and allowed, according to the Quenes Maiesties Iniunctions.  1560.'[2]

The same title, practically word for word, appears in the English edition of 1561, the only known copy of which is in the library of the Society of Antiquaries, where it is bound up together with a Bible of 1553. It bears Day's name as printer and the date. It contains, moreover, an *Introduction to learn to sing*, a feature hitherto unknown in Sternhold, but not unfrequently occurring afterwards. Although no mention is made of them in the title, the edition of 1560 includes metrical versions of three of the Evangelical Hymns, the ten Commandments, the Lord's Prayer and the Creed. The practice of repeating the tunes begins here, for though the number of Psalms has been increased, the number of tunes has diminished. There are only forty-two, of which twenty-four have been taken on from the previous edition ; the rest are new. Among the new tunes will be found six adopted from the French Psalter, in the manner described above. They are as follows : the tunes to the French 50th, 121st, 124th, 127th, 129th and 130th have been set to the same Psalms in the English version ; the French 107th has been compressed to suit the English 120th. The tune for the metrical commandments is the same in both versions.

Twenty-three more translations were added in another edition brought out in 1561 at Geneva :[3]

' Foure score and seven Psalmes of David in English Mitre, by Thomas Sterneholde and others : conferred with the Hebrewe, and in certeine places corrected, as the sense of the Prophet requireth.  Whereunto are added the Songe of Simeon, the then commandments and the Lord's Prayer.  1561.'

From the ' Forme of Prayers,' etc., bound up with it, we gather that it was ' printed at Geneva by Zacharie Durand.' The number of tunes had now been largely increased, and raised to a point beyond which we shall find it scarcely advanced for many years afterwards. The exact number

---

[1] The discovery of a copy of the second edition was described in *The Times*, Sept. 19, 1902.

[2] A copy, without name of place or printer, and imperfect at the end, is in the library of Christ Church, Oxford.
[3] The unique copy of this book is in the Library of St. Paul Cathedral.

is sixty-two; of which twenty-four had appeared in both previous editions, fourteen in the edition of 1560 only and two in the edition of 1556 only. The rest were new. Among the new tunes will again be found several French importations. The tunes for the English 50th and 104th are the French tunes for the same Psalms. The 100th is the French 134th from Claudin le Jeune's collection, Leyden, 1633,

the 113th is the French 36th, the 122nd the French 3rd, the 125th the French 21st, the 126th the French 90th. Thus far there is no sign of any other direct influence. The imported tunes, so far as can be discovered, are all French; and the rest are English imitations in the same style.[1]

Before we enter upon the year 1562, which saw the completion of Sternhold's version, it is necessary that some account should be given of another Psalter, evidently intended for the public, which had been in preparation for some little time, and actually printed in 1567 or 1568 according to John Daye's license granted by the Stationers' Company, but which was never issued — the Psalter of Archbishop Parker. The title is as follows :

'The whole Psalter translated into English metre, which contayneth an hundreth and fifty psalmes. Imprinted at London by John Daye, dwelling over Aldersgate beneath S. Martyn's. Cum gratiâ et privilegio Regiae maiestatis, per decennium.'

The privilege sufficiently proves the intention to publish. It seems at first sight curious, that while it has been necessary to speak of the copies of published works hitherto referred to as

unique, it should be possible to say of this, which was never given to the public, that at least eight examples are in existence. The reason, however, is no doubt to be found in the fact that the few copies struck off as specimens were distributed to select persons, and so, finding their way at once into careful hands, were the better preserved. The existing copies, so far as they have been compared, correspond exactly ; and show that the work was complete, lacking nothing except the date, for which a blank space was left at the foot of the title-page. The verse of this translation, which is in various metres, is in every way far superior to that of Sternhold's ; but, though the author has evidently aimed at the simplicity and directness of his original, he is frequently obscure. The suppression of the work, however, was probably not due to any considerations of this kind, but either to the enormous popularity of Sternhold's version, which was every day becoming more manifest, or, as it has been sometimes supposed, to a change in the author's opinion as to the desirability of psalm-singing. In any case, it is much to be regretted, since it involved the suppression of nine tunes specially composed by Tallis, in a style peculiar to himself. which, if the work had been published, would at all events have once more established the standard of an English tune in four parts, broad, simple and effective, and suitable for congregational use ; and, from the technical point of view, finer than anything of the kind that has been done since. Whether it would have prevailed or not, it is impossible to say. We have seen how, in the case of Tye, the influence of Geneva triumphed over the beauty of his music ; and that influence had become stronger in the interval. On the other hand, the tendency to florid descant, so hateful to the reformers, was absent from the work of Tallis. The compositions in this book are printed, in the manner then customary, in separate parts, all four being visible at once. They are in nearly plain counterpoint ; the final close is sometimes slightly elaborated, but generally the effect— which is one of great richness, solemn or sweet according to the nature of the particular scale— is obtained by very simple means. Eight of the tunes are in the first eight modes, and are intended for the Psalms ; the ninth, in Mode XIII., is supplementary, and is set to a translation of Veni Creator. Two of them have been revived, and are now well known. One appears in our hymnals as 'Tallis,' and is the supplementary tune in Mode XIII. ; the other, generally set to Bishop Ken's evening hymn, and known as 'Canon,' is the tune in Mode VIII. With regard to the latter, it should be mentioned that in the original it is twice as long as in the modern form, every section being repeated before proceeding to the next. With this exception the melodies appear as they were

---

1 The imported tunes sometimes underwent a slight alteration, necessitated by the frequency of the feminine rhymes in the French version. By this method a new character was often given to the tune.

written ; but, as regards the three other parts,
only such fragments have been retained as have
happened to suit the taste or convenience of
compilers.  In the original, too, the tenor leads
in the canon ; this is reversed in the modern
arrangement.  The tune in Mode I., given as
No. 78 in *The English Hymnal* (1906), transposed a third higher, is in a more severe and
solemn strain than the two just mentioned.
The treatment of the sixth—natural in the
first half of the tune and flat in the latter
half—is in the finest manner of Dorian harmony.  The instruction with regard to the
tunes is as follows :

'The tenor of these partes be for the people when
they will syng alone, the other parts, put for greater
queers, or such as will syng or play them privatlye.'

The method of fitting the Psalms to appropriate tunes is very simple.  At the head of
each Psalm stands an accent—grave, acute or
circumflex—indicating its nature as sad, joyful
or indifferent, according to the author's notion :
the tunes bear corresponding accents.  The
work is divided into three parts, each containing
fifty Psalms ; and since it is only in the third
part that these accents appear (together with
a rather ingenious system of red and black
brackets, showing the rhyming structure of the
verse), we may perhaps conclude that the work
was not all printed at once, and that it was only
towards the end—possibly after the promulga-
tion of Elizabeth's injunctions—that it was
thought desirable to have tunes composed.

The first complete edition of the Sternhold
and Hopkins version, containing the whole
Psalms, the Evangelical Hymns and the
Spiritual Songs, was published in 1562.[1]  The
second edition followed in 1563 and the third
in 1564 ; the title is as follows :

'The whole booke of Psalms collected into Englysh
Meter, by T. Sternhold, I. Hopkins, and others, conferred with the Ebrue, with apt notes to singe them
withal.  Faithfully perused and alowed according to
thorder appointed in the Queene's maiestie's Iniunctions. . . .  Imprinted at London by John Day
dwelling over Aldersgate. . . . 1562.'

The number of tunes in this edition is sixty-
five, including a few duplicates ; of which ten
had appeared in all the previous editions, nine
in the editions of 1560 and 1561 only, seven
in the edition of 1561 only, and four in the
edition of 1560 only.  The rest were new.  It
will have been observed that a considerable
rearrangement of the tunes had hitherto taken
place in every new edition ; the tunes which
were taken on from previous editions generally
remained attached to the same Psalms as before,
but the number of new tunes, as well as of
those omitted, was always large.  Now, however, the compilers rested content ; and henceforward, notwithstanding that a new edition
was published almost yearly, the changes were
so gradual that it will only be necessary to take
note of them at intervals.  The tunes are

printed without bars, and in notes of unequal
length.  Semibreves and minims are both used,
but in what seems at first sight so unsystematic
a way—since they do not correspond with the
accents of the verse—that few of the tunes,
as they stand, could be divided into equal sections ; and some could not be made to submit
to any time - signature whatever.  In this
respect they resemble the older ecclesiastical
melodies.  The idea of imitation, however, was
probably far from the composer's mind, and the
object of his irregularity was no doubt variety
of effect ; the destruction of the monotonous
swing of the alternate eight and six with
accents constantly recurring in similar positions.  To the eye the tunes appear somewhat
confused ; but upon trial it will be found that
the long and short notes have been adjusted
with great care, and, taking a whole tune
together, with a fine sense of rhythmical
balance.  The modes in which these compositions are written are such as we should expect
to meet with in works of a popular, as opposed
to an ecclesiastical, character.  The great
majority of the tunes will be found to be in
the modes which have since become our major
and minor scales.  The exact numbers are as
follows : twenty-eight are in Modes XIII. and
XIV., twenty-three in Modes IX. and X., twelve
in Modes I. and II., one in Mode VII., and one
in Mode VIII.  All these modes, except the
last two, are used both in their original and
transposed positions.

A knowledge of music was at this time so
general that the number of persons able to sing
or play these tunes at sight was probably very
considerable.  Nevertheless, as in the edition
of 1560, so also in 1561, 1562, 1564 and again
in 1577 and 1581, there was published *An
Introduction to Learn to Sing*, consisting of the
scale and a few elementary rules, for the benefit
of the ignorant.  The edition of 1607 contained
a more elaborate system of rules, and ' like,
those of 1570, 1573, 1583, 1584, 1588, 1590,'
had the sol-fa joined to every note of the tunes
throughout the book.

For competent musicians, a four-part setting
of the ' church tunes ' was also provided by the
same publisher :

'The whole psalmes in foure partes, which may
be song to al musicall instrumentes, set forth for the
encrease of vertue, and abolishyng of other vayne
and triflyng ballades.  Imprinted at London by John
Day, dwelling over Aldersgate, beneath Saynt Mar-
tyns.  Cum gratia et privilegio Regiae Maiestatis, per
septennium.  1563.'[2]

Notwithstanding this title, only the first
verse of each Psalm is given ; enough to accompany the notes once, and no more : it is therefore only a companion to Sternhold ; not, like
almost all subsequent works of the kind, a
substitute.  But in other respects it was designed on a much larger scale than anything

---

[1] A copy is in the John Rylands Library at Manchester.

[2] A second edition was published in 1565.

that appeared afterwards. It is in four volumes, one for each voice. Every composition, long or short, occupies a page; and at the head of each stands one of the fine pictorial initial letters which appear in all Day's best books about this time. But it is as regards the quantity of the music that it goes furthest beyond all other collections of the same kind. The composers of subsequent Psalters thought it quite sufficient, as a rule, to furnish each of the sixty-five 'church tunes' with a single setting; but here, not only has each been set, but frequently two and sometimes three and four composers have contributed settings of the same tune; and as if this were not enough, they have increased the work by as many as thirty tunes, not to be found in Sternhold, and for the most part probably original. The total result of their labours is a collection of 141 compositions, of which four are by N. Southerton, eleven by R. Brimle, seventeen by J. Hake, twenty-seven by T. Causton and eighty-one by W. Parsons. It is worthy of remark that while all the contemporary musicians of the first rank had already been employed upon contributions to the liturgical service—not only by way of MSS., but also in the printed work, 'Certayne notes,' etc., issued by Day in 1560—the composers to whom the publisher had recourse for this undertaking are all, except one, otherwise unknown.[1] Nor is their music, though generally respectable and sometimes excellent, of a kind that requires any detailed description: it will be sufficient to mention a few of its most noticeable characteristics, interesting chiefly from the insight they afford into the practice of the average proficient at this period. The character of these compositions in most cases is much the same as that of the simple settings of the French Psalter[2] by Goudimel and Claude le Jeune, the parts usually moving together, and the tenor taking the tune. The method of Causton, however, differs in some respects from that of his associates: he is evidently a follower of Tye, showing the same tendency towards florid counterpoint, and often indeed using the same figures. He is, as might be expected, very much Tye's inferior in invention, and, moreover, still retains some of the objectionable collisions, inherited by the school of this period from the earlier descant, which Tye had refused to accept.[3] Brimle offends in the same way, but to a far greater extent: indeed, unless he has been cruelly used by the printer, he is sometimes unintelligible. In one of his compositions, for instance, having to accommodate his accompanying voices to a

1 Causton, a gentleman of the Chapel Royal, had been a contributor to 'Certayne notes.'
2 Concerning those composed by Franc for the Psalter of 1565, see Vol. II. p. 292.
3 He frequently converts passing discords into discords of percussion, by repeating the bass note; and his ear, it seems, could tolerate the prepared ninth at the distance of a second, when it occurred between inner parts.

difficult close in the melody, he has written as follows[4]:

The difficulty arising from the progression of the melody in this passage was one that often presented itself during the process of setting the earliest versions of the 'church tunes.' It arose whenever the melody, in closing, passed by the interval of a whole tone from the seventh of the scale to the final. When this happened, the final cadence of the mode was of course impossible, and some sort of expedient became necessary. Since, however, no substitute for the proper close could be really satisfactory—because, no matter how cleverly it might be treated, the result must necessarily be ambiguous—in all such cases the melody was sooner or later altered. As these expedients do not occur in subsequent Psalters, two other specimens are here given of a more rational kind than the one quoted above.

MODE IX. Transposed (Final, D).          W. PARSONS.

MODE I. Transposed (Final, G).          J. HAKE.

4 This passage, however, will present nothing extraordinary to those who may happen to have examined the examples, taken from Bisby, Pigott and others, in Morley's Plaine and Easie Introduction to Practicall Musick. From those examples it appears that the laws which govern the treatment of discords were not at all generally understood by English musicians, even as late as the beginning of Henry the Eighth's reign: it is quite evident that discords (not passing) were not only constantly taken unprepared, but, what is more strange, the discordant note was absolutely free in its progression. It might either rise or fall at pleasure: it might pass by skip or by degree, either to concord or discord; or it might remain to become the preparation of a suspended discord. And this was the practice of musicians of whom Morley says that 'they were skilful men for the time wherein they lived.'
5 In East's Psalter the tune of No. 1 has already been altered, in order to make a true final close possible, in the manner shown below. The tune containing No. 2 does not occur again, but here also an equally simple alteration brings about the desired result.

W. COBBOLD.

T

Both Parsons[1] and Hake appear to have been excellent musicians. The style of the former is somewhat severe, sometimes even harsh, but always strong and solid. In the latter we find more sweetness; and it is characteristic of him that, more frequently than the others, he makes use of the soft harmony of the imperfect triad in its first inversion. It should be mentioned that of the seventeen tunes set by him in this collection, seven were 'church tunes,' and ten had previously appeared in Crespin's edition of Sternhold, and had afterwards been dropped. His additions, therefore, were none of them original. One other point remains to be noticed. Modulation, in these settings, is extremely rare; and often, when it would seem—to modern ears at least—to be irresistibly suggested by the progression of the melody, the apparent ingenuity with which it has been avoided is very curious. In the tune given to the 22nd Psalm, for instance, which is in Mode XIII. (final, C), the second half begins with a phrase which obviously suggests a modulation to the dominant:

but which has been treated by Parsons as follows:[2]

The importance of this Psalter, at once the first and the most liberal of its kind, entitles it to a complete example of its workmanship. The tune chosen is that to the 137th Psalm, an excellent specimen of the English imitations of the French melodies, and interesting also as being one of the two tunes which, appearing among the first printed—in Crespin's edition of

[1] W. Parsons must not be confounded with R. Parsons, a well-known composer of this period. J. Hake may possibly have been the 'Mr. Hake,' a singing man of Windsor, whose name was mentioned by Testwoode in one of the scoffing speeches for which he was afterwards tried (with Merbecke and another) and executed.

[2] Nothing is more interesting than to trace the progress of a passage of this kind through subsequent Psalters, and to notice how surely, sooner or later, the modulation comes:

MODE XIII. Transposed.

W. COBBOLD (Este's Psalter, 1592).

T. MORLEY (Barley's Psalter).

Sternhold—are in use at this day. It was evidently a favourite with Parsons, who has set it three times; twice placing it in the tenor, and once in the upper voice. The latter setting is the one here given[3]:

MODE XIV. Transposed.

Psalm cxxxvii. W. PARSONS.

When as we sat in Ba - bi - lon,

the ry - vers round a - bout: And in re - mem -

braunce of Si - on, the teares for grief burst out:

We hanged our harpes and in - stru - ments, the

wil - low trees up - on: For in that place men

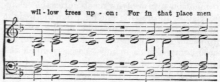

for their use, had plant - ed ma - ny one.

At the end of the book are to be found a few miscellaneous compositions, some in metre and some in prose, probably not specially intended for this work, but adopted into it. Some of these are by the musicians employed upon the Psalter; but there are also two by Tallis, and one each by Shephard and Edwards.

The ample supply of four-part settings contained in Day's great collection seems to have so far satisfied the public craving that during the next sixteen years no other publication of the

[3] It must be confessed that the tune is more beautiful without its setting. Parsons has not only avoided every kind of modulation, but has even refused closes which the ear desires, and which he might have taken without having recourse to chromatic notes. It remained for later musicians to bring out the beauty of the melody.

same kind was attempted. Nor had the work which appeared at the end of that period been composed with any kind of desire to rival or succeed the existing one ; it had, in fact, never been intended for the public, and was brought out without the permission, or even the knowledge, of its author. Its title was as follows :

'The Psalmes of David in English meter with notes of foure partes set unto them by Guilielmo Daman, for John Bull, to the use of the godly Christians for recreatyng themselves, instede of fond and unseemely Ballades. Anno 1579 at London Printed by John Daye. Cum privilegio.'

The circumstances of this publication, as they were afterwards related, were shortly these. It was Damon's custom, on the occasion of each of his visits to his friend, John Bull, to compose, and leave behind him, a four-part setting of some one of the 'church tunes'; and these, when the collection was complete, Bull gave to the printer, without asking the author's consent. The preface, by one Edward Hake, is a kind of apology, partly for the conduct of the above-mentioned John Bull, ' citizen and goldsmith of London,' and partly for the settings themselves, of which he says that they were ' by peece meale gotten and gathered together from the fertile soyle of his honest frend Guilielmo Damon one of her Maiesties Musitions,' who ' never meant them to the use of any learned and cunnyng Musition, but altogether respected the pleasuryng of his private frend.' The settings —one only to each tune—are very much of the kind that might be expected from the circumstances. They are in plain counterpoint, with the tune in the tenor ; evidently the work of a competent musician, but without special merit. The book contains fourteen tunes not to be found in Day, and among these are the first of those single common measure tunes which later quite took the place in popular favour of all but a few of the older double kind. They had not as yet been named, but they were afterwards known as Cambridge, Oxford, Canterbury and Southwell. Two of the 'church tunes' have been dropped ; and it should also be remarked that in many tunes the value of the notes has been altered, the alteration being, in all cases, the substitution of a minim for a semibreve.

Warton mentions a small publication, ' VII Steppes to heauen, alias the vij [penitential] Psalmes reduced into meter by Will Hunnys,'[1] which he says was brought out by Henry Denham in 1581 ; and ' Seuen sobs of a sorrowfull soule for sinne,' published in 1585, was, according to the same authority, a second edition of the same work with a new title. The later edition contains seven tunes in double common measure, in the style of the ' church tunes,' exceedingly well written, and quite up to the average merit of their models. Burney and

[1] B.M. and Bodl.

Lowndes both mention a collection of settings with the following title :

' Musicke of six and five parts made upon the common tunes used in singing of the Psalmes by John Cosyn, London by John Wolfe, 1585.'

Another work, called by Canon Havergal the ' Psalter of Henrie Denham,'[2] is said to have been published in 1588.

Damon seems to have been considerably annoyed to find that compositions which he thought good enough for Bull, had been by Bull thought good enough for the public ; and, as a protest against the injustice done to his reputation, began, and lived long enough to finish, two other separate and complete settings of the ' church tunes,' in motet fashion ; the tunes in the first being in the tenor, and in the second in the upper voice. They were brought out after his death by a friend, one William Swayne, from whose preface we learn the particulars of the publication of 1579. The titles are as follows:

1. 'The former booke of the Musicke of M. William Damon late one of her maiesties Musitions : conteining all the tunes of David's Psalmes, as they are ordinarily soung in the Church : most excellently by him composed into 4 parts. In which sett the Tenor singeth the Church tune. Published for the recreation of such as delight in Musicke : by W. Swayne Gent. Printed by T. Este, the assigne of W. Byrd. 1591.'

2. ' The second Booke of the Musicke of M. William Damon, late one of her maiesties Musitions ; conteining all the tunes of David's Psalmes, as they are ordinarily soung in the Church ; most excellently by him composed into 4 parts. In which Sett the highest part singeth the Church tune. Published for the recreation of such as delight in Musicke : By W. Swayne, Gent. Printed by T. Este, the assigne of W. Byrd, 1591.'

In both these works the compositions are in the same rather ornate style ; points of imitation are frequently taken upon the plain-song, the parts from time to time resting, in the usual manner of the motet. Their whole aim is, in fact, more ambitious than that of any other setting of the ' church tunes.' Fourteen of the original tunes have been dropped, and five added —among them the tune afterwards known as Windsor or Eton. (See WINDSOR TUNE.)

East (Este), the publisher of these two works, must have been at the same time engaged upon the preparation of his own famous Psalter, for in the course of the next year it was brought out, with the following title :

' The whole booke of psalmes : with their wonted Tunes, as they are song in Churches, composed into foure parts : All which are so placed that foure may sing ech one a seueral part in this booke. Wherein the Church tunes are carefully corrected, and thereunto added other short tunes usually song in London, and other places of this Realme. With a table in the end of the booke of such tunes as are newly added, with the number of ech Psalme placed to the said Tune. Compiled by sondry avthors who haue so laboured herein, that the vnskilfull with small practice may attaine to sing that part which is fittest for their voice. Imprinted at London by Thomas Est, the assigné of William Byrd : dwelling in Aldersgate streete at the signe of the Black Horse and are there to be sold. 1592.'[3]

[2] This and the above were not examined by the writer.
[3] A second edition was published in 1594 and a third in 1604. The work was reprinted by the Musical Antiquarian Society in 1844.

It seems to have been part of East's plan to ignore his predecessor. He has dropped nine of the tunes which were new in Daman's Psalters, and the five which he has taken on appear in his 'Note of tunes newly added in this booke.' Four of these five were those afterwards known as Cambridge, Oxford, Canterbury and Windsor, and the first three must already have become great favourites with the public, since Cambridge has been repeated thirty-one times, Oxford twenty-six times, and Canterbury thirty-three times. The repetition, therefore, is now on a new principle: the older custom was to repeat almost every tune once or twice, but in this Psalter the repetition is confined almost entirely to these three tunes. Four really new tunes, all in single common measure, have been added. To three of these, names, for the first time, are given; they are ' Glassenburie,' ' Kentish ' (afterwards Rochester) and 'Chesshire.' The other, though not named as yet, afterwards became Winchester.

For the four-part settings East engaged ten composers, ' being such,' he says in his preface, ' as I know to be expert in the Arte and sufficient to answere such curious carping Musitions, whose skill hath not been employed to the furthering of this work.' This is no empty boast: seventeen of the settings are by John Farmer; twelve by George Kirbye; ten by Richard Allison; nine by Giles Farnaby; seven by Edward Blancks; five by John Douland; five by William Cobbold; four by Edmund Hooper; three by Edward Johnson, and one by Michael Cavendish. It will be observed that though most of these composers are eminent as madrigalists, none of them, except Hooper, and perhaps Johnson, are known as experts in the ecclesiastical style: a certain interest therefore belongs to their settings of plain-song; a kind of composition which they have nowhere attempted except in this work.[1] The method of treatment is very varied: in some cases the counterpoint is perfectly plain; in others plain is mixed with florid; while in others again the florid prevails throughout. In the plain settings no great advance upon the best of those in Day's Psalter will be observed. Indeed, in one respect — the melodious progression of the voices—advance was scarcely possible; since equality of interest in the parts had been, from the very beginning, the fundamental principle of composition. What advance there is will be found to be in the direction of harmony. The ear is gratified more often than before by a harmonic progression appropriate to the progression of the tune. Modulation in the closes, therefore, becomes more frequent; and in some cases, for special reasons, a partial modulation is even introduced in the middle of a section. In all styles, a close containing the prepared fourth, either struck or suspended, and accompanied by the fifth, is the most usual termination; but the penultimate harmony is also sometimes preceded by the sixth and fifth together upon the fourth of the scale. The plain style has been more often, and more successfully, treated by Blancks than by any of the others. He contrives always to unite solid and reasonable harmony with freedom of movement and melody in the parts; indeed, the melody of his upper voice is often so good that it might be sung as a tune by itself. But by far the greater number of the settings in this work are in the mixed style, in which the figuration introduced consists chiefly of suspended concords (discords being still reserved for the closes), passing notes, and short points of imitation between two of the parts at the beginning of the section. It is difficult to say who is most excellent in this manner. Farmer's skill in contriving the short points of imitation is remarkable, but one must also admire the richness of Hooper's harmony, Allison's smoothness, and the ingenuity and resource shown by Cobbold and Kirbye. The last two, also, are undoubtedly the most successful in dealing with the more florid style, which, in fact, and perhaps for this reason, they have attempted more often than any of their associates. They have produced several compositions of great beauty, in which most of the devices of counterpoint have been introduced, though without ostentation or apparent effort.

Farnaby and Johnson were perhaps not included in the original scheme of the work, since they do not appear till late, Johnson's first setting being Ps. ciii. and Farnaby's Ps. cxix. They need special, but not favourable, mention; because, although their compositions are thoroughly able, and often beautiful—Johnson's especially so—it is they who make it impossible to point to East's Psalter as a model throughout of pure writing. The art of composing for concerted voices in the strict diatonic style had reached, about the year 1580, probably the highest point of excellence it was capable of. Any change must have been for the worse, and it is in Johnson and Farnaby that we here see the change beginning.[2]

[1] Farmer had published, in the previous year, forty canons, two to one, upon one plain-song. These, however, were only contrapuntal exercises.

[2] Johnson (Ps. cxi.) has taken the fourth unprepared in a chord of the 6-4, and the imperfect triad with the root in the bass. Farnaby so frequently abandons the old practice of making all the notes upon one syllable conjunct, that one must suppose he actually preferred the leap in such cases. The following variants of a well-known cadence, also, have a kind of interest, since it is difficult to see how they could for a moment have borne comparison with their original:

G. FARNABY.        E. JOHNSON.

Johnson, though sometimes licentious, was also sometimes even prudish  In taking the sixth and fifth upon the fourth of the

There is, however, one Psalter which can be said to show the pure Elizabethan counterpoint in perfection throughout. It is entirely the work of one man, Richard Allison, already mentioned as one of East's contributors, who published it in 1599, with the following title :

'The Psalmes of David in Meter, the plaine song beeing the common tunne to be sung and plaide upon the Lute, Orpharyon, Citterne or Base Violl, severally or altogether, the singing part to be either Tenor or Treble to the instrument, according to the nature of the voyce, or for fowre voyces. With tenne short Tunnes in the end, to which for the most part all the Psalmes may be usually sung, for the use of such as are of mean skill, and whose leysure least serveth to practize. By Richard Allison Gent. Practitioner in the Art of Musicke, and are to be solde at his house in the Dukes place neere Alde-Gate London, printed by William Barley, the asigne of Thomas Morley. 1599.'

The style of treatment employed by Allison in this work—in which he has given the tune to the upper voice throughout—is almost the same as the mixed style adopted by him in East's Psalter. Here, after an interval of seven years, we find a slightly stronger tendency towards the more florid manner, but his devices and ornaments are still always in perfectly pure taste.[1] The lute part was evidently only intended for use when the tune was sung by a single voice, since it is constructed in the manner then proper to lute accompaniments to songs, in which the nótes taken by the voice were omitted. Sir John Hawkins, in his account of the book, makes a curious mistake on this point. He says, 'It is observable that the author has made the plain-song or church tune the cantus part, *which part being intended as well for the lute or cittern as the voice, is given also in those characters called the tablature which are peculiar to those instruments.*' That the exact opposite is the case [2] will be seen from the translation of a fragment of the lute part, here given :

VOICES.
When as we sat in Ba- bi- -lon.

The next Psalter to be mentioned is one which seems to have hitherto escaped notice.

It was issued without date ; but since we find that it contains tunes not existing in the third edition of East (1604), it may perhaps be supposed to be later than that edition ; and since we know that its printer, W. Barley, brought out nothing after the year 1614, it would be natural to assume that it was published in the interval between those two dates. Its title is as follows :

'The whole Booke of Psalmes. With their woonted Tunes, as they are sung in Churches, composed into foure parts. Compiled by sundrie Authors, who have so laboured herein, that the unskilful with small practise may attaine to sing that part, which is fittest for their voice. Printed at London in little S. Hellens by W. Barley, the assigne of T. Morley, and are to be sold at his shop in Gratious street. Cum privilegio.'

From this title, and from the fact that Morley was the successor to Byrd, whose assignee East was, it would be natural to infer that the work was a further edition of East's Psalter : and from its contents, it would seem to put forward some pretence to be so. But it differs in several important respects from the original. East's Psalter was a beautiful book, in octavo size, printed in small but perfectly clear type ; the voice parts separate, but all visible at once, and all turning the leaf together. Barley's Psalter is reduced to duodecimo size, becoming in consequence inconveniently thick ; it is badly printed ; and the parts, though separate, do not always turn the leaf together. Worse than this, in almost all the settings, *the two upper voice parts are omitted,* and the remaining parts —the tune and the bass—being separate are rendered useless even to the organist, the only person who could have turned two parts to any sort of account. The work, therefore, is so unsatisfactory as to be scarcely worthy of notice, did it not contain ten new and admirable settings, of which four are by Morley himself, five by John Bennet, and one by Farnaby. These not only save the book, but render it valuable ; for in Ravenscroft's Psalter, published a few years later, only four of them—two by Morley and two by Bennet—survive. This work, therefore, contains six compositions by eminent musicians which are not to be found elsewhere. They are of course printed entire, as are also the settings of the two established and often-repeated favourites above referred to, Oxford and Cambridge tunes, and a few others, which, however, though they have escaped mutilation, have not escaped alteration, considerable changes being sometimes made in the parts. In some of the mutilated settings, also, the bass part has been altered, and in some a new bass has been substituted for the old one, while the editor has allowed the name of the original composer to stand above the tune. Examples of extreme carelessness in editing might also be given, were it worth while to do so. On the whole, the book is somewhat of a puzzle. There would be nothing

scale, his associates accompanied them, in the modern way, with a third ; Johnson, however, refuses this, and, following the strict Roman practice, doubles the bass note instead.

[1] It was by a chance more unfortunate even than usual that Dr. Burney selected this Psalter—on the whole the best that ever appeared—as a victim to his strange prejudice against our native music. His slighting verdict is that 'the book has no merit, but what was very common at the time it was printed ' : which is certainly true ; but Allison, a musician of the first rank, is not deserving of contempt on the ground that merit of the highest kind happened to be very common in his day.

[2] Hawkins has evidently been misled by the clumsily worded title.

surprising in its peculiarities had it been some unauthorised or piratical edition of East ; but when we remember that the printer was working under the royal patent granted to Morley, and that Morley himself, and another musician almost as distinguished, contributed to it some of the best settings of church tunes ever composed, it becomes difficult to account for its badness.[1] Besides the new settings of old tunes, it also contains one new tune set by Blancks, afterwards called by Ravenscroft a Dutch tune.

Ravenscroft's Psalter, which comes next in order, was published in 1621, with the following title :

' The whole Booke of Psalmes with the Hymnes Evangelicall and Songs Spirituall. Composed into four parts by sundry authors, to such severall tunes, as have been, and are generally sung in England, Scotland, Wales, Germany, Italy, France, and the Netherlands : never as yet before in one volume published. . . . Newly corrected and enlarged by Thomas Ravenscroft Bachelar of Musicke. Printed at London, for the Company of Stationers.' [2]

This Psalter contains a larger number of compositions than any other except that of Day ; but the number in excess of the ' church tunes ' is not made up, as in Day, by alternative settings, but by the addition of new tunes, almost all of which are single common measure tunes of the later kind, with names. They appear in the index under the heading—' such tunes of the Psalmes usually sung in Cathedrall Churches, Collegiat Chapels, &c.,' and are divided broadly into three classes, one of which contains those named after the English Cathedrals and Universities, while the other two are called respectively Scotch and Welsh, and the tunes named accordingly. The whole subject of these names, and how they are to be understood, has been gone into at some length by Canon Havergal in the preface to his quasi-reprint of this Psalter ; and his conclusion is probably the right one, namely, that the tunes were in most cases designated according to the localities in which they were found in use, but that this does not necessarily imply a local origin. We have already referred to Ravenscroft's description of the old double common measure tunes, and need add nothing here with respect to them. Under the heading ' forraigne tunes usually sung in Great Brittaine ' will be found, for the French, only the few tunes taken from the Geneva Psalter, enumerated above ;

[1] One explanation only can be suggested at present. The work may never have been intended to rank with four-part psalters at all. The sole right to print Sternhold's version, with the ' church tunes,' had just passed into the hands of the Stationers' Company ; and it is possible that this book may have been put forward, not as a fourth edition of East, but in competition with the company : the promoters hoping, by the retention of the complete settings of a few favourite tunes, and the useless bass part of the rest, to create a technical difference, which would enable them to avoid infringement of the Stationers' patent. The new settings of Morley and Bennet may have been added as an attractive feature. If, however, the announcement in the title of the third edition of East (1604), ' printed for the companie of Stationers,' should mean that the company had acquired a permanent right to that work, Barley's publication would seem no longer to be defensible, on any ground. Further research may make the matter more clear.

[2] A second edition was published in 1633. It was also several times reprinted, either entirely or in part, during the 18th century.

with regard to other sources, the magnificent promise of the title-page is reduced to three German tunes, two Dutch, and one Italian.

Of the 105 settings in this work, 28 had appeared in previous ones. All the musicians engaged upon East's Psalter are represented here ; a large proportion of their compositions have been taken on, and Dowland has contributed a new one ; Dowland's is the setting of the 100th Psalm here given. Also, one of Parsons' settings has been taken from Day's Psalter, though not without alteration. The four settings by Morley and Bennet, from Barley's Psalter, have already been mentioned, and in addition there is a new one by Morley, a setting of the 1st Psalm. Tallis's tune in Mode VIII is also given here from Parker's

*' French tune,' from Ravenscroft's ' Booke of Psalmes,' 1621.*

Psalter (to a morning hymn), in the shortened form, but with the tenor still leading the canon.

New composers appear, whose names and contributions are as follows : R. Palmer, 1 ; J. Milton, 2 ; W. Harrison, 1 ; J. Tomkins, 1 ; T. Tomkins, 2 ; W. Cranfield or Cranford, 1 ; J. Ward, 1 ; S. Stubbs, 2 ; Martin Pierson. 1 ; and Ravenscroft, 51. In the work of all these composers is to be seen the same impurity of taste which was visible in the settings made for East by Farnaby and Johnson. The two cadences given above in a note, as examples of a kind of aberration, are here found to have become part of the common stock of music ; and an inferior treatment of conjunct passages in short notes, in which the alternate crotchet is dotted, finds, among other disimprovements, great favour with the editor. Ravenscroft and Milton appear to be by far the best of the new contributors. The variety shown by the former in his methods of treatment is remarkable : he seems to have formed himself upon East's Psalter, to have attempted all its styles in turn, and to have measured himself with almost every composer. Notwithstanding this, it is evident that he had no firm grasp of the older style, and that he was advancing as rapidly as any musician of his day towards the modern tonality and the modern priority of harmonic considerations in part-writing. Milton's two settings are fine, notwithstanding the occasional use of the degraded cadence, and on the whole worthy of the older school, to which indeed he properly belonged. The rest, if we except Ward, may be briefly dismissed. They were inferior men, working with an inferior method.

Two years later appeared the work of George Wither :

'The Hymnes and Songs of the Church, Divided into two Parts. The first Part comprehends the Canonicall Hymnes, and such parcels of Holy Scripture as may properly be sung : with some other ancient Songs and Creeds. The second Part consists of Spirituall Songs, appropriated to the severall Times and Occasions, observable in the Church of England. Translated and composed by G. W. London, printed by the assignes of George Wither, 1623. Cum privilegio Regis Regali.'

This work was submitted during its progress to James the First, and so far found favour that the author obtained a privilege of fifty-one years, and a recommendation in the patent that the book should be 'inserted in convenient manner and due place in every English Psalm book in metre.' The king's benevolence, however, was of no effect ; the Company of Stationers, considering their own privilege invaded, declared against the author, and by every means in their power, short of a flat refusal, avoided the sale of the book. Here again, as in the case of Parker's Psalter, the virtual suppression of the work occasioned the loss of a set of noble tunes by a great master. Sixteen compositions by Orlando Gibbons had been made for it, and were printed with it. They are in two-part counterpoint, nearly plain, for treble and bass, the treble being the tune, and the bass, though not figured, probably intended for the organ. In style they resemble rather the tunes of Tallis than the imitations of the Geneva tunes to which English congregations had been accustomed, it being possible to accent them in the same way as the words they were to accompany ; syncopation, however, sometimes occurs, but rarely, and more rarely still in the bass. The harmony often reveals very clearly the transitional condition of music at this period. For instance, in Modes XIII. and XIV.[1] a sectional termination in the melody on the second of the scale was

always, in the older harmony, treated as a full close, having the same note in the bass ; here we find it treated in the modern way, as a half close, with the fifth of the scale in the bass.

In 1632 an attempt was made to introduce the Geneva tunes complete into this country. Translations were made to suit them, and the work was brought out by Thomas Harper. It does not seem, however, to have reached a second edition. The enthusiasm of earlier days had no doubt enabled the reformers to master the exotic metres of the few imported tunes ; but from the beginning the tendency had been to simplify and, so to speak, to anglicise them ; and since the Geneva tunes had remained unchanged, Harper's work must have presented difficulties which would appear quite insuperable to ordinary congregations.

The Scottish Psalter of 1635 was reprinted in full, with dissertations, etc., by the Rev. Neil Livingston, at Glasgow, in 1864.

We have now arrived at the period when the dislike which was beginning to be felt by educated persons for the abject version of Sternhold was to find practical expression. Wither had intended his admirable translation of the Ecclesiastical Hymns and Spiritual Songs to supersede the older one, and in 1638 George Sandys, a son of the Archbishop, published the complete Psalter, with the following title :

'A paraphrase upon the Divine Poems, by G. S. Set to new tunes for private devotion ; and a thorough bass, for voice or instrument. By Henry Lawes, gentleman of His Majesty's Chapel Royal.'[2]

The tunes, twenty-four in number, are of great interest. Lawes was an ardent disciple of the new Italian school ; and these two-part compositions, though following in their outline the accustomed Psalm-tune form, are in their details as directly opposed to the older practice as anything ever written by Peri or Caccini. The two parts proceed sometimes for five or six notes together in thirds or tenths ; the bass is frequently raised a semitone, and the imperfect fifth is constantly taken, both as a harmony and as an interval of melody. The extreme poverty of Lawes's music, as compared with what was afterwards produced by composers following the same principles, has prevented him from receiving the praise which was certainly his due. He was the first English composer who perceived the melodies to which the new system of tonality was to give rise ; and in this volume will be found the germs of some of the most beautiful and affecting tunes of the 17th and 18th centuries : the first section of the famous St. Anne's tune, for instance, is note for note the same as the first section of his tune to the 9th Psalm. Several of these tunes, complete, are to be found in our modern hymnals.

---

[1] These tunes, with four-part harmony, are included in the 1904 edition of *Hymns Ancient and Modern.* Eleven examples of Gibbons's tunes are included in the *English Hymnal,* 1906.

[2] These works were reprinted by John Russell Smith in 1856 and 1872 respectively.

The translation of Sandys was intended, as the title shows, to supersede Sternhold's in private use ; but several others, intended to be sung in the churches, soon followed. Besides the translation of Sir W. Alexander (published in Charles the First's reign), of which King James had been content to pass for the author, there appeared, during the Commonwealth, the versions of Bishop King, Barton and Rous. None, however, require more than a bare mention, since they were all adapted to the 'church tunes' to be found in the current editions of Sternhold, and have therefore only a literary interest. Nothing requiring notice here was produced until after the Restoration, when, in 1671, under circumstances very different from any which had decided the form of previous four-part Psalters, John Playford brought out the first of his well-known publications :

'Psalms and Hymns in solemn musick of foure parts on the Common Tunes to the Psalms in Metre : used in Parish Churches. Also six Hymns for one voyce to the Organ. By Iohn Playford. London, printed by W. Godbid for J. Playford at his shop in the Inner Temple. 1671.'

This book contains only forty-seven tunes, of which thirty-four were taken from Sternhold (including fourteen of the single common measure tunes with names, which had now become ' church tunes '), one from Wither, and twelve were new. But Playford, in printing even this comparatively small selection, was offering to the public a great many more than they had been of late accustomed to make use of. The tunes in Sternhold were still accessible to all ; but not only had the general interest in music been steadily declining during the reigns of James and Charles, but the authorised version itself, from long use in the churches, had now become associated in the minds of the puritans with the system of Episcopacy, and was consequently unfavourably regarded, the result being that the number of tunes to which the Psalms were now commonly sung, when they were sung at all, had dwindled down to some half-dozen. These tunes may be found in the appendix to Bishop King's translation, printed in 1651. According to the title-page, his Psalms were ' to be sung after the old tunes used in yᵉ churches,' but the tunes actually printed are only the Old 100th, 51st, 81st, 119th, Commandments, Windsor, Southwell and the Lamentations. ' There be other tunes,' adds the author, ' but being not very usuall are not here set down.' The miserable state of music in general at the Restoration is well known, but, as regards Psalmody in particular, a passage in Playford's preface so well describes the situation, and some of its causes, that it cannot be omitted here :

' For many years, this part of divine service was skilfully and devoutly performed, with delight and comfort, by many honest and religious people ; and is still continued in our churches, but not with that reverence and estimation as formerly ; some not affecting the translation, others not liking the music : both, I must confess, need reforming. Those many tunes formerly used to these Psalms, for excellency of form, solemn air, and suitableness to the matter of the Psalms, were not inferior to any tunes used in foreign churches ; but at this day the best, and almost all the choice tunes are lost, and out of use in our churches ; nor must we expect it otherwise, when in and about this great city, in above one hundred parishes, there is but few parish clerks to be found that have either ear or understanding to set one of these tunes musically as it ought to be : it having been a custom during the late wars, and since, to choose men into such places, more for their poverty than skill or ability ; whereby this part of God's service hath been so ridiculously performed in most places, that it is now brought into scorn and derision by many people.'

The settings are all by Playford himself. They are in plain counterpoint, and the voices indicated are alto, countertenor, tenor and bass, an arrangement rendered necessary by the entire absence, at the Restoration, of trained trebles.

This publication had no great success, a result ascribed by the author to the folio size of the book, which he admits made it inconvenient to ' carry to church.' His second Psalter, therefore, which he brought out six years later, was printed in 8vo. The settings are here again in plain counterpoint, but this time the work contains the whole of the ' church tunes.' The title is as follows :

' The whole book of Psalms, collected into English metre by Sternhold Hopkins, &c. With the usual Hymns and Spiritual Songs, and all the ancient and modern tunes sung in Churches, composed in three parts, Cantus Medius and Bassus. In a more plain and useful method than hath been heretofore published. By John Playford. 1677.'

Apart from the reasons given by Playford for setting the tunes in three parts only, we know that this way of writing was much in favour with English composers after the Restoration, and remained so till the time of Handel. Three-part counterpoint had been much used in earlier days by the secular school of Henry the Eighth's time, but its prevalence at this period was probably due to the fact that it was a favourite form of composition with Carissimi and his Italian and French followers, whose influence with the English school of the Restoration was paramount.

This was the last complete setting of the ' church tunes,' and for a hundred years afterwards it continued to be printed for the benefit of those who still remained faithful to the old melodies and the old way of setting them. In 1757 the book had reached its 20th edition.

Playford generally receives the credit, or discredit, of having reduced the ' church tunes ' to notes of equal value, since in his Psalters they appear in minims throughout, except the first and last notes of sections, where the semibreve is retained ; but it will be found, on referring to the current editions of Sternhold, that this had already been done, probably by the congregations themselves, and that he has taken the tunes as he found them in the authorised version. His settings also have often been blamed, and it must be confessed that, compared with most of his predecessors, he is only a tolerable musician ; but this being admitted, he is still deserving of praise for having made, in the publication of his Psalters, an intelligent attempt to assist in the general work of reconstruction; and if he failed to effect the permanent restoration of the older kind of Psalmody, it was in fact not so much owing to his weakness as to the natural development of new tendencies in the art of music.

The new metrical translations afterwards brought out were always intended, like those of the Commonwealth, to be sung to the ' church tunes ' ; and each work usually contained a small selection, consisting of those most in use, together with a few new ones. Concurrently with these appeared a large number of publications—Harmonious Companions, Psalm Singers' Magazines, etc., which contained all the favourite tunes, old and new, set generally in four parts. Through one or other of these channels most of the leading musicians of this and the following century contributed to the popular Psalmody. Both tunes and settings now became very various in character, and side by side with settings made for East's Psalter might be found compositions of which the following fragment will give some idea :

Harmonious Companion, 1732.

Tune.

The   Lord goes   up . . . . . a . .

- - bove          the          sky.

On the next page of the ' Harmonious Companion ' is the original setting of the 44th Psalm by Blancks.

The fact most strongly impressed upon the mind after going through a number of these publications, extending over a period of one hundred and fifty years, is that the quality and character of the new tunes and settings in no way depends, as in the case of the old Psalters, upon the date at which they were written. Dr. Howard's beautiful tune, ' St. Bride,' for instance, was composed thirty or forty years after the strange production given above ; his tune, however, must not be taken as a sign of any general improvement, things having rather gone from bad to worse. The truth seems to be that the popular tradition of Psalmody having been hopelessly broken during the Commonwealth, and individual taste and ability having become the only deciding forces in the production of tunes, the composers of the 17th and 18th centuries, in the exercise of their discretion, chose sometimes to imitate the older style and sometimes to employ the inferior methods of contemporary music. To the public the question of style seems to have been a matter of the most perfect indifference.

Sternhold continued to be printed as an authorised version until the second decade of the 19th century. The version of Tate and Brady remained in favour twenty or thirty years longer, and was only superseded by the hymnals now in actual use.        H. E. W.

(See an interesting article on the French Huguenot Psalters, by H. Kling, professor in the Conservatoire of Geneva, in the R.M.I., vol. vi. p. 496. On the Puritan use of Psalters, see Mus. T., 1901, p. 453.)

**PSALTERY** (ψαλτήριον ; Old Eng. sautry ; Fr. psaltérion ; Ger. Psalter ; Ital. salterio). A dulcimer, played with the fingers or a plectrum instead of by hammers. There exists a classic sculptured representation of the Muse Erato, holding a long ten-stringed lyre, with the name ΨΑΛΤΡΙΑΝ cut on its base. From this it has been inferred that the strings of this lyre were touched by the fingers without the usual plectrum of ivory or metal. Chaucer's ' sautrie ' in the Miller's Tale [1] came direct from the East, perhaps imported by returning Crusaders, its kinship to the Persian and Arabic santir and kanun being unmistakable. The psaltery was the prototype of the spinet and harpsichord, particularly in the form which is described by Praetorius in his Organographia, as the ' istromento di porco,' so called from its likeness to a pig's head.

Notwithstanding the general use of keyed instruments in 1650 we read in the Musurgia of Athanasius Kircher that the psaltery played with a skilled hand stood second to no other instrument, and Mersenne, about the same date, praises its silvery tone in preference to that of any other, and its purity of intonation, so easily controlled by the fingers.

No ' istromento di porco ' being now known to exist, we have to look for its likeness in painted or sculptured representations. The earliest occurs in a 13th-century MS. in the library at Douai. It is there played without a plectrum. From the 14th century there remain frequent examples, notably at Florence, in the famous Organ Podium of Luca della Robbia, a cast of which is in the Victoria and Albert Museum at South Kensington.

But other forms were admired. (See PLATE XXVIII. No. 5.) Exactly like an Arabic kanun is a psaltery painted A.D. 1348 by that loving

1 ' And all above ther lay a gay sautrie
On which he made on nightes melodie,
So swetely, that all the chambre rong,
And Angelus ad virginem he song.'

delineator of musical instruments, Orcagna, himself a musician, in his 'Trionfo della Morte,' at Pisa. The strings of the instrument are in groups of three, each group, as in a grand piano, being tuned in unison to make one note. Sometimes there were groups of four, a not unfrequent stringing in the DULCIMER. There is a good coloured lithograph of Orcagna's fresco in *Les Arts au moyen âge* by Paul Lacroix (Paris, 1874, p. 282); it is there called 'Le Songe de la Vie.' A fine representation of such a psaltery, strung in threes, by Orcagna, will be found in the National Gallery, London.          A. J. H.

PUCCINI, GIACOMO ANTONIO DOMENICO MICHELE SECONDO MARIA (*b.* Lucca, June 22, 1858 ; *d.* Brussels, Nov. 29, 1924), belonged to a family which for a century and a half had produced an uninterrupted line of musicians. His great-great-grandfather, Giacomo (*b.* 1712), was maestro di cappella to the republic of Lucca, wrote highly respectable church music, and was the master of Guglielmi. Antonio, the son of Giacomo the elder (*b.* 1747), was less famous as a composer than as a theorist. Domenico (*b.* 1771), the grandfather of the subject of this article, attained distinction as a church composer, but was more famous for his operas. Michele, his son (*b.* 1813), won more than local notoriety. His sacred music was admired throughout North Italy, and his death in 1864 was honoured by the composition of a Requiem by Pacini.

With so distinguished a genealogy it was not surprising that Giacomo Puccini should show precocious signs of musical talent. When Lucca had taught him all that he could learn, his name won him a pension from the Queen of Italy, which enabled him to enter the Milan Conservatorio. While he was still a student, his first orchestral work, a 'Sinfonia-Capriccio,' was performed at the school with considerable success. His chief instructor was Amilcare Ponchielli, at whose suggestion he undertook the composition of 'Le Villi,' a 1-act opera, the libretto of which was by Fontana. The opera was written for a competition organised by the paper *Teatro illustrato*. The committee which examined the works submitted did not consider 'Le Villi' worthy even of mention. But some friends of Puccini, amongst whom was Arrigo Boïto, heard the score and soon discovered its worth. On their recommendation the opera was performed on May 31, 1884, at the Dal Verme theatre, and so well received that an enlarged edition was prepared for La Scala, where again it met with success in the following year. The score, though immature, shows remarkable melodic invention and no little imaginative power, and the symphonic movements are scored in masterly fashion. After 'Le Villi,' Puccini was silent until 1889, when his 'Edgar' was produced at La Scala, Apr. 21. It is founded upon Alfred de

Musset's wild melodrama *La Coupe et les lèvres*. Puccini's music is always melodious and often vigorous and impressive, but the book was too much for him, and 'Edgar' was a complete failure. 'Manon Lescaut,' produced at the Teatro Regio, Turin, Feb. 1, 1893, atoned in some measure for this failure. The libretto is the work of the composer and a committee of friends. The music shows a remarkable development of style, and many of the scenes—notably that of the embarkation of the *filles de joie* at Havre—are designed with graphic decision and handled with real power.

With 'La Bohème' (Teatro Regio, Turin, Feb. 1, 1896) Puccini surpassed all his previous triumphs, and placed himself definitely at the head of the younger Italian composers. The librettists, Giacosa and Illica, wisely made no attempt to construct a dramatic whole from Murger's novel, but chose four scenes, each complete in itself and all admirably contrasted one with another, which together give a capital picture of Bohemian life in Paris about 1830. Puccini's music reflects the alternate gaiety and pathos of Murger's novel with a truth and sincerity to which no name but that of genius can be applied. 'Tosca,' produced at the Teatro Costanzi, Rome, Jan. 14, 1900, unquestionably revealed fresh aspects of his genius. The libretto, founded by Illica and Giacosa upon Sardou's famous drama, is a prolonged orgy of lust and crime, which lends itself but ill to musical illustration. Yet the skill with which Puccini fastened upon everything in the story that had a spark of lyrical feeling showed the quality of his musical instinct. Much of 'Tosca' is hardly more than glorified incidental music, as indeed, given the nature of the subject, was only to be expected, but whenever the libretto gave him a chance Puccini showed that the hand which wrote 'La Bohème' had gained in strength and certainty of touch. The passions treated in 'Tosca' are often crude and sometimes monstrous, and have little in common with the quick play of chequered feeling that characterises 'La Bohème,' yet such passages as Cavaradossi's air in the first act, Tosca's air in the second and almost the whole of the last act, which rises to a wonderful height of lyric rapture, show that Puccini's power of expressing certain aspects of emotion was maturing in a very remarkable manner.          R. A. S. ; rev. F. B.

'Madama Butterfly,' founded on a magazine story by John Luther Long, dramatised by the author and David Belasco, and turned into a libretto by Illica and Giacosa, is the opera which first showed a change in the attitude of the Italian public, which had hitherto idolised Puccini. It was given at La Scala on Feb. 17, 1904, and the performance ended in a complete fiasco. Various reasons have been given to explain the set-back, especially since a revised

## LXI

*By courtesy of Messrs. Schott & Co.*

SGAMBATI

PUCCINI

From a photograph by Attilio Badodi, Milan

version, first given at Brescia in May of the same year, reversed the verdict of the Milanese and opened up a career of success not less definite than that of ' Tosca ' and ' Bohème.' Undoubtedly the introduction of singers wearing lounge suits had an unfavourable impression on the audience. The two acts of which the opera then consisted were also much longer than Italian traditions demand. But it is probable that the chief cause of the first failure lay in a more critical frame of mind of an audience determined not to be intoxicated by the charm of passionate melody. Having been praised for ' Bohème ' and ' Tosca, in terms which knew no measure, he was now blamed more than any weakness of the opera justified. Certainly ' Butterfly ' even in the revised edition we now know is not a flawless work. It was Puccini's habit in setting to music a foreign subject to embody songs and airs of the country in order to secure local colour. This was the procedure he adopted in ' Butterfly ' and also in ' The Girl of the Golden West.' But he had not the genius of the symphonic writer which can turn a common tune into a thing of tragedy or pathos. The American and Japanese tunes in ' Butterfly ' remain to the end foreign elements, and the strength of the opera is in those scenes in which the composer has forgotten both East and West and devoted himself wholly to the description of the heroine and her tragic story. In these the warm, passionate nature of his music, the fine sense of theatrical needs and effects, have exercised a profound appeal on all audiences, including the English audience which first heard ' Butterfly ' at Covent Garden in 1905.

With the next opera, ' The Girl of the Golden West ' (Ital. ' La fanciulla del West '), Puccini opens up a new epoch in his career, an epoch of experiments to bring his technique up-to-date, and to assimilate to some extent the reforms advocated by the moderns. In this he was not quite successful. ' The Girl of the Golden West ' (the libretto of which was drawn from a play of Belasco by G. Civinini and G. Zangarini) had a triumphant reception on its first performance in New York on Dec. 10, 1910. Elsewhere, however, it has been received more coolly and critically. The new manner, the improved technique, is not nearly as convincing as the old manner was. He has learnt to use subtler or more modern harmonic combinations, but not to use them in such a way as to make them appear inevitable. Similarly, ocal colour is obtained by the use of local melodies which are never remoulded so as to harmonise with the composer's more characteristic style. In spite of some excellent and typical pages, ' The Girl of the Golden West ' has not proved a worthy successor to ' Butterfly.'

Even less successful was ' La Rondine,' Puccini's next venture. It was undertaken at the request of a Viennese publisher anxious to persuade Puccini to write musical comedy. Puccini had then a disagreement with his publishers, Ricordi, and, after demurring for a while, accepted the proposal to write the operetta for which he was to receive 200,000 Austrian crowns on a libretto by Wilner, the librettist of Lehar. The Italian translator, Adami, was already at work converting the musical comedy book into comic opera when war broke out. The original contract was cancelled, the book remodelled, and the opera sold to an Italian publisher. It was performed at Monte Carlo on Mar. 27, 1917. It was very well received, but that verdict was not confirmed elsewhere, and the opera has failed to hold its place in the Puccinian repertory.

Of the three 1-act operas which make up the Trittico (New York, Dec. 14, 1918), the first, ' Il tabarro,' is tragic to the point of melodrama ; the second, ' Suor Angelica,' is supposed to represent a mystic subject ; the third, ' Gianni Schicchi,' is comedy. The contrast is most effective, and there is no question that in this triptych the composer's technique is more elaborate than in ' Butterfly,' but complexity is no longer an impediment to natural expression. Not all the three operas, however, have equal merit. ' Il tabarro ' has pages of fine dramatic writing, and in ' Suor Angelica ' the melody has at times greater strength if less luscious beauty than in any other opera of Puccini. But the subject of the first is somewhat sordid, and in ' Suor Angelica ' the librettist has attempted to condense too many episodes for a homogeneous work of one act. The final scene, moreover, in which a miracle is represented, is merely theatrical and does not carry conviction. The third opera, ' Gianni Schicchi,' on the other hand had delighted by its deftness, skill and *vis comica* even those who found little to praise in any other work of Puccini. The action fits admirably the requirements of the 1-act play. It is swift, varied, interesting, and the music aids it at every point. It adds lyrical charm to the by-play of the two young lovers, and it gives zest to the adventure of the Florentine rogue who turns the greed of Donati's heirs to his advantage. Thus vivacity, wit and humour rob the story of whatever gruesome feature it might have, had it been less ably told.

Puccini's last opera, ' Turandot,' was almost finished when he was attacked by the disease of which he died. He carried the sheets of the last duet to Brussels, where he went to be operated upon for cancer of the throat. The operation was successful, but his heart did not stand the shock, and he died on Nov. 29, 1924. ' Turandot ' was produced at La Scala, Milan under the direction of Toscanini on

April 25, 1926. The score was completed by F. ALFANO.

BIBL.—WAKELING DRY, *Giacomo Puccini* (*Living Masters of Music*). London, 1906; FAUSTO TORREFRANCA, *Puccini e l' opera internazionale* (Turin, 1913); ONORATO ROUX, *Memorie giovanili autobiografiste* (Florence); GINO MONALDI, *Puccini e la sua opera* (Libreria Montegazza, Rome); ADOLF WEISSMAN, *Giacomo Puccini* (Munich, 1922); ARNALDO FRACCAROLI, *La vita di G. Puccini* (Milan, 1925); article by PIZZETTI, in *Musicisti contemporanei* (Milan).

F. B.

PUCCITTA, VINCENZO (*b*. Civitavecchia, 1778; *d*. Milan, Dec. 20, 1861), pupil of Fenaroli and Salò at the Conservatorio dei Turchini, Naples. He was in great demand as an opera composer in his time, and visited all the principal towns of Europe, for which he wrote 30 operas. He wrote with great facility, but without depth of thought or feeling (*Q.-L.*; *Riemann*).

PUENTE, GUISEPPE DEL (*b*. Naples; *d*. New York, 1894 or 1895), Italian baritone, was the Escamillo when, in 1878 at the rebuilt Her Majesty's Theatre, ' Carmen ' was heard for the first time in England. According to Mapleson, Del Puente was no better pleased with his part before the rehearsals than Campanini was with that of Don José, but when the eventful night came both singers triumphed.

Del Puente enjoyed at that time a well-established reputation in London. Under Mapleson at Drury Lane he made a most successful first appearance as Rigoletto in 1873, and in 1874 he was a member of the brilliant cast that strove to put life into Balfe's ' Il talismano.' He was again at Drury Lane —in Harris's memorable season—in 1887, singing, among other parts, Valentine to Jean de Reszke's Faust. Late in his career he sang in America with Gilmore's band.　S. H. P.

PUGET, LOISA (*b*. Paris, *c*. 1810), though an amateur, achieved an extraordinary popularity in the reign of Louis Philippe by her songs, composed to Gustave Lemoine's words. Among the best known of these were ' À la grâce de Dieu,' ' Ave Maria,' ' Le Soleil de ma Bretagne,' ' Ta Dot,' ' Mon Pays,' ' Les Rêves d'une jeune fille,' etc. Musically speaking, they are inferior to those of Panseron, Labarre or Masini ; but the melodies were always so natural and so well suited to the words, and the words themselves were so full of that good *bourgeois* character which at that time was all the fashion in France, that their vogue was immense. Encouraged by her success, Puget aspired to the theatre. She took lessons from Adolphe Adam, and on Oct. 1, 1836, produced at the Opéra-Comique a one-act piece, ' Le Mauvais Œil,' which was sung to perfection by Ponchard and Mme. Damoreau. In 1842 she married Lemoine, and, finding the popularity of her songs on the wane, had the tact to publish no more. She broke silence only once again with an operetta called ' La Veilleuse, ou les Nuits de Milady,' produced at the Gymnase, Sept. 27. 1869.　G. C.

PUGNANI, GAETANO (*b*. Turin, Nov. 27, 1731 ; *d*. there, June 15, 1798), celebrated violinist, one of the best representatives of the Piedmontese school of violin-playing.

Being a pupil first of Somis, who studied under Corelli, and afterwards of Tartini, he combined the prominent qualities of the style and technique of both these great masters. He was appointed first violin to the Sardinian court in 1752, and began to travel in 1754. He made lengthened stays at Paris and in London, where he was for a time leader of the opera band, produced an opera of his own (Burney, *Hist*. iv. 494), and published trios, quartets, quintets and symphonies. In 1770 Burney found him at Turin, and there he remained as leader, conductor, teacher and composer for the rest of his life.

To Pugnani more than to any other master of the violin appears to be due the preservation of the pure grand style of Corelli, Tartini and Vivaldi, and its transmission to the next generation of violinists. Apart from being himself an excellent player, he trained a large number of eminent violinists—such as Conforti, Bruni, Polledro and, above all, Viotti. He was also a prolific composer : he wrote a number of operas and ballets, which, however, appear not to have been very successful. Fétis gives the names of nine, and a list of his published instrumental compositions : one violin-concerto (out of nine), three sets of violin-sonatas, duos, trios, quartets, quintets, and twelve symphonies for strings, oboes and horns.　P. D.

PUGNO, STÉPHANE RAOUL (*b*. Paris, June 23, 1852 ; *d*. Moscow, Jan. 3, 1914), pianist and composer, was a pupil of the Conservatoire, where he won the first piano prize in 1866, first harmony prize, and first medal for solfège in 1867, and first organ prize in 1869. He was organist of Saint Eugène (1872–92), chorus-master at the Théâtre Ventadour in 1874, professor of harmony (1892–96) and of the piano (1896–1901) in the Conservatoire.

He gained a world - wide reputation as a pianist, and his playing of Mozart in particular was a thing of exquisite quality. His first appearance in London took place on May 28, 1894, at a recital of his own, and his subsequent appearances here were frequent. His sonata recitals in conjunction with Ysaÿe, and his playing of the works of César Franck with orchestra were alike noteworthy.

His first important composition was an oratorio, ' La Résurrection de Lazare ' (1879), after which he wrote a three-act féerie, ' La Fée Cocotte ' ; ' Les Papillons,' a ballet (Palace Theatre, 1881) ; an opéra-comique, ' Ninetta ' (Renaissance, 1882) ; a five-act ballet, 'Viviane' (Eden Theatre, 1886) ; a three-act opéra-bouffe, ' Le Sosie ' (Bouffes-Parisiens, 1887) ; a three - act opéra - comique, ' Le Valet de

&#1072;oeur' (Bouffes, 1888); 'Le Retour d'Ulysse' Bouffes, 1889); 'La Vocation de Marius,' four acts (Nouveautés, 1890); 'La petite Poucette' (Renaissance, 1891); 'La Danseuse de corde,' three-act pantomime (Nouveau Théâtre, 1892); 'Pour le Drapeau,' mimodrame in three acts (Ambigu, 1895); 'Le Chevalier aux fleurs,' ballet in collaboration with Messager (Folies-Marigny, 1897); 'Mélusine,' 'Les Pauvres Gens,' and other things, such as songs, a pianoforte sonata, and a set of four piano pieces 'Les Nuits.' His last work was music to the *Città Morte* (*Ville Morte*) of d'Annunzio, written in collaboration with Nadia Boulanger. **G. F.**

PUJOL, JOAN (JOHANNES) (*b.* Barcelona, 1573; *d.* there, 1626), Spanish composer. He was maestro de capilla at Tarragona, 1593–95, Saragossa (Cathedral of El Pilar), 1595–1612, and Barcelona, 1612–26. In 1600 he was ordained priest. His church music shows both the severity of the mid. 16th century and the dramatic feeling of the 17th; he sometimes employs a continuo, and his MSS. provide interesting examples of how chromatic alteration was practised in his time. Many of his works were written for St. George's Day and other festivals in the chapel of St. George, patron of Catalonia, and are dedicated to the *diputats* (deputies) of the General Catalan Assembly. MSS. are preserved in Barcelona (Bibl. de la Diputació, Orfeó Català, the church of Santa María del Mar and the Cathedral Archives), Cardona (Communal Archives), Gandía, Montserrat, Saragossa (both cathedrals), Vich. Secular works with Spanish words are to be seen at Munich (Staatsbibl., MS. E. 200), Madrid (Bibl. Nac., M. 1370–2, and Bibl. Medinaceli, MS. 13,231).

A complete edition (by H. Anglès) is in course of publication at Barcelona. Publ. del Depart. de Musica, III.) **J. B. T.**

PULIASCHI, GIOVANNI DOMENICO, a 16th-17th-century singer of the Papal Chapel (1600) with a voice of extraordinary compass, of whom Solerti says that he sang contralto, tenor and bass. G. F. Anerio dedicated to him his 'Gemme musicali,' and edited also Puliaschi's songs (1620) (*Riemann*).

PULITI, GABRIELLO (*b.* Montepulciano, near Arezzo, late 16th cent.), Franciscan monk, held a number of posts as organist, including an appointment at Trieste Cathedral. He wrote several books of motets, madrigals, and other sacred and secular songs, including sacred songs for a solo voice with bass (1618) (*Q.-L.*).

PUNTO, see STICH, Joh. Wenzel.

PUPPO, GIUSEPPE (*b.* Lucca, June 12, 1749; *d.* Florence, Apr. 19, 1827), eminent violinist, was a pupil of the Conservatorio at Naples, and when still very young gained considerable reputation in Italy as a virtuoso.

He came to Paris in 1775; thence he went to Spain and Portugal, where he is reported to

have amassed a fortune. After having stayed for some years in England he returned to Paris in 1784, and remained there till 1811, occupying the post of leader, first at the Théâtre de Monsieur, which was then under Viotti's direction, then at the Théâtre-Feydeau, and finally conducting the band at the Théâtre-Français. As he was an excellent accompanist, he was much in request in musical circles, and might have secured for himself a competence if it had not been for his eccentricity and unsteadiness, which brought him into constant troubles. In 1811 he suddenly left Paris, abandoning his wife and children for ever. Arrived at Naples he was lucky enough to secure the leadership of the band at a theatre. He, however, did not stay long, but went to Lucca, thence to Florence, and finally found employment as teacher at a music school at Pontremoli. After two years he threw up this appointment and returned to Florence; was there found, utterly destitute, by Edward Taylor, Gresham Professor of Music, and by his generosity was placed in a hospice, where he died. His published compositions include three concertos, eight studies, duets for violin and pianoforte pieces. **P. D.**

PURCELL, the name of a family of musicians in the 17th and 18th centuries, which included amongst its members the greatest and most original of English composers.

(1) The name of 'Pursell,' presumably HENRY PURCELL the elder (*d.* Aug. 11, 1664), is first found in Pepys's *Diary*, under date Feb. 21, 1659–60, where he is styled 'Master of Musique.' He is said [1] to have acted in 'The Siege of Rhodes' in 1656, and to have doubled the part of Mustapha with Thomas Blagrove. Upon the re-establishment of the Chapel Royal (1660) Henry Purcell was appointed one of the Gentlemen. He was also Master of the Choristers of Westminster Abbey. On Dec. 21, 1663, he succeeded Signor Angelo as one of the King's Band of Music. His sons are numbered below as Edward (3), Henry (4) and Daniel (5). He died Aug. 11, 1664, and was buried in the east cloister of Westminster Abbey, Aug. 13. There is a three-part song, 'Sweet tyranness, I now resign my heart,' in Playford's 'Musical Companion,' 1667, which is probably of his composition, although it is sometimes attributed to his more celebrated son. It was reprinted in Burney's *History*, iii. 486.

His brother, (2) THOMAS (*d.* July 31, 1682), was appointed Gentleman of the Chapel Royal in 1660. In 1661 he was lay-vicar of Westminster Abbey and copyist. On Aug. 8, 1662, he was appointed, jointly with Pelham Humfrey, Composer in Ordinary for the Violins to His Majesty, and on Nov. 29 following, 'Musician in Ordinary for the Lute and Voice

[1] W. H. Cummings, *Mus. T.* 1895, p. 730.

in the room of Henry Lawes, deceased.' In May 28, 1666, he supplicated [1] for arrears of payment. In 1672 he was, with Humfrey, made Master of the King's Band of Music. He was buried in the cloisters of Westminster Abbey, Aug. 2, 1682. He had probably been long before in ill-health, as on May 15, 1681, he granted a power of attorney to his son Matthew to receive his salary as Gentleman of the Chapel Royal. He was the composer of several chants, one of which (printed by Burney, *History*, iii. 477) has remained in constant use. A pencil portrait on vellum by Thos. Foster of ' Colonel Purcell' (Holburne Museum, Bath) may represent him.     w. h. h., with addns.

(3) EDWARD (*b.* 1653 ; *d.* June 2, 1717), son of Henry (1) was Gentleman Usher to Charles II. He afterwards entered the army and served with Sir George Rooke at the taking of Gibraltar, and the Prince of Hesse at the defence of it. Upon the death of Queen Anne he retired and resided in the house of the Earl of Abingdon, where he died. He was buried in the chancel of the church of Wytham, near Oxford.

(4) HENRY (*b.* 1658–59 ; *d.* Westminster, Nov. 21, 1695), the famous composer, is discussed below.

(5) DANIEL (*b. circa* 1660 ; *d.* Nov. 1717), was in 1688 appointed organist of Magdalen College, Oxford, remaining there until 1695, when he resigned his appointment in order to live in London. It may have been as a consequence of his illustrious brother's illness and death in that year that he came to London, as in the last year of his brother's life he had written a masque in the fifth act of ' The Indian Queen,' and had added to the music of ' Pausanias.' In 1693 he had set to music Yalden's ' Ode for St. Cecilia's Day.' After his brother's death, Daniel Purcell seems to have been greatly in request for music for plays. He wrote music for ' The Patriot ' and ' The Northern Lass.' In 1696 he wrote music for Mary Pix's ' Ibrahim XIII.,' possibly also for her ' Spanish Wives,' as well as for the anonymous ' Neglected Virtue,' and the ' opera ' ' Brutus of Alba,' the published songs from which bear the imprint 1696, though the piece was not produced till 1697 – 98. Cibber's ' Love's Last Shift ' has music written by Purcell in the same year, and so has Lord Lansdowne's ' She Gallants.' In 1697 he wrote instrumental and vocal music to D'Urfey's ' Cynthia and Endymion,' and collaborated with Jeremiah Clark in Settle's ' World in the Moon.' In 1698 he wrote music for Gildon's ' Phaeton, or the Fatal Divorce,' Cibber's ' Love makes a Man ' and Lacy's ' Sawney the Scot ' (an alteration of ' The Taming of the Shrew '), and set odes for the Princess Anne's birthday and St. Cecilia's

Day. About this time he set Nahum Tate's ' Lamentation on the Death of Henry Purcell.' Other odes for St. Cecilia's Day were written in later years. In 1699 he wrote music for Motteux's ' Island Princess ' with Jeremiah Clark and Leveridge. In 1700 he wrote music for Oldmixon's ' The Grove, or Love's Paradise,' and gained the third of the prizes offered for musical settings of Congreve's ' Judgment of Paris.' (See ECCLES ; FINGER ; and WELDON.) The plays furnished for the year were Farquhar's ' Constant Couple ' ; D'Urfey's ' Masaniello ' ; ' The Pilgrim ' (Beaumont and Fletcher) ; Burnaby's ' Reformed Husband ' and Cibber's ' Careless Husband.' In 1701 he provided some of the music for Lee's ' Rival Queens,' Finger having written some before him ; Baker's ' Humours of the Age ' and Mrs. Trotter's ' Unhappy Penitent ' ; in 1702, Steele's ' Funeral,' and in 1703, Farquhar's ' Inconstant ' and Steele's ' Tender Husband ' were the plays for which he wrote music. For the opening of Vanbrugh's theatre in the Haymarket (1705) he wrote an ' opera ' on ' Orlando Furioso ' ; in Mar. 1706–07 he contributed music to Farquhar's ' Beau's Stratagem,' and in the latter year set a St. Cecilia Ode for Oxford. A masque, ' Orpheus and Eurydice,' [2] is mentioned in 1707, and among plays for which dates are not forthcoming are J. Hughes's ' Amalasont,' D'Urfey's ' The Bath ' and ' The Campaigners,' Motteux's ' Younger Brother,' and a revival of ' Macbeth,' all of which had music by Daniel Purcell. In 1712 he gave a concert of ' vocal and instrumental musick entirely new,' at Stationers' Hall, and in 1713 he was appointed organist of St. Andrew's, Holborn,[3] a post which he retained until his death.[4] On Dec. 12, 1717, the *Daily Courant* contained an advertisement of Edward Purcell's application for the post of organist ' in the room of his uncle, Mr. Daniel Purcell, deceased.' Daniel Purcell's works include

' The Psalmes set full for the Organ or Harpsichord as they are Plaid in Churches and Chappels in the manner given out ; as also with their Interludes of great Variety.'

One of the ' givings out ' and an ' interlude ' are printed in *Mus. T.*, 1905, p. 162. There are six anthems in Magdalen College, Oxford, and songs, etc., are in ' Harmonia sacra,' ' The Banquet of Musick,' ' Thesaurus musicus ' and ' Deliciae musicae.' Some sonatas for flute and some for violin with bass were published, as well as ' Six Cantatas for a Voice.'

(6) EDWARD (*d.* July 1, 1740 [5]), youngest, but only surviving, son of the great Henry Purcell, was baptized in Westminster Abbey,

[1] *Cal. of State Papers*, ch. ii. 1665-66, Ent. Books. xiv. p. 96.

[2] By Dennis, printed in *The Muses' Mercury*, 1707.    w. b. s
[3] For this appointment see 7th Report Historical MSS. Commission, Appx. p. 689b (Rev. T. W. Webb's Papers), ' Report of Serjeant Pengelly as to ye organist of St. Andrews, Holborn.'
                                           w. b. s.
[4] See *Mus. T.*, 1905, p. 158.
[5] See *Ibid.*, Aug. 1905, p. 517.

Sept. 6, 1689. He was therefore (like his father) only 6 years old when his father died. When 16 years old he lost his mother, who by her nuncupative will stated that,

' according to her husband's desire, she had given her deare son good education, and she alsoe did give him all the Bookes of Musick in generall, the Organ, the double spinett, the single spinett, a silver tankard, a silver watch, two pairs of gold buttons, a hair ring, a mourning ring of Dr. Busby's, a Larum clock, Mr. Edward Purcell's picture, handsome furniture for a room, and he was to be maintained until provided for.'

Embracing the profession of music, he became organist of St. Clement's, Eastcheap. He applied for the post of organist of St Andrew's, Holborn (see above, under Daniel (5)), but was unsuccessful, both at that time, when Maurice Greene was appointed, and a few months afterwards, when the post became vacant again owing to Greene's appointment to St. Paul's. On July 8, 1726, he was appointed organist of St. Margaret's, Westminster. There is a song by him in the ' Monthly Mask ' for Sept. 1717.[1] He left a son,

(7) EDWARD HENRY (d. circa 1770), who was a chorister of the Chapel Royal under Bernard Gates. He succeeded his father as organist of St. Clement's, Eastcheap. He was organist of St. Edmund's, Lombard Street, and of St. John's, Hackney, from 1753–64. His name is among the subscribers to H. Burgess's songs.

## LIFE OF HENRY PURCELL

HENRY (b. circa 1658–59 ; d. Westminster, Nov. 21, 1695), younger son of Henry Purcell the elder, is traditionally said to have been born in Little St. Ann's Lane, Old Pye Street, Westminster, but no authoritative evidence as to the birthplace is as yet forthcoming. Nor can the date be certainly fixed ; the inscription on the tombstone, ' Anno Aetatis suae 37mo,' may be taken as proving him to have been born between Nov. 21, 1658, and Nov. 20, 1659 (see below, and Mus. T., 1895, p. 733). From 1661 till the death of Henry Purcell the elder in 1664, the family lived in ' the Great Almonry South.' The arms on the monument, and those below the portrait in the ' Sonnata's of Three Parts ' (1683) seem to connect the composer with the family of Purcell of Onslow, Shropshire, but on this point nothing certain has been found. The statement that he lost his father before he was 6 years old (Aug. 11, 1664), if it can be accepted, still further limits the time of his birth, which must therefore have taken place between Nov. 21, 1658, and Aug. 11, 1659. On his father's death he was adopted by his uncle, Thomas Purcell (2), and was admitted a chorister of the Chapel Royal, under Captain Cooke, the master of the children. Cooke was succeeded in 1672 by Pelham HUMFREY (q.v.), and it is assumed that Purcell learnt from Humfrey the new French style of

1 Cf. also Mus. T., Aug. 1905.

music which Humfrey had learnt from Lully. As early as 1670 Purcell is said [2] to have composed music for an ' Address of the Children of the Chapel Royal to the King.' On the theory that the famous Macbeth Music is by Purcell, we are driven to suppose it to have been written in Purcell's 14th year, in 1672. If the song, ' Sweet tyranness,' ascribed to Henry Purcell the elder, is by Henry the younger it must date from this time.

On the breaking of his voice, he seems to have been retained as a supernumerary, and to have become a pupil of John Blow for composition. It is more than likely that he composed anthems during this period, but at present the dates of his earlier anthems have not been established. From 1676–78, and again from 1688–90, he held the post of copyist at Westminster Abbey. In 1676 he contributed a song to the new edition of bk. i. of Playford's ' Choice Ayres,' etc., and in 1677 composed an elegy on the death of Matthew Locke, printed in bk. ii. of the ' Choice Ayres,' 1679 ; other songs by him appeared in the same book. That he was composing anthems about this time is clear from a letter [3] written by his uncle, Thomas Purcell, to John Gostling, the famous bass singer, at Canterbury, on Feb. 8, 1678–79, in which reference is made to Gostling's exceptionally low notes ; it has been supposed that the anthem, ' They that go down to the sea in ships,' was written at this time, as it was undoubtedly intended for Gostling, but there is no direct evidence as to this. (See list below.)

In 1679 [4] Purcell succeeded Blow as organist of Westminster Abbey : it has been generally held that Blow resigned his place voluntarily, resuming it again after Purcell's death ; but the act of magnanimity is by no means certain, and here again direct evidence is wanting. In 1680 began the long series of dramas in which music by Purcell played a more or less important part.[5] About the same year Purcell wrote a number of ' Fantazias ' for strings [6] in various numbers of parts, which are preserved (B.M. Add. MSS. 30,930) ; a comparison of them with his ' Sonnata's ' of 1683 shows that the former were modelled rather on those of Orlando Gibbons than on those of the Italian masters who were copied in the later set. In that year, too, began the series of odes and ' welcome songs ' which form no unimportant section of the composer's work from this time

2 Cummings's Life.
3 See Ibid., p. 28.
4 1680 has been generally accepted, but a re-examination of the Abbey records establishes 1679 ; see West, Cath. Org. p. 144.
5 Downes, Roscius Anglicanus, p. 49, states ' Theodosius or The Force of Love wrote by Mr Nathaniel Lee [cast given], all the parts in it being perfectly performed with several entertainments of singing composed by the famous master Mr Henry Purcell (being the first he ever composed for the stage), made it a living and gainful play to the company ; the Court, especially the Ladies by their daily charming preference gave it great encouragement.'
6 The nine 4-part Fantazias are dated from June 10 to Aug. 31, 1680. The Three, four and five part Fantasies for Strings were first published in score and parts by Curwen in 1927 ; edited by P Warlock and A. Mangeot.

forth until the end of his life. 'Welcome, Vicegerent of the mighty King' was written to greet Charles II. on his return from Windsor in 1680. Another ode of this year, 'to welcome the Duke of York on his return from Scotland,' is mentioned by Cummings,[1] but is not otherwise known. On July 14, 1682, he was appointed organist of the Chapel Royal in place of Edward Lowe, deceased. A year or more before this appointment he had married, and his eldest son was born on Aug. 9, 1682. Some songs are said to have been written for the inauguration of the Lord Mayor, Sir William Pritchard, on Oct. 29 of the same year. The following year, 1683, saw the publication of Purcell's first printed composition, the twelve 'Sonnata's of III. Parts : two viollins and basse : to the Organ or Harpsecord. Composed by Henry Purcell, Composer in Ordinary to his most Sacred Majesty, and Organist of his Chappell Royall.'[2]
It is quite clear from the preface that Purcell 'faithfully endeavour'd a just imitation of the most fam'd Italian Masters,' and it is an interesting question what were his exact models ; it has been supposed that Bassani's sonatas were known to Purcell ; but if this were so, the 'Balletti, correnti, gighe e sarabande,' the only work of his which was printed early enough (1677) are all on such a very simple, recurrent pattern that the theory can hardly be upheld. In that same year, 1677, the Opera quinta, also called 'Sonatas,' of Giovanni Battista Vitali, appeared at Bologna, and there is in their design and character so great a resemblance to Purcell's work that it is difficult to resist the conclusion that these may have been the Englishman's models.[3] The opportunity for becoming acquainted with these Italian works was very probably due to Purcell's court appointment ; but whatever the circumstances of their origin, there can be no doubt that the sonatas reach a far higher point of power and originality than had been previously attained in England, and that they are far more vigorous than the works from which they were imitated. The sonatas were printed in four partbooks, with one for the continuo part, or thorough-bass.[4] It is perhaps fanciful to see in the name of Purcell's eldest son, 'John Baptista,' another imitation of Italian models.
The first of the odes on St. Cecilia's Day was composed in this same year (1683), and he seems to have written three for the same festival, one in Latin, 'Laudate Ceciliam.' The score of one, to words by Christopher Fishburn, 'Welcome to all the pleasures,' was

published in the following year. In 1684 Purcell, with Blow, took part in the famous organ competition at the Temple Church, playing the organ by 'Father' SMITH, the rival instrument, by Renatus HARRIS, being played by Draghi. At the time of the coronation of James II. Purcell received £34 : 12s. from the secret-service money for superintending the erection of an organ in the Abbey especially for the coronation. One of the anthems, 'My heart is inditing,' is held to have been composed for the occasion ; the other, 'I was glad,' to have been composed before.[5] In 1687 an 'Elegy on John Playford' was written, and, as well as a birthday ode, 'Sound the Trumpets,' in which occurs 'a duet for altos, "Let Caesar and Urania live," which continued so long in favour that succeeding composers of odes for royal birthdays were accustomed to introduce it into their own productions until after the middle of the 18th century.'[6]
By this time Purcell had provided music for about nine plays (see list below), and so had gained some stage experience. Still, none of the plays were such as required much skill of dramatic writing, and the marvel of the production of 'Dido and Aeneas' remains as great when it is assigned to its proper period of time in the composer's career as when the earlier dates of its origin were universally accepted.[7]
The history of this problem may be briefly summarised as follows : Hawkins,[8] apparently reasoning from the fact that Tate's play 'Brutus of Alba' was first called 'Dido and Aeneas,' and that therefore the play with the latter title preceded 'Brutus of Alba' (pubd. 1678), suggested 1677 as the latest possible date for Purcell's music, and treated the work as that of a youth of 19. Prof. Taylor, in the Musical Antiquarian Society's edition, put it still further back, to 1675, but the discovery, in 1842, of a copy of the original libretto,[9] showed —although it is not dated—that the work was written for Mr. Josias Priest's boarding-school at Chelsea. As Priest removed to Chelsea in 1680, that date was accepted by Rimbault and others following him, who were anxious to place the composition of the opera as early as possible, for Purcell's credit. In D'Urfey's 'New Poems' (1690) is an epilogue spoken at the performance 'by Lady Dorothy Burk.' Squire, though unable to find more exact evidence for Lady Dorothy's age than can be

---

[1] *Life*, p. 32.
[2] See Purcell Society, vol. v., where the title-page is given in facsimile.
[3] Bridge, quoting Roger North, held that Nicola MATTEIS (*q.v.*) was Purcell's principal model. See *Mus. Ass. Proc.* 1915–16, p. 4, also *Twelve Good Musicians*, p. 128. Barclay Squire has drawn attention to a first-hand piece of evidence from the 12th edition of Playford's 'Introduction to the Skill of Musick,' which Purcell edited. Purcell has there introduced a passage from a work by 'the famous Lelio Calista, an Italian,' as an example of fugue in the composition of a sonata. See CALISTA.
[4] See preface to the sonatas, Purcell Society, vol. v., and *Mus. T.*, 896, p. 10.

[5] On the chronology of Purcell's Church Music, see G. E. P. Arkwright, *Mus. Ant.* i. 63, 234 ; also prefaces to the several volumes of the Purcell Society. See also A. Hughes-Hughes, *Mus. T.*, 1896, pp. 81-3, for an attempt to establish two periods from the evidence of the composer's handwriting.
[6] See Husk, article 'Purcell,' in 1st edition of this Dictionary.
[7] Barclay Squire established the date of the first performance as taking place between 1688 and 1690 (see *Sammelb. Int. Mus. Ges.* vol. v. pp. 506-14).
[8] *History*, edition of 1853, p. 745.
[9] Printed in facsimile in vol. iii. of the Purcell Society publications.

based on a Treasury Paper containing a petition which shows that Lady Dorothy was a Protestant though her father was a Catholic, deduced from the fact that her father, the eighth earl of Clanricarde, succeeded in 1687 (and that therefore she would not be 'Lady Dorothy' until that year) the theory that the opera could not have been produced before that year, while a line in the epilogue, 'we are Protestants and English nuns,' and the phrase 'turning times,' point to the revolution of 1688 as being past, so that the date is limited to the time between 1688 and 1690, when the epilogue was published in D'Urfey's poems. Squire further pointed to internal evidence tending to confirm the comparatively late date of this most interesting work. For in dramatic directness, characterisation, adaptation of means to ends, feeling for climax, as well as actual beauty, the opera [1] is as much alive in the 20th century as are any of Gluck's. Every student is familiar with the poignant farewell of Dido, 'When I am laid in earth,' on Purcell's favourite foundation of a ground-bass; and the succeeding chorus of cupids is hardly less affecting, while the witches' music and all the rest is full of dramatic life and originality.

In 1689 Purcell was involved in a dispute concerning the fees paid for seats in the organ-gallery at the Abbey for the coronation of William and Mary; these fees had been considered by Purcell as his lawful perquisite, but an order was made that unless he refunded the money his place would be declared null and void. As he retained his place until his death, it is probable that he gave back the fees. In 1690 was produced, and in 1691 was published, the music to 'Dioclesian,' Betterton's adaptation of Beaumont and Fletcher's 'Prophetess,' the printed copies of which, issued at so low a price that the composer lost by the transaction, were all corrected by him with his own hand. The music would rank with the other theatrical productions were it not for the elaborate masque in the fifth act; the rest consists of act-tunes and a song or two. The whole is more elaborately scored than anything we have yet met with of Purcell's, trumpets and oboes (including a tenor oboe) being introduced. A chaconne before the third act, in which two flutes have a canon above the recurrent bass, is singularly beautiful, the song, 'What shall I do to show how much I love her!' has remained in favour until the present day, and the final chorus, 'Triumph, victorious Love,' is a remarkably fine, sustained piece of music. In spite of its want of commercial success, the music to 'Dioclesian' seems to have won for the composer the favour of Dryden.[2]

Of far greater importance was the next work in which Purcell was associated with Dryden, the so-called opera of 'King Arthur' (1691). The musical numbers in this piece, though far more numerous than those in 'Dioclesian,' are still a kind of adjunct to the main scheme of the play; the singing parts are quite distinct from the personages of the drama, and the music, as a whole, might be most properly described as a series of *intermezzi*. Individual scenes, such as the sacrificial scene, the wonderfully effective 'frost scene,' and the whole of the concluding masque, are full of beauty and originality; but there is so little connexion with the play that a performance of the music alone (such as was given at the Birmingham [3] Festival of 1897) must necessarily seem rather wanting in continuity. Whether, after uniting all the separate portions preserved in various MSS. and printed editions, we possess all the music that Purcell wrote, as he wrote it, cannot as yet be decided; but music has been found for all the portions in which music is required, and what we have now is probably something very like what Purcell produced. The 'Ayres for the Theatre,' which is the authority for many of the instrumental numbers, were only published for stringed instruments, and there may have been other instruments added to these for the performance, as other instruments take part in the body of the work.

The chief work of 1692 was in connexion with an anonymous adaptation of *A Midsummer Night's Dream*, called 'The Fairy Queen,' and produced at Dorset Gardens Theatre in the spring of that year. The 'Select Songs' published by Heptinstall in 1692 are the only part of the music that appeared in Purcell's lifetime; by Oct. of 1700 the score had been lost, and the patentees of the theatre offered a reward of £20 for its recovery. By a most fortunate accident the theatre copy of the music was discovered in 1901 in the library of the R.A.M., and the whole work, edited by Mr. J. S. Shedlock, was published in the Purcell Society's edition (1903). It is conjectured that the volume was in the hands successively of Dr. Pepusch, William Savage and R. J. S. Stevens.[4] Like the other 'operas,' the piece contains a number of beautiful things quite unconnected with the original play of Shakespeare, and it is curious to notice that no word of Shakespeare's is here set to music by Purcell. The songs of the seasons, culminating in the splendid bass song, 'Next Winter comes slowly,' the beautiful soprano air, 'O let me weep,' and other things, are justly famous. The ode for St. Cecilia's Day of the same year, set to words by Brady, 'Hail, bright Cecilia!' is the most elaborate of the compositions for

---

[1] On the question as to the completeness or incompleteness of the present score see the *Zeitschrift* of the Int. Mus. Ges. vi. 56.
[2] See his Epistle Dedicatory to *Amphitryon* (1690), quoted by Cummings, *Life*, p. 55.

[3] See the preface to the vocal score of 'King Arthur' edited by Fuller Maitland for this festival (Boosey, 1897).
[4] *Mus. T.*, 1901, pp. 388 and 472.

this festival, and the ode for Queen Mary's birthday in this year, Sedley's ' Love's Goddess sure was blind,' contains a song, ' May her blest example chase,' in connexion with which a story is told by Hawkins to the effect that Purcell, nettled by the Queen's asking Mrs. Arabella Hunt to sing the Scots song, ' Cold and Raw,' on some occasion when he was present, introduced it in the next birthday ode, making it the bass of the air just mentioned. The story may or may not be true, but the song is a striking instance of Purcell's love for a moving bass and his skill in treating basses of this kind, whether melodic in themselves, or recurrent, as in the numberless ' ground-basses ' of fine quality that exist of his.

In 1693 Purcell wrote music for a great many plays, and set Tate's ode for the Queen's birthday, ' Celebrate this Festival.' He must have composed in this year the ode for the centenary commemoration of Trinity College, Dublin, ' Great Parent, hail ' in connexion with the celebration held on Jan. 9. 1694.[1] In 1694 Purcell revised the twelfth edition of Playford's *Introduction to the Skill of Musick*, and while altering the earlier part of the book in many ways, he completely rewrote the treatise at the end.[2] The opening words of the section for which he is responsible are curious when taken in connexion with Purcell's own way of treating the bass.

' Formerly they used to Compose from the *Bass*, but Modern Authors Compose to the *Treble* when they make *Counterpoint* or *Basses* to Tunes or Songs.'

The whole passage which follows is of the utmost interest to the student of Purcell's music. The great work of this year was the splendid Te Deum and Jubilate for St. Cecilia's Day, which, after its publication by Purcell's widow in 1697, was annually performed at the Festival of the Sons of the Clergy (*q.v.*) until Handel wrote his Utrecht Te Deum in 1713, after which the two works were performed alternately till 1743, when Handel's Dettingen Te Deum displaced both the others. (See also Three Choirs Festival.) In a mistaken desire to bring Purcell's work into accordance with the pre-vailing Handelian fashion of his day, Boyce rearranged it in such a manner that its char-acter was spoilt, and the work was not available in its original form until, in 1895, for the Purcell Bicentenary, Sir J. F. Bridge, who possessed the autograph score,[3] brought out a purified edition of it.

Queen Mary died of smallpox at Kensington, Dec. 28, 1694, and was buried on Mar. 5, 1694/95, in Henry VII.'s chapel in West-minster Abbey. The funeral was of rare magnificence, and various accounts of it were

published ; it is now certain that Purcell composed for it the beautiful anthem, ' Thou knowest, Lord, the secrets of our hearts,' as well as two pieces for ' flatt trumpets '; but the evidence for the assumption that the second anthem was his ' Blessed is the man ' rests on a very slight foundation. Barclay Squire has given the text[4] of the ' March ' and ' Canzona ' that were played ; the former was adapted from the music to ' The Libertine ' written about two years before. The instruments on which the pieces were played were almost undoubtedly ' sackbuts ' or trombones. The anthem became so famous that in after-years, when Croft (*q.v.*) composed the music for the Burial Service, he incorporated Purcell's music, instead of setting these words anew. Two elegies for the Queen were written in 1695, which were published in a collection, together with one by Blow. In this same year, the last of the composer's life, he wrote music for the ' operatic ' version of Howard and Dryden's *Indian Queen*, when it underwent the usual process of adaptation for music, *i.e.* the addition of numbers which could be set to music quite independently of the original play. It has been shown by Squire[5] that the work belongs to this last year of Purcell's life, and it is con-jectured that to his illness was due the fact that the final masque was composed by his brother, Daniel Purcell. An extraordinary piece of literary piracy was achieved in regard to this music. Messrs. May and Hudgebutt not only brought out the music, but had the impertinence to prefix to it a dedication to Purcell himself, in which they admit and excuse their theft. Another work for the stage, probably dating from the same year, was in connexion with Shadwell's adaptation of *The Tempest* into ' an opera '; this had first ap-peared in 1673, but there is no evidence of any of Purcell's music being written before 1695, in which year a song, ' Dear pretty Youth,' was published, in ' Deliciae musicae ' (see Tempest). There is a strange lack of con-temporary MSS. of the music.[6] Cummings had an old theatre copy, and another is in the British Museum ; Goodison's edition is the principal source for the music, but is un-trustworthy as to dates. Yet another work for the stage, produced in the same year, ' Don Quixote, part iii ,' contained what was no doubt Purcell's last composition, the song ' From rosie Bow'rs.' This was also printed in ' Orpheus Britannicus ' with the heading, ' This was the last Song that Mr. *Purcell* Sett, it being in his Sickness.' There is apparently nothing else of Purcell's in the production. Purcell died on Nov. 21, 1695, probably at his house in Marsham Street, Westminster.[7] The

---

[1] The score (30 pages) for voices and strings preserved in the Library of Trinity College, Dublin, is entitled ' Commemoration Ode Performed at Christ Church in Dublin, Jan. 9, 1694.' L. L. M'C. D.
[2] See *Sammelb.* Int. Mus. Ges. vi. 521.
[3] Now in the British Museum.

[4] See the *Sammelb.* Int. Mus. Ges. iv. 225.
[5] *Sammelb.* Int. Mus. Ges. v. 529.
[6] See Dent, Preface to ' The Indian Queen ' and ' The Tempest,' Purcell Society, vol. xix. ; also Squire, *Sammelb.* Int. Mus. Ges. pp. 551-5.
[7] *Mus. T.*, 1895, p. 734.

early deaths of three of his children suggest that there was a consumptive tendency in the family, and in any case there is no need to attach any importance to the tradition reported by Hawkins, that the composer caught cold from being kept waiting for admittance into his house late at night. He was buried Nov. 26, 1695, beneath the organ in Westminster Abbey, and a tablet was erected on a pillar near the grave by Annabella, Lady Howard, who may have written the inscription:

'Here lyes HENRY PURCELL Esqr. Who left this Life And is gone to that Blessed Place Where only his Harmony can be exceeded. Obijt 2jmo die Novembris Anno Aetatis suae 37mo. Annoq Domini j695.'

Over the grave was placed the following epitaph :

'Plaudite, felices superi, tanto hospite, nostris
   Praefuerat, vestris addite ille choris :
Invida nec vobis Purcellum terra reposcat,
   Questa decus sêcli, deliciasque breves.
Tam cito decessisse, modo cui singula debet
   Musa, prophana suos religiosa suos.
Vivit Io et vivat, dum vicina organa spirant,
   Dumque colet numeris turba canora Deûm.'

This, having become totally defaced, was renewed in 1876.

Purcell had six children, three of whom died before him, viz. John Baptista, baptized Aug. 9, 1682, buried Oct. 17 following ; Thomas, buried Aug. 3, 1686; and Henry, baptized June 9, 1687, buried Sept. 23 following.

His eldest daughter was FRANCES (bapt. Westminster Abbey, May 30, 1688 ; d. 1724). In 1706 her mother appointed her her residuary legatee and her executrix, when she should reach the age of 18. She proved the will July 6, 1706. She married, shortly after her mother's death, Leonard Welsted, poet and dramatist. Her only daughter was FRANCES (b. 1708 ; d. unmarried 1726). Another daughter of Purcell, MARY PETERS (bapt. Westminster Abbey, Dec. 10, 1693), it is presumed, survived her father, but predeceased her mother, as she is not named in the latter's will. For EDWARD, the only son who survived his parents, see (6) above.

The composer's widow survived him till Feb. 1706, when she died at Richmond, being buried on the 14th in the north aisle of Westminster Abbey. The works of Purcell published posthumously are as follows :

' Ten Sonatas in Four Parts ' (1697), for the same combination of instruments as the set published in 1683, and containing the famous ' Golden Sonata.'
' Lessons for the Harpsichord or Spinnet ' (1696).
' A Collection of Ayres for the Theatre ' (1697), containing act-tunes, etc., for many of the plays.
' Orpheus Britannicus,' a collection of Purcell's songs, bk. i. 1698, bk. ii. 1702, second edition of bk. i. 1706, second edition of bk. ii. 1711. A third edition of both books, or more probably the ' remainder' of the stock, furnished with a new title-page, was issued in 1721, but is very rare.

By way of exception to the usual course of composers' reputations, there has always been a tradition of Purcell's greatness, and a more or less continuous stream of editions of his works. Even the vogue of Handel was not enough to obliterate all trace of Purcell's

fame. The influence of the Englishman's music upon the German master is quite unmistakable ; before Handel came to England the massive choral effects, produced by means of the utmost simplicity, are not to be found in any of his works ; they are the distinguishing mark of Purcell's choruses, although Purcell's are very short as compared with Handel's.[1] Among the most important issues of Purcell's music must be reckoned Vincent Novello's four volumes of the Sacred Music (1829–32), which contain all the anthems and services, etc , then accessible. Unfortunately the edition, and those which base their read-ings upon it without reference to better authorities, are so inaccurate that very little idea can be obtained of the true characteristics of the composer's genius. The Musical Antiquarian Society did useful work in publishing many of the most important of Purcell's compositions ; but it was not until the foundation of the PURCELL SOCIETY (q.v.) in 1878 that a really methodical issue of the music could be begun.                                      M.

PORTRAITS.—The following is a list of the portraits of Purcell as to which there can be no doubt.

(i.) Oval, head and shoulders, turned to the left, as a young man, by Sir Godfrey Kneller. This picture was given by Purcell to John Church (1675 ?–1741), from whom it descended to his son, the Rev. John Church (d. 1785), rector of Boxford, Suffolk. The latter's daughter (Mrs. Strutt) gave it to Joah Bates (1741–99), who owned it in 1793. In 1846 it was owned by Edward Bates, when it was engraved by W. Humphreys from a drawing by Edward Novello for Vincent Novello's edition of Purcell's sacred music. It was bought from the Bates family by Henry Littleton, and from him passed to his son Alfred H. Littleton, after whose death (1915) it was bought by W. Barclay Squire (see PLATE LXII.).

(ii.) A drawing or sketch of (i.), formerly in the possession of Dr. Burney, later in that of Archdeacon Burney, now in the Print Room, British Museum.

(iii.) At the age of 24. Engraving by R. White in the Sonatas of Three Parts, published in 1683. No original of this is known.

(iv.) A painting (oval, half-length) by John Closterman, in the National Portrait Gallery (No. 1352). This is the original of the engraving in ' Orpheus Britannicus ' (1698), and was probably painted after the composer's death. A copy or replica is preserved at Dyrham Park, Chippenham, and a small version is in the collection of Mr. A. F. Hill. According to Hawkins (History of Music, 1853, ed. ii. p. 747, and also in the Universal

1 See E. D. Rendall, Mus. T. 1895, p. 293, on the influence of Purcell on Handel's ' Acis and Galatea.'

*Magazine,* Dec. 1777), a tavern formerly existed in Wych Street with the sign of 'The Purcell's Head.' This sign was 'a half-length; the dress a brown full-bottomed wig, and a green night-gown, very finely executed.' The description agrees with the Closterman portrait, and possibly one of the two above-mentioned versions was originally the tavern-sign.

As to the following, doubts have been raised whether they represent Henry or Daniel Purcell.

(v.) A small half-length, seated at a harpsichord, on which is an open music-book containing part of a 'Sonata Settima'; the left hand points to a miniature held in the right hand. By John Closterman (National Portrait Gallery, No. 1463). This picture formerly belonged to Dr. Burney. Another version of it (belonging to Miss Done, Worcester) has a different portrait in the miniature, and the music-book contains 'Britons, strike home' (from 'King Arthur'). A sketch for this picture is at Christ Church, Oxford (Walpole, Soc. vol. v. p. 2). Sir Charles Holmes (*Burlington Magazine,* Aug. 1915) considers that these pictures represent Daniel Purcell.

(vi.) Half-length, holding a roll of music. By John Closterman (Royal Society of Musicians). Belonged to the composer's son Edward and his grandson, Edward Henry, from whom it was bought by Dr. Boyce. At the death of the latter it was sold to Redmond Simpson, who bequeathed it to the directors of the Ancient Concerts, with remainder to the Royal Society of Musicians. Engraved (mezzotint) by G. Zobel. Sir Charles Holmes (*Burlington Magazine,* Aug. 1915) considers that this represents Daniel Purcell; the original is certainly the same as that of No. v.

(vii.) A fine oil painting now at the R.C.M. bears the inscription, 'Henri Purcell A° Dni 1693.'

All the prints and engravings are copied from or based on Nos. (i.), (ii.), (iii.). (i.) From this and the sketch for it there are prints or engravings by S. Harding, engraved by W. N. Gardiner, published by E. and S. Harding in 1794 as from 'an original picture at Dulwich College'; by W. Pinnock, 1823, and as the frontispiece to Novello's edition of Purcell's Sacred Music. From (iii.) there is a print 'finely engraved from an original Painting' in the *Universal Magazine,* Dec. 1777, and by C. Grignion in Hawkins. From (iii.), besides the frontispiece to 'Orpheus Britannicus,' there is a small engraving by H. Adlard.

A bust of Purcell was formerly in the Music School, Oxford, but has disappeared. In the *Dictionary of National Biography* it is stated that a portrait (called 'Thomas Clark') in the Board Room, Dulwich College, represents Purcell. The picture is still there, and certainly is not a portrait of the composer.

The *Mus. T.* for Sept. 1920 published reproductions of three alleged portraits of Purcell, but in the best opinion these are not contemporary, nor is anything said about their origin.                              w. b. s.

## CHARACTERISTICS OF PURCELL'S ART

It remains to make some examination of the grounds on which Purcell has been styled 'the greatest and most original of English composers.' In recent years his claim to that title has been questioned in view of the increased knowledge of the great Elizabethans, notably Byrd and Weelkes, and the fuller and richly deserved homage paid to them. They stand at the summit of a great artistic epoch; Henry Purcell began a new era. He was born into a society which had to recreate traditions from the ruins of old ones, to build up new institutions and prove the efficacy of untried tools. It was Purcell who, more than any other, did all these things for the London of the Restoration period, and in doing so set his seal on the music of the Church, the theatre, the concert room and the chamber. In only the first of these is it possible to institute a comparison between Purcell and his Elizabethan predecessors which may be partly to his detriment (see ANTHEM and SERVICE). Even here, however, the comparison is not very pertinent. It is true that the Restoration re-established practically the same liturgy in the English Church as that which had belonged to the first Caroline era, but the appearance of identity is deceptive. There was a deeper cleavage between the Church of Purcell and Orlando Gibbons than between that of Gibbons and Taverner, although Taverner had composed for a Latin Office and Gibbons for an English one which virtually was that of Purcell's day. Despite the destruction of the monasteries the English cathedral service had maintained, up to Gibbons's day, much of the monastic ideal, expressed musically in a polyphony which was the combination of modal melodies. It was the puritan revolt which swept away the reflective artistic culture of the monasteries.

CHURCH MUSIC.—Purcell served a thoroughly secularised church, and its music was based on the secular methods deliberately imported by Charles II. through HUMFREY (*q.v.*). In the Chapel Royal, in which Purcell was brought up and for which the majority of his anthems were written, music was regarded as a discreet entertainment for the men and women of fashion who composed the court. Purcell's methods in his numerous 'verse' anthems with accompaniments, including long ritornelli for strings, are those of the theatre and the chamber sonata, the parts moving harmonically over a THOROUGH-BASS (*q.v.*). Their words are most frequently taken from the Psalms, occa-

## LXII

HENRY PURCELL

From the painting by Sir Godfrey Kneller, bequeathed by the late W. Barclay Squire to the
National Portrait Gallery

sionally from the Prophets, and in one famous instance, ' My beloved spake,' from the Song of Solomon. The Christian religion is sedulously avoided ; save where the Judaic texts are occasionally rounded off with a ' Gloria Patri,' his anthems would be as suitable to a synagogue as to a Christian Church. What he did was to dramatise the sentiments of the Psalmist, just as he dramatised his theatrical librettists, and he produced in these works a series of cantatas bristling with points of interest, quickly achieved moments of vivid expression between combined solo voices (generally male alto, tenor and bass) filled out with ingeniously wrought instrumental music.

The survival of Purcell's anthems in the daily cathedral services of later generations damaged his reputation far more than the temporary neglect of all his admittedly secular work. Their instrumental parts were omitted ; their rhythms were flattened out by the droning voices of ' lay clerks ' and their *tempi* were slowed down to suit conceptions of propriety which had never troubled him in their composition. Purcell's church music cannot be properly understood until it is taken at his own valuation, performed as he intended it to be, frankly and fearlessly and without, as it were, an eye on the stately tread of the Dean's verger. An example may be quoted from ' In thee, O Lord, do I put my trust.' It begins with a fine symphony for strings on a ground-bass, and the whole is carried on in a series of ' verses ' for men's voices alternating with symphonies in which the themes are developed instrumentally. The following air for alto voice is a typical example of Purcell's vocal cantilena above a flowing instrumental bass.

Obviously this moves freely at a fairly quick pace, which will make the ' Alleluja ' trio at the same pace very fast indeed. The entry of the bass voice with this phrase,

may sound shockingly jovial, but that is the pace at which it must go if Purcell is to be rightly interpreted, and when so sung the movement is a brilliant scherzo. It is that sort of thing which has earned Purcell the reputation for frivolity in church circles, but his anthems are anything but frivolous. Next to his capacity for happiness is his capacity for poignant expression produced by an interval of melody or an unexpected conjunction of harmonies, the latter especially where the words suggest a hint of mystery. Such a moment occurs earlier in the same anthem in the words ' Thou art He that took me out of my mother's womb,' where the chord (D, B♭ and F♯) following on F major harmony is extraordinarily arresting.

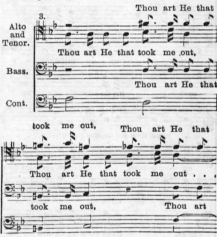

But the fact that such things as these were the basis of his style does not mean that he was oblivious of the broader effects of choral voices in the mass or unable to draw on the resources of polyphony when necessary. The spacious handling of ' Let every thing that hath breath ' (finale to the anthem, ' O Praise God in his holiness '), where ten real parts, two violins and eight voices, employ the arts both of polyphony and of homophonic groups of chords, shows his command, and we have only to quote the ending of the beautiful ' Save me, O God ' to realise that Purcell was a master of the strict contrapuntal style (see overleaf).

The quotation further shows how strong was the influence of modal melody on Purcell, and throughout his works it gains an added interest by its conjunction with the clearly defined notions of major and minor tonalities which had become established in his generation. In the final cadence of 'Save me, O God' (Ex. 4)

we get a particularly striking instance of that employment of both the major and minor thirds in a chord which had been a special characteristic of the English polyphonists in the madrigal, and Purcell was wont to get many of his most trenchant effects by the daring employment of such discords. A different use of a similar device deserves attention. It occurs in one of the recitatives which Purcell delighted to write for GOSTLING (q.v.), the famous bass of the Chapel Royal.

The harmonic accompaniment of such a passage (it is unfigured) presents a nice problem to the organist.

LANGUAGE IN SONG.—The passage leads naturally to a consideration of that which is universally acknowledged to give Purcell his strongest claim to be regarded as first among English composers, his power of setting the English language in SONG (q.v.). He it was who completed what John MERBECKE (q.v.) had begun a hundred years before Purcell's birth, when he first attempted to express the syllabic values of English in a quasi-mensural plain-song. John Dowland, Orlando Gibbons and Henry Lawes were contributors to an art which reached perfection in the so-called recitative of Purcell as found in the anthems, the odes, the theatre pieces and most particularly in the only complete opera, 'Dido and Aeneas.' Purcell's recitative, unlike the *recitativo secco* of the Italian opera, gains its maximum of effect when it is sung in strict time. It then gives with extraordinary fidelity the accentual value to the words which belongs to good speaking, and emphasises the broad sense of the text in a way to carry it through the aisles of the cathedral or across the footlights of the theatre. In the passage quoted above (Ex. 5) the preacher might lay more stress on the pronouns; Purcell shows the true orator's sense in perceiving that the greatness of mercy (not *His* mercy) is the theme here, and he gets his justification when he reaches the climax of the movement in the phrase,

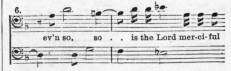

where the declamatory repetition of 'so,' and the placing of the word 'Lord' on an E♭ never touched elsewhere in the movement, clinches the matter. In such ways Purcell gives to his recitatives a melodic form which makes them musical works of the first order. They are singularly free from that desultory wandering from phrase to phrase and the repetition of harmonic and melodic *clichés* which deface the recitatives of the 18th century, even those of the greatest composers. To get the full measure of his power in this direction a careful study should be made of the soliloquy of Aeneas which ends the second act of ' Dido.'

It must be admitted that his eloquence is sometimes limited (though not in ' Dido,' his greatest piece of vocal declamation) by a tendency to seek expressiveness through a strained use of vocal ornament. Certainly he uses to excess such dotted note rhythms as

in both the anthems and the odes, and in a way which gives the feeling of a forced cheerfulness becoming at times irritating. But the reliance on such rhythms is the only sign of anything which can be called a *cliché* in the whole of Purcell's work. Sometimes his ornaments are unsuccessful only because of their extreme venturesomeness. The song ' 'Tis Nature's Voice,' in the Ode on Saint Cecilia's Day (1692), said to have been ' sung with incredible graces by Mr. Purcell himself,' [1] pushes to its furthest limit the art of decorative word-painting.[2] That it was written for his own voice shows that Purcell must have been himself a very highly accomplished countertenor (alto) singer, and lets us into the supreme secret of his composition. Whatever he writes for the voice, from the most artless melody, tavern song or catch to the most elaborate piece of vocalisation such as this, has behind it the sure instinct of the singer.

It was this singer's instinct which made Purcell the greatest master of the ground-bass used as a song form. The ground-bass of the Chaconne type, wherever it appears in musical history, in the operas of Lully, the violin solo sonata of Bach, or the fourth symphony of Brahms, has the inherent weakness that the music tends to get cut into phrase lengths corresponding with the repetitions of the ground. That is equally a characteristic of Purcell's use of it for dance purposes in his stage works.[3] Where, however, he adopts the ground-bass as a structural principle in song the voice part is entirely unfettered in rhythm by the measure of the bass. In ' Dido and

Aeneas ' there are three such songs of which the last has become the most famous on account of its extraordinary intimacy of expression. Both the others, however, ' Ah ! Belinda ' and ' Oft she visits ' are more subtle examples of Purcell's way of crossing the 4-bar rhythm of the ground-bass with vocal phrases of unequal length, overlapping the cadences and producing melodic contours as free as those of unaccompanied recitative. The music of ' Dido ' is now so generally accessible [4] that quotation here is unnecessary.

THEATRE MUSIC.—Romain Rolland, in one of the most penetrating studies of Purcell's art which has appeared in recent years,[5] says :

' Presque partout, il resta incomplet ; il ne chercha pas à briser les dernières barrières qui le séparaient de la perfection.'

The general truth of this must be admitted, but in ' Dido ' we have the one work which makes the qualification of the statement necessary. The more it is studied the more confidently can we assert its flawlessness as one of the masterpieces of music-drama and the only English one. The special circumstances of its production (see LIFE OF HENRY PURCELL above) made it possible for Purcell to write here as he willed and not in accordance with the demands made by fashion. We have seen how largely his church music was conditioned by fashion, and the Restoration theatre was even more fettered than the Restoration Church. That which was called ' opera ' meant a stage work designed to appeal to the eye rather than to the ear, a hybrid of the spoken drama and the MASQUE (*q.v.*). Music ranked with dancing, scenery and ' machines ' as one of the attractive accessories of the production, not as its *raison d'être*. Matthew LOCKE (*q.v.*) in his preface to ' Psyché ' (1675) exposes the whole position with frankness, bitterly contrasting the English conception of opera with that of the Italians, and claiming with justice that he had done more than any other to raise the musical status of the entertainment which passed by that name. Purcell at a later date also expresses his view of the matter in a preface,[6] that to ' The Fairy Queen ' (1692), where, like Locke, he draws an unfavourable comparison between the position of English opera and opera in Italy and France, and raises what is probably the first plea for a subsidised opera - house. This preface, written after the private production of ' Dido ' at Chelsea,[7] defines opera as ' a story sung with proper action,' which is just what ' Dido ' is and ' The Fairy Queen ' is not. All that

---

[1] *Gentleman's Journal and Monthly Miscellany*, Nov. 1692.
[2] Compare the passage on the word ' Grieve ' with the weeping of St. Peter in Bach's St. John Passion.
[3] See, for example, the Chaconne, ' Dance for a Chinese man and woman ' in ' The Fairy Queen,' but compare with this the sonata No. 6 of the ' Ten Sonatas in Four Parts ' discussed below.

[4] There are two editions of the vocal score, that edited by W. H Cummings (Novello) and one, embodying more recent research (1926), edited by E. J. Dent (Oxford Univ. Press), with a German translation by Anton Mayer.
[5] *Encyclopédie de la musique et dictionnaire du Conservatoire*; *L'Opéra au XVIIe siècle—Angleterre.*
[6] Reprint in Purcell Society's edition, vol. xii.
[7] ' Dido ' itself seems to have been an attempt to follow up the experiment, also privately made, of Blow's ' Venus and Adonis.'

Purcell was ever able to do in his works written for the public stage was to secure the continuity of the music through certain scenes (generally those having to do with supernatural characters) interpolated into the spoken play. 'The Fairy Queen,' 'King Arthur,' 'The Tempest' and 'The Indian Queen' may be regarded as operas in this limited sense, but no one of them is, to use his own term, 'a perfect opera.' The masques in 'Dioclesian' and in 'Timon of Athens' also have sufficient continuity to be considered as belonging to the operatic category. The rest are a more or less fortuitous collection of pieces, overtures, curtain tunes, dances and songs, hastily thrown off to meet the requirements of incidental music. Except as evidence of Purcell's almost Schubertian fund of melody they are unimportant.

FESTIVAL ODES.—The fashion of producing odes set to elaborate music for combined voices and instruments whenever a festival of any sort, public or private, was to be celebrated is historically interesting for us, because it marks the beginning of that form of concert-giving which has been most characteristic of the English people through two succeeding centuries. Handel discerned the national genius for such choral singing and exploited it in his oratorios from which many developments spring (see THREE CHOIRS FESTIVAL). In Purcell's day the institution of the festivals of St. CECILIA (*q.v.*, subsection CECILIAN FESTIVALS) were the most public occasions of the kind and the most worthy to engage the powers of the artist. The praise of music was a theme calculated to inspire a composer; Purcell's contributions to it are all interesting, and culminate in the masterpiece of 1692, 'Hail, bright Cecilia,' for which Nicholas Brady provided him with at least a fairly serviceable libretto. Its central chorus 'Soul of the World' stands beside the final chorus of 'Dido' and the anthem 'Save me, O God' as evidence of Purcell's power to rise to the expression of a supreme emotion when he was deeply stirred. Apart from this moment the work is full of subtle strokes of the kind in which he excelled; the declamation of ''Tis Nature's Voice,' the ground-bass song 'Wondrous Machine,' and the handling of *obbligato* instruments, flutes, oboes and violins, in several numbers are all Purcell in his finest and most delicate vein. Particularly it is worth while to note the duet (alto and tenor), 'In vain the am'rous flute,' where he quotes the ground-bass of Dido's Lament but does not use it as a ground. This treatment shows his freedom from stereotyped formulae. Apart from the St. Cecilian celebrations, however, the production of odes for every conceivable occasion, especially royal occasions, was part of the routine duty of a composer who, young as he was, was the acknowledged leader of his time and who held royal appointments. In the long series of birthday and welcome odes, with their fulsome compliments to thoroughly uninteresting dignitaries, it is quite evident that Purcell is often forced to simulate an enthusiasm which he does not feel. He schools himself to sentiment for Queen Mary's birthday year by year; compare the following from 'Now does the glorious day appear' (1689) with the very similar movement of 'Oft she visits' in 'Dido,' and the difference between art and artifice is instantly apparent.

A year later the martial prowess of Dutch William sinks him to

We know that Purcell had a sense of humour. The drunken poet, supposed to be a caricature of D'Urfey, in 'The Fairy Queen,' sufficiently shows that. Is it possible that he apostrophised his sovereign with his tongue in his cheek? A sincerer form of patriotism, the love of country, could rouse Purcell to write sturdy British songs as different in tone from this bombast as they are from the delicate artistry of 'Dido' and 'Hail, bright Cecilia.' Chief among the odes in this vein is the robust 'Yorkshire Feast Song' whose ballad tunes and bucolic choruses belong to the same category as those of the patriotic opera 'King Arthur.' In such things Purcell shows that he can say the obvious thing in music without fear of vulgarity. That power alone goes far to establish him as the greatest of English composers.

INSTRUMENTAL MUSIC.—There remains to be considered one field of his art in which his position is certainly unique, that of pure instrumental music. For practical purposes that is covered by the fantasies for strings and the sonatas for strings and harpsichord. His suites for harpsichord solo were written for educational purposes, many of the single dance pieces for harpsichord are arrangements from theatre tunes and songs, and only the toccata in A stands out from these things as a work conceived in the grand manner for virtuoso performance. It has been suggested that this was intended for the organ, but a comparison of it with the few desultory organ pieces by him which survive makes the suggestion seem more than doubtful. Certainly no intelligent editor would have included any of them among the doubtful works of J. S. Bach, as the toccata was included by the editors of the Bachgesellschaft edition. With this solitary example of big work one wonders the more at the lack of enterprise shown by Purcell in writing for the keyboard instruments. He did nothing to revive for the harpsichord or the organ the glories of the old English virginal school (see VIRGINAL MUSIC), and this toccata shows that he could have done something.

With his string music, however, the case is very different. The 'Fantazias' of 1680 show him working on the lines of the old English consort of viols which had been the instrumental counterpart to the madrigal in an earlier generation (see FANCY). The twelve 'Sonnata's of III Parts,' published three years later, make a definite break with the past. In them the composer revises his technical style in the light of what he had gleaned from whatever source of the methods of the Italians. The counterpoint now rests on the foundation of the THOROUGH-BASS (q.v.), and the three parts, two violins and bass viol, are accompanied by a keyboard instrument. Each sonata consists of a group of movements arranged to give direct contrasts of *tempi*, fast and slow. Their number varies from four to seven, and each (except generally the first movement) is marked by one of the Italian terms, *adagio*, *grave*, *largo*, *presto*, *allegro*, *vivace*, which are explained according to his own interpretation of them in the preface. It is quite clear from the internal evidence of style that the opening movements are always intended to have dignity and weight of utterance, and demand a moderate *tempo*. The *largo* is always in a triple time and has the character of a saraband, though neither that nor any other dance-form name is employed by Purcell in his sonatas. In fact the only generic title used is 'canzona,' which appears in eight out of the twelve sonatas. The canzona is the movement of greatest contrapuntal energy. An incisive subject introduced fugally sets the rhythmic pattern of the movement. Sometimes imitations on the principal theme form the chief source of thematic interest, as in the canzona of sonata No. 4 in F major; at other times (*e.g.* the canzona in No. VI., C major), after a sufficient development of the first idea Purcell leaves it for another one in a care-free fashion. A certain looseness of texture in the canzonas, and indeed

elsewhere, remains as a legacy from the style of the Fancy, as described by Morley. The principle of recapitulation which the Italians early made the basis of their form (see FORM and SONATA) is hardly recognised by Purcell. The short *grave* and *adagio* movements which separate these larger forms and are sometimes employed as finales are very personal. It is in them that we get most of those astringent harmonies which he uses in moments of strong feeling, alike in the music of the Church and the stage. Such passages as the following give an interest and colour to these sonatas, which more than replaces the suavity of melody on which the Italians relied.

10.

This from sonata No. IX., one of the finest of the whole series, is typical, and it should be noticed that a peculiarly vivid sense of contrast is here produced by the fact that this striking chromatic cadence precedes a finale in 12-8 time, which is in effect, though not in name, one of the most light-hearted of jigs. In this instance, as in others which approach dance movement types, the form is thoroughly organised and balanced.

Burney's general criticism of the style of these sonatas, that 'the passages all come from the head and not from the hand,'[1] is a pertinent one. His comparison, to Purcell's disadvantage in this respect, is with Corelli, whose first set was published in Italy simultaneously with Purcell's, and therefore was not among the latter's Italian models. But the defect which Burney discovers has nothing to do with models of composition but with the fact that a violinist instinctively gravitates towards passages which belong to the technique of his instrument (see BOWING and FINGERING), and one searches in vain

1 *General History of Music*, vol. iii. p. 507.

through Purcell for any **evidence** that the composer was a violinist. The note *c'''* is the limit of his upward compass, arpeggio passages of the kind which lie across strings tuned in fifths are not sought out, no emphasis is laid on the contrasts of tone between one string and another, bowing is hardly considered.[1] In general the counterpoint might be as well played on flute or organ stops as on the strings. This is sufficient to explain why Purcell, with far more original genius than Corelli, failed to found a school of concerted chamber music in England. His sonatas appealed, as they still do, to those ' who carry musical souls about them,' but much less to those who carried violins about them. They neither advanced the technique of the student nor served to display the achievements of the virtuoso.

What care Purcell bestowed on the musical scheme of these sonatas, which it must be remembered were his first important publication, is shown by the fact that no two of the twelve are in the same key. They are arranged in pairs, a minor key being followed by a major one throughout, the first eight being in a sequence of a minor followed by its relative major.[2] The implication is that he set himself to exhibit all the keys which the unequal temperament of the harpsichord made it convenient to use. He may even have contemplated pursuing the matter further on the lines of Bach's 'Wohltemperirtes Clavier,'[3] since the ' Ten Sonatas in Four Parts ' published posthumously by his widow begin with two further keys,[4] which would accord with this scheme.

It has generally been assumed that the ' Ten Sonatas in Four Parts '[5] represent a later phase of Purcell's art, but there is no evidence, either external or internal, to support this idea. Indeed Frances Purcell's remark in the dedication to Lady Rhodia Cavendish, that the collection had ' already found many friends,' shows that at any rate they were not new. It is even possible that some were already written when Purcell himself made his choice of twelve in contrasted keys for his first publication. There is little in the way of either scope or handling which can be pointed to as signs of greater maturity in the composer. Occasionally a subject, such as that of the opening movement of No. 4 in D minor or the *largo*

[1] Very occasionally Purcell uses slurs to indicate bowing, but only in a tentative fashion. In the final *largo* of sonata No. 1 in G minor a passage is first marked *piano* with slurred bowing and then repeated without slurs.
[2] The keys are, G minor, B♭ major, D minor, F major, A minor, C major, E minor, G major, C minor, A major, F minor, D major.
[3] It has been suggested that Father Smith's introduction of the so-called ' Quarter Tones ' into the organ of the Temple Church (*i.e.* the division of the notes G♯-A♭ and D♯-E♭) may have originated with Purcell himself. If so, it shows that Purcell, like J. S. Bach, was exercised about the question of temperament. See Andrew Freeman, *Father Smith* (1926).
[4] These are B minor and E♭ (relatives to D major and C minor). The other keys of the 1697 set repeat those of 1683 ; they are, A minor, D minor, three in G minor (a favourite violin key), C major, F major and D major
[5] The part-writing is the same as in the 1683 set, only here the thorough-bass is accounted a part, and Purcell says of the 1683 set that the engraving of the thorough-bass was ' a thing quite beside his first resolutions.'

of No. 8 in G minor, leads him to a more expansive development than is usual, but such things are no more than examples of those sudden strokes of genius which are to be met with throughout Purcell's work.[6] The sonata No. 9 in F major has attained a peculiar fame under the title of the ' Golden Sonata.' It is one of Purcell's larger works, consisting of an opening movement, a *largo*, *canzona*, *grave* and *allegro*, all very firmly knit in design and distinct from one another in character, but it is difficult to see why it should have been thus crowned above its companions, and one is tempted to suspect that the chance of its having received the golden crown of its title has persuaded posterity to invent reasons for the distinction.[7] The one sonata of the ten which stands apart from all its companions is No. 6, and it does so by reason of the fact that it is not really a sonata at all in Purcell's usual acceptation of the term, but virtually a chaconne built on a ground-bass of five bars, as follows :

11.

The form is one after Purcell's own heart. The five-bar measure of the bass gives him unlimited scope for weaving melodies of varying lengths between the two violin parts, and applying that art which we have seen was the peculiar property of his songs on a ground-bass. It is an exceptionally spacious piece of writing, and in the course of 42 repetitions of the bass Purcell manages to cover an extraordinary emotional range ; there is never a dull or perfunctory moment, and each thought leads so naturally to the next that the whole strikes the ear as one great piece of symphonic design.

From this cursory view of Purcell's output, undertaken to exhibit prevailing characteristics rather than to provide a commentary on particular works, one broad fact emerges. His view of music was identical with that of the modern musician. We may compare such a movement as the above with Bach or Brahms and test his theatre music by the principles of Gluck and Wagner, not in order to assert that he was as great as the greatest, but as a means of discovering where he is great at all. The method is inapplicable to any composer of an earlier generation save in a few particular instances. To put Byrd's Mass for five voices beside Bach's in B minor, or Bull's variations beside those of Beethoven on a theme of Diabelli would be a manifest futility. We have

[6] C. V. Stanford, in editing the ' Ten Sonatas in Four Parts ' for the Purcell Society, enriched them with a brilliantly written piano part which materially adds to their importance. But this is an example of Stanford's genius, not of Purcell's.
[7] Fuller Maitland, in editing the 1683 set for the Purcell Society, declares that ' among the Twelve Sonatas we look in vain for a rival to the famous "Golden Sonata,"' but J. F. Bridge (*Twelve Good Musicians*, p. 130) thinks it inferior to No. 4 (also in F) in the first set.

for the most part to be conversant with a whole set of conditions embodied in a now obsolete theory of music before we can measure the stature of each individual work of Byrd's and Bull's time. But Purcell belongs to our world, the world made for us by two centuries of great masters intervening between his life and our own. We can apply familiar criteria to every department of his work and discover by their means his successes and his failures. In doing so a large proportion of his output will drop off as perfunctory or damaged by the social or other material conditions in which he produced it. But his best stands the test triumphantly and shows him to have been a man of first-rate creative power, a mind of vivid imagination and keen sensitiveness, of the same order, if not of the same calibre, as the masters who have made music the subtly expressive agent of human feeling which it has become in modern times.        c.

## Summary of Works

The following list of Purcell's works is necessarily only an attempt, as many of the anthems, etc., cannot at present be authoritatively dated, or even ascribed to certain periods in the composer's career. The list of plays for which he wrote music is based on that given in Squire's article in the *Sammelbände* of the Int. Mus. Ges. (v. 489 ff.).

### 1. SACRED MUSIC

#### ANTHEMS AND CHURCH MUSIC

The main source for the bulk of these anthems, etc., is Vincent Novello's edition of 'Purcell's Sacred Music.' His versions are for the most part quite untrustworthy, but until the work of editing them with care and reverence shall have been completed it is convenient to use his collection as indicating the number, etc., of extant works. A list of the anthems already published by the Purcell Society will be found on p. 301.

Ah ! few and full of sorrows.
Beati omnes. S.S.A.B.
Be merciful unto me. Verse, A.T.B.
Behold, I bring you glad tidings. Verse, A.T.B.
Behold now, praise the Lord. Verse, A.T.B.
Blessed are they that fear. Verse, S.S.A.B. (before 1688).
Blessed be the Lord my strength. A.T.B.
Blessed is he that considereth the poor. A.T.B.
Blessed is he whose unrighteousness. Verse, S.S.A.T.T.B.
Blessed is the man that feareth the Lord.
Bow down Thine ear. Verse, 4 vv.
By the waters of Babylon. Verse, T.T.B.
Early, O Lord, my fainting soul.
Gloria Patri. Three compositions in canon.
Hear my prayer. Full, 8 vv.
Hear me, O Lord, and that soon. Verse, A.S.A.T.B.
Hear me, O Lord, the great support. A.T.B.
In Thee, O Lord, do I put my trust. A.T.B.
It is a good thing to give thanks. A.T.B.
I was glad. Verse, A.T.B.
I will sing unto the Lord. Full, S.S.A.T.B.
I will give thanks. Verse, T.B.B.
Jehovah, quam multi (or Jehovah, how many). S.S.A.T.B.
Laudate Dominum. Canon, a 3.
Let God arise. Verse, TT.
Lord, how long wilt Thou be angry ? Full, S.S.A.T.B.
Lord, I can suffer Thy rebukes.
Lord, who can tell ? Verse, T.T.B.
Man that is born of a Woman. (Funeral sentences, containing 'Thou knowest, Lord,' as a verse.)
My beloved spake. Verse, A.T.B.B.
My heart is fixed. Verse, A.T.B.
My heart is inditing. Verse, a 8 [1685].
My song shall be alway. Verse, S.
O all ye people.
O all ye people, clap your hands. S.S.T.B.
O consider my adversity. Verse, A.T.B.
O give thanks. Verse, a 4.
O God, Thou art my God. Full, S.S.A.T.B.
O God, Thou hast cast us out. Full, S.S.A.T.B.
O happy man.
O Lord God of hosts. Full, a 8.
O Lord, grant the King a long life.
O Lord, our Governour.
O Lord, our Governour. Verse, S.S.S.B.B.
O Lord, rebuke me not. Verse, S. or T.
O Lord, Thou art my God. Verse, A.T.B.

O miserable man.
O praise God in His holiness. a 8.
O praise the Lord, all ye heathen. T.T. [early].
O sing unto the Lord. Verse, a 4 [1688].
Out of the Deep. Verse, S.A.B.
Praise the Lord, O Jerusalem.
Praise the Lord, O my soul. a 6.
Praise the Lord, O my soul, O Lord my God. Verse, A.B. [1687].
Rejoice in the Lord ('The Bell Anthem,' so called from its chiming figure in the bass). Verse, A.T.B.
Remember not, Lord, our offences. Full, S.S.A.T.B.
Save me, O God. Full, S.S.A.T.B. [c. 1690].
Sing unto God, O ye kingdoms of the earth. Verse, B.
The Lord is my light. Verse, A.T.B.
The Lord is King. Verse, B.
The way of God is an undefiled way. Verse, A.A.B.
They that go down to the sea in ships. Verse, A.B. [1685].
Thou knowest, Lord. (The well-known funeral sentences, a 4, different from those in 'Man that is born of a Woman.')
Thy way, O God, is holy. Verse, A.B.
Thy word is a lantern. Verse, A.T.B.
Turn Thee again, O Lord. a 4.
Turn Thou us, O good Lord. Verse, A.T.B.
Turn Thou us, O good Lord. A.T.B.
Unto Thee will I cry. Verse, A.T.B.
Who hath believed our report ? Verse, A.T.T.B.
Why do the heathen ? Verse, A.T.B.

#### SERVICES

Te Deum and Jubilate in D.
Te Deum, Benedictus, Kyrie, Creed, in B flat.
Benedicite, and Jubilate, in B flat. ('Second Morning Service.')
Magnificat and Nunc Dimittis, in B flat.
Cantate and Deus misereatur, in B flat.
Evening Service in G minor.

#### HYMNS, ETC., IN PLAYFORD'S 'HARMONIA SACRA,' AND NOVELLO'S 'PURCELL'S SACRED MUSIC.'

(For solo voices, unless otherwise stated ; frequently a 'chorus' is added for two voices.)

Arise, my darkened melancholy soul.
Awake, and with attention hear.
Awake, ye dead (two voices).
Begin the song.
Close thine eyes and sleep secure (two voices).
Full of wrath (for the Conversion of St. Paul).
Great God, and just.
How have I stray'd.
How long, great God ('The Aspiration').
In guilty night (trio, 'Saul and the Witch of Endor').
In the black dismal dungeon.
Let the night perish ('Job's Curse').
Lord, what is man ?
Now that the sun (Evening Hymn).
O I'm sick of life. A.T.B.
O Solitude !
Plung'd in the confines of despair. T.T.B. (Add. MS. 30,930.)
Since God so tender a regard. T.T.B.
Tell me, some pitying Angel ('The Blessed Virgin's Expostulation ').
The earth trembled ('On our Saviour's Passion ').
The night is come (Evening Hymn).
Thou wakeful Shepherd (Morning Hymn).
We sing to Him, whose wisdom.
With sick and famish'd eyes.
Hymn-tune 'Burford,' and settings of several psalm-tunes in Playford's *Introd.* (1694) ; see the *Sammelbände* of the Int. Mus. Ges. vi. 521.

### II. SECULAR MUSIC

#### ODES AND WELCOME SONGS

1. 1680. Welcome, Vicegerent.
2. 1681. Swifter, Isis.
3. 1682. What shall be done.
4. 1682. The Summer's Absence unconcern'd we bear.
5. 1683. Fly, bold Rebellion.
6. 1683. Welcome to all the pleasures.
7. 1683. Raise the voice. } for St. Cecilia's Day.
8. 1683. Laudate Cecilium.
9. 1683. From Hardy Climes (Marriage Ode for Princess Anne).
10. 1684. From these serene.
11. 1685. Why are all the muses mute ?
12. 1686. Ye tuneful Muses.
13. 1687. Sound the Trumpet.
14. 1689. Now does the glorious day appear (Queen Mary's Birthday).
15. 1689. Celestial Music.
16. 1690. Arise my Muse (Queen Mary's Birthday).
17. 1690. Of old when Heroes (Yorkshire Feast Song).
18. 1691. Welcome, glorious morn (Queen Mary's Birthday).
19. 1692. Love's Goddess sure was blind (Queen Mary's Birthday)
20. 1692. Hail bright Cecilia (Ode on St. Cecilia's Day).
21. 1693. Celebrate this festival (Queen Mary's Birthday).
22. 1694. Great Parent, hail (Dublin Commemoration Ode).
23. 1694. Come, ye sons of Art (Queen Mary's Birthday).
24. 1695. Who can from joy refrain ? (Duke of Gloucester's Birthday).

#### Odes of uncertain date

25. If ever I more riches did desire (to words by Cowley).
26. Hark, Damon, hark.
27. Hark, how the wild musicians sing (words by Cowley).
28. How pleasant is this flowery plain (words by Cowley).
29. We reap all the pleasures (words by Cowley).

#### INCIDENTAL MUSIC TO PLAYS, 'OPERAS,' ETC.

1680. Theodosius, and The Virtuous Wife.
1681. King Richard the Second, and Sir Barnaby Whigg.
1682 ? The Double Marriage.
1683 ? The English Lawyer.
1685 ? Circe, and Sophonisba.
1686. The Knight of Malta.

1688. The Fool's Preferment.
1688–90 ? Dido and Aeneas.
1690. Dioclesian, Distressed Innocence, Pausanias, Sir Anthony Love, Amphitryon, and The Massacre of Paris.
1691. King Arthur, The Gordian Knot untied, The Indian Emperor, The Wives' Excuse.
1692. Cleomenes, The Fairy Queen, The Marriage-Hater Match'd, Regulus, The Libertine, Henry the Second, Aureng-Zebe, and Oedipus.
1693. The Old Bachelor, The Richmond Heiress, The Maid's Last Prayer, The Female Vertuosoes, The Double Dealer, Epsom Wells, and Rule a Wife and Have a Wife.
1694. Don Quixote part i., Love Triumphant, The Married Beau, The Fatal Marriage, Canterbury Guests, Don Quixote part ii., Timon of Athens, The Spanish Friar, and (?) Tyrannick Love.
1695. Abdelazer, Bonduca, The Indian Queen, The Mock Marriage, The Rival Sisters, Oroonoko, The Tempest, and Don Quixote part iii.

SONGS, DUETS, TRIOS AND CATCHES (upwards of 200)

It is at present impossible to catalogue these, as in many cases such questions as authenticity, sources, etc., have yet to be settled. The Purcell Society's publications will eventually contain the complete works in these forms.

INSTRUMENTAL MUSIC

Fantasias in 3, 4, 5, 6, 7 and 8 parts. (B.M. Add. MS. 30,930.)
Twelve Sonatas of Three Parts, 1683.
Ten Sonatas of Four Parts, 1697.
Sonata for violin and bass, from a MS. formerly in the possession of Mr. Taphouse, printed in A. Moffat's ' Meisterschule.'
Overtures, etc.
Organ music : Four voluntaries (a) on the 100th Psalm Tune, (b) in D minor, (c) in D minor ' for the Double Organ,' and (d) in C, ascribed to Purcell.
Harpsichord Music : ' A Choice Collection c. Lessons for the Harpsichord or Spinnet,' 1696, contains eight suites, March, Trumpet Tune, Chacone, Jig and Trumpet Tune called the Cebell.
' Musick's Handmaid,' part ii., contains (1689) Song Tune, Lesson, March, three Minuets, a new Scotch Tune, a new Ground, a new Irish Tune (' Lilliburlero '), Rigadoon, Sefauchi's Farewell (' Sefauchi ' is for ' Sifaco ' ; see that article), Minuet.
From various sources : Air, Ground in Gamut, Lesson, Voluntary, A Verse, Trumpet Tune, Air, Rondo, Ground, Prelude, Air, Toccata,[1] Hornpipe, Almand, Corant, Air, Gavott, Minuet, Ground, Prelude, Almain and Borry, Overture, Air and Jig in G, Gamut b.

M.

## PURCELL CLUB, THE (1836–63), was

constituted at a meeting held in Aug. 1836 : the first members were Turle (conductor), King, Bellamy, Fitzwilliam, J. W. Hobbs and E. Hawkins (secretary). The club was limited to twenty professional and twenty non-professional members, who met twice a year ; on the second Thursday in February, when they dined together, and on the last Thursday in July, when they assembled in Westminster Abbey, at the morning service, by permission of the Dean, for the purpose of assisting in such Purcell music as might be selected for the occasion. On the evening of the same day the members again met to perform secular music composed by Purcell ; the soprano parts were sung by the chorister-boys from Westminster Abbey, the Chapel Royal, and St. Paul's Cathedral, but ladies were admitted amongst the audience.

On Feb. 27, 1842, a special meeting was held, when EDWARD TAYLOR (q.v.) was elected President, and the dates of meeting were changed to Jan. 30 and the first Thursday in July. Interesting performances of many of Purcell's works were given year by year, and a book of words of 194 pages was privately printed for the use of the members, under the editorship of Taylor. The Club was dissolved in 1863, and the valuable library, which had been acquired by gift and purchase, was deposited at Westminster Abbey, under the guardianship of the organists of Westminster Abbey and St. Paul's Cathedral.    W. H. C.

[1] This Toccata was printed from a MS. formerly in the possession of Fr. Knuth, and Wm. Rust, as a doubtful work of J. S. Bach in the B.-G. edition, vol. xlii. p. 250.

PURCELL COMMEMORATION. (1) The bicentenary of Henry Purcell's birth was commemorated in London on Jan. 30, 1858. The members of the PURCELL CLUB (q.v.) and a large number of musicians and amateurs assembled in the evening at the Albion Tavern, Aldersgate Street, London, when, after a banquet, a selection of Purcell music was performed, and addresses were given by Edward TAYLOR (q.v.), who presided. The programme consisted entirely of music composed by Purcell, and was as follows : Grace, ' Gloria Patri ' ; anthems, ' O give thanks,' ' O God, thou hast cast us out,' ' O sing unto the Lord ' ; song and chorus, ' Celebrate this festival ' ; a selection from ' King Arthur' ; cantata, 'Cupid, the slyest rogue alive ' ; song, ' Let the dreadful engines ' ; chorus, ' Soul of the world, inspired by thee.'

W. H. C.

(2) In Nov. 1895 the bicentenary of the composer's death was celebrated by a performance of ' Dido and Aeneas ' by the pupils of the R.C.M. at the Lyceum Theatre, Nov. 20 ; a special service in Westminster Abbey on Nov. 21, at which the following anthems were sung— ' O all ye people,' ' O give thanks,' ' Praise the Lord, O my soul,' ' Remember not, Lord,' ' O sing unto the Lord,' ' Thou knowest, Lord,' ' Praise the Lord, O Jerusalem ' ; and by a special concert of the Philharmonic Society in the Queen's Hall on Nov. 21, at which the 1692 ' Ode on St. Cecilia's Day ' was revived, and a miscellaneous programme gone through. At the preceding Leeds Festival an ' Invocation to Music,' by Parry, was produced, with special reference to the bicentenary, and at the following Birmingham Festival, in 1897, ' King Arthur ' was given.    M.

PURCELL OPERATIC SOCIETY, see SHAW, (2) MARTIN.

PURCELL SOCIETY, THE. Founded Feb. 21, 1876, ' for the purpose '—in the words of the prospectus—' of doing justice to the memory of Henry Purcell, firstly by the publication of his works, most of which exist only in MS., and secondly by meeting for the study and performance of his various compositions.' [2] The original committee consisted of the Rev. Sir F. A. G. Ouseley, Bart., G. A. Macfarren, Sir Herbert S. Oakeley, Sir John Goss, Sir George Elvey, Joseph Barnby, Joseph Bennett, J. F. Bridge, W. Chappell, W. H. Cummings, J. W. Davison, E. J. Hopkins, John Hullah, Henry Leslie, A. H. Littleton, Hon. Secretary, Walter Macfarren, Julian Marshall, E. Prout, E. F. Rimbault, Henry Smart, John Stainer, Rev. J. Troutbeck, James Turle.

The subscription is one guinea per volume. In 1887 the scheme, which had fallen into abeyance for some years, was reorganised, W. H. Cummings undertaking the duties of editor, and W. Barclay Squire becoming

[2] This part of the scheme was soon given up.

## LXIII

OPENING BARS OF PURCELL'S 'GOLDEN SONATA,' 1683.

BEGINNING OF A PRELUDE from Part II. of Johann Sebastian Bach's
'Das Wohltemperirte Klavier,' 1744.

British Museum                    *By permission of the Superintendent.*

PART OF A CONCERTO BY HANDEL, identical with the chorus 'And the Glory
of the Lord' (from 'Messiah,' 1741)

honorary secretary. In 1923 Gerald Cooper became honorary secretary.

The following volumes have appeared :

1. The Yorkshire Feast Song (1689), ed. Cummings. 1878.
2. The Masque in ' Timon of Athens,' ed. Sir F. A. Gore Ouseley (assumed date 1678, probable date 1694). 1882.
3. Dido and Aeneas, ed. Cummings (assumed date 1680, probable date 1688–89). 1889.
4. Duke of Gloucester's Birthday Ode. ' Who can from joy refrain ? ' ed. Cummings (1695). 1891.
5. Twelve ' Sonnata's of Three Parts ' (1683), ed. J. A. Fuller Maitland. 1893.
6. Harpsichord Music, ed. W. B. Squire, and Organ Music, ed. Dr. E. J. Hopkins. 1895.
7. Ten Sonatas of Four Parts (1697), ed. Sir C. V. Stanford. 1896.
8. Ode on St. Cecilia's Day, 1692, ed. J. A. Fuller Maitland. 1897.
9. Dioclesian (1690), ed. Sir J. F. Bridge and John Pointer. 1900.
10. Three Odes for St. Cecilia's Day. (' Welcome to all the pleasures,' 1683 ; ' Raise the Voice,' probably 1683, and ' Laudate Ceciliam,' 1683), ed. G. E. P. Arkwright. 1899.
11. Birthday Odes for Queen Mary, part i. (' Now does the glorious day appear,' 1689 ; ' Arise, my muse,' 1690 ; ' Welcome, welcome, glorious morn,' 1691), ed. Arkwright. 1902.
12. The Fairy Queen, ed. J. S. Shedlock. 1903.
13 (a). Sacred Music, Part I. Eight Anthems. Two Funeral Sentences: (1) ' In the midst of life,' (2) ' Thou knowest, Lord ' ; ' Who hath believed our report ? ' ; ' My beloved spake ' (earliest version) ; ' Behold now, praise the Lord ' ; ' Save me, O God ' ; ' Blessed is he whose unrighteousness' ; ' Hear me, O Lord ' (earliest version of opening verse, later version) ; ' Bow down thine ear,' ed. by G. E. P. Arkwright. 1921.
13 (b). Sacred Music, Part I. Early Anthems (not yet published, 1926).
14. Sacred Music, Part II. Anthems, ' It is a good thing,' ' O praise God in His holiness,' ' Awake, put on thy strength,' ' In Thee, O Lord,' ' The Lord is my light,' ' I was glad,' ' My heart s fixed,' ' Praise the Lord, O my soul,' ' Rejoice in the Lord alway,' ed. Wooldridge and Arkwright. 1904.
15. Welcome songs, Part I. ' Welcome, Vicegerent of the mighty King,' on his Majesty's return from Windsor, 1680 ; ' Swifter, Isis, swifter flow,' 1681 ; ' What shall be done on behalf of the man,' on the Duke of York's return from Scotland, 1682 ; ' The Summer's Absence unconcerned we bear,' for the King's return from Newmarket, 1682 ; ' Fly, bold Rebellion,' 1683, on the discovery of the Rye House Plot, ed. R. Vaughan Williams, 1905.
16. Dramatic Music, Part I. ' Abdelazar,' ' Amphitryon,' ' Aureng-Zebe,' ' Bonduca,' ' The Canterbury Guests,' ' Circe,' ' Cleomenes,' ' Distressed Innocence,' ' The Comical History of Don Quixote ' Parts I., II. and III., ' The Double Dealer,' ' The Double Marriage,' ' The English Lawyer,' ed. by Alan Gray. 1906.
17. Sacred Music, Part III. Anthems, ' Why do the heathen,' ' Unto Thee will I cry,' ' I will give thanks,' ' My heart is inditing,' ' O sing unto the Lord,' ' Praise the Lord, O Jerusalem,' ' Praise the Lord, O my soul,' ed. by H. E. Wooldridge and G. E. P. Arkwright. 1907.
18. Welcome Songs, Part II. ' From those serene and rapturous joys,' performed to His Majesty in 1684 ; ' Why, why are all the muses mute ? ' being the first song performed to King James II., 1685 ; ' Ye tuneful Muses,' 1686 ; ' Sound the trumpet,' 1687 ; ed. by R. Vaughan Williams. 1910.
19. The Indian Queen,' ' The Tempest,' ed. Edward J. Dent. 1912.
20. Dramatic Music, Part II. ' The Fatal Marriage'; ' The Female Vertuosos'; ' A Fool's Preferment'; ' The Gordian Knot untied' ; ' Henry the Second'; ' The Indian Emperor'; ' King Richard the Second'; ' The Knight of Malta'; ' The Libertine'; ' Love Triumphant'; ' The Maid's Last Prayer'; ' The Marriage-hater Match'd'; ' The Married Beau'; ' The Massacre of Paris'; ' The Mock Marriage,' ed. by Alan Gray. 1916.
21. Dramatic Music, Part III. ' Oedipus'; ' The Old Bachelor'; Oroonoko'; ' Pausanias'; ' Regulus'; ' The Richmond Heiress'; The Rival Sisters'; ' Rule a Wife and Have a Wife'; ' Sir Anthony Love'; ' Sir Barnaby Whigg'; ' Sophonisba'; ' The Spanish Friar'; ' Theodosius'; ' Tyrannick Love'; ' The Virtuous Wife'; ' The Wives' Excuse'; Music in an unidentified play, ed. by Alan Gray. 1917.
22. Catches and Rounds, ed. by W. Barclay Squire ; Two Part and Three Part Songs, ed. by J. A. Fuller Maitland. 1922.
23. Services. Morning and Evening in B♭ ; Evening in G mi. ; Te Deum and Jubilate in D (with accomp. for 2 trpts. and strings), ed. by Alan Gray. 1923.
24. Birthday Odes for Queen Mary, Part II. ' Love's Goddess sure ' (1692) ; Celebrate this festival (1693) ; ' Come ye sons of art ' (1694), ed. by Geoffrey Shaw. 1926.
The following volumes, still unpublished (1926), are expected to complete the series : Secular Songs and Cantatas (ed. by G. Shaw) ; Sacred Music (ed. by Alan Gray) ; Anthems (ed. by G. E. P. Arkwright) ; King Arthur (ed. by Dennis Arundell) ; Miscellaneous Odes and Choral pieces ; Miscellaneous Instrumental Music and Supplements.

PURDAY, a London family largely connected with music and music-publishing.

(1) PURDAY & BUTTON were the direct successors to the large firm of THOMPSON (q.v.) who had held business premises at 75 St. Paul's Churchyard from about 1750. Purday went into partnership with S. J. Button about 1805, but retired about 1808, when the firm took the name BUTTON & WHITAKER (q.v.). Purday was probably the father of (2) ZENAS TRIVETT

PURDAY who, taking over JOHN BLAND'S (q.v.) old shop, in succession to William Hodsoll, in 1831 established a large music trade, principally in numerous sheet songs. He ceased business about 1855–60.

(3) THOMAS EDWARD PURDAY, of the same family, was, from 1836 to after 1855, doing a similar trade in sheet songs in St. Paul's Churchyard.

(4) CHARLES HENRY PURDAY (b. Folkestone, Jan. 11, 1799 [1] ; d. London, Apr. 23, 1885), well known as a composer and a writer, was a lecturer on musical matters, and at one time a vocalist of some repute. He directed much energy to the amendment of the law in relation to musical copyright, and he acted for some time as conductor of psalmody to the Scotch Church in Crown Street, Covent Garden, composing and editing a number of works of sacred music. Some of his secular songs, and his fine tune to ' Lead, kindly light,' attained considerable popularity. He was a contributor to the first edition of this Dictionary.     F. K.

PURDIE, ROBERT, the founder of an extensive music-publishing business in Edinburgh. He is first heard of in 1804 as a music-teacher in Jollie's Close, Edinburgh, off the Canongate, but in 1805 he had removed to a better district, St. James's Square. In 1808 he opened a music shop at 35 Princes Street, and here he began the issue of sheet music. In 1813 the number of the premises changed to 71, and in 1828 it was again renumbered as 83.

He quickly became the leading music-publisher in the Scottish capital ; and besides a great deal of sheet music his imprint is on a well-known collection of Scottish songs, ' The Scotish Minstrel,' in six vols., edited by R. A. Smith, ' The Irish Minstrel,' and on similar works. On the failure of Nathaniel Gow, Purdie, in conjunction with Alexander Robertson, another Edinburgh publisher, reissued the Gow publications. Robert Purdie was succeeded near the year 1837 by his son John, and the business was carried on until about 1887.     F. K.

PURFLING, the inlaid line of plane wood, formed of three slips, of which the centre one is stained black, the two outer being left white, following the outlines of musical instruments of the violin and guitar type, which, owing to its utility in preserving the edges from chipping, is all that is left of the redundant ornamentation so skilfully employed by the ancient lute and viol makers. Some of the earlier makers, notably Jacobs of Amsterdam, purfled with whalebone, but the true artists used, and still use, the three strips sunk together into a carefully cut groove, and finished off when the glue is dry with a small gouge. ' Purfling ' may be bought ready made, i.e. the three strips ready glued together for inlaying, but this

[1] Brit. Mus. Biog.

strains and buckles at the sharper bends with deplorable results upon the ultimate effect. (See VIOLIN-MAKING.) Some of the lavish decoration, purfled and otherwise, of former times is to be seen on modern Italian guitars and mandolines. The great makers could not wholly resist these graceful adornings. Gasparo da Salò made a violin, we are told, of which the head, finger-board, tailpiece and bridge were carved by Benvenuto Cellini. Maggini strove to replace the ebony and ivory embellishments by purfled designs of elegant patterns, within the regula-tion line of purfling as we know it to-day. Amati made a couple of violins which were decorated at each corner and on the sides, at the blocks, with designs in black, of a *fleur-de-lys*, inlaid with precious stones, while other instruments, notably some of Andreas Amati, bear painted armorial bearings and inscriptions. Even Stradivarius himself ornamented some of his best violins with beautiful designs painted in black, or inlaid with ebony, and also, as in the case of the ' Rode ' (1722), with a double line of purfling, enclosing a diamond pattern in mother-of-pearl.

BIBL.—HILL, *Antonio Stradivari*; HART, *The Violin*; HERON-ALLEN, *Violin-making*; MEREDITH MORRIS, *British Violin-makers*; MAUGIN and MAIGNE, *Manuel du Luthier*.        E. H.-A.

PURITANI DI SCOZIA, I, opera in 2 acts; words by Count Pepoli, music by Bellini; pro-duced Théâtre des Italiens, Paris, Jan. 25, 1835; King's Theatre, as ' I Puritani ed i Cavalieri,' May 21, 1835; New York, Palmo's Opera House, Feb. 1844.        G.

PURITAN'S DAUGHTER, THE, opera in 3 acts; words by J. V. Bridgeman, music by Balfe. Produced Covent Garden, London, Nov. 30, 1861 (Pyne and Harrison).        G.

PUSCHMANN, ADAM ZACHARIAS (b. Görlitz, 1532; d. Breslau, Apr. 4, 1600), one of the most remarkable of the latest ' Meistersinger ' and a pupil of Hans Sachs. He wrote ' Gründ-licher Bericht des deutschen Meistergesanges ' (1574), containing some of his own songs. The MS. collection of his songs, containing also some by M. Behaim and Hans Sachs, was published in 1906 by Georg Münzer (*Riemann*).

PYE, KELLOW JOHN (b. Exeter, Feb. 9, 1812; d. Exmouth, Sept. 22, 1901 [1]), entered the R.A.M., in Feb. 1823, immediately after its foundation, and took the first pianoforte lesson ever given within its walls. This was from Cipriani Potter. He also studied harmony, counterpoint and composition there, under Dr. Crotch, the Principal, and remained a pupil till 1829. He returned in 1830 to Exeter, and for some years enjoyed considerable local fame in the south-west of England. In 1832 he gained the Gresham medal for his full anthem, ' Turn Thee again, O Lord ' (Novello), which with other anthems of his is in use in the Cathedrals. In 1842 he took the degree of Mus.B. at Oxford.

[1] *Mus. T.* 1901, p. 756.

He was a member of the Philharmonic Society from 1846, and in 1853 gave up the professional career, and went into business (in the firm of Plasket & Co., wine merchants) in London, where he retained his connexion with the art by joining the direction of the R.A.M., succeed-ing Sir G. Clerk as chairman of the committee of management (1864–67). He was also a mem-ber of the Executive and Finance Committees of the National Training School of Music; he joined the committee of the Bach Choir on its foundation in 1876, and was on the council of the R.C.M. from the beginning of that institu-tion in 1883. He was an active member of the Madrigal Society, its treasurer in 1856, and vice-president in 1891. Madrigals of his own gained the Society's prize in 1888 and 1891. He was on the committee of the Mendelssohn Scholar-ship Foundation. His published works, besides those mentioned, comprise ' Stray Leaves,' 12 Nos. (Lamborn Cock & Co.), 4 Full Anthems (Novello), 3 Short Full Anthems (Do.), Songs, etc.        G.

PYGOTT, RICHARD (late 15th and early 16th cent.), English choir trainer and composer. As early as 1517 he was master of the children of Cardinal Wolsey's Chapel. He thus held this post while William CORNYSHE (*q.v.*) was similarly employed at the Chapel Royal, and, like him, was much favoured by Royal prefer-ments and payments. Dean Pace, who suc-ceeded Colet as Dean of St. Paul's in 1519, in various letters to Wolsey, compliments the Cardinal on the excellence of his chapel, inti-mating that it was better than that of the King. He even quotes Cornyshe himself as extolling Pygott for his good training, and refers to ' his sure and cleanly singing . . . [and] . . . good and crafty discant.' In 1524 Pygott became a gentleman of the Chapel Royal, but kept his post in Wolsey's Chapel until the Cardinal's fall in 1529. During this period (as appears from a payment made to him in 1527) he was deputy master at the Royal Chapel. In 1532 he was given a corrody in the monastery of Coggeshall, Essex, and the next year was pre-sented to the canonry and prebend of Tam-worth. After the dissolution of the monas-teries, Pygott was granted a pension to be paid out of the confiscated property at Coggeshall (1538), and also received some further monies from the Abbey of Tower Hill. His name ap-pears regularly in the royal pensions list during 1540–47. On Oct. 31, 1541, he was given a sub-stantial sum for his house at Greenwich, and in 1545 was restored to his prebend at Tamworth, which he had apparently left because he was not in Orders (a royal letter instructs the Dean and Chapter of Wells ' to suffer Richard Pygot of the Chapel to reside upon his pre-bend there, notwithstanding his laity '). His name appears as a gentleman of the Chapel Royal in the last year of Henry VIII.'s reign

(1547), and two payments to him, in 1551 and 1552, show that Edward VI. still retained his services.[1]

He is mentioned by Morley in his *Plaine and Easie Introduction* (1597) as a 'Practicioner' in music. A 4-part Carol (' By-by ') by him is included in Wynkyn de Worde's Song-book, 1520, the only known copy of which is the bassus part in the British Museum.

Missa. 'Veni Sancte Spiritus.' PH.; B.M. Add. MSS. 34,191/4b. Tenor part only.
Carols, a 4. 'Qui petis, o filli'
'The moder full manerly' ⎫ B.M. Add. MSS
'I mene this by Mary' ⎬ 31,92ạ/112b.
'Musyng on her maners' ⎭
Motets. 'Gaude pastore.' B.M. Add. MSS. 34,191/23. Tenor part only.
'Salve Regina.' Harl. MSS. 1709/26. Medius part only.
J. M^K.

PYNE, LOUISA FANNY (*b.* Aug. 27, 1832; *d.* London, Mar. 20, 1904), daughter of George Pyne, alto singer (*b.* 1790; *d.* Mar. 15, 1877), and niece of James Kendrick Pyne, tenor singer (*d.* Sept. 23, 1857). She studied singing under Sir George Smart, and in 1842 appeared successfully in public with her elder sister, Susan (afterwards the wife of F. H. Standing, a baritone singer, known professionally as Celli). In 1847 the sisters performed in Paris. In Aug. 1849 Louisa made her first appearance on the stage at Boulogne as Amina in ' La Sonnambula.' On Oct. 1 following she began an engagement at the Princess's Theatre as Zerlina, in an English version of ' Don Juan.' Her first original part was Fanny in Macfarren's ' Charles the Second,' produced Oct. 27, 1849. On Mar. 1850 she sang at the Philharmonic ; was engaged the same year at Liverpool, and in 1851 at the Haymarket. On Aug. 14, 1851, she performed the

[1] See W. H. Grattan Flood, *Early Tudor Composers.*

Queen of Night in ' Il Flauto Magico ' at the Royal Italian Opera. She also sang in oratorios and at concerts.

In Aug. 1854 she embarked for America in company with her sister Susan, W. Harrison and Borrani. She performed in the principal cities of the United States for three seasons, being received everywhere with the greatest favour. On her return to England in 1856 she, in partnership with Harrison, formed a company for the performance of English operas, which they gave first at the Lyceum and afterwards at Drury Lane and Covent Garden Theatres, until 1864, when the partnership was dissolved. (See HARRISON, WILLIAM.) Miss Pyne subsequently appeared at Her Majesty's Theatre. In 1868 she was married to Frank Bodda, the baritone singer. She retired from public life, and devoted herself to teaching. Her voice was a soprano of beautiful quality and great compass and flexibility ; she sang with great taste and judgment, and excelled in the florid style, of which she was a perfect mistress. She received a pension from the Civil List in 1896.                              W. H. H.

PYROPHONE, see KASTNER (2).

PYSING (PISING), WILLIAM, 17th-century English composer of church music. A man of this name was a lay clerk of Canterbury Cathedral from 1635-83 (G. E. P. Arkwright, *Catalogue of Mus. in Ch. Ch.*). A verse anthem by Pysing, ' I will magnify thee,' is in Barnard's MS. collection (R.C.M. 1045-51), and is also in Tcnb.O.B./66b. Another verse anthem by him, ' The Lord heare thee,' is in Ch. Ch. 61-6.                              J. M^K.

# Q

QUADRILLE (Ger. *Kontretanz*), a dance executed by an equal number of couples drawn up in a square. The name (which is derived from the Ital. *squadra*) was originally not solely applied to dances, but was used to denote a small company or squadron of horsemen, from three to fifteen in number, magnificently mounted and caparisoned to take part in a tournament or carousal.[1] The name was next given to four, six, eight or twelve dancers, dressed alike, who danced in one or more companies in the elaborate French ballets[2] of the 18th century. The introduction of 'contredanses' into the ballet, which first took place in the fifth act of Rousseau's 'Fêtes de Polymnie' (1745), and the consequent popularity of these dances, are the origin of the dance which, at first known as the 'Quadrille de contredanses,' was soon abbreviated into 'quadrille.'

The quadrille was settled in its present shape at the beginning of the 19th century, and it has undergone but little change, save in the simplification of its steps. It was very popular in Paris during the Consulate and the first Empire, and after the fall of Napoleon was brought to England by Lady Jersey, who in 1815 danced it for the first time at Almack's[3] with Lady Harriet Butler, Lady Susan Ryde, Miss Montgomery, Count St. Aldegonde, Montgomery, Montague and Standish. The English took it up with the same eagerness which they displayed with regard to the polka in 1845, and the caricatures of the period abound with amusing illustrations of the quadrille mania. It became popular in Berlin in 1821.

The quadrille consists of five distinct parts, which bear the name of the 'contredanses' to which they owe their origin. No. 1 is 'Le Pantalon,' the name of which is derived from a song which began as follows :

> 'Le pantalon
> De Madelon
> N'a pas de fond,'

and was adapted to the dance. The music consists of 32 bars in 6–8 time. No. 2 is 'L'Été,' the name of a very difficult and graceful 'contredanse' popular in the year 1800 ; it consists of 32 bars in 2–4 time. No. 3 is 'La Poule' (32 bars in 6–8 time) which dates from the year 1802. For No. 4 (32 bars in 2–4 time) two figures are danced, 'La Trénise,' named after the celebrated dancer Trenitz, and 'La Pastourelle,' perhaps a survival of the old 'Pastorale.' No. 5 — 'Finale' — consists of three parts repeated four times. In all these figures (except the Finale, which sometimes ends with a coda) the dance begins at the ninth bar of the music, the first eight bars being repeated at the end by way of conclusion. The music of quadrilles is scarcely ever original ; operatic and popular tunes are strung together, and even the works of the great composers are sometimes made use of.[4] The quadrilles of Musard, with some by Strauss, are almost the only exceptions.    W. B. S.

The 'Quadrille des Lanciers' was invented in 1856 at Paris by the dancer Laborde. It is composed of five figures : 'les tiroirs,' 'les lignes,' 'les moulinets,' 'les visites,' 'les lanciers,' the latter giving its name to the whole quadrille. Each figure consists of 24 bars, except the third one with only 16.    M. L. P.

QUAGLIATI, PAOLO (b. *circa* 1560), was a musician living in Rome, who in 1608 is indicated as holding the position of organist at the Liberian Basilica of Santa Maria Maggiore. In 1585 he edited a collection of Spiritual Canzonets for three voices, containing, besides sixteen numbers by himself, some contributions by Marenzio, Nanino and Giovanelli. His other publications before 1600 consist of two books of Secular Canzonets *a* 3. Two Canzonets *a* 4 with cembalo and lute accompaniment appear in Verovio's collection of 1591, which has been republished complete by Alfred Wotquenne. After 1600 he appears to have followed with interest the twofold direction in music emanating from Florence and Venice respectively, the Florentine *stile rappresentativo* for solo voices, and the Venetian concerted style with basso continuo. In 1606 he composed an opera with libretto by his pupil Pietro della Valle, entitled 'Carro di fedeltà d'amore,' which was performed on a Carnival car in the streets of Rome. It has five solo voices, and was published in 1611, with the addition of several Arie *a* 1-3. His other works are a book of Concerted Madrigals *a* 4 for voices and instruments, with a separate book for Basso Continuo, some other books of Spiritual Madrigals *a* 1-3, and two books of Sacred Motets and Dialogues for two and three choirs in the concerted style with Basso Continuo (Rome, 1612–27). In Diruta's 'Il Transilvano' there appears a toccata by Quagliati for organ or clavier, which has been republished by L. Torchi in *L'arte musicale in Italia*, vol. iii.    J. R. M.

QUALITY. The characteristic feature by which the notes of the different instruments of the orchestra can be distinguished from each

1 Compare the use of the Spanish equivalent, *cuadrilla*, for the party of four *banderilleros* associated with each *torero* in a bull-fight, and the familiar name of a card-game once very popular.
2 The Ballets were divided into five acts, each act into three, six, nine, or twelve 'entrées,' and each 'entrée' was performed by one or more 'quadrilles' of dancers.
3 See Captain Gronow's *Reminiscences* (1861).

4 The clever 'Bologna Quadrilles' on themes from Rossini's Stabat Mater, were published shortly after the appearance of that work. The plates of these quadrilles were destroyed on the publishers learning the source from which the author (popularly supposed to be J. W. Davison) had obtained the melodies. Hans von Bülow wrote a set of quadrilles on airs from Berlioz's 'Benvenuto Cellini.'

other is called the quality of the notes. In popular language the word tone is commonly used with the same meaning. (See ACOUSTICS, subsection QUALITY.)          J. W. C.

QUANTITY, see METRE.

QUANTZ, JOHANN JOACHIM (*b.* Oberscheden, near Göttingen, Jan. 30, 1697 [1]; *d.* Potsdam, July 12, 1773), celebrated flute-player and composer. His father, a blacksmith, urged him on his death-bed (1707) to follow the same calling, but, in his own words, ' Providence, who disposes all for the best, soon pointed out a different path for my future.' From the age of 8 he had been in the habit of playing the double-bass with his elder brother at village fêtes, and judging from this that he had a talent for music, his uncle Justus Quantz, Stadtmusikus of Merseburg, offered to bring him up as a musician. He went to Merseburg in Aug. 1708,[2] but his uncle did not long survive his father, and Quantz passed under the care of the new Stadtmusikus, Fleischhack, who had married his predecessor's daughter. For the next five and a half years he studied various instruments, Kiesewetter being his master for the pianoforte. In Dec. 1713 he was released from his apprenticeship, and soon after became assistant, first to Knoll, Stadtmusikus of Radeberg, and then to Schalle of Pirna near Dresden. Here he studied Vivaldi's violin-concertos, and made the acquaintance of Heine, a musician in Dresden, with whom he went to live in Mar. 1716. He now had opportunities of hearing great artists, such as Pisendel, Veracini, Sylvius Weiss, Richter and Buffardin, the flute-player. In 1717 he went, during his three months' leave, to Vienna, and studied counterpoint with Zelenka, a pupil of Fux. In 1718 he entered the chapel of the King of Poland, which consisted of twelve players, and was stationed alternately in Warsaw and Dresden. His salary was 150 thalers, with free quarters in Warsaw, but finding no opportunity of distinguishing himself either on the oboe, the instrument for which he was engaged, or the violin, he took up the flute, studying it with Buffardin. In 1723 he went with Weiss to Prague, and the two played in Fux's opera ' Costanza e fortezza,' performed in honour of the coronation of Charles VI. Here also he heard Tartini. In 1724 Quantz accompanied Count Lagnasco to Italy, arriving in Rome on July 11, and going at once for lessons in counterpoint to Gasparini, whom he describes as a ' good-natured and honourable man.' In 1725 he went on to Naples, and there made the acquaintance of Scarlatti, Hasse, Mancini, Leo, Feo and other musicians of a similar stamp. In May 1726 we find him in Reggio and Parma, whence he travelled by Milan, Turin, Geneva and Lyons to Paris,

arriving on Aug. 15. In Paris—where his name was remembered [3] as ' Quouance '—he remained seven months, and occupied himself with contriving improvements in the flute, the most important being the addition of a second key, as described by himself in his *Versuch einer Anweisung die Flöte . . . zu spielen,* vol. iii. chap. 58 (Berlin, 1752). He was at length recalled to Dresden, but first visited London for three months. He arrived there on Mar. 20, 1727, when Handel was at the very summit of his operatic career, with Faustina, Cuzzoni, Castrucci, Senesino, Attilio and Tosi in his train. He returned to Dresden on July 23, 1727, and in the following March re-entered the chapel, and again devoted himself to the flute. During a visit to Berlin in 1728 the Crown Prince, afterwards Frederick the Great, was so charmed with his playing that he determined to learn the flute, and in future Quantz went twice a year to give him instruction. In 1741 his pupil, having succeeded to the throne, made him liberal offers if he would settle in Berlin, which he did, remaining till his death. He was Kammermusicus and court-composer, with a salary of 2000 thalers, an additional payment for each composition, and 100 ducats for each flute which he supplied. His chief duties were to conduct the private concerts at the Palace, in which the king played the flute, and to compose pieces for his royal pupil. He left in MS. 300 [4] concertos for one and two flutes—of which 277 are preserved in the Neue Palais at Potsdam—and 200 other pieces ; flute solos, and dozens of trios and quatuors, of which 51 are to be found at Dresden. His printed works are three—' Sei Sonate ' dedicated to Augustus III. of Poland, op. 1, Dresden, 1734 ; ' Sei duetti,' op. 2, Berlin, 1759 ; six sonatas for two flutes, op. 3, of doubtful authenticity, London, Walsh ; five sonatas for flutes, also op. 3, Paris, Boivin ; a Method [5] for the flute—*Versuch einer Anweisung die Flöte traversière zu spielen*— dedicated to Frederick ' Könige *in* Preussen,' Berlin, 1752, 4to, with twenty-four copper-plates. This passed through three (or four) German editions, and was also published in French and Dutch. He left also a serenata, a few songs, music to twenty-two of Gellert's hymns, ' Neue Kirchenmelodien,' etc. (Berlin, 1760), and an autobiography (in Marpurg's *Beiträge*). Three of the Melodien are given by von Winterfeld, *Evang. Kircheng.* iii. 272. Besides the key which he added to the flute, he invented the sliding top for tuning the instrument. His playing, which was unusually correct for the imperfect instruments of the day, delighted not only Frederick, but

[1] According to his autobiography in Marpurg's *Beiträge zur Aufnahme der Musik.*
[2] Not 1707, as Mendel states.
[3] In Boivin's *Catalogue.*
[4] But see *Q.-L.* p. 99, on this number.
[5] A new edition of the *Versuch,* by A. Schering, appeared at Leipzig in 1906. The work is much more than a Method for the flute, almost what we should now call a handbook of ' musical appreciation.' The pages devoted to the flute only number about an eighth of the whole work.

Marpurg, a more fastidious critic. He married, not happily, in 1737 ; and died in easy circumstances and generally respected.

All details regarding him may be found in *Leben und Werken*, etc., by his grandson Albert Quantz (Berlin, 1877).    F. G.

QUARENGHI, GUGLIELMO (*b.* Casalmaggiore, Oct. 22, 1826 ; *d.* Milan, Feb. 4, 1882), violoncellist and composer. He studied at the Milan Conservatoire, 1839–42, occupied the post of first violoncello at La Scala Theatre in 1850 ; became professor of his instrument at the Milan Conservatoire in 1851, and in 1879 maestro di capella at the Milan Cathedral. As a composer he contributed an opera entitled 'Il dì di Michel' ; published in 1863 some church music and transcriptions, as well as an interesting method for the violoncello ; a valuable treatise upon the origin of bow instruments precedes this *Metodo di violoncello* (Milan, 1876), in which he compares the earliest forms with the various barbaric and semi-barbaric instruments previously in use amongst primitive nations. In addition the author gives the 'Personaggi' of Monteverdi's 'Orfeo,' and the tuning of the earliest viols. (*Riemann* ; *Baker.*)    E. H.-A.

QUARLES, CHARLES, Mus.B. (*d.* York early in 1727), graduated at Cambridge in 1698. He was organist of Trinity College, Cambridge, from 1688–1709. He was appointed organist of York Minster, June 30, 1722. 'A Lesson' for the harpsichord by him was printed by Goodison about 1788.    W. H. H.

QUARTET (Fr. *quatuor* ; Ger. *Quartett* ; Ital. *quartetto*), a composition for four instruments or voices.

STRING QUARTET.—The leading instrumental quartet is that written for two violins, viola and violoncello, and down to the close of the 19th century it conformed in the main to the structure of the symphony or sonata. Indeed the development of the sonata form can be traced quite clearly in the string quartet. At first it concerned itself chiefly with melody played by the first violin and accompanied by the other instruments, but composers were not long in seeing the possibilities opened out by the establishment of a combination which possessed in its four members a similarity in tone-quality and an equally distributed flexibility in musical expression. Thus Haydn's quartets, even those written at Weinzirl known as op. 1, whether originally intended for quartet or string orchestra, show an increasing perception of how to distribute the interest of the writing and make each instrument in turn take a part of equal importance. Mozart's greater skill and feeling for polyphonic writing carried matters much further, while in the work of Beethoven the quartet reached the climax of the purely classical style. The 'romantic' period left its mark upon the quartet in the evident desire for in-

creasing the richness of the tone, and we find in the quartets of Schubert, Schumann, Mendelssohn and Brahms attempts to replace pure polyphony by massed tonal effects, the frequent use of double-stopping and the *tremolo* ; in fact the character of independent part-writing sometimes disappears, and the writing approaches that of the orchestra both in point of view and sound. Still more has the orchestral influence been noticeable in later developments where a far more extensive use of the various 'colour' effects of which the instruments are capable has been made. Eventually also other forms than the strict sonata form were taken up, as had already been done with the symphony and the orchestra, and we thus get quartets in one movement of the 'FANTASY' (*q.v.*) type, or short 'character' movements described as 'pictures,' 'sketches' and the like.

The main classical repertory is as follows : Haydn, 83, of which the very early examples were possibly intended for string orchestra ; Mozart, 26 ; Beethoven, 16, and Fugue, op. 133, originally intended as finale to op. 130 ; Schubert, 3 ; Schumann, 3 ; Mendelssohn, 6 ; Brahms, 3 ; Dvořák, 8 ; Tchaikovsky, 3 ; Glazounov, 6 ; Borodin, 2 ; Reger, 4 ; Stanford, 5 ; S. Taneiev, 5 ; Smetana, 2 ; Verdi, Franck, Grieg, Wolf and Debussy each left one. More recent quartets are those of Bartok, Bax, Bloch, Bridge, Busoni, Elgar, Gibbs, Hindemith, Holbrooke, Honegger, Jarnach, McEwen, Milhaud, Novák, Pfitzner, Pizzetti, Ravel, Respighi, Schönberg, Scott, Smyth, Suk, Taillefere, Tovey, Turina, Vaughan Williams, Gerrard Williams and Charles Wood.

PIANOFORTE QUARTET.—Next in importance to the quartet for strings alone is that for pianoforte and strings (violin, viola and violoncello). Having its origin in the accompanied sonatas for one or more stringed instruments, the combination was found with the development of the piano and of the technique of piano playing to possess valuable qualities for musical expression. Obviously the effects are of a different nature from those of the strings alone, and while there must always be a disadvantage in the association of a fixed-tone instrument with those whose tones are free, this is compensated for by the difference in quality and the harmonic support which the pianoforte supplies.

There are two pianoforte quartets of Mozart, four of Beethoven, three of which were early works and bear no opus-number, and Mendelssohn's opp. 1, 2 and 3, the combination practically coming into prominence with Schumann's op. 47 in E flat and the opp. 25, 26 and 60 of Brahms. There are also examples by Dvořák, 2 ; Fauré, 2 ; Holbrooke, Novák, Parry, Reger, Saint-Saëns, Stanford.

Other quartet combinations are of course possible, such as that of Mozart for oboe, violin, viola and violoncello. (See CHAMBER MUSIC.)

VOCAL QUARTETS are so called whether accompanied or not. Both types have been greatly exploited in oratorio, alone and in combination with chorus, while the ensemble of a quartet of protagonists in opera was a regular feature of the older schools wherein the composer was often called on to show his skill in portraying simultaneously four different lines of thought or types of characterisation. The self-existing vocal quartet, soprano, alto, tenor and bass, with or without accompaniment, has, if one excepts the madrigal, a curiously small repertory. In point of fact, many madrigals and partsongs are equally suitable for a small choir. Otherwise outstanding works of this class are the two sets of ' Liebeslieder-Walzer,' opp. 52 and 65, the ' Gypsy Songs,' op. 103, and quartets, opp. 64, 92 and 112, of Brahms, Schumann's ' Spanisches Liederspiel,' Henschel's 'Serbisches Liederspiel,' Fauré's 'Pavane' and 'Madrigal'; and from English writers there may be mentioned ' Six Pastorals ' and ' Nursery Rhymes ' (two sets) of H. Walford Davies, ' Songs of the River ' of T. F. Dunhill, songs from ' The Princess ' of Stanford and five songs from 'England's Helicon' of Ernest Walker.                                    N. C. G.

QUARTET ASSOCIATION, THE (1852–1855). A Society for the performance of chamber music, started in 1852 by Sainton, Cooper, Hill and Piatti, with such eminent artists as Sterndale Bennett, Mlle. Clauss, Mme. Pleyel, Arabella Goddard, Pauer, Hallé, etc., at the pianoforte. They gave six concerts each season at Willis's Rooms, but ended with the third season. The programmes were selected with much freedom, embracing English composers—Bennett, Ellerton, Loder, Macfarren, Mellon, etc.; foreign musicians then but seldom heard—Schumann, Cherubini, Hummel, etc., and Beethoven's posthumous quartets. The pieces were analysed by G. A. Macfarren.                                    G.

QUART-GEIGE, see VIOLINO PICCOLO.

QUART-POSAUNE, see TROMBONE.

QUASI, as if—i.e. an approach to. ' Andante quasi allegretto ' or ' Allegretto quasi vivace ' means a little quicker than the one and not so quick as the other—answering to poco allegretto, or più tosto allegro.          G.

QUATRE FILS AYMON, LES, opéracomique; words by Leuven and Brunswick, music by Balfe. Produced Opéra-Comique, Paris, July 15, 1844; Princess's Theatre, London, as ' The Castle of Aymon, or The Four Brothers,' in 3 acts, Nov. 20, 1844. G.

QUAVER (Fr. croche; Ger. Achtelnote, whence the American term, Eighth note; Ital. croma): half the value of a crotchet, and the eighth part of a semibreve. It is written, when single ♪, when joined ♫. Its rest is ♩.

QUEEN OF SHEBA, see KÖNIGIN VON SABA, DIE; REINE DE SABA, LA.

QUEEN'S HALL. This hall in Langham Place was built in 1893 by private enterprise and was opened to the public on Dec. 2 of that year, when a choral and orchestral concert was conducted by Cowen, the programme including Mendelssohn's ' Hymn of Praise.' The actual first concert, however, was that given on Nov. 27 by the Royal Amateur Orchestral Society conducted by George Mount, at which the Prince of Wales was present, the Duke of Edinburgh occupying his post as leader; a private view had been held on Nov. 25 with various musical performances, including those of the band of the Coldstream Guards. April 8, 1894, saw the first Sunday afternoon concert, an organ recital, while on Apr. 7, 1895, there took place the first Sunday evening orchestral concert, conducted by Randegger. In the following August the PROMENADE CONCERTS (q.v.) began (see also NEW QUEEN'S HALL ORCHESTRA), and in October the first regular series of Sunday afternoon orchestral concerts, which for two seasons were conducted by Randegger and subsequently by Henry Wood. These were continued regularly down to the autumn of 1924. It was in 1897 that the Sunday Concert Society was formed to undertake the responsibilities of these concerts and meet the objections raised by the London County Council regarding the profits over Sunday entertainments, the Sunday Musical Union taking its place in 1918; in this connexion it may be stated that about £3000 has been given to various philanthropic institutions, besides the endowment of a Musician's Bed at the Middlesex Hospital.

The main hall, for there are really two under the one roof, with its seating capacity of 2492 and central situation, became London's principal musical centre after the closing of the St. James's Hall in 1905. Intimately connected with Henry Wood and the New Queen's Hall Orchestra, it has been the scene of many important events, such as the three visits in 1896–97 of the Lamoureux Orchestra from Paris, Robert Newman's Musical Festivals, 1899, 1902, besides countless recitals and orchestral concerts given by the leading musicians of the day. It should be added that the small hall with a seating capacity of over 500 was formerly much used for recitals. The hall was designed by T. E. Knightley, structural features being the 17 exits into 3 streets and the fact that the grand circle is on the street level. The organ is by Hill. In Dec. 1902 Messrs. Chappell became lessees of the hall.                                    N. C. G.

QUEEN'S HALL ORCHESTRA, see NEW QUEEN'S HALL ORCHESTRA.

QUEEN SQUARE SELECT SOCIETY, see ALSAGER, Thos. Massa.

QUEISSER, CARL TRAUGOTT (b. Döben, near Leipzig, Jan. 11, 1800; d. Leipzig, June 12, 1846), a great trombone-player, born of poor parents. His turn for music showed itself early, and he soon mastered all the ordinary orchestral instruments. He ultimately confined himself to the viola, and to the trombone. In 1817 he was appointed to play the violin and trombone in the town orchestra, and by 1830 had worked his way into the other orchestras of Leipzig, including that of the Gewandhaus. He played the viola in Matthäi's well-known quartet for many years ; was one of the founders of the Leipzig ' Euterpe,' and led its orchestra for a long time ; and in short was one of the most prominent musical figures in Leipzig during its best period.

As a solo trombone-player he appeared frequently in the Gewandhaus Concerts, with concertos, concertinos, fantasias and variations, many of them composed expressly for him by C. G. Müller, F. David, Meyer, Kummer and others ; and the reports of these appearances rarely mention him without some term of pride or endearment. ' For fulness, purity and power of tone, lightness of lip, and extraordinary facility in passages,' says his biographer, ' he surpassed all the trombone players of Germany.' [1] There was a Leipzig story to the effect that at the first rehearsal of the 'Lobgesang,' Queisser led off the Introduction as follows : ·

to Mendelssohn's infinite amusement. *Se non è vero, è ben trovato.*

Queisser was well known throughout Germany, but never appears to have left his native country.                                    G.

QUERCU, Simon de (van Eijcken) (*b.* Brabant, late 15th cent.), cantor at the court of Milan. He accompanied Maximilian and Francesco Sforza, sons of the Duke, to Vienna, where he was still living in 1513, and brought out his *Opusculum musices*, etc., an essay on elementary musical theory for students, in 1509 (other editions, 1513, 1516, 1518) ; also *Vigiliae cum vesperis et exequiis mortuorum* (1513).                    E. v. d. s.

QUICK-STEP, see March.

QUILTER, Roger (*b.* Brighton, Nov. 1, 1877), composer, is known chiefly by his songs, graceful settings of English lyrics.

He was educated at Eton and studied composition at Frankfort with Iwan Knorr. He first made his mark with settings (voice and piano) of Shakespeare, particularly the songs from *Twelfth Night* and *As You Like It*, which beside showing a gift for vocal melody had a certain distinction of touch. He continued writing in the same *genre*, ranging in his choice of poets from the Elizabethans to Tennyson. The latter's ' Now sleeps the crimson petal ' is

among the most charming. Quilter has been fortunate in the fact that his work has appealed to such singers as Elwes (who produced his cycle, ' To Julia,' and many other songs), Plunket Greene and John Coates.

Several of his orchestral works, slight in quality but, like his songs, graceful and spontaneous, have been produced by Wood at Queen's Hall, and include a Serenade (1907), ' Three English Dances ' (small orchestra) and a ' Children's Overture ' based on tunes from Crane's book of nursery rhymes, *Baby's Opera*. Quilter wrote incidental music for the fairy play ' Where the Rainbow ends ' (Savoy, 1911), as well as for a production of *As You Like It* (1922). (For list, see *B.M.S. Ann.*, 1920).                                        c.

QUINAULT, Jean Baptiste Maurice (called Quinault l'Aîné) (*d.* Gien, 1744), dramatic composer, singer at the Théâtre-Français from 1712–18, afterwards actor at the Comédie Française until 1723. He composed ballets, divertissements, incidental music and songs for comedies, etc. His ballet, ' Les Amours des déesses,' was performed at the Opéra in 1728. His sister, Marie Anne, made her début at the Opéra in 1709, but afterwards became a member of the Comédie Française.                                  e. v. d. s.

QUINIBLE, see Quintoyer.

QUINT, an organ stop which causes the fifth above a given note to sound as well as the note belonging to the key which is pressed down. From the note and its fifth there arises a differential tone an octave below the note. By this mixture an organ with 16-ft. pipes can be made to sound as if with 32-ft. pipes ; that is the pitch of the lowest note, but with far less energy than if properly produced with a 32-ft. pipe.                            T. E.

QUINTA FALSA (False fifth). The forbidden interval between Mi in the Hexachordon durum, and Fa in the Hexachordon naturale— the diminished fifth of modern music. (See Mi contra Fa.)                          w. s. r.

QUINTE, the name given in France, during the 17th and part of the 18th centuries, to the now obsolete five-stringed tenor viol, and also to one of the members of the violin family, ' Quinte,' or ' taille de violon,' the modern so-called ' alto ' (English, viola). The origin of the word ' Quinte ' may be traced to the fact that its strings were tuned a fifth lower than those of the violin, or, more probably, it originated with the instrumental writing in 5 parts, then usual. When 4-part writing came into use, the word ' Quinte ' was retained, whilst ' taille,' became obsolete. The instrument retained its old name in France until the beginning of the 19th century, when it was replaced by the Italian ' alto.'

Five-stringed viols were amongst the earliest in use. Praetorius (*Organographia*, 1619) says hey were employed in ancient times, and Agricola (*Musica instrumentalis*, 1532) gives the tuning of the five-stringed viols then in vogue. Although composers of vocal music during the 16th century not infrequently called their tenor part ' Quinte ' or ' Quintus,' viols of that denomination remained under the title of tenor until a later period ; and probably the first instance where ' Quintus ' designates a musical instrument occurs in the overture to Monteverdi's ' Orfeo ' (Venice, 1609–13). *L'État de France*, in 1683, gives the name of ' Fossart,' who played the ' Quinte de violon ' in the Queen's band, and in 1712–13 the Paris opera orchestra included two ' Quintes ' amongst the instruments. In 1773 there were four ' Quintes ' amongst the musicians of the ' Grande Chapelle,' and ' Quintes ' were employed in all the orchestras. Jean-Jacques Rousseau (*Dictionnaire de musique*, Paris, 1708) gives a good deal of information concerning the ' Quinte.' Under ' Viole ' he says that in France the ' Quinte ' and the ' Taille ' (a large six-stringed tenor viol), contrary to the Italian custom, played the same part, and under ' Partie ' mentions that the ' Quinte ' and ' Taille ' were united under the name ' Viole.' The highest and lowest notes of these instruments, according to the same writer, were—

Quinte or Viola.       Taille.

from which it is to be inferred that the tuning was the same as that given by Agricola in 1532, *i.e.*

Alto and Tenor.

In England the two tenor viols which formed a part of the ' Chests of six Viols,' so much in vogue during the 17th and beginning of the 18th centuries, were probably identical with the ' Quinte ' and ' Taille ' ; but the French title was never adopted in this country. The bulky size of the ' Quinte ' rendered it such an awkward instrument to play upon that its dimensions gradually diminished from century to century, and when the violin came into more general use, it melted into the ' Haute Contre ' (alto viol). In the second half of the 18th century it developed into a tenor violin with four strings, and adopted the C clef on the third line which was formerly the clef of the ' Haute Contre' or alto viol. (See VIOL FAMILY.)

BIBL.—AGRICOLA (Martinus), *Musica instrumentalis* ; PRAETORIUS, *organographia* ; J.-J. ROUSSEAU, *Dictionnaire de musique* ; LA BORDE, *Essai sur la musique* ; LAURENT GRILLET, *Les Ancêtres du violon* ; HART, *The Violin.*      E. I.-A. ; addn. M. L. P.

QUINTET (Fr. *quintette* ; Ger. *Quintett* ; Ital. *quintetto*), a composition for five instruments or voices. The ideal instrumental quintet is that for strings alone. It generally consists of two violins, two violas and violoncello. As the tone of the violoncello is far more powerful than that of the viola, this combination is considered superior to that in which the numbers of viola and violoncello are reversed, as in the notable work of Schubert. A double-bass has been tried in the 34 quintets of Onslow ; here, however, one begins to get outside the domain of true chamber-music and to approach that of the small orchestra. Dvořák's op. 77 is for this combination. Beethoven left one quintet (two violas) and Brahms two. The quintets of Parry, Schillings and Vaughan Williams may also be mentioned.

The addition of the pianoforte to the string quartet dates from the ' romantics,' and the rich effect of combining two distinct tone-colourings, each one capable of harmonic independence, has been widely exploited since the famous example of Schumann appeared. This form of quintet is very popular, and many composers have written them. The list includes Bax, Brahms, Dohnányi, Dvořák, Elgar, Fauré, Franck, Goossens, Hindemith, Pfitzner, Reger, Scott, Stanford, Tovey and Turina. Schubert's ' Trout ' quintet is for piano, violin, viola, violoncello and double-bass.

Other combinations have been employed. There are quintets for clarinet and strings of Mozart, Brahms, Holbrooke, Howells, Reger and Weber, and one for horn and strings of Mozart ; Weingartner has written for clarinet, strings and pianoforte, and for two oboes, two violins and violoncello ; there are harp and strings quintets of Bax and Harrison, pianoforte strings and horn of Draeseke, pianoforte and wind of Beethoven (or for pianoforte and strings), Mozart, Rubinstein and Spohr, and for wind alone of Fibich and Hindemith. (See CHAMBER MUSIC.)

The addition of another part to the vocal quartet has a singularly rich effect, the nature of that part in opera necessarily depending upon the characters assembled at the moment where such an *ensemble* becomes possible. There are two quintets in Mozart's ' Die Zauberflöte,' for example, in which three women's voices are supported by a tenor and bass ; the same arrangement occurs in Spohr's ' Azor and Zemira,' while in Wagner's ' Die Meistersinger ' there are two tenors. Compare songs of four and five parts in the ENGLISH MADRIGAI SCHOOL.       N. C. G.

QUINTON, a five-stringed TREBLE VIOL. (See *PLATE LXXXVII.* No. 6 ; also VIOL, TREBLE 3.)

QUINTOYER (Old Eng. ' Quinible '), to sing in fifths—a French verb, in frequent use among extempore organisers during the Middle Ages. (See ORGANUM ; PART-WRITING.)     W. S. R.

QUINTUPLE TIME, the measure of five beats. As a rule quintuple time has two accents, one on the first beat of the bar, and the other on either the third or fourth, the bar being thus divided into two unequal parts, when it can be regarded as a compound of duple and triple, employed alternately.

Quintuple time produces an effect sufficiently characteristic and interesting to have induced various composers to make experiments therein, the earliest attempt of any importance being a symphony in the second act of Handel's 'Orlando' (1732), in which the hero's perturbation[1] is represented by this peculiar time. The same rhythm occurs in an air to the words 'Se la sorte mi condanna' in the opera of 'Ariadne' by Adolfati, written in 1750, and it is also found in the folk-music of many countries. Thus Reicha, in a note to No. 20 of his set of 36 fugues (each of which embodies some curious experiment in either tonality or rhythm), states that in a certain district of the Lower Rhine, named Kochersberg, the airs of most of the dances have a well-marked rhythm of five beats, and he gives as an example the following waltz :

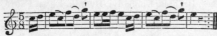

In the above example the second accent falls on the third beat, the rhythm being that of 2–8 followed by 3–8, and the same order is observed in a charming movement by Hiller, from the trio, op. 64.

In Reicha's fugue above referred to, the reverse is the case, the fourth beat receiving the accent, as is shown by the composer's own time-signature, as well as by his explicit directions as to performance. The following is the subject :

Instances of quintuple time in compositions of the early 19th century are to be found in a trio for strings by K. J. Bischoff, for which a prize was awarded by the Deutsche Tonhalle in 1853 ; in Chopin's sonata in C minor, op. 4 ; in Hiller's 'Rhythmische Studien,' op. 52 ; in 'Viens, gentille dame' ; in Boïeldieu's 'La Dame blanche'; Löwe's Ballad 'Prinz Eugen'; a number in Rubinstein's 'Tower of Babel,' etc.

Another characteristic example occurs in the 'Gypsies' Glee,' by W. Reeve (1796). This may fairly be considered an example of genuine quintuple rhythm, for instead of the usual division of the bar into two parts, such as might be expressed by alternate bars of 3–4 and 2–4, or 2–4 and 3–4, there are five distinct beats in

1 Burney, *History*, iv. 364, describes it as 'a division of time which can only be borne in such a situation'

every bar, each consisting of an accent and a non-accent. The same true quintuple time, as distinguished from a combination of triple and duple time, distinguishes the second movement of Tchaikovsky's 'Pathetic' symphony. The passage in the third act of 'Tristan und Isolde,' occurring at a most exciting moment in the drama, is apt to escape the attention of many hearers who are only conscious of the impatient effect it produces.

In the 20th century quintuple time has been so freely exploited as to have become almost a mannerism of the age. It may be said to have spread west over Europe since the Russian nationalists, who consciously based their style on folk-songs, were drawn to use it. In England, Gustav Holst has made a particularly extensive use of it.

F. T., rev. ; with addns. M. and C.

QUINTUS (the Fifth), the fifth part in a composition for five voices ; called also Pars quinta and Quincuplum. In music of the 15th and 16th centuries, the fifth part always corresponded exactly in compass with one of the other four ; it would, therefore, have been impossible to describe it as first or second cantu-altus, tenor or bassus.    W. S. R.

QUIRE, see CHOIR.

QUITTARD, HENRI (b. Clermont-Ferrand, Puy de Dôme, May 13, 1864 ; d. Paris, July 21, 1919), a French musical historian whose name stands high. A *licencié es lettres* at 24, he came to Paris, and, following the advice of E. Chabrier, studied music with C. Franck. He soon devoted himself to the history of music, and his first studies appeared in 1898. His special domain was the French musicians of the 16th and 17th centuries, but he investigated French musical history from the 13th century in a striking way. The lutenists of France were of great interest to him ; with M. Brenet he was one of the first to demonstrate their importance. His activity shows itself in the numerous articles published in the *Revue internationale de musique, Revue musicale, Tribune de St. Gervais*, publications of the International Musical Society, etc. For list see *Bulletin de la Société Française de Musicologie*, No. 5, Dec. 1919, obituary article by L. de La Laurencie. His last articles, *Notes sur Guillaume de Machaut et son œuvre*, were published in the *Bulletin* of the above-named Society (1918–19).

His few separate published works are : *Un Musicien en France au XVIIe siècle : Henri du Mont* (Paris, 1906, *Mercure du France*); *Mes-langes divers* on the same, and on G. Bouzignac. (Schola, Paris); *Le Trésor d'Orphée* of Antoine Francisque (lute transcription) (Paris *S.I.M.* editions). He left in preparation an important work on G. de Machaut, and an edition of harpsichord pieces by L. Couperin. His private collection of lute music, transcriptions, etc., which he himself built up, has been bequeathed to the Conservatoire Library. H. Quittard was lecturer at the École des Hautes Études Sociales, archivist at the Opéra, 1912 until his death, musical critic to *Le Matin*, and from 1909 to *Le Figaro*.     M. L. P.

QUODLIBET (Lat. 'What you please '), also called QUOTLIBET (' As many as you please '), and in Italian MESSANZA or MISTI-CHANZA (' A mixture '). This was a kind of musical joke in the 16th and early part of the 17th centuries, the fun of which consisted in the extempore juxtaposition of different melodies, whether sacred or secular, which were incongruous either in their musical character, or in the words with which they were associated; sometimes, however, the words were the same in all parts, but were sung in snatches and scraps, as in the quodlibets of Melchior Franck.[1] There were two ways of performing this : one was to string the melodies together simply and without any attempt at connecting them by passages such as those found in modern ' fantasias '; the other, the more elaborate method, consisted in singing or playing the melodies simultaneously, the only modifications allowed being those of time.

This pastime was a favourite one with the Bachs, at whose annual family gatherings the singing of quodlibets was a great feature.[2] Sebastian Bach himself has left us one delightful example of a written-down quodlibet, at the end of the ' 30 variations ' in G major, for a detailed analysis of which see Spitta. The two tunes used in it are ' Ich bin so lang bei dir nicht gewest,' and ' Kraut und Rüben, Haben mich vertrieben.' One of the best modern examples, although only two themes are used, is in Reinecke's variations for two pianos on a gavotte of Gluck's, where, in the last variation, he brings in simultaneously with the gavotte the well-known musette of Bach which occurs in the third ' English '

[1] See Praetorius, *Syntagma musicum*. tom. iii. cap. v.
[2] See Spitta, *J. S. Bach* (Engl. transl.), i. 154, iii. 172-6.

suite. A good instance, and one in which the extempore character is retained, is the singing of the three tunes ' Polly Hopkins,' ' Buy a Broom ' and ' The Merry Swiss Boy ' together, which was formerly sometimes done for a joke. A very interesting specimen of a 16th-century quodlibet by Johann Göldel, consisting of five chorale-tunes—viz. (1) ' Erhalt uns, Herr, bei deinem Wort,' (2) ' Ach Gott von Himmel,' (3) ' Vater unser im Himmelreich,' (4) ' Wir glauben all,' (5) ' Durch Adams Fall'—is given as an appendix to Hilgenfeldt's *Life of Bach*. We quote a few bars as an example of the ingenuity with which the five melodies are brought together :

M.

Parry's music to *The Clouds* of Aristophanes (see GREEK PLAYS, MUSIC TO) contains a brilliant modern example of the quodlibet, and his music of this kind makes liberal use of the principle without necessarily employing the name.     C.

# R

**RAAFF,** Anton (*b.* Holzem, near Bonn, 1714; *d.* Munich, May 27, 1797), one of the most distinguished tenors of his day ; educated for the priesthood at the Jesuit College at Cologne. His fine voice so struck the Elector, Clement Augustus, that he took him to Munich, where Ferrandini brought him forward in an opera. After studying for a short time with Bernacchi at Bologna, Raaff became one of the first tenors of his time. In 1738 he sang at Florence on the betrothal of Maria Theresa, and followed up this successful début at many of the Italian theatres. In 1742 he returned to Bonn, and sang at Vienna in Jommelli's ' Didone ' (1749), to Metastasio's great satisfaction. In 1752 he passed through Italy to Lisbon ; in 1755 he accepted a summons to Madrid, where he remained under Farinelli's direction, enjoying every favour from the court and public. In 1759 he accompanied Farinelli to Naples. In 1770 he entered the service of the Elector, Karl Theodor, at Mannheim. In 1778 he was in Paris with Mozart, and in 1779 he followed the court to Munich, where Mozart composed the part of Idomeneo for him. Mozart in his letters speaks of him as his ' best and dearest friend,' especially in one from Paris, dated June 12, 1778. He composed for him in Mannheim the air, ' Se al labbro mio non credi ' (Köchel, 295).     C. F. P.

**RABAN,** Edward (*d.* 1658), was an Englishman who, having fought in the wars of the Netherlands, from the year 1600, settled at Edinburgh, at the Cowgate Port, as a printer, in 1620. One work with the Edinburgh imprint alone remains, and in the same year he removed to St. Andrews, and finally to Aberdeen in 1622. In this place he was under the patronage of the town dignitaries, and had the friendship of Bishop Forbes. It was, presumably, these circumstances that enabled him to carry on his craft unmolested, unlike John Forbes of the same city who, at a later date, suffered fine and imprisonment for infringing the monopoly held by the King's printer in Scotland. Raban at once started the printing of liturgical works, including a prayer-book, dated 1625, which is stated to have the music to the Psalms. In 1629 he printed two editions of *CL. Psalmes of the princelie prophet David,* a quarto for binding with Bibles and a 16mo edition. Also, in 1633, two editions of *The Psames of David in prose and metre according to the Church of Scotland. . . . In Aberdene, imprinted by Edward Raban for David Melvill,* 1633, 8°. These have the music to the Psalms printed from movable type. Though probably not so well executed as the music of Andro Hart of Edinburgh, these are of great interest in the history of Scottish music-printing. Raban gave up business in 1649.     F. K.

**RACHMANINOV,** Sergeï Vassilievich (*b.* in the Government of Novgorod, Apr. 1-Mar. 20, O.S., 1873), distinguished pianist and one of the most talented of the Moscow school of composers. At 9 years of age he entered the St. Petersburg Conservatoire, where he remained three years, making the pianoforte his chief study. Three years later, in 1885, he was transferred to the Conservatoire at Moscow. Here he studied the pianoforte, first with Tchaikovsky's friend, Zvierev, and afterwards with Siloti. His masters for theory and composition were Taneiev and Arensky. The musical influences of Moscow are clearly evident in the works of Rachmaninov. In 1892 he won the gold medal for composition, and on quitting the Conservatoire, in the same year, started on a long concert tour through the chief towns of Russia. In 1899 Rachmaninov appeared in London at one of the concerts of the Philharmonic Society, and made a good impression in the threefold capacity of composer, conductor and pianist. In 1893 he was appointed professor of pianoforte to the Maryinsky Institute for Girls, in Moscow. From 1897-98 he directed the Private Opera in Moscow. His first symphony was given at a concert of the Royal Philharmonic Society, in May 1909, under Nikisch ; the second, in E minor, at the Leeds Festival, 1910, conducted by the composer. Since the Russian revolution he has spent much of his time in America, revisiting Europe for concert tours. Several of Rachmaninov's songs and pianoforte pieces, especially the famous prelude in C♯ minor, have attained immense popularity. His compositions are as follows :

### ORCHESTRAL

' The Rock,' fantasia, op. 7 ; Gipsy Capriccio, op. 12 ; Symphony No. 1, op. 13 (1895) ; No. 2, in E minor, op. 27 ; symphonic poem, ' The Isle of Death ' (after Böcklin), Promenade Concerts, Aug. 25, 1915.

### PIANOFORTE

Three Concertos, opp. 1, 18 and 30 ; two Suites, opp. 5 and 17 ; six pieces for four hands, op. 11 ; five pieces for two hands, op. 3 (including the C♯ minor prelude) ; seven pieces, op. 10 ; six Moments Musicaux, op. 16 ; variations on the theme of Chopin's Prelude in C minor, op. 22.

### CHAMBER MUSIC

Elegiac trio (in memory of Tchaikovsky) for pianoforte, violin and violoncello, op. 9 (1893) ; sonata for violoncello and pianoforte, op. 19 ; two pieces for violin and pianoforte, op. 6 ; two pieces for violoncello and pianoforte, op. 2.

### VOCAL

Six choruses for female voices, op. 15 ; humorous chorus for mixed voices ; cantata, ' Spring,' for chorus, baritone solo and orchestra, op. 20 ; six songs, op. 4 ; six ditto, op. 8 ; 12 ditto, op. 14 ; ' Fate ' (to Beethoven's Fifth Symphony), op. 17 ; ' The Bells ' (Edgar Allan Poe) for chorus and orchestra, Birmingham Fest. Choral Soc. 1921, Liverpool 1922, conducted by Sir Henry J. Wood.

### OPERATIC

' Aleko,' one act, Imp. Opera, Moscow, 1892 ; ' The Avaricious Knight,' Moscow ; ' Francesca da Rimini ' (1906) — both revived in Moscow, 1913.     R. N.

**RACKET,** Rackett or Rankett (Fr. *cervelat*) ; also known as sausage-bassoon, an obsolete instrument of small cylindrical bore, played with a double reed of the bassoon type.

It is described both by Praetorius and by Mersenne, and was made both of wood and ivory. The *apparent* length of the instrument was very small, as the bore doubled many times upon itself, the true length being thus disguised. In addition to the holes or ventages closed by the tips of the fingers in the usual way, the doubling of the tube allowed of the piercing of several holes which were closed by other joints of the fingers, or soft parts of the hand. According to Praetorius the rackets were made in families, the compass of a set of four extending from C to *d'*. (See *PLATE IV*. No. 3.)      D. J. B.

RADESCA DI FOGGIA, ENRICO, organist from *c.* 1605 of the cathedral, and a citizen of Turin, chamber musician in the ducal chapel there, of which he became the ' maestro ' in 1615. He composed a book of masses *a* 4 v., and 7 books of motets, madrigals, canzonets, etc. (list in *Q.-L.*).

RADFORD, ROBERT (*b.* Nottingham, May 13, 1874), bass singer. This versatile and capable artist, after his successful début at the Norwich Festival in 1899, secured and maintained a high position among contemporary British vocalists. He was trained chiefly at the R.A.M., where he studied under Alberto Randegger, Frederic King and Battison Haynes. Possessing a voice of rich and resonant quality with the timbre and compass of a genuine basso, he was able by combined intelligence and industry to make the most of his natural musical gifts ; and his progress, as he gained experience both in opera and in concert work, was proportionately rapid. He developed a sound and dignified oratorio style, and during many years was engaged as the leading English bass soloist at all the chief provincial festivals, the Handel Festivals, etc. At the same time his bent as a dramatic artist early marked him out for a career on the operatic stage. He made his first appearance at Covent Garden, on the opening night of the summer season of 1904, in the small but important rôle of the Commendatore in ' Don Giovanni,' Emmy Destinn making her début on the same occasion, with Hans Richter as conductor. He next took part in the English cycles of the ' Ring ' given in the winter of 1908 under the same distinguished conductor, filling with credit the parts of Fasolt and Hunding. This was really the start of his long and successful labours in connexion with opera sung in the vernacular, first under the Grand Opera Syndicate at Covent Garden, then under Sir Thomas Beecham at the same house, at Drury Lane, and His Majesty's ; and subsequently with the BRITISH NATIONAL OPERA COMPANY (*q.v.*), of which he was a founder and director from its inception in 1921. He added steadily to his repertory, and among the parts in which he became especially popular were, besides the

Wagnerian, those of Sarastro, Osmin, Mephistopheles, the Father in ' Louise,' and ' Boris Godounov.' Alike in the older and the more modern operas his excellent enunciation and diction stood him in good stead, and the same valuable quality lent a notable weight and impressiveness to his declamation in the part of Elijah and the oratorios of Handel and Haydn.      H. K.

RADICATI, FELICE ALESSANDRO (*b.* Turin, 1778 ; *d.* Vienna,[1] Apr. 14, 1823), violinist and composer. His parents belonging to the poor nobility of Italy, the child's singular interest in music was encouraged the more, and he began his studies at a very early age. Pugnani taught him the violin. Profiting by the precepts of this great master, Radicati acquired many of Pugnani's finer qualities, and, on reaching manhood, toured with unqualified success in Italy, France and England.[2] The love of his native land, however, and the additional inducement of a post at the court of King Victor Emanuel V., drew him back to Italy, whither he returned, accompanied by his accomplished wife, Teresa BERTINOTTI. In the year 1815 the town of Bologna announced a competition for the post of leader of the town orchestra—at that time celebrated ; but when it came to be known that Radicati had entered the lists, no one would contend against him ; with the result that he was elected to the post on Mar. 31, 1815, without contest. After this his talents obtained for him the appointments of director of the great orchestra of the Basilica di S. Pietro, and professor of the violin at the famous Liceo Filarmonico of Bologna. His career was calamitously cut short, in the prime of life, by a fatal carriage accident.

The authorities on the subject of Radicati's career give but few dates. According to *Q.-L.* he was in London 1806–07, and toured in Lombardy [3] in 1816. His principal biographer, Carlo Pancaldi—a Bolognese lawyer—wrote an eulogy in his memory, but unfortunately mentions but one date, that of his election at Padua on Mar. 31, 1815. As a violinist his qualities appear to have been those of a musician rather than those of a virtuoso. Pancaldi tells us that his style was dignified and his tone sonorous, that he counted Haydn, Beethoven and Romberg among his friends, and that he was well educated in other respects than music. As a composer he devoted himself especially to perfecting the quartet, which at that time—in spite of Boccherini's influence—was less thought of in Italy than in other countries. Besides his numerous contributions to chamber music, Radicati wrote six or seven operas, among which are included his ' Ricardo Cuor di Leone,' produced at Bologna ;

[1] *Q.-L.*
[2] He had a season of Italian Opera at Crow Street Theatre, Dublin, Aug.-Sept. 1911.      W. H. G. F.
[3] *Fétis.*

a couple of farces, 'I due prigionieri,' 'Il medico per forza'; a concerto for violin, and a number of small 'Arias,' 'Cavatinas,' etc. All these were in the possession of his son in 1828. The most complete list of his compositions—published and MS.—is probably that given in Q.-L. Radicati's wife and his son Karolus, who became a lawyer, erected a monument to his memory in the Campo Santo at Bologna.

BIBL.—CARLO PANCALDI, *Cenni intorno Felice Radicati*, Bologna, 1828; Q.-L.; Fétis; Baker. E. H.-A.

RADZIWILL, ANTON HEINRICH, Prince of, Royal Prussian 'Statthalter' of the Grand Duchy of Posen (b. Wilna, June 13, 1775; d. Berlin, Apr. 7, 1833), married in 1796 the Princess Luise, sister of that distinguished amateur, Prince Louis Ferdinand of Prussia. Radziwill was known in Berlin not only as an ardent admirer of good music, but as a fine violoncello player, and 'a singer of such taste and ability as is very rarely met with amongst amateurs.'[1] Beethoven was the great object of his admiration. He played his quartets with devotion, made a long journey to Prince Galitzin's on purpose to hear the Mass in D, was invited by Beethoven to subscribe to the publication of that work, and indeed was one of the seven who sent in their names in answer to that appeal. To him Beethoven dedicated the overture in C, op. 115 (known as 'Namensfeier'), which was published as 'Grosses Ouverture in C dur *gedichtet*,' etc., by Steiner of Vienna in 1825.

Radziwill was not only a player, a singer and a passionate lover of music, he was also a composer of no mean order. Whistling's *Handbuch* (1828) names three Romances for voice and PF. (Peters), and songs with guitar and violoncello (B. & H.), and Mendel mentions duets with PF. accompaniment, a 'Complaint of Maria Stuart,' with PF. and violoncello, and many partsongs (still in MS.) composed for Zelter's Liedertafel, of which he was an enthusiastic supporter.[2] But these were only preparations for his great work, entitled 'Compositions to Goethe's dramatic poem of Faust.' This, which was published in score and arrangement by Trautwein of Berlin in Nov. 1835, contains twenty-five numbers, occupying 589 pages. A portion was sung by the Singakademie as early as May 1, 1810; the choruses were performed in May 1816, three new scenes as late as Nov. 21, 1830, and the whole work was brought out by that institution after the death of the composer. The work was repeatedly performed during several years in Berlin, Danzig, Hanover, Leipzig, Prague and many other places.[3] It made its appearance in a performance at Hyde Park College,

[1] *A.M.Z.* 1831, July 27. See also 1809, June 28; 1814, Sept. 28.
[2] Zelter's *Correspondence with Goethe* teems with notices of the Prince.
[3] See Index to *A.M.Z.* For an analysis of the work see *A.M.Z.* 1836, pp. 601, 617.

London, on May 21, 1880, under the direction of L. Martin-Eiffe. G.

RAFF, JOSEPH JOACHIM (b. Lachen, Lake of Zurich, May 27, 1822; d. Frankfort, June 24/5, 1882), received his early education at Wiesenstetten in Würtemberg, in the home of his parents, and then at the Jesuit Lyceum of Schwyz, where he carried off the first prizes in German, Latin and mathematics. Want of means compelled him to give up his classical studies and become a schoolmaster, but he stuck to music, and, though unable to afford a teacher, made such progress not only with the piano and the violin, but also in composition, that Mendelssohn, to whom he sent some MSS., gave him in 1843 a recommendation to Breitkopf & Härtel, who published his early pianoforte pieces. Amidst privations which would have daunted any one of less determination he worked steadily on, and at length having fallen in with Liszt, was treated by him with the kindness which always marked his intercourse with rising or struggling talent, and was taken by him on a concert-tour. Meeting Mendelssohn for the first time at Cologne in 1846, and being afterwards invited by him to become his pupil at Leipzig, he left Liszt for that purpose. Before he could carry this project into effect, however, Mendelssohn died, and Raff remained at Cologne, occupying himself *inter alia* in writing critiques for Dehn's *Cäcilia*. Later, in 1854, he published *Die Wagnerfrage*, a pamphlet which excited considerable attention. Liszt's endeavours to secure him a patron in Vienna in the person of Mecchetti the publisher, were frustrated by Mecchetti's death while Raff was actually on the way to see him. Undismayed by these repeated obstacles he devoted himself to a severe course of study, partly at home and partly at Stuttgart, with the view to remedy the deficiencies of his early training. At Stuttgart he made the acquaintance of Bülow, who became deeply interested in him, and did him a great service by taking up his new Concertstück, for PF. and orchestra, and playing it (Jan. 1, 1848).

By degrees Raff attached himself more and more closely to the new German school, and in 1850 went to Weimar to be near Liszt. Here he remodelled an opera, 'König Alfred,' which he had composed in Stuttgart three years before, and it was produced at the court theatre, where it was often performed. Other works followed—a string quartet in 1855, and the first sonata for PF. and violin (E minor) in 1857. In the meantime he had engaged himself to Doris Genast, daughter of the well-known actor and manager, and herself on the stage; and in 1856 he followed her to Wiesbaden, where he was soon in great request as a pianoforte teacher. In 1858 he composed the incidental music for *Bernhard von Weimar*, a drama by Wilhelm Genast, the overture to which speedily became a favourite, and was much played throughout Germany. In 1859 he married. In 1863 his first symphony,[1] 'An das Vaterland,' obtained the prize offered by the Gesellschaft der Musikfreunde in Vienna. In 1870 his comic opera, 'Dame Kobold,' was produced at Weimar. Other operas for which he himself wrote the libretti have not been performed in public. In 1877 he was appointed with much éclat director of the Hoch Conservatorium at Frankfort, a post he held until his death. Since his death his music has passed, alike in Germany and England, into an oblivion which cannot excite surprise in those who realise the inherent weaknesses of the composer; and the sudden change on the part of the public, from a widespread admiration to almost complete neglect, is of itself a severe criticism on his work. A detailed analysis of the first six of his symphonies appeared in the *Monthly Musical Record* for 1875, and a good idea may be gathered therefrom of Raff's style.

A complete catalogue of Raff's works appeared in earlier editions of this Dictionary; the greater number of them are for pianoforte solo. The following are his more important compositions:

Sonatas for vln. and PF, opp. 73 (E minor), 78 (A), 128 (D), 129 (G minor), 'Chrom. Sonate in einem Satze,' 145 (C minor).
PF. Trios, opp. 102, 112 (G minor), 155, 158 (D).
String Quartets, opp. 77 (D minor), 90 (A), 136 (E minor), 137 (A minor), 138 (G), 192, No. 1 (C minor); No. 2 (D), 'Die schöne Mullerin'; No. 3 (C), in canon-form.
PF. Quartets, op. 202, Nos. 1 and 2.
PF. Quintet, op. 107 (A minor).
String Sextet, op. 178.
String Octet, op. 176.
PF. and orch., opp. 76, 'Ode au printemps'; op. 185, Concerto (C minor); op. 200, Suite (E flat).
Violin and orch., Suite, op. 180.
Concertos for vln., opp. 161 (B minor), and 206 (A minor).
Concerto for vcl., op. 193 (D minor).
Suites and Overtures, op. 101, Suite; op. 103, Jubilee Overture; op. 117, Festival Overture; op. 127, 'Ein' feste Burg' Overture; op. 204, Suite (B flat).
Symphonies, 'An das Vaterland,' op. 96; (C), op. 140; 'Im Walde,' op. 153; (G minor), op. 167; 'Lenore,' op. 177; 'Gelebt, gestrebt, gelitten, gestritten, gestorben, umworben (D minor), op. 189; 'In the Alps,' (B flat), op. 201; 'Frühlingsklänge' (A), op. 205; 'Im Sommer' (E minor), op. 208; 'Zur Herbstzeit,' op. 213; 'Der Winter,' op. 214 (left unfinished, and revised by Erdmannsdörfer).
Sinfonietta for wind instruments, op. 188.
Voices and orch., 'Wachet auf,' op. 80; Psalm 130, 'De profundis,' op. 141; 'Die Tageszeiten,' op. 209; 'Weltende—Gericht—neue Welt,' oratorio, op. 212.
Comic Opera, 'Dame Kobold,' op. 154.

F. G., rev. and abridged.

**RAG TIME.** A modern term, of American origin, signifying, in the first instance, broken rhythm in melody, especially a sort of continuous syncopation. 'Rag time tunes' is a name given to those airs which are usually associated with the so-called 'coon' songs or lyrics, which are supposed to depict negro life in modern America.　　　　　F. K.

**RAICK,** DIEUDONNÉ (*b.* Liège, 1702; *d.* Antwerp, Nov. 30, 1764), a vicar-choral of Notre Dame (Cathedral), after filling organist posts there as well as at Louvain and Ghent. He composed 12 suites and 3 sonatas for harpsi-

chord, 6 'petites suites' for harpsichord, flute or violin, and a number of harpsichord pieces.
　　　　　　　　　　E. v. d. s.

**RAIF,** OSKAR (*b.* Zwolle, Holland, July 31, 1847; *d.* Berlin, July 29, 1899), was a pupil of Tausig, and occupied a post as pianoforte teacher in the Royal Hochschule at Berlin, with the title of Königlicher Professor, from 1875 till his death.　　　　　H. V. H.

**RAIMONDI,** IGNAZIO (*b.* Naples, *c.* 1735; *d.* London, Jan. 14, 1813), Neapolitan violinist and composer. Judging by the fact that he went to Amsterdam in 1760, and there produced his first compositions, we may infer that he was born about 1735 or 1740. He died in London at his own house, 74 Great Portland Street. From 1762–80 he was director of concerts at Amsterdam, and produced his symphony entitled 'The Adventures of Telemachus.' From Amsterdam he went to Paris, where his opera, 'La Muette,' was performed, and about 1780 he came to London, where he received sufficient encouragement to induce him to' make it his permanent home. His compositions became very popular in England, particularly a symphony entitled 'The Battle' (1785). On June 1, 1791, he gave a benefit concert at the Hanover Square Rooms, at which he figured both as violinist and composer; he was assisted by Signor Pacchierotti, Madame Mara, Lord Mornington and Monsieur Dahmer.[2] The following year he gave a series of 12 subscription concerts at Willis's Rooms, and at these he both played solos and led the orchestra. Emanuele Barbella is said to have taught Raimondi the violin, but whether this be fact or no, we may infer from Dr. Burney[3] who calls Raimondi a 'worthy disciple' of Barbella, that this artist's technique was of the then greatly admired Tartini school. Raimondi's published compositions include two symphonies—besides the 'Telemachus' above mentioned, a number of quartets for two violins, viola and violoncello, two sets of six trios for two violins and violoncello, and some sonatas for two violins, violin and violoncello, and violin and viola.

BIBL.—BURNEY, *History of Music*; W. T. PARK, *Musical Memoirs*; *Fétis*; *Q.-L.*; *The Gentleman's Magazine*, Jan. 1813; *The Times*, May 14, 1800.　　　E. H.-A., with addns.

**RAIMONDI,** PIETRO (*b.* Rome, Dec. 20, 1786; *d.* there, Oct. 30, 1853), came of poor parents and at an early age passed six years in the Conservatorio of the Pietà de' Turchini at Naples. After many wanderings, mostly on foot—from Naples to Rome, from Rome to Florence, from Florence to Genoa—and many years, he at length found an opportunity of coming before the public with an opera entitled 'Le bizzarrie d' amore,' which was performed at Genoa in 1807. After three years there,

---

[1] The dates of composition of later symphonies are as follows: 2nd and 3rd, 1869; 4th, 1871; 5th, 1872. 6th, 1876; 7th, 1877; 8th, 1878; 9th, 1880.

[2] See *Morning Chronicle*, June 1, 1791.
[3] *History of Music*. vol. iii. 570.

each producing its opera, he passed a twelve-month at Florence, and brought out two more. The next twenty-five years were spent between Rome, Milan, Naples and Sicily, and each year had its full complement of operas and ballets. In 1824 he became director of the royal theatres at Naples, a position which he retained till 1832. In that year the brilliant success of his opera buffa, 'Il ventaglio' (Naples, 1831), procured him the post of professor of composition in the Conservatorio at Palermo. Here he was much esteemed, and trained several promising pupils. In Dec. 1852, he was called upon to succeed Basili as maestro di cappella at St. Peter's. Shortly before this, in 1848, he had after four years of toil completed three oratorios, 'Potiphar,' 'Pharaoh' and 'Jacob,' which were not only designed to be performed in the usual manner, but to be played all three in combination as one work, under the name of 'Joseph.' On Aug. 7, 1852, the new maestro brought out this work at the Teatro Argentina. The success of the three single oratorios was moderate, but when they were united on the following day—the three orchestras and the three troupes forming an *ensemble* of nearly 400 musicians—the excitement and applause of the spectators knew no bounds, and so great was his emotion that Raimondi fainted away.

The list of his works is astonishing, and embraces 62 operas; 21 grand ballets, composed for San Carlo between 1812 and 1828; 8 oratorios; 4 masses with full orchestra; 2 ditto with 2 choirs *a cappella*; 2 Requiems with full orchestra; 1 ditto for 8 and 16 voices; a Credo for 16 voices; the whole Book of Psalms, for 4, 5, 6, 7 and 8 voices; many Te Deums, Stabats, Misereres, Tantum ergos, psalms and litanies; two books of 90 *partimenti*, each on a separate bass, with three different accompaniments; a collection of figured basses with fugued accompaniments as a school of accompaniment; 4 fugues for 4 voices, each independent but capable of being united and sung together as a quadruple fugue in 16 parts; 6 fugues for 4 voices capable of combination into 1 fugue for 24 voices; a fugue for 16 choirs; 16 fugues for 4 voices; 24 fugues for 4, 5, 6, 7 and 8 voices, of which 4 and 5 separate fugues will combine into one. A fugue in 64 parts, for 16 four-part choirs, is said to exist. Besides the above feat with the three oratorios he composed an opera seria and an opera buffa which went equally well separately and in combination. Such stupendous labours are, as Fétis remarked, enough to give the reader the headache: what must they have done to the persevering artist who accomplished them? But they also give one the heartache at the thought of their utter futility. Raimondi's compositions, with all their ingenuity, belong to a past age, and we may safely say that they will never be revived.      G.

RAINFORTH, ELIZABETH (*b.* Nov. 23, 1814; *d.* Redland, Bristol, Sept. 22, 1877), studied singing under George Perry and T. Cooke, and acting under Mrs. Davison, the eminent comedienne. After having gained experience at minor concerts, she appeared upon the stage at the St. James's Theatre, Oct. 27, 1836, as Mandane, in Arne's 'Artaxerxes,' with complete success. She performed there for the remainder of the season, and then removed to the English Opera-House. Subsequently to her public appearance she took lessons from Crivelli. In 1837 she sang in oratorio at the Sacred Harmonic Society, and continued to do so for several years. She made her first appearance at the Philharmonic, Mar. 18, 1839. In 1840 she sang at the Antient Concerts, and in 1843 at the Birmingham Festival. After performing at Covent Garden from 1838–43 she transferred her services to Drury Lane, where she made a great hit by her performance of Arline, in Balfe's 'Bohemian Girl,' on its production, Nov. 27, 1843. In the previous year she had a most successful season in Dublin, and repeated her visits to Ireland in 1844 and 1849. She was engaged at the Worcester Festival of 1845, and in this year (Crosby Hall, London, Jan. 8) sang the soprano solo in Mendelssohn's 'Hear my prayer' at its first performance. She continued to perform in the metropolis until about 1852, when she removed to Edinburgh, where she remained until about 1856. She then retired, and in 1858 went to live at Old Windsor, and taught music in the neighbourhood until her complete retirement in Mar. 1871, when she removed to her father's at Bristol. Her voice was a high soprano, even and sweet in quality.     W. H. H.

RAISON, ANDRÉ, a late 17th-century organist at Ste- Geneviève and the Jacobin Church, Paris; one of the great French organmasters. He composed 'Livre d'orgue' (1687), republished by Guilmant; 'Offerte du 5e- ton,' addition to former (1688); 2nd book of 'Livre d'orgue' (1714).     E. V. D. S.

RALLENTANDO, RITARDANDO, RITENENTE, RITENUTO—'Becoming slow again,' 'Slackening,' 'Holding back,' 'Held back.' The first two of these words are used quite indifferently to express a gradual diminution of the rate of speed in a composition, and although the last is commonly used in exactly the same way, it seems originally and in a strict sense to have meant a uniform rate of slower time, so that the whole passage marked *ritenuto* would be taken at the same time, while each bar and each phrase in a passage marked *rallentando* would be a little slower than the one before it. That there exists a difference in their uses is conclusively proved by a passage in the quartet op. 131 of Beethoven, where in the 7th movement (allegro) a phrase of three recurring minims, which is repeated in all five times, has the direction 'Espressivo, poco ritenuto' for its first three appearances, which are separated by two bars *a tempo*, and for the last two times has *ritardando*, which at length leads into the real *a tempo*, of which the former separating fragments were but a presage. This is one of the very rare instances of the use of the word *ritenuto* by Beethoven. The conclusion from it is confirmed by a passage in Chopin's Rondo, op. 16, consisting of the four bars which immediately precede the entry of the second subject. Here the first two bars consist of a fragment of a preceding figure which is repeated, so that both these bars are exactly the same ; the last two bars, however, have a little chromatic cadence leading into the second subject. The direction over the first two bars is ' poco ritenuto,' and over the last two ' rallentando,' by which we may be quite sure that the composer intended the repeated fragment to be played at the same speed in each bar, and the chromatic cadence to be slackened gradually.

*Ritenente* is used by Beethoven in the PF. sonata, op. 110, about the middle of the first movement, and again in the sonata, op. 111, in the first movement, in the seventh and fifteenth bars from the beginning of the *allegro con brio*. It would seem that the same effect is intended as if ' ritenuto ' were employed ; in each case, the words ' meno mosso ' might have been used. Beethoven prefers *ritardando* to *rallentando,* which latter is common only in his earlier works.      M.

RAMANN, (1) LINA (*b.* Mainstockheim, near Kitzingen, Bavaria, June 24, 1833 ; *d.* Munich, Mar. 30, 1912), musical writer and educationist. It was not till her seventeenth year that she had any instruction in music. At that time her parents removed to Leipzig, and from 1850-53 she there enjoyed the advantage of pianoforte lessons from the wife of Dr. F. Brendel, herself formerly a scholar of Field's. From this period she adopted the career of a teacher of music, and studied assiduously, though without help, for that end. After a period of activity in America, she opened (in 1858) an institute in Glückstadt (Holstein) for the special training of music-mistresses, and maintained it till 1865, in which year she founded a more important establishment, the Music School at Nuremberg, in conjunction with Frau Ida Volkmann of Tilsit, and assisted by a staff of superior teachers, under Frl. Ramann's own superintendence. The school was transferred to Aug. Göllerich in 1890, when Frl. Ramann moved to Munich. She published two works—*Die Musik als Gegenstand der Erziehung* (Leipzig : Merseburger, 1868), and *Allgemeine Erzieh- und Unterrichtslehre der Jugend* (Leipzig : H. Schmidt, 1869 ; 2nd ed. 1873), which were both received with favour by the German press. From 1860 she was musical correspondent of the Hamburg *Jahreszeiten.*

A volume of her essays contributed to that paper has been collected and published, under the title of *Aus der Gegenwart* (Nuremberg : Schmid, 1868). In the early part of 1880 she published a study of Liszt's ' Christus '(Leipzig, Kahnt), and later in the year the first volume of a *Life of Liszt*,[1] completed in 1894 (Leipzig, Breitkopf). The first portion was translated by Mrs. S. H. Eddy, Chicago, and by Miss E. Cowdery, and published in two vols. in 1882. This is an important work. It suffers somewhat from over-enthusiasm, but it is done with great care, minuteness and intelligence, and obviously profited largely by direct information from Liszt himself. She also edited Liszt's writings (1880–83, in six volumes). Her cousin,

(2) BRUNO (*b.* Erfurt, Apr. 17, 1832 ; *d.* Dresden, Mar. 13, 1897), was brought up to commerce, but his desire and talent for music were so strong, that in 1857 or 1858 he succeeded in getting rid of his business and put himself under Dr. F. Brendel and Riedel for regular instruction. He then for five years studied under Hauptmann at Leipzig, and was a teacher and composer at Dresden from 1867 until his death. His works are numerous, but they consist almost entirely of songs for one or more voices, and of small and more or less sentimental pieces for the pianoforte. He also wrote poetry and some dramatic pieces. G.

RAMEAU, JEAN PHILIPPE (*b.* Dijon, Oct. 23, 1683 [2] ; *d.* Paris, Sept. 12, 1764), eminent composer and writer on the theory of music, born in the house of the former ' Cour de Saint-Vincent,' actually 5 and 7 rue Vaillant, and baptized in the Collegiate church of St. Étienne, Sept. 25, 1683. In this church his father, Jean [3] was organist. He held similar posts at the Cathedral, Sainte Bénigne and Notre-Dame, after the birth of his son. He intended Jean Philippe, the eldest of his three sons, to be a magistrate, but his strong vocation for music and obstinacy of character frustrated these views. According to his biographers he played the harpsichord at 7, and read at sight any piece of music put before him : music indeed absorbed him to such an extent when at the Jesuit College that he neglected his classical studies, and was altogether so refractory that his parents were requested to remove him. Henceforth he never opened a book, unless it were a musical treatise. He quickly mastered the harpsichord, and studied the organ and violin with success, but there was no master in Dijon capable of teaching him to write music, and he was left to discover for himself the laws of harmony and composition. At the age of 17 he fell in love with a young

---

[1] Vol. i., 1880 ; vol. ii. part i., 1887 ; vol. ii. part ii., 1894.
[2] The date of birth is taken from the composer's monument at Dijon : the first edition of this Dictionary gives the more usual date, Sept. 25, 1683.
[3] His mother's name was Claudine de Martinécourt.

widow in the neighbourhood, who indirectly did him good service, since the shame which he felt at the bad spelling of his letters drove him to write correctly. To break off this acquaintance his father sent him, in 1701, to Italy, where, however, he did not remain long, a mistake which, in after life, he regretted. He liked Milan, and indeed the attractions of such a centre of music must have been great. The story goes that he left with a theatrical manager whom he accompanied as first violin to Marseilles, Lyons, Nîmes, Montpellier and other places in the south of France. It is known that in 1702 he became temporary music-master at the Metropolitan church of Avignon, and in the same year he was organist at Clermont-Ferrand (until 1705). From his ' Premier Livre de pièces de clavecin ' (Paris, 1706) we learn that he was then living in Paris, at a wig-maker's in the Vieille Rue du Temple, as Haydn did at Keller's, though without the disastrous results which followed that connexion. Meantime he was organist of the Jesuit convent in the Rue St. Jacques, and of the chapel of the Pères de la Merci. Up to 1708 he remained in Paris, but took his father's place at Notre Dame, Dijon, from 1709–14, in which year he was nominated organist at the Jacobins, Lyons, till 1715, when he again started for Clermont-Ferrand, becoming cathedral organist there, and composing his *Traité de l' harmonie*. It has been stated that his brother Claude resigned the post of organist there in his favour, but this is incorrect, his brother being then at Dijon.[1] In this secluded mountain town, with a harsh climate predisposing to indoor life, he had plenty of time for thought and study. The defects of his education drove him to find out everything for himself. From the works of Descartes, Mersenne, Zarlino and Kircher he gained some general knowledge of the science of sound, and taking the equal division of the monochord as the starting-point of his system of harmony, soon conceived the possibility of placing the theory of music on a sound basis. Henceforth he devoted all his energies to drawing up his *Traité de l'harmonie*, and as soon as that important work was finished he determined to go to Paris and publish it. His engagement with the Chapter of Clermont had, however, several years to run, and there was great opposition to his leaving, owing to the popularity of his improvisations on the organ, in which his theoretical studies, far from hampering his ideas, seemed to give them greater freshness and fertility.

Once free he started immediately for Paris,

and brought out his *Traité de l'harmonie* (Ballard, 1722, 4to, 432 pp.).[2] The work did not at first attract much attention among French musicians, and yet, as Fétis observes, it laid the foundation for a philosophical science of harmony. Rameau's style is prolix and obscure, often calculated rather to repel than attract the reader, and the very boldness and novelty of his theories excited surprise and provoked criticism. His discovery of the law of inversion in chords was a stroke of genius, and led to very important results, although in founding his system of harmony on the sounds of the common chord, with the addition of thirds above or thirds below, he put both himself and others on a wrong track. In the application of his principle to all the chords he found himself compelled to give up all idea of tonality, since, on the principles of tonality he could not make the thirds for the discords fall on the notes that his system required. Fétis justly accuses him of having abandoned the tonal successions and resolutions prescribed in the old treatises on harmony, accompaniment and composition and the rules for connecting the chords based on the ear for a fixed order of generation, attractive from its apparent regularity, but with the serious inconvenience of leaving each chord disconnected from the rest.

Having rejected the received rules for the succession and resolution of chords which were contrary to his system, Rameau perceived the necessity of formulating new ones, and drew up a method for composing a fundamental bass for every species of music. The principles he laid down for forming a bass different from the real bass of the music, and for verifying the right use of the chords, are arbitrary, insufficient in a large number of cases and, as regards many of the successions, contrary to the judgment of the ear. Finally, he did not perceive that by using the chord of the 6-5-3 both as a fundamental chord and an inversion he destroyed his whole system, as in the former case it is impossible to derive it from the third above or below.[3] After more study, however, particularly on the subject of harmonics, Rameau gave up many of his earlier notions and corrected some of his most essential mistakes. The development and modification of his ideas may be seen by consulting his works, of which the following is a list : *Nouveau système de musique théorique . . . pour servir d'introduction au traité d'harmonie* (1726, 4to) ; *Génération harmonique*, etc. (1737, 8vo) ; *Démonstration du principe de l'harmonie* (1750, 8vo) ; *Nouvelles réflexions sur la démonstration du principe de l'harmonie* (1752, 8vo) ; *Extrait*

---

[1] His younger brother, Claude (b. Dijon ; d. Autun, May 20, 1761) a man of indomitable spirit, succeeded his father as organist at Dijon, and only left his native town in 1755, being engaged as organist at Autun Cathedral on Mar. 8, 1755 (*Bulletin de la Société française de Musicologie*, 1921, No. 8). His son Jean François, a gifted musician, but a dissipated man, is admirably portrayed by Diderot in his *Neveu de Rameau*. He published in 1766 a poem in five cantos called *Le Raméide*, followed in the same year by *La Nouvelle Raméide*, a parody by his schoolfellow Jacques Cazotte. He is mentioned by Mercier in his *Tableau de Paris*.

[2] The third part of this was translated into English fifteen years later with the title *A Treatise of Music containing the Principles of Composition*. London, no date, 8vo, 180 pp.

[3] Fétis has explained, detailed and refuted Rameau's system in his *Esquisse de l'histoire de l'harmonie*, which has been used by the writer, and to which he refers his readers.

*d'une réponse de M. Rameau à M. Euler sur
l'identité des octaves*, etc. (1753, 8vo)—all published in Paris. To these specific works, all
dealing with the science of harmony, should
be added the *Dissertation sur les différentes
méthodes d'accompagnement pour le clavecin ou
pour l'orgue* (Paris, Boivin, 1732, 4to), and
some articles which appeared in the *Mercure de
France* and in the *Mémoires de Trévoux*.

The mere titles of these works are a proof
of the research and invention which Rameau
brought to bear on the theory of music ; but
what was most remarkable in his case is that
he succeeded in lines which are generally opposed to each other, and throughout life
occupied the first rank not only as a theorist,
but as a player and composer.  Just when his
*Traité de l'harmonie* was beginning to attract
attention he arranged to make music for the
little pieces which his fellow-countryman, Alexis
Piron, was writing for the Théâtre de la Foire,
and accordingly, on Feb. 3, 1723, they produced 'L'Endriague,' in three acts, with dances,
divertissements and 'grand airs,' as stated in
the title. In Jan. 1724 he obtained the
privilege of publishing his cantatas and various
instrumental compositions, amongst others his
'Pièces de clavecin, avec une méthode pour la
mécanique des doigts,' etc., republished as
'Pièces de clavecin, avec une table pour les
agréments '[1] (Paris, 1731 and 1736, oblong
folio).

As a favourite music-master Rameau's
position and prospects now warranted his
taking a wife, and on Feb. 25, 1726, he was
united to Marie Louise Mangot, a good
musician, with a pretty voice.  The disparity
of their ages was considerable, the bride being
only 18, but her loving and gentle disposition
made the marriage a very happy one.

A few days later, on Feb. 29, Rameau produced at the Théâtre de la Foire a one-act
piece called ' L'Enrôlement d'Arlequin,' followed in the autumn by ' Le Faux Prodigue,'
two acts, both written by Piron.  Such small
comic pieces as these were obviously composed, by a man of his age and attainments (he
was now 42), solely with the view of gaining
access to a stage of higher rank, but there was
no hope of admission to the theatre of the
Académie without a good libretto, and this it
was as difficult for a beginner to obtain then
as it is now.  There is a remarkable letter,
still extant, from Rameau to Houdar de
Lamotte, dated Oct. 1727, asking him for a
lyric tragedy, and assuring him that he was no
novice, but one who had mastered the ' art of
concealing his art.'  The blind poet refused his
request, but aid came from another quarter.
La Popelinière, the *fermier général*, musician,
poet and artist, whose houses in Paris and at

Passy were frequented by the most celebrated
artists, French and foreign, had chosen Rameau
as his clavecinist and conductor of the music
at his fêtes, and before long placed at his disposal the organ in his chapel, his orchestra and
his theatre.  He did more, for through his
influence Rameau obtained from Voltaire the
lyric tragedy of ' Samson,' which he promptly
set to music, though the performance was prohibited on the eve of its representation at the
Académie—an exceptional stroke of ill-fortune.[2]

In 1727 a competition took place for the post
of organist at the church of St. Paul, and
Rameau was among the candidates. Marchand,
then at the head of the organists in Paris,
was naturally one of the examiners ; and either
from fear of being outshone by one whom he
had formerly patronised, or for some other
reason, he used his whole influence in favour of
Daquin, who obtained the post.

In 1732 Rameau was organist at Sainte-Croix
de la Bretonnerie and in 1736 at the church of
the Jesuits' College.  His first dramatic work
of importance, for which the Abbé Pellegrin
agreed to furnish a libretto, was ' Hippolyte et
Aricie,' founded on Racine's *Phèdre*.  The Abbé
compelled Rameau to sign a bill for 500 livres
as security in case the opera failed, but showed
more sagacity and more heart than might have
been expected from one

' Qui dînait de l'autel et soupait du théâtre,
  Le matin catholique et le soir idolâtre,'

for he was so delighted with the music on its
first performance at La Popelinière's that he
tore up the bill at the end of the first act.  The
world in general was less enthusiastic, and after
having overcome the ill-will or stupidity of
the performers, Rameau had to encounter the
astonishment of the crowd, the prejudices of
routine and the jealousy of his brother artists.
Campra alone recognised his genius, and it is to
his honour that when questioned by the Prince
de Conti on the subject he replied, ' There is
stuff enough in " Hippolyte et Aricie " for ten
operas ; this man will eclipse us all.'

The opera was produced at the Académie de
Musique on Oct. 1, 1733.  Rameau was then
turned 50 years of age, and the outcry with which
his work was greeted suggested to him that he
had possibly mistaken his career ; for a time he
contemplated retiring from the theatre, but was
reassured by seeing his hearers gradually accus-
toming themselves to the novelties which at
first shocked them.  The success of ' Les Indes
galantes ' (Aug. 23, 1735), of ' Castor et Pollux,'
his masterpiece (Oct. 24, 1737) and of ' Les
Fêtes d'Hébé ' (May 21, 1739), however,
neither disarmed his critics, nor prevented
Rousseau from making himself the mouthpiece
of those who cried up Lully at the expense of
the new composer.  But Rameau was too well

---

[1] Both Fétis and Pougin have fallen into the mistake of considering this a separate work.

[2] On the history of this work, see Hugues Imbert's *Symphonis*
(1891), and for a résumé of the facts, see *Mus. T.*, 1898, p. 279 ff.

**aware** of the cost of success to be hurt by epigrams, especially when he found that he could count both on the applause of the multitude and the genuine appreciation of the more enlightened.

His industry was immense, as the following list of his operas and ballets produced at the Académie de Musique in twenty years will show:

| | |
|---|---|
| Dardanus, five acts and prologue (Oct. 19, 1739). | Naïs, three acts and prologue (Apr. 22, 1749). |
| Les Fêtes de Polymnie, three acts and prologue (Oct. 12, 1745). | Zoroastre, five acts (Dec. 5, 1749). |
| Le Temple de la Gloire, Fête in three acts and prologue (Feb. 1745). | La Guirlande, ou les Fleurs enchantées, one act (Sept. 21, 1751). |
| Zaïs, four acts and prologue (Feb. 29, 1748). | Acante et Zéphise, three acts (Nov. 19, 1751). |
| Pygmalion, one act (Aug. 27, 1748). | Les Surprises de l'Amour, three acts (July 12, 1757). (First performed, Versailles, 1748.) |
| Les Fêtes de l'Hymen et de l'Amour, three acts and prologue (Mar. 15, 1747). | Les Paladins, three acts (Feb. 12, 1760). |
| Platée, three acts and prologue (Feb. 4, 1749). (First performed Versailles, Mar. 31, 1745.) | Nélée et Myrthis, pastorale in one act. |
| | Abaris, ou les Boréades, ' tragédie,' in five acts. |

Besides these, Rameau found time to write divertissements for ' Les Courses de Tempé,' a pastoral (Théâtre - Français, Aug. 1734), and ' La Rose ' (Théâtre de la Foire, Mar. 1744), both by Piron. From 1740–45 the director of the Opéra gave him no employment, and in this interval he published his ' Nouvelles Suites de pièces de clavecin ' and his ' Pièces de clavecin en concert avec un violon ou une flûte ' (1741), remarkable compositions which have been reprinted by Mme. Farrenc (' Le Trésor des pianistes ') and Poisot. He also accepted the post of conductor of the Opéra-Comique, of which Monnet[1] was manager, probably in the hope of attracting public attention and forcing the management of the Opéra to alter their treatment of him. Finally he composed for the Court ' Lysis et Délie,' ' Daphnis et Églé,' ' Les Sybarites ' (Oct. and Nov. 1753) ; ' La Naissance d'Osiris,' and ' Anacréon ' (Oct. 1754), all given at Fontainebleau. Some years previously, on the occasion of the marriage of the Dauphin with the Infanta, he had composed ' La Princesse de Navarre ' to a libretto of Voltaire (three acts and prologue, performed with great splendour at Versailles, Feb. 23, 1745). This was the most successful of all his *opéras de circonstance*, and the authors adapted from it ' Les Fêtes de Ramire,' a one-act opera-ballet, also performed at Versailles (Dec. 22, 1745).

In estimating Rameau's merits we cannot in justice compare him with the great Italian and German masters of the day, whose names and works were then equally unknown in France ; we must measure him with contemporary French composers for the stage. These writers had no idea of art beyond attempting a servile copy of Lully, with overtures, recitatives, vocal pieces and ballet airs, all cast in one sterotyped form. Rameau made use of such a variety of means as not only attracted the attention of his hearers, but retained it. For the placid and

[1] See Monnet's *Supplément au roman comique*, p. 51. This fact seems to have escaped all Rameau's biographers.

monotonous harmonies of the day, the trite modulation, insignificant accompaniments and stereotyped ritornelles, he substituted new forms, varied and piquant rhythms, ingenious harmonies, bold modulations and a richer and more effective orchestration. He even ventured on enharmonic changes, and instead of the time-honoured accompaniments with the strings in five parts and flutes and oboes in two, and with *tutti* in which the wind simply doubled the strings, he gave each instrument a distinct part of its own, and thus imparted life and colour to the whole. Without interrupting the other instruments, he introduced interesting and unexpected passages on the flutes, oboes and bassoons, and thus opened a path which has been followed up with ever-increasing success. He also gave importance to the orchestral pieces, introducing his operas with a well-constructed overture, instead of the meagre introduction of the period, in which the same phrases were repeated *ad nauseam*. (See ORCHESTRATION.) Nor did he neglect the chorus ; he developed it, added greatly to its musical interest and introduced the syllabic style with considerable effect. Lastly, his ballet-music was so new in its rhythms, and so fresh and pleasing in melody, that it was at once adopted and copied in the theatres of Italy and Germany.

We have said enough to prove that Rameau was a composer of real invention and originality. His declamation was not always so just as that of Lully ; his airs have not the same grace, and are occasionally marred by eccentricity and harshness and disfigured by roulades in doubtful taste ; but when inspired by his subject Rameau found appropriate expression for all sentiments, whether simple or pathetic, passionate, dramatic or heroic. His best operas contain beauties which defy the caprices of fashion and will command the respect of true artists for all time.

But if his music was so good, how is it that it never attained the same popularity as that of Lully ? In the first place, he took the wrong line on a most important point ; and in the second, he was less favoured by circumstances than his predecessor. It was his doctrine that for a musician of genius all subjects are equally good, and hence he contented himself with uninteresting fables written in wretched style, instead of taking pains, as Lully did, to secure pieces constructed with skill and well versified. He used to say that he could set the *Gazette de Hollande* to music. Thus he damaged his own fame, for a French audience will not listen even to good music unless it is founded on an interesting drama.

Much as Rameau would have gained by the co-operation of another Quinault, instead of having to employ Cahusac, there was another reason for the greater popularity of Lully,

Under Louis XIV. the King's patronage was quite sufficient to ensure the success of an artist ; but after the Regency, under Louis XV., other authorities asserted themselves, especially the 'philosophes.' Rameau had first to encounter the vehement opposition of the Lullists ; this he had succeeded in overcoming, when a company of Italian singers arrived in Paris, and at once obtained the attention of the public and the support of a powerful party. The partisans of French music rallied round Rameau, and the two factions carried on what is known as the 'Guerre des Bouffons,' but when the struggle was over, Rameau perceived that his victory was only an ephemeral one, and that his works would not maintain their position in the repertory of the Opéra beyond a few years. With a frankness very touching in a man of his gifts, he said one evening to the Abbé Arnaud, who had lately arrived in Paris, 'If I were twenty years younger I would go to Italy, and take Pergolesi for my model, abandon something of my harmony and devote myself to attaining truth of declamation, which should be the sole guide of musicians. But after sixty one cannot change ; experience points plainly enough the best course, but the mind refuses to obey.' No critic could have stated the truth more plainly. Rameau never attained complete skill in writing for the voice ; he is in consequence only the first French musician of his time, instead of taking his rank among the great composers of European fame. But for this, he might have effected that revolution in dramatic music which Gluck accomplished some years later.[1]

But even as it was, his life's work is one of which any man might have been proud ; and in old age he enjoyed privileges accorded only to talent of the first rank. The directors of the Opéra decreed him a pension ; his appearance in his box was the signal for a general burst of applause, and at the last performance of 'Dardanus' (Nov. 9, 1760) he received a perfect ovation from the audience. At Dijon the Académie elected him a member in 1761, and the authorities exempted himself and his family for ever from the municipal taxes. The King had named him composer of his chamber music in 1745 ; his patent of nobility was registered, and he was on the point of receiving the order of St. Michel, when, already suffering from the infirmities of age, he took typhoid fever and died.[2] All France mourned for him ; Paris

gave him a magnificent funeral, and in many other towns funeral services were held in his honour. Such marks of esteem are accorded only to the monarchs of art.

Having spoken of Rameau as a theorist and composer, we will now say a word about him as a man. If we are to believe Grimm and Diderot, he was hard, churlish and cruel, avaricious to a degree and the most ferocious of egotists. The evidence of these writers is, however, suspect ; both disliked French music, and Diderot, as the friend and *collaborateur* of d'Alembert, would naturally be opposed to the man who had had the audacity to declare war against the Encyclopedists.[3] It is right to say that, though he drew a vigorous and scathing portrait of the composer, he did not publish it.[4] As to the charge of avarice, Rameau may have been fond of money, but he supported his sister Catherine[5] during an illness of many years, and assisted more than one of his brother artists —such as Dauvergne and the organist Balbâtre. He was a vehement controversialist, and those whom he had offended would naturally say hard things of him. Tall, and thin almost to emaciation, his sharply marked features indicated great strength of character, while his eyes burned with the fire of genius. There was a decided resemblance between him and Voltaire, and painters have often placed their likenesses side by side. Amongst the best portraits of Rameau may be specified those of Benoit (after Restout), G. Dagoty, Masquelier and Carmontelle (full length) ; also a bust by J. J. Caffieri and a drawing of it engraved by Saint-Aubin.[6] (See *PLATE XLIV*.) In the fine oil-painting in the Museum of Dijon (in which it is difficult to recognise Rameau), and a work by Chardin,[7] he is represented seated, with his fingers on the strings of his violin, the instrument he generally used in composing. The bust which stood in the *foyer* of the Opéra was destroyed when the theatre was burnt down in 1781 ; that in the Paris Conservatoire is by Destreez (1865). A bronze statue by Guillaume was erected at Dijon in 1880.

Rameau had one son and two daughters, none of them musicians. He left in MS. four

---

[1] 'Rameau,' writes L. de La Laurencie, 'may be considered as one of the ancestors of the modern orchestra, and doubtless as one of the precursors of the symphony. Such pieces as the overtures to 'Zoroastre' and 'Naïs' rank him amongst those who opened the way to Haydn and Mozart. As for his dance airs, Diderot justly said of them, that they would last eternally. Above all, he is a great and profound musician, a complete artist ; and it cannot be imputed to him that in his time the only field of action opened to composers was operatic production.'
In France, the growing taste for old music and the development of its practice have gradually replaced Rameau in the position he deserves to occupy. The work of divulgation undertaken by the Schola Cantorum, and the modern publication of his music, have greatly contributed to this result.     M. L. P.
[2] In the Rue des Bons Enfants. He was buried at Saint-Eustache.

[3] Rameau was asked to correct the articles on music for the *Encyclopédie*, but the MSS. were not submitted to him. He published in consequence: *Erreurs sur la musique dans l'Encyclopédie* (1755) ; *Suite des Erreurs*, etc. (1756) ; *Réponse de M. Rameau à MM. les éditeurs de l'Encyclopédie sur leur Avertissement* (1757) ; *Lettre de M. d'Alembert à M. Rameau, concernant le corps sonore, avec la réponse de M. Rameau* (undated, but apparently 1759)—all printed in Paris. He also wrote other theoretical works : *Nouveau Système de musique théorique.* . . (1726) ; *Dissertation sur les différentes méthodes d'accompagnement pour le clavecin* (1732) ; *Génération harmonique ou traité de musique harmonique* . . . (1737) ; *Nouvelles Réflexions sur la démonstration au principe d'harmonie* . . . (1752), etc.
[4] We refer to Diderot's violent satire on the morals and philosophic tendencies of the 18th century, entitled *Le Neveu de Rameau.* It is a curious fact that this brilliantly written dialogue was only known in France through a re-translation of Goethe's German version. The first French edition, by Saur, appeared in Paris only in 1821.
[5] A good player on the harpsichord ; she lived in Dijon, and died there, 1762.
[6] Jal, *Dictionnaire critique de biographie et d'histoire* (2nd ed. Paris, 1872, p. 1037).
[7] *Revue de musicologie*, 1923, (pp. 175-6) ; and L. de La Laurencie, *L'École française de violon de Lulli à Viotti*.

cantatas, three motets with chorus and fragments of an opera ' Roland,' all which are now in the Bibliothèque Nationale. None of his organ pieces have survived ; and some cantatas, mentioned by the earlier biographers, besides two lyric tragedies, ' Abaris ' and ' Linus,' and a comic opera, ' Le Procureur dupé,' are lost ; but they would have added nothing to his fame.

See the March No., 1921, of the *Bulletin de la Société de Musicologie*, which contains several studies relative to the Rameau family.

G. C. ; rev. M. L. P.

#### PRINCIPAL REPRINTS

HARPSICHORD MUSIC—Farrenc, ' Trésor des pianistes ' ; Méreaux, ' Les Clavecinistes ' ; L. Diémer, ' Les Clavecinistes français ' ; Pauer, ' Alte Klaviermusik ' ; ' Alte Meister ' ; ' Œuvres complètes de Jean-Philippe Rameau,' published under the direction of C. Saint-Saëns (Paris, Durand), begun in 1894, reached its 18th vol. in 1924 (' Naïs,' revised by Reynalds Hahn). For a list of works published in this edition see *Encycl. de la Musique et Dictionnaire du Conservatoire : France XVIIe–XVIIIe siècles.*

#### BIBLIOGRAPHY

L. DE LA LAURENCIE, (1) *Rameau* (Paris, 1908) ; (2) *L'École française de violon de Lully à Viotti* (Paris, 1922–24) ; *Bulletin de la Société française de Musicologie* (1921) (articles by J. C. PROD'HOMME, L. DE LA LAURENCIE, TIERSOT) ; PIERRE LASSERRE, *L'Esprit de la musique française de Rameau à l'invasion wagnérienne* (Paris, 1817) ; PAUL-MARIE MASSON, *L'Opéra de Rameau* (in prep. 1826).

**RAMIN**, GÜNTHER (b. Carlsruhe, Oct. 15, 1898), organist and composer. At the age of 11 he entered the Thomasschule at Leipzig and in 1914 joined the Leipzig Conservatorium, where he studied the organ with Straube, piano with Teichmüller, theory and composition with Krehl. In 1918, when less than 20, he succeeded Straube as organist of the famous Thomaskirche at Leipzig, and in 1921 assumed the additional duties of organ-teacher at the Conservatorium. He is the most brilliant of Straube's many brilliant organ-pupils, and has already established a wide renown in Germany and other countries as one of the first organists of the day. His virtuosity is controlled by a fine taste and musicianship, and his gift of improvisation is in no way inferior to his remarkable powers of interpretation of the great masters. His compositions include organ pieces, a piano and violin sonata and a 4-part motet. Mention should also be made of his exquisite accompanying on the pianoforte, and of his skill as a choral conductor.

H. B.

**RAMIREZ DE ARELLANO**, ALONSO (18th cent.), Spanish composer, author of a ' Canon, Recte & Retro for 48 voices,' printed in London (by Welcker) in 1765. (B.M. ; Liceo, Bologna.)

J. B. T.

**RAMONDON**, LEWIS, presumably a Frenchman, and at first a singer in the pre-Handelian Italian operas in London. He appeared in ' Arsinoë,' 1705 ; in ' Camilla,' 1706 ; and ' Pyrrhus and Demetrius,' 1709. He sometimes took Leveridge's parts in these operas, but about 1711 he ceased to be a public singer, and turned his talents to composition. He brought out the series called ' The Lady's Entertainment ' in 1709, 1710, 1711 and 1738.

He arranged for the harpsichord the song-tunes in ' Camilla,' using, perhaps for the first time in music notation for this instrument, a five instead of a six-line stave, and giving as the reason—' that the lessons being placed on five lines renders them proper for a violin and a base.' His vocal compositions were in high favour, and half a dozen or so may be seen in Walsh's ' Merry Musician, or a Cure for the Spleen,' vol. i., 1716 ; others are on the single song sheet of the period. A tune of his, ' All you that must take a leap in the dark,' attained some degree of popularity by being sung by Hacheath in the ' Beggar's Opera.' It is probable that he died about 1720, as his name does not appear after that date.

F. K.

**RAMOS** (RAMIS) **DE PAREJA**, BARTOLOMÉ (b. Baeza, c. 1440 ; d. ? Rome, after 1491 ; perhaps in 1521), a learned Spanish musician, who first propounded the theory of equal temperament. He lectured in Salamanca and then removed to Bologna, where he resided from 1480–82. He was living in Rome in 1491. His *Musica practica* was published at Bologna in 1482 ; a Latin version of a (hypothetical) Spanish original, said to have been written at Salamanca. It has been reprinted by Joh. Wolf (*Beiheft* 2, I.M.G., 1901).

Spanish musicians consider that Ramos de Pareja arrived at the theory of equal temperament from observing the practice of players on the GUITAR and VIHUELA (q.v.), in which the scales are formed of equal semitones and the frets are placed a semitone apart.

That this was the custom in Spain not long after Ramos de Pareja is shown by Juan BERMUDO, who states in his *Declaracion de Instrumentos* (1st ed., 1549) that the frets must be placed so that from one to the other is a semitone, ' so that the semitone is formed of two frets, the tone of three.' Again, tuning (he says) is accomplished by getting two notes in unison on different strings, touching the lower string on the 5th fret while the upper one is sounded ' open '—as is the custom to-day. Clearly the system of tuning by equal semitones has been practised in Spain from very early times ; and Ramos de Pareja's theory, which caused such astonishment, may have been merely a generalisation from familiar practice in his own country. Two motets and a Magnificat by him were printed by Eslava.

J. B. T.

**RAMPOLLINI**, MATTIO, of Florence, where he contributed songs to the wedding festivities of the Duke in 1539. He composed a book of canzone, words by Petrarca, published by Jacque Moderne [1] ; also songs in various collective volumes (E. Vogel ; *Q.-L.*).

**RAMSEY**, ROBERT (1st half of 17th cent.), English organist and composer. He took his Mus.B. degree at Cambridge in 1616, and was

<hr>

[1] 1550 or 1560 ? (See *Q.-L.*)

required to compose a ' Canticum ' to be performed at St. Mary's Church. He was organist of Trinity College, Cambridge, 1628-44, and master of the children there, 1637-44.[1] B.M. Add. MSS. 11,608/26 contains a song by Ramsey, 'Wnat teares, deere Prince,' apparently written on the occasion of the death of Henry, Prince of Wales (1612). Three madrigals by him, ' Wilt thou, unkind, now leave me ' (a 6), ' O how fortunate they ' (a 5) and ' Since no desert can move thee,' are also in the British Museum (the first is Add. MSS. 17,786-91, and the treble, bassus and quintus parts of the 2nd and 3rd in Add. MSS. 29,366-8). The British Museum also contains (Harl. 7337) 3 canons, ' Hast thee, O Lord ' (3 in 1), ' Music devine ' (3 in 1) and ' She weepeth sore in yᵉ night ' (4 in 1), by Ramsey ; but Hilton elsewhere attributes the first to Thomas Ford, and the third to William Lawes. A dialogue between Saul, the witch of Endor, and ' Samuell's ghost,' beginning, ' In guiltie night ' (and later set by Purcell), was also set by Ramsey, and is in B.M. Add. MSS. 11,608/23b, score ; and Add. MSS. 29,396/113, single part and words only. Besides the following list the words of an anthem are given in Clifford's ' Collection ' (1663), while Davey (Hist. Eng. Mus.) refers to an autograph copy of some services and anthems at Anderson's College, Glasgow.

SERVICES, ETC.

Service ' of 4 parts ' (T.D. ; J. ; K. ; Gloria tibi ; M. ; N.D. ; L.), PII.
Whole Service in F. Harl. 7340/65. Score.
T.D. in A min. B.M. Add. MSS. 29,289/66. Altus part only.
Latin T.D. and J. PH.
Do. in F. PH.
Latin Litany in G. PH.

ANTHEMS

Hear my prayer. B.M. Add. MSS. 29,366-8. Cantus, bassus and quintus parts only.
I heard a voice. PH. 34/124. Incomp.
My song shall be alway. PH.
O come let us sing. Yk.
When David hard a 6. B.M. Add. MSS. 29,427/32b. Altus part only.
COLLECTS for Ascension Day, All Saints Day, Annunciation, Christmas Day, Easter Day, Purification, Trinity Sunday, Whitsunday. PH.

MOTETS

Inclina Domine. Yk.
O Sapientia. PH.           J. Mᴷ.

**RANDALL, John,** Mus.D. (b. 1715 ; d. Cambridge, Mar. 18, 1799), was a chorister of the Chapel Royal under Bernard Gates. He was one of the boys who shared in the representation of Handel's ' Esther ' at Gates's house, Feb. 23, 1732, he himself taking the part of Esther. He graduated as Mus.B. at Cambridge in 1744, his exercise being an anthem. In 1743 he was appointed organist of King's College, and on the death of Dr. Greene in 1755 was elected professor of music at Cambridge. In 1756 he proceeded Mus.D. He composed the music for Gray's Ode for the Installation of the Duke of Grafton as Chancellor of the University in July 1767, and some church

1 Davey, Hist. Eng. Mus., refers to him as holding this latter post in 1631.

music. He was organist of Trinity College in 1777. Two fine hymn tunes attributed to him are reprinted in the ' English Hymnal ' (Nos. 93 and 250).        w. H. H., addn.

**RANDALL, (1) P.,** a London music-seller and publisher, who had a shop at the sign of ' Ye Viol and Lute,' at Paul's Grave, without Temple Bar, in 1707, and for some years later. He may have been related, by marriage, to John Walsh, senior, the great music-publisher of this period. Before 1710 he was a partner with Walsh, and had abandoned his own place of business for Walsh's address in Katherine Street, Strand. His name, in conjunction with Walsh's, appears on many imprints of Walsh's publications. Later issues of these publications have Randall's name erased, and before 1720 his name entirely disappears from them.

(2) WILLIAM (d. circa 1780), is presumed to be a son of the preceding. At the death of John Walsh, junior, Jan. 15, 1766, William Randall succeeded to the extensive business in Katherine Street, and shortly afterwards was for a couple of years or less in partnership with a person named Abell. Randall & Abell issued in large folio in 1768 what is practically the first complete edition of the ' Messiah,' as well as some minor issues. Randall was in business alone in 1771, and besides reprinting the Walsh publications, he published many interesting works. One of these was a reissue in 1771 of Morley's Plaine and Easie Introduction. Collections of Vauxhall or other songs came forth, country dances, and the like. William Randall died about 1780, and his widow, Elizabeth, carried on the business until it was taken over, about 1783, by Wright & Wilkinson, who made a great business almost solely by reprinting Handel's works from the original plates.        F. K.

**RANDEGGER, ALBERTO** (b. Trieste, Apr. 13, 1832 ; d. London, Dec. 18, 1911), composer, conductor and singing-master. He began the study of music at the age of 13, under Lafont for the PF. and L. Ricci for composition, soon began to write, and by the year 1852 was known as the composer of several masses and smaller pieces of church music, and of two ballets, both produced at the Teatro Grande of his native town. In the latter year he joined three other of Ricci's pupils in the composition of a buffo opera to a libretto by Gaetano Rossi, entitled ' Il lazzarone,' which had much success, first at the Teatro Mauroner at Trieste, and then elsewhere. In the next two years he was occupied as musical director of theatres at Fiume, Zara, Sinigaglia, Brescia and Venice. In the winter of 1854 he brought out a tragic opera in four acts, called ' Bianca Capello,' at the chief theatre of Brescia. At this time he was induced to come to London, where he became widely known as a teacher of singing, conductor and composer. In 1864 he produced at the Theatre Royal, Leeds, 'The Rival Beauties,' a comic operetta in two acts. In 1868 he became professor of singing at the R.A.M., and was made an honorary member and director of that institution and a member of the Committee of Management. He was also a professor of singing at the R.C.M. and on the Board of Professors there. In the autumn of 1857 he conducted a series of Italian operas at St. James's Theatre; in 1879–85 for the Carl Rosa Company, and for Harris at Drury Lane and Covent Garden in 1887–98. He conducted the Queen's Hall Choral Society in 1895–97, and also the first two seasons of symphony concerts at Queen's Hall (*q.v.*); but his most important position of this kind was the conductorship of the Norwich Festival, which he held from 1881–1905 inclusive.

Randegger's published works comprise a dramatic cantata (words by Mme. Rudersdorff), entitled 'Fridolin,' composed for the Birmingham Festival, and produced there, Aug. 28, 1873; the 150th Psalm, for soprano, solo, chorus, orchestra and organ, for the Boston Festival, 1872; Funeral Anthem for the death of the Prince Consort; a scena, 'The Prayer of Nature,' sung by Edward Lloyd at a Philharmonic concert in 1887; and a large number of songs and concerted vocal music for voice and orchestra or PF. He wrote the *Primer of Singing* in Novello's series. (See the *Mus. T.* for 1899, p. 653 ff.)　　G., rev. with addns.

RANDHARTINGER, BENEDICT (*b.* Ruprechtshofen, Lower Austria, July 27, 1802; *d.* Vienna, Dec. 22, 1893), an Austrian musician, memorable for his connexion with Schubert. At 10 years old he came to the Convict school at Vienna, and was then a pupil of Salieri's. He afterwards studied for the law, and for ten years was secretary to Count Széchényi, an official about the court. But he forsook this line of life for music; in 1832 entered the court chapel as a tenor singer; in 1844 became vice-court-Kapellmeister, and in 1862, after Assmayer's death, entered on the full enjoyment of that dignity. His compositions are more then 600 in number, comprising an opera, 'König Enzio'; 20 masses; 60 motets; symphonies; quartets, etc.; 400 songs, 76 4-part songs, etc. Of all these, 124, chiefly songs, are published; also a volume of Greek national songs, and a volume of Greek liturgies.

His acquaintance with Schubert probably began at the Convict, and at Salieri's; though as he was Schubert's junior by five years, they can have been there together only for a short time; but there are many slight traces of the existence of a close friendship between them. He was present, for example, at the first trial of the D minor string quartet (Jan. 29, 1826), and he was one of the very few friends who visited Schubert in the terrible loneliness of his last illness. But for Randhartinger it is almost certain that Schubert's 'Schöne Müllerin' would never have existed. He was called out of his room while Schubert was paying him a visit, and on his return found that his friend had disappeared with a volume of Müller's poems which he had accidentally looked into while waiting, and had been so much interested in as to carry off. On his going the next day to reclaim the book, Schubert presented him with some of the now well-known songs, which he had composed during the night. This was in 1823. It is surely enough to entitle Randhartinger to a perpetual memory.

He had a brother JOSEF, of whom nothing is known beyond this—that he was probably one of the immediate entourage of Beethoven's coffin at the funeral. He, Lachner and Schubert are said to have gone together as torch-bearers (Kreissle von Hellborn's *Schubert*, p. 266).　　G.

RANDLES, ELIZABETH (*b.* Wrexham, Aug. 1, 1800; *d.* Liverpool, 1829), an extraordinary infant musical prodigy and performer on the pianoforte. She played in public before she was fully 2 years of age. Her father, a blind harper and organist of Wrexham, of some degree of local fame (1760–1820), placed her under John Parry the harper, and afterwards took her on tour to London, where she attracted much attention, and was made a pet of by the royal family. A second visit to London was undertaken in 1808, and a concert for her benefit given in the Hanover Square rooms. At this Madame Catalani and other singers and instrumentalists gave their gratuitous services, Sir George Smart conducting. She settled in Liverpool as a music teacher about 1818.　　F. K.

RANELAGH HOUSE AND GARDENS were situated on the bank of the Thames, eastward of Chelsea Hospital. They were erected and laid out about 1690 by Richard Jones, Viscount (afterwards Earl of) Ranelagh, who resided there until his death in 1712. In 1733 the property was sold in lots, and eventually the house and part of the gardens came into the hands of a number of persons who converted them into a place of public entertainment. In 1741 they began the erection of a spacious Rotunda (185 feet external, and 150 feet internal diameter), with four entrances through porticos. Surrounding it was an arcade, and over that a covered gallery, above which were the windows, sixty in number. In the centre of the interior and supporting the roof was a square erection containing the orchestra, as well as fireplaces of peculiar construction for warming the building in winter. Forty-seven boxes, each to contain eight persons, were placed round the building, and in these the company partook of tea and coffee. In the garden was a Chinese building, and a canal upon which the visitors were rowed about in boats. Ranelagh was opened with a public breakfast, Apr. 5, 1742. The admission was 2s. including breakfast. On May 24 following it was opened for evening concerts; Beard was the principal singer, Festing the leader, and the choruses were chiefly from oratorios. Twice a week ridottos were given, the tickets for which were £1 : 1s. each, including supper. Masquerades were shortly afterwards introduced, and the place soon became the favourite resort of the world of fashion. Ranelagh was afterwards opened about the end of Feb. for breakfasts, and on Easter Monday for the evening entertainments. On Apr. 10, 1746, a new organ by Byfield was opened at a public morning rehearsal of the music for the season, and Parry, the celebrated Welsh harper, appeared. In 1749, in honour of the Peace of Aix-la-Chapelle, an entertainment called ' A Jubilee Masquerade in the Venetian manner,' was given, of which Horace Walpole, in a letter to Sir Horace Mann, dated May 3, 1749, gives a lively description.

This proved so attractive that it was repeated several times in that and succeeding years, until the suppression of such entertainments in 1755. In 1751 morning concerts were given twice a week, Signora Frasi and Beard being the singers. At that date it had lost none of its charm. ' You cannot conceive,' says Mrs. Ellison, in Fielding's *Amelia*, ' what a sweet elegant delicious place it is. Paradise itself can hardly be equall to it.' In 1754 an entertainment of singing, recitation, etc. was given under the name of ' Comus's Court,' which was very successful. In 1755 a pastoral, the words from Shakespeare, the music by Arne, was produced; Beard and Miss Young were the singers; Handel's ' L' Allegro ed Il Pensieroso ' was introduced on Beard's benefit night, and Stanley was the organist. In 1759 Bonnell Thornton's burlesque ' Ode on St. Cecilia's Day ' was performed with great success. In 1762 Tenducci was the principal male singer. In 1764 a new orchestra was erected in one of the porticos of the rotunda, the original one being found inconvenient from its height. On June 29, 1764, Mozart, then 8 years old, performed on the harpsichord and organ several pieces of his own composition for the benefit of a charity. In 1770 Burney was the organist. Fireworks were occasionally exhibited, when the price of admission was raised to 5s. In 1777 the fashionable world played one of its strange, unreasoning freaks at Ranelagh. Walpole wrote on June 18 :

' It is the fashion now to go to Ranelagh two hours after it is over. You may not believe this, but it is literal. The music ends at ten, the company go at twelve.'

This practice caused the concert to be started at a later hour than before. In 1790 a representation of Mount Etna in eruption, with the Cyclops at work in the centre of the mountain, and the lava pouring down its side, was exhibited. The mountain was 80 feet high. In 1793 the Chevalier d'Éon fenced in public with a French professor, and about the same time regattas on the Thames in connexion with the place were established. In 1802 the Installation Ball of the Knights of the Bath was given at Ranelagh, and also a magnificent entertainment by the Spanish ambassador. These were the last occurrences of any importance ; the fortunes of the place had long been languishing, and it opened for the last time July 8, 1803. On Sept. 30, 1805, the proprietors gave directions for taking down the house and rotunda ; the furniture was soon after sold by auction, and the buildings removed. The organ was placed in Tetbury Church, Gloucestershire. No traces of Ranelagh remain ; the site now forms part of Chelsea Hospital garden.                    w. h. h.

**RANK.** A rank of organ-pipes is one complete series or set, of the same quality of tone and kind of construction from the largest to the smallest, controlled by one draw-stop, acting on one slider. If the combined movement of draw-stop and slider admits air to two or more such series of pipes, an organ-stop is said to be of two or more ranks, as the case may be. Occasionally the twelfth and fifteenth, or fifteenth and twenty-second, are thus united, forming a stop of two ranks ; but, as a rule, only those stops whose tones are reinforcements of some of the higher upper-partials of the ground-tone are made to consist of several ranks, such as the Sesquialtera, Mixture, Furniture, etc. These stops have usually from three to five ranks each, reinforcing (according to their special disposition) the ground-tone by the addition of its 17th, 19th, 22nd, 24th, 26th, 29th—that is, of its 3rd, 5th and 8th in the third and fourth octave above. (See Sesquialtera ; Mixture.)    j. s.

**RANSFORD**, (1) Edwin (*b.* Bourton-on-the-Water, Gloucestershire, Mar. 13, 1805 ; *d.* London, July 11, 1876), baritone singer, song-writer and composer. He first appeared on the stage as an ' extra ' in the opera-chorus at the King's Theatre, Haymarket, and was afterwards engaged in that of Covent Garden Theatre. During Charles Kemble's management of that theatre he made his first appearance as Don Caesar in ' The Castle of Andalusia,' on May 27, 1829, and was engaged soon afterwards by Arnold for the English Opera-House (now the Lyceum). In the autumn of 1829, and in 1830, he was at Covent Garden. In 1831 he played leading characters under Elliston at the Surrey Theatre, and became a general favourite. In 1832 he was with Joe Grimaldi at Sadler's Wells, playing Tom Truck, in Campbell's nautical drama ' The Battle of Trafalgar,' in which he made a great hit with

Neukomm's song 'The Sea.' At this theatre he sustained the part of Captain Cannonade in Barnett's opera 'The Pet of the Petticoats.' He afterwards fulfilled important engagements at Drury Lane, the Lyceum and Covent Garden. At Covent Garden he played the Doge of Venice in 'Othello,' Mar. 25, 1833, when Edmund Kean last appeared on the stage, and Sir Harry in *The School for Scandal* on Charles Kemble's last appearance as Charles Surface. His final theatrical engagement was with Macready at Covent Garden in 1837–38. He wrote the words of many songs, his best being perhaps 'In the days when we went gipsying.' In later years his entertainments, 'Gipsy Life,' 'Tales of the Sea' and 'Songs of Dibdin,' etc., became deservedly popular. As a genial *bon camarade* he was universally liked. He was also a music-seller and publisher, and during the 'forties and 'fifties issued a great number of the popular songs of the day. His shop was in Charles Street, Soho, but in 1850 he moved to 461 Oxford Street.

In 1869 he went into partnership with his son, (2) WILLIAM EDWIN (*d*. Sept. 21, 1890), at 2 Princes Street, Cavendish Square. The son, who continued the business after his father's death, was a tenor vocalist of ability.

w. h. ; addns. f. k.

RANTZAU, I, opera in 4 acts ; text by G. Targioni-Tazzetti and G. Menasci ; music by Mascagni. Produced Pergola, Florence, Nov. 10, 1892 ; Covent Garden, July 7, 1893.

RANZ DES VACHES (*Kuhreihen, Kuhreigen* ; Appenzell patois *Chüereiha*), a strain of an irregular description, which in some parts of Switzerland is sung or blown on the Alpine horn in June, to call the cattle from the valleys to the higher pastures. Several derivations have been suggested for the words *ranz* and *reihen* or *reigen*. *Ranz* has been translated by the English 'rant,' and the French 'rondeau,' and has been derived from the Gaelic root *riunce* or *raun*, which may also be the derivation of *reihen*, in which case both words would mean the 'procession or march of the cows.' Stalder (*Schweizerisches Idiotikon*) thinks that *reihen* means 'to reach,' or 'fetch,' while other authorities say that the word is the same as *reigen* (a dance accompanied by singing), and derive *ranz* from the Swiss patois 'ranner,' to rejoice.

The Ranz des Vaches are very numerous, and differ both in music and words in the different cantons. They are extremely irregular in character, full of long cadences and abrupt changes of tempo. It is a curious fact that they are seldom strictly in tune, more particularly when played on the Alpine horn, an instrument in which, like the BAGPIPE, the note represented by F is really an extra note between F and F♯. This note is very characteristic of the Ranz des

Vaches ; passages like the following being repeated and varied almost *ad infinitum*.

The most celebrated Ranz des Vaches is that of Appenzell, a copy of which is said to have been sent to our Queen Anne, with whom it was a great favourite. The first work in which it was printed is Georg Rhau's *Bicinia* (Wittenberg, 1545). It is also to be found in a dissertation on Nostalgia in Zwinger's *Fasciculus dissertationum medicarum* (Basle, 1710). Rousseau printed a version in his *Dictionnaire de musique*, which Laborde arranged for four voices in his *Essai sur la musique*.[2] It was used by Grétry in his overture to 'Guillaume Tell,' and by Adam in his *Méthode de piano du Conservatoire*. It has been also arranged by Webbe, Weigl, Rossini ('Guillaume Tell') and Meyerbeer.                    w. b. s.

RAOUL, JEAN MARIE (*b.* Paris, *c.* 1766 ; *d.* there, 1837), a government official and an excellent violoncellist. He composed sonatas, studies, solos and a tutor for the violoncello. Having acquired the famous *Duiffoprucgar* viola da gamba (now in Brussels Conservatoire Museum) he decided, *c.* 1810, to revive that instrument, and had a 7-stringed gamba of a modified model constructed by Vuilleaume, which figured in the exhibition of that year under the name of 'Heptacorde.' He contributed a *Notice sur l'heptacorde* to the *Annales de la littérature*, etc., which appeared also as a pamphlet.        e. v. d. s.

RAPPOLDI, EDUARD (*b.* Vienna, Feb. 21, 1831 ; *d.* Dresden, May 16, 1903), made his first appearance in his 7th year as violinist, pianist and composer. His talent for the pianoforte was so great as to induce the Countess Banffy to put him under Mittag, Thalberg's teacher. But the violin was the instrument of his choice, and he succeeded in studying it under Jansa, who induced him to go to London in 1850. Here he made no recorded appearance. On his return to Vienna he was so far provided for by the liberality of the same lady, that he became a pupil of the Conservatorium under Hellmesberger from 1851–54. He then put himself

[1] There is a curious analogy between the above and the following strain, which was sung with infinite variations in the agricultural districts near London to frighten away the birds from the seed. In both passages the F is more nearly F♯.

[2] Other examples and descriptions will be found in the following works : Cappeller's *Pilati Montis historia* (1757) ; Stolberg's *Reise in Deutschland, der Schweiz, etc.* (1794) ; Ebel's *Schilderung der Gebirgsvölker der Schweiz* (1798) ; Sigmund von Wagner's *Acht Schweizer Kuhreihen* (1805) ; the article on Viotti in the *Décade philosophique* (An 6) ; Castelnau's *Considérations sur la nostalgie* (1806) ; Edward Jones's *Musical Curiosities* (1811) ; *Recueil de ran des vaches et de chansons nationales suisses*, 3rd edition, Berne, 1818. also Tarenne's *Sammlung von Schweizer Kuhreihen und Volksliedern* (1818) ; Huber's *Recueil de ranz des vaches* (1830) ; and Tobler's *Appenzellischer Sprachschatz* (1837).

under Böhm, and shortly began to travel, and to be spoken of as a promising player. The first real step in his career was conducting a concert of Joachim's at Rotterdam in 1866, where he had been Konzertmeister since 1861. At the end of that year he went to Lübeck as Kapellmeister, in 1867 to Stettin in the same capacity, and in 1869 to the Landestheater at Prague. During this time he was working hard at the violin, and also studying composition with Sechter and Hiller. From 1871–77 he was a colleague of Joachim at the Hochschule at Berlin—where he proved himself a first-rate teacher—and became a member of the JOACHIM QUARTET (q.v.). In 1876 he was made Royal Professor, and in 1877 became joint Konzertmeister with Lauterbach at the Dresden opera, and chief teacher in the Conservatorium there. He retired in 1898, after which time he only taught a few favoured pupils. Though a virtuoso of the first rank, he followed in the footsteps of Joachim by sacrificing display to the finer interpretation of the music, and succeeded in infusing a new spirit into chamber music at Dresden. He composed symphonies, quartets, sonatas and songs, some of which have been printed. They are distinguished for earnestness, and for great beauty of form, and a quartet was performed in Dresden in the winter of 1878 which aroused quite an unusual sensation. In 1874 Rappoldi married Laura KAHRER (q.v.).     G.

RASELIUS, ANDREAS (b. Hahnbach, near Amberg, Upper Palatinate, between 1562 and 1564 ; d. Heidelberg, Jan. 6, 1602), son of a Lutheran preacher, who had studied at Wittenberg under Melanchthon, and whose original name, Rasel, Melanchthon latinised into Raselius. From 1581–84 Andreas attended the then Lutheran University of Heidelberg, taking his degree as Magister Artium in the latter year. In the same year he was appointed cantor and teacher at the Gymnasium of Ratisbon, then conducted under Lutheran auspices. In his capacity as cantor he published in 1589 a musical instruction book with the title *Hexachordum seu Quaestiones musicae practicae sex capitibus comprehensae*, which was still in use at Ratisbon in 1664. In 1599 appeared his 'Regenspurgischer Kirchen-Contrapunkt,' 'which contains simple settings a 5 of 51 of the older Lutheran psalm tunes and Chorals. The full title describes them as set so that the congregation may easily sing the Choral tune while the trained choir provide the harmonies. The Choral tune is in the upper part, but the harmonies are not always mere note-for-note counterpoint as in a modern hymn tune. A few specimens of these settings are given in Schöberlein's *Schatz*. Other published works of Raselius are ' Teutsche Sprüche aus den sonntäglichen Evangelia . . .,' 53 German motets a 5 (Nuremberg, 1594), and ' Neue Teutsche Sprüche auf die . . . Fest und

Aposteltage . . .,' 22 motets a 5-9, described as composed on the 12 modes of the Dodecachordon (Nuremberg, 1595). Besides these published works there remain in MS. several collections of Latin and German motets and Magnificats by Raselius. He is also known as the author of a historical work, a chronicle of Ratisbon, originally written both in Latin and German, of which only the German edition survives. Raselius remained at Ratisbon till 1600, when he received a pressing invitation from the Elector Palatine Frederick IV. to return to Heidelberg as Hofkapellmeister. This higher post of honour he held till his death in 1602. A monograph on Raselius by J. Auer, of Amberg, appeared as a Beilage to Eitner's *Monatshefte* of 1892.     J. R. M.

RASI, FRANCESCO (b. Arezzo, late 16th cent.), of a Tuscan noble family, singer, poet and composer ; pupil of Caccini. From the end of the 16th century to 1620 he was at the court of Mantua. He composed ' Musica di camera e di chiesa,' dedicated to the Archbishop of Salzburg (1612) ; also madrigals, songs, dialogues (1608, 1610, 1620). (Particulars in *Q.-L.* and *Mendel.*)

RASOUMOWSKY,[1] ANDREAS KYRILLOVITSCH (b. Oct. 22, 1752), a Russian nobleman to whom Beethoven dedicated the ' Rasoumowsky quartets ' (op. 59). He was the son of Kyrill Rasum, a peasant of Lemeschi, a village in the Ukraine, who, with his elder brother, was made a Count (Graf) by the Empress Elisabeth of Russia. Andreas served in the English and Russian navies, rose to the rank of admiral, and was Russian ambassador at Venice, Naples, Copenhagen, Stockholm and Vienna. In England his name must have been familiar, or Foote would hardly have introduced it as he has in *The Liar* (1762). At Vienna he married, in 1788, Elisabeth, Countess of Thun, one of the ' three Graces,' elder sister of the Princess Carl Lichnowsky (see LICHNOWSKY) ; and on Mar. 25, 1792, had his audience from the Emperor of Austria as Russian ambassador, a post which he held with short intervals for more than twenty years. He was a thorough musician, an excellent player of Haydn's quartets, in which he took second violin, not improbably studying them under Haydn himself. That, with his connexion with Lichnowsky, he must have known Beethoven is obvious; but no direct trace of the acquaintance is found until May 26, 1806 (six weeks after the withdrawal of ' Fidelio '), which Beethoven —in his usual polyglot—has marked on the first page of the quartet in F of op. 59, as the date on which he began it—' Quartetto angefangen am 26ten May 1806.'

In 1808 the Count formed his famous quartet party—Schuppanzigh, first violin ; Weiss,

---

[1] Rasumoffsky and Rasoumoffsky are forms used by Beethoven in various dedications.

**viola**; Lincke, violoncello; and he himself second violin—which for many years met in the evenings and performed, among other compositions, Beethoven's pieces, 'hot from the fire,' under his own immediate instructions.

In Apr. 1809 appeared the C minor and 'Pastoral' symphonies (Nos. 5 and 6), with a dedication (on the parts) to Prince Lobkowitz and 'son excellence Monsieur le Comte de Rasumoffsky' (Breitkopf & Härtel). These dedications doubtless imply that Beethoven was largely the recipient of the Count's bounty, but there is no direct evidence of it, and there is a strange absence of reference to the Count in Beethoven's letters. His name is mentioned only once—July 24, 1813—and there is a distant allusion in a letter of a much later date (Nohl, *Briefe B.*, 1865, No. 354). In the autumn of 1814 came the Vienna Congress (Nov. 1, 1814–June 9, 1815), and as the Empress of Russia was in Vienna at the time, the Ambassador's Palace was naturally the scene of special festivities. It was not, however, there that Beethoven was presented to the Empress, but at the Archduke Rodolph's.[1] The Count's hospitalities were immense, and, vast as was his palace, a separate wooden annexe had to be constructed capable of dining 700 persons.

On June 3, 1815, six days before the signature of the final Act of the Congress, the Count was made Prince (Fürst), and on the 31st of the following December the dining-hall just mentioned was burnt down. The Emperor of Russia gave 400,000 silver roubles (£40,000) towards the rebuilding, but the misfortune appears to have been too much for the Prince; he soon after sold the property, pensioned his quartet, and disappears from musical history. The quartet kept together for many years after this date, Sina playing second violin. Beethoven mentions them apropos of the Galitzin quartets in the letter to his nephew already referred to, about 1825.      A. W. T.

RATAPLAN, like Rub-a-dub, is an imitative word for the sound of the drum, as Tan-ta-ra is for that of the trumpet, and Tootle-tootle for the flute.[2] It is hardly necessary to mention its introduction by Donizetti in the 'Fille du régiment,' or by Meyerbeer in the 'Huguenots'; and every Londoner is familiar with it in Sergeant Bouncer's part in Sullivan's 'Cox and Box.' 'Rataplan, der kleine Tambour' is the title of a Singspiel by Pillwitz, which was produced at Bremen in 1831, and had a considerable run both in north and south Germany between that year and 1836.
     G.

RATTI, (1) BARTOLOMEO (called 'il Moro') (b. Padua, 1593), second (afterwards first) maestro di cappella of S. Antoniana, Padua. He composed church motets and psalms, and

3 books of secular madrigals and canzonets. (2) LORENZO, of Perugia, maestro di cappella at the German College, Rome, 1628; S. Loretto, 1630. He composed motets and other church music between 1615 and 1632 (*Q.-L.*; *Fétis*).

RAUGEL, FÉLIX (b. Saint-Quentin, Nov. 27, 1881), conductor and musician. He was a pupil of Henri Libert in Paris, and, at the Schola Cantorum, of Albert Roussel, Decaux and Vincent d'Indy. He founded in 1908 La Société G. F. Haendel, which he directed from 1908–14. He has been maître de chapelle at the church of St. Eustache since 1911 and conductor of the Chorale Française, founded in 1922. His chief publications are:

*Les Orgues de l'Abbaye de Saint-Mihiel* (1919, Hérelle); *Recherches sur quelques maîtres de l'ancienne facture française* (Hérelle); *Les Organistes* (1923, Laurens); *Les Grandes Orgues des églises de Paris*; *Les Anciennes Orgues de Seine-et-Oise* (Fischbacher); *Haendel Encyclopédie Delagrave*); *Palestrina* (Laurens;.

RAUPACH, (1) CHRISTOPH (b. Toudern, Silesia, July 5, 1686), an excellent organist and writer on music at Hamburg in 1701. From May 1, 1703, he was organist of St. Nicolas, Stralsund. (2) HERMANN FRIEDRICH (b. Stralsund, c. 1726), son and pupil of Christoph, went to Russia, c. 1756, as conductor of the Imperial Opera, and produced several operas of his composition. He settled afterwards at Paris, where he brought out 6 sonatas for pianoforte with violin, c. 1776.      E. v. d. S.

RAUZZINI, (1) VENANZIO (b. Rome, 1747; d. Bath, Apr. 8, 1810), made his début at Rome in 1765, captivating his audience by his fine voice, clever acting and prepossessing appearance. In 1766 or 1767 he was at Munich, where Burney heard him in 1772, and where four of his operas were performed. He sang at various places during this period. In London he made his first appearance in 1774, in Corri's 'Alessandro nell' Indie.' His appearance in a pasticcio of 'Armida' in the same year has resulted in the attribution to him of an opera of that name dated 1778.[3] He distinguished himself as an excellent teacher of singing, Miss Storace, Braham, Miss Poole (afterwards Mrs. Dickons) and Incledon being among his pupils. In 1778 and 1779 he gave subscription concerts with the violinist Lamotte, when they were assisted by such eminent artists as Miss Harrop, Signor Rovedino, Fischer, Cervetto, Stamitz, Decamp and Clementi. He also gave brilliant concerts in the new Assembly Rooms (built 1771) at Bath, where he took up his abode on leaving London. Here he invited Haydn and Dr. Burney to visit him in 1794. On this occasion Haydn wrote a four-part canon (or more strictly a round) to an epitaph on a favourite dog buried in Rauzzini's garden (see HAYDN). Rauzzini's operas performed in London were 'Piramo e Tisbe' (Mar. 16, 1775, and afterwards in Vienna), 'Le ali d' Amore'

---

1 Schindler, i. 233 (quoted by Thayer, iii. 321).
2 Other forms are Patapataplan, Palalalalan, Bumberumbumbum. See the *Dictionnaire encyclopédique* of Sachs & Villatte.

3 The error was copied into many dictionaries from the first edition of this work.

'Feb. 27, 1776); 'Creusa in Delfo' (1783); 'La regina di Golconda' (1784); and 'La Vestale' (1787). 'L' eroe cinese,' originally given at Munich in 1771, was performed in London in 1782.[1] He composed string quartets, sonatas for PF., Italian arias and duets, and English songs; also a Requiem produced at the little Haymarket Theatre in 1801, by Dr. Arnold and Salomon. A miniature by J. Hutchinson (monochrome) is in the Victoria Museum at Bath. His brother,

(2) MATTEO (b. Rome, 1754; d. 1791) made his first appearance at Munich in 1772, followed his brother to England, and settled in Dublin, where he produced an opera, 'Il rè pastore,' in 1784. He had written 'Le finte gemelli' for Munich in 1772 and 'L' opera nuova' for Venice in 1781. He employed himself in teaching singing.                    c. f. p., with addns.

RAVAL, SEBASTIAN (fl. 1580–1603), Spanish madrigalist who lived in Italy and set Italian words instead of Spanish. He was a knight of the order of St. John of Jerusalem, and served various patrons: firstly, Marcantonio Colonna, the victor of Lepanto (1573) and Viceroy of Sicily, 1577–82. Then, after some years with Cardinal Ascanio Colonna, he went to Urbino, where he is described as being among the magnifici virtuosi at the ducal court of Francesco Maria II. At the end of 1592 he was in Rome, under the protection of Cardinal Alessandro Peretti (Jan. 15, 1593) and (May 10, 1593) of Marcantonio Colonna, nephew and namesake of his former patron. In the palace of this Roman patrician he extemporised counterpoints before a number of musicians, among whom was MARENZIO; and encouraged by their praises he published in one year three sets of madrigals. However, his boasting led to the intervention of Giov. Maria NANINO and Francesco SORIANO, who challenged him to a contest and ignominiously routed him. In the next year (1594) he appropriately published a set of Lamentations; but remained in Rome till after 1598, when, through the Duke of Maqueda (a Spaniard like himself), he obtained the post of maestro at Palermo. Here (in 1600) his boastfulness had the same consequences as in Rome. He was challenged by a Calabrian musician, Achille Falcone, of Cosenza; but came off victorious. Nanino and Soriano were appealed to, but before the rival compositions could be submitted to them Falcone was dead (Nov. 9, 1600), v. G. Radiciotti, Sammelbd. I.M.G. xiv. 185 ff. (1912).

Raval published the following works:

Motectorum, 5 ꞁ. Rome, 1593. (Barcelona; Ratisbon; Verona.)
Il primo libro di Canzonette a 4 v. Venice, G. Vincenti, 1593. (Bologna.)
Il primo libro de' Madrigali a 5 v. Venice, G. Vincenti, 1593. (Bologna.)
Lamentationes Hieremiæ Prophetæ, 5 v. Rome, 1594. (Rome: St. Cecilia.)

[1] These dates are from the Public Advertiser.

Madrigali a 3 v. . . . . con 2 Madrigali a 5 v & un a 8 v. Rome, 1595. (Bologna.)
Libro de' Motetti a 3 . . . 8 v. Palermo, 1601. (Ratisbon, incomplete.)

Six madrigals by Raval are included in the Madrigali a 5 di Achille Falcone. Venice, G. Vincenti, 1603.                    J. B. T.

RAVEL, MAURICE (b. Ciboure, near St. Jean de Luz, Basses-Pyrénées, France, Mar. 7, 1875). His mother's lineage was Basque; his father's partly French-Swiss. At the age of 12 he was taken to Paris, where his first teachers were H. Ghis (piano) and Charles René (theory). In 1889 he entered, at the Paris Conservatoire, Anthiome's preparatory piano class. In 1891 he passed into de Bériot's class (where among his companions was Ricardo Viñes, who was to be the first to make his works known). He studied harmony with Pessard, and, from 1897 onwards, counterpoint with Gédalge and composition with Fauré. His interest in contemporary production led him to study the music of Chabrier, of Satie, of Liszt, and of various Russians, which influenced him considerably. His own creative outlook, however, was definite and individual from the very outset. We have it from his early master Charles René (quoted by R. Manuel, vide infra) that his first attempts at composition, a set of variations and a sonata movement, showed the conception of music by which he was guided later to have been altogether instinctive, and well outlined from the first. And his earliest known compositions, 'Menuet antique,' 1895, 'Sites auriculaires,' 1895, 'Sainte,' 1896 (published 1907 only) and 'Deux Épigrammes de Clément Marot,' 1896), show his individuality already unmistakable, and mature or very nearly.

The first public performances of his music ('Sites auriculaires,' 1898, overture 'Shéhérazade,' 1899) was unfavourably noticed by the few critics who noticed it at all, and contributed to create the legend that Ravel was a dangerous revolutionist—a legend which spread quickly among official musical circles, and proved detrimental to the young composer; for, after being awarded the second Grand Prix de Rome in 1901, he was refused the higher reward in 1902 and 1903, and in 1905 declared ineligible on the strength of the results of the usual preliminary competition. At that time not only his 'Jeux d'eau' and 'Pavane' for piano, but his string quartet had been performed and published—so that there could be no doubt that his technical ability reached the required standard. The jury's decision provoked an outburst of indignation even among the critics who had been, and long afterwards continued to be, hostile to Ravel's music.

From that time onwards, the only landmarks in his biography are the dates of composition and performance of his works

During the first period, that is, up to 1914, his line of evolution remained remarkably un-

swerving. From the time of the 'Jeux d'eau'
(1901) onwards, his harmonic idiom and style of
writing for the piano, both highly original and
effective, are further developed in ' Miroirs '
(1905) and 'Gaspard de la nuit' (1908). The less
exuberantly picturesque vein of the ' Menuet '
and ' Pavane' is further exemplified in the
'Sonatina,' the first movement of which was
written towards the end of 1903 (for a competition opened by a periodical, and eventually
cancelled) and the remainder in 1905 and in
the delightful 'Ma Mère l'oye' (first written as
a piano duet with one very easy part in 1908 ;
arranged into ballet form and orchestrated,
1912).

Many of Ravel's best songs were written
during the years 1903–06 : the set 'Shéhérazade,'
first published with piano accompaniment and
shortly afterwards orchestrated ; the ' Noël des
jouets ' ; and the ' Histoires naturelles.'

Accidental circumstances turned his attention, with admirable results, to the harmonisation of folk-songs. The first was a request to
provide accompaniments for Greek folk-songs
selected to illustrate a lecture (' Cinq Chansons
populaires grecques,' 1905) ; the second was
a competition opened by the Moscow ' Maison
du Lied ' at which four of his settings were
awarded the first prize.

From the first example of Ravel's orchestral
music, the ' Shéhérazade ' Overture, to the
works of his full maturity, the line is equally
direct. A curious fact is that although he is a
born orchestrator, and his command of the
orchestral medium is unsurpassed, he wrote
comparatively little for the orchestra ; and of
that little a large proportion consists of re-
arrangements of piano versions. These are :
' Barque sur l'océan ' (1907) and 'Alborada del
gracioso ' (1912), both from the set ' Miroirs ' ;
'Pavane pour une infante défunte ' (1908) ; the
' Shéhérazade ' song-set, and ' Ma Mére l'oye,'
already mentioned. In 1912 Ravel likewise
orchestrated and turned into a ballet, under the
title ' Le Langage des fleurs,' his piano ' Valses
nobles et sentimentales,' published the previous
year (and first performed at a concert of the
Société Musicale Indépendante at which the
authorship of all the new works on the programme was kept secret). The only concert
works of his which first appeared in orchestral
form are the ' Rhapsodie espagnole ' (1907)—
one movement, however, the ' Habanera,'
is an orchestral version of one of the ' Sites
auriculaires ' of 1895—and ' La Valse ' (1920).
But Ravel's skill proves so thorough, his sense
of fitness so unerring, that in all these instances
none of the shortcomings usually inseparable
from adaptations are to be noticed, either from
the æsthetic point of view or from the technical:
both available versions possess all the characteristics of versions originally conceived in
view of the very medium in which they are

carried out. The clearest case in point is
perhaps, the 'Alborada del gracioso ' from the
earlier version of which there is as much to be
learnt on the art of writing for the piano as
there is on the art of writing for the orchestra
from the later version.

The number of works first written by him for
stage purposes is equally small. For a long
time he intended to set to music A. Ferdinand
Hérold's French translation of Hauptmann's
Versunkene Glocke ; and the preliminary work
was far advanced when he finally relinquished the idea. In 1907 a little farce by
Franc-Nohain, which had been performed at
the Odéon without attracting much attention,
took his fancy and he set it to music. This was
' L'Heure espagnole ' (first performed in 1911),
one of the most brilliantly successful of his
achievements in a light vein. In 1909 he was
commissioned to write the ballet ' Daphnis et
Chloé ' for Diaghilev's Russian Company. This
work (first performed in 1912) constitutes so
far the high-water mark in his orchestral production. Since then his only original work for
the stage is ' L'Enfant et les sortilèges ' (text
by Messrs. Colette. Monte Carlo, 1925).

The ' Trois Poèmes de Mallarmé,' for voice
and 8 instruments (1913), may be taken as
standing on the boundary between the first and
second period. They are one of Ravel's most
subtle and recondite achievements, and exemplify his growing tendency towards abstraction and simplification. Henceforth he devotes his attention more and more to line
(never neglected in his earlier work) and less
to colour. This may be due, partly, to the
influence of Saint-Saëns's music, which at that
time he used to study with ever-increasing interest. Roland Manuel[1] rightly calls attention
to analogies between Ravel's trio (1915) and
Saint-Saëns's first trio and third symphony.
And there may be something that recalls Saint-
Saëns as well as Chabrier in the quality and treatment of the orchestral ' La Valse ' (1920). ' Le
Tombeau de Couperin,' a piano suite (1914–17,
four parts were orchestrated in 1918), and the
sonata for violin and violoncello (1920–22), are
the other signal works of the later period. The
sonata especially is a remarkably fine achievement, in which simplification is carried to the
utmost, and extraordinary resourcefulness is
shown in the accomplishment of the difficult
task of achieving variety and fullness within a
scheme almost entirely restricted to lines.

In all his works Ravel stands revealed as a
typical product of French culture, essentially
intelligent, versatile, although he deliberately
restricts his field, purposeful, and uniformly
keen in investigating the possibilities of music.
He is, first and last, a pure musician, whose
sensitive ear and alert sense of proportion lead
him always to judge, and to be guided, by the

[1] Revue musicale, Apr. 1925.

properties of musical substance, never by any other consideration. He is more interested in problems of quality than in problems of pure form; but his sense of form is unerring. He sets great store by restraint; but the genuine emotion which permeates, for instance, the beginning of 'Asie,' 'L'Indifférent,' 'Le Martin-pêcheur' (in the 'Histoires naturelles '), 'Le Gibet ' (in ' Gaspard de la nuit '), ' Oiseaux tristes,' the 'Forlane ' in 'Le Tombeau de Couperin' and the slow movement of the quartet is never lacking even in works of his which, on the surface, may convey an impression of detachment. In his musical humour the sympathetic quality is as striking as the wit.

His style is characterised by sharp definition of contours, by finish, point and piquancy down to the utmost detail. One critic [1] has described him as always interested in achieving the seemingly impossible. From the technical point of view the remark is true enough. But it is always an artistic end, not a merely technical, that he has in view.

His preference for working on a small scale has given occasion to much adverse criticism. That he is quite capable of dealing with broader schemes is shown by ' Daphnis et Chloé,' and in a large measure by ' Gaspard de la nuit.' If he has not done so more often, it is by virtue of a deliberate, carefully thought out æsthetic choice, or of what his adverse critics (who are almost as numerous as his fervent admirers) usually describe as ' a sense of his own limitations.' But there can be no doubt that few composers have succeeded in achieving more thoroughly exactly what they aimed at achieving. In his native country he speedily won recognition in spite of relentless opposition. And he is now acknowledged everywhere as one of France's most representative composers.

He is an excellent teacher, but only a few private pupils have received lessons from him. He has written a small number of critical articles, which are very characteristic of him. Most of these are to be found in the files of two French periodicals, *S.I.M.* and *Comoedia Illustré*, for the years 1912–14.

### LIST OF WORKS

#### PIANO

Sérénade grotesque. (Before 1894.) Unpubl.
Menuet antique. (1895.)
Sites auriculaires. (Duet for 2 PF.) Unpubl.
   Habanera (1895) ; Entre cloches (1896).
Pavane pour une infante défunte. (1899.)
Jeux d'eau. (1901)
Miroirs. (1905.)
   Noctuelles—Oiseaux tristes—Une Barque sur l'océan—Alborada del gracioso—La Vallée des cloches.
Sonatine. (1903–05 )
Gaspard de la nuit. (1908.)
   Ondine—Le Gibet—Scarbo.
Ma Mère l'Oye. Duet. (1908.)
   Pavane de la Belle au Bois Dormant—Petit Poucet—Laideronette, impératrice des pagodes—Le Jardin féerique.
Menuet sur le nom d'Haydn. (1909.)
Valses nobles et sentimentales. (1911.)
Prélude. (1913.)

[1] Vuillermoz, *Musiques d'aujourd'hui*.

A la manière de . . . (1913.)
   Borodine—Chabrier.
Le Tombeau de Couperin. (1914–17.)
   Prélude—Fugue—Forlane—Rigaudon—Menuet—Toccata.
Sur le nom de Gabriel Fauré. (1922.)

#### CHAMBER MUSIC

String Quartet, F major. (1902–03.)
Introduction et Allegro, for harp, string quartet, flute and clarinet. (1906.)
Piano Trio, A minor. (1915.)
Sonata for violin and violoncello. (1920–22.)
'Tzigane,' rhapsody for violin and piano. (1924.)

#### ORCHESTRAL

Shéhérazade, overture (1898.) Unpubl.
Pavane pour une infante défunte. (1899.)
Rhapsodie espagnole. (1907.)
   Prélude—Malagueña—Habanera—Feria.
Une Barque sur l'océan. (1908.)
Daphnis et Chloé. Ballet. (1909–11.)
Alborada del gracioso. (1912.)
'Ma Mère l'oye,' ballet. (1912.)
' Adélaïde ou le Langage des fleurs.' (1912.)
Le Tombeau de Couperin. (1919.)
   Prélude—Forlane—Menuet—Rigaudon.
La Valse, poème chorégraphique. (1920.)

#### VOCAL

##### Songs with Piano Accpt.

Ballade de la reine morte d'aimer (R. de Marés). (1894.) Unpubl.
Un Grand Sommeil noir (Verlaine). (1895.) Unpubl.
Sainte (Mallarmé). (1896.)
Deux Épigrammes (Marot). (1896.)
   D'Anne jouant de l'épinette—D'Anne qui me jecta de la neige.
Si morne (Verhaeren). (1899.) Unpubl.
Manteau de fleurs (Gravollet). (1903.)
*Shéhérazade (Klingsor). (1903.)
   Asie—La Flûte enchantée—L'Indifférent.
*Noël des jouets (Ravel). (1905.)
Cinq Mélodies populaires grecques. (1905.)
   Le Réveil de la mariée—Là-bas, vers l'église—Quel galant. Chanson des cueilleuses de lentisque—Tout gai.
Les Grands Vents venus d'outremer (H. de Régnier). (1906.)
Histoires naturelles (J. Renard). (1906.)
   Le Paon—le Grillon—le Cygne—le Martin-pêcheur—La Pintade.
Sur l'herbe (Verlaine). (1907.)
Vocalise en forme d'Habanera. (1907.)
Quatre Chants populaires. (1910.)
   Espagnol—Français—Italien—Hébraïque.
*Deux Mélodies hébraïques. (1914.)
   Kaddisch—L'Énigme éternelle.
Ronsard à son âme (Ronsard). (1924.)
   The songs marked * exist with orchestral accompaniment.

##### Songs with Instr. Accpt.

Trois Poèmes de Mallarmé. (1913.) (For voice, piano, string quartet, 2 flutes and 2 clarinets.)

#### PARTSONGS

Trois Chansons, mixed choir, unacc. (Ravel). (1916.)

#### LYRIC PLAYS

L'Heure espagnole (Franc-Nohain). (1907.)
L'Enfant et les sortilèges (Colette). (1924–25.)

#### BIBLIOGRAPHY

M. D. CALVOCORESSI: *Maurice Ravel* (*Mus. T.*, Dec. 1913); *Les Histoires naturelles et l'imitation Debussyste*. (*Grande Revue*, May 1907.)
A. CŒUROY : *La Musique française moderne*. (Paris, 1922.)
G. DYSON : *The New Music*. (London, 1924.)
C. GRAY : *A Survey of Contemporary Music*. (London, 1925.)
ROLAND MANUEL : *Maurice Ravel*. (Paris, 1914.)
J. MARNOLD: *Musiques d'autrefois et d'aujourd'hui*. (Paris, 1911.)
R. O. MORRIS : *Maurice Ravel*. (*Music and Letters*, July 1921.)
SHERA : *Debussy and Ravel*. (London, 1925.)
Special Ravel number of the *Revue musicale* (Apr. 1925.)

                                M. D. C.

**RAVENSCROFT, JOHN** (*d. circa* 1745), one of the Tower Hamlets waits and violinist at Goodman's Fields Theatre, was noted for his skill in the composition of hornpipes, a collection of which he published. Two of them are printed in Hawkins's *History*, and another in vol. iii. of ' The Dancing Master.' A set of sonatas for two violins and violone or archlute were printed at Rome in 1695.

                                W. H. H.

**RAVENSCROFT, THOMAS, B.Mus.** (*b. circa* 1590; *d. circa* 1633 [2]), English composer and

[2] A Thomas Ravenscroft (*d.* 1630) is buried at Barnet. w. B. S.

editor of various musical publications. In one of the prefaces to his *Brief Discourse* (1614) his age is given as 22, but this would make him only 15 when he became B.Mus. at Cambridge in 1607, and 17 when he published 'Pammelia' and 'Deuteromelia.' He was a chorister at St. Paul's under Edward Pearce, and from 1618–22 was music‑master at Christ's Hospital.

His publications are :

1609. 'Pammelia. Musick's Miscellanie ; or, Mixea Varietie of Pleasant Roundelays, and delightful Catches of 3, 4, 5, 6, 7, 8, 9, 10 Parts in one. None so ordinarie as musicall, none so musicall, as not to all, very pleasing and acceptable.' (Reprinted 1618.)

1609. 'Deuteromelia : or the Second part of Musick's Melodie, or melodius Musicke of Pleasant Roundelais ; K.H. Mirth,[1] or Freemens Songs and such delightful Catches.' 'Qui canere potest, canat.' Catch that catch can. 'Ut Melos, sic Cor melos afficit et reficit.' (See CATCH.)

1611. 'Melismata. Musicall Phansies : Fitting the Court, Citie and Countrey Humours. To 3, 4 and 5 Voyces.'

1614. 'A Brief Discourse of the true (but neglected) use of Charact'ring the Degrees, by their Perfection, Imperfection and Diminution in Measurable Musicke, against the Common Practise and Custome of these Times. Examples whereof are exprest in the Harmony of 4 Voyces, concerning the Pleasure of 5 usuall Recreations. 1. Hunting. 2. Hawking. 3. Dancing. 4. Drinking. 5. Enamouring.'

1621. 'The Whole Booke of Psalmes : With the Hymnes Evangelicall and Spirituall. Composed into four parts by Sundry Authors with severall Tunes as have been and are usually sung in England, Scotland, Wales, Germany, Italy, France and the Netherlands.' (2nd edition, 1633. See PSALTER, THE ENGLISH METRICAL.)

'Pammelia' is of some importance as the earliest English printed collection of this kind of music. It contains 100 rounds and catches,[2] some with sacred words, either Latin or English texts of the metrical psalm type, but the majority are settings of stanzas or fragments of a traditional or popular character (such as the famous canon, 'Robin, lend me thy bowe,' which is included). 'Deuteromelia' is a collection of 31 pieces, 7 of which are 'Freemen's Songs' for 3 voices. Seven others are 'Freemen's Songs' for 4 voices ; the remainder are rounds for 3 and 4 voices. 'Three blind mice' here appears among the rounds, perhaps for the first time in print, as well as the catch, 'Hold thy peace, knave,' sung in Shakespeare's *Twelfth Night*. The 'Freemen's Songs' again are settings of poems (often with verse and chorus) chiefly of a popular, humorous or broad character ; one of them, 'Wee be Souldiers three,' is printed in Hawkins's *History*. 'Melismata' is a similar collection of 23 settings indexed as follows : 6 Court Varieties, 4 Citie Rounds, 4 Citie Conceits, 5 Country Rounds and 4 Country Pastimes. With the exception of the 9 'Citie' and Country Rounds, these are all short madrigals which, both in their words and music, express the 'humour' they are intended to illustrate. An excellent setting of the well-known 'Three Ravens' ballad appears under 'Country Pastimes.'

[1] The expression 'K.H. Mirth' in this title has been thought by some to stand for 'King Henry's Mirth,' but it has been suggested (E. H. Fellowes, *Eng. Madr. Composers*) that it is meant for 'King's Head,' and as such would stand either for a tavern of that name in Cheapside, or for a house in Greenwich known later to Pepys as 'the great musicke house.'

[2] For quotations see article on Thomas Ravenscroft by the writer, *Mus. T.*, Oct. 1924, p. 881.

*A Briefe Discourse*, dedicated to the senators and guardians of Gresham College, begins with an 'apologie' which deprecates the breaking of rules (chiefly with respect to time and 'prolations') by contemporary musicians and minstrels, and is followed by the 'Discourse' proper which seeks to define the 'Divisions of Moode, Time and Prolation' in Measurable Music' by quotations from such authorities as Glareanus, Ornithoparcus, Sebaldus, Heydon, Dunstable and Morley. Whereas in his 1609 and 1611 publications there is no evidence to show that Ravenscroft composed any of the music himself, many of the 'examples' appended to the *Briefe Discourse* are by him. The most notable among these is really a song‑cycle in 4 parts, and is possibly the first thing of its kind to appear in this country (but see NICHOLSON, Richard). The poem is in dialect, 'Hodge Trillindle to his Zweet hort Malkyn' ; the first part is Hodge's declaration, the second Malkyn's answer, the third their 'Gonglusion' and the last 'their Wedlocke.' The last named is set by John Bennet.[3] Other numbers were contributed by his master, Edward Pearce, and by John Bennet. Another 'Treatise of Musick' by Ravenscroft is in B.M. Add. MSS. 19,578/19. This, besides giving the substance of *A Briefe Discourse*, divides music into 'Practive and Speculative,' describes the gamut and gives an account of the intervals.

A study of these four publications of Ravenscroft establishes him in a peculiar position among Elizabethan composers. A learned and serious musician (if not a pedant in some respects), he was nevertheless determined to satisfy all tastes by his 'Court, City and Country' humours. While demonstrably capable of writing madrigals and anthems in the usual style, his tavern songs and catches, his hunting and hawking songs and his 'Hodge and Malkyn' are an indication of his broad sympathies and of his ability to express them in music. All four books are in the British Museum (K. 1, e 8-11) ; separate numbers are in B.M. Add. MSS. 31,420, 33,933, 5336, 29,386, 29,291 ; also in R.C.M. 722, 814, 821.

Ravenscroft is, however, best known by his 1621 publication, usually referred to as 'Ravenscroft's Psalter,' fully described under PSALTER. This contains 100 harmonisings, of which 48 are his own, but most of them which are still in use are only 'sadly garbled' versions of the originals. The remaining settings are by Richard Allison, Edward Blancks, John Bennet, Michael Cavendish, William Cranford, John Dowland, Giles Farnaby, John Farmer, William Harrison, Edmund Hooper, George Kirby, John Milton, Thomas Morley, Robert Palmer, William Parsons, Martin Peerson,

[3] See E. H. Fellowes, *English Madrigal Verse*.

Simon Stubbs, Thomas Tallis, John Tomkins and Thomas Tomkins.

ANTHEMS

[1] Ah helpless wretch, *a* 5.   B.M. Add. MSS. 29,372-7 and 29,427/25. Altus part only.
[1] All laud and praise, *a* 5   B.M. Add. MSS. 29,372-7 and 29,427/25. Altus part only.
In Thee, O Lord.  Verse anthem, *a* 5.  Ch. Ch. 56-60.  Bass part wanting.
[1] O Jesu meek, *a* 5.   B.M. Add. MSS. 29,372-7.
O Jesu sweet.  B.M. Add. MSS. 29,427/23.  Altus part only.
O let me hear.  Verse anthem, *a* 5.  Durh. ; B.M. Add. MSS. 30,478-9.  Tenor cantoris part only ; Ch. Ch. 56-60.  Bass part wanting.
O Lord, in Thee is all my trust, *a* 5.  B.M. Add. MSS. 29,427/29. Altus part only.
O woful ruines, *a* 5.  Ch. Ch. 56-60.  Bass part wanting.
This is the day.  Verse anthem, *a* 5.  Ch. Ch. 56-60.  Bass part wanting.

J. M[K].

RAVINA, JEAN HENRI (*b.* Bordeaux, May 20, 1818 ; *d.* Paris, Sept. 30, 1906), pianoforte composer. His mother was a prominent musician at Bordeaux. At the instance of Rode and Zimmermann the lad was admitted to the Conservatoire of Paris in 1831. His progress was rapid—second prize for PF. in 1832 ; first prize for the same in 1834 ; first for harmony and accompaniment in 1835 ; a joint professorship of PF., Nov. 1835. In Feb. 1837 he left the Conservatoire and embarked on the world as a virtuoso and teacher. He resided exclusively at Paris, with the exception of a journey to Russia in 1853, and Spain in 1871. He received the Legion of Honour in 1861. His compositions are almost all salon pieces. He also published a 4-hand arrangement of Beethoven's nine symphonies. (See Pougin's supplement to *Fétis*.)          G.

RAWLINGS (RAWLINS), (1) THOMAS (*b. circa* 1703 ; *d.* 1767), was a pupil of Dr. Pepusch, and a member of Handel's orchestra at both opera and oratorio performances. On Mar. 14, 1753, he was appointed organist of Chelsea Hospital.

His son, (2) ROBERT (*b.* 1742 ; *d.* 1814), was a pupil of his father, and afterwards of Barsanti. At 17 he was appointed musical page to the Duke of York, with whom he travelled on the Continent until the Duke's death. In 1767 he returned to England and became a violinist in the King's band and Queen's private band.

His son, (3) THOMAS A. (*b.* 1775 ; *d.* mid-19th cent.), studied music under his father and Dittenhöfer. He composed some instrumental music performed at the Professional Concerts, became a violinist at the Opera and the best concerts, and a teacher of the pianoforte, violin and thorough-bass. He composed and arranged many pieces for the pianoforte, and some songs.                          w. h. h.

RAYMAN, JACOB, see VIOLIN FAMILY, subsection ENGLISH MAKERS.

RE, the second note of the major scale in the nomenclature of France and Italy : See D ; HEXACHORD ; SOLMISATION.

REA, WILLIAM (*b.* London, Mar. 25, 1827 ; *d.* Newcastle, Mar. 8, 1903), when about 10

[1] These 3 anthems were contributed to Thomas Myriell's collection, 'Tristitiae remedium' (1616), which also contains a motet, ' Ne laeteris inimica mea,' *a* 5, by Ravenscroft.

years old learnt the pianoforte **and organ from** Josiah Pittman, for whom he acted as deputy for several years. In or about 1843 he was appointed organist to Christchurch, Watney Street, St. George's-in-the-East, and at the same time studied the pianoforte, composition and instrumentation under Sterndale Bennett, appearing as a pianist at the concerts of the Society of British Musicians in 1845. On leaving Christchurch he was appointed organist to St. Andrew Undershaft. In 1849 he went to Leipzig, where his masters were Moscheles and Richter ; he subsequently studied under Dreyschock at Prague. On his return to England, Rea gave chamber concerts at the Beethoven Rooms, and became (1853) organist to the Harmonic Union. In 1856 he founded the London Polyhymnian Choir, to the training of which he devoted much time, and with excellent results ; at the same time he conducted an amateur orchestral society. In 1858 he was appointed organist at St. Michael's, Stockwell, and in 1860 was chosen by competition organist to the corporation of Newcastle-on-Tyne, where he also successively filled the same post at three churches in succession, and at the Elswick Road Chapel. At Newcastle Rea, besides weekly organ and pianoforte recitals, formed a choir of eighty voices, which in 1862 was amalgamated with the existing Sacred Harmonic Society of Newcastle. In 1867 he began a series of excellent orchestral concerts which were carried on every season for nine years, when he was compelled to discontinue them, owing to the pecuniary loss which they entailed. In 1876 he gave two performances of 'Antigone' at the Theatre Royal, and devoted much of his time to training his choir (200 voices), the Newcastle Amateur Vocal Society, and other Societies on the Tyne and in Sunderland, besides giving concerts at which the best artists performed. His published works comprise four songs, three organ pieces and some anthems. At the close of 1880 he was appointed organist of St. Hilda's, S. Shields ; in 1888 he resigned the corporation appointment. He was an honorary Fellow of the R.C.O., and in 1886 received the honorary degree of Mus.D. from the University of Durham. He composed a 'Jubilee Ode' for the Newcastle Exhibition of 1887. An account of his life and works is in *Mus. T.*, Apr. 1903. His wife, EMMA MARY (*née* Woolhouse) (*d.* May 6, 1893), was an accomplished musician, actively connected with the musical life of Newcastle.          w. b. s. ; addns. F. K.

READ, FREDERICK JOHN (*b.* Faversham, Dec. 1857 [2] ; *d.* Chichester, Jan. 28, 1925), was organist of Chichester Cathedral during two periods, 1886–1902 and 1921–25. His first important post was at Christ Church, Reading, where he made his mark as a choral conductor

[2] West, *Cath. Org.*

as well as a church organist. Similarly at Chichester during his first period he introduced many important works as conductor of the Chichester Musical Society. At that time he was also a teacher of harmony and counterpoint at the R.C.M. ; he was an examiner for the Associated Board of the R.A.M. and R.C.M., and for the R.C.O. Among many compositions, mostly for church use, his madrigal ' Love wakes and weeps ' deserves mention, since it won the prize of the MADRIGAL SOCIETY (q.v.). For an appreciation of Read by Sir Hugh P. Allen (formerly his pupil) see *Mus. T.*, Mar. 1925.          C.

READE, CHARLES (b. June 8, 1814 ; d. Apr. 11, 1884), English dramatist and novelist, claims a notice in his capacity of expert connoisseur, and one of the earliest collectors of old violins. He devoted much time to the study of violin construction, and—as his sons put it—acquired ' as keen a scent for the habitat of a rare violin as the truffle dog for fungus beneath the roots of the trees.' He gathered much of this accurate knowledge from one Henri, a player and a maker to boot, resident in Soho, with whom he engaged in experiments in varnish, and in the business of importing fiddles from abroad for the English dealers. Frequent visits to Paris, in the latter connexion, resulted sometimes in profit and at other times in financial catastrophe ; but they succeeded in bringing to England some of the finest specimens of Cremona instruments that are known to-day. They were in Paris buying a stock of thirty fiddles when the Revolution of 1848 broke out, and Henri threw aside fiddle-dealing and joined the revolutionists. He was shot before his friend's eyes at the first barricade, and Charles Reade escaped with difficulty, leaving the fiddles behind. These were found stored away in a cellar after the Revolution, and eventually reached Reade, who records that he sold one of them for more than he paid for the whole lot. At the time of the Special Loan Exhibition of Musical Instruments held at the South Kensington Museum in 1872, Reade wrote a series of letters on Cremona fiddles in the *Pall Mall Gazette*, in which he propounded the theory that the ' Lost Cremona Varnish ' was a spirit varnish laid over an oil varnish. Coming as it did from so noted a connoisseur, there were many who accepted the theory as the solution of the question. These letters were privately reprinted by G. H. M. Muntz, under the title *A Lost Art Revived : Cremona Violins and Varnish* (Gloucester, 1873), and again in the volume entitled *Readiana* (Chatto & Windus, 1882). In later life Charles Reade abandoned fiddles and fiddle-trading, but we find traces of his infatuation in his writings. The adventurous career of John Frederick Lott, the violin-maker, is told by him, somewhat romantically,

in his novel *Jack of all Trades* ; whilst interesting matter concerning the violin comes into *Christie Johnstone* and his collection of tales entitled *Cream*.

BIBL.—CHARLES L. and Rev. COMPTON READE, *Charles Reade*; JOHN COLEMAN, *Charles Reade*; SUTHERLAND-EDWARDS, *Personal Recollections*; G. HART, *The Violin*; D.N.B.
                                        E. H.-A.

READING, JOHN. There were three musicians of this name, all organists.

(1) JOHN (d. 1692), appointed Junior Vicar-Choral of Lincoln Cathedral, Oct. 10, 1667, Poor Vicar, Nov. 28, 1667, and master of the choristers, June 7, 1670. He succeeded Randolph Jewett as organist of Winchester Cathedral in 1675, and retained the office until 1681, when he was appointed organist of Winchester College. He was the composer of the Latin Graces sung before and after meat at the annual College election times, and the well-known Winchester School song, ' Dulce Domum ' ; all printed in Dr. Philip Hayes's ' Harmonia Wiccamica.'

(2) JOHN, organist of Chichester Cathedral, 1674–1720. Several songs included in collections published between 1681 and 1688 are probably by one or other of these two Readings.

(3) JOHN (b. 1677 ; d. Sept. 2, 1764) was a chorister of the Chapel Royal under Dr. Blow. In 1696–98 he was organist of Dulwich College.[1] He was appointed Junior Vicar and Poor Clerk of Lincoln Cathedral, Nov. 21, 1702, master of the choristers, Oct. 5, 1703, and instructor of the choristers in vocal music, Sept. 28, 1704. He appears to have resigned these posts in 1707, and to have returned to London, where he became organist of St. John, Hackney (in 1708), St. Dunstan in the West, St. Mary Woolchurchhaw, Lombard Street, and St. Mary Woolnoth. He published ' A Book of New Songs (after the Italian manner) with Symphonies and a Thorough Bass fitted to the Harpsichord, etc.,' and (about 1709) ' A Book of New Anthems.'

There was another person named Reading who was a singer at Drury Lane in the latter part of the 17th century. In June 1695 he and Pate, another singer at the theatre, were removed from their places and fined 20 marks each for being engaged in a riot at the Dog Tavern, Drury Lane, but were soon after reinstated.

A Rev. John Reading, D.D., Prebendary of Canterbury Cathedral, preached there a sermon in defence of church music, and published it in 1663.          W. H. H.

REAL FUGUE, see FUGUE.

REAY, SAMUEL (b. Hexham, Mar. 17, 1822 ; d. Newark, July 21 or 22, 1905), was noted for his fine voice and careful singing as a chorister at Durham Cathedral. After leaving the choir he had organ lessons from Stimpson of Birmingham, and then became successively

---

[1] Information from Dr. W. H. Cummings.

## LXIV

MUSICAL INSTRUMENTS — ENGLAND (c. 1175)

(University Libr., Glasgow)

Above: Chimebells.    Centre: Harp.    Below: Rebec, Panpipes, Recorder and Viol.
Medallions: Psaltery, Handbells and Organistrum.

organist at St. Andrew's, Newcastle (1845); St. Peter's, Tiverton (1847); St. John's Parish Church, Hampstead (1854); St. Saviour's, Warwick Road (1856); St. Stephen's, Paddington; Radley College (1859, succeeding Dr. E. G. Monk); Bury, Lancashire (1861); and in 1864 was appointed 'Song-schoolmaster and organist' of the parish church, Newark, retiring from the latter post in 1901, but retaining that of Song-schoolmaster on the Magnus foundation until his death. In 1879 he distinguished himself by producing at the Bow and Bromley Institute, London, two comic cantatas of J. S. Bach (' Caffee-Cantate ' and ' Bauern-Cantate '), which were performed there —certainly for the first time in England—on Oct. 27, under his direction, to English words of his own adaptation. Reay published a Morning and Evening Service in F, several anthems and two madrigals (all Novello); but was best known as a writer of partsongs, some of which (' The clouds that wrap,' ' The dawn of day,' written for the Tiverton Vocal Society) were deservedly popular.       G.

REBAB (REBABA), a bowed instrument in popular use in Egypt and northern Africa: it has a rectangular body and one or two strings of twisted horsehair. (*PLATE LXXXVII.* No. 1; see VIOL FAMILY.)       F. W. G.

REBEC (Ital. *ribeca, ribeba*; Span. *rabé, rabel*), the French name (said to be of Arabic origin) of that primitive stringed instrument which was in use throughout western Europe in the Middle Ages, and was the parent of the viol and violin, and is identical with the German ' Geige ' and the English ' fiddle '; in outline something like the mandoline, of which it was probably the parent. It was shaped like the half of a pear, and was everywhere solid except at the two extremities, the upper of which was formed into a peg-box identical with that still in use, and surmounted by a carved human head. The lower half was considerably cut down in level, thus leaving the upper solid part of the instrument to form a natural finger-board. The portion thus cut down was scooped out, and over the cavity thus formed was glued a short pine table, pierced with two trefoil-shaped sound-holes, and fitted with a bridge and sound-post (see *PLATE LXXXVII.* No. 3). The player either rested the curved end of the instrument lightly against the breast, or else held it like the violin, between the chin and the collar-bone, and bowed it like the violin. It had three stout gut strings, tuned the lower strings of the violin (A, D, G). Its tone was loud and harsh, emulating the female voice, according to a French poem of the 13th century.

> ' Quidam rebecam arcuabant,
> Muliebrem vocem confingentes.' [1]

[1] D'Aymeric de Peyrat; see Du Cange's *Glossarium*, s.v. Bandora.'

An old Spanish poem speaks of ' el rabé gritador,' [2] or the ' squalling rebec.' This powerful tone made it useful in the mediæval orchestra; and Henry the Eighth employed the rebec in his state band. It was chiefly used, however, to accompany dancing; and Shakespeare's musicians in *Romeo and Juliet*, Hugh Rebeck, Simon Catling (Catgut) and James Soundpost were undoubtedly rebec-players. After the invention of instruments of the viol and violin type it was banished to the streets of towns and to rustic festivities, whence the epithet ' jocund ' applied to it in Milton's *L' Allegro*. It was usually accompanied by the drum or tambourine. It was in vulgar use in France in the 18th century, as is proved by an ordinance issued by Guignon in his official capacity as ' Roi des Violons ' in 1742, in which street-fiddlers are prohibited from using anything else:

> ' Il leur sera permis d'y jouer d'une espèce d'instrument à trois cordes seulement, et connu sous le nom de rebec, sans qu'ils puissent se servir d'un violon à quatre cordes sous quelque prétexte que ce soit.'

A similar order is extant, dated 1628, in which it is forbidden to play the treble or bass violin ' dans les cabarets et les mauvais lieux,' but only the rebec. The rebec was extinct in England earlier than in France. It is now totally disused, and no specimen was known until, at the Exhibition of Musical Instruments at Milan in 1881, six genuine specimens were shown. Representations of it in sculpture, painting, manuscripts, etc., are abundant.

The custom of playing songs in unison with the voice, which came into vogue in the 15th century, resulted in the classification of rebecs into definite ' sets ' answering in pitch to the treble, alto, tenor and bass voices. Martin Agricola, in his *Musica instrumentalis*, 1528, gives woodcuts of a ' set ' of rebecs which he calls discant, altus, tenor and bassus.       E. J. P.; addn. E. H.-A.

REBEL, (1) JEAN-FÉRY (b. Paris, Apr. 1666; d. there, Jan. 2, 1747), the son of JEAN, a singer in the service of the French court from 1661 to his death in 1692. He was a pupil of Lully, and probably entered the Académic Royale de Musique as violinist in 1700. After a precocious childhood he entered the Opéra as a violinist. In 1703 he produced ' Ulysse,' opera in five acts with prologue, containing a *pas seul* for François Prévôt to an air called ' Le Caprice,' for violin solo. The opera failed, but the caprice remained for years the test-piece of the *ballerine* at the Opéra. After this success Rebel composed violin solos for various other ballets, such as ' La Boutade,' ' Les Caractères de la danse ' (1715), ' Terpsichore ' (1720), ' La Fantaisie ' (1727), ' Les Plaisirs champêtres ' and ' Les Éléments.' Several of these were engraved, as were his sonatas for the violin.

[2] Don Ant. Rod. de Hita; see Vidal, *Les Instruments à archet*.

In 1713 he was accompanist at the Opéra, and in 1717 was one of the ' 24 violons,' and by 1720 ' compositeur de la chambre ' to the king. This latter office he resigned in 1727 in favour of his son François, and later passed on to him the duties of conductor of the Opéra, which he had fulfilled for many years. He was buried on Jan. 3, 1747.

His sister, (2) ANNE-RENÉE (b. 1662; d. 1722), became one of the best singers of the court, and from the age of 11 years appeared in the ballet, etc. She was married in 1684 to Michel Richard de LALANDE (q.v.).

Jean - Féry's son, (3) FRANÇOIS (b. Paris, June 19, 1701; d. there, Nov. 7, 1775), at 13 played the violin in the Opéra orchestra. It seems to have been at Prague, during the festivities at the coronation of Charles VI. in 1723, that he became intimate with François Francœur ; the two composed conjointly, and produced at the Opéra, the following operas: ' Pyrame et Thisbé ' (1726) ; ' Tarsis et Zélie ' (1728) ; ' Scanderbeg ' (1735) ; Ballet de la paix ' (1738) ; ' Les Augustales ' and ' Le Retour du roi ' (1744) ; ' Zélindor,' ' Le Trophée ' (in honour of Fontenoy, 1745) ; ' Ismène ' (1750) ; ' Les Génies tutélaires ' (1751) ; and ' Le Prince de Noisy ' (1760), most of which were composed for court fêtes or public rejoicings. Rebel seems to have been the sole author of a 'Pastorale héroïque' (1730).

From 1733–44 Rebel and Francœur were joint leaders of the Opéra orchestra, and in 1753 were appointed managers. They soon, however, retired in disgust at the petty vexations they were called upon to endure. Louis XV. made them surintendants of his music, with the Order of St. Michel. In Mar. 1757 these inseparable friends obtained the privilege of the Opéra, and directed it for ten years on their own account with great administrative ability.

Rebel composed some cantatas, a Te Deum and a De Profundis, performed at the Concert Spirituel, but all his music is now forgotten, excepting a lively air in the first finale of ' Pyrame et Thisbé ' which was adapted to a much-admired pas seul of Mlle. de Camargo, thence became a popular contredanse—the first instance of such adaptation—and in this form is preserved in the ' Clé du caveau,' under the title of ' La Camargo.' A very interesting account of the family, with detailed notices of the music of J. F. Rebel, appeared in the Sammelbände of the Int. Mus. Ges. vol. vii. p. 253, by M. L. de La Laurencie. This work established the high importance, in the history of French instrumental music, of the works which he has there catalogued :

1. Vln. pieces with basso continuo, divided into a series of tunes. (1705.)
2. Caprice. (1711.)
3. Boutade. (1712.)
4. Collection of 12 sonatas, for 2 and 3 parts, with basso continuo. (1712–13.) (Original date, 1695.)

5. Vln. sonatas, together with many pieces for the vla. (1713.)
6. ' Caractères de la danse.' (1715.)
7. ' La Terpsichore,' sonata. (1720.)
8. ' Fantaisie.' (1729.)
9. ' Les Plaisirs champêtres.' (1734.)
10. ' Les Éléments, symphonie nouvelle.' (1737.)

BIBL.—L. de LA LAURENCIE, L'École française de violon de Lully à Viotti, i. (1922), pp. 71-102. Portrait.

G. C. ; addns. M. P.

REBELLO, João Soares (or João Lourenço) (b. Arcos, or Caminha, 1610 ; d. near Lisbon, Nov. 16, 1661), Portuguese composer, fellow-student of King John IV. At 14 he entered the choir of the ducal chapel at Villa Viçosa, and was not forgotten when John IV. ascended the throne. He was choirmaster, received titles and honours, and it was to him that the king dedicated his Defence of Modern Music. The works of ' Rebellinho ' were printed, in accordance with a clause in the King's will.

' Psalmi tum vesperarum tum completarum. Item Magnificat, Lamentationes et Miserere.' Rome, 1657. (Bibl. Nac., Lisbon ; partbooks of 2nd choir, only.)

Other works in MS. for 4 to 17 v. are mentioned, but are apparently lost.         J. B. T.

REBER, Napoléon-Henri (b. Mülhausen, Oct. 21, 1807 ; d. Paris, Nov. 24, 1880), entered at 20 the Paris Conservatoire, studying counterpoint and fugue under Seuriot and Jelensperger, and composition under Lesueur. Circumstances led him to compose chamber music, after the success of which he attempted opera. His music to the second act of the charming ballet ' Le Diable amoureux ' (Sept. 23, 1840) was followed at the Opéra-Comique by ' La Nuit de Noël,' three acts (Feb. 9, 1848), ' Le Père Gaillard,' three acts (Sept. 7, 1852), ' Les Papillotes de M. Benoît,' one act (Dec. 28, 1853) and ' Les Dames capitaines,' three acts (June 3, 1857). In these works he strove to counteract the tendency towards noise and bombast then so prevalent both in French and Italian opera, and to show how much may be made out of the simple natural materials of the old French opéra-comique by the judicious use of modern orchestration.

In 1851 he was appointed professor of harmony at the Conservatoire, and in 1853 the well-merited success of ' Le Père Gaillard ' procured his election to the Institut as Onslow's successor. Soon after this he renounced the theatre and returned to chamber music. He also began to write on music, and his well-known Traité d'harmonie (1862) went through many editions.

In 1862 Reber succeeded Halévy as professor of composition at the Conservatoire ; since 1871 he was also inspector of the succursales or branches of the Conservatoire. He died after a short illness and was succeeded as member of the Institut by Saint-Saëns. He was made chevalier of the Légion d'Honneur in 1855, and officier in 1870.

His compositions comprise four symphonies, a quintet and three quartets for strings, one PF. ditto, seven trios, duets for PF. and violin, and

PF. pieces for two and four hands. Portions of his ballet ' Le Diable amoureux ' have been published for orchestra, and performed at concerts. In 1875 he produced a cantata called ' Roland,' but ' Le Ménétrier à la cour,' opéra-comique, and ' Naïm,' grand opera in five acts, were never performed, though the overtures are engraved.    G. C. ; addns. M. L. P.

REBHUHN (REPHUN), PAUL, an early 16th-century (? Saxon) poet-composer. He wrote dramas to which he composed the music (introduction, songs, choruses). A modern edition was published by the Litterarische Verein, Stuttgart, 1859 (vol. 49 ; other ed. in Q.-L.). His ' Susanna,' first published at

secco was played on a harpsichord and pianoforte from a figured bass ; during the earlier half of the 19th century the practice arose, more especially in England, of using double-bass and violoncello, the former playing the basso continuo, the latter the harmonies arpeggiando (see DRAGONETTI and LINDLEY). It is recorded that Lindley often embellished his share by the introduction of figures and ornamental passages ; but, however ingenious this may have been, it was entirely at variance with the effect intended by the composer, which was simply to give support to the vocal line and to conjoin the modulations of the music :

Zwickau in 1536, is a good example of his attempt to bring order into the rhythmical construction of his rhymes on classical lines, and in this he was a precursor of Opitz (A. Koberstein, Gesch. der deutschen National-literatur ; Q.-L.).

RECITA (Ital.), ' performance.'

RECITAL, a term which has come into use in England to signify a performance of solo music by one performer. It was probably first used by Liszt at his performance at the Hanover Square Rooms, June 9, 1840, though as applying to the separate pieces and not to the whole performance. The advertisement of the concert says that ' M. Liszt will give Recitals on the Pianoforte of the following pieces.' The name was afterwards adopted by HALLÉ (q.v.) and others, and is in the present day often applied to concerts when two or more soloists take part.    G.

RECITATIVE (Fr. récitatif ; Ger. Recitativ ; Ital. recitativo ; from the Latin recitare) is the name given to the declamatory portions of an opera, oratorio or cantata as opposed to the lyrical. Recitativo secco denotes the type of recitative where the rhythm is free to follow the verbal accentuation, the interest thus lying in the vocal part, the accompaniment being reduced to the merest frame ; recitativo stromentato, on the other hand, has a more elaborate instrumental part, the music necessarily becoming of a more rhythmical pattern (see OPERA). Recitative in one form or another must always be a part of the opera structure ; it is here that the necessary explanations and formal dialogue are dealt with, and there is no difference in essentials between such passages in latter-day works and those of Peri and Monteverdi. For a long time the recitativo

For a discussion of the English recitative see under PURCELL : CHARACTERISTICS OF PURCELL'S ART, subsection LANGUAGE IN SONG.

BIBL.—CHARLOTTE SPITZ, Die Entwickelung des ' Stile Recitativo.' A.M., Apr. 1921, pp. 237-44.    N. C. G.

RECITING-NOTE (Lat. repercussio, nota dominans), a name sometimes given to that important note in a Gregorian tone on which the greater portion of every verse of a psalm or canticle is continuously recited. As this particular note invariably corresponds with the dominant of the mode in which the psalm tone is written, the terms dominant and reciting-note are frequently treated as interchangeable. (See MODES ; PSALMODY.)

    W. S. R.

The term is similarly applied to the corresponding notes of the Anglican chant. (See CHANT and CHANTING.)

RECORDER, see FIPPLE FLUTE (1).

RECTE ET RETRO, PER (Lat. imitatio cancrizans, imitatio per motum retrogradum, imitatio recurrens ; Ital. imitazione al rovescio, o alla riversa ; Eng. retrograde imitation). A peculiar kind of imitation, so constructed that the melody may be sung backwards as well as forwards ; as shown in the following two-part canon, which must be sung by the first voice from left to right, and by the second from right to left, both beginning together, but at opposite ends of the music.

The earliest known instances of Retrograde Imitation are to be found among the works of the Flemish composers of the 15th century, who delighted in exercising their ingenuity, not only upon the device itself, but also upon the Inscriptions prefixed to the canons in which it was employed. The Netherlanders were not, however, the only musicians who indulged successfully in this learned species of recreation. Probably the most astonishing example of it on record is the motet,[1] 'Diliges Dominum,' written by William Byrd for four voices— treble, alto, tenor and bass—and transmuted into an eight-part composition, by adding a second treble, alto, tenor and bass, formed by singing the four first parts backwards. It is scarcely possible to study this complication attentively, without feeling one's brain turn giddy ; yet, strange to say, the effect produced is less curious than beautiful.

There is little doubt that the idea of singing music from right to left was first suggested by

reversed, as well as the sequence of the notes, is called 'Retrograde Inverse Imitation' (Lat. imitatio cancrizans motu contrario ; Ital. imitazione al contrario riverso). It might have been thought that this would have contented even Flemish ingenuity. But it did not. The partbooks had not yet been turned upside-down ! In the subjoined example we have endeavoured to show, in a humble way, the manner in which this most desirable feat may also be accomplished. The two singers, standing face to face, hold the book between them ; one looking at it from the ordinary point of view, the other, upside-down, and both reading from left to right—that is to say, beginning at opposite ends. The result, if not strikingly beautiful, is, at least, not inconsistent with the laws of counterpoint. (For other examples see INSCRIPTION.)

Retrograde Imitation has survived in more

Lau - da - te Dominum, om - nes     gen - tes,     om - nes     gen - tes, lau - da - te Do - mi - num.

those strange oracular verses [2] which may be read either backwards or forwards, without injury to words or metre ; such as the well-known pentameter—

'Roma tibi subito motibus ibit amor,'

or the cry of the Evil Spirits—

'In girum imus noctu ecce ut consumimur igni.'

The canons were frequently constructed in exact accordance with the method observed in these curious lines ; and innumerable quaint conceits were invented, for the purpose of giving the singers some intimation of the manner in which they were to be read. 'Canit more Hebraeorum' was a very common motto. 'Misericordia et veritas obviaverunt sibi' indicated that the singers were to begin at opposite ends, and meet in the middle. In the second Agnus Dei of his 'Missa Graecorum,' Hobrecht wrote, 'Aries vertatur in Pisces'— Aries being the first sign of the Zodiac, and Pisces the last. In another part of the same Mass he has given a far more mysterious direction—

'Tu tenor cancriza et per antifrasin canta, Cum furcis in capite antifrasizando repete.'

This introduces us to a new complication ; the secret of the motto being, that the tenor is not only to sing backwards, but to invert the intervals ('per antifrasin canta'), until he reaches the 'horns'—that is to say, the two cusps of the semicircular time-signature—after which he is to sing from left to right, though still continuing to invert the intervals. This new device, in which the intervals themselves are

than one very popular form. In the year 1791 Haydn wrote for his Doctor's degree, at the University of Oxford, a 'Canon cancrizans, a tre' ('Thy Voice, O Harmony'), which will be found in Vol. II. p. 574, and he has also used the same device in the minuet of one of his symphonies. (Cf. ROVESCIO, AL.) But perhaps it has never yet appeared in a more popular form than that of the well-known double chant by Dr. Crotch :

Sir John Stainer wrote a hymn-tune 'Per Recte et Retro' in 1898 for the Church Hymnary (No. 381) ; it is also No. 81 of Novello's edition of the composer's hymns. It reads backwards in all the parts.    w. s. r.

REDFORD, JOHN (b. circa 1485 ; d. circa 1545), English organist, composer and dramatist. He is said [3] to have received his early training in the choir school of St. Paul's Cathedral, and later to have been appointed a vicar - choral there. He subsequently became organist, almoner and master of the choristers, although there is no record of him in any such capacity before 1530. Thomas Tusser was taken into St. Paul's choir school about 1535, and was thus a pupil of Redford. In the former's One Hundred Points of Husbandrye (1557), an autobiographical poem, which describes how he was 'impressed' as a choir - boy from Wallingford and ultimately

---

1 Reprinted by Hawkins, History, ch. 96.
2 Versus recurrentes, said to have been first invented by the Greek poet, Sotades, during the reign of Ptolemy Philadelphus. The examples we have quoted are, however, of much later date ; the oldest of them being certainly not earlier than the 7th century.

3 W. H. Grattan Flood, Early Tudor Composers, p. 96.

got into St. Paul's choir, he gives the following eulogy of Redford :

> 'But mark the chance, myself to vance,
> By friendship's lot to Paul's I got.
> So found I grace a certain space.
>     Still to remaine.
> With Redford there—the like nowhere
> For cunning such and vertue much,
> By whom some part of music's art
>     So did I gaine.'

Redford was fortunate in being at St. Paul's while Pace and Sampson were there. Pace succeeded Colet as dean, 1519, and Sampson succeeded Pace, 1536. Pace was an excellent musician (see PYGOTT), while SAMPSON (*q.v.*) was himself a composer. Redford no doubt received some encouragement from them, not only, perhaps, in his church composition, but also in the preparation of choir - boy plays (usually with music), which was one of his duties as choirmaster. The children of the Chapel Royal and of St. George's Chapel, Windsor, were similarly employed, and besides Redford, such men as Gilbert Banastir, Cornyshe, Heywood, Richard Edwardes and William Hunnis, in their capacities as masters of the children, set up a standard of excellence in these plays which soon came to threaten the interests of adult professional actors, and finally resulted in the famous 'boys and players' controversy of Shakespeare's time. Grattan Flood, quoting from the *Calendar of Letters and Papers of Henry VIII.*, refers to an occasion on Nov. 10, 1527, when 'the children of Paules' presented at Greenwich a Latin-French play for the entertainment of the French nobles. Redford was no doubt in charge of this, but more definite evidence as to his activities in this direction is provided by his Morality play 'Wyt and Science,' [1] (B.M. Add. MSS. 15,233). This was printed by Halliwell for the Shakespeare Society in 1848, and, besides its 1000 or so lines of dialogue contains the words of three songs (' Gyve place to honest recreacion,' ' Welcum myne owne ' and ' Exceedyng mesure '), which Redford no doubt set himself. That other music was also provided is shown by a note at the end :

'Heere cumth in fowre wyth violes and sing "remembraunce," and at the last quere (verse) all make cur(t)sye and so goe forth syngyng.'

The play itself is made up of the usual rather dreary didactic dialogue, but it was adapted in more than one Elizabethan interlude (see J. Seifert, *Wit and Science Moralitäten*, 1892). The last page of another Morality by Redford is also in the MS. ; at the end is the note, 'Here the(y) syng "Hey nony, nonye," and so go furth syngyng.'

Redford's name is included in the list of 'Practicioners' in music given in Morley's *Plaine and Easie Introduction*, 1597. His

[1] Grattan Flood gives the date of its performance as 1538–39, but Brandl dates the play between 1541 (when the 'gaillard,' which is mentioned, was first danced in England), and the death of Katherine Parr in 1548. (See E. K. Chambers, *Medieval Stage*, vol. ii. p. 454.)

anthem, ' Rejoice in the Lord alway,' is still known and sung ; it was first printed in the appendix to Hawkins's *History* ; later by the Motet Society ; and in 1894 by Novello (edited by Sir G. C. Martin). A 4-part motet by ' Redfurde,' ' Christus resurgens,' is in the British Museum (Add. MSS. 17,802 - 5), and another '[Lumbi] vestri precincti,' *a* 6, at Oxford (Ch. Ch. 979-83, tenor part wanting). But the great bulk of what remains to us of Redford's music is in the form of what is usually described in library catalogues as organ ' solos ' or ' voluntaries.' Seeing that these pieces usually have Latin titles, it is much more probable that they were reductions in score of what were originally motets for voices. The reduction is not necessarily a complete one (particularly in the ' full,' as opposed to the ' verse ' parts), and was no doubt used chiefly to support the voices. B.M. Add. MSS. 30,513 is in the hand of Thomas Mulliner, a later choirmaster at St. Paul's, and contains twenty or so of these motet arrangements by Redford, on two staves of from 5 to 8 lines each, or on a single stave of from 11 to 13 lines. These are enumerated below :

* ' Aurora luxis,' ' Christe qui lux ' (2), * ' Eterne rerum conditor,' ' Eterne Rex altissime,' * ' Exultet celum laudibus,' ' Glorificamus,' * ' Iste Confessor ' (2), ' Jam lucis,' * ' Lucem tuam ' (2), * ' Miserere,'' O Lux ' (' on the fabourden '), * ' O Lux,' * ' Salvator ' (2), ' Te per orbem terrarum,' ' Veni Redemptor,' * ' Verbum supernum,' ' Sine Nomine ' and ' A meane.'
B.M. Add. MSS. 15,233, besides the ' Eterne Rerum ' of above, also contains five others by Redford as below :
    ' Primo dierum,' ' Ad cenam Agni providi,' T.D.' ' Alme siderum conditor ' and ' Tui sunt ceh.'
B.M. Add. MSS. 29,996 is a similar collection of some 91 pieces. Nos. 1-50 appear to be in Redford's hand. He is probably author of all the anonymous pieces among these, but only the following (apart from motets already enumerated) bear his name :
    ' A solis ortus cardine,' ' Christe Redemptor,' ' Deus Creator omnium,' ' Felix namque ' (2), ' Justus et palma,' ' Lucis Creator,' ' Precatus est Moyses.'
Besides these, Ch. Ch. (1034) contains an isolated ' organ voluntary ' (probably a motet ' sine nomine '), and organ scores of the following (Ch. 371) :
    Agnus, ' Anguelare [*sic*] fundamentum,' Miserere (2) and ' Veni Redemptor.'
*N.B.*—Roy. MSS. 31-35 is a 16th-century collection of 33 motets for 4, 5, 6, 7 and 8 v., possibly all by Derick GERARDE (*q.v.*) ; vol. iii. contains the following note : ' finis qd. master Redford.' Redford, a contemporary of Gerarde, may thus be the composer of some of these, but none of them is in his hand (cf. B.M. Add. MSS. 29,996).

                                                    J. M[K].

REDHEAD, RICHARD (*b.* Harrow, Mar. 1, 1820 ; *d.* Hallingley, Sussex, Apr. 27, 1901), was a chorister at Magdalen College, Oxford, 1829–36, having received his musical education there from Walter Vicary, the organist. He was organist at Old Margaret Chapel (now All Saints' Church), Margaret Street, in 1839-1864, and from the latter date at St. Mary Magdalene, Paddington, a post he held till his death. His works are almost exclusively written or compiled for use in the Church of England, viz. ' Church Music,' etc., 1840, ' Laudes Diurnae, the Psalter and Canticles in the Morning and Evening Service,' 1843, Music for the Office of the Holy Communion,' 1853 ; ' O My people,' anthem for Good Friday ; ' Church Melodies, a collection of short pieces and Six Sacred Songs,' 1858 ; ' The Cele

* Described as being ' withe a meane.'

brant's Office Book,' 1863 ; 'Ancient Hymn Melodies, Book of Common Prayer with Ritual music, Canticles at Matins and Evensong, pointed as they are to be sung in churches and adapted to the Ancient Psalm Chants, and Parish Tune Book and Appendix,' 1865 ; 'The Universal Organist, a Collection of Short Classical and Modern Pieces,' 1866–81 ; 'Litany with latter part of Commination Service, Music to the Divine Liturgy during the Gradual, Offertorium and Communion, arranged for use throughout the year,' 1874 ; Festival Hymns for All Saints and St. Mary Magdalene Days, Hymns for Holy Seasons, Anthems, etc.    A. C.

REDI, TOMASO (b. Siena, 2nd half of 17th cent. ; d. circa 1735), maestro di cappella of S. Casa di Loretto, Rome, at the time of his death, which position he had filled for about forty years. He composed masses and other church music of excellence. His controversy with Padre Martini about the resolution of a canon by Animuccia has been reported in various places. (See Q.-L. and Fétis.)

REDOUTE, public assemblies at which the guests appeared with or without masks at pleasure. The word is French, and is explained by Voltaire and Littré as being derived from the Italian ridotto—perhaps with some analogy to the word ' resort.'

Such assemblies soon made their way to Germany and England. They are frequently mentioned by Horace Walpole under the name ' Ridotto,' and were one of the attractions at Vauxhall and Ranelagh in the middle of the 18th century. In Germany and France the French version of the name was adopted. The building used for the purpose in Vienna, erected in 1748, and rebuilt in stone in 1754, forms part of the Burg or Imperial Palace, the side of the oblong facing the Josephs-Platz. There was a grosse and a kleine Redoutensaal. In the latter Beethoven played a concerto of his own at a concert of Haydn, Dec. 18, 1795. The rooms were used for concerts till about 1870. The masked balls were held there during the Carnival, from Twelfth Night to Shrove Tuesday, and occasionally in the weeks preceding Advent ; some being public, i.e. open to all on payment of an entrance fee, and others private. Special nights were reserved for the court and the nobility. The ' Redoutentänze '—Minuets, Allemandes, Contredanses, Schottisches, Anglaises and Ländler—were composed for full orchestra, and published (mostly by Artaria) for pianoforte. Mozart,[1] Haydn, Beethoven,[2] Hummel, Woelfl, Gyrowetz and others, have left dances written for this purpose.    C. F. P.

REDOWA, a Bohemian dance which was introduced into Paris in 1845, and quickly

1 See Köchel's Catalogue, No. 599, etc.
2 See Nottebohm's Thematic Catalogue, Section ii. pp. 135-7.

attained for a short time great popularity, both there and in London, although it is now never danced. In Bohemia there are two variations of the dance, the Rejdovák, in 3–4 or 3–8 time, which is more like a waltz, and the Rejdovacka, in 2–4 time, which is something like a polka. The ordinary Redowa is written in 3–4 time (M.M. |=160). The dance is something like a Mazurka, with the rhythm less strongly marked. The following example is part of a Rejdovák which is given in Köhler's ' Volkstänze aller Nationen '—

W. B. S.

REED (Fr. anche ; Ger. Blatt, Rohr ; Ital. ancia). The speaking part of many instruments, both ancient and modern ; the name being derived from the material of which it has been immemorially constructed. The plant used for it is a tall grass or reed, the Arundo donax or sativa, growing in the south of Europe. The substance in its rough state is commonly called ' cane,' though differing from real cane in many respects. The chief supply is now obtained from Fréjus on the Mediterranean coast. Many other materials, such as lance-wood, ivory, silver and ' ebonite,' or hardened india-rubber, have been experimentally substituted for the material first named ; but hitherto without success. Organ reeds were formerly made of hard wood, more recently of brass, German silver and steel. The name Reed is, however, applied by organ-builders to the metal tube or channel against which the vibrating tongue beats, rather than to the vibrator itself.

Reeds are divided into the ' Free ' and the ' Beating '; the latter again into the ' Single ' and the ' Double ' forms. The free reed is used in the harmonium and concertina, its union with beating reeds in the organ not having proved successful. The vibrator, as its name implies, passes freely through the long slotted brass plate to which it is adapted ; the first impulse of the wind tending to push it within the slot and thus close the aperture. In ' percussion ' harmoniums the vibrator is set suddenly in motion by a blow from a hammer connected with the keyboard (see HARMONIUM). The beating reed in its single form is that of the organ and the clarinet. In this the edges of the vibrator overlap the slot leading into the resonating pipe or tube, and so close it periodically during vibration. The reed, which is a thin blade or lamina, has roughly the form of a long parallelogram, and it is firmly secured for a portion of its length to the bed or table of the tube or mouthpiece in which the slot is cut. In the organ reed the necessary opening for the entrance of the wind at the free end is obtained by giving a slight curvature to the blade or reed; the pressure of the wind tends to close this opening, and vibration is thus set up. In the clarinet the same result is obtained by giving a slight curvature to the bed of the mouthpiece towards its tip, the under side of the reed itself being left perfectly flat (see CLARINET).

The double reed, as used in the oboe and the bassoon, is constructed of two segments united in a tubular form at one end, and splayed out and flattened at the other so as to leave a slight opening in shape like the section of a double-convex lens. The bassoon reed is placed directly upon the 'crook' of the instrument, but the oboe reed is built up upon a small tube or 'staple.' The exact appearance of both single and double reeds will be gathered better from the drawings than from a more detailed description.

Single Reed : 1. Clarinet reed, as held to the mouthpiece by a metal ligature.
Double Reeds : 2. Bassoon reed. 3. Bassoon reed, foreshortened to show the opening between the two blades. 4. Oboe reed.

The single reed is used also on the saxophone, and the double reed for the chaunter of the Highland bagpipe, but the drones of the bagpipe are sounded by single reeds of a most rudimentary character. It is possible to replace the double reed of the oboe and bassoon by a single reed of the clarinet type fitted to a small mouthpiece. The old dolcino, alto-fagotto or tenoroon (see BASSOON, 3) was so played in the band of the Coldstream Guards by Henry Lazarus when a boy. The idea has been revived of late years as a novelty, but neither the oboe nor the bassoon is capable of improvement in this way, although the saxophone, also a

conical tube, is well adapted to the single reed, being an instrument of wider calibre. (See MOUTHPIECE.)      W. H. S. ; addns. D. J. B.

REED, THOMAS GERMAN (b. Bristol, June 27, 1817 ; d. Upper East Sheen, Surrey, Mar. 21, 1888). His father was a musician, and the son first appeared, at the age of 10, at the Bath concerts as a PF. player with John Loder and Lindley, and also sang at the concerts and at the Bath Theatre. Shortly after, he appeared at the Haymarket Theatre, London, where his father was conductor, as PF. player, singer and actor of juvenile parts. In 1832 the family moved to London, and the father became leader of the band at the Garrick Theatre. His son was his deputy, and also organist to the Roman Catholic Chapel, Sloane Street. German Reed was an early member of the Society of British Musicians, he studied hard at harmony, counterpoint and PF. playing, composed much, gave many lessons, and took part in all the good music he met with. His work at the theatre consisted in great measure of scoring and adapting, and getting up new operas, such as 'Fra Diavolo' in 1837. In 1838 he became musical director of the Haymarket Theatre, a post which he retained till 1851. In 1838 he also succeeded Tom Cooke as Kapellmeister at the Royal Bavarian Chapel. Beethoven's Mass in C was produced there for the first time in England, and the principal Italian singers habitually took part in the Sunday services. At the Haymarket, for the Shakespearean performances of Macready, the Keans, the Cushmans, etc., he made many excellent innovations, by introducing, as overtures and entr'actes, good pieces, original or scored by himself, instead of the rubbish usually played at that date. During the temporary closing of the theatre, Reed produced Pacini's opera of 'Sappho' at Drury Lane (Apr. 1, 1843). In 1844 he married Miss Priscilla Horton, and during the next few years directed the production of English opera at the Surrey, managed Sadler's Wells during a season of English opera, with his wife, Miss Louisa Pyne, Harrison, etc., conducted the music at the Olympic under Wigan's management, and made prolonged provincial tours.

In 1855 he started a new class of performance which, under the name of 'Mr. and Mrs. German Reed's Entertainment,' [1] made his name widely known in England. Its object was to provide good dramatic amusement for a large class of society who, on various grounds, objected to the theatres. It was opened at St. Martin's Hall, Apr. 2, 1855, as 'Miss P. Horton's Illustrative Gatherings,' with two pieces called 'Holly Lodge' and 'The Enraged Musician' (after Hogarth), written by W. Brough, and presented by Mrs. Reed, with the aid of her

[1] Detailed lists of these entertainments were given in previous editions of this Dictionary.

husband only, as accompanist and occasional actor. In Feb. 1856 they removed to the Gallery of Illustration, Regent Street. They then engaged John Parry, and later were joined by Miss Fanny Holland and Arthur Cecil, and soon after by Corney Grain and Alfred Reed. The repertory during this later period included various operettas and 'Opere di camera' of Offenbach, Sullivan ('Cox and Box,' and others with texts written by Gilbert). While the entertainment still remained at the Gallery of Illustration, Reed became lessee of St. George's Hall for the production of comic opera. He engaged an orchestra of forty and a strong chorus, and 'The Cóntrabandista' (Burnand and Sullivan), 'L'Ambassadrice' (Auber) and the 'Beggar's Opera' were produced, but without the necessary success. Reed then gave his sole attention to the Gallery of Illustration, in which he was uniformly successful, owing to the fact that he carried out his entertainments with talent, tact and judgment, and constant variety.

When the lease of the Gallery of Illustration expired, the entertainment was transferred to St. George's Hall, and there many more entertainments were produced both under Reed and under Corney Grain and Alfred Reed.

The librettists included F. C. Burnand, W. S. Gilbert, G. Grossmith, Gilbert à Beckett, A. Law, Comyns Carr and Walter Frith; and the composers German Reed, Molloy, King Hall, Corney Grain, Cotsford Dick, Eaton Faning, A. J. Caldicott, E. Solomon and Walter Slaughter. A. C.

The accompaniments were played on a pianoforte and harmonium. For many years the 'Musical Sketches' of Corney Grain were a principal attraction of the entertainment. German Reed died in 1888, and in 1895 the entertainments came to an end with the deaths of Alfred German Reed, Mar. 10, and Corney Grain, Mar. 16. An attempt was made to revive the enterprise, but without effect.

Mrs. GERMAN REED, née PRISCILLA HORTON (b. Birmingham, Jan. 1, 1818; d. Bexley Heath, Mar. 18, 1895), showed from a very early age unmistakable qualifications for a theatrical career, in a fine strong voice, great musical ability and extraordinary power of mimicry. She made her first appearance at the age of 10 at the Surrey Theatre, under Elliston's management, as the Gipsy Girl in 'Guy Mannering.' After this she was constantly engaged at the principal metropolitan theatres in a very wide range of parts. Her rare combination of great ability as a singer, with conspicuous gifts as an actress, and most attractive appearance, led to an engagement in 1837 with Macready for his famous performances at Covent Garden and Drury Lane, in which she acted Ariel, Ophelia, the Fool[1] in

[1] See *Macready's Reminiscences*, by Sir F. Pollock, ii. 97.

'Lear,' the Attendant Spirit in 'Comus, Philidel in 'King Arthur' and Acis in 'Acis and Galatea.' Miss Horton then became the leading spirit in Planché's graceful burlesques at the Haymarket Theatre. On Jan. 20, 1844, she married German Reed, and the rest of her career has been related under his name. She died a few days after her son and Corney Grain. G.

REED, WILLIAM HENRY (b. Frome, July 29, 1876), violinist, has been a member of the London Symphony Orchestra from its formation (1904), and its leader since 1912.

Reed studied under Sauret at the R.A.M., where he also worked at composition and theoretic studies with Corder and Prout. He is accomplished both as a solo and chamber music player, and took part in the first performances of Elgar's chamber works (see ELGAR). He is a teacher at the R.C.M., and has done much work as a conductor. Reed is a skilful composer for the orchestra, and his tone poems 'The Lincoln Imp' (Hereford, 1921) and 'Aesop's Fables' (Hereford, 1924) are full of ingenious quips of humorous instrumentation. His works further include a set of variations for strings (Worcester, 1911), 'Will o' the Wisp' (orch.) (Gloucester, 1913), 'Two Somerset Idylls' for small orchestra (Worcester, 1926), a violin concerto in A minor, a Rhapsody for violin and orchestra and chamber music. C.

REED-STOP. When the pipes of an organ, controlled by a draw-stop, produce their tone by means of a vibrating tongue striking the face of a reed, the stop is called a reed-stop. (See REED; and ORGAN, Vocabulary of Stops.)

REEL (Anglo-Saxon hreol, connected with the Suio-Gothic rulla, 'to whirl'), an ancient dance the origin of which is enveloped in much obscurity. The fact of its resemblance to the Norwegian Hallung, as well as its popularity in Scotland, and its occurrence in Denmark, the north of England and Ireland, has led most writers to attribute to it a Scandinavian origin. although its rapid movements and lively character are opposed to the oldest Scandinavian dance rhythms. The probability is that the reel is of Celtic origin, perhaps indigenous to Britain, and from there introduced into Scandinavia. In Scotland the reel is usually danced by two couples; in England—where it is now almost only found in connexion with the Sword Dance, as performed in the North Riding of Yorkshire—it is danced by three couples. The figures of the reel differ slightly according to the locality; their chief feature is their circular character, the dancers standing face to face and describing a series of figures of eight. The music consists of 8-bar phrases, generally in common time, but occasionally in 6-4. The Irish reel is played much faster than the Scottish; in Yorkshire an ordinary hornpipe tune is used. The following example, 'Lady

Nelson's Reel,' is from a MS. collection of dances in the possession of the present writer :

An example of the Danish reel will be found in Engel's 'National Music' (London, 1866).

One of the most characteristic Scottish reels is the Reel of Tulloch (Thulichan):

Others, equally good, are 'Colonel M'Bean's Reel,' ' Ye're welcome, Charlie Stuart,' ' The Cameronian Rant,' ' Johnnie's friends are ne'er pleased' and 'Flora Macdonald.'

For the slow reel, see STRATHSPEY.

W. B. S.

In *News from Scotland* (1591) it is stated that ' Giles Duncan did go before them playing a *reill* or dance upon a small trump.' The Irish reel, which is apparently alluded to here, is in 2–4, or common time, and is always danced singly : the first eight bars, danced in steps, are followed by a round for the next eight bars, when the original steps are resumed, but reversed.

W. H. G. F.

REEVE, WILLIAM (*b.* 1757 ; *d.* June 22, 1815), after quitting school, was placed with a law stationer in Chancery Lane, where his fellow-writer was Joseph Munden, afterwards the celebrated comedian. Determined, however, upon making music his profession, he became a pupil of Richardson, organist of St. James's, Westminster. In 1781 he was appointed organist of Totnes, Devonshire, where he remained till about 1783, when he was engaged as composer at Astley's. He was next for some time an actor at the regular theatres. In 1791, being then a chorus singer at Covent Garden, he was applied to, to complete the composition of the music for the ballet pantomime of 'Oscar and Malvina,' left unfinished by Shield, who, upon some differences with the manager, had resigned his appointment. Reeve thereupon produced an overture and some vocal music, which were much admired, and led to his being appointed composer to the theatre. In 1792 he was elected organist of St. Martin,

Ludgate. In 1802 he became part proprietor of Sadler's Wells Theatre. His principal dramatic compositions were :

' Oscar and Malvina ' and ' Tippoo Saib,' 1791 ; ' Orpheus and Eurydice,' partly adapted from Gluck, 1792 ; ' The Apparition,' ' British Fortitude,' ' Hercules and Omphale ' and ' The Purse, 1794 ; ' Merry Sherwood ' (containing Reeve's best-known song, ' I am a Friar of orders grey '), 1795 ; ' Harlequin and Oberon,' 1796 ; ' Bantry Bay,' ' The Round Tower ' and ' Harlequin Quixote,' 1797 ; ' Joan of Arc ' and ' Ramah Droog ' (with Mazzinghi), 1798 ; ' The Turnpike Gate ' (with Mazzinghi), ' The Embarkation ' and ' Thomas and Susan,' 1799 ; ' Paul and Virginia ' (with Mazzinghi) and ' Jamie and Anna,' 1800 ; ' Harlequin's Almanack ' and ' The Blind Girl ' (with Mazzinghi), 1801 ; ' The Cabinet ' (with Braham, Davy and Moorehead) and ' Family Quarrels ' (with Braham and Moorehead), 1802 ; ' The Caravan,' 1803 ; ' The Dash ' and ' Thirty Thousand ' (with Davy and Braham), 1804 ; ' Out of Place ' (with Braham) and ' The Corsair,' 1805 ; ' The White Plume,' ' Rokeby Castle ' and ' An Bratach,' 1806 ; ' Kais ' (with Braham), 1808 ; ' Tricks upon Travellers ' (part), 1810 ; and ' The Outside Passenger ' (with Whitaker and D. Corri), 1811.

He wrote music for some pantomimes at Sadler's Wells ; amongst them ' Bang up,' by C. Dibdin, jun., containing the favourite Clown's song, ' Tippitywitchet,' for Grimaldi. He was also author of *The Juvenile Preceptor, or Entertaining Instructor*, etc.    W. H. H.

REEVES, JOHN SIMS (*b.* Woolwich, Sept. 26,[1] 1818 ; *d.* Worthing, Oct. 25, 1900), tenor singer, son of a musician in the Royal Artillery, received his early musical instruction from his father, and at 14 obtained the post of organist at North Cray Church, Kent.

Upon gaining his mature voice he determined on becoming a singer, and, after a year spent in studying for the medical profession, in 1839 made his first appearance at the Newcastle-upon-Tyne Theatre as the Gipsy Boy in ' Guy Mannering,' and subsequently performed Dandini in ' La Cenerentola,' and other baritone parts. The true quality of his voice, however, having asserted itself, he placed himself under J. W. Hobbs and T. Cooke, and in the seasons of 1841–42 and 1842–43 was a member of Macready's company at Drury Lane, as one of the second tenors, performing such parts as the First Warrior in Purcell's ' King Arthur,' Ottocar in ' Der Freischütz,' and the like. He then went, to prosecute his studies, first to Paris under Bordogni, and subsequently to Milan under Mazzucato ; he appeared at La Scala as Edgardo in Donizetti's ' Lucia di Lammermoor ' with marked success. Returning to England he appeared at Vincent Wallace's benefit concert (Drury Lane, May 17, 1847) and other concerts, and was engaged by Jullien for the stage of Drury Lane, where he made his first appearance on Monday, Dec. 6, 1847, as Edgar in ' The Bride of Lammermoor,' and at once took position as an actor and singer of the first rank. A fortnight later he performed his first original part, Lyonnel in Balfe's ' Maid of Honour.' Berlioz, who conducted the performance, engaged him for the performance of two parts of ' La Damnation de Faust' at Drury Lane, Feb. 7, 1848. In 1848 he was engaged at Her Majesty's Theatre, and

<hr>

[1] *Memoirs of the Royal Artillery Band*, by H. G. Farmer (1904), p. 74 ff.  He entered his name in a birthday book, however, as born on Oct. 21.

came out as Carlo in Donizetti's 'Linda di Chamounix,' appearing also as Florestan in 'Fidelio.' His operatic career was more or less overshadowed by the great place he made for himself in oratorio ; he sang the part of Faust when Gounod's opera was given for the first time in English, at Her Majesty's Theatre, and for a few performances he sang Braham's old part of Sir Huon in 'Oberon.' Captain Macheath, in 'The Beggar's Opera,' was one of the last operatic parts in which he appeared.

In the autumn of 1848 he was engaged at the Norwich Musical Festival, where he showed his ability as an oratorio singer by an extraordinarily fine delivery of 'The enemy said' in 'Israel in Egypt.' On Nov. 24 following he made his first appearance at the Sacred Harmonic Society in Handel's 'Messiah.' The rapid strides which he was then making towards perfection in oratorio were shown—to take a few instances only—by his performances in 'Judas Maccabaeus' and 'Samson,' 'Elijah,' 'St. Paul' and 'Lobgesang,' and 'Eli' and 'Naaman' (both composed expressly for him). But his greatest triumph was achieved at the Handel Festival at the Crystal Palace in 1857, when, after singing in 'Messiah' and 'Judas Maccabaeus' with increased reputation, he gave 'The enemy said' in 'Israel in Egypt' with such remarkable power, fire and volume of voice, breadth of style and evenness of vocalisation, as completely electrified his hearers. He repeated this wonderful performance at several succeeding festivals, and in the Handelian repertory nothing was more striking than his delivery of 'Total Eclipse' from 'Samson.' He sang in Bach's 'St. Matthew Passion' under Sterndale Bennett in 1862.[1] His farewell concert took place at the Albert Hall on May 11, 1891, but he sang afterwards at Covent Garden and at music halls. In the quarter of a century during which his voice was at its best, he sang with Jenny Lind, Clara Novello, Tietjens, Adelina Patti and Christine Nilsson, and held his own with them all. No one could with greater certainty find the exact tone to fit the most varied emotions. It was a comprehensive talent indeed that could range at will from the levity of Captain Macheath's songs to the poignant pathos of Handel's 'Deeper and deeper still,' the emotional warmth of Beethoven's 'Adelaide' or the cycle 'An die ferne Geliebte.'

Sims Reeves married, Nov. 2, 1850, Miss EMMA LUCOMBE (d. Upper Norwood, June 10, 1895), soprano singer, who had been a pupil of Mrs. Blane Hunt, and appeared at the Sacred Harmonic Society's concert of June 19, 1839, and sang there and at other concerts until 1845, when she went to Italy. She returned in 1848, and appeared in opera as well as at concerts.

[1] This was the fourth performance of the work in London. See *Life of Sterndale Bennett*, by his son, p. 319, and Appendix A.

She retired from public life and occupied herself as a teacher of singing, for which she had a deservedly high reputation. After her death in 1895 Reeves married his pupil, Miss Maud Rene, with whom he went on a successful concert tour in South Africa in 1896. His son HERBERT, after a careful education under his father and at Milan, made his successful début at one of Ganz's concerts (June 12, 1880), and met with considerable favour from the public.

w. h. h. ; addns. *D.N.B.*, s. h. p., etc.

BIBL.—*Sims Reeves, by Himself.* (London, 1888.)

**REFORMATION SYMPHONY, THE,** Mendelssohn's symphony in D minor, op. 107, No. 36 of the posthumous works ; completed in 1830. Produced Berlin, Nov. 1832, under his own direction ; Crystal Palace, Nov. 30, 1867.

**REFRAIN** (Fr. *refrain* ; Ger. *Reimkehr*). This word is used in music to denote what in poetry is called a 'burden,' *i.e.* a short sentence or phrase which recurs in every verse or stanza. It was probably first employed in music in order to give roundness and unity to the melody, and was then transferred to the poetry which was written especially for music. Such collections as the 'Échos du temps passé' give an abundance of examples in French music, where songs with refrains are most frequently to be found. 'Lilliburlero' may be cited as one English instance out of many. Schubert's four Refrain-Lieder were published as op. 95.

M.

**REGAL,** a small portable organ furnished in its earlier form with reed-pipes only. It was probably invented about the year 1460, when Henry Traxdorff of Nuremberg constructed an organ of which the sound 'resembled that of the shawm.' The reeds are of the 'beating' or clarinet type and not 'free' reeds of the harmonium type (see REED). The origin of the name has little, if anything, to do with royalty ; in English orthography of the 16th century it is spelt Rigol or Regol, and this suggests that it is a contraction of the Latin *regula*, and that the instrument was employed in the first instance to 'rule' or 'regulate' the chanting of the monks in choir (compare such derivatives from the Latin *regula* as the Old German *Rigol* and *Regul*, or the Italian *rigola* and *regolo*). Some, however, consider that the word is a contraction of *rigabello*, a name given to an instrument used in Italian churches before the introduction of the organ, but of which no particular information is forthcoming (cf. CHENG or SHENG).

Such was the popularity of the new instruments that, under the name regal, its reed pipes were soon added to the flue pipes of the large organs and became the first 'reed stop' of which we have any definite record. In the first part of the 16th century the instrument itself was enlarged by the addition of flue pipes ; for instance, Henry VIII. possessed a single

## LXV

1. BIBLE REGAL (*c.* 1700).     2. PORTATIVE ORGAN (as used *c.* 1500).
3. POSITIVE ORGAN or REGAL (J. Loosemore, 1650).

1, 2. Galpin Collection.     3. Blair Atholl Castle.

regal having 'one stoppe pipe of tinne, one Regall of tinne and a cimball'; another regal had 'one stoppe of pipes of wood with a cimball of tinne and the Regall of papire.' The tin, the wood and the paper were of course for the body of the pipes; the 'cimball' was a small 'mixture.' A fine example of a large English regal bearing the initials I.L. (John Loosemore of Exeter) and the date 1650 is preserved at the castle, Blair Atholl; it has five stops: Stopt Diapason, Principal, Twelfth, Fifteenth and Trumpet, the last the old regal stop (*PLATE LXV*. No. 3). Mace's table organ, as described in his *Musick's Monument* (1676), had a regal stop, which with the 'Hoboy' stop, worked by a foot pedal, produced the 'Voice Humaine.'

A specimen of the regal with reed pipes only, once the property of the late A. J. Hipkins, is in the collection of the R.C.M.; its compass is 4 octaves (short octave in bass), and the date 1629. Towards the end of the 16th century George Voll of Nuremberg rendered the instrument yet more portable, for he made the bellows in the shape of a book, the keyboard and pipes being enclosed therein after performance: this form became known as the 'Bible' or 'Book Regal,' and specimens are very rare and valuable. There are at the present time (1926) three examples in England: one at the R.C.M. and lately the property of Mrs. Pagden and Miss Ferrari; another is in the possession of Mr. Spencer Portal at Bere Hill, Whitchurch, Hants; and the third is in the writer's own collection (see *Old English Instruments of Music*, Methuen): they are all of late 17th century or early 18th century date (*PLATE LXV*. No. 1).

The regal was not only employed in the churches but was in general use for entertainments and dramatic performances. In Edward's 'Damon and Pythias' (1565) there is a stage direction, 'here the regales play a mourning song' as Pythias is borne off to prison. In 1562 at the feast of the Guild of Parish Clerks there was after dinner 'a goodlie playe of the children of Westminster with waits and regales and singinge'; whilst in the mystery and morality plays it figures largely, being carefully distinguished in the accounts from the organ. In the 16th century William Tresorer held the court appointment of regal-maker at the annual salary of £10, and as late as 1684 we find Henry Purcell enjoying a similar office as 'keeper, maker, repairer and tuner of the King's Regalls, Virginals and Organs.' In 1695 it was divided between Dr. John Blow and Bernard (Father) Smith, 'and the longer liver to enjoy the whole place.' In 1779 the tuner of the regalls 'received £56 per annum, though it is commonly stated that Bernard Gates, who died in 1773, was the last to hold this historic post.

In the inventory of the musical instruments belonging to King Henry VIII. we find double regals as well as single regals mentioned, and also combined instruments such as 'an instrument with a single Virginal and a single Regal,' and another, 'with a Double Virginal and a Double Regal.' Many explanations have been given of the meaning of the words 'single' and 'double' in this particular association. Some would refer it to the number of bellows, but the virginal required no bellows at all, and the terms are as frequently applied to that and other keyboard stringed instruments. Dr. Rimbault (*The Organ*, 1870) considered that it referred in part to the rows or ranks of pipes, single regals having but one rank, double regals more than that number: but in the inventory above mentioned there are single regals with 2, 3 and even 4 stops requiring 2, 3 or 4 ranks of pipes. Sir George Grove and A. J. Hipkins held that it referred wholly to the number of keyboards, the single regal or virginal having one manual or keyboard, the double two keyboards; but whilst it is true that a two-manual virginal or clavicymbal appears at the end of the 16th century, introduced for the first time by Hans Ruckers, there is no example on record at all of a two-manual regal: moreover, two of King Henry's double regals had only 2 stops, and what need of just 2 stops for a two-manual instrument?

Surely the terms 'single' and 'double' as used in the 16th century relate to the *compass* of the instrument, whether regal or virginal? Playford (*Introduction to the Skill of Music*, 1661) states that notes 'below the gamut in the Basses [*i.e.* Bass G] are called double notes,' and adds, 'I have therefore expressed them with double letters.' A single regal or virginal therefore descended to single C (tenor C) or to G (Gamut), and a double regal or virginal an octave lower to double C or to double G. Specimens of instruments made in the first half of the 16th century having such a compass are still in existence. Moreover, we have an interesting confirmation of the writer's view given us by Praetorius (1618), for he tells us that in England the fagotto (bassoon) descending to single G (Gamut) was called the 'single courtal,' and that reaching double C the 'double courtal.'

In the 17th and later centuries, when two-manual organs and harpsichords were in common use, the terms single and double were then transferred to the number of keyboards.                              F. W. G.

REGAN, ANNA, soprano singer. (See SCHIMON.)

REGENT'S BUGLE, see BUGLE.

REGER, MAX (*b.* Brand, Bavaria, Mar. 19, 1873; *d.* Leipzig, May 11, 1916), was the son of a teacher at Brand. A year after his birth the father was transferred to Weiden, where subsequently the boy's musical education was begun, first in piano-playing by his mother, and later by a young teacher, Adalbert Lindner. His rapid progress—from 1886–89 he was organist at the Weiden Catholic church —led the parents to consult Hugo Riemann, then living at Sondershausen, and in 1890 young Reger went to him as pupil, following him the next year to Wiesbaden and soon becoming a teacher in the same conservatoire as his master. His studies (which hitherto had been chiefly of pianoforte music from Beethoven to Liszt, while a hearing of ' Die Meistersinger ' and ' Parsifal ' at Bayreuth had made a lasting impression) were directed by Riemann to the works of Brahms and Bach, and his leaning towards strict and definite musical forms was thereby specially accentuated. In 1896 Reger performed his military service in Wiesbaden, in the course of which he suffered a serious illness which occasioned his discharge. Moreover, the mode of life there had obviously assumed a character which threatened to lead to spiritual and physical ruin. He was brought home by his sister and again received by his parents in Weiden, where he stayed from 1898–1901. Here his creative output experienced an enormous increase, especially of works for organ, chamber music and songs. In 1901, wishing to support himself by his work, he went to Munich, where he began to encounter serious strife with the whole of the German musical world. Having already renounced the influence of Riemann, he now intended to wage war under the banner of ' progress,' and was then attacked from every camp. The conquests which, however, he soon made among the public he owed chiefly to his pianoforte-playing, which attracted great attention on account of its extremely delicate musical qualities.

Reger appeared before the public less as a soloist (and then as a rule with the piano works of Bach and Mozart) than as an accompanist or performer of chamber music. Thus, through his recitals, his songs and chamber music became more and more known, although at first they seemed abnormal and strange, and their great beauty was but gradually recognised. He found the most opposition amongst the critics, who attacked him with extreme obstinacy, and in many cases to the end of his life. Soon, however, more and more voices spoke in his behalf, and his concert tours brought him ever wider appreciation throughout Germany, as well as in Prague and Vienna. He could no longer be overlooked, as, owing largely to the support of the great organist, Karl STRAUBE (q.v.), he had now for long enjoyed the reputation which was due to him in his own domain, composition for the organ. Reger swiftly paralleled for the organ the magnificent development which orchestral music had undergone in the 19th century. He was a Roman Catholic by up-

bringing, but his great fantasias on Protestant hymns, and on his deeply venerated B-A-C-H with their mighty closing fugues, and the great fantasia inspired by Dante's *Inferno*, together with the ' Variations on an Original Theme,' show that he had imbibed other traditions and created a prominent landmark in the development of organ music.

Soon after his arrival in Munich, Reger married Elsa von Bagensky, whom he had first met in Wiesbaden. His financial position was by no means secured, though his compositions, after a long period of neglect by the publishers, again began to appear. Neither they nor the concerts, however, brought him much money at first, so that he was forced to take up teaching work, in the course of which he steadily laid stress on the old masters, on clear and sure moulding, and thorough command of technique. He sharply reproved any laxities of harmony, his own theory of harmony being, as a result of Riemann's teaching, strictly logical.

With ever-increasing confidence Reger now took his place in the musical world, his keen sense of humour enabling him to overcome many difficulties, and the tone of the concluding fugues which so frequently crown his work became increasingly sure. His sonata in C major for violin and piano, in which, as in some earlier work, he once more expresses his despair and defiance, was the cause of renewed hostility, but it also attracted widespread attention. Some piano works of monumental structure, the ' Variations on a Theme from Bach,' for two hands, then the beautiful ' Variations on a Theme from Beethoven,' and the titanic ' Passacaglia and Fugue ' for four hands on two pianos, and later the triumphant violin sonata in F sharp minor, already met with wide admiration.

Musical circles awaited his first orchestral work with great eagerness. It was his opus 90, though it must be remembered that a large number of his youthful works, being unpublished, are not counted, and that in a majority of cases an opus number includes a whole series of works, often on a large scale. This, Reger's first orchestral work, ' Sinfonietta,' appeared in 1906, when he was 33 years of age. He did not wish to begin with a big heroic symphony, and while in the accompaniment to a chorus, ' The Song of the Glorious,' he had, like Strauss, made the greatest possible use of wind-instruments, in the ' Sinfonietta ' he employed a smaller orchestra with but one trombone. But he wove a wonderful texture of music with all the voices, determined to get the maximum of sound and melody, so that the result had nothing at all in common with modern ' orchestral effects.' Reger held two appointments in Munich—the Akademie der Tonkunst (Academy of Music) had appointed him its teacher in composition, theory and organ, and pupils came streaming to him ; the Porges Choral Society entrusted him with the direction of its concerts. But in neither of these posts could he find a satisfactory permanent occupation. He was still the object of too much jealousy and hostility, and he never in his life acquired the ability to face the world with the cool diplomacy which is necessary in posts of the kind.

In 1907 he was appointed Musical Director at the University of Leipzig, but soon relinquished the post, finding the duties connected with it uncongenial. But the teaching post at the Leipzig Conservatory, which he undertook at the same time, he retained to the end of his life. Even on the day of his death he gave instruction at this institution. Strangely enough, he composed no organ music during the Leipzig period, but several choral pieces, partly with and partly without orchestral accompaniment. Amongst them were ' Die Nonnen ' (The Nuns), ' Der römische Triumphgesang ' (Roman Hymn of Triumph), ' Die Weihe der Nacht ' (Sacredness of Night), his wonderful motets, written for the Thomaner-Chor, and the prodigious ' Psalm 100 ' for choir and orchestra, with its gigantic concluding fugue. For orchestra alone he had already written in Munich, besides ' Sinfonietta,' the light but thoughtful ' Serenade,' and the majestic and humorous ' Variations on a Theme from Hiller'; to these he added in Leipzig the violin concerto and piano concerto, with the ' Symphonic Prologue to a Tragedy,' the deepest and most powerful of his orchestral compositions, and the ' Comedy Overture,' short and sprightly, like a filigree. He resumed the composition of chamber music, piano-pieces and ballads. At Munich Reger had already begun to compose, besides his larger and more difficult works, small pieces which were less likely to prove a strain on performers and audiences. He continued the long series of ' Schlichte Weisen,' sonatinas, and the piano-pieces ' Aus meinem Tagebuch ' (From my Diary). Some of the ' Schlichte Weisen ' soon found their way abroad and made a name for Reger with the wider public. At this time, too, he turned to a form of music which he had cultivated in Weiden, and wrote a number of notable sonatas for the violin alone—a type of composition which had not been successfully attempted since Bach.

In 1911 Reger was invited by the aged Duke George to be director of the court orchestra at Meiningen. He was faced with the task of reviving the fame of the Meiningen orchestra, which it had owed chiefly to Hans von Bülow and Fritz Steinbach. In the preceding years Reger had achieved great results as a conductor in various cities, both with his own works and those of other composers, above all through the subtlety of his interpretation and his ability to establish in the orchestra complete understanding of his own musical feeling. In Meiningen he was now able further to develop his method of direction, by constant work with an absolutely first-rate orchestra. He also engaged in minute study which considerably influenced his own orchestral compositions. He continually strove to attain greater ' transparency.' His ideal for orchestral music became in an ever-increasing degree the perfect clearness of Mozart. But he did not scorn to attempt also the modern sound-experiments of a Debussy. He composed in Meiningen a series of orchestral works which record the various phases of his work—' Das Konzert im alten Stil ' (Concerto in the old style), the ' Romantische Suite,' ' Böcklin Suite,' the ' Ballet Suite,' and later ' Variations on a Theme from Mozart.' In these works he betook himself for a time to the field of descriptive ' programme ' music, in order to test in every way the resources of the orchestra. Reger's concert tours with the Meiningen orchestra became triumphal progresses. He now cultivated the greatest simplicity as a conductor, the main effects being achieved by elaboration in the rehearsals, and the performances made a profound impression. It was always the music, and the music alone, that the conductor threw into relief, and not himself or the artistry of his orchestra. The result was that works often heard before now appeared as a new revelation.

Reger's activities at Meiningen came to an end after only two years. The death of Duke George brought to a close this brilliant epoch in the artistic life of the city. Reger went to reside at the university town of Jena, where, far from the madding crowd of the great cities, and yet in a centre of intellectual stimulus, he wished to devote himself to composition, enjoying the society of gifted men, as he had earlier done at Leipzig. He wished to give only occasional concerts in the large musical centres. In Jena he wrote a whole series of works, including chamber music, pieces for choir and orchestra, for the piano and for the organ, hymns and unaccompanied choral songs, besides ' Kinderlieder ' and other songs with piano accompaniment. The composer was turning over in his mind plans for a great oratorio and for a symphony. What he had already accomplished he conceived only as a preparation for the great works he had planned. Before he could attempt these he was cut off suddenly in 1916 at the age of 43. He succumbed to a heart attack in his bed at Leipzig, whither he used to travel every week to teach at the Conservatoire.

His life had been laborious and full of strife, but in his later years full of success also. The outward honours which fell to him—he was Generalmusikdirektor, Hofrat, Professor and Honorary Doctor of two universities—had but little charm for him. That his works, owing as they did so little to outward sensation and so much to inward concentration, brought him comparatively wide recognition in his own lifetime, no doubt meant far more to him. To him, his life was an uninterrupted period of study and labour, and the only merit he saw in his successes was that due to unremitting toil. To the great masters of the past he looked up with the deepest veneration. Whether he would ever be counted of their number, he left calmly to the test of time. He loved his native country as a matter of course, and declined the most attractive offers of permanent posts abroad. Concert tours in Holland and Russia brought him great success, but failed to induce him to undertake such journeys frequently or for extended periods. He visited England in 1909, and took part in chamber concerts in London, which introduced many of his works of the kind to a public which had previously known him chiefly through his organ music played by Walter Parratt and other English organists. To everybody who was not hostile to him, he was kind and affectionate, while with persons of rank or influence he was open and unconstrained. A human side to his nature was a strong, pithy sense of humour, with regard to which a large number of anecdotes were current in Germany. Everything which was not perfectly honest and straightforward was repugnant to him. Reverence for all things divine was one of his chief characteristics, and shines forth clearly in his music. If this trait in his music could help to awaken an echo in the whole world, he would have attained the greatest and most beautiful of all human purposes.

K. H. (transl. Cecil Lewis).

Op.
1. Sonata No. 1 for vln. and PF., in D min.
2. Trio for PF., vln. and vla., B min.
3. Sonata No. 2 for vln. and PF., in D.
4. Six Songs.
5. Sonata No. 1 for v'cl. and PF., in F min.
6. Songs for 4 voices with PF.
7. Three Organ pieces.
8. Five Songs.
9. 'Walzer Kapricen' (PF. pieces for 4 hands).
10. 'Deutsche Tänze' (PF. pieces for 4 hands).
11. Seven Waltzes for PF. solo.
12. Five Songs.
13. 'Lose Blätter,' PF. solo.
14. Five Duets for soprano and alto, with PF.
15. Ten Songs.
16. Suite in E min., for organ.
17. 'Aus der Jugendzeit,' twenty pieces for PF. solo.
18. 'Improvisation,' PF. solo.
19. Two Sacred Songs, with organ.
20. Five Humoresken for PF. solo.
21. { Hymn, 'An der Gesang,' male chorus and orch.
     { Pianoforte Quintet,[1] C min. (MS.)
22. Six Waltzes for PF. (4 hands).
23. Four Songs, with vln. and PF.
24. Six Pieces for PF. solo.
25. Aquarellen for PF. solo.
26. Seven Fantasiestücke for PF. solo.
27. Fantasie for organ on 'Ein' feste Burg.'
28. Sonata No. 2 for PF. and v'cl., in G min.
29. Fantasie and Fugue, C min., for organ.
30. Fantasie for organ on 'Freu' dich sehr, o meine Seele.'
31. Six Songs.
32. Seven Characteristic Pieces for PF. solo.
33. Sonata for Organ, F sharp min.
34. 'Pièces pittoresques' for PF. (4 hands).
35. Six Songs.
36. 'Bunte Blätter,' nine small pieces for PF. solo.
37. Five Songs.

---

[1] *Riemann*; other authorities give quartet.

Op.
38. { Two volumes of Folk-songs for male chorus (a 5–9).
     { Two volumes of Folk-songs for mixed chorus (a 6–8).
     { Sacred German Folk-songs (a 7–12).
     { Seven Choruses for male voices.
39. Three Six-part Choruses for mixed voices.
40. { I. Fantasie on 'Wie schön leucht't uns der Morgenstern.'
     { II. Ditto on 'Straf mich nicht in deinem Zorn' (both for organ).
41. Sonata No. 3 in A for vln. and PF.
42. Four Sonatas for vln. alone in D min., A, B min. and G min.
43. Eight Songs.
44. Ten Pieces for PF.
45. Six Intermezzi for PF.
46. Phantasie and Fugue on B A C H for organ.
47. Six Trios for organ.
48. Seven Songs.
49. Two Sonatas for clar. and PF. (A flat maj. and F sharp min.).
50. Two Romances in G and D, vln. and orch.
51. Twelve Songs.
52. { Organ Fantasie on 'Alle Menschen müssen sterben.'
     { Ditto. 'Wachet auf, ruft uns die Stimme.'
     { Ditto. 'Halleluja, Gott zu loben.'
53. Seven 'Silhouetten' for PF.
54. Two String Quartets in G min. and A.
55. Fifteen Songs.
56. Five easy Preludes and Fugues for organ.
57. Symphonic Fantasie and Fugue for organ.
58. Six Burlesken for PF. (4 hands).
59. Twelve Pieces for organ.
60. Sonata for organ in D min.
61. { 'Palmsonntagmorgen' (5 voices a cappella).
     { 'Der evangelische Kirchenchor' (for 4 voices), forty Easy Compositions for church performance.
62. Sixteen Songs.
63. Twelve Monologues for the organ.
64. Quintet in C min., PF. and strings.
65. Twelve Pieces for organ.
66. Twelve Songs.
67. Fifty-three Easy 'Choral Vorspiele.'
68. Six Songs.
69. Ten Organ Pieces.
70. Seventeen Songs.
71. 'Gesang der Verklärten' (for 5-voiced choir and orch.).
72. Sonata No. 4 for PF. and vln., C maj.
73. Variations and Fugue on an original theme for organ.
74. String Quartet No. 3 in D min.
75. Eighteen Songs.
76. Fifteen 'Schlichte Weisen' for PF. and voice.
77. { (a) Serenade in D for flute, vln. and vla.
     { (b) Trio in A min. for vln., vla. and v'cl.
78. Sonata No. 3 for v'cl. and PF., in F.
79. Fourteen volumes of Pieces for PF., for organ, for PF. and vln., for PF. and v'cl., and songs.
80. Five Easy Preludes and Fugues, Bach's Two-part Inventions arranged as organ trios (with K. Straube) and Twelve Pieces for organ.
81. Variations and Fugue on a theme of J. S. Bach, for PF. solo.
82. Twelve small pieces for PF. solo, 'Aus meinem Tagebuche.'
83. Songs for male chorus.
84. Sonata No. 5 for PF. and vln., in F sharp min.
85. Four Preludes for the organ.
86. Variations and Fugue on a theme by Beethoven for two PFs.
87. Two Compositions for vln. and PF.
88. Four Songs.
89. Two Sonatas (E min. and D) for PF. solo.
90. Sinfonietta for orch.
91. Seven Sonatas for vln. alone.
92. Suite in G min. for organ.
93. Two Suites for PF. and vln., F maj. (in old style).
94. Six Pieces for PF.
95. Serenade, G maj., orch.
96. Introduction, Passacaglia and Fugue, two PFs.
97. Four Songs.
98. Five Songs.
99. Six Preludes and Fugues for PF.
100. Variations on a theme of J. A. Hiller, orch.
101. Vln. Concerto, A maj.
102. Trio, PF., vln. and v'cl.
103. { (a) Suite for PF. and vln., A min.
      { (b) Two Sonatinas, vln. and PF.
104. Six Songs.
105. Sacred Songs, with organ.
106. Psalm 100, choir, orch. and organ.
107. Sonata No. 3, clar. and PF., B flat maj.
108. Symphonic Prologue to a Tragedy.
109. String Quartet No. 4, E flat.
110. Sacred Songs, with organ.
111. { (a) Duets, soprano and alto, with PF.
      { (b) and (c) Choruses for women's voices.
112. 'Die Nonne,' chorus and orch.
113. PF. Quartet, D min.
114. Concerto, PF. and orch., F min.
115. 'Episodes,' PF.
116. Sonata No. 4, v'cl., A min.
117. Preludes and Fugues, vln. alone.
118. Sextet for strings, F maj.
119. 'Die Weihe der Nacht,' alto solo, male chorus and orch.
120. Comedy Overture, orch.
121. String Quartet No. 5, F sharp min.
122. Sonata No. 6, PF. and vln.
123. Concerto in the olden style.
124. 'An die Hoffnung,' alto solo and orch.
125. Romantic Suite, orch.
126. 'Römischer Triumphgesang,' male chorus and orch.
127. Introduction, Passacaglia and Fugue, organ.
128. Four Tone-poems after Böcklin, orch.
129. Nine Pieces for organ.
130. Ballet-suite, orch.
131. Preludes and Fugues, vln. alone; Duos, Canons and Fugues for vlns.; Three Suites, v'cl. alone; Three Suites, vla. alone.
132. Variations on a theme of Mozart, orch.

Op.
133. PF. Quartet, A min.
134. Variations on a theme of Telemann, for PF.
135. Choral Preludes and Fantasia and Fugue in D min. for organ.
136. 'Hymn der Liebe,' baritone solo and orch.
137. Twelve Sacred Songs.
138. Eight Sacred Songs for mixed choir.
139. Sonata No. 7, PF. and vln., C min.
140. 'Vaterländische,' Overture, orch.
141. (a) Serenade, string trio, G min.; (b) string trio, D min.
142. Five Nursery Rhymes for soprano.
143. Twelve Pieces for PF.
144. 'Requiem' and 'Der Einsiedler,' songs for mixed chorus and orch.
145. Seven Pieces for organ.  (Reger's last composition.)
146. Quintet, clar. and strings, A maj.
147. Andante and Rondo Capriccioso, vln. and orch., unfinished.

Without opus numbers are :—
 Four 'Heitere Lieder.'
 Four Sacred Songs.
 Piano Transcriptions of songs by Hugo Wolf, Jensen, Brahms and Richard Strauss.
 Piano Transcription (4 hands) of Bach's Orchestral Suites and Brandenburg Concertos; Wolf's 'Penthesilea' and 'Italian Serenade,' etc.
 Cantatas, 'O wie selig' for mixed choir and congregation, with accompaniment of strings and organ; for Good Friday, 'O Haupt voll Blut und Wunden,' for alto and tenor (or soprano) soli, mixed choir, vln. solo, oboe solo and organ; 'Von Himmel hoch'; 'Meinen Jesum Christ nicht.'
 For male chorus :—
  Nine Volkslieder.
  Five Volkslieder.
  Twelve Madrigals.
 For mixed choir :—
  Eight Volkslieder.
  Six Volkslieder.
  Twelve German Sacred Songs (in three books).
  'Komm, heiliger Geist.'
  'Es fiel ein Thau,' for 5-part choir.
  'Vom Himmel hoch,' for 4-part chorus, two solo vlns., choir and congregation, with organ or harmonium.
 For organ :—Schule des Triospiels (arrangements of Bach's 2-part Inventions, with K. Straube).
  Variations on 'Heil unser'm König, Heil,' and 'Heil dir im Siegerkranz.'
  Prelude and Fugue, G sharp min.
  Romanze (also for harmonium).
  Songs with organ or piano.
  Arrangements of fifteen of Bach's clavier works for organ.
  Arrangements of songs for harmonium.
  Prelude and Fugue, vln. alone.
 PF. and vln. :—Petite Caprice, Romanze (G maj.) and Wiegenlied.
 For PF. and v'cl. :—Caprice.
 For voice and PF. :—Sixteen Songs.
 PF. solo :—Perpetuum mobile, Elegie, Humoreske, Romanze, Moment musical, Scherzino, Albumblatt, Frühlingslied, Mélodie, two Humoresken, Nachtstück.
  Canons in all maj. and min. keys—Book I. in two parts, Book II. in three parts.
  Four special studies for left hand alone :—Scherzo, Humoreske, Romance and Prelude and Fugue.
  Five PF. studies (arrangements of Chopin's works).
  Regiments-Marsch der ehemaligen Hannoverschen Armee (arrangement).
 Literary work :—Beiträge zur Modulationslehre (Contribution to the Rules of Modulation).

BIBLIOGRAPHY

W. Altmann : Reger-Katalog : vollständiges Verzeichnis sämtlicher im Druck erschienenen Werke, Bearbeitungen und Ausgaben Max Regers, etc.  (Berlin, 1917.)
Karl Hasse : Max Reger. (Leipzig, 1921.)
Adalbert Lindner : Max Reger, ein Bild seines Jugendlebens und künstlerischen Werdens.  (Stuttgart, 1922.)  (Lindner was Reger's first teacher.)
H. Poppen : Max Reger.  (Leipzig, 1921, 16mo.)
The Max-Reger Gesellschaft publishes Mitteilungen every half-year.  The first appeared in 1921.
Eugen Segnitz : Max Reger.  Abriss seines Lebens und Analyse seiner Werke.  (Leipzig, 1922.)
Richard Würz : Max Reger.  Eine Sammlung von Studien aus dem Kreise seiner persönlichen Schüler.  Edited by R. Würz. (Munich, 1920, etc.)

REGGIO (b. Genoa, first quarter of 17th cent.; d. London, July 23, 1685 [1]), was private musician (lutenist and singer) to Queen Christina of Sweden after her abdication. After her final departure from Rome, Reggio came to England and settled at Oxford, where, in 1677, he published A Treatise to sing well any Song whatsoever. Evelyn heard him sing in Sept. 1680 and July 1684, and says that he had set some of Abraham Cowley's poems to music. In 1680 he issued a book of songs dedicated to the king, and containing the earliest setting of 'Arise, ye subterranean

[1] Hawkins.

winds,' from Shadwell's 'Tempest,' afterwards set by Purcell. (See Sammelbände of the Int. Mus. Ges. v. 553.) Seven Italian songs are in the British Museum in MS., two duets in the Fitzwilliam Museum at Cambridge, and a three-part motet at Ch. Ch., Oxford. Reggio was buried in St. Giles's in the Fields.      M.

REGINO (d. Treves, 915), abbot of the Benedictine Monastery of Prüm, Eiffel, in 892, and of St. Maximin at Treves, c. 899. He wrote a treatise, De harmonica institutione; also Tonarius sive octo toni cum suis differentiis. (For republications see Q.-L.; biogr. in Fétis.)

REGIS, Jean, a Flemish musician of the latter part of the 15th century, usually reckoned along with Busnois, Caron, Obrecht and Okeghem as belonging to the transitional school of composers between Dufay and Binchois on the one hand, and Josquin des Prés on the other. Tinctoris mentions him with special distinction. He was for a time master of the choir-boys in Antwerp Cathedral, and is also supposed to have been in personal relation with Dufay. Though he does not appear, like Dufay, to have ever been a member of the Papal Choir, two of his masses were copied into the great choir-books of the Sistine Chapel, which are so far interesting as showing the curious custom of the time in combining different liturgical texts. Thus in one of them, while the two upper voices sing the usual words of the Mass, the tenor sings the 'Ecce ancilla Domini' and the bass 'No timeas Maria,' which would seem to show that this Mass was specially composed for the festival of the Annunciation. In the other the alto and tenor sing 'Dum sacrum mysterium cerneret Joannes,' which would imply the work to be intended for the festival of St. John the Evangelist. Regis is also the author of a Mass, 'L'omme arme,' in the archives of Cambrai, and of a few other pieces in the collections of Petrucci. The setting of a popular song, 'S'il vous plaisait,' a 4, transcribed by Kiesewetter in his Schicksale und Beschaffenheit des welt lichen Gesanges, serves to show the skill of Regis as a contrapuntal harmonist of the time in a very favourable light.      J. R. M.

REGISTER, (1) of an organ. Literally a set of pipes as recorded or described by the name written on the draw-stop; hence, in general, an organ-stop. The word 'register' is, however, not quite synonymous with 'stop,' for we do not say 'pull out, or put in, a register,' but 'a stop,' although we can say indifferently 'a large number of registers' or 'of stops.' The word is also used as a verb; for example, the expression 'skill in registering' or 'registration' means skill in selecting various combinations of stops for use. The word 'stop' is, however, never used as a verb in this sense. (See Organ; Organ-Playing; Registration.)
      J. S.

(2) Of the voice; a classification of parts of the voice according to method of production, as 'head register,' 'chest register.' (See SINGING, pp. 768, 769.)

(3) The term is also used, though not very satisfactorily, of parts of the scale according with the general pitch of voices, e.g. 'soprano register,' 'tenor register.'

REGISTRATION. The art of combining and contrasting the tones produced from the several stops (registers) of the organ.

There is no doubt whatever that as soon as organs contained any considerable number of stops or registers, the practice of contrasting, combining and blending them became recognised as one of the most valuable elements in the organist's art. The specifications of the Italian organs of the 16th and 17th centuries show us that very little could have been done on them in the direction of tone-colour, and the works of Frescobaldi (1583–1643), organist of St. Peter's, Rome, bear out this assumption. They are for the most part vivacious toccatas and slow canzoni which would be played on the flue-work of one manual for a whole movement, possibly followed by a movement on the other manual. There is ample evidence that in both France and Germany, for nearly a century before Bach's time, the effective use of the stops was regarded as something both of an art and a science. Before Buxtehude's time, the pedal was being used in an extraordinarily free way for the 'giving-out' of the melody and also for 2-part work (double pedal). The latter, when used for a chorale prelude, as in the partita, 'Jesus Christus unser Heiland,' of Tunder (1614–67), who preceded Buxtehude at Lübeck, always indicates the use of 8-foot stops on the pedal.

The Lübeck organ in Buxtehude's time was a magnificent instrument with 3 manuals and a pedal-organ, which contained 2 stops of 32 ft., 2 of 16 ft., an 8-ft., 2 of 4 ft., a Decembass, 2 mixtures and 4 reeds; and although there are no details of his registration, there is every reason to believe that Bach's method was founded to a large extent on Buxtehude's. At any rate, the rapid changes of manuals in Bach's music are in the same style as Buxtehude's. Bach always kept his mind very alert with regard to French music; for Paris had a school of organists whose art was by no means immature; and their organs were well supplied with varied stops. Couperin's organ at St. Gervais, Paris, still exists. It has five manuals (2 short ones) and a pedal-organ. Its best stops are the Cromhorne (clarinet), the Bassoon-hautbois, the Cornet (a soft 8-ft. with delicious mixtures on the récit.), the Flute and the Trumpet on the echo. The Viole, referred to so frequently in Couperin's music, is now missing. Records of the music of the period show that the practice of 'echoing' was a

frequent device. A 'Qui tollis' by Nicolas Gigault (b. circa 1645) exists, in which an elaborately figured melody is given to an 8-ft. trumpet on the pedals, accompanied by 4-part counterpoint on the Plein Jeu. Nicolas de Grigny (c. 1671–1703), organist of Rheims cathedral (one of the composers whose works the young Bach copied out for study), in his 'Livre d'orgue' (published 1701), marked many passages for Trompette or Cromorne 'en taille' in the bass, with the Tierce or Cornet in the right hand. We notice at once that this was a combination very similar to that frequently used by Bach. In his specification for the restoration of the organ at Mühlhausen, Bach particularly wished a Tierce added to the Quint, so as to make a beautiful Sesquialtera, which 'will be useful for the execution of all kinds of inventions.'[1] He asked for extra wind-pressure in order to make the new 32 Untersatz (Sub-bass) speak properly. This stop, he says, must have a special wind-chest. The Bombarde is to be given a rounder tone. He replaces the Trumpet on the great-organ by a 16-foot Fagotto of delicate scale, again 'to serve for all kinds of new inventions, as well as pour la musique' (in French; i.e. for playing the basso continuo with the orchestra). He replaces the Gemshorn with an 8-foot Viol di Gamba, a favourite stop with him, and he asks for the tremulant stop to be made regular in its vibration.

Authentic details of Bach's own registration are sparse, but those that exist are very significant. They point to a highly original method of tone-colouring, one scarcely known to us at the present day. From his pupil Walther's copy, brought away from Bach's opening recital on the restored organ at Mühlhausen, it is easy to reconstruct Bach's registration of the Choral-prelude 'Ein' feste Burg' (Peters VI., No. 22). The piece is wholly in the spirit of the virtuoso which Bach undoubtedly was. He opened with the left hand on a combination including a delicate 16-foot Fagotto; the right hand entered in bar 3 (or 4) on another manual with a combination which included the Sesquialtera. Bars 20 to 24 were played with both hands on the 2nd manual with soft pedal stops (including the new 32-ft. Sub-bass). He would go back to the duet arrangement in bar 24, letting the pedal proclaim the chorale in the bass. At bar 35, he would go to the 3rd manual, the right hand returning to the first for the chorale in bar 41; and the full Great would be used for both hands from bar 48 to the end. It is a most stimulating thing to play through this wonderful piece with the Mühlhausen specification on the organ-desk. The set of chorale-preludes published by Schübler afford other significant examples. The two, 'Kommst

---

[1] The organ at St. Thomas's, Leipzig, possessed three sesquialtera stops, the one on the Positif being added between 1730–31 by Scheibe.

ʒu nun, Jesu' (Peters VII. p. 16) and 'Wer nur den lieben Gott lässt walten' (Peters VII. p. 76) are both marked 'Ped. 4 Fuss,' doubtless a 4-foot pedal-reed, probably Schalmei. The 'Wo soll ich fliehen hin'(Peters VII. p. 84) is marked 1 'Clav. 8 Fuss; 2 Clav. 16 Fuss'; and 'Ped. 4 Fuss.' The 3 canonic preludes in the Little Organ Book are marked as follows: 'Gottes Sohn ist kommen' (canon at 8ve) for 2 manuals and pedals. R.H. 'Principal 8 F., Ped. Tromp. 8 F.' The Christmas Hymn, 'In dulci jubilo' (canon 4 in 2 at 8ve) has an 8-foot reed indi- cated for the pedals; but if the pedal-board does not rise to the high F-sharp, then a 4-foot reed must be used and the part played an octave lower. For 'O Lamm Gottes un- schuldig' (canon at 5th) the pedal is also marked 8-foot reed, and the remarkable phras- ing is Bach's own marking. The rapid changes of manual which Bach marked in the dorian toccata and in the chorale prelude 'Christ lag in Todesbanden,' etc., were the continuation of an old tradition. Such contrasts occur frequently in Buxtehude's works and were even more elaborate with the early French organists.

The most important record of Bach's regis- tration is to be found in the organ concerto in D minor composed by his eldest son, Wilhelm Friedemann. This work exists in a copy actually made by his father, who also added the directions for the stops. There we find the organ used in a most surprising way. The first movement, which starts in a low register, is marked R.H. on Oberwerk, Octava 4 F. L.H. on Brustpositif Octava 4 F. and Pedal Principal 8 F. At bar 21, the Sub-bass 32 F. is added to the pedal, and an 8 ft. Principal to the Oberwerk. The *Grave* movement (and apparently the fugue) is marked *Pleno*; the *Largo* is directed to be played with the *spiccato* touch and the series of effective manual changes is most artistically arranged in the finale.

The term *Organo pleno* which occurs at the head of some of Bach's work and in the course of others, is used in two senses. At the head of a work, it merely indicates that the piece is laid out for an organ of 3 manuals and a pedal of full compass. In the course of a piece, it means the same as the French term *Plein-Jeu*, a combination of all the great and pedal flues, mutation stops and mixtures, with 16 and 32-ft. reeds (no. 8 or 4) on the pedals only.

After Bach's time, organ-playing declined; little progress was made and instruments were neglected. The works of Merkel and Rhein- berger as regards registration were affected by their own meagre instruments. Only Mendelssohn sought to revive the true Bach spirit; but little progress in registration was made with REGER. The organ works of Liszt, so full of colour, were little known; but the coming of KARG-ELERT covered all the lost

ground and more. No one, perhaps, has done more to elevate the art of organ-registration, which is surely quite as important to organ music as is the art of instrumentation to orchestral work.

It is time to come to the work of the English organists. Even so late as the 17th century, the chief English organs were small 2-manual instruments without compound, flute or reed stops. After the Restoration, the advent of these stops and the addition of an 'Echo' organ in the work of Bernhard Schmidt created a stir; but it was not until Renatus Harris's 4-manual organ in Salisbury cathedral was built (in 1710) that we find any wide range of tone. Even so, no very great advantage could be taken of it, so long as there was no pedal organ. It is not until 1790 that we find the first pedal organ installed at St. James, Clerkenwell (by G. P. England). Even then it had no pipes of its own, but merely drew down the manual notes. When proper pipes for an octave of pedals were installed, progress was hampered by the use of a GGG compass. But the Eng- lish organs could never be seriously regarded as *solo* instruments, until about 1834, when Hill introduced a 2-octave CC pedal-board in the York Minster organ.

Amongst the chief English players of the last century were the two WESLEYS, W. T. BEST and Walter PARRATT. Of these, Best did the most for the advance of registration. His numberless arrangements afford an accurate knowledge of his system on the St. George's Hall organ at Liverpool. E. H. LEMARE carried on Best's custom of transcribing orches- tral works. By transferring Wagner's music to the organ, he discovered many new combina- tions and invented a new style of organ treat- ment, which had far-reaching results when absorbed into the American cinema playing. The English organists, on the whole, still suffer from the fact that the pedal organ did not arrive here until the harmonic period had set in; in consequence they have never regarded the pedals exactly as a separate manual. On the other hand, their pedal-boards have always been the most practical in form. The exhibi- tion of French organs in London in 1856 awakened English interest in the beauty of harmonic flutes, gambas and reeds on different pressures, and English organ-builders soon rivalled the Continental builders in the beauty of their instruments. The English pedal organ still remains behind in completeness of registers, but such specifications as those at Liverpool Cathedral and Albert Hall, London (both 1924; the first by Willis, the second by Harrison) are significant as harbingers of a new state of things. The English treatment of the four manuals, too, having its roots in accompanimental methods, has not reached that true democratising of the manuals which is the chief feature in the playing of the finest French and American recitalists.[1]

Progress in organ-registration can only be brought about by collaboration between players and artist-builders. The reason that France was for a long period in the forefront, was due to the long collaboration between the builder CAVAILLÉ-COLL and the organists, WIDOR and GUILMANT. The latter was to the modern harmonic school what Bach was to the contrapuntal. Joseph BONNET carried his master's ideas still further, especially as regards poetic treatment of the pedal; and Marcel DUPRÉ's application of the full resources of the technique of modern composition to his wonderful extemporary playing seems to have almost exhausted the possibilities of the French organ.

The modifying conditions are too numerous to enable one to lay down any hard and fast rules regarding the application of tone-colours; but a rather more scientific treatment of the subject would make for progress. The art of registration does not depend entirely on the number of stops at the player's command; for often a real artist will secure very fine results from quite a small instrument. Regard should be paid to the various classes of organ-tone: diapason, flute, gedackt, gamba, organ reed-tone, whose qualities and properties must be thoroughly understood before blending, shading and balancing can be obtained. The gedackt and flute classes are pleasing to the ear in themselves, and will blend easily with other classes; but diapason-tone is always better when pure. Gamba-tone has had a stigma placed on it during the last half-century; but in its more delicate forms it is not wearing to the ear; and Bach was extremely fond of it. There are many colours which are variations of the main classes, such as dulciana, dolcan, dolce, horn-diapasons, etc. (all diapason family); grossflöte, clarabella, hohlflöte, waldflute, philomena, flauto d' amore (all flute family); bourdon, doppelflöte, lieblich gedacht, quintaten, etc., all of which make shading, colouring and mixing easier. (See ORGAN: Vocabulary of Stops.) On small instruments much can be done by playing an octave (or two) higher on 16-ft. stops, or an 8ve (or two) lower on 4-ft. (or 2-ft.), and by the frequent use, when possible, of a pedal 8-ft. to take the lowest part of manual work. The large and ever-growing families of orchestral flutes, strings, reeds and brass, and even percussion stops, are used chiefly along the lines of orchestration.

With regard to the handling of the tone-colouring, a curious anomaly is that the stops in French instruments are arranged in the least convenient manner of all — in long terraces,

and not in columns: and the jambs, too, are so long, that assistants are always necessary. The English system with short jambs and slanting stop-frames is vastly superior; though these are now surpassed by the more compact system of 'stop-keys.'

The early organists indicated their stops by name, until the time when certain combinations became taken for granted. Mendelssohn, Merkel and Rheinberger satisfied themselves with indicating the manuals to be used and the use of the ordinary terms *ppp* to *fff*. When a move forward became imperative, the stops were again indicated by name (see Widor's organ symphonies, etc.), but the dangers of such a method are only too apparent in the numerous arrangements of W. T. Best, where the stops mentioned, from his own organ at Liverpool, are hardly ever suitable on other organs. A similar criticism may be levelled at the very elaborately marked Bach volume (II.) in Peters edition, by Karl Straube, of Leipzig. Karg-Elert's system of marking 16, 8, 4 (2 ft.; if very soft), etc., has been productive of good results; but the soundest system of indication is along the broader lines of indicating merely the power, class and quality of the stops needed, such as string-tone, flute-tone, etc., modified by the marks *ppp* to *fff*, and even by such descriptions as lugubrious, bright, ringing, etc.

For new ideas we must cross to America. The enormous wealth of colour and other devices at the player's disposal in such organs as those at the Eastman Theatre, Rochester, U.S.A., and at the Wanamaker Building, Philadelphia, U.S.A., opens up endless new territories. The Rochester organ contains great, swell, choir, solo, orchestral, echo and special string organs, besides a pedal of 47 stops. The total number of stops is 180, to which may be added 83 couplers and other contrivances. On these two organs all the manuals (with the exception of part of the Great) are boxed, and special solo-stops are found on all. The orchestral organ, too, can be played from all manuals. Notable additions to the large concert and cinema organs are the pianoforte, harpsichord and harp, celeste and carillon effects on several of the manuals. These additions give an altogether new character to the softer side of organ-playing. High pressure stops are no longer confined to the solo manual, nor low-pressures to choir and swell. The whole of the stops on one manual may often be transferred to another, and the way forward seems to lie in the abandonment of the old-fashioned prerogatives of the different manuals, and the true democratising of all the manuals and pedals. (See ORGAN-PLAYING.)

BIBL.—W. GOODRICH, *Organ in France* (Boston Music Co.); E. E. TRUETTE, *Organ Registration* (Thompson & Co., Boston); A. EAGLEFIELD-HULL, *Organ Playing, its Technique and Expression*

[1] But compare with this the statement of the English view as put forward by Dr. P. C. Buck in the article ORGAN-PLAYING.

A. E.-H.

REGNART, surname of a family of Flemish musicians who flourished towards the end of the 16th century.  There were five brothers, one of whom, AUGUSTIN (not August, as given by Eitner, which would correspond to Augustus in Latin but not to Augustinus), was a canon of the Church of St. Peter, Lille (not Douai, as Eitner suggests in *Q.-L.*, forgetting the words of the dedication partly quoted by himself in his *Bibliographie*, p. 216).[1]

In 1590 Regnart edited and published at Douai a Collection of thirty-nine Motets, *a* 4-6, composed by his four brothers FRANCIS, JACOB, PASCHASIUS and CHARLES REGNART.  The work appropriately bears on its title-page the motto, 'Ecce quam bonum et quam jucundum fratres habitare in unum,' Psal. 132.  The full title is :

* Novae Cantiones Sacrae, 4, 5 et 6 vocum tum instrumentorum ouivis generi tum vivae voci aptissimae, authoribus Francisco, Jacobo, Pascasio, Carolo Regnart, fratribus germanis.' [2]

Of the four brothers only two attained any real position or eminence as composers, Francis and Jacob.  The other two are only represented by three motets apiece in this Collection, and of their careers nothing is known with any certainty.

Of FRANCIS, Augustin tells us that he had pursued his studies at the University of Douai and the Cathedral of Tournai.  Besides the twenty-four motets in the Collection above mentioned, Francis Regnart is chiefly known by a book of fifty chansons *a* 4-5, 'Poésies de Ronsard et autres,' originally published at Douai by Jean Bogaerd in 1575, and afterwards at Paris by Le Roy and Ballard in 1579.  These chansons have now been republished in modern score by H. Expert in his collection 'Les Maîtres musiciens de la renaissance française.'  Fétis mentions a book of Missae tres *a* 4-5, by Francis Regnart, published by Plantin in 1582, but there is no trace of such a publication in Goovaert's *Bibliographie*, and Eitner knows nothing of it.

Of the life and works of JACOB (*d.* Prague, 1600) we have fuller information.  He was early received as an Alumnus of the Imperial Chapel at Vienna and Prague.  In 1564 he is designated as tenor singer in the chapel, and as a member of the chapel accompanied the Emperor to the Augsburg Diet of 1566.  In 1573 he is mentioned as musical preceptor to

1 See also Goovaert's *Bibliographie*, p. 268 ; but he contradicts himself by elsewhere (p. 52) describing Augustin Regnart as Canon of St. Peter's, Louvain.

2 Another incidental mistake of Eitner is that of taking the word ' germanis ' as indicative of nationality, and explaining it on the ground that Flanders was then part of Germany, while all that the word really implies is that the brothers were full brothers.

the boys of the choir, and before 1579 became the vice-Kapellmeister.  In 1580 he was offered by the Elector of Saxony the post of Kapellmeister at Dresden vacant by the death of Scandelli, but declined.  In 1582, however, he left the imperial service to enter that of the Archduke Ferdinand at Innsbruck, where he remained as Kapellmeister till 1595.  He then returned to Prague, where he died.  Shortly before his death, in the dedication of a book of masses to the Emperor, Rudolf II., which, however, was not published till afterwards, he recommended to the care of the Emperor his wife and six children.  The widow, a daughter of Hans Vischer, the famous bass singer in the Electoral Chapel at Munich under Orlando Lassus, returned to Munich, where she occupied herself in preparing for publication in 1602-03 three volumes of her husband's masses, containing altogether 29 *a* 5, 6, 8 and 10, also a book of 'Sacrae cantiones,' *a* 4-12, 35 Nos.  The other sacred works of Regnart which appeared during his lifetime were a book of 'Sacrae cantiones,' *a* 5-6, 1575, and one *a* 4, 1577 ; also one entitled *Mariale*, 1588, Marian motets composed by way of thanksgiving for recovery from severe illness.

He was, however, even more widely known by his secular works, which consist of (1) two books of 'Canzone italiane,' *a* 5 (1574-81), (2) two books entitled 'Threni Amorum,' German secular songs, *a* 5 (1595), and (3) several collections, *a* 3, 4, 5, entitled 'Kurtzweilige teutsche Lieder nach Art der Neapolitanen oder welschen Villanellen' (1576-91).  Of the latter, the collection of 67 *a* 3 was republished by Eitner in modern score in 1895.  They are written in the simple melodious Italian canzonet style, without any artificiality of counterpoint.  In some introductory lines of verse the composer apologises for his frequent intentional employment of consecutive fifths in the harmony as being in accordance with the simple popular character he wished to give these songs.  The melody of one of them, 'Venus du und dein Kind,' has become, with a slight alteration in the first line, the Choral tune well-known later, 'Auf meinen lieben Gott.'  Two of Regnart's other songs, *a* 5, which have something more of imitative counterpoint, have been reprinted in Commer's selection of 'Geistliche und weltliche Lieder aus der xvi-xvii Jahrh.'  None of his Latin motets have been reprinted, with the exception of one which found admission into the *Evangelical Gotha Cantional* of 1655, whence it has been reproduced in Schöberlein's *Schatz*.  His masses, several of them based on the themes of German popular songs, must have been popular in their day, judging from the MS. copies of them enumerated in Eitner as surviving in various church archives.  A Passion according to St. Matthew, *a* 8, by Regnart survives only in MS., of which some account is given in Kade, *Die ältere Passions-kompositionen*, pp. 60-62.　　　　　　J. R. M.

REPRINTS.—H. EXPERT, *Maîtres Musiciens de la Renaissance française*, No. 15 (Paris); *Extraits des maîtres musiciens de la Renaissance française* (Paris); *La Fleur des musiciens de P. de Ronsard*, contained in *La Fleur des poésies de P. de Ronsard, gentilhomme vendômois* (Paris, Cité des Livres, 1923).

BIBL.—ALFRED WASSERMANN, *Die weltlichen Werke Jakob Regnarts*. Vienna Dissertation, 1919.

REGONDI, GIULIO (b. Geneva, 1822; d. May 6, 1872). His father took him to every court of Europe, excepting Madrid, before he was 9 years old. They arrived in England in June 1831; and Giulio seems never to have left the United Kingdom again except for two concert tours in Germany, one with Lidel, the violoncellist, in 1841, the other with Mme. Dulcken in 1846. On the former of these tours he played both the guitar and the melophone, and evoked enthusiastic praises from the correspondents of the *A.M.Z.* in Prague and Vienna for his extraordinary execution on both instruments. The CONCERTINA (q.v.) was patented by Sir Charles Wheatstone in 1829, but did not come into use till Regondi took it up. He wrote two concertos for it, and a very large number of arrangements and original compositions. He also taught it largely, and at one time his name was to be seen in almost all concert programmes. He was a great friend of Molique's, who wrote for him a concerto for the concertina (in G) which he played with great success at the concert of the Musical Society of London, Apr. 20, 1864. When he went abroad for his second tour, his performance and the effect which he got out of so unpromising an instrument astonished the German critics. (See *A.M.Z.*, 1846, p. 853.)　　　　　　G.

REHEARSAL (Fr. *répétition*, Ger. *Probe*), the occasions in which music, particularly ensemble music, is studied previous to the performance. The continental practice of admitting the public to full rehearsals (Fr. *répétition générale*, Ger. *Haupt-probe* or *General-probe*) is little followed in England except at certain of the older festivals, notably the Three Choirs and Handel Festivals.　　　　　　c.

REICHA, ANTON (b. Prague, Feb. 27, 1770; d. May 28, 1836), lost his father before he was a year old; his mother not providing properly for his education, he left home, and took refuge with his grandfather at Glattow, in Bohemia. The means of instruction in this small town being too limited, he went on to his uncle JOSEPH REICHA (b. Prague, 1746; d. Bonn, 1795), a violoncellist, conductor and composer, who lived at Wallerstein in Bavaria. His wife (a native of Lorraine speaking nothing but French) had no children, so they adopted the nephew, who thus learned to speak French and German besides his native Bohemian. He now began to study the violin, pianoforte and flute in earnest. On his uncle's appointment, in 1788, as musical director to the Elector of Cologne, he followed him to Bonn, and entered

the band of Maximilian of Austria as second flute. The daily intercourse with good music roused the desire to compose, and to become something more than an ordinary musician, but his uncle refused to teach him harmony. He managed, however, to study the works of Kirnberger and Marpurg in secret, gained much practical knowledge by hearing the works of Handel, Mozart and Haydn, and must have learned much from his constant intercourse with Beethoven, who played the viola in the same band with himself and was much attached to him. At length his perseverance and his success in composition conquered his uncle's dislike. He composed without restraint, and his symphonies and other works were played by his uncle's orchestra.[1]

On the dispersion of the Elector's court in 1794, Reicha went to Hamburg, where he remained till 1799. There the subject of instruction in composition began to occupy him, and there he composed his first operas, ' Godefroid de Montfort,' and ' Oubaldi, ou les Français en Égypte ' (two acts). Though not performed, some numbers of the latter were well received, and on the advice of a French émigré, he started for Paris towards the close of 1799, in the hope of producing it at the Théâtre Feydeau. In this he failed, but two of his symphonies, an overture and some ' Scènes italiennes,' were played at concerts. After the successive closing of the Théâtre Feydeau and the Salle Favart, he went to Vienna, and passed six years (1802–08) in renewed intimacy with Beethoven, and making friends with Haydn, Albrechtsberger, Salieri and others. The patronage of the Empress Maria Theresa was of great service to him, and at her request he composed an Italian opera, ' Argina, regina di Granata.' During this happy period of his life he published symphonies, oratorios, a Requiem, six string quintets, and many solos for PF. and other instruments. He himself attached great importance to his ' 36 Fugues pour le piano,' dedicated to Haydn, but they are not the innovations which he believed them to be; in placing the answers on any and every note of the scale he merely reverted to the ricercari of the 17th century, and the only effect of this abandonment of the classic laws of ' real fugue ' was to banish tonality.

The prospect of another war induced Reicha to leave Vienna, and he settled finally in Paris in 1808. He now realised the dream of his youth, producing first ' Cagliostro ' (Nov. 27, 1810), an opéra-comique composed with Dourlen; and at the Opéra, ' Natalie ' (three acts, July 30, 1816), and ' Sapho ' (Dec. 16, 1822). Each of these works contains music worthy of respect, but they had not sufficient dramatic effect to take with the public.

Reicha's reputation rests on his chamber

[1] See an interesting notice by Kastner, quoted by Thayer, *Beethoven*, i, 188.

music, and on his theoretical works. Of the former the following deserve mention : a diecetto for five strings and five wind instruments ; an octet for four strings and four wind instruments ; twenty-four quintets for flute, oboe, clarinet, horn and bassoon ; six quintets and twenty quartets for strings ; one quintet for clarinet and strings ; one quartet for PF., flute, violoncello and bassoon ; one do. for four flutes ; six do. for flute, violin, tenor and violoncello ; six string trios ; one trio for three violoncellos ; twenty-four do. for three horns ; six duets for two violins ; twenty-two do. for two flutes ; twelve sonatas for PF. and violin, and a number of sonatas and pieces for PF. solo. He also composed symphonies and overtures. These works are more remarkable for novelty of combination and striking harmonies than for abundance and charm of ideas. Reicha's faculty for solving musical problems brought him into notice among musicians when he first settled in Paris, and in 1818 he was offered the professorship of counterpoint and fugue at the Conservatoire. Among his pupils there were Boilly, Jelensperger, Bienaimé, Millaut, Lefebvre, Elwart, Pollet, Lecarpentier and Dancla.

His didactic works, all published in Paris, are : *Traité de mélodie*, etc. (4to, 1814) ; *Cours de composition musicale*, etc. (1818) ; *Traité de haute composition musicale* (first part 1824, second 1826), a sequel to the other two ; and *Art du compositeur dramatique*, etc. (4to, 1833).

Czerny published a German translation of the *Traité de haute composition* (Vienna, 1834, four vols. folio), and in his *Art d'improviser* obviously made use of Reicha's *Art de varier*—fifty-seven variations on an original theme.

Reicha married a Parisian, was naturalised in 1829, and received the Legion of Honour in 1831. He presented himself several times for election to the Institut before his nomination as Boieldieu's successor in 1835. He only enjoyed his honours a short time, dying of inflammation of the lungs in 1836. A life-like portrait, somewhat spoiled by excessive laudation, is contained in the *Notice sur Reicha* (Paris, 1837, 8vo), by his pupil Delaire.          G. C.

See also ERNST BÜCKEN, *Anton Reicha als Theoretiker*. *Z.M.W.*, Dec. 1919, pp. 156-69.

REICHARDT, ALEXANDER (*b.* Packs, Hungary, Apr. 17, 1825 ; *d.* Boulogne, 1860), tenor singer, made his first appearance at the age of 18 at the Lemberg theatre as Rodrigo in Rossini's 'Otello.' His success there led him to Vienna, where he was engaged at the court Opera, and completed his education under Gentiluomo, Catalani, etc. At this time he was much renowned for his singing of the Lieder of Beethoven and Schubert, and was in request at all the soirées ; Prince Esterhazy made him his Kammersänger. In 1846 he made a tour through Berlin, Hanover, etc., to Paris, returning to Vienna. In 1851 he made his first appearance in England, singing at the Musical Union, May 6, at the Philharmonic, May 12, at many other concerts, and before Queen Victoria. In the following season he returned and sang in Berlioz's 'Romeo and Juliet,' at the new Philharmonic Concert of Apr. 14, also in the Choral Symphony, Berlioz's 'Faust' and the 'Walpurgisnacht,' and enjoyed a very great popularity. From this time until 1857 he passed each season in England, singing at concerts, and at the Royal Opera, Drury Lane, and Her Majesty's Theatre, where he filled the parts of the Count in 'The Barber of Seville,' Raoul in 'The Huguenots,' Belmont in the 'Seraglio,' Don Ottavio in 'Don Juan,' and Florestan in 'Fidelio.' He also appeared with much success in oratorio. In 1857 he gave his first concert in Paris, in the Salle Erard, and the following sentence from Berlioz's report of the performance will give an idea of his style and voice. 'M. Reichardt is a tenor of the first water—sweet, tender, sympathetic and charming. Almost all his pieces were re-demanded, and he sang them again without a sign of fatigue.' In 1860 he settled in Boulogne. After he retired from the active exercise of his profession he organised a Philharmonic Society at Boulogne ; he was president of the Académie Communale de Musique, and his occasional concerts for the benefit of the hospital—where one ward is entitled 'Fondation Reichardt'—were among the chief musical events of the town. Reichardt was a composer as well as a singer. Several of his songs were very popular in their day.                               G.

REICHARDT, (1) JOHANN FRIEDRICH (*b.* Königsberg, Prussia, Nov. 25, 1752 ; *d.* Giebichenstein, near Halle, June 17, 1814), composer and writer on music ; son of a musician.

His education was more various than precise, music he learnt by practice rather than by any real study. His best instrument was the violin, on which he attained considerable proficiency under Veichtner, a pupil of Benda ; but he was also a good pianist. Theory he learned from the organist Richter. On leaving the University of Königsberg he started on a long tour, ostensibly to see the world before choosing a profession, though he had virtually resolved on becoming a musician. Between 1771 and 1774 he visited Berlin, Leipzig, Dresden, Vienna, Prague, Brunswick and Hamburg, made the acquaintance of the chief notabilities—musical, literary and political—in each place, and became himself in some sort a celebrity, after the publication of his impressions in a series of *Vertraute Briefen eines aufmerksamen Reisenden*, in two parts (1774 and 1776). On his return to Königsberg he went into a government office, but hearing of the death of Agricola of Berlin, he applied in person to Frederick the Great for the vacant post of Kapellmeister and court composer, sending him his opera 'Le feste galanti,' and though barely 24 obtained it in 1776. He at once began to introduce reforms, both in the Italian opera and the court orchestra, and excited much opposition from those who were more conservative than himself. While thus occupied he was indefatigable as a composer, writer and conductor. In 1783 he founded the Concerts Spirituels for the performance of unknown works, vocal and instrumental, which speedily gained a high reputation. He published collections of little-known music, with critical observations, edited newspapers, wrote articles and critiques in other periodicals, and produced independent works. But enemies, who were many, contrived to annoy him so much in the exercise of his duties, that in 1785 he obtained a long leave of absence, during which he visited London and Paris, and heard Handel's oratorios and Gluck's operas, both of which he heartily admired. In both places he met with great success as composer and conductor, and was popular for his social qualities ; but neither of his two French operas ' Tamerlan' and ' Panthée,' composed for the Opéra, was performed. On the death of Frederick the Great (1786) his successor confirmed Reichardt in his office, and he produced several new operas, but his position became more and more disagreeable. His vanity was of a peculiarly offensive kind, and his enemies found a weapon ready to their hand in his avowed sympathy with the doctrines of the French Revolution. The attraction of these views for a buoyant, liberal mind like Reichardt's, always in pursuit of high ideals, and eager for novelty, is obvious enough ; but such ideas are dangerous at court, and after further absence (from 1791) which he spent in Italy, Hamburg, Paris and elsewhere, he received his dismissal from the Kapellmeistership in 1794.[1] He retired to his estate, Giebichenstein, near Halle, and occupied himself with literature and composition, and occasional tours. In 1796 he became inspector of the salt works at Halle. After the death of Frederick William II. he produced a few more operas in Berlin, but made a greater mark with his Singspiele, which are of real importance in the history of German opera. In 1808 he accepted the post of Kapellmeister at Cassel to Jerome Bonaparte, refused by Beethoven, but did not occupy it long, as in the same year we find him making a long visit to Vienna. On his return to Giebichenstein he gathered round him a pleasant and cultivated society, and there, in the midst of his friends, he died.

Reichardt has been, as a rule, harshly judged ; he was not a mere musician but rather

a combination of musician, littérateur and man of the world. His overweening personality led him into many difficulties, but as a compensation he was endued with great intelligence, and with an ardent and genuine desire for progress in everything—music, literature and politics. As a composer his works show cultivation, thought and honesty : but have not lived, because they want the necessary originality. This is specially true of his instrumental music, which is entirely forgotten. His vocal music, however, is more important, and a good deal of it might well be revived, especially his Singspiele and his Lieder. Mendelssohn was no indulgent critic, but on more than one occasion he speaks of Reichardt with a warmth which he seldom manifests even towards the greatest masters. He never rested until he had arranged for the performance of Reichardt's Morning Hymn, after Milton, at the Düsseldorf Festival of 1835 ; and his enthusiasm for the composer, and his wrath at those who criticised him, are delightful to read.[2] Years afterwards, when his mind had lost the ardour of youth, and much experience had sobered him, he still retained his fondness for this composer, and few things are more charming than the genial appreciation with which he tells Reichardt's daughter of the effect which her father's songs had had, even when placed in such a dangerous position as between works of Haydn and Mozart, at the Historical Concert at the Gewandhaus in Feb. 1847. It is the simplicity, the naïveté, the national feeling of this true German music that he praises, and the applause with which it was received shows that he was not alone in his appreciation. Amongst Reichardt's numerous works are eight operas ; eight Singspiele, including four to Goethe's poems, ' Jery und Bätely ' (1789), ' Erwin und Elmire,' ' Claudine von Villabella ' and ' Lilla ' ; five large vocal works, including Milton's ' Morning Hymn,' translated by Herder, his most important work, in 1835 ; a large number of songs, many of which have passed through several editions, and been published in various collections.

Reichardt's writings show critical acumen, observation and judgment. Besides the letters previously mentioned, he published — *Das Kunstmagazin*, eight numbers in two vols. (Berlin, 1782 and 1791) ; *Studien für Tonkünstler und Musikfreunde*, a critical and historical periodical with thirty-nine examples (1792) ; *Vertraute Briefe aus Paris*, three parts (1804) ; *Vertraute Briefe auf einer Reise nach Wien*, etc. (1810)[3] ; fragments of autobiography in various newspapers ; and innumerable articles, critiques, etc. The *Briefe* are specially interesting from the copious details they give, not only on the music, but on the politics, literature and society of the various

---

[1] There was apparently some dissatisfaction with Reichardt's efficiency as a musician as well as with his political opinions, for Mozart's remark that ' the King's band contains great virtuosi, but the effect would be better if the gentlemen played together,' certainly implied a reflection on the conductor. Neither does Reichardt seem to have appreciated Mozart (Jahn's *Mozart*, ii. 410).

[2] Letters, Dec. 28, 1833 ; Apr. 3, 1835.
[3] New edition by Gustav Gugitz, 2 vols. (Munich, 1918.)

places he visited. For list of compositions and writings, see *Q.-L.*                                A. M.

BIBLIOGRAPHY
Autobiography. *Berlinischen musikalischen Zeitung.* 1805.
H. M. SCHLETTERER: *Biography* (1865, incomplete).
P. LANGE: *J. F. Reichardt.* (Halle, 1902.)
WALTHER PAULI: *J. F. Reichardt, sein leben, etc.* (Berlin, 1903.)
GEORG HEINRICKS: *Joh. Freidrich Reichardts Beziehungen zu Cassel und zu Georg Christoph Grosheim in Cassel,* pp. 36. (Homberg, 1922.)
HERMANN VON HASE: *Beiträge zur Breitkopfschen Geschäftsgeschichte.* *Z.M.W.,* May 1920, pp. 465-9 : *Reichardt.*
GUSTAV GUGITZ: *Unbekanntes zu Johann Friedrich Reichardts Aufenthalt in Österreich.* *Z.M.W.,* June 1920, pp. 529-34.

(2) LOUISE (*b.* Berlin, 1780; *d.* Hamburg, Nov. 17. 1826), daughter and pupil of Johann Friedrich, made her début as a singer in 1794 in Berlin. She accompanied her father in his wanderings, and after his death, in 1814, settled at Hamburg and opened a vocal academy with Clasing. The loss of her fiancé shortly before the wedding, and the loss of her voice, cast a shadow over her life. She wrote a considerable number of songs, of which some are still popular favourites. (*Q.-L.*; *Mendel.*)

REICHER-KINDERMANN, HEDWIG (*b.* Munich, July 15, 1853; *d.* Trieste, June 2, 1883), the daughter of the celebrated baritone, KINDERMANN (*q.v.*). She was taught the piano first by her mother, and at the School of Music, but abandoned the same in favour of singing, on the advice of Franz Wüllner. She received her vocal instruction from her father, and made her début at the Munich Opera as one of the boys in the 'Meistersinger,' and next played small parts in the opera, drama and ballet, besides singing in the chorus, in order to gain experience. She sang the alto part in Franz Lachner's Requiem at Leipzig in 1871 with such success that she became engaged at Carlsruhe. She played 'as guest' at Berlin as Pamina, June 5, and Agathe, June 9, 1874; she then returned to Munich, and sang Daniel in Handel's 'Belshazzar,' Apr. 14, 1875. Soon after she married Emanuel Reicher, an actor at the Gärtnerplatz Theatre, and for a time sang there in opéra bouffe, but returned to opera and played Grimgerde in the 1st Cycle, and Erda in the 2nd Cycle, at Bayreuth in 1876. She next played at Hamburg, Vienna (where she appeared as Leah on the production of Rubinstein's 'Maccabees'), and again at Munich. Having received instruction for the purpose from Faure and Jules Cohen at Paris, she sang in French at Monte Carlo in 1880 with such success that she received an offer to sing at La Scala, Milan, but declined it in favour of an engagement under Neumann at Leipzig, where she made her début as Fidelio, May 12, 1880. She became a great favourite, and remained there until 1882. She played in Neumann's company in the 'Ring' at Berlin and other German towns, in London, and lastly at Trieste. (See Neumann's *Erinnerungen, etc.*, 1907.) She made a great impression at Her Majesty's Theatre as Fricka on the production of 'Rheingold,' May 5, and of 'Walküre,'

May 6, 1882, and still more as Brünnhilde in the 2nd Cycle.                                A. C.

REICHMANN, THEODOR (*b.* Rostock, Mar. 15, 1849; *d.* Marbach, Lake of Constance, May 22, 1903), was taught to sing at first by Mantius, and subsequently by Lamperti in Milan. He made his début as a baritone at Magdeburg in 1869, and sang at Berlin, Rotterdam, Strassburg (1872), Hamburg (1873), Munich (1875), and was a member of the Court Opera at Vienna in 1882-89. In 1882 he sang the part of Amfortas at Bayreuth for the first time, and was identified with it for some ten years, after which differences with the authorities resulted in his non-appearance there until 1902. In the seasons between 1889 and 1891 he sang in New York, and in the latter year returned to Vienna, becoming once more a member of the Opera company in 1893. In that year he sang the part of Creon in 'Medea' at an operatic festival at Gotha. He appeared in London at Covent Garden in 1884, and at Drury Lane and Covent Garden in 1892, singing the parts of Wotan, Hans Sachs, Flying Dutchman, Pizarro, and the Trompeter von Säkkingen. He was far more popular in Germany than in England, where he had to stand comparisons with voices of far more beautiful quality than his.    M.

REID, GENERAL JOHN (*b.* Feb. 13, 1721; *d.* London, Feb. 6, 1807), the son of Alexander Robertson of Straloch, Perthshire, was educated at Edinburgh University, and entered Lord Loudoun's regiment of Highlanders in 1745. He subsequently adopted the surname by which he is known. After the quelling of the Jacobite rebellion, he saw active service in Flanders, Martinique, Havana and North America. He was in the 42nd Highlanders in 1751-70, was promoted colonel in 1777 and major-general in 1781. In 1794 he became colonel of the 88th foot, and general in 1798, dying possessed of a fortune of £50,000. By his will, made in 1803, he directed his trustees, in the event of his daughter dying without issue, to found a professorship of music in the University of Edinburgh,

'For the purpose also, after completing such endowment as hereinafter is mentioned, of making additions to the library of the said University, or otherwise promoting the general interest and advantage of the University in such . . . manner as the Principal and Professors . . . shall . . . think most fit and proper.'

In a codicil, dated 1806, he adds :

'After the decease of my daughter . . . I have left all my property . . . to the College of Edinburgh where I had my education . . . and as I leave all my music books to the Professor of Music in that College, it is my wish that in every year after his appointment he will cause a concert of music to be performed on the 13th of February, being my birthday.'

He also directed that at this annual 'Reid Concert' some pieces of his own composition should be performed 'by a select band.'
When by the death of General Reid's

daughter in 1838 some £70,000 became available, it seems to have been handed over to the University authorities without sufficient attention to the italicised portion of the following instruction in the will :

'That . . . my said Trustees . . . shall and do, *by such instrument or instruments as may be required by the law of Scotland* make over the residue of my . . . personal estate to the Principal and Professors of the said University.'

And as no particular sum was specified for foundation and maintenance of the Chair of Music, considerable latitude being allowed to the discretion of the University authorities, the secondary object of the bequest received far greater care and attention than the primary one, and for years the Chair was starved. In 1851, anticipating Professor Donaldson's intention of petitioning Parliament, the Edinburgh Town Council, as ' Patrons ' of the University, raised an action against the Principal and Professors for alleged mismanagement and misappropriation of the Reid Fund. A long litigation followed, and by decree of the Court of Session in 1855 the University authorities were ordered to devote certain sums to the purchase of a site and the erection of a building for the class of music. The class-room and its organ were built in 1861, and the professor's salary—which had been fixed at the very lowest sum suggested by the founder, viz. £300—as well as the grant for the concert, were slightly raised, and a sum set apart, by order of the Court, for expenses of class-room, assistants, instruments, etc. See EDINBURGH and PROFESSOR.

                                   H. S. O. ; addns. *D.N.B.*

REID CONCERTS, see EDINBURGH.

REIMANN, (1) IGNAZ (*b.* Albendorf, district of Glatz, Dec. 27, 1820 ; *d.* June 17, 1885), became principal teacher and choirmaster at Rengersdorf in Silesia, having been a pupil of the Breslau Seminary. He was an excessively diligent and fluent composer of church music, and wrote no fewer than 74 masses, of which only 18 were published. His son,

(2) HEINRICH (*b.* Rengersdorf, Mar. 14, 1850 ; *d.* Charlottenburg, May 24, 1906), received musical instruction from his father. He passed the Gymnasium at Glatz, and studied philology at Breslau from 1870–74, graduated the following year, and taught at the gymnasia of Strehlen, Wohlau, Berlin, Ratibor and Glatz, for a year in each place successively, till in 1885 he became director of that at Gleiwitz, in Upper Silesia. There he quarrelled with the authorities, threw up his post, became a Protestant, and thenceforth devoted himself entirely to music. He became known during 1879 and 1880 as musical reporter to the *Schlesicher Zeitung*, and by other literary works (*Nomos*, 1882 ; *Prosodies*, 1885–1886). After he took definitely to music, he published some vocal and organ compositions (sonatas, studies, etc.), and a biography of Schumann, which was published by Peters in

1887, and in that year he moved to Berlin to act as musical critic for the *Allgemeine Musikalische Zeitung*. For a time he was occupied at the Royal Library, besides being teacher of organ-playing and theory at the Scharwenka-Klindworth Conservatorium till 1894, and organist of the Philharmonic till 1895, in which year the Kaiser appointed him to the great church in the Augusta-Victoriaplatz, erected to the memory of the Emperor William I., where he enjoyed a great reputation as an organ virtuoso, and directed some impressive performances of oratorios, masses, and church music generally. In 1897 he received the title of Professor, and in 1898 founded a Bach Society.

His compositions include duets for female voices ; love scenes in waltz form for four voices ; a chorus for four male voices ; an album of children's songs for solo voice; toccata for organ in E minor (op. 23) ; piano duets ; two wedding songs for bass voice ; arrangements of twenty-five German songs, ' Das deutsche Lied,' of the 14th to the 19th centuries, also for bass voice ; a prelude and triple fugue in D minor for the organ ; and ciacona for organ in F minor. His writings include a contribution on the theory and history of Byzantine music (1889) ; two volumes of musical retrospects, *Wagneriana-Lisztiana* ; an opening volume to his own collection of lives of celebrated musicians, being the biography of Schumann already mentioned, to which he added those of Bülow and J. S. Bach.

                                                H. V. H.

REIMANN, MATTHIEU (Matthias Reymannus) (*b.* Löwenberg, 1544 ; *d.* Prague, Oct. 21, 1597), a Doctor of Law and Imperial Councillor under Rudolf II. ; wrote two works for the lute ; the one entitled ' Noctes musicae ' appeared in 1598, and the other, ' Cithara sacra psalmodiae Davidis ad usum testudinis,' in 1603.                                          H. V. H.

REINA, FRA SISTO, of Saronno, Lombardy, Franciscan monk, from 1648 organist at Beata Vergine de Miracoli del Borgo, Saronno ; in 1660 maestro di cappella of S. Francis, Piacenza ; in 1662 organist and maestro di cappella of S. Bartolomeo, Modena ; in 1664 mentioned only as organist of that church. He wrote masses and other church music. His ' La danza delle voci ' (Psalms, Te Deum, etc.), op. 9, published in 1664, contains 2 sonatas for 4 violins (*Q.-L.*).

REINACH, THÉODORE (*b.* St. Germain en Laye, July [1] 3, 1860), barrister from 1881–86, professor at the Collège de France, archæologist and historian, member of the French *Parlement* (1906–14) and of the Institut, is an authority in the domain of Hellenism and of Greek music. In the *Revue des études grecques* (editor since 1888) he has published, 1892–1901, *Notes sur les problèmes musicaux d'Aristote* (with

[1] Not June, as in some Dictionaries.

d'Eichthal), 1894; *La Guitare dans l'art grec*
(1396), etc.; *La Musique des sphères* (1901).
He has contributed to the *Dictionnaire des
antiquités grecques et romaines* (Lyra, Musica,
Tibia, etc.); *L'Ami des monuments : Note sur
l'hymne à Apollon* (1894); *Bulletin de Correspondance hellénique : La Musique des hymnes de
Delphes, Un nouvel hymne delphique* (1893,
1894); to the *Revue critique* (1887), *Revue
archéologique* (1919), *Revue musicale* (1904,
1922), *Revue de Paris, Revue bleue, Revue de
musicologie*, etc. He has published with
H. Weil: *Plutarque : De la musique* (trans.)
(Paris, 1900, Leroux), and a book, *La Musique
grecque* (Paris, Payot, 1926). He is the author
of ' Salamine,' lyric drama (after Aeschylus's
' Persae '), music by M. Emmanuel, not yet
performed, and of ' La Naissance de la lyre '
(after Sophocles), music by A. Roussel, performed at the Opéra (1925).          M. L. P.

REINAGLE, (1) JOSEPH (*b.* near Vienna ?),
said to have served in the Hungarian army.
In 1762 he was at Portsmouth, where his sons
were born. By the influence of the Earl of
Kelly, he was appointed in 1762 trumpeter to
the King, presumably in Scotland, as he appears
to have at that time removed to Edinburgh.
(See SCHETKY.)

(2) ALEXANDER (*b.* Portsmouth, 1756;
*d.* Maryland, Baltimore, U.S.A., Sept. 21,
1809) was probably his eldest son. He accompanied his younger brother, Hugh (4), to
Lisbon, and after his death went to America
about 1786. His name is attached to

' A Collection of the most Favourite Scots tunes with Variations
for the Harpsichord by A. Reinagle, London, printed for and sold
by the author,' folio.

This scarce and rudely printed volume is advertised in Aird's ' Selection,' vol. ii. 1782, and
though bearing ' London ' as an imprint was
most likely issued from Glasgow. In Philadelphia, where the greater part of his American
life was spent, he became a musician of importance. In 1793 he formed a company with
Thomas Wignell, built the New Theatre in
Chestnut Street, and was pianist in the
orchestra. Both plays and operas were produced there for which in some cases he wrote
music. Some sonatas by him are in the
Library of Congress at Washington.

BIBL.—SONNECK, *Early Concert Life, Early Opera*, pp. 113, 118;
*Sammelb.* Int. Mus. Ges. vi. 465, 486-9.

The second son, (3) JOSEPH (*b.* Portsmouth,
1762; *d.* Oxford, Nov. 12, 1825), was first
intended for the navy, and next apprenticed to
a working jeweller in Edinburgh. He took up
music as a profession, and studied the French
horn and the trumpet under his father and
subsequently the violoncello under J. G. C.
SCHETKY (*q.v.*), who had married his sister.
He became a noted player at the Edinburgh
concerts, but abandoned the instrument as a
consequence of his brother's superior skill on it,
resuming it after Hugh's death. He became

violin and viola player and leader of the
orchestra at St. Cecilia's Hall, Edinburgh. He
came to London, and was one of the second
violins at the Handel Commemoration in 1784.
In the following year he became associated
with Haydn and Salomon and played at their
concerts. Early in the 19th century he re
moved to Oxford, and died there. His published works include ' Twenty-four progressive
lessons for the pianoforte ' (1796), ' Duets for
the Violoncello,' quartets for strings, besides
an *Introduction to the Art of Playing the Violoncello*, which ran through several editions. In
Gow's ' Fifth Collection of Strathspey Reels '
are some airs by Joseph Reinagle ; one,
' Dumfries Races,' became well known.

The third son, (4) HUGH (*d.* Lisbon, Mar. 19,
1785), became a proficient violoncellist, went
to Lisbon for the benefit of his health in 1784,
and died there of consumption.

(5) ALEXANDER ROBERT (*b.* Brighton, Aug.
21, 1799; *d.* Kidlington, near Oxford, Apr. 6,
1877), the son of the younger Joseph (3),
settled with his father in Oxford, where he
became teacher, organist and a well-known
figure in musical circles. He was organist of
the church of St. Peter in the East. He composed a number of sacred pieces, including the
well-known ' St. Peter ' psalm-tune. He also
wrote and compiled many books of instruction
for the violin and violoncello.

His wife, (6) CAROLINE (*née* ORGER) (*b.* London, 1818; *d.* Mar. 11, 1892), married Reinagle
(5) in 1846. She was associated with her
husband as a teacher, and wrote some technical works for the pianoforte, besides a concerto and several chamber compositions. She
also attained some success as a pianist.

F. K.; addns. *Mus. T.*, 1906, pp. 541,
617, and 683, *Amer. Supp.*, etc.

REINCKEN (REINKEN), JOHANN ADAM
(JAN ADAMS REINCKEN) (*b.* Wilshausen, Lower
Alsace, Apr. 27, 1623; *d.* Nov. 24, 1722),
eminent organist, pupil of Heinrich Scheidemann, became in 1654 organist of the church
of St. Catherine at Hamburg, and retained the
post till his death. He was a person of some
consideration at Hamburg, both on account of
his fine playing, and of his beneficial influence
on music in general, and the Hamburg Opera
in particular, but his vanity and jealousy of his
brother artists are severely commented on by
his contemporaries. So great and so widespread was his reputation that Sebastian Bach
frequently walked to Hamburg from Lüneburg
(1700–03), and Cöthen (1720), to hear him play.
Reincken may be considered the best representative of the North German school of
organists of the 17th century, whose strong
points were, not the classic placidity of the
South German school, but great dexterity of
foot and finger, and ingenious combinations
of the stops. His compositions are loaded with

passages for display, and are defective in form, both in individual melodies and general construction. His works are very scarce ; ' Hortus musicus,' for two violins, viola da gamba and bass (Hamburg, 1704) is reprinted as No. XIII. of the publications of the Maatschappij tot bevordering der Toonkunst (Amsterdam, 1887). No. XIV. of the same publication consists of Reincken's ' Partite diverse ' (variations), but even in MS. only very few pieces are known—two on Chorals, one toccata, and two sets of variations (for clavier).[1] Of the first of these, one—on the Choral ' An Wasserflüssen Babylons '—is specially interesting, because it was by an extempore performance on that Choral at Hamburg in 1720 that Bach extorted from the venerable Reincken the words, ' I thought that this art was dead, but I see that it still lives in you.' (Cf. EXTEMPORISATION.) Two organ fugues, a toccata in G, variations on Chorals and on a ' ballet,' etc. are in MSS. at Dresden, Leipzig and Darmstadt. (See the *Tijdschrift* of the Vereeniging voor N.-Nederlands Muziekgeschiedenis, vi. pp. 151-8, *Q.-L.*, etc.)    A. M.

BIBL.—W. STAHL, *Zur Biographie Johann Adam Reinkens.* A.M., Apr. 1921, pp. 232-6.

REINECKE, CARL HEINRICH CARSTEN (*b.* Altona, June 23, 1824 ; *d.* Leipzig, Mar. 10, 1910), composer, conductor and performer, director of the Gewandhaus concerts at Leipzig, the son of a musician, was from an early age trained by his father, and at 11 performed in public.

As a youth he was a first-rate orchestral violin-player. At 18 he made a concert tour through Sweden and Denmark, with especial success at Copenhagen. In 1843 he settled in Leipzig, where he studied diligently, and eagerly embraced the opportunities for cultivation afforded by the society of Mendelssohn and Schumann, with a success which amply shows itself in his music. In 1844 he made a professional tour with Wasielewski to Riga, returning by Hanover and Bremen. He was already in the pay of Christian VIII. of Denmark, and in 1846 he again visited Copenhagen, remaining there for two years. On both occasions he was appointed court pianist. In 1851 he went with the violinist Otto von Königslöw to Italy and Paris ; and on his return Hiller secured him for the professorship of the piano and counterpoint in the Conservatorium of Cologne. In 1854 he became conductor of the Konzertgesellschaft at Barmen, and in 1859 Musikdirector to the University of Breslau. On Julius Rietz's departure from Leipzig to Dresden in 1860, Reinecke succeeded him as conductor at the Gewandhaus, and became at the same time professor of composition in the Conservatorium. Between the years 1867 and 1872 he made extensive tours ; in England he

[1] Spitta's *Bach*, Eng. transl. i. 197-9.

played at the Musical Union, Crystal Palace, and Philharmonic, on the 6th, 17th and 19th of Apr. 1869, respectively, and met with great success both as a virtuoso and a composer. He reappeared in this country in 1872, and was equally well received. In 1895 he resigned the post of conductor of the Gewandhaus concerts, but kept his position in the Conservatorium, being appointed in 1897 director of musical studies until 1902, when he retired altogether.

Reinecke's industry in composition was great, his best works, as might be expected, being those for piano ; his three PF. sonatas indeed are excellent compositions, on the lines of Mendelssohn's technique ; his pieces for two PFs. are also good ; his PF. concerto in F♯ minor, once a well-established favourite both with musicians and the public, was followed by two others in E minor and C respectively. Besides other instrumental music—a wind octet, quintets, four string quartets, seven trios, concertos for violin and violoncello, etc.—he composed an opera in five acts, ' König Manfred,' and two in one act each, ' Der vierjährige Posten ' (after Körner) and ' Ein Abenteuer Händels ' ; ' Auf hohen Befehl ' (1886) and ' Der Gouverneur von Tours ' (1891) ; incidental music to Schiller's ' Tell ' ; an oratorio, ' Belsazar ' ; cantatas for men's voices ' Hakon Jarl ' and ' Die Flucht nach Ägypten ' ; overtures, ' Dame Kobold,' 'Aladdin,' ' Friedensfeier,' an overture, ' Zenobia,' and a funeral march for the Emperor Frederick (op. 200) ; two masses, and three symphonies (op. 79 in A, op. 134 in C minor, and op. 227 in G minor) ; and a large number of songs and of pianoforte pieces in all styles, including valuable studies and educational works. Of his settings of fairy tales as cantatas for female voices, 'Schneewittchen,' 'Dornröschen,' ' Aschenbrödel ' and several others became very popular. His style was refined, and he wrote with peculiar clearness and correctness. Various contributions to musical literature will be found enumerated in *Riemann*.

BIBL.—J. W. VON WASIELEWSKI, *Karl Reinecke* (1893). See E. SEGNITZ, *Carl Reinecke* (1900).    F. G.

REINE DE SABA, LA, opera in 4 acts ; words by Barbier and Carré ; music by Gounod. Produced Opéra, Feb. 28, 1862 ; in concert form as ' Irene ' (H. B. Farnie), Crystal Palace, Aug. 12, 1865 ; as opera, F. Archer Co., Apr. 21, 1880, Theatre Royal, Manchester. See also KÖNIGIN VON SABA (Goldmark).

REINER (RENER), ADAM (*b.* Liège, late 15th cent.), an important early 16th-century composer who was ranked with Moralis. He composed masses, other church music and songs, two of which appeared in a modern edition. (See list in *Q.-L.*)

REINER, AMBROSIUS (*b.* Altdorf - Weingarten, Dec. 7, 1604 ; *d.* Innspruck, July 5, 1672). Between 1643-56 he was first organist, then Kapellmeister, at the archducal court, Innspruck. He composed masses, psalms, litanies, odes and sacred songs (*Q.-L.*; *Riemann*).

REINER, FRITZ (*b.* Budapest, Dec. 19, 1888), orchestral conductor, was educated at the Landesmusik-Akademie in Budapest, became conductor of the Landestheater at Laibach (1910), and of the Volks Oper at Budapest in 1911. In 1914 he was conductor at the Hof Oper at Dresden, and in 1921 he followed Ysaÿe as director of the Cincinnati Symphony Orchestra (see CINCINNATI). He visited London, conducting the London Symphony Orchestra in Elena Gerhardt's concert on May 27, 1924.                C.

REINER, JACOB (*b.* Altdorf, Würtemberg, *c.* 1559 or 1560 ; *d.* Aug. 12, 1606), was brought up at the Benedictine Monastery of Weingarten, where he also received his first musical training. We have it on his own authority that he was afterwards a pupil of Orlando Lassus at Munich, where also his first publication, a volume of motets *a* 5-6, appeared in 1579. Incidentally it may be mentioned that in 1589 Lassus dedicated a book of six masses, the eighth volume of the *Patrocinium musices*, to the Abbot of Weingarten. Reiner himself returned to Weingarten, and from at least 1586 to his death in 1606 was engaged as lay singer and choirmaster at the monastery. His publications are fairly numerous, and consist of several volumes of motets, masses and Magnificats, which need not here be specified in detail (especially since partbooks are frequently missing), also two volumes of German songs *a* 3-5. Three settings *a* 5 of the Passion exist in MS., of a similar character to those by Lassus. The first volume of Reiner's motets was reproduced in lithograph score by Otto-mar Dresel in 1872, and one of the numbers also appears in the supplement to Proske's ' Musica divina,' edited by F. X. Haberl in 1876.                J. R. M.

REINE TOPAZE, LA, opéra-comique in 3 acts ; words by Lockroy and Battes, music by Victor Massé. Produced Théâtre-Lyrique, Dec. 27, 1856. In English, Her Majesty's Theatre, Dec. 24, 1860.                G.

REINHARD, ANDREAS (REINHARDUS), organist and notary at Schneeberg, Saxony, wrote 3 treatises : *Musica* (Leipzig, 1604), *De harmoniae limbo* (1610), *Methodus de arte musica* (MS. *c.* 1610, in Erfurt Library ?) (*Riemann*).

REINHARD, JOHANN GEORG (*b. circa* 1677 ; *d.* Vienna, Nov. 6, 1742). From Jan. 1, 1708, he was imperial court organist ; from 1734–40 also court composer of ballets and serenatas. He composed an opera and church music (*Q.-L.*).

REINHOLD, HUGO (*b.* Vienna, Mar. 3, 1854), was a choir-boy of the Hofkapelle of his native city and a pupil of the Conservatorium der Musikfreunde till 1874, where he worked with Bruckner, Dessoff and Epstein under the endowment of the Duke of Saxe-Coburg and Gotha, and obtained a silver medal. His many compositions include piano music and songs, a string quartet (op. 18 in A major), a suite in five movements for piano and strings, and a Prelude, Minuet and Fugue for stringed orchestra. The two latter were performed at the Vienna Philharmonic Concerts of Dec. 9, 1877, and Nov. 17, 1878, respectively, and were praised by the Vienna critic of the *Monthly Musical Record* for their delicate character and absence of undue pretension. The quartet was executed by Hellmesberger.                H. V. H.

REINHOLD, THEODOR CHRISTLIEB (*b.* 1682 ; *d.* 1755), was the teacher of Johann Adolf Hiller (Hüller), the composer of numerous motets, and cantor of the Kreuzkirche at Dresden from 1720 till his death.                H. V. H.

REINHOLD, (1) THOMAS (*b.* Dresden, *c.* 1690 ; *d.* Chapel Street, Soho, 1751), was the reputed nephew, or, as some said, son, of the Archbishop of Dresden. He had an early passion for music, and having met Handel at the Archbishop's residence conceived so strong a liking for him that after a time he quitted his abode and sought out the great composer in London, where he appeared in various works of Handel's, after making his first appearance in July 1731 at the Haymarket Theatre as a singer in ' The Grub Street Opera.'

His son, (2) FREDERICK CHARLES (*b.* 1737 ; *d.* Somers Town, Sept. 29, 1815), received his musical education first in St. Paul's and afterwards in the Chapel Royal. On Feb. 3, 1755, he made his first appearance on the stage at Drury Lane as Oberon in J. C. Smith's opera ' The Fairies,' being announced as ' Master Reinhold.' He afterwards became organist of St. George the Martyr, Bloomsbury. In 1759 he appeared as a bass singer at Marylebone Gardens, where he continued to sing for many seasons. He afterwards performed in English operas, and sang in oratorios, and at provincial festivals, etc. He was especially famed for his singing of Handel's song, ' O ruddier than the cherry.' He was one of the principal bass singers at the Commemoration of Handel in 1784. He retired in 1797. See *Mus. T.*, 1877, p. 273.                W. H. H.

REINTHALER, KARL MARTIN (*b.* Erfurt, Oct. 13, 1822 ; *d.* Bremen, Feb. 13, 1896), conductor of the Private Concerts at Bremen, was early trained in music by G. A. Ritter, then studied theology in Berlin, but after passing his examination, devoted himself entirely to music, and studied with A. B. Marx. His first attempts at composition, some psalms sung by the Cathedral choir, attracted the attention of King Frederick William IV., and procured him a travelling grant. He visited Paris, Milan, Rome and Naples, taking lessons

in singing from Geraldi and Bordogni.  On his
return in 1853 he obtained a post in the Conservatorium of Cologne, and in 1858 became
organist in the Cathedral of Bremen, and conductor of the Singakademie.  He had already
composed an oratorio, 'Jephta' (performed in
London by Hullah, Apr. 16, 1856, and published with English text by Novello), and in
1875 his opera 'Edda' was played with success
at Bremen, Hanover and elsewhere.  His
'Bismarck-hymn' obtained the prize at Dort-
mund, and he composed a symphony and a
large number of partsongs.  He was a member
of the Berlin Academy from 1882, and had the
title of Royal Professor in 1888.  His cantata
'In der Wüste' had a great success, and his
opera 'Käthchen von Heilbronn' received a
prize at Frankfort.  He retired from the
Singakademie in 1890.　　F. G., with addns.

REISSIGER, KARL GOTTLIEB (b. Belzig,
near Wittenberg, Jan. 31, 1798 ; d. Nov. 7,
1859), son of Christian Gottlieb Reissiger, who
published three symphonies for full orchestra
in 1790.

His father was cantor at Belzig.  He became
in 1811 a pupil of Schicht at the Thomasschule,
Leipzig.  In 1818 he removed to the university
with the intention of studying theology, but
some motets composed in 1815 and 1816 had
already attracted attention, and the success
of his fine baritone voice made him determine
to devote himself to music.  In 1821 he went
to Vienna and studied opera thoroughly.  Here
also he composed 'Das Rockenweibchen.'  In
1822 he sang an aria of Handel's, and played
a PF. concerto of his own composition at a
concert in the Kärnthnerthor Theatre.  Soon
after he went to Munich, where he studied with
Peter Winter, and composed an opera, 'Dido,'
which was performed several times at Dresden
under Weber's conductorship.  At the joint
expense of the Prussian government and of
his patron von Altenstein, a musician, he undertook a tour in 1824 through Holland, France
and Italy, in order to report on the condition
of music in those countries.  On his return he
was commissioned to draw up a scheme for a
Prussian national conservatorium, but at the
same time was offered posts at the Hague and
at Dresden.  The latter he accepted, replacing
Marschner at the Opera, where he laboured
hard, producing both German and Italian
operas.  In 1827 he succeeded C. M. von
Weber as conductor of the German Opera at
Dresden.  Among his operas, 'Ahnenschatz'
(1824), 'Libella,' 'Turandot,' 'Adèle de Foix'
and 'Der Schiffbruch von Medusa' had great
success in their day.  The overture to the
'Felsenmühle,' a spirited and not uninteresting
piece, was occasionally played.  Masses and
church music, an oratorio, 'David,' a few
Lieder, numerous chamber compositions (particularly some graceful and easy trios for

PF.. violin and violoncello) made his name very
popular for a period.  He was the composer of
the piece known as 'Weber's Last Waltz.'  This
is No. 5 of his 'Danses brillantes pour le
pianoforte' written in 1822, and published
by Peters at Leipzig in 1824.  On his death
Reissiger was succeeded at Dresden by Julius
Rietz.　　　　　　　　　　　　　　　F. G.

BIBL.—KURT KREISER, *Carl Gottlieb Reissiger.  Sein Leben, nebst
einigen Beiträgen zur Geschichte des Konzertwesens in Dresden,* pp. iv
118.  (Dresden 1918.)

REISSMANN, AUGUST (b. Frankenstein,
Silesia, Nov. 14, 1825 ; d. Berlin, Dec. 1, 1903),
musician and writer on music, was grounded
in music by Jung, the cantor of his native
town.  In 1843 he removed to Breslau, and
there had instruction from Mosewius, Baum-
gart, Ernst Richter, Lüstner and Kahl in
various branches, including pianoforte, organ,
violin and violoncello.  He at first proposed
to become a composer, but a residence in
1850–52 at Weimar, where he came in contact
with the new school of music, changed his
plans and drove him to literature.  His first
book was *Von Bach bis Wagner* (Berlin, 1861) ;
rapidly followed by a historical work on the
German song, *Das deutsche Lied*, etc. (1861),
rewritten as *Geschichte des deutschen Liedes*
(1874).  This, again, was succeeded by his
General History of Music—*Allg. Geschichte der
Musik* (3 vols., Leipzig, 1864), with a great
number of interesting examples ; *Allg. Musik-
lehre* (1864) ; and *Lehrbuch der musik. Kompositionen* (3 vols. Berlin, 1866–71).  His later
works were of a biographical nature, attempts
to show the gradual development of the life
and genius of the chief musicians—Schumann
(1865), Mendelssohn (1867), Schubert (1873),
Haydn (1879), Bach (1881), Handel (1882),
Gluck (1882), Weber (1883).  In 1877 he
published a volume of lectures on the history
of music, delivered in the Conservatorium of
Berlin, where he resided from 1863.  His chief
employment from 1871 was the completion of
the *Musik-Conversationslexikon*, in which he
succeeded Mendel as editor, after the death of
the latter.  The 11th volume, completing the
work, appeared in 1879.

As a practical musician Reissmann was
almost as industrious as he was in literature.
The operas 'Gudrun' (Leipzig, 1871), 'Die
Bürgermeisterin von Schorndorf' (Leipzig,
1880) and 'Das Gralspiel' (Düsseldorf, 1895),
a ballet, 'Der Blumen Rache' (1887), a work
for singing and speaking soloists, with choir
and piano, 'König Drosselbart' (1886),
dramatic scenas, an oratorio, 'Wittekind'
(1888), a concerto and a suite for solo violin
and orchestra ; two sonatas for pianoforte and
violin ; and a great quantity of miscellaneous
pieces for piano solo and for the voice are
mentioned.  In 1881 he edited an Illustrated
History of German Music.　　　　　　G.

RELATIVE is the word used to express the connexion between a major and a minor key which have the same signature ; A minor is the ' relative ' minor of C, C the ' relative ' major of A minor.                                   M.

RELFE, JOHN (b. Greenwich, 1763 ; d. London, c. 1837), studied under his father, Lupton Relfe,fifty years organist at Greenwich Hospital, and under Keeble.  He was a member of the King's Band in 1810 and a teacher of harmony and PF.  He composed a cantata, numerous songs, PF. sonatas, etc., and wrote several books on musical theory, and *Remarks on the Present State of Musical Instruction* (1819).

                                        E. v. d. s.

RELLSTAB, (1) JOHANN KARL FRIEDRICH (b. Berlin, Feb. 27, 1759 ; d. Charlottenburg, Aug. 19, 1813).  His father, a printer, wished him to succeed to the business, but from boyhood his whole thoughts were devoted to music. He was on the point of starting for Hamburg to complete, with Emanuel Bach, his musical studies begun with Agricola and Fasch, when the death of his father forced him to take up the business.  He added a music-printing and publishing branch ; was the first to establish a musical lending library (1783) ; founded a Concert Society, on the model of Hiller's at Leipzig, and called it ' Concerts for connoisseurs and amateurs.'  The first concert took place Apr. 16, 1787, at the Englisches Haus, and in course of time the following works were performed ; Salieri's ' Armida,' Schulz's ' Athalia,' Naumann's ' Cora,' Hasse's ' Conversione di San Agostino,' Bach's ' Magnificat ' and Gluck's ' Alceste,' which was thus first introduced to Berlin.  The Society at last merged in the Singakademie.  He wrote musical critiques for the Berlin paper, signed with his initials ; and had concerts every other Sunday during the winter at his own house, at which such works as Haydn's ' Seasons ' were performed ; but these meetings were stopped by the entry of the French in 1806, when he frequently had twenty men and a dozen horses quartered on him ; lost not only his music but all his capital, and had to close his printing-press.  In time he resumed his concerts ; in 1809 gave lectures on harmony ; in 1811 travelled to Italy.  Not long after his return he was struck with apoplexy while walking at Charlottenburg, and was found dead on the road some hours afterwards.  As a composer he left three cantatas, a ' Passion,' a Te Deum and a Mass.  Also an opera ; songs too numerous to specify ; vocal scores of Graun's ' Tod Jesu ' and Gluck's ' Iphigénie ' ; and a German libretto of Gluck's ' Orphée,' apparently from his own pen.  Of instrumental music he published—marches for PF., symphonies and overtures ; a series of pieces with characteristic titles, ' Obstinacy,' ' Sensibility,' etc. ; twenty-four short pieces for PF., violin and

bass, etc.  Also *Versuch über die Vereinigung der mus. und oratorischen Deklamation* (1785) ; *Über die Bemerkungen einer Reisenden . . .* (1789) (see REICHARDT) ; and *Anleitung für Clavierspieler* (1790).  These works, for the most part bibliographical curiosities, are very instructive.

Rellstab had three daughters, of whom (2) CAROLINE (b. Apr. 18, 1794 ; d. Feb. 17, 1813) was a singer, distinguished for her extraordinary compass.  His son,

(3) HEINRICH FRIEDRICH LUDWIG (b. Berlin, Apr. 13, 1799 ; d. there, Nov. 27, 1860), though delicate in health, and destined for practical music, was compelled by the times to join the army, where he became ensign and lieutenant. In 1816, after the peace, he took lessons on the piano from Ludwig Berger, and in 1819 and 1820 studied theory with Bernhard Klein. At the same time he taught mathematics and history in the Brigadeschule till 1821, when he retired from the army to devote himself to literature, ultimately settling in Berlin (1823). He also composed much part-music for the ' Jüngere Liedertafel,' which he founded in conjunction with G. Reichardt in 1819, wrote a libretto, ' Dido,' for B. Klein, and contributed to Marx's *Musikzeitung*.  A pamphlet on Madame Sontag (*Henriette, oder die schöne Sängerin*) procured him three months' imprisonment in 1826, on account of its satirical allusions to a well-known diplomatist.  In 1826 he joined the staff of the *Vossische Zeitung*, and in a short time completely led the public opinion on music in Berlin.  His first article was a report on a performance of ' Euryanthe,' Oct. 31, 1826.  Two years later he wrote a cantata for Humboldt's congress of physicists, which Mendelssohn set to music.

Rellstab quarrelled with Spontini over his ' Agnes von Hohenstauffen ' (Berlin *Musikalische Zeitung* for 1827, Nos. 23, 24, 26 and 29), and the controversy was maintained with much bitterness until Spontini left Berlin, when Rellstab, in his pamphlet *Über mein Verhältniss als Kritiker zu Herrn Spontini* (1827), acknowledged that he had gone too far.

Rellstab's novels and essays are to be found for the most part in his *Gesammelte Schriften*, 24 vols. (Leipzig, Brockhaus).  A musical periodical, *Iris im Gebiet der Tonkunst*, founded by him in 1830, survived till 1842.  His recollections of Berger, Schroeder - Devrient, Mendelssohn, Klein, Dehn and Beethoven (whom he visited in Mar. 1825), will be found in *Aus meinem Leben* (2 vols. Berlin, 1861).

                                             F. G.

REMBT, JOHANN ERNST (b. Suhl, Thüringer-Wald, 1749 or 1750 ; d. there, Feb. 26, 1810), was appointed organist at Suhl in 1773 and remained till his death.  He was distinguished as a performer, and, devoting himself to the study of the works of Sebastian Bach, he worthily upheld the more solid traditions of the Bach school of organ-playing against the prevailing shallowness of his time. Breitkopf & Härtel still retain in their catalogue some of his works originally published by them, such as his six fugued Choral-preludes, six organ trios and various Choral-preludes in trioform. Various fughettas for the organ also appear in Volkmar's ' Orgel-Album.'

J. R. M.

REMÉNYI, EDUARD (real name HOFFMANN) (b. Heves,[1] Hungary, 1830 ; d. San Francisco, May 15, 1898), a famous violinist, received his musical education at the Vienna Conservatorium during the years 1842–45, where his master on the violin was Joseph Böhm, the famous teacher of Joachim. In 1848 he took an active part in the insurrection, and became adjutant to the famous general Görgey, under whom he took part in the campaign against Austria. After the revolution had been crushed he had to fly the country, and went to America, where he resumed his career as a virtuoso. He toured in Germany, taking Brahms [2] with him, in 1852–53. In 1853 he went to Liszt in Weimar, who at once recognised his genius and became his artistic guide and friend. In the following year he came to London and was appointed solo violinist to Queen Victoria. In 1855 he was in America, and in 1860 he obtained his amnesty and returned to Hungary, where some time afterwards he received from the Emperor of Austria a similar distinction to that granted him in England. After his return home he seems to have retired for a time from public life, living chiefly on an estate he owned in Hungary. In 1865 he appeared for the first time in Paris, where he created a perfect furore. Repeated tours in Germany, Holland and Belgium further spread his fame. In 1875 he settled temporarily in Paris, and in the summer of 1877 came to London, where also he produced a sensational effect in private circles. The season being far advanced he appeared in public only once, at Mapleson's benefit concert at the Crystal Palace, where he played a fantasia on themes from the ' Huguenots.' In the autumn of 1878 he again visited London, and played at the Promenade Concerts. He was on his way to America, where he gave concerts and took up his residence. In 1887 he undertook a tour of the world, in the course of which he appeared in private in London in 1891 and 1893. As an artist he combined perfect mastery over the technical difficulties of his instrument with a strongly pronounced individuality. His soul was in his playing, and his impulse carried him away as he warmed to his task, the impression produced on the audience being accordingly in an ascending scale. Another

[1] According to another account at Miskolc.
[2] For details of this tour see Florence May, *Life of Brahms* vol. i. pp. 92–104.

important feature in Reményi's playing was the national element. He strongly maintained against Liszt the genuineness of Hungarian music, and showed himself thoroughly imbued with that spirit by writing several ' Hungarian melodies,' which have been mistaken for popular tunes and adopted as such by other composers. The same half-Eastern spirit was observable in the strong rhythmical accentuation of Reményi's style, so rarely attained by artists of Teutonic origin. Reményi's compositions are of no importance, being mostly confined to arrangements for his instrument, and other pieces written for his own immediate use. Reményi died during a concert at which he was playing at San Francisco.    E. H.-A.

RÉMY, W. A. (b. Prague, June 10, 1831 ; d. there, Jan. 22, 1898), the name by which an eminent musician and teacher in Prague preferred to be known. His real name was Wilhelm Mayer, and he was the son of a lawyer in Prague. A pupil of C. F. Pietsch, he appeared at the age of 17 years as the composer of an overture to Sue's ' Fanatiker in den Cevennen ' ; but in obedience to the parental desires, he studied law, took the degree of Dr.Jur. in 1856, and did not take up music as his profession until 1862, when he became conductor of the Steiermärkische Musikverein, and earned experience as an orchestral director. He kept the post till 1870, composing many orchestral works during the period, among them an overture to ' Sardanapalus ' and a symphonic poem, ' Helena,' as well as his first symphony in F. The three works made their way as far as Leipzig, where they were received with great success. From the date of his resignation he lived as an unofficial teacher, and devoted himself to composition, until his death. His works include two more symphonies (in F and E flat), a ' Phantasiestück ' for orchestra, given at the Vienna Philharmonic Concerts under Dessoff ; a ' Slawische Liederspiel ' for soli and chorus, with accompaniment of two pianos, another work of the same kind, ' Östliche Rosen,' a concert-opera, ' Waldfräulein,' and many songs, etc. Among his most eminent pupils may be mentioned Busoni, Kienzl, Heuberger, von Reznicek and Felix Weingartner. (*Neue Musik-Zeitung*, 1890, p. 261.)    M.

RENALDI (RINALDI), GIULIO (b. Padua, early 16th cent., still living there, 1569), composed 3 books of madrigals and canzone, two of which were published in 1567 and one in 1569.    E. V. D. S.

RENAUD, MAURICE ARNOLD (b. Bordeaux, 1862), studied singing at the Conservatoire, Paris, and subsequently at that of Brussels. From 1883–90 he sang at the Monnaie, Brussels, in a variety of parts, making a great impression ; on Jan. 7, 1884, as the High Priest in Reyer's ' Sigurd,' and on Feb. 10, 1890, as

Hamilcar in Reyer's ' Salammbô,' on production of these operas. On Oct. 12, 1890, he made his début at the Opéra-Comique, Paris, as Karnac in ' Le Roi d'Ys,' and sang on Dec. 3 as the hero of Diaz's new opera ' Benvenuto.' On July 17, 1891, he made a very successful début at the Opéra as Nelusko, and remained there until 1902. On leave of absence, on June 23, 1897, he made his début at Covent Garden as Wolfram and De Nevers in selections from ' Tannhäuser ' and ' Huguenots,' at the State performance in honour of the Diamond Jubilee of Queen Victoria ; and in the same season he sang the above parts, Don Juan and Juan in D'Erlanger's ' Inez Mendo.' He fully confirmed his Parisian reputation by his fine voice and presence, and excellent singing and acting. From 1898–1905 he reappeared here frequently at the above theatre, singing the part of Henri VIII. in Saint-Saëns's opera, July 19, 1898, that of Hares in De Lara's ' Messaline,' July 13, 1899 ; and appearing as Hamlet, Rigoletto, Valentine, Escamillo, etc. He sang at Monte Carlo in 1907 in Bruneau's ' Nais Micoulin.' He was considered one of the best representatives of Beckmesser.

A. C.

RENCONTRE IMPRÉVUE, LA; ou les Pèlerins de la Mecque (Ger. *Die Pilgrime von Mekka*), comic opera, words by Dancourt from a farce by Lesage ; music by Gluck. Produced Schönbrunn, in French in 1764, in German in 1766, and revived 1780; in German at Vienna in 1776, and in Paris, as ' Les Fous de Medina,' in 1790.      G.

RENDANO, Alfonso (*b.* Carolei, near Cosenza, Apr. 5, 1853), studied first at the Conservatorio at Naples, then with Thalberg, and lastly at the Leipzig Conservatorium. He played at the Gewandhaus with marked success on Feb. 8, 1872. He then visited Paris and London, performed at the Musical Union (Apr. 30, 1872), the Philharmonic (Mar. 9, 1873), the Crystal Palace and other concerts, and much in society ; and after a lengthened stay returned to Italy. He became professor of pianoplaying at the Naples Conservatorio, and settled later in Rome. An opera by him, ' Conmelo,' was produced at Turin in 1902, and also given at Stuttgart.      G., with addns.

RENIÉ, Henriette (*b.* Paris, 1876), harpist and composer, gained first prize for harp at the Paris Conservatoire, awarded unanimously, in 1887 (at the age of 11 years). From this time she had such a vogue that the Queen of Belgium came to Brussels to hear her. Composers (Gounod amongst others) encouraged her to pursue her theoretical studies, and she afterwards gained a prize for harmony (Lenepveu's class) and composition. In 1901 she appeared as a virtuoso in the Concerts Lamoureux in a concerto of her own composition. The combination of harp with orchestral accompaniment was at that time a novelty. Since then she has been well received in all the Parisian symphony concerts and elsewhere in Europe. She is unquestionably, since the death of Hasselmans, the most important of the French school of harpists.

As a composer, in addition to the concerto already mentioned, she has written an ' Élégie ' for harp and orchestra (Lamoureux, 1907), a trio for harp, violin and violoncello, a sonata for PF. and violoncello, 2 pieces for violin and harp, a number of pieces for harp solo (Ballades, Contemplation, Légende, etc.) and some songs. In the matter of transcription she has successfully created a repertory for the harp out of the works of numerous old masters of the clavecin, without ever doing violence to their thought.

M. P.

RENNES, Catharina Van (*b.* Utrecht, Aug. 2, 1858), Dutch singer and composer, was a pupil of Richard Hol and Johannes Messchaert. Her parents were musical, though not in any professional sense, and she was encouraged to sing and play from her earliest infancy. After a schooling abroad she settled in Utrecht as a teacher of singing and piano, where she had considerable success. Later she taught at Hilversum and at The Hague and numbered among her pupils the Princess Juliana, only daughter of the Queen of the Netherlands.

As a composer she has been extremely popular in her own country, particularly for her children's songs and cantatas, which are written to Dutch words. Many of the solo songs are settings of German poems, and in these she sometimes rises to considerable heights. Instrumental music, except simple pianoforte pieces connected with children's stories, she has left practically untouched. Her style is graceful and melodious, the music being always well fitted to the words, while the pianoforte part is rarely more than a simple and suggestive accompaniment written in a somewhat conservative manner.      H. A.

RENVOYSY, Richard de, a 16th-century canon, and master of the children of the chapel of the Sainte Chapelle, Dijon, one of the best lutenists of his time, who composed Psalms of David, 4 v., and the ' Odes of Anacreon,' *a* 4 (both published in 1581). He was burned at the stake on Mar. 6, 1586, for immorality in connection with the school (*Q.-L.*).

RE PASTORE, IL, dramatic cantata to Metastasio's words (with compressions), composed by Mozart at Salzburg in 1775, in honour of the Archduke Maximilian. First performed Apr. 23, 1775.      G.

REPEAT, REPETIZIONE, REPLICA (Fr. *reprise* ; Ger. *Wiederholung*). The sign

is used to show that the music is to be repeated either from the beginning of the movement or from some point where the same sign appears, but in a reversed form : ☰☷

Compare DA CAPO.                        M.

RÉPÉTITION (Fr.), see REHEARSAL.

REPETITION (PIANOFORTE). The rapid reiteration of a note is called repetition ; a special touch of the player facilitated by mechanical contrivances in the pianoforte action ; the earliest and most important of these having been the invention of Sébastien ERARD. (See the diagram and description of Erard's action under PIANOFORTE.)            A. J. H.

REPORTS (the word seems not to be used in the singular), an old English and Scottish term for points of imitation. From the eight examples in the Scottish Psalter of 1635 (reprinted in the Rev. Neil Livingston's edition, 1864) it would seem that the term was used in a more general sense, of a setting of certain tunes in which the parts moved in a kind of free polyphony, not in strictly imitative style. In Purcell's revision of the treatise which appears in the third part of Playford's *Introduction to the Skill of Musick* (12th edition, 1694), the term is mentioned but not explained further than as being synonymous with ' imitation ' : ' The second is *Imitation* or *Reports*, which needs no Example.' (See *Sammelbände* of the Int. Mus. Ges. vi. p. 562.)       M.

REPRISE, repetition ; a term which is occasionally applied to any repetition in music, but is most conveniently confined to the recurrence of the first subject of a sonata movement after the conclusion of the working out or development. (See FORM and SONATA.) In Couperin, Rameau and other French composers the term is used of a short refrain at the end of a movement, which was probably intended to be played over more than twice, as sometimes it contains the ordinary marks of repetition within the passage covered by the word. G.

REQUIEM (Fr. *messe des morts* ; Ital. *messa per i defunti* ; Lat. *missa pro defunctis* ; Ger. *Todtenmesse*), a solemn Mass, sung annually in Commemoration of the Faithful Departed on All Souls' Day (Nov. 2) ; and, with a less general intention, at funeral services, on the anniversaries of the decease of particular persons, and on such other occasions as may be dictated by feelings of public respect or individual piety.

The Requiem takes its name [1] from the first word of the Introit—' Requiem aeternam dona eis, Domine.' When set to music, it naturally arranges itself in nine principal sections : (1) The Introit—' Requiem aeternam ' ; (2) the Kyrie ; (3) the Gradual and Tract—' Requiem aeternam ' and ' Absolve, Domine ' ; (4) The Sequence or Prose—Dies irae ; (5) The Offertorium—' Domine Jesu Christi ' ; (6) the Sanc-

[1] That is to say, its name as a special Mass. The music of the ordinary Polyphonic Mass always bears the name of the canto fermo on which it is founded.

tus ; (7) the Benedictus ; (8) the Agnus Dei ; and (9) the Communio—' Lux aeterna.' To these are sometimes added (10) the Responsorium—' Libera me,' which, though not an integral portion of the Mass, immediately follows it on all solemn occasions ; and (11) the Lectio—' Taedet animam meam,' of which we possess at least one example of great historical interest.

The plain-song melodies adapted to the nine divisions of the Mass will be found in the Gradual, together with that proper for the Responsorium. The Lectio, which really belongs to a different service, has no proper melody, but is sung to the ordinary ' Tonus Lectionis.' (See INFLEXION.) The entire series of melodies is of rare beauty, and produces so solemn an effect, when sung in unison by a large body of grave equal voices, that most of the great polyphonic composers have employed its phrases more freely than usual in their Requiem Masses, either as canti fermi, or in the form of unisonous passages interposed between the harmonised portions of the work. Compositions of this kind are not very numerous ; but most of the examples we possess must be classed among the most perfect productions of their respective authors.       W. S. R.

What has been said of the effect of secular influences on the composition of music to the MASS (*q.v.*) applies *mutatis mutandis* to the Requiem Mass. Famous compositions of the text mentioned under their composers' names are those of PALESTRINA, VICTORIA, FRANCESCO ANERIO, ORAZIO VECCHI of the polyphonic period ; MOZART, GOSSEC, CHERUBINI (2 settings), BERLIOZ, BRUCKNER, BRUNEAU, VERDI and DVOŘÁK.              C.

RESIN, see COLOPHANE ; ROSIN.

RESINARIUS, BALTHASAR (*b.* Jessen, early 16th cent.), is possibly, but not certainly, identical with Balthasar Harzer or Hartzer. He took holy orders and became Bishop of Leipa, in Bohemia, about 1543. He had been a chorister in the service of the Emperor Maximilian I. He is said to have been a pupil of Isaac, and he published at Wittenberg in 1543 ' Responsorium numero octoginta de tempore et festis . . . libri duo.'

RESOLUTION is the process of relieving dissonance by succeeding consonance. See HARMONY.

RESPIGHI, OTTORINO (*b.* Bologna, July 9, 1879), one of the most prominent Italian musicians of the present day. He studied music at first with his father, then at the Liceo Musicale of Bologna, which he entered in 1892. His teachers were Federico Sarti (violin) and Giuseppe Martucci (composition). He left that institution in 1899, obtaining first the diplomas of both the violin and the composition schools. His interest in composition soon gained the upper hand, and when Martucci left Bologna for

Naples (1902) Respighi decided to gain an insight into the methods of foreign composers. With this purpose in view he went to St. Petersburg, attracted by the fame of Rimsky-Korsakov, whose pupil he became. After some time he went on to Berlin to study awhile under Max Bruch. Respighi is now professor of composition at the Royal Liceo di S. Cecilia in Rome, to which office he was appointed in 1913. In Jan. 1924, by the unanimous vote of a Government Commission, which included Puccini and Cilèa, Respighi was appointed principal of the Liceo S. Cecilia of Rome in succession to Enrico Bossi.

If not quite as prolific as some of his less successful Italian contemporaries, Respighi has already contributed much both to the theatre and to chamber music. From his Russian masters he undoubtedly learnt to look upon opera as something different from what it was to the Italians who preceded him in that field. While they have shown a marked preference for highly dramatic situations, Respighi is attracted by situations in which the ironic and comic spirits have also their share. This is the case in particular of his latest and most successful opera, ' Belfagor,' where the characterisation is both subtler and truer than is usually the case in opera. If he undoubtedly owes much to the teaching and the example of Rimsky-Korsakov, he remains nevertheless individual in feeling and expression. There is also much beautiful melody in all Respighi's works, but lyricism is no longer the tyrant forcing the composer's hand. If Respighi does not allow intellectualism to clog the wheels of imagination, he also refuses to admit anything which does not reach a high intellectual standard. Above all, his music, although modern in every sense, is free from sheer eccentricity. His main concern is never to astonish, but to express his own ideas and emotions in such a way that they represent most faithfully an intellectual conception.

The list of his compositions up to the present is as follows :

#### FOR THE THEATRE

Re Enzo,' comic opera in 3 acts (text by A. Dorsini). Bologna, 1905.
' Semirama,' opera in 3 acts (text by A. Cerè). Bologna, 1910.
' Maria Vittoria,' opera in 4 acts (text by A. Guiraud). Not yet performed.
' Scherzo veneziano,' a mimic action of I. Leonidoff. Rome, 1920.
' La Boutique fantasque ' (arrangement of Rossini's music for the Russian Ballet). London, 1919.
' Belfagor,' opera. Milan, 1923.
' La bella addormentata,' fable for marionettes. Rome 1922.
' Aretusa,' for soprano and orchestra. Bologna, 1911.

#### ORCHESTRAL MUSIC

Suite for strings and organ. Rome, 1914.
' Sinfonia drammatica.' Rome, 1915.
' Le fontane di Roma,' symphonic poem. Rome, 1916.
' Ballata delle gnomidi,' symphonic poem. Rome, 1920.
' Antiche danze ed arie.' Rome, 1924.
' La primavera,' poema lirico, soli, choir and orchestra. Rome, 1923.
' Pini di Roma,' symphonic poem. Rome, 1924.

#### CHAMBER MUSIC

' Sonata ' in B minor for violin and pianoforte. Naples, 1918.
String Quartet ' in D major. Bologna, 1907.
Quintet.'

' Lamento di Arianna ' of Monteverdi (arrangement).
' Transcription ' of toccate and fugues of Frescobaldi's for piano.
' Concerto Gregoriano ' for violin and orchestra. 1922.
' Songs.'
Quartetto Dorico. London, 1924.      F. B.

**RESPOND** (Lat. *responsorium*), a form of ecclesiastical chant which grew out of the elaboration of the primitive RESPONSORIAL PSALMODY. Some of the Responds have been frequently treated in the polyphonic style with very great effect, not only by the great masters of the 16th century, but even as late as the time of Colonna, whose Responsoria of the Office for the Dead, for eight voices, are written with intense appreciation of the solemn import of the text.

A large collection of very fine examples, including an exquisitely beautiful set for Holy Week, by Victoria, will be found in vol. iv. of Proske's ' Musica divina.'     W. S. R.

**RESPONSE**, in English church music, is in its widest sense any musical sentence sung by the choir at the close of something read or chanted by the minister.

The musical treatment of Versicles and Responses offers a wide and interesting field of study. There are great varieties of plainsong settings to be met with, gathered from Sarum and other uses. Merbecke's *Booke of Common Praier noted* provided a plain-song for the English text. Building on this, Tallis, Byrd and others wrote harmonised settings to responses of the daily Offices, including the Litany. Examples are to be found among 17th-century composers also founded on the plain-song in the tenor voice, but many later settings abandoned this sound principle. Some of these survive in certain cathedrals. Specimens, both of the earlier and later settings, are to be found in Jebb's ' Choral Responses.'

The medial accent is used in Versicles and Responses when the last word is a polysyllable, thus :

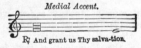

*Medial Accent.*

℟ And grant us Thy salva-tion.

When the last word is a monosyllable or is accented on its last syllable, there is an additional note, thus :

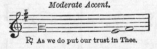

*Moderate Accent.*

℟ As we do put our trust in Thee.

In comparing our Versicles and Responses with the Latin from which they were translated, it is important to bear this rule as to the ' final word ' in mind ; because the Latin and English of the same Versicle or Response will frequently take different ' accents ' in the two languages. For example, the following

Versicle takes in the Latin the *medial accent,* but in the translation will require the *moderate accent*:

*Latin form.*

Ab inimicis nostris defende nos Chris - te.

*English form.*

From our enemies defend us, O   Christ.

The Litany is in binary form. Its opening sentences or Invocations are each divided by a colon and take this form:

used without variation for all the Invocations. It happens that each of the sentences of Invocation contains in our English version a monosyllable before the colon; but it is not the case in the Latin, therefore both Versicle and Response differ from our use, thus:

{ O God the / Father, of } heaven: { have mercy upon / us, miser- } a-ble sinners.

*Latin.*

Pater de coelis De - us.     etc.

In the Petitions of the Litany the whole sentence of music stands thus:

(Petition chanted by    (Response by Choir and
Priest.)            People.)

It only remains to say a few words on (1) Amens, (2) Doxology to Gospel, (3) Responses to the Commandments.

(1) Since the Reformation two forms of *Amen* have been chiefly used in the English Church, the monotone and the approach by a semitone, generally harmonised thus:

A - men.         A - men.

(2) The Doxology to the Gospel is in the same tone and should be sung at the same pitch as the Gospel. This is the most familiar form, but few singers can recite the Gospel on C, so it is set too high. When the Gospel is inflected with the drop of a minor third (C to A)

instead of C to B, the response of the choir should follow suit.

{ Glory / Thanks } be to Thee, O Lord.

(3) The Responses to the Commandments are an expansion of the ancient

> ' Kyrie eleison,
> *Christe eleison,*
> Kyrie eleison,'

made to serve as *ten* responses instead of being used as one responsive prayer. The ancient form appears in Merbecke (1550), and the so-called Merbecke's Kyrie now used is an editorial manipulation.     J. S.; rev. and abridged.

**RESPONSORIAL PSALMODY** is the earliest form in which psalms have been sung in the Christian Church. It is a development from inflected monotone (see INFLEXION). In the earliest Christian days the recitation of the psalms was carried out by a single soloist, who monotoned the greater part of the psalm, but inserted various cadences or inflexions at certain points of distinction in the verse. This was very probably but the carrying on of what had long been current in the Synagogue. (See PLAIN-SONG; HEBREW MUSIC.) It was very advisable not to leave the whole of the performance of the psalm to the soloist; and it became customary for the congregation to interject some small response at the close of each verse. Such a response was known among the Greeks as an acrostic (ἀκροστίχιον or ἀκροτελεύτιον), and the technical word in Latin for this performance by the congregation was *Respondere*; hence this form of psalmody was called Responsorial Psalmody. The refrain was originally very brief—an Amen or an Alleluia, a short text like the ' For his mercy endureth for ever ' of Psalm cxxxvi. or some pregnant sentence drawn from the psalm which was being sung. In the earliest days the soloist's text was very little removed from monotone, but already by the time of St. Augustine it had become more elaborate, and the ancient simplicity was looked upon as an archaism. The result was a performance somewhat resembling the familiar Litany. The psalmody remained such a short time in this comparatively simple stage that very few actual monuments of it have survived. The Responsorial Psalmody that exists is of the elaborate sort. Partly as a result of the growing artistic feeling, partly also in consequence of the existence of trained singers in the great Song School at Rome, the music, alike of the soloist who sang the verses of the psalm and of the choir who responded, was elaborated to a very high pitch. Then, since it was impossible to sing the whole psalm to a highly ornate chant habitually, certain verses were selected from the psalm for this elaborate treatment; and there grew up, therefore, the musical form called the Respond, which consisted in its simplest shape of a choral melody (called the Respond proper), alternating with one or more Verses sung by the soloist. This form is found both in the music of the Mass and in that of Divine Service, and mainly as an interlude between the reading of lessons. In the former it is called for distinction's sake *Responsorium Graduale* or the Gradual. In the latter case

the second mode, and are decorated with similar melodic themes.

The music falls into eight divisions, each of which consists of (a) an intonation, (b) the recitation in inflected monotone, (c) the cadence or *pneuma* or *melisma*. There are in all fifteen different texts set to this scheme of music; the *Justus ut palma* is given here as being the best representative of the group; but in two of the divisions another text is given as well, in order to reveal the structure the more clearly.

The same plan holds good with the responds of the Office which are found for the most part

it is simply called *Responsorium*; for the lesser Offices, which came to be sung without musical elaboration, there came to be a few simple forms of Responsorial music, modelled on the elaborate responds of Matins but differing from them in being simpler in texture. This brief form was then called *Responsorium breve* as distinct from the *Responsorium prolixum*.

The highest development of elaboration was reached in the Gradual; but even there, in spite of all the embroidery, the primitive monotone around which everything else centres is still traceable; and careful analysis will show that with all its elaboration the chant is still an inflected monotone. This statement can most easily be proved by the study of a single group of Graduals which are ordinarily ascribed to

in the service of Matins. It is visible more plainly in the verses of the responds than in the responds themselves. Those of the Office use a set of invariable psalm melodies, one belonging to each mode; in these the monotone is very clear, and yet there is much elaboration in the cadences, and the forms are so plastic that they can by certain well-defined rules be readily adapted to the various texts of the verses. (See PSALMODY.) The Graduals in the Mass do not utilise these common forms for their Verses; each Verse is peculiar to the Gradual; but even so there is much similarity observable amongst them both in general structure and in detail. In decadent days even the responds of the Office have their Verses set to a special melody and not to the common one.

As regards liturgical (as distinct trom musical) structure the respond of the Office is like the Gradual-Respond of the Mass, but not identical. In neither case is it common now to find more than one Verse, but the Respond in the Office is often accompanied by the *Gloria patri* as well, in the early shape in which it consisted of one phrase, not two. Further, it became customary in France to repeat after the Verse not the whole of the Respond but only a part of it ; and this custom spread till it was universal.

The following Respond, then, which belongs to Matins of the First Sunday in Advent and stands at the head of the series, may be taken as representing this form of composition in an unusually full shape.

Three boys sing the Respond—

A boy sings the first Verse to the psalm melody of the seventh mode (see PSALMODY)—

'Quique terrigenae et filii hominum, simul in unum dives et pauper' (Ps. xlix. 2).

The choir repeats the Respond from *Ite* onwards. A second boy sings a second Verse as before—

'Qui regis Israel intende, qui deducis velut ovem Joseph' (Ps. lxxx. 1).

The choir repeats the Respond from *Nuncia*. A third boy sings a third Verse—

Excita domine potentiam tuam, et veni ut salvos facias nos.'

The R̷ is repeated from *Qui regnaturus*. The three boys sing the *Gloria patri* (down to *Sancto* only) to the same psalm melody, and the choir repeats the closing section of the Respond—*In populo Israel*.     W. H. F.

RESPONSORIUM, see RESPOND ; RESPONSORIAL PSALMODY.

REST (Fr. *silence, pause* ; Ger. *Pause* ; Ital. *pausa*), the sign of silence in music. The duration of the silence, equivalent to a note value, is shown by the form of the character employed to denote it. (See NOTATION, Vol. III. p. 658.)

RESULTANT TONES (Fr. *sons résultants* ; Ger. *Combinationstöne*) are produced when any two loud and sustained musical sounds are heard at the same time. There are two kinds of resultant tones, the 'Differential' and the 'Summational.' The 'Differential tone' is so called because its number of vibrations is equal to the difference between those of the generating sounds. The 'Summational tone' is so called because its number of vibrations is equal to the sum of those of the generating sounds. The following diagram shows the pitches of the differential tones of the principal consonant intervals when in perfect tune :

Generators.

Differentials.

If the interval be wider than an octave, as in the last two examples, the differential is intermediate between the sounds which produce it. These tones can be easily heard on the ordinary harmonium, and also on the organ. They are not so distinct on the piano, because the sounds of this instrument are not sustained. By practice, however, the resultant tones can be distinguished on the piano also.

Dissonant as well as consonant intervals produce resultant tones. Taking the minor seventh in its three possible forms, the differentials are as follows :

The first form of minor seventh is obtained by tuning two fifths upwards (C–G–D) and then a major third downwards (D–B♭); its differential tone is *I*A♭, an exact major third below C. The second form is got by two exact fourths upwards (C–F–B♭) : the differential is then *I*A♭, which is flatter than the previous *I*A♭ by the interval 35 : 36. The third form is the so-called 'Harmonic seventh' on C, whose differential is G, an exact fourth below C. Of the marks \, /, here used to distinguish notes which are confused in the ordinary notation, it may be briefly explained that the acute sign / refers to notes arrived at in an ascending series of fifths, the grave sign \ to those in a descending series of fifths.

Hitherto we have spoken only of the differential tones which are produced by the fundamentals or prime PARTIAL TONES (q.v.) of musical sounds. But a differential may also arise from the combination of any upper partial of one sound with any partial of the other sound ; or from the combination of a differential with a partial, or with another differential. Thus the major third C–E may have the following differential tones :

All these tones are heard simultaneously; but for convenience the differentials of the first, second, third and fourth orders are written in notes of different length. We see, then, that the number of possible resultant tones is very great ; but only those which arise from the primes of musical sounds are sufficiently strong to be of practical importance.

In enabling the ear to distinguish between consonant and dissonant intervals, the differential tones are only less important than the upper partials. Thus if the chord G–E–C be accurately tuned as 3 : 5 : 8, the differential of G–C coincides with E, and that of E–C with G. But if the intervals be tempered the differentials are thrown out of tune, and give rise to beats. These beats are very loud and harsh on the ordinary harmonium, tuned in equal temperament. Again, in the close triad C–E–G the differentials of C–E and of E–G coincide and give no beats if the intervals be in perfect tune. On a tempered instrument the result is very different. If we take C to have 264 vibrations, the tempered E has about 332 and the tempered G about 395½ vibrations. The differential of C–E is then 68½, and that of E–G 63. These two tones beat 5½ times each second, and thus render the chord to some extent dissonant.

In the minor triad, even when in just intonation, several of the resultant tones do not fit in

with the notes of the chord, although they may be too far apart to beat. In the major triad, on the contrary, the resultant tones form octaves

with the notes of the chord. To this difference Helmholtz attributes the less perfect consonance of the minor triad, and its obscured though not inharmonious effect.

The origin of the differential tones has been the subject of much discussion. Thomas Young held that when beats became too rapid to be distinguished by the ear, they passed into the resultant tone. This view prevailed until the publication in 1856 of Helmholtz's investigations, in which many objections to Young's theory were brought forward. The later mathematical theory given by Helmholtz is too abstruse to admit of popular exposition. (See ACOUSTICS.)

As a consequence of his theory, Helmholtz deduced a different series of resultant tones, which he calls summational tones, because their number of vibrations is the sum of those of the generators. The existence of the summational tones, which Helmholtz believed he verified experimentally, has been called in question by Dr. Preyer.

Not only the origin but also the discovery of differential tones has been disputed. The earliest publication of the discovery was made by a German organist named Sorge in 1745. Then came Romieu, a French savant, in 1751. Lastly, the great Italian violinist, Tartini, made the phenomenon the basis of his treatise on harmony in 1754. But Tartini explicitly claims priority in these words :

' In the year 1714, when about twenty-two years of age, he discovered this phenomenon by chance on the violin at Ancona, where many witnesses who remember the fact are still living. He communicated it at once, without reserve, to professors of the violin. He made it the fundamental rule of perfect tuning for the pupils in his school at Padua, which was commenced in 1728 and which still exists ; and thus the phenomenon became known throughout Europe.' [1]

Tartini in some cases mistook the pitch of the differential tone ; but there does not appear to be any reason for taking from him the credit of the discovery which has so long been associated with his name.          J. L.

RESZKE, DE, (1) EDOUARD (b. Warsaw, Dec. 23, 1855 ; d. Poland, May 25, 1917), was taught singing by his brother Jean, Ciaffei, Steller and Coletti, and made his début Apr. 22, 1876, as the King in 'Aïda,' on its production at the Italiens, Paris. He sang there with success for two seasons, and afterwards went to Italy, where, in 1880, at Turin, he made a success in two new parts—the King in Catalani's ' Elda,' Jan. 31, and Charles V. in Marchetti's ' Don Giovanni d' Austria,' Mar. 11, and appeared at Milan on the production of Ponchielli's ' Figliuol prodigo,' Dec. 26. From 1880–84 he was engaged in London with the Royal Italian Opera until its collapse. He made his début on Apr. 13, 1880, as Indra (' Roi de Lahore '), but his success as a foremost lyric artist was established

1 De' principii dell' armonia musicale, Padua, 1767, p. 36.

by his admirable performances of St. Bris, the Count in 'Sonnambula' and other important parts. He appeared as Hagen, on production of Reyer's 'Sigurd,' July 15, 1884, etc. In 1883–1884 he reappeared in Paris at the Italian Opera (Théâtre des Nations), with great success, in 'Simone Boccanegra'; in Massenet's 'Hérodiade,' on its production in Paris; in Dubois's 'Aben Hamet,' Dec. 16, 1884, and in other operas. He was engaged at the Opéra, where he first appeared Apr. 13, 1885, as Mephistopheles, a part he sang subsequently in the 500th performance of 'Faust.' He appeared as Leporello in the centenary performance of 'Don Juan,' Nov. 4, 1887. He played at the Italian Opera at Drury Lane in 1887 the part of Ramfis in 'Aïda,' and sang during the season as Basilio, St. Bris, Mephistopheles and Henry the Fowler ('Lohengrin'). From 1888 to 1900 he sang every season (except 1899), and added to his repertory the parts of Almaviva, Marcel, the Mefistofele of Boïto, and, most important of all, the Wagnerian parts of Hans Sachs, King Mark, Kurwenal, Hunding and Hagen. From 1890, for many seasons, he sang in America with his brother, with the greatest success. He sang at the Mozart (concert) Festival at the Nouveau Théâtre in Paris in the spring of 1906, under the direction of Reynaldo Hahn. In Feb. 1907 he advertised his intention of opening a school of singing in London, and appeared there on June 13.

His brother, (2) JEAN (more correctly JAN MECZISLAW) (b. Warsaw, Jan. 14, 1850 [1]; d. Nice, Apr. 3, 1925), the eldest son of the controller of the government railways, was taught singing by his mother, a distinguished amateur, and at the age of 12 sang solos in the cathedral there. He was taught later by Ciaffei, Cotogni and Sbriglia. Under the name 'De Reschi' he made his début at Venice as a baritone in 'Favorita' in Jan. 1874, according to an eye-witness, with success.[2] He made his début at Drury Lane on Apr. 11 of the same year, and in the same part, and played there two seasons as Don Giovanni, Almaviva, De Nevers and Valentine. A contemporary [3] spoke of him as one of whom the highest expectations might be entertained, having a voice of delicious quality; he phrased artistically and possessed sensibility, but lacked experience such as would enable him to turn his vocal gifts to greater account and to become an effective actor. It is interesting to find that the quality of the organ was even then considered to be more of the robust tenor timbre than a baritone. Under his own name he made his début at the Italiens as Fra Melitone ('Forza del destino'), Oct. 31, 1876, with some success, and as Severo (Donizetti's 'Poliuto'), Dec. 5; Figaro ('Barbiere'), Dec. 19.

He made his tenor début as 'Robert' at Madrid in 1879 with great success, and was engaged at the Théâtre des Nations in 1884. He played there the part of St. John the Baptist on the production of 'Hérodiade' so much to the satisfaction of Massenet, that he procured him an engagement at the Opéra to create the title-part of 'Le Cid,' in which he made his début on its production, Nov. 30, 1885. He was engaged there for four years, and sang the usual tenor parts, notably Don Ottavio ('Don Juan' centenary) and Romeo (in 1888, on the production of Gounod's opera at the Opéra). On June 13, 1887, he reappeared at Drury Lane as Radames, and sang as Lohengrin, Faust and Raoul. He worthily fulfilled his early promise by the marked improvement both in his singing and acting, and by his ease and gentlemanly bearing, the improvements being almost entirely due to his own hard work and exertions. On June 4, 1888, as Vasco de Gama, he made his first appearance at Covent Garden, and from that season dates the revival of opera as a fashionable amusement in London. Till 1900, inclusive, he sang nearly every year in England, his parts including John of Leyden, the Duke in 'Un ballo,' Don José, Phoebus in Goring Thomas's 'Esmeralda,' Lancelot in Bemberg's 'Elaine,' Werther (in Massenet's opera). In the great parts of Wagner, such as Walther, Tristan and Siegfried, he was unrivalled, throwing new light upon the music by his wonderful power of interpreting the dramatic side, without losing sight of vocal purity. He sang for several seasons in America with his brother, and at Warsaw and St. Petersburg. On Dec. 11, 1890, he assisted gratuitously in the performance of 'Carmen' at the Opéra-Comique in Paris, where Mme. Galli-Marié reappeared in her original part, and Melba and Lassalle were in the cast. He reappeared at intervals at the Paris Opéra, singing in 'Siegfried' and 'Pagliacci' on the Paris production of those operas. He was announced in Reyer's 'Sigurd' in 1904, but was unable to appear through illness. He spent the latter part of his life in Paris, and from 1919 at his villa at Nice,[4] and devoted himself to teaching.

Their sister, (3) JOSEPHINE (d. Warsaw, Feb. 22, 1891), educated at the Conservatorium of St. Petersburg, attracted the notice of Halanzier at Venice, and was engaged by him at the Opéra, where she made her début as Ophelia, June 21, 1875. She sang there with success for some time, where she was the original Sita ('Roi de Lahore'), Apr. 27, 1877. Later she was very successful at Madrid, Lisbon, etc.; sang at Covent Garden as Aïda, Apr. 18, 1881, and again in Paris at the Théâtre des Nations as Salomé ('Hérodiade'), Mar. 13, 1884. She retired from public life

[1] See Truth, July 15, 1897.
[2] Letter of Michael Williams in Musical World, Jan. 31, 1874.
[3] Athenæum, Apr. 18, and July 25, 1874.

[4] For an appreciation of Jean de Reszke as a teacher see M. and L. vol. vi. No. 3.

in her marriage with Leopold de Kronenburg of Warsaw.          A. C.

BIBL.—H. DE CURZON, *Nouvelle Revue*, July 15, 1921, *Jean de Reszke*; *Lyrica*, Mar. 1925, *Les Gloires du chant*: *Jean de Reszke*; *Music and Letters*, vol. vi. No. 3, Essays by several English writers.

RETARDATION is a word used by some theorists to distinguish a small group of discords which are similar in nature to suspensions, but resolve upwards, as in the following example :

C. H. H. P.

REUBKE, (1) ADOLF, a famous German organ-builder, 1805–75. His principal achievement appears to be the organ of 88 stops in Magdeburg Cathedral.

(2) JULIUS (*b.* Hausniendorf, Mar. 23, 1834 ; *d.* Pillnitz, June 3, 1858), second son of the above, pianist and composer. His works, published posthumously, comprise a sonata and various pieces for PF., songs and an organ sonata, ' The Ninety-fourth Psalm.' Of these only the last-named is widely known. Reubke was a favourite pupil of Liszt, who regarded him as a composer of unusual promise. The organ sonata, however, is a work of far more than mere promise : it shows a ripeness and imaginative power truly remarkable in a youth barely out of his 'teens. It is also of considerable importance in the history of organ music, as it undoubtedly led to the composition of a good many important organ works based on a ' programme.' It is in one continuous movement, falling into three sections—a fantasia and a very free fugue divided by a brief adagio, one theme serving as a basis of the three sections. The portions of the Psalm dealt with are vv. 1, 2, 3, 6, 7, 17, 19, 22, 23 of the English Prayer Book version. No indication is given as to the connexion between text and music, but the following appears to be the scheme : First section, vv. 1, 2, 3, 6, 7 ; adagio, 17, 19 ; fugue, 22, 23. The influence of Liszt is apparent, not only in the metamorphoses of theme, but in harmony and figuration. The sources of some of its most striking passages are to be found in Liszt's fugue on ' Ad nos.' But this does not detract from its merit ; and its genuine originality, power and effectiveness have established it firmly in the repertory.          H. G.

REULX (RIEU, REUX), ANSELME DE, an early 16th-century Netherlander, singer, *c.* 1524, in the Spanish chapel of Charles V. ; composed 2 books of madrigals (1543 and 1546), single madrigals in collective volumes (*Q.-L.*).

REUSNER, ESAJAS (*b.* Löwenberg, in Silesia, Apr. 29, 1636 ; *d.* Cölln on the Spree, May 1. 1679), of a patrician family, was a pupil of his father (also called ESAJAS), a lutenist who arranged a book of sacred songs for the lute (published 1645). Esajas, jun., was in 1651 at the court of the Polish Princess Radziwill, where he was instructed in the art of composition by a French lutenist. In 1655 he became court lutenist at Liegnitz-Brieg, and on Feb. 5, 1674, was at the court of Brandenburg. He composed 4 books of suites of dances, beginning with a prelude or sonatina. One of these, ' Musikalische Taffel-Erlustigung ' (Brieg, 1688), shows on the title-page the remark : ' Arranged in 4 parts (1 vln., 2 violas, Bc.) in the French manner by J. G. Stanley.' The latter, also a chamber musician at Brieg, was apparently an Englishman. Esajas arranged 100 sacred melodies for the lute, the latest of his published works, in 1676 (*Riemann*; *Q.-L.*).

REUTTER, (1) GEORG (*b.* Vienna, 1656 ; *d.* Aug. 29, 1738), became in 1686 organist of St. Stephen's, and in 1700 Hof- and Kammer-organist. He also played the theorbo in the Hofkapelle from 1697 to 1703. In 1712 he succeeded Fux as Kapellmeister to the Gnadenbild in St. Stephen's, and in 1715 became Kapellmeister of the cathedral itself. His church music (see *Q.-L.*), was sound without being remarkable. Some of his instrumental music for organ or harpsichord has been published in *D.T.Ö.* XIII. ii. On Jan. 8, 1695, he was knighted in Rome by Count Francesco Sforza, on whose family Pope Paul III. had bestowed the privilege of conferring that honour in 1539. His son,

(2) JOHANN ADAM KARL GEORG (*b.* Vienna, Apr. 6, 1708 [1] ; *d.* Mar. 12, 1772), became court-composer in 1731, and succeeded his father in 1738 as Kapellmeister of the cathedral. In 1746 he was appointed second court Kapellmeister, his duty being to conduct the music of the Emperor's church, chamber and dinner-table. On Predieri's retirement in 1751 Reutter exercised the functions of chief court Kapellmeister, but did not receive the title till the death of the former in 1769. As an economical measure he was allowed the sum of 20,000 gulden (£2000) to maintain the court Kapelle (the whole body of musicians, vocal and instrumental), and he enjoys the melancholy distinction of having reduced the establishment to the lowest possible ebb. Reutter composed for the court numerous operas, cantatas *d'occasion* and Italian oratorios for Lent ; also a Requiem and smaller dramatic and sacred works. His masses are showy, with rapid and noisy instrumentation, so much so that ' rushing (rauschende) violins *à la Reutter* ' became a proverb. Burney heard one of them during his visit to Vienna in 1772, and says ' it was dull, dry stuff ; great noise and little meaning characterised the whole performance.'[2]

[1] According to the cathedral register.
[2] *Present State of Music in Germany*, i. 261.

A symphony by Reutter is published in *D.T.Ö.* XV. ii. In 1731 Reutter married THERESE HOLZHAUSER (*d.* 1782), a court singer of merit. He was much favoured at court owing to his great tact ; and Maria Theresa ennobled him in 1740 as ' Edler von Reutter.' His name is inseparably associated with that of Haydn, whom he heard sing as a boy in the little town of Hainburg, and engaged for the choir of St. Stephen's, where he sang from 1740–48. His treatment of the poor chorister, and his heartless behaviour when the boy's fine voice had broken, are mentioned under HAYDN.

BIBL.—STOLLBROCK's biography in the *Vierteljahrsschrift*, 8, p. 165 ff. ; *Q.-L.*, where a list of his compositions will be found ; NORBERT HOFER, *Die beiden Reutter als Kirchenkomponisten.* Vienna Dissertation, 1915.           C. F. P.

RÊVE, LE, lyric drama in 4 acts, text by Louis Gallet after Zola ; music by Alfred Bruneau. Produced Opéra-Comique, Paris, June 18, 1891 ; Covent Garden, Oct. 29, 1891.

RÉVEILLÉ, see MILITARY SOUNDS AND SIGNALS.

REVERSE, see RECTE ET RETRO ; ROVESCIO.

REY, JEAN - BAPTISTE (*b.* Tarascon, *circa* 1760 ; *d.* Paris, 1822), is said to have taught himself the harpsichord, violin and violoncello ; occupied the post of maître de musique at the cathedrals of Viviers and Uzes, and went to Paris in 1785, establishing himself there as a professor of music. A year later he was admitted into the Opéra orchestra, and held an appointment as violoncellist until his death. A potpourri (op. 1) of his for pianoforte was published by Leduc in Paris, and Nadermann of Paris brought out his *Cours élémentaire de musique et de piano.* In 1807 the same firm published his *Exposition élémentaire de l'harmonie ; théorie générale des accords d'après les différents genres de musique.* *Q.-L.* mentions twelve sonatas for violoncello, op. 4.

BIBL.—J. B. WECKERLIN, *Bibl. du Conservatoire Nat. de Musique et de Déclamation* ; Catal. de la Réserve ; *Fétis.*
           E. H.-A.

REY, (1) JEAN-BAPTISTE (*b.* Lauzerte, now Tarn-et-Garonne, France, Dec. 18, 1734 ; *d.* Paris, July 15, 1810). His musical studies began at an early age at Toulouse, where later he became *chef d'orchestre* at the Opéra. Until the age of 40 he filled similar posts at Montpellier, Marseilles, Bordeaux and Nantes. It was at the last-named town that a summons to Paris to assist in the production of Gluck's ' Alceste ' reached him in 1776. Three years later Louis XVI. appointed him master of his private music with a salary of 2000 frs. In the same year the King decorated him with the Order of Saint Michel and appointed him Surintendant de la Chapelle. In 1781 he was appointed conductor at the Opéra, replacing Francœur. According to Fétis and Michel Brenet, Rey conducted the orchestra of the Concert Spirituel between 1782 and 1786, and some of his compositions were performed there. In 1794 he became a member of the jury of the Institut National de Musique. After the French Revolution he was elected a member of the Committee of Administration for the Affairs of the Opéra, and in May 1799 was nominated professor of harmony at the Conservatoire. It was there that F. J. Fétis became a pupil of Rey, and was instructed by him according to the complicated principles of Rameau. So staunch was his adherence to bygone traditions that he became involved in the turbulent discussions which were roused by Catel's innovations. Finally his championship of his friend Lesueur brought about his dismissal from the Conservatoire in 1802. Napoleon soothed his wounded feelings by nominating him his maître de chapelle two years later. As a conductor Rey was closely associated with all the great composers of his day and assisted in the productions of the masterpieces of Piccinni, Gluck, Paisiello, Grétry, Lemoine and Méhul. Sacchini, on his death-bed, entrusted the completion of his opera ' Arvire et Evelina ' to his friend Rey. This commission was conscientiously executed by him, and the opera was produced Apr. 29, 1788. He is also said to have written all the ballet music in the same composer's opera ' Œdipe à Colone ' and in Salieri's ' Tarare.'

His original compositions comprise some MS. motets with orchestra, several of which were performed in the Chapelle du Roi, and some solfège studies which are included in the third part of the ' Solfèges du Conservatoire de Paris.' His two-act opera ' Diane et Endymion ' was produced in Paris in 1791, and the opera in one act, entitled ' Apollon et Coronis,' was performed at the Opéra in 1781. This last was written in conjunction with his brother,

(2) LOUIS CHARLES JOSEPH (*b.* Lauzerte, Oct. 26, 1738 ; *d.* Paris, May 12, 1811), a chorister at the Abbey of St. Sernin, Toulouse. He became a violoncellist in the theatre orchestra at Montpellier, and came to Paris in 1755 to profit by Berteau's teaching. Two years later he occupied the post of violoncellist at the principal theatre in Bordeaux, an appointment which he held for nine years. At the end of the year 1766 he became a member of the Paris Opéra orchestra, and in 1772 was admitted into the orchestra of the Chapelle du Roi. After forty years' service Rey retired from the orchestra with a pension in 1806. Fétis says that he cut his throat in delirium caused by a nervous fever. He wrote some trios for two violins and violoncello ; some duos for violin and violoncello, etc., and a brochure entitled : *Mémoire justicatif des artistes de l'Académie Royale de Musique ou response à la lettre qui leur a été adressée le 4 Sept. 1789.* This last was a reply to Papillon de la Ferté's complaints

of the behaviour of the members of the Opéra orchestra.

BIBL.—MICHEL BRENET, *Les Concerts en France* ; SAINT LAURENT, *Dictionnaire encyclopédique* ; *Nouvelle Biographie générale*, Paris, 1843 ; FÉTIS, *Biog. des mus.; Journal de Paris*, July 19, 1810.

E. H.-A. ; rev. M. L. P.

REY COLAÇO, ALEJANDRO (*b.* Tangier, Apr. 1854), Portuguese musician. He studied at Madrid, Paris and Berlin, and returned to Lisbon as a teacher of the PF. He has done much to encourage the performance of chamber music; but is chiefly remarkable for his interest in *fados* and other forms of Portuguese national song, which in his hands appear as genuine music. He has edited one or two collections of Portuguese folk-songs and dances.    J. B. T.

REYER, ERNEST (*b.* Marseilles, Dec. 1, 1823 ; *d.* Levandou, Hyères, Jan. 15, 1909) whose real name was Louis Ernest Etienne Rey, best known to fame as the composer of the opera 'Sigurd,' learnt the elements of music as a child at the free school of music founded at Marseilles by the Florentine Barsoti. At this age, though he had made up his mind to become a professional musician, he did not display more than an average aptitude for the task ; so that his father, seeing no reason to suppose that he would earn a livelihood by music, and hoping to cure him of his ambitions, sent him at the age of 16 to Algiers, where the boy's uncle was a government official. Neither his uncle nor his comparative ignorance of scholastic harmony and counterpoint prevented him from composing songs and other works on a small scale, some of which became popular successes, and he even succeeded in having a Mass performed in the cathedral at Algiers to celebrate the return to the city of the governor-general, the Duc d'Aumale. This composition, which was dedicated to the Duchess, has never been heard again and has remained unpublished ; but its performance opened the eyes of his parents, and when, on the outbreak of the revolution in 1848 Reyer found himself deprived of his patron's support and obliged to return to Paris, no further objections were raised to his making music his career, and he settled down to hard study under his aunt Mme. Louise FARRENC, herself a composer of some distinction.

He made many literary friends at this time, amongst them being Flaubert, Gautier, Louis de Cormenin, Méry and others who had then, common Oriental interests. The east was as it is now, a ready source of inspiration to the romantics, and it influenced Reyer in his choice of libretti throughout his career. Two of his first works, written after he had emerged from his technical studies with Mme. Farrenc, were on Oriental subjects and both were provided by Gautier. These were 'Le Sélam' a symphonic ode in 4 parts on the model of Félicien David's 'Le Désert,' which was produced with

success at the Théâtre-Ventadour on Apr. 5, 1850, and 'Sacountala' a ballet-pantomime in 2 acts which was given in July 1858 at the Opéra, where another dramatic cantata 'Victoire' saw the light just a year later. Both 'Le Sélam' and 'Sacountala' were favourably criticised by Berlioz, who praised the young composer for the beauty and restraint of his orchestration and commented on the fact that his instruments of ' percussion ' were not instruments of ' persecution.' Between these two works he had written a one-act opéra-comique with a libretto by Méry, 'Maître Wolfram' (Théâtre-Lyrique, May 20, 1854, revived Opéra-Comique, 1873), and this again was warmly praised by Berlioz as well as by Halévy and ran for many nights. His next opera 'La Statue,' based on a subject in the 'Arabian Nights,' showed signs of maturity in its understanding of the technique of the theatre, and the individual character and melodiousness of the music attracted the notice of Bizet. Originally in 3 acts it was produced at the Théâtre-Lyrique, in Apr. 1861, two years after the appearance of Gounod's 'Faust,' revised for the Opéra-Comique in Apr. 1878 ; with recitatives to take the place of spoken dialogue so that it might conform to the conventions of opera-houses outside France, and rewritten in 5 acts for the Opéra in Mar. 1903. In 1862, the year after the original production of ' La Statue,' a 2-act opera 'Érostate' was given at Baden (Aug. 21), along with Berlioz's 'Béatrice et Bénédict,' and was revived for two nights only at the Opéra in Oct. 1871.

Meanwhile Reyer was meditating another opera on a legend drawn from the Nibelungen cycle by his friends Du Locle and Alfred Blau. For the moment, however, this was to remain only in his head, as he found it easier to earn a living by writing musical criticism than grand opera. Twenty years previously he had tried his hand at journalism in the columns of the *Presse*, the *Revue Française* and the *Courrier de Paris*, and now after various vicissitudes he was offered the post of critic to the *Débats* in place of d'Ortigue, who had succeeded Berlioz. He went out to Cairo for the paper to see the first night of Verdi's 'Aïda,' in Dec. 1871, and then returned to Paris to break lances on behalf of Wagner, Berlioz, Frank, Bizet, Lalo and other composers of the young French school. Many of these articles were subsequently published in the volume *Notes de musique* (Paris, Charpentier, 1875) and in the posthumous *Quarante ans de musique* (Paris, Calmann-Lévy, 1909), the material for which was selected by Emile Henriot from articles which had appeared between 1857 and 1897.

Reyer's election to the Institut, where he succeeded Félicien David in 1876, was naturally a stimulus to his musical as distinct from his literary activities, as it was a definite official recognition of his merits as a composer. But there were many obstacles to the production of the new opera ‘ Sigurd,’ and for years the work remained unheard except for a few excerpts and the overture, which Pasdeloup introduced to the public at his popular concerts. At last, in 1883, the management of the Théâtre de la Monnaie at Brussels offered to mount it, and here it received its first performance in January of the following year. In the following July it was produced at Covent Garden and again in Jan. 1885 at Lyons, and then on June 12 of that year it was heard at Paris at the Opéra, but in a truncated version which the composer refused to remain in the house to hear. Brussels, which had welcomed ‘ Sigurd,’ also saw the first production, in Feb. 1890, of ‘ Salammbô ’ (based on Flaubert’s novel), which reached the Paris Opéra in May 1892. The parts of Brunehild and Salammbô in these two operas were taken in Brussels and also in Paris by Mme. Rose Caron, and both works quickly won their way into popular favour, which they retained until after Reyer’s death. The musical idiom in which they are couched, whilst owing more than a little to Wagner and Berlioz and even to Gluck and Weber, is fresh and attractive ; the use of leitmotiv is judicious and free from monotony ; the conventional tricks and repetitions of the operas in vogue in his day are generally avoided, the orchestration is picturesque and the musical phrases fit the natural declamation of the words. As a literary critic, too, Reyer was undoubtedly effective. He wrote with vigour and with sympathy for his subject (he said of his own criticism that though he had keen predilections he was without prejudice), and his admirable use of irony combined with a playful wit makes many of his articles thoroughly readable to-day.

In addition to the works for the theatre mentioned above, Reyer composed a number of songs, a few small pieces for pianoforte, three unaccompanied male-voice choruses, ‘ Le Chant des paysans,’ ‘ Chœur de buveurs,’ and ‘ Chœur des assiégés ’ ; three sacred pieces, Ave Maria, Salve Regina, and O Salutaris ; a hymn, ‘ L’Union des arts,’ for the inauguration of a musical society (Marseilles, 1862) ; ‘ Le Hymne du Rhin,’ for soprano, choir and orchestra (Baden, 1865) ; and ‘ La Madeleine au désert ’ (a scène lyrique first sung by M. Bouhy at a Pasdeloup concert in 1874). He also edited and harmonised a volume of ‘ 40 Vieilles Chansons.’　　　　L. W. H.

BIBLIOGRAPHY

G. Servières : (1) La Musique française moderne (Paris, 1896).
　(2) Les Relations d’ Ernest Reyer et de Th. Gautier (Revue d’histoire littéraire, Jan.-May 1917).
A. Pougin : Musiciens du XIXe siècle (Paris, 1911).

H. de Curzon : (1) La Légende de Sigurd dans l’Edda ; L’Opéra d’Ernest Reyer.
　(2) Salammbô (de Reyer) ; le poème et l’opéra (Paris, 1923), with list of works.
　(3) Ernest Reyer, sa vie et ses œuvres, 1823-1909 (Paris, 1924).
A. Jullien : (1) Reyer (Paris, 1909).
　(2) Reyer intime d’après des lettres inédites (Revue musicale, (1924, No. 3).
Charles Vincens : Éloge d’Ernest Reyer (Marseilles, 1909).

REZNIČEK, Emil Nikolaus von (b. Vienna, May 4, 1860), composer, was at first destined for a legal career, and for that purpose was entered as a law student at Graz, where he contrived to pursue some musical studies under Prof. Wilhelm Mayer. He made the acquaintance of Busoni and Weingartner, and at the age of 21 married the latter’s kinswoman, Milka Thurn. Rebelling against the irksomeness of legal studies he became, a year later, a student at the Leipzig Conservatorium under Reinecke and Jadassohn. A year’s hard work sufficed to perfect his knowledge of the art of composition, and he wrote several important works, including a symphonic suite in E minor (1883).

Being drawn towards the dramatic side of music, Rezniček undertook the duties of theatre conductor at Graz, Zürich, Stettin, Berlin, Jena, Bochum and Mainz, the last appointment alone giving him something like the scope he desired. Then, branching out in a different direction, he obtained an appointment as military conductor in Prague.

Rezniček’s first opera, ‘ The Maid of Orleans,’ was composed in 1886, and two other works for the stage, ‘ Satanella ’ and ‘ Emmerich Fortunat,’ followed in 1887 and 1888. All these operas were produced in Prague. But his greatest theatrical success came in 1894, when the comic opera, ‘ Donna Diana,’ was written within a few weeks, and given for the first time in Prague on Dec. 16. The scene is laid in the castle of Don Diego at Barcelona, at the period of the independence of Catalonia ; the libretto is by Moreto. Rezniček had in the meantime retired from his military post. Another important work belonging to the Prague period is the Requiem in D minor for Schmeykal, for chorus, orchestra and organ.

For a short time Rezniček was court Kapellmeister at Weimar, and in 1896-99 held a similar post at Mannheim. His folk-opera ‘ Till Eulenspiegel,’ dealing with the pranks of the well-known German comic character, was produced at Carlsruhe in 1901, and revived in Berlin in 1903. In 1902 he removed to Berlin, where he founded the Kammer-Orchester-Konzerte for works requiring small orchestral combinations. He also directed the monthly concerts of the Warsaw Philharmonic Society, and made frequent journeys to Russia, where he was as highly appreciated as in Berlin. He became teacher of composition at the Klindworth-Scharwenka Conservatorium in 1906. In Nov. 1907 he conducted two concerts in London, introducing his symphony in D major to an English audience　For the next two seasons he was conductor at the Opera in Warsaw, a post he lost when a new management was installed in 1909. Rezniček then became conductor at the Komische Oper in Berlin.

After an orchestral fugue in C sharp minor, written in 1906, Rezniček composed little until his Berlin appointment came to an end in 1911, when the Komische Oper closed down ; but now a number of important works followed each other in rapid succession, including a symphony in F minor, a violin concerto, incidental music to a play by Strindberg, a choral work entitled ' Vater unser,' and the opera ' Ritter Blaubart,' finished in 1918.

In Mar. 1919 Rezniček was made a member of the Akademie der Künste in Berlin, and he retired from public life.

In addition to the works already referred to, the following may be mentioned :

Mass in F for the Jubilee of the Emperor Francis Joseph II. (1898) ; ' Ruhm und Ewigkeit,' a poem by Nietzsche set for tenor voice and orchestra ; a Comedy Overture ; a Symphonic Suite in D major ; Idyllic Overture (Berlin, Nikisch, 1903) ; Tragic Symphony in D minor (Berlin, Weingartner, 1904) ; 3 Volkslieder for voice and small orchestra (Kammer-Orchester-Konzerte, 1905) ; Ironic Symphony, B major (do.) ; String Quartet in C sharp minor (Berlin, Dessau Quartet, 1906) ; ' Nachtstück ' for violoncello, with accompaniment for harp, four horns and string quartet ; Serenata for strings ; Introduction and Valse Caprice for violin and orchestra (Kammer-Orchester-Konzerte, 1906).

D. H. ; addns. E. B.

BIBL.—MAX CHOP, E. N. v. Rezniček, sein Leben und seine Werke (Vienna, 1920) ; RICHARD SPECHT, E. N. v. Rezniček, eine vorläufige Studie (Vienna, 1923).

RHAMES, a family of Dublin music publishers. (1) AARON was issuing sheet music in Dublin c. 1729–32. His son (2) BENJAMIN was in an extensive way of trade and was established in 1753 at 16 Upper Blind Quay at the sign of the Sun, and published great quantities of single sheet songs, mainly of contemporary English music. He was succeeded by his widow, (3) ELIZABETH, about 1773 or 1775. In the year 1776 the name Upper Blind Quay was altered into Exchange Street, and the later imprints of Elizabeth Rhames bear the new address with the same number, 16. She remained in business until about the year 1790, when (4) FRANCIS, her son, took over the concern and greatly increased the output of music sheets. In 1809 Paul Alday bought the business and remained at the same address until 1823 or 1824, removing then to 10 Dame Street. Elizabeth Rhames and her son published, among other Irish works, pieces by Sir John Stevenson, the copyright of which, after being held by Alday, was transferred to James Power of London.

F. K. ; information from W. H. G. F.

RHAPSODY. The Greek Rhapsodist (ῥαψῳδός) was a professional reciter or chaunter of epic poetry. ῥαψῳδία is the Greek title of each book of the Homeric poems, the first book of the Iliad being ῥαψῳδία A, and so forth. The Rhapsody was the song of the Rhapsode ; a sequel of Rhapsodies when sung in succession or written down so as to form a series, con-

stituted an epic poem, and when a long poem was chanted in sections at different times and by different singers it was said to be rhapsodised. The usual derivation of ῥαψῳδία is ῥάπτω = I sew, and ᾠδή = song, ode.

Musicians might speak, in Hamlet's phrase, of a ' rhapsody of words,' or of tunes—that is to say, of a string of melodies arranged with a view to effective performance in public, but without regular dependence of one part upon another. Such a description would seem to apply pretty closely to Liszt's fifteen ' Rapsodies hongroises,' and to his ' Reminiscences d'Espagne ' (a fantasia on two Spanish tunes, ' Les Folies d'Espagne ' and ' La Jota aragonesa,' 1844–45), which, in 1863, he republished as a ' Rhapsodie espagnole.' The history of the latter piece is similar to that of the Hungarian rhapsodies—portions of which were originally published under the title of ' Mélodies hongroises — Ungarische Nationalmelodien '—short transcriptions of Hungarian tunes as they are played by the wandering bands of gipsies, the national musicians of Hungary. The prototype of these ' melodies ' in all probability was Schubert's ' Divertissement à la Hongroise,' in G minor, op. 54—a piece Liszt was always fond of, and of which he produced several versions—as of the whole for pianoforte solo, and of the march in C minor for orchestra.[1] Liszt's ten sets of ' Mélodies hongroises ' date from 1839–47 ; the fifteen so-called ' Rhapsodies hongroises ' from 1853–54.

In 1859 Liszt published a book in French, Des Bohémiens et de leur musique en Hongrie— a late and overgrown preface, as he confesses, to the Rhapsodies. In this brilliant, though at intervals somewhat meretricious work,[2] an effort is made to claim for the set of Rhapsodies the dignity of an Hungarian Epic sui generis. Be this as it may, the term ' Rhapsodie ' remains as one of Liszt's many happy hits in the way of musical nomenclature.

Brahms has adopted the term ' Rhapsodie ' both in Liszt's sense and in that of the Greek Rhapsodists ; and, as usual with him, he has added weight to its significance. His original ' Rhapsodien,' op. 79, for pianoforte solo—in B minor and G minor—are abrupt, impassioned aphoristic pieces of simple and obvious structure, yet solidly put together. The ' Rhapsodie ' in C, op. 53, for contralto, male chorus and orchestra, justifies its title, in the Greek sense, inasmuch as it is a setting—a recitation, a rhapsody—of a portion of Goethe's poem ' Harzreise im Winter ' ; it, also, is a compact and carefully balanced piece. The last pianoforte piece, in op. 119, is a noble Rhapsody, in which there is perhaps rather more of the quality that is usually called ' rhapsodical '

[1] He played his version of the march in London, Apr. 1886.
[2] Like Liszt's Chopin, this book is on good authority reported to be the joint production of himself and certain female friends.

than is to be found in Brahms's other rhapsodies.

The term has become a favourite one with later composers. E. D.

RHAU (RHAW), GEORG (b. Eisfeld, Franconia, c. 1488 ; d. Wittenberg, Aug. 6, 1548), was cantor at the Thomasschule at Leipzig till 1520, after which he settled at Eisleben as a schoolmaster, and subsequently at Wittenberg, where he became a printer, issuing books both in ordinary typography (including many first editions of Luther's writings) and in musical notes, including his own works, *Enchiridion musices ex variis musicorum libris*, etc., 1518 (often reprinted), *Enchiridion musicae mensuralis*, 1520, etc. He also brought out many collections of musical works (see Q.-L.) ; Winterfeld ascribes some Chorals to him.

RHEINBERGER, JOSEF GABRIEL (b. Vaduz, Liechtenstein, Mar. 17, 1839; d. Munich, Nov. 25, 1901), composer, organist and teacher. Unusually gifted as a child, he had acquired considerable fame when only 5 years old ; received at about this time lessons in theory, pianoforte and organ from Sebastian Pohly, a retired schoolmaster at Schlanders (a special pedal - board being made for him); and was appointed organist at Vaduz Parish Church at the age of 7. A few incidents of his childhood are worth relating, as evidence of his precocity, and as early manifestations of the exacting standard and refusal to compromise that throughout life marked his attitude towards his art. The public performance of his first composition, a Mass, when he was only 8 years old, roused so much interest that the Bishop of Chur asked for the boy to be brought to the cathedral, in order that his gifts might be demonstrated. Josef was set to accompany on the organ a Salve Regina for male voices, the singers being the Bishop and clergy. He soon stopped the performance, however, with the remark, ' But, my Lord Bishop, you are singing out of tune ! ' His opinions as to quality in music were expressed no less frankly, and in the most practical of ways. The congregation at Vaduz was alarmed one day at the sudden appearance of clouds of smoke. The source proved to be a stove into which the eight-year-old organist had thrust the copies of some masses by Bühler that did not meet with his approval.

A trifling incident in his tenth year had an important bearing on his future. Turning over the music for the leader of a string quartet— an amateur named Schrammel—Josef remarked during the tuning, ' Your A string sounds a semitone higher than my pianoforte at home.' This proved to be the case, and the violinist was so struck by the boy's acuteness that he persuaded his father to allow him to live at Feldkirch, in order that he might receive tuition from the choir-director, Philip Schmut-

zer. Here he stayed two years, retaining his organist's post at Vaduz, and making the weekly journey of ten miles on foot. In 1850 he left Feldkirch, and a year later entered the Conservatoire at Munich, where he remained till 1854, studying under Leonhard (piano), Herzog (organ) and Maier (counterpoint). On leaving the Conservatoire, where he had greatly distinguished himself, he settled in Munich and became a pupil of Lachner, ekeing out his slender income by teaching In 1859 he succeeded Leonhard as pianoforte professor at the Conservatoire, becoming professor of composition about a year later. At the dissolution of the Conservatoire Rheinberger was given the post of ' Repetitor ' at the court theatre, where he early created a sensation by playing and transposing at first sight ' The Flying Dutchman.' He found theatrical work uncongenial, however, and retired in 1867. During this period (1860–66) he was organist at the court church of St. Michael; in 1864 he became conductor of the Munich Choral Society, after acting as its accompanist since 1854 ; and in 1867, on the reorganisation, under von Bülow, of the Conservatoire, he was made professor of organ and composition, and ' Inspector ' of instrumental and theory classes, the title of Royal Professor being conferred shortly after. These positions he held with increasing distinction during the remainder of his life. As a teacher his fame extended far, pupils coming to him from England and America. In 1877 he declined an offer of the directorship of the newly founded Hoch - Conservatorium at Frankfort —for which decision Ludwig II. gave him the order of knighthood of St. Michael. In the same year Rheinberger resigned his post as conductor of the Munich Choral Society, and succeeded Wüllner as director of the court church music. This appointment led him to compose many ecclesiastical works, among them an eight-part Mass dedicated to Pope Leo XIII., who conferred on him a knighthood of Gregory the Great. On his sixtieth birthday, in 1899, Rheinberger received from the University of Munich the degree of Doctor *honoris causa*. His later years were clouded by ill-health, exposure during a mountaineering tour in the Tyrol having brought about an incurable lung disease. He married (about 1867) Frau von Hoffnaass, *née* Jägerhüber (b. Oct. 1822 ; d. Dec. 31, 1892), a gifted singer and writer, who supplied the texts for many of her husband's choral works.

Rheinberger was a prolific composer in almost every field, but, beyond some of the chamber music, certain of the PF. soli, and his organ music, little of his very large output achieved popularity in this country. To-day practically everything but his organ music is forgotten. Sincerity and impeccable workmanship distinguished all he wrote, but emotional impulse is often lacking, and it must be confessed that, save in one department, he said little that was not more powerfully expressed by the greater of his contemporaries—especially Brahms. The exception, however, is important. There can be no doubt that Rheinberger found in the organ the medium above all suited to his temperament and genius. He was a fine player from childhood, serious in mood, severe in taste, and a composer exceptionally skilled in counterpoint and in all the devices that belong traditionally to organ music; small wonder that his reputation as a writer for the organ has steadily grown as his position in other respects has declined. Originally regarded as an orchestral, choral and chamber-music composer who also wrote organ music, he is now firmly established as an organ writer of the first rank, who made many less successful excursions into other fields. Did Rheinberger himself feel something of this in his latter years ? The thought is suggested by a glance at his list of works, in which the organ appears with increasing frequency towards the end. Thus, from opus numbers 142 to 197 appear twelve of the twenty sonatas,[1] sixty pieces, twelve trios, one concerto, and two suites for organ and strings. This growing preoccupation with the instrument is significant, even when allowance is made for the fact that from 1877 his post as director of the church music at the court no doubt increased his interest in church and organ composition.

The great bulk of German organ music written during the past century is strongly reminiscent of Bach so far as the letter is concerned, but the spirit is too often absent. Rheinberger gives us an example of the reverse state of things. Save for some reminders of 'The Wedge' prelude and fugue in the first sonata, his idiom hardly ever recalls that of Bach, but there is a truly Bach-like spaciousness and architectural quality about his finest movements. Like Bach, too, his music depends for its effect very little on registration.[2] It rarely calls for more than judicious changes of power, and the simple type of variety obtainable from the alternation of manua's balanced in power and contrasted in colour; and in page after page no expression marks appear. This point in common between Bach and Rheinberger is due to the same cause. The average German organ of Rheinberger's day had made little advance on that of Bach so far as mechanical accessories were concerned. Rheinberger's own organ, for example, had not even a swell-box ! This explains the extra-

ordinary fact that in all his organ music the sign ⸺ occurs only once—in the 19th sonata, where the increase is evidently intended to be made through stops gradually added, the left hand being given a rest for that purpose. This lack of registration facilities no doubt influenced the style of Rheinberger, as it did that of Bach. Their continuity was, of course, primarily the result of the contrapuntal texture that was their normal medium ; but in part it must have owed something to their necessary disregard of any but the simplest kinds of registration. Given a choice between breaking the flow, and a disturbance of it for the purpose of such effects as soloing, or subtle gradations of power, their decision was clearly on the side of the purely musical interest. As the loss of tonal variety is generally more than compensated by the continuity, it is clear that any registration that interrupts the flow is to be deprecated as being fatal to one of the music's finest qualities.

Rheinberger's affinity to Bach ends here. In melodic style, idiom, figuration, rhythm and construction he derives rather from Beethoven, Schumann and Brahms. His fugues hardly ever recall Bach, and he is surely unique among German organ composers in that he wrote only one Choral prelude,[3] and that a very little one. As a Roman Catholic, he had, of course, no official concern with the Choral. Plain-song[4] also appears to have attracted him very little as a basis for organ music.

Apart from their intrinsic value, the sonatas contain much of interest and importance on the structural side. Although many of the movements are in 'sonata form,' there is almost always a good deal of modification. Evidently Rheinberger felt that an instrument so lacking in variety as the organ (especially *his* organ) was ill-suited to the customary 'working out' and recapitulation. Hence his avoidance of lengthy development, and his habitual shortening of the recapitulation, the balance being made good by increasing the importance of the coda, and by liberality in regard to subject matter. The Preludio in No. 7, for example, contains five subjects, almost all equally important, any two of which would provide ample material for ordinary 'first movement' development. Continuity and variety are ensured by such devices as the merging of the opening section into the working-out ; by basing the latter either wholly or partly on some new material ; and by making the second subject an extension of the first, rather than a definite, self-contained theme. Sometimes there is no working-out section, its place being taken by some development near

---

[1] As the twenty sonatas are all in different keys, ten major and ten minor, we may assume that the composer aimed at a set of twenty-four.
[2] It should be added, as evidence of the small part played by registration in the conception of the sonatas, that Nos. 2-20 were arranged by Rheinberger himself for pianoforte duet.

[3] Monologue No. 6 consists of Schumann-like arabesques over the Passion Choral used as a bass.
[4] In Sonata No. 3 he uses *Tonus Peregrinus*; and in No. 4 the Eighth Tone is introduced as a second subject in the fugue.

the end of the movement. In fact, the student of composition, especially where form is concerned, will find in the sonatas a wealth of interest and instruction.

No fewer than seventeen of the sonatas contain a fugue, and in addition there are about thirty shorter examples among the various sets of pieces. Here, by common consent, Rheinberger is at his best. His invention moves freely under the restrictions of the form—indeed, a striking point about the sonata fugues is that, on the whole, they show more emotional power and imagination than do the nominally free movements. (Rheinberger's ability to use the stricter forms as a medium for original and expressive music—surely one of the tests of a composer—is shown no less strikingly elsewhere. The two sets of trios contain some delightful canons, and there are five admirable ground-bass treatments in the miscellaneous pieces, and a truly noble specimen in the Passacaglia of the 8th sonata.) In the sonata fugues Rheinberger makes many interesting and almost invariably successful experiments in construction. Perhaps the happiest is his method of combining fugue and sonata form by the introduction of an important theme—generally of a harmonic or broadly melodic character—to serve as second subject.[1] When this second subject is a quotation from an earlier movement in the sonata, as is the case in the B flat minor, G major, B major and A flat fugues, the procedure is even more striking, though, of course, its full effect is made only when the entire sonata is played. In the D minor fugue the stately second subject is evolved from the opening of the preceding Intermezzo ; in the E flat minor, vivid contrast is provided by important new material of an agitated character ; in the ' Ricercare ' in D the long and apparently unrelated middle section in F, marked ' Intermezzo,' is derived from an inversion of the first six notes of the fugue subject ; and so forth. But whatever the source of the non-fugal matter, it is fitted into the scheme so skilfully that the interest is enhanced, or at least maintained. There can be no doubt that in the successful working of this device, Rheinberger has solved the problem which Bach set himself in one or two of the organ fugues, notably in the ' Wedge,' i.e. the introduction of a long middle section, independent in character, yet falling well into the scheme, and increasing the interest of the fugal matter on its resumption in the final section. As Parry says,[2] the fact of the ' Wedge ' giving an impression of being ' singularly loose in structure,' proves that Bach had not solved the difficulty of ' relieving the extreme insistence on the striking subject.' Moreover, his adoption in the ' Wedge ' of the *da capo* form (one of the

very few cases in fugal writing) cannot be said to be a success, because it is opposed to the spirit of a form which demands cumulative interest. Rheinberger avoids both pitfalls, the independent matter being at least as significant as the fugal context, and the interest of the final section of the fugue being increased by a wealth of new treatment. His one misfire in experimenting with the fugue form is in the E minor fugue, in which a short quiet theme is introduced three times, with rondo-like effect. It fails because it merely breaks into the progress of the fugue without contributing anything to the scheme as a whole.

The other important new departure in Rheinberger's fugues is the coda, which often takes the place of the conventional *stretti* and pedal point. Usually Rheinberger employs for this purpose a broad theme from an earlier part of the sonata[3] ; but even more successful (especially when the fugue is played alone) is the device of rounding off the movement with a triumphant statement of the subject richly harmonised.[4] With all this structural freedom there is little room for the time-honoured scientific devices of fugue, and in only two—the C minor and the Ricercare in D—does Rheinberger concern himself much with *stretti*, augmentation, inversion, etc. So intent is he on freedom that he even eschews the use of a regular counter subject. It is worth noting that much of the success of the fugues is due to their bold and striking subjects.

The slow movements of the sonatas deserve a word. The best of them brought into organ music a touch of romance and colour that had hitherto been generally absent. Mendelssohn gave a lead in this way in his 2nd, 4th and 5th sonatas, but Rheinberger extended the scope of the slow movement, making liberal use of sonata, rondo and variation forms. His frequent introduction of a loud and animated middle section is not always an advantage, for the movement is apt to fail as a contrast to its companions. He has good precedent in the classical symphony, of course, but there is a world of difference between the great varieties of *f* and *ff* of the orchestra and the limited scope and unyielding tone of the organ. Despite this fault (which a player of discretion can easily modify) the slow movements contain many delightful pages in which the composer shows himself to be a genuine tune-writer. The Cantilene (No. 11), Idyll (No. 14), Canzona (No. 13), Pastorale (No. 12) and the charming Theme and Variations (No. 10), for example, are among the most attractive things in organ music, being as melodious as the typical French ' Cantilene,' without its too frequent superficiality.

---

1 'Subject' is used here in its sonata sense, not as indicating a theme for fugal treatment.
2 *Johann Sebastian Bach*, p. 511.

3 Fugues in E flat minor, F sharp major, D major, etc.
4 Fugues in C minor, E minor, B flat and F major.

Rheinberger's miscellaneous pieces are apparently the only extensive set of short organ works by a German composer in which the Choral plays no important part. They cover a great range of style and mood, and in almost all of them the composer's invention is at its happiest. Their nearest analogy is in the short piano works of Schumann and Brahms. They show Rheinberger as a late-Romantic in the use of such titles as 'Vision,' 'Contemplation,' 'Evening Rest,' 'Lamento,' 'Riposo,' 'Aspiration,' etc., and by reason of a certain intimacy of style they take a place in the repertory near to the 'Little Organ Book' of Bach.

It will be seen from the above discussion that Rheinberger's organ music makes considerable demands on both player and hearer. Much of it will be dismissed as dull by those who look to the organ for little more than saccharine andantes, cheerful marches, or transcriptions and imitations of orchestral music. Dull moments there are, as is inevitable in so large an output. But they are few, and are mainly confined to the later sonatas, which, judged as complete works, lack the sustained invention and energy of Nos. 3 to 14. Nor are the later works free from turgidity and prolixity. But these blemishes—due apparently to failing health—do not materially affect the value of a mass of work that, in artistic purity, dignity, skill and general interest, deserves a high place amongst music written for instrumental solo.

H. G. ; incorporating material from J. W. N.

LIST OF COMPOSITIONS

Op.
1. 4 Pieces, pf.
2. 5 Partsongs.
3. 7 Songs.
4. 5 Songs.
5. 3 Small pf. pieces.
6. 3 Studies, pf.
7. 3 Characteristic pieces, pf.
8. 'Waldmärchen,' pf.
9. 5 Studies, pf.
10. 'Wallenstein,' symphony.
11. 5 Pieces, pf.
12. Toccata, pf.
13. 'Tarantella,' pf., 4 hands.
14. 24 Preludes, pf.
15. Duo, 2 pfs.
16. 'Stabat Mater,' soli, chorus and orch.
17. 2 Four-part Ballads.
18. Overture, 'Taming of the Shrew.'
19. Toccatina, pf.
20. 'Die sieben Raben,' romantic opera in 3 acts.
21. 'Wasserfee,' vocal quartet and pf.
22. 4 Songs.
23. Fantasia, pf.
24. 4 Vocal quartets.
25. 'Lockung,' vocal quartet and pf.
26. 7 Songs.
27. 1st Organ Sonata, in C minor.
28 4 Humoresken, pf.
29. 'Aus Italien,' 3 pf. pieces.
30. 7 Pf. duets (from the music to 'Der wunderthätige Magus').
31. 5 Partsongs.
*32. 'Daughter of Jairus,' cantata for children.
33. Prelude and fugue, pf.

Op.
34. Trio, pf. and strings.
35. Hymn for female choir, organ and harp.
36. 9 Duets, pf. (from the music to 'Die unheilbringende Krone').
*37. 'Poor Henry,' comic opera for children.
38. Quartet, pf. and strings, in E flat.
39. 6 Pf. pieces, in fugal form.
40. 5 Motets, choir.
41. 7 Songs.
42. Étude and fugato, pf.
43. Capriccio giocoso, pf.
44. 3 Male choruses.
45. 2 Pf. studies on a theme by Handel.
46. 'Passion Music,' choir and organ.
47. Symphonic sonata, pf.
48. 4 Male choruses.
49. 10 Organ trios.
50. Ballad, 'Das Thal des Espingo,' male chorus and orch.
51. Improvisation on a theme from 'Die Zauberflöte,' pf.
52. 5 Partsongs.
53. 3 Studies, pf.
54. 4 Hymns, mezzo-soprano and organ (or pf.)
55. 8 Songs.
56. 4 Vocal quartets, with strings and pf.
57. 7 Songs.
58. 6 Hymns, choir.
59. Pf. study.
60. Requiem, soli, chorus and orch.
61. Theme and variations, pf.

* Works possessing English text.

Op.
62. Mass for one voice and organ.
63. 8 Part-songs.
*64. 'May Day,' 5 three-part female choruses, with pf.
65 2nd Organ sonata in A flat.
66. 3 Studies, pf.
67. 6 Preludes, pf.
68. 6 Pieces, in fugal form.
69. 3 Sacred partsongs.
70. 'Thurmers Töchterlein,' comic opera in 4 acts.
71. Ballad, 'König Erich,' chorus with pf.
72. 'Aus den Ferientagen,' 4 pf. duets.
73. 5 Male choruses.
74. 5 Male choruses.
*75. 2 Vocal quartets, with pf.
*76. 'Toggenburg,' soli, chorus and pf.
77. Sonata, vln. and pf., or v'cello and pf.
78. 3 Pf. pieces.
79. Fantasia, orch. or pf., 4 hands.
80. 5 Partsongs.
81. 'Die todte Braut,' romance, mezzo-soprano, choir and orch. (or pf.)
82. String quintet, in A minor (or pf. duet).
83. Missa brevis in D minor, choir.
84. Requiem in E flat, choir.
85. 7 Male choruses.
86. 4 Epic songs, male choir.
87. Symphony ('Florentine') in F.
88. 3rd Organ sonata ('Pastoral') in G (or pf. duet).
89. String quartet in C minor.
90. 'Vom Rheine,' 6 male choruses.
91. 'Johannisnacht,' male choir and pf.
92. Sonata, pf. and v'cello, in C (or vln. and pf.).
93. Theme and variations, string quartet in G minor (or pf. duet).
94. Concerto, pf. and orch. in A flat.
95. 2 Choruses with orch. (or pf.)
96. 3 Latin hymns, three-part female choir and organ.
*97. Ballad, 'Clarice of Eberstein,' soli, chorus and orch.
98. 4th Organ sonata, 'tonus peregrinus,' in A minor (or pf. duet).
99. Pf. sonata in D flat.
100. 7 Songs, male choir.
101. 3 Studies, pf.
102. Ballad, 'Wittekind,' male chorus and orch. (or pf.)
103. 3 Vocal duets, sop., bass, and pf.
104. Toccata, pf.
105. Sonata, vln. and pf., in E minor.
106. 2 Romantic songs, choir and orch. (or pf.)
107. 5 Hymns for choir.
108. 'Am Strom,' 6 partsongs.
109. Mass in E flat for double choir, ded. to Leo XIII.
110. Overture to Schiller's 'Demetrius' (or pf. duet).
111. 5th Organ sonata in F sharp (or pf. duet).
112. 2nd Trio, pf., vln. and v'cello, in A.
113. 6 Studies for pf. (left hand).
114. Quintet, pf. and strings, in C.
115. Toccata, pf. in C minor.
116. 4 Songs, male choir.
117. 'Missa Sanctissimae Trinitatis,' choir, in F.
118. 6 Two-part hymns, with organ
119. 6th Organ sonata, in E flat minor (or pf. duet).
*120. Legend, 'Christophorus,' soli, chorus and orch. (or pf.)
121. Trio, pf. and strings, in B flat.
122. Sonata, C minor, pf., 4 hands (or 2 pfs., 8 hands).
123. 24 Fughetten for organ.
124. 8 Partsongs.
125. 7 Male choruses.
126. Mass, three-part female choir, in A.
127. 7th Organ sonata in F minor (or pf. duet).
128. 4 Elegiac songs, with organ.

Op.
129. 3 Italian songs.
130. 6 Male choruses.
131. 6 Female choruses.
132. 8th Organ sonata, in B minor (or pf. duet).
133. 4 Motets, six-part choir.
134. Easter hymn, double choir.
135. Pf. sonata, in E flat.
136. 14 Songs.
137. Organ concerto in F, with orch. (or pf. duet).
138. Stabat Mater, choir, string orch. and organ.
139. Nonet, wind and strings (or pf. duet).
140. 5 Hymns, choir and organ.
141. 6 Male choruses.
142. 9th Organ sonata, in B flat minor (or pf. duet).
143. 'Die Rosen von Hildesheim,' male chorus and wind instruments.
144. 3 Male choruses.
145. 'Montfort,' soli, chorus and orch.
146. 10th Organ sonata, in B minor (or pf. duet).
147. String quartet in F.
148. 11th Organ sonata in D minor (or pf. duet).
149. Suite, organ, violin, v'cello and string orch.
150. 6 pieces, violin and organ, or v'cello and organ.
151. Mass in G.
152. 30 Children's songs.
153. 'Das Zauberwort,' Singspiel, in 2 acts, for children.
154. 12th Organ sonata, in D flat (or pf. duet).
*155. Mass, three-part female choir and organ.
156. 12 Characteristic pieces for organ.
157. 6 Sacred songs, with organ.
158. 8 Soprano (or baritone) songs.
159. Mass, four-part choir and organ, in F minor.
160. 7 Male choruses.
161. 13th Organ sonata, in E flat (or pf. duet).
162. 'Monologue,' 12 organ pieces.
*163. 5 Motets, five-part choir.
*164. 'Star of Bethlehem,' Christmas cantata, soli, chorus and orch. (or pf.)
165. 14th Organ sonata, in C (or pf. duet).
166. Suite, vln. and organ, in C minor.
167. 'Meditations,' 12 organ pieces.
168. 15th Organ sonata, in D (or pf. duet).
169. Mass, soli, choir and orch., (or strings and organ).
170. 8 Four-part songs, 'Sturm und Frieden.'
*171. 'Marianische Hymnen' voice and organ (or pf.)
172. Mass, male choir with organ (or wind instruments.)
173. 4 Male choruses.
174. 12 Organ pieces.
175. 16th Organ sonata, in G sharp minor (or pf. duet).
176. 9 Advent-Motetten, choir.
177. 2nd Concerto for organ and orch., in G minor (or pf. duet).
178. Sonata for horn and pf.
179. 'Hymnus an die Tonkunst,' for male chorus and orch.
180. 12 Characteristic pieces for pf.
181. 17th Organ sonata in B.
182. 'Vom goldenen Horn,' Türkisches Liederspiel with pf.
183. 12 Studies, pf.
184. Romantic sonata for pf., in F sharp minor.
185. 7 Male choruses.
186. 8 Four-part songs, 'Jahreszeiten.'
*187. Mass, for female voices and organ, in G minor.
188. 18th Organ sonata, in A.
189. 12 Organ trios.
190. Mass, for male choir and organ, in F.
191. Trio, for pf., vln. and v'cello, in F.
192. Mass, 'Misericordias Domini,' choir and organ, in E.
193. 19th Organ sonata, in G minor.

RHEINECK, Christoph (b. Memmingen, Nov. 1, 1748; d. there, July 29, 1797), was successful with some operas in Lyons and other French towns, but returned to Memmingen on the death of his father to take over the management of the latter's hotel. He brought out another opera ('Rinaldo') at that town in 1779, and wrote a large number of songs which count among the best of their time; some appeared in Bossler's 'Blumenlese' (*Riemann*; *Q.-L.*).

RHEINGOLD, Das, see RING DES NIBELUNGEN.

RHINE FESTIVALS, see NIEDERRHEINISCHE MUSIKFESTE.

RHUBEBA, see REBEC.

RHYTHM. Italy, France and Germany have meant by 'rhythm' the larger distributions of metre, the composition of the phrase and the period. *Il ritmo, le rhythme, die Rhythmik* have to do with such questions as the proper barring and balance of the phrase, its division into groups, how much of the preliminary group (*anakrousis*), if any, is essential or accidental, and the like. Books such as R. Westphal's *Allgemeine Theorie der musikalischen Rhythmik*, 1880, a closely reasoned account of phrasing drawn up on the lines of Greek theory, and Mathis Lussy's *Le Rhythme musical*, 1884, full of æsthetic vision and critical insight, supply a large number of pertinent instances and illuminate them. Those who may wish to seize quickly the point of view of each of these writers may compare their account of Beethoven's op. 26 (Westphal, p. 117, Lussy, p. 11); the former is inclined to find an *anakrousis* everywhere, the latter to judge each phrasing on its merits.

In English 'rhythm' means something more personal. A living sense of rhythm is based on an experience of actual failure and success; books cannot teach it.

AN ACT OF FUSION.—If rhythm is the 'life' of time in all its aspects, if it redeems time from a clock-like precision, adapting it constantly to changed conditions, bridging what separates the mechanical from the human and eventually, as we may believe, the finite from the infinite, it does all this by holding two, or more, discrepant elements together as one. A melody—an Irish reel, perhaps—is in strict time, or people could not dance to it correctly; but if it

had not also rhythm, they would not dance to it passionately. Rhythm seems in this case to hold together with 'the time' a number of minute, unverifiable accelerandos and ritardandos, or else to refuse resolutely to admit them. Whichever it does, it is that one fiddler's 'reading' or 'expression' of the music, the outcome of all the musicality that is in him, his special creation, inimitable, and not recoverable perhaps, even by him, again. But where did he get this *rubato* from ? He got it from the ups and downs of the melody. What these put into the strict time is, as Lussy pointed out, pathos—' la nature douloureuse de nos sentiments.' So that in this case rhythm is, in precise language, the effect of pitch upon duration.

That is the performer's rhythm, or one instance of it; it consists in a creative act which reconciles in a flash the claims of the two warring constituents of melody, time and pitch.

COMPOSER'S RHYTHM.—When the music is harmonised, when in fact there is more than one simultaneous melody, there may be two times, or two accents, or two metres to reconcile. In this rhythm the composer shares, for he put them there (cf. POLYPHONY: PRINCIPLES OF THE 16TH CENTURY). The performer's part is to feel them all, and to decide instantaneously which, if any, of them is to be given greater value. He can do this only by establishing a level which they may rise above and fall below, and the greatest artists are those who can consistently maintain this level.

The composer has a level to maintain too—the consistency of his work as a whole. His greatest danger is anticlimax, the 'bathos' of literature—raising expectations and not fulfilling them. To avoid that he husbands his resources. If he has established a given motion (time), he does not change it capriciously; his dynamic changes (accent) have a sense of proportion; his variation of a melodic figure (metre)—from simple to complex or, as Beethoven often proceeds, from complex to simple—is part of a considered development; his greatest merit is—as it is also of the conductor's, among performers—to have kept 'the line.'

OTHER USES OF THE WORD.—The idea of rhythm, being arrived at only after some experience, is naturally subject to misconception. We speak euphemistically of the rhythm being wrong when it was the 'time' that was at fault. We call *Adagio* a slow 'rhythm' when we should say PACE. 'Rhythm' has been applied to groups of bars for which PERIOD would be a better word. It has been defined as 'the systematic grouping of notes with regard to duration, which includes, quite against the author's intention, the metrical distribution within the bar; that is a correct definition of METRE, but not of rhythm. Rhythm is, as has been said, time, pace, metre, and other things rolled into one, and it is not surprising that it has been used to name each of them singly.

Like good reading aloud, the true rhythmical performance of music is a verdict based on the knowledge of much else besides the matter in hand.        A. H. F. S.

RHYTHMIC MODES. Composers of the 13th and 14th centuries adapted the plain-song or other themes (tenors) of their motets in accordance with a system or series of forms known as the Rhythmic Modes. These were six in number, founded on the *feet* of classical poetry. In the *quantitative* age of Latin verse, *i.e.* up to the time of St. Ambrose (4th century) the foot was governed by the length of vowel, not by the accent; thus:

—◡|—–|—◡◡|—◡|—◡

Integer vitae scelerisque purus

is made up of five feet, the first and the last two being trochees, the second a spondee and the third a dactyl (see METRE). In the days of mediæval music this rhythm would be entirely altered in accordance with the needs of pronunciation (a sign of advance, not of decadence), and would become

|·· |⌣·|·|⌣·||·|⌣·||·

Integer vitae scelerisque purus,

*i.e.* a dactyl followed by four trochees. The foot is therefore to be taken, musically, as an *accentual* unit, and not in the same sense as in the classical Latin verse system.

The earliest POLYPHONY (*q.v.*) was nothing more than a ' double plain-song,' two parts in free rhythm kept together by certain technical conventions. Before long, however, the need of some mensurate system to ensure uniformity, and to increase the possibilities of composition, was recognised.

Musicians therefore began to cast their plain-songs into one or other of these six rhythmic moulds:

| No. | Old classical scansion, now represented by accent. | Foot. | Time-value (notation halved). |
|---|---|---|---|
| 1. | — ◡ | Trochee | ♩ ♪ |
| 2. | ◡ — | Iambus | ♪ ♩ |
| 3. | — ◡ ◡ | Dactyl | ♩. ♪ ♩ |
| 4. | ◡ ◡ — | Anapaest | ♪ ♩ ♩. |
| 5. | — — — | Molossus | ♩. ♩. ♩. |
| 6. | ◡ ◡ ◡ | Tribrach | ♪ ♪ ♪ (rarely used) |

The third and fourth Rhythmic Modes are divided, it will be observed, in triple time, not in duple as we might expect. This is explained (*after* the event) by the mediæval writers as symbolic of the Blessed Trinity. But the cause is earlier than the explanation, and it is probably due to the fact that a unit or *tempus* of this form is more workable, being divisible in more ways than the forms ◯ ♩ ♩ and ♩ ♩ ◯.

These rules were also applied (sometimes with less strictness) to the upper parts of the motet: the motet being the dominating form of composition during these centuries. The modes of the various voices were not usually identical; thus (from *Oxf. Hist. Mus.* i. 169):

Mode 1 (Trochaic).

Mode 3 (Dactylic).

The system lasted, roughly, from 1150 or 1200–1350, but its influence may be traced later. It began to die out with the widespread revival of duple time about 1300, and finally disappeared with the growth of freedom in composition which marks the 15th century.        A. H.

RIAÑO, JUAN FACUNDO (*b.* Granada, Nov. 24, 1828; *d.* Madrid, Feb. 27, 1901), a leading authority on the history of Spanish art, who belongs to musical history through his remarkable *Critical and Bibliographical Notes on Early Spanish Music* (London, 1887). Riaño's exact references and accurate bibliographical descriptions of mediæval musical MSS. are in striking contrast to the vague inaccuracy of Soriano Fuertes. He held that the neumes in the Visigothic (Mozarabic) MSS. were based upon a form of the Visigothic alphabet consisting of cursive characters, rarely used, but found in the signatures to Spanish documents of the 10th-12th centuries. His theory, though it has not received much attention, is developed with great learning and acuteness. The book is also of importance in the study of early Spanish instruments.

Riaño became a Senator, Privy Councillor and member of various academies; but he gave real help and encouragement to the study of the fine arts in Spain, and was founder and director of the *Museo de reproducciones artisticas*. His publications (in English) besides the *Notes on Early Spanish Music*, include a *Classified and Descriptive Catalogue of the Art Objects of Spanish Production in the S. Kensington Museum* (1872), and a *Manual of Spanish Industrial Arts* (1879).        J. B. T.

RIBATTUTA (re-striking), an ornamental device in which the alternation of two notes was developed by the process of acceleration into a trill, thus :

 etc

Grove said of the Ribattuta, ' Beethoven has preserved it for ever in the overture "Leonora III." (bar 75 of *Allegro*).'

RIBERA, ANTONIO DE (early 16th-cent.), Spanish church musician ; a member of the Cappella Pontificia, Rome, from 1514–22. He composed some of the music sung annually in the Mystery of ELCHE.        J. B. T.

RIBERA, BERNADINO DE (mid.-16th cent.), Spanish church musician, choirmaster at Toledo in 1563, but replaced in the following year. Eslava printed 2 motets and a Magnificat; the Toledo MSS. include a Mass, ' De Beata Virgine,' and Magnificats.        J. B. T.

RIBIBLE, an obsolete instrument played by a bow. It is mentioned by Chaucer and other early writers, and appears to have been either the rebec itself, or a particular form of it. Sometimes it is spelled ' rubile.' It has been suggested that both ' rebec ' and ' ribible ' are derived from the Moorish word ' rebeb ' or ' rehab,' which seems to have been the name of a somewhat similar musical instrument. (See REBEC.)        F. K.

RIBS (Fr. *éclisses* ; Ger. *Zarge*), the sides of stringed instruments of the violin type, connecting the back and the table. They consist of six (sometimes only five) pieces of maple, and should be of the same texture as the back, and if possible cut out of the same piece. The flatter the model, the deeper the ribs require to be ; hence the viol tribe, having perfectly flat backs and tables of slight elevation, are very deep in the ribs. The oldest violins were often very deep in the ribs, but many of them have been since cut down. Carlo Bergonzi and his contemporaries had a fashion of making shallow ribs, and often cut down the ribs of older instruments, thereby injuring their tone beyond remedy.        E. J. P.

RICCATTI, CONTE GIORDANO (b. Castel Franco, near Treviso, Feb. 28, 1709 ; d. Treviso, July 20, 1790), mathematician, architect, musical amateur ; wrote a number of essays and treatises on the harmonic systems of Rameau, Tartini and Vallotti, a book on counterpoint, contributions to Cologera's *Raccolta* (on acoustics, etc.) and a biography of Agostino Steffani.        E. V. D. S.

RICCI, (1) LUIGI (b. Naples, June 8, 1805 ; d. Prague, Dec. 31, 1859), entered in 1814 the Royal Conservatorio, then under Zingarelli, of which he became in 1819 one of the sub-professors together with Bellini.

His first opera, ' L' impresario in angustie,' was performed by the students of the Con-

servatorio in 1823, and enthusiastically applauded. In the following four years he wrote ' La cena frastornata,' ' L' abate Taccarella,' ' Il Diavolo condannato a prender moglie,' and ' La lucerna d' Epitteto,' all for the Teatro Nuovo. In 1828 his ' Ulisse,' at the San Carlo, was a failure. In 1829 ' Il colombo ' in Parma and ' L' orfanella di Ginevra ' in Naples were both successful. The winter of 1829–30 was disastrous for Ricci, his four new operas (' Il sonnambulo,' ' L' eroina del Messico,' ' Annibale in Torino ' and ' La neve ') being all unsuccessful. In the autumn of 1831 he produced at La Scala, Milan, ' Chiara di Rosemberg,' and this opera, performed by Grisi, Sacchi, Winter, Badioli, etc., was greatly applauded, and soon became successful in all the theatres of Italy. ' Il nuovo Figaro ' failed in Parma in 1832. In it sang Rozer, who afterwards married Balfe. The same fate attended ' I due sergenti ' at La Scala in 1833, where the following year he gave ' Un' avventura di Scaramuccia,' which was a very great success, and was translated into French by Flotow. The same year ' Gli esposti,' better known as ' Eran due ed or son tre,' was applauded in Turin, whilst ' Chi dura vince,' like Rossini's immortal Barbiere,' was hissed at Rome. It was afterwards received enthusiastically at Milan and in many other opera-houses of Europe. In 1835 ' Chiara di Montalbano ' failed at La Scala, while ' La serva e l' ussero ' was applauded in Pavia. Ricci had thus composed twenty operas when only 30 years old ; and although many of his works had met with a genuine and well-deserved success, he was still very poor and had to accept the post of musical director of the Trieste Cathedral and conductor of the Opera. In 1838 his ' Nozze di Figaro ' was a fiasco in Milan, where Rossini told him that its fall was due to the music being *too serious*. For the next six years Ricci composed nothing. In 1844 he married Lidia Stoltz, by whom he had two children, ADELAIDE, who in 1867 sang at the Théâtre des Italiens in Paris, but died soon after, and LUIGI, who settled in London.

' La solitaria delle Asturie ' was given in Odessa in 1844 ; ' Il birraio di Preston ' in Florence in 1847 ; and in 1852 ' La festa di Piedigrotta ' was very successful in Naples. His last opera, ' Il Diavolo a quattro,' was performed in Trieste in 1859. He composed in collaboration with his brother FEDERICO ' Il colonnello,' given in Rome, and ' M. de Chalumeaux,' in Venice, in 1835 ; in 1836 ' Il disertore per amore ' for the San Carlo in Naples, and ' L'amante di richiamo,' given in Turin in 1846. Of these four operas, ' Il colonnello ' alone had a well-deserved reception. But the opera which placed him in a very high rank among Italian composers is

' Crispino e la comare,' written in 1850 for Venice, and to which his brother Federico partly contributed. This opera, one of the best comic operas of Italy, enjoyed a long success all the world over.

Shortly after the production of ' Il Diavolo a quattro' in 1859, however, symptoms of insanity showed themselves, and the malady soon became violent. He was taken to an asylum at Prague, his wife's birthplace, and died there. At Trieste a funeral ceremony was followed by a performance of selections from his principal works, his bust was placed in the lobby of the Opera-house, and a pension was granted to his widow.

He published two volumes of vocal pieces entitled ' Mes Loisirs' and ' Les Inspirations du thé' (Ricordi), and he left in MS. a large number of compositions for the cathedral service. His brother,

(2) FEDERICO (b. Naples, Oct. 22, 1809; d. Conegliano, Italy, Dec. 10, 1877) entered the Royal Conservatorio of that town, where his brother was then studying, and received his musical education from Bellini and Zingarelli. In 1837 he gave ' La prigione d' Edimburgo' in Trieste. The barcarola of this opera, ' Sulla poppa del mio brick,' was for long one of the most popular melodies of Italy. In 1839 his ' Duello sotto Richelieu' was only moderately successful at La Scala, but in 1841 ' Michelangelo e Rolla' was applauded in Florence. In it sang Signora Strepponi, who afterwards married Verdi. ' Corrado d' Altamura' was given at La Scala in the same year. At the personal request of Charles Albert he composed in 1842 a cantata for the marriage of Victor Emmanuel, and another for a court festival. In 1843 his ' Vallombra' failed at La Scala. ' Isabella de' Medici ' (1844) in Trieste, ' Estella' (1846) in Milan, ' Griselda' (1847) and ' I due ritratti' (1850) in Venice, were all failures. ' Il marito e l'amante' was greatly applauded in Vienna in 1852, but his last opera, ' Il paniere d' amore,' given there the following year, did not succeed. He was then named musical director of the imperial theatres of St. Petersburg, which post he occupied for many years. Of the operas written in collaboration with his brother we have already spoken.

He brought out at the Fantaisies-Parisiennes, Paris, ' Une Folie à Rome,' Jan. 30, 1869, with great success. Encouraged by this he produced an opéra-comique in three acts, ' Le Docteur rose' (Bouffes-Parisiens, Feb. 10, 1872), and ' Une Fête à Venise,' a reproduction of his earlier work, ' Il marito e l' amante' (Athénée, Feb. 15, 1872). Shortly after this Federico retired to Conegliano in Italy. He was concerned partially or entirely in nineteen operas. He also left two masses, six albums or collections of vocal pieces (Ricordi), and many detached songs.      L. R.

RICCI, PASQUALE (b. Como, c. 1733), pupil of Vignati, Milan; entered a religious order and received the title ' abbate.' He travelled in Holland, England and France, where his symphonies, concertantes, quintets, quartets, trios, duets, sonatas, etc., were published and well received. He returned eventually to Como as maestro di cappella of the cathedral (Q.-L.; Riemann).

RICCIO, TEODORO (d. 1603 or 1604), a native of Brescia, who after holding the post of choirmaster at one of the churches of Brescia was in 1576 invited by George Frederick, Margrave of Brandenberg - Anspach, to be his Kapellmeister at Anspach. When in 1579 George Frederick became also Duke of Prussia, Riccio accompanied him as Kapellmeister to his new capital Königsberg, where, like Scandello, also a native of Brescia, in similar circumstances at Dresden, Riccio became a Lutheran, and seems to have settled for the rest of his life, with an occasional visit to Anspach. His adoption of Lutheranism made little difference to the nature of his compositions for use in church, as Latin was still largely used in the services of Lutheran court chapels, and so we find that his publications mainly consist of various volumes of Latin masses, motets and Magnificats a 4 to 8 or 12. Probably Johann Eccard, who was called to be his coadjutor at Königsberg from 1581, provided the music required for German texts. Besides the Latin works Q.-L. mentions two incomplete books of madrigals a 5 and 6, and one book of Canzone alla napolitana. Riccio is supposed to have died between 1603 and 1604, since in the latter year Eccard is known to have succeeded him definitely as Kapellmeister.    J. R. M.

RICERCARE (RICERCATA) (from ricercare, ' to search out'), an Italian term of the 17th century, signifying a fugue of the closest and most learned description. Frescobaldi's Ricercari (1615), which are copied out in one of Dr. Burney's note-books (B.M. Add. MSS. 11,588), are full of augmentations, diminutions, inversions and other contrivances, in fact recherchés or full of research. J. S. Bach has affixed the name to the 6-part fugue in his ' Musikalisches Opfer,' and the title of the whole contains the words in its initial—Regis Iussu Cantio Et Reliqua Canonica Arte Resoluta.

But the term was also employed for a fantasia on some popular song, street-cry, or such familiar theme. Dr. Cummings possessed a MS. book, dated 1580–1600, containing twenty-two ricercari by Cl. da Coreggio, Gianetto Palestina (sic), A. Vuillaert (sic), O. Lasso, Clemens non Papa, Cip. Rore and others —compositions in four and five parts, on ' Ce moy de May,' ' Vestiva i colli,' ' La Rossignol,' ' Susan un jour,' and other apparently popular songs. This use of the word appears to have been earlier than the other, as pieces of the kind by Adriano (1520–67) are quoted.    G.

RICH, JOHN (b. circa 1682; d. Nov. 26, 1761), son of Christopher Rich, patentee of Drury Lane Theatre. His father, having been compelled to quit Drury Lane, had erected a new theatre in Lincoln's Inn Fields, but died in 1714 when it was upon the eve of being opened. John Rich, together with his brother Christopher, then assumed the management and opened the house about six weeks after his father's death. Finding himself unable to contend against the superior company engaged at Drury Lane, he had recourse to the introduction of a new species of entertainment—pantomime—in which music, scenery, machinery[1] and appropriate costumes formed the prominent features. In these pieces he himself, under the assumed name of Lun, performed the part of Harlequin[2] with such ability as to extort the admiration of even the most determined opponents of that class of entertainment. (See BALLAD OPERA; BEGGAR'S OPERA; LINCOLN'S INN FIELDS THEATRE; PANTOMIME.) Encouraged by success he at length decided upon the erection of a larger theatre, the stage of which should afford greater facilities for scenic and mechanical display, and accordingly built the first Covent Garden Theatre, which he opened Dec. 7, 1732. Hogarth produced a caricature on the occasion of the removal to the new house, entitled ' Rich's Glory, or his Triumphal Entry into Covent Garden,' copies of which will be found in Wilkinson's Londina illustrata, and in H. Saxe Wyndham's Annals of Covent Garden Theatre, vol. i. He conducted the new theatre with great success until his death, relying much upon the attraction of his pantomimes and musical pieces, but by no means neglecting the regular drama. In his early days he had attempted tragic acting, but failed. He was buried Dec. 4, 1761, in Hillingdon churchyard, Middlesex. (For list of productions, etc., see D.N.B.)           W. H. H.

RICHAFORT, JEAN, a Flemish musician of the earlier part of the 16th century, whom we know on the authority of the poet Ronsard to have been a pupil of Josquin des Prés. He was one of the more distinguished composers of the period immediately after Josquin, in which with the retention of what was valuable in the older technique of contrapuntal artifice there was, as Wooldridge observes, a greater approach made towards purity of sound and beauty of expression. The only known dates of Richafort's career are that between 1543 and 1547 he was choirmaster of the church of St. Gilles, Bruges, but this is supposed to have been

towards the end of his life, since as early as 1519 a motet of his composition appears in one of the collections of Petrucci, the Motetti de la Corona, lib. ii. His works appeared only in the collections of the time, and specially in those of Attaingnant and Modernus between 1530 and 1550. Two masses are specially mentioned, one, ' O genetrix gloriosa,' published by Attaingnant 1532, and afterwards copied into the Sistine Chapel and other choir-books; the other, ' Veni Sponsa Christi,' 1540, based on one of his own motets, which Ambros describes as the finest of the collection of motets in which it appears. The motet has been reprinted in Maldeghem's ' Trésor.' A Requiem a 6 would seem from the account which Ambros gives of it to be on the whole more curious than beautiful, though it testifies to the aim after intensity of expression. While the other voices sing the ritual text, the two tenor sing in canon ' Circumdederunt me gemitus mortis,' and also reply to each other as if with exclamations of personal sorrow, ' c'est douleur non pareille.' If some of Richafort's works retain a character of antique severity, others, as Eitner observes, are remarkable for their wonderful beauty, clearness and simplicity. Several of his motets Ambros singles out for high praise. Of one which he mentions, ' Quem dicunt homines,' the opening portion is given by Wooldridge in the Oxf. Hist. Mus. vol. ii. pp. 269-70. Glarean gives in full Richafort's motet ' Christus resurgens ' as a good example of the polyphonic treatment of the Ionic mode. Of the fifteen chansons of Richafort in various collections, two fine specimens are accessible in modern reprints, ' De mon triste déplaisir ' in Commer Collectio xii., and ' Sur tous regrets ' in Eitner's re-publication of Ott's ' Liederbuch,' 1544.

            J. R. M.

RICHARD, LEWIS, master of the Queen's music under Elizabeth, organist of Magdalen College, Oxford.[3] He composed music to Davenant's masque, ' Salmacida spolia,' performed at Whitehall, Jan. 21, 1639.

            E. V. D. S.

RICHARD CŒUR DE LION, opéra-comique in 3 acts; words by Sedaine; music by Grétry. Produced Opéra-Comique Oct. 21, 1784.[4] Two versions were made for the English stage; General Burgoyne's was acted at Drury Lane in 1786, and Leonard MacNally's at Covent Garden in the same year. Thomas Linley adapted Grétry's music to one of them and the opera remained a standard work for many years.      G. ; addns. F. K.

RICHARDS, HENRY BRINLEY (b. Carmarthen, Nov. 13, 1817; d. London, May 1, 1885), son of Henry Richards, organist of St. Peter's, Carmarthen, was intended for the medical

---

[1] Most of Rich's machinery was invented by John Hoole, the translator of Tasso, and his father, Samuel Hoole, an eminent watchmaker.

[2] He played Harlequin in ' Cheats, or the Tavern Bilkers,' a pantomime by John Weaver (adapted from ' Les Fourberies de Scapin '), with music by Dr. Pepusch, in 1716–17.    W. H. G. F.

[3] Fétis's dates are questionable.

[4] See Beethoven for the variations on ' Une fièvre brûlante.' Another set attributed to Mozart is now considered spurious.

profession, but became a pupil of the R.A.M., where he obtained the King's scholarship in 1835, and again in 1837. He soon gained a high position in London as a pianist. As a composer he was financially very successful, his song 'God bless the Prince of Wales' (published in 1862) having reached a high pitch of popularity, even out of England, and his sacred songs, partsongs and pianoforte pieces having been most favourably received. An overture in F minor was performed in 1840. He composed additional songs for the English version of Auber's 'Crown Diamonds,' when produced at Drury Lane in 1846. He especially devoted himself to the study of Welsh music (upon which he lectured), and many of his compositions were inspired by his enthusiastic love for his native land. He exerted himself greatly in promoting the interests of the South Wales Choral Union on its visits to London in 1872 and 1873, when they successfully competed at the National Music Meetings at the Crystal Palace. (Addns. D.N.B.)                                    w. h. h.

RICHARDS, HENRY WILLIAM, Mus.D. Dunelm (b. London, Apr. 16, 1865), was for 35 years organist and choirmaster of Christ Church, Lancaster Gate (1886–1921), where he maintained a high musical standard. A professor of the organ and member of the Committee of Management of the R.A.M., he became Warden (virtually vice-principal) of that institution in 1924. He is examiner to and member of the Associated Board of the R.A.M. and R.C.M., and was president of the R.C.O. (1924). He is the author of Organ Accompaniment of the Church Services and Choir Training.                                    c.

RICHARDSON, ALFRED MADELEY 'b. Southend-on-Sea, June 1, 1868), organist, was educated at the R.C.M. and Keble College, Oxford, where he took the degree of Mus.D. in 1897. From that year until 1908 he was organist of Southwark Cathedral, where he did much to establish the high reputation of the cathedral music. In 1909 he went to America as organist of St. Paul's Church, Baltimore, and since 1912 has been on the teaching staff of the Institute of Musical Art, New York. His publications include church music and works on the technique of organ playing and choir training.                                    c.

RICHARDSON, FERDINAND (real name FERDINANDO HEYBOURNE) (b. circa 1558; d. Tottenham, Middlesex, June 4, 1618), pupil of Tallis, groom of the Privy Chamber in 1587; pensioned, 1611. Eight pieces of his are in the 'Fitzwilliam Virginal Book,' others are in B.M. Add. MSS. 30,485. A Latin poem of his is in 'Cantiones sacrae' by Tallis and Byrd (1575).                                    e. v. d. s.

RICHARDSON, JOSEPH (b. 1814; d. Mar. 22, 1862), eminent flute-player. He was engaged in most of the London orchestras, was solo-player at Jullien's concerts for many years, and afterwards became principal flute in the Queen's private band. He played at the Melodists' Club and the Società Armonica in 1836, and was a member of the Liszt concert party in 1841. His neatness and rapidity of execution were extraordinary, and were the great features of his playing. He composed numerous fantasias for his instrument, usually extremely brilliant.       G.; addn. w. h. g. f.

RICHARDSON, VAUGHAN (b. London, latter half of 17th cent.; d. before June 26, 1729), was in 1675[1] a chorister of the Chapel Royal, under Dr. Blow. He was possibly a nephew of Thomas Richardson (alto singer, gentleman of the Chapel Royal from 1664 to his death, July 23, 1712, lay-vicar of Westminster Abbey), and a brother of Thomas Richardson, who was his fellow-chorister. In June 1692 he was appointed organist of Winchester Cathedral. In 1701 he published 'A collection of Songs for one, two and three voices, accompany'd with instruments.' He was author of some church music: a fine anthem, 'O Lord God of my salvation,' and an Evening Service in C (composed in 1713), are in the Tudway Collection (Harl. MSS. 7341 and 7342), and another anthem, 'O how amiable,' also in Tudway, and printed in Page's 'Harmonia sacra'; others are in the books of different cathedrals. He was also composer of 'An Entertainment of new Musick, composed on the Peace' (of Ryswick), 1697; 'A Song in praise of St. Cecilia,' written for a celebration at Winchester about 1700, and a 'set of vocal and instrumental music,' written for a like occasion in 1703. An autograph volume of music, containing fourteen anthems, a 'Song for the King' (1697), six sonatas for strings, etc., was in the possession of J. S. Bumpus.

w. h. h.

RICHARDSON, WILLIAM (b. late 17th cent.; d. circa 1731–32), a chorister in the Chapel Royal under Blow; organist of St. Nicholas, Deptford, in 1697. He composed Lessons for the harpsichord or spinet (London, 1708); 'The Pious Recreation,' containing 'A new sett of Psalm-tunes' (1729); among the latter appears the popular psalm-tune 'Greenwich' (Brown & Stratton; Q.-L.).

RICHAULT, (1) CHARLES SIMON (b. Chartres, May 10, 1780; d. Paris, Feb. 20, 1866), head of a family of celebrated French music-publishers, came early to Paris, and served his apprenticeship in the music-trade with J. J. Momigny. From him he acquired a taste for the literature of music and chamber compositions; and when he set up for himself at No. 7 Rue Grange Batelière in 1805, the first works he published were classical. He soon perceived that there was an opening in Paris for editions of the best works of German musicians, and the early efforts of French composers of promise. Accordingly he was the first to publish Beethoven's symphonies and Mozart's concertos in score; to make known in France the oratorios of Bach and Handel, and the works of Schubert, Mendelssohn and Schumann; to bring out the first operas of Ambroise Thomas and Victor Massé; to encourage Berlioz when his 'Damnation de Faust' was received with contempt, and to welcome the orchestral compositions of Reber and Gouvy. His business increased rapidly, and he was soon obliged to move into larger premises in the Boulevard Poissonnière, first at No. 16, and then at No. 26. Here he published Mozart's concertos in 8vo score, and other works of the classical composers of Germany, and acquired the bulk of the stock of the firms of Frey, Naderman, Sieber, Pleyel, Petit, Erard and Delahante. He moved in 1862 to No. 4 in the Boulevard des Italiens. In this house he died. His son,

(2) GUILLAUME SIMON (b. Paris, Nov. 2, 1806; d. Feb. 7, 1877), had long been his father's partner, and continued in the old line of serious music. He bought the stock of the publisher Pacini. On his death his son,

(3) LÉON (b. Paris, Aug. 6, 1839; d. there, Apr. 7, 1895), resolved to give a fresh impetus to the firm, which already possessed 18,000 publications. His intelligent administration of his old and honourable business procured him a silver medal at the International Exhibition of 1878, the highest recompense open to music-publishers, the jury having refused them the gold medal. The music stock belonging to this firm is now in the possession of the publishers, Costallat, Paris.    G. C.

RICHTER, ERNST FRIEDRICH EDUARD (b. Gross-schönau, Lusatia, Oct. 24, 1808; d. Leipzig, Apr. 9, 1879), son of a schoolmaster. From his eleventh year he attended the Gymnasium at Zittau, managed the choir, and arranged independent performances. In 1831 he went to Leipzig to study with Weinlig, the then cantor, and made such progress that soon after the foundation of the Conservatorium, in 1843, he became one of the professors of harmony and counterpoint. Up to 1847 he conducted the Singakademie; he was afterwards organist successively of the Peterskirche (1851) and the Neukirche and Nicolaikirche (1862). After Hauptmann's death, Jan. 3, 1868, he succeeded him as cantor of the Thomasschule. Of his books, the Lehrbuch der Harmonie (afterwards called Praktische Studien zur Theorie), (12th ed. 1876), has been translated into Dutch, Swedish, Italian, Russian, Polish and English. The Lehre von der Fuge has passed through three editions, and Vom Contrapunct through two. The English translations of all these are by Franklin Taylor, and

were published by Cramer & Co. in 1864, 1878 and 1874 respectively. Richter also published a Catechism of Organ-building. Of his many compositions de circonstance the best known is the cantata 'Dithyrambe,' for the Schiller Festival in 1859. Other works are—an oratorio, 'Christus der Erlöser' (Mar. 8, 1849), masses, psalms, motets, organ-pieces, string-quartets and sonatas for PF. He became one of the King's Professors in 1868, and on his death was succeeded as cantor by W. Rust.    F. G.

RICHTER, FERDINAND TOBIAS (b. Würzburg, 1649; d. Vienna, 1711), succeeded Alessandro Poglietti as Imperial court organist at Vienna in 1683. In Q.-L. he is wrongly said to have been the teacher in composition of the Emperor Leopold I., but he was undoubtedly music teacher to Leopold's children, the future Emperor Joseph I. and the three Archduchesses. Richter enjoyed a high reputation as organ-player and composer. Several even of Pachelbel's pupils at Nuremberg came afterwards to Vienna to perfect themselves in organ-playing by further instructions from Richter, and Pachelbel himself must have held Richter in high esteem, since in 1699 he dedicated to him along with Buxtehude his organ or clavier work entitled 'Hexachordum Apollinis.' It is all the more remarkable that so few organ works of Richter have been preserved. D.T.Ö. xiii. 2 contains three clavier suites out of a set of five, and an organ toccata with short fugued versetti out of a set of five on the church tones intended for liturgical use, and printed for the first time, but these hardly suffice to explain his great reputation. The State (Imperial) Library at Vienna preserves in MS. two serenatas by Richter evidently intended for court festivities, 'L' Istro ossequioso' and 'Le promesse degli Dei'; also five spiritual dramas composed for performance by the pupils of the Jesuit college at Vienna. There are also some instrumental works, a sonata a 7 (described as for two trombe, one timpano, two violini, two viole da braccio e cembalo), along with some balletti a 4 and a 5, also two sonatas a 8.    J. R. M.

RICHTER, FRANZ XAVER (b. Höllischau, Moravia, Dec. 1 or 31,[1] 1709; d. Sept. 12, 1789). His first official post was that of Kapellmeister to the Abbot of Kempten, which he held from 1740–50, when difficulties appear to have arisen with the authorities as the result of his duplication of posts. He had been a bass-singer at the court of Mannheim since 1747, and no doubt this was the cause of his dismissal from Kempten. He is stated by F. Walter, Geschichte des Theaters, etc. (1898), to have appeared in operatic performances in

---

[1] Gerber's Lexikon, followed by Riemann, in his Lexikon, and in his preface to the Denkm. volume containing works by Richter, gives Dec. 1 as the date of birth: Q.-L. follows Lobstein's Beiträge, etc., in giving Dec. 31 as the date.

1748 and 1749. He was also engaged as leader of the second violins in the orchestra. An oratorio, ' La deposizione della croce,' was performed at Mannheim in 1748. He left Mannheim for Strassburg in 1769, becoming Kapellmeister at the Minster, and spending the remainder of his life there. On his death he was succeeded by Ignaz Pleyel, who, according to Fétis, had acted as his assistant for six years. Burney, in his *Present State (Germany)*, ii. 327, speaks of the great reputation Richter enjoyed, and of the want of real individuality in his music.[1] He speaks of his frequent employment of the device called ROSALIA. He left sixty-four symphonies, of which the themes of sixty-two are given in the volume devoted to the Mannheim school of symphonists in the *D.D.T.* (2nd series), iii. 1. Three of the symphonies are printed in full, and the preface contains a detailed account of the composer. *D.D.T.* (2nd series), vii. 1, contains a further example of Richter's symphonic work. An enormous mass of church music is ascribed to him in *Riemann*, such as 28 masses, 2 Requiems, 16 psalms, 38 motets, etc. *Q.-L.* gives a more limited list of extant works, and contains many doubtful statements concerning the composer.        M.

RICHTER, HANS (*b.* Raab, Hungary, Apr. 4, 1843; *d.* Bayreuth, Dec. 5, 1916), celebrated conductor. His father was Kapellmeister of the cathedral at Raab. His mother, *née* Josephine Csazinsky (*d.* Oct. 20, 1892), sang the part of Venus in ' Tannhäuser ' at the first performance in Vienna in 1857; she was afterwards a very successful teacher of singing in Vienna. The father died in 1853, and Hans was then placed at the Löwenburg Convict-School in Vienna. Thence he went into the choir of the court chapel, and remained there for four years. In 1860 he entered the Conservatorium, and studied the horn under Kleinecke, the violin under Heissler and theory under Sechter.

After a lengthened engagement as horn-player in the orchestra of the Kärnthnerthor Opera he was recommended by Esser to Wagner, went to him at Lucerne, remained there from Oct. 1866 to Dec. 1867, and made the first fair copy of the score of ' Die Meistersinger.' In 1868 he accepted the post of conductor at the Hof- und National Theater, Munich, and remained there for a year. He next visited Paris, and after a short residence there, proceeded to Brussels for the production of ' Lohengrin ' (Mar. 22, 1870). He then returned to Wagner at Lucerne, assisted at the first performance of the ' Siegfried Idyll ' (Dec. 1870), and made the fair copy of the score of the ' Der Ring des Nibelungen ' for the engraver. In Apr. 1871 he went to Pest as chief conductor of the National Theatre, a post to which he

---

[1] A string quartet in D played by the Lener Quartet (London, 1925) contains a conspicuously beautiful slow movement. Riemann mentions six string quartets.     C.

owed much of his great practical knowledge of the stage and stage business. In Jan. 1875 he conducted a grand orchestral concert in Vienna, which had the effect of attracting much public attention to him, and accordingly, after the retirement of Dessoff from the court opera, Richter was invited to take the post, which he entered upon in the autumn of 1875, concurrently with the conductorship of the Philharmonic concerts. In 1884–90 he conducted the concerts of the Gesellschaft der Musikfreunde.

He had conducted the rehearsals of ' Der Ring des Nibelungen ' at Bayreuth, and in 1876 he directed the whole of the rehearsals and performances of the Festival there, and, at the close of the third set of performances, received the Order of Maximilian from the King of Bavaria, and that of the Falcon from the Grand Duke of Weimar. In 1877 he produced ' Die Walküre ' in Vienna, and followed it in 1878 by the other portions of the trilogy. In 1878 he was made court Kapellmeister, and received the Order of Franz Josef. The high standard and position of the band of the Vienna opera-house is due to him.

His first introduction to English audiences was at the famous Wagner Concerts given in the Albert Hall in 1877, when he shared the duties of conductor with Wagner himself. In 1879 (May 5-12), 1880 (May 10-June 14) and 1881 (May 9-June 23) were started what were at first called ' Orchestral Festival Concerts,' but afterwards the ' Richter Concerts,' in London, which excited much attention, chiefly for the conductor's knowledge of the scores of Beethoven's symphonies and other large works, which he conducted without book. The Richter Concerts went on for many years with great success, but after Richter went to live in Manchester in 1897, as director of the Hallé Orchestra, the London concerts were given less regularly. They were succeeded by the concerts of the LONDON SYMPHONY ORCHESTRA (*q.v.*) (1904 *et seq.*). In 1882 and 1884 he conducted important performances of German operas in London, introducing ' Die Meistersinger ' and ' Tristan ' to the London public. Special performances of German opera at Covent Garden were conducted by Richter from 1904 until his retirement, and amongst all the activities in concert room and opera-house by which he furthered musical development in England his performances of ' The Ring of the Nibelungs ' in English for the first time (1909) are specially worthy of record as a landmark. Those performances laid the foundations of many successful careers of English singers. Richter conducted the triennial festival at BIRMINGHAM (*q.v.*) from 1885–1909, and continued his work at MANCHESTER (*q.v.*) until 1911. In that year he conducted ' Die Meistersinger ' at Bayreuth for the last time. He then lived in retirement at Bayreuth.     F. G. ; with addns. C.

RICOCHET. The employment of the bounding staccato—*staccato à ricochet*—is thus indicated in violin music. As the best examples of this bowing are to be found in the works of the French and Belgian composers, it is probable that it owes its invention to the father of virtuosity—Paganini. The same system which governs the flying staccato—so brilliantly applied by Paganini, de Bériot, Wieniawski, Vieuxtemps and latter-day virtuosi to the execution of swift chromatic passages—dominates the ricochet, but being thrown upon the strings less rapidly, and with more force, the effect is heavier. To accomplish this style of bowing neatly, the stick should be held so that the full breadth of the hair at the upper part shall fall upon the strings accurately. The wrist must remain flexible, while the fingers grip the bow firmly and relax to allow the bow to rebound. Two graceful examples of the application of the ricochet are to be found in the Bolero of de Bériot's ' Scène de ballet,' and in the Polonaise of Vieuxtemps's ' Ballade et Polonaise.'
         O. R.

RICORDI, (1) GIOVANNI (*b.* Milan, 1785 ; *d.* there, Mar. 15, 1853), founder of the well-known music-publishing house in Milan. He made his first hit with the score of Mosca's ' Pretendenti delusi.' Since that time the firm has published for all the great Italian *maestri,* down to Verdi and Boïto, and has added to them a large catalogue of modern works of all classes. The *Gazzetta musicale,* edited with great success by Mazzucato, had much influence on its prosperity. It possesses the whole of the original scores of the operas it has published—a most interesting collection. Giovanni's son and successor, (2) TITO (*b.* Oct. 29, 1811 ; *d.* Sept. 7, 1888), further enlarged the business. His son, (3) GIULIO DI TITO (*b.* Dec. 19, 1840 ; *d.* June 6, 1912), was a practised writer, a skilled draughtsman, a composer of drawing-room music, under the pseudonym of Burgmein, and in all respects a thoroughly cultivated man. On his death the firm came under the management of Dr. Carlo Clausetti, with whom Renzo Valcarenghi became associated in 1919. (See PERIODICALS.)
         F. G., with addns.

RIDDELL (RIDDLE), JOHN (*b.* Ayr, Sept. 2, 1718 ; *d.* Apr. 5, 1795), composer of Scottish dance music. It is stated in ' The Ballads and Songs of Ayrshire,' 1846, that Riddell was blind from infancy, also that he was composer of the well-known tune ' Jenny's Bawbee.' This latter statement is not authenticated. Burns mentions him as ' a bard-born genius,' and says he is composer of ' this most beautiful tune ' (' Finlayston House ').

Riddell published about 1766 his first ' Collection of Scots Reels, or Country Dances, and Minuets,' and a second edition of it, in oblong folio, in 1782.     F. K.

RIDDELL, ROBERT (*d.* Friars' Carse, Apr. 21, 1794), a Scottish antiquary, and friend of Robert Burns. He was an army (or Volunteer) captain, and resided on the family estate Glenriddell, Dumfriesshire. He was an amateur composer of Scottish dance music, and wrote the music to one or two of Burns's songs. His most interesting publication (1794) is ' A Collection of Scotch, Galwegian, and Border Tunes . . . selected by Robert Riddell of Glenriddell, Esq.,' folio.     F. K.

RIDOTTO, see REDOUTE.

RIEDEL, CARL (*b.* Kronenberg, Rhine provinces, Oct. 6, 1827 ; *d.* Leipzig, June 3, 1888). Though always musically inclined he was educated for trade, and was at Lyons in the silk business until 1848, when he determined to devote himself to music as a profession. He returned home and at once began serious study under the direction of Carl Wilhelm, then an obscure musician at Crefeld, but destined to be widely known as the author of ' Die Wacht am Rhein.' Late in 1849 Riedel entered the Leipzig Conservatorium, where he made great progress under Moscheles, Hauptmann, Becker and Plaidy. He practised and performed in a private society at Leipzig Astorga's Stabat, Palestrina's ' Improperia ' and Leo's Miserere, and this led him to found a singing society of his own, which began on May 17, 1854, with a simple quartet of male voices, and was the foundation of the famous Association which, under the name of the ' Riedelsche Verein,' became celebrated in Leipzig. The first public concert was held in Nov. 1855, and its first great achievement was a performance of Bach's B minor Mass, Apr. 10, 1859. In the list of the works performed by the Verein we find Beethoven's Mass in D, Kiel's ' Christus,' Berlioz's ' Messe des morts,' and Liszt's ' Graner Messe ' and ' St. Elizabeth.' Riedel was one of the founders of the ' Beethovenstiftung,' and an earnest supporter of the Wagner performances at Bayreuth in 1876. His own compositions are chiefly partsongs for men's voices, but he edited several important ancient works by Praetorius, Franck, Eccard and other old German writers, especially a ' Passion ' by Heinrich Schütz, for which he selected the best portions of four Passions by that master —a proceeding certainly deserving all that can be said against it.     G.

RIEDER, AMBROSIUS (*b.* Döbling, near Vienna, Oct. 10, 1771 ; *d.* Perchtoldsdorf, near Vienna, Nov. 19, 1855), was ' regens chori ' at the time of his death. He was a pupil of Albrechtsberger, and a prolific composer, credited with having written 427 works, including masses and other church music, chamber music and numerous organ fugues, preludes, etc. His ' Ecce panis ' is still in use in the Feast of Corpus Christi. He also wrote instruction books for thorough-bass playing, improvising and fugal playing. Rieder was a friend of Schubert's brother, Ferdinand, and of S. Sechter (*Riemann*; *Q.-L.*).

RIEMANN, KARL WILHELM JULIUS HUGO (*b.* Grossmehlra, near Sondershausen, July 18, 1849; *d.* Leipzig, July 10, 1919), one of the most famous of German musical historians in the 19th century, studied law, etc., at Berlin and Tübingen. He saw active service in the Franco-German war, and afterwards devoted his life to music, studying in the Leipzig Conservatorium.

After some years' residence at Bielefeld as a teacher, he was appointed to the post of ' Privatdozent ' in the University of Leipzig, which he held from 1878–80, going thence to Bromberg; in 1881–90 he was teacher of the piano and theory in the Hamburg Conservatorium, and subsequently (after a three months' stay at the Conservatorium of Sondershausen) was given a post at the Conservatorium of Wiesbaden (1890–95). In the latter year he returned to Leipzig, as a lecturer in the University, and in 1901 was appointed professor.

Riemann was amazingly active as a writer on every branch of musical knowledge, but his work was as thorough as if it had been small in extent. First in public importance among his works stands the *Musiklexikon* (1882), which attained to eight editions during his life (see DICTIONARIES OF MUSIC), and beside it may be mentioned the useful *Opernhandbuch* (1884 – 93) and the *Handbuch der Musikgeschichte* (see list below). On the teaching of harmony, on musical phrasing and the peculiarities of notation required for explaining his system to students, he strongly supported various innovations, most of them due to his own inventive faculty. As a practical illustration of his excellent method of teaching the art of phrasing, his editions of classical and romantic pianoforte music, called ' Phrasierungsausgaben,' may be mentioned. He edited many masterpieces of ancient music, notably in several volumes of the second series (Bayern) of *D.D.T.* (*q.v.*). His original compositions—for he found time to write music as well as musical literature—are numerous but not very important, being mainly of an educational kind.

The following is a chronological list of Riemann's more important literary works on the theory and history of music :

*Vom musikalischen Hören.* 1873.
*Musikalische Syntaxis.* 1877.
*Studien zur Geschichte der Notenschrift.* 1878.
*Die Entwickelung unserer Notenschrift.* 1881.
*Musiklexikon.* 1882. (Trans. English 1893, French 1896, Russian, Danish, abbrev.)
*Die Natur der Harmonik.* 1882. (Trans. English.)
*Neue Schule der Melodik.* 1883.
*Vergleichende Klavierschule.* 1883.
*Der Ausdruck in der Musik.* 1883.

*Musikalische Dynamik und Agogik.* 1884. (Trans. Russian.)
*Opernhandbuch.* 1884–93.
*Praktische Anleitung zum Phrasieren.* 1886.
*Handbuch der Harmonielehre.* 1887. (Trans. French, Italian.)
*Systematische Modulationslehre.* 1887. (Trans. Russian.)
*Lehrbuch des einfachen, doppelten und imitierenden Kontrapunkts.* 1888. (Trans. English.)
*Katechismus der Musik.* 1888. (Trans. Czech.)
*Musikinstrumente.* 1888. (Trans. English.)
*Katechismus der Musikgeschichte.* 1888. (Trans. English, Italian, Czech Russian.)
*Katechismus der Klavierspiel.* 1888. (Trans. English, Russian, Czech.)
*Katechismus der Kompositionslehre.* 1889.
*Generalbassspiel.* 1889.
*Musikdiktat.* 1889.
*Katechismus der Harmonielehre.* 1890.
*Katechismus der Fuge.* (Analysis of Bach's ' 48 ' and Art of Fugue.) 1890–91.
*Katechismus der Gesangskomposition.* 1891.
*Vereinfachte Harmonielehre.* 1893. (Trans. English, French, Russian.)
*Notenschrift und Notendruck.* 1896.
*Geschichte der Musiktheorie im 9-19 Jahrh.* 1898.
*Epochen und Heroen der Musikgeschichte.* 1900.
*Geschichte der Musik seit Beethoven.* 1901
*Grosse Kompositionslehre.* 1902–3.
*Orchestrierung.* 1902. (Trans. English, Czech.)
*Partiturspiel.* 1903. (Trans. English.)
*Das Problem des harmonischen Dualismus.* 1905.
*Handbuch der Musikgeschichte.* Published in parts as follows :
    I. (i.) Early Period. 1901.
    I. (ii.) The Middle Ages. 1905.
    II. (i.) Renaissance, 1300–1600. 1907
    II. (ii.) The Thoroughbass Epoch, 1600–1700. 1911.
    II. (iii.) The Great German Masters. 1912
*Kleines Handbuch der Musikgeschichte.*
*Die byzantinische Notenschrift im 10-15 Jahrh.* 1909.
*Folkloristische Tonalitätsstudien.* 1916.

BIBL.—MENNICKE, *Riemann Festschrift*, 1909; WILIBALD GURLITT, *H. Riemann und die Musikgeschichte*, Z.M.W., 1919.

M. ; addns. from *Riemann*, etc.

RIEMSDIJK, J. C. M. VAN (*b.* 1843 ; *d.* Utrecht, June 30, 1895), was a member of an aristocratic family, and an enthusiastic amateur musician. He was a cultivated scholar, and devoted himself to editing the old songs of the Netherlands with marked success. He became Technical Director of the State railway. His house was always open to any artists, and his welcome was always ready for those who followed music as a profession.

He was chairman of the ' Vereeniging voor N.-Nederlands Musikgeschiedenis ' (Society of Musical History in the North Netherlands), in which capacity he doubtless had many facilities for collecting old Netherland Folk-Songs, of which he availed himself in the most able manner. His works are as follows :

1881. *State Music School of Utrecht*, 1631–1881 (a complete history of the Art of Music in the Netherlands between those dates).
*1882. Netherland Dances arranged for PF. duet.
1888. The two first music books of Tylman Susato (*c.* 1545), a collection of Netherland Folk-Songs of the 16th century.
*1888. Hortus Musicus of J. A. Reincken (1623–1722) for two violins, viola and bass (translation into Dutch).
*1890. Twenty-four Songs of the 15th and 16th centuries with PF. accompaniment.
1896. Folk-Song book of the Netherlands (posthumous).

The works marked thus * are among the publications of the Vereeniging voor N.-Nederlands Musikgeschiedenis.

D. H.

RIENZI, DER LETZTE DER TRIBUNEN (the last of the Tribunes), opera in 5 acts ; words founded on Bulwer's novel ; music by Wagner. Produced Dresden, Oct. 20, 1842 ; in French (Nuitter and Guillaume), Théâtre-Lyrique, Apr. 16, 1869 ; New York, Academy of Music, 1878 ; in English, Her Majesty's Theatre (Carl Rosa), Jan. 27, 1879.

G.

RIEPEL, JOSEPH (*b.* Horschlag, Austria, 1708; *d.* Ratisbon, Oct. 23, 1782), Kapellmeister to the Prince Thurn and Taxis. He composed church music, operas, concertos and chamber music, which remained mostly in MS. His theoretical works, which were all published, enjoyed a great reputation as works of sterling value. A list of these is given in *Q.-L.* and *Riemann*.

RIES. A distinguished family of musicians.

(1) JOHANN (*b*. Benzheim on the Rhine, 1723 ; *d*. Cologne, 1784) was appointed court trumpeter to the Elector of Cologne at Bonn, with a salary of 192 thalers, May 2, 1747, and violinist in the chapel, Mar. 5, 1754.

On Apr. 27, 1764, his daughter (2) ANNA MARIA was appointed singer. In 1774 she married Ferdinand Drewer, violinist in the band, and remained first soprano till the break-up in 1794.

Her brother (3) FRANZ ANTON (*b*. Bonn, Nov. 10, 1755 ; *d*. Nov. 1, 1846) was an infant phenomenon on the violin ; learned from J. P. Salomon ; and was able to take his father's place in the orchestra at the age of 11. His salary began when he was 19, at 25 thalers a year ; he occupied the post until 1774. In 1779 he visited Vienna, and made a great success as a solo and quartet player. But he elected to remain, on poor pay, in Bonn, and was rewarded by having Beethoven as his pupil and friend. On Mar. 2, 1779, he petitioned the Elector Maximilian for a post, and received it on May 2. During the poverty of the Beethoven family, and through the misery caused by the death of Ludwig's mother in 1787, Franz Ries stood by them like a real friend. In 1794 the French arrived, and the Elector's establishment was broken up. Some of the members of the band dispersed, but Ries remained, and documents are preserved which show that after the passing away of the invasion he was to have been court-musician.[1] Events, however, were otherwise ordered ; he remained in Bonn, and at Godesberg, where he had a little house, till his death ; held various small offices, culminating in the Bonn city government in 1800, taught the violin, and brought up his children well. He assisted Wegeler in his Notices of Beethoven, was present at the unveiling of Beethoven's statue in 1845, had a Doctor's degree and the Order of the Red Eagle conferred on him.

Franz's son (4) FERDINAND (*b*. Bonn, Nov.[2] 1784 ; *d*. Aix-la-Chapelle, Jan. 13, 1838), who with the Archduke Rudolph enjoys the distinction of being Beethoven's pupil, was brought up from his cradle to music. His father taught him the pianoforte and violin, and B. Romberg the violoncello. In his childhood he lost an eye through small-pox. After the break-up of the Elector's band he remained three years at home, working very hard at theoretical and practical music, scoring the quartets of Haydn and Mozart, and

[1] See the curious and important lists and memorandums, published for the first time in Thayer's *Beethoven*, i. 248.
[2] Baptized Nov. 28.

arranging the 'Creation,' the 'Seasons' and the Requiem with such ability that they were all three published by Simrock.

In 1801 he went to Munich to study under Winter, in a larger field than he could command at home. Here he was so badly off as to be driven to copy music at 3d. a sheet. But poor as his income was he lived within it, and when after a few months Winter left Munich for Paris Ries had saved seven ducats. With this he went to Vienna in Oct. 1801, taking a letter from his father to Beethoven. Beethoven received him well, and when he had read the letter said, ' I can't answer it now ; but write and tell him that I have not forgotten the time when my mother died ' ; and, knowing how miserably poor the lad was, he on several occasions gave him money unasked, for which he would accept no return. The next three years Ries spent in Vienna. Beethoven took a great deal of pains with his pianoforte-playing, but would teach him nothing else. He, however, prevailed on Albrechtsberger to take him as a pupil in composition. The lessons cost a ducat each ; Ries had in some way saved up twenty-eight ducats, and therefore had twenty-eight lessons. Beethoven also got him an appointment as pianist to Count Browne, the Russian *chargé d'affaires*, and at another time to Count Lichnowsky. The pay for these services was probably not over-abundant, but it kept him, and the position gave him access to the best musical society. As to Ries's relations with Beethoven see BEETHOVEN, Vol. I. p. 283 ; they are fully laid open in Ries's own invaluable notices. He had a great deal to bear, and, considering the secrecy and imperiousness which Beethoven often threw into his intercourse with every one, there was probably much unpleasantness in the relationship. Meantime Ries must have become saturated with the music of his great master ; a thing which could hardly tend to foster any little originality he may ever have possessed.

As a citizen of Bonn he was amenable to the French conscription, and in 1805 was summoned to appear there in person. He left in Sept. 1805, made the journey on foot *via* Prague, Dresden and Leipzig, reached Coblenz within the prescribed limit of time, and was then dismissed on account of the loss of his eye. He then went on to Paris, and existed in misery for apparently at least two years, at the end of which time he was advised to try Russia. On Aug. 27, 1808, he was again in Vienna, and soon afterwards received from Reichardt an offer of the post of Kapellmeister to Jerome Bonaparte, King of Westphalia, at Cassel, which Reichardt alleged had been refused by Beethoven. Ries behaved with perfect loyalty and straightforwardness in the matter. Before replying, he endeavoured to find out from Beethoven himself the real state of the case; but Beethoven, having adopted the idea that Ries was trying to get the post over his head, would not see him, and for three weeks behaved to him with an incredible degree of cruelty and insolence. When he could be made to listen to the facts he was sorry enough, but the opportunity was gone.

The occupation of Vienna (May 12, 1809) by the French was not favourable to artistic life. Ries, however, as a French subject, was free to wander. He accordingly went to Cassel, possibly with some lingering hopes, played at court, and remained till the end of Feb. 1810, very much applauded and fêted, and making money—but had no offer of a post. From Cassel he went by Hamburg and Copenhagen to Stockholm, where we find him in Sept. 1810, making both money and reputation. He had still his eye on Russia, but between Stockholm and St. Petersburg the ship was taken by an English man-of-war, and all the passengers were turned out upon an island in the Baltic. In St. Petersburg he found Bernhard Romberg, and the two made a successful tour, embracing places as wide apart as Kiev, Reval and Riga. The burning of Moscow (Sept. 1812) put a stop to his progress in that direction, and we next find him again at Stockholm in Apr. 1813, *en route* for England. By the end of the month he was in London.

Here he found his countryman and his father's friend, Salomon, who received him cordially and introduced him to the Philharmonic Concerts. His first appearance there was Mar. 14, 1814, in his own PF. Sextet. His symphonies, overtures and chamber works frequently occur in the programmes, and he himself appears from time to time as a PF. player, but rarely if ever with works of Beethoven. Shortly after his arrival he married an English lady of great attractions, and he remained in London till 1824, one of the most conspicuous figures of the musical world. ' Mr. Ries,' says a writer in the *Harmonicon* of Mar. 1824,

' is justly celebrated as one of the finest pianoforte performers of the day ; his hand is powerful and his execution certain, often surprising ; but his playing is most distinguished from that of all others by its romantic wildness.'

His sojourn here was a time of herculean labour. His compositions numbered at their close nearly 180, including 6 fine symphonies ; 4 overtures ; 6 string quintets, and 14 do. quartets ; 9 concertos for PF. and orchestra ; an octet, a septet, 2 sextets and a quintet, for various instruments ; 3 PF. quartets and 5 do. trios ; 20 duets for PF. and violin ; 10 sonatas for PF. solo ; besides a vast number of rondos, variations, fantasias, etc., for the PF. solo and duet. Of these 38 are attributable to the time of his residence here, and they embrace 2 symphonies, 4 concertos, a sonata and many smaller pieces. As a pianist and teacher he

was very much in request. He was an active member of the Philharmonic Society. His correspondence with Beethoven during the whole period is highly creditable to him, proving his gratitude towards his master, and the energy with which he laboured to promote Beethoven's interests. That Beethoven profited so little therefrom was no fault of Ries's.

Having accumulated a fortune adequate to the demands of a life of comfort, he gave a farewell concert in London, Apr. 8, 1824, and removed with his wife to Godesberg, near his native town, where he had purchased a property. Though a loser by the failure of a London bank in 1825–26, he was able to live independently. About 1830 he removed to Frankfort. His residence on the Rhine brought him into close contact with the Lower Rhine Festivals, and he directed the performances of the years 1825, 1829, 1830, 1832, 1834 and 1837, as well as those of 1826 and 1828 in conjunction with Spohr and Klein respectively. In 1834 he was appointed head of the town orchestra and Singakademie at Aix-la-Chapelle. But he was too independent to keep any post, and in 1836 he gave this up and returned to Frankfort. In 1837 he assumed the direction of the Cecilian Society there on the death of Schelble, but this lasted a few months only, for on Jan. 13, 1838, he died after a short illness.

The principal works which he composed after his return to Germany are ' Die Räuberbraut,' which was first performed in Frankfort probably in 1829, then in Leipzig, July 4, and London, July 15, of the same year, and often afterwards in Germany ; another opera, known in Germany as ' Liska,' but produced at the Adelphi, London, in English, as ' The Sorcerer,' by Arnold's company, Aug. 4, 1831, and a third, ' Eine Nacht auf dem Libanon ' ; an oratorio, ' Der Sieg des Glaubens ' (The Triumph of the Faith), apparently performed in Dublin for the first time in 1831[1] and then at Berlin, 1835 ; and a second oratorio, ' Die Könige Israels ' (The Kings of Israel), Aix-la-Chapelle, 1837. He also wrote much chamber music and six symphonies. All these works, however, are dead. Beethoven once said of his compositions, ' he imitates me too much.' He caught the style and the phrases, but he could not catch the immortality of his master's work. One work of his will live—the admirable *Biographical Notices of Ludwig van Beethoven*, which he published in conjunction with Dr. Wegeler (Coblenz, 1838). The two writers, though publishing together, have fortunately kept their contributions quite distinct ; Ries's occupies from pp. 76 to 163 of a little duodecimo volume, and of these the last thirty-five pages are occupied by Beethoven's letters. The work is translated into French by Le

1 Information from L. M'C. L. Dix, Esq.

Gentil (Dentu, 1862), and partially into English by Moscheles, as an Appendix to his version of Schindler's *Life of Beethoven*.

A. W. T.

(5) PIETER JOSEPH (*b*. Bonn, Apr. 6, 1791; *d*. London, Apr. 6, 1882), a brother and devoted admirer of FERDINAND, whose compositions were cherished by him until death, when they passed into the care of A. J. Hipkins, who later restored them to the Ries family.

Ries was also a musician, but his active life was spent partly in the Broadwood House as the foreign correspondent; and earlier with the East India Company during the period of Charles Lamb.[1] Although a busy man, he gave his spare time either to teaching or playing music, and also to finding a ready market for the eau de Cologne of his countrymen and friends the Farinas.

He was a staunch Roman Catholic and a good friend. He did not marry. Young as he was in the bitter winter of 1794, he well remembered the advent of the French, and of the soldiers billeted on his father's crowded home, and of their helpfulness in fetching water, in chopping wood, and in amusing the children; perhaps, most of all, Napoleon, and the compelling glance of his eyes.    E. J. H².

(6) HUBERT (*b*. Bonn, Apr. 1, 1802; *d*. Berlin, Sept. 14, 1886), youngest brother of Ferdinand, made his first studies as a violinist under his father, and afterwards under Spohr. Hauptmann was his teacher in composition. From 1824 he lived at Berlin. In that year he entered the band of the Königstadt Theatre, Berlin, and in the following year became a member of the royal band. In 1835 he was appointed director of the Philharmonic Society at Berlin. In 1836 he was nominated Konzertmeister, and in 1839 elected a member of the Royal Academy of Arts. In 1851 he became a teacher at the Kgl. Theaterinstrumentalschule, from which he retired with a pension in 1872. A thorough musician and a solid violinist, he was held in great esteem as a leader, and more especially as a methodical and conscientious teacher. His Violin-School for beginners is a very meritorious work, eminently practical and widely used. He published two violin-concertos, studies and duets for violins, and some quartets. An English edition of the Violin-School appeared in 1873 (Hofmeister). Three of his sons gained reputation as musicians :

(7) LOUIS (*b*. Berlin, Jan. 30, 1830; *d*. London, Oct. 3, 1913), violinist, pupil of his father and of Vieuxtemps, settled in 1853 in London, where he enjoyed deserved reputation as violinist and teacher. He was a member of the Quartet of the Musical Union from 1855–

1870, and held the second violin at the Monday Popular Concerts from their beginning in 1859 until his retirement in 1897.

(8) ADOLPH (*b*. Berlin, Dec. 20, 1837; *d*. Apr. 1899), pianist, was a pupil of Kullak for the piano, and of Boehmer for composition, and lived in London as a pianoforte teacher. He published a number of compositions for the piano, and some songs.

(9) FRANZ (*b*. Berlin, Apr. 7, 1846), the youngest son of Hubert (6), studied the violin with his father and with Massart and Vieuxtemps in Paris. In 1870 he visited London, appearing at the Crystal Palace. His promising career as a violinist had to be abandoned owing to nerve trouble, and he went into business (Ries und Erler) in Berlin. His compositions include orchestral and chamber works. He edited the sonatas of Corelli and instrumented works of Schumann, etc.

A. W. T.; addns. E. H.-A., W. W. C., *Riemann*, etc.

RIETER-BIEDERMANN, an eminent German firm of music-publishers. The founder was JACOB MELCHIOR RIETER-BIEDERMANN (*b*. May 14, 1811; *d*. Jan. 25, 1876), who in June 1849 opened a retail business and lending-library at Winterthur. Since the first work was published in 1856, the business continually improved and increased. In 1862 a publishing branch was opened at Leipzig, which eventually became the headquarters of the firm. In 1917 it was acquired by Peters. The stock catalogue of the firm included music by Berlioz, Brahms (PF. concerto, PF. quintet, 'Requiem,' 'Magelone-Lieder,' etc.); A. Dietrich; J. O. Grimm; Gernsheim; von Herzogenberg; F. Hiller; Holstein; Kirchner; Lachner; F. Marschner; Mendelssohn (op. 98, Nos. 2, 3; opp. 103, 105, 106, 108, 115, 116); Raff; Reinecke; Schumann (opp. 130, 137, 138, 140, 142); etc.    G.

RIETI, VITTORIO (*b*. Alexandria, Jan. 28, 1898), composer, of Italian parentage and up bringing, had some teaching from G. Frugatta at Milan and O. Respighi at Rome. He is reported to have destroyed all his compositions written before 1920. Since then works by him have been produced at the festivals of the International Society for Contemporary Music, namely, a concerto for wind with orchestra (Prague, 1924), a suite from a ballet, 'Noah's Ark' (Prague, 1925), and a transcription for modern performance of a 'Sonata' by Monteverdi (Venice, 1925). His ballet 'Barabau' was produced by Diaghilev in London (Coliseum, Dec. 11, 1925).    C.

RIETZ (originally RITZ[2]), (1) EDUARD (*b*. Berlin, Oct. 17, 1802; *d*. Jan. 23, 1832), the elder brother of Julius Rietz, an excellent violinist, studied first under his father, a member of the royal band, and afterwards, for

---

[1] To Ries, Lamb's wit was incomprehensible. Once, on extolling the beauties of the Rhine, Lamb, who was peeling an apple, tossed him the paring, saying, ' There's the *rine* for you.' Evidently Ries was not aware of the British vernacular for ' rind.'

[2] Uniformly so spelt by Mendelssohn.

some time, under Rode. He died too young to acquire more than a local reputation, but Mendelssohn had the highest possible opinion of his powers as an executant.[1] It was for Rietz that he wrote the octet which is dedicated to him, as well as the sonata for PF. and violin, op. 4. For some years Rietz was a member of the royal band, but as his health failed him in 1824 he had to quit his appointment and even to give up playing. He founded and conducted an orchestral society at Berlin, with considerable success; he died of consumption. Mendelssohn's earlier letters teem with affectionate references to him, and the news of his death affected him deeply.[2] The Andante in Mendelssohn's string quintet, op. 18, was composed at Paris ' in memory of E. Rietz,' and is dated on the autograph ' Jan. 23, 1832,' and entitled ' Nachruf.'

(2) JULIUS (b. Berlin, Dec. 23, 1812; d. Dresden, Sept. 12, 1877), younger brother of the preceding, violoncellist, composer and eminent conductor. Brought up under the influence of his father and brother, and the intimate friend of Mendelssohn, he received his first instruction on the violoncello from Schmidt, a member of the royal band, and afterwards from Bernhard Romberg and Moritz Ganz. Zelter was his teacher in composition. He obtained, at the age of 16, an appointment in the band of the Königstadt Theater, where he also achieved his first success as a composer by writing incidental music for Holtei's drama, ' Lorbeerbaum und Bettelstab.' In 1834 he went to Düsseldorf as second conductor of the opera. Mendelssohn, who up to his death showed a warm interest in Rietz, was at that time at the head of the opera, and on his resignation in the summer of 1835, Rietz became his successor. He did not, however, remain long in that position, for, as early as 1836, he accepted, under the title of ' Städtischer Musikdirector,' the post of conductor of the public subscription concerts, the principal choral society, and the church-music at Düsseldorf. In this position he remained for twelve years. During this period he wrote some of his most successful works—incidental music to dramas of Goethe, Calderon, Immermann and others; music for Goethe's Liederspiel ' Jery und Bätely,' his first symphony in G minor; three overtures—' Hero and Leander,'[3] concert overture in A major, Lustspiel-overture, the ' Altdeutscher Schlachtgesang ' and ' Dithyrambe '—both for men's voices and orchestra. He was six times chief conductor of the Lower Rhine Festivals—in 1845, 1856 and 1869 at Düsseldorf; in 1864, 1867 and 1873 at Aix.

In 1847, after Mendelssohn's death, he took leave of Düsseldorf, leaving Ferdinand Hiller as his successor, and went to Leipzig as conductor of the opera and the Singakademie. He gave up the post at the opera in 1854. From 1848 we find him also at the head of the Gewandhaus orchestra, and teacher of composition at the Conservatorium. In this position he remained for thirteen years. Two operas, ' Der Corsar ' and ' Georg Neumark,' were failures, but his symphony in E♭ had a great and lasting success. At this period he began also to show his eminent critical powers by carefully revised editions of the scores of Mozart's symphonies and operas, of Beethoven's symphonies and overtures for Breitkopf & Härtel's complete edition, and by the work he did for the Bach and (German) Handel Societies. An edition of Mendelssohn's complete works closed his labours in this respect.

In 1860 the King of Saxony appointed him conductor of the Royal Opera and of the music at the Hofkirche at Dresden. He also accepted the post of Artistic Director of the Dresden Conservatorium. In 1874 the title of General-Musikdirector was given to him. The University of Leipzig had already in 1859 conferred on him the honorary degree of Doctor of Philosophy.

Rietz was for some time one of the most influential musicians of Germany. He was a good violoncellist, but soon after leaving Düsseldorf he gave up playing entirely. As a composer he showed a complete mastery of all technicalities, yet few of his works have shown any vitality.      P. D.

BIBL.—P. A. MERBACH, Briefwechsel zwischen Eduard Devrient und Julius Rietz, etc. A.M., July 1921.

RIGADOON (Fr. rigadon or rigaudon), a lively dance, which most probably came from Provence or Languedoc, although its popularity in England has caused some writers to suppose that it is of English origin. It was danced in France in the time of Louis XIII., but does not seem to have become popular in England until the end of the 17th century. According to Rousseau it derived its name from its inventor, one Rigaud, but others connect it with the English ' rig,' i.e. wanton or lively.

The Rigadoon was remarkable for a peculiar jumping step (which is described at length in Compan's Dictionnaire de la danse, Paris, 1802); this step survived the dance for some time. The music of the Rigadoon is in 2-4 or C time, and consists of three or four parts, of which the third is quite short. The number of bars is unequal, and the music generally begins on the third or fourth beat of the bar. The following example is from the third part of Henry Playford's ' Apollo's Banquet ' (sixth edition, 1690). The same tune occurs in ' The Dancing

---

[1] ' I long earnestly,' says he, in a letter from Rome, ' for his violin, and his depth of feeling; they come vividly before my mind when I see his beloved neat handwriting.'
[2] Mendelssohn's Letters from Italy and Switzerland, English translation, p. 327.
[3] See Mendelssohn's Letters, ii. p. 234 (Eng. ed.).

Master,' but in that work the bars are incorrectly divided:

RIGBY, George Vernon (b. Birmingham, Jan. 21, 1840), tenor singer, first appeared in London (Mar. 4, 1861) at the Alhambra, Leicester Square (then a concert room, managed by E. T. Smith), and in Aug. following at Mellon's Promenade Concerts at Covent Garden. In 1865 he sang in the provinces as a member of H. Corri's Opera Company, until November, when he went to Italy and studied under Sangiovanni at Milan, where, in Nov. 1866, he appeared at the Carcano Theatre as the Fisherman in ' Guglielmo Tell.' He next went to Berlin, and in Jan. 1867 appeared at the Victoria Theatre there, in the principal tenor parts in ' Don Pasquale,' ' La sonnambula ' and ' L' Italiana in Algieri.' He then accepted a three months' engagement in Denmark, and performed Almaviva in the ' Barbiere,' the Duke in ' Rigoletto ' and other parts, in Copenhagen and other towns. He returned to England in Sept. 1867, sang the part of Samson (Handel) at the Gloucester Festival (1868) in place of Sims Reeves, and was immediately engaged by the Sacred Harmonic Society, where he appeared, Nov. 27, 1868, with signal success. In 1869 he appeared on the stage of the Princess's Theatre as Acis in Handel's ' Acis and Galatea.'

RIGHINI, Vincenzo (b. Bologna, Jan. 22, 1756 ; d. there, Aug. 19, 1812), composer, singer and conductor.

As a boy he was a chorister at San Petronio and had a fine voice, but owing to injury it developed into a tenor of so rough and muffled a tone, that he turned his attention to theory, which he studied with Padre Martini. In 1776 he sang for a short time in the Opera Buffa at Prague, then under Bustelli's direction, but was not well received. He made a success there, however, with three operas of his composition, ' La vedova scaltra,' ' La bottega del caffè ' and ' Don Giovanni,' also performed in Vienna (Aug. 1777), whither Righini went on leaving Prague in 1780. There he became singing-master to Princess Elisabeth of Würtemberg, and conductor of the Italian opera. He next entered the service of the Elector of Mainz (1788–92) and composed for the Elector of Treves ' Alcide al Bivio ' (Coblenz) and a missa solennis (1790). In April 1793 (owing to the success of his ' Enea nel Lazio ') he was invited to succeed Alessandri at the Italian Opera of Berlin, with a salary of 3000 thalers (about £450). Here he produced ' Il trionfo d' Arianna ' (1793), ' Armida ' (1799), ' Tigrane' (1880), ' Gerusalemme liberata ' and ' La selva incantata ' (1802). The last two were published after his death with German text (Leipzig, Herklotz).

In 1793 Righini married Henriette Kneisel (b. Stettin, 1767 ; d. Berlin, Jan. 25, 1801), a charming blonde, and according to Gerber, a singer of great expression. She died of consumption. After the death of Friedrich Wilhelm II. (1797) his post became almost a sinecure, and in 1806 the opera was entirely discontinued. As a composer his best point was his feeling for ensemble, of which the quartet in ' Gerusalemme ' is a good example. He was a successful teacher of singing, and counted distinguished artists among his pupils. After the loss of a promising son in 1810, his health gave way, and in 1812 he was ordered to try the effects of his native air at Bologna. His own Requiem (score in the Berlin Library) was performed by the Singakademie in his honour.

Besides 20 operas, of which a list is given by Fétis (13 are mentioned in Q.-L. as still extant), Righini composed church music—a Te Deum and a Missa Solennis were published—several cantatas, and innumerable scenas, Lieder and songs ; also a short ballet, ' Minerva belebt die Statuen des Dädalus ' (1802), and some instrumental pieces, including a serenade for two clarinets, two horns and two bassoons (1799, Breitkopf & Härtel). One of his operas, ' Il convitato di pietra, ossia il dissoluto,' will always be interesting as a forerunner of Mozart's ' Don Giovanni.' It was produced at Vienna, Aug. 21, 1777 (ten years before Mozart's), and is described by Jahn (Mozart, ii. 333). His best orchestral work is his overture to ' Tigrane,' which was often played in Germany and England. Breitkopf & Härtel's Catalogue shows a tolerably long list of his songs, and his exercises for the voice (1804) are amongst the best that exist. English amateurs will find a duet of his, ' Come oprima,' from ' Enea nel Lazio,' in the ' Musical Library,' vol. i. p. 8, and two airs in Lonsdale's ' Gemme d' antichità.' He was one of the sixty-three composers who set the words ' In questa tomba oscura,' and his setting was published in 1878 by Ritter of Magdeburg.

RIGOLETTO, opera in 3 acts; libretto by Piave (founded on V. Hugo's *Le Roi s'amuse*); music by Verdi. Produced Teatro Fenice, Venice, Mar. 11, 1851; in Italian, Covent Garden, May 14, 1853, and Italiens, Paris, Jan. 19, 1857; New York, Academy of Music; Nov. 4, 1857.                    G.

RILLÉ, FRANÇOIS ANATOLE LAURENT DE (*b.* Orleans, 1828; *d.* Paris, Aug. 26, 1915), the composer of an enormous number of partsongs and other small choral works. He was at first intended to be a painter, but altered his purpose and studied music under an Italian named Comoghio, and subsequently under Elwart. His compositions, of which a list of the most important is given in the supplement to *Fétis*, have enjoyed a lasting popularity with 'orphéoniste' societies, and have that kind of vigorous effectiveness which is exactly suited to their purpose. A large number of operettas of very slight construction have from time to time been produced in Paris, and the composer has made various more or less successful essays in the department of church music.     M.

RIMBAULT, EDWARD FRANCIS, LL.D. (*b.* Soho, June 13, 1816; *d.* Sept. 26, 1876), son of Stephen Francis Rimbault, organist of St. Giles in the Fields, received his first instruction in music from his father, but afterwards became a pupil of Samuel Wesley. At 16 years old he was appointed organist of the Swiss church, Soho.

He early directed his attention to the study of musical history and literature, and in 1838 delivered a series of lectures on the history of music in England. In 1840 he took an active part in the formation of the Musical Antiquarian and Percy Societies, of both which he became secretary, and for both which he edited several works.[1] In 1841 he was editor of the musical publications of the Motet Society. In the course of the next few years he edited a collection of Cathedral Chants; 'The Order of Daily Service according to the use of Westminster Abbey'; a reprint of Lowe's *Short Direction for the performance of Cathedral Service*; Tallis's Responses; Merbecke's 'Book of Common Prayer Noted' a volume of unpublished Cathedral Services; Arnold's Cathedral Music; and the oratorios of 'Messiah,' 'Samson' and 'Saul,' for the Handel Society. In 1842 he was elected F.S.A. and member of the Academy of Music in Stockholm, and obtained the degree of Doctor in Philosophy. He was offered, but declined, the appointment of professor of music in Harvard University, U.S.A. In 1848 he received the honorary degree of LL.D. from the University of Oxford. He lectured on music at the Collegiate Institution, Liverpool; the Philosophic Institute, Edinburgh; the

Royal Institution of Great Britain, and elsewhere. He published *The Organ, its History and Construction* (1855) (in collaboration with E. J. Hopkins); *Notices of the Early English Organ Builders* (1865); *History of the Pianoforte* (1860); *Bibliotheca madrigaliana* (1847); *Musical Illustrations of Percy's Reliques*; *The Ancient Vocal Music of England*; *The Rounds, Catches and Canons of England* (in conjunction with Rev. J. P. Metcalfe); two collections of Christmas Carols; 'A Little Book of Songs and Ballads,' etc., etc. He edited North's *Memoirs of Musick* (1846), Sir Thomas Overbury's Works (1856), the *Old Cheque Book of the Chapel Royal* (1872), and two Sermons by Boy Bishops. He arranged many operas and other works, was author of many elementary books, and an extensive contributor to periodical literature. His compositions were but few, the principal being an operetta, 'The Fair Maid of Islington' (1838), music to *The Castle Spectre* (1839), and a posthumous cantata, 'Country Life.' His pretty little song, 'Happy Land,' had an extensive popularity. After his resignation of the organistship of the Swiss church, he was successively organist of several churches and chapels, such as St. Peter's, Vere Street. He died, after a lingering illness, and was buried at Highgate Cemetery, leaving a fine musical library, which was sold by auction at Sotheby's on July 3, 1877, and following days. See an account of the library in the *Musical World*, 1877, p. 539. An obituary notice appeared in the *Mus. T.*, 1877, p. 427, and other papers. The most complete list of his works is in *Brit. Mus. Biog.*               W. H. H.

RIMSKY-KORSAKOV, NICHOLAS ANDREIEVICH (*b.* Tikhvin, Government of Novgorod, Mar. 18,[2] 1844; *d.* St. Petersburg, June 21, 1908), one of the most brilliant of the Russian Nationalist group of composers.

The child's earliest musical impressions were derived from a small band, consisting of four Jews employed upon the family estate. These musicians mustered two violins, cymbals and a tambourine, and were often summoned to the house to enliven the evenings when there was company or dancing. At 6 years old the boy began to be taught the piano, and at 9 he made his first attempts at composition. His talent for music was evident to his parents, but being of aristocratic family he was destined for one of the only two professions then considered suitable for a young man of good birth. In 1856 Rimsky-Korsakov entered the Naval College in St. Petersburg, where he remained until 1862. This period of his life was not very favourable to his musical development, but he managed on Sundays and holidays to receive some instruction in the violoncello from Ulich, and in the pianoforte from an excellent teacher, Fedor Kanillé. His acquaintance with

---

[1] His editions of early English music, though useful in their day, are not now (1927) accepted as authoritative.     C.

[2] O.S. Mar. 6.

Balakirev, dating from 1861, was the decisive moment in his career.

Intercourse with the young but capable leader of the new Russian school of music, and with his disciples, Cui, Moussorgsky and Borodin, awoke in the young naval cadet an ambition to study the art to more serious purpose. He had only just begun to profit by Balakirev's teaching when he was sent abroad ; but, undaunted by the interruption, during this cruise, which lasted three years (1862–65), he completed a symphony, op. 1. From the letters which he wrote at this time to César Cui it is evident that he composed under great difficulties, but the work was completed in spite of them, and, movement by movement, the manuscript was sent to Balakirev for advice and correction. The symphony was performed for the first time in Dec. 1865, when Balakirev conducted it at one of the concerts of the Free School of Music, St. Petersburg. The public, who gave it a hearty reception, were surprised when a youth in naval uniform appeared to acknowledge their ovation. Rimsky-Korsakov now remained in St. Petersburg, and was able to renew his musical studies and his close association with the circle of Balakirev.

The compositions which followed the first symphony—the symphonic poem ' Sadko ' (1867), and the opera ' Pskovitianka ' (' The Maid of Pskov ')—called the attention of all musical Russia to this promising composer. In 1871 he was appointed professor of composition and instrumentation in the St. Petersburg Conservatoire. He retired from the navy, which can never have been a congenial profession, in 1873, and at the wish of the Grand Duke Constantine Nicholaevich was appointed inspector of naval bands, a post which he held until it was abolished in 1884. From 1883–1884 he was assistant director to the court chapel under Balakirev. Succeeding to Balakirev, he became director and conductor of the Free School Concerts from 1874–81, and conducted the Russian Symphony Concerts, inaugurated in St. Petersburg by Belaiev, from 1886 to 1900. His gifts in this respect were highly appreciated in Paris and Brussels. Rimsky-Korsakov's career remained closely associated with St. Petersburg, which was the scene of his earliest successes, and on more than one occasion he declined the directorship of the Moscow Conservatoire. His pupils number some distinguished names : Liadov, Ippolitov-Ivanov, Sacchetti, Grechaninov and Glazounov all studied under him for longer or shorter periods. In 1873 Rimsky-Korsakov married Nadejda Nicholaevna Pourgold, a gifted pianist, who proved a helpmeet in the truest sense of the word. This lady and her sister, A. P. Molas, played important parts in the history of the modern Russian school ; the former by her clever pianoforte arrangements of many of the great orchestral works, while the latter, gifted with a fine voice and dramatic instinct, created most of the leading female rôles in the operatic works of Cui, Moussorgsky and Borodin, before they obtained a hearing at the Imperial Opera.

ORCHESTRAL WORKS. — Rimsky - Korsakov had already composed his symphonic works ' Sadko ' and ' Antar,' and his opera ' Pskovitianka,' and had been appointed professor at the St. Petersburg Conservatoire, when his ' ideal conscientiousness ' awoke in him some doubts as to the solidity of his early musical education. Admirably as the system of self-education had worked in his case, he still felt it a duty to undergo a severe course of theoretical study in order to have at his disposal that supreme mastery of technical means in which all the great classical masters excelled. Accordingly he began to work at fugue and counterpoint, thereby calling forth from Tchaikovsky, in 1875, this tribute of admiration : ' I do not know how to express all my respect for your artistic temperament. . . . I am a mere artisan in music, but you will be an artist in the fullest sense of the word.' Most of Rimsky-Korsakov's early works were revised after this period of artistic discipline. In the earlier phases of his career he was obviously influenced by Glinka and Liszt, and in a lesser degree by Schumann and Berlioz. The imitative period was, however, of short duration, and perhaps no composer of his generation could boast a more individual and distinctive utterance than Rimsky-Korsakov. But its distinctiveness lies in extreme refinement and restraint rather than in violent and sensational expression. He wins but does not force our attention. A lover of musical beauty rather than musical truth—or, to put it more justly, believing truth to lie in idealistic rather than realistic methods of creation, he was never deeply influenced by the declamatory and naturalistic style of Dargomijsky and Moussorgsky. Like Tchaikovsky, he divided his career between operatic and symphonic music, but with a steadily increasing tendency towards the former. After his first symphony, written on more or less conventional lines, he showed a distinct preference for the freer forms of programme music, as shown in the symphonic poem ' Sadko,' the Oriental Suite ' Antar,' and the symphonic suite ' Scheherezade.' In the sinfonietta upon Russian themes, and the third symphony in C major, he returned to more traditional treatment. Almost without exception Rimsky-Korsakov's symphonic works are distinguished by a poetic and tactful expression of national sentiment. His art was rooted in the Russian soil, and the national element pervades it like a subtle but unmistakable aroma.

His music invariably carries the charm of expressive orchestration. Taking it up where Glinka left it in his ' Jota Aragonese ' and incidental music to ' Prince Kholmsky,' Rimsky-Korsakov developed this characteristic quality of Russian musicians beyond any of his contemporaries, without, however, overstepping the bounds of what sane minds must still regard as legitimate effect. He was at his best in descriptive orchestration—in the suggestion of landscape and atmospheric conditions. But his clear objective outlook lead him to a luminous and definite tone-painting quite different from the subtle and dreamy impressionism of Debussy. The musical pictures of Rimsky-Korsakov are mostly riant and sunny ; sometimes breezy and boisterous, as in the sea - music of ' Sadko ' and ' Scheherezade ' ; often full of a quaint pastoral grace, as in the springtide music in his opera ' The Snow Maiden.' His harmony has freshness and individuality. He makes considerable use of the old church modes and Oriental scales.

OPERAS. — All Rimsky - Korsakov's operas, except ' Mozart and Salieri,' are based upon national subjects, historical or legendary. Tales from the Slavonic mythology, which combine poetical allegory with fantastic humour, exercised the greatest attraction for him. In his first opera, ' The Maid of Pskov,' he evidently started under the partial influence of Dargomijsky's ' The Stone Guest,' for the solo parts consist chiefly of mezzo-recitativo, the dryness of which is compensated by the orchestral colour freely employed in the accompaniments. In the two operas which followed, ' A Night in May ' and ' The Snow Maiden,' the dramatic realism of his first work for the stage gives place to lyrical inspiration and the free flight of fancy. ' Mozart and Salieri '—a setting of Poushkin's dramatic duologue—and ' The Boyarina Vera Sheloga ' show a return to the declamatory style, while ' Sadko,' which appeared in 1896, is a skilful compromise between lyrical and dramatic forms, and may be accepted as the mature expression of his artistic creed. Of all his operatic works, ' The Snow Maiden,' founded upon Ostrovsky's poetical legend of the springtide, has perhaps the most characteristic charm, but the last of his operas, ' The Golden Cockerel ' (' Le Coq d'or ') has through force of circumstances won peculiar favour outside Russia and particularly in England. ' Sadko,' the thematic material for which is partly drawn from the symphonic poem of the same name, is more epic in character and full of musical interest. It must be surmised that it is only the peculiarly national character of the libretto which has hindered this remarkable work from becoming more widely known. Most of Rimsky-Korsakov's operas combine with this strong national element that also of the neighbouring East.

SONGS.—As a song-writer Rimsky-Korsakov takes a high place in a school which has shown itself pre-eminent in this branch of art. He composed about eighty songs, remarkable for an all-round level of excellence, for few are really poor in quality, while the entire collection comprises such lyrical gems as ' Night,' the Hebrew song (' Awake, long since the dawn appeared '), ' A Southern night,' ' Spring,' and ' Come to the kingdom of roses and wine.' In his songs, as in his operas, he inclined more to the lyrical grace of Glinka than to the declamatory force of Dargomijsky. His melodies are not lacking in distinction and charm, especially when they approach in style to the melodies of the folk-songs ; but in this respect he is somewhat lacking in impassioned inspiration and copious invention. The richness and picturesqueness of his accompaniments make the characteristic interest of his songs.

GENERAL CHARACTERISTICS.—A close study of the works of Rimsky-Korsakov reveals a distinguished musical personality ; a thinker, a fastidious and exquisite craftsman, an artist of that refined and discriminating type who is chiefly concerned in satisfying the demands of his own conscience rather than the tastes of the general public. Outside Russia he was for a time censured for his exclusive devotion to national ideals. On the other hand, some Russian critics accused him of opening the door to Wagnerism in national opera. This was only true in so far as he grafted upon the older lyrical forms the use of some modern methods, notably the occasional enployment of the *leitmotif*. As regards instrumentation he had a remarkable faculty for the invention of new and brilliant effects, and was a master in the skilful use of onomatopœia. Given a temperament, musically endowed, which *sees* its subject with the direct and observant vision of the painter, instead of dreaming it through a mist of subjective exaltation, we get a type of mind that naturally tends to a programme which is clearly defined. Rimsky-Korsakov belonged to this class. We feel in all his music the desire to depict, which so often inclines us to the language of the studio in attempting to express the quality of his work. His music is entirely free from that tendency to melancholy unjustly supposed to be the characteristic of all Russian art. The folk-songs of Great Russia—the source from which the national composers have drawn their inspiration—are pretty evenly divided between the light and shade of life ; it was the former aspect which made the strongest appeal to the vigorous, optimistic, but highly poetical temperament of this musician.

Many gifted members of the new Russian school were prevented by illness, by the enforced choice of a second vocation, and by the imperfect conditions of artistic life of their time, from acquiring a complete musical education. Rimsky-Korsakov, out of the fulness of his own technical equipment, was ever ready to sacrifice time and labour in the interest of his fellow - workers. Thus, he orchestrated 'The Stone Guest' which Dargomijsky endeavoured to finish on his deathbed; part of Borodin's 'Prince Igor' and Moussorgsky's operas 'Khovantshina' and 'Boris Godounov.'

In 1889, during the Parıs Exhibition, he conducted two concerts devoted to Russian music given in the Salle Trocadéro. In 1890 and again in 1900 he conducted concerts of Russian music in the Théâtre de la Monnaie, Brussels.

In Mar. 1905, in consequence of a letter published in the *Russ*, in which he advocated the autonomy of the St. Petersburg Conservatoire, hitherto under the management of the Imperial Russian Musical Society, and complained of the too stringent police supervision to which the students were subjected, Rimsky-Korsakov was dismissed from his professorship. This high-handed action on the part of the authorities was deeply resented by all his colleagues, and Glazounov, Liadov and Blumenfeld immediately resigned their posts by way of protest. By the autumn of the same year the Conservatoire had actually wrested some powers of self-government from the Musical Society, and having elected Glazounov as director, the new committee lost no time in reinstating Rimsky-Korsakov in the professorship of composition and instrumentation which he had honourably filled since 1871. The following is a list of Rimsky-Korsakov's numerous compositions :

### ORCHESTRAL

Symphony No. 1, E♭ minor, op. 1, afterwards transposed into E minor ; Symphony No. 2, 'Antar,' op. 9, afterwards entitled 'Oriental Suite' ; Symphony No. 3, C minor, op. 32, 1873, revised 1884 ; Sinfonietta on Russian themes, A minor, op. 31. Overture on Russian themes, op. 28 ; 'Easter,' overture, op. 36, 1888 ; 'Sadko,' musical picture, op. 5, 1867, revised 1891 ; Serbian Fantasia, op. 6 ; 'A Tale,' op. 29, subject from the Prologue of Poushkin's 'Russian and Lioudmilla' ; Capriccio on Spanish themes, op. 34, 1887 ; Symphonic Suite 'Scheherezade' (from the *Arabian Nights*), op. 35, 1888; Suites from the operas 'The Snow Maiden' and 'Tsar Saltana,' and the opera-ballet 'Mlada,' op. 57 ; prelude 'At the Grave,' op. 61 ; 'suite from the opera 'Christmas Eve' (chorus *ad lib.*).

### CHAMBER MUSIC

String quartet, F major, op. 12 ; string sextet, A major (MS.) ; quintet for piano, flute, clarinet, horn and bassoon ; first movement of the string quartet on the theme B-la-f (Belaiev) ; third movement of the quartet 'For a Fête Day' ; allegro of the string quartet in the collection 'Fridays' ; Serenade for violoncello and pianoforte, op. 37.

### ORCHESTRA AND SOLO INSTRUMENTS

Pianoforte concerto, C♯ minor, op. 30 ; Fantasia on Russian themes for violin and orchestra.

### PIANOFORTE

Six variations on the theme B-a-c-h, op. 10 ; four pieces, op. 11 ; three pieces, op. 15 ; six fugues, op. 17 ; eight variations on a folktune (no op. number) ; five variations for the 'Paraphrases' (see BORODIN).

### CHORAL WITH ORCHESTRA

Folk-song, op. 20 , 'Slava,' op. 21 ; cantata for soprano, tenor, and mixed chorus, op. 44 ; 'The Fir and the Palm' (from op. 3) for baritone ; two ariosos for bass, 'Anchar' (The Upas Tree) and 'The Prophet,' op. 49 ; trio for female voices, op. 53 ; 'The Ballad o the Doom of Oleg,' for tenor and bass soli, male choir and orchestra

(performed at the Newcastle Festival, 1909) ; cantata for soli and chorus, op. 58 ; 'Fragment from Homer,' cantata for three 'female voices and chorus, op. 60.

### CHORUS ONLY

Two trios for female voices, op. 13 ; four variations and a fughetta for female quartet, op. 14 ; six choruses a cappella, op. 16 ; twe mixed choruses, op. 18 ; fifteen Russian folk-songs, op. 19 ; four trios for male voices, op. 23.

### SONGS, ETC.

Four songs, op. 2 ; four songs, op. 3 ; four songs, op. 4 ; four songs op. 7 ; six songs, op. 8 ; two songs, op. 25 ; four songs, op. 26 ; four songs, op. 27 ; four songs, op. 39 ; four songs, op. 40 ; four songs, op. 41 ; four songs, op. 42 ; four songs, op. 43 ; four songs, op. 45 ; five songs, op. 46 ; two duets, op. 47 ; four duets, op. 50 ; five duets, op. 51 ; two duets, op. 52 ; four duets for tenor, op. 55 : two duets, op. 56.

### SACRED MUSIC

The liturgy of St. John Chrysostom (a portion only), op. 22 ; six transpositions, including the psalm 'By the waters of Babylon,' op. 22 *a* ; 'We praise Thee, O God ' (MS. 1883).

### OPERAS

'The Maid of Pskov ' (' Pskovitianka '), libretto from a drama by Mey (1870–72 ; performed St. Petersburg, 1873, revised in 1894) ; 'A Night in May,' text from Gogol (1878, St. Petersburg, 1880) ; 'The Snow Maiden,' text from Ostrovosky (1880–81, St. Petersburg, 1882); 'Mlada,' fairy opera-ballet (St. Petersburg, 1893); 'Christmas Eve,' legendary opera, text from Gogol, 1874 (Maryinsky Theatre, St. Petersburg, 1895) ; 'Sadko,' epic-opera, 1895–96 (Private Opera, Moscow, 1897 ; St. Petersburg, 1901) ; 'Mozart and Salieri,' dramatic scenes, op. 48, 1898 (Private Opera, Moscow, 1898) ; 'Boyarina Vera Sheloga,' musical dramatic prologue to 'The Maid of Pskov,' op. 54 (Private Opera, Moscow, 1899 ; St. Petersburg, 1902) ; 'The Tsar's Bride,' 1898 (Private Opera, Moscow, 1899 ; St. Petersburg, Maryinsky Theatre, 1902) ; 'The Tale of Tsar Saltana, etc.', 1899–1900 (Private Opera, Moscow, 1900) ; 'Servilia ' (Maryinsky Theatre, St Petersburg 1902) ; 'Kostchei the Immortal,' an autumn legend (Private Opera, Moscow, 1902) ; ' Pan Voyevoda,' 'The Tale of the Invisible City of Kitezh and the Maiden Fevronia ' ; ' The Golden Cockerel ' (Moscow, 1910).

One hundred Russian folk-songs, op. 24 (1877) ; forty Russian folk-songs (1882) ; *A Practical Guide to the Study of Harmony* (1888).

### LITERARY WORKS

*History of my Musical Life* (trans. French and English). ; *Collected Essays and Sketches* ; *The Foundations of Instrumentation* (trans. French and English).

BIBL.—STASSOV, *Rimsky-Korsakov* (1890) ; ROSA NEWMARCH, *The Russian Opera* (1914) ; MONTAGU-NATHAN, *Biography* and *History of Russian Music* (1915).                                    R. N.

RINALDO. (1) Handel's first opera in England ; composed in a fortnight, and produced at the King's Theatre in the Haymarket, Feb. 24, 1711. The libretto was founded on the episode of Rinaldo and Armida in Tasso's *Gerusalemme liberata* (the same on which Gluck based his ' Armida '). Rossi wrote it in Italian, and it was translated into English by Aaron Hill.

(2) Cantata for male voices, set to Goethe's words, by Johannes Brahms (op. 50). First performed by the Akademisches Gesangverein, Vienna, Feb. 28, 1869.

RINALDO DI CAPUA, an Italian composer of the 18th century. Burney made his acquaintance in Rome in 1770, and since he describes him as an old man we may suppose him to have been born about 1700–10. Fétis gives 1715 as the year of his birth, and Rudhardt 1706, but neither writer states his authority for the date. According to Burney he was

' the natural son of a person of very high rank in that country [*i.e.* the kingdom of Naples], and at first studied music only as an accomplishment ; but being left by his father with only a small fortune, which was soon dissipated, he was forced to make it his profession.'

It has been assumed that he was born at Capua, and took his name from that place ; but it may be noted that whether Rinaldo had a legitimate claim to it or not, Di Capua was a fairly common surname in the neighbourhood of Naples at that time. He composed his first opera at the age of 17, at Vienna, according to Burney ; Spitta showed that no opera by Rinaldo was ever produced at Vienna, but thought it probable that he had some connexion with that city, since Metastasio's ' Ciro riconosciuto,' which formed the libretto of an opera by Rinaldo produced at Rome in 1737, was set to music for the first time by Caldara for performance at Vienna on Aug. 28, 1736. A further connexion with the imperial court is shown by the fact that he composed a special work to celebrate the election of Francis I. in 1745. It seems, therefore, not unreasonable to take Burney's words literally, and to understand that the opera ' Ciro riconosciuto,' though performed in Rome, was composed in Vienna. If this was his first opera, it would settle 1720 as the year of Rinaldo's birth. Spitta was, however, not aware of the existence of a few airs from a comic opera, the title of which has not been preserved, produced at the Teatro Valle in Rome in the autumn of 1737. Burney informs us that

' in the course of a long life he has experienced various vicissitudes of fortune ; sometimes in vogue, sometimes neglected.'

Most of his operas were given at Rome, a few being produced at Florence and Venice ; although described in some libretti as a Neapolitan, no opera of his is known to have been performed in Naples. The Bouffons Italiens performed an intermezzo of his, ' La zingara ' (La Bohémienne), at Paris in 1753, in a version which included songs by other composers ; among these was the well-known ' Tre giorni son che Nina,' generally ascribed to Pergolesi, and on this account attributed to Rinaldo by Spitta. The song has, however, been recently proved to be by another composer (see CIAMPI). When Burney knew him he was in somewhat impoverished circumstances, owing to the indifference of the public which had once applauded him. He had collected his works with a view to making provision for his old age, but at the moment when they were required discovered that his son had sold them for waste paper. Burney mentions an intermezzo composed for the Capranica theatre in 1770 (' I finti pazzi ') when he was already an old man. Another opera, ' La donna vendicativa ' (ascribed by Clément and Larousse to 1740, though on no apparent authority), was performed in Rome in 1771, and this was probably his last work. After this date we know only of ' La giocondina ' (Rome, 1778), which was probably a revival of an earlier work. Burney, with characteristic kindliness, recommended him as a teacher to William Parsons, who had studied at a Neapolitan conservatorio, where

according to his own account he learnt nothing. Parsons became Master of the King's Musick in 1786, to the great disappointment of Burney, to whom the post had been promised. Another pupil of Rinaldo was Antonio Aurisicchio.

Rinaldo was supposed to have been the inventor of accompanied recitative ; Burney pointed out that this invention belonged to Alessandro Scarlatti. Rinaldo himself only claimed

' to have been among the first who introduced long *ritornellos* or symphonies into the recitatives of strong passion and distress, which express or imitate what it would be ridiculous for the voice to attempt.'

An example from ' Vologeso ' is in the Fitzwilliam Museum. His musical education having been that of an amateur, his technique of composition was sometimes defective ; but, apart from this slight weakness of harmony, he was one of the best composers of his period for dramatic power and melodic beauty. He was especially successful in brilliant coloratura, but was also capable of producing most attractive light operas. To judge from the few fragments of his work that remain, ' Ciro riconosciuto ' and ' Vologeso ' seem to have been his most important dramatic works.

CATALOGUE OF EXTANT WORKS OF RINALDO DI CAPUA

OPERAS

A comic opera, name unknown (Rome, T. Valle, 1737). Fragments : Palermo R.C.M.
Ciro riconosciuto (Rome, T. Tordinona, 1737 ; revived Rome, 1739). Fragments : formerly in possession of Spitta ; Brit. Mus. ; Münster.
La commedia in commedia (Rome, T. Valle, 1738). Libretto : Brussels Conservatoire. Fragments : Palmero R.C.M. Revived at Venice (T. San Cassiano, 1749). Libretto : Venice, Bibl. Marc.
The opera was also performed in London ; Walsh printed five airs as 'The favourite Songs in the Opera call'd La Comedia in Comedia.' Rinaldo's name is not mentioned, and the work was probably a pasticcio ; one song, however, 'Non so la prole mia,' is in the Palermo collection, which bears Rinaldo's name
Farnace (Venice, T. S. Giovanni Grisostomo, 1739). Libretto : Venice, Bibl. Marc.
Vologeso re de' Parti (Rome, T. Argentina, 1739). Libretto : Bologna, Lic Mus. Fragments : Brit. Mus. ; Brussels Cons. ; Cambridge, Fitz. Mus. ; Dresden ; Münster ; New York, in possession of H. E. Krehbiel, Esq.
La libertà nociva (Rome, T. Valle, 1740). Libretto : Bologna ; Brussels Cons. Fragments : Brit. Mus. ; Cambridge, Fitz. Mus. Revived in Florence (T. Cocomero, 1742), Bologna (T Formagliari, 1743). Libretti : Bologna. Also at Venice (T. San Cassiano, 1744). Libretto : Bologna ; Venice.
Turno Herdonio Aricino (Rome, T. Capranica, 1743). Libretto : Bologna ; Brussels Cons.
Le nozze di Don Trifone (Rome, T. Argentina, 1743) Libretto : Bologna.
L' ambizione delusa (Venice, T. S. Cassiano, 1744). Libretto : Bologna ; Venice. Revived at Milan (T. Ducale, 1745). Libretto : Bologna.
La forza del sangue (intermezzo), (Florence, T. Pallacorda, 1746). Libretto : Brussels Cons.
Il bravo è il bello (intermezzo), (Rome, T. Granari, 1748). Libretto : Brussels Cons.
Mario in Numidia (Rome, T. Dame, 1749). Libretto : Bologna. Fragments : Brit. Mus. ; Dresden ; Munich.
Il bravo burlato (intermezzo), (Florence, T. Pallacorda, 1749). Libretto Brussels Cons.
A comic opera (Rome ? 1750) Fragments : Dresden.
Il ripiego in amore (Rome, T. Valle, 1751). Libretto : Bo'ogna.
Il cavalier Mignatta ( intermezzi), (Rome, T. Capranica, 1751). Il galloppino ) Libretto ' Brussels Cons.
La donna superba (intermezzo), (Paris, Opéra, 1752). Libretto : Brussels Cons. Fragments (with French words): Brussels Cons.
La forza della pace (Rome, T. Pace, 1752). Libretto : Bologna.
La zingara (intermezzo), Paris, Opéra, 1753). Libretto : Brussels Cons. Score, printed in Paris, Brussels Cons. Revived at Pesaro, 1755, as ' Il vecchio amante e la zingara.' Libretto : Bologna.
La serva sposa (Rome, T. Valle, 1753). Libretto : Bologna.
La Chiavarina (Rome, T. Valle, 1754). Libretto : Bologna.
Attalo (Rome, T. Capranica, 1754). Libretto : Brussels Cons. Rinaldo di Capua appears here under the pseudonym of Cleofante Doriano.
Adriano in Siria (Rome, Argentina, 1758). Libretto : Brussels Cons. Fragments : Brit. Mus.
La smorfiosa (Florence, T. Cocomero, 1758). Libretto : Bologna.

Le donne ridicole (intermezzo), (Rome, T. Capranica, 1759). Libretto : Brussels Cons.

Il caffè di Campagna (farsetta), (Rome, T. Pace, 1764). Libretto : Bologna ; Brussels Cons.

I finti pazzi per amore (farsetta), (Rome, T. Pace, 1770). Libretto : Bologna ; Brussels Cons.

La donna vendicativa (farsetta), (Rome, T. Pace, 1771). Libretto : Bologna. Score : Brit. Mus.

La giocondina (farsetta), (Rome, T. Pace, 1778). Libretto : Brussels Cons.

(La statua per puntiglio, ascribed to R. di Capua by Eitner, is by Marcello di Capua.)

SACRED MUSIC

Cantata per la Natività della Beata Vergine (Rome, Collegio Nazareno, 1747). Score : Münster. Paris, Bibl. Nat. ? (Eitner).

A few other works are mentioned by Eitner : symphonies, probably opera overtures, and cantatas (Venice) ascribed to Cavaliere Rinaldi, who may have been a different composer.

Airs from operas as yet unidentified are at Cambridge, Fitz. Mus., Münster, and Montecassino.

The writer is indebted to the late H. E. Krehbiel for notice of the airs in his possession ; the MS. from which they are taken formerly belonged to Thomas Gray, the poet, and is described in Krehbiel's *Music and Manners in the Classical Period*. Other authorities consulted : Burney's *Present State of Music in France and Italy* (1771) ; an article by Spitta in the *Vierteljahrsschrift für Musikwiss.*, vol. iii. (1887), and A. Wotquenne's *Catalogue* of the library of the Brussels Conservatoire, vol. i. (1898). The two latter works give fuller bibliographical details than we have space for here.

E. J. D.

RINCK (RINK), JOHANN CHRISTIAN HEINRICH (*b*. Elgersburg, Saxe-Gotha, Feb. 18, 1770 ; *d*. Darmstadt, Aug. 7, 1846), celebrated organist and composer for his instrument. His talent developed itself at an early period, and, like Johann SCHNEIDER, he had the advantage of a direct traditional reading of the works of Sebastian Bach, having studied at Erfurt (in 1786–89) under Kittel, one of the great composer's best pupils. Rinck, having sat at the feet of Forkel at the University of Göttingen, obtained in 1790 the organistship of Giessen, where he held several other musical appointments. In 1805 he became organist at Darmstadt, and ' professor ' at its college ; in 1813 was appointed court organist, and in 1817 chamber musician to the Grand Duke (Ludwig I.). Rinck made several artistic tours in Germany, his playing always eliciting much admiration. At Trèves, in 1827, he was greeted with special honour. He received various decorations—in 1831 membership of the Dutch Society for Encouragement of Music ; in 1838 the cross of the first class from his Grand Duke ; in 1840 ' Doctor of Philosophy and Arts ' from the University of Giessen. Out of his 125 works a few are for chamber, including sonatas for PF., violin, and violoncello, and PF. duets. But his reputation is based on his organ music, or rather on his ' Practical Organ School,' a standard work. Rinck's compositions for his instrument show no trace of such sublime influence as might have been looked for from a pupil, in the second generation, of Bach ; throughout them fugue-writing is conspicuous by its absence, but his organ-pieces contain much that is interesting to an organ student. Amongst his works the more important are the ' Practical Organ School,' in six divisions (op. 55, re-edited by Otto Dienel, 1881), and numerous ' Preludes for Chorales,' issued at various periods. He also composed for the church a Pater Noster for four voices with organ (op. 59) ; motets, ' Praise the Lord ' (op. 88) and ' God be merciful ' (op. 109) ; twelve

Chorals for men's voices, etc. His valuable library was purchased in 1852 by Lowell Mason of Boston, Mass., and since given to Yale.

H. S. O.

RINFORZANDO, ' reinforcing ' or increasing in power. This word, or its abbreviations, *rinf.* or *rfz*, is used to denote a sudden and brief *crescendo*. It is applied generally to a whole phrase, however short, and has the same meaning as *sforzando*, which is only applied to single notes. It is sometimes used in concerted music to give a momentary prominence to a subordinate part, as for instance in the Beethoven quartet, op. 95, in the Allegretto, where the violoncello part is marked *rinforzando* when it has the second section of the principal subject of the movement.

M.

RING DES NIBELUNGEN, DER, a tetralogy or sequence of four music-dramas (more correctly a ' trilogy ' with a preludial drama), words and music by Wagner.

DAS RHEINGOLD. Produced Munich, Sept. 22, 1869 ; London, Her Majesty's Theatre, May 5, 1882 ; New York, Metropolitan Opera House, 1889 ; in English, Covent Garden (Richter), Jan. 27, 1908 ; Paris, Opéra, 1909.

DIE WALKÜRE. Produced Munich, June 25, 1870 ; New York, Academy of Music, but incomplete, Apr. 2, 1877 ; London, Her Majesty's Theatre, May 6, 1882 ; Opéra, Paris, May 6, 1893 ; in English, Covent Garden (Hedmondt season), Oct. 16, 1895.

SIEGFRIED. Produced Bayreuth, Aug. 16, 1876 ; London, Her Majesty's Theatre, May 8, 1882 ; New York, Metropolitan Opera House, Nov. 9, 1887 ; in French, Brussels, June 12, 1891 ; in English, Carl Rosa Co., Manchester, 1901.

GÖTTERDÄMMERUNG. Produced Bayreuth, Aug. 17, 1876 ; Her Majesty's Theatre, May 9, 1882 ; New York, Metropolitan Opera House, Jan. 25, 1888 ; Paris, Château d'Eau, 1902 ; in English, Covent Garden (Richter), Feb. 1, 1908.

The whole cycle was first produced at BAYREUTH (*q.v.*), 1876 ; London, 1882 ; New York, 1889 ; Paris, 1911 ; and in English, Covent Garden, 1908.

RINNUCINI, OTTAVIO (*b*. Florence ; *d*. there, 1621), a poet who wrote the first opera librettos for Peri, Caccini, Monteverdi and Gagliano. He was a great favourite of Maria di Medici, and was honoured by Henry IV. on his repeated visits to the French court between 1600 and 1605.

E. V. D. S.

RIOS, ALVARO DE LOS (*d*. ? Madrid, 1623), Spanish composer, appointed *musico de camera* to the queen, Doña Margherita de Austria, on Aug. 10, 1607. He was highly praised by the dramatist Tirso de Molina (author of the first play on the subject of Don Juan), who describes a performance of another play of his,

*El Vergonzoso en palacio*, at Toledo with music by Alvaro de los Rios and others. The Sablonara MS. at Munich (Staatsbibl., E. 200), and Madrid (Bibl. Nac., M. 1263, a somewhat inaccurate modern copy) contains 8 compositions by him.                J. B. T.

RIOTTE, PHILIPP JACOB (*b.* St. Mendel, Trèves, Aug. 16, 1776; *d.* Aug. 20, 1856), was taught music by André of Offenbach, and made his first appearance at Frankfort in Feb. 1804. In 1806 he was music-director at Gotha. In 1808 he conducted the French operas at the Congress of Erfurt. In Apr. 1809 his operetta 'Das Grenzstädtchen' was produced at the Kärnthnerthor theatre, and thenceforward Vienna was his residence. In 1818 he became conductor at the Theater an-der-Wien, beyond which he does not seem to have advanced. The list of his theatrical works is immense. His biography in Wurzbach's *Lexicon* enumerates, between 1809 and 1848, no less than forty-eight pieces, operas, operettas, ballets, pantomimes, music to plays, etc., written mostly by himself, and sometimes in conjunction with others. In 1852 he wound up his long labours by a cantata 'The Crusade,' which was performed in the great Redoutensaal, Vienna, with much applause. He wrote an opera called 'Mozart's Zauberflöte' at Prague about 1820. He left also a symphony (op. 25), nine solo-sonatas, six do. for PF. and violin, three concertos for clarinet and orchestra, but these are defunct. He became very popular by a piece called 'The Battle of Leipzig,' for PF. solo, which was republished over half Germany, and had a prodigious sale.       G.

RIPA, ALBERTO DA (also called Alberto Mantovano) Seigneur de Carrois (*b.* Mantua, 1529; *d.* 1551), was a famous virtuoso of the lute at the French court.

RIPFEL, C. (*b.* Mannheim, 1790; *d.* Frankfort-on-M., Mar. 8, 1876), was engaged at Frankfort for forty-five years as principal violoncello at the theatre. B. Romberg declared him to be the greatest virtuoso on his instrument, but nervousness caused him to retire from the concert platform. He was a composer of great merit, but refused to publish any of his compositions (E. van der Straeten, *Hist. of the Violoncello*).

RIPIENO, 'supplementary,' the name given in the orchestral concertos of the 17th and 18th centuries to the accompanying instruments which were only employed to fill in the harmonies and to support the solo or 'concertante' parts. (See CONCERTANTE; CONCERTINO.)             M.

RIPPON, (1) JOHN (*b.* Tiverton, Apr. 29, 1751; *d.* London, Dec. 17, 1836 [1]). He was a doctor of divinity, and had a meeting-house for a number of years in Carter Lane, Tooley

[1] *Brit. Mus. Biog.*

Street. His 'Selection of Psalm and Hymn Tunes,' from the best authors, in three and five parts (1791) was a tune-book in much request for congregational singing, and ran through a large number of editions. In its compilation and arrangement he was assisted by T. Walker.            F. K.

His nephew, also (2) JOHN RIPPON, was composer of an oratorio 'The Crucifixion,' published in 1837.          W. H. G. F.

RISELEY, GEORGE (*b.* Bristol, Aug. 28, 1845), was elected chorister of Bristol Cathedral in 1852, and in Jan. 1862 articled to John Davis Corfe, the cathedral organist, for instruction in the organ, pianoforte, harmony, and counterpoint. During the next ten years he was organist at various churches in Bristol and Clifton, at the same time acting as deputy at the cathedral. In 1870 he was appointed organist to the Colston Hall, Bristol, where he started weekly recitals of classical and popular music, and in 1876 succeeded Corfe as organist to the cathedral. In 1877 he started his orchestral concerts, which won for him a well-deserved reputation. Notwithstanding considerable opposition, and no small pecuniary risk, he continued, during each season, to give fortnightly concerts, at which the principal works of the classical masters were well performed, and a large number of interesting novelties by modern writers, both English and foreign, produced. In 1878 he was appointed conductor of the Bristol Orpheus Society, and enlarged its scope and greatly increased its reputation. He conducted the Bristol Society of Instrumentalists, and was the founder of the Bristol Choral Society in 1889. He retired with a pension from the cathedral appointment in 1898, and was appointed conductor of the Alexandra Palace, and of the Queen's Hall Choral Society. In 1896 he conducted his first Bristol Festival with great success, and was the conductor of these triennial festivals up to 1911, since when they have not been given (see BRISTOL). His compositions include a Jubilee Ode (1887), part-songs, etc. See an interesting article on him in *Mus. T.*, 1899, p. 81 ff.           W. B. S.

RISLER, JOSEPH EDOUARD (*b.* Baden, Feb. 23, 1873), studied at the Paris Conservatoire, where he gained, among other distinctions, first medals in solfège and elementary piano in 1887, a first piano prize (in Diémer's class) in 1889, a second harmony prize in 1892, and the first prize for accompaniment in 1897. On leaving the Conservatoire, Risler made further studies with Dimmler, Stavenhagen, D'Albert, and Klindworth. In 1896 and 1897 he was one of the 'Assistenten auf der Bühne' at Bayreuth, and took part as 'répétiteur' in preparing the 'Meistersinger' for the Paris Opéra. In 1906 he was appointed a member of the Conseil Supérieur of the Paris

Conservatoire. From 1907–09 he was pianoforte professor there. Risler has given many pianoforte recitals in France, Germany, Holland, Russia, Spain, etc. His first appearance in England took place at Prince's Hall, May 17, 1894, when he played two sonatas of Beethoven. He played the thirty-two sonatas of Beethoven in London in 1906. He has written a concert-transcription of Strauss's 'Till Eulenspiegel,' etc.                                    G. F.

RISPOSTA (Lat. *comes* ; Eng. ' Answer '), the answer to the subject of a Fugue, or point of imitation. (See PROPOSTA ; FUGUE.)

RIST, JOHANN (*b.* Ottensen, near Hamburg, Mar. 8, 1607 ; *d.* Wedel-on-Elbe, Aug. 31, 1667), preacher and church-councillor, was also a musician, and a poet of distinction. He was made poet-laureate by the Emperor in 1644, and raised to the rank of nobility in 1653. Rist was the founder of the Hamburg Lieder-school, on whose behalf he enlisted the interest of many of the best song composers of his time, who set to music his vast number of sacred and secular poems, of which he composed a fair number himself. In this way he exercised a considerable influence upon the evolution of the Lied as well as upon the musical taste of the people. Some of his hymns are still favourites throughout Germany (*Q.-L.* ; *Riemann*).

RISTORI, GIOVANNI ALBERTO (*b.* Bologna, 1692 ; *d.* Dresden, Feb. 7, 1753), composer. He came to Dresden in 1715 with his father, the leader of an Italian theatrical company. In 1717 he became composer to the Royal Italian theatre in Dresden, and director of the Polish chapel ; in 1733 he was private organist to the court (Kammerorganist) ; in 1750 he was appointed, with J. H. Hasse, as vice Kapellmeister. Ristori composed chiefly operas and church music. Of 17 known operas twelve manuscripts are in existence. A number of his manuscripts are in the Dresden State Library, including 3 oratorios, 15 masses, 3 Requiems, a beautiful Stabat Mater in C minor, dated 1730, numbers of motets and other church works. In the British Museum there is a soprano cantata, 'Verdi Colli.'        R. M<sup>G</sup>.

RITARDANDO, RITEMENTE, RITENUTO, see RALLENTANDO.

RITORNELLO (abbrev. *ritornel., ritor.* ; Fr. *ritournelle*). (1) An Italian word, literally signifying a little return or repetition ; but more frequently applied, in a conventional sense, (*a*) to a short instrumental melody played between the scenes of an opera, or even during the action, either for the purpose of enforcing some particular dramatic effect or of amusing the audience during the time occupied in the preparation of some elaborate ' set-scene ' (early instances are found in Peri's ' Euridice ' and Monteverdi's ' Orfeo ') ; and (*b*) to the symphonies introduced between the

vocal phrases of a song or anthem. The opera and church music of the 17th and 18th centuries affords innumerable instances of this latter use of the term.

(2) An ancient form of Italian verse, in which each strophe consists of three lines, the first and third of which rhyme with each other, after the manner of the *Terza rima* of Dante. Little folk-songs of this character are still popular, under the name of ' ritornelli ' or ' stornelli,' among the peasants of the Abruzzi and other mountain regions of Italy.                    W. S. R., abridged.

RITTER, ALEXANDER (*b.* Narva, Russia, June 7, 1833 ; *d.* Munich, Apr. 12, 1896), of parents of German extraction, was a prominent figure in the circle of those who fought for Wagner's music, and for the advanced side of the art generally. He learnt the violin from Franz Schubert the Dresden teacher, and in 1849–51 was a pupil of the Leipzig Conservatorium. He married a niece of Richard Wagner, Franziska Wagner, an actress, in 1854, and went to live at Weimar in that year in the company of the earlier pupils and friends of Liszt. In 1856 he was made conductor at the town theatre of Stettin, and after several changes of residence and employment, settled at Würzburg in 1863, establishing a music-shop there which he managed from 1875–82, when he joined the Meiningen orchestra under Bülow. On Bülow's retirement from the post of conductor in 1886, Ritter went to live in Munich. His op. 1 was a string quartet of some merit ; two operas, ' Der faule Hans ' (1885) and ' Wem die Krone ? ' (1890), were finished and produced in Munich and Weimar respectively. Several symphonic poems are mentioned in detail in *Riemann*, and in the article on Ritter by F. Rösch in *Musikalisches Wochenblatt* for 1898.                                            M.

RITTER, FRÉDÉRIC LOUIS (*b.* Strassburg, June 22, 1834 ; *d.* Antwerp, July 22, 1891), Alsatian conductor, teacher and writer on music. His musical studies were begun at an early age under Hauser and Schletterer, were continued at Paris under Kastner, and were completed in Germany. At the age of 18 he was made professor of music in the Protestant Seminary of Fénéstrange, Lorraine. In 1856 he went to Cincinnati, Ohio, and there organised the Cecilia (choral) and the Philharmonic (orchestral) Societies, and at the concerts of these two organisations many important works were performed for the first time in America. In 1861 he moved to New York, there becoming conductor of the Sacred Harmonic Society and of the Arion Choral Society (male voices). In 1874 he went to Poughkeepsie, N.Y., as director of music at Vassar College. The University of New York conferred on him the degree of Mus.D. in 1878.

Ritter is chiefly known to-day through his

writings. These include : *A History of Music*
(2 vols., 1870–74) ; *Music in England* (1883) ;
*Music in America* (1883) ; and *Music in its
Relation to Intellectual Life* (1891).   w. s. s.

RITTER, HERMANN (*b.* Wismar, Mecklenburg, Sept. 26, 1849 ; *d.* Würzburg, Jan.
1926), attracted considerable public interest
in Germany during the latter half of the
19th century by his performances on the
'viola alta,' an instrument which he claimed
to be his own invention.   While studying
history and art at the Heidelberg University,
Ritter became deeply interested in the history
of musical instruments, and the desire to
improve the muffled tone of the ordinary viola
induced him to attempt the construction
of a similar instrument which should possess
the acute resonant qualities of the violin.
According to his own account, this consumma-
tion was effected by the aid of the rules laid
down by Antonio Bagatella in his pamphlet
entitled *Regole per la costruzione di violini,
viole, violoncelli, e violoni,* etc., etc., Padua,
1786, of which a second edition appeared in
Padua in 1883, and German translations at
Padua in 1786 and Leipzig in 1806.   In point
of fact Hermann Ritter's viola alta was in
reality a revival of the large tenor viol, that
direct descendant of those *instruments de
remplissage* the quinte and haute contre, which
he methodised into a tenor of extra large
proportions constructed on the scientific
acoustical basis appertaining to the violin.
His public appearances with the instrument
began in 1876.   They attracted the consideration of many eminent composers, and Wagner,
who was at that time occupied with his
'Ring des Nibelungen,' invited his aid for the
production of that opera in the same year.
After completing this engagement Ritter
travelled for several years, touring in Germany, Austria, Switzerland, Holland, Russia,
England and Scotland, and in 1879 he was
appointed professor of musical history and
æsthetics, as well as of the viola, at the Royal
School of Music at Würzburg.   There his
talents and personal influence were the means
of attracting a vast number of students, who
assisted in spreading the fame of his invention,
and in 1889 five of his pupils were playing in
the orchestra of the Bayreuth festival.   In
1889 he was learnedly advocating the use of a
three-footed binder in a pamphlet entitled *Der
dreifüssige oder Normal-Geigensteg* (Würzburg,
G. Hartz).

The Grand Duke of Mecklenburg appointed
Ritter his 'Court Chamber Virtuoso,' and the
Emperor Ludwig II. of Bavaria gave him the
title of 'Court Professor.'   He married the
singer Justine Haecker in 1884.   He wrote
and arranged an immense amount of music for
his viola alta and traced its history in his
book entitled *Die Geschichte des Viola alta*

(Leipzig, Merseburg).   (See VIOLIN FAMILY,
subsection SUBSIDIARY MEMBERS, 7.)

E. H.-A.

BIBL.—G. ADEMA, *Hermann Ritter und seine Viola alta* (Würzburg
1881, 2nd edition, 1890) ; HERMANN RITTER, *Die Viola alta oder
Allgeige* (Leipzig, 1885), 1st edition, Heidelberg, 1876 ; 2nd edition
Leipzig, 1877.   (RIEMANN.)

RITTER, PETER (*b.* Mannheim, July 2,
1763 ; *d.* there, Aug. 1, 1846), studied the
violoncello under Fitz and Danzi, and composition under Vogler, and toured as a violoncello prodigy.   In 1784 he succeeded Franz
Danzi in the Mannheim orchestra, and became
Kapellmeister there in 1803.   He was a composer of great merit, who produced successfully
21 singspiele, an oratorio, quartets, trios, concertos and sonatas for violoncello, also church
music.   His fine popular hymn, 'Lord of
Glory,' was used by Humperdinck in 'The
Miracle' (E. van der Straeten, *Hist. of the
Violoncello*).

RITTER (properly BENNET), THEODORE
(*b.* near Paris, Apr. 5, 1841 ; *d.* there, Apr. 6,
1886), was a pupil of Liszt and wrote a number
of successful drawing-room pieces (' Chant dᵘ
braconnier,' 'Sylphes,' etc.).   He produceu
two operas (' Marianne,' at Paris in 1861, and
' La dea risorta,' at Florence, 1865).

RIVARDE, SERGE ACHILLE (*b.* New York,
Oct. 31, 1865), violinist.   His father was
Spanish ; his mother American.   He lived in
America till the age of 11, receiving lessons successively from Felix Simon, Henri Wieniawski
and Joseph White (a man of colour).   Coming
to Europe he entered the Paris Conservatoire,
to become a pupil of Charles Dancla.   He won
a first prize in July 1879, sharing the same with
Franz Ondříček.   In 1881 he returned to
America, where he stayed three years, and then
gave up violin-playing entirely for a time.   In
1885 he came back to Paris and entered
Lamoureux's orchestra, in which he remained
for five years as principal violin, and occasional soloist.   He gave up the appointment in
1891 and made his début in London in 1894.

In 1899 he took the post of violin professor
at the R.C.M.   He is occasionally heard as
soloist in London and abroad, being the possessor of an exceptionally pure style, but spends
most of his time in teaching.   In 1924 he
started a school of his own for violin-playing in
London, but without abandoning his work at
the R.C.M., where as a teacher of solo and en
semble playing he has earned a high reputation.
He published (1922) a small manual of his
method, *Violin-playing*.                 w. w. c.

RIZZIO (RIZZI, RICCI), DAVID (*b.* Turin,
Italy, early 16th cent. ; *d.* Holyrood Palace,
Scotland, Mar. 9, 1566), the son of a professional
musician and dancing master.   He obtained a
post at the court of the Duke of Savoy, and
came over to Scotland in the train of the
ambassador in 1561.   With his brother Joseph
he remained in the service of Mary Queen of

Scots in the first instance as a bass singer, receiving £80 per year. He so won his way into her favour (no doubt primarily by his ability in connexion with court masques, of which she was fond), that he became, in 1564, her foreign secretary. By this he aroused political and other feelings, and he was stabbed to death, almost in the Queen's presence, in Holyrood Palace, on the evening of Mar. 9, 1566.

There is no doubt that Rizzio exercised some influence on the music then fashionable in Scotland (or at least in Edinburgh), and there appears to have been a very strong tradition that he was the composer of several of the well-known Scots tunes. In 1725 William Thomson in the 'Orpheus Caledonius' puts this tradition into definite form by affixing a mark to seven of the airs there engraved, stating them to be the composition of Rizzio (see ORPHEUS CALEDONIUS). James Oswald and others have in one or two instances also assigned other airs to Rizzio with probably less of tradition to justify them.     F. K.

ROBARTT, of Crewkerne, was an 'orgyn maker' who let out organs to churches by the year. The Mayor of Lyme Regis, in 1551, paid him ten shillings for his year's rent.     V. DE P.

ROBERDAY, FRANÇOIS (d. circa 1695), a learned Paris organist of the 17th century. He was attached to the music of Queen Anne of Austria and Queen Marie-Thérèse, was known as one of the masters of Lully, and was organist of the church of the Petits-pères. His 'Fugues et caprices' (pub. 1660) show him to have been influenced by the German and Italian musicians, especially by Frescobaldi and Frohberger. This work was republished in the 'Archives des maîtres de l'orgue,' by Guilmant and Pirro.     F. R^L.

ROBERT BRUCE, a pasticcio adapted by Niedermeyer from four of Rossini's operas— 'Zelmira,' the 'Donna del lago,' 'Torvaldo e Dorliska' and 'Bianca e Faliero.' Produced without success at the Académie Royale, Dec. 30, 1846. It is published in Italian as 'Roberto Bruce' by Ricordi.     G.

ROBERT LE DIABLE, opera in 5 acts; words by Scribe; music by Meyerbeer. Produced Opéra, Paris, Nov. 21, 1831; in English, imperfectly, as 'The Demon, or the Mystic Branch,' Drury Lane, Feb. 20, 1832, and as 'The Fiend Father, or Robert of Normandy,' Covent Garden, the day following; as 'Robert the Devil,' Drury Lane (Bunn), Mar. 1, 1845; in French, Her Majesty's, June 11, 1832; in Italian, Her Majesty's, May 4, 1847; New York, Park Theatre (English), Apr. 7, 1834.     G.

ROBERTO DEVEREUX, CONTE D'ESSEX. (1) Opera in 3 acts, text by Romani (from Corneille), music by Mercadante. Produced Milan, Mar. 10, 1833 (2) Opera in 3 acts;

libretto by Camerano from Corneille's 'Comte d'Essex,' music by Donizetti. Produced Naples in 1837; Italiens, Paris, Dec. 27, 1838; Her Majesty's Theatre, June 24, 1841.     G.

ROBERTS, HENRY, a music and an ornamental engraver, who issued several notable books of songs with music, now much sought after, mainly on account of their decorative character. In these works the pieces are headed with pictorial embellishments. The earliest of Roberts's publications is 'Calliope, or English Harmony,' in two volumes octavo. It was issued by and for the engraver in periodical numbers of 8 pp. and began late in the year 1737. Twenty-five numbers formed the first volume, which was completed in 1739. The second volume began in this year, but from some cause now unknown the publication came to a standstill when half through, and was not resumed until 1746, when it was met with the imprint of John Simpson (q.v.). This volume contains 'God save the King,' which, from the date 1739 appearing on some of the plates, has been hastily assumed to be prior to the copy in the Gentleman's Magazine of 174.. this, however, is not the case, for ample proof exists that this portion of the volume was not issued before the spring of 1746. The plates of 'Calliope,' thirty or forty years afterwards, came into possession of Longman & Broderip, who reprinted from them. Roberts's other famous work is 'Clio and Euterpe,' precisely similar in style, which, issued in two volumes, bears the dates 1758 and 1759. A later edition has a third volume added, and is dated 1762. A fourth was again added when re-issued by John Welcker. Henry Roberts kept a music and a print-shop in Holborn 'near Hand Alley almost opposite Great Turnstile.' His name is attached as engraver to several pieces of decorative engraving on music-sheets.     F. K.

ROBERTS, JOHN (b. Wales, Dec. 22, 1822; d. May 6, 1877), composer of sacred music. Before 1839 he had adopted the name 'Ieum Gwyllt.' He removed to Liverpool and became editor of a Welsh newspaper, besides writing upon musical matters. In 1858 he again returned to Wales, and at Aberdare set up as a music teacher. On Jan. 10, 1859, he founded there the first of a long series of Welsh musical festivals, and in the same year published a tune-book, 'Llyfr Tonau,' which was much used throughout Wales, and passed through many editions. Roberts was a strong advocate of temperance, and preached as a Calvinistic Methodist.

Information principally from D.N.B.;     F. K.

ROBERTS, JOHN HENRY (b. Penzallt, Wales, 1849; d. Liverpool, July 30, 1924), attained distinction among his countrymen as a composer of hymn-tunes, partsongs, etc.

He became organist of a Welsh chapel at the age of 12, attracted the favourable notice of

S. S. Wesley, who offered him an organistship at Gloucester, spent four years (from 1870) at the R.A.M., where he studied with Sterndale Bennett, and then returned to Wales to become organist at Bethesda and Carnarvon. Later he became principal of the Liverpool Cambrian School of Music, and did much work as adjudicator at Eisteddfodau, where many of his partsongs became popular as test pieces. (See obit. notice, *Liverpool Post*, July 31, 1924.)

ROBERTS, JOHN VARLEY, Mus.D. (*b.* Stanningley, near Leeds, Sept. 25, 1841 ; *d.* Oxford, Feb. 9, 1920), was for 37 years organist and choirmaster of Magdalen College, Oxford, during which time the musical services of the chapel attained a high reputation.

He early exhibited much ability for music, and at 12 was appointed organist of S. John's, Farsley, near Leeds. In 1862 he became organist of S. Bartholomew's, Armley, and in 1868 organist and choirmaster of the parish church, Halifax. In 1871 he graduated Mus.B., and in 1876 Mus.D., at Christ Church, Oxford. During his organistship at Halifax, upwards of £3000 was raised to enlarge the organ, originally built by Snetzler—the instrument upon which Sir William Herschel, the renowned astronomer, formerly played. In 1876 Dr. Roberts became a Fellow of the R.C.O., London. In 1882 he was elected organist at Magdalen College, Oxford, succeeding Sir Walter Parratt. He retired from this in 1919. In 1884 the University Glee and Madrigal Society was founded under his conductorship. In 1885–93 he was organist of St. Giles's, Oxford, and in the former year was appointed examiner in music to the Oxford Local Examinations, and also became conductor of the Oxford Choral Society. In 1883 he was appointed one of the University examiners for musical degrees. In 1916 he was given the degree of M.A. Oxon. *honoris causa.* In 1907 he presented a new organ to his native village. His compositions include sacred cantatas, ' Jonah,' for voices and orchestra ; ' Advent,' ' The Story of the Incarnation,' ' The Passion,' for church choirs ; Psalm ciii. for voices and orchestra ; six Services, one an Evening Service in C written for the London Church Choir Association Festival in 1894 ; about fifty anthems, besides part-songs and organ pieces. His *Practical Method of Training Choristers*, 1898, 1900 and 1905, is very useful.          W. B. S.

ROBIN DES BOIS. The title of the first French version of ' Der FREISCHÜTZ ' (*q.v.*).

ROBIN HOOD. An opera in 3 acts ; words by John Oxenford ; music by G. A. Macfarren. Produced Her Majesty's Theatre, London, Oct. 11, 1860, and had a very great run. G.

Other operas on the same subject have been produced, besides many masques of the 16th and 17th centuries, more or less associated with the May Day games and observances ; of these early pieces little record as to detail has survived.

A ballad opera of the name was acted at Lee & Harper's great booth, at St. Bartholomew's Fair, in 1730 ; the music and libretto of this was published by John Watts in the year of production. A different ' Robin Hood,' by Moses Mendez, was performed at Drury Lane in 1750, the music being supplied by Charles (afterwards Dr.) Burney. Another English ballad opera in 3 acts, which attained some degree of fame, was entitled ' Robin Hood, or Sherwood Forest.' This was written by Leonard MacNally, with the music selected, arranged and composed by William Shield. It was produced at Covent Garden Theatre in 1784, the principals being Mrs. Kennedy, Mrs. Martyr, Mrs. Banister and Miss Kemble, while the male singers were Banister, Johnstone and Edwin. The piece had a considerable run, and several of the songs lasted in popularity long after the opera itself was dead.     F. K.

ROBINSON, (1) ANASTASIA (*b. circa* 1698 ; *d.* Bevis Mount, Southampton, Apr. 1755) was daughter of a portrait painter, who, becoming blind, was compelled to qualify his children to gain their own livelihood. Anastasia received instruction from Dr. Croft, Pier Giuseppe Sandoni, and the singer called The BARONESS (*q.v.*), successively. She appeared in ' Creso ' in 1714 ; as Ariana in Handel's ' Amadigi,' May 25, 1715 ; and in 1720 at the King's Theatre as Echo in Domenico Scarlatti's opera, ' Narciso.' She afterwards sang in the pasticcio of ' Muzio Scevola,' in Handel's ' Ottone,' ' Floridante,' ' Flavio ' and ' Giulio Cesare ' ; in Bononcini's ' Crispo ' and ' Griselda,' and other operas. Her salary was £1000 for the season, besides a benefit-night. She possessed a fine voice of extensive compass, but her intonation was uncertain. She quitted the stage in 1724, having two years previously been privately married to the Earl of Peterborough, who did not avow the marriage until shortly before his death in 1735, although, according to one account, she resided with him as mistress of the house, and was received as such by the Earl's friends. According to another account, she resided with her mother in a house at Parson's Green, which the Earl took for them, and never lived under the same roof with him, until she attended him in a journey in search of health, a short time before his death. She was buried at Bath Abbey. There is a fine portrait of her by Faber after Bank, 1727.

Her younger sister, (2) ELIZABETH intended for a miniature painter, preferred being a singer. She studied under Bononcini, and afterwards at Paris under Rameau ; but though an excellent singer, was said to have been prevented by timidity from ever appearing in public.[1] A fortunate marriage, however, relieved her from the necessity of obtaining her own subsistence.    w. h. h. ; addns. *D.N.B.*

ROBINSON, (1) Francis, was an eminent professor of music in Dublin, and in 1810 was mainly instrumental in founding 'The Sons of Handel,' probably the earliest society established there for the execution of large works. He was the father of four sons, all musicians. The eldest, (2) Francis, Mus.D. (*b. circa* 1799 ; *d.* Oct. 1872), had a tenor voice of great beauty and sympathetic quality ; was a vicar-choral of the two Dublin Cathedrals ; and, at the Musical Festival in Westminster Abbey in June 1834, sang a principal part. Another son, (3) William, had a deep bass of exceptional volume ; while (4) John (*b. circa* 1812; *d.* 1844), the organist of both Cathedrals and of Trinity College, had a tenor ranging to the high D. The four brothers formed an admirable vocal quartet, and were the first to make known the German partsongs then rarely heard either in England or Ireland. (5) Joseph, the youngest (*b.* Aug. 20, 1815 ; *d.* Aug. 23, 1898), was a chorister of St. Patrick's at the early age of 8, and afterwards a member of all the choirs, where his fine delivery of recitative was always a striking feature. He also played in the orchestra of the Dublin Philharmonic. But it is as a conductor that his reputation is best established. In 1834 he founded the Antient Concert Society (see Dublin) of which he was conductor for twenty-nine years, and which ceased to exist soon after his resignation. It began its meetings in his own house, then took a large room, now the Royal Irish Academy, and in 1843 had made such progress that it purchased and remodelled the building since known as the Antient Concert Rooms. Amongst the last things written by Mendelssohn was the instrumentation of his 'Hear my Prayer' (originally composed for voices and organ only), expressly for Robinson to produce at the 'Antients.' It did not reach him till after the composer's death. (See Mendelssohn, Vol. III. p. 407, n. 1.) In 1837 he became conductor of the University Choral Society, founded by the students. At one of its concerts the music of 'Antigone' was given for the first time out of Germany. He continued to conduct the Society for ten years. In 1849 he married Miss Fanny Arthur (see below). In 1852, at the opening of the Cork Exhibition, Robinson conducted the music, which was on a large scale, and included a new cantata by Robert Stewart. In 1853 an International Exhibition was opened in Dublin ; there he assembled 1000 performers, the largest band and chorus yet brought together in Ireland.

In 1856 efforts were made to revive the

Irish Academy of Music, founded in 1848, but languishing for want of funds and pupils. (See Dublin, subsection Royal Irish Academy.) Mr. and Mrs. Robinson joined as professors, and nearly all the Irish artists, both vocal and instrumental, who appeared during their time, owed both training and success to their teaching ; and when, after twenty years, Robinson resigned, the institution was one of importance and stability. In 1859, for the Handel Centenary, he gave the 'Messiah,' with Jenny Lind and Belletti among the principals. The net receipts amounted to £900, an unprecedented sum in Dublin. In 1865 the large Exhibition Palace was opened by the Prince of Wales, and Robinson conducted the performance with a band and chorus of 700.

After the cessation of the 'Antients,' there was no Society to attempt systematically the worthy production of great works. To remedy this a chorus was trained by Robinson, and established in 1876 as the Dublin Musical Society. The last concert conducted by Robinson was on Dec. 6, 1888, previous to which the members presented him with an address and a purse of 100 sovereigns. The purse was returned[2] by him with warm expressions of gratitude, but with the characteristic words :

'While I think a professional man should expect his fair remuneration, yet his chief object may be something higher and nobler—the advancement of art in his native city.'

The Society was revived in 1889, under the conductorship of Dr. Joseph Smith, but collapsed after some years. Robinson wrote a variety of songs, concerted pieces and anthems, besides arranging a number of standard songs and Irish melodies. In 1881 he married for the second time.

In 1849 a young pianist, Miss Fanny Arthur (*b.* Sept. 1831 ; *d.* Oct. 31, 1879), arrived in Dublin from Southampton, and made her first successful appearance there—Feb. 19, 1849. She had studied under Sterndale Bennett and Thalberg. Robinson and she were married July 17 following, and she continued for thirty years to be an extraordinary favourite. Her first appearance in London was at the Musical Union, June 26, 1855, when she played Beethoven's sonata in F (op. 24) with Ernst, and received the praises of Meyerbeer ; also at the New Philharmonic in 1856, where she played Mendelssohn's concerto in D.

Mrs. Robinson passed a very active musical life, though it was often interrupted by nervous illness. In teaching she had a peculiar power of infusing her own ideas into others. She played from time to time at concerts of a high class, and herself gave a very successful concert

[1] A 'Miss Robinson, jun.' appeared at Drury Lane, Jan. 2, 1729, as Ariel in 'The Tempest.' It is possible that this was Margaret Robinson.

[2] In Apr. 1898 Robinson was granted a Civil List Pension.

in Paris, at the Salle Erard (Feb. 4, 1864). Her pianoforte compositions are numerous and graceful. Her sacred cantata, ' God is Love,' was repeatedly performed throughout the kingdom. She met a sudden and tragic end, which caused profound regret.

L. M'C. L. D.; addns. *Brit. Mus. Biog.*, *Mus. T.* Sept. 1898, p. 609, and W. H. G. F. (See also an article by Sir C. V. Stanford in *Cornhill Magazine*, June 1899, and *Studies and Memories*.)

ROBINSON, JOHN (*b.* 1682; *d.* Apr. 30, 1762), was a chorister of the Chapel Royal under Dr. Blow. He became organist of St. Lawrence, Jewry, in 1710, and St. Magnus, London Bridge, in 1713. Hawkins, in his *History*, describes him as ' a very florid and elegant performer on the organ, inasmuch that crowds resorted to hear him '; and elsewhere says :

'In parish churches the voluntary between the Psalms and the first Lesson was anciently a slow, solemn movement, tending to compose the minds and excite sentiments of piety and devotion. Mr. Robinson introduced a different practice, calculated to display the agility of his fingers in *allegro* movements on the cornet, trumpet, sesquialtera, and other noisy stops, degrading the instrument, and instead of the full and noble harmony with which it was designed to gratify the ear, tickling it with mere airs in two parts, in fact solos for a flute and a bass.'

On Sept. 30, 1727, Robinson was appointed to succeed Dr. Croft as organist of Westminster Abbey. He had an extensive practice as a teacher of the harpsichord, and will be long remembered by his double chant in E♭. He was buried, May 13, 1762, in the north aisle of Westminster Abbey. He married, Sept. 6, 1716, Ann, youngest daughter of William Turner, Mus.D. She was a singer, and appeared at the King's Theatre in 1720 in Domenico Scarlatti's opera ' Narciso,' being described as ' MRS. TURNER-ROBINSON ' to distinguish her from Anastasia Robinson, who sang in the same opera. She died Jan. 5, and was buried Jan. 8, 1741, in the west cloister of Westminster Abbey. Robinson had a daughter, who was a contralto singer and the original representative of Daniel in Handel's oratorio ' Belshazzar,' 1745 ; she also sang in others of his oratorios.      W. H. H.

ROBINSON, THOMAS, was author of a curious work published at London in folio in 1603, bearing the following title—*The Schoole of Musicke : wherein is taught the perfect method of the true fingering of the Lute, Pandora, Orpharion and Viol de Gamba*. In 1609 he published ' New Citharen Lessons.'

        W. H. H.

ROBLEDO, MELCHOR (*d.* Saragossa, 1587), Spanish church - musician, who, after some years spent in Rome, returned to Spain (1569) and became choirmaster of the old cathedral (*la Seo*) in Saragossa. His reputation was such that the chapters of both cathedrals (the *Seo*

and the *Pilar*) decided, with unusual artistic insight, that the only church-music to be sung should be drawn from the works of Morales, Victoria, Palestrina and Robledo—a practice which, unfortunately, is no longer followed. Eslava printed 4 motets. Other works in MS. are found in the Sistine Chapel (Mass, 5 v., and motet, 5 v.); Bologna (Lamentations, 4 v.); Valencia, Patriarca, Mass, 5 v.; Saragossa.        J. B. T.

ROBSON, JOSEPH (*d.* 1876), organ-builder. See APOLLONICON ; FLIGHT.

ROCHE, EDMOND (*b.* Calais, Feb. 20, 1828 ; *d.* Paris, Dec. 16, 1861), began life as a violin-player, first as Habeneck's pupil at the Conservatoire, but quickly relinquished music for literature. Roche undertook the translation of the libretto of ' Tannhäuser ' for its representation at the Opéra, Mar. 13, 1861, and in a preface to his *Poésies posthumes* (Paris, Lévy, 1863) Sardou has described the terrible persistence with which Wagner kept his translator to his task. (See Pougin's supplement to Fétis.) In Jullien's *Richard Wagner*, 1887, the facts of the case were made public ; it seems that Roche, not knowing German, had recourse to the services of a friend named Lindau, and the translation, when sent to the director of the Opéra, was rejected, as it was in blank verse ; the necessary alteration into rhyme was made by Roche, Nuitter and Wagner in collaboration. On this Lindau brought an action against Wagner, to enforce the mention of his name as one of the translators ; the case was heard on Mar. 6, 1861, a week before the first representation of the opera, and it was decided that no name but that of Wagner should appear in the books. So that Roche had not even the satisfaction of seeing his name in print in connexion with the work, for even Lajarte (*Bibl. Mus. de l'Opéra*, ii. 230) gives Nuitter as the author of the French words. Besides the poems contained in the volume cited, Roche contributed critical articles to several small periodicals.     M.

ROCHLITZ, JOHANN FRIEDRICH (*b.* Leipzig, Feb. 12, 1769; *d.* Dec. 16, 1842), critic, and founder of the *Allgemeine musikalische Zeitung*.

His fine voice procured his admission at 13 to the Thomasschule, under the cantorship of Doles, where he spent six years and a half. He began to study theology in the University, but want of means compelled him to leave and take a tutorship, which he supplemented by writing. For the titles of his non-musical works see *Riemann*. He also attempted composition, and produced a Mass, a Te Deum, some partsongs for male voices, a setting of Ps. xxiii., and a cantata, ' Die Vollendung des Erlösers.' In 1798 he founded the *Allgemeine musikalische Zeitung* (Breitkopf & Härtel), and edited it till 1818, during which period his articles largely contributed to the improved general appreciation in North Germany of the works of Haydn, Mozart and Beethoven. The best of them were afterwards republished by himself under the title of *Für Freunde der Tonkunst*, in four vols. (1824–32, reprinted later by Dörffel, third edition, 1868). It contains, amongst other matter, an interesting account of a visit to Beethoven at Vienna in 1822. Another important work was a collection in three vols. (Schott, 1838–40) of vocal music, from Dufay to Haydn, entitled 'Sammlung vorzüglicher Gesangstücke vom Ursprung gesetzmässiger Harmonie bis auf die neue Zeit.'[1] The first two volumes of the *A.M.Z.* contain a series of anecdotes on Mozart, whose acquaintance he made during Mozart's visit to Leipzig; but Jahn, in the preface to his *Mozart*, has completely destroyed the value of these as truthful records. Rochlitz was a good connoisseur of paintings and engravings. In 1830 he was one of the committee appointed by the Council of Leipzig to draw up a new hymn-book, and some of the hymns are from his own pen. He also wrote the librettos for Schicht's 'Ende des Gerechten,' Spohr's 'Last Judgment' and 'Calvary,' and for Bierey's opera 'Das Blumenmädchen.' He was a Hofrath of Saxony. F. G.

ROCK, MICHAEL (d. Mar. 1809), was appointed organist of St. Margaret's, Westminster, June 4, 1802, in succession to William Rock, junr., who had filled the office from May 24, 1774. He composed some popular glees— 'Let the sparkling wine go round' (which gained a prize at the Catch Club in 1794), 'Beneath a churchyard yew,' etc. w. h. h.

ROCKSTRO (originally RACKSTRAW), WILLIAM SMITH (b. North Cheam, Surrey,[2] Jan. 5, 1823; d. London, July 2, 1895), was distinguished as a student of modal music and an important contributor to this Dictionary. The form of his surname by which he was known was an older style resumed after 1846.

He was successively pupil of John Purkis, the blind organist, of Sterndale Bennett, and at the Leipzig Conservatorium, where he studied from 1845–46. He enjoyed the special friendship and tuition of Mendelssohn, and was with Hauptmann for theory and with Plaidy for pianoforte. For some years after his return to England he was active as a teacher and performer in London, being regular accompanist at the 'Wednesday concerts,' where Braham and other eminent singers were to be heard. At this period he wrote his most popular and beautiful song, 'Queen and huntress'; and his pianoforte editions of classical and other operas led the way in popularising that class of music in an available form for the use of those who could not read full scores; and in his indications of the orchestral instruments

[1] The complete contents of this collection was given in previous editions of this Dictionary.
[2] Baptized at Morden Church.

above the music-staves he did much to point the way towards a general appreciation of orchestral colour. In the early sixties he left London for Torquay on account of his mother's health and his own, and on her death in 1876 he became a Roman Catholic.

He had been organist and honorary precentor at All Saints' Church, Babbacombe, from 1867, and won a high position as a teacher. He published, with T. F. Ravenshaw, a 'Festival Psalter, adapted to the Gregorian Tones,' in 1863, and 'Accompanying Harmonies to the Ferial Psalter' in 1869. These were the first-fruits of his assiduous study of ancient music, on which he became the first authority of his time in England. A couple of textbooks on harmony (1881) and counterpoint (1882) had a great success, and in the latter part of the first edition of this Dictionary he wrote a large number of articles on musical archæology generally. Later research has superseded his, but at the time he wrote, his contributions to such subjects as the music of the period which closed in 1600 were important. He was too ardent a partisan to be an ideal historian, but his *History of Music for Young Students* (1879) and his larger work, *A General History of Music* (1886), contain much that is of permanent value. His *Life of Handel* (1883) and *Mendelssohn* (1884) are fine examples of eulogistic biography, though they are hardly to be recommended as embodying a calmly critical estimate of either composer. In his larger *History* he showed that he was, nevertheless, not above owning himself in the wrong, and his recantation of certain excessive opinions expressed by him in the Dictionary against Wagner's later works was due to true moral courage. He conducted a concert of sacred music of the 16th and 17th centuries at the Inventions Exhibition of 1885, and in 1891 gave up Torquay for London, giving lectures at the R.A.M. and R.C.M., and holding a class for counterpoint and plain-song at the latter institution. As a singing-master and teacher of the pianoforte his method of imparting instruction was remarkably successful. As a composer, he never quite freed himself from the powerful influences engendered by his studies: the lovely madrigal, 'O too cruel fair,' was judged unworthy of a prize by the Madrigal Society on the ground that it was modelled too closely on Palestrina; and his oratorio, 'The Good Shepherd,' produced at the Gloucester Festival of 1886 under his own direction, was found to bear too many traces of Mendelssohnian influence to deserve success. In 1891 he collaborated with Canon Scott Holland in writing the life of his old friend, Jenny Lind-Goldschmidt; an abbreviated edition came out in 1893, and with Otto Goldschmidt he wrote a still shorter book, *Jenny Lind, her Vocal Art and Culture* (partly reprinted from the biography). For many years his health had been bad, and he had many adverse circumstances to contend with. He fought bravely for all that he held best in art, and boundless enthusiasm carried him through. (*D.N.B.* etc.)        M. ; rev. C.

RODA, CECILIO DE (*b.* Albuñol, Granada, Oct. 24, 1865 ; *d.* Madrid, Nov. 27, 1912), Spanish musical historian, author of valuable papers on the songs, dances and instruments of the time of ' Don Quixote '—*Ilustraciones del Quijote : Los instrumentos músicales y los danzas* (Madrid, Ateneo, 1905) ; on Spanish secular music in the time of Charles V., 1516–56 (*Rev. Mus. de Bilbao*, 1912, Nos. 5-11) ; and on Spanish instruments in the 13th century (*Report of 4th Congress of Int. Mus. Society*; London, 1912, pp. 62, 332). He also described a sketch-book of Beethoven (opp. 130, 132 and 133) which had come into his possession, and did much to make the last quartets and PF. sonatas better known in Madrid.    J. B. T.

RODE, JACQUES PIERRE JOSEPH (*b.* Bordeaux, Feb. 16, 1774 ; *d.* there, Nov. 25, 1830), a great violinist. When 8 years of age he came under the tuition of Fauvel aîné, a well-known violinist of his native town, and studied under him for six years. In 1788 he was sent to Paris. Here Punto (or Stich), the famous horn-player, heard him, and, being struck with the boy's exceptional talent, gave him an introduction to Viotti, with whom he studied for two years. In 1790 he made his first public appearance, when he played Viotti's 13th concerto at the Théâtre de Monsieur with complete success. Although then but 16 years of age, he was appointed leader of the second violins in the excellent band of the Théâtre Feydeau. In this position, appearing at the same time frequently as soloist, he remained till 1794, and then started for his first tour to Holland and the north of Germany. His success, especially at Berlin and Hamburg, was great. From the latter place he sailed for his native town, but the vessel was compelled by adverse winds to make for the English coast. So Rode came to London ; but he only once appeared in public, at a concert for a charitable purpose, and left England again for Holland and Germany. Finally he returned to France and obtained a professorship of the violin at the newly established Conservatoire at Paris. He was solo violin at the Opéra until Nov. 1799. In 1799 he went to Spain, and at Madrid met Boccherini, who is said to have written the orchestration for Rode's earlier concertos, especially for that in B minor. On his return to Paris in 1800 he was appointed solo violinist to the First Consul, and it was at that period that he achieved his greatest success in the French capital. In 1803 he went with Boieldieu to St. Petersburg. Spohr heard him on his passage through Brunswick,

and was so impressed that for a considerable time he made it his one aim to imitate his style and manner as closely as possible. Arrived at the Russian capital, Rode met with a most enthusiastic reception, and was at once attached to the private music of the Emperor with a salary of 5000 roubles (about £750). But the fatigues of life in Russia were so excessive that from this period a decline of his powers appears to have set in. On his return to Paris in 1808 his reception was less enthusiastic than in former times, and even his warmest friends and admirers could not but feel that he had lost considerably in certainty and vigour. From 1811 we find him again travelling in Germany. Spohr, who heard him in 1813 at Vienna, tells in his *Selbstbiographie* (i. 178) of the disappointment he felt at Rode's playing, which he now found mannered, and deficient in execution and style.

In Vienna Rode came into contact with Beethoven, who finished the great sonata in G, op. 96, expressly for him. It was played by Rode and the Archduke Rudolph, Beethoven's pupil, at a private concert, but, as far as the violin part was concerned, not much to the composer's satisfaction. Soon afterwards, at any rate, Beethoven requested the Archduke to send the violin part to Rode that he might play it over before a second performance, and he adds : ' He will not take it amiss ; certainly not ! would to God there were reason to beg his pardon for doing so.' [1] Fétis's statement that Beethoven wrote a Romance for Rode probably rests on a confusion of the G major sonata with the Romanza in the same key.

In 1814 Rode went to Berlin, married, and remained for some time. He then retired to his native place. At a later date he made an ill-advised attempt to resume a public career. But his appearance at Paris proved a complete failure, and Mendelssohn, writing from thence in Apr. 1825, says that he was fixed in his resolution never again to take a fiddle in hand.[2] This failure he took so much to heart that his health began to give way, and he died at Bordeaux, Nov. 25, 1830.

Rode was no mere virtuoso, but a true artist. His truly musical nature shows itself equally in his compositions. His concertos have a noble dignified character and considerable charm of melody, while, it need hardly be added, they are thoroughly suited to the nature of the violin, even though they hardly show high creative power.

He published ten concertos (three more were issued after his death) ; five sets of quartets ; seven sets of variations ; three books of duos for two violins, and the well-known twenty-four caprices.

Of his concertos, the 7th in A minor is still

1 Thayer, *Life of Beethoven*, iii. p. 223.
2 *Die Familie Mendelssohn*, i. p. 149.

in the repertory of some eminent violinists. The variations in G major—the same which the famous singer Catalani and other celebrated vocalists after her made their *cheval de bataille* —are occasionally heard. But above all, his ' 24 caprices or études ' will always, along with Kreutzer's famous forty caprices, hold their place as indispensable for a sound study of the violin.                                    P. D.

RODIO, ROCCO (*b.* Calabria, *c.* 1530), wrote a book on counterpoint which appeared in three editions (1600, 1609, 1626) ; a book of masses (1580), including one in 5 parts, which could be sung also in 4 or even 3 parts by the omission of quintus and treble ; also 2 books of madrigals *a* 4 v. (2nd book in 1587) (*Q.-L.* ; *Riemann*).

RODOLPHE (RUDOLPH), JEAN JOSEPH (*b.* Strassburg, Oct. 14, 1730 ; *d.* Paris, Aug. 18, 1812), studied the horn and violin under his father, and went to Paris in 1746, where he became Leclair's pupil on the violin. After several provincial engagements he entered the chapel of the Duke of Parma in 1754, cultivating chiefly the horn. He studied composition under Traëtta, continuing under Jommelli, when he joined the Stuttgart court chapel in 1761. In 1767 he entered the private music of Prince Conti in Paris, where in 1669 he became solo horn at the Opéra and member of the Royal Chapel in 1770. In the latter year he appeared also in London ; in 1784 he became teacher of harmony at the Paris Conservatoire, where under the reconstruction in 1799 he became professor ' des solfèges ' (elements of music), and resigned in 1802. Mozart and Grétry speak of him with great respect. He composed several operas, ballets, horn concertos and pieces, violin duets, etc., and two instruction books (*Solfèges* and *Théorie d'accompagnement*), which were widely used (*Riemann* ; *Q.-L.* , *Fétis*).

RODRÍGUEZ DE HITA, ANTONIO (*d.* Madrid, Feb. 21, 1787), Spanish composer. He is first heard of in 1757 as choirmaster at Palencia in Old Castille, publishing in a pamphlet of 36 pages [1] as sound advice to his pupils as any teacher could give. He was probably rewarded with the post of musical director of the Convent of the Incarnation at Madrid ; the date of his appointment is sometimes given as 1754 or 1755, though on the title-pages of his pamphlet he describes himself as being still maestro de capilla at Palencia in 1757. His Hymns for 4 and 8 v. (Bibl. Nac. Madrid), probably belonging to this period, are notable for their elegance and nobility of style. Ten years later he made the acquaintance of the Spanish dramatist Don Ramón de la Cruz (1731–96), and the two produced a series of remarkable works in the style of the national lyric

[1] An abstract will be found in Mitjana, *Encl. de la musique: Espagne*, p. 2118.

theatre of Spain, which had suffered under the popularity and efficiency of Italian opera.

' Briseida ' was produced on July 10, 1768, at the Teatro del Príncipe, Madrid. It was an attempt to write an Italian opera with Spanish words and Spanish music ; it was also one of the first public performances in Spain which were given at night. (The overture, some arias and a concerted number were performed under Pedrell in 1896, for the centenary of Ramón de la Cruz.) ' Briseida ' was followed in the autumn of 1768 by ' Las segadoras de Vallecas,' a comic opera on popular lines, in which Spanish rustics were freely introduced ; and this showed the way to the composer's masterpiece, ' Las labradoras de Murcia ' (1769), revived by Pedrell in 1896. The plot is a comedy of Spanish country life and manners. An extremely effective moment depends upon the old belief that silkworms must on no account be allowed to hear the thunder ; and here they are prevented from doing so (as is often actually the case) by a number of people singing and playing upon native instruments. The score is notable for its independent viola-parts, unusual in operatic music of that date, and particularly so in Spain. The music of Rodríguez de Hita (preserved in the Bibl. del Ayuntamiento, Madrid) is remarkable for its thoroughness as well as its real imaginative and dramatic talent.          J. B. T.

RODWELL, GEORGE HERBERT BONAPARTE (*b.* Nov. 15, 1800 ; *d.* Upper Ebury Street, Pimlico, Jan. 22, 1852), brother of J. T. G. Rodwell, part proprietor and manager of the Adelphi Theatre, London, and author of several dramatic pieces, was for many years music director of the Adelphi. On the death of his brother, in Mar. 1825, he succeeded to his share in the theatre. He was a pupil of Vincent Novello and Henry Bishop, and became in 1828 professor of harmony and composition at the R.A.M. He was the composer of very many operettas and other dramatic pieces, of which the following are the principal :

' The Flying Dutchman' (Adelphi, 1826) ; ' The Cornish Miners ' (English Opera-House, 1827) ; ' The Bottle Imp ' and ' The Mason of Buda ' (partly adapted from Auber's ' Le Maçon,' 1828) ; ' The Spring Lock,' ' The Earthquake ' and ' The Devil's Elixir ' (1829) ; ' The Black Vulture ' (1830) ; ' My Own Lover ' and ' The Evil Eye ' (1832) ; ' The Lord of the Isles ' (1834) ; ' Paul Clifford ' (with Blewitt), (1835) ; ' The Spirit of the Bell ' (Lyceum, 1835) ; ' The Sexton of Cologne ' (1836) ; ' Jack Sheppard ' (1839) ; and ' The Seven Sisters of Munich ' (1847).

In 1836 he was director of the music at Covent Garden, where he brought out many adaptations of operas, etc., ' anticipating the repertory of Drury Lane ' (*D.N.B.*). He was author of several farces and other dramatic pieces, amongst which were *Teddy the Tiler* (written in 1830 for Tyrone Power, and eminently successful), *The Chimney-Piece*, *The Pride of Birth*, *The Student of Lyons* and *My Wife's Out* ; of three novels, *Old London Bridge*, *Memoirs of an Umbrella* and *Woman's Love* ;

and of *The First Rudiments of Harmony,*
1831. He composed also two collections of
songs: ' Songs of the Sabbath Eve ' and
' Songs of the Birds ' (1827). For many years
he persistently advocated the establishment
of a National Opera. He married the daughter
of Liston, the comedian. He was buried at
Brompton Cemetery. W. H. H.

ROECKEL, (1) PROFESSOR JOSEPH AUGUST
(*b.* Neumburg vorm Wald, Upper Palatinate,
Aug. 28, 1783 ; *d.* Anhalt-Cöthen, Sept. 1870).
He was originally intended for the church,
but in 1803 entered the diplomatic service of
the Elector of Bavaria as Private Secretary to
the Bavarian Chargé d'Affaires at Salzburg.
On the recall of the Salzburg Legation in 1804,
he accepted an engagement to sing at the
Theater an-der-Wien, where, Mar. 29, 1806,
he appeared as Florestan in the revival of
' Fidelio.' [1] In 1823 Roeckel was appointed
professor of singing at the Imperial Opera ; in
1828 he undertook the direction of the opera
at Aix-la-Chapelle, and in the following year
made the bold experiment of producing German operas in Paris with a complete German
company. Encouraged by the success of this
venture, Roeckel remained in Paris until 1832,
when he brought his company to London,
and produced ' Fidelio,' ' Der Freischütz ' and
other masterpieces of the German school, at
the King's Theatre ; the principal artists
being Schröder-Devrient and Haitzinger, with
Hummel (Roeckel's brother-in-law) as conductor. In 1835 he retired from operatic life,
and in 1853 finally returned to Germany,
where he died.

(2) AUGUST (*b.* Graz, Dec. 1, 1814 ; *d.* Buda-
Pest, June 18, 1876), his eldest son, was
music director at Bamberg, at Weimar (1838–
1843), and lastly was music director at the
Dresden Opera in 1843–49, and so a colleague of
Richard Wagner ; being, like the latter, involved in the Revolution of 1848 (he had also
witnessed the Paris Revolution of 1830), he
abandoned music and devoted himself entirely to politics. He spent thirteen years in
prison (1849–62), and on his release became
editor of various newspapers at Coburg
Frankfort, Munich and Vienna successively.
He published an account of his imprisonment
(*Sachsens Erhebung,* etc.). Wagner's letters
to him were published in 1894, and translated
into English by Miss E. C. Sellar shortly afterwards. From admiration of Wagner's genius,
Roeckel withdrew an opera of his own, ' Farinelli,' which had been accepted for performance
at Dresden. See also Praeger's *Wagner as I
knew him,* p. 119 ff.

(3) EDWARD (*b.* Trèves, Nov. 20, 1816 ;
*d.* Bath, Nov. 2, 1899), the 2nd son of Joseph
Roeckel (1), received his musical education

from his uncle, J. N. Hummel. He came to
London in 1835, and gave his first concert in
1836 at the King's Theatre. He subsequently
went on a concert tour in Germany, and performed with great success at the courts of
Prussia, Saxony, Saxe-Weimar, Anhalt-Dessau,
etc. In 1848 he settled in England, and
resided at Bath, where he succeeded Henry
Field. He published a considerable quantity
of pianoforte music.

(4) JOSEPH LEOPOLD (*b.* London, Apr. 11,
1838 ; *d.* Vittel, Vosges, June 20, 1923), the
youngest son, studied composition at Würzburg
under Eisenhofer, and orchestration under
Götze at Weimar. He also settled in England,
and lived at Clifton ; he was well known as a
teacher and a voluminous composer of songs.
His cantatas ' Fair Rosamond,' ' Ruth,' ' The
Sea Maidens,' ' Westward Ho,' ' Mary Stuart,'
' The Victorian Age ' (1887) and many others
were received with much favour. The
first of these was performed at the Crystal
Palace in 1871, and a baritone scena with
orchestra, ' Siddartha,' was produced at the
Bristol Festival of 1896. A song-cycle was
brought forward at the same festival in 1902.
In 1864 Roeckel married Miss JANE JACKSON
(*b.* 1834 ; *d.* Clifton, Aug. 26, 1907), a successful
pianist, who did much good work as a teacher
at Clifton, and wrote pianoforte pieces, etc.,
under the name of Jules de Sivrai. W. B. S.

RÖLLIG, JOHANN GEORG (*b.* Berg-Giess-
hübel, Saxony, 1710 ; *d.* Vienna, 1804), studied
at Dresden, chiefly under Zelenka, becoming
violoncellist in the court chapel at Zerbst,
where he still was in 1761. as Konzertmeister,
and as famous teacher. He composed church
music, cantatas, etc. (*Q.-L.* ; *Riemann*).

RÖLLIG, KARL LEOPOLD, from 1764–73
conductor of Ackermann's theatrical company
at Hamburg, was an improver of and virtuoso
on the glass-harmonica, and inventor of the
orphica and Xänorphica (improved PF. and
archi-PF). In 1797 he was appointed at the
Imperial Library, Vienna. He composed concertos and pieces for the above instruments;
also interlude for orchestra, songs and theoretical works, etc. (*Q.-L.* ; *Riemann*).

RÖNTGEN, (1) ENGELBERT (*b.* Deventer,
Holland, Sept. 30, 1829 ; *d.* Leipzig, Dec. 12,
1897), entered the Conservatorium at Leipzig
in 1848, as a pupil of David for violin and of
Hauptmann for theory. Upon graduating at
the Conservatorium, Röntgen was engaged as
a first violin both in the Opera orchestra and
in the famous Gewandhaus orchestra. In
1869 he became professor of the violin at the
Conservatorium; second Konzertmeister of the
Gewandhaus orchestra, and, on the death of his
illustrious master, David, in 1873 he was made
first Konzertmeister in his place. Röntgen
was a fine violinist although he never adopted
the career of a virtuoso, and his careful editing

---

[1] For Roeckel's own account of his intercourse with Beethoven
see Thayer, vol. ii. p. 294, and vol. iii. p. 269.

of Beethoven's quartets proves him to have been a scholarly musician. He married a daughter of Moritz Klengel, Konzertmeister at the Gewandhaus.

BIBL.—A. EHRLICH, *Celebrated Violinists* ; BACHMANN, *Le Violon*; LAHEE, *Famous Violinists* ; ETHEL SMYTH, *Impressions that Remained*, ii. p. 252.    E. H.-A.

RÖNTGEN, JULIUS (b. Leipzig, May 10, 1855), composer, the child of Dutch parents. His father was Engelbert Röntgen, leader of the Gewandhaus Orchestra, Leipzig. In 1877 Röntgen came to Amsterdam, where he lived till 1924, working as a pianist, teacher, conductor and, since 1914, director of the Conservatoire.

Röntgen is a very gifted and prolific composer, in the romantic style, and he has also made his mark through his arrangements and editions of old Dutch songs and dances. Amongst his compositions, his chamber works take the most important place. He has composed also several operas, songs, choral works and orchestral music, including a symphony, a pianoforte concerto, and a charming ballade based on a Norwegian folk-tune. He has published *Brahms's Correspondence with Th. Engelmann* (1918). His own interesting correspondence with his friend Edvard Grieg he has not yet made public.    R. MᶜG.

ROGEL, JOSÉ (b. Orihuela, Alicante, Dec. 24, 1829; d. Cartagena, Feb. 25, 1901), Spanish conductor and composer, began music under Cascales, and Gil, organist and conductor of the cathedral, and made great progress, till sent to Valencia by his father to study law. Under the guidance of Pascual Perez, a musician of ability, he learned composition and other branches of practical music. After completing his legal course and taking his degree at Madrid, Rogel was able to indulge his taste, and acted as conductor and composer to several theatres. His earliest opera publicly performed was 'Loa a la Libertad' (Madrid, 1854). Between this date and 1881 he wrote or collaborated in 81 theatrical works (mainly *Zarzuelas*), of which 'El joven Telémaco' was the most popular. In some he collaborated with BARBIERI (q.v.). The titles of his pieces are of all characters, ranging from 'Revista de un muerto' and 'Un viage de mil demonios' to 'El General Bumbum.'    G. ; addns. J. B. T.

ROGER, ESTIENNE, an Amsterdam music publisher who was in a very extensive way of business from 1696 to 1722. His work is of the highest class of music printing and engraving, and is from copperplates. It is said that he was one of the first to introduce the practice of punching the notes on the copper as a substitute for engraving. Walsh and Hare are stated to have taken this idea from him and to have used pewter, a cheaper and a more ductile metal. He translated the *Traité de la composition* of de Nivers into Flemish (1697).

Among other works Roger issued, circa 1720, a fine edition of Corelli's four sets of sonatas, and also of the same composer's concertos. Several collections of miscellaneous works are mentioned in Q.-L.

Roger either died or gave up business about 1725 (his last dated publication is 1722), leaving as his successor Michel Charles Le Céne, who reissued many of his predecessor's publications.    F. K.

ROGER, GUSTAVE HIPPOLITE (b. La Chapelle-Saint-Denis, Paris, Dec. 17, 1815 ; d. Paris, Sept. 12, 1879), eminent French singer. He entered the Conservatoire in 1836, and after studying for a year under Martin carried off the first prizes both for singing and opéra-comique. He obtained an immediate engagement, and made his début at the Opéra-Comique, Feb. 16, 1838, as Georges in 'L'Éclair.' To a charming voice and distinguished appearance he added great intelligence and stage tact, qualities which soon made him the favourite tenor of the Parisian world, and one of the best comedians of the day. Ambroise Thomas composed for him 'Le Perruquier de la Régence' and 'Mina,' Halévy gave him capital parts in 'Les Mousquetaires de la Reine' and 'Le Guitarrero,' and Auber secured him for 'Le Domino noir,' 'La Part du Diable,' 'La Sirène' and 'Haydée.' Meyerbeer declared him to be the only French artist capable of creating the part of John of Leyden. In consequence, after ten years of uninterrupted success, Roger left the Opéra-Comique for the Opéra, where on Apr. 16, 1849, he created an immense sensation with Mme. Viardot, in 'Le Prophète.' During the next ten years he was invaluable at the Opéra, creating new parts in the 'Enfant prodigue,' the 'Juif errant' and many more. His best creation after John of Leyden, and his last part at the Opéra, was Hélios in David's 'Herculanum' (Mar. 4, 1859). In the following autumn he lost his right arm while shooting, by the bursting of a gun ; he reappeared with a false one, but with all his skill and bravery he could not conceal his misfortune, and found himself compelled to bid farewell to the Opéra and to Paris.

He went once more to Germany, which he had been in the habit of visiting since 1850, and where he was invariably successful, partly owing to his unusual command of the language. After this he sang in the principal provincial theatres of France, and in 1862 reappeared at the Opéra-Comique in his best parts, especially that of Georges Brown in 'La Dame blanche,' but it was evident that the time for his retirement had arrived. He then took pupils for singing, and in 1868 accepted a professorship at the Conservatoire, which he held till his death.

Roger was the author of the French translation of Haydn's 'Seasons,' and of the words of several romances and German Lieder. His book, *Le Carnet d'un ténor* (Paris, Ollendorff, 1880), is a portion of his autobiography. It contains an account of his visits to England in 1847 (June) and 1848 (June-Nov.), when he sang at the Royal Italian Opera, and made an artistic tour in the provinces with Mlle. Jenny Lind and other artists.          G. C.

ROGER-DUCASSE, see DUCASSE.

ROGERS, BENJAMIN, Mus.D. (*b.* Windsor, 1614 ; *d.* June 1698), son of Peter Rogers, lay-clerk of St. George's Chapel, Windsor, was a chorister of St. George's under Dr. Giles, and afterwards a lay-clerk there. He succeeded Jewett in 1639 as organist of Christ Church, Dublin, where he continued until the rebellion in 1641, when he returned to Windsor and obtained a lay-clerk's place there ; but on the breaking up of the choir in 1644 he taught music in Windsor and its neighbourhood, and obtained some compensation for the loss of his appointment. In 1653 he composed some airs in four parts for violins and organ, which were presented to the Archduke Leopold, after-wards Emperor of Germany, and favourably received by him. In 1658 he was admitted Mus.B. at Cambridge.[1] In 1660 he composed a 'Hymnus Eucharisticus' in four parts, to words by Dr. Nathaniel Ingelo, which was performed at Guildhall when Charles II. dined there on July 5.[2] About the same time he became organist of Eton College. On Oct. 21, 1662, he was reappointed a lay-clerk at St. George's, Windsor, his stipend being augmented by half the customary amount ; and he also received out of the organist's salary £1 per month as deputy organist. On July 22, 1664, he was appointed Informator Choristarum and organist of Magdalen College, Oxford. On July 8, 1669, he proceeded Mus.D. at Oxford. In Jan. 1685 he was removed from his place at Magdalen College on account of irregularities,[3] the College, however, assuring to him an annuity of £30 for life. He survived until June 1698, on the 21st of which month he was buried at St. Peter-le-Bailey. His widow, whom the College had pensioned with two-thirds of his annuity, survived him only seven months, and was laid by his side Jan. 5, 1699.

Rogers composed much church music ; four services are printed in the collections of Boyce, Rimbault and Ouseley ; another, an Evening Verse Service in G, is at Ely in MS. Some anthems were printed in 'Cantica sacra,' 1674, and by Boyce and Page ; and many others are in MS. in the books of various cathedrals and college chapels. Four glees are contained in Playford's 'Musical Companion,' 1673, and many instrumental compositions in 'Courtly Masquing Ayres,' 1662. Some MS. organ com-positions are in the R.C.M., and J. S. Bumpus

possessed a volume in the handwriting of Dr. Philip Hayes, containing the whole of Rogers's compositions for the church. His 'Hymnus Eucharisticus' (the first stanza of which, beginning 'Te Deum Patrem colimus,' daily sung in Magdalen College Hall by way of grace after dinner, is printed in the Appendix to Hawkins's *History*) is sung annually on the top of Magdalen tower at five in the morning of May 1 in lieu of a Requiem which, before the Reformation, was performed in the same place for the soul of Henry VII. His service in D and some of his anthems, which are pleasing and melodious in character, are still sung in cathedrals.        W. H. H.

ROGERS, JOHN (*b.* London ; *d.* Aldersgate, London, *c.* 1663), a famous lutenist, was attached to the household of Charles II. in 1661–63. He lived near Aldersgate.        W. H. H.

ROGERS, SIR JOHN LEMAN, Bart. (*b.* Apr. 18, 1780 ; *d.* Dec. 10, 1847), succeeded his father in the baronetcy in 1797. He became a member of the Madrigal Society in 1819, and in 1820 was elected its permanent presi-dent (being the first so appointed), and held the office until 1841, when he resigned on account of ill-health. He composed a cathe-dral service, chants, anthems, madrigals, glees and other vocal music. He was an ardent admirer of the compositions of Tallis, and by his exertions an annual service was held for several years in Westminster Abbey, the music being wholly that of Tallis.        W. H. H.

ROGERS, ROLAND, Mus.D. (*b.* West Brom-wich, Staffordshire, Nov. 17, 1847), was ap-pointed organist of St. Peter's Church, West Bromwich, in 1858. He studied under S. Grosvenor, and in 1862 obtained by competition the post of organist at St. John's, Wolver-hampton. In 1867 he similarly obtained the organistship of Tettenhall parish church, and in 1871 was appointed organist and choir-master of Bangor Cathedral, a post which he resigned at the end of 1891. He took the Oxford degree of Mus.B. in 1870, and that of Mus.D. in 1875. Dr. Rogers's published works are 'Prayer and Praise,' a cantata, a prize cantata, 'The Garden' (Llandudno, 1896), Evening Services in B♭ and D, anthems, part-songs, organ solos and songs ; a symphony in A, a psalm 'De Profundis,' and several anthems and services are still in MS.        W. B. S.

ROGIER, PHILIP (*b.* Arras, 1562/3 (?) ; *d.* Madrid, Feb. 29, 1596), first heard of as a choir-boy in Madrid (June 15, 1572) ; and a member of the Chapel Royal again from 1586. He was appointed maestro de capilla in 1587, vice-master of the singers in 1590. In 1609 he was succeeded by Mateo Romero, his pupil. His printed works include :

Sacrarum Modulationum quas vulgo motecta appellant, 4, 5, 6 et 8 v. Lib. I. Naples, 1595. (Valladolid.)
Missæ Sex . . . Madrid, 1598. (Madrid, Bibl. Nac. ; Toledo, Cathedral ; Milan, Cathedral ; Tournai Publ. Library.)

---

[1] See Carlyle's *Oliver Cromwell*, v. 243, 244 (People's edition).
[2] The hymn was different from that, bearing the same title, which Rogers afterwards set for Magdalen College, Oxford.
[3] See West's *Cath. Org.* p. 120.

This contains 5 masses by Rogier and one by his pupil, G. de Ghersem. In the Mass ' Philippus secundus Rex Hispaniae,' these words are sung by the tenor to the canto fermo throughout the work (cf. MORALES). MSS. of Philip Rogier are preserved in the Escurial and at the new cathedral (El Pilar), Saragossa.    J. B. T.

ROGNONE-TAEGIO (ROGNONI), (1) RIC-CARDO, a 16th-century musician at Milan, composed Canzonette alla napolitana, a 3-4 v. (1586); passagi . . . nel diminuire (for playing divisions) (1592); pavane et balli, etc. (4-5 parts, 1603). His sons were (2) GIOVANNI DOMENICO, organist and Ducal maestro di cappella at Milan, c. 1620; composed organ canzonas (1605), 2 books of madrigals (1605, 1619), a Requiem Mass (1624). (3) FRANCESCA, an early 17th-century maestro di cappella of St. Ambrogio, Milan; composed masses, motets, madrigals, fauxbourdons, correnti e gagliarde, aggiunta dello scolare di violino, selva di varij passagi, etc. (embellishments in singing and playing), (between 1610-24) (Q.-L.; Riemann).

ROGUES' MARCH, THE, originally a military quickstep, which from some cause has become appropriate to use when offenders were drummed out of the army. When, from theft, or other crime, it was decided to expel a man from the regiment, the buttons bearing the regimental number, and other special decorations, were cut from his coat, and he was then marched, to the music of drums and fifes playing ' The Rogues' March,' to the barrack gates, and kicked or thrust out into the street.

The writer, though he has made diligent search, cannot find traces of the tune before the middle of the 18th century, although there can be but little doubt that the air, with its association, had been in use long before that time. About 1790, and later, a certain more vocal setting of the air was used for many popular humorous songs. ' Robinson Crusoe,' ' Abraham Newland ' and the better-known ' Tight little Island,' are among these. The latter song, as ' The Island,' was written by Thomas Dibdin about 1797,[1] and sung by a singer named Davies at Sadler's Wells in that year.

The original ' Rogues' March ' stands thus—

[1] Dibdin's Memoirs.

It is found in many 18th-century collections of fife and flute music; the above copy is from ' The Compleat Tutor for the Fife,' London, printed for and sold by Thompson & Son, 8vo, circa 1759-60.    F. K.

ROHR FLUTE (ROHRFLÖTE), see FLUTE-WORK.

ROI DE LAHORE, LE, opera in 5 acts, text by Louis Gallet; music by Jules Massenet. Produced Opéra, Paris, Apr. 27, 1877; Covent Garden, June 28, 1879.

ROI DES VIOLONS—' king of the violins ' —a title of great interest as illustrating the struggle between art and authority. On Sept. 14, 1321, the ménestriers or fiddlers of France formed themselves into a regular corporation, with a code of laws in eleven sections, which was presented to the Prévôt of Paris, and by him registered at the Châtelet. The Confraternity, founded by thirty-seven jongleurs and jongleresses, whose names have been preserved, prospered so far as in 1330 to purchase a site and erect on it a hospital for poor musicians. The building was begun in 1331, finished in 1335, and dedicated to St. Julien and St. Genest. The superior of this ' Confrérie of St. Julien des ménétriers ' was styled ' king,' and the following were ' Rois des ménétriers ' in the 14th century: Robert Caveron, 1338; Copin du Brequin, 1349; Jean Caumez, 1387; and Jehan Portevin, 1392.

In 1407 the musicians, vocal and instrumental, separated themselves from the mountebanks and tumblers who had been associated with them by the statutes of 1321. The new constitution received the sanction of Charles VI., Apr. 24, 1407, and it was enacted that no musician might teach or exercise his profession without having passed an examination, and been declared suffisant by the ' Roi des ménestrels ' or his deputies. These statutes continued in force down to the middle of the 17th century. History, however, tells but little about the new corporation. The only ' rois ' whose names have been preserved in the charters are—Jehan Boissard, called Verdelet, 1420; Jehan Facien, the elder, and Claude de Bouchardon, oboes in the band of Henri III., 1575; Claude Nyon, 1590; Claude Nyon, called Lafont, 1600; François Rishomme, 1615; and Louis Constantin, ' roi ' from 1624 to 1655. Constantin (d. Paris, 1657), was a distinguished artist, violinist to Louis XIII. and composer of pieces for strings in five and six parts, several of which are preserved in the valuable collection already named under PHILIDOR.

In 1514 the title was changed to ' roi des ménestrels du royaume.' All provincial musicians were compelled to acknowledge the authority of the corporation in Paris, and in the 16th century branches were established in the principal towns of France under the title of ' Confrérie de St. Julien des ménétriers.' In

Oct. 1658 Louis XIV. confirmed Constantin's successor, Guillaume Dumanoir I., in the post of ' Roi des violons, maîtres à danser, et joueurs d'instruments tant haut que bas,' ordaining at the same time that the ' Roi des violons ' should have the sole privilege of conferring the mastership of the art throughout the kingdom ; that no one should be admitted thereto without serving an apprenticeship of four years, and paying sixty livres to the ' roi,' and ten livres to the masters of the Confrérie ; the masters themselves paying an annual sum of thirty sous to the corporation, with a further commission to the ' roi ' for each pupil. The masters alone were privileged to play in taverns and other public places, and in case this rule were infringed the ' roi ' could send the offender to prison and destroy his instruments. This formidable monopoly extended even to the king's band, the famous ' twenty-four violons,' who were admitted to office by the ' roi ' alone on payment of his fee. (See VINGT-QUATRE VIOLONS.)

So jealously did Guillaume Dumanoir I. guard his rights that in 1662 he began an action against thirteen dancing-masters, who, with the view of throwing off the yoke of the corporation, had obtained from Louis XIV. permission to found an ' Académie de danse.' The struggle gave rise to various pamphlets,[1] and Dumanoir was beaten at all points. He bequeathed a difficult task to his son Michel Guillaume Dumanoir II., who succeeded him as ' roi ' in 1668, and endeavoured to enforce his supremacy on the instrumentalists of the Opéra, but, as might have been expeedct, was overmatched by Lully. After his difficulties with the director of the Opéra, Dumanoir II., like his father, came into collision with the dancing-masters. In 1691 a royal proclamation was issued by which the elective committee was abolished, and its place filled by hereditary officials, aided by four others appointed by purchase. Against this decree the corporation and the thirteen members of the Académie de Danse protested, but the Treasury was in want of funds, and declined to refund the purchase money. Finding himself unequal to such assaults Dumanoir resigned in 1693, and died in Paris in 1697. He delegated his powers to the privileged committee of 1691, and thus threw on them the onus of supporting the claims of the Confrérie over the clavecinists and organists of the kingdom ; a parliamentary decree of 1695, however, set free the composers and professors of music from all dependence on the corporation of the ménétriers. This struggle was several times renewed. When Pierre Guignon

[1] Of these the principal are *Établissement de l'Académie royale de dance* [sic] *en la ville de Paris, avec un discours académique pour prouver que la dance, dans sa plus noble partie, n'a pas besoin des instruments de musique, et qu'elle est en tout absolument indépendante du violon* (Paris, 1663, 4to), and *Le Mariage de la musique st de la dance* [sic], *contenant la réponce* [sic] *au livre des treize prétendus académiciens touchants ces deux arts* (Paris, 1664, 12mo).

(b. 1702 ; d. 1774), a good violinist, and a member of the King's chamber-music and of the Chapel Royal, attempted to reconstitute the Confrérie on a better footing, it became evident that the musicians as a body were determined to throw off the yoke of the association. Guignon was appointed ' Roi des violons ' by letters patent, June 15, 1741, was installed in 1742, and in 1747 endeavoured to enforce certain new enactments, but a parliamentary decree of May 30, 1750, put an end to his pretended authority over clavecinists, organists and other serious musicians. The corporation was maintained, but its head was obliged to be content with the title of ' Roi et maître des ménétriers, joueurs d'instruments tant haut que bas, et hautbois, et communauté des maîtres à danser.' Roi Guignon still preserved the right of conferring on provincial musicians the title of ' lieutenants généraux et particuliers' to the ' roi des violons,' but even this was abrogated by a decree of the Conseil d'État, Feb. 13, 1773. The last ' roi des violons ' at once resigned, and in the following month his office was abolished by an edict of the King dated from Versailles.          G. C.

BIBL.—*Abrégé historique de a Ménestrandie* (Versailles, 1774, 12mo) ; *Statuts et règlements des maîtres de danse et joueurs d'instruments . . . registrés au Parlement le 22 Août 1659* (Paris, 1753) ; *Recueil d'édits, arrêts du Conseil du roi, lettres patentes, . . . en faveur des musiciens du Royaume* (Ballard, 1774, 8vo) ; A. VIDAL, *Les Instruments à archet* (i. and ii., Paris, 1876, 1877, 4to). B. BERNARD, *Recherches sur l'histoire de la Corporation des Ménétriers* (Bibliothèque de l'École des Chartes, v.) ; R. THOINAN, *Louis Constantin, roi des violons* (Paris, 1878) ; LA LAURENCIE, *Guignon* (*L'École française de violon*, ii. (1923, pp. 40–76).

ROI D'YS, LE, opera in 3 acts, text by Édouard Blau ; music by Lalo, produced Opéra-Comique, Paris, May 7, 1888 ; Covent Garden, July 17, 1901.

ROI L'A DIT, LE, opéra-comique in 3 acts ; text by Edm. Gondinet ; music by Delibes. Produced Opéra-Comique, May 24, 1873 ; in English, Prince of Wales's Theatre, by the R.C.M., Dec. 13, 1894.

ROI MALGRÉ LUI, LE, opéra-comique in 3 acts ; text by Emile de Najac and Paul Burani ; music by Chabrier. Produced Opéra-Comique, Paris, May 18, 1887.

ROITZSCH, F. AUGUST (b. Gruna, near Görlitz, Dec. 10, 1805 ; d. Leipzig, Feb. 4, 1889), won a high reputation as a careful editor of old music, and more especially of Bach's instrumental compositions, in the valuable cheap editions of the firm of Peters.

          M.

ROKITANSKY, (1) HANS, FREIHERR VON (b. Vienna, Mar. 8, 1835 ; d. Laubegg, Nov. 1909), eldest son of Carl Freiherr von Rokitansky (1804–78), an eminent medical professor. He studied singing chiefly at Bologna and Milan, and first appeared in England at concerts in 1856. In 1862 he made his début at Prague in ' La Juive,' and fulfilled a very successful engagement there of two years. In 1863 he sang the same part at Vienna, in 1864 obtained an engagement there, and was a member of the opera company for many years, retiring in 1892. His voice was a basso-profondo of great compass and volume, very equal in all its range ; he had a commanding presence, and was an excellent actor. On June 17, 1865, he reappeared in London at Her Majesty's as Marcel with very great success, and then sang there and at Drury Lane for four consecutive seasons, and was greatly esteemed. He returned for the seasons of 1876 and 1877 in some of his old parts, and played for the first time the King in 'Lohengrin,' and Giorgio in 'I Puritani.' He retired from public life at the end of 1894, and became a professor in the Vienna Conservatorium.

(2) VICTOR (b. July 9, 1836 ; d. Vienna, July 17, 1896), a younger brother of the above, and a fashionable singing-master at Vienna. From 1871–80 he filled the post of professor of singing at the Conservatorium of Vienna ; he published *Über Sänger und Singen* in 1894.

A. C.

ROLFE & CO., pianoforte-makers. William Rolfe was at 112 Cheapside in 1796 as a music-seller and publisher of minor musical works, also as maker of musical instruments. Before this date he was partner in a small music-publishing firm, Culliford, Rolfe, & Barrow, at the same address, about 1790. With Samuel Davis, Rolfe took out a patent for improvements in pianofortes on Jan. 31, 1797, and his pianofortes had some degree of reputation. His business continued until 1806, when the firm was William Rolfe & Sons, and in 1813 they had additional premises at 28 London Wall. Rolfe & Sons (or Co.) remained in Cheapside for many years. In 1850 the number had been changed to 61, and the London Wall premises to 31 and 32. They removed to 12 Great Marlborough Street (1869), and then (1878) to 11 Orchard Street. During the 'eighties their place of business was at 6 Lower Seymour Street, but after 1890 no traces of them can be found.    F. K.

ROLL (Ger. *Wirbel*), the name given to a tremolo effect on the DRUM (q.v.).

ROLLA, (1) ALESSANDRO (b. Pavia, Apr. 22, 1757 ; d. Milan, Sept. 15, 1841), violinist and composer. He first studied the pianoforte, but soon exchanged it for the violin, which he learned under Renzi and Conti. He had also a great predilection for the viola, and wrote and performed in public concertos for that instrument. In 1782–1802 he was leader of the band at Parma, and it was there that PAGANINI (q.v.) was for some months his pupil. In 1802 he went to Milan as leader and conductor of the opera at La Scala, in which position he gained a great reputation. He became in 1805 a professor at the Conservatorio of Milan. His compositions had considerable success in their time ; they consist

of a large number of violin duets, some serenades, trios, quartets and quintets for stringed instruments, and concertos for the violin and for the viola, as well as songs. (See Q.-L.)

His son and pupil, (2) ANTONIO (b. Parma, Apr. 18, 1798 ; d. Dresden, May 19, 1837), was leader of the Italian Opera band at Dresden from 1823–35. He published concertos and other solo pieces for the violin.    P. D.

ROLLAND, ROMAIN (b. Clamecy, Nièvre, Jan. 29, 1866), writer on music. He was a pupil at the École Normale Supérieure (1886–89), an *agrégé* in history, pupil at the École française at Rome (1889–91), *chargé de mission* in Italy (1892–93). He was made 'docteur ès lettres,' June 19, 1895, and presented a musical thesis (the first to follow that of Jules Combarieu)—*Les Origines du théâtre lyrique moderne : histoire de l'opéra en Europe avant Lulli et Scarlatti*. His Latin thesis was entitled : *Cur ars picturœ apud Italos xvi. sœculi deciderit ?*

Rolland became president of the musical section of the École des Hautes-Études Sociales (1901), and gave a course of lectures on the history of music at the École Normale Supérieure ; and in 1903 at the Sorbonne.[1] He resigned this instructional work for reasons of health, and has lived in Switzerland since 1913.

Rolland wrote for the *Revue de Paris*, *Revue d'art dramatique*, and *Revue musicale* of J. Combarieu, the *S.I.M.*, the *Encyclopédie musicale* of Lavignac ; and has published the following works : *Beethoven* (1903) ; *Paris als Musikstadt* (1905); *Haendel* (1910) ; *Des Études sur l'opéra au XVIIe siècle* (*Encyclopédie* Lavignac). He has collected a certain number of studies in *Musiciens d'aujourd'hui* and *Musiciens d'autrefois* (2 vols. 1908 ; 2nd ed. 1925 ; Eng. transl. 1915), and in *Voyage au pays du passé* (1919 ; 2nd ed. 1920). The novel, *Jean-Christophe* (1904–12), in which the hero is a musician, must be included among the musical works of Rolland.

As a dramatist Rolland has produced or published between 1897 and 1925 a certain number of works collected together under the title *Théâtre de la Révolution* and *Théâtre de l'âme*. He has published in addition *François Millet* (London, 1902), *Le Théâtre du peuple* (1903), *La Vie de Michel-Ange* (1905), the *Vie de Tolstoi* (1911) ; also various novels of a philosophical and social nature : *Colas Breugnon* (1914 : publ. 1918), *Clérambault, L'Âme enchaînée*, collections of articles (*Au-dessus de la mêlée*, 1917, etc.). Many of his works have been translated into other languages.

Rolland, whose works and ideas, of great individuality, have been much discussed since the war, is laureate of the French Académie

[1] It may be recalled that it was Professor Lionel Dauriac who first lectured on musical æsthetics at the Sorbonne (1896–1903).

(grand prix de littérature, 1913 ; grand prix Nobel, 1916).

BIBLIOGRAPHY

JEAN BONNEROT: (1) *Romain Rolland ; extraits de son œuvre* (Nevers, *Cahiers nivernais*, 1909) ; (2) *Romain Rolland, sa vie, son œuvre* (1921, with very complete bibliography).
PAUL SEIPPEL ' *Romain Rolland, l'homme et l'œuvre* (1913).
MARTINET : *Pages choisies de Romain Rolland* (about 1920).
P. J. JOUVE : *Romain Rolland vivant* (1920).
STEFAN ZWEIG : *Roman Rolland, der Mann und das Werk* (Frankfort-on-M. 1921 ; with bibliography).
The Review *Europe*, of Feb. 15, 1926, is entirely devoted to Rolland.
                                                    J. G. P.

ROLL-CALL, see MILITARY SOUNDS AND SIGNALS.

ROLLE. A German musical family. The father, (1) CHRISTIAN FRIEDRICH (*d.* Magdeburg, 1751), was town musician of Quedlinburg and of Magdeburg in 1721. Of his three sons, (2) CHRISTIAN CARL (*b.* Quedlinburg, 1714) was cantor cf the Jerusalem Church, Berlin, about 1760. He had sons, of whom (3) FRIEDRICH HEINRICH left a biography of his father ; while (4) CHRISTIAN CARL (the younger) succeeded him as cantor.

(5) JOHANN HEINRICH (*b.* Quedlinburg, Dec. 23, 1718; *d.* Magdeburg, Dec. 29, 1785), third son of Christian Friedrich (1) (the second son is un-named) held the post of organist at St. Peter's, Magdeburg, in 1732 when only 14 years old (*Q.-L.*). He was at the Leipzig University in 1736, and migrated to Berlin in hopes of some legal post ; but this failing he adopted music as his career, and about 1740 entered the court chapel of Frederick the Great as a chamber musician (viola-player). There he remained till 1746, and then took the organist's place at the Johanniskirche, Magdeburg, as town musician, and worked there with uncommon zeal and efficiency. His industry seems almost to have rivalled that of Bach himself. He left several complete annual series of church music for all the Sundays and Festivals ; cantatas for Easter, Whitsuntide and Christmas, of which many are in the State Library at Berlin ; five Passions, and at least sixty other large church compositions. Besides these there exist twenty-one large works of his, of a nature between oratorio and drama, such as ' Saul, or the power of Music,' ' Samson,' ' David and Jonathan,' ' The Labours of Hercules,' ' Orestes and Pylades,' ' Abraham on Moriah,' ' The Death of Abel,' etc. The last two were for many years performed annually at Berlin, and were so popular that the editions had to be renewed repeatedly. In addition to these he left many songs and compositions for organ, orchestra, and separate instruments. (See *Q.-L.* for list.)                              G.

ROLLI, PAOLO ANTONIO, an Italian poet, a Florentine, who was employed by the managers of the Italian opera to supply the libretti for several of the operas put before the English public in the early years of the 18th century. It is said that he was originally a pastry-cook, but, coming to England about 1718, his pro-

ductions pleased the public, and he became much noticed. In 1727 he issued a small book of canzonets and cantatas, with the music, dedicated to the Countess of Pembroke. At a later date he set up as teacher of the Italian language, and left England for Italy in 1744. Two stanzas of his poem, ' Se tu m' ami,' were set by Pergolesi, and three by J. J. Rousseau ; and his whole book of canzonets and cantatas was adapted to new music by William De Fesch about 1745–46, and published with a fresh dedication to Lady Frances Erskine.
                                                    F. K.

ROMANCE (Ger. *Romanze*). A term of very vague signification, answering in music to the same term in poetry, where the characteristics are rather those of personal sentiment and expression than of precise form. The Romanze in Mozart's D minor PF. concerto differs (if it differs) from the slow movements of his other concertos in the extremely tender and delicate character of its expression ; in its form there is nothing at all unusual : and the same may be said of Beethoven's two Romances for the violin and orchestra in G and F (opp. 40 and 50), and of Schumann's ' Drei Romanzen ' (op. 28). Schumann has also affixed the title to three movements for oboe and PF. (op. 94), and to a well-known piece in D minor (op. 32, No. 3), just as he has used the similar title, ' in Legendenton.'

In vocal music the term is obviously derived from the character or title of the words. In English poetry we have few ' romances,' though such as Moore's melodies as ' She is far from the land where her young hero sleeps ' might well bear the title. But in France they abound, and some composers (such as Puget and Panseron) have derived nine-tenths of their reputation from them. ' Partant pour la Syrie ' may be named as a good example. Mendelssohn's ' Songs without Words ' are called in France ' Romances sans paroles.'                              G.

ROMANI, FELICE (*b.* Genoa, Jan. 31, 1788 ; *d.* Moneglia, Riviera, Jan. 28, 1865), a famous Italian littérateur, was educated for the law, but soon forsook it for more congenial pursuits, and was in early life appointed to the post of poet to the royal theatres, with a salary of 6000 lire. The fall of the French government in Italy drove him to his own resources. He began with a comedy, ' L' amante e l' impostore,' which was very successful, and the forerunner of many dramatic pieces. But his claim to notice in a dictionary of music rests on his opera-libretti, in which he was for long the favourite of the Italian composers (see LIBRETTO). For Simone Mayr he wrote ' Medea ' (1812), ' La rosa bianca e la rosa rossa ' and others ; for Rossini, ' Aureliano in Palmira ' and ' Il Turco in Italia ' ; for Bellini, ' Bianca e Faliero,' ' La straniera,' ' La sonnambula,' ' Il pirata,' ' Norma,' ' I Capuletti ' and 'Beatrice di Tenda'; for Donizetti, 'Lucrezia,' 'Anna Bolena,' 'L'elisir d'amore' and 'Parisina'; for Mercadante, 'Il Conte d'Essex'; for Ricci, 'Un avventura di Scaramuccia'; and many others, in all fully a hundred. As editor for many years of the *Gazzetta Piemontese*, he was a voluminous writer.

In the latter part of his life he became blind, and was pensioned by Government, and spent his last years in his family circle at Moneglia, on the Riviera.                           G.

ROMANTIC, the antithesis of CLASSICAL (*q.v.*). Both terms were taken from literature, and brought into musical æsthetics during the early years of the 19th century, and have remained in use as convenient labels for certain kinds of musical expression. Roughly speaking, by classical we mean Bach, Mozart, Haydn, Beethoven, Schubert, Mendelssohn and Brahms; by romantic, Weber, Berlioz, Chopin, Schumann, Liszt and Wagner. Nowadays it is seen that it is not possible to draw a clean dividing line; all the composers named in the classical group can be shown to possess romantic qualities, but at the time the idea of the romanticists really meant no more than modernity, the spirit of unrest and desire for progress which appears at the close of every epoch. Pater says that Rousseau's statement 'I am different from all men I have seen. If I am not better, at least I am different' is representative of the whole movement. Beethoven's death closed the epoch which brought with it the solidification of structure. But he had opened the way to the expression of a strongly personal note, and the fact that the forms were settled left composers the freer to work in their own way. The point of view changed; it became possible to open up less elevated and simpler paths; in opera the subject drawn from Greek and Roman mythology gave way to the homely, the national and the fantastic; the SYMPHONIC POEM (*q.v.*) took the place of the symphony, while the range of musical expression through the means of the pianoforte became greatly widened in the hands of Chopin and Schumann. In effect music became more democratic, and the demands for more colour and variety, synchronising with improvements in certain musical instruments, notably the pianoforte and the brass instruments (see VALVE), had far-reaching results. (Cf. also ABSOLUTE MUSIC; PROGRAMME MUSIC.)      N. C. G.

ROMBERG, a German family of musicians. The founders were (1) ANTON and (2) HEINRICH, a pair of inseparable brothers, who dressed alike and lived together in Bonn. They were still alive in 1792. (3) ANTON (*b.* Westphalia, Mar. 6, 1742; *d.* Dec. 14, 1814), a bassoon-player, lived at Dinklage (Duchy of Oldenburg), gave concerts at Hamburg, and

lived long enough to play a concerto for two bassoons with his youngest son, (4) ANTON (*b.* 1777).

(5) BERNHARD (*b.* Dinklage, Nov. 12, 1767; *d.* Hamburg, Aug. 13, 1841), eldest son of Anton (3) is regarded as head of the school of German violoncellists. When only 14 he attracted considerable attention in Paris during a visit there with his father; from 1790–1793 he was in the band of the Elector of Cologne at Bonn at the same time with Ferdinand Ries, Reicha and the two Beethovens. During the French invasion he occupied himself in a professional tour in Italy, Spain and Portugal, and was well received, especially in Madrid, where Ferdinand VII. accompanied him on the violin. His cousin Andreas went with him, and on their return through Vienna late in 1796 they gave a concert at which Beethoven played (Thayer, ii. 16). After his return Bernhard married Catherine Ramcke at Hamburg. From 1801–03 he was a professor in the Paris Conservatoire, and we next find him in the King's band at Berlin. Spohr (*Autob.* i. 78) met him there at the end of 1804, and played quartets with him. Perhaps the most remarkable fact he mentions is that after one of Beethoven's early quartets (op. 18) Romberg asked how Spohr could play 'such absurd stuff' (*barockes Zeug*). It is of a piece with the well-known anecdote of his tearing the copy of the first Rasoumowsky quartet from the stand and trampling on it.

The approach of the French forces in 1806 again drove Romberg on the world, and in 1807 he was travelling in South Russia, but returned to Berlin, and was court Kapellmeister 1815–19, when he retired into private life at Hamburg. In 1814 he visited England, giving a concert under the patronage of Prince Blucher and the Hetman of the Cossacks, at Willis's Rooms, June 27. In 1822 he went to Vienna, in 1825 to St. Petersburg and Moscow, to Frankfort ir 1836, and in 1839 to London [1] and Paris, where his *Method for the Violoncello* (Berlin, Trautwein, 1840) was adopted by the Conservatoire.

Bernhard Romberg materially extended the capabilities of the violoncello. His concertos may be said to contain implicitly a complete theory of violoncello-playing, and there are few passages known to modern players the type of which may not be found there. It may be gathered from the character of his compositions that his tone was not so full and powerful as that of artists who confine themselves more to the lower register of the instrument and to passages of less complication. As an indication that this view agrees with that which prevailed during his lifetime, we find him,

[1] He does not seem to have played on this occasion; but a slight trace of his presence is perhaps discoverable in an overture of his nephew's, which closes the Philharmonic programme of June 17 1839.

for instance, spoken of as follows by a correspondent of the *A.M.Z.* for 1817, who had heard him play at Amsterdam :

'The visit of B. Romberg had long been eagerly looked for. The immense reputation which preceded him caused his first concert to be crowded to excess. He played a concerto (' die Reise auf den Bernhardsberg ') and a capriccio on Swedish national airs. In regard to the perfection and taste of his performance, to the complete ease and lightness of his playing, our great expectations were far exceeded—but not so in respect of tone—this, especially in difficult passages, we found much weaker than the powerful tone of our own Rauppe, and indeed scarcely to compare with it.'

At a second concert Romberg played his well-known Military Concerto, and the same view was reiterated.

Bernhard Romberg composed violoncello solos of various kinds ; string quartets ; PF. quartets ; a funeral symphony for Queen Louise of Prussia ; a concerto for two violoncellos (Breitkopf & Härtel), his last work ; and operas—' Die wiedergefundene Statue,' words by Gozzi von Schwick (1790), and ' Der Schiffbruch ' (1791, Bonn), ' Don Mendoce,' with his cousin Andreas (Paris), ' Alma,' ' Ulysses und Circe ' (July 27, 1807) and ' Rittertreue,' three acts (Jan. 31, 1817, Berlin). His son (6) KARL, also a violoncellist (*b.* St. Petersburg, Jan. 17, 1811), played in the court band there from 1832–42, and afterwards lived at Vienna.

Anton Romberg (3), the father of Bernhard, had a brother (7) GERHARD HEINRICH (*b.* Aug. 8, 1745), a clarinet-player, and music director at Münster, who lived with him for some time at Bonn, and had several children, of whom the most celebrated was (8) ANDREAS JAKOB, a violinist (*b.* Vechta, near Münster, Apr. 27, 1767; *d.* Gotha, Nov. 10, 1821). When only 7 he played in public with his cousin Bernhard, with whom he remained throughout life on terms of the closest friendship. At 17 he excited great enthusiasm in Paris, and was engaged for the Concert Spirituel (1784). In 1790 he joined his cousin at Bonn, played the violin in the Elector's band, and accompanied him to Italy in 1793. In Rome they gave a concert at the Capitol (Feb. 17, 1796) under the patronage of Cardinal Rezzonico. Andreas then made some stay in Vienna, where Haydn showed great interest in his first quartet. In 1797 he went to Hamburg, and in 1798 made a tour alone. In 1800 he followed Bernhard to Paris, and composed with him ' Don Mendoce, ou le Tuteur portugais.' The opera failed, and the success of their concerts was but partial, so Andreas left for Hamburg, where he married, and remained for fifteen years. He next became court Kapellmeister at Gotha, where he died in very great destitution. Concerts were given in various towns for the benefit of his widow and children. The university of Kiel gave him a degree of Doctor of Music. He composed six symphonies, quartets, quintets and

church music ; a Te Deum, Psalms, a Dixit, Magnificat and Hallelujah, in four, five, eight and sixteen parts ; several operas—' Das graue Ungeheuer ' (1790, Bonn), ' Die Macht der Musik ' (1791), ' Der Rabe,' operetta (1792), ' Die Grossmuth des Scipio ' and ' Die Ruinen zu Paluzzi '—the two last not performed. His best-known work is the music for Schiller's ' Lay of the Bell ' which kept its place in concert programmes for many years. ' The Transient and the Eternal,' ' The Harmony of the Spheres,' ' The Power of Song ' and a Te Deum (in D), as well as ' The Lay of the Bell,' were all published with English words by Novello. His Toy-symphony is now and then played as an alternative to Haydn's, and was chosen for performance by an extraordinary company, embracing most of the great artists of London, May 14, 1880. Two sons, (9) CYPRIAN (*b.* Hamburg, Oct. 28, 1807 ; *d.* there, Oct. 14, 1865) and (10) HEINRICH are mentioned in the *A.M.Z.* The former, a violoncellist, pupil of his uncle, made concert-tours, became a member of the court orchestra of St. Petersburg, and published compositions for his instrument (*Riemann*). Andreas's brother, (11) BALTHASAR (*b.* 1775; *d.* 1792), was educated for a violoncellist. His sister (12) THERESE (*b.* 1781) had a considerable reputation as a pianist.                    F. G. ; note by A. F. H.

ROME. The early music schools of Rome, from the time of St. Sylvester to that of Palestrina, were so closely connected with the papacy that their history may be read in the article SISTINE CHOIR. Whether or not Guido d' Arezzo founded a school of singing at Rome in the first half of the 11th century is only a matter of conjecture (see GUIDO D' AREZZO).

The Sistine Chapel was not the only one which had a school or college of music attached to it, though it was by far the earliest. In 1480 Sixtus IV. proposed the formation of a ' cappella musicale ' in connexion with the Vatican, distinct from the Sistine ; his idea was not, however, realised till the time of Julius II., when the ' Cappella Giulia ' was founded (in 1513) for twelve singers, twelve scholars and two masters for music and grammar. Arcadelt was the first ' maestro de' Putti ' (in 1539) and Palestrina the first ' maestro della cappella della basilica vaticana ' (1551–54). Among celebrated ' maestri ' in later days were Tommaso Bai (1713–15) and Domenico Scarlatti (1715–19). The ' Cappella musicale nella protobasilica di S. Giovanni in Laterano ' was founded in 1535 by Cardinal de Cupis ; one of the earliest ' maestri de' Putti ' was Lasso (1541) ; Palestrina held the office of ' maestro di cappella ' here after his exclusion from the Vatican Chapel (1555–61). The ' Cappella di musica nella basilica liberiana ' (or Sta. Maria Maggiore) was founded about the same time as the Lateran Chapel, and numbers among its maestri Palestrina (1561–71), Giov. Maria Nanini (1571–75) and Alessandro Scarlatti (1703–09).

Besides these exclusively ecclesiastical schools, others were established by private individuals. The first man who is known to have kept a public music school at Rome was a certain Gaudio Mell, whose school is supposed to have been founded about the year 1539 ; and among his earliest pupils were Palestrina, Giovanni Animuccia and Giovanni Maria Nanini. In 1549 Nicola Vicentino, the would-be restorer of the ancient Greek modes, opened a small private school at Rome, into which a few select pupils were admitted. But it was not till a quarter of a century later that a public music school was opened by an Italian. Whether Nanini was inspired by his master's example, or was stirred by the musical agitation of the day, is of little importance ; but it is certain that the year to which the opening of his school is attributed was the same which saw the foundation of the order of Oratorians, who in the person of their leader, St. Filippo Neri, were then doing so much for the promotion of music. Nanini soon induced his former fellow-pupil, Palestrina, to assist him in teaching, and he appears to have given finishing lessons. Among their best pupils were Felice Anerio and Gregorio Allegri. After Palestrina's death Nanini associated his younger brother Bernardino with him in the work of instruction, and it was probably for their scholars that they wrote jointly their treatise on counterpoint. Giovanni Maria dying in 1607 was succeeded by Bernardino, who was in his turn succeeded by his pupil and son-in-law Paolo Agostini. It must have been this school that produced the singers in the earliest operas and oratorios of Peri, Caccini, Monteverdi, Cavaliere, Gagliano, etc.

In the second quarter of the 17th century a rival school was set up by a pupil of B. Nanini, Domenico Mazzocchi, who, with his younger brother Virgilio, opened a music school which was soon in a very flourishing condition ; this was due in a great measure to the fact that the masters were themselves both singers and composers. Their curriculum differed but slightly from that of the Nanini school. In the morning one hour was given daily to practising difficult passages, a second to the shake, a third to the study of literature, and another hour to singing with the master before a mirror ; in the afternoon an hour was occupied in the study of the theory of music, another in writing exercises in counterpoint, and another in literature ; the remainder of the day (indoors) was employed in practising the harpsichord and in composition. Outside the school the pupils used sometimes to give their services at neighbouring churches. In 1662 Pompeo Natale kept a music school, at which Giuseppe

Ottavio Pitoni, the reputed master of Durante and Leo, learnt singing and counterpoint. G. A. Angelini-Buontempi, a pupil of the Mazzocchis, writing in 1695, says that Fedi, a celebrated singer, had opened the first school exclusively for singing at Rome. His example was soon followed by Giuseppe Amadori, with equal success ; the latter was a pupil of P. Agostini and no doubt had not entirely forgotten the teachings of the old school : but by the end of the 17th century its traditions were gradually dying out, to be replaced by the virtuosity of the 18th century.

We must now retrace our steps and give some account of the most important musical institution at Rome of past or present time— the ' Congregazione dei Musici di Roma sotto l' invocazione di Sta. Cecilia.' It was founded by Pius V. in 1566, but its existence is usually dated from 1584, when its charter was confirmed by Gregory XIII.; almost all the masters and pupils of the Palestrina-Nanini school enrolled their names on its books, and their example has been since followed by over 4000 others, including every Italian of note, and in the 19th century many illustrious foreigners, such as John Field, Wagner, Liszt, Gounod, etc. etc.

The officers originally appointed were a Cardinal Protector, a ' Primicerio ' or president, usually a person of high position, a ' Consiglio dirigente ' of four members (representing the four sections—composition, the organ, singing and instrumental music), a secretary, a chancellor, twelve counsellors, two prefects, etc. ; there were also professors for almost every branch of music ; Corelli was head of the instrumental section in 1700. Those qualified for admission into the institution were maestri di cappelle, organists, public singers and well-known instrumentalists. By a papal decree of 1689 all musicians were bound to observe the statutes of the Academy ; and by a later decree (1709) it was ordained that its licence was necessary for exercising the profession. Soon after this the Congregation began to suffer from an opposition, which, though covert, was none the less keenly felt ; and in 1716 a papal decree unfavourable to the institution was passed. In 1762 it was flourishing again, for in that year we find that a faculty was granted to the Cardinal Protector to have the general direction of all ecclesiastical music at Rome. By another decree of 1764 it was enacted that none but those skilled in music should be in future admitted as members. The entrance-fee was, as it has continued to be, a very small one. The demands made upon members were also very slight. At first they were only expected to assist, by their compositions or performances, in the grand annual festival in honour of the patron saint. Towards the close of the 17th century were added one or two annual services in memory of benefactors; in 1700 a festival in honour of St. Anna; and in 1771 a ' *piccola* festa di Sta. Cecilia.'

The Congregation originally took up its quarters at the College of Barnabites (afterwards Palazzo Chigi) in the Piazza Colonna, where they remained for nearly a century; thence they moved to the Convent of Sta. Maria Maddalena, and again to another college of Barnabites dedicated to San Carlo a Catinari. Here they resided for the greater part of two centuries, and, after the temporary occupation of premises in the Via Ripetta, finally, in 1876, settled at their present quarters, formerly a convent of Ursuline nuns, in the Via dei Greci. Besides the hostility which the Congregation had to undergo at the beginning of the 18th century—which was repeated in another form as late as 1836—it has had its financial vicissitudes. Indeed at the end of the 18th century the funds were at a very low ebb, from which they have been gradually recovering. The institution was dignified with the title of Academy of Gregory XVI. in 1839. Two years later Rossini's Stabat Mater was performed for the first time in Italy in its entirety by the members of the Academy. Pius IX., who became Pope in 1846, though he founded several other schools for singing, such as that of ' S. Salvatore in Lauro,' did little more for the Academy than to bestow upon it the epithet ' Pontificia.'                                A. H. H.

During the early years of his reign two attempts were made to found a Liceo Musicale or music school in connexion with the Accademia. The first, in 1847, received encouragement and sympathy from the pontiff, but efforts to obtain a Government subsidy for the purpose failed owing to the political disturbances of 1848–49. Another endeavour by Professor Filippo Bornia in 1857 had no better result. It was not until 1869, when two young associates of the institute, Giovanni Sgambati and Ettore Pinelli, opened gratuitous classes for pianoforte and violin on the premises of the Accademia that a practical start was made in this direction. In the following year the two professors sought and obtained from Cardinal Di Pietro, Protector of the Accademia, official sanction for their venture. This was given in a decree, dated May 23, 1870, establishing the classes on a recognised footing as belonging to and dependent upon the institution. The fresh departure received further impetus later in the same year. Soon after the fall of the pontifical government in September the associates of the Accademia, now a ' Royal ' institution, expressed in general assembly unanimous approval of the classes and entrusted a provisional committee, with Professor Bornia at its head, with the task of formally constituting a Liceo Musicale.

From this period the energies of the Accademia, which until now had been little more than a body of examiners and licentiates, became centred in the new development, and its history identified with that of the daughter-institute of which the classes formed by Sgambati and Pinelli were the nucleus, and of which, therefore, they are rightly considered the founders. Meanwhile the music school had been rapidly growing. Sgambati had engaged three assistants for pianoforte teaching. Alessandro Orsini with a sub-professor had opened classes for singing, and violoncello and brass instruments were being taught. At length after seven years of careful preparation the Liceo Musicale was formally constituted under the direction of a ' Commissione disciplinare ' and a ' Comitato tecnico,' with a staff of twenty-nine professors. The new institute was launched on March 3, 1877, in the presence of the Crown Prince and Princess (Umberto and Margherita) of Italy.

The Accademia now occupied itself with the compilation of a statute for the Liceo, and in accordance with the wishes of the Government the ' Commissione disciplinare ' was substituted, in 1886, by an administrative council. On this the Government, the Province of Rome and the Municipality, as contributors to the maintenance of the Liceo, were represented, while its director was nominated by the Accademia itself.

Every branch of practice and theory is taught, besides Italian literature and the history of music.

To its premises in the Via dei Greci the Accademia, assisted by contributions from the Government and Queen Margherita, has added a spacious concert-hall with an organ, opened in 1895. Here, during winter and spring, public orchestral and chamber concerts are given.

The Library also constitutes an increasingly important branch of its influence. Originally small, the collection of books and MSS. was increased by the musical library of Gregory XVI. bequeathed in 1846. It was still further enriched in 1875 by the Orsini collection, and later by the musical works which had formerly belonged to the dissolved monasteries. In 1882 were added copies of all modern musical publications since 1500 (see LIBRARIES).

Quite apart from the Accademia, which with its Liceo is the musical centre of Rome, much has been done for the improvement of the popular taste in music. Orchestral concerts are given frequently at the Augusteo Hall, where all the most celebrated European conductors have appeared and have familiarised the Roman public with classical and modern works. As an operatic centre, however, Rome lacks the prestige of Milan and Naples, the chief theatres of opera being the Argentina and the Costanzi. Puccini's 'Tosca' and 'Trittico' were produced for the first time at the Costanzi Theatre.   H. A. W. ; rev., with addns., F. B.

BIBL.—GIULIA DE DOMINICIS, *Roma centro musicale nel Settecento, R.M.I.,* 1923, pp. 511–528 ; GIUSEPPE PAVAN, *Saggio di cronistoria del teatro musicale romano. Il teatro Capranica. Catalogo cronologico delle opere rappresentate nel secolo xviii, R.M.I.,* anno 29, 1922, pp. 425–444.

ROMEO AND JULIET. A subject often set by opera composers ; *e.g.*—

(1) Roméo et Juliette ; 3 acts ; words by de Ségur, music by Steibelt. Théâtre-Feydeau, Paris, Sept. 10, 1793.

(2) 'Giulietta e Romeo ' ; opera seria in 3 acts, words by Giuseppe Foppa, music by Zingarelli.   Produced La Scala, Milan, Jan. 30, 1796.

(3) 'Giulietta e Romeo,' 3 acts, words by Romani, music by Vaccaj. Produced Teatro della Canobbiana, Milan, Oct. 31, 1825 ; King's Theatre, London, Apr. 10, 1832.

(4) 'I Capuletti ed i Montecchi,' in 3 acts ; libretto by Romani, music by Bellini. Produced Venice, Mar. 11, 1830 ; Paris, Jan. 10, 1833.   King's Theatre, London, July 20, 1833 ; usually given with a fourth act taken from Vaccaj's version.

(5) 'Les Amants de Vérone,' 5 acts, text and music by the Marquis d'Ivry (under the pseudonym of Richard Yrvid), written in 1864, performed privately in 1867, and publicly at the Salle Ventadour, Oct. 12, 1878. At Covent Garden, May 24, 1879.

(6) 'Roméo et Juliette,' in 5 acts ; words by Barbier and Carré, music by Gounod. Produced Théâtre-Lyrique, Apr. 27, 1867 ; Covent Garden, in Italian, July 11, 1867 ; in English, Carl Rosa Co., Liverpool, Jan. 15, 1890 ; New York, Academy of Music, Nov. 15, 1867.

(7) 'Romeo and Juliet,' a setting of the entire Shakespeare text by J. E. Barkworth, produced Middlesborough (Harrison - Frewin Co.), Jan. 7, 1916, and Surrey Theatre, 1920.

(8) 'Giulietta e Romeo,' 3 acts, music by Zandonai.   Rome 1922.

(9) In addition to these it has been made the subject of a work by Berlioz, his fifth symphony—'Roméo et Juliette. Symphonie dramatique avec chœurs, solos de chant, et prologue en récitatif choral,' op. 17 ; produced Conservatoire, Nov. 24, 1839 ; the first part under Berlioz's direction, New Philharmonic Concert, Mar. 24, 1852, and the entire work, Philharmonic Society (Cusins), Mar. 10, 1881.

(10) A symphonic poem by Tchaikovsky ; produced at the Musical Society in Moscow, Mar. 4, 1870.

ROMER, EMMA (*b.* 1814 ; *d.* Margate, Apr. 14, 1868), soprano singer, pupil of Sir George Smart, made her first appearance at Covent Garden, Oct. 16, 1830, as Clara in 'The Duenna.' She met with a favourable reception, and for several years filled the position of prima donna at Covent Garden, the English Opera-House, and Drury Lane, with great credit. In 1852 she took the management of the Surrey Theatre, with a company containing Miss Poole and other good singers, and brought out a series of operas in English.   Miss Romer was rarely heard in the concert-room, but appeared at the Westminster Abbey Festival in 1834. She was the original singer of the title-parts in Barnett's 'Mountain Sylph ' and 'Fair Rosamond.'  Her performance of Amina in the English version of Bellini's 'Sonnambula ' was much admired.   She married a Mr. Almond.   W. H. H.

ROMERO, MATEO ('MAESTRO CAPITAN ') (*d.* Madrid, May 10, 1647). Born in Flanders, or of Flemish origin (his name is said to have been originally 'Rosmarin '), he joined the Chapel Royal, Madrid, in 1594 as cantor, becoming maestro in 1598. There were at that time two choirs, the Spanish and the Flemish, *Capilla Española* and *C. Flamenca*. Romero belonged to the latter and was a pupil of Philip ROGIER (*q.v.*)  His name appears again in a list dated 1604 ; in 1609 he succeeded Rogier and was ordained priest, being appointed to a chaplaincy (*capellanía*) at Toledo (Capilla de los Reyes Nuevos) in 1624.  In 1633 he retired on a pension, being succeeded in the choirmastership by PATIÑO, while in 1638 he was sent, rather against his will, on a musical mission to the Duke of Braganza in Portugal. The duke, on his accession to the throne of Portugal in 1640, rewarded him with the title of *Capellán cantor de la Corona,* and mentioned him (after his death) in his *Defence of Modern Music,* published in 1649.

Romero ('El Maestro Capitan,' as he was usually called) had an immense reputation in the Peninsula. The 'Cancionero de Sablonara ' (MS. Munich and a copy at Madrid) contains 22 compositions by him for 3 and 4 v., including settings of poems by the great dramatist Lope de Vega. Other works by him are included in the 'Libro de tonos humanos,' collected by Diego Pizarro (Madrid, Bibl. Nac., M. 1262), while church-music by him is preserved at Saragossa, Seville and other cathedrals.  A motet ('Libera me ') for 2 choirs was printed by Eslava (*v.* Mitjana, *Rev. de Filol. españ.,* 1919, vi. 241 ff.   J. B. T.

RONALD, SIR LANDON (*b.* London, June 7, 1873), conductor and composer, has been Principal of the GUILDHALL SCHOOL OF MUSIC (*q.v.*) since Nov. 1910.

The son of Henry RUSSELL (*q.v.*), Landon Ronald was educated at St. Marylebone and All Souls Grammar School and also at Margate. At the early age of 11 (1884) he entered the R.C.M. as a student, where his teachers during the next five years included Hubert Parry (composition), Franklin Taylor (piano) and Henry Holmes (violin). He had left the R.C.M. when in 1891 he attracted attention by his skilful performance of the piano solo music to the much-discussed wordless play, ' L'Enfant prodigue' (see WORMSER). He went on tour in the provinces with this play. Mancinelli, then conductor at Covent Garden, next secured him an engagement with Augustus Harris as *maestro al piano* for the season of 1891, and his work there with the famous singers of the day and under Mancinelli gave him a thorough education in the traditions of opera, which in any other country but England would have determined his subsequent career as an operatic conductor. Ronald toured as conductor with Harris's Italian Opera Company through two seasons, and subsequently directed some English opera performances at Drury Lane, maintaining, however, his close connexion with Covent Garden till after the death of Harris. He also during this period (1894) toured in America as piano accompanist to Mme. Melba. When he left Covent Garden the fact that this country offered practically no other opportunities for operatic conducting caused him to accept for a time a post as conductor of musical comedy at the Lyric Theatre, and it is a regrettable fact that the special experience gained by him in these formative years has never been used in any way commensurate with his powers.

Ronald, however, was a man to make his own opportunities. He turned to concert work, accepted a summer engagement for orchestral concerts at Blackpool and there decisively proved his power of handling an orchestra. The formation of the LONDON SYMPHONY ORCHESTRA (*q.v.*) in 1904 brought him before the London public in symphonic work, and his position was consolidated by an invitation to Berlin. His brilliant performance with the Berlin Philharmonic Orchestra, by gaining him the applause of the foreigner, increased the respect of his countrymen. In Vienna, Leipzig, Bremen and ultimately in Rome, where (1909) he gave the first performance there of Elgar's first symphony at a concert of the Academy of St. Cecilia, Ronald won the applause of continental audiences. At home his work was continued in several seasons at Blackpool, in promenade concerts at Birmingham and in the north with the SCOTTISH ORCHESTRA (*q.v.*). In 1909 he became permanent conductor of the New Symphony Orchestra, now the ROYAL ALBERT HALL ORCHESTRA (*q.v.*), and his Sunday Concerts at the Albert Hall and the series of symphony concerts at Queen's Hall were a regular feature of the London season until 1914. In spite of the mass of educational and executive work which his appointment at the G.S.M. necessarily entails, Ronald has continued his connexion with the Royal Albert Hall Orchestra, and has also frequently undertaken single concerts of the Royal Philharmonic Society.

The most conspicuous characteristic of Ronald's art as a conductor is the complete-

ness and care with which he controls his forces. Everything is accomplished with the utmost deftness, and in concerto work with soloists he is the ideal accompanist. His most distinguished interpretations are in the symphonic work of Elgar, with whose music he displays a peculiar sympathy founded on a long personal friendship with the composer. Ronald's compositions are numerous, but must be regarded as a secondary activity in his career. They include

Incidental music to *The Garden of Allah* (Drury Lane, 1921).
An Orchestral Suite from the same.
'A Birthday Overture' for orch.
Scena, 'Adonais' (Shelley), voice and orch.
Scena, 'The Lament of Shah Jehan,' voice and orch.
Many songs and PF. pieces.

His songs have been highly successful with a wide public; one of them, 'Down in the forest,' having attained that almost embarrassing popularity which falls to the lot of the fluent writer, generally when he least expects it. Ronald was knighted in 1922; in the autumn of that year he published a book of reminiscences, *Variations on a Personal Theme*. In 1924 he was made F.R.C.M.     c.

RONCONI, (1) DOMENICO (*b.* Lendinaradi-Polesine, Venice, July 11, 1772; *d.* St. Petersburg, Apr. 13, 1836). He first appeared on the stage in 1797 at La Fenice, Venice, and obtained great renown both as a singer and actor there and in other Italian cities, sang in Italian opera at St. Petersburg (1801–05), was director of the Italian opera in Vienna in 1809, sang in Paris in 1810, and was engaged at Munich in 1819–29, becoming a teacher of singing there. He founded a vocal school in 1829 at Milan. Of his three sons,

(2) FELICE (*b.* Venice, 1811; *d.* St. Petersburg, Sept. 10, 1875), under the direction of his father, devoted himself to instruction in singing, and became a professor in 1837 at Würzburg, at Frankfort, and, in 1844–48, at Milan. He was similarly engaged for some years in London, and finally at St. Petersburg. He was the author of a method of teaching singing and of several songs. His elder brother,

(3) GIORGIO (*b.* Milan, Aug. 6, 1810; *d.* Madrid, Jan. 8, 1890), celebrated baritone, received instruction in singing from his father, and began his dramatic career in 1831, at Pavia, as Arturo in 'La Straniera.' He played in some of the small Italian cities, then at Rome, where Donizetti wrote for him 'Il furioso,' 'Torquato Tasso' and 'Maria di Rohan,' in which last, as the Duc de Chevreuse, he obtained one of his greatest triumphs—also at Turin, Florence and Naples, where on Oct. 8, 1837, he married Signorina Elguerra Giannoni, who, according to some accounts, had recently sung with success at the Lyceum and King's Theatres, London. He began his career in England at Her Majesty's, Apr. 9, 1842, as Enrico in 'Lucia,' and was well received

during the season in that character and in those of Filippo ('Beatrice di Tenda'), Belcore ('L'elisir'), Basilio, Riccardo ('Puritani'), Tasso, etc. In the last opera his wife played with him, but neither then, nor five years later as Maria di Rohan, did she make the least impression on the English public. He then made a provincial tour with her, Thalberg and John Parry. In the winter he played at the Italiens, Paris, with such success that he was engaged there for several subsequent seasons, and at one time was manager of the theatre, and was also engaged at Vienna, Pest, Madrid (where he was manager), Barcelona and Naples. He reappeared in England, Apr. 13, 1847, at Covent Garden, as Enrico, and also played Figaro ('Barbiere'), May 8, De Chevreuse on the production in England of 'Maria di Rohan,' and the Doge on the production of Verdi's 'I due Foscari,' June 19, in which 'by his dignity and force he saved the opera . . . from utter condemnation.'[1] He sang at the Italian Opera every season until 1866 inclusive, excepting in 1855 and 1862. His Rigoletto was unrivalled, but his Don Juan was a disappointment. He sang in America (1866–74) with great success, and on his return to Europe he became a teacher of singing at the Conservatorio at Madrid. In 1863 he founded a school of singing at Granada. A warm appreciation of his powers appears in Santley's *Student and Singer*.

(4) SEBASTIANO (*b*. Venice, May 1814), the other son, also a baritone, received instruction from his father and the elder Romani, and made his first appearance in 1836, at the Teatro Pantera, Lucca, as Torquato Tasso, in which part throughout his career he made one of his greatest successes. He enjoyed considerable popularity in his own country, at Vienna, and in Spain, Portugal and America, as an able artist in the same line of parts as his brother —unlike him in personal appearance, being a tall thin man, but like him in the capability of his face for great variety of expression. He appeared in England on Dec. 17, 1836, at the Lyceum, as Cardenio in Donizetti's 'Furioso,' and also sang for a few nights at the King's Theatre, as well as at the Philharmonic, Feb. 27, 1837. He reappeared in 1860 at Her Majesty's, as Rigoletto, Masetto and Griletto ('Prova d'un opera seria'). He retired from public life after a career of thirty-five years, and settled in Milan as a teacher of singing.[2] A. C.

RONDEAU, a French name for a short poem of six or eight lines, containing but two rhymes, and so contrived that the opening and closing lines were identical, thus forming as it were a circle or *round*. The name has come to be used in music for a movement constructed on a somewhat corresponding plan. (See RONDO.) G.

[1] Chorley.
[2] He supplied much of the above information with regard to his family. The date of his death is unknown.

RONDEÑA, see FANDANGO; and SONG, subsection SPAIN (4).

RONDINE, LA, comic opera on a libretto of Wilner translated by Adami; music by Puccini. Produced (in French) Monte Carlo, Mar. 27, 1917; Buenos Ayres, the same year; (in Italian), San Carlo, Naples, Feb. 26, 1918.

RONDO (Fr. *rondeau*), a piece of music having one principal subject, to which a return is always made after the introduction of other matter, so as to give a symmetrical or *rounded* form to the whole.

From the simplicity and obviousness of this idea it will be readily understood that the rondo-form was the earliest and most frequent definite mould for musical construction. For a full tracing of this point see FORM. Later on there grew out of the free section a second subject in a related key, and still later a third, which allowed the second to be repeated in the tonic. This variety closely resembles the first-movement form, the third subject taking the place of the development of subjects, which is rare in a rondo. The chief difference lies in the return to the first subject immediately after the second, which is the invariable characteristic of the rondo. The fully developed rondo-form of Beethoven and the modern composers may be thus tabulated:

1st sub. (dominant). 2nd sub. 1st sub. 3rd sub. 1st sub. 2nd sub. (tonic). Coda.

In the case of a rondo in a minor key, the second subject would naturally be in the relative major instead of in the dominant. The finale of Beethoven's 'Sonate pathétique' (op. 13) affords an exceptionally clear instance of this use of rondo form.

Beethoven's rondos will all be found to present but slight modifications of the above form. Sometimes a 'working-out' or development of the second subject will take the place of the third subject, as in the sonata in E minor (op. 90), but in every case the principal subject will be presented in its entirety at least three times. But as this was apt to lead to monotony—especially in the case of a long subject like that in the sonata just quoted— Beethoven introduced the plan of varying the theme slightly on each repetition, or of breaking off in the middle. In the rondo of the sonata in E♭ (op. 7) again, we find the main subject cut short on its second appearance, while on its final repetition all sorts of liberties are taken with it; it is played an octave higher than its normal place, a free variation is made on it, and at last we are startled by its being thrust into a distant key—E♮. F. C.

RONG, WILHELM FERDINAND (*b. circa* 1720; *d.* after 1821), chamber musician of Prince Henry of Prussia, after whose death he settled at Berlin as teacher of singing, piano, violin and guitar, and lecturer on musical theory. He invented a kind of lyre which he called 'Appolina pour les Dames.' According to his own statement he was 80 years old in 1800 (Ledebur, *Berliner Tonkünstlerlexikon*, p. 479), which makes it all the more wonderful that he still wrote songs to celebrate the delivery of his country from the French in 1815 and 1816. He composed a Mass and other church music, a duo-drama in 1 act, and a number of secular songs, wrote several books on the elements of music and musical theory, and invented some musical games to teach these subjects (Ledebur; *Q.-L.* ; *Riemann*).        E. V. D. S.

RONZI, SIGNORA, see BEGNIS, DE (2).

ROOKE, WILLIAM MICHAEL (*b.* South Great George's Street, Dublin, Sept. 29, 1794 ; *d.* Oct. 14, 1847), son of John Rourke, or O'Rourke, a Dublin tradesman, studied, almost unaided, so assiduously that in 1813 he took to music as a profession (having altered the form of his name), learned counterpoint under Dr. Cogan, a Dublin professor, and became a teacher of the violin and pianoforte. Among his pupils on the former instrument was Balfe, then a boy. In 1817 he was appointed chorus-master and deputy leader at the theatre in Crow Street, Dublin, and soon afterwards composed a polacca, ' Oh Glory, in thy brightest hour,' which was sung by Braham, and met with great approbation. In 1818 he composed his first opera, ' Amilie,' and in 1821 he removed to England, where he became chorus-master at Drury Lane Theatre, under Tom Cooke, and, in 1830-33, leader at Vauxhall, under Sir Henry Bishop. In 1826 he was leading oratorios at Birmingham, and in the same year came to London, and sought the appointment of chorus-master at Drury Lane, and established himself as a teacher of singing. His opera, ' Amilie, or The Love Test,' was at last brought out at Covent Garden, Dec. 2, 1837, with decided success. He immediately began the composition of a second opera, and on May 2, 1839, produced at Covent Garden ' Henrique, or, The Love Pilgrim,' which, although most favourably received, was withdrawn after five performances on account of a misunderstanding with the manager. He composed two more entitled ' Cagliostro ' and ' The Valkyrie,' which have never been performed. He was buried in Brompton Cemetery.

        W. H. H. ; addn. W. H. G. F.

ROOT, a term much used by 19th-century theorists as an aid to harmonic classification. The system which employed it postulated (*a*) that all chords were derived from triads (major and minor) ; (*b*) that triads in a key were those which had as bass note one contained in the diatonic scale of that key.

Hence the root of every chord would be the bass note of the triad from which the chord was derived, and the discovery of the root would be an indication of the key of the music at the moment at which the chord was used. The system became inadequate from the moment at which chords not referable to a triad in a key became current in the musical vocabulary. (See HARMONY.)        C.

ROOT, GEORGE FREDERICK (*b.* Sheffield, Mass., U.S.A., Aug. 30, 1820 ; *d.* Bailey's Island, Maine, Aug. 6, 1895), American popular composer. He studied under Webb of Boston and afterward in Paris. In 1859-71 he was a music-publisher in Chicago. With Lowell Mason he was active in popularising music in American public schools. He wrote numerous cantatas, but he is known and remembered as the composer of certain songs much sung during and after the American Civil War, in particular, ' The Battle Cry of Freedom ' ; ' Just Before the Battle, Mother ' ; and the spirited ' Tramp, Tramp, Tramp, the Boys are Marching,' also known as ' God Save Ireland.'

        W. S. S.

ROOTHAM, (1) DANIEL WILBERFORCE (*b.* Cambridge, Aug. 15, 1837 ; *d.* Bristol, Mar. 1922), the son of a bass singer in the choirs of Trinity and St. John's Colleges, Cambridge (1815 till his death in 1852), himself sang as a chorister in the same choirs from the age of 8, and from 1850 for four years studied the piano, organ and harmony under T. A. Walmisley. On the death of his father he removed to Bristol, where his elder brother was a lay-clerk in the cathedral ; he soon got a similar position, and also studied singing in London under Schira. In 1865 he succeeded J. D. Corfe, the cathedral organist, as conductor of the Bristol Madrigal Society. The former post he retained till 1877, and held the post of organist at St. Peter's, Clifton Wood, from 1866 for 27 years. The conductorship of the Madrigal Society he retained till his retirement in 1915. He did important work for the furtherance of music in BRISTOL (*q.v.*). His son,

(2) CYRIL BRADLEY, Mus.D. (*b.* Bristol, Oct. 5, 1875), was educated at Bristol Grammar School and Clifton College. Winning scholarships and various honours, he went to St. John's College, Cambridge, in 1894, and graduated in the Classical Tripos in 1897 ; he took the Mus.B. degree at Cambridge in 1900 and the M.A. degree in 1901. In his third year at Cambridge he undertook all Dr. Garrett's musical duties ; on leaving Cambridge he went to the R.C.M., studying under Stanford, Parratt, Barton and others. In 1898 he succeeded Walford Davies as organist of Christ Church, Hampstead, in 1901 was made organist of St. Asaph Cathedral, and in the same year returned to St. John's College, Cambridge, as organist and musical director. This post he still (1927) holds. His career has been not only personally distinguished but important to the musical life of the university, which has been much advanced by his many activities. He conducted

the performance of 'The Magic Flute' in 1911 (see DENT, E. J., and CAREY, Clive), became conductor of the Cambridge University Musical Society (1912), University Lecturer in Music (1913) and was made a Fellow of St. John's (1914).

He has composed much, and his opera 'The Two Sisters' (3 acts), text by Marjorie Fausset, founded on the ballad 'The Twa Sisters o' Binnorie,' was performed at Cambridge in Feb. 1922. His works of concerted chamber music, including three string quartets (one in C was produced by the Philharmonic String Quartet in 1915) and a string quintet in D, have qualities of refined scholarship and charm, but it is by several short choral works with orchestra that he has made his chief mark. These include 'Andromeda' for soli, choir and orchestra (Bristol Festival, 1908), 'Coronach' for baritone solo, choir and orchestra, 'For the Fallen,' a setting of Binyon's poem, somewhat overshadowed by Elgar's more famous one (published 1914, first performed Cambridge, 1919) and 'Brown Earth' (published in Carnegie Collection). This last, a setting of a poem by Thomas Moult, was first performed at the Albert Hall, London (Mar. 14, 1923), at a concert given by the combined musical societies of Oxford and Cambridge Universities. Rootham has further produced from time to time several works in the smaller forms for orchestra alone, but in the choral works, and especially in 'Brown Earth,' the stimulus of words brings out the more delicate and poetic qualities of his mind and gives distinction to his music.

(For fuller list see *B.M.S. Ann.* 1920.) C.

ROOY, ANTONIUS MARIA JOSEPHUS VAN, known as ANTON (*b.* Rotterdam, Jan. 1, 1870). According to *Baker*, he sang treble in a church choir, but after mutation his voice became a fine baritone, on account of which he left a cigar business and studied singing with Stockhausen at Frankfort. After singing in concerts he was engaged at Bayreuth in 1897, through the recommendation of Frau Wagner's daughter Frau Prof. Thode, who had heard him sing very finely at a concert 'Wotan's Farewell.' At Bayreuth he made an instant success as Wotan in the three parts of the Trilogy, on account of his commanding presence, his sonorous voice and his dignified acting. In the winter he sang these parts at Berlin, and on May 11, 1898, he made his début at Covent Garden as Wotan in 'Die Walküre' with great success. Subsequently he sang at that theatre almost every season until 1913, being identified with the Wagner parts, Wolfram, Kurwenal, Hans Sachs, etc. For many years he sang these parts also in America, besides Escamillo and Valentine. Van Rooy was also an admirable Lieder singer, and in 1899 and 1900 gave two recitals at St. James's Hall with Carl Friedberg the pianist,

when he sang the entire 'Dichterliebe' of Schumann, and songs ranging from Haydn to Richard Strauss and Hugo Wolf.        A. C.

ROPARTZ, JOSEPH GUY MARIE (*b.* Guingamp, Côtes du Nord, June 15, 1864), came of an old Breton family. His studies, diligently pursued at Rennes, Vannes and Angers, would have qualified him to follow a literary career, but he preferred music. He was a pupil of Th. Dubois (2d 'accessit' in harmony) and of Massenet in the Paris Conservatoire, afterwards of César Franck, who has strongly influenced him. Though his life has been devoted to composition, he has directed, since 1894, the Conservatoire of Nancy with great success and gave a strong impulse to the symphonic concerts of that town. He has occupied the same position at Strassburg since 1919, and also that of director of the Conservatoire. Like his master, César Franck, he is a teacher. He has composed dramatic and so-called absolute music. His dramatic production includes: 'Le Diable couturier' (1894); 'Marguerite d'Écosse' (both in one act); incidental music to 'Pêcheur d'Islande' (1891) (Loti and Tiercelin), played in Paris in 1893; and to 'Œdipe à Colonne'; 'Le Miracle de Saint-Nicolas,' a legend in two parts (1905). 'Le Pays,' a musical drama in 3 acts (1908–10), (poem by Charles Le Goffic), performed at Nancy, Feb. 1913, and at Paris (Opéra-Comique), Apr. 15 of the same year, his chief dramatic work, aroused the greatest interest. Of French inspiration solely, its musical conception is characteristic of the composer's manner. 'The music,' writes E. Burlingame Hill, 'is tensively dramatic, effective stylistically and strongly original. The orchestra reinforces the stage situation admirably by its varied and highly coloured sonority." But J. G. Ropartz is, as V. d'Indy has termed it, a born symphonic musician.

The general character of the musical production of Ropartz recommends itself by its close alliance to the popular melody of his native Brittany, combined with a somewhat religious inspiration, and to a strong predilection for classic form in the spirit of César Franck.

LIST OF WORKS

ORCHESTRAL.—Four symphonies (1895, 1900, 1906, 1910); the first one, 'Symphonie sur un choral breton,' the third one (E maj.) obtaining the 'Prix Cressent'; 'Paysage de Bretagne' (originally written for a theatre of 'ombres chinoises') 'Les Landes' (1888); 'Dimanche breton' (1894); 'La Cloche des morts' (1902); 'A Marie endormie' (1912); 'La Chasse du Prince Arthur'; 'Soir sur les chaumes' (1913).

CHAMBER MUSIC.—Two sonatas for PF. and vln. (1908, 1918)[1] two for PF. and vcl. (1904, 1919); one trio for PF. (1919); two str. quartets (1894, 1912). For the PF. alone: 'Ouverture Variations et Finale' (1904), 'Choral varié,' 'Dans l'ombre de la montagne,' 'Musiques au jardin,' three Nocturnes, 'Croquis d'été' (1918), etc.

He has composed a number of songs: 'Quatre poèmes' (1894), 'Veilles de départ,' 'Le Rêve sur le sable' (1914, first performed, 1917), 'Quatre Odelettes' (1917), etc.

CHURCH MUSIC.—A setting of Psalm cxxxvi. for choir, organ and orch. (1897); Motets, Ave Maria, 12 Cantiques bretons, 'Messe de Saint Odile,' 'Messe de Saint Anne,' etc., etc.

ORGAN MUSIC.—'Versets pour les Vêpres des Saintes femmes,' 'Thème varié Chorals,' 'Au pied de l'autel' (60 pieces), 'Douze Pièces pour orgue,' etc.

---

[1] The dates are those of publication of the works.

CHORUSES, transcriptions, arrangements of popular songs, two military marches, etc.
MUSICAL LITERATURE —*Notations artistiques* (1891) ; *V. Massé* ; and volumes of poems, *Adagiettes, Modes mineurs, Les Muances*, etc.

### BIBLIOGRAPHY

GUSTAVE DORET : *Musique et musiciens.* (Lausanne, 1915.)
A. COEUROY : *La Musique française moderne* (1st and 2nd ed. 1922, 1924.)
*Revue musicale* : 1924, No. 8. M. Boucher : *Guy Ropartz.*
EDWARD BURLINGAME HILL : *Modern French Music* (Houghton Mifflin Company, 1924.)       M. L. P.

RORE, CIPRIANO DE (*b*. Mechlin or Antwerp, *c*. 1516 ; *d*. Parma, end of 1565), composer of the Venetian school. He studied under Willaert,[1] maestro di cappella of St. Mark's, Venice, and was probably in early life a singer in that cathedral. In 1542 he brought out his first book of madrigals *a* 5, and in 1550 his first book *a* 4 appeared, a work long held in favour,[2] and for the next seven or eight years published continually.[3] About 1550 [4] he appears to have left Venice for the court of Hercules II., Duke of Ferrara, and for some years we hear nothing of him.[5] In 1558 he was given leave of absence to visit his parents at Antwerp, and soon afterwards visited the court of Margaret of Austria, Governess of the Netherlands, whose husband, Duke Ottavio Farnese, engaged him as his maestro di cappella at Parma. On the death of Willaert he was appointed his successor, Oct. 18, 1563. He resigned this position almost immediately, and returned to the court of Parma in July 1564, where he died, in the autumn of 1565. He was buried in the cathedral of that city, and the following epitaph gives an authentic sketch of his life :

> Cypriano Roro, Flandro
> Artis Musicae
> Viro omnium peritissimo,
> Cujus nomen famaque
> Nec vetustate obrui
> Nec oblivione deleri poterit,
> Hercules Ferrariens. Ducis II.
> Deinde Venetorum,
> Postremo
> Octavi Farnesi Parmae et Placentiae
> Ducis II Chori Praefecto.
> Ludovicus frater, fil. et haeredes
> Moestissimi posuerunt.
> Obiit anno MDLXV. aetatis vero suae XLIX.

---

[1] See title-page ' Fantesie e recerchari, etc., composti da lo Eccell. A. Vugliart e *Cipriano suo Discepolo*, etc., Venetiis, 1549 ' (B.M. A. 287).
[2] The Fétis library at Brussels contains important copies of three editions, 1552, 1569 and 1582. The edition in the B.M. is 1575.
[3] The following list of books of motets and madrigals is taken from Fétis's *Biographie*, Eitner's *Bibliographie*, *Q.-L.* and the catalogues of the B.M. and Fétis libraries. Some contain work by other composers, but in all cases they bear Cipriano's name, and he is the chief contributor. The date given is that of the supposed first edition : —
*Motets.* Bk. i. *a* 5, Venice, 1544 (B.M.) ; bk. ii. *a* 4 and 5, Venice, 1547 (Fétis, *Biogr.*) ; bk. iii. *a* 5, Venice, 1549 (Eitner).
*Madrigals.* Bk. i. *a* 5, Venice, 1542 ; bk. ii. *a* 5, Venice, 1544 (B.M., *Q.-L.* gives 1552 as the first edition) ; bk. iii. *a* 5, Venice, 1544. The 1562 edition in B.M. ; bks. iv. and v. (1557 and 1566). (The fifth book contains an ode to the Duke of Parma, and from the events of the composer's life we may assume this volume to be one of his latest publications.) For the first book of madrigals *a* 4, see above ; the second was printed in 1557, and in 1565 came out a selection of the four- and five-part madrigals, as ' Le vive fiamme,' etc. A large number of the four-part madrigals were brought out in score in 1577.
*Chromatic madrigals.* Bk. i. *a* 5, 1544 (B.M. ; the word ' ristampato ' on title-page shows that this is not the first edition. The first book was reprinted as late as 1593 (Fétis library). Burney has inserted one number in his *History*.
[4] In this year a reprint of his first book of madrigals was brought out at Ferrara.
[5] Except the publication of two Passions (Paris, 1557) with the following curious titles : ' Passio N. J. Christi in qua solus Johannes canens introducitur cum quatuor vocibus ' and ' Passio . . . in qua introducuntur Jesus et Judaei canentes, cum duabus et sex vocibus.'

The position to which Rore attained at St. Mark's, and the rank as a musician which contemporary writers assigned him, point to his having been something of an innovator, and a really original composer. His sacred and secular compositions were frequently reprinted,[6] and were included in many collections of the time.[7] (See *Q.-L.* for these and for MS. copies.) We know that they were held in high esteem in the court chapel at Munich, and were constantly performed there under Lassus's direction.[8] Duke Albert of Bavaria caused a superb copy of Rore's motets to be made for his library, where it remains to this day, with a portrait of the composer on the last page, by the court painter Mielich.

J. R. S.-B.

ROSA (ROSE), CARL AUGUST NICOLAS (*b*. Hamburg, Mar. 22, 1842 ; *d*. Paris, Apr. 30, 1889), was educated as a violin-player and made such progress as to be sent to the Leipzig Conservatorium, which he entered in 1859. He afterwards studied at the Paris Conservatoire, and obtained the post of Konzertmeister at Hamburg in 1863. In 1866 he came to England and appeared as a solo player at the Crystal Palace on Mar. 10. After a short stay in London he joined Bateman in a concert-tour in the United States, and there met Madame Parepa (see PAREPA-ROSA), whom he married at New York, in Feb. 1867. His wife's success on the stage led to the formation of a company under the management and conductorship of Rose, which, during its early campaigns could boast such names as Parepa, Wachtel, Santley, Ronconi and Formes among its artists.

Early in 1871 Rose—who by this time had changed his name to Rosa to avoid mistakes in pronunciation—returned to England with his wife, and then made a lengthened visit to Egypt for health. After this they again returned to London, but Madame Parepa-Rosa died almost immediately, Jan. 21, 1874. Rosa, however, was resolved to test the fortunes of English opera in London, and on Sept. 11, 1875, he opened the Princess's Theatre with a company including Miss Rose Hersee as prima donna, Santley and other good singers.

G.

Rosa's subsequent career was bound up with the fortunes of the opera company which he directed till his death (see CARL ROSA OPERA COMPANY).

ROSA, SALVATOR (*b*. Arenella, near Naples, July 21, 1615 ; *d*. Rome, Mar. 15, 1673). His father Vito Antonio de Rosa sent him to be educated at the college of the padri Somaschi. He soon began to study music, and became an

---

[6] His collected madrigals *a* 4 were published in score, Venice, 1577.
[7] Fétis mentions a book of Cipriano's masses *a* 4, 5, 6 (Venice, 1566) on the authority of Draudius's *Bibliotheca classica*. This is probably ' Liber Missarum ' *a* 4, 5, 6 (Venice, 1566), to which Cipriano only contributes the first Mass ' Doulce memoyre.'
[8] *Discorsi delli triomphi, etc. nelle nozze dell' illustr. duca Gugl. etc. da Massimo Trojano* (Monaco, Berg. 1568).

expert player of the lute, improvising accompaniments and interludes to his own verses. His ambition to go to Rome and devote himself seriously to painting seemed on the point of being fulfilled in 1635, when he visited Rome for the first time. But becoming ill, he returned to Naples at the end of six months, and there became a pupil of the painter, Aniello Falcone, until 1637. Then again he went to Rome, and accompanied a friend, Mercurio, in the service of the Cardinal Brancaccio, to Viterbo, where he received a commission to paint an altar-piece.

After a visit to Naples, he was again in Rome in 1638 until Sept. 1640, when he went to Florence to take an appointment as painter to the court of the Medici, a post he held for nearly nine years. During this time he met Filippo Lippi, poet and painter, and Cesti, the musician, and wrote *La strega*, to which Cesti composed the music, and *Il lamento*, later on set to music by Bandini. It was probably towards the end of 1640 that he wrote the satire *La musica*, a violent attack on the depraved taste shown in Italian church music. It was not published till some years after Rosa's death, and evidently caused much agitation. It was answered with a bitterness almost equal to its own by Mattheson in his *Mithridat wider den Gift einer welschen Satyre, genannt la Musica*, Hamburg, 1749; in which a German translation of the satire is given, with pages of comments and annotations. The six satires, *La Musica, La Poesia, La Pittura, La Guerra, La Babilonia* and *L' Invidia*, written by Rosa between 1640 and 1669, were probably first published in Rome in 1695; the title-page, without date, and with Amsterdam falsely indicated as the printing place, is as follows: *Satire de Salvator Rosa dedicate a settano. In Amsterdam presso Severo Prothomastix*, 12mo, p. 161. It was followed by numberless unauthorised editions. The first dated edition of 186 pages was printed in Amsterdam by J. F. Bernard in 1719, the second edition is dated 1781, and the third 1790. In 1770 there was an edition *Con note di A. M. Salvini*, printed at Florence, but with Amsterdam on the title page; this was reprinted in 1781, 1784 and 1787.

Rosa on leaving Florence was in Volterra for a time, and then returned to Rome in Feb. 1649. The year 1647 was certainly passed peaceably in Tuscany, in spite of the legend which has it that Rosa was at Naples during the insurrection in July 1647, and was one of the 'compagnia della morte' under the leadership of the painter Falcone. To begin with, no such company existed, and secondly, there are letters preserved, written by Rosa to his friend Maffei, one from Pisa, on Jan. 9, 1647, and another from Florence, on Sept. 26, 1647, in which the tumults at Naples are not even

alluded to (Cesareo, *Poesie e lettere*, 1892, p. 55). In 1650 Rosa again visited Florence, Pisa and Siena, returning to Rome in December, where he worked at his painting, finding relaxation in writing songs to which either he or his friend Cavelli, then in Rome, composed the airs.

Rosa was buried in the church of Santa Maria degli Angioli alle Terme di Diocleziano. Little of his music is known, with the exception of the songs published in the 'Gemme d' antichità' and other modern collections. His position, however, was one of some musical interest. A personal friend of some of the leading composers of the time—Cavalli, Cesti, Bandini and others—he was so far in touch with the new ideas just germinating, as to adopt the method of writing for a single voice with *bassc continuo* accompaniment.

In 1770 Dr. Burney acquired from a great-grand-daughter of Rosa, occupying the same house on the Monte Santa Trinità in Rome in which he had lived and died, a musical manuscript in Rosa's handwriting, containing, besides airs and cantatas by Cesti, Rossi, etc., eight cantatas written and composed by Rosa himself. The airs are melodious and vivacious, and have a good deal of charm. Burney (*Hist. of Music*, iv. pp. 165-8) gives the music of a certain number of them; they were also included by N. d' Arienzo in his paper on Rosa in the *R.M.I.*, 1894, i. 389.

The better-known airs are ' Vado ben spesso,' printed by Dr. Crotch in *Specimens of Various Styles*, 1808. Edited by H. Bishop in ' Gemme d' antichità,' No. 26, and in *La scuola antica*, No. 24, also in Marx's *Gluck und die Oper*, 1863. Beilage, No. 2. ' Star vicino,' edited by W. H. Callcott, ' Gemme,' No. 27. And ' Selve voi che,' edited by J. Pittmann, London, 1878. A manuscript copy of the latter is in the Vienna Imperial Library, No. 19,242 in Mantuani's catalogue.    c. s.

ROSALIA. This name has been given to the identical repetition of a melody a tone higher, keeping the exact intervals of the notes. It comes from an old popular song, ' Rosalia, mia cara,' which begins :

etc.

The objection to this is that at the third bar the key changes abruptly from G to A, with an effect of—

etc.

thus suggesting consecutive fifths between the 1st and 3rd, and consecutive octaves between the 2nd and 4th bars, at the distance, at which they most matter, of a whole tone.

There are some SEQUENCES (*q.v.*) which, without being exactly rosalias, have almost as repellent an effect. A slight change in the melody and harmony just saves Schumann's Arabeske ; a slight change in the harmony fails to save ' Salve, dimora.' A. H. F. S.

ROSAMOND, opera, text by Joseph Addison ; music by Thomas Clayton ; produced Drury Lane Theatre, Mar. 4, 1707.

Arne, many years later, took the libretto for one of his early musical efforts ; produced Little Theatre, Haymarket, Mar. 7, 1733.
F. K.

ROSAMUNDE FÜRSTIN VON CYPERN (Rosamund, Princess of Cyprus), romantic play in 4 acts ; written by Wilhelmine Christine von Chezy, the overture and incidental music by Schubert (op. 26). Produced Theater an-der-Wien, Vienna, Dec. 20, 1823, and only performed twice. The overture (in C), known as the ' Overture to Rosamunde ' (op. 26) was composed for the melodrama of the ' Zauber-harfe,' or Magic Harp. See SCHUBERT.

ROSE or KNOT (Fr. *rosace* ; Fr. and Ger. *Rosette* ; Ital. *rosa*), the ornamental device or scutcheon inserted in the sound-hole of the table of stringed instruments, such as the lute, guitar, mandoline, dulcimer or harpsichord, serving not only a decorative purpose, but— in the Netherlands especially—as the maker's ' trade mark.' In the harpsichord and spinet there was usually but one sound-hole with its rose ; but owing to the origin of these keyboard instruments from the psaltery, their analogy with the lute, and the fact of the Roman lutes having three, several sound-holes were sometimes perforated. In fact, a harpsichord dated 1531 was seen in Italy by the eminent art critic, T. J. Gullick, which possessed no less than five, each with a rose inserted. From the analogy above referred to, the old Italian harpsichord makers named the bottom of the instrument ' cassa armonica ' (sound-chest) ; as if its office were like that of the back of the lute or viol, while the belly was the ' piano armonico ' (sound-flat).[1] The Flemings, retaining the sound-hole, doubtless adhered more or less to this erroneous notion of a sound-chest. The Hitchcocks in England (1620 and later) appear to have been the first to abandon it ; no roses are seen in their instruments. Kirkman in the next century still adhered to the rose and trade scutcheon, but Shudi did not. In the *Giornale de' Litterati d' Italia* (Venice, 1711, tom. v.), Scipione Maffei, referring to Cristofori, who had recently invented the pianoforte, approves of his retention of the principle of the rose in his ordinary harpsichords, although contemporary makers for the most part had abandoned it. But Cristofori, instead of a large rose, to further, as

he thought, the resonance, used two small apertures in the front. Under the head RUCKERS will be found illustrations of the rose or *rosace*, as used by those great makers.
A. J. H.

ROSÉ, ARNOLD JOSEF (*b.* Oct. 24, 1863), a distinguished violinist, who, in 1881, became Konzertmeister to the Vienna court orchestra. He founded the Rosé Quartet (with R. C. Fischer, A. Ruzitska, F. Buxbaum), and has led its consistently fine performances in many European tours. J. Walther became violoncellist of the Quartet in 1921.

ROSE, JOHANN HEINRICH VIKTOR (*b.* Quedlinburg, Dec. 7, 1743 ; *d.* there, Mar. 9, 1820). After studying several instruments with his father, a town-musician (waits), 1756, the Princess Amalia of Prussia took him to Berlin to study the violoncello under Mara and Graul ; in 1763 he became chamber musician to the Prince of Anhalt-Bernburg, and in 1772, through the influence of Princess Amalia, organist at Quedlinburg Cathedral. He was an excellent teacher and composed 3 sonatas for violoncello, op 1, and melodies for the Quedlinburg Hymn Book (1791). E. v. d. s.

ROSEINGRAVE (ROSINGRAVE), (1) DANIEL (*d.* Golden Lane, Dublin, May 1727), church musician and organist. He received his early musical education as one of the children of the Chapel Royal ; though whether before 1660, under Captain Cook, or after that date, under Pelham Humfrey, is uncertain. He is stated subsequently to have studied under Dr. John Blow and Henry Purcell. He was organist of Gloucester Cathedral from 1679–81, of Winchester Cathedral from 1682–92, of Salisbury Cathedral from 1692–98, was appointed organist and vicar-choral of St. Patrick's Cathedral, Dublin, in 1698, and organist and stipendiary of Christ Church Cathedral, Dublin, in the same year. Hawkins said that he retired from the organistship of St. Patrick's in 1719 in favour of his son Ralph, but remained organist of Christ Church until his death. This is inaccurate ; he made an application to the Chapter to this effect, but instead Ralph was appointed vicar and probably did duty for his father.[2] He married Ann, daughter of the Rev. Thomas Washbourne, D.D., who survived him, and by whom he had several children, including his sons Thomas and Ralph, who were also distinguished musicians. There appear to have been Roseingraves in Ireland before Daniel Roseingrave's time, as mention is made in the Chapter Acts of Christ Church Dean and Chapter to one Ralph Roseingrave in 1661.

Daniel Roseingrave succeeded Robert Hodge as organist of St. Patrick's. Hodge, who resigned the post of organist, was thereupon appointed ' Master of the song to the Quire,'

[1] In modern Italian we more frequently meet with 'tompagno,' 'tavola armonica,' and 'fondo,' meaning ' belly,' or ' sound-board.'

[2] Information from w. b. s.

apparently as a *solatium* for losing the post of organist. The arrangement does not appear to have been a happy one, for in 1699 we find a Chapter Act in the following words :

'The said Dean and Chapter having received information that Mr. Hodge and Mr. Rosingrave, two of the Vicars-choral, gave each other very scurrilous language in Christ Church, Dublin, and after went together to the taverne and there fought, upon which the said Hodge and Roseingrave were ordered to appear before the said Dean and Chapter to answer in their places touching such their misdemeanours. And upon hearing what they could severally say for themselves touching the matter. And it thereupon appearing to the said Dean and Chapter that Mr. Roseingrave was ye first and chief aggressor, and that also the said Mr. Hodge was to blame. It was thereupon ordered by the aforesaid Dean and Chapter that the said Mr. Daniell Roseingrave should forthwith pay into the hands of ye steward of the said Vicars choralls the sume of three pounds and the said Mr. Hodge the sume of 20s. sterling for a penall mulct for such their offences, the same to be disposed of as the said Dean shall think fitt, and that the said Mr. Roseingrave should then and there beg publick pardon of the said Mr. Hodge for the scurillous language hee gave him as aforesaid, which was accordingly done in the presence of the said Dean and Chapter.'

Robert Hodge, it may be mentioned, had previously, when organist of Wells Cathedral (1688), been corrected and admonished for breaking windows.

At Christ Church Cathedral Roseingrave appears to have been equally combative. By a Chapter Act in 1700 the Dean and Chapter, on hearing the Petition of Daniel Roseingrave complaining of assault by Mr. Thomas Finell,

'ordered on hearing the Petition of Daniel Roseingrave and examination of several witnesses that the said Daniel Roseingrave and Thomas Finell be and are hereby suspended *ab officio et beneficio* ' ;

and further ordered

'that from henceforth no Vicar or Stipendiary of this Church do wear a sword under the penalty of expulsion.'

This suspension was subsequently removed on payment of ' mulcts ' by the offending parties.

By his will, dated Oct. 21, 1724, Daniel Roseingrave left the house in Peter Street, Dublin, in which he then dwelt, to his ' second son Ralph,' [1] to whom he also left the residue of his property, subject to his providing an annuity of £20 for his (Daniel's) wife, the said Ann Roseingrave. To his ' eldest son Thomas ' he only left five shillings. Daniel Roseingrave died at Golden Lane (the same street where, fifty-five years later, John Field was born), and was buried in the churchyard of St. Bride's Church. His widow died in 1732–33, and was buried in the old churchyard in St. Patrick's Cathedral.

Although Daniel Roseingrave seems to have written a great deal of church music, and is

highly spoken of as a composer by Burney and Hawkins, very little of his music is now extant. One of his anthems, ' Lord, Thou art become gracious,' is preserved in manuscript in the library of Christ Church, Oxford, and another, ' Haste Thee, O Lord,' in the Bodleian Library. J. S. Bumpus had autograph scores of four other anthems of his.

By a Chapter Act of Christ Church, Dublin, dated Dec. 15, 1699, it is ordered ' that the Proctor do pay unto Mr. Daniel Roseingrave three pounds as a gratuity for his writing three services and two Creeds for the use of the Church.' Unfortunately all traces of these compositions have long since disappeared.

(2) Thomas (*b.* Winchester, 1690 ; *d.* Dunleary, June 23, 1766), second son of Daniel Roseingrave. At the age of 7 he came with his father to Dublin, and from him received his early education in music. Thomas Roseingrave entered Trinity College, Dublin, in 1707, and his then age is given in the College Register as 16. He did not, however, proceed to his degree in Arts.

In a Chapter Act of St. Patrick's Cathedral, dated Dec. 14, 1709, it is ordered by the Dean and Chapter

'that whenever Thomas Rosseingrave sonn of Daniell Rossingrave, the present organist of the said Cathedrall, being minded to travell beyond seas to improve himself in the art of music, and that hereafter he may be useful and serviceable to the said Cathedrall, yt tenne guineas be by the Proctor of the said Canonry given him as a guift from the said Canonry towards bearing his charges.'

He went to Italy in 1710, and at Venice made the acquaintance of the Scarlattis, Alessandro and Domenico. For the latter he appears to have formed a great admiration. Burney [2] says that he

'followed him to Rome and Naples, and hardly ever quitted him while he remained in Italy, which was not till after the Peace of Utrecht [1713], as appears by an anthem which he composed at Venice in 1713, " Arise, shine, for thy light is come." '

The manuscript of this anthem, which he wrote with orchestral accompaniment, is preserved in the Tudway collection (Harl. MS. 7342). Burney says of it, ' There is much fire in the introductory symphony, which is of a very modern cast.' How long he continued abroad is not exactly known, but in 1720 we find him in London, where he produced, at the Haymarket Theatre, Domenico Scarlatti's opera, ' Narciso,' with two additional songs and two duets of Roseingrave's own composition.

As a composer and organist he appears to have been held in high estimation, his powers of reading at sight and of improvising being especially dwelt on by his contemporaries.

In 1725 he was appointed the first organist of St. George's, Hanover Square. There were seven other competitors, all of whom had to give a performance on the organ before Dr.

---

[1] Although in his will Daniel describes Ralph as his ' second son,' his eldest son was Daniel, Junior (*b.* Winchester, 1685 ; *d.* before 1724), entered Trinity College, Dublin, in 1702, obtained a scholarship in 1705, and took out his B.A. degree in 1707. He was, doubtless, the ' young Roseingrave ' who appears by the College Register to have been appointed organist of Trinity College Chapel in 1705, as in that year Thomas was only fourteen, and Ralph still younger. In 1707 he was given leave of absence for one year, ' in order to improve himself in music.' He had probably died some years before 1724, the date of his father's will.

[2] *History of Music,* iv. p. 263.

Greene, Dr. Pepusch and Galliard, who acted as judges. Burney says that Roseingrave's performance of the set pieces was by no means good, but that when he was asked to improvise on given themes, he ' treated the subjects with such science and dexterity, inverting the order of notes, augmenting and diminishing their value, introducing counter subjects, and treating the themes to so many ingenious purposes, that the judges were unanimous in declaring him the victorious candidate.'

Archdeacon Coxe, in his *Anecdotes of George Frederick Handel and John Christopher Smith*, speaking of Roseingrave at this time, says :

' His reputation was at this period so high that on commencing teaching he might have gained one thousand pounds a year, but an unfortunate event reduced him to extreme distress. Among Roseingrave's scholars was a young lady to whom he was greatly attached, and whose affections he had gained, but her father, who intended to give her a large fortune, did not approve of her marrying a musician, and forbade Roseingrave his house. This disappointment affected his brain, and he never entirely recovered the shock. He neglected his scholars and lost his business. He lived upon fifty pounds per annum, which his place produced, and was often in indigence. He was perfectly rational upon every subject but the one nearest his heart ; whenever that was mentioned he was quite insane.'

In 1737–38 he was compelled to give up the organistship, and lived for some time at Hampstead. Thence he removed [1] to Dublin, where he probably lived with his nephew, William Roseingrave (*b.* 1725), a son of RALPH (3), who at this time (1753) held the office of Chief Chamberlain of the Exchequer Court.

Mrs. Delany, in her memoirs, under date Jan. 12, 1753, writes :

' Mr. Roseingrave, who was sent away from St. George's Church on account of his mad fits, is now in Ireland, and at times can play very well on the harpsichord.' [1]

Faulkner's *Dublin Journal* of Feb. 3, 1753, contains an announcement that

' the celebrated Opera of " Phaedra and Hippolitus," composed by Mr. Roseingrave lately arrived from London, will be performed at the Great Music Hall in Fishamble Street, and conducted by himself on Tuesday the 6th of March. Between the acts Mr. Roseingrave will perform Scarlatti's " Lessons on the Harpsichord," with his own additions, and will conclude with his celebrated " Almand." '

And in the same Journal of Feb. 27, we read :

' Yesterday there was a public rehearsal of Mr. Roseingrave's Opera of " Phaedra and Hippolytus " at the great Music Hall in Fishamble Street, to a numerous audience, which met the highest applause, the connoisseurs allowing it to exceed any musical performance ever exhibited here, in variety, taste, and number of good songs.'

One wonders if the writer of this notice had been at the production of the ' Messiah ' in the same hall eleven years earlier.

Two anthems of Thomas Roseingrave (' Great is the Lord ' and ' One Generation ') are included in the manuscript collection of anthems in the R.C.M. He was an enthusiastic admirer of Palestrina, and is said to have

[1] W. H. G. F. gives the date as 1749.
[2] *Correspondence*, iii. 194.

adorned the walls of his bedroom with scraps of paper containing extracts from the works of that master.

He was buried on June 26, 1766, in the churchyard of St. Patrick's Cathedral, in the same grave with his brother Ralph. The inscription on the tombstone adds that he died in the 78th year of his age, ' a most celebrated musician and accomplished man.' Although an inscription added to this tombstone at a later date (1802) states that his wife, Mrs. Jane Roseingrave, is also buried there, this is incorrect, as the Jane Roseingrave in question was the wife of the before-mentioned William Roseingrave, who died in 1780, and is buried in an adjoining grave. Thomas Roseingrave does not appear to have been married.

The most important of his published compositions are : Fifteen voluntaries and fugues for the organ or harpsichord ; six double fugues for the organ or harpsichord ; the opera ' Phaedra and Hippolytus ' ; eight suits of lessons for the harpsichord or spinet ; six cantatas (Italian words) ; the additional songs and duets sung with Scarlatti's opera ' Narciso ' ; and twelve solos for the German flute with thorough-bass for the harpsichord. He edited the ' Forty-Two Suits of Lessons for the Harpsichord by Domenico Scarlatti,' prefixing an introductory movement in G minor.

(3) RALPH (*b.* Salisbury, *c.* 1695 ; *d.* 1747), the youngest son of Daniel Roseingrave, received his musical education from his father. In 1718–19 Daniel Roseingrave petitioned the Dean and Chapter of St. Patrick's Cathedral, Dublin, to allow him to resign the post of organist in favour of his son Ralph, who appears to have been forthwith appointed vicar-choral, but did not formally succeed his father as organist until 1726. On his father's death in 1727 he also succeeded him as organist of Christ Church Cathedral, Dublin, at a salary of fifty pounds per annum. He appears to have written a good deal of church music. Eight of his anthems and two Services in C and F are preserved at Christ Church, and some of them are still sung there. Another anthem of his, ' O God of Truth,' is published in Hullah's Part Music, and an old organ book in the possession of J. S. Bumpus contains a Service of his in F with a setting of the Benedicite. He is buried in the churchyard of St. Patrick's Cathedral. The headstone mentions that his wife Sarah, who died in 1746, and four of their children, are buried with him, as are also his mother Ann Roseingrave, and his brother Thomas. Ralph Roseingrave is sometimes mentioned as having taken part as a soloist in the production of the ' Messiah ' on Apr. 13, 1742, but Dr. J. C. Culwick, in his pamphlet on the original *Word Book of Handel's ' Messiah '* (1891), points out the improbability of his having done so.        L. M'C. L. D.

ROSELLEN, Henri (b. Paris, Oct. 13, 1811 ; d. there, Mar. 18, 1876), son of a PF. maker, took a second PF. prize at the Conservatoire, 1827, and a first harmony prize, 1828. He was a pupil and imitator of Herz. He published nearly 200 works for PF., including a 'Méthode de piano' (Heugel), a collection of progressive exercises entitled 'Manuel des pianistes' (Ibid.), a trio for piano and strings, and many separate pieces of drawing-room character, one of which, a Rêverie (op. 32, No. 1), enjoyed an extraordinary popularity for many years over the whole of Europe.                            G.

ROSENHAIN, Jacob (b. Mannheim, Dec. 2, 1813 ; d. Baden-Baden, Mar. 21, 1894), eldest son of a banker. His teachers were Jacob Schmitt, Kalliwoda and Schnyder von Wartensee. His first appearance as a pianoforte-player was in 1823 at Frankfort, where his success induced him to take up his residence. A one-act piece of his, 'Der Besuch im Irrenhause,' was produced at Frankfort, Dec. 29, 1834, with great success ; his second, 'Liswenna,' three acts, was never performed in its original form. In 1837 he came to London, played at the Philharmonic, Apr. 17, and was much heard in the concerts of the day. After this he took up his abode in Paris, where he became very prominent, giving chamber concerts in combination with Alard, Ernst and other eminent players, and carrying on a school of pianoforte-playing in conjunction with J. B. Cramer. His early opera 'Liswenna' was provided with a new libretto (by Bayard and Arago), and brought out at the Opéra as 'Le Démon de la nuit,' Mar. 17, 1851. It had, however, but a moderate success, and was withdrawn after four representations, though it was afterwards occasionally played in Germany. Another one-act piece, 'Volage et jaloux,' produced at Baden-Baden, Aug. 3, 1863, completes the list of his works for the stage. In instrumental music he was much more prolific. He composed three symphonies—in G minor (op. 42), played at the Gewandhaus, Leipzig, under Mendelssohn's direction, Jan. 31, 1846 ; in F minor (op. 43), played at Brussels, and at the Philharmonic, London, Apr. 24, 1854 ; 'Im Frühling,' in F major (op. 61), rehearsed at the Conservatoire, and played at a Concert Populaire ; four trios for PF. and strings ; one PF. concerto ; three string quartets ; two violoncello sonatas ; twelve characteristic studies (op. 17) and twenty-four 'Études mélodiques' (op. 20), both for PF. solo ; a PF. concerto, op. 73 ; sonata, op. 74 ; do. PF. and violoncello, op. 98 ; 'Am Abend' for quartet, op. 99. Also various pieces for piano entitled 'Poèmes,' 'Rêveries,' etc. ; a biblical cantata, and various songs, etc. Schumann criticised several of his pieces with kindness and liberality.          G.

ROSENKAVALIER, DER, opera in 3 acts ; text by H. von Hofmannsthal ; music by Richard Strauss. Produced Royal Opera, Dresden, Jan. 26, 1911 ; Covent Garden, Jan. 1, 1913 ; New York, Metropolitan Opera House, Dec. 9, 1913 ; in English (Denhof Opera Co.), Prince of Wales's Theatre, Birmingham, Sept. 20, 1913.

ROSENMÜLLER, Johann (b. Pelsnitz, Vogtland of Saxony, c. 1619 ; d. Wolfenbüttel, Sept. 10 or 11, 1684). In spite of the poverty of his parents the arrangements of the time enabled him to obtain a good general education, and in 1640 his name appears inscribed in the Matriculation-book of the University of Leipzig. In 1642 he became collaborator or assistant-master at the Thomasschule. In musical matters he would appear to have been mainly a pupil of Tobias Michael, who then held the important office of cantor at the school. In 1645 Rosenmüller published his first work, a work for instruments entitled 'Paduanen, Alemanden, Couranten, Balletten, Sarabanden mit 3 Stimmen und ihrem Basso pro Organo.' A more important work was his 'Kernsprüche,' published in two parts, 1648 and 1652-53, each part consisting of twenty Latin and German motets on Scripture and other church texts for three to seven voices, mostly with accompaniment of two violins, and also occasionally trombones and other instruments with basso continuo. When Tobias Michael became too infirm to discharge adequately his duties as cantor, Rosenmüller acted as his deputy, and in this position gave such satisfaction to the city council as to obtain the promise of succession to the cantorship. In 1651 he also held the post of organist at the Nikolaikirche. But in May 1655 his prospects of further promotion were blighted by an accusation made against him of some grave moral offence, for which he was temporarily imprisoned. He succeeded in effecting his escape, and betook himself for a time to Hamburg. From Hamburg he is said to have addressed a 'Supplication' to the Elector of Saxony, Johann Georg I., along with a setting of the Hymn of Albinus, 'Straf mich nicht in deinem Zorn.' This would almost seem to be an admission of his guilt, although Winterfeld in his Evangelischer Kirchengesang endeavours to prove him innocent of the charge made against him. However the case may be, Rosenmüller did not feel himself safe in Hamburg, but fled to Italy, and settled in Venice as a teacher of music for a considerable number of years.

Of his stay in Venice little would have been known if Johann Philipp Krieger, who was afterwards Kapellmeister at Weissenfels, had not sought him out and become his pupil in composition. A large number of works existing only in MS., consisting of

Latin motets, Vesper Psalms, Lamentations, and various parts of the Mass, must be referred to this Venetian stay. The only work published in Venice was one for instruments, entitled 'Sonate da camera cioe Sinfonie, Alemande, Correnti, Balletti, Sarabande da suonare con 5 strom. da arco et altri' . . . 1670. This work was dedicated to Duke Johann Friedrich of Brunswick, who became acquainted with the composer on the occasion of one of his visits to Venice. It has been republished, *D.D.T.* vol. xviii., where also in his introduction the editor, Karl Nef, traces the influence of the Venetian opera-symphonies upon Rosenmüller's style of instrumental composition. The acquaintance with Duke Johann Friedrich had important consequences for Rosenmüller. It led to his recall to Germany. Duke Johann Friedrich recommended him to his brother the reigning Duke Anton Ulrich, who was an enlightened patron of literature and music, and himself a hymn-writer of some reputation. In 1674 Duke Anton Ulrich appointed Rosenmüller Kapellmeister at Wolfenbüttel, where he remained for the rest of his life. Only one other work was published in this later period of his life, 'Sonate a 2, 3, 4, e 5 stromenti da arco et altri . . . Nuremberg, 1682,' dedicated to his patron Duke Anton Ulrich. A large number of German motets and cantatas belonging to this time remained unpublished. None of Rosenmüller's vocal works has yet been republished in modern editions, with the exception of two Choral-tunes and settings—'Straf mich nicht in deinem Zorn' and 'Welt ade, ich bin dein müde.' The former of these tunes indeed seems far less suitable to its original German words than to those of the Easter hymns to which it has been so successfully adapted in English hymn-books, 'Christ the Lord is risen again.' Of Rosenmüller's 5-voice setting of 'Welt ade' it would appear that Sebastian Bach thought so highly that he took it over bodily from Vopelius' 'Leipziger Gesangbuch,' 1682, to incorporate it into his own church-cantata of 1731, 'Wer weiss, wie nahe mir mein Ende.' This led to both tune and setting being afterwards ascribed to Bach in earlier editions of his 'Choral-gesänge.'

J. R. M.

ROSENTHAL, MORIZ (*b.* Lemberg, Dec. 18, 1862), pianist. His father was a professor in the chief Academy at Lemberg. From him Rosenthal obtained the solid foundation of the philosophical turn of mind which early in his career became very fully developed. At 8 years of age the boy began the study of the pianoforte under a certain Galoth. In 1872 Carl Mikuli, then director of the Lemberg Conservatorium, took charge of Rosenthal's education, and within the same year played in public with him Chopin's rondo in C for two

pianos. When, in 1875, the family moved to Vienna, Rosenthal became a pupil of Joseffy, who set to work systematically to ground the boy on Tausig's method. The results were astonishing enough, since in 1876 Rosenthal played at his first public recital Beethoven's thirty-two variations, Chopin's F minor concerto, and some Liszt and Mendelssohn. Promptly a tour followed through Roumania, where at Bucharest the king created the 14-year-old lad court pianist. In the next year Liszt came into Rosenthal's life, and henceforth played a great part therein, and in 1878 and subsequently they were together in Weimar and Rome. As Liszt's pupil Rosenthal then appeared in Paris, St. Petersburg and elsewhere.

Meanwhile the philosophical studies were by no means neglected, for in 1880 Rosenthal qualified at the Staatsgymnasium in Vienna to take the philosophical course at the University, where he studied with Zimmermann, Brentano and Hanslick (musical æsthetics). Six years elapsed before he resumed public pianoforte-playing. Then there followed in quick succession, after a triumph in the Liszt Verein at Leipzig, a long series of concert tours, in America and elsewhere, which brought him ultimately to England in 1895 and to America again later. As a master of technique Rosenthal is not surpassed by any pianist of his time, while as an interpreter, especially of music of the modern composers and of Schubert, he earned a prodigious reputation. To his great technical accomplishment he adds a beautiful touch, and to those who know him personally he is a musician of unquestionable distinction. R. H. L.

ROSE OF CASTILE, opera in 3 acts; compiled by Harris & Falconer (from 'Le Muletier de Tolède'), music by Balfe. Produced Lyceum Theatre (Pyne and Harrison), London, Oct. 29, 1857. G.

ROSE OF PERSIA, THE, comic opera in 2 acts; text by Basil Hood; music by Sullivan; produced Savoy Theatre, Nov. 29, 1899.

ROSES, JOSE (*b.* Barcelona, Feb. 9, 1791; *d.* there, Jan. 2, 1856), priest and musician, learned music from Sampere, maestro de capilla at Barcelona; was first organist of the monastery of San Pablo and then succeeded his master at Santa Maria del Pino, a post which he held for thirty years. During this time he composed a large quantity of music—masses, requiems, motets, graduals, etc., which are preserved in MS. in the church. Among his pupils may be mentioned Calvo, Puig, Rius, Casanovas, etc.

G.

ROSIERS (ROZIERS), ANDRÉ DE, SIEUR DE BEAULIEU, a 17th-century French composer of 16 books, 'Les libertez de . . . à 4 parties' (dessus, haute-contre, taille, basse-contre) published between 1634 and 1672 ; ' Alphabet de chanson pour danser et pour boire,' book iv., Paris, 1646.

ROSIERS, CHARLES, a 17th-century violinist, afterwards vice-Kapellmeister of the Elector of Cologne, at Bonn ; composed a book of motets (1688) ; ' Pièces choisies à la manière italienne,' for flute, violin and other instruments (1691) ; 14 ' Sonate per le violino et le hautbois,' à 6 parties (2 dessus, haut-contre, bassus, basso continuo et trompette), and a guitar tutor (1699) ; symphonies by him were advertised at Amsterdam in 1691.

E. v. d. s.

ROSIN (RESIN) (Fr. colophane), a preparation applied to the hair of the violin bow to give it the necessary ' bite ' upon the strings. Rosin is the residuary gum of turpentine after distillation. The ordinary rosin of commerce is a coarse, hard substance, quite useless to the fiddler, for whom the rough material undergoes a process of refinement. The ancient English recipe was to boil rough rosin down in vinegar, a process no longer in vogue, as excellent French rosin is now to be had at a very trifling cost. It is prepared by dissolving the rough article in a glazed earthen vessel over a slow charcoal fire. As it melts, it is strained through coarse canvas into a second vessel also kept at a moderate heat, from which it is poured into pasteboard or metal moulds. Some players affect to prefer the rosin of Gand, others that of Vuillaume, but both are made of the same material and at the same factory. Rosin should be transparent, of a darkish yellow colour in the mass, and quite white when pulverised : it ought to fall from the bow, when first applied to the strings, in a very fine white dust : when crushed between the fingers it ought not to feel sticky. The best rosin is made from Venetian turpentine. The same sort of rosin serves for the violin, viola and violoncello. The double-bass bow requires a stiffer preparation than pure rosin, and accordingly double-bass rosin is made of ordinary rosin and white pitch in equal proportions. Emery powder and other matters are sometimes added in the composition of rosin, but are quite unnecessary, and even injurious to the tone. A liquid rosin, applied to the bow with a camel's-hair brush, has its advocates. (See COLOPHANE.)

E. J. P.

ROSINA, an English ballad opera, of the 18th century, which attained an extraordinary degree of popularity, holding the boards, as a stock piece, for nearly half a century. The libretto, written by Mrs. Brooke, is founded on the Scriptural story of Ruth and Boaz ; or of Palemon and Lavina, in Thomson's ' Seasons,' a subject which has inspired numbers of theatrical pieces.

The opera was first produced at Covent Garden in 1783, and its music was written,

selected and arranged by William Shield. Miss Harper took the title-rôle ; Mrs. Martyr, Phœbe ; and Mrs. Kennedy the hero, William, while the rest of the male characters were taken by Banister, Brett and Davies.

F. K.

ROSKOŠNÝ, JOSEF RICHARD (b. Prague, Sept. 21, 1833 ; d. there, 1913), a Czech composer. He was a successful pianist, touring in Austria-Hungary, Italy, Serbia and Roumania, and composed a good deal of brilliant music for his instrument, as well as many songs in a light folk style. It was, however, as a composer of popular operas that he made a more lasting reputation. The influence of Smetana somewhat strengthened his earlier style, which was coloured by the eroticism of Gounod and the facile side of Mendelssohn. Later in his career the Italian realists came in for a share of his admiration, and the result was his opera ' Stoja,' unique in this respect. His agreeable eclecticism proves that he had no great independence of thought ; but his operatic music tells effectively, thanks to his sense of stagecraft. ' Popelka ' (Cinderella) continues to keep its place in the repertory of Czech opera. The admirable libretto is by Otakar HOSTINSKÝ (q.v.), and the music echoes the popular style with a grace not unworthy of a disciple of Smetana.

Operas: ' Mikuláš ' (Nicholas), 1870 ; ' Svatojanské proudy ' (The Rapids of St. John), 1871 ; ' Popelka ' (Cinderella), 1885 ; ' Stoja,' 1894 ; ' Satanella,' 1898 ; ' Černé jezero ' (The Black Lake), 1905. Pianoforte pieces and songs.

R. N.

ROSLAVETZ, NIKOLAI ANDREIVICH (b. Surai, Government of Chernigov, Dec. 24, 1880, O.S.), composer, of peasant origin. He received his musical education at the Moscow Conservatoire, where he won a silver medal for a cantata ' Heaven and Earth ' (after Byron). His compositions include :

A symphony (1922) ; two symphonic poems ; a quintet for harp, oboe, two violas and violoncello ; 5 string quartets ; 2 PF. trios ; 5 violin sonatas ; 2 violoncello sonatas ; songs.

R. N.

ROSS, JOHN (b. Newcastle-upon-Tyne, Oct. 12, 1763 ; d. Aberdeen, July 28, 1837), was placed in his 11th year under Hawdon, organist of St. Nicholas Church, a disciple of Charles Avison, with whom he studied for seven years. In 1783 he was appointed organist of St. Paul's Chapel, Aberdeen, where he remained until his death. He composed ' An Ode to Charity,' pianoforte concertos and sonatas, songs, canzonets, hymns, waltzes, etc.

W. H. H. ; addns. Brit. Mus. Biog.

ROSSELLI (ROSELLI, ROSSELLO, ROUSSEL, RUSELLO), FRANCESCO, maestro di cappella at St. Peter's, Rome, in 1548, and master of the boys of the cappella Giulia. He retired in 1550. He composed motets and other church music, all in MS.; 2 books of madrigals, 5 v. (1562–63); 1 book madrigals, 4 v. (1565); chansons nouvelles, 4-6 v. (Paris, 1577) ; also chansons and madrigals in collective volumes (Q.-L.).

ROSSETER, PHILIP (b. circa 1575, d. London, May 5, 1623), lutenist and song-writer. In 1601 was published :

'A Booke of Ayres, set foorth to be song to the Lute, Orpherian and Base Violl, by Philip Rosseter Lutenist : And are to be solde at his house in Fleestreete neere to the Grayhound. At Lonond [sic] Printed by Peter Short, by the assent of Thomas Morley.' (Eng. Sch. of Lutenist Song-writers.)

This book differs from all the other song-books of the English lutenists in that it really consists of two separate books of twenty-one songs each ; the first by Campian and the second by Rosseter. There is only one title-page, and the dedication to Sir Thomas Monson and the Address to the Reader are Rosseter's. In the first section the words as well as the music are admittedly by Campian ; there is no positive evidence that Campian also wrote the words of Rosseter's songs, but it is commonly assumed that he did so. All the songs in the volume were written as solo-songs without an alternative version for four voices. All Rosseter's songs are simple in construction, but they are very melodious and admirably vocal. In the Address to the Reader Rosseter says some interesting things about song, and he was evidently one of those who did not approve of the complexity of contrapuntal writing.

In 1609 he published a set of

'Lessons for the Consort : made by sundrie excellent Authors and set to sixe severall instruments.'

Rosseter's association with Kingham, Reeve and Robert Jones for training ' the Children of the Revels to the Queen ' is described in the article on Robert JONES, q.v. Campian seems to have been the life-long friend of Rosseter ; lying in 1620, he bequeathed him all his property, amounting to about £20, expressing a wish ' that it had bin farr more.' Rosseter died in Fetter Lane, and was buried on May 7, at St. Dunstan's in the West, where Campian also was buried. He left a widow and two sons ; his brother Hugh is also mentioned in his will (P.C.C., 41 Swann).     E. H. F.

ROSSETTO (ROSETO, ROSETUS), STEFFANO (b. Nice), lived in 1565 in Florence. In 1567 he was musician of Cardinal de Medici there ; 1579–80 organist of Munich court chapel ; and, according to Riemann, maestro di cappella at Novara. He composed 1 book madrigals, 4 v. (1560) ; 2 books madrigals, 5 v. (1560, 1566) ; 1 book madrigals, 6 v. (1566) ; a madrigal cycle, ' Il lamento di Olimpia,' with 1 canzona, 5-10 v. (1567). All these were published at Venice. 1 book motets, 5-6 v., so contrived that they may be used for all manner of instruments (Nüremberg, 1573), dedicated to Archduke Ferdinand of Austria. Eitner in Q.-L. says that his name in the documents of the Munich court chapel appears once as Joseph N. Roseto, and in another place as Steffan Roseto ; this appears rather to suggest two different people.     E. V. D. S.

ROSSI. No fewer than twenty-eight musicians of this name are enumerated in Q.-L., and as there are motets and other works in various libraries attributed to ' Rossi ' without further identification, there is still a large field open for careful research before the facts can be absolutely ascertained. Of these older bearers of the name there are seven who may be distinguished as important : (1) SALOMONE, a Jewish musician, was at the court of Mantua from 1587–1628, when he appears to have died. He enjoyed such high favour with two successive dukes that he was privileged to dispense with the yellow badge that all Jews were ordered to wear. He issued madrigals and canzonets in 1589, 1600, 1602, 1603, 1610, 1614 and 1628, but his most important works were instrumental, being contained in four books, called ' Sinfonie e gagliarde ' and ' Sonate ' (1607, 1608, 1623 and 1636). He wrote 28 compositions (a 4-8) to Hebrew psalms, published in two editions, in Hebrew and Italian, in 1623. The authority for his life is Birnbaum's Jüdische Musiker am Hofe zu Mantua A selection from his vocal music was published in 1877 by S. Naumburg and Vincent d'Indy, and examples of his instrumental music are included in Riemann's ' Alte Kammermusik.'

(2) GIOVANNI BATTISTA (b. Genoa), a monk, who published in 1618 at Venice a book on mensural notation, Organo de cantori per intendere da se stesso ogni passo difficile, etc., containing cantilene a 2-5, and a book of four-part masses in the same year.     M.

(3) MICHAEL ANGELO, a Roman musician of the earlier part of the 17th century, was a pupil of Frescobaldi for organ-playing. He is known as the composer of an opera entitled ' Erminia sul Giordano,' [1] which in 1635 or 1637 [2] was performed with all stage accessories in the Palace of Taddeo Barberini, Prefect of Rome and Prince of Palestrina. It was published in 1637, and dedicated to the Signora Anna Colonna Barberina, the Princess of Palestrina. A full account of the opera, the libretto of which is based on an episode in Tasso's Gerusalemme liberata, is given in H. Goldschmidt's Studien zur Geschichte der italienischen Oper, with some specimens of the music. Like most of the Roman operas of the period, the music would appear to be utterly wanting in any dramatic power ; the form of the drama is merely an excuse for scenic decorations and occasional graceful pastoral music. Rossi is better known as a composer for clavier. He published a collection of Toccate e Correnti for organ or cembalo (second edition, Rome, 1657, first edition without date). These are now generally accessible in Torchi's ' L' arte musicale in Italia,' vol. iii. They are modelled on the style of the pieces of the same name by

[1] Words by Giulio Rospighosi, afterwards Clement IX.   W. B. S.
[2] Fétis and Clément, Dictionnaire lyrique, erroneously give the date 1625.

Frescobaldi, but show no advance either in technique or treatment, though the correnti are melodious enough. Previous to this republication by Torchi, there used to appear in various modern collections of older music, such as L. Köhler's ' Maîtres du clavecin,' Pauer's ' Alte Meister ' and others, an Andantino and Allegro ascribed to Rossi, which have now been proved to be spurious,[1] their whole style showing them to belong to the following century.    J. R. M.

(4) LUIGI (b. Torre Maggiore, 1598; d. Rome, Feb. 19, 1653), was, about 1620, in the service of Cardinal Barberini in Rome as a singer. Through Mazarin's influence he was invited to Paris, where on Mar. 2, 1647, his opera ' Le Mariage d'Orphée et Euridice ' was given, being the first Italian opera performed in Paris. Five years before he had composed a dramatic work, ' Il palagio d' Atlante,' to words by G. Rospighosi (a copy in the R.C.M. has the title ' Il pallazzo incantato '). Gevaert edited a selection of thirteen cantatas by him. Some of his compositions are in the Bibliothèque Nationale : ' Recueil d' airs italiens.' He was buried at Santa Maria in the Via Lata at Rome.[2]

BIBL.—ROMAIN ROLLAND, Musiciens d'autrefois (Paris, 1908); H. PRUNIÈRES, L'Opéra italien en France avant Lully (Paris, 1913).

(5) FRANCESCO, an Abbate, a native of Apulia (Fétis gives Bari as his birthplace), who brought out several operas in Venice between 1686 and 1689, viz. ' Il Sejano moderno ' (1686), ' La Clorilda ' and ' La pena degl' occhi ' in 1688, and ' Mitrane ' in 1689. The last work contains the beautiful air, ' Ah ! rendimi quel core,' by which alone his name is known in the present day. An oratorio, ' La caduta dei Giganti,' is in MS.

(6) GIUSEPPE (d. Rome, c. 1719) was successively maestro di cappella at the Castle of St. Angelo, Rome, Pistoia and San Loreto, Rome. A Mass in 12 parts, divided into three choirs, and two settings of Dixit Dominus for 12 and 16 voices respectively, are preserved at Bologna, where the latter are ascribed to the later Giuseppe Rossi.

(7) GIUSEPPE, maestro in the cathedral of Terni, and the composer of an opera, ' La sposa in Livorno,' given in Rome in 1807. He published a treatise, Alli intendenti di contrappunto, in 1809, and several of his motets are at Bologna.    M.

There are, furthermore, three later opera-composers of the name, as follows :

(8) LAURO (b. Macerata, Feb. 19, 1810 ; d. Cremona, May 5, 1885), a pupil of Crescentini, Furno and Zingarelli at Naples. He began to write at once, and at 18 had his first two operas—' Le contesse villane ' and

' La villana contessa ' — performed at the Fenice and Nuovo Theatres of Naples respectively. Other pieces followed : one of them, ' Costanza ed Oringaldo,' being written expressly for the San Carlo at the request of Barbaja. On the recommendation of Donizetti, Rossi was engaged for the Teatro Valle at Rome, and there he remained for 1832 and 1833, and composed four operas and an oratorio. In 1834 he moved to Milan, and brought out ' La casa disabitata ' (or ' I falsi monetari '), which, though but moderately successful at La Scala, was afterwards considered his chef-d'œuvre, and spoken of as ' Rossi's Barbiere di Siviglia.' It pleased Malibran so much that she induced Barbaja to bespeak another opera from Rossi for the San Carlo, in which she should appear. The opera was composed, and was named ' Amelia ' (produced at Naples, Dec. 4, 1834) ; but owing to her caprice was a failure. She insisted on having a pas de deux inserted for her and Mathis. The theatre was crowded to the ceiling to see the great singer dance ; but her dancing did not please the public, and the piece was damned. This disappointment, though somewhat alleviated by the success of his ' Leocadia ' (1834) seems to have disgusted Rossi with Italy ; he accepted an engagement from Mexico, left Europe, Oct. 15, 1835, and arrived at Vera Cruz the 6th of the following January. From Mexico he went to the Havannah, New Orleans and Madras ; married in 1841, and returned to Europe, landing at Cadiz, Feb. 3, 1843. He began again at once to compose—' Cellini a Parigi ' (Turin, 1845), etc., but with very varying success. In 1846 he reappeared at La Scala at Milan with ' Azema di Granata,' ' Il borgomastro di Schiedam,' and three or four other operas in following years. His great success, however, appears to have been made with ' Il domino nero,' at the Teatro Canobbiana, Sept. 1849. In 1850 he was called to be director of the Conservatorio at Milan. For this institution he published a Guida di armonia pratica orale (Ricordi, 1858), and between 1850 and 1859 composed a great many operas, and detached pieces for voices and for instruments. After the death of Mercadante in 1870, Rossi succeeded him as head of the Conservatorio at Naples. This office he resigned in 1878, and he went to Cremona in 1880, dying there on May 5, 1885. Lists of his works are given by Florimo (Cenni Storici, pp. 948-962), Riemann and Pougin. They comprise 29 operas, a Mass, and a dozen miscellaneous compositions, including six fugues for strings, two sets of vocal exercises, and the Guide to Harmony already mentioned. His best works are ' Cellini a Parigi,' ' I falsi monetari,' ' La contessa di Mons ' and ' Il domino nero.' One of his operas, ' La figlia di Figaro,' is said to have been produced at the Kärnthnerthor theatre.

---

[1] Ernst von Werra was the first to prove, by examination of the genuine works of Rossi previously unknown, the anachronism of this attribution (M.f.M. xxviii. pp. 123 ff.).
[2] Romain Rolland, Musiciens d'autrefois (Paris, 1908).

Vienna, Apr. 17, 1846 ; and another, ' Biorn,' was announced for performance at the Queen's Theatre, London, Jan. 17, 1877—English libretto by Frank Marshall ; but no notice of either performance can be found. An oratorio, ' Saul,' elegies on Bellini and Mercadante, a Mass and other works, are mentioned by Riemann.              G.

(9) GIOVANNI GAETANO (b. Borgo San Donnino, Parma, Aug. 5, 1828 ; d. Parma, Mar. 30, 1886) studied at the Milan Conservatorio, was leader of the orchestra in the theatre at Parma, and organist of the court chapel there, from 1852–73, and director of the Parma Conservatorio in 1864–73. In 1873 he became conductor at the Teatro Carlo Felice, Genoa, until 1879. His operas were : ' Elena di Taranto ' (Parma, 1852), ' Giovanni Giscala ' (Parma, 1855), ' Nicolò de' Lapi ' (Ancona, 1865), ' La contessa d'Altemberg ' (Borgo San Donnino, 1872) and ' Maria Sanz ' (Bergamo, 1895). A symphony, ' Saul,' won a prize in Paris in 1878, and Rossi wrote besides three masses, an oratorio and a requiem.

(10) CESARE (b. Rivarolo, near Mantua, Jan. 20, 1858) has won success as a teacher of the piano, as director of the music school and conductor at Trent, and as a composer in many branches of art, his opera ' Nadeja ' having been received with much favour at Prague in 1903 (Riemann, etc.).     M.

ROSSIGNOL, LE, opera in 3 acts, by Igor Stravinsky, founded on a Hans Andersen story. Produced Paris, 1914 ; Drury Lane, June 18, 1914 ; in English (Beecham), Covent Garden, Nov. 12, 1919.

ROSSINI, GIOACCHINO ANTONIO (b. Pesaro, Feb. 29, 1792 ; d. Passy, Nov. 13, 1868), was the only child of Giuseppe Rossini, town-trumpeter (trombadore) of Lugo and inspector of slaughter-houses. In the political struggles of 1796 the father declared himself for the French and for republican government, and was sent to gaol. His wife was thus driven to turn her voice to account and went with her little Gioacchino to Bologna, making her début as ' prima donna buffa ' with such success as to procure her engagements in various theatres of the Romagna during the Carnival. Meantime the trombadore had regained his liberty and was engaged as horn-player in the bands of the theatres in which his wife sang. The child was left at Bologna in the charge of a pork butcher, where he acquired a little musical knowledge from a certain Prinetti of Novara, who gave him harpsichord lessons for three years, and later from Angelo Tesei, a clever master, able to make singing and practical harmony interesting to his pupil. In a few months Rossini learned to read, to accompany and to sing well enough to take solos in church at the modest price of three pauls per service. He was thus able, at the age of 10, to assist his parents, who, owing

to a sudden change in his mother's voice, were again in misfortune.

At the age of 13 Rossini was a sufficiently good singer to be well received at the theatre ; he also played the horn by his father's side, and had a fair reputation as accompanist. At this time the Chevalier Giusti, commanding engineer at Bologna, took a great affection for the lad, read and explained the Italian poets to him, and opened his fresh and intelligent mind to the comprehension of the ideal ; and it was to the efforts of this distinguished man that he owed the start of his genius, and such general knowledge as he afterwards possessed. After three years with Tesei he put himself under a veteran tenor named Babbini to improve his singing. On Mar. 20, 1807, he was admitted to the counterpoint class of Padre Mattei at the Liceo Communale of Bologna, and soon after to that of Cavedagni for the violoncello.

Before he entered Mattei's class he had composed a variety of things—little pieces for two horns, songs of Zambini, and even an opera, called ' Demetrio,' for his friends the Mombellis. Mattei, who was a pedant, saw no reason for modifying his usual slow mechanical system to suit the convenience of an able scholar, and after a few months of discouraging labour Gioacchino began to look to instinct and practice for the philosophy, or at least the rhetoric, of this art. It is said that when Mattei explained that the amount of counterpoint which his pupil had already acquired was sufficient for a composer in the ' free style ' but that for church-music much severer studies were required, the boy cried, ' What, do you mean that I know enough to write operas ? ' ' Certainly,' was the reply. ' Then I want nothing more, for operas are all that I desire to write.' Meantime it was necessary that he and his parents should live, and he therefore dropped counterpoint and returned to his old trade of accompanist, gave lessons, and conducted performances of chamber-music.

At the end of his first year at the Liceo his cantata ' Il pianto d' armonia per la morte d' Orfeo ' was not only rewarded with the prize, but was performed in public, Aug. 8, 1808. It was followed, not by a symphony, as is sometimes said, but by an overture in the fugued style, in imitation of that to ' Die Zauberflöte,' but so weak, that after hearing it played he destroyed it. The same fate probably attended some pieces for double bass and strings, and a Mass, both written at the instance of an amateur of the double bass.

VENICE AND MILAN.—Through the Marquis Cavalli, who had promised him his interest whenever it should be wanted, Rossini received an invitation to compose an opera from the manager of the San Mosè theatre at Venice, and ' La cambiale di matrimonio ' or the ' Matrimonial market,' an opera-buffa in one act, was produced there in the autumn of 1810 and sung by Morandi, Ricci, De Grecis and Raffanelli. Returning to Bologna, he composed for Esther Mombelli's benefit a cantata called 'Didone abbandonata,' and in 1811 he wrote for the Teatro del Corso an opera-buffa in two acts, 'L' equivoco stravagante.'

'Demetrio e Polibio' was brought out at the Teatro Valle by his old friends the Mombellis in 1811. Early in 1812 he produced at the San Mosè theatre, Venice, two buffa operas —'L' inganno felice,' and 'L' occasione fa il ladro, ossia il Cambio della valigia.' After the Carnival he went to Ferrara, and there composed an oratorio, 'Ciro in Babilonia,' which was brought out during Lent and proved a fiasco.[1] Another failure was 'La scala di seta,' an opera-buffa in one act, produced at Venice in the course of the spring. While the Mombellis were engaged on his serious opera, he flew off to Milan to fulfil an engagement which Marcolini had procured for him, by writing, for her, Galli, Bonoldi and Parlamagni, a comic piece in two acts called 'La pietra del paragone,' which was produced at La Scala during the autumn of 1812 with immense success. It was his first appearance at this renowned house, and the piece is underlined in the list as 'musica nuova di Gioacchino Rossini, di Pesaro.' It has a finale which is memorable as the first occasion of his employing the *crescendo*, which he was ultimately to use and abuse so copiously. Mosca has accused Rossini of having borrowed this famous effect from his 'Pretendenti delusi,' produced at La Scala the preceding autumn, forgetting that Mosca himself had learned it from Generali and other composers. Such accusations, however, were of little or no importance to Rossini, who had already made up his mind to adopt whatever pleased him, wheresoever he might find it. In the meantime he took advantage of his success to pass a few days at Bologna with his parents, *en route* for Venice; and thus ended the year 1812, in which he had produced no less than six pieces for the theatre.

The year 1813 began with a joke. He had accepted a commission of 500 francs for a serious opera for the Grand Theatre at Venice, but the manager of San Mosè, furious at his desertion, in pursuance of some former agreement, forced on him a libretto for that theatre, 'I due Bruschini, o il figlio per azzardo,' which, if treated as intended, would inevitably have been the death of the music. From this dilemma Rossini ingeniously extricated himself by reversing the situations and introducing all kinds of tricks. The second violins mark each bar in the overture by a stroke of the bow on the lamp shade ; the bass sings at the top of his register and the soprano at the bottom of hers ; a funeral march intrudes itself into one of the

most comical scenes ; and in the finale the words 'son pentito' are so arranged that nothing is heard but 'tito, tito, tito.' Those of the audience who had been taken into the secret were in roars of laughter, but the strangers who had paid for their places in good faith were naturally annoyed and hissed loudly. But no complaints were of any avail with Rossini, he only laughed at the success of his joke. 'I due Bruschini' disappeared after the first night, and the remembrance of it was very shortly wiped out by the appearance of 'Tancredi' produced at the Fenice during the Carnival, and sung by Manfredini, Malanotte, Todran and Bianchi. This work, full of spirit and melody, was received with enthusiasm, and nobody had time to notice various plagiarisms from Paisiello and Paër. All Venice, and very soon all Italy, was singing or humming 'Mi rivedrai, ti rivedro.' One must read the accounts of the day to understand the madness —for it was nothing else—which 'Tancredi' excited among the Venetians. 'I fancied,' said Rossini, with his usual gaiety, 'that after hearing my opera they would put me into a mad-house—on the contrary, they were madder than I.' Henceforward he was as much fêted for his social qualities as for his music.

His next work was 'L' Italiana in Algeri,' an opera-buffa produced at the San Benedetto theatre, Venice, in the summer of 1813. 'Aureliano in Palmira' and 'Il Turco in Italia' were both brought out at La Scala, Milan, the first in Dec. 1813, the second in Aug. 1814, before an audience somewhat more critical than that at Venice. 'Aureliano,' though it contains some fine things, which were afterwards utilised in 'Elisabetta' and the 'Barbiere,' was a fiasco. The 'Turco,' too, was not received with the applause which it afterwards commanded. Rossini, however, was greatly fêted during his stay in Milan, and among his 'amiable protectresses'—to use the expression of Stendhal—was the Princess Belgiojoso, for whom he composed a cantata entitled 'Egle ed Irene.' After the production of his next opera, 'Sigismondo,' written for the Fenice at Venice, in the Carnival of 1815, Rossini returned to his home at Bologna. There he encountered Barbaja, who from being a waiter at a coffee-house had become the farmer of the public gaming-tables and impresario of the Naples theatre, and engaged with him to take the musical direction of the San Carlo and Del Fondo theatres at Naples, and to compose annually an opera for each. For this he was to receive 200 ducats (about £35) per month, with a small share in the gaming-tables, amounting in addition to some 1000 ducats per annum, for which, however, he obtained no compensation after the tables were abolished in 1820.

NAPLES AND ROME.—During Murat's visit to Bologna in Apr. 1815 Rossini had composed a

---

[1] It was performed as 'Cyrus in Babylon' at Drury Lane Theatre (Lent Oratorios), Jan. 30, 1823, under Smart.

cantata in favour of Italian independence, but politics were not his line, and he arrived in Naples fully conscious of this, and resolved that nothing should induce him to repeat the experiment. The arrival of a young composer with so great a reputation for originality was not altogether pleasing to Zingarelli, the chief of the Conservatorio, or to the aged Paisiello. But no intrigues could prevent the brilliant success of ' Elisabetta, regina d' Inghilterra,' which was produced before the court for the opening of the autumn season, 1815, in which Mlle. Colbran, Dardanelli, Manuel Garcia and Nozzari took the principal parts. The libretto was by a certain Schmidt, and it is a curious fact that some of its incidents anticipate those of ' Kenilworth,' which was not published till January 1821. ' Elisabetta ' is the first opera in which Rossini so far distrusted his singers as to write in the ornaments of the airs; and it is also the first in which he replaced the *recitativo secco* by a recitative accompanied by the string quartet. The overture and the finale to the first act of ' Elisabetta ' are taken from ' Aureliano.'

Shortly before Christmas Rossini left Naples for Rome to write and bring out two works for which he was under engagement. The first of these, ' Torvaldo e Dorliska,' produced at the Teatro Valle, Dec. 26, 1815, was coldly received, but the second, ' Almaviva, ossia l' inutile precauzione,' founded on Beaumarchais' ' Barbier de Séville,' by Sterbini, which made its first appearance at the Argentina, Feb. 5, 1816, was unmistakably damned. The cause of this was the predilection of the Romans for Paisiello, and their determination to make an example of an innovator who had dared to reset a libretto already treated by their old favourite. Rossini, with excellent taste and feeling, had inquired of Paisiello, before adopting the subject, whether doing so would annoy the veteran, whose ' Barbiere ' had been for a quarter of a century the favourite of Europe, and not unnaturally believed that after this step he was secure from the ill-will of Paisiello's friends and admirers.[1] However, although hissed on the first night, ' Almaviva ' was listened to with patience on the second, and ended by becoming, under the title of ' Il barbiere di Siviglia,' one of the most popular comic operas ever composed. The cast was as follows :

| | | |
|---|---|---|
| Rosina | . . | Giorgi-Righetti. |
| Berta | . . | Rossi. |
| Figaro | . . | Zamboni. |
| Almaviva | . . | Garcia. |
| Bartolo | . . | Botticelli. |
| Basilio | . . | Vitarelli. |

The opening of the cavatina ' Ecco ridente ' is borrowed from the opening of the first chorus in ' Aureliano.' The air of Berta ' Il vecchietto

[1] We have Rossini's own authority for this, and for the opera having been written in thirteen days, in his letter to Scitivaux. See *Musical World*, Nov. 6, 1875, p. 751.

cerca moglie ' was suggested by a Russian tune, and the eight opening bars of the trio ' Zitti, zitti ' are notoriously taken note for note from Simon's air in Haydn's ' Seasons.'

On his return to Naples after the Carnival of 1816, and the gradual success of the ' Barbiere,' Rossini composed a grand cantata entitled ' Teti e Peleo ' for the marriage of the Duchesse de Berry, and then dashed off a two-act comic opera entitled ' La gazzetta ' to a libretto by Tottola, which was produced at the Teatro dei Fiorentini, Naples, with Chambrand, Pellegrini and Casaccia in the cast. ' Otello ' was brought out at the Teatro del Fondo, Naples, Dec. 4, 1816, with Isabella Colbran, Nozzari, Davide, Cicimarra and Benedetti as its interpreters, but the tragic termination of the whole was very distasteful to the public, and when the opera was taken to Rome it was found necessary to invent a happy ending.

The machinery and power of rapidly changing the scenes were at that time so very imperfect in the smaller Italian theatres that Rossini would only accept the subject of Cinderella, when proposed to him by the manager of the Teatro Valle at Rome, on condition that the supernatural element was entirely omitted. A new comic piece was therefore written by Ferretti under the title of ' Cenerentola, ossia la bontà in trionfo '; Rossini undertook it, and it was produced at the Carnival of 1817 with unmistakable success. In the profusion and charm of its ideas this delicious work is probably equal to the ' Barbiere,' but it is inferior in unity of style. No doubt this is partly owing to the fact that many of the pieces appeared originally in other works such as ' La pietra del paragone,' ' La gazzetta ' and ' Turco in Italia.' Such repetitions answered their purpose at the moment, but while thus extemporising his operas Rossini forgot that a day would arrive when they would all be published, and when such discoveries as those we have mentioned, and the identity of the principal motif of the duet of the letter in ' Otello ' with the *agitato* of an air from ' Torvaldo e Dorliska,' would inevitably be made. As he himself confessed in a letter about this time, he thought he had a perfect right to rescue any of his earlier airs from operas which had either failed at the time or become forgotten since. Whatever force there may be in this defence, the fact remains that ' Cenerentola ' and the ' Barbiere ' share between them the glory of being Rossini's *chefs-d'œuvre* in comic opera.

From Rome he went to Milan, to enjoy the triumph of the ' Gazza ladra '—libretto by Gherardini,—which was brought out on May 31, 1817, at La Scala. The Milanese found no difference between the really fine parts of the opera and those which are mere padding—of which the ' Gazza ladra ' has several.

From Milan he returned to Naples, and produced ' Armida ' during the autumn season, a grand opera in three acts, with ballet, which was mounted with great splendour, and enjoyed the advantage of very good singers. This work had hardly made its appearance before Rossini had to dash off two more— ' Adelaide di Borgogna,' sometimes known as ' Ottone Rè d' Italia,' and an oratorio—' Mosè in Egitto.' ' Adelaide' was produced at the Argentina at Rome, in the Carnival of 1818, was well sung and warmly received. ' Mosè' was written for the San Carlo at Naples, which Barbaja had rebuilt after the fire of 1816, and brought out there in Lent with Isabella Colbran, Benedetti, Porto and Nozzari. Here for the first time Rossini was so much pressed as to be compelled to call in assistance, and employed his old and tried friend Carafa in the recitatives and in Pharaoh's air ' Aspettar mi.' [1]

As some relaxation after this serious effort, he undertook, in the summer of 1818, a one-act piece ' Adina, o il Califfo di Bagdad,' for the San Carlos Theatre, Lisbon ; and immediately after, ' Ricciardo e Zoraide ' for San Carlo, Naples, which was sung to perfection at the autumn season there by Isabella Colbran, Pisaroni, Nozzari, Davide and Cicimarra.

' Ricciardo ' was extraordinarily full of ornament, but ' Ermione,' which was produced at San Carlo in the Lent of 1819, went quite in the opposite direction, and affected an unusual plainness and severity. Though splendidly sung, ' Ermione ' did not please, and the single number applauded was the one air in which there was any ornamentation. An equally poor reception was given to a cantata written for the re-establishment of the health of the King of Naples, and sung at the San Carlo, Feb. 20, 1819. It consisted of a cavatina for Isabella Colbran, and an air with variations, which was afterwards utilised in the ballet of the ' Viaggio a Reims.' The piece was hastily thrown off, and was probably of no more value in the eyes of its author than was an opera called ' Edoardo e Cristina ' which was brought out at the San Benedetto, Venice, this same spring, and was in reality a mere pasticcio of pieces from ' Ermione,' ' Ricciardo ' and other operas hitherto unheard in Venice, attached to a libretto imitated from Scribe. Fortunately the opera pleased the audience, and sent Rossini back to Naples in good spirits, ready to compose a new cantata for the visit of the Emperor of Austria. The new work was performed on May 9, 1819, at the San Carlo, and was sung by Colbran, Davide and Rubini, to the accompaniment of a military band. This Rossini probably accepted as a useful experience for his next new opera, the ' Donna del lago,' in the march of which we hear the results of his experiments in writing for a wind band.

[1] Omitted in the Italian score published in Paris.

The production on Oct. 4, 1819, with Colbran, Pisaroni, Nozzari, Davide and Benedetti, was simply one long torture of disappointment to the composer, who was possibly not aware that the storm of disapprobation was directed not against him so much as against Barbaja the manager, and Colbran his favourite.

On the following evening the hisses became *bravos*, but of this Rossini knew nothing, as by that time he was on his road to Milan. La Scala opened on Dec. 26, 1819, for the Carnival season with ' Bianca e Faliero,' libretto by Romani, which was admirably sung by Camporese and others. No trace of it, however, now remains except a duet and quartet, which were afterwards introduced in the ' Donna del lago,' and became very popular at concerts.

His engagement at Milan over, he hurried back to Naples to produce the opera of ' Maometto secondo,' before the close of the Carnival. It had been composed in great haste, but was admirably interpreted by Colbran, Chaumel (afterwards Madame Rubini), Nozzari, Cicimarra, Benedetti and F. Galli. It was the last opera that Rossini was destined to give at Naples before the revolt of July 20, 1820, of the Carbonari, under Pepe, which obliged the King to abandon his capital, ruined Barbaja by depriving him at once of a powerful patron and of the monopoly of the gambling-houses, and drove Rossini to make important changes in his life. Having for the moment no engagement for La Scala, he undertook to write ' Matilda di Ciabrano ' (' Mathilde di Shabran ') for Rome. Torlonia the banker had bought the Teatro Tordinone, and was converting it into the Apollo ; and it was for the inauguration of this splendid new house that Rossini's opera was intended. The opening took place on the first night of the Carnival of 1821. The company, though large, contained no first-rate artists, and Rossini was therefore especially careful of the *ensemble* pieces. The first night was stormy, but Rossini's friends were in the ascendancy, Paganini conducted in splendid style, and the result was a distinct success.

On his return to Naples, Rossini learned from Barbaja his intention of visiting Austria, and taking his company of singers to Vienna. Rossini's next opera, ' Zelmira,' was therefore to be submitted to a more critical audience than those of Italy, and with this in view he applied himself to make the recitatives and harmonies interesting, and to throw as much variety as possible into the form of the movements. He produced the opera at the San Carlo before leaving, in the middle of Dec. 1821. It was sung by Colbran, Cecconi, Davide, Nozzari, Ambrosi and Benedetti. On the 27th of the same month he took his benefit, for which he had composed a special cantata entitled ' La riconoscenza ' ; and the day after left for the north. He was accompanied by Isabella

Colbran, with whom he had been in love for years, whose influence over him had been so great as to make him forsake comedy for tragedy, and to whom he was married on his arrival at Bologna. The wedding took place in the chapel of the Archbishop's palace, and was celebrated by Cardinal Opizzoni. Rossini has been accused of marrying for money, and it is certain that Colbran had a villa and £500 a year of her own, that she was seven years older than her husband, and that her reputation as a singer was on the decline.

VIENNA.—After a month's holiday the couple started for Vienna, where they arrived about the end of Feb. 1822. He seems to have made his début before the Vienna public on Mar. 30 as the conductor of his 'Cenerentola,' in the German version, as 'Aschenbrödel,' and his *tempi* were found somewhat too fast for the 'heavy German language.' 'Zelmira' was given at the Kärnthnerthor opera-house on Apr. 13, with a success equal to that which it obtained at Naples. Rossini was not without violent opponents in Vienna, but they gave him no anxiety, friends and enemies alike were received with a smile, and his only retort was a good-humoured joke. He is said to have visited Beethoven, and to have been much distressed by the condition in which he found the great master. The impression which he made on the Viennese may be gathered from a paragraph in the Leipzig *A.M.Z.*[1] of the day, in which ne is described as 'highly accomplished, of agreeable manners and pleasant appearance, full of wit and fun, cheerful, obliging, courteous and most accessible. He is much in society, and charms every one by his simple, unassuming style.' After the close of the Vienna season the Rossinis returned to Bologna, where his parents had resided since 1798. There, at the end of September, he received a flattering invitation from Prince Metternich, entreating him to come to Verona, and he accordingly arrived at the Congress in time for its opening, Oct. 20, 1822. Rossini's contribution to the Congress was a series of cantatas, which he poured forth without stint or difficulty. The best known of these is 'Il vero omaggio'; others are 'L' augurio felice,' 'La sacra alleanza' and 'Il bardo.'

The Congress at an end, he began to work at 'Semiramide,' which was brought out at the Fenice, Venice, Feb. 3, 1823, with Madame Rossini, the two Marianis, Galli and Sinclair the English tenor, for whom there were two airs. The opera was probably written with more care than any of those which had preceded it; and possibly for this very reason was somewhat coldly received.

PARIS AND LONDON.—Rossini was not unnaturally much disappointed at the result of his labour, and resolved to write no more for the theatres of his native country. The resolution was hardly formed when he received a visit from the manager of the King's Theatre, London (Benelli), and a proposal to write an opera for that house, to be called 'La figlia dell' aria,' for the sum of £240—£40 more than he had received for 'Semiramide,' a sum at the time considered enormous. The offer was promptly accepted, and the Rossinis started for England without delay, naturally taking Paris in their road, and reaching it Nov. 9, 1823. Paris, like Vienna, was then divided into two hostile camps on the subject of the composer. Berton always spoke of him as 'M. Crescendo,' and he was caricatured on the stage as 'M. Vacarmini'; but the author of the 'Barbiere' could afford to laugh at such satire, and his respectful behaviour to Cherubini, Lesueur and Reicha, as the heads of the Conservatoire, his graceful reception of the leaders of the French School, his imperturbable good temper and good spirits, soon conciliated every one. A serenade, a public banquet, triumphant receptions at the opera-house, a special vaudeville ('Rossini à Paris, ou le Grand Dîner')—everything in short that could soothe the pride of a stranger—was lavished upon him from the first. On Dec. 13, 1823, Rossini and his wife arrived in London. They were visited immediately by the Russian ambassador, M. de Lieven, who gave the composer barely time to recover from the fatigues of the journey before he carried him off to Brighton and presented him to the King. George IV. received Rossini in the most flattering manner. 'Zelmira' was brought out at the Opera on Jan. 24, 1824; and the royal favour naturally brought with it that of the aristocracy, and a solid result in the shape of two grand concerts at Almack's, at two guineas admission. The singers on these occasions were Mme. Rossini, Mme. Catalani, Mme. Pasta and other first-rate artists, but the novelty, the attraction, was to hear Rossini himself sing the solos [2] in a cantata (or 'ottavino') which he had composed for the occasion, under the title of 'Il pianto delle Muse in morte di Lord Byron.' He also took part with Catalani in a duet from Cimarosa's 'Matrimonio' which was so successful as to be encored three times. He appeared at the so-called 'Cambridge Festival' again with Catalani, in July 1824. The opera manager was unable to finish the season, and became bankrupt before discharging his engagements with Rossini. Nor was this all. Not only did he not produce the 'Figlia dell' aria,' but the music of the first act unaccountably vanished, and has never since been found. It was in vain for Rossini to sue the manager; he failed to obtain either his MS. or a single penny of the advantages guaranteed to him by the contract. True, he enjoyed a considerable set-off to the loss just mentioned

[1] May 8, 1822, reporting the early part of March.

[2] This recalls the visit of a great composer in 1746, when Gluck gave a concert at the King's Theatre, at which the great attraction was his solo on the musical glasses! (See GLUCK.)

in the profits of the countless soirées at which he acted as accompanist at a fee of £50. At the end of five months he found himself in possession of £7000 ; and just before his departure was honoured by receiving the marked compliments of the King at a concert at the Duke of Wellington's, for which His Majesty had expressly come up from Brighton.[1] He left England on July 26.

Through the Prince de Polignac, French ambassador in England, Rossini had already concluded an agreement for the musical direction of the Théâtre Italien, Paris, for eighteen months at a salary of £800 per annum. In order to be near his work he took a lodging at No. 28 Rue Taitbout, and at once set about getting younger singers for his company. Knowing that Paër was his enemy, and would take any opportunity of injuring him, he was careful to retain him in his old post of *maestro al cembalo* ; but at the same time he engaged Hérold (then a young man of 25) as chorus-master, and as a check on the pretensions of Madame Pasta he brought to Paris Esther Mombelli, Schiassetti, Donzelli and Rubini, successively. To those who sneered at his music he replied by playing it as it was written, and by bringing out some of his operas which had not yet made their appearance in Paris, such as ' La donna del lago ' (Sept. 7, 1824), ' Semiramide ' (Dec. 8, 1825), and ' Zelmira ' (Mar. 14, 1826). And he gave much éclat to his direction by introducing Meyerbeer's ' Crociato '—the first work of Meyerbeer heard in Paris — and by composing a new opera, ' Il viaggio a Reims, ossia l' Albergo del giglio d' oro,' which he produced on June 19, 1825, during the fêtes at the coronation of Charles X. This work, in one act, and three parts, was written for fourteen voices, and was sung by Mmes. Pasta, Schiassetti, Mombelli, Cinti, Amigo, Dotti and Rossi ; and by Levasseur, Zucchelli, Pellegrini, Graziani, Auletta, Donzelli, Bordogni and Scudo—a truly magnificent assemblage. In the ballet he introduced an air with variations for two clarinets, borrowed from his Naples cantata of 1819, and played by Gambaro (a passionate admirer of his) and by F. Berr. In the hunting scene he brought in a fanfare of horns, and the piece winds up with ' God save the King,' ' Vive Henri Quatre,' and other national airs, all newly harmonised and accompanied. After the Revolution of 1848 the words were suitably modified by H. Dupin, and the piece appeared in two acts at the Théâtre-Italien as ' Andremo noi a Parigi ' on Oct. 26 of that year.[2]

After the expiration of Rossini's agreement as director of the Théâtre-Italien, the Intendant of the Civil List conferred upon him the sinecure posts of ' Premier Compositeur du Roi ' and ' Inspecteur Général du Chant en France,' with an annual income of 20,000 francs, possibly in the hope that he might settle permanently at Paris, and in time write operas expressly for the French stage. This was also an act of justice, since in the then absence of any law of international[3] copyright his pieces were public property, and at the disposal not only of a translator like Castil-Blaze, but of any manager or publisher in the length and breadth of France who chose to avail himself of them. The step was justified by the event. The opera of ' Maometto '—originally written by the Duke of Ventagnano, and produced at Naples in 1820 —had never been heard in France. Rossini employed Soumét and Balocchi to give the libretto a French dress ; he revised the music, and considerably extended it ; and on Oct. 9, 1826, it was produced at the Opéra as ' Le Siège de Corinthe,' with a cast which included Nourrit and Mlle. Cinti, and with great success. For the new opera Rossini received 6000 francs from Troupenas.

After this feat Rossini turned to another of his earlier works, as not only sure of success but eminently suited to the vast space and splendid *mise en scène* of the Opéra. This was ' Mosè.' He put the revision of the libretto into the hands of Étienne Jouy and Balocchi, and arranged for Cinti, Nourrit and Levasseur to be in the cast. ' Moïse ' was produced Mar. 25, 1827, and created a profound impression. True, it had been heard in its original form at the Italiens five years before, but the recollection of this only served to bring out more strongly the many improvements and additions in the new version—such as the introduction to the first act ; the quartet and chorus ; the chorus ' La Douce Aurore ' ; the march and chorus, etc. The airs de ballet were largely borrowed from ' Armida ' (1817) and ' Ciro in Babilonia' (1812). This work gave Rossini a sort of imperial position in Paris. But it was necessary to justify this, and he therefore resolved to try a work of a different character. With this view he employed Scribe and Poirson to develop a vaudeville which they had written in 1816 to the old legend of ' Le Comte Ory,' adapting to that lively piece some of his favourite music in the ' Viaggio a Reims.' ' Le Comte Ory ' was produced at the Opéra, Aug. 20, 1828, and the principal characters were taken by Mme. Damoreau-Cinti, Mlles. Jawurek and Mori, Adolphe Nourrit, Levasseur and Dabadie. The introduction is based on the old song which gives its name to the piece. The best thing in the second act is borrowed from the *Allegretto scherzando* of Beethoven's eighth symphony. Rossini was at that time

---

[1] See *Mus. T.*, 1900, pp. 18 ff.
[2] The score of ' Andremo noi a Parigi ' is in the Library of the Conservatoire, but the finale of the ' Viaggio,' which we have mentioned as containing national airs, is not there, and all trace of this curious feat seems to have vanished.

[3] The custom in Italy in those days was to sell an opera to a manager for two years, with exclusive right of representation ; after that it became public property. The only person who derived no profit from this arrangement was the unfortunate composer.

actually engaged with Habeneck, the founder of the Concerts du Conservatoire, and his intimate friend, in studying the symphonies of Beethoven.

The study of Beethoven was at any rate not a bad preparation for the very serious piece of work which was next to engage him, and for a great portion of which he retired to the château of his friend Aguado the banker at Petit-Bourg. Schiller had recently been brought into notice in France by the translation of de Barante ; and Rossini, partly attracted by the grandeur of the subject, partly inspired by the liberal ideas at that moment floating through Europe, was induced to choose the liberator of the Swiss Cantons as his next subject. He accepted a libretto offered him by Etienne Jouy, Spontini's old librettist, who in this case was associated with Hippolyte Bis. Their words, however, were so unmusical and unrhythmical that Rossini had recourse to Armand Marrast, at that time Aguado's secretary, and the whole scene of the meeting of the conspirators was rewritten by him.

'Guillaume Tell' was produced at the Opéra on Aug. 3, 1829, with the following cast :

| Arnold | . | . | Nourrit. |
| Walter Fürst | . | . | Levasseur. |
| Tell | . | . | Dabadie. |
| Ruodi | . | . | A. Dupont. |
| Rodolphe | . | . | Massol. |
| Gessler | . | . | Prévost. |
| Leutold | . | . | Prévôt. |
| Mathilde | . | . | Damoreau-Cinti. |
| Jemmy | . | . | Dabadie. |
| Hedwige | . | . | Mori. |

It was to have been the first of a series of five operas, for, being anxious to visit once more the city in which his mother died in 1827, and where his father, who had soon tired of Paris, was awaiting him, he had resigned his office as inspector of singing in France, and made an arrangement with the Government of Charles X., dating from the beginning of 1829, by which he bound himself for ten years to compose for no other stage but that of France, and to write and bring out an opera every two years, receiving for each such opera the sum of 15,000 francs. In the event of the Government failing to carry out the arrangement he was to receive a retiring pension of 6000 francs. But political and domestic circumstances prevented this plan from being carried out. Having left Paris for Bologna he was considering the subject of 'Faust,' with a view to his next work, when he received the sudden news of the abdication of Charles X. and the revolution of July 1830. The blow shattered his plans and dissipated his fondest hopes.

He flattered himself that he had regenerated the art of singing in France. What would become of it again under a king who could tolerate no operas but those of Grétry ? Anxious to know if his friend Lubbert was still at the head of the Académie de Musique, and if the new Intendant of the Civil List would acknowledge the engagements of his predecessor, he returned to Paris in Nov. 1830 ; and, intending only to make a short stay, took up his quarters in the upper storey of the Théâtre des Italiens, of which his friend Severini was then director. Here, however, he was destined to remain till Nov. 1836. The new Government repudiated the agreement of its predecessor, and Rossini had to carry his claim into the law-courts. Had his lawsuit alone occupied him, it would not have been necessary to stay quite so long, for it was decided in his favour in Dec. 1835. But there was another reason for his remaining in Paris, and that was his desire to hear ' The Huguenots ' and ascertain how far Meyerbeer's star was likely to eclipse his own. It is impossible to believe that a mere money question could have detained him so long at a time when almost every day must have brought fresh annoyances. After reducing ' Guillaume Tell ' from five acts to three, the management carried love of compression so far as to give only one act at a time, as a *lever de rideau*, or accompaniment to the ballet. This was indeed adding insult to injury. ' I hope you won't be annoyed,' said the director of the Opéra to him one day on the boulevard, ' but to-night we play the second act of "Tell." ' ' The whole of it ? ' was the reply. How much bitter disappointment must have been hidden under that reply ! During the whole of this unhappy interval he only once resumed his pen, namely in 1832 for the ' Stabat Mater,' at the request of his friend Aguado, who was anxious to serve the Spanish minister Señor Valera. He composed at that time only the first six numbers, and the other four were supplied by Tadolini. The work was dedicated to Valera, with an express stipulation that it should never leave his hands. In 1834 he allowed Troupenas to publish the ' Soirées musicales,' twelve vocal pieces, several of which have still retained their charm.

The rehearsals of ' The Huguenots ' lingered on, and it was not till Feb. 29, 1836, that Rossini could hear the work of his new rival. He returned to Bologna shortly after, taking Frankfort in his way, and meeting Mendelssohn.[1] He had not been long in Bologna before he heard of the prodigious success of Duprez in the revival of ' Guillaume Tell ' (Apr. 17). Such a triumph might well have nerved him to fresh exertions. But it came a year too late ; he had already taken an irrevocable resolution never again to break silence. It would be very wrong to conclude from this that he had lost his interest in music. The care which he bestowed on the Liceo of Bologna, of which he was honorary director, shows that the art still exercised all its claims on him. He was especially anxious to improve the singing

1 See Hiller's *Mendelssohn*, and M.'s own letter, July 14, 1836.

of the pupils, and among those who are indebted to his care Marietta Alboni held the first rank.

Rossini's father died Apr. 29, 1839, and he soon afterwards learned to his disgust that the MS. of the ' Stabat ' had been sold by the heirs of Señor Valera, and acquired by a Paris publisher for 2000 francs. He at once gave Troupenas full power to stop both publication and performance, and at the same time completed the work by composing the last four movements, which, as we have already said, were originally added by Tadolini. The first six movements were produced at the Salle Herz, Paris, Oct. 31, 1841, amidst very great applause. Troupenas [1] bought the entire score for 6000 francs. He sold the right of performance in Paris during three months to the Escudiers for 8000, which they again disposed of to the director of the Théâtre Italien for 20,000. Thus three persons were enriched by this single work. It was performed complete for the first time at the Salle Ventadour, Jan. 7, 1842, by Grisi, Albertazzi, Mario and Tamburini.

But at the very moment that the ' Stabat ' was making its triumphant progress round the world, Rossini began to suffer tortures from the stone, which increased to such an extent as to force him, in May 1843, to Paris, where he underwent an operation which proved perfectly satisfactory. We next find him writing a chorus to words by Marchetti for the anniversary festival of Tasso at Turin, on Mar. 13, 1844. On the 2nd of the following September ' Othello ' was produced in French at the Opéra with Duprez, Barroilhet, Levasseur and Mme. Stoltz. Rossini, however, had nothing to do with this adaptation, and the divertissement was arranged entirely by Benoist from airs in ' Mathilde de Sabran ' and ' Armida.' While ' Othello ' was thus on the boards of the opera, Troupenas brought out ' La Foi, l'Espérance et la Charité ' (Faith, Hope and Charity), three choruses for women's voices, the first two composed many years previously for an opera on the subject of Œdipus. These choruses are hardly worthy of Rossini. They justify Berlioz's sarcasm—' his Hope has deceived ours ; his Faith will never remove mountains ; his Charity will never ruin him.' It is fair to say that Louis Engel, in his book From Mozart to Mario, states that Rossini repudiated them. Troupenas also brought out a few songs hitherto unpublished, and these re-attracted the attention of the public in some degree to the composer. His statue was executed in marble [2] by Etex, and was inaugurated at the Académie de Musique, June 9, 1846. A few months later (Dec. 30), by his

permission, a pasticcio adapted by Niedermeyer to portions of the ' Donna del lago,' ' Zelmira ' and ' Armida,' and entitled ' Robert Bruce,' was put on the stage of the Opéra, but it was not successful, and Mme. Stoltz was even hissed. From his seclusion at Bologna Rossini kept a watchful eye upon the movements of the musical world, and during his long residence there he only broke his vow of silence for the ' Inno popolare a Pio IX.' The beginning of this was adapted to an air from ' La donna del lago,' and its peroration was borrowed from ' Robert Bruce,' which gives ground for supposing that he himself was concerned in the arrangement of that opera, and explains his annoyance at its failure.

The political disturbances which agitated the Romagna at the end of 1847 compelled Rossini to leave Bologna. He quitted the town in much irritation. After the death of his wife (Oct. 7, 1845), he married (in 1847) Olympe Pélissier, with whom he had become connected in Paris at a time when she was greatly in public favour, and when she sat to Vernet for his picture of ' Judith and Holofernes.' In fact at this time the musician had to a great extent disappeared in the voluptuary. From Bologna he removed to Florence, and there it was that this writer visited him in 1852. He lived in the Via Larga, in a house which bore upon its front the words *Ad votum.* In the course of a long conversation he spoke of his works with no pretended indifference, but as being well aware of their worth, and knowing the force and scope of his genius better than any one else. He made no secret of his dislike to the violent antivocal element in modern music, or of the pleasure he would feel when ' the Jews had finished their Sabbath.' It was also evident that he had no affection for the capital of Tuscany, the climate of which did not suit him.

At length, in 1855, he crossed the Alps and returned to Paris, never again to leave it. His reception there went far to calm the nervous irritability that had tormented him at Florence, and with the homage which he received from Auber and the rest of the French artists his health returned. His house, No. 2 in the Rue Chaussée d'Antin, and, at a later date, his villa at Passy, were crowded by the most illustrious representatives of literature and art, to such an extent that even during his lifetime he seemed to assist at his own apotheosis. Was it then mere idleness which made him thus bury himself in the Capua of his past successes ? No one who, like the present writer, observed him coolly, could be taken in by the comedy of indifference and modesty that it pleased him to keep up. We have already said that, after Meyerbeer's great success, Rossini had taken the resolution of writing no more for the Académie de Musique and keeping silence. The latter part of this resolution he did not,

---

[1] We have mentioned that he paid 6000 francs for the ' Siège de Corinthe.' For ' Moïse ' he gave only 2400 ; but, on the other hand, the ' Comte Ory ' cost him 12,000, and ' Guillaume Tell ' 24,000.

[2] It represented him seated in an easy attitude. It was destroyed when the opera-house was burnt down in 1873.

however, fully maintain. Thus he authorised the production of ' Bruschino ' at the Bouffes Parisiens on Dec. 28, 1857, though he would not be present at the first representation. ' I have given my permission,' said he, ' but do not ask me to be an accomplice.' The discovery of the piece—which is nothing else but his early farce of ' Il figlio per azzardo ' (Venice, 1813)—was due to Prince Poniatowski, and some clever librettist was found to adapt it to the French taste. A year or two later Méry with difficulty obtained his permission to transform ' Semiramide ' into ' Sémiramis,' and in its new garb it was produced at the Opéra, July 9, 1860, with Carlotta Marchisio as Semiramis, her sister Barbara as Arsace, and Obin as Assur. In this transformation Rossini took no ostensible part. Carafa at his request arranged the recitatives, and wrote the ballet music. These were mere revivals. Not so the sacred work which he brought out at the house of Pillet-Will the banker on Mar. 14, 1864, and at the rehearsals of which he presided in person; this was the ' Petite messe solennelle,' which though so called with a touch of Rossinian pleasantry is a Mass of full dimensions, lasting nearly two hours in performance. This work, comprising soli and choruses, was written with the accompaniment of a harmonium and two pianos. On this occasion it was sung by the two Marchisios, Gardoni and Agnesi, and was much applauded. Rossini afterwards scored it with slight alterations for the full orchestra, and in this shape it was performed for the first time in public at the Théâtre-Italien, on the evening of Sunday, Feb. 28, 1869 on the seventy-eighth anniversary of the composer's birth as nearly as that could be, seeing that he was born in a leap year on Feb. 29.

In the last years of his life Rossini affected the piano, spoke of himself as a fourth-rate pianist, and composed little else but pianoforte pieces, most of which were in some sense or other *jeux d'esprit.* For the Exposition Universelle of 1867, however, he wrote a cantata, which was performed for the first time at the ceremony of awarding the prizes on July 1, and was also executed at the Opéra at the free performances on Aug. 15, 1867 and 1868. It opens with a hymn in a broad style, but winds up with a vulgar quick-step. The title, which we give from the autograph, seems to show that Rossini was quite aware of the character of the finale of his last work.

À Napoléon III.
et
à son vaillant Peuple.

Hymne
avec accompagnement d'orchestre et musique militaire
pour baryton (solo), un Pontife,
chœur de Grands Prêtres
chœur de Vivandières, de Soldats, et de Peuple.
À la fin
Danse, Cloches, Tambours et Canons.
Excusez du peu ! !

The final touch is quite enough to show that Rossini to the last had more gaiety than propriety, more wit than dignity, more love of independence than good taste. He preferred the society of artists to any other, and was never so happy as when giving free scope to his caustic wit or his Rabelaisian humour. His *bons mots* were abundant, and it is surprising that no one has yet attempted to collect them. One or two may find place here. One day, in a fit of the spleen, he cried out, ' I am miserable ; my nerves are wrong, and every one offers me string instead.' D'Ortigue, the author of the *Dictionnaire liturgique,* had been very severe on him in an article in the *Correspondant* on ' Musical royalties,' and an enthusiastic admirer of the Italian School having replied somewhat angrily, Rossini wrote to him, ' I am much obliged to you for your vigorous treatment (*lavement*) of the tonsure of my friend the Curé d'Ortigue.' A number of friends were disputing as to which was his best opera, and appealed to him. ' You want to know which of my works I like best ? " Don Giovanni " ! ' He took extreme delight in his summer villa at Passy, which stood in the Avenue Ingres, and had a fine garden of about three acres attached to it. In that house he died on Friday Nov. 13, 1868, at 9 P.M., after a long day of agony. His funeral was magnificent. As Foreign Associate of the Institute (1833) ; Grand Officer of the Legion of Honour (1864), and the orders of St. Maurice and St. Lazare ; commander of many foreign orders, and honorary member of a great number of Academies and musical institutions—Rossini had a right to every posthumous honour possible. The funeral took place at the Church of the Trinité on Saturday Nov. 21 ; it was gorgeous, and was attended by several deputations from Italy. Tamburini, Duprez, Gardoni, Bonnehée, Faure, Capoul, Belval, Obin, Delle Sedie, Jules Lefort, Agnesi, Alboni, Adelina Patti, Nilsson, Krauss, Carvalho, Bloch and Grossi, with the pupils of the Conservatoire, sang the Prayer from ' Moïse.' Nilsson gave a fine movement from the 'Stabat' of Pergolesi, but the most impressive part of the ceremony was the singing of the 'Quis est homo' from Rossini's own 'Stabat Mater' by Patti and Alboni.

Rossini bequeathed to the Bologna Institute an annual sum of 6000 francs (£240) for a competition both in dramatic poetry and composition, specifying particularly that the object of the prize should be to encourage composers with a turn for melody. The greater part of his property Rossini devoted to the foundation and endowment of a Conservatorio of Music at his native town Pesaro, of which A. Bazzini and Mascagni were successively directors.

In order to complete this sketch it is necessary to give as complete a list as possible of his works. N.B.—In the column after the names, (1) signifies that the score has been engraved; (2) that it is published for voices and piano; (3) that it is still in manuscript.

## I. OPERAS

| Title. | 1 = Full Score. 2 = PF. do. 3 = MS. | First representation. | First performance in London at King's Theatre. |
|---|---|---|---|
| Adelaide di Borgogna, or Ottone Rè d' Italia | — 2, 3 | Rome, Car. 1818 | |
| Adina (farsa) | — 2, 3 | Lisbon, 1818 | |
| Armida | — 2, 3 | Naples, Aut. 1817 | |
| Assedio di Corinto, L' | — 2, 3 | Milan, Dec. 26, 1828 | June 5, 1834 |
| Aureliano in Palmira | — 2, 3 | Milan, Dec. 26, 1813 | June 22, 1826 |
| Barbiere di Siviglia, Il | — 2, 3 | Rome, Feb. 5, 1816 | Jan. 27, 1818 |
| Barbier de Séville, Le | 1, 2, — | Paris, May 6, 1824 | |
| Bianca e Faliero | — 2, 3 | Milan, Dec. 26, 1819 | |
| Bruschini, I due (farsa) | — | Venice, 1819 | |
| Bruschini | — | Paris, Dec. 28, 1857 | |
| Cambiale di matrimonio, La (farsa) | — 2, 3 | Venice, Aut. 1810 | |
| Cambio della valigia, Il, or L' occasione, etc. (farsa) | — 2, 3 | Venice, 1812 | |
| Cenerentola, La | — 2, 3 | Rome, Car. 1817 | Jan. 8, 1820 |
| Comte Ory, Le | 1, 2, — | Paris, Aug. 20, 1828 | Feb. 28, 1829 |
| Dame du lac, La | 1, — | Paris, Oct. 21, 1825 | |
| Demetrio e Polibio | — 2, 3 | Rome, 1812 | |
| Donna del lago, La | — 2, 3 | Naples, Oct. 4, 1819 | Feb. 18, 1823 |
| Edoardo e Cristina | — 2, 3 | Venice, Car. 1819 | |
| E'isabetta | — 2, 3 | Naples, Aut. 1815 | Apr. 20, 1818 |
| Equivoco stravagante | — 2, 3 | Bologna, Aut. 1811 | |
| Ermione | — 2, 3 | Naples, Lent, 1819 | |
| Figlio per azzardo, Il. See Bruschini | | | |
| Gazza ladra, La | — 2, 3 | Milan, May 31, 1817 | Mar. 10, 1821 |
| Gazzetta, La | — 2, 3 | Naples, 1816 | |
| Guillaume Tell | 1, 2, — | Paris, Aug. 3, 1829 | July 11, 1839 |
| Inganno felice, L' (farsa) | — 2, 3 | Venice, Car. 1812 | July 1, 1819 |
| Isabelle, adapted from do. | — 2, — | | |
| Italiana in Algeri, L' | — 2, 3 | Venice, 1813 | Jan. 27, 1819 |
| Maometto Secondo | — 2, 3 | Naples, Car. 1820 | |
| Matilda di Shabran | — 2, 3 | Rome, Car. 1821 | July 3, 1823 |
| Mathilde de Sabran | — 2, — | Paris, 1857 | |
| Moïse | 1, 2, — | Paris, Mar. 25, 1827 | |
| Mosè in Egitto (2 or 4 acts) | — 2, 3 | Naples, Lent, 1818 | (Pietro l' Eremita) Apr. 23, 1822 |
| Do. 2nd Italian libretto | | Paris, 1827 | |
| Occasione fa il ladro, L', or Il cambio, etc. (farsa) | | Venice, 1812 | |
| Otello | — 2, 3 | Naples, Dec. 4, 1816 | May 16, 1822 |
| Otello, ou le More de Venise (Castil-Blaze) | | Lyons, Dec. 1, 1823 | |
| Othello (Royer & Waez) | — 2, — | Paris, Sept. 2, 1844 | |
| Ottone Rè d' Italia. See Adelaide | | | |
| Pietra del paragone, La | — 2, 3 | Milan, Sept. 26, 1812 | |
| Pie voleuse, La | 1, — | Paris, 1822 | |
| Riccardo e Zoraide | — 2, 3 | Naples, Aut. 1818 | June 5, 1823 |
| Robert Bruce | | Paris, Dec. 30, 1846 | |
| Scala di seta La (farsa) | — 2, 3 | Venice, Car. 1812 | |
| Semiramide | — 2, 3 | Venice, Feb. 3, 1823 | July 15, 1824 |
| Sémiramis | — 2, 3 | Paris, July 9, 1860 | |
| Siège de Corinthe, Le | 1, 2, — | Paris, Oct. 9, 1826 | |
| Sigismondo | — 2, 3 | Venice, Car. 1815 | |
| Tancredi | — 2, 3 | Venice, Feb. 6, 1813 | May 4, 1820 |
| Torvaldo e Dorliska | — 2, 3 | Rome, Dec. 26, 1815 | |
| Turco in Italia, Il | — 2, 3 | Milan, Aug. 14, 1814 | May 19, 1821 |
| Viaggio a Reims, Il | | Paris, June 19, 1825 | |
| Zelmira | — 2, 3 | Naples, Dec. 1821 | Jan. 24, 1824 |

## II. CANTATAS

Il pianto d' armonia, Bologna, 1808.
Didone abbandonata, Bologna. 1811.
Egle ed Irene, 1814.
Teti e Peleo, 1816.
Igea, 1819.
Partenope, 1819.
La riconoscenza, 1821.
Il vero omaggio, Verona, 1823.

L' augurio felice, Verona, 1823.
La sacra alleanza, Verona, 1823.
Il bardo, Verona, 1823.
Il ritorno, 1823.
Il pianto delle Muse, London, 1823.
I pastori, Naples, 1825.
Il serto votivo, Bologna, 1829.

## III. SACRED MUSIC

Oratorio, 'Ciro in Babilonia,' Ferrara, Lent, 1812.
'Saul' (for the Oratory, Rome, 1834).
Stabat Mater, 1832-41. 1, 2, 3.
Petite messe solennelle, 1864. 1, 2, 3.
Tantum ergo, for 2 tenors and bass, with orchestra. 1, 2, 3. Composed at Bologna, and per-

formed Nov. 28, 1847, for the re-establishment of the services in the church of S. Francesco dei Minori conventuali.
Quoniam, bass solo and orchestra, 1, 2, 3.
O Salut.ris, 4 solo voices. Published at Paris in La Maîtrise and reproduced in facsimile by Azevedo in his Rossini.

## IV. MISCELLANEOUS VOCAL MUSIC

Gorgheggi e solfeggi. A collection of exercises for the voice.
Non posso, o Dio, resistere. Cantata.
Oh quanto son grate. Duettino.
Ridiamo, cantiamo, a 4.
Alle voci della gloria. Scena ed Aria.
Les Soirées musicales. 8 ariettas and 4 duets.

Inno populare, on the accession of Pius IX. Chorus.
Dall' Oriente l'.astro del giorno a 4.
Cara Patria. Cantata.
Chant des Titans. Chorus.
Se il vuol la Molinara.—Rossini's first composition.
La separazione. Dramatic song.

Various other airs and pieces, thirty or forty in number, will be found in the catalogues of Ricordi, Lucca, Brandus (Troupenas), and Escudier, which it is hardly necessary to enumerate here. Probably no composer ever wrote so much in albums as did Rossini. The number of these pieces which he threw off while in London alone is prodigious. They are usually composed to some lines of Metastasio's, beginning 'Mi lagnerà tacendo della sorte amara,' which he is said to have set more than a hundred times. The famous aria, 'Pietà, Signore,' which credulous amateurs still regard as Stradella's, was, according to Piatti, written as a joke by Rossini.

We have stated that during the latter years of his life Rossini composed a great quantity of music for the PF. solo, both serious and comic. These pieces were sold by his widow en masse to Baron Grant for the sum of £4000. After a time the whole was put up to auction in London and purchased by Ricordi of Milan, Paul Dalloz, proprietor of a periodical entitled La Musique, at Paris, and other persons.

## V. INSTRUMENTAL MUSIC

Le Rendezvous de chasse. A fanfare for 4 trumpets, composed at Complègne in 1828 for M. Schickler, and dedicated to him.
3 Marches for the marriage of H.R.H. the Duke of Orleans. Arranged for PF. a 4 mains.

March (Pas redoublé) composed for H.I.M. the Sultan Abdul Medjid. Arranged for PF. solo (Benedict) and a 4 mains.
5 String quartets, arranged as sonatines for the PF. by Mockwitz (Breitkopf & Härtel).

To enumerate and elucidate all the biographical and critical notices of Rossini would require a volume; we shall therefore confine ourselves to mentioning these of importance either from their authority, their ability, or the special nature of their contents; and for greater convenience of reference we have arranged them according to country and date.

### BIBLIOGRAPHY

#### I. ITALIAN

G. CARPANI : Lettera all' anonimo autore dell' articolo sul ' Tancredi di Rossini. Milan, 1818, 8vo.
Le Rossiniane, ossia Lettere musico-teatrali. Padua, 1824, 130 pages. 8vo. Portrait.
NIC. BETTONI : Rossini e la sua musica. Milan, 1824, 8vo.
P. BRIGHENTI : Della musica rossiniana e del suo autore. Bologna, 1830, 8vo.
LIB. MUSUMECI : Parallelo tra i maestri Rossini e Bellini. Palermo, 1832, 8vo.
ANON. : Osservazioni sul merito musicale dei maestri Bellini e Rossini, in riposta ad un Parallelo tra i medesimi. Bologna, 1834, 8vo. This pamphlet was translated into French by M. de Ferrer, and published as Rossini et Bellini. Paris, 1835, 8vo.
ANON. : Rossini e la sua musica; una passeggiata con Rossini. Florence, 1841, 16mo.
ANON. : Dello Stabat Mater di Gioachino Rossini, lettere storicocritiche di un Lombardo. Bologna, 1842, 8vo.
GIOV. RAFFAELLI. Rossini, canto. Modena, 1844, 8vo.
FR. REGLI : Elogio di Gioachino Rossini. We have not been able to discover how far Regli (1804-66) has used this work in his Dizionario biografico (1860).
E. MONTAZIO : Gioachino Rossini. Turin, 1862, 18mo. Portrait.
GIUL. VANZOLINI : Della vera patria di G. Rossini. Pesaro, 1873, 8vo.

VERRUCCI : *Giudizio perentorio sulla verità della patria di G. Rossini impugnata dal Prof. Giul. Vanzolini.* Florence, 1874 ; an 8vo pamphlet of 20 pages.
SETT SILVESTRI : *Della vita e delle opere di G. Rossini.* Milan, 1874, 8vo ; with portrait and facsimiles.
ANT. ZANOLINI : *Biografia di Gioachino Rossini.* Bologna, 1875, 8vo ; with portrait and facsimiles.
R. GANDOLFI : *Onoranze fiorentine a Gioacchino Rossini.* 1902.
V. CAVAZZANI-MALANTI : *Rossini a Verona durante il Congresso del 1822.* Verona, 1922.
G. MALERBI : *Gioacchino Rossini. Pagine segrete.* Bologna, 1922.
GIUSEPPE RODICIOTTI : *La famosa lettera al Cecognara non fu scritta dal Rossini. R.M.I.*, 1923.

II. FRENCH

PAPILLON : *Lettre critique sur Rossini.* Paris, 1823, 8vo.
STENDHAL : *Vie de Rossini.* Paris, 1823, 8vo. Stendhal, whose real name was Henri Beyle, compiled this work from Carpani. In many passages in fact it is nothing but a translation, and Beyle's own anecdotes are not always trustworthy. It was translated into English (London, 12mo, 1826) and German (Leipzig, 1824), in the latter case by Wendt, who has added notes and corrections.
BERTON : *De la musique mécanique et de la musique philosophique.* Paris, 1824, 8vo ; 24 pages.
Ditto, followed by an *Épitre à un célèbre compositeur français* (Boieldieu). Paris, 1826, 8vo ; 48 pages.
IMBERT DE LAPHALEQUE : *De la musique en France : Rossini, 'Guillaume Tell.'* (*Revue de Paris*, 1829.)
J. D'ORTIGUE : *De la guerre des dilettanti ou de la révolution opérée par M. Rossini dans l'opéra français.* Paris, 1829, 8vo.
N. BETTONI : *Rossini et sa musique.* Paris, Bettoni, 1836, 8vo.
ANON : *Vie de Rossini*, etc. Antwerp, 1839, 12mo, 215 pages. (By M. Van Damme, who in his turn has borrowed much from Stendhal.)
J. DE LOMÉNIE : *M. Rossini, par un homme de rien.* Paris, 1842, 8vo.
AULAGNIER : *Quelques observations sur la publication du 'Stabat mater' de Rossini.* Paris, 1842, 4to.
ANON. *Observations d'un amateur non dilettante au sujet du 'Stabat' de M. Rossini.* Paris, 1842, 8vo.
E. TROUPENAS : *Résumé des opinions de la Presse sur le 'Stabat' de Rossini.* Paris, 1842, 8vo ; 75 pages.
ESCUDIER FRÈRES : *Rossini, sa vie et ses œuvres.* Paris, 1854, 12mo ; 338 pages.
EUG. DE MIRECOURT : *Rossini.* Paris, 1855, 32mo.
A. AZEVEDO : *G. Rossini, sa vie et ses œuvres.* Paris, 1865, large 8vo ; 310 pages, with portraits and facsimiles. This is the most complete and eulogistic work on Rossini. It appeared originally in the *Ménestrel*, but was discontinued there, the editor not approving of a violent attack on Meyerbeer, which Azevedo included in it.
VIRMAÎTRE ET ÉLIE FRÉBAULT : *Les Maisons comiques de Paris.* 1868, 12mo. One chapter is devoted to the house of Rossini.
N. ROQUEPLAN. *Rossini.* Paris, 1869, 12mo ; 16 pages.
E. BEULÉ : *Éloge de Rossini.* Paris, 1869.
A. POUGIN : *Rossini : Notes, impressions, souvenirs, commentaires.* Paris, 1870, 8vo ; 91 pages. The detailed and annotated chronological list mentioned on p. 8 has not yet been published.
O. MOUTOU : *Rossini et son 'Guillaume Tell.'* Bourg, 1872, 8vo.
VAN DER STRAETEN. *La Mélodie populaire dans l'opéra 'Guillaume Tell' de Rossini.* Paris, 1879, 8vo.
J. SITTARD : *Rossini.* 1882.
E. MICHOTTE : *La Visite de R. Wagner à Rossini.* Brussels, 1906.
L. DAURIAC : *Rossini.* Paris, 1907.
PIERRE LASSERRE : *L'Esprit de la musique française de Rameau à l'invasion wagnérienne.* Paris, 1917.
H. DE CURZON : *Rossini.* Paris 1920.

III. GERMAN

OETTINGER : *Rossini, komischer Roman.* Leipzig, 1847. A satirical work translated into Danish by Marlow (Copenhagen, 1849, 2 vols. 8vo ; into Swedish by Landberg (Stockholm, 1850, 2 vols. 8vo) ; and into French by Royer, *Rossini, l'homme et l'artiste* (Brussels, 1858, 3 vo s. 16mo).
OTTO GUMPRECHT *Musikalische Charakterbilder.* Leipzig, 1869, 8vo.
FERD. HILLER : *Plaudereien mit Rossini.* Inserted (with date 1856 in Hiller's *Aus dem Tonleben unserer Zeit* (Leipzig, 1868), translated into French by Ch. Schwartz in *La France musicale* 1855 ; and into English by Miss M. E. von Glehn in *Once a Week* 1870.
A. STRUTH : *Rossini, sein Leben, seine Werke und Charakterzüge.* Leipzig.
LA MARA : *Musikalische Studienköpfe*, vol. ii. Leipzig, 1874-76, 2 vols. 12mo.

IV. ENGLISH

HOGARTH : *Memoirs of the Musical Drama.* London, 1838, 2 vols. 8vo.
H. S. EDWARDS : *Rossini's Life.* London, 1869, 8vo ; portrait.—*History of the Opera*, Ib. 1862, 2 vols. 8vo.—*Rossini and his School*, 1881.

Portraits of Rossini are frequent at all periods of his life. Marochetti's statue, in which he is represented sitting, was erected in his native town in 1864. There is a good bust by Bartolini of Florence. In the 'foyer' of the old opera-house in the Rue Le Peletier, Paris (now destroyed), there was a medallion of Rossini by Chevalier ; a duplicate of this is in the possession of the editor of the *Ménestrel*. The front of the present opera-house has a

bronze-gilt bust by Évrard. A good early engraving of him is that from an oil-painting by Mayer of Vienna (1820). Of later ones may be mentioned that by Thévenin after Ary Scheffer (1843) : still later, a full-length drawn and engraved by Masson, and a photograph by Erwig, engraved as frontispiece to the PF. score of 'Sémiramis' (Heugel). A drawing by L. Dupré is reproduced on *PLATE XLIX*. Among the lithographs the best is that of Grévedon ; and of caricatures the only one deserving mention is that by Dantan.

G. C., rev. and abridged.

ROSTH (ROSTHIUS), JOHANN KASPAR NIKO-LAUS (*b.* Weimar, latter 16th century), studied theology and music at Torgau, was in the Electoral Chapel, Heidelberg, 1583 ; Kapell-meister at the court of Altenburg, 1593 ; discantist at Weimar, 1594 ; and pastor at Cos-menz, Altenburg, 1606. He composed 1 book of motets, 6 and 8 v. (1613) ; 1 book of songs ('Frölche neuwe teutsche gesäng '), sacred and secular, 4, 5, 6 v. (1583) ; 2 books, xxx. newer lieblicher Galliardt (4-part songs), 1st part, 1593, 2nd part, 1594 ; 'A Resurrection' and other sacred music in MS. (*Q.-L.*).

ROTA, (1) see ROTTE.
(2) The name *rota* is applied to the famous round, 'SUMER IS ICUMEN IN' (*q.v.*), and may have been a generic name for what we now call ROUND.
M.

ROTA, ANDREA (*b.* Bologna, *c.* 1553 ; *d.* 1597), was appointed, in 1583, choir-master to the church of San Petronio in that city. His publications consist of three books of madrigals, two *a* 5 (Venice, 1579–89), one *a* 4 (1592) ; two books of motets *a* 5-10 (1584, 1595) ; and one book of masses *a* 4-6 (1595). A very pleasing madrigal *a* 5 is republished in Torchi's 'L' arte musicale in Italia,' vol. i. ; also an Agnus Dei *a* 7 with double canon, and a Dixit Dominus *a* 8. Padre Martini's *Esem-plare* contains a Da Pacem by Rota, and Paolucci's 'L' arte prattica,' a motet *a* 10.

J. R. M.

ROTTE (ROTE), a form of the ancient lyre prevalent in Northern Europe from pre-Christian to mediæval times. Diodorus Siculus (*c.* 25 B.C.) states that the Celtic bards accom-panied their songs upon instruments 'like lyres.' Amongst the Britons it was known as the 'Crot' (see CRWTH). And Venantius Fortunatus (*c.* A.D. 600) alludes to it under the latinised form *Chrotta*, for which *Rotta* is substituted in one of the versions of his poem.

It was apparently derived—like the Greek and Roman lyres—from the early home of the Aryan race on the plains of Western Asia. Illustrations are found on the Irish crosses of the 8th and 9th centuries, and in a manuscript of the 12th or 13th century found by Abbot Gerbert in the monastery of S. Blasius it is depicted under the title *Cythara teutonica* as a lyre with rounded angles, slightly incurved sides and seven strings.

In the 8th century an English abbot, writing to the Archbishop of Mainz, asked him to send to him a musician ' who can play upon the instrument (*cithara*) that we call a Rotte, because I have an instrument but I have no performer.'

An actual specimen of the Rotte of this period was discovered in the Black Forest in the grave of a German warrior and is now preserved in the Ethnographical Museum at Berlin. It is about 30 ins. in length (*PLATES XXXI.* and *LXVI.*).

In English manuscripts from the 8th to the 11th centuries the Rotte is frequently illustrated, as for instance in the British Museum MS. Vesp. A. i. : the Anglo-Saxon name seems to have been *Cytere*. Chaucer spells the name as Rote, in which he is followed by Spenser, though probably by the end of the 16th century the word was but a poetical fancy. Owing to this later spelling confusion has been caused with the word *Rota*, a name given by Latin writers to the Organistrum or Hurdy-gurdy, which was played by turning a wheel (*rota*) and thus setting the strings in vibration (see HURDY-GURDY).                               F. W. G.

ROUART - LEROLLE, publishers. This house, of great importance in the movement of French contemporary music, dates from 1905. It was in this year that Alexis Rouart (1869–1921) acquired the publications of Meuriot and Baudoux. He went into partnership, in 1908, with Jacques Lerolle (*b.* 1880), son of the painter and nephew of Ernest Chausson, the composer, who brought publications of Gregh, dating from 1840, into the partnership. Under the management of Rouart and Lerolle, the old stock chiefly composed of light music and of monologues, gave place to a series of works of very different nature, either great classics, or the works of the most modern composers.

Since the death of A. Rouart (1921) the firm has been under the direction of J. Lerolle, with Mme. Rouart (the widow) as partner, and with François Hepp (*b.* 1887), son-in-law of A. Rouart, as co-director.                               M. P.

ROUGET DE LISLE, CLAUDE JOSEPH (*b.* Montaigu, near Lons-le-Saulnier, May 10, 1760; *d.* Choisy-le-Roy, June 26-7, 1836), author of the ' Marseillaise.' He entered the School of Royal Engineers (' École Royale du Génie ') at Mezières in 1782, and left it two years later with the rank of ' aspirant-lieutenant.' Early in 1789 he was made second lieutenant, and in 1790 he rose to be first lieutenant, and was moved to Strassburg, May 1, 1791, where he soon became very popular in the triple capacity of poet, violin-player and singer. His hymn, ' à la Liberté,' composed by Ignace Pleyel, was sung at Strassburg at the fête of Sept. 25, 1791. While there he wrote three pieces for the theatre, one of which, ' Bayard en Bresse,' was produced at Paris, Feb. 21, 1791, but without success. In Apr. 1792 he wrote the ' MARSEILLAISE ' (*q.v.*). As the son of royalist parents, and himself belonging to the constitutional party, Rouget de Lisle refused to take the oath to the constitution abolishing the crown; he was therefore stripped of his military rank, denounced and imprisoned, only to escape after the fall of Robespierre in 1794, an event he celebrated in a ' Hymne dithyrambique,' etc. ' Le Chant des vengeances ' (1798) and ' Le Chant des combats ' (1800) (poem and music by Rouget de Lisle) were performed at the Théâtre de la République et des Arts, 1798 and 1800. He also wrote a ' Hymne à la Raison,' a ' Hymne du 9 Thermidor,' and ' Les Héros du Vengeur.' He re-entered the army, and made the campaign of La Vendée under General Hoche; was wounded, and at length, under the Consulate, returned to private life at Montaigu, where he remained in the depth of solitude and of poverty till the second Restoration. His brother then sold the little family property, and Rouget was driven to Paris; and there would have starved but for a small pension granted by Louis XVIII. and continued by Louis Philippe, and for the care of his friends Béranger, David d'Angers, and especially M. and Mme. Voïart, in whose house, at Choisy-le-Roi, he died.

Besides the works already mentioned, he published in 1797 a volume of *Essais en vers et en prose* (Paris, F. Didot, 5th year of the Republic), dedicated to Méhul, and now extremely rare ; so also is his ' Cinquante chants français ' (1825, 4to), with PF. accompaniment. One of these songs, ' Roland à Roncevaux,' was written in 1792, and its refrain—

'Mourir pour la patrie,
C'est le sort le plus beau, le plus digne d'envie '—

was borrowed by the authors of the ' Chant des Girondins,' which was set to music by Varney, and played a distinguished part in the Revolution of 1848. He wrote another set of twenty-five romances with violin obbligato, and two opera-libretti, ' Jacquot, ou l'école des mères ' for Della Maria, and ' Macbeth ' for Chelard, produced in 1827. His ' Relation du désastre de Quiberon ' is in vol. ii. of the *Mémoires de tous.*

There exists a fine medallion of Rouget by David d'Angers, which is engraved in a pamphlet by his nephew, entitled *La Vérité sur la paternité de la Marseillaise* (Paris, 1865).

G. C. ; addns. M. L. P.

BIBL.—J. TIERSOT, (1) *Rouget de Lisle, son œuvre, sa vie* (Paris, 1892) ; (2) *Histoire de la Marseillaise* (Paris, 1915).

ROULADE, an *agrément* of the French school, left to the judgment of the executant. It is composed on the following formula :

E. B^L.

## LXVI

MUSICAL INSTRUMENTS — ENGLAND, c. 1025

(University Libr., Cambridge)

1. Crowd.    2. Rotte.    3. Cornett.    4. Panpipes and Clappers.
Centre: Harp.

ROUND. (1) ' A species of canon in the unison, so called because the performers begin the melody at regular rhythmical periods, and return from its conclusion to its beginning, so that it continually passes round and round from one to another of them.'[1] Rounds and Catches, the most characteristic forms of English music, differ from canons in only being sung at the unison or octave, and also in being rhythmical in form. Originating at a period of which we have but few musical records, these compositions have been written and sung in England with unvarying popularity until the present day. The earliest extant example of a round is the well - known ' SUMER IS ICUMEN IN ' (q.v.). Amongst early writers on music, the terms ' round ' and ' catch ' were synonymous, but at the present day the latter is generally understood to be what Hawkins (vol. ii.) defines as that species of round

' wherein, to humour some conceit in the words, the melody is broken, and the sense interrupted in one part, and caught again or supplied by another,'

a form of humour which easily adapted itself to the coarse tastes of the Restoration, at which period rounds and catches reached their highest popularity. That catches were immensely popular with the lower classes is proved by the numerous allusions to 'alehouse catches' and the like in the dramas of the 16th and 17th centuries. According to Drayton (*Legend of Thomas Cromwell*, Stanza 29) they were introduced into Italy by the Earl of Essex in 1510.

The first printed collection of rounds was that edited by Thomas Ravenscroft, and published in 1609 under the title of ' Pammelia. Musickes Miscellanie.' For full title and list of subsequent publications see CATCH. This interesting collection contains many English, French and Latin rounds, etc., some of which are still popular. Amongst them there is also a curious ' Round of three Country Dances in one ' for four voices, which is in reality a Quodlibet on the country-dance tunes ' Robin Hood,' ' Now foot it ' and ' The Crampe is in my purse.' ' Pammelia ' was followed by two other collections brought out by Ravenscroft, ' Deuteromelia ' in 1609, and ' Melismata ' in 1611, and the numerous publications of the Playfords, the most celebrated of which is ' Catch that catch can, or the Musical Companion ' (1667), which passed through many editions. The most complete collection of rounds and catches is that published by Warren in thirty-two monthly and yearly numbers, from 1763–94, which contains over 800 compositions, including many admirable specimens by Purcell, Blow and other masters of the English school. It is to be regretted that they

are too often disfigured by an obscenity of so gross a nature as to make them now utterly unfit for performance. A good specimen of the round proper is Hayes's ' Wind, gentle evergreen.' The Round has never been much cultivated by foreign composers. One or two examples are, however, well known, amongst them may be mentioned Cherubini's ' Perfida Clori.'

(2) Any dance in which the dancers stood in a circle was formerly called a round or roundel.[2] The first edition of the ' Dancing Master ' (1651) has thirteen rounds, for six, eight or ' as many as will.' Subsequent editions of the same book have also a dance called ' Cheshire Rounds,' and Part II. of Walsh's ' Compleat Country Dancing Master ' (1719) has Irish and Shropshire rounds. These latter dances are, however, not danced in a ring, but ' longways,' *i.e.* like ' Sir Roger de Coverley.' In Jeremiah Clarke's ' Choice Lessons for the Harpsichord or Spinett ' (1711), and similar contemporary publications, the word rondo is curiously corrupted into ' Round O.'    w. b. s.

ROUND, CATCH AND CANON CLUB (1843–1911). A society founded in London in 1843, by Enoch Hawkins, for the purpose of singing the new compositions of the professional members and others, written in the form of Round, Catch and Canon ; hence the title of the Club. Among the original members were Enoch Hawkins, Hobbs, Bradbury, Handel Gear, Henry Phillips, Addison, D'Almaine and F. W. Collard. The meetings were originally held at the Crown and Anchor Tavern whence the Club removed to the Freemasons' Tavern, thence to the Thatched House, again to Freemasons' Tavern, and to St. James's Hall, where, until the demolition of the building, it assembled every fortnight from the first Saturday in November until the end of March, ten meetings being held in each season. Its meetings were subsequently held in the Criterion Restaurant, and took place on Monday evenings instead of Saturdays. In the earlier years of its existence the number both of professional and non-professional members at each dinner rarely exceeded eighteen, but in the later years of the Club's prosperity from sixty to seventy dined together. The management of the Club was in the hands of the officers, who were the proprietors, and each of whom in turn took the chair, and was alone responsible for the entertainment. The musical programmes latterly consisted mainly of glees, although an occasional catch was introduced. The last session of the Club was that which ended in March 1911.    c. m., addns.

ROUNDS, a term used by bell-ringers to denote the ringing of bells in the order of the

---

[1] ' The Rounds, Catches and Canons of England ; a Collection of Specimens of the sixteenth, seventeenth and eighteenth centuries adapted to Modern Use. The Words revised, adapted or re-written by the Rev. J. Powell Metcalfe. The Music selected and revised, and An Introductory Essay on the Rise and Progress of the Round, Catch, and Canon ; also Biographical Notices of the Composers, written by Edward F. Rimbault, LL.D.,' from which work much of the information contained in the above article has been derived.

[2] ' Come now a roundel and a fairy song.
*Midsummer Night's Dream*, Act ii. sc. 2.

successive notes of the major scale, beginning with the highest note (treble) and concluding with the lowest (tenor) (see CHANGE RINGING).                                    w. w. s.

ROUSSEAU, JEAN, a late 17th-century viol da gambist in Paris; pupil of Sainte Colombe. Fétis mentions 2 books of ' Pièces de viole,' by him, but does not say where they are to be found. His *Traité de la viole* (1687) is well known as a book of great interest with regard to the history as well as the technique of the instrument ; he wrote also a ' Méthode claire, certaine et facile, pour apprendre à chanter la musique,' etc. (1691).              E. v. d. s.

ROUSSEAU, JEAN JACQUES (*b.* Geneva, June 28, 1712 ; *d.* Ermenonville, near Paris, July 3, 1778). The details of his life are given in his *Confessions* ; we shall here confine ourselves to his compositions, and his writings on music.

Rousseau studied music with a maître de chapelle from 1727–30 but remained to the end a poor reader and an indifferent harmonist, though he exercised a great influence on French music. He contributed an air to the *Mercure de France* (June 1737). He is found as a musician at Chambéry between 1735 and 1737.[1] Immediately after his arrival in Paris he read a paper before the Académie des Sciences (Aug. 22, 1742) on a new system of musical notation, which he afterwards extended and published under the title of *Dissertation sur la musique moderne* (Paris, 1743, 8vo). His method of representing the notes of the scale by figures—1, 2, 3, 4, 5, 6, 7—had been already proposed by Souhaitty, but Rousseau's combinations, and especially his signs of duration, are so totally different as entirely to redeem them from the charge of plagiarism. A detailed analysis and refutation of the system may be found in Raymond's *Des principaux systèmes de notation musicale* (Turin, 1824, 8vo), to which the reader is referred.

Copying music had been Rousseau's means of livelihood, and this led him to believe that the best way to learn an art is to practise it ; at any rate he composed an opera, ' Les Muses galantes ' (1747), which was produced at the house of La Popelinière, when Rameau, who was present, declared that some pieces showed the hand of a master, and others the ignorance of a schoolboy. Not being able to obtain access to any of the theatres, Rousseau undertook to write the articles on music for the *Encyclopédie*, a task which he accomplished in three months, and afterwards acknowledged to have been done hastily and unsatisfactorily. We have mentioned in the article RAMEAU, the exposé by that great musician of the errors in the musical articles of the *Encyclopédie* ; Rousseau's reply was not published till after his death, but it is included in his complete works.

[1] According to W. H. Grattan Flood.

Three months after the arrival in Paris of the Italian company who popularised the ' Serva padrona '[2] in France, Rousseau produced ' Le Devin du village ' before the King at Fontainebleau, on Oct. 18 and 24, 1752. The piece, of which both words and music were his own, pleased the court, and was quickly reproduced in Paris. The first representation at the Opéra took place Mar. 1, 1753, and the last in 1829, after more than 400 performances, when some wag[3] threw an immense powdered perruque on the stage and gave it its deathblow. It is curious that the representations of this simple pastoral should have coincided so exactly with the vehement discussions to which the performances of Italian opera gave rise. We cannot enter here upon the literary quarrel known as the ' Guerre des Bouffons,' or enumerate the host of pamphlets to which it gave rise,[4] but it is a strange fact, only to be accounted for on the principle that man is a mass of contradictions, that Rousseau, the author of the ' Devin du village,' pronounced at once in favour of Italian music.

His *Lettre sur la musique française* (1753) raised a storm of indignation, and not unnaturally, since it pronounces French music to have neither rhythm nor melody, the language not being susceptible of either ; French singing to be but a prolonged barking, absolutely insupportable to an unprejudiced ear ; French harmony to be crude, devoid of expression, and full of mere padding ; French airs not airs, and French recitative not recitative. ' From which I conclude,' he continues, ' that the French have no music, and never will have any ; or that if they ever should, it will be so much the worse for them.' To this pamphlet the actors and musicians of the Opéra replied by hanging and burning its author in effigy. His revenge for this absurdity, and for many other attacks, was the witty *Lettre d'un symphoniste de l'Académie royale de musique à ses camarades de l'orchestre* (1753), which may still be read with pleasure. The æsthetic part of the *Dictionnaire de musique* which he finished in 1764 at Motiers-Travers, is admirable both for matter and style. He obtained the privilege of printing it in Paris, Apr. 15, 1765, but did not make use of the privilege till 1768 ; the Geneva edition, also in one vol. 4to, came out in 1767. In spite of mistakes in the didactic, and serious omissions in the technical portions, the work became very popular, and was translated into several languages ; the English edition (London, 1770, 8vo) being by William Warin (see DICTIONARIES OF MUSIC).

[2] It has been generally supposed that the ' Serva padrona ' was not heard in Paris before 1752 ; this, however, is a mistake ; it had been played so far back as Oct. 4, 1746, but the Italian company who performed it was not satisfactory, and it passed almost unnoticed.
[3] Supposed to have been Berlioz, but he exculpates himself in his *Memoirs*, chap. xv.
[4] See Chouquet's *Histoire de la musique dramatique*, pp. 134 and 434.

Rousseau's other writings on music are : *Lettre à M. Grimm, au sujet des remarques ajouteés à sa Lettre sur Omphale* (1752), belonging to the early stage of the 'Guerre des Bouffons' ; *Essai sur l'origine des langues*, etc. (1753), containing chapters on harmony, on the supposed analogy between sound and colour and on the music of the Greeks ; *Lettre à M. l'Abbé Raynal au sujet d'un nouveau mode de musique inventé par M. Blainville*, dated May 30, 1754, and first printed in the *Mercure de France* ; *Lettre à M. Burney sur la musique, avec des fragments d'observations sur l'Alceste italien de M. le chevalier Gluck*, an analysis of 'Alceste' written at the request of Gluck himself ; and *Extrait d'une réponse du Petit Faiseur à son Prête-Nom, sur un morceau de l'Orphée de M. le chevalier Gluck*, dealing principally with a particular modulation in 'Orphée.' From the last two it is clear that Rousseau heartily admired Gluck, and that he had by this time abandoned the exaggerated opinions advanced in the *Lettre sur la musique française*. The first of the above was issued in 1752, the rest not till after his death ; they are now only to be found in his complete works.

On Oct. 30, 1775, Rousseau produced his 'Pygmalion' at the Comédie-Française ; it is a lyric piece in one act, and caused some sensation owing to its novelty. Singing there was none, and the only music consisted of orchestral pieces in the intervals of the declamation. He also left fragments of an opera 'Daphnis et Chloé' (published in score, Paris, 1780, folio), and a collection of about a hundred romances and detached pieces, to which he gave the title 'Consolations des misères de ma vie' (Paris, 1781, 8vo) ; in the latter collection are the graceful 'Rosier,' often reprinted, and a charming setting of Rolli's 'Se tu m' ami.' Rousseau was accused of having stolen the 'Devin du village' from a musician of Lyons named Granet, and the greater part of 'Pygmalion' from another Lyonnais named Coigniet. Among his most persistent detractors was Castil-Blaze (see *Molière musicien*, ii. 409), but he says not a word of the 'Consolations.' Now any one honestly comparing these romances with the 'Devin du village,' will inevitably arrive at the conviction that airs at once so simple, natural and full of expression, and so incorrect as regards harmony, not only may, but must have proceeded from the same author. There is no doubt, however, that the instrumentation of the 'Devin' was touched up, or perhaps wholly re-written, by Francœur, on whose advice, as well as on that of Jelyotte the tenor singer, Rousseau was much in the habit of relying. An air (' de trois notes ') and a duettino, melodious and pretty but of the simplest style, are given in the *Musical Library*, vol. iii.    G. C.

BIBL.—JULIEN TIERSOT, *Jean-Jacques Rousseau* ; G. CUCUEL, *Les Créateurs de l'Opéra-comique*. Both these are in the *Collection des maitres de la musique* (Paris, 1912) ; *Correspondence générale de J.-J. Rousseau* (published by Th. Dufour and P. P. Plan (vols. i., ii. Paris, 1924).    M. L. P.

ROUSSEAU, (1) SAMUEL ALEXANDRE (*b.* Neuve-Maison, Aisne, June 11, 1853; *d.* Paris, Oct. 1, 1904), studied at the Paris Conservatoire, where he gained successively the first organ prize in 1877, in César Franck's class, and the Grand Prix de Rome in 1878 with 'La Fille de Jephté.' In the latter year the Prix Cressent was awarded to his opéra-comique, 'Dianora,' which was produced at the Opéra-Comique, Dec. 22, 1879. Works sent from Rome, and executed at the Conservatoire, were 'Sabnius' (1880), 'Kaddir' (1881), 'La Florentine' (1882). He was for some years maître de chapelle in Sainte-Clotilde, and chorus-master of the Société des Concerts du Conservatoire. He wrote a great quantity of church music, two Masses, motets, organ pieces, etc. ; secular choral works, pieces for piano, harmonium, violin, small orchestra, etc. and songs. He was president of the Société des Compositeurs, and vice-president of the Association de la critique musicale et dramatique. His most famous work was the opera, 'La Cloche du Rhin,' in three acts, brought out at the Paris Opéra, June 8, 1898 ; another three-act opera, 'Mérowig,' was crowned by the City of Paris in 1891, and was first performed in concert-form at the Grand Théâtre, Paris (Salle de l'Éden), Dec. 12, 1892. His lyrical drama, in four acts, 'Leone,' to a libretto by George Montorgueil, was produced posthumously at the Opéra-Comique, Paris, Mar. 7, 1910.    G. F. ; rev. M. L. P.

His son (2) MARCEL AUGUSTE LOUIS, called Marcel Samuel Rousseau (second Grand Prix de Rome in 1905, harmony professor at the Conservatoire), has composed : 'Berenice,' incidental music ; 'Le Roi Arthur,' lyric poem (1903) ; 'Tarass-Boulba,' musical drama, performed in Paris at the Théâtre Lyrique du Vaudeville in 1919 ; 'Le Hulla,' 'conte lyrique,' performed at the Opéra-Comique, Paris, March 9, 1923, also piano compositions.    M. L. P.

ROUSSEAU'S DREAM, a very favourite air in England in the early part of the 19th century. Its first appearance under that name is presumably as 'an Air with Variations for the Pianoforte, composed and dedicated to the Rt. Hon. the Countess of Delaware, by J. B. Cramer. London, Chappell,' 1812.

But it is found (with very slight changes) a quarter of a century earlier, under the title of 'Melissa. The words by Charles James, Esq., adapted to the Pianoforte, Harp, or Guitar. London, J. Dale, 1788.' The melody occurs in the 'Pantomime' in Scene 8 of the 'Devin du village,' where its form is as follows:

The tune, no doubt, made its way in England through the adaptation of the opera by Dr. Burney, as 'The Cunning Man,' in 1766. It seems to have been first adapted to a hymn in Thomas Walker's 'Companion to Dr. Rippon's Tunes' (1825), and after its appearance in 'Sacred Melodies' (1843), with the name 'Rousseau' attached to it, became widely popular as a hymn-tune. The origin of the title 'Dream' is not forthcoming.

G.; addns. w. h. g. f.

ROUSSEL, ALBERT (b. Tourcoing, Dept. Nord, Apr. 5, 1869), composer, lost his parents at the age of 7, and was brought up by his grandfather, who was Mayor of Tourcoing. Later on he was sent to the Collège Stanislas in Paris, where he prepared himself for the Naval School, and made a special study of mathematics. At the same time he took piano lessons from the organist of St. Ambroise, Stolz. In 1887 he joined the training ship *Borda* off Brest. Having afterwards served on various ships, he sailed to French Indo-China on the *Styx*. On his return to France he received a commission on the *Melpomène*, where he composed his first tentative work, a fantasia for violin and piano. Later, on board the *Victorieuse*, he essayed a piece for violin, viola, violoncello and organ, but so small was his technical knowledge that he wrote the viola part in the treble clef. It was in 1893 that his fellow-officer, Calvé, a brother of the famous singer, induced him to submit a 'Marche nuptiale' to Édouard Colonne. While on leave the following year, he showed his music to Koszul, the director of the Conservatoire of Roubaix, who saw in it enough promise to encourage him to study systematically. Roussel resigned from the Navy, and began to work seriously under Gigout in Paris. On being introduced to Vincent d'Indy in 1896, he became one of that master's first pupils at the then newly-founded Schola Cantorum.

In 1898, 2 madrigals for four voices were performed and gained the prize of the Société des Compositeurs. The first published work of

Roussel's, 'Des heures passent,' for piano, belongs to the same year. After six years of study, he became professor at the Schola in Oct. 1902. The same year saw the composition of the trio (op. 2), and in 1903 followed the orchestral prelude inspired by Tolstoy's 'Resurrection' (op. 4). Between 1904–06 the first Symphony, 'Le Poème de la forêt,' was written. Although separate movements were occasionally heard in Paris, the work was not given in its complete form until 1908, in Brussels. Paris followed suit the next year. The incidental music to G. Jean-Aubry's 'Le Marchand de sable qui passe' was composed in 1908 and performed at Havre in December.

Roussel revisited Cochin China and saw India in 1909, and the outcome of his impressions was the composition of the 'Évocations,' three symphonic poems written in 1910–11. 'Le Festin de l'araignée,' a ballet with a scenario by Gilbert de Voisins based on the 'Souvenirs entomologiques' of Henri Fabre, was written in 1912, and produced at the Théâtre des Arts on Apr. 3, 1913.

Another work inspired by the visit to India is the opera-ballet, 'Padmâvatî,' on a libretto by Louis Laloy, which was begun in 1914 but not finished until after the war, in which Roussel was anxious to take an active part. His health not having permitted his remaining in the naval reserves, he tried to join the army, but was rejected for the same reason. He served, however, with the Red Cross, and carried medicaments and cash to the hospitals at the front during the battle of the Marne. Afterwards he joined the motor transport service with a commission corresponding to his old naval degree and went through the siege of Verdun and the battle of the Somme. In Jan. 1918, with his health completely undermined, he was discharged and retired to Perros-Guirec in Brittany, where he finished 'Padmâvatî,' which was produced at the Paris Opéra on June 1, 1923. The orchestral piece 'Pour une fête de printemps' (op. 22) and the second Symphony (op. 23) were composed in 1919–20, and the latter was first performed at the Pasdeloup Concerts on Mar. 4, 1922. A work for the stage, 'La Naissance de la lyre,' to a libretto by Théodore Reinach based on Sophocles was written between 1921–23.

As a composer Roussel possesses almost every quality but that of spontaneous invention; his work is fastidious and distinctive, full of colour, poetry and decorative refinement, but seldom inspired in a purely musical sense. He conjures up images which appeal by their delicacy and individuality to the hearer's æsthetic perception rather than to his ear. Roussel is an artist first and a musician afterwards. He might equally well have developed into a poet or painter. In the latter case he would have been an artist for whom colour is of vastly greater importance than design.

Nevertheless, a great perception of form, as distinct from formality, is discernible in Roussel's work from the beginning. In the early chamber music he adhered loosely, but in his own way logically, to the cyclic form of the Franck school. In the later works he gains a feeling of symmetry by placing various sections or movements next to each other in a definitely planned order. To make this mode of construction completely successful, each section would, however, have to be a homogeneous musical unity, and this Roussel does not fully achieve. His gift of building up musical continuity is limited to the expedient of repeating his thematic material in new keys and with varied instrumental treatment, and to that of carrying his music forward by means of new matter which has no organic affinity with what has gone before.

In his treatment of Eastern subjects Roussel is extraordinarily successful. In spite of his occasional use of Oriental material, the ' Évocations ' and ' Padmâvatî ' record a European's impressions of the East in his own native terms. They are not photographic reproductions of things seen, but a recreation of the experiences and feelings, an evocation (no better title could have been found for the 3 symphonic poems) of dreams and memories of the Orient.

In the songs Roussel compensates for his lack of melodic inspiration by a faithful adherence to the poetic declamation and by highly interesting and illuminating piano parts ; but he is rarely quite convincing in this branch of his art.

His later works, notably the second symphony, show a certain hardness and angularity which point to the influence of Stravinsky, but, as is the case with all influences which have claimed a passing tribute from him, he has merely taken possession of certain of Stravinsky's idiomatic devices as a new asset and absorbed them into his own personality. He is entirely without any settled method or system, and could undergo even Debussy's strong influence without falling a victim to that master's mannerisms.

WORKS

Op.
1. Suite, ' Des heures passent ' (PF.).  (1898.)
2. Trio (vln., vcl. and PF.).  (1902.)
3. 4 Poems by Henri de Régnier (voice and PF.).  (1903.)
4. ' Resurrection ' (Tolstoy), Prelude (orch.).  (1903.)
5. Rustiques, 3 Pieces (PF.).  (1904–06.)
6. Divertissement (PF. and 5 wind instr.).  (1906.)
7. ' Le Poème de la forêt,' Symphony No. 1 ( rch.).  (1904–06.)
8. 4 Poems by Henri de Régnier (voice and PF.).  (1907.)
9. ' La Menace,' Poem (voice and orch.).  (1907.)
10. ' Flammes ' (voice and PF.).  (1908.)
11. Sonata (vl. and PF.).  (1907–08.)
12. 2 Songs from the Chinese (voice and PF.).  (1907–08.)
13. Incidental Music for ' Le Marchand de sable qui passe' (G. Jean-Aubry) (small orch.).  (1908.)
14. Suite (PF.).  (1909–10.)
15. ' Évocations,' 3 Symphonic Poems (orch.; No. 3 with chorus).  (1910–11.)
16. Sonatina (PF.).  (1912.)
17. ' Le Festin de l'araignée,' Ballet by Gilbert de Voisins.  (1912.)
18. Padmâvatî, Opera-Ballet by Louis Laloy.  (1914–18.)
19. 2 Songs.  (1918.)
20. 2 Songs.  (1919.)
21. Impromptu (harp).  (1919.)

Op.
22. ' Pour une fête de printemps ' (orch.).  (1920.)
23. Symphony No. 2, B flat (orch.).  (1919–20.)
24. ' La Naissance de la lyre,' Opera by Théodore Reinach (after Sophocles).  (1921–23.)
25. ' Madrigal aux Muses (3 female voices, unaccomp.).  (1923.)
    ' L'Accueil des Muses ' (PF.), for ' Le Tombeau de Debussy.'  (1920.)

Among early works no longer acknowledged by the composer, are a horn quintet, a violin sonata and a symphonic sketch, ' Vendanges.'
E. B.

ROUX, GASPARD LE (b. Paris, c. 1660 ; d. circa 1705–10). Practically nothing is known of the life of this Parisian composer, who won fame but who disappeared quite young, leaving only one large work in manuscript. He was, says Sébastien de Brossard, a celebrated master of the clavecin and an excellent musician.

The career of Gaspard Le Roux appears to have been at the earliest from 1685 to 1710 at the latest.  In 1690 the Mercure published an ' Air spirituel ' in which the basso continuo is indicated as having been written by ' M. le Roux, fameux maître de musique.'  In 1692 his name appears amongst the Parisian professors of the clavecin in the ' Livre d'adresses ' of Blegny du Pradel.  In 1695, in the list of organists and clavecinists established for taxation, he appears to hold a good position, for he is taxed at the highest rate.  He paid 15 livres like Couperin, Garnier, Marchand, Le Bègue and some others.

In 1701 he published in the collection of ' Airs sérieux et à boire ' (Ballard) an ' Air sérieux ' of delicate grace, written in a key more instrumental than vocal (F♯ minor).  In 1705 he took a copyright of ten years (Apr. 21), for the impression and the rights of sale of his principal work : a collection of his ' Pièces de clavessin ' which appeared in that year, and which did not pass unnoticed, for the book was soon pirated by a Dutch editor.  In his preface the author gives no details about himself.  He announces that he will include ' d'autres morceaux de musique plus grands et plus relevéz,' probably his motets, of which some are preserved in Brossard's copies.  The promise was not kept, and after the appearance of the ' livre de clavecin ' no trace of Le Roux's existence is to be found.

This clavecinist did not merit the oblivion into which he fell immediately after his death.  If, in their traditional form, his pieces belong to the first school of French clavecin music, the school of Chambonnières, and Le Bègue, they show by certain signs of style that they are the work of a contemporary of Couperin who knew and appreciated the Italian sonatas.

The melodic themes, on the other hand, suggest a personal style ; they show a fine sensibility and are quite modern at times.  Keys rare at that time are employed for choice.  The harmonies are subtle and have racial characteristics.  The book of Gaspard Le Roux, in some ways in advance of his time, is certainly one of the best which appeared in

France between those of Chambonnières and those of Couperin.

It should be noted that Le Roux's pieces can be played, following his own indications, in three different ways : (1) On the clavecin alone ; (2) on two clavecins, an arrangement which Couperin also advocated ; (3) as instrumental trios (violins and bass) in which the three separate parts are usually printed at the foot of the pages, below the clavecin version.

Le Roux's motets, in the classic French style inaugurated by Du Mont and Lully, and illustrated by Lalande, are also works of value, to judge by the three specimens in the Brossard Collection. Those for two or three voices with single *basso continuo* are brilliantly and expressively written.

### WORKS

1. 'Air spirituel.' (*Mercure*, Mar. 1690.)
2. 'Air sérieux, Beaux Déserts, charmants boccages,' for vln., voice and basso continuo. 'Airs sérieux et à boire.' (Paris, 1701, Aug.)
3. Pièces de clavecin (a) ' Pièces de clavessin composées par Gaspard le Roux avec la manière de les joüer.' (Paris, 1705.) (b) ' Pièces de clavessin, propres à joüer sur un et deux clavessins, composées par Gaspard le Roux avec la manière de les joüer.' (Amsterdam, without date).
4. Motets (a) ' Thuris odor volet ad auras ' ; (b) ' Beati qui habitant in domo tua ' ; (c) ' Alma redemptoris mater.' (Bibl. Nat. de Paris : Brossard Collection.)

(4) Pietro (b. Bergamo, Feb. 6, 1793 ; d. there, Sept. 8, 1838), who received his first lessons, both in violin-playing and the general science of music, from his grandfather. By an influential patron he was sent to Paris to study under R. Kreutzer, and his playing attracted much attention there. On his father's appointment to Weimar he joined him for a time. At the end of 1814 we find him at Munich, playing with great applause. He remained there for some years, and was made ' Royal Bavarian chamber-musician ' and ' first concerto-player.' In Feb. 1817 he was playing at Vienna ; there he married Micheline, daughter of E. A. Förster, and a fine PF.-player, and in 1819 went on to Bergamo, took the place once occupied by his grandfather, and seems to have remained there, suffering much from bad health, till his death. (See *A.M.Z.*, Dec. 26, 1838.)

G.

ROVESCIO, AL, a term used, in instrumental music, to express two different things. (1) An imitation by contrary motion, in which every descending interval in the leading part is imitated by an ascending one, and *vice versa*; see Moscheles's étude ' La forza,' op. 51.

*Menuetto al Rovescio.*

[The Repeat, as played after the Trio.]

MODERN REPRINTS.—' Quatre pièces et sarabande diversifiée,' (Ed. Paul Brunold, publ. Sénart, Paris) ; ' Six pièces,' and ' Air sérieux, Beaux Déserts ' (Brunold), *Revue musicale, Supp.*, Mar. 1924.

BIBL.—Du Pradel, *Livre commode des adresses de Paris, 1692* (reprinted by E. Fournier, Paris, 1878) ; Pérachon, *Le Faux Satyrique puni et le mérite couronné* (Lyons, 1696) ; Jules Écorcheville, *Vingt Suites d'orchestre du XVIIe siècle français* (Paris, 1906) ; André Pirro, *L'Esthétique de J. S. Bach* (Paris, 1907) ; *Les Clavecinistes* (Paris, 1925) ; André Tessier, *L'Œuvre de Gaspard le Roux* ; *Note bibliographique* (*Revue de musicologie*, Dec. 1922) ; *Un Claveciniste français, Gaspard le Roux* (*Revue musicale*, Mar. 1924).

MANUSCRIPTS.—Paris. Archives Nationales : *Rolle des sommes qui seront payées par les organistes et professeurs de clavecins*, 1695 ; Bibliothèque Nationale : Brossard Collection.

A. T.

ROVELLI, a family of eminent Italian musicians. (1) Giovanni Battista was first violin in the orchestra of the church of S. Maria Maggiore of Bergamo, at the beginning of the 19th century.

(2) Giuseppe (b. Bergamo, 1753 ; d. Parma, Nov. 12, 1806), his son, was a violoncellist.

(3) Alessandro was at one time director of the orchestra at Weimar, and was the father of—

(2) A phrase or piece which may be played backwards throughout. It is then synonymous with Cancrizans. An interesting example occurs in the minuet of a sonata for PF. and violin by Haydn, in which, on the repetition after the trio, the minuet is played backwards, so as to end on the first note, Haydn's indication being *Menuetto D.C. wird zurückgespielt.* (See Rectf et Retro.)

F. T.

ROVETTA, Prete Giovanni (b. Venice, end of 16th cent. ; d. there, Aug. 1668), was first a choirboy at St. Mark's, Venice, where he was appointed as bass, Dec. 17, 1623 ; then priest at San Fantino and S. Silvestro ; Nov. 22, 1627, vice-maestro di cappella ; and after Monteverdi's death, Feb. 21, 1644, first maestro. He wrote a large number of masses, psalms, motets, etc., and 3 books of madrigals, 2-8 parts, of which the first book, op. 2, appeared in four editions ; he composed also some operas ; a list is given in *Q.-L.* (more particulars in *Mendel*). A number of his madrigals (*a* 2, 3 and 4) are in MS. (possibly autograph) at St. Michael's College, Tenbury.

ROWE, WALTER, a 16th-17th-century English viol da gamba and viola bastarda player, before 1614 at Hamburg; 1614–21 in the court chapel, Berlin, where a 'Walter Rowe, Junior' appears in the latter year, who was still there in 1641, and was teacher of the Princesses Louise Charlotte and Hedwig Sophia. One W. Rowe died 1671 at Berlin, probably the younger, whom Heinrich Albert mentions as a 'famous musician' and Chrysander as having been engaged at the court of Güstrow. Some gamba pieces probably by the elder Rowe are preserved in collective MS. vols. in various German libraries (*Q.-L.*).

ROY (LEROY), ADRIEN LE, was a singer, lute-player and composer, and one of the most celebrated music printers of the 16th century.

He worked with the types of Le Bé (cut in 1540), as Attaingnant had done before him with those of Hautin. Fétis states that he worked by himself for some time, but cites no evidence. In 1551 Le Roy married the sister of R. Ballard, who was already occupying himself with music printing, and was attached to the court; they joined partnership and obtained a patent, dated Feb. 16, 1552, as sole printers of music to Henri II. In 1571 he received Orlando Lasso as his guest, and published a volume of 'moduli' for him, with a dedication to Charles IX. (See LASSUS.) Le Roy's name disappears from the publications of the firm in 1589, and it may be inferred that he died then. His instruction [1] book for the lute, 1557, was translated into English in two different versions, one by Alford, London, 1568, and one by 'F. K. Gentleman' (*Ib.* 1574). A second work of his was a short and easy instruction book for the 'Guiterne,' or guitar (1578); and a third is a book of 'airs de cour' for the lute, 1571, in the dedication of which he says that such airs were formerly known as 'voix de ville.' Besides these the firm published, between 1551 and 1568, twenty books of 'Chansons' for four voices. (See BALLARD.)  G.

ROY, BARTHOLOMEO LE, musician at Rome, 1582, maestro di cappella to the Viceroy of Naples, 1585. A Mass of his was published, together with one by Palestrina (Venice, 1585). He wrote also madrigals, songs, and an instrumental movement. (See *Q.-L.*)

ROY, RENÉ LE (*b.* Maisons-Laffitte, Seine-et-Oise, Mar. 4, 1898), flautist. At 9 years of age he began to study the flute with Hennebains, entered the Paris Conservatoire in 1916, in Lafleurance's class, and took a brilliant first-

[1] *Instruction de partir toute musique des huit tons divers en tablature de luth.* The copy of 1557 mentioned by Fétis is not extant.

class prize in 1918. He then became a pupil of Philippe Gaubert, whom he succeeded as soloist in the Société des Instruments à Vent, founded by Taffanel. He has since founded a new group, the Quintette Instrumental de Paris. Both alone and with this group he has made numerous concert tours through Europe with a growing success. A number of pieces have been heard for the first time played by him, of which the last in date is the 'Sérénade' dedicated to him by Albert Roussel (1925).  M. P.

ROYAL ACADEMY OF MUSIC, 1720–28, see HANDEL.

ROYAL ACADEMY OF MUSIC. The original plan for this institution was proposed by Lord Westmorland (then Lord Burghersh) at a meeting of noblemen and gentlemen held at the Thatched House Tavern, London, on July 5, 1822. The proposal meeting with approval, at a second meeting, July 12, rules and regulations were drawn up, and a committee was appointed to carry out the undertaking. According to the rules adopted, the constitution of the new Academy was to be modelled upon the British Institution. The King was announced as the principal Patron, the government was to consist of a committee of twenty-five directors and a sub-committee of nine subscribers, and the school was to be supported by subscriptions and donations. There was also to be a Board, consisting of the Principal and four professors, and the number of pupils was not to exceed forty boys and forty girls, to be admitted between the ages of 10 and 15, and all to be boarded in the establishment. A sub-committee, the members of which were Lord Burghersh, Sir Gore Ouseley, Count St. Antonio, Sir Andrew Barnard, Sir John Murray and the Hon. A. Macdonald, was empowered to form the Institution. Dr. Crotch was appointed the first Principal, and by September 1 the sum of £4312 : 10s. had been collected, including an annual subscription of 100 guineas from George IV., which was continued by his successors, William IV. and Queen Victoria. In November the house, No. 4 Tenterden Street, Hanover Square, was taken for the new school, but the opening was deferred until Mar. 1823, on the 24th of which month the first lesson was given by Cipriani Potter to Kellow Pye.

The Academy began its labours with the following staff: Head Master—Rev. John Miles. Governess—Mrs. Wade. Principal—Dr. Crotch. Board of Professors — Attwood, Greatorex, Shield and Sir George Smart. Supplementary members of the Board—Horsley and J. B. Cramer. Professors—Anfossi, Andrew, Bishop, Bochsa, Crivelli, F. Cramer, Clementi, Coccia, Cerruti, Dragonetti, Dizi, Griesbach, Hawes, Ireland, C. Kramer, Liverati, Lindley, Loder, Mori, Macintosh, Nicholson, Cipriani Potter,

Puzzi, Ries, H. Smart, Spagnoletti, Watts, Willmann and Caravita.[1]

The Foundation students who were first elected were the following : Girls—M. E. Lawson, C. Smith, M. Chancellor, S. Collier, E. Jenkyns, M. A. Jay, C. Bromley, H. Little, J. Palmer, C. Porter. Boys—W. H. Holmes, H. A. M. Cooke,[2] A. Greatorex, T. M. Mudie, H. G. Blagrove, Kellow J. Pye, W. H. Phipps, A. Devaux, C. Seymour, E. J. Neilson and C. S. Packer. The pupils were divided into two classes, those on the foundation paying ten guineas per annum, while extra students paid twenty guineas, or if they lodged and boarded in the establishment, thirty - eight guineas. Although the first report of the Committee (June 2, 1823) was satisfactory, yet financial difficulties soon made themselves felt. In Mar. 1824 the Committee reported a deficiency for the current year of £1600, if the institution were conducted on the same plan as before. To meet this, the difference between the students' payments was abolished, and the fees were fixed for all at £40, the professors at the same time giving their instruction gratis for three months. Lord Burghersh also applied to the Government for a grant, but without effect. In 1825 further alterations were made as to the admission of students, by which the numbers amounted in four months' time to a hundred, and Lord Burghersh made another appeal for a Government grant. In spite of this, the year's accounts still showed an unsatisfactory financial condition. During the latter part of the year Moscheles was included among the staff of professors. Early in 1826 the increased number of students compelled the Academy to enlarge its premises, the lease [3] of No. 5 Tenterden Street was bought, and the two houses were thrown into one. In February the Government were petitioned for a charter. In reply it was stated that though unwilling to give a grant, they were ready to defray the cost of a charter. In 1827 the financial condition of the Academy was so disastrous that it was proposed to close the institution ; but a final appeal to the public procured a loan of £1469, beside further donations, enabling the directors to carry on the undertaking on a reduced scale and with increased fees. Henceforward the state of things began to mend. The charter was granted on June 23, 1830. By this document the members of the Academy and their successors were incorporated and declared to be, and for ever hereafter to continue to be by the name of the ' Royal Academy of Music,' under the government of a Board of Directors, consisting of thirty members, with power to

[1] Although the above was published in the *Morning Post* as the list of professors, instruction seem only to have been given by the following : Dr. Crotch, Lord, Potter, Haydon, Crivelli, F. Cramer, Spagnoletti, Lindley, Bochsa, Cooke, Caravita, Cicchetti, Goodwin, J. B. Cramer, Beale and Finart ; and by Mmes. Biagioli, Reguandin and Miss Adams. (See First Report of the Committee, June 2, 1823.)
[2] Known as ' Grattan Cooke.'
[3] Relinquished in or before 1853.

make rules and regulations ; a Committee of Management, with full power over the funds and both students and professors ; and a Treasurer.

In 1832 Dr. Crotch resigned his post of Principal, and was succeeded by Cipriani Potter, who retained office until his resignation in 1859. The financial position of the Academy, although not prosperous, remained on a tolerably secure footing. In 1834 William IV. directed that a quarter of the proceeds of the Musical Festival held in Westminster Abbey should be handed over to the institution. This sum, amounting to £2250, was devoted by the Committee to the foundation of four King's Scholarships, to be competed for by two male and two female students. Instead, however, of being invested separately, the fund was merged in the general property of the Academy, a mistake which eventually led to the discontinuance of the scholarships. For the next ten years the financial condition of the Academy continued to fluctuate. In July 1853 the Committee of Management (which was totally unprofessional in its constitution) summoned the professors, revealed to them the decline of the funded property, and asked their counsel as to the remedies to be adopted. The professors advised that the management should be made entirely professional. This course was so far adopted that a Board of Professors was appointed to advise the Committee.

The first act of this Board (Sept. 1853) was to recommend the discontinuance of the practice of students lodging and boarding on the premises. This recommendation was adopted, and since that time the Academy only receives day students. The Board formed in 1853 was disbanded by Lord Westmorland in 1856, but after his death in 1859 a new Board was formed ; this, however, found itself obliged to resign in 1864. Before its resignation it drew up a memorial to Government, praying for an annual grant. After a conference with a deputation of professors, Mr. Gladstone, then Chancellor of the Exchequer, inserted in the estimates for the year a sum of £500 ' to defray the charge which will come in course of payment during the year ending Mar. 31, 1865, for enabling the Directors of the Royal Academy of Music to provide accommodation for the Institution.' In 1866, upon the change of Administration, suggestions were made to the Committee on the part of the Government, and were renewed personally in 1867 by the then Chancellor of the Exchequer, in consequence of which the Committee was induced to expend the whole of its funds, in order to accommodate the institution to the designs in which it was invited to participate. In 1867, Lord Beaconsfield (then Mr. Disraeli), in reply to a question as to the grant, announced in the House of Commons that ' the Government were of opinion that they would not be authorised in recommending any enlargement of the grant, the results of the institution not being in fact of a satisfactory character.' This was followed by the total withdrawal of the grant, in order (to quote from an official letter addressed to Sir W. Sterndale Bennett) ' simply to give effect to the opinion that it was not so expedient to subsidise a central and quasi-independent association, as to establish a system of musical instruction under the direct control of some Department of Government.' In this emergency the Committee decided to close the establishment. The funds (including the sum devoted to the King's Scholarships) were totally exhausted. The professors met in 1868 to consider what could be done, and generously offered to accept a payment *pro rata*. It was then, however, announced that the Committee had resigned the Charter into the hands of the Queen. Upon this the professors obtained a legal opinion, to the effect that the Charter could not be resigned without the consent of every member of the Academy. As many of the members protested at the time against the resignation of the Charter, it was returned, and by great exertions on the part of the professors, a new Board of Directors was formed under the presidency of the Earl of Dudley, who appointed a new Committee of Management, in which the professional element formed an important ingredient.

From the time of this change the institution has continued to prosper. In 1868, on the return to office of the Liberal Ministry, Mr. Gladstone restored the annual grant of £500. In 1876 the number of pupils had so increased that the lease of the house adjoining the premises in Tenterden Street, No. 5, had to be repurchased out of the savings of the institution. This house was joined on to the original premises, and a concert-room was formed out of part of the two houses, which though small proved a great boon not only to the students for their regular concerts, but to many concert-givers for whose purposes the more extensive rooms of St. James's Hall, Exeter Hall, etc., were too large. In July 1880 William Shakespeare was appointed conductor of the Students' concerts, *vice* Walter Macfarren. He was succeeded in 1886 by Barnby, by Mackenzie in 1888 and by Henry Wood in 1923. It was since the appointment of Mackenzie as Principal in Feb. 1888 that the real tide of prosperity for the institution set in, 6 Tenterden Street and 12 and 13 Dering Street being added to the premises in 1892 and 1898 respectively, and in 1903 the upper part of 3 Tenterden Street, to meet the increase of accommodation required.

In 1911 the lease expired and the Academy moved to its present site, York Gate, Marylebone Road, the new buildings being formally opened[1] on June 22, 1912. A junior department was opened in 1914.

In 1922 there came the centenary celebrations, lasting from July 10 to July 22, during which at the Queen's, Æolian and Duke's Halls, a large amount of music by past and present Academy students was performed, including revivals of Goring Thomas's 'Nadeshda,' Sullivan's ' Yeomen of the Guard ' and Mackenzie's ' Cricket on the Hearth.'

The Duke's Hall, it may be added, is the Academy's own concert-hall, with a seating capacity of 800 and an organ by Norman & Beard which was presented by Mrs. Thomas Threlfall as a memorial to her husband, who for many years was a patron of the institution and chairman of the committee of management.

In 1924, on the retirement of Mackenzie at the end of 30 years of office, J. B. McEwen became Principal.

The following have been the Principals of the Academy from its foundation to the present time :

Crotch (1823–32), Cipriani Potter (1832–59), Charles Lucas (1859–66), William Sterndale Bennett (1866–75), George Alexander Macfarren (1875–87), Alexander Campbell Mackenzie (1888–1924), John Blackwood McEwen (1924).

The Academy is supported by the Government grant, subscriptions, donations and fees from students. It is under the direction of a President (H.R.H. the Duke of Connaught and Strathearn, K.G.), four vice-presidents, about twenty directors, and a Committee of Management, consisting partly of professors of the institution and partly of well-known business men who are so good as to place their powers at the service of the institution. It was Mackenzie's wish that his office as Principal and that of Chairman of this Committee should be separate functions, and accordingly since 1890 this has been the case. Thomas Threlfall was elected to the latter post in 1890, and filled it with zeal and distinguished success till his death in February 1907, when his place was taken by P. L. Agnew. A staff of professors and sub-professors (students) gives instruction in every branch of music, besides which there are classes for languages, diction, elocution, opera, dancing, drama, fencing, and deportment. Students cannot enter for less than a year, nor for a single subject ; the normal course is three years, and all pupils receive an all-round musical training. The library of the institution has been noticed under LIBRARIES.

There are between 60 and 70 scholarships and exhibitions open to competition (not all awarded annually) ; but mention should be made of the noble foundation, by the late Mrs. Ada Lewis Hill, of the fifteen scholarships bearing her name, five of which are awarded each year and tenable for three years. Deserving

[1] An extension of the building, including a well-equipped theatre for operatic rehearsal, was opened by the Duke of Connaught, Oct. 19, 1926.

but indigent musical ability is also assisted by the Students' Aid Fund, of which the interest is appropriated, at the Committee's discretion, towards the reduction of the fees of talented pupils.

Public performances have been given by the pupils of the R.A.M. at various intervals from the date of its foundation. Their locality was sometimes in the Hanover Square Rooms and sometimes at Tenterden Street. The present custom is to have fortnightly concerts of chamber and organ music in the Duke's Hall, and one chamber concert and one orchestral concert at the Queen's Hall every term. Public operatic and dramatic performances are also given from time to time, these being sometimes of works by the students themselves.

For many years the R.A.M. held Local Examinations throughout the kingdom. In 1889 it combined with the R.C.M. for this purpose. See ASSOCIATED BOARD.

The R.A.M. continues its own separate Examination in London (independent of Academy Teaching) of music teachers and performers. This is known as the ' Metropolitan Examination.' Successful candidates at this Examination, which increases annually in popular estimation, receive diplomas certifying to their proficiency, and are created by the directors, Licentiates of the Royal Academy of Music, L.R.A.M.

w. B. S.; with addns. by F. C. and others.

ROYAL ALBERT HALL. This hall originated in a scheme laid before the Commissioners of the Exhibition of 1851 for the erection of a suitable building for the purposes of art and science and to serve as a completion of the memorial to the Prince Consort. The Commissioners gave the site and a guarantee towards the cost of building, which was raised in the main by public subscription. It was formally opened on Mar. 29, 1871. In June of that year a choral concert was given to inaugurate the opening of the International Exhibition held on adjacent ground. This was conducted by Gounod, who had come to England as a consequence of the Franco-Prussian war, and the choir then formed shortly became the ROYAL CHORAL SOCIETY (*q.v.*). Further musical performances of various kinds were given during and in connexion with the exhibition of 1873. In 1874 an important series of choral and orchestral concerts took place, given in conjunction with Messrs. Novello, at which an attempt was made to popularise the best music. For a short time these were given daily and, amongst other things, did a good deal towards making known the music of Wagner. They came to an end with the production in England of Verdi's ' Requiem ' in 1875. Another notable event was the series of 8 Wagner concerts in 1877. Meanwhile the hall was gradually being used for other purposes

than music, and in 1878 an exhibition of fine arts was held. The year 1880 saw the beginning of the ' benefit ' concert and the suitability of the large auditorium for recitals of artists of the greatest public renown, and in 1881 Sims Reeves gave a series of ' farewell ' oratorio concerts.

By raising temporarily the level of the arena, balls on a large scale became practicable, and the hall has been greatly used for these and such things as, in later days, cinema exhibitions and boxing-matches. In 1926 C. B. Cochran undertook the management of the hall.

In 1885, in connexion with the Inventions Exhibition, an important display of musical instruments was on view, the largest and most extensive known. Various ' farewell ' concerts may be mentioned : Prosper Sainton, 1883; Christine Nilsson, 1888; Sims Reeves, 1891; Edward Lloyd, 1900; Patti, 1906; Santley, 1907; and Albani, 1911. The jubilee of the opening of the hall was celebrated by a special concert, attended by the King and Queen, on May 7, 1921. The seating capacity of the hall is about 10,000 ; its inside measurements are : length, 264 ft., and width, 231 ft., while the height of the dome from the floor of the arena is 132 ft. 6 in. The fine organ is by Willis. (See article by H. Klein in *Mus. T.*, Apr., May and June 1921.)　　　　　　N. C. G.

ROYAL ALBERT HALL ORCHESTRA. This organisation was formed under the title of New Symphony Orchestra in 1905 by John Saunders, who acted as leader, Eli Hudson, a prominent flautist of the day, and Charles Draper, the clarinettist, and made its first appearance at a series of Sunday afternoon concerts at the Coronet Theatre, Notting Hill Gate, beginning Oct. 29, and under the conductorship of E. Howard Jones. In 1906 Beecham became conductor, and concerts were given at the Queen's Hall and in many provincial cities, at which numerous British works were produced. In Nov. 1907, the orchestra was incorporated as a limited company, and a provincial tour was made with Kubelik, Landon Ronald conducting. At the close of this, Ronald was appointed permanent conductor, and in March 1909 a series of symphony concerts was begun at the Queen's Hall, which lasted till 1914. In Oct. 1909 the first series of Sunday afternoon concerts was given at the Royal Albert Hall, the last of these being that of the season 1918–19. A short series of Promenade concerts at the Royal Albert Hall, conducted by Beecham and Ronald, May-June 1915, may be mentioned. On Oct. 30, 1920, four more series of Sunday concerts were given by the orchestra at the same hall, but under the title it now bears. For official purposes the original title remains unchanged.

N. C. G.

ROYAL AMATEUR ORCHESTRAL SOCIETY, THE, was established in 1872 by

H.R.H. the Duke of Edinburgh (late Duke of Coburg), who was the first president and leader of the orchestra for many years. J. R. Gow was honorary secretary, and George Mount acted as conductor for the first twenty-six years of the Society's existence, retiring in 1897, when Ernest Ford was appointed. Sir Arthur Sullivan conducted the first concert in 1873, and took a lifelong interest in the institution, which has done much to raise the standard of amateur proficiency in London.          M.

ROYAL ARTILLERY BAND. The band of the Royal Regiment of Artillery was formed in 1762, and may thus claim to be the oldest permanent musical organisation in the country. Antony Rocca appears to have been the first bandmaster, succeeded on his death in 1774 by Georg Kuhler (later known as George Kealer). In 1777 Frederick Wielle was appointed, and O. Schnuphass in 1802, George M'Kenzie, 1805, William G. Collins, 1845, James Smyth, 1854, Cavaliere Ladislao Zavertal, 1881, and E. C. Stretton, the present bandmaster, 1907. The band is maintained by the officers of the Royal Artillery and has, from its inception, been double-banded, that is, a string and military band. In strength it has risen from the modest eight players of 1762 to the full symphony orchestra, or military band, of 107 of the present day. A regular series of vocal, chamber and orchestral concerts was instituted in 1810, at which the performance of classical music was undertaken. These concerts took place at Woolwich. In 1889 there was started the system of giving symphony concerts in London in addition to those at Woolwich, and from Jan. 1895 to May 1905 the band appeared regularly at the Royal Albert Hall on Sunday afternoons. Concerts are now also given from time to time at various R.A. stations. In 1913–14 the band represented British military music at the Auckland Exhibition, and also at the Gothenburg Exhibition of 1924.

ROYAL CHORAL SOCIETY. This choir grew out of the one organised by Gounod on the opening of the Royal Albert Hall in 1871, being taken over in the following year by Barnby (who amalgamated with it his own choir), and giving its first concert on Feb. 12, 1873, a performance of Bach's ' St. Matthew Passion.' It was known at first as the ' Royal Albert Hall Choral Society,' the name being changed to the present title by consent of Queen Victoria in 1888. The repertory of the choir has necessarily been confined in the main to works of great public appeal : ' Messiah,' performed regularly twice annually, formerly three times, ' Elijah,' Berlioz's ' Faust,' Sullivan's ' Golden Legend,' for some years a very popular work, and, in later days, Coleridge-Taylor's ' Hiawatha ' and Elgar's ' Dream of Gerontius.' But during a period of over fifty years many notable choral works have been revived, and some heard

either for the first time, or for the first time in London. Mention may be made of Bach's B minor Mass, Beethoven's Mass in D and ' Choral ' symphony, Brahms's ' Requiem,' Coleridge-Taylor's ' Hiawatha ' first performed in complete form, Dvořák's ' Stabat Mater,' Elgar's ' Apostles,' ' Kingdom ' and ' Dream of Gerontius,' Gounod's ' Redemption,' once a great favourite, many oratorios of Handel and Mendelssohn, Parry's ' Job,' ' King Saul,' ' War and Peace,' ' Blest Pair of Sirens,' and other works, Rossini's ' Stabat Mater,' Saint-Saëns's ' Samson and Delilah,' Smyth's Mass, Stanford's ' Revenge,' ' Voyage of Maeldune,' etc., Vaughan-Williams's ' Sea Symphony,' Verdi's ' Requiem,' (given under the composer's direction at one of the concerts organised in the hall by Messrs. Novello in 1875), and Wagner, ' Parsifal,' the whole work in concert form in 1884, and various operatic selections. Barnby was succeeded on his death in 1896 by Frederick Bridge, who held the post till his retirement in 1922. He was succeeded in turn by H. L. Balfour, who had for some years acted as chorus-master. His appointment was that of general conductor to the society, guest conductors being invited to take charge of a certain proportion of the concerts in each season.

The orchestra employed for the society's concerts was at first composed of the Royal Amateur Orchestral Society augmented by professional players. Difficulties over rehearsals led to the engagement of a professional band only, composed of London's chief instrumentalists.

When the society was first formed the management was largely controlled by the Commissioners of the Exhibition of 1851, through whose instrumentality the hall was built (see ROYAL ALBERT HALL) ; in the autumn of 1875 an independent committee was formed, with the Duke of Edinburgh as its first president. The present governing body consists of amateurs and professional musicians under the presidency of the Duke of Connaught. (See an article on the Royal Albert Hall and Choral Society, by H. Klein, *Mus. T.*, Apr., May and June 1921.)
                                                  N. C. G.

ROYAL COLLEGE OF MUSIC. For information as to the inception of this institution, see NATIONAL TRAINING SCHOOL FOR MUSIC. The R.C.M. was founded by the Prince of Wales at a meeting held at St. James's Palace, Feb. 28, 1882, and was opened by the Prince himself on May 7 of the following year. Negotiations took place with the R.A.M. with the object of uniting the two institutions, but the project came to nothing. The object of the foundation may best be described in the words of the Royal Charter, by which it was incorporated May 23, 1883 :

' *First*, the advancement of the Art of Music by means of a central working and examining body charged with the duty of providing musical instruction of the highest class, and of rewarding with academical degrees and certificates of proficiency and otherwise persons whether educated or not at the College, who on examination may prove themselves worthy of such distinctions and evidences of attainment ;

'Secondly, the promotion and supervision of such musical instruction in schools and elsewhere as may be thought most conducive to the cultivation and dissemination of the Art of Music in the United Kingdom ;

'Lastly, generally the encouragement and promotion of the cultivation of Music as an Art throughout our dominions.'

Like its predecessor, the R.C.M. rests on the basis of endowed scholarships lasting normally three years with the possibility of extension. The funds for these are provided by the interest of money subscribed throughout the country and permanently invested. The College opened with 50 scholars elected by competition, 15 of whom received a maintenance grant in addition to their free musical education. The number of scholarships has been considerably enlarged since. A large number of Council Exhibitions and other valuable prizes are competed for annually. The first number of paying students was 42 ; in 1925 the number was about 600. The Government of the R.C.M., of which the King is Patron, consists of a Council presided over by the Prince of Wales. King Edward VII. as Prince of Wales was the first President ; the Council is divided into Finance and Executive Committees. The Executive head of the R.C.M. is termed Director. The first staff consisted of :

Director : Sir George Grove, D.C.L. ; Board of Professors : J. F. Bridge, Mus.D., H. C. Deacon, Henry Holmes, Mme. Lind Goldschmidt (Jenny Lind), Walter Parratt, C. Hubert H. Parry, Mus.D., Ernest Pauer, C. V. Stanford, Mus.D., Franklin Taylor, A. Visetti. Other principal teachers : Mme. A. Goddard, J. F. Barnett, G. C. Martin, Mus.D., R. Gompertz, O. H. Howell, F. E. Gladstone, Mus.D., J. Higgs, Mus.B., G. Garcia. Registrar : G. Watson, jun.

In 1894, on the resignation of Grove, Parry was appointed Director and filled the post with great distinction until his death in 1918, when Hugh P. Allen, Mus.D. (the present, 1927, Director), was appointed. Other officials of the R.C.M. at this date are George A. Macmillan, D.Litt. (Hon. Secretary), Claude L. C. Aveling, M.A. (Registrar), E. J. N. Polkinhorne, Hon. R.C.M. (Bursar), and Miss Beatrix Darnell (Lady Superintendent).

When the accommodation in the original building, now occupied by the ROYAL COLLEGE OF ORGANISTS (q.v.), became insufficient a new site was granted in Prince Consort Road, and the first stone of the new building was laid on July 8, 1890. The structure, erected by the generosity of the late Mr. Samson Fox, M.I.C.E., was formally opened on May 2, 1894. To this a large concert-room was subsequently added and opened on June 13, 1901. It contains a fine organ, the gift of Sir Hubert Parry. Other important acquisitions to the property of the R.C.M. are the Library of the SACRED HAR-

MONIC SOCIETY (q.v.), acquired through the exertions of Sir P. Cunliffe Owen, and that of the CONCERTS OF ANCIENT MUSIC, given by Queen Victoria (see LIBRARIES). In 1894 Sir George Donaldson presented a large collection of musical instruments, preserved as the Donaldson Museum. (See COLLECTIONS OF MUSICAL INSTRUMENTS.) In 1903 Sir S. Ernest Palmer founded the PATRON'S FUND (q.v.). Other endowments from the same source are the Berkshire Scholarship, and in 1924 the Ernest Palmer Opera Study Fund. Two memorials of Sir Hubert Parry's directorship have been added : the Parry Opera Theatre (Council's memorial) and the Parry Room, a reading-room for students and others in the library, the memorial of members of the College. Both were opened in 1921.

From 1885–1914 the Opera Class gave annual performances in London theatres, which included revivals of several important works. In the earlier years of the R.C.M.'s history numerous orchestral concerts were given in the public concert halls of London and elsewhere. Both these activities were undertaken as a means of fulfilling the last of the three objects named in the Charter. In recent years the performances, both of opera and concert, have been given within the building, and more as a part of the education of the students than as an appeal to the general public. The growth of the R.C.M. itself, as well as changes in general conditions of the art in England, have induced a more intensive policy.

In 1889 the R.C.M. joined with the R.A.M. in forming the ASSOCIATED BOARD (q.v.) for the purpose of conducting local examinations throughout the Empire. The degrees and diplomas conferred by the R.C.M. independently are as follows : G.R.C.M. (Graduate) is granted to pupils of the College of at least three years' standing, who have attained high honours in certain branches of the Associateship examination. A.R.C.M. (Associate) is conferred by examination on candidates from all sources in various branches of the art. F.R.C.M. (Fellow) is conferred by the Council to mark appreciation of services rendered to the art of music and to the College ; the number is limited to 50. Hon. R.C.M. is similarly conferred. The Council has power to create degrees, Doctor and Bachelor of Music. (See DEGREES IN MUSIC.)     C.

ROYAL COLLEGE OF ORGANISTS, an association founded in 1864 on the initiative of R. D. Limpus, with a view (1) to provide a central organisation in London of the profession of organist ; (2) to provide a system of examinations and certificates for the better definition and protection of the profession, and to secure competent organists for the service of the Church ; (3) to provide opportunities for intercourse amongst members of the profession and the discussion of professional topics ; (4) to encourage the composition and study of sacred music.

A council was chosen, and the College was opened at Queen Square, Bloomsbury, and afterwards was located successively at 95 Great Russell Street, Hart Street, Bloomsbury, and Kensington Gore, when, after the opening of the new building of the R.C.M., the old building of that school passed into the tenure of the R.C.O. The College is incorporated under the Companies' Acts ; it consists of a President, Vice-Presidents, Musical Examiners, Hon. Treasurer, Hon. Secretary, Hon. Librarian, Hon. Auditors (two), Fellows, Associates, Hon. Members and Ordinary Members. The Archbishops of Canterbury and York and the Bishop of London are Patrons of the College, and the names of some notable musicians appear among the office-bearers from the beginning up to the present time. A council of not less than 30 Fellows, with the Hon. Secretary and Hon. Treasurer, hold the reins of government, retiring annually ; two-thirds of the number are re-elected with other Fellows who have not served during the preceding year. At the general meeting every July the retiring council present their report on the state of the College.

Arrangements are made for the half-yearly holding of examinations in organ - playing, general knowledge of the organ, harmony, counterpoint, composition, sight-reading and general musical knowledge, after passing which a candidate is entitled to a diploma admitting him to a fellowship in the College. This examination is only open to candidates who have previously been examined for and obtained the certificate of associateship, and to musical graduates of the English Universities. To Dr. E. H. TURPIN (q.v.), for many years Hon. Secretary, was due the proposal to establish a Pension Fund for organists incapacitated by age or illness. Other features of the College work are the Organists' Register, and the prizes for composition. The College was incorporated by Royal Charter in 1893.

The *Calendar of the Royal College of Organists*, issued annually, contains a short history of the College with full information as to its current activities and particularly the regulations for its examinations.      L. M. M., rev.

ROYAL HARMONIC INSTITUTION, see ARGYLL ROOMS.

ROYAL IRISH ACADEMY OF MUSIC, see DUBLIN.

ROYAL MILITARY SCHOOL OF MUSIC, Whitton, Twickenham. Kneller Hall is established on the site of the original mansion of Sir Godfrey Kneller, one time court painter.

Before 1857 bands in the army were not officially recognised, and the bands that then existed were financed and controlled entirely by their own officers. Units competed with one another in the appearance of the band, (dressing their bandsmen in multi-coloured uniforms), and in the number of instruments and capable musicians each possessed. The result of this was that army bands were in a state of chaos, and massed band performances were impossible owing to the different instrumentation and various pitches of these bands. (See PITCH.)

British army bands compared most unfavourably with continental bands at this period, and attention was drawn to the very poor pay given to our bandsmen and the absence of any opportunity to advance their position, which caused bandsmen to purchase their discharge as soon as they acquired a fair proficiency on an instrument, so that they could obtain more lucrative positions in civil life. Musicians obtained the interest of the Duke of Cambridge in military bands. They represented that a bandsman's pay should be increased and that he was capable of being trained as a bandmaster. (At this time bandmasters were, with few exceptions, foreigners.)

The result of these representations was the official recognition of army bands and the establishment of the Royal Military School of Music (1857), to train instrumentalists and bandmasters for army bands.

The institution began in a modest way with four professors, including Herr Schallehn, the Principal or Resident Instructor, and was open ' to the sons of sailors and soldiers who are intended for either service and have shown musical aptitude.'

Later in 1875 the institution was formally taken over by the Government—accommodation was provided for more pupils and the staff of professors increased. The official head of the institution is the Commandant, whose tenure of office is four years, who has a small military staff, including the Director of Music, Lieut. H. E. Adkins, Mus.Bac., L.R.A.M., A.R.C.M. (who is the permanent musical head), and a teaching staff of sixteen professors. The establishment provides for 36 students for training as bandmasters and 144 pupils for training as soloists.

Pupils sent to Kneller Hall must be in possession of an Army Second-Class Certificate of Education, and be good performers on their instruments. In addition to their training on a wind instrument, pupils may be taught a string instrument or the pianoforte. Instruction is also given in the elements of music, elementary harmony, aural training, and an elementary knowledge of military band instrumentation. The pupil's course is for one year.

Candidates for a student's course must be N.C.O.'s, soloists on their instruments, in possession of a First-Class Army Certificate of

Education, and be strongly recommended by their Commanding Officers. Candidates have to pass a qualifying examination in the elements of music, elementary harmony, free counterpoint, musical history and elementary band instrumentation.

A successful candidate on joining Kneller Hall serves a probationary period of six months, and if he proves in any way unsuitable he is returned to his unit. He is first prepared for examination in advanced harmony, free counterpoint, canon and fugue, military band instrumentation and aural training. This examination is conducted by representatives of the War Office, R.A.M. and R.C.M.

When the student qualifies in this examination he turns his attention to conducting, the training and rehearsing of a military band, orchestral concert work, training of a male voice choir, church services, and advanced arranging of compositions for the military band and orchestra.

Each student has to compose a Quick March for a military band, church voluntaries for the orchestra, and a short choral work for male voices. In addition, students attend a comprehensive course which includes an outline of world history, advanced English, correspondence, accounts, the preparation and delivery of lectures, and lessons on musical subjects, and the pronunciation of the names of composers, musical works, and musical terms in German, Italian and French, under the Education Instructor.

During his course at Kneller Hall the student studies in succession the technique of every instrument in the military band.

He is expected to be a fair performer on each, so that he can give elementary instruction in these instruments.

At the end of this course, which lasts about three years, the qualified students are appointed bandmasters to army bands as vacancies occur.

H. E. A.

ROYAL PHILHARMONIC SOCIETY, see PHILHARMONIC SOCIETY.

ROYAL SOCIETY OF MUSICIANS OF GREAT BRITAIN. This Society was founded by the exertions of FESTING (q.v.), and Wiedemann the flautist, who were struck by the appearance of two little boys driving milch asses, who proved to be orphans of a deceased oboe-player named Kytch. They immediately raised subscriptions to relieve the family, and feeling that some permanent establishment was required to meet similar cases, induced the most eminent music-professors of the day to associate themselves together as a Society for that purpose. This excellent work was formally accomplished on April 19, 1738, and amongst its first members were Handel, Boyce, Arne, Christopher Smith, Carey, Cooke, Edward Purcell, Leveridge, Greene, Reading, Hayes, Pepusch and Travers.

In 1739 the members of the Society executed a 'deed of trust,' which was duly enrolled in the Court of Chancery; the signatures of the members, 226 in number, include the most eminent professors of music of the time. The deed recites the rules and regulations for membership and for the distribution of the funds, and provides for regular monthly meetings at the sign of Saint Martin, in St. Martin's Lane. Handel took an especial and active interest in the welfare of the Society, composing concertos and giving concerts for the benefit of its funds, and at his death bequeathing to it a legacy of £1000. The Handel Commemoration held in Westminster Abbey in 1784 brought a further addition of £6000. In 1789 George III. granted the Society a charter, by virtue of which its management is vested in the hands of the ' Governors ' and ' Court of Assistants.' In 1804 the funds of the Society not being in a flourishing condition, the king gave a donation of 500 guineas. Considerable sums have been given or bequeathed to the Society by members of the music profession, amongst them being Signora Storace £1000, Crosdill £1000, Begrez £1000, Schulz £1000, Thomas Molineax, a Manchester bassoon and double-bass player, 1000 guineas.

The Society pays away annually a considerable sum to relieve distress, which amount is provided by donations from the public, subscriptions and donations of members of the Society, and interest on the Society's funded property.

Members of the Society must be professional musicians, and are now of both sexes. The Royal Society of Female Musicians was established in 1839 by several ladies of distinction in the musical profession, amongst others Mrs. Anderson, Miss Birch, Miss Dolby and Miss Mounsey (Mrs. Bartholomew), in consequence of the Royal Society of Musicians having made no provision in their laws for the admission of female members. The two societies were amalgamated in 1886.

There is, says Dr. Burney, ' no lucrative employment belonging to this Society, excepting small salaries to the secretary and collector, so that the whole produce of benefits and subscriptions is net, and clear of all deductions or drawbacks.' The large staff of physicians, surgeons, counsel, solicitors, give their gratuitous services to the Society. The present (1926) secretary is J. F. C. Bennett. The Society's rooms are at No. 12 Lisle Street, Leicester Square, and contain some interesting memorials of music, as well as a collection of portraits, including Handel, two portraits by Hudson and Van der Myn (?); Haydn; Corelli, by Howard; Geminiani, by Hudson; Purcell, by Closterman; C. E. Horn, by Pocock; John Parry, the elder; Sir W. Parsons; J. Sinclair, by Harlowe; Gaetano Crivelli, by Partridge;

Domenico Francesco Maria Crivelli ; J. S. Bach, by Clark of Eton ; Beethoven, a print with autograph presenting it to C. Neate ; W. Dance, a drawing by his brother ; a life-size painting of George III. by Gainsborough ; W. H. Cummings, George Smart and various less distinguished members of the Society, and a plaster bust of Gounod by A. Gilbert, R.A.

w. h. c.

ROYAL VICTORIA HALL, see OLD VIC.

ROYER, JOSEPH NICOLAS PANCRACE (*b.* Bourgogne, *c.* 1700 ; *d.* Paris, Jan. 11, 1755), of noble family, settled in Paris in 1725 as teacher of the harpsichord. He became a musician-in-ordinary to the king, and in 1753 bought from B. de Bury the place of Maître de musique de la chambre du Roy. In 1741 he became conductor at the Opéra, in 1743 inspector and in 1748 director and lessee of the concert spirituel. He composed several operas and ballets, 1 book of sonatas (1740), and 1 book of pièces de clavecin, 1er livre (1746).

E. v. d. s.

ROZE, MARIE HIPPOLYTE, *née* PONSIN (*b.* Paris, Mar. 2, 1846 ; *d.* near Paris, June 21, 1926), received instruction in singing from Mocker at the Conservatoire, and in 1865 gained first prizes in singing and comic opera. She made her début Aug. 16 of that year at the Opéra-Comique as Marie, in Hérold's opera of that name, and at once concluded an engagement for the next three years there. She created the part of Djelma in ' Le Premier jour de Bonheur ' of Auber, at his request, on Feb. 15, 1868. After further instruction from Wartel she appeared at the Opéra as Marguerite in ' Faust ' (Jan. 2, 1870), returned to the Opéra-Comique to create the part of Jeanne in Flotow's ' L'Ombre,' July 7, 1870. After the war she sang for a season at Brussels and elsewhere, and on Apr. 30, 1872, first appeared in England at the Italian Opera, Drury Lane, as Marguerite, and as Marcelline in ' Les Deux Journées,' on its production (for one night only), June 20, 1872. The ensuing seasons, until 1881 (except 1878 and 1880) she sang at that theatre or at Her Majesty's, becoming a great favourite. In 1874 she married an American bass singer, Julius Edson Perkins, who died in the following year at Manchester. In the winter of 1877 she made a highly successful visit to America, returning in 1879 to Her Majesty's Theatre. After singing at the Birmingham Festival of 1882 with great success, she joined the Carl Rosa Company from 1883–89 ; in that time she added to her repertory Fidelio and Elsa, and was the first representative in England of Manon Lescaut in Massenet's opera of that name. Her impersonation of Carmen was her greatest success, as it was full of delicate detail, and presented Bizet's music in an ideal way. She sang the part first in Italian in 1879 in America and

afterwards in London. Scarcely less effective was her Manon in Massenet's opera, first sung by her in English at Liverpool, Jan. 17, 1885, and at Drury Lane on May 7. In 1890 she settled in Paris as a teacher of singing, reappearing at long intervals in London and the English provinces in concerts. She made a farewell tour in 1894 ; her last appearance in London was as late as 1903, when she sang at a concert given by one of her pupils.

A. C.

RUBATO. The word means ' robbed ' (time), and the thing may be defined as the effect of pitch upon duration, a definition which holds also if we extend pitch to mean a cluster of pitches, in counterpoint, harmony or orchestration. In music everything is relative ; no element enters in without modifying, however slightly, other elements. A note held for a certain length at one pitch does not affect us in the same way as when held at another, and this difference of affection is expressed by altering slightly the duration. This alteration is a matter of nice judgment, and the act of *rubato* is a golden opportunity for the exercise of economy, without which it is apt to defeat its own end.

The term has suffered from a misconception. The rule has been given and repeated indiscriminately that the ' robbed ' time must be ' paid back ' within the bar. That is absurd, because the bar line is a notational, not a musical, matter (see BAR). But there is no necessity to pay back even within the phrase : it is the metaphor that is wrong. *Rubato* is the free element in time, and the more it recognises the norm the freer it is. The law which it has to recognise is the course of the music as a whole ; not a bar but a page, not a page but a movement. If it does not do this it becomes spasmodic and unmeaning, like correspondence which is too much underlined.

BIBL.—LUCIAN KAMIENSKI, *Zum ' Tempo Rubato' A. M.* ; HENRY T. FINCK, *Musical Progress : the Disgraceful Tempo Rubato Muddle*, Philadelphia, 1923, with quotations from the preface to some Toccatas by Frescobaldi ; and from Mace's *Musick's Monument* (1676).

A. H. F. S.

RUBEBE (RYBYBE), a mediæval instrument of the viol family. It was larger than the REBEC (*q.v.*) but, like it, came into England from Southern Europe, having been in use under Moorish influence in Spain from the 10th century. It was doubtless evolved from the Arabian Rebaba. During performance the instrument was usually rested on the knee or between the knees, as shown in the Norman carvings of the 12th century, but in the early 14th century we find it played at the shoulder. The body was oval—not pear-shaped like the Rebec —and without the incurvations or waist found in the viol or ' Fithele,' popular at the same period. Jerome of Moravia (*c.* 1260) has left us instructions as to its tuning and fingering : the strings, four in number, were arranged in two pairs and tuned in fifths (tenor G and C) : the compass was an octave and one note, shifts being unknown. A dance tune of the late 13th century (Bodl. Donce, 139) was no doubt originally written for this instrument. Before the Middle Ages closed it was merged into the VIOL (*q.v.*).      F. W. G.

RUBINELLI, GIOVANNI BATTISTA (*b.* Brescia, 1753 ; *d.* there, 1829), celebrated singer, made his first appearance on the stage at the age of 18, at Stuttgart, in Sacchini's ' Calliroe.' For some years he was attached to the Duke of Würtemberg's chapel, but in 1774 he sang at Modena in Paisiello's ' Alèssandro nelle Indie ' and Anfossi's ' Demofoönte.' During the next few years he performed at all the principal theatres in Italy, and in 1786 he came to London. He made a successful début in a pasticcio called ' Virginia,' his own part in which was chiefly composed by Tarchi. He next sang with Mara, in ' Armida,' and in Handel's ' Giulio Cesare,' revived for him, with several interpolations from Handel's other works. These are said to have been most admirably sung by Rubinelli.

After his season in London he returned to Italy, where he had enormous success at Vicenza and Verona, in 1791 and 1792, in ' La morte di Cleopatra ' of Nasolini, and ' Agesilao ' of Andreozzi. In 1800 he left the stage, and settled at Brescia.      F. A. M.

RUBINI, GIOVANNI BATTISTA (*b.* Romano, near Bergamo, Apr. 7, 1795 ; *d.* there, Mar. 2, 1854), one of the most celebrated tenor singers.

After a period of youthful discouragements he got a small engagement at Pavia, then another at Brescia for the Carnival ; he next appeared at the San Moisè theatre at Venice, and lastly at Naples, where the director, Barbaja (according to Escudier), engaged him to sing with Pellegrini and Nozzari, in two operas written for him by Fioravanti. (The name of one of these operas, ' Adelson e Salvina,' is identical with that of an early work of Bellini's, produced about this time.) With the public Rubini was successful, but so little does Barbaja appear to have foreseen his future greatness that he wished to part with him at the end of the first year's engagement, and only consented to retain his services at a reduced salary. Rubini preferred making some sacrifice to leaving Naples, where he was taking lessons of Nozzari, and he acceded to Barbaja's conditions, which very soon, however, had to be rescinded, owing to Rubini's brilliant successes at Rome (in ' La gazza ladra ') and at Palermo. Some time in 1819 he married Mlle. Chomel, known at Naples as La Comelli, a singer of some contemporary celebrity, a Frenchwoman by birth, and pupil of the Paris Conservatoire.

His first appearance at Paris was on Oct. 6, 1825, in the ' Cenerentola,' and was followed by others in ' Otello ' and ' La donna del

lago.' He was hailed unanimously as ' King of Tenors,' but he was still bound by his engagement with Barbaja, who only yielded him for six months to the Théâtre-Italien, claiming him back at the end of that time to sing at Naples, then at Milan and at Vienna.

Up to this time his laurels had been won in Rossini's music, on which his style was first formed, but Rubini was the foundation and *raison d'être* of the whole phase of Italian opera that succeeded the Rossinian period. He and Bellini were said to have been born for one another. During the whole composition of ' Il pirata,' Rubini stayed with Bellini, singing each song as it was finished. Donizetti, again, achieved no great success until the production of ' Anna Bolena,' his *thirty-second* opera, in which the tenor part was written expressly for Rubini, who achieved in it some of his greatest triumphs. It was followed by ' Lucia,' ' Lucrezia,' ' Marino Faliero ' and others, in which a like inspiration was followed by the same result.

Rubini first came to England in 1831, when freed from his engagement with Barbaja, and from that time till 1843 he divided each year between Paris and this country, singing much at concerts and provincial festivals, as well as at the Opera, and creating a *furore* wherever he went.

In 1843 he started with Liszt on a tour through Holland and Germany, but the two separated at Berlin, and Rubini went on alone to St. Petersburg, where he created an enthusiasm verging on frenzy. By his first concert alone he realised 54,000 francs. The Emperor Nicholas made him ' Director of Singing ' in the Russian dominions, and a colonel into the bargain.

In the summer of this year Rubini went to Italy, giving some representations at Vienna by the way. He returned to Russia in the winter of 1844, but finding his voice permanently affected by the climate resolved to retire from public life. He bought a property near Romano, where he died.

Rubini's voice extended from E of the bass clef to B of the treble, in chest notes, besides commanding a falsetto register as far as F or even G above that. A master of every kind of florid execution, and delighting at times in its display, no one seems ever to have equalled him when he turned these powers into the channel of emotional vocal expression, nor to have produced so magical an effect by the singing of a simple, pathetic melody, without ornament of any kind. He indulged too much in the use of head-voice : some of his greatest effects were produced by an excessive use of strong contrasts between *piano* and *forte*, and he was the earliest to use that thrill of the voice known as the *vibrato*. To him, too, was originally

PASTA

From a water-colour drawing by A. E. Chalon, R.A.,
in the Victoria and Albert Museum

RUBINI

From a water-colour drawing by A. E. Chalon, R.A., bequeathed
by the late W. Barclay Squire to the R.C.M.

due that species of musical sob produced by the repercussion of a prolonged note before the final cadence, which, electrifying at first as a new effect, has become one of the commonest of vocal vulgarisms. But such was his perfection of finish, such the beauty of his expression, such his thorough identification of himself, not with his dramatic impersonations but with his songs, that his hold on the public remained unweakened to the last, even when his voice was a wreck and his peculiarities had become mannerisms.          F. A. M., abridged.

RUBINI, NICOLO, of Modena, pupil of Orazio Vecchi, from 1607–25 cornettist in Modena court chapel. He wrote a book on counterpoint ; composed 2 books of madrigals (1610, 2 v., 1615, 5 v., 1 book motets, 4-10 v. 1606), and 1 book canzone, 3 v. (1613) (Q.-L.).

RUBINSTEIN, (1) ANTON GREGOR (b. Wechwotynetz, Volhynia, Russia, Nov. 28, 1830[1] ; d. Peterhof, Nov. 20, 1894), an eminent composer of Jewish parentage, and one of the greatest pianists the world has ever seen. He received his first musical instruction from his mother, and afterwards from a pianoforte-teacher in Moscow named Villoing. As early as 1839 he made his first public appearance in Moscow, and in the following year undertook a concert-tour with his teacher, journeying to Paris, where he made the acquaintance of Liszt, who was then teaching in that city, and under whose advice he there pursued his studies. A year later he made a more extended tour, going to England (1842), and thence to Holland, Germany and Sweden. In 1845 he went to study composition with Dehn in Berlin. From 1846–48 he passed in Vienna and Pressburg, teaching on his own account. In 1848 he returned to Russia, where the Grand Duchess Helen nominated him Kammervirtuos. After studying diligently in St. Petersburg for eight years he appeared as a fully-fledged artist with piles of original compositions, first in Hamburg and then all over Germany, where he found enthusiastic audiences and willing publishers. His early operas, to Russian words, were performed as follows : ' Dimitri Donskoi,' 1852 ; ' Die sibirischen Jäger,' 1852 ; ' Toms der Narr,' 1853, and ' Hadji-Abrek ' were not performed. From this time his fame as a pianist and composer spread rapidly over Europe and America. He again visited England in 1857, and made his first appearance at the Philharmonic on May 18. In 1858 he returned home again, gave brilliant concerts in St. Petersburg, Moscow, etc., and settled in the former city. At this period he was appointed imperial concert-director, with a life-pension. Thenceforward he worked in conjunction with

[1] Nov. 30 is given in most books of reference, as the equivalent of Nov. 18 (O.S.). In his Autobiography (see below) he declares Nov. 16 (O.S.) to be the actual day, but that the 18th had been so long regarded as his birthday that he had no intention of changing it. Nov. 16 (O.S.) is the equivalent of Nov. 28.

his friend Carl Schuberth for the advancement of music in Russia, and had the merit of being the founder of the St. Petersburg Conservatorium in 1862, remaining its principal until 1867.

On leaving Russia he made another triumphant tour through the greater part of Europe, which lasted till the spring of 1870. When in his native country, in 1869, the Emperor decorated him with the Vladimir Order, which raised him to noble rank. In 1870 he rested awhile, and expressed the intention of retiring from public life ; but it was not likely that this desire could be fulfilled. He held the directorship of the · Philharmonic Concerts and Choral Society in Vienna for the next year or two, and this was followed by fresh concert tours. In 1872–73 he toured in America. Every year the same threat of retirement was made, but the entreaties of the public, and, probably, the desire of providing for his wife and family, brought the gifted genius before us again and again. He gave a set of farewell recitals all over Europe in 1885–1887, and in 1887–90 he again undertook the direction of the St. Petersburg Conservatorium, and from the latter year lived for a time in Dresden. In 1889 he celebrated his artistic jubilee and published an Autobiography.

We have said that Rubinstein's first visit to London was in 1842. He was then only just 12. Mendelssohn and Thalberg were both there, and the Philharmonic was thus already occupied. Mention of him is to be found in Moscheles's Diary for 1842 (Leben, ii. 90), where he is spoken of as ' a rival to Thalberg . . . a Russian boy whose fingers are as light as feathers, and yet as strong as a man's.' In the Musical and Dramatic Review of May 28, 1842, he is mentioned. He did not return to this country till 1857, when he appeared at the Philharmonic on May 18, playing his own concerto in G. He came back in the following year, played again at the Philharmonic on June 7, and at the Musical Union, May 11. In 1869 he came a fourth time, and played at the Musical Union only (May 18, June 1). In 1876 he made his fifth visit, played at the Philharmonic, May 1, and gave four recitals in St. James's Hall. In 1877 he again gave recitals, and conducted his · ' Ocean ' symphony (six movements) at the Crystal Palace, Apr. 21 ; he conducted his ' Dramatic ' symphony, and played Beethoven's concerto in G, at the Crystal Palace on June 4. In 1881 he gave another series of recitals at St. James's Hall : his opera ' The Demon ' was brought out in Italian at Covent Garden on June 21, and his ' Tower of Babel,' with other music, at the Crystal Palace on June 11. In May and June 1886, he gave a final set of seven historical recitals in St. James's Hall.

Rubinstein's playing was not only remarkable for the absolute perfection of *technique*, in which he was the only rival Liszt ever had, but there was the fire and soul which only a true and genial composer can possess. He could play a simple piece of Haydn or Mozart so as positively to bring tears into the eyes of his hearers, but, on the other hand, he would sometimes fall a prey to a strange excitement which caused him to play in the wildest fashion. An example (though hardly a commendable one) of his perfect mastery over tone is to be found in his performance of the Funeral March of Chopin's sonata in B♭ minor. Regardless of the composer's intentions, he began it *ppp*, proceeding *crescendo*, with perfect gradation, up to the trio, after which he began again *ff* and with an equally long and subtle *diminuendo* ended as softly as he began.

The compositions of Rubinstein may be considered as the legitimate outcome of Mendelssohn; they contain a fine broad vein of melody supported by true and natural harmony, and thorough technical skill. But they show also the fatal gift of fluency, and the consequent lack of self-criticism and self-restraint. Rubinstein wrote in every department of music, but his songs and chamber music are all that can be called really popular, although his ' Ocean Symphony ' was during his life known all over the world.[1] This is undoubtedly one of his best works, the ideas throughout being vivid and interesting, while the workmanship shows unusual care. From the composer's having added an extra Adagio and Scherzo after the first appearance of this symphony we may presume he had a particular regard for it, though to risk wearying an audience by inordinate length is scarcely the way to recommend a work to their favour. The ' Dramatic ' symphony (op. 95) was formerly admired. His pianoforte concertos are very brilliant and effective, especially that in G (op. 45); his violin concerto (op. 46) is a fine work, though but little known. The Persian Songs (op. 34) are perhaps the most popular of his vocal works, but there are many very striking and successful specimens among his other songs— ' Es blinkt der Thau ' and ' Die Waldhexe ' for instance—and the duets are full of beauty and passion. The numerous drawing-room pieces which he wrote for the piano are far superior to most of their class, his writing for the instrument being invariably most brilliant, as is but natural in so great a pianist. In his chamber-music he was apt to give the piano an undue prominence; the quintet in F (op. 55) is almost a pianoforte concerto in disguise. His operas and oratorios met with qualified success; he had a preference for sacred subjects, which are but ill fitted for the stage.

[1] First performed in London by Musical Art Union (Klindworth), May 31, 1861; with extra movements, Crystal Palace, Apr. 12, 1877; Philharmonic, June 11, 1879.

List of dramatic works (including the oratorios, or sacred operas, which were all intended for stage-performance) :

Dimitri Donskoi. St. Petersburg, 1852.
Sibirskije Ochotnikie. St. Petersburg, 1852. (' Die sibirischen Jäger.')
Foma Duratchok (' Toms, der Narr '). St. Petersburg, 1853.
Mest (' Die Rache '). St. Petersburg, 1858.
Hadji-Abrek (apparently not performed).
Die Kinder der Haide, five acts. Vienna, 1861.
Feramors (Lalla Rookh), three acts. Dresden, 1863.
Der Thurm zu Babel (' The Tower of Babel '). Königsberg, 1870 (see op. 80).
Der Dämon, three acts. St. Petersburg, 1875. As ' Il Demonio,' Covent Garden, 1881.
Die Makkabäer, three acts. Berlin, 1875.
Das verlorene Paradies (Düsseldorf, 1875). A preliminary performance had taken place in 1855 under Liszt at Weimar (see op. 54).
Nero, four acts. Hamburg, 1879.
Kalashnikov Moskovski Kupets (' Der Kaufmann von Moskau '). St. Petersburg, 1880.
Die Rebe (' La Vigne '), 1882.
Sulamith. Hamburg, 1883.
Unter Räubern, one act (Hamburg, 1883, played before ' Sulamith ').
Der Papagei, one act. Hamburg, 1884.
Moses (1887), see op. 112.
Gorjushka (' Die Kummervolle '). St. Petersburg, 1889.
Christus. Berlin, 1888, Bremen, 1895, on the stage (see op. 117).

The complete list of Rubinstein's numbered works is as follows :

| Op. | | Op. | |
|---|---|---|---|
| 1. | 6 little Songs in Low German dialect. Voice and PF. Schreiber. | 32. | 6 Songs from Heine. Voice and PF. Kistner. |
| 2. | 2 Fantasias on Russian themes. PF. solo. Schreiber. | 33. | 6 Songs. Voice and PF. Kistner. |
| 3. | 2 Melodies for PF. solo (F, B) Schreiber. | 34. | 12 Persian Songs. V. and PF. Kistner. |
| 4. | Mazourka-Fantaisie. PF. solo (G). Schreiber. | 35. | 2nd PF. Concerto (F). Schreiber. |
| 5. | Polonaise, Cracovienne and Mazurka. PF. solo. Schreiber. | 36. | 12 Songs from the Russian. Voice and PF. Schreiber. |
| 6. | Tarantelle, PF. solo (B). Schreiber. | 37. | Akrostichon (Laura) for PF. solo. Schreiber. |
| 7. | Impromptu-Caprice, ' Hommage à Jenny Lind ' PF. solo (A minor). Schreiber. | 38. | Suite (10 Nos.) for PF. solo. Schreiber. |
| 8. | 6 Songs (words from the Russian). Voice and PF. Senff. | 39. | 2nd Sonata for PF. and Vcello (G). B. & H. |
| 9. | Octet in D for PF. V., Viola, Vcello, Bass, Fl., Clar., and Horn. Peters. | 40. | 1st Symphony for Orchestra (F). Kahnt. |
| | | 41. | 3rd Sonata for PF. solo (F). B. & H. |
| 10. | Kamennoi-Ostrow. 24 Portraits for PF. Schott. | 42. | 2nd Symphony, ' Ocean ' (C). Senff. |
| 11. | 3 Pieces for PF. and V.; 3 do. for PF. and Vcello; 3 do. for PF. and Viola. Schuberth. | 43. | Triumphal Overture for Orchestra. Schott. |
| | | 44. | ' Soirées de St.-Pétersbourg.' for PF. solo (6 pieces). Kahnt. |
| 12. | 1st Sonata for PF. solo (E). Peters. | 45. | 3rd PF. Concer to (G). B. B. |
| 13. | 1st Sonata for PF. and V. (G). Peters. | 46. | Concerto, Violin and Orch. (G). Peters. |
| 14. | ' The Ball,' Fantasia in 10 Nos. for PF. solo. B. B.[2] | 47. | 3 String Quartets (Nos. 4, 5, 6, E min., B♭, D min.). B. & H. |
| 15. | 2 Trios. PF., V., and Vcello (F, G min.). Hofmeister. | 48. | 12 Two-part Songs (from the Russian) with PF. Senff. |
| 16. | Impromptu, Berceuse and Serenade. PF. solo. Hofmeister. | 49. | Sonata for PF. and Viola (F min.). B. & H. |
| | | 50. | 6 ' Charakter-Bilder.' PF. duet Kahnt. |
| 17. | 3 String Quartets (G, C min., F). B. & H.[3] | 51. | 6 Morceaux for PF. Senff. |
| 18. | 1st Sonata for PF. and Vcello (D). B. & H. | 52. | 3rd Trio. PF. and Strings (B♭). Senff. |
| 19. | 2nd Sonata for PF. and V. (A min.). B. & H. | 53. | 6 Preludes and Fugues in free style. PF. solo. Peters. |
| 20. | 2nd Sonata for PF. solo (C min.). B. & H. | 54. | ' Paradise Lost.' Sacred Opera after Milton, in 3 parts. Senff. |
| 21. | 3 Caprices for PF. solo (F♯, D, E♭). B. & H. | 55. | Quintet for PF. and Wind (F). Schuberth. |
| 22. | 3 Serenades for PF. solo (F, G min., E♭). B. & H. | 56. | 3rd Symphony (A). Schuberth. |
| 23. | 6 Études for PF. solo. Peters. | 57. | 6 Songs. Voice and PF. Senff. |
| 24. | 6 Preludes for PF solo. Peters. | 58. | Scena ed Aria, ' E dunque vero ? ' Sop. and Orch. Schott. |
| 25. | 1st PF. Concerto (E min.). Peters. | 59. | String Quintet (F). Senff. |
| 26. | Romance and Impromptu. PF. solo (F, A minor). Schreiber. | 60. | Concert Overture in B♭. Senff. |
| | | 61. | 3 Partsongs for Male Voices. Schreiber. |
| 27. | 9 Songs (words from Russian). Voice and PF. Schreiber. | 62. | 6 Partsongs for Mixed Voices. Schreiber. |
| 28. | Nocturne (G♭) and Caprice (E♭) for PF. solo. Kistner. | 63. | ' Die Nixe.' Alto Solo, Female Chorus, and Orch. Senff. |
| 29. | 2 Funeral Marches. PF. solo. —1. For an Artist (F min.); 2. For a Hero (C min.). Kistner. | 64. | 5 Fables by Kriloff. Voice and PF. Senff. |
| | | 65. | 1st Concerto for Vcello and Orch. (A min.). Senff. |
| 30. | Barcarolle (F. min.); Allº Appass. (D min.) for PF. solo. Kistner. | 66. | Quartet. PF. and Strings (C). Senff. |
| 31. | 6 4-part Songs for Male Voices. Kistner. | 67. | 6 Two-part Songs with PF. Senff. |

[2] B.B. = Bote & Bock.    [3] B. & H. = Breitkopf & Härtel.

Op.
68. 'Faust.'    Musical portrait, for Orch. Siegel.
69. 5 Morceaux for PF. solo. Siegel.
70. 4th PF. Concerto (D min.). Senff.
71. 3 Morceaux. PF. solo. Siegel.
72. 6 Songs for a Low Voice and PF. Senff.
73. Fantaisie for 2 Pianos (F). Senff.
74. 'Der Morgen.' Cantata for Male Voices and Orch. (from the Russian). Senff.
75. 'Album de Peterhof.' 12 Pieces. PF. solo. Senff.
76. 6 Songs for Voice and PF. Senff.
77. Fantaisie for PF. (E min.). Senff.
78. 12 Songs from the Russian. Voice and PF. Senff.
79. 'Ivan the Terrible.' Musical portrait for Orch. B.B.
80. 'The Tower of Babel.' Sacred opera in one act. Senff. Chappell.
81. Études for PF. solo. B.B.
82. Album of National Dances (6) for PF. solo. B.B.
83. 10 Songs. Voice and PF. B.B.
84. Fantasia for PF. and Orch. (C). Senff.
85. 4th Trio. PF. and Strings (A). Lewy.
86. Romance and Caprice for Violin and Orch. Senff.
87. 'Don Quixote.' Musical portrait. Humoreske for Orch. Senff.
88. Theme and Variations for PF. solo (G). Senff.
89. Sonata for PF. duet (D). Senff.
90. 2 String Quartets (Nos. 7, 8, G min., E min.). Senff.
91. Songs and Requiem for Mignon (from Goethe's 'Wilhelm Meister') for Solos, Chorus, and PF. Senff.
92. 2 Scenas for Contralta and Orchestra. No. 1. 'Hecuba'; No. 2. 'Hagar in the desert.' Senff.

Op.
93. 9 Books of Miscellaneous Pieces (12) for PF. solo. Senff.
94. 5th PF. Concerto (Eb). Senff.
95. 4th Symphony, 'Dramatic' (D min.). Senff.
96. 2nd Concerto. Vcello and Orch. Senff.
97. Sextuor for Strings (D).Senff.
98. 3rd Sonata. PF. and V. (B min.). Senff.
99. Quintet. PF. and Strings (G min.). Senff.
100. 4th Sonata for PF. solo (A min.). Senff.
101. 12 Songs. Voice and PF. Senff.
102. Caprice russe. PF. and Orch. Senff.
103. Bal costumé. Set of characteristic pieces (20) for PF. 4 hands. B.B.
104. Élégie; Variations; Étude PF. solo. B.B.
105. A series of Russian songs. Voice and PF. B.B.
106. 2 String Quartets (Nos. 9, 10, Ab, F min.).
107. 5th Symphony (G min.). In memory of the Grandduchess Hélène Paulowna. Senff.
108. 5th Trio for PF. and Strings in C minor.
109. Soirées Musicals. 9 PF. pieces.
110. Eroica, Fantasia for PF. and Orchestra.
111. 6th Symphony (A minor).
112. 'Moses,' a Biblical opera in 8 tableaux. Part I. containing four tableaux (Bilder), was published by Senff, 1888.
113. Concertstück for PF. and Orch.
114. Akrostichon, for PF. solo.
115. Songs.
116. Concert-overture, 'Antony and Cleopatra.'
117. Christus, Biblical Opera.
118. Six PF. solos.
119. Suite in Eb for orchestra, in six movements.

Without opus numbers appeared the following:
Symphonic poem, 'Russij.' Moscow, 1882.
Fantasia eroica for orchestra.
Ouverture solenuelle, for orchestra, with organ and chorus (posth.). Three barcarolles (A minor, G, and C minor).
Pianoforte pieces :—' Valse caprice,' E flat, and ' Ungarische Phantasie,' ' Russische Serenade,' ' Phantasie,' 3 ' Morceaux caractéristiques,' 6 preludes, cadenzas to Beethoven's pianoforte concertos, and to Mozart's concerto in D minor, arrangement of the march in Beethoven's ' Ruins of Athens.'

BIBLIOGRAPHY

Autobiography (German, 1889; trans. English by Aline Delano, 1890).
Other writings by A. Rubinstein include *Die Musik und ihre Meister* (1892); *Erinnerungen aus 50 Jahren* (Russian, 1892; trans. German by E. Kretschmann, 1895); *Gedankenkorb* (supplement to *Die Musik und ihre Meister*, 1897).
Biographies by W. Baskin (1886). N. Lissowski (1889), A. MacArthur (1889), and Sandra Droucker (1904).

(2) NICHOLAS, his younger brother (b. Moscow, June 2, 1835; d. Paris, Mar. 23, 1881), was also a fine pianist and no mean composer, though overshadowed by the fame of his great brother. He studied under Kullak and Dehn in Berlin during 1844-46. In 1859 he founded at Moscow the Russian Musical Society, which gave twenty concerts each year; and in 1864 the Conservatorium, and was head of both till his death. He it was who brought forward Tchaikovsky's early compositions and the latter's trio was dedicated to his memory (see TCHAIKOVSKY). In 1861 he visited England, and played twice at the Musical Union (June 4, 18). In 1878 he gave four orchestral concerts of Russian music in the Trocadéro at Paris with great success. He died of consumption on his way to Nice for his health. Among his most famous pupils were

TANEIEV, SILOTI and SAUER. The Musical Society gave annual concerts in his memory, on the anniversaries of his birth and death.[1]

RUBINSTEIN, JOSEPH—no relation of the foregoing (b. Staro Konstantinov, Russia, Feb. 8, 1847; d. Lucerne, Sept. 15, 1884)—acquired some fame as a pianist and composer of drawing-room music. He also obtained an unenviable notoriety through certain newspaper articles in the *Bayreuther Blätter* signed with his name, and attacking Schumann and Brahms in a most offensive and vindictive manner. He made some good pianoforte transcriptions of the works of Wagner, of whom he was an ardent if not very judicious propagandist. He committed suicide.

F. C.

RUCKERS, harpsichord-makers of Antwerp, who were working as masters between 1579 and 1667 or later, the first of whom, Hans Ruckers, is always credited with great improvements in keyboard instruments. It is certain that the tone of the Ruckers harpsichords has never been surpassed for purity and beauty of tone-colour, and from this quality they remained in use in England, as well as in France and the Netherlands, until harpsichords and spinets were superseded, at the end of the 18th century, by the pianoforte. The art of harpsichord-making, as exemplified in London by Kirkman and Shudi, was directly derived from Antwerp and the Ruckers. Time seemed to have no effect with the Ruckers instruments. They were decorated with costly paintings in this country and France, when a hundred years old and more. New keys and new jacks replaced the old ones; so long as the sound-board has stood, the 'silvery sweet' tone has lasted. As a record we have catalogued all the existing instruments we have seen or can hear of, appending the list to this notice.

In John Broadwood's books, 1772-73, are several entries concerning the hiring of Ruker, Rooker and Rouker harpsichords to his customers; to the Duchess of Richmond, Lady Pembroke, Lady Catherine Murray, etc. etc. In 1790 Lord Camden bought a 'double Ruker': in 1792 Mr. Williams bought another, the price charged for each being twenty-five guineas. These entries corroborate the statement of James Broadwood (*Some Notes*, 1838, printed privately 1862) that many Ruckers harpsichords were extant and in excellent condition fifty years before he wrote. He specially refers to one that was twenty years before in possession of Mr. Preston, the publisher, reputed to have been Queen Elizabeth's, and sold when Nonsuch Palace was demolished. To have been hers Hans Ruckers the elder must be credited with having made it.

[1] The articles on both the Rubinsteins were unsigned in the first edition and their authorship is unknown. They were considerably remodelled for the second edition and have been subjected to further revision for this one.

If the tone caused, as we have said, the long preservation of the Ruckers clavecins, on the other hand the paintings which adorned them not unfrequently caused their destruction. A case in point is the instrument of the Parisian organist, Balbâtre, whom Burney visited when on his famous tour. Burney says it was painted inside and out with as much delicacy as the finest coach or snuff-box he had ever seen. Inside the cover was the story of Rameau's 'Castor and Pollux,' the composer, whom Burney had seen some years before, being depicted crowned with a wreath. He describes the tone as delicate rather than powerful (he would be accustomed in London to the sonorous pompous Kirkmans, which he so much admired), and the touch, in accordance with the French practice of quilling, as very light. This instrument was then more than a hundred years old, perhaps more than a hundred and fifty. On the front board above the keys is inscribed a complete piece of clavecin music, ' Pastorale par Mr. Balbastre, le 6 Aoust, 1767,' beginning:

etc.

The stand for this instrument is rococo, and gilt. We learn more of its fate from Rimbault,[1] who tells us that it became the property of Mr. Goding, of London, who sacrificed Ruckers's work to display the paintings by Boucher and Le Prince that had adorned it on a new grand piano made for the purpose by Zeitter. This maker showed respect for his predecessor by preserving the sound-board, which he converted into a music-box, the inscription 'Joannes Ruckers me fecit Antverpiae' being transferred to the back. This box ultimately became Rimbault's ; the piano was sold at Goding's sale by Christie & Manson in 1857. In the same house (Carlton House Terrace), and sold by auction at the same time for £290, was an Andries Ruckers harpsichord that had also been made into a pianoforte by Zeitter. In this instrument the original sound-board, dated 1628, was preserved. The sound-hole contained the rose (No. 6) of this maker. The present compass of the piano is five octaves F—F. Inside the top is a landscape with figures, and outside, figures with musical instruments on a gold ground. Round the case on gold are dogs and birds, a serpent and birds, etc. All this decoration is 18th-century work. The instrument is on a Louis Quinze gilt stand.

It was this intimate combination of the decorative arts with music that led to the clavecin and clavichord makers of Antwerp becoming members of the artists' guild of St. Luke in that city. They were enrolled in the first instance as painters or sculptors. We must however, go farther back than Hans Ruckers and his sons to estimate truly their position

[1] The Pianoforte, 1860, p. 76.

and services as clavecin makers. For this retrospect the pamphlet of the Chevalier Léon de Burbure — Recherches sur les facteurs de clavecins et les luthiers d'Anvers (Brussels, 1863), supplies valuable information. We learn that at the end of the 15th and beginning of the 16th centuries, precisely as in England and Scotland at the same period, the clavichord was in greater vogue than the clavecin ; possibly because clavecins were then always long and sometimes trapeze-shaped. It must be remembered that the names Clavicordio in Spain, Clavicordo in Italy and Clavicorde in France, have been always applied to the quilled instruments. We are not, therefore, sure whether old references to the clavichord are to be taken as describing a plectrum or a tangent keyboard instrument. About the year 1500 the clavecin had been made in the clavichord shape in Venice, and called spinet. (See SPINET.) This new form must have soon travelled to the Low Countries, and have superseded the clavichord as it did in England and France about the same epoch.

A clavecin maker named Josse Carest was admitted in 1523 to the St. Luke's guild as a sculptor and painter of clavichords (literally ' Joos Kerrest, clavecordmaker, snyt en scildert ').[2] Another Carest had been accepted in 1519 as an apprentice painter of clavecins (' Goosen Kareest, schilder en Klavecimbelmaker, gheleert by Peeter Mathys '). This is an earlier instance of the name Clavecin than that quoted by M. de Burbure as the oldest he had found in Belgium, viz. a house in the parish of Notre Dame, Antwerp, which, in 1532, bore the sign of ' de Clavizimbele.' No doubt at that time both clavecins and clavichords were in use in Antwerp, but in a few years we hear of the latter no more ; and the clavecin soon became so important that, in 1557, Josse Carest headed a petition of the clavecin-makers to be admitted to the privileges of the guild as such, and not, in a side way, merely as painters and sculptors of their instruments. Their prayer was granted and the ten petitioners were exempted from the production of ' masterworks,' but their pupils and all who were to come after them [3] were bound to exhibit masterworks, being clavecins, oblong or with bent sides ('viercante oft gehoecte clavisimbale,' square or grand as we should say), of five feet long or more ; made in the workshops of master experts, of whom two were annually elected ; and to have the mark, design or scutcheon, proper to each maker (syn eygen marck, teecken, oft wapene), that is, a recog-

[2] See De Liggeren en andere Historische Archieven der Antwerpsche Sint Lucasgilde. Rombouts en Van Lerius. 2 vols. Baggerman, Antwerp ; Nijhoff, The Hague. In the Museum of the Conservatoire of Music, Brussels, there is a spinet inscribed IOES KAREST DE COLONIA with the date 1548 (No. 1587). The case is in the trapeze shape of the Italian instruments, as in A.4 by Hans Ruckers the elder (1591).
[3] Later on, tuners also became members of the guild. For instance Michel Colyns, Claversingelstelder, in 1631–32 ; who was, however, the son of a member.

nised trade-mark on each instrument. We will give these trade-marks of the members of the Ruckers family from sketches kindly supplied by (the late) Abel Régibo, of Renaix in Belgium; three, belonging to Hans and his two sons, having been already published by Edmond van der Straeten in his monumental work *La Musique aux Pays-Bas*, vol. iii. (Brussels, 1875).[1] It is at once evident that such regulations tended to sound work. The trade-marks we have more particularly described under Rose. They were usually made of lead, gilt, and were conspicuous in the sound-holes of the instruments.

Some of the contemporary Italian keyboard-instruments might be taken to give a general idea of what the Antwerp ones were like prior to the improvements of Hans Ruckers the elder. In the preparation of the sound-boards the notion of the sound-chest of Lute and Psaltery prevailed. Ruckers adhered to this principle, but being a tuner and perhaps a builder of organs, he turned to the organ as a type for an improved clavecin, and while holding fast to *timbre* as the chief excellence and end of musical instrument making, introduced different tone colours and combined them after organ analogies and by organ contrivances of added keyboards and registers. It is doubtful what changes of construction Hans Ruckers made in the harpsichord—perhaps the octave strings only. Yet a clavicembalo by Domenico di Pesaro, dated 1590, in the Victoria and Albert Museum, has the octave strings with two stops. Ruckers's great service may after all have only been to improve what others had previously introduced. It is nearly certain that harpsichords with double keyboards and stops for different registers existed before his time, and their introduction may be attributed to the great favour the Claviorganum, or combined spinet and organ, was held in during the 16th century. The researches of M. Edmond van der Straeten[2] have done much to bring into prominence the great use of the Claviorganum at an early time; see Rabelais, who, before 1552, described Carêmeprenant as having toes like an 'épinette órganisée.' The merit of Hans Ruckers,[3] however, traditionally attributed to him, was his placing the octave as a fixture in the long clavecin, boldly attaching the strings to hitch-pins on the sound-board (strengthened beneath for the purpose) and by the addition of another keyboard, also a fixture, thus establishing a model which remained dominant for large instruments until the end of the clavecin manufacture.[4]

[1] Burney refers to these marks when writing about the Ruckers.
[2] *La Musique aux Pays-Bas*, vol. viii. Brussels, 1885.
[3] On the inventions of H. Ruckers the elder, see Hipkins's *Pianoforte Primer*, p. 81.
[4] The end of the manufacture for Antwerp is chronicled by M. de Burbure in one seen by him—he does not say whether single or double—made by a blind man, and inscribed 'Joannes Heineman me fecit A° 1795, Antwerpiae.' The latest harpsichord made (apart from modern revivals) seems to be an instrument by Clementi, dated 1802, and shown at the Bologna Exhibition of 1888.

An interesting chapter is devoted to the Ruckers family by M. Edmond van der Straeten in the work already referred to (vol. iii. p. 325, etc.). He has gathered up the few documentary notices of the members of it discovered by MM. Rombouts and Van Lerius, by M. Génard and by M. Léon de Burbure, with some other facts that complete all that is known about them.

The name Ruckers, variously spelt Rukers, Rueckers, Ruyckers, Ruekaers, Rieckers and Rikaert, is really a contraction or corruption of the Flemish Ruckaerts or Ryckaertszoon, equivalent to the English Richardson. (1) Hans the elder was certainly of Flemish origin, being the son of Francis Ruckers of Mechlin. He can hardly have been born later than 1555. Married at Notre Dame (the cathedral), Antwerp, June 25, 1575, as Hans Ruckaerts, to Naenken Cnaeps, he was admitted as Hans Ruyckers, 'clavisinbalmakerre,' to the guild of St. Luke in 1575. It appears strange that he was not enrolled a citizen until 1594, but this may have been, as M. de Burbure suggests, a readmission, to repair the loss of a record burnt when the Spaniards sacked the Hôtel de Ville in 1576. In those troubled times there could have been but little to do in clavecin-making. May we see in this a reason for his acquiring that knowledge of the organ which was to lead ultimately to his remodelling the long clavecin? The date of his death will be dealt with in a special note at the end of the article.

He had four sons, Francis, Hans, Andries and Anthony. It is only with (2) Hans (baptized Jan. 15, 1578)[5] and (3) Andries (baptized August 30, 1579) that we are concerned, since they became clavecin-makers of equal reputation with their father. We learn that in 1591 Hans Ruckers the elder became tuner of the organ in the Virgin's chapel of the Cathedral, and that in 1593 he added fourteen or fifteen stops to the large organ in the same church. In 1598 and 1599 either he or his son Hans (the records do not specify which) had charge of the organs of St. Bavon, and from 1617–23 of St. Jacques. A Hans Ruckers died in 1642. We believe that this date refers to the son, as the latest clavecin we have met with of his make is the Countess of Dudley's beautiful instrument dated that year (list, B. 23); the latest certain date of the father's clavecins at present found being 1616.

Of the instruments catalogued below, it will be observed that twenty-three are probably by Hans the elder. The long ones are provided with the octave stop and, with a few exceptions, have the two keyboards identified with him as the inventor. But it is interesting to observe the expedients agreeing with the statement of

[5] Fétis (*Biog. universelle*, art. 'Ruckers') puts July for January in error.

Prætorius, that octave instruments [1] were employed with and in the oblong clavecins. These expedients doubtless originated before Hans Ruckers; indeed in the Museum at Nuremberg there is an oblong clavecin of Antwerp make, signed 'Martinus Vander Biest,' and dated 1580, that has on the right hand an octave spinet in it.[2] 'Merten' Vander Biest entered the Guild in Antwerp, as one of the ten clavecin makers, in 1558, and was a witness at Hans Ruckers's marriage in 1575. The first instrument recorded for Hans Ruckers (dated 1581) is also of this type, but the smaller instrument is to the left (see A. 1), as is found too in another double virginal bearing his mark (A. 18) now in America. In the Museum of the Conservatoire, Brussels, there is an oblong clavecin by Hans the elder (A. 8), wherein the octave spinet is above and not by the side of the fixed one — according to Victor Mahillon a later addition, though the work of the maker himself. This curious instrument formerly belonged to Fétis (who sold the paintings that adorned it), and is dated 1610. While on the subject of these removable octave spinets we will refer to two with keyboards side by side, made by Hans the younger (B. 3 and B. 6) and dated 1619 and 1623 respectively. Another long clavecin, also by Hans the younger (B. 31), not dated, now in the Hochschule, Berlin, has the octave spinet fixed in the angle side, precisely as in a more modern one, made by Coenen of Ruremonde, which may be seen in the Plantin Museum, Antwerp. The same construction is found in a harpsichord by Hans the elder (A. 5) and in one by his son (B. 32), with a two-keyboard clavecin and a spinet. A double virginal by Andreas Ruckers (C. 26) is in the Heyer Musikhistorisches Museum formerly at Cologne, now at Leipzig.

Hans Ruckers the younger—known to the Belgian and French 'musicologists' as Jean, because he used the initials I. R. in his rose, while the father, as far as we know, used H. R. —was, as we have said, the second son.

We have given the date of his baptism in the cathedral in 1578, but have no further details to record beyond the ascertained facts that he was married to Marie Waelrant, of the family of the musician Hubert Waelrant,[3] in the cathedral, Nov. 14, 1604, and that he was employed to tune the organ of St. Jacques from 1631 until 1642. There is also evidence as to his having died in that year. Thirty-two instruments attributed to him as sole maker are listed below.

Van der Straeten has, however, brought us nearer Hans the younger, by reference to Sainsbury's collection of *Original unpublished papers illustrative of the life of Sir Peter Paul Rubens* (London, 1859, p. 208, etc.), wherein are several letters which passed in 1638 between the painter, Balthazar Gerbier, at that time at Brussels and the private secretary of Charles I., Sir F. Windebank. They relate to the purchase of a good virginal from Antwerp for the King of England. Be it remembered that up to this time, and even as late as the Restoration, all clavecins in England, long or square, were called virginals. (See VIRGINAL.) Gerbier saw one that had been made by Hans Ruckers, the younger ('Johannes Rickarts'), for the Infanta. He describes it as having a double keyboard placed at one end, and four stops; exactly what we should now call a double harpsichord. There were two paintings inside the cover, the one nearest the player by Rubens; the subject Cupid and Psyche. The dealer asked £30 for it, such instruments without paintings being priced at £15. After some correspondence it was bought and sent over. Arrived in London it was found to be wanting six or seven keys, and to be insufficient for the music,[4] and Gerbier was requested to get it exchanged for one with larger compass. Referring to the maker, Gerbier was informed that he had not another on sale, and that the instrument could not be altered. So after this straightforward but rather gruff answer Gerbier was written to not to trouble himself further about it. Van der Straeten inquires what has become of this jewel? We agree with him that the preservation of the pictures has probably long since caused the destruction of the instrument. With such decoration it would hardly remain in a lumber-room. Van der Straeten himself possessed a Jean Ruckers single harpsichord (now in the Berlin Hochschule), restored by Ch. Meerens, of which he has given a heliotype illustration in his work. It is a splendid specimen of Hans the younger. (See B. 8, below.)

Andries Ruckers (the elder, to distinguish him from his son Andries), the third son of Hans, was, as we have said, baptized in 1579, and was a master in 1610–11.[5] As a member of the Confraternity of the Holy Virgin in the cathedral he tuned the chapel organ gratuitously in 1644. His work, notwithstanding Burney's impression about the relative excellence of his larger instruments, was held in as great esteem as that of his father and brother. In 1671, Jean Cox, choirmaster of the cathedral, left by will, as a

---

[1] We hesitate to accept Prætorius's statement literally as to such spinets being tuned a fifth as well as an octave higher. This more likely originates in the fact that the F and C instruments had before his time been made at one and the same pitch, starting from the lowest key, although the disposition of the keyboards and names of the notes were different; as in organs, where pipes of the same measurement had been actually used for the note F or the note C. See SHORT OCTAVE; Arnold Schlick's *Spiegel der Orgelmacher*, 1511.

[2] A woodcut of this rare instrument is given in Part ix. of Dr. A. Reissmann's *Illustrirte Geschichte der deutschen Musik*, Leipzig, 1881. Both keyboards, side by side, are apparently original, with white naturals and compass of four octaves C—C. It is the right-hand keyboard that is tuned the octave higher, and is removable like a drawer. A full description of this double instrument is reproduced in Reissmann's work, copied from the *Anzeiger für Kunde der deutschen Vorzeit* (Nuremberg, 1879, No. 9).

[3] Dr. John Bull succeeded Rumold Waelrant as organist of the cathedral in 1617, and retained the post until his death in 1628. He must have known Hans Ruckers and his two sons well, and been well acquainted with their instruments.

[4] The Hitchcocks were active in the latter half of the 17th century and early in the 18th, making spinets in London with five octaves, G—G.

[5] The Guild year ran from Sept. 18, 1610 to Sept. 18, 1611.

precious object, an André Ruckers clavecin. Within the writer's recollection there have been three honoured witnesses in London to this maker's fame, viz. that said to be Handel's (C. 30), dated 1651, given by Messrs. Broadwood to the Victoria and Albert Museum (see *PLATE* XXXII. No. 2); Mr. Howard Head's (C. 4), dated 1614; and one belonging to the late Miss Twining, a single keyboard one (C. 25), dated 1640.[1] A tradition exists that Handel had also played upon both the last-named instruments. We do not know when Andries Ruckers the elder died. He was certainly living in 1651, since that date is on his harpsichord at South Kensington. Forty-four instruments are listed under his name.

Of (4) ANDRIES Ruckers the younger, the information is most meagre. Born in 1607, he probably became a master in 1637–38. The Christian name is wanting in the entry in the ledger, but as the son of a master, the son of Andries the elder is apparently indicated. The researches of Génard have proved the birth of a daughter to Hans the younger, but not that of a son. It might be Christopher, could we attribute to him a master for a father. Regarding him, however, as living earlier, we are content to believe that Andries the younger then became free of the Guild; but as his known instruments are of late date, it is possible that he worked much with his father. We know from a baptism in 1665 that the younger Andries had married Catherina de Vriese, perhaps of the family of Dirck or Thierri de Vries, a clavecin-maker whose death is recorded in 1628. Fétis (*Biog. univ.*, 2nd edit. vii. 346 *b*) says he had seen a fine clavecin made by Andries the younger, dated 1667. M. Régibo possessed undoubted instruments by him, and has supplied a copy of his rose. Five instruments of his make are recorded.

A virginal by a Christopher Ruckers is recorded and Van der Straeten refers to another in the Museum at Namur. We cannot determine Christopher's relationship to the other Ruckers, but he might have been the Her Christofel Ruckers, organist and clockmaker of Termonde, where he set up a carillon in 1549—possibly a priest; at least the title 'Her' would indicate a person regarded with veneration. The same writer, in the 5th vol. p. 393 of *La Musique aux Pays-Bas*, continues, 'who knows if this Christopher did not own a workshop for clavecin making? The priest was everything at that epoch, and a scholar, an organ or spinet-builder seems to us quite natural and normal.' More probably he was his son or grandson, his work appearing to be of the earlier part of the 17th century, c. 1620. Two instruments only

[1] This instrument formerly belonged to the Rev. Thomas Twining, Rector of St. Mary, Colchester, who died in 1804. A learned scholar (he translated Aristotle's *Poetics*) and clever musician, he enjoyed the friendship of Burney and valued highly his favourite harpsichord, on which the great Handel had played. Charles Salaman used both this instrument and Messrs. Broadwood's in his admirable lectures given in 1855–56 in London and the provinces.

appear under his name. On his 'rose' the winged figure is standing, not seated.     A. J. H.

Upon reference to the following list [2] it will be observed that in Section A under the name of HANS RUCKERS many instruments have been included bearing the inscription of his son IOANNES (JEAN), in one case linked with the name of another son, ANDREAS or ANDRIES. This opens up the debated question of the date of death of HANS RUCKERS the elder, which has been placed as early as 1598, though we find his trade mark with the initials H. R. upon instruments made as late as 1616. It is important to remember that, by the rules of the Guild of St. Luke, which regulated the craft, this mark was much more than the trade mark of a firm : it was a personal 'escutcheon' belonging solely to the 'free' maker who had been admitted to the Guild. Young makers were required to work under some such 'free' master, who was responsible for wood and tools etc., used, until such time as they themselves were admitted. Under these strict regulations it would have been impossible for the sons to have used for 18 years the personal mark of their deceased father : during that period they must have served as apprentices in his workshop. So, taking the dates of their instruments as recorded in the list, we find that Andries obtained the right to use his own 'free' maker's mark in 1610–11 (C. 1) : and this date bears out the true meaning of the entry on the Rolls of the Guild for that period 'Hans Rukers sone claversigmaker,' that is 'Hans Ruckers's son clavecinmaker,' the Christian name being omitted.[3]

On the other hand Jean Ruckers, who still worked with his father, did not seek admission or receive his 'free' maker's mark till 1617 (B. 1). Unfortunately no reference can be made to the Rolls, as they are lost from 1616 to 1629. In 1617 Hans Ruckers, the father, probably retired from active business and was appointed to the care of the organs at the collegiate Church of St. Jacques in Antwerp, a post which he held till 1623 when the engagement was terminated as stated in the church

[2] The few alterations made in the above article written by A. J. Hipkins mainly consist of amended references to the new list of Ruckers instruments, corrections of one or two misprints and slight omissions required by more recent information. Thanks will ever be due to the late MM. Mahillon, Meerens, Van der Straeten and Régibo for their assistance in the compilation of the first list ; but we desire to acknowledge our personal indebtedness to Miss Hipkins, Mr. Howard Head, Miss F. Morris (New York), Herr G. Kinsky (Cologne), M. Ernest Closson (Brussels), and the Messrs. Steinert for their valuable assistance towards the present revision. We have had the opportunity of research in Paris and Antwerp, and the use of the detailed catalogues of the valuable collections at Brussels, Cologne, Berlin and New York. This has enabled us to correct several discrepancies in the last list (1902) and to prevent, as far as possible, the duplication of descriptions of the same instrument. We have renumbered the sections, but have added references to the numbers in the 2nd edition. Where known, we have given the names of former owners, but the difficulty of tracing present ownership has been very great; and from insufficiency of data, in some cases impossible.

[3] It is unfortunate that the editors of the Rolls (MM. Rombouts and Van Lerius) have inserted commas which do not exist in the original script. De Burbure read it correctly in 1863. These Rolls have at times been but loosely kept ; in places, no name but only the address of the newly enrolled member is entered. There is, moreover, no need to repeat the word ' son ' as referring to Hans Ruckers the younger (Jean), because the heading of the short list of admissions states that all were ' sons of masters.'

records. He must then have been about 70 years of age, and probably died soon afterwards, say, in 1625. It is interesting to notice that his name is inscribed on two existing instruments made in 1610 (A. 8 and 9), the year in which Andries his son was applying for admission to the Guild: it may have been required by the rules.[1]　　　　F. W. G.

[1] We therefore have no hesitation in accepting Herr Kinsky's strong reasons for believing that Hans Ruckers the elder died ' après 1623 ' and not in 1598 (taken from the burial payment for a certain Hans Rycaedt), although we had not the opportunity of reading his interesting paper in *La Guide musicale* (1911) before our opinion, based upon the above facts, was formed.

## A LIST OF 106 RUCKERS VIRGINALS AND HARPSICHORDS PRESUMED TO BE STILL EXISTING IN 1926

(1)

*JAHSc*

Extreme measurements of length and width are given, and references to the numbering in the second edition (1902).

The paintings on the sound-boards are devices, generally of fruits, birds, flowers and foliage.

### A. HANS RUCKERS (THE ELDER)
#### c. 1550–c. 1625

Free maker's mark—a winged figure seated and holding a harp, with the initials H. R., as in Rose No. 1.

In two instances a second geometrical rose.

| No. | No. 2nd Edition. | Date. | Shape. | Size. | General Description. | Former Owners. | Present Owner. |
|---|---|---|---|---|---|---|---|
| 1 | | 1581 | Oblong | ft. in.　ft. in.<br>5　9 × 1　7 | A double virginal: 2 keyboards side by side, the smaller octave instrument to the left removable: on both the compass 4 octaves (C—C) with bass short octave: white natural keys. Inscribed HANS RUCKERS ME FECIT, 1581. On larger instrument H. R. rose: on smaller a geometrical rose. Outside of case undecorated: painted on lid within, a Fête Champêtre of the 16th cent.: sound-board painted with flowers, etc. Over keyboard of larger instrument plaster medallions of Philip II., King of Spain and his fourth wife, Doña Ana of Austria. On the front board MUSICA DULCIS LABORUM LEVAMEN. Illustrated in the *Connoiseur*, London, July, 1916. This instrument with its tone preserved and in very good condition was found in the chapel of a country estate near Cuzco once belonging to the Oropesa family. The case had been mistaken for that of a long candle box. The stand is missing. It is said to have been presented by King Philip to the Marquise of Oropesa, a descendant of the Incas. | The Marquises of Oropesa, Cuzco, Peru. | S. G. B. (Peru). |
| 2 | 1 | 1590 | Bentside. | 7　4 × 2　9 | 2 keyboards, not original: compass 4¾ oct. (G—E), chromatic: black naturals: finely painted. H. R. rose. | Abel Régibo, Renaix. Collection dispersed, 1897. | .. |
| 3 | 2 and 3 | 1590 | Bentside. | 7　9 × 2　10½ | 2 keyboards, not original: compass 5 oct., chromatic: black naturals. Inscribed HANS RUCKERS ME FECIT, 1590. H. R. rose. Compass extended by Blanchet of Paris (*c.* 1750).* 5 stops worked by the knees (à genouillère). Case decorated with Chinese subjects in lacquer. | Château de Pau, France. | Musée du Conservatoire de Musique, Paris (No. 326). |
| 4 | 4 | 1591 | Trapeze. | 5　7 × 1　11 | 1 keyboard: 4 oct. (C—C) with bass short octave: white naturals: H. R. rose. Decorated in red and black on a yellow ground: on cover, 1591. Inscribed SCIENTIA NON HABET INIMICUM NISI IGNORANTEM. | T. J. Canneel, Director Académie Royale, Ghent. | .. |
| 5 | 5 | 1594 | Oblong. | 5　11 × 2　6 | A one-keyboard harpsichord with an octave instrument placed in the hollow of the bentside. The principal keyboard 4 oct. (C—C): 3 stops on right hand (original): H. R. rose. The smaller instrument 3½ oct. (C—A) with bass short octave and highest G♯ omitted: a geometrical rose. White naturals. Inside lid a painting, said to be by Hieronymus Jannsens, of a similar instrument. Inscribed HANS RUCKERS ME FECIT ANTVERPIAE, 1594. See the similar instruments by IOANNES RUCKERS (B. 31 and 32). | Kunstgewerbe Museum, Berlin. | Schloss Museum, Berlin. |

* It was believed by MM. Snoeck, Van der Straeten, Régibo and V. Mahillon, that few of the Ruckers clavecins were of the original compass of keys. The statements of compass in this list and also in KEYBOARD should be qualified by this remark. The increase was, however, made long ago, and in some instances possibly by the maker himself. M. van der Straeten, p. 348, has a passage quoted from Van Blankenburg : ' This was at the time when clavecins had still a narrow keyboard. In the present day (1739 ?) it would be difficult to meet with one of this kind : all the keyboards having been lengthened.' Again, white naturals are believed to be original in these instruments. Upon very old alterations it is not easy to decide. We are of opinion that black naturals and ivory sharps were occasionally substituted when the paintings were done. In dealing with these questions, however, it is best to refrain from generalising ; many errors having arisen from too hasty conclusions.

| No. | No. 2nd Edition. | Date. | Shape. | Size. | General Description. | Former Owners. | Present Owner. |
|---|---|---|---|---|---|---|---|
| | | | | ft. in. ft. in. | | | |
| 6 | 6 | 1598 | Oblong. | 5 9 ×1 8 | 1 keyboard to the left : 4½ oct. (G—C) with bass short octave : white naturals (not original). Inscribed IOHANNES (sic) RUCKERS FECIT ANTVERPIAE. H. R. rose. Sound-board painted with flowers, etc. Inside lid DULCISONUM REFICIT TRISTIA CORDA MELOS, with date 1598. Exhibited Paris Exhibition, 1900, and illustrated in Le Musée rétrospectif. | .. | Mlle. Jeanne Lyon, Paris. |
| 7 | 7 | 1604 | Oblong. | 4 8 ×1 7½ | 1 keyboard : original compass 4 oct. (C—C) with bass short octave : now 3¾ oct. (E—C) chromatic. White naturals. Inscribed IOANNES ET ANDREAS RUCKERS FECERUNT. H. R. rose. Painted sound-board with date 1604. Outside of case painted in grisaille. | A. Régibo, Renaix. C. Snoeck, Ghent. | Musée du Conservatoire de Musique, Brussels (No. 2927). |
| 8 | 8 | 1610 | Oblong. | 5 7 ×1 7 | 2 keyboards, one above the other, the lower coupled to the upper (an octave instrument added at a little later date). Compass 4½ oct. (C—F). White naturals. Inscribed HANS RUCKERS ME FECIT ANTVERPIAE, 1610. H. R. roses in both sound-boards. | F. J. Fétis, Brussels. | Musée du Conservatoire, Brussels (No. 275). |
| 9 | 9 | 1610 | Oblong. | 1 3 ×0 9 | 1 keyboard : 2½ octaves : white naturals. Inscribed at back of case, HANS RUCKERS ME FECIT ANTVERP, 1610. Case ebony inlaid with ivory : on the lid LAUDABO NOMEN DEI CUM CANTICO ET MAGNIFICABO EUM IN LAUDE. A small octave virginal. | J. Audéoud. | Musée du Conservatoire de Musique, Paris (No. 1080). |
| 10 | .. | 1610 | Oblong. | 5 6 ×1 8 | 1 keyboard : 4 oct. (C—C) with bass short octave : white naturals. Inscribed IOANNES RUCKERS ME FECIT ANTVERPIAE. H.R. rose. Case dark green with a painting inside front boards : decorated sound-board with date 1610. | A. Sol, Tournai. | J. Hel, Lille. |
| 11 | 10 | 1611 | Oblong. | 5 6 ×1 7½ | 1 keyboard : 4 oct. (C—C) with bass short octave. Inscribed IOANNES RUCKERS FECIT ANTVERPIAE, 1611. H. R. rose. Case decorated with patterned paper. Reported by E. van der Straeten and V. Mahillon as in the Steen Museum, Antwerp : but no longer there nor in the Vleeschhuis Museum. See C. 44. | Musée du Steen, Antwerp. | .. |
| 12 | 11 | 1612 | Bentside. | 7 6 ×2 11 | 2 keyboards : nearly 5 octaves (G—F) chromatic. Keyboards put in by Messrs. Broadwood in 1885. Inscribed IOANNES RUCKERS ME FECIT ANTVERPIAE, 1612. H.R. rose. 3 stops. Black case : painted sound-board : no stand. Found at Windsor Castle, 1883, and supposed by some to be the ' large harpsichord ' left by Handel to Smith, and given by the latter to King George III. See C. 30. Exhibited at the Inventions Exhibition, London, 1885. | .. | H.M. The King. |
| 13 | 12 | 1612 | Bentside. | 7 6 ×3 0 | 2 keyboards : 5 octaves (F—F) chromatic : 5 stops : black naturals : no maker's name : on painted sound-board date 1612, with H. R. rose. Inscribed ' Mis en ravalement par Pascal Taskin, 1774,' meaning that the compass of the keyboard was extended by this Parisian maker. The instrument painted inside and out with Louis XIV. subjects by Van der Meulen, and said to have belonged to Marie Antoinette. Exhibited at the Inventions Exhibition, 1885. | Torlini, Rome, 1842. Viscount Powerscourt. | Edgar Speyer, New York. |
| 14 | .. | 1613 | Bentside. | 7 4½ ×2 10 | 2 keyboards, the upper one an octave higher. 4½ oct. (G—C) with bass short octave. 2 stops. Black naturals. Leather plectra. Painted sound-board with date 1613. H. R. rose. Case finely decorated in lacquer with Chinese figures within and without. An elaborately carved stand with six legs. | M. Planchet, Paris. | Louis Steinert, Providence, U.S.A. |
| 15 | 13 | 1614 | Oblong. | 5 5½ ×1 7½ | 1 keyboard : 4 oct. (C—C) with bass short octave. H. R. rose. Sound-board and case badly repainted : no date now visible. | C. Snoeck, Ghent. | Musée du Conservatoire, Brussels (No. 2930). |
| 16 | 14 | 1614 | Bentside. | 7 4½ ×3 3 | 2 keyboards : 5 oct. and a note (F—G), not original. White naturals : 4 stops. 2 knee levers (genouillères) and a ' mute ' stop of the 18th cent. H. R. rose, and the date 1614. Lid painting c. 1700. | C. Snoeck, Ghent. | Museum der Hochschule für Musik, Berlin (No. 2229). |
| 17 | .. | 1616 | Bentside. | 7 4 ×2 7 | 2 keyboards : 4½ oct. (C—F). H. R. rose. Much restored. | .. | M. Costil, Paris. |
| 18 | 16 and 19 | Undated. | Oblong. | 5 7 ×1 5½ | A double virginal : 2 keyboards side by side, the left-hand one removable. Present compass 4 oct. (C—C) chromatic, the smaller instrument an octave higher. According to Hipkins the original keys (now lost) had a compass from B—B (4 octaves). Inscribed on each instrument IOANNES RUQUERS ME FECIT. H. R. rose. Lid painting, contest of Apollo and | Messrs. Chappell. G. Donaldson, London. Morris Steinert, Newhaven, U.S.A. | Miss B. Skinner, Holyoake, Mass., U.S.A. |

| No. | No. 2nd Edition. | Date. | Shape. | Size. | General Description. | Former Owners. | Present Owner. |
|---|---|---|---|---|---|---|---|
| | | | | ft. in.  ft. in. | | | |
| 19 | .. | .. | Bentside. | 9  4 × 2  10½ | Marsyas.   Stand with six arcaded balusters.  Exhibited at the Inventions Exhibition, 1885, and illustrated in Hipkins's *Musical Instruments*, 1888. 2 keyboards : 4½ oct. (C—A) with bass short octave : 4 stops.  No maker's name, but H. R. rose.  Sound-board painted with arabesques in gold, blue and red : outside and inside of case decorated with paintings, amongst them Orpheus charming the animals and Louis XIV. as Apollo surrounded by the Nine Muses.  The framed stand with eight legs.  Illustrated in Museum Cat. Vol. IV. | .. | Musée du Conservatoire, Brussels (No. 2510). |
| 20 | 17 | .. | Bentside. | 7  4 × 2  7 | N.B.—The following instruments are attributed to Hans Ruckers (the Elder). 2 keyboards : 4½ oct. (C—F) chromatic : originally C—C with bass short octave.  4 stops (one mere ornament).  No rose or inscription, but attributed by the late C. Snoeck to Hans Ruckers. | A. Régibo. C. Snoeck. | Musée du Conservatoire, Brussels (No. 2934). |
| 21 | .. | .. | Oblong. | 1  2½ × 0  8 | 1 keyboard : 2⅔ oct. (G—E), the lowest G♯ and highest D♯ omitted.  Boxwood naturals.  Case painted with hunting scenes.  Inscribed DUCERE UXOREM EST VENDERE LIBERTATEM.  Painted sound-board : decorated with gilt ornaments.  An octave virginal attributed to Hans Ruckers.  Illustrated in Museum Catalogue, 1910.  See No. 9. | .. | Heyer Museum, formerly Cologne now at Leipzig (No. 35). |
| 22 | .. | .. | Oblong. | 1  7½ × 0  10½ | 1 keyboard : 3½ oct. (D—A) with bass short oct.  Upper G♯ key omitted.  White naturals.  Case inlaid with ebony and ivory.  Lid painting—a harvest scene.  An octave virginal attributed to Hans Ruckers.  See No. 9.  Illustrated on *PLATE XC.* | .. | Heyer Museum, formerly Cologne now at Leipzig (No. 36). |
| 23 | 18 | .. | Bentside. | .. | Now converted into a grand pianoforte by Zeitter.  Case decorated with paintings of classical subjects by Boucher and Le Prince.  Original sound-board with the name board IOANNES RUCKERS ME FECIT ANTVERPIAE made nto a box for music.  Attributed by Hipkins to Hans Ruckers (the Elder).  See Art. RUCKERS. (Nos. 15 and 20 (2nd edition) transferred to Andreas Ruckers, C. 16 and C. 44.) | M. Balbastre, Paris. James Goding. Panmure Gordon, London. | .. |

## B. JOANNES RUCKERS (HANS THE YOUNGER), 1578–1642

Free maker's mark—a winged figure seated and holding a harp with the initials I. R.

(2)

(3)

(4)

Three varieties : (a) figure with face to right ; (b) facing front ; (c) with face to left, as in Roses Nos. 2, 3, 4.

| No. | No. 2nd Edition. | Date. | Shape. | Size. | General Description. | Former Owners. | Present Owner. |
|---|---|---|---|---|---|---|---|
| | | | | ft. in.  ft. in. | | | |
| 1 | 21 | 1617 | Bentside. | 6  8 × 3  7 | 2 keyboards : white naturals.  Paintings in Vernis Martin : lately removed. | M. Pilette, Brussels, 1878.  Since sold, Hôtel Drouot. | .. |
| 2 | 22 | 1618 | Oblong. | 2  8½ × 1  3 | 1 keyboard : 4 oct. (C—C) with bass short octave : white naturals.  Inscribed IOANNES RUCKERS FECIT.  I. R. rose (No. 2).  Decorated sound-board with date 1618. | A. Colin, Paris. | Musée du Conservatoire de Musique, Paris (No. 317). |
| 3 | 23 | 1619 | Oblong. | 7  4 × 2  7 | A double virginal : 2 keyboards, side by side : the larger instrument with 4 stops, the smaller tuned an octave higher.  4½ oct. (C—F).  White naturals.  I. R. roses (No. 4). | A. Régibo, Renaix. | .. |
| 4 | 24 | 1619 | Oblong. | 3  5 × 1  8½ | 1 keyboard : 4 oct. (C—C) with bass short octave.  White naturals.  I. R. rose (No. 2). | A. Régibo. | .. |

| No. | No. 2nd Edition. | Date. | Shape. | Size. | | General Description. | Former Owners. | Present Owner. |
|---|---|---|---|---|---|---|---|---|
| | | | | ft. in. | ft. in. | | | |
| 5 | 25 | 1622 | Oblong. | 5 7 | × 1 7½ | 1 keyboard : 4½ oct. (C—F) : chromatic. White naturals. Inscribed IOANNES RUCKERS FECIT ANTVERPIAE. On lid, OMNIS SPIRITUS LAUDET DOMINUM. Painted sound-board with date in ink ' Anno 1622.' I. R. rose. Exhibited at Inventions Exhibition, London, 1885, and illustrated in Hipkins's *Musical Instruments*, 1888. | V. Mahillon, Brussels. | .. |
| 6 | .. | 1623 | Oblong. | 5 8 | × 1 8 | A double virginal. 2 keyboards, side by side : the smaller octave instrument removable. 4 oct. (C—C) with bass short octave. White naturals. Inscribed IOANNES RUCKERS ME FECIT. I. R. roses (No. 2). Case with patterned paper. Painted sound-board with date 1623 on lid : AUDI, VIDE ET TACE, SI VIS VIVERE IN PACE. On front board : OMNIS SPIRITUS LAUDET DOMINUM. | .. | M. and A. Salomon, Paris. |
| 7 | 26 | 1626 | Oblong. | 4 3 | × 1 7 | 1 keyboard. Inscribed IOANNES RUCKERS FECIT ANTVERPIAE, 1626. | Pley Collection, Brussels (dispersed 1906). | .. |
| 8 | 27 | 1627 | Bentside. | 6 0 | × 2 7½ | 1 keyboard : 4½ oct. (C—E). 2 stops : white naturals. Inscribed IOANNES RUCKERS FECIT ANTVERPIAE. I. R. rose (No. 4). Painted sound-board with date 1627. Lid painting—an Italian coast scene : motto MUSICA DONUM DEI. Illustrated by Van der Straeten (*Musique aux Pays-Bas*, Vol. 3) and Museum Catalogue (Plate 7), 1922. | E. van der Straeten. C. Snoeck, Ghent. | Museum der Hochschule für Musik, Berlin (No. 2227). |
| 9 | .. | 162(7) | Bentside. | 7 7 | × 3 1 | 2 keyboards : nearly 5 oct. (F—E) chromatic : black naturals. 3 stops. Inscribed IOANNES (*sic*) RUCKERS ME FECIT ANTVERPIAE, 162 . I. R. rose (No. 2). Sound-board elaborately painted with flowers and foliage. Over the keys a floral design with cartouche bearing the words : H. RUKKERS (*sic*) ANTVERPIAE, and beneath ' Refait par Blanchet Facteur du Roi à Paris, 1756.' Lid paintings—pastoral scenes, ascribed to Boucher (1703–70). Outside of case painted with sprays of flowers : stand 18th cent. Obtained in America from a French family in whose possession it had been from the time of Louis XIV. Restored by Arnold Dolmetsch, 1908. (The date on the jack rail has been mutilated by subsequent additions : the present owner places it at 1600 : but the third figure certainly 2, and the fourth probably 7. The I. R. rose was not in use before 1617.) | .. | Miss B. Skinner, Holyoake, Mass., U.S.A. |
| 10 | 28 and 29 | 1628 | Oblong. | 5 9 | × 1 7½ | 1 keyboard : 4½ oct. (C—F) with lowest C♯ omitted : white naturals. Compass originally 4 oct. (C—C) with bass short octave. A ' mute ' stop ' à genouillère.' Dated ' Anno 1628 ' in ink. I. R. rose. Lid painting—a trophy of musical instruments. Exhibited at Brussels Exhibition, 1880. | L. Jouret, Brussels. C. Snoeck, Ghent. | Musée du Conservatoire, Brussels (No. 2926). |
| 11 | 30 | 1629 | Bentside. | 7 4 | × 3 0 | 2 keyboards : nearly 5 oct. (G—F). I. R. rose (No. 4). | Gerard de Prins, Louvain. | .. |
| 12 | .. | 1629 | Oblong. | 4 3 | × 1 7 | 1 keyboard : 4 oct. and one tone (C—D) with bass short octave. Inscribed IOANNES RUCKERS FECIT ANTVERPIAE, 1629. Painted sound-board : case decorated with patterned paper. I. R. rose. On lid : OMNIS SPIRITUS LAUDET DOMINUM. | .. | Musée du Conservatoire, Brussels (No. 2511). |
| 13 | 31 | 1630 | Bentside. | 4 10½ | × 2 10 | 2 keyboards : 4½ oct. (G—E) : black naturals. Inscribed IOANNES RUCKERS ME FECIT ANTVERPIAE. Case in gold and black lacquer. Lid painting—a woodland scene, ascribed to Lancret. Stand with six legs, decorated with carving in relief. Illustrated in *L'Illustration*, 1858, and L. de Burbure's *Recherches sur les facteurs de clavecins d'Anvers*, 1862. | F. Pigeory, Paris. | Baroness J. de Rothschild, Paris. |
| 14 | 32 | 1632 | Bentside. | 8 2 | × 3 3 | 2 keyboards : 5 octaves and one tone (F—G) : white naturals. 4 stops ' à genouillère.' I. R. rose (No. 3). | C. Snoeck, Ghent | .. |
| 15 | 33 | 1632 | .. | .. | | ' Top painted : rose not described : the date inclines us to attribute it to Hans the Younger.' A. J. Hipkins. | M. de Breyne, Ypres. | .. |
| 16 | 34 | 1634 | Bentside. | 7 3 | × 3 2 | 2 keyboards : 4½ oct. (G—E) : white naturals. Inscribed IOANNES RUCKERS FECIT ANTVERPIAE. I. R. rose. On lid ACTA VIRUM PROBANT, 1634 : on flap SOLI DEO GLORIA. Case painted in marbled red and white with green and black border : large decorative hinges. | .. | Earl of Dysart, Ham House, Richmond. |
| 17 | 35 | 1636 | Oblong. | 5 9 | × 1 8 | 1 keyboard. Inscribed IOANNES RUCKERS FECIT ANTVERPIAE, 1636. Original stand. | Pley Collection, Brussels. | .. |

| No. | No. 2nd Edition. | Date. | Shape. | Size. ft. in. ft. in. | General Description. | Former Owners. | Present Owner. |
|---|---|---|---|---|---|---|---|
| 18 | 36 | 1637 | Oblong. | 5 7 ×1 8 | 1 keyboard: 4 oct. (C—C) with bass short octave: white naturals. On sound-board, date 1637 with I. R. rose. On lid, AUDI, VIDE ET TACE SI VIS VIVERE IN PACE. Case decorated with patterned paper. Illustrated in Snoeck's Catalogue, 1894. | C. Snoeck, Ghent. | Museum der Hochschule für Musik, Berlin (No. 2236). |
| 19 | 37 | 1637 | Bentside. | 6 1 ×2 9½ | 1 keyboard: 4¾ oct. (A—F): white naturals. Inscribed as No. 13, with date 1637. Exhibited at the Inventions Exhibition, London, 1885. | J. C. Horsley, R.A., London. | .. |
| 20 | 38 | 1638 | Oblong. | 5 9 ×1 7 | 1 keyboard: 4 oct. and one tone (C—D). Original compass 4 oct. (C—C) with bass short octave: white naturals. Inscribed IOANNES RUCKERS FECIT ANTVERPIAE, 1638. I. R. rose (No. 2). On lid, MUSICA MAGNORUM EST SOLAMEN DULCE LABORUM. | C. Snoeck, Ghent. | Musée du Conservatoire, Brussels (No. 2933). |
| 21 | 39 | 1638 | Bentside. | 7 4½×2 6 | 2 original keyboards: the lower 4½ oct. (C—F) with bass short octave: the upper 4 oct. (C—C) with bass short octave. The upper has prolongations on the lowest F♯ and G♯ keys at an angle to touch the fourths below, in order to preserve the semitonal succession after the short octave of the lower keyboard, while securing the short octave of the upper. Below the C of the upper keyboard is a wooden block as described by Von Blankenburg (see Hipkins, *Pianoforte Primer*, p. 82). Two rows of jacks and the 2 stops have been removed, so that the instrument is now two independent harpsichords, an eleventh apart in pitch. Painted sound-board with date 1638. Inscribed IOANNES RUCKERS FECIT ANTVERPIAE. Case black and gold: paintings inside the lid: old stand. Keyboards illustrated in Hipkins's *Pianoforte Primer*, 1896. | E. Spence, Florence. The late Right Hon. Sir Bernhard Samuelson and Lady Samuelson (sold 1915). | In America. |
| 22 | 40 | 1639 | Bentside. | 5 9 ×2 7 | 1 keyboard: no keys: 4 stops. I. R. rose (No. 4). Case black and gold. | Messrs. Kirkman, London. | Victoria and Albert Museum, South Kensington (No. 1739). |
| 23 | 41 | 1642 | Bentside. | 7 4½×2 8 | 2 keyboards: 4½ oct. (G—D) with bass short octave: 4 stops. I.R. rose (No. 4). Lid painting—mythological subjects after Rubens. Case decorated with gilding in arabesques. Exhibited at Inventions Exhibition, 1885, and illustrated in Catalogue of Musicians Company's Exhibition, 1904 (Novello). | .. | The Countess of Dudley. |
| 24 | 42 | Undated. | Bentside. | 7 11 ×3 0 | 2 keyboards: 5 oct. (F—F) chromatic, having been completed and extended. I. R. rose (No. 3). Paintings outside by Brouwer or Teniers the younger, those within the lid attributed to Paul Bril or Jan Breughel. | L. Clapisson, Paris. | Musée du Conservatoire, Paris (No. 327). |
| 25 | 43 | .. | Bentside. | 7 1 ×2 7 | 1 keyboard: 4½ oct. (G—D): black naturals. I. R. rose (No. 4): blackwood case with incrusted ivory and, according to M. du Sommerard, Italian work. | .. | Musée de l'Hôtel de Cluny, Paris (No. 2825). |
| 26 | 45 | .. | Bentside. | 5 11 ×2 7½ | 4½ oct. (C—E): white naturals: 'superb paintings.' | C. Snoeck, Ghent. | .. |
| 27 | 46 | .. | Bentside. | 6 0 ×2 7 | 1 keyboard: 4½ oct. (C—F): 5 keys added in treble: white naturals: 3 stops. I. R. rose (No. 2). Painting of Orpheus playing a bass viol. | A. Régibo, Renaix. | .. |
| 28 | 47 | .. | Bentside. | .. | 1 keyboard: 4½ oct. (C—F): 4 keys added in treble. I. R. rose (No. 3) cut in hardwood. | A. Régibo, Renaix. | .. |
| 29 | 51 | .. | Bentside. | 7 3 ×2 11 | 1 keyboard: 4¾ oct. (F—D) chromatic: 3 stops. I. R. rose (No. 3). Case painted in marbled green. | .. | Musée der Steen, Antwerp (No. P. 28). |
| 30 | 48 | .. | Oblong. | 4 4 ×1 4½ | 1 keyboard: 5 oct. and a tone (F—G): extended. I. R. rose. | C. Snoeck, Ghent. | Museum der Hochschule für Musik, Berlin (No. 2222). |
| 31 | 44 | .. | Oblong. | 5 11 ×2 5½ | A one-keyboard harpsichord with an octave instrument placed in the hollow of the bentside: compass of both instruments 4 oct. (C—C) with bass short octave. Principal keyboard with 2 stops: white naturals. I. R. roses (Nos. 2 and 4). Inscribed IOANNES RUCKERS FECIT ANTVERPIAE. On the end flap GLORIA DEO: on the side flap OMNIS SPIRITUS LAUDET DOMINUM. Lid painting—a Turkish battle. See A. 5. Illustrated in the Museum Catalogue, 1922. | C. Snoeck, Ghent. | Museum der Hochschule für Musik (No. 2232). |
| 32 | 50 | .. | Oblong. | 7 3 ×2 8 | A two-keyboard harpsichord with an octave instrument placed in the hollow of the bentside as in No. 31. Principal keyboard 4½ oct. (G—C) with bass short octave: 4 stops. Smaller instrument 4 oct. (C—C) with bass short octave. I. R. roses (Nos. 2 and 4). Case decorated with patterned paper. Lid painting—a modern copy of a painting, representing Apollo and the Nine Muses, by Martin de Vos (Antwerp, 1532–1603) | C. Snoeck, Ghent. | Musée du Conservatoire, Brussels (No. 2935). |

| No. | No. 2nd Edition. | Date. | Shape. | Size. | General Description. | Former Owners. | Present Owner. |
|---|---|---|---|---|---|---|---|
| | | | | | in the Old Museum, Brussels. Framed stand with eight turned legs. Illustrated in the Conservatoire Museum Catalogue, Vol. V. p. 150. A similar instrument in the Musée Plantin at Antwerp inscribed Iohannes Iosephus Coenen—Aᵒ 1735. [No. 49 (2nd edition) referred to A. 7.] | | |

(6)

(5)

### C. ANDREAS RUCKERS (THE ELDER)
### 1579–c. 1652

Free maker's mark—a winged figure seated and holding a harp, with the initials A. R., as in Rose No. 6. In one instance a geometrical rose— No. 5.

| No. | No. 2nd Edition. | Date. | Shape. | Size. | General Description. | Former Owners. | Present Owner. |
|---|---|---|---|---|---|---|---|
| | | | | ft. in. ft. in. | | | |
| 1 | 32 | 1610 | Oblong. | 4 4 × 1 6 | 1 keyboard : 4 oct. (C—C) with bass short octave : white naturals. Inscribed ANDREAS RUCKERS ME FECIT ANTVERPIAE. A. R. rose (No. 6). On lid, OMNIS SPIRITUS LAUDET DOMINUM. Case with patterned paper : sound-board painted with flowers and foliage, and date 1610. A 'mute' stop added in the 18th cent. Exhibited at the Crystal Palace Exhibition, London, 1900, and illustrated in Galpin's *Old Musical Instruments* (Methuen), 1911. | Canon F. W. Galpin, Witham, Essex. | The Museum of Fine Arts, Boston, U.S.A. |
| 2 | 53 | 1613 | Oblong. | 3 8½ × 1 4½ | 1 keyboard : 4 oct. (C—C) with bass short octave : white naturals. Inscribed as No. 1, with date 1613. Sound-board formerly painted. | Matthias van der Gheyn, 1740. Chev. X. van Elevyck, Louvain. | Musée du Conservatoire de Musique, Brussels (No. 274). |
| 3 | 54 | 1613 | Oblong. | 3 8½ × 1 5½ | 1 keyboard : 4 oct. (C—C) with bass short octave. Inscribed as No. 1, with date 1613. | M. Havaux, Rebecq-Rognon. C. Snoeck, Ghent. | Musée du Conservatoire, Brussels (No. 2928). |
| 4 | 55 | 1614 | Bentside. | 7 6 × 2 8 | 2 keyboards : 4¾ oct. (A—F) : white naturals. 4 stops, the 'lute' an addition : pedal not original : case veneered and compass extended 18th cent. Inscribed as No. 1. A. R. rose (No. 6). Lid painting attributed to Van der Meulen. Exhibited at Inventions Exhibition, London, 1885. | Dr. Blow of Bath. General Hopkinson. J. Kendrick Pyne. Boddington Collection, Manchester. Howard Head, London. | W. C. Priestley, Bath. |
| 5 | 56 | 1615 | Bentside. | 4 0 × (2 5) | 1 keyboard : 50 keys : 4 stops. Case painted outside with draped designs : patterned paper within. Painted sound-board. On lid, CONCORDIA RES PARVAE CRESCUNT DISCORDIA MAXIMAE DILABUNTUR. Reported by Chev. de Burbure in 1863 but now lost : was in dilapidated condition. If size given (1 m. 22 c.) is correct, this was a harpsichord of the smallest size, made probably for special portability : the width has been inserted from similar instruments. | Church of St. Jacques, Antwerp. | .. |
| 6 | 57 | 1618 | Bentside. | 7 4 × 2 10 | 1 keyboard : 4½ oct. (C—F) extended : white naturals. 2 stops. Inscribed SOLI DEO GLORIA, 1618. A. R. rose (No. 6). | C. Snoeck. | Museum der Hochschule für Musik, Berlin (No. 2224). |
| 7 | 58 | 1619 | Bentside. | 8 10½ × 2 10 | 2 keyboards : 5 oct. (C—C), the lowest note 8ve below vlc. C : sound-board gilt and diapered in Moorish style : outside, a painting of Orpheus. Inscribed as No. 1, with date 1619. A. R. rose (No. 5). | A. Régibo, Renaix. | .. |
| 8 | 59 | 1620 | Bentside. | 5 10 × 2 8 | 2 keyboards : nearly 5 oct. (G—F) with bass short octave : 4 stops. A. R. rose (No. 6). Case painted in grisaille : decorated sound-board with date 1620. Lid painting—a town scene. | C. Snoeck. | Museum der Hochschule, Berlin (No. 2230). |
| 9 | 60 | 1620 | Oblong. | 3 7 × 1 5 | 1 keyboard : 4 oct. (C—C) with bass short octave : white naturals. Inscribed as No. 1. On lid, SIC TRANSIT GLORIA MUNDI. Illustrated in Steinert Collection Catalogue, 1893. | Morris Steinert, Newhaven, Conn., U.S.A. | H. Worch, Washington, U.S.A. |
| 10 | 61 | 1620 | Oblong. | 5 8 × 1 7½ | 1 keyboard : 4 oct. (C—C) chromatic, the short octave extended : white naturals. Inscribed as No. 1. On lid, OMNIS SPIRITUS LAUDET DOMINUM. Decorated sound-board with date 1620. Illustrated in Museum Catalogue, Vol. III. | V. and J. Mahillon, Brussels. | Musée du Conservatoire, Brussels (No. 1597). |
| 11 | 62 | 1620 | Oblong. | 4 1 × 1 3½ | 1 keyboard : 4 oct. (C—C) with bass short octave : white naturals. Inscribed as No. 1. On lid, SIC TRANSIT GLORIA MUNDI. Exhibited at Brussels Exhibition, 1880. | A. Campo, Brussels. | .. |

| No. | No. 2nd Edition. | Date. | Shape. | Size. | | General Description. | Former Owners. | Present Owner. |
|---|---|---|---|---|---|---|---|---|
| | | | | ft. in. | ft. in. | | | |
| 12 | 63 | 1623 | Oblong. | 5 7½ × 1 | 7½ | 1 keyboard : 4 oct. (C—C) : white naturals. Inscribed as No. 1, with date 1623. | V. and J. Mahillon, Brussels. | .. |
| 13 | 64 | 1624 | Bentside. | 7 9 × 3 | 1 | 2 keyboards : 5 oct. (F—F) : white naturals : 3 stops : pedal not original. Case veneered and compass extended 18th cent. A.R. rose (No.6). | John Hullah, London. | Mrs. J. Cyriax, London. |
| 14 | 65 | 1624 | Bentside. | 8 0 × 2 | 10 | 5 oct. (F—F) : 3 stops. Inscribed MUSICA LAETITIAE COMES, MEDICINA DOLORUM. | .. | Musée Archéologique, Bruges. |
| 15 | 66 | 1626 | Oblong. | 4 0 × 3 | 1½ | 1 keyboard : 3½ oct. and 2 notes : compass extended 18th cent. Inscribed as No. 1. On lid, SIC TRANSIT GLORIA MUNDI. Stand a row of five balusters. | E. van der Straeten. | .. |
| 16 | 15 | 1628 | Bentside. | 7 7½ × 3 | 6½ | Width increased for extended compass : sound-board painted with flowers and foliage. A. R. rose (No. 6). | W. H. Burns and Captain Hall. | .. |
| 17 | .. | 1628 | Bentside. | | .. | Converted into a pianoforte of 5 oct. (F—F) by Zeitter. A. R. rose (No. 6). Outside of case decorated with figures and musical instruments on a gold ground and surrounded by animals and birds. Lid painting—a landscape with figures. All 18th-cent. work. A Louis Quinze gilt stand. | James Goding, London (sold 1857). | .. |
| 18 | 67 | 1632 | Oblong. | 5 8 × 1 | 7½ | 1 keyboard to right hand of front : 4½ oct. (C—F) : white naturals. A. R. rose (No. 6). On lid, MUSICA MAGNORUM SOLAMEN DULCE LABORUM. | A. Régibo. | .. |
| 19 | 68 | 1633 | Oblong. | 2 1½ × 1 | 6 | 1 keyboard to left hand of front : 4½ oct. (C—F) : white naturals. A. R. rose (No. 6). Hardwood jacks of double thickness : painting inside lid. | A. Régibo. | .. |
| 20 | 69 | 1633 | Bentside. | 7 0 × 2 | 3 | 1 keyboard : 4 oct. and a tone (C—D) with lowest C♯ omitted. Originally with unison and octave strings : altered at later date to two unison strings (see Nos. 39, 40). White naturals. Inscribed ANDREAS RUCKERS IN ANTVERPEN, ANNO 1633. Stand in rococo style. Illustrated in P. de Wit's Perlen (1892) and Heyer Museum Catalogue (1910). | Paul de Wit, Leipzig. | Heyer Museum, formerly Cologne now at Leipzig (No 71). |
| 21 | 70 | 1634 | .. | | .. | Inscribed ANDREAS RUCKERS ANTVERPIAE. Reported by E. van der Straeten. | In Flanders. | .. |
| 22 | 71 | 1636 | Bentside. | | .. | 2 keyboards : 5 oct. (F—F) : black naturals : extended compass stops, and stand legs like Taskin's work : beautifully painted. Inscribed as No. 1 with date 1636. Reported by E. van der Straeten. | At Dijon. | M. Girard ? Paris. |
| 23 | 72 | 1636 | Bentside. | 7 8 × 3 | 1 | 2 keyboards : 5 oct. (F—F) : black naturals : 5 stops, 4 à genouillère. Over the keys, ANDRE RUKUERS, ANNEE 1636. Near the wrest-pins, ' Fait par Paschal Taskin à Paris, 1782.' Extended compass but with original painted sound-board. A. R. rose (No. 6). Case decorated with lacquer in Chinese style. Exhibited at the Inventions Exhibition, London, 1885. | Queen Marie Clotilde of France, wife of Emmanuel IV., King of Sardinia. | Museo Civico, Turin. |
| 24 | 73 | 1639 | Bentside. | 6 4 × 2 | 9 | 2 keyboards : 4½ oct. (G—D) : white naturals. 3 stops. Case dark green powdered with gold. Painted sound-board. A. R. rose (No. 6). | C. Cramp. J. Morley, London. | D. F. Scheurleer, The Hague. |
| 25 | 74 | 1640 | Bentside. | 6 0 × 2 | 5 | 1 keyboard : 4 oct. and a tone (C—D) : white naturals. 2 stops. Inscribed ANDREAS RUCKERS, 1640. A. R. rose (No. 6). On lid, MUSICA LAETITIAE COMES, MEDICINA DOLORUM. On flap, CONCORDIA MUSIS AMICA. Case with patterned paper. | Rev. Thomas Twining, Colchester, 1800. Miss Twining, Twickenham. | Miss B. Skinner, Holyoake, Mass., U.S.A. |
| 26 | .. | 1644 | Oblong. | 7 4 × 1 | 8 | A double virginal : 2 keyboards, side by side, the octave instrument a modern replacement. 4 oct. with added low C♯. A. R. rose (No. 6). Painted sound-board with date 1644. Case with patterned paper : on lid, OMNIS SPIRITUS LAUDET DOMINUM. | Prince de Caraman Chimay. | Heyer Museum, formerly Cologne now at Leipzig (No. 1093). |
| 27 | 75 | 1644 | Oblong. | 5 8 × 1 | 8 | 1 keyboard : 4 oct. (C—C). Inscribed ANDREAS RUCKERS, ANNO 1644. | V. Mahillon, Brussels. | .. |
| 28 | 76 | 1646 | Bentside. | 7 5 × 3 | 0 | 2 keyboards : extended to 5 oct. Black naturals : inscribed as No. 1 with date 1646. A. R. rose (No. 6). | Paul Endel, Paris. | .. |
| 29 | .. | 1648 | Bentside. | 6 0 × 2 | 6 | 1 keyboard : 4 oct. and one tone (C—D) chromatic, having been completed. 3 stops. Inscribed as No. 1. A. R. rose (No. 6). Painted sound-board with date 1648. Case dark green with arabesques. On front board, SOLI DEO GLORIA. On lid, ACTA VIRUM PROBANT and SIC TRANSIT GLORIA MUNDI. The numerals 69 are written inside the case in ink inside, and are supposed to give the age of the maker : if so, they are correct. | .. | Otto van Koppenhagen, New York. |
| 30 | 77 | 1651 | Bentside. | 6 8 × 3 | 0 | 2 keyboards (not original) : nearly 5 oct. (G—F) lowest G♯ omitted. White naturals. Inscribed as No. 1 with date 1651 (also on sound-board). A. R. rose (No. 6). Black case : on lid, SIC TRANSIT GLORIA MUNDI : on | Christopher Smith. Lady Rivers. Mr. Wickham. Canon Hawtrey. Dr. Chard. Messrs Broadwood. | Victoria and Albert Museum, South Kensington (No. 1079). |

| No. | No. 2nd Edition | Date. | Shape. | Size. | | General Description. | Former Owners. | Present Owner. |
|---|---|---|---|---|---|---|---|---|
| | | | | ft. in. | ft. in. | | | |
| | | | | | | flap, MUSICA DONUM DEI, and formerly on front board, ACTA VIRUM PROBANT. Painted sound-board with flowers and a concert of monkeys. No stand. Said to have been Handel's 'large harpsichord,' given by him to his pupil Christopher Smith : but see A. 12. Illustrated in the Museum Catalogues (1874 and 1908) and also on *PLATE* . | | |
| 31 | 78 | Undated. | Oblong. | 2 7 | ×1 3½ | 1 keyboard in the middle of the front : 4 oct. (C—C). White naturals. A. R. rose (No. 6). | A. Régibo. | .. |
| 32 | 79 | .. | Bentside. | 7 6 | ×2 7 | 2 keyboards : lower, 4½ oct. (G—C) with bass short octave : upper, 4 oct. (C—C) with bass short octave. 3 stops : no name or rose, and jack rail missing : no keys and in dilapidated condition. Style of Andreas Ruckers. On lid, OMNIS SPIRITUS LAUDET DOMINUM and CONCORDIA RES PARVAE CRESCUNT, DISCORDIA MAXIMAE DILABUNTUR. Fine arcaded stand. | .. | Musée du Steen, Antwerp (No. P. 3). |
| 33 | 80 | .. | Bentside. | 7 3 | ×2 11 | 2 keyboards : 5 oct. (F—F) : black naturals. Inscribed as No. 1. Date of extension and renovation (1758) marked on a jack : fine paintings attributed to Watteau : carved and gilt stand. Exhibited at Brussels Exhibition, 1880. | .. | Baron de Göer, Château de Velu, Pas de Calais, France. |
| 34 | 81 | .. | Oblong. | 3 8 | ×1 5 | 1 keyboard : 4½ oct. (C—F) chromatic, having been extended : white naturals. Inscribed as No. 1. A. R. rose (No. 6). Case with patterned paper. On lid, SIC TRANSIT GLORIA MUNDI. | .. | Musée du Conservatoire, Brussels, (No. 1593). |
| 35 | 82 | .. | Bentside. | 6 6 | ×2 8 | 2 keyboards : nearly 5 oct. (G—F) with bass short octave : white naturals. Name and rose missing : attributed to Andreas Ruckers by the work. | C. Snoeck. | .. |
| 36 | 83 | .. | Oblong. | 3 8 | ×1 4 | 1 keyboard : 4 oct. (C—C) with bass short octave. A. R. rose (No. 6). | C. Snoeck. | .. |
| 37 | 84 | .. | Bentside. | 6 1 | ×2 10 | 1 keyboard : 4 oct. (C—C) without lowest C♯ : white naturals A. R. rose (No. 6). On lid—a hunting scene. | G. de Prins, Louvain. | .. |
| 38 | 85 | .. | Four-cornered. | 2 8 | ×1 0½ | 1 keyboard, projecting 4 in. : 4 oct. and one tone (C—D) with bass short octave. White naturals. Inscribed as No. 1. A. R. rose. Inside painted with curved design in black on white ground with red line Georgian mahogany case. | W. H. Hammond Jones, Witley, Godalming. | .. |
| 39 | 86 | .. | Bentside. | 6 0 | ×2 5 | 1 keyboard : 4 oct. and one tone (C—D) with bass short octave : probably white naturals, but only one black sharp key left. A. R. rose (No. 6). On lid—a stag hunt with floral designs. 2 stops : originally unison and octave : later two unisons : now unison and octave. Case green. | .. | Musée du Steen, Antwerp (No. P. 26). |
| 40 | 87 | .. | Bentside. | 6 0 | ×2 5 | 1 keyboard : 4 oct. (C—C) chromatic : white naturals. A. R. rose (No. 6). Case painted in marbled green. On lid, SIC TRANSIT GLORIA MUNDI. 2 stops altered and rearranged as in No. 39. Also an inserted ' mute ' stop. | Musée du Steen, Antwerp (No. P. 27). | Museum Vleeschhuis, Antwerp. |
| 41 | 88 | .. | Bentside. | 6 4 | ×2 9 | 2 keyboards : 4½ oct. (G—D) chromatic : white naturals. 3 stops. Inscribed as No. 1. Case covered with dark-green paper spotted with gold : parts of interior and front board gilded. A. R. rose in painted sound-board. Illustrated in Boddington Collection Catalogue, 1888. | J. Kendrick Pyne. Boddington Collection, Manchester. Howard Head, London. | .. |
| 42 | .. | .. | Bentside. | 7 8 | ×3 1½ | 2 keyboards : 5½ oct. (C—F), extended compass with bass short octave, but now tuned from bass E chromatically : black naturals. A. R. rose (No. 6). 2 stops. Outside of case green with panels in old gold. Inside of lid red lacquer : painted sound-board. Stand (18th cent.) with seven legs. | .. | Albert Steinert, Providence, U.S.A. |
| 43 | .. | .. | Bentside. | 5 6 | ×3 0 | 2 keyboards : nearly 4 oct. (G—F) : white naturals Inscribed as No. 1 with date (illegible). A. R. rose (No. 6). Outside of case decorated with paintings and large ornamental hinges : inside with lacquer. Painted sound-board. | .. | Alexander Steinert, Boston, U.S.A. |
| 44 | 20 | .. | Oblong. | 5 7½ | ×1 7½ | 1 keyboard : 4 oct. (C—C) with bass short octave : white naturals. A. R. rose (No. 6). Case with patterned paper : outside painted in panels. On lid—a view of Antwerp in oils. Original stand with arcaded pillars. This instrument is certainly the work of Andreas Ruckers, but a badly-fitting jack-rail from some other instrument, inscribed ' Ioannes Ruckers fecit Antwerpiae,' has been introduced. The present lid is 3 ins. | A. Jacobs-Wens, Antwerp. Musée du Steen, Antwerp (No. P. 2). | Museum Vleeschhuis, Antwerp. |

| No. | No. 2nd Edition. | Date. | Shape. | Size. | General Description. | Former Owners. | Present Owner. |
|---|---|---|---|---|---|---|---|
| | | | | | too short for the case. Originally in the Steen Museum, it corresponds closely in size and compass to the virginal A. 11 now missing : but it is undated and bears the A. R. rose. In 1619 Andreas Ruckers made a large harpsichord for the Guild of St. Luke, and in 1638 a costly instrument for the Archduchess Isabella of Austria and the Netherlands. E. van der Straeten reported an instrument dated 1613 by this maker as in the Steen Museum, but it is now missing : and Herr Kinsky considers that the small octave virginal, dated 1617, in the Musée du Conservatoire de Musique, Paris (No. 316), and labelled Italian, should be attributed to this maker. Blondel (*Hist. anecdotique du piano*) mentions a Ruckers clavecin painted by Gravelot. In the Brownsea Collection (Dorset) there is an Andreas (undated), now a piano. | | |

(7)

## D. ANDREAS RUCKERS (THE YOUNGER), 1607–*c.* 1670

Free maker's mark—a winged figure seated and holding a harp, with the initials A. R., as in Rose No. 7

| No. | No. 2nd Edition. | Date. | Shape. | Size. | General Description. | Former Owners. | Present Owner. |
|---|---|---|---|---|---|---|---|
| | | | | ft. in.  ft. in. | | | |
| 1 | 89 | 1655 | Bentside. | .. . | Case painted in blue camaieu in rococo style : attributed to the younger Andreas from its late date. | M. Lavignée (from the Château de Perceau, près Cosne). | .. |
| 2 | 90 | 1656 | Bentside. | 5  4½ × 2  2½ | 1 original keyboard : 4 oct. (C—C) : white naturals. Painting inside lid. A. R. rose (No. 7). | M. Régibo, Renaix. | .. |
| 3 | 91 | 1659 | Bentside. | 5  10 × 2  4 | 1 original keyboard : 4 oct. (C—C) : white naturals. A. R. rose (No. 7). | M. Régibo. | .. |
| 4 | .. | 1667 | Bentside. | .. | 'Un beau clavecin.' Reported by F. J. Fétis, 1865. | .. | .. |
| 5 | 92 | Undated. | Oblong. | 4  9 × 1  5½ | 1 original keyboard to the left : 4 oct. and a tone (D—E) : white naturals. A. R. rose No. 7. | M. Régibo. | .. |

(8)

## E. CHRISTOPHER (CHRISTOPHEL, CHRISTOFEL) RUCKERS, *c.* 1620

Free maker's mark—a winged figure standing and holding a harp, with the initials C. R., as in Rose No. 8

| No. | No. 2nd Edition. | Date. | Shape. | Size. | General Description. | Former Owners. | Present Owner. |
|---|---|---|---|---|---|---|---|
| | | | | ft. in.  ft. in. | | | |
| 1 | 93 | Undated. | Oblong. | 3  7 × 1  5½ | 1 original keyboard to the right : 4½ oct. (C—E) with bass short octave and upper D♯ omitted. White naturals. C. R. rose. Painted case with patterned paper inside. Painted sound-board. On lid, ACTA VIRUM PROBANT. Framed stand with turned legs. Illustrated in Museum 'Handbook of Keyboard Instruments,' 1903. | A. Régibo, Renaix. A. Pley, Brussels. | Metropolitan Museum of Art, New York (No. 2344). |
| 2 | 94 | .. | .. | .. | An instrument by Christophel Ruckers stated by E. van der Straeten to be in the Museum at Namur. | .. | Museum, Namur. |

RUDDIGORE; OR, THE WITCH'S CURSE (originally spelt RUDDYGORE), comic opera in 2 acts ; words by W. S. Gilbert, music by Sullivan. Produced Savoy Theatre, Jan. 22, 1887.

RUDERSDORFF, HERMINE (*b.* Ivanowsky, Ukraine, Dec. 12, 1822 ; *d.* Boston, Feb. 26, 1882). Her father, Joseph Rudersdorff, a distinguished violinist (afterwards of Hamburg), was then engaged at Ivanowsky. She learned singing at Paris from Bordogni, and at Milan from de Micherout, also master of Clara Novello, Catherine Hayes, etc. She first appeared in Germany in concerts, and sang the principal soprano music at the production of Mendelssohn's 'Lobgesang' at Leipzig, June 25, 1840. The next year she appeared on the stage at Carlsruhe with great success, and then at Frankfort—where in 1844 she married Dr. Küchenmeister, a professor of mathematics— and at Breslau, Berlin, etc. Her repertory was large, and included both dramatic and coloratura parts. On May 23, 1854, she first appeared in England in German opera at Drury Lane, as Donna Anna, and was fairly well received in that and her subsequent parts of Constance in Mozart's 'Entführung,' Agatha, Fidelio and Margaret of Valois, and in English as Elvira in 'Masaniello.' She took up her residence in England for several years, only occasionally visiting Germany for concerts and festivals. She sang at the Royal Italian Opera in 1855, also from 1861–65, as Donnas Anna and Elvira, Jemmy, Bertha, Natalia (' L'Étoile du nord '), etc. ; and in English at St. James's Theatre for a few nights in Loder's opera, 'Raymond and Agnes.' But it was as a concert-singer that she was best appreciated, her very powerful voice (not always pleasing), combined with admirable powers of declamation, certainty of execution and thorough musicianship, having enabled her to take high rank as a singer of oratorio. She was engaged at the Boston Festivals of 1871 and 1872, and finally settled in that city, becoming a teacher of singing there. For the Birmingham Festival of 1873 she wrote the libretto of Randegger's cantata 'Fridolin,' founded on Schiller's 'Gang nach dem Eisenhammer.' She had previously introduced, in 1869, at the Gewandhaus concerts, Leipzig, the same composer's scena 'Medea,' which she sang also at the Crystal Palace and in 1872 at Boston.    A. C.

RUDHALL, a family of bell-founders who carried on business in Bell Lane, Gloucester, from 1648 until late in the 18th century. Its successive members were Abraham, sen., Abraham, jun., Abel, Thomas and John. From catalogues published by them it appears that from 1648 to Lady Day, 1751, they had cast 2972 bells 'for sixteen cities ' and other places ' in forty-four several counties,' and at Lady Day 1774 the number had increased to 3594. During the foundry's existence 4521 bells were cast. Up to 1774 the business prospered, but after this date it declined, and the foundry was closed in 1830. The principal metropolitan peals cast by them were those of St. Bride, St. Dunstan-in-the-East, and St. Martin-in-the-Fields. The Rudhalls cast no large bells ; their largest is of 50 cwts. at Wells Cathedral, and their second largest at Bath Abbey, 38 cwts. With two exceptions, the tenors of all their peals are under 30 cwts. The most eminent member of the family was Abraham, jun. (*b.* 1657; *d.* Jan. 25, 1736). He was ' famed for his great skill, beloved and esteemed for his singular good nature and integrity,' and brought the art of bell-casting to great perfection. He was buried in Gloucester Cathedral. His daughter, Alicia, married William HINE, the cathedral organist. The last of the Rudhalls, the 3rd Abraham, a mercer, left the foundry to his daughter. She, in 1829, transferred her interest to Thomas MEARS, bell-founder of Whitechapel, into whose business it was merged.

              W. H. H. and W. W. S.

RUDOLPH JOHANN JOSEPH RAINER, ARCHDUKE OF AUSTRIA (*b.* Florence, Jan. 8, 1788; *d.* Baden, Vienna, July 24, 1831), was the youngest child of Leopold of Tuscany and Maria Louisa of Spain. Music was hereditary in his family. His great-grandfather, Carl VI., so accompanied an opera by Fux that the composer exclaimed : ' Bravo ! your Majesty might serve anywhere as chief Kapellmeister ! ' ' Not so fast, my dear chief Kapellmeister,' replied the Emperor ; ' we are better off as we are ! ' His grandmother, the great Maria Theresa, was a fine singer ; her children, from very early age, sang and performed cantatas and little dramas, to words by Metastasio, on birthdays and fêtes. His uncle, Max Franz, was Elector of Cologne, viola-player, and organiser of the splendid orchestra at Bonn, to which the Rombergs, Rieses, Reichas and Beethovens belonged. It was his father, Leopold, who, after the first performance of Cimarosa's ' Matrimonio segreto,' gave all those who took part in the production a supper, and then ordered the performance to be repeated ; and it was his aunt, Marie Antoinette, who supported Gluck against Piccinni at Paris.

Like the other children of the imperial family, Rudolph was instructed in music by Anton Teyber, and tradition says that as early as 12 or 14 he gave ample proof of more than ordinary musical talent and taste ; as soon as he had liberty of choice he exchanged Teyber for Beethoven. The precise date and circumstances attending this change have eluded investigation ; but it seems probable that the connexion between Rudolph, a youth of 16, and Beethoven, a man of 34, began in the winter of 1803–04.

Ries relates that Beethoven's **breaches of**

court etiquette were a constant source of trouble
to his pupil's chamberlains, who strove in vain
to enforce its rules on him. He at last lost
all patience, pushed his way into the young
Archduke's presence, and, excessively angry,
assured him that he had all due respect for his
person, but that the punctilious observance of
all the rules in which he was daily tutored
was not his business. Rudolph laughed good-
humouredly and gave orders that for the future
he should be allowed to go his own way.

Beethoven's triple concerto, op. 56 (1804),
though dedicated to Prince Lobkowitz, was
written, says Schindler, for the Archduke,
Seidler and Kraft. The work does not require
great execution in the piano part, but a youth
of 16 able to play it must be a very respectable
performer.

The weakness of the Archduke's constitution
is said to have been the cause of his entering
the Church. The coadjutorship of Olmütz
secured to him the succession; and the income
of the position was probably not a bad one;
for, though his allowance as Archduke in a
family so very numerous was of necessity comparatively small, yet in the spring of 1809, just
after completing his 21st year, he subscribed
1500 florins to Beethoven's annuity. In 1818
Beethoven determined to compose a Solemn
Mass for the installation service of his pupil, a
year or two later. On Sept. 28, 1819, the Cardinal's insignia arrived from the Pope, and the
installation was at length fixed for Mar. 9,[1] 1820.
But the Mass had assumed such gigantic proportions that the ceremony had passed nearly
two years before it was completed.[2] Instead of
it, the music performed was a Mass in B♭, by
Hummel; a Te Deum in C, by Preindl; ' Ecce
Sacerdos magnus,' by a ' Herr P. v. R.'; and
Haydn's Offertorium in D minor.

Apart from the annuity, Rudolph's purse was
probably often opened to his master; but the
strongest proofs of his respect and affection are
to be found in his careful preservation of Beethoven's most insignificant letters; in the zeal
with which he collected for his library everything published by him; in his purchase of
the caligraphic copy of his works made by
Haslinger[3]; and in his patience with him, often
in trying circumstances. For Beethoven, notwithstanding all his obligations to his patron,
chafed under the interference with his perfect
liberty, which duty to the Archduke-Cardinal
occasionally imposed. There are passages in
his letters to Ries and others (suppressed in
publication), as well as in the conversation-
books, which show how galling even this light
yoke was to Beethoven; and one feels in

perusing those addressed to the Archduke how
frivolous are some of the excuses for not attending him at the proper hour, and how hollow
and insincere are the occasional compliments,
as Rudolph must have felt. That Beethoven
was pleased to find the Forty Variations dedicated to him by ' his pupil, R. E. H.' (Rudolph
Erz-Herzog), was probably the fact; but it is
doubtful whether his satisfaction warranted the
superlatives in which his letter of thanks is
couched. Other letters again breathe throughout nothing but a true and warm affection for
his pupil. Köchel sensibly remarks that the
trouble lay in Beethoven's

' aversion to the enforced performance of regular
duties, especially to giving lessons and teaching the
theory of music, in which it is well known his strength
did not lie, and for which he had to prepare himself.'

When the untamed nature of Beethoven, and
his deafness, are considered, together with his
lack of worldly wisdom and his absolute need of
a Maecenas, one feels deeply how fortunate he
was to have attracted and retained the sympathy and affection of a man of such sweet and
tender qualities as Archduke Rudolph.

We can hardly expect an Archduke-Cardinal
to be a voluminous composer, but the Forty
Variations already mentioned, and a sonata for
PF. and clarinet, composed for Count Ferdinand
Troyer, both published by Haslinger, are good
specimens of his musical talents and acquirements. There is also a set of Variations on a
theme of Rossini, corrected by Beethoven in
MS. He was for many years the ' protector '
of the great Gesellschaft der Musikfreunde at
Vienna, and bequeathed to it his very valuable
musical library. An oil portrait in the possession of his son shows a rather intellectual face,
of the Hapsburg type, but its peculiarities so
softened as to be more than ordinarily pleasing,
and even handsome.[4]

The Archduke's published works are the two
alluded to above: Theme by L. van Beethoven,
with Forty Variations—for PF. solo (Haslinger); Sonata for PF. and clarinet, op. 2, in
A (Haslinger).                               A. W. T.

RUDORFF, ERNEST (b. Berlin, Jan. 18,
1840; d. there, Dec. 31, 1916), composer,
pianist and teacher. His family was of Hanoverian extraction. At the age of 5 he received
his first musical instruction from a god-daughter
of C. M. von Weber, an excellent pianist and
of a thoroughly poetical nature. From his 12th
to his 17th year he was a pupil of Bargiel in
PF. playing and composition. A song and a
PF. piece composed at this period he afterwards
thought worthy of publication (op. 2, No. 1;
op. 10, No. 4). For a short time in 1858
he had the advantage of PF. lessons from
Mme. Schumann, and from his 12th to his
14th year learned the violin under Louis Ries.
In 1857 he entered the Friedrichs Gymnasium,

---

[1] This date is from the report of the event in the *Wiener musikalische Zeitung* of Mar. 25, 1820.
[2] Beethoven announces its completion in a letter to the Archduke,
Feb. 27, 1822.
[3] These, a splendid series of red folio volumes beautifully copied,
are conspicuous in the Library of the Gesellschaft der Musikfreunde
at Vienna.

[4] For a more detailed notice see the *Musical World*, Apr. 2, 1881.

whence in 1859 he passed to the Berlin university. During the whole of this time his thoughts were bent on the musical profession. When Joachim visited Berlin in 1852 Rudorff had played before him, and had made such a favourable impression that Joachim advised his being allowed to follow the profession of music. His father at length consented that he should go at Michaelmas, 1859, and attend the Conservatorium and the university at Leipzig. After two terms of theology and history he devoted himself exclusively to music, and on leaving the Conservatorium in 1861, continued his musical studies for a year under Hauptmann and Reinecke. Rudorff went to Stockhausen early in 1864, conducted those of the Choral Society's concerts in which Stockhausen himself sang, and finally made concert tours with him. In 1865 he became professor at the Cologne Conservatorium, and there in 1867 he founded the Bach Society, whose performance at their first concert in 1869 gave such satisfaction to Rudorff that he at first refused an appointment as professor in the new Hochschule at Berlin under Joachim's direction. He afterwards changed his mind, and from Oct. 1869 to 1910, when he retired, was first professor of PF.-playing and director of the piano classes in that institution, besides conducting part of the orchestral practices, and in Joachim's absence directing the public performances. In the summer of 1880, on Max Bruch's appointment as director of the Liverpool Philharmonic Society, Rudorff succeeded him as conductor of the Stern Singing-Society in Berlin, but without resigning his post at the Hochschule. He retained the direction of this Society till 1890.

He had talent for piano-playing, though an unfortunate nervousness prevented him from exercising it much in public. His tone was beautiful, his conception poetical, and he possessed considerable power of execution, never degenerating into mere display. He was an excellent teacher; but his greatest gifts were shown in composition. His musical style was founded throughout upon the romantic school of Chopin, Mendelssohn and Schumann, and especially of Weber. His partsongs interest by their elegance and thoughtfulness, but few, if any, leave a pleasant impression on the mind. This is true also of his solo songs. He had an almost feminine horror of anything rough or common, and often carried this to such a pitch as seriously to interfere with simplicity and naturalness. He deeply imbibed the romantic charm of Weber's music, but the bold easy mirth which at times does not shrink from trivialities was unfortunately utterly strange to him. His early songs opp. 1 and 2 foliow, it is true, closely in Schumann's steps, but they are among the most beautiful that have been written in his style.

Rudorff's works are for the most part of great technical difficulty, and many of them are over-elaborated, a fact which has kept his works from being as well known as they deserve. The following is a list of his principal works :

| Op. | | Op. | |
|---|---|---|---|
| 1. | Variations for two PF. | | from Tieck, for soli, |
| 2. | Six songs. | | chorus and orchestra. |
| 3. | Six songs from Eichendorff. | 20. | Serenade for orchestra. |
| 4. | Six duets for PF. | 22. | Six three-part songs for |
| 5. | Sextet for strings (played at | | female voices. |
| | the Popular Concerts in | 24. | Variations on an original |
| | Apr. 1900 and Jan. 1903). | | theme for orchestra. |
| 6. | Four partsongs for mixed | 25. | Four six-part songs. |
| | voices. | 26. | 'Gesang an die Sterne,' by |
| 7. | Romance for violoncello and | | Rückert, for six-part |
| | orchestra. | | chorus and orchestra. |
| 8. | Overture to 'Der blonde Ek- | 27. | Six four-part songs. |
| | bert' for orchestra. | 29. | Two études for PF. |
| 9. | Six partsongs for female | 30. | Four partsongs for mixed |
| | voices. | | choir. |
| 10. | Eight Fantasiestücke for PF. | 31. | Symphony in B flat. |
| 11. | Four partsongs for mixed | 38. | Kinderwalzer for PF. duet. |
| | voices. | 40. | Symphony in G minor (1891). |
| 12 | Overture to 'Otto der Schütz' | 45. | Romantic overture for orch. |
| | for orchestra. | 54. | Pieces for PF. duet. |
| 13. | Four partsongs for mixed | 55. | Variations. |
| | voices. | | Symphonic variations for |
| 14. | Fantasie for PF. | | orchestra. |
| 15. | Ballade for full orchestra. | | Scherzo capriccioso for |
| 18. | 'Der Aufzug der Romanze,' | | orchestra. |

He also arranged Schubert's 4-hand fantasia in F minor (op. 103) for orchestra.

P. S., with addns.

BIBL.—*Briefwechsel* (see BRAHMS and JOACHIM).

RUE, PIERRE DE LA, also known as Pierchon, Perisson, Pierson, Pierzon, Pierozon and Petrus Platensis (b. Picardy, mid. 15th cent.; d. Courtrai, Nov. 20, 1518), fellow-pupil of Josquin des Prés in the school of Okeghem. State records prove that he was in the service of the court of Burgundy in the years 1477, 1492, 1496, 1499, 1500 and 1502. In 1501 he was a prebend of Courtrai, and later held a similar benefice at Namur, which he resigned in 1510. He was in the service of Charles V. until 1512, when he entered that of Margaret of Austria, 'gouvernante' of the Netherlands.

Writers on music have accorded him a position as a contrapuntal composer scarcely second to that of Josquin, and the magnificent copies of his masses made by order of the Princess Margaret of Austria, and now in the libraries of Vienna and Brussels, testify to the value set upon his works by those he served. Indeed, considering his great reputation, it is somewhat surprising that so little is known of the events of his life, and that so little of his music has been printed. Of the thirty-six masses now existing Petrucci printed five in the composer's lifetime ('Misse Petri de la Rue'; Venetiis, 1503), and a few more in later collections. Twenty-three remain in MS. Of motets, only twenty-five (though thirty-eight have been identified), and of secular pieces no more than ten, are to be found in the publications of the 16th century—a small result compared with the long catalogue of Josquin's printed works. Burney, Forkel and Kiesewetter give short examples from Pierre de la Rue's compositions. (See *Q.-L.* for list of works in MS.)

J. R. S. B., with addns.

BIBL.—E. DROZ and G. THIBAULT: *Bibliographie des recueils de chansons du XVe siècle.*
REPRINTS.—H. EXPERT: 'Les Maîtres musiciens de la Renaissanc française': Missa, 'Ave Maria' (vol. 8): 'Extraits des maître

musiciens de a Renaissance française': 'Ma Mère hélas! mariez-moy'; 'O Salutaris Hostia' (Paris, Sénart). CH. BORDES: (1) Trois chansons du 15e siècle à 3 voix'; 'Il me fait mal de vous voir languir' (Paris, Rouart et Lerolle). (2) 'Anthologie des maîtres religieux primitifs ' (Paris, Bureau d'édition de la Schola Cantorum): 'O Salutaris Hostia.'

**RÜBEZAHL**, opera in 2 acts; words by J. G. Rhode; music by WEBER, q.v.      G.

**RÜCKAUF, ANTON** (b. Prague, Mar. 13, 1855; d. Schloss Alt-Erlaa, Sept. 19, 1903), was a pupil of Proksch, and studied at the same time at the Prague Organ School. He taught for a time at Proksch's Institute till he went, at the expense of the state, to further his studies in Vienna, where, advised by Brahms, he learnt counterpoint with Nottebohm, and with Navratil when Nottebohm died. His connexion with Gustav Walter, whose permanent accompanist he was, had a great influence over his development as a composer of songs. His compositions are of various sorts, including songs, ' Balladen,' settings to five Minnelieder of Walter con der Vogelweide, gipsy songs, duets, choral songs with PF. accompaniment and also a cappella, besides a violin sonata (op. 7), a PF. quintet (op. 13), some piano solos and duets, and an opera, ' Die Rosenthalerin,' which was produced at Dresden in 1897, and attracted a considerable amount of attention.      H. V. H.

**RUEDA,** see SONG, subsection SPAIN (3).

**RÜHLING,** (1) HANS (b. Borna, Saxony, c. mid. 16th cent.), from 1572–75 organist at Geithain, Saxony; organist at Döbeln, c. 1572; and from c. 1582 at Groitzsch, near Leipzig. He wrote ' Tabulaturbuch auf Orgeln und Instrument,' etc. (1583), containing 86 German and Latin sacred songs, arranged in organ tablature, with names of the original composers.

His son, (2) SAMUEL (b. Groitzsch, c. 1586; d. Dresden, June 1626), was cantor at the Pauliner church, Leipzig, and from Sept. 17, 1612, at the ' Kreuzkirche,' Dresden; also poet laureate and Archdean. He composed motets, 8, 9 v., which remained in MS.      E. V. D. S.

**KÜHLMANN, FRANS** (b. Brussels, Jan. 11, 1868), conductor. He was a pupil at the Brussels Conservatoire, and took part in the orchestra of the Théâtre de la Monnaie for seven years. After conducting at Rouen, Liège, Antwerp, Brussels, etc., he was engaged at the Opéra-Comique, in place of Büsser, and conducted for the first time (' Carmen '), Sept. 6, 1905. He succeeded Luigini (d. July 29, 1906) as principal conductor, and has been conductor of the Paris Opéra since 1914. He is also principal conductor at the Concerts Colonne, and has conducted the popular concerts at Antwerp since 1920.      J. G. P.

**RUFFO, VINCENZO,** a member of a noble Veronese family, who flourished as a composer in the 16th century. His name is included by Baini in his list of the ' good musicians ' of his fourth epoch. Unless a fifth-part Magnificat, stated to have been published at Venice in 1539 and to exist at Lüneburg, be a genuine work, his first publication would seem to be a book of motets dated 1542, where he is described as ' musico ' (i.e. castrato) in the service of the Marchese Alfonso d' Avalli. In 1554 he became maestro di cappella at the cathedral of Verona, and in 1563 was appointed to a similar post at the cathedral of Milan. In 1574–79 he was at Pistoia in the same capacity, and in 1580 we find him again at Milan. His last publication, a book of masses, dated 1592, contains no mention of any official post, and it is argued that he therefore held none in his latest years. The other masses appeared in 1557, 1574 and 1580; motets in 1542, 1555 and 1583; settings of the Magnificat in 1578, and psalms a 5 in 1574. His madrigals were published in 1545, 1554, 1555, 1556 and 1560. The psalms and a Mass were written for his patron Saint Carlo Borromeo in accordance with the decrees of the Council of Trent. An Adoramus is printed by Lück, and a madrigal, ' See from his ocean bed,' edited by Oliphant, is in Hullah's Part Music. Torchi, in his ' Arte musicale in Italia,' vol. i., gives two movements from masses, a motet and two madrigals. The libraries of Ch. Ch. and the R.C.M. contain specimens of his works in MS., and for others the article in Q.-L. and an interesting monograph by Luigi Torri in R.M.I. iii. 635, and iv. 233, should be consulted.      M.

**RUGGI, FRANCESCO** (b. Naples, Oct. 21, 1767: d. there, Jan. 23, 1845), was a pupil of Fenaroli at Conservatorio S. Maria di Loreto; in 1795 deputy maestro di cappella of Naples; in 1825 successor of Tritto as professor of counterpoint and composition at the Conservatorio of S. Pietro a Majella, where Bellini and Carafa were among his pupils. He composed 5 operas, an oratorio, numerous masses and other church and secular music (Q.-L.; Mendel; Riemann).

**RUGGIERI,** the name of a celebrated family of violin-makers, who flourished at Cremona and Brescia. The eldest was (1) FRANCESCA, commonly known as 'Ruggieri il Per ' (the father), whose instruments date from 1668–1720 or thereabouts; (2) GIOVANNI BAPTISTA (1700–25), and (3) PIETRO (1700–20), who form the second generation of the family, were probably his sons; Giovanni Baptista (2) (called ' il buono '), who was indisputably the best maker in the family, claims to have been a pupil of Nicolo Amati. Besides these, we hear of (4) GUIDO and (5) VINCENZO, both of Cremona, early in the 18th century. The instruments of the Ruggieri, though differing widely among themselves, bear a general resemblance to those of the Amati family.      E. J. P.

RUIMONTE (RIMONTE), PEDRO (*b.* Saragossa), Spanish madrigalist, brought from Spain by the Infanta Isabella at the time of her marriage to the Archduke Albert, Governor of the Netherlands. From 1603–05 he was *maestro musico de camera* at the archducal court at Brussels. In 1614 he received a sum of money to enable him to return to Spain, but was apparently in Brussels once more in 1618. His madrigals, published in the same year, are the only examples of the later chromatic madrigal with Spanish words. He also set a few popular Spanish villancicos, with a verse of 2 or 3 v. ; and refrain for 5 or 6 v. His printed works are as follows :

Cantiones sacræ 4, 5, 6 et 7 v. et Hieremiæ Prophetæ Lamentationes 6 v. Antwerp, 1607. Phalèse. (Wolfenbüttel : tenor only.)
Missæ, 6 v. Antwerp, 1614. Phalèse (B.M.).
Parnaso Español de Madrigales y Villancicos a 4, 5 y 6. Antwerp, 1614. Phalèse. (Christ Church, Oxford, sextus missing; Bibl. Nat., Paris ; Bibl. de la Diputació, Barcelona, quintus only. Two of the 6-part madrigals, without words, in B.M. Add. MSS. 30,816-19.)
                     J. B. T.

RUINS OF ATHENS, THE, dramatic piece (Nachspiel) written by Kotzebue, with an overture and eight numbers composed by Beethoven (op. 113) in 1811, for the opening of a new theatre at Pest, Feb. 9, 1812. The overture to 'The Ruins of Athens' and the Turkish March No. 4 were published in 1823, but the rest of the music remained in MS. till 1846.                G.

RUIZ DE RIBAYAZ, LUCAS (*b.* near Burgos, 17th cent.), Spanish guitarist, prebendary of the Collegiate Church of Villafranca del Bierzo, who published a book of tablature entitled

Luz y Norte musical para caminar por las cifras de la Guitarra Española. y Arpa. . . . Madrid. 1677. (B.M. ; Brussels, Conservatoire ; Madrid, Bibl. Nac., Bibl. Medinaceli.)

It is of considerable interest owing to the number of 17th - century Spanish dances it contains.                J. B. T.

RULE, BRITANNIA ! Song composed by Arne for his masque of 'Alfred' (the words by Thomson and Mallet), and first performed at Cliefden House, Maidenhead, Aug. 1, 1740. Cliefden was then the residence of Frederick, Prince of Wales, and the occasion was to commemorate the accession of George I. and the birthday of Princess Augusta. The masque was repeated on the following night, and published by Millar, Aug. 19, 1740.

Dr. Arne afterwards altered the masque into an opera and it was so performed at the Smock Alley Theatre, Dublin, on Mar. 10, 1744. In the advertisement it is announced that 'Alfred' will conclude with a

'favourable Ode in honour of Great Britain, beginning "When Britain first at Heaven's command." '

It was not heard in London till Mar. 20, 1745, when it was given at Drury Lane for the benefit of Mrs. Arne.

The year 1745, in which the opera was produced, is memorable for the Jacobite rising in the North, and in 1746 Handel produced his

'Occasional Oratorio,' in which he refers to its suppression, 'War shall cease, welcome Peace,' adapting those words to the opening bars of 'Rule, Britannia !'—in itself a great proof of the popularity of the air.[1]

War shall cease,        wel - come Peace.

'Rule, Britannia !' was first published by Henry Waylett as an appendix (with another song) to Arne's 'Music in the Judgment of Paris.' The copyright privilege is dated Jan. 29, 1740–41.    w. c. abridged ; addns. F. K.

BIBL.—J. CUTHBERT HARRIS, *The Nineteenth Century*, Dec. 1896 ; CHURTON COLLINS, *The Saturday Review*, Feb. 20, 1897 ; CHAPPELL, *Popular Music of the Olden Times.*

RUMFORD, ROBERT KENNERLEY (*b.* London, Sept. 2, 1870), a baritone singer who, after study with Henschel and Alfred Blume, made a successful first appearance at one of Henschel's symphony concerts at St. James's Hall, Feb. 16, 1893.

In 1894 he studied with Georges Sbriglia in Paris, and subsequently in England made his reputation in works of a serious kind, such as Bach's 'St. Matthew Passion' (Bach Festival at Queen's Hall, Apr. 6, 1897) and Brahms's 'Ernste Gesänge' (St. James's Hall Popular Concert, Jan. 31, 1898). After his marriage with Clara BUTT (*q.v.*) his career changed its course, and he was associated with her in popular concerts of a different type from those of the old St. James's Hall. Their 'Grand Concerts' at the Albert Hall have been repeated in tours all over the English-speaking world, and were interrupted only by the war, when Rumford served in France (1914–17), and later in the Special Intelligence Department of the War Office.                C.

RUMMEL, a German musical family.

(1) CHRISTIAN FRANZ LUDWIG FRIEDRICH ALEXANDER (*b.* Brichsenstadt, Bavaria, Nov. 27, 1787 ; *d.* Wiesbaden, Feb. 13, 1849) was educated at Mannheim, and seems to have had instruction from the Abbé Vogler. In 1806 he took the post of bandmaster to the 2nd Nassau infantry, made the Peninsular Campaign, married in Spain, was taken prisoner, released, and served with his regiment at Waterloo. He was then employed by the Duke of Nassau to form and lead his court orchestra, which he did with great credit to himself till 1841, when it was dissolved. He was not only an able conductor and a composer of much ability and industry, but a fine clarinettist and a good pianist. His works are numerous, and embrace pieces for military band, concertos, quintets and other pieces for clarinet, many pianoforte compositions, especi-

---

[1] By a singular anachronism, Schoelcher. in his *Life of Handel* (p. 299), accuses Arne of copying these and other bars in the song from Handel, instead of Handel's quoting them from Arne.

ally a sonata for four hands (op. 20), waltzes, variations, etc., and a Method for the PF.

His daughter, (2) JOSEPHINE (b. Manzanares, Spain, May 12, 1812 ; d. Dec. 19, 1877), was pianist at the court at Wiesbaden.

His son, (3) JOSEPH (b. Wiesbaden, Oct. 6, 1818; d. London, Mar. 25, 1880), was educated by his father in music generally, and in the clarinet and PF. in particular, on both of which he was a good player. He was for many years Kapell-meister to the Prince of Oldenburg, then residing at Wiesbaden—a post in which he was succeeded by Adolph Henselt. Up to 1842 he lived in Paris, and then removed to London for five years. In 1847 he returned to Paris, and remained there till driven back to London by the war in 1870 ; and in London he resided till his death. Joseph Rummel wrote no original music, but he was one of the most prolific arrangers of operas and operatic selections for the PF. that ever existed. For nearly forty years he worked incessantly for the houses of Schott and Escudier, publish-ing about 400 pieces with each house under his own name, besides a much larger number under noms de plume. His arrangements and tran-scriptions amount in all to fully 2000. He wrote also a series of exercises for Augener & Co., and for Escudier.

Joseph's sister, (4) FRANZISKA (b. Wiesbaden, Feb. 4, 1821), was educated by her father until she went to Paris to study singing under Bordogni, and afterwards to Lamperti at Milan. She became principal singer at the court of Wiesbaden, and at length married Peter Schott, the well-known music publisher at Brussels, who died in 1873.

Another son, (5) AUGUST (b. Wiesbaden, Jan. 14, 1824; d. London, Dec. 14, 1886), a capable pianist, became a merchant in London.

His son, (6) FRANZ (b. London, Jan. 11, 1853; d. Berlin, May 2, 1901), at the age of 14 went to Brussels to study the PF. under Brassin, first as a private pupil and afterwards in the Conservatoire. He took the first prize for PF.-playing there in 1872, and afterwards became one of the staff of teachers. He made his first public appearance at Antwerp, Dec. 22, 1872, in Henselt's PF. concerto ; in July 1873 played Schumann's concerto at the Albert Hall Concerts, London ; and again at Brussels, before the King and Queen of the Belgians, with great distinction. He remained at the Con-servatoire as professor till 1876, when on the advice of Rubinstein he threw up his post and began to travel, playing in the Rhine provinces, Holland and France. Early in 1877 he came to London, and played at the Crystal Palace on Apr. 7. Next year he went to America, where he met with great success, though interrupted by a serious accident. He returned in 1881, and played again at the Crystal Palace on Apr. 30. He was for a long time a teacher

in the Stern Conservatorium at Berlin. He afterwards lived at Dessau.      G.

RUMMEL, WALTER (b. Berlin, July 19, 1887), son of Franz Rummel, Anglo-German pianist, studied under Fabian in Washington, and went thence to Berlin, where he was trained by Godowski and Kaun. In 1908 he proceeded to Paris, where he belonged to the 'Inner Circle' of Debussy. As a pianist he has toured all countries of Europe, becoming well known by his cycles of ' one composer ' recitals which he repeated in many capitals. He married (1912) the French pianist Thérèse Chaigneau, and appeared with her in recitals for two piano-fortes in 1913. A pianist of strong creative power and fine artistry, he specialises in Bach, and has transcribed and arranged several cantatas by Bach, as well as many pieces by Bach's forerunners. As a composer Rummel combines the charm of Debussy with the romantic dreaminess of Schumann, and a strong influence of Wagner and César Franck.

WORKS.—'Invocation to Wagner' (vln. and orch.); 'Invocation to the God of the Earth' (alto and orch.); 'From the Depths' (str. quartet); 'To a Memory' (vln. sonata); 6 Nature Studies (PF.); Little Fairy Suite (PF.); Prelude in B, many old Troubadour songs; Etain's Song from the 'Immortal Hour' (Boughton, 2 fl. and str.); several Transcriptions and Arrangements of 'Old Masters.'      H. J. K.

RUNGENHAGEN, CARL FRIEDRICH (b. Ber-lin, Sept. 27, 1778; d. there, Dec. 21, 1851), became in 1815 second director of the Sing-akademie, and in 1833 succeeded Zelter as first director. In 1843 he received the title of professor : he wrote four operas, three ora-torios, a Mass, a Stabat Mater for female voices, a great deal of church music, many songs, and orchestral and chamber music, all of which is now forgotten. (Riemann.)      M.

RUPPELT, MILOŠ (b. Liptó Sv. Mikuláš, Slovakia, 1881), administrator of the Slovak Music School, Bratislava : composer of songs and pianoforte music.      R. N.

RUSSELL, (1) HENRY (b. Sheerness, Dec. 24, 1812 ; d. London, Dec. 8, 1900), went to Bologna in 1825 to study music, was for a time a pupil of Rossini in Naples, appeared as a singer at the Surrey Theatre in 1828, and went to Canada about 1833. He was organist of the Presbyterian church, Rochester, N.Y., and travelled in America till 1841, when he returned to England and gave entertainments by himself and in company with Charles Mackay. The first took place at the Hanover Square Rooms, Mar. 8, 1842. In his particular style he had no rival. His songs ' I'm afloat,' ' A life on the ocean wave ' (which in 1889 was authorised as the march of the Royal Marines), ' Cheer, boys, cheer ' (the only air played by the regimental drum and fife band when a regiment goes abroad), ' Woodman, spare that tree,' etc., are still familiar, and some of his dramatic songs, as ' The Dream of the Reveller,' ' The Maniac,' ' The Gambler's Wife,' etc., were immensely popular in their day. It may certainly be said that over 800 songs were either written or composed by him. At a time when Australia, Tasmania and New Zealand were almost unknown, Henry Russell was instrumental, through the Canadian government, in sending over thousands of poor people who are now wealthy. A memoir was published in 1846, and a book of reminiscences, *Cheer, Boys, Cheer*, in 1895. He retired from public life in 1865, and was fêted at a special concert given in his honour by Sir A. Harris in Covent Garden Theatre, Oct. 12, 1891. *L' amico dei cantanti* is a treatise on the art of singing. Two of his sons have attained distinction in music.

(2) HENRY, a singing-master and operatic impresario, and (3) LANDON RONALD (*q.v.*).

J. H. D. ; addns. *D.N.B.* (suppl.), *Mus. T.* Jan. 1901, etc.

RUSSELL, WILLIAM, Mus.B. (*b.* London, Oct. 6, 1777; *d.* Nov. 21, 1813), son of an organ-builder and organist. He was successively a pupil of Cope, organist of St. Saviour's, Southwark, Shrubsole, of Spa Fields Chapel, and Groombridge, Hackney and St. Stephen's, Coleman Street. In 1789 he was appointed deputy to his father as organist of St. Mary, Aldermanbury, and continued so until 1793, when he obtained the post of organist at the chapel in Great Queen Street, Lincoln's Inn Fields, which he held until 1798, when the chapel was disposed of to the Wesleyan body. In 1797 he became a pupil of Dr. Arnold, with whom he studied for about three years. In 1798 he was chosen organist of St. Ann's, Limehouse. In 1800 he was engaged as pianist and composer at Sadler's Wells, where he continued about four years. In 1801 he was engaged as pianist at Covent Garden and appointed organist of the Foundling Hospital Chapel. He took his Mus.B. degree at Oxford in 1808. He composed three oratorios, ' The Deliverance of Israel,' ' The Redemption ' and ' Job ' (1826) ; a Mass in C minor, an ' Ode to Music,' an ' Ode to the Genius of Handel,' Christopher Smart's ' Ode on St. Cecilia's Day,' and an ' Ode to Harmony,' several glees, songs and organ voluntaries, and about twenty dramatic pieces, chiefly spectacles and pantomimes. He edited in 1809 ' Psalms, Hymns and Anthems for the Foundling Chapel.' He was much esteemed both as pianist and organist. W. H. H.

RUSSIAN BASSOON (Fr. *basson russe*), an obsolete brass instrument similar in pattern to the BASS-HORN (*q.v.*). Its name was misleading as it has no connexion with the bassoon, although, like that instrument, its tube was doubled back on itself. The Russian Bassoon and the bass-horn were superseded by the ophicleide.

RUSSIAN SYMPHONY ORCHESTRA, see NEW YORK.

RUSSLAN I LIOUDMILLA, romantic opera, in 5 acts, based on a poem by Poushkin,

music by Glinka. Produced St. Petersburg, Nov. 27, 1842. G.

RUST, a distinguished German musical family. (1) FRIEDRICH WILHELM (*b.* Wörlitz, Dessau, July 6, 1739 ; *d.* there, Mar. 28, 1796). His father was a person of eminence, and he received a first-rate education. He was taught music by his elder brother, Johann Ludwig Anton, who as an amateur had played the violin in J. S. Bach's orchestra at Leipzig ; and at 13 he played the whole of the ' Wohl-temperirtes Clavier ' without book. Composition, organ and clavier he learned from Friedemann and Emanuel Bach, and the violin from Höckh and F. Benda ; and in 1765, during a journey to Italy, from G. Benda, Tartini and Pugnani. In 1766 he returned to Dessau, and became the life and soul of the music there. On Sept. 24, 1774, a new theatre was opened through his exertions, to which he was soon after appointed music-director. He married his pupil, Henriette Niedhart, a fine singer, and thenceforward, with a few visits to Berlin, Dresden, etc., his life was confined to Dessau. His compositions include a Psalm for solo, chorus and orchestra ; several large church cantatas; duodramas and monodramas ; operas; music to plays ; prologues and occasional pieces, etc. ; odes and songs (2 collections) ; sonatas [1] and variations for the PF.,[2] solo— ' 4 dozen ' of the former and many of the latter—concertos, fugues, etc. etc. ; and three sonatas for violin solo. That in D minor was often played at the Monday Popular Concerts. His last composition was a violin sonata for the E string, thus anticipating Paganini. A list of his works, with every detail of his life, extending to 6½ large pages, is given in Mendel. A monograph on him, with list of works, etc., was published in 1882 by W. Hofäus, and Dr. E. Prieger published a pamphlet, *F. W. Rust, ein Vorgänger Beethovens*. His eldest son was drowned ; the youngest,

(2) WILHELM KARL (*b.* Dessau, Apr. 29, 1787 ; *d.* there, Apr. 18, 1855) began music very early ; and besides the teaching he naturally got at home, he learned thorough-bass with Türk while at Halle University. In Dec. 1807 he went to Vienna, and in time became intimate with Beethoven, who praised his playing of Bach, and recommended him strongly as a teacher. Amongst other pupils he had Baroness Ertmann and Maximilian Brentano. His letters to his sister on Beethoven are given by Thayer, iii. 35-6. He remained in Vienna till 1827, when he returned to his native place and lived there till his death.

[1] The sonatas are analysed in Shedlock's *Pianoforte Sonata*, p. 152 f.
[2] A selection of these works was republished by the composer's grandson Wilhelm (3) and much edited. On these editions a high claim was put forward for Rust as a forerunner of Beethoven. Vincent D'Indy edited ' 12 sonates pour piano ' of F. W. Rust, following Wilhelm Rust's estimate. The original texts were examined by Ernest Neufeldt, and the conclusions drawn from the edited texts were controverted by him in *Die Musik*. See also *Sammelbände*, Int. Mus. Ges., 1913, and article by M. D. Calvocoressi, *Mus. T.*, 1914.

(3) WILHELM (b. Dessau, Aug. 15, 1822; d. Leipzig, May 2, 1892), nephew of the foregoing and grandson of Friedrich Wilhelm (1), himself an advocate, and a fine amateur player on both violin and pianoforte, learned music from his uncle and F. Schneider. After a few years' wandering he settled in Berlin, where he soon joined the Singakademie. He played at the Philharmonic Society of Berlin, Dec. 5, 1849, and was soon much in request as a teacher. In Jan. 1861 he became organist of St. Luke's Church, and twelve months afterwards director of Vierling's Bach Society, which he conducted till 1874, performing a large number of fine works by Bach and other great composers, many of them for the first time. The list of occasional concerts conducted by him is also very large. In 1870 he undertook the department of counterpoint and composition in the Stern Conservatorium at Berlin, in 1878 was appointed organist of the Thomaskirche, Leipzig, and in 1880 succeeded E. F. E. Richter as cantor of the Thomasschule. He was connected with the Leipzig Bachgesellschaft from 1850, and edited vols. v., vii., ix.-xxiii. and xxv. His original works have reached op. 33, of which eight are for the PF. and the rest for voices. A biography appeared in the *Musikal. Wochenblatt* for 1890.       G.

RUTHERFORD, DAVID; a Scotch music publisher in London who worked in St. Martin's Court, near Leicester Fields, ' at the sign of the Violin and German Flute,' about 1745. His publications consist principally of minor works for the violin or flute, such as country dances, minuets and books of airs. He republished in octavo William M'Gibbon's ' Scotch Airs,' and issued song-sheets, etc. He was publisher, and probably author, of several quaint instruction books, as

*The Fiddle new model'd, or a useful introduction for the violin, exemplified with familiar dialogues,* circa 1750, 8vo, and *The art of playing on the violin, showing how to stop every note exactly.*

He was succeeded at the same address by John Rutherford, who issued a similar class of works, and who remained in business until 1783 or later.       F. K.

RUTINI, (1) GIOVANNI MARCO (b. Florence, c. 1730; d. there, c. 1797), studied at the Conservatorio di S. Orofrio a Capuana, Naples; went to Germany in 1754 and resided at Vienna, Prague and Nuremberg, returning to Italy after a number of years. In 1766 he was maestro di cappella at the court of Modena, where his opera ' Gli sposi in maschera ' was performed; afterwards he was maestro di cappella at the court of Tuscany. He wrote a number of operas, PF. sonatas and some church music. His son, (2) FERDINANDO (b. Modena, c. 1767; d. Florence, 1827), was maestro di cappella, after holding a similar position at Macerata, c. 1812. He composed operas and cantatas.[1]

        [1] Mendel.

RUTINI, GIOVANNI PLACIDO, who is frequently confused with Giov. Marco, was in Prague about the same time (1756) as the latter, and went to St. Petersburg in Aug. 1758. Their distinct individuality is clearly proved by title-pages of their respective works, and Giov. Marco's letter of 1771 printed in his sonatas of 1765. Of Giov. Placido's work only cantatas, canzone, arie and PF. sonatas (three of which appeared in a modern edition by E. Pauer) are known. The arias appear to be taken from operas of his; but Eitner (*Q.L.*) thinks it doubtful whether the sonatas are his or Giov. Marco's.       E. v. d. s.

RUTTER, (?) RICHARD (early 16th cent.), English composer of church music. B.M. Egerton MS. 2604/1 contains a record of a payment to a Richard Rutter as ' drumslade,' or drummer, to Henry VIII. in 1526. The Bodl. Mus. Sch. includes a Mass by Rutter; there is also an anthem by him, ' Blessed is the man that feareth,' at Durham Cathedral, the tenor cantoris part of which is in B.M. Add. MSS. 30,478-9.       J. Mᴷ.

RUY BLAS, an overture in C minor (op. 95) and a chorus for soprano voices and orchestra (op. 77, No. 3), composed by Mendelssohn to Victor Hugo's play. Produced Leipzig, Mar. 11, 1839. The overture produced in London, May 25, 1849.       G.

RUYNEMAN, DANIEL (b. Amsterdam, Aug. 8, 1886), Dutch composer. He was originally intended for a commercial career and started the study of music comparatively late and without a teacher, what instruction he has received being of a desultory nature. This has resulted in a certain degree of awkwardness in some of his writing, though he has a strong personality and has made a number of very successful experiments make, in fact, his strongest claim to notice, and although he has written a number of works in more or less classical form and of considerable beauty, his chief works are out of the ordinary in form, in the instruments employed and in psychological expression. He started in this direction with what he called three ' Pathematologies,' or studies in psychology, and his latest work he calls ' a psycho-symbolic play,' with music for a vocal and instrumental orchestra. The most notable, however, is a set of ' Hieroglyphs,' written for three flutes, harp, cup-bells, celesta, piano, 2 mandolines and two guitars. The cup-bells are his own invention, and give out a rich boom or tone that continues in a manner suggestive of the Eastern atmosphere which it may be presumed he wishes to achieve. The list of his works is as follows (published by Chester and by Noske, The Hague) :

Sonata in G major for piano and violin.
Sonatina for piano.
3 Pathematologien for piano (1. Hallucination ; 2. The Voice from the Past ; 3. Impression).

2 Sacred Songs (words by Rabindranath **Tagore**).
Chinese Songs (two sets to ancient words).
Liedeken, for voice and piano.
Winterabend, for voice and p¹ano.
Trois Mélodies, for voice and piano.
Hieroglyphs, for chamber orchestra.
Klaaglied van een Slaaf, for violin and piano.
'The Clown,' a psycho-symbolic play with music for a vocal and instrumental orchestra.

                                    **H. A.**

RYAN, MICHAEL DESMOND (*b.* Kilkenny, Mar. 3, 1816; *d.* Dec. 8, 1868), dramatic and musical critic, son of Dr. Michael Ryan. On the completion of his academical education at an early age he entered the University of Edinburgh, early in the year 1832, for the purpose of studying medicine. He remained in Edinburgh for some three years, after which he determined to quit Edinburgh and try his fortune in London. Here he arrived in 1836, by chance met with J. W. Davison, and began an intimate and lifelong friendship. Ryan now entered upon his literary career in earnest, writing articles and poems for *Harrison's Miscellany*, etc., and producing verses for songs. A set of twelve sacred songs, versified from the Old Testament and set to music by Edward Loder (D'Almaine), may also be mentioned. The 'Songs of Ireland' (D'Almaine), in which, in conjunction with F. N. Crouch, new verses were fitted to old melodies, is another example of effective workmanship. In 1844 Ryan became a contributor to the *Musical World*, and two years later subeditor, a post which he filled as long as he lived. For years he was a contributor to the *Morning Post, Court Journal, Morning Chronicle* and other periodicals. In 1849 he wrote the opera libretto of ' Charles II.' for G. A. Macfarren. The subject was taken from a well-known comedy by Howard Payne, rendered popular at Covent Garden by Charles Kemble's acting some quarter of a century before. A short time afterwards Ryan was commissioned by Jullien to provide the libretto of a grand spectacular opera on the subject of Peter the Great—brought out at the Royal Italian Opera on Aug. 17, 1852, under the title of ' Pietro il Grande.' With the late Frank Mori, Ryan collaborated in an opera called ' Lambert Simnel,' originally intended for Sims Reeves, but never performed. In 1857 he formed his first association with the *Morning Herald* and its satellite the *Standard*, and became permanently connected with those journals in 1862 as musical and dramatic critic.

                                  **D. L. R.**

RYBNER, PETER MARTIN CORNELIUS (*b.* Copenhagen, Denmark, Oct. 26, 1855), Danish-American teacher and composer. He studied with Gade, Hartmann, Reinecke and David, and later with von Bülow and Rubinstein. As a concert pianist he toured throughout Europe. In 1904 he succeeded MacDowell as head of the music department of Columbia University (New York); he retired from that position in 1919. His compositions include a symphonic poem; an overture and other orchestral pieces; a violin concerto; a three-act ballet, ' Prince Ador ' (Karlsruhe, 1903); and many pieces in the smaller forms.

                                  **W. S. S.**

SAAR, Louis Victor (*b.* Rotterdam, Dec. 10, 1868), Dutch-American composer and teacher. A graduate of the Strassburg Gymnasium and later of the Munich Conservatory, he came to New York in 1894 as accompanist at the Metropolitan Opera House ; later he taught theory at various institutions in that city and elsewhere in the United States. His compositions include an orchestral suite, 'From the Kingdom of the Great Northwest,' 'Three Silhouettes' and other orchestral pieces ; 'The 128th Psalm,' for solo, chorus and orchestra, and other choral pieces ; chamber music, violin and pianoforte pieces and songs.

W. S. S.

SABANEIEV, Leonid Leonidovich (*b.* Moscow, 1871), Russian composer and musical critic, studied under Serge Taneiev (*q.v.*) at the Moscow Conservatoire, and took his degree (mathematics) at the Moscow University (1908). He has made a special study of Scriabin's music and musical philosophy, and his book and numerous articles form the standard authorities on this composer.

R. N.

SABATA, Victor de (*b.* Trieste, 1892), son of the choirmaster at La Scala, entered the Milan Conservatoire in 1902, where he studied with M. Saladino (theory) and G. Orefice (composition). He left the Conservatoire in 1910, having won the first prize and a special encomium for the composition of a suite for orchestra. He has since become known as composer and conductor. His compositions include an orchestral poem 'Juventus,' quartets and two operas : 'Lisistrata' and 'Il macigno.' The last was performed with some success at La Scala in 1916.

F. B.

SABATIER, see Unger, Caroline.

SABBATINI, Galeazzo, of Pesaro, was probably maestro di cappella there for some years before 1626 ; this is indicated at any rate in the preface to the 'Sacrae laudes,' Venice, 1626.[1] On the title-pages of his works he is called maestro di cappella di camera to the Duke of Mirandola in 1630 and again in 1636. The dates of his publications range from 1625–40. In G. B. Doni's *Annotazioni*, published in 1640, the 'Discorso primo dell' inutile osservanza de tuoni' (p. 234) is dedicated to 'Signor Galeazzo Sabbatini a Bergamo.' Sabbatini is highly commended by Kircher[2] for his scientific knowledge of music :

'rarus musicus, qui tria genera novo ausu ad arithmeticas leges revocans, multo plura sanè invenit, quorum diversis in locis huius operis mentio fiet, et inter coetera abacum novum ordinavit exactissimè quicquid in musica desiderari potest referentem, omnibus harmoniis exibendis perfectissimum,' etc.

Sabbatini published one theoretical work, on the thorough-bass or basso continuo, which

1 Parisini, *Catalogo*, ii. 492.
2 *Musurgia universalis*, Rome, 1650, tom. i. p. 460.

Burney[3] criticises as inadequate because it only treats of common chords given to every note of the scale. The title is :

'Regola facile e breve per sonare sopra il basso continuo, nel-l' organo, manacordo, ò altro simile stromento. Composta da Galeazzo Sabbatini. Dalla quale in questa prima parte ciascuno se stesso potrà imparare da i primi principii quello che sarà necessario per simil'effetto. Venetia per il Salvatori, 1628, 4to.'

The second edition, dated 1644, is in the British Museum, and a third edition was published in Rome in 1669. No 'seconda parte' of the work is known. Sabbatini's published compositions were as follows :

1 Il primo libro de' madrigali di Galeazzo de Sabbatini da Pesaro. Concertati a due, tre, e quattro voci. Opera prima. Nouamente composta, e data in luce. Venetia, Aless. Vincenti, 1625, 4to. A second edition was issued in 1627, and a third in 1639.
2. Il secondo libro de' madrigali di G. S., concertati a 2, 3, et 4 voci. Con la risposta a quattro voci e due violini ad alcuni versi che incominciano quando la Donna si dimostra altiera, posti nel terzo de' madrigali a 6 del Sig. Steffano Bernardi, etc. Opera seconda. Nouamente composta et data in luce. Venetia, Aless. Vincenti, 1626, 4to. Second edition in 1636.
3. Sacrae Laudes musicis concentibus a G. S. contextae, 2, 3, 4, et 5 vocibus concinendae. Una cum bassus continuus pro organo, etc. Opus tertium, liber primus. Venetiis, A. Vincentium, 1626, 4to. Second edition, 1637 : another edition, Antwerp, 1642.
4. Madrigali concertati a cinque voci con alcune canzoni concertate anc' esse diuersamente con sinfonie e ritornelli, e nel fine una canzonetta con voci, e instromenti, che si concerta in tempo imperfetto, ò in proportione minor perfetta, cioè ò in numero binario, ò in numero ternario. Di G. S. Opera quarta, de' madrigali libro terzo. Nouamente composti e dati in luce. Venetia, Aless Vincenti, 1627, 4to. Second edition in 1634.
5. Madrigali concertati a 2, 3, 4, e 5 voci. Con alcune canzoni concertate, e tramezzate diuersamente con sinfonie e ritornelli. Di G. S. maestro di cappella di camera dell' eccell. sig. duca della Mirandola. Opera quinta, de' madrigali libro quarto. Nouamente composti e dati in luce. Venetia, A. Vincenti, 1630, 4to. Second edition, 1637.
6. Madrigali concertati a 2, 3, e 4 voci, con alcune canzonette concertate con instromenti, di G. S. mastro di capella di camera dell' eccell. sig. duca della Mirandola, etc. Opera sesta, de' madrigali libro quinto. Nouamente composti e dati in luce, et a sua eccellenza illustrissima dedicati. Veneti, A. Vincenti, 1636, 4to.
7. Sacrarum laudum musicis conceptibus a Galeatio Sabbatino contextarum 2, 3, 4, et 5 vocibus ad organum concinendarum. Liber secundus. Opus septimum, etc. Venetiis, A. Vincentium, 1637, 4to. Another edition was published at Antwerp in 1641.
8. Deiparae Virginis Laudes a G. S. musicis conceptibus cum 3, 4, 5, et 6 vocibus contextae, etc. Opus octavum. Venetiis, A. Vincentium, 1638. 4to.
9. Sacre lodi concerto a voce sola, C.A.T.B. Con la parte continua da sonare di G. S. Opera nona. Venetia, A. Vincenti, 1640, 4to. These are the 'Motetti a voce sola di G. S. lib. primo.'
10. Libro de' madrigali di G. S. concertati a 2, 3, e 4 voci, con la risposta a quattro voci, e due violini ad alcuni versi che incominciano quando la donna si dimostra altiera. Posti nel terzo de' madrigali a 6 del sig. Steffano Bernardi. Con il basso continuo. Nouamente ristampati. In Anversa presso i heredi di Pietro Phalesio al Re David, 1640, obl. 4to. A reprint of the second volume of madrigals published in 1626.
Compositions in other publications :
A motet and a mass 'dal sig. Galeazzo Sabbatini, maestro dell' autore,' in Raniero Scarselli's Sacrarum modulationum, Venice, 1637.
'Laudate pueri' for three voices, in Marcello Minozzi's Salmi, Venice, 1638. Minozzi in the preface mentions that Sabbatini was his teacher, ' huomo di quel grido che particolarmente è noto a gli intendenti dell' arte.' (Parisini, ii. 275.)
'O nomen Jesu' for three voices, in Ambr. Profius's Ander Theil geistlicher Concerten, Leipzig, 1641 ; 'Jesu Domine' for two voices, in the Dritter Theil, 1642 ; 'Laudate pueri,' 'Omnes sancti' and a Missa, all for four voices, in the Vierdter und letzter Theil, 1646.
One motet in Profius's Cunis solennib. Jesuli recens-nati, 1646.
'Nos autem gloriari' for three voices, in Benedetto Pace's Motetti d' autori eccellentissimi, Loreto, 1646.
'Hò perso il mio core,' in Florido concento di madrigali, Rome, 1653.
*MSS.* In the Berlin Staats Bibliothek : MS. 1100, 'Amare desidero.' In the Upsala Univ.-Bibliothek : 'Io amo,' one of the Madrigali concertati a cinque voci, published 1627.
In the Westminster Abbey Library : 'Amor porta ' for voice with basso continuo, in a 17th-century folio manuscript.

C. S.

SABBATINI, Luigi Antonio (*b.* Albano Laziale, near Rome, 1732 ; *d.* Padua, Jan. 29, 1809), was educated at Bologna in the Franciscan monastery of minori conventuali, where he studied music under Padre G. B. Martini. There is a manuscript in Sabbatini's hand-

3 *Hist. of Music*, iii. p. 538.

writing in the Bologna Liceo Musicale, which contains the

' Regole per accompagnare del pre. G. B. Martini, min. conle. maestro di cappella di San Francesco in Bologna, 1761. Per uso di Fra Luigi Ant. Sabbatini, min. conle.' [1]

He remained there eight years, according to a long and interesting letter which he wrote to Martini from Albano on Nov. 2, 1766, now preserved in the library of the Accademia filarmonica, Bologna.[2] He was afterwards in the Franciscan monastery at Padua, where Vallotti gave him lessons in composition. Eventually he was appointed maestro di cappella at the church of the SS. Apostoli in Rome; a letter in the Bologna collection, written to Martini from Rome, is dated July 17, 1776.[3]

Before Vallotti, maestro di cappella of S. Antonio, Padua, died in Jan. 1780, he expressed a wish that Sabbatini should be his successor. Sabbatini was offered the post, but, unwilling to leave Rome, he suggested that Agostino Ricci would be a suitable candidate. Ricci was therefore appointed on Apr. 26, 1780, and remained in Padua for six years; but when he left for Assisi, Sabbatini was persuaded to reconsider his decision, and was finally appointed to the post on Apr. 22, 1786, which he held until his death. During these twenty-three years of his life he enriched the archives of S. Antonio with many compositions, writes Gonzati,[4] among which may be especially mentioned his Salmi di Terza, four masses, a vespero, and a Compieta breve, all composed for four voices.

Sabbatini was elected one of the eight members of the music section of the Accademia Italiana in May 1807. In 1887 a bust of Sabbatini was placed in the Piazza Feoli, Albano; this tribute to his memory was due to Signor Cesare de Sanctis, also an Albano musician.

The larger part of Sabbatini's church music remains in manuscript in the archives of S. Antonio,[5] but Tebaldini, who gives a list of eighty-six compositions, has published some examples for four voices with orchestra, which he considers show that Sabbatini instinctively tried for new combinations, new effects, and that he sometimes lent his music quite an individual character by giving the canto fermo to the alto or soprano part instead of the tenor. Sabbatini was generally recognised as a sound and erudite theorist; Gervasoni[6] testifies to his profound knowledge no less than to his great personal charm.

Some other manuscript compositions are in the Bologna Liceo Musicale; autograph scores of twelve pieces of sacred music for two and four voices with orchestral accompaniment, in one volume, and three Kyrie, two Gloria, two Credo and 'Qui habitat,' all for four voices

with orchestral accompaniment, in another volume[7]; as well as twenty-one pieces of sacred music for four voices with figured bass; and 'Atto di contrizione' for two voices with basso continuo. The nineteenth volume of the Martini correspondence in the same library consists entirely of letters from Sabbatini.

In the Vienna Hofbibliothek in MS. 16,217 there is a Mass for four voices with organ accompaniment; and in MS. 19,103 a treatise on music:

' Trascritto ad litteram nell' anno 1791 Dal p. L. A. Sabbatini, min. con. maestro di capella nella sacra Basilica del Santo in Padova.' [8]

The following theoretical works were published:

*Elementi teorici della musica colla pratica de' medesimi, in duetti e terzetti a canone, ecc. di fra L. A. Sabbatini, min. con. già maestro di cappella nella Basilica Costantiniana de' SS. XII. Apostoli in Roma .d al presente in quella del Santo in Padova.* In Roma, 1789–90, obl. folio. In three books. A second edition was published at Rome in 1795.

*La vera idea delle musicali numeriche segnature ecc. dal fra L. A. S. m.c. maestro di cappella nella Basilica di S. Antonio di Padova.* Venezia, 1799, presso Seb. Valle, 4to, p. 179. A manuscript of Sabbatini's inscribed *Trattato di contrappunto,* which is in the Padua Library, would appear to be the first sketch for this more elaborate work.

*Trattato sopra le fughe musicali di Fra L. A. S. m.c. corredato da copiosi saggi del suo antecessore P. Franc. Ant. Vallotti.* Venezia, 1802, presso Seb. Valle, 4to. In two books. An analysis of Vallotti's fugues with examples taken from his church music.

*Solfèges ou leçons élémentaires de musique, etc. en canon avec basse continue.* Par le R. P. Luigi A. Sabbatini, etc. Publié par M. Alex. Chorom, Paris, *circa* 1810, 8vo, pp. 120. Consists of music taken from *Elementi teorici,* 1789. Another edition was published in 1834.

Besides these works Sabbatini also published a life of Vallotti: *Notizie sopra la vita e le opere del R. P. Fr. Ant. Vallotti* (Padua, 1780): and edited a collection of Marcello's psalms which was published at Venice in 1801. (*Fétis.*)

C. S.

**SABBATINI,** PIETRO PAOLO, was a native of Rome. The dates of his published works range from 1628–57, and from their title-pages it is to be gathered that in 1628 he was maestro di cappella dell' Archiconfraternità della morte et oratione di Roma; 1630–31 maestro di cappella di S. Luigi de' francesi, Rome; and in 1650 professore di musica. Catalisano alludes to him in his *Grammatica armonica,* 1781, p. xii: ' Per esprimere quanto mai sia tenuto a questi celebri maestri di cappella . . . P. P. Sabbatini,' etc. His published works were:

1. Il sesto di Pietro Paolo Sabbatini maestro di cappella del l' archiconfraternità della morte et oratione di Roma. Opera VIII. In Bracciano, per And. Fei, stampatore ducale, 1628, folio, pp. 23. Contains songs for one, two and three voices, some with guitar accompaniment.

2. Intermedii spirituali di P.P.S., etc., as above. Libro I. Opera IX. In Roma appresso Paolo Masotti, 1628, folio, pp. 27. Contains three Intermedii.

3. Psalmi magnificat cum quatuor antiphonis ad Vespera, cum Lettaniis B.V. octonis vocibus uno cum Basso ad organum decantandi. Auctore P.P.S. romano in Ecclesia S. Aloysii Gallicae nationis musices moderatore, Liber I. Opus XII. Romae, P. Masottum, 1630, 4to.

4. Il terzo di P.P.S. maestro di cappella di S. Luigi de' francesi in Roma. In Roma, appresso P. Masotti, 1631, folio, pp. 19. Contains villanelle for one, two and three voices.

5. Il quarto de Villanelle a una, due e tre voci. Del Sig. P.P.S. etc., as above. Roma, G. B. Robletti, 1631, folio, pp. 19. The dedication is written by Pietro Simi, a pupil of Sabbatini, from Rom May 1, 1631. He states that he rescues from oblivion these villarelle by P. P. Sabbatini.

6. Canzoni spirituali a una, a due, et a tre voci da cantarsi, e sonarsi sopra qualsivoglia istromento, Libro II. Opera XIII. de P.P.S. In Roma, appresso Lod. Grignani, 1640, folio, pp. 32.

7. Varii capricci, e canzonette a una e tre voci da cantarsi sopra qualsivoglia istromento con l' alfabeto della chitarra spagnuola, di P.P.S. Romano, Libro VII. Opera XIV. Roma, Vinc. Bianchi, 1641, folio, pp. 32.

8. Prima scelta di villanelle a due voci composte da P.P.S. da sonarsi in qualsivoglia instromento con le lettere accomodate alla chitarra spagnola in quelle più à proposito. In Roma, Vitale Mascardi, 1652, folio, pp. 19.

9. Ariete spirituali a una, doi e tre voci di P.P.S. in diversi stili da cantarsi in qualsivoglia instromento, Libro V. Opera XXI. Roma, Jacomo Fei del q. Andrea, 1657, folio, pp. 24.

---

1 Parisini, *Catalogo,* i. 282.
2 Succi, *Mostra internazionale,* Bologna, 1888.
3 Masseangeli, *Catalogo della collezione de' autografi,* Bologna, 1881.
4 *La Basilica di S. Antonio di Padova,* 1853, ii. p. 453.
5 *L' Archivio mus. della cappella Antoniana,* 1895, p. 51.
3 *Nuova teoria di musica,* Parma, 1812, p. 285.

7 Parisini, *Catalogo,* ii. pp. 136, 306.
8 Mantuani's *Catalogue.*

The following treatise was also published :
    Toni ecclesiastici colle sue intonazioni, all' uso romano. Modo per sonare il basso continuo, chiavi corrispondenti all' altre chiavi generali, et ordinarie, etc., da P.P.S. Professore della musica. Libro I. Opera XVIII. Roma, Lod. Grignani, 1650, 4to.        C. S.

SACCHETTI, Liberio Antonovich (*b.* Kenzar, near Tambov, Aug. 30, 1852 ; *d. circa* 1912–13), an authority on musical history and æsthetics. His father—of Italian descent—was a music teacher at Kenzar. In 1866 Sacchetti began to study the violoncello under C. Davidov in St. Petersburg. From 1868–74 he continued his studies at the Conservatoire, still making the violoncello his first consideration. Later on he turned his attention to musical theory and entered Rimsky-Korsakov's class. In 1886 he was the first to fill the newly created chair of Musical History and Æsthetics in the St. Petersburg Conservatorium. These lectures proved so popular that he was requested to give similar courses to the students of the Academy of Arts (1889–94). Sacchetti was appointed assistant to Vladimir Stassov, director of the Art Department of the Imperial Public Library, in 1895. He was sent as delegate of the Imperial Russian Musical Society to the musical exhibition at Bologna in 1888 ; and was also chosen to read a paper at the Paris exhibition of 1900 upon ' Russian Church Music.' His most popular works are : *A Sketch for a Universal History of Music* (St. Petersburg, 1883, 3rd edition, 1900) ; *A Short Historical Chrestomathy of Music* (1906, 3rd edition, 1900) ; *From the Spheres of Æsthetics and Music* (collected essays, 1896).        R. N.

SACCHI, Barnabite Giovenale (*b.* Milan, 1726 ? ; *d.* there, Sept. 27, 1789), a learned member of the congregation of St. Paul called Barnabites, whence he took the additional name of Barnabite. He was a member of several societies and academies of science and art, and a copious writer on music. A list of his works appears in *Q.-L.*, including his biographies of Carlo Broschi and Benedetto Marcello.        E. v. d. S.

SACCHINI, Antonio Maria Gaspere (*b.* Pozzuoli, near Naples, July 23, 1734; *d.* Paris, Oct. 7, 1786). This ' graceful, elegant and judicious composer,' as Burney calls him, who enjoyed great contemporary fame and was very popular in this country, was the son of poor fisher people who had no idea of bringing him up to any life but their own. It chanced, however, that Durante heard the boy sing some popular airs, and was so much struck with his voice and talent that he got him admitted into the Conservatorio of San Onofrio at Naples. Here he learned the violin from Niccolo Forenza, and acquired a considerable mastery over the instrument, which he subsequently turned to good account in his orchestral writing. He studied singing with Gennaro Manna ; harmony and counterpoint with Durante himself, who esteemed him highly, holding him up to his other pupils, among whom were Jommelli,

Piccinni and Guglielmi, as their most formidable rival. Durante died in 1755, and in the following year Sacchini left the Conservatorio, but not until he had produced an intermezzo in two parts, ' Fra Donato,' very successfully performed by the pupils of the institution. For some years he supported himself by teaching singing and writing little pieces for minor theatres, till, in 1762, he wrote a serious opera, ' Semiramide,' for the Argentina theatre at Rome. This was so well received that he remained for seven years attached to the theatre as composer, writing operas not only for Rome but many other towns. Among these, ' Alessandro nelle Indie,' played at Venice in 1768, was especially successful, and obtained for its composer, in 1769, the directorship of the Ospedaletto school of music there. He seems to have held this office for little more than a year, but during that time formed some excellent pupils, among whom may be mentioned Gabrieli, Canti and Pasquali.

Before 1770 he left Venice, and proceeded by way of Munich, Stuttgart and other German towns to England, arriving in London in Apr. 1772. For Munich he wrote ' Scipione in Cartagena ' and ' L' eroë cinese ' in 1770, and for Stuttgart ' Calliroë.' His continental fame had preceded him to this country, and a beautiful air of his, ' Care luci,' introduced by Guarducci into the pasticcio of ' Tigrane ' as early as 1767, had, by its popularity, paved the way for his music. True, a strong clique existed against the new composer, but he soon got the better of it.

In addition to the ' Cid ' and ' Tamerlano,' mentioned by Burney, he produced here ' Lucio Vero ' and ' Nitetti e Perseo ' (1773–74). His perfect comprehension of the art of writing for the voice, and the skill with which he adapted his songs to their respective exponents, contributed an important element to the success of his music, even indifferent singers being made to appear to advantage. His popularity, however, was undermined, after a time, from a variety of causes. Jealousy led to cabals against him. He would probably have lived down calumny, prompted by personal spite, but his idle and dissolute habits estranged his friends, impaired his health and got him deeply into debt, the consequence of which was that he left this country and settled in Paris—Burney says in 1784 ; Fétis in 1782. It seems probable that this last date is correct, as several of his operas were produced in the French capital during 1783–84. He had been there on a visit in 1781, when his ' Isola d' Amore,' translated by Framéry and adapted to the French stage, was played there successfully, having been played under the name of ' La Colonie ' in 1775. His ' Olimpiade ' had been given in 1777. Burney says that in Paris Sacchini was almost adored. He started with an apparent advantage in the patronage of Joseph II. of Austria, who was in Paris at the time, and recommended the composer to the protection of his sister, Marie Antoinette. Thanks to this, he obtained a hearing for his ' Rinaldo ' (rearranged and partly rewritten for the French stage as ' Renaud ') and for ' Il gran Cid,' which, under the name of ' Chimène,' was performed before the court at Fontainebleau. Both of these works contained great beauties, but neither had more than a limited success. ' Dardanus,' a French opera, was not more fortunate in 1784. ' Œdipe à Colone ' was finished early in 1785, and performed at Versailles, Apr. 4, 1786. This, his masterpiece, brought him his bitterest disappointment. The Queen had promised that ' Œdipe ' should be the first opera at the royal theatre during the court's next residence at Fontainebleau. The time was approaching, but nothing was said about it, and Sacchini remarked with anxiety that the Queen avoided him and seemed uneasy in his presence. Suspense became intolerable, and he sought an audience, when the Queen unwillingly and hesitatingly confessed the truth :

'My dear Sacchini, I am accused of showing too much favour to foreigners. I have been so much pressed to command a performance of M. Lemoine's "Phèdre" instead of your "Œdipe" that I cannot refuse. You see the situation; forgive me.'

Poor Sacchini controlled himself at the moment, but on arriving at home gave way to despair. The Queen's favour lost, he believed his only chance gone. He took to his bed then and there, and died three months afterwards.

It is very difficult to form a just estimate of this composer, whose merits were great, yet whose importance to the history of Art seems now so small. Among the second-rate writers of this transition period, Sacchini must rank first. A little more force, perhaps a little less facility, and he might have been a great, instead of a clever or a ' graceful, elegant and judicious ' composer. In his later works the influence of Gluck's spirit is unmistakable. There is a wide gulf between such early Italian operas as ' L' isola d' Amore,' consisting of the usual detached series of songs, duets and concerted pieces, and the ' Œdipe à Colone,' where each number leads into the next, and where vigorous accompanied recitative and well-contrasted dialogued choruses carry on and illustrate the action of the drama, while keeping alive the interest of the hearer. Burney remarks that Sacchini,

'observing how fond the English were of Handel's oratorio choruses, introduced solemn and elaborate choruses into some of his operas; but, though excellent in their kind, they never had a good effect ; the mixture of English singers with the Italian, as well as the awkward figure they cut as actors, joined to the difficulty of getting their parts by heart, rendered those compositions ridiculous which in still life would have been admirable.' [1]

[1] *History*, iv. p. 241, note.

In Paris they managed these things better, for in all the operas of Sacchini which were composed or arranged for the French stage, choruses are used largely and with admirable effect, while in ' Œdipe ' they are the principal feature. The ' Œdipe ' was continuously on the boards of the Opéra for fifty-seven years (from 1787–1844). During this time it had 583 representations. It was revived in July 1843, and was performed six times in that year and once in May 1844.

Sacchini understood orchestral as well as choral effect. His scores are small, oboes, horns and sometimes trumpets and bassoons being the only additions to the string quartet, but the treatment is as effective as it is simple. His part-writing is pure and good, while the care and finish evident in his scores are hard to reconcile with the accounts of his idle and irregular ways. The same technical qualities are shown in his compositions for the church, which in other ways are less distinguished than his operas from contemporary works of a similar kind.

Much of Sacchini's music is lost. Four oratorios, a Mass and various motets, etc., are mentioned in *Q.-L.*; Fétis gives a list of twenty - one sacred compositions, and the names of forty-one operas, the chief of which have been mentioned here ; but Burney puts the number of these much higher (twenty-seven are given as still extant in *Q.-L.*). The last of them, ' Arvire et Evelina,' was left unfinished. It was completed by J. B. Rey, and performed with success after the composer's death (Apr. 29, 1788). He also left two symphonies in D, six trios for two violins and bass ; six quartets for two violins, tenor and bass ; and two sets, each of six harpsichord sonatas, with violin, as well as twelve violin sonatas (opp. 3 and 4) for clavier solo. These were all published in London. One of the sonatas, in F, was included in Pauer's ' Alte Meister.' A couple of cavatinas are given by Gevaert in his ' Gloires d'Italie,' and an antiphon for two voices by Choron in his ' Journal de Chant.'

F. A. M.

SACKBUT, an early name for the trombone, probably derived from the Spanish *sacabuche* (' draw-tube '), *i.e. sacar* ' to draw,' and *bucha* ' a pipe,' originally of boxwood (cf. Portuguese *sacabuxa*), the name being also given to a form of pump. In Egypt the Arabic *bûq* is still used to denote a kind of trumpet. Other derivations, however, are from O.F. *saquier-boter* (' to pull and to push ') or Sp. *sacar del buche* (' to exhaust the chest '). The form first appears in Spanish literature of the 14th century, the trombone having been evolved from the trumpet about the year 1300. At the beginning of the next century the French form *saqueboute* is found, and at the close of the same century, when the instrument was introduced into England, it was known as the *shakbusshe* and subsequently as the *saykebud, sackbut* or *sagbut.* One of the earliest uses of the word in English literature occurs in Hawes's *Passetyme of Pleasure.* (1506). The so-called representation of a 9th-century sackbut in the Boulogne Psalter (MS. No. 20) is an error, the instrument depicted being a fanciful delineation of the sambuke, an ancient four-stringed lyre. The phrase ' tuba ductilis,' applied in later times to the Sackbut, originally meant a trumpet of metal beaten or drawn out by the hammer, *i.e.* not cast (*PLATE LXVIII.* No. 4). For details of the instrument see TROMBONE.

BIBL.—MAHILLON, *Le Trombone,* Brussels, 1906 ; GALPIN, *The Sackbut, its Evolution and History, Mus. Assoc. Proceedings,* 1907.

F. W. G.

SACRED HARMONIC SOCIETY (1832–1882). This Society was originated by Thomas Brewer, Joseph Hart, W. Jeffreys, Joseph Surman and Cockerell, who first met, with a view to its establishment, on Aug. 21, 1832. Its practical operations did not, however, begin until Nov. 20 following. Its first meetings were held in the chapel in Gate Street, Lincoln's Inn Fields, where the first concert was given on Tuesday evening, Jan. 15, 1833. The programme comprised selections from Handel's ' Messiah ' and ' Funeral Anthem,' and from Perry's ' Fall of Jerusalem ' and ' Death of Abel,' with Attwood's coronation anthem ' O Lord, grant the king a long life,' and the hymn ' Adeste fideles.' The names of the principal singers were not published : Thomas Harper was engaged as solo trumpeter. The then officers of the Society were John Newman Harrison, president ; Thomas Brewer, secretary ; J. G. Moginie, treasurer ; Joseph Surman, conductor ; George Perry, leader of the band ; and F. C. Walker, organist. In Nov. 1833, the permission to meet in the chapel being suddenly withdrawn, the Society removed to a chapel in Henrietta Street, Brunswick Square, and shortly afterwards to a room belonging to the Scottish Hospital in Fleur de Lys Court, Fleet Street ; but at Midsummer 1834 it migrated to Exeter Hall, which was its home until Michaelmas 1880. The concerts were for the first two years given in the minor hall, and consisted principally of selections, in which a few short complete works were occasionally introduced, such as Handel's ' Dettingen Te Deum,' Haydn's ' Mass,' No. 1. The Society having on June 28, 1836, given a concert in the large hall in aid of a charity, with very great success, was shortly afterwards induced to give its own concerts there, and at the same time an important change in its policy was effected— the abandonment of miscellaneous selections for complete oratorios. Up to that period, even at the provincial festivals, it was very rarely that any complete oratorio, except Handel's ' Messiah,' was performed, whilst the programmes of the so-called ' Oratorios ' at

the two patent theatres on the Wednesdays and Fridays in Lent were a mongrel mixture of oratorio songs and choruses, secular songs of all kinds, and instrumental solos. The first concert given in the large hall on the Society's own account was Handel's ' Messiah,' on Dec. 20, 1836, with about 300 performers. In 1837 Mendelssohn's ' St. Paul ' (Mar. 7) was given for the first time in London. On Sept. 12 another performance of ' St. Paul ' was given, in the composer's presence (see MENDELSSOHN). During the year the number of performers was increased to 500. In the same year the formation of a musical library was begun, and Robert Kanzow Bowley appointed honorary librarian. During the seasons 1838–41 various revivals of Handel oratorios took place. A new organ, built for the Society by Walker, was opened Jan. 23, 1840, with a performance by Thomas Adams. In 1843 Spohr's ' Fall of Babylon ' was produced, conducted by the composer, who was then on a visit to England ; Mendelssohn's ' Hymn of Praise ' was introduced, and also Handel's ' Deborah.' In 1844 the season was chiefly distinguished by two performances of Mendelssohn's ' St. Paul,' conducted by the composer. The year 1847 was an important epoch in the Society's annals with a revival of Handel's ' Belshazzar ' and the production for the first time in its improved form of Mendelssohn's ' Elijah,' under his own personal direction. Subsequently Spohr visited this country at the invitation of the Society and conducted two performances of his ' Fall of Babylon ' and one of his ' Christian's Prayer ' and ' Last Judgment ' (the last for the only time in England under his direction), and produced his ' 84th Psalm, Milton's version,' composed expressly for the occasion. In this year dissatisfaction with the conductor Joseph Surman led to the appointment of Costa in 1848 ; pending this appointment the remaining concerts of the season were conducted by Perry. Costa strengthened and improved both band and chorus, the number of performers being augmented to nearly 700. The performances of the season consisted principally of more effective renderings of the stock pieces, but Mendelssohn's music for ' Athalie ' was introduced with great success. In 1850 nothing new was given but Mendelssohn's ' Lauda Sion ' in an English dress. The year 1851 was chiefly remarkable for the number of concerts given —thirty - one ; ' Messiah,' ' Elijah ' and the ' Creation ' having been performed alternately, one in each week, from May to September for the gratification of visitors to the Great Exhibition in Hyde Park. Later in the year Haydn's ' Seasons ' was introduced for the first time. In 1852 Spohr's ' Calvary ' and the fragments of Mendelssohn's ' Christus ' were introduced. In 1853 some changes took place in the officers of the Society ; R. K. Bowley became treasurer,

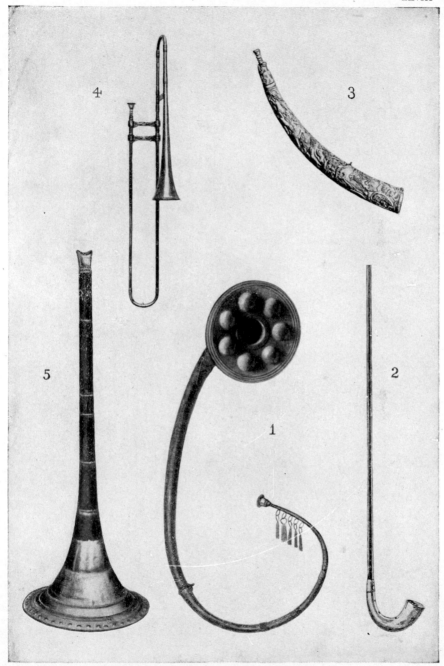

## LXVIII

1. PREHISTORIC LUR (Denmark, *c.* 1500 B.C.)—a copy.
2. ROMAN LITUUS (*c.* 100 B.C.)—a copy.     3. ENGLISH OLIPHANT (1712).
4. NUREMBERG SACKBUT (J. Neuschel, 1557).     5. ENGLISH VAMPHORN (*c.* 1800).

1, 2, 4. Galpin Collection.     3. Heyer Museum, formerly Cologne, now Leipzig.     5. Braybrooke Church, Northants.

and W. H. Husk succeeded him as librarian : Mozart's Requiem was first brought forward this year. The year 1854 was distinguished by two performances of Beethoven's Mass in D, and the Society undertook the performance of the music at the opening of the Crystal Palace on May 10. In 1856 Costa's ' Eli ' was performed for the first time in London. In 1857 Rossini's Stabat Mater was introduced, and the Society undertook the musical arrangements for the first Handel Festival at the Crystal Palace. (See HANDEL FESTIVAL.) In 1862 Beethoven's ' Mount of Olives ' was given with its proper libretto. In 1870 Beethoven's Mass in D was again performed. The Society sustained the loss, by death, of three of its principal officers : J. N. Harrison, president ; R. K. Bowley, treasurer ; and T. Brewer, secretary and, for a few weeks, president. They were replaced by D. Hill, president ; W. H. Withall, treasurer ; and J. F. Puttick, secretary. In 1873 the last-named died, and E. H. Mannering was appointed in his stead. Bach's ' St. Matthew Passion ' was given for the first time. Mozart's Litany in B♭, in an English dress, was introduced in 1877. In 1878 Rossini's ' Moses in Egypt ' was restored to its original position as an oratorio. Owing to a change in the proprietorship of Exeter Hall, the Society had to quit that building, and the concerts of the season 1880–81 were given in St. James's Hall, the number of performers being reduced, on account of the limited space of the orchestra, to about 300. The first concert was on Dec. 3. Sullivan's ' Martyr of Antioch ' (first time in London) and Cherubini's Requiem in C minor were brought out during the season.

The Society's library was the largest collection of music and musical literature ever gathered together by a musical body in England. A printed catalogue was issued in 1872. It was acquired for the R.C.M. at the dissolution of the original Society. (See LIBRARIES.) The Society also possessed some interesting original portraits, statuary and autograph letters. It was in constitution an essentially amateur body, none but amateurs being eligible for membership, and the governing committee being chosen by and from the members. The most eminent professors were engaged as principal vocalists and instrumentalists, the rest of the band and the whole of the chorus being amateurs. The members were comparatively few in number, the majority of the amateurs being assistants, who gave their gratuitous services, but paid no subscription. The subscription of members, originally £1, was afterwards £2 : 2s. per annum. The original Society was dissolved in 1882, its last concert being a performance of ' Solomon ' on Apr. 28 of that year. Some members of the committee determined to resuscitate the Society, and the new institution was incorporated in

1882. Charles Hallé was appointed conductor, and in 1885 was succeeded by W. H. Cummings, who had, up to that time, acted as assistant conductor. In the autumn of 1888 the new Society ceased to exist.

The Benevolent Fund of the Society was instituted Mar. 14, 1855, for the aid of necessitous persons who had at any time been connected with the Sacred Harmonic Society. The management of the fund was entrusted to an independent committee, chosen by the governors of the fund from the members of the Sacred Harmonic Society. w. h. h.

SACROBUSCO (SACROBOSCO), JOHANNES DE. A 12th- or 13th-century MS. in the Bibl. Vallicelliana, Rome, contains a *Tractatus de sphaera* by this author, which was copied at Padua in 1418, with other treatises, in a codex ; now in the Liceo Mus., Bologna. La Fage says that Sacrobusco was an Englishman.

           E. v. d. s.

SADKO, ' legendary ' opera in 7 tableaux. Composed by Rimsky-Korsakov. Produced Moscow, Dec. 1897.

SADLER'S WELLS, a place of entertainment near the New River Head, Pentonville, much associated with music from the end of the 17th century.

In a garden belonging to a person named Sadler an ancient well was discovered in 1683. The water of the well was chalybeate and ferruginous, and Sadler, who owned a sort of tavern, having attached a wooden Music House, exploited the medicinal qualities in rivalry of the waters at Tunbridge and at Epsom. He laid out the grounds and engaged tumblers and musicians, and the place was much frequented for its open-air concerts. In 1699 James Miles and a Francis Forcer, the latter a musician, were proprietors, and the place became known also as ' Miles's Music House.' Miles having died in 1724, Francis Forcer, junior, increased the attractions, and Forcer dying in 1743, the gardens passed into the hands of one Rosoman, who made many alterations, rebuilding the Music House in brick. This brick structure, erected in 1765, formed part of Sadler's Wells theatre until late in the 19th century. Mrs. Lampe, Thomas Lowe and other vocalists of repute sang at Sadler's Wells, and at a later date Miss Romanzini (Mrs. Bland) and Braham were among the performers engaged there. Mrs. Mountain, the singer, whose parents were engaged at Sadler's Wells, was named after Rosoman the proprietor. Charles Dibdin the elder, and his sons Thomas and Charles, were all more or less closely connected with Sadler's Wells, writing plays and musical pantomimes for production there. The younger Dibdins were proprietors and managers. Grimaldi's connexion with this theatre, and that of other pantomimists, tumblers, rope - dancers and actors, do not concern the musical records of it. The theatre has seen many changes, and became a music-hall.[1]

BIBL.—A collection of scraps relating to Sadler's Wells, bound in fourteen volumes, formed by Percival, is in the British Museum. *London Pleasure Gardens*, by W. and A. E. WROTH, *Old and New London*.

         F. K.

SAETA, see SONG, subsection SPAIN (4).

SAFFO, see SAPPHO.

ṢAFI ED-DÍN, 'ABD EL-MÚMIN AL-BAGH-DÁDÍ (13th cent.), a celebrated Arab musician who flourished at Baghdad during the reign of the last 'Abbásid caliph, al-Musta'ṣim (1242–1258). He was a talented performer on the lute, and during the sack of Baghdad in 1258 his skill saved him; Hulágú Khán, the Mongol leader, hearing him play, gave orders that he, his family and his goods should be spared. He had been tutor to the son of a vizier; and to his pupil he dedicated an important treatise on the theory of music (Bibl. Nat., Paris), which has been translated into French by Carra de Vaux.[2] It is a shortened and simplified version of the work of AL-FÁRÁBÍ, clearer than the original and differing from it in certain points. On the difference of sound from noise, for example, al-Fárábí had written: 'Musical sound is a simple noise, persisting during an appreciable time in the body in which it is produced.' Avicenna had proposed the definition: 'Sound is noise which has an appreciable duration and a certain pitch.' Ṣafi ed-Dín, observing that noise also has pitch as well as duration, explained the difference thus: 'Noises have the character of sounds when it is possible to measure the relations between their respective pitches.' The Arabs, following the traditions of Pythagoras and Euclid, determined pitch from the length of a vibrating string. The other works of Ṣafi ed-Dín include an Epistle on music (Paris; Vienna) and a treatise on rhythm, *The Book of the Periods* (Brit. Mus.).

         J. B. T.

SAFONOV, VASSILY ILICH (*b.* Itsyoursky, Terek, Northern Caucasus, Feb. 6—O.S. Jan. 25—1852; *d.* Mar. 1918), the son of a Cossack general living in the village of Its-yoursky, in the district of Terek in the northern Caucasus, on the banks of the romantic river Terek, sung by the poets Poushkin and Lermontov. His education was carried on at the Alexandrovsky Lycée in St. Petersburg, and during this time he took pianoforte lessons from Leschetizky. On completing his course in the above institution he decided to devote himself entirely to music, and entered the Conservatorium in 1878, where he became a pupil of Sieke and Zaremba for theory, and continued his pianoforte studies under Louis Brassin. He left the Conservatorium, a gold medallist, in 1880, and began his career as a pianist by a long tour in northern Europe,

[1] In 1925 a project was started to secure the theatre for dramatic and operatic entertainment on the lines of the 'Old Vic.'
[2] *Journ. Asiatique*, 1891, xviii. p. 279 f.

Austria and Hungary, in company with the famous violoncellist Carl Davidov. On his return he held a sub-professorship for a short time in the St. Petersburg Conservatorium, but was soon called to fill a more important post in the sister institution in Moscow. He eventually succeeded Taneiev as director of the Moscow Conservatorium in 1889. Here he did some admirable work in reorganisation; while his indomitable energy still found an outlet in teaching, and the orchestral, choral and ensemble classes remained under his personal supervision.

He first became known as a conductor in 1889, when he organised a series of local concerts at popular prices for the townsfolk, and in 1890 he was appointed to the Moscow branch of the Russian Musical Society in this capacity. Safonov first visited England in Feb. 1906, when he conducted one of the concerts of the London Symphony Orchestra. After a brilliant success in Vienna, he visited New York, where he was offered the conductorship of the Philharmonic Orchestra, and made his first appearance in that capacity on Mar. 5, 1904. He held this position till Mar. 1909. In October of that year he made his first appearance at an English provincial festival, conducting most of the concerts of the first Musical Festival held at Newcastle-upon-Tyne. Safonov was occasionally spoken of as 'the batonless conductor.' Having on one occasion forgotten to take it to a rehearsal, he became convinced that its use was unnecessary and resolved henceforward to direct his players by the movements of his hands alone. Far more important from the artistic point of view than this innovation are the great services he rendered to Russian music; particularly to that of Tchaikovsky, by his intimate and impressive readings of his symphonies. Safonov was not, however, merely a Slavonic specialist. His interpretations of Haydn, Beethoven and Brahms showed him to be a conductor of many sympathies, with a decided leaning to the classic.

The fact that he was once known as a pianist of exceptional ability is likely to be forgotten in the brilliant success of his later career, but he numbered among his pupils several artists who continued the traditions of his peculiarly finished and delicate style.

         R. N.

SAGE DE RICHÉE, PHILIPP FRANZ LE, lutenist, in the service of Baron van Neidhardt at Breslau, 1695; master of Joh. Kasp. Kropfganss; known by the work: Philipp Franz Le Sage de Richée | Cabinet | Der | Lauten | In Welchem zu finden, 12 Neue Partien | etc. (described in *M.f.M.* 21, pp. 10 and 11, with musical examples; also *Q.-L.*).

SAGGIO DI CONTRAPPUNTO, see MARTINI, GIOV. BATT.

**SAINT ANNE'S TUNE,** a famous hymn tune,[1] first found in ' A Supplement to the New Version of the Psalms,' sixth edition, much enlarged, 1708. Dr. Croft's name is not mentioned in the work, but he is believed to have been the musical editor of this edition of the ' Supplement '; the name of the tune is probably derived from that of the parish, St. Anne's, Westminster, of which church he was then organist, and the tune itself is directly ascribed to him by his contemporaries,[2] viz. Philip Hart in ' Melodies proper to be sung to any of yᵉ Versions of yᵉ Psalms of David,' 1719, and John Church in his ' Introduction to Psalmody,' 1723. The tune appears in the ' Supplement ' in the following form :

Psalm xlii.  *St. Anne's Tune.*

Some doubt has been thrown on the authorship of the tune from its having been found in Abraham Barber's ' Book of Psalm Tunes,' a Yorkshire collection, of which the licence bears date Feb. 14, 1687, when Croft was but ten years of age. Here the tune appears under the name of ' Leeds,' and is ascribed to ' Mr. Denby,' whose name some editors of hymnals have too hastily substituted for that of Croft. The edition, however, of Barber's Psalms which contains the tune is the seventh, dated 1715, or seven years after the publication of the 'Supplement' already mentioned. This edition contains, besides tunes for canticles, psalms, etc., twenty - eight hymn tunes arranged in four parts, with the melody in the tenor. Of these tunes three only have a composer's name prefixed, and these three, which bear the names of northern towns (' Leverpool,' ' Hallifax ' and ' Leeds '), are all ascribed to ' Mr. Denby.' It may be observed that while the melody of ' Leeds ' is identical with that of St. Anne's in the ' Supplement,' the modulation at the end of the third strain is different.

1 J. S. Bach's organ fugue in E flat is in England commonly called ' St. Anne's' from a fortuitous likeness between the subject of the fugue and the first line of this hymn tune.
2 See *Mus. T.*, 1900, p. 585, where the tune is given in facsimile and Croft's authorship discussed.

*Leeds Tune.*          MR. DENBY.

The supposition that ' Leeds ' was originally in Barber's Psalm-book was disproved by the discovery of a copy of an early edition of the collection, which from the evidence of the preface appears to be either the third or fourth, and to have been published about 1696.[3] The title-page is unfortunately missing. This volume, a smaller book than the edition of 1715, contains but twelve hymn tunes arranged in two parts, and neither the tune in question nor Denby's name occurs in it. Until, therefore, an edition of Barber's Psalms is found containing ' Leeds,' and of earlier date than 1708, Denby must be regarded as merely the author of a rearrangement of Croft's tune.

That some confusion existed respecting the authorship may perhaps be inferred from the fact that Dr. Miller, organist of Doncaster Parish Church, in his ' Psalms of David,' 1790, gives ' St. Ann's, Dr. Croft ' on one page, and opposite to it ' Leeds, Denby,' in triple time and as a different tune. On the other hand, it may be noticed that in another Yorkshire collection, John and James Green's ' Collection of choice Psalm Tunes ' (Sheffield, 3rd ed., 1715), St. Anne's tune is quoted under that name.          G. A. C.

**SAINT-AUBIN,** (1) JEANNE CHARLOTTE SCHRŒDER (*b.* Paris, Dec. 9, 1764 ; *d.* there, Sept. 11, 1850), a remarkable opera singer. She was daughter of a theatrical manager, began to act as a mere child, and, when only 9, charmed Louis XV. by her precocious talent. In 1782 she married Saint-Aubin, an actor in Mlle. Montansier's company, and in 1786 made her first appearance at the Opéra in ' Colinette à la cour,' but perceiving that she was not qualified for so large a stage, had the good sense to transfer herself to the Comédie-Italienne. There her expressive face, graceful acting and good singing could be properly appreciated, and she speedily became a favourite. She sang romances with great charm, and became the acknowledged star of the company and its most profitable member.

At her farewell benefit (Apr. 2, 1808) she took

3 The preface speaks of ' former editions,' and adds—' since the Psalms in metre are this last year much refin'd as to the English by some good grave Divine Persons who hath only left out all the old words and made the meter good English.' The preface to the seventh edition is a different one.

the part of Mme. Belmont in this work, leaving Rosine, her own creation, to her second daughter, Alexandrine. Her modest pension of 1900 francs was increased by Louis XVIII. to 3000. She took her final farewell, assisted by her elder daughter, Mme. Duret, on Nov. 7, 1818, in 'Une heure de mariage,' and was as much applauded as ever.

Three of her children distinguished themselves; the son, (2) JEAN DENIS (b. Lyons, 1783; d. Paris, 1810), was a violinist and composer of great promise.

The elder daughter, (3) CÉCILE (b. Lyons, 1785), a pupil of Garat, made her début in 1805 at the Opéra-Comique in 'Le Concert interrompu,' but went back to the Conservatoire to study, and did not reappear till 1808. Under the name of Mme. Duret she rose for a short time to distinction as the favourite singer of Nicolo Isouard, who composed several important and difficult parts for her. Her best creations were in 'Le Billet de loterie' and 'Jeannot et Colin.' She retired in 1820.

Her sister, (4) ALEXANDRINE (b. Paris, 1793), made a brilliant début at the Théâtre Feydeau in 1809, and in the following year excited great enthusiasm in Isouard's 'Cendrillon.' This was, however, the only original part in which she distinguished herself, and on her marriage with an actor at the Vaudeville in 1812 she retired from the stage.      G. C.

SAINT CECILIA'S HALL, see EDINBURGH.

SAINTE-COLOMBE, SIEUR DE (d. before 1701), a famous French bass-viol player who died about the time of publishing his *Tombeau* in the 2nd book of his 'Pièces de viole.' He was a pupil of Hotman, and teacher of Marin Marais. Together with his two daughters he used to give concerts for 3 gambas.

     E. V. D. S.

SAINT-GEORGES, JULES HENRI VERNOY, MARQUIS DE (b. Paris, Nov. 7, 1801; d. there, Dec. 23, 1875)—not to be confounded with the notorious Chevalier de Saint-Georges (b. 1739; d. 1799)—writer of novels, and author of numerous librettos for operas and opérascomiques, was the favourite collaborator of Halévy. Among his 120 librettos we need only specify those for Donizetti's 'Fille du régiment'; Adolphe Adam's 'La Marquise,' 'Cagliostro,' 'Le Bijou perdu,' operas; and 'Giselle,' 'La Jolie Fille de Gand' and 'Le Corsaire,' ballets; Auber's 'L'Ambassadrice,' 'Zanetta' and 'Les Diamants de la couronne,' with Scribe; Grisar's 'Lady Melvil,' 'Le Carillonneur de Bruges' and 'Les Amours du diable'; Clapisson's 'La Fanchonnette'; and Halévy's 'L'Éclair,' 'Les Mousquetaires de la reine,' 'Le Val d'Andorre,' 'La Fée aux roses,' 'Le Juif errant,' 'Le Nabab' and 'Jaguarita l'Indienne.'

From this list it will appear that Saint-Georges was the most prolific, as he was the ablest, of all French contemporary librettists after Scribe.      G. C.

SAINT-HUBERTY,[1] ANTOINETTE CÉCILE (b. Toul, c. 1756; d. Barnes, near Richmond, July 22, 1812), an eminent French operatic actress whose real surname was Clavel. Her father, who had previously served in the army, became stage manager to a French opera company at Mannheim, and afterwards at Warsaw, where she studied for four years with Lemoyne, conductor of the orchestra. Her first public appearance was in an opera of his, 'Le Bouquet de Colette.' She then went to Berlin, and is said to have been married there to a certain Chevalier de Croisy, of whom, however, nothing is heard in her subsequent history. For three years she sang at Strassburg as Mlle. Clavel, and thence went to Paris and made her début at the Opéra as 'un démon, un plaisir' in the first performance of Gluck's 'Armide' (Sept. 23, 1777). For a considerable time she only played in subordinate parts. Her first great success was as Angélique in Piccinni's 'Roland,' and was followed by others in Floquet's 'Le Seigneur Bienfaisant,' Gossec's 'Thésée' (Mar. 1, 1782) and Edelmann's 'Ariane' (Sept. 24, 1782), all tragic parts; while as Rosette in Grétry's 'L'Embarras des richesses' (Nov. 26, 1782) she showed all the versatility and vivacity necessary for comedy. As Armide (in Sacchini's 'Renaud'), in 'Didon,' 'Chimène,' 'Les Danaïdes,' 'Alceste' and 'Phèdre' she had a succession of triumphs. 'Didon,' Piccinni's masterpiece, made no impression till she undertook the title rôle, and the composer declared that, without her, his opera was 'without Dido.' On her first appearance in that part (Jan. 16, 1784) she was crowned upon the stage.

In 1785 she made a journey to Marseilles which resembled a royal progress, but on her return to Paris she found new rivals to dispute her sway. She failed, too, as Clytemnestra, a part altogether unsuited to her. It ended four years later by her marrying the Comte d'Entraigues, of strong royalist sympathies, in which she participated warmly. In 1790 he had emigrated to Lausanne, and there their marriage took place, at the end of that year. It was only acknowledged, however, in 1797, after the Count, imprisoned at Milan by Bonaparte, had been released by his wife, who found means of enabling him to escape and of preserving his portfolio, full of political papers. For this service she was rewarded by Louis XVIII. with the Order of St. Michel and, it seems, by her husband with the recognition of their marriage.

The Count afterwards entered the Russian diplomatic service and was employed on secret missions. The peace of Tilsit changed his tactics. He possessed himself in some manner of a copy of the secret articles of the Treaty.

---

[1] How she obtained this name is not known.

and hastened with them to England to communicate them to the Government. For this he is said to have received a pension. He established himself, with his wife, at Barnes, near Richmond, where they were assassinated by their servant, who stabbed them as they were getting into their carriage, and blew out his own brains afterwards.      F. A. M.

SAINT JAMES'S HALL CONCERT ROOMS (1858–1905) were erected, at the cost of a company with limited liability, from designs by Owen Jones. Messrs. Lucas were the builders.

The project was taken up by two of the music-publishing firms, Beale & Chappell of Regent Street, and Chappell & Co. of New Bond Street; and the company was formed mainly by them, and among their friends. T. F. Beale and W. Chappell became the tenants of the Crown for the land, holding it in trust for the company. The capital was fixed at £40,000, because the original estimate for the new building was £23,000 and the remainder was supposed to be an ample sum for compensations, working expenses, etc. It was then unknown that between Regent Street and Piccadilly was the ancient boundary of Thorney Island with its quicksand, but this was encountered in the course of the building, and had to be saturated with concrete at great cost, in order to make a sure foundation. Other demands raised the cost of the building to beyond £70,000. The great hall was opened to the public on Mar. 25, 1858, with a concert for the benefit of the Middlesex Hospital, given in presence of the Prince Consort.

The principal entrance to the great hall was originally from Regent Street, and that to the minor hall from Piccadilly. The dimensions of the great hall were 139 feet in length, 60 in height and 60 in breadth. It seated on the ground floor 1100; in the balcony 517; in the gallery 210; in the orchestra 300; total 2127. Under the platform end of the great hall was the minor hall, 60 feet by 57, having also a gallery, an orchestra and a small room. This was occupied for many years by the Christy (Moore & Burgess) Minstrels. Under the Regent Street end of the great hall was one of the dining-rooms, 60 feet by 60, and on the Regent Street level was another dining-room, 40 feet by 40, with a large banqueting-room on the floor above, etc.

In 1860 alterations and additions were made to the restaurant attached to the concert-rooms, at a further outlay of £5000. The company was eventually enabled to pay these charges, through the uncovenanted liberality of some of the directors in accepting personal responsibility to mortgagees and bankers, while they diminished the debt annually through the receipts of the hall. Many concerts were given for the express purpose of engaging the hall on off nights, especially the Monday Popular Concerts (see POPULAR CONCERTS), which were originally started by Chappell & Co. to bring together a new public to fill the hall on Monday nights. In 1874 three more houses in Piccadilly were purchased to add to the restaurant. The rebuilding of these entailed a further expenditure of £45,000, so that the total cost exceeded £120,000      W. C.

In much later days important alterations were made in the approaches to the hall, a fine marble staircase leading direct from the Piccadilly entrance. In spite of these, there was an element of danger from the presence of kitchens and the Christy Minstrels' hall below, and in spite of the beautiful acoustics of the great hall and its wonderful artistic associations, it was not wholly a misfortune when it was determined to pull it down and use the site for a hotel. The last concert took place on Feb. 11, 1905.      M.

SAINT JOHN'S EVE, opera in one act; text by Eleanor Farjeon; music by Mackenzie. Produced (British National Opera Co.) Liverpool, Apr. 16, 1924.

SAINT-LAMBERT, MICHEL DE, lived in Paris at the end of the 17th and the beginning of the 18th centuries. Nothing is known of the life of this clavecinist. The name of Michel, even, is only given here in accordance with Fétis, and there is reason to believe that it may not have been his real Christian name.

As far as we can judge from his two didactic works published in the first years of the 18th century, Saint-Lambert appears to have been a competent professor of the clavecin, having a good method of teaching and a very open mind, more cultivated than the majority of musicians of that epoch. There is extant a set of well-turned verses written in praise of Marchand, which appears at the beginning of the 2nd volume of Marchand's clavecin pieces, who must have been among his friends.

He enunciates in his *Principes* the first rules of music, and his method of playing the clavecin is remarkably apt and well directed. His chapter on 'Ornaments' will be specially useful to modern clavecinists. He relies in this exposition on the only three French masters whose books of pieces existed in his time: Chambonnières, Le Bègue and d'Anglebert. He also makes use of the organ pieces of Nivers, and does not hesitate to vary some of the ornaments, or even to invent them anew, like that which he calls 'aspiration,'

*Written.*      *Played.*

and which has nothing in common with the ornament of the same name invented by Couperin.

His *Traité de l'accompagnement* is also remarkably clear. The harmonic theory of the period is set out more simply than it is by d'Andrieu. But because of the accuracy of his commentaries Saint-Lambert remains as valuable for historians of actual music as he was for the students of accompaniment in his own day. His two sagacious propositions of reform also show him to have been in advance of his time. One, explained in his *Principes* (and adopted by Montéclair), relates to the reduction of the number of clefs, of which several had become useless and worrying to teach. Saint-Lambert proposed to reduce them to three, placing always the same note on each line of the stave but in different octaves. This simplification of clefs was realised little by little in practice, with less logic, and it is permissible to regret it. The other proposition, which he expounds in the preface to his *Traité*, passed rapidly into practice. Saint-Lambert noticed that, in his time, the usual sharps and flats of the minor tones always included a flat less than they ought to hold. He declares (and he offers an example in his book) that

'tout ton qui a le mode mineur a la sixième de sa finale essentiellement mineure,'

and that he would

'mettre le bémol à la clef, et non pas dans le courant de l'air comme accidentel, ainsi qu'il se pratique ordinairement ; ce qui est une erreur considérable qui n'a pas été reconnuĕ jusqu'à présent.'

### WORKS

*Les Principes du clavecin, contenant une explication exacte de tout ce qui concerne la tablature et le clavier.* (Paris, 1702 ; reprinted Amsterdam, without date.)
*Nouveau Traité de l'accompagnement du clavecin, de l'orgue et des autres instruments.* (Paris, 1707 ; reprinted Amsterdam, without date.)
Italian translations of some works exist in MS. in the library of the Liceo Musicale at Bologna. Fétis thinks that these were only second editions ; that the first of the *Principes* would be dated 1697, and of the *Traité*, 1680. No example can be shown to bear these dates, and Fétis's assertion would appear to be contradicted by many passages in Saint-Lambert's prefaces.

BIBL.—*Mémoires de Trévoux.* (July 1708.)                A. T.

SAINT-LÉON, (1) CHARLES VICTOR ARTHUR (real name MICHEL) (*b.* Paris, Apr. 17, 1821 ; *d.* there, Sept. 2 or 5, 1870), violinist, composer, dancer and French choregraphist, son of a ballet-master at the Theatre Royal of Stuttgart. He was a pupil of Paganini and Mayseder, making his début at the age of 14 at Munich as dancer and violinist. He toured from 1838, and gave a performance in Italy of 'La Vivandière et le postillon' (1843), when he danced with Fanny Cerrito, whom he married in 1845 at Paris. He made his first appearance at the Paris Opéra in 1846, and gave there performances of 'La Fille de marbre,' which he danced with his wife (Oct. 20, 1847), 'La Vivandière ' (Oct. 20, 1848), 'Le Violon du diable,' *ballet fantastique*, which he played on the violin (Jan. 19, 1849), 'Stella ' (Feb. 22, 1850) (the music of all these by Pugni) ; 'Pâquerette ' (libretto by Théophile Gautier, music by Benoit, Jan. 15, 1851), 'Les Nations ' (ode by Théodore de Banville, music by Ad. Adam for the delegates of the Great Exhibition in London). He appeared later, as author,

violinist and dancer, at the Théâtre-Lyrique in 'Le Lutin de la vallée' (Jan. 22, 1853), 'Le Danseur du roi ' (Oct. 22, 1853 ; music by Eug. Gautier). He reappeared at the Opéra in 1853, travelled in England, Germany (1853), Russia (1854, 1864), and directed the dancing at the Royal Theatre at Lisbon. From 1864–1870 he again directed, at the Paris Opéra, the following ballets of Minkous and Delibes, in which it is said he collaborated in the music : 'Néméa ' (1864), 'La Source ' (1866), 'Coppélia ' (1870). Marie Louise, Archduchess of Parma, created Saint-Léon chamber violinist in 1844.

He was an artist of unusual intelligence, speaking fluently several languages. H. Quittard said of him : Saint-Léon, 'a contribué à rendre les pas de ballet moins solennels peut-être, mais plus vivants et plus pittoresques qu'ils ne l'étaient avant lui.'

His wife, (2) FRANCESCA (called FANNY) CERRITO (*b.* Naples, Mar. 11, 1821 ; still living in 1895), known as 'quatrième Grâce,' an Italian dancer, made her début at the San Carlo Theatre in 1835, appeared in Rome, Florence, Turin, Milan (1838), Vienna (1838–1840), London (1840–45) and Paris, where she took the leading parts in her husband's ballets. Her success in London was considerable : she danced a *pas de quatre* with Marie Taglioni, Carlotta Grisi and Lucie Graban, reappearing to make herself a name beside those dance celebrities of the 19th century. Having separated from her husband about 1850, she was re-engaged at the Opéra in 1852, leaving it the following year. She lived from that time in Paris. In 1854 she collaborated with Théophile Gautier in the ballet 'Gemma ' (music by Count Gabrielli), in which she also danced.

### BIBLIOGRAPHY

SAINT-LÉON : *La Sténochorégraphie, ou art d'écrire promptement la danse, avec portraits et biographies des plus célèbres maîtres de ballets anciens et modernes*, dedicated to H.M. Nicolas I. (Paris, 1852). *De l'état actuel de la danse* (Lisbon, Apr. 5, 1856).
J. D. D. S. : *Biographie de M. et Mme. Cerrito-Saint-Léon* (*La Renommée*, 1850).
DE LAJARTE : *Bibliothèque musicale de l'Opéra*, vol. ii.
FÉTIS : Suppt. II.
DE BOIGNE : *Petits Mémoires de l'opéra* (1857, chap. xxii.).
HORACE DE VIEL-CASTEL : *Mémoires* (1883).
VAPEREAU : *Dict. des contemporains* (1895).
*Grande Encyclopédie*, art. by QUITTARD.                J. G. P.

SAINTON, PROSPER PHILIPPE CATHERINE (*b.* Toulouse, June 5, 1813 ; *d.* Oct. 17, 1890), an eminent violin-player whose father was a merchant at Toulouse. He received his education at the College of Toulouse and was destined for the law, but in Dec. 1831 he entered the Conservatoire at Paris and studied the violin under Habeneck, taking the first prize in 1834. For two years after this he was a member of the orchestra of the Société des Concerts, and the Opéra ; and then made an extended tour through Italy, Germany, Russia, Finland, Sweden, Denmark and Spain, with great success. In 1840 he was appointed professor of the violin in the Conservatoire of his native city. In 1844 he made his first visit to England, and played at the Philharmonic on June 10 and July 8 of that memorable season, under the baton of Mendelssohn. The following year he returned, was appointed professor at the R.A.M., and settled in London. He took the first and second violin alternately with Sivori, Ernst, Molique and Vieuxtemps, at the performances of Beethoven's quartets at the house of ALSAGER (q.v.) in 1845 and 1846, which resulted in the ' Beethoven Quartet Society.' He was also a constant leader at the performances of the Musical Union, the Quartet Association, the Monday Popular Concerts, etc. etc. On the establishment of the Royal Italian Opera at Covent Garden, Apr. 6, 1847, Sainton became leader of the orchestra, a post which he held until 1871, when he accompanied Sir Michael Costa to the rival house and remained there till 1880. He was leader of the Philharmonic band from 1846–54 inclusive, and of the Sacred Harmonic Society from 1848, conducting the performances of the latter society in the absence of his chief, as he did those of the Opera. He was also for many years leader of the Birmingham Festivals and other provincial musical performances. From 1848–55 he was conductor of the State band and violin solo to the Queen, resigning the post of his own accord. At the opening of the International Exhibition of 1862 Sainton conducted the performance of Sterndale Bennett's Ode (to Tennyson's words), and was presented by the composer with the autograph of the work as a token of his gratitude and consideration. Among the many pupils whom he formed during his long career as professor of the violin at the R.A.M. may be mentioned H. Weist-Hill, F. Amor, A. C. Mackenzie, A. Burnett, Gabrielle Vaillant, W. Sutton. His works comprise two concertos for the violin with orchestra ; a solo de concert ; a rondo mazurka ; three romances ; several airs with variations ; and numerous fantasias on operas. In 1860 Sainton married Miss Dolby (see SAINTON-DOLBY). His farewell concert took place at the Albert Hall on June 25, 1883.       G.

SAINTON - DOLBY, CHARLOTTE HELEN (b. London, May 17, 1821 ; d. there, Feb. 18, 1885), contralto singer.

Her earliest instructress was a Mrs. Montague, from whom she received pianoforte lessons. On the death of her father Miss Dolby determined to adopt the musical profession, and in Jan. 1834 entered the R.A.M., where she first studied under J. Bennett and Elliott. and then under Crivelli. In 1837 she was elected a King's Scholar. She remained at the Academy for three years. She made her first appearance at the Philharmonic in a quartet, June 14, 1841, and in a solo, Apr. 14, 1842. In the winter of 1845–46 Mendelssohn, who had been delighted by her singing in ' St.

Paul,' obtained for her an engagement at the Gewandhaus Concerts at Leipzig, where her first appearance took place Oct. 25, 1845, and on Dec. 6 she sang in a duet with Jenny Lind. About this time Mendelssohn dedicated to her his Six Songs [1] (op. 57), besides writing the contralto music in ' Elijah ' with the special view to her singing it. Her success in Leipzig was followed by several concert tours in France and Holland, in both of which countries Miss Dolby established her reputation as a singer of the first rank. In 1860 she married Prosper SAINTON (q.v.), and ten years later she retired from public life. In 1872 Mme. Sainton opened her Vocal Academy, at which she successfully trained many excellent artists in the admirable school of pure vocalisation, of which she was herself so distinguished an example. Mme. Fanny Moody was her most eminent pupil. Mme. Sainton also appeared before the world as a composer. Her cantatas ' The Legend of St. Dorothea ' and ' The Story of the Faithful Soul,' produced respectively at St. James's Hall on June 14, 1876, and Steinway Hall on June 19, 1879, have been performed in the provinces and the colonies with unvaried success. A fairy cantata for female voices, ' Florimel,' was published after her death, which took place at 71 Gloucester Place, Hyde Park, London. She was buried at Highgate Cemetery, the great concourse of persons assembled testifying to the estimation in which the singer was held. The R.A.M. founded, shortly after her death, a scholarship in her memory.          W. B. S.

SAINT PAUL (Ger. PAULUS), Mendelssohn's first oratorio, op. 36, Produced Lower Rhine Festival, Düsseldorf, May 22, 1836 ; Liverpool, Oct. 7, 1836 ; Sacred Harmonic Society, Mar. 7, 1837 ; Birmingham Festival, Mendelssohn conducting, Sept. 20, 1837.

SAINT PETER, an oratorio in 2 parts ; words by Chorley, music by Sir Julius Benedict. Produced Birmingham Festival, Sept. 2, 1870.          G.

SAINT-SAËNS, CHARLES CAMILLE (b. Paris, Oct. 9, 1835 ; d. Algiers, Dec. 16, 1921). His father (d. Dec. 1835) was of peasant origin, his mother of a bourgeois family. It was from her and from her great-aunt, Charlotte Masson, that he received, during his earliest infancy, his first musical lessons. From the outset he displayed a great fondness for music, an uncommon ability in piano-playing, a sensitive ear, great musical memory and an unerring sense of pitch. Nature, indeed, was generous with him, endowing him not only with intellect and talent, but also with energy, buoyancy and an inexhaustible capacity for work. At the age of 7 he became a pupil of Stamaty for the piano, and of Pierre Maleden (himself a pupil of Gottfried Weber) for harmony. At that time he had already began to compose ;

[1] Also dedicated to Mme. Livia Frege.

and in 1840 he performed before an audience, with the Belgian violinist Bessems, one of Beethoven's violin sonatas. In 1846 he gave his first piano recital at the Salle Pleyel; in 1848 he entered Eugène Benoit's organ class at the Paris Conservatoire, in which he obtained the second prize the following year and the first in 1851, after which he passed into Halévy's composition class. It was at this period that he first met Liszt, whose music was to exercise so great an influence upon him.

In 1852 he entered the competition for the Prix de Rome, but without success. The same year his ' Ode à Sainte Cécile ' won the first prize at a competition opened by the Société Sainte-Cécile of Paris. This work was performed in Dec. 1852 and again in 1854.

In 1853 he was appointed organist of the Church Saint Merry; he occupied this post until Dec. 1857, when he was appointed organist of the Madeleine. His first symphony (published in 1855) was performed by the Société Sainte-Cécile in 1853, and again in 1856 and 1857.

In 1856 he wrote his second symphony for a competition opened by the Société Sainte-Cécile of Bordeaux. This work took the first prize, and was performed at Paris the following February. In 1861 he was appointed piano professor at the École Niedermeyer. He held this post four years. This was the only period of his life devoted to teaching. Fauré, Gigout and Messager were among his pupils.

During all this early period of his career he composed sedulously and achieved fame as a virtuoso. His playing was, and always remained, remarkable for purity, perspicuity and ease; the only qualities not displayed by him were poetic intensity and fervour.

Soon his ambition to write for the theatre began to assert itself. But he found no encouragement with directors. So he resolved again to compete for the Prix de Rome (1864), but failed a second time in the attempt. Soon afterwards Auber persuaded Carvalho, the director of the Théâtre Lyrique, to try him with a libretto. And so he wrote (1864–65) his first opera, ' Le Timbre d'argent,' which was to be produced only in 1877—the year when the most popular of his dramatic works, ' Samson et Dalila,' was first performed at Weimar.

His early operas, beginning with ' La Princesse Jaune ' (Paris, 1872), were not very successful at the outset. Even ' Samson et Dalila ' was rejected by the Paris directors— a fate shared by his ' Étienne Marcel ' (produced at Lyons, 1879).

He had sowed the seed of suspicion through enlisting among the champions of modern art. In 1871, to protest against the almost universal antipathy evinced towards living French composers—and especially those who wrote instrumental music—he joined Romain Bussine as a founder of the Société Nationale de Musique, whose object was to produce new works of the French school.

Despite the hostility manifested in certain quarters, he was not long in finding recognition as a writer of instrumental music. His four symphonic poems, in which he skilfully followed Liszt's lead without imitating him slavishly (' Le Rouet d'Omphale,' 1871; ' Phaëton,' 1873; 'La Danse macabre,' 1874; 'La Jeunesse d'Hercule,' 1877); his chamber music (quintet, 1858; first trio, 1863; piano quartet, 1875), confirmed the favourable impression created by his early symphonies and his first religious compositions—among which is the Mass op. 4, written in 1856. Other works of special interest from the point of view of form are the concertos, and especially the piano concertos, of which Saint-Saëns wrote five: the first was first performed at Leipzig in 1865; the second at Paris, Rubinstein conducting, in 1868; the third at Leipzig (Gewandhaus) in 1869; the fourth at Paris (Concerts Colonne) in 1875; and the fifth at Paris in 1896, at a special concert commemorating the fiftieth anniversary of the composer's début. On all these occasions the composer played the piano part himself.

The first performance of the first violin concerto took place at Paris in 1873 (soloist, Sarasate); that of the second violin concerto in the same city, 1880 (soloist, Marsick); that of the violoncello concerto in 1873 (Paris Conservatoire; soloist, Tolbecque).

Indeed, from the middle 'sixties onwards, his career was one of almost uninterrupted progress and success. In 1871 he visited London for the first time, giving organ recitals at the Albert Hall; in 1875 he began a series of triumphant tours, visiting, among other countries, Russia and Austria. As early as 1868 he had received the order of the Legion of Honour, the first of the many official distinctions, French and foreign, which came to him in the course of his career. In 1881 he was elected a member of the French Institut, and thenceforward all the Paris theatres were opened to his works. ' Henri VIII ' was produced at the Opéra in 1883. Then came ' Proserpine ' (Opéra-Comique, 1887); ' Ascanio ' (Opéra, 1890); ' Les Barbares ' (Opéra, 1901); ' Parysatis ' (Béziers, 1902); ' Hélène ' (Monte Carlo, 1905); ' L'Ancêtre ' (Monte Carlo, 1906); ' Déjanire ' (Opéra, 1911). In 1892 he received the honorary degree of Mus.D. from the University of Cambridge.

He left hardly any branch of musical art untouched. The catalogue of his output comprises piano and organ music, symphonic and chamber music of all descriptions, cantatas, oratorios, songs and choral works, incidental music, operettas, operas, a ballet, transcriptions and arrangements. He was the general

## LXIX

SAINT-SAËNS
From a heliogravure by Dujardin

AMBROISE THOMAS
From a tinted pen-and-ink drawing bequeathed by the late W. Barclay Squire to the R.C.M.

editor of Rameau's complete works published by Durand, Paris ; he also edited the score of Gluck's ' Écho et Narcisse,' and Marc Antoine Charpentier's incidental music to Molière's *Le Malade imaginaire*.

He was fond of dabbling in literature and science. He wrote a book of poems, a few farces, and various papers on scientific topics. Part of his many essays on music and the theatre appeared in book form (*Harmonie et mélodie*, 1885 ; *Portraits et souvenirs*, 1899).

His place among French composers of his time was from the outset unique in several respects ; and unique it remained, after a fashion, until the end of his long and active career. His greatest merit is to have been a pioneer of progress and a champion of instrumental music at a moment when musical France stood in great need of the influence which he exerted so powerfully. With Berlioz, Gounod and Lalo he stands out as a promoter of the wonderful revival of French music ; and when further headway was made under the influence of Franck, Fauré and Chabrier, his influence continued to carry weight, although it ceased to predominate as it had done during the first stages of the revival.

No composer played so great a part in the formation and towards the recognition of the modern French school of symphony : for his music set high standards in form, style and workmanship ; his output was abundant and regular ; his combative activity was uncompromising and tireless. But although—sharing the fate of the other leaders of the French school—he was often denounced as an anarchist, he was essentially classical and moderate in tastes and tendencies. This idiosyncrasy accounts for the curious fact that he gradually passed from the leadership of the progressive party to that of the conservative. He remained strictly faithful to his ideals, and was at the close of his career exactly what he was at the outset. As early as 1874 he foretold (in the *Nouvelle Revue*) that a new and fertile era was opening for music, following upon the breaking-up of the major-minor tonal system ; but although since then French music progressed exactly as he had foretold, he became more and more dissatisfied with the way in which things were moving around him, and was wont to express his hostility most forcibly. He exercised a sound moderating influence at a time when Wagner's music was threatening to sweep many French composers and a great fraction of the French public off their feet. He stood for the maintenance of French measure and French perspicuity. As early as 1888 one of his admirers, Hughes Imbert, described him as ' holding his own among the independent and intelligent spirits who did not fear to confront new ideas, but were not daring enough to attempt capital reforms.' Later,

Romain Rolland (in *Musiciens d'aujourdhui*) wrote :

' He is tormented by no passions, and nothing perturbs the lucidity of his mind. At times, his music seems to carry us back to Mendelssohn, to Spontini, to the school of Gluck. He brings into the midst of our present restlessness something of the sweetness and clarity of past periods, something that seems like fragments of a vanished world.'

So far as regards skill and technical knowledge, Saint-Saëns ranks remarkably high. His command of orchestration is supreme ; and the same may be said of his sense of form—exemplified at its best in the symphonic poems and in the third symphony (first performed at the Royal Philharmonic Society in May 1886), his instrumental masterpiece. It has often been remarked that his music is more brilliant than moving, and characterised by a certain coldness ; and that he remained indifferent to the quality of his ideas. Indeed, his imagination asserts itself far more in the treatment of his materials than in actual invention. It is perhaps chiefly for this reason that only a small portion of his big output survives.    M. D. C.

LIST OF SAINT-SAËNS'S COMPOSITIONS

Op.
1. Three pieces for harmonium.
2. First symphony, Eb (published 1855).
3. PF. solos, bagatelles.
4. Mass for soli, choir, organ and orch.
5. Tantum ergo for 8-part choir with organ.
6. Tarantelle for flute, clarinet and orch.
7. Rhapsodies on Breton themes for organ.
8. Six duets for harmonium and PF.
9. Bénédiction nuptiale for organ.
10. Scena from Horace.
11. Duettino in G for PF.
12. Oratorio de Noël.
13. Élévation for harmonium.
14. Quintet, A minor, for PF. and strings.
15. Serenade for PF., organ, vln. and viola or v'cl.
16. Suite for PF. and v'cl.
17. First PF. concerto in D.
18. Trio, PF. and strings in F.
19. Les Noces de Prométhée, cantata.
20. First violin concerto, A minor.
21. First mazurka for PF.
22. Second PF. concerto, G minor.
23. Gavotte for PF.
24. Second mazurka for PF.
25. March for PF., ' Orient et Occident,' 4 hands.
26. Mélodies persanes for voice.
27. Romance for PF., organ and vln.
28. Introduction and rondo capriccioso for vln. and orch
29. Third PF. concerto, Bb.
30. La Princesse Jaune, opera.
31. Le Rouet d'Omphale, symphonic poem.
32. Sonata in C minor, PF. and v'cl.
33. Violoncello concerto, A minor.
34. Marche héroïque for orch.
35. Variations for two PF.'s on a theme of Beethoven.
36. Romance, horn or v'cl. and orch. in F.
37. Romance for flute or vln. in D flat.
38. Berceuse in B flat, PF. and vln.
39. Phaëton, symphonic poem.
40. Danse macabre, symphonic poem.
41. Quartet for PF. and str. in B flat.
42. Ps. xix. (vulg. xviii.), ' Coeli enarrant,' for soli, choir and orch.
43. Allegro appassionato for PF. and v'cl.
44. PF. concerto in C minor.
45. Le Déluge, biblical opera.
46. Les Soldats de Gédéon, for double male chorus, unaccomp.
47. Samson et Dalila, opera.
48. Romance, vln. and orch.
49. Suite for orch.
50. La Jeunesse d'Hercule, symphonic poem.
51. Romance in D, PF. and v'cl.
52. Six études for PF.
53. Chanson de grand-père for two female voices, and Chanson d'ancêtre, male choir baritone solo ; accompt. orch. or PF.
54. Requiem for soli, choir and orch.
55. Second symphony, A minor.
56. Minuet and valse for PF.
57. La Lyre et la harpe, soli, choir and orch.
58. Second violin concerto in C.
59. Ballade for PF., 4 hands.
60. Suite algérienne for orch.
61. Third violin concerto, B minor.
62. Morceau de concert, vln. and orch.
63. Une nuit à Lisbonne, barcarolle for orch.
64. Jota aragonese for orch.
65. Septet for PF., 5 stringed instruments and trumpet.
66. Third mazurka, B minor, for PF.
67. Romance for horn (from op. 16).
68. Two choruses with *ad lib.* PF. accompaniment.

Op.
69. Hymne à Victor Hugo for orch. and chorus *ad lib*
70. Allegro appassionato for PF. and orch.
71. Two choruses for male voices.
72. PF. album.
73. Rhapsodie d'Auvergne for PF. and orch.
74. Saltarelle for male choir, unaccompanied.
75. Sonata for PF. and vln., D minor.
76. Wedding Cake, caprice valse for PF. and str.
77. Polonaise for two PF.'s.
78. Third symphony in C minor, orch., organ, PF., 4 hands.
79. Caprice for PF. and three wind instruments, on Danish and Russian airs.
80. Souvenir d'Italie, for PF.
81. Albumblatt for PF. 4 hands.
82. La Fiancée du timballer (Victor Hugo's ballade), voice and orch.
83. Havanaise for PF. and vln.
84. Les Guerriers, for male chorus, unaccompanied.
85. Les Cloches du soir, PF.
86. Pas redoublé for PF., 4 hands.
87. Scherzo for two PF.'s, 4 hands.
88. Valse canariote for PF.
89. Africa, fantaisie, PF. and orch.
90. Suite, PF.
91. Chant saphique, v'cl. and PF.
92. Second trio, E minor, PF. and str.
93. Sarabande and rigaudon for orch.
94. Concertstück for horn.
95. Fantaisie for harp.
96. Caprice arabe for two PF.'s, 4 hands.
97. Thème varié for PF.
98. Pallas Athene, hymn for sop. and orch.
99. Three preludes and fugues for organ.
100. Souvenir d'Ismailia, PF.
101. Fantaisie for organ.
102. Second sonata, PF. and vln., E♭.
103. Fifth PF. concerto in F.
104. Valse Mignonne for PF.
105. Berceuse for PF., 4 hands.
106. Caprice héroïque.
107. Marche religieuse, organ.
108. Barcarolle, vln., v'cl., organ and PF.
109. Three preludes and fugues.
110. Valse nonchalante.
111. Six études.
112. First string quartet.
113. Chant d'automne, 4 male voices.
114. La Nuit, sop., solo and choir.
115. Le Feu céleste, cantata.
116. Lola, dramatic scene.
117. Coronation march.
118. Romance du soir, partsong.
119. Second v'cl. concerto.
120. Valse langoureuse.
121. A la France, choral ode.
122. Caprice andaloa.
123. Second v'cl. sonata.
124. Duet, vln. and harp.
125. Sur les bords du Nil, military march.
126. La Gloire de Corneille.
127. Psalm cl., double choir and orch.
128. L'Assassinat du Duc de Guise.
129. Valse gaie.
130. La Foi, incidental music.
131. La Gloire, cantata.
132. La Muse et le poète.
133. Ouverture de fête.
134. Aux aviateurs.
135. Six PF. études, left hand only.
136. Triptych, vln. and PF.
137. Aux mineurs.
138. Hymne au printemps.
139. Valse gaie.
140. Overture from an unfinished comic opera.
141. Two partsongs.
142. Hymne aux travailleurs.
143. Elegy, vln. and PF.
144. Cavatina, tenor trombone.
145. Ave Maria, *a cappella*.
146. Cendre rouge.
147. Tu es Petrus, *a cappella*.
148. Quam dilecta.
149. Laudate Dominum.
150. Seven improvisations, organ.
151. Three partsongs, female voices.
152. Études, PF.
153. Second string quartet.
154. Morceau de concert, harp.
155. Marche interalliée.
156. Cyprès et lauriers, organ and orch.
157. Third organ fantasy.
158. Prière, v'cl. and organ.
159. Hymne à la paix.
160. Second elegy, vln. and PF.
161. Six fugues, PF.
162. Odelette, flute.
163. March.
164. Les Conquérants de l'air.
165. Le Printemps.
166. Oboe sonata.
167. Clarinet sonata.
168. Bassoon sonata.
169. Feuillet d'album, PF.

Works without opus numbers—
Fantaisie for vln. and harp (1907).
Twenty-five motets; songs, partsongs, etc.
Transcriptions of his own and other music.

BIBL.—JEAN BONNEROT, *Saint-Saëns* (the new edition, Paris, 1923, may be described as the official biography); ARTHUR HERVEY, *Saint-Saëns* (London, 1921); G. SERVIÈRES, *Saint-Saëns* (Paris, 1923).

SAINT-SÉVIN, see ABBÉ.

SALA, NICOLA (*b.* near Benevento, Naples, 1701; *d.* 1800), was brought up in the Conservatorio della Pietà de' Turchini under Fago, Abos and Leo. He devoted the whole of a long life to his Conservatorio, in which he succeeded Fago as second master about 1764, and Cafaro in 1787, as first master. The great work to which all his energies were devoted was his *Regole del contrappunto prattico* in three large volumes, containing methodical instruction in the composition of fugues, canons, etc., which was published in 1794. During the disturbances in Italy the engraved plates vanished for a time and were supposed to be lost. Choron then reprinted the work (Paris, 1808), but the plates were afterwards discovered. Both editions are in the R.C.M. Sala wrote little besides this work. Three operas, 'Vologeso,' 1737; 'Zenobia,' 1761; and 'Merope,' 1769; an oratorio, ' Giuditta,' 1780 ; three ' Prologues ' on the births of kings of Naples ; a Mass, a Litany and a few smaller pieces are mentioned by Florimo (*Cenno storico*, p. 562).      G.

SALAMAN, CHARLES KENSINGTON [1] (*b.* London, Mar. 3, 1814; *d.* there, June 23, 1901), began music early—violin, PF. and composition. In 1824 he became a student of the R.A.M., but soon left it and studied under Charles Neate, the friend of Beethoven. He made his first public appearance at Blackheath, in 1828, as a PF.-player ; then went to Paris and took lessons of Herz, and in the following summer returned to London and began teaching, playing and writing.

In 1830 he played a 'rondeau brillant' of his own in London, and composed an ode for the Shakespeare commemoration, which was performed at Stratford-on-Avon, Apr. 23, and was repeated in London. From 1833–37 he gave annual orchestral concerts in London, at one of which he played Mendelssohn's G minor concerto for the third time in England—the former two performances having been by the composer himself. In 1835 he instituted, with Henry Blagrove and others, the Concerti da Camera. He was an associate of the Philharmonic Society from 1837–55. In 1846, 1847 and 1848 he resided at Rome, and while conducting Beethoven's symphony No. 2 (for the first time in Rome), the concert was interrupted by the news of Louis Philippe's flight from Paris. He was made a member of the Academy of St. Cecilia in 1847. He founded an amateur choral society in London in 1849. On Mar. 18, 1850, he played at the Philharmonic. In 1855 he began a series of lectures on the history of the pianoforte and other musical subjects, which he continued both in London and the country for several years. In 1858 he was one of the founders of the MUSICAL SOCIETY OF LONDON, and acted as its

[1] He assumed this name in 1867 at the desire of his father, who had been born in Kensington in 1789.

honorary secretary until 1865: He was one of the founders of the MUSICAL ASSOCIATION, and its secretary until 1877. Besides the popular 'I arise from dreams of thee,' he composed many songs, some to Hebrew, Greek and Latin words; psalms (the 84th, 29th); anthems, choral works, in Hebrew for the service of the synagogue, and various PF. pieces. He contributed to various musical journals. An interesting obituary notice appeared in *Mus. T.*, 1901, p. 530. Addns. from that article and from *Brit. Mus. Biog.*                    G.

SALAMMBÔ, opera in 3 acts; text by du Locle, music by E. Rèyer. Produced Brussels, Feb. 9, 1890; New York, Metropolitan Opera House, Mar. 20, 1901.

SALBINGER (SLABLINGER; in 1548 he signs his name 'Salminger'), SIGISMUND, an early 16th-century Franciscan monk of Munich. He left his order, married and went with his wife to Augsburg *c.* 1526–27, and joined the moderate anabaptists, but was forced, by imprisonment and torture, to recant in 1530. He was driven out of Augsburg in 1531, but later was allowed to return, and in 1537 he was schoolmaster and afterwards also town musician. In 1544 he started a bookshop, and in 1561–62 was in the service of the Fuggers. He published the first complete metric German version of the Psalms (1537), and also several collective volumes, containing in all 210 songs by various important masters (1540–49).

SALCIONAL, see SALICIONAL.

SALE (SOLE), FRANCISCUS (*d.* Prague, ? 1599), a Belgian (?) musician; Kapellmeister (*magister chori*) of the Austrian Princess Magdalena at Hall-on-the-Inn, 1589; singer in the Imperial Chapel at Prague under Phil. de Monte, 1593. He composed 1 book of 5-6 part masses (1589), motets, canzonets, songs to the Virgin Mary and other church music. (See list in *Q.-L.*; also *Riemann.*)

SALE, (1) JOHN (*b.* Gainsborough, Mar. 19, 1734; *d.* Oct. 2, 1802), was admitted in 1766 a lay-clerk of St. George's Chapel, Windsor, and held that post until his death.

His son, (2) JOHN (*b.* London, 1758; *d.* Westminster, Nov. 11, 1827), was in 1767 admitted a chorister of St. George's Chapel, Windsor, and Eton College under William Webb, and so continued until 1775. In 1777 he obtained a lay-clerk's place in both choirs. On July 12, 1788, he was admitted a gentleman of the Chapel Royal in the room of Nicholas Lade or Ladd; in 1794 he succeeded John Soaper as vicar-choral of St. Paul's; and in 1796 John Hindle as lay-vicar of Westminster Abbey. At Christmas 1796 he resigned his appointments at Windsor and Eton. In 1800 he succeeded Richard Bellamy as almoner and master of the choristers of St. Paul's. On Jan. 14, 1812, he was appointed successor to Samuel Webbe as secretary to the Catch Club, and soon afterwards

resigned his places of almoner and master of the choristers of St. Paul's. He was also conductor of the Glee Club. He possessed a rich, full and mellow-toned bass voice, and sang with distinct articulation and energetic expression. He was for thirty years a principal singer at the Concerts of Ancient Music and other leading concerts in London, and at various provincial festivals. He composed several glees (published in 1800), and some which were included, with glees by Lord Mornington and other composers, in collections published by him. He left two sons, viz. :

(3) JOHN BERNARD (*b.* Windsor, June 24, 1779; *d.* Westminster, Sept. 16, 1856) was admitted a chorister of St. George's Chapel, Windsor, and Eton College in 1785. He was in the chorus of the Ancient Concerts in 1792, and in 1794 was principal soprano at the Three Choirs Festival at Hereford. In 1800 he succeeded Richard Bellamy as lay-vicar of Westminster Abbey; on Jan. 19, 1803, was admitted a gentleman of the Chapel Royal, in the place of Samuel Champness, and in 1806, on the death of Richard Guise, obtained a second lay-vicar's place at Westminster Abbey.[1] On Mar. 30, 1809, he succeeded Michael Rock as organist of St. Margaret's, Westminster. About 1826 he was appointed musical instructor to the Princess Victoria. In 1838 he was admitted organist of the Chapel Royal on the death of Attwood. His voice was a powerful bass, and his style of singing refined; he excelled in anthems, glees and other part-music. He was for many years principal second bass at the Concerts of Ancient Music. He long enjoyed a high reputation as a teacher of singing and the pianoforte. His compositions were few, consisting only of some chants, psalm tunes, Kyries, glees, songs and duets. One of his duets, 'The Butterfly,' was long in favour. In 1837 he published a collection of psalm and hymn tunes, chants, etc., with a concise system of chanting. Of his three daughters, MARY ANNE and SOPHIA (*d.* May 3, 1869) were organists and teachers of music. The youngest, LAURA, was the wife of William John Thoms, the antiquary, and originator of *Notes and Queries.*

The other son, (4) GEORGE CHARLES (*b.* Windsor, 1796; *d.* Jan. 23, 1869), was admitted a chorister of St. Paul's under his father in 1803. He afterwards became a skilful organist; in 1817 succeeded Dr. Busby as organist of St. Mary, Newington, and in 1826 was appointed organist of St. George's, Hanover Square.

W. H. H.

SALES, PIETRO POMPEO (*b.* Brescia, 1729; *d.* Hanau, 1797). An earthquake in his native town drove him to Germany, where he held appointments at various courts, being in the service of the Bishop of Augsburg in 1763,

[1] In order to understand how one person could perform the duties of two in the same choir it is necessary to explain that by long-standing custom each lay-vicar attends during six months of the year only, *i.e.* in each alternate month.

whence he went to Padua to produce one of his
operas. He returned, however, to Augsburg,
as in 1765 he still calls himself Kapellmeister
of the Prince-Bishop of Augsburg. After this
he visited England, but returned to Germany
in 1768, and became Kapellmeister and court
councillor of the Elector at Coblenz, where
he still was in 1778, and where Burney met
him in 1772. There he produced a number
of operas which were performed in Germany
as well as in London, where in 1776 he appeared
also as a virtuoso on the viola da gamba (Pohl,
ii. 374). In 1797 he fled before the invading
French to Hanau, where he died soon after.
He composed operas, oratorios, church music,
symphonies and concertos and a sonata for
PF. His wife was an excellent opera singer
(*Riemann*; *Q.-L.*).

SALÉZA, ALBERT (*b*. Bruges, Basses-Pyré-
nees, Oct. 18, 1867), operatic tenor. He studied
at Paris Conservatoire with Bax and Obin, and
carried off the 1st prize for singing and 2nd
prize for opera in 1888. He made a successful
début the same year at the Opéra-Comique as
Mylio in ' Le Roi d'Ys,' and remained until
engaged for the Opéra, appearing there Jan. 1,
1892. In the following May he created the chief
tenor rôle in Reyer's ' Salammbô ' ; and in 1894
that of Otello, when Verdi's opera was first given
in Paris ; besides singing the Cid, Siegmund,
Sigurd, Roméo, etc. At Nice he also sustained
the leading parts in Berlioz's ' Prise de Troie '
and Salvayre's ' Richard III.' His début at
Covent Garden took place in 1898, when he sang
Roméo to the Juliette of Miss Suzanne Adams
(also a débutante) and won an immediate success. His singing was marked by admirable
taste and dramatic feeling ; his clear, strong
tone filled the theatre ; and he proved himself
a capital actor. His impersonation closely resembled that of Jean de Reszke, whose stage
career was then drawing to an end. He was
also a good Faust, and created here the rôle of
the hero in Mancinelli's opera, ' Ero e Leandro.'
He sang at Covent Garden until 1902 and for a
few seasons at the Metropolitan Opera House,
New York.                                       H. K.

SALICIONAL (SALICET), a soft - toned
organ-stop of a reedy quality. The pipes are of
a very small scale. The mouth is also much
more ' cut up ' than that of a diapason pipe.
The origin of the word Salicet is plain ; to this
day country boys make toy wind-instruments
out of ' withy ' ; but withy is also called ' sally,'
and ' sally ' is *salix*, a willow. In some counties
a willow is called (by combining both names)
a ' sally-withy.' A Salicet is therefore a stop
made to imitate a rustic ' willow-pipe.' The
introduction of the Salicional or Salicet was
later than that of the Dulciana (said to have
been invented by Snetzler), and it must be
considered merely as a variety of that stop. It
is of 8 ft. or unison pitch.            J. S.

SALICOLA, MARGHERITA, a distinguished
opera singer, was at the court of Mantua in
1685. The Elector of Saxony, who heard her
at Venice, abducted her, and took her to
Dresden, as one of the first female singers on
the German operatic stage. In 1693 she sang
at Vienna.

SALIERI, ANTONIO (*b*. Legnago, Veronese
territory, Aug. 19, 1750 ; *d*. Vienna, May 7,
1825), court Kapellmeister at Vienna, son of a
wealthy merchant. He learnt music early from
his brother Franz, a pupil of Tartini. After
the death of his parents a member of the
Mocenigo family took him to Venice, where he
continued his studies, and made the acquaintance of Gassmann, composer and late Kapellmeister to the Emperor, who became much
interested in him, and took him to Vienna
in June 1766. Here Gassmann continued
his fatherly care, provided his protégé with
teachers, and himself instructed him in composition, made him acquainted with Metastasio,
and introduced him to the Emperor Joseph,
whose chamber concerts he henceforth attended, and often took an active part in.
While Gassmann was in Rome, composing an
opera for the Carnival of 1770, Salieri conducted
the rehearsals for him, and composed his own
first comic opera, ' Le donne letterate,' which
received the approval of Gluck and Calzabigi,
and was performed with success at the Burgtheater. On Gassmann's death in 1774 Salieri
returned his paternal kindness by doing all in
his power for the family, and educating the two
daughters as opera singers. In the same year
the Emperor appointed him court composer,
and on Bonno's death in 1788 he became court
Kapellmeister. He was also a director of the
opera for twenty-four years, till 1790, when he
resigned, and out of compliment to him the
post was given to his pupil Weigl. In 1778
Salieri was in Italy, and composed five operas
for Venice, Milan and Rome. For the Emperor's
newly founded National Singspiel he wrote
' Der Rauchfangkehrer ' (1781), and for a fête
at Schönbrunn ' Prima la musica, poi le parole '
(1786).[1] When the Académie de Musique in
Paris requested Gluck to suggest a composer
who could supply them with a French opera
in which his own principles should be carried
out, he proposed Salieri, who accordingly
received the libretto of ' Les Danaïdes ' from
Moline, worked at it under Gluck's supervision,
and personally superintended its production in
Paris (Apr. 26, 1784).[2] He was entrusted with
librettos for two more operas, and returned
with a great increase of fame to Vienna, where
he composed an opera buffa, ' La grotto di
Trofonio ' (Oct. 12, 1785), the best of its kind

[1] Mozart's ' Schauspieldirector ' was given the same evening.
[2] The play-bill of the first twelve performances described it as
an opera by Gluck and Salieri, in accordance with a stipulation of
the publisher Deslauriers, but before the thirteenth representation
Gluck publicly stated in the *Journal de Paris* that Salieri was the
sole author.

and one of his finest works, which had an extraordinary success, and was engraved by Artaria. In 1787 he again visited Paris, where the first of his operas, ' Les Horaces,' had failed (Dec. 7, 1786), owing to a variety of untoward circumstances, a failure amply retrieved, however, by the brilliant success of ' Axur, Re d'Ormus' (June 8, 1787), or ' Tarare,' as it was first called. This, which has remained his most important work, was first performed in Vienna, Jan. 8, 1788. Another work composed in Vienna for Paris was a cantata, ' Le Dernier Jugement ' [1] (libretto by Chevalier Roger), ordered by the Société d'Apollon, and performed there and at the Concert Spirituel with great applause from the connoisseurs. In 1801 Salieri went to Trieste to conduct an opera composed for the opening of a new opera-house. This was his last Italian opera, and Die Neger ' (Vienna, 1804) his last German one, for owing to his dislike to the change of taste in dramatic music, he devoted himself chiefly to church music, composing also a few instrumental pieces, choruses, and canons in various parts, published as ' Scherzi armonici.' On June 16, 1816, he celebrated the fiftieth anniversary of the beginning of his career in Vienna, when he was decorated with the gold ' Civil-Ehrenmedaille ' and chain, and honoured by a fête, at which were performed special compositions by each of his pupils, including Schubert.[2] Salieri was also vice-president of the Tonkünstler Societät, and till 1818 conducted nearly all the concerts. For the twenty-fifth anniversary of its foundation (1796) he composed a cantata ' La Riconoscenza,' and for the fiftieth (1821) a partsong, ' Zu Ehren Joseph Haydn,' to whom the society was largely indebted. Salieri was also a generous contributor to the funds. He took great interest in the foundation of the Conservatorium (1817), and wrote a singing-method for the pupils. He lost his only son in 1805, and his wife in 1807, and never recovered his spirits afterwards. On June 14, 1824, after fifty years of service at court, he was allowed to retire on his full salary.

His biographer, Edler von Mosel,[3] describes him as a methodical, active, religious-minded, benevolent, and peculiarly grateful man, easily irritated, but as quickly pacified. We have seen how he discharged his obligations to Gassmann. He gave gratuitous instruction and substantial aid of various kinds to many poor musicians, and to the library of the Tonkünstler Societät he bequeathed forty-one scores in his own handwriting (thirty-four operas, and

seven cantatas), now in the Hofbibliothek. In accordance with his own wish his Requiem was performed after his death at the Italian church. He remained throughout on cordial terms with Haydn, whose two great oratorios he often conducted, and Beethoven dedicated to him in 1799 three sonatas for PF. and violin, op. 12. Nottebohm [4] has printed ten Italian vocal pieces, submitted by Beethoven to Salieri, with the corrections of the latter. These chiefly concern the arrangement of the notes to the words, so as to conform to the rules of Italian prosody, and produce the best effect. The pieces are undated, but internal evidence fixes them to the period between 1793 and 1802. It appears that as late as 1809 the great composer consulted his old adviser as to the arrangement of his Italian, probably in the ' Four Ariettas and Duet ' of op. 82 ; and that even then, when Beethoven was so fiercely independent of all other musicians, their relations were such that he voluntarily styled himself ' Salieri's pupil.' [5] As regards Mozart, Salieri cannot escape censure, for though the accusation of having been the cause of his death has been long ago disproved, it is more than possible that he was not displeased at the removal of so formidable a rival. At any rate, though he had it in his power to influence the Emperor in Mozart's favour, he not only neglected to do so, but even intrigued against him, as Mozart himself relates in a letter to his friend Puchberg.[6] After his death, however, Salieri befriended his son, and gave him a testimonial, which secured him his first appointment.

His works were too much in accordance with the taste, albeit the best taste, of the day to survive. He drew up a catalogue of them in 1818. They comprise five Masses, a Requiem, three Te Deums, and several smaller church works ; four oratorios (including ' La Passione di Gesù Cristo,' performed by the Tonkünstler Societät in 1777) ; one French, three Italian, and two German cantatas, and five patriotic partsongs ; several instrumental pieces ; two operas to French, and thirty-seven to Italian words ; one German Singspiel, three German operas, and numerous vocal pieces for one or more voices, choruses, canons, fragments of operas, etc. (See Q.-L. for detailed list.)

C. F. P.

SALIMBENE, Fra, a Minorite friar, of Parma, who began his life early in the 13th century, and seems to have lived through the greater part of the same century (achieving a good deal of distinction in his order), and whose extremely curious Cronaca or Diary throws considerable interesting side-light on musical affairs in his time. He was a skilled and passionate music-lover. He gives us our accounts of two or three distinguished Franciscan

---

[1] The following anecdote is connected with this cantata. Salieri was talking over the difficulties of the work with Gluck, especially as to the voice to be assigned to the part of Christ, for which he finally proposed a high tenor. Gluck assented, adding, half in joke, half in earnest, ' Before long I will send you word from the other world in what key our Saviour speaks.' Four days later, Nov. 15, 1787, he was dead.
[2] The autograph of Schubert's Cantata—both words and music by him—was sold by auction in Paris, May 14, 1881.
[3] Über das Leben und die Werke des Anton Salieri, Vienna, 1827.

[4] Beethoven's Studien, Rieter-Biedermann, 1873, vol. i.
[5] See Moscheles's Life, i. 10.
[6] Nottebohm's Mozartiana, p. 64.

composers and singers of his day, including the once-famous Fra Enrico da Pisa, and Fra Vita da Lucca, who were in great demand during their careers. The *Cronaca* was found in the Vatican Library in the middle of the 19th century. It has been printed (though never completely) in the original Latin, and in a translation into Italian made by Cantarelli, and published by Battei, at Parma in 1882.    E. I. P. S.

SALINAS, FRANCISCO DE (*b.* Burgos, Mar. 1, 1513; *d.* Salamanca, Jan. 13, 1590), a writer on the theory of music, professor at the University of Salamanca and friend of the poet Luis de León. Salinas was the first Spanish musician to write down folk-songs as they were sung in his own time.

He was the son of Juan de Salinas, a Treasury official under the Emperor Charles V.; and losing his sight at the age of 10, he was dedicated by his parents to the study of music. Having attained a certain proficiency on the organ, he gave music lessons in exchange for instruction in grammar, and then passed to the University of Salamanca, where he became a familiar of the Archbishop, Don Pedro Sarmiento. This prelate took him first to Santiago, and then on becoming a cardinal brought him to Rome (1538). Salinas became acquainted with the lutenist Francesco da Milano (author of numerous books in tablature published at Venice and elsewhere between 1536 and 1563); the composer he admired most was Orlando Lasso. In 1558 he was organist in the private chapel of the Spanish Viceroy at Naples, which at that time was directed by Diego ORTIZ (*q.v.*). The Viceroy (the great Duke of Alba) afterwards persuaded the Pope (Paul IV.) to confer on Salinas the benefice of the Abbey of San Pancrazio in Rocca Scalegna. He returned to Salamanca in 1561, and was elected professor of music (1567) with the obligation to lecture for one hour daily on the theory and practice of the art; his retirement took place in 1587 when he had occupied the chair for 21½ years. He became acquainted with the poet Luis de León, who since 1561 had held one of the chairs of theology in the university. In 1573, giving evidence before the Inquisition, he deposed to having known Luis de León for at least six years, and admitted that the poet often came to his house and discoursed on philosophy, poetry and the arts. Salinas published *De musica libri septem* in 1577 (2nd ed. 1592). He takes up the position held by Zarlino in *Le istitutioni harmoniche* (1562); but the chief interest of his book lies in the number of Spanish popular songs, together with a few heard in Rome and Naples, with which he illustrated his chapters on music in relation to classical prosody. The importance of these was first pointed out by Burney,[1] who quoted

[1] *Hist.* iii. 306 ff.

several of them, while a hundred years later PEDRELL based some of his studies of Spanish musical folk-lore on these melodies. They include several old Spanish ballads and a number of popular songs, some of which relate to historical events. One of the finest tunes (' Yo me iba, mi madre ') is found 200 years earlier in the ' Llibre vermell,' a MS. of pilgrims' songs from Montserrat. Another (' No

SALINAS (1577).

Yo me i-ba, mi ma-dre, a  Vi-lla-re-a-le, er-ra-ra yo el ca-mi-no en fuer-te lu-ga-re.

me digays, madre ') is the earliest known tune for the old Portuguese dance, the FOLÍAS (*q.v.*). A third (' Rey don Alonso ') was originally a Moorish song and dance, ' Qalbi bi qalbi, qalbi 'arabí (' My heart, oh my heart, is the heart of an Arab '), frequently referred to in old Spanish literature; it is the first Arab tune to be noted in western musical notation. Salinas was famous as an organist; his playing has been immortalised by Luis de León in one of the finest poems in the Spanish language. (See *M. and L.*, vol. viii. No. 1).    J. B. T.

SALLANTIN, ANTOINE (*b.* Paris, 1754; *d.* there, after 1813), member of a numerous family of musicians, and a famous oboist. He was a pupil of J. Chr. Fischer in London, 1790–1792, and from 1794–1813 was oboe-teacher at the Paris Conservatoire. He did much to raise the standard of oboe-playing in France. A flute concerto which appeared under his name is probably by his son CHARLES (le jeune), an excellent flute-player (*Fétis*; *Riemann*; *Q.-L.*).

SALMON, (1) MRS. (maiden name, ELIZA MUNDAY) (*b.* Oxford, 1787; *d.* 33 King's Road East, Chelsea, June 5, 1849). Her mother's family had produced several good musicians; her uncle, William Mahon (*b.* 1753; *d.* Salisbury, May 2, 1816), was the best clarinettist of his day; her aunts, Mrs. Warton, Mrs. Ambrose and Mrs. Second, were capable singers.

She was a pupil of John Ashley, and made her first appearance at Covent Garden in the Lenten concerts given by him under the name of ' oratorios,' Mar. 4, 1803. On Feb. 11, 1806, she married James Salmon, and went to reside at Liverpool, where she became distinguished as a concert singer, occasionally appearing in London, and rapidly attaining the highest popularity. In 1812 she sang at the Gloucester Festival, and in 1815 at the Ancient Concerts. From that time to the close of her career her services were in constant request at nearly all the concerts, oratorios and festivals in town and country. Her voice was a pure soprano of the most beautiful quality, of extensive compass, very brilliant tone and extraordinary flexibility. She excelled in songs of agility. She unfortunately gave way to intemperance, which eventually occasioned derangement of the nervous system, and in 1825 she suddenly lost her voice. She married again, a clergyman named Hinde, who died leaving her totally destitute. A concert was given for her relief, June 24, 1840, which proved a complete failure. She gradually sank into a state of the greatest poverty; in 1845 an effort was made to raise a fund to purchase an annuity for her, but it was only partially successful. Her death was registered in the names of Eliza Salmon Hinde.

Her husband, (2) JAMES SALMON (d. West Indies), son of (3) JAMES SALMON (gentleman of the Chapel Royal, Nov. 30, 1789, vicar-choral of St. Paul's, and lay-clerk of St. George's Chapel, Windsor, d. 1827), received his early musical education as a chorister of St. George's, Windsor. In 1805 he was appointed organist of St. Peter's, Liverpool, and was in much esteem as a performer. In 1813, having fallen into embarrassed circumstances (by some attributed to his wife's extravagance, and by others to his own irregularities), he enlisted, and went with his regiment to the West Indies, where he died.

(4) WILLIAM (b. 1789; d. Windsor, Jan. 26. 1858), another son of James (3), was also a chorister of St. George's. He was admitted a gentleman of the Chapel Royal, May 28, 1817, and was also lay-vicar of Westminster Abbey and lay-clerk of St. George's, Windsor.

w. h. h.

SALMON, THOMAS (b. Hackney, Middlesex, June 24, 1648; d. Mepsal, Bedfordshire, July 1706), was on Apr. 8, 1664, admitted a commoner of Trinity College, Oxford. He took the degree of M.A. and became rector of Mepsal or Meppershall. In 1672 he published

'An Essay to the Advancement of Musick, by casting away the perplexity of different Cliffs, and uniting all sorts of Musick in one universal character.'

A quotation from the Essay will be found in the article SPINET.

Matthew LOCKE (q.v.) criticised the scheme with great asperity, and the author published a Vindication of it, to which Locke and others replied. In 1688 he wrote a book on Temperament, A Proposal to perform Music in Perfect and Mathematical Proportions; he lectured before the Royal Society on Just Intonation, in July 1705; and in the following December approached Sir Hans Sloane with a view of making researches into the Greek enharmonic music. He was buried at Mepsal, Aug. 1, 1706. For his non-musical works see D.N.B.

w. h. h.

SALÒ, (1) GASPARO DA (b. circa 1542; d. Brescia, Apr. 14, 1609), a celebrated violin-maker of Brescia. The career of this maker rested entirely upon conjecture, until the keeper of the Brescian State Archives, Cavaliere Livi, undertook to investigate da Salò's life, and published the result of his researches in the Nuova antologia, on Aug. 16, 1891. The documentary evidence there quoted has proved Gasparo da Salò to have been a member of an artistic family; that his legitimate name was Gasparo di Bertolotti; that his grandfather was a lute-maker of Polepenazze, named Santino di Bertolotti; and that his father was a painter, Francesco di Bertolotti, who was apparently called 'Violino' by his intimate friends. Owing to the loss of certain requisite pages of the parish registers of Salò, the exact date of this violin-maker's birth is still unknown, but calculating by the income-tax returns of Brescia, which declare him to be 26 in 1568, and 45 in 1588, his birth locates itself with some degree of accuracy in the year 1542. It is supposed that da Salò learnt his art partly from his grandfather and partly from a Brescian viol-maker who stood sponsor to his son Francesco, named Girolamo Virchi. Whether Virchi was da Salò's master or not is merely surmise, but what is certain is that the great Brescian master's earliest efforts met with such small encouragement that he contemplated removing to France, but was turned from his purpose by a loan of 60 lire from a certain brother Gabriel of St. Pietro. This advance was apparently the turning-point in da Salò's career; it was the moment when hazardous venture gave place to definite aim. In 1568 da Salò was renting a house and shop in the Contrada del Palazzo Vecchio, Brescia, at £20 per annum. He then possessed the title of 'Magistro di violino,' and owned a stock of musical instruments which he valued at £60. In 1579 there is an added title of 'Magistro a cittari,' and in 1583 'Artifice d' istrumenti di Musica.' Five years later, 1588, and twenty after his first establishment in the Contrada del Palazzo Vecchio, he changed his residence to the Contrada Cocere, where he valued his stock of finished and unfinished violins at £200, and styled himself 'Magister instrumentorum musice.' In 1599 he bought a house in Brescia, in a street called St. Peter the Martyr; and between 1581 and 1607 owned some small properties about Calvagese, near Salò. Although all trace of the place of his interment is lost, it is known that he was buried at Santo Joseffo in Brescia. His wife's Christian name was Isabella (b. 1546).

G. da Salò's son, (2) FRANCESCO (b. Brescia, 1565; d. there, ? 1614), was married to Signorina Fior of Calvagese, near Salò, in his twenty-third year. He followed the fiddle-making profession during his father's lifetime, but ceased to do so after his death. It is probable that he sold his business to his father's pupil Paolo Maggini, and retired. In any case he apparently left Brescia in 1614, and nothing further is known of him after that date.

Gasparo da Salò was one of the earliest makers of stringed instruments who employed the pattern of the violin as distinguished from that of the viol. His works are of a primitive pattern, more advanced than that of Zanetto and other old Brescian makers, but totally different from that of the contemporary Amati family. The model varies, being sometimes high, sometimes flat; the middle curves are shallow, and the sound-holes straight and angular. The wood is generally well chosen, and the thicknesses are correct; and the tone of the instrument, when of the flat model and in good preservation, peculiarly deep and penetrating. He made many instruments, especially basses, of pear wood as well as sycamore wood. His selection of timber was most careful; indeed, the remarkable regularity of the grain in the tables of his instruments bears evidence to this particular trait of the Brescian master. His varnish is principally deep yellow, and rich in tone, though some of his instruments are much darker in colour; in fact some are almost black, an effect doubtless due to age. The sound-holes are long, parallel and pointed in form, and in the gambas and viols still retain the more simple C shape; yet in spite of their length they are in perfect harmony with the form of the instrument. The purfling is usually single, and the general appearance of his work is bold, but not highly finished. His tickets run as follows: ' Gasparo da Salò: In Brescia,' and are undated.

The pattern of Gasparo da Salò was partially revived in the 18th century, owing no doubt to its great tone-producing capacity, by the celebrated Joseph GUARNERIUS (q.v.), and to a less extent by some of the French makers. As a maker of tenors and double-basses Gasparo da Salò has never had an equal, and his instruments of these classes are eagerly sought after. The objection to his tenors is their great size, but their effect in a quartet is unrivalled. Two remarkably fine specimens, formerly in the possession successively of Dr. Stewart of Wolverhampton, and of John Adam of Blackheath, came subsequently into the possession of J. A. Torrens Johnson. The most perfect specimen of a da Salò viola ever seen by the writer was the one which belonged to Edward Withers in 1884. This was a fine primitive instrument, and another perfect specimen was the property of Tyssen Amherst, an English amateur of celebrity. At the Special Loan Exhibition of Musical Instruments at the Fishmongers' Hall in 1904 there were three of da Salò's masterpieces. One was a viola of 1570, the property of E. A. Sandermann; another a viola da gamba of the same date, lent by W. E. Hill & Sons; and a third was a viol of 1565,

belonging to F. Pengrie. (The dates quoted are according to the catalogue.) At the Victoria and Albert Museum there are two Gasparo da Salò viole da gamba. One is mounted with seven strings, an innovation attributed to Marais in the 17th century. The sound-holes are in the C form, the ribs curve into the neck in the true viol fashion, the wood of the belly is even in grain, and the varnish is brownish yellow. Its complete length is 4 feet, and it was bought at the sale of the Engel collection for £8. The other gamba by this maker is mounted for six strings. The neck terminates in a well-carved grotesque head of an old woman; the wood of the table is even in grain; the sound-holes are in the C form; the varnish is slightly darker than the instrument mentioned above. The finger-board is ornamented with ivory and tortoise-shell, and bound with catgut frets. The purfling is in one single broad line. It is labelled within ' Gasparo da Salò: In Brescia.' The length measures 3 feet 9 inches, and it was bought at the sale of the Engel collection for £10. The well-known violin-maker, August Reichers of Berlin, possessed a small-sized violoncello by this maker in 1894 (probably a cut-down bass), and Dragonetti possessed three or four double-basses by da Salò. The most celebrated of these instruments was presented to him by the monks of the monastery of St. Marco, Venice, about the year 1776, and was returned to the donors after his death. It would appear that this bass has disappeared. Another of Dragonetti's basses was bequeathed by him to the Duke of Leinster, and a third was in the possession of the Rev. G. Leigh Blake in 1875. In the same year John Hart owned a Gasparo da Salò bass (small size) in an exceptional state of preservation.

The most renowned instrument of this maker is the violin which was made by him to the order of the Cardinal Aldobrandini, a noble patron of the fine arts in Rome, who paid da Salò 3000 Neapolitan ducats for his work, and presented it to the treasury of Innspruck, where it was preserved as a curiosity. The head of this curious violin is said to have been carved by Benvenuto Cellini; it represents an angel's face carved and coloured, surrounded by flowing locks of hair. Behind this there leans a little mermaid, the human form of which terminates in scales of green and gold. The tail-piece is another mermaid, in bronze colour, and the finger-board is ornamented with arabesques in blue and gold; while the bridge is delicately carved in the form of two intertwining fish, similar to the zodiacal sign of the month of February. The belly is made of an exceedingly rare species of Swiss pine, which grows on the Italian side of the Swiss Alps, and is even-grained. When Innspruck was taken by the French in 1809, this violin was carried to Vienna and sold to a wealthy Bohemian amateur named Rahaczek, who was a well-known collector. Ole Bull saw it at Rahaczek's house during a visit to Vienna in 1839, and tried to persuade his host to part with it, but this he refused to do. However, after his death Rahaczek's sons offered it to Bull at a price, and he purchased it from them in the year 1841. At the death of Ole Bull this violin became the property of an American amateur resident in the United States. Gasparo's violins, which are mostly of small size, are not in request for practical purposes.

Fétis, in *A. Stradivari* (1864), mentions a very remarkable violin of da Salò which was sold at Milan in 1807 ; and that Baron de Bagge also possessed one in the year 1788, of which Rudolph Kreutzer spoke with admiration. Another violin he states to be in the possession of T. Forster, an English amateur, and the owner of a numerous collection of violins, which bore the inscription ' Gasparo da Salò : In Brescia, 1613,' but either the ticket or instrument was doubtless counterfeit. On Apr. 21, 1907, commemorative tablets in honour of Gasparo da Salò and G. P. Maggini were placed in the façade of the church of San Giuseppe, and of a house near the Palazzo Vecchio, at Brescia.

BIBL.—VON LUTGENDORFF, *Die Lauten-und Geigenmacher* ; J. M. FLEMING, *The Fiddle Fancier's Guide* ; EDMUND SCHEBEK, *Der Geigenbau in Italien und sein deutscher Ursprung* ; H. WEUSTENBERG, *Die alten italienischen Geigenmacher* ; G. HART, *The Violin, Harper's Magazine*, No 368, Jan. 1881 (No. 2, vol. i., English edition) ; SARA BULL, *Ole Bull : A Memoir* ; P. GUERRINI, *La Cappella musicale del Duomo di Salò. R.M.I.*, anno 29, 1922, fasc. 1.            E. H.-A.

SALOMÉ, ' drama ' in one act, founded on the French play by Oscar Wilde ; German version by Frau Hedwig Lachmann ; music by Richard Strauss. Produced Dresden, Dec. 9, 1905 ; Théâtre du Châtelet, Paris, in German, May 8, 1907 (it had previously been given in Brussels, in French) ; Covent Garden, Dec. 8, 1910 ; New York, Metropolitan Opera House, 1907. ' Salomé ' was the title under which Massenet's, ' HÉRODIADE ' (*q.v.*) was given in London.

SALOMÉ, THÉODORE CÉSAR (*b.* Paris, Jan. 20, 1834 ; *d.* Saint Germain-en-Laye, July 1896), received his education at the Conservatoire, where he obtained various prizes for harmony, counterpoint and organ, and gained the second Prix de Rome in 1861. For many years he was organist of the small organ in the church of the Trinité, in 1872–73 taught solfège in the Conservatoire, and was maître de chapelle at the Lycée Saint-Louis, etc. He wrote various organ pieces which became popular, and several interesting orchestral works, performed by the Société Nationale in 1877.

G. F.

SALOMON, JOHANN PETER (*b.* Bonn,[1] 1745 ; *d.* London, Nov. 25, 1815), a name inseparably connected with that of Haydn, early became an expert violinist, and in 1758 was admitted into

[1] The Salomons' house was 515 Bonngasse, the same in which Beethoven was born. Salomon was christened Feb. 2.

the orchestra of the Elector Clement August. In 1765 he made a concert tour to Frankfort and Berlin ; and Prince Henry of Prussia, who had an orchestra and a small French opera company at Rheinsberg, made him his Konzertmeister, and composer of operettas. He had already shown his appreciation for Haydn by introducing his symphonies whenever he could. On the prince's sudden dismissal of his band, Salomon went to Paris, where he was well received, but being so near London he determined to go on there, and on Mar. 23, 1781, made his first appearance at Covent Garden Theatre. The pieces on this occasion were Mason's ' Elfrida,' set to music by Dr. Arne, and Collins's ' Ode on the Passions,' with soli and choruses by Dr. Arnold, both of which he led, besides playing a solo in the middle. From this time he frequently appeared at concerts as soloist, quartet-player (violin and viola) and conductor. He quarrelled with the directors of the Professional Concerts, soon after their foundation, and thenceforward took an independent line. During Mara's first season in London, in 1784, he conducted and played solos at all her concerts. In 1786 he gave a series of subscription concerts at the Hanover Square Rooms, and produced symphonies by Haydn and Mozart. From that time he contented himself with an annual benefit concert, but acted as leader at others, both in London, as at the Academy of Ancient Music in 1789, and elsewhere, as at the Oxford Commemoration, Winchester and Dublin. A grand chorus composed by him in honour of the King's recovery, performed by the New Musical Fund in 1789, and repeated at his own concert, was his one successful vocal piece. He removed in 1790 to No. 18 Great Pulteney Street, in which house Haydn stayed with him in the following year. The two had long been in correspondence, Salomon endeavouring in vain to secure the great composer for a series of concerts ; but as he was at Cologne on his way from Italy, where he had been to engage singers for the Italian Opera, he saw in the papers the death of Prince Esterhazy, hurried to Vienna, and carried Haydn back in triumph with him to London. Haydn's two visits to England in 1791 and 1794 were the most brilliant part of Salomon's career as an artist, and after the return of the former to Vienna the two continued the best of friends. It was at Salomon's suggestion that Haydn undertook to write ' The Creation.' Salomon's most important composition was an opera, ' Windsor Castle,' composed for the Prince of Wales's wedding, Apr. 8, 1795. In 1796 Salomon resumed his concerts, at which he was assisted by Mara, the young tenor Braham, and his own promising pupil Pinto. On Apr. 21, 1800, he produced Haydn's ' Creation ' at the King's Theatre, though not for the first time in England, as he had been forestalled by John Ashley (Covent Garden, Mar. 28). Salomon's active career closes with the foundation of the Philharmonic Society, in which he took a great interest, playing in a quintet by Boccherini, and leading the orchestra, at the first concert in the Argyll Rooms, Mar. 8, 1813. Up to the last he was busy planning an Academy of Music with his friend Ayrton. A fall from his horse caused a long illness, from which he died at his house, No. 70 Newman Street. He was buried Dec. 2, 1815, in the south cloister of Westminster Abbey. He bequeathed his house to the Munchs of Bonn, his next of kin; £200 to F. Ries, for the benefit of his brother Hubert ; and his Stradivarius violin (said to have belonged to Corelli, and to have his name upon it) to Sir Patrick Blake, Bart., of Bury St. Edmunds.[1]

Salomon was, on the whole, a first-rate solo-player, but his special field was the quartet, in which he showed himself a solid and intelligent musician. Haydn's last quartets were composed especially to suit his style of playing.

He was a man of much cultivation, and moved in distinguished society. Bland published an engraving of him by Facius from Hardy's picture. Another portrait by Lansdale was sent by Salomon himself to the Museum at Bonn. A pencil drawing by Dance is in the R.C.M. His best epitaph is contained in a letter from Beethoven to his pupil Ries in London (Feb. 28, 1816) : ' Salomon's death grieves me much, for he was a noble man, and I remember him ever since I was a child.' [2]    c. f. p. ; addns. *D.N.B.*, etc.

SALPINX. The Greek name for the straight military trumpet. (See TUBA ROMAN.)

SALTANDO, see SAUTILLÉ.

SALTARELLO (SALTARELLA) (Latin *saltare*, to jump).

(1) In 16th-century collections of dance tunes the melodies usually consist of two distinct divisions, the first of which is written in common time, the second in 3 time. The former was probably danced like our English country-dances (*i.e.* the dancers standing in two lines facing each other) and bore the distinguishing name of the dance, while the latter was like the modern round dance and was variously entitled Nachtanz, Proportio, Hoppeltanz or Saltarello, the first three being the German and the last the Italian names for the same movement. Thus in Bernhard Schmidt's *Tabulaturbuch* (Strassburg, 1577) are found the following dances : ' Possomezzo Comun ' with ' Il suo saltarello ' ; ' Ein guter Hofdantz ' with ' Nachdantz ' ; ' Alemando novello : Ein guter neuer Dantz ' with ' Proportz darauf,' and ' Ein guter neuer Dantz '

with ' Hoppeldantz darauf.' Similarly in the Fitzwilliam Virginal Book (i. 306) there is an elaborate ' Galiarda Passamezzo ' by Peter Philips (dated 1592) which consists of ten 8-bar ' divisions,' the ninth of which is entitled ' Saltarella.' The Saltarello, or Proportio, was always founded on the air of the first part of the dance, played in triple time with a strong accent on the first beat of the bar. The manner in which this was done will be seen by examining the following example, from the second book of Caroso da Sermoneta's ' Nobiltà di dame ' (Venice, 1600). It is part of a balletto, ' Laura Soave,' the second part of which (a Gagliarda) and the last forty bars of the Saltarello are not printed here for want of space.

*Si torna à far un altra volta.*

*Gagliarda.*    *Saltarella.*

etc.

(2) A popular Roman dance, in 3–4 or 6–8 time, danced by one or two persons, generally a man and a woman, the latter of whom holds up her apron throughout the dance. The step is quick and hopping, and the dance gradually increases in rapidity as the dancers move round in a semicircle, incessantly changing their position, and moving their arms as violently as their legs. The music is generally in the minor, and is played on a guitar or mandoline, with tambourine accompaniment. The finale to Mendelssohn's Italian symphony contains two Saltarello themes, in each of which the jumping or hopping step is very apparent. In contrast to these is a Tarantella, used as a third subject, a continuous flow of even triplets.    w. b. s.

SALTATO, see SAUTILLÉ.

SALTZMAN-STEVENS, MINNIE (*b.* Bloomington, Ill., U.S.A., 1878), operatic soprano. She sang first as a contralto in Chicago churches, then studied four years with Jean de Reszke in Paris (1905–09). Her début as Brünnhilde in ' Die Walküre ' at Covent Garden, in Jan. 1909, was her first appearance on the stage, this being a special winter season of one month, consisting mainly of Wagner revivals conducted by Hans Richter. She sang the same part in the remaining sections of the ' Ring,' and in all alike created a highly satisfactory impression by her intelligence of gesture and declamation and the general smoothness and finish of her singing. Her voice proved to be of sympathetic quality,

[1] See the *Westminster Abbey Registers*, by J. L. Chester, D.C.L. Sir P. Blake's property was sold after his death, and nothing is now known by the family about the violin.
[2] Pohl's *Haydn in London*, pp. 73-85. *Beethoven's Sämmtliche Briefe*, No. 411.

and of adequate power and range for the requirements of these rôles. Later she sang here in English as well as German, and was also heard to advantage as Isolde (1911) and Sieglinde (1912). After her initial success in London she was engaged for Bayreuth and appeared there for two seasons as Kundry and Sieglinde. After further experience at Berlin, Frankfort and Brussels she returned to her native land and joined the Chicago Opera Company, with which she sang from 1911–14.

BIBL.—*International Who's Who in Music*; NORTHCOTT, *Covent Garden and the Royal Opera.*     H. K.

SALVAYRE, GERVAIS BERNARD, called GASTON (*b.* Toulouse, Haute-Garonne, June 24, 1847; *d.* St. Ague, Toulouse, May 16, 1916), was brought by Ambroise Thomas to the Paris Conservatoire, where he studied the organ with Benoist, and composition and fugue with Thomas and Bazin. He gained the first prize for organ in 1868, and competed for the Prix de Rome every year from 1867–72, gaining it at last by sheer force of perseverance. Many of his compositions date from this time, notably his opera of ' Le Bravo,' and his sacred symphony in four movements, ' Le Jugement dernier,' of which the first two movements were performed at the Concerts du Châtelet, Mar. 19, 1876. It was given in its entirety at the same concerts on Dec. 3, 1876, under the title of ' La Résurrection,' and again, under a third title, ' La Vallée de Josaphat,' at Lamoureux's concert on Apr. 7, 1882. The remaining works written by Salvayre for the concert-room are an ' Ouverture symphonique,' performed on his return from Rome at the Concerts Populaires, Mar. 22, 1874 ; a Stabat Mater (1876), given under the Administration des Beaux-Arts (performed in London, Apr. 23, 1879, at one of Mme. Viard-Louis's concerts) ; a setting of Ps. cxiii. for soli, chorus and orchestra ; and an air and variations for strings, performed in 1877, all the last given as the fruits of his residence in Italy. On his return to Paris he was appointed chorus-master at the Opéra Populaire which it had been attempted to establish at the Théâtre du Châtelet, and he then wrote ballet music for Grisar's ' Amours du Diable,' revived at this theatre Nov. 18, 1874. Three years later he made his real début with his grand opera, ' Le Bravo ' (Théâtre-Lyrique, Apr. 18, 1877), a noisy and empty composition. His little ballet ' Fandango ' (Opera, Nov. 26, 1877), in which he made use of some highly characteristic Spanish melodies, was a decided advance in point of instrumentation ; but his grand opera, ' Richard III.,' performed at St. Petersburg, Dec. 21, 1883, was a dead failure, and ' Egmont,' produced at the Opéra-Comique, Dec. 6, 1886, was only performed a few times. Salvayre was commissioned to set to music Dumas's drama ' La Dame de Monsoreau,' a

subject little fitted for musical treatment. It was produced at the Opéra, Jan. 30, 1888, and was wholly unsuccessful. ' Solange ' was produced at the Opéra-Comique, Mar. 10, 1909. Salvayre was decorated with the Légion d'honneur in July 1880. He was musical critic to *Gil Blas.*      A. J.

SALVE REGINA, one of the most celebrated Latin antiphons. It does not belong to the classical Gregorian plain-song, but both words and music were written in the 11th century. They have been ascribed to various authors, but are with greatest probability assigned to Hermann Contractus (1013–54), the crippled monk of St. Gall and Reichenau, composer and writer on musical theory and practice. Originally an independent antiphon, this was afterwards assigned a special place of its own and became one of the antiphons of the Blessed Virgin sung after Compline. The music opens thus—

Sal - ve   Re - gi - na mi-se-ri-cor-di - æ, etc.

and continues in pure Dorian classical style. In this respect it is unlike the companion antiphon *Alma Redemptoris mater*, also attributed to Hermann, which shows signs of modern or popular tonality from the very start.

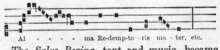

Al - - - ma Re-demp-to - ris ma - ter, etc.

The *Salve Regina*, text and music, became speedily popular. The words were the subject of sets of sermons by the end of the century, and soon St. Bernard and others still more widely established their popularity. In some rites the antiphon was admitted into the Office itself on one of the festivals of the Blessed Virgin ; it was then naturally associated with the First Tone. In the present Roman Breviary the text has been altered, and many incorrect forms of the music prevail. Apart from the plain-song setting the words have frequently been set in the motet style by Palestrina and others. These antiphons of the Blessed Virgin were among the earliest texts to be set in ' prick-song,' partly because elaboration was especially connected with such services, and partly because the antiphon at the close of Compline, being extra-liturgical, gave scope for polyphonic treatment, and in fact was among the first to develop into an ' anthem ' in the modern sense of the word. Their popularity has survived down to the present time, and many composers great and small have set the *Salve Regina*, the *Alma Redemptoris*, the *Regina coeli*, etc.      W. H. F.

SALZILLI, CRESCENTINO, an early 17th·

century Neapolitan composer of three books of madrigals and three books of canzonets, published at Naples between 1607 and 1616.

SAMARA, SPIRO (b. Corfu, Nov. 29, 1861; d. Athens, Apr. 1917), the son of a Greek father and an English mother, began his musical education at Athens under Enrico Stancampiano, a former pupil of Mercadante, and afterwards studied at the Paris Conservatoire, where his principal master was Léo Delibes. An introduction to the publisher Sonzogno led to the production of his first opera, 'Flora mirabilis,' which was given at the Teatro Carcano, Milan, May 16, 1886. 'Flora mirabilis,' which was written to a fantastic libretto by Ferdinando Fontana on a subject possibly suggested by the scene of the flower-maidens in the recently produced 'Parsifal,' was a kind of compromise between opera, ballet and spectacle. The legendary atmosphere of the tale appealed strongly to the young composer's imagination, and his music, though unequal, showed remarkable promise. Unfortunately that promise was never redeemed. 'Flora mirabilis,' after a brief period of popularity, dropped into oblivion, and none of Samara's subsequent operas has won anything like permanent success. 'Medgé' (Rome, 1888), a revised edition of an opera written before the production of 'Flora mirabilis,' was followed by 'Lionella' (Milan, 1891). 'La Martire' (Naples, 1894) won a certain measure of success owing to the clever if somewhat brutal treatment of certain realistic scenes, notably that of a café-concert, and still more from the remarkably powerful performance of Mme. Bellincioni in the part of the heroine, but the sheer musical value of 'La Martire' was very small. Samara's next two works, 'La furia domata' (Milan, 1895), an operatic version of Shakespeare's Taming of the Shrew, and 'Storia d' amore' (Milan, 1903), were completely unsuccessful, but 'Mademoiselle de Belle-Isle' (Genoa, 1905) was more favourably received. Subsequent productions were 'Rhéa' (Florence, 1908) and 'La guerra in tempo di guerra' (Athens, 1914).

R. A. S., with addns.

SAMAROFF, OLGA (b. San Antonio, Tex., U.S.A., Aug. 8, 1882), American pianist of distinction (née HICKENLOOPER). The first American of her sex to be admitted to piano classes at the Paris Conservatoire, she obtained most of her musical education at that institution, later studying with Ernest Hutcheson, and with Jedliczka in Berlin. Her début was made in 1905, with the New York Symphony Society under Walter Damrosch. Since then she has made numerous and extensive tours in America and Europe, and has appeared as soloist with most of the leading orchestras of those continents. In 1911 she married Leopold

STOKOWSKI; they were divorced 12 years later.    W. S. S.

SAMMARCO, MARIO (b. Palermo, 1873), operatic baritone, was taught singing at Palermo by Antonio Cantelli, made his first appearance at the Dal Verme Theatre, Milan, in Puccini's opera 'Le Villi,' and soon established his position. He came to London in 1904 with a high reputation, and his first appearance as Scarpia in 'Tosca,' Oct. 19, at Covent Garden, proved that report had not exaggerated his merits. He displayed a beautiful baritone voice, high in range—easily reaching g'—rich and sweet throughout its compass and under perfect control. He sang annually at Covent Garden till 1914, was engaged by Hammerstein for the Manhattan Opera House in New York in the winter of 1907, and returned to the same theatre in the two following years. In the autumn season at Covent Garden in 1907 he played Don Giovanni for the first time on any stage. He could not look the part and lacked distinction of manner, but he sang Mozart's music with great fluency and finish. His favourite characters, according to his own statement, are Rigoletto, Don Giovanni, Falstaff (which he has never sung in London), Iago and Tonio (' Pagliacci '). Sammarco has sung in many modern operas, among them the 'Andrea Chénier' of Giordano, 'Germania' of Franchetti, 'La Zaza' of Leoncavallo, and Saint-Saëns's 'Henry VIII.' At various times he has appeared in Moscow, St. Petersburg, Naples, Madrid and Buenos Ayres.

S. H. P.

SAMMARTINI, (1) GIUSEPPE (GIOSEFFE) (b. Milan, c. 1693; d. circa 1750), a musician whose works, with those of his brother, were in great vogue in England during the first half of the 18th century. He came to England, according to Burney,[1] in 1723, and according to Hawkins in 1729. Quantz heard him in Milan in 1726, and he published 12 sonatas in London, Oct. 26, 1727.[2] He was well received by Bononcini, Dr. Greene and others, and was by the influence of the first-named appointed as oboe-player at the Opera. With Arrigoni he gave some concerts at Hickford's Room in 1732.[2] His performance on the instrument surpassed all that had been before heard, and raised it to a great importance. It was thought that much of the fine quality he obtained was by a secret method of manipulating the reed before its insertion. Sammartini, having left the Opera, was patronised by Frederick Prince of Wales and his wife, holding in their household the position of musical director of the Chamber Concerts. The precise date of his death is uncertain. Burney[3] records his performance at Hickford's Room as late as 1744. Sammartini

1 Martini's first public performance in England was at a benefit concert for Signor Piero at the little theatre in the Haymarket. Burney, Hist. iv. 649.
2 Information from w. h. g. f.
3 Hist. iv. 663.

composed many sets of sonatas for flutes and for violins.

To distinguish him from his brother he is frequently named in contemporary references ' St. Martini of London,' his brother being ' of Milan.' His first publication was a set of sonatas for two flutes, issued in 1738. The sale of these being slow he destroyed the plates and the unsold copies, though they were afterwards reissued by Johnson of Cheapside. In the same year six concerti grossi were published. His next work, dedicated to the Princess of Wales, was twelve sonatas for the violin (Walsh, c. 1740). Others issued by Simpson are : ' Six Concertos for violins, etc., in 7 parts,' eight overtures, six more concerti grossi, harpsichord concertos, ' Six Solos for a German flute,' and ' Six Sonatas for two German flutes or violins.' Scattered pieces by him are often found in collections of airs (' Martini's Minuet ' being long a favourite), but it is difficult to distinguish them from work by his brother or from that of many other musicians who bore the same surname. (See Q.-L.)

(2) GIOVANNI BATTISTA (b. Milan, 1700/01 ; d. there, Jan. 15, 1775 [1]), his younger brother, remained in Italy, and became a prolific composer both for instruments and voices. J. Simpson of London published (1744) of his works ' Six Sonatas for two violins and a bass,' and Burney [2] says that between 1740 and 1770, in which latter year he saw him in Milan, he produced for the violin ' an incredible number of spirited and agreeable compositions,' and in 1770 ' he was maestro di cappella to more than half the churches in the city, for which he furnished massos upon all the great festivals.' Many motets, etc., and a great number of concertos, symphonies, overtures, trios, sonatas, etc., are mentioned in Q.-L.    F. K., addns.

BIBL.— R. SONDHEIMER, G. B. Sammartini, with numerous examples in music type (Z.M.W., Nov. 1920) ; G. DE SAINT-FOIX, La Chronologie de l'œuvre instrumentale de Jean Baptiste Sammartini (Sammelbände der Internationalen Musikgesellschaft, 1914).

SAMMONS, ALBERT EDWARD (b. London, Feb. 23, 1886), violinist, a pupil of his father, an amateur musician. He had a few desultory lessons from John Saunders and Frederick Weist-Hill. He must mainly be considered as a self-taught artist, yet can command a fine, apparently effortless technique which places him among the most capable of living violinists.

Happening to attract the attention of Sir Thomas Beecham, who heard him play the Mendelssohn concerto at the Waldorf Hotel (1908), he received an engagement as leader of the Beecham orchestra, a post he retained for five years, during which he took part in some fifty operas and ballets.

His early successes as a soloist included appearances at a Patron's Fund Concert at Queen's Hall (Max Bruch concerto), at the Harrogate Symphony Concert (Mendelssohn), and at the Philharmonic Society, of which he became leader, making a favourable impression by his playing of the solo in Strauss's ' Heldenleben.' In 1912 he played before the King in the Saint-Saëns concerto, the composer being present.

He toured in Germany in the spring of 1913 with the Russian ballet under Monteux, passing the summer season of the same year at the Dieppe casino, where he had some useful experience in concerto-playing. Later he won great distinction in London and the provinces by his interpretation of the Elgar concerto, a work singularly suited to his temperament and mentality, and also by his competent quartet leading. He was for nine years leader of the LONDON STRING QUARTET (q.v.), playing in first performances of works by Schönberg, Goossens, Waldo Warner, McEwen, Ethel Smythe and others. He also introduced several new works at a series of sonata recitals given in conjunction with William Murdoch (pianist).

He has edited the Delius concerto and partly rewritten the violin part. His own compositions include a Phantasy quartet for strings (Cobbett prize), several violin soli and books of studies.

At a Cobbett competition among British violin-makers, held at the Æolian Hall on Feb. 19, 1923, he played behind a screen upon a new violin by Alfred Vincent against a Strad, the former, upon which he now habitually plays, gaining the suffrage of the audience. w. w. c.

SAMPSON, RICHARD, LL.D. (b. circa 1470 ; d. Eccleshall, Sept. 25, 1554), English ecclesiastic and composer of church music. He was appointed proctor at Tournay in 1517, and Dean of St. Stephen's, Westminster, 1520. Two years later he became a canon of St. Paul's Cathedral, and was later appointed Dean of the Chapel Royal. He was holding this latter post when, in 1533, he became Dean of Lichfield. On Feb. 20, 1536, during Dean Pace's illness, Cromwell made him Vice-Dean of St. Paul's, and in May of that year, when Pace died, he succeeded him as Dean. A few months after this he became Bishop of Chichester. He was deprived of his deanery of the Chapel Royal, but on Mar. 3, 1543, he was promoted by Henry VIII. to the see of Lichfield and Coventry.[3]

Like his predecessor at St. Paul's, Sampson was a musician (for details of Pace's musical activities see PYGOTT and REDFORD). Two motets by Sampson, ' Quam pulchra es, amica,' a 5, and ' Psallite felices protecti culmine rose purpuree,' a 4, are in the Roy. Lib. B.M. 11 E x1/11b. The latter is a long setting of a Latin song in honour of Henry VIII. There

1 Death certificate. See G. de Saint-Foix, Histoire musicale ; une découverte. R.M.I., 1921, p. 316. According to burial certificate Bulletin de la Société Française de Musicologie, No. 9—Documents). Hist. iii. 573.

3 His ecclesiastical career is described with some fullness in Grattan Flood's Early Tudor Composers.

is a drawing of the Tudor rose on folio 2 in the MS.                                    J. M<sup>K</sup>.

SAMSON, oratorio by Handel; words compiled by Newburgh Hamilton from Milton's 'Samson Agonistes,' 'Hymn on the Nativity' and 'Lines on a Solemn Musick.' The autograph of the work is in the Roy. Lib. B.M., and contains the following dates : End of first part, 'Sept. 29, 1741'; end of second part, '⊙ (i.e. Sunday) Oct. 11, 1741'; end of chorus 'Glorious hero,' 'Fine dell' Oratorio,' S.D.G., London, G. F. Handel, 𝄇 (i.e. Thursday) Oct. 29, 1741'; then the words 'Fine dell' oratorio' have been struck out, and 'Come, come,' 'Let the bright,' and 'Let their celestial' added, with a note at end, 'S.D.G.—G. F. Handel, Oct. 12, 1742.' Produced Covent Garden, Lent, 1743; revived by the Sacred Harmonic Society, Nov. 14, 1838.                          G.

SAMSON ET DALILA, opera in 3 acts, text by Ferdinand Lemaire, music by Saint-Saëns; produced Weimar under Liszt, Dec. 2, 1877; Rouen, 1890; Covent Garden (in concert form), Sept. 25, 1893; as opera, Covent Garden, Apr. 26, 1909; in English, Theatre Royal, Dublin (Moody-Manners Co.), Jan. 11, 1910.

SAMUEL, HAROLD (b. London, May 23, 1879), a pianist who has made a special study of Bach, was educated at the R.C.M. under Dannreuther and Stanford. His playing of the major works of Bach early attracted the attention of musicians, but it was not until 1921, when he gave a week of daily concerts of Bach in London, that his powers were appreciated by a wider public. He has since given several such weeks, and has toured with success in America. He is a musician of wide sympathies, and his interpretative gifts have been shown in the playing of compositions of many schools and times.                      C.

SAN CARLO, see NAPLES.

SANCES, GIOVANNI FELICE (b. Rome, c. 1600; d. Vienna, Nov. 24, 1679), one of the first who used the word 'cantata' for vocal compositions in several parts for a solo voice. He entered the Imperial Chapel, Vienna, as tenor singer in 1637, became vice-Kapellmeister, Oct. 1, 1649, and Kapellmeister, Oct. 1, 1669. He was a prolific composer who wrote so much that J. J. Fux wrote to the Emperor in 1715 : 'The greater part of the chapel is still filled with his compositions.' Among these were : 3 operas, 4 oratorios, 4 books of 'Cantate a voce sola,' 'Capricci poetici' and 'Trattenimenti musicali per camera' (I.M.G. xv. 116; Q.-L.; Riemann).

SANCTUS. The angelic hymn based on Isaiah vi. 3 and St. Matt. xxi. 9, sung in all Liturgies at the beginning of the Anaphora or central section of the service. In the Latin rite it is introduced by the Preface, sung by the celebrant, while the hymn itself is sung by the clergy and congregation, or by the choir,

according to later usage. The original setting was in the simplest style of recitative like that of the Preface. Later plain-song settings were more elaborate (see PLAIN-SONG, p. 201).

Various specimens survive of the setting of the Sanctus in prick-song. The first stage here, as elsewhere, was the setting of an Organum or free voice part against the plain-song, as in the following instance from the latter part of the Sanctus :

The original may be seen in facsimile in Early English Harmony (Plain-song Soc.), pl. xl. It belongs to the 14th century. This was but a step on the way to developed polyphony. Another Sanctus in three parts written by John Benet in the first half of the 15th century is given at pp. 51, 52 of the same volume, and this may be cited as marking an intermediate stage on the way to the great masters of the 16th century. (See MASS.)                    W. H. F.

SANDBERGER, ADOLF (b. Würzburg, Dec. 19, 1864), has achieved most important work in musical research and has also been an assiduous composer.

After prolonged study in the principal cities of Europe, he became curator of the musical department of the State Library at Munich and teacher of musical science at the University of Munich in 1894, becoming professor of the University in 1900. His most important work has been as editor of the Denkmäler der Tonkunst in Bayern (see DENKMÄLER). He has written much on general musical subjects, his work ranging from Leben und Werke des Dichtermusikers Peter Cornelius, to Beiträge zur Geschichte der bayrischen Hofkapelle unter Orlando di Lasso. He is editor of the complete edition of the works of Lassus.          C.

SANDERSON, JAMES (b. Workington, Durham, 1769; d. circa 1841), had from early childhood a passion for music, and, without the assistance of masters, so qualified himself that in 1783 he was engaged as violinist at the Sunderland Theatre. In 1784 he went to Shields as a teacher of the violin and pianoforte, and met with much success. In 1787 he was engaged as leader at the Newcastle-upon-Tyne Theatre, and in 1788 at Astley's Amphitheatre. In 1789 he made his first attempt at dramatic composition by writing instrumental interludes to illustrate the several parts of Collins's ' Ode on the Passions,' which the eminent tragedian, George Frederick Cooke, was to recite on his benefit night at Chester. His next work was ' Harlequin in Ireland ' at Astley's in 1792. In 1793 he was engaged at the Royal Circus, afterwards the Surrey Theatre, as composer and music director, a post which he retained for many years. His principal productions during that period were ' Blackbeard,' 1798 ; ' Cora,' 1799 ; ' Sir Francis Drake,' 1800 (in which was the song, ' Bound 'prentice to a waterman,' which became so great a favourite with stage representatives of British sailors that it was constantly introduced into pieces in which a seaman formed one of the characters for fully half a century), and ' Hallowe'en.' His 'Angling Duet,' originally composed for ' The Magic Pipe,' a pantomime produced at the Adelphi, also enjoyed a long popularity. He composed many pieces for the violin.          w. h. h.

In these pantomimes and operas he was associated with J. C. Cross, who wrote most of the words and contrived the scenic effects. The song ' Gin a body meet a body ' is claimed by Chappell as originally appearing in one of these productions, ' Harlequin Mariner,' 1795–96, but the air is found in print in Scottish collections long before this, and there is sufficient evidence to show that Cross and Sanderson had merely adapted the song to London requirements.          F. K.

SANDERSON, SIBYL (b. Sacramento, California, Dec. 7, 1865 ; d. Paris, May 16, 1903), American dramatic soprano, chiefly associated with the operas of Massenet. Educated in San Francisco, at the age of 19 she entered the Paris Conservatoire and there studied under Sbriglia and Mme. Marchesi. She made her début in the title-rôle of Massenet's ' Manon ' at The Hague in 1888. Massenet, much impressed by her voice with its range of three octaves, wrote for her ' Esclarmonde ' and later ' Thaïs ' ; in the former she made her first appearance in Paris, at the Opéra-Comique, in 1889. Although she also sang in Brussels, St. Petersburg, Moscow, London and New York, her popularity was chiefly confined to Paris. Massenet in his memoirs called her an ' ideal ' Manon and an ' unforgettable ' Thaïs.

w. s. s.

SANDONI, see CUZZONI, Francesca.

SANDYS, WILLIAM, F.S.A. (b. 1792 ; d. Feb. 18, 1874), was educated at Westminster School,

and afterwards called to the Bar. He is entitled to mention here as editor of

' Christmas Carols, Ancient and Modern, including the most popular in the West of England, with the tunes to which they are sung. Also specimens of French Provincial Carols,' 1833 ;

author of *Christmastide, its History, Festivities and Carols*, with twelve carol tunes, 1852 ; and joint author with Simon Andrew Forster of *The History of the Violin and other Instruments played on with the Bow. . . . Also an Account of the Principal Makers, English and Foreign*, 1864.          W. H. H.

SANG SCHOOLS, see SONG SCHOOLS.

SAN MARTINI, see SAMMARTINI.

SANTA CHIARA, opera in 3 acts ; words by Mme. Birch Pfeiffer, music by H.R.H. Ernest, Duke of Saxe-Coburg-Gotha. Produced Coburg, Oct. 15, 1854 ; Opéra, Paris (French translation by Oppelt), Sept. 27, 1855 ; Covent Garden (in Italian), June 30, 1877.          G.

SANTA MARIA, FR. THOMAS DE (b. Madrid ; d. 1580). Spanish organist and Dominican monk. In 1565 he published

Libro llamado Arte de tañer fantasia, assi para tecla como para vihuela y todo instrumento, en que se pudiere tañer a 3 y a 4 voces y a mas. Valladolid, 1565. (B.M. ; Madrid : Bibl. Nac., Bibl. Medinaceli and Bibl. Escurial ; Barcelona, Bibl. Univ ; Berlin.)

It is an introduction to ' the art of playing fantasies, both on keyboard instruments and on the *vihuela* (Spanish lute) and every instrument in which it is possible to place 8 in 3 or 4 parts or more.' See the study by O. Kinkeldey, *Orgel u. Klavier in der Musik des 16. Jahrhunderts*. Leipzig, 1919, with transcriptions of several fantasias in modern notation. Also P. Villalba, *Antología de organistas Españoles*, i. (Madrid), and Pedrell.          J. B. T.

SANTI, FATHER ANGELO DE (b. Trieste, July 12, 1847), Italian ecclesiastic and writer, entered young the Jesuit Order, his knowledge of music being almost entirely the fruit of self-education. He graduated in letters at Innsbruck University. His success as a director of music in various Jesuit colleges brought him to the notice of Pope Leo XIII., who encouraged his ideas of a complete reform of religious music. He was instrumental in founding the Schola Cantorum of the Vatican Seminary, where the whole repertory consists almost entirely of works of the classical school of Palestrina. Father De Santi was the prime mover of the Gregorian celebrations held in Rome in 1891, on which occasion he published various articles which aroused a good deal of opposition. Pope Leo stood his friend, but it was only during the pontificate of Pius X. that the reforms of De Santi were applied and embodied in the famous *Motu proprio* on church music. In 1910, Pius X., on the advice of De Santi, decided to create in Rome a centre for the study of sacred music, and a school was opened in the following year. De Santi, who was elected in 1909, and again in 1920, President of the Italian Association St. Cecilia, has written also much on historical and literary subjects. Most of his articles on music have appeared in *Civiltà Catholica* and *Rassegna Gregoriana*.                              F. B.

SANTI, ORLANDI (*d.* Mantua, July 1619), maestro di cappella of Cardinal Ferd. Gonzaga, Florence, temporary maestro in 1608, and maestro di cappella at Mantua as Monteverdi's successor in 1612. He composed 5 books of madrigals (1602–09), arias, duets and an opera ' Galatea,' produced at Mantua, 1617, which has been lost.                  E. v. d. s.

SANTINI, FORTUNATO (*b.* Rome, Jan. 5, 1778; *d.* there, 1862), Abbé, a learned musician who early lost his parents, and was brought up in an orphanage. He showed such talent for music that he was put to study with Jannaconi, and received into the Collegio Salviati. During his stay there (until 1798) he occupied himself in copying and scoring the church music of the great masters, and after his ordination in 1801 devoted his life to music, copying, collating and compiling with unwearied industry. As an ecclesiastic he had the *entrée* to many libraries and collections generally inaccessible, and set himself to the task of scoring all important works then existing only in parts. In 1820 he issued a catalogue (46 pp., 1000 Nos.) of his music, the MS. of which, containing more than the printed one, was in the collection of the writer.[1] A MS. copy of a *Catalogo della musica antica, sacra, e madrigalesca, che si trova in Roma via dell' anima no. 50 presso Fortunato Santini*, is in the Fétis collection at Brussels, No. 5166. His learning, and practical knowledge of church music, made his assistance invaluable to all engaged in musical research. He did much to make German music known in Italy, translating Rammler's ' Tod Jesu ' into Italian, and helping the introduction of Graun's music. Mendelssohn writes (*Letters*, Rome, Nov. 2, 1830) :

' The Abbé has long been on the look-out for me, hoping I should bring the score of Bach's " Passion." '

And again (Nov. 8) :

' Santini is a delightful acquaintance ; his library of old Italian music is most complete, and he gives or lends me anything and everything.'

Then he tells how Santini is trying to get Bach's composition performed at Naples, and goes on (Nov. 16) :

' Old Santini continues to be courtesy personified ; if some evening in company I praise anything, or say I do not know such and such a piece, the very next morning he comes knocking gently at my door with the identical piece folded up in his blue handkerchief. Then I go to him in the evenings, and we are really fond of each other.'

Santini composed pieces in five, six and eight real parts. A Requiem *a* 8 is at Bologna, where are numerous other church compositions. (See *Q.-L.*) The Singakademie of Berlin elected him an honorary member. On the death of his sister he sold his valuable collection,

stipulating, however, for the use of it for life. His library is in the Museum of Christian Antiquities at Münster in Westphalia. A pamphlet, *L'Abbé Santini et sa collection musicale à Rome* (Florence, 1854), giving a useful résumé of its contents, was published by the Russian, Vladimir Stassov.    F. G.

SANTLEY, SIR CHARLES (*b.* Liverpool, Feb. 28, 1834 ; *d.* Sept. 22, 1922), baritone singer, son of William Santley, a teacher of music. He was a chorister in early life, and, after various appearances as an amateur, he went to Italy to have his beautiful voice trained. Here, at Milan, he was under Gaetano Nava from Oct. 1855.

He made a début before very long, as the Doctor in ' La Traviata,' at Pavia, and after singing some other small parts, returned to England in Oct. 1857, and pursued his studies under Manuel Garcia. His first appearance before an English audience was at St. Martin's Hall on Nov. 16, 1857, when he sang the part of Adam in ' The Creation ' ; he next sang three times at the Crystal Palace, and again in ' The Creation ' (taking the parts of Raphael and Adam), at the Sacred Harmonic Society, Jan. 8, 1858. In March of the same year he undertook, at the same society's concert, the part of Elijah, with which he was afterwards so closely identified. In the following autumn he sang at the first Leeds Festival, taking the bass part of Rossini's Stabat Mater, and other works. His first appearance on the English stage was at Covent Garden, with the Pyne and Harrison Company, as Hoel in ' Dinorah,' in Sept. 1859 ; he sang with the same company in ' Trovatore,' ' Lurline ' and other operas. He took part in a concert performance of ' Iphigénie en Tauride,' under Hallé, about this time. In the winter of 1860–61 he sang in English opera at Her Majesty's Theatre, in ' Robin Hood,' ' La Reine Topaze,' ' Fra Diavolo,' etc. In 1861 he sang for the first time at the Birmingham Festival, and in the winter again at Covent Garden, in ' The Lily of Killarney,' and other things. He first appeared in the Italian opera in England at Covent Garden in 1862 in ' Il Trovatore,' and later in the same season he joined the company of Her Majesty's Theatre under Mapleson, appearing as the Count in ' Figaro,' and Nevers in ' Les Huguenots.' In 1863 he sang the part of Valentine on the production of ' Faust ' in England with such success that Gounod wrote the song ' Even bravest heart ' (' Dio possente ') especially for him, and for the English performance of the work in 1864. He sang at Barcelona in the winter of 1864–65, adding Rigoletto to the number of his characters. At Manchester in Sept. 1865 he sang the part of Don Giovanni for the first time, and later on appeared in London as Caspar in ' Der Freischütz.' In 1870, after singing the part of the

1 His address is there given Roma, Via Vittoria, No. 49, while in the Fétis collection it is Via dell' anima, No. 50.

Dutchman for the first time in England (as 'L' Olandese dannato'), he gave up Italian opera, and sang at the Gaiety Theatre under Hollingshead, as Zampa, Peter the Shipwright, and Fra Diavolo. In 1871 he made a very successful tour in America in opera and concerts. In 1875 he joined the Carl Rosa Company at the Princess's Theatre; he appeared as Figaro on the opening night of the season, continuing with the company in 1876, when he sang the Flying Dutchman in English at the Lyceum.

After his first festival performance at Birmingham in 1861, he was in request at all the autumnal festivals, singing, for the first time at the Three Choir Meetings, at Worcester in 1863. He had previously sung at the Handel Festival in 1862, and until 1906 he appeared regularly at these triennial meetings. From about this time his position in oratorio and concert work was ever more and more important. On Apr. 9, 1859, he had married Gertrude Kemble, daughter of John Mitchell Kemble, the eminent Anglo-Saxon scholar, and grand-daughter of Charles Kemble. She appeared as a soprano singer at St. Martin's Hall in the 'Messiah,' but retired from public life on her marriage. Their daughter, EDITH, had a short but brilliant career as a concert singer (soprano), before her marriage in 1884 with the Hon. R. H. Lyttelton.

Though the versatility of his genius allowed him to express any emotion to the full, yet Santley's singing was identified with certain characteristics in the minds of those who knew it best. The quality of the voice was less remarkable for richness or sonority than for its eloquence of expression, and had a timbre which in love-music more easily represented fiery passion than soft languor. This fire was never more perfectly in its place than in 'Elijah,' where it was prominent from the opening recitative until the end. His distinct enunciation and power of varying the tone-colour were among his technical merits; but beyond and above these was the informing spirit of energy finely held in control. This made his singing of songs as dramatic as if they were scenes on the stage, although he never fell into the error of making lyrics sound operatic. His performance of the 'Erl King' (which he always sang in English) can never be forgotten in this respect, and in a kindred mood Hatton's 'To Anthea' became exclusively his own. His interpretation of Handel's 'O ruddier than the cherry' was masterly in delineation and humour. Among the oratorios in which he made the greatest impression, apart from 'Elijah,' must be mentioned 'The Redemption' (Birmingham, 1882) and 'The Spectre's Bride' (Birmingham, 1885). He found time in the intervals of a wonderfully successful and busy career to compose several works for the

service of the Roman Church (which he joined about 1880), such as a Mass in A flat, an Ave Maria, and other things. A berceuse for orchestra was performed at Sydney in 1890, when Santley was on a tour in Australia. In 1887 he was created a Knight Commander of St. Gregory the Great by Pope Leo XIII. In 1892 he published an amusing and valuable volume of reminiscences, *Student and Singer*. On May 1, 1907, the 'jubilee' of his artistic career was celebrated at a concert at the Albert Hall, when he appeared with many eminent artists. A money presentation, referred to on that occasion, was made some time afterwards. He was knighted later in the year. He took part in a benefit given for him at Covent Garden on May 23, 1911, when he sang in Dibdin's 'The Waterman,' and made his last appearance in 1915 at the Mansion House at a concert in aid of Belgian refugees. He published *The Singing Master*, 1900, *The Art of Singing*, 1908, and *Reminiscences of my Life*, 1909.                                    M.

SANTOLIQUIDO, FRANCESCO (*b.* San Giorgio a Cremano, Naples, Aug. 6, 1883), composer, received his musical education at the Liceo Santa Cecilia in Rome, where one of his professors was Stanislao Falchi. In his aims and sympathies he belongs to the younger, progressive Italian school, but his long absence from his country kept him somewhat aloof from the activities of his colleagues. Having written an orchestral work, 'Crepuscolo sul mare,' in his student days, and conducted it at Nuremberg in 1909, and produced an opera, 'La favola di Helga,' at the Teatro dal Verme in Milan in 1910, he emigrated to Tunisia the following year, taking up his residence at a remote little Arab village. This voluntary exile was not without influence on his music. Although he wrote a 'Symphony in F major in the Classical Style' in 1916, several of his works are impregnated with Oriental feeling. A second opera, 'Ferhuda,' based on scenes from Arab life, was produced at Tunis in 1919, and an orchestral piece, 'Il profumo delle oasi sahariane,' on popular Arab tunes, was written on the edge of the desert, and first performed at Tunis and Algiers in 1918 by an orchestra of Serbian refugees. Another work on an Eastern subject is the mimed drama 'La bajadera della maschera gialla,' produced in Rome in 1923. Santoliquido now lives in the Italian capital, but still spends much of his time in North Africa. Among his works not mentioned above are: an unpublished opera, 'L' ignota'; 'La morte di Tintagiles,' 'Paesaggi' and 'Acquarelle' for orchestra; some settings of Japanese and Persian poetry for voice and piano; and several piano pieces, including 'Due acqueforti tunisine' and 'Ex humo ad sidera.'                                    E. B.

SANTUCCI, MARCO (*b.* Camaiore, Toscana,

July 4, 1762 ; *d.* Lucca, Nov. 29, 1843), studied at the Conservatorio di Loreto, Naples, took holy orders in 1794, and became maestro di cappella at S. Giovanni, Lateran, Rome. In 1808 he was made a canon at Lucca Cathedral. He was a noted contrapuntist who wrote sacred choral works up to 48 parts. He also wrote 12 sonatas in fugal style for PF. Lists of his works are given in *Q.-L.*, and by *Fétis* and *Riemann*. He published also some theoretical essays which Fétis considers of no value.

                              E. v. d. s.

SANZ, GASPAR (*b.* Calanda, 17th cent.), Spanish guitarist. After taking degrees in philosophy and theology at Salamanca, he passed to Naples, where he is said (on doubtful authority) to have studied with Christoforo Carisani (Caresana), though Carisani may have been several years older than Sanz and have succeeded him as maestro de capilla to the Spanish viceroy. He published a book of tablature entitled

Instruccion de musica sobre la guitarra española. . . . Saragossa, 1674. (Madrid, Bibl. Nac. ; Munich.) Also 1697. (B.M. ; Paris, Conservatoire ; Brussels, Conservatoire ; Barcelona, Diputació.)

It is interesting from the contemporary Spanish dance music it contains.      J. B. T.

SAPELLNIKOFF, VASSILY (*b.* Odessa, Nov. 2, 1868), was a student of the Conservatorium at Odessa under L. Brassin and Sophie Menter ; became professor of the pianoforte at the Moscow Conservatorium in 1897 ; but after a few years took up his residence in Germany, living for a time at Leipzig, and subsequently at Munich. His career as a pianist has been one of continuous success. He made his début at Hamburg in 1888 when he played Tchaikovsky's concerto in B flat minor under the composer's direction. This work he introduced into England. His first appearance here was at the Philharmonic Concert on Apr. 11, 1889, and he has returned repeatedly since. M. ; addns. C.

SAPPHO. (1) Saffo. Opera in 3 acts ; text by Cammarano ; music by Giov. Pacini. Produced Naples, Nov. 27, 1840 ; Drury Lane, English version by Serle, Apr. 1, 1843.

(2) Sapho. Opera in 3 acts ; words by Émile Augier ; music by Gounod. Produced Opéra, Apr. 16, 1851 ; reduced to 2 acts, and reproduced July 26, 1858 ; as 'Saffo,' Covent Garden (in Italian), Aug. 9, 1851 ; afterwards remodelled, extended to 4 acts, and produced Opéra, Apr. 2, 1884.

(3) Sapho. Opera in 5 acts ; text by Henri Cain and Arthur Bernède, music by Massenet. Produced Opéra-Comique, Paris, Nov. 27, 1897 ; New York, 1909.      G.

SARABAND, a stately dance, once very popular in Spain, France and England. Its origin and derivation have given rise to many surmises. Fuertes [1] says that the dance was invented in the middle of the 16th century by a dancer called Zarabanda, who, according

[1] *Historia de la musica española*, Madrid, 1859.

to other authorities, was a native of either Seville or Guayaquil, and after whom it was named. Others connect it with the Spanish Sarao (an entertainment of dancing), and Sir William Ouseley,[2] in a note to a Turkish air called 'Ser-i-Kháneh,' or 'the top of the house,' has the following :

'Some tunes are divided into three parts and are marked *Kháne-i śáni* "the second part," and *Kháne-i śáliś* "the third part"; near the conclusion of several we also find the Persian words *ser-band*, from which, without doubt, our *sara-band* has been derived.'[3]

Whatever its origin may have been, it is found in Europe at the beginning of the 16th century, performed in such a manner as to render its Oriental source highly probable. This may be gathered from the following extract from chapter xii., 'Del baile y cantar llamado Zarabanda,' of the *Tratado contra los Juegos Publicos* (*Treatise against Public Amusements*) of Mariana (1536–1623) :

'Entre las otras invenciones ha salido estos años un baile y cantar tan lascivo en las palabras, tan feo en los meneos, que basta para pegar fuego aun á las personas muy honestas' ('Amongst other inventions there has appeared during late years a dance and song, so lascivious in its words, so ugly in its movements, that it is enough to inflame even very modest people').

This reputation was not confined to Spain, for Marini in his poem *L'Adone* (1623) says :

'Chiama questo suo gioco empio e profano Saravanda, e Ciaccona, il nuovo Ispano.'[4]

Padre Mariana, who believed in its Spanish origin, says that its invention was one of the disgraces of the nation, and other authors attribute its invention directly to the devil. The dance was attacked by Cervantes and Guevara, and defended by Lope de Vega, but it seems to have been so bad that at the end of the reign of Philip II. it was for a time suppressed. It was soon, however, revived in a purer form, and was introduced at the French court in 1588, where later on Richelieu, wearing green velvet knee-breeches, with bells on his feet, and castanets in his hands, danced it in a ballet before Anne of Austria.

In England the Saraband was soon transformed into an ordinary country-dance. The first edition of Playford's *Dancing Master* (1651) has two examples, one to be danced 'longwayes for as many as will' (*i.e.* as 'Sir Roger de Coverléy' is danced), and the other, 'Adson's Saraband,' to be danced 'longwayes for six.' It was at about this time that the Saraband, together with other dances, found its way into the Suite, of which it formed the slow movement, placed before the concluding Gigue. In this form it is remarkable for its strongly accentuated and majestic rhythm, generally as follows :

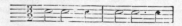

[2] *Oriental Collections*, 1728, vol. ii. p. 197, misquoted by Mendel, under 'Saraband.'
[3] In a MS. collection of dances in the Music School at Oxford is a Saraband by Coleman, entitled 'Seribran.'
[4] 'New Spain' is Castile.

It is written either in the major or the minor key, in 3–2 or 3–4 time, although Walther (*Lexikon*, 1732) says that it may be also written in 2–4 time. It usually consists of two 8- or 12-bar divisions, begins on the down-beat, and ends on the second or third beat. Bach, in the 'Clavierübung,' Pt. I. (B.-G. iii. 76), has a Saraband beginning on the up-beat, and Handel (Suite XI.) has one with variations. Those by Corelli do not conform to the established rules, but are little more than Sicilianas played slowly (see BEAT 3).

The following Saraband for the guitar is printed in Fuertes' *Historia de la musica española*.

Handel's noble air 'Lascia ch' io pianga,' in 'Rinaldo,' is taken with no material alteration from a Saraband in his earlier opera of 'Almira,' in which the majestic rhythm mentioned reigns in all its dignity. See Chrysander's *Händel*, i. 121.                    W. B. S.

BIBL.—J. ÉCORCHEVILLE, *Vingt suites du 17e siècle français* (Paris).

SARADIEV, CONSTANTINE SOLOMONOVICH (*b.* Derbent, Darghestan, Caucasus, Sept. 26, 1877), conductor and violinist, studied first at the Moscow Conservatoire under Hřímalý (violin) and Taneive (theory) ; from 1905–06 was a pupil of Nikisch at Leipzig, and also worked under Ševčík in Prague. He taught the violin at the Synodal School, Moscow, 1898–1907, and conducted the Sokolniky Concerts there in 1908, 1910 and 1911. He was associated with various movements to bring music within reach of the masses. He is now director of the State Institute of Theatrical Art, Moscow.        R. N.

SARANGI, see INDIAN MUSIC, subsection INSTRUMENTS.

SARASATE.  PABLO MARTIN MELITON SARASATE Y NAVASCUES (*b.* Pamplona, Mar. 10, 1844 ; *d.* Villa Navarra, Biarritz, Sept. 21,

1908), celebrated violinist, came to France as a child, and entered the Paris Conservatoire, Jan. 1, 1856. The following year he became the favourite pupil of Alard, and gained the first prizes for solfège and violin. He then entered Reber's harmony class, and secured a *premier accessit* in 1859, but shortly after relinquished the study of composition for the more tempting career of a concert player. His beautiful tone, retentive memory, immense execution and certainty of finger, added to the singularity of his manners and appearance, ensured his success in Paris, the French provinces and the Peninsula. The Spaniards naturally honoured an artist whom they looked upon as their own countryman, but Sarasate aspired to make his name known wherever music was appreciated, as well as in the two countries especially his own by birth and adoption. Besides making his way through Europe, from the remotest corner of Portugal to Norway, and from London to Moscow, he visited America, North and South. In all his wanderings he contrived to carry on his cultivation, and develop his great natural gifts. To London his first visit was in 1861, when he played at St. James's Hall on May 22 ; he came again in 1874, when he played at the Philharmonic Concert, May 18, and at the Musical Union, June 9, etc. He returned in 1877 (Crystal Palace, Oct. 13) and 1878 (Philharmonic, Mar. 28), and frequently afterwards. In 1885 and 1886 he gave sets of orchestral concerts conducted by Cusins, and at the Birmingham Festival of 1885 played a concerto written for him by Mackenzie.

Sarasate's distinguishing characteristics were not so much fire, force and passion, though of these he had an ample store, as purity of style, charm, brightness of tone, flexibility and extraordinary facility. He had a large repertory, comprising the concertos of German masters and the works of the French and Belgian schools. The concertos of Saint-Saëns and Lalo (who wrote his first violin concerto for Sarasate), and the 'Symphonie espagnole' of the latter, were favourites with him. Bruch wrote his second concerto and the 'Scottish Fantasia' for him. He generally avoided the music of Paganini and his followers, partly for want of taste for it, and partly because of the long stretches required, his hand being very small. But he will always be remembered for his rendering of the solos he wrote for himself, and played so exquisitely, giving the spirit of Spanish dance translated into terms of the violin virtuoso. He possessed two fine Stradivari violins, one of which, dated 1724, was presented to him when a boy by Queen Isabella of Spain. This instrument was one of those brought from the Chapelle Royale at Naples by Charles III. (for whom Boccherini composed his quintets), and upon it he mainly played throughout his career. A successful copy of it was made by Vuillaume, and was sometimes used by him at rehearsals. Later in life he acquired from the Boissier collection an exceptionally beautiful instrument, bearing date 1713. Sarasate composed for his instrument romances, fantaisies, and especially transcriptions of Spanish airs and dances, all calculated to display his skill as a virtuoso. His 'Zigeunerweisen,' 'Jota Aragonesa' and the four books of Spanish dances are among the most popular violin soli in existence.    G. C.; addns. W. W. C., etc.

SARDANA, see SONG, subsection SPAIN (2).

SARGENT, HAROLD MALCOLM WATTS (b. Stamford, Lincolnshire, Apr. 29, 1895), has made a distinct mark as a conductor both in concert work and opera.

Sargent took his A.R.C.O. diploma while still a pupil of Stamford School, in 1911 he was articled to Dr. Keeton of Peterborough Cathedral, and became organist of Melton Mowbray parish church in 1914. During the war he served with the 27th Durham Light Infantry, but was able to take his degree Mus.D. at Durham in 1919. The opportunity of conducting an orchestral composition of his own, 'Impressions of a Windy Day,' at a Queen's Hall Promenade Concert in 1921 showed where his special gifts lay. He was subsequently appointed to the teaching staff of the R.C.M. as junior orchestral conductor, and soon undertook work for the B.N.O.C. His success in carrying through the first public performance of Vaughan Williams's opera, 'Hugh the Drover' (His Majesty's Theatre, July 1924), showed unusual ability, and he later conducted Holst's 'At the Boar's Head' at Manchester, as well as a fairly large repertory of standard works with the B.N.O.C. In 1925 he was invited by the Royal Philharmonic Society to conduct a programme of English orchestral works, which included the first performance of Herbert Howells's PF. concerto and Vaughan Williams's pastoral symphony. He has been constantly in request for special performances in many parts of the country; his regular engagements have included the season of the Llandudno Orchestra, several series of valuable children's concerts at Westminster, and the London season (1926) of the D'Oyly Carte Opera Company.    C.

SARRO (SARRI), DOMENICO (b. Trani, Naples, c. 1678; d. ? Naples, after 1739), studied at the Conservatorio de' Turchini, 1688–1697; was vice-maestro in 1712, and afterwards maestro of the Chapel Royal, Naples. As an opera composer he established a European reputation, although he himself apparently never left Naples. In addition to 36 operas, performed in all the principal European theatres, he wrote oratorios, masses and other church music, cantatas, serenades, arias; also

a concerto for 2 vlns., flute, viola, violoncello and bass (Q.-L.; Riemann).

SARRUSOPHONE, a brass instrument of conical bore, played with a double reed, designed in 1863 by Sarrus, a bandmaster in the French army. The scheme of the inventor comprised a whole family of instruments ranging in pitch from soprano to contra-bass, and his expectation was that they might well take the place of oboes and bassoons in military bands. As regards the contra-bass models, Sarrus was to some extent anticipated by Stehle of Vienna in 1835, who brought out a contra-bassoon in brass, of simple fingering, and whose model has been further developed by Cerveny of Königgratz, and Mahillon of Brussels; but to Sarrus belongs the credit of designing a whole family of double-reed instruments as possible substitutes for the oboe and bassoon groups. The objection that has been raised to them is that they fail to produce the delicate and distinctive qualities of the wooden double-reed instruments. (See PLATE V. No. 2.)

The complete family of sarrusophones comprises the sopranino in $e'\flat$, soprano in $b\flat$, alto in $e\flat$, tenor in $B\flat$, baritone in $E\flat$, bass in $B_{,}\flat$, contra-bass in $E_{,}\flat$, and the contra-bassoon in $C_{,}$ or $B_{,,}\flat$. All these have a compass from one tone below the pitch note, to a fifth above its double octave, $b\flat$ to $f'''$, agreeing in this respect with the oboe, and the general scheme of fingering is much like that of the oboe. The tube of all but the small instruments is bent back upon itself, so as to reduce the length to a convenient compass.

The actual use of the sarrusophone in the orchestra has been very limited, but Saint-Saëns appears to have thought highly of the contra-bass instrument as an alternative to the double-bassoon, and used it on several occasions. Jules Massenet introduced it in his 'Esclarmonde' with great effect, and other composers have followed his example. It is possible that the bass and contra-bass members of the family may be kept alive, as they have distinctive qualities, but the treble and alto instruments can be regarded only as interesting experiments.    D. J. B.

SARTI, GIOVANNI VINCENZO, of St. Agata, was maestro di cappella at Forli Cathedral c. 1643, and at the Metropolitan church at Ravenna, 1648. He composed 6 books of 'Concerti sacri,' 2-6 v., Litanies, 8 v., and 2 books of psalms, between 1643 and 1655 (Q.-L.).

SARTI, GIUSEPPE (b. Faenza, Dec. 1, 1729 [1]; d. Berlin, July 28, 1802), opera composer, was the son of a jeweller who played the violin in the cathedral. He early learned music, and had lessons in composition — from Vallotti according to his own family, from Padre

[1] A date differing from that given by most of his biographers, but furnished by Sarti's own grandson to the writer, who took great pains to verify it.

Martini according to his biographers. Whether at Padua or at Bologna (the respective homes of the two masters), he completed his studies at an early age, for we learn from the Chapter archives, still preserved in the library of Faenza, that he was organist of the cathedral from 1748 to Apr. 1750, and director of the theatre from 1752. In 1751 he composed his first opera, 'Pompeo in Armenia,' which was enthusiastically received by his fellow-townsmen, and followed by several more serious works, and 'Il rè pastore' (Venice, 1753), which had an immense success. So quickly did his fame spread that when he was only 24 the King of Denmark (Frederick V.) invited him to Copenhagen as Kapellmeister to the Prince Royal, and director of the Italian opera ; and, on the closing of the latter in two years, made him court Kapellmeister. In the summer of 1765 the King determined to reopen the opera, and Sarti went back to Italy to engage singers after an absence of twelve years ; but his plans were upset by the deaths first of the King in 1766 and then of his own mother in 1767, so that it was not till 1768 that he returned to Copenhagen. These three years of trouble were not unfruitful, as he composed five operas, of which two, 'I contratempi' (1767) and 'Didone abbandonata,' were given in Venice, where he seems chiefly to have resided.

Overskou's carefully compiled *History of the Danish Stage* [1] informs us that Sarti directed the Danish court theatre from 1770 to May 20, 1775, when he was summarily dismissed. A favourite with Christian VII., and the protégé of Struensee and Queen Caroline Matilda, he was too artless and straightforward to curry favour with the Queen Dowager and the ambitious Ove Gulberg ; so after the catastrophe of 1772 he found his position gradually becoming worse and worse, and when the oligarchical party had secured the upper hand, imprisoning the Queen, and reducing the King to a mere cipher, he had, with other court favourites, to endure much ill treatment, and was finally banished. During this second stay at Copenhagen he married Camilla Pasi, by whom he had two daughters.

Returning to Italy in the summer of 1775, he went first to Venice, became at once director of the Ospedaletto Conservatorio, and administered it with great success for four years. In 1779 the post of maestro di cappella of the cathedral of Milan fell vacant through the death of Fioroni, and Sarti was pronounced successful at a competition held before the Conservatorio of Naples. This victory over Paisiello and other eminent musicians greatly increased his reputation, and procured him many distinguished pupils, Cherubini among the number, who indeed was not only his

pupil, but for some years his assistant.[2] In 1784 he received an invitation from Russia too advantageous to be refused, but the nine years spent in Milan were the most brilliant of his whole career, and the most prolific, including as they did his most successful operas, 'Le Gelosie villane'[3] and 'Farnace' (Venice, 1776) ; 'Achille in Sciro' (Florence, Oct. 1779) ; 'Giulio Sabino' (Venice, 1781), and 'I due litiganti' (Milan, 1782). To complete the list, at least ten more operas and several cantatas on a large scale should be added, works for the cathedral choir, including several masses, a Miserere *a* 4, and some important motets.

On his way to St. Petersburg, Sarti made some stay at Vienna, where Joseph II. received him graciously, and granted him the proceeds of a performance of 'I due litiganti,' which had long maintained its place at the Burgtheater, and had helped to fill its coffers, as the monarch politely told the composer. He there made the acquaintance of Mozart, then in the very prime of life, who speaks of him as an 'honest, good man,' and who not only played to him a good deal, but adopted an air from his 'I due litiganti' as the theme of a set of Variations (Köchel, 460), and as a subject in the second finale of 'Don Juan.' His pleasure in Mozart's playing did not, however, place him on Mozart's level ; and when the famous six quartets were published, Sarti was one of the loudest to complain of their 'barbarisms.' His examination remains mostly in MS., but some extracts are given in the *A.M.Z.* for 1832 (p. 373), including nineteen serious errors in thirty-six bars, and showing how difficult it is even for a very clever composer to apprehend the ideas of one greater than himself.

Catherine II. received him with even greater marks of favour than Joseph, which he repaid by composing several important works for her own choir, and by bringing the Italian opera into a state of efficiency it had never attained before. Among his sacred compositions of this period may be mentioned an oratorio for two choirs, full orchestra and band of Russian horns ; a Te Deum for the taking of Otchakow by Potemkin ; and a Requiem in honour of Louis XVI. It was in the Te Deum that Sarti employed fireworks and the discharge of cannon to heighten the martial effect of the music. Among his operas produced at St. Petersburg were 'Armida' (1786), which had an immense success, and was sung to perfection by the celebrated Todi ; and 'Olega,' the libretto of which was by the Empress herself. In this opera Sarti endeavoured to imitate the music of the ancient Greeks, and made use of some of their modes. A skilled mathematician and physicist, he was fond of explaining to the

[1] Thomas Overskou, *Den danske Skueplads in dens Historie*, 8vo. Copenhagen, 1854, etc.

[2] See Cherubini's preface to the Catalogue of his works.
[3] Mozart, in 1791, wrote a final chorus for this, of which, however, nothing has survived but the five bars in his autograph catalogue. (See Köchel, 615.)

Empress his theories of acoustics, which he illustrated by many ingenious experiments. He invented a machine for counting the vibrations of sounds, and fixed 436 vibrations [1] for the A, as the normal pitch for his orchestra. For this invention he was elected an honorary member of the Academy of Science in St. Petersburg. Many other honours were conferred upon him, including those of councillor of the University, chief maître de chapelle to the court and nobility of the first class. Todi's intrigues caused him temporary inconvenience, but he consoled himself for a short period of disgrace by going to a village in the Ukraine, given him by Prince Potemkin, and founding there a school of singing which turned out some remarkable singers. In 1793 the Empress restored him completely to favour, and placed him at the head of a Conservatoire planned after the model of those in Italy. After her death and that of her son Paul I., Sarti determined to revisit his native land, and in the spring of 1802 left Russia, where he had lived for eighteen years without a break. At Berlin he formed an intimacy with the court Kapellmeister, Noël Mussini (b. Bergamo, 1765; d. Florence, 1837), who fell in love with his daughter Giuliana, and became his son-in-law.[2] Immediately after the marriage the kind and gentle Sarti fell seriously ill of gout, and died July 28, 1802. He was buried in the Catholic church of St. Edwige, where his ashes still remain.

From some unexplained cause, very few of Sarti's compositions have been engraved. His Te Deum was printed with Russian words at St. Petersburg, and Breitkopf & Härtel have published two of his sacred pieces, one in eight, the other in six real parts. A French translation of the 'Nozze di Dorina' (identical with 'I due litiganti'), apparently the only opera of his that has been engraved, appeared in Paris; but Ricordi of Milan has copies of 'Armida e Rinaldo,' 'I finti eredi,' 'Le gelosie villane,' 'Nitteti' and 'Vologeso.' These scores, as well as those of 'Adriano in Sciro,' 'Alessandro,' 'Gli amanti consolati,' 'Castore e Polluce,' 'I Contratempi,' 'Didone abbandonata,' 'Erifile,' 'I due litiganti,' 'Giulio Sabino,' 'Idalide,' 'Ifigenia,' 'Il Medonte,' 'Il militare bizzarro,' 'Mitridate' and 'Scipione,' and also of nearly all his sacred works, are in the library of the Paris Conservatoire, from which circumstance the writer is able to pronounce upon his style. The part-writing is eminently vocal, and the most difficult combinations are mastered with ease, but the scientific element is never unduly forced into notice, owing to Sarti's gift of fresh and

[1] The 'diapason normale' fixes 435 vibrations for the same note. See PITCH.
[2] The articles on Sarti and Mussini in *Fétis* are full of errors and omissions. We have corrected the most glaring mistakes from family papers kindly furnished by the distinguished painter, L. Mussini, director of the Museo at Siena, and grandson of the composer.

spontaneous melody. Most of his operas contain numbers well constructed with a view to stage effect, and full of expression and charm; indeed so much of his music might still be heard with pleasure that it seems strange that no great artist has attempted to revive it.

His masses alone retain their hold on public favour, and one was performed on Easter Day 1880 in Milan Cathedral, which still has all the MSS.

Sarti left six sonatas for clavier solo (London, 1762). An Allegro from these was included in Pauer's 'Alte Meister.' Cherubini quotes a 'Cum sancto' a 8 of his in his *Counterpoint*; and Fétis a Kyrie from the same Mass in his treatise. Breitkopf published a fugue for eight voices, a hymn and a Miserere, and the overture to 'Ciro riconosciuto.' A rondo for mezzo-soprano will be found in Gevaert's 'Gloires d' Italie,' and a cavatina, from 'Giulio Sabino,' in the 'Gemme d' antichità.'

The Mussini family possess a fine oil-painting of the composer, taken in 1786 by Tonci, an Italian painter settled in St. Petersburg. *Le Chevalier Sarti*, a novel by P. Scudo, appeared first in the *Revue des Deux Mondes*, and has since been published separately (Paris, Hachette, 1857).　　　　　　　　　　　　　G. C.

SARTORIO (SERTORIJ), ANTONIO (b. Venice, c. 1620), was Kapellmeister at the court of Brunswick until 1676; from then till c. 1681 (when he was succeeded by Legrenzi) he was maestro di cappella at St. Mark's, Venice. He is one of the chief representatives of Venetian opera after Cavalli and Cesti. Apart from a number of operas he composed 8-part psalms, cantatas, solo cantatas, motets and canzonets (Q.-L.; Fétis).

SARTORIS, MRS., see KEMBLE, Adelaide.

SARTORIUS, PAUL, organist to the Archduke Maximilian of Austria, 1599, residing at Nuremberg. He composed masses, sonetti spirituali, 6 v. (1601), madrigals a 5 (1600), 'Neue teutsche Liedlein' (new German songs) after the manner of canzonets (1601), motets, 6-12 v. (1602) (Q.-L.).

SASLAVSKY, ALEXANDER (b. Kharkov, Russia, Feb. 9, 1876; d. San Francisco, Aug. 20, 1924), violinist. After study in his birthplace and at Vienna he toured in Canada (1893) and then joined the New York Symphony Orchestra, of which in 1903 he became leader and assistant conductor under Walter DAMROSCH (q.v.). He was one of the founders (1904) of the Russian Symphony Orchestra in New York. In 1919 he became leader of the New Philharmonic Orchestra in Los Angeles, and in California he conducted a string orchestra bearing his own name. (*Amer. Supp.*)

SASS, MARIE CONSTANCE (b. Ghent, 1838; d. Sainte-Perine, 1907), one of the outstanding sopranos of her day. She has two special claims to be remembered. Known at that time as Marie Saxe, she was the Elisabeth in the ill-fated performances of 'Tannhäuser' at Paris in 1861, and at Paris in 1865 she played Selika at the production of 'L'Africaine.'

She was a pupil of Mme. Ugalde, and from all accounts had an exceptional voice. Appearing first in Paris at the Théâtre-Lyrique in 1859, she was at the Opéra between 1860–70. After the Franco-German war she sang in Italy and Spain, and also at Brussels. One of her parts at the Opéra was Donna Anna, which she sang at a special revival to Faure's Don Juan. She died in great poverty. Her husband—the union only lasted from 1864–67 —was M. Castelmary, who was well known in London, singing for Mapleson at Drury Lane in 1873, and for Harris at Covent Garden.

S. H. P.

SATANELLA, OR THE POWER OF LOVE, opera in 4 acts ; words by Harris and Falconer ; music by Balfe. Produced Lyceum Theatre (Pyne and Harrison), Dec. 20, 1858.    G.

SATIE, ERIK ALFRED LESLIE (*b.* Honfleur, Calvados, Mar. 17, 1866 ; *d.* Paris, July 2, 1925), composer. His father was a composer and music publisher in Paris, and his mother, of British origin, composed pianoforte pieces, under the name of Eugénie Satie-Barnetsche.

Having spent a year at the Conservatoire (1883–84), Satie brought out his 'Ogives' (1886 ; publ. 1889), a series of works of which the strange titles and the novelty of expression provoked some astonishment : 'Sarabandes' (1887), 'Gymnopédies' (1888 ; Nos. 1 and 3 orchestrated by Debussy) ; 'Gnossiennes' (1890). He collaborated in the rites imagined by the poet Joséphin Péladan ('Le Sâr'), the music for the scene of the 'Fils des Étoiles' (1891), etc. ; wrote a prelude for Jules Bois, for 'La Porte héroïque du Ciel' (1894) ; and composed some 'Danses gothiques' (1893), etc. But he collaborated also with the Montmartre song-writer Hyspa, and composed for the music-hall singer Paulette Darty (Mme. de Bardy) some waltz songs ('Je te veux,' 'Poudre d'or,' etc.), which had some vogue.

Becoming friends, towards 1890, with Claude Debussy, it is claimed that Satie exercised a certain amount of influence over him, and that he counselled him to ask Maeterlinck for a dramatic poem.

Between 1905–08, Satie, at the age of 40, took it into his head to study at the Schola Cantorum, where he had for masters V. d'Indy and Albert Roussel. In spite of his attendance at this institution, Satie, who had published 'Pièces froides' (1897), 'Pièces en forme de poire' (1903), etc., continued to compose such works as 'Trois Valses du précieux dégoûté,' 'Choses vues à droite et à gauche' (with the 'Fugue à tâtons'), 'Chapitres tournés en tous sens,' 'Croquis et agaceries d'un homme de bois,' 'Les Pantins dansent,' 'Descriptions automatiques,' 'Véritables préludes flasques' (for a dog), 'Aperçus désagréables' (with a fugue), 'Heures séculaires et instantanées,' 'En habit de cheval' (2 preludes, 1 choral), etc. : the greater part of these works were published in 1913 (Demets ; republished Rouart-Lerolle) ; 'Pièces montées' (1920), etc.

Satie was considered as a pioneer by some young musicians who 'discovered' him about 1910, and he became a kind of leader of a school, l'École d'Arcueil (Satie lived in this locality). He had attempted compositions of greater dimensions : 'Parade' (Russian Ballets, 1917), 'Relâche' (Swedish Ballets, 1924), 'Mercure' (Soirées de Paris, 1924), 'Socrate,' symphonic drama in three parts, with voice, on the dialogues of Plato, translated by Victor Cousin (1919, for the Société Nationale ; adapted for the stage, Prague, 1925) ; 'Le Piège de Méduse,' lyric comedy (1921) ; recitatives for 'Le Médecin malgré lui' of Gounod (Monte Carlo, 1924). He left a score of 'Paul et Virginie' (libretto by R. Radiguet and J. Cocteau).

An incomplete musician, Satie, partly by chance, partly consciously, outstripped by forty years contemporary polytonalists and atonalists. A humorist, literary rather than musical, he searched for unusual titles for his compositions (imitated in this respect by other composers, such as Ravel and Florent Schmitt) ; fanciful, mystifying, with a natural facility for provoking astonishment and a sense of the grotesque, with a simplicity of means which perhaps shows his natural limitation, Satie occupies a place apart in the history of contemporary music.

'C'est sa singularité outrancière et paradoxale qui a empêché le succès direct de ses efforts, mais c'est bien elle aussi qui eut le mérite de la découverte. Si l'absurde de 1886 est devenu la réalité de 1910, si les trouvailles d'un simple ont rénové le langage des habiles, l'histoire de la musique doit le savoir, comme le savent quelques initiés.' (J. Écorcheville.)

BIBL.—E. SATIE, *Mémoires d'un amnésique* (*S.I.M.*, 1912) ; *Notes sur la musique moderne* (*L'Humanité*, Oct. 11, 1919) ; Contribution to the *Almanach de Cocagne pour 1920* ; J. ÉCORCHEVILLE, *Erik Satie* (*Revue music. S.I.M.*, Mar. 15, 1911). L. LALOY (*Comœdia*, Oct. 8, 1913). RUDHYAR D. CHENNEVIÈRE, *Erik Satie and the Music of Irony* (*Mus. Quarterly*, Oct. 1919). *Revue musicale*, Mar. 1924, arts. by R. KOECHLIN, G. AURIOL, J. COCTEAU, illustrated ; and Aug. 1925, art. by J. COCTEAU and AURIC. *Arts et lettres d'aujourdhui* (Brussels, Mar. 16, 1924), art. by PAUL COLLAER. *Il Pianoforte*, Aug. 1925, art. by H. PRUNIÈRES. A. CŒUROY, *Musiciens français modernes*, 1922.

J. G. P.

SATURDAY POPULAR CONCERTS, see POPULAR CONCERTS.

SATZ, the German term for MOVEMENT (*q.v.*).

SAUER, EMIL (*b.* Hamburg, Oct. 8, 1862), was a pupil of Nicolas Rubinstein at the Moscow Conservatorium in 1876–81, and subsequently studied under Liszt and Deppe. From 1882 he made frequent and successful concert tours as a virtuoso pianist. He first appeared in England at eight recitals of his own, in Nov. 1894, and rapidly attained great success in this country, maintained through many visits. In 1901 he was appointed head of one department of the pianoforte branch of the

Vienna Conservatorium, which he gave up in Apr. 1907, going to live at Dresden. He resumed his position in Vienna in 1915. His technique is wonderfully neat and accurate, and his playing, though occasionally rather wanting in breadth, is always agreeable. He has written a 'Suite moderne,' 24 concert études, 2 sonatas and many slighter pieces for the pianoforte, as well as two concertos in E minor and C minor. He has also published a volume of reminiscences, *Meine Welt* (1901).

M.; addns. Riemann.

SAUL. (1) An oratorio; words attributed both to Jennens and Morell, music by Handel. The composition was begun July 23, 1738. The second act was completed Aug. 28, and the whole on Sept. 27, of the same year. First performance at the King's Theatre, Tuesday, Jan. 16, 1739; at Dublin, May 25, 1742. Revived by the Sacred Harmonic Society, Mar. 20, 1840. The autograph is in the Roy. Lib. B.M.

(2) 'King Saul.' An oratorio; composed by C. H. H. Parry, produced Birmingham Festival of 1894.                              G.

SAUNDERS, JOHN (*b.* Dec. 23, 1867; *d.* Oct. 7, 1919), violinist, studied at the G.S.M. under J. T. Carrodus and Benoît Hollander. Though his services were much in request for orchestral playing (he led the orchestra of the Royal Philharmonic Society in 1910, and that of the Russian ballet in 1918–19) it is as a chamber music player that he will be best remembered. His purity of style made him an ideal leader of quartets in classic mould, and he was perhaps the most appreciated of all the performers at the SOUTH PLACE CONCERTS (*q.v.*). His first appearance there was on Dec. 20, 1891, his last on Jan. 5, 1919, and his total number of appearances 239, a truly remarkable record. The audiences showed their appreciation by subscribing over £300 for the establishment of a John Saunders Memorial Scholarship.                              w. w. c.

SAURET, ÉMILE (*b.* Dun-le-Roi, Cher, France, May 22, 1852; *d.* London, Feb. 12, 1920), violinist, soon attracted the notice of de Bériot, and became his pupil, the last he ever had. He began to travel at an early age, playing in the chief towns of France and Italy, in Vienna and in London, where he played at the International Exhibition of 1862 and also at the Alhambra. More important was his appearance at Alfred Mellon's Concerts, Covent Garden, Aug. 27, 1866. He played often at the French court in the last days of the Second Empire. In 1872 he made his first visit with Strakosch to the United States, and his second in 1874, remaining there till Jan. 1876. In New York he made the acquaintance of von Bülow and Rubinstein, and on his return to Leipzig was welcomed by the latter, then engaged in the rehearsals of his 'Paradise

Lost.' Sauret made his début in the Gewandhaus in May 1876 in Mendelssohn's concerto, and was most warmly received. He took lessons in composition from Jadassohn. He, however, returned immediately to America, and it was not till he came back again in 1877, and went through Germany and Austria in two long and most successful tours, that his reputation was established in his native country. In England he reappeared in 1880, and played at the Crystal Palace, Apr. 24, and Philharmonic (Bruch's concerto, No. 1) on the 28th.

Liszt showed him much kindness, and they often played together. In 1872 he married Teresa Carreño, the marriage being dissolved a few years later. In 1879 he married Emma Hotter of Düsseldorf, and being appointed professor of the violin at Kullak's Academy in Berlin, he settled in that city, remaining there nearly ten years. He relinquished this post, however, in 1890, when the R.A.M. invited him to fill the vacancy caused by the death of the principal violin professor, Prosper Sainton. In 1903 Sauret again gave up this second professorship for a similar position at the Chicago Musical College, where he remained until July 1906. For a time he lived in Geneva, giving private lessons to a small coterie of pupils, many of whom followed him from America. As a virtuoso Sauret obtained a greater degree of popularity in America than here. His playing was distinguished by the grace and elegance of the French school, to which was added a conscientious handling of the classics. He wrote a large amount of music, including an excellent Method for the violin.

His published works include a concerto in G minor; a Ballade, a Légende; and a Serenade in G—all for solo violin and orchestra; Caprice de Concert in D; Scherzo fantastique; Valse-caprice; Barcarolle-mazurka, and many other drawing-room pieces, as well as transcriptions from Mendelssohn, Rubinstein, Wagner, etc.

He also wrote a concerto in E major for violin and orchestra, a *Gradus ad Parnassum du violiniste* (Leipzig, 1894), and a number of études, small pieces and transcriptions for the violin, with and without orchestra.

BIBL.—LAHEE, *Famous Violinists*; MASON CLARKE, *Dictionary of Fiddlers*; *Baker*; *Mus. T.*, 1900, p. 9.
G.; addns. E. H.-A.

SAUTILLÉ (Ital. *saltato*), a technical term in violin and violoncello music whereby the executant understands that a certain skipping motion of the bow is to be employed. To the school of classical composers from Corelli to Spohr, *sautillé* was either unknown or by them ignored; but with the advent of Paganini this brilliant embellishment came into vogue. (See BOWING.)                              O. R.

SAUZAY, CHARLES EUGÈNE (*b.* Paris, July 14, 1809; *d.* there, Jan. 24, 1901), eminent French violinist. In 1823 he entered the

Conservatoire, and in his second year became the pupil of Baillot and of Reicha. He obtained the second violin prize in 1825, the first violin prize and the second for fugue in 1827. A few years later he joined Baillot's quartet, first as second violin and then as tenor, *vice* Urhan, married Mlle. Baillot, and continued one of her father's party till its dissolution in 1840. He soon rose rapidly both in society and as a professor. In 1840 he was made first violin to Louis Philippe, and afterwards leader of the second violins to the Emperor Napoleon III. In 1860 he succeeded Girard as professor at the Conservatoire. His own quartet party started after the termination of Baillot's, including his wife and Boëly as pianists, Norblin and Franchomme; and gave its concerts, sometimes with and sometimes without orchestra, in the Salle Pleyel. Sauzay is mentioned by Hiller as one of Mendelssohn's acquaintances during his stay in Paris in 1830. He was greatly sought after both as a player and a teacher. His publications are not important, and consist of incidental music to ' Georges Dandin ' and ' Le Sicilien,' cleverly written in the style of Lully to suit the date of the pieces ; fantasias and romances ; a PF. trio ; a string trio ; songs; *Haydn, Mozart, Beethoven ; Étude sur le quatuor* (Paris, 1861), a disappointing work from the pen of a musician of so much eminence and experience ; *L'École de l'accompagnement* (Paris, 1869), a sequel to the foregoing. He also composed a series of ' Études harmoniques ' for the violin.                                G.

SAVAGE, WILLIAM (*b. circa* 1720 ; *d.* London, July 27, 1789), was a pupil of Pepusch, and became a gentleman of the Chapel Royal in 1744. He was almoner, vicar-choral and master of the choristers at St. Paul's Cathedral in 1748, and was the master of Battishill and Stevens. He wrote some chants and church music of little importance. (*Brit. Mus. Biog.*)

SAVART, FÉLIX (*b.* Mézières, June 30, 1791 ; *d.* Mar. 17,[1] 1841), a French doctor of medicine who abandoned his profession and devoted himself to investigating the theory of the vibration of surfaces and strings. He was the son of Gérard Savart, a mathematical instrument maker of repute, director of the *ateliers* of the École d'Artillerie, and the author of several useful innovations, including an ingenious contrivance for dividing circles.

Originally established at Metz, he left Paris in 1819, where he was made conservateur de physique at the Collège de France, and in 1827 was elected a member of the Académie des Sciences. Following in the steps of Chladni, he made many investigations in acoustics, which are recorded in the several publications bearing his name. He appears particularly to have thrown light on the nature of that complicated relation between a vibrating body

[1] Death certificate.

which is the source of sound, and other bodies brought into connexion with it, by virtue of which the original sound is magnified in intensity and modified in quality ; well-known examples of such an arrangement being furnished by the *sound-boards* of the violin tribe and the pianoforte.

In his *Mémoire sur la construction des instruments à cordes et à archet,* published in Paris in 1819, he explains the series of experiments which led him to construct his ' Trapezoid Violin,' familiarly known in England as Savart's ' Box Fiddle.' The exhaustive tests therein described are the most renowned and convincing that have ever been undertaken. Clearly and distinctly he proved that wood arched in the form ordinarily employed for stringed instruments of the violin tribe does not vibrate in every part of its length and breadth equally ; that there are points where the vibrations decrease, and points—*i.e.* the bouts, corner-blocks and sound-holes—where the vibrations cease ; finally, that a flat piece of wood vibrates more readily and evenly than an arched one. Taking these facts for his basis, he constructed a violin in the form of a box, narrower at the upper than at the lower end. The two tables were flat, planed on the inner side and slightly raised on the outer so as to support the increased pressure of the strings caused by the bridge, which was necessarily higher than usual, so as to allow the bow a free passage across the strings, which would otherwise be hindered by the straight sides of the instrument. In contrast with the customary curved sound - holes of the ordinary violin, Savart cut his straight ; and their position in the belly, and distance apart, he determined by a series of practical experiments which are minutely described in his book. He tried two bass-bars, one placed down the centre joint of the violin, the other crescent-shaped, only touching the table at a point just below the bridge. Curiously enough, both these forms produced apparently identical effects. The sides of the instrument were $\frac{1}{12}$ in. in thickness, and no side linings were employed. The sound-post was placed behind the bridge, but a little more to the right than is customary. To prevent the excessive pull of the strings on the tender part of the table (inseparable from a tail-piece attached in the ordinary way), Savart carried his strings over a hardwood or ivory nut at the end of the violin and attached them to the tail-pin, which was set slightly below the centre. A jury of the Académie des Sciences, composed of Biot, Charles, Haüy and De Prony, together with four members of the Académie des Arts, Berton, Catel, Le Sueur and Cherubini, were appointed to consider the merits of this violin. The eminent violinist Lefebvre played alternately on a fine Cremona and Savart's violin before this jury, and eventually the latter was pronounced to be equal, if not superior, to the Italian masterpiece.

Savart's name is also connected with an ingenious little device for measuring, in a manner easily appreciable by a lecture audience, the number of vibrations corresponding to a given musical note. A wheel, caused to rotate quickly by ordinary mechanical contrivances, is furnished on its circumference with teeth or ratchets, against which a tongue of pasteboard or some other elastic substance is brought into contact. The passage of each tooth gives a vibration to the tongue, and if the wheel revolve fast enough, the repetition of these vibrations will produce a musical sound. Hence, as the number of rotations of the wheel in a given time can be easily counted, the number of vibrations corresponding to the note produced can be experimentally ascertained with tolerable precision. This mode of determining vibration numbers has been since superseded by the more elegant instrument, the SIREN, and by other modes known to modern acoustic physicists, but from the simplicity of its demonstrations it is still often used. Savart also investigated with some attention and success the acoustical laws bearing on wind instruments and on the production of the voice.

He wrote *Mémoire sur la voix humaine*, published in 1825, and also *Sur la voix des oiseaux*, 1826. His complete works were published in the *Annales de Physique et de Chimie*, 1819–40.

BIBL.—P. DAVIDSON, *The Violin*; HERON-ALLEN, *Violin-making*; J. GALLAY, *Luthiers italiens*; LÉON MORDRET, *La Lutherie artistique*; J. A. OTTO, *Über den Bau und die Erhaltung der Geige*; F. SAVART, *Mémoire sur la construction des instruments*, etc. (a condensed German translation of this work was published in Leipzig in 1844); F. J. FÉTIS, *Biographical Notice of Nicolo Paganini, The Repository of Arts, Literature, and Fashion*, etc., vol. xi., 2nd Series, Jan. 1, 1821, No. 6, pp. 21 and 80; *Nouvelle Biographie générale publiée par Firmin Didot*; *Nouveau Larousse illustré*; Fétis, *Biog. des Mus.*

W. P. ; addns. E. H.-A.

SAVETTA, ANTONIO (*b*. Lodi, late 16th cent.), composed masses, Magnificats, motets, 6-12 v., madrigals between 1608–10, and 'Salmi ariosi e brevi ' (short and tuneful psalms), 8 v., lib. 3, op. 14 (1636).

SAVILE, JEREMY, a composer of the middle of the 17th century, some of whose songs are included in ' Select Musicall Ayres and Dialogues,' 1653, is now only known by ' Here's a health unto his Majesty,' and his four-part song, ' The Waits,' printed in Playford's ' Musical Companion,' by long-standing custom the last piece sung at the meetings of the Madrigal Society and similar bodies.      W. H. H.

SAVIONI, MARIO, of Rome, pupil of Vincent Ugolini, entered the Papal Chapel as contralto in 1643, and was maestro thereof in 1659 and 1668. He composed concerti morali e spirituali (1660), motets for solo voice (1676), madrigals, 5 v. (1668), madrigali e concerti *a* 3 (1672); various songs in collective volumes (*Q.-L.*).

SAVITRI, chamber opera in one act ; text and music by Gustav Holst. First public per-

formance Lyric Theatre, Hammersmith, June 23, 1921.

SAVONAROLA, opera in a prologue and 3 acts ; words by Gilbert à Beckett ; music by Stanford. Produced Stadt-Theater, Hamburg (words translated by Ernst Frank), Apr. 18, 1884 ; Covent Garden (German Opera, under Richter), July 9 of the same year.     M.

SAVOY, see OLD HUNDREDTH.

SAVOY THEATRE, see CARTE ; SULLIVAN.

SAX, (1) CHARLES JOSEPH (*b*. Dinant, Belgium, Feb. 1, 1791 ; *d*. Paris, Apr. 26, 1865), a Belgian musical-instrument maker of the first rank. He was first a cabinet-maker, then a mechanic in a spinning-machine factory, and then set up in Brussels as a maker of wind instruments. He had served no apprenticeship to the trade, and his only qualification was that he could play the serpent ; he was therefore obliged to investigate for himself the laws concerning the bore of instruments ; but as he had great manual dexterity, and a turn for invention, he was soon able to produce serpents and flutes of fair quality. He quickly attracted notice by his clarinets and bassoons, which gained him a medal at the Industrial Exhibition of 1820, and the title of musical-instrument maker to the court of the Netherlands, which also encouraged him by advancing him capital. In 1822 he began to make all kinds of wind instruments, brass and wood, and in 1824 invented an ' omnitonic horn,' which he continued to perfect till 1846. This instrument could be adjusted to any key by means of a piston sliding backwards or forwards on a graduated scale of about half an inch long, which set the body of the instrument in communication with tubes of different lengths corresponding to all the major keys. On a separate elbow was a movable register which the player fixed opposite the number of the key he wished to use, and the tube of that key being at once brought into position, the instrument was played exactly like an ordinary horn. Sax also invented brass instruments producing every note in the scale, without crooks, pistons or cylinders. He took out patents for a keyed harp, a piano and a guitar on a new system, but his efforts were mainly directed to perfecting the clarinet, especially the bass clarinet, and discovering new methods of boring brass and wood wind instruments with a view to make them more exactly in tune. His exertions were crowned with success, and he obtained gratifying distinctions at the Brussels Industrial Exhibition of 1835.

Charles Sax was the father of eleven children, of whom two sons were distinguished in the same line. The eldest of these,

(2) ANTOINE JOSEPH, known as ADOLPHE SAX (*b*. Dinant, Nov. 6, 1814 ; *d*. Paris, Feb. 4, 1894), was brought up in his father's workshop, and as a child was remarkable for manual skill, and

love of music. He entered the Brussels Conservatoire and studied the flute and clarinet—the latter with Bender, who considered him one of his best pupils. Like his father his efforts were directed mainly to the improvement of that instrument, especially the bass clarinet, and he even designed a double-bass clarinet in B♭. In the course of his endeavours to improve the tune of his favourite instrument he invented an entire family of brass instruments with a new quality of tone, which he called SAXOPHONE (*q.v.*). The hope of making both fame and money led him to Paris; he arrived in 1842 and established himself in the Rue St. Georges, in small premises which he was afterwards forced to enlarge. He had no capital beyond his brains and fingers, which he used both as a manufacturer and an artist; but he had the active support of Berlioz, Halévy and G. Kastner, and this soon procured him money, tools and workmen. He exhibited in the French Exhibition of 1844, and obtained a silver medal for his brass and wood wind instruments, a great stimulus to a man who looked down upon all his rivals, and aimed not only at eclipsing them, but at securing the monopoly of furnishing musical instruments to the French army. In 1845 he took out a patent for the SAXHORN (*q.v.*), a new kind of bugle, and for a family of cylinder instruments called SAXO-TROMBA, intermediate between the saxhorn and the cylinder trumpet. On June 22, 1846, he registered the saxophone, which has remained his most important discovery. A man of such inventive power naturally excited much jealousy and ill-feeling among those whose business suffered from his discoveries, but his tact and wisdom made numerous and powerful friends, among others Général de Rumigny, Aide-de-camp to Louis Philippe, and a host of newspaper writers who were perpetually trumpeting his praises. He lost no opportunity of vaunting the superiority of his instruments over those in use in the French military bands, at a special competition held between the two; and the superiority, whether deserved or not, soon resulted in a monopoly, the first effect of which was to banish from the military bands all horns, oboes and bassoons.

The Paris Industrial Exhibition of 1849, at which Sax obtained a gold medal, brought his three families of instruments still more into notice; and he received the Council Medal at the Great Exhibition of 1851. In spite of these merited honours, he became bankrupt in 1852. He soon, however, made an arrangement with his creditors, and on re-starting business entered for the Paris Exhibition of 1855, and gained another gold medal. When the pitch was reformed in 1859 every orchestra and military band in France had to procure new wind instruments—an enormous advantage, by which any one else in Sax's place would have

made a fortune; but with all his ability and shrewdness he was not a man of business, and his affairs became more and more hopelessly involved. There was full scope for his inventive faculties under the Second Empire, and he introduced various improvements into the different piston instruments, only one of which need be specified, viz. the substitution of a single ascending piston for the group of descending ones. This principle he adapted to both conical and cylindrical instruments. He also invented instruments with seven bells and six separate pistons; instruments with rotatory bells for altering the direction of the sound, and a host of smaller improvements and experiments, all detailed in Fétis's *Rapports de l'Exposition* and *Biographie universelle*.

At the London International Exhibition of 1862, Sax exhibited cornets, saxhorns and saxotrombas, with 3 pistons, and with 2, 3, 4 and 5 keys; and at Paris in 1867 he took the Grand Prix for specimens of all the instruments invented or improved by him. He afterwards lost his powerful patrons and declined in prosperity year after year. He was obliged to give up his vast establishment in the Rue St. Georges and to sell (Dec. 1877) his collection of musical instruments. The printed catalogue contains 467 items, and though not absolutely correct is interesting, especially for the view it gives of the numerous infringements of his patents. The typical instruments of the collection were bought by the Museum of the Paris Conservatoire, the Musée Instrumental of Brussels and the late César Snoeck of Renaix, a wealthy Belgian collector.

Among the numerous works written to advertise the merits of Adolphe Sax's instruments we need only mention two—Comettant's *Histoire d'un inventeur au XIXme siècle* (Paris, 1860, 552 pp. 8vo, with a fair likeness of Sax); and Pontécoulant's *Organographie* (Paris, 1861, 2 vols. 8vo).

(3) ALPHONSE, worked with his brother for some years, and seems to have devoted his attention especially to ascending pistons. He set up for himself in the Rue d'Abbeville (No. 5 *bis*), but did not succeed. He published a pamphlet, *Gymnastique des poumons*; *la musique instrumentale au point de vue de l'hygiène et la création des orchestres féminins* (Paris, 1865), which is merely a disguised puff.

G. C.

SAXHORN (SAXTUBA), a brass valve instrument of the bugle type, invented by Adolphe SAX (*q.v.*), played with a cup mouthpiece. (See *PLATE LXXXIV*. No. 3.)

It is built in at least seven different pitches, so as to provide a range of somewhat similar tone-colour of about five octaves. The saxhorn family naturally divides itself into two groups, the soprano and alto (flügelhorns) in E♭ and B♭ respectively, and the tenor in E♭ and baritone in E♭ (althorns), forming the upper and speaking from the second harmonic 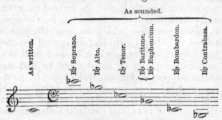 sounding a minor third, and a whole tone lower, while the bass in B♭ (equivalent to the euphonium) and bass tuba in E♭ (bombardon) and contrabass, an octave below the B♭ bass, form the lower and speak from the fundamental 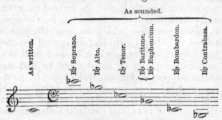. (See TUBA.) The tone-colour of the lower group is broader and heavier than that of the upper. The difference between the baritone and the euphonium, both in B♭ and of the same pitch and compass, may be compared to the difference between the baritone and bass voices. Although the lower group can take three octaves easily, the average easy compass of the upper is about two octaves.

The valve system of the saxhorn is arranged in such manner that the depression of the second valve flattens the pitch a semitone, the depression of the first valve flattens it a tone, and the third valve a tone and a half. Whatever the normal pitch of the instrument, the second note of the harmonic series is written as middle c′ when the treble clef is used, but when the bass clef is employed the notes are written as sounded. The harmonic scale obtained from the unaltered length of the instrument is supplemented when three valves are used singly and in combination, by six other similar scales, and by this means a complete chromatic scale can be produced.

are required, and to obtain them a fourth valve, altering the pitch two and half tones, is usually employed. (For explanation of certain inaccuracies due to the use of valves in combination see VALVE.)

The instruments are sometimes pitched in F instead of E♭ and in C instead of B♭ when required for use in the orchestra. As stated above, the second note in the harmonic series is written as middle C when the treble clef is used, the actual pitch of the note for each of the instruments named being as here shown:

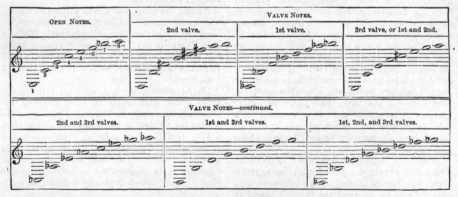

In every case, however, the note written as middle C is known as the 'low C' of the instrument, the octave below is the 'pedal C,' and the octave above, or No. 4 in the harmonic series, is known as 'middle C.' 'Top C' or No. 8 in the harmonic series is rarely passed.

There can be no doubt that the inventor of the saxhorn added greatly to the compass, richness and flexibility of the military brass and reed bands. (See WIND BAND.) But it is

SCHEME OF FINGERING FOR THE SAXHORN

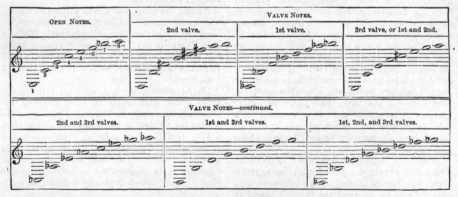

It will be observed, on comparing the notes on the first and last groups of the scheme, that there is a gap between the open pedal C (No. 1) and the G♭ above it, produced by the combined use of the 1st, 2nd and 3rd valves, but this is of no practical consequence on the alto, tenor and baritone instruments, as the quality of the extreme low notes is poor. With the basses (euphoniums and tubas), however, the case is different, as the notes of the pedal octave

a question whether the tone of these powerful auxiliaries blends so well with the stringed instruments as that of the trumpet, French horn and trombone—and hence their comparative neglect.

Sax's first advice to players exhibits the power of his new instruments—that, namely, of playing in every key without using 'crooks,' as in the French horn and trumpet. (See HORN.) He also attacked the problem of true intonation in valve instruments, by means of what he terms a compensator. Besides these improvements he planned all the tubes and mechanism on a far sounder acoustical basis than had been attempted in the fortuitous and disconnected contrivances of former periods. The valve or piston was indeed known, but was open to the objection stated above, and was at best but a clumsy machine. He unquestionably simplified it by causing fewer turns and corners to interfere with the free course of the vibrating column of air. It is to be noted, however, that all the instruments of the Sax family, like the ordinary cornet-à-pistons, utilise the harmonic octave below that in which the natural trumpet and French horn speak; indeed, as said, the three lowest can speak from the fundamental, and thus obtain power and facility somewhat at the expense of quality.

Sax did not aim at designing or improving instruments of the trumpet and horn qualities only, but rather at adapting improved valves systematically to brass instruments of the bugle type ranging in pitch from soprano to contrabass, the lower pitched members of the family being substitutes for the imperfect serpents, ophicleides and other bass horns then in use. The power and facility of tone production of the instruments known as saxhorns, whether made by Sax or by other makers who have followed up his ideas, should therefore be compared with that obtainable on these keyed instruments, rather than with the quality of French horns and trumpets. The cornet is an instrument standing by itself, as a hybrid between the trumpet and the flügel-horn, and its analogy with saxhorns, as now understood, cannot be pushed beyond the fact that the free use of the second octave in the harmonic series is common to it and to them.

It is to open-air music that we must look to understand the change that has been brought about by the introduction of the saxhorns. Granting that with the exception of the bass tubas, nothing distinctive has been added to the orchestra by them, it yet remains that popular music has been revolutionised, for military bands have been reorganised, and the brass bands which are so largely instrumental in introducing good music to the masses have become possible. w. h. s.; addns. d. j. b.

SAXOPHONE, an instrument invented by Adolphe Sax about 1840, introduced officially into the French army bands, July 31, 1845, and registered by Sax, June 22, 1846. It consists essentially of a conical brass tube furnished with about twenty lateral orifices covered by keys, and with six studs or finger-plates for the first three fingers of either hand, and is played by means of a mouthpiece and single reed of the clarinet kind. (See *PLATE XVII.* Nos. 1, 2.) In addition to lateral holes giving the scale, two

small holes opened by keys, and known as 'pipes' or 'speakers,' are also provided, and are used for the production of the octaves. The saxophones generally in use are the soprano in $b\flat$, the alto in $e\flat$, the tenor in B$\flat$, the baritone in E$\flat$, and the bass in B$\flat$. A sopranino in $e'\flat$ is sometimes made, and $c$ and $f$ are occasionally used for the pitch notes instead of $b\flat$ and $e\flat$ respectively. Those most used are the alto and tenor varieties. In French military bands, however, five or more are in use ; having to a great degree superseded the more difficult but more flexible clarinet, and having quite replaced the bassoon. (See WIND BAND.)

The compass of the saxophone as generally recognised is from $b$ to $f'''$, but all the members of the family are frequently made with an extension of the bell for $b\flat$, which note is obtained by the closing of an extra open-standing key. The two highest keys, giving $e'''$ and $f'''$, are, however, seldom fitted to any but the alto and tenor instruments. The key-system for the right hand is similar to that of the Boehm flute, but for the left hand approaches more nearly to that of the ordinary oboe. The fundamental sounds from $b\flat$ or $b\natural$ to $c''\sharp$ are obtained by the successive opening of the lateral holes, and by means of the two octave or 'pipe' keys the compass is carried up from $d''$ to $c'''\sharp$. The four highest notes, $d'''$, $e'''\flat$, $e'''$ and $f'''$, are produced by four keys on the upper part of the instrument, used exclusively for these notes. Since its introduction, many improved or alternative fingerings have been designed for and adopted on the saxophone; among these are, an extension downwards to A$\natural$ by means of a second open-standing key, shake keys from $e'$ to $f'$, $f'\sharp$ to $g'\sharp$, $b'\flat$ to $b'\natural$, and a key giving the fourth from $c'''$ to $f'''$. The tenor saxophone in C is also in growing use as a melody instrument.

The saxophone, though inferior in compass, quality and power of articulation to the clarinet and basset-horn, and especially to the bassoon, has great value in military combinations. It reproduces on a magnified scale something of the violoncello quality, and gives great sustaining power to the full chorus of brass instruments, by introducing a mass of harmonic overtones wanting in Sax's other contrivance. The tone of the soprano saxophone is somewhat strident, but the general quality of all combines the 'vocal' and the 'string' characteristics, and undoubtedly bridges over the gap between the older established 'reed' instruments and the 'brass.' There is a growing use of the instrument in British military bands, consequent upon a revised scheme of instrumentation authorised by Col. Somerville, Commandant of the Royal Military School of Music in 1923 ; while for the performance of popular dance music it has had a great vogue in recent years.

In the orchestra it has not been much employed except in France, where it was introduced by Kastner in 1844 in 'Le dernier roi de Juda,' and subsequently by Meyerbeer, Thomas, Saint-Saëns, Bizet and Vincent d'Indy. Strauss employed a quartet of saxophones in his 'Domestic Symphony.' Joseph Holbrooke has written for them a good deal.

D. J. B.

SAXO-TROMBA. In addition to the Saxhorn (q.v.), Adolphe Sax also designed a family of brass valve instruments, having, as the title suggests, a tube mainly cylindrical so as to produce the effect of a valve trombone. They were originally made in the model of the baritone, upright, so as to be suitable for mounted military bands, but have quite fallen out of use. The tone-quality lay between that of the bugle and the trumpet.     N. C. G.

SAYVE, LAMBERT DE (b. ? Liège, c. 1549; d. Prague, Feb. 1614), court musician of Archduke Charles of Austria in 1582; Kapellmeister of the Emperor Mathias in Hungary, 1600, in Vienna and Prague from 1612. He composed motets, 4-16 v.; Teutsche Liedlein, 4 v. (1602; other ed., 1611); 1 lib. delle Canzoni Alla Napolitana, 5 v. (1582); MS. masses, Vienna, Hofburg libr.     E. V. D. S.

SCACCHI, MARCO (b. Rome, late 16th cent.; d. Galese, before 1687 [1]), pupil of Francesco Felice, was Kapellmeister and composer at the Polish court, Warsaw, 1623–48, but retired in 1648 to Galese in Italy, where he lived to the time of his death. He is better known to posterity by his controversy with SIEFERT (q.v.) than by his compositions, which consist of masses, motets, madrigals, etc. (See list in Q.-L. and Fétis.)     E. V. D. S.

SCALA, LA, see MILAN.

SCALCHI, SOFIA (b. Turin, Nov. 29, 1850), received instruction in singing from Augusta Boccabadati, and made her début at Mantua in 1866 as Ulrica in 'Un ballo in maschera.' She afterwards sang at Verona, Bologna, Faenza, Nice, etc., and in England for the first time, Sept. 16, 1868, at the Promenade Concerts, Agricultural Hall, with great success. At the Royal Italian Opera, Covent Garden, she first appeared, Nov. 5 of the same year, as Azucena, and after that as Pierrotto ('Linda'), Urbano, Un Caprajo ('Dinorah'), etc. She sang there every year till 1890 inclusive. Her voice was of fine quality in compass, two octaves and a half from low F to b'', enabling her to take both the mezzo-soprano and contralto parts in a great number of operas. One of her most successful impersonations was Wania in Glinka's 'Vie pour le Czar.' She had frequent engagements in Italy, St. Petersburg, Moscow, Vienna, North and South America, etc. In Sept. 1875 she married Signor Lolli, a gentleman of Ferrara.     A. C.

[1] According to Fetis.

SCALE (Lat. and Ital. scala = ladder; Fr. gamme; Ger. Tonleiter = sound-ladder). A scale is a theoretical statement of the notes employed by convention in music. Scale is in itself an intimate fusion of melody and harmony. The music of any period tends to fall into certain accepted melodic figures (melody), and these are related to a central tonic note (harmony). These two constitute a convention, which alters as time goes on, and scale therefore has a history. (See HARMONY.)

Almost all the peoples of the earth have recognised the fourth as a starting-point. This

they filled in variously, and, as their musical experience grew, they extended their compass by means of a second fourth similarly filled.

The point at which they unconsciously aimed was to have the maximum number of notes consonant, and that is brought about by having the two tetrachords similar. The Greeks, among others, realised this, though they also recognised other 'mixed' scales in which the tetrachords were dissimilar. (See GREEK MUSIC.) Their typical scale was

and though their tonic was originally E or A, they found before long that any note could be the tonic. The music of the Latin Church (10th to 16th centuries), from which grew the whole body of later European music, adopted, or at any rate coincided with, the Greek in a general way, and their scales were arranged in a system of Modes or Tones. (See MODES, ECCLESIASTICAL.) These we may rearrange in a harmonic order. (The tonic in each case is C, with the dominant to the right of it, and the subdominant to the left.)

Of the two extreme modes, the Lydian as such was practically never used, and the Phrygian was rare in polyphonic music. The others

settled down into two groups : (1) The Mixo-
lydian and Ionian, in which we recognise our
major scale,

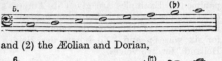

and (2) the Æolian and Dorian,

in which, if the leading note (B) is optionally
sharpened, we find our three minors—the
' descending ' with A♭, B♭ ; the ' ascending '
with A♮, B♮ ; and the ' harmonic ' with A♭,
B♮. That is the state of things in the Handel-
Bach period, when a good deal of major is
really Mixolydian and a good deal of minor is
really Dorian.

The classical period—say, from the ' B minor
Mass ' to the ' Deutsches Requiem '—definitely
fixed major and minor, whose exact intonation is given under INTERVAL. Since then
the scale seems to some to have altered,
but whether the terms ' Whole Tone ' and
' duodecimal,' by which that alteration is
described, are anything more than a change
of nomenclature, it is too soon to say. It
should be remembered that EQUAL TEMPERA-
MENT (q.v.), to which they appeal for their
justification, was in full swing during the
classical period, and yet that Mozart entirely,
and Beethoven for the most part, wrote with
Just Intonation for their premiss. Equal temperament is only a melodic alteration which,
without making the harmonic basis un-
recognisable, permits modulation on a keyboard which cannot adjust itself to the needs
of the moment ; but voices and strings, which
can adjust, recur to JUST INTONATION (q.v.)
whenever the harmonic import outweighs the
melodic. (Cf. HARMONY.)      A. H. F. S.

SCALETTA, ORAZIO (b. Crema, mid - 16th
cent. ; d. Mantua, c. 1630). He stood in high
repute as a composer, and received many marks
of distinction from ruling sovereigns, while
the Duke Gonzaga had a medal struck in his
honour. In 1611 he was maestro di cappella at
the principal church of Salo. A small book of
his on musical theory for the use of students
appeared in a large number of editions. He
composed masses, madrigals, motets, sacred
and secular songs. (See list in Q.-L.) He
died of the plague.      E. v. d. s.

SCANDELLO (SCANDELLIUS, SCANDELLI),
ANTONIO (b. Brescia, 1517 ; d. Dresden, Jan.
18, 1580). In 1553 he was already resident
in Dresden and a member of the Hofkapelle,
but he often returned to visit his native
place ; in 1567, on account of the plague, he
and his family left Dresden and spent four
months in Brescia. In 1555 six Italians are
mentioned as being members of the Dresden

Hofkapelle : ' welsche Instrumentisten in der
Musica,' among them Anthonius Scandellus,
his brother Angelus Scandellus and Benedict
Tola, the painter, whose daughter Agnes
became Scandello's second wife in June 1568.[1]
The Italians, receiving higher pay than the
Germans, were even then arousing feelings of
jealousy, which later resulted in open quarrels
and opposition.[2] In 1555, Scandello, with
250 fl. 16 grs. 9 pf. a year, was receiving a
larger salary than the Kapellmeister, Matthias
Le Maistre, who had only 204 fl. 7 grs. 9 pf. It
is also curious to note that the Italian players
were paid on a higher scale than singers from
the Netherlands, the highest salary to the
latter only amounting to 120 fl.[3] It is true that
the player was expected to show facility on a
large variety of instruments ; Scandello himself was a noted zinke (or cornett) player,
besides being already a composer of some
repute.

In 1566 Scandello became assistant Kapellmeister to the ageing Le Maistre, and on his
retirement was appointed Kapellmeister, Feb.
12, 1568, when his salary altogether amounted
to 400 fl. a year, a large sum for those days.
A letter addressed to the Kapellmeister on
Jan. 13, 1579, gives leave to his brother Angelo
to go to Venice for three months, to collect
some debts. He retained his post until his
death. One of his sons, AUGUST, was also a
member of the Dresden Hofkapelle.

Three motets for six voices, dated 1551, in
a manuscript in the Dresden Library, are probably Scandello's earliest compositions. Next
comes the Mass for six voices, in commemoration of the death of the Elector Moritz of
Saxony, July 9, 1553, at the battle of Sievers-
hausen. In the ' Inventarium ' of the Kapelle
music drawn up by the Dresden Kapellmeister,
Johann Walther, Oct. 16, 1554, for the use of
his successor, Matthias Le Maistre, this Mass
is mentioned as being in six little printed partbooks : ' VI. kleine gedruckt Partes in per-
gament, darinnen das Epitaphium Electoris
Mauricii Antonii Scandelli.'[4] At the present
time only a manuscript copy of it is known,
made in Torgau, in 1562, by one Moritz
Bauerbach of Pirna, tenorist in the Dresden
Kapelle ; very possibly it was owing to the
suggestion of Johann Walther, then living in
retirement at Torgau, that Bauerbach wrote
it. The manuscript[5] was formerly in the
Pirna Stadt-Bibliothek, but is now in the
Dresden Staat-Bibliothek.

Especial mention must be made of the
Passion music[6] and the story of the Resurrection, which were in all probability composed

1 *Monatshefte*, 1877, p. 255.
2 Fürstenau, *Zur Geschichte*, i. 26.
3 Fürstenau, *Archiv für die sächs. Geschichte*, iv., 1866.
4 W. Schäfer, *Sachsen-Chronik*, 1853, p. 320.
5 A large part of the Mass was scored by Otto Kade and published
in Ambros's *Geschichte der Musik*, 1889, vol. v.
6 See O. Kade, *Die ältere Passionskomposition*, 1893, p. 191, a
reprint of the Passion music, pp. 306-44.

before 1561. Scandello some years later refers to them in a document dated July 15, 1573; they were therefore in existence some fifty years before Heinrich Schütz's great works were published, his ' Auferstehung ' in 1623, and his ' Passionen nach Johannis ' not until 1664. A manuscript copy of Scandello's work, dated 1593, formerly at Grimma, now in the Dresden Library, is entitled ' Passio et Resurrectio Domini nostri Jesu Christi ab Antonio Scandello compositae '; the scribe was Johann Gengenbach of Colditz. It only gives the tenor part of the choruses; the music is otherwise complete. The manuscript of the tenor partbook now in the same library, but formerly at Löbau, contains the ' Johannispassion ' and the ' Auferstehungsgeschichte,' without mention of the composer's name. Another Löbau manuscript contains a complete copy of the ' Auferstehung '; this part of the composition was the first to appear in print. It was published by Samuel Besler at Breslau, 1612, with the title,

' Gaudii paschalis Jesu Christi redivivi in Gloriosissimae Resurrectionis ejus laetam celebrationem. Relatio historia à quatuor Evangelistis consignata, etc., durch Samuelem Beslerum, etc.'

Besler alludes in the preface to the composer, Antonius Scandellus, ' der berhümbte musicus.' It was again published in an adapted form by O. S. Harnisch in 1621. In the same year Besler published the Passion music:

' Ant. Scandelli . . . Passio, Das Leyden unsers Herrn Jesu Christi nach dem H. Evangelisten Johanne. Durch S. B. mit der Chorstimme vermehrt,' Breslau, 1621.

It is from this edition that the chorus parts, missing in the manuscripts, have been filled in. The Passion opens with the words in four-part writing, ' Das Leyden unsers Herrn Jesu Christi wie das der heilige Evangelist Johannes beschreibet.' Throughout, each individual character is represented by a duo, trio or quartet, with the exception of the Evangelist, who is given the traditional recitative. The words of Christ are invariably set as a solo quartet, those of Peter as a trio, and so on. The concluding chorus and the short, quick outcries of the people are all in five-part writing; possibly the opening chorus should be the same. There is no accompaniment (see PASSION MUSIC). For a comparison of the Schütz and Scandello works see SCHÜTZ, also *M.f.M.* 1882, p. 37, where also the identity of the anonymous ' Auferstehung ' published by Vopelius in the *Neu Leipziger Gesangbuch*, 1682, pp. 311-65,[1] with that of Scandello's is pointed out. Scandello was the first composer to set the story of the Resurrection to music, and he followed very closely the lines laid down in his Passion music.

As to his other compositions, it may be noted that although his Italian madrigals, published 1566 and 1577, are purely vocal works with

no accompaniment, the German Lieder, both sacred and secular, published 1568, 1570 and 1575, may be sung to an instrumental accompaniment. Examples are given in Ambros's *Geschichte der Musik.* v., ' Bonzorno, madonna,' for four voices; ' Der Wein der schmeckt mir ' for six voices; and ' Nu komm der Heiden Heiland ' for five voices.

### LIST OF PUBLISHED WORKS

Missa sex vocum super Epitaphium Mauricii Ducis et Electoris Saxoniae ab Anthonio Scandello, Italo, composita, 1553. Walther (1732) states that it was published at Nuremberg, by Georg Fabricius, in 1558.

El primo libro de le canzoni napoletane a IIII voci, composti per Messer Antonio Scandello musico del illus et eccel. sig. Duca Augusto Elettor di Sassonia. Novamente datti in luce. Noribergae excudebant Ulricus Neuberus et Th. Gerlatzen, 1566, obl. 4to. Four partbooks. The dedication to the Elector August is dated from Augsburg. Contains twenty-four canzoni. Later editions were issued at Nuremberg in 1572 and 1583.

Melodia Epithalami in honorem . . . Martini Henrici et filiae Barbarae viri Joh. Schildbergii . . . sex vocum. Witebgrgae, 1568.

Epithalamia, in honorem . . . Nicolai Leopardi, symphoniacorum puerorum illustrissimi ac serenis. principis Georgii Friderici, marchionis Brandeburgensis . . . praeceptoris, et pudicissimae virginis ac sponsae Kunigundae . . . composita per Ant. Scandellum, Matthaeum Le Maistre, etc. Noribergae apud Th. Gerlatzerum, 1568. Text: Beati omnes qui timent; in two movements, for six voices.

Newe Teutsche Liedlein mit vier und fünff Stimmen, welche gantz lieblich zu singen, und auff allerley Instrumenten zugebrauchen. Durch Anthonium Scandellum, Churfürstlicher G. zu Sachsen Kappelmeister verfertigt. Gedruckt zu Nürnberg, durch Dietrich Gerlatz, inn Johann von Bergs seligen Druckerey, 1568, obl. 4to. Four partbooks, containing twelve sacred songs. Includes the well-known Choral ' Lobet den Herrn,' which took a permanent place in church song, and was reprinted in Joachim Magdeburg's ' Christliche u. tröstliche Tischgesänge,' Erfurt, 1571; the Dresdener Gesangbuch, 1593; J. C. Kühnau's Vierstimmige alte u. neue Choralgesänge,' 1790, ii. p. 140; Lützel's Kirchliche Chorgesänge, 1861, No. 11; and with the song ' Allein zu dir ' for six voices, in Winterfeld's *Evangelische Kirchengesang*, 1842, Nos. 38 and 39.

Nawe und lustige weltliche Deudsche Liedlein, mit vier, fünff, und sechs Stimmen, auf allerley Instrumenten zugebrauchen, und lieblich zu singen. Durch Ant. Scandellum, etc. von ihme selbst corrigiret, und in Druck vorfertiget. Gedruckt zu Dresden durch Matthes Stöckel und Gimel Bergen, 1570, obl. 4to. Five partbooks, containing twenty songs. A later edition of 1578 had the title-page as above with the exception of the tenor partbook, dated a year later, as follows: Schöne, weltliche und geistliche, nawe, deudsche Liedlein mit vier, fünff und sechs Stimmen, 1578.

Epithalamium in honorem . . . Christophori Waltheri, illustriss. Flectoris Saxoniae . . organistae insignis: prudentiss. viri Joannis Waltheri, consulis Dresdensis, ac fautoris musicae singularis . . . filii, et honestissimae foeminae Catherinae Tolae, sponsae ipsius, Benedicti Tolae, musici et pictoris . . . relictae filiae. Compositum sex vocibus ab illus. Electoris Saxoniae . . . musici chori magistro, Antonio Scandello, 1574, 4to. Six partbooks.

Nawe schöne ausserlesene Geistliche Deudsche Lieder, mit fünff und sechs Stimmen, gantz lieblich zu singen und auff allerley Instrumenten zugebrauchen, sampt einem Dialogo mit acht Stimmen. Durch Ant. Scandellum, etc. componirt, auch von ihme selbst corrigirt, und in Druck vorfertiget. Dresden, Gimel Bergen, 1575, obl. 4to. Contains twenty-three compositions, ' meist über ältere Kirchenmelodien.'

Missae sex, quarum priores tres quinque. posteriores vero sex vocum sunt, compositum super has cantionumseil. 1, super: avec que vous; 2. Io mi son giovenetta; 3. Ad aequales; 4. Maria Magdalena; 5. Au premier jour; 6. O passi sparsi. Authore Ant, Scandello Electoris Saxoniae musices praefecto. Monachi, 1576.

Il secondo libro de le canzoni napolitane, a quatro et a cinque voci. Composte per Ant. Scandello, maestro de la capella del illus. et eccel. sig. Elettore di Sassonia, etc. Novamente date in luce. Stampate in Monacho per Adam Berg, 1577, obl. 4to. Five partbooks, containing twenty-four canzoni.

#### COMPOSITIONS IN OTHER PUBLICATIONS

Thesaurus musicus. Noribergae, 1564.
' Imperium Augusti sit foelix,' ' Magnificat,' ' Noe, noe, exultemus,' all for eight voices, in the first volume; ' Alleluia noli flere Maria ' for seven voices, in the second.

Beati omnes, Psalmus 128 Davidis. . . . Per Cl. Stephani Buchariensem. Noribergae, 1569. Includes Scandello's setting of the psalm for six voices (see his Epithalamia, 1568). A manuscript copy is in the Vienna Hofbibliothek, No. 15,591.

Das erste Buch . . . schöner Lautenstück . . . mit vier und fünff Stimmen. Getruckt durch Bernhard Jobin, bürger zu Strassburg, 1572. Includes ' Ich weis mir ein fest gebautes hauss ' for five voices, in lute tablature.

Ein new kunstlich Tabulaturbuch . . . durch Eliam Nicolaum Ammorbach, bürger und Organist in Leipzig zu Sanct Thomas Leipzig, 1575. ' Ich weis mir,' ' Den liebsten Buhlen,' ' Gros lief hat,' ' Kein lieb ohn leid,' ' Von deinetwegen,' all for five voices, in lute tablature.

Selectae Cantiones octo et septem vocum, etc. Argentorati, 1578. ' Noe, noe exultemus,' for eight voices.

Schöne ausserlesene . . . Teutsche Lieder XX. Durch J. Pühlerum Schvuandorffensem. München, 1585.
' Mancher der spricht,' for four voices.

Corollarium Cantionum sacrarum . . . F. Lindneri, Noribergae, 1590. No. 22. Antonius Scandellus; ' Christus vere languores ' in two movements, for five voices. On a manuscript copy in the Zwickau Library is written, ' Ultima cantio Anthonii Scandelli qui

---

[1] Reprinted by Riegel and Schöberlein, *Kirchliche Chorgesänge*, 1868, ii. pp. 619-47.

18 Januarii die vesperi hora 7, anno 80, aetatis suae 63 obiit' (Kade, *Le Maistre*, p. 3). MSS. are also in the Basle, Dresden and Liegnitz libraries.

Musikalischer Zeitvertreiber, das ist Allerley seltzame lecherliche Vapores und Humores, etc., Nürnberg, 1609. Contains songs for 4, 5, 6, 7 and 8 voices; two compositions are by Scandello.

Triumphi di Dorothea . . . das ist geistliches musicalisches Triumph Cräntzlein . . . durch M. Rinckhardum. Leipzig, 1619. Contains 'Ich weis mir ' for five voices.

Engelmann's Quodlibetum novum latinum quinque vocum. Leipzig, 1620. Compositions by Scandello in Part I.

Cantionale sacrum, das ist, Geistliche Lieder mit 3, 4, 5 oder mehr Stimmen unterschiedlicher Autorum. Gotha, 1646–48, 3 volumes. One composition by Scandello, also in the edition of 1651–55–57.

Joh. G. Ebeling's edition of P. Gerhardi geistliche Andachten, 1667. With Scandello's melody to ' Lobet den Herrn.'

A. Neithardt, Sammlung religiöser Gesänge, vii. No. 11. ' Lasset die Kindelein ' for five voices.

Franz Commer, Geistliche u. weltliche Lieder. 1870, Nos. 11, 12, ' Ich ruf zu dir ' and ' Gelobet seist du,' both for five voices; other motets in " Musica sacra," vols. 15, 19 and 20.

Franz Wüllner, Chorübungen der Münchener Musikschule, 1893, Nos. 63, 99. ' Auf dich trau ich ' and ' Mit Lieb bin ich,' both for four voices.

MSS. In Augsburg Library, No. 21, Lib. I. Sacrarum missarum sex vocum variorum authorum haud vulgarium, 1595. Missa super : Maria Magdalena. (Schletterer's *Catalogue*.) Basle Universitäts-Bibliothek, No. 33, Magnificat VIII toni, in tablature, date about 1585. (Richter's *Catalogue*.) Berlin. Königl. Bibliothek, many sacred songs in score (Eitner).

Breslau Stadtbibliothek, No. 2 (date 1573) in score, and No. 5 in separate partbooks, ' Alleluia noli flere ' for seven voices. No. 6 (date 1567) and No. 11 (date 1583), ' Noe, noe exultemus ' for eight voices. Both in Thes. mus. 1564. No. 11 and No. 14 (date about 1600). ' Ein Kindelein so lieblich ' for six voices, and ' Gelobet seist du ' for five voices, both from ' Nawe sch. auss. geistl.' 1575. No. 10, five partbooks, nine Italian madrigals from Scandello's second book, 1577. No. 94, six folio partbooks, late 16th century, Missae super : Aueeque vous ; Io mi son giovenetta ; Ad aequales ; all for five voices, and Missae super : Maria Magdalena ; Au premier jour ; O passi sparsi, all for six voices. The six masses published at Munich in 1576, see above. A MS. copy of the Mass ' O passi sparsi ' is also in the Vienna Hofbibliothek, date about 1560. (Bohn's *Catalogue*.)

Brieg Gymnasial-Bibliothek. No. 36, six partbooks, date 1592, ' Lobet den Herrn ' for four voices (see 1568 publication). In Nos. 40, 51, 52, imperfect sets of partbooks, ' Ach edler Wein ' for five voices ; ' Schöns lied ' ; ' S' io canto,' and ' Se per sentir ' (from Lib. I. of Canzoni, 1572), all for four voices. (Kuhn's *Catalogue*.)

Dresden State Library, No. 1270. Three motets for six voices : ' Christus dicit ad Thomam ' dated 1551, ' Hodie Christus natus est ' 1551, and ' Illuminare Jerusalem.' (Kade's *Catalogue*.)

Munich State Library, No. 34 (Mus. MS. 509), date 1602, Missa super : O passi sparsi, and Missa super : Au premier jour, both for six voices. No. 207 (Mus. MS. 1501), ' Ich weis mir ' for five voices, and ' Ach Gott wem soll ich's ' for four voices. No. 132 (Mus. MS. 1536), date 1553, an incomplete set of partbooks ; two Magnificats, and two motets for eight voices ; one motet for seven, and one for six voices (Maier's *Catalogue*.) Grimma Library MS. motets written between 1593 and 1595, some for four and five voices by Scandello.

Liegnitz Ritterakademie Bibl. MS. 19, many motets by Scandello.

Pirna Stadtkirche 16th-century MS. 'Auf dich trau ich ' for four voices (from 1568 work). Another MS. with ' Dies sanctificatus ' for six voices.

Zwickau Ratsschulbibliothek No. 39, date about 1600, in tablature, ' Mit Lieb bin ich ' for four voices (from ' Nawe und lustige Liedlein,' 1578). No. 678, date before 1580, five folio partbooks ' Nun kommt der Heiden Heiland ' for five voices. No. 679, incomplete set of partbooks, Missa super : Germania plange, for six voices. No. 680, incomplete set of partbooks, ' Magnus Dominus ' in two movements (which was included in Walther's *Inventarium* in 1554), and ' Allein zu dir,' both for six voices. (Vollhardt's *Catalogue*.)

C. S.

SCARIA, EMIL (*b.* Graz, Styria, Sept. 18, 1840 ; *d.* Blasewitz, near Dresden, July 22, 1886), studied at the Conservatorium, Vienna, under Gentiluomo, made his début at Pest as St. Bris in the ' Huguenots,' and afterwards sang at Brunn and Frankfort. In 1862 he came to London for the purpose of further study under Garcia, and sang at the Crystal Palace, on Apr. 5, and at a concert given later by Franz Abt, who procured him an engagement at Dessau. He next played at Leipzig (1863–65) and from 1865–72 at Dresden. From 1872–86 he was engaged at Vienna, where he established his reputation as a versatile singer and actor in both baritone and bass parts, but best in the latter, as his

' carefully deadened high notes form so great a contrast to the vigorous notes of his lower and middle register.' [1]

On leave of absence he sang in the principal German cities, in Italian opera in Russia, etc.

[1] Hanslick.

He sang the part of Escamillo to the Carmen of Bertha Ehnn, Oct. 23, 1875, when Bizet's opera was first given outside France. Among his later parts were Hans Sachs (' Meistersinger '), Wotan (' Nibelungen '), for which character he was originally selected by Wagner for Bayreuth, and which he sang at Her Majesty's Theatre in 1882, Micheli (' Wasserträger '), Marcel, Bertram and (1879) Seneschal (' Jean de Paris '). Finest of all was his Gurnemanz in ' Parsifal,' which he created at Bayreuth in 1882 ; he sang it at the concert performance of the work in the Albert Hall, London, in 1884. He became insane in 1886, and died the same year. A. Neumann's *Erinnerungen an Richard Wagner*, 1907, gives many amusing stories of him.　　　　　A. C.

SCARLATTI, (1) ALESSANDRO (*b.* Palermo, Sicily, 1659 [2] ; *d.* Naples, Oct. 24, 1725). It has generally been assumed that his birthplace was Trapani, on the strength of an alleged autograph score of his opera ' Pompeo,' which both Fétis and Florimo professed to have seen while in the possession of Gaspare Selvaggi of Naples. Selvaggi's library was bought by the Marquis of Northampton, and presented by him in 1843 to the British Museum ; but no score of ' Pompeo ' is to be found there now, nor is it included in the MS. catalogue of the collection drawn up for the donor at the time. The only known score of ' Pompeo ' is in the Royal Library at Brussels, and formerly belonged to Fétis ; but it is not autograph, and does not bear the inscription mentioned. This inscription, by the way, is given by Fétis as ' Musica del Signor Alessandro Scarlatti da Trapani,' and by Florimo as ' Pompeo del Cav. Alessandro Scarlatti di Trapani.' Florimo's version can hardly be accepted as genuine, since ' Pompeo ' appeared in 1683, while the composer did not receive the title of Cavaliere until many years later. The official record of his birth or baptism has hitherto eluded the most careful research. The fact, however, that he was born in Sicily is proved conclusively by statements in the printed libretti of his early operas, and in MS. chronicles which record their performance, and speak of the composer as a Sicilian. A number of documents have recently been discovered which prove beyond dispute that he always described himself as a native of Palermo. His father, who may probably have been a musician, since all his children except the eldest daughter are known to have been musicians, was named Pietro ; his wife's name was Eleonora d'Amato. He left Palermo in 1672 with his five children, and established himself at Rome ; the two youngest sons, Francesco and Tommaso, were not taken to Rome, but left at Naples, where both remained until they were grown up. This suggests that Pietro or his wife may have had

[2] Or possibly 1658, as may be deduced from the statement of his age engraved on his tombstone.

relatives at Naples who would take charge of them. Alessandro is traditionally supposed to have been a pupil of Carissimi in Rome, although that master died when Scarlatti was 15 years old. His early compositions show the influence of Legrenzi, and more especially of Stradella, whose best work has been shown to have been done in Rome; and his early chamber cantatas, of which some are probably earlier in date than even his first operas, are generally to be found in MS. alongside of similar music by composers who worked in Rome and northern Italy.

Pietro did not live long after his migration to Rome. He was already dead when Alessandro married Antonia Anzalone, a native of Rome, in the church of S. Andrea delle Fratte on Apr. 12, 1678. His eldest son, who as usual bore his grandfather's name, PIETRO FILIPP (5), was born on Jan. 5, 1679. Another son, Benedetto Bartolomeo, was born at Rome on Aug. 24 of the following year; he died at Naples in 1684. A third son, Raimondo, seems also to have been born at Rome; nothing is known of him except that he was living in Rome in 1717, when he acted for his brother Domenico in a legal matter. His daughter Flaminia was probably born at Rome, and possibly also Cristina, who was presumably a daughter of Alessandro, as she stood god-mother to one of his grand-daughters in 1714. At what date Scarlatti migrated to Naples it is difficult to ascertain. He stated himself that he lived 'seven or eight years' in Rome; but his sister Melchiorra, who was the eldest of the family, says that she went to live in Naples in Oct. 1682, and it might seem probable that they went there together. But the Neapolitan libretto of 'Pompeo' (Feb. 1684) still describes Scarlatti as maestro di cappella to the Queen of Sweden.

His first known opera was 'L'errore innocente ovvero Gli equivoci nel sembiante,' produced Feb. 8, 1679, in Rome at the Collegio Clementino. This work won him the interest of Christina Queen of Sweden, who even asserted her protection of him in defiance of the Papal representatives, Scarlatti being in bad odour at the Vatican on account of the misconduct of his sister with an ecclesiastic. In the libretto of his second opera, 'L'honestà negli Amori' (1680), he is described as maestro di cappella to Queen Christina. Both these operas are on a small scale; 'Pompeo' (Rome, 1683) was probably his first attempt at *opera seria* in the grand manner. In Feb. 1684 'Pompeo' was given at Naples, where 'Gli equivoci' had also been heard, and on the 17th of the same month he was appointed maestro di cappella to the Viceroy, his brother FRANCESCO (2) receiving a post as violinist in the same chapel royal. The two brothers owed their appointments to the influence of their sister, Anna Maria, an

opera singer, who was the mistress of a court official; and the affair seems to have caused some indignation at Naples, not so much on grounds of morality as from motives of chauvinism. That Scarlatti was regarded as a stranger in Naples seems a sufficient proof that he did not receive his musical education there, as Neapolitan historians of music have tried to maintain. His famous son GIUSEPPE DOMENICO (3) was born at Naples, Oct. 26, 1685, and three more children, Caterina, Carlo and Gian Francesco, in 1690, 1692 and 1695. From this time to 1702 he remained at Naples, occupied principally in the composition of operas for production at the royal palace or at the royal theatre of San Bartolomeo. He was also much in demand as a composer of music for aristocratic entertainments, and soon fell into a popular and hasty style of work. His chamber music, however, shows that even at this time his artistic ideals were much higher, and by 1702 Naples had become so irksome to him, both for musical and financial reasons, that he determined to try his fortunes elsewhere. His salary was in arrear, and the political disturbances consequent on the War of the Spanish Succession rendered his position still more insecure. On June 14 he went with Domenico to Florence, where they enjoyed the patronage of Ferdinand III., son of the Grand Duke of Tuscany, a prince who was enthusiastically devoted to music. For his private theatre at Pratolino Scarlatti composed several operas, and the Archivio Mediceo at Florence contains a very interesting correspondence between the prince and the musician on the subject of these works. Ferdinand, however, was not disposed to offer him any permanent post, and Scarlatti, being resolved not to return to Naples, accepted the humble position of assistant maestro di cappella at the church of S. Maria Maggiore in Rome. This was obtained for him by Cardinal Pietro Ottoboni, who had taken an interest in him for some twelve years or more, and who also made him his private maestro di cappella. Nevertheless, Scarlatti seems to have been no happier in Rome than in Naples, judging from the contempt for both places which he expresses in his letters to Ferdinand. He had been forced to write down to the level of a Spanish viceroy's taste for the opera-house at Naples; at Rome the Popes had done their best to suppress opera altogether on grounds of public morality. This must, no doubt, have been a severe blow to Scarlatti, whose real genius sought expression in dramatic music, although it found vent in chamber music when its natural outlet was obstructed.

On Apr. 26, 1706, Scarlatti was admitted a member of the Arcadian Academy, under the name of *Terpandro Politeio*, Corelli and Pasquini being elected at the same time. Crescimbeni [1] gives a charming account of their musical

---

[1] *Arcadia*, Lib. vii. Prosa v.

## LXX

DOMENICO SCARLATTI

ALESSANDRO SCARLATTI

From a painting ascribed to Francesco Solimena in the
R. Conservatorio di Musica, Naples

performances at these pastoral assemblies. To this period of Scarlatti's activity belong many of his beautiful chamber cantatas, and a certain amount of church music. In May 1707 Antonio Foggia died, and Scarlatti succeeded him as principal maestro at the church of S. Maria Maggiore. He continued to compose operas for Ferdinand de' Medici while living in Rome, but although his voluminous correspondence about these works has been preserved, the scores of them have unfortunately disappeared. In spite of all his efforts to write pleasing music, he seems to have been too severe for the prince's taste, and in 1707 he was dropped in favour of Perti.

In this year he produced two operas, ' Mitridate Eupatore ' and ' Il trionfo della Libertà,' at Venice (Teatro S. Giovanni Crisostomo), going there in person to direct them. These works are on a larger scale than any of his previous operas, and the first is one of the best that he ever wrote ; the second has come down to us in so fragmentary a condition that it is hardly possible to form a fair judgment upon it. In all probability Scarlatti remained at Venice to the end of the Carnival, and thence made his way to Urbino, travelling, there is reason to believe, by way of Ferrara. The reigning pope (Clement XI.) was a native of Urbino, and the Albani family, to which he belonged, were nobles of great importance in that country. The resident representative of the family, Cardinal Orazio Albani, was interested in music, and although no trace of Alessandro Scarlatti is now to be found there, the Albani library possesses several libretti of Domenico's operas, as well as a few musical treasures of an earlier date. Scarlatti remained at Urbino until September, but probably returned to Rome for Christmas, since he wrote a Mass with orchestral accompaniment for this festival.

Although Scarlatti had left Naples in June 1702, his post at the royal chapel was not filled up until Oct. 1704, when a certain Gaetano Veneziano was appointed. In Dec. 1707 he was succeeded by Francesco Mancini ; but towards the end of 1708, Cardinal Grimani, the Austrian Viceroy, made an attempt to persuade Scarlatti to return. It seems that Scarlatti, as might have been expected, declined to accept the post of deputy first organist, which was offered him, having been at the head of the chapel for nearly twenty years, and did not return until he had been restored to the office of maestro di cappella, with an increased stipend. Mancini was compensated with the title of Vice-maestro, and the right of succeeding eventually to the post held by Scarlatti. It is doubtful, however, whether he re-established himself definitely at Naples until 1713. Although described in the libretti of ' L' Amor volubile e tiranno ' (1709) and ' La principessa fedele ' (1710) as Maestro della Real Cappella,

he does not appear to have written anything more for Naples during the next three years, and on May 27, 1713, the new Viceroy, Count Daun, made a special confirmation of the appointment given him by Cardinal Grimani. This action secured him for Naples for the next few years.

During this second period of work in Naples Scarlatti was at the height of his fame. He produced operas on a magnificent scale at the court theatre ; ' Tigrane ' (1715) and its contemporaries, though less interesting than his later operas, are brilliant and effective—the leisured work of a man mellowed by success, not the hurried output of one struggling to retain the favour of his patrons at any sacrifice of artistic ideals. To this period also belong some oratorios, notably ' San Filippo Neri ' (1713), and several serenatas for state occasions. The honour of knighthood, which is first vouched for by the appearance of his name with the title Cavaliere in the libretto of ' Carlo Rè d' Alemagna ' (1716), was probably conferred upon him in recognition of the serenata and opera which he composed to celebrate the birth of the Archduke Leopold. It has been suggested that he received the order of the Golden Spur from the Pope, at the request of Cardinal Ottoboni ; but if this were the case it is only natural to suppose that it would have been conferred upon him while in the Cardinal's service, or even under the pontificate of the Cardinal's uncle, Alexander VIII. It may, however, be pointed out that in this year, 1716, he composed a Mass (known as ' Missa Clementina II.') for Clement XI. In 1718 he made his one attempt at pure comic opera, ' Il trionfo dell'onore,' performed at the Teatro dei Fiorentini.

The interest of the Neapolitans in Scarlatti's music seems to have waned about this time. After ' Cambise ' (1719) no more of his operas were heard there, and it is probable that he established himself in Rome, since his stipend as maestro di cappella at Naples was not paid to him any more, although he retained the title. At Rome he had a number of admirers sufficient to undertake the production of a series of operas which exhibit the composer in a still more advanced phase of artistic development. The first of these was ' Telemaco ' (1718), which was followed by ' Marco Attilio Regolo ' (1719), ' Tito Sempronio Gracco ' and ' Turno Aricino ' (1720), apparently not so much revivals as entire recompositions of two earlier operas, and finally his 114th and last opera, ' Griselda ' (1721). Since the autograph score of this last informs us that it was composed for Prince Ruspoli, we may suppose that that nobleman (who had interested himself in Scarlatti's work when he was living in Rome before) was the principal organiser of the performances, which took place at the ' Sala degli illustrissimi Signori Capranica.' In 1721

Clement XI. was succeeded by Innocent XIII., and in November of that year Scarlatti was commissioned by the Portuguese Ambassador to compose a pastorale for the Pope's formal entrance into the Vatican. This appears to have been his last work for Rome, where he had distinguished himself in sacred music as well as in opera, producing a fine Mass with orchestra and other works for St. Cecilia's Day at the request of Cardinal Acquaviva, who had a special interest in the church of St. Cecilia in Trastevere. In 1722 he seems to have visited Loreto, where he is supposed to have composed a setting of the psalm ' Momento Domine David' and an Ave Maria. The following year probably saw him back at Naples. He set to work on a serenata for the marriage of the Prince of Stigliano, but appears to have left it unfinished, as the first part only has come down to us. There is every reason to suppose that he was now living in complete retirement, forgotten by his own generation, and regarded as a crabbed and eccentric harmonist by even so learned a musician as the German theorist Heinichen.

In 1724 J. A. Hasse, having quarrelled with Porpora, came to Scarlatti as a pupil; the old man was attracted by the boy's amiable disposition, and during the few remaining months of Scarlatti's life the two musicians regarded each other with the affection of father and son. Quantz visited Naples in 1725 and stayed with Hasse, whom he begged to introduce him to Scarlatti; Scarlatti, however, merely replied to Hasse's request, ' My son, you know that I cannot endure players of wind instruments, for they all blow out of tune.' Hasse succeeded eventually in inducing him to receive Quantz, who heard him play the harpsichord ' in a learned manner '; Scarlatti even accompanied him in a solo and composed a couple of flute pieces for him. He died on Oct. 24 of the same year, and was buried in the church of Montesanto. His epitaph is said to have been written by Cardinal Ottoboni, and runs as follows:

HEIC · SITVS · EST
EQVES · ALEXANDER · SCARLACTVS
VIR · MODERATIONE · BENEFICIENTIA
PIETATE · INSIGNIS
MVSICES · INSTAVRATOR · MAXIMVS
QVI · SOLIDIS · VETERVM · NVMERIS
NOVA · AC · MIRA · SVAVITATE
MOLLITIIS
ANTIQVITATI · GLORIAM · POSTERITATI
IMITANDI · SPEM · ADEMIT
OPTIMATIBVS · REGIBVSQ
APPRIME · CARVS
TANDEM · ANNOS · NATVM · LXVI · EXTINXIT
SVMMO · CVM · ITALIAE · DOLORE
IX · KAL$^{AS}$ · NOVEMBRIS · CIƆIƆCCXXV
MORS · MODIS · FLECTI · NESCIA

Scarlatti is one of the most important figures, not only in the history of opera, but in the entire history of music. He is the most im-

portant of that group of composers who succeeded the first pioneers of the monodic style, based upon the modern tonal system, and who moulded and developed a musical idiom which served as the language of musical expression down to the days of Beethoven. In his early work he is naturally under the influence of older composers—Carissimi, Luigi Rossi, Stradella and Legrenzi ; indeed, the vague tradition of his having studied in Parma might associate him with the last-named composer as a pupil. His first operas and his early cantatas and church music have, moreover, a certain harshness and crudity which reveals the beginner ; Stradella's operas and Rossi's cantatas, though old-fashioned in their phraseology, are much more mature and finished in their execution. It is interesting to compare Scarlatti with Purcell, who was his exact contemporary : Purcell was also under Italian influence, and we find in the young Scarlatti many points of resemblance to him, notably in the treatment of harmony—both composers showing a tendency to think polyphonically, though melodiously, and being either indifferent to, or more probably taking a positive pleasure in, the painful dissonances resulting from their unbending logic. But with his appointment as maestro di cappella at Naples, Scarlatti modified his style. Here he was forced to work with the utmost rapidity, and to work for popular success. The fine detail of his earlier work is swept aside ; the curious forms, derived in part from the ground-bass, in which he had once delighted, are abandoned, and he poured forth a long series of operas in which the grace and vigour of his best moments eventually degenerated into insipidity and vulgarity. Three important features characterise this somewhat unfortunate period of his career. The *da capo* aria in ternary form (ABA), though of course not an invention of Scarlatti, is now definitely established as the only type of operatic aria, to the entire exclusion of all other forms. The form of overture known as the ' Italian ' overture was introduced in 1696 for the revival of an earlier opera, ' Dal male il bene,' and, though subject to much development, remains constant in its main outlines to the end of the Metastasio period of Italian opera ; and lastly, the opera ' Olimpia vendicata ' (1686) presents us with the earliest known example of accompanied recitative. From about 1686–96 Scarlatti's operas have a facile grace that is often far removed from triviality ; the operas ' La Statira ' (1690), ' La Rosaura ' (1690) and ' Pirro e Demetrio ' (1694), which was performed in London in an English adaptation in 1708, were deservedly popular in their day, and contain music which has even survived down to our own. About 1697 a change comes over Scarlatti's style, due in all probability to the influence of Giovanni Bononcini, whose 'Trionfo di Camilla' was performed at Naples in that year. Bononcini had a certain genius for airs of a spirited martial type—'L' esperto nocchiero' from 'Astarto' is a good specimen—and no doubt they pleased the court, since they were easy to understand, and even a viceroy could beat time to them. Scarlatti, either on his own initiative or more probably in obedience to orders from above, set to work on the same lines, and from 1697–1702 turned out a number of inferior operas, full of airs that are either sugary and cloying or pompous and stilted. Their only redeeming features, as a rule, are the comic scenes, which are trivial but certainly humorous. Of this phase 'Eraclea' (1700) and 'Laodicea e Berenice' (1701) are the best examples.

There can be little doubt that Scarlatti's most serious work was being put into the operas which he composed for Ferdinand de' Medici. His letters give a detailed account of the composition of 'Turno Aricino' (1704), 'Lucio Manlio' (1705) and 'Il Gran Tamerlano' (1706). He speaks with enthusiasm of Stampiglia's libretto to the second of these, and appears to have considered the opera the best that he had hitherto composed, although each act was written in a fortnight. The scores of these operas, however, have entirely disappeared, and not even scattered fragments of them can be traced. To what great height he was capable of rising at this stage may be seen in the opera 'Mitridate Eupatore,' composed for Venice in 1707. Although the interest is not equally sustained all through, the work is a very remarkable example of the classical manner at its grandest. The libretto is also remarkable, as depending entirely upon its political interest. There are no love scenes at all; but the devotion of the heroine for her lost brother is expressed with a passionate sincerity that far transcends anything that Scarlatti had written before. J. S. Bach at his best has hardly surpassed the dignified recitative 'O Mitridate mio,' followed by the magnificent aria 'Cara tomba' in Act iv.

With his return to Naples in 1709 Scarlatti entered upon yet another stage of development. The deep poetic intention of 'Mitridate' is indeed seldom apparent; but the experience of former years had given the composer command of every resource, and the honour in which he was held at the Austrian court enabled him to write in a style more worthy of himself. We may regret the loss of that tender charm so characteristic of his early work, but we must admit the wonderful vigour and brilliance of such operas as 'La principessa fedele' (1710), 'Il Ciro' (Rome, 1712), 'Scipione nelle Spagne' (Naples, 1714) and, above all, 'Tigrane' (1715). In these operas we may notice not only the more extended development of the ternary aria

forms, but also an advance towards a more modern treatment of the orchestra. Scarlatti's early operas are generally scored for a band of strings, supported, of course, by the harpsichord and other harmonic instruments, such as the lute, playing from the basso continuo, which in this case we can hardly call the 'figured' bass, since Italian accompanists were so fluent in improvisation that the composer could generally spare himself the trouble of indicating the harmony in the conventional shorthand. To this band are added occasionally trumpets, flutes, oboes and bassoons, not as regular constituents of the orchestra, but treated more as obbligato instruments, with a view to special colour effects. The burden of the accompaniment rested on the harpsichord. Violin-playing was at the close of the 17th century still so primitive that the strings of an opera band could seldom be trusted with the delicate task of supporting a singer. In most cases they enter only to play the final noisy ritornello at the close of an air; sometimes they are given a share in the accompaniment, but treated as a group antiphonal to the harpsichord. Scarlatti, however, was evidently interested in the development of violin-playing, and as time went on he allotted to the strings a more important share of the work, stimulated, no doubt, by the influence of Corelli, who was thought by his contemporaries to be distinguished more as a conductor than as a composer. As early as 'Mitridate Eupatore' (1707) we may observe the tendency to reverse the principle of the earlier work; it is the strings (generally without double-basses) that accompany the voice, and the harpsichord that is reserved to add power and brilliance to the ritornelli. Moreover, Scarlatti's whole outlook becomes gradually less and less aggressively contrapuntal, the harsh dissonances of his boyhood are soon smoothed away, and the general scheme of his musical thought tends more to melody supported by harmony, although he showed to the end of his life that he regarded free counterpoint as the most intellectual style of expression. This point of view naturally influences his instrumentation, and causes his later scores to have much more affinity to the modern style of treating the orchestra.

A fifth and final period is exemplified in the series of operas written for Rome that began with 'Telemaco' and ended with 'Griselda.' Twenty years earlier Scarlatti had bitterly lamented the impossibility of producing operas in the city that had witnessed his first triumphs. But the passion for opera, which had attacked Rome no less than other Italian cities during the baroque period, was too serious to be stifled by the protests of clerical prudery, and Rome now showed him that here at last was an audience which could appreciate the full maturity of the genius which she had been the first to encourage. In these latest operas we see not only the furthest development of technical resource, but also the ripened fruits of emotional experience. Here at last is the whole Scarlatti; here at last he was able to place upon the stage something of that passionate tenderness and serious musical reasoning that he had for so many years brought to utterance only in the intimacy of his chamber cantatas, and exhibit the whole in all the glory of variegated orchestration, lighted up by the blaze of vocal *coloratura*.

Scarlatti has been remembered in modern times chiefly on account of his operas ; but we cannot understand his complete development without a study of his chamber music. The chamber cantata was to the age of Rossi and Scarlatti what the pianoforte sonata or violin sonata was to the age of Beethoven and Brahms —the most intimate and the most intellectual form of music that could be produced. The degraded age of vocal virtuosity had not yet arrived ; the singers were not merely the most agile performers upon the most perfect of instruments, but the most intellectual exponents of the art of music. Scarlatti, the greatest and almost the last of the great writers of chamber cantatas, practised in this form, as Beethoven did in the pianoforte sonata, from his earliest years to that of his death. Over five hundred of his cantatas have come down to us, representing every period of his life, and we may often see that for any given period, as with Beethoven's pianoforte sonatas, they represent the highest intellectual achievement of the moment. It is unfair to judge them by the standard of Schumann's ' Lieder ' ; they are not lyrical outbursts, sacrificing formality to the personal emotion of the poet, much less scenes taken out of operas, as has been suggested, but carefully designed studies in composition, often depending for their main interest on the working out of some interesting problem of modulation or of thematic development. Thus in 1712 he sent Gasparini two settings of the cantata ' Andate o miei sospiri ' which had been set by Gasparini and sent to him by the composer. The first of these two settings is a beautiful specimen of Scarlatti's work at this period ; the second was designed with a view to puzzling his correspondent with the most difficult modulations, both in the recitatives and in the airs. The work is difficult even to the modern reader, but only on account of the terseness of its thought. 'Awkward ' and ' experimental ' are epithets that could hardly ever be applied to Scarlatti, and his music often fails to interest the modern romantic reader because of the absolute mastery with which he solves his problems.

His instrumental chamber music is of less value. It was apparently traditional to treat this branch of art in a more archaic style ; the four ' Sonate a quattro ' (string quartets), and even the twelve symphonies for small orchestra (1715), are more primitive in their methods than the sonatas of Corelli. He composed a certain amount of music for the harpsichord and organ, but it is for the most part straggling and ineffective, interesting only as showing a certain influence on the early work of his son. His best work for the harpsichord is a set of variations on the theme of Corelli's ' Follia.' [1]

As a church composer Scarlatti is not at his best. The story of his having set the Mass two hundred times may be dismissed as a fable. Considering the vast quantity of other music o. his that has survived, it can hardly be believed that as many as 190 masses should have been lost. Quantz is the only authority for this statement, and as he never mentions a single composition of Scarlatti's by name, his information deserves little credit. Of the ten surviving masses, the majority are in the strict style kept up to the end of the 18th century and called ' alla Palestrina,' though breaking gradually away from the manner of its illustrious model. Scarlatti treats discords with more freedom, and occasionally shows a more modern feeling for fugue ; but his strict masses are on the whole uninteresting. Two masses with orchestra are important in the history of modern church music. The first (1707) is somewhat crude and ineffective, but the second (1720) is a worthy ancestor of the great masses of Bach and Beethoven. The miscellaneous church music calls for little comment. Roger of Amsterdam printed a collection of ' Concerti sacri ' (about 1710), characterised by a Jesuitical brilliance which is meretricious, but certainly attractive ; three motets for double choir, ' Tu es Petrus,' ' O magnum mysterium ' and ' Volo, Pater ' (about 1707), are broad and dignified ; the little ' Laetatus sum ' for four voices (printed by Proske) is a model of counterpoint in Leo's manner. The oratorios and secular serenatas are of very varying value, and show the same sort of tendencies as the operas. (See ORATORIO.)

Mention must also be made of Scarlatti as a teacher. The *Regole per principianti*, a MS. treatise on accompaniment, is of interest, as showing that its author was always liberal in his views on the theory of his art. He allows various harmonies (*e.g.* the use of a second inversion of a dominant seventh) which his contemporaries did not, admitting that not everybody would agree with him, but defending himself on the principle that such progressions sound well. To what extent he taught at Naples is not clear. The tendency of modern research is to indicate that the

[1] Modern edition by Aless. Longo, published by Ricordi.

younger generation of composers at Naples were trained for the most part by Nicola Fago and Gaetano Greco ; Hasse seems to have been almost the only one who came into intimate relations with him. His frequent absence from Naples must have been a serious interruption to teaching work, and in his latter years he was evidently quite forgotten by the Neapolitan public.

Nevertheless, Alessandro Scarlatti must certainly be regarded as the founder of the Neapolitan school of the 18th century. He was, of course, not the first teacher nor the first opera composer that appeared in Naples ; but Provenzale, a man far inferior to his Venetian and Roman contemporaries, was much too insignificant to be the leader of a new movement. The real celebrity of Naples as an operatic centre dated from Scarlatti's appointment in 1683, and the long series of his operas performed there from 1683–1702, and from 1709–1719, during which periods he almost monopolised the stage of S. Bartolomeo, caused his artistic influence to be paramount there. But the unfortunate, though natural, consequence was that the younger generation of composers imitated him not at his ripest but at his most successful phase, so that, in spite of the earnest effort of Leo, the later Italian opera proceeded rapidly to that state of decadence against which Gluck finally led the reaction. For this reason Scarlatti has too often been represented as the first composer who took the downward step towards empty formalism and the prostitution of opera to the vanity of singers. This is gross injustice. We may regret that adverse circumstances compelled him to produce much that was unworthy of his best ideals ; but the mass of chamber cantatas and the later operas show him to have been a thoroughly intellectual musician, a complete master of form in its minutest details, who made as severe demands upon the brains of his interpreters as upon their technical powers.

Scarlatti indeed is the founder of that musical language which has served the classical composers for the expression of their thoughts down to the close of the Viennese period. Thematic development, balance of melodic phrase, chromatic harmony—all the devices which the 17th century had tentatively introduced, are by him woven into a smooth and supple texture, which reached its perfection in one who, although he never knew his true master, was yet his best pupil—Mozart.

E. J. D.

BIBL.—E. J. DENT, *Alessandro Scarlatti, his Life and Works* (London, 1905) ; CHARLES VAN DEN BORREN, *Alessandro Scarlatti et l'esthétique de l'opéra napolitaine* (Brussels, 1922) 14 pp. only ; ULISSE PROTA-GIURLEO, *Alessandro Scarlatti 'il Palermitano'* (Naples, 1926).

(2) FRANCESCO (*b.* ? Palermo, 1668), a brother of Alessandro, spent his early life at Naples, where he became violinist in the royal band in 1684. He married Rosalina

Albano in 1690, and in 1691 obtained leave to go to Palermo. He was in Vienna in 1715 and applied without success for the post of vice-Kapellmeister, in spite of the support of Fux. He was on the staff of the Royal Chapel in Naples again in 1719, but shortly afterwards came to London, where he gave a concert mainly of his own compositions, in Sept. 1720, at Hickford's Room. A Mass and Dixit Dominus by him, *a* 16, are in the Bodleian Library, dated 1702 and 1703 respectively. A Miserere *a* 5 is in the court library at Vienna, and some opera airs and cantatas in the Fitzwilliam Museum, Cambridge, and elsewhere. (See *Q.-L.*) E. J. D.

(3) GIUSEPPE DOMENICO (*b.* Naples, Oct. 26, 1685 ; *d.* there, 1757), son of Alessandro, first learned from his father, and later from Gasparini. He has been called a pupil of Bernardo Pasquini, but that seems most improbable, seeing that Pasquini was of the school of Palestrina, and wrote entirely in the contrapuntal style, whereas Domenico Scarlatti's chief interest is that he was the first composer who studied the peculiar characteristics of the free style of the harpsichord. Shedlock's suggestion that he was taught, or at least largely influenced, by Gaetano Greco is far more likely. His bold style was by no means appreciated in Italy, for Burney remarks[1] that the harpsichord was so little played that it had not affected the organ, which was still played in the grand old traditional style. The first work on which Domenico is known to have been engaged was that of remodelling for Naples, in 1704, Polaroli's opera 'Irene' (Venice, 1695). At Naples Alessandro wrote to Ferdinand de' Medici on May 30, 1705 :

'His talent found scope indeed, but it was not the sort of talent for that place. I send him away from Rome also, since Rome has no roof to shelter music that lives here in beggary. This son of mine is an eagle whose wings are grown ; he ought not to stay idle in the nest, and I ought not to hinder his flight. Since the *virtuoso* Nicolino, of Naples, is passing through Rome on his way to Venice, I have thought fit to send Domenico with him ; and under the sole escort of his own artistic ability (which has made great progress since he was able to be with me and enjoy the honour of obeying Your Royal Highness's commands in person, three years ago), he sets forth to meet whatever opportunities may present themselves for making himself known—opportunities for which it is hopeless to wait in Rome nowadays.'

Domenico duly presented himself to the Prince with this letter, which is now in the Medici archives at Florence, and presumably continued his journey with Nicolino, at any rate as far as Venice. In 1708 he was in Venice studying with Gasparini, and making the acquaintance of Handel. Domenico seems to have accompanied Handel to Rome, for Cardinal Ottoboni held a kind of competition between the two, at which the victory was undecided on the harpsichord, but when it came to the organ,

---

[1] *State of Music in France and Italy.*

Scarlatti was the first to acknowledge his rival's superiority, declaring that he had no idea such playing as Handel's existed. The two became fast friends from that day ; they remained together till Handel left Italy, and met again in London in 1720.

In 1709 he entered the service of Marie Casimire, Queen of Poland, and composed for her private theatre in Rome several operas : a *dramma pastorale* ' Sylvia ' (libretto in the Paris Bibliothèque Nationale), which was followed by ' Orlando ' (1711), ' Fatide in Sciro ' (1712), ' Ifigenia in Aulide ' and ' in Tauride ' (1713), ' Amor d' un' ombra ' and ' Narciso ' (1714), and ' Amleto ' (1715, Teatro Capranica), interesting as the first musical setting of that subject. Even in extreme old age Handel spoke with pleasure of D. Scarlatti, and Mainwaring [1] relates that when Scarlatti was in Spain, if his own playing was admired, he would turn the conversation on Handel's, crossing himself at the same time as a sign of his extreme reverence. In Jan. 1715 he succeeded Baj as maestro di cappella of St. Peter's in Rome, where he composed masses, Salve Reginas, etc. On Jan. 28, 1717, he obtained legally, somewhat against his father's wishes, his ' emancipation,' *i.e.* his full legal independence of his father's control. This was probably in view of his journey to London. In 1719 he went to London, where his ' Narciso ' was performed (May 30, 1720), and in 1721 to Lisbon, where he became a court favourite. The longing for home and kindred, however, drove him back to Naples, where Hasse heard him play the harpsichord in 1725.

In 1729 he was invited to the Spanish court, and appointed music-master to the Princess of the Asturias, whom he had formerly taught in Lisbon. Details of the later part of Scarlatti's life are curiously few, but a visit to Dublin [2] in the autumn of 1740, made perhaps at the suggestion of T. Roseingrave who had been in Italy, has been established. Two benefit concerts were arranged for him there early in 1741, and the fact that he contributed songs to two pasticcio operas, ' Alessandro in Persio ' and ' Merope,' in London, 1741 – 42, marks his return. According to the *Gazetta musicale* of Naples (Sept. 15, 1838) he returned to Naples in 1754, and died there in 1757. Being an inveterate gambler he left his family in great destitution, but Farinelli came to their assistance.[3]

As we have said, Scarlatti was in some sense the founder of modern execution, and his influence may be traced in Mendelssohn, Liszt and many other masters of the modern school. He made great use of the crossing of the hands, and produced entirely new effects by this means. His pieces, unlike the suites of Handel and his

predecessors, were all short. Santini possessed 349 of them. Of these Scarlatti himself only published one book of thirty pieces, entitled ' Esercizii per gravicembalo,' etc., printed according to Burney in Venice, but at any rate before Aug. 1746, when the Prince of the Asturias, whose name is on the title-page, ascended the throne. In the Fétis collection is a Paris edition, ' Pièces pour le clavecin,' two vols., published by Mme. Boivin (*d.* Sept. 1733) and Le Clerc.[4] ' 42 Suits [5] of Lessons ' were printed by John Johnson (at the Harp and Crown, Cheapside), London, under the supervision of Scarlatti's friend Roseingrave (between 1730 and 1737, when Roseingrave went out of his mind). In 1752 John Worgan obtained the sole licence to print certain new works by Domenico Scarlatti, and published them (at J. Johnson's, facing Bow Church, Cheapside). These were twelve sonatas, most of them new to England. Czerny's edition (Haslinger, Vienna, 1839), containing 200 pieces, was re-edited (Paris, Sauer, Girod) and revised by Mme. Farrenc from Roseingrave's edition and MSS. then in possession of Rimbault. There are also 130 pieces in Farrenc's ' Trésor des pianistes ' (1864); sixty sonatas are published by Breitkopf ; and eighteen pieces, grouped as Suites by von Bülow, by Peters, and an edition of ' Esercizi per gravicembalo ' by Paul Dukas. Tausig arranged several of the sonatas to suit the requirements of modern pianists, but the greatest boon to lovers of Domenico Scarlatti is the publication of a complete edition of his sonatas by Ricordi under the editorship of Alessandro Longo. Besides these famous works and the operas, among which last are to be included contributions to various pasticcios, Domenico Scarlatti wrote a Stabat Mater for ten voices and organ, and a Salve Regina for a single voice, stated to be his last composition.

F. G. ; addns. E. J. D., etc.

(4) PIETRO FILIPPO (*b.* Rome, Jan. 5, 1679 ; *d.* Naples, Feb. 22, 1750), eldest son of Alessandro, appears to have studied in Rome along with his brother Domenico. He returned with his father to Naples in 1708, being then married to Vittoria Glieri and father of two sons. Cardinal Grimani, the viceroy, gave him the post of supernumerary organist in the Royal Chapel, and he succeeded Vignola as organist in 1712. He seems to have inherited little of his father's ability, for in 1744 he applied for the post of maestro di cappella on the death of Leo and was refused it. He left his children badly off. After his death the three, Domenico, Alessandro and Anna, presented a petition to the King that Alessandro might be appointed to succeed his father, but it was not granted. A sum of 30 ducats was granted to Anna in

1 *Memoirs*, p. 61.
2 Sacchi's *Vita di Don Carlo Broschi*.
3 See notes from W. H. G. F. *Mus. Ant.* i. 178.

4 No. 10 in vol. ii. is an organ fugue by Alessandro Scarlatti.
5 Which are not ' Suites,' but single movements.

1753, in consideration of her extreme destitution. She died Feb. 7, 1779, and was buried by charity.                          E. J. D.

(5) TOMMASO, brother of Alessandro (b. Palermo, c. 1670; d. Naples, Aug. 1, 1760), entered the Conservatorio di S. Onofrio at the age of 10, and became a tenor singer. He sang the comic parts in several of his brother's operas. He married Antonia Carbone in 1701 and had ten children, of whom the youngest was

(6) GIUSEPPE (b. Naples, June 18, 1723; d. Vienna, Aug. 17, 1777), nephew, therefore, not grandson, as has been formerly stated, of Alessandro. At one time he seems to have been maestro at Pavia, and in the text-book of 'I portentosi effetti,' revived at Berlin in 1763, he is styled maestro di cappella in Naples. He settled in Vienna in 1757, before which date he had produced the following operas: 'Merope,' Rome, 1740 (repeated at Naples, 1755); 'Dario,' Turin, 1741; 'Pompeo in Armenio,' Rome, 1747; 'Adriano in Siria,' Naples, 1752; 'Ezio,' Naples, 1754; 'I portentosi effetti della natura,' Venice, 1754; 'Antigone,' Milan, 1756; 'Chi tutto abbraccia nulla stringe,' Venice, 1756. In Vienna he brought out at the court theatre: 'Il mercato di malmantile' and 'L' isola disabitata,' 1757; 'La serva scaltra,' 1759; 'Issipile' and 'La clemenza di Tito,' 1760; 'Artaserse,' 1763; 'Li stravaganti,' 1765; 'La moglie padrona,' 1768. (See Q.-L.)     C. F. P.; rev. E. J. D.

SCENA (Gr. Σκηνή; Lat. scena; Ital. scena, teatro, palco; Fr. scène, théâtre; Eng. scene, stage; Ger. Bühne, Auftritt), a term which, in its oldest and fullest significance, applies equally to the stage, to the scenery it represents, and to the dramatic action which takes place upon it. Hence the long array of synonyms placed at the beginning of this article.

(1) Classical authors most frequently use the word in its first sense, as applying to that part of a Greek or Roman theatre which most nearly answers to what we should now call the stage; and the classical tendencies of the Renaissance movement led to its similar use in the 16th century.

(2) In its second sense the word is commonly applied, in England, to those divisions of a drama which are marked by an actual change of scenery; a method of arrangement which is even extended to English translations of foreign works.

(3) In the Italian, German and French theatres the word is more frequently used, in its third sense, to designate those subordinate divisions of an act [1] which are marked by the entrance or exit of one or more members of the 'Dramatis Personae,' a new scene being always added to the list when a new character

appears upon or quits the stage, though it be only a messenger with half a dozen words to say or sing.                          W. S. R.

(4) In a more limited sense the term scena is applied to an operatic movement generally, though not always, for solo voices which differs from the ordinary recitative and aria by its dramatic rather than lyrical or reflective character. In the older types it consisted of accompanied recitative, either interspersed with passages of rhythmic melody or followed by a regular aria. In the former case the word was generally used alone—and always in its Italian form: in the latter the composition was sometimes called 'scena ed aria.' (See OPERA.)

In later operatic developments the differentiation between lyrical and dramatic expression has become less marked in a formal sense, while the tendency to avoid soliloquy has naturally limited the introduction of moments to which the term scena might be properly applied.

Besides the operatic scena, notable examples of which are to be found in Mozart ('Fidelio') and Weber, the term is also applied to certain detached movements of Mozart, to Beethoven's 'Ah! perfido' and Mendelssohn's 'Infelice.' Spohr used the title 'scena cantante' for a work for violin and orchestra.

SCENARIO, an Italian term meaning a preliminary sketch of the scenes and main points of an opera libretto.                          G.

SCHABLONE, the German term for a stencil or pattern, and thence in musical criticism applied to music written with too much adherence to mechanical form or manner, whether the composer's own or some one else's—made on a cut-and-dried pattern. The term Kapellmeister-Musik is used by the German critics for a similar thing. With a slightly different metaphor we should say, 'cast in the same mould.'                          G.

SCHACK (Žak), BENEDICT (b. Mirovice, Bohemia, 1758; d. Munich, 1826), the first Tamino, and one of the party [2] who stood round Mozart's bed the night before his death, and at his request sang the completed portions of the Requiem as far as the first bars of the 'Lacrimosa,' when he broke into violent weeping at the thought that he should never finish it. Schack was a man of general cultivation, a thorough musician and a good flute-player. He composed several operas for Schikaneder's theatre. Mozart was on intimate terms with him, and would often come and fetch him for a walk, and, while waiting for Schack to dress, would sit down at his desk and touch up his scores. Schack's voice was a fine tenor, flexible and sonorous, and his execution thoroughly artistic, but he was a poor actor.[3] In 1787 he was taking second parts only; in 1792 he sang Tamino, Count Almaviva and Don Ottavio

---

[1] Ital. atto; Fr. acte; Ger. Aufzug—in allusion to the raising of the curtain.

[2] The others were Mozart's brother-in-law, Hofer, the violinist, and Franz Xaver Gerl, a bass singer, and the first Sarastro. Mozart himself sang the alto.     [3] Jahn's Mozart, ii. p. 510.

(Don Gonsalvo in the German translation), after which we hear no more of him as a singer. In 1780 he was Kapellmeister to a nobleman, and in 1805 retired on a pension. A Mass by him was finished by Mozart.[1] His operas or Singspiele came between 1789 and 1793 ; some were written with Gerl.[2]        C. F. P.

SCHADE (SCHADAEUS), ABRAHAM (b. Senftenberg), studied at Leipzig in 1564; was cantor at Torgau, 1613–14, and afterwards at Bautzen, where he became rector, and retired in 1617. He edited the famous collection of motets in 4 volumes, ' Promptuarium musicum,' of which a detailed account appears in Eitner's Bibliographie, p. 251.        E. v. d. s.

SCHÄFER, DIRK (b. Rotterdam, Nov. 5, 1873), pianist and composer. He was a pupil at the Cologne Conservatoire, 1891–94 ; he won in 1894 the Mendelssohn Prize in Berlin ; he then came to The Hague and moved in 1904 to Amsterdam. Amongst his compositions the most notable are his chamber works. They include a piano quintet, a string quartet and several violin sonatas. He has written for orchestra a ' Suite pastorale ' and a ' Javaansche Rapsodie.' In his own country Schäfer is acclaimed as a fine pianist.        R. MᶜG.

SCHAEFFER, PAUL, town musician in Gora from 1617 to c. 1620 and from 1621 at Breslau, where he still was in 1645. Between 1617 and 1626 he composed 8 volumes of sacred and secular music, including 1 book of 4-part dance tunes (1622).        E. v. d. s.

SCHAFFRATH, CHRISTOPH (b. Hohenstein, near Dresden, 1709 ; d. Berlin, Feb. 17, 1763), a famous harpsichord player, and composer of distinct merit. In 1733 he was in the service of the Polish Prince Sangusko. He competed unsuccessfully with Wilhelm Friedemann Bach for the post of organist at the Sophienkirche, Dresden. In 1735 he became chamber musician to the Crown Prince of Prussia, on whose accession to the throne as Frederic II. (the Great) he remained attached to the court, and was afterwards musician to Princess Amalia. He composed symphonies, overtures, concertos for harpsichord and for violin, and a large amount of chamber music of every kind. (List in Q.-L.)        E. v. d. s.

SCHAFHAEUTL, KARL FRANZ EMIL (b. Ingolstadt, Feb. 16, 1803 ; d. Munich, Feb. 25, 1890), a scientist who made valuable researches in acoustics (see Riemann, 1923). (See BELLY ; SOUNDBOARD.)

SCHALE, see CYMBALS.

SCHALE, CHRISTIAN FRIEDRICH (b. Brandenburg, 1713 ; d. Berlin, Mar. 2, 1800), an excellent violoncellist, organist, and distinguished composer of songs and instrumental music. He was a pupil of Christ. E. Rôlle.

In 1742 he was royal chamber virtuoso, organist of Berlin Cathedral (Dom) in 1764, and in 1749 he founded with others the first amateur concert at Berlin, ' Die musikausübende Gesellschaft,' at the house of the then cathedral organist, Sack. Burney made his acquaintance at Berlin. (For list of works, see Q.-L.)        E. v. d. s.

SCHALK, FRANZ (b. Vienna, May 27, 1863), conductor, was a pupil of Anton Bruckner, and had gained a lengthy and varied experience, chiefly in Vienna, before succeeding Ferdinand Löwe as chief conductor at the Hofoper in that city. He paid two visits to London, namely, during the winter of 1907 and the autumn of 1911, both short German seasons at Covent Garden. During the latter, when he was sole conductor, he earned unqualified commendation by his artistic direction of ' Der Ring ' (three cycles) and a finished production of Humperdinck's ' Königskinder.' After the war (1914–18) he had Richard Strauss for some years as his associate at the Vienna Imperial Opera ; but differences arose between them and reached an acute stage in 1924, when Strauss ultimately resigned and left his colleague in sole control. (See VIENNA.)        H. K.

SCHALMEI, see SHAWM.

SCHARWENKA, (1) LUDWIG PHILIPP (b. Samter, near Posen, East Prussia, Feb. 16, 1847 ; d. July 16, 1917). His father was an architect in Samter. His taste for music showed itself early, but he was unable to cultivate it seriously till the removal of his family to Berlin in 1865, when he entered Kullak's ' New Academy,' studying under Wüerst and Heinrich Dorn, having previously completed his studies at the Gymnasium in Posen, where his parents settled in 1859. On completing his course at the Academy he remained on the staff as a teacher of theory till 1881, when he became teacher of composition at his brother's newly opened Conservatorium, the direction of which he undertook with Hugo Goldschmidt on his brother's emigration to America in 1891. In 1880 he married the well-known violinist Marianne Stresow (d. Oct. 24, 1918). Besides having made a good name for himself with a long list of interesting compositions, Scharwenka was an accomplished caricaturist.

The compositions of Philipp Scharwenka include a vast number of piano pieces—Ländler, waltzes, minuets, mazurkas, etc.—of which ' Album polonais ' (op. 33) is best known, many songs, three concert pieces for violin and PF. (op. 17), studies for violin, studies for violoncello, three sonatas for pianoforte (op. 61) ; two choral works with soli and orchestra, ' Herbstfeier ' (op. 44) and ' Sakuntala ' ; a choral work with pianoforte accompaniment ad lib.,' Dörpertanzweise ' ; a PF. trio in C♯ minor (op. 100) ; and some orchestral works, two symphonies, a Serenade (op. 19), a Fantasiestück ' Liebes-

---

[1] See the Harmonicon, vol. ix. p. 298.
[2] Gerl sang ' Osmin ' in 1797 at the same theatre in the Freihaus, where was produced in 1797 his comic opera in three acts, ' Die Maskerade,' by ' a former member of this theatre.'

nacht,' a Festival Overture (op. 43), an 'Arcadian Suite' (op. 76), Symphonic Poems, 'Frühlingswogen' (op. 87), 'Traum und Wirklichkeit' (op. 92), a Violin Concerto (op. 95) and Symphonia Brevis in E flat (op. 115).

H. V. H.

His brother, (2) FRANZ XAVER (*b.* Samter, Jan. 6, 1850 ; *d.* Berlin, Dec. 8, 1924), pianist and composer, was, like his brother, at Kullak's Academy in Berlin, where he was well known, while still a pupil, for his PF. playing and composition, which he studied under Kullak and Wüerst respectively. He made his first appearance in public in Berlin at the Singakademie in 1869, and remained for some time at Kullak's as a teacher, until compelled to leave it for his military duties in 1873. After this he began to travel, and was soon renowned as a fine and brilliant player, and a ' young composer of remarkable endowments.' In 1877 he produced his first concerto for the PF. (in B♭ minor, op. 32), playing it to the meeting of German musicians at Hanover in May ; it was played in England for the first time by Edward Dannreuther at the Crystal Palace, Oct. 27, 1877. In 1878, Feb. 14, Scharwenka himself played it at the Gewandhaus, Leipzig. In 1879 he made his first appearance in England, playing the same work at the Crystal Palace, Mar. 1, and played at the Musical Union, Apr. 29. In 1880 he returned and played his B♭ minor concerto at the Philharmonic, Feb. 19, and the Beethoven E♭ concerto on June 9. In 1881 he made a third visit and played his second concerto (in C minor, op. 56), which he had produced at the Gesellschaftskonzert at Vienna, Feb. 24 ; but his stay was shortened by his recall to Germany for his military duties, though he found time to appear several times, and deepened the favourable impression he had previously made. In 1899 he made another visit to England and played his third concerto (C♯ minor, op. 80).

On Oct. 1, 1881, Scharwenka opened his own Conservatorium in Berlin (staff including his brother Philipp's wife, *née* Marianne Stresow, Albert Becker, Philipp Rüfer, J. Kotek, O. Lessmann, W. Langhans, M. Röder, W. Jähns, A. Hennes and Philipp Scharwenka), which became amalgamated with that of Klindworth in 1893, subsequently known as the Klindworth-Scharwenka Conservatorium (and School for Opera and Drama), and run under the artistic direction of the brothers Scharwenka and Kapellmeister Robitschek and the administration of the latter, with Xaver Scharwenka as principal.

In 1891, answering a call to found and direct a branch of his Conservatorium in New York, Xaver Scharwenka, his wife and family, with all their belongings, emigrated to the States, where they remained seven years ; he, however, crossing to Europe and back no less than seven times during that period. In the New World he

made numerous tours, and to his astonishment discovered that in the West he had already earned a reputation as a pianist through a former pupil of his brother, who had adopted his name and given concerts for two years without his identity being discovered. He toured in America as late as 1914. In that year he left the Klindworth - Scharwenka Conservatorium to found a school of his own in Berlin.

As a pianist Xaver Scharwenka was renowned above all his other qualifications for the beautiful quality of his tone. If he was a specialist as interpreter of one composer rather than another it was of Chopin, whose nationality he partly shared, but of the other great masters his readings were always grand and musicianly, while to hear him play a waltz of Strauss was as dance-inspiring as the magic bells of Papageno. His compositions, which possess energy, harmonic interest, strong rhythm, many beautiful melodies and much Polish national character, include a symphony in C minor (op. 60) ; four PF. concertos in B♭ minor, C minor, C♯ minor and F minor (opp. 32, 56, 80 and 82) ; two PF. trios in F♯ minor and A minor (opp. 1 and 42) ; two v'cello sonatas in D minor and E minor (opp. 2 and 46) ; a PF. quartet in F (op. 37) ; two PF. sonatas in C♯ minor and E♭ (opp. 6 and 36) ; very many piano pieces, mostly Polish dances, but also a scherzo in G, a ballade (op. 8), a concert menuet in B (op. 18), a theme and variations, studies and some songs, besides some books of technical exercises of great value to the pianist (*Methodik des Klavierspiels*, 1908). An opera without opus number, in 4 acts, to a libretto by Dr. Ernst Koppel, 'Mataswintha' (from the novel of Felix Dahn, *Ein Kampf um Rom*), was produced at Weimar, Oct. 4, 1896, under Stavenhagen, and at the Metropolitan Opera House, New York, Apr. 1, 1897, under the composer's direction.

Xaver Scharwenka was Royal Professor, Imperial and Royal ' Kammervirtuos,' ordinary member and senator of the Royal Prussian Academy of Arts, president of the ' Musik pädagogische ' Association, Doctor of Music (America), and bore the title of Ritter hoher Orden. He published *Klänge aus meinem Leben. Erinnerungen eines Musikers* (Leipzig, 1922).

H. V. H.

SCHAUSPIELDIREKTOR, DER, 'Comödie mit Musik in 1 Act,' containing an overture and four numbers ; words by Stephanie, jun., music by Mozart. Produced at a court festival at Schönbrunn, Feb. 7, 1786. Over the terzet (No. 3) is the date Jan. 18, 1786. It was adapted to a French libretto by Léon Battu and Ludovic Halévy under the name of ' L' impresario,' and produced in Paris, Bouffes-Parisiens, May 20, 1856. A careful version of the entire piece from the German original, by W. Grist, was brought out at the Crystal Palace, London, on Sept. 14, 1877, as ' The Manager.'  G.

SCHEBEK, EDMUND (*b.* Petersdorf, Moravia, Oct. 22, 1819; *d.* Prague, Feb. 11, 1895), a distinguished and influential Austrian amateur, Doctor of Law, imperial councillor and secretary to the Chamber of Commerce at Prague. He began his musical career as head of a society at Olmütz, and continued it at Prague, where, in conjunction with Weiss, the superior of the Capuchins, and Krejci he revived much of the best old Italian church music. He devoted his attention specially to the construction of the violin, in relation to which he published very interesting treatises—*On the Orchestral Instruments in the Paris Exhibition of 1855* [1]; *On the Cremonese Instruments, à propos of the Vienna Exhibition of 1873*, and *The Italian Violin Manufacture and its German Origin.*[2] He also published a valuable little pamphlet on Froberger (1874). Dr. Schebek possessed a fine collection of ancient stringed instruments, Beethoven autographs, etc.       G.

SCHEBEST, AGNES (*b.* Vienna, Feb. 15, 1813; *d.* Stuttgart, Dec. 22, 1869), became attached at a very early age to the court theatre at Dresden, first in the chorus, and then as singer of small solo parts. Here she had the inestimable advantage of frequently hearing and seeing the great Schroeder-Devrient. In 1833 she left Dresden for Pest, and from 1836–41 starred throughout Germany with very great applause. Her voice was a fine mezzo-soprano; her style and method were good, her best parts heroic, with much energy and passion. In 1841 she married the great theologian Dr. David Strauss (himself a keen amateur, and author of an interesting paper on Beethoven's ninth symphony). She left an account of her career—*Aus dem Leben einer Künstlerin* (1857), and *Rede und Gebärde* (1862).       G.

SCHECHNER-WAAGEN, NANETTE (*b.* Munich, 1806; *d.* Apr. 30, 1860), dramatic singer. She was employed in the opera at Munich in a minor capacity, and, on the occasion of Madame Grassini's visit, was chosen to second her in some selections from Cimarosa's 'Gli Orazii e Curiazii.' Schechner's beautiful voice made a great impression, and won for her a patroness in the Queen of Bavaria. After some study in singing and in Italian, she appeared in Italian opera in Munich until 1827, after which she devoted herself to German opera. In 1826 she was in Vienna, if a curious story, related by Schindler, of a scene in the theatre there, apropos of an air written for her by SCHUBERT (*q.v.*), may be believed. It is related by Fétis that, when she first appeared in Berlin in Weigl's 'Schweizerfamilie,' the first act was played to an almost empty house; but such enthusiasm did her Emmeline arouse

in the few listeners, that the report of it spread to the neighbouring cafés during the entr'acte, a large audience was drawn to the theatre for the rest of the performance, and the singer's success was complete. Her Donna Anna, Euryanthe, Fidelio, Reiza, Vestalin and Iphigenie in Tauris excited great admiration in Berlin and Munich. In 1832 she married Waagen, a lithographer and painter. She took a place in the first rank of German singers, but her brilliant career lasted no longer than ten years. A severe illness injured her voice, and she retired from the stage in 1835.

Mendelssohn heard her at Munich in 1830, and while he found her voice much gone off and her intonation false, says. that her expression was still so touching as to make him weep.[3]       L. M. M.

SCHEIBE, JOHANN ADOLPH (*b.* Leipzig, May 1708; *d.* Copenhagen, Apr. 22, 1776), the son of an organ-builder, was educated for the law at the Nikolaischule, and at the University, where Gottsched was at the time professor. In 1735 he set out to try his fortune as a musician, visiting Prague, Gotha, Sondershausen, and settling in 1736 at Hamburg as a teacher. He composed incidental music to various plays, and wrote a grand opera which only reached the stage of being twice rehearsed. In 1737 he began the publication by which he is famous in the history of German opera. *Der critische Musikus*, as it was called, came out as a weekly periodical, and carried further the war against Italian operatic conventions which Gottsched had declared in his *Vernünftigen Tadlerinnen*. In 1740 he was appointed Kapellmeister to the Margrave of Brandenburg - Culmbach, and also visited Copenhagen, where he settled two years later, and in 1742 became director of the court opera, retaining this post till 1749, when he was succeeded by the Italian Sarti. He next devoted himself to literature and composition, becoming for a time head of a music-school at Sonderburg in Holstein. In 1745 he published a second edition of the *Critischer Musikus* (see below), and in 1754 wrote an *Abhandlung vom Ursprung und Alter der Musik*. He contributed a treatise on recitative, in the composition of which he was a proficient, to the *Bibliothek der schönen Wissenschaften und freien Künste* (vols. xi. and xii.), 1764–65. In 1773 appeared the first of four projected volumes on composition, *Über die musikalische Composition*, but no more was finished, as the author died in 1776. Apart from his championship of German opera, he obtained an unenviable notoriety by an attack on Sebastian Bach, published in the sixth number of his periodical, under date May 14, 1737. He had competed for the post of organist to the Nikolaikirche in 1729, and Bach, one of the judges, had not

1 *Die Orchester-Instrumente auf der Pariser Weltausstellung im Jahre 1855* (Vienna, Staatsdrückerel, 1858).
2 *Der Geigenbau in Italien und sein deutscher Ursprung* (Vienna, 1872 and 1874).
3 Letter, June 6, 1836.

approved his playing; furthermore, it seems probable that Bach, in his cantata 'Der Streit zwischen Phöbus und Pan,' had intended the character of Midas as a reference to Scheibe. It is only fair to say that Scheibe recanted his errors in the second edition of the *Critischer Musikus*, issued in 1745. Scheibe wrote an opera, 'Thusnelda,' which was published (with an introductory article on vocal music) at Copenhagen in 1749; two oratorios, 'Die Auferstehung' and 'Der wundervolle Tod des Welterlösers'; masses, secular cantatas, church compositions to the number of 200; 150 flute concertos; 70 quartets or symphonies, trios, sonatas, existed, for the most part in MS.

BIBL.—*Q.-L.*; *Riemann*: *Sammelbände* of the Int. Mus. Ges. ii. 654 f. SPITTA, *J. S. Bach* (Eng. trans.), ii. 645-7, iii. 522-5.

M.

SCHEIBLER, JOHANN HEINRICH (*b.* Montjoie, near Aix-la-Chapelle, Nov. 11, 1777; *d.* Nov. 20, 1838), a silk manufacturer who, after many travels, settled down at Crefeld, where he was first-assistant Bürgermeister. He made some interesting experiments with JEW'S-HARPS (*q.v.*), and in 1812–13 turned his attention to the imperfections of existing means of tuning. He first tried a monochord, but finding that he could not always get the same note from the same division of his monochord, he endeavoured to help himself by beats, and discovered that each beat corresponded to a difference of two simple vibrations or one double vibration in a second. His plan was to fix the monochord by finding the stopped length which would give a note beating four times in a second with his own fork. Then, after endless trials and calculations, he found similar places for all the divisions of the scale, and finally from the monochord made forks for each note of the equally tempered scale. By repeated comparisons with his forks he found that it was impossible to make a mathematically accurate monochord, or to protect it from the effects of temperature. He then hit upon the plan of inserting forks between the forks of his scale, from the lowest A of the violin to the open A, and counting the beats between them. It was this counting that was the trouble, but by highly ingenious mechanical contrivances he was enabled to complete the count of his fifty-two forks within from ·0067 to ·00083 beats or double vibrations in a second, and hence to tune a set of twelve forks so as to form a perfectly equal scale for any given pitch of A. The particulars of his forks and the mode of counting them are contained in his little pamphlet *Der physikalische und musikalische Tonmesser* (Essen, Bädeker, 1834, p. 80, with lithographic plates),[1] from which the preceding history has been gathered. During his life-

[1] *The physical and musical Tonometer, which proves visibly, by means of the pendulum, the absolute numbers of vibrations of musical tones, the principal kinds of combinational tones, and the most rigid exactness of equally tempered and mathematical just chords.*

time he issued four smaller tracts, showing how to tune organs by beats, which were collected after his death as *H. Scheibler's Schriften*, etc. (Crefeld, Schmüller, 1838). These pamphlets form part of the interesting bequest left to A. J. Hipkins by A. J. Ellis, and have since completed Hipkins's gift to the Royal Institution in memory of his friend Dr. Ellis Scheibler's wonderful tonometer of fifty-two forks has completely disappeared. But another one, of fifty-six instead of fifty-two forks, which belonged to Scheibler, still exists, and was inherited by his daughter and grandson, who lent it to Amels, formerly of Crefeld, who again lent it to A. J. Ellis, who counted it and, having checked his results by means of M'Leod's and Mayer's machines for measuring pitch, gave the value of each fork in the *Journal of the Society of Arts* for Mar. 5, 1880, p. 300, correct to less than one-tenth of a double vibration. The two extreme forks of this fifty-six-fork tonometer agree in pitch precisely with those of the fifty-two-fork tonometer; but no other forks are alike, nor could the forks of the fifty-two-fork tonometer have been easily converted into those of the other one. In 1834, at a congress of physicists at Stuttgart, Scheibler proposed with approval the pitch A 440 at 69° F. (=A 440·2 at 59° F.) for general purposes, and this has been consequently called the Stuttgart pitch.[2] (Cf. PITCH.)   A. J. H.

SCHEIDEMANN, the name of a family of organists in Hamburg in the 16th and 17th centuries. (1) DAVID, probably an uncle of (2) HEINRICH, was in 1585 organist of St. Michael's Church, Hamburg. He is chiefly noteworthy as associated with three other Hamburg organists of repute, Jacob and Hieronymus Praetorius and Joachim Decker, in the compilation of what we should now call a Choralbuch, though this name was not in general use then,[3] a book of the usual hymn tunes or Chorals of the Lutheran Church, simply harmonised in four parts for congregational singing. This book appeared in 1604. Its original title is:

'Melodeyen-Gesangbuch, darein Dr. Luthers und ander Christen gebräuchlichste Gesänge, ihren gewöhnlichen Melodien nach . . . in vier Stimmen übergesetzt.'

The example first set by Lucas Osiander, in 1586, of uniformly giving the melody to the

[2] He selected it as the mean of the variation of pitch in pianos as then tuned at Vienna, and not from the fact that it enables the scale of C major, in just intonation, to be expressed in whole numbers, as has been sometimes said.

[3] It is worth while noting that the word Choral (in English usually spelt Chorale), as now restricted to the melodies of German metrical hymns, really originated in a misunderstanding of what Walther meant when he spoke of Luther as having called the 'deutscher Choralgesang' into life. What both Luther and Walther meant by 'Choralgesang' was the old cantus choralis or plain-song of the Latin Church, which Luther himself wished to retain; and his merit consisted in the adaptation of the chief parts of the Latin Choral to German words, his work in this respect corresponding to Merbecke's 'Book of Common Prayer Noted' with us in England. All the older Lutheran church musicians, such as Lucas Lossius and Michael Praetorius, used the words Choral and Choralgesänge in this sense of the old plain-song melodies to the graduals, sequences and antiphons, whether sung to Latin or adapted to German words. It was only when German metrical hymns gradually superseded in common use the other choral parts of the service, that the name Choral in course of time became restricted to the melodies of these hymns. See Winterfeld, *Ev. Kirch.* i. pp. 151, 152.

soprano part and not to the tenor, as the older practice was, is here followed, and in the preface attention is called to the greater convenience of this for congregational singing. Of the eighty-eight tunes in the book, David Scheidemann harmonised thirteen or fourteen ; among them there appears for the first time harmonised ' Wie schön leuchtet der Morgenstern.' Gerber, confusing David with Heinrich, attributes both the melody and the setting of this Choral to Heinrich. But Winterfeld shows (*Ev. Kirch.* i. p. 90) that the melody belongs to neither, but seems to be taken from an old secular song beginning with similar words (' Wie schön leuchten die Äugelein '), to the metre of which Philip Nicolai in 1599 wrote the words of his hymn ' Wie schön leuchtet der Morgenstern.' It should be mentioned, however, that Wackernagel (*Das deutsche Kirchenlied*, Bd. i. pp. 618-19), after giving the words of the secular song in full, adduces reasons for believing that in this case the secular song is a later parody of Nicolai's hymn, not *vice versa*. Winterfeld praises Scheidemann's settings of the Chorals for their fresh animated character, and for the happy way in which the rhythmical peculiarities of the old melodies are brought out. Chorals were not then sung as now, all in slow uniform rhythm, but many of the older melodies had curious changes of rhythm, as from common to triple time, in successive lines. (See the specimens of Scheidemann in Winterfeld, Part i. Nos. 70, 71.)

(2) HEINRICH (*b. circa* 1596; *d.* 1654 [1]) was the son of Hans Scheidemann, organist of St. Catherine's Church, Hamburg, who instructed him in his art until *c.* 1613-14, when the church administrators, recognising his talent, sent him with Jacob Praetorius, the younger, to Amsterdam, to be initiated into a higher style of organ-playing under the tuition of the then most famous organ-player of Europe, Peter Sweelinck. Heinrich succeeded his father on his death in 1625 as organist of St. Catherine's, and became one of the greatest organists of his time. Mattheson says of Scheidemann that his organ-playing and compositions were like himself, popular and agreeable, easy and cheerful, with no pretence or desire for mere show. Some of his organ pieces have been discovered in MS. tablature at Lüneburg, for an estimate of which see Seiffert's *Geschichte der Klaviermusik*, vol. i. pp. 117-19. In 1641 he was called to Lübeck to examine and give his verdict about the new organ. Heinrich Scheidemann was again associated with Jacob Praetorius in contributing melodies to Rist's ' Himmlische Lieder,' which were published in 1641-42. Praetorius composed ten to the 4th

part of Rist's book, Scheidemann ten to the 5th part, entitled ' Höllenlieder.' One of Scheidemann's melodies in this collection, ' Frisch auf und lasst uns singen,' continued for a while in church use, as it appears again in Vopelius's ' Leipziger Gesangbuch ' of 1682. Among Scheidemann's pupils were Werner Fabricius, Matthias Weckmann and Joh. Adam Reincken, the last of whom became his successor as organist of St. Catherine's, Hamburg, in 1654.

J. R. M. ; addns. and corr., E. v. d. S.

SCHEIDEMANTEL, KARL (*b.* Weimar, Jan. 21, 1859; *d.* there, Oct. 1923), was taught singing by Bodo Borchers, and on Sept. 15, 1878, made his début at Weimar as Wolfram. He remained there until 1886, having in the meantime received further instruction from Stockhausen at Frankfort. In 1884, on leave from Weimar, he sang in German at Covent Garden, June 4, as Kothner, as the Minister (' Fidelio '), Herald (' Lohengrin '), Kurwenal, Wolfram and, July 9, Rucello, on the production of Stanford's ' Savonarola.' He made a very favourable impression, both on account of his fine baritone voice and his excellent singing and acting. In 1886 he sang at Bayreuth as Klingsor, Amfortas (a remarkable performance) and Kurwenal ; after which he made his débuts at Dresden as the Dutchman, and the Templar and Hans Heiling of Marschner, as a permanent member of the company there, as successor to Degele, the result of a successful ' Gastspiel ' the previous year. Here he remained till 1911, and gained great popularity in a large number of parts.

On Dec. 12, 1896, he sang with great success as the hero in Bungert's ' Odysseus' Heimkehr,' on Jan. 29, 1898, in ' Kirke,' on Mar. 21, 1901, in ' Nausikaa ' (the second and third parts respectively of the Homeric tetralogy), and on May 21, 1901, in Paderewski's ' Manru,' on the production of that opera. On leave of absence, in 1888, he sang as Hans Sachs at Bayreuth ; in 1893, at the Gotha Opera Festival, as Rodolph in the revival of Boieldieu's ' Petit Chaperon Rouge.' On May 27, 1899, he sang again at Covent Garden, as Hans Sachs a performance remarkable both on account of his fine acting and for the refinement of his singing and declamation. In 1909 he brought out a new edition of ' Così fan tutte ' (' Dame Kobold '), and published *Stimmbildung* (1907) and *Gesangbildung* (1913, Eng. trans. Carlyle).

After his retirement from the Dresden stage he taught for a time at Weimar, and from 1920-1922 he directed the Landesoper at Dresden.

A. C.

SCHEIDT, SAMUEL (*b.* Halle, 1587 ; *d.* there, Mar. 30,[2] 1654), one of the celebrated three S's (the other two being Heinrich Schütz

---

[1] Max Seiffert, in the *Sammelbände* of the Int. Mus. Ges. ii. p. 117, gives the date of Scheidemann's death as 1663, but *Q.L.* gives reasons for adhering to the previously accepted date, 1654, as there is no doubt that Reincken succeeded him in that year.

[2] Entry in church register. *Riemann.*

and Johann Hermann Schein, his contemporaries), was the best German organist of his time.

His father, Conrad Scheidt, was master or overseer of salt-works at Halle. The family must have been musical, as some works are still preserved of Gottfried, Samuel's brother, which A. G. Ritter[1] says show considerable musical ability. Samuel owed his training as an organist to the then famous ' Organistenmacher,' Peter Sweelinck of Amsterdam. About 1605 he betook himself to Amsterdam, and became a pupil of Sweelinck. In 1608 or 1609 he became organist in the Moritzkirche in Halle, and in 1620 at least, if not earlier, he had received the appointment of organist and Kapellmeister to Christian Wilhelm, Markgraf of Brandenburg, and then Protestant administrator of the archbishopric of Magdeburg. In this capacity Scheidt officiated not at Magdeburg but in the Hofkirche at Halle. The troubles of the Thirty Years' War and the misfortunes of his patron, the siege and sack of Magdeburg in 1631, and the abdication of Christian Wilhelm in 1638, seem to have made no difference to Scheidt's official position at Halle, though his income and means of living must have suffered ; the service in the Hofkirche ceased after 1625, and the Moritzkirche was destroyed by fire in 1637. We have no record as to his personal relations with Christian's successors in the administration of the Magdeburg archbishopric, but Chrysander[2] prints a letter from Scheidt to Duke Augustus of Brunswick in 1642, which seems to imply that he was then looking for some patronage or assistance from that art-loving prince. Scheidt never left Halle, however, and his circumstances may have improved, as in his will he bequeathed some money for the sake of the organ in the St. Moritzkirche at Halle.

Scheidt's first published work appeared at Hamburg in 1620 (' Cantiones sacrae octo vocum '), and consists of thirty-nine vocal compositions, fifteen of which are settings of Lutheran Chorals. In 1621–22 appeared the first part of his sacred concertos, in 2-12 vocal parts with instrumental accompaniment. This was followed by successive books of similar pieces, published in 1631, 1634, 1635 and 1640. His fame, however, rests not on his vocal compositions but on his works for the organ. His next work, also published at Hamburg in 1624, is considered epoch-making in the history of organ music. It consists of three parts, but the whole work bears the general title ' Tabulatura nova ' (republished *D.D.T.* vol. i.) ; the same title, indeed, as many earlier works of the same kind in Germany (*e.g.* Ammerbach, 1571 ; B. Schmid, 1577 ; Paix, 1583 ; Woltz,

1617), from all of which, however, it differs widely both in aim and style, and indeed marks the beginning of a new and better treatment of the organ both with regard to playing and to composition. From 1570 to about 1620 organ - playing in Germany almost entirely consisted in what was known as the art of ' coloriren,' the art of ' colouring ' melodies sacred or secular by the inserting of meaningless passages, all framed on one and the same pattern, between each note or chord of the melody. These earlier Tablature-books were all compiled simply to teach this purely mechanical art of ' colouring ' melodies for the organ. The music was written in the so-called German tablature, *i.e.* with letters instead of notes.[3] (For a full account of these German ' Coloristen '[4] of the 16th and 17th centuries, see A. G. Ritter's *Geschichte der Orgelmusik*, pp. 111-39.) Scheidt's ' Tabulatura nova ' put an end to this miserable style of playing and composing for the organ, as well as to the old German tablature. The music in his book is noted in score of four staves, with five lines to the stave, so far differing from the notation both of Frescobaldi and Sweelinck, the former using two staves of six and eight lines respectively, the latter two staves both of six lines. To give an idea of the contents of Scheidt's work, we transcribe in full the separate titles of the three parts :

I. Tabulatura Nova, continens variationes aliquot Psalmorum, Fantasiarum, Cantilenarum, Passamezo et Canones aliquot, in gratiam Organistarum adornata a Samuele Scheidt Hallense, Reverendiss. Illustrissimique Principis ac Domini, Christiani Guilielmi Archiepiscopi Magdeburgensis, Primatis Germaniae Organista et Capellae Magistro. Hamburgi . . . MDCXXIV.
II. Pars Secunda . . . continens Fugarum, Psalmorum, Cantionum et Echus Tocatae variationes varias et omnimodas. Pro quorumvis Organistarum captu et modulo. . . .
III. Tertia et ultima pars, continens Kyrie Dominicale, Credo in unum Deum, Psalmum de Coena Domini sub Communione, Hymnos praecipuorum Festorum totius anni, Magnificat 1–9 toni, modum ludendi pleno Organo et Benedicamus . . . In gratiam Organistarum, praecipue eorum qui musice pure et absque celerrimis coloraturis Organo ludere gaudent . . .

The last words mark an important difference between the third part and the two preceding. In the first two parts the composer appears to wish to show how he could beat the ' Colourists ' on their own ground, his figures and passages, however, not being like theirs, absolutely meaningless and void of invention, but new and varied, and having an organic connexion with the whole composition to which they belong. He shows himself still as virtuoso, desirous to extend the technique of organ-playing, while at the same time displaying his contrapuntal mastery. So far as technique is concerned, there is to be noticed in Scheidt the extended use of the pedal, so different from Frescobaldi's occasional use of it for single notes merely, also the imitation of orchestral effects, such as what he himself terms ' imitatio violistica,' the imitation of the effects of the different ways of bowing on the

---

[1] *Geschichte der Orgelmusik.*
[2] *Jahrbücher für musikalische Wissenschaft,* i. p. 158.

[3] For an example of German organ tablature see Schlecht, *Geschichte der Kirchenmusik,* p. 377 f.
[4] ' Geschmacklose Barbaren ' (tasteless barbarians), as Ambros calls them.

violin, and the imitation of an organ tremulant itself by the rapid interchange of the fingers of the two hands on one and the same key (' Bicinium imitatione tremula organi duobus digitis in una tantum clave manu tum dextra, tum sinistra '). The first two parts contain a mixture of sacred and secular pieces, the secular pieces, however, being marked off as for domestic rather than for church use by the absence of a pedal part. The sacred pieces consist of ten fantasias or sets of variations on Choral melodies, with a few fugues or fantasias on another motive, among which is a ' fantasia fuga quadruplici ' on a madrigal by Palestrina which Ritter describes as a masterpiece of contrapuntal art, four subjects from the madrigal being treated first singly and then together, and with contrary motion and other devices. The secular pieces consist chiefly of variations on secular melodies, among which appears one entitled an English song ' de fortuna ' (i.e. the famous ' Fortune, my foe ').

The third part of the ' Tabulatura nova ' stands, however, on a higher level than the first two. The composer expressly renounces the virtuoso ; he writes, as the title-page says, for those who delight to play the organ purely musically, and without mere ornamental and passage work. In this third part he gives very full directions with regard to registering both for manuals and pedal. It is intended entirely for church use, and both by the choice of pieces and the manner in which they are arranged, it gives us an insight into the way in which the organ was very frequently employed in the church services of those days. It was not then generally used to accompany or sustain the voices of the choir or congregation, but rather to alternate with them. Thus, for instance, between each verse of the Magnificat sung by the choir without accompaniment, the organ would come in independently with some variation or changing harmonies on the plain-song melody. A further use of the organ was even to take the place of the choir in making the responses to the ecclesiastical intonations of the officiating clergy when there was no proper choir to do this. Frescobaldi's works (especially ' Fiori musicali,' 1635) furnish instances of this use of the organ in the Catholic ritual. Thus when the priest had intoned the Kyrie of the Mass, in the absence of a proper choir, the organist would answer, as Ambros [1] expresses it when speaking of Frescobaldi's works of the kind, ' with a kind of artistically ennobling and enriching echo ' (' mit einer Art von künstlerisch-veredelnden und bereichernden Echo '), that is to say, the organist, taking up the plain-song theme, would not just harmonise it note by note, but treat it in the form of a short

[1] See the quotations from Frescobaldi in Ambros's *Geschichte der Musik*, iv. pp. 444-50.

polyphonic composition for the organ. The third part of Scheidt's ' Tabulatura ' shows that this usage was retained for a considerable time in the Lutheran service. It opens with twelve short movements based on the plain-song of the different sections of the Kyrie and Gloria of the Mass, and the remark, or rubric, as we might call it, ' Gloria canit pastor,' shows that they were expressly intended as responses made by the organ to the intonation of officiating clergy. The Magnificat follows, in all the church tones, one verse sung by the ecclesiastic and every alternate verse arranged to be played by the organ in lieu of a choir. This way of treating the Magnificat prevailed in Lutheran churches even up to Pachelbel's time (1706), though the plain-song was more and more put into the background, and the practice became simply an excuse for interludes on any motive. After the Magnificat came a series of hymns common to both Catholic and Lutheran churches, with their plain-song melodies treated in a similar fashion. The book further contains Luther's version of the Creed (' Wir glauben All' an einen Gott ') with its Doric melody, John Huss's Communion Hymn, arranged to be played instead of being sung during Communion. The two last pieces in the book are 6-part movements for the full organ, meant to be played at the end of Vespers. Interwoven with the last is the liturgical melody of the Benedicamus. In all these compositions Scheidt has faithfully adhered to the original plain-song melodies when they appear as cantus firmus, but in the further working-out has not been content simply to harmonise them according to the laws of the church modes, but has so far altered them in accordance with the new ideas of harmony then beginning to make way. But there is still wanting in him a consistent system of modulation. The chromatic semitones are still employed by him rather in a haphazard sort of way.

Twenty-six years later, viz. in 1650, Scheidt published another work for the organ, his second and last, which shows a different conception as to the use of the organ in the services of the Church, and probably marks a change which was then going on gradually in the practice of the Lutheran Church. The congregational singing of metrical hymns was gradually superseding the older liturgical music, and the organ had more and more to surrender its independence to accommodate itself to the simple accompaniment in 4-part harmony of the melodies of these hymns, which now began to assume exclusively the name of Choralmusik. This, which was at first a loss, became in time a gain, as it deepened the sense of the value of harmony for its own sake : and besides, out of this originated the new art form of the Choral-Vorspiel of later days. Scheidt's last organ work was intended to meet the new requirements. Its title sufficiently explains its object :

*'Tabulatur-Buch 100 geistlicher Lieder u. Psalmen D. Martini Lutheri und anderer gottseliger Männer für die Herren Organisten mit der Christlichen Kirchen u. Gemeine auf der Orgel, desgleichen auch zu Hause zu spielen u. zu singen, auf alle Fest- u. Sonn-tage durchs ganze Jahr mit 4 Stimmen componirt ... Gedruckt zu Görlitz ... im 1650 Jahr.'*

This work is dedicated to the Magistrates and Town Council of Görlitz, and the composer seems to imply that it had been undertaken at their special desire. In this, as in his previous work, there is noticeable, as Ritter points out, the same undecided struggle in the composer's mind between attachment to the old and inclination to the new. Thus, while he strictly adheres to the original rhythms of the old melodies, he harmonises according to the rules of modern musical accent, and thus the rhythm of the melody is not in agreement with the rhythm implied by the harmony. See for illustration his setting of ' Ein' feste Burg ' in Ritter, *Geschichte der Orgel-Musik*, p. 19, the first two bars of which may here be given :

One Choral appears in this book for the first time, viz. ' O Jesulein süss, O Jesulein mild,' which has been adapted in later Choral-books to the words ' O heiliger Geist, O heiliger Gott.' As harmonised by Scheidt it is given in Winterfeld, *Ev. K. G.* ii. No. 218, and Schöberlein, *Schatz des Chorgesangs*, ii. No. 457.

If it is his organ works that now entitle Scheidt to honourable remembrance, and give him a distinct position of his own amongst composers, it was not his organ works, but his vocal compositions, that procured him the esteem of his contemporaries, and caused him to be ranked as one of the celebrated three S.'s. Of his vocal works, besides the ' Sacrae cantiones ' of 1620, mentioned above, there are mentioned ' Liebliche Krafft-Blümlein Conzertweise mit 2 Stimmen sampt dem General-Basse,' Halle, 1625. Another work should also be recorded, consisting of ' Paduana, Galliarda,' etc., for four and five voices, 1621, the second part of which was called ' Ludorum musicorum prima et secunda pars,' and published in 1622.

It is natural to draw comparisons, as Ritter does in his history above quoted, between Scheidt and Frescobaldi, whose lives covered nearly the same period of time, and who may both be regarded as the true founders of modern organ music, or rather, the Italian of clavier music generally, the German of specifically organ music. Of the two, Frescobaldi is the greater genius, showing greater force of imagination in the invention of new forms and the solution of difficult problems ; Scheidt

is more laborious and painstaking, showing greater study of the capabilities of his instrument, as for instance in the use of the pedal, and in registering generally, with neither of which did Frescobaldi concern himself. As Ritter points out, while Scheidt has thus greater command of all the resources of expression, Frescobaldi has more of real poetic expression in his music itself. For more detailed comparison of the two masters it will be sufficient to refer to Ritter's work.

BIBL.—MAX SEIFFERT, preface to vol. i. of *D.D.T.* containing Scheidt's *Tabulatura nova*; *Vierteljahrsschrift für Musikwiss.* vii. p. 188 f. ; ARNO WERNER, *Sammelbände*, Int. Mus. Ges. i. p. 401, where a detailed study of Samuel and Gottfried Scheidt is to be found ; list of works in *Q.-L.*; CHRISTIAN R. MAHRENHOLZ, *Samuel Scheidt, sein Leben, seine Werke* (Göttingen Dissertation, 1923).
J. R. M.

SCHEIFFELHUT, JAKOB, musical director at St. Anne's, Augsburg, c. 1682. Apart from a few vocal compositions with instrumental accompaniment, he is chiefly known by his instrumental pieces. (See *Q.-L.*)

SCHEIN, JOHANN HERMANN (b. Grunhain, Saxony, Jan. 20, 1586; d. Leipzig, Nov. 19, 1630). His father was Lutheran pastor at Grunhain. Having lost his father at an early age, he was taken to Dresden and became a chorister in the court chapel there in 1599. His further education was received at the Gymnasium of Schulpforta in 1603 and the University of Leipzig (1607). Of his further musical training we have no details. In 1615 he was invited to be Kapellmeister at Weimar, but held this post for only two years. On the death of Seth Calvisius in Nov. 1615 he obtained the appointment of cantor to the Thomasschule in Leipzig, which post he held till his death.

Schein is chiefly known to later times by his Cantional, first published in 1627. Its original title is :

*'Cantional oder Gesangbuch Augspurgischer Confession, in welchem des Herrn D. Martini Lutheri vnd anderer frommen Christen, auch des Autoris eigne Lieder vnd Psalmen. . . . So im Chur- vnd Fürstenthümern Sachsen, insonderheit aber in beiden Kirchen und Gemeinen allhier zu Leipzig gebräuchlich, verfertiget und mit 4, 5, 6 Stimmen componirt.'*

A second (enlarged) edition appeared in 1645, after Schein's death. As the title shows, it consists of Choral-melodies, both old and new, harmonised for ordinary church use, mostly note against note. Schein himself appears in this book in three capacities, viz. as poet, melodist and harmonist. Of the 200 and odd Choral-melodies in the book about 80 are Schein's own, a few of which have still held their ground in modern Choral-books, though some appear to be attributed to him by mistake. Schein's book differs from Crüger's similar book of later date (1648) in retaining the old irregular rhythm of Choral-melodies, while Crüger has transformed their rhythms according to more modern ideas. But if Schein still retains the old rhythm in the melodies, in his harmonies he has almost entirely lost, as Winterfeld points out, the feeling for the peculiarities of the old church modes in which these melodies are written, though otherwise his harmonies are serious and dignified. With Michael Praetorius and Heinrich Schütz, and probably through their influence, Schein was one of the pioneers in Germany of the new movement in music proceeding from Italy at the beginning of the 17th century. Naturally his other works show this more plainly than the Cantional, as many of them are avowedly written in imitation of Italian models. These other works are as follows :

1. Venus-Kränzlein mit allerley lieblichen und schönen Blumen gezieret und gewunden, oder Neue Weltliche Lieder mit 5 Stimmen, neben etlichen Intraden, Gagliarden und Canzonen . . . Leipzig, 1609. This work consists of sixteen secular strophic songs *a* 5 and one *a* 8, in the simplest Italian canzonetta style, homophonic throughout, besides eight instrumental pieces *a* 5 and 6.

2. Cymbalum Sionium sive Cantiones Sacrae 5, 6, 8, 10 et 12 vocum. Leipzig, 1615. This work contains thirty sacred motets, some to Latin texts, some to German, besides an instrumental canzone *a* 5 as Corollarium.

3. Banchetto Musicale, neuer anmuthiger Padouanen, Gagliarden, Courenten und Allemanden *a* 5 auf allerley Instrumenten, bevorans auf Violen nicht ohne sonderbare *gratia* lieblich und lustig zu gebrauchen . . . Leipzig, 1617. This work was dedicated to Duke Johann Ernst of Weimar and contains twenty instrumental suites consisting of Paduanas, Gagliardas, Courentes *a* 5 and Allemande and Tripla *a* 4, with two separate pieces at the end.

4. Opella Nova, erster Theil Geistlicher Concerten mit 3, 4 und 5 Stimmen zusampt dem General-Bass auf jetzo gebräuchliche italienische Invention componirt. Leipzig, 1618. This work contains thirty sacred compositions on German texts in the new Italian style, with instrumental basso continuo, which, however, seems to be purely *ad libitum*.

5. Musica Boscareccia, Waldliederlein auf Italien-Villanellische Invention, Beides für sich allein mit lebendiger Stim, oder in ein Clavicembel, Spinet, Tiorba, Lauten, etc. This work appeared in three parts published in 1621, 1626, 1628 respectively, and contains altogether fifty secular compositions *a* 3 on poems by Schein himself written in the artificial pastoral style of the time. These pieces are more polyphonic in their character than those of the 'Venus-Kränzlein,' and, as the title indicates, they may be sung by voices alone or with the substitution of instruments for one or other of the vocal parts or instrumental accompaniment generally. A new edition of the work appeared in 1644, with the substitution of sacred texts for the original secular.

6. Fontana d' Israel, Israels Brünlein auserlesener Kraft-sprüchlein altes und neuen Testaments von 5 und 6 Stimmen sambt dem General Bass auf eine sonderbare anmutige Italien-Madrigalische Manier sowol für sich allein mit lebendiger Stim und Instrumenten als auch in die Orgel Clavicembel bequemlich zugebrauchen. Leipzig, 1623. This work consists of twenty-six sacred pieces *a* 5 and 6 on German texts, composed in the later freer madrigal style of Monteverdi and others, allowing greater boldness of harmonic progression.

7. Diletti pastorali, Hirten Lust von 5 Stim. zusampt dem General-Bass auf Madrigal Manier. Leipzig, 1624. 15 Nos.

8. Studenten-Schmaus *a* 5. Leipzig, 1626. 5 Nos.

9. Opella Nova, Ander Theil Geistlicher Concerten. Leipzig, 1626. Contains thirty-two sacred pieces, twenty-seven with German texts, five with Latin.

Besides these works and the Cantional of 1627, *Q.-L.* enumerates a large number of occasional compositions for weddings and funerals, many of which, however, Schein himself incorporated into the publications above specified.

In 1895 Arthur Prüfer published a monograph on Schein's Life and Works,[1] by way of preparation for an edition of his works which has since been completed in 8 volumes.

J. R. M.

SCHELBLE, JOHANN NEPOMUK (*b.* Hüfingen, Black Forest, May 16, 1789 ; *d.* Frankfort, Aug. 7, 1837), a thoroughly excellent and representative German musician, whose father was superintendent of the House of Correction at Hüfingen. His strict musical education was begun in a monastery of Marchthal 1800–1803, and continued at Donaueschingen under Weisse. He then spent some time, first with Vogler at Darmstadt and then with Krebs, a

distinguished singer, at Stuttgart, and there, in 1812, he filled the post of elementary teacher in the Royal Musical Institution, a very famous and complete school of those times.[2] In 1813 he went to Vienna, lived in intimate acquaintance with Beethoven, Moscheles, Weigl, Spohr, etc., composed an opera and many smaller works, and went on the stage, where, however, his singing, though remarkable, was neutralised by his want of power to act. From Austria in 1816 he went to Frankfort, which became his home. Here the beauty of his voice, the excellence of his method, and the justness of his expression, were at once recognised. He became the favourite teacher, and in 1817 was made director of the Musical Academy. This, however, proved too desultory for his views, and on July 24, 1818, he formed a society of his own, which developed into the famous Caecilian Society of Frankfort, and at the head of which he remained till his death. The first work chosen by the infant institution was the ' Zauberflöte ' ; then Mozart's Requiem ; then one of his Masses ; and then works by Handel, Cherubini, Bach, etc. In 1821 the Society assumed the name of the ' Cäcilienverein '; the repertory was increased by works of Palestrina, Scarlatti and other Italian masters, and at length, on Mar. 10, 1828, Mozart's ' Davidde penitente ' and the Credo of Bach's Mass in B minor were given ; then, May 2, 1829 (stimulated by the example of Mendelssohn in Berlin), the Matthew Passion ; and after that we hear of ' Samson ' and other oratorios of Handel, Bach's motets and choruses of Mendelssohn, whose genius Schelble was one of the first to recognise, and whose ' St. Paul ' was suggested to him by the Caecilian Association, doubtless on the motion of its conductor. Whether the Society ever attempted Beethoven's Mass does not appear, but Schelble was one of the two private individuals who answered Beethoven's invitation to subscribe for its publication.

His health gradually declined, and at length, in the winter of 1835, it was found necessary to make some new arrangement for the direction of the Society. Mendelssohn was asked,[3] and undertook it for six weeks during the summer of 1836. Mendelssohn's fondness and esteem for the man whose place he was thus temporarily filling is evident in every sentence referring to him in his letters of this date. Schelble's great qualities as a practical musician, a conductor and a man, are well summed up by Hiller[4] in his book on Mendelssohn, to which we refer the reader.

BIBL.—VON WEISSMANN, *J. N. Schelble* (Frankfort, 1838) ; K. LANGE, *Die gehörsentwicklungmethode von Schelble* (1873).
G.

SCHELLE, JOHANN (*b.* Geissingen, Meissen, Sept. 6, 1648 ; *d.* Leipzig, Mar. 10, 1701),

[1] See the lengthy review by Karl Hasse of Bd. vi. (1919) of *Scheins sämtliche Werke*, edited by Arthur Prüfer in *Z.M.W.*, July 1920. pp. 578-95.

[2] See the *A.M.Z.*, 1812, p. 234.
[3] *Letters*, Feb. 18, 1836.
[4] *Mendelssohn*, translated by Miss M. E. von Glehn, p. 8.

studied at Leipzig, was cantor at Eilenburg in
1672, and in 1676 succeeded Knüpfer as cantor
of St. Thomas, Leipzig. Only some songs of
his were published in Feller's ' Andächtige
Student ' and Vopelius's song-book. Twenty-
five MS. cantatas, with instrumental accompaniments, are in the Berlin Library (*Q.-L.*;
*Riemann*; A. Schering, *Über die Kirchen Kan-
taten vorbachischer Thomas Kantoren*).

SCHELLER, JAKOB (*b.* Schettal, Rakonitz,
Bohemia, May 16, 1759; *d.* 1803), a very
clever violinist. He was thrown on his own
resources from a very early age, and we hear
of him at Prague, Vienna and Mannheim, where
he remained for two years playing in the court
band, and learning composition from Vogler.
After more wandering he made a stay of three
years in Paris, studying the school of Viotti.
He then, in 1785, took a position as Konzertmeister in the Duke of Würtemberg's band at
Montbeliard. This forced him to resume his
wandering life, and that again drove him to
intemperance, till after seven or eight years
more he ended miserably, being even obliged
to borrow a fiddle at each town he came to.[1]
He was celebrated more for his tricks and *tours
de force* than for his legitimate playing. Spohr[2]
speaks of his flageolet-tones, of variations on
one string, of pizzicato with the nails of the
left hand, of imitations of a bassoon, an old
woman, etc. ; and Fétis mentions a trick in
which by loosening the bow he played on all
four strings at once.          G.

SCHELLING, ERNEST (*b.* Belvidere, New
Jersey, July 26, 1876), American pianist and
composer. A pianistic prodigy in Philadelphia at the age of 4, he studied, 1882–85,
with Mathias at the Paris Conservatoire and
later with Moszkowski, Bruckner, Leschetizky,
Huber, Barth and Paderewski. He has given
recitals throughout Europe and South America
as well as in the United States, and has played
with most of the leading orchestras and with
various chamber-music organisations. He was
a captain in the American Expeditionary Forces
during the war (1918). Since 1924 he has been
lecturing to juvenile audiences on orchestral
music and orchestral instruments. His orchestral compositions have been widely played. His
works include :

Symphony, C minor.
' Fantastic Suite,' pianoforte and orchestra.
Impressions from an Artist's Life,' pianoforte and orchestra.
' Symphonic Legend.'
' A Victory Ball,' orchestral fantasy.
Concerto, violin.
' Divertimento,' pianoforte and string quartet.
Other chamber music, pianoforte pieces and songs.          W. S. S.

SCHEMELLI, GEORG CHRISTIAN (*b.* Herz-
berg, *c.* 1678), was a pupil of the Thomasschule at Leipzig from 1695, and was cantor of
the castle at Zeitz. In 1736 he published a

' Musicalisches Gesang-Buch, Darinnen 954 geistreiche, sowohl
alte als neue Lieder und Arien, mit wohlgesetzten Melodien, in
Discant und Bass, befindlich sind . . .'

1 Rochlitz, *Für Freunde der Tonkunst*, ii.
2 *Selbstbiog.* i. 280.

In the preface the compiler states that the
tunes in his book were partly newly composed,
partly improved, by J. S. Bach. Various
authorities on the life of Bach have spent much
labour in investigating which were the tunes
newly composed by him, and which were
merely revised and corrected by him. While
Spitta attributes 29 out of the 69 tunes to
Bach, F. Wüllner, the editor of the volume of
the Bach Gesellschaft (xxxix.) in which the
hymns appear, considers that only 24 are
Bach's ; while *Q.-L.* assigns only 22 to Bach.
His name, curiously enough, is appended to
only one of the sacred songs of which the collection mainly consists (the beautiful ' Vergiss
mein nicht,' above which is written ' di J. S.
Bach, D. M. Lips.' See S. Spitta, *J. S. Bach*,
Eng. trans. i. 367-70 ; iii. 109-14).          M.

SCHENK, JOHANN, was a viola da gamba
player in the service of the Elector Palatine at
Düsseldorf in the latter part of the 17th century.
He was afterwards at Amsterdam, where he
published numerous works for his instrument,
and other compositions. The following are
known to have existed, but only a few of them
are still extant, according to *Q.-L.* :

Op.
1. Airs from an opera, ' Ceres en Bachus.'
2. Konstoeffeningen (sonatas or suites).
3. Il giardino armonico, sonate da camera a 4 (two vlns., gamba and continuo).
4. Koninklyke Harpliederen, 150 airs for one or two voices, with a prelude and postlude.
6. Scherzi musicali, for viola da gamba and bass.
7. Eighteen sonatas for violin and bass.
8. La ninfa del Reno, twelve sonatas or suites.
9. L'Echo du Danube, sonatas.
10. Les Fantaisies bizarres de la goutte, twelve sonatas for viola da gamba.

E. van der Straeten's *History of the Violoncello* contains a very full account of Schenk ;
*Q.-L.*; *Riemann.*

SCHENK, JOHANN (*b.* Wiener Neustadt,
Lower Austria, Nov. 30, 1761[3]; *d.* Dec. 29,
1836), mainly interesting from his connexion
with Beethoven, at an early age was admitted
into the Archbishop's choir at Vienna. In
1774 he was a pupil of Wagenseil. In 1778 he
produced his first Mass, which he followed by
other sacred pieces and by many Singspiele and
operas, beginning with ' Die Weinlese,' 1785,
and ' Die Weihnacht auf dem Lande,' 1786,
and ending with ' Der Fassbinder,' 1802,
which gained him a considerable name, and
rank with those of Dittersdorf and Wenzel
Müller. In addition he wrote symphonies,
concertos, quartets, Lieder, etc. The autographs of many of these are in the Gesellschaft
der Musikfreunde at Vienna, with that of a
theoretical work, *Grundsätze des Generalbasses*.
In 1794 he was appointed music director to
Prince Carl von Auersperg ; in 1795 his
' Achmet und Almanzine ' was brought out at
Vienna, and finally ' Der Dorfbarbier ' was
produced at the Kärnthnerthor Theatre, Nov.
7, 1796, a work that was always popular, and
kept its position in the repertory for many

3 Date given by *Q.-L.* which Riemann accepts.

years. Between this, his masterpiece, and the 'Fassbinder,' already mentioned, came 'Der Bettelstudent' (1796) and 'Die Jagd' (1797). The anecdote of his kissing Mozart's hand during the overture on the first night of the 'Zauberflöte' has been already related (see MOZART). His first meeting with Beethoven is told in Bauernfeld's biographical sketch of Schenk in the *Wiener Zeitschrift für Kunst* for 1837 (Nos. 5, 6 and 7). Gelinek mentioned to Schenk that he had found a young man whose playing excelled anything ever heard before, excepting Mozart's, and who had been studying counterpoint for six months with Haydn, but to so little purpose that it would be a great kindness if Schenk would give him some help. A meeting was arranged at Gelinek's house, when Beethoven improvised for over half an hour in so remarkable and unusual a manner that, forty years afterwards, Schenk could not speak of it without emotion. Schenk next went to see the young artist. Himself a model of neatness, he was rather taken aback by the disorderliness of the room, but Beethoven's reception was cordial and animated. On the desk lay some short exercises in counterpoint, in which on the first glance Schenk detected a few errors. Beethoven's troubles soon came out. He had come to Vienna aware of his own ability, but anxious to learn; had at once put himself in the hands of the first master to be got, and yet was making no progress. Schenk at once agreed to help him, and took him through Fux's *Gradus ad Parnassum*, with which indeed Haydn was familiar enough. As it was essential that Haydn should not be entirely thrown over, Beethoven copied exercises partly corrected by Schenk,[1] and Haydn was then able to congratulate himself on the progress of his hot-headed pupil. The affair was of course kept strictly secret; but Beethoven having fallen out with Gelinek, the latter gossiped, and Schenk was deeply annoyed. Beethoven, however, when on the point of following Haydn to Eisenstadt, wrote very gratefully to Schenk,[2] and the two remained on pleasant terms. It is interesting to know that besides Mozart and Beethoven, Schenk was acquainted with Schubert. Bauernfeld introduced them, and so congenial were they that after an hour's talk they parted like old friends.

Very unassuming in his ways, Schenk was respected as a thorough though somewhat pedantic teacher of the piano and composition. His portrait, in the museum of the Gesellschaft der Musikfreunde in Vienna, shows a pleasing countenance. Two cantatas, 'Die Huldigung'

[1] This surely says a great deal for Beethoven's patience, and for his desire not to offend Haydn.
[2] 'I wish I were not starting to-day for Eisenstadt. I should like to have had more talk with you. In the meantime you may count upon my gratitude for the kindness you have shown me. I shall do all in my power to return it. I hope to see you and enjoy your society again soon. Farewell, and do not forget your Beethoven.'

and 'Die Mai,' his last complete compositions, date from 1819, and at an advanced age he set about remodelling his 'Jagd,' for which he got Bauernfeld to write him a new libretto. He had finished the first act when he died.

BIBL.—ERNST ROSENFELD-RÖMER, *Johann Schenk als Opernkomponist* (Vienna Dissertation, 1921).

C. F. P., with addns.

**SCHERER,** SEBASTIAN ANTON (*bapt.* Ulm, Oct. 4, 1631; *d.* there, Aug. 26, 1712), was town musician in 1653; second organist, 1664; director of music, 1668; organist at Ulm Cathedral (successor of Tob. Eberlin), 1671. He composed masses, psalms and motets with instruments, two books of organ pieces in tablature highly spoken of by Fétis, sonatas for 2 violins and viola da gamba, suites for lute. Eitner states that he was appointed organist at St. Thomas, Strassburg, Nov. 4, 1684 (*Q.-L.*; *Riemann*).

**SCHERING,** ARNOLD (*b.* Breslau, Apr. 2, 1877), holds an important place amongst German research students, having devoted himself particularly to the rise of the classical style in oratorio and sonata, as well as the early vocal music of Germany.

Schering graduated D.Ph. at Leipzig in 1902 with the study of the early violin concerto. In 1907 he became teacher at the University of Leipzig and in due course professor. Since 1909 he has held courses in musical history at the Conservatoire, and since 1920 has been professor of the University of Halle. Since 1904 he has edited the *Bachjahrbuch* of the Neuen Bachgesellschaft. His publications on oratorio, early chamber music, organ music, etc., are numerous. He edited Hasse's oratorio, 'La conversione di S. Agostino,' for the *D.D.T* (see DENKMÄLER), and has produced many editions of old works. In 1908 he discovered the parts of the lost 'Christmas Oratorio' of Heinrich Schütz (*q.v.*) and edited their publication as a supplement to the complete works.

C.

**SCHERZANDO** (SCHERZOSO), 'playful,' 'lively'; a direction of frequent occurrence, indicating a passage of a light and cheerful character. It is occasionally used, in combination with some other direction, to indicate the style of a whole movement, as *Allegro scherzando*, *Allegretto scherzando* (Beethoven, symphony No. 8), etc., but its more usual and characteristic application is to a phrase which is to be played in a lively manner, in contrast to the rest of the movement or to some other phrase. The word is found, where one would least expect it, in the old editions of Beethoven's Mass in D, near the beginning of the 'Et vitam venturi'; but on reference to Breitkopf & Härtel's complete edition it turns out to have been read in error for *sforzando*!    M.

**SCHERZO,** an Italian word signifying 'jest' or 'joke.' Its application in music is extensive and—as is the case with many other musical titles—often incorrect.

The term (Scherzando) seems to have been first employed merely as a direction for performance, but there are early instances of its use as a distinctive title. The light Italian canzonets popular in Germany in the 17th century were called 'Scherzi musicali.' Late in the 17th century Johann Schenk published some 'Scherzi musicali per la viola di gamba.' Later, when each movement of an instrumental composition had to receive a distinctive character, the directions *Allegretto scherzando* and *Presto scherzando* became common, several examples occurring in the sonatas of Ph. Em. Bach. But even in the 'Partitas' of his great father we find a scherzo preceded by a burlesca and a fantaisie.

Coming to the period of the SYMPHONY (*q.v.*), it may be as well to remind the reader that the presence of the minuet or scherzo in works of the symphonic class is a matter of natural selection or survival of the fittest. In the old suites the minuet, being of rather shorter rhythm than the other dances, was seized upon, perhaps unconsciously, by the great masters who tied themselves down to the old form, and was exaggerated out of all recognition for the sake of contrast. When we come to Haydn the term minuet ceases to have any meaning; the stateliness and character of the dance are quite gone. But with the true instinct of an artist, Haydn felt that, in a work containing such subtleties as the ordinary first movement and slow movement, a piece of far lighter character was imperatively demanded. So lighter and quicker and more sportive grew the minuets, till Beethoven crowned the incongruous fashion with the minuet of his first symphony. The minuets of many of the string quartets of Haydn exhibit indeed those quaint and fanciful devices of unexpected reiteration, surprises of rhythm and abrupt terminations which are the leading characteristics of the Scherzo, and are completely opposed to the spirit of the true minuet. One which begins and ends each part with these bars

*8ve basso.*

is a strong instance in point.

Beethoven quickly gave the Scherzo the permanent position in the symphony which it now occupies. He also settled its form and character (see FORM, under SUBSIDIARY FORMS OF THE SONATA: (2) MINUET AND SCHERZO). It is a good answer to those who consider the classical forms worn out and irksome to the flow of inspiration to point out that in the Scherzo, where full rein is given to the individual caprice of the musician, there is as much attention given to construction as anywhere. In fact, either the bold and masculine first-movement form, or its sister the weaker and more feminine rondo form, must be the backbone of every piece of music with any pretensions to the name. But, lest the light and airy character of the Scherzo should be spoilt by the obtrusion of the machinery, the greater composers have sought to obscure the form artistically by several devices, the most frequent and obvious being the humorous persistent dwelling on some one phrase, generally the leading feature of the first subject. Witness the scherzo of Beethoven's ninth symphony, where the opening phrase for the drums is used as an accompaniment to the second subject—indeed as a persistent 'motto' throughout. Apart from this there is not the slightest departure from rigid first-movement form in this great movement.

The trio, which is a relic of the minuet and takes the position of third subject or middle section in a rondo, survives because of the naturally felt want of a contrast to the rapid rhythm of the Scherzo. Many modern composers affect to dispense with it, but there is usually a central section answering to it, even though it be not divided off from the rest by a double bar. Mendelssohn was most successful in writing scherzos without trios. The main idea was to have a movement in extremely short and marked rhythm, for which purpose triple time is generally the best. In the pianoforte sonatas, the scherzo to that in E♭ (op. 31, No. 3) is the only instance where Beethoven has employed 2–4. The trios to the scherzos of the Pastoral and Choral Symphonies are 2–4 and C for special reasons of effect and contrast. It may be worth noticing that Beethoven invariably writes 3–4 even where 6–8 or 3–8 could equally well have been employed. Amongst Beethoven's endless devices for novelty should be noticed the famous treatment of the scherzo in the C minor symphony—its conversion into a weird and mysterious terror, and its sudden reappearance, all alive and well again, in the midst of the tremendous jubilation of the finale. Symphony No. 8, too, presents some singular features. The second movement is positively a cross between a slow movement and a scherzo, partaking equally of the sentimental and the humorous. But the finale is nothing else than a rollicking scherzo, teeming with eccentricities and practical jokes from beginning to end, the opening jest (and *secret* of the movement) being the sudden unexpected entry of the basses with a tremendous C sharp, afterwards turned into D flat, and the final one, the repetition of the chord of F at great length as if for a conclusion, and then, when the hearer naturally thinks that the end is reached, a start off in another direction with a new coda and wind-up.

Humour is more unexpected in Schubert than in Beethoven, and perhaps because of its unexpectedness we appreciate it the more. The scherzo of the C major symphony is full of happy thoughts and surprises, as fine as any of Beethoven's, and yet distinct from them. The varied changes of rhythm in two, three and four bars, the piquant use of the wood wind, and above all the sudden and lovely gleam of sunshine

combine to place this movement among the things imperishable. The scherzos of the octet, the quintet in C, and above all, the PF. duet in C, which Joachim restored to its rightful dignity of symphony, are all worthy of honour. The last-named, with its imitations by inversion of the leading phrase, and its grotesque bass, is truly comical:

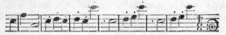

It is much to be regretted that later composers lost sight of the true bearing of the Scherzo so completely. Mendelssohn indeed has given it an elfish fairy character, but though this is admirable in the 'Midsummer Night's Dream,' it is perhaps a little out of place elsewhere. Lightness and airy grace his scherzos possess to admiration, in common with his capriccios, which they closely resemble ; but neither he nor his successors realised the musical humour which vents itself in unexpected rhythms and impudent upstartings of themes in strange places. Mendelssohn has not used the title 'scherzo' to either of his five symphonies, though the 'Vivace non troppo' of the 'Scotch,' the 'Allegretto' of the 'Lobgesang' and the 'Allegro Vivace' of the 'Reformation' are usually called scherzos. It is sufficient to name the string octet, the two PF. trios and the two quintets for strings, as a few of his works which contain the most striking specimens in this line.

With Schumann we find ourselves again in a new field. Humour, his music seldom, if ever, presents, and he is really often far less gay in his scherzos than elsewhere. He introduced the innovation of two trios in his B♭ and C symphonies, PF. quintet and other works, but although this practice allows more scope to the

fancy of the composer in setting forth strongly contrasted movements in related rythm, it is to be deprecated as tending to give undue length and consequent heaviness to what should be the lightest and most epigrammatic of music. Beethoven has repeated the trios of his fourth and seventh symphonies, but that is quite another thing. Still, though Schumann's scherzos are wanting in lightness, their originality is more than compensation. Several of his Kreisleriana and other small PF. pieces are to all intents and purposes scherzos.

Unlike Schubert and Beethoven, Brahms seldom wrote a really bright scherzo, but he published one for PF. solo (op. 4) which is very odd and striking. The second symphony has a movement which is a combination of minuet and scherzo, and certainly one of his most charming ideas. On somewhat the same principle is the scherzo of the second string sextet (op. 36) which begins in 2-4 as a kind of gavotte, while the trio is 3-4 presto, thus reversing the ordinary practice of making the trio broader and slower than the rest of the piece.

Quite on a pedestal of their own stand the four scherzos for piano by Chopin. They are indeed no joke in any sense ; the first has been entitled ' Le Banquet infernal,' and all four are characterised by a wild power and grandeur to which their composer seldom attained.

The position of the Scherzo in the symphony —whether second or third of the four movements—is clearly a matter of individual taste, the sole object being contrast.        F. C.

SCHETKY, JOHANN GEORG CHRISTOFF (b. Hesse-Darmstadt, 1740 ; d. Edinburgh, Nov. 29, 1824), a composer, and an excellent performer on the violoncello. He was the son of Louis Schetky, secretary and musician to the Landgrave there.

J. G. C. Schetky was intended for the law, but developed musical abilities and became locally famous. He travelled to Italy and France, and obtained recognition and patronage at various courts. He returned to Hesse-Darmstadt, but after the death of the Landgrave set out for London. Robert Bremner, the music publisher, having been commissioned by the gentlemen directors of St. Cecilia's Hall, Edinburgh, to engage a first violoncellist for the concerts held there, met Schetky at Lille and brought him to Edinburgh, where he arrived in Feb. 1772, and there spent the remainder of a long life. He played at the Edinburgh concerts, and became associated with the musical life there. He was a friend of Robert Burns, and at the latter's request set to music his song ' Clarinda, mistress of my soul,' printed with the music in the second volume of Johnson's *Scots Museum*, 1788. In 1774 Schetky married the daughter of Joseph REINAGLE (*q.v.*), senior, an Austrian musician who was then settled in Edinburgh. He had several children by this marriage, one of whom, John Christian, was marine painter to George IV. and to Queen Victoria. Schetky, the musician, died in Edinburgh aged 84, and was buried in the Canongate burial-ground. His published works consist of concertos, duets, trios, etc., for strings, and some harpsichord sonatas. They were principally, if not all, published by Robert Bremner. A MS. oratorio, ' Die verschmachtende Verspottung des zum Tode verurtheilten Heylandes,' is at Darmstadt. For some details of his life see *Life of John C. Schetky, late Marine Painter,* by his daughter, and *St. Cecilia's Hall,* by David Fraser Harris, Edinburgh, 1899.      F. K.

SCHEURLEER, DR. DANIEL FRANÇOIS (*b.* The Hague, Nov. 13, 1855), a banker by profession, has devoted his considerable wealth to the collection of a fine library of books about music and a museum of ancient and modern musical instruments (see COLLECTIONS), and to the study on his own part and the encouragement of the study by others, of music in its historical aspects.

An enthusiastic member of the International Musical Society, after the dissolution of that body he started in 1920 the Union Musicologique, in which he had the assistance of an eminent international committee. A *Bulletin* is issued twice each year containing reports from various countries, and articles by W. Barclay Squire, Ch. van den Borren, Prof. Max Seiffert, Dr. Guido Adler, J. G. Prod'homme and others (see PERIODICALS). He wrote and published in 1878 an essay on *Twee Titanen der 19e eeuw : Hector Berlioz en Antoine Wiertz,* but most of his writing has been concerned with the music of the Netherlands. He was for some years president of the Vereeniging voor Noord-Nederlandsch Muziek Geschiedenis, and received the honorary degree of Doctor in 1910. His principal works are Catalogues of his own library (see LIBRARIES, subsection HOLLAND), a new edition of Jan Fruytier's *Ecclesiasticus, oft de wijse sproken Iesu des soons Syrach, nu eerstmael deurdeelt ende ghestelt in liedekens, op bequame en ghemeyne voisen naer wtwijsen der musijck-noten daer by ghevoecht,* and of the 16th-century ' Een devoot ende Profitelijck Boexken,' an Introduction to Röntgen's ' Dutch dances of the 16th century,' *Muziekleven in Nederland in de 2de helft der 18e eeuw,* and *Muziekleven te 's-Gravenhage in de 2de helft der 18de eeuw.*     H. A.

SCHICHT, JOHANN GOTTFRIED (*b.* Reichenau, Zittau, Sept. 29, 1753 ; *d.* Feb. 16, 1823), owed his education to an uncle ; went to Leipzig University in 1776, intending to study law, but gradually adopted music, and was soon chosen by Adam Hiller as solo clavier-player at his concerts. On Hiller's retirement he succeeded him in 1785, and at length in 1810 rose to the head of his profession as cantor of the Thomasschule. He died, leaving many large works (three oratorios, much church and chamber music), as well as a translation of the PF. Schools of Pleyel and Clementi, and of Pellegrini-Celoni's Singing Method, etc., but his most important legacy was an edition of J. S. Bach's motets (B. & H. 1802–03).    G.

SCHICK, (1) MARGARETE LUISE (*née* HAMEL) (*b.* Mainz, Apr. 26, 1773 ; *d.* Berlin, Apr. 29, 1809), a famous singer, especially as interpreter of Gluck's works ; daughter of a bassoon-player, pupil of Stephani at Würzburg and Righini at Mainz. She made her début at Mainz in 1788. When Mozart heard her at the coronation of Leopold II. at Frankfort-on-the-Main, he said, ' Now I do not want to hear any other singing.' In 1791 she married the violinist Ernst Schick, went to Hamburg in 1793, and thence to Berlin, where Frederick William II. had engaged both for the Schlosstheater. Margarete was allowed, however, to sing at the National Theatre also, where she appeared in operas by Gluck and Mozart, which suited her more serious nature and deep and intense feeling. Unfortunately, when singing after a long illness in Righini's Te Deum the effort proved too much ; she had a relapse, and the rupture of an artery in the throat caused her death. A bust by Wichmann of this great artist decorates the concert-room of the Schauspielhaus, Berlin. Her husband, (2) ERNST (*b.* The Hague, 1756 ; *d.* Berlin, Feb. 10, 1815), studied the violin under Kreusser, taking Esser and Lolli as his models. In 1793 he instituted chamber concerts with Bohrer at Berlin, where they produced chiefly lesser known classical compositions. Schick composed 6 violin concertos and some Masonic songs. Both his daughter Julie and his granddaughter Pauline von Schätzel were noted singers (*Mendel*).

SCHICKHARD (SCHICKARD), JOHANN CHRISTIAN, a composer resident at Hamburg about 1730. His works were chiefly published at Amsterdam, but were republished by the elder John Walsh in England. They comprise instrumental pieces, including : soli for a flute and bass, op. 17 ; concertos for flutes, op. 19 ; soli for German flute, hautboy or violin, op. 20 ; sonatas for two violins and a bass, op. 5 ; sonatas for two German flutes and a bass, op. 10 ; and some others. These were all published by Walsh and reissued by Randall.     F. K.

SCHIEDERMAYR (SCHIEDERMAIER), JOHANN BAPTIST (*b.* Pfaffenmünster, near Straubing, June 23, 1779 ; *d.* Linz, Jan. 6, 1840), organist of Linz Cathedral. He was a prolific composer of masses and other church music, Singspiele, symphonies, chamber music. He brought out an abbreviated edition of Leopold Mozart's violin Tutor, and an instruction book for the singing of Chorals in Roman Catholic churches (*Q.-L.* ; *Riemann*).

**SCHIEDMAYER.** Two firms of this name in Stuttgart have enjoyed wide reputation as pianoforte-makers, viz. ' Schiedmayer & Sons ' and ' Schiedmayer Pianofortefabrik ; vormals, J. & P. Schiedmayer.'

(1) JOHANN DAVID SCHIEDMAYER (*d.* Nuremberg, 1806) towards the close of the 18th century was a musical instrument maker at Erlangen, and afterwards at Nuremberg. His son, (2) JOHANN LORENZ (*b.* 1786 ; *d.* 1860), went after this for two years to Vienna as a workman, and in 1809 established a business at Stuttgart in partnership with C. F. Dieudonné (*d.* 1825). Before that time pianoforte-making was virtually unknown in Stuttgart, those who required satisfactory instruments obtaining them from Vienna. Lorenz Schiedmayer's intelligence and aptness for business gained a position for his firm, and it soon became one of the first in Germany. In 1845 Lorenz united his two eldest sons, (3) ADOLF (*b.* 1820 ; *d.* 1890) and (4) HERMANN (*d.* 1861), to himself, and ' Schiedmayer & Sons ' soon became as well known in foreign countries as in Würtemberg. The sons of the brothers Adolf and Hermann, bearing the same Christian names, were for many years the directors of this firm, which has made both concert and ordinary instruments, and has competed with success in London and Paris and other exhibitions.

The two younger sons of Johann David, (5) JULIUS (*b.* Feb. 17, 1822 ; *d.* Feb. 1878) and (6) PAUL (*d.* June 18, 1890), at first devoted themselves to harmonium - making, then of recent introduction, a practical knowledge of which had been gained by Paul in Paris. They started together in 1854, but after the death of the father in 1860, turned to pianoforte-making in competition with the elder firm, and the younger firm became known as ' Schiedmayer Pianofortefabrik.'

Special mention must be made of Julius Schiedmayer's prominence as an expert in the juries of the great Exhibitions of London, 1862; Paris, 1867 ; Vienna, 1873 ; and Philadelphia, 1876.                                    A. J. H.

BIBL.—A. EISENMANN, *Schiedmayer und Söhne.* 1909.

**SCHIEVER, ERNST** (*b.* Hanover, Mar. 23, 1844 ; *d.* there, 1915), violinist, studied under Joachim, 1860–64. In 1868 he joined the Müller Quartet, with which he travelled as leader until its dissolution in 1869, and became in the same year a teacher at the Hochschule and a member of the Joachim Quartet. He remained in Berlin two years, organising with Hermann Franke (second violin), Leonhard Wolff (viola) and Robert Hausmann (violoncello) another quartet party, which was engaged subsequently by Count Hochberg, and became known as the Gräflich Hochberg

Quartet of Schloss Rohnstock, near Striegau, in Silesia. In 1878 he came to England, making Liverpool his headquarters and undertaking the leadership of the Richter orchestra, with which he was connected for nearly thirty years. The Schiever Quartet, in which he was associated with A. Ross (second violin), Carl Courvoisier (viola) and Walter Hatton (violoncello), was an institution favourably known in the north of England.                          W. W. C.

**SCHIKANEDER, EMMANUEL** (*b* Ratisbon, Jan. 3, 1748 [1]; *d.* Vienna, Sept. 21, 1812), theatrical manager, playwright, actor and singer. He began life as a poor wandering musician, joined some strolling players at Augsburg in 1773, married the adopted daughter of the manager, and at length undertook the direction himself. In 1780 his wanderings brought him to Salzburg, where he fell in with the Mozarts, and at once began to make a profit out of Wolfgang's talents. In 1784 we find him in Vienna, giving with Kumpf a series of excellent performances of German opera, comedy, etc., at the Kärnthnerthor theatre. He appeared on the boards both here and at the Burgtheater, where, however, he did not succeed. He next took the management of the theatre at Ratisbon, but was recalled to Vienna by his wife, who had undertaken the little theatre lately built in the grounds of Prince Starhemberg's house in the suburb of Wieden, for which Schikaneder received a *privilegium* or licence.[2] He had no scruples as to the means to be adopted to make a hit, but in spite of large receipts was continually in difficulty. On one such occasion (Mar. 1791) he had recourse to Mozart, whom he implored to set to music a libretto adapted by himself from a piece by Giesecke, a member of his company. Mozart, always good-natured, especially to a brother Mason, consented, and from that moment till its completion Schikaneder stuck closely to him, and did all he could to keep him amused over his work. The history of the ' Zauberflöte ' is well known; Schikaneder made various suggestions in the composition, took the part of Papageno, and found himself saved from ruin by the success of the opera ; but he showed little gratitude to Mozart, and after his death, instead of helping the widow of the man by whom he had benefited so materially, contented himself with loud and vain lamentations. In 1800 he entered into partnership with a merchant named Zitterbarth, who, at a short distance from the small theatre just mentioned, built the ' Theater-an-der-Wien,' opened June 13, 1801 (see BEETHOVEN). Zitterbarth then bought the *privilegium* from Schikaneder, who managed it for him till 1806. His next project was to build, with the assistance of some wealthy friends, a new theatre in the Joseph-

[1] *Riemann.*
[2] It was popularly called Schikaneder's theatre.

stadt suburb, but this he did not carry out. On his way to Pest, whither he had been invited to undertake a theatre, he went mad, was brought back to Vienna, and died in great misery.

Schikaneder wrote the librettos for many popular operas, Singspiele and fairy pieces, the list of which, with year of performance, is here published for the first time :

' Anton der dumme Gärtner ' (Schack and Gerl), 1789 ; ' Die beiden Antons ' (with 4 sequels), ' Jakob und Nannerl ' and ' Der Stein der Weisen,' or ' Die Zauberinsel ' (Schack and others), 1790 ; ' Die Zauberflöte ' (Mozart), 1791 ; ' Der wohlthätige Derwisch,' or ' Die Schellenkappe ' (Schack, Gerl and others), 1792 ; ' Die Eisenkönigin,' ' Die Waldmänner ' and ' Der Zauberpfeil ' (Lickl), 1793 ; ' Der Spiegel von Arkadien ' (Süssmayer) and ' Die Hirten an Rhein,' 1794 ; ' Der Scheerenschleifer ' (Henneberg), ' Der Königssohn aus Ithaka ' (A. F. Hoffmeister) and ' Der Höllenberg ' (Woelfl), 1795 ; ' Der Tyroler Wastel ' (Haibel) and a second part ' Österreich's treue Brüder,' 1796 ; ' Das medizinische Consilium ' (Haibel), ' Der Löwenbrunnen ' (Seyfried) and ' Babylons Pyramiden ' (Act i. Gallus, Act ii. Peter Winter), 1797 ; ' Das Labyrinth,' or ' Kampf mit den Elementen ' (second part of ' Zauberflöte,' Winter), 1798 ; ' Die Ostindier vom Spittelberg ' (Seyfried, Stegmayer, etc.), ' Conrad Langbarth,' or ' Der Burggeist ' (Henneberg), ' Minna und Peru,' or ' Königspflicht ' (Act i. Henneberg, Act ii. Seyfried), and ' Der Wundermann am Wasserfall ' (Seyfried), 1799 ; ' Amors Schifchen ' (Seyfried), 1800 ; at the Theater-an-der-Wien—opening night— ' Alexander ' (Teyber), ' Thespis Traum ' and ' Proteus und Arabiens Söhne ' (Stegmayer), 1801 ; ' Tsching ! Tsching ! ' (Haibel), 1802 ; ' Die Entlarvten,' a continuation of the ' Waldmänner ' (Anton Fischer), and ' Pfändung und Personalarrest ' (Teyber), 1803 ; ' Der Stein der Weisen ' (Schack and others), 1804 ; ' Swetards Zauberthal ' (Fischer), 1805 ; ' Die Eisenkönigin ' (Henneberg) and ' Die Kurgäste am Sauerbrunnen ' (Anton Diabelli), Schikaneder's last piece, given for his benefit, 1806.

C. F. P.

BIBL.—E. V. KOMORZYNSKI, E. Schikaneder, 1901 ; A. W. THAYER, Beethoven ; E. J. DENT, The Magic Flute, its History and Interpretation, 1911.

SCHILDT, MELCHIOR (b. Hanover (?), 1592 ; d. there, May 22, 1667), a pupil of Sweelinck, organist at the principal church at Wolfenbüttel from 1623–26, court organist at Copenhagen from 1626–29, and from 1629 to his death organist at the Market church, Hanover, as successor to his father and brother. Of his valuable compositions only one cantata, 4 v., and a few organ and harpsichord pieces in MS. are preserved (Q.-L. ; Riemann).

SCHILLING, DR. GUSTAV (b. Schwiegershausen, Hanover, Nov. 3, 1803 ; d. Nebraska, U.S.A., Mar. 1881), author of a book much esteemed in Germany, though little known in England—Encyclopädie der gesammten musikalischen Wissenschaften oder Universal Lexikon der Tonkunst (7 vols. 8vo, Stuttgart, 1835–40). His father was a pastor at Schwiegershausen. He was brought up at Göttingen and Halle, and in 1830 settled in Stuttgart as director of Stöpel's Music School. In 1857 he went to America. He published several other works bearing on music, but none of the importance of that already mentioned. (For list see Riemann.)

G.

SCHILLINGS, MAX VON (b. Düren, Rheinland, Apr. 19, 1868), studied under K. Joseph Brambach and O. F. von Königslow at Bonn. From the former he derived the traditions of both Hummel and Beethoven, as shown through the medium of the teaching of Hiller, whose pupil Brambach was ; while from the latter he inherited, musically, the methods of David the violinist, and Moritz Hauptmann the distinguished theorist. On leaving Bonn,

Schillings continued his studies at Munich, where, after three years spent in perfecting himself in all branches of his art, he decided to settle. He was appointed chorus-master at Bayreuth in 1902, having acted as one of the assistant stage conductors there in 1892. In the autumn of 1908 he became musical assistant to the intendant of the Stuttgart court theatre, conductor of the royal concerts and director of operatic productions. From 1911–18 he was general musical director at Stuttgart, and received from the King of Würtemberg the title ' Von ' in 1912, the year of the opening of the new opera-house of Stuttgart. Other events of this period were his production of a condensed version of Berlioz's ' Les Troyens ' (1913), and the production of his own opera ' Mona Lisa ' on Sept. 26, 1915. In 1919 he became director of the Staatsoper at BERLIN (q.v.). His compositions, fairly numerous, show a high order of talent ; but the composer was at first considered to be decidedly dominated by the influence of Wagner. The opus numbers not mentioned in the following list are for the most part filled with songs, partsongs and other small works.

LIST OF PRINCIPAL WORKS

Op.
3. ' Ingwelde.'  Opera.  3 acts.  (Prod. Carlsruhe, 1894.)
5. Improvisation.  PF. and vln.
6. ' Meergruss ' and ' Seemorgen.'  Symphonic fantasies for orch.
8. ' Ein Zwiegespräch.'  Vln. and v'cello soli with small orch.
9. ' Kassandra ' and ' Das elenosiche Fest.'  Recitations with orch.
10. ' Der Pfeifertag.'  Opera.  (Prod. Schwerin, 1901.)
11. Symphonic prologue, ' Oedipus.'
12. ' Orestes.'  Incidental music.  (1900.)
15. ' Hexenlied ' (orch. music to Wildenbruch).
20. ' Moloch.'  Musical tragedy.  (Dresden, 1906.)
21. ' Dem Verklärten ' (Schiller).  Baritone solo, ch. and orch.
22. ' Glockenliedes.'  Tenor solo and orch.
24. Music to Goethe's Faust (I.).  (1908.)
25. Violin concerto, A minor.
26. ' Hochzeitslied.'  Soli, ch. and orch.
27. March for military band.
28. ' Jung Olaf.'  Recitation with orch. or PF.
31. ' Mona Lisa.'  Opera.  2 acts.  (Stuttgart, 1915.)
32. String quintet in E flat.
33. ' Die Perle ' (Goethe).  Duet with orch.
34. String quartet in E minor.

D. H. ; addns. Riemann, etc.

SCHIMON, (1) ADOLF (b. Vienna, Feb. 29, 1820 ; d. Leipzig, June 21, 1887), son of an Austrian artist, well known for his portraits of Beethoven, Weber, Spohr, etc. At 16 he went to Paris and entered the Conservatoire as a pupil of Berton and Halévy. In 1844 he brought out an opera called ' Stradella,' at La Pergola in Florence. In 1850 he was in London, and took a provincial tour with Balfe, Reeves and Clara Novello. From 1854–59 he was attached to the Italian opera in Paris, and in 1858 produced a comic opera, ' List um List,' which was successful in North Germany. In 1872 we find him again at Florence, where he married Anna REGAN. From 1874–77 he was teacher of singing in the Conservatorium at Leipzig, and from thence was called to Munich, where he was professor of singing in the Royal Music School until 1886, when he returned to Leipzig. His original compositions embrace quartets, trios and solos for the PF., and songs in various languages, and he edited many vocal pieces by Scarlatti, Porpora, Paradies and other old Italian masters.

His wife, (2) ANNA REGAN-SCHIMON (b. Aich, near Carlsbad, Sept. 18, 1841 ; d. Munich, Apr. 18, 1902), was brought up in the house of Dr. Anger in Carlsbad till 1859, when she was placed as a pupil with Mme. Schubert (née Maschinka-Schneider) in Dresden. In the following year she accompanied Mme. Sabatier-Ungher, the great contralto, to Florence, where she remained under the care of that eminent artist till Feb. 1864. During this time she made her first attempts on the stage at Siena, her success in which encouraged her in further study. From 1864–67 she was engaged at the court theatre at Hanover ; then as Kammersängerin to the Grand Duchess Helena in St. Petersburg, where she sang at three of the seven concerts given by Berlioz. In 1869 she visited London in company with her old friend and teacher Mme. Sabatier, sang twice at the Philharmonic and three times at the Crystal Palace, and at Hallé's Recitals, etc. From this time till 1875 she was frequently in England, widely known and much liked for her exquisite delivery of Schubert's and other songs. In 1870 and 1871 she visited Vienna with great success, and in 1872 married Dr. Schimon. She made two brilliant tours with Mombelli, Sivori, Trebelli, etc., in the winters of 1872 and 1873, and from that time till her death only appeared occasionally at the Gewandhaus Concerts at Leipzig. After her husband's death she accepted a post in the Royal Music School at Munich.                                          G.

SCHINDELMEISSER, LOUIS (b. Königsberg, Dec. 8, 1811 ; d. Darmstadt, Mar. 30, 1864), was educated at the Gymnasium at Berlin. He learned music from a French musician named Hostié, and from Gährich. He first adopted the clarinet, but afterwards took a wider range. From 1832–37 he filled Kapellmeisters' posts at Salzburg, Innsbruck, Graz, Berlin (Königstadt Theatre) and Pest, where he remained for nine years. Finally he was court Kapellmeister at Darmstadt. His works embrace six operas—'Mathilde,' 'Ten happy Days,' 'Peter von Szapary' (Pest, 1839), 'Malvina' (Pest, 1851), 'The Avenger,' 'Melusine' (1861) ; an oratorio, 'S. Boniface' ; an overture to 'Uriel Acosta' and incidental music to various plays ; a concerto for clarinet and orchestra, and a concertante for four clarinets and orchestra ; songs, PF. pieces, etc.                                          G.

SCHINDLER, ANTON (b. Medl, Neustadt, Moravia, 1796 ; d. Bockenheim, near Frankfort, Jan. 16, 1864), the devoted friend and biographer of Beethoven. His father was cantor and schoolmaster at Medl. He began the study of music and the violin early in life. While quite young he entered the Vienna University to study law, and assiduously kept up his music by practice in an amateur orchestra. His introduction to Beethoven took place accidentally in 1814, when he was asked to take a note from Schuppanzigh to the great composer. Later in the year he played in Beethoven's two concerts of Nov. 29 and Dec. 2. He and the master met often, and the intimacy increased until, early in 1819, on the recommendation of Dr. Bach he became a kind of secretary to Beethoven, and at length, in 1822, took up residence in his house. He then became conductor at the Josephstadt Theatre, where he studied several of Beethoven's great works under his own direction. Beethoven, however, at last began to tire of his young friend, and after much unpleasantness, in 1824 after the failure of the concert of May 23, the breach came. Beethoven behaved with great violence and injustice, and Schindler was driven from him till Dec. 1826, when he arrived in Vienna from Gneixendorf, to die. Schindler at once resumed his position, attended him with devotion till his death, wrote several letters [1] to Moscheles on the details of the event, and in company with Breuning took charge of Beethoven's papers. Breuning died, and then the whole came into Schindler's hands.

In 1831 he wrote some interesting articles on Beethoven and Schubert in Bäuerle's *Theaterzeitung*. In December he left Vienna and became Kapellmeister to the cathedral at Münster, a post which he exchanged four years later for that of music-director at Aix-la-Chapelle. After some years he relinquished this, became first a private teacher and then went entirely into private life. He lived in various towns of Germany, and at length in Bockenheim.

His book on Beethoven is entitled *Biographie von Ludwig van Beethoven. Mit dem Porträt Beethovens und zwei Facsimilen* (Münster, 1840, 1 vol. 8vo). [2] This was followed by *Beethoven in Paris . . . ein Nachtrag zur Biographie Beethoven's*, etc. (Münster, 1842 ; 1 thin vol. 8vo), and that by a second edition of the *Biographie* with additions (Münster, 1845, 1 vol. 8vo). The third and last edition appeared in 1860. Being so long about Beethoven, he accumulated many autographs and other papers and articles of interest, and these he disposed of to the library at Berlin for an annuity. His sister was a singer, who in the year 1830 was engaged at the Königstadt Theatre, Berlin.

Schindler has been the object of much obloquy and mistrust, but it is satisfactory to know, on the authority of A. W. Thayer, that this is unfounded, and that his honesty and intelligence are both to be trusted.    G.

SCHINDLER, KURT (b. Berlin, Feb. 17,

---

[1] Printed in Moscheles' *Life*, i. 145-79.
[2] This is the book which was translated or adapted by Moscheles (London, Colburn, 1841), strange to say with no mention of Schindler on the title-page.

1882), German-American conductor and composer. He studied extensively at the universities of Munich and Berlin, as well as piano with
Zieler, Gernsheim, L. C. Wolf and Ansorge, and
composition with Bussler and Thuille. After
various engagements as a conductor in Germany, he went to New York in 1905 as assistant
conductor of German opera at the Metropolitan
Opera House, a post he held for three seasons.
In 1909 he founded in that city the MacDowell
Chorus, which in 1912 became the Schola
Cantorum, now one of the most significant of
American choral organisations (see NEW YORK).
A skilful and ingenious translator and arranger
of songs and choral music, he has also to his
credit more than 50 compositions in various
vocal forms.                  w. s. s.

SCHIRA, FRANCESCO (b. Malta, Sept. 19,
1815 ; d. London, Oct. 16, 1883), received his
early education at Milan, and was placed, at
the age of 9, in the Conservatorio, where he
learned counterpoint under Basily, principal of
that institution. At 17, having completed his
studies, Francesco was commissioned to write
an opera for La Scala, which was produced
Nov. 17, 1832. That ' Elena e Malvina ' won
favourable recognition may be inferred from
the fact that a Lisbon impresario, being at
Milan with the object of forming a company for
the Santo Carlos, contracted an engagement
with Schira for the forthcoming season as
Maestro Direttore, Compositore e Conduttore
della Musica. He remained eight years at
Lisbon, where he was also appointed professor
of harmony and counterpoint at the Conservatorio, composing ' I cavalieri di Valenza ' and
' Il fanatico per la musica ' for the Santo
Carlos, besides ballets, cantatas, etc.

In Jan. 1842 Schira quitted Lisbon for Paris,
with the idea of obtaining some book in the
French language which he might set to music.
In Paris he made the acquaintance of Maddox,
then in quest of artists for the Princess's
Theatre. This led to an offer from the London
manager, and Schira was appointed director of
music and orchestral chief at that establishment. On Monday, Dec. 26, 1842, the Princess's opened as a lyric theatre, and Schira's
appearance at the conductor's desk was his
first introduction to the English public. The
opera chosen was an English version of ' La
Sonnambula.' Among notable incidents during
Schira's term of conductorship may be specified
the production of two operas by Balfe, originally composed for the Paris Opéra-Comique—
' Le Puits d'Amour,' called ' Geraldine ' (Aug.
1843), and ' Les Quatre Fils d'Aymon,' called
' The Castle of Aymon ' (Nov. 1844). At the
end of 1844 Schira accepted an engagement
from Alfred Bunn, then lessee of Drury Lane,
to fill the place left vacant by Benedict, who
resigned immediately after Balfe's ' Daughter
of St. Mark ' was brought out. At Drury Lane

he remained until the spring of 1847, when
Bunn seceded from the management, the committee having entertained the proposal of
Jullien to become future lessee ; and here
several adaptations of foreign operas, besides
a good number of works by English composers,
were produced. From the latter it will suffice
to name Wallace's ' Maritana ' and ' Matilda
of Hungary,' Macfarren's ' Don Quixote,'
Benedict's ' Crusaders,' Lavenu's ' Loretta '
(composed for Mme. Anna Bishop), Balfe's
' Enchantress,' etc.; among the former, Flotow's
' Stradella ' and ' Martha.' In Sept. 1848
Bunn took Covent Garden Theatre, and
Schira was again appointed conductor. The
season only lasted two months, but comprised
the engagement of Sims Reeves and an entirely
new opera called ' Quentin Durward,' the
composition of Henri Laurent. The success
of the enterprise was not in proportion to
the expectations of the manager ; ' Quentin
Durward ' was by no means a hit, and though
Bunn had lowered his prices the house was
prematurely closed. Thus an opera entitled
' Kenilworth,' from Schira's own pen, which
had already been put into rehearsal with Sims
Reeves in the part of Leicester, was lost to the
public, and no more English opera was heard
at Covent Garden until Pyne and Harrison
migrated there from the Lyceum.

Although he had severed his connexion with
the Princess's as musical director, in which
position his worthy successor was Edward
Loder, Schira wrote two original works for the
theatre in Oxford Street—' Mina,' produced in
1845, and ' Theresa, or the Orphan of Geneva,'
in 1850, both, the latter especially, received
with marked favour. Schira was once more
engaged as conductor at Drury Lane, and the
theatre opened on Jan. 23, 1852, with an
English version of ' Robert le Diable,' succeeded by ' Fra Diavolo,' with Sims Reeves in
the title part. The principal incident that
marked the season was the production of ' The
Sicilian Bride,' by Balfe, in no respect one of
his most successful efforts. From this time
Schira devoted himself specially to giving instructions in the vocal art. He nevertheless
did not neglect composition, as testified in a
number of charming songs, duets, trios, etc.,
some of which have attained wide popularity.
He also was busily employed in the composition
of a grand opera called ' Niccolò de' Lapi,'
performed with marked applause at Her
Majesty's Theatre in May 1863. For the
Carnival at Naples, two years later, he wrote
another grand opera entitled ' Selvaggia,'
which was given with brilliant success, and
represented at Milan, Barcelona and elsewhere.
The reception accorded to ' Selvaggia ' led to
his being asked to write another opera, ' Lia,'
for Venice. This, also brought out during
the Carnival, was hardly so much to the taste

of the Venetians as its precursor. Nevertheless there are amateurs who regard 'Lia' as Schira's best work.

The managers of the Birmingham Festival commissioned Schira to write a cantata for the meeting of 1873, and he wrote a piece entitled 'The Lord of Burleigh,' the libretto, by Desmond Lumley Ryan, being founded upon Tennyson's well-known poem, though not a line was appropriated save the motto which heads the title-page of the printed edition. An operetta entitled 'The Ear-ring' was performed at the St. George's Hall Theatre. In his own country and elsewhere abroad he held the insignia of several orders of merit, tho most prized of which was that of Commendatore della Corona d' Italia—prized the more because conferred by King Humbert *motu proprio*.

J. W. D.

SCHIRMER, G., is the corporate name under which is carried on the music-publishing business, now one of the largest and most important of its kind, that was established in New York by GUSTAV SCHIRMER (*b.* Saxony, 1829 ; *d.* Eisenach, 1893). Schirmer went to New York in 1837, and in 1861, with B. Beer, he took over Breusing's music business, of which he had for some time been manager. Later Schirmer obtained complete control, and the house increased steadily in standing and in importance. On the death of Gustav Schirmer in 1893 the business was incorporated by his heirs, and its management undertaken by his two sons, now both deceased

After this incorporation the business continued to expand, particularly in the department of publication. The firm has its own engraving and printing plant, one of the few maintained by American music - publishing houses. The principal circulating music library in the United States was established and for many years maintained by G. Schirmer ; in 1906 it was transferred to the Institute of Musical Art. Since 1891 the Boston Music Company has been affiliated with G. Schirmer as a branch house. Since 1915 the house of G. Schirmer has published *The Musical Quarterly* (see PERIODICALS), under the editorship of O. G. SONNECK (*q.v.*).        R. A.

SCHLAGINSTRUMENTEN (Ger.), instruments of percussion.

SCHLANGENROHR, see SERPENT.

SCHLEIFER, see SLIDE.

SCHLEPPEN (Ger.), to drag. A frequent direction in modern scores is ' Nicht schleppend '—Do not drag.

SCHLESINGER, the name of two famous music-publishing firms, one in Berlin the other in Paris.

The Berlin firm ('Schlesingerschen Buch- und Musikalienhandlung ') was founded in 1810 by (1) ADOLF MARTIN SCHLESINGER (*d.* 1839), a man of original character and great ability.

Among the principal works issued by him was the edition of Bach's ' Matthew Passion,' one of the fruits of Mendelssohn's revival of it,[1] which Schlesinger brought out, according to his favourite expression, ' for the honour of the house.' It was announced in Sept. 1829, and published soon afterwards both in full and PF. score. He also founded the *Berliner A.M.Z.*, which under the editorship of A. B. Marx had for seven years (1824–30) much influence for good in Germany.

His second son, (2) HEINRICH (*b.* 1807 ; *d.* Dec. 14, 1879), carried on the business till his death. He founded the *Echo* in 1851, a periodical which remained in his hands till 1864, when it was sold to R. Lienau. ·

The eldest son, (3) MORITZ ADOLF (*d.* Baden-Baden, Feb. 1871), left Berlin, and in 1819 entered the bookselling house of Bossange père at Paris. In 1823 he endeavoured to found a similar business for himself. Police difficulties prevented him from carrying out his intention, and he founded, in 1834, a music business instead which soon took a leading place among French publishers. He brought his German tastes with him, and an unusual degree of enterprise. His first serious effort was an edition of Mozart's operas in PF. score, for which Horace Vernet designed the title-page. This was followed by editions of the complete works of Beethoven, Weber, Hummel, etc., and a ' Collection de chefs-d'œuvre ' in twenty-four volumes. He published also the full scores of Meyerbeer's ' Robert ' and ' Les Huguenots '; Halévy's ' L'Éclair,' ' La Juive,' ' Les Mousquetaires,' ' La Reine de Chypre,' ' Guido et Ginevra,' ' Charles VI ' ; Donizetti's ' La Favorite ' ; Berlioz's ' Symphonie fantastique,' and overture to the ' Carnaval romain '; the arrangements of Wagner ; the chamber music of Onslow, Reissiger, and a host of other pieces of all descriptions for which the reader must be referred to the catalogue of the firm. Amongst the educational works the ' Méthode des méthodes ' is conspicuous. On Jan. 5, 1834, he issued the first number of the *Gazette musicale*, which in a few months was united to the *Revue musicale* and ran a useful and successful course till its expiry in 1880. In 1846 Schlesinger sold the business to Brandus and Dufour, and retired to Baden-Baden. The music stock is now in the possession of Joubert of Paris.        G.

SCHLICK, ARNOLT, the elder (*b.* Bohemia, *c.* 1460 ; *d.* after 1517). Like Paumann of Nuremberg he was blind, a fine organist and a lute-player. He was a member of the Hofkapelle at Heidelberg before 1511, holding the post of organist to the Count Palatine.

In the fourth book of the ' Micrologus,' 1517, dedicated to Schlick, ' musico consummatissimo, ac Palatini Principis organiste

<hr>

[1] Mar. 11, 1829. See Marx's *Erinnerungen.* ii. pp. 50. 87.

probatissimo,' Ornithoparcus thus apostrophises him :

'From your sentence no man will enter appeale ; because there is no man either learneder, or subtiler in this art, than your selfe, who besides the practice, hast wisdome, eloquence, gentlenesse, quicknesse of wit, and in all kinds of musicke a divine industry, and further the knowledge of many other sciences. Thou wantest the bodily lamp, but in thy mind shineth that golden light ; . . wherefore not only by thy princes, who are to thee most gracious, but even of all men (like Orpheus and Amphion) art thou loved ' [1]

Schlick himself states in the preface to his 'Tabulaturen' that he made tours through Germany and Holland, winning much renown as an organist, and that he was in Worms in 1495, at the time that the Reichstag was held there. Two of Schlick's works are still in existence, the first on organs and organists, the second, a volume of organ and lute pieces in tablature. The former was called :

'Spiegel der Orgelmacher vnd Organisten allen Stifften vnd Kirchen so Orgel halten oder machen lassen hochnützlich, durch den hochberümpten vnd kunstreichen meyster Arnolt Schlicken, Pfalzgrauischen Organisten artlich verfasst,' etc. (1511), small 4to, 00 pages (' Mirror of organ-builders and organists, very useful to all foundations and churches which possess or order organs, excellently composed by the celebrated and gifted master A. S., organist to the Palatinate ').

The only copy known lacks the page at the end which would have given the name of the publisher, but there is little doubt that it was printed by Peter Schöffer at Mainz. Eitner reprinted the whole work in the *M.f.M.*, 1869, giving a facsimile of the engraved title-page. It deals with the materials to be used for the construction of an organ, its erection, the tuning of the pipes, and other technical and theoretical matters, to which is added a description of the organs then in existence, and some allusions to the music of the period. Ellis, in his paper on the history of musical pitch read before the Society of Arts, Mar. 3, 1880 (see PITCH), referred to this book as being of great use in showing the relation between very high and very low church pitch, and the method of tuning before the invention of the mean-tone temperament. He notes also the curious fact that Schlick recommended both the very sharp and the very flat pitch, and for the same reason, consideration of the convenience of both singer and organist using the old ecclesiastical tones, that is, consideration of the compass of the voice and of ease in fingering. This appears to account for the high and low pitches in the earlier period of church pitch.

Schlick's work is mentioned in Virdung's *Musica getutscht*, 1511 (see Eitner's reprint, page E, IV. v.) :

'Dann ich neulich ein tractetlin han gelesen, das ist der spiegel aller organisten vnn orgelmacher intituliert oder genannt, darin find ich in dem andern capitel, das er spricht der organist well dann per fictam musicam spilen, weste der selb von den dreyen geschlechten zu sagen er wurd sye, nit fictam musicam nennen, dann das er maynt fictam musicam syn, das ist cromaticum genus . . . man soll ihn aber verzeihen dann er hat es übersehen, ists augen schuld, oder der spiegel ist dunckel worden,' etc.

These remarks on his use of the term ' musica ficta ' did not at all please Schlick, and in return he made a long attack on Virdung in his preface to the ' Tabulaturen,' published the year after ; there are only two copies known of this important work, one in the Leipzig Stadtbibliothek, the other, without title-page, is in the Berlin Königl. Bibliothek. The full title is

' Tabulaturen etlicher lobgesang vnd lidlein vff die orgeln vn lauten, ein theil mit zweien stimen zu zwicken vn die drit dartzu singen, etlich on gesangk mit dreien, von Arnolt Schlicken Pfalzgrauischen Churfürstlichen Organisten tabulirt, vn in den truck in d'vrsprungkilchen stadt der truckerei zu Meintz wie hie nach volgt verordnet. (On last page) Getruckt zu Mentz durch Peter Schöffern. Vff Sant Mattheis Abent.' Anno 1512, small obl. 4to, 83 pages unnumbered.

It contains fourteen organ pieces, twelve songs with lute accompaniment, and three pieces for lute. Eitner reprinted (*M.f.M.*, 1869) all the organ and two lute compositions. They are preceded by a letter from Schlick's son Arnolt, asking his father to make him a collection of organ and lute music ; it is dated St. Catherine's Day, 1511, and an answer from his father promising to do so, although he has become blind, is dated St. Andrew's Day, 1511. Some satirical verses about Virdung follow. Schlick's method of arranging songs, some with one-voice part and two lutes accompanying, others for three lutes only, is noted by Ambros [2] as being rather remarkable at that early date. Two examples were transcribed and published by Wilhelm Tappert.[3] Schlick's volume is also the earliest appearance in print of the German tablature, for Ammerbach's ' Tabulaturbuch ' was not published until 1571, and Bernh. Jobin's work in 1572. The organ pieces are all taken from sacred vocal compositions, but are arranged with intelligence and artistic feeling, and with a musicianly touch that shows a genuine sense of instrumental composition ; the next step in advance was to be taken later on by Buus, Willaert and others, in their ' Ricercari ' for the organ.[4] No. 10 from ' Tabulaturen,' an organ arrangement in three-part writing of ' Maria zart,' was published in A. G. Ritter's *Zur Geschichte des Orgelspiels*, 1884, ii. 96. In the Heilbronn Gymnasial-bibliothek is a MS. partbook with the bass only of a three-part song, ' Mi, mi,' by Arnolt Schlick. A manuscript, *Mus. Theoret.* 40, 57, written between 1533 and 1540, in the Berlin Königl. Bibliothek, contains a treatise, *De musica poetica*, which has been ascribed to Arnolt Schlick the younger, because of the initials A. S. attached to it. It is described by H. Bellermann,[5] who gives a facsimile of one of the musical examples in it, a four-part setting by Heinrich Isaac ; it is interesting because of the different parts being distinguished by different colours, the soprano and bass being written in red, the alto in green, and the tenor in black ink.      c. s.

[1] Dowland's translation, 1609.

[2] *Geschichte der Musik*, iii. 440.
[3] *Sang u. Klang aus alter Zeit*, Berlin, 1906.
[4] Wasielewski, *Geschichte der Instrumentalmusik im XVI. Jahrhundert*, 1878.
[5] *Der Contrapunct*, 1862, p. 28.

SCHLICK, JOHANN KONRAD (b. Münster, c. 1759; d. Gotha, c. 1825), an excellent violoncellist at the Episcopal Chapel, Münster, until 1776, when he went to Gotha as court musician. He toured a great deal as virtuoso, and married in 1785 the violin virtuoso Regina STRINASACCHI (q.v.). Joh. Schlick composed symphonies, chamber music, concertos, etc., but only a few of his concertos and sonatas for violoncello and three string quartets are still extant. (Mendel; Q.-L.; E. van der Straeten, Hist. of the Violoncello.) E. V. D. S.

SCHLICK, RUDOLF, a doctor of medicine who lived in Meissen, published the following work :

‘ Rodholfi Schlickii R Exercitatio, qua musices origo prima, altus antiquissimus, dignitas maxima, et emolumenta, quae tam animo quam corpori humano confert summa, breviter ac dilucide exponuntur. Spirae, typis Bernardi Albini, 1588, 8vo, pp. 48.’

A copy is in the Bodleian Library, with ‘ Robertus Burton, 1600,’ on the fly-leaf, probably the author of the Anatomy of Melancholy. C. S.

SCHLOESSER, (1) LOUIS (b. Darmstadt, 1800 ; d. there, Nov. 17, 1886), learnt music from Rinck at Darmstadt, and from Seyfried, Salieri and Mayseder in Vienna. In due time he entered the Conservatoire at Paris, and attended the violin class of Kreutzer and the composition class of Lesueur. He then went to Darmstadt and became first leader and then conductor of the court band. His works comprise five operas, among them ‘ Das Leben ein Traum ’ (1839) and ‘ Die Braut des Herzogs ’ (1847), a melodrama, music to ‘ Faust,’ a Mass, a ballet and a quantity of instrumental music of all descriptions. His son, (2) CARL WILHELM ADOLPH (b. Darmstadt, Feb. 1, 1830 ; d. Great Bookham, Nov. 10, 1913), was educated by his father, and in 1847 established himself at Frankfort. In 1854 he went to England and settled in London as an esteemed teacher. He was a professor at the R.A.M. until his retirement in 1903. He published both in England and Germany a great number of PF. works, both soli and duets, including a suite dedicated to Cipriani Potter and a set of twenty-four studies ; many songs and vocal pieces; and many larger works are in MS. His ‘ Schumann Evenings ’ in 1868 were well known, and did much to advance the knowledge of Schumann in England. G.

SCHMEDES, ERIK (b. Gyentofte, near Copenhagen, Aug. 27, 1868), operatic tenor, studied with various teachers in Germany and Austria and with Padilla in Paris, before making a brilliant début at Wiesbaden in 1891. Singing as a light or lyric tenor, he went on to Nuremberg in 1894 and to Dresden in 1896 ; but two years later, when he began his long career at the Vienna Imperial Opera, he attacked the heavier dramatic and Wagnerian parts with signal success. The result was his engagement for Bayreuth in 1899, and he sang there for several years. His production and style were remarkable for ease and polish, the quality of his voice very pleasing ; and he was an excellent actor.

BIBL.—International Who's Who in Music. H. K.

SCHMELTZL (SCHMELTZEL), WOLFGANG, a native of Kemnat in the Upper Palatinate, was at first a Protestant cantor at Amberg, where he married, but eventually forsook his wife and children and became a Roman priest. About 1540 he was a schoolmaster in Vienna, and in 1544 issued the book by which he is known, a collection of ‘ Quodlibets ’ for four and five voices, as well as folk-songs of the time. The title is :

‘ Guter seltzamer vnd kunstreicher teutscher Gesang, sonderlich etliche künstliche Quodlibet, Schlacht (bei Pavia), vnd dergleichen mit 4 oder 5 stimmen. . . .’

It was printed at Nuremberg in four part-books. Copies are at Berlin, in the British Museum, and elsewhere.

BIBL.—Q.-L.; EITNER, Deutsches Lied, vol. i.; and M.f M. iii. 201. A long account of the book is given in the Sammelbände of the Int. Mus. Ges. vi. 80, by ELSA BIENENFELD. M.

SCHMELZER, AB EHRENRUEFF, JOHANN HEINRICH (b. circa 1630 ; d. Vienna, June 1680), chamber musician in the Imperial Court Chapel, Oct. 1, 1649–70 ; vice-Kapellmeister, Jan. 1, 1671 ; Kapellmeister, Oct. 1, 1679. He wrote the ballets for the operas given at the court, especially to those by Draghi ; composed vocal and instrumental pieces which remained in MS., including many sonatas for violin with and without other instruments (Q.-L. ; Riemann).

SCHMID, ANTON (b. Pihl, near Leipa, Bohemia, Jan. 30, 1787 ; d. Salzburg, July 3, 1857), custos of the Hofbibliothek in Vienna, entered the Imperial Library at Vienna in 1818, became scriptor in 1819 and custos in 1844. His department as a writer was the history and literature of music and hymns. He contributed to the following works : Dr. Ferdinand Wolf's Über die Lais, Sequenzen, und Leiche (Heidelberg, 1841) ; Becker's Darstellung der musikalischen Literatur (supplement, Leipzig, 1839) ; A. Schmidt's Allg. Wiener musik. Zeitung (from 1842–48) ; Dehn's Cäcilia (from 1841–48 ; Mayence, Schott) ; and the Österreich. Blätter für Lit. und Kunst (1844. 1845). His independent works are Ottaviano dei Petrucci of Fossombrone, the inventor of movable metal types for printing music, and his successors (Vienna, Rohrmann, 1845) ; Joseph Haydn und Nicolo Zingarelli, proving that Haydn was the author of the Austrian national hymn (Vienna, Rohrmann, 1847) ; Christoph Willibald Ritter von Gluck (Leipzig, Fleischer, 1854) ; also a work on chess, Tschaturangavidjá (Vienna, Gerold, 1847).

To Schmid in the first instance is due the orderly and systematic arrangement of the musical archives of the Hofbibliothek. To recognition of his unwearied industry and research he was made a member of many learned societies in different parts of Europe.

C. F. P.

SCHMID, (1) BERNHARD (b. Strassburg, 1520; d. there, ? 1592), organist at St. Thomas, Strassburg, 1560, and from 1564–92 at the cathedral. He wrote 2 books of organ pieces (1577) in tablature, including arrangements of motets by Lassus, Crecquillon, Arcadelt, etc.; (2) BERNHARD, son of the former (b. Strassburg, 1548), succeeded his father in both positions, and published a book in organ tablature of preludes, toccatas, motets, canzonets, madrigals and fugues in 4, 5 and 6 parts (1607) (Q.-L.; Riemann).

SCHMIDT, BERNHARD, see SMITH (' Father Smith ').

SCHMIDT, JOHANN CHRISTOPH (b. Hohenstein, 1664; d. Dresden, Apr. 13, 1728). After holding appointments as teacher of the choir-boys and second organist at the Dresden court, he was sent to Italy for further studies. In 1696 he became vice-Kapellmeister, and succeeded Strungk as Kapellmeister in 1698. He was entrusted with the entire management of the Electoral Chapel, was court composer, and honoured with the title of Ober Kapellmeister in 1717. Joh. Seb. Bach appears to have thought well of him, as he copied one of his motets. He composed masses, motets and other sacred and secular vocal and instrumental music, which remained mostly in MS. (Q.-L.).

SCHMITT, a German musical family founded by a cantor at Obernburg in Bavaria.

The son, (1) ALOYS (b. Erlenbach-on-Main, Aug. 26, 1788; d. Frankfort, July 25, 1866), was taught to play by his father. He then learned composition from André of Offenbach, and in 1816 established himself in Frankfort as a PF. teacher. After a few successful years there—during which, among others, he had taught Ferdinand Hiller—and much travelling, he migrated to Berlin, then to Hanover, where he held the post of court organist (1825–29), and lastly back to Frankfort. His reputation as a teacher was great, though he had a passion for journeys, and his pupils complained of his frequent absences. He composed more than 100 works of all descriptions, including masses, four operas, two oratorios and string quartets, besides some useful PF. studies.

His brother, (2) JAKOB (b. Obernburg, Nov. 2, 1803; d. June 1853), was a pupil of Aloys. He settled in Hamburg, where he brought out an opera (' Alfred der Grosse ') and a prodigious amount of music, including many sonatas for the piano, solo and with violin, variations, three books of studies, etc., in all more than 300 works.

(3) GEORG ALOYS (b. Hanover, Feb. 2, 1827; d. Dresden, Oct. 15, 1902), son of Aloys (1), was

at Heidelberg University, and put himself under Vollweiler for serious study of counterpoint. His first attempt was an operetta called ' Trilby,' which was performed at Frankfort in 1850 with great success. He then passed some years in various towns of Germany, and at length, in 1856, was called by Flotow to Schwerin as court Kappellmeister. He retired on a pension in 1892, and in the following year became head of the Mozartverein in Dresden. In 1860 he visited London and played before Queen Victoria. He wrote operas, music to plays, and orchestral and other works. He edited and completed Mozart's Mass in C minor (1901). Emma BRANDES (Mme. Engelmann), the eminent pianist, was his pupil.

G.

SCHMITT, FATHER JOSEPH, an 18th-century Cistercian monk in the monastery of Eberbach, Rheingau; an excellent violinist and prolific instrumental composer. He left the monastery before 1780 and went to Amsterdam, where he started a music engraving and publishing business which was taken over by J. J. Hummel. Driven out by the French Revolution, he went to Frankfort-on-Main in 1803, where he became musical director of the theatre. A list of his works is given in Q.-L. His youngest son, FRIEDRICH, was an operatic tenor and well-known singing-master.

E. V. D. S.

SCHMITT, FLORENT (b. Blâmont, Meurthe-et-Moselle, Sept. 28, 1870), French composer. He began his musical studies at Nancy, 1887, entering two years later the Paris Conservatoire, where he was a pupil of Dubois and Lavignac (harmony), and Massenet and G. Fauré (composition). He won the Grand Prix de Rome in 1900. He was director of the Conservatoire, Lyons, 1922–24.

Florent Schmitt has composed much and in many styles; but he is first and foremost a symphonic composer, loving great and deeply-felt poems, solidly planned, imposingly eloquent and decorated with the most dazzling orchestral colours. His music overflows with life and colour. The power of his eloquence upon the public cannot be doubted, since it acclaims the formidable Psalm xlvi., the powerful ' Tragédie de Salomé' or the symphonic episodes of ' Antoine et Cléopâtre.' The music of Florent Schmitt is specially remarkable for the vigour of its style, the inexhaustible variety of its writing, and the skill of the composer in drawing out his vocal and orchestral masses. For the rest, Florent Schmitt has written numerous critical musical articles in La France (1913–14), and since 1919 in the Courrier musical.

WORKS

Numerous pieces for PF. (Hamelle, Leduc, Rouart-Lerolle, Mathot, Heugel, Durand).
Collections of songs: op. 39, ' Chansons à 4 voix,' 4 v. and orch. (Mathot); op. 40, ' Deux chœurs à capella' (1908); ' Cinq motets' (written for the army during the war, Durand); op. 47, ' Danse des Devadasis,' chor. and orch. (1900, Durand; ' Chant de guerre' (1915, Durand); etc.

Symphonic music: op. 38, Psalm xlvi., with chor. (1904, Mathot);
op. 44, 'Musique de plein-air' (Durand); op. 49, 'Le Palais
hanté,' symphonic study (1904, Durand); op. 65, 'Rêves'
(1918, Durand); op. 66, 'Légende' for saxophone and orch.
(1918, Durand); op. 'The Dionysiaques,' etc.
Chamber music: op. 52, Quintet, PF. and strings (1901–08,
Mathot); op. 54, 'Lied et scherzo' for double wind quintet (1910,
Durand); op. 68, 'Sonate libre,' vln. and PF. (Durand);
'Andante et scherzo,' chromatic harp and string quartet
(Durand).
Theatre: op. 50, 'La Tragédie de Salomé,' drama without words,
in 2 acts and 7 scenes (first production, Théâtre des Arts,
Nov. 9, 1907); 'Antoine et Cléopâtre,' symphonic preludes
and interludes for the drama of André Gide, after Shakespeare
(Opéra, 1920); 'Le Petit Elfe Ferme-l'œil' (Opéra-Comique,
1924), a ballet after Hans Andersen's tale; 'Salambô,' com-
posed for the cinematograph film (Opéra, 1925).

BIBLIOGRAPHY

M. D. Calvocoressi, *New Music Review*, 1911; Séré, *Musiciens
français d'aujourd'hui*; A. Cœuroy, *La Musique française moderne*
(Paris, 1922); E. Vuillermoz, *Musique d'aujourd'hui* (Paris, 1923);
P. O Ferroud, *Revue musicale*, Apr. 1924.
F. R<sup>L</sup>.

SCHMITTBAUR, Joseph Aloys (*b*. Bam-
berg, Nov. 8, 1718; *d*. Karlsruhe, Oct. 24, 1809).
He was a pupil of Jommelli and prolific composer, who became Kapellmeister at Karlsruhe
in 1772. He was looked upon as one of the
greatest vocal composers of his time, and his
masses were performed in all the great Catholic
cathedrals, especially in the Rhineland and
in Cologne, where they were still in use during
the first half of the 19th century. His numerous symphonies and chamber music works
were of a superficial nature, like the products of
the younger Mannheim school. (See list in
*Q.-L.*)    E. v. d. S.

SCHMULLER, Alexander (*b*. Mozyr,
Russia, Dec. 5, 1880), violinist, a pupil of Ševčik,
Hřimalý and Auer. He settled in Berlin in
1908; in 1914 he accepted a post at the Conservatoire of Amsterdam, from which place he
undertakes extensive concert tours. Schmuller
is one of the most versatile violinists of our
time, especially in the excellence of his interpretation of modern music. He played for a
number of years with Max Reger, the value of
whose compositions he was amongst the first to
recognise.    R. M<sup>G</sup>.

SCHNABEL, Joseph Ignaz (*b*. Naumburg
a/Queis, May 24, 1767; *d*. Breslau, June 16, 1831).
The son of a cantor and himself a schoolmaster,
he gained a wide reputation for the singing of
his pupils. In 1797 he went to Breslau as
organist of St. Clara and violinist at St.
Vincent. In 1805 he became Kapellmeister of
the cathedral; in 1812 musical director of the
University, director of the Royal Institute for
church music, and teacher of music at the
Catholic seminary. He composed masses and
other church and secular vocal and instrumental music (*Q.-L.*; *Riemann*).

SCHNEIDER, (1) Georg Abraham (*b*. Darmstadt, Apr. 9, 1770; *d*. Berlin, Jan. 19, 1839),
became a proficient on the horn, and studied
theory with Portmann, whose daughter he afterwards married. He was successively oboist in
a Hessian regiment, horn-player in the court
bands of Darmstadt, Schwerin, Rheinsberg
and Berlin. In 1812 or 1814 he undertook the
duties of theatrical conductor at Reval, but
went back to Berlin in 1816, and in 1820 was

made Kapellmeister of the court opera and
director of military bands. He had a rare
knowledge of musical instruments of all kinds,
and wrote a large number of operettas, masses,
cantatas, an oratorio, 'Die Pilgrime auf
Golgotha,' symphonies, concertos and chamber
music of all kinds. (*Q.-L.*; *Riemann*.)    M.

(2) Louis (*b*. Berlin, Apr. 29, 1805; *d*. Potsdam, Dec. 16, 1878), son of the above, published
*Geschichte der Oper und des Königlichen Opern-
hauses zu Berlin*, 1852. (*Riemann*.)

SCHNEIDER, (1) Johann Christian Friedrich (*b*. Alt-Waltersdorf, near Zittau, Jan. 3,
1786; *d*. Nov. 23, 1853), composer, teacher and
conductor, composed a symphony at the age
of 10. In 1798 he entered the Gymnasium
of Zittau, and studied music with Schönfelder
and Unger. In 1804 he published three PF.
sonatas, and having entered the University of
Leipzig in 1805, carried on his musical studies
to such purpose that in 1807 he became organist
of St. Paul's, in 1810 director of the Seconda
opera, in 1812 organist of the Thomaskirche,
and in 1817 director at the Stadt Theater.
There he remained till 1821, when he became
Kapellmeister to the Duke of Dessau, whose
music he much improved, and founded in the
town a Singakademie, a schoolmasters' choral
society and a Liedertafel. In 1829 he founded
a musical institute, which succeeded well, and
educated several excellent musicians, Robert
Franz among the number. Schneider was also
an industrious composer, his works comprising:

Oratorios—'Die Höllenfahrt des Messias' (1810), 'Das Weltgericht' (1819), 'Totenfeier' (1821), 'Die Sündfluth' (1823),
'Verlorne Paradies' (1824), 'Jesu Geburt' (1825), 'Christus das
Kind,' 'Pharao' and 'Gideon' (1829), 'Absalom' (1830), 'Das
befreite Jerusalem' (1835), 'Salomonis Tempelbau' (1836),
'Bonifazius' (1837) 'Christus der Erlöser' (1838), 'Gethsemane
und Golgotha' (1838); 14 masses; various settings of Gloria and
Te Deum; 25 cantatas; 5 hymns; 13 psalms; 7 operas; 23 symphonies; 60 sonatas; 6 concertos; 400 Lieder for men's voices,
and 200 ditto for a single voice.

Schneider directed the musical festivals of
Magdeburg (1825), Nuremberg (1828), Strassburg (1830), Halle (1830 and 1835), Halberstadt
(1830), Dessau (1834), Wittenberg (1835),
Coethen (1838 and 1846), Coblenz and Hamburg (1840), Meissen (1841), Zerbst (1844) and
Lübeck (1847). He also published didactic
works—*Elementarbuch der Harmonie und Ton-
setzkunst* (1820), translated into English
(London, 1828); *Vorschule der Musik* (1827);
and *Handbuch des Organisten* (1829–30). The
oratorio of the 'Sündfluth' was translated
into English as 'The Deluge' by E. Taylor,
published in London, and performed at the
Norwich Festival of 1833.

Schneider was a doctor of philosophy and
a member of the Berlin and several other
academies. Some traits of his curious jealous
temper will be found in Schubring's Reminiscences of Mendelssohn, in *Daheim* for 1866,
No. 26. He was vexed with Mendelssohn for
his revival of Bach's Passion—but the feeling
passed away; and in the *Signale* for 1866,
Nos. 46, 47, 48, there are eight letters, 1829–45

'translated in *The Musical World*, Dec. 29, 1866, and Jan. 5, 1867), from Mendelssohn to him showing that they were on very good terms.[1] When Mendelssohn's body passed through Dessau on its way to Berlin, Schneider met it at the station with his choir, and a lament was sung which he had purposely composed, and which will be found in the *A.M.Z.* for 1847, No. 48.

BIBL.—ALFRED FAST, *Friedrich Schneider in seinen Sinfonien und Ouvertüren.* Halle Dissertation, 1921.　　　　　　F. G.

(2) JOHANN GOTTLOB (*b.* Alt-Gersdorf, Oct. 28, 1789 ; *d.* Dresden, Apr. 13, 1864), celebrated Dresden organist, brother of the preceding, was at 22 organist of the Leipzig University church, and by 1820 was recognised as one of the first organists living. To his fine playing at a Magdeburg festival in 1825 he owed his Dresden appointment of court organist, which he held till his death. From the organ-loft of the Hofkirche he made his influence felt ; how widely, may be gathered from the mere names of his pupils, amongst whom were Mendelssohn, Schumann, Liszt, Merkel, Töpfer, Van Eycken. The last four were amongst the thirty old pupils who composed and presented to him that graceful offering, the ' Jubel Album für die Orgel,' in 1861, the fiftieth year of his artistic career. Schumann's studies with him permanently influenced the composer, and directly inspired or helped to inspire the Pedal Pianoforte Studies, and Fugues on the name of Bach ; and Mendelssohn confessed a like obligation and admiration. Schneider's reading of Bach—derived straight from him by direct descent in only three removes—was the best weapon in his equipment as a teacher. He always ended a lesson by playing one of the great fugues or, especially, ' organ Chorals.' Sir Herbert Oakeley (Schneider's last pupil) used to talk much of his playing of these compositions. He liked playing some of ' the 48 ' on his deep-toned Silbermann organ.

Schneider's few published works include an ' answer of thanks ' to the ' Jubel Album,' a masterly fantasia and fugue in D minor (op. 3), etc.　　　　　　E. M. O.

Another brother, (3) JOHANN GOTTLOB (*b.* Alt-Gersdorf, July 19, 1797 ; *d.* Aug. 4, 1856), was organist of the Kreuzkirche at Hirschberg. (*Riemann.*)

SCHNELLER, the German name for the short trill or inverted mordent (see PRALL-TRILLER).

Written.　Played.

SCHNETZLER, JOHANN, see SNETZLER, JOHN.

SCHNORR VON CAROLSFELD, LUDWIG (*b.* Munich, July 2, 1836 ; *d.* Dresden, July 21, 1865), tenor singer, the son of the painter Julius Schnorr von Carolsfeld. He first received instruction in music from Julius Otto at Dresden, where, in 1846, his father became director of the Kunst Akademie. In 1854 he was for a short time at the Leipzig Conservatorium, and later in the year studied for the stage under Eduard Devrient at Carlsruhe, where he became engaged. He made his début in the modest part of Napthali in Méhul's ' Joseph,' and later made a great success as Robert (Meyerbeer). About this period he married the singer Malwina Garrigues (*b.* Dec. 7, 1825 ; *d.* Vincentius Hospital, Carlsruhe, Feb. 8, 1904). On leave of absence, he sang in opera at Wiesbaden and Frankfort, and at festivals at Mainz and Düsseldorf. From 1860–65 he was engaged at Dresden, where he increased his popularity. In 1862 Wagner heard him when singing at Carlsruhe as Lohengrin, and was so struck with his performance that he determined to confide to him the part of Tristan whenever the opera was produced. Schnorr had been warmly recommended to the composer earlier, both by Tichatschek the singer, and Devrient, but for a time Wagner was not prepossessed in Schnorr's favour, on account of his unromantic figure, in spite of his talent and his enthusiasm for Wagner and his music.[2] On June 10, 1865, Schnorr and his wife created the parts of Tristan and Isolde, when the opera was produced at Munich, at the express instance of the composer. Their leave of absence being limited, they returned to Dresden, July 15, and the tenor died six days after, of a chill and rheumatism, caught at the first performance of the opera. He was a clever all-round musician, an excellent pianist and extempore player, a composer, and arranger of songs of Bach, Gluck and the old Italian school. He was also a painter and a writer of poetry. In 1867 his widow published a volume of poems by herself and her husband. After his death she was engaged at Hamburg, and finally at Carlsruhe, where, on her retirement, she became a teacher of singing.　　A. C.

SCHNÜFFIS, see LAURENTIUS VON SCHNÜF-FIS.

SCHOBERLECHNER, (1) FRANZ (*b.* Vienna, July 21, 1797 ; *d.* Berlin, Jan. 7, 1843). Hummel composed for him his second pianoforte concerto in C, which he performed in public with success when only 10 years old. The precocious child was taken under the patronage of Prince Esterhazy, and sent to Vienna to study under Forster. From 1814 he travelled in Austria and Italy. While at Florence he composed a Requiem and a *buffa* opera, ' I virtuosi teatrali.' In the next year, having been appointed maestro di cappella to the Duchess of Lucca, he wrote ' Gli Arabi

[1] See also Hauptmann's letters to Spohr.

[2] See ' Meine Erinnerungen an L. S. v. C.,' *Neue Zeitschrift für Musik*, Nos. 24 and 25, 1868.

nelle Gallie,' and subsequently, at Vienna in 1820, ' Der junge Onkel.' In 1823 he went to Russia. He seems to have written to Beethoven before starting, for letters of introduction, which the composer refused.[1] At St. Petersburg he recommended himself to dall' Occa, a professor of singing, whose daughter he married in 1824. After travelling in Germany and Italy, the pair returned to St. Petersburg in 1827, where Mme. Schoberlechner was engaged for three years at the Italian Opera at a salary of 20,000 roubles. Her husband composed for her an opera, ' Il Barone di Dolzheim,' which had some success. In 1831 Schoberlechner retired to a country house near Florence. His last opera was ' Rossane,' produced at Milan, Feb. 9, 1839.

(2) MADAME SOPHIE SCHOBERLECHNER, daughter of Signor dall' Occa (b. St. Petersburg, 1807 ; d. Florence, 1863), till 1827 appeared only in concerts, but was then engaged at the Italian Opera of St. Petersburg. She had a very beautiful voice, and for twelve or thirteen years sang with unvarying success in almost all the principal towns of Germany and Italy. In 1840 she left the stage and retired to her husband's property in Tuscany.

F. A. M.

SCHOBERT,[2] JOHANN (JEAN) (b. circa 1720, d. Sept. 1767), a player on the harpsichord, was brought up at Strassburg. He was at one time organist at Versailles, but was dismissed for negligence. He settled in Paris in 1760, in which year his first works were published there, where he was in the service of the Prince de Conti. On the occasion of his death, Grimm, no mean judge of music, inserts in his Correspondance a very high eulogium on his merits as a player. He praises him for

'his great ability, his brilliant and enchanting execution, and an unequalled facility and clearness. He had not the genius of our Eckard, who is undoubtedly the first master in Paris ; but Schobert was more universally liked than Eckard, because he was always agreeable, and because it is not every one who can feel the power of genius.'

He left 17 sonatas for clavier and violin ; 11 for clavier, violin and violoncello ; 3 quartets for clavier, 2 violins and violoncello ; 6 ' sinfonies ' for clavier, violin and two horns ; 6 clavier concertos, and 4 books of sonatas for clavier solo.[3] These seem to have been originally published in Paris, but editions of many of them appeared in London between 1770 and 1780. The particulars of his death are given by Grimm. It was occasioned by eating some fungi which he gathered near Paris, and which killed his wife, his children, a friend, the servant, and himself.[4] Crotch included two of Schobert's pieces in his ' Specimens,' vol. iii. A minuetto and allegro

[1] See note to Beethoven's Letters, translated by Lady Wallace, vol. ii. p. 115.
[2] ' Chobert ' in Mozart's orthography. Letter, Oct. 17, 1777.
[3] Weitzmann, Geschichte des Clavierspiels.
[4] Grimm (new ed.), vii. 422.

molto in E♭ have been reprinted in Pauer's ' Alte Meister ' (the former has been ' freely arranged ' in L. Godowsky's ' Renaissance '), other movements in the ' Maîtres du clavecin,' and a sonata, so-called, in the Musical Library. A more important reprint, however, is that of D.D.T. vol. xxxix., where a large selection of his works has been edited by Riemann. Burney (Hist. iv. 591, 597) remarks that his music is essentially harpsichord music, and that he was one of the few composers who were not influenced by Emanuel Bach.

BIBL.—GEORGES DE SAINT-FOIX, Jean Schobert, 1740–1767. (With music) Revue musicale, Aug. 1922.       G., rev.

SCHÖFFER, PETER (the younger), an early 16th-century printer, son of the partner of Gutenberg and Fust, one of the earliest German music printers, whose work rivals that by Petrucci in every respect. He worked at first at Mainz, where in 1512 he published Arnold Schlick's organ tablature, and in 1513 the first 4-part song-book. Thence he went to Worms, and from 1534–37 was at Strassburg in partnership with Apiarius, who soon after went to Berne. In 1539 he was again working on his own account, and in 1540 was printer at Venice (Q.-L. ; Riemann).

SCHŒLCHER, VICTOR (b. Paris, July 21, 1804 ; d. Harville, Seine-et-Oise, Dec. 24, 1893), French writer and politician, son of a manufacturer of china, was educated at the Collège Louis le Grand, and well known as an ultra - republican. On the accession of the Emperor Napoleon III. he was expelled both from France and Belgium, but took refuge in London, where he brought out his Histoire des crimes du 2 décembre (1853), and an English pamphlet entitled Dangers to England of the Alliance with the Men of the Coup d'État (1854).

Schœlcher remained in England till Aug. 1870, returning to Paris immediately before the Revolution of Sept. 4. As staff-colonel of the Garde Nationale he commanded the Legion of Artillery throughout the siege of Paris. After Jan. 31, 1871, he was elected to the Assemblée Nationale by the Department of the Seine, Martinique and Cayenne, and sat for Martinique till elected a life senator (Dec. 16, 1875).

His claim to a place in this work, however, is as a distinguished amateur. His devotion to art of all kinds was proved by his articles in L'Artiste (1832) and La Revue de Paris (1833), and he made during his travels a most interesting collection of foreign musical instruments. His long stay in England had a still more remarkable result in his enthusiasm for Handel. He accordingly made a collection of Handel's works, and of books and pamphlets bearing on his life and music, a list of which he gives in the beginning of his book. To the autographs in Buckingham Palace and the Fitzwilliam Museum at Cambridge, and to the copies by Smith formerly in possession of H. B. Lennard, he obtained access, and thus provided, published *The Life of Handel, by Victor Schœlcher*, London, Trübner, 8vo, 1857. The author was materially assisted by Rophino Lacy,[1] whose labours are amply acknowledged in the preface (p. xxii). The work was written by Schœlcher in French, and translated by James Lowe. It contains much information beyond what is indicated in the title, especially with regard to Italian opera and music in general in England during the 18th century. The French MS., *Handel et son temps*, was handed over to *La France musicale*, which (Aug. 19, 1860) published the first four chapters and the beginning of the fifth (Nov. 2, 1862), but there broke off, doubtless for political reasons. The MS. was supposed to have been destroyed, till May 25, 1881, when it was offered for sale by Charavay, and at once bought for the library of the Conservatoire, thus completing Schœlcher's magnificent gift (Nov. 1872) of all the works, in print or MS., used by him in preparing the book, and his collection of foreign instruments. He later added a quantity of music and rare books bearing on the history of Italian opera in London, and on singing and pianoforte-playing in the United Kingdom. The *Fonds Schœlcher*, as it is called, contains in all 500 volumes uniformly bound with the initials of the donor, and has already been of immense service to French artists and musicologists.

G. C.

SCHÖNBERG, ARNOLD (b. Vienna, Sept. 13, 1874), Austrian composer, was attracted to composition from his earliest school days, when he wrote short duets for his violin lessons. He subsequently taught himself the violoncello, and composed several trios and a string quartet for a group of his schoolfellows with whom he played chamber music. At the age of 16 his father died, and the boy was left in straitened circumstances. He continued his musical pursuits, but remained entirely self-taught in composition until a friend showed some of his work to Alexander von Zemlinsky, who was so favourably impressed that he offered to teach him. This, the only tuition Schönberg had, was the foundation of an intimate personal friendship which was converted into relationship by his marriage, in 1901, with Zemlinsky's sister Mathilde. Meanwhile, in 1897, Schönberg, besides making a piano arrangement of his friend's opera ' Sarema,' wrote a string quartet which, after drastic revision, was performed the following winter and attracted favourable attention. This work, the first to be heard in public, is unfortunately lost, but twelve of the larger number of songs which followed (1898–1900) were published as opp. 1-3. Some of these were included by Prof. Gärtner at a song recital (Dec. 1900) and provoked the

---

[1] M. Schœlcher's statement as to Mr. Lacy's assistance should materially modify our inferences from his account of his own part in the examination of Handel's MSS. (p. xxi).

first of the hostile demonstrations which have dogged the successive stages of the composer's evolution. His next work was the well-known string sextet ' Verklärte Nacht ' (op. 4), which was composed in three weeks (Sept. 1899) during a sojourn with Zemlinsky at Payerbach. He then engaged upon the composition of the ' Gurre-Lieder ' (without op. no.), a vast work for soli (one of whom is a reciter), chorus and orchestra, of which a laudatory review by Ernest Newman appeared in the *Mus. T.* of Jan. 1914. It was completed by Mar. 1901, and the scoring begun the following August, but owing to the pressure of professional occupations it had to be put aside, and the third section of the work was not orchestrated until 1910–11, when, however, no important changes were made in the composition. It was first performed at Vienna on Feb. 23, 1913, under Franz Schreker.

From 1901, the year of his marriage, to July 1903 Schönberg lived in Berlin, at first conducting the Überbrettl performances, afterwards scoring, sometimes conducting, a number of operettas. During this period he wrote the symphonic poem ' Pelleas and Melisande' (op. 5). In the autumn following his return to Vienna (1903) he took up teaching, to which he has since devoted close and constant attention. After writing six songs with orchestra (op. 8), he engaged upon the string quartet in D minor (op. 7) which was begun at Mödling in the summer of 1904, and completed a year later at Gmunden. It was followed by eight songs (op. 6), the last three of which are dated Oct. 1905. The following year (1906) is represented by the ballad ' Jane Grey ' (op. 12, no. 1), the chamber symphony in E major (op. 9) and the greater part of a second chamber symphony which he subsequently (1911) discarded. On Mar. 9, 1907, he completed, for a competition, the chorus ' Friede auf Erden ' (op. 13), and the same day began the composition of the string quartet in F sharp minor, the first movement of which was completed at Gmunden on Sept. 1. In the early part of that year first the D minor quartet, and then the chamber symphony, had been performed by the Rosé Quartet in the face of violent hostile demonstrations. About this time he wrote the second ballad of op. 12 and, a little later, the songs op. 14. The second quartet was completed in the summer of 1908, and a third sketched which was, however, abandoned. Then followed the Stefan-George cycle ' Die hängenden Gärten ' which was completed in the autumn. The first performance of the F sharp minor quartet took place in December amid wild scenes. Frau Gutheil-Schoder, of the Opera, sang the Stefan-George poems which are set with its third and fourth movements.

The following year (1909) appeared the first compositions belonging definitely to the new style, to which recent works, notably the quartet (op. 10), and the songs (opp. 14 and 15) had perceptibly been leading. These consisted of the three piano pieces (op. 11), the five orchestral pieces (op. 16), both of which provoked a world-wide discussion, and the monodrama ' Erwartung,' which was composed in sixteen days (Aug. 27–Sept. 12, 1909), but was not performed until the Prague International Festival of May 1924, Zemlinsky conducting and Marie Gutheil-Schoder taking the part of the woman. The text of this, written by Marie Pappenheim at Schönberg's suggestion, is a monodrama—a drama of one character. A woman wanders through a forest anxiously seeking her lover. Her forebodings are realised and she finds him dead, slain near the house of the woman who has taken him from her. Schönberg has employed a large orchestra, and the soprano part is of enormous difficulty. After this he engaged upon a second dramatic work, ' Die glückliche Hand ' (The Lucky Hand), op. 18, which was, however, not completed until Nov. 18, 1913. The action is sustained throughout by one character, a man, but there are two others, a a man and a woman, and a chorus of six men and six women. The subject is symbolical and might be described as the pursuit of happiness, but the dramatic means employed are strange. At the rise of the curtain the stage is almost in darkness. At the front lies a man. On his back crouches a monstrous cat-like creature which appears to be biting him. At the back are dark violet hangings through which appear in a green light the twelve faces of the chorus, who describe the fate of the man who seeks earthly happiness whilst spiritual happiness awaits him in the end. The subsequent episodes are concerned with spurious forms of happiness. It was first performed at Vienna in Oct. 1924.

In 1910 Schönberg began to write his *Treatise on Harmony*, and to score the third part of the 'Gurre-Lieder.' For three years previously he had been turning his attention to another medium of expression, and painted a large number of pictures. In the autumn of 1910, on his return from a Berlin performance of ' Pelleas and Melisande,' an exhibition of these was held in Heller's Gallery, in connexion with which Rosé gave performances of both quartets. The following spring (1911) he wrote the six small pieces for piano (op. 19). Later in the year he migrated once more to Berlin, where he completed the *Harmony Treatise* and the scoring of the ' Gurre-Lieder,' and set ' Herzgewächse ' (Maeterlinck) for high soprano, celesta, harmonium and harp (op. 20). In 1912, between Mar. 20 and Sept. 9, he wrote the cycle ' Pierrot Lunaire,' the first performance of which was given that autumn in Berlin, and

followed by a tour in Germany and Austria. ' Pierrot Lunaire ' consists of twenty-one poems (in three cycles of seven each) by Albert Giraud in a translation by Otto Erich Hartleben, set for declamation with five instruments in constantly varied combinations : piano, flute (alternating with piccolo), clarinet (alternating with bass clarinet), violin (alternating with viola) and violoncello. To English readers, the poems recall the mood of the literary 'nineties as represented for instance by Ernest Dowson, and it is interesting to note that another poet to whom Schönberg has been strongly attracted, Stefan George, is Dowson's German translator. Except at a few points the part of the reciter is notated, but clear indications are given that it is not to be either sung or delivered in a sing-song form of speaking voice. The composer makes the distinction that in song the pitch of each note is unalterably fixed, whereas the speaking voice gives each note but immediately leaves it upwards and downwards. The rhythm is, however, to be maintained as strictly as in song. Performers are further requested not to seek to define the mood and character of the pieces from the text. So far as the composer intended the incidents and emotions described to be expressed, his purpose is achieved in the music as written. Two actresses have given interpretations, notably in Austria, Germany and Holland, which earned the composer's approval : Albertine Zehme in the first performances, and Erika Wagner since the war. These rendered the music in strictest accordance with the composer's views. Marya Freund, who took part in other performances, mainly in France, Italy and England, never forgot that she was a singer. Hence her rendering is not considered strictly orthodox, but its excellence has nevertheless contributed materially to the attention which the work has everywhere received.

Next began a series of foreign appearances. In Nov. 1912 he conducted ' Pelleas and Melisande ' at Amsterdam with great success. Returning to Vienna he had the satisfaction of hearing the integral performance of the ' Gurre-Lieder ' on Feb. 23, 1913, and conducted an orchestral concert on Mar. 30, attended by the usual disturbance. Meanwhile Sir Henry Wood, who had conducted the first London performance of the five orchestral pieces on Sept. 3, 1912, had invited him to direct the second, which he did in Feb. 1914, journeying afterwards to Leipzig for the ' Gurre-Lieder ' and Amsterdam for the five pieces. When war broke out the only composition in addition to the above which was finished was the orchestral song ' Seraphita,' to which, by the end of 1914, he had added three others to form op. 22. Then occurs a long interval, interrupted during

**1915-17** by spells of military service, but otherwise occupied with the poems of a projected trilogy of oratorios, and the composition, as yet unfinished, of its third section, ' Die Jakobsleiter.' Early in 1918 he returned to Vienna, teaching and directing as president the activities of the Verein für Musikalische Privat-Aufführungen. From about 1920 he came again into international prominence with numerous performances everywhere. In the summer of 1922, at the suggestion of Josef Stransky, then conductor of the New York Philharmonic Society, he scored for orchestra two Bach Choral-Preludes : 'Schmücke dich' and 'Komm, Gott, Schöpfer, heiliger Geist.' They were first played in Carnegie Hall the following December. During 1923 he completed three works which showed that in the long interval his style had reached a further stage of evolution. These were the five piano pieces (op. 23) begun in 1920, the serenade for seven instruments (op. 24) begun in 1921 and a suite of dance movements Prelude, Gavotte and Musette, Intermezzo, Minuet and Gigue) for piano (op. 25). Since then has appeared the quintet for wind instruments (op. 26), composed 1923-24.

The sequence of works is given above in some detail, because it has considerable bearing upon the stages of the composer's development. For instance, the sensational *volte-face* which is often alleged to have taken place between op. 10 and 11 acquires a less revolutionary aspect when one realises that several works intervened in which a gradual transition, begun in the quartet op. 10, can be traced until it reaches the definite stage of op. 11. Nevertheless the occurrence of such turning points permits Schönberg's work to be divided into three distinct periods. The first comprises opp. 1-10 and 12-15, of which all but the earliest have a transitional character, which becomes conspicuous from op. 10 onwards. The second is represented by opp. 11 and 16-22, the third by opp. 23-26.

Mastery of, and emancipation from, accepted forms was progressively the goal of the first. Starting with the melodic-harmonic apparatus of the Romantic Movement in the sextet 'Verklärte Nacht,' and the 'Gurre-Lieder,' the composer soon carried chromaticism to the very limits of tonality, by chromatic alteration, and especially by the use of the vacillating (*schwebende*) chords, among which those resulting from an equal division of the octave, or generally symmetrical intervals, have the most disintegrating effect upon tonality. In the chamber symphony the use of the whole-tone scale, and, at the opening, of four superimposed fourths, sap the main tonality of E major, and in the last movement of the F sharp minor quartet there are whole passages in which the key remains fluid and indefinite. In regard to

this period it is useful to consult the authoritative and detailed analytical guides to the 'Gurre-Lieder,' 'Pelleas and Melisande' and the chamber symphony which are the work of Schönberg's pupil, Alban BERG (*q.v.*). In the George-Lieder (op. 15) the composer finally dispenses with the aid of tonality and commits himself to the new path. From this point also the old view of consonance and dissonance gives way to a new, for the most part contrapuntal, mode of writing.

In the second period Schönberg develops the newly-found independence, the first effect of which is a drastic restriction of the dimensions of his works and of the means employed in them. Where nothing is written as a mere product of the context, and consequently every note has its full significance, the texture would naturally be considerably lightened. But whilst the formal principles derived from tonality were discarded, others were not only retained but further developed. For instance, the second cycle of ' Pierrot Lunaire' opens with a passacaglia, ' Die Nacht' to which Roland Tenschert has devoted a careful analytical study in *Die Musik* (May 1925). ' Der Mondfleck,' in the same work, contains a double canon *cancrizans*. 'Pierrot Lunaire,' for a reciter and five instruments is the best known work of this period, though in England it has had fewer performances than the five orchestral pieces. The composer's admirers are a little inclined to distrust its relative popularity, fearing lest it may be attributable more to its literary evocations than to an understanding of its strictly musical qualities.

In the third period Schönberg establishes new formal principles to govern the new material and new experience acquired in the second. These principles have been described by Erwin Stein in an essay, *Neue Formprinzipien*, which is included in the special Schönberg number with which the *Musikblätter des Anbruch* celebrated his fiftieth birthday, and also in a compilation *Von neuer Musik* (Marcan, Cologne 1925). Schönberg himself is preparing a treatise on this new method which he terms *Komposition mit zwölf Tönen*, which he envisages as the continuation of his *Treatise on Harmony*. Its basis is the twelve-note scale, but, as Stein points out, if this is to create a form it must be differentiated, and that can only happen by means of a limitation of some kind. This is done by arranging the twelve notes (or a portion of them) into a basic shape (*Grundgestalt*), of which a composition may have one or more. These note-shapes can be inverted, and both the original and the inversion horizontally reversed (*cancrizans*), giving four variants of each. These again may be transposed at any interval. Thus is constituted the material of the composition, which may be used horizontally, with the consecutive notes in one part or distributed, and vertically, furnishing therefore both line and texture. Stein gives a detailed explanation on these lines of opp. 23, 24 and 25, and in the *Anbruch* of Feb. 1925 a corresponding analysis of the wind quintet (op. 26) is given by the composer's son-in-law, Felix Greissle, who conducted the first performance, Sept. 16, 1924, at Vienna. The serenade (op. 24) was given at the Venice (1925) Festival of the International Society for Contemporary Music.

Schönberg's *Treatise on Harmony*, revised and now in its third edition, embodies the substance of his teaching as imparted to his pupils, of whom there have been many, including Anton von Webern, Alban Berg, Heinrich Jalowetz, Erwin Stein, Egon Wellesz, Karl Horwitz, Paul A. Pisk and Hans Eisler. Its preface opens : 'This book I have learned from my pupils.' His poems for 'The Lucky Hand,' and for the projected trilogy of oratorios, 'Totentanz der Prinzipien, Requiem, Die Jakobsleiter,' have been published as 'Texte.' His other writings comprise an article on musical criticism (*Der Merker*, 1909, II.), a memorial tribute to Mahler (*ibid.* 1911, V.), problems of art-education (*Musik. Taschenbuch*, Vienna, 1911), 'Parsifal' and copyright (*Konzert-Taschenbuch*, 1912), the relation to the text (*Blaue Reiter*, 1913), *Gewissheit* (included in a vol. of *Confessions*, published by Reiss, Berlin), music (*Richtlinien für ein Kunstamt*, Ad. Loos, Vienna, 1919, reprinted in *Von neuer Musik*, Marcan, Cologne, 1925), a new twelve-note notation (*Anbruch*, Jan. 1925), tonality and form (*Christian Science Monitor*, Dec. 1925) and *Gesinnung oder Erkenntnis* (*Annual of the Universal Edition*, Vienna, 1926). In the last-mentioned he refers to a volume *Der musikalische Gedanke und seine Darstellung*, upon which he is engaged.

There is a rapidly growing Schönberg literature. The most detailed account of the composer and his works is contained in a monograph by Dr. Egon Wellesz (Tal, Vienna, 1921 ; English translation by W. H. Kerridge, Dent, London, 1925), to which the present writer is indebted for some dates and biographical information. A shorter monograph by Dr. Paul Stefan has been issed by the same publisher (Tal, Vienna, 1924). Then there are two compilations, one a collection of essays inscribed to him by his pupils and published under his name (R. Piper, Munich, 1912), and the other consisting partly of essays and partly of complimentary addresses issued as a special number of the *Anbruch* (Aug. - Sept. 1924) on the occasion of the composer's fiftieth birthday as mentioned above. Besides the various writings to which the reader has been referred (analytical guides by Alban Berg, articles by Tenschert, Stein and Greissle) should be mentioned further an article *Arnold Schönberg*, contributed by Paul Bekker to *Kritische Zeitbilder*; Arnold

*Schönberg und Wien*, by D. I. Bach (*Merker* 1921, II.) ; and *Pierrot Lunaire*, by Erwin Stein (*Il Pianoforte*, Apr. 1924). But the performance of his most discussed works has led everywhere to numerous articles, appreciative or polemical, and most books on modern music devote a special chapter to his methods.

## WORKS

Op.
1. Two songs with PF.
2. Four songs with PF.
3. Six songs with PF.
4. ' Verklärte Nacht ' Sextet, for 2 vlns., 2 vlas. and 2 vcls. (also for str. orch.).
5. ' Pelleas and Melisande,' symph. poem for orch.
6. Eight songs with PF.
7. Str. Quartet I. in D min.
8. Six songs with orch.
9. Chamber symphony in E maj. for 15 solo instr.
10. Str. Quartet II. in F sharp min., with sopr. in 3rd and 4th movements.
11. Three pieces for PF.
12. Two ballads, v. and PF.
13. ' Friede auf Erden,' mixed choir *a cappella*.
14. Two songs with PF.
15. Fifteen poems from Stefan George, ' Buch der hängenden Garten,' for v. and PF.
16. Five pieces for orch.
17. ' Erwartung,' monodrama.
18. ' Die glückliche Hand,' drama with music.
19. Six small pieces for PF.
20. ' Herzgewächse,' for high sopr., celesta, harmonium and harp.
21. Three cycles of seven poems each from Albert Giraud's ' Pierrot Lunaire ' as declamation with five instr. (PF., fl., alternating with piccolo, clar. with bass clar., vln. with vla., and vcl.)
22. Four songs with orch.
23. Five pieces for PF.
24. Serenade for 7 instr. (clar., bass clar., mandoline, guitar vln., vla. and vcl.), and, in 1 number, a bass voice.
25. Suite for PF.
26. Quintet for wind instr. (fl., oboe, clar., horn and bassoon).

WITHOUT OP. NOS.

Gurre-Lieder for soli, choir, and orch.
Two chorale-preludes (Bach), arranged for orch.

EDITIONS

Cembalo-part to symphony in A maj., concerti for clavicembalo in G min. and D maj., and for vcl., by Matthias Georg Monn, and a divertimento by Johann Christoph Monn.

POEMS

' Die glückliche Hand,' ' Requiem,' ' Totentanz der Prinzipien,' ' Die Jakobsleiter,' published together as ' Texte.'

THEORETICAL WRITINGS.

*Harmonie-Lehre* and essays enumerated above.

E. E.

SCHÖNBERGER, BENNO (*b*. Vienna, Sept. 12, 1863), was a pupil of Anton Door for piano, Bruckner for counterpoint and Volkmann for composition at the Vienna Conservatorium until 1874, when he played at recitals, and with the Hellmesberger Quartet. He went for a time to study with Liszt, and in 1878 undertook an extended tour in Russia, Germany, Austria and Belgium. From 1880–85 he taught in Vienna, and after a journey to Sweden in 1886 settled in London, making his first appearance at a recital of his own, in Jan. 1887. From that time he held an honourable place among the pianists who appear regularly in London, and his interpretations of the classics were always sound and interesting, while his tone and technique were of remarkable excellence. He went to America on tour in 1894. Later he has made frequent appearances in England, and toured in Europe. He has published numerous piano pieces, including three sonatas and songs. (*Baker*, etc.)     M.

SCHOLA CANTORUM. (1) For the history of the ancient Papal Choir school of this name see SISTINE CHOIR; (2) an important music school in PARIS (*q.v.*) ; (3) a choral society in NEW YORK (*q.v.*). See also SCHINDLER, Kurt.

SCHOLZ, (1) BERNHARD E. (b. Mainz, Mar. 30, 1835 ; d. Munich, Dec. 26, 1916), studied the piano with Ernst Pauer (at that time director of the Liedertafel in that city) and theory with S. W. Dehn, became teacher of theory in the Royal School of Music at Munich in 1856, was Kapellmeister at the Hanover Court Theatre from 1859–65, when he went to live in Berlin, until he was summoned to Breslau in 1871 as director of the Orchester-verein. On Apr. 1, 1883, he became Raff's successor as director of Dr. Hoch's Conserva-torium at Frankfort. There he met with much opposition, and in spite of endless intrigue succeeded in ensuring a prosperous future for the Conservatorium. From 1884 he also directed the Gesangverein founded in Mainz by Fried. Wilhelm Rühl. He retired in 1908 and subsequently lived at Florence and Munich.

Scholz's many compositions include songs, string quartets (opp. 46 and 48), and a quintet (op. 47), a piano concerto, a symphony in B♭ (op. 60) entitled 'Malinconia,' some pieces for orchestra, soli and chorus, ' Das Siegesfest,' ' Das Lied von der Glocke,' overtures to Goethe's 'Iphigenie' and 'Im Freien,' a Requiem, and the operas 'Carlo Rosa' (Munich, 1858) ; 'Zietensche Husaren' (Bres-lau, 1869) ; 'Morgiane' (Munich, 1870) ; 'Genoveva' (Nuremberg, 1875) ; 'Der Trom-peter von Säkkingen' (Wiesbaden, 1877) ; 'Die vornehmen Wirte' (Leipzig, 1883) ; 'Ingo' (Frankfort-on-M., 1898) ; 'Anno 1757' (Berlin, 1903) ; and Mirandolina (Darmstadt, 1907).         H. V. H.

His son, (2) HANS (b. Breslau, Mar. 7, 1879), educated at Frankfort, became teacher of har-mony and counterpoint in Munich Univer-sity. In 1914 he produced a German transla-tion of Berlioz's Memoirs.

SCHOP (SCHOPP), JOHANN (d. circa 1664 or 1665), a skilful player on the lute, violin and trombone, who entered the court band at Wolfenbüttel in 1615, was a violinist at the Danish court in 1618–19 (according to one account he went to Denmark in 1615, so that his stay at Wolfenbüttel must have been very short), and in 1621 became director of the Ratsmusik at Hamburg, being appointed later on organist to the town and to the church of St. James. Although he was chiefly renowned as an instrumentalist (Mattheson speaks of him as incomparable in his way), he is at present known mainly as a composer of Choral-tunes, in virtue of his contributions to Rist's hymn-book, published in 1641 as 'Himmlische Lieder.' No copy seems to exist of his 'Neue Paduanen, Galliarden, Allemanden,' published in six parts at Hamburg in 1633–40 ; his 'Geistliche Concerten' appeared in 1643, and many occasional compositions, such as con-gratulatory odes on weddings, are extant.

Besides Rist's book, already alluded to, the following contain tunes by Schop : Rist's 'Frommer und gottseliger Christen alltägliche Hausmusik' (1654), Philip von Zesen's 'Jugend- und Liebes-Flammen,' 1651 and 1653, and from these books the melodies were copied into later collections. (Q.-L. etc.)     M.

SCHOTT, ANTON (b. Castle Staufeneck, Swabian Alps, June 25, 1846 ; d. Stuttgart, Jan. 8, 1913), was educated at the military academy at Ludwigsburg, Würtemberg, and served as an artillery officer through the war of 1866. Some time after, his voice attracted the attention of Pischek, and of Frau SCHEBEST, from the latter of whom he had much instruc-tion preparatory to his appearance on the stage. On May 8, 1870, Schott made his début at Frankfort as Max in 'Der Freischütz,' with such success that he determined to abandon the army in favour of music, though prevented for a time by the outbreak of the war of 1870, through which he served and obtained his captaincy. At the end of 1871 he was engaged at Munich, and subsequently at Berlin, Schwerin and Hanover. At the last place he created the part of Benvenuto Cellini on the revival of Berlioz's opera there under Bülow. He sang in England, June 16, 1879, at piano recitals given by von Bülow at St. James's Hall, and at a New Philharmonic concert, in all of which he was well received. He ap-peared Jan. 10, 1880, at Her Majesty's Theatre (Carl Rosa), as Rienzi, and afterwards as Lohengrin, with only moderate success, owing to his faulty intonation. He had a fine presence and a good voice. He received further instruc-tion from Blume, and created the part of Azim in Stanford's 'Veiled Prophet' on Feb. 8, 1881, at Hanover. In 1882 he sang with Neumann in Wagner's company in Italy, and in 1884 in Leopold Damrosch's company in America. He afterwards devoted himself exclusively to con-cert-singing. In his day he was considered one of the best 'heroic tenors' in Germany.        A. C.

SCHOTT (B. SCHOTT UND SÖHNE), the well-known firm of music-publishers at Mainz. This business was founded in 1773 by BERNHARD SCHOTT, and carried on after his death in 1817 by his sons ANDREAS (b. 1781 ; d. 1840) and JOHANN JOSEPH (b. 1782 ; d. 1855), who in the early part of the 19th century set up a house of their own at Antwerp (afterwards removed to Brussels) which gave them an ad-vantage both in suppressing pirated editions, and in dealing with the French and Italian com-posers then in vogue. In 1838 they founded a branch in London, superintended by a third brother, ADAM (who was afterwards a band-master in Canada and India, dying in the latter country), and conducted with great success since 1849 by J. B. Wolf (b. 1815 ; d. 1881), and, after his death, by Carl Volkert. Another branch in Paris soon followed. PETER (*d.* Paris, Sept. 20, 1894), grandson of Bernhard, lived in Brussels and managed the business of the branches there and in Paris, forwarding at the same time the circulation of the Mainz publications. Besides these four independent houses the firm had depôts in Leipzig, Rotterdam and New York. FRANZ PHILIPP (*b.* 1811 ; *d.* Milan, 1874), elder grandson of Bernhard, took part in the business from 1825, and managed it after the death of his father Andreas, first in partnership with his uncle Johann Joseph, and after his death by himself. After his death the business was carried on with the old traditions by PETER SCHOTT (a son of the Brussels Peter), FRANZ VON LANDWEHR (a nephew of the family), and DR. L. STRECKER.

At a time when the book and music trade was regulated by no fixed laws, the correct and elegant editions of Mainz found a ready entrance into foreign countries, and the firm was thus stimulated to keep ahead of rivals by making constant improvements in music-printing and engraving. They were the first to use lithography for this purpose, an important turning-point in the printing of music. Their copyright publications included Beethoven's latest quartets, Ninth Symphony and Mass in D, nearly all the operas of Donizetti, Rossini, Adam and Auber, most of Rink's organ-music, 'Der Choralfreund,' in nine volumes ; 'École pratique de la modulation,' op. 99 ; 'Gesangstudien' (vocalises, méthode de chant, etc.) by Bordèse, Bordogni, Concone, Fétis, Gavaudé, Garcia, Lablache, Abbé Mainzer, Rossini, Rubini, Vaccaj, etc. ; in later times, Wagner's 'Meistersinger,' 'Ring des Nibelungen' and 'Parsifal.' The establishment has been enlarged by the addition of a printing-office (where have been printed, among others, Gottfried Weber's theoretical works, the periodical *Cäcilia,* 1824–48, etc.), and in 1829 of a piano factory, which, however, was given up in 1860 on account of the extension of the main business.

The Schotts, besides innumerable services to art and artists, did good work in a smaller circle by fostering music in Mainz itself. Franz and his wife Betty (*née* von Braunrasch, *b.* 1820 ; *d.* 1875) left a considerable sum for the maintenance of a permanent orchestra and conductor of eminence, in order that Mainz might hold its own in music with the richer cities of the Rhine provinces.    C. F. P.

SCHOTTISCHE ('The Scots dance'), a round dance very similar to the polka. It must not be confounded with the Écossaise, which was a country dance of Scottish origin introduced into France towards the end of the 18th century. The Schottische was first danced in England in 1848, when it was also known as the German Polka. It does not seem to have been danced in Paris, as Cellarius (*La Danse des salons,* Paris, 1847) does not include it amongst the dances he describes. The music is almost the same as that of the polka, but should be played rather slower. The following is the tune to which it was originally danced in England :

W. B. S.

SCHRADIECK, HENRY (*b.* Hamburg, Apr. 29, 1846 ; *d.* Brooklyn, Mar. 25, 1918), violinist, received his first lesson from his father on his fourth birthday, and already made public appearances in his sixth year. In 1854 Teresa Milanollo heard and took considerable interest in him, putting him into the hands of Léonard at the Conservatoire in Brussels, where he stayed for four years, and gained the first prize. Afterwards he studied under David at Leipzig (1859–61), obtaining his first important engagement in 1863 as soloist in the so-called 'Private Concerts,' conducted by Reinthaler at Bremen. The following year he was appointed professor of the violin at the Moscow Conservatorium, but in 1868 returned to Hamburg to take the post vacated by Auer as Konzertmeister of the Philharmonic Society. After six years he moved (in 1874) to Leipzig, becoming Konzertmeister at the Gewandhaus concerts, professor at the Conservatorium and leader of the theatre orchestra. His pupils became very numerous, and at length he found himself overburdened with so many duties, and accepted an appointment as conductor and teacher of the violin at the College of Music at Cincinnati. Here he worked until 1889, and then returned to his native town, taking his old position as Konzertmeister of the Philharmonic Society, besides teaching at the Hamburg Conservatorium. Subsequently he went to New York as principal violin professor at the National Conservatoire, moving in 1899 to Philadelphia, where he taught at the S. Broad Street Conservatoire.

Amongst his important studies for the violin are 25 Grosse Studien for violin alone, three volumes of Technical Studies, Scale Studies, Guide to the Study of Chords, Finger Exercises and 'The First Position.' He also interested himself in questions connected with the making of violins.    W. W. C.

SCHRAMM, MELCHIOR (*b.* Silesia, *c.* mid.

';6th cent.), was in the chapel of Count Karl of Hohenzollern-Sigmaringen in 1574; organist at Offenburg, Baden, ? 1595. He was a distinguished composer, who was ranked with Lassus and Kerle. He composed motets and songs (*Q.-L.*; *Riemann*; *Fétis*).

SCHREIDER - TRNAVSKY, MIKULÁŠ (*b.* Trnava, 1881), Slovak composer. He studied music for a year at the Academy of Music, Budapest, then entered the Vienna Conservatoire, and finally worked for two years with Karel Stecker in Prague. On leaving the Prague Conservatoire he did a year's military service as 'volunteer.' His first musical post was at a Serbian church at Great Bečkerck. He toured for a time with the singer Boža Oumirov, visiting Berlin and Paris, where his songs in the national style had considerable success. In 1909 he became director of the choir of the Collegiate Church, Trnava. He had to serve in the army from 1914–18, when he was appointed by the Government to be the inspector of singing in Slovak schools. His 'Collection of National Songs,' published by the Slovak society Detvan (1908), has been commended by specialists (2nd edition, F. Chadim, Prague). A further instalment of Slovak songs was published later at Turčansky Sv. Martin (2nd edition, Mojmír Urbánek, Prague). His work is highly characteristic and musicianly. Besides these collections of genuine national songs, he has written the chorus 'Up, brothers,' some church music, a pianoforte quintet and a 'School of Singing.'

R. N. and A. Kᴷ.

SCHREKER, FRANZ (*b.* Monaco, Mar. 23, 1878) is the most conspicuous melodramatic figure since Wagner, though utterly unlike him in sentiments and ideas. He studied in Vienna under Robert Fuchs. In 1911 he founded and became conductor of the Philharmonic Choir in Vienna, where he was also teacher of composition at the Imperial Academy of Music. In 1920 he was appointed director of the Academy of Music in Berlin. A thoroughly modern composer, his strongest powers lie within the melodramatic field, this vein being apparent even in his orchestral works. Fascination of tone, rich colouring, sensuous melodies, great contrasts, half-completed *Motive*, characterise his musical style. As a dramatist, Schreker moves between naturalism (Wedekind) and mysticism (E. T. A. Hoffmann). His libretti are based on sex - psychological ideas derived from the School of Freud and Weininger.

WORKS.—Two songs (for vln. and PF.); five songs (for vln. and PF.); five poems (for vln. and PF.); two songs on 'The Death of a Child'; Psalm cxvi. (1st perf. Vienna with Phil. Orch.); pieces for orch. (str. orch. and harp), lost; andante for orch. (perf. Conservatory, Vienna, 1900); 'Ave Maria' (for vln. and organ), Der Merken 1, 2; eight songs (for vln. and PF.); Intermezzo (for str. orch.); 'Flames' (a 1 act opera); 'Swan Song' (for mixed chor. and orch.); 'Ekkehard' (symphonic overture for orch.); Romantic Suite (for orch.); Fantastic Overture (for orch.); 'Der Geburtstag der Infantin' (music to dance-pantomime by Oscar Wilde (1st perf. Promenade Concerts, Wood, Sept. 1925); 'The Wind' dance allegory (for o ch.); Dance Suite (for full orch.);

'Der ferne Klang,' opera (Frankfort, Aug. 18, 1912); five songs; (vln. and PF.); 'Entführung' (for vln. and PF.), Der Merker iii, 4; 'Das Spielwerk und die Prinzessin,' opera (Vienna, 1913), (later converted into 'Das Spielwerk,' Munich, Oct. 30, 1920); 'The Red Death' (Edgar Allan Poe); 'Die Gezeichneten,' opera, (Frankfort, Apr. 25, 1918); 'Die tönenden Sphären,' opera 1915); Chamber Symphony (for 23 solo instruments), (given at Queen's Hall under Wood, Oct. 27, 1923); 'Der Schatzgräber,' opera (Frankfort, Jan. 24, 1920); 'Memnon,' operatic poem; 'Irrelohe' opera (Cologne, Mar. 27, 1924).

He has also published two books of his 'Poems for Music.'       H. J. K.

SCHREYER, CHRISTIAN HEINRICH (*b.* Dresden, Dec. 24, 1751; *d.* there, Jan. 24, 1823), Pastor of Ortrand near Dresden. He is valued as a composer of Lieder; he also wrote instrumental music and some theoretical works (*Riemann*; *Q.-L.*).

SCHRIDER (SCHREIDER, SCHRÖDER), CHRISTOPHER, was one of Father Smith's workmen, and previous to 1708 had become his son-in-law. After Smith's death he succeeded to his business, and in 1710 was organ-builder to the Royal Chapels. His organs do not appear to be very numerous, that of Westminster being his *chef-d'œuvre*. It was built for the coronation of George II. in 1727, and was presented to the Abbey by the King.[1] He put up another organ in Henry the Seventh's Chapel for the funeral of Queen Caroline, Dec. 17, 1737.[2] An amusing epitaph is quoted in Scott's *Gleanings from Westminster Abbey*, 2nd ed. p. 279.       V. de P.

SCHRÖDER - DEVRIENT, WILHELMINE (*b.* Hamburg, Dec. 6, 1804[3]; *d.* Coburg, Jan. 21, 1860), a highly - gifted dramatic singer. Her father, Friedrich Schröder—who died in 1818—had been an excellent baritone singer, a favourite in many operas, especially in Mozart's 'Don Juan,' which he was the first to act in German. Her mother was Antoinette Sophie Bürger, a celebrated actress, sometimes called 'the German Siddons.'

Wilhelmine was the eldest of four children. She enjoyed great advantages of training; dancing lessons, and public appearances in ballets in early childhood, helped her to mastery of attitude and elasticity of movement; afterwards, when her parents' wanderings led them to Vienna, she took such parts as Ophelia, and Aricia (Schiller's 'Phädra'), at the Hofburg-theater, receiving careful instruction in gesture and delivery from her mother, who afterwards superintended her study of operatic parts.

In 1821 Wilhelmine made a brilliant first appearance at the Vienna opera-house as Pamina in 'Die Zauberflöte.' The freshness of her well-developed soprano, her purity of intonation and certainty of attack, astonished the public. Other early triumphs were Emmeline (Weigl's 'Schweizerfamilie'), Marie Grétry's 'Barbe bleu'[4]), and Agathe ('Der

---

[1] Chrysander's *Händel*, ii. 174, note.
[2] *Ibid.* p. 437, note; Stanley's *Westminster Abbey*, p. 166.
[3] According to her own account, as quoted in Glümer's *Erinnerungen*, and not in Oct. 1805, as stated by Fétis.
[4] 'Raoul Barbe bleu' (1789), Germanised into 'Raoul der Blaubart.'

Freischütz '), in which part she appeared under Weber's direction at Vienna, Mar. 7, 1822. But her great achievement was the creation of the part of Leonore, on the revival of ' Fidelio ' at Vienna later in the year. Her impersonation of the heroine, besides laying the foundation of her own fame, won for the work the praise so long withheld, and achieved its ultimate position by repeated performances in Germany, London and Paris. Beethoven was present at the first performance. ' He sat behind the conductor, and had wrapped himself so closely in the folds of his cloak that only his eyes could be seen flashing from it.[1] Afterwards he smilingly patted her cheek, thanked her, and promised to write an opera for her.

In 1823 she went to Dresden to fulfil a contract to sing at the court theatre for two years, at a salary of 2000 thalers. (At a later period she received 4000 thalers at the same house, for her connexion with Dresden never entirely ceased as long as she was on the stage.) She married Karl Devrient, an excellent actor whom she met in Berlin during an engagement there that year. Four children were born, but the marriage was not a happy one, and was dissolved in 1828. During the next eight years she delighted her audiences by her appearance in the leading classical and romantic characters which ever remained her most successful parts. Yet no less did she succeed, in Paër's comic opera, ' Sargino,' in singing with so much finish, and acting with so much humour, that it became a matter of dispute whether tragedy or comedy was her forte.

In 1830 she passed through Weimar and sang to Goethe on her way to Paris to join Röckel's German company. With an exalted sense of the importance of her mission, she wrote :

' I had to think not only of my own reputation, but to establish German music. My failure would have been injurious to the music of Beethoven, Mozart and Weber.'

This date was an epoch in the history of music in Paris. Bouquets—then an extraordinary manifestation of approval — were showered upon the triumphant singer. In her subsequent visits to Paris, 1831 and 1832, she sang in Italian opera.

In 1832 Schröder-Devrient was heard at the King's Theatre in London, engaging with Monck Mason to sing ten times monthly during May, June and July, for £800 and a benefit. Chelard was conductor. ' Fidelio,' ' Don Juan ' and Chelard's ' Macbeth ' were repeatedly given.[2] The ' Queen of Tears ' (so she was styled) was heard next season in ' Der Freischütz,' ' Die Zauberflöte,' ' Euryanthe ' and ' Otello.' The engagement was to sing for Bunn at Covent Garden twenty-four times at £40 a night, and once for the benefit of the speculators. However, all London was under the

spell of Taglioni and of Fanny Elsler. Malibran and Schröder-Devrient in the English opera ; Pasta, Cinti-Damoreau, Rubini and Tamburini, in the Italian opera, sang to empty houses. Again in 1837, after Malibran's death, Bunn engaged Schröder-Devrient at a double salary. ' Fidelio,' ' La Sonnambula ' and ' Norma ' were performed in English. She broke down in health before the season was over, but was able, however, to give a farewell performance of ' Fidelio,' with the last act of the ' Montecchi e Capuletti,' and then discovered that Bunn had declared himself bankrupt and could pay her nothing. In his book, *The Stage both before and behind the Curtain*, Bunn complains of the singer's attempts at extortion ; says that she demanded the fourth part of the proceeds of each night, but on this sum proving to fall short of the fixed salary, asked for £100.

From 1837 a gradual decline in power was observed in Mme. Schröder-Devrient, though she continued to delight her audiences all over Germany. Of Wagner's operas she only appeared in ' Rienzi ' as Adriano Colonna, in ' Der fliegende Holländer ' as Senta and in ' Tannhäuser ' as Venus.[3] Gluck's masterpieces were among her latest studies. Her last appearance in Dresden was in his ' Iphigenie in Aulis,' in 1847 ; her last appearance on any stage took place at Riga, where she played Romeo. Her concert-singing was greatly admired, and one of the liveliest passages in Mendelssohn's letters [4] describes the *furore* caused by her impromptu execution of ' Adelaide ' in her ordinary travelling dress at the Gewandhaus Concert of Feb. 11, 1841.

She had made a second marriage with von Döring, a worthless person, who immediately seized upon his wife's earnings and pension, and left her almost destitute, to recover what she could in a long lawsuit. The marriage was dissolved at her wish. In 1850 she married von Bock, a man of culture, who took her to his property in Livonia. Passing through Dresden she was arrested on account of the sympathy she had shown with the revolution of 1848. An examination in Berlin resulted in her being forbidden to return to Saxony ; in the meantime she was exiled from Russia. Her husband's exertions and sacrifices secured a reversal of this sentence. In 1856 she visited some German towns, singing Lieder in public concerts. Her interpretations of Beethoven's ' Adelaide ' and of Schubert's and Schumann's songs were immensely admired, though by some thought too dramatic. When at Leipzig her strength succumbed to a painful illness. She was devotedly nursed by a sister and a friend at Coburg, where she died.

Even in her best days her voice was of no

---

1 See Glümer's *Erinnerungen an Wilhelmine Schröder-Devrient.*
2 See Chorley's *Musical Recollections.*

3 For Wagner's enthusiastic impressions of her see *My Life* (Eng. trans.), p. 44, etc.
4 Letter, Feb. 14, 1841.

extraordinary compass, but, to the last, the tones of the middle notes were of exceptionally fine quality. Mazatti's teaching, with further instruction from Radichi and from Miksch (the Dresden chorus-master), had not been sufficient training for the young girl, who had besides been disinclined to the drudgery of scale-singing. The neglect of system and of careful vocal exercise resulted in faulty execution and too early loss of the high notes. But there seemed a discrepancy between the delicate organisation of her voice and the passionate energy of her temperament. By force of will she accomplished more than was warranted by her natural powers. It was the dramatic genius of this artist which won for her a European reputation. She infused a terrible earnestness into the more pathetic impersonations, while an almost unerring instinct of artistic fitness, combined with a conscientious study of the parts, secured a perfection of performance which reached every detail of by-play.

BIBL.—CHORLEY, *Modern German Music* (i. 341); BERLIOZ, letters in the *Journal des Débats* (1843); RELLSTAB (*Ges. Schriften*, ix.); A. VON WOLZOGEN, *Wilh. Schröder-Devrient* (Leipzig, 1863); WAGNER, *Über Schauspieler und Sänger*.

L. M. M., abridged.

SCHROETER, CHRISTOPH GOTTLIEB (*b.* Hohenstein, Saxony, Aug. 10, 1699; *d.* Nordhausen, 1782), long enjoyed in Germany the honour of having invented the pianoforte. His claims, first published by himself in Mizler's *Musikalische Bibliothek* (Leipzig, 1738) and repeated in Marpurg's *Kritische Briefe* (Berlin, 1764), have been examined and set aside in favour of Cristofori. (See PIANOFORTE.) We learn from Schroeter's autobiography that at 7 years of age he was placed as a chorister at Dresden, under Kapellmeister Schmidt, and that Graun was his companion. The clavichord early became his greatest pleasure. When he lost his voice he entered the Kreuzschule to study thorough-bass, that is, accompaniment as then practised, and learned to quill and tune harpsichords, which led him to the monochord and systems of temperament. On the wish of his mother that he should study theology, he went to Leipzig for that purpose in 1717, but after her death resumed music, returned to Dresden, and was accepted by Lotti to copy for him and write his middle parts. According to Schroeter's own account, it was Hebenstreit's PANTALEON (*q.v.*) which led him at this time to attempt to combine the characteristics of the harpsichord and clavichord, by inventing two hammer actions, the models of which he deposited at the Saxon court in 1721; but immediately afterwards he left Dresden, taking service with a Baron whom he does not name, to travel in Germany, Holland and England. In 1724 he went to the University of Jena and began writing upon musical subjects; in 1726 he took the organist's place at Minden, removing in 1732 to Nord-

hausen, where he remained until his death. He published a treatise, *Deutliche Anweisung zum General-Bass*, in 1772 at Halberstadt, and his *Letzte Beschäftigung mit musikalischen Dingen* appeared posthumously in 1782. A list of his polemical pamphlets is given in *Q.-L.* and elsewhere.     A. J. H., with addns.

SCHRÖTER, (1) CORONA ELISABETH WILHELMINE (*b.* Guben, Jan. 14, 1751[1]; *d.* Ilmenau, Aug. 23, 1802), a celebrated singer of the Weimar court in its most brilliant days, was the daughter of a musician, Johann Friedrich Schröter, oboist in the royal orchestra. The family shortly after her birth migrated from Guben to Warsaw, and finally to Leipzig. Corona's voice was trained by her father, and she sang when she was but 14 at a Leipzig Grosses Konzert (1765). From the following year until 1771 she was engaged at these concerts, Schmehling (La Mara) being retained as principal vocalist. She then came to London with her family, see below Johann Samuel (3). Goethe had become acquainted with Schröter in 1766; ten years later he conveyed to her the offer of the post of Kammersängerin to the Dowager Duchess of Weimar. Here she made her first appearance Nov. 23, 1776, and soon became the idol of the place. Associated with Goethe himself in the production of his dramas, she created amongst others the part of Iphigenia, completely realising the poet's ideal (see *Auf Miedings Tod*). Her co-operation in 'Die Fischerin' included the composition of all the music. It was on July 22, 1782, that she was heard as Dortchen, and that 'Der Erlkönig,' with which the play opens, was sung for the first time. In 1782-84 she sang at the Gewandhaus in Leipzig. After 1786 Schröter sang little in public, but devoted herself to composition, painting, and a few dramatic pupils. Schiller heard her read Goethe's 'Iphigenie' in 1787, and Charlotte von Schiller, a year or two later, found much to praise in the musical settings of 'Der Taucher' and 'Würde der Frauen,' and their expressive rendering by the famous artist.

Her songs were published in two books. They are melodious and simple settings of poems by Herder, Matthison, Klopstock, etc. Book I. (25 Lieder, Weimar, 1786) contains Goethe's 'Der neue Amadis' and 'Der Erlkönig.' The second collection of songs was published at Weimar, 1794. Besides the life by Keil, Düntzer's *Charlotte von Stein und Corona Schröter* may be consulted for details of her social and artistic successes. In 1778 Schröter handed to Goethe her MS. autobiography, which has never been made public, perhaps has not yet been discovered among his papers, although Goethe noted the receipt of it in his diary.

[1] According to her biographer, Keil (*Vor hundert Jahren*, Leipzig, 1875).

(2) JOHANN HEINRICH, her brother, violinist, visited England, and published some duos for two violins and for violin and violoncello, in 1782.　　　　　　　　　　　L. M. M.

(3) JOHANN SAMUEL (b. Warsaw, c. 1750; d. Pimlico, Nov. 2, 1788), another brother, pianoforte-player and composer for that instrument. About 1763 he accompanied his father and sister to Leipzig, and sang there in the Gewandhaus Concerts. On the breaking of his voice he devoted himself entirely to the piano, and travelled with his father, brother and sister, performing as they went, through Holland to London. There they made their début in the concerts of Bach and Abel at the Thatched House, St. James's Street, May 2, 1772, Schröter playing a concerto on the 'Forte Piano,' which J. Christian Bach had first performed in 1767, the brother Johann Heinrich on the violin, and the sister, Corona, singing. In 1773 we find evidence of his performance on the harpsichord, as Broadwood's books show that a harpsichord was sent to Haberdashers' Hall on Mar. 4, for J. S. Schröter. After J. C. Bach's death in 1782, he succeeded him as music-master to the Queen. 'Six Sonatas for the harpsichord or piano forte' are announced by W. Napier in the *Public Advertiser* in 1776 as his op. 1. This was followed in 1778 by op. 3, 'Six Concertos with an accompaniment for two violins and a bass'; and this again by three concertos with string accompaniments, op. 4; three, op. 5 (Berlin); op. 6 (Paris); op. 2, six trios (Amsterdam); op. 9, two trios (Amsterdam). Many other compositions—quintets, trios, sonatas with and without accompaniment—are enumerated in *Q.-L.* The *A B C Dario* (p. 144) says of him:

'He has composed the harpsichord parts of some concertos; the accompaniments are by Bach; they are neither new nor very striking. He plays in an elegant and masterly style; his cadences are well imagined, and if his *penchant* was not rather to play rapidly than *al core*, he would excel on the pianoforte.'

Burney, on the other hand (in Rees), says:

'He became one of the neatest and most expressive players of his time, and his style of composition, highly polished, resembles that of Abel more than any other. It was graceful and in good taste; but so chaste as sometimes to seem deficient in fire and invention.'

He did not remain long before the public in consequence of his marriage with one of his pupils, a young lady of birth and fortune, after which he played only at the concerts of the Prince of Wales and a few others of the nobility. He died on Sunday, Nov. 2, 1788, in his own house at Pimlico, having lost his voice some years before by a severe cold. His marriage was a clandestine one, and brought him into collision with his wife's family, the result of which was his surrendering all his rights for an annuity of £500. She is the lady who took lessons from Haydn during his residence in London, and fell violently in love with him.

Haydn spoke of her many years after as a very attractive woman, and still handsome, though over sixty. 'Had I been free,' said the patriarch, 'I should certainly have married her'—she was then a widow. He dedicated to her three clavier trios (B. & H., Nos. 1, 2, 6).
　　　　　　　　　C. F. P.; addns. A. J. H.

SCHROETER, LEONARD (b. Torgau, mid. 16th cent.; d. circa 1600 [1]), became cantor of the cathedral of Magdeburg about 1564, in succession to Gallus Dressler, also a composer of some importance. Schroeter's chief work is 'Hymni sacri,' Erfurt, 1587, and consists of 4- and 5-part settings of those Latin church hymns which had been received into the worship of the Lutheran Church. Winterfeld says of these hymns that they belong to the best musical works of the time; the harmony is rich, clear and dignified, and shows an unmistakable advance on the path of the older masters. They are in the same style as the hymns of Palestrina and Victoria, only the choral melody is mostly given to the upper voice. Some of these hymns, as well as some of the German psalms of Gallus Dressler, Schroeter's predecessor, are republished in Schöberlein and Riegel's *Schatz des liturgischen Chorgesangs*, Göttingen, 1868–72. Earlier publications of hymn-tunes by Schroeter were published in 1562, 1576, 1584, etc. (See *Q.-L.* for list.) Four Weihnachts-Liedlein by Schroeter are received into the repertory of the Berlin Dom-Chor, and are published in Schlesinger's 'Musica sacra,' No. 11. A German Te Deum for double choir by Schroeter, originally published in 1576, has been printed by Otto Kade in the Notenbeilagen to Ambros's *Gesch. der Musik*, No. 28. J. R. M.

SCHUBART, CHRISTIAN FRIEDRICH DANIEL (b. Obersontheim, Suabia, 1739 [2]; d. Stuttgart, Oct. 10, 1791), was brought up (not as a musician) at Nördlingen, Nuremberg and Erlangen. In 1768 we find him as organist at Ludwigsburg. His life seems to have been a very wild and irregular one, but he must have been a man of great talent and energy to justify the eulogies on him so frequent in the early volumes of the *A.M.Z.* of Leipzig, and the constant references of Otto Jahn in his *Life of Mozart*. He lived in Mannheim, Munich, Augsburg and Ulm; founded a *Deutsche Chronik* in 1774; was more than once in confinement for his misdeeds, and at length was imprisoned from 1777–87 at Hohenasperg. On his release he was appointed director of the court theatre; his paper changed its title to *Vaterlands-Chronik*, and appeared from 1787 until the year of his death. An autobiography, written in prison, appeared in 1791–93. His compositions are few and unimportant. They include a set of 'Musikalische Rhapsodien,' a

---

[1] *Riemann* gives 1595; his successor was appointed in 1600.
[2] The day is given in *Q.-L.* as Mar. 26, and in *Riemann* as Apr. 13.

Salve Regina, variations and other clavier pieces. A work of his on musical æsthetics, *Ideen zu einer Ästhetik der Tonkunst*, was published after his death by his son Ludwig (Vienna, 1806). From the notices of it in the *A.M.Z.* (viii. 801, xiii. 53, etc.) and Jahn's citations, it appears to be partly a dissertation on the styles, abilities and characteristics of great musicians and artists. It also contains some fanciful descriptions of the various keys, which Schumann notices (*Ges. Schriften*, i. 180) only to condemn. But Schubart will always be known as the author of the words of one of F. Schubert's most favourite songs—' Die Forelle ' (op. 32). The words of 'An den Tod' and ' Grablied auf einen Soldaten ' are also his. His son further published two volumes of his *Vermischte Schriften* (Zürich, 1812).          G.

SCHUBAUR, JOHANN LUKAS (bapt. Lechfeld, Swabia, Dec. 23, 1749; *d.* Munich, Nov. 15, 1815), studied medicine and became a physician of high repute. From his early youth he had studied music, and the teaching of music was at times his only means of subsistence. As a composer he was one of the most successful representatives of the German Singspiel, which had not long come into existence ; he also composed some cantatas and the 107th Psalm in Moses Mendelssohn's translation (*Riemann* ; *Q.-L.*).

SCHUBERT, (1) FERDINAND (*b.* Vienna, Oct. 19, 1794 ; *d.* Feb. 28, 1859), one of the elder brothers of Franz SCHUBERT, second son of his father. After passing the two-years' course at the Normal School of St. Anna in 1807–08, he became his father's assistant at the school in the Lichtenthal. In Nov. 1810 he was installed as assistant (Gehilfe), and in 1816 teacher, at the Imperial Orphan House (Waisenhaus) in Vienna, where he continued till Mar. 1820, devoting himself specially to the Bell-Lancastrian method. He was then appointed principal teacher and choirmaster to the school at Altlerchenfeld, Vienna, till 1824, when he was nominated to be head teacher of the Normal School of St. Anna, which he held from Jan. 22, 1824, till his appointment as director of the same establishment on Mar. 15, 1854. This position he retained till his death. His merits were recognised by the bestowal of the Gold Cross of Merit (Verdienstkreuze), with the Crown. During this long period of useful and efficient service he was twice married, and had in all seventeen children, of whom Ferdinand, Rudolf and Hermann were living in Vienna in 1882. His daughter Elise married Linus Geisler, and their daughter, Caroline Geisler-Schubert, had a successful career in Vienna as a player and teacher. Between 1819 and 1853 Ferdinand published twelve school-books on various branches of learning, which came into general use. Music he learnt from his father and from Holzer, and left more than forty

works, of which the following were published : Regina Cœli, *a* 4 and orch. (op. 1) ; German Requiem, *a* 4 with organ (op. 2) ; 4 Waisenlieder (op. 3) ; Cadenzas for PF. in all keys (op. 4) ; Requiem *a* 4 and orch. (op. 9) ; Mass in F *a* 4 and orch. (op. 10) ; Salve Regina in F *a* 4 and orch. (op. 11) ; Salve Regina *a* 4 and wind (op. 12) ; original March and Trio. The MS. works contain various other pieces of church music. Of the two Requiems the first is mentioned in his brother's letter of Aug. 24, 1818 ; the second was performed a few days before Franz's death, and was possibly the last music he heard. The library of the Musikverein at Vienna contains the autograph of Franz Schubert's Mass in G, with oboes (or clarinets) and bassoons, added by Ferdinand, July 23, 1847.

Ferdinand's love for his brother and care of his memory are often referred to in the article on the latter. (See SCHUBERT, Franz Peter.) An interesting evidence of their attachment is afforded by a letter [1] of his to Franz, dated Vienna, July 3, 1824, and containing the following passage in regard to a clock at the Ungarische Krone in Vienna, which played his brother's music :

' This clock delighted me not a little, when one day at dinner for the first time I heard it play some of your waltzes. I felt so strange at the moment that I really did not know where I was ; it was not only that it pleased me, it went regularly through my heart and soul with a fearful pang and longing, which at last turned into settled melancholy.'

This may be fanciful, but it is the language of passionate affection, which evidently animated Ferdinand's whole intercourse with his great brother. Franz's reply (July 16-18, 1824) is quite in the same strain. (The above article is indebted to Wurzbach's *Biographisches Lexicon*.)          G.

SCHUBERT, (1) FRANZ (*b.* Dresden, July 22, 1808 ; *d.* there, Apr. 12, 1878), a violinist, came of a musical family. He was a pupil of Lafont, and rose through various grades to succeed Lipinski in 1861 as first Konzertmeister in his native city. He retired in 1873, on the fiftieth anniversary of his entrance into the orchestra. His published works include studies, a duo for violin and piano, and two concertante for violin and violoncello (with Kummer). His little piece, ' L'Abeille ' is often to be found on violinists' programmes.

Schubert's wife, (2) MASCHINKA (*b.* Aug. 25, 1815 ; *d.* Dresden, Sept. 20, 1882), daughter of Georg Abraham SCHNEIDER (*q.v.*), was a distinguished bravura singer, appeared at the German opera in London in 1832, and was subsequently engaged at Milan and Dresden.          G.

(3) GEORGINE (*b.* Dresden, Oct. 28, 1840 ; *d.* Potsdam, Dec. 26, 1878), singer, daughter of the above, was her mother's pupil, and also studied with Jenny Lind and Manuel Garcia.

1 I owe this letter to Miss Geisler-Schubert.   3.

She made her début (1859) at Hamburg, sang in many German cities as well as Prague, Florence and Paris, when she was engaged at the Théâtre Lyrique. At the Monday Popular Concerts of London (1875) she had a considerable success. (*Riemann*.)

SCHUBERT,[1] FRANZ PETER (*b*. Vienna, Jan. 31, 1797; *d*. there, Nov. 19, 1828). The one great composer native to Vienna, was born in the district called Lichtenthal, at the house which is now numbered 54 of the Nussdorfer Strasse,[2] on the right, going out from Vienna. There is now a grey marble tablet over the door, with the words ' Franz Schuberts Geburtshaus ' in the centre ; on the left side a lyro crowned with a star, and on the right a chaplet of leaves containing the words, ' 31 Jänner 1797.'

He came of a country stock, originally belonging to Zukmantel in Austrian Silesia. His father, Franz, the son of a peasant at Neudorf in Moravia, was born about 1764, studied in Vienna, and in 1784 became assistant to his brother, who kept a school in the Leopoldstadt. His ability and integrity raised him in 1786 to be parish schoolmaster in the parish of the ' Twelve holy helpers ' in the Lichtenthal, a post which he kept till 1817 or 1818, when he was appointed to the parish school in the adjoining district of the Rossau, and there he remained till his death, July 9, 1830. He married early, while still helping his brother, probably in 1783, Elisabeth Vitz, or Fitz, a Silesian, who was in service in Vienna, and was, like Beethoven's mother, a cook. Their first child, Ignaz, was born in 1784. Then came a long gap, possibly filled by children who died in infancy—of whom they lost nine in all ; then, Oct. 19, 1794, another boy, FERDINAND (*q.v.*) ; then in 1796, Karl, then Franz, and lastly, a daughter, Theresia, Sept. 17, 1801, who died Aug. 7, 1878. The hardworked mother of these fourteen children lived till 1812. Soon after her death her husband was married again, to Anna Klayenbök, a Viennese, and had a second family of five children, of whom three grew up, viz. Josefa (*d.* 1861), Andreas, an accountant in one of the public offices, and Anton, a Benedictine priest, Father Hermann [3]—the last two living in 1881.

Ignaz and Ferdinand followed their father's calling, and inherited with it the integrity, frugality and modesty, which had gained him such respect. Of the former we do not hear much ; the one letter by him that is preserved (Oct. 12, 1818), shows him very free-thinking, very tired of schoolmastering, very much attached to his home and his brother.[4] He remained at the Rossau school till his death in 1844. Ferdinand, on the other hand, rose to be director of the chief normal school of St. Anna in Vienna, and played a considerable part in the life of his celebrated brother, by whom he was fondly loved, to whom he was deeply attached, and whose eyes it was given to him to close in death.

Little Franz was no doubt well grounded by his father, and to that early training probably owed the methodical habit which stuck to him more or less closely through life, of dating his pieces, a practice which makes the investigation of them doubly interesting.[5] As schoolmasters the father and his two eldest sons were all more or less musical. Ignaz and Ferdinand had learned the violin with other rudiments from the father, and Franz was also taught it by him in his turn, and the ' Clavier ' (*i.e.* probably the pianoforte—for Beethoven's op. 31 was published before Schubert had passed his sixth year) by Ignaz, who was twelve years his senior. But his high vocation quickly revealed itself ; he soon outstripped these simple teachers, and was put under Michael Holzer, the choirmaster of the parish, for both violin and piano, as well as for singing, the organ and thorough-bass. On this good man, who long outlived him, he made a deep impression. ' When I wished to teach him anything fresh,' he would say, ' he always knew it already. I have often listened to him in astonishment.' [6] Holzer would give him subjects to extemporise upon, and then his joy would know no bounds, and he would cry ' The lad has got harmony at his fingers' ends.' [7] Such astonishment was natural enough, but it would have been far better if he had taught him counterpoint. Ignaz too—and an elder brother is not always a lenient judge of his junior — bears similar testimony. ' I was much astonished,' says he,

' When after a few months he told me that he had no more need of help from me, but would go on by himself ; and indeed I soon had to acknowledge that he had far surpassed me, beyond hope of competition.'

SCHOOL DAYS.—Before he became eleven he was first soprano in the Lichtenthal choir, noted for the beauty of his voice and the appropriate-

---

[1] The following abbreviations are used in the notes to this article :
*K.H.* = Kreissle von Hellborn's biography. The first reference to the German editon ; the second, in brackets, to Coleridge's translation.
*Ferd.* = Ferdinand Schubert, in his biographical sketch in Schumann's *Neue Zeitschrift für Musik*, x. p. 129, etc.
*A.M.Z.* = *Allgemeine musikalische Zeitung.*
*N.Z.M.* = *Neue Zeitschrift für Musik.*
*W.Z.K.* = *Wiener Zeitschrift für Kunst,* etc.
[2] The Nussdorfer Strasse runs north and south. At the time of Schubert's birth it was called ' Auf dem Himmelpfortgrund,' and the house was No. 72. The Himmelpfortgasse (' the street of the gr .e of heaven ') was a short street running out of it westwards towards the fortifications—the same which is now the ' Säulengasse.' The present Schubertgasse did not then exist beyond the opening into the main street. I find all this on a large map of the date in the British Museum.
[3] Author of a sermon on the 1400th anniversary of the birth of St. Benedict (Vienna, 1880), in which he is styled ' Capitularpriester des Stiftes Schotten ; Curat und Prediger an der Stiftspfarre ; Besitzer des gold. Verdienstkreuzes m. d. Krone.'

[4] *K.H.* p. 146 (i. 149).
[5] His usual practice was to write the title of the piece, the date, and his name, '*Frz Schubert Mpia*' (*manu propriâ*), at the head of the first page, on beginning to compose. In his earlier years he added the full date of completion at the end, even when it was the same day. See Nos. 1, 2 and 5 of the ' 6 Lieder ' (Müller)—all three belonging to 1813, as given in Nottebohm's *Catalogue*, p. 243. Sometimes he has dated each movement, as in the string quartet in Bb (op. 168), described under 1814. With 1815, however, this minute dating in great measure ceases, and as a rule we find the year or at most the month stated. [6] *N.Z.M.* [7] *K.H.* .. 5 (i. 5).

.less of his expression. He played the violin solos when they occurred in the service, and at home composed little songs and pieces for strings or for pianoforte. ] For a child so gifted, of people in the position of the Schuberts, the next step was naturally the Imperial *Convict*, or school [1] for educating the choristers for the court-chapel; and to the *Convict* accordingly Franz was sent in Oct. 1808, when eleven years and eight months old. He went up with a batch of other boys, who, while waiting, made themselves merry over his grey suit, calling him a miller, and otherwise cracking jokes. But the laugh soon ceased when the ' miller ' came under the examiners, the court Kapellmeister Salieri and Eybler, and Korner the singing-master. He sang the trial-pieces in such a style that he was at once received, and hence-forth the grey frock was exchanged for the gold-laced uniform of the imperial choristers. The music in the *Convict* had been a good deal dropt in consequence of the war, but after the signing of the treaty of peace, Oct. 14, 1809, it regained its old footing, and then Franz soon took his right place in the music-school. There was an orchestra formed from the boys, which practised daily symphonies and overtures of Haydn, Mozart, Krommer, Kozeluch, Méhul, Cherubini, etc., and occasionally Beethoven. Here his home practice put him on a level with older boys than himself. The leader of the band, behind whom he sat, several years his senior, turned round the first day to see who it was that was playing so cleverly, and found it to be ' a small boy in spectacles named Franz Schubert.' [2] The big fellow's name was Spaun, and he soon became intimate with his little neighbour. Franz was extremely sensitive, and one day admitted to his friend, very con-fused and blushing deeply, that he had already composed much ; that indeed he could not help it, and should do it every day if he could afford to get music-paper. Spaun saw the state of matters, and took care that music-paper should be forthcoming ; for which and other kindnesses his name will be long re-membered. Franz in time became first violin, and when Ruzicka, the regular conductor, was absent, he took his place. The orchestral music must have been a great delight to him, but we only hear that he preferred Kozeluch to Krommer, and that his particular favourites were some adagios of Haydn's, Mozart's G minor symphony, in which he said ' You could hear the angels singing,' and the overtures to ' Figaro ' and ' Die Zauberflöte.' It is also evident from his earliest symphonies that the overture to ' Prometheus ' had made its mark on his mind. On Sundays and holidays he went home, and then the great delight of the

family was to play quartets, his own or those of other writers, in which the father took the violoncello, Ferdinand and Ignaz the first and second violins, and Franz the viola, as Mozart did before him, and Mendelssohn after him. The father would now and then make a mistake ; on the first occasion Franz took no notice, but if it recurred he would say with a smile, in a timid way, ' Herr Vater, something must be wrong there.'

The instruction in the *Convict* was by no means only musical. There was a Curator, a Director (Rev. Innocenz Lang), a Sub-director, an Inspector, a staff of preachers and catechists ; and there were teachers of mathematics, history and geography, poetry, writing, draw-ing, French and Italian.[3] In fact it was a school, apart from its music department. Franz of course took his part in all this instruc-tion, and for the first year is said to have ac-quitted himself with credit, but his reputation in the school fell off as it increased in the musical department. The extraordinary thirst for composition, which is so remarkable through-out his life, began to assert itself at this time, and appears to have been limited only by his power of obtaining paper ; and it not unnatur-ally interfered with his general lessons.

His first pianoforte piece of any dimensions, and apparently his earliest existing composition, was a four-hand fantasia, containing more than a dozen movements, all of different characters, and occupying thirty-two pages of very small writing. It is dated Apr. 8–May 1, 1810, and was followed by two smaller ones.[4] His brother remarks that not one of the three ends in the key in which it began. The next is a long vocal piece for voice and PF., called ' Hagars Klage ' —Hagar's lament over her dying son—dated Mar. 30, 1811, also containing twelve move-ments, with curious unconnected changes of key ; and another, of even grimmer character, attributed to the same year, is called ' Leichen-fantasie,' or Corpsefantasia, to the words of Schiller's gruesome juvenile poem of the same name. This has seventeen movements, and is quite as erratic in its changes of key and disre-gard of the compass of the voice as the preced-ing.[5] The reminiscences of Haydn's 'Creation,' Mozart's opera airs, and Beethoven's andantes, are frequent in both. A fourth is ' Der Vater-mörder '—the Parricide—for voice and PF., ' 26 Dec. 1811,' a pleasant Christmas piece ! a decided advance on the two previous songs in individuality of style, and connection. 1811 also saw the composition of a quintet-overture, a string quartet, a second fantasia for four hands, and many songs.[6] For 1812 the list is more instrumental. It contains an overture

[1] In the Piaristengasse in the Josephstadt. See a very full and interesting account of this school in Hanslick's excellent book, *Geschichte des Concertwesens in Wien* (Vienna, 1869), p. 141.
[2] From a sketch by von Köchel, entitled *Nachruf an Joseph von Spaun*, Vienna (privately printed), 1866.

[3] See the list of names in *K.H.* p. 13 (i. 13).
[4] *Ferd.* p. 133. Reissmann (p. 7) gives the inscriptions—' Den 8. Aprill angefangen. Den 1. May vollbracht, 1810.'
[5] The autographs of both are in possession of Herr Nicholas Dumba of Vienna.
[6] *Ferd.* p. 138.

for orchestra in D ; a quartet overture in B♭ ; string quartets in C, B♭ and D [1] ; a sonata for PF., violin and violoncello [2] ; variations in E♭, and an andante, both for PF. ; a Salve Regina and a Kyrie. In 1813 an octet [3] for wind ; three string quartets in C, B♭, E♭ and D ; minuets and trios for orchestra and for PF. ; a third fantasia for the PF., four hands ; several songs, terzets and canons ; a cantata in two movements, for three male voices and guitar, for his father's birthday, Sept. 27—both words and music his own ; and his first symphony in D,[4] intended to celebrate the birthday of Dr. Lang, and finished on Oct. 28. With this very important work his time at the *Convict* ended. He might have remained longer ; for it is said that the Emperor, who took an interest in the lads of his chapel, had specially watched the progress of this gifted boy with the lovely voice and fine expression, and that a special decision had been registered in his favour on Oct. 21, assuring him a foundation scholarship in the school, provided that during the vacation he should study sufficiently to pass an examination.[5] To this condition, however, he refused to submit ; and at some time between Oct. 26 and Nov. 6 he left the *Convict* and returned home.[6] His mother died in 1812, but we hear nothing of the event, unless the octet just named refers to it. The father married again in about a year, and the new wife, as we shall see, did her duty to her stepson Franz fully, and apparently with affection.

Franz was now just completing his seventeenth year, and what has been rightly called the first period of his life. The *Convict* has much to answer for in regard to Schubert. It was entrusted with the most poetical genius of modern times, and it appears to have allowed him to take his own course in the matter of composition almost unrestrained. Had but a portion of the pains been spent on the musical education of Schubert that was lavished on that of Mozart or of Mendelssohn, we can hardly doubt that even his transcendent ability would have been enhanced by it, that he would have gained that control over the prodigious spontaneity of his genius which is his only want, and have risen to the very highest level in all departments of composition, as he did in song-

writing. But though Eybler and Salieri were the conductors of the choir in chapel, it does not appear that they had any duties in the school, and Ruzicka, the thorough-bass master, like Holzer, was so prostrated by Schubert's facility as to content himself with exclaiming that his pupil already knew all he could teach him, and must have ' learned direct from heaven.' If all masters adopted this attitude towards their pupils, what would have become of some of the greatest geniuses ? The discomforts of the school appear to have been great even for that day of roughness. One of the pupils speaks of the cold of the practice-room as ' dreadful ' (*schauerlich*) ; and Schubert's own earliest letter, dated Nov. 24, 1812, to his brother Ferdinand, shows that these young growing lads were allowed to go without food for 8½ hours, between ' a poor dinner and a wretched supper.' There was not even sufficient music-paper provided for the scholars, and Schubert was, as we have seen, dependent on the bounty of the richer pupils.

On the other hand, the motets and masses in the service, the rehearsals in the school, such teaching as there was, and the daily practisings, must have been both stimulating and improving, and with all its roughness a good deal of knowledge could not but have been obtainable. One advantage Schubert reaped from the *Convict*—the friends which he made there, many of them for life, Spaun, Senn, Holzapfel, Stadler and others, all afterwards more or less eminent, who attached themselves to him as every one did who came into contact with him ; a band of young adorers, eager to play, or sing, or copy anything that he composed ; the earnest of the devoted friends who surrounded him in later years, and helped to force his music on an ignorant and preoccupied public. Nor did the enthusiasm cease with his departure ; for some years afterwards the orchestral pieces which he had written while at the school were still played by the boys from his own MS. copies.

EARLY MUSICAL IMPRESSIONS.—Outside the school he had sometimes opportunities of going to the opera. The first opera which he is said to have heard was Weigl's ' Waisenhaus,' played Dec. 12, 1810 ; but this was eclipsed by the ' Schweizerfamilie ' of the same composer, July 8, 1811 ; that again by Spontini's ' Vestalin,' with Milder, Oct. 1, 1812 ; and all of them by Gluck's ' Iphigenie auf Tauris,' which he probably heard first Apr. 5, 1815, with Milder and Vogl in the two principal parts, and which made a deep and ineffaceable impression upon him, and drove him to the study of Gluck's scores.[7] During the same years there were also many concerts, including those at which Beethoven produced his 5th, 6th and 7th symphonies, the ' Choral Fantasia,' portions of the Mass in C, the overture to ' Coriolan,' and others of

---

[1] Kreissle expressly states this (p. 550) and gives the date—' Nov. 19, 1812.'

[2] See Alfred Orel, ' Franz Schubert's "Sonate" für Klavier, Violine und Violoncello aus dem Jahre 1812,' *Z.M.W.* Jan.-Feb. 1923, pp. 209-18. The work has been published by the Wiener Philh. Verlag.

[3] This octet, dated Sept. 19, is said to be mentioned by Ferdinand Schubert as ' Franz Schubert's Leichenbegängniss ' (funeral ceremony). It is supposed by Kreissle (p. 31) to have been composed for the funeral of his mother ; but it is difficult to believe that the words which he wrote for his father's birthday ode, eight days later, would have had no reference to the mother's death—which they certainly have not—if it had occurred at that date.

[4] Adagio and allegro vivace (D, ; andante (G) ; minuet and trio (D) ; finale, allegro vivace (D). The work was played from MS. at the Crystal Palace, Feb. 5, 1881. The autograph is in possession of Herr Dumba, Vienna.

[5] *K.H.* p. 33 (i. 33).

[6] It is stated on Spaun's authority that Schubert was led to this decision by the advice of the poet Theodor Körner. But Körner, in whose correspondence there is no mention of Schubert, left Vienna at the beginning of this year and died at Gadebusch in August.

[7] From Bauernfeld, in *W.Z.K.*

his greatest compositions. Schubert probably heard all these works, but it is very doubtful whether he heard them with the same predilection as the operas just mentioned. We might infer with certainty from the three earliest of his symphonies, that Beethoven's style had as yet taken but little hold on him, notwithstanding the personal fascination which he seems to have felt for the great master from first to last. But, indeed, we have his own express declaration to that effect. Coming home after a performance of an oratorio of Salieri's, June 16, 1816, he speaks of the music in terms which can only refer to Beethoven, as

'Of simple natural expression, free from all that *bizarrerie* which prevails in most of the composers of our time, and for which we have almost solely to thank one of our greatest German artists; that *bizarrerie* which unites the tragic and the comic, the agreeable and the repulsive, the heroic and the petty, the Holiest and a harlequin; infuriates those who hear it instead of dissolving them in love, and makes them laugh instead of raising them heavenwards.'

Mozart was at the time his ideal composer; this, too, is plain from the symphonies, but here also he leaves us in no doubt. Three days earlier we find in the same diary,[1] apropos of one of the quintets of that great master:

'Gently, as if out of the distance, did the magic tones of Mozart's music strike my ears. With what inconceivable alternate force and tenderness did Schlesinger's masterly playing impress it deep, deep, into my heart! Such lovely impressions remain on the soul, there to work for good, past all power of time or circumstances. In the darkness of this life they reveal a clear, bright, beautiful prospect, inspiring confidence and hope. O Mozart, immortal Mozart! what countless consolatory images of a bright better world hast thou stamped on our souls.'

There is no doubt to which of these two great masters he was most attached at the time he wrote this.[2]

POST SCHOOLDAYS.—We have seen what a scourge the conscription proved in the case of Ries, and the uneasiness of Mendelssohn's family till the risk of it was over in his case (Vol. III. p. 384). To avoid a similar danger[3] Schubert elected to enter his father's school, and after the necessary study for a few months at the Normal School of St. Anna, did so, and actually remained there for three years as teacher of the lowest class. The duties were odious, but he discharged them with strict regularity, and not with greater severity than might reasonably be expected from the irritable temperament of a musician condemned to such drudgery. The picture of Pegasus thus in vile harness, and the absence of any remark on the anomaly, throws a curious light on the beginnings of a great composer. Out of school hours, however, he had his relaxations. There was a family in the Lichtenthal named Grob—a mother, son and daughter—whose relations to him were somewhat like those of the Breunings to Beethoven (Vol. I. pp. 260-61). The house was higher in the scale than his father's, and he was quite at home there. Therese, the daughter, had a fine high soprano voice, and Heinrich Grob played both pianoforte and violoncello; the mother was a woman of taste, and a great deal of music was made. It is not impossible that Therese inspired him with a softer feeling.[4] The choir of the Lichtenthal church, where his old friend Holzer was still choirmaster, was his resort on Sundays and feast days, and for it he wrote his first Mass, in F—begun May 17, finished July 22, 1814—a fitting pendant to the symphony of the previous October. He was not yet eighteen, and the Mass is pronounced by a trustworthy critic[5] to be the most remarkable first mass ever produced, excepting Beethoven's in C, and as striking an instance of the precocity of genius as Mendelssohn's overture to the 'Midsummer Night's Dream.' It seems to have been first performed on Oct. 16, the first Sunday after St. Theresa's day, 1814—Mayseder, then twenty-five and an acknowledged virtuoso, leading the first violins; and was repeated at the Augustine church ten days after. This second performance was quite an event. Franz conducted, Holzer led the choir, Ferdinand took the organ, Therese Grob sang, the enthusiasm of the family and friends was great, and the proud father presented his happy son with a five-octave piano.[6] Salieri was present and loud in his praises, and claimed Schubert as his pupil. He had indeed begun to take some interest in the lad before[7] he left the *Convict*, and continued it by daily lessons 'for a long time.'[8] That interest was probably much the same that he had shown to Beethoven fifteen years before, making him write to Metastasio's words, and correcting the prosody of his music. But there must have been some curious attraction about the old man to attach two such original geniuses as Beethoven and Schubert to him, and make them willing to style themselves 'scholars of Salieri.'[9] His permanent influence on Schubert may be measured by the fact that he warned him against Goethe and Schiller, a warning which Schubert attended to so far as to compose sixty-seven songs of the one poet, and fifty-four of the other !

Franz's next effort was an opera—a light and absurd supernatural 'opéra-comique' in three acts, 'Des Teufels Lustschloss,' words by Kotzebue. He probably began it while at the *Convict*, the first act having been completed

1 Quoted by *K.H.* pp. 103, 101 (l. 105, 103).
2 At the same time it is fair to add that even now his allegiance was divided. In the instrumental compositions of this period, though the style is modelled on Mozart, the subjects are occasionally reminiscent of Beethoven's ideas; and there is a significant story that when a friend praised some of his settings af Klopstock, and hailed him already as one of the great masters of composition, he answered diffidently, 'Perhaps, I sometimes have dreams of that sort, but who can do anything after Beethoven?' W. H. HW.
3 He was three times summoned to enlist. See *Ferd.* p. 133.

4 See *K.H.* pp. 141 (i. 144).
5 Prout, in *Monthly Musical Record*, Jan. and Feb. 1871.
6 *Ferd.* p. 1336. 7 *K.H.* i. 27 *note*.
8 Bauernfeld, in *W.Z.K.*, June 9, 1829.
9 For Beethoven see Vol. I. p. 265. Schubert so styles himself on the title-pages of his 'Fernando' and 'Claudine von Villabella.'

Jan. 11, 1814; the second, Mar. 16; and the third, May 15. Two days afterwards he began the Mass. That over, he had leisure to look again at the earlier work. The experience gained in writing the Mass probably revealed many an imperfection in the opera. He at once rewrote it, and finished the revision of it on Oct. 22. The work was never performed. With all these and other labours he found time to visit the *Convict*[1] in the evenings, take part in the practices, and try over his new compositions. Besides the pieces already mentioned, the productions of 1814 embrace a Salve Regina for tenor and orchestra. Also two string quartets in D and C minor respectively, and a third in B♭, published as op. 168, and remarkable for the circumstances of its composition. It was begun as a string trio, and ten lines were written in that form. It was then begun again and finished as a quartet. The movements are more fully dated than usual.[2] Also five minuets and six ' Deutsche ' (or waltzes) for strings and horns; and seventeen songs, among them ' Gretchen am Spinnrade ' (Oct. 19) and Schiller's ' Der Taucher,' a composition of enormous length, begun Sept. 1813 and finished in the following Aug. On Dec. 10 he began his second symphony, in B♭.[3] The autograph shows that the short introduction and allegro vivace were finished by the 26th of the same month, but its completion falls in 1815.

Before the year closed he made the acquaintance of Mayrhofer, a man of eccentric, almost hypochondriac, character, and a poet of grand and gloomy cast, who became his firm friend, and fifty-four of whose poems (besides the operas of ' Adrast ' and ' Die beiden Freunde von Salamanka '), fortunately for Mayrhofer's immortality, he set to music—some of them among his very finest songs. The acquaintance began by Schubert's setting Mayrhofer's ' Am See.' He composed it on Dec. 7, and a few days afterwards visited the poet at his lodgings in the Wipplinger Strasse 420 (since destroyed), a small dark room rendered illustrious by being the residence of Theodor Körner, and afterwards of Schubert, who lived there in 1819 and 1820. The visit was the beginning of a friendship which ended only with Schubert's death.

RAPID COMPOSITION.—The year 1815 is literally crowded with compositions. Two orchestral symphonies of full dimensions, Nos. 2 and 3 (that in B♭ ended Mar. 24, that in D,[4] May 24—

July 19); a string quartet in G minor (Mar. 25–Apr. 1); PF. sonatas in C, F, E (Feb. 11) and E (Feb. 18); an adagio in G (Apr. 8): twelve Wiener Deutsche, eight Écossaises (Oct. 3), and ten variations for PF. solo; two Masses, in G[5] (Mar. 2–7) and B♭ (Nov. 11–); a new ' Dona.'[6] for the Mass in F; a Stabat Mater in G minor (Apr. 4); a Salve Regina (July 5); five large dramatic pieces: ' Der vierjährige Posten,' one-act operetta (ended May 16); ' Fernando,' one-act Singspiel (July 3–9); ' Claudine von Villabella,' three-act Singspiel (Act 1, July 26–Aug. 5), originally composed complete, but Acts 2 and 3 were used by an officious maid-servant for lighting fires; ' Die beiden Freunde von Salamanka,' a two-act Singspiel by Mayrhofer (Nov. 18–Dec. 31); ' Der Spiegelritter,' three-act opera, of which eight numbers are with the Gesellschaft des Musikfreunde at Vienna; perhaps also a Singspiel called ' Die Minnesänger,' and ' Adrast,' an opera by Mayrhofer, of which but seven numbers exist.[7]

In addition to all these there are no less than 146 songs. In Aug. alone there are over thirty, and in Oct. over twenty, of which eight are dated the 15th and seven the 19th! And of these 146 songs some are of such enormous length as would seem to have prevented their publication. ' Minona ' (MS., Feb. 8), the first one of the year, contains sixteen, and ' Adelwold and Emma ' (MS., June 5) no less than fifty-five, closely written sides. Of those published, ' Die Bürgschaft ' (' Aug. 1815 ') fills twenty-two pages of Litolff's edition, ' Elysium ' thirteen and ' Loda's Gespenst ' fifteen of the same. It was the length of such compositions as these—' pas une histoire, mais des histoires '—that caused Beethoven's exclamation on his deathbed: ' Such long poems, many of them containing ten others,' by which he meant as long as ten. And this mass of music was produced in the mere intervals of his school drudgery! Well might his brother say that the rapidity of his writing was marvellous.

Amidst all this work and, one might be tempted to believe, all this hurry, it is astonishing to find that some of the songs of these boyish years are amongst the most permanent of his productions. ' Gretchen am Spinnrade,' a song full of the passion and experience of a lifetime, was written (as we have said) in Oct. 1814, when he was 17. ' Der Erl König ' itself

---

[1] *K.H.* p. 18 (i. 19).

[2] The allegro has at beginning, ' 5 Sept. 1814 '; at end, ' den 6 Sept. in 4 Stunden angefertigt,' apparently implying that it was dashed off before and after twelve o'clock at night. Andante, at beginning, ' den 6 Sept. 1814 '; at end, ' den 10 Sept. 1814.' Minuet, at end, ' 11 Sept. 1814.' Finale, at end, ' den 13 Sept. 1814.' Autograph with Spina.

[3] At beginning, ' 10 Dec. 1814 '; at end of allegro, ' 26 Dec. 1814 '; at beginning of finale, ' 25 Feb. 1815 '; and at end, ' 24 Mar. 1815.' The movements are largo and allegro vivace (B♭); andante (E♭); minuet and trio (C minor); finale, presto vivace (B♭). Played from MS. at the Crystal Palace, Oct. 20, 1877. Autograph with Herr Dumba.

[4] It is in the usual number of movements: adagio maestoso and

allegro con brio (D); allegretto (G); minuet and trio (D); finale, presto vivace (D). Dates: allegro, at beginning, ' 24 May 1815 '; end, ' July 12, 1815.' Allegretto, at beginning, ' July 15, 1815.' End of finale, ' July 19, 1815.' Autograph with Herr Dumba.

[5] Published by M. Berra, of Prague, in 1846, as the composition of R. Führer. (See Vol. II. p. 319.) The fraud was not exposed till 1847, when it was announced by Ferd. Schubert in the *Allg. Wiener Musikzeitung* of Dec. 14. Ferdinand mentions this Mass in his list under 1815. A copy, evidently copied closely from the autograph, but with the addition of oboes (or clarinets) and bassoons by Ferd. Schubert (July 23, 1847), is in the library of the Gesellschaft der Musikfreunde.

[6] Mentioned by Ferdinand, p. 139a.

[7] Autographs of Fernando, Teufels Lustschloss and Adrast are with Herr Dumba.

ın its original form (with a few slight differences)[1] belongs to the winter of 1815, and the
immortal songs of the ' Haidenröslein,' ' Rastlose Liebe,' ' Schäfers Klagelied,' the grand
Ossian songs and others of his better-known
works fall within this year. The Mass in G,
too, though composed for a very limited orchestra, and not without tokens of hurry, is a
masterpiece. The dramatic works contain many
beautiful movements and are full of striking
things, but the librettos are so bad that in their
present condition they can never be put on the
stage. The symphonies, though not original,
are not without original points ; and are so sustained throughout, so full of fresh melody and
interesting harmony, and so extraordinarily
scored considering their date, that in these
respects a man of double Schubert's age might
be proud to claim them.

The habit of writing to whatever words came
in his way was one of Schubert's characteristics,
especially in the earlier part of his career. With
his incessant desire to sing ; with an abundant
fountain of melody and harmony always well-
ing up in him and endeavouring to escape, no
wonder that he grasped at any words and tried
any forms that came in his way and seemed to
afford a channel for his thoughts. If good,
well ; if bad, well too. The reason why he
wrote eight operas in one year was no doubt in
great measure because he happened to meet
with eight librettos ; had it been four or twelve
instead of eight the result would have been the
same. The variety in the productions even of
this early year is truly extraordinary. A glance
at the list is sufficient to show that he tried
nearly every form of composition, whilst the
songs which he set range from gems like
Goethe's ' Meeresstille ' and ' Freudvoll und
leidvoll' to the noisy ballads of Bertrand ;
from Mayrhofer's stern classicality and the
gloomy romance of Ossian to the mild sentiment of Klopstock. No doubt, as Schumann
says, he could have set a placard to music.[2] The
spectacle of so insatiable a desire to produce has
never before been seen ; of a genius thrown
naked into the world and compelled to explore
for himself all paths and channels in order to
discover by exhaustion which was the best—
and then to die.

During this year he taught diligently and
punctually in his father's school, and attended
Salieri's lessons. His relations to the Lichtenthal remained as before. The Mass in G, like
that in F, was written for the parish church, and
according to the testimony of one[3] of his old

friends was especially intended for those of his
companions who had been pupils of Holzer's
with him. A pleasant relic of his home life
exists in a piece of music written for his father's
birthday, Sept. 27, 1815, for four voices and
orchestra—' Erhabner, verehrter Freund der
Jugend.'[4] He kept up his intercourse also
with the Convict, and when he had written anything special it was one of the first places to
which he would take it. There possibly his
symphonies were tried, though it is doubtful if a
juvenile orchestra would contain clarinets, bassoons, trumpets and horns, all which are present
in the scores of the first four symphonies.

There, thanks to the memorandum of another
old ' Convicter,' we can assist at the first hearing
of ' Der Erl König.' Spaun happened to call
one afternoon, in this very winter, at the elder
Schubert's house in the Himmelpfortgrund, and
found Franz in his room, in a state of inspiration
over Goethe's ballad, which he had just seen for
the first time. A few times' reading had been
sufficient to evoke the music, which in the rage
of inspiration he was whelming down[5] on to
the paper at the moment of Spaun's arrival ;
indeed it was already perfect except the mere
filling in of the accompaniment. This was
quickly done ; and it was finished in the form
in which we can now see it in the Berlin
Library.[6] In the evening Schubert brought it
to the Convict, and there first he and then Holzapfel sang it through. It was not altogether
well received. No wonder ; the form was too
new, the dramatic spirit too strong, even for
that circle of young Schubert admirers. At the
words ' Mein Vater, mein Vater, jetzt fasst er
mich an !' where G♭, F♮ and E♭ all come together, there was some dissent, and Ruzicka,
as teacher of harmony, had to explain to his
pupils, as best he might, a combination which
now seems perfectly natural and appropriate.

INTERVENTION OF SCHOBER.—1816 was
passed much as 1815 had been, in a marvellous
round of incessant work. The drudgery of the
school, however, had become so insupportable
that Schubert seized the opportunity of the
opening of a Government school of music at
Laibach, near Trieste, to apply for the post of
director, with a salary of 500 Vienna florins—
£21 a year. The testimonials which he sent in
in April from Salieri, and from Joseph Spendou,
Chief Superintendent of Schools, were so cold in
tone as to imply that however much they valued
Schubert, they believed his qualifications not to
be those of the head of a large establishment.[7]
At any rate he failed, and the post was given, on
the recommendation of Salieri, to a certain

---

[1] The Berlin Library possesses an autograph of the earlier form.
All the versions are in the complete edition.
[2] ' Qu'on me donne la Gazette de Hollande,' says Rameau. But
Schubert could have thrown poetry into an advertisement ! ' Give
me the words,' said Mozart, ' and I'll put the poetry to them.'
[3] Herr Doppler. I cannot refrain from mentioning this gentleman, who in 1867 was shopman at Spina's (formerly Diabelli's). I
shall never forget the droll shock I received when on asking him if
he knew Schubert, he replied : ' Know him ? I was at his christen-
ing !' Kreissle's Life is indebted to him for many a trait which
would otherwise have been lost.

[4] Now in the Imperial Library, Berlin. No doubt there was one
every year, though that of 1814 has been lost.
[5] Hinzuwühlend is Kreissle's word, doubtless from Spaun's lips.
[6] If indeed this be the actually first original. The omission of
bar 8, and its subsequent insertion, however, as well as the clean
regular look of the whole, seem to point to its being a transcript.
The various versions of this song, and the stages of its growth,
can be seen in the complete edition of Breitkopf & Härtel.
[7] K.H. p. 107 (i. 109).

Jacob Schaufl.  Schubert found compensation, however, in the friendship of Franz von Schober, a young man of good birth and some small means, who had met with his songs at the house of the Spauns at Linz, and had ever since longed to make his personal acquaintance.  Coming to Vienna to enter the university, apparently soon after the Laibach rebuff, he called on Schubert, found him in his father's house, overwhelmed with his school duties, and with apparently no time for music.  There, however, were the piles of manuscript—operas, masses, symphonies, songs — heaped up around the young schoolmaster-composer, and Schober saw at once that some step must be taken to put an end to this cruel anomaly and give Schubert time to devote himself wholly to the art of which he was so full.  Schober proposed that his new friend should live with him ; Franz's father—possibly not oversatisfied with his son's performances as a teacher of the alphabet to infants [1]—consented to the plan, and the two young men (Schober was some four months Franz's junior) went off to keep house together at Schober's lodgings in the Landkrongasse. A trace of this change is found on two MS. songs in the Musikverein at Vienna, ' Leiden der Trennung ' and ' Lebenslied,' inscribed ' In Herr v. Schober's lodging ' and dated Nov. 1816.  Schubert began to give a few lessons, but soon threw them up,[2] and the household must have been maintained at Schober's expense, since there was obviously as yet no sale for Schubert's compositions.  He had good friends, as Beethoven had at the same age, though not so high in rank—Hofrath von Kiesewetter, Matthäus von Collin, Graf Moritz Dietrichstein, Hofrath Hammer von Purgstall, Pyrker, afterwards Patriarch of Venice and Archbishop of Erlau, Frau Caroline Pichler—all ready and anxious to help him had they had the opportunity.  But Schubert never gave them the opportunity.  He was a true Viennese, born in the lowest ranks, without either the art or the taste for ' imposing ' on the aristocracy (Beethoven's[3] favourite phrase) that Beethoven had ; loving the society of his own class, shrinking from praise or notice of any kind, and with an absolute detestation of teaching or any other stated duties.  But to know him was to love and value him.

CANTATAS FOR SEVERAL OCCASIONS.—Three little events, which slightly diversify the course of this year, are of moment as showing the position which Schubert took amongst his acquaintances.  The first was the 50th anniversary of Salieri's arrival in Vienna, which he had entered as a boy on June 16, 1766.  (See SALIERI, p. 509.)  On Sunday, June 16, 1816, the old Italian was invested with the Imperial gold medal and chain of honour, in the presence

of the whole body of court musicians ; and in the evening a concert took place at his own house, in which, surrounded by his pupils, Weigl, Assmayer, Anna Fröhlich, Schubert and many others,[4] both male and female, he snuffed up the incense of his worshippers and listened to compositions in his honour by his scholars past and present.  Among these were pieces sent by Hummel and Moscheles, and a short cantata, both words and music by Schubert.[5]

Eight days afterwards, on July 24, there was another festivity in honour of the birthday of a certain Herr Heinrich Watteroth,[6] a distinguished official person, for which Schubert had been employed to write a cantata on the subject of Prometheus, words by Philipp Dräxler, another official person.  The cantata has disappeared ; but from a description of it by Leopold Sonnleithner, communicated to Zellner's Blätter für Theater, etc. (No. 19), and reprinted[7] separately, it seems to have been written for two solo voices, soprano (Gäa) and bass (Prometheus), chorus and orchestra, and to have contained a duet in recitative, two choruses for mixed and one for male voices (the disciples of Prometheus).  This last is described as having been in the form of a slow march, with original and interesting treatment.  The performance took place in the garden of Watteroth's house in the Erdberg suburb of Vienna.  As all the persons concerned in the festivity were people of some consideration, and as the music was very well received, it may have been an important introduction for the young composer.  A congratulatory poem by von Schlechta, addressed to Schubert, appeared a day or two later in the Theaterzeitung.  Schubert had already, in the previous year, set a song of Schlechta's—' Auf einem Kirchhof '— and he promptly acknowledged the compliment by adopting one of more moment from Schlechta's ' Diego Manzanares,' ' Wo irrst du durch einsame Schatten ? ' his setting of which is dated July 30, 1816.[8]  Schubert evidently was fond of his cantata.  It was performed at Innsbruck by Gänsbacher, and at Vienna by Sonnleithner in 1819.  Schubert wished to give it at the Augarten in 1820, and had sent it somewhere for performance at the time of his death. He was paid 100 florins Vienna currency (or £4) for it, and he notes in his journal that it was the first time he had composed for money.

The third event was the composition of a

[4] There was a Liszt among Salieri's pupils at this time, but hardly the future Abbé, who was then but five years old.  Franz Liszt and Schubert met once—in the curious collection of variations on Diabelli's waltz, to which fifty Austrian composers contributed. Beethoven's contribution being the thirty-three variations, op. 120. Liszt's variations is No. 24, and Schubert's No. 38.  Liszt was throughout an indefatigable champion for Schubert.
[5] The autograph of this little curiosity was sold in Paris, by auction, May 14, 1881.  The words are given by Kreissle, p. 82 (i. 83), but are not worth quoting.  They do not possess the individuality of thought which makes Schubert's later verses so interesting, in spite of the crudity of their expression.
[6] His birthday was July 12, but the performance was put off on account of the weather.
[7] I am indebted for this reprint to my ever-kind friend Mr. C. F. Pohl, of the Gesellschaft der Musikfreunde, Vienna.
[8] He returned to this poet in 1820, 1825, 1826, 1828.

[1] There is ground for this supposition.
[2] Bauernfeld, W.Z.K.        [3] Imponiren.  Thayer, ii. 313.

cantata on a larger scale than either of the ~thers. It was addressed to Dr. Joseph Spendou, in his character of Founder and Principal of the Schoolmasters' Widows' Fund, and contained eight numbers, with solos for two sopranos and bass, a quartet and choruses, all with orchestral accompaniment. Whether it was performed or not is uncertain,[1] but it was published in 1830 in PF. score by Diabelli, as op. 128.

The other compositions of the year 1816 are ts numerous as usual. There is a fine trio for S.S.A. and PF. to the words of Klopstock's 'grosses Halleluja' (Lf. 41, No. 2); a Salve Regina in F, to German words, for four voices and organ [2] (Feb. 21, 1816), another, to Latin words, for unaccompanied chorus (Feb. 1816), and a Stabat Mater in F minor (Feb. 28, 1816) to Klopstock's translation of the Latin hymn. The last of these is written for soprano, tenor and bass solo and chorus, and for an orchestra of the usual strings, two flutes, two oboes, two bassoons, one contra-bassoon, two horns, three trombones, two trumpets and drums. These, however, are not uniformly employed; the trumpets and drums only appear for a few chords in Nos. 9 and 12; No. 5, an eight-part chorus, is accompanied by the wind alone; and No. 6, a tenor air, by the strings, with oboe solo. This work was performed in 1841 by the Musik-verein of Vienna, and in 1863 at the Altlerchen-felder church, but was not published until the appearance of Breitkopf & Härtel's edition.

Among other works of this year are a setting of the Angels' Chorus from 'Faust'—'Christ ist erstanden' (June 1816); a fragment of a Requiem in E♭ [3] (July 1816), which ends with the second bar of the second Kyrie; a Tantum ergo in C (Aug.); a Magnificat in C (Sept.); and a duet, 'Auguste jam coelestium' (Oct.), strongly tinctured by Mozart.[4]

Of operas we find only one in 1816, probably because only one libretto came in his way. It is called 'Die Bürgschaft,' and is in three acts. The author of the words is not known; and the quotations in Kreissle show that they are in great part absolute rubbish. Schubert con-tinued his task to the third act, fifteen numbers, and there stopped. The autograph, in Herr Dumba's possession, is dated May 1816.

The symphonies of 1816 are two—the fourth, in C minor, entitled 'Tragic symphony,' and dated Apr. 1816 [5]; and the fifth, in B♭, for small orchestra, dated Sept. 1816–Oct. 3, 1816.[6]

The first of these is a great advance on its pre-decessors; the andante is individual and very beautiful, and the finale wonderfully spirited. The other, though full of Mozart, is as gay and untrammelled as all Schubert's orchestral music of that day. It is sometimes entitled 'With-out Trumpets or Drums,' and is said to have been composed for the orchestra at the Gundel-hof, which grew out of the Schubert Sunday afternoon quartets.[7] Both were often played at the Crystal Palace, under Manns's direction, and were among the favourite works in the repertory of that establishment. A string quartet in F; a string trio in B♭, apparently very good; a rondo in A for violin solo and quartet (June 1816); a violin concerto in C; three sonatinas for PF. and violin (op. 137); a PF. sonata in F; two movements of another in E; various marches for PF.; twelve Deutsche (waltzes); six Écossaises, with the inscriptions 'Composed while a prisoner in my room at Erd-berg' and 'Thank God'—probably the relic of some practical joke—are still existing.

SONG COMPOSITION.—Very little of the above, however interesting, can be said to be of real, first-rate, permanent value. But when we approach the songs of 1816 the case is altered. There are not quite so many with this date as there were with that of 1815, but there are over a hundred in all, and among them are some of his finest settings of Goethe, the three songs of the Harper, in 'Wilhelm Meister' (op. 12, Sept. 6), Mignon's 'Sehnsucht' song (op. 62, No. 4); 'Der Fischer'; 'Der König in Thule' (op. 5, No. 5), 'Jägers Abendlied' and 'Schäfers Klagelied' (op. 3), 'Wanderer's Nachtlied' (op. 4),—'An Schwager Kronos' (op. 19). Of Schiller there are the beautiful 'Ritter Toggenburg,' Thekla's song (op. 58), etc., and to name only one other, the far-famed 'Wan-derer,' by Schmidt of Lubeck.

These magnificent pieces are well known to every lover of Schubert, but they are not more valued than such exquisitely simple and touch-ing little effusions as 'An eine Quelle' of Claudius (op. 109, No. 3), 'Der Abend' of Kosegarten (op. 118, No. 2) or 'Der Leidende' of Hölty (Lief. 50, No. 2), all equally bearing his stamp.

The lists of the songs of these two years throw a curious light on Schubert's musical activity and mode of proceeding. Dr. Johnson was said when he got hold of a book to 'tear the heart out of it,' and with Schubert it was very much the same. To read a poem and at once to fasten upon it and transcribe it in music seems to have been his natural course; and having done one he went at once to the next. A volume of Hölty, or Claudius, or Kosegarten came into his hands; he tore from it in a moment what struck him, and was not content with one song, but must have three, four or

---

[1] Kreissle, i. 88, says that it was.
[2] Nottebohm's *Catalogue*, p. 226.
[3] First printed by Schumann as Appendix to his newspaper, the *N.Z.M.*, for June 18, 1839.
[4] This paragraph is contributed by W. H. HW. The autograph of the last named was in Brahms's possession. The date is quoted from the *Catalogue* of the accurate Nottebohm. Brahms judged it to be later than 1816.
[5] Apr. 1816.—Adagio molto and allegretto vivace in C minor; andante in A♭; menuet and trio in E♭; finale in C. The auto-graph has vanished.
[6] Sept. 1816.—Fine den 3 Oct. 1816. Allegro, B♭; andante con moto, E♭; menuet and trio, G minor and G major; finale, allegretto vivace, B♭. Autograph with Peters & Co.

[7] Hanslick *Concertwesen*, p. 142.

five. Thus, in the summer of 1815, he evidently meets with Kosegarten's poems, and, in July, sets twenty of them. In March 1816 he sets five songs by Salis; in May, six by Hölty; in Nov., four by Claudius, three by Mayrhofer and so on. To read these lists gives one a kind of visible image of the almost fierce eagerness with which he attacked his poetry, and of the inspiration with which the music rushed from his heart and through his pen—'everything that he touched,' says Schumann, 'turning into music.' Thus, at a later date, calling accidentally on Randhartinger, and his friend being summoned from the room, Schubert, to amuse himself in the interval, took up a little volume which lay on the table. It interested him; and as his friend did not return he carried it off with him. Anxious for his book, Randhartinger called next morning at Schubert's lodgings, and found that he had already set several pieces in it to music. The volume was Wilhelm Müller's poems; the songs were part of the 'Schöne Müllerin.' A year or two after this, in July 1826—it is his old friend Doppler who tells the story—returning from a Sunday stroll with some friends through the village of Währing, he saw a friend sitting at a table in the beer-garden of one of the taverns. The friend, when they joined him, had a volume of Shakespeare on the table. Schubert seized it and began to read; but before he had turned over many pages pointed to 'Hark, hark, the lark!' and exclaimed: 'Such a lovely melody has come into my head, if I had but some music paper.' Some one drew a few staves on the back of a bill of fare, and there, amid the hubbub of the beer-garden, that beautiful song, so perfectly fitting the words, so skilful and so happy in its accompaniment, came into perfect existence. Two others from the same poet not improbably followed in the evening.[1]

It seems that the quartet afternoons at the house of Schubert the elder had gradually extended themselves into performances of Haydn's symphonies, arranged as quartets and played with doubled parts; players of ability and name joined, and a few hearers were admitted. After a time the modest room became inconveniently crowded, and then the little society migrated to the house of a tradesman named Frischling (Dorotheengasse 1105), wind instruments were added, and the smaller works of Pleyel, Haydn and Mozart were attacked. In the winter of 1815 another move became necessary, to the house of Otto Hatwig, one of the violins of the Burgtheater, at the Schottenthor, and in the spring of 1818 to his new residence in the Gundelhof, and later still at Pettenkofer's house in the Bauernmarkt. The band now contained some good professional players, and could venture even on Beethoven's

first two symphonies and the overtures of Cherubini, Spontini, Boieldieu, Weigl, etc. Schubert belonged to it all through, playing the viola, and it was probably with the view to their performance by the society that he wrote the two symphonies of 1816 (Nos. 4 and 5), two overtures in the winter of 1817 and his sixth symphony in the spring of 1818.

VOGL'S ESTIMATE OF THE SONGS.—Schober and Mayrhofer were Schubert's first friends outside the immediate circle of his youthful associates. He was now to acquire a third, destined to be of more active service than either of the others. This was Vogl. He was twenty years Franz's senior, and at the time of their meeting was a famous singer at the Vienna Opera, admired more for his intellectual gifts than for the technical perfection of his singing, and really great in such parts as Orestes in 'Iphigenie,' Almaviva in 'Figaro,' Creon in 'Medea' and Telasko in the 'Vestalin.' About the year 1816—the date is not precisely given—Vogl was induced by Schober to come to their lodgings and see the young fellow of whom Schober was always raving, but who had no access to any of the circles which Vogl adorned and beautified by his presence. The room as usual was strewed with music. Schubert was confused and awkward; Vogl, the great actor and man of the world, gay, and at his ease. The first song he took up—probably the first music of Schubert's he had ever seen—was Schubert's 'Augenlied.' He hummed it through and thought it melodious, but slight—which it is. 'Ganymed' and the 'Schäfers Klage' made a deeper impression; others followed and he left with the somewhat patronising but true remark: 'There is stuff in you; but you squander your fine thoughts instead of making the most of them.' But the impression remained; he talked of Schubert with astonishment, soon returned, and the acquaintance grew and ripened till they became almost inseparable, and until in their performances of Schubert's songs 'the two seemed,' in Schubert's own words, 'for the moment to be one.' In those days songs were rarely if ever sung in concert-rooms; but Vogl had the *entrée* to all the great musical houses of Vienna, and before long his performances of the 'Erl King,' the 'Wanderer,' 'Ganymed,' 'Der Kampf,' etc., with the composer's accompaniment, were well known. What Vogl's opinion of him ultimately became may be learnt from a passage in his diary:

' Nothing shows so plainly the want of a good school of singing as Schubert's songs. Otherwise, what an enormous and universal effect must have been produced throughout the world, wherever the German language is understood, by these truly divine inspirations, these utterances of a musical *clairvoyance*! How many would have comprehended, probably for the first time, the meaning of such expressions as "speech and poetry in music," "words in harmony," "ideas clothed in music," etc., and would have learnt

---

[1] The drinking-song from 'Antony and Cleopatra' (marked 'Währing, July 26'), and the lovely 'Sylvia' ('July 1826'). The anecdote is in Kreissle.

that the finest poems of our greatest poets may be enhanced and even transcended when translated into musical language ? Numberless examples may be named, but I will only mention "The Erl King," "Gretchen," "Schwager Kronos," the Mignon and Harper's songs, Schiller's "Sehnsucht," "Der Pilgrim" and "Die Bürgschaft."'

This extract shows how justly Vogl estimated Schubert, and how, at that early date, his discernment enabled him to pass a judgment which even now it would be difficult to excel. The word *clairvoyance*, too, shows that he thoroughly entered into Schubert's great characteristic. In hearing Schubert's compositions it is often as if one were brought more immediately and closely into contact with music itself than is the case in the works of others ; as if in his pieces the stream from the great heavenly reservoir were dashing over us, or flowing through us, more directly, with less admixture of any medium or channel, than it does in those of any other writer—even of Beethoven himself. And this immediate communication with the origin of music really seems to have happened to him. No sketches, no delay, no anxious period of preparation, no revision appear to have been necessary. He had but to read the poem, to surrender himself to the torrent, and to put down what was given him to say as it rushed through his mind. This was the true 'inspiration of dictation,' as much so as in the utterance of any Hebrew prophet or seer. We have seen one instance in the case of the 'Erl King.' The poem of the Wanderer attracted him in the same way, and the song was completed in one evening. In a third case, that of Goethe's 'Rastlose Liebe,' the paroxysm of inspiration was so fierce that Schubert never forgot it, but, reticent as he often was, talked of it years afterwards.[1] It would seem that the results did not always fix themselves in the composer's memory as permanently as if they had been the effect of longer and more painful elaboration. Vogl tells an anecdote about this which is very much to the point.[2] On one occasion he received from Schubert some new songs, but being otherwise occupied could not try them over at the moment. When he was able to do so he was particularly pleased with one of them, but as it was too high for his voice he had it copied in a lower key. About a fortnight afterwards they were again making music together, and Vogl placed the transposed song before Schubert on the desk of the piano. Schubert tried it through, liked it, and said, in his Vienna dialect : 'I say ! the song's not so bad ; *whose is it* ?' so completely, in a fortnight, had it vanished from his mind ! Sir Walter Scott attributed a song of his own to Byron ; but this was in 1828, after his mind had begun to fail.[3]

INFLUENCE OF ROSSINI.—1817 was comparatively an idle year. Its great musical event was the arrival of Rossini's music in Vienna. 'L' Inganno felice ' was produced at the Hoftheater, Nov. 26, 1816, and 'Tancredi,' Dec. 17 ; 'L' Italiana in Algeri,' Feb. 1, 1817, and 'Ciro in Babilonia,' June 18 ; and the enthusiasm of the Viennese—like that of all to whom these fresh and animated strains were brought—knew no bounds. Schubert admired Rossini's melody and spirit, but rather made fun of his orchestral music, and a story is told —not impossibly apocryphal [4]—of his having written an overture in imitation of Rossini, before supper, after returning from 'Tancredi.' At any rate he has left two ' Overtures in the Italian style ' in D and C, dated Sept.[5] and Nov. 1817 respectively, which were much played at the time. Schubert made four-hand PF. arrangements of both, and that in C has been since published in score and parts as op. 170, and has been played at the Crystal Palace (Dec. 1, 1866, etc.) and elsewhere. Its caricature of Rossini's salient points, including of course the inevitable *crescendo*, is obvious enough ; but nothing could transform Schubert into an Italian, and the overture has individual and characteristic beauties which are immediately recognisable. The influence of Rossini was no mere passing fancy, but may be traced in the sixth symphony, mentioned below, and in music of his later life—in the two marches (op. 121), the finale to the quartet in G (op. 161) and elsewhere.

A third overture in D belongs to 1817, and, though still in MS., has also been played at the Crystal Palace (Feb. 6, 1869, etc.). It is in two movements, adagio and all°. giusto, and the former is almost a draft of the analogous movement in the overture known as 'Rosamunde' (op. 26), though really the 'Zauberharfe.' There the resemblance ceases. What led Schubert to the pianoforte this year in so marked a manner is not known, but his devotion to it is obvious, for no fewer than six sonatas belong to this period, viz. three with opus numbers—op. 122, in E♭ ; op. 147,[6] in B (Aug.) ; op. 164, in A minor [7] ; and three others, in F, A♭ and E minor (June).

Schubert's sixth symphony, in C,[8] completed in Feb. 1818, appears to have been begun in the preceding October. It is the first one which he has marked as 'Grosse Sinfonie,' though hardly with reason, as both in form and orchestra it is the same as the early ones. It is an advance on the others, and the scherzo shows the first decided signs of Beethoven's influence. Passages may also be traced to Rossini and the Italian opera.

The catalogue of the instrumental com-

---

1 Bauernfeld, *W.Z.K.*    2 In *Kreissle*, p. 119 (i. 123).
3 Lockhart's *Life of Scott*, vii. 129.

4 *K.H.* 129 (i. 133).
5 Kreissle says May.   September is Nottebohm's date : but there is another overture in D, and it seems doubtful which of the two is dated May and which September.
6 Autograph in possession of Brahms.
7 Published by Spina as ' 7th sonata.'
8 Adagio and allegro in C ; andante in F ; scherzo in C and trio in E major ; finale in C.

positions of this year closes with a string trio [1] and a polonaise for the violin. In the number of the vocal compositions of 1817 there is an equal falling off. Rossini's popularity for the time shut the door against all other composers, and even Schubert's appetite for bad libretti was compelled to wait. Not only, however, are there no operas this year, there is no church music, and but forty-seven songs. In quality, however, there is no deterioration in the songs. The astonishing 'Gruppe aus dem Tartarus' and the 'Pilgrim' of Schiller; the 'Ganymed' of Goethe; the 'Fahrt zum Hades,' 'Memnon' and 'Erlafsee' of Mayrhofer; and 'An die Musik' of Schober are equal to any that come before them. Among the MS. songs is one showing the straits to which Schubert was sometimes put, either by the want of materials or by the sudden call of his inspiration. It is the beginning of a setting of Schiller's 'Entzückung an Laura,' and is written on the front page of the second violin part of a duet-fugue by Fux, the words 'Fuga. Duetto. Violino: Secundo. Del: Sing:[2] Fux' appearing in the copyist's formal handwriting through Schubert's hasty notes. It is superscribed 'Entzückung an Laura Abschied August 1817. Schubert Mpia'—interesting as showing that in 'Abschied' he has added his own comment to Schiller's words; that he dated his pieces at the moment of beginning them; and that he sometimes signed his name without the 'Franz.'

His circle of intimate friends was increased about this date by Anselm and Joseph Hüttenbrenner and Joseph Gahy. Anselm, four years his senior, was a pupil of Salieri's, and there they had met in 1815. With the younger brother, Joseph, he became acquainted in the summer of 1817.[3] Both were men of independent means, and Anselm was a musician by profession. Gahy was in the Government employment, an excellent pianoforte-player, of whom Schubert was for long very fond. The younger Hüttenbrenner was bewitched by Schubert, much as Krumpholz and Schindler were by Beethoven; and was ever ready to fetch and carry for his idol, and to praise whatever he did, till the idol would turn on his worshipper and be so cruel as to get the nickname of 'The Tyrant' from the rest of the set.

How Schubert existed since he threw up his place at the school and left his father's house is a point on which we are in entire ignorance. His wants were few, but how even those few were supplied is a mystery. We have seen that he lived rent-free with Schober for a few

months in 1816, but the return of Schober's brother put an end to the arrangement,[4] and from that date he must have been indebted to Spaun, or some friend better off than himself, for lodgings, for existence and for his visits to the theatre, for there is no trace of his earning anything by teaching in 1817, and the few pounds paid him for the Watteroth cantata is the only sum which he seems to have earned up to this date.

THE ESTERHAZY FAMILY.—In the summer of 1818, however, on the recommendation of Unger, the father of Mme. Unger-Sabatier the great singer (see UNGER, Caroline), Schubert accepted an engagement as teacher of music in the family of Count Johann Esterhazy, to pass the summer at his country seat at Zselész, in Hungary, on the Waag, some distance east of Vienna, and the winter in town. He was to be a member of the establishment and to receive two gulden for every lesson. The family consisted of the count and countess, two daughters—Marie, thirteen, and Caroline, eleven—and a boy of five. All were musical. The count sang bass, the countess and Caroline contralto, Marie had a fine soprano, and both daughters played the piano. Baron von Schönstein, their intimate friend, slightly older than Schubert, a singer of the highest qualities, with a noble baritone voice, made up the party, which certainly promised all the elements of enjoyment. It was a pang to Schubert to part from the circle of his companions, to whom he was devoted, but it is not difficult to imagine how pleasant he must have found the comfort and generous living of the Esterhazy house, while at the same time there would be opportunities of retirement and abundant means of diversion in a beautiful country, a new people and the Hungarian and gipsy melodies.

When they left town does not appear.[5] Schubert's Mass in C,[6] his fourth, written like the others for Holzer, is dated 'July 1818'; but there is nothing to show whether it was finished in Vienna or in the country. A set of MS. solfeggi for the Countess Marie, also dated July, is perhaps evidence that by that time they were settled at Zselész. Two letters to Schober are printed by Bauernfeld,[7] and are dated Aug. 3 and Sept. 18, 1818. The first is addressed to his home circle, his 'dearest fondest friends . . Spaun, Schober, Mayrhofer and Senn . . . you who are everything to me.' There are messages also to Vogl, and to Schober's mother and sister, and to 'all possible

---

[1] In B♭, in one movement.
[2] For 'Sign.' A facsimile is given by Reissmann.
[3] So *Kreissle*, i. 128. But does not the dedication of the song, 'Die Erwartung,' composed Feb. 27, 1815—' to his friend,' J. H.—show that the acquaintance was of much earlier date? True, it was not published till the April after Schubert's death; and the song may have been prepared by him for publication shortly before, and the dedication added then.

[4] *K.H.* 109 (l. 112).
[5] There is an interesting autograph copy of the 'Forelle' song dated at A. Hüttenbrenner's lodgings (in Vienna), midnight, Feb. 21, 1818, and besprinkled with ink instead of sand. It has been published in photography. But the 'Forelle' really dates from 1817. (Nottebohm, in the *Them. Catalogue*.)
[6] Published in 1826 as op. 48. Schubert wrote a new and most beautiful Benedictus to it in 1828, only a few months before his death.
[7] In *Die Presse*, Vienna, Apr. 17, 1869. Reprinted in the *Signale*, Nov. 15, 1869.

acquaintances,' and an urgent entreaty to write soon—'every syllable of yours is dear to me.' He is thoroughly well and happy, and 'composing like a god... Mayrhofer's Einsamkeit is ready, and I believe it to be the best thing I have yet done, for I was *without anxiety*' (*ohne Sorge*—the italics are his own). 'Einsamkeit' is a long ballad, filling nineteen close pages of print, with a dozen changes of tempo and as many of signature; perhaps not quite coming up to his own estimate of it, though both words and music are often very striking. The length of this and other ballads will probably always hinder their wealth of melody, dramatic effects and other striking beauties from being known by the world at large.

The other letter, seven weeks later, throws more light on his position at Zselész 'as composer, manager, audience, everything in one.'

'No one here cares for true Art, unless it be now and then the Countess; so I am left alone with my beloved, and have to hide her in my room, or my piano, or my own breast. If this often makes me sad, on the other hand it often elevates me all the more. Several songs have lately come into existence, and I hope very successful ones.'

He is evidently more at home in the servants' hall than the drawing-room:

'The cook is a pleasant fellow; the ladies'-maid is thirty; the housemaid very pretty, and often pays me a visit; the nurse is somewhat ancient; the butler is my rival; the two grooms get on better with the horses than with us. The Count is a little rough; the Countess proud, but not without heart; the young ladies good children. I need not tell you, who know me so well, that with my natural frankness I am good friends with everybody.'

The letter ends with an affectionate message to his parents.

The only songs which can be fixed to this autumn, and which are therefore doubtless those just referred to, besides the great 'Einsamkeit,' are the 'Blumenbrief,' 'Blondel und Maria,' 'Das Marienbild' and 'Litaney,' 'Das Abendroth'—for a contralto, evidently composed for the countess; 'Vom Mitleiden Mariä,' and three sonnets from Petrarch. The Hungarian national songs left their mark in the '36 original dances,' or 'First Waltzes' (op. 9), some of which were written down in the course of the next year. The 'Divertissement à la hongroise' and the quartet in A minor (op. 29), in which the Hungarian influence is so strong, belong—the first apparently, the second certainly—to a much later period.

A third letter of this date, hitherto unprinted, with which the writer has been honoured by the granddaughter [1] of Ferdinand Schubert, to whom it was addressed, is not without interest, and is here printed entire. The Requiem referred to was by Ferdinand, and had evidently been sent to his brother for revision. The letter throws a pleasant light on the strong link existing between Franz and his old home, and

suggests that assistance more solid than 'linen' may often have reached him from his fond step-mother in his poverty in Vienna. In considering the pecuniary result of the engagement, it must be remembered that the florin was at that time only worth a franc, instead of two shillings. The month's pay therefore, instead of being £20, was really only about £8. Still, for Schubert that was a fortune.

'24 Aug. 1818.

'DEAR BROTHER FERDINAND,

'It is half-past 11 at night, and your Requiem is ready. It has made me sorrowful, as you may believe, for I sang it with all my heart. What is wanting you can fill in, and put the words under the music and the signs above. And if you want much rehearsal you must do it yourself, without asking me in Zelész. Things are not going well with you; I wish you could change with me, so that for once you might be happy. You should find all your heavy burdens gone, dear brother; I heartily wish it could be so.—My foot is asleep, and I am mad with it. If the fool could only write it wouldn't go to sleep!

'Good morning, my boy, I have been asleep with my foot, and now go on with my letter at 8 o'clock on the 25th. I have one request to make in answer to yours. Give my love to my dear parents, brothers, sisters, friends and acquaintances, especially not forgetting Carl. Didn't he mention me in his letter! As for my friends in the town, bully them, or get some one to bully them well, till they write to me. Tell my mother that my linen is well looked after, and that I am well off, thanks to her motherly care. If I could have some more linen I should very much like her to send me a second batch of pocket-handkerchiefs, cravats and stockings. Also I am much in want of two pair of kerseymere trousers. Hart can get the measure whenever he likes. I would send the money very soon. For July, with the journey-money, I got 200 florins.

'It is beginning already to be cold, and yet we shall not start for Vienna before the middle of October. Next month I hope to have a few weeks at Freystadt, which belongs to Count Erdödy, the uncle of my count. The country there is said to be extraordinarily beautiful. Also I hope to get to Pesth while we are at the vintage at Bosczmedj, which is not far off. It would be delightful if I should happen to meet Herr Administrator Taigele there. I am delighted at the thought of the vintage, for I have heard so much that is pleasant about it. The harvest also is beautiful here. They don't stow the corn into barns as they do in Austria, but make immense heaps out in the fields, which they call *Tristen*. They are often 80 to 100 yards long, and 30 to 40 high, and are laid together so cleverly that the rain all runs off without doing any harm. Oats and so on they bury in the ground.

'Though I am so well and happy, and every one so good to me, yet I shall be immensely glad when the moment arrives for going to Vienna. Beloved Vienna, all that is dear and valuable to me is there, and nothing but the actual sight of it will stop my longing! Again entreating you to attend to all my requests, I remain, with much love to all, your true and sincere

'FRANZ Mpia.

'A thousand greetings to your good wife and dear Resi, and a very hearty one to aunt Schubert and her daughter.'

RETURN TO VIENNA. — The inscription 'Zelész, Nov. 1818' on the song 'Das Abendroth' shows that the return to Vienna was not till nearly the end of the year. He found the theatre more than ever in possession of Rossini. To the former operas, 'Elisabetta' was added in the autumn and 'Otello' early in Jan. 1819. But one of the good traits in Schubert's character was his freedom from jealousy and his determination to enjoy what was good, from whatever quarter it came, or however much it was against his own interest

---

[1] Fräulein Caroline Geisler, daughter of Linus Geisler and Ferdinand's second daughter, Elise.

A letter of his to Hüttenbrenner, written just after the production of 'Otello,' puts this in very good light:

'"Otello" is far better and more characteristic than "Tancredi." Extraordinary genius it is impossible to deny him. His orchestration is often most original, and so is his melody; and except the usual Italian gallopades, and a few reminiscences of "Tancredi," there is nothing to object to.'

But he was not content to be excluded from the theatre by every one, and the letter goes on to abuse the 'canaille of Weigls and Treitschkes' and ' other rubbish, enough to make your hair stand on end,' all which were keeping his operettas off the boards. Still, it is very good-natured abuse, and so little is he really disheartened that he ends by begging Hüttenbrenner for a libretto; nay, he had actually just completed a little piece called 'Die Zwillingsbrüder' ('The Twins'), translated by Hofmann from the French—a Singspiel in one act, containing an overture and ten numbers. He finished it on Jan. 19, 1819, and it came to performance before many months were over.

Of his daily life at this time we know nothing. We must suppose that he had regular duties with his pupils at the Esterhazys' town house, but there is nothing to say so. We gather that he joined Mayrhofer in his lodgings, 420 in the Wipplingerstrasse, early in the year.[1] It was not a prepossessing apartment. 'The lane was gloomy; both room and furniture were the worse for wear; the ceiling drooped; the light was shut out by a big building opposite—a worn-out piano, and a shabby bookcase.' The only relief is the name of the landlady—Sanssouci, a Frenchwoman. No wonder that Mayrhofer's poems—he was ten years Schubert's senior—were of a gloomy cast.

The two friends were on the most intimate terms, and addressed each other by nicknames. What Mayrhofer's appellation may have been we do not know, but Schubert, now and later, was called ' the Tyrant,' for his treatment of Hüttenbrenner; also ' Bertl,' ' Schwammerl,' and, best of all, ' Kanevas '—because when a stranger came into their circle his first question always was, ' Kann er was ? ' (' Can he do anything ? ') Their humour took all sorts of shapes, and odd stories are told of their sham fights, their howls, their rough jokes and repartees.[2] Mayrhofer was a Government employé and went to his office early, leaving his fellow-lodger behind. Schubert began work directly he awoke, and even slept in his spectacles to save trouble; he got at once to his writing, sometimes in bed, but usually at his desk. It was so still when Hiller called on him eight years later.'[3] 'Do you write much?' said the boy, looking at the manuscript on the

standing desk—they evidently knew little in north Germany of Schubert's fertility. 'I compose every morning,' was the reply; 'and when one piece is done I begin another.' And yet this was the *musicien le plus poète que jamais*—it might have been the answer of a mere Czerny! Add to this a trait, communicated to the writer by Schubert's friend, Franz Lachner, of Munich, that when he had completed a piece, and heard it sung or played, he locked it up in a drawer and often never thought about it again.

This close work went on till dinner-time—two o'clock—after which, as a rule, he was free for the day, and spent the remainder either in a country walk with friends or in visits—as to Sofie Müller and Mme. Lacsny Buchwieser, whom we shall encounter farther on; or at Schober's rooms, or some coffee-house—in his later days it was Bogner's Café in the Singerstrasse, where the droll cry of a waiter was a never-ending pleasure to him. But no hour or place was proof against the sudden attack of inspiration when anything happened to excite it. An instance occurs at this very time, Nov. 1819, in an overture for four hands in F (op. 34), which he has inscribed as 'written in Joseph Hüttenbrenner's room at the City Hospital in the inside of three hours; and dinner missed in consequence.'[4] If the weather was fine he would stay in the country till late, regardless of any engagement that he might have made in town.

The only compositions that can be fixed to the spring of 1819 are five songs dated Feb. and one dated Mar.; a very fine quintet for equal voices, to the 'Sehnsucht' song in 'Wilhelm Meister'—a song which he had already set for a single voice in 1816, and was to set twice more in the course of his life (thus rivalling Beethoven, who also set the same words four times); an equally fine quartet for men's voices, 'Ruhe, schönstes Glück der Erde,' dated Apr.; four sacred songs by Novalis, dated May; and a striking overture in E minor, in series ii. of the complete edition.

HOLIDAY WITH VOGL.—The earnings of the previous summer allowed him to make an expedition this year on his own account. Mayrhofer remained in Vienna, and Vogl and Schubert appear to have gone together to Upper Austria. Steyr was the first point in the journey, a town beautifully situated on the Enns, not far south of Linz. They reached it early in July; it was Vogl's native place, and he had the pleasure of introducing his friend to the chief amateurs of the town, Paumgartner, Koller, Dornfeld, Schellmann — substantial citizens of the town, with wives and daughters, 'Pepi Koller,' 'Frizi Dornfeld,' 'the eight Schellmann girls,' etc., who all welcomed the

---

[1] In a letter to Mayrhofer from Linz, dated Aug. 19, 1819, he says, 'Let the bearer have my bed while he stays with you.' *K.H.* p. 159 (i. 160). The bed must have been his before he left town.
[2] *K.H.* p. 51 (i. 51).     [3] In Hiller's *Künstlerleben*, p. 49.

[4] *K.H.* p. 160 (i. 162).

musician with real Austrian hospitality, heard his songs with enthusiasm, and themselves helped to make music with him. His friend Albert Stadler was there also with his sister Kathi. How thoroughly Schubert enjoyed himself in this congenial *bourgeois* society, and in such lovely country — he mentions its beauties each time he writes—we have ample proof in two letters.[1] Among other drolleries the ' Erl King ' was sung with the parts distributed amongst Vogl, Schubert and Pepi Koller. Perhaps, too, Schubert gave them his favourite version of it on a comb. Vogl's birthday (Aug. 10) was celebrated by a cantata in C, containing a terzet, two soprano and two tenor solos, and a finale in canon, pointed by allusions to his various operatic triumphs, words by Stadler, and music by Schubert.[2] After this the two friends strolled on to Linz, the home of the Spauns, and of Kenner and Ottenwald, whose verses Franz had set in his earlier days ; and thence perhaps to Salzburg, returning to Steyr about the end of the month. Nor did the joviality of these good Austrians interfere with composition. Besides the impromptu cantata just mentioned, the well-known PF. quintet (op. 114), in which the air of ' Die Forelle ' is used as the theme of the andantino, was written at Steyr, possibly as a commission from the good Paumgartner, and was performed by the Paumgartner party. Schubert achieved in it the same feat which is somewhere ascribed to Mozart, of writing out the separate parts without first making a score, and no doubt played the pianoforte part by heart. The date of their departure, Sept. 14, is marked by an entry in the album of Miss Stadler, when Schubert delivered himself of the following highly correct sentiment : ' Enjoy the present so wisely, that the past may be pleasant to recollect, and the future not alarming to comtemplate.' This may pair off with a sentence written by Mozart, in English, in the album of an English Freemason, which has not yet been printed : ' Patience and tranquillity of mind contribute more to cure our distempers as the whole art of medicine. Wien, den 30te März 1787.' [3]

A few days more saw them again settled in Vienna. Each of the two letters preserved from the journey contains an obvious allusion to some love affair ; but nothing is known of it. He could hardly have adopted a more effectual diversion from such sorrows than the composition of a Mass, on an extended scale ; that, namely, in A♭—his fifth—which he began this month under the serious title of ' Missa Solemnis ' ; but he seems to have dawdled over it more than over any other of his works, as it was not finished till Sept. 1822 and contains many marks of indecision.

[1] *K.H.* pp. 158-9 (i. 159-60).
[2] Published to other words, ' Herrlich prangt,' as op. 158.
[3] I owe this to my good friend Mr. Pohl of Vienna.   G.

The most pregnant musical event of this year is the fact that on Feb. 28, 1819, a song of Schubert's was sung in public—the ' Schäfers Klagelied,' sung by Jäger at Jäll's concert at 5 P.M. at the ' Römische Kaiser,' Vienna. It was Schubert's first appearance before the public as a song-writer,[4] and is not'ced by the Leipzig *A.M.Z.* in these terms :

' Goethe's Schäfers Klagelied set to music by Herr Franz Schubert —the touching and feeling composition of this talented young man was sung by Herr Jäger in a similar spirit.'

Such is the first utterance of the press on one who has since evoked so much enthusiasm ! In the course of this year Schubert appears to have forwarded the three songs ' Schwager Kronos,' ' Über Thal ' (Mignon) and ' Ganymed '—afterwards published as op. 19 — to Goethe ; but no notice was taken by the poet of one who was to give some ·of his songs a wider popularity than they could otherwise have enjoyed, a popularity independent of country or language ; nor does Schubert's name once occur in all the six volumes of Goethe's correspondence with Zelter.

OPERAS.—1820 was again a year of great activity. Owing to Vogl's influence Schubert was gradually attracting the attention of the managers. The ' Zwillingsbrüder ' had been written for the Kärnthnerthor Theatre (see p. 594), and it was not long before the *régisseur* of the rival opera-house, the Theatre an-der-Wien, suggested to him a libretto called the ' Zauberharfe,' or ' Magic harp,' a melodrama in three acts, by the same Hofmann who had translated the former piece. To receive such a proposal and to act upon it was a matter of course with Schubert, and the ' Zauberharfe ' is said to have been completed in a fortnight.[5] But before this, early in the year, he had met with the works of A. H. Niemeyer, Professor of Theology at Halle, and had adopted the poem of ' Lazarus, or the Feast of the Resurrection,' for an Easter cantata. Easter fell that year on Apr. 2, and his work is dated ' Feb.,' so that he was in ample time. The poem—or drama, for there are seven distinct characters—is in three parts. 1. The sickness and death. 2. The burial and elegy. 3. The resurrection. Of these the first and a large portion of the second were completed by Schubert, apparently without the knowledge of any of his friends. Ferdinand mentions the first part in his list,[6] but the existence of the second was unknown till, through the instrumentality of Thayer, it was unearthed in 1861.[7]

On June 14 the ' Zwillingsbrüder,' or ' Zwillinge,' was produced at the Kärnthnerthor Theatre. It is a comic operetta (' Posse '), with spoken dialogue, in one act, containing an

[4] One of the ' Italian ' overtures had been given on Mar. 1, 1818, at one of Jäll's concerts.
[5] Autograph in Herr Dumba's collection.
[6] *N.Z.M.* p. 139a.
[7] Performed in 1863 and published by Spina in 1866.

overture and ten numbers, and turns on the plot that has done duty many times before, the confusion between two twin-brothers, who were both acted by Vogl. The overture was encored on the first night, and Vogl's two songs were much applauded, but the piece was virtually a *fiasco* and was withdrawn after six representations. Schubert took so little interest in its production that, like Mendelssohn at the 'Wedding of Camacho,' he did not even stay in the house, and Vogl had to appear instead of him in front of the curtain. The libretto, though overburdened with characters, is sadly deficient in proportion, and contains very little action. Schubert's music, on the other hand, is light, fresh and melodious, pointed, unusually compact and interesting throughout. In the concerted numbers there is evidence of great dramatic power. To condemn it, as the critics of the day do, as wanting in melody, and constantly striving after originality, is to contradict Schubert's most marked characteristics and is contrary to the facts. There is possibly more justice in the complaint that the accompaniments were too loud, though that is certainly not the fault in his masses, his only other published works with orchestral accompaniments anterior to this date. The work has been published in vocal score by Peters (1872).

On Aug. 19 the 'Zauberharfe' was produced at the Theatre an-der-Wien. It consists chiefly of chorus and melodrama, with only a few solo passages. There is a fine overture (in C), original, characteristic and full of beauty, which was published before 1828 as op. 26, under the name of 'Rosamunde,' to which it seems to have no claim.[1] The piece was occasionally brought forward till the winter and was then dropped. These three vocal works appear so far to have whetted Schubert's appetite that in the autumn he attacked the more important libretto of 'Sakontala,' a regular opera in three acts, by P. H. Neumann, founded on the Indian drama of that name. He sketched two acts, and there it remains; the MS. is in Herr Dumba's possession. Another important and very beautiful piece is the 23rd Psalm,[2] set for two sopranos and two altos with PF. accompaniment, at the instigation of the sisters Frölich, and dated at the beginning '23 Dec. 1820'—perhaps with a view to some private concerts given, now or later, at the old hall of the Musikverein. Another is the 'Gesang der Geister über den Wassern' of Goethe (op. 167). This fine and mystical poem had a strong attraction for Schubert. He set it for four equal voices in 1817; then he reset it for four tenors and four basses with two violas, two violoncellos and bass in Dec. 1820; and lastly revised

this in Feb. 1821. It was first produced on Mar. 7, 1821, and found no favour, to Schubert's disgust. It was again performed on Mar. 30, before a more receptive audience, with a far better result. It was revived at Vienna in 1858 by Herbeck, and in England was performed with success on Mar. 22, 1881, under the direction of Prout. It is enormously difficult, and, though perfectly in character with the poem, will probably never be attractive to a mixed audience. Another work of 1820 were some antiphons (op. 113) for Palm Sunday (Mar. 26), composed for Ferdinand, who had been recently appointed choirmaster at the Altlerchenfelder church, and found the duties rather too much for him. They are written with black chalk on coarse grey wrapping paper; and the tradition is that they and two motets were written in great haste, just in time for the service. On Easter Sunday Franz attended and conducted the Mass for his brother.

The fantasia in C for PF. solo (op. 15), containing variations on Schubert's own 'Wanderer,' is probably a work of this year. It was written for von Liebenberg, a PF.-player, to whom Schubert dedicated it. This fine piece was brought into vogue by Liszt's arrangement of it for PF. and orchestra as a concerto; but it is doubtful if it is improved by the process. Schubert never could play it; he always stuck fast in the last movement, and on one occasion jumped up and cried 'Let the devil himself play it!' Another piece is an allegro for strings in C minor, dated Dec. 1820, the first movement of a quartet, of which there exist besides forty-one bars of the andante, in A♭. The allegro is of first-rate quality, and Schubert in every bar. It was published in 1868 by Senff. The MS. was in Brahms's fine collection of autographs.

The songs of 1820, seventeen in all, though not so numerous as those of previous years, are very fine. They contain 'Der Jüngling auf dem Hügel' (op. 8, No. 1), 'Der Schiffer,' 'Liebeslauschen,' three grand songs to Mayrhofer's words, 'Orest auf Tauris,' 'Der entsühnte Orest,' and 'Freiwilliges Versinken,' and four Italian canti, written for Frl. von Romer, who afterwards married Schubert's friend Spaun, and since published with one which was probably written under Salieri's eye as early as 1813. The most remarkable of all is 'Im Walde,' or 'Waldesnacht,' a very long song of extraordinary beauty, variety, force and imagination.

SONG PUBLICATION BEGUN.—With Feb. 1821 Schubert entered his 25th year, and it was a good omen to receive such a birthday present as the three testimonials of this date which Kreissle has[3] preserved. The first is from von Mosel, then court secretary; the second from Weigl, director of the court Opera, Salieri and von Eichthal; the third from Moritz, Count

---

[1] The overture played to the 'Rosamunde' music is in D minor, and was afterwards published as 'Alfonso & Estrella.' There is, perhaps, another in existence. See the letter to von Mosel quoted farther on.     [2] To Moses Mendelssohn's translation.

[3] *K.H.* p. 201 (i. 203).

Dietrichstein, whom Beethoven addresses as 'Hofmusikgraf' and who appears to have been a sort of Jupiter-Apollo with general sway over all court music. These influential personages warmly recognise his eminent ability, industry, knowledge, feeling and taste, and profess the best intentions towards him. The three documents were enclosed by the Count in a letter to Vogl, full of good wishes for the future of his friend. Still more gratifying was the prospect, which now at last opened, of the publication of his songs. It was the first good epoch in Schubert's hitherto struggling life. He had now been writing for more than seven years, with an industry and disregard of consequences which are really fearful to contemplate ; and yet, as far as fame or profit were concerned, might almost as well have remained absolutely idle. Here at length was a break in the cloud. It was not less welcome because it was mainly due to his faithful friends the Sonnleithners, who had made his acquaintance through the accident of Leopold Sonnleithner's being at school with him, and ever since cherished it in the most faithful and practical way, Ignaz, the father, having, since 1815, had large periodical music meetings of artists and amateurs in his house at the Gundelhof, which were nothing less than Schubert propaganda. Here, before large audiences of thoroughly musical people, Schubert's pieces were repeatedly performed, and at length, on Dec. 1, 1820, the ' Erl King ' was sung by Gymnich, a well-known amateur, with a spirit which fired every one of the audience with the desire to possess the song, and appears to have suggested to Leopold and Gymnich the possibility of finding a publisher for the inspirations which had for so long been their delight and astonishment. They applied to Diabelli and Haslinger, the leading houses of Vienna, but without success ; the main objections being the insignificance of the composer and the difficulty of his pianoforte accompaniments. On this they resolved to take the matter into their own hands ; and, probably not without misgivings, had the ' Erl King ' engraved. The fact was announced at the next concert at the Gundelhof, and a hundred copies were at once subscribed for in the room—sufficient to defray the cost of the engraving and printing and of engraving a second song as well. Meantime the ' Erl King ' had been sung in public (for the concerts at the Gundelhof were, strictly speaking, private, limited to the friends of the host) by Gymnich, at an evening concert of the Musikverein, in one of the public rooms of the city, on Jan. 25, 1821, Schubert himself appearing on the platform and playing the accompaniment. Everything was done by the young enthusiasts to foster the Schubert *furore*, even to the publication of a set of ' Erl King waltzes ' by A. Hüttenbrenner, which at any rate must have made the name familiar, though they pro-

voked Schubert, and drew from Kanne some satirical hexameters and pentameters which may be read in Kreissle.[1] On Feb. 8 the programme of the Musikverein concert included three songs of his, the ' Sehnsucht ' by Schiller, ' Gretchen am Spinnrade' and ' Der Jüngling auf dem Hügel ' ; and on Mar. 8 the ' Gruppe aus dem Tartarus.' On Mar. 7 the ' Erl King ' was again sung, this time by Vogl himself, at an unmistakable public concert at the Kärnthnerthor Theatre, a concert supported by all the most distinguished ladies of the court, who received the song with loud applause. Think what the first appearance of these godlike pieces must have been ! It was the rising of the Sun ! He is now an everyday sight to us ; but how was it the first time that he burst in all his brightness on the eyes of mortals ? In the midst of all this enthusiasm the ' Erl King ' was published on Apr. 1, 1821, by Cappi and Diabelli, on commission. It was dedicated to Count Moritz Dietrichstein, whose kindness well deserved that recognition. On Apr. 30 ' Gretchen am Spinnrade ' appeared as op. 2. The succeeding publications—each made to depend on the success of the last—were as follows :

May 29. Op. 3. Schäfers Klagelied ; Meeres-Stille ; Heidenröslein ; Jägers Abendlied.
Do.    Op. 4.   Der Wanderer ; Morgenlied ; Wanderers Nachtlied.
July 9. Op. 5. Rastlose Liebe ; Nähe des Geliebten ; Der Fischer ; Erster Verlust ; Der König in Thule.
Aug. 23. Op. 6. Memnon ; Antigone und Œdip ; Am Grabe Anselmos.
Nov. 27. Op. 7. Die abgeblühte Linde ; Der Flug der Zeit ; Der Tod und das Mädchen.

Here the publication by commission stopped, the Diabellis being evidently convinced that the risk might be profitably assumed ; and accordingly op. 8 appears on May 9, 1822, as ' the property of the publishers.' The dedications of the first seven numbers no doubt furnish the names of Schubert's most influential supporters : 1. Graf von Dietrichstein ; 2. Reichsgraf Moritz von Fries ; 3. Ignaz von Mosel ; 4. Johann Ladislaus Pyrker, Patriarch of Venice ; 5. Salieri ; 6. Michael Vogl ; 7. Graf Ludwig Széchényi. It must be admitted that the above are very good lists, and that if Schubert had waited long for the publication of his works, the issue of twenty songs in eight months, under the patronage of seven such eminent personages, was a substantial compensation. We do not hear, however, that much money came into his hands from the publication. The favourable impression made by the publication may be gathered from the long, intelligent and sympathetic criticism, ' Blick auf Schuberts Lieder, by F. von Hentl, which appeared in the *Wiener Zeitschrift für Kunst*, etc.—a periodical belonging to Diabelli's rivals, Steiner & Co. — for Mar. 23, 1822.

---

[1] Hanslick, *Concertwesen*, p. 234 ; and *K.H.* p. 60 (i. 60).

Schubert was now a good deal about the theatre, and when it was determined to produce a German version of Hérold's 'Clochette,' as 'Das Zauberglöckchen,' at the court opera, he was not unnaturally called upon to insert a couple of pieces to suit the Vienna audience. It was what Mozart often did for the Italian operas of his day—what indeed we know Shakespeare to have done in more than one case. The opera was produced on June 20. The interpolated pieces were a long air for tenor,[1] in three movements—maestoso, andante and allegro—full of passion and imagination, and a comic duet between the princes B flat and C natural (Bedur and Cedur). They were more applauded than anything else in the work, but Schubert's name was not divulged; the opera as a whole did not please and was soon withdrawn.

The little variation which he contributed, as No. 38, to Diabelli's collection of fifty variations—the same for which Beethoven wrote his thirty-three (op. 120)—should not be overlooked. Though not published till 1823, the autograph, now in the Hofbibliothek at Vienna, is dated 'March 1821.' The variation is fresh and pretty in the minor of the theme, but is more noticeable from its situation than from its own qualities. A few dances for PF. solo are dated '8th March' and 'July' in this year, and a collection of thirty-six, containing those alluded to and others of 1816 and 1819, was published by Cappi and Diabelli on Nov. 29, as op. 18. Some of these are inscribed on the autograph 'Atzenbrucker Deutsche, July 1821,' indicating a visit to Atzenbruck, the seat of an uncle of Schober's, near Abstetten, between Vienna and St. Pölten, where a three days' annual festivity was held, to which artists of all kinds were invited, and where Schubert's presence and music were regarded as indispensable.

THE SYMPHONY IN E.—Whether after this he and Schober returned to Vienna we know not, no letters remain; but the next event of which any record remains is the composition of a symphony, his seventh,[2] in E, which is marked, without note of place, as begun in August He did not complete the writing of it, and indeed it is probable that it did not occupy him more than a few hours; but the autograph, which is in the writer's possession,[3] is a very curious manuscript, probably quite unique, even among Schubert's feats of composition. It occupies 167 pages of 42 sheets (10 quires of 4 and 1 of 2), and is in the usual movements —adagio in E minor and allegro in E major;

andante in A; scherzo in C and trio in A.[4]; and allegro giusto in E major. The introduction and a portion of the allegro are fully scored and marked; but at the 110th bar— the end of a page—Schubert appears to have grown impatient of this regular proceeding and from that point to the end of the work has made merely memoranda. But these memoranda are, in their way, perfectly complete and orderly to the end of the finale. Every bar is drawn in; the *tempi* and names of the instruments are fully written at the beginning of each movement; the *nuances* are all marked; the very double bars and flourishes are gravely added at the end of the sections, and 'Fine' at the conclusion of the whole; and Schubert evidently regarded the work as no less complete on the paper than it was in his mind. And complete it virtually is; for each subject is given at full length, with a bit of bass or accompaniment-figure or *fugato* passage. There is not a bar from beginning to end that does not contain the part of one or more instruments; at all crucial places the scoring is much fuller; and it would no doubt be possible to complete it as Schubert himself intended.[5]

'ALFONSO UND ESTRELLA.'—We next find the two friends at the castle of Ochsenburg, a few miles south of St. Pölten, the seat of the Bishop, who was a relative of Schober's; and there and in St. Pölten itself they passed a thoroughly happy and healthy holiday of some weeks in September and October. The Bishop and Baron Mink, a local magnate, were congenial hosts, and the visit of the two clever young men was the signal for various festivities, in which all the aristocracy of the country-side —'a princess, two countesses and three baronesses,' in Schober's enumeration—took part, and in which the music and drollery of Schubert and his friend delighted every one. The great result of the visit, however, was the composition of an opera to Schober's words, on a romantic subject of battles, love, conspiracy, hunting, peasant life and everything else, so natural in opera librettos, so impossible in real life. It was called 'Alfonso und Estrella,' and two acts were completed before their return to town. The first act is dated at the end of the autograph Sept. 20, and the second Oct. 20. A week later they were back again in Vienna.

The songs composed in 1821 are very important, and comprise some of his very finest, and in the most various styles. It is sufficient to name among the published ones 'Grenzer

---

[1] Introduced into 'Alfonso und Estrella' in 1881 by Joh. Fuchs.
[2] The seventh in order of undertaking, but in the complete edition of Schubert's works the great Symphony in C, which Grove called No. 10, is numbered seven, being the last of the completed symphonies. The 'Unfinished' (B minor) symphony is there numbered eight, which accords with Grove's numbering. He regarded the problematical 'Gastein' symphony as No. 9.                           c.
[3] I received it in 1868 from the late Paul Mendelssohn, Felix's brother, into whose hands it came after his brother's death. Felix Mendelssohn had it from Ferdinand Schubert direct.          g.

[4] The change in this symphony from the scherzo in C to the trio in A, by an E in octaves in the oboes lasting four bars, is an anticipation of the similar change in the same place in the great C major symphony of 1828, and a curious instance of the singular way in which many of Schubert's earlier symphonies lead up to his crowning effort.                                          G.
[5] It is said that the sketch was submitted to Mendelssohn, who refused to complete it. In later days, at the suggestion of Sir George Grove, J. F. Barnett undertook the task, and the symphony, scored by him from Schubert's indications, was produced at the Crystal Palace on May 5, 1883. See Barnett's *Musical Reminiscences and Impressions*, pp. 312-22.            W. H. F"

der Menschheit ' (Feb.) ; ' Geheimes ' (Mar.) ; Suleika's two songs (opp. 14, 31) ; ' Sei mir gegrüsst ' (op. 20, No. 1) ; and ' Die Nachtigall,' for four men's voices (op. 11, No. 2)—all of the very highest excellence, of astonishing variety, and enough of themselves to make the fame of any ordinary composer. A fine setting of ' Mahomet's song,' by Goethe, for bass (possibly for Lablache), was begun in March.

The third act of ' Alfonso und Estrella ' was finished on Feb. 27, 1822. The fact that a thoroughly worldly, mercenary, money-making manager like Barbaja, who was at the same time a firm believer in Rossini, had become lessee of the two principal theatres of Vienna, augured badly for Schubert's chance of success in that direction. But indeed the new piece seems to have been calculated to baffle any manager, not only in Vienna but everywhere else. It caused, as we shall see, a violent dispute, eighteen months later, between Schubert and Weber, which but for Schubert's good temper would have led to a permanent quarrel. Anna Milder, to whom Schubert sent a copy of the work in 1825, tells him, in a letter full of kindness and enthusiasm, that the libretto will not suit the taste of the Berliners, ' who are accustomed to the grand tragic opera or the French opéra-comique.' Nor was the libretto the only drawback. Schubert, like Beethoven in ' Fidelio,' was in advance of the modest execution of those days. At Graz, the abode of the Hüttenbrenners, where there was a *foyer* of Schubert enthusiasts, the opera got as far as the rehearsal, and would probably have reached the stage, if the accompaniments had not proved impossible for the band.[1] No performance took place until twenty-six years after poor Schubert's death, namely, at Weimar, on June 24, 1854, under the direction of Liszt, who, with all his devotion to the master, had to reduce it much for performance. It was very carefully studied, and yet the success, even in that classical town, and with all Liszt's enthusiasm and influence, seems to have been practically *nil*. At last, however, its time came. Twenty-five years later, in 1879, it was again taken in hand by Kapellmeister Johann Fuchs of the court opera, Vienna, who entirely rewrote the libretto and greatly curtailed the work ; and in this form it was brought to performance at Carlsruhe in Mar. 1881, with great success.

RELATIONS WITH BEETHOVEN.—But to return to Schubert and 1822. Early in the year he made the acquaintance[2] of Weber, who spent a few weeks of Feb. and Mar. in Vienna to arrange for the production of his ' Eury-

anthe.' No particulars of their intercourse on this occasion survive. With Beethoven Schubert had as yet hardly exchanged words. And this is hardly to be wondered at, because, though Vienna was not a large city, yet the paths of the two men were quite separate. Apart from the great difference in their ages, and from Beethoven's peculiar position in the town, his habits were fixed, his deafness was a great obstacle to intercourse, and, for the last five or six years, what with the lawsuits into which his nephew dragged him and the severe labour entailed by the composition of the Mass in D, and of the sonatas opp. 106, 109, 110 and 111—works which by no means flowed from him with the ease that masses and sonatas did from Schubert—he was very inaccessible. Any stranger arriving from abroad with a letter of introduction was seen and treated civilly. But Schubert was a born Viennese, and, at the time of which we speak, Beethoven was as much a part of Vienna as St. Stephen's tower, and to visit him required some special reason and more than special resolution.

A remark of Rochlitz's[3] in the July of this year shows that Schubert was in the habit of going to the same restaurant with Beethoven, and worshipping at a distance ; but the first direct evidence of their coming into contact occurs at this date. On Apr. 19, 1822, he published a set of variations on a French air as op. 10, and dedicated them to Beethoven as ' his admirer and worshipper ' (*sein Verehrer und Bewunderer*). The variations were written in the winter of 1820–21, and Schubert presented them in person to the great master. There are two versions of the interview,[4] Schindler's and J. Hüttenbrenner's. Schindler was constantly about Beethoven. He was devoted to Schubert, and is very unlikely to have given a depreciating account of him. There is therefore no reason for doubting his statement, especially as his own interest or vanity were not concerned. It is the first time we meet Schubert face to face. He was accompanied by Diabelli, who was just beginning to find out his commercial value, and would naturally be anxious for his success. Beethoven was at home, and we know the somewhat overwhelming courtesy with which he welcomed a stranger. Schubert was more bashful and retiring than ever ; and when the great man handed him the sheaf of paper and the carpenter's pencil provided for the replies of his visitors, could not collect himself sufficiently to write a word. Then the variations were produced, with their enthusiastic dedication, which probably added to Beethoven's good humour. He opened them and looked through them, and, seeing something that startled him, naturally pointed it out.

---

[1] *K.H.* p. 249 (i. 252).
[2] For their meeting we have the authority of Weber's son in his biography, ii. 420. But his statement that Schubert was alienated from Weber by Weber's criticism on ' Rosamunde ' is more than doubtful, because ' Rosamunde ' was probably not composed till some nineteen months later, and because it was not Schubert's habit to take offence at criticism.

[3] *Für Freunde der Tonkunst*, iv. 352. See the life-like and touching picture by Braun von Braun given in Nohl's *Beethoven*, iii. 682.
[4] Schindler's *Beethoven*, ii. 176.

At this Schubert's last remnant of self-control seems to have deserted him and he rushed from the room. When he got into the street, and was out of the magic of Beethoven's personality, his presence of mind returned, and all that he might have said flashed upon him, but it was too late. The story is perfectly natural, and we ought to thank Beethoven's Boswell for it.[1] Which of us would not have done the same ? Beethoven kept the variations and liked them ; and it must have been some consolation to the bashful Franz to hear that he often played them with his nephew. Hüttenbrenner's [2] story is that Schubert called, but found Beethoven out ; which may have been an invention of Diabelli's to shield his young client.

This autumn Schubert again took up the Mass in A♭, which was begun in 1819 ; finished it, and inscribed it ' *im* 7♭ 822 *beendet*.' [3] Not that that was the final redaction ; for, contrary to his usual practice—in fact it is almost a solitary instance—he took it up again before his death and made material improvements [4] both in the position of the voice-parts and in the instrumentation, as may be seen from the autograph score now in the library of the Gesellschaft der Musikfreunde.

This year seems to have been passed entirely in Vienna, at least there are no traces of any journey ; and the imprisonment in the broiling city, away from the nature he so dearly loved, was not likely to improve his spirits. What events or circumstances are alluded to in the interesting piece called ' My Dream,' [5] dated ' July 1822,' it is hard to guess. It may not improbably have been occasioned by some dispute on religious subjects of the nature of those hinted at in his brother Ignaz's letter of Oct. 12, 1818.[6] At any rate it is deeply pathetic and poetical.

The 'Unfinished' Symphony.—During this summer Joseph Hüttenbrenner was active in the cause of his friend. He made no less than four endeavours to bring out the ' Teufels Lustschloss '—at the Josefstadt and court theatres of Vienna, at Munich and at Prague. At Prague alone was there a gleam of hope. Hollbein, the manager there, requests to have the score and parts sent to him, at the same

time regretting that during a month which he had passed in Vienna Schubert had not once come near him. Hüttenbrenner also urged Schubert on Peters, the publisher, of Leipzig, who in a tedious egotistical letter, dated Nov. 14, 1822, gives the usual sound reasons of a cautious publisher against taking up with an unknown composer—for in north Germany Schubert was still all but unknown. One is sorry to hear of a little rebuff which he sustained at this time from the Gesellschaft der Musikfreunde of Vienna, to whom he applied to be admitted as a practising member (on the viola), but who refused him on the ground of his being a professional and therefore outside their rules.[7] A somewhat similar repulse was experienced by Haydn from the Tonkünstler Societät. (See Vol. II. p. 571.) On the other hand, the musical societies both of Linz and Graz elected him an honorary member. To the latter of these distinctions we owe the two beautiful movements of the symphony No. 8, in B minor, which was begun at Vienna on Oct. 30, 1822, and intended as a return for the compliment. The allegro and andante alone are finished,[8] but these are of singular beauty and the greatest originality. In them, for the first time in orchestral composition, Schubert exhibits a style absolutely his own, untinged by any predecessor, and full of that strangely direct appeal to the hearer of which we have already spoken. It is certain that he never heard the music played, and that the new and delicate effects and orchestral combinations with which it is crowded were the result of his imagination alone. The first movement is sadly full of agitation and distress. It lay hidden at Graz for many years, until obtained from Anselm Hüttenbrenner by Herbeck, who first produced it in Vienna at one of the Gesellschaft concerts in 1865.[9] It was published by Spina early in 1867 ; was played at the Crystal Palace, Apr. 6, 1867, and elsewhere in England, and always with increasing success. In fact no one can hear it without being captivated by it.

The songs composed in 1822—fourteen printed and two in MS.—comprise ' Epistel von Collin ' (Jan.) ; ' Heliopolis ' (Apr.) ; ' Todesmusik,' with a magnificent opening (op. 108, No. 2 ; Sept.) ; ' Schatzgräbers Begehr ' (op. 23, No. 4 ; Nov.) with its stately bass ; ' Willkommen und Abschied ' (op. 56, No. 1 ; Dec.) ; ' Die Rose ' (op. 73) ; and ' Der Musensohn ' (op. 92). The concerted pieces,' Constitutionslied ' (op. 157 ; Jan.), ' Geist der Liebe ' (op. 11, No. 3), ' Gott in der Natur ' (op. 133) and ' Des Tages Weihe ' (op. 146), all belong to this year.

---

[1] But see *Krehbiel*, iii. 79 where Schindler's story is rejected in favour of Hüttenbrenner's.　　　　　　　　　　　　　　　c.

[2] *K.H.* p. 261 (i. 264).

[3] 7♭ stands for September.

[4] This was kindly pointed out to the writer by Johannes Brahms, who had an early copy of the score, made by Ferdinand Schubert from the autograph in its original condition. In this shape Brahms rehearsed the Mass, but found many portions unsatisfactory, and was interested to discover subsequently from the autograph that Schubert had altered the very passages alluded to and made them practicable. He made three attempts at the ' Cum sancto ' before succeeding, each time in fugue, and always with a different subject. Of the first, there are four bars ; of the second, 199 ; the third is that printed in Schreiber's edition. This edition is unfortunately very incorrect. Not only does it swarm with misprints, but whole passages, and those most important ones (as in the horns and trombones of the Dona), are clean omitted. The nuances also are shamefully treated.

[5] First printed by R. Schumann in the *Neue Zeitschrift für Musik* for Feb. 5, 1839. See also *K.H.* p. 333 (ii. 16).

[6] *K.H.* p. 146 (i. 148).

[7] *K.H.* p. 280 (i. 283).

[8] The autograph in possession of the Gesellschaft der Musikfreunde in Vienna contains nine bars of the scherzo in full score and sketches of the scherzo and beginning of the trio in short score. See the facsimile of the whole published by the Drei Masken Verlag, 1924.　　　　　　　　　　　　　　　c.

[9] See Hanslick, *Concertsaal*, p. 350.

Publication went on in 1822, though not so briskly as before. The variations dedicated to Beethoven (op. 10) were first to appear, on Apr. 19. They were followed by op. 8 (four songs) on May 9, and op. 11 (three partsongs) on June 12. Then came a long gap till Dec. 13, on which day opp. 12, 13 and 14, all songs, appeared at once. We have not space to name them. But with such accumulated treasures to draw upon, it is unnecessary to say that they are all of the first class. The pecuniary result of the publications of 1821 had been good; 2000 gulden were realised, and of the 'Erl King' alone more than 800 copies had been sold; and if Schubert had been provident enough to keep his works in his own possession he would soon have been out of the reach of want. This, however, he did not do. Pressed by the want of money, in an incautious moment he sold the first twelve of his works [1] to Diabelli for 800 silver gulden (£80), and entered into some injudicious arrangement with the same firm for future publications. His old and kind friend Count Dietrichstein about this time offered him a post as organist to the court chapel,[2] but he refused it, and he was probably right, though in so doing he greatly distressed his methodical old father. His habits, like Beethoven's, made it absurd for him to undertake any duties requiring strict attendance.

FURTHER DRAMATIC WORKS.—The Vienna theatre being closed to 'Alfonso und Estrella,' Schubert turned his thoughts in the direction of Dresden, where his admirer Anna Milder was living, and where Weber was director of the Opera; and we find him in a letter of Feb. 28, 1823 (published in 1881 for the first time) [3] asking his old patron Herr von Mosel for a letter of recommendation to Weber. He is confined to the house by illness, and apologises for not being able to call. There are no traces of reply to this application, but it probably led to nothing, for, as we shall see, the score of the opera was still in his hands in October. He was evidently now set upon opera. In the letter just mentioned he implores von Mosel to entrust him with a libretto 'suitable for his littleness'; and though he never seems to have obtained this, he went on with the best he could get, and 1823 saw the birth of no less than three dramatic pieces. The first was a one-act play with dialogue, adapted from the French by Castelli, and called 'Die Verschworenen,' or 'The Conspirators.' The play was published in the *Dramatic Garland*—an annual collection of dramas—for 1823. Schubert must have

seen it soon after publication, and by April had finished the composition of it. The autograph, in the British Museum, has at the end the words 'Aprill 1823. F. Schubert, Ende der Oper.' It contains an overture and eleven numbers, and appears from Bauernfeld's testimony to have been composed with a view to representation at the court theatre. The libretto is a very poor one, with but few dramatic points, and confines the composer mainly to the chorus. The licensers changed its title to the less suspicious one of 'Der häusliche Krieg,' or 'The Domestic Struggle,' and it was duly sent in to the management, but it returned in twelve months without examination. It did not come to performance at all during Schubert's lifetime, nor till 1861. In that year it was given, under Herbeck's direction, by the Musikverein, Vienna, on Mar. 1 and 22; and on the stage at Frankfort on Aug. 29; since then at the court theatre, Vienna, at Munich, Salzburg and other German towns; in Paris, Feb. 3, 1868, as 'La Croisade des Dames'; and at the Crystal Palace, Sydenham, Mar. 2, 1872, as 'The Conspirators.' In less than two months after throwing off this lively Singspiel, Schubert had embarked in something far more serious, a regular three-act opera of the 'heroico-romantic' pattern—also with spoken dialogue—the scene laid in Spain, with Moors, knights, a king, a king's daughter and all the usual furniture of these dreary compilations. The libretto of 'Fierrabras,' by Josef Kupelwieser—enough of itself to justify all Wagner's charges [4] against the opera-books of the old school—was commissioned by Barbaja for the court theatre. The book was passed by the Censure on July 21; but Schubert had by that time advanced far in his labours, and had in fact completed more than half of the piece. He began it, as his own date tells us, on May 25. Act 1, filling 304 pages of large oblong paper,[5] was completely scored by the 31st of the month; Act 2, in five days more, by June 5; and the whole three acts, fully 1000 pages, and containing an overture and twenty-three numbers, were entirely out of hand by Oct. 2. And all for nothing! Schubert was not even kept long in suspense, for early in the following year he learnt that the work had been dismissed. The ground for its rejection was the badness of the libretto; but knowing Barbaja's character, and seeing that Kupelwieser was secretary to a rival house (the Josefstadt), it is difficult not to suspect that the commission had been given by the wily Italian, merely to facilitate the progress of some piece of business between the two establishments.

It is, as Liszt has remarked, extraordinary that Schubert, who was brought up from his youth on the finest poetry, should have unhesi-

---

[1] So say the books; but the works published on commission were opp. 1–7, containing twenty songs.
[2] The evidence for this transaction is very obscure, and the story may have become confused with a proposed application in 1825. See below, p. 607.  W. H. HW.
[3] In the *Neue Freie Presse* of Vienna, Nov. 19, 1881. The letter, though formal in style, is curiously free in some of its expressions. It mentions the overture to the 1st Act of 'Alfonso and Estrella.' What can this be? The overture known under that name (op. 69) is dated 'Dec. 1823,' and is said to have been written for 'Rosamunde.'

[4] Hanslick, *Concertsaal*, p. 150.
[5] The autograph was shown to Sullivan and the writer by that energetic Schubert apostle, Johann Herbeck, in 1868.

tatingly accepted the absurd and impracticable librettos which he did, and which have kept in oblivion so much of his splendid music. His devotion to his friends, and his irrepressible desire to utter what was in him, no doubt help to explain the anomaly, but an anomaly it will always remain. It is absolutely distressing to think of such extraordinary ability, and such still more extraordinary powers of work, being so cruelly thrown away, and of the sickening disappointment which these repeated failures must have entailed on so simple and sensitive a heart as his. Fortunately for us the strains in which he vents his griefs are as beautiful and endearing as those in which he celebrates his joys.

' DIE SCHÖNE MÜLLERIN.'—His work this summer was not, however, to be all disappointment. If the theatre turned a deaf ear to his strains there were always his beloved songs to confide in, and they never deceived him. Of the song in Schubert's hands we may say what Wordsworth so well says of the sonnet :

> ' With this key
> Shakespeare unlocked his heart ; the melody
> Of this small lute gave ease to Petrarch's wound.

> .    .    .    .    .    ' and when a damp
> Fell round the path of Milton, in his hand
> The thing became a trumpet, whence he blew
> Soul-animating strains, alas too few !'

—with the notable difference that it was given to Schubert to gather up and express, in his one person and his one art, all the various moods and passions which Wordsworth has divided amongst so many mighty poets.

And now, in the midst of the overwhelming tumult and absorption which inevitably accompany the production of so large a work of imagination as a three-act opera, brought into being at so extraordinarily rapid a pace, he was to stop and to indite a set of songs, which, though not of greater worth than many others of his, are yet so intelligible, so expressive, address themselves to such universal feelings, and form so attractive a whole, that they have certainly become more popular, and are more widely and permanently beloved, than any similar production by any other composer. We have already described the incident through which Schubert made acquaintance with the *Müllerlieder* [1] of Wilhelm Müller, twenty of which he selected for the beautiful series so widely known as the ' Schöne Müllerin.' We have seen the enduring impatience with which he attacked a book when it took his fancy, and the eagerness with which he began upon this particular one. We know that the Müllerlieder were all composed this year ; that some of them were written in hospital ; that No. 15 is dated

'October'; that a considerable interval elapsed between the second and third act of ' Fierrabras '—probably the best part of July and August. Putting these facts together, it seems to follow that the call on RANDHARTINGER (*q.v.*) and the composition of the first numbers of the ' Schöne Müllerin' took place in May, before he became immersed in ' Fierrabras.' Then came the first two acts of that opera ; then his illness, and his sojourn in the hospital, and more songs ; then the third act of the opera ; and lastly the completion of the ' Lieder.'

WEBER AND THE OPERA.—Be this as it may, there was no lack of occupation for Schubert after he had put ' Fierrabras ' out of hand. Weber arrived in Vienna late in Sept. 1823, and on Oct. 3 began the rehearsals of ' Euryanthe ' ; and for a month the musical world of Austria was in a ferment. After the first performance, on Oct. 25, Weber and Schubert came somewhat into collision. Schubert, with characteristic frankness, asserted that the new work wanted the geniality and grace of ' Der Freischütz,' that its merit lay mainly in its harmony,[2] and that he was prepared to prove that the score did not contain a single original melody. Weber had been much tried by the rehearsals, by the growing conviction that his work was too long, and by the imperfect success of the performance ; and with a combination of ignorance and insolence which does him no credit replied, ' Let the fool learn something himself before he criticises me.' Schubert's answer to this was to go off to Weber with the score of ' Alfonso und Estrella.' When they had looked through this, Weber returned to Schubert's criticisms on ' Euryanthe,' and, finding that the honest Franz stuck to his point, was absurd enough to lose his temper and say, in the obvious belief that the score before him was Schubert's first attempt, ' I tell you the first puppies and the first operas are always drowned.' Franz, it is unnecessary to say, bore no malice, even for so galling a speech, and it is due to Weber to state that he took some pains later to have the work adopted at the Dresden theatre.[3]

Schubert did not yet know the fate which awaited ' Fierrabras '; all was at present *couleur de rose* ; and the fascination of the theatre, the desire innate in all musicians, even one so self-contained as Schubert, to address a large public, sharpened not improbably by the chance recently enjoyed by the stranger, was too strong to be resisted, and he again, for the third time in ten months, turned towards the stage. This time the temptation came in the shape of ' Rosamunde, Princess of Cyprus,' a play of ultra-romantic character, by Madame von Chezy, authoress of ' Euryanthe,' a librettist whose lot seems to have been to

---

[1] The *Müllerlieder*, twenty-three in number, with Prologue and Epilogue in addition, are contained in the 1st vol. of the *Gedichte aus den hinterlassenen Papieren eines reisenden Waldhornisten* (poems found among the papers of a travelling French horn-player), which were first published at Dessau, 1821. Schubert has omitted the Prologue and Epilogue, and three poems—' Das Mühlenleben' after ' Der Neugierige '; ' Erster Schmerz, letzter Scherz' after ' Eifersucht und Stolz '; and ' Blümlein Vergissmein' after ' Die böse Farbe.'

[2] See Mendelssohn's opinion in *The Mendelssohn Family*, i. 237.
[3] *K.H.* p. 246 (i. 249) *note*.

drag down the musicians connected with her. The book of ' Rosamunde ' must have been at least as inefficient as that with which Weber had been struggling, to cause the failure of such magnificent and interesting music as Schubert made for it. The drama has disappeared, but Kreissle gives the plot,[1] and it is both tedious and improbable. It had, moreover, the disadvantage of competition with a sensational spectacular piece, written expressly to suit the taste of the suburban house, the Theatre an-der-Wien, at which ' Rosamunde ' was produced, and which, since the time when Schikaneder induced Mozart to join him in the ' Magic Flute,'[2] had a reputation for such extravaganzas. Schubert completed the music in five days.[3] It consists of an overture in D,[4] since published as ' Alfonso und Estrella,' op. 69 ; three entr'actes ; two numbers of ballet music ; a little piece for clarinets, horns and bassoons, called a ' Shepherds' melody,' of bewitching beauty ; a romance for soprano solo ; and three choruses. The romance (op. 26), the shepherds' chorus, the entr'acte in B♭ and the air de ballet in G are not only very beautiful but very attractive; and the entr'acte in B minor, of a grand, gloomy and highly imaginative cast, is one of the finest pieces of music existing. The play was brought out on Dec. 20, 1823 ; the overture, though the entire orchestral part of the music had only one rehearsal of two hours, was twice redemanded, other numbers were loudly applauded, and Schubert himself was called for at the close ; but it only survived one more representation, and then the parts were tied up and forgotten till the year 1867, when they were discovered by two English travellers in Vienna.[5] (See GROVE, Vol. II. p. 467.)

Besides the Müllerlieder several independent songs of remarkable beauty belong to 1823. Conspicuous among these are ' Viola ' (Schneeglöcklein ; op. 123), a long composition full of the most romantic tenderness and delicacy, with all the finish of Meissonnier's pictures, and all his breadth and dignity. Also the ' Zwerg ' (op. 22, No. 1), by Matthias von Collin, in which Schubert has immortalised the one brother, as Beethoven, in his overture to ' Coriolan,' did the other. This long, dramatic and most pathetic ballad, which but few can hear unmoved, was written absolutely à l'improviste, without note or sketch, at the top of his speed, talking all the while to Randhartinger, who was waiting to take him out for a walk.[6] Equal, if not superior, to these in merit, though of smaller dimensions, are

' Dass sie hier gewesen ' (op. 59, No. 2) ; ' Du bist die Ruh ' (op. 59, No. 3) ; the Barcarolle, ' Auf dem Wasser zu singen ' (op. 72), to which no nearer date than ' 1823 ' can be given. Below these again, though still fine songs, are ' Der zürnende Barde ' (Feb.) ; ' Drang in die Ferne ' (op. 71 ; Mar. 25) ; ' Pilgerweise ' (Apr.) ; ' Vergissmeinnicht ' (May). The fine sonata in A minor for PF. solo, published as op. 143, is dated Feb. 1823, and the sketch of a scena for tenor solo and chorus of men's voices, with orchestra, dated May 1823. The latter was completed by Herbeck and published in 1868 by Spina as ' Rüdiger's Heimkehr.'

Ten works (opp. 15 to 24) were published in 1823. The earliest was a collection of dances, viz. twelve waltzes, nine Écossaises and seventeen Ländler, op. 18, published Feb. 5 ; the PF. fantasia, op. 15, followed on Feb. 24. The rest are songs, either solo—op. 20, Apr. 10 ; op. 22, May 27 ; op. 23, Aug. 4 ; op. 24, Oct. 7 ; op. 16, Oct. 9 ; op. 19, twenty-one (no dates)— or partsongs, op. 17, Oct. 9. With op. 20 the names of Sauer & Leidesdorf first occur as publishers.

THE OCTET.—The year 1824 began almost exclusively with instrumental compositions. An introduction and variations for PF. and flute (op. 160), on the ' Trockne Blumen ' of the ' Schöne Müllerin,' are dated ' Jan.,' and were followed by the famous octet (op. 166) for clarinet, horn, bassoon, two violins, viola, violoncello and contrabass, which is marked as begun in Feb. and finished on Mar. 1. It was written—not, let us hope, without adequate remuneration, though that was probably the last thing of which its author thought—for Count F. von Troyer, chief officer of the household to the Archduke Rudolph, Beethoven's patron. In this beautiful composition Schubert indulges his love of extension. It contains, like Beethoven's septet, eight movements ; but, unlike the septet, it occupies more than an hour in performance. But though long, no one can call it tedious.[7] The Count played the clarinet, and must have been delighted with the expressive melody allotted to him in the andante. The work was performed immediately after its composition, with Schuppanzigh, Weiss and Linke, three of the famous Rasoumowsky quartet, amongst the players. His association with the members of this celebrated party may well have led Schubert to write string quartets ; at any rate, he himself tells us that he had written two before Mar. 31, and these are doubtless those in E♭ and E (op. 125), since the only other quartet bearing the date of 1824—that in A minor—has so strong a Hungarian flavour as to point to his visit to Zselész later in the year. How powerfully his

---

[1] K.H. p. 285 (l. 288), etc.
[2] Produced at the Theatre an-der-Wien, Sept. 30, 1791.
[3] So says Wilhelm von Chezy, the son of the librettist, who was on terms with Schubert. See his journal, Erinnerungen, etc., 1863.
[4] The autograph is dated ' Dec. 1823.'
[5] It is hardly necessary to remind the reader that the two travellers were Sir George Grove and Sir Arthur Sullivan. See C L. Graves, Life of Sir George Grove, p. 147.                                C.
[6] Kreissle, Sketch. p. 154 note.

[7] Published by Spina in 1854.

thoughts were running at present on orchestral music is evident from the fact that he mentions both octet and quartets as studies for ' the Grand Symphony,' [1] which was then his goal, though he did not reach it till eighteen months later.

A bitter disappointment, however, was awaiting him in the rejection of ' Fierrabras,' which, as already mentioned, was returned by Barbaja, ostensibly on account of the badness of its libretto.   Two full - sized operas — this and ' Alfonso und Estrella '—to be laid on the shelf without even a rehearsal !   Whatever the cause, the blow must have been equally severe to our simple, genuine composer, who had no doubt been expecting, not without reason, day by day for the last four months, to hear of the acceptance of his work.   His picture of himself under this temporary eclipse of hope is mournful in the extreme, though natural enough to the easily depressed temperament of a man of genius.   After speaking of himself as ' the most unfortunate, most miserable being on earth,' he goes on to say :

' Think of a man whose health can never be restored, and who from sheer despair makes matters worse instead of better.   Think, I say, of a man whose brightest hopes have come to nothing, to whom love and friendship are but torture, and whose enthusiasm for the beautiful is fast vanishing ; and ask yourself if such a man is not truly unhappy.

My peace is gone, my heart is sore,
Gone for ever and evermore.

This is my daily cry ; for every night I go to sleep hoping never again to wake, and every morning only brings back the torment of the day before.   Thus joylessly and friendlessly would pass my days, if Schwind did not often look in and give me a glimpse of the old happy times. . . . Your brother's opera '— [this is a letter to Kupelwieser the painter, and the allusion is to ' Fierrabras ']—' turns out to be impracticable, and my music is therefore wasted. Castelli's "Verschworenen" has been set in Berlin by a composer there, and produced with success.   Thus I have composed two operas for nothing.'

This sad mood, real enough at the moment, was only natural after such repulses.   It was assisted, as Schubert's depression always was, by the absence of many of his friends, and also, as he himself confesses, by his acquaintance with Leidesdorf the publisher (in Beethoven's banter ' Dorf des Leides,' a very ' village of sorrow '), whom he describes as a thoroughly good, trustworthy fellow, ' but so very melancholy that I begin to fear that I may have learnt too much from him in that direction.'   It must surely have been after an evening with this worthy that he made the touching entries in his journal which have been preserved ; e.g.

' Grief sharpens the understanding and strengthens the soul : Joy on the other hand seldom troubles itself about the one, and makes the other effeminate or frivolous.'   ' My musical works are the product of my genius and my misery, and what the public most relish is that which has given me the greatest distress.'

Fortunately, in men of the genuine composer temperament, the various moods of mind follow one another rapidly.   As soon as they begin to

compose the demon flies and heaven opens That gloomy document called ' Beethoven's Will,' to which even Schubert's most wretched letters must yield the palm, was written at the very time that he was pouring out the gay and healthy strains of his second symphony.

COMPOSITIONS AT ZSELÉSZ.—Schubert left town with the Esterhazys in a few weeks after these distressing utterances, and for a time forgot his troubles in the distractions of country life in Hungary.   At Zselész he remained for six months, but his life there is almost entirely a blank to us.   We can only estimate it by the compositions which are attributable to the period, and by the scanty information conveyed by his letters, which, though fuller of complaint than those of 1818, are even less communicative of facts and occurrences.   To this visit is to be ascribed that noble composition known as the Grand Duo ' (op. 140), though designated by himself as ' Sonata for the PF. for four hands. Zselés, June 1824 ' ; a piece which, though recalling in one movement Beethoven's second, and in another his seventh, symphony, is yet full of the individuality of its author ; a symphonic work in every sense of the word, which, through Joachim's instrumentation, has now become an orchestral symphony, and a very fine one.   To Zselész also are due the sonata in B♭ (op. 30, May or June), the variations in A♭ (op. 35, ' middle of 1824 '), two waltzes (in op. 33, ' 1824, July '), and four Ländler (' July 1824,' Nott. p. 215)—all for PF. four hands ; other waltzes and Ländler in the same collections for two hands ;   and the ' Gebet ' of Lamotte Fouqué (op. 139a), signed ' Sept. 1824, at Zelész in Hungary '—all evidently arising from the necessity of providing music for the Count's family circle.   The young Countesses were now nineteen and seventeen, and doubtless good performers, as is implied in the duet form of the pianoforte works.   We are probably right in also attributing the lovely string quartet in A minor (op. 29) and the four-hand ' Divertissement à la hongroise ' (op. 54) to this visit, at any rate to its immediate influence. Both are steeped in the Hungarian spirit, and the divertissement contains a succession of real national tunes, one of which he heard from the lips of a maidservant as he passed the kitchen with Baron Schönstein in returning from a walk. For the Baron was at Zselész on this as on the last occasion, and frequent and exquisite must have been the performances of the many fine songs which Schubert had written in the interval since his former visit.

The circumstances attending the composition of the vocal quartet (' Gebet,' op. 139) just mentioned are told by Kreissle, probably on the authority of Schönstein, and they give a good instance of Schubert's extraordinary facility. At breakfast one morning, in Sept. 1824, the Countess produced Lamotte Fouqué's poem,

[1] ' In this manner I shall prepare the way to the Grand Symphony (zur grossen Sinfonie).' Letter to L. Kupelwiezer, K.H. p. 321 (ii. 5).

and proposed to Schubert to set it for the family party. He withdrew after breakfast, taking the book with him, and in the evening, less than ten hours afterwards, it was tried through from the score at the piano. The next evening it was sung again, this time from separate parts, which Schubert had written out during the day. The piece is composed for quartet, with solos for Mme. Esterhazy, Marie, Schönstein and the Count, and contains 209 bars. A MS. letter of Ferdinand's,[1] dated July 3, full of that strong half-reverential affection which was Ferdinand's habitual attitude towards his gifted brother, and of curious details, mentions having sent him Bach's fugues (never-cloying food of great composers) and an opera-book, ' Der kurze Mantel.' Strange fascination of the stage, which thus, in despite of so many failures, could keep him still enthralled !

The country air of the Hungarian mountains, and no doubt the sound and healthy living and early hours of the château, restored Schubert's health completely, and in a letter of Sept. 21 to Schober he says that for five months he had been well. But he felt his isolation and the want of congenial Vienna society keenly ; speaks with regret of having been ' enticed ' into a second visit to Hungary, and complains of not having a single person near to whom he could say a sensible word. How different from the exuberant happiness of the visits to Steyr and St. Pölten, when every one he met was a demonstrative admirer, and every evening brought a fresh triumph !

Now, if ever, was the date of his tender feeling for his pupil Caroline Esterhazy, which his biographers have probably much exaggerated. She was 17 at the time, and Bauernfeld represents her as the object of an ideal devotion which soothed, comforted and inspirited Schubert to the end of his life. Ideal it can only have been, considering the etiquette of the time and the wide distance between the stations of the two ; and the only occasion on which Schubert is ever alleged to have approached anything like a revelation of his feelings is that told by Kreissle—on what authority he does not say, and it is hard to conceive—when on her jokingly reproaching him for not having dedicated anything to her, he replied, ' Why should I ? everything I ever did is dedicated to you.' True, the fine fantasia in F minor, published in the March following his death as op. 103, is dedicated to her ' by Franz Schubert,' a step which the publishers would hardly have ventured upon unless the MS.—probably handed to them before his death—had been so inscribed by himself. But it is difficult to reconcile the complaints of isolation and neglect already quoted from his letter to Schober with the existence of a passion which must have been fed every time

he met his pupil or sat down to the piano with her. We must be content to leave each reader to decide the question for himself.

Vocal composition he laid aside almost entirely in 1824. The only songs which we can ascertain to belong to it are four—the fine though gloomy ones called 'Auflösung ' and ' Abendstern,' both by Mayrhofer ; another evening song ' Im Abendroth ' by Lappe, all three in March ; and the bass song, ' Lied eines Kriegers,' with which he closed the last day of the year.[2] Of partsongs there are two, both for men's voices ; one a ' Salve regina,' written in April before leaving town ; and the other, the ' Gondelfahrer,' or Gondolier, a very fine and picturesque composition, of which Lablache is said to have been so fond that he encored it on first hearing and himself sang in the encore (Spaun). A sonata for PF. and arpeggione, in A minor, dated Nov. 1824, was probably one of his first compositions after returning to town.[3]

The publications of 1824 embrace opp. 25 to 28 inclusive, all issued by Sauer & Leidesdorf. Op. 25 is the ' Schöne Müllerin,' 20 songs in five numbers, published Mar. 25 ; op. 26 is the vocal music in ' Rosamunde,'[4] the romance and three choruses ; op. 27, three fine ' heroic marches,' for PF. four hands ; op. 28, ' Der Gondelfahrer,' for four men's voices and PF., Aug. 12.

VIENNA AGAIN.—1825 was a happy year to our hero—happy and productive. He was back again in his dear Vienna, and exchanged the isolation of Zselész for the old familiar life, with his congenial friends Vogl, Schwind, Jenger, Mayrhofer, etc. (Schober was in Prussia and Kupelwieser still at Rome), in whose applause and sympathy and genial conviviality he rapidly forgot the disappointments and depression that had troubled him in the autumn. Sofie Müller, one of the great actresses of that day, evidently a very accomplished, cultivated woman, was then in Vienna, and during Feb. and Mar. her house was the resort of Schubert, Jenger and Vogl, who sang or listened to her singing of his best and newest Lieder—she herself sang the ' Junge Nonne ' at sight on Mar. 3—and lived a pleasant and thoroughly artistic life.[5] Others, which she mentions as new, and which indeed had their birth at this time, are ' Der Einsame ' and ' Ihr Grab.' The ' new songs from the Pirate,' which she heard on Mar. 1, may have been some from the ' Lady of the Lake,' or ' Norna's song,' or even ' Anna Lyle,' usually placed two years later. Schubert published some important works early in this year—the overture in F for four hands (op. 34) ; also the sonata in B♭ (op. 30) and the variations in A♭ (op. 35), both for four hands ; and the string quartet in A minor (op. 29)—fruits of his

1 For which I again gladly acknowledge the kindness of Frl. Caroline Geisler-Schubert, Schubert's grandniece.

2 The autograph, so dated, belonged to C. J. Hargitt, London.
3 Gotthard, 1871. Autograph in Musikverein.
4 Besides the vocal music, the overture was published about 1828, and the entr'actes and ballet music in 1866.
5 See her interesting journal, in her *Leben und nachgelassene Papiere* herausg. von Johann Grafen Majláth (Vienna, 1832).

sojourn in Hungary. The last of these, the only quartet he was destined to publish during his life, is dedicated ' to his friend I. Schuppanzigh,' a pleasant memorial of the acquaintance cemented by the performance of the octet a twelvemonth before. And as on such publications some amount of money passes from the publisher to the composer, this fact of itself would contribute to enliven and inspirit him. In addition to these instrumental works some noble songs were issued in the early part of 1825—' Die zürnende Diana ' and the ' Nachtstück,' of Mayrhofer ; ' Der Pilgrim ' and ' Der Alpenjäger,' of Schiller ; and Zuleika's second song. The two beautiful solo sonatas in A minor and in C—the latter of which he never succeeded in completely writing out, but the fragment of which is of first-rate quality—also date from this time.

A SUMMER TOUR.—As if to revenge himself for his sufferings at the Esterhazys', he planned an extensive tour for this summer, in his favourite district and in the company of his favourite friend. Vogl, on Mar. 31, started for his home at Steyr. Schubert soon followed him, and the next five months, to the end of Oct., were passed in a delightful mixture of music, friends, fine scenery, lovely weather and absolute ease and comfort, in Upper Austria and the Salzkammergut, partly amongst the good people who had welcomed him so warmly in 1819, partly among new friends and new enthusiasm. Taking Steyr as their *point d'appui,* they made excursions to Linz, Steyreck, Gmunden, Salzburg and even as far as Gastein, etc., heartily enjoying the glorious scenery by day, received everywhere on arrival with open arms, and making the best possible impression with their joint performances. The songs from ' The Lady of the Lake ' were either composed before starting or on the road. At any rate they formed the chief programme during the excursion. If the whole seven were sung or not is uncertain [2]; but Schubert particularly mentions the ' Ave Maria,' apropos of which he makes an interesting revelation. ' My new songs,' says he,

' from Walter Scott's " Lady of the Lake," have been very successful. People were greatly astonished at the devotion which I have thrown into the Hymn to the Blessed Virgin, and it seems to have seized and impressed everybody. I think that the reason of this is that I never force myself into devotion, or compose hymns or prayers unless I am really overpowered by the feeling ; that alone is real, true devotion.'

It is during this journey, at Salzburg, that he makes the remark, already noticed, as to the performance of Vogl and himself. At Salzburg, too, it was the ' Ave Maria ' that so riveted his hearers :

' We produced our seven pieces before a select circle, and all were much impressed, especially by the Ave Maria, which I mentioned in my former letter.

The way in which Vogl sings and I accompany, so that for the moment we seem to be one, is something quite new and unexpected to these good people.'

Schubert sometimes performed alone. He had brought some variations and marches for four hands with him, and, finding a good player at the convents of Florian and Kremsmünster, had made a great effect with them. But he was especially successful with the lovely variations from the solo sonata in A minor (op. 42) ; and here again he lets us into his secret:

' There I played alone, and not without success, for I was assured that the keys under my hands sang like voices, which if true makes me very glad, because I cannot abide that accursed thumping, which even eminent players adopt, but which delights neither my ears nor my judgment.'

He found his compositions well known throughout Upper Austria. The gentry fought for the honour of receiving him, and to this day [3] old people are found to talk with equal enthusiasm of his lovely music and of the unaffected gaiety and simplicity of his ways and manners.

GASTEIN AND A ' GRAND SYMPHONY.'—The main feature of the tour was the excursion to Gastein in the mountains of East Tyrol. To Schubert this was new ground, and the delight in the scenery which animates his description is obvious. They reached it about Aug. 18, and appear to have remained three or four weeks, returning to Gmunden about Sept. 10. At Gastein, among other good people, he found his old ally Ladislaus Pyrker, Patriarch of Venice, and composed two songs to his poetry, ' Heimweh ' and ' Allmacht ' (op. 79). But the great work of this date was the ' Grand Symphony ' [4] which had been before him for so long. We found him eighteen months ago writing quartets and the octet as preparation for it, and an allusion in a letter [5] of Schwind's shows that at the beginning of Aug. he spoke of the thing as virtually done. That it was actually put on to paper at Gastein at this date we know from the testimony of Bauernfeld,[6] who also informs us that it was a special favourite with its composer. Seven songs in all are dated in this autumn, amongst them two fine scenes from a play by W. von Schütz called ' Lacrimas ' (op. 124), not so well known as they deserve.

The letters of this tour, though not all preserved, are unusually numerous for one who so much disliked writing. One long one to his father and mother ; another, much longer, to Ferdinand ; a third to Spaun ; and a fourth to Bauernfeld, are printed by Kreissle, and contain passages of real interest, showing how keenly he observed and how thoroughly he enjoyed nature, and displaying throughout a vein of good sense and even practical sagacity,[7]

---

[1] For the dates of the early part of the tour, see *K.* ii. 21.
[2] Schubert speaks of them as ' unsere sieben Sachen ' (letter to Ferdinand, *Kreissle,* p 363) ; but Nos. 3 and 4 are for chorus.

[3] Written in 1881.
[4] Grove pinned his faith to the existence of the Gastein symphony, but it has not been discovered. See his own note and that of w. H. HW. on p. 608, note 6.    c.
[5] *K.H.* p. 358 (ii. 43). ' To your Symphony we are looking forward eagerly,' implying that Schubert had mentioned it in a former letter.        [6] *W.Z K.,* June 9-13, 1829.
[7] See his shrewd reasons for not at once accepting Bauernfeld's proposition that he, Schwind and Schubert should all live together. *K.H.* p. 370 (ii. 57). Also the whole letter to Spaun.

and a facility of expression, which are rare in him.

At length the summer and the money came to an end, Vogl went off to Italy for his gout, and Schubert, meeting Gahy at Linz, returned with him and the MS. symphony to Vienna in an *Einspänner*, to find Schober and Kupelwieser both once more settled there. The first thing to be done was to replenish his purse, and this he soon did by the sale of the seven songs from 'The Lady of the Lake,' which he disposed of on Oct. 29 to Artaria for 200 silver gulden—just £20! Twenty pounds, however, were a mine of wealth to Schubert; and even after repaying the money which had been advanced by his father, and by Bauernfeld for the rent of the lodgings during his absence, he would still have a few pounds in hand.

During Schubert's absence in the country his old friend Salieri died, and was succeeded by Eybler. The court organist also fell ill, and Schwind wrote urging him to look after the post; but Schubert made no sign, and evidently did nothing in the matter, though the organist died on Nov. 19. He obviously knew much better than his friends that he was absolutely unfit for any post requiring punctuality or restraint. In the course of this year he was made 'Ersatzmann,' or substitute—whatever that may mean—by the Musikverein or Gesellschaft der Musikfreunde. Of what happened from this time till the close of 1825 we have no certain information. He set two songs by Schulze in Dec.; and it is probable that the PF. sonata in D (op. 53) and the noble funeral march for the Emperor of Russia (op. 55), whose death was known in Vienna on Dec. 14, both belong to that month. What gave him his interest in the death of Alexander is not known, but the march is an extraordinarily fine specimen. A piece for the piano in F, serving as accompaniment to a recitation from a poem by Pratobevera, a series of graceful modulations in arpeggio form, also dates from this year.[1]

The compositions of 1825 may be here summed up: Sonata for PF. solo in A minor (op. 42); ditto in D (op. 53); ditto in A (op. 120); unfinished ditto in C ('Reliquie,' Nott. p. 211); a funeral march, four hands, for the Emperor Alexander of Russia (op. 55). Songs —'Des Sängers Habe,' by Schlechta, and 'Im Walde,' by E. Schulze; seven from 'The Lady of the Lake' (op. 52); another from Scott's 'Pirate'[2]; 'Auf der Bruck,' by Schulze; 'Fülle der Liebe,' by Schlegel; 'Allmacht' and 'Heimweh,' by Pyrker; two scenes from 'Lacrimas,' by W. von Schütz; and 'Abendlied für die Entfernte,' by A. W. Schlegel; 'Die junge Nonne,' 'Todtengräbers Heimweh' and 'Der blinde Knabe,' all by Craigher; 'Der Einsame,' by Lappe; and, in Dec.,

'An mein Herz' and 'Der liebliche Stern,' both by Ernst Schulze. It is also more than probable that the string quartet in D minor was at least begun before the end of the year.

The publications of 1825 are: In Jan., opp. 32, 30, 34; Feb. 11, opp. 36 and 37; May 9, op. 38; July 25, op. 43; Aug. 12, op. 31; and, without note of date, opp. 29 and 33. Op. 29 is the lovely A minor quartet; and it is worthy of note that it is published as the first of 'Trois quatuors.' This was never carried out. The two others were written, as we have already seen (p. 603), but they remained unpublished till after the death of their author.

1826 was hardly eventful in any sense of the word, though by no means unimportant in Schubert's history. It seems to have been passed entirely in Vienna. He contemplated a trip to Linz with Spaun and Schwind, but it did not come off. The weather of this spring was extraordinarily bad, and during April and May he composed nothing.[3] The music attributable to 1826 is, however, of first-rate quality. The string quartet in D minor, by common consent placed at the head of Schubert's music of this class, was first played on Jan. 29, and was therefore doubtless only just completed.[4] That in G (op. 161) Schubert himself has dated as being written in ten days (June 20 to June 30), a work teeming with fresh vigour after the inaction of the preceding two months, as full of melody, spirit, romance, variety and individuality as anything he ever penned, and only prevented from taking the same high position as the preceding by its great length—due to the diffuseness which Schubert would no doubt have remedied had he given himself time to do so. One little point may be mentioned *en passant* in both these noble works—the evidence they afford of his lingering fondness for the past. In the D minor quartet he goes back for the subject and feeling of the andante to a song of his own of 1816, and the finale of the G major is curiously tinged with reminiscences of the Rossini fever of 1819.

The 'Rondeau brillant' in B minor for PF. and violin (op. 70), subsequently such a favourite in the concert-room, also belongs to this year, though it cannot be precisely dated; and so does a piece of still higher quality, which is pronounced by Schumann to be its author's 'most perfect work both in form and conception,' the sonata in G major for PF. solo, op. 78, usually called the 'Fantasia,' owing to a freak of the publisher's. The autograph is inscribed, in the hand of its author, 'IV. Sonate für Pianoforte allein. Oct. 1826, Franz Schubert'; above which, in the writing

---

[1] Printed by Reissmann in his book.
[2] So says Sofie Müller (under date of Mar. 1); but perhaps it was her mistake for Norman's song in 'The Lady of the Lake.'

[3] See his letter to Bauernfeld and Mayrhofer, in *Die Presse*, Apr. 21, 1869.
[4] *K.H.* p. 391 (ii. 77). The finale was voted too long, to which Schubert, after a few minutes' consideration, agreed, and 'at once cut out a good part.' (Hauer's information.) The autograph has disappeared.

of Tobias Haslinger, stands the title ' Fantasie, Andante, Menuetto und Allegretto.' [1] We may well say with Beethoven, ' O Tobias ! '

By the side of these undying productions the ' Marche héroïque,' written to celebrate the accession of Nicholas I. of Russia, and the andantino and rondo on French *motifs*—both for PF., four hands—are not of great significance.

An attack of song-writing seems to have come upon him in March, which date we find attached to six songs ; or, if the rest of those to Seidl's words, forming opp. 105 and 80, and marked merely ' 1826,' were written at the same time (as, from Schubert's habit of eviscerating his books, they not improbably were) —twelve. Three Shakespeare songs are due to this July — ' Hark ! hark ! the lark,' [2] from *Cymbeline* ; ' Who is Sylvia ? ' from the *Two Gentlemen of Verona* ; and the Drinking-song in *Antony and Cleopatra* — the first two perhaps as popular as any single songs of Schubert's. The circumstances of the composition, or rather creation, of the first of these have already been mentioned (p. 500). The fact of three songs from the same volume belonging to one month (not improbably to one day, if we only knew) is quite *à la Schubert*. A beautiful and most characteristic piece of this year is the ' Nachthelle,' or ' Lovely night,' written to words of Seidl's—not improbably for the Musikverein, through Anna Fröhlich—for tenor solo, with accompaniment of four men's voices and pianoforte, which would be a treasure to singing societies for its truly romantic loveliness but for the inordinate height to which the voices are taken and the great difficulty of executing it with sufficient delicacy. A song called ' Echo ' (op. 130), probably written in 1826, was intended to be the first of six ' humorous songs ' for Weigl's firm.[3]

We hear nothing of the new symphony during the early part of this year. No doubt it was often played from the MS. score at the meetings of the Schubert set, but they say no more about it than they do of the octet, or quartets, or sonatas, which were all equally in existence ; and for aught we know it might have been ' locked in a drawer,' which was often Schubert's custom after completing a work—' locked in a drawer and never thought about again.' [4] It was, however, destined to a different fate. On Sept. 9, 1826, at one of the first meetings of the Board of the Musikverein after the summer recess, Hofrath Kiesewetter reports that Schubert desires to dedicate a symphony to the society ; upon which the sum of 100 silver florins (£10) is voted to him, not in payment for the work, but as a token

of sympathy and as an encouragement. The letter conveying the money is dated the 12th, and on or even before its receipt Schubert brought the manuscript and deposited it with the society. His letter accompanying it may here be quoted :

' To the Committee of the Austrian Musical Society. —Convinced of the noble desire of the Society to give its best support to every effort in the cause of art, I venture, as a native artist, to dedicate this my Symphony to the Society, and most respectfully to recommend myself to its protection. With the highest esteem. Your obedt.          FRANZ SCHUBERT.'

In accordance with this, the MS. probably bears his formal dedication to the Verein, and we may expect to find that, though so long talked of, it bears marks of having been written down as rapidly as most of his other productions.[5] At present, however, all trace of it is gone ; not even its key is known. There is no entry of it in the catalogue of the society's library, and except for the minute and letter given above, and the positive statements of Bauernfeld quoted below,[6] it might as well be non-existent. That it is an entirely distinct work from that in C, written two and a half years later, can hardly admit of a doubt.

MISCELLANEOUS PUBLICATIONS. — Of the publications of 1826, the most remarkable are the seven songs from ' The Lady of the Lake,' for which Artaria had paid him 200 florins in the preceding Oct., and which appeared on the 5th of this Apr., in two parts, as op. 52. They were succeeded immediately, on Apr. 8, by the PF. sonata in D (op. 53) and the ' Divertissement à la hongroise ' (op. 54), both issued by the same firm. For these two splendid works Schubert received from the penurious Artaria only 300 Vienna florins, equal to £12. Songs issued fast from the press at this date ; for on Apr. 6 we find op. 56 (three songs) announced by Pennauer,

---

[1] See an interesting letter from Ernst Perabo, the owner of the MS. with an extract from the andante, in the *Monthly Musical Record* for Apr. 1888.

[2] Entitled ' Serenade,' but more accurately an ' Aubade.

[3] See Nottebohm's *Catalogue* under op. 130.

[4] Lachner's expression to my friend Mr. C. A. Barry in 1881.

[5] The documents on which these statements are based are given by Herr C. F. Pohl in his *History of the Gesellschaft der Musikfreunde* —or Musikverein—Vienna, 1871, p. 16 ; and by Ferdinand Schubert in the *Neue Zeitschrift für Musik* for Apr. 30, 1839, p. 140.

[6] Bauernfeld, in an article ' Über Franz Schubert ' in the *Wiener Zeitschrift für Kunst, Literatur, Theater und Mode* for 9, 11, 13 June 1829 (Nos. 69, 70, 71), says as follows : ' To the larger works of his latter years also belongs a Symphony written in 1825 at Gastein, for which its author had an especial predilection. . . . At a great concert given by the Musik Verein shortly after his death a Symphony in C was performed, which was composed as early as 1817 [1818], and which he considered as one of his less successful works. . . . Perhaps the Society intends at some future time to make us acquainted with one of the later symphonies, possibly the Gastein one already mentioned.' [N.B. The two movements of the B minor symphony (1822) were not at this time known, so that by ' later symphonies ' Bauernfeld must surely intend the two of 1825 and 1828.] At the end of the article he gives a ' chronological list of Schubert's principal works not yet generally known.' Amongst these are ' 1825, Grand Symphony.' . . . ' 1828, Last Symphony '— ' Grand ' (*grosse*) being the word used by Schubert himself in his letter to Kupelwieser referred to above (p. 604). It is plain, therefore, that at this time, seven months after Schubert's death, the Gastein symphony of 1825, and that in C major of 1828, were known as distinct works. The present writer has collected the evidence for the existence of the symphony in a letter to the London *Athenæum* of Nov. 19, 1881.          G.

This note is left as Sir George Grove wrote it. But the existence of the Gastein symphony rests at present on very imperfect evidence. There is no mention of it in Ferdinand Schubert's catalogue, or in Kreissle von Hellborn's biography, or in the testimony of any one who claims to have seen the score. The symphony accepted by the Gesellschaft der Musikfreunde and performed by them in the year of Schubert's death is the C major, written in 1818 and incorrectly dated, in a Gesellschaft programme, 1825. No copy of the work in question has revealed itself to the most careful research. It is probable that the so-called Gastein symphony is Schubert's ' No. 6,' possibly retouched during the holiday of 1826 and offered to the Gesellschaft in the following year.          W. H. HW.

and opp. 57 and 58 (each three songs) by Weigl; on June 10, op. 60 ('Greisengesang' and 'Dithyrambe') by Cappi and Czerny; in Sept. op. 59 (four songs, including 'Dass sie hier gewesen,' 'Du bist die Ruh' and 'Lachen und Weinen') by Leidesdorf; and op. 64 (three partsongs for men's voices) by Pennauer; and on Nov. 24, op. 65 (three songs) by Cappi and Czerny. Some of these were composed as early as 1814, 1815, 1816; others again in 1820, 1822 and 1823. The Mass in C (op. 48) and three early pieces of church music, 'Tantum ergo' (op. 45), 'Totus in corde' (op. 46) and 'Salve regina' (op. 47) were all issued in this year by Diabelli. Of dances and marches for piano there are eight numbers: a galop and eight Écossaises (op. 49); thirty-four 'Valses sentimentales' (op. 50); 'Hommage aux belles Viennoises' (sixteen Ländler and two Écossaises, op. 67); three marches (four hands, op. 51)—all published by Diabelli; the two Russian marches (opp. 55, 56), by Pennauer; six polonaises (op. 61), Cappi and Czerny; and a divertissement, or 'Marche brillante et raisonnée,' on French *motifs* (op. 63), Weigl. In all, twenty-two publications, divided among six publishers, and containing 106 works.

PRECARIOUS CONDITIONS.—We have been thus particular to name the numbers and publishers of these works, because they show conclusively how much Schubert's music was coming into demand. Pennauer and Leidesdorf were his personal friends, and may possibly have printed his pieces from chivalrous motives; but no one can suspect hard and experienced men of business like Diabelli and Artaria of publishing the music of any one at their own risk unless they believed that there was a demand for it. The list is a remarkable one, and will compare for extent and variety with that of most years of Beethoven's life. And even at the incredibly low prices [1] which his publishers gave for the exclusive copyright of his works, there is enough in the above to produce an income sufficient for Schubert's wants. But the fact is that he was mixed up with a set of young fellows who regarded him as a Crœsus,[2] and who virtually lived upon his carelessness and good-nature, under the guise of keeping house in common. Bauernfeld, in an article in the Vienna *Presse* of Apr. 17, 1869, has given us the account with some *naïveté*. A league or partnership was made between himself, Schwind the painter and

Schubert. They had nominally their own lodgings, but often slept all together in the room of one. The affection between them was extraordinary. Schubert used to call Schwind 'seine Geliebte'—his *innamorata*! A kind of common property was established in clothes and money; hats, coats, boots and cravats were worn in common, and the one who was in cash paid the score of the others. As Schwind and Bauernfeld were considerably younger than Schubert, that duty naturally fell on him. When he had sold a piece of music he seemed to this happy trio to 'swim in money,' which was then spent 'right and left' in the most reckless manner, till it was all gone, and the period of reverse came. Under these circumstances life was a series of fluctuations, in which the party were never rich, and often very poor. On one occasion Bauernfeld and Schubert met in a coffee-house near the Kärnthnerthor Theatre, and each detected the other in ordering a *mélange* (*café au lait*) and biscuits, because neither had the money to pay for dinner. And this in Schubert's twenty-ninth year, when he had already written immortal works quite sufficient to make a good livelihood!

Outside the circle of this trio were a number of other young people, artists and literary men—Schober, Jenger, Kupelwieser, etc.—attracted by Schubert's genius, good-nature and love of fun, and all more or less profiting by the generosity of one who never knew what it was to deny a friend. The evenings of this jolly company were usually passed in the Gasthaus, and then they would wander about till daybreak drove them to their several quarters, or to the room of one of the party. It would be absurd to judge Vienna manners from an English point of view. The Gasthaus took the place of a modern club, and the drink consumed probably did not much exceed that which some distinguished Vienna artists now imbibe night after night, and does not imply the excess that it would infallibly lead to in a northern climate; but it must be obvious that few constitutions could stand such racket, and that the exertion of thus trying his strength by night and his brain by day must have been more than any frame could stand. In fact his health did not stand the wear and tear. We have seen that in Feb. 1823 he could not leave the house; that in the summer of the same year he was confined to the hospital; that in Mar. 1824 he speaks of his health as irrecoverably gone; and the dedication of the six four-hand marches, op. 40, to his friend Bernhardt, doctor of medicine, 'as a token of gratitude,' is strong evidence that in 1826, the year of their publication, he had had another severe attack.[3]

---

[1] It is said by Schindler that the prices agreed on with him were ten Vienna gulden per Heft of songs, and twelve per pianoforte piece. (The Vienna gulden was then worth just one franc. 'Heft' meant a single song, not a 'Part' of two or three. This is conclusively proved by Ferdinand Schubert's letter of 1824. These prices were not adhered to. Thus for the seven 'Lady of the Lake' songs he had 500 paper gulden = £20, or nearly £3 per song. Even that is low enough. On the other hand, F. Lachner told Mr. Barry that in the last year of Schubert's life he took half a dozen of the 'Winterreise' songs to Haslinger at Schubert's request and brought back one gulden a piece (= 10d.) for them!

[2] The expression is Bauernfeld's.

[3] See Otto Erich Deutsch, 'Schuberts Krankheit. Neue Mitteilungen' (*Z.M.W.*, Nov 1921, pp. 100-106), and Waldemar Schweisheimer, 'Der kranke Schubert' (*Z.M.W.*, June/July 1923, pp. 552-61)        c.

It was probably a sense of the precarious nature of such a life that led some of his friends in the autumn of 1826 to urge Schubert to stand for the post of vice-Kapellmeister in the Imperial court, vacant by the promotion of Eybler to that of principal Kapellmeister ; but the application, like every other of the same kind made by him, was a failure, and the place was given to Joseph Weigl by the Imperial decree of Jan. 27, 1827.

Another opportunity of acquiring a fixed income was opened to him during the same autumn by the removal of Karl August Krebs from the conductorship of the Court theatre to Hamburg. Vogl interested Duport, the administrator of the theatre, in his friend, and the appointment was made to depend on Schubert's success in composing some scenes for the stage. Madame Schechner, for whom the principal part was intended, a young débutante who was making her first appearance in Vienna, objected at the pianoforte rehearsals to some passages in her air, but could not induce the composer to alter them. The same thing happened at the first orchestral rehearsal, when it also became evident that the accompaniments were too noisy for the voice. Still Schubert was immovable. At the full-band rehearsal Schechner fairly broke down, and refused to sing any more. Duport then stepped forward, and formally requested Schubert to alter the music before the next meeting. This he refused to do ; but, taking the same course as Beethoven had done on a similar occasion, said loudly, ' I will alter nothing,' took up his score and left the house. After this the question of the conductorship was at an end. Schubert's behaviour in this matter has been strongly censured, but we do not see much in it. Such questions will always depend on the temperament of the composer. Had it been either Mozart or Mendelssohn we cannot doubt that all would have gone smoothly ; the prima donna would not only not have been ruffled, but would have felt herself complimented, and the music would have been so altered as to meet every one's wish, and yet sound as well as before. On the other hand, had it been Beethoven or Schumann we may be equally sure that not a note would have been changed, and that everything would have ended in confusion. With all Schubert's good-nature, when his music was concerned he was of the same mind as Beethoven and Schumann. There are other instances of the same stubbornness, which will be noticed later.

Some set-off to these disappointments was afforded by the ready way in which his Gastein symphony [1] was received by the Musikverein, and the sympathetic resolution and prompt donation which accompanied its acceptance, although no attempt to perform or even

rehearse it can now be traced. The beautiful ' Nachthelle,' already referred to, which he composed in September, was rehearsed during the early winter months, and performed by the Society on Jan. 25, 1827.

Some little gratification also he not improbably derived from the letters which during this year he began to receive from publishers in the north. Probst of Leipzig—one of Beethoven's publishers, predecessor of the firm of Senff—was the first to write. His letter is dated August 26, and is followed by one from Breitkopf & Härtel of Sept. 7. True, neither are very encouraging. Probst speaks of his music as too often ' peculiar and odd,' and ' not intelligible or satisfactory to the public ' ; and begs him to write so as to be easily understood ; while Breitkopf stipulates that the only remuneration at first shall be some copies of the works. Still, even with this poor present result, the fact was obvious that he had begun to attract attention outside of Austria.

THE ' WINTERREISE ' CYCLE.—As to Schubert's life in the early part of 1827 we have little to guide us beyond the scanty inferences to be drawn from the dated compositions. The first of these of any moment are eight variations (the eighth very much extended) on a theme in Hérold's opera ' Marie,' for PF. four hands (op. 82). ' Marie ' was produced on the Vienna boards Jan. 18, 1827 ; and Schubert's variations are dated ' February,' and are dedicated to one of his friends in Upper Austria, Prof. Cajetan Neuhaus of Linz. The next and still more important work is the first half of the ' Winterreise,' twelve songs (' Gute Nacht ' to ' Einsamkeit '), marked as begun in Feb. 1827. Franz Lachner remembers that ' half a dozen ' of them were written in one morning, and that Haslinger gave a gulden (that is a franc) apiece for them. The poems which form the basis of this work are by Wilhelm Müller, the poet of the ' Schöne Müllerin,' which the Winterreise closely approaches in popularity, and which it would probably equal if the maiden of the Winterwalk were as definite a creation as the miller's daughter is. They are twenty-four in all, and appear under their now immortal name in the second volume of the work of which vol. i. contained the ' Schöne Müllerin,' and which has the quaint title already quoted (p. 602).[2] The second volume was published at Dessau in 1824, and did not at once attract Schubert's notice. When it did, he made short work of it. Another important composition of this month (dated Feb. 28) is the Schlachtlied (battle-song) of Klopstock, set for two choirs of male voices, sometimes answering in eight real parts, of immense force and vigour, and marked by that dogged adherence to rhythm so characteristic of Schubert.

---

[1] But see note above, p. 608. c.

[2] The order of the songs is much changed in the music.

BEETHOVEN'S RECOGNITION OF SCHUBERT.
—He can scarcely have finished with this before
the news that Beethoven was in danger spread
through Vienna. The great musician got back
to his rooms in the Schwarzspanierhaus from
his fatal expedition to Gneixendorf in the first
week of December, became very ill, and during
Jan. was tapped for the dropsy three times.
Then Malfatti was called in, and there was a
slight improvement. During this he was allowed to read, and it was then that Schindler,
a zealous Schubert propagandist, took the
opportunity to put some of Schubert's songs
into his hands.[1] He made a selection of about
sixty, in print and MS., including 'Iphigenie,'
'Grenzen der Menschheit,' 'Allmacht,' 'Die
junge Nonne,'[2] 'Viola,' the 'Müllerlieder,' etc.
Beethoven up to this time probably did not
know half a dozen of Schubert's compositions,
and his astonishment was extreme, especially
when he heard that there existed at least 500
of the same kind. 'How can he find time,'
said he, 'to set such long poems, many of them
containing ten others?' i.e. as long as ten
separate ones; and said over and over again,
'If I had had this poem I would have set it
myself'; 'Truly Schubert has the divine fire
in him.' He pored over them for days, and
asked to see Schubert's operas and P.F. pieces,
but the illness returned and it was too late.
But from this time till his death he spoke often
of Schubert, regretting that he had not sooner
known his worth, and prophesying that he
would make much stir in the world.[3] Schubert
was sure to hear of these gratifying utterances,
and they would naturally increase his desire to
come into close contact with the master whom
he had long worshipped at a distance. It is
possible that this emboldened him to visit the
dying man. He seems to have gone twice;
first with Anselm Hüttenbrenner and Schindler.
Schindler told Beethoven that they were there,
and asked whom he would see first. 'Schubert
may come in first' was the answer. At this
visit, perhaps, if ever, it was that he said, in
his affectionate way, 'You, Anselm, have my
mind (Geist), but Franz has my soul (Seele).'[4]
The second time he went with Josef Hüttenbrenner and Teltscher the painter. They
stood round the bed. Beethoven was aware
of their presence, and fixing his eyes on them,
made some signs with his hand. No one, however, could explain what was meant, and no
words passed on either side. Schubert left
the room overcome with emotion. In about
three weeks came the end, and then the funeral.
Schubert was one of the torch-bearers. Franz

1 Schindler, Beethoven, i. 136.
2 Schindler's list of the songs perused by Beethoven differs in his
two accounts. Compare his Beethoven, ii. 136, with K.H. p. 264
(i. 266).
3 Schindler, in Bäuerle's Theaterzeitung (Vienna), May 3, 1831.
4 See von Leitner, Anselm Hüttenbrenner, Graz, 1868, p. 5 The
story has an apocryphal air, but Hüttenbrenner was so thoroughly
trustworthy that it is difficult to reject it. At any rate, Beethoven
is not likely to have thus expressed himself before he had made
acquaintance with Schubert's music.

Lachner and Randhartinger walked with him
to and from the cemetery. The way back lay
by the Himmelpfortgrund, and close by the
humble house in which he had drawn his first
breath. They walked on into the town, and
stopped at the 'Mehlgrube,' a tavern in the
Kärnthnerthorstrasse, now the Hotel Munsch.
There they called for wine, and Schubert drank
off two glasses, one to the memory of Beethoven,
the other to the first of the three friends who
should follow him. It was destined to be
himself.

Lablache was also one of the torch-bearers at
the funeral. This and the part which he took
in the Requiem for Beethoven (Vol. I. p. 303)
may have induced Schubert to write for him
the 'three Italian Songs for a Bass voice,' which
form op. 83, and are dedicated to the great
Italian basso.

Hummel and Hiller were in Vienna during
Mar. 1827, and Hiller describes meeting Schubert and Vogl at Madame Lacsny-Buchwieser's,
and his astonishment at their joint performance. 'Schubert,' says Hiller,[5]

'Had little technique, and Vogl but little voice;
but they had both so much life and feeling, and went
so thoroughly into the thing, that it would be impossible to render these wonderful compositions more
clearly and more splendidly. Voice and piano became as nothing; the music seemed to want no
material help, but the melodies appealed to the ear
as a vision does to the eye.'

Not only did the boy think it the deepest
musical impression he had ever received, but
the tears coursed down the cheeks even of the
veteran Hummel. Either then or a few evenings afterwards, Hummel showed his appreciation by extemporising on Schubert's 'Blinde
Knabe,' which Vogl had just sung—to Franz's
delight.

In April Schubert wrote the beautiful
'Nachtgesang im Walde' (op. 139b) for four
men's voices and four horns; and a 'Spring
Song,' also for men's voices. In July we have
the very fine and characteristic serenade
'Zögernd leise' (op. 135) for alto solo and
female voices, a worthy pendant to the
'Nachthelle,' and written almost à l'improviste.[6]
A fête was to be held for the birthday of a young
lady of Döbling. Grillparzer had written some
verses for the occasion, and Schubert, who was
constantly in and out of the Fröhlichs' house,
was asked by Anna to set them for her sister
Josephine and her pupils. He took the lines,
went aside into the window, pushed up his
spectacles on to his brow, and then, with the
paper close to his face, read them carefully
twice through. It was enough: 'I have it,'
said he, 'it's done, and will go famously.' A
day or two afterwards he brought the score, but
he had employed a male chorus instead of a
female one, and had to take it away and trans-
pose it. It was sung in the garden by moon-

5 Künstlerleben (1880), p. 49.     6 K.H. p. 474 (ii. 160).

light, to the delight of every one, the villagers thronging round the gate. He alone was absent.

1827 witnessed another attempt at an opera —the ' Graf von Gleichen,' written by Bauernfeld, apparently in concurrence[1] with Mayrhofer. Schubert had the libretto in August 1826, submitted it to the management of the Royal Opera-house, and arranged with Grillparzer, in case the Censure should cause its rejection, to have it accepted by the Königstadt Theatre. Owing possibly to the delay of the Censure it was nearly a year before he could begin the composition. The MS. sketch,[2] is dated at the beginning ' 17 Juni 1827.' The opera is sketched throughout, and he played portions of it to Bauernfeld. Forty years later the sketch came into the hands of Herbeck, and he began to score it after Schubert's indications— of which there are plenty—but was prevented by death.

VISIT TO GRAZ.—A correspondence had been going on for long between the Schubert circle at Vienna and the Pachler family in Graz, the capital of Styria, as to an expedition thither by Schubert, and at length it was arranged for the autumn of this year. Carl Pachler was one of those cultivated men of business who are such an honour to Germany ; an advocate, and at the head of his profession, yet not ashamed to be an enthusiastic lover of music and musicians, and proud to have them at his house and to admit them to his intimate friendship. Amongst his circle was Anselm Hüttenbrenner, the brother of Schubert's friend Josef, himself an earnest admirer of Franz, whose last visit to Vienna had been to close the eyes of his old friend Beethoven. The house was open to painters, singers, actors and poets, ' the scene of constant hospitalities, the headquarters of every remarkable person visiting Graz.' Such was the family whose one desire was to receive Schubert and Jenger. The journey was an affair of two days and a night, even in the fast coach. They left on Sunday morning, Sept. 2, and reached Graz on Monday night.

The next three weeks were spent in the way which Schubert most enjoyed, excursions and picnics by day through a beautiful country, and at night incessant music ; good eating and drinking, clever men and pretty women, no fuss, a little romping, a good piano, a sympathetic audience and no notice taken of him—such were the elements of his enjoyment. The music was made mostly by themselves, Schubert singing, accompanying and playing duets with Jenger, and extemporising endless dance tunes. He does not appear to have composed anything of great moment during the visit. A galop and twelve waltzes, published under the titles of the ' Grätzer Waltzer ' (op. 91) and the ' Grätzer

Galoppe '[3] ; three songs (op. 106, 1, 2, 3—the last a particularly fine one) to words by local poets—and the ' Old Scottish Ballad ' by Herder (op. 165, No. 5), were probably all that he penned during this festive fortnight ; unless perhaps some of those exquisite little pieces published in 1828 and 1838 as ' Impromptus ' and ' Moments musicals ' are the result of this time. Two songs, written a couple of years before, ' Im Walde,' and ' Auf der Bruck,' of the purest Schubert, proved, and justly proved, such favourites that he had them lithographed and published in the place.[4] The visit is further perpetuated by the titles of the dances just mentioned, and by the dedication to Mme. Pachler of op. 106, a collection of four songs, the three already named and the lovely ' Sylvia.' Schubert seems to have had this set of songs lithographed without name of place or publisher, shortly after his return, on purpose for his hostess.[5]

The journey home was a triumphal progress, and by the 27th they were back in Vienna. Schubert then wrote the second part of the ' Winterreise ' (Nos. 13-24), completing that immortal work. The shadows lie much darker on the second than on the first part, and the ' Wegweiser,' ' Das Wirthshaus,' ' Die Krähe,' ' Die Nebensonnen,' and ' Der Leiermann,' are unsurpassed for melancholy among all the songs. Even in the extraordinary and picturesque energy of ' Die Post ' there is a deep vein of sadness. Schubert here only followed faithfully, as he always does, the character of the words.

On Oct. 12 he wrote a little four-hand march as a souvenir for Faust Pachler, the son of his host, a trifle interesting only from the circumstances of its composition. In the same month he composed his first PF. trio, in B♭ (op. 99), and in November the second, in E♭ (op. 100). They were both written for Bocklet, Schuppanzigh, and Lincke, and were first heard in public, the one early in January, the other on Mar. 26, 1828. The year was closed with an Italian cantata, dated Dec. 26, ' alla bella Irene,' in honour of Frl. Kiesewetter (afterwards Mme. Prokesch v. Osten), the daughter of his friend the Hofrath, sponsor to the Gastein symphony (p. 608). It is probably more interesting for its accompaniment for two pianos than for anything else.

The communications with Probst of Leipzig went on. There is a letter from him dated Jan. 15, and he himself paid a visit to Vienna later in the season, and made Schubert's[6] personal acquaintance, but the negotiations were not destined to bear fruit till next year.

1 See Schubert's letter (May 1826) with Bauernfeld's statements in the Presse of Apr. 21, 1869, and Signale, Nov. 1869.
2 In Dumba's collection.
3 Published by Haslinger, as No. 10 of the ' Favorite Galops,' 1828.
4 They stood originally in B♭ minor and A♭, but on republication by Diabelli after his death, as op. 93, the keys were changed to G minor and G major.
5 Compare Jenger's letter in K.H. (ii. 103, note), with Nottebohm's notice under op. 106.
6 K.H. p. 421 (ii. 107).

But a proof that Schubert was making his mark in North Germany is afforded by a letter from Rochlitz, the critic—editor of the Leipzig *Allgemeine musikalische Zeitung*, and a great personage in the musical world of Saxony—dated Nov. 7, 1827, proposing that Schubert should compose a poem by him, called 'Der erste Ton,' or 'The first Sound,' a poem which Weber had already set without success, and which Beethoven had refused. Rochlitz's letter was probably inspired by the receipt of three of his songs set by Schubert as op. 81, and published on May 27. The proposition, however, came to nothing.

Coincident with these communications from abroad came a gratifying proof of the improvement in his position at home, in his election as a member of the representative body of the Musical Society of Vienna. The date of election is not mentioned : but Schubert's reply, as given by Pohl,[1] is dated Vienna, June 12, 1827, and runs as follows :

'The Managing Committee of the Society of Friends of Music of the Austrian Empire having thought me worthy of election as a Member of the Representative Body of that excellent Society, I beg herewith to state that I feel myself greatly honoured by their choice, and that I undertake the duties of the position with much satisfaction.     FRANZ SCHUBERT, Compositeur.'

We have mentioned the more important compositions of 1827. There remain to be named two songs by Schober (op. 96, No. 2) ; and one by Reil (op. 115, No. 1) ; a comic trio, 'Die Hochzeitsbraten' (op. 104), also by Schober ; and an allegretto in C minor for PF. solo, written for his friend Walcher, 'in remembrance of Apr. 26, 1827,' and not published till 1870.

The publications of 1827 are as follows : the overture to 'Alfonso und Estrella' (op. 69) ; 'Rondeau brillant,' for PF., and violin (op. 70) ; songs—'Der Wachtelschlag' (op. 68, Mar. 2), 'Drang in die Ferne' (op. 71, Feb.), 'Auf dem Wasser zu singen' (op. 72, Feb.), 'Die Rose' (op. 73, May 10)—all four songs previously published in the Vienna *Zeitschrift für Kunst* ; four polonaises, for PF. four hands (op. 75) ; overture to 'Fierrabras,' for PF. four hands, arranged by Czerny (op. 76) ; twelve 'Valses nobles,' for PF. solo (op. 77, Jan.) ; Fantasie, etc. for PF. in G (op. 78) ; two songs, 'Das Heimweh,' 'Die Allmacht' (op. 79, 'May 16 '); three songs (op. 80, May 25) ; three ditto (op. 81, May 28) ; variations on theme of Hérold's (op. 82, Dec.) ; three Italian songs (op. 83, Sept. 12) ; four songs (op. 88, Dec. 12).

LAST COMPOSITIONS.—We have now arrived at Schubert's last year, 1828. It would be wrong to suppose that he had any presentiment of his end ; though, if a passion for work, an eager use of the 'day,' were any sign that the 'night' was coming 'in which no man could work,' we might also be justified in doing so.

[1] *Die Gesellschaft der Musikfreunde*, etc., p. 16.

We hear of his suffering from blood to the head, but it was not yet enough to frighten any one. He returned to the extraordinary exertions, or rather to the superabundant productions of his earlier years, as the following full list of the compositions of 1828, in order, as far as the dates permit, will show.

Jan.   Songs, 'Die Sterne' (op. 96, No. 1) ; 'Der Winterabend.'
Mar.   Symphony in C.
       Oratorio, Miriam's Siegesgesang.
       Song, 'Auf dem Strom,' voice and horn (op. 119).
May.   Lebensstürme, PF. duet (op. 144).
       Hymn to the Holy Ghost (op. 154), for two choirs and wind.
       2 Clavierstücke.
       Song, 'Widerschein.'
June.  Mass in E♭ (begun)
       Fugue in ɛ minor, PF. duet, op. 152 ('Baden, Juny, 1828 ')
       Grand Rondeau, PF. duet (op. 107).
July.  Psalm 92, in Hebrew, for baritone and chorus.
Aug.   Songs, 'Schwanengesang,' Nos. 1-13.
Sept.  PF. Sonata in C minor.
       Ditto in A.
       Ditto in B♭ ('Sept. 26 ').
Between Aug. and Oct.  Tantum ergo in E♭, and Offertorium in B♭, for tenor solo, chorus and orchestra.   Published 1890 by Peters.
Oct.   Song, 'Schwanengesang,' No. 14.
       New Benedictus to Mass in C.
       'Der Hirt auf den Felsen,' voice and clarinet (op. 129).
'1828 ' only.  String Quartet in C (op. 163).

This truly extraordinary list includes his greatest known symphony, his greatest and longest mass, his first oratorio, his finest piece of chamber music, three noble PF. sonatas and some astonishingly fine songs. The autograph of the symphony, 218 pages in oblong quarto, is now one of the treasures of the Library of the Musikverein at Vienna. It has no title or dedication, nothing beyond the customary heading to the first page of the score 'Symfonie März 1828, Frz. Schubert Mpia,' marking the date at which it was begun. If it may be taken as a specimen, he took more pains this year than he did formerly. In the first three movements of this great work there are more afterthoughts than usual. The subject of the introduction and the first subject of the allegro have both been altered. In several passages an extra bar has been stuck in—between the scherzo and the trio, two bars ; in the development of the scherzo itself sixteen bars of an exquisite episode—first sketched in the octet—have been substituted. The finale alone remains virtually untouched.[2] But such alterations, always rare in Schubert, are essentially different from the painful writing and erasing and rewriting, which we are familiar with in the case of Beethoven's finest and most spontaneous music. This, though the first draft, is no rough copy ; there are no traces of sketches or preparation ; the music has evidently gone straight on to the paper without any intervention, and the alterations are merely a few improvements *en passant*.[3] It is impossible to look at the writing of the autograph, after Schubert has warmed to his work, especially that of the finale, and not see that it was put down as an absolute *impromptu*, written as fast as the pen could travel on the paper.

[2] See details by the present writer in Appendix to the *Life of Schubert*, translated by A. D. Coleridge, vol. ii. p. 320.
[3] The original MS. orchestral parts show at any rate that the alterations in the score were made before they were copied from it. C. V. Stanford kindly examined them for me with that view.

It seems that Schubert's friends used to lecture him a good deal on the diffuseness and want of consideration which they discovered in his works, and were continually forcing Beethoven's laborious processes of composition down his throat. This often made him angry, and when repeated, evening after evening, he would say, 'So you're going to set upon me again to-dav ! Go it, I beg you !' But, for all his annoyance, the remonstrances appear to have had some effect ; and after Beethoven's death he asked Schindler to show him the MS. of 'Fidelio.'[1] He took it to the piano, and pored over it a long time, making out the passages as they had been, and comparing them with what they were ; but it would not do ; and at last he broke out and exclaimed that for such drudgery he could see no reason under any circumstances ; that he thought the music at first just as good as at last ; and that for his part he had really no time for such corrections. Whether the amendments to the great symphony were a remorseful attempt on Schubert's part to imitate Beethoven and satisfy the demands of his friends we cannot tell ; but if so they are very unlike the pattern.

The autograph of the E♭ Mass, in the Bibliothek at Berlin, does not show at all the same amount of corrections as that in A♭ (see p. 600), nor do the fugal movements appear to have given any special trouble. True, the 'Cum Sancto' was recommenced after the erasure of seven bars,[2] but apparently merely for the sake of changing the tempo from C to ₵, and the larger part of the movement was evidently written with great rapidity. In the 'Et vitam 'there are barely a dozen corrections, and the 'Osanna' has every mark of extreme haste. Some of the erasures in this work are made with the penknife—surely an almost unique thing with Schubert! The four-hand PF. fugue in E minor (op. 152, dated 'Baden, June 1828 ') is not improbably a trial of counterpoint with reference to this Mass.

The songs of 1828 are splendid. It does not appear that the fourteen which were published after his death with the publisher's title of 'Schwanengesang—'the Swan's song'—were intended by him to form a series of the same kind as the 'Schöne Müllerin' and 'Winterreise'; but no lover of Schubert can dissociate them, and in the 'Liebesbotschaft,' 'Aufenthalt,' 'Ständchen,' etc., we have some of the most beautiful, and in the 'Atlas,' 'Am Meer,' 'Doppelgänger,' etc., some of the most impressive, of his many songs. The words of some are by Rellstab, and the origin of these is thus told by Schindler.[3] Schubert had been much touched by Schindler's

efforts to make Beethoven acquainted with his music, and after the great master's death the two gradually became intimate. Schindler had possession of many of Beethoven's papers, and Schubert used to visit him in familiar style, to look over them. Those which specially attracted him were the poems and dramas sent in at various times for consideration ; amongst others a bundle of some twenty anonymous lyrics which Beethoven had intended to set, and which therefore attracted Schubert's particular notice.[4] He took them away with him, and in two days brought back the 'Liebesbotschaft,' 'Kriegers Ahnung,' and 'Aufenthalt,' set to music. This account, which is perfectly natural and consistent, and which Mr. Thayer allows me to say he sees no reason to question, has been exaggerated [5] into a desire expressed by Beethoven himself that Schubert should set these particular songs ; but for this there is no warrant. Ten more quickly followed the three just mentioned; and these thirteen—seven to Rellstab's and six to Heine's words (from the *Buch der Lieder* [6]), were, on Nottebohm's authority, written in August. The last is by Seidl ; it is dated 'Oct. 1828,' and is probably Schubert's last song.

But it is time to return to the chronicle of his life during its last ten months. Of his doings in January we know little more than can be gathered from the following letter to Anselm Hüttenbrenner, the original of which is in the British Museum (Add. MS. 29,804, *f.* 24).

'VIENNA, *Jan.* 18, 1828.
'MY DEAR OLD HÜTTENBRENNER—You will wonder at my writing now ? So do I. But if I write it is because I am to get something by it. Now just listen ; a drawing-master's place near you at Graz is vacant, and competition is invited. My brother Karl, whom you probably know, wishes to get the place. He is very clever, both as a landscape-painter and a draughtsman. If you could do anything for him in the matter I should be eternally obliged to you. You are a great man in Graz, and probably know some one in authority, or some one else who has a vote. My brother is married, and has a family, and would therefore be very glad to obtain a permanent appointment. I hope that things are all right with you, as well as with your dear family, and your brothers. A Trio of mine, for Pianoforte, Violin, and Violoncello, has been lately performed by Schuppanzigh, and was much liked. It was splendidly executed by Boklet, Schuppanzigh, and Link. Have you done nothing new ? Apropos, why doesn't Greiner,[7] or whatever his name is, publish the two songs ? What's the reason ? Sapperment !

'I repeat my request ; recollect, what you do for my brother, you do for me. Hoping for a favorable answer, I remain your true friend, till death.
'FRANZ SCHUBERT Mpia, of Vienna.'

The expression 'till death,' which appears here for the first time in his letters, and the words 'of Vienna,' added to his name, are both singular.

---

[1] Schindler, *Erinnerungen*, in *Niederrheinische Musikzeitung*, 1857, pp. 73-8, 81-8.
[2] The omission of the words 'Jesu Christe' at the end of the Quoniam,' and other omissions, show that he had not conquered the carelessness so frequent in his early Masses as to the treatment of the words.
[3] Schindler, *Erinnerungen*, etc., as before.

[4] They proved afterwards to be by Rellstab.
[5] See Rellstab's *Aus m. Leben,* ii. 245.
[6] Baron Schönstein relates—*K.H.* p. 447 (ii. 135)—that he found Heine's 'Buch der Lieder ' on Schubert's table some years before this date, and that Schubert lent them to him with the remark ' that he should not want them again.' But such reminiscences are often wrong in point of date : the fact remains ineffaceable in the mind, the date easily gets altered. In fact Heine's 'Buch der Lieder ' was first published in 1827. The six songs which Schubert took from it are all from the section entitled 'Die Heimkehr.'
[7] A publisher in Graz. His name was Kienreich, and the two songs, 'Im Walde ' and ' Auf der Bruck ' (op. 93), appeared in May.

On the 24th, at an evening concert at the Musikverein, the serenade for contralto solo and female chorus just mentioned was performed, and is spoken of by the correspondent of the Leipzig *A.M.Z.* as 'one of the most charming works of this favourite writer.' In February we find three letters from North Germany, one from Probst of Leipzig and two from Schott. They show how deep an impression Schubert was making outside Austria. Both firms express warm appreciation of his music, both leave the terms to be named by him, and Schott orders a list of nine important pieces.

On March 26 Schubert gave, what we wonder he never gave before, an evening concert on his own account in the hall of the Musikverein. The following is the programme exactly reprinted from the original:

firmly in opera and symphony. This rests on the authority of Kreissle [2]; the silence of Pohl in his history of the society shows that its minute-books contain no express mention of the reception of the work, as they do that of the symphony in October 1826. There is no doubt, however, that it was adopted by the society, and is entered in the Catalogue, under the year 1828, as xiii. 8024.[3] But this prodigious work was far beyond the then powers of the chief musical institution of Vienna. The parts were copied and some rehearsals held; but both length and difficulty were against it, and it was soon withdrawn, on Schubert's own advice, in favour of his earlier symphony, No. 6, also in C. Neither the one nor the other was performed till after his death.

March also saw the birth of the interesting

Einladung
zu dem Privat Concerte, welches Franz Schubert am
26. März, Abends 7 Uhr im Locale des österreichischen Musikvereins
unter den Tuchlauben No. 558 zu geben die Ehre haben wird.

Vorkommende Stücke.

1. Erster Satz eines neuen Streich Quartetts vorgetragen von
den Herren Böhm, Holz, Weiss, und Linke.

2. *a.* Der Kreutzzug, von Leitner          ⎫ Gesänge mit Begleitung des
   *b.* Die Sterne,      von demselben       ⎪ Piano Forte, vorgetragen von
   *c.* Fischerweise,    von Bar. Schlechta  ⎬ Herrn Vogl, k. k. pensionirten
   *d.* Fragment aus dem Aeschylus           ⎭ Hofopernsänger.

3. Ständchen von Grillparzer, Sopran-Solo und Chor, vorgetragen von
Fräulein Josephine Fröhlich und den Schülerinnen des Conservatoriums.

4. Neues Trio für das Piano Forte, Violin und Violoncelle,
vorgetragen von den Herren Carl Maria von Boklet, Böhm und **Linke.**

5. Auf dem Strome von Rellstab. Gesang mit Begleitung
des Horns und Piano Forte, vorgetragen von den Herren
Tietze, und Lewy dem Jüngeren.

6. Die Allmacht, von Ladislaus Pyrker, Gesang mit Begleitung
des Piano Forte, vorgetragen von Herren Vogl.

7. Schlachtgesang von Klopstock, Doppelchor für Männerstimmen.

Sämmtliche Musikstücke sind von der Composition des Concertgebers.
Eintrittskarten zu fl. 3. W. W. sind in den Kunsthandlungen
der Herren Haslinger, Diabelli und Leidesdorf zu haben.

This programme attracted 'more people than the hall had ever before been known to hold,' and the applause was very great. The net result to Schubert was 800 gulden, Vienna currency, equal to about £32. This put him in funds for the moment, and the money flowed freely. Thus, when, three days later, Paganini gave his first concert in Vienna, Schubert was there, undeterred, in his wealth, by a charge of five gulden. Nay, he went a second time, not that he cared to go again, but that he wished to treat Bauernfeld, who had not five farthings, while with him 'money was as plenty as blackberries.' [1]

This month he wrote, or began to write, his last and greatest symphony, in C. He is said to have offered it to the society for performance, and in so doing to have expressed himself to the effect that henceforth he wished to have nothing more to do with songs, as he was now planted

oratorio 'Miriam's Song of Victory,' to Grillparzer's words.[4] It is written, as so many of Schubert's choral pieces are, for a simple pianoforte accompaniment; but this was merely to suit the means at his disposal, and is an instance of his practical sagacity. It is unfortunate, however, since the oratorio has become a favourite, that we have no other orchestral accompaniment than that afterwards adapted by Lachner, which is greatly wanting in character, and in the picturesque elements so native to Schubert.[5] A song to Rellstab's words, 'Auf dem Strom' (op. 119), for soprano, with obbligato horn and PF. accompaniment, written for Lewy, a Dresden horn-player, belongs to this month and was indeed first heard at Schubert's own concert, on

---

[1] See Bauernfeld's Letter in the *Presse*, Apr. 17, 1869. *Häckerling*, chaff,' is Schubert's word.

[2] *K.H.* p. 445 (ii. 132).
[3] See Pohl's letter to *The Times*, of Oct. 17, 1881.
[4] Kreissle, p. 609 (ii. 285), says that it was produced in the Schubert Concert, Mar. 1828. But this is contradicted by the Programme which is printed above. It was first performed Jan. 30, 1829, at a concert for erecting Schubert's headstone.
[5] It has been performed (with Lachner's orchestration) at the Crystal Palace several times, at the Leeds Festival 1880, and elsewhere in England.

the 26th and afterwards repeated at a concert of Lewy's, on April 20, Schubert himself playing the accompaniment each time.

To April no compositions can be ascribed unless it be the quintet in C for strings (op. 163), which bears only the date ' 1828.' This is now universally accepted not only as Schubert's finest piece of chamber music, but as one of the very finest of its class. The two violoncellos in themselves give it distinction ; it has all the poetry and romance of the G major quartet, without the extravagant length which will always stand in the way of that noble production ; while the adagio is so solemn and yet so beautiful in its tone, so entrancing in its melodies, and so incessant in its interest, and the trio of the scherzo, both from itself and its place in the movement, is so eminently dramatic, that it is difficult to speak of either too highly.

In May we have a grand battle-piece, the ' Hymn to the Holy Ghost,' for eight male voices, written for the Concert Spirituel of Vienna, at first with PF. in October scored by the composer for a wind band, and in 1847 published as op. 154. Also a ' Characteristic Allegro ' for the PF. four hands, virtually the first movement of a sonata — issued some years later with the title ' Lebensstürme ' (op. 144) ; an allegro vivace and allegretto, in E♭ minor and major, for PF. solo, published in 1868 as first and second of ' 3 Clavierstücke ' ; and a song ' Widerschein.'

In June, probably at the request of the publisher, he wrote a four-hand rondo for PF. in A, since issued as ' Grand Rondeau, op. 107 ' ; and began his sixth Mass, that in E♭. In this month he paid a visit to Baden— Beethoven's Baden—since a fugue for four hands in E minor is marked as written there in ' June 1828.' In the midst of all this work a letter [1] from Mosewius of Breslau, a prominent Prussian musician, full of sympathy and admiration, must have been doubly gratifying as coming from North Germany.

In July he wrote the 92nd Psalm in Hebrew for the synagogue at Vienna, of which Sulzer was precentor. In August, notwithstanding his declaration on completing his last symphony, we find him (under circumstances already described) composing seven songs of Rellstab's, and six of Heine's, afterwards issued as ' Schwanengesang.'

He opened September with a trifle in the shape of a short chorus,[2] with accompaniment of wind band, for the consecration of a bell in the church of the Alservorstadt. A few days after, the memory of Hummel's visit in the spring of 1827 seems to have come upon him like a lion, and he wrote off three fine PF. solo sonatas, with the view of dedicating them to

that master. These pieces, though very unequal and in parts extraordinarily diffuse, are yet highly characteristic of Schubert. They contain some of his finest and most original music, and also his most affecting (*e.g.* andantino, scherzo and trio of the A minor sonata) ; and, if full of disappointment and wrath and the gathering gloom of these last few weeks of his life, they are also saturated with that nameless personal charm that is at once so strong and so indescribable. The third of the three, that in B♭, dated Sept. 26, has perhaps more of grace and finish than the other two. The sonatas were not published till a year after Hummel's death, and were then dedicated by Diabelli-Spina to Robert Schumann, who acknowledges the dedication by a genial though hardly adequate article in his *Ges. Schriften*, ii. 239. The second part of the ' Winterreise ' was put into Haslinger's hands for engraving before the end of this month.[3]

In October, prompted by some occasion which has eluded record, he wrote a new ' Benedictus ' to his early Mass in C, a chorus of great beauty and originality in A minor, of which a competent critic [4] has said that ' its only fault consists in its immeasurable superiority to the rest of the Mass.' To the same period may be assigned a fine offertorium, ' Intende voci orationis meae,' and an extremely beautiful ' Tantum ergo ' in E♭, for chorus and orchestra. For some other occasion, which has also vanished, he wrote accompaniments for thirteen wind instruments to his grand ' Hymn to the Holy Ghost ' ; a long scena or song for soprano—probably his old admirer, Anna Milder—with pianoforte and obbligato clarinet (op. 129) ; and a song called ' Die Taubenpost ' (' The carrier pigeon ') to Seidl's words. The succession of these pieces is not known. It is always assumed that the Taubenpost, which now closes the Schwanengesang, was the last. Whichever of them was the last was the last piece he ever wrote.

The negotiations with Probst and Schott, and also with Brüggemann of Halberstadt, a publisher anxious for some easy PF. pieces for a series called ' Mühling's Museum,' by no means fulfilled the promise of their commencement. The magnificent style in which the Schotts desired Schubert to name his own terms [5] contrasts badly with their ultimate refusal (Oct. 30) to pay more than 30 florins (or about 25s.) for the PF. quintet (op. 114) instead of the modest sixty demanded by him. In fact the sole result was an arrangement with Probst to publish the long and splendid E♭ trio, which he did, according to Nottebohm,[6]

[1] *K.H.* p. 428 (ii. 114).
[2] *K.H.* p. 443 (ii. 131). This piece, ' Glaube, Hoffnung, und Liebe,' is not to be confounded with one of similar title for a solo voice published, Oct. 6, 1828, as op. 97.

[3] Schubert's letter to Jenger, Sept. 25. *K.H.* p. 437 (ii. 124).
[4] E. Prout in the *Monthly Musical Record* for 1871, p. 56.
[5] *K.H.* p. 424 (ii. 109)
[6] Probst announces two long lists of new music in the *A.M.Z.* for Oct., but makes no mention of the trio. It is reviewed most favourably in the *A.M.Z.* for Dec. 10, 1828. Alas ! he was then beyond the reach of praise or blame.

ın September, and for which the composer received the incredibly small sum of 21 Vienna florins, or just 17s. 6d. ! Schubert's answer to Probst's inquiry as to the ' Dedication ' is so characteristic as to deserve reprinting :

'VIENNA, *Aug.* 1.

' Euer Wohlgeboren, the opus of the Trio is 100. I entreat you to make the edition correct ; I am extremely anxious about it. The work will be dedicated to no one but those who like it. That is the most profitable dedication. With all esteem,
'FRANZ SCHUBERT.'

The home publications of 1828 are not so important as those of former years. The first part of the ' Winterreise ' (op. 89) was issued in January by Haslinger ; Mar. 14, three songs by Sir W. Scott (opp. 85, 86) by Diabelli ; at Easter (Apr. 6) six songs (opp. 92 and 108), and one set of ' Moments musicals,' by Leidesdorf ; in May, two songs (op. 93) by Kienreich [1] of Graz ; in June or July (' Sommer '), four songs (op. 96) by Diabelli ; Aug. 13, four Refrain-Lieder (op. 95), Weigl. Also the following, to which no month can be fixed : ' Andantino varié and Rondeau brillant ' (op. 84), PF. four hands, on French *motifs*, forming a continuation of op. 63, Weigl ; three songs (op. 87), Pennauer ; four impromptus (op. 90), and twelve Grätzer Waltzer (op. 91) for PF. solo, Diabelli ; Grätzer Galoppe, do. Haslinger ; four songs (op. 106) lithographed without publisher's name.

POVERTY.—There is nothing in the events already catalogued to have prevented Schubert's taking an excursion this summer. In either Styria or Upper Austria he would have been welcomed with open arms, and the journey might have given him a stock of health sufficient to carry him on for years. And he appears to have entertained the idea of both.[2] But the real obstacle, as he constantly repeats, was his poverty.[3] ' It's all over with Graz for the present,' he says, with a touch of his old fun, ' for money and weather are both against me.' Franz Lachner, at that time his constant companion, told the writer that he had taken half a dozen of the ' Winterreise ' songs to Haslinger and brought back half a dozen gulden—each gulden being then worth a franc. Let the lover of Schubert pause a moment, and think of the ' Post ' or the ' Wirthshaus ' being sold for tenpence ! of that unrivalled imagination and genius producing those deathless strains and being thus rewarded ! When this was the case, when even a great work like the Eb trio, after months and months of negotiation and heavy postage, realises the truly microscopic amount of ' 20 florins 60 kreutzers ' (as with true Prussian businesslike minuteness Probst specifies it), of 17s. 6d. as our modern currency has it—not even Schubert's fluency and rapidity could do more than keep body

and soul together. It must have been hard not to apply the words of Müller's ' Leiermann' to his own case—

' Barfuss auf dem Eise
Wankt er hin und her,
*Und sein kleiner Teller*
*Bleibt ihm immer leer.*'

In fact so empty was his little tray that he could not even afford the diligence-fare to Pest, where Lachner's ' Bürgschaft ' was to be brought out, and where, as Schindler reminds him, he would be safe to have a lucrative concert of his own music, as profitable as that of Mar. 26. Escape from Vienna by *that* road was impossible for him this year.

LAST RESIDENCE.—Schubert had for some time past been living with Schober at the ' Blaue Igel ' (or Blue Hedgehog), still a well-known tavern and resort of musicians in the Tuchlauben ; but at the end of August he left and took up his quarters with Ferdinand in a new house in the Neue Wieden suburb, then known as No. 694 Firmian, or Lumpert,[4] or Neugebauten, Gasse, now (1881) No. 6 Kettenbrücken Gasse ; a long house with three rows of nine windows in front ; a brown sloping tiled roof ; an entry in the middle to a quadrangle behind ; a quiet, clean, inoffensive place. Here, on the second floor, to the right hand, lived Schubert for the last five weeks of his life, and his death is commemorated by a stone tablet over the entry, placed there by the Männergesang Verein in Nov. 1869, and containing these words :

' In diesem Hause starb am 19 November 1828 der Tondichter Franz Schubert.'

Ferdinand had removed there, and Franz went there too. He made the move with the concurrence of his doctor, von Rinna, in the hope that as it was nearer the country—it was just over the river in the direction of the Belvedere—Schubert would be able to reach fresh air and exercise more easily than he could from the heart of the city. The old attacks of giddiness and blood to the head had of late been frequent, and soon after taking up his new quarters he became seriously unwell. However, this was so far relieved that at the beginning of October he made a short walking tour with Ferdinand and two other friends to Über-Waltersdorf, and thence to Haydn's old residence and grave at Eisenstadt, some 25 miles from Vienna. It took them three days, and during that time he was very careful as to eating and drinking, regained his old cheerfulness, and was often very gay. Still he was far from well, and after his return the bad symptoms revived, to the great alarm of his friends. At length, on the evening of Oct. 31, while at supper at the Rothen Kreuz in the Himmelpfortgrund, an eating-house much frequented by himself and his friends, he took some fish on his plate, but at the first mouthful threw down

---

1 Whom Schubert parodies as ' Greiner,' *i.e.* grumbler.
2 Jenger's and Traweger's letters, *K.H.* pp. 416, 427, 431, etc.
3 Letters, *K.H.* p. 437 (ii. 124), etc

4 *K.H.* p 453 *note.*

the knife and fork, and exclaimed that it tasted
like poison. From that moment hardly anything but medicine passed his lips; but he
still walked a good deal. About this time
Lachner returned from Pest in all the glory of
the success of his opera; and though only in
Vienna for a few days, he called on his friend,
and they had two hours' conversation. Schubert was full of plans for the future, especially
for the completion of 'Graf von Gleichen,'
which, as already mentioned, he had sketched
in the summer of 1827. He discussed it also
with Bauernfeld during the next few days, and
spoke of the brilliant style in which he intended
to score it. About this time Carl Holz, Beethoven's old friend, at Schubert's urgent
request, took him to hear the great master's
C♯ minor quartet, still a novelty in Vienna. It
agitated him extremely. 'He got (says Holz)
into such a state of excitement and enthusiasm
that we were all afraid for him.'[1]  On Nov. 3,
the morrow of All Souls' day, he walked early
in the morning to Hernals—then a village, now
a thickly built suburb outside the Gürtel-
strasse—to hear his brother's Latin Requiem in
the church there. He thought it simple, and
at the same time effective, and on the whole
was much pleased with it. After the service
he walked for three hours, and on reaching
home complained of great weariness.

ILLNESS AND DEATH.—Shortly before this
time the scores of Handel's oratorios had come
into his hands—not impossibly some of the set
of Arnold's edition given to Beethoven before his
death, and sold in his sale for 102 florins; and
the study of them had brought home to him his
deficiencies in the department of counterpoint.
'I see now,' said he[2] to the Fröhlichs, 'how
much I have still to learn; but I am going to
work hard with Sechter, and make up for lost
time'—Sechter being the recognised authority
of the day on counterpoint. So much was he
bent on this that on the day after his walk to
Hernals, i.e. on Nov. 4, notwithstanding his
weakness, he went into Vienna and, with
another musician named Lanz, called on
Sechter to consult him on the matter, and
they actually decided on Marpurg as the text-
book and on the number and dates of the
lessons.[3] But he never began the course.
During the next few days he grew weaker and
weaker; and when the doctor was called in it
was too late. About the 11th he wrote a note[4]
to Schober—doubtless his last letter.

'DEAR SCHOBER,
'I am ill. I have eaten and drunk nothing for
eleven days, and am so tired and shaky that I can
only get from the bed to the chair, and back. Rinna
is attending me. If I taste anything, I bring it up
again directly.

'In this distressing condition, be so kind as to help me
to some reading. Of Cooper's I have read The Last of
the Mohicans, The Spy, The Pilot and The Pioneers.
If you have anything else of his, I entreat you to leave
it with Frau von Bogner at the Coffee house. My
brother, who is conscientiousness itself, will bring it to
me in the most conscientious way. Or anything else.
Your friend,                    SCHUBERT.'

What answer Schober made to this appeal is
not known. He is said to have had a daily
report of Schubert's condition from the doctor,
but there is no mention of his having called.
Spaun, Randhartinger,[5] Bauernfeld and Josef
Hüttenbrenner are all said to have visited
him; but in those days there was great dread
of infection, his new residence was out of the
way, and dangerous illness was such a novelty
with Schubert that his friends may be excused
for not thinking the case so grave as it was. After
a few days Rinna himself fell ill, and his place
was filled by a staff-surgeon named Behring.

On the 14th Schubert took to his bed.[6]  He
was able to sit up a little for a few days longer,
and thus to correct the proofs of the second
part of the 'Winterreise,' probably the last
occupation of those inspired and busy fingers.
He appears to have had no pain, only increasing
weakness, want of sleep and great depression.
Poor fellow! no wonder he was depressed!
everything was against him, his weakness, his
poverty, the dreary house, the long lonely
hours, the cheerless future—all concentrated
and embodied in the hopeless images of Müller's
poems, and the sad gloomy strains in which he
has clothed them for ever and ever—the 'Letzte
Hoffnung,' the 'Krähe,' the 'Wegweiser,' the
'Wirthshaus,' the 'Nebensonnen,' the 'Leiermann'—all breathing of solitude, broken
hopes, illusions, strange omens, poverty, death,
the grave! As he went through the pages, they
must have seemed like pictures of his own life;
and such passages as the following from the
'Wegweiser' (or Signpost), can hardly have
failed to strike the dying man as aimed at
himself:

'Einen Weiser seh' ich stehen,
Unverrückt vor meinem Blick,
Eine Strasse muss ich gehen,
Die noch keiner ging zurück.'

Alas! he was indeed going the road which
no one e'er retraces! On Sunday the 16th the
doctors had a consultation; they predicted a
nervous fever, but had still hopes of their
patient. On the afternoon of Monday, Bauernfeld saw him for the last time. He was in very
bad spirits, and complained of great weakness
and of heat in his head, but his mind was still
clear and there was no sign of wandering; he
spoke of his earnest wish for a good opera-
book. Later in the day, however, when the
doctor arrived, he was quite delirious, and
typhus had unmistakably broken out. The

[1] Quoted by Nohl, Beethoven, iii. 964. Holz says it was the last music that poor Schubert heard. Ferdinand claims the same for his Requiem. At any rate, both were very near the end.
[2] Kreissle's Sketch, p. 152.
[3] K.H. p. 451 (ii. 138), expressly on Sechter's authority.
[4] Given by Bauernfeld, in Die Presse, Apr. 21, 1869.
[5] Fräulein Geisler-Schubert informs me that Ferdinand's wife (still living, 1882) maintains that Randhartinger was the only one who visited him during his illness; but it is difficult to resist the statements of Bauernfeld (Presse, Apr. 21, 1869) and of Kreissler's informants, p. 452 (ii. 140).
[6] Ferdinand, in the N.Z.M. p. 143.

next day, Tuesday, he was very restless throughout, trying continually to get out of bed, and constantly fancying himself in a strange room. That evening he called Ferdinand on to the bed, made him put his ear close to his mouth, and whispered mysteriously, ' What are they doing with me ? ' ' Dear Franz,' was the reply, ' they are doing all they can to get you well again, and the doctor assures us you will soon be right, only you must do your best to stay in bed.' He returned to the idea in his wandering—' I implore you to put me in my own room, and not to leave me in this corner under the earth ; don't I deserve a place above ground ? ' 'Dear Franz,' said the agonised brother, ' be calm ; trust your brother Ferdinand, whom you have always trusted, and who loves you so dearly. You are in the room which you always had, and lying on your own bed.' ' No,' said the dying man, ' that's not true ; Beethoven is not here.' So strongly had the great composer taken possession of him ! An hour or two later the doctor came, and spoke to him in the same style. Schubert looked him full in the face and made no answer : but turning round clutched at the wall with his poor tired hands, and said in a slow earnest voice, ' Here, here, is my end.' At three in the afternoon of Wednesday, Nov. 19, 1828, he breathed his last, and his simple earnest soul took its flight from the world. He was thirty-one years, nine months and nineteen days old. There never has been one like him, and there never will be another.

His death, and the letters of the elder Franz and of Ferdinand, bring out the family relations in a very pleasant light. The poor pious bereaved father, still at his drudgery as ' school teacher in the Rossau,' ' afflicted, yet strengthened by faith in God and the Blessed Sacraments,' writing to announce the loss of his ' beloved son, Franz Schubert, musician and composer ' ; the good innocent Ferdinand, evidently recognised as Franz's peculiar property, clinging to his brother as the one great man he had ever known ; thinking only of him, and of fulfilling his last wish to lie near Beethoven—these form a pair of interesting figures. Neither Ignaz nor Carl appear at all in connection with the event, the father and Ferdinand alone are visible.

The funeral took place on Friday Nov. 21. It was bad weather. but a number of friends and sympathisers assembled. He lay in his coffin, dressed, as the custom then was, like a hermit, with a crown of laurel round his brows. The face was calm, and looked more like sleep than death. By desire of the family Schober was chief mourner. The coffin left the house at half-past two, and was borne by a group of young men, students and others, in red cloaks and flowers, to the little church of S. Joseph in

Margarethen, where the funeral service was said, and a motet by Gänsbacher, and a hymn of Schober's, ' Der Friede sey mit dir, du engelreine Seele '—written that morning in substitution for his own earlier words, to the music of Schubert's ' Pax vobiscum '—were sung over the coffin. It was then taken to the Ortsfriedhof in the village of Währing, and committed to the ground, three places higher up than the grave of Beethoven.[1] In ordinary course he would have been buried in the cemetery at Matzleinsdorf, but the appeal which he made almost with his dying breath was naturally a law to the tender heart of Ferdinand, and through his piety and self-denial his dear brother rested if not next, yet near, to the great musician whom he so deeply reverenced and admired. Late in the afternoon Wilhelm von Chezy, son of the authoress of ' Euryanthe ' and ' Rosamunde,' who though not in Schubert's intimate circle was yet one of his acquaintances, by some accident remembered that he had not seen him for many months, and he walked down to Bogner's coffee-house, where the composer was usually to be found between five and seven, smoking his pipe and joking with his friends, and where the Cooper's novels mentioned in his note to Schober were not improbably still waiting for him. He found the little room almost empty, and the familiar round table deserted. On entering he was accosted by the waiter—' Your honour is soon back from the funeral ! ' ' Whose funeral ? ' said Chezy in astonishment. ' Franz Schubert's,' replied the waiter, ' he died two days ago, and is buried this afternoon.' [2]

He left no will. The official inventory [3] of his possessions at the time of his death, in which he is described as ' Tonkünstler und Compositeur '—musician and composer—is as follows :

' Three dress coats, 3 walking coats, 10 pairs of trousers, 9 waistcoats—together worth 37 florins ; 1 hat, 5 pairs of shoes and 2 of boots—valued at 2 florins ; 4 shirts, 9 cravats and pocket handkerchiefs. 13 pairs of socks, 1 towel, 1 sheet, 2 bedcases—8 florins ; 1 mattress, 1 bolster, 1 quilt—6 florins ; a quantity of old music valued at 10 florins—63 florins (say £2 : 10s.) in all. Beyond the above there were no effects.'

Is it possible, then, that in the ' old music, valued at 8s. 6d., ' are included the whole of his unpublished manuscripts ? Where else could they be but in the house he was inhabiting ?

The expenses of the illness and funeral amounted in all to 269 silver florins, 19 kr. (say £27). Of this the preliminary service cost 84 fl. 35 kr. ; the burial 44 fl. 45 kr. ; and the ground 70 fl. ; leaving the rest for the doctor's fees and incidental disbursements. Illness and

1 Next to Beethoven came ' Freiherr von Wssehrd ' ; then ' Joh. Graf Odonel and Gräfin O'Donnell.' and then Schubert.
2 Wilhelm von Chezy, *Erinnerungen aus meinen Leben* (1863), pp. 182, 183.
3 Given at length by Kreissle (p. 457)—but entirely omitted in the translation—and materially misquoted by Gumprecht (p. 15).

death were truly expensive luxuries in those days.

On Nov. 27, the Kirchenmusikverein performed Mozart's Requiem in his honour; and on Dec. 23 a Requiem by Anselm Hüttenbrenner was given in the Augustine church. On Dec. 14, his early symphony in C, No. 6, was played at the Gesellschaftskonzert, and again on March 12, 1829. At Linz on Christmas Day there was a funeral ceremony with speeches and music. Articles in his honour appeared in the *Wiener Zeitschrift* of Dec. 25 (by von Zedlitz), in the *Theaterzeitung* of Vienna of the 20th and 27th (by Blahetka); in the Vienna *Zeitschrift für Kunst* of June 9, 11, 13, 1829 (by Bauernfeld); in the Vienna *Archiv für Geschichte* by Mayrhofer); and memorial poems were published by Seidl, Schober, and others. On Jan. 30, 1829, a concert was given by the arrangement of Anna Fröhlich in the hall of the Musikverein; the programme included 'Miriam,' and consisted entirely of Schubert's music, excepting a set of flute variations by Gabrielsky, and the first finale in 'Don Juan'; and the crowd was so great that the performance had to be repeated shortly afterwards. The proceeds of these concerts and the subscriptions of a few friends sufficed to erect the monument which now stands at the back of the grave. It was carried out by Anna Fröhlich, Grillparzer and Jenger. The bust was by Franz Dialler, and the cost of the whole was 360 silver florins, 46 kr. The inscription [1] is from the pen of Grillparzer:

DIE TONKUNST BEGRUB HIER EINEN REICHEN BESITZ
ABER NOCH VIEL SCHOENERE HOFFNUNGEN.
FRANZ SCHUBERT LIEGT HIER.
GEBOREN AM XXXI. JÆNNER MDCCXCVII.
GESTORBEN AM XIX. NOV. MDCCCXXVIII.
XXXI JAHRE ALT.[2]

The allusion to fairer hopes has been much criticised, but surely without reason. When we remember in how many departments of music Schubert's latest productions were his best, we are undoubtedly warranted in believing that he would have gone on progressing for many years, had it been the will of God to spare him.

In 1863, owing to the state of dilapidation at which the graves of both Beethoven and Schubert had arrived, the repair of the tombs, and the exhumation and reburial of both, were undertaken by the Gesellschaft der Musikfreunde. The operation was begun on the 12th of October and completed on the 13th. The opportunity was embraced of taking a cast and a photograph of Schubert's skull, and of measuring the principal bones of both skeletons.

1 We have given the inscription exactly as it stands on the monument. Kreissle's version (p. 463), followed by Gumprecht and others, is incorrect in almost every line.

2 MUSIC HAS HERE ENTOMBED A RICH TREASURE,
BUT MUCH FAIRER HOPES.
FRANZ SCHUBERT LIES HERE.
BORN JAN. 31, 1797;
DIED NOV. 19, 1828;
31 YEARS OLD.

The lengths in Schubert's case were to those in Beethoven's as 27 to 29,[3] which implies that as Beethoven was 5 ft. 5 in. high, he was only 5 ft. and $\frac{1}{2}$ an inch. Schubert was reburied in the central cemetery of Vienna on Sept. 23, 1888.

Various memorials have been set up to him in Vienna. The tablets on the houses in which he was born and died have been noticed. They were both carried out by the Männergesang Verein, and completed, the former Oct. 7, 1858, the latter in Nov. 1869. The same Society erected by subscription a monument to him in the Stadt-Park, a sitting figure in Carrara marble by Carl Kuntmann, with the inscription ' Franz Schubert, seinem Andenken der Wiener Männergesangverein, 1872.' It cost 42,000 florins, and was unveiled May 15, 1872.

POSTHUMOUS PUBLICATIONS.—Outside of Austria his death created at first but little sensation. Robert Schumann, then 18, is said to have been deeply affected, and to have burst into tears when the news reached him at Leipzig; Mendelssohn too, though unlike Schubert in temperament, circumstances and education, doubtless fully estimated his loss; and Rellstab, Anna Milder and others in Berlin who knew him, must have mourned him deeply; but the world at large did not yet know enough of his works to understand either what it possessed or what it had lost in that modest reserved young musician of thirtyone. But death always brings a man, especially a young man, into notoriety, and increases public curiosity about his works: and so it was now; the stream of publication at once began and is even yet flowing,[4] neither the supply of works nor the eagerness to obtain them having ceased. The world has not yet recovered from its astonishment as, one after another, the stores accumulated in those dusky heaps of music paper (valued at 8s. 6d.) were made public, each so astonishingly fresh, copious and different from the last. As songs, masses, partsongs, operas, chamber-music of all sorts and all dimensions—pianoforte-sonatas, impromptus and fantasias, duets, trios, quartets, quintet, octet, issued from the press or were heard in manuscript; as each season brought its new symphony, overture, entr'acte, or ballet-music, people began to be staggered by the amount.

' A deep shade of suspicion is beginning to be cast over the authenticity of posthumous compositions. All Paris has been in a state of amazement at the posthumous diligence of the song-writer, F. Schubert, who, while one would think that his ashes repose in peace in Vienna, is still making eternal new songs.' [5] We know better now, but it must be confessed that the doubt was not so unnatural then.

3 See *Actenmässige Darstellung der Ausgrabung und Wiederbeeinsetzung der irdischen Reste von Beethoven und Schubert*, Vienna, Gerold, 1863.
4 The critical edition of Schubert's works was not completed till 1897. See List at the end of this article.          G.
5 *The Musical World* of Jan. 24, 1839, p. 150.

Of the MS. music—an incredible quantity, of which no one then knew the amount or the particulars, partly because there was so much of it, partly because Schubert concealed, or rather forgot, a great deal of his work—a certain number of songs and pianoforte pieces were probably in the hands of publishers at the time of his death, but the great bulk was in the possession of Ferdinand, as his heir. A set of four songs (op. 105) was issued on the day of his funeral. Other songs—opp. 101, 104, 106, 110-112, 116-118; and two PF. duets, the fantasia in F minor (op. 103) and the 'Grand Rondeau' (op. 107)—followed up to April 1829. But the first important publication was the well-known 'Schwanengesang,' so entitled by Haslinger—a collection of fourteen songs, seven by Rellstab, six by Heine, and one by Seidl—unquestionably Schubert's last. They were issued in May 1829, and, to judge by the lists of arrangements and editions given by Nottebohm, have been as much appreciated as the 'Schöne Müllerin' or the 'Winterreise.' A stream of songs followed—for which we must refer the student to Nottebohm's catalogue.

The early part of 1830 [1] saw the execution of a bargain between Diabelli and Ferdinand, by which that firm was guaranteed the property of the following works : opp. 1-32, 35, 39-59, 62, 63, 64, 66-69, 71-77, 84-88, 92-99, 101-104, 106, 108, 109, 113, 115, 116, 119, 121-124, 127, 128, 130, 132-140, 142-153 ; also 154 songs ; 14 vocal quartets ; the canons of 1813 ; a cantata in C for three voices ; the 'Hymn to the Holy Ghost'; Klopstock's 'Stabat Mater' in F minor, and 'Grosses Halleluja'; Magnificat in C; the string quintet in C; four string quartets in C, Bb, G, Bb ; a string trio in Bb ; two sonatas in A and A minor, variations in F, an adagio in Db, and allegretto in C♯—all for PF. solo; sonata for PF. and Arpeggione ; sonata in A, and fantasie in C—both for PF. and violin ; rondo in A for violin and quartet ; adagio and rondo in F for PF. and quartet ; a concert-piece in D for violin and orchestra ; overture in D for orchestra ; overture to third act of the 'Zauberharfe'; 'Lazarus'; 'Tantum ergo' in Eb for four voices and orchestra ; an offertorium in Bb for tenor solo, chorus and orchestra.

Another large portion of Ferdinand's possessions came, sooner or later, into the hands of Dr. Eduard Schneider, son of Franz's sister Theresia. They comprised the autographs of symphonies 1, 2, 3 and 6, and copies of 4 and 5; Autographs of operas: The 'Teufels Lustschloss,' 'Fernando,' 'Der vierjährige Posten,' 'Die Freunde von Salamanka,' 'Die Bürgschaft,' 'Fierrabras,' and 'Sakontala'; the Mass in F;

and the original orchestral parts of the whole of the music to 'Rosamunde.' [2]

On July 10, 1830, Diabelli began the issue of what was entitled 'Franz Schuberts nachgelassene musikalische Dichtungen'; and continued it at intervals till 1850, by which time 50 Parts (*Lieferungen*), containing 137 songs, had appeared. In 1830 he also issued the two astonishing 4-hand marches (op. 121) ; and a set of 20 waltzes (op. 127) ; whilst other houses published the PF. sonatas in A and Eb (opp. 120, 122) ; the two string quartets of the year 1824 (op. 125) ; the D minor quartet, etc. For the progress of the publication after this date we must again refer the reader to Nottebohm's invaluable *Thematic Catalogue* (Vienna, Schreiber, 1874), which contains every detail, and may be implicitly relied on; merely mentioning the principal works, and the year of publication : 'Miriam,' Mass in Bb, three last sonatas and the Grand Duo, 1838 ; symphony in C, 1840 ; fantasie in C, PF. and violin, 1850 ; quartet in G, 1852 ; quintet in C, and octet, 1854 ; 'Gesang der Geister,' 1858 ; 'Verschworenen,' 1862 ; Mass in Eb, 1865 ; 'Lazarus,' 1866 ; symphony in B minor, 1867 ; Mass in Ab, 1875.

There were many other publications of songs, pianoforte pieces, etc., for which the reader is referred to Nottebohm's *Thematic Catalogue*. Of the songs two collections may be signalised as founded on the order of opus numbers : that of Senff of Leipzig, edited by Julius Reitz, 361 songs in 20 vols. and that of Litolff of Brunswick—songs in 10 vols. But neither of these, though styled 'complete' are so. For instance, each omits opp. 83, 110, 129, 165, 172, 173 ; the six songs published by Müller, the forty by Gotthard ; and Litolff also omits opp. 21, 60. A complete edition of Schubert's works was announced by Breitkopf & Härtel on 'Schubert's death-day 1884.' It appeared between 1885 and 1897. For its classification see p. 636.

SCHUMANN'S PROPAGANDA. — Schumann's visit to Vienna in the late autumn of 1838 formed an epoch in the history of the Schubert music. He saw the immense heap of MSS. which remained in Ferdinand's hands even after the mass bought by Diabelli had been taken away, and amongst them several symphonies. Such sympathy and enthusiasm as his must have been a rare delight to the poor desponding brother. His eagle eye soon discovered the worth of these treasures. He picked out several works to be recommended to publishers, but meantime one beyond all the rest riveted his attention—the great symphony of March 1828 (was it the autograph, not yet deposited in the safe keeping of the Gesellschaft der Musikfreund, or a copy ?) and he arranged with Ferdinand to send a transcript of it to Leipzig to Mendelssohn for the Gewandhaus Concerts, where it was

---

[1] The list which follows is taken from *Kreissle*, p. 566 (fl. 245), who apparently had the original document before him. The only date given by Kreissle is 1830, but it must have been early in that year, since op. 121, which forms part of the bargain, was issued in February. Some of the numbers in the list had already been issued as the property of the publishers.

[2] The greater part of these came into the possession of Nicholas Dumba of Vienna.

produced Mar. 21, 1839,[1] and repeated no less than three times during the following season. His chamber-music was becoming gradually known in the North, and as early as 1833 is occasionally met with in the Berlin and Leipzig programmes. David, who led the taste in chamber music in the latter place, was devoted to Schubert. He gradually introduced his works, until there were few seasons in which the quartets in A minor, D minor (the score of which he edited for Senff), and G, the string quintet in C (a special favourite), the octet, both trios, the PF. quintet and the 'Rondeau brillant,' were not performed amid great applause at his concerts. Schumann had long been a zealous Schubert propagandist. From an early date his *Zeitschrift* contains articles of more or less length, always inspired by an ardent admiration ; Schubert's letters and poems and his brother's excellent short sketch of his life, printed in vol. x. (Apr. 23 to May 3, 1839) —obvious fruits of Schumann's Vienna visit —are indispensable materials for Schubert's biography ; when the symphony was performed he dedicated to it one of his longest and most genial effusions,[2] and each fresh piece was greeted with a hearty welcome as it fell from the press. One of Schumann's especial favourites was the E♭ trio ; he liked it even better than that in B♭, and has left a memorandum of his fondness in the opening of the adagio of his symphony in C, which is identical, in key and intervals, with that of Schubert's andante. The enthusiasm of these prominent musicians, the repeated performances of the symphony and its publication by Breitkopf (in Jan. 1850), naturally gave Schubert a strong hold on Leipzig, at that time the most active musical centre of Europe ; and after the foundation of the Conservatorium in 1843 many English and American students must have carried back the love of his romantic and tuneful music to their own countries.

SPREAD OF SCHUBERT'S MUSIC.—Several performances of large works had taken place in Vienna since Schubert's death, chiefly through the exertions of Ferdinand and of a certain Leitermayer, one of Franz's early friends ; such as the E♭ Mass at the parish church of Maria Trost on Nov. 15, 1829 ; 'Miriam,' with Lachner's orchestration, at a Gesellschaft concert in 1830 ; two new overtures in 1833 ; an overture in E, the chorus of spirits from 'Rosamunde,' the 'Grosses Halleluja,' etc., early in 1835, and four large concerted pieces from 'Fierrabras' later in the year ; an overture in D ; the finale of the last symphony ; a march

and chorus, and an air and chorus, from 'Fierrabras,' in April 1836 ; another new overture, and several new compositions from the 'Remains,' in the winter of 1837–38. As far as can be judged by the silence of the Vienna newspapers, these passed almost unnoticed. Even the competition with North Germany failed to produce the effect which might have been expected. It did indeed excite the Viennese to one effort. On the 15th of the December following the production of the symphony at Leipzig its performance was attempted at Vienna, but though the whole work was announced,[3] such had been the difficulties at rehearsal that the first two movements alone were given, and they were only carried off by the interpolation of an air from 'Lucia' between them.

But symphonies and symphonic works can hardly be expected to float rapidly ; songs are more buoyant, and Schubert's songs soon began to make their way outside, as they had long since done in his native place. Wherever they once penetrated their success was certain. In Paris, where spirit, melody and romance are the certain criterions of success, and where nothing dull or obscure is tolerated, they were introduced by Nourrit, and were so much liked as actually to find a transient place in the programmes of the concerts of the Conservatoire, the stronghold of musical toryism.[4] The first French collection was published in 1834, by Richault, with translation by Bélanger. It contained six songs—'Die Post,' 'Ständchen,' 'Am Meer,' 'Das Fischermädchen,' 'Der Tod und das Mädchen,' and 'Schlummerlied.' The 'Erl King' and others followed. A larger collection, with translation by Emil Deschamps, was issued by Brandus in 1838 or 1839. It is entitled 'Collection des Lieder de Franz Schubert,' and contains sixteen—'La jeune religieuse,' 'Marguérite,' 'Le roi des aulnes,' 'La rose,' 'La sérénade,' 'La poste,' 'Ave Maria,' 'La cloche des agonisants,' 'La jeune fille et la morte,' 'Rosemonde,' 'Les plaintes de la jeune fille,' 'Adieu,' 'Les astres,' 'La jeune mère,' 'La Berceuse,' 'Éloge des larmes.'[5] Except that one—'Adieu'[6]—is spurious, the selection does great credit to Parisian taste. This led the way to the 'Quarante mélodies de Schubert' of Richault, Launer, etc., a thin 8vo volume, to which many an English amateur is indebted for his first acquaintance with these treasures of life. By 1845 Richault had published as many as 150 with French words.

[1] Mar. 22 in the *Allg. Mus. Zeitung*, Mar. 21 in Schumann's paper. The symphony was repeated Dec. 12, 1839, Mar. 12, and Apr. 3, 1840. Mendelssohn made a few cuts in the work for performance.

[2] *Ges. Schriften*, iii. 195. Schumann's expressions leave no doubt that the symphony in C was in Ferdinand's possession at the time of his visit. This and many others of his articles on Schubert have been translated into English by Miss M. E. von Glehn and Mrs. Ritter.

[3] The MS. parts in the possession of the Musikverein show the most cruel cuts, possibly with a view to this performance. In the finale, one of the most essential and effective sections of the movement is clean expunged.

[4] 'La jeune religieuse' and 'Le roi des aulnes' were sung by Nourrit, at the concerts of Jan. 18 and Apr. 26, 1835, respectively —the latter with orchestral accompaniment. On Mar. 20, 1836 'Marguérite' was sung by Mlle. Falcon, and there the list stops.

[5] This list is copied from the Paris correspondence of the *A.M.Z.* 1839, p. 394.

[6] This song is made up of phrases from Schubert's songs and will probably always be attributed to him. It stands even in Pauer's edition. But it is by A. H. von Weyrauch, who published it himself in 1824. See Nottebohm's *Catalogue*, p. 254.

Some of the chamber music also soon obtained a certain popularity in Paris, through the playing of Tilmant, Urhan and Alkan, and later of Alard and Franchomme. The trio in B♭, issued by Richault in 1838, was the first instrumental work of Schubert's published in France. There is a 'Collection complète' of the solo PF. works published by Richault in 8vo, containing the Fantasie (op. 15), ten sonatas, the two Russian marches, Impromptus, Moments musicals, five single pieces, and nine sets of dances. Liszt and Heller kept the flame alive by their transcriptions of the songs and waltzes. Habeneck attempted to rehearse the symphony in C in 1842, but the band refused to go beyond the first movement, and Schubert's name up to this date (1881) appears in the programmes of the concerts of the Conservatoire attached to three songs only. Pasdeloup introduced the symphony in C and the fragments of that in B minor.

Liszt's devotion to Schubert was great and unceasing We have already mentioned his production of 'Alfonso und Estrella' at Weimar in 1854, but it is right to give a list of his transcriptions, which have done a very great deal to introduce Schubert into many quarters where his compositions would otherwise have been a sealed book. His first transcription— 'Die Rose,' op. 73—was made in 1834, and appeared in Paris the same year.[1] It was followed in 1838 by the 'Ständchen,' 'Post,' and 'Lob der Thränen,' and in 1839 by the 'Erl King' and by twelve Lieder. These again by six Lieder ; four 'Geistliche Lieder ; ' six of the 'Müllerlieder' ; the 'Schwanengesang,' and the 'Winterreise.' Liszt also transcribed the 'Divertissement à la hongroise,' three marches and nine 'Valses-caprices,' or 'Soirées de Vienne,' after Schubert's op. 67. All the above are for PF. solo. He also scored the accompaniment to the 'Junge Nonne,' 'Gretchen am Spinnrade,' 'So lasst mich scheinen' and the 'Erl King,' for a small orchestra ; adapted the 'Allmacht' for tenor solo, male chorus and orchestra, and converted the fantasie in C (op. 15) into a concerto for PF. and orchestra. Some will think these changes indefensible, but there is no doubt that they are done in a masterly manner, and that many of them have become very popular. Heller's arrangements are confined to six favourite songs.

ENGLISH PUBLICATIONS AND PERFORMANCES. —England made an appearance in the field with the 'Moment musical' in F minor in 1831, followed in 1832 by the 'Erl King' and the 'Wanderer.' In 1836 Mr. Ayrton printed 'The Letter of Flowers' and 'The Secret,' in the Musical Library, to Oxenford's translation. Mr. Wessel (Ashdown & Parry) had begun his 'Series of German Songs' earlier than this, and

by 1840, out of a total of 197, the list included 38 of Schubert's, remarkably well chosen, and including several of the finest though less known ones, e.g. 'Ganymed,' 'An den Tod,' 'Sei mir gegrüsst,' 'Die Rose,' etc. etc. Ewer's 'Gems of German Song,' containing many of Schubert's, were begun in Sept. 1837. Schubert's music took a long time before it obtained any public footing in this country. The first time it appears in the Philharmonic programmes—then so ready to welcome novelties—is on May 20, 1839, when Ivanoff sang the Serenade in the 'Schwanengesang' to Italian words, 'Quando avvolta.' Staudigl gave the 'Wanderer,' May 8, 1843. On June 10, 1844, the overture to 'Fierrabras' was played under Mendelssohn's direction, and on June 17 the 'Junge Nonne' was sung to French words by M. de Revial, Mendelssohn playing the magnificent accompaniment. We blush to say, however, that neither piece met with approval.[2] Mendelssohn conducted the last five Philharmonic concerts of that season (1844), and amongst other orchestral music new to England had brought with him Schubert's symphony in C and his own overture to 'Ruy Blas.' At the rehearsal on June 10, however, the behaviour of the band towards the symphony—excited, it is said, by the continual triplets in the finale—was so insulting that he refused either to go on with it or to allow his own overture to be tried. But the misbehaviour of our leading orchestra did not produce the effect which it had done in Paris ; others were found to take up the treasures thus rudely rejected, and Schubert has had an ample revenge.

The centres for his music in England have been—for the orchestral and choral works, the Crystal Palace, Sydenham and Hallé's Concerts, Manchester ; and for the chamber music, the Popular Concerts and Hallé's Recitals. At the Crystal Palace the symphony in C was in the repertory of the Saturday Concerts from Apr. 5, 1856 ; the two movements of the B minor symphony were first played Apr. 6, 1867, and constantly repeated. The six other MS. symphonies were obtained from Dr. Schneider in 1867 and since, and have been played at various dates, a performance of the whole eight in chronological order forming a feature in the series of 1880–81. The 'Rosamunde' music was first played Nov. 10, 1866, and the 'air de ballet' in G, Mar. 16, 1867. Joachim's orchestration of the Grand Duo (op. 140) was given Mar. 4, 1876. The overtures to 'Alfonso und Estrella,' 'Fierrabras,' 'Freunde von Salamanka,' 'Teufels Lustschloss' and that 'in the Italian style' have been frequently heard. 'Miriam's Song' was first given Nov. 14, 1868 (and three times since) ; the 'Conspirators,' Mar. 2, 1872 ; the 23rd Psalm, Feb. 21, 1874 ; the E♭ Mass, Mar. 29,

---

[1] These particulars are taken partly from Miss Ramann's *Life of Liszt*, and partly from Liszt's *Thematic Catalogue*. The third No of the 'Apparitions' is founded on a waltz melody of Schubert's.

[2] *The Musical World*, 1844, p. 197.

1879.[1] At the Popular Concerts a beginning was made May 16, 1859, with the A minor quartet, the D major sonata and the 'Rondeau brillant.' Afterwards the D major and G major quartets, many sonatas and other PF. pieces were added, and the octet, the quintet in C and the two trios were repeated season by season, and enthusiastically received. The quartet in B♭, the trio in the same key, the sonata for PF. and arpeggione, etc., were brought to a hearing. A large number of songs were made familiar to the subscribers to these concerts through the fine interpretation of Stockhausen, Mme. Joachim, Miss Sophie Löwe, Santley, Henschel and other singers. At Hallé's admirable recitals at St. James's Hall, from their commencement in 1861 all the published sonatas were repeatedly played; not only the popular ones, but of those less known none were given less than twice; the fantasia in C, op. 15, three times; the PF. quintet, the fantasia for PF. and violin, the impromptus and Moments musicals, the '5 pieces,' the '3 pieces,' the adagio and rondo, the valses nobles, and other numbers of this fascinating music were heard again and again.

The other principal publications in England are the vocal scores of the six masses, the PF. accompaniment arranged from the full score by Ebenezer Prout, published by Augener—the 1st, 2nd, 3rd, 4th in 1871, the 6th (E♭) in 1872, and the 5th (A♭) in 1875.[2] The masses have been also published by Novello, both with Latin and English words ('Communion Service'); and the same firm published 'Miriam,' in two forms, and the 'Rosamunde' music, both vocal score and orchestral parts. Augener also published editions of the PF. works, and of a large number of songs, by Pauer.

PORTRAITS.—Schubert was not sufficiently important during his lifetime to attract the attention of painters, and although he had more than one artist in his circle there are but three portraits of him known. 1. A poor stiff head by Leopold Kupelwieser, full face, taken July 10, 1821, photographed by Mietke and Wawra of Vienna, and wretchedly engraved as the frontispiece to Kreissle's biography. 2. A very characteristic half-length, three-quarter-face, in water-colours, by W. A. Rieder, taken in 1825, in possession of Dr. Granitsch of Vienna.[3] A *replica* by the artist, dated 1840, is now in the Musikverein. It has been engraved by Passini, and we here give the head, from a photograph expressly taken from the original (*PLATE LXXI.*). 3. The bust on the tomb, which gives a very prosaic version of his features.

PERSONALIA.—His exterior by no means answered to his genius. His general appearance was insignificant. As we have already said, he was probably not more than 5 feet and 1 inch high, his figure was stout and clumsy, with a round back and shoulders (perhaps due to incessant writing) fleshy arms and thick short fingers. His complexion was pasty, nay even tallowy; his cheeks were full, his eyebrows bushy and his nose insignificant. But there were two things that to a great extent redeemed these insignificant traits—his hair, which was black,[4] and remarkably thick and vigorous,[5] as if rooted in the brain within; and his eyes, which were truly 'the windows of his soul,' and even through the spectacles he constantly wore were so bright as at once to attract attention.[6] If Rieder's portrait may be trusted—and it is said to be very faithful, though perhaps a little too *fine*—they had a peculiarly steadfast penetrating look, which irresistibly reminds one of the firm rhythm of his music. His glasses are inseparable from his face. One of our earliest glimpses of him is 'a little boy in spectacles' at the *Convict*; he habitually slept in them; and within eighteen months of his death we see him standing in the window at Döbling, his glasses pushed up over his forehead, and Grillparzer's verses held close to his searching eyes. He had the broad strong jaw of all great men, and a marked assertive prominence of the lips. He had a beautiful set of teeth (Benedict). When at rest the expression of his face was uninteresting, but it brightened up at the mention of music, especially that of Beethoven. His voice was something between a soft tenor and a baritone. He sang 'like a composer,' without the least affectation or attempt.[7]

A CHARACTER STUDY.—His general disposition was in accordance with his countenance. His sensibility, though his music shows it was extreme, was not roused by the small things of life. He had little of that jealous susceptibility which too often distinguishes musicians, more irritable even than the 'irritable race of poets.' His attitude towards Rossini and Weber proves this. When a post which he much coveted was given to another,[8] he expressed his satisfaction at its being bestowed on so competent a man. Transparent truthfulness, good-humour, a cheerful contented evenness, fondness for a joke and a desire to remain in the background—such were his prominent characteristics in ordinary life. But we have seen how this apparently impassive man could be moved by a poem which appealed

---

[1] This list of achievements was primarily due to the enthusiasm of Grove himself, who as secretary of the Crystal Palace inspired the pioneer work done by Manns and his orchestra. See C. L. Graves, *Life of Sir George Grove*, p. 52.

[2] Reviewed by E. Prout in *Concordia* for 1875, pp. 8, 29, 109, etc.

[3] He bought it in Feb. 1881 for 1205 florins, or about £120. It is about 8 inches high, by 6 wide. It was taken, or begun, while Schubert took refuge in the artist's house from a storm (Pohl).

[4] We have three hairs of Schubert's (given to my brother by his great-niece Caroline Geisler Schubert, a pianist long resident in London); they are by no means *black*, rather of a warm auburn tint.

E. J. H[5].

[5] All three portraits agree in this. An eminent surgeon of our own day is accustomed to say, 'Never trust a man with a great head of black hair, he is sure to be an enthusiast.'

[6] W. v. Chezy, *Erinnerungen—*' with eyes so brilliant as at the first glance to betray the fire within.'

[7] Bauernfeld.

[8] Weigl.

## LXXI

WEBER

From a sketch made in London in 1826, now in the R.C.M.

SCHUBERT

From a lithograph by J. Kriehuber

to him, or by such music as Beethoven's C♯ minor quartet.[1] This unfailing good-nature, this sweet lovableness, doubtless enhanced by his reserve, was what attached Schubert to his friends. They admired him ; but they loved him still more. Ferdinand perfectly adored him, and even the derisive Ignaz melts when he takes leave.[2] Hardly a letter from Schwind, Schober, or Bauernfeld, that does not amply testify to this. Their only complaint is that he will not return their passion, that ' the affection of years is not enough to overcome his distrust and fear of seeing himself appreciated and beloved.'[3] Even strangers who met him in this *entourage* were as much captivated as his friends. J. A. Berg of Stockholm, who was in Vienna in 1827, as a young man of twenty-four, and met him at the Bogners', speaks of him[4] with the clinging affection which such personal charm inspires.

He was never really at his ease except among his chosen associates. When with them he was genial and compliant. At the dances of his friends he would extemporise the most lovely waltzes for hours together, or accompany song after song. He was even boisterous—playing the ' Erl King ' on a comb, fencing, howling and making many practical jokes. But in good society he was shy and silent, his face grave ; a word of praise distressed him, he would repel the admiration when it came, and escape into the next room, or out of the house, at the first possible moment. In consequence he was over-looked, and of his important friends few knew, or showed that they knew, what a treasure they had within their reach. A great player like Bocklet, after performing the B♭ trio, could kneel to kiss the composer's hand in rapture, and with broken voice stammer forth his homage, but there is no trace of such tribute from the upper classes. What a contrast to Beethoven's position among his aristocratic friends—their devotion and patience, his contemptuous be-haviour, the amount of pressing necessary to make him play, his scorn of emotion and love of applause after he had finished ! (See Vol. I. p. 265.) The same contrast is visible in the dedications of the music of the two—Beethoven's chiefly to crowned heads and nobility, Schubert's in large proportion to his friends. It is also evident in the music itself, as we shall endeavour presently to bring out.

He played, as he sang, ' like a composer,' that is, with less of technique than of knowledge and expression. Of the virtuoso he had absolutely nothing. He improvised in the intervals of throwing on his clothes, or at other times when the music within was too strong to be resisted, but as an exhibition or performance never, and there is no record of his playing any music but his own. He occasionally accompanied his songs

at concerts (always keeping very strict time), but we never hear of his having extemporised or played a piece in public in Vienna. Notwith-standing the shortness of his fingers, which some-times got tired,[5] he could play most of his own pieces, and with such force and beauty as to compel a musician[6] who was listening to one of his latest sonatas to exclaim, ' I admire your playing more than your music,' an exclamation susceptible of two interpretations, of which Schubert is said to have taken the unfavourable one. But accompaniment was his *forte*, and of this we have already spoken (see pp. 606, 611, etc.). Duet-playing was a favourite recreation with him. Schober Gahy and others were his companions in this, and Gahy has left on record his admiration of the clean rapid playing, the bold conception and perfect grasp of expression, and the clever droll remarks that would drop from him during the piece.

His life as a rule was regular, even monotonous. He composed or studied habitually for six or seven hours every morning. This was one of the methodical habits which he had learned from his good old father ; others were the old-fashioned punctilious style of addressing strangers which struck Hiller[7] with such consternation and the dating of his music. He was ready to write directly he tumbled out of bed, and remained steadily at work till two. ' When I have done one piece I begin the next ' was his explanation to a visitor in 1827 ; and one of these mornings produced six of the songs in the 'Winterreise' ! At two he dined—when there was money enough for dinner—either at the Gasthaus, where in those days it cost a 'Zwanziger' (8½d.), or with a friend or patron ; and the afternoon was spent in making music, as at Mme. Lacsny-Buchwieser's (p. 611), or in walking in the environs of Vienna. If the weather was fine the walk was often prolonged till late, regardless of engage-ments in town ; but if this was not the case, he was at the coffee-house by five, smoking his pipe and ready to joke with any of his set ; then came an hour's music, as at Sofie Müller's (p. 605) ; then the theatre, and supper at the Gasthaus again, and the coffee-house, sometimes till far into the morning. In those days no Viennese, certainly no young bachelor, dined at home ; so that the repeated visits to the Gasthaus need not shock the sensibilities of any English lover of Schubert. (See p. 609.) Nor let any one be led away with the notion that he was a sot, as some seem prone to believe. How could a sot—how could any one who even lived freely, and woke with a heavy head or a disordered stomach—have worked as he worked, and have composed nearly 1000 such works as his in eighteen years, or have performed the feats of

. See pp. 587, 618.    [2] *K.H.* p. 149 (i. 151).
[3] Schwind, in *K.H.* p. 345 (ii. 28).    [4] In a letter to the writer.

[5] Bauernfeld.    [6] Horzalka.    *K.H.* p. 128 (i. 132).
[7] *Künstlerleben*, p. 49. ' Schubert I find mentioned in my journal as a *quiet man*—possibly not always so, though it was only amongst his intimates that he broke out. When I visited him in his modest lodging he received me kindly, but so respectfully, as quite to frighten me.'

rapidity that Schubert did in the way of opera, symphony, quartet, song, which we have enumerated? No set could write six of the 'Winterreise' songs—perfect, enduring works of art—in one morning, and that no singular feat! Your Morlands and Poes are obliged to wait their time, and produce a few works as their brain and their digestion will allow them, instead of being always ready for their greatest efforts, as Mozart and Schubert were. Schubert—like Mozart—loved society and its accompaniments; he would have been no Viennese if he had not; and he may have been occasionally led away; but such escapades were rare. He does not appear to have cared for the other sex, or to have been attractive to them as Beethoven was notwithstanding his ugliness. This simplicity curiously characterises his whole life; no feats of memory are recorded of him as they so often are of other great musicians; the records of his life contain nothing to quote. His letters, some forty in all, are evidently forced from him. 'Heavens and Earth,' says he, 'it's frightful having to describe one's travels; I cannot write any more.' 'Dearest friend'—on another occasion —'you will be astonished at my writing: I am so myself.' [1] Strange contrast to the many interesting epistles of Mozart and Mendelssohn, and the numberless notes of Beethoven! Beethoven was well read, a politician, thought much and talked eagerly on many subjects. Mozart and Mendelssohn both drew; travelling was a part of their lives; they were men of the world, and Mendelssohn was master of many accomplishments. Schumann too, though a Saxon of Saxons, had travelled much, and while a most prolific composer, was a practised literary man. But Schubert has nothing of the kind to show. He not only never travelled out of Austria, but he never proposed it, and it is difficult to conceive of his doing so. To picture or work of art he very rarely refers. He expressed himself with such difficulty that it was all but impossible to argue with him.[2] Besides the letters just mentioned, a few pages of diary and four or five poems are all that he produced except his music. In literature his range was wide indeed, but it all went into his music; and he was strangely uncritical. He seems to have been hardly able—at any rate he did not care—to discriminate between the magnificent songs of Goethe, Schiller and Mayrhofer, the feeble domesticities of Kosegarten and Hölty and the turgid couplets of the authors of his librettos. All came alike to his omnivorous appetite. But the fact is that, apart from his music, Schubert's life was little or nothing, and that is its most peculiar and most interesting fact. Music and music alone was to him all in all. It was not his *principal* mode of expression, it was his *only* one; it swallowed up every other.

His afternoon walks, his evening amusements, were all so many preparations for the creations of the following morning. No doubt he enjoyed the country, but the effect of the walk is to be found in his music and his music only. He left, as we have said, no letters to speak of, no journal; there is no record of his ever having poured out his soul in confidence, as Beethoven did in the 'Will,' in the three mysterious letters to some unknown Beloved, or in his conversations with Bettina. He made no impression even on his closest friends beyond that of natural kindness, goodness, truth and reserve. His life is all summed up in his music. No memoir of Schubert can ever be satisfactory, because no relation can be established between his life and his music; or rather, properly speaking, because there is no life to establish a relation with. The one scale of the balance is absolutely empty, the other is full to overflowing. In his music we have fluency, depth, acuteness and variety of expression, unbounded imagination, the happiest thoughts, never-tiring energy and a sympathetic tenderness beyond belief. And these were the result of natural gifts and of the incessant practice to which they forced him; for it seems certain that of education in music—meaning by education the severe course of training in the mechanical portions of their art to which Mozart and Mendelssohn were subjected—he had little or nothing. As we have already mentioned, the two musicians who professed to instruct him, Holzer and Ruzicka, were so astonished at his ability that they contented themselves with wondering and allowing him to go his own way. And they are responsible for that want of counterpoint which was an embarrassment to him all his life, and drove him, during his last illness, to seek lessons. (See p. 618.) What he learned, he learned mostly for himself, from playing in the *Convict* orchestra, from incessant writing, and from reading the best scores he could obtain; and, to use the expressive term of his friend Mayrhofer, remained a 'Naturalist' to the end of his life. From the operas of the Italian masters, which were recommended to him by Salieri, he advanced to those of Mozart, and of Mozart abundant traces appear in his earlier instrumental works. In 1814 Beethoven was probably still tabooed in the *Convict*; and beyond the 'Prometheus' music and the first two symphonies, a pupil there would not be likely to encounter anything of his.

## A STUDY OF THE MUSIC

INSTRUMENTAL.—The first symphony dates from 1814 (his 18th year), and between that and 1818 we have five more. These are all much tinctured by what he was hearing and reading—Haydn, Mozart, Rossini, Beethoven (the last but slightly, for reasons just hinted at). Now and

---

[1] *K.H.* p. 368 (ii. 55); p. 417 (ii. 104).
[2] Seyfried, in Schilling's *Lexicon*.

then—as in the second subjects of the first and last allegros of symphony 1, the first subject of the opening allegro of symphony 2, and the andante of symphony 5, the themes are virtually reproduced — no doubt unconsciously. The treatment is more his own, especially in regard to the use of the wind instruments, and to the 'working out' of the movements, where his want of education drives him to the repetition of the subject in various keys, and similar artifices, in place of contrapuntal treatment. In the slow movement and finale of the 'Tragic' symphony, No. 4, we have exceedingly happy examples, in which, without absolutely breaking away from the old world, Schubert has revealed an amount of original feeling and an extraordinary beauty of treatment which already stamp him as a great orchestral composer. But whether always original or not in their subjects, no one can listen to these first six symphonies without being impressed with their *individuality*. Single phrases may remind us of other composers, the treatment may often be traditional, but there is a fluency and continuity, a happy cheerfulness, an earnestness and want of triviality and an absence of labour, which proclaim a new composer. The writer is evidently writing because what he has to say must come out, even though he may occasionally couch it in the phrases of his predecessors. Beauty and profusion of melody reign throughout. The tone is often plaintive but never obscure, and there is always the irrepressible gaiety of youth and of Schubert's own Viennese nature, ready and willing to burst forth. His treatment of particular instruments, especially the wind, is already quite his own—a happy *conversational* way which at a later period becomes highly characteristic. At length, in the B minor symphony (Oct. 30, 1822), we meet with something which never existed in the world before in orchestral music—a new class of thoughts and a new mode of expression which distinguish him entirely from his predecessors, characteristics which are fully maintained in the 'Rosamunde' music (Christmas 1823), and culminate in the great C major symphony (March 1828).

The same general remarks apply to the other instrumental compositions—the quartets and PF. sonatas. These often show a close adherence to the style of the old school, but are always effective and individual, and occasionally, like the symphonies, varied by original and charming movements, as the trio in the E♭ quartet, or the minuet and trio in the E major one (op. 125, 1 and 2), the sonata in A minor (1817), etc. The visit to Zselész in 1824, with its Hungarian experiences, and the pianoforte proclivities of the Esterhazys, seem to have given him a new impetus in the direction of chamber music. It was the immediate or proximate cause of the 'Grand Duo'—that

splendid work in which, with Beethoven in his eye, Schubert was never more himself—and the 'Divertissement à la hongroise'; as well as the beautiful and intensely personal string quartet in A minor, which has been not wrongly said to be the most characteristic work of any composer; ultimately also of the D minor and G major quartets, the string quintet in C, and the last three sonatas, in all of which the Hungarian element is strongly perceptible—all the more strongly because we hardly detect it at all in the songs and vocal works.

Here then, at 1822 in the orchestral works, and 1824 in the chamber music, we may perhaps draw the line between Schubert's mature and immature compositions. The step from the symphony in C of 1818 to the unfinished symphony in B minor, or to the 'Rosamunde' entr'acte in the same key, is quite as great as Beethoven's was from No. 2 to the Eroica, or Mendelssohn's from the C minor to the Italian symphony. All trace of his predecessors is gone, and he stands alone in his own undisguised and pervading personality. All trace of his youth has gone too. Life has become serious, nay cruel; and a deep earnestness and pathos animate all his utterances. Similarly in the chamber music, the octet stands on the line, and all the works which have made their position and are acknowledged as great are on this side of it—the Grand Duo, the Divertissement à la hongroise,' the PF. sonatas in A minor, D and B♭, the fantasie-sonata in G; the impromptus and moments musicals; the string quartets in A minor, D minor and G; the string quintet in C; the 'Rondo brillant'—in short, all the works which the world thinks of when it mentions Schubert (we are speaking now of instrumental music only) are on this side of 1822. On the other side of the line, in both cases, orchestra and chamber, are a vast number of works full of beauty, interest and life; breathing youth in every bar, absolute Schubert in many movements or passages, but not completely saturated with him, not of sufficiently independent power to assert their rank with the others, or to compensate for the diffuseness and repetition which remained characteristics of their author to the last, but which in the later works are hidden or atoned for by the astonishing force, beauty, romance and personality inherent in the contents of the music. These early works will always be more than interesting; and no lover of Schubert but must regard them with the strong affection and fascination which his followers feel for every bar he wrote. But the judgment of the world at large will probably always remain what it now is.

He was, as Liszt so finely said, ' *le musicien le plus poète que jamais* '—the most poetical musician that ever was; and the main characteristics of his music will always be its vivid personality, fullness and poetry. In the case of other great composers, the mechanical skill and ingenuity, the very ease and absence of effort with which many of their effects are produced, or their pieces constructed, is a great element in the pleasure produced by their music. Not so with Schubert. In listening to him one is never betrayed into exclaiming 'How clever!' but very often 'How poetical, how beautiful, how intensely Schubert!' The impression produced by his great works is that the means are nothing and the effect everything. Not that he had no technical skill. Counterpoint he was deficient in, but the power of writing whatever he wanted he had absolutely at his fingers' end. No one had ever written more, and the notation of his ideas must have been done without an effort. In the words of Macfarren,[1] 'the committing his works to paper was a process that accompanied their composition like the writing of an ordinary letter that is indited at the very paper.' In fact we know, if we had not the manuscripts to prove it, that he wrote with the greatest ease and rapidity, and could keep up a conversation, not only while writing down but while inventing his best works; that he never hesitated; very rarely revised—it would often have been better if he had; and never seems to have aimed at making innovations or doing things for effect. For instance, in the number and arrangement of the movements, his symphonies and sonatas never depart from the regular Haydn pattern. They rarely show æsthetic artifices, such as quoting the theme of one movement in another movement,[2] or running them into each other; changing their order, or introducing extra ones; mixing various times simultaneously — or similar mechanical means of producing unity or making novel effects, which often surprise and please us in Beethoven, Schumann, Mendelssohn and Spohr. Nor did he ever indicate a programme, or prefix a motto to any of his works. His matter is so abundant and so full of variety and interest that he never seems to think of enhancing it by any devices. He did nothing to extend the formal limits of symphony or sonata, but he endowed them with a magic, a romance, a sweet naturalness, which no one has yet approached (see SONATA and SYMPHONY). And as in the general structure so in the single movements. A simple canon, as in the Eb trio, the andante of the B minor or the scherzo of the C major symphonies; an occasional round, as in the masses and partsongs;—such is pretty nearly all the science that he affords. His vocal fugues are notoriously weak, and the symphonies rarely show

those piquant *fugatos* which are so delightful in Beethoven and Mendelssohn. On the other hand, in all that is necessary to express his thoughts and feelings, and to convey them to the hearer, he is inferior to none. Such passages as the return to the subject in the andante of the B minor symphony, or in the ballet air in G of 'Rosamunde'; as the famous horn passage in the andante of the C major symphony—which Schumann happily compares to a being from the other world gliding about the orchestra—or the equally beautiful violoncello solo farther on in the same movement, are unsurpassed in orchestral music for felicity and beauty, and have an emotional effect which no learning could give. There is a place in the working-out of the Rosamunde Entr'acte in B minor (change into G♯) in which the combination of modulation and scoring produces a weird and overpowering feeling quite exceptional, and the change to the major near the end of the same great work will always astonish. One of the most prominent beauties in these orchestral works is the exquisite and entirely fresh manner in which the wind instruments are combined. Even in his earliest symphonies he begins that method of dialogue by interchange of phrases, which rises at last to the well-known and lovely passages in the overture to 'Rosamunde' (2nd subject), the trios of the Bb entr'acte, and the 'Air de ballet' in the same music, and in the andantes of the B minor and C major symphonies. No one has ever combined wind instruments as these are combined. To quote Schumann once more—they talk and intertalk like human beings. It is no artful concealment of art. The artist vanishes altogether, and the loving, simple, human friend remains. It were well to be dumb in articulate speech with such a power of utterance at command! If anything were wanting to convince us of the absolute inspiration of such music as this it would be the fact that Schubert never can have heard either of the two symphonies which we have just been citing.

But to return to the orchestra. The trombones were favourite instruments with Schubert in his later life. In the fugal movements of his two last masses he makes them accompany the voices in unison with a persistence which is sometimes almost unbearable for its monotony. In portions of the C major symphony also some may possibly find them too much used.[3] But in other parts of the masses they are beautifully employed, and in the introduction and allegro of the symphony they are used with a noble effect, which not improbably suggested to Schumann the equally impressive use of them in his Bb symphony. The accompaniments to his subjects are always of great ingenuity and originality, and full of life and

---

[1] Philharmonic programme, May 22, 1871
[2] Instances may be quoted from the 'Rondo brillant,' op. 70, where part of the introduction is repeated in the Rondo, and from the PF. trio in E flat, op. 100, where the principal theme of the slow movement is repeated in the finale. The Wanderer fantasia is the most conspicuous instance.    C.

[3] There is a tradition that he doubted this himself, and referred the score to Lachner for his opinion.

maracter. The triplets in the finale to the C major symphony, which excited the *mal à propos* merriment of the Philharmonic orchestra (see p. 623), are a very striking instance. Another is the incessant run of semiquavers in the second violins and violas which accompany the second theme in the finale of the Tragic symphony. Another, of which he is very fond, is the employment of a recurring monotonous figure in the inner parts:

often running to great length, as in the andantes of the Tragic and B minor symphonies; the moderato of the B♭ sonata; the fine song 'Viola' (op. 123, at the return to A♭ in the middle of the song), etc. etc. In his best PF. music, the accompaniments are most happily fitted to the leading part, so as never to clash or produce discord. Rapidly as he wrote he did these things as if they were calculated. But they never obtrude themselves or become prominent. They are all merged and absorbed in the gaiety, pathos, and personal interest of the music itself, and of the man who is uttering through it his griefs and joys, his hopes and fears, in so direct and touching a manner as no composer ever did before or since, and with no thought of an audience, of fame, or success, or any other external thing. No one who listens to it can doubt that Schubert wrote for himself alone. His music is the simple utterance of the feelings with which his mind is full. If he had thought of his audience, or the effect he would produce, or the capabilities of the means he was employing, he would have taken more pains in the revision of his works. Indeed the most affectionate disciple of Schubert must admit that the want of revision is often but too apparent.

In his instrumental music he is often very diffuse. When a passage pleases him he generally repeats it at once, almost note for note. He will reiterate a passage over and over in different keys, as if he could never have done. In the songs this does not offend; and even here, if we knew what he was thinking of, as we do in the songs, we might possibly find the repetitions just. In the E♭ trio he repeats in the finale a characteristic accompaniment which is very prominent in the first movement and which originally belongs perhaps to the A♭ impromptu (op. 90, No. 4)—and a dozen other instances of the same kind might be quoted.[1] This arose in great part from his imperfect

education, but in great part also from the furious pace at which he dashed down his thoughts and feelings, apparently without previous sketch, note, or preparation; and from his habit of never correcting a piece after it was once on paper. Had he done so he would doubtless have taken out many a repetition and some trivialities which seem terribly out of place amid the usual nobility and taste of his thoughts. It was doubtless this diffuseness and apparent want of aim, as well as the jolly, untutored *naïveté* of some of his subjects (rondo of D major sonata, etc.), and the incalculable amount of modulation, that made Mendelssohn shrink from some of Schubert's instrumental works, and even go so far as to call the D minor quartet *schlechte Musik*—i.e. 'nasty music.' But unless to musicians whose fastidiousness is somewhat abnormal—as Mendelssohn's was—such criticisms only occur afterwards, on reflection; for during the progress of the work all is absorbed in the intense life and personality of the music. And what beauties there are to put against these redundances! Take such movements as the first allegro of the A minor sonata or the B♭ sonata; the G major fantasia-sonata; the two characteristic marches; the impromptus and Moments musicals; the minuet of the A minor quartet; the variations of the D minor quartet; the finale of the B♭ trio; the first two movements, or the trio, of the string quintet; the two movements of the B minor symphony, or the wonderful entr'acte in the same key in 'Rosamunde'; the finale of the last symphony—think of the abundance of the thoughts, the sudden surprises, the wonderful transitions, the extraordinary pathos of the turns of melody and modulation, the absolute manner (to repeat once more) in which they bring you into contact with the affectionate, tender, suffering personality of the composer—and who in the whole realm of music has ever approached them? For the magical expression of such a piece as the andantino in A♭ (op. 94, No. 2), any redundance may be pardoned.

In Schumann's words,

'he has strains for the most subtle thoughts and feelings, nay even for the events and conditions of life; and innumerable as are the shades of human thought and action, so various is his music.'[2]

Another equally true saying of Schumann's is that, compared with Beethoven, Schubert is as a woman to a man. For it must be confessed that one's attitude towards him is almost always that of sympathy, attraction and love, rarely that of embarrassment or fear. Here and there only, as in the 'Rosamunde' B minor entr'acte, or the finale of the last symphony, does he compel his hearers with an irresistible power; and yet how different is this compulsion from the strong, fierce, merciless coercion with which

1 For a comparison of his sonatæ with those of other masters see SONATA.

2 *Ges. Schriften*, i. 206.

Beethoven forces you along, and bows and bends you to his will, in the finale of the eighth or, still more, that of the seventh symphony.

THE SONGS.—We have mentioned the gradual manner in which Schubert reached his own style in instrumental music (see pp. 626-8). In this, except perhaps as to quantity, there is nothing singular, or radically different from the early career of other composers. Beethoven began on the lines of Mozart, and Mendelssohn on those of Weber, and gradually found their own independent style. But the thing in which Schubert stands alone is that while he was thus arriving by degrees at individuality in sonatas, quartets and symphonies, he was pouring forth songs by the dozen, many of which were of the greatest possible novelty, originality and mastery, while all of them have that peculiar *cachet* which is immediately recognisable as his. The chronological list of his works shows that such masterpieces as the 'Gretchen am Spinnrade,' the 'Erl King,' the Ossian Songs, 'Gretchen im Dom,' 'Der Taucher,' 'Die Bürgschaft,' were written before he was nineteen, and were contemporary with his very early efforts in the orchestra and chamber music; and that by 1822—in the October of which he wrote the two movements of his eighth symphony, which we have named as his first absolutely original instrumental music—he had produced in addition such ballads as 'Ritter Toggenburg' (1816), and 'Einsamkeit' (1818); such classical songs as 'Memnon' (1817), 'Antigone und Oedip' (1817), 'Iphigenie' (1817), 'Ganymed' (1817), 'Fahrt zum Hades' (1817), 'Prometheus' (1819), 'Gruppe aus dem Tartarus' (1817); Goethe's 'Wilhelm Meister' songs, 'An Schwager Kronos' (1816), 'Grenzen der Menschheit' (1821), Suleika's two songs (1821), 'Geheimes' (1821); as well as the 'Wanderer' (1816), 'Sei mir gegrüsst' (1821), 'Waldesnacht' (1820), 'Greisengesang' (1822), and many more of his very greatest and most immortal songs.

And this is very confirmatory of the view already taken in this article (p. 590) of Schubert's relation to music. The reservoir of music was within him from his earliest years, and songs being so much more direct a channel than the more complicated and artificial courses and conditions of the symphony or the sonata, music came to the surface in them so much the more quickly. Had the orchestra or the piano been as direct a mode of utterance as the voice, and the forms of symphony or sonata as simple as that of the song, there seems no reason why he should not have written instrumental music as characteristic as his eighth symphony, his sonata in A minor and his quartet in the same key, eight years earlier than he did; for the songs of that early date prove that he had then all the original power, imagination and feeling that he ever had. That it should have

been given to a comparative boy to produce strains which seem to breathe the emotion and experience of a long life is only part of the wonder which will also surround Schubert's songs.

After 1822, when his youth was gone and health had begun to fail, and life had become a terrible reality, his thoughts turned inwards, and he wrote the two great cycles of the 'Müllerlieder' (1823) and the 'Winterreise' (1827); the Walter Scott and Shakespeare songs; the splendid single songs of 'ImWalde' and 'Auf der Bruck,' 'Todtengräbers Heimweh,' 'Der Zwerg' 'Die junge Nonne'; the Barcarolle, 'Du bist die Ruh,' and the lovely 'Dass sie hier gewesen'; the 'Schiffers Scheidelied,' those which were collected into the so-called 'Schwanengesang' and many more.

It is very difficult to draw a comparison between the songs of this later period and those of the earlier one, but the difference must strike every one, and it resides mainly perhaps in the subjects themselves. Subjects of romance—of ancient times and remote scenes, and strange adventures and desperate emotion—are natural to the imagination of youth. But in maturer life the mind is calmer, and dwells more strongly on personal subjects. And this is the case with Schubert. After 1822 the classical songs and ballads are rare, and the themes which he chooses belong chiefly to modern life and individual feeling, such as the 'Müllerlieder' and the 'Winterreise,' and others in the list just given. Walter Scott's and Shakespeare's form an exception, but it is an exception which explains itself. We no longer have the exuberant dramatic force of the 'Erl King,' 'Ganymed,' the 'Gruppe aus dem Tartarus,' 'Cronnan,' or 'Kolma's Klage'; but we have instead the condensation and personal point of 'Pause,' 'Die Post,' 'Das Wirthshaus,' 'Die Nebensonnen,' the 'Doppelgänger' and the 'Junge Nonne.' And there is more maturity in the treatment. His modulations are fewer. His accompaniments are always interesting and suggestive, but they gain in force and variety and quality of ideas in the later songs.

In considering the songs themselves somewhat more closely, their most obvious characteristics are: Their number; their length: the variety of the words; their expression, and their other musical and poetical peculiarities.

1. Their number. The published songs, that is to say the compositions for one and two voices, excluding offertories and songs in operas, amount to 603.[1]

2. Their length. This varies very much. The shortest, like 'Klage um Aly Bey,' 'Der Goldschmiedsgesell,' and 'Die Spinnerin' (op. 118, 6), are strophic songs (that is, with the same melody and harmony unchanged verse

[1] This is the number included in the complete edition, Series XX. in 10 books.　　　　　　　　　　　　　　　　　　　　G.

after verse), in each of which the voice part is only eight bars long, with a bar or two of introduction or ritornel. The longest is Bertrand's ' Adelwold und Emma ' (June 5, 1815), a ballad the autograph of which contains fifty-five pages. Others of almost equal length and of about the same date are : ' Minona,' ' Die Nonne,' 'Amphiaraos,' etc. Another is Schiller's ' Der Taucher,' which fills thirty-six pages of close print. Schiller's ' Bürgschaft ' and the Ossian-songs are all long, though not of the same extent as ' Der Taucher.' These vast ballads are extremely dramatic ; they contain many changes of tempo and of signature, dialogues, recitatives, and airs. The ' Ritter Toggenburg ' ends with a strophic song in five stanzas. ' Der Taucher ' contains a long pianoforte passage of sixty bars, during the suspense after the diver's last descent. ' Der Liedler ' contains a march. The ballads mostly belong to the early years, 1815, 1816. The last is Mayrhofer's ' Einsamkeit,' the date of which Schubert has fixed in his letter of Aug. 3, 1818. There are long songs of later years, such as Collin's ' Der Zwerg ' of 1823 ; Schober's ' Viola ' and ' Vergissmeinnicht ' of 1823, and ' Schiffers Scheidelied ' of 1827, and Leitner's ' Der Winterabend ' of 1828 ; but these are essentially different from the ballads ; they are lyrical, and evince comparatively few mechanical changes.

It stands to reason that in 603 songs collected from all the great German poets, from Klopstock to Heine, there must be an infinite variety of material, form, sentiment and expression. And one of the most obvious characteristics in Schubert's setting of this immense collection is the close way in which he adheres to the words.[1] Setting a song was no casual operation with him, rapidly as it was often done ; but he identified himself with the poem, and the poet's mood for the time was his. Indeed he complains of the influence which the gloom of the ' Winterreise ' had had upon his spirits. He does not, as is the manner of some song-composers, set the poet at naught by repeating his words over and over again. This he rarely does ; but he goes through his poem and confines himself to enforcing the expression as music alone can do to poetry. The music changes with the words as a landscape does when sun and cloud pass over it. And in this Schubert has anticipated Wagner, since the words to which he writes are as much the absolute basis of his songs as Wagner's librettos are of his operas. What this has brought him to in such cases as the ' Erl King,' the ' Wanderer,' ' Schwager Kronos,' the ' Gruppe aus dem Tartarus,' the Shakespeare songs of

[1] It is strange to find his practice in the masses so different. There—a critic has pointed out—in every one of the six, words are either omitted or incorrectly jumbled together (Prout, *Concordia*, 1875, p. 110a). Was this because he understood the Latin words imperfectly ?

' Sylvia ' and ' Hark, hark, the lark ! ' those of Ellen and the Huntsman in ' The Lady of the Lake,' even Englishmen can judge ; but what he did in the German literature generally may be gathered from the striking passage already quoted from Vogl (p. 590), and from Mayrhofer's confession—doubly remarkable when coming from a man of such strong individuality —who somewhere says that he did not understand the full force even of his own poems until he had heard Schubert's setting of them.

One of his great means of expression is modulation. What magic this alone can work may be seen in the trio of the sonata in D. As in his PF. works, so in the songs, he sometimes carries it to an exaggerated degree. Thus in the short song ' Liedesend ' of Mayrhofer (Sept. 1816), he begins in C minor, and then goes quickly through E♭ into C♭ major. The signature then changes, and we are at once in D major ; then C major. Then the signature again changes to that of A♭, in which we remain for fifteen bars. From A♭ it is an easy transition to F minor, but a very sudden one from that again to A minor. Then for the breaking of the harp we are forced into D♭, and immediately, with a further change of signature, into F♯. Then for the King's song, with a fifth change of signature, into B major ; and lastly, for the concluding words,

'Und immer näher schreitet
Vergänglichkeit und Grab—'

a sixth change, with eight bars in E minor, thus ending the song a third higher than it began.

In Schiller's ' Der Pilgrim ' (1825), after two strophes (four stanzas) of a Choral-like melody in D major, we come, with the description of the difficulties of the pilgrim's road—mountains, torrents, ravines—to a change into D minor, followed by much extraneous modulation, reaching A♭ minor, and ending in F, in which key the first melody is repeated. At the words ' näher bin ich nicht zum Ziel '—we have a similar phrase and similar harmony (though in a different key) to the well-known complaint in the ' Wanderer,' ' Und immer fragt der Seufzer, Wo ? ' The signature then changes, and the song ends very impressively in B minor.

These two are quoted, the first as an instance rather of exaggeration, the second of the mechanical use of modulations to convey the natural difficulties depicted in the poem. But if we want examples of the extraordinary power with which Schubert wields this great engine of emotion, we would mention another song which contains one of the best instances to be found of propriety of modulation. I allude to Schubart's short poem to death, 'An den Tod,' where the gloomy subjects and images of the poet have tempted the composer to a series of successive changes so grand, so sudden, and yet so easy and so thoroughly in keeping with the subject, that it is impossible to hear them unmoved.

But modulation, though an all-pervading means of expression in Schubert's hands, is only one out of many. Scarcely inferior to the wealth of his modulation is the wealth of his melodies. The beauty of these is not more astonishing than their variety and their fitness to the words. Such tunes as those of ' Ave Maria,' or the serenade in the ' Schwanengesang,' or ' Ungeduld,' or the ' Grünen Lautenband,' or ' Anna Lyle,' or the ' Dithyrambe,' or ' Geheimes,' or ' Sylvia,' or the ' Lindenbaum,' or ' Du bist die Ruh,' or the ' Barcarolle,' are not more lovely and more appropriate to the text than they are entirely different from one another. One quality only, spontaneity, they have in common. With Beethoven, spontaneity was the result of labour, and the more he polished the more natural were his tunes. But Schubert read the poem, and the appropriate tune, married to immortal verse (a marriage, in his case, truly made in heaven), rushed into his mind, and to the end of his pen. It must be confessed that he did not always think of the compass of his voices. In his latest songs, as in his earliest (see p. 583), we find him taking the singer from the low B♭ to F, and even higher.

The tune, however, in a Schubert song is by no means an exclusive feature. The accompaniments are as varied and as different as the voice-parts, and as important for the general effect. They are often extremely elaborate, and the publishers' letters contain many complaints of their difficulty.[1] They are often most extraordinarily suitable to the words, as in the ' Erl King,' or the beautiful ' Dass sie hier gewesen,' the ' Gruppe aus dem Tartarus,' the ' Waldesnacht ' (and many others) ; where it is almost impossible to imagine any atmosphere more exactly suitable to make the words grow in one's mind than is supplied by the accompaniment. Their unerring certainty is astonishing. Often, as in ' Heliopolis,' or ' Auflösung,' he seizes at once on a characteristic impetuous figure, which is then carried on without intermission to the end. In ' Anna Lyle,' how exactly does the sweet monotony of the repeated figure fall in with the dreamy sadness of Scott's touching little lament ! Another very charming example of the same thing, though in a different direction, is found in ' Der Einsame,' a fireside piece, where the frequently-recurring group of four semi-quavers imparts an indescribable air of domesticity to the picture.[2] In the ' Winterabend ' —the picture of a calm moonlit evening—the accompaniment, aided by a somewhat similar little figure, conveys inimitably the very breath

[1] Op. 57, containing three songs by no means difficult, was published with a notice on the title-page that care had been taken (we trust with Schubert's consent) to omit everything that was too hard.
[2] A similar mood is evoked in the andante of the Grand Duo (op. 140).

of the scene. Such atmospheric effects as these are very characteristic of Schubert.

The voice-part and the accompaniment sometimes form so perfect a whole that it is impossible to disentangle the two ; as in ' Sylvia,' where the persistent dotted quaver in the bass, and the rare but delicious ritornel of two notes in the treble of the piano-part (bars 7, 14, etc.), are essential to the grace and sweetness of the portrait, and help to place the lovely English figure before us. This is the case also in ' Anna Lyle ' just mentioned, where the ritornel in the piano-part (bar 20, etc.) is inexpressibly soothing and tender in its effect, and sounds like the echo of the girl's sorrow. The beautiful serenade in the ' Schwanengesang,' again, combines an incessant rhythmical accompaniment with ritornels (longer than those in the last case), both uniting with the lovely melody in a song of surpassing beauty. In the ' Liebesbotschaft,' the rhythm is not so strongly marked, but the ritornels are longer and more frequent, and form a charming feature in that exquisite love-poem. Schubert's passion for rhythm comes out as strongly in many of the songs as it does in his marches and scherzos. In the two just named, though persistent throughout, the rhythm is subordinated to the general effect. But in others, as ' Suleika,' ' Die Sterne,' the ' Nachtgesang im Walde,' ' Erstarrung,' or ' Frühlingssehnsucht,' it forces itself more on the attention.

Schubert's basses are always splendid, and are so used as not only to be the basis of the harmony but to add essentially to the variety and effect of the songs. Sometimes, as in ' Die Krähe,' they are in unison with the voice-part. Often they share with the voice-part itself in the melody and structure of the whole. The wealth of ideas which they display is often astonishing. Thus in ' Waldesnacht,' a very long song of 1820, to a fine imaginative poem by F. Schlegel, describing the impressions produced by a night in the forest, we have a splendid example of the organic life which Schubert can infuse into a song. The pace is rapid throughout ; the accompaniment for the right hand is in arpeggios of semiquavers throughout, never once leaving off ; the left hand, where not in semiquavers also, has a succession of noble and varied rhythmical melodies, independent of the voice, and the whole is so blended with the voice-part—itself extraordinarily broad and dignified throughout ; the spirit and variety and the poetry of the whole are so remarkable, and the mystery of the situation is so perfectly conveyed, as to make the song one of the finest of that class in the whole Schubert collection. The same qualities will be found in ' Auf der Bruck ' (1825).

We do not say that this is the highest class of his songs. The highest class of poetry, and of music illustrating and enforcing poetry, must always deal with human joys and sorrows, in their most individual form, with the soul loving or longing, in contact with another soul, or with its Maker ; and the greatest of Schubert's songs will lie amongst those which are occupied with those topics, such as ' Gretchen am Spinnrade,' the ' Mignon ' songs, the ' Wanderer,' the ' Müllerlieder,' and ' Winterreise,' and perhaps highest of all, owing to the strong religious element which it contains, the ' Junge Nonne.' [1] In that wonderful song the personal feelings and the surroundings are so blended— the fear, the faith, the rapture, the storm, the swaying of the house, are so given, that for the time the hearer becomes the Young Nun herself. Even the convent bell, which in other hands might be a burlesque, is an instrument of the greatest beauty.

We have spoken of the mental atmosphere which Schubert throws round his poems ; but he does not neglect the representation of physical objects. He seems to confine himself to the imitation of natural noises, and not to attempt things which have no sound. The triplets in the ' Lindenbaum ' may be intended to convey the fluttering leaves of the lime-tree, and the accompaniment-figure in ' Die Forelle ' may represent the leaps of the trout ; but there are other objects about which no mistake can be made. One imitation of the bell we have just referred to. Another is in the ' Abendbilder,' where an F♯ sounds through sixteen bars to represent the ' evening bell ' ; in the ' Zügenglöcklein ' the upper E is heard through the whole piece ; and the bell of St. Mark's is a well-known feature in the partsong of the ' Gondelfahrer.' The post-horn forms a natural feature in ' Die Post,' and the hurdy-gurdy in ' Der Leiermann.' Of birds he gives several instances ; the nightingale in ' Ganymed ' and ' Die gefangene Sänger ' ; the raven in ' Abendbilder,' and perhaps in ' Frühlingstraum ' ; the cuckoo in ' Einsamkeit,' the quail in ' Der Wachtelschlag ' ; and the cock in ' Frühlingstraum.'

That hesitation between major and minor which is so marked in Beethoven is characteristic also of Schubert, and may be found in nearly every piece of his. A beautiful instance may be mentioned *en passant* in the trio of the G major fantasia sonata (op. 78), where the two bars in E minor which precede the E major have a peculiarly charming effect. Another is supplied by the four bars in A minor, for the question which begins and ends the beautiful fragment from Schiller's ' Gods of ancient Greece.' He also has an especially happy way —surely peculiarly his own—of bringing a minor piece to a conclusion in the major. Two instances of it, which all will remember, are in the romance from ' Rosamunde ' :

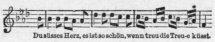

Du süsses Herz, es ist so schön, wenn treu die Treu-e küsst.

and in the ' Moment musical,' No. 3, in F minor. This and the ritornels already spoken of strike one like personal features or traits of the composer. But apart from these idiosyncrasies, the changes from minor to major in the songs are often superb. That in the ' Schwager Kronos ' (astonishing production for a lad under twenty), where the key changes into D major, and farther on into F major, to welcome the girl on the threshold, with the sudden return to D minor for the onward journey and the sinking sun—can be forgotten by no one who hears it, nor can that almost more beautiful change to D major in the ' Gute Nacht ' on the mention of the dream. This latter, and the noble transition to F major in the ' Junge Nonne ' are too familiar to need more than a passing reference, or that to G major in the ' Rückblick,' for the lark and nightingale and the girl's eyes, or to D major in the Serenade. ' Irdisches Glück ' is in alternate stanzas of major and minor. In Schiller's ' Rose ' (op. 73) every shade in the fate of the flower is thus indicated ; and this is no solitary instance, but in almost every song some example of such faithful painting may be found. A word will often do it. With Schubert the minor mode seems to be synonymous with trouble, and the major with relief ; and the mere mention of the sun, or a smile or any other emblem of gladness is sure to make him modulate. Some such image was floating before his mind when he made the beautiful change to A major near the beginning of the A minor quartet (bar 23).

I end my imperfect sketch of the life and works of this wonderful musician, by recalling the fact that Schubert's songs, regarded as a department of music, are absolutely and entirely his own. Songs there were before him, those of Schulz for instance, and of Zumsteeg, which he so greatly admired, and of Haydn and Mozart—touching, beautiful expressions of simple thought and feeling. But the song, as we know it in his hands—full of dramatic fire, poetry and pathos ; set to no simple Volkslieder, but to long complex poems, the best poetry of the greatest poets, and an absolute reflection of every change and breath of sentiment in that poetry ; with an accompaniment of the utmost force, fitness and variety—such songs were his and his alone. With one exception. Beethoven left but one song of importance, his ' Liederkreis ' (op. 98), but that is of superlative excellence. The ' Liederkreis,' however, was not published till Dec. 1816, and even if Schubert made its acquaintance immediately, yet a reference to the chronological List will show that by that time his style was formed, and many of his finest songs written.

He may have gained the idea of a connected series of songs from Beethoven, though neither the ' Schöne Müllerin ' nor the ' Winterreise ' have the same intimate internal connection as the ' Liederkreis ' ; but the character and merits of the single songs remain his own. When he wrote ' Loda's Gespenst ' and ' Kolma's Klage ' in 1815, he wrote what no one had ever attempted before. There is nothing to detract from his just claim to be the creator of German song as we know it, and the direct progenitor of those priceless treasures in which Schumann, Mendelssohn and Brahms have followed his example.

SUMMARY.—Of Schubert's religion it is still more difficult to say anything than it was of Beethoven's, because he is so much more reticent. A little poem of Sept. 1820, one of two preserved by Robert Schumann (*Neue Zeitschrift für Musik*, Feb. 5, 1839), is as vague a confession of faith as can well be imagined.

THE SPIRIT OF THE WORLD

Leave them, leave them, to their dream
   I hear the Spirit say :—
It and only it can keep them
   Near me on their darkling way.

Leave them racing, hurrying on
   To some distant goal,
Building creeds and proofs upon
   Half-seen flashes in the soul.

Not a word of it is true.
   Yet what loss is theirs or mine ?
In the maze of human systems
   I can trace the thought divine.

The other, three years later, May 8, 1823, is somewhat more definite. It calls upon a ' mighty Father' to look upon His son lying in the dust ; and implores Him to pour upon him the everlasting beams of His love ; and, even though He kill him, to preserve him for a purer and more vigorous existence. It expresses—very imperfectly, it is true, but still unmistakably—the same faith that has been put into undying words in the prologue to *In Memoriam*.

Franz may not have gone the length of his brother Ignaz [1] in vulgar scoffing at religious forms and persons, which no doubt were very empty in Vienna at that date ; but still of formal or dogmatic religion we can find no traces, and we must content ourselves with the practical piety displayed in his love for his father and Ferdinand, and testified to by them in their touching words and acts at the time of his death (pp. 618, 619) ; and with certainty that, though irregular after the irregularity of his time, Schubert was neither selfish, sensual, nor immoral. What he was in his inner man we have the abundant evidence of his music to assure us. Whatever the music of other composers may do, no one ever rose from hearing a piece by Schubert without being benefited by it. Of his good-nature to those who took the bread out of his mouth we have already spoken. Of his modesty we may be allowed to

[1] See his letter in *Kreissle*, p. 147 (i. 149).

say that he was one of the very few musicians who ever lived who did not behave as if he thought himself the greatest man in the world.[2] And these things are all intrinsic parts of his character and genius.

That he died at an earlier age [3] even than Mozart or Mendelssohn, or our own Purcell, must be accounted for on the ground partly of his extraordinary exertions, but still more of the privations to which he was subjected from his very earliest years. His productions are enormous, even when measured by those of the two great German composers just named, or even of Beethoven, who lived to nearly double his years. At an age when Beethoven had produced one symphony he had written ten,[4] besides a mass of works great and small. ' Fairer hopes ' ? Had he lived, who can doubt that he would have thrown into the shade all his former achievements ? But as we have endeavoured to explain, his music came so easily and rapidly that it was probably not exhausting. It was his privations, his absolute poverty and the distress which he naturally felt at finding that no exertions could improve his circumstances, or raise him in the scale of existence, that in the end dragged him down. Nearly the first distinct glimpse we catch of him is in the winter of 1812, supplicating his brother for a roll, some apples, or a few halfpence, to keep off the hunger of the long fast in the freezing rooms of the *Convict*. Within a year of his death we catch sight of him again, putting up with coffee and biscuits because he has not $8\frac{1}{2}$d. to buy his dinner with ; selling his great trio for 17s. 6d. and his songs at 10d. each, and dying the possessor of effects which were valued at little more than two pounds. Beside this the poverty of Mozart —the first of the two great musicians whom Vienna has allowed to starve—was wealth.

Such facts as these reduce the so-called friendship of his associates to its right level. With his astonishing power of production the commonest care would have ensured him a good living ; and that no one of his set was found devoted enough to take this care for him, and exercise that watch over ways and means which Nature had denied to his own genius, is a discredit to them all. They prate of their devotion to their friend, when not one of them had the will or the wit to prevent him from starving ; for such want as he often endured

[2] This modesty comes out in a letter to Ferdinand of July 16-18, 1824, where Schubert says, 'It would be better to play some other quartets than mine ' (probably referring to those in E and E♭), ' since there is nothing in them except perhaps the fact that they please you, as everything of mine pleases you. True,' he goes on, ' you do not appear to have liked them so much as the waltzes at the Ungarische Krone,' alluding to a clock at that eating-house of which Ferdinand had told him, which was set to play Franz's waltzes. The clock shows how popular Schubert was among his own set, and I regret having overlooked the fact in its proper place.
[3] The following are among the musicians, poets and painters who have died in the fourth decade of their lives : Shelley, 30 ; Sir Philip Sidney, 32 ; Bellini, 33 ; Mozart, 35 ; Byron, 36 ; Raffaelle, 37 ; Burns, 37 ; Purcell, 37 ; Mendelssohn, 38 ; Weber, 39 ; Chopin, 40.
[4] This number includes the sketch in E major, the ' Gastein ' symphony and the unfinished symphony in B minor.   c.

must inevitably have injured him, and we cannot doubt that his death was hastened by the absence of those comforts, not to say necessaries, which should have nursed and restored the prodigal expenditure of his brain and nerves.

We are accustomed to think of Beethoven's end as solitary and his death as miserable, but what was his last illness compared to Schubert's. Officious friends, like Pasqualati, sending him wine and delicacies; worshipping musicians, like Hummel and Hiller, coming to his death-bed as if to a shrine; his faithful attendants, Schindler, Hüttenbrenner and Breuning, waiting on his every wish; the sense of a long life of honour and renown; of great works appreciated and beloved; the homage of distant countries, expressed in the most substantial forms—what a contrast to the early death-bed and the apparent wreck of such an end as Schubert's! Time has so altered the public sense of his merits that it is all but impossible to place oneself in the forlorn condition in which he must have resigned himself to his departure, and to realise the darkness of the valley of the shadow of death through which his simple, sincere, guileless soul passed to its last rest, and to the joyful resurrection and glorious renown which have since attended it. *Then* an intelligent and well-informed foreign musician could visit the Austrian capital and live in its musical circles without so much as hearing Schubert's name.[1] *Now* memorials are erected to him in the most public places of Vienna, institutions are proud to bear his name, his works go through countless editions and publishers grow rich upon the proceeds even of single songs, while faces brighten and soften, and hands are clasped, as we drink in the gay and pathetic accents of his music.

For even his privations and his obscurity have now been forgotten in the justice since done to him, and in the universal affection with which he was regarded as soon as his works reached the outside world—an affection which, as we have conclusively shown, has gone on increasing ever since his death. In the whole range of composers it may be truly said that no one is now so dearly loved as he, no one has the happy power so completely of attracting both the admiration and the affection of his hearers. To each one he is not only a great musician, not only a great enchanter, but a dear personal friend. If in his ' second state sublime ' he can know this, we may feel sure that it is a full compensation to his affectionate spirit for the many wrongs and disappointments that he endured while on earth.

The very wide field over which Schubert

---

ranged in poetry has been more than once alluded to in the foregoing. It would be both interesting and profitable to give a list of the poems which he has set. Such a list, not without inaccuracies, will be found in Wurzbach's *Biographisches Lexicon*, vol. xxxii. p. 94. Here we can only say that it includes over 600 poems by 100 authors, of whom the principal are :

Goethe, 72 ; Schiller, 54 ; Mayrhofer, 48 ; W. Müller, 44 ; Hölty, 25 ; Matthisson, 27 ; Kosegarten, 20 ; F. Schlegel, 19 ; Klopstock, 19 ; Körner, 16 ; Schober, 15 ; Seidl, 15 ; Salis, 14 ; Claudius, 13 ; Walter Scott, 10 ; Rellstab, 9 ; Uz, 8 ; Ossian, 7 ; Heine, 6 ; Shakespeare, 3 ; Pope, 1 ; Colley Cibber, 1 ; etc. etc.

G., with addns. (chiefly in footnotes)<br>w. h. h<sup>w</sup>. and c.

BIBLIOGRAPHY

1. The first place must be given to Ferdinand Schubert's sketch, entitled ' Aus Franz Schuberts Leben,' four short papers which appeared in Schumann's periodical, the *Neue Zeitschrift für Musik*, in Nos. 33 to 36 (Apr. 23-May 3), 1839. These are written with great simplicity and apparently great exactness ; but might have been extended to double the length with great advantage.

2. Mayrhofer contributed a short article of recollections, *Erinnerungen*, to the *Neues Archiv für Geschichte . . . Literatur und Kunst* (Vienna) Feb. 23, 1829 ; and Bauernfeld a longer paper, *Über Franz Schubert*, to Nos. 69, 70, 71, of the *Wiener Zeitschrift für Kunst, Literatur, Theater, und Mode*, for June 9, 11, 13, 1829. These papers, written so shortly after Schubert's death by men extremely intimate with him, are very valuable.

3. Bauernfeld also made two interesting communications to the *Freie Presse* of Vienna, for Apr. 17 and 21, 1869, containing six letters and parts of letters by Schubert, and many anecdotes. These latter articles were reprinted in the Leipzig *Signale* for Nov. 15, 22, 26, 28, 1869 ; translated in the *Musical World*, Jan. 8, 15, Feb. 5, 19, 1870, and in Bauernfeld's *Gesammelte Schriften*, vol. xii. (Vienna, 1873). But recollections written so long after the event must always be taken *cum grano*.

4. Schindler wrote an article in *Bäuerle's Wiener Theaterzeitung*, for May 3, 1831, describing Beethoven's making acquaintance with Schubert's songs on his death-bed ; and other articles in the *Niederrheinische Musikzeitung*, for 1857. He also mentions Schubert in his *Life of Beethoven*, 3rd ed., ii. 136.

5. Schumann printed four letters (incomplete), two poems, and a Dream, by Schubert, as ' Reliquien ' in his *Neue Zeitschrift für Musik* for Feb. 1 and 5, 1839.

6. One of the same letters was printed complete in the *Signale*, No. 2, for 1878.

7. The *Diary* of Sofie Müller (Vienna, 1832), the *Unvergessenes* of Frau von Chezy (Leipzig, 1858), and the *Erinnerungen* of her son W. von Chezy (Schaffhausen, 1863), all afford original facts about Schubert by those who knew him.

8. Ferd. Hiller's *Künstlerleben* (Cologne, 1880), contains a paper—' Vienna 52 years since '—embodying a few interesting and lifelike notices of the year 1827. Of all these, use has been made in the foregoing pages.

9. The first attempt to write a life of Schubert was made by von Kreissle, who, in 1861 published a small 8vo pamphlet of 165 pages entitled *Franz Schubert, eine biografische Skizze* ; von Dr. Heinrich von Kreissle. This is a very interesting little book, and though not nearly so long as the second edition, it contains some facts which have dropped out of that.

10. The second edition, *Franz Schubert*, von Dr. Heinrich Kreissle von Hellborn (Vienna, Gerold, 1865), is a large 8vo of 619 pages, with portrait after Kupelwieser. This is a thoroughly honest, affectionate book ; but it is deformed, like many German biographies, by a very diffuse style and a mass of unnecessary matter in the shape of detailed notices of every one who came into contact with Schubert ; and some of the letters appear to be garbled ; but the analyses of the operas and the lists of works are valuable, and there are some interesting facts gathered from the Fröhlichs, Ferdinand Schubert, Spaun, Hüttenbrenner and others. It has been translated into English by Mr. A. D. Coleridge (two vols. 8vo, Longman, 1869), with an Appendix by the present writer, containing the themes and particulars of the MS. Symphonies and other MS. music of Schubert, as seen by Arthur Sullivan and him in Vienna in 1867. A résumé of the work is given in English by Wilberforce, *Franz Schubert*, etc. (London, 1866).

11. Both Kreissle's works have been largely utilised by H. Barbedette, in *F. Schubert, sa vie*, etc. (Paris, 1866). This contains an atrocious version of Rieder's portrait, and one new fact—a facsimile of Schober's song ' An die Musik,' valuable because, being dated Apr. 24, 1827 (while the song was composed in 1817), it shows that Schubert did not confine his dates to the original autographs.

12. The chief value of Reissmann's book, *Franz Schubert, sein Leben u. seine Werke* (Berlin, 1873), consists in the extracts from the juvenile MS. songs, Quintet overture (pp. 12-30), the comparisons of early songs with later revisions of the same (pp. 24, 154, etc.), five pieces printed for the first time, and facsimile of a MS. page.

13. Gumprecht, La Mara, and others have included sketches of Schubert in their works.

14. The article on Schubert in Wurzbach's *Biographisches*

1 The allusion is to E. Holmes, the biographer of Mozart, who passed some time in Vienna in the spring of 1827, evidently with the view of finding out all that was best worth knowing in music, and yet does not mention Schubert's name. (See his *Ramble among the Musicians of Germany*.)

*Lexicon* (Part 32, pp. 30-110 ; Vienna, 1876) is a good mixture of unwearied research, enthusiasm for his hero and contempt for those who misjudge him (see for example, p. 98b). The copious lists are extremely interesting and useful. Unfortunately they cannot always be trusted, and the quotations are sometimes curiously incorrect. Thus Mr. Arthur Duke Coleridge is raised to the peerage as ' Herzog Arthur von Coleridge,' etc., etc. Still all students of Schubert should be grateful for the article.

15. The facsimile of the ' Erl King ' in its first form has been mentioned in the body of the article (p. 586). Further consideration convinces me that the original of this cannot be the first autograph, but must be a copy made afterwards by Schubert.

Two documents must be mentioned.

16. *Actenmässige Darstellung der Ausgrabung und Wiederbeinsetzung der irdischen Reste von Beethoven und Schubert* (Vienna, 1863).

17. *Vom Wiener Männergesangverein. Festschrift zur Enthüllung des Schubert Denkmales am 15. Mai, 1872*, an account of the unveiling of the statue in the Stadt Park, containing a capital sketch of Schubert's Life, Lists, and many other welcome facts. Herr Dumba's speech on the occasion and poems by Bauernfeld and Weilen were printed separately. Good photographs of the statue are published by Löwy of Vienna.

18. Since writing the foregoing I have seen the *Life and Works of Schubert*, by A. Niggli, which forms No. 15 of Breitkopf & Härtel's *Musikalische Vorträge* (1880). It appears to be an excellent and generally an accurate compilation,[1] with a great deal of information in small compass, but wants a list of works to make it complete.

19. A *Life* by H. F. Frost in *The Great Musicians*, edited by Francis Hueffer (London, 1881), is readable and intelligent, and has a list of works year by year.

The articles on Schubert's masses by Professor Prout, in the *Monthly Musical Record* for 1871, and the *Concordia* for 1875, are too important and interesting to be omitted. Among other articles on Schubert may be specially mentioned those in the *Monthly Musical Record* for Feb. 1897 ; those in the *Musical Times* for Aug. 1893, Jan. and Feb. 1897, Sept. and Oct. 1901, and an interesting critical study by Antonín Dvořák and H. T. Finck in *The Century* for July 1894. *The Romantic Composers*, by Daniel Gregory Mason (1907), contains a very interesting article on Schubert.

G., with addn. W. H. HW.

## THEMATIC CATALOGUES

1. *Thematisches Verzeichniss im Druck erschienenen Compositionen von Franz Schubert* (Vienna, Diabelli) [1852], contains the works from Opus 1 to 160 ; Schwanengesang ; Lieferungen 1 to 50 ; and thirty songs (included in the foregoing) of a series entitled ' Immortellen.'

2. *Thematisches Verzeichniss der im Druck erschienenen Werke von Franz Schubert*, herausgegeben von G. Nottebohm. Vienna, F. Schreiber, 1874, pp. 1 to 288. This admirable work is as comprehensive and accurate as the previous publications of its author would imply its being. Under the head of printed works it comprises : (1) Works with opus numbers 1 to 173. (2) Nachgelassenen Mus. Dichtungen, Lieferungen 1 to 50. (3) Works without opus numbers for orchestra, chamber music, etc. (4) Doubtful and spurious compositions ; works still in MS. ; books, portraits, etc. (5) Index, list of songs, etc.

The information under each piece is not confined to the name and date of publication, but gives in most cases the date of composition and frequently also such facts as the first time of performance, etc. It is in fact, like all the author's publications, a model of what such a catalogue should be.

G.

## LIST OF WORKS

The collected edition, *Kritisch durchgesehene Gesammtausgabe*, of Schubert's works (1885–97) issued by Breitkopf & Härtel is complete in 22 Series. The following list shows the classification and summarises the contents :

SERIES I.—EIGHT SYMPHONIES

No. 1 in D (1813) ; No. 2 in B♭ (1814) ; No. 3 in D (1815) ; No. 4, ' Tragic ' in C min. (1816) ; No. 5 in B♭ (1816) ; No. 6 in C (1817) ; No. 7 in C (1828) ; No. 8, unfinished, in B min. (1822).

SERIES II.—OVERTURES FOR ORCHESTRA

Overture in D to the ' Lustspiel ' ; ' Der Teufel als Hydraulicus ' ; Overture in D ; Overture in B♭ ; Overture in D ; Overture in D (in Italian style) ; Overture in C (in Italian style) ; Overture in E min. ; Five Minuets with six Trios ; Five ' Deutsche ' with Coda and Seven Trios ; Minuet. (See also Series XXI.)

SERIES III.—OCTETS

Op. 166, Octet for 2 vlns., vla., double bass, clar., horn and fag. ; Minuet and Finale of an Octet for 2 oboes, 2 clar., 2 horns and 2 fag. ; ' Eine kleine Trauermusik ' for 2 clar., 2 fag., contra-fag., 2 horns and 2 trombones.

SERIES IV. TO VI.—CHAMBER MUSIC FOR STRINGS

Quintet (op. 163) in C (1828), 2 vlns., vla., v'cl. Quartets—No. 1, Quartet (1812) ; No. 2, Quartet in C (1812) ; No. 3, Quartet in B♭ (1812) ; No. 4, Quartet in C (1813) ; No. 5, Quartet in D (1813) ; No. 6, Quartet in D (1813) ; No. 7, Quartet in D (1814) ; No. 8, Quartet in B♭, op. 168 (1814) ; No. 9, Quartet in G min. (1815) ; No. 10, Quartet in E♭, op. 125, No. 1 (c. 1817) ; No. 11, Quartet in E, op. 125, No. 2 (c. 1817) ; No. 12, Quartett-Salz in C min. (1820) ; No. 13, Quartet in A min., op. 27 (1824) ; No. 14, Quartet in D min. (1826) ; No. 15, Quartet in G, op. 161 (1826). (See also Series XXI.)

SERIES VII.—CHAMBER MUSIC FOR PF. AND STRINGS

Quintet (op. 114), ' Die Forelle,' PF., vln., vla., v'cl., double bass ; Adagio and Rondo concertante, PF., vln., vla., v'cl. ; First trio, in B♭ (op. 99), PF., vln., v'cl. ; Second trio, in E♭ (op.100), PF., vln., v'cl. ; Notturno (op. 148), PF., vln., v'cl.

[1] I am sorry to find the inscription on the tomb very incorrectly given.

G.

SERIES VIII.—WORKS FOR PF. WITH ONE OTHER INSTRUMENT

Rondo (op. 70), PF., vln. ; Sonata in D (op. 137, No. 1) ; Sonata in A min. (op. 137, No. 2) ; Sonata in G min. (op. 137, No. 3), all PF., vln. ; Phantasie (op. 159), PF., vln. ; Sonata in A (op. 162), PF., vln. ; Introduction and variations on a theme 'Ihr Blümlein allen ' from the ' Müllerlieder,' PF., flute (op. 160) ; Sonata, PF. and arpeggione or v'cl.

SERIES IX.—PF. 4 HANDS

Three Marches (marches héroïques), op. 27 ; Six Marches, op. 40 ; Three Military Marches, op. 51 ; Funeral March for Emperor Alexander I. of Russia, op. 55 ; Heroic March for Emperor Nicholas I., op. 66 ; Two Characteristic Marches, op. 121 ; Children's March in G ; Overture in F, op. 34 ; Overture in C ; Overture in D ; Sonata in B♭, op. 30 ; Sonata in C, op. 140 ; Rondo in A, op. 107 ; Rondo in D, op. 138 ; Variations in E min. on a French song, op. 10 ; Variations in A♭ on an original theme, op. 35 ; Variations in C on a theme (' Was einst vor Jahren ') from Herold's opera ' Marie,' op. 82, No. 1 ; Introduction and Variations in B♭ from an original theme, op. 82, No. 2 ; ' Divertissement à la hongroise ' in G min., op. 54 ; Divertissement in E min. on French motives, op. 63 ; Andantino varie in B min. on French motives, op. 84, No. 1 ; Rondo brillant in E min. on French motives, op. 84, No. 2 ; Lebenstürme in A min., op. 144 ; Phantasie in F min., op. 103 ; 6 Polonaises, op. 61 ; 4 Polonaises, op. 75 ; 4 Ländler ; Fugue in E min., op. 152 ; Allegro Moderato in C and Andante in A min. ; Three Phantasies (1810–13).

SERIES X.—PF. SOLO SONATAS

Sonata in E (1815) ; Sonata in C (1815) ; Sonata in A♭ (1817) ; Sonata in E min. (1817) ; Sonata in B, op. 147 (1817) ; Sonata in A min., op. 122 (1817) ; Sonata in A min., op. 142 (1823) ; Sonata in A min., op. 42 (1825) ; Sonata in A, op. 120 (1825) ; Sonata in D, op. 53 (1825) ; Sonata in G, op. 78 (1826) ; Sonata in C min. (1828) ; Sonata in A (1828) ; Sonata in B♭ (1828). (See also Series XXI.)

SERIES XI.—MISCELLANEOUS WORKS FOR PF.

Phantasie (' The Wanderer '), op. 15 ; 4 impromptus, op. 90 ; 4 impromptus, op. 142 ; Moments Musicals, op. 94 ; Adagio and Rondo, op. 145 ; Ten Variations ; Variations on a theme by A. Hüttenbrenner ; Variation on a waltz by Diabelli ; Andante in C ; Klavierstück in A♭ ; Adagio in E ; Allegretto in C min. ; 3 Klavierstücke ; 5 Klavierstücke ; 2 Scherzi ; March in E.

SERIES XII.—DANCES FOR PF.

Original Dances, op. 9 ; Waltzes, Ländler and Ecossaisen, op. 18 ; German Dances and Ecossaisen, op. 33 ; Valses sentimentales, op. 50 ; Viennese, Damenländler and Ecossaisen, op. 67 ; Valses nobles, op. 77 ; ' Grätzer Walzer,' op. 91 ; 20 Waltzes, op. 127 ; 12 Ländler, op. 171 ; many other sets of German Dances, Ländler, etc.

SERIES XIII.—MASSES

Mass in F ; Mass in G ; Mass in B♭ ; Mass in C ; Mass in A♭ ; Mass in E♭ ; ' Gesänge zur Feier des heiligen Opfers der Messe.'

SERIES XIV.—OTHER CHURCH WORKS

*A. With Accompaniment*

First Offertorium for sopr. or ten., op. 46 ; Second Offertorium for sopr., op. 47 ; Salve Regina (Third Offertorium) for sopr., op. 153 ; Offertorium ' Tres sunt ' for chor. ; Graduale ' Benedictus es, Domine,' for chor., op. 150 ; Tantum Ergo (3 settings) for chor., op. 45 ; Salve Regina for ten. ; Duet ' Auguste jam coelestium,' for sopr. and ten. ; Magnificat, for soli and chor. ; Stabat Mater for chor. ; Stabat Mater (of F. G. Klopstock) for soli and chor. ; Kyrie (3 settings), for chor. ; Salve Regina (' Hymne an die heilige Mutter Gottes '), for chor.

*B. Without Accompaniment*

Antiphones for Palm Sunday, for mixed choir ; Salve Regina for 4 male voices ; Salve Regina, for mixed choir ; Kyrie, for mixed choir.

Draft of a Tantum Ergo for soli, chor. and orch. (short score). (See also Series XXI.)

SERIES XV.—OPERAS AND OTHER STAGE WORKS

' Des Teufels Lustschloss,' opera in 3 acts ; ' Der vierjährige Postin,' singspiel in 1 act ; ' Fernando,' singspiel in 1 act ; ' Die beiden Freunde von Salamanka,' singspiel in 2 acts ; ' Die Zwillingsbrüder,' singspiel in 1 act ; ' Die Verschworenen,' singspiel in 1 act ; ' Die Zauberharfe,' melodrama in 3 acts ; music to ' Rosamunde von Cypern,' op. 26 ; ' Alfonso und Estrella,' opera in 3 acts, op. 69 ; ' Fierrabras,' heroic-romantic opera in 3 acts, p. 76 ; Fragments : ' Claudine von Villa Bella,' singspiel ; ' Der Spiegelritter,' operetta ; ' Die Bürgschaft,' opera ; ' Adrast,' opera ; addition to Herold's ' Das Zauberglöcken.'

SERIES XVI.—WORKS FOR MALE VOICES

*A. With Accompaniment for Strings or Wind Instruments*

' Nachtgesang im Walde,' op. 139b ; ' Hymne,' op. 154 ; ' Gesang der Geister über den Wasser,' op. 167.

*B. With PF. Accompaniment*

Das Dörfchen, op. 11, No. 1 ; Die Nachtigall, op. 11, No. 2 ; Geist der liebe, op. 11, No. 3 ; Frühlingsgesang, op. 16, No. 1 ; Naturgenuss, op. 16, No. 2 ; Der Gondelfahrer, op. 28 ; Bootgesang, op. 52, No. 3 ; Zur guten Nacht, op. 81, No. 3 ; Widerspruch, op. 105, No. 1 ; Nachthelle, op. 134 ; Ständchen, op. 135 ; Im Gegenwärtigen Vergangenes ; Trinklied ; Trinklied ; Bergknappenlied ; La Pastorella.

*C. Without Accompaniment*

Jünglingswonne, op. 17, No. 1 ; Liebe, op. 17, No. 2 ; Zum Rundetanz, op. 17, No. 3 ; Die Nacht, op. 17, No. 4 ; Wehmuth, op. 64, No. 1 ; Ewige Liebe, op. 64, No. 2 ; Flucht, op. 64, No. 3 ; Mondenschein, op. 102 ; Schlachtlied, op. 151 ; Trinklied, op. 155 ; Nachtmusik, op. 156 ; Frühlingsgesang ; Der Geistertanz ; Gesang der Geister über den Wassern ; Lied im Freien ; Sehnsucht ; Ruhe, schönstes Glück der Erde ; Wein und Liebe ; Der Entfernten ;

Die Einsiedelei ; An den Frühling ; Grab und Mond ; Hymne ; Wer ist gross ? ; Beitrag zur Jubelfeier Salieris ; Gesang der Geister über den Wassern ; Das Dörfchen.

### SERIES XVII.—WORKS FOR MIXED VOICES

#### A. With Orch. Accompaniment

'Lazarus,' religious drama in 3 parts (incomplete) ; Cantata in honour of Joseph Spendon, op. 128 ; Cantata on the Emperor's birthday, op. 157 ; ' Namensfeier ' Cantata ; ' Glaube, Hoffnung und Liebe.'

#### B. With PF. Accompaniment

Gott im Ungewitter ' ; ' Gott der Weltschöpfer ' ; ' Hymne an den Unendlichen,' op. 112, No. 3 ; ' Miriams Siegesgesang,' op. 136 ; ' Gebet,' op. 139 ; Quartet, op. 146 ; ' An die Sonne ' ; ' Lebenslust ' ; ' Der Tanz ' ; Cantata for Irene Kiesewetter ; ' Begräbnisslied ' ; ' Osterlied.'

#### C. Without Accompaniment

' Christ ist erstanden ' ; Psalm 92.

### SERIES XVIII.-XIX.—WORKS FOR FEMALE VOICES AND SMALLER CHORAL PIECES

Coronach, op. 52, No. 4 ; Psalm 23, op. 132 ; Gott in der Natur, op. 133 ; Ständchen, op. 135 ; Das Leben ; Klage um Ali Bey.

### SERIES XX.—SONGS

Ten books (603 Nos. in all), the contents arranged chronologically with full alphabetical index in the first book.

### SERIES XXI.—SUPPLEMENT

Containing miscellaneous works both instrumental and vocal. The instrumental music includes 2 Overtures for orch. ; Concert-stück, vln. and orch. ; Rondo, vln. and str. quartet ; Trio in B♭, vln., vla. and v'cl. (1817) ; 2 Overtures, PF. 4 hands ; 7 Sonatas for PF. ; and many dance pieces for PF. ; Vocal music includes Tantum Ergo, chor. and orch. ; Offertorium, ten., solo, chor. and orch. ; several pieces for male voices ; and a draft of a Cantata ' Die Schlacht.'

### SERIES XXII.

Additional matter (Revisions Bericht) relating to all the series and including sketches and fragments.

### ADDITIONAL BIBLIOGRAPHY

#### ENGLISH

EDMONDSTOUNE DUNCAN : Schubert, containing catalogue based on the collected edition.
W. H. HADOW : Oxf. Hist. Mus., vol. v., The Viennese Period.

#### GERMAN

OTTO ERICH DEUTSCH : Franz Schubert. Die Dokumente seines Lebens und Schaffens. 3 Bd. (Munich, 1905-13.) Deutsch has a life of Schubert on a large scale in preparation.
Franz Schubert's Briefe und Schriften. Mit den zeitgenössischen Bildnissen, drei Handschriftproben und anderen Beilagen. Edited by Otto Erich Deutsch, pp. iv. 15.) (Munich, 1919.)
R. H. BARTSCH : Schwammerl : ein Schubert-Roman. (Leipzig, 1910.)
MORITZ BAUER : Die Lieder Franz Schuberts. Bd. i. (Leipzig, 1915.) Bd. 2 has not yet been published.
WILLI KAHL : ' Das lyrische Klavierstück Schuberts und seiner Vorgänger seit 1810.' A.M.Z., Jan. 1921 and Apr. 1921.
HERMANN VON DER PFORDTEN : Franz Schubert und das deutsche Lied. (Leipzig, 1916, 2nd ed., 1920.)
HEINRICH KASPAR SCHMID : ' Franz Schubert's neuentdecktes Quartett. Ein offener Brief.' Z.M.W., Dec. 1918, pp. 183-8.
RUDOLFINE KROTT : Die Singspiele Schuberts. Vienna Dissertation 1921.
RICHARD HEUBERGER : Franz Schubert. 3. Auflage, durchgesehen und ergänzt von Hermann von der Pfordten. pp. 118. (Berlin, 1920.) (Berühmte Musiker, Bd. 14.) First published in 1902.
A. FARCANU : Leopold von Sonnleithners Erinnerungen an Franz Schubert. Z.M.W., May 1919, pp. 466-83.
MORITZ BAUER : ' Johann Mayrhofer ' (studied in his relation to and influence on Schubert). Z.M.W., Nov. 1922, p. 79, et seq.

#### FRENCH

TH. GEROLD : Schubert. (Paris, 1923.). With an extensive biblio-graphy.

SCHUBERT, LOUIS (b. Dessau, Jan. 27, 1828 ; d. Dresden, Sept. 17, 1884), violinist and singing-master, went in his eighteenth year to St. Petersburg, and then as Konzertmeister to Königsberg, where he remained till 1862. He then returned to Dresden, where he enjoyed a great reputation as a teacher of singing. He published a method of singing in the form of songs, and four of his operettas became favourites.    G.

SCHUBERTH, (1) GOTTLOB (b. Carsdorf, Aug. 11, 1778 ; d. Feb. 18, 1846), received his musical education at Jena, and learnt the violin from Stamitz. In 1804 he went to Magdeburg, resided there for some years, and was dis-tinguished as an excellent clarinet and oboe player. In 1833 he moved to Hamburg. His eldest son,

(2) JULIUS FERDINAND GEORG (b. Magde-burg, July 14, 1804 ; d. Leipzig, June 9, 1875), was the founder of the well-known firm of J. Schuberth & Co. in Leipzig and New York. After learning the business of a music publisher in Magdeburg, he started in 1826 on his own account at Hamburg, whence he was enabled to found branch establishments at Leipzig (1832) and New York (1850). In 1854 he gave up the Hamburg business to his brother FRIEDRICH (5) and devoted himself entirely to Leipzig and New York. Besides his publishing business, Julius was an indefatigable student of language, literature and music. He was publisher, editor and proprietor of a Musikalisches Conversations-lexicon (which has gone through ten editions, and from which the details of the present article have been obtained), the Kleine Hamburger Musik Zeitung (1840-50), the New York Musik Zeitung (1867), and Schuberths kleiner Musik Zeitung (1871-72). In 1840 he founded the Norddeutscher Musikverein and Preis Institut at Hamburg. He received many decorations from the crowned heads of Germany in recognition of his services to music. In 1874 he settled at Leipzig. His business, which in 1877 comprised over 6000 publications, was carried on after his death with increasing success by his widow and nephew until 1891, when it was bought by F. Siegel.

(3) LUDWIG (b. Magdeburg, Apr. 18, 1806 ; d. St. Petersburg, 1850), the second son of Gottlob, studied under his father and C. M. von Weber, and when only 16 was music-director at the Stadt Theater of his native town. He was subsequently court Kapellmeister at Oldenburg, and after living at Riga and Königsberg (1835) became (1845) conductor of the German Opera at St. Petersburg. His compositions include some published chamber music, besides operas and symphonies which remain in MS. His younger brother,

(4) CARL (b. Magdeburg, Feb. 25, 1811 ; d. Zürich, July 22, 1863), learnt the piano from his father, and the violoncello from L. Hesse. In 1825 he was placed under Dotzauer at Dresden, and in 1828 made his first concert tour to Ludwigslust and Hamburg. In 1829 he played at Copenhagen and Gothenburg, but a series of misfortunes drove him back to Magdeburg, where he occupied the post of first violoncello in the theatre orchestra. In 1833 he again played in Hamburg with success, and during the next few years gave concerts in all the principal towns of North Germany, Belgium and Holland, besides visiting Paris and London (1835). In the autumn of the latter year he was appointed solo violoncellist to the Czar. He remained for twenty years at St. Petersburg, occupying the posts of musical director at the University, conductor of the Imperial Court Orchestra, and inspector of the Imperial Dramatic College. His compositions include

chamber music and concertos for the violoncello, etc.

(5) FRIEDRICH WILHELM AUGUST (b. Magdeburg, Oct. 27, 1817), fifth son of Gottlob Schuberth, was the head of the firm of ' Fritz Schuberth' at Hamburg from 1853.    W. B. S.

SCHUCH, ERNST VON (b. Graz, Nov. 23, 1847; d. Dresden, May 3, 1914), was at first intended for the legal profession, but music was too strong (he had appeared as a violinist at the age of 7, and at 9 years old played solos on the piano and violin in public), and he received instruction from Eduard Stoltz at Graz, and afterwards from Dessoff in Vienna. In 1867 he was appointed conductor of Lobe's theatre at Breslau, and after short engagements at Würzburg, Graz and Basle he was engaged by Pollini to conduct a series of Italian operas in different parts of Germany. In Mar. 1872 he conducted his first opera in Dresden, and in August following was appointed Kapellmeister there. In 1873 he was made court Kapellmeister, and very soon his great gifts began to make the Dresden opera famous throughout the world for the catholicity of its repertory, the broad views of its conductor, and the excellence of individual performances. Schuch always gave due regard to the art of the bel canto, and as an operatic conductor he had few rivals. In 1897 he was ennobled by the Emperor of Austria, and in 1899 he was given the title of privy councillor.

In 1875 he married the singer Clementine SCHUCH-PROSKA (her maiden name was accurately Procházka) (b. Vienna, Feb. 12, 1853), a pupil of Mme. Mathilde Marchesi at the Vienna Conservatoire, and a member of the opera company at Dresden from 1873. Her voice was a light soprano, and she sang florid music with great skill. She appeared in London at some of the early Richter Concerts, and at the Crystal Palace ; she sang the part of Aennchen in ' Der Freischütz' at the German Opera under Richter in 1884, with much success, and also appeared as Eva in ' Die Meistersinger.' She retired from the stage in 1895.    M.

BIBL.—P. SAKOLOWSKI, E. Schuch, 1901.

SCHÜRMANN, GEORG CASPAR (b. circa 1672; d. Wolfenbüttel, Feb. 25, 1751 [1]), one of the early composers of German opera, was the son of a Lutheran pastor in Hanover. He early showed a decided talent for music, first as singer and afterwards as composer. From 1693-97 he was engaged as falsetto singer at the Hamburg Opera, and also for church services. In 1697 the Duke of Brunswick invited him to Wolfenbüttel, and shortly afterwards, at the Duke's expense, he visited Italy for the further cultivation of his musical talent. From 1702-1707, with the Duke of Brunswick's permission, he entered the service of the Duke of Meiningen,

but in the latter year he was recalled to Wolfenbüttel, where he remained till his death, busily engaged in the composition and production of German operas, in which he himself took a leading part as alto singer, and also from time to time acted as Kapellmeister. Many of these operas [2] were also produced at Hamburg, but none of them were ever printed during his lifetime, and most of them are only known from their libretti. Of a few only has the music survived. One of them, entitled ' Ludovicus Pius,' or ' Ludewig der fromme,' first produced in 1726, has now been reprinted, though not complete, by Dr. Hans Sommer, from a MS. in his possession, and appears as Band xvii. in Eitner's Publikation älterer Musikwerke. As a Beilage to the Monatshefte of 1885, Eitner has also printed an aria from another opera of Schürmann's, entitled ' Henricus Anceps,' or ' Heinrich der Vogler,' besides a complete Church Cantata for the New Year, both of which are calculated to give a very favourable idea of Schürmann's powers as a composer. Eitner is disposed to assign him a very high place even in association with Handel and Bach, both for genuine feeling and contrapuntal skill.

J. R. M.

BIBL.—E. STIER, Musik, iii. (1904); G. F. SCHMIDT, G. K. Schürmann (Munich Dissertation, 1913).

SCHÜTT, EDUARD (b. St. Petersburg, Oct. 22, 1856), was intended for a mercantile career, but relinquished it for music, which he learned from Petersen and Stein sufficiently to pass the examination at the St. Petersburg Conservatoire, with honour, in 1876. He then entered the Conservatorium at Leipzig, passed the final examination there in 1878, and went to Vienna, where he was elected conductor of the Akademische Wagner-Verein. In Jan. 1882 he played his concerto (op. 7) in G minor, before the Russian Musical Society at St. Petersburg. It was performed at the Crystal Palace, Sydenham, Apr. 15, 1882, by Mme. Frickenhaus. Later, he composed a second piano concerto, op. 47, in F minor, also a comic opera, ' Signor Formica.' His published works include — Serenade for strings, op. 6 ; Variations for 2 pianos, op. 9 ; numerous songs, piano pieces, transcription of songs by Brahms, Strauss's Fledermaus waltz, etc.    G., with addns.

SCHÜTZ, HEINRICH (name sometimes latinised SAGITTARIUS) (b. Köstritz, Saxony, Oct. 8, 1585 ; d. Dresden, Nov. 6, 1672), ' the father of German music,' as he has been styled. His father and grandfather occupied a good social position at Weissenfels, whither his father removed with his family on the death of the grandfather in 1591. Admitted in 1599 as a chorister into the chapel of the Landgraf Maurice of Hesse-Cassel, Schütz had, besides a thorough musical training, the advantage of a good general education in the arts and sciences

[1] Riemann.

[2] Riemann gives names and dates of about 20 operas.

## LXXII

SWEELINCK

From an engraving by J. Muller (1624)

SCHÜTZ

From a painting in the University Library, Leipzig

of the time, which enabled him in 1607 to proceed to the University of Marburg, where he pursued with some distinction the study of law. The Landgraf, when on a visit to Marburg, observing in his *protégé* a special inclination and talent for music, generously offered to defray the expense of his further musical cultivation at Venice under the tuition of Giovanni Gabrieli, the most distinguished musician of the age. Schütz accordingly proceeded to Venice in 1609, and already in 1611 published the first-fruits of his studies under Gabrieli, a book of 5-part madrigals dedicated to his patron. On the death of Gabrieli in 1612, Schütz returned to Cassel and was appointed organist to the Landgraf, but, either uncertain himself as to his real vocation for music, or induced by his friends, he had still some thoughts of taking up again the profession of law. Perhaps the Landgraf's chapel was too narrow a sphere for him to work in ; it was fortunate therefore that in 1614 he received the invitation to undertake the entire direction of the Kapelle of the Elector Johann Georg of Saxony at Dresden, at a salary of 400 gulden.. The Landgraf was unwilling to part with him, and would at first only allow him to accept this position temporarily. He recalled Schütz in 1616, but on the earnest petition of the Elector finally consented to his remaining permanently at Dresden. Schütz's first endeavour at Dresden was to reorganise the electoral music, and, indeed, as he had been engaged to do, on the Italian model, for the purpose of introducing the new concerted style of music, vocal and instrumental. He procured good Italian instruments and players, and sent qualified members of the Kapelle to Italy for a time to perfect themselves in the new style of singing and playing.

His first work of importance appeared in 1619, ' Psalmen Davids sammt etlichen Motetten und Concerten mit 8 und mehr Stimmen,' a work which shows the influence of the new monodic or declamatory style which Schütz had learned in Italy.

For his purpose Schütz uses the means of expression afforded by contrast of different choirs, or contrast of solo voices with full choir, or contrast of voices with instruments, either the simple basso continuo, *i.e.* for organ, lute or theorbo, or strings with occasional trumpets, etc. His next work, in 1623, was an oratorio on the subject of the Resurrection, entitled

' Historia der fröhlichen und siegreichen Auferstehung unsers einigen Erlösers unde Seligmachers Jesu Christi.'

The occasion for the composition of this work would seem to have been the practice, still kept up at Dresden, Leipzig and other churches in Saxony, of singing the story of the Resurrection at Easter as that of the Passion in Holy Week. A ' Geistliches Gesangbuch ' of 1612 informs us that ' Every year on Easter-day at Vespers, before the sermon, there is sung in

our Christian congregations the Resurrection, so splendidly set by Antonius Scandellus.' This Antonius Scandellus, Scandello or Scandelli, had been one of Schütz's own predecessors at Dresden from 1568–80, and had written both a Passion and a Resurrection. (See SCANDELLO.) His ' Resurrection ' must have continued in use even beyond Schütz's time, since it even appears in Vopelius's ' Leipziger Gesangbuch ' of 1682. It may be seen in Schöberlein and Riegel's ' Schatz des liturgischen Chorgesang,' ii. 619-47.[1] Schütz's ' Resurrection ' follows the line of Scandello's ; only whereas Scandello's composition is purely vocal, that of Schütz is adapted to instrumental accompaniment. Both works begin with a setting (in Scandello 5-part, in Schütz 6-part) of the words ' Die Auferstehung unsers Herrn Jesu Christi, wie uns die von den Evangelisten beschrieben wird,' and conclude with a setting (Scandello 5-part, Schütz 8-part) of the words ' Gott sei Dank, der uns den Sieg gegeben hat,' etc. In Scandello, the part of the Evangelist is altogether liturgical; but in Schütz, while it is mostly based on the liturgical melody, the more important passages have given to them a more characteristic and expressive form of declamation, which sometimes rises up to actual melody in the more modern sense of the term, and the Evangelist's part is accompanied throughout either by the organ or preferably by four viole da gamba, which are called upon at certain pauses in the narrative to execute appropriate runs or passages (' Zierliche und appropriirte Läufe oder Passaggi machen '). The words of other personages are set for two or more voices, according to their number—as, for instance, the words of the three Maries as a trio, of the two angels as a duet, of the eleven disciples as a 6-part chorus ; only that usually for single personages two parts are employed (as in Scandello), though Schütz permits one of these parts to be taken, as he expresses it, *instrumentaliter*.

This work of Schütz is altogether remarkable, as being a highly successful endeavour to unite dramatic expressiveness with reverence for ecclesiastical tradition. The same spirit is shown in another form in his next work of importance, ' Cantiones sacrae,' for four voices with bass accompaniment for organ. The endeavour here is to unite the older form of the motet with the newer form of the concerto, and the diatonic church modes with the use of chromatic harmonies.

In 1627 Johann Georg I. of Saxony wished to signalise the occasion of the marriage of his daughter to the Landgraf of Hesse-Darmstadt by giving the first performance of opera in Germany. The opera had just sprung into life in connexion with the new musical

[1] With regard to the authorship, compare O. Kade's remarks in the Vorwort to the Notenbeilagen to Ambros's *Geschichte*. xlvi.

movement in Italy, as a supposed revival of the antique music-drama. Schütz was commissioned to procure from Italy Peri's opera ' Dafne.' The poet Opitz was set to the task of translating the Italian text by Rinuccini into German, and as it was found that Peri's music would not quite fit the new German words, Schütz had to adapt them to new music of his own. The opera ' Dafne,' as thus set by Schütz, was performed at Torgau on Apr. 13, 1627. Unfortunately the music of this first German opera has not been preserved, and no further account of it has been given. It is probable, however, that Schütz did little else on this occasion than rearrange Peri's music and add something in exactly the same style. In any case, the result was not such as to induce Schütz to make any further attempts in music for the theatre, if we except another occasional piece, a ballet, ' Orpheus und Euridice,' written in 1638, the music of which appears also to be lost. In 1625 appeared his ' Geistliche Gesänge,' and in 1628 Schütz, having lost his wife, found some comfort in his sorrow, as he tells us, by occupying himself with the task of composing melodies with simple 4-part harmony to a rhymed version of the Psalms by Dr. Cornelius Becker. This version by Becker was meant to be a Lutheran rival to an earlier Calvinistic version by Lobwasser, based on the French Psalter of Marot and Beza, and adapted to the same melodies. Later on, Johann Georg II., with a view to the introduction of the Becker Psalter in place of Lobwasser's in the schools and churches of Saxony, urged Schütz to complete his composition of melodies for the work. The task was hardly congenial to our composer, as he himself confesses in the preface to the complete work when it appeared in 1661. Two further editions, however, of this Psalter, with Schütz's melodies, appeared in 1676 and 1712. Some of these melodies passed into later Cantionals, though none has ever taken the same place in general use or esteem that similar work by less eminent composers has done.

Partly to distract himself from his great sorrow, partly to familiarise himself with the still newer development of music in Italy, with which the name of Claudio Monteverdi is chiefly associated, Schütz set out on a second visit to Italy in 1629. He found musical taste in Venice greatly changed since the time of his first visit (1612), ' modern ears were being regaled with a new kind of sensation ' (' recente titillatione '). The new style consisted in the greater prominence given to solo singing, and to intensity of expression in solo singing, the freer use of dissonances, and greater richness and variety in instrumental accompaniment. In a series of works entitled ' Symphoniae sacrae,' Schütz endeavoured to turn to account the new experiences he had gained, without,

however, like his new Italian models, turning his back upon his earlier polyphonic training. He never altogether forgot to unite the solidity of the old school with the piquancy of expression of the new. The first part of ' Symphoniae sacrae ' appeared at Venice in 1629, and consists of 20 settings of Latin texts, chiefly from the Psalms and the Song of Songs. A second part of ' Symphoniae sacrae,' with the subtitle ' Deutsche Concerten,' appeared at Dresden in 1657 ; a third part also at Dresden in 1650. The two later parts are settings of German Bible texts. They may be described as brief dramatic cantatas for various combinations of voices and instruments, and in virtue of them Schütz may be considered joint-founder with Carissimi of the dramatic oratorio. Winterfeld [1] singles out for special notice from the first part, ' Fili, fili mi, Absalom ' (David's lament over Absalom), written for bass solo with accompaniment of four trombones, and from the third part, ' Saul, Saul, was verfolgst du mich ? ' (a cantata for the festival of the Conversion of St. Paul), and ' Mein Sohn, warum hast du uns das gethan ? ' (for the first Sunday after Epiphany).

In 1631 and following years Saxony became the scene of war, and one result was the complete disorganisation of the Elector's Kapelle, means failing for the payment of musicians, and the attention of the Elector and his court being occupied with more serious matters than music. Schütz obtained leave in 1633 to accept an invitation to Copenhagen from King Christian IV. of Denmark. The years 1635–41 were spent in wanderings to and fro between different courts with occasional returns to Dresden, Schütz being still nominally in the service of the Elector. The chief works worthy of notice published during these years are two sets of Geistliche Concerte for one to five voices, with basso continuo (1636, 1639), the second set being especially remarkable by the composer's frequent directions for the securing of proper expression in his music. (It is to be remembered that marks and terms of expression were not then in common use.) In 1641 Schütz returned to Dresden to make an effort to reorganise the music, but from want of means his efforts were not crowned with anything like success till 1645 or 1647. A work of importance was written and produced about 1645, though strangely enough it was never printed or published in Schütz's lifetime, and only appeared in print for the first time in 1873, edited by Carl Riedel of Leipzig. It is a small Passion oratorio on the Seven Words from the Cross. This work is of importance as contributing some new elements to the development of the later Passion music. First, the part of the Evangelist is no longer based on the liturgical intonation,

[1] *Gabrieli*, vol. iii. pp. 82, etc., also *Evang. Kir. Gesang.* vol. ii. p. 315.

as in the ' Resurrection ' oratorio of 1623, but takes the form of the new ' Arioso recitative.' For the sake of variety Schütz divides this part among different solo voices, and sets it twice in the form of a quartet. Next, the work is opened and concluded with a chorus (5-part with basso continuo) expressive of the feelings of Christians at the contemplation of our Lord upon the Cross. After the opening, and again before the concluding chorus, there occurs a short 5-part instrumental symphony, which has been aptly described as an ideal raising and dropping of the curtain before and after the action. The instruments to be used are not specified, but strings are probably more intended than anything else. The part of our Lord differs from the other parts in having a 3-part instrumental accompaniment. This probably originated out of the custom in previous ' Passions ' (as followed in Scandello's ' Resurrection,' for instance), of setting the words of our Lord in four vocal parts. Schütz here improved upon the idea, first timidly suggested by himself in his ' Resurrection,' of giving the words of a single character to a single voice, for the sake of dramatic consistency, and assigning the accompanying parts to the instruments. The way in which this accompaniment is carried out deserves to be noticed. It is neither in the old style nor in the new, but a curious combination of both ; the lower part is identical with the basso continuo for sustaining the harmony throughout : the other two parts are written in the polyphonic style with the voice, consisting of imitations either preceding or following the vocal phrase. It is well known how Bach in his ' Matthew-Passion ' developed this idea of a special accompaniment to the words of our Lord, surrounding Him as it were with a halo. Naturally there are no arias in the modern sense in Schütz's work, all is in the form of expressive recitative. A touching simplicity and tenderness distinguish the whole work. (See PASSION MUSIC.)

In 1648 appeared his ' Musicalia ad Chorum sacrum,' a work in quite a different style from those last mentioned, and showing a reaction in Schütz's mind against the exclusive claims of the modern ' Manier.' It consists of twenty-nine pieces to German words, for five, six and seven voices, in the old motet or strictly polyphonic style, in which the bassus generalis or continuus may be dispensed with (as the title says, ' Wobei der Bassus Generalis auf Gutachten und Begehren, nicht aber aus Nothwendigkeit zugleich auch zu befinden ist '). In the preface he expresses the opinion that no one will become a capable musician who has not first acquired skill in strict contrapuntal work without the use of the basso continuo. Personal reasons to some extent combined with artistic reasons to produce the reaction in favour of the older school of music as against the new, to

which we have referred. From 1647 onwards, in spite of the many personal sacrifices he had made on behalf of the Elector's Kapelle, as for instance by paying or increasing out of his own salary the salaries of others of the musicians, he appears to have suffered so many annoyances in connexion with it as caused him to have almost a disgust for the further cultivation of music at Dresden, and induced him to solicit over and over again in 1651–55 dismissal from the Elector's service. The new Italian element in the chapel was very different from the old ; Schütz was getting involved in continual differences and squabbles with a new Italian colleague Bontempi. Italian art was losing its earlier seriousness of purpose, turning its back upon its older traditions, and aiming simply at the amusement of princes and their courts, and thus acquiring a popularity dangerous to higher ventures of art. The Elector, however, refused to accept the resignation of his Kapellmeister, and after 1655 affairs improved somewhat, so far as Schütz was personally concerned, so that he continued quietly at his post for the remaining sixteen years of his life.

In 1657 he published ' Zwölf geistliche Gesänge ' a 4 for small choirs, a work which we might call a German Communion and Evening Service, consisting, as it does, mainly of settings of the chief portions of the liturgy in order, viz. the Kyrie, Gloria, Nicene Creed, Words of Institution (usually appointed to be sung in early Lutheran liturgies), a Communion Psalm, Post-Communion Thanksgiving, then a Magnificat and Litany, etc. From 1657–61 our composer would seem to have been occupied with the task enjoined on him by the new Elector, that of composing additional melodies for Becker's Psalter, already mentioned ; work which apparently gave him more trouble than it was worth, and hindered him from devoting himself to other more congenial work. In the preface to this Psalter, 1661, he says that ' to confess the truth, he would rather have spent the few remaining years of his life in revising and completing other works which he had begun, requiring more skill and invention ' (' mehr sinnreichen Inventionen ').

In 1664, at the instance of the Elector Johann Georg II., Schütz composed what may be described as a Christmas Oratorio. Its original title is ' Historia der freuden-und gnaden-reichen Geburt Gottes und Mariens Sohn Jesu Christi,' etc. It is a work conceived on a larger scale—vocal and instrumental—than his other works of the kind, but, unfortunately, Schütz only had printed the part of the Evangelist in recitative with figured bass. In this imperfect form it was republished by Philipp Spitta in 1885 in the first volume of his complete edition of the works of Schütz. Since then the other vocal and nearly all the instrumental parts have been discovered in MS.

in the university library of Upsala in Sweden. The introduction, consisting of the title 'Die Geburt,' etc., is set for four vocal and five instrumental parts. This is followed by 'The Message of the Angel,' set for soprano solo with accompaniment of two violettas and one violone, introducing a simple cradle song; the 'Chorus of Angels,' for six voices with violins and violas; the words of the Shepherds set for three alto voices accompanied by two flutes and bassoon; the words of the Wise Men, for three tenor voices with two violins and bassoon; the High Priests for four bass voices and two trombones; and so on with the rest of the work to its conclusion with a Thanksgiving Chorus. The whole work has now been edited in score for practical use by A. Schering as a supplement to Spitta's complete edition.

The last work of Schütz preserved to us, and perhaps his most famous work, is his setting of the story of the Passion, four settings in all, after the four Evangelists, 'Historia des Leidens und Sterbens unserer Herrn und Heylandes Jesu Christi' (1665–66). This work was never published in his own lifetime, and the only original copy extant is that of the St. John Passion, presented by the composer himself to the Duke of Wolfenbüttel, and now in the library at Wolfenbüttel. The only copy of the other settings is that made by a later hand in 1690, regarding which see below in list of Schütz's works. As we now have the work, it is for voices alone without instruments. It is, therefore, as if the composer here wished to renounce the mere external advantages of the newer concerted and dramatic style for the sake of showing how the spirit of it could be retained and applied to the purely vocal and older polyphonic style. For what specially distinguishes this Passion Music is the series of brief choruses of surprising dramatic energy and truth of expression, yet never overstepping the bounds of devout reverence inspired by the subject. Otherwise the work is more purely liturgical than later Passions, not having arias and Chorals to interrupt the narrative and give that variety of interest so needed for modern concert performance. Each Passion is opened according to old custom with a setting of the title (' the Passion, etc.') and closed with a devotional chorus in motet style, the text taken from some familiar church hymn. The rest of the work is written in unaccompanied recitative, though parts of it may have been meant to be accompanied in the manner suggested by Schütz himself in his 'Resurrection.' In the 'St. Matthew' the recitative has more of melodic expressiveness than in the other Passions. The 'St. Mark' is peculiar in combining the greatest monotony of recitative with the richest dramatic character in the choruses. Spitta, the editor of the complete edition of Schütz's works, is inclined, on this

and other grounds, to doubt the authenticity of the 'St. Mark Passion' (see his Preface, pp. xx, xxi). But the fact of its being joined with the other undoubtedly authentic Passions without anything to indicate its being by a different author, is sufficient to outweigh mere suspicions. These 'Passions,' compressed by Carl Riedel and so far adapted to the requirements of modern performance, have been repeatedly produced with considerable success by the Riedelsche Verein of Leipzig.

In his later years Schütz's powers began to fail, especially his sense of hearing; and we are told, when he could no longer go out, he spent the most of his time in the reading of Holy Scripture and spiritual books. His last attempts at composition were settings of portions of the 119th Psalm; and no verse indeed of that Psalm could have been more fittingly chosen as the motto of both his personal life and his art-work than that on which he was last engaged, but left unfinished: 'Thy statutes have been my songs in the house of my pilgrimage.' He is the true predecessor of Handel and Bach, not so much in the mere form of his work as the spirit. If in the dramatised Biblical scenes of his 'Symphoniae sacrae' he is more especially Handel's predecessor, in his Passion Music he is Bach's. Both Handel and Bach simply brought to perfection what lay in germ in Heinrich Schütz. His great merit consists in this, that at a time when the new dramatic style was threatening the complete overthrow of the older polyphonic style, he saw how to retain the advantages of both, and laboured to engraft the one upon the other. The rather singular coincidence of Schütz's birth-year being exactly a hundred years earlier than the birth-year of Handel and Bach, brought about, on the occasion of the keeping of the bicentenary of the two latter, in 1885, a great revival of interest in the work of their forerunner, which has had this practical result at least, the publication of a monumental edition of his works by Breitkopf & Härtel of Leipzig.

The following is a list of Schütz's works, based on Eitner, *M.f.M.* xviii. p. 47 ff., and *Q.-L.*

### I. WORKS PUBLISHED IN LIFETIME

1. Il primo libro de Madrigali de Henrico Sagitario Alemanno. Venice, 1611. Dedicated to Landgraf Moritz of Hesse-Cassel. Contains 18 Madrigals *a* 5, and 1 Dialogo *a* 8.
2. 3 Pièces d'occasion, entitled 'Concerte,' published separately. Dresden, 1618.
3. Die Worte Jesus Syrach; Wol dem der ein tugends. Weib, 1618.
4. Concerto in two parts. 1618.
5. Psalmen Davids sampt etlichen Moteten und Concerten mit acht und mehr Stimmen, nebenst andern zweien Capellen dass dero etliche auf drei und vier Chor nach Beliebung gebraucht werden können, wie auch mit beigefügten Basso Continuo vor die Orgel, Lauten, Chitaron, etc. Dresden, 1619. Contains 26 Psalms.
6. Psalm cxxxiii., for 8 voices with Basso Continuo, composed for his brother's wedding. Leipzig, 1619.
7. Syncharma Musicum tribus Choris adornatum, etc. A pièce d'occasion for the restoration of peace in Silesia. Breslau, 1621.
8. Historia der fröhlichen und siegreichen Auferstehung unsers einigen Erlösers und Seligmachers Jesu Christi. In fürstlichen Capellen oder Zimmern um die Osterliche zeit zu geistlicher Recreation füglichen zu gebrauchen. Dresden, 1623. An Oratorio on the Resurrection of Christ. The title shows that it was intended as well for chamber performance as for church.

9. Elegy on the Death of 'Fürstin Frau Sophia, Herzogin zu Sachsen.' Melody with Basso Cont. Text by Schütz himself. Freiberg, 1623.

10. Cantiones sacrae quatuor vocum, cum Basso ad Organum. Freiberg, 1625. Contains 41 pieces *a* 4 with Latin words.

11. De vitae fugacitate, Aria quinque vocum supra Bassum Con-'inuum. Freiberg, 1625. A pièce d'occasion.

12. Psalmen Davids, in Teutsche Reimen gebrachte durch D. Cornelium Beckern . . . nach gemeiner Contrapunctsart in 4 Stimmen gestellt . . . Freiberg, 1628. Contains 92 new melodies by Schütz himself and 11 others harmonised by him. An edition, Güstrow, 1640, was published for use in Mecklenburg-Schwerin. A later enlarged edition, with melodies for all the Psalms, appeared, Dresden, 1661.

13. Symphoniae sacrae . . . variis vocibus ac Instrumentis accommodatae a 3, 4, 5, 6. Opus ecclesiasticum secundum. Venice, 1629. Dedicated to the Elector of Saxony. Contains 20 settings of Latin texts.

14. 'Das ist je gewisslich wahr.' A motet for 6 voices in memory of Johann Hermann Schein, died 1631. Dedicated to Schein's widow and children. Dresden, 1631.

15. Erster Theil Kleiner geistlichen Concerten, mit 1, 2, 3. 4 und 5 Stimmen sammt beigefügten Basso Cont. Leipzig, 1636. Contains 17 pieces to German words.

16. Musicalische Exequien . . . mit 6, 8 und mehr Stimmen zu gebrauchen. Dresden, 1636. Contains 3 funeral pieces.

17. Anderer Theil Kleiner geistlichen Concerten, mit 1, 2, 3, 4 und 5 Stimmen, sammt beigefügten Basso Continuo vor die Orgel. Dresden, 1639. Contains 31 pieces, texts German and Latin.

18. Symphoniarum sacrarum Secunda Pars . . . Deutsche Concerte mit 3, 4, 5 nämlich einer, zwo, dreien Vocal- und zweien Instrumental-Stimmen. . . . Opus Decimum. Dresden, 1647. Dedicated to Christian V. of Denmark. Contains 27 pieces. German words.

19. Danck-Lied für die hocherwiesene fürstliche Gnade in Weymar, 1647.

20. Musicalia ad Chorum sacrum. Geistliche Chor-Musik mit 5, 6, 7 Stimmen, beides Vocaliter und Instrumentaliter zu gebrauchen . . . Opus Undecimum. Dresden, 1648. Dedicated to the Bürgermeister, etc., of Leipzig, out of respect for the Choir of the Thomas-Schule. Contains 29 motets to German words.

21. Symphoniarum sacrarum Tertia Pars. Deutsche Concerte mit 5, 6, 7, 8, nämlich 3, 4, 5, 6. Vocal- und zweien Instrumental-Stimmen. . . . Opus Duodecimum. Dresden, 1650.

22. Canticum B. Simeonis. German text of Nunc Dimittis, 2 settings for 6 voices. (Not perfectly preserved.)

23. Zwölf geistliche Gesänge a 4. Für kleine Cantoreien. Opus Decimum Tertium. Dresden, 1657.

24. Historia der Freuden- und Gnaden-reichen Geburt Gottes und Marien Sohnes, Jesu Christi . . . Vocaliter und Instrumentaliter in die Musik versetzt. Dresden, 1664. A Christmas Oratorio, but only imperfectly preserved.

**II. WORKS UNPUBLISHED IN LIFETIME**

1. Die Sieben Worte unsers lieben Erlösers und Seligmachers Jesu Christi, so Er am Stamm des heiligen Kreuzes gesprochen, ganz beweglich gesetzt. . . . Parts in manuscript preserved in the Library at Cassel, discovered in 1855 by O. Kade, and first published in Score and adapted for modern performance by Carl Riedel, Leipzig, 1873.

2. Historia des Leidens und Sterbens unsers Herrens Jesu Christi. (*a*) Nach dem Evangelisten St. Matthaeus. (*b*) Nach St. Marcus. (*c*) Nach St. Lucas. (*d*) Nach St. Johannes. An older form of the Johannes Passion exists in MS. 1665. Of the four Passions together there exists only a copy made by J. Z. Grundig in 1690, now in the Leipzig Stadt Bibliothek.

3. Various single motets and concerted pieces, enumerated by Eitner, *M.f.M.* xviii. pp. 62, 67-70, and in the *Q.-L.*

**III. WORKS LOST**

1. 'Dafne.' Opera, performed 1627. German text by Opitz, after the original by Rinuccini.

2. A Ballet with Dialogue and Recitative, composed for the marriage of Johann Georg II. of Saxony, 1638. (Another Ballet, 'Von Zusammenkunft und Wirkung der VII. Planeten,' existing in MS., is conjecturally ascribed to Schütz in Eitner's List, *M.f.M.* xviii. p. 69.)

All Schütz's MS. remains at Dresden were destroyed by fire, 1760. The same fate befell in 1794 what he may have left at Copenhagen.

**IV. DOUBTFUL WORKS**

Ballet, 'Von Zusammenkunft und Wirkung der VII Planeten,' found in MS. at Dresden. (See above.)

**V. COMPLETE EDITION IN SCORE**

Begun on the Tercentenary of the composer's Birthday, 1885. Heinrich Schütz, Sämmtliche Werke, edited by Friedrich Chrysander and Philipp Spitta, and published by Messrs. Breitkopf & Härtel, Leipzig (1885–94).

Vol. 1 contains the 'Resurrection' Oratorio, the Passions-Musik after the four Evangelists, the Seven Words from the Cross, and in an Appendix the imperfect Christmas Oratorio, and the older form of the Johannes-Passion.

Vols. 2 and 3 contain the Psalms and Motets of 1619.

Vol. 4, Cantiones sacrae, 1625.

Vol. 5, Symphoniae sacrae, Part I. 1629.

Vol. 6, Geistliche Concerte of 1636 and 1639.

Vol. 7, Symphoniae sacrae, Part II. 1647.

Vol. 8, Musicalia ad Chorum sacrum, 1648.

Vol. 9, Italian Madrigals, 1611.

Vols. 10 and 11, Symphoniae sacrae, Part III. 1630.

Vol. 12, Gesammelte Motetten, Concerte, Madrigals, and Arien, i. (containing Nos. 14, 16 and 22, besides other things).

Vol. 13, Ditto. ii. Pss. 24, 8, 7, 85, 127, 15 and motets.

Vol. 14, Ditto. iii. 14 Compositions, including No. 6.

Vol. 15, Ditto. iv. 12 Compositions, including No. 7.

Vol. 16, Psalms for Becker's hymn-book.

Supplement edited by A. Schering (see above).

**BIBLIOGRAPHY**

P. SPITTA : Biography of Schütz (*Allg. d. Biographie*, etc., 1894).
F. SPITTA : *Gedächtnissrede auf Schütz. Die Passionen nach den vier Evangelien von H. Schütz.* (1886.)
F. CHRYSANDER : *Geschichte der Braunschweig-Wolfenbüttelschen Kapelle und Oper* (1863). (*Jahrb. für mus. Wissenschaft*).
A. PIRRO : *H. Schütz* (Paris, 1913). *Encyclopédie de la musique* (*Allemagne, XVIIe et XVIIIe siècles*).
A. EINSTEIN : *Schütz-Miszellen*, i. (*Z.M.W.*, May 1923, pp. 432, 433).
HANS JOACHIM MOSER : *Heinrich Schütz. Gedenkrede* (*Z.M.W.*, Nov. 1922, pp. 65-74).
JULIUS SMEND : *Zur Wortbetonung des Lutherischen Bibeltextes bei Heinrich Schütz* (*Z.M.W.*, Nov. 1922, pp. 75-8).

J. R. M.

**SCHULHOFF,** (1) JULIUS (*b.* Prague, Aug. 2, 1825 ; *d.* Berlin, Mar. 13, 1898), once dear to player and dancer for his Galop di Bravura, Impromptu Polka and many more brilliant and clever PF. pieces. He learned the piano from Kisch, and counterpoint from Tomaschek, and before he was 14 made a successful appearance as a player. Notwithstanding his success, the boy's ambition was too great to allow him to remain in Prague, and in 1842 he went to Paris, then a hotbed of pianoforte virtuosity. Here a fortunate interview with Chopin gave him his opportunity. He played in public (Nov. 2, 1845) and published his first two works, of which op. 1, an Allegro Brillant, was dedicated to Chopin. After a lengthened residence in Paris he took a very extended tour through France, Austria (1849–50), England, Spain (1851) and even south Russia and the Crimea (1853). He lived in Dresden from 1870, and in Berlin from about 1897. A sonata in F minor and twelve études are among his more earnest compositions. G.

(2) ERWIN (*b.* Prague, June 8, 1894), great-grandnephew of the above, studied at the Conservatoires of Prague, Vienna, Leipzig and Cologne and is a pianist who devotes himself to the furtherance of modern art and a composer who aims at naturalism. He has published much piano music and composed a considerable quantity of chamber music. His op. 26 is a symphony for soprano voice and orchestra, his op. 28 one for alto and orchestra (*Riemann*.)

**SCHULTHEISS,** BENEDICT (*d.* Mar. 1, 1693), was the younger son of Hieronymus Schultheiss (1600–69) and his second wife, whom he married in 1648. Benedict became organist at S. Egidius, Nuremberg, but he died at a comparatively early age. He published first a set of clavier pieces :

'Muth und Geist ermunternder Clavier-Lust. Erster Theil, Nürnberg, 1679 ; Ander Theil, 1680.'

Later he seems to have devoted himself entirely to church music, and composed many Chorals which are still included in the evangelical church-song ; they will be found in the following works, all published in his lifetime :

Heiliger Sonntags-Handel und Kirch-Wandel . . . durch Sigmund von Birken. Nürnberg, 1681. Contains two melodies with figured bass by 'Ben. Schulth.'
Der geistlichen Erquick-Stunden des . . . Heinr. Müllers . . . Poetischer Andacht-Klang von denen Blumgenossen verfasset, anjetzo mitt 60 Liedern vermehret, und von unterschiedlichen Ton-Künstlern in Arien gesetzt. Nürnberg, 1691. Contains thirteen melodies with figured bass by Schultheiss.
Gott-geheiligter Christen nützlich-ergetzende Seelen-Lust . . . mit lieblich in Noten gesetzten neuen Arien . . . vorgestellet von W. C. D. [W. C. Dessler]. Nürnberg, 1692.

It contains twenty-five melodies with figured bass ; Zahn included nine of them in his great work *Die Melodien der deutschen evangelischen Kirchenlieder*, 1893, and thinks Schultheiss composed all twenty-five, although only the first eleven are initialled *B. S.*    C. S.

SCHULTHESIUS, JOHANN PAUL (*b.* Fechheim, Saxe-Coburg, Sept. 14, 1748 ; *d.* Leghorn, Apr. 18, 1816), received his first lessons in music from his father, a schoolmaster ; in 1764 he entered the local college to follow a course of theology, became a member of the choir, and remained there six years, acquiring a thorough knowledge of music. From 1770–73 he was at the University of Erlangen, where he completed his theological studies, while he was able to obtain organ lessons from Kehl, an excellent organist. He was then offered a post at Leghorn, as Protestant minister to the colony of Germans and Dutch settled there ; he accepted and went to Italy, where he remained for the rest of his life. Checchi was organist at that time, and gave him lessons in counterpoint and composition. Schulthesius was an excellent performer on the clavier, and in 1782 he was called upon to play some of his own compositions before the Grand Duke of Tuscany, and was very favourably received. He became one of the most erudite musicians of his time, and in 1807 was nominated secretary of the fourth class of the Accademia di scienze, lettere ed arti di Livorno. His treatise on the quality and character of church music :

*Sulla musica da chiesa.* Memoria di Gio. Paolo Schulthesius. Livorno, presso Tommaso Masi. 1810, 4to,

was also published in the first volume of the *Proceedings* of his Accademia. Letters of his to Marco Santucci are in existence ; in one of them he mentions his work, and expresses his desire to hear Santucci's opinion of it. The following compositions were also published :

Tre sonate per il Cimbalo o piano-forte con l' accompagnamento d' un violino obbligato. Composte da Gio. Paolo Schulthesius. Opera 1. Livorno, 1780, obl. folio. A copy of the second edition is in the British Museum.
Sonate a solo per il cembalo o pianoforte. Op. 2. Livorno, obl. fol.
Deux quatuors pour piano, violon, viola et violoncello. Op. 3, London, 1785.
Otto variazioni facili sopra un Andantino per il cimbalo o pianoforte, violino, viola e violoncello obbligato. Op. 4. Livorno. Four oblong folio partbooks.
Allegretto avec 12 variations pour le Clavecin ou pianoforte, violon, viola et violoncello obbligato. Op. 6. Augsburg (Gombart).
Andante grazioso de Pleyel varié pour le clavecin ou pianoforte, violon et violoncello obbligato. Op. 7. Augsburg (Gombart).
Andantino original, avec huit variations pour le piano. Op. 8. Augsburg (Gombart).
Sept variations pour le forte-piano. Op. 9. Augsburg (Gombart). 1797. Dedicated to Joh. Nic. Forkel.
Huit variations sur un air russe pour piano. Op. 10. Livorno.
Douze variations sur l'air de *Malbrouk* pour piano, violon, viola et violoncello. Op. 11. Florence (Nicola Pagni).
La reconciliazione di due amici, tema con variazioni. Op. 12. Augsburg (Gombart). It was dedicated to Haydn.
Otto variazioni sentimentali sopra un tema originale intitolato L' Amicizia per pianoforte, dedicate al signore Carlo Mozart, figlio maggiore del Gran Mozart. Op. 14. Leipzig. Breitkopf.
C. S.

SCHULTZ, see PRAETORIUS.

SCHULTZ (SCHULTZE), CHRISTOPH (*b.* Sorau, 1606 ; *d.* Delitzsch, Aug. 28, 1683), a pupil of Schein at Leipzig, cantor at the Neumarkt Halle, and in 1633 cantor at Delitzsch. He composed several books of sacred songs, some in madrigal form, and a Passion according to St. Luke (1653) (*Riemann* ; *Q.-L.*).

SCHULTZ (SCULTETUS), JOHANN (*b.* Lüneburg, late 16th cent. ; *d.* Dannenberg, Brunswick, Feb. 1653), was organist to the Prince of Brunswick, Lüneburg. He composed several books of motets, madrigals, etc., and instrumental pieces (*Riemann* ; *Q.-L.* ; Dr. Rob. Siebeck).

SCHULZ (SCHULZ - BEUTHEN), HEINRICH (*b.* Beuthen, June 19, 1838 ; *d.* Dresden, Mar. 12, 1915), was a voluminous composer of works on a large scale, which, however, have not gained any very widespread acceptance.

He studied at the Leipzig Conservatorium (1862–65) and privately with Karl Riedel, and at that time composed Psalm xxix. for three choirs, wind and organ, with other choral settings of psalms and two symphonic poems. He then settled (1866) as a teacher in Zürich, where six of his eight symphonies were written, together with many other works both vocal and instrumental. A nervous break - down brought a temporary cessation of composition. From 1881 he lived in Dresden, from 1893–95 in Vienna, when he returned to Dresden again, and in 1911 was made Royal Professor. The works of his first Dresden period include four operas (not, apparently, performed), a Requiem (ch. and orch.), and further symphonic poems. His eighth symphony (' Sieges-sinfonie ') and movements for further symphonies belong to his second Dresden period. Most of his larger works remain in M.S.

C. (information from *Riemann*).

SCHULZ, JOHANN ABRAHAM PETER (*b.* Lüneburg, Mar. 30, 1747 ; *d.* Schwedt, June 10, 1800), son of a baker. His master was Schmugel, a local organist of ability, whose descriptions of Berlin and of Kirnberger's labours so excited him that at the age of 15, without money and against the wish of his family, he went thither and put himself under the protection of Kirnberger, who was very good to him, under whom he studied and to whom he became greatly attached. In 1768 he was fortunate enough to travel in France, Italy and Germany under good auspices. In 1773 he returned to Berlin, and found his old master and Sulzer at work on their *Allgem. Theorie der schönen Künste*, and undertook the musical portion of it from S to the end. In 1776–78 he was also Kapellmeister to the French theatre at Berlin, and afterwards to the private theatre of the Crown Princess at Berlin and that of Prince Henry at Reinsberg, where he stayed for seven years from Apr. 1, 1780. His choruses to 'Athalia,' produced while there, were translated and brought out at Copenhagen, and the result was an offer from the King of Denmark to be his Kapellmeister at a salary of 2000 thalers. This he accepted and held for eight years, from 1787, with great credit and advantage to the place. His health at length obliged him to leave, and he departed, Sept. 29, 1795, for

Hamburg, Lüneburg and Berlin. He lost his wife, and at length died at Schwedt deeply and widely lamented. Schulz was a prolific composer; his operas are 'Clarisse' (1775), 'La Fée Urgèle' (1782), 'Minona,' and 'Le Barbier de Séville' (1786), 'Aline' (1789); besides, he wrote music to plays, and sacred music such as 'Christi Tod,' 'Maria und Johannes,' etc. Q.-L. gives the names of many church and chamber works, as well as of his important song collections. His literary works include a treatise on a new mode of writing music. He also edited Kirnberger's *Wahre Grundsätze zum Gebrauch der Harmonie* (1783). But his true claim to notice rests on his songs. He was the first to give the Volkslied an artistic turn. He was very careful to get good words, and as a considerable move was taking place among the poets at that date (1770–80), and Bürger, Claudius, Hölty, and others were writing, he had good opportunities, and many of his settings were published in the Göttingen *Musenalmanach* and Voss's *Almanach*. He published also 'Lieder in Volkston bey dem Klavier zu singen' (1782), containing forty-eight songs, 2nd ed. (1785) in two parts, and a third part in 1790. (See Reissmann, *Gesch. d. deutschen Liedes*, p. 149.)　　　　　　　　G.

BIBL.—MAX SEIFFERT, *J. A. P. Schulz's ' dänische' Oper.*, A.M. 13, 1919; HERMANN VON HASE, *Beiträge zur Breikopfschen Geschäftsgeschichte*, Z.M.W., May 1920, pp. 463-5 : *Schulz.*

SCHULZ (SCHULZE), JOHANN PHILIPP CHRISTIAN (b. Langensalza, Thüringia, Feb. 1, 1773 ; d. Leipzig, Jan. 30, 1827), was a student at Leipzig University and studied music under Engler and Schicht. From 1795 he conducted the performances of Sekonda's theatrical company, and on July 31, 1810, was appointed director and conductor of the Gewandhaus concert, which position he held to the time of his death. He composed overtures, marches, etc., for orchestras and a number of vocal compositions for chorus as well as for solo voices. His music library, including the MS. of Beethoven's 'Wiener Tänze,' he bequeathed to the School of St. Thomas (*Riemann* ; *Q.-L.*).

SCHULZE, J. F. & SONS, a firm of organbuilders, whose founder, (1) J. F. SCHULZE (b. Milbitz-bei-Paulinzella, Thuringia, 1794 ; d. 1858), began his manufactory in his birthplace, 1825. His first organs were for Horba (with ten stops) and Milbitz (twenty-one stops). In 1825 he moved to Paulinzella, where his business largely increased. At this period his principal organs were those for Bremen Cathedral and Solingen. In 1851 the firm sent an organ to the International Exhibition in Hyde Park, which obtained a prize medal and was the beginning of much work done for England. In 1854 they built the great organ in the Marienkirche at Lübeck.

J. F. Schulze was succeeded by his three sons, the most distinguished of whom was (2) HEINRICH EDMUND (b. circa 1824; d. 1878),

who introduced many improvements. On the rebuilding of the parish church of Doncaster, after the fire in 1853, the organ was rebuilt by the Schulze firm, with great success. Besides this fine instrument, their most important organs are in Bremen, Düsseldorf, Söst and Aplerbeck. H. E. Schulze died at the age of 54, and shortly after, on the death of the surviving brother, the firm ceased to exist.

The Schulzes' organs are most celebrated for their flute-pipes, which are constructed so as to admit as much wind as possible. In order to do this the feet are opened very wide, and the pipes are in consequence cut up unusually high. By this means, with a comparatively low pressure of wind an extraordinarily rich quantity of tone is produced. The Schulzes carried the same principles into their wooden flute pipes. Their organs are also celebrated for their string-toned stops, but the drawback in all of these is a certain slowness in their speech. Besides the organs at Doncaster and Northampton, the Schulzes have instruments in England at churches at Armley ; Leeds (in conjunction with Hill) ; Hindley, Wigan ; Tyne Dock, South Shields ; Harrogate ; also at Northampton Town Hall ; Charter-house School, Godalming ; Seaton Carew (Thos. Walker, Esq.).　　　　　　　　　　　W. B. S.

SCHUMANN, CLARA JOSEPHINE (b. Leipzig, Sept. 13, 1819 ; d. Frankfort, May 20, 1896), wife of Robert Schumann, one of the greatest pianoforte-players that the world has ever heard, was the daughter of Friedrich WIECK (q.v.).

She began the pianoforte at a very early age under her father's guidance ; and on Oct. 20, 1828, when she had just completed her ninth year. made her début in public at a concert of Frl. Perthaler's, where she played with Emilie Reinhold in Kalkbrenner's 4-hand variations on the march from 'Moïse.' The notices in the Leipzig *Tageblatt* and A.M.Z. show that she was already an object of much interest in the town. At this time she was accustomed to play the concertos of Mozart and Hummel with orchestra by heart, and thus early did she lay the foundation of that sympathy with the orchestra which so distinguished her. On Nov. 8, 1830, when just over 11, she gave her first concert at the Gewandhaus under the good old name of 'Musikalische Akademie'; and her performance is cited by the A.M.Z. as a proof of how far application and good teaching can bring great natural gifts at so early an age. Her solo pieces were 'Rondo brillant' (op. 101), Kalkbrenner; 'Variations brillantes' (op. 23), Herz ; and variations of her own on an original theme ; and she is praised by the critic just referred to for already possessing the brilliant style of the greatest players of the day. Her next appearance was on May 9, 1831, in pieces by Pixis and Herz—still bravura music.

In the same year a set of four polonaises by her was published by Hofmeister. About this time she was taken to Weimar, Cassel and Frankfort, and in the spring of 1832 to Paris, where she gave a concert on Apr. 9 at which she extemporised for the first time in public. Mendelssohn was there at the time, but was suffering from an attack of cholera, and thus the meeting of these two great artists— destined to become such great friends—was postponed. On July 9, and July 31, 1832, she gives two other ' Musikalische Akademien ' in Leipzig, at which, besides Pixis and Herz, we find Chopin's variations on ' La ci darem ' (op. 2), a piece which, only a few months before, Robert Schumann had welcomed with his first and one of his most spirited reviews. At the former of these two concerts Frl. Livia Gerhardt (Mme. Frege) sang in public for the first time.

On Sept. 30, 1832, Clara Wieck seems to have made her début at the Gewandhaus concerts in Moscheles's G minor concerto, and from that time forward her name is regularly found in the programmes of those famous subscription concerts, as well as of others held in the same hall. In the winter of 1837 she made her first visit to Vienna, and remained during the winter playing with great success, and receiving the appointment of ' Kk. Kammer-virtuosin.'

Schumann had been on a very intimate footing in the Wiecks's house for some years, but it was not till the end of 1835 that his attachment to Clara was openly avowed, and it was not till Sept. 12, 1840 (the eve of her birthday), after a series of delays and difficulties which are sufficiently touched upon in the article on Robert Schumann, that they were married. For eighteen months after this event Mme. Schumann remained in Leipzig. We find her name in the Gewandhaus programmes attached to the great masterpieces, but occasionally playing more modern music, as on Dec. 6, 1841, when she twice played with Liszt in a piece of his for two pianos. In the early part of 1842 she and he husband made a tour to Hamburg, which she continued alone as far as Copenhagen. Early in 1844 they went together to St. Petersburg, and at the end of the year Schumann's health made it necessary to leave Leipzig and remove to Dresden, where they resided till 1850. During all this time Mme. Schumann's life was bound up with her husband's, and they were separated only by the exigencies of her profession. She devoted herself not only to his society, but to the bringing out of his music, much of which—such as the PF. concerto, the quintet, quartet and trios, etc.— owed its first reputation to her. In 1846 she met Jenny Lind for the first time at Leipzig, and in the winter of the same year they met again at Vienna, when the two great artists appeared together at a concert in December.

England, though at one time in view, was reserved to a later day. At Paris she never played after the early visit already spoken of. The trials which this faithful wife must have undergone during the latter part of her husband's life, from his first attempt at self-destruction to his death, July 29, 1856, need only be alluded to here. It was but shortly before the fatal crisis that she made her first visit to England, playing at the Philharmonic on Apr. 14 and 28, at the Musical Union on four separate occasions, and elsewhere, her last appearance being on June 24. On June 17 she gave an afternoon 'Recital' at the Hanover Square rooms, the programme of which is worth preserving.

1. Beethoven, Variations in E♭ on theme from the Eroica ; 2. Sterndale Bennett, Two Diversions (op. 17), Suite de pièces (op. 24. No. 1) ; 3. Clara Schumann, Variations on theme from Schumann's ' Bunte Blätter ' ; 4. Brahms, Sarabande and Gavotte in the style of Bach ; 5. Scarlatti, Piece in A major ; 6. R. Schumann's Carnaval (omitting Eusebius, Florestan, Coquette, Replique, Estrella and Aveu).

She returned from London to Bonn just in time to receive her husband's last breath (July 29, 1856).

After this event she and her family resided for some years in Berlin with her mother, who had separated from Wieck and had married a musician named Bargiel; and in 1863 she settled at Baden-Baden, in the Lichtenthal, which then became her usual headquarters till 1874.

Her reception in this conservative country was hardly such as to encourage her to repeat her visit ; she appeared again at the Philharmonic on June 29, 1857, and on June 27, 1859. In a few years the appreciation of Schumann's music had greatly increased on this side the Channel ; and the anxiety of amateurs to hear an artist whose fame on the Continent was so great, became so loudly expressed, that Mme. Schumann was induced to make another visit. She played at the Philharmonic, May 29, 1865, Musical Union, Apr. 18, 25, and June 6, etc. etc. In 1867 she returned again, and after this her visit became an annual one up to 1882, interrupted only in 1878, 1879, 1880, when health and other circumstances did not permit her to travel. She came again in 1885, 1886, 1887 and 1888. In 1886 she again visited Austria, and gave six concerts at Vienna ; and any coldness that the Viennese may have previously shown towards her husband's compositions was then amply atoned for.

In 1878 she accepted the post of principal teacher of the pianoforte in the Conservatoire founded by Dr. Hoch at Frankfort, where she lived and worked with great success until the end of her life.

This is not the place or the time to speak of the charm of Madame Schumann's personality, of the atmosphere of noble and earnest simplicity which surrounded her in private life no less than in her public performance. Those who had the privilege of her acquaintance do not need such description, and for those who had not it is unnecessary to make the attempt. She was deeply and widely beloved, and at a time when there appeared to be a prospect of her being compelled by ill-health to abandon her public appearances, the esteem and affection of her numerous friends took the practical form of a subscription, and a considerable sum of money was raised in Germany and England for her use.

As an artist,[1] Mme. Schumann's place was indubitably in the very first rank; indeed she may perhaps be considered to stand higher than any of her contemporaries, if not as regards the possession of natural or acquired gifts, yet in the use she made of them. Her playing was characterised by an entire absence of personal display, a keen perception of the composer's meaning, and an unfailing power of setting it forth in perfectly intelligible form. These qualities would lead one to pronounce her one of the most intellectual of players, were it not that that term has come to imply a certain coldness or want of feeling, which was never perceived in her playing. But just such a use of the intellectual powers as serves the purposes of true art, ensuring perfect accuracy in all respects, no liberties being taken with the text, even when playing from memory, and above all securing an interpretation of the composer's work which is at once intelligible to the listener—this certainly formed an essential element of her playing, and it is worth while insisting on this, since the absence of that strict accuracy and perspicuity is too often mistaken for evidence of deep emotional intention. With all this, however, Mme. Schumann's playing evinced great warmth of feeling, and a true poet's appreciation of absolute beauty, so that nothing ever sounded harsh or ugly in her hands; indeed it may fairly be said that after hearing her play a fine work (she never played what is not good), one always became aware that it contained beauties undiscovered before. This was, no doubt, partly due to the peculiarly beautiful quality of the tone she produced, which was rich and vigorous without the slightest harshness, and was obtained, even in the loudest passages, by pressure with the fingers rather than by percussion. Indeed, her playing was particularly free from violent movement of any kind; in passages, the fingers were kept close to the keys and squeezed instead of striking them, while chords were grasped from the wrist rather than struck from the elbow. She founded her technique on the principle laid down by her father, F. Wieck, who was also her instructor, that 'the touch [i.e. the blow of the finger upon the key] should never be audible, but only the musical sound,'

[1] This appreciation of Mme. Schumann's style and works was supplied to Sir G. Grove by Franklin Taylor.

an axiom the truth of which there is some danger of overlooking, in the endeavour to compass the extreme difficulties of certain kinds of modern pianoforte music.

Mme. Schumann's repertory was very large, extending from Scarlatti and Bach to Mendelssohn, Chopin and Brahms, and it would be difficult to say that she excelled in her rendering of any one composer's works rather than another's, unless it be in her interpretation of her husband's music. And even here, if she was pronounced by general opinion to be greatest in her playing of Schumann, it is probably because it was to her inimitable performances that we owe, in this country at least, the appreciation and love of his music now happily become universal, and thus the player shared in the acknowledgment she won for the composer.

Mme. Schumann's compositions, though not very numerous, evince that earnestness of purpose which distinguished her work in general. Even her earliest essays, which are short pianoforte pieces written for the most part in dance-form, are redeemed from any approach to triviality by their interesting rhythms, and in particular by the freshness of their modulations, the latter being indeed in some cases original even to abruptness. Their general characteristic is that of delicacy rather than force, their frequent staccato passages and the many skipping grace-notes which are constantly met with requiring for their performance a touch of the daintiest lightness; although qualities of an opposite kind are occasionally shown, as in the 'Souvenir de Vienne,' op. 9, which is a set of variations in bravura style on Haydn's Austrian Hymn. Among her more serious compositions of later date are a trio in G minor for pianoforte, violin and violoncello, op. 17, which is thoroughly musicianlike and interesting, three charming cadenzas to Beethoven's concertos, opp. 37 and 58, and a set of three Preludes and Fugues, op. 16, which deserve mention not only on account of their excellent construction, but as forming a most valuable study in *legato* part-playing. There is also a piano concerto, op. 7, dedicated to Spohr, of which the passages (though not the modulations) remind one of Hummel; but it is a short work and not well balanced, the first movement being reduced to a single solo, which ends on the dominant, and leads at once to the andante.

In the later works, as might naturally be expected, there are many movements which bear traces of the influence of Schumann's music both in harmony and rhythm, but this influence, which first seems perceptible in the 'Soirées musicales,' opp. 5, 6, is afterwards less noticeable in the pianoforte works than in the songs, many of which are of great beauty, and some of which (see op. 12) were incorporated into collections by Schumann. Her 'Liebst du um Schönheit' is one of the most expressive songs in existence. Schumann himself has made use of themes by Mme. Schumann in several instances, namely in his Impromptus, op. 5 (on the theme of her Variations, op. 3, which are dedicated to him), in the andantino of his sonata in F minor op. 14, and (as a 'motto') in the 'Davidsbündlertänze,' op. 6. The following is a list of Mme. Schumann's compositions:

| Op. | | Op. | |
|---|---|---|---|
| 1. | Quatre Polonaises. | 15. | Four pièces fugitives. |
| 2. | Caprices en forme de Valse. | 16. | Three preludes and fugues. |
| 3. | Romance variée. | 17. | Trio, PF. and strings, G |
| 4. | Valses romantiques. | | minor. |
| 5, 6. | Soirées musicales, 10 Pièces | 18. | (?) |
| | caractéristiques. | 19. | (?) |
| 7 | Concerto for pianoforte in | 20. | Variations on a theme by |
| | A minor. | | Robert Schumann.[1] |
| 8. | Variations de Concert, in | 21. | Three romances. |
| | C, on the Cavatina in 'Il | 22. | Three romances for PF and |
| | pirata.' | | violin. |
| 9. | Souvenir de Vienne in E♭, | 23. | 6 Lieder from Rollet's 'Ju- |
| | impromptu. | | cunde.' |
| 10. | Scherzo, D minor. | | 'Liebeszauber,' Lied by Geibel. |
| 11. | 3 Romances (Mechetti). | | Andante and Allegro, PF. solo. |
| 12. | 3 Songs in R. Schumann's | | Cadenzas to Beethoven's Con- |
| | op. 37 (Nos. 2, 4 11). | | certos in C minor and G, |
| 13. | 6 Lieder. | | and to Mozart's in G |
| 14. | 2nd Scherzo, in C minor. | | minor. |
| | | | G. |

BIBL.—B. LITZMANN, *Clara Schumann* (Biography, 3 vols., 1902, 1906, 1908); English translation (abridged) by G. E. HADOW, 2 vols. (London, 1913); F. MAY, *The Girlhood of Clara Schumann* (London, 1912); W. KLEEFELD, *Clara Schumann* (Bielefeld, 1920); (see also Robert Schumann Bibliography).

**SCHUMANN,** GEORG ALFRED (*b.* Königstein on the Elbe, Oct. 25, 1866), was taught the violin by his father, Clemens Schumann (*d.* 1918), the town musical director there, and the organ by his grandfather, with such good results that at 9 years old he played in the orchestra, and at 12 did the organist's duty. At 15 he played the piano in public, and after learning from some Dresden masters, he went to the Leipzig Conservatorium, remaining there from 1881-88. In 1891-96 he was conductor of a choral society at Danzig, and from 1896 to 1899 director of the Philharmonic orchestra and choir in Bremen. In 1900 he was appointed Royal Professor, and made head of the Berlin Singakademie (see BERLIN). In 1913 he followed Bruch as head of the composition school of the Academy of Arts and was made Doctor of Philosophy of Berlin University in 1916. His compositions are in all the larger forms excepting opera. His op. 3 is a choral work, 'Amor und Psyche'; a symphony in B minor won a prize; his first published work for orchestra was a suite, 'Zur Karnevalszeit,' op. 22. Op. 24 is a set of symphonic variations on 'Wer nur den lieben Gott lässt walten,' for organ and orchestra, and op. 30, 'Variationen und Doppelfuge über ein lustiges Thema für grosses Orchester,' shows much humour and technical skill; a serenade, op. 34, and an overture, 'Liebesfrühling,' are among the orchestral works which have reached their climax in a symphony in F minor, op. 42. This symphony was played in London under Landon Ronald in 1909, and his oratorio 'Ruth' (op. 50) was given at the Sheffield Festival under Wood in 1911.

[1] From 'Bunte Blätter,' op. 90, No. 4; also varied by Brahms' op. 9.

Two other choral works, the 'Totenklage,' op. 33, and 'Sehnsucht,' op. 40, deserve mention, and his chamber music includes variations and fugue on a theme of Beethoven for two pianos, a quintet for piano and strings in E minor, op. 18, a violoncello sonata, op. 19, two trios, in F and G, two violin sonatas in E minor and C sharp minor, and a pianoforte quartet for piano and strings in F minor, op. 29. Schumann belongs to the more conservative group of German composers, and his sound musicianship, the originality of his ideas and the skill of their treatment, mark him as a worthy member of the party which most strenuously resists the attitude of the ultra-modern writers. (Paul Hielscher, in *Monographen moderner Musiker*; *Riemann.*)　　　　　　　　　　　M., addns.

**SCHUMANN,** ROBERT ALEXANDER (*b.* Zwickau, Saxony, June 8, 1810; *d.* Endenick near Bonn, July 29, 1856), was the youngest son of Friedrich August Gottlob Schumann (*b.* 1773), a bookseller, whose father was a clergyman in Saxony; the composer's mother, Johanna Christiana (*b.* 1771), was the daughter of Herr Schnabel, Rathschirurgus (surgeon to the town council) at Zeitz.

Schumann cannot have received any incitement towards music from his parents; his father, however, took a lively interest in the *belles lettres*, and was himself known as an author. He promoted his son's leanings towards art in every possible way, with which, however, his mother seems to have had no sympathy. In the small provincial town where Schumann spent the first eighteen years of his life there was no musician capable of helping him beyond the mere rudiments of the art. There was a talented town-musician, who for several decades was the best trumpeter in the district,[2] but, as was commonly the case, he practised his art simply as a trade. The organist of the Marienkirche, J. G. Kuntzsch, Schumann's first pianoforte teacher, after a few years declared that his pupil was able to progress alone, and that his instruction might cease. He was so impressed with the boy's talent, that when Schumann subsequently resolved to devote himself wholly to art, Kuntzsch prophesied that he would attain to fame and immortality, and that in him the world would possess one of its greatest musicians. Some twenty years later, in 1845, Schumann dedicated to him his studies for the pedal-piano, op. 56.

[His gift for music showed itself early. He began to compose, as he tells us himself, before he was 7. According to this he must have begun to play the piano, at latest, in his sixth year.] When he was about 11, he accompanied at a performance of Friedrich Schneider's 'Weltgericht,' conducted by Kuntzsch, standing up at the piano to do it. At home, with the

[2] Schumann, *Gesammelte Schriften*, ii. 126 (1st ed.).

aid of some young musical companions, he got up performances of vocal and instrumental music which he arranged to suit their humble powers. In more extended circles, too, he appeared as a pianoforte-player, and is said to have had a wonderful gift for extempore playing. His father took steps to procure for him the tuition of C. M. von Weber, who had shortly before (1817) been appointed Kapellmeister in Dresden. Weber declared himself ready to undertake the guidance of the young genius, but the scheme fell through for reasons unknown. From that time Schumann remained at Zwickau, where circumstances were not favourable to musical progress; he was left to his own instruction, and every inducement to further progress must have come from himself alone. Under these circumstances, a journey made when he was 9 years old to Carlsbad, where he first heard a great pianoforte-player—Ignaz Moscheles—must have been an event never to be forgotten; and indeed during his whole life he retained a predilection for certain of Moscheles's works, and a reverence for his person. The influence of the pianoforte technique of Moscheles on him appears very distinctly in the variations published as op. 1.

At the age of 10 he entered the fourth class at the Gymnasium (or Academy) at Zwickau, and remained there till Easter, 1828. He had then risen to the first class, and left with a certificate of qualification for the University. During this period his devotion to music seems to have been for a time rather less eager, in consequence of the interference of his schoolwork and of other tastes. Now, at the close of his boyhood, a strong interest in poetry, which had been previously observed in him, but which had meanwhile been merged in his taste for music, revived with increased strength; he rummaged through his father's book-shop, which favoured this tendency, in search of works on the art of poetry; poetical attempts of his own were more frequent, and at the age of 14 Robert had already contributed some literary efforts to a work brought out by his father and called *Bildergallerie der berühmtesten Menschen aller Völker und Zeiten*. That he had a gift for poetry is evident from two Epithalamia given by Wasielewski.[1] In 1827 he set a number of his own poems to music, and it is worthy of note that it was not by the classical works of Goethe and Schiller that Schumann was most strongly attracted. His favourite writers were Schulze, author of 'Die bezauberte Rose'; the unhappy Franz von Sonnenberg; Byron, and, above all, Jean Paul, with whose works he made acquaintance in his seventeenth year (at the same time as with the compositions of Franz Schubert). These poets represent the cycle of views,

sentiments, and feelings, under whose spell Schumann's poetical taste, strictly speaking, remained throughout his life. And in no musician has the influence of his poetical tastes on his music been deeper than in him.

STUDENT DAYS.—On Mar. 29, 1828, Schumann matriculated at the University of Leipzig as *Studiosus Juris*. It would have been more in accordance with his inclinations to have devoted himself at once wholly to art, and his father would no doubt have consented to his so doing; but he had lost his father in 1826, and his mother would not hear of an artist's career. Her son dutifully submitted, although he was decidedly averse to the study of jurisprudence. Before actually joining the university he took a short pleasure trip into South Germany, in April 1828. He had made acquaintance in Leipzig with a fellow-student named Gisbert Rosen; and a common enthusiasm for Jean Paul soon led to a devoted and sympathetic friendship. Rosen went to study at Heidelberg, and the first object of Schumann's journey was to accompany him on his way. In Munich he made the acquaintance of Heine, in whose house he spent several hours. On his return journey he stopped at Bayreuth to visit Jean Paul's widow, and received from her a portrait of her husband.

During the first few months of his university life, Schumann was in a gloomy frame of mind. A students' club to which he belonged for a time, struck him as coarse and shallow, and he could not make up his mind to begin the course of study he had selected. A large part of the first half-year had passed by and still—as he writes to his friend—he had been to no college, but 'had worked exclusively in private, that is to say, had played the piano and written a few letters and Jean Pauliads.'[2]

In this voluntary inactivity and solitude the study of Jean Paul must certainly have had a special charm for him. That writer, unsurpassed in depicting the tender emotions, with his dazzling and even extravagant play of digressive fancy, his excess of feeling over dramatic power, his incessant alternations between tears and laughter, has always been the idol of sentimental women and ecstatic youths. 'If everybody read Jean Paul,' Schumann writes to Rosen, 'they would be better-natured, but they would be unhappier; he has often brought me to the verge of desperation, still the rainbow of peace bends serenely above all the tears, and the soul is wonderfully lifted up and tenderly glorified.' Even in his latest years Schumann would become violently angry if any one ventured to doubt or criticise Jean Paul's greatness as an imaginative writer, and the close affinity of their natures is unmistakable. Schumann himself tells us how once, as

---

[1] *Biographie*, 3rd ed., Bonn, 1880, p. 305.

[2] On the defects and excesses of Schumann's student days see Nieck's *Robert Schumann*, chap. v.

a child, at midnight, when all the household were asleep, he had in a dream and with his eyes closed, stolen down to the old piano, and played a series of chords, weeping bitterly the while. So early did he betray that tendency to over-strung emotion which found its most powerful nourishment in Jean Paul's writings.

Music, however, is a social art, and it soon brought him back again to human life. In the house of Professor Carus [1] he made several interesting acquaintances, especially that of Marschner, who was then living in Leipzig, and had brought out his 'Vampyr' there in the spring of 1828. His first meeting with Wieck, the father of his future wife, took place in the same year; and Schumann took several piano-forte lessons from him. Several music-loving students met together there, and all kinds of chamber music were practised. They devoted themselves with especial ardour to the works of Schubert, whose death, on Nov. 19, 1828, was deeply felt by Schumann. Impelled by Schubert's example, he wrote at this time eight polonaises for four hands; also a quartet for piano and strings, and a number of songs to Byron's words; all of which remain un-published. Besides these occupations, he made a more intimate acquaintance with the clavier works of Sebastian Bach. It is almost self-evident that what chiefly fascinated Schumann in Bach's compositions was the mysterious depth of sentiment revealed in them. Were it not so, it would be impossible to conceive of Bach in connexion with the chaotic Jean Paul; and yet Schumann himself says that in early life Bach and Jean Paul had exercised the most powerful influence upon him. Considering the way in which his musical education had been left to itself, the fact of his so thoroughly appreciating the wealth and full-ness of life in Bach's compositions at a time when Bach was looked upon only as a great contrapuntist, is clear evidence of the greatness of his own genius, which indeed had some affinity to that of Bach. The ingenuity of outward form in Bach's works was neither strange nor unintelligible to him. For although Schumann had hitherto had no instructor in composition, it need scarcely be said that he had long ago made himself familiar with the most essential parts of the composer's art, and that constant practice in composition must have given him much knowledge and skill in this branch of his art.

At Easter, 1829, Schumann followed his friend Rosen to the University of Heidelberg. The young jurists were perhaps tempted thither by the lectures of the famous teacher, A. F. J. Thibaut; but it is evident that other things contributed to form Schumann's resolution: the situation of the town—a perfect Paradise—

[1] 'Patientibus Carus, sed clarus inter doctos.' (Berlioz, Voyage musical, Letter IV.)

the gaiety of the people, and the nearness of Switzerland, Italy and France. A delightful prospect promised to open to him there: 'That will be life indeed!' he writes to his friend; 'at Michaelmas we will go to Switzerland, and from thence who knows where?' On his journey to Heidelberg chance threw him into the society of Willibald Alexis. Alexis had trodden the path which Schumann was destined to follow, and had reached art by way of the law. No doubt this added to Schumann's interest in the acquaintance. It cannot be denied that even in Heidelberg Schumann carried on his legal studies in a very desultory manner, though Thibaut himself was a living proof that that branch of learning could co-exist with a true love and comprehension of music. Only a few years before (in 1825) Thibaut had published his little book, *Über Reinheit der Tonkunst*, a work which at that time essentially contributed to alter the direction of musical taste in Germany. Just as in his volume Thibaut attacks the degenerate state of church music, Schumann, at a later date was destined to take up arms, in word and deed, against the flat insipidity of concert and chamber music. Nevertheless the two men never became really intimate; in one, no doubt, the *doctor* too greatly preponderated, and in the other the artist. Thibaut himself subsequently advised Schumann to abandon the law, and devote him-self entirely to music.

Indeed, if Schumann was industrious in any-thing at Heidelberg it was in pianoforte-play-ing. After practising for seven hours in the day, he would invite a friend to come in the evening and play with him, adding that he felt in a particularly happy vein that day; and even during an excursion with friends he would take a dumb keyboard with him in the carriage. By diligent use of the instruction he had re-ceived from Wieck in Leipzig, he brought him-self to high proficiency as an executant; and at the same time increased his skill in improvisa-tion. One of his musical associates at this time used afterwards to say that from the playing of no other artist, however great, had he ever ex-perienced such ineffaceable musical impressions; the ideas seem to pour into the player's mind in an inexhaustible flow, and their profound originality and poetic charm already clearly foreshadowed the main features of his musical individuality. Schumann appeared only once in public, at a concert given by a musical society at Heidelberg, where he played Moscheles's variations on the 'Alexandermarsch' with great success. He received many requests to play again, but refused them all, probably, as a student, finding it not expedient.

It will no doubt be a matter of surprise that Schumann could have justified himself in thus spending year after year in a merely nominal study of the law, while in fact wholly given up to his favourite pursuit. A certain lack of determination, a certain shrinking from anything disagreeable, betray themselves during these years as his general characteristics, and were perhaps an integral part of his nature. At the same time his conduct is to a certain extent explicable, by the general conditions of German student life. Out of the strict discipline of the Gymnasium the student steps at once into the unlimited freedom of the University. It was the intoxicating poetry of the student life which Schumann drank in deep draughts. Its coarseness was repellent to his refined nature, and his innate purity and nobility guarded him against moral degradation ; but he lived like a rover rejoicing in this bright world as it lies open to him, worked little, spent much, got into debt, and was as happy as a fish in the water. Besides its tender and rapturous side, his nature had a vein of native sharpness and humour. With all these peculiarities he could live his student's life to the full, though in his own apparently quiet and unassertive way. The letters in which he discusses money matters with his guardian, Herr Rudel, a merchant of Zwickau, show how he indulged his humorous mood even in these : ' Dismal things I have to tell you, respected Herr Rudel,' he writes on June 21, 1830 :

' In the first place, that I have a *repetitorium* which costs eighty gulden every half-year, and secondly, that within a week I have been under arrest by the town (don't be shocked) for not paying thirty gulden of other college dues.'

And on another occasion, when the money he had asked for to make a journey home for the holidays did not arrive :

' I am the only student here, and wander alone about the streets and woods, forlorn and poor, like a beggar, and with debts into the bargain. Be kind, most respected Herr Rudel, and only this once send me some money—only money—and do not drive me to seek means of setting out which might not be pleasant to you.'

The reasons he employs to prove to his guardian that he ought not to be deprived of means for a journey into Italy are most amusing :

' At any rate I shall have made the journey : and as I *must* make it once, it is all the same whether I use the money for it now or later.'

His compositions, too, plainly show how deeply the poetical aspect of student life had affected him, and had left its permanent mark on him. I need only remind the reader of Kerner's ' Wanderlied ' (op. 35, No. 3), dedicated to an old fellow-student at Heidelberg, and of Eichendorff's ' Frühlingsfahrt ' (op. 45, No. 2). Among German songs of the highest class, there is not one in which the effervescent buoyancy of youth craving for distant flights has found such full expression, at once so thoroughly German and so purely ideal, as in this ' Wanderlied,' which indeed, with a different tune, is actually one of the most favourite of student songs. 'Frühlingsfahrt ' tells of two young comrades who

quit home for the first time, one of whom soon finds a regular subsistence and a comfortable home, while the other pursues glittering visions, yields to the thousand temptations of the world, and finally perishes ; it is a portrait of a German student drawn from the life, and the way in which Schumann has treated it shows that he was drawing on the stores of his own experience.

Several journeys also served to infuse into Schumann's student life the delight of free and unrestrained movement. In Aug. 1829 he went for a pleasure trip to North Italy, quite alone, for two friends who had intended to go failed him. But perhaps the contemplative and dreamy youth enjoyed the loveliness of the country and the sympathetic Italian nature only the more thoroughly for being alone. Nor were little adventures of gallantry wanting. Fragments of a diary kept at this time, which are preserved (Wasielewski, p. 325), reveal to us the pleasant sociableness of the life which Schumann now delighted in. The Italian music which he then heard could indeed do little towards his improvement, except that it gave him, for the first time, the opportunity of hearing Paganini. The deep impression made by that remarkable player is shown by Schumann's visit to Frankfort (Easter, 1830) with several friends to hear him again, and by his arrangement of his ' Caprices ' for the pianoforte (opp. 3 and 10). Shortly after this he seems to have heard Ernst also in Frankfort. In the summer of 1830 he made a tour to Strassburg, and on the way back to Saxony visited his friend Rosen at Detmold.

When Schumann entered upon his third year of study, he made a serious effort to devote himself to jurisprudence ; he took what was called a *Repetitorium*, that is, he began going over again with considerable difficulty, and under the care and guidance of an old lawyer, what he had neglected during two years. He also endeavoured to reconcile himself to the idea of practical work in public life or the government service. His spirit soared up to the highest goal, and at times he may have flattered his fancy with dreams of having attained it ; but he must have been convinced of the improbability of such dreams ever coming true ; and indeed he never got rid of his antipathy to the law as a profession, even in the whole course of his *Repetitorium*. On the other hand, it must be said, that if he was ever to be a musician, it was becoming high time for it, since he was now 20 years old. Thus every consideration urged him to the point. Schumann induced his mother, who was still extremely averse to the calling of a musician, to put the decision in the hands of Friedrich Wieck. Wieck did not conceal from him that such a step ought only to be taken after the most thorough self-examination, but if he had already examined himself, then Wieck could only advise him to take the step. Upon this his mother yielded, and Robert Schumann became a musician.

Music Study.—The delight and freedom which he inwardly felt when the die was cast, must have shown him that he had done right. At first his intention was only to make himself a great pianoforte-player, and he reckoned that in six years he would be able to compete with any pianist. But he still felt very uncertain as to his gift as a composer ; the words which he wrote to his mother on July 30, 1830—' Now and then I discover that I have imagination, and perhaps a turn for creating things myself ' —sound curiously wanting in confidence, when we remember how almost exclusively Schumann's artistic greatness was to find expression in his compositions.

He quitted Heidelberg late in the summer of 1830, in order to resume his studies with Wieck in Leipzig. He was resolved, after having wasted two years and a half, to devote himself to his new calling with energetic purpose and manly vigour. And faithfully did he keep to his resolution. The plan of becoming a great pianist had, however, to be given up after a year. Actuated by the passionate desire to achieve a perfect technique as speedily as possible, Schumann devised a contrivance by which the greatest possible dexterity of finger was to be attained in the shortest time. By means of this ingenious appliance the third finger was drawn back and kept still, while the other fingers had to practise exercises. But the result was that the tendons of the third finger were overstrained, the finger was crippled, and for some time the whole right hand was injured. This most serious condition was alleviated by medical treatment.[1] Schumann recovered the use of his hand, and could, when needful, even play the piano ; but the third finger remained useless, so that he was for ever precluded from the career of a virtuoso.

Although express evidence is wanting, we may assume with certainty that this unexpected misfortune made a deep impression upon him ; he saw himself once more confronted with the question whether it was advisable for him to continue in the calling he had chosen. That he answered it in the affirmative shows that during this time his confidence in his own creative genius had wonderfully increased. He soon reconciled himself to the inevitable, learned to appreciate mechanical dexterity at its true value, and turned his undivided attention to composition. He continued henceforth in the most friendly relations with his pianoforte-master, Wieck ; indeed until the autumn of 1832 he lived in the

same house with him (Grimmaische Strasse No. 36), and was almost one of the family. For his instructor in composition, however, he chose Heinrich Dorn, at that time conductor of the Opera in Leipzig, subsequently Kapellmeister at Riga, Cologne and Berlin, who lived till 1892. Dorn was a clever and sterling composer ; he recognised the greatness of Schumann's genius, and devoted himself with much interest to his improvement.[2] It was impossible as yet to confine Schumann to a regular course of composition : he worked very diligently, but would take up now one point of the art of composition and now another. In 1836 he writes to Dorn at Riga that he often regrets having learnt in too irregular a manner at this time ; but when he adds directly afterwards that, notwithstanding this, he had learnt more from Dorn's teaching than Dorn would believe, we may take this last statement as true. Schumann was no longer a tyro in composition, but had true musical genius, and his spirit was already matured. Under such circumstances he was justified in learning in his own way.

In the winter of 1832–33, he lived at Zwickau, and for a time also with his brothers at Schneeberg. Besides a pianoforte concerto, which still remains a fragment, he was working at a symphony in G minor, of which the first movement was publicly performed in the course of the winter both at Schneeberg and Zwickau. If we may trust the evidence of the *Musikalisches Wochenblatt*, Leipzig, 1875, p. 180, the whole symphony was performed at Zwickau in 1835, under Schumann's own direction, and the last movement was almost a failure.

At all events the symphony was finished, and Schumann expected it to be a great success ; in this he must have been disappointed, for it has never been published. The first performance of the first movement at Zwickau took place at a concert given there on Nov. 18, 1832, by Wieck's daughter Clara, who was then 13 years of age. Even then the performances of this gifted girl, who was so soon to take her place as the greatest female pianist of Germany, were astonishing, and by them, as Schumann puts it, ' Zwickau was fired with enthusiasm for the first time in its life.' It is easily conceivable that Schumann himself was enthusiastically delighted with Clara, adorned as she was with the twofold charm of childlike sweetness and artistic genius. ' Think of perfection,' he writes to a friend about her on Apr. 5, 1833, ' and I will agree to it.' And many expressions in his letters seem even to betray a deeper feeling, of which he himself did not become fully aware until several years later.

Schumann's circumstances allowed him to

[1] For the testimony of Wieck (*Clavier und Gesang*) and of his daughter, Marie Schumann, on the nature of the accident see Niecks, *Rob. Sch.* p. 102. Niecks, referring to this article (p. 105), notes that ' the lamed finger is called the third, in accordance with English nomenclature, in which the hand has a thumb and four fingers.'

[2] Schumann's gratitude to him is thus expressed : ' The man who first gave a hand to me as I climbed upwards, and, when I began to doubt myself, drew me aloft so that I should see less of the common herd of mankind, and more of the pure air of art.'

revisit Leipzig in Mar. 1833, and even to live there for a time without any definite occupation. He was not exactly well off, but he had enough to enable him to live as a single man of moderate means. The poverty from which so many of the greatest musicians have suffered never formed part of Schumann's experience. He occupied himself with studies in composition chiefly in the contrapuntal style, in which he had taken the liveliest interest since making the acquaintance of Bach's works; besides this his imagination, asserting itself more and more strongly, impelled him to the creation of free compositions. From this year date the impromptus for piano on a romance by Clara Wieck, which Schumann dedicated to her father, and published in August 1833, as op. 5. In June he wrote the first and third movements of the G minor sonata (op. 22), and at the same time began the F♯ minor sonata (op. 11) and completed the toccata (op. 7), which had been begun in 1829. He also arranged a second set of Paganini's violin caprices for the piano (op. 10), having made a first attempt of the same kind (op. 3) in the previous year. Meanwhile he lived a quiet and almost monotonous life. Of family acquaintances he had few, nor did he seek them. He found a faithful friend in Frau Henriette Voigt, who was as excellent a pianist as she was noble and sympathetic in soul. She was a pupil of Ludwig Berger, of Berlin, and died young in the year 1839. Schumann was wont as a rule to spend his evenings with a small number of intimate friends in a restaurant. These gatherings generally took place at the ' Kaffeebaum ' (Kleine Fleischergasse, No. 3). He himself, however, generally remained silent by preference, even in this confidential circle of friends. Readily as he could express himself with his pen, he had but little power of speech. Even in affairs of no importance, which could have been transacted most readily and simply by word of mouth, he usually preferred to write. It was, moreover, a kind of enjoyment to him to muse in dreamy silence. Henriette Voigt told W. Taubert that one lovely summer evening, after making music with Schumann, they both felt inclined to go on the water. They sat side by side in the boat for an hour in silence. At parting Schumann pressed her hand and said, ' To-day we have perfectly understood one another.'

FOUNDATION OF THE ' ZEITSCHRIFT.'—It was at these evening gatherings at the restaurant in the winter of 1833–34 that the plan of starting a new musical paper was matured. It was the protest of youth, feeling itself impelled to new things in art, against the existing state of music. Although Weber, Beethoven and Schubert had only been dead a few years, though Spohr and Marschner were still in their prime, and Mendelssohn was beginning to be celebrated, the general characteristic of the music of about the year 1830 was either superficiality or else vulgar mediocrity. ' On the stage Rossini still reigned supreme, and on the pianoforte scarcely anything was heard but Herz and Hünten.' Under these conditions the war might have been more suitably carried on by means of important works of art than by a periodical about music. Musical criticism, however, was itself in a bad way at this time. The periodical called Caecilia, published by Schott, which had been in existence since 1824, was unfitted for the general reader both by its contents and by the fact of its publication in parts. The Berliner allgemeine musikalische Zeitung, conducted by Marx, had come to an end in 1830. The only periodical of influence and importance in 1833 was the Allgemeine musikalische Zeitung, published by Breitkopf & Härtel of Leipzig, and at that time edited by G. W. Fink. But the narrow view taken of criticism in that periodical, its inane mildness of judgment—Schumann used to call it ' Honigpinselei ' or ' Honey-daubing '—its lenity towards the reigning insipidity and superficiality, could not but provoke contradiction from young people of high aims. And the idea of first bringing the lever to bear on the domain of critical authorship, in order to try their strength, must have been all the more attractive to these hot-headed youths, since most of them had had the advantage of a sound scholarly education and knew how to handle their pens. On the other hand, they felt that they were not yet strong enough to guide the public taste into new paths by their own musical productions ; and of all the set Schumann was the most sensible of this fact.

Such were the grounds on which, on Apr. 3, 1834, the first number of the Neue Zeitschrift für Musik saw the light. Schumann himself called it the organ of youth and movement. As its motto he even chose this passage from the prologue to Shakespeare's Henry VIII. :

> ' Only they
> Who come to hear a merry bawdy play,
> A noise of targets, or to see a fellow
> In a long motley coat guarded with yellow,
> Will be deceived—'

a passage which sufficiently expresses his intention of contending against an empty flattering style of criticism, and upholding the dignity of art. ' The day of reciprocal compliments,' says the preliminary notice, ' is gradually dying out, and we must confess that we shall do nothing towards reviving it. The critic who dares not attack what is bad, is but a half-hearted supporter of what is good.' The doings of ' the three arch-foes of art—those who have no talent, those who have vulgar talent, and those who, having real talent, write too much,' are not to be left in peace · ' their latest phase, the result of a mere cultivation of executive technique,' is to be opposed as inartistic. 'The older time,' on the other hand, ' and the works it produced, are to be recalled with insistence, since it is only at these pure sources that new beauties in art can be found.' Moreover, the *Zeitschrift* is to assist in bringing in a new 'poetic' period by its benevolent encouragement of the higher efforts of young artists, and to accelerate its advent. The editing was in the hands of Robert Schumann, Friedrich Wieck, Ludwig Schunke and Julius Knorr.

Of all these Schunke alone was exclusively a musician. That gifted pianist, who belonged to a widely dispersed family of esteemed musicians, came to Leipzig in 1833, and became a great friend of Schumann, but died at the end of the following year at the early age of 24. The three other editors were by education half musicians and half *littérateurs*, even Julius Knorr (*b.* 1807) having studied philology in Leipzig. Schumann co-operated largely in Schunke's contributions (signed with the figure 3), for handling the pen was not easy to him. Hartmann of Leipzig was at first the publisher and proprietor of the *Zeitschrift*, but at the beginning of 1835 it passed into the hands of J. A. Barth of Leipzig, Schumann becoming at the same time proprietor and sole editor. He continued the undertaking under these conditions till the end of June 1844 ; so that his management of the paper extended over a period of above ten years. On Jan. 1, 1845, Franz BRENDEL (*q.v.*) became the editor, and after the summer of 1844 Schumann never again wrote for it, with the exception of a short article[1] on Johannes Brahms to be mentioned hereafter.

THE ' DAVIDSBÜNDLER.'—Schumann's own articles are sometimes signed with a number— either 2 or some combination with 2, such as 12, 22, etc. He also concealed his identity under a variety of names—Florestan, Eusebius, Raro, Jeanquirit. In his articles we meet with frequent mention of the Davidsbündler, a league or society of artists or friends of art who had views in common. This was purely imaginary, a half-humorous, half-poetical fiction of Schumann, existing only in the brain of its founder, who thought it well fitted to give weight to the expression of various views of art, which were occasionally put forth as its utterances. The characters which most usually appear are Florestan and Eusebius, two personages in whom Schumann endeavoured to embody the dual sides of his nature. The vehement, stormy, rough element is represented by Florestan ; the gentler and more poetic by Eusebius. These two figures are obviously imitated from Vult and Walt in Jean Paul's *Flegeljahre* ; indeed Schumann's literary work throughout is strongly coloured with the manner of Jean Paul, and frequent reference is made to his writings. Now and then, as moderator between these an-

tagonistic characters, who of course take opposite views in criticism, ' Master Raro ' comes in. In him Schumann has conceived a character such as at one time he had himself dreamed of becoming. The explanation of the name 'Davidsbündler' is given at the beginning of a ' Shrove Tuesday discourse ' by Florestan in the year 1835. ' The hosts of David are youths and men destined to slay all the Philistines, musical or other.' In the college-slang of Germany the ' Philistine ' is the non-student who is satisfied to live on in the ordinary routine of everyday life, or—which comes to the same thing in the student's mind—the man of narrow, sober, prosaic views, as contrasted with the high-flown poetry and enthusiasm of the social life of a German university. Thus, in the name of Idealism, the ' Davidsbündler ' wage war against boorish mediocrity, and when Schumann regarded it as the function of his paper to aid in bringing in a new 'poetical phase' in music he meant just this. Though Schumann was himself the sole reality in the 'Davidsbündlerschaft,' he indulged his fancy by introducing personages of his acquaintance whose agreement with his views he was sure of. He quietly included all the principal co-operators in the *Zeitschrift*, and even artists such as Berlioz, whom he did not know, but in whom he felt an interest, and was thus justified in writing to A. von Zuccalmaglio in 1836 : ' By the Davidsbund is figured an intellectual brotherhood which ramifies widely, and I hope may bear golden fruit.' He brings in the brethren, who are not actually himself, from time to time in the critical discussions : and the way in which he contrives to make this motley troop of romantic forms live and move before the eyes of the reader is really quite magical. He could say with justice : ' We are now living a romance the like of which has perhaps never been written in any book.' We meet with a Jonathan, who may perhaps stand for Schunke (on another occasion, however, Schumann designates himself by this name) ; a Fritz Friedrich probably meant for Lyser[2] the painter, a lover of music ; Serpentin is Carl Banck, a clever composer of songs, who at the outset was one of his most zealous and meritorious fellow-workers ; Gottschalk Wedel is Anton von Zuccalmaglio, then living in Warsaw, who had made a name by his collection of German and foreign Volkslieder ; Chiara is of course Clara Wieck, and Zilia (apparently shortened from Cecilia) is probably the same. Felix Mendelssohn appears under the name of Felix Meritis, and the name Walt occurs once (in 1836, *Aus den Büchern der Davidsbündler*, ii. Tanzlitteratur). It cannot be asserted that any particular person was meant, still his direct reference to Jean Paul's *Flegeljahre* is interesting. There is also a certain Julius among the 'Davids-

[1] *Neue Bahnen*, Oct. 28. 1853.

[2] Author of the sketch of Beethoven engraved at p. 268 of Vol. I of this Dictionary.

bündler,' probably Julius Knorr. The name occurs in Schumann's first essay on music, 'Ein opus ii.' This is not included in the *Neue Zeitschrift*, but appears in No. 49 of the *Allgemeine musikalische Zeitung* for 1831 (then edited by Fink). The editor has prefixed a note to the effect that 'it is by a young man, a pupil of the latest school, who has given his name,' and contrasts it with the anonymous work of a reviewer of the old school discussing the same piece of music. The contrast is indeed striking, and the imaginative flights of enthusiastic young genius look strange enough among the old-world surroundings of the rest of the paper.

SCHUMANN AS EDITOR.—Schumann placed this critique—which deals with Chopin's variations on 'La ci darem'—at the beginning of his collected writings, which he published towards the close of his life (*Gesammelte Schriften*, 4 vols. Georg Wigand, Leipzig, 1854). It is a good example of the tone which he adopted in the *Neue Zeitschrift*. His fellow-workers fell more or less into the same key, not from servility, but because they were all young men, and because the reaction against the Philistine style of criticism was just then in the air. This may be plainly detected, for instance, in a critique written by Wieck for the periodical called *Caecilia*, on Chopin's airs with variations. It is easy to understand that the total novelty of the style of writing of the *Neue Zeitschrift* should have attracted attention to music ; the paper soon obtained a comparatively large circulation ; and as, besides the charm of novelty and style, it offered a variety of instructive and entertaining matter, and discussed important subjects earnestly and cleverly, the interest of the public was kept up, and indeed constantly increased, from year to year. The influence exerted by Schumann on musical art in Germany through the medium of this paper cannot but be regarded as very important.

It has been sometimes said that Schumann's literary labours must have done him mischief, by taking up time and energy which might have been better employed in composition. But this view seems to me untenable. Up to the period at which we have now arrived, Schumann, on his own statement, had merely dreamed away his life at the piano. His tendency to self-concentration, his shyness, and his independent circumstances, placed him in danger of never achieving that perfect development of his powers which is possible only by vigorous exercise. Now the editing of a journal is an effective remedy for dreaming ; and when, at the beginning of 1835, he became sole editor, however much he may have felt the inexorable necessity of satisfying his readers week after week, and of keeping his aim constantly in view, it was no doubt a most beneficial exercise for his will and energies. He

was conscious of this, or he certainly would not have clung to the paper with such affection and persistency ; and it is a matter of fact that the period of his happiest and most vigorous creativeness coincides pretty nearly with that during which he was engaged on the *Zeitschrift*. Hence, to suppose that his literary work was any drawback to his artistic career is an error, though it is true that as he gradually discovered the inexhaustible fertility of his creative genius, he sometimes complained that the details of an editor's work were a burden to him. Besides, the paper was the medium by which Schumann was first brought into contact and intercourse with the most illustrious artists of his time ; and living as he did apart from all the practically musical circles of Leipzig, it was almost the only link between himself and the contemporary world.

Nor must we overlook the fact that certain peculiar gifts of Schumann found expression in his writings on musical subjects, gifts which would otherwise scarcely have found room for display. His poetic talent was probably neither rich enough nor strong enough for the production of large independent poems ; but, on the other hand, it was far too considerable to be condemned to perpetual silence. In his essays and critiques, which must be regarded rather as poetic flights and sympathetic interpretations than as examples of incisive analysis, his poetical gift found a natural outlet, and literature is by so much the richer for them. Nay, it is a not unreasonable speculation whether, if his imaginative powers had not found this vent they might not have formed a disturbing and marring element in his musical creations. Even as it is, poetical imagery plays an important part in Schumann's music, though without seriously overstepping the permissible limits. This, too, we may safely say, that in spite of his silent and self-contained nature, there was in Schumann a vein of the genuine *agitator*, in the best and noblest sense of the word ; he was possessed by the conviction that the development of German art, then in progress, had not yet come to its final term, and that a new phase of its existence was at hand. Throughout his writings we find this view beautifully and poetically expressed, as for instance,

'Consciously or unconsciously a new and as yet undeveloped school is being founded on the basis of the Beethoven-Schubert romanticism, a school which we may venture to expect will mark a special epoch in the history of art. Its destiny seems to be to usher in a period which will nevertheless have many links to connect it with the past century.'

Or again :

'A rosy light is dawning in the sky ; whence it cometh I know not ; but in any case, O youth, make for the light.'

SCHUMANN'S CRITICISM.—To rouse fresh interest and make use of that already existing for the advancement of this new movement was one of his deepest instincts, and this he largely accomplished by means of his paper. From his pen we have articles on almost all the most illustrious composers of his generation—Mendelssohn, Taubert, Chopin, Hiller, Heller, Henselt, Sterndale Bennett, Gade, Kirchner and Franz, as well as Johannes Brahms, undoubtedly the most remarkable composer of the generation after Schumann.  On some he first threw the light of intelligent and enthusiastic literary sympathy ; others he was actually the first to introduce to the musical world ; and even Berlioz, a Frenchman, he eulogised boldly and successfully, recognising in him a champion of the new idea.  By degrees he would naturally discern that he had thus prepared the soil for the reception of his own works.  He felt himself in close affinity with all these artists, and was more and more confirmed in his conviction that he too had something to say to the world that it had not heard before.  In the *Zeitschrift* he must have been aware that he controlled a power which would serve to open a shorter route for his own musical productions.

' If the publisher were not afraid of the editor, the world would hear nothing of me—perhaps to the world's advantage.  And yet the black heads of the printed notes are very pleasant to behold.'
' To give up the paper would involve the loss of all the reserve force which every artist ought to have if he is to produce easily and freely.'

So he wrote in 1836 and 1837.  But at the same time we must emphatically contradict the suggestion that Schumann used his paper for selfish ends.  His soul was too entirely noble and his ideal aims too high to have any purpose in view but the advancement of art ; and it was only in so far as his own interests were inseparable from those of his whole generation, that he would ever have been capable of forwarding the fortunes of his own works.  The question even whether, and in what manner, his own works should be discussed in the *Neue Zeitschrift* he always treated with the utmost tact.  In one of his letters he clearly expresses his principles on the subject as follows :

' I am, to speak frankly, too proud to attempt to influence Härtel through Fink (editor of the *Allgemeine mus. Zeitung*) ; and I hate, at all times, any mode of instigating public opinion by the artist himself.  What is strong enough works its own way.'

His efforts for the good cause indeed went beyond essay-writing and composing.  Extracts from a note-book published by Wasielewski prove that he busied himself with a variety of plans for musical undertakings of general utility.  Thus he wished to compile lives of Beethoven and of Bach, with a critique of all their works, and a biographical dictionary of living musicians on the same plan.  He desired that the relations of operatic composers and managers should be regulated by law.  He wished to establish an agency for the publication of musical works, so that composers might derive greater benefit from their publications, and gave his mind to a plan for founding a Musical Union in Saxony, with Leipzig as its headquarters, to be the counterpart of Schillings's Deutscher National Verein für Musik.

RECEPTION OF PF. COMPOSITIONS.—In the first period of his editorship, before he had got into the way of easily mastering his day's labour, and when the regular round of work had still the charm of novelty, it was of course only now and then that he had leisure, or felt in the mood, for composing.  Two great pianoforte works date from 1834 (the ' Carnaval,' op. 9, and the ' Études symphoniques,' op. 13), but in 1835 nothing was completed.  After this, however, Schumann's genius began again to assert itself, and in the years 1836 to 1839 he composed that splendid set of pianoforte works of the highest excellence, on which a considerable part of his fame rests, viz. the great fantasia (op. 17), the F minor sonata (op. 14), Fantasiestücke (op. 12), Davidsbündlertänze, Novelletten, Kinderscenen, Kreisleriana, Humoreske, Faschingsschwank, Romanzen and others.  The fount of his creative genius flowed forth ever clearer and more abundantly.  ' I used to rack my brains for a long time,' writes he on March 15, 1839,

' but now I scarcely ever scratch out a note.  It all comes from within, and I often feel as if I could go playing straight on without ever coming to an end.'

The influence of Schumann the author on Schumann the composer may often be detected.  Thus the ' Davidsbündler ' come into his music, and the composition which bears their name was originally entitled ' Davidsbündler, dances for the Pianoforte, dedicated to Walther von Goethe by Florestan and Eusebius.'  The title of the F♯ minor sonata, op. 11, which was completed in 1835, runs thus : ' Pianoforte Sonata. Dedicated to Clara by Florestan and Eusebius.'  In the ' Carnaval,' a set of separate and shorter pieces with a title to each, the names of Florestan and Eusebius occur again, as do those of Chiarina (the diminutive of Clara), and Chopin ; the whole concluding with a march of the Davidsbündler against the Philistines.

The reception of Schumann's works by the critics was most favourable and encouraging, but the public was repelled by their eccentricity and originality ; and it was not till after the appearance of the ' Kinderscenen ' (1839) that they began to be appreciated.  Opp. 1 and 2 actually had the honour of a notice in the Vienna *Musikalische Zeitung* of 1832, by no less a person than Grillparzer the poet.  Fink designedly took hardly any notice of Schumann in the *Allgemeine musikalische Zeitung*.  But Liszt wrote a long, discriminating, and very favourable article in the *Gazette musicale* of 1837 upon the impromptus (op. 5), and the sonatas in F♯ minor and F minor.  Moscheles wrote very sympathetically on the two sonatas in the *Neue Zeitschrift für Musik* itself (vols. 5 and 6), and some kind words of recognition of Schumann's genius were published subsequently from his diary.[1] Other musicians, though not expressing their sentiments publicly, continued to hold aloof from him. Hauptmann at that time calls Schumann's pianoforte compositions ' pretty and curious little things, all wanting in proper solidity, but otherwise interesting.' [2]

RELATIONS WITH MENDELSSOHN.—In October 1835 the musical world of Leipzig was enriched by the arrival of Mendelssohn. It was already in a flourishing state : operas, concerts and sacred performances alike were of great excellence, and well supported by the public. But although the soil was well prepared before Mendelssohn's arrival, it was he who raised Leipzig to the position of the most musical town of Germany. The extraordinarily vigorous life that at once grew up there under the influence of his genius, drawing to itself from far and near the most important musical talent of the country, has shown itself to be of so enduring a character that even at the present day its influences are felt. Schumann too, who had long felt great respect for Mendelssohn, was drawn into his circle. On Oct. 4, 1835, Mendelssohn conducted his first concert in the Gewandhaus ; the day before this there was a musical gathering at the Wiecks', at which both Mendelssohn and Schumann were present, and it seems to have been on this occasion that the two first came into close personal intercourse.[3] On Oct. 5, Mendelssohn, Schumann, Moscheles, Banck, and a few others, dined together. In the afternoon of the 6th there was again music at Wieck's house ; Moscheles, Clara Wieck and L. Rakemann from Bremen, played Bach's D minor concerto for three claviers, Mendelssohn putting in the orchestral accompaniments on a fourth piano. Moscheles had come over from Hamburg, where he was staying on a visit, to give a concert in Leipzig. Schumann had already been in correspondence with him, but this was the first opportunity he had enjoyed of making the personal acquaintance of the man whose playing had so delighted him in Carlsbad when a boy of nine. Moscheles describes him as ' a retiring but interesting young man,' and the F♯ minor sonata, played to him by Clara Wieck, as ' very laboured, difficult and somewhat intricate, although interesting.'

A livelier intimacy, so far as Schumann was concerned, soon sprang up between him and Mendelssohn. When Mendelssohn had to go to Düsseldorf in May 1836, to the first performance of ' St. Paul ' at the Niederrheinische Musikfest, Schumann even intended to go with him, and was ready months beforehand, though when the time arrived he was prevented from going. They used to like to dine together, and gradually an interesting little circle was formed around them, including among others Ferdinand David, whom Mendelssohn had brought to Leipzig as leader of his orchestra. In the early part of January 1837 Mendelssohn and Schumann used in this way to meet every day and interchange ideas, so far as Schumann's silent temperament would allow. Subsequently when Mendelssohn was kept more at home by his marriage, this intercourse became rarer. Schumann was by nature unsociable, and at this time there were outward circumstances which rendered solitude doubly attractive to him. Ferdinand Hiller, who spent the winter of 1839–40 in Leipzig with Mendelssohn, relates that Schumann was at that time living the life of a recluse and scarcely ever came out of his room. Mendelssohn and Schumann felt themselves drawn together by mutual appreciation. The artistic relations between the two great men were not as yet, however, thoroughly reciprocal. Schumann admired Mendelssohn to the point of enthusiasm. He declared him to be the best musician then living, said that he looked up to him as to a high mountain-peak, and that even in his daily talk about art some thought at least would be uttered worthy of being graven in gold. And when he mentions him in his writings, it is in a tone of enthusiastic admiration, which shows in the best light Schumann's fine ideal character, so remarkable for its freedom from envy. And his opinion remained unaltered : in 1842 he dedicated his three string quartets to Mendelssohn, and in the ' Album für die Jugend ' there is a little piano piece called ' Erinnerung,' dated Nov. 4, 1847, which shows with eloquent simplicity how deeply he felt the early death of his friend. It is well known how he would be moved out of his quiet stillness if he heard any disparaging expression used of Mendelssohn. Mendelssohn, on the contrary, at first only saw in Schumann the man of letters and the art-critic. Like most productive musicians, he had a dislike to such men as a class, however much he might love and value single representatives, as was really the case with regard to Schumann. From this point of view must be regarded the expressions which he makes use of now and then in letters concerning Schumann as an author.[4] If they sound somewhat disparaging, we must remember that it is not the personal Mendelssohn speaking against the personal Schumann, but rather the creative artist speaking against the critic, always in natural opposition to him. Indeed it is obviously impossible to take such remarks in a disadvantageous sense, as

[1] *Moscheles' Leben*, Leipzig, 1873, vol. ii. p. 15 ; English translation by A. D. Coleridge, vol. ii. pp. 19, 20.
[2] See Hauptmann's *Letters to Hauser*, Leipzig, 1871, vol. i. .p. 255.
[3] *Moscheles' Leben*, vol. i. p. 301 ; English translation, vol. i. p. 322.
[4] See Mendelssohn's *Briefe*, ii. 116 ; Lady Wallace's translation, ii. 97 (hardly recognisable, owing to *Die musikalische Zeitung* (Schumann's paper) being rendered ' The musical papers ') ; and Hiller's *Felix Mendelssohn Bartholdy*, Cologne, 1878, p. 64.

Schumann quite agreed with Mendelssohn on the subject of criticism.[1] One passage in his writings is especially remarkable in this respect. He is speaking of Chopin's pianoforte concerto, and Florestan exclaims,

' What is a whole year of a musical paper compared to a concerto by Chopin ? What is a magister's rage compared to the poetic frenzy ? What are ten complimentary addresses to the editor compared to the Adagio in the second Concerto ? And believe me, Davidites, I should not think you worth the trouble of talking to, did I not believe you capable of composing such works as those you write about, with the exception of a few like this concerto. Away with your musical journals ! It should be the highest endeavour of a just critic to render himself wholly unnecessary ; the best discourse on music is silence. Why write about Chopin ? Why not create at first hand—play, write and compose ? ' [2]

True, this impassioned outburst has to be moderated by Eusebius. But consider the significance of Schumann's writing thus in his own journal about the critic's vocation! It plainly shows that he only took it up as an artist, and occasionally despised it. But with regard to Schumann's place in art, Mendelssohn did not, at that time at all events, consider it a very high one, and he was not alone in this opinion. It was shared, for example, by Spohr and Hauptmann. In Mendelssohn's published letters there is no verdict whatever on Schumann's music.[3] The fact, however, remains that in Schumann's earlier pianoforte works he felt that the power or the desire for expression in the greater forms was wanting, and this he said in conversation. He soon had reason to change his opinion, and afterwards expressed warm interest in his friend's compositions. Whether he ever quite entered into the individualities of Schumann's music may well be doubted ; their natures were too dissimilar.

VIENNA.—Schumann's constant intimacy in Wieck's house had resulted in a tender attachment to his daughter Clara, now grown up. It was in the latter part of 1835 that this first found any definite expression. His regard was reciprocated, and in September 1837 he preferred his suit formally to her father.[4] Wieck, however, did not favour it ; possibly he entertained loftier hopes for his gifted daughter. At any rate he was of opinion that Schumann's means and prospects were too vague and uncertain to warrant his setting up a home of his own. Schumann seems to have acknowledged the justice of this hesitation, for in 1838 he made strenuous efforts to find a new and wider sphere of work. With the full consent of Clara Wieck he decided on settling in Vienna, and bringing out his musical periodical in that city. The glory of a great epoch still cast a light over the musical life of the Austrian capital—the

epoch when Gluck, Haydn, Mozart, Beethoven and Schubert were living and working there. In point of fact, all genuine music had vanished even during Beethoven's lifetime, and had given way to a trivial and superficial taste. Rossini and his followers were paramount in opera ; in orchestral music there were the waltzes of Strauss and Lanner ; and in vocal music the feeble sentimentalities of Proch and his fellow-composers. So far as solo-playing was concerned, the fourth decade of the century saw it at its highest pitch of executive brilliancy, and its lowest of purpose and feeling—indeed it may be comprehensively designated as the epoch of Thalberg. Thus Schumann would have found in Vienna ample opportunity for doing good work, for the Viennese public was still as ever the most responsive in the world, and one to justify sanguine hopes. Schumann effected his move with the assistance of Professor Joseph Fischhof, his colleague on the paper ; settling himself in October 1838 in the Schönlaterngasse, No. 679. Oswald Lorenz edited the *Zeitschrift* as Schumann's deputy, and for a time it was still to be issued in Leipzig. Schumann hoped to be able to bring it out in Vienna by January 1839, and made every effort to obtain the prompt permission of the authorities, as well as the support of influential persons for himself and his journal. But the consent of the censor's office and the police were long withheld ; and he was required to secure the co-operation of an Austrian publisher, in itself a great difficulty. It is hard to believe that in the great city of Vienna no strictly musical newspaper then existed, and that a small catalogue, the *Allgemeine musikalische Anzeiger*, published weekly by Tobias Haslinger, and almost exclusively devoted to the business interests of his firm, was the only publication which could pretend to the name. But the publishers were either too indolent or too timid to attempt any new enterprise, and sought to throw impediments in Schumann's way.

His courage and hopefulness were soon much reduced. The superficially kind welcome he met everywhere could not conceal the petty strife of coteries, the party spirit and gossip of a society which might have been provincial. The public, though keenly alive to music, was devoid of all critical taste. He ' could not get on with these people,' he writes to Zuccalmaglio as early as Oct. 19, 1838 ; their utter insipidity was at times too much for him, and while he had hoped that on its appearance in Vienna the *Zeitschrift* would have received a fresh impulse, and become a medium of intercourse between North and South, he was forced as early as December to say : ' The paper is evidently falling off, though it must be published here ; this vexes me much.' Sterndale Bennett, who was residing in Leipzig during 1837–38, and who, Schumann hoped, would

[1] See Niecks, *Rob. Sch.* p. 303, where this passage is specifically discussed. Cf. *ibid.* p. 146 *et seq.*
[2] *Gesammelte Schriften,* i. 276 ; Engl. trans. in *Music and Musicians,* series i. p. 205.
[3] See Mme. Schumann's statement that the letters of Mendelssohn to herself referring to her husband which she offered for publication were returned. Niecks, *Rob. Sch.* p. 150.
[4] These dates are now finally settled by Litzmann's *Clara Schumann,* vol. i. p. 123, etc.

settle with him in Vienna, was obliged to relinquish his intention ; and in Vienna itself he sought in vain for an artist after his own heart,

'one who should not merely play tolerably well on one or two instruments, but who should be a *whole man*, and understand Shakespeare and Jean Paul.'

At the same time he did not abandon the scheme of making a wide and influential circle of activity for himself ; he was unwilling to return to Leipzig, and when in Mar. 1839 he made up his mind to do so, after trying in vain to carry on the journal in Vienna, it was with the intention of remaining there but a short time. He indulged in a dream of going to England never to return ! What the anticipations could have been that led him to cherish such an idea we know not ; perhaps his friendship for Bennett may have led to it ; but, in point of fact, he never set foot on English ground.

As far, therefore, as making a home for himself went, his half-year's stay in Vienna was without result. But without doubt Schumann received impulses and incitements towards further progress as a musician through his acquaintance with Vienna life. A work which is to be referred directly to this influence is the 'Faschingsschwank aus Wien' (op. 26, published by Spina in 1841). In the first movement, which seems to depict various scenes of a masquerade, there springs up quite unnoticed the melody of the ' Marseillaise ' (p. 7, bar 40, etc. ; Pauer's edition, vol. iii. p. 596, l. 1), at that time strictly forbidden in Vienna. Schumann, who had been much worried by the government officials on account of his newspaper, took this opportunity of playing off a good-tempered joke upon them.

It was very natural that, with his enthusiastic admiration for Schubert, he should take pains to follow out the traces of that master, who had now been dead just ten years. He visited the Währing cemetery, where Schubert is buried, divided by a few intervening graves from Beethoven. On the tomb of the latter a steel pen was lying ; this Schumann took possession of, and being always fond of symbolical associations and mystic connexions, used on very special occasions. With it he wrote his symphony in B♭ (op. 38), and the notice of Schubert's C major symphony, which is found in the *Zeitschrift* for 1840.[1] And here we encounter one of the chief benefits which Schumann received from his stay in Vienna. He visited Franz Schubert's brother Ferdinand, who showed him the artistic remains of his too early lost brother, and among them the score of the C major symphony. This he had composed in Mar. 1828, but never lived to hear it performed entire, and no one had since cared to take any trouble about it. Schumann

[1] See also the *Gesammelte Schriften*, iii. 195.

arranged for the score to be sent to Leipzig, and there on Mar. 21, 1839, it was performed for the first time under Mendelssohn's direction. Its success was very striking, and was of great influence on the more thorough and widespread appreciation of Schubert's genius. Schumann retained pleasant memories of Vienna throughout his life, in spite of the little notice he attracted on this occasion, and the meagre success of a concert consisting of his own works, which he gave with his wife on a subsequent visit in the winter of 1846. In the summer of 1847 he even wished to apply for a vacant post on the board of direction at the Conservatorium, but when the year 1848 came, he was extremely glad that the plan had come to nothing.

COURTSHIP AND MARRIAGE.—At the beginning of April 1839 Schumann returned to his old life in Leipzig. He devoted himself with new zest to the interests of the journal, and delighted in once more being associated with prominent and sympathetic musicians. In the summer he paid a short visit to Berlin, which pleased and interested him from its contrast to Vienna.

Unfortunately Wieck's opinion as to the match between Schumann and his daughter remained unchanged, and his opposition to it became even stronger and more firmly rooted. Since persuasion was unavailing, Schumann was forced to call in the assistance of the law, and Wieck had to account for his refusal in court. The case dragged on for a whole year, but the final result was that Wieck's objections to the marriage were pronounced to be trivial and without foundation. A sensitive nature such as Schumann's must have been deeply pained by these difficulties, and the long-delayed decision must have kept him in disastrous suspense. His letters show signs of this. For the rest, his outward circumstances had so much improved, that he could easily afford to make a home without the necessity of such a round of work as he had attempted in Vienna. ' We are young,' he writes on Feb. 19, 1840, ' and have hands, strength and reputation ; and I have a little property that brings in 500 thalers a year. The profits of the paper amount to as much again, and I shall get well paid for my compositions. Tell me now if there can be real cause for fear.' One thing alone made him pause for a time. His bride-elect was decorated with different titles of honour from the courts at which she had played in her concert tours. He himself had, it is true, been latterly made a member of several musical societies, but that was not enough. In the beginning of 1840 he executed a scheme which he had cherished since 1838, and applied to the University of Jena for the title of Doctor of Philosophy. Several cases in which the

German universities had granted the doctor's diploma to musicians had lately come under Schumann's notice; for instance the University of Leipzig had given the honorary degree to Marschner in 1835, and to Mendelssohn in 1836, and these may have suggested the idea to him. Schumann received the desired diploma on Feb. 24, 1840. As he had wished, the reason assigned for its bestowal is his well-known activity not only as a critical and æsthetic writer, but as a creative musician. At last, after a year of suspense, doubts and disagreements, the marriage of Robert Schumann with Clara Wieck took place on Sept. 12, 1840, in the church of Schönefeld, near Leipzig.

The 'Davidsbündlertänze,' previously mentioned, bore on the title-page of the first edition an old verse—

'In all und jeder Zeit
Verknüpft sich Lust und Leid :
Bleibt fromm in Lust, und seyd
Beim Leid mit Muth bereit.'

And when we observe that the two first bars of the first piece are borrowed from a composition by Clara Wieck (op. 6, No. 5), we understand the allusion. Schumann himself admits that his compositions for the piano written during the period of his courtship reveal much of his personal experience and feelings, and his creative work in 1840 is of a very striking character.

SONG.—Up to this time, with the exception of the symphony in G minor, which has remained unknown, he had written only for the piano ; now he suddenly threw himself into vocal composition, and the stream of his invention rushed at once into this new channel with such force that in that single year he wrote above one hundred songs. Nor was it in number alone, but in intrinsic value also, that in this department the work of this year was the most remarkable of all Schumann's life. It is not improbable that his stay in Vienna had some share in this sudden rush into song, and in opening Schumann's mind to the charms of pure melody. But still, when we look through the words of his songs, it is clear that here more than anywhere, love was the prompter —love that had endured so long a struggle, and at last attained the goal of its desires. This is confirmed by the 'Myrthen' (op. 25), which he dedicated to the lady of his choice, and the twelve songs from Rückert's *Liebesfrühling* (op. 37), which were written conjointly by the two lovers. 'I am now writing nothing but songs great and small,' he says to a friend on Feb. 19, 1840 ;

'I can hardly tell you how delightful it is to write for the voice as compared with instrumental composition, and what a stir and tumult I feel within me when I sit down to it. I have brought forth quite new things in this line.'

With the close of 1840 he felt that he had worked out the vein of expression in the form of song with pianoforte accompaniment, almost to perfection. Some one expressed a hope that after such a beginning a promising future lay before him as a song-writer, but Schumann answered, 'I cannot venture to promise that I shall produce anything further in the way of songs, and I am satisfied with what I have done.' And he was right in his firm opinion as to the peculiar character of this form of music. 'In your essay on song-writing,' he says to a colleague in the *Zeitschrift*, 'it has somewhat distressed me that you should have placed me in the second rank. I do not ask to stand in the first, but I think I have some pretensions to a place *of my own*.'

As far as anything human can be, the marriage was perfectly happy. Besides their genius, both husband and wife had simple domestic tastes, and were strong enough to bear the admiration of the world without becoming egotistical. They lived for one another, and for their children.[1] He created and wrote for his wife, and in accordance with her temperament ; while she looked upon it as her highest privilege to give to the world the most perfect interpretation of his works, or at least to stand as mediatrix between him and his audience, and to ward off all disturbing or injurious impressions from his sensitive soul, which day by day became more and more irritable. Now that he found perfect contentment in his domestic relations, he withdrew more than ever from intercourse with others, and devoted himself exclusively to his family and his work. The deep joy of his married life produced the direct result of a mighty advance in his artistic progress. Schumann's most beautiful works in the larger forms date almost exclusively from the years 1841-45.

ORCHESTRAL COMPOSITION.—In 1841 he turned his attention to the symphony, as he had done in the previous year to the song, and composed, in this year alone, no fewer than three symphonic works. The B♭ symphony (op. 38) was performed as early as Mar. 31, 1841, at a concert given by Clara Schumann in the Gewandhaus at Leipzig. Mendelssohn conducted it, and performed the task with so much zeal and care as truly to delight his friend. The other two orchestral works were given at a concert on Dec. 6 of the same year, but did not meet with so much success as the former one. Schumann thought that the two together were too much at once ; and they had not the advantage of Mendelssohn's able and careful direction, for he was spending that winter in Berlin. Schumann put these two works away for a time, and published the B♭ symphony alone. The proper title of one of these was 'Symphonistische Phantasie,' but

[1] Eight in all : Marie, Elise, Julie, Enid, Ludwig, Ferdinand, Eugenie, Felix.

## LXXIII

ROBERT AND CLARA SCHUMANN

After a Daguerreotype taken in Hamburg in 1850

it was performed under the title of 'Second Symphony,' and, in 1851, the instrumentation having been revised and completed, was published as the 4th symphony (D minor, op. 120). The other was brought out under an altered arrangement, which he made in 1845, with the title 'Ouverture, Scherzo, et Finale' (op. 52); and it is said that Schumann originally intended to call it 'Sinfonietta.' Besides these orchestral works the first movement of the pianoforte concerto in A minor was written in 1841. It was at first intended to form an independent piece with the title of 'Fantasie.' As appears from a letter of Schumann to David, it was once rehearsed by the Gewandhaus orchestra in the winter of 1841–42. Schumann did not write the last two movements which complete the concerto until 1845.

CHAMBER MUSIC.—The year 1842 was devoted to chamber music. The three string quartets deserve to be first mentioned, since the date of their composition can be fixed with the greatest certainty. Although Schumann was unused to this style of writing, he composed the quartets in about a month—a certain sign that his faculties were as clear as his imagination was rich. In the autograph,[1] after most of the movements is written the date of their completion. The adagio of the first quartet bears the date June 21, 1842; the finale was 'finished on St. John's day, June 24, 1842, in Leipzig.' In the second quartet the second movement is dated July 2, 1842, and the last July 5, 1842, Leipzig. The third is dated as follows: first movement, July 18, second July 20, third July 21, and the fourth Leipzig, July 22, all of the same year. Thus the two last movements took the composer only one day each. These quartets, which are dedicated to Mendelssohn, were at once taken up by the Leipzig musicians with great interest. The praise bestowed upon them by Ferdinand David called forth a letter from Schumann, addressed to him, which merits quotation, as showing how modest and how ideal as an artist Schumann was:

'Härtel told me how very kindly you had spoken to him about my quartets, and, coming from you, it gratified me exceedingly. But I shall have to do better yet, and I feel, with each new work, as if I ought to begin all over again from the beginning.'

In the beginning of October of this year the quartets were played at David's house; Hauptmann was present, and expressed his surprise at Schumann's talent, which, judging only from the earlier pianoforte works, he had fancied not nearly so great. With each new work Schumann now made more triumphant way—at all events in Leipzig. The same year witnessed the production of the quintet for pianoforte and strings (op. 44). The first public performance took place in the Gewandhaus on Jan. 8, 1843, his wife, to whom it is

[1] In the possession of Herr Raymund Härtel, of Leipzig.

dedicated, taking the pianoforte part. Berlioz, who came to Leipzig in 1843, and there made Schumann's personal acquaintance, heard the quintet performed, and carried the fame of it to Paris. Besides the quintet, Schumann wrote, in 1842, the pianoforte quartet (op. 47) and a pianoforte trio. The trio, however, remained unpublished for eight years, and then appeared as op. 88, under the title of 'Phantasiestücke' for pianoforte, violin and violoncello. The quartet too was laid aside for a time; it was first publicly performed on Dec. 8, 1844, by Madame Schumann, in the Gewandhaus, David taking the violin part, and Niels W. Gade, who was directing the Gewandhaus concerts that winter, playing the viola.

CHORAL WORKS.—With the year 1843 came a total change of style. The first work to appear was op. 46, the variations for two pianos, which are now so popular, and to which Mendelssohn may have done some service by introducing them to the public, in company with Mme. Schumann, on August 19, 1843. The principal work of the year, however, was 'Paradise and the Peri,' a grand composition for solo voices, chorus and orchestra, to a text adapted from Moore's 'Lalla Rookh.' The enthusiasm created by this work at its first performance (Dec. 4, 1843), conducted by the composer himself, was so great that it had to be repeated a week afterwards, on Dec. 11, and on the 23rd of the same month it was performed in the Opera House at Dresden. It will be easily believed that from this time Schumann's fame was firmly established in Germany, although it took twenty years more to make his work widely and actually popular. Having been so fortunate in his first attempt in a branch of art hitherto untried by him, he felt induced to undertake another work of the same kind, and in 1844 began writing the second of his two most important choral works, namely, the music to Goethe's 'Faust.' For some time, however, the work consisted only of four numbers. His uninterrupted labours had so affected his health that in this year he was obliged for a time to forgo all exertion of the kind.

CONCERT TOURS.—The first four years of his married life were passed in profound retirement, but very rarely interrupted. In the beginning of 1842 he accompanied his wife on a concert tour to Hamburg, where the B♭ symphony was performed. Madame Schumann then proceeded alone to Copenhagen, while her husband returned to his quiet retreat at Leipzig. In the summer of the same year the two artists made an excursion into Bohemia, and at Königswart were presented to Prince Metternich, who invited them to Vienna. Schumann at first took some pleasure in these tours, but soon forgot it in the peace and comfort of domestic life, and it cost his wife great trouble to induce him to make a longer journey to Russia in the beginning of 1844. Indeed she only succeeded by declaring that she would make the tour alone if he would not leave home. ' How unwilling I am to move out of my quiet round,' he wrote to a friend, ' you must not expect me to tell you. I cannot think of it without the greatest annoyance.' However, he made up his mind to it, and they started on Jan. 26. His wife gave concerts in Mitau, Riga, St. Petersburg and Moscow ; and the enthusiasm with which she was everywhere received attracted fresh attention to Schumann's works, the constant aim of her noble endeavours. Schumann himself, when once he had parted from home, found much to enjoy in a journey which was so decidedly and even brilliantly successful. At St. Petersburg he was received with undiminished cordiality by his old friend Henselt, who had made himself a new home there. At a soirée at Prince Oldenburg's Henselt played with Mme. Schumann her husband's variations for two pianos. The symphony in B♭ was also performed under Schumann's direction at a soirée given by the Counts Joseph and Michael Wielhorsky, highly esteemed musical connoisseurs ; and it is evident that the dedication of Schumann's PF. quartet (op. 47) to a Count Wielhorsky was directly connected with this visit.

In June they were once more in Leipzig, and so agreeable were the reminiscences of the journey that Schumann was ready at once with a fresh plan of the same kind—this time for a visit to England with his wife in the following year ; not, indeed, as he had once intended, with a view to permanent residence, but merely that she might win fresh laurels as a player, and to make himself known as a composer. He proposed to conduct parts of ' Paradise and the Peri ' in London, and anticipated a particular success for it because the work ' had, as it were, sprung from English soil, and was one of the sweetest flowers of English verse.' On June 27, 1844, he writes to Moscheles concerning the project, which had the full support of Mendelssohn ; but the scheme ultimately came to nothing, chiefly because of the refusal of Buxton, the proprietor of the publishing firm of Ewer & Co., to bring out ' Paradise and the Peri ' with English words. Still Schumann, even long after, kept his eye steadily fixed on England. He was delighted at being told that Queen Victoria often listened to his music, and had had the symphony in B♭ [1] played by the private band at Windsor, and he contemplated dedicating his Manfred music (op. 115) to Her Majesty, but the idea was given up.

Instead of going to England, they at length paid a visit to Vienna in the winter of 1846. Here again Schumann conducted his symphony

[1] The first performance of the B♭ symphony in England was at the Philharmonic Concert, June 5, 1854.

in B♭ and his wife played his pianoforte concerto. This was on Jan. 1, 1847. But the public were perfectly unsympathetic, and justified an earlier utterance of Schumann that ' The Viennese are an ignorant people, and know little of what goes on outside their own city.' Nor were matters much more satisfactory in Berlin, whither they went from Vienna to conduct ' Paradise and the Peri ' ; while in Prague, where they performed on their way, they met with the warmest reception.

REMOVAL TO DRESDEN.—The year 1844 was the last of Schumann's residence in Leipzig ; for in October he left the town where he had lived and worked with short intervals for fourteen years, and moved to Dresden. He had given up the editorship of the Neue Zeitschrift in July, and from April 3, 1843, had held a professor's chair in the Conservatorium. founded at Leipzig by Mendelssohn's exertions, and opened on that date. (See LEIPZIG ; also MENDELSSOHN, Vol. III., p. 405.) He was professor of pianoforte-playing and composition ; but his reserved nature was little suited to the duties of a teacher, though his name and the example afforded by his work were no doubt highly advantageous to the infant institution. Schumann had no disciples, properly speaking, either in the Conservatorium or as private pupils. In a letter to David from Dresden he incidentally mentions Carl Ritter as having instruction from him, and as having previously been a pupil of Hiller's ; and he writes to Hiller that he has brought young Ritter on a little. But what the style of Schumann's teaching may have been cannot be told ; and a single exception only proves the rule.

The move to Dresden seems to have been chiefly on account of Schumann's suffering condition. His nervous affection rendered change of scene absolutely necessary to divert his thoughts. He had overworked himself into a kind of surfeit of music, so much so that his medical attendant forbade his continually hearing it. In the musical world of Leipzig such a prohibition could not be strictly obeyed, but at Dresden it was quite different. ' Here,' he writes to David on Nov. 25, 1844,

' one can get back the old lost longing for music. there is so little to hear ! It just suits my condition, for I still suffer very much from my nerves, and everything affects and exhausts me directly.'

Accordingly he at first lived in Dresden in the strictest seclusion. A friend sought him out there and found him so changed that he entertained grave fears for his life. On several occasions he tried sea-bathing, but it was long before his health can be said to have radically improved. In February 1846, after a slight improvement, he again became very unwell, as he did also in the summer of the following year. He observed that he was unable to remember the melodies that occurred to him, when composing; the effort of invention fatiguing his mind to such a degree as to impair his memory. As soon as a lasting improvement took place in his health, he again devoted himself wholly to composition. He was now attracted more powerfully than before to complicated contrapuntal forms. The 'Studies' and 'Sketches' for the pedal-piano (opp. 56 and 58), the six fugues on the name of 'Bach' (op. 60) and the four piano fugues (op. 72) owe their existence to this attraction. The greatest work of the years 1845–46, however, was the C major symphony (op. 61), which Mendelssohn produced at the Gewandhaus in Leipzig, Nov. 5, 1846. Slight intercourse with a few congenial spirits was now gradually resumed. Among those whom he saw was the widow of C. M. v. Weber, whose fine musical feeling was highly valued by Schumann. The first year in Dresden was spent with Ferdinand Hiller, who had been living there since the winter of 1844. Their intercourse gradually grew into a lively and lasting intimacy. When Hiller was getting up subscription concerts in the autumn of 1845, Schumann took an active share in the undertaking. With Richard Wagner, too, then Kapellmeister at Dresden, he was on friendly terms. He was much interested in the opera of 'Tannhäuser' and heard it often, expressing his opinion of it in terms of great though not unqualified praise. But the natures of the two musicians differed too widely to allow of any real sympathy between them. (See WAGNER, Vol. V. p. 589.) Wagner was always lively, versatile and talkative, while Schumann's former silence and reserve had increased since his illness, and even intimate friends, like Moscheles and Lipinski, had to lament that conversation with him was now scarcely possible.

OPERA.—At the end of Schumann's collected works we find a *Theaterbüchlein* (1847–50), in which are given short notes of the impressions made upon him by certain operas. From this we learn that in 1847 he went comparatively often to the theatre; the reason being that at that time he himself was composing an opera. He had long cherished the idea. So early as Sept. 1, 1842, he writes, 'Do you know what is my morning and evening prayer as an artist? *German Opera. There* is a field for work.' He concludes a critique of an opera by Heinrich Esser in the number of the *Zeitschrift* for September 1842 with these significant words:

'It is high time that German composers should give the lie to the reproach that has long lain on them of having been so craven as to leave the field in possession of the Italians and French. But under this head there is a word to be said to the German poets also.'

In 1844 he composed a chorus and an aria for an opera on Byron's *Corsair*. The work, however, went no farther, and the two pieces still remain unpublished. He also corresponded with his friend Zuccalmaglio as to the subject for an opera, which he wished to find ready on his return from Russia; and made notes on more than twenty different subjects of all kinds, periods and nationalities; but none of these were found suitable, and circumstances led to the abandonment of the project.

At length, in 1847, he decided on the legend of St. Geneviève. The two versions of the story contained in the tragedies of Tieck and Hebbel (principally that of Hebbel) were to serve as the basis of the text. The treatment of the words he persuaded Robert Reinick, the poet, who had been living in Dresden since 1844, to undertake. Reinick, however, failed to satisfy him, and Hebbel, who came to Dresden at the end of July 1847, could not say that he thought it a satisfactory text, though he declined to assist in remedying the deficiencies and bringing it into the desired form. This, however, was from no lack of interest in Schumann himself. On the contrary Hebbel always preserved the highest esteem for him, and subsequently dedicated to him his drama of *Michael Angelo*, accepting in return from Schumann the dedication of his 'Nachtlied' (op. 108). But it was repugnant to him to see his work mutilated in the way which Schumann considered necessary for an opera. The composer was at last obliged to trust to his own poetic powers, and construct a text himself from those already mentioned.

By August 1848 the music for the opera was so far complete that Schumann thought he might take steps for its performance. His first thought was of the theatre at Leipzig, where he knew that he was most warmly remembered. Wirsing was at that time the director, Julius Rietz the conductor, and the opera was to have been brought out in the spring of 1849, but it came to nothing. In June, when the preparations were to have begun, Schumann was detained by domestic circumstances, and the rest of the year slipped away with constant evasions and promises on the part of the director of the theatre. Even the promise, 'on his honour,' that the opera should be performed at the end of February 1850, at latest, was not kept. And so in this, his very first attempt at dramatic work, Schumann made acquaintance with the shady side of theatrical management in a way which must have disgusted his upright and honourable spirit. In his indignation, he would have made the director's breach of faith public, by invoking the aid of the law; but his Leipzig friends were happily able to dissuade him from this course. At last, on June 25, 1850, the first representation of 'Genoveva' actually took place under Schumann's own direction. But the time was unfavourable. 'Who,' he writes to Dr. Hermann Härtel, 'goes to the theatre in May or June, and not rather into the woods?'

However, the number of his admirers in Leipzig was great, and the first opera by so famous a master excited great expectations; the house was full, and the reception by the public, though not enthusiastic, was honourable to the composer.

Still, artists and connoisseurs were tolerably unanimous in thinking that Schumann lacked the special genius for writing opera. His almost entire exclusion of recitative was very widely disapproved of. No one but the venerable Spohr, who had attended many of the rehearsals, gave a really favourable verdict upon the work. In his last opera, 'The Crusaders,' Spohr himself had adopted similar methods of making the music follow the plot closely without ever coming to. a standstill, and he was naturally delighted to find the same in Schumann's work. After three representations (June 25, 28, 30) 'Genoveva' was laid aside for the time. Schumann, already vexed by the tedious postponements of the first performance, and disappointed by the cold reception of the work, was greatly annoyed by the discussions in the public prints, especially by a critique from Dr. E. Krüger, one of the collaborateurs in the *Neue Zeitschrift*. A letter from Schumann to Krüger, in stronger terms than might have been expected from him, put an end for ever to their acquaintance.

GOETHE'S 'FAUST.'—Schumann derived far more gratification from the reception of his music to 'Faust.' In 1848 he completed the portion he had originally intended to write first, viz. the salvation of Faust, which forms the end of the second part of Goethe's poem, and the music of which is called the 'third part.' On June 25, 1848, the first performance took place among a limited circle of friends, upon whom it made a deep impression. The most cultivated portion of the audience was of opinion that the music made the meaning of the words clear for the first time, so deeply imbued was the composer with the poet's inmost spirit. As the 100th anniversary of Goethe's birthday was approaching (August 28, 1849) it was decided to give a festival concert in Dresden, at which this 'Faust' music and Mendelssohn's 'Walpurgisnacht' should form the programme. When the Leipzig people heard of this intention, they would not be behind Dresden, and also got up a performance of the same works on August 29. In Weimar too the 'Faust' music was performed for the same festivity. Schumann was exceedingly delighted that his work had been employed for so special an occasion. He writes to Dr. Härtel : 'I should like to have Faust's cloak, and be able to be everywhere at once, that I might hear it.' In Dresden the success of the work was very considerable, but it made less impression at its first performance in Leipzig. Schumann took this quite calmly. 'I hear different accounts,' says he in a letter,

'of the impression produced by my scenes from "Faust"'; some seem to have been affected, while upon others it made no definite impression. This is what I expected. Perhaps an opportunity may occur in the winter for a repetition of the work, when it is possible that I may add some other scenes.'

This repetition, however, did not take place in Schumann's lifetime. He fulfilled his scheme of adding several scenes ; and in 1853 prefixed an overture to the whole work, which was divided into three parts. It was not published complete until two years after his death.

In the meantime, Schumann's health had again improved, as was evident from his augmented creative activity. Indeed his eager desire for work increased in a way which gave rise to great apprehensions. In the year 1849 alone he produced thirty works, most of them of considerable extent. It had never seemed so easy to him to create ideas and bring them into shape. He composed as he walked or stood, and could not be distracted, even by the most disturbing circumstances. Thus he wrote Mignon's song 'Kennst du das Land' at Kreischa, near Dresden, in the midst of a group of his noisy children. And in a restaurant near the post office, much frequented by the artistic society of Dresden, where he used to drink his beer in the evening, he would usually sit alone, with his back to the company and his face to the wall, whistling softly to himself, and developing his musical ideas all the time. No preference for any particular form of art can be traced in Schumann's work at this time. Pianoforte works and chamber trios, songs and vocal duets, choruses, choral works with orchestra, concertos with orchestra, compositions for horn, clarinet, oboe, violoncello or violin, with pianoforte accompaniment, even melodramatic music—all these thronged as it were out of his imagination in wild and strange succession. Among all the beautiful and important works produced at this time, the music to Byron's *Manfred* deserves especial mention. The first stage performance of it was given by Franz Liszt in Weimar on June 13, 1852. For that occasion the drama was adapted for the stage by Schumann himself, in an arrangement which is printed as a preface to the score of the work. The first performance of the music at a concert took place at Leipzig on Mar. 24, 1859.

CHORAL CONDUCTING.—Dresden was Schumann's place of residence until 1850.[1] In the latter years of his stay there his outward life was more active than before. No journeys of note were made, it is true, with the exception of those to Vienna and Berlin already mentioned, and a longer expedition undertaken in 1850 to Bremen and Hamburg, where many concerts were given. He avoided the passing disturbance occasioned by the Dresden insurrection of 1849, by leaving the town with his family. Though no revolutionary, like Richard Wagner,

---

[1] The formation of the BACH GESELLSCHAFT (*q.v.*), in which Schumann took a prominent part, belongs to this year.

scarcely even a politician, Schumann loved individual liberty and wished others to enjoy it also. But what gave a different aspect to his life as a musician in the last years of his stay in Dresden, was his occupation as a conductor. Ferdinand Hiller had conducted a choral society for men's voices ; and when he left Dresden to go to Düsseldorf as municipal director of music, Schumann succeeded him in his post. He conducted the society for some time with great interest, and was glad to find that his capacity for conducting was not so small as he had generally fancied it to be. He was even induced to write a few works for male chorus. Three songs of War and Liberty (Kriegs- und Freiheitslieder, op. 62) and seven songs in canon-form, to words by Rückert (op. 65), were written in 1847, and a grand motet for double chorus of men's voices (op. 93) in 1849. But a nature like Schumann's could not thrive in the atmosphere of a German singing-club. He was in all respects too refined for the tone of vulgar comfort, and often even of low senti-mentality, which pervades these assemblies, and they could not but be irksome to him. ' I felt myself,' he says, in a letter to Hiller written on Apr. 10, 1849, after his withdrawal, ' out of my element : they were such nice (*hübsch*) people.' This is even noticeable in his com-positions for male chorus ; they are not of the right kind, and have in consequence never been much sung. Of greater artistic importance was a society of mixed voices which was con-stituted in January 1848, and of which Schu-mann was asked to take the lead. It was not very large—in 1849 it numbered only sixty or seventy members—but these were efficient, and Schumann was able ' to perform correctly any music he liked with pleasure and delight.' It was this society that gave the first performance of the third part of ' Faust ' in June 1848, at a private party ; Schumann was induced to write many new compositions for them, and they did much service in promoting a knowledge of his music in Dresden by two performances of ' Paradise and the Peri ' on Jan. 5 and 12, 1850. They even succeeded in drawing him into social amusements. In August 1848 a general ex-cursion was arranged, in which Schumann took what was, for him, a lively interest.

That Schumann, after so successful a begin-ning in the art of conducting, considered him-self fitted to undertake the direction of perform-ances on a larger scale, is evident from the following circumstance. After Mendelssohn's death the Gewandhaus concerts were conducted by Julius Rietz, who until 1847 had been at work in Düsseldorf. In the summer of 1849 a report reached Dresden that Rietz was going to succeed O. Nicolai as royal Kapellmeister at Berlin. Schumann thereupon applied for the post of concert director at the Gewandhaus. Dr. Hermann Härtel was to be the medium of

communication, and Schumann, with a well-founded expectation that the choice would fall upon him, gave himself up for a time with great pleasure to the idea of becoming the successor of the honoured Mendelssohn. ' It would give me great pleasure,' he wrote :

' if the thing came to pass. I long for regular duty, and though I can never forget the last few years, during which I have lived exclusively as a composer, and know that so productive and happy a time may perhaps never be mine again, yet I feel impelled towards a life of active work, and my highest endeavour would be to keep up the renown which the institution has so long enjoyed.'

This wish was not realised, for Rietz remained in Leipzig. But Schumann's desire for a more extended field of work as a conductor was to be satisfied in another way in the following year.

DÜSSELDORF.—In 1850 Hiller gave up his post in Düsseldorf to obey a call to Cologne as Kapellmeister to that city. He suggested that Schumann should be his successor, and opened negotiations with him. Some efforts were made to keep him in Dresden and to obtain his ap-pointment as Kapellmeister to the King of Saxony ; but the attempt was unsuccessful, and Schumann accepted the directorship at Düsseldorf that summer, though he left his native place with deep regret, and not without some suspicions as to the condition of music in Düsseldorf, of which he had heard much that was unfavourable from Mendelssohn and Rietz. In his new post he had the direction of a vocal union and of an orchestra, and a number of concerts to conduct in the course of the winter. He arrived at Düsseldorf, Sept. 2, 1850, and the first winter concert was in some sort a formal reception of him, since it consisted of the over-ture to ' Genoveva,' some of his songs and Part I. of ' Paradise and the Peri.' It was under the direction of Julius Tausch, Schu-mann himself appearing as conductor for the first time on Oct. 24.

He was very well satisfied with his new sphere of work. The vocal resources, as is the case with all the choirs of the Rhine towns, were admirable ; Hiller had cultivated them with special zeal, and he and Rietz had left the orchestra so well drilled that Schumann, for the first time in his life, enjoyed the inestimable advantage of being able to hear everything that he wrote for the orchestra performed imme-diately. The concerts took up no more of his time than he was willing to give, and left him ample leisure for his own work. Chamber music was also attainable, for in J. von Wasie-lewski there was a good solo violinist on the spot. Schumann and his wife were at once welcomed in Düsseldorf with the greatest respect, and every attention and consideration was shown to them both. It might be said that their position here was one of special ease, and they soon formed a delightful circle of intimate acquaintants. Little as his music was then known in the Rhine cities, Schumann's advent in person seems to have given a strong impulse to the public feeling for music in Düsseldorf. The interest in the subscription concerts during the winter of 1850 was greater than it had ever been before; and the board of directors was able, at the close of the usual series of six concerts, to undertake a second series of three or four. At Schumann's instance one of the winter concerts was entirely devoted to the works of living composers, an idea then perfectly novel, and showing that he had remained faithful to his desire—manifested long before through the *Zeitschrift*—of facilitating the advancement of young and gifted composers.

At first Schumann's direction gave entire satisfaction. If some performances were not perfectly successful, they were compensated for by others of special excellence; and the execution of Beethoven's symphony in A at the third concert even seemed to show that he was a born conductor. But it was not so in reality; indeed he was wholly wanting in the real talent for conducting; all who ever saw him conduct or who played under his direction are agreed on this point. Irrespective of the fact that conducting for any length of time tired him out, he had neither the collectedness and prompt presence of mind, nor the sympathetic faculty, nor the enterprising dash, without each of which conducting in the true sense is impossible. He even found a difficulty in starting at a given *tempo*; nay, he sometimes shrank from giving any initial beat; so that some energetic pioneer would begin without waiting for the signal, and without incurring Schumann's wrath. Besides this, any thorough practice bit by bit with his orchestra, with instructive remarks by the way as to the mode of execution, was impossible to this great artist, who in this respect was a striking contrast to Mendelssohn. He would have a piece played through, and if it did not answer to his wishes, had it repeated. If it went no better the second, or perhaps even a third time, he would be extremely angry at what he considered the clumsiness or even the ill-will of the players; but detailed remarks he never made.

Any one knowing his silent nature and his instinctive dislike to contact with the outer world, might certainly have feared from the first that he would find great difficulty in asserting himself as a director of large masses. And as years went on his incapacity for conducting constantly increased, as the issue showed, with the growth of an illness, which, after seeming to have been completely overcome in Dresden, returned in Düsseldorf with increasing gravity. His genius seemed constantly to shrink from the outside world into the depths of his soul. His silence became a universally accepted fact, and to those who saw him for the first time he seemed apathetic. But in fact he was any-

thing rather than that; he would let a visitor talk for a long time on all kinds of subjects without saying a word, and then when the caller rose to leave, 'not to disturb the master longer,' he would discover that Schumann had followed the one-sided 'conversation' with unfailing interest. When sitting for an hour, as he was accustomed of an evening, with friends or acquaintances at the restaurant, if anything was said that touched or pleased him he would give the speaker a radiant, expressive glance, but without a word; and the incessant creative labours, to which he gave himself up so long as he was able, are the best proof of the rich vitality which constantly flowed from the deepest sources of his soul.

In the family circle he was a different man; there he could be gay and talkative to a degree that would have surprised a stranger. He loved his children tenderly, and was fond of occupying himself with them. The three piano sonatas (op. 118) composed for his daughters Julie, Elise and Marie, the Album for beginners (op. 68); the Children's Ball (op. 130), and other pieces, are touching evidence of the way in which he expressed this feeling in music.

LATE COMPOSITIONS.—The first great work of the Düsseldorf period was the symphony in E♭ (op. 97), marked by the composer as No. 3, although it is really the fourth of the published ones, that in D minor preceding it in order of composition. If we call the overture, scherzo and finale (op. 52) a symphony too, then the symphony in E♭ must rank as the fifth. It would seem that Schumann had begun to work at it before his change of residence. As soon as he conceived the project of leaving Saxony for the Rhine, he bethought himself of the great musical festival which ever since 1818 had been held in the lower Rhine districts (see NIEDER-RHEINISCHE FEST), and was inspired by the idea of assisting at one of these in the capacity of a composer. He wrote down this great work with its five movements between Nov. 2 and Dec. 9, 1850. He has told us that it was intended to convey the impressions which he received during a visit to Cologne; so that its ordinary name of the 'Rhenish Symphony' may be accepted as correct. It was first performed at Düsseldorf on Feb. 6, 1851, and then at Cologne on Feb. 25, both times under the direction of the composer, but was coldly received on both occasions.[1]

Although Schumann had had no pleasant experiences in connexion with the opera 'Genoveva,' he was not to be deterred from making another essay in dramatic composition. In Oct. 1850 he received from Richard Pohl, at that time a student in the Leipzig University, Schiller's 'Bride of Messina,' arranged as an

[1] Its first performance in England was at a concert of Signor Arditi's, Dec. 4, 1865.

opera libretto. Schumann could not make up his mind to set it to music; but in Dec. 1850 and Jan. 1851 he wrote an overture to the 'Braut von Messina' (op. 100), which showed how much the material of the play had interested him, in spite of his refusal to set it. He inclined to a more cheerful, or even a comic subject, and Goethe's 'Hermann und Dorothea' seemed to him appropriate for an operetta. He consulted several poets concerning the arrangement, and having made out a scheme of treatment, wrote the overture at Christmas 1851 (op. 136). The work, however, progressed no farther. He subsequently turned his attention to Auerbach's 'Dorfgeschichten,' but without finding any good material, and no second opera from his pen ever saw the light.

He completed, however, a number of vocal compositions for the concert-room, in which his taste for dramatic music had free play. A young poet from Chemnitz, Moritz Horn, had sent him a faery poem, which greatly interested him. After many abbreviations and alterations made by Horn himself at Schumann's suggestion, 'The Pilgrimage of the Rose' (Der Rose Pilgerfahrt, op. 112) was really set to music between April and July 1851. The work, which both in form and substance resembles 'Paradise and the Peri,' except that it is treated in a manner at once more detailed and more idyllic, had at first a simple pianoforte accompaniment, but in November Schumann arranged it for orchestra. June 1851 is also the date of the composition of Uhland's ballad 'Der Königssohn' (op. 116), in a semi-dramatic form, to which indeed he was almost driven by the poem itself. Schumann was much pleased with his treatment of this ballad, which he set for solo, chorus and orchestra. In the course of the next two years he wrote three more works of the same kind: 'Des Sängers Fluch' (op. 139), a ballad of Uhland's; 'Vom Pagen und der Königstochter' (op. 140), a ballad by Geibel; and 'Das Glück von Edenhall' (op. 143), a ballad by Uhland.

In the last two poems he made alterations of more or less importance, to bring them into shape for musical setting, but the 'Sängers Fluch' had to be entirely remodelled—a difficult and ungrateful task, which Richard Pohl carried out after Schumann's own suggestions.

At that time this young man, a thorough art enthusiast, kept up a lively intercourse with Schumann, both personally and by letter. They devised together the plan of a grand oratorio. Schumann wavered between a Biblical and an historical subject, thinking at one time of the Virgin Mary, at another of Ziska or Luther. His final choice fell upon Luther. He pondered deeply upon the treatment of his materials. It was to be an oratorio suitable both for the church and the concert-room, and in its poetical form as dramatic as possible. In point of

musical treatment he intended the chorus to predominate, as in Handel's 'Israel in Egypt,' of which he had given a performance in the winter of 1850. Moreover, it was not to be complicated and contrapuntal in style, but simple and popular, so that 'peasant and citizen alike should understand it.' The more he pondered it the more was he inspired with the grandeur of the subject, although by no means blind to its difficulties. 'It inspires courage,' he says, 'and also humility.' He could not, however, coincide with his poet's opinion as to the extent of the work, the latter having formed the idea of a sort of trilogy, in oratorio form, while Schumann wished the work to be within the limit of one evening's performance, lasting about two hours and a half. In this way the few years of creative activity that were still granted to him slipped away, and the oratorio remained unwritten. The impossibility of satisfying, by the oratorio on Luther, the inclination for grave and religious music which became ever stronger with increasing years, is partly the reason of his writing in 1852 a Mass (op. 147), and a Requiem (op. 148). But to these he was also incited by outward circumstances. The inhabitants of Düsseldorf are mostly Catholics, the organ-lofts in the principal churches are too small to hold a large choir and orchestra, and the regular church music was in a bad condition. The choral society which Schumann conducted was accustomed, as a reward for its labours, to have several concerts of church music, or at least sacred compositions, every year; and Schumann was probably thinking of this custom in his Mass and his Requiem, but he was not destined ever to hear them performed.

In the summer of 1851 he and his family made a tour in Switzerland, which he had not visited since the time of his student life in Heidelberg; on his return he went to Antwerp, for a competitive performance by the Belgian 'Männergesangverein,' on August 17, at which he had been asked to aid in adjudging the prizes. Two years later, towards the end of 1853, he and his wife once more visited the Netherlands, and made a concert tour through Holland, meeting with such an enthusiastic reception that he could not help saying that his music seemed to have struck deeper root there than in Germany. In March 1852 they revisited Leipzig, where, between the 14th and the 21st, a quantity of his music was performed; the Manfred overture and the 'Der Rose Pilgerfahrt' at a public matinée on the 14th; the sonata in D minor for pianoforte and violin (op. 121) in a private circle, on the 15th; the symphony in E♭ at a concert at the Gewandhaus on the 18th; the pianoforte trio in G minor (op. 110) at a chamber concert on the 21st. On Nov. 6, 1851, the overture to the 'Braut von Messina' was also performed at the

Gewandhaus. The public had thus, during this season, ample opportunity of becoming acquainted with the latest works of this inexhaustible composer. But although he had lived in Leipzig for fourteen years, and had brought out most of his compositions there, besides having a circle of sincerely devoted friends in that city, he could not on this occasion boast of any great success ; the public received him with respect and esteem, but with no enthusiasm. But in this respect Schumann had lived through a variety of experience ; ' I am accustomed,' he writes to Pohl, Dec. 7, 1851, when speaking of the reception of the overture to the ' Braut von Messina,' ' to find that my compositions, particularly the best and deepest, are not understood by the public at a first hearing.' Artists, however, had come to Leipzig from some distance for the ' Schumann-week ' ; among them Liszt and Joachim.

In August 1852 there was held in Düsseldorf a festival of music for men's voices, in which Schumann assisted as conductor, though, owing to his health, only to a very limited extent. He took a more important part at Whitsuntide 1853, when the 31st of the Lower Rhine Festivals was celebrated in Düsseldorf on May 15, 16 and 17. He conducted the music of the first day, consisting of Handel's ' Messiah ' and of his own symphony in D minor, which was exceedingly well received. In the concerts of the two following days, which were conducted chiefly by Hiller, two more of Schumann's larger compositions were performed; the pianoforte concerto in A minor, and a newly composed Festival Overture with soli and chorus on the ' Rheinweinlied ' (op. 123). But although Schumann appeared in so brilliant a way as a composer, and as such was honoured and appreciated in Düsseldorf, yet there was no concealing the fact that as a conductor he was inefficient. The little talent for conducting that he showed on his arrival in Düsseldorf had disappeared with his departing health. It was in fact necessary to procure some one to take his place. An attempt was made after the first winter concert of the year (Oct. 27, 1853) to induce him to retire for a time from the post of his own accord. But this proposal was badly received. The fact, however, remains, that from the date just mentioned all the practices and performances were conducted by Julius Tausch, who thus became Schumann's real successor. No doubt the directors of the society were really in the right; though perhaps the form in which Schumann's relation to the society was expressed might have been better chosen. The master was now taken up with the idea of leaving Düsseldorf as soon as possible, and of adopting Vienna, for which he had preserved a great affection, as his permanent residence. But fate had decided otherwise.

THE ARRIVAL OF BRAHMS.—The dissatisfaction induced in his mind by the events of the autumn of 1853 was, however, mitigated partly by the tour in Holland already mentioned, and partly by another incident. It happened that in October a young and wholly unknown musician arrived, with a letter of introduction from Joachim. Johannes Brahms—for he it was—immediately excited Schumann's warmest interest by the genius of his playing and the originality of his compositions. In his early days he had always been the champion of the young and aspiring, and now as a matured artist he took pleasure in smoothing the path of this gifted youth. Schumann's literary pen had lain at rest for nine years ; he now once more took it up, for the last time, in order to say a powerful word for Brahms to the wide world of art. An article entitled *Neue Bahnen* (New Paths) appeared on Oct. 28, 1853, in No. 18 of that year's *Zeitschrift*. In this he pointed to Brahms as the artist whose vocation it would be ' to utter the highest ideal expression of our time.' He does not speak of him as a youth or beginner, but welcomes him into the circle of masters as a fully equipped combatant. When before or since did an artist find such words of praise for one of his fellows ? It is as though, having already given so many noble proofs of sympathetic appreciation, he could not leave the world without once more, after his long silence, indelibly stamping the image of his pure, lofty and unenvious artist-nature on the hearts of his fellow-men.

So far as Brahms was concerned, it is true that this brilliant *envoi* laid him under a heavy debt of duty, in the necessity of measuring his productions by the very highest standard ; and at the time Schumann was supposed to have attributed to Brahms, as he did to the poetess Elisabeth Kulmann, gifts which he did not actually possess. We know now that Schumann's keen insight did not deceive him, and that Brahms verified all the expectations formed of him. His intercourse with the young composer (then twenty years old), in whom he took the widest and most affectionate interest, was a great pleasure to Schumann.

At that time, too, Albert Dietrich (afterwards Hofkapellmeister at Oldenburg) was staying in Düsseldorf, and Schumann proved to the utmost the truth of what he had written only a few months previously of Kirchner, that he loved to follow the progress of young men. A sonata for pianoforte and violin exists in MS. which Schumann composed during this month (Oct. 1853) in conjunction with Brahms and Dietrich. Dietrich begins with an allegro in A minor ; Schumann follows with an intermezzo in F major ; Brahms—who signs himself *Johannes Kreissler junior*—adds an allegro (scherzo) in C minor ; and Schumann winds up the work with a finale in A minor, ending in A major. The title of the sonata is worth noting.

Joachim was coming to Düsseldorf to play at the concert of Oct. 27, so Schumann wrote on the title-page :

'In anticipation of the arrival of our beloved and honoured friend Joseph Joachim, this sonata was written by Robert Schumann, Albert Dietrich and Johannes Brahms.' [1]

This interesting intimacy cannot have continued long, since in November Schumann went to Holland with his wife, and did not return till Dec. 22. But he met Brahms again in Hanover in Jan. 1854 at a performance of 'Paradise and the Peri,' where he found also Joachim and Julius Otto Grimm. A circle of gifted and devoted young artists gathered round the master and rejoiced in having him among them, little imagining that within a few months he would be suddenly snatched from them for ever.

MENTAL COLLAPSE. — Schumann's appearance was that of a man with a good constitution ; his figure was above the middle height, full and well-built ; but his nervous system had always shown extreme excitability, and even so early as his twenty-fourth year he suffered from a nervous disorder which increased to serious disease. At a still earlier date he had shown a certain morbid hypertension of feeling, in connexion with his passionate study of Jean Paul, of whom he wrote, even in his eighteenth year, that he often drove him to the verge of madness. Violent shocks of emotion, as for instance the sudden announcement of a death, or the struggle for the hand of Clara Wieck, would bring him into a condition of mortal anguish, and the most terrible state of bewilderment and helplessness, followed by days of overwhelming melancholy. A predisposition to worry himself, an 'ingenuity in clinging to unhappy ideas,' often embittered the fairest moments of his life. Gloomy antic.pations darkened his soul ; 'I often feel as if I should not live much longer,' he says in a letter to Zuccalmaglio of May 18, 1837, 'and I should like to do a little more work ' ; and later, to Hiller—' man must work while it is yet day.' The vigour of youth for a time conquered these melancholy aberrations, and after his marriage the calm and equable happiness which he found in his wife for a long time expelled the evil spirit. It was not till 1844 that he again fell a prey to serious nervous tension This was evidently the result of undue mental strain, and for a time he was forced to give up all work, and even the hearing of music, and to withdraw into perfect solitude at Dresden. His improvement was slow and not without relapses ; but in 1849 he felt quite re-established, as we gather from his letters and from the work he accomplished ; and his condition seems to have remained satisfactory till about the end of 1851. Then the symptoms of disease reappeared ; he

[1] The MS. was in Joachim's possession, and he permitted the publication of the movement by Brahms, which appeared in 1907.

had, as usual, been again working without pause or respite, and even with increased severity ; and was himself so much alarmed as to seek a remedy. Various eccentricities of conduct betrayed even to strangers the state of nervous excitability in which he was. By degrees delusions grew upon him, and he fancied that he incessantly heard one particular note, or certain harmonies, or voices whispering words of reproof or encouragement. Once in the night he fancied that the spirits of Schubert and Mendelssohn brought him a musical theme, and he got up and noted it down. He was again attacked by that 'mortal anguish of mind ' of which he had had former experience, and which left him perfectly distracted. Still, all these symptoms were but temporary, and between the attacks Schumann was in full possession of his senses and self-control. He himself expressed a wish to be placed in an asylum, but meanwhile worked on in his old way. He wrote some variations for the piano on the theme revealed to him by Schubert and Mendelssohn, but they were his last work, and remained unfinished.

On Feb. 27, 1854, in the afternoon, in one of his fits of agony of mind, he left the house unobserved and threw himself from the bridge into the Rhine. Some boatmen were on the watch and rescued him, and he was recognised and carried home. Unmistakable symptoms of insanity now declared themselves, but after a few days a peculiar clearness and calmness of mind returned, and with it his irrepressible love of work. He completed the variation on which he had been at work before the great catastrophe. These last efforts of his wearied genius remain unpublished, but Brahms has used the theme for a set of 4-hand variations which form one of his most beautiful and touching works (op. 23), and which he has dedicated to Schumann's daughter Julie.

The last two years of Schumann's life were spent in the private asylum of Dr. Richarz at Endenich, near Bonn. His mental disorder developed into deep melancholy ; at times—as in the spring of 1855—when for a while he seemed better, his outward demeanour was almost the same as before. He corresponded with his friends and received visits, but gradually the pinions of his soul drooped and fell, and he died in the arms of his wife, July 29, 1856, only 46 years of age.

Soon after Schumann's death his music achieved a popularity in Germany which will bear comparison with that of the most favourite of the older masters. When once the peculiarities of his style grew familiar, it was realised that these very peculiarities had their origin in the deepest feelings of the nation. The desire of giving outward expression to the love which was felt towards him soon asserted itself more and more strongly. Schumann was buried at

Bonn, in the churchyard opposite the Sternen-thor, and it was resolved to erect a monument to him there. On Aug. 17, 18 and 19, 1873, a Schumann festival took place at Bonn, consisting entirely of the master's compositions. The conducting was undertaken by Joachim and Wasielewski, and among the performers were Madame Schumann, who played her husband's pianoforte concerto, and Stockhausen. The festival was one of overwhelming interest, owing to the sympathy taken in it, and the manner in which that sympathy was displayed. The proceeds of the concerts were devoted to a monument to Schumann's memory, which was executed by A. Donndorf of Stuttgart, erected over the grave, and unveiled on May 2, 1880. On this occasion also a concert took place, consisting of compositions by Schumann and Brahms's violin concerto (op. 77), conducted by himself and played by Joachim.

---

THE LITERARY ARTIST.—Schumann, with his activity both as an author and as a composer, was a new phenomenon in German music. It is true that he had had a predecessor in this respect in C. M. von Weber, who also had a distinct gift and vocation for authorship, and whose collected writings form a literary monument possessing far more than a merely personal interest. Still, Weber was prevented by circumstances and by his own natural restlessness from fully developing his literary talent, while Schumann benefited by the restraint and discipline of his ten years of editorship. In 1854 he had his *Gesammelte Schriften über Musik und Musiker* published in four volumes by Wigand in Leipzig, and it was not long in reaching its second edition, which appeared in two volumes in 1871. This collection, however, is not nearly complete, and the essays it includes have been much altered. A full and correct edition of his writings is still a desideratum.

It must not, however, be imagined that Schumann's aim as an author was to lay down the principles on which he worked as a composer ; it is indeed hardly possible to contrast the critical and the productive elements in his works. His authorship and his musical compositions were two distinct phases of a creative nature, and if it was by composition that he satisfied his purely musical craving it was by writing that he gave utterance to his poetical instincts. His essays are for the most part rather rhapsodies on musical works or poetical imagery lavished on musical subjects than criticisms properly speaking ; and the cases where he writes in the negative vein are very rare exceptions. A high ideal floats before his mind, and supported by the example of the greatest masters of the art, his one aim is to introduce a new and pregnant period of music in contrast to the shallowness of his own time. Again and

again he speaks of this as the ' poetic phase '— and here we must guard against a misunderstanding. The term ' poetic music ' is often used in antithesis to ' pure music,' to indicate a work based on a combination of poetry and music ; as, for instance, a song, which may be conceived of either as a purely musical composition founded on the union of definite feelings and ideas, or as intended to express the preconceived emotions and ideas of the poet. But it was not anything of this kind that Schumann meant to convey ; he simply regarded poetry as the antithesis to prose, just as enthusiasm is the antithesis to sober dullness, the youthful rhapsodist to the Philistine, the artist with his lofty ideal to the mechanical artisan or the superficial dilettante. His aim is to bring to birth a living art, full of purpose and feeling, and he cannot endure a mere skeleton of forms and phrases. In this key he pitches his writings on music, and their purport is always the same. He once speaks of reviewers and critics under a quaint simile—' Music excites the nightingale to love-songs, the lap-dog to bark.' Nothing could more accurately represent his own attitude in writing on music than the first of these images. From his point of view a piece of music ought to rouse in the true critic sympathetic feeling, he ought to absorb and assimilate its contents, and then echo them in words—Schumann was in fact the singing nightingale. Though we may not feel inclined to apply his other comparison to every critic who does not follow in his steps, we may at least say that the difference between Schumann's style and that of the musical periodicals of his day was as great as that between a nightingale and a lap-dog. And how strange and new were the tones uttered by this poet-critic ! A considerable resemblance to Jean Paul must be admitted, particularly in his earlier critiques: the ecstatic youthful sentiment, the humorous suggestions, the highly wrought and dazzling phraseology are common to both ; but the style is quite different. Schumann commonly writes in short and vivid sentences, going straight at his subject without digressions, and indulging in bold abbreviations. There is a certain indolence of genius about him, and yet a sure artistic instinct throughout. Nor has he a trace of Jean Paul's sentimental ' luxury of woe,' but we everywhere find, side by side with emotional rhapsody, the refreshing breeziness of youth and health.

It has already been said that Schumann connects certain definite characteristics with different feigned names (Florestan, Eusebius, Raro, etc.), a device which none but a poet could have hit on. Indeed, it would be a hindrance to the writing of calm criticism, which must have a fixed and clearly defined position as its basis. But it often introduces a varied and even dramatic liveliness into the discussion, which is very attractive, and leads to a deeper consideration of the subject. Schumann, however, could use still more artificial forms in his critiques. Thus he discusses the first concert conducted by Mendelssohn at the Gewandhaus, Oct. 1835, in letters addressed by Eusebius to Chiara in Italy ; and within this frame the details of the concert are gracefully entwined with ingenious reflections and fanciful ideas which add brilliance to the picture. On another occasion, when he was to write about a mass of dance music, Schumann has recourse to the following fiction : the editor of a certain musical paper gives an historical fancy ball. Composers are invited, young lady amateurs and their mothers, music publishers, diplomatists, a few rich Jewesses, and—of course—the Davidsbündler ; the dance programme includes the music to be criticised, to which the couples whirl about during the whole evening. Hence arise all sorts of humorous incidents—satirical, whimsical and sentimental outpourings, in which a criticism of the compositions is brought in unperceived. On another occasion, the Davidsbündler have met, and the new compositions are played in turns ; during the playing the rest carry on a variety of amusements which culminate in a magic lantern, throwing the figures of a masked ball on the wall, which Florestan, standing on the table, explains, while Zilia plays Franz Schubert's 'Deutsche Tänze.' Anything more vivid, charming and poetical than this essay [1] has never been written on music ; a little work of art in itself ! Once, in reviewing a concert given by Clara Wieck, he gives us a real poem.[2] In this he combines his own tender sentiments with a skilful characterisation of all that was peculiar in the performance. For sketching character-portraits Schumann shows a conspicuous talent; the articles in which he has characterised Sterndale Bennett, Gade and Henselt are unsurpassed by anything since written concerning these artists. He seems to have penetrated with the insight of a seer to the core of their natures, and has set forth his conclusions in a delicate and picturesque manner that no one has succeeded in imitating.

The foundation of Schumann's critiques lay in kindness ; his fastidious character would simply have nothing to do with anything bad enough to demand energetic reproof. The most cutting and bitter article [3] he ever wrote was the famous one on Meyerbeer's 'Huguenots.' In its violence it has no doubt somewhat overshot the mark ; but nowhere perhaps do the purity and nobleness of Schumann's artistic views shine forth more clearly than in this critique and in the one immediately follow-

ing on Mendelssohn's 'St. Paul.' It was the great success of the 'Huguenots' which infused the acid into Schumann's antagonism ; for when dealing with inoffensive writers he could wield the weapons of irony and ridicule both lightly and effectively. But he is most at his ease when giving praise and encouragement ; then words flow so directly from his heart that his turns of expression have often quite a magical charm. As an example we may mention the article [4] on Field's seventh concerto. Anything more tender and full of feeling was never written under the semblance of a critique than the remarks on a sonata in C minor by Delphine Hill-Handley—formerly Delphine Schauroth.[5] Schumann has here given us a really poetical masterpiece in its kind, full of intelligent appreciation of the purport of the work, and giving covert expression to its maidenly feeling, even in the style of his discussion ; it must delight the reader even if he does not know a note of the composition. Schumann had fresh imagery always at command, and if in a generally meritorious work he found something to blame, he contrived to do it in the most delicate manner. His amiable temper, his tender heart and his conspicuous talents for literary work combined never left him at a loss in such cases for some ingenious or whimsical turn. Sometimes, though rarely, in his eager sympathy for youthful genius in difficulty he went too far ; Hermann Hirschbach, for instance, never fulfilled the hopes that Schumann formed of him ; and even in his remarks on Berlioz, he at first probably said more than he would afterwards have maintained.

In later years Schumann's flowery and poetic vein gave way to a calm and contemplative style. His opinions and principles remained as sound as ever, but they are less keenly and brilliantly expressed than at the earlier period when he took peculiar pleasure in turning a flashing phrase.[6] Still, the practical musician always predominates, and Schumann himself confesses that 'the curse of a mere musician often hits higher than all your aesthetics'[7] Here and there, however, we come upon a profound aesthetic axiom, the value of which is in no degree diminished by our perception that it is the result rather of intuition than of any systematic reflection. It is universally acknowledged that by his essay 'on certain corrupt passages in classical works'[8] Schumann gave a real impetus to the textual criticism of music ; historical clues and comparisons are frequently suggested, and though these indications are not founded on any comprehensive historical knowledge, on all important subjects they show a happy instinct for the right conclusion, and are always worthy of attention.

1 It is in the *Ges. Schriften*, vol. ii. p. 9 ; and it is partly translated in *Music and Musicians*, vol. i. p. 102.
2 'Traumbild, am 9. September, 1838, Abends,' vol. ii. p. 233.
3 *Ges. Schriften*, vol. ii. p. 220; translated in *Music and Musicians*, vol. i. p. 302.
4 *Ibid.* vol. i. p. 268 ; *Music and Musicians*, vol. i. p. 267.
5 *Ibid.* vol. i. p. 92. 6 *Ibid.* vol. i. pp. 27, 208.
7 *Ibid.* vol. ii. p. 246.
8 *Ibid.* vol. iv. p. 59 ; *Music and Musicians*, vol. i. p. 26.

It may be said of Schumann's literary work in general that it was not calculated to attract attention merely for the moment, though it did in fact open up new paths, but that it took the form of writings which have a high and permanent value. They will always hold a foremost place in the literature of music, and may indeed take high rank in the literature of art. For analytical acumen they are less remarkable. Schumann cannot be called the Lessing of music, nor is it by the display of learning that he produces his effects. It is the union of poetic talent with musical genius, wide intelligence and high culture that stamps Schumann's writings with originality and gives them their independent value.

Schumann's literary work was connected with another phase of the musical world of Germany, as new in its way as the twofold development of his genius—the rise of party feeling. No doubt Schumann gave the first impetus to this movement, both by his imaginary 'Davidsbündlerschaft' and by that Radical instinct which was part of his nature. Schumann's principles as an artist were the same which have been professed and followed by all the greatest German masters; what was new in him was the active attempt to propagate them as principles. So long as he conducted the Zeitschrift he could not of course lend himself to party feeling; the standard he had assumed was so high that all who took a serious view of art were forced to gather round him. But the spirit of agitation was inflamed, and when he retired from the paper other principles of less general application were put forward. It was self-evident that Schumann was the only contemporary German composer who could stand side by side with Mendelssohn, and they were of course compared. It was asserted that in Mendelssohn form took the precedence of meaning, while in Schumann meaning predominated, striving after a new form of utterance. Thus they were put forward as the representatives of two antagonistic principles of art, and a Mendelssohn party and a Schumann party were formed. In point of fact there was scarcely any trace of such an antagonism of principle between the two composers; the difference was really one of idiosyncrasy; and so, being grounded more or less on personal feeling, the parties assumed something of the character of cliques. The literary Schumannites, having the command of an organ of their own, had an advantage over the partisans of Mendelssohn, who, like Mendelssohn himself, would have nothing to do with the press. Leipzig was for a time the headquarters of the two parties. There, where Mendelssohn had worked for the delight and improvement of the musical world, it was the fate of his art to be first exposed to attack and detraction, which, to the discredit of the German nation, rapidly spread through wider and wider circles, and was fated too to proceed first from the blind admirers of the very master for whom Mendelssohn ever felt the deepest attachment and respect. That Schumann himself must have been painfully affected by this spirit is as clear as that it could only result in hindering the unprejudiced reception of his works; and the process thus begun with Schumann has been carried on, in a greater degree, in the case of Wagner.

PIANOFORTE MUSIC.—As a composer Schumann started with the pianoforte, and until the year 1840 wrote scarcely anything but pianoforte music. For some time he used to compose sitting at the instrument, and continued to do so even until 1839, though he afterwards condemned the practice (in his Musikalische Haus- und Lebens-regeln). At all events it had the advantage of making him write from the first in true pianoforte style. If ever pianoforte works took their origin from the innermost nature of the pianoforte, Schumann's did so most thoroughly. His mode of treating the instrument is entirely new. He develops upon it a kind of orchestral polyphony, and by means of the pedal, of extended intervals, of peculiar positions of chords, of contractions of the hands and so forth he succeeds in bringing out of it an undreamt-of wealth of effects of tone. How deeply and thoroughly Schumann had studied the character of the instrument may be seen from the detailed preface to his arrangement of Paganini's caprices (op. 3). Even in his earliest pianoforte works he nowhere shows any inclination to the method of any of the older masters, except in the variations, op. 1, which betray the influence of the school of Hummel and Moscheles. But it is evident that he knew all that others had done, and the time and attention devoted in his writings to works of technical pianoforte study were no doubt deliberately given. Notwithstanding this his compositions are scarcely ever written in the bravura style; for he seldom cared to clothe his ideas in mere outward brilliancy. Sometimes one is constrained to wonder at his reluctance to use the higher and lower registers of the pianoforte.

As is the case with the technical treatment of the piano, so it is from the beginning with the substance and form of his compositions. Few among the great German masters show such striking originality from their very first compositions. In the whole range of Schumann's works there is scarcely a trace of any other musician. At the outset of his course as a composer he preferred to use the concise dance or song form, making up his longer pieces from a number of these smaller forms set together as in a mosaic, instead of at once casting his thoughts in a larger mould. But the versatility with which the small forms are treated is a testimony to the magnitude of his creative faculty. The predominance of the small forms is explained by his earlier method of composing. Diligent and constant though he was in later years, in early life his way of working was fitful and inconstant. The compositions of this period seem as if forced out of him by sudden impulses of genius. As he subsequently says of his early works, 'the man and the musician in me were always trying to speak at the same time.' This must indeed be true of every artist; if the whole personality be not put into a work of art, it will be utterly worthless. But by those words Schumann means to say that as a youth he attempted to bring to light in musical form his inmost feelings with regard to his personal life-experiences. Under such circumstances it is but natural that they should contain much that was purely accidental and inexplicable by the laws of art alone; but it is to this kind of source that they owe the magic freshness and originality with which they strike the hearer. The variations, op. 1, are an instance of this. The theme is formed of the notes A, B(♭), E, G, G. Meta Abegg was the name of a beautiful young lady in Mannheim, whose acquaintance Schumann, when a student, had made at a ball. Playful symbolism of this kind is not unfrequent in him. To a certain extent it may be traced back to Sebastian Bach, who expressed his own name in a musical phrase; as Schumann afterwards did Gade's. (See 'Album für die Jugend,' op. 68, No. 41.) In the same way (*Ges. Schriften*, ii. 115) he expresses the woman's name 'Beda' in musical notes, and also in the 'Carnaval' made those letters in his own name which stand as notes—*s* (*es*), *c*, *h*, *a*—into a musical phrase. But the idea really came from Jean Paul, who is very fond of tracing out such mystic connexions. Schumann's op. 2 consists of a set of small pianoforte pieces in dance form under the name of 'Papillons.' They were written partly at Heidelberg, partly in the first years of the Leipzig period which followed. No inner musical connexion subsists between them. But Schumann felt the necessity of giving them a poetical connexion, to satisfy his own feelings, if for nothing else, and for this purpose he adopted the last chapter but one [1] of Jean Paul's *Flegeljahre*, where a masked ball is described at which the lovers Wina and Walt are guests, as a poetic background for the series. The several pieces of music may thus be intended to represent partly the different characters in the crowd of maskers, and partly the conversation of the lovers. The finale is written designedly with reference to this scene in Jean Paul, as is plain from the indication written above the notes found near the end—

[1] In a letter to his friend Henriette Voigt, Schumann calls it the *last chapter*. This, although obviously a slip of the pen, has led several writers to wonder what ground or fanciful idea lurks behind the 'Papillons.'

'The noise of the Carnival-night dies away. The church clock strikes six.' The strokes of the bell are actually audible, being represented by the A six times repeated. Then all is hushed, and the piece seems to vanish into thin air like a vision. In the finale there are several touches of humour. It begins with an old Volkslied, familiar to every household in Germany as the GROSSVATERTANZ (*q.v.*).

In contrast to these two old-fashioned love-tunes is placed the soft and graceful melody of No. 1 of the 'Papillons,' which is afterwards worked contrapuntally with the 'Grossvater-tanz.' The name 'Papillons' is not meant to indicate a light, fluttering character in the pieces, but rather refers to musical phases which, proceeding from various experiences of life, have attained the highest musical import, as the butterfly soars upwards out of the chrysalis. The design of the title-page in the first edition points towards some such meaning as this; and the explanation we have given corresponds with his usual method of composing at that time. There exists, however, no decisive account of it by the composer himself.

In a kind of connexion with the 'Papillons' is the 'Carnaval,' op. 9. Here again Schumann has depicted the merriment of a masquerade in musical pictures, and a third and somewhat similar essay of the same kind is his 'Faschings-schwank [2] aus Wien,' op. 26. The 'Carnaval' is a collection of small pieces, written one by one without any special purpose, and not provided either with collective or individual titles until later, when he arranged them in their present order. The musical connexion between the pieces is that with few exceptions they all contain some reference to the succession of notes *a, es, c, h* (A, E♭, C, B) or *as, c, h* (A♭, C, B). Now Asch is the name of a small town in Bohemia, the home of a Fräulein Ernestine von Fricken, with whom Schumann was very intimate at the time of his writing this music. The same notes in another order, *s* (or *es*), *c*, *h*, *a*, are also the only letters in Schumann's own name which represent notes. This explains the title 'Sphinxes,' which is affixed to the ninth number on p. 13 of the original edition. The pieces are named, some from characters in the masked ball—Pierrot, Arlequin, Pantalon and Colombine—and some from real persons. In this last category we meet with the members of the Davidsbund—Florestan, Eusebius and Chiarina; Ernestine von Fricken, under the name Estrella, Chopin and Paganini; there is also a 'Coquette,' but it is not known for whom this is intended. Besides these, some of the pieces are named from situations and occurrences at the ball; a recognition, an avowal of love, a promenade, a pause in the dance (Reconnaissance, Aveu, Promenade, Pause);

[2] *Fasching* is a German word for the Carnival.

2 X

between these are heard the sounds of waltzes, and in one of the pieces the letters A-S-C-H and S-C-H-A, 'Lettres dansantes,' themselves dance boisterously and noisily, and then vanish like airy phantoms. A piece called 'Papillons' rushes by like a hasty reminiscence, and in the numbers entitled 'Florestan' an actual passage from No. 1 of the 'Papillons' (op. 2) is inserted. The finale is called 'March of the Davidsbündler against the Philistines.' The symbol of the Philistines is the 'Grossvater-tanz,' here called by Schumann a tune of the 17th century. The fact of the march being in 3-4 time has perhaps a humorous and symbolic meaning.

The 'Davidsbündlertänze' (op. 6), the 'Fan-tasiestücke' (op. 12), 'Kinderscenen' (op. 15), 'Kreisleriana' (op. 16), 'Novelletten' (op. 21), 'Bunte Blätter' (op. 99) and 'Albumblätter' (op. 124), the contents of which all belong to Schumann's early period, and, of the later works, such pieces as the 'Waldscenen' (op. 82), all bear the impress of having originated, like the 'Papillons' and the 'Carnaval,' in the personal experiences of Schumann's life. They are *poésies d'occasion* (Gelegenheitsdichtungen), a term which, in Goethe's sense, designates the highest form that a work of art can take. As to the 'Davidsbündlertänze,' the 'Kreisleriana' and the 'Novelletten,' Schumann himself tells us that they reflect the varying moods wrought in him by the contentions about Clara Wieck. In the 'Davidsbündlertänze' the general arrangement is that Florestan and Eusebius appear usually by turns, though some-times also together. The expression 'dance' does not, however, mean, as is sometimes supposed, the dances that the Davidsbündler led the Philistines, but merely indicates the form of the pieces, which is, truth to say, used with scarcely less freedom than that of the march in the finale to the 'Carnaval.' The 'Kreisleriana' have their origin in a fantastic story with the same title by E. T. A. Hoffmann, contained in his *Fantasiestücke in Callots Manier* (Bamberg, 1814, p. 47). Hoffmann was a follower of Jean Paul, who indeed wrote a preface to *Fantasiestücke*. Half musician, half poet, Schumann must have looked on him as a kindred spirit; and in the figure of the wild and eccentric yet gifted 'Kapellmeister Kreisler,' drawn by Hoffmann from incidents in his own life, there were many traits in which Schumann might easily see a reflection of him-self. Of the 'Novelletten,' Schumann says that they are 'long and connected romantic stories.' There are no titles to explain them, although much may be conjectured from the indications of time and expression. But the rest of the works we have just mentioned nearly always have their separate component parts, headed by names which lead the imagination of the player or hearer, in a clear and often

deeply poetic manner, in a particular and definite direction. This form of piano piece was altogether a very favourite one with Schu-mann. He is careful to guard against the supposition that he imagined a definite object in his mind, such as a 'pleading child' (in op. 15) or a 'haunted spot in a wood' (in op. 82), and then tried to describe it in notes. His method was rather to invent the piece quite independently and afterwards to give it a particular meaning by a superscription. His chief object was always to give the piece a value of its own, and to make it intelligible of itself. This principle is undoubtedly the right one, and, by adopting it, Schumann proved himself a genuine musician, with faith in the independent value of his art. Nevertheless, had he considered the poetical titles utterly unimportant, he would hardly have employed them as he has in so large a majority of his smaller pianoforte pieces. His doing so seems to evince a feeling that in the composition of the piece alone he had not said everything that struggled within him for expression. Until a particular mood or feeling had been aroused in the hearer or the player, by means of the title, Schumann could not be sure that the piece would have the effect which he desired it to have. Strictly speaking, poetry and music can only be really united by means of the human voice. But in these pianoforte pieces with poetical titles Schumann found a means of expression which hovered as it were between pure instrumental music on the one hand and vocal music on the other, and thus received a certain indefinite and mysterious character of its own, which may most justly be called romantic, but which is entirely apart from any connexion with what is now called PRO-GRAMME MUSIC (*q.v.*).

Among the compositions consisting of small forms we must count the variations. Schu-mann treated the variation-form freely and fancifully, but with a profuse wealth of genius and depth of feeling. For the impromptus on a theme by Clara Wieck (op. 5), Beethoven's so-called 'Eroica Variations' (op. 35), apparently served as a model; they remind us of them both in general arrangement and in the employ-ment of the bass as a theme, without being in any way wanting in originality. In the andante and variations for two pianofortes (op. 46), one of the most charming and popular of Schu-mann's pianoforte works, he treated the form with such freedom that they are not so much variations as fantasias in the style of variations.[1] His most splendid work in this form is his op. 13 (the 'Études symphoniques'), a work of the grandest calibre, which alone would be sufficient to secure him a place in the first rank of com-posers for the pianoforte, so overpowering is the

---

[1] They were at first intended to be accompanied by two violon-cellos and horn, and this version is in the supplementary volume of the Breitkopf edition.

display of his own individual treatment of the pianoforte—frequently rising to the highest limits of the bravura style of execution—of his overflowing profusion of ideas, and his boldness in turning the variation-form to his own account. In the finale the first two bars only of the theme are employed, and these only occasionally in the 'working-out section.' In other respects the proud edifice of this elaborately worked number has nothing in common with a variation.[1] It contains, however, a delicate reference to the person to whom the whole work is dedicated, William Sterndale Bennett. The beginning of the chief subject is a fragment of the celebrated romance in Marschner's 'Templer und Jüdin' (' Du stolzes England, freue dich,' etc.). It is an ingenious way of paying a compliment to his beloved English composer.[2]

Schumann had made early attempts at works of larger structure, but it cannot be denied that they were not at first successful. The sonata in F♯ minor (op. 11) teems with beautiful ideas, but is wanting in unity to a remarkable degree, at least in the allegro movements. That in F minor (op. 14) shows a decided improvement in this respect, and the sonata in G minor (op. 22) is still better, although not entirely free from a certain clumsiness. Schumann afterwards showed himself quite aware of the faults of these sonatas in regard to form. They offer the most striking example of his irregular and rhapsodical method of working at that period. The second movement of the sonata in G minor (see SONATA) was written in June 1830, the first and third in June 1833, the fourth in its original form in Oct. 1835, and in its ultimate form in 1838, the whole sonata being published in 1839. The sonata in F♯ minor was begun in 1833 and not completed till 1835. That in F minor, finished on June 5, 1836, consisted at first of five movements—an allegro, two scherzos (one after the other), an andantino with variations and a prestissimo. When the work was first published, under the title of 'Concerto sans orchestre,' Schumann cut out the two scherzos, apparently intending to use them for a second sonata in F minor. This, however, was not carried out, and in the second edition of the work he restored the second of the scherzos to its place.[3] When we observe how he took up one sonata after another, we see how impossible it is that any close connexion can subsist between the several parts, or that there should be any real unity in them as a whole.

The allegro for pianoforte (op. 8) is somewhat disjointed in form, while the toccata (op. 7), a

bravura piece of the greatest brilliance and difficulty in perfect sonata-form, exhibits a great degree of connexion and consequence. In the great fantasia (op. 17) we are led by the title to expect no conciseness of form. The classical masters generally gave to their fantasias a very clearly defined outline, but Schumann in this case breaks through every restriction that limits the form, especially in the first movement, where he almost seems to lose himself in limitless freedom. In order to give unity to the fantastic and somewhat loosely connected movements of this work of genius, he again had recourse to poetry, and prefaced the piece with some lines by F. Schlegel as a motto:

| | |
|---|---|
| Durch alle Töne tönet | Through all the tones that vibrate |
| Im bunten Erdentraum, | About earth's mingled dream, |
| Ein leiser Ton gezogen | One whispered note is sounding |
| Für den der heimlich lauschet. | For ears attent to hear, |

The 'earth's mingled dream' is in a manner portrayed in the substance of the composition. Schumann means that 'the ear attent to hear' will perceive the uniting-tones that run through all the pictures which the imagination of the composer unrolls to his view. Schlegel's motto seems almost like an excuse offered by Schumann. The original purpose of this fantasia was not, however, to illustrate these lines. About Dec. 17, 1835, an appeal having been made from Bonn for contributions to a Beethoven memorial, Schumann proposed to contribute a composition; and this was the origin of the work now called 'Fantasia,' the three movements of which were originally intended to bear the respective inscriptions of 'Ruins,' 'Triumphal Arch' and 'The Starry Crown.' By these names the character both of the separate parts and of the whole becomes more intelligible. In order to get into the right disposition for the work Schumann's four articles [4] on Beethoven's monument should be read.

Although few of Schumann's pianoforte works of the first period are without defects of form, yet their beauties are so many that we easily forget those defects. In certain ways the compositions of the first ten years present the most characteristic picture of Schumann's genius. In after life he proposed and attained loftier ideals in works worthy of the perfect master. But the freshness and charm of his earlier pianoforte works was never surpassed, and in his later years was but rarely reached. A dreamy imaginative nature was united in Schumann's character with a native solidity that never descended to the commonplace. From the first his music had in it a character which appealed to the people—nay, which was in a way national. After Beethoven, Schumann is the first master who possesses the power of giving full and free expression to the humorous element in instrumental music. Both in his writings and compositions he allows it to have full play, and it is in his earlier PF. works

---

[1] The five variations left out in the published edition are included in the supplementary volume of Breitkopf's edition.
[2] H. E. Krehbiel pointed out that the theme of the finale is based on an inversion of the principal theme. Schumann's intention to quote from Marschner in honour of Bennett has been questioned.
[3] The first appeared in 1866 as No. 12 of the posthumous works published by Rieter-Biedermann, together with the discarded finale of the sonata in G minor as No. 13. Both are in the supplementary volume of the B. & H. edition (1893).

[4] *Ges. Schriften*, vol. i. p. 215.

that it is most prominent. One of his freshest and fullest works is the Humoreske (op. 20), the most wonderful portrayal of a humorous disposition that it is possible to imagine in music. Schumann's thorough individuality is prominent alike in harmonies, rhythm and colouring, and in the forms of the melodies. It is, however, characteristic of his early pianoforte works that broad bold melodies rarely occur in them, though there is a superabundance of melodic fragments—germs of melody, as they might be called, full of a deep expression of their own. This music is pervaded by a spring-like animation and force, a germ of future promise, which gives it a peculiar romantic character; a character strengthened by the admixture of poetic moods and feelings. Schumann was both musician and poet, and he who would thoroughly understand his music must be first imbued with the spirit of the German poets who were most prominent in Schumann's youth; above all others Jean Paul and the whole romantic school, particularly Eichendorff, Heine and Rückert. And just as these poets were specially great in short lyrics, revealing endless depths of feeling in a few lines, so did Schumann succeed, as no one had done before, in saying great things, and leaving unutterable things to be felt, in the small form of a short pianoforte piece.

Schumann's enthusiastic admiration and thorough appreciation of Bach have been already described (see BACH GESELLSCHAFT). He shared this with Mendelssohn, but it is certain that he entered more thoroughly than Mendelssohn did into the old master's mysterious depth of feeling. It would therefore have been wonderful if he had not attempted to express himself in the musical forms used by Bach. His strong natural inclination towards polyphonic writing is perceptible even in his earliest pianoforte works, but it was not until 1840 that it comes prominently forward. His six fugues on the name 'Bach' (op. 60), the four fugues (op. 72), the seven pianoforte pieces in fughetta form (op. 126), the studies in canon form for the pedal piano (op. 56), and the other separate canons and fugues scattered up and down his pianoforte works—all form a class in modern pianoforte music just as new as do his pianoforte works in the free style. The treatment of the parts in the fugues is by no means always strictly according to rule, even when viewed from the standpoint of Bach, who allowed himself considerable freedom. In employing an accompaniment of chords in one part, he also goes far beyond what had hitherto been considered allowable. But yet, taken as a whole, these works are masterpieces; no other composer of his time could have succeeded as he did in welding together so completely the modern style of feeling with the old strict form, or in giving that form a new life and vigour by

means of the modern spirit. In these pieces we hear the same Schumann whom we know in his other works; his ideas adapt themselves as if spontaneously to the strict requirements of the polyphonic style, and these requirements again draw from his imagination new and characteristic ideas. In short, though a great contrapuntist he was not a pedantic one, and he may be numbered among the few musicians of the last hundred years to whom polyphonic forms have been a perfectly natural means of expressing their ideas.

SONG WRITING.—As a composer of songs Schumann displays a more finely cultivated poetic taste than Schubert, with a many-sided feeling for lyric expression far greater than Mendelssohn's. Many of his melodies are projected in bold and soaring lines, such as we meet with in no other composer but Schubert; for instance, in the well-known songs 'Widmung' (op. 25, No. 1), 'Lied der Braut' (op. 25, No. 12), 'Liebesbotschaft' (op. 36, No. 6), 'Stille Thränen' (op. 35, No. 10) and others. Still more frequently he throws himself into the spirit of the German Volkslied, and avails himself of its simpler and narrower forms of melody. Indeed his songs owe their extraordinary popularity chiefly to this conspicuously national element. The reader need only be reminded of the song ' O Sonnenschein ' (op. 36, No. 4), of Heine's ' Liederkreis ' (op. 24), and of the Heine songs ' Hör' ich das Liedchen klingen,' 'Allnächtlich im Traume,' 'Aus alten Märchen ' (op. 48, Nos. 10, 14, 15), of most of the songs and ballads (opp. 45, 49, 53), and above all of the ' Wanderlied ' (op. 35, No. 3), which sparkles with youthful life and healthy vigour. Besides these there are many songs in which the melody is hardly worked out, and which are—as is also frequently the case with his pianoforte works—as it were, mere sketches, or germs, of melodies. This style of treatment, which is quite peculiar to Schumann, he was fond of using when he wished to give the impression of a vague, dreamy, veiled sentiment; and by this means he penetrated more deeply than his contemporaries into the vital essence and sources of feeling. Such songs as ' Der Nussbaum ' (op. 25, No. 3), or ' Im Walde ' (op. 39, No. 11) are masterpieces in this kind. Besides this, Schumann always brought a true poet's instinct to bear on the subtlest touches and most covert suggestions in the poems which he chose for setting, and selected the musical expression best fitted to their purport. He was the first who ventured to close on the dominant seventh when his text ended with a query (as in op. 49, No. 3). With him also the vocal part often does not end on the common chord, but the true close is left to the accompaniment, so as to give an effect of vague and undefined feeling. The part filled by the pianoforte in Schumann's songs is a very important one. It was evidently of moment in the history of his art that Schumann should have come to the work of writing songs after ten years' experience as a composer for the pianoforte, and after instituting an entirely new style of pianoforte music. This style supplied him with an immense variety of delicate and poetic modes and shades of expression, and it is owing to this that he displays such constant novelty in his treatment of the pianoforte part. The forms of phrase which he adopts in his ' accompaniments ' are infinitely various, and always correspond with perfect fitness and ingenuity to the character of the verses. In some cases the pianoforte part is an entirely independent composition, which the voice merely follows with a few declamatory phrases (op. 48, No. 9, ' Das ist ein Flöten und Geigen '); while in others, in contrast to this, the voice stands almost alone, and the pianoforte begins by throwing in a few soft chords which nevertheless have their due characteristic effect (op. 48, No. 13, ' Ich hab' im Traum '). In Schumann's songs the proper function of the pianoforte is to reveal some deep and secret meaning which it is beyond the power of words, even of sung words, to express ; and he always disliked and avoided those repetitions of the words of which other composers have availed themselves in order to fill out in the music the feeling to which the words give rise. When he does repeat he always seems to have a special dramatic end in view rather than a musical one, and often makes the piano supplement the sentiment aroused by the text, while the voice is silent. He is particularly strong in his final symphonies, to which he gave a value and importance, as an integral portion of the song, which no one before him had ventured to do, often assigning to it a new and independent musical thought of its own. Sometimes he allows the general feeling of the song to reappear in it under quite a new light ; sometimes the musical phrase suggests some final outcome of the words, opening to the fancy a remote perspective in which sight is lost (a beautiful example is op. 48, No. 16, ' Die alten bösen Lieder '). Or he continues the poem in music ; of which a striking instance is the close of the ' Frauenliebe und -Leben ' (op. 42), where by repeating the music of the first song he revives in the fancy of the lonely widow the memory of her early happiness. The realm of feeling revealed to us in Schumann's songs is thoroughly youthful, an unfailing mark of the true lyric ; the sentiment he principally deals with is that of love, which in his hands is especially tender and pure, almost maidenly. The set of songs called 'Frauenliebe und -Leben' gives us a deep insight into the most subtle and secret emotions of a pure woman's soul, deeper indeed than could have been expected from any man, and in fact no composer but Schumann would have been capable of it.

Schumann also found musical equivalents and shades of colour for Eichendorff's mystical views of nature ; his settings of Eichendorff's poems may be called absolutely classical, and he is equally at home in dealing with the bubbling freshness or the chivalrous sentiment of the poet. Many of Schumann's fresh and sparkling songs have a touch of the student's joviality, but without descending from their high distinction; never under any circumstances was he trivial. Indeed he had no sympathy with the farcical, though his talent for the humorous is amply proved by his songs. A masterpiece of the kind is the setting of Heine's poem ' Ein Jüngling liebt ein Mädchen ' (op. 48, No. 11), with its strange undercurrent of tragedy. It was principally in dealing with Heine's words that he betrays this sense of humour ; ' Wir sassen am Fischerhause' (op 45, No. 3) is an example, and still more ' Es leuchtet meine Liebe ' (op. 127, No. 3), where a resemblance to the scherzo of the A minor string quartet is very obvious. A thing which may well excite astonishment as apparently quite beside the nature of Schumann's character, is that he could even find characteristic music for Heine's bitterest irony (op. 24, No. 6) ' Warte, warte, wilder Schiffsmann,' and many of the ' Dichterliebe.'

THE SYMPHONIES.—Schumann's symphonies may be considered as the most important in their time since Beethoven. Though Mendelssohn excels him in regularity of form, and though Schubert's C major symphony is quite unique in its wealth of beautiful musical ideas, yet Schumann surpasses both in greatness and force. He is the man, they the youths ; he has the greatest amount of what is demanded by that greatest, most mature, and most important of all forms of instrumental music. He comes near to Beethoven, who it is quite evident was almost the only composer that he ever took as a model. No trace whatever of Haydn or Mozart is to be found in his symphonies, and of Mendelssohn just as little. A certain approximation to Schubert is indeed perceptible in the ' working out ' (*Durchführung*) of his allegro movements. But the symphonies, like the pianoforte works, the songs, and indeed all that Schumann produced, bear the strong impress of a marvellous originality, and a creative power all his own. Even the first published symphony (in B♭, op. 38) shows a very distinct talent for this branch of composition. We do not know that Schumann had ever previously attempted orchestral compositions, except in the case of the symphony written in the beginning of 1830, which still remains in MS. In 1839 he writes to Dorn : ' At present it is true that I have not had much practice in orchestral writing, but I hope to master it some day.' And in his next attempt he attained his object. In a few passages in the B♭ symphony, the effects of the instruments are indeed not rightly calculated. One great

error in the first movement he remedied after
the first hearing. This was in the two opening
bars, from which the theme of the allegro is
afterwards generated, and which were given to
the horns and trumpets. It ran originally thus,
in agreement with the beginning of the allegro
movement :

which, on account of the G and A being stopped
notes, had an unexpected and very comic effect.
Schumann himself was much amused at the
mistake ; when he was at Hanover in January
1854 he told the story to his friends, and it was
very amusing to hear this man, usually so grave
and silent, regardless of the presence of strangers
(for the incident took place at a public restaurant), sing out the first five notes of the subject
quite loud, the two next in a muffled voice, and
the last again loud. He placed the phrase a
third higher, as it stands in the printed score :

Another, but less important passage for the
horns has remained unaltered. In bar 17 of
the first allegro, Schumann thought that this
phrase

ought to be made more prominent than it
usually was on the horns, and requested both
Taubert and David, when it was in rehearsal
at Berlin and Leipzig in the winter of 1842, to
have it played on the trombones.

But in general we cannot but wonder at the
certain mastery over his means that he shows
even in the first symphony. His orchestration
is less smooth and clear than that of either
Mendelssohn or Gade, and in its sterner style
reminds us rather of Schubert. But this stern
power is suited to the substance of his ideas,
and there is no lack of captivating beauty of
sound. We even meet in his orchestral works
with a number of new effects of sound such as
only true genius can discover or invent. Instances of these are the treatment of the three
trumpets in the ' Manfred ' overture, the use
made of the horns in the second movement of
the symphony in E♭, the violin solo introduced
into the Romanza of the D minor symphony,
etc. etc. It is hard to decide which of Schumann's four symphonies (or five, counting op.
52) is the finest. Each has individual beauties
of its own. In life and freshness and the feeling
of inward happiness, the symphony in B♭
stands at the head. Schumann originally intended to call it the ' Spring Symphony ' ; and
indeed he wrote it, as we learn from a letter to
Taubert, in Feb. 1841, when the first breath of

pring was in the air. The first movement was
to have been called ' Spring's Awakening,' and
the finale (which he always wished not to be
taken too fast) ' Spring's Farewell.' Many
parts of the symphony have an especial charm
when we thus know the object with which they
were written. The beginning of the introduction evidently represents a trumpet summons
sent pealing down from on high ; then gentle
zephyrs blow softly to and fro, and everywhere
the dormant forces awake and make their way
to the light (we are quoting from the composer's
own programme). In the allegro the spring
comes laughing in, in the full beauty of youth.[1]
This explains and justifies the novel use of the
triangle in the first movement—an instrument
not then considered admissible in a symphony.
An enchanting effect is produced by the Spring
song at the close of the first movement, played
as though sung with a full heart ; and it is an
entirely new form of coda (see p. 67 of the
score). In publishing the symphony, Schumann omitted the explanatory titles, because
he believed that the attention of the public is
distracted from the main purpose of a work by
things of that kind. We may well believe,
moreover, that a good part of the spring-like
feeling in this symphony comes from the deep
and heart-felt joy which Schumann felt at being
at last united to his hard-won bride. The
same influence is seen in the D minor symphony
(op. 120), written in the same year with that
just described, and immediately after it. It is
entirely similar to its predecessor in its fundamental feeling, but has more passion. The
form too is new and very successful ; the four
sections follow each other consecutively without
any pauses, so that the work seems to consist
of only one great movement. The subjects of
the Introduction reappear in the Romanze,
with different treatment, and the chief subject
of the first allegro is the foundation of that of
the last. The second part of the first allegro
is in quite an unusual form, and before the last
allegro we find a slow introduction—imaginative, majestic and most original. As has been
already mentioned, Schumann intended to call
the work ' Symphonic Fantasia.' Here, too,
poetic pictures seem to be hovering round him
on every side.

His third symphonic work of the year 1841
is also irregular, but only in form, and has as
good a right as the second to the name of ' Symphony.' It appeared, however, under the name
' Overture, Scherzo and Finale ' as op. 52. Of
this work, which is charming throughout, the
first movement offers us the only example to be
found in Schumann of the influence of Cherubini, a master for whom he had a great reverence. Perhaps the most lovely movement is the
highly poetic scherzo in gigue-rhythm, which

[1] Schumann intended the *più vivace* of the Introduction to be
taken distinctly faster at once, so that the time might glide im
perceptibly into the allegro.

might constitute a type by itself among symphony-scherzos. His other scherzos approximate in style to those of Beethoven, whose invention and speciality this form was, and who had no successor in it but Schumann. The characteristic of the C major symphony (op. 61) is a graver and more mature depth of feeling ; its bold decisiveness of form and overpowering wealth of expression reveal distinctly the relationship in art between Schumann and Beethoven. The form, too, as far as regards the number and character of the movements, is quite that of the classical masters, while in the last symphony (E♭, op. 97) Schumann once more appears as one of the modern school. This is divided into five separate movements, including a slow movement in sustained style, and of a devotional character, between the andante and the finale. Schumann originally inscribed it with the words ' In the style of an accompaniment to a solemn ceremony ' (im Charakter der Begleitung einer feierlichen Ceremonie), and we know that it was suggested to him by the sight of Cologne Cathedral, and the festivities on the occasion of Archbishop von Geissel's elevation to the Cardinalate. The other movements are powerful, and full of variety and charm, and the whole symphony is full of vivid pictures of Rhineland life. Perhaps the gem of the whole is the second movement (scherzo), in which power and beauty are mingled with the romance which in every German heart hovers round the Rhine and its multitude of songs and legends. Although written in 1850, when Schumann's imagination was becoming exhausted, the work bears no trace of any diminution of power. (For a study of the position taken by Schumann's symphonies in the development of the form, see SYMPHONY.)

The poetical concert-overture, a form invented by Mendelssohn, and practised by Bennett and Gade, was one never cultivated by Schumann. His overtures are really ' opening pieces,' whether to opera, play, or some festivity or other. In this again he follows Beethoven. His overtures, like those of Beethoven, are most effective in the concert-room, when the drama or occasion for which they were composed is kept in mind. It is so even with the wonderful ' Genoveva ' overture, which contains something of Weber's power and swing ; but more than all is it true of the overture to Byron's *Manfred*, so full of tremendous passion. None of the overtures subsequently written by Schumann reached this perfection, least of all his ' Faust ' overture, though that to the ' Braut von Messina ' (op. 100) is not much inferior to ' Manfred.' In the last year of his productive activity Schumann was much occupied with this form, but the exhausted condition of his creative powers cannot be disguised, either in the ' Faust ' overture or in those to

Shakespeare's *Julius Caesar* (op. 128) and Goethe's *Hermann und Dorothea* (op. 136), which last he had intended to set as an opera. The festival overture on the ' Rheinweinlied ' (op. 123) is cleverly worked, and a very effective *pièce d'occasion*.

CONCERTED CHAMBER MUSIC.—It was in the spring of 1838 that Schumann made his first attempt, so far as we know, at a string quartet. It was scarcely successful, for he was too much immersed in pianoforte music ; at any rate the world has hitherto seen nothing of it. In June and July 1842 he was much more successful. The three string quartets (op. 41), written at this time, are the only ones that have become known. They cannot be said to be in the purest quartet style ; but as Schumann never played any stringed instrument, this is not surprising. They still retain much of the pianoforte style ; but by this very means Schumann attains many new and beautiful effects. At the time of writing the A minor quartet Schumann had become acquainted with Marschner's G minor trio (op. 112), and speaks of it in the *Zeitschrift*. The fine scherzo of that work struck him very much, and in his own scherzo it reappears, in a modified form certainly, but yet recognisable enough. In spite of this plagiarism, however, we must allow the quartet to be in the highest degree original, and full of richness and poetry. It contains much enchanting beauty, never surpassed even by Schumann. He seems here to have resumed his practice of mixing up poetic mysticism with his music. What other reason could there be for proposing to use the four bars of modulation from the first quartet (bars 30-34), exactly as they stand, for an introduction to the second quartet ? He afterwards struck them out, as may be seen in the autograph. The other quartets also arrived at their present form only after manifold alterations. The slow introduction to the quartet in A minor was at first intended to be played *con sordini*. The third quartet began with a chord of the 6-5 on D, held out for a whole bar. The greatest alterations were made in the first allegro of the A minor and in the variations in A♭ of the F major quartets. Whole sections were rewritten and modified in various ways. But Wasielewski is mistaken in saying (3rd ed. p. 178, note) that the *più lento* over the coda in these variations is a misprint for *più mosso*. Schumann wrote *più lento* quite plainly, and evidently meant what he wrote. He may possibly have changed his mind afterwards, for in regard to *tempo* he was often moved by the opinions of others.

Of the works for strings and pianoforte, the quintet (op. 44) is the finest ; it will always keep its place in the first rank of musical masterpieces. It claims the highest admiration, not only because of its brilliant originality, and its innate power—which seems to grow with every movement, and at the end of the whole leaves the hearer with a feeling of the possibility of never-ending increase—but also because of its gorgeous beauty of sound, and the beautiful and well-balanced relations between the pianoforte and the strings. Musicians like Carl Reinecke of Leipzig, who at the time of its appearance were in the most susceptible period of youth, told the writer of the indescribable impression the work made upon them. It must have seemed like a new paradise of beauty revealed to their view. The pianoforte quartet (op. 47) only wants animation, and a more popular character in the best sense of the word, to make it of equal merit with the quintet. There is much in it of the spirit of Bach, as is perhaps most evident in the wonderful melody of the andante. A high rank is taken by the trios in D minor (op. 63) and F major (op. 80), both, as well as the quintet and quartet, written in one and the same year. In the first a passionate and sometimes gloomy character predominates, while the second is more cheerful and full of warmth in the middle movements. The canonic style is employed in the adagios of both trios with new and powerful effect. The treatment of the strings with respect to the pianoforte may here and there be considered too orchestral in style; but it must not be forgotten that it was adopted to suit the piano style, which in Schumann is very different from that of the classical masters. The two trios, however, are wanting in that expression of perfect health which is so prominent in both the quintet and the quartet. They show traces of the hurry and breathless haste which in his later years increases the complication of his rhythms. The third and last trio (G minor, op. 110) is far inferior to the others. There is still the same artistic design, and in isolated passages the noble genius of the master still shines clearly out; but as a whole this trio tells of exhaustion. The same may be said of most of the other chamber works of Schumann's latest years. Among them are two sonatas for piano and violin, gloomy, impassioned compositions, which can hardly be listened to without a feeling of oppression. There are also a number of shorter pieces for different instruments, among which the ' Märchenbilder für Pianoforte und Viola ' (op. 113) are prominent.

No one who bears in mind Schumann's ultimate fate can hear without emotion the last of these ' Märchenbilder,' which bears the direction ' Langsam, mit melancholischem Ausdruck.'

THE CONCERTOS.—In the sphere of the concerto Schumann has left an imperishable trace of his genius in the pianoforte concerto in A minor (op. 54). It is one of his most beautiful and mature works. In addition to all his peculiar originality it has also the

qualities, which no concerto should lack, of external brilliancy, and striking, powerful, well-rounded subjects. The first movement is written in a free form with happy effect ; the cause being that Schumann had at first intended it to stand as an independent piece, with the title ' Fantasia.' He did not add the other two movements until two years afterwards.—The ' Introduction und Allegro appassionato,' for pianoforte and orchestra (op. 92), is a rich addition to concerto literature. In Schumann there is a deeper connexion between the pianoforte and orchestra than had before been customary, though not carried to such a point as to interfere with the contrast between the two independent powers. He was far from writing symphonies with the pianoforte *obbligato*. His other works in concerto form, written in the last years of his life, do not attain to the height of the concerto. Among them is an unpublished violin concerto written between Sept. 21 and Oct. 3, 1853, and consisting of the following movements : (1) D minor alla breve, ' Imkräftigen, nicht zu schnellen Tempo'; (2) B♭ major, common time, ' Langsam ' ; (3) D major, 3–4, ' Lebhaft, doch nicht zu schnell.' The autograph was in the possession of Joachim. A fantasia for violin and orchestra, dedicated to the same great artist, is published as op. 131. The violoncello concerto (op. 129) is remarkable for a very beautiful slow middle movement. There is also a concerto for four horns and orchestra (op. 86). Schumann himself thought very highly of this piece, partly because, as he wrote to Dr. Härtel, ' it was quite curious.' It is indeed the first attempt made in modern times to revive the form of the old *Concerto grosso* which Sebastian Bach had brought to perfection in his six so-called ' Brandenburg' concertos. As these concertos of Bach were not printed until 1850, and Schumann can scarcely have known them in manuscript, it is a remarkable and interesting coincidence that he should thus have followed Bach's lead without knowing it. The piece is particularly hard for the first horn, because of the high notes. When well rendered it has a peculiarly sonorous, often very romantic effect, to which, however, the ear soon becomes insensible from the tone of the four horns.

CHORAL COMPOSITIONS.—In his account of Marschner's ' Klänge aus Osten,' a work performed in Leipzig on Oct. 22, 1840, Schumann expresses great admiration for the form, in which it was possible to make use for concert performances of romantic stories, which had hitherto been only used on the stage. He was the first to follow this example in his ' Paradise and the Peri.' The text was taken from Moore's poem, of which Schumann shortened some parts to suit his purpose, while he lengthened others by his own insertions. It was his first work for voices and orchestra, and is one of his greatest and most important. The subject was happily chosen. The longing felt by one of those ideal beings created by the imagination from the forces of nature, to attain or regain a higher and happier existence, and using every means for the fulfilment of this longing, is of frequent occurrence in the German popular legends, and is still a favourite and sympathetic idea in Germany. It is the root of the legends of the Fair Melusina, of the Water Nixie and of Hans Heiling. Schumann's fancy must have been stimulated by the magic of the East, no less than by Moore's poem, with its poetic pictures displayed on a background of high moral sentiment. The fact of Schumann's having retained so much of Moore's narrative is worthy of all praise ; it is the descriptive portions of the poem that have the greatest charm, and the music conforms to this. True, there will always be a certain disadvantage in using a complete self-contained poem as a text for music, a great deal of which will inevitably have been written without regard to the composer. Much that we pass over lightly in reading has, when set to music, a more definite and insistent effect than was intended. In other places again, the poem, from the musician's point of view, will be deficient in opportunities for the strong contrasts so necessary for effect in music. This is very obvious in Schumann's composition. The third portion of the work, although he took much trouble to give it greater variety by additions to the poetry, suffers from a certain monotony. Not that the separate numbers are weaker than those of the former parts, but they are wanting in strong shadows. But there is something else that prevents the work from producing a really striking effect upon large audiences, and that is, if we may say so, that there is too much music in it. Schumann brought it forth from the fullness of his heart, and threw, even into its smallest interludes, all the depth of expression of which he was capable. The beauties are crowded together, and stand in each other's light. If they had been fewer in number they would have had more effect. But, with all these allowances, ' Paradise and the Peri ' is one of the most enchanting musical poems in existence. All the choruses in ' Paradise and the Peri,' perhaps with the exception of the last, are fine, original and effective. But it must be admitted that choral composition was not really Schumann's strong point. In many of his choruses he might even seem to lack the requisite mastery over the technical requirements of choral composition, so instrumental in style, so impracticable and unnecessarily difficult do they seem. But if we consider Schumann's skill in polyphonic writing, and recall pieces of such grand conception and masterly treatment as the beginning of the last chorus of the ' Faust ' music, we feel convinced that the true reason of the defect lies deeper.

The essential parts of a chorus are large and simple subjects, broad and flowing development, and divisions clearly marked and intelligible to all. In a good chorus there must be something to speak to the heart of the masses. Schumann took exactly the opposite view. The chorus was usually an instrument unfitted for the expression of his ideas. His genius could have mastered the technical part of choral composition as quickly and surely as that of orchestral composition. But since the case was otherwise, the chief importance of ' Paradise and the Peri ' is seen to be in the solos and their accompaniments, especially in the latter, for here the orchestra stands in the same relation to the voice as the pianoforte does in Schumann's songs.

In the fairy-tale of ' The Pilgrimage of the Rose ' (op. 112) Schumann intended to produce a companion picture to ' Paradise and the Peri,' but in less definite outline and vaguer colours. The idea of the poem is similar to that of the former work, but Horn's execution of the idea is entirely without taste. Schumann was possibly attracted by its smooth versification and a few really good musical situations. The music contains much that is airy and fresh, as well as a beautiful dirge. On the other hand, it is full of a feeble sentimentality utterly foreign to Schumann's general character, and ascribable only to the decay of his imagination. The insignificant and wholly idyllic subject was quite inadequate to give employment to the whole apparatus of solo, chorus and orchestra, and Schumann's first idea of providing a pianoforte accompaniment only was the right one. His other works in this form consist of four ballads : ' Der Königssohn ' (op. 116), ' Des Sängers Fluch ' (op. 139), ' Das Glück von Edenhall ' (op. 143), all by Uhland ; and ' Vom Pagen und der Königstochter ' (op. 140), by Geibel. It is painfully evident that these poems were not really written for music. The way the principal events of the story are described, and the whole outward form of the verses, imply that they were intended to be recited by a single person, and that not a singer but a speaker. If necessary to be sung, the form of a strophic song should have been chosen, as is the case with ' Das Glück von Edenhall,' but this would confine the varieties of expression within too narrow a range. It is as though Schumann's pent-up desire for the dramatic form were seeking an outlet in these ballads ; especially as we know that in the last years of his creative activity he was anxious to meet with a new opera libretto. The faults of texts and subjects might, however, be overlooked, if the music made itself felt as the product of a rich and unwearied imagination. Unfortunately, however, this is seldom the case. It is just in the more dramatic parts that we detect an obvious dullness in the music, a lameness in rhythm, and a want of fresh and happy contrasts. It must be remarked, however, that isolated beauties of no mean order are to be met with ; such as the whole of the third part and the beginning and end of the second, in the ballad ' Vom Pagen und der Königstochter,' These works, however, taken as a whole, will hardly live.

On the other hand, there are some works of striking beauty for voices and orchestra in a purely lyrical vein. Among these should be mentioned the ' Requiem for Mignon ' from ' Wilhelm Meister ' (op. 98b), and Hebbel's ' Nachtlied ' (op. 108). The former of these was especially written for music, and contains the loveliest thoughts and words embodied in an unconstrained and agreeable form. Few composers were so well fitted for such a work as Schumann, with his sensitive emotional faculty and his delicate sense of poetry ; and it is no wonder that he succeeded in producing this beautiful little composition. But it should never be heard in a large concert-room, for which its delicate proportions and tender colouring are utterly unfitted. The ' Nachtlied ' is a long choral movement. The peculiar and fantastic feeling of the poem receives adequate treatment by a particular style in which the chorus is sometimes used only to give colour, and sometimes is combined with the orchestra in a polyphonic structure, in which all human individuality seems to be merged, and only the universal powers of nature and of life reign supreme.

Schumann's music to ' Faust ' is not intended to be performed on the stage as the musical complement of Goethe's drama. It is a piece for concert performance, or rather a set of pieces, for he did not stipulate or intend that all three parts should be given together. What he did was to take out a number of scenes from both parts of Goethe's poem, and set music to them. It follows that the work is not self-contained, but requires for its full understanding an accurate knowledge of the poem. From the First Part he took the following : (1) Part of the first scene in the garden between Gretchen and Faust ; (2) Gretchen before the shrine of the Mater dolorosa ; (3) The scene in the Cathedral. These three form the first division of his Faust music. From the Second Part of the play he adopted : (1) The first scene of the first act (the song of the spirits at dawn, the sunrise, and Faust's soliloquy) ; (2) The scene with the four aged women from the fifth act ; (3) Faust's death in the same act (as far as the words, ' Der Zeiger fällt—Er fällt, es ist vollbracht '). These form the second division of the music. Schumann's third division consists of the last scene of the fifth act (Faust's glorification) divided into seven numbers. The experiment of constructing a work of art, without central point or connexion in itself, but entirely dependent for these on another work of art, could only be

successful in the case of a poem like ' Faust ' ; and even then, perhaps, only with the German people, with whom Faust is almost as familiar as the Bible. But it really was successful, more particularly in the third division, which consists of only one great scene, and is the most important from a musical point of view. In this scene Goethe himself desired the co-operation of music. Its mystic import and splendid expression could find no composer so well fitted as Schumann, who seemed, as it were, predestined for it. He threw himself into the spirit of the poem with such deep sympathy and understanding, that from beginning to end his music gives the impression of being a commentary on it. To Schumann is due the chief meed of praise for having popularised the second part of ' Faust.' In musical importance no other choral work of his approaches the third division of his work. In freshness, originality and sustained power of invention it is in no way inferior to ' Paradise and the Peri.' Up to about the latter half of the last chorus it is a chain of musical gems, a perfectly unique contribution to concert literature, in the first rank of those works of art of which the German nation may well be proud. The second division of the ' Faust ' music, is also of considerable merit. It is, however, evident in many passages that Schumann has set words which Goethe never intended to be sung. This is felt still more in the scenes from the First Part, which are, moreover, very inferior in respect of the music. The overture is the least important of all ; in fact the merit of the work decreases gradually as we survey it backwards from the end to the beginning ; a circumstance corresponding to the method pursued in its composition, which began in Schumann's freshest, happiest and most masterly time of creativeness, and ended close upon the time when his noble spirit was plunged in the dark gloom of insanity.

DRAMATIC WORKS.—There exist only two dramatic works of Schumann intended for the theatre : the opera of ' Genoveva ' and the music to Byron's Manfred. The text of the opera may justly be objected to, for it scarcely treats of the proper legend of Genoveva at all ; almost all that made the story characteristic and touching being discarded, a fact which Schumann thought an advantage. This may perhaps be explained by remembering his opinion that in an opera the greatest stress should be laid on the representation of the emotions, and that this object might most easily be attained by treating the external conditions of an operatic story as simply and broadly as possible. He also probably felt that a great part of the Genoveva legend is epic rather than dramatic. He was mistaken, however, in thinking that after the reductions which he made in the plot, it would remain sufficiently interesting to the general public. He himself, as we have said, arranged his own libretto. His chief model was Hebbel's ' Genoveva,' a tragedy which had affected him in a wonderful way ; though he also made use of Tieck's ' Genoveva.' Besides these he took Weber's ' Euryanthe' as a pattern. The mixture of three poems, so widely differing from one another, resulted in a confusion of motives and an uncertainty of delineation which add to the uninteresting impression produced by the libretto. The character of Golo, particularly, is very indistinctly drawn, and yet on him falls almost the chief responsibility of the drama. The details cannot but suffer by such a method of compilation as this. A great deal is taken word for word from Hebbel and Tieck, and their two utterly different styles appear side by side without any compromise whatever. Hebbel, however, predominates. Tieck's work appears in the finale of the first act, and in the duet (No. 9) in the second act, e.g. the line ' Du liebst mich, holde Braut, da ist der Tag begonnen.' Genoveva's taunt on Golo's birth is also taken from Tieck, although he makes the reproach come first from Wolf and afterwards from Genoveva herself, but without making it a prominent motive in the drama. Beside this several Volkslieder are interspersed. This confusion of styles is surprising in a man of such fine discrimination and delicate taste as Schumann displays elsewhere. The chief defect of the opera, however, lies in the music. In the opera of ' Genoveva,' the characters all sing more or less the same kind of music ; that which Schumann puts to the words is absolute music, not relative, i.e. such as would be accordant with the character of each individual. Neither in outline nor detail is his music sufficiently generated by the situations of the drama. Lastly, he lacks appreciation for that liveliness of contrast which appears forced and out of place in the concert-room, but is absolutely indispensable on the stage. ' Genoveva ' has no strict recitatives, but neither is there spoken dialogue ; even the ordinary quiet parts of the dialogue are sung in strict time, and usually accompanied with the full orchestra. Schumann considered the recitative a superannuated form of art, and in his other works also makes scarcely any use of it. This point is of course open to dispute ; but it is not open to dispute that in an opera, some kind of calm, even neutral form of expression is wanted, which, while allowing the action to proceed quickly, may serve as a foil to the chief parts in which highly wrought emotions are to be delineated. The want of such a foil in ' Genoveva ' weakens the effect of the climaxes, and with them, that of the whole. As in the formation of the libretto Schumann took ' Euryanthe ' as his model, so as a musician he intended to carry out Weber's intentions still farther, and to write, not an opera in the old-fashioned ordinary sense, but a music-drama, which should be purely national.

At the time when ' Genoveva ' was written, he was utterly opposed to Italian music, not in the way we should have expected him to be, but exactly as Weber was opposed to it in his time. ' Let me alone with your canary-bird music and your tunes out of the waste-paper basket,' he once said angrily to Weber's son, who was speaking to him of Cimarosa's ' Matrimonio segreto.' But although he may not have succeeded in producing a masterpiece of German opera, we may appreciate with gratitude the many beauties of the music, the noble sentiment pervading the whole, and the constant artistic feeling, directed only to what is true and genuine. The finest part of the work is the overture, a masterpiece in its kind, and worthy to rank with the classical models.

The music to Byron's *Manfred* (op. 115) consists of an overture, an entr'acte, melodramas, and several solos and choruses. Byron expressly desired the assistance of music for his work, though not so much of it as Schumann has given. Schumann inserted all the instrumental pieces in the work, with the exception of the tunes on the shepherd's pipe in the first act; also the Requiem heard at Manfred's death, sounding from the convent church. On the other hand, it is remarkable that he left the song of ' The captive usurper ' in Act. ii. Scene iv. without music. The whole work consists of sixteen numbers, including the overture ; this Schumann composed first of all, and probably without intending to write music for the drama itself. Even here he does not evince any special gift for dramatic writing. Byron's drama has been frequently performed upon the stage with Schumann's music, and its effectiveness can thus be tested. The music hardly ever serves to intensify the dramatic effects, and yet this is all that is necessary in a drama. It appears rather to be the outcome of the impression produced on Schumann by Byron's poem. There is one peculiarity about the ' Manfred ' music. On the stage it loses a great part of its effect, just as, in my opinion, the poem loses half its fantastic and weird magic by being dressed in the clumsy and palpable illusions of a scenic representation. The overture is a piece of music of the most serious character, and much more fitted for concert performance than for assembling an audience in a theatre. This is still more true of all the other pieces, so delicate in construction and subtle in feeling, the closing Requiem by no means excluded. And yet in the concert-room the music does not make its due effect ; partly because the hearer is withdrawn from the influence of the action, which is indispensable to the full understanding of the whole work ; and also because in the melodramas the spoken words and the music which accompanies them disturb one another more than when performed on the stage.

From these remarks it might be imagined that the ' Manfred ' music is an inferior work; but strange to say that is by no means the case. It is a splendid creation, and one of Schumann's most inspired productions. It hovers between the stage and the concert-room; and, paradoxical as it may seem, the deepest impression is produced by reading the score, picturing in one's mind the action and the spoken dialogue, and allowing the music to sink deep into the ears of one's mind. Perhaps the most striking parts of it all are the melodramas, and among them the deeply touching speech of Manfred to Astarte; and these all stand out with a peculiar purity and unity, when read as just described. They are in a manner improvements upon those highly poetic piano pieces of Schumann with superscriptions; and we ought to think of the words when hearing the piece. In this music, if nowhere else, is revealed Schumann's characteristic struggle after the inward, to the disregard of the outward; and we see how diametrically opposed to his nature was the realisation of dramatic effects where all is put into visible and tangible form. But he devoted himself to the composition of the ' Manfred ' music just as if he had been fitted for it by nature. The poet and the composer seem to have been destined for one another as truly as in the case of the ' Faust ' music, but in a different way. Byron had no idea of stage representation in writing *Manfred*; he only wished his poem to be read. Its romantic sublimity of thought, spurning all firm foothold or support on the earth, could only find its due completion in music such as this, which satisfies the requirements of neither stage nor concert-room. That a work of art, mighty and instinct with life, can be produced with a sublime disdain of all limits set by circumstance, provided only genius is at work upon it, is amply proved by Byron and Schumann in this their joint production. It has been already remarked more than once that the gloomy, melancholy and passionate intensity of strife in Byron's *Manfred*, heightened by contrast with the splendid descriptions of nature, corresponded to the conditions of Schumann's spirit at the time when the music was written. And indeed a deep sympathy speaks in every bar. But there was in Schumann a longing for peace and reconciliation, which is wanting in Byron. This comes out very plainly in different passages in the music, of which the most striking is the Requiem at the close, which sheds over the whole work a gentle gleam of glory.

In January 1851 Schumann wrote to a friend:

' It must always be the artist's highest aim to apply his powers to sacred music. But in youth we are firmly rooted to the earth by all our joys and sorrows; it is only with advancing age that the branches stretch higher, and so I hope that the period of my higher efforts is no longer distant.'

He is here speaking emphatically of ' sacred,' not of church music. Church music he never wrote, his Mass and his Requiem notwithstanding. It should be adapted to the church services, and calculated to produce its effect in combination with the customary ceremonial; but sacred or religious music is intended to turn the mind of the hearers, by its own unaided effect, to edifying thoughts of the eternal and divine. Of compositions of this class we possess several by Schumann; nor was it in 1851 that he first began writing them. There is an Advent hymn for solo, chorus and orchestra (op. 71), written in 1848; a motet for men's voices with organ, subsequently arranged for orchestra (op. 93), of 1849, and a New Year's hymn for chorus and orchestra (op. 144) of the winter of the same year; all three settings of poems by Friedrich Rückert. The Mass (op. 147) and the Requiem (op. 148), on the other hand, were composed in 1852, and Schumann may have been thinking mainly of works of this kind when he wrote the letter quoted above. As a Protestant his relations to the Mass and Requiem were perfectly unfettered; and in the composition of these works he can have had no thought of their adaptation to divine service, since even in form they exhibit peculiarities opposed to the established order of the Mass. It may, however, be assumed that it was the Catholic feeling of Düsseldorf which suggested them, and that he intended the works to be performed on certain occasions at church concerts. The words of the Mass will always have a great power of elevating and inspiring an earnest artist; but irrespective of this the composition of a Mass must have had a peculiar attraction for Schumann on other grounds. A poetical interest in the Catholic Church of the Middle Ages was at that time widely prevalent in Germany, particularly in circles which were most influenced by romantic poetry, and found in the Middle Ages the realisation of their most cherished ideals. Schumann shared in this tendency; a vein of mystical religionism, which otherwise might have lain dormant, often shows itself in his later compositions. For instance, under the name Requiem we find the setting of a hymn, ascribed to Héloise, the beloved of Abélard (op. 90, No. 7),

' Requiescat a labore
Doloroso, et amore,' etc.

Other instances are the poems of Mary Stuart (op. 135) and the Requiem for Mignon. In the Mass he has, contrary to custom, introduced an offertorium, *Tota pulchra es, Maria, et macula non est in te.*

In judging of Schumann's sacred music it is necessary to repeat that, though the chorus is not, strictly speaking, the musical means by which he was best able to express himself, yet both custom and the character and importance of the subject urged him to make considerable use of it in these works. Thus they contain a contradiction in themselves; they are all nobly and gravely conceived, but as choral music are only very rarely satisfactory. The Mass, no doubt, ranks highest, and contains much that is very beautiful; the 'Kyrie,' the 'Agnus,' the beginning and end of the 'Sanctus' and part of the 'Credo' being among Schumann's very best choral works. Unfortunately there is less to be said for the Requiem; we should have expected the mere idea of a Mass for the dead to have inspired such a genius as Schumann's, even without recollecting the wonderful tones which he has found for the final Requiem in 'Manfred.' But this work was undoubtedly written under great exhaustion; and the first romantic chorus alone makes a uniformly harmonious impression. It closes the list of Schumann's works, but it is not with this that we should wish to complete the picture of so great and noble a master. He once said with reference to the Requiem, 'It is a thing that one writes for oneself.' But the abundant treasure of individual, pure and profound art which he has bequeathed to us in his other works is a more lasting monument to his name, stupendous and imperishable.

### BIBLIOGRAPHY

Among the published works that treat of Schumann's life and labours, that by Wasielewski deserves the first mention (*Robert Schumann, eine Biographie*, VON JOSEF W. VON WASIELEWSKI; Dresden, R. Kunze, 1858; ed. 3, Bonn, E. Strauss, 1880). Though in time it may yet receive additions and revision, it has still the enduring merit of giving from accurate acquaintance the broad outlines of Schumann's life. AUGUST REISSMANN's *Robert Schumann, sein Leben und seine Werke* (1865, 1871 and 1879) contains analysis of many works. Other valuable contributions to his biography have been written by F. HUEFFER, *Die Poesie in der Musik* (Leipzig, 1874); by R. POHL, *Erinnerungen an R. Schumann*, *Deutsche Revue*, vol. iv., Berlin, 1878 (pp. 169-81 and 306-17); by MAX KALBECK, *R. Schumann in Wien*, forming the feuilletons of the *Wiener allgemeine Zeitung* of Sept. 24, 29, and Oct. 5, 1880. An accurate and sympathetic essay on Schumann, *Robert Schumanns Tage und Werke* was contributed by A. W. AMBROS to the *Culturhistorische Bilder aus dem Musikleben der Gegenwart* (Leipzig, Matthes, 1860; pp. 51-96). Schumann's literary work was reviewed by H. Deiters in the *Allg. musik. Zeitung* (Leipzig, Breitkopf & Härtel, 1865, Nos. 47-49). The *Gesammelte Schriften* reached their third edition in 1883; and were translated by FANNY RAYMOND RITTER; *Die Davidsbündler* by F. G. JENSEN (1883) is full of interest. A collection of the master's *Jugendbriefe*, edited by CLARA SCHUMANN, appeared in 1885, and was translated in 1888; F. G. JENSEN's *Neue Folge* of letters (1886) appeared as *The Life of Robert Schumann told in his Letters*, translated by MAY HERBERT (1890). Litzmann's biography of Clara Schumann contains much new information. A large selection from all the letters was published by DR. KARL STOROK in 1907, and translated by HANNAH BRYANT. FREDERICK NIECKS's *Robert Schumann, a Supplementary and Corrective Biography*, edited by his widow, CHRISTINA NIECKS, was published in 1924, and is referred to in footnotes added to this article in the present edition. ROBERT PITROU's *La Vie intérieure de R. Schumann* (Paris, 1925) may be compared. The literary works of Schumann have been translated into French by H. de Curzon.

Schuberth & Co. published in 1860—1 a Thematic Catalogue of Schumann's printed works, extending to op. 143 only. A complete index to all the published compositions of Schumann, with careful evidence as to the year in which each was written, published and first performed, and their different editions and arrangements, was compiled by Alfred Dörffel as a supplement to the *Musikalisches Wochenblatt* (Leipzig, Fritzsch, 1875). It is impossible to indicate all the shorter notices of Schumann in books and periodicals. The author of this article has had the advantage of seeing a considerable number of his unpublished letters and of obtaining much information at first hand from persons who were in intimate relations with him.

### CATALOGUE OF SCHUMANN'S PUBLISHED WORKS

The complete edition of Breitkopf & Härtel in thirty-four volumes, edited by Clara Schumann and others, was completed in 1893 by a supplementary volume edited by Brahms.

(All works down to op. 23, inclusive, are for pianoforte solo.)

Op.
1. Variations on the name 'Abegg.'
2. Papillons, twelve pieces.
3. Six studies after Paganini's Caprices.
4. Intermezzi, six pieces.
5. Impromptus (Variations) on a theme of Clara Wieck.
6. Davidsbündlertänze, eighteen pieces.
7. Toccata.
8. Allegro.

Op.
9. Carnaval, twenty-one pieces.
10. Six studies after Paganini's Caprices.
11. Sonata in F sharp minor.
12. Fantasiestücke, eight pieces.
13. Études en forme de variations (Études symphoniques).
14. Sonata in F minor.
15. Kinderscenen, thirteen pieces.
16. Kreisleriana, eight pieces.
17. Fantasia in C.
18. Arabeske.
19. Blumenstück.
20. Humoreske.
21. Novelletten, eight pieces.
22. Sonata in G minor.
23. Nachtstücke, four pieces.
24. Liederkreis, nine songs.
25. Myrthen, twenty-six songs.
26. Faschingsschwank aus Wien, PF. solo.
27. Lieder und Gesänge (5).
28. Three Romances for PF. solo.
29. Three poems by Geibel (the first for two sopranos, the second for three sopranos and the third, Zigeunerleben—'Gipsy Life,' for small chorus, triangle and tambourines *ad lib.*).
30. Three songs to Geibel's words.
31. Three songs to Chamisso's words.
32. Scherzo, Gigue, Romanza and Fughetta, for PF. solo.
33. Six four-part songs for men's voices.
34. Four duets for sopr. and tenor.
35. Twelve songs to words by Kerner.
36. Six songs to words by Reinick.
37. Twelve songs from Rückert's 'Liebesfrühling.' (Three numbers, 2, 4 and 11, are by Clara Schumann.)
38. Symphony in B flat.
39. Liederkreis, twelve poems by Eichendorff.
40. Five songs.
41. Three string quartets in A minor, F and A.
42. Frauenliebe und -Leben, songs by Chamisso.
43. Three two-part songs.
44. Quintet for PF. and strings in E flat.
45. Three Romanzen und Balladen, voice and PF.
46. Andante and variations for two pianos.
47. Quartet for PF. and strings in E flat.
48. Dichterliebe, sixteen songs by Heine.
49. Three Romanzen und Balladen, voice and PF.
50. Paradise and the Peri, cantata for solo voices, chorus and orch.
51. Five songs.
52. Overture, Scherzo, and Finale for orch.
53. Three Romanzen und Balladen, voice and PF.
54. Concerto for PF. and orch.
55. Five songs by Burns for mixed chorus.
56. Studies for the pedal piano, six pieces in canon.
57. Belsatzar, ballad by Heine.
58. Four sketches for pedal piano.
59. Four songs for mixed chorus.
60. Six fugues on the name Bach, for PF. or organ.
61. Symphony in C, for orch.
62. Three songs for male chorus.
63. Trio for PF. and strings in D minor.
64. Three Romanzen und Balladen, voice and PF.
65. Ritornellen, canons for male chorus.
66. Bilder aus Osten, for PF., four hands.
67. Five Romanzen und Balladen, for chorus.
68. Album for the young (forty pieces).
69. Six Romances, for female chorus.
70. Adagio and allegro, for PF. and horn (or violoncello or violin).
71. Adventlied, for chorus and orch.
72. Four fugues for piano.
73. Three Fantasiestücke for PF. and clarinet (violin or violoncello).
74. Spanisches Liederspiel, for vocal quartet, with PF. acct.
75. Five Romanzen und Balladen, for chorus.
76. Four marches for PF.
77. Five songs.
78. Four duets for sopr. and tenor.
79. Lieder-album, twenty-eight songs for the young.
80. Trio for PF. and strings in F.
81. Genoveva, opera in four acts.
82. Waldscenen, nine pieces for PF.
83. Three songs.
84. A Parting Song (' Es ist bestimmt '), chorus and orch.
85. Twelve PF. duets, 'für kleine und grosse Kinder.'
86. Concertstück, for four horns and orch.
87. Der Handschuh, ballad for voice and PF.
88. Four Phantasiestücke for PF. and violin and violoncello.
89. Six songs.
90. Seven songs.
91. Six Romances for female chorus.
92. Introduction and allegro appassionato, PF. and orch.
93. Motet, 'Verzweifle nicht,' double male chorus with organ acct.
94. Three Romances for oboe and PF. (or violin or violoncello).
95. Three songs from Byron's Hebrew melodies, with acct. of harp or PF.
96. Five songs.
97. Symphony in E flat.
98a. Nine songs from 'Wilhelm Meister.'
98b. Requiem für Mignon, from the same, for chorus and orch.
99. Bunte Blätter for PF. (fourteen pieces).
100. Overture to *Die Braut von Messina*.
101. Minnespiel for solo voices and PF.
102. Five Stücke im Volkston for violoncello (or violin) and PF.
103. Mädchenlieder, vocal duets.
104. Seven songs.
105. Sonata for PF. and violin, A minor.
106. Schön Hedwig, ballad for declamation with PF. acct.
107. Six songs.
108. Nachtlied, for chorus and orch.
109. Ballscenen, nine pieces for PF. duet.
110. Trio for PF. and strings in G minor.
111. Three Fantasiestücke for PF.
112. Der Rose Pilgerfahrt (Pilgrimage of the Rose) for soli, chorus and orch.
113. Märchenbilder, for PF. and viola (or violin).
114. Three songs for female chorus.

Op.
115. Music to Byron's *Manfred*.
116. Der Königssohn, ballad for soli, chorus and orch.
117. Four Husarenlieder, for voice and PF.
118. Three PF. sonatas for the young.
119. Three songs.
120. Symphony in D minor.
121. Sonata for PF. and violin, D minor.
122. Two ballads for declamation, with PF. acct.
123. Festival overture on the Rheinweinlied, for orch.
124. Albumblätter, twenty PF. pieces.
125. Five songs.
126. Seven pieces in fughetta form for PF.
127. Five songs.
128. Overture to *Julius Caesar*.
129. Concerto for violoncello and orch.
130. Kinderball, six pieces for PF. duet.
131. Phantasie for violin and orch.
132. Märchenerzählungen, four pieces for PF., clarinet (or violin) and viola.
133. Gesänge der Frühe, five PF. pieces.
134. Concert-allegro with introduction, for PF. and orch.
135. Five Gedichte der Maria Stuart, for voice and PF.
136. Overture to *Hermann und Dorothea*.
137. Five hunting-songs for male chorus, with acct. of four horns.
138. Spanische Liebeslieder, for soli, with acct. of PF. duet.
139. Des Sängers Fluch, for soli, chorus and orch.
140. Vom Pagen und der Königstochter, four ballads for soli, chorus and orch.
141. Four songs for double chorus.
142. Four songs.
143. Der Glück von Edenhall, for soli, chorus and orch.
144. Neujahrslied, for chorus and orch.
145. Five Romanzen und Balladen, for chorus.
146. Five Romanzen und Balladen, for chorus.
147. Mass, for chorus and orch.
148. Requiem, for chorus and orch.

WITHOUT OPUS NUMBERS

Scenes from Goethe's *Faust* for soli, chorus and orch.
Der deutsche Rhein, song with chorus.
PF. accompaniments to Bach's suites for violin alone.

The following are in the supplementary volume of the complete edition:
1. Andante and variations for two pianofortes, two violoncelli and horn.
2. An Anna, song.
3. Im Herbste, song.
4. Hirtenknabe, song.
5. Sommerruh', duet with PF. acct.
6. Five extra variations for op. 13.
7. Scherzo for PF. (suppl. to op. 14).
8. Presto for PF. (suppl. to op. 22).
9. Thema in E flat for PF.

P. S.

SCHUMANN - HEINK, ERNESTINE (*née* ROESSLER) (*b.* Lieben, near Prague, June 15, 1861), was taught singing by Marietta Leclair at Graz, and on Oct. 13, 1878, made her début at Dresden as Azucena, remaining there four years. In 1883 she was engaged at Hamburg, where she remained many years. In 1892, as Frl. Heink, she sang with the Hamburg Company both at Covent Garden and Drury Lane, making her début June 8 (Covent Garden) as Erda in ' Siegfried.' Later she sang as Fricka, Waltraute, and, July 8, as the Countess in the production in England at Drury Lane of Nessler's ' Trompeter von Säkkingen.' She made a great impression, on account of her fine voice, combining mezzo and contralto, and of her excellent singing and acting. From 1897–1900 inclusive she sang again at Covent Garden, principally in Wagner parts ; July 11, 1898, the music of the Prologue, on the production of Mancinelli's ' Ero e Leandro.' From 1896–1906 she was in continued request at Bayreuth. From 1898 she was engaged at the Berlin Opera, and she purchased her release from this engagement in order to follow up her success in America. She had first appeared in America at Chicago (Nov. 7, 1898) and New York (Jan. 9, 1899). She sang frequently at the Metropolitan till 1904, and became an American citizen in 1905. She created the part of Clytemnestra in Strauss's ' Elektra ' at

Dresden, Jan. 25, 1909. She has been three times married : first in 1883 to Heink ; secondly, in 1893, to Paul Schumann ; thirdly, on May 27, 1905, to William Rapp, son of a publisher in Chicago, her business manager.

A. C., with addns.

SCHUNKE, LOUIS (LUDWIG) (*b.* Cassel, Dec. 21, 1810 ; *d.* Dec. 7, 1834), pianoforte-player and composer, of a musical family. His progress was so rapid that at 10 he could play the concertos of Mozart and Hummel with ease. In 1824 he visited Munich and Vienna, and then Paris, where he put himself under Kalkbrenner and Reicha. After some wandering to Stuttgart, Vienna (1832), Prague and Dresden he came to Leipzig, where he made the acquaintance of Schumann, and an intimate friendship was the result. Schunke died at the early age of not quite 24, to the great grief of Schumann, who indulged his affection in several interesting papers (*Ges. Schriften*, i. 92, 325 ; ii. 56, 277) full of memorials of his friend's characteristics. Schunke was one of the four who edited the *Neue Zeitschrift für Musik* on its first appearance. His articles are signed with the figure 3. His published compositions are for the piano, and show considerable ability.

G.

SCHUPPANZIGH, IGNAZ (*b.* Vienna, 1776 ; *d.* Mar. 2, 1830), celebrated violinist. His father was a professor at the Realschule, Vienna. He adopted music as a profession about the end of 1792, and that he early became known as a teacher we gather from an entry in Beethoven's diary for 1794, ' Schuppanzigh three times a week, Albrechtsberger three times a week.' Beethoven was studying the viola which was at that time Schuppanzigh's instrument, but he soon after abandoned it for the violin. Before he was 21 he had made some name as a conductor, and in 1798 and 1799 directed the Augarten concerts. The *A.M.Z.* of May 1799, after describing the concerts, remarks that

' the zeal shown by Herr Schuppanzigh in interpreting the compositions produced, makes these concerts models worth following by all amateur associations of the kind, and by many conductors.'

Beethoven, who had also appeared at the Augarten concerts, kept up a singular kind of friendship with Schuppanzigh. They were so useful to each other that, as Thayer says, they had a great mutual liking, if it did not actually amount to affection. Schuppanzigh was goodlooking, though later in life he grew very fat, and had to put up with many a joke on the subject from Beethoven. ' My lord Falstaff '[1] was one of his nicknames. The following piece of rough drollery, scrawled by Beethoven on a blank page at the end of his sonata op. 28, is here printed for the first time :

---

[1] Letter to Archduke in Nohl, *Neue Briefe*, p. 75.

*Lob auf den Dicken.*

Schuppanzigh was a great quartet-player, and belonged to the party which met every Friday during 1794 and 1795 at Prince Carl Lichnow-sky's, where he took the first violin, the Prince himself, or a Silesian named Sina, the second, Weiss the viola, and Kraft, a thorough artist, the violoncello—occasionally changing with Beethoven's friend Zmeskall. Towards the close of 1808 Schuppanzigh founded the Rasoumowsky Quartet, to which he, Mayseder and Linke remained attached for life. Weiss again took the viola. Beethoven's quartets were the staple of their performances. In the meantime Schuppanzigh had married a Fräulein Kilitzky, the sister of a well-known singer, who sang with little success 'Ah perfido!' at a concert of Beethoven's in 1808, instead of Anna Milder. On this occasion the great joker writes to Graf Brunswick, 'Schuppanzigh is married—they say his wife is as fat as himself—what a family.'[1] When the Rasoumowsky palace was burnt down in 1815 Schuppanzigh started on a tour through Germany, Poland and Russia, and did not return till early in 1824, when the quartets were resumed with the same band of friends (see Beethoven's letters to his nephew, 1825). One of the first events after his return was the performance of Schubert's octet, which is

marked as finished on Mar. 1, and was doubtless played very shortly after. The acquaintance thus begun was cemented by Schubert's dedication of his lovely quartet in A 'to his friend I. Schuppanzigh,' a year later. Schuppanzigh was a member of the court chapel, and for some time director of the court opera. He died of paralysis. Of his compositions the following were printed : 'Solo pour le violon avec quatuor' (Diabelli), 'Variationen über ein russisches Lied' (Cappi), and 'Variationen über ein Thema aus Alcina' (Mollo).    F. G.

**SCHUSTER**, JOSEPH (*b.* Dresden, Aug. 11, 1748; *d.* there, July 24, 1812). In 1765 Schuster and his friend Seydelmann went with Naumann to Italy to study composition. They remained there until 1768, and Schuster produced several operas. In 1772 both were appointed church composers to the Elector. From 1774–76 and again from 1778–82 Schuster was in Italy partly to study with Padre Martini, partly to produce some operas which he had written to order for various Italian theatres. In Naples his success was so great that the king appointed him his honorary maestro di cappella. He wrote about 25 Italian and German operas, masses, oratorios, secular vocal music, symphonies, chamber music, etc. (See list in *Q.-L.* ; see also *Riemann* ; *Mendel*.)

**SCHUYT** (SCUTIUS), CORNELIS (*b.* Leyden ; *d.* there, June 1616 ²), went to Italy at the town's expense to perfect himself. In 1593 he was appointed organist at the Begijnenhof (nunnery), Leyden. He composed several books of madrigals and a book of pavans, galliards and instrumental canzone (*Q.-L.*).

**SCHWANENBERG** (SCHWANENBERGER), JOHANN GOTTFRIED (*b.* Wolfenbüttel, Dec. 23, 1740; *d.* Brunswick, Apr. 5, 1804), studied in Italy chiefly under Hasse, and was court Kapellmeister at Brunswick from 1762. He composed operas, cantatas, symphonies, sonatas, etc. (list in *Q.-L.* ; also *Riemann*).

**SCHWARBROOK**, THOMAS, a German, was in the employ of Renatus Harris the organ-builder. Early in the 18th century he left London to live at Warwick, and built many noble instruments. His masterpiece was the organ of St. Michael's, Coventry, built in 1733, which cost £1400. The latest mention of him is in 1752, when he improved the organ of Worcester Cathedral.    V. de P.

**SCHWARTZENDORF**, J. P. A., see MARTINI IL TEDESCO.

**SCHWEITZER**, ALBERT (*b.* Upper Alsace, Jan. 14, 1875), became famous in the musical world through his writing on J. S. Bach, which, together with that of Pirro, has had a marked influence on the modern estimate of that master.

Schweitzer studied the organ both at Strassburg and in Paris (with Widor) together with theology and medicine, but, contrary to the usual practice of those who have made a name in music, art had no triumph in his case over the learned professions. He became a teacher of theology in the University of Strassburg in 1913, and if one interest may be said to have absorbed him more than others it has been his work as a medical missionary in equatorial Africa, where he now lives and works. It was in the Congo that he began his work on J. S. Bach. His *Jean Sébastien Bach, le musicien-poète* was published in Paris 1905 and expanded in a subsequent German edition (Leipzig, 1907). The latter has been translated into English by Ernest Newman. The emphasis laid on Bach's realism and his use of type figures of melody to illustrate ideas was an individual contribution to the study of Bach's æsthetic standpoint, and Schweitzer has probably been more quoted than any authority since Spitta. He engaged with Widor on an edition of Bach's organ works (still incomplete), was organist of the Société J. S. Bach in Paris, which he helped to found, and in 1922, after more than four years in Africa, he gave a number of organ recitals in European cities (including one at Westminster Abbey), devoting the proceeds to the medical mission which he had established in Africa.            c.

SCHWEITZER, ANTON (*bapt.* Coburg, June 6, 1735; *d.* Gotha, Nov. 23, 1787), received his musical education at the expense of the Duke of Coburg, who sent him to Kleinknecht at Bayreuth. He then went to Hildburghausen as Kapellmeister at the court and conductor of Seiler's theatrical company. After further studies in Italy he became musical director at the Ducal Theatre, Weimar, and when that was burnt down, in 1774, went to Gotha, where he became Benda's successor at the court. He composed several serious operas to librettos which Wieland had specially written for him, and which are among the first German operas; but his greatest success lay in his ' Singspiele,' in which genre he was foremost among all who cultivated it. So great was the ignorance of the public that he was placed above Gluck by his contemporaries (*Q.-L.* ; *Riemann*).

SCHWEMMER, HEINRICH (*b.* Gumbertshausen, near Hallburg, Lower Franconia, Mar. 28, 1621; *d.* May 26, 1696). In his younger years war and the pestilence obliged his family to seek refuge first at Weimar, then at Coburg. According to Gerber he first visited Nuremberg in 1641 as a pupil of the St. Sebald School, and received his musical instruction from the organist Johann Erasmus Kindermann. But the first documentary evidence we have of his presence at Nuremberg is in connexion with a great musical festival and banquet held there in 1649, in honour of the Swedish Field-Marshal, after the Peace of Westphalia. Schwemmer appears among the singers on that occasion,

though not yet holding any appointment. The year 1650 is the date of his first appointment at Nuremberg as an assistant master at the St. Laurence School. In 1656 he is described as *Director Chori musici* at the Frauenkirche; but with this post, which he seems to have retained till his death, he was obliged, in accordance with the custom of the time, to combine certain duties of ordinary school instruction at the St. Sebald School. Like greater musicians after him Schwemmer appears to have found his ordinary school duties somewhat irksome, and for an occasional negligence in them came under the censure of the town authorities. In spite of this he was recognised as the best musical teacher in Nuremberg, and the most distinguished of later Nuremberg musicians, such as Pachelbel, Johann Krieger, and Baltazar Schmidt, were his pupils. He was also the musician most sought after for such occasional compositions as wedding and funeral anthems. *Q.-L.* enumerates twenty of such works for voices and instruments. He was also the composer of a large number of melodies for the various Nuremberg hymn-books of the time. In *D.D.T.* (2nd series, Bayern) vi. there is printed for the first time an Easter Motet by him for voices and instruments, which is characterised by much of the Handelian simplicity and directness of choral effect. Only a few other church works by him remain in MS.            J. R. M.

SCHWENKE (SCHWENCKE), a German musical family, whose founder, (1) JOHANN GOTTLIEB (*b.* Breitenau, Saxony, Aug. 11, 1744; *d.* Hamburg, Dec. 7, 1823), was a famous bassoonist and a ' Rathsmusikus.' His son (2) CHRISTIAN FRIEDRICH GOTTLIEB (*b.* Wachenhausen, Harz, Aug. 30, 1767; *d.* Hamburg, Oct. 28, 1822) was a proficient clavier-player, and appeared in public at Hamburg in a concerto by his father in 1779, when eleven and a half years old. Emanuel Bach interested himself in the boy's career, and was instrumental in getting him sent to Berlin (1782), where he studied under Kirnberger. He tried for an organist's post at Hamburg in 1783, but was unsuccessful, although Emanuel Bach was a judge. In 1787 and 1788 he studied at the University of Leipzig and Halle, and after the dispute which followed on Emanuel Bach's death in 1789, Schwenke was appointed to succeed him as town cantor, but the new conditions attached to the post were so irksome that he devoted himself mainly to mathematical problems. As a composer his main importance was in the stress he laid on good accentuation. He set Klopstock's ' Vaterunser ' and ' Der Frohsinn ' to music, and was a friend of the poet's. Various cantatas for solo and chorus with orchestra, six organ fugues, a concerto for oboe, and clavier sonatas are mentioned in *Q.-L.*, from which most of the above information is derived. He was bold enough to rescore the 'Messiah' and Bach's B minor Mass.

Two of his sons were musicians: the elder, (3) JOHANN FRIEDRICH (b. Hamburg, Apr. 30, 1792; d. there, Sept. 28, 1852), was a player on the organ, violoncello and clarinet, was appointed to the Nikolaikirche in Hamburg in 1829 and composed cantatas with organ accompaniment, arrangement, etc., of Chorals, a septet for five violoncellos, double-bass and drums, and orchestrated Beethoven's 'Adelaide' and 'Wachtelschlag,' among other things. The younger, (4) KARL (b. Hamburg, Mar. 7, 1797), was a clever pianist and an industrious composer; three sonatas for piano duet, and one for violin, appeared, as well as a symphony performed at the Paris Conservatoire in 1843, and at Hamburg. From 1870 when he lived near Vienna, all trace of him is lost. Johann Friedrich's son and pupil, (5) FRIEDRICH GOTTLIEB (b. Hamburg, Dec. 15, 1823; d. there, June 11, 1896), was his successor in the Nikolaikirche, had success as a pianist and organist in Paris (1855) and elsewhere. Two fantasias for organ, trumpet, trombones and drums, are his most important compositions. He re-edited his father's collection of Chorals, and wrote preludes to them. (*Riemann*; *Q.-L.*)          M.

SCHWINDL (SCHWINDEL), FRIEDRICH (d. Carlsruhe, Aug. 10, 1786), was a skilful player on the violin, flute and clavier, in the 18th century. He was at the Hague about 1770, where Burney met him, and in Geneva and Mülhausen, where he brought out some operettas; finally he settled at Carlsruhe, where he died holding the position of *Markgräflich badischer Konzertmeister*. He was one of the followers of the Mannheim school; his numerous symphonies, quartets, trios, etc., appeared at Amsterdam, Paris, and London (where his music enjoyed great popularity), from 1765 onwards. A Mass in E minor for four voices and orchestra is in MS. at Milan. (*Riemann*; *Q.-L.*, etc.)          M.

SCHYTTE, (1) LUDWIG THEODOR (b. Aarhus, Jutland, Denmark, Apr. 28, 1848; d. Berlin, Nov. 10, 1909), was originally a chemist, and gave up that business for music in 1870, when he studied the pianoforte under Anton Rée and Edmund Neupert, and composition with Gebauer and Gade, finally going to Taubert in Berlin, and Liszt at Weimar. He had one of the advanced piano classes in Horák's Academy in Vienna in 1887–88, and subsequently resided there, being distinguished as a player, composer and teacher. A very large number of graceful and effective compositions for pianoforte testified to his industry, and many have become widely popular, such as op. 22, 'Naturstimmungen'; op. 30, 'Pantomimen' for PF. duet; op. 53, sonata. A pianoforte

concerto is op. 28, and among his many songs, a cycle, 'Die Verlassene,' deserves mention. A comic opera, 'Fahrendes Volk,' was not performed; but 'Hero,' a one-act opera, was given at Copenhagen in 1898, and an operetta, 'Der Mameluk,' at Vienna in 1903. (*Riemann*; *Baker*.) His brother, (2) HENRIK BISSING (b. Aarhus, May 4, 1827; d. Copenhagen, Feb. 22, 1909), was a violoncellist, musical critic to several Danish papers, editor of *Musikbladet* (1884–93) and of a *Nordisk Musiklexikon*.          M.

SCIOLTO, CON SCIOLTEZZA, 'freely'; an expression used in nearly the same sense as *ad libitum*, but generally applied to longer passages, or even to whole movements. It is also applied to a fugue in a free style. Thus what Beethoven, in the last movement of the sonata in B♭, op. 106, calls 'Fuga con alcune licenze,' might otherwise be called 'Fuga sciolta.'          M.

SCONTRINO, ANTONIO (b. Trapani, Sicily, May 17, 1850; d. Florence, Jan. 7, 1922). His father, a carpenter by trade, was an ardent lover of music, playing the violin and guitar as well as singing, and constructing violins, guitars, violoncellos, double-basses and even pianofortes. With his children and brothers this keen amateur formed an orchestra in which, at the age of 7 years, Antonio was persuaded to take part as double-bass, playing on a violoncello adapted for the purpose, and provided with three strings only.

In 1861 he took up music in earnest, and entered the Palermo Conservatorio to study the instrument which chance, rather than choice, had made his own. For harmony he was a pupil of Luigi Alfano, and for counterpoint and composition of Platania, the director of the institution. In 1870 he left the Conservatorio and toured as a virtuoso on the double-bass throughout southern Italy; in the following year he obtained the libretto of an opera from Leopoldo Marenco, but the work, 'Matelda,' was not produced until 1876. Aided by a grant from the municipality and province of Trapani, Scontrino went in 1872 to Munich, where for two years he studied German music. In 1874 he came to England as a member of Mapleson's orchestra, and afterwards settled in Milan as a teacher of instrumental, vocal and theoretical music. In 1891 he was appointed professor of counterpoint and composition in the Palermo Conservatorio, and in 1892 a similar professorship was gained by him in competition, at the Reale Istituto Musicale at Florence.

His works include five operas: 'Matelda,' 4 acts (Milan, Teatro Dal Verme, 1876); 'Il progettista,' 1 act (Rome, 1882); 'Sortilegio,' 3 acts (Turin, 1882); 'Gringoire,' 1 act (Milan, 1890); and 'Cortigiana,' 4 acts (Milan, 1895–1896). Among his more important orchestral compositions are an overture to Marenco's 'Celeste,' incidental music to D' Annunzio's 'Francesca da Rimini,' a 'Sinfonia marinesca' and 'Sinfonia romantica.' Three string quartets and a prelude and fugue for the same instruments ; various pieces for violin, violoncello and double-bass with piano accompaniment, and several sets of pianoforte soli are among his instrumental works ; and his songs, which number about fifty, include two cycles, La Vie intérieure ' to words by Sully Prud'homme, and ' Intima vita ' to words by E. Panzacchi. An O Salutaris and Salve Regina for two voices with organ accompaniment, a motet, ' Tota Pulcra,' for vocal quartet, and a Gloria, an eight-part fugue for solo voices, are his sacred compositions.           M.

SCORDATURA (mis-tuning), a term used to designate some abnormal tunings of the violin which are occasionally employed to produce particular effects.

The scordatura originated in the lute and viol, which were tuned in various ways to suit the key of the music. Their six strings being commonly tuned by fourths, with one third in the middle, the third was shifted as occasion required, and an additional third or a fifth was introduced elsewhere, so as to yield on the open strings as many harmonies as possible ; in old lute music the proper tuning is indicated at the beginning of the piece. This practice survives in the guitar. The normal tuning being as at (a), very striking effects in the key of E major,

for instance, may be produced by tuning the instrument as at (b). The scordatura was formerly often employed on the violin. (1) The tuning (c) is extremely favourable to simplicity of fingering in the key of A. It is employed by Tartini in one of his soli, and by Castrucci in a well-known fugue : its effect is noisy and monotonous. It is frequently employed by Scotch reel-players, and in their hands has a singularly rousing effect. The following strain from ' Kilrack's Reel ' is to be read by the player as if tuned in the ordinary way, so that the first phrase sounds in the key of A :

The reel called ' Appin House ' and the lively Strathspey called ' Anthony Murray's Reel ' are played in the same tuning. (2) The tuning (d) employed by BIBER (q.v.) is a modification of (c), a fourth being substituted for a fifth on the first string ; and (3) the tuning (e), also employed by Biber, is a similar modification of the

normal tuning by fifths. In these tunings the viol fingering must be used on the first strings. On Biber's use of the scordatura in the eleventh sonata of his second book (reprinted in D.T.Ö. xii. 2) see the Zeitschr. of the Int. Mus. Ges. viii. p. 471, and ix. p. 29 (both 1907). (4) The tuning (f), employed by Nardini in his Enigmatic Sonata, is the reverse of the last, being a combination of the common tuning for the first two strings with the viol tuning in the lower ones. (5) The tuning (g) is employed by Barbella in his ' Serenade ' and by Campagnoli in his ' Notturno,' to imitate the viola d' amore, from the four middle strings of which it is copied. Thick first and second strings should be used, and the mute put on. The effect is singularly pleasing : but the G and A on the second string are flat and dull. (6) The tuning (h) employed by Lolli, is the normal tuning except the fourth string, which is tuned an octave below the third. If a very stout fourth string is used, a good bass accompaniment is thus obtainable.

Such are a few of the abnormal tunings employed by the old violinists. The scordatura is seldom used by modern players except on the fourth string, which is often tuned a tone higher, as at (i). (De Bériot, Mazas, Prume, etc.). This device may always be employed where the composition does not descend below A ; the tone is much increased, and in some keys, especially D and A, execution is greatly facilitated. Paganini tuned his fourth string higher still, as at (j) and (k), with surprising effect ; the B♭ tuning was a favourite one with De Bériot. Paganini's tuning in flats (l) cannot

be called scordatura, as it consists in elevating the violin generally by half a tone for the sake of brilliancy. The same device was employed by Spohr in his duets for harp and violin, the harp part being written in flats a semitone higher. The fourth string is rarely lowered : but Baillot sometimes tuned it a semitone lower, as at (m), to facilitate arpeggios in the sharp keys.

The scordatura (n) is employed by Bach in his fifth sonata for the violoncello. It corresponds to the violin tuning (e). This depression of the first string, if a thick string is used, is not unfavourable to sonority. When the scordatura is used, suitable strings should be obtained. Thicker ones are necessary where the pitch is depressed, and thinner ones where it is elevated : and the player will find it best to keep a special instrument for any tuning which he frequently employs.        E. J. P.

In engraved music of Scottish reels, etc., the scordatura was marked at the beginning of the piece by the word ' Scordatura ' and the tuning in notes. In manuscript music, however, it was frequently more carelessly indicated, or even left without indication. It must be remembered that although all notes on the mistuned strings are affected, yet the notation throughout the piece always stood as if the tuning were normal, and consequently allowance for this must be made in playing on the piano, etc., and in transcripts. In scordatura of the lowest string the sound A is represented by the note G, the sound B by the note A, and so on. For a curious instance of the Scottish scordatura see SIR ROGER DE COVERLY.                    F. K.

BIBL.—ANDREAS MOSER, *Die Violin-Skordatur.* *A.M.* 14, 1919. (16 pp.)

SCORE (Fr. *partition*; Ger. *Partitur*; Ital. *partitura, partizione, partitino, sparta, spartita*; Lat. *partitio, partitura, partitura cancellata*.

a 'short' score, a 'vocal' score, or a 'piano' score, should properly be reserved for the system which presents on separate staves all the parts that are to be performed simultaneously, commonly spoken of as 'full score.' The oldest known form of score would seem to be that in the pseudo-Hucbald *Musica enchiriadis*, a treatise of the 11th century. A specimen will be found under NOTATION.

An interesting early score is in the B.M. Harl. MS. 978—the volume which contains the famous Reading *rota* 'Sumer is icumen in.' Below the three voice-parts here shown there is a supplementary *quadruplum*, written on a separate stave, which has no concern with our present purpose. This composition shows that in the first half of the 13th century the essential feature of a score was realised in England.

A series of staves on which the different parts of a piece of music are written one above another, so that the whole may be read at a glance.

The English name is derived from the practice of dividing the music by bars or lines *scored* through the entire series of staves. The Latin term, *partitura cancellata* owes its origin

In Arundel MS. No. 248, fol. 153*a*, 154*b*, 155*a* and 201*a*, there are two-part compositions regularly scored on staves of eight and nine lines. In the last of these, now nearly illegible, two staves, each consisting of four black lines, are separated by a red line. In the other case the staves consist of eight uniform and equidistant black lines. The following is from

to the compartments or *cancelli*, into which the page is divided by the vertical scorings. The word score, though often misapplied in the present day to what is more correctly called

fol. 155*a* of the MS., and the lower part of the same facsimile is another hymn 'Salue uirgo uirginū,' for three voices, on a stave of twelve equidistant black lines. The MS. dates from about the middle of the 13th century. A score of the same kind, about the same date, is referred to by Ambros as being in the Bibliothèque Nationale, Paris.　　　　　w. s. r.

It will be observed that in these examples care is taken that the notes which synchronise in time are in the same vertical line. In the *rota* (see Frontispiece to Vol. V.) and in the 15th century carols edited by J. A. Fuller Maitland and W. S. Rockstro ; although the parts are superimposed, yet there is no attempt to make the page really a score.

One of the first printed scores, properly so-called, is that of Cipriano de Rore's madrigals of 1577 ; and one of the first printed orchestral scores, if not the very first, was that of the ' Ballet comique de la Royne ' (Paris, 1582). From the system then adopted to the complicated scores now in use, the process is one of natural development. Down to the days of Bach and Handel, and for some time after them, the orchestral instruments were used rather as an accretion of obbligato parts than as a complex whole ; but from the time that the orchestra became a recognised constitution, some system of grouping instruments of the same class near each other has been followed. The basso continuo or thorough-bass, whether figured or not, always occupied the lowest stave, and its inseparable companion, the violoncello part, was placed immediately above it. In purely orchestral music the viola comes next and the two violin parts ; but in vocal music, whether for soli or choruses, the voice-parts, with or without an organ part below them, occupy the position immediately above the violoncello. Sometimes in a concerto the solo instrument has this place, as in the first organ concerto of Handel ; but more often, and in modern music almost universally, the solo instrument in such a composition is placed above the strings.

Having arrived at the line for the first violin[1] or violin solo part, it will be most convenient to describe the constitution of the score from the top downwards. In certain instances, such as Beethoven's C minor symphony, Mozart's ' Jupiter ' symphony, Schumann's in E flat, etc., the drums occupy the top line ; but in far the greater number of cases the piccolos or flutes head the score as the top of the group of ' wood-wind ' instruments. Next come the oboes with the cor anglais, then the clarinets of all types ; the bassoons with double bassoon generally end the group of ' wood.' Some composers have written their horn - parts between the clarinet and bassoons, but the modern plan is to let them head the division of ' brass,' and below them to place

trumpets, trombones and tubas. Upon the staves between the last of the brass instruments and the first violin lines are placed the instruments of percussion, generally beginning with the ordinary drums, and including such things as triangles, tambourines, big drum, side drum, cymbals, etc. The staves for the harp or harps are generally placed in this division, often below the big drum line. As a rule assistance is given to the reader's or conductor's eye by not carrying the bar-lines through all the staves, but leaving spaces in the vertical lines between the various groups of instruments. In a well-edited score, while the whole is joined together at the beginning of each page and the groups are indicated by thicker vertical lines, the bar-divisions will be continuous from the piccolo line to that of the double bassoon, and from the first horn line to that of the bass tuba ; each instrument of percussion will have its own bar-lines to itself, and the three upper strings will be joined in their bar-lines. If solo parts and a double chorus are employed, each solo part will have its separate bar-lines, and each choir will have joined bar-lines. Lastly, the violoncello and double-bass part will be barred together. With every kind of difference in detail, this arrangement has continued in use from the classical days to our own, the change of place in the drum-line being the most important alteration.

The following arrangement (with English nomenclature) of the score of Gustav Holst's suite ' The Planets ' (' Mars ') is representative of modern practice :

2 Piccolos.
2 Flutes.
2 Oboes.
English horn (cor anglais).
Bass oboe.
3 Clarinets in B♭.
Bass clarinet in B♭.
3 Bassoons.
Double bassoon.
6 horns in F 　{ I., II., III., / IV., V., VI. } (2 staves).
4 trumpets in C 　{ I., II., / III., IV. } (2 staves).
2 Tenor trombones.
Bass trombone.
Tenor tuba in B♭.
Bass tuba.

6 Timpani (two players). 　(These notes showing the tuning placed outside the score. Bass clef implied.)

Side drum ⎫
Cymbals ⎪
Bass drum ⎬ (Single line each.)
Gong ⎭
Harp I. ⎫
Harp II. ⎬ (2 braced staves each.)
Organ (2 braced staves.)
Strings (1st vlns., 2nd vlns., vlas., v'celli., double basses : 5 staves).

For specimens of arrangement of scores for military band see WIND BAND. (Compare also ORCHESTRATION.)　　　　m. ; addns. c.

SCORING, the art of ORCHESTRATION (*q.v.*).

SCOTCH SNAP or CATCH is the name given to the reverse of the ordinary dotted note which has a short note after it—in the snap the short note comes first and is followed by the long one. It is characteristic of the slow STRATHSPEY (*q.v.*), rather than of vocal music,

[1] The grouping of the strings at the foot of the score was by no means invariable even as late as the 19th century. The autograph of Schubert's unfinished symphony has the following arrangement, reading from top to bottom : Vlns., vla., ii., ob., clar., fag., corni, clarinii (trumpets), tymp., tromboni, v'cl., bass. (See facsimile, Drei Masken Verlag.)　　　c.

though as Burns and others wrote songs to some of these dance-tunes, it is not infrequently found in connexion with words. 'Green grow the rashes,' 'Roy's wife,' and 'Whistle o'er the lave o't,' contain examples of the snap.

It was in great favour with many of the Italian composers of the 18th century, for Burney—who seems to have invented the name —says in his account of the Italian Opera in London, in 1748, that there was at this time too much of the 'Scots catch or cutting short of the first of two notes in a melody.' He blames Cocchi, Perez and Jommelli 'all three masters concerned in the opera " Vologeso "' for being lavish of the snap.                    J. M. W.

In the hands of Hook and the other purveyors of the pseudo-Scottish music, which was in vogue at Vauxhall and elsewhere in the 18th century, it became a senseless vulgarism, and with the exception of a few songs, such as those mentioned above, and the Strathspey reel in which it is an essential feature, its presence may generally be accepted as proof that the music in which it occurs is not genuine.     M.

SCOTCH SYMPHONY, THE, Mendelssohn's own name for his A minor symphony (op. 56) ; produced at a Gewandhaus Concert, Mar. 3, 1842 ; Philharmonic Society, London, June 13, 1842, Mendelssohn conducting.

SCOTT, CHARLES KENNEDY (b. Romsey, Nov. 16, 1876), has done important work as a choral conductor in London.

Scott studied at the Brussels Conservatoire where he took a first prize in organ-playing (1897). From the time that he settled in London (1898) he subordinated his personal career as performer or composer to the furtherance of English music, particularly of choral music. He founded the Oriana Madrigal Society in 1904, associated with it a scheme for the publication of English Madrigals (the 'Euterpe Series') and published a *Manual of Madrigal Singing*. Under his direction the Oriana Madrigal Society soon earned a high reputation as a small choir of picked voices pursuing a definite artistic ideal. The programmes devised by Scott have brought together the old music and the new, for his aim has been to perform whatever is of musical value irrespective of age or idiom. Scott took an active part in schemes for the advancement of national music, notably the concerts of Balfour GARDINER (q.v.) and the Glastonbury productions of opera by Rutland BOUGHTON (q.v.). In 1919 he formed and conducted the PHILHARMONIC CHOIR (q.v.), primarily for the performance of larger choral works with the Royal Philharmonic Society. Here his excellent training in choral technique has placed in the hands of visiting conductors a vocal body of equal competence with the Society's orchestra, but the choir has also given important programmes under his direction.     C.

SCOTT, CYRIL (b. Oxton, Cheshire, Sept. 27, 1879), composer and poet, began to play the piano by ear at a very early age. By the time he had reached his seventh year and learnt musical notation, he began to write down his immature attempts at composition. His mother, an excellent amateur musician, advocated a musical career for him, although his father was at first opposed to the idea.

At the age of 12 Scott was sent to Frankfort-on-Main, where he began to study the piano seriously at the Hoch Conservatoire, his general education being entrusted to a tutor. On his return to England this mode of instruction was continued at Liverpool, where he also perfected his piano-playing under Steudner-Welsing. At 16 he returned to Frankfort in order to take up the study of composition under Ivan Knorr. Among his fellow-students were Percy Grainger, Norman O'Neill and Roger Quilter. It was still the fashion at that time to send young British musicians to study in Germany, but Scott and his companions escaped the influence of a one-sided academicism by being placed under a professor whose sympathies extended beyond national boundaries, and especially to the Slavonic schools. Another influence which affected the young artist's outlook was that exercised on him by the poet Stefan George.

In 1898 Cyril Scott left Frankfort for the second time and took up his residence in Liverpool, where he gave a piano recital and received a few pupils. Here began a warm friendship with Charles Bonnier, at that time professor of French literature at the university, who made Scott acquainted with modern poetry and first awakened in him a desire to devote himself actively to that art. Scott wrote his first verses about 1900, and at that time his 'Heroic Suite' was performed by Richter at Liverpool and Manchester, and his first symphony at Darmstadt. Both works, together with some chamber music written at Frankfort, were later destroyed by the composer as unrepresentative.

The first London production of a work by Cyril Scott was that of the piano quartet in E minor at St. James's Hall in 1901, Kreisler playing the violin part. In 1903 Henry J. Wood produced the second symphony at the Promenade Concerts. Scott now began to produce a good deal of work, and was soon encouraged in his activities by the firm of Elkin & Co., who entered into contract with him for the publication of his songs and smaller piano pieces. Schott & Co. followed suit in 1909 with an agreement covering violin pieces and piano works on a larger scale.

It is by no means irrelevant to mention the deep interest which the composer began to take in Oriental philosophy and theosophy about this time, for with it his musical style underwent a marked change. Tonality, diatonic scales and regular rhythmic periods were not discarded for good and all, since Scott desired to enlarge his means of expression rather than to éxchange old conventions for new formulas, but they were regarded by him as inessential, and he began to write music without any key signature and with an elaborate method of irregular barring that fixed down the main accents of his long and free melodic lines. The first important works in this new style were the sonata for violin and piano, written between 1908–10, and the sonata for piano, which belongs to the same period. About this time Scott began a composition on a still larger scale, the ' Nativity Hymn ' for chorus and orchestra, which is preceded by the ' Christmas Overture ' for orchestra alone. The ' Aubade ' for orchestra and the ' Tallahassee Suite ' for violin and piano belong to the year 1911, and the reconstruction of the piano quintet from an older sextet is approximately contemporary with these two works.

In 1913 Scott was invited to Vienna by Gustav Mahler's widow, and the overture to Maeterlinck's ' Princesse Maleine ' was given there with such success that a performance of the ' Nativity Hymn ' and ' Christmas Overture ' was contemplated for the following year, but frustrated by the European War.

At the British Music Festival organised in London by Thomas Beecham in 1915, the piano concerto, written in 1913–14, was heard for the first time, with the composer in the solo part. The same conductor introduced the ' Two Passacaglias on Irish Themes ' at one of the Royal Philharmonic Society's concerts in 1916. A setting of Keats's ' La Belle Dame sans Merci ' for chorus and orchestra was composed in 1915–16. Scott afterwards entered, for the first time in his career, upon a phase of operatic composition. The first of his operas to be performed was ' The Alchemist,' produced at Essen on May 28, 1925, under the direction of Felix Wolfes.

The art of Cyril Scott in its mature stages has an unmistakably personal quality that is at once its merit and its limitation. He rightly prefers to achieve self-expression in a somewhat constricted idiom to the imitation of even the greatest models at the expense of his individuality, but it must be confessed that he does not always escape the danger of his idiosyncrasies hardening into mechanical mannerisms or of going over the same ground several times with only a surface appearance of striking out in a new direction. It is no doubt his way of applying principles which are new and highly distinctive at first, but afterwards tend to become stereotyped formulas, that has deluded some critics into making too much of a supposed likeness between his art and that of Debussy : in actual fact, though their manner of envisaging their tasks may be the same, its results are utterly dissimilar in practice.

The secret of a certain sameness of flavour almost throughout Scott's work lies probably in its predominantly harmonic character. His treatment of each note in the chromatic scale as a unit not dependent on a certain position in relation to a tonic root is immensely fertile in novel chord formations and chord sequences, but his music is on the other hand comparatively poor in variety of texture. Even in the string quartet, the medium to which contrapuntal writing is most indispensable, there is an extraordinary amount of part-writing in vertically parallel groupings. But it must be borne in mind that these limitations are part and parcel of the particular nature of his work : he is by no means incapable of submitting his characteristic methods to the discipline of the most exacting forms of thematic treatment, as is proved by such things as the two ' passacaglias ' for orchestra and the fugue in t<sup>h</sup> second suite for piano, where he adapts elaborate polyphonic devices to his special requirements with a mastery that is none the less complete for its independence of classical models.

Scott has a highly developed sense of secondary and tertiary harmonic colours. He blends his chords and lets them succeed each other with such subtlety that to an ear once accustomed to his idiom the apparently most daring combinations appear not as dissonances, but as a new and finely calculated euphony. His melodic invention, when it is not made subordinate to the harmony, is little inferior to the latter. In his songs he often achieves a tunefulness that is both attractive and distinctive, and the long-drawn melodic curves in some of his larger works, which breathe freely under the composer's unrestricted barring, are highly original in contour, phrasing and accentuation.

In respect of form, Scott's work rests on a solid classical foundation, but he applies the conventional patterns of the sonata, the rondo, the passacaglia, etc., to his own uses by accommodating them to the need of each work. He may leave himself free to string together what movements he pleases by making use of the suite, or he may organise a sonata form that varies the classical model according to a no less logical plan of his own. The cyclic sonata form has also advanced in his hands, as may be seen from the finale in the violin sonata, where he does not merely recall a motto theme, but sums up much of the principal material previously used. In the matter of orchestral colour, Scott is often fastidious to the verge of preciosity. The curious orchestration of his piano concerto, for instance, where harp, celesta and glockenspiel reinforce almost incessantly the cold glitter of the solo part, may seem as cloying to some temperaments as a perpetual redolence of incense. But though one may be enervated by the languorous scents that frequently pervade Scott's orchestration as well as his harmony, it is impossible ever to call their quality in question. He is too much of a sensitive musical poet to indulge in cheap effects · there is on the contrary a certain over-refinement about his style which at times imparts to it an almost morbid delicacy.

Many of Scott's smaller works, especially among the piano pieces and songs, have become exceedingly popular in Great Britain, but his larger compositions have been more frequently produced abroad, especially in Germany and Austria. His dramatic work is interesting for its independence of Wagnerian or any other models. The only published score so far (1926) is that of 'The Alchemist,' which shows a laudable tendency to return to a purely musical treatment that avoids any kind of pictorial duplication of what is already sufficiently clearly conveyed by the action.

E. B.

### LIST OF WORKS

EARLY WORKS NOW WITHDRAWN.—'Heroic Suite,' orch. ; Overture to 'Aglavaine et Sélysette' ; Overture to 'Pelléas et Mélisande' ; Symphony No. 1 ; Symphony No. 2 (now 'Three Symphonic Dances ') ; Trio, vln., v'cl. and PF.

ORCHESTRA.—'Aubade' ; 'Christmas Overture' ; Concerto, PF. and orch. ; Concerto. vln. and orch. ; Two Passacaglias on Irish Themes ; Rhapsody ; 'Souvenir de Vienne' ; 'Three Symphonic Dances' (new version of 2nd Symphony).

VOCAL WORKS WITH ORCHESTRA.—'La Belle Dame sans Merci,' chorus and orch. ; Nativity Hymn, chorus and orch. ; Overture to 'Princesse Maleine,' orch. and final chorus ; 'The Ballad of Fair Helen of Kirkconnel,' bar. and orch.

CHAMBER MUSIC.—Quartet, E minor, vln., vla., v'cl. and PF. ; Quintet, PF. and strs. (originally a sextet) ; String Quartet (suite) ; Trio, vln., v'cl. and PF.

VIOLIN AND PIANO. — 'Trois Danses tristes' ; Two Preludes ; Settings of 'Cherry Ripe' and 'The Gentle Maiden' ; Sonata ; Two Sonnets ; 'Tallahassee' Suite, etc.

VIOLA AND PIANO.—Fantasia.

VIOLONCELLO AND PIANO.—'Pierrot amoureux.'

FLUTE AND PIANO.—'Scotch Pastoral' ; 'The Ecstatic Shepherd.'

PIANO SOLO.—'Egypt,' Suite ; Two Etudes ; Handelian Rhapsody ; 'Impressions from the Jungle Book' ; 'Indian Suite' ; Modern Finger Exercises ; 'Pastoral Suite' ; Five Poems ; 'Rondeau de Concert' ; 'Russian Suite' ; Sonata ; 2nd Suite ; and about 100 small pieces, including 'Two Alpine Sketches,' 'Chimes,' 'Columbine,' 'Danse nègre,' 'Diatonic Study,' 'Irish Reel,' 'Lotus Land,' 'Over the Prairie,' 'Pierrette,' 'Prélude solennel,' 'Rainbow Trout,' 'Sphinx,' 'Vesperale,' 'Water-Wagtail' etc.

SONGS.—About 80 Songs including 'A Blackbird Song,' 'A Gift of Silence,' 'An Old Song ended,' 'And so I made a Villanelle,' 'Two Chinese Songs,' 'Daffodils,' 'Love's Aftermath,' 'Love's Quarrel,' 'Lullaby,' 'My Captain,' 'Old Songs in New Guise,' Pierrot and the Moon Maiden,' 'Scotch Lullaby,' etc.

VOICE AND SOLO INSTRUMENTS.—'Idyll,' voice and flute ; 'Idyllic Fantasy,' voice, oboe and v'cl.

DRAMATIC WORKS.—' Smetse Smee,' play with incidental music on Dutch and Flemish folk-songs ; 'The Alchemist,' opera ; 'The Incompetent Apothecary,' ballet ; 'The Saint of the Mountain,' opera ; 'The Shrine,' opera.

BIBL.—A. EAGLEFIELD HULL, *Cyril Scott, Composer, Poet and Philosopher* ; CYRIL SCOTT, *My Years of Indiscretion* ; *The Philosophy of Modernism in its Connection with Music.*

SCOTT, JOHN (*b. circa* 1776 ; *d.* Spanish Town, Jamaica, 1815), nephew of John Sale, jun., was a chorister of St. George's Chapel, Windsor, and Eton College ; afterwards studied the organ under William Sexton, organist of St. George's, Windsor, and became deputy for Dr. Arnold at Westminster Abbey. He was also chorus-master and pianist at Sadler's Wells. On the erection of the first organ in Spanish Town, Jamaica, he went out as organist, and died there. He was composer

of a well-known anthem, 'Praise the Lord, O Jerusalem,' and a famous comic song, 'Abraham Newland,'[1] has been ascribed to him (see ROGUE'S MARCH). This composition, however, was more commonly ascribed to Tipton, a Vauxhall writer, and was written about the end of the 18th century. W. H. H. ; rev. F. K.

SCOTT, LADY JOHN DOUGLAS (*b.* 1810 ; *d.* Spottiswoode, Mar. 12, 1900), an amateur composer of Scottish songs. Born Alicia Ann Spottiswoode, she was the eldest daughter of John Spottiswoode, of Spottiswoode in Berwickshire. On Mar. 16, 1836, she married Lord John Montague-Douglas Scott (son of the fourth Duke of Buccleuch, *d.* 1860). In 1870, under the will of her father, she resumed her maiden name.

Her best claim to remembrance, musically, is her composition of the song 'Annie Laurie,' which was first published without composer's name in the third volume of Paterson and Roy's 'Vocal Melodies of Scotland' in 1838. So popular was the song during the Crimean War, that a letter from the composer herself, in her last years, by mistake refers to it as being composed about that period. It may be added that the words are altered from a song first published in *A Ballad Book* collected by Charles Kirkpatrick Sharpe, and privately issued in 1824. A few other of her songs gained but scant favour, although she is sometimes credited with being the composer or adapter of 'The Banks of Loch Lomond,' a Scottish song still much sung.

Throughout her life she upheld the ancient Scottish customs in a manner verging on eccentricity. F. K.

SCOTT-GATTY, SIR ALFRED SCOTT (*b.* Ecclesfield, Yorks, Apr. 26, 1847 ; *d.* London, Dec. 18, 1918), Garter Principal King-of-Arms, was an amateur musician, whose songs had a great vogue in their day by reason of their unaffected melody and simple, if untutored, style. His earliest work appeared in *Aunt Judy's Magazine,* edited by his mother, Mrs. Alfred Gatty. He contributed to the German Reed entertainments, and later brought out several musical plays for children and the more ambitious 'Tattercoats,' produced for charity at the Savoy Theatre in 1900. He founded the MAGPIE MADRIGAL SOCIETY (*q.v.*) in 1886. He was appointed Rouge Dragon Pursuivant of Arms at the College of Heralds in 1880, becoming York Herald in 1886 and Garter in 1904, and was knighted the same year.

N. C. G.

SCOTTI, ANTONIO (*b.* Naples, 1869), baritone singer, made his first appearance on the stage at Malta on Nov. 1, 1889. He steadily won the favour of the public, and following upon successful engagements in Milan, Rome, Buenos Ayres and Madrid he came to London

[1] Abraham Newland was the Chief Cashier of the Bank of England.

in 1899, and appeared at Covent Garden as Don Giovanni on June 8. In that winter he went to New York, appeared at the Metropolitan in the same part on Dec. 27 and in his first season firmly established his position as one of the leading baritones of the day. For the next fifteen years his career was divided between London and New York, where, particularly in association with Caruso, his fame increased in a great variety of parts, notably Rigoletto, Iago, Amonasro (in ' Aïda '), the Baron Scarpia in ' Tosca,' Tonio in ' Pagliacci ' and the Count in ' Le Nozze di Figaro.' Subsequently New York became his headquarters, and besides singing constantly at the Metropolitan he toured with his own company in 1919–20.

Scotti was taught singing by Madame Trifari Payanini (*d.* 1908)—herself a pupil of the elder Lamperti—and has expressed in print his great indebtedness to her skill. Like many other singers before him he was a little impatient at being kept back in his young days, but when at last the opportunity of doing heavy dramatic work came to him he recognised the wisdom of his teacher's methods, his carefully placed voice being equal to all reasonable demands upon it. s. h. p. ; rev. o.

**SCOTTISH NATIONAL MUSIC.** Of Scottish national or folk music no specimens exist before the early part of the 17th century. That Scotland was a musical nation there is no denying, and we have every reason to believe that it was in no way lacking in musical beauty as the later examples show. Indeed there is strong evidence that many of the tunes which did not see the light of print until the 18th century are of a very much earlier date though lack of printed or manuscript notation leaves us in the dark for positive proof.

There are many early entries in royal and other accounts showing that musical performances were frequent, but there is nothing to show that these performances were of native music ; the contrary seems to be the case, and that English, French or other fashionable compositions were rendered. Meanwhile we have the strong belief that Scottish folk-music, ran as it did in England, a silent stream ignored by the cultured musician.

The first light we have on Scottish national music is provided by the Skene Manuscript, a set of seven small volumes now bound together which belonged to John Skene of Hallyard who died in 1644. It is probable that he was responsible for the notation of the tunes. It is believed to have been written between the years 1615 and 1635. It is written in tablature for a lute with six strings. It is now in the Advocates' Library, Edinburgh ; it contains 114 airs. (See LIBRARIES.)

The next early manuscript of Scottish music is the Straloch Manuscript, also in tablature, dated 1627. There are several other manu-scripts of lesser importance. The Straloch MS. was formerly in the possession of Burney and a copy of the Scottish airs in it was made by G. F. Graham in 1839, since which time the original has disappeared. Graham's copy is in the Advocates' Library.

It must be premised that the Straloch and the Skene manuscripts do not contain only Scottish airs. There are many tunes which are English and some nondescript pieces which have no historical value. It was not until the early years of the 18th century that Scottish tunes began to be preserved in any quantity. The late John Glen possessed an important manuscript book, ' Margaret Sinkler's Book,' 1710, which contains over 100 early versions of Scottish airs. Some other manuscripts might be mentioned, but historically they are not so important as the above named.

There are two early works that bear upon the subject of Scottish Song : Wedderburn's 'Complainte of Scotland,' 1548, and ' Ane Compendious Booke of Godly and Spirituall Songs,' 1621. In the first is a list of names of songs sung by shepherds, some of which are English. The second is a collection of hymns set to secular tunes, mostly Scottish. In Verstegan's *Restitution of Decayed Intelligence*, 1605, there is mentioned a Scottish woman ' dandling her child to sing " Bothwell Bank thou blumest fayre." '

Several more instances of early Scottish songs might be cited, but little can be gathered regarding the music fitted to the songs.

In 1662 John Forbes of Aberdeen published his *Cantus Songs and Fancies, to three, foure or five parts.* Later editions bear the dates 1666 and 1682. The book has extracts from some English publications and has really little bearing upon Scottish national music.

Towards the end of the 17th century Scottish songs began to appear on half-sheets engraved by T. Cross, and in the early editions of *Pills to purge Melancholy* and elsewhere many attempts to produce songs in the Scots manner came forth. It was quite a fashionable craze and the best musicians of to-day composed songs in this manner.

The first printed book of Scottish tunes was issued by Henry Playford in 1700 with a second edition dated 1701. Its title runs :

' A collection of original Scotch tunes (full of the highland humours) for the violin being the first of this kind yet printed, 1700.'

There are 39 tunes contained in the volume.

In 1724 Allan Ramsay issued the first volume of his *Tea Table Miscellany* which contains a selection of Scottish songs. In 1726 he published a small oblong work, *Musick for Allan Ramsay's Collection of Scots Songs.* In 1725 appeared the first collection of Scottish songs fitted to the music. This is, *Orpheus Caledonius,* arranged by William Thomson, a singer under court favour. There are fifty airs with an added bass and the long list of subscribers shows that the singing of Scottish songs was popular.

In 1733 he published a second edition in two volumes, containing 100 songs and airs.

In the first edition of *Orpheus Caledonius* there are several tunes marked as by Rizzio. This assumption has been ridiculed, but further consideration will show that though the airs claimed are quite unlikely to be the composition of Rizzio, yet there can be but little doubt that Rizzio as a favoured court musician may have had a certain influence upon the style of composition. In fact some of the tunes are far more scholarly than those which have come from a peasant class.

The bibliography appended to the end of the article will show that a great deal of Scottish national music took the form of REELS and STRATHSPEYS (*q.v.*), the national dances of the country. Many of the Scottish fiddlers issued collections of these dances of their own composition and of traditional airs.

The Gow family were the principal of these and their collections are extremely valuable as they contain not only the composition of the family but many beautiful airs which have come down traditionally.     F. K.

### SCOTTISH SCALES AND THEIR MELODIES

The existence of Scottish airs constructed on the series 1, 2, 3, 5, 6 of a major diatonic scale is well known.[1] These are not by any means numerous, though their characteristic leap between the third and fifth, and sixth and eighth of the scale, is so common in Scottish melody, that many persons not only believe the greater part of our airs to be pentatonic, but do not admit any others to be Scottish. However the taste for this style may have arisen, the series of notes was a very convenient one, for an instrument possessing the major diatonic scale in one key only could play these airs correctly in the three positions of the scale where major thirds are found, that is, on the first, fourth, and fifth degrees. In the key of C, these are as shown below, adding the octave to the lowest note of the series in each case.

*Pentatonic scale in three positions, without change of signature.*

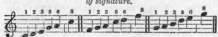

If, reversing the order of the notes given above, we begin with the sixth, and passing downwards add the octave below, the feeling of a minor key is established, and keys of A, D, and E minor seem to be produced. Besides tunes in these six keys, a few others will be found, which begin and end in G minor (signature two flats), though also played with natural

[1] This pentatonic scale is the basis of much primitive folk-music. Cf. NEGRO MUSIC.

notes; for B and E being avoided in the melody neither of the flats is required.

A curious peculiarity of tunes written in this series is, that from the proximity of the second and third positions phrases move up and down from one into the other, thus appearing to be alternately in the adjoining keys a full tone apart, moving for example from G into F and *vice versa*. The following are good examples of the style :

(1) *Gala Water.*

(2) *Were na my heart licht I wad die.*

(3) *The bridegroom grat.*

When the sheep are in the fauld & the kye at hame, And
a' the warld to sleep are gane, The waes o' my heart fa' in
show'rs frae my e'e, While my gudeman lies sound by me.

The first, 'Gala Water,' is one of the most beautiful of our melodies. The modern version of it contains the seventh of the scale more than once, but Oswald has preserved the old pentatonic version in his *Caledonian Pocket Companion* (1759–65). That version is here given in the large type, the small type showing the modern alterations. The air may be played correctly beginning on E, on A, or on B, representing the third of the keys of C, F and G ; but neither flat nor sharp is required in any of the positions, the notes being all natural throughout.

The second is the melody to which Lady Grizel Baillie wrote (1692) her beautiful ballad, 'Were na my heart licht, I wad die.' It is a very simple, unpretending tune, and is given chiefly on account of its close ; indeed, both of these tunes are peculiar, and worth more detailed discussion that can be given them here.

The third is the old tune which was so great a favourite with Lady Anne Lyndsay that she wrote for it her celebrated ballad ' Auld Robin Gray.' Although it has been superseded by a very beautiful modern English air, it ought not to be entirely forgotten.

Another exceedingly beautiful pentatonic melody is that to which Burns wrote ' O meikle thinks my love o' my beauty.' It will be found in E minor in the ' Select Songs of Scotland,' by Sir G. A. Macfarren ; but it may also be played in D minor and A minor, in each case without either flat or sharp being required in the melody.

The use of the pentatonic scale in our early music must gradually have ceased, through acquaintance with the music of the church service, which had its singularly complete diatonic system of modes. The complete diatonic scale, which we find in the simple shepherd's pipe or recorder, is really that on which our older melodies are formed. The pitch note might be D or G, or any other, but the scale would be the ordinary major diatonic with the semitones between the 3rd and 4th and 7th and 8th degrees. The key of C is that adopted in the following remarks. With scarcely an exception the old tunes keep steadily to this scale without the use of any accidental. It will also be seen that the pathos produced by means of the 4th of the key, is a clever adaptation of a necessity of the scale. ' The Flowers of the Forest'—fortunately preserved in the Skene MS. —is a fine example of the skill with which the composer used the means at his disposal. The first strain of the air is in G major, as will be seen if it be harmonised, though no F sharp was possible on the instrument ; in the second strain, no more affecting wail for the disaster of Flodden could have been produced than that effected by the use of the F♮, the 4th of the

*The Flowers of the Forest.*    Ancient Version.

scale of the instrument, the minor 7th of the original key. With his simple pipe the composer has thus given the effect of two keys.

It may be objected that the voice was not tied down to the notes of an imperfect instrument, and could take semitones wherever it felt them to be wanted ; but in the process of transmission the untutored singers, happily ignorant of musical science, adhere rigidly to the original forms of the scales in which they sing.

The same effect of playing in two keys occurs in ' O waly waly ! love is bonnie, a little while when it is new,' but in most modern versions of

the melody both the F♮ and F♯ are found : this was not possible on the primitive instrument, though easy on the lute or violin.

*O waly waly.*

Any air which has the natural as well as the altered note may be set down as either modern, or as having been tampered with in modern times. The major seventh in a minor key is also a fairly good sign of modern writing or modern meddling. In a tune written otherwise in the old tonality, the occurrence of the major seventh sounds weak and effeminate when compared with the robust grandeur of the full tone below.

A few more examples may be given to show the mingling of the pentatonic with the completed scale. ' Adieu Dundee '—also found in the Skene MS.—is an example of a tune written as if in the natural key, and yet really in the Dorian mode.

*Adew Dundee.*

Another example is 'The wauking of the fauld,' which, played in the same key, has the same peculiarity in the 13th bar ; this, however, is the case only in modern versions of the air, for that given by Allan Ramsay in the *Gentle Shepherd* (1736) is without the E.

### Of the Gaelic Music

If the difficulty of estimating the age of the music of the Lowlands is great, it is as nothing compared to what is met with in considering that of the Highlands.

The Celts certainly had music even in the most remote ages, but as their airs had been handed down for so many generations solely by tradition, it may be doubted whether this music bore any striking resemblance to the airs collected between 1760 and 1780 by the Rev. Patrick Macdonald and his brother. The specimens given of the most ancient music are interesting mainly in so far as they show the kind of recitative to which ancient poems were chanted, for they have little claim to notice as melodies. The example here given is said to be ' Ossian's soliloquy on the death of all his contemporary heroes.'

Slow.

There are, however, many beautiful airs in the collection; they are simple, wild, and irregular; but their beauty has not a very wide appeal on a first hearing. Of the style of performance the editor says:

' These airs are sung by the natives in a wild, artless and irregular manner. Chiefly occupied with the sentiment and expression of the music, they dwell upon the long and pathetic notes, while they hurry over the inferior and connecting notes, in such a manner as to render it exceedingly difficult for a hearer to trace the measure of them. They themselves while singing them seem to have little or no impression of measure.'

This is more particularly the case with the very old melodies, which wander about without any attempt at rhythm, or making one part answer to another. The following air is an excellent example of the style:

*Wet is the night and cold.*

Slow.

In contrast to these are the ' Luinig ' and ' Jorram,' the former sung by the women at their work, the latter boat-songs.

Patrick Macdonald says ' the very simplicity of the music is a pledge of its originality and antiquity.' Judged by this criticism his versions of the airs seem much more authentic than those of his successors. Captain Fraser of Knockie, who published a very large and important collection of Highland airs in 1816, took much pains, in conjunction with a musical friend, to form what he terms a ' standard.' As he had no taste for the old tonality, he introduces the major seventh in minor keys, and his versions generally abound in semitones. He professed a liking for simplicity, and is not sparing of his abuse of MacGibbon and Oswald for their departures from it; yet his own turns and shakes and florid passages prove that he did not carry his theory into practice. As, however, a large portion of his volume is occupied with tunes composed during the latter part of the 18th and the beginning of the 19th century, in these it would be affectation to expect any other than the modern tonality. A specimen of what he calls an ancient Ossianic

air is given as a contrast to that selected from Patrick Macdonald. In style it evidently belongs to a date nearer to the times of MacPherson than to those of Ossian. Compare the ' soliloquy ' given above with the following:

*An air to which Ossian is recited.*

Slow.

It cannot be denied that though by his alterations of the forms of Gaelic melody Fraser may have rendered them more acceptable to his contemporaries, he has undoubtedly shorn the received versions of much of their claim to antiquity. The volume published by the Gaelic Society of London in 1876, though not faultless in regard to modern changes, has restored some of the old readings; one example ought to be quoted, for the air ' Mairi bhan og ' is very beautiful, and the F♮ in the fourth bar gives us back the simplicity and force of ancient times.

*Mairi bhan og.*   (Mary fair and young.)

Captain Fraser stigmatises the previous collections of Patrick Macdonald and Alexander Campbell (*Albyn's Anthology*) as very incorrect. But Fraser's own versions have in many cases been much altered in the second edition (1876), while more recent works differ most remarkably from earlier copies. The airs are evidently still in a plastic state—every glen, almost every family, seems to have its own version.

It is evident from the examples given by Patrick Macdonald that in the most ancient times Gaelic music was devoid of rhythm. The Ossianic chants are short and wild. They are succeeded by longer musical phrases, well suited it may be to heighten the effect of the Gaelic verse, but, apart from that, formless to a modern ear. From these emerge airs still wild and irregular, but with a certain sublimity arising from their very vagueness. Even when they become more rhythmic the airs do not at once settle down into phrases of twos and fours, but retain an easy indifference to regularity ; two alternating with three, four with five bars, and this in so charming a way that the ease and singularity are alone apparent. The air ' Morag ' may be cited ; other examples may be found in *Albyn's Anthology*, 1816–18, and in ' Orain na h-Albain,' an excellent collection of Gaelic airs made by Miss Bell and edited by Finlay Dun.                    J. M. W. ; addn. F. K.

### LATER COLLECTIONS

George THOMSON (*q.v.*) employed Pleyel, Kozeluh, Haydn, Beethoven, Weber and Hummel to harmonise and supply symphonies to the Scottish songs which comprised his published collections. The choice in all these instances was not very good. Beethoven appears to have been under the impression that the ' Scotch snap ' was characteristic of all Scottish music, whereas, really, it only naturally belongs to the strathspey, the reel and the Highland fling. Haydn, who seems truly to have had a liking for, and some knowledge of, Scottish vocal music, was certainly better fitted for the task ; he also arranged the two volumes of Scottish songs issued by Whyte in 1806–07.

Sir G. A. Macfarren's collection has already been spoken of, and an excellent set of twelve Scottish songs arranged by Max Bruch was published by Leuckart of Breslau. ' Songs of the North,' with the music arranged by Malcolm Lawson, had a great popularity, but many of the airs suffered a good deal in transmission, and several of them are to be found in a purer form in Macleod's 'Songs of a Highland Home.'

The virulent attack made by the late William Chappell on the claims advanced for the Scottish origin of certain airs cannot in every case be considered justifiable. There is much truth in what he advances, *i.e.* that a number of Anglo-Scottish songs of the 17th and 18th centuries have been too readily claimed as Scottish folk-songs, in spite of the fact that they have been sufficiently well ascertained to be the composition of well-known English musicians.[1]

It is, however, quite evident that Chappell's irritation has, on some points, led him astray,[2] for some of his statements can be proved to be wrong ; those for instance regarding ' Jenny's Bawbee,' ' Gin a body ' and ' Ye Banks and Braes ' and some others. That STENHOUSE (*q.v.*), up to Chappell's time the chief writer on the history of Scottish song, makes many lamentably incorrect assertions in his commentary on Johnson's *Scots Musical Museum* cannot be denied, but that he did so wilfully is quite unlikely. It must be remembered that Stenhouse was handicapped by being

four hundred miles from the British Museum Library, a storehouse which supplied Chappell so well, and, besides, Stenhouse's work was a pioneer, for his notes were begun in 1817.

Another class of music which now constitutes part of the national music of Scotland was the compositions of professional or semi-professional musicians. As the fiddle is the national instrument of Scotland, so the reel and the strathspey reel are the national dances. A great number of country musicians, particularly in the northern part of Scotland, composed and played these dance tunes for local requirements. These they named either after some patron or gave them a fanciful title. In many instances, by the aid of subscription, the musician was enabled to publish one or a series of his compositions, and so favourite dance tunes from these works were frequently reprinted and rearranged by other musicians.

Isaac Cooper of Banff, Daniel Dow, William Marshall and many other lesser-known composers, along with the Gow family, have thus enriched Scottish music. We must also remember that where one of this type of musicians has succeeded in getting his compositions into print, there may be many whose tunes have passed into local tradition namelessly, so far as composer is concerned. While there are a great many beautiful and purely vocal airs, yet these instrumental melodies have largely been used by song-writers in spite of their great compass ; this is one of the factors which makes Scottish song so difficult of execution to the average singer. ' Miss Admiral Gordon's Strathspey,' ' Miss Forbes' Farewell to Banff,' ' Earl Moira's welcome to Scotland,' with others, are well-known examples, and have been selected by Burns and other song-writers for their verses. Another notable one is ' Caller Herring,' which, composed by Nathaniel Gow as a harpsichord piece (one of a series) intended to illustrate a popular Edinburgh Cry, had its words fitted twenty years afterwards by Lady Nairne.

About 1820–30 many now well-known songs in the Scottish vernacular had their birth, possibly owing to the Waverley novels. Allan Ramsay was the first to collect the Scots songs into book form from tradition, and from printed ballad sheets and garlands. His first volume of *The Tea-Table Miscellany* was issued in 1724, three others following later. It is rather unfortunate, from an antiquarian point of view, that Ramsay and his friends were not content to leave them as collected, but imparted to many a then fashionable artificial flavour, while boasting in his dedication of the charming simplicity of the Scotch ditties.

In 1769 and 1776 David Herd rendered a more trustworthy account of traditional Scots song in the two volumes he published ; while Johnson's *Scots Musical Museum* of six hundred

---

[1] See Chappell, *Popular Music*, old edition, pp. 609-16, etc.
[2] John Glen in his *Early Scottish Melodies* has much to say regarding Chappell's attack.

songs, with the music, was the principal collection of the 18th century.

The following list comprises all the important collections of Scottish national music, including some early manuscripts which contain Scottish airs :

### BIBLIOGRAPHY

#### MANUSCRIPTS

*c.* 1612–28. The Rowallan MS. In lute tablature on a six-line stave, 50 pp. It belonged to, and was probably written by, Sir William Mure of Rowallan between the dates 1612 and 1628. It contains several Scottish airs, and is in the library of the Edinburgh University.

*c.* 1627–29. The Straloch MS. In lute tablature on a six-line stave. Contained Scottish and other airs. The original manuscript is now lost, but a copy of a portion of it was made by G. F. Graham and is in the Advocates' Library, Edinburgh (see STRALOCH MS.).

16——? The Skene MS. In tablature on a four-line stave. In the Advocates' Library (see SKENE MS.).

*c.* 1675–80. The Guthrie MS. In tablature; contains a number of Scottish airs, or, rather, as the late Mr. Glen pointed out, accompaniments for them. In the Edinburgh University.

1683–92. The Blaikie MSS. These two, in tablature for the viol da gamba, belonged to Andrew Blaikie of Paisley, a music-engraver, early in the 19th century. They bore dates as in the margin, but both manuscripts are now lost. Transcripts of portions of them are in the Wighton Library, Dundee.

16——? The Leyden MS. In tablature for the lyra viol. It belonged to Dr. John Leyden and is now lost. A transcript made by G. F. Graham is in the Advocates' Library. The contents are much the same as one of the Blaikie MSS. and is apparently of the same date. Another Leyden MS. is in the Advocates' Library, dated 1639, but this does not appear to contain Scottish airs.

1704. Agnes Hume's MS. dated 1704. In the Advocates' Library, ordinary notation.

1709. Mrs. Crockat's MS. Referred to by Stenhouse who once possessed it ; it is said to have been dated 1709, but it is now lost.

1710. Margaret Sinkler's MS. An oblong quarto volume of about a hundred airs, which formerly belonged to the late Mr. John Glen. It bears the date 1710, and is in ordinary notation.

1723–24. Cumming MS. A small volume of airs for the violin, dated 1723 on first leaf and 1724 on last, with the name of its original compiler, ' Patrick Cumming, Edinburgh.' It contains a number of Scotch airs, up to its date unpublished. In the possession of the present writer.

#### PRINTED AND ENGRAVED COLLECTIONS

Many Scots and Anglo-Scottish airs appear in Playford's ' Dancing Master,' 1650–1728, and other of Playford's publications; also in D'Urfey's ' Pills to purge Melancholy,' 1698–1720. At later dates a great number are also to be found in the London country-dance books of various publishers.

1662, 1666, 1682. Forbes. ' Cantus : Songs and Fancies to three, foure or five parts, both apt for voices and viols.' John Forbes, Aberdeen, 1662 ; 2nd ed., 1666 ; 3rd, 1682. The first book of secular music printed in Scotland. Contains several Scottish songs. A reprint of the 1682 ed. was issued by Gardner of Paisley in 1879.

1700–1. H. Playford. ' A Collection of Original Scotch Tunes (full of the Highland Humours) for the Violin.' London, H. Playford, 1700. 4to.
(A second edition with four more tunes issued with date of 1701. This is the first collection of Scottish airs named as such. There appears to be only one copy of each in existence. Mr. Inglis of Edinburgh holds the 1700 edition, and the British Museum Library the second edition. The work is printed from movable type.)

*c.* 1700–5. ' A Collection of Original Scotch Tunes for the Violin, the whole pleasant and comical, being full of the Highland Humour.' London, John Young.
(This, and another, with the same title published by John Hare, London, are obviously imitations of Playford's work. The one published by Young is in the library of an Edinburgh gentleman, and the other by Hare is mentioned and its contents noted in *Notes and Queries*, 5th series, vol. v. p. 503.)

1725. ' Orpheus Caledonius or a Collection of the best Scotch Songs set to musick by W. Thomson.' London, for the author. Folio, n.d.
(Entered at Stationers' Hall, Jan. 5, 1725. The first collection of Scotch songs with their airs. The book contains fifty songs. See separate article, Vol. III. p. 774.)

*c.* 1726. Musick for Allan Ramsay's Collections of Scots Songs set by Alexander Stuart.' Edinburgh. Sm. ob., n.d.
(This was intended to provide the airs for the songs in the *Tea-Table Miscellany*.)

1730. Craig. ' A Collection of the choicest Scots Tunes adapted for the Harpsichord or Spinnet . . . by Adam Craig.' Edinburgh, 1730. Ob. folio.

1733. ' Orpheus Caledonius.' Second edition, Edinburgh, 1733. 2 vols. 8vo. [100 songs.]
(The first volume is practically identical with the first edition. The second volume is additional matter, being fifty more songs with the music.)

1740. Oswald, James. ' A Curious Collection of Scots Tunes for a Violin, Bass viol or German flute . . . by James Oswald, musician in Edinbr.' Ob. folio, *c.* 1740.
(This is, in all probability, the first of the many volumes

of Scots music issued by Oswald. When he arrived in London this work was re-engraved, and with another volume published by John Simpson.)

*c.* 1742. ' A Collection of Curious Scots Tunes for a Violin, German flute or Harpsichord.' By Mr. James Oswald. London, J. Simpson.
' A Second Collection of Curious Scots Tunes for a Violin, etc.' (see above ; both were advertised in 1742).

*c.* 1742–60. Oswald, James. ' The Caledonian Pocket Companion.' London. 12 books, 8vo.
(This important publication of Scottish airs was commenced about 1742–43, and ultimately reached to twelve books about 1760. The first numbers were published by J. Simpson, others by the author, and the whole was reprinted by Straight and Skillern.)

17——? Oswald. ' A Collection of 43 Scots Tunes with Variations . . . by James Oswald.' London, Bland and Weller.
(Originally issued at a much earlier date than these publishers.)

*c.* 1761–62. Oswald. ' A Collection of the best old Scotch and English Songs set for the voice . . . by James Oswald, chamber composer to His Majesty.' London, n.d.

1742. Barsanti. ' A Collection of old Scots Tunes, with a bass for Violoncello or Harpsichord . . . by Francis Barsanti.' Edinburgh, n.d. 4to.

1742, 1746, 1755. M'Gibbon. ' A Collection of Scots Tunes. Some with variations for a Violin, Hautboy or German Flute . . . by Wm. M'Gibbon.' Edinburgh. Ob. folio, 1742. Second collection, 1746. Third, 1755.
(Afterwards reprinted by N. Stewart, Bremner and Rutherford.)

*c.* 1745. Twelve Scotch and Twelve Irish Airs with variations . . . . by Mr. Burk Thumoth.' London, J. Simpson. 8vo.

1757. Bremner, Robert. ' Thirty Scots Songs for a voice and harpsichord . . . the words by Allan Ramsay.' Edinburgh, R. Bremner. Folio, n.d.
' A Second set of Scots Songs.' Bremner. *c.* 1759.
(These two, originally published at Edinburgh, were afterwards reprinted with Bremner's London imprint, and again reprinted by Stewart of Edinburgh with a 3rd vol. added.)

1759. Bremner, R. ' A Collection of Scots Reels and Country Dances.' Ob. 4to, n.d.
(Issued in numbers 1759 to 1761.)

1759. Bremner, R. ' A Curious Collection of Scots Tunes.' Edinburgh, R. Bremner. Ob. folio, n.d.
(Afterwards reprinted by Ding of Edinburgh.)

1762. Peacock. ' Fifty favourite Scots Airs for a Violin . . . with a Thoroughbass for the Harpsichord.' Francis Peacock, Aberdeen. Folio, n.d.

1761–62. Stewart, Neil. ' A Collection of the newest and best Reels and Country Dances.' Edinburgh, Neil Stewart. Ob. 4to, n.d.

*c.* 1762. A New Collection of Scots and English Tunes, adapted to the Guitar.' Edinburgh, N. Stewart. Ob. 4to.
' A Collection of Scots Songs adapted for a Voice and Harpsichord.' Edinburgh, N. Stewart. Folio.

1772. M'Lean. ' A Collection of favourite Scots Tunes with Variations for the Violin . . . by Chs. M'Lean and other eminent masters.' Edinburgh, Stewart. Ob. folio.

*c.* 1775. ' A Collection of Ancient Scots Music for the Violin, Harpsichord or German Flute, never before printed.' Daniel Dow, Edinburgh. Ob. folio.
(Dow published about this time two other collections of his own compositions, ' Thirty-seven Reels ' and ' Twenty Minuets.')

1780. Cumming, Angus. ' A Collection of Strathspey or Old Highland Reels by Angus Cumming.' Edinburgh. Ob. folio, 1780.
(A later edition is dated 1782.)

1780. M'Glashan. ' A Collection of Strathspey Reels,' by Alexander M'Glashan. Ob. folio.

1781. ——' A Collection of Scots Measures.' Alexander M'Glashan. Ob. folio.

1786. ——' A Collection of Reels.' Alex. M'Glashan. Ob. folio.

1775? Aird, James. ' A Selection of Scotch, English, Irish and Foreign airs adapted to the fife, violin or German flute.' Glasgow, Jas. Aird. 6 books, small oblong.
(This series of books is important in the matter of Scottish and Irish music. The first two were issued about 1775, the 3rd in 1782, the 4th 1788, 5th 1794, 6th 1797 and the 7th early in the 19th century.)

1787–1803. Johnson, James. ' The Scots Musical Museum.' Edinburgh, James Johnson. 6 vols. 8vo.
(This important work consists mainly of Scots songs collected by Johnson and his friends from printed and other sources. Burns interested himself in the publication, and some of his songs were here first issued with music. The first vol. was published in 1787, 2nd 1788, 3rd 1790, 4th 1792, 5th 1797, 6th 1803.)

Gow. (The publications of the Gow family have a strong bearing on the subject of Scottish music. Niel Gow the father and Nathaniel the son composed, arranged and adapted a great deal of what now constitutes Scottish national music. Their sheet publications are innumerable, and their collections of Strathspey reels and vocal melodies are named in Vol. II. at p. 427 of the present work.)

Later collections of Scottish songs with music were those issued by Wm. Napier, 3 vols., 1790–92 ; Corri, 2 vols., *c.* 1790 ; Urbani, 6 vols., *c.* 1792, 1794, 1799, 1800, 1805 ; Dales, ' Sixty Favourite Scottish Songs,' 3 vols. (180 songs), *c.* 1794–95 ; George Thomson's collections, 1793, etc. (see separate articles) ; Whyte, 2 vols., 1806–07 ; J. Elouis, 2 vols., 1806–07 ; R. A. Smith, ' Scotish Minstrel,' 6 vols., 1820–24, 8vo ; Paterson and Roy, ' Vocal Melodies of Scotland,' 4 vols., 1837–38. Among annotated collections of Scottish music, the following are noteworthy : ' Scotish Songs in two Volumes [Joseph Ritson], 1794, 8vo (reprinted in 1869) ; Wood's Songs of Scotland,' edited by G. F. Graham, 3 vols. 1848, etc., 8vo ; ' The Lyric Gems of Scotland,' Cameron, Glasgow, 2 vols., sm. 4to, 1856 ; ' The Select Songs of Scotland,' Hamilton, Glasgow, folio, 1857 ; ' The Songs of Scotland, prior to Burns,' Chambers, 1862, 8vo.

* The Minstrelsy of Scotland,' Alfred Moffat, Augener, 1895 ; ' Early Scottish Melodies,' John Glen, 1900, 8vo ; ' The Glen Collection of Scottish dance music,' 1891–95; John Glen, 2 vols., folio. Jacobite songs are best represented in Hogg's ' Jacobite Relics,' 1819–21, 2 vols. 8vo (reprinted in 1874) ; Gaelic music is found scattered through Gow's publications and other collections of Scottish dance music, and elsewhere, but the best-known gatherings into volume form are—Rev. Peter M'Donald's ' Highland Airs,' folio [1783] ; Simon Fraser's ' Airs and Melodies, peculiar to the Highlands and Islands of Scotland,' 1816, folio (reprinted 1876) ; Alexander Campbell's ' Albyn's Anthology,' 1816–18, 2 vols., folio ; ' Orain na h-Albain,' collected by Miss G. A. Bell, Edinburgh, c. 1840 ; ' A Treatise on the Language, Poetry and Music of the Highland Clans,' Donald Campbell, Edinburgh, 1867, 8vo ; ' Ancient Orkney Melodies, collected by Col. Balfour,' 1885 ; ' The Minstrelsy of the Scottish Highlands,' Alfred Moffat, Bayley and Ferguson, Glasgow, 1907 ; ' Songs of the Hebrides ' (3 vols. Eng. and Gaelic text), 1909, 1917, 1921, collected by Marjorie Kennedy Fraser ; ' Last Leaves of Traditional Ballads and Ballad Airs,' collected in Aberdeenshire by the late Gavin Greig, 4to (The Buchan Club, Aberdeen, 1925), a very valuable book.

The above bibliography represents but a tithe of what might justly be included in it. Although there is much traditional Scottish music found among the quantity of dance collections issued by individual Scottish musicians it is difficult to classify it. Besides the Scottish publications enumerated above, the London country-dance books from the early part of the 18th century onward contain much interesting matter in connexion with both Scottish and Irish music. Walsh and others issued collections of Scottish songs and airs, but they were mainly taken from Thomson's ' Orpheus Caledonius.' His ' Caledonian country dances ' and those published by John Johnson are, however, of much antiquarian interest.

The attention recently paid to folk-song has brought forth enough evidence to show that the published Scottish national music is but a small proportion of what, even now, exists in a traditionary form. Gavin Greig, Miss Lucy Broadwood and other workers have, without much search, brought to light a wealth of Gaelic music of a purely traditional kind. In the Lowlands of Scotland folk-song exists as it does in England, and much of this lowland Scottish folk-song is either almost identical with that found in different parts of England or consists of variants of it. There is, of course, a certain proportion which may be classed as purely confined to Scotland.

One of the first of the modern attempts to tap this stream of traditional music was made by Dean Christie, who published his two volumes of *Traditional Ballad Airs* in 1876 and 1881. This collection of between three and four hundred tunes, noted down with the words in the north of Scotland, would have been much more valuable if the Dean had been content to present them exactly as noted. Another valuable contribution to the publication of Scottish folk-song is Robert Ford's *Vagabond Songs of Scotland,* first and second series, 1899 and 1900. In both these works folk-song as known in England is largely present. The New Spalding Club of Aberdeen in 1903 made an initial movement towards the rescue of traditional Scottish song. Gavin Greig (who is also a grantee under the Carnegie Trust given to the universities of Scotland for research work) was

commissioned to collect systematically in the north-east of Scotland. Greig's able paper, *Folk-Song in Buchan,* being part of the *Transactions of the Buchan Field Club,* gives some of the results of his labours. The Scottish National Song Society has also turned its attention to folk-song research.       F. K.

SCOTTISH ORCHESTRA, THE. The Scottish Orchestra Company, Limited, was formed in 1891 with the object of fostering the study and love of orchestral music in Scotland, and for the purpose of organising and maintaining an efficient orchestra available for concerts throughout Scotland. To this end a fully equipped band of eighty performers, named ' The Scottish Orchestra,' was recruited in 1893 under the leadership of Maurice Sons, and conducted by George Henschel. Its headquarters are in Glasgow ; and during the autumn and winter season concerts are given not only in Glasgow, but also in Edinburgh (in the latter city at the series of concerts under the management of Paterson & Sons), and less frequently at Aberdeen, Dundee, Dunfermline, Paisley, Greenock, and in many other towns, by this fine combination of players.

Apart from the presentation of purely orchestral compositions, the Scottish orchestra has frequently been associated with the principal Scottish choral societies in the production of important choral works. In 1895 Henschel resigned the post of conductor, and was succeeded first by Wilhelm Kes (1895–98), and later by Max Bruch (1898–1900), Frederic Cowen (1900–10), Mlynarski (1910–16), Landon Ronald (1916–20), Julius Harrison (1920–23). A system of inviting several conductors to take part in each season was then adopted until 1926, when TALICH (*q.v.*) undertook the winter season.

In the absence of the regular conductor, the Scottish Orchestra has played under the direction of many famous conductors, including Richard Strauss, Fritz Steinbach, Edouard Colonne, Hans Richter, Henry J. Wood, and others, and though, in accordance with the purpose for which it was founded, the appearances of this band are appropriately confined mainly to the country north of the Tweed, it has played in London, Leeds, Newcastle, Huddersfield and elsewhere.       R. F. M<sup>C</sup>E.

SCRIABIN, ALEXANDER NICHOLAEVICH, (*b.* Moscow, Jan. 10, 1872, O.S. Dec. 29, 1871 ; *d.* there, Apr. 1/14, 1915), composer and pianist.

He received his early education in the Cadet Corps, but afterwards, abandoning the military career for music, entered the Moscow Conservatoire, where he studied composition under Taneiev and piano under Safonov and gained a gold medal in 1892. Having completed his course at the Conservatoire he went abroad, and won considerable reputation both as pianist and composer in Paris. Brussels. Amsterdam and other cities. From 1898–1904 he was professor of pianoforte at the Moscow Conservatoire, but after that date devoted himself almost exclusively to composition, and soon came to be regarded as one of the most gifted of the younger Russian composers. Like Chopin, by whom he was influenced in early life, he seemed at first to be attracted to the smaller musical forms. His early pianoforte works are delicate and poetical. In his larger compositions he followed the orchestration of Wagner rather than of Glinka. Literary influences counted for a great deal in his development. Vague religious, philosophical and æsthetic ideas were disseminated in Russia at the beginning of the century by the modernist movement, led by Merejskovsky and the poet Vyacheslav - Ivanov. They found their way into painting through the musician-painter Churlianis, and into music through Scriabin. But although the influence of Ivanov may have set Scriabin on the path of esoteric inquiry and æsthetic experimentalism, it did not, as in the case of some of the poet's disciples, chill lyrical glow and joyousness which were temperamental qualities in the composer. Following at first along Wagnerian lines, he evolved the idea of a fresh synthesis of all the arts which was to culminate in a masterpiece : a 'Mystery' designed to knit up every art, not as with Wagner in the service of drama, but of religion. From this point his music became inextricably involved with his religious or philosophical creed : a form of theosophy in close alliance with oriental mysticism. From the symphony in E, op. 26, onward, his works may be regarded as a succession of efforts towards this supreme end. For this reason his tendencies are totally different from those of the nationalist group who derived from Glinka and Dargomijsky; but his vision and restless quest of spiritual revelation, as well as his pre-occupation with esoterics, were shared in common with many Russians of genius.

For the better expression of his ideology Scriabin devised a harmonic system based upon a 'synthetic' chord (a thirteenth, minor seventh and augmented ninth) derived from the upper partials 8, 9, 10, 11, 12, 13, 14— usually disposed in fourths.

He is still feeling after this new principle in the compositions which, roughly speaking, lie between op. 30 and op. 60, as may be observed most easily in the pianoforte works—the fourth and fifth sonatas; the 'Poème satanique,' op. 34; the Études, op. 42, etc. He uses the system with more complete confidence in the later piano sonatas; in the three Études, op. 65, in fifths, sevenths and ninths; in 'Vers la flamme,' op. 72; and in 'Prometheus.' Scriabin was a consummate pianist, and has added much to the modern technique of the instrument.

The musical writer Sabaneiev, who was Scriabin's close confidant in æsthetic matters, tells us that the first symphony, op. 26, in E major, is a hymn to art as religion ; the third, 'The Divine Poem,' op. 43, is the self-affirmation of personality—the emancipation of the soul from its fetters ; the 'Poem of Ecstasy,' op. 54, expresses the joy of creative activity. 'Prometheus : the Poem of Fire,' presses still nearer to the composer's ultimate aim. Here he makes a definite step towards the reunion of the arts by associating sounds and colours. The 'keyboard of light,' which he contrived for the purpose, proved a failure in practice. 'Prometheus' was produced at Queen's Hall on Feb. 1, 1913, under Sir Henry J. Wood, and repeated the following year, Mar. 14, 1914, when the composer played the important piano part. Nothing is forthcoming of the 'Mystery' beyond the text of the introduction, entitled 'Propylæa' (the porches), and a few musical notes.

Whether, as Safonov once prophesied to the writer, Scriabin would have strangled his creative gift in the noose of his self-made formulas, or whether in his passionate zeal for a more supersensitised art he would, in his upward flight, have dropped some of those hierophantic pretensions and complexities which threatened the sources of pure musical inspiration, must, because of his untimely death, remain a debatable question. It seems probable that when his theosophical programmes are forgotten, some of his music will still appeal because of its winged, ecstatic quality and a joyousness rare in the art of his period—and these aspects are most subtly expressed by him through the medium of the piano. (See Sonata, p. 839.)

At the time of Scriabin's visit to London, in the spring of 1914, he was suffering from a swelling on the lip which indicated a form of blood poisoning. Eventually it disappeared, but the poison was only in abeyance, and returned in a fatally acute form a few months later. The composer died in Moscow, after a short illness, at the age of 44.      R. N.

LIST OF WORKS
PIANO WORKS

Op 1, Valse in F minor ; op. 2, Three Pieces ; op. 3, Ten Mazurkas ; op. 4, Allegro appassionato ; op. 5, Two Nocturnes ; op. 6, Sonata No. 1, F minor (1895) ; op. 7, Two Impromptus à la Mazur ; op. 8, Twelve Studies ; op. 9, Prelude and Nocturne ; op. 10, Two Impromptus ; op. 11, Twenty-four Preludes ; op. 12, Two Impromptus ; op. 13, Six Preludes ; op. 14, Two Impromptus ; op. 15, Five Preludes ; op. 16, Five Preludes ; op. 17, Seven Preludes ; op. 18, Allegro de Concert, B flat minor ; op. 19, Sonata No. 2, G sharp minor (Sonate-fantaisie) ; op. 20, Concerto, F sharp minor, for piano and orchestra ; op. 21, Polonaise ; op. 22, Four Preludes ; op. 23, Sonata No. 3, F sharp minor ; op. 25, Nine Mazurkas—all the above date from the 'nineties. Op. 27, Two Preludes ; op. 28, Fantaisie ; op. 30, Sonata No. 4 in F sharp major ; op. 31, Four Preludes ; op. 32, Two Poems ; op. 33, Four Preludes ; op. 34, Tragödie (Tragic poem) ; op. 35, Three Preludes ; op. 36

'Poème satanique'; op. 37, Four Preludes; op. 38, Valse, A flat major; op. 39, Four Preludes; op. 40, Two Mazurkas; op. 41, Poem, D flat major; op. 42, Eight Études; op. 44, Two Poems; op. 45, Three Pieces: op. 46, Scherzo, C major; op. 47, Quasi-valse; op. 48, Four Preludes; op. 49, Three Pieces; op. 50, unpublished; op. 51, Four Pieces; op. 52, Three Pieces; op. 53, Sonata No. 5; op. 55, unpublished; op. 56, Four Pieces; op. 57, Two Pieces; op. 58, Feuillet d'album; op. 59, Two Pieces; op. 61, Poème-nocturne; op. 62, Sonata No. 6; op. 63, Two Poems; op. 64, Sonata No. 7; op. 65, Three Études; op. 66, Sonata No. 8; op. 67, Two Preludes; op. 68, Sonata No. 9; op. 70, Sonata No. 10; op. 71, Two Poems; op. 72, Vers la flamme; op. 73, Two Dances; op. 74 Five Preludes.

ORCHESTRAL WORKS

'Reverie,' op. 24; Symphony No. 1, in E major, with chorus, op. 26 (1900); Symphony No. 2, in C minor, op. 29 (1903); Symphony No. 3, in C, The Divine Poem, op. 43; Le Poème de l'extase, op. 54 (1908); Prometheus: the Poem of Fire, op. 60, for orchestra, piano, organ, choir and colour keyboard (1913). The majority of Scriabin's early works were published by Belaïev; those dating about 1911–13 by the Russian Music Publishing Co.; most of them from op. 65 onward by Jurgenson, Moscow.

BIBLIOGRAPHY

Monographs by SABANÉIEV, JUNST and KARATAGYN; special number of the *Muzykalny Sovremennik* (4-5, 1916); *A Russian Tone-Poet*, A. EAGLEFIELD HULL (London, Kegan Paul); ROSA NEWMARCH, *Scriabin and Contemporary Russian Music* (*The Russian Review*, Feb. 1913), and the analysis of 'Prometheus' (authorised by the composer), Queen's Hall programmes, Feb. 1, 1913, and Mar. 14, 1914; see also *Russia of the Russians*, by HAROLD WILLIAMS, Ph.D., Pitman & Sons (1915).

**SCRIBE,** AUGUSTIN-EUGÈNE (*b.* Paris, Dec. 25, 1791; *d.* there, Feb. 21, 1861), the most prolific of French dramatists, and the best librettist of his day. He lost his parents early, and the well-known advocate Bonnet urged him to take to the Bar; but he was irresistibly drawn to the stage, and from his début at 20 at the Théâtre du Vaudeville till his death, he produced for the different theatres of Paris a rapid succession of pieces which have served as models to a host of imitators. He originated the *comédie-vaudeville*, and attained to high comedy in 'Une Chaîne'; but it is in opéra-comique and lyric tragedy that he has given the most striking proofs of his imagination and knowledge of the stage. For half a century he produced on an average ten pieces a year, many, it is true, written conjointly with various authors, but in these 'mariages d'esprit' Scribe was always the head of the firm.

Meyerbeer's 'Huguenots,' 'Robert,' 'Prophète,' 'L'Étoile du nord,' and 'L'Africaine'; Auber's 'Fra Diavolo,' 'Gustave III,' 'Cheval de bronze,' 'Domino noir,' and 'Diamants de la couronne'; Auber's 'Muette de Portici'; and Verdi's 'Vêpres siciliennes' are the most famous of his libretti.

Scribe died suddenly. He had been a member of the French Academy since 1836, and had acquired a large fortune. His complete works have been published (1874–85; 76 vols.), and there are several editions of his stage-pieces. That of 1855 comprises 2 vols. of operas, and 3 of opéras-comiques; and that of Calmann Lévy (1874–81), 6 vols. 12mo of ballets and operas, and 20 of opéras-comiques. A perusal of these gives a high idea of his fertility and resource.              G. C.

BIBL.—EUGÈNE LEGONNÉ, *Scribe* (1874).

**SCRIPTORES.** There are several great collections of ancient writers on musical theory, both Greek and Latin. In 1652 Meibomius printed a valuable collection of Greek writers

which long held the field. It is now, however, superseded by the following:

*Musici scriptores Graeci*, ed. C. Janus (Teubner, 1895), contains, with elaborate prolegomena, the following authors:

1. Aristotle. 'Loci de musica.'
2. Pseudo-Aristotle. 'De rebus musicis problemata.'
3. Euclides. 'Sectio canonis.'
4. Cleonides. Εἰσαγωγὴ ἁρμονική.
5. Nicomachus Gerasenus. Ἁρμονικὸν ἐγχειρίδιον & Excerpta.
6. Bacchius. Εἰσαγωγὴ τέχνης μουσικῆς.
7. Gaudentius. Ἁρμονικὴ εἰσαγωγή.
8. Alypius. Εἰσαγωγὴ μουσική.
9. 'Excerpta Neapolitana.'
10. 'Carminum Graecorum reliquiae.'

The *De musica* of ARISTIDES QUINTILIANUS is not included above, because it had been edited separately by A. Jahn (Berlin, 1882). The *Harmonic Elements* of Aristoxenus are best studied in Macran's edition (Oxford, 1902).

The later Greek writers are to be found as published by Wallis, either separately or in his *Opera mathematica* (Oxford, 1699), of which vol. iii. contains Ptolemy, *Harmonica*; Porphyry, *Commentary on Ptolemy*; and Bryennius, *Harmonica*. To these may be added a less important anonymous work, *De musica*, ed. Bellermann (Berlin, 1841).

For Latin authors reference must first be made to the great collection of Martin Gerbert, *Scriptores ecclesiastici de musica*, 3 vols., 1784 (and reproduced in facsimile 1905). It contains the following:

VOL. I.

1. S. Pambo. 'Geronticon' (in Greek and Latin).
2. 'Monacho qua mente sit Psallendum.'
3. 'Instituta Patrum de modo Psallendi' (? Cistercian).
4. S. Nicetius of Treves. 'De bono Psalmodiae.'
5. Cassiodorus. 'Institutiones musicae.'
6. S. Isidore. 'Sententiae de musica.'
7. Alcuin. 'Musica.'
8. Aurelian. 'Musica disciplina.'
9. Remigius. 'Musica.'
10. Notker. 'De musica.'
11. Hucbald. 'De musica.'
    (Pseudo-Hucbald.) 'Musica enchiriadis, Commemoratio brevis de tonis et psalmis modulandis.'
12. Regino. 'De harmonica Institutione.'
13. Odo. 'Tonarius,' 'Dialogus de musica.'
14. Adelbold. 'Musica.'
15. Bernelin. 'Divisio monochordi.'
16. Various anonymous pieces.

VOL. II.

1. Guido d' Arezzo. 'De disciplina artis musicae,' 'Regulae musicae rhythmicae,' 'De ignoto cantu,' 'Tractatus correctorius multorum errorum,' 'De tropis sive tonis.'
2. Berno of Reichenau. 'De varia Psalmorum atque cantuum modulatione,' 'De consona tonorum diversitate,' 'Tonarius.'
3. Hermann Contractus. 'Musica,' 'Explicatio signorum,' 'Versus ad discernendum cantum.'
4. William of Hirschau. 'Musica.'
5. Theoger of Metz. 'Musica.'
6. Aribo Scholasticus. 'Musica.'
7. John Cotton. 'De musica.'
8. S. Bernard. 'Tonal.'
9. Gerlandus. 'De musica.'
10. Eberhard of Freisingen. 'De mensura fistularum.'
11. Anonymous. 'De mensura fistularum.'
12. Engelbert of Admont. 'De musica.'
13. Joh. Ægidius. 'Ars musica.'

VOL III.

1. Franco. 'Ars cantus mensurabilis.'
2. Elias Salmon. 'Scientia artis musicae.'
3. Marchetti of Padua. 'Lucidarium musicae planae,' 'Pomerium musicae mensuratae.'
4. Jean de Muris. 'Summa musicae,' 'Musica speculativa,' 'De numeris,' 'Musica practica,' 'Questiones super partes musicae,' 'De discantu,' 'De tonis,' 'De proportionibus.'
5. Arnulph. 'De differentiis cantorum.'
6. John Keck. 'Introductorium musicae.'
7. Adam da Fulda. 'Musica.'
8. 'Constitutiones capellae Pontificiae' (1545).
9. Τεχνὴ ψαλτικὴ seu Ars Psallendi aut cantandi Graecorum.

A continuation of Gerbert was gathered by Coussemaker under the title *Scriptores de musica medii aevi* (1864–76). It contains the following works :

### Vol. I.

1. Fra Jerome of Moravia. 'De musica.' With extracts from 'Positio vulgaris.' John de Garlandia, 'De musica mensurabili'; Franco of Cologne, 'Ars cantus mensurabilis'; Peter Picard, 'Musica mensurabilis.'
2. Franco. 'Compendium discantus.'
3. John de Garlandia. 'Introductio musicae.'
4.     „        'De musica mensurabili.'
5. Walter de Odington 'De speculatione musice.'
6. Aristotle. 'De musica' (12th or 13th century).
7. Petrus de Cruce. 'De tonis.'
8. John Balloc. 'Abbreviatio Franconis.'
9. Anonymus. 'De consonantiis musicalibus.'
10.     „        'De discantu.'
11.     „        'Cantu mensurabili.'
12.     „        'De mensuris et discantu.'
13.     „        'De discantu.'
14.     „        'De figuris sive de notis.'
15.     „        'De musica.'
16. Robert Handlo. 'Regulae.'
17. John Hanboys. 'Summa super musicam.'

### Vol. II.

1. Regino of Prüm. 'Tonarius.'
2. Hucbald. 'Musica encheiriadis' (a bit unpublished by Gerbert).
3. Guido d' Arezzo, 'De modorum formulis.'
4.     „        'De sex motibus vocum.'
4. Odo. 'Intonarium.'
5. Guido in Caroli-loco Abbas. 'Opusculum.'
6. Jean de Muris. 'Speculum musicae' (books vi. and vii.).
7. A Carthusian. 'De musica plana.'
8. Anonymus. 'De musica.'

### Vol. III.

1. 'Marchetti of Padua. 'Brevis compilatio' (see Gerbert).
2. John de Garlandia. 'Introductio de contrapuncto.'
3. Philip de Vitry. 'Ars nova.'
4.     „        'Ars contrapuncti.'
5.     „        'Ars perfecta.'
6.     „        'Liber musicalium.'
7. Jean de Muris. 'Libellus cantus mensurabilis.'
8.     „        'Ars contrapuncti.'
9.     „        'Ars discantus.'
10. Henry of Zeland. 'De cantu perfecto et imperfecto.'
11. Philoppotus Andreas. 'De contrapuncto.'
12. Philip de Caserta. 'De diversis figuris.'
13. Giles de Murino. 'Cantus mensurabilis.'
14. Johannes Verulus de Anagnia. 'De musica.'
15. Theodore de Campo. 'Musica mensurabilis.'
16. Prosdocimus de Beldemandis. 'De contrapuncto.'
17.     „        „        „        'Tractatus practice cantus mensurabilis.'
18.     „        „        „        'Do. ad modum Italicum.'
19.     „        „        „        'Libellus monochordi.'
20.     „        „        „        'Summula proportionum.'
21. Nicasius Weyts, Carmelite. 'Regulae musicae.'
22. Christian Saze of Flanders. Tractatus.'
23. Gulielmus Monachus. 'De praeceptis artis musicae.'
24. Antonius de Leno. 'Regule de contrapanto.'
25. John de Hothby. 'Regulae super proportionem.'
26.     „        'De cantu figurato.'
27.     „        'Regulae supra contrapunctum.'
Anonymous works, 28-40 (pp. 334-498).

### Vol. IV.

1. John Tinctoris. (1) 'Expositio manus'; (2) 'De natura et proprietate tonorum'; (3) 'De notis et pausis'; (4) 'De regulari valore notarum'; (5) 'Liber imperfectionum'; (6) 'Tractatus alterationum'; (7) 'Super punctis musicalibus'; (8) 'De arte contrapuncti'; (9) 'Proportionale musices'; (10) 'Diffinitorium musices.'
2. Simon Tunstede. 'Quatuor principalia musices.'
3. Johannes Gallicus. 'Ritus canendi'; 'Introductio.'
4. Antonius de Luca. 'Ars cantus figurati.'
5. Anonymus. 'De musica figurata.'

For Boethius's *De institutione musica* recourse may be had to his works in Migne's *Patrologia Latina* or in Teubner's *Bibliotheca* (ed. Friedlein). Note also *Ein anonymer Musiktractat* (ed. J. Wolf), Leipzig, 1893, and a valuable little early tract printed by Wagner in *Rassegna Gregoriana*, iv. 482 (1904).

W. H. F.

SCUDO, PIETRO (*b.* Venice, June 6, 1806; *d.* Blois, Oct. 14, 1864), was brought up in Germany. Some circumstance led him to Paris, and in 1816 he entered Choron's school, and studied singing there at the same time with Duprez. He never became a good singer, and after taking a secondary part in Rossini's 'Il viaggio a Reims' left the boards, returned to Choron's school, and there picked up a slender knowledge of music. After the re-

volution of 1830 he played second clarinet in a military band. Returning to Paris he made his way into society, set up as a teacher of singing, and a composer of romances. He took to writing, and published *Physiologie du rire* and *Les Partis politiques en province* (1838). He gradually restricted himself to musical criticism, but as long as he wrote only for the *Revue de Paris,* the *Réforme* and the *Revue indépendante,* he was unknown outside certain cliques in Paris. As musical critic to the *Revue des deux mondes,* he became a man of mark. Scudo's articles are worth reading as specimens of French musical criticism before Berlioz was known, and while Fétis occupied a field without a rival. They have been mostly republished under the following titles : *Critique et littérature musicale* (1850, 8vo ; 1852, 12mo), 2nd series (1859, 12mo) ; *La Musique ancienne et moderne* (1854, 12mo) ; *L'Année musicale,* 3 vols. (Hachette, 1860, 1861, and 1862) ; *La Musique en 1862* (Hetzel, 1863) ; and *Le Chevalier Sarti* (1857, 12mo), a musical novel taken from Italian and German sources, of which a continuation, *Frédérique,* appeared in the *Revue des deux mondes,* but was not republished. All his works were printed in Paris. Scudo finally became insane, and died in an asylum at Blois.

G. C.

SEASONS, THE — 'Die Jahreszeiten'— Haydn's last oratorio. The book was compiled in German from Thomson's 'Seasons' by Van Swieten, who induced Haydn to undertake its composition immediately after the success of the 'Creation'; and the music was written between Apr. 1798 and Apr. 24, 1801, on which day the first performance took place at the Schwarzenberg palace, Vienna.

The score was published in 1802–03 (without date) at Vienna ; a barbarous English version accompanied the German text. In 1813 Clementi published a vocal score with a better version. The Rev. John Webb followed with a further improvement in 1840 or 1841, Professor E. Taylor made a fourth.

G.

SEBASTIANI, JOHANN (*b.* Weimar, Sept. 30, 1622 ; *d.* 1683), is said to have studied music in Italy. He is next heard of as settled at Königsberg in Prussia about 1650, where also in 1661 he was appointed cantor to the Domkirche in the Kneiphof quarter of the town, and in 1663 became Kapellmeister to the electoral Schlosskirche. He retired on a pension in 1679. He is chiefly known as the composer of a Passion music, which occupies an important place in the development of the form. The full title of the work is :

'Das Leyden und Sterben unsers Herrn und Heylandes J. Chr. nach dem heiligen Matthaeo. In eine recitirende Harmoni von 5 singenden und 6 spielenden Stimmen nebst dem Basso continuo gesetzet. Worinnen zu erweckung mehrer Devotion unterschiedliche Verse aus denen gewöhnlichen Kirchenliedern mit eingeführet. . . Königsberg, 1672.'

The work is dedicated to Frederick William, Elector of Brandenburg. As the title indicates, it is a Passion with instrumental accompaniment *a* 6 and chorus *a* 5. The instrumental parts are for first and second violins, three for viola da gamba or da braccio, and one for viola bassa. But the full accompaniment is only reserved for the dramatic choruses in the work. Elsewhere the distinction is made that while the violas alone accompany the words of the Evangelist and other single characters sung by solo voices, the first and second violins alone with basso continuo accompany the utterances of our Lord. There are also short symphonic interludes for violas alone, and the Choral verses are intended to be sung by a solo voice with the accompaniment of violas. The conclusion consists of a hymn of thanksgiving, the first four verses of which are sung solo, and only the last verse tutti. The whole interesting work has now been reprinted in the *D.D.T.* xvii. (See PASSION MUSIC.) Other works of Sebastiani, enumerated in *Q.-L.*, are two collections of 'geistliche und weltliche Lieder' bearing the title 'Parnass-blumen,' published at Hamburg 1672 and 1675, also a large number of occasional compositions for weddings and funerals. A few sacred compositions in the concerted style for voices and instruments remain in MS.          J. R. M.

SECHTER, SIMON (*b.* Friedberg, Bohemia, Oct. 11, 1788; *d.* Sept. 12, 1867), a famous theoretician and composer.

In 1804, after a moderate musical education, he went to Vienna, where he applied himself with ardour to theoretical studies. In 1809, while Vienna was in the hands of the French, he made the acquaintance of Dragonetti—then living in concealment under the curious apprehension that Napoleon would oblige him to go to Paris—for whom he wrote the pianoforte accompaniments to his concertos for the double bass. In 1810 Sechter became teacher of the piano and singing at the Blind Institute, for which he wrote many songs and two masses. During the whole of this time he pushed forward his studies, working more especially at Bach and Mozart. He found a good friend in Abbé Stadler, through whose means three of Sechter's masses were performed at the court chapel. A Requiem of his and a chorus from Schiller's 'Bride of Messina' were also executed at the Concert Spirituel with success. In 1824 he became court organist, first as subordinate, and in 1825, on the death of Worzischeck, as chief, an office which he retained till his death. His fame as a theoretical teacher attracted numerous scholars, amongst others the great Schubert, who was on the point of taking lessons from him when attacked by his last illness. (See SCHUBERT.) Amongst his pupils may be mentioned, Preyer, Nottebohm, the Princess Czartorijska, Sucher, Bibl, Rosa Kastner (Escudier), Rufinatscha, Bruckner, Otto Bach, Döhler, Schachner, Filtsch, S.

Bagge, Benoni, Vieuxtemps, Pauer, C. F. Pohl and Thalberg. The Emperor Ferdinand conferred upon him the large gold medal for a Mass dedicated to his Majesty, which was shortly followed by the order of St. Louis from the Duke of Lucca. In 1850 he became professor of composition in the Conservatorium at Vienna. His Aphorisms, etc., which he communicated to the Vienna *A.M.Z.*, show him to have been a profound thinker, and give many instructive hints both to teachers and scholars. His most intimate friends were Staudigl, Lutz and Hölzel, for whom he wrote a quantity of humorous Volkslieder in contrapuntal style, as well as many comic operettas, ballads, etc. His diligence in study was astonishing. No day passed in which he did not write a fugue. A few years before his death he had the misfortune, through his own good nature, to lose almost everything, and died in poverty and privation.

His unpublished works in the Imperial Library and the Musikverein at Vienna contain four oratorios, operas and large cantatas, music for voice, organ, and pianoforte, including 104 variations on an original theme of 104 bars; also a complete theoretical treatise ready for publication, in two portions, first on acoustics, second on canon. Among his published works are an edition of Marpurg *On Fugue*, with many additions; *Grundsätze der musik. Composition* (3 vols. B. & H.); twelve masses; *Practical Examples of Accompaniment from Figured Bass*, op. 59; *Practical School of Thorough Bass*, opp. 49, 98; preludes for the organ, in four books; fugues, hymns, choral preludes; four fugues for PF., op. 5, dedicated to Beethoven; fugue in C minor, to the memory of Schubert, op. 43; etc. Sechter completed the grand fugue for orchestra in D major left unfinished by Mozart.
                                                   C. F. P.

SECOND, the smallest interval in the scale used for musical purposes. It is described by notes which are next to each other on the stave or by letters which lie next each other in the alphabet, as A B, B C, C D♯, E♭ F♯.

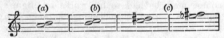

Three kinds can be practically distinguished. The minor second, which is equal to a semitone, as at (*b*) in the example; the major second, which is equal to a tone (but of which there are two kinds, grave and acute—see below), as at (*a*); and the augmented second, which is equal to three semitones, as at (*c*).—The numerical ratios of the several intervals in just intonation are given as follows: the minor second, 16 : 15; the grave major second, 10 : 9; the acute major second, 9 : 8; and the augmented second, 75 : 64. (See SEMITONE; INTERVAL.)
                                                   C. H. H. P.

SECONDO, the second player in a duet. (See PRIMO.)

SEDIE, ENRICO DELLE (b. Leghorn, June 17, 1824[1]; d. Paris, Nov. 28, 1907), baritone singer, son of a merchant of Leghorn. In the year 1848 he volunteered in the army of Charles Albert of Piedmont, and fought against the Austrians in the war for Italian independence. He was taken prisoner at the battle of Curtatone but afterwards released, and at the close of the campaign of the following year retired from the army with the rank of lieutenant. Under the direction of his fellow-citizen, Orazio Galeffi, he then devoted himself to the study of singing, and in 1851 made his début at Pistoia[2] in Nabucco.

From 1854, when he made a great success as Rigoletto in Florence, his position was secure. He appeared with unvarying success at Rome, Milan, Vienna, Paris and London, and though possessed of so little voice as to gain the sobriquet of Il baritono senza voce, he made up by dramatic accent and purity of style for the shortcomings of nature. In 1867, at the earnest request of Auber, he accepted a professorship at the Conservatoire of Paris on the most advantageous terms hitherto offered. Under him a commission was appointed for the entire remodelling of that institution, but the death of Auber and the outbreak of the Franco-Prussian War compelled the Government to abandon their intention. In 1874 he published a large work upon the art of singing and musical declamation, under the title of L'Art lyrique. Translations of this and other vocal treatises are published in New York as A Complete Method of Singing.

Delle Sedie was Cavalieri of the Order of the Crown of Italy, for his military services in the campaigns of 1848, 1849; Cavaliere of the Order of SS. Maurizio and Lazzaro; and member of many societies and academies both of Italy and France. For some time he lived in Paris, and devoted himself entirely to the teaching of his art.                    J. C. G.

SEEGR (SEEGER, SEGER, SAGER, SEGERT, ZECKERT), JOSEPH FERDINAND NORBERT (b. Repin near Melnik, Bohemia, Mar. 21, 1716; d. Apr. 22, 1782), eminent organist and composer. Educated at Prague, where he graduated Master of Philosophy, he was alto singer at St. James's Church in that city, and later, organist at St. Martin's. In 1735 he was first violinist at the Tein Church, but was appointed organist in 1741, which position he retained until his death. In addition, he held the appointment of organist at the Kreuzherrenkirche in the Old Town for thirty-seven years (1745-1782). In this church Joseph II. heard Seegr play, and was so delighted with the masterly performance that he at once determined to give him a court appointment at Vienna. Seegr

died, however, before the official document arrived which contained this preferment. Amongst his pupils were the principal Bohemian musicians of that time, viz.: Kozeluh, Maschek, Mysliwecek, Gelinek, Brixi, Kucharz, etc.

That Seegr was well known to Bach is testified by the fact that the latter advised Count Millesimo to place Mathias Sofka under Master Seegr, remarking that he could not entrust him to a better teacher. Burney (Present State of Music, Germany, vol. ii. pp. 13-14) mentions him as being a fine organ-player, a good linguist and an excellent musician. The unanimous testimony of his contemporaries proclaims Seegr as one of the finest organists of his time. At his death his compositions were acquired by Ernst, Konzertmeister of Gotha. Daniel Gottlob Turk, music director of Halle, was employed to edit the first posthumous instalment of these compositions—'Eight Toccatas and Fugues' for the organ (Breitkopf, 1793), which are up to the present his best-known works. The toccatas are in reality preludes—with the exception of No. 5, the style of which is more in accordance with its title. His other compositions consisted of many masses, psalms, litanies, etc., printed copies of which do not exist. After the lapse of nearly a century and a quarter, Messrs. Novello & Co. have issued Nos. 1, 5 and 7, edited by Dom Samuel Gregory Ould, and adapted to the requirements of the modern organ.                    W. W. S.

SEELING, HANS (b. Prague, 1828; d. there, May 26, 1862), pianist and composer. Ill-health obliged him to go to Italy in 1852, and in 1856 he toured in the East, returning to Italy in 1857. After settling in Paris, 1859, he made his home in Germany. An excellent pianist, he met with unfailing success on his tours. Seeling composed a number of brilliant pieces and studies for the piano, of which the best known are the 'Barcarolle,' the 'Lorelei' (op. 2), the 'Concert Studies' (op. 10), and the 'Memories of an Artist' (op. 13). These compositions are highly effective, and their character partakes of Henselt on the one hand and Bendel on the other.                    D. H.

SEGNO, i.e. the sign 𝄋. (See DAL SEGNO.)

SEGRETO DI SUSANNA, IL, opera in one act; text by Enrico Golisciani; music by Wolf-Ferrari. Produced Hofoper, Munich, Nov. 4, 1909; New York, Metropolitan Opera House, Mar. 14, 1911; Covent Garden, July 11, 1911; Costanzi Theatre, Rome, Nov. 27, 1911; in English (Beecham) Covent Garden, Nov. 12, 1919.

SEGUE, 'follows'—as segue l' aria, 'the aria follows'; a direction frequently found at the end of recitatives. It is thus equivalent to the more modern word attacca. It is also found occasionally at the foot of a page where a space is left after one movement in order that the next may begin at the top, to avoid turning over in the middle. It then indicates that no stop is to be made between the two movements.                                      M.

SEGUIDILLA (SIGUIDILLA), a popular national dance of Spain. The origin of both name and dance are uncertain; it existed in La Mancha in the time of Cervantes (see *Don Quixote*, part ii. chap. 38), but there is no evidence to show whether it is indigenous, or introduced into Spain by the Moors. It is, however, certain that from La Mancha it spread all over Spain, and it is still danced in both town and country. Seguidillas are divided into three kinds—Seguidillas Manchegas, the original form of the dance, in which it assumes a gay and lively character; Seguidillas Boleras,[1] more measured and stately; and Seguidillas Gitanas, danced very slowly and sentimentally. To these some writers add a fourth kind, the Seguidillas Taleadas, said to be a combination of the original Seguidilla with the Cachucha. The music is written in 3-4 or 3-8 time, usually in a minor key, and is performed on the guitar with occasionally a flute, violin or castanet accompaniment. The *coplas*, or words sung by the musicians, are written in couplets of four short lines followed by an *estrevillo* or refrain of three lines, but some coplas want this latter feature. Both music and words often partake of the character of an improvisation, the former remarkable for strange and sudden modulations, and the latter treating of both serious and comic subjects.

A collection of coplas was published at the end of the 18th century by N. Zamacola, writing under the pseudonym of Don Preciso. From the introduction to this book the following quaint description of the Seguidilla is translated:

' So soon as two young people of the opposite sexes present themselves standing face to face at a distance of about two varas [2] in the middle of the room, the "ritornelo" or prelude of the music begins; then the seguidilla is insinuated by the voice—if it be a manchega, by singing the first line of the copla; if it be a bolera, by singing two lines, which must only take up four bars. The guitar follows, playing a pasacalle [3]; and at the fourth bar the seguidilla begins to be sung. Then the dance breaks out with castanets or crotolas,[4] running on for a space of nine bars, with which the first part concludes. The guitar continues playing the pasacalle, during which the dancers change to opposite positions by means of a very deliberate and simple promenade (*paseo*). While singing again, at the beginning of the fourth bar, each goes on for nine bars more, making the variations and differences of their respective schools, which forms the second part. Again they change places, and upon each dancer returning to the spot where they began to dance, the third part goes on in the same way as the second, and on arriving at the ninth bar, the voice, the instrument, and the castanets cease all at once, and as if impromptu, the room remaining in silence, and the dancers standing immovable in various beautiful attitudes, which is what we call " well stopped " (*Bien parado*).'

Space will not allow us to give an example of the music which accompanies this beautiful

dance. In Book IV. of Luigi Borghi's ' Opera Dances ' (London, 1783) is a seguidilla modified for theatrical representation, and in the first act of ' Carmen ' there is a Spanish air which Bizet has entitled ' Seguidille.' Better examples than these will be found in Mendel's *Lexicon* (sub voce Seguidilla), and in the Appendix to Part I. of Marino Soriano Fuertes's *Historia de la musica española* (Madrid, 1855–59), in which specimens are given of the varieties of the dance. With regard to the words, the following copla (from Don Preciso's *Colleccion de Coplas*, Madrid, 1799) may serve as an example:

' El Lunes me enamoro,
Mártes lo digo,
Miércoles me declaro,
Júeves consigo:
Viérnes doy zelos
Y Sabado y Domingo
Busco Amor nuevo.' [5]

(See SONG, subsection SPAIN 4.)          W. B. S.

SEGUIN, (1) ARTHUR EDWARD SHELDEN (*b.* London, Apr. 7, 1809; *d.* New York, Dec. 9, 1852), of Irish descent, received his musical education at the R.A.M., and first appeared in public in 1828 at concerts and performances of Italian operas given by its pupils. His voice was a deep bass, of very extensive compass, and he met with a very favourable reception. In 1829 he sang at the Exeter Festival. In 1831 he appeared at the theatre in Tottenham Street as Polyphemus in ' Acis and Galatea.' In 1832 he sang at the Concert of Ancient Music. In 1833 and 1834 he was engaged at Covent Garden, and in the latter year appeared at the King's Theatre as Il Conte Robinson in Cimarosa's ' Matrimonio segreto,' and also sang at the Festival in Westminster Abbey. From 1835–37 he was engaged at Drury Lane. In Aug. 1838 he appeared at the English Opera House in Macfarren's ' Devil's Opera,' and soon afterwards quitted England for America, made his first appearance at the National Theatre, New York, as the Count in Rooke's ' Amilie ' on Oct. 15, 1838, and was extremely well received. He afterwards formed an opera company named ' The Seguin Troupe,' who performed at various places in the United States and Canada. Amongst other distinctions he was elected a chief by one of the Indian tribes, and received an Indian name, signifying ' The man with the deep mellow voice,' an honour which had never before been conferred on any Englishman except Edmund Kean, the tragedian.

His wife, ANN CHILDE (*b.* London, 1814; *d.* New York, Aug. 1888), was also a pupil of the R.A.M., and appeared in public as a soprano singer in 1828 in the same performances as her future husband, and with equal success. In 1832 she sang at the Concert of Ancient Music, and in 1834 at the Westminster Abbey Festival. After performing for two or three seasons at

---

1 Not to be confounded with the Bolero, said to have been invented in 1780 by Don Sebastian Zerezo.
2 1 vara= 34 inches.
3 Literally ' street-pass '; any popular street-song. (See PASSACAGLIA.)          4 A kind of castanet.

5 Translation: ' On Monday I fall in love, on Tuesday I say so, Wednesday I declare myself, Thursday I succeed: Friday I cause jealousy, and Saturday and Sunday I seek a fresh love.'

the King's Theatre as 'seconda donna,' she appeared on the English stage at Drury Lane, Nov. 3, 1837, as Donna Anna in the English version of Mozart's 'Don Giovanni.' She accompanied her husband to America and performed in opera until his death, when she retired from the stage and taught music in New York.

Seguin's younger brother, (2) WILLIAM HENRY (b. London, 1814 ; d. Dec. 28, 1850), also a pupil of the R.A.M., possessed a light bass voice and was a concert singer and member of the choir of the Temple Church. He married Miss GOOCH, soprano singer, a fellow-pupil at the R.A.M., who survived him a few years only.

His sister, (3) ELIZABETH (b. London, 1815 ; d. London, 1870), was also a singer, and was the mother of Mme. PAREPA-ROSA (q.v.).

W. H. H.

SEIDEL, FRIEDRICH LUDWIG (b. Treuenbrietzen, July 14, 1765 ; d. Charlottenburg, May 8, 1831), a pupil of Friedrich Benda at Berlin, while Reichardt took him into his house and supplied his personal wants. In 1792 he was organist at St. Mary's; in 1801 assistant conductor at the National Theatre; in 1808 musical director of the Royal Chapel; and in 1822 court Kapellmeister. He was pensioned in 1830. He composed a Mass, Requiem and other church music, an oratorio, operas, music for plays, overtures, a sextet, PF. and wind, pieces for PF. and songs (Riemann ; Q.-L.).

SEIDL, ANTON (b. Pest, May 7, 1850 ; d. New York, Mar. 28, 1898), was entered as a pupil at the Leipzig Conservatorium in Oct. 1870. Early in 1872 he went to Bayreuth, and was there employed by Wagner to make the first copy of the score of the Nibelungen trilogy. He also assisted at the festival in Aug. 1876. In 1879, through Wagner's recommendation, he obtained the post of conductor at the Leipzig Opera-House, and remained there until 1882, when he went upon a long tour through Germany, Holland, England, Italy, etc., in the capacity of conductor of Angelo Neumann's 'Nibelungen' opera troupe. The performances were not altogether faultless : it is true that the vocalists were good, but the great music drama was reproduced in a sadly mutilated condition. Yet Seidl proved himself to be an energetic conductor, and was personally successful. In 1883 he became conductor at the Bremen Opera-House. Early in 1885 he married the well-known soprano singer Frl. Kraus, and in September of that year accepted the post of conductor of German opera at the New York Metropolitan Opera-House, which post he filled with great distinction. He also succeeded THOMAS (q.v.) as conductor of the New York Philharmonic Society (1891), and conducted the first performance of Dvořák's symphony, 'From the New World' (1893). In 1895–97 he

again conducted German opera in New York, and in 1897 he conducted at Covent Garden.

C. A.

BIBL.—H. E. KREHBIEL, Anton Seidl, 1898 ; Anton Seidl, Memorial by his Friends, New York, 1899.

SEIDL, ARTHUR (b. Munich, June 8, 1863), distinguished critic and littérateur, graduated D.Phil. (1887) at Leipzig University with a thesis, Vom Musikalisch-Erhabenen. He concentrated his attention primarily on modern music and its problems, as the titles of his many publications show. Riemann gives a list which includes further works on æsthetics, on Wagner, Richard Strauss, Hans Pfitzner (1921) and other men and matters.

In 1898–99 at Weimar Seidl was engaged in editing Nietzsche's works and letters ; in 1904 he became teacher of musical history, literature and æsthetics in Leipzig University, and concurrently with this (1903–19) was musical manager to the Hoftheater at Dessau. Later, at Dessau, he has held private courses in musical science.

BIBL.—L. FRANKENSTEIN, A. Seidl, 1913 ; B. SCHUHMANN, Musik und Kultur (Festschrift for Seidl's fiftieth birthday) ; Riemann.

C.

SEIFFERT, MAX (b. Beeskow on the Spree, Feb. 9, 1868), was educated at his native place and at the Joachimsthal Gymnasium at Berlin. He studied musical science and literature under Philipp Spitta, and wrote a treatise on Sweelinck for the doctor's degree in 1891 (printed in the Vierteljahrsschrift of that year). Besides many contributions to that periodical, to the Allg. deutsche Biographie, the Tijdschrift of the Dutch Vereeniging, etc., he issued a revised and enlarged edition of C. F. Weitzmann's Geschichte der Klaviermusik in 1899, and was editor of the complete works of Sweelinck issued in twelve volumes, and of several volumes of the various series of D.D.T. (q.v.). From April 1904 till 1914 he was editor-in-chief of the Internationale Musikgesellschaft, and from 1918 he edited the Archiv für Musikwissenschaft, which as far as Germany was concerned took up the task of the Int. Mus. Ges. (Riemann.)

M., with addns.

SEISS, ISIDOR WILHELM (b. Dresden, Dec. 23, 1840 ; d. Cologne, Sept. 25, 1905), was at first a pupil of F. Wieck for piano and of Julius Otto for theory. In 1858–60 he studied at Leipzig under Hauptmann. He had a success as a pianist in the following year, and issued several compositions. In 1871 he was appointed a piano-teacher at the Cologne Conservatorium, and in 1878 received the title of professor. He had a long and successful career there, and conducted the Musikalische Gesellschaft. His compositions, chiefly educational works for the piano, are tasteful and of high aim ; his clever arrangement of Beethoven's 'Contre-danses' and 'Danses allemandes' are among his most famous productions, as well as a revised version of Weber's E flat concerto. A 'Feierlich

Szene und Marsch' are for orchestra. (*Rie-mann*.)                                    M.

SÉJAN, NICOLAS (*b.* Paris, Mar. 19, 1725; *d.* there, Mar. 16, 1819), a famous organist. In 1760 he was at St. André des Arts; in 1772 successor of Daquin at Notre Dame; in 1789 successor of L. A. Couperin at the Royal Chapel and teacher of singing at the École Royale de Chant. He lost his position through the Revolution. In 1807 he was organist at the Dôme des Invalides, and in 1814 again at the Royal Chapel. He composed 3 PF. trios, 6 violin sonatas, PF. and organ pieces (*Riemann*; *Q.-L.*).

SEKLES, BERNHARDT (*b.* Frankfort-on-Main, June 20, 1872), pupil of Uzielli, Knorr, and Scholz, at the Hochs Conservatorium. He was for some time Kapellmeister in Heidelberg and Mainz, but later became teacher of theory at the Hochs Conservatorium, Frankfort. His works are full of exotic charm, beauty and colour, and have a certain affinity with the compositions of Cyril Scott. They include:

Songs for soprano (opp. 2, 3, 8, 15); songs for tenor; songs for baritone (opp. 1, 7, 11); 'Aus den Gärten der Semiramis,' symph. poem; serenade (for 11 solo instruments); passacaglia and fugue (for orch. and organ); 'Kleine Suite' (for orch.); 'Die Temperamente' (for orch.); passacaglia and fugue (for str. quartet); sonata (for vcl. and PF.); Dance-Play, 'Der Zwerg und die Infantin' (Frankfort, 1913); opera, 'Schahrazade' (Mannheim, 1917); Burlesque, 'Die Hochzeit des Faun' (Wiesbaden, 1921); PF. pieces (opp. 4, 5, 10).          K. D. H.

SELBY, BERTRAM, LUARD- (*b.* Ightham, Kent, Feb. 12, 1853; *d.* Jan.[1] 1919), received his musical education at the Leipzig Conservatorium under Reinecke and Jadassohn; became organist of St. Barnabas, Marylebone, and Highgate School in 1876, and gave chamber concerts in London before his appointment to the post of organist of Salisbury Cathedral in 1881, a post he retained for two years. He was next organist at St. John's, Torquay, in 1884, and of St. Barnabas, Pimlico, in 1886. He was appointed organist of Rochester Cathedral in succession to Dr. John Hopkins, in 1900. His most important works are incidental music to 'Helena in Troas,' performed in London, May 1886, and 'Weather or No,' a musical duologue, produced at the Savoy Theatre in Aug. 1896. An orchestral 'Idyll' was played at one of Henschel's London Symphony Concerts on Mar. 11, 1897. This, two quintets for piano and strings, a suite for violin and piano, many piano pieces and an opera 'The Ring' (1886) remain unpublished. The list of printed works includes 'The Waits of Bremen,' 'The Dying Swan,' 'Summer by the Sea,' short cantatas, part-songs, 'The Hag,' 'It was a Lover and his Lass,' trios, etc., for female voices, a violin sonata in B minor, some sixteen anthems, ten services, very numerous organ pieces and some songs, all of which show great taste and refinement of treatment.                         M.

SELLE, THOMAS (*b.* Zörbig, Saxony, Mar. 23, 1599; *d.* Hamburg, July 2, 1663), was first

[1] See *Mus. T.,* Feb. 1919.

rector at Wesselburen; in 1624 at Heide; in 1625 at Wesselburen-Itzehoe; in 1634 cantor at Itzehoe; in 1637 cantor at Johanneum, Hamburg; and in 1641 town cantor, minor canon and musical director at Hamburg Cathedral. He composed a large number of concerts, madrigals, motets, sacred and secular songs, including a number of settings of poems by Rist, the various books bearing the long florid titles customary at that time (*Q.-L.*; *Riemann*).

SELLINGER'S ROUND, a 16th-century tune and round dance, of unknown authorship, which had immense popularity during the 16th and 17th centuries. The original form of the title was doubtless 'St. Leger's Round.' The delightful vigour and unusual character of the air are felt to-day, when played before a modern audience, as fully as in its own period. It is frequently referred to in 16th- and 17th-century literature, including *Bacchus Bountie*, 1593; Morley's *Plaine and Easie Introduction*, 1597, and elsewhere. In some cases the sub-title 'or the Beginning of the World' is found added to it, and this is partly explained in a comedy named 'Lingua,' 1607. An excellent version of the tune, arranged with variations by William Byrd, is found in 'The Fitzwilliam Virginal Book,' and other copies of the air are in Lady Neville's Virginal Book and William Ballet's Lute-book. (See VIRGINAL MUSIC.)

Printed copies, which differ considerably, and are not so good as those referred to, appear in some of the Playford publications, including early editions of 'The Dancing Master,' on 'Musick's Handmaid,' and 'Musick's delight the Cithren.' The original dance has probably been a maypole one, and this is borne out by a rude wood-cut on the title-page of a 17th-century 'Garland,' where figures are depicted dancing round a maypole, and 'Hey for Sellinger's Round' inscribed above them.

The following is the air, without the variations and harmony, as given in the 'Fitzwilliam Virginal Book':

F. K.

SELNECCER (SELENECCER), NIKOLAUS (*b.* Hersbruck, near Nuremberg, Dec. 6, 1528; *d.* Leipzig, May 24, 1592), was organist of the Burgkapelle in that city, at the age of 12. and

studied at Wittenberg from 1540.  From 1557–
1561 he was court preacher and tutor in Dresden, and subsequently held professional posts
in Jena (1561–68), Leipzig (1568–70), Wolfenbüttel (1570–74), Leipzig again (1574–88).  In
the latter year he was deprived of his offices and
became Superintendent at Hildesheim, until at
the death of the Elector Christian of Saxony he
was reinstated.  He was an eminent theologian,
and wrote the words and music of many hymns ;
his great work in this direction was published
at Leipzig in 1587, under the title ' Christliche
Psalmen, Lieder, vnd Kirchengesenge,' set for
four voices, Selneccer's own compositions being
marked with his initials.  Specimens of his
music are given in several of the hymn-books of
the 17th century.  (Q.-L.)                   M.

SELVA, BLANCHE MARIE (b. Brive, Corrèze,
Jan. 29, 1884), French pianist, was rewarded
with a first-class medal in the preparatory pianoforte class at the Paris Conservatoire (1895), and
became a pupil of V. d'Indy.  She studied at
the Schola Cantorum, taught piano there for
many years, and afterwards at the Strassburg
and Prague Conservatoires.  Her concert career
began at the age of 13 ; at 20 she had performed all Bach's works in 17 concerts.  Since
1902 she has devoted her remarkable talent to
the works of modern French composers, which
she played at the Société Nationale de Musique,
and at the Libre Esthétique, Brussels.

Her works relating to PF. teaching and
musical interpretation are : La Sonate (Paris,
Rouart et Lerolle, 1913) ; Quelques mots sur la
sonate (Paris, Mellotée, 1914) ; L'Enseigne-
ment musical de la technique du piano, comprising two preparatory books (book 1, 1922), and
3 volumes (vol. 3 in 2 parts).  (Paris, Rouart
et Lerolle).                             M. L. P.

SEMBRICH, MARCELLA (b. Wisniewczyk,
Galicia, Feb. 15, 1858), distinguished Polish-
American soprano.  The daughter of a musician, Kasimir Kochanski, Sembrich adopted
her mother's maiden name.  Taught by her
father, at the age of 12 she played both the
violin and the piano in public ; later she received further instruction on these instruments
from Wilhelm Stengel (whom she afterwards
married) and Brustermann, then went to
Vienna for the completion of her studies, but
' discovering ' her voice she determined to
adopt a vocal career.  Accordingly she studied
at Vienna singing under Rokitansky, and later
at Milan under Lamperti the younger, and on
June 7, 1877, made her début at Athens in
' I Puritani.'

Further study of the German repertory fol-
lowed, under Richard Lewy.  In October, 1878,
Sembrich made a highly successful début at
Dresden as Lucia.  There she remained until
the spring of 1880, singing coloratura parts.  In
June, 1880, she made her first appearance in
England, at the Royal Italian Opera, singing
the part of Lucia and subsequently other rôles.
She returned there for the seasons of 1881–84.
During the succeeding years she sang in Paris,
Russia, Spain and the United States, and in
1895 reappeared in London, at Covent Garden,
as Susanna.  Thereafter her appearances in
opera were confined to Austria and the United
States, where she was long a member of the
Metropolitan Opera Company, retiring in 1909.
She continued active in concert singing on both
sides of the Atlantic until 1917, when she per-
manently retired and made her home in New
York.

Sembrich's voice, singularly perfect in
quality, with a compass from $c'$ to $f'''$,
was also capable of true expressiveness.  As
a singer of songs she achieved a combination
of beautiful tone with musical intelligence.

A. C. ; rev. W. S. S.

SEMELE, a secular oratorio by Handel, composed in 1743, between June 3 and July 4.  The
libretto is slightly altered from an opera-book
of Congreve's, written in 1707.  ' Semele ' is
termed by Arnold ' A Dramatic Performance,'
by Mainwaring ' An English opera [1] but called
an Oratorio,' while it was announced at different
times in the General Advertiser as ' Semele, after
the manner of an Opera,' and ' Semele, after the
manner of an Oratorio.'  The first performance
took place on Feb. 10, 1744, at Covent Garden
Theatre ; the following December, with additions and alterations, King's Theatre, Haymarket ; revived by Smith and Stanley in
1762, and Cambridge University Musical
Society, Nov. 27, 1878.  The original MS. is in
the Roy. Lib. B.M., and there are some interesting sketches (principally of Act iii.) in the Fitzwilliam Museum at Cambridge.        W. B. S.

SEMET, THÉOPHILE (b. Lille, Sept. 6, 1824 ;
d. Corbeil, near Paris, Apr. 15, 1888), opera
composer.  The prizes he gained at the local
Conservatoire procured him a grant from the
municipality to study in Paris, and he entered
Halévy's class for composition.  His first work
was merely a few songs and some charming
orchestral music for 'La Petite Fadette,' vaudeville in two acts (Variétés, Dec. 28, 1850), but
he at length procured a better opportunity, and
his ' Nuits d'Espagne,' two acts (May 26), and
' La Demoiselle d'honneur,' three acts (Dec. 30),
were both produced in 1857 with success at the
Théâtre Lyrique ; ' Gil Blas ' (Mar. 26, 1860),
an opéra-comique in five acts, and ' Ondine,'
three acts (Jan. 7, 1863), followed at the same
theatre, and his next work, ' La Petite Fadette '
(Sept. 11, 1869), was produced at the Opéra-
Comique.

Besides his operas he composed songs for a
piece called ' Constantinople ' (1854) ; songs ;
a cantata (performed at the Opéra, Aug. 15,
1862) ; airs de ballet for ' Les Pirates de la

[1] It was given as an opera at the new theatre, Cambridge, by
members of the University and others, under the direction of Dr
C. B. ROOTHAM (q.v.), on Feb. 10, 1925.

Savane ' (1867), and many partsongs, some of
which, especially ' La Danse des Sylphes,' are
remarkable. He was drummer at the Opéra
for many years. G. C.

SEMIBREVE (Fr. *ronde*; Ger. *Taktnote,
ganze Note*, whence the American term *whole
note*; Ital. *semibreve*) : the half of a breve
(whence its name) and equal to two minims. It
is written ○, and its rest is —, a block-stroke
placed below a line of the stave (see NOTATION).

SEMICHORUS, *i.e.* Half-chorus ; a word
used to denote a kind of antiphonal effect produced by employing half the number of voices
at certain points, and contrasting this smaller
body of sound with the full chorus. M.

SEMICROMA (Lat. *semichroma* ; Eng.
*quaver*, or *semiquaver*), the Italian name for
the semiquaver. Old writers, however, sometimes apply the term croma to the crotchet, and
semicroma to the quaver. (See NOTATION,
subsection LESSER NOTE VALUES ; QUAVER.)
W. S. R.

SEMIFUSA, the Latin name for the semiquaver ; but sometimes applied to the quaver
also. (See NOTATION.) W. S. R.

SEMIMINIMA MAJOR and MINOR (Eng.
*greater* and *lesser half - minim*=crotchet and
quaver ; Ital. *croma e semicroma*; Ger. *Viertel
und Achtel*; French *noire et croche*). (See
NOTATION, subsection LESSER NOTE VALUES.)

SEMIQUAVER (Fr. *double croche*; Ger.
*Sechzehntel*, whence the American term *Sixteenth note*; Ital. *semicroma, biscroma*) : the
half of a quaver, and the sixteenth of a semibreve. It is written, when single ♪, when
joined ♫. Its rest is ᶻ (see NOTATION).

SEMIRAMIDE (*i.e.* Semiramis, Empress of
Nineveh) ; a favourite subject with Italian
writers of operas. Libretti upon it were written
by Moniglia, Apostolo Zeno and Silvani ; and
Clément's *Dictionnaire lyrique* contains a list
of twenty-one operas composed to one or other
of these by the masters of the 18th century.
Voltaire's play on the same subject was adapted
to music and set by Graun (Berlin, 1754) and
Catel (1802). Rossini's version was written to
a libretto by Rossi, and produced Venice, Feb. 3,
1823 ; King's Theatre, July 15, 1824 ; New
York, Apr. 25, 1826 ; in French, as ' Semiramis,'
Paris, July 9, 1860. — SEMIRAMIDE RICONO-
SCIUTA, words by Metastasio, was set by Vinci,
Porpora, Cocchi, Sarti, Traetta, Meyerbeer
and Gluck—the last of these at Vienna in
1748. G.

SEMITONE (from the Greek ἡμιτόνιον). Half
a tone ; the smallest interval in the ordinary
musical scales. The semitone may be of different
kinds, each of which has a different theoretical
magnitude.

Since the invention of the diatonic scale the
natural interval of the fourth has been subdivided
artificially into two tones and a semitone. In the
ancient Greek time the two tones were both what
are now called *major* tones, and the hemitone
had a magnitude determined by the difference
between their sum and the fourth ; but when
harmony began to prevail, one of the tones was
diminished to a *minor* tone, and this gave the
modern semitone a little greater value. The
semitone, so formed, as belonging to the diatonic
scale (from B to C, or from E to F, for example)
is called a *diatonic* semitone.

The introduction of chromatic notes gave rise
to a third kind of semitone, as from C to C♯ or
from G to G♭ ; this is called a *chromatic* semitone and has a less magnitude than the diatonic
one.

Finally came the great simplification of music
by dividing the octave into twelve equal
intervals, each of which was called a *mean* semitone, thus abolishing practically the difference
between the diatonic and the chromatic values.
A semitone may now be considered, in practical
use, as simply the interval between the sounds
given by any two adjoining keys on a well-
tuned piano.

The relations between the theoretical magni-
tudes of the different kinds of semitones are
about as follows : If we represent the magnitude
of a mean semitone by 25, the true magnitude of
a diatonic semitone will be about 28 ; of a chromatic semitone about 18 ; and of the ancient
Greek hemitone about 23. W. P.

SEMPLICE, ' simple ' ; a direction denoting
that the passage so marked is to be performed
without any adornment or deviation from the
time, used particularly in passages of which the
character might possibly be misunderstood.
The arietta which forms the subject of the
variations in Beethoven's last PF. sonata, op.
111, is marked ' Adagio molto semplice cantabile.' Variants of the term, suggesting less
formality, are ' semplicemente ' and ' con sem-
plicità.' M.

SEMPRE, ' always,' a word used in conjunction with some other mark of time or expression
to signify that such mark is to remain in force
until a new direction appears. Its purpose is
to remind the performer of the directions which
might otherwise be forgotten—as in the scherzo
of the Eroica Symphony, where the direction
*Sempre pp. e staccato* is repeated again and again
throughout the movement. M.

SENAILLÉ, JEAN BAPTISTE (*b.* Paris, Nov.
23, 1687 ; *d.* there, Oct. 15, 1730), a violinist of
eminence, at one time member of the band of
Louis XV., was born in the parish of Saint
Germain l'Auxerrois, Paris. His father, Jean
Senaillé, was one of the 24 *violons du roi*. He
received his earliest violin instruction from
Queversin, a member of the famous ' Vingt-
quatre violons,' and during his period of study
with this master assisted a *maître à danser*
named Bonnefons. His next teacher was
Corelli's excellent pupil, Jean Baptiste Anet,

generally known as Baptiste, whose teaching imbued him with such a longing to visit Italy that he travelled to Modena, where he became a pupil of Tommaso Antonio Vitali. According to the account of Senaillé given by Jacques Lacombe in his *Dictionnaire portatif des beaux-arts* (Paris, 1752), Anet's teaching enabled his pupil to surpass the Italian violinist; for on his arrival at Modena, during the time of the annual fair held in the month of May, the composer of the opera then being performed begged him to play in his orchestra, and on gaining his consent installed him with ceremony in a place prepared for him above the other members of the band. After the performance, he was presented to the Duke and Duchess of Modena: played several of his own sonatas before them and their guests with unqualified success, eventually receiving an appointment in the music of the court. In 1720 he settled in Paris, where the special recommendation of the Duchess of Modena, daughter of the Duc d'Orléans—at that time Regent of France—procured him a position in the court band. He performed frequently with great success in the Concert Spirituel from its foundation. A similar appointment was accorded him in the private band of Louis XV., and he held this until his death, when he was succeeded by Joseph Francœur.

Senaillé ranked as one of the best performers of his time in France. His importation of the Italian methods of playing influenced the French school—at that time in its first state of development—almost as much as did Leclair. Through his two best pupils Guignon and Guillemain, his traditions were transmitted and preserved. His compositions show the influence of Corelli; they comprised five books of sonatas for violin alone, and were published in books of 10 sonatas in the following years: 1710, 1712, 1716, 1721, 1727. A selection of 13 sonatas by him appeared, taken from his violin works (Le Cène, Amsterdam), under the title 'Sonates de Senaillé ajustées pour les musettes et les vielles,' fol. s. d. (M. Pincherle's Collection, Paris). An aria of his for PF. and vln. is included in G. Jensen's 'Classische Violin-Musik,' Heft iii. A sarabande and allemanda (sonate à violon seul) is arranged by Alfred Moffat. A sonata in G edited by Alfred Moffat is in Simrock's 'Meister-Schule für Violine mit Begleitung des Pianoforte.' Alard includes Senaillé's Ninth Sonata in his 'Maîtres classiques de violon' (1862), and G. Jensen has arranged the same sonata for piano and violin, which is published in 'Classische Violin-Musik,' 1890. A composition by Senaillé is also to be found in E. M. E. Deldevez's 'Pièces diverses choisies' (Paris, Richault, 1858).

BIBL.—A. VIDAL, *Les Instruments à archet*; G. HART, *The Violin and its Music*; CHORON ET FAVOLLE, *Dict. hist. des mus.*; FÉLIX HUËT, *Études sur les différentes écoles de violon*; FÉTIS, *Biog. des mus.*; J. LACOMBE. *Dictionnaire des beaux-arts*; CLARKE, *Dict. of Fiddlers*; TITON DU TILLET, *Parnasse françois, premier supplément*

(pp. 673-4); L. J. VALDRIGHI, *Capelle, concerti e musiche di Casa d'Este ..tti e memorie delle R. R. Deputazioni di storia patria per le provincie modenesi* (series iii., ii., 434); L. DE LA LAURENCIE, *L'École française de violon*, i. (1922, pp. 165-79).

E. H.-A.; addns. M. P.

**SÉNART, MAURICE** (*b.* Jan. 29, 1878), music publisher, founded, in 1908, in partnership with Roudanez, a music-publishing business which set out to make the best classical works accessible to the public. In this a large edition was undertaken, under the artistic direction of Vincent d'Indy, of which each number cost only 25 centimes. Then came the vocal works edited by Henry Expert, and an anthology of popular songs.

In 1912 were published 'Maîtres contemporains de l'orgue' (8 vols.). This same year Sénart was alone at the head of the firm, which was changed in 1920 into the Société anonyme des Éditions Maurice Sénart, with its business address at 20 rue du Dragon. By his efforts since then, the publication of 'La Musique de chambre' has been carried on, a vast periodic collection of instrumental and vocal music, of which three-quarters are devoted to modern music and one-quarter to old music. From its foundation to Dec. 1925 the Société had published more than 5000 works or about 40,000 engraved pages.          M. P.

**SENESINO**, FRANCESCO BERNARDI (*b.* Siena, *c.* 1680; *d. circa* 1750), one of the most famous of the sopranists who flourished in the 18th century. He derived his name from his native town. He received his musical education from Bernacchi, at Bologna. In 1719 he was singing at the court theatre of Saxony, and when Handel came to Dresden in quest of singers was engaged by him for London. His first appearance in this country (Nov. 1720) was in Bononcini's opera 'Astarto,' which at once established him in public favour. He sang next in a revival of Handel's 'Floridante,' and in the celebrated 'Muzio Scævola'; afterwards in Handel's 'Ottone,' 'Flavio' and 'Giulio Cesare' (1723), 'Tamerlano' (1724), 'Rodelinda' (1725), 'Scipio' and 'Alessandro' (1726), and in various operas and pasticcios by other composers. In 'Giulio Cesare' his declamation of the famous accompanied recitative 'Alma del gran Pompeo' created a special sensation. A writer in the *London Magazine* (Feb. 1733) relates an amusing anecdote of Senesino in this opera:

'When I was last at the opera of "Julius Cæsar," a piece of the machinery tumbled down from the roof of the theatre upon the stage, just as Senesino had chanted forth these words "Cesare non seppe mai che sia timore" (Cæsar never knew fear). The poor hero was so frightened that he trembled, lost his voice, and fell crying. Every tyrant or tyrannical minister is just such a Cæsar as Senesino.'

'Alessandro' had a run of two months, and its last performance, advertised for June 7, was prevented by the sudden illness of Senesino, who, as soon as he was able to travel, set off for Italy, for the recovery of his health, promising to return the next winter. This promise, however, was not kept in time to enable the Opera-house to open before Christmas.

Senesino reappeared in Handel's 'Admeto,' early in 1727. This was followed in the same year by 'Riccardo Imo,' and in 1728 by 'Siroë' and 'Tolomeo,' in which a great effect was made by the echo song, 'Dite che fa,' sung by Cuzzoni, with many of the passages repeated behind the scenes by Senesino. But now, after several unprosperous seasons, the society called the Royal Academy was dissolved. Hawkins attributes to this time the quarrel which ended in a final rupture between Senesino and the great composer. But this is disproved by the fact that Senesino returned to sing for Handel in 1730. That there was, however, much discord in the company before it separated is true enough.

He rejoined the Haymarket company, under Handel's management, at a salary of 1400 guineas, and appeared on Feb. 2, 1731, in 'Poro,' then considered a great success. In the same year were revived 'Rodelinda' and 'Rinaldo.' 'Ezio' and 'Sosarme' were produced in 1732. Besides singing in all these, Senesino took part (May 2, 1732) in 'Esther,' Handel's first oratorio, described as 'a new species of exhibition at the Opera-house,' and on June 10, in a curious performance, under the composer's own direction, of 'Acis and Galatea.' Several airs and three choruses were interpolated on this occasion, from Handel's early Neapolitan serenata on the same subject, and the piece was sung partly in English and partly in Italian.

The last of Handel's operas in which Senesino appeared was 'Orlando' (Jan. 1733), but he took part later in the same season in 'Deborah,' described then as an opera, and performed (as was 'Esther') on opera nights. The long impending quarrel now came to a crisis. Accordingly, says Burney,

'the nobility and gentry opened a subscription for Italian operas at Lincoln's Inn Fields, inviting Porpora thither to compose and conduct, and engaging Senesino, Cuzzoni, Montagnana, Segatti, Bertolli, and afterwards Farinelli, to perform there.'

There Senesino remained till 1735, when he returned to Siena, with a fortune of £15,000, and built himself a house.

Senesino's voice was a mezzo-soprano, or, according to some, a contralto. Although limited in compass it was considered by many good judges to be superior in quality even to that of Farinelli. It was clear, penetrating and flexible, his intonation faultless, his shake perfect. Purity, simplicity and expressiveness were the characteristics of his style, while for the delivery of recitative 'he had not his fellow in Europe.'

In 1739 Senesino was living at Florence and sang a duet with the Archduchess Maria Theresa there.                                  F. A. M.

SENFF, Bartholf (b. Friedrichshall, Coburg, Sept, 2, 1815 ; d. Badenweiler, June 25, 1900), an eminent German music-publisher. He founded the house which bears his name, in Leipzig, in 1850, and his catalogue contains original editions of Mendelssohn, Schumann, Brahms (opp. 5, 6, Gavotte by Gluck, 5 Studien für PF.), Gade, Hiller, Reinecke, Reitz, Rubinstein, and other masters, as well as the excellent educational works of Louis Köhler.

Senff was founder, editor and proprietor of the well-known musical periodical Signale für die musikalische Welt. (See Periodicals, Musical.)                                  G.

SENFL (Senfel), Ludwig (b. Zürich, end of 15th cent. ; d. Munich, c. 1555). A volume of MS. songs in the Vienna library contains some verses, written and set to music by Senfl himself, describing his early enthusiasm for music, his education under Heinrich Isaac, and his gratitude to that master. At an early age he entered the court chapel of Maximilian I., ultimately succeeded Isaac as Kapellmeister, and held that office till the emperor's death (Jan. 1519), on which occasion he wrote music to the words 'Quis dabit oculis nostris fontem lacrimarum.' In 1520 he was at Augsburg, received a present of fifty gulden from Charles V. on Feb. 19, and in the following November personally edited the 'Liber selectarum cantionum,' one of the first music books printed in Germany. Thence he went to Munich, though in what capacity is uncertain. On one title-page (1526) he is called 'Musicus intonator,' on another (1534) 'Musicus primarius,' of the Duke of Bavaria, while in his own letters he subscribes himself simply 'Componist zu München.' In Forster's collection of Liedlein (preface dated Jan. 31, 1556) he is spoken of as 'L. S. seliger' (i.e. dead); and if the title 'musicus primarius' stands for Kapellmeister he must have died or retired some years before, since Ludwig Daser had held that office for some years when Lassus went to Munich in 1557.

The well-known letter from Luther to Senfl [1] is no evidence that the composer had worked specially for the Lutheran Church, though the existence of the correspondence has given rise to that idea. Indeed his connexion with the strictly Catholic court of Munich would, as Fétis points out, render it most improbable.[2] Four letters written by Senfl to the Margrave Albrecht of Brandenburg and to Georg Scultheis are printed in the A.M.Z. for Aug. 12, 1863.

A portrait engraved on a model by Hagenauer of Augsburg, with the inscription 'Ludovvicus Senfel,' and on the reverse 'Psallam deo meo quamdiu fuero 1529,' is in the collection of coins and medals at Vienna.

1 Dated Coburg, Oct. 4, 1530. The letter is printed in Dr. M. Luthers Gedanken über die Musik, F. A. Beck (Berlin, 1828), p. 58.
2 Biographie des musiciens, vi. 44.

The state library at Munich contains the manuscript church service books begun by Isaac and completed by Senfl, as well as manuscript masses by the latter. These have been published in *D.D.T.* (second series) III. ii. The most important publications during his life are:

(1) ' Quinque salutationes D. N. Hiesu Christi,' etc. (Norimbergae, 1526).
(2) ' Varia carminum genera, quibus tum Horatius, tum alii egregii poetae . . . harmoniis composita ' (*Id.* 1534).
(3) ' 121 newe Lieder ' (*Id.* 1534), with 81 nos. by L. S.
(4) ' Magnificat octo tonorum,' *a* 4, 5 (*Id.* 1537).
(5) ' 115 guter newer Liedlein ' (*Id.* 1544), with 64 nos. by L. S.

Besides these Eitner[1] names above 100 separate pieces printed in various collections of the 16th century. (See *Q.-L.*) Nine sacred pieces (*a* 4) are given by Winterfeld in *Der evangelische Kirchengesang* (Leipzig, 1843), and five Lieder by Liliencron in *Die historischen Volkslieder der Deutschen* (Leipzig, 1865–69).     J. R. S.-B.

SENNET—also written SENET, SENNATE, SYNNET, CYNET, SIGNET or SIGNATE—a word which occurs in stage-directions in the plays of the Elizabethan dramatists, and is used to denote that a particular fanfare is to be played. The name is probably derived from Seven, and may indicate a flourish of seven notes, as suggested in Stainer and Barrett's *Dictionary of Musical Terms*. It is a technical term, and what particular notes were played is now unknown. A Sennet was distinguished from a Flourish, as is proved by a stage-direction in Dekker's *Satiromastix*, ' Trumpets sound a florish, and then a sennate.' (Nares's *Glossary*.)

                        W. B. S.

SENZA, ' without '—as *senza organo*, ' without organ ' ; a direction of frequent occurrence throughout Handel's organ concertos ; *senza repetizione*, ' without repeat ' (see REPEAT) ; *senza tempo*, ' without time,' which occurs in Schumann's Humoreske, op. 20, in the movement marked Precipitoso. The right hand is marked *come senza tempo* (' Wie ausser tempo,' in German), while the left remains *in tempo*. The same direction is employed at the end of Chopin's Nocturne, op. 9, No. 3. In the ' Sanctus ' of Verdi's Requiem both the terms *senza misura* and *senza tempo* occur.    M.

SEPTAVE, the compass of seven diatonic notes reckoned upward from the tonic or keynote. The term is occasionally employed by organ-builders.             T. E.

SEPTET (Fr. *septuor* ; Ger. *Septett* ; Ital. *septetto*), a composition for seven instruments or voices.

Instrumental septets are comparatively few in number. As noted under SEXTET the addition of extra instruments to the quartet of strings tends to go beyond the domain of chamber-music. T. F. Dunhill in his treatise on Chamber Music notes the existence of a single work for strings alone, otherwise composers have looked to the possibilities of the variety afforded by the inclusion of pianoforte

[1] *Bibliographie* (Berlin, 1877).

and wind instruments in the combination. Among such are Beethoven's op. 20 for violin, viola, violoncello, double-bass, clarinet, bassoon and horn ; D'Indy and Schönberg have written for strings and wind ; Ravel for strings, wind and harp ; Hummel, Saint-Saëns and Spohr for pianoforte, strings and wind, and Onslow and Pijper for pianoforte, wind and double-bass. (See CHAMBER MUSIC.)

The vocal septet occurs in opera where the dramatic situation may allow for the ensemble of the protagonists. One will be found in the last act of Goetz's ' Taming of the Shrew.'

                        N. C. G.

SEQUENCE, (*a*) the repetition of a definite group of notes or chords in different positions of the scale, like regular steps ascending or descending, as in the following outlines :

The device has been a favourite one with composers, from Corelli, Bach and Handel to Schumann, Brahms and Wagner. The reason is partly that it is so thoroughly intelligible without being commonplace. The mind is easily led from point to point by recognising each successive step after the first group of chords has been given, and is sufficiently interested by the slight amount of diversity which prevails at each repetition. It thus supplies a vital element of form in a manner which in some cases has certain advantages over simple exact repetition, especially when short phrases are repeated in juxtaposition. It was consequently made much use of by early composers of sonatas, and instrumental works of like nature, such as Corelli and his immediate successors ; and in many cases examples make their appearance at analogous points in different movements, indicating the recognition of formal principles in their introduction. This occurs, for instance, near the beginning of the second half in the following movements from Corelli's Opera Quarta : Corrente and Allemanda of Sonata 1, Allemanda and Corrente of Sonata 2, Corrente of Sonata 3, Corrente and Giga of Sonata 4, Gavotte of Sonata 5, Allemanda and Giga of Sonata 6, and so forth. A large proportion of both ancient and modern sequences are diatonic ; that is, the groups are repeated analogously in the same key series, without consideration of the real difference of quality in the intervals ; so that major sevenths occasionally answer minor sevenths, and diminished fifths perfect fifths, and so forth ; and it has long been considered allowable to introduce intervals and combinations, in those circumstances, which would otherwise have been held inadmissible. Thus a triad on the leading note would in ordinary circumstances be considered as a discord, and would be limited in progression accordingly; but if it occurred in a sequence, its limitations were freely obviated by the preponderant influence of the established form of motion. Such diatonic sequences, called also sometimes diatonic successions, are extremely familiar in Handel's works. A typical instance is a capriccio in G major, published in Pauer's 'Alte Meister,' which contains at least fifteen sequences, some of them unusually long ones, in four pages of allegro. The subject itself is a characteristic example of a sequence in a single part; it is as follows :

A kind of sequence which was early developed, but which is more characteristic of later music, is the modulatory sequence, sometimes also called chromatic. In this form accidentals are introduced, sometimes by following exactly the quality of the intervals where the diatonic series would not admit of them, and sometimes by purposely altering them to gain the step of modulation. This will be easily intelligible from the following example :

The usefulness of the device in such circumstances is, if anything, even more marked than it is in a single key, because of the greater breadth of range which it allows, and the closeness and cogency of the successive transitions which it renders possible. A compact and significant example to the point is the following from a fugue by Cherubini in C major :

Beethoven made very remarkable use of this device, especially in the great sonata in B♭, op. 106, from which an example is quoted in the article MODULATION. The 'working out' portion of the first movement of the same sonata is an almost unbroken series of sequences of both orders; and the introduction to the final fugue is even more remarkable, both for the length of the sequence and the originality

of its treatment. The first-mentioned, which is from the slow movement, is further remarkable as an example of a peculiar manipulation of the device by which composers have obtained very impressive results. This is the change of emphasis in the successive steps of which it is composed. For instance, if the characteristic group consists of three chords of equal length, and the time in which it occurs is a square one, it is clear that the chord which is emphatic in the first step will be weakest in the next, and *vice versa*. This form will be most easily understood from an outline example :

A passage at the beginning of the presto at the end of Beethoven's Leonora overture, No. 3, is a good example of a sequence of this kind in a single part. It begins in the following quotation at * :

(See ACCENT.)

The extension of the characteristic group of a sequence is almost unlimited, but it will be obvious at once that in harmonic sequences the shorter and simpler they are the more immediately they will be understood. In long-limbed sequences the hearer may soon perceive that there is a principle of order underlying what he hears, though its exact nature may always elude his apprehension, and in respect of the larger branches of form this is a decided advantage. Among short-limbed emphatic sequences in modern music, the one of eight steps which occurs towards the end of the first full portion of the overture to 'Die Meistersinger' is conspicuous, and it has the advantage of being slightly irregular. The long-limbed sequences are sometimes elaborately concealed, so that the underlying source of order in the progression can only with difficulty be unravelled. A remarkable example of a very complicated sequence of this kind is a passage in Schumann's fantasia in C major (op. 17), in the movement in E♭, marked 'Moderato con energia,' beginning at the 58th bar. The passage is too long to quote, but the clue to the mystery may be extracted somewhat after this manner :

In order to see how this has been manipulated reference must be made to the original.

Another species of sequence is that in which a figure or melody is repeated a tone higher; this has been termed a ROSALIA (*q.v.*). Another, which is equally characteristic, is a repetition of a figure or passage a semitone higher; an example from the Eroica Symphony is quoted in Vol. III. p. 486 of this Dictionary.

The device has never been bound to rigid exactness, because it is easy to follow, and slight deviations seasonably introduced are often happy in effect. In fact, its virtue does not consist so much in the exactness of transposition as in the intelligibility of analogous repetitions. If the musical idea is sufficiently interesting to carry the attention with it, the sequence will perform its function adequately even if it be slightly irregular both in its harmonic steps and in its melodic features; and this happens to be the case both in the example from the slow movement of Beethoven's sonata in B♭, and in the passage quoted from Schumann's fantasia. It is not so, however, with the crude harmonic successions which are more commonly met with; for they are like diagrams, and if they are not exact they are good for nothing.     C. H. H. P.

(*b*) (Lat. *Sequentia, Prosa.*) A hymn of peculiar structure, which owes its name to its position in the Mass; it appears there as the continuation or sequence of the Gradual and Alleluia. It originally was a long jubilus or melody without words, attached to the *a* of the Alleluia. (See TROPE.) In the 9th century in France words were adapted to the notes, and these were called a ' Prose,' because they followed the lines of the music and not any scheme of metre. When these compositions had thus won a place for themselves, fresh ones came to be written in regular metre, and the old name Prose being unsuitable gave way to the new name Sequence. From the 12th century to the 15th century such compositions were most popular; and many of the most beautiful specimens we possess were written by the great hymnologists who flourished during these productive periods. Mediæval Office-Books contain innumerable sequences of striking originality; but at the last revision of the Roman liturgy, by direction of the Council of Trent, the greater number of these were expunged. Five, however, have been retained in the current missal; and these five occupy a very prominent position in the services in which they are incorporated, as well as in the history of ecclesiastical music.

(1) The sequence appointed for Easter Sunday is Victimae paschali, the oldest now in use, and in reality a Prose, attributed to Wipo in the first half of the 11th century.

(2) The sequence for Whitsunday, Veni Sancte Spiritus, in rhymed triplets of Trochaic Dimeter Catalectic, has been attributed[1] to Innocent III. at the end of the 12th century; it is called by mediæval writers, The Golden Sequence.

(3) For the festival of Corpus Christi, S. Thomas Aquinas wrote the celebrated sequence, Lauda Sion, which is generally believed to date from about the year 1261.

(4) To Innocent III. is also attributed the Stabat Mater, sung since 1727 on the Feasts of the Seven Dolours of Our Lady (the Friday in Passion Week, and the third Sunday in September). The authorship, however, has not been certainly ascertained; and many are inclined to attribute it to Jacobus de Benedictis (Jacopone). (See STABAT MATER.)

(5) Even more celebrated than any of these is the Dies irae written, during the latter half of the 12th century or beginning of the 13th century, by Thomas of Celano, and sung in the Requiem, or Mass for the Dead. In the triple stanzas of this wonderful poem the rhymed Latin of the Middle Ages attained its highest perfection; and, though the Stabat Mater is frequently said to be second only to it in beauty, the distance between the two is very great.

The plain-chant melodies of sequences differ from hymn melodies in their structure. The ancient jubilus was divided into sections, each of which is sung twice, and consequently a sequence melody properly consists of a series of phrases each of which is repeated. Similarly a sequence is a series of verses each dual in structure and consisting of strophe and antistrophe. They may be represented by the formula $aa' : bb' : cc'$, etc. In the early rhythmical proses $a$, $b$, $c$, etc., are usually unlike one another; in the later metrical proses for the most part the same scheme runs throughout the words though the music varies. The Dies irae is irregular and does not conform to the usual type, because it was not originally a sequence at all.    W. S. R.; revised W. H. F.

SERAFINO, SANTO (SANCTUS SERAPHIN), and GIORGIO (uncle and nephew), two celebrated violin-makers of Venice. The uncle, as his label informs us (' Sanctus Seraphin Utinensis fecit Venetiis '), was originally of Udine, a town in the Venetian territory towards the mountains of Carinthia, and probably of Jewish extraction. His nephew, if we may judge from the style of his instruments, worked with the uncle many years, and appears to have succeeded him in the business. The instruments of Santo Serafino occupy a middle place between the Italian and the Tyrolese school. As far as external appearance goes, the maker seems to vacillate between the model of Stainer and that of Nicolo Amati. But in the essential particulars of the art, in the selection

[1] For attribution to Stephen Langton of Canterbury, see the *Tablet*, May 22, 1926.

of wood of the finest and most sonorous quality, in the proper calculation of the proportions, and the solidity and finish of the parts, he worked on the principles of the Cremona makers. Few equalled him as a workman. Those who wish to see how far mechanical perfection can be carried should examine his purfling with a magnifying glass. In Serafino's earlier years the Stainer character predominates in his instruments ; in his later years he leaned to the Amati model. His instruments are famous for their perfect finish (reminding forcibly of the style of Stradivarius), their remarkably lustrous deep red varnish and fine mellow tone.

The period of Santo Serafino's activity extends from about 1678–1735. He worked in Udine for nearly twenty years, and during that time he employed an engraved label of large dimensions which runs : ' Sanctus Seraphinus Nicolai Amati Cremonensis Allumnus faciebat : Udine A. 16 .' It is worthy of note that the dates on Serafino's labels are in accordance with the rest of his work, neatly written in, and not bungled, as is frequently the case with his contemporaries. The Venetian label quoted at the beginning of this article is larger than any label to be found in a Cremona instrument. The legend on Serafino's ticket is framed by a design composed on three sides of graceful curving strokes, while the upper side is formed of two fern leaves and elegant curves. On either side there are some rolls of music and a violin. Representations of this ticket are given by Laurent Grillet in his *Ancêtres du violon* and also in von Lutgendorff's *Die Geigen- und Lautenmacher*. One of the finest known examples of this maker's work was a violoncello lent to the South Kensington Special Loan Exhibition by its owner H. B. Heath in 1872.

Georgio Serafino followed his uncle's later model with such precision that it is difficult to find any point of difference. Like his uncle, he finished his instruments to a degree which amounts to a fault, depriving them, as it does, of character and individuality. Like his uncle, he used a large copper-plate label (nearly all the Italian makers used letterpress labels) bearing the inscription ' Georgius Seraphin Sancti nepos fecit Venetiis (1743).' Both makers branded their instruments at the tail-pin.

A superb violin of Santo Serafino which belonged to Barré and Bayly's collection realised £280, at a sale by auction in 1894, while a violoncello by the same maker, the property of James Goding, was sold in a like manner for £56 : 14s. in 1857. According to Von Lutgendorff, George Seraphin was not Sanctus Seraphin's nephew but his grandson.

BIBL. — VON LUTGENDORFF, *Die Geigen- und Lautenmacher*; CHARLES READE, *A Lost Art Revived*; ALBERTO BACHMANN, *Le Violon*; J. M. FLEMING, *Old Violins*: LAURENT GRILLET, *Les Ancêtres du violon*; G. HART, *The Violin*; A. VIDAL, *Les Instruments à archet*.

E. J. P. ; addns. E. H.-A.

SERAGLIO, THE. (1) The English title of Mozart's ENTFÜHRUNG AUS DEM SERAIL (*q.v.*).

(2) An opera by Charles Dibdin under this title was produced at Covent Garden, Nov. 14, 1776. Dibdin being then in France, Dr. Arnold, composer to the theatre, had some share in the musical part of it, but it contains Dibdin's fine song ' Blow high, blow low ' sung in the opera by Reinhold, and afterwards introduced by Bannister into Arne's opera ' Thomas and Sally.' The opera had very little success, but both libretto and music were published. Harris, the Covent Garden manager, altered the piece considerably for acting purposes.    F. K.

SERAPHINE. The seraphine has already been referred to as a precursor of Debain's HARMONIUM (*q.v.*). It was an English free-reed instrument resembling the German Physharmonica, which latter was brought to England by the Schulz family in 1826. In 1828 a similar instrument, but named aeol-harmonica, was played by young Schulz at a Philharmonic Concert (Concertante for aeol-harmonica and two guitars, Apr. 28). In 1833, John Green, who had been Clementi's traveller, and had a shop in Soho Square, brought out the seraphine. Green engaged Samuel Wesley to give weekly performances upon the seraphine at his shop, and managed for some time to dispose of his instruments at 40 guineas each. But the seraphine was harsh and raspy in tone, and never found favour with sensitive musicians. The wind apparatus, similar to the organ, was a dead-weighted bellows giving a uniform pressure, and a swell was produced by opening a shutter of a box placed over the reeds.

In the year 1841 W. E. Evans invented the ' organo harmonica,' the improvements in the seraphine consisting of thin steel reeds artistically voiced, and coiled springs in the reservoir to enable the player to produce a rapid articulation with a small wind pressure, and to increase the power of tone as the reservoir filled. Eminent musicians publicly pronounced Evans' instrument more valuable than the seraphine as a substitute for the organ, but neither the one nor the other was capable of what is now known as ' dead expression.'

Patents for various improvements of the seraphine were taken out by Myers and Storer in 1839, by Storer alone in 1846 and by Mott in the same year. There is further reference to it in patents of Pape 1850, and Blackwell 1852. About the last-named date it was superseded by the harmonium. (See *PLATE XV*. No. 4.)    A. J. H.

SERENADE (Fr. *sérénade* ; Ger. *Ständchen* ; Ital. *serenata*), evening song, from the Italian *sera*. Hence the word has been applied, indiscriminately, to many different kinds of music intended to be sung or played at night in the open air ; and so generally has this connexion of ideas been accepted that, by common consent, the term 'serenade' has identified itself in many languages with the song sung by a lover standing beneath his mistress's window, or the concert of instrumental music substituted for it by an admirer with 'no voice for singing.'

To be true to nature, a serenade of this kind should be simple, melodious, sensuous in expression, and accompanied by some kind of instrument which the lover might carry in his hand. All these conditions are fulfilled in the most perfect example of the style that ever has been, or is ever likely to be, written—' Deh vieni alla finestra,' in ' Don Giovanni.' The melody of this is as artless as a folk-song, yet capable of breathing the very soul of voluptuous passion.

W. S. R.

If Mozart created the perfect type of vocal serenade in the song just mentioned, such things as his ' Hafner Serenade ' have served as the model of the instrumental serenade, which, like the *divertimento*, is generally in a large number of short movements. The two serenade trios of Beethoven (opp. 8 and 25) are illustrious specimens of the forms in which each section is of the most concise structure and built upon melodic themes that are easily recognisable by the untutored ear. Two serenades by Brahms are among his earlier works ; the first, op. 11, is for full orchestra, in D ; and the second, op. 16, in A, has no violins. It does not appear that the German equivalent, *Ständchen*, has found much favour with the composer of instrumental serenades.　　　　　　　　　　　M.

SERENATA (Fr. *sérénade* ; Ger. *Serenade* ; Ital. *serenata*). Though the terms serenata and serenade are generally regarded as interchangeable—so nearly synonymous that we have no choice but to give the one as the translated equivalent of the other—they mean, in musical language, two very different things.

The vocal serenata may be considered as a form of cantata, which may be either dramatic or imaginative, or even a simple ode on any subject not actually sacred. Handel applied the term to his Italian pastoral, ' Aci, Galatea, e Polifemo,' written at Naples in 1709 ; to the ode composed for the birthday of Anne of Denmark in 1712 ; and to the English pastoral ' Acis and Galatea,' [1] written at Cannons in 1720.

We must not omit mention of a serenata by Stradella in which two lovers, each with his orchestra *in a coach*, serenade a lady, a work which is famous because Handel appropriated a great deal of it in ' Israel.' It was republished as No. 3 of Chrysander's *Supplemente* to the edition of Handel.

The form of the instrumental serenata is much more clearly defined, and comprised within much narrower limits. It was very popular during the latter half of the 18th century ; and,

[1] Called also, in early copies, ' Opera,' ' Mask ' and ' Pastoral.'

for some considerable time, occupied a position midway between those of the orchestral suite which preceded and the symphony which followed it. From the former it borrowed the multiplicity, and from the latter the colouring, of the long series of lightly developed movements of which it usually consisted. Neither the sequence nor the structure of these movements was subject to any very rigid law. Two forms, however, were considered so necessary that they may almost be described as indispensable—the march and the minuet. With the former almost every serenata of any consequence began or ended. The latter was almost always interposed between two allegros, or an allegro and an andante, or, indeed, between any two movements of any other kind ; and used so freely that it frequently made its appearance several times in the course of a composition of importance. The gavotte and bourrée so freely used in the older suite were completely banished from the serenata. When wind instruments were alone employed, the composition was often called ' Harmoniemusik ' ; and this term was so generally received that music for wind instruments is popularly called ' Harmonie ' in Germany to the present day　The term cassation was also frequently applied to works of this kind, whether written for the full orchestra or for wind instruments alone ; and many pieces, not differing very much from these, were called divertimenti. Sometimes the number of instruments employed was very small, for the serenata was almost always intended for private performance, and it was a matter of necessity that it should accommodate itself to the resources of the particular establishment for which it was intended.　　　W. S. R.

SERES, WILLIAM, an early music-printer associated with John Day and others, had a privilege for printing psalters, etc. He was working in 1548, and was one of the early members of the Stationers' Company, filling the offices of Warden and Master. His shop was ' at the signe of the Hedge Hogg.' One of his noteworthy works is Francis Seagar's ' Certayne Psalms select out of the Psalter of David, drawn into English metre with notes to every Psalm in iiij parts to Synge,' 1553.　　F. K.

SERGEANT - TRUMPETER, see TRUMPETER.

SERINETTE, a miniature barrel organ with 10 to 13 high - pitched pipes employed in teaching the canary (*serin*) to whistle popular melodies. It was much used in France, and during the course of instruction the cage was covered with a cloth and the same tune played constantly until learnt by the bird. (See MECHANICAL APPLIANCES.)　　F. W. G.

SERMISY, CLAUDE DE (*b. circa* 1490 ; *d.*1562), one of the group of French musicians connected with the Chapelle du Roi early in the 16th century.

Sermisy is first heard of in 1508,[1] when he was appointed 'clerc musicien' in the Sainte-Chapelle du Palais at Paris; his name appears in the Sainte-Chapelle registers as Claude de Cermisy. He was there for a short period, as before 1515 he became a ' chanteur ' in the Chapelle de musique du Roi, at that time Louis XII. This post was equivalent to the English 'gentleman of the Chapel Royal,' and as a chanteur his name occurs in a list of the musicians who were present at the funeral of Louis XII. He eventually succeeded Antoine de Longueval as sous-maître of the Chapelle. In the accounts of payments to the various members of the Chapelle in 1533 there are some entries concerning Claude de Sermisy. As sous-maître he received the sum of 400 livres tournois ( = 2400 francs), his wages for the said year, and a sum of 1080 livres tournois ( = 6480 francs) for the feeding and maintenance of the children of the Chapelle Royale for the year, and another sum of 240 l.t. ( = 1440 francs) for care of the books belonging to the Chapelle and for the procuring of singing boys, ' pour envoyer quérir des chantres.' This shows his position as sous-maître to have been similar to that of the English master of the children of the Chapel Royal, who also received like payments, and fees for journeys made to ' press ' children for the service of the Chapel.

On Sept. 20, 1533, Sermisy was made a canon of La Sainte-Chapelle, which gave him a residence and a large salary, and only imposed the obligation of officiating at certain ceremonies ; he retained therefore his post of sous-maître, although he and Louis Hérault are mentioned as joint possessors of the office in 1547, when François I. died. They continued to hold it under Henri II. As a member of the Chapelle du Roi, Sermisy was present on three historical occasions, first at the meeting of François I. with Pope Leo X. at Bologna in 1515, when the French singers vied with the Papal Choir ; then in 1520 when François I. and Henry VIII. met at the Field of Cloth of Gold, and again in 1532 when they met at Boulogne ; on both occasions the English and the French musicians delighted their hearers with their performances.

A work published in 1554, the *Rudiments de musicque* by Maximilien Guilliaud, was dedicated to the

'excellent musicien Monsieur Maistre Claude de Sermisy, maistre de la Chapelle du Roy, et chanoine le la Sainte-Chapelle du Palais Royal à Paris ; 15 Septembre, 1552.'

Sermisy probably resigned the post of sous-maître soon after this date, but retained his connexion with La Sainte - Chapelle until Aug. 16, 1561, his name then appearing for the last time on the rolls of the Chapter meetings.

Four partbooks containing 28 motets composed by Sermisy were published in 1542 :

[1] Information based on researches of Michel Brenet. See *Sammelb.* Int. Mus. Ges. 1904.

' Nova et prima motectorum editio 6, 5, 4, 3 et 2 vocum, Lib. 1, 2, 3, Paris.' Pierre Attaingnant.

Claude de Sermisy, or Claudin as he is almost invariably called in music - books, shows an extraordinarily wide range as a composer ; love songs, masses, motets were published in rapid succession, and retained their popularity for many years after his death, if one may judge by the number of reprints of his works.

Upwards of 200 of his chansons were included in the various collections of the period.

The set of song-books published by Pierre Attaingnant in Paris, beginning in January 1529 with the ' Trente et huyt chansons musicales à quatre parties,' which were continued until 1535, contained ninety - two chansons by Claudin. The same publishers began a new series in 1538, ' Premier livre contenant xxv chansons nouvelles à quatre parties '; in this set, up to the ' vingtseptiesme livre ' in 1548, there were thirty-five chansons by Claudin. About the same time Jacques Moderne in Lyons was publishing the various volumes of ' Le Parangon des chansons,' and in the 2nd, 3rd, 4th, 7th, 9th and 10th volumes (1538–43), which were often reprinted, Claudin was represented by about twelve different songs. In Venice the ' Primo libro de le canzoni francese,' published by Scotto in 1535, included ' Faict ou failly ' for four voices by Claudin. While at Anvers, Tylman Susato printed, in 1544, Claudin's ' O combien est malheureux,' in the ' Quatriesme livre des chansons à quatre parties.' In Paris, Attaingnant's song-books were being replaced by Nicolas du Chemin's publications ; the Premier, Second and the ' Quart livre du recueil contenant . . . chansons à quatre parties,' in 1551, contained altogether fifteen of Claudin's chansons. Shortly before his death, Adrian Le Roy and Robert Ballard of Paris, the widely-known ' imprimeurs du roy,' who published much of the music of the 16th century, produced the ' Livre de meslanges, contenant six vingtz chansons des plus rares . . . soit des autheurs antiques, soit des plus memorables de notre temps,' 1560, which contained Claudin's ' Peine et travail me faut ' for six voices.

Claudin's claim to be a pupil of the great Josquin rests on a phrase in the preface to this volume : 'Josquin des Prez, hennuyer de nation, et ses disciples, Mouton, Claudin, Jaquet,' etc. The same publishers also issued in 1571 the 'Second recueil . . . de chansons à quatre parties,' in which were eight chansons by Claudin. There is one song in Granjon's 'Trophée, livre 2'; there are four in ' Il primo libro di madrigali d'Archadelt a tre voci' (Venetia, Gardano, 1559); another, 'On en dire ce qu'on,' in the 'Troisième livre delle Muse a tre voci' (Venice, Scotto, 1562), and three more in the ' Primo libro de canzoni francese a due voci ' (Venice, Antonio Gardano, 1564).

In 1532 Attaingnant issued seven volumes of masses by various composers. These included the following by Claudin for four voices :

Liber  I. Secunda est ' Philomena praevia.'
„   II. Secunda est ' Missa IX lectionum.'
„  III. Prima est ' Missa plurium motetarum.'
„  IV. Secunda est ' Missa pro defunctis.'
„  VII. Prima est ' Domini est terra.'

In 1534 Attaingnant published :

Missarum musicalium ad quatuor voces, pares, Liber II.  ' Tota pulchra,' Claudin ;  ' Missa ad placitum,' Claudin ; etc.
Liber III.  ' Missa Dominus quis habitabit,' Claudin.  Paris, 1540.

In 1556 Nicolas du Chemin published in Paris a great collection of masses, among them :

Missa cum quatuor vocibus.  Ad imitationem moduli : 'Ab initio' condita . . . auctore D. Claudio de Sermisy Regio Symphoniacorum ordini praefecto et in regali parisiensis palatii sacello canonico.
Missa cum quatuor vocibus.  Ad imitationem cantionis : 'Voulant l'honneur' condita, etc.
Missa cum quatuor vocibus paribus.  Ad imitationem moduli : ' Tota pulchra es ' condita, etc.
Missa cum quinque vocibus.  Ad imitationem moduli : ' Quare fremuerunt gentes ' condita, etc.

Three of the masses printed in 1532 were reissued :

Missae tres Claudio de Sermisy Regii Sacelli magistro, praestantissimo musico auctore . . . cum quatuor vocibus . . . 'Novem lectionum' fol. 2 ; ' Philomena praevia ' fol. 13 ; ' Domini est terra ' fol. 23.
Lutetiae 1558 apud Adrianum Le Roy et Robt. Ballard, folio.

There was another edition in 1583. The same publishers in the ' Missae tres a Claudio de Sermisy, Joannes Maillard, Claudio Goudimel, cum quatuor vocibus conditae,' 1558, included Claudin's ' Missa plurium modulorum.' His motets were published in such collections as the ' Fior de motetti ' (? 1526), the ' Motetti del fiore ' (1532). Rhau's ' Tricinia ' (1542) and Ochsenkuhn's ' Tabulatur Buch ' (1558).

MS. copies of Claudin's music are to be found in different foreign libraries, in Rome, Berlin, Cambrai, Bologna, in the Dresden State Library, MS. 1270, No. 5, a ' Laudate Dominum ' for six voices by Claudin ; in the Munich State Library, MSS. 69, 92 and 132 contain motets and MSS. 202, 204, 205 and 207 various chansons—all were published in the 16th century.

Of modern reprints, Henry Expert's publication ' Les Maîtres musiciens' includes Attaingnant's 'Trente et un chansons' (1529), of which eleven were composed by Claudin. Three chansons are in vol. 23 of the ' Publikation älterer prakt. und theoret. Musikwerke,' Leipzig, 1899. Commer (' Coll. op. mus.' vol. xii.) reprints three, the melodies of which were used for Psalms lxxii., ciii. and cxxviii., in the ' Souter Liedekens,' Antwerp, 1540. Otto Kade in his book Die ältere Passionskomposition, Gütersloh, 1893, treats very fully of Claudin's Passion music, published by Attaingnant in 1534. Further reprints are, Extraits des maîtres musiciens de la Renaissance (H. Expert, Paris) 4 chansons ; Chansonnier du XIVe siècle (Ch. Bordes, Paris) 2 chansons.

BIBL.—MICHEL BRENET, Les Musiciens de la Sainte-Chapelle du Palais (Paris, 1910).
        C. S. ; addns. M. L. P.

SEROV, ALEXANDER NICHOLAEVICH (b. St. Petersburg, Jan. 23, 1820; d. there, Feb. 1 —Jan. 20, O.S.—1871), composer and critic, was the son of a government official, educated at the School of Jurisprudence, where he only made one intimate friend, Vladimir Stassov, destined afterwards to be his stoutest opponent in matters of art.

In his Reminiscences of the School of Jurisprudence Stassov has given an interesting account of Serov's student days. He left the institution with a decided hankering after an artistic career, but accepted a clerkship in a government office in obedience to his father's wish. He found, however, some leisure for musical pursuits, studied the violoncello and was busy with the project of composing an opera. From his correspondence with Stassov we gather that he cherished vague, ambitious plans which were hindered by lack of technical training and by the unsympathetic attitude of his father. In 1848 he was transferred from the capital to the dull provincial town of Simferopol, which proved fatal to his musical schemes. Nevertheless his determination to acquire further technical knowledge was unshaken. Through Stassov he obtained an introduction to the famous theorist Hunke, then living in St. Petersburg, who undertook to instruct him in counterpoint by correspondence. The method was not very successful, and Serov's progress was slow. It is evident that he was often tempted to throw up his official position for art's sake, but his father sternly discountenanced such a proceeding. Nevertheless, his feeling for music continued to assert itself, and as his ideas assumed more definite shape, he turned to criticism, which at that time was at a low ebb in Russia. His first articles in the Russian Contemporary in 1851 created something like a sensation, because he brought to bear upon his æsthetic criticism a highly cultivated intelligence, a distinctive style and an effective, if ponderous, irony. His early articles dealt with Mozart, Beethoven, Donizetti, Rossini, Meyerbeer and Spontini, and in discussing the last named he explained and defended the historical ideal of the music-drama. Considering that at this time Serov was practically ignorant of Wagner's works, the conclusions which he draws do credit to his reflection and foresight. His writings have now lost much of their value because of their polemical character. With one hand Serov pointed to the great musical movement in Western Europe ; with the other he sought to blind the eyes of Russian society to the awakening which was taking place within.

It was not until after his visit to Germany in 1858, from which—in his own words—he returned ' Wagner mad,' that he took up a distinctly hostile attitude to the New Russian School which was striving to express in music the spirit of the race. Then followed that long polemic between Serov and Stassov which was only a side episode in that greater conflict between Western and Slavophil. In spite of great popular authority, Serov's position in 1860 was in many respects an isolated and unenviable one. There was neither place nor need for an ardent Wagnerian propaganda in Russia. Between his ungenerous depreciation of the new school and his lukewarm attitude towards Rubinstein, Serov's influence began to wane. Serov had passed his fortieth year before he set to work upon his first opera, 'Judith.' With extraordinary energy and determination he surmounted all technical difficulties, and completed his opera in the spring of 1862. In Mar. 1863 Wagner visited St. Petersburg, and Serov submitted to him the score of 'Judith.' Wagner more particularly praised the orchestration, in which he cannot have failed to see the reflection of his own influence. 'Judith' was produced in the course of the season 1863–64, on a scale of magnificence hitherto unknown in the production of national opera, and immediately took the public by storm. The subject was well adapted to Serov's opulent and sensational manner. In general style the work recalls the early Wagnerian operas, with some curious reminiscences of Meyerbeer. As regards picturesque effect, 'Judith' is admirable, although the dramatic colour is occasionally coarse and flashy. The many technical defects were easily overlooked by the public in an opera which made so direct an appeal to their sensuous enjoyment. Serov's long apprenticeship to musical criticism taught him what was attractive and practicable for the stage, just as he had acquired from the study of Wagner a considerable power of effective orchestration. 'Judith' fascinated not only the uncritical public, but many of the young musical generation, including Tchaikovsky, who refers to it as one of his 'first loves' in music.

Serov lost no time in following up his first success, and 'Rogneda' was completed and performed in the autumn of 1865. Its success was unprecedented. In 'Rogneda' Serov almost discards the Wagnerian influence for that of Meyerbeer. We look in vain in this work for the higher purpose, the effort at psychological delineation and comparative solidity of execution which are occasional features of 'Judith.' Tchaikovsky writes :

'Serov knew how to catch the crowd, and if this opera suffers from poverty of melodic inspiration, want of organic sequence, weak recitative and declamation, and from harmony and instrumentation that are purely decorative—yet what sensational effects the composer succeeds in piling up ! . . . The whole thing literally crackles with them. Serov had only a mediocre gift, united to great experience, remarkable intellect and extensive erudition ; therefore it is not astonishing to find in "Rogneda" numbers —rare oases in a desert—in which the music is excellent.'

Tchaikovsky stood somewhat apart from the heated conflict with national tendencies in which Serov was constantly involved, therefore his judgment may be accepted as less biassed than that of the majority of his contemporaries. After the triumph of 'Rogneda' Serov rested awhile upon his laurels. The balm of success seems to have done something to soften his hostility to the national school, for the lectures on Glinka and Dargomijsky which he delivered before the Russian Musical Society in 1866 are valuable not only for clearness of exposition, but for fairness of judgment.

For the subject of his third opera Serov turned to contemporary national life as depicted in Ostrovsky's strong, but somewhat sordid, play 'The Power of Evil.' His correspondence reveals his intentions with regard to this work. 'Ten years ago,' he says,

'I wrote much about Wagner. Now it is time to act. To embody the Wagnerian theories in a music-drama written in Russian on a Russian subject. . . . In this work, besides observing as far as possible the principles of dramatic truth, I aim at keeping more closely than has yet been done to the forms of Russian popular music as preserved in our folk-songs.'

He is seeking in fact to fuse the methods of Glinka with those of Wagner, and produce a Russian music-drama. Serov was a connoisseur of Russian folk-songs, but he had not the genius of Glinka ; moreover, with all his knowledge of the popular music he was never penetrated by the national spirit as was his great predecessor. In creating this Russo-Wagnerian work Serov created something purely artificial : a hybrid which could bring forth nothing in its turn. The work never attained the popularity of 'Judith' and 'Rogneda.'

Serov died of heart disease in 1871. The orchestration of 'The Power of Evil' was completed by one of his most talented pupils, Soloviev. At the time of his death he was busy with a fourth opera based upon Gogol's 'Christmas Eve Revels,' but this work did not progress beyond a first sketch, from which his widow afterwards arranged an orchestral suite, published in 1877. Other compositions, all belonging to his later years, are : Stabat Mater, Ave Maria, incidental music to 'Nero' (1869), 'A Christmas Song' and two or three orchestral works, including a 'Gopak' and 'Dance of the Zaporogne Cossacks.' Serov married Valentina Semenovna Bergman, a talented pupil of the St. Petersburg Conservatoire, and the composer of several operas, one of which, 'Uriel Acosta' (Moscow, 1885), brought her some success. She was also a constant contributor to the reviews, and in later years devoted her energies to the popularising of music among the masses.    R. N.

BIBL.—ROSA NEWMARCH, *The Russian Opera*, 1913 ; OSKAR VON RIESEMANN, *Monographien zur russischer Musik*, vol. i. (*Die Musik in Russland vor Glinka, M. J. Glinka, A. S. Dargomyski, A. N. Sseroff*), 1923.

**SERPENT** (Eng. and Fr. ; Ger. *Schlangenrohr* ; Ital. *serpentone*), a now obsolete instru-

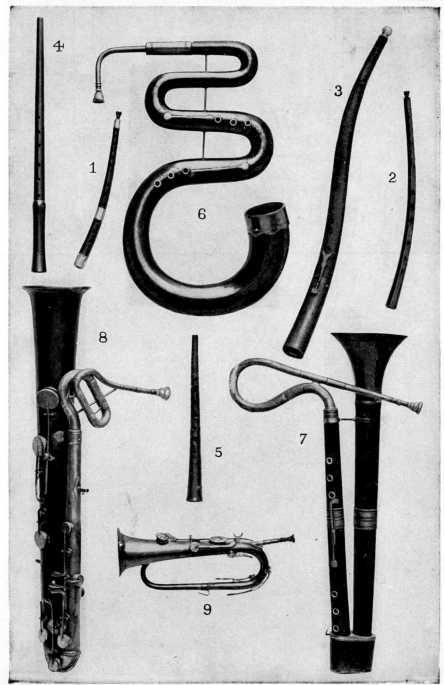

1. HIGH TREBLE CORNETT (1518).     2. TREBLE CORNETT (*c.* 1600).
3. GREAT CORNETT (*c.* 1600).     4. MUTE CORNETT (17th cent.).     5. STRAIGHT CORNETT
6. SERPENT (*c.* 1780).     7. ENGLISH BASS HORN (*c.* 1800).     8. OPHICLEIDE (*c.* 1830).
9. ENGLISH KEYED or KENT BUGLE (*c.* 1820).

ment forming the natural bass of the ancient cornet family, played with a cupped mouthpiece similar to that of the bass trombone. (See *PLATE LXXIV.* No. 6.) It consisted of a wooden tube about 8 feet long, increasing conically from ⅝ of an inch in diameter at the mouthpiece to 4 inches at the open end. The name is obviously derived from the curved form into which the tube was contorted. There were six holes on the front of the instrument, to be stopped by the three middle fingers of either hand ; those for the left hand on the third descending branch ; those for the right on the fourth ascending branch towards the bell. The holes were set in groups of three, within reach of the outstretched fingers.

The serpent consisted of three parts : (1) the mouthpiece, (2) the crook, or curved brass tube leading into (3) the wooden body, which is built up of several pieces held together by a leathern covering. The whole of the instrument was, however, sometimes made of brass or copper. It is usually said to have been invented by a canon of Auxerre, named Edmé Guillaume, in 1590. However that may be, there can be no doubt that about this period clerical musicians employed bass reed and brass instruments for the accompaniment of ecclesiastical plain-song. Indeed Mersenne, who gives a remarkably good and complete account of the serpent, notices that ' even when played by a boy it is sufficient to support the voices of twenty robust monks.' The ' Serpent d'Église ' was a recognised functionary in French churches, and for many years the instrument was an indispensable member of the primitive orchestras which accompanied the singing in rural churches in England.

The scale of the serpent was capricious, and indeed fortuitous. Mersenne gives it a compass of seventeen diatonic notes from 8-foot D upwards, and intimates that the intervening chromatics can be obtained by half-stopping. He does not name the device of cross-fingering so largely employed on the bassoon. Berlioz, who speaks slightingly of it, states that it is in B♭, and that parts for it ' must be written a whole tone above the real sound.' Old parts, however, used in England were invariably in C.

The serpent produced the usual harmonic series of notes. These in Mersenne's work seem limited to the fundamental, its octave and twelfth. There would be no difficulty in obtaining a far larger compass. Lichtenthal,[1] who, as an Italian, highly values the serpent, gives its compass as no less than four full octaves from the *Do bassissimo*, which ' does not exist on the pianoforte (1826), but on the pedal of the organ of 16 feet,' up to the *Do* of the violin on the third space. He states, moreover, that the lowest sound of *Do* can only be used from time

[1] *Dizionario della musica*, tom. i. p. 193.

to time, ' avendo bisogno di una particolare buona imboccatura '—requiring a specially good lip. As the fundamental note, pedal, or lowest proper tone of the serpent was the 8-feet C, just as it is on the trombone, euphonium, or ophicleide in C, the statement of Lichtenthal can only be explained by admitting that certain players, by a peculiarly loose embouchure, could produce notes of a forced or constrained pitch one octave lower than due to the length of tube. The compass given in the scales and tutors is three octaves from C to *c*″, with a possible extension downwards, by slackening the lips, to B, and B,♭.

It will be seen from the plate that one hand being applied to an ascending, and the other to a descending branch, the usual sequence of fingering is inverted in the two hands ; the scale proceeding downwards in the left and upwards in the right. The serpent is probably the only instrument exhibiting so quaint and unscientific a device. This fact, and the different lengths of sounding-tube intervening between the holes, indicate the great imperfection of the instrument mechanically considered, and point to the conclusion that a good player must have relied more on his dexterity and on the strength of his embouchure, as mentioned above, than on the resources of the instrument itself. Later makers, however, added a multiplicity of keys, both above and below, which only complicated without facilitating performance. A part for it is to be found in the score of Mendelssohn's overtures ' The Calm Sea and Prosperous Voyage ' and ' St. Paul,' in the overtures to ' Masaniello,' ' The Siege of Corinth ' (between the second and third trombones), and ' Rienzi.' It is also found in the score of ' I Vespri siciliani.' It is usually replaced in performance by the tuba. A Yorkshireman of Richmond, named Hurworth, who played in the private band of George III., could execute elaborate flute variations with perfect accuracy on this unwieldy instrument.

A *Method for the Serpent*, containing studies and duets, was published by Cocks. The only concerted music set down to it seems to have been originally intended for the bassoon.

A ' contra-serpent ' was shown in the Exhibition of 1851, made by Jordan of Liverpool. It was in E♭ of the 16-foot octave. It was, however, too unwieldy to be carried by the player, and required independent support. Another modification of this instrument was invented by Beacham and played on by Prospère in Jullien's orchestra. It was named the serpentcleide, and was essentially an ophicleide with a body of wood instead of brass.

　　　　　　　　　　　w. h. s. ; addns. d. j. b.

SERPETTE, Henri Charles Antoine Gaston (*b.* Nantes, Nov. 4, 1846 ; *d.* Paris, Nov. 3, 1904), French composer, began life as an advocate, but gave up the bar for music. He was a pupil of Ambroise Thomas at the Conservatoire, and took the Grand Prix de Rome in 1871 for a cantata (' Jeanne d'Arc ') of great promise.  On his return from Italy, despairing of acceptance at the Opéra-Comique, he closed with the Bouffes Parisiens, and produced ' La Branche cassée ' (three acts, Jan. 23, 1874), with a success which induced him to go on composing works of the same slight character. The following is a list of his theatrical works :

' Le Manoir du pic tordu ' (May 28, 1875) ; ' Le Moulin du vert galant ' (Apr. 12, 1876) ; ' La Petite Muette ' (Oct. 3, 1877), all in three acts and given in Paris ; ' La Nuit de St. Germain ' (Mar. 1880) in Brussels ; ' Madame le Diable,' ' Fanfreluche ' (1882, 1883) ; ' Le Château de Tire-larigot ' (1884) ; ' Cendrillonette ' (1890) ; ' La Demoiselle du téléphone ' (1891) ; ' Cousin-Cousine ' (1893) ; ' La Dot de Brigitte ' (1895) ; ' Le Capitole,' an opéra-comique (1895) ; ' Le Carnet du diable,' a fantastic piece (1895) ; ' Le Carillon ' (1896) ; ' Le Royaume des femmes,' an operette (1896) ; ' Shakespeare,' an opéra-bouffe (1899).       G. C.

SERRANO, EMILIO (b. Vitoria, Spain, 1850), court pianist to the Infanta Isabel (Countess of Girgenti), director of the Royal Opera and professor of the Conservatoire of Madrid, composed much music, including grand operas, of which ' Irene de Otranto ' (1891) and ' Gonzalo de Córdoba ' (1898) were produced with great success in Madrid.       H. V. H.

SERRES, MARIE FRANÇOIS LOUIS ARNAL DE (b. Lyons, Rhône, Oct. 8, 1864), French composer, entered the Paris Conservatoire in 1884 and joined the organ class of César Franck, becoming his private pupil from 1885–90. He studied harmony in the class of Taudou (1st ' accessit ' 1888).  He is one of the most active colleagues of Ch. Bordes and V. d'Indy at the Schola, was professor there from 1900 (chamber music, lyric declamation choir-class, general inspector of studies), and organist of the Paris Irish Chapel (St. Joseph).  He has composed orchestral music : ' Les Caresses,' performed at the Société Nationale, ' Les Heures claires ' (voice and orchestra).  His choral music, sacred and secular (' Nuit d'été,' ' Le Jour des morts,' motets, French and Latin, ' Ave verum,' etc.), is of special interest.  His songs (' Toi,' ' Sub urbe,' ' L'Éveil de Pâques,' ' Le Jardin clos,' 6 poems, etc.) are characteristic of the tradition of Duparc and Chausson.  De Serres's delicate and expressive manner of writing was much appreciated by César Franck.       M. L. P.

SERVAIS, (1) ADRIEN FRANÇOIS (b. Hal, near Brussels, June 6, 1807 ; d. there, Nov. 26, 1866), a great violoncellist, became a pupil of Platel in the Brussels Conservatoire, where he rapidly rose to the first rank.  On the advice of Fétis he went to Paris, where his success was great.  In 1835 he visited England, and on May 25 played a concerto of his own at the Philharmonic concert, where he was announced as ' principal violoncello to the King of the Belgians.'  He then returned home, and wisely resolved to study for a year, and it was during this period that he formed the style by which he was afterwards known.  In 1836 he reappeared

in Paris, and the next dozen years were occupied in a series of long tours through Germany, Holland, Austria, Norway, Russia, and even Siberia.  In 1842 he married in St. Petersburg. In 1848 he settled in Brussels as professor in the Conservatoire, and formed many distinguished pupils.  He died of an illness contracted during his third visit to St. Petersburg.  His works comprise three concertos and sixteen fantasies for violoncello and orchestra ; six études for violoncello and PF.—with Grégoir ; fourteen duos for ditto ; three duets for violin and violoncello—with Léonard ; one duet for ditto —with Vieuxtemps.  A biography of Servais was published at Hal by Vanderbroeck Desmeth, 1866.  Interesting reminiscences of him are published in the *Guide musical* of June 2, 1907, à propos of the centenary of his birth.

His eldest son, (2) JOSEPH (b. Hal, Nov. 28, 1850 ; d. there, Aug. 29, 1885), succeeded his father in June 1872 as professor of the violoncello at the Brussels Conservatoire. He appeared first at Warsaw with his father, and the pair excited the greatest enthusiasm.  In 1868 he was appointed solo violoncellist at Weimar and remained two years.  In 1875 he played for the first time in Paris at one of Pasdeloup's Popular Concerts, when some of the journals spoke in terms of extravagant praise of his performance. The instrument used by both father and son was a fine Stradivarius presented by the Princess Yousoupoff.  A second son, (3) FRANÇOIS MATTHIEU (d. near Paris, Jan. 14, 1901), a successful pianist and composer, was a pupil in the same Conservatoire.  His opera ' Jon ' was produced at Carlsruhe, 1899.  (See VIOLONCELLO-PLAYING.)       T. P. P.

SERVA PADRONA, LA—' the maid turned mistress.'  An Italian intermezzo, in two acts ; words by Nelli ; music by Pergolesi.  Written and produced, Naples, Aug. 23, 1733 ; Paris, first on Oct. 4, 1746, at the Hôtel de Bourgogne ; revived by the ' Bouffons-Italiens,' Aug. 1, 1752, occasioning the ' Guerre des Lullistes et des Bouffonistes.'  See RAMEAU and ROUSSEAU. Revived, Aug. 13, 1862, Opéra-Comique ; given in London, Royalty, Mar. 7, 1873.—An imitation of Nelli's libretto, with the same title, was composed by Paisiello during his stay at St. Petersburg.       G.

SERVICE.  This word is used in the English language with a great variety of meaning. It has a special use for church musicians in reference to the free and somewhat elaborate musical settings of the canticles and certain other details contained in the *Book of Common Prayer*.  Among its many meanings the word ' service ' is defined in the *New English Dictionary* as signifying the action of serving a master ; hence it is employed with a religious significance to describe the celebration of public worship in a general way as ' Divine Service ' ; in a more limited sense it denotes a ritual or series of words and ceremonies prescribed for public worship, often coupled with a defining word, such as marriage-service, burial-service, etc. It is but one step further to the special meaning already mentioned with which it is used by musicians.

These musical settings are to be grouped under three main headings : (*a*) The Office for the Holy Communion ; (*b*) Morning Prayer ; (*c*) Evening Prayer. The portions of the Communion Office that may be set to music are the *Kyrie*, the Creed, the *Sanctus* and the *Gloria in excelsis*. The *Benedictus* and *Agnus Dei* have no place in the *Book of Common Prayer*,[1] but since the middle of the 19th century they have come into such general use that composers now commonly include them in their 'Communion Services.' There are five canticles in the Morning Service of the Prayer Book which may be set to music : *Venite, Te Deum, Benedictus*, with the alternatives *Benedicite* and *Jubilate*. The evening canticles are *Magnificat* and *Nunc Dimittis*, with the alternatives, *Cantate Domino* and *Deus misereatur*. Church musicians employ the term 'Service' for a musical setting of any of the three groups, and there are many examples of these compositions which are limited to a single one of them ; a few settings include both alternatives among the canticles, but it has been a very general practice to deal with all three groups as a single composition, usually styled a 'Full Service,' and in such instances it is conventional to write all the several numbers in the same key. It has become the custom to refer to a service not only by the name of the composer but also by the key in which it is written ; thus, for example, 'Stanford in B flat' is understood to comprise his setting in B flat of the canticles for Morning and Evening Prayer as well as the music for the Communion Office. 'Walmisley in D minor' is an example of an Evening Service alone, and 'Boyce in C' is a setting of the morning canticles alone. There are also numerous settings of the Communion Service which have no Morning or Evening Service connected with them.

In considering the history and development of the service it will be convenient to discuss the settings of the Communion Office first. It is not proposed here to deal with the musical settings of the Latin Mass. (See MASS.) Even before the appearance of the *First Prayer Book of Edward VI.* the Mass was being celebrated with English words in the place of Latin, and English versions of the Office are to be found, for example, in Marshall's *Primer* of 1535, Hilsey's *Primer* of 1539 and Henry VIII.'s *Primer* of 1545. But attention has been drawn[2] to the fact that complete musical settings of these English versions of the Holy Communion Office were written for practical use at much the

1 As in force in 1926.
2 Editors of the Carnegie edition of 'Tudor Church Music.'

same date. Some of these were adaptations ; thus two of Taverner's masses, 'Sine Nomine' and 'Small Devotion,' are to be found adapted to English words in the Bodleian MSS. Mus. Sch. E420-422 ; the importance of this discovery is enhanced by the possibility, subsequently suggested by Dom Anselm of Pershore, that these partbooks are in Taverner's autograph. This same set of books contains ten more complete English Communion Services set to original music by various composers, although their names are not recorded in the MSS., and all these settings included the *Gloria in excelsis*, Creed, *Sanctus*, *Benedictus* and *Agnus Dei*. One of these Communion Services was the work of John Heath, and was subsequently printed by John Day in 1560 in his 'Certaine Notes set forth in foure and three parts to be song at the morning, Communion, and evening praier.' But in the interval the progress of religious controversy had led to the exclusion of the *Benedictus* and *Agnus Dei*, so that Heath's settings of these were omitted by Day.

In the meanwhile many notable composers set themselves to provide music for the newly authorised *Book of Common Prayer*, and in dealing with the Communion Office they confined themselves to settings of the *Kyrie*, as a response to the Commandments, and the Nicene Creed, in accordance with the later usage of Elizabeth's reign. The *Benedictus, Agnus Dei* and *Gloria in excelsis* were entirely dropped, and few, if any, genuine settings of the *Sanctus* are to be found in the works of the Elizabethan composers. The *Sanctus* in Gibbons's service is certainly spurious, and so, almost equally certainly, is that sometimes attached to Byrd's 'short' service. Byrd's 'short' service and 'great' service alike include only the *Kyrie* and Creed. The music of the Communion Office continued to be thus limited until the Restoration period, when it again became customary to sing the *Sanctus* in connexion with the 'ante-Communion' Service which customarily followed Morning Prayer at that date every Sunday. It is interesting, however, to note that in three or four cathedrals, among them Durham and Exeter, the full Communion Service was celebrated chorally once a month, with scarcely any interruption through the three centuries that succeeded the Reformation. An example of a complete Communion Service, written in the 18th century, is that of Kempton of Ely ; it is a very feeble composition, but considerable historical interest is attached to it.

No further change took place until the middle of the 19th century, when, as one of the effects of the 'Oxford movement,' choral celebration of the Holy Communion came into general vogue ; this led to an immediate demand for music for the *Gloria in excelsis* in addition to the *Kyrie*, Creed and *Sanctus* ; and at a rather later date the *Benedictus* and *Agnus Dei* were also re-introduced. Thus a full modern Communion Service will usually contain a *Kyrie* (either the nine-fold Greek *Kyrie*, or the Response to the Commandments; or both), Creed, *Sanctus, Gloria in excelsis, Benedictus* and *Agnus Dei*. In some instances composers have also added to their Communion Services special introits, settings of the Offertory sentences, elaborate *Amens* and other minor features.

The disestablishment of the daily choral celebration of the Mass in the English cathedrals and collegiate churches, which was one of the features of the Reformation movement, led immediately to the establishment of the elaborate choral performances of Morning and Evening Prayer which have formed such a distinctive feature of English church music during the past four centuries. It seems to have been clearly felt that the great traditions of the famous choirs must be maintained, and that if the daily singing of the Mass was proscribed it behoved them to perform the substituted services with all the dignity that the best music and the best singing could lend to them. Thus, as soon as the *Book of Common Prayer* came into use, and even rather earlier, a demand was created for musical settings of the canticles and for English anthems (see ANTHEM), as well as for harmonised adaptations of the old plain-song for the litany preces and responses and for chants for the Psalms, the prayers being chanted or invariably 'intoned' by the Priest. The Bodleian MSS. Mus. Sch. E 420-422 contain several settings of the morning and evening canticles in English, some of which are at least as early as the Prayer Book. A new musical tradition was thus constructed on the old foundations, and this has not only provided the means of a continuous expression of dignified worship day by day in our great cathedral churches, but also has proved of incalculable value to the growth and prosperity of English music as a whole, seeing that the large majority of notable English musicians since the Reformation received their earliest training as choristers; Henry Purcell provides a conspicuous illustration of this truth. But whereas the music of the Mass formed the basis of the music of the English Communion Service as regards both form and style, there was little to serve as a model for setting the English canticles of Morning and Evening Prayer. It is probable that the pioneers looked to the Latin settings of *Te Deum* and *Magnificat* for guidance, but the needs of the cathedrals called for something of a simple character, and, in addition, the suggestion was made by Cranmer that in setting the canticles ' the song should not be full of notes, but, as near as may be, for every syllable a note so that it may be sung distinctly and devoutly.'[1] This led to the straightforward type of setting

[1] Letter to Henry VIII. See MERBECKE.

which the Elizabethan composers styled the 'short' service. But in spite of injunctions and orders the composers could not be entirely restrained, and many of them wrote more elaborate settings which they described as 'great,' or sometimes 'high' services. In these 'great' services verbal phrases were frequently repeated and much ingenuity was shown in contrapuntal device. Far the finest of all the 'great' services is that of Byrd; Tallis also wrote a service on these lines, but only fragments have survived and its value cannot be judged from these. The practice of composing 'great' services continued into the 17th century. It should be mentioned that a feature which uniformly characterises the settings of the service, from the time of the Reformation to the present date, is the antiphonal treatment by which sections of the music are allotted alternately to the two sides of the choir, the sides being denoted *Decani* (that of the Dean) and *Cantoris* (that of the Precentor).

The Elizabethan musicians usually set *Venite* in similar style to the other canticles, but the custom of singing *Venite* to a chant in the daily cathedral usage has long superseded this form. The Elizabethans almost invariably set *Benedictus* rather than the alternative *Jubilate* which was inserted in the second Prayer Book in 1552 as a concession to Puritan demands. Early examples of settings of *Jubilate* are those of John FARRANT in D minor and GIBBONS in D minor (Gibbons's more elaborate service). After the Restoration *Jubilate* was set in preference to *Benedictus* in a very large majority of services. In the present century *Benedictus* is commonly preferred, but *Jubilate* cannot be entirely banished from the daily cathedral lists without also consigning many excellent settings of *Te Deum* to unmerited neglect The *Benedicite* has seldom been set in ' service - form at any period.

The two evening canticles are *Magnificat* and *Nunc Dimittis*. In 1552 the psalms *Cantate Domino* and *Deus misereatur* were introduced as alternatives for the same reason as *Jubilate*. No settings of these alternative canticles are found much before the Restoration period, but from that time until the close of the 19th century there are many examples. Child, Blow, Purcell and Croft are among the earlier composers who wrote settings of *Cantate Domino* and *Deus misereatur*.

It remains to discuss briefly the development of the service during the past four centuries. The Edwardine examples in the Bodleian Library have already been mentioned. These are of a very simple and mainly homophonic character, and must be regarded for the most part as experiments rather than as suitable for modern use. Tye and Tallis are among the great pioneers of the service; Tallis's 'short' service is still in constant use ; it shows a decided advance upon the earlier works of the kind, especially as regards the thematic material ; it is almost entirely homophonic and conforms to Cranmer's view. It was left to Byrd to raise the service to that degree of excellence that enables it to appeal to modern ears as a thing of beauty quite apart from any feeling of antiquarian interest ; his ' short ' service is remarkable for its subtlety in the treatment of the verbal rhythm as well as for its melodic beauty and the balance of the phrasing. Byrd's ' great ' service stands as the finest of all English services : the several sections are treated with much elaboration and rare contrapuntal skill, the salient features of each canticle being brought into prominence by special devices. The *Gloria Patri* to the *Nun Dimittis* of this service is of unrivalled dignity and beauty. Two other Evening Services by Byrd have survived. Of these his ' Second Service with verses to the organs ' represents an important development in service-form ; it is the earliest service, as far as is known, in which there are passages for a solo voice with an independent organ accompaniment. Morley wrote an elaborate service with ' verses ' and independent organ accompaniment, but the most important service-writers of this school after Byrd were Weelkes and Tomkins. Weelkes wrote as many as 10 settings of the *Magnificat* and *Nunc Dimittis*, and to 6 of these there is a corresponding Morning Service. Unfortunately of only one of these has sufficient text survived to make satisfactory reconstruction practicable ; the missing alto part in the 4-part service can easily be supplied, but this is the least interesting of Weelkes's services. All the others are for ' verse ' and chorus, and some exhibit much originality in structure, notably that 5-part service which is described in the manuscripts as ' for two trebles.' In this service each verse of the words is given alternately to solo voices with independent accompaniment and to 5-part chorus ; this device is even followed in the *Gloria*. One of Weelkes's services is ' of seven parts.' Another is described as ' Mr. Weelkes's *in medio chori* ' ; the exact meaning of this term, which is to be found in connexion with more than one service in Batten's organ-book (Tenbury MS. 791), has not been satisfactorily explained. Tomkins wrote 5 settings of the Morning and 7 of the Evening Service. The first two, which include *Venite, Kyrie* and Creed together with the morning and evening canticles, are unaccompanied settings, of the ' short ' service type, in four parts. The third service includes *Te Deum, Jubilate, Magnificat* and *Nunc Dimittis* ; it is mainly in 5 parts, but there are sections in 7, 8 and 9 parts. This service is of an elaborate character, but can be sung unaccompanied. The 4th service is styled a

' great ' service, and is also elaborate, but the organ part forms an indispensable part of the composition. The evening canticles of this service are laid out in alternate sections of solo and 5-part chorus, much like Weelkes's service ' for two trebles.' Tomkins's 5th service is less elaborated, but contains passages for bass solo together with other verse sections alternating with 4-part choral writing. There are two evening services by Tomkins in Batten's organ-book (Tenbury MS. 791) which were not published in *Musica Deo sacra*.

Orlando Gibbons's services are of special interest ; his ' short ' service in F is far less homophonic than those of Byrd and Tallis, for the four voices rarely coincide in singing the words. Yet there is little repetition of the words. The *Gloria* of the *Nunc Dimittis* is in canon, but it is very smooth and melodious, especially in the concluding phrases. His second service is extended in form like a ' great ' service, but, like that of Tomkins, it differs from the ' great ' service of Byrd in having an independent organ part and many solo and ' verse ' passages. The form of the *Jubilate* in this service is like that of Weelkes's ' for two trebles,' in that alternate sections are for solo and chorus. Among other service-writers of this school were the Farrants, the Mundys, Adrian Batten and Nathaniel Giles.

The services of these Elizabethan and Jacobean composers have been discussed here at some length because it is important to emphasise the originality as well as the sterling merit of their work in the light of what followed. For, strange to say, in a period of nearly 200 years that followed, the service, instead of advancing in interest and developing in form, stood absolutely still and in many respects deteriorated. None of the experiments of Byrd, Weelkes or Gibbons as regards form were followed up ; the ' great ' services were neglected, and almost exclusively the ' short ' service became the accepted model. Benjamin Rogers and Child in the mid-17th century followed the design of the ' short ' service exclusively ; moreover, their work is conventional and lacks the inspiration and interest which characterises that of their predecessors.

What is more surprising is that the composers of the Restoration school did nothing of any real value for the service. This was the period in which the development of the anthem was very pronounced, especially as regards accompaniment. But the services even of Blow and Purcell show no similar advance ; they can be sung without accompaniment and are designed on the ' short ' service model. Purcell's big *Te Deum* in D does not, of course, belong to this class of work at all (see CECILIA, ST., subsection CECILIAN CELEBRATIONS) ; it was never intended for daily cathedral use. Neither Croft nor Aldrich, nor any other of this school of composers, added anything to the service. During the 18th century the standard of achievement sank lower and lower, and the services of that date are, with scarcely any exception, entirely lacking in subtlety of verbal expression and accentuation. King's services were absolutely commonplace, Travers in his more florid style was little better, whereas the work of Kent and Nares is of the feeblest character. The services of Boyce are slightly more robust, but are much inferior to his best anthems, and the close of the century brought with it the bombastic and vulgar style of which Cooke's service in G is typical. The close of the 18th century saw the turn of the tide. Attwood and the elder Wesley were among those who first pointed to better things, but it was T. A. Walmisley and Sebastian Wesley who really set up a new standard and laid the foundation of the modern service ; and the most important feature of their work was the use they made of the organ, not merely for the reinforcement and duplication of the vocal parts, but as being able to contribute something of an independent nature to the composition which could not be supplied by the voices alone. A mere glance at the scores of Walmisley in D minor and Wesley in E will suffice to prove the value as well as the originality of these two composers in this particular field of work.

Little further need be said ; once the possibilities had been discovered of using the organ for this type of accompaniment, the floodgates were opened, for not only was there far greater scope for the composers' imagination, but fresh and almost endless variety of device was immediately made available ; it followed also in the natural course of things that services should be written for special occasions with full orchestral accompaniment. The new features were necessarily abused by many composers, but the cathedral repertory of services has been much enriched since the days of Walmisley and Wesley ; and standing first among a distinguished group of modern service-writers is Charles Villiers Stanford. Stanford's name is certain to live in connexion with his services even if all his other work should perish, and it is probable that his B flat service is more widely known than any English service written since the Reformation.    E. H. F.

SESQUI, a Latin word signifying, literally, the whole *plus* its half.

In musical terminology, the prefix Sesqui is used in combination with certain numeral adjectives, to express the proportion, either of harmonic intervals or of rhythmic combinations. (See PROPORTION and NOTATION.)    W. S. R.

SESQUIALTERA, a compound organ stop consisting of several ranks of pipes, sometimes as many as five. Various combinations of intervals are used, but they only represent different positions of the third, fifth, and eighth of the

ground-tone in the third or fourth octave above. The sesquialtera thus gives brilliance to the tone by reinforcing these upper partials.    J. S.

SESTET, see SEXTET.

ŠEVČÍK, OTTAKAR (b. Horazdowitz, Bohemia, Mar. 22, 1852), violinist and pedagogue, of Czech nationality. His father, a teacher of the violin, after giving him elementary lessons, sent him in 1866 to the Conservatorium in Prague, where he studied under Anton Bennewitz until 1870, and then accepted an appointment as Konzertmeister of the Mozarteum in Salzburg. This engagement, varied by the organising of self-supporting concerts at Prague, lasted until 1873, in which year he made his début as a soloist at Vienna, becoming eventually Konzertmeister of the Komische Oper in that city. At the closing of the operahouse he gave concerts in Moscow, and in 1875 was appointed professor at the Imperial Music School in Kiev, remaining there till 1892, when he accepted an invitation from Anton Bennewitz, then director of the Prague Conservatorium, to return to Bohemia and fill the post of principal professor of the violin at that institution. Thenceforward, although he occasionally played in public (for the last time in 1898), he mainly devoted himself to teaching. His appointment happened to synchronise with the entry, as a pupil, of Jan KUBELIK, then 12 years of age, and possessed of a marvellous gift for technique. Ševčík taught him for six years, moulding him in accordance with his own special theories of teaching, to which Kubelik's success first drew the world's attention. This success was thought, however, to be very largely due to the young violinist's own natural ability, and it was not until, first, Kocian, and then, in a still greater degree, Marie Hall, confirmed, by the brilliance of their performances, the effectiveness of his system of training, that his reputation became established abroad. Pupils offered themselves in such great numbers, mainly from England and America, that only a small proportion of them could be accepted. Among them were the sons of Wilhelmj and Hugo Heermann, the daughter of Wieniawski, Zacharewitsch, Michel de Sicard, Walter Schulze, Vivien Chartres, Leon Sametini, Zimbalist, Daisy Kennedy, and many others more locally known, who, after studying under Ševčík, received teaching appointments at various music schools. Under the Ševčík system nothing is left undone that methodical training of ear or muscles can accomplish. Ševčík's principles are embodied in his *Method*, which is a monument of patient toil that will secure him fame after his pupils are forgotten. It consists of four books. Book I. is a Violin Method for Beginners (in seven parts, op. 6). In this he has adopted for the early stages of practice what he calls his ' Semitone System.' Whereas in the ordinary diatonic scale the stoppings are unequal, the semitones which occur being produced on almost every string with the aid of different fingers, in this book scales are placed before the beginner, in which all the stoppings are the same on each string. This helps him to acquire quickly pure intonation, and enables him to devote his entire attention to the holding of the violin and the handling of the bow. Book II. contains Studies preparatory to the shake and for developing the touch (in two parts, op. 7). Changes of position and preparatory scale studies, op. 8, and Preparatory Studies in double stopping, op. 9. Book III. is a School of Violin Technique (in four parts, op. 1), for more advanced pupils, and is Ševčík's magnum opus. Book IV. is a School of Bowing Technique (in six parts, op. 2), in which appear some 4000 varieties of bowing in progressive order, with metronome marks, and exhaustive directions tending to the development of the bow arm.

His publications include a series of 'Bohemian dances' for violin solo. In 1886 the Czar Alexander II. conferred upon him the Order of St. Stanislaus for pedagogic services.

W. W. C.

**ŠEVČÍK-LHOTSKY QUARTET.** A Czech string quartet originally founded in Warsaw, in 1903, by three pupils of Otakar Ševčík : Bohuslav Lhotsky (*b.* Libochovice, 1879), Karel Procházka (*b.* Domažlice, 1878) and Karel Moravec. The original violoncellist, Boguslav Váska, was succeeded by Ladislav Zelenka in 1911, who eventually joined the BOHEMIAN (CZECH) STRING QUARTET (*q.v.*), his place in Lhotsky's Quartet being filled by Antonio Fingerland. The quartet is permanently fixed in Prague, from which centre frequent tours have been made in Europe. England was visited in 1913 and 1923.     R. N.

**SEVENTH**, the intervals which contain seven notes comprise some of the most important chords in music, and such as have been peculiarly conspicuous in musical history. They are divided mainly into three classes—major sevenths, minor sevenths, and diminished sevenths ; as

(See INTERVAL ; HARMONY.)     C. H. H. P.

**SÉVÉRAC**, JOSEPH MARIE DÉODAT DE (*b.* St. Félix de Caraman-Lauraguais, July 20, 1873 ; *d.* Céret, Pyrenées Orientales, Mar. 23, 1921). He first studied solfège and harmony at the Conservatoire of Toulouse, and in 1896 came to Paris, where he entered the Schola Cantorum, studying counterpoint with A. Magnard, and composition with V. d'Indy, until 1907. Highly gifted and profoundly musical, possessing the sense of colour and life, he was one of the most original musicians of his genera-

tion. His premature death was a great loss to the musical art of his country. His artistic personality affirms itself in striking fashion in his PF. works : 'Le Chant de la terre' (1900), 'En Languedoc' (1904), 'Baigneuses au soleil' (1908), 'Cerdaña' (1910), 'En vacances' (1910), 'Sous les lauriers roses' (1919), 'Le Soldat de plomb' (easy piece for four hands).

His songs are remarkable and attractive for the quality of their musical expression. For the stage he wrote 'Le Cœur du moulin' (1903-1908) (Opéra-Comique, Dec. 8, 1909), a lyric, poem in two acts ; 'Héliogabale' (Béziers, Aug. 21, 1910), 'Hélène de Sparte' (incidental music) (Théâtre du Châtelet, May 5, 1912), etc. He composed organ and chamber music, motets, many unpublished compositions (list in Seré), and harmonised a number of 'Chansons anciennes.' His temperament somewhat resembled that of Ch. Bordes. De Séverac possessed a special aptitude for translating into music the atmosphere of nature in general, and specially that of his native country.    M. L. P.

BIBL.—O. SÉRÉ, *Musiciens français d'aujourd'hui*, 1921 (with bibliography) ; *Revue musicale*, Oct. 1921 (E. ROUART) ; *Mus. T.*, July 1919 (LEIGH HENRY) ; *Music and Letters* (Apr. 1922) ; E. BURLINGAME HILL, *Modern French Music* (Houghton Mifflin Company, Boston, New York, 1924).

**SEVERI**, FRANCESCO (*b.* Perugia ; *d.* Rome, Dec. 25, 1630), was from Dec. 31, 1613, a singer in the Papal Chapel. He composed 'Salmi passegiati . . . sopra i falsobordoni' (1615) ; 1-3 part arie to sing to the guitar, harpsichord, etc. (1626).

**SEVERN**, THOMAS HENRY (*b.* London, Nov. 5, 1801 ; *d.* Wandsworth, Apr. 15, 1881), brother of Joseph Severn the painter, the intimate friend of Keats, Leigh Hunt, etc., became, after many difficulties, manager of Farn's music-business at 72 Lombard Street. He was the first conductor of the City of London Classical Harmonists, started in 1831. He was virtually self-taught, and his knowledge of music was derived from study of the scores of the great masters, and from practice. Severn was the author of an opera, and of various songs which were very popular in their time ; a cantata, 'The Spirit of the Shell' ; two Te Deums (Novello & Co.), etc. etc.    G.

**SEVILLANA**, see SONG, subsection SPAIN (4).

**SEXT** (Lat. *officium* (*vel oratio*) *ad horam sextam* ; *ad sextam*), the last but one of the 'Lesser Hours' in the Roman Breviary.

The plain-song music for Sext will be found in the Antiphonal.    W. S. R.

**SEXTET** (or SESTET) (Fr. *sextuor* ; Ger. *Sextett* ; Ital. *sestetto*), a composition for six instruments or voices. The instrumental sextet for strings alone or for strings and wind or pianoforte is apt to encroach somewhat upon the domain of the small orchestra. If the string quartet is the ideal combination for combined solo-playing, it follows that the addition of parts tends to defeat its object, for the ear cannot take in more than a certain amount of multiplicity of detail, while masses of rich tone-colour, whether the writing is polyphonic or harmonic in its main outline, take one beyond the medium. Nevertheless, Brahms's sextets for two violins, two violas and two violoncellos are notable examples, both of the form and of his own style. String sextets have also been written by Dvořák, Goossens (three violins, viola and two violoncellos), Holbrooke, Reger, Schönberg and Tchaikovsky. Haydn's ' Echo ' sextet is for four violins and two violoncellos.

Other combinations have been employed : Beethoven's op. 81b is for strings and two horns,[1] and his op. 71 is for clarinets, horns and bassoons.[2] Holbrooke has written for pianoforte and wind and for pianoforte and strings, including double-bass, and there is the well-known pianoforte and wind sextet of Thuille and a similar work by Pijper. (See CHAMBER MUSIC.)

Vocal sextets occur in operas where the situation makes them possible. In the older operas the concerted finales are often found to be built up upon the vocal combination of the protagonists ; that at the close of ' Don Giovanni ' being especially noteworthy, as in the usual version of the opera this section is omitted.

N. C. G.

SEXTOLET (Fr. sextolet ; Ger. Sextole ; Ital. sestina), a group of six notes of equal length, played in the time of four ordinary notes of the same species. To distinguish them from regular notes of like form the number 6 is placed above or below the group. The true sextolet is formed from a triplet, by dividing each note into two, thus giving six notes, the first of which alone is accented ; but there is also a similar group of six notes, far more frequently used than the real sextolet, in which a slight accent is given to the fourth note as well as the first. This group, which really consists of two triplets, is properly known as the double triplet, and should be marked with the figure 3 over the second and fifth notes, though it is frequently marked with 6, and called a sextolet. The difference is well shown in the following two extracts from the Largo of Beethoven's concerto in C, op. 15. (See also TRIPLET.)

Double Triplets.

Sextolets.

To ensure correct accentuation such passages are better grouped thus :

F. T.

SEXTUS (Pars sexta, sextuplum ; Eng. the sixth voice, or part). In the partbooks of the 15th and 16th centuries four voices only were, as a general rule, mentioned by name, the cantus, altus, tenore and bassus. When a fifth voice was needed, it was called quintus, or pars quinta, and corresponded exactly in compass with one of the first four. When yet another voice was added, it was called sextus, or pars sexta, and corresponded in compass with another original voice-part. The extra part, therefore, represented sometimes an additional treble, sometimes an alto, sometimes a tenor, and sometimes a bass ; and always corresponded in compass with some other part in equal importance with itself.    W. S. R.

SEYFRIED, IGNAZ XAVER, RITTER VON (b. Vienna, Aug. 15, 1776 ; d. Aug. 26, 1841), was originally intended for the law, but his talent for music was so decided that, encouraged by Peter Winter, he determined to become a professional musician. In this his intimacy with Mozart and subsequent acquaintance with Beethoven were of much use. His teachers were Kozeluh for the PF. and organ, and Haydn for theory. In 1797 he became joint conductor of Schikaneder's theatre with Henneberg, a post he retained in the new Theatre ' an-der-Wien ' from its opening in 1801 till 1826. The first work he produced there was a setting of Schikaneder's comic opera ' Der Löwenbrunnen ' (1797), and the second, a grand opera ' Der Wundermann am Rheinfall ' (1799), on which Haydn wrote him a very complimentary letter. These were succeeded by innumerable operas great and small, operettas, Singspiele, music for melodramas, plays (including some by Schiller and Grillparzer), ballets, and pantomimes. Specially successful were his biblical dramas, ' Saul, König von Israel ' (1810), ' Abraham ' (1817), ' Die Maccabäer,' and ' Die Israeliten in der Wüste.' The music to ' Ahasverus ' (1823) he arranged from piano pieces by Mozart, and the favourite Singspiel, ' Die Ochsenmenuette ' (1823) (an adaptation of Hofmann's vaudeville ' Le Menuet du bœuf ') was similarly a pasticcio from Haydn's works. His church music, widely known and partly printed, included many masses and Requiems, motets, offertoires, graduales, a ' Libera ' for men's voices composed for Beethoven's funeral, etc. (See Q.-L.) Seyfried also contributed articles to Schilling's Universal Lexicon der Tonkunst, Schumann's Neue Zeitschrift für Musik, the Leipziger allg. Zeitung, and Cäcilia, besides editing Albrechtsberger's complete works—the Generalbass-Schule, Compositionslehre, and a Supplement in three volumes on playing from score (Haslinger)— and Beethoven's *Studies in Counterpoint* (1832). Nottebohm's critical investigations reduced this last work to its proper value.

Seyfried was elected an honorary or a corresponding member of innumerable musical societies at home and abroad. His pupils included Louis Schlösser, Karl Krebs, Heinrich Ernst, Skiwa, Baron Joseph Pasqualati, Carl Lewy, Heissler, Kessler, J. Fischhof, Sulzer, Carl Haslinger, Parish - Alvars, R. Mulder, S. Kuhe, Walther von Goethe, Baron Hermann Löwenskiold, F. von Suppé, Köhler and Basadona.

His closing years were saddened by misfortune. He was buried in the Währinger cemetery (Ortsfriedhof), near Beethoven and Schubert.                 C. F. P.

SFOGATO (open, airy), a word used in rare instances by Chopin (as in the 'Barcarole') in certain of those little cadenzas and ornaments that he is so fond of using, to indicate what may be called his own peculiar touch, a delicate and, as it were, ethereal tone, which can only be produced upon the pianoforte, and then only by skilful performers. 'Exhalation' is the only word that conveys an idea of this tone when it is produced. A 'Soprano sfogato' is a thin, acute voice.             M.

SFORZANDO (SFORZATO), 'forced'; a direction usually found in its abbreviated form *sf*. or *sfz*. referring to single notes or groups of notes which are to be especially emphasised. It is nearly equivalent to the accent >, but is less apt to be overlooked in performance, and is therefore used in all important passages.  M.

SGAMBATI, GIOVANNI (*b*. Rome, May 28, 1843; *d*. Dec. 15, 1914), a remarkable pianist and composer. His mother, an Englishwoman, was the daughter of Joseph Gott the sculptor, a native of London, who had for many years practised his art in Rome. Giovanni was intended for his father's profession, that of an advocate, and he would have been educated with that view but for his strong turn for music. He took his first lessons in pianoforte-playing at the age of 5 from Amerigo Barberi, author of a treatise on harmony, who used to pride himself on the fact that his own teacher had been a pupil of Clementi. After the death of his father in 1849 young Sgambati's mother migrated with her two children to Trevi in Umbria, where she married again. Here Giovanni's lessons, supplemented by a course of harmony, were continued under Natalucci, a former pupil of Zingarelli, at the Conservatorio of Naples. From the age of 6 the boy often played in public, sang contralto in church, conducted small orchestras, and was known as the author of several sacred pieces. In 1860 he settled in Rome and soon became famous for his playing, and for the classical character of his programmes.

His favourite composers were Beethoven, Chopin and Schumann, and he was an excellent interpreter of the fugues of Bach and Handel. Shortly after this he was on the point of going to Germany to study when the arrival of Liszt in Rome saved him from that necessity. With him Sgambati studied long and diligently. He soon began to give orchestral concerts in the 'Galleria Dantesca,' which, as the 'Sala Dante,' was for many years the only concert-hall in Rome. Here, under Sgambati's direction, the symphonies and concertos of the German masters, until then unknown in the papal city, at length found a hearing. Beethoven's 'Eroica' was introduced to the Roman public and the 'Emperor' concerto was played to them by Sgambati for the first time, just as later they learned at his hands to know and appreciate Brahms, Saint-Saëns and later writers.

At the same time Sgambati was busy with his compositions. In 1864 he wrote a string quartet; in 1866, a pianoforte quintet (F minor, op. 4), an overture for full orchestra to Cossa's 'Cola di Rienzi,' together with other works, and in the same year he conducted Liszt's 'Dante' symphony (Feb. 26) with great success and credit to himself.

In company with Liszt, he visited Germany in 1869, and at Munich heard Wagner's music for the first time. Sgambati's talent naturally attracted the notice of von Keudell, the well-known amateur and German ambassador in Rome. At the orchestral concerts which he conducted at the embassy many of his works were first heard. Here also, in 1876, he made the acquaintance of Wagner, in whose honour the ambassador one evening gave a concert consisting entirely of Sgambati's compositions, including two pianoforte quintets and several songs. Wagner, much surprised to find in Rome a composer who made music of this kind, expressed a wish to hear it again, and on the following evening the programme was privately repeated for the delectation of the master, who immediately wrote to the publishing-house of Schott, advising them to purchase and print Sgambati's works without delay. The firm then published the two quintets, as well as a prelude and fugue for pianoforte.

Encouraged by this well-merited recognition Sgambati wrote a Festival-overture and a concerto for pianoforte and orchestra, his symphony in D, produced at a concert in the 'Sala Dante' early in 1881 and repeated on Mar. 28 of that year at the Quirinal, being the first work of the kind ever given at the Italian court, in the presence of King Humbert and his Consort, Queen Margherita, to whom it was dedicated. In 1882 Sgambati paid his first visit to England and played his pianoforte concerto at the Philharmonic concert of May 11. His symphony was given at the Crystal

Palace on June 10 under the composer's direction. Both works were well received, but the symphony made much the greater impression of the two.

His quartet for strings in D flat, printed about this time, is one of the works by which Sgambati is best known. First played in London by the Kneisel Quartet of Boston, it was afterwards included by Joachim and Piatti, along with his second pianoforte quintet, in the repertory of the Popular Concerts, and eventually attained wide popularity throughout Europe. Two years later (1884) Sgambati conducted the symphony in Paris, where he had been invited as representative of Italy at the International Concerts given in the Trocadéro. In 1886 he was named one of the five corresponding members of the French Institute to fill the place vacated by Liszt. In 1887 he was invited to conduct his second symphony, in E flat (written in 1883), and to execute his first quintet at the great musical festival of the Tonkünstler-Versammlung in Cologne.

In the same year he wrote, in honour of the wedding of the Duke of Aosta, an ' Epitalamio sinfonico,' which takes the form of a suite, though considerably more developed than is usually the case in compositions so described. After its production at Turin the author conducted performances of the work in Milan and Rome, and brought it to London on the occasion of his second visit in 1891, when it was given at a Philharmonic concert. During the same season he gave a concert of his own compositions at Princes' Hall, and was commanded to Windsor, where he played before QueenVictoria. One of the most memorable journeys made by Sgambati to foreign countries included a visit to Russia in the autumn of 1903. Received with enthusiasm, he gave concerts, consisting chiefly of his own works, at St. Petersburg, Moscow and other places in Northern Europe, with such conspicuous success that they would have welcomed him gladly another year.

To commemorate the death of King Humbert he wrote a ' Messa da Requiem ' for chorus, baritone solo and orchestra, which was produced at the Pantheon, Jan. 17, 1896, and several times repeated. It was also given in Germany, at Cologne in Nov. 1906, in the composer's presence, and at Mayence in Mar. 1907. The Requiem is a fine piece of religious writing, in strict conformity with the spirit of the sacred text, modern without extravagance of any kind, and its themes well developed, though not so diffusely as to render it unsuitable for performance on liturgical occasions.

Sgambati devoted the energies of his best years to teaching ; and, as a result, must be considered the founder, with his colleague Pinelli, of the Liceo Musicale in connexion with the Accademia di S. Cecilia in ROME (q.v.). Beginning with a free class for the pianoforte

in 1869 he persevered in giving instruction of the soundest description.

His success as a writer for the pianoforte was due to his rare knowledge of its resources, to his facility in producing required effects with the simplest means, to his complete command of harmonic combinations of the subtlest kind, and to the exquisite finish given to even the least of his inspirations. With Sgambati device is rarely evident. His figures of accompaniment are as spontaneous as the melodies they sustain. Certain of his minor compositions, such as the beautiful intermezzo in op. 21 and certain numbers in his ' Pièces lyriques ' (op. 23) and in his ' Mélodies poétiques ' (op. 36), may be cited as reaching a level which in little descriptive pieces of the kind has rarely been surpassed. His more important pianoforte pieces, his chamber-music and his orchestral writings, taken together, place him at the head of those Italian musicians of the latter part of the 19th century, who, not writing for the stage, have moulded their work on classic models.

His native city owes him a lasting debt as its apostle of classical music, as teacher, performer and director. His efforts did not go unrecognised in high places. His influence was felt and appreciated at the Italian court, where he was appointed pianist and director of Queen Margherita's Quintet, and named, by *motu proprio* of King Victor Emmanuel III. in 1903, Commendatore of the Order of SS. Maurice and Lazarus.

Some of the works mentioned above are still unprinted ; his published works include the following :

Op.
1. Album of five songs.
2. Album of ten songs.
3. Notturno for pf.
4. Quintet, pf. and strings, F minor.
5. Quintet, pf. and strings, B flat.
6. Prelude and fugue for pf. in E flat minor.
10. Two Études for pf., D flat and F sharp minor, written for the Method of Lebert and Stark, Stuttgart.
12. Fogli volanti for pf., 8 pieces.
14. Gavotte for pf.   Easy edition arranged by author.
15. Concerto, pf. and orchestra, in G minor.
16. Symphony in D.
17. Quartet in D flat for strings.
18. Quattro pezzi for pf.   Preludio, Vecchio minuetto, Nenia, Toccata.
19. Four Italian songs.
20. Tre notturni for pf.
21. Suite for pf. (Prelude, Valse, Air, Intermezzo, Étude mélodique)
22. Passiflore, voice and pf.
23. Pièces lyriques (6) for pf.
24. Due pezzi for violin and piano.
25. Te Deum laudamus, andante solenne, for strings and organ. The same for full orchestra.
29. Gondoliera for violin and piano.
30. Benedizione nuziale for organ.
31. Fifth Nocturne for pf.
32. Melodie liriche, four songs.
33. Sixth Nocturne for pf.
34. ' Versa est in luctum cythara mea.' Motet for baritone, organ and strings (included in opus 38).
35. Quattro melodie per una voce e pf.
36. Mélodies poétiques (12) for pf.
37. ' Tout bas,' Melodia per canto.
38. Messa da Requiem per coro, baritone solo, orchestra ed organe (*ad lib.*).

(The following are without opus number.)
Serenata, per canto e pianoforte.
Ballata, per tenore.
Stornello toscano, per una voce e pianoforte.
Romanza senza parole, pf.
' Il faut aimer,' Gavotte chantée.
La mia stella, Melodia.
Melodie liriche (five, and a duet).
Two songs—
1. Fior di siepe.
2. Fuori di porta.

TRANSCRIPTIONS

Liszt. Die Ideale, pf. four hands.
Chopin. Canzone lituana, pf. solo.
Gluck. Melodia dell' Orfeo, pf. solo.
'Separazione,' old Italian folk-song (edited and provided with accompaniment by G. Sgambati).

                G. ; addns. H. A. W.

BIBL.—FRITZ VOLBACH, *Giovanni Sgambati. Katalog seiner hauptsächlichsten Werke bis auf die Neuzeit vervollständigt, m! ausführlichen Erläuterungen, Kritiken von Aufführungen und einer Einleitung.* (Schott, Mainz, 1913.)

**SHAKE OR TRILL** (Fr. *trille,* formerly *tremblement, cadence*; Ger. *Triller*; Ital. *trillo*). The shake, one of the earliest in use among the ancient graces, is also the chief and most frequent ornament of modern music, both vocal and instrumental. It consists of the regular and rapid alternation of a given note with the note above, such alternation continuing for the full duration of the written note.

The shake is the head of a family of ornaments, all founded on the alternation of a principal note with a subsidiary note one degree either above or below it. (See MORDENT; PRALLTRILLER; RIBATTUTA; ORNAMENTS.)

The sign of the shake in modern music *tr.* (generally followed by a waved line ∿∿∿∿ if over a long note), and in older music *tr.* ∿∿, ⋆⋆⋆, and occasionally +, placed over or under the note ; and it is rendered in two different ways, beginning with either the principal or the upper note, as in Example 1 :

1. *Written.*   *Performed.*      *Or thus.*

These two modes of performance differ considerably in effect, because the accent, which is always perceptible, however slight it may be, is given in the one case to the principal and in the other to the subsidiary note, and it is therefore important to ascertain which of the two methods should be adopted in any given case. Most of the earlier masters, including C. P. E. Bach, Marpurg, Türk, etc., held, what was the absolute rule of the classical French school up to the end of the 18th century, that all trills should begin with the upper note, while 19th-century authorities such as Hummel, Czerny and Moscheles have preferred to begin on the principal note. This diversity of opinion indicates two different views of the very nature and meaning of the shake ; according to the latter, it is a trembling or pulsation—the reiteration of the principal note, though subject to continual momentary interruptions from the subsidiary note, gives a certain undulating effect not unlike that of the tremulant of the organ ; according to the former, the shake is derived from the still older APPOGGIATURA (*q.v.*), and consists of a series of appoggiaturas with their resolutions—is in fact a kind of elaborated appoggiatura,—and as such requires the accent to fall upon the upper or subsidiary note. Marpurg says

'the trill derives its origin from an appoggiatura (*Vorschlag von oben*) and is in fact a series of descending appoggiaturas executed with the greatest rapidity,' and Emanuel Bach, speaking of the employment of the shake in ancient (German) music, says 'formerly the trill was usually only introduced after an appoggiatura,' and he gives the following example :

2.

Nevertheless, the theory which derives the shake from a trembling or pulsation, and therefore places the accent on the principal note, in which manner most shakes in modern music are executed, has the advantage of considerable, if not the highest antiquity. Compare Caccini's *trillo* and *gruppo* quoted under ORNAMENTS.

Playford, in his *Introduction to the Skill of Musick* (1655), quotes an anonymous treatise on 'the Italian manner of singing,' in which precisely the same two graces are described.[1] Commenting on the shake, Playford says :

'I have heard of some that have attained it after this manner, in singing a plain-song of six notes up and six down, they have in the midst of every note beat or shaked with their finger upon their throat, which by often practice came to do the same notes exactly without.'

It seems then clear that the original intention of a shake was to produce a trembling effect, and so the custom of beginning with the principal note may be held justified.

In performing the works of the great masters from the time of Bach to Beethoven then, it should be understood that, according to the rule laid down by contemporary teachers, the shake begins with the upper or subsidiary note, but it would not be safe to conclude that this rule is to be invariably followed. In some cases we find the opposite effect definitely indicated by a small note placed before the principal note of the shake, and on the same line or space, thus—

3. MOZART (ascribed to), 'Une fièvre,' Var. 3.

and even when there is no small note it is no doubt correct to perform all shakes which are situated like those of the above example in the same manner, that is, beginning with the principal note. So therefore a shake at the beginning of a phrase or after a rest (Ex. 4), or after a downward leap (Ex. 5), or when preceded by a note one degree below it (Ex. 6) should begin on the principal note.

---

[1] The author of this treatise is said by Playford to have been a pupil of the celebrated Scipione della Palla, who was also Caccini's master.

4.    BACH, Prelude No. 16, Book I.

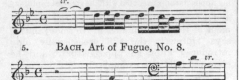

5.    BACH, Art of Fugue, No. 8.

6.    BACH, Sonata for PF. and Flute, No. 6.

It is also customary to begin with the principal note when the note bearing the shake is preceded by a note one degree above it (Ex. 7), especially if the tempo be quick (Ex. 8), in which case the trill resembles the PRALLTRILLER (*q.v.*), the only difference being that the three notes of which it is composed are of equal length, instead of the last being the longest.

7.    BACH, Organ Fugue in F.

8.    MOZART, Sonata in F.

If, however, the note preceding the shake is slurred to it (Ex. 9 *a*), or if the trill note is preceded by an appoggiatura (Ex. 9 *b*), the trill begins with the upper note ; and this upper note is *tied* to the preceding note, thus delaying the entrance of the shake in a manner precisely similar to the bound Pralltriller (cf. PRALLTRILLER, Ex. 3).    A trill so situated is called in German *der gebundene Triller* (the bound trill).

9.    (*a*) BACH, Concerto for two Pianos.

Played.

(*b*) HAYDN, Trio in E minor.

Played.

When the note carrying a shake is preceded by a short note of the same name (Ex. 10), the upper note always begins, unless the antici-pating note is marked staccato (Ex. 11), in which case the shake begins with the principal note.

10.    BACH, Chromatic Fantasia.

Played.

11.    MOZART, Sonata in C minor.

Certain later composers, when a trill begin-ning with the subsidiary note is required, have indicated it by a small grace-note, written immediately before the trill-note (Ex. 12). This grace-note is occasionally met with in older music (see Clementi, sonata in B minor), but its employment was objected to by Türk, Marpurg and others, as liable to be confused with the real appoggiatura of the bound trill, as in Ex. 9.    This objection does not hold in modern music, since the bound trill is no longer used.

12.    BEETHOVEN, Sonata, Op. 53, Finale.

etc.

Immediately before the final note of a shake a new subsidiary note is generally introduced, situated one degree *below* the principal note. This and the concluding principal note together form what is called the *turn* of the shake, though the name is not strictly appropriate, since it properly belongs to a separate species of ornament of which the turn of a shake forms in fact the second half only.[1]    (See TURN.) The turn is variously indicated, sometimes by two small grace-notes (Ex. 13), sometimes by notes of ordinary size (Ex. 14), and in old music by the signs ⁓, ⁓ or ⁓.

13.    CLEMENTI,       14.    HANDEL, Gigue
      Sonata in C.                (Suite 14).

Sometimes the turn is not indicated at all, but it has nevertheless to be introduced if the shake is followed by an accented note (Ex. 15). If, however, the next following note is un-accented, no turn is required, but an extra

_____
[1] The turn of a trill is better described by its German name *Nachschlag*, or after-beat.

principal note is added to the last couple of
notes, that the trill may end as well as begin
with the principal note (Ex. 16). When the
trill is followed by a rest, a turn is generally
made, though it is perhaps not necessary unless
specially indicated (Ex. 17).

15. MOZART, ' Lison dormait,' Var. 8.

16. CLEMENTI, Sonata in G.

17. BEETHOVEN, Trio, Op. 97.

When a note ornamented by a shake is
followed by another note of the same pitch, the
lower subsidiary note only is added to the end
of the shake, and the succeeding written note
serves to complete the turn. Even when the
trill-note is tied to the next following, this
extra lower note is required, provided the
second written note is short, and occurs on an
accented beat (Ex. 18). If the second note is
long, the two tied notes are considered as forming one long note, and the shake is therefore
continued throughout the whole value.

18. BACH, Fugue No. 15, Vol. II.

Very similar is the rendering of a shake on a
dotted note : the turn ends on the dot, which
thus takes the place of the second of the two
notes of the same pitch. Thus the effect of the
two modes of writing shown in Ex. 19 a and b
would be the same. If, however, the dotted
note is followed by a note a degree lower, no
turn is required (Ex. 20).

19. HANDEL, Suite 10. Allemande.

Rendering of both.

20. HANDEL, Suite 10. Allegro.

Trills on very short notes require no turn,
but consist merely of a triplet.

Besides the several modes of ending a shake,
the beginning can also be varied by the
addition of what is called the upper or lower
prefix. The upper prefix is not met with in
modern music, but occurs frequently in the
works of Bach and Handel. Its sign is a tail
turned upwards from the beginning of the
ordinary trill mark, and its rendering is as
follows—

21. BACH, Partita No. 1, Sarabande.

The lower prefix consists of a single lower subsidiary note prefixed to the first note of a shake
which begins with the principal note, or of two
notes, lower and principal, prefixed to the first
note of a shake beginning with the upper note.
It is indicated in various ways, by a single small
grace-note (Ex. 22), by two (Ex. 23), or three
grace-notes (Ex. 24), and in old music by a tail
turned downwards from the beginning of
the trill mark (Ex. 25), the rendering in all
cases being that shown in Ex. 26.

From a composer's habit of writing the
lower prefix with one, two or three notes, his
intentions respecting the beginning of the
ordinary shake *without* prefix, as to whether it
should begin with the principal or the subsidiary note, may generally be inferred. For
since it would be incorrect to render Ex. 23 or
24 in the manner shown in Ex. 27, which involves the repetition of a note, and a consequent
break of legato—it follows that a composer who
chooses the form Ex. 23 to express the prefix
intends the shake to begin with the upper note,
while the use of Ex. 24 shows that a shake
beginning with the principal note is generally
intended.

27.

That the form Ex. 22 always implies the
shake beginning with the principal note is not
so clear (although there is no doubt that it
usually does so), for a prefix is possible which

leaps from the lower to the upper subsidiary note. This exceptional form is frequently employed by Mozart, and is marked as in Ex. 28. It bears a close resemblance to the DOUBLE APPOGGIATURA (q.v.).

28.    MOZART, sonata in F.    Adagio.

Among later composers, Chopin and Weber almost invariably write the prefix with two notes (Ex. 23) ; Beethoven uses two notes in his earlier works (see op. 2, No. 2, Largo, bar 10), but afterwards generally one (see op. 57).    F. T.

SHAKESPEARE, WILLIAM (b. Croydon, June 16, 1849), composer, vocalist, pianist. At the age of 13 he was appointed organist at the church where formerly he had attracted attention in the choir. In 1862 he began a three years' course of study of harmony and counterpoint under Molique ; but after that master's death, having in 1866 gained the King's Scholarship at the R.A.M., continued his studies there for five years under Sir W. Sterndale Bennett. Whilst at the R.A.M. he produced and performed at the students' concerts a pianoforte sonata, a pianoforte trio, a capriccio for pianoforte and orchestra, and a pianoforte concerto ; and attracted some notice as a solo-player.

He was elected Mendelssohn Scholar in 1871, for composition and pianoforte-playing, and in accordance with the wish of the Committee entered the Conservatorium at Leipzig. There, whilst under the instruction of the director, Carl Reinecke, he produced and conducted in the Gewandhaus a symphony in C minor. Having discovered himself to be the possessor of a tenor voice, he was sent by the Mendelssohn Scholarship Committee to study singing with Lamperti at Milan, and there remained for two and a half years. But though singing was his chief pursuit he did not neglect composition, and while in Italy wrote two overtures, two string quartets and other works.

In 1875 he returned to England, and entered upon the career of a concert and oratorio singer. He was appointed in 1878 professor of singing, and in 1880 conductor of the concerts, at the R.A.M. This latter office he resigned in 1886, but as a teacher of singing both at the R.A.M. and privately he has enjoyed a wide reputation. In 1924 he published Plain Words on Singing (Putnam).

J. C. G.

SHALIAPIN, FEDOR J., see CHALIAPIN.

SHAMUS O'BRIEN, romantic comic opera in 2 acts ; text by G. H. Jessop (after J. Sheridan Le Fanu) ; music by Stanford, op. 61. Produced Opéra-Comique Theâtre, London, Mar. 2, 1896.

SHANTY (CHANTY), a song used chiefly by sailors to give time to the pulling of a rope, or other matter where a united exertion is essential. It is doubtful as to derivation, whether from the French root, ' chant,' or whether by reason of its coming from a section of men in the ' lumber ' trade in America or Canada, who, living in ' shanties ' or roughly built wooden huts, are sometimes called ' shanty men.' In American publications the spelling ' shanty ' [1] for the song is generally employed.

It must be also noticed that most of the modern ' chanties ' appear to have crossed the Atlantic and to have a distinctly American influence.

The sailor's shanty is different in all respects from the song he sings to amuse himself or his comrades. It is a work song and not a play song. The shanty must now be almost spoken of in the past tense, as an obsolete portion of sea life, for the use of steam has obviated much of the pulling and hauling on ships. In steamers sails are seldom used, and the raising of the anchor, the pumping of the bilgewater from the ship, with many other things that formerly were done by manual labour, are now the work of the donkey-engine. In the old sailing vessels where every sail had to be raised by hand, many a time with the wind pulling adversely at the canvas, the task of a ship's crew was no light affair. The mate, probably seeing the futile efforts of the men to raise the heavy-yard, would call for a shanty. This would be responded to by the ' shanty-man,' as the general leader was usually called. He would sing some kind of familiar nonsense-verses, the crew joining in with a recognised chorus at certain words where the united pull would come, as for instance :

*Haul the Bowline.*

*Solo.*—We'll haul on the bowline
So early in the morning.
We'll haul on the bowline
The bowline haul.

*Chorus.*—We'll haul on the bowline
The bully ship 's a-rolling.
We'll haul on the bowline
The bowline haul, etc.

The musical rhythm is found to be a great help in getting the united effort at the required instant.

Shanties are divided into different classes. One of them is recognised as the ' bunt ' shanty, which is or was used in reefing sail. The men on the yard with their feet in the foot-ropes have to pull in the ' bunt ' or loose

1 The form has been generally adopted in England since it indicates the traditional pronunciation.

sail, reefing it by knotting together the reef lines attached to the sail. The general bunt chant was

> 'We'll tauten the bunt, and we'll furl, hey !
> And pay Paddy Doyle for his boots.'

The pumping shanties were generally more of a connected narrative song, as the pumping being merely a monotonous up and down motion, required a prolonged rather than a great strain. This may be said of the capstan shanties, the men walking round the capstan and thrusting against the capstan bars to raise the anchor.

While many of these shanties are universal in English-speaking ships, yet there are considerable differences in the tunes and versions of the words used.

The familiar ones are : ' Whisky for my Johnnie,' ' The Rio Grande,' ' The Wide Missouri,' ' Reuben Ranzo,' ' Old Storm Along,' ' Blow the man down,' ' Tom's gone to Ilo,' and some others. As before stated, there are a great number that mention American localities, ' Mobile Bay,' ' The Banks of the Sacramento,' and others, which have emanated from America and got diffused among ships.

' Leave her, Johnnie, leave her,' is sometimes used as a shanty, but its original purpose was to describe the vessel and its officers as the men were paid off. For instance it might run :

> 'Oh, the captain he is a very good man,
> Leave her, Johnnie, leave her,
> But the mate isn't worth an old tin pan,
> Sing leave her, Johnnie, leave her.'

and so forth. ' Outward Bound,' beginning :

> 'To Liverpool docks we bade adieu
> To Sall, and Susie, and Kitty too.
> The anchor's weigh'd, the sail's unfurl'd
> We're bound to cross the watery world.
> For don't you see we're outward bound,
> Hurrah ! we're outward bound, etc.,'

may be used as a capstan shanty. The docks mentioned will, of course, vary with the port of departure. Shanties, though not so named, have been in use in all nations, savage and civilised, for the same purpose that the British shanty is or was employed, to give a measured rhythm for the pulling of oars and other matters connected with the working of a vessel. The Nile boat-songs, the Italian barcaroles, the Highland boat-songs, as well as the Chinese and Canadian, have all had old specimens musically noted down.

The sailors' shanty has been dealt with in American and English magazine articles, while Miss L. A. Smith's ' Music of the Waters' contains an interesting collection of this class of music.          F. K.

The following are chief among the published collections of shanties :

DAVIS and TOZER : *Sailors' Songs and Chanties.* The words by Fredk. Davis, R.N.R., the music composed and arranged upon traditional sailor airs by Ferris Tozer.
Ditto. A more extended edition.
SMITH, LAURA A. : *The Music of the Waters.* A collection of the sailors' shanties or working songs of the sea. (1888.)
BRADFORD and FAGGE : *Old Sea Chanties.* Collected and arranged by John Bradford and Arthur Fagge. (1904.)

SHARP, CECIL J : *Pulling Chanties.* Collected and arranged by Cecil J. Sharp. Music and words.
*Capstan Chanties* Collected and arranged by Cecil J. Sharp. Music and words.
BECKETT : *Shanties and Forebitters.* Collected and arranged by Mrs. C. Beckett. (1914.)
BULLEN and ARNOLD : *Songs of Sea Labour.* Music and words by Frank T. Bullen and W. F. Arnold.
TREVINE : *Deep Sea Chanties.* Collection of 15. Words and tunes by Owen Trevine.
KEMP, H. : *Chanteys and Ballads, Sea Chantys, Tramp Ballads and other Ballads.* H. Kemp. (1922.)
WHALL : *Ships' Sea Songs and Shanties.* Collected by W. B. Whall, master mariner. (1910.)
Another and enlarged edition. (1912.)
TERRY, SIR RICHARD : *The Shanty Book.* Part I. Sailor shanties collected and edited, with pianoforte accompaniment, by Richard Runciman Terry. (1921.) Part II. (1926.)
*Journal of the Folk-song Society :* A certain number of shanties have been collected by members, and appear in the Journals of the Folk-song Society.

SHARP (Fr. *dièse*, Ger. *Kreuz*, Ital. *diesis*) ♯ : the sign for raising a note by a semitone. Placed immediately after the clef they govern every occurrence of the note they affect throughout the composition ; thus the keys with one sharp or more in the signature are known as the sharp keys. When introduced in the course of the music they hold good until the end of the bar in which they occur, unless cancelled by a natural.

In the notation of the 17th and early 18th centuries the sharp had a slightly different form, ♯ or ×. The latter is now become the sign of the double sharp.

F♯, C♯, etc., are termed in French *Fa dièze*, *Ut dièze*, etc. ; in German *Fis*, *Cis*, etc. In Germany the ♯ was at one time used to express the major key. Beethoven inscribed the Leonora Overture No. 1 (in C major) ' Ouvertura in C♯.' This custom is now happily disused.

The term ' sharp ' and its derivatives are also used to express a raising of the pitch, intentional or otherwise. (See ACCIDENTALS ; INTONATION ; SIGNATURE.)     S. T. W.

SHARP, CECIL JAMES (*b.* London, Nov. 22, 1859 ; *d.* there, June 23, 1924), was eminent as a student of English folk-song and dance. His researches not only added enormously to the musician's knowledge of these subjects, but his life devoted to them in what may be called a missionary spirit resulted in a popular revival which seems destined to produce far-reaching results.

Sharp, the son of a city merchant whose hobby was architecture, early imbibed from his father a knowledge and love of the English cathedrals. They were the starting-point of his subsequent passionate devotion to the life and indigenous art of his country. He was educated at Uppingham and at Clare College, Cambridge (whence he took the degree B.Mus.), then went to Australia where at twenty-four he became Associate to the Chief Justice of Southern Australia. Music also claimed him there, for he was (1889–92) organist of the cathedral at Adelaide where he also established a music school. Returning to England he was (1896–1905) principal of the Hampstead Conservatoire, and during these years the main preoccupation of his life began. In 1899 he first saw the Morris danced at Headington

(Oxfordshire), and the realisation that in the songs and dances of the countryside there still lingered a national art unrecognised by townsmen caused him to undertake innumerable journeys to record with notebook and pencil whatever might be gleaned. He recognised that others had been before him in this quest,[1] but he brought to it an ardour greater than that of most of his forerunners. His acquisitions were issued in the several collections of 'Folk-songs from Somerset' (1904–09) and in a sketch of the general field of research issued as *English Folk-song, some Conclusions* (1907). He investigated the sword dance of the North and the country dance of the Midlands, and interpreted Playford's *Dancing Master* (see PLAYFORD) in the light of his experience of the latter. The chief of his publications in these directions are enumerated below. Meantime he had become a member of the already existing FOLK-SONG SOCIETY (*q.v.*), and in 1911 he founded the English Folk Dance Society for the revival of the art. He gathered round him a number of young men and women who entered into his enthusiasm; among them was George BUTTERWORTH (*q.v.*) who collaborated in many of his publications. Amongst his minor services was the adaptation of music and dance from traditional English sources for Granville Barker's production of 'A Midsummer Night's Dream' (Savoy, 1914). The war, which claimed the younger members of Sharp's fraternity for other duties, broke up the team work of what had become a powerful movement, but his own activities were unabated. He visited America in order to collect the songs and dances which had lived on in the Southern Appalachian mountains, since their transportation there from England by the first settlers. He found there many primitive forms of the songs already noted in England with others. His 'English Folk-songs from the South Appalachians' (some of them collected by Olive Dame Campbell, 1917) contains nearly 500 songs, etc. His last years were spent in consolidating his work by reissues of selected editions of his songs, with the revision of accompaniments thereto and by re-establishing the work of the Folk Dance Society particularly in connexion with the competitive festivals. He was engaged on a translation of Thoinot Arbeau's *Orchésographie* (see ARBEAU) and a *History of the Dance* when he died. The following is a list of Sharp's principal publications:

*A Book of British Song.* 1902.
*Folk-songs from Somerset* (5 series, with C. L. Marson). 1904–09.
*English Folk-songs for Schools* (with S. Baring Gould). 1906.
*Country Dance Tunes* (11 parts, with G. S. K. Butterworth). 1906, etc.
*The Country Dance Book* (6 parts with Butterworth and Maud Karpeles).
*English Folk-song, some Conclusions.* 1907.
*The Morris Book* (5 parts, with Butterworth and H. MacIlwaine, 1907–13.

[1] See *English Folk-song, some Conclusions*, Introduction.

*English Folk Carols.* 1911.
*The Sword Dances of Northern England* (3 parts). 1911.
*Folk Dancing in Schools.* 1913.
*English Chanteys.* 1914.
*Folk Singing in Schools.* 1914.
Incidental music to *A Midsummer Night's Dream.* 1914.
*100 English Folk-songs.* 1916.
*English Folk-songs from the Southern Appalachians.* 1917.
*Folk-songs, Chanteys and Singing Games* (with C. H. Farnsworth).
*A Collection of Selected Folk-songs* (with R. Vaughan Williams). 1918.
(See also ENGLISH FOLK-SONG, Bibliography.)

C.

SHARPE, ETHEL, see HOBDAY (3).

SHARPE, (1) HERBERT FRANCIS (*b.* Halifax, Mar. 1, 1861; *d.* S. Kensington, London, Oct. 14, 1925), won a pianoforte scholarship at the opening of the National Training School, where he afterwards succeeded Eugène d'Albert as Queen's Scholar. He appeared as a finished pianist in 1882, and gave many concerts in the provinces as well as in London, where he organised several series of very interesting trio concerts in 1899–1902. He was appointed a professor at the R.C.M. in 1884, and in 1890 became an examiner for the Associated Board. In such work the greater part of his life was spent, and he was actively engaged in teaching up to the time of his sudden death. He wrote a comic opera in three acts (still in MS.), a concert overture for orchestra, pieces for one and two pianos, for flute or piano, for violin and piano, etc., besides partsongs, vocal trios, and songs. An excellent 'Pianoforte School' is his op. 60 (*Brit. Mus. Biog.*). M.

His son, (2) CEDRIC (*b.* London, Apr. 13, 1891), violoncellist, gained a scholarship at the R.C.M. (1907) where he studied under W. H. Squire. He has made his mark as a leading player in London orchestras and as a fine chamber music-player, more especially with the Philharmonic String Quartet. C.

SHARP (or ACUTE) MIXTURE, an organ stop consisting chiefly of pipes representing the higher partial tones, overtones or harmonics.

According to Dr. E. J. Hopkins, a sharp mixture is one of four ranks giving a sharp clear tone, consisting of the following intervals in relation to the unison: 19th, 22nd, 26th, 29th, or $g'$, $c''$, $g''$, $c'''$, in relation to CC or 8 ft. C. T. E.

SHAW (1) GEOFFREY TURTON (*b.* London, Nov. 14, 1879) was a chorister of St. Paul's Cathedral under Sir George Martin, and later organ scholar at Caius College, Cambridge, where he studied under Sir Charles Stanford and Dr. Chas. Wood. He is an inspector of music to the Board of Education and has devoted himself to the furtherance of popular organisations, both in the schools and training colleges and by means of such unofficial activities as summer schools for teachers and competitive festivals. He followed his brother as organist of St. Mary's, Primrose Hill. His compositions include partsongs and unison songs (for list see *B.M.S. Ann.* 1920) and he has co-operated with his brother in editing song books.

(2) MARTIN (b. London, Mar. 9, 1876), brother of the above, studied at the R.C.M. and held several posts as a church organist. He founded the Purcell Operatic Society, which began its activities with ' Dido and Æneas ' at the Hampstead Conservatoire, May 18, 1900, and subsequently at the Coronet Theatre. The masque from ' Diocletian ' was given at Queen Street Theatre, Kingsway, and although the society was short-lived, it did important work in reviving public interest in Purcell's dramatic music.

As organist of St. Mary's, Primrose Hill, he worked for a purer style of church music, and identified himself with every movement in the direction of national revival. He edited ' Songs of Britain,' ' The English Carol Book,' ' League of Nations Song Book,' and with his brother, the ' Motherland Song Book,' and published (1921) *The Principles of English Church Music Composition.*

His own compositions are numerous, and he has been particularly successful as a song writer. His ballad opera, ' Mr. Pepys,' libretto by Clifford Bax, was produced at the Everyman Theatre, Hampstead, in 1926. C.

SHAW, MARY (MRS. ALFRED SHAW) (b. 1814 ; d. Hadleigh Hall, Suffolk, Sept. 9, 1876), daughter of John Postans, messman at the Guard Room, St. James's Palace, was a student at the R.A.M. from Sept. 1828 to June 1831, and afterwards a pupil of Sir George Smart. Miss Postans appeared in public as a contralto singer in 1834, and at the Amateur Musical Festival in Exeter Hall in November of that year attracted great attention by the beauty of her voice and the excellence of her style. In 1835 she was engaged at the Concert of Ancient Music and the York Festival, and about the end of the year became the wife of Alfred Shaw, an artist of some repute. In 1836 she appeared at the Norwich and Liverpool Festivals, at the latter of which she sang the contralto part in ' St. Paul,' on its first performance in England. In 1837 she was engaged at the Philharmonic and Sacred Harmonic Societies and Birmingham Festival. In 1838, after fulfilling an engagement at the Gloucester Festival, she left England and appeared at the Gewandhaus concerts, under Mendelssohn. A letter from him to the directors of the Philharmonic Society, dated Jan. 19, 1839, speaks of Clara Novello and Mrs. Shaw as ' the best concert-singers we have had in this country for a long time.' From Germany she proceeded to Italy, and appeared at La Scala, Milan, Nov. 17, 1839, in Verdi's ' Oberto.' She returned to England in 1842, and appeared at Covent Garden with Adelaide Kemble ; in 1843 at the Sacred Harmonic Society with Clara Novello ; and afterwards at the Birmingham Festival. Her brilliant career was suddenly arrested by a heavy visitation. Her husband

became deranged, and the calamity so seriously shocked her whole system that the vocal organs became affected, and she was unable to sing in tune. She resorted to teaching, for three or four years appearing in public at an annual benefit concert. After her husband's death in 1847 she married J. F. Robinson, a country solicitor, and retired from the profession.

w. H. H.

SHAWM, a wind instrument of the oboe type, with a double reed but a larger conical bore and a wide bell. The name is generally said to be a corruption of the French *chalumeau,* but it would be more correct to say that both words have been derived from the same source, the Lat. *calamus,* ' a reed,' through the diminutive *calamellus.* In mediæval times the word appears as *calamel, chalamelle* or *chalemie* in France ; *caramillo* and *charamella* in Spain and Italy ; *Schalmei* or *Schalmey* in Germany ; and *shalmele, shalm* or *shawm* in England. It is not until the 16th century that the form *chalumeau* occurs, and in the next century it was used to denote a distinct instrument with cylindrical bore and single reed, the precursor of the modern clarinet. As shown by an ancient fresco in the British Museum, an instrument similar to the shawm was known to the Romans, but its popularity in Europe is traceable to the Arabic and Saracenic influences of the 12th and 13th centuries (see PIPES, EVOLUTION OF). In the 16th century shawms were made of various sizes from high treble to contra-bass, the larger forms being generally known on the Continent under the names Pommer and Bombardt. In England the title shawm included all sizes ; hence Drayton (*Polyolbion,* vol. iv.) speaks of the ' shrillest Shawm,' and an old proverb of the time of Henry VIII., formerly inscribed on the walls of Leckingfield Manor House, Yorkshire, states that :

' A shawme makethe a swete sounde for he tunythe
   [the] basse :
It mountithe not to hy but kepithe rule and space :
Yet yf it be blowne withe to a vehement wynde,
It makithe it to mysgoverne oute of his kynde.
    (MS. copy Brit. Mus. Bib. Reg. 18 D. ii.) '

In the Privy Purse Expenses of Henry VIII. is the following entry :

' 1530. For ij sagbuttes ij *Tenor* Shalmes and two
   trebull Shalmesse x li. x s.'

Illustrations of the various kinds of shawms are given by Virdung (*Musica Getutscht,* 1511), Praetorius (*Sciagraphia,* 1620) and Mersenne (*Harmonie universelle,* 1635) ; also of existing instruments in Day's *Musical Instruments in the Military Exhibition* (1891), Kappey's *Military Music* and in *Mus. T.,* Aug. 1906. (See *PLATE LXXV.* Nos. 5-8).'

The high treble shawm is still used on the continent with the bagpipe (cornemuse) by itinerant musicians ; in Brittany it is called bombardt and in Italy cionnamella or cenna mella (see PIFFERO). The word shawm disappeared from general use in England during the early part of the 17th century, in favour of the title hoboy, though this name appears as early as 1561 in the opera 'Ferrex and Porrex.' In 1607 the Edinburgh town musicians consisted of players on 'chalmis and howboyis,' from which it may be inferred that by that time the two instruments had become distinct.

For the term 'wayghte' as applied to the shawm see WAITS, and for the subsequent history of the instrument see OBOE.    F. W. G.

SHEDLOCK, JOHN SOUTH (b. Reading, Sept. 29, 1843 ; d. London, Jan. 9, 1919), musical critic, was a pupil of Lübeck for the piano and of Edouard Lalo for composition.  Before going to Paris for his musical studies he had taken the degree of B.A. at the London University in 1864.  From the time of his return to England he was active as a teacher, and occasionally played in public.  In 1879 he was appointed critic of The Academy, in succession to Prout, and became engaged almost exclusively in musical literature.  He was appointed critic of The Athenæum in 1901, retiring in 1916.  He was also editor of the Musical Monthly Record for many years.  Besides journalistic work, he did much of an archæological kind.  A series of articles on Beethoven's sketch-books (Mus. T., 1892) led to his discovery of a copy of Cramer's studies annotated by Beethoven, at Berlin.  This was published as 'The Beethoven-Cramer Studies' in 1893.  Other works on Beethoven consisted of two volumes of letters translated into English (reissued in an abridged edition, 1 vol., 1926) and Beethoven's Pianoforte Sonatas, the Origins and Respective Values of various Readings.  In 1895 he edited two of Kuhnau's 'Biblischen Sonaten,' and a selection of harpsichord pieces by Pasquini and others.  In the same year appeared his most important work, a treatise on The Pianoforte Sonata, which was translated two years afterwards into German by Olga Stieglitz.  His chief composition is a quartet for pianoforte and strings, written in 1886.    M., with addns.

SHEFFIELD.  The Sheffield festival came rapidly into the first rank by reason of its magnificent chorus-singing, due to the exceptional choir-training skill of Henry COWARD (q.v.).  This notable Yorkshire music-meeting originated in a very modest way, nothing more than a performance of Mendelssohn's 'Elijah' in 1895, conducted by Coward.  In the following year (1896) the first festival proper, lasting two days, was held, when the works performed included 'Elijah,' 'The Golden Legend' (Sullivan), 'Faust' (Berlioz) and 'Job' (Parry).

It was not, however, until the meeting of 1899 (three days) that the singing of the chorus made the fame of the Sheffield Festival.  On that occasion the programme included :

'Messiah,' 'King Olaf' (Elgar), 'Samson and Delilah' (Saint-Saëns), 'The Golden Legend,' 'The Choral Symphony,' 'King Saul' (Parry), and the 'Hymn of Praise.'

August Manns conducted on both occasions.

At the festival of 1902 the following works were performed, under the conductorship of Henry J. Wood :

'Elijah,' 'Gareth and Lynette' (a cantata composed for the occasion by Coward), 'Triumphlied' (Brahms), 'The Dream of Gerontius' and 'Coronation Ode' (Elgar), 'Wanderer's Sturmlied' (Richard Strauss), 'Israel in Egypt' (selection), 'Stabat Mater' (Dvořák), 'Jesu, priceless Treasure' (Bach), 'Meg Blane' (Coleridge-Taylor), 'Easter,' symphonic poem for organ and orchestra (Fritz Volbach), 'Blest Pair of Sirens' (Parry), and 'The Hymn of Praise.'

Weingartner conducted the 1905 festival, at which Cliffe's 'Ode to the North-East Wind' and Nicholas Gatty's 'Fly, envious Time' were heard for the first time, and two 8-part choruses by Weingartner, 'The House of Dreams' and 'The Song of the Storm,' had their first performance in England.  Bach's B minor Mass, Mozart's Requiem and Schumann's 'Paradise and the Peri' were included in the programme.

The 1908 festival was under Henry J. Wood's conductorship.  There were no actual novelties, but the 'Sea Drift' of Delius was heard for the first time in England, and Debussy rescored his early cantata, 'L'Enfant prodigue,' for the occasion.  The 'St. Matthew' Passion, Beethoven Choral Symphony, Berlioz's Te Deum, Franck's 'Béatitudes,' and Walford Davies's 'Everyman,' were among the more important works in the programme.

For the 1911 festival the time was changed from Oct. to Apr., and Henry J. Wood resumed the conductorship, which Coward, who had acted in that capacity from the beginning, resigned. There was nothing new in the programme, but Georg Schumann's oratorio 'Ruth' was given for the first time in this country, Bach's B minor Mass and 'St. Matthew Passion' were included in the programme, and native music was represented by the first part of Bantock's 'Omar Khayyam.'

Preparations were made for a festival in 1914, but the war intervened, and since then the festival has been in abeyance, and is understood to be awaiting the erection of a City Hall, for which a site has been secured and plans drawn up.

None of the existing musical societies of Sheffield are of very long standing, and the oldest seems to be the AMATEUR MUSICAL SOCIETY, which was founded in 1864 as a singing class, and for some years gave private concerts to which only members and their friends were admitted.  The first conductor was an amateur, H. W. Ibbotson, and he was followed in about five years' time by F. Schöllhammer; in 1904 Henry J. Wood and J. A. Rodgers were joint conductors, and in 1921 J. F. Staton followed them.  The Society introduced to Sheffield Brahms's 'Song of Destiny' (1876), Bach's 'Magnificat' (1877), Elgar's 'Kin

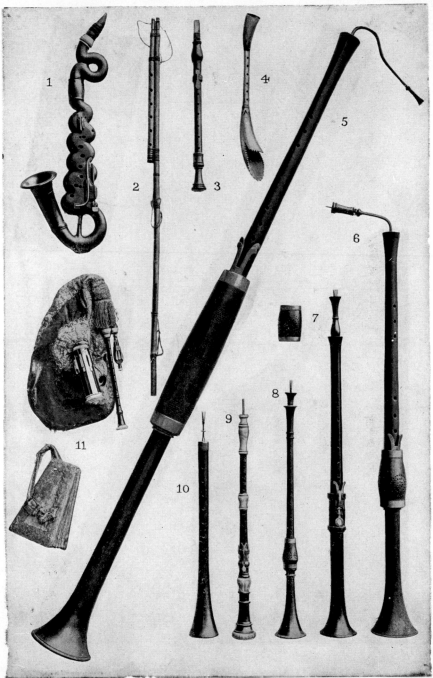

 By permission of Walter Scott Publishing Co.

1. BASS CLARINET (N. Papalini, *c.* 1800).    2. EGYPTIAN ARGHOOL.
3. CHALUMEAU (as used *c.* 1700).    4. WELSH PIBGORN or HORNPIPE.
5-8. A SET OF SHAWMS (as used *c.* 1600).    9. ENGLISH HAUTBOY (*c.* 1675).
10. ARABIAN ZAMR.    11. FRENCH MUSETTE (with bellows, *c.* 1700).

Olaf,' Harty's 'Mystic Trumpeter,' M'Cunn's 'Scottish Border Ballads' and Holst's 'Cloud Messenger,' and among the more important works given are the 'St. Matthew' and 'St. John' Passions, Vaughan Williams's 'Sea Symphony,' Elgar's 'Gerontius,' and a programme of Byrd's works in commemoration of his tercentenary.

The Society which bulks largely in the music of Sheffield is the MUSICAL UNION, founded in 1876, and thence onwards to now (1927) under the conductorship of Coward. Among the long list of works given during the half-century of its existence may be mentioned the B minor Mass, and 'St. Matthew' Passion of Bach, Beethoven's Mass in D and Choral Symphony, and many native compositions, such as Elgar's 'Gerontius,' etc., Parry's 'Judith,' 'Job,' etc., Bantock's 'Atalanta' and 'Vanity of Vanities,' Macmillan's 'England' (composed at Ruhleben), Holst's 'Hymn of Jesus' and Ethel Smyth's Mass in D. The Musical Union has acquired a more than local reputation by its extensive tours. It visited London in 1902 (under Weingartner) and on many later occasions, Germany in 1906, and again in 1910, Canada in 1908, circumnavigated the world in a six months' tour (these foreign experiences being shared by some Leeds singers), and took a prominent part in the Paris International Festival of 1912. From 1897 it has furnished a contingent to the Handel Festivals.

Perhaps the most remarkable results produced by the local resources of Sheffield have been the annual performances of the Sheffield and district GRAND OPERA SOCIETY, which since its foundation in 1920 has given, on a complete scale, remarkably efficient performances of (inter alia) 'Tannhäuser,' 'Lohengrin,' 'Aïda,' 'Carmen' and 'Esmeralda.' Staton was the conductor up to 1925, when he was succeeded by John Cope.

Sheffield has been so exclusively interested in choral music that it has proved a difficult task to arouse much enthusiasm for orchestral music. An attempt was made in 1909 to form a permanent local orchestra, and 'Promenade' concerts were given from then to 1915 under the conductorship of J. A. Rodgers, on whose death they were continued under Wood in 1919 to 1920–21. The financial results were not commensurate with their artistic success, and their place was taken by two concerts by the Queen's Hall Orchestra included in the Subscription Series. In helping to create a taste for orchestral music the University String Orchestra, under Mr. Linfoot, which began its operations in 1919, is doing a useful work.

In chamber music the 'Five o'clock' Concerts, organised during the war and carried on ever since, by the Misses Foxon, have filled a too conspicuous gap in Sheffield music. With the aid chiefly of local musicians, supplemented by distinguished artists from outside Sheffield, about eight concerts are given each season, the programmes of which are invariably of great artistic interest, and are seldom without some feature that is rare or at least unfamiliar. The University mid-day recitals, organised by Mrs. J. B. Leathes, also deserve mention in this connexion.          H. T.

SHENSHIN, ALEXANDER ALEXEIEVICH (b. Nov. 19, 1890), composer, studied under Glière, Grechaninov and Javorsky. He was appointed professor at the Moscow State Conservatoire in 1922, and composer to the Children's Theatre, Moscow (1920). He has written an orchestral poem, op. 5; a PF. quintet in D min. (both MS.), songs and PF. pieces (Russian State Music Publishing Department).          R. N.

SHEPHERD, ARTHUR (b. Paris, Idaho, U.S.A., Feb. 19, 1880), American conductor and composer. He studied at the New England Conservatory, with Dennée and Faelten in piano, with Goetschius and Chadwick in composition. In 1897–1908 he taught and conducted in Salt Lake City, Utah; in 1908–20 he taught at the New England Conservatory and was for a time conductor of the Cecilia Society (choral) of Boston. Since 1920 he has been associate conductor of the Cleveland Symphony Orchestra. His compositions include several overtures and orchestral suites; a Fantasia for pianoforte and orchestra; choral pieces; a piano sonata; and smaller piano pieces and songs.          W. S. S.

SHEPHERD (SHEPHEARD, SHEPPARD, SHEPPERD), (1) JOHN (b. early part of 16th cent.; d. (?) 1563), was a chorister of St. Paul's under Thomas Mulliner. In 1542 he was appointed instructor of the choristers and organist of Magdalen College, Oxford, which office he resigned in 1543, was reappointed to it in 1545, and held it until 1547. He was a Fellow of the College from 1549–51 and was in the Royal Chapel of Queen Mary. On Apr. 21, 1554, having then been a student in music for 20 years, he supplicated for the degree of Mus.D., but it does not appear whether he actually took the degree. John Day's 'Certain Notes,' etc., 1560, contains two anthems a 4 by him—'I give you a new commandment,' and 'Submit yourselves.' Another book of Day's, the 'Whole Psalms in foure parts,' 1563, has a 'Prayer' by him, 'O Lord of hostes.' Barnard prints a four-part anthem, 'Haste thee.' Hawkins prints a motet in three parts by him, 'Steven first after Christ for Gods worde his blood spent,' and a melodious little 'Poynte'— a fugal piece for four voices of seven bars length. Burney[1] complains that the motet is not a good specimen, and prints another, 'Esurientes,' for five voices from the Christ

1 *History*, ii. 565.

Church MSS., on which he pronounces Shepherd to have been superior to any composer of the reign of Henry VIII. In the Durham part-books, the anthem ' O Lord the maker of all thing ' usually assigned to Henry VIII., is accredited to Shepherd. It is more probably by William Mundy. Much of his church music is preserved in the Music School, Oxford ; the MSS. at Christ Church contain five complete portions of the Magnificat and some motets, also complete. The great majority of Shepherd's motets in the library are incomplete, as the tenor partbook is wanting. A ' Deus misereatur ' and Gloria in short score, written on two six-lines staves and barred with twelve minims to the bar, is in a MS. organ-book, (6). In the British Museum (Add. MSS. 15,166, 29,289. 30,480) are treble parts of many of his English compositions, amongst them 2 M. and E. Services with Creed ; 2 Te Deums and Magnificats, 2 Creeds and 7 Anthems. Add. MSS. 4900, 29,246, contain four pieces with lute accompaniment, and Add. MSS. 17,802-5 have no fewer than four Masses [1]—' The western wynde,' ' The French Masse,' ' Be not afraide,' and ' Playn song Mass for a Mene ' ; four Alleluias, and ten Latin Motets, all for four voices complete. The R.C.M. possesses four Latin motets, and a ' First Service ' by him. Morley in his *Introduction* includes him amongst ' famous Englishmen.'

Another (2) JOHN SHEPHERD, possibly a son of the above, was sworn a gentleman of the Chapel Royal, Dec. 1, 1606. (Rimbault's *Old Cheque-book*, p. 43.) Perhaps it was he who added a Kyrie to Johnson's service in G, in the Cathedral Library, Ely. (See Dickson's *Catalogue*, 32, 37.) Perhaps, also, he is the ' Thos. Shepherd ' of Tudway (iv. 72).      W. H. H.

SHEPHERD, WILLIAM (*d.* Jan. 19, 1812), an Edinburgh composer, violinist and music-publisher. About 1793 he issued a ' Collection of Strathspey Reels ' dedicated to Miss Abercromby, and a similar one about 1802–03. In 1796 he entered into partnership with Nathaniel Gow, in a music-publishing business, at 41 North Bridge, Edinburgh, removing before 1804 to 16 Princes Street.

Gow and Shepherd were unfortunate in their speculations, and Shepherd appears to have been deeply involved at his death.      F. K.

SHEPHERD'S PIPE,[2] a name given to the pastoral oboe or musette. It was an instrument with a double reed like that of the bagpipe chanter, and was sometimes combined with a windbag. (See BAGPIPE, subsection MUSETTE). It was made in several sizes, constituting a family or 'consort' similar to the viols, recorders and other instruments. Its origin in the simple

[1] The Masses of Shepherd with certain of the Motets have been scored by Sir Richard Terry and sung at Westminster Cathedral.
[2] There is a fine specimen of this very rare Shepherd or Lowland pipe at the R.C.M. It was bequeathed by Charles Keene, the *Punch* artist (with his Northumbrian pipes, in 1891) to A. J. Hipkins.      E. J. H⁵.

reed is well given in Chappell's *History of Music*, vol. i. p. 259.

An excellent drawing of its various forms, with the method of holding it, is to be found in a *Traité de la musette*, by Jean Girin of Lyons, 1572, where it is distinguished from the ' Cromorne ' and ' Hautbois.' The bagpipe form with drones and windbag is also engraved.
      W. H. S.

SHERARD, JAMES, a 17th-century apothecary and excellent amateur violinist. He composed 2 books of sonatas for 2 violins and bass, which are of distinct merit (E. v. d. Straeten, *Eighteenth Century Violin Sonatas ; The Strad*).

SHEREMETIEV, ALEXANDER DMITRIEVICH, Count (*b.* 1859). His ancestor, Peter Borisov, had been one of the first noblemen to establish a private choir in the 17th century, while his father's church choral choir had become widely famous under the baton of Lomakin. Count Alexander Sheremetiev started his choir in 1884, under the conductorship of Archangelsky. In 1882 he had already organised a symphony orchestra. In 1898 he began to give national concerts in St. Petersburg, which gradually acquired the character of symphony concerts at popular prices, and were very highly rated from the artistic point of view. In 1902 Count Sheremetiev became intendant of the Imperial court chapels.
      R. N.

SHERIDAN, MARGARET (*b.* Castlebar, Co. Mayo, Oct. 15, 1889), operatic soprano. An orphan from the age of 4, she was brought up at a convent until she was 17, when she attracted notice by her successes at a Dublin competition festival. A subscription was raised for her vocal education, and in Sept. 1909 she entered the R.A.M., where she became a pupil of William Shakespeare and remained until the end of 1911, having won a silver medal. After further study in Italy she made a successful début in opera and appeared several times at La Scala. In 1919 she made her first appearance during the summer season at Covent Garden as Madama Butterfly. The part proved somewhat beyond her powers, but her pleasing voice and artistic training enabled her to create a favourable impression, and this was enhanced later in the season by her sympathetic impersonation of the heroine in Mascagni's opera, ' Iris,' then given for the first time in England. Subsequently, besides going the round of the principal Italian theatres, she was engaged to sing at the Chicago Opera House in 1923–24, and there again met with considerable success.      H. K.

SHERRINGTON, see LEMMENS, MME.

SHERWOOD, PERCY (*b.* Dresden, May 23, 1866), was a pupil of the Conservatorium of his native place, studying the pianoforte and composition under Draeseke, W. Roth, etc., in

1885–88. In 1889 he won the Mendelssohn prize with a Requiem for voices and orchestra. He was appointed a teacher in the Dresden Conservatorium in 1893, and professor in 1911. He won considerable success both as a pianist and composer in Germany. His works include a piano concerto, 2 symphonies, overtures, a violin sonata (C minor), 2 sonatas for violoncello, music for piano, organ, etc., as well as songs. In Feb. 1907 he gave a concert of unpublished compositions of his own, in the Palmengarten, Dresden, the programme of which consisted of a sonata for two pianos, a suite for clarinet and piano, and a quintet for piano and strings. (*Brit. Mus. Biog.*; *Riemann*.)

M., with addns.

SHERYNGHAM (15th or early 16th cent.), English composer. The scores of 6 4-part carols by him are included in B.M. Add. MSS. 5465-67b, which also contain compositions by Gilbert Banastir (*sic*), William Cornyshe and other early English composers : ' Ah gentill Jhesu,' ' Uppon the cross nailed,' ' My blody wownds,' ' I hade on petur and mawdlen pyte,' ' Thynk agayne, pride,' and ' Lord, on all synfull.'

A 2-part madrigal, ' My wofull hart,' by Sheryngham, is in B.M. Add. MSS. 11,583-4b, and was printed by Burney (*Hist.* vol. ii.).

J. Mᴷ.

SHE STOOPS TO CONQUER, opera, in 3 acts; adapted by E. Fitzball from Goldsmith's comedy; music by G. A. Macfarren. Produced Covent Garden (Pyne & Harrison), Feb. 11, 1864.

G.

SHIELD, WILLIAM (*b.* Whickham, Durham, Mar. 5, 1748; *d.* Berners Street, London, Jan. 25, 1829), composer of opera, etc., son of a singing-master. He received his first musical instruction when 6 years old, from his father, but, losing his parent three years later, he was apprenticed to a boat-builder at South Shields. His master, however, permitted him to pursue his musical studies, and he obtained some lessons in thorough-bass from Charles Avison, and occasionally played the violin at music meetings in the neighbourhood. On the expiration of his apprenticeship, having acquired sufficient knowledge to lead the subscription concerts at Newcastle, he determined upon making music his profession, and removed to Scarborough, where he became leader at the theatre and concerts. Whilst there he produced his first composition, an anthem for the opening of a new church at Sunderland. Having been heard by Fischer and Borghi, they recommended him to Giardini, by whom he was engaged in 1772 as a second violin in the Opera band. In 1773 he was promoted to the post of principal viola which he held for eighteen years, and which he also filled at all the principal concerts.

In 1778 he produced, at the Haymarket, his first dramatic piece, the comic opera ' The Flitch of Bacon.' This led to his being engaged as composer to Covent Garden Theatre, a post which he occupied until his resignation, 1791. During his engagement he composed many operas and other pieces. In 1791 he made the acquaintance of Haydn, and was wont to say that in four days, during which he accompanied Haydn from London to Taplow and back, he gained more knowledge than he had done by study in any four years of his life. In the same year he visited France and Italy. In 1792 he was re-engaged as composer at Covent Garden, in which capacity he acted until 1797. In 1807 he gave up all connexion with the theatre. He was appointed master of the King's Musick in 1817.

He published at various times, ' A Collection of Favourite Songs, To which is added a Duet for two Violins ' ; ' A Collection of Canzonets and an Elegy ' ; and ' A Cento, consisting of Ballads, Rounds, Glees, etc.' ; likewise ' Six Trios for two Violins and Bass,' and ' Six Duos for two Violins.' He was also author of *An Introduction to Harmony*, 1800 ; and *Rudiments of Thorough Bass*, about 1815. His dramatic compositions, consisting of operas, musical farces and pantomimes, were as follow :

' The Flitch of Bacon,' 1778 ; ' Lord Mayor's Day,' 1782 ; ' The Poor Soldier,' ' Rosina,' ' Harlequin Friar Bacon,' 1783 ; ' Robin Hood,' ' The Noble Peasant,' ' Fontainebleau,' ' The Magic Cavern,' 1784 ; ' Love in a Camp,' ' The Nunnery,' ' The Choleric Fathers,' ' Omai,' 1785 ; ' Richard Cœur de Lion,' ' The Enchanted Castle, 1786 ; ' The Highland Reel,' ' Marian,' ' The Prophet,' ' Aladdin, 1788 ; ' The Crusade,' ' The Picture of Paris,' 1790 ; ' The Woodman,' ' Oscar and Malvina ' (with Reeve), 1791 ; ' Hartford Bridge,' 1792 ; ' Harlequin's Museum,' ' The Deaf Lover,' ' The Midnight Wanderers,' ' Sprigs of Laurel,' 1793 ; ' Arrived at Portsmouth,' ' The Travellers in Switzerland,' ' Netley Abbey,' 1794 ; ' The Mysteries of the Castle,' 1795 ; ' Abroad and at Home,' ' Lock and Key,' 1796 ; ' The Italian Villagers,' ' The Village Fête,' ' Wicklow Gold Mines,' 1797 ; ' The Farmer,' 1798 ; ' Two Faces under a Hood,' 1807.

In many of his pieces he introduced songs, etc., selected from the works of other composers, English and foreign ; and was thereby the means of making the general public acquainted with many beautiful melodies of which they would otherwise have remained ignorant.

Shield's melodies charm by their simple, natural beauty ; at once vigorous and refined, they appeal directly to the hearts of Englishmen. But he also wrote songs of agility, to display the powers of Mrs. Billington and others. Among his most popular songs are ' The Thorn,' ' The Wolf,' ' The Heaving of the Lead,' ' Old Towler,' ' The Ploughboy ' and ' The Post Captain ' ; but these are but some of the most prominent. Shield died at his residence, 31 Berners Street, and was buried on Feb. 4 in the south cloister of Westminster Abbey. With the exception of his fine tenor viola, reputed a Stainer, which he bequeathed to George IV. (who accepted the gift, but directed that its utmost value should be paid to the testator's presumed widow), he left his whole estate to his ' beloved partner, Ann [Stokes], Mrs. Shield upwards of forty years.' His valuable musical library was sold in July 1829. On Oct. 19, 1891, a memorial cross was erected to his memory in Whickham Churchyard, Durham, and a slab in Westminster Abbey (1892), both due to the efforts of John Robinson of Sunderland.    w. h. h., with addns.

SHIFT (1). In playing the violin, or any of the instruments belonging to that family, an executant effects a ' shift ' when the left hand passes from one established position to another. Thus, when the hand moves up or down the finger-board the player was said to be ' on the shift.' The term was also used to denote the positions themselves, the second position being known as the ' half-shift,' the third position as the ' whole-shift,' and the fourth position as the ' double-shift.'

This technical acquirement, which is now an exact and indispensable means of reaching every note within the compass of the violin (see FINGERING, VIOLIN), evidently originated in Italy. There is a certain amount of ambiguity surrounding its use by viol-players previous to its introduction among violinists ; but it is quite certain that before the 17th century there are no indications of any such custom. During the 17th century, however, there is little doubt that it was employed by the best viol-players of the day. Christopher Simpson clearly demonstrates its use in *The Division Viol* (second edition, London, 1667), wherein he states, under ' *The ordering of the fingers in gradual notes*,' that

' in any point of Division which reaches to the lower Frets or *beyond them* ; the highest note thereof is always stopt either with the third or fourth finger.'

The first tentative advances towards the adoption of the ' shift ' took the form of an extension of the little finger in the first position, and the feat of touching the first C on the *chanterelle* of the violin by this means was looked upon as a daring undertaking. As a natural consequence, the executant's ability rested almost entirely upon his manner of playing *l'ut*, and so sensational was the effect of its advent upon the listeners that an involuntary murmur of ' Gare l'ut ' was wont, it is said, to escape from the lips of his listeners. Beyond a doubt, many professional violinists could shift in the first three positions by the year 1655, for Mersenne (*Harmonie universelle*) speaks with admiration of those players who could mount up to the octave of each string. Then in 1658 Anthony Wood in his *Life* describes the wonderful playing of Thomas Baltzar—the Paganini of his day—whom he saw

' run up his fingers to the end of the finger-board of the violin and run them back insensibly and all with alacrity and in very good tune, which I am sure any in England never saw the like before.'

To Mattaei — who came to England in 1672— is accorded the invention of the ' half-shift,'

or second position. But although the ' shift ' was favoured by professional players of exceptional ability at this period, its adoption was far from general, owing to the confused methods of holding the violin which continued well into the next century. Lully, who was himself a violinist, gives an idea of the capacity of the ordinary orchestral technique by choosing a test piece for those desiring to gain the ' dignus est intrare ' of his band in which no C on the *chanterelle* occurred. For thirty years the entr'acte from his opera of ' Atys ' served this purpose. Even in Leopold Mozart's time the question of holding the violin was far from settled, for, in his *Violin School* (1756), he mentions that there are two ways of holding the violin, the first being ' against the breast ' — which position he regards as an obstacle to ' shifting '—and the second is to place the violin under the chin and rest it on the shoulder. The best professional players adopted the latter method, and their example finding favour with lesser artists was the means of abolishing the ' breast position ' and bringing the ' shift ' into general use.

The ' shift ' on the violoncello was doubtless derived from the violin, and is governed by the same rules. The ' thumb movement,' or ' shifting of the thumb ' which was the means of facilitating the use of the high positions on the violoncello, was first employed—and it is said invented—by the French artist Berteau in the first half of the 18th century.

BIBL.—FELIX HUET, *Étude sur les différentes écoles de violon*, Châlons-sur-Marne, 1880 ; A. MENGY, *Quelques Observations sur l'art du violon*, Paris, 1888 ; G. KOECKERT, *Les Principes rationnels de la technique du violon*, Leipzig, 1904 ; ANON., *The Violin, How to master it*, Edinburgh, 1889 ; CARL COURVOISIER, *Technics of Violin-Playing*, London, 1899.                                    O. R.

(2) In trombone-playing, ' shift ' signifies an alteration in position of the movable slide, by means of which the fundamental length of the instrument is increased. The home position of the slide is known as the No. 1 ' position,' and the successive shifts, lowering the pitch by successive semitones, give respectively the second, third, fourth, fifth, sixth and seventh ' positions,' the number of the ' position ' being thus always one higher than the number of semitones by which the pitch is lowered (see TROMBONE).                            D. J. B.

SHINNER, EMILY (*b.* Cheltenham, July 7, 1862 ; *d.* July 17, 1901), began the study of the violin at the age of 7. In 1874 she went to Berlin, and for two years studied under H. Jacobsen, a pupil of Joachim, female violinists not being at that time admissible to the Hochschule. In 1876 this restriction was taken away, and Miss Shinner was among the first admitted. In Oct. 1877 she became a pupil of Joachim, and remained with him for three years. In Feb. 1881 she came to London, and after being heard at several private concerts (among others at one given by the Bach Choir), made her début at a concert given by H. R. Bird in the Kensington Town Hall, in Brahms's sonata in G, etc. At the London Musical Society's concert of June 29, 1882, she played David's concerto in E minor with great success, and from that time held a high position among English artists, her style being pure and refined, and her power of interpreting works of a high intellectual order being very remarkable. She appeared at the Popular Concert on Feb. 9, and at the Crystal Palace on Mar. 8, 1884 ; in 1887 she organised a successful quartet party of women. In Jan. 1889 she married Capt. A. F. Liddell.

M.

SHIRREFF, JANE (b. 1811 ; d. Kensington, Dec. 23, 1883), soprano singer, pupil of Thomas Welsh, appeared at Covent Garden with great success, Dec. 1, 1831, as Mandane in Arne's ' Artaxerxes.' In 1832 she sang at the Concert of Ancient Music, the Philharmonic Concert and Gloucester Festival, and in 1834 at the Westminster Abbey Festival. Her engagement at Covent Garden continued from 1831–1835. In 1835 she was engaged at Drury Lane, but in 1837 returned to Covent Garden. In 1838 she went to America in company with Wilson, E. Seguin and Mrs. E. Seguin, where she became a universal favourite. On her return to England she married J. Walcott, and retired into private life. Her voice was full-toned, and powerful in the higher, but somewhat weak in the lower notes ; her intonation was perfect, and she was a much better actress than the generality of singers.          W. H. H.

SHIRREFFS, ANDREW (b. 1762 ; d. circa 1807), an Aberdeen musician and poet. He wrote a once popular pastoral musical comedy ' Jamie and Bess, or the Laird in Disguise ' in five acts, modelled upon Allan Ramsay's Gentle Shepherd. This was published in 1787 ; and the musical part of it advertised as for sale in 1788. He was composer of ' Forty Pieces of Original Music,' published by Stewart & Co., Edinburgh. Shirreffs was M.A. of Marischal College, Aberdeen (1783), and edited the Aberdeen Chronicle and the Caledonian Magazine. He came to London in 1798. He was originally a bookbinder, was lame, and his portrait is prefixed to his volume of poems, 1790. Burns mentions having met him, and refers to him as ' a little decreped body, with some abilities.'

F. K.

SHOFAR (SHOPHAR; Heb. Šofar), the Jewish ram's-horn instrument, used in the synagogue worship. The natural horn is flattened in section, and a cup mouthpiece is formed at the small end (see PLATE LXXXIII. No. 2). The instrument, or an imitation of its effect, is introduced into the scores of Macfarren's ' John the Baptist ' and Elgar's ' Apostles.' (See HEBREW MUSIC.)          D. J. B.

SHORE, (1) MATHIAS (d. 1700), was one of the trumpeters in ordinary to James II. in 1665,

and a few years afterwards was promoted to the post of Sergeant Trumpeter, in which he distinguished himself by the rigorous exaction of his fees of office. (See TRUMPETER.) He left three children :

(2) WILLIAM (d. Dec. 1707), also one of the King's trumpeters in ordinary, succeeded his father as Sergeant Trumpeter. He was buried at St. Martin's-in-the-Fields. He followed his father's example in the severe exaction of fees.

(3) CATHERINE (b. circa 1668 ; d. circa 1730) was a pupil of Henry Purcell for singing and the harpsichord. In 1693 she became the wife of Colley Cibber, without consent of her father, whose resentment was not, however, of very long duration, as when he made his will, Mar. 5, 1695–96, he bequeathed to her one-third of the residue of his property. Shortly after her marriage Mrs. Cibber appeared on the stage as a singer, and, among other songs, sang the second part of Purcell's air ' Genius of England ' (' Don Quixote,' Part II.), to her brother John's trumpet accompaniment.

(4) JOHN (d. Nov. 20, 1752), the most celebrated trumpeter of his time, in 1707 succeeded his brother William as Sergeant Trumpeter. Purcell composed for him obbligato parts to many songs, which may be seen in the ' Orpheus Britannicus,' and which fully attest his skill. His playing is highly commended in the Gentleman's Journal for Jan. 1691–92, where in an account of the celebration on St. Cecilia's Day in the preceding November, we read :

' Whilst the company is at table the hautboys and trumpets play successively. Mr. Showers hath taught the latter of late years to sound with all the softness imaginable ; they plaid us some flat tunes made by Mr. Finger with a general applause, it being a thing formerly thought impossible upon an instrument designed for a sharp key.'

His name appears in 1711 as one of the twenty-four musicians to Queen Anne, and also as lutenist to the Chapel Royal.[1] He is said to have been the inventor of the tuning-fork, and also to have split his lip in sounding the trumpet, thereby incapacitating himself for performing. In 1749 he married a Mrs. Speed with a fortune of £15,000.[2] He died at the alleged age of 90, but it is very probable that his age was overstated.          W. H. H.

SHORT, PETER, an early London music printer and publisher, who printed a number of madrigal books and some early musical treatises. He worked ' at the sign of the Starre ' on Bread Street Hill from about 1584, and his issues include Morley's Plaine and Easie Introduction to practical Musick, 1597 ; Holborne's Cittharn Schoole, 1597 ; ' Seuen Sobs of a Sorrowfull Soule for Sin,' 1597 ; Dowland's ' First Booke of Songes,' 1597 ; Morley's ' Canzonets,' 1597 ; Farnaby's ' Canzonets,' 1598 ; Cavendish's ' Ayres,' 1599, and some other

1 In the Cheque Book of the Chapel Royal he is said to have been appointed lutenist in 1715, but the entry was evidently not made until some time later, and probably from memory only.
2 London Magazine, Feb. 1749.

works. He was succeeded in business at the same address, between 1603 and 1608, by Humfrey Lowndes, who reissued Morley's *Introduction*.    F. K.

SHORT OCTAVE. In the early days of harmony, and indeed until the whole circle of keys was made available in practical music, the chromatic notes in the lowest octave of the keyboard were not wanted, since they were not required as basses. The evidence of pictorial representations shows that as early as the 14th century the expedient was adopted of omitting some of the strings or organ pipes belonging to such keys, and letting their places be taken by strings and pipes tuned to notes below the apparent notes. Various systems of these effecting a saving of space in the organ will be found explained under ORGAN, Vol. III. p. 748. For similar expedients in the SPINET see that article, Vol. V. p. 93. The 'Fitzwilliam Virginal Book' contains indirect evidence that 'short octaves' were in general use early in the 17th century; in one piece, the player's left hand is required to strike this chord ♩♩, which is of course impossible on a full keyboard; on one with a short octave in which the low G sharp key is attached to the string tuned to the low E, the chord does not exceed the limit of the ordinary player's hand.    M.

SHORT SCORE, a term meaning the condensation of a vocal or instrumental score into an *ad libitum* part for piano or organ.

SHRUBSOLE, WILLIAM (*b.* Canterbury, Jan. 1760; *d.* London, Jan. 18, 1806), organist and hymn composer, was for seven years chorister at the Cathedral there. He studied the organ during this time, and was in 1782 appointed organist to Bangor Cathedral. While here he gave great offence to the Dean and Chapter by his association with dissenters, and by 'frequenting conventicles'; this led to his dismissal in 1784. He came to London, and immediately got a post as organist at Lady Huntingdon's Chapel, Spafields, Clerkenwell, which he held till his death. He was buried in Bunhill Fields, and his monument was restored in 1892, mainly by the exertions of F. G. Edwards.

Shrubsole is best remembered by the composition of the fine hymn tune 'Miles Lane,' which appeared in the *Gospel Magazine* as early as 1779.    F. K.

SHUDI, BURKAT (*b.* Schwanden, Glarus, Switzerland, Mar. 13, 1702; *d.* London, Aug. 19, 1773), famous harpsichord-maker and founder of the house of Broadwood. Burkat Shudi, as he inscribed his name upon his instruments, was properly BURKHARDT TSCHUDI, and was a cadet of a noble family belonging to Glarus in Switzerland.[1] He came to England

in 1718 as a simple journeyman joiner.[2] When he turned to harpsichord-making is not known, but we are told by Burney, who knew Shudi and old Kirkman well, that they were both employed in London by Tabel[3] (a Fleming who had settled in Swallow Street with all the traditions of his famous countrymen, the Ruckers), and Burney calls them Tabel's foremen, perhaps meaning his principal workmen. The anecdote given by Burney, in Rees's *Cyclopædia*, of Kirkman's hasty wedding with his master's widow, and acquisition with her of Tabel's stock-in-trade, gives no information about Shudi, who, according to the *Daily Advertiser*, Oct. 5, 1742, 'removed from Meard's Street in Dean Street, Soho, to Great Pulteney Street, Golden Square' (the house occupied by his descendants, the Broadwoods, until 1904). Shudi was then styled 'Harpsichord Maker to H.R.H. the Prince of Wales.' The earliest business record of Shudi occurs in the diary of John Hervey, 1st Earl of Bristol (1688–1742), under date '11th April, 1733. Paid B. Shudi for tuning the harpsichord, 17/6,' which looks like the previous year's tunings, seven in all. The earliest known double harpsichord of his in existence was acquired by Paul de Wit, of Leipzig, in Rome in 1901, bearing in it the name of 'Anna Strada, 1731,' a singer made famous by Handel, who, as a personal friend of Shudi, may have given it to her. (See BROADWOOD; KIRKMAN.)

Kirkman had the King's Arms for the sign of his business in Broad Street, Carnaby Market; Shudi, the Plume of Feathers at the house now 33 Great Pulteney Street. We may trace the choice of signs of these old colleagues and now rival makers to the divided patronage of the King (George II.) and Prince of Wales, who were notoriously unfriendly. No doubt Handel's friendship was of great value to Shudi; few harpsichords were then made, as owing to the relatively high price, and the great expense and trouble of keeping them in order, they were only for the rich. But the tuning and repairing alone would keep a business going; harpsichords lasted long, and were submitted to restoration and alteration that would surprise the amateur of the present day.[4]

The Shudi harpsichord, formerly Queen Charlotte's, now in Windsor Castle, is dated 1740. It has a 'Lute' stop, a pleasing variation of *timbre*, and, like the pedal, of English invention in the previous century.

---

[1] Of the Schwanden branch, Heinrich (*b.* 1074; *d.* 1149), made Feodary of Glarus by the Lady Gutta, Abbess of Seckingen, was the first to adopt the surname Schudi (*sic*). The family tree goes back to Johann, Mayor of Glarus (*b.* about 870). Sir Walter Scott, in his ballad of the *Battle of Sempach*, extols the deeds of 'Albert Tschudi of Zürich' (Minnesänger and warrior), who fought in this patriotic war (9th July, 1386).

[2] See *Schweizerische Lexicon*, Zürich, 1795, art. 'Tschudi.'

[3] Broadwood's books of 1777 mention a second-hand harpsichord by Tabel (written Table). A harpsichord by Tabel with two manuals, and very like a Kirkman, is in the possession of Helena, Countess of Radnor.

[4] While pianofortes are now kept in tune by yearly contracts, the researches of William Dale, in Broadwood's old books, show that harpsichords in the 18th century were tuned by *quarterly* contracts.

James Shudi Broadwood (MS. notes, 1838) accredits his grandfather Shudi with the gift of a harpsichord to Frederick the Great, Shudi being a staunch Protestant and regarding Frederick as the leader and champion of the Protestant cause. Broadwood, moreover, believed that a portrait of Shudi, which remained until a few years since in one of the rooms in Great Pulteney Street, represented him as engaged in tuning the identical harpsichord thus bestowed. Shudi's first wife [1] and two sons are also in the picture, a reproduction of which serves as the frontispiece to Rimbault's *History of the Pianoforte.* The elder boy, apparently nine years old, was born in 1736. This synchronises the picture with Frederick's victory and the peace concluded the

exist, are of the soundest possible workmanship, discrediting Burney's assertion of the want of durability of his harpsichords,[2] a reproach, however, which Burney goes on to say could not be alleged against Shudi's son-in-law and successor, Broadwood. He, however, praises Shudi's tone as refined and delicate. The Potsdam harpsichords were made with Shudi's Venetian swell, for which the pedals still exist, but it was probably not to the German taste of the time and was therefore removed. Hopkins, in his comprehensive work upon the organ, says the original organ swell was the ' nagshead,' a mere shutter, invented by Abraham Jordan in 1712. But to imitate its effect in the harpsichord we know that Plenius about 1750, and also in

| No. | Date. | Signature. | Present or Recent Owner. | Remarks. |
|---|---|---|---|---|
| ? | 1729 | Burkat Shudi. | Herr Paul de Wit, Leipzig. | Belonged to Anna Strada in 1731. Gift of Handel. |
| 94 | 1740 | ,, | H.M. the King, Windsor Castle. | Removed from Kew Palace in 1875. |
| 103 | 1740 | ,, | Mrs. Delany. | Still at Llanover, Wales. |
| ?144 | 1749 | ,, | Mr. Warre. | Double. Is a wreck. 5½ C-F, 5 stops, no machine nor pedals. |
| ?229 | 1749 | ,, | F. Fairley, Esq., Newcastle-on-Tyne. | Single keyboard. 5 oct., F-F, with lowest F sharp omitted. 2 stops. |
| 260 | 1751 | ,, | | |
| 407 | 1760 | ,, | W. Dale, Esq. | Double. 5 oct., F sharp. Usual stops, added swell on a chest of drawers. |
| 423 | 1761 | ,, | Miss Fanny Davies. | Single. Bought in London, 1911. |
| 427 | 1761 | | | |
| 428 | 1761 | | | |
| 511 | 1766 | B. Tschudi. | Hohenzollern Museum, Berlin. | Made for Frederick the Great, described by Burney and Hipkins. Both of 5½ octs., C-F. |
| 512 | 1766 | ,, | ,, | |
| 529 | 1766 | Burkat Schudi. | Harry Hodge, Esq. | Overhauled by Dolmetsch in 1896. |
| ?625 | 1770 | ,, | W. Dale, Esq. | Was in David Hartley's family. 6 stops, 2 pedals, as have nearly all these instruments. |
| 639 | 1771 | ,, | John Broadwood & Sons. | Played upon by Moscheles, Pauer and Hipkins in their historical performances. |
| 671 | 1772 | B. S. and J. Broadwood. | Miss Margaret H. Glyn. Ewell. | |
| 686 | 1773 | ,, ,, | Ditto. Lent to the Rev. Sir F. A. G. Ouseley, Bart., Tenbury. | Bought of T. W. Taphouse, 1861. |
| 691 | 1773 | ,, ,, | M. Victor Mahillon, Brussels. | Sent to ' the Empress ' (Maria Theresa) Aug. 20, 1773. Obtained by M. Mahillon from Vienna. |
| 708 | ? | | | |
| ?750 | 1775 | ,, ,, | Messrs. Price & Sons, Yeovil. (In 1901 it was on sale in London.) | Made for Lady Stavordale, Redlynch, Bruton. |
| 762 | 1775 | ,, ,, | Musikverein, Vienna. | Was Joseph Haydn's, and subsequently Herbeck's. |
| 787 | 1776 | ,, ,, | | |
| 789 | 1776 | ,, ,, | | |
| 862 | 1779 | | | |
| 899 | 1781 | B. S. and Johannes B. | The late T. W. Taphouse, Oxford. | 5 oct., F-F, 7 stops, 2 pedals. Came from Mrs. Anson's, Sudbury Rectory, Derby. |
| 902 | 1781 | ,, ,, | The late Dr. C. Harford Lloyd. | 5 oct., F-F. Restored by Mr. Taphouse. |
| 919 | 1782 | ,, ,, | Stephen Stratton, Esq., Birmingham. | Belonged to the Wrottesley family. |
| 955 | 1789 | | | |
| | 1789 | | Knabe & Co., Baltimore. | Once belonged to Chas. Carrol of Carrolton, one of the signees of the Declaration of Independence. |
| 1015 | 1785 | | Mrs. Mackail, daughter of Burne Jones. | |
| 1137 | 1790 | ,, | | Instr. mentioned in A. J. Hipkins's notes in the appendix of the 1st edit. of this Dictionary. |
| 1148 | 1791 | | Dr. Henry Watson, Manchester. | |
| 1155 | 1793 | | | |

following year (1745). But the writer could not find this instrument either in Potsdam or Berlin in 1881. The tradition about it is, however, strengthened by the fact that in 1766 Frederick obtained from Shudi two special double harpsichords for his new palace at Potsdam, and which are now in the Hohenzollern Museum. Instead of the anglicised 'Shudi,' they are accurately inscribed 'Tschudi.' One has silver legs, etc.; the other rests upon a partially gilded stand. Following Burney, who, however, only describes the first one, they appear to have been placed in the apartments of the Princess Amelia and the Prince of Prussia. These instruments, like all Shudi's which still

London, by a pedal movement, gradually raised and lowered a portion of the top or cover. This, coming into general use, Shudi improved upon it by his important invention of the ' Venetian swell ' on the principle of a Venetian blind, which he patented Dec. 18, 1769. He probably delayed taking out the patent until it became necessary by his partnership with John Broadwood, who had also become his son-in-law,[3] earlier in the same year. This invention was subsequently transferred to the organ. (See SWELL.)

In Pohl's *Mozart in London* (Vienna, 1867)

[1] Catherine Wild, also of Schwanden (*b.* 1704 ; *d. circa* 1758). See Shudi's will, where the settlement is mentioned, on his second wife, Eliz. Meier, and is dated Feb. 23, 1759. Kubli-Müller discovered from the Zürich archives that she was a descendant of Anna Zwingli, sister of the famous Protestant reformer.

[2] Burney gives as his authority Snetzler the organ-builder, who attached organs to some of Shudi's harpsichords, and was, moreover, Shudi's intimate friend and executor. Shudi left him his ring, containing a portrait of Frederick the Great.

[3] By his marriage with Barbara Shudi, *bapt.* Mar. 12, 1748 ; married to John Broadwood, Jan. 2, 1769 ; *d.* July 8, 1776. The first wife of John Broadwood, she was the mother of James Shudi Broadwood (*b.* Dec. 20, 1772 ; *d.* Aug. 8, 1851 ; and grandmother of Henry Fowler Broadwood and Walter Stewart Broadwood.

' Herr Thudy ' is credited with the invention of the ' machine stop ' [1]; but, as he did not patent it, perhaps he was not the actual inventor.

In a Kirkman harpsichord of 1758 there is neither swell nor machine pedal, nor even a ' Buff stop ' ; but Kirkman was conservative, Shudi progressive, and his harpsichords were less powerful but sweeter in tone than those of Kirkman.

A harpsichord exists inscribed with the joint names of Shudi and Broadwood, dated 1770, although Shudi made harpsichords for himself after that date and independent of the partnership, as we know by existing instruments and by his will. The last harpsichord made at Pulteney Street (Mar. 1793) was made for Henry de la Maine, of Cork, with his cipher, £84. About 1772 he retired to a house in Charlotte Street, leaving the business premises to his son-in-law, John Broadwood, and died Aug. 19, 1773. The next day a harpsichord was shipped to 'the Empress,' ordered by Joseph II. for Maria Theresa. The harpsichord that was Haydn's, acquired for the museum at Vienna at a cost of £110 sterling, was also a ' Shudi and Broadwood,' but this was the younger Burkat Shudi, who was in partnership with John Broadwood from 1773 to about 1782 and died in 1803.

A list of the existing harpsichords by Shudi and Shudi & Broadwood, as far as is known,[2] is given on the preceding page: all but one are double harpsichords. The price of a single harpsichord about 1770 was 35 guineas; with octava (i.e. octave string), 40 guineas; with octava and swell, 50 guineas. A double harpsichord with swell was 80 guineas.[3]

A. J. H. ; addns. and rev. E. J. H[s].

SHUDI, Joshua, harpsichord - maker and pupil of Burkat Shudi, appears from his advertisement in the Gazetteer of Jan. 12, 1767, to have set up for himself about that time at the Golden Guitar, Silver Street, Golden Square, London. An advertisement of his widow, Mary Shudi, then of Berwick Street, St. James's, in the Public Advertiser of Jan. 16, 1775, announces his death and her continuance of the business, and as there is a fine harpsichord still existing, said to have a romantic history and bearing the name and date of Joshua Shudi, 1779, it is evident that she continued to use her late husband's name, or dated instruments of his make when she sold them.　　　A. J. H.

SHUTTLEWORTH, Obadiah (d. circa 1735), son of Thos. Shuttleworth of Spitalfields, who had acquired some money by vending MS. copies of Corelli's works before they were published in England. He was an excellent violinist, and was principal violin at the Swan

Tavern concerts, Cornhill, from their beginning in 1728 until his death. He was also a skilful organist, and in 1724 succeeded Philip Hart as organist of St. Michael's, Cornhill, and a few years afterwards was appointed one of the organists of the Temple Church. He composed twelve concertos and some sonatas for the violin, which he kept in MS., his only printed compositions being two concertos adapted from the first and eleventh concertos of Corelli. These were published by Joseph Hare, at the Viol and Flute in Cornhill, and were engraved by T. Cross : the date is about 1726.

w. h. h. ; addn. f. k.

SI, the seventh note of the major scale in the nomenclature of France and Italy : =B. (See Hexachord ; Solmisation.)

SIBELIUS, Jean (b. Tavastehus, Finland, Dec. 8, 1865), composer, descends from purely Finnish parentage on both sides, his father, a well-known doctor, springing from old peasant stock and his mother from a clerical family. He differs in this respect from his immediate forerunners who laid the foundations of a national school of Finnish music, but who were either settlers from North Germany or partly Swedish by race (see Song, section Finland).

Although Sibelius evinced a remarkable musical talent at an early age, he was given a classical education and studied law at the university of Helsingfors. But the call of his chosen art proved too urgent, and he entered the conservatoire of that city, studying for three years under Wegelius, then the leader of the national movement, standing half-way between Pacius, who only ventured on a somewhat timid racial expression in comparatively simple songs and male-voice choruses, and Kajanus, the first to interpret Finnish folk-lore through the medium of instrumental music. Sibelius afterwards went to Berlin, where he came under the tuition of Bargiel and Becker, and subsequently to Vienna, where he finished his studies with Goldmark and Robert Fuchs. It was perhaps because he never came under the influence of any dominant foreign master that his strong individuality revealed itself at once in the first works written after his return to his native country in 1893. Even then he already had in his possession a symphony for solo voices, chorus and orchestra, ' Kullervo,' the first work of his based on the Finnish national epic, the Kalevala, which, however, he did not allow to be published. An opera, ' The Maid in the Tower,' was produced at Helsingfors in 1896. In little more than three years after his return home, during which time he taught the violin and theory at the Helsingfors conservatoire, he won such recognition as a national composer that a life grant was offered him by the state in 1897, on which he was able to retire and to devote himself entirely to a creative career. His life has since been outwardly

[1] Left-hand stop and pedal, which releases all registers when a climax is essential.
[2] Additions to the original list are here made from the MS. notes left by A. J. Hipkins.
[3] The altered value of money should be borne in mind in comparing these prices with those of modern pianofortes.

uneventful, interrupted only by periodical journeys abroad and a visit to the U.S.A., where in 1914 he resumed his teaching activities for a short time at the New England Conservatoire in Boston. He paid several visits to England, the two most important occurring in 1912, when the fourth symphony was produced at the Birmingham Festival, and in 1921, when he appeared several times at Queen's Hall at the invitation of Sir Henry J. Wood, introducing to London the fifth symphony and 'The Oceanides' (written in 1914 for the combined New York and Boston symphony orchestras). Both his 50th and 60th birthdays were celebrated in Helsingfors as events of national importance. On the former occasion the fifth symphony was produced and on the latter the seventh. (See list below.)

Sibelius is regarded by his compatriots with the veneration which only so highly cultured, united and sanely democratic a people, and perhaps only a small people, can accord to a creative artist of their own race. He is in the fullest sense of the term a musical patriot and has enriched Finnish music, both officially and spontaneously, with a large number of works likely to form part of Finland's national art treasures for all time. Among the works due to his sense of public duty may be mentioned the tone poem, 'Finlandia' (op. 26), 'The Origin of Fire' (op. 32), written for the inauguration of the Finnish National Theatre in 1902, the Marches for the Finnish Infantry and the Scouts (op. 91) and the Carillon (op. 65) for the new church of Berghäll, a modern suburb of Helsingfors. But the composer's real significance as a national tone poet reveals itself in the music based on the country's rich store of ancient saga and due only to the inner promptings of his creative imagination. To this category belong, first and foremost, the symphonic works inspired by the *Kalevala*, including the 'Kullervo' symphony, and 'The Origin of Fire' for male voices and orchestra already mentioned, as well as the orchestral Legends, 'The Swan of Tuonela' and 'Lemminkäinen's Homefaring,' (op. 22), the symphonic fantasia, 'Pohjola's Daughter' (op 49) and the three piano pieces on the 'Kyllikki' episode (op. 41). No less profoundly national, though more indefinite as regards the poetic basis, are the tone poems for orchestra, 'Night Ride and Sunrise' (op. 55) and 'The Bard' (op. 64), the suite for strings, 'Rakastava' (op. 14), the 'Spring Song' for orchestra (op. 16) which depicts the pathos of the sudden outburst of the brief northern summer season, the funeral march 'In Memoriam' (op. 59) and works for chorus and orchestra such as the 'Impromptu' (op. 19), 'The Ferryman's Brides' (op. 33) and 'The Captive Queen' (op. 48), the latter plainly symbolic of Finland's dependence and yearning for liberty.

The most popular, however, of all these patriotic works, and those which were the first to establish Sibelius's reputation outside his own country, are the symphonic poem, 'En Saga' (op. 9) and the somewhat external and frankly popular 'Finlandia' (op. 26). The latter reproduces so faithfully the outward features and the spirit of Finnish folk-song that it was at first found hard to believe in the originality of the thematic material. The tunes were all the composer's own, but the work has by this time become the treasured possession of his compatriots and the typical musical manifestation of Finnish patriotism for the rest of the world. Still national, but more localised, are the 'Karelia' overture and suite (opp. 10 & 11), which characterise the inhabitants of the south-eastern province of Finland, a type distinguished by a gayer, livelier and more amiable, but less steadfast, temperament than that of the western and northern Finn, the Tavast.

For Sibelius this temporary visit to Karelia was only one of his many excursions, some of which, in the artistic sense, took him even farther afield. In his incidental music especially he transplants himself temporarily to foreign soil and shows himself as a versatile artist by no means always narrowly confined to his native earth. In the music to Adolf Paul's 'King Christian II' (op. 27) and in that to Strindberg's 'Svanehvit' (op. 54) he is attracted respectively by Swedish history and Swedish fairy-tale; Maeterlinck's 'Pelléas et Mélisande' (op. 46) takes him to mid-Europe, and Procopé's 'Belshazzar's Feast' (op. 51) to the east. The 'Scènes historiques' for orchestra (opp. 25 & 66) touch upon various mediæval countries. His occasional predilection for classical subjects, as in the symphonic poem, 'The Oceanides' (op. 73), the orchestral dance intermezzi 'The Dryad' (op. 45, No. 1) and 'Pan and Echo' (op. 53), and the 'Song of the Athenians' (op. 31), go far to support Mrs. Rosa Newmarch's assertion that she detects a pre-natal Hellenic strain in the composer. In all his temperamental complexity, which is indeed characteristic of the Finn and explained by the chequered racial and political history to which he is heir, Sibelius represents the type of the Tavast, with his intense love of the native soil, his brooding melancholy and sullen obstinacy in the face of oppression and climatic rigour, which can at times blaze into fierce anger or seek relief in reckless enjoyment of the hour. The predominant traits of his most representative works are an almost passionate adoration of nature, a patriotism that is never vainglorious, and a resoluteness tempered at times by a deep and genuine tenderness free from sentimental ostentation. All this is almost incessantly accompanied by a ground bass that plays up and down the gamut of a fundamental sorrow varying between dreamy sadness and utter despair.

SYMPHONIES.—In content and form the symphonies are entirely personal creations evincing a powerful mentality unrestrained by historical precedent and uncomplicated by æsthetic preconceptions. Sibelius uses just as much of the traditional symphonic form as will hold his ideas together without in any way constraining them. His characteristic method of working with short motives in a kind of mosaic style rather than with elaborate themes which take their recognised places as first, second and auxiliary subjects, would not readily fall into the orthodox formula. He is averse to thematic developments which merely sustain the framework of a movement without expressing anything of vital importance ; all that concerns him is a lucid statement of what is uppermost in his mind, without any explanatory parentheses and oratorical perorations. This elliptical manner may disconcert the hearer who expects a certain amount of relaxation into decorative or transitional passages in a symphonic movement, and to him Sibelius may seem almost brutally abrupt and cursory, but familiarity with this compact and pithy style makes it appear immensely satisfying to those who can accustom themselves to understand the general statement of a syllogism without the adduction of minor premises and conclusions.

It is difficult to give decided preference to any one of the seven symphonies, which differ greatly from each other. No. 1 (op. 39) will give most satisfaction to those who insist on purity of classical form regardless of its suitability to the subject-matter. In Nos. 2 and 3 (opp. 43 and 52) a successive advance towards personal freedom may be traced, and in No. 4 (op. 63), with its mystical and almost primitive nature worship, complete maturity in the way of adjusting matter and manner is reached. Most akin in spirit to this work, although less free and fantastic, is the equally admirable No. 6[1] (op. 104), which again seems to have grown from the primeval soil of Finland, while No. 5 (op. 82) is distinguished by a simplicity and comparative gaiety that will probably make it the most readily accessible and popular in time to come. No. 7 (op. 105), in one continuous movement, is distinguished by an almost Beethoven-like grandeur and solemnity that indicates a work written for a special occasion.

The violin concerto (op. 47) may be grouped with the symphonies, with which it has the characteristic freedom of form in common. The solo part, though extremely difficult, gives little opportunity for purely technical display; it is closely interwoven with the symphonic tissue, and the work is therefore neglected by the average virtuoso.

[1] First heard in England under Sir Henry Wood at Queen's Hall, Nov. 20, 1926.

CHAMBER MUSIC, ETC.—The only important chamber work by Sibelius is the string quartet, 'Voces intimae' (op. 56), cast in suite rather than sonata form. It affords an interesting example of the composer's manner of sustaining one mood throughout a whole movement, in spite of great variety in detail.

Sibelius does not write particularly well for the piano, and although some of his genre pieces may be ranked with similar small works by Grieg or MacDowell, he has contributed nothing of vital significance to keyboard literature. The 'Kyllikki' pieces (op. 41) and the sonata (op. 12) are the most interesting of the piano works, and the 3 sonatinas (op. 67) contain much that is highly characteristic. His writing for violin and violoncello is more congenial to the instruments, but most of the pieces are quite unimportant ; notable exceptions are the two works for violin and orchestra (opp. 69 and 77) and 'Malinconia' (op. 20) for violoncello and piano.

VOCAL MUSIC stands next in importance to Sibelius's orchestral works on folk-lore subjects and to the symphonies. The works for chorus and orchestra have already been mentioned, but to a country that cultivates unaccompanied choral singing so extensively as Finland does, his output of partsongs, although small, is of even greater consequence. The three partsongs for male voices (op. 18) are among his best and most individual work, and the Latin Hymn (op. 21) must also be singled out.

The songs of Sibelius are not far short of 100 in number and cover a truly Schubertian variety of subjects. Although the poetry he set is chiefly in the Swedish tongue, it is culled almost exclusively from his native soil, for, owing to Finland's extensive Swedish culture, the native poets Runeberg, Rydberg, Topelius, Tavaststjerna and others on whose work Sibelius has drawn wrote in the Scandinavian language. The songs are predominantly melodic, and in the piano parts mere accompanying on the one side and undue symphonic or pictorial elaboration on the other are avoided with equal felicity. The music illuminates and intensifies the mood and feeling of the poetry without duplicating its verbal imagery.

There is no need to deal at length with the popular aspects of Sibelius's work. Such things as 'Finlandia,' the 'Valse triste' the 'Romance' in D♭ for piano, and songs like 'Black Roses' and 'The Tryst' have become so familiar that they are liable to obscure the larger and profounder works.

Immaturity and dependence on other composers' influences are, strange to say, absent from the beginning. Whatever procedures he may have learnt, as, for instance, from the French impressionists, he absorbed entirely into his musical personality, and affinities with

Grieg and other Scandinavian composers are due to environment rather than to conscious imitation. At weak moments, indeed, there is something of a familiar type of mild northern balladry about his music. Curiously enough, there is little change of outlook or steady progress to be discerned in his chronological catalogue. The early 'En Saga' seems as mature and complete to-day as the last two symphonies, and the latest piano pieces are no better than, and not essentially different from, the first 'six impromptus.'

In summing up the art of Sibelius, it might be said that it takes its root in the soil of his native country, but becomes individualised in its growth by contact with the composer's experience of life, which is never impeded by æsthetic prepossessions. He has a strong personal bias which, combined with his racial consciousness, eschews convention by the substitution of an artistic code of his own. His work is neither deliberately modern nor studiedly archaic; it is simply, in its most characteristic manifestations, unlike any other music.

The following list includes all the works by Sibelius published up to 1925:

Op.
5. 6 Impromptus, PF.
9. 'En Saga,' symphonic poem, orch.
10. 'Karelia' overture, orch.
11. 'Karelia' suite, orch.
12. Sonata, F major, PF.
13. 7 Songs.
14. 'Rakastava' (The Lover), suite, str. and timp.
16. 'Spring Song,' orch.
17. 7 Songs.
18. 3 Partsongs for male voices.
19. 'Impromptu,' female voices and orch.
20. 'Malinconia,' vcl. and PF.
21. Hymn, 'Natus in curas,' male voices.
22. Legends for orch.: 'The Swan of Tuonela,' and 'Lemminkäinen's Homefaring.'
23. Cantata for the year 1897, mixed chorus.
24. 10 Pieces, PF.
25. 'Scènes historiques,' Set I., orch.
26. 'Finlandia,' tone poem, orch.
27. Incidental Music for 'King Christian II.,' by Adolf Paul.
31. 'Song of the Athenians,' men's and boys' voices, 7 horns and percussion.
32. 'The Origin of Fire' (' Ukko the Fire-Maker '), bar. solo, male voices and orch. (1902.)
33. 'The Ferryman's Brides.' bar. or mezzo-sopr. and orch.
34. 8 Pieces, PF.
35. 2 Songs.
36. 6 Songs.
37. 5 Songs.
38. 5 Songs.
39. Symphony No. 1, E minor. (1899.)
40. 'Pensées lyriques,' 7 Pieces, PF.
41. 'Kyllikki,' 3 Pieces, PF.
42. Romance, C major, str. orch.
43. Symphony No. 2, D major. (1902.)
44. Incidental Music for 'Kuolema,' by Arvid Järnefelt (including 'Valse triste ').
45. 2 Tone Poems, orch.: No. 1, 'The Dryad '; No. 2, 'Dance Intermezzo.
46. Incidental Music for Maeterlinck's 'Pelléas et Mélisande.'
47. Concerto, D minor, vln. and orch.
48. 'The Captive Queen,' chorus and orch.
49. 'Pohjola's Daughter,' symphonic fantasia, orch.
50. 6 Songs.
51. Incidental Music for 'Belshazzar's Feast,' by Hjalmar Procopé.
52. Symphony No. 3, C major. (1907.)
53. 'Pan and Echo,' Dance intermezzo, orch.
54. Incidental Music to Strindberg's 'Svanehvit,' small orch.
55. 'Night Ride and Sunrise,' orch.
56. String Quartet, 'Voces Intimae.' (1908.)
57. 8 Songs.
58. 10 Pieces, PF.
59. 'In Memoriam,' Funeral March, orch.
60. 2 Songs from Shakespeare's 'Twelfth Night,' with PF. or guitar.
61. 8 Songs.
62. (a) 'Canzonetta,' str. orch.; (b) 'Valse romantique,' small orch.
63. Symphony No. 4, A minor. (1912.)
64. 'The Bard,' tone poem, orch.
65. Carillon for the Church of Berghäll.
66. 'Scènes historiques,' Set II., orch.
67. 3 Sonatinas, PF.

Op.
68. 2 Rondinos, PF.
69. 2 Serenades, vln. and orch.
70. 'Luonnotar,' tone poem, sopr. and orch.
71. Music for the pantomime 'Scaramouche.'
72. 6 Songs.
73. 'The Oceanides,' symphonic poem, orch. (1914.)
74. 4 Lyric Pieces, PF.
75. 5 Pieces, PF.
76. 13 Pieces, PF.
77. (a) 'Laetare anima mea '; (b) 'Devotion,' vln. and orch.
78. 2 Pieces, vln. and PF.
79. 6 Pieces, vln. and PF.
80. Sonatina, vln. and PF.
81. 3 Pieces, vln. and PF.
82. Symphony No. 5, E flat major. (1915.)
85. 5 Pieces, PF.
86. 6 Songs.
87. 'Impromptu,' orch.
88. 6 Songs.
89. 3 Humoresques, vln. and PF.
90. 6 Songs.
91. (a) March of the Finnish Infantry; (b) Scout March. Various arrangements.
94. 6 Pieces, PF.
96. (a) 'Valse lyrique'; (b) 'Autrefois; (c) Valse chevaleresque, orch.
97. 6 Bagatelles, PF.
98. 'Suite champêtre,' PF.
99. 8 Pieces, PF.
102. 'Novelette,' vln. and PF.
104. Symphony No. 6, D minor. (1923.)
105. Symphony No. 7, C major. (1925.)
'Carminalia,' 3 Latin satires, chorus S.A.B.
6 Finnish Folk-songs, arranged for PF.
Incidental Music for 'The Language of the Birds,' by Adolf Paul.
'Kullervo,' Symphony, orch. with solo voices and chorus (1892.) (Unpublished.)
'The Maid in the Tower,' opera. (1896.) (Unpublished.)

                                 E. B.

BIBL.—E. FURUHJELM, Jean Sibelius. Hans tondiktning och drag u. hans liv. (Stockholm, 1917); WALTER NIEMANN, Jean Sibelius (Leipzig, 1917). With a list of Sibelius's compositions.

SIBONI, (1) GIUSEPPE (b. Forli,[1] Jan. 27, 1780; d. Copenhagen, Mar. 29, 1839), made his début as a tenor singer at Florence in 1797, and after singing in Genoa, Milan and Prague, appeared at the King's Theatre, London, in 1806, and sang for the following three seasons. In 1810, 1811, 1812, 1813 and 1814 he was in Vienna, where he sang at the first performances of Beethoven's 'Wellington's Sieg' and 'Tremate empi.' In 1813 he sang at Prague, and after engagements at Naples and St. Petersburg (1818) settled at Copenhagen in Oct. 1819, where he lived for the rest of his life, occupying the post of director of the Royal Opera and of the Conservatorium. He was married three times, his second wife being a sister of Schubert's friend, von Schober. Many of Paër's tenor parts were written for him.

BIBL.—A. MONTI, Giuseppe Siboni, tenore, musicista, forlivese. Forli, 1922.

(2) ERIK ANTON WALDEMAR (b. Copenhagen, Aug. 26, 1828; d. there, Feb. 22, 1892), son of the above, learnt the pianoforte from Courländer and Goetze, composition from F. Vogel, and harmony from J. P. E. Hartmann. In Sept. 1847 he went to Leipzig, and studied under Moscheles and Hauptmann, but on the outbreak of the Schleswig-Holstein insurrection he enlisted as a volunteer in the Danish army, and took part in the campaign of 1848. In 1851 he went to Vienna, and studied counterpoint under Sechter until 1853, when he returned to Copenhagen, visiting Paris on his way. Among his pupils at this time were our own Queen Alexandra, her sister, the Empress of Russia, and the Landgrave

---

[1] Fétis gives his birthplace as Bologna, and the date as 1782, but the above details are from autobiographical notes supplied by his son.

Frederick William of Hesse Cassel. In 1864 Siboni was appointed organist and professor of music at the Royal Academy of Music of Sorö, in Seeland, a post he resigned on account of health in 1883; he returned to Copenhagen. The following are his chief compositions:

### 1. PUBLISHED

Three Impromptus for PF. for 4 hands (op. 1); Organ Preludes; Quartet for PF. and Strings (op. 10); Tragic Overture in C minor. (op. 14); Songs and PF. pieces.

### 2. UNPUBLISHED

Two Danish operas—'Loreley,' in 1 act; 'Carl den Andens Flugt,' in 3 acts (Libretto on subject from English History by Professor Thomas Overskou), successfully performed at the Royal Theatre of Copenhagen in 1861; Psalm cxi. for Bass Solo, Chorus and Orchestra; 'Stabat Mater,' for Soli, Chorus, Orchestra and Organ; Cantata, 'The Battle of Murten,' for Soli, Male Chorus and Orchestra; 'The Assault of Copenhagen,' Cantata for Soli, Chorus and Orchestra; two Symphonies; Concert Overture; PF. Concerto; String Quartets; PF. Trio; Duet for 2 PFs., Sonatas for PF. and Violin, and PF. and Violoncello, etc., many of them performed at concerts in Copenhagen.

**SICARD,** LAURENT, a 17th-century tenor singer, attached to the Sainte-chapelle under Louis XIII. He edited 17 books of ' Airs serieux et à boire,' 2 and 3 v., with basso continuo, published by Ballard between 1666 and 1683.                                     E. v. d. s.

**SICILIANA,** SICILIANO, SICILIENNE, a dance rhythm closely allied to the Pastorale. The name is derived from a dance-song popular in Sicily, analogous to the Tuscan Rispetti.[1] Walther (*Lexicon*, 1732) classes these compositions as canzonettas, dividing them into Neapolitan and Sicilian, the latter being like jigs, written in rondo form, in 12–8 or 6–8 time. The Siciliana was sometimes used for the slow movement of suites and sonatas (as in Bach's violin sonata in G minor), but is of more frequent occurrence in vocal music, in which Handel, following the great Italian masters, made great use of it. Amongst later composers, Meyerbeer has applied the name to the movement ' O fortune, à ton caprice ' in the finale to Act I. of ' Robert le Diable,' although it has little in common with the older examples. The Siciliana is generally written in 6–8, but sometimes in 12–8 time, and is usually in a minor key. In the bar of six quavers, the first note is usually a dotted quaver, and the fourth a crotchet, followed by two semiquavers. The Siciliana is sometimes in one movement, but usually ends with a repetition of the first part. It should be played rather quickly, but not so fast as the Pastorale, care being taken not to drag the time and to avoid all strong accentuation, smoothness being an important characteristic of this species of composition.                          w. b. s.

**SICILIAN BRIDE,** THE, opera in 4 acts; words translated by Bunn from St. Georges, music by Balfe. Produced Drury Lane Theatre, Mar. 6, 1852.                          G.

**SIDE-DRUM** (Fr. *caisse roulante*), see DRUM (3). (*PLATE XXIV*. No. 4.)

**SIEBENHAAR,** MALACHIAS (*b*. Creibitz, Mar. 6, 1616; *d*. Magdeburg, Jan. 6, 1685), studied at Wittenberg, where he became the

friend of Phil. von Zesen. In 1644 he was cantor at the town-school, Magdeburg; in 1656 second preacher at St. Ulrich, there. He composed motets and songs, and collaborated in von Zesen's collections of songs (*Q.-L.*; *Riemann*).

**SIÉBER** (1), JEAN GEORGES (*b*. Franconie, 1734; *d*. 1815), horn-player and music publisher, came to Paris in 1758. He was French horn-player at the Comédie Française in 1763, then at the Opéra. It would appear that on the advice of J. C. Bach he took up music publishing in 1771, succeeding Huberty.

(2) His son, GEORGES JULIEN (*d*. 1834), took over the business (Hôtel d'Aligre, 123 rue Saint Honoré).

The Siébers have published a considerable number of the works of Boccherini, J. C. Bach, Borghi, Gaviniès, St. Georges, Gossec, Haydn, Krumpholz, Mozart, Pugnani, Stamitz, Vanhall, etc. They have greatly aided in the spread of new symphonic works, not only in Paris, but also in Mannheim and Vienna.

BIBL.—G. CUCUEL (*Sammelb*. I.M.G. xiii. 2 and xiv. 2).
                                              M. P.

**SIEFERT,** PAUL (*b*. Danzig, 1586; *d*. there, May 6, 1666), a pupil of Sweelinck, at first member of the chapel of Sigismund III. at Warsaw. In 1623 he was organist at St. Mary's, Danzig. He was a prolific composer, who was always quarrelling with the Kapellmeisters for not doing justice to the performance of his works. This led to a published controversy between him and Marco SCACCHI (*q.v.*), who in 1640 had criticised his psalms. Only 2 books of Psalms 4-8 v., a Te Deum, etc., and some organ pieces of his are still in existence (*Q.-L.*; *Riemann*).

**SIÈGE DE CORINTHE,** LE, lyric tragedy in 3 acts; words by Soumet and Balocchi, music by Rossini. Produced Opéra, Oct. 9, 1826. It was an adaptation and extension of ' MAOMETTO SECONDO ' (*q.v.*).                          G.

**SIEGE OF ROCHELLE,** THE, opera in 3 acts; words by Fitzball, music by Balfe. Produced Drury Lane Theatre, Oct. 29, 1835. G.

**SIEGFRIED,** see RING DES NIBELUNGEN.

**SIFACE,** GIOVANNI FRANCESCO GROSSI, (*b*. La Chiesina, near Pescia, Feb. 12, 1653; *d*. May 29, 1697), sopranist, is said to have been a pupil of Redi. If so, this must have been Tommaso Redi, who became maestro di cappella at Loreto towards the end of the 17th century, although, as he was Siface's contemporary, it seems improbable that he should have been his instructor. Siface was admitted into the Pope's chapel in Apr. 1675. He would seem at that time to have been already known by the sobriquet which has always distinguished him, and which he owed to his famous impersonation of Siface or Syphax in some opera.[2]

---

[1] For an account of these Sicilian songs see G. Pitrè, *Sui canti popolari Siciliani*, Palermo, 1868.

[2] See Dent's *Scarlatti*, p. 37.

Siface's voice, an artificial soprano, was full and beautiful ; his style of singing broad, noble and very expressive. Mancini extols his choir-singing as being remarkable for its excellence. In 1679 he was at Venice for the Carnival, acting with great success in the performances of Pallavicini's ' Nerone,' of which a description may be found in the *Mercure galant* of the same year. After this he came to England, and Hawkins mentions him as pre-eminent among all the foreign singers of that period. He was for a time attached to James II.'s chapel,[1] but soon returned to Italy. In the second part of Playford's collection, ' Musick's Handmaid ' (1689), there is an air by Purcell, entitled ' Sefauchi's farewell,' which refers to Siface's departure from this country.

This great singer was murdered by the brothers of the Marchesa Marsili,[2] while travelling from Bologna to Ferrara.[3] He is referred to in Durfey's ' Fool's Preferment ' (1688), Act. I. Sc. i.     F. A. M. ; rev. W. B. S.

SIGISMONDO D' INDIA, CAVALIERE (*b.* Palermo, end of 16th cent.), director of the chamber music of the Duke of Savoy ; from 1612 maestro di cappella of the Cardinal Maurice of Savoy. In 1627 the cardinal is called Sabandia. Sigismondo lived at Turin ; he composed two books of church concerts for voices, 1 book of motets, 8 books of madrigals, 2 books of vilanelle, etc.  (*See Q.-L.*)

SIGNA, opera in 2 acts, libretto (founded on Ouida's story) by G. à Beckett, H. Rudall, and F. E. Weatherley ; Italian version by G. Mazzucato. Music by F. H. Cowen. Produced (in Italian) Teatro dal Verme, Milan, Nov. 12, 1893, in 4 acts, reduced to 3, and ultimately to 2 ; Covent Garden, June 30, 1894.    M.

SIGNALS, see MILITARY SOUNDS AND SIGNALS.

SIGNATURE. (1) KEY - SIGNATURE (Fr. *armure, armature* ; *signes accidentales* ; Ger. *Vorzeichnung*, properly *reguläre Vorzeichnung*). The group of sharp or flat signs placed at the beginning of a composition, immediately after the clef, or in the course of a composition generally after a double-bar. They affect all notes of the same names as the degrees on which they stand, and thus define the key, major or minor, of the composition (cf. KEY, SCALE, ACCIDENTAL).

The following is a table of key signatures :

*Sharp Signatures.*

| | | | | | | |
|---|---|---|---|---|---|---|
| Major— | G | D | A | E | B | F sharp | C sharp. |
| Minor— | E | B | F sharp | C sharp | G sharp | D sharp | A sharp |

*Flat Signatures.*

| | | | | | | |
|---|---|---|---|---|---|---|
| Major— | F | B flat | E flat | A flat | D flat | G flat | C flat |
| Minor— | D | G | C | F | B flat | E flat | A flat |

(See NOTATION, Vol. III. p. 662.)

(2) TIME-SIGNATURE (Lat. *signum modi, vel temporis, vel prolationis* ; Ger. *Taktzeichen*). A sign placed after the clef and key signature (where one is used) in order to give notice of the time in which a composition is written.

These signs and their evolution are fully described under NOTATION, Vol. III. p. 656. (See also TIME.)

SIGNORUCCI, POMPEO, maestro di cappella, 1794, and organist at Borgo San Sepolcro (Toscana, Arezzo) ; in 1608 maestro di cappella at Pisa Cathedral and Accademico Unisono of Perugia. Banchieri[4] calls him maestro di cappella of Siena. He wrote several books of masses, psalms, madrigals and church concerts, some motets and canzone in collective volumes (*Q.-L.*).

SIGTENHORST MEYER, BERNHARD VAN DER (*b.* Amsterdam, June 17, 1888), one of the most independent and most distinctively national composers among the younger Dutch school. He was a pupil of Bernard Zweers, Daniel de Lange and J. B. C. de Pauw, besides studying the methods of French masters in Paris. Any tendencies towards a French style of writing were quickly removed by his determination to retain his Dutch nationality as a composer and by a journey to Java and the East where he received many impressions subsequently expressed in his music. Himself a pianist of considerable ability, a large proportion of his music consists of pieces for his own instrument describing his impressions of various places. Technically there is little of the ' impressionist ' in his work, and besides the pianoforte pieces he has attempted many other forms. His one opera, ' De Verzoeking van Boeddha ' (The Temptation of Buddha) to words by Rient van Santen, is written for soli, women's chorus, string orchestra, harps and celesta.

The following is a list of his works :

' De Witte Reiger ' and ' Het Naardermeer,' two songs published before his op. 1 and without opus number.

Op.
1. Van de Bloemen, four pieces for piano.
2. Het Oude China, four pieces for piano.
3. By den Tempel, 3 liederen
4. Van de Vogels, 3 pieces for piano.
5. Fluisteringen, 3 liederen.
6. Stemmingen, 3 liederen.
7. Stabat Mater for vocal quartet or mixed choir a capella.
8. De Verzoeking van Boeddha, opera.
9. 6 Gezichten op den Fuji, for piano.
10. Doode Steden, 2 liederen.
11. De Maas, 3 pieces for piano.
12. St. Quentin, 2 pieces for piano.
13. 1st String Quartet (in 5 movements : The Worship of the Magi, The Flight into Egypt, The Driving of the Money Changers out of the Temple, The Burial, and The Angels by the Grave)
14. Oude Kasteelen, 3 pieces for piano.
15. Veltdeuntjens (words by P. C. Hooft).
16. Prelude for piano.

---

1 Evelyn heard him there, Jan. 30, 1687, and on Apr. 19 following at Pepys's house. He speaks of him in highly commendatory terms.
2 Cf. C. Ricci, *Frastoria and Leggenda*, p. 124.
3 Cf. C. Nardini's *Il musico Siface e l' ambassatore di Francia a Roma, 1683*. Florence, 1791.

                    4 *Lettera Armon.* fol. 142.

H. A.

SIGUIRIYA GITANA, see CANTE HONDO ;
SONG, subsection SPAIN (4).

SIGURD, opera in 5 acts; text by Du Locle
and A. Blau, music by Ernest Reyer. Produced
Brussels, Jan. 7, 1884 ; Covent Garden, July 15
of the same year ; Opéra, Paris, June 12, 1885.

SILAS, ÉDOUARD (b. Amsterdam, Aug. 22,
1827 ; d. London, Feb. 8, 1909), pianist and
composer. His first teacher was Neher, one of
the court orchestra at Mannheim. He first
appeared in public at Amsterdam in 1837 ; he
studied the piano in 1839 with Lacombe, in
1842 he was placed under Kalkbrenner at Paris,
and soon afterwards entered the Conservatoire
under Benoist for the organ and Halévy for
composition. In 1849 he obtained the first prize
for the former. In 1850 he came to England ;
played first at Liverpool, and made his first
appearance in London at the Musical Union,
May 21. From that date Silas was established
in London as teacher, and as organist of the
Roman Catholic chapel at Kingston-on-Thames.
His oratorio ' Joash ' (words compiled by G.
Linley) was produced at the Norwich Festival
of 1863. A symphony in A (op. 19) was
produced by the Musical Society of London,
Apr. 22, 1863 ; repeated at the Crystal Palace,
Feb. 20, 1864 ; and afterwards published. A
concerto for PF. and orchestra in D minor is
also published. A fantasia and an Élégie,
both for PF. and orchestra, were given at the
Crystal Palace in 1865 and 1873. Three
Mythological Pieces for orchestra were played
at a Philharmonic Concert in 1888. In
1866 he received the prize of the Belgian competition for sacred music for his Mass for four
voices and organ.

Silas is the author of a Treatise on Musical
Notation, and an Essay on a new method
of Harmony—both unpublished. An English
opera, ' Nitocris ' ; overture and incidental
music to ' Fanchette ' ; a musical comedietta,
' Love's Dilemma ' ; a Cantata; an Ave Verum ;
O Salutaris (2) ; a symphony in C major ; and
other compositions remained unpublished. The
list of his published instrumental works is very
large, and includes many organ pieces which
became popular, PF. pieces, among which the
best known are gavotte in E minor, bourrée in
G minor, ' Malvina ' (romance), suite in A minor,
op. 103, six duets, etc. etc.

Silas was for many years a teacher of harmony at the G.S.M. and the London Academy
of Music.                             G., addns.

SILBERMANN, a family of organ-builders,
clavichord and pianoforte makers, of Saxon
origin, of whom the most renowned were
(1) ANDREAS (b. Kleinbobritzsch. near Frauen-

stein, Saxony, May 16, 1678 ; d. Mar. 16, 1734 [1]),
who built the Strassburg Cathedral organ, and
(2) GOTTFRIED, who built the organs of
Freiberg and Dresden, and was the first to
construct the pianoforte in Germany. His
work receives special notice below. Following Gerber's Lexicon, they were sons [2] of Michael
Silbermann, a carpenter at Kleinbobritzsch.
Andreas was brought up to his father's craft,
and travelled, according to the custom of the
country, in 1700. He learnt organ-building,
and in 1703 we find him settled in that vocation
at Strassburg. According to Hopkins and
Rimbault [3] he built the Strassburg organ—
his greatest work of 29 recorded by them—in
1714-16. He had nine sons, of whom three
were organ-builders, and after the father's
death carried on the business in common. Of
the three, (3) JOHANN ANDREAS, the eldest
(b. Strassburg, June 26, 1712 ; d. Feb. 11, 1783),
built the Predigerkirche organ at Strassburg,
and that of the Abbey of St. Blaise in the Black
Forest. In all he built fifty-four organs, in addition to writing a history of the city of Strassburg,
published 1775. His son (4) JOHANN JOSIAS
(d. June 3, 1786) was a musical instrument
maker. The next son of Andreas, (5) JOHANN
DANIEL (b. Mar. 31, 1717 ; d. Leipzig, May 6,
1766), was employed by his uncle (2) GOTTFRIED,
and was intrusted after his uncle's death
with the completion of the famous organ (in
the Hofkirche) in Dresden. Mooser,[4] however,
who claims to follow good authorities, attributes
the completion of this instrument to Zacharias
Hildebrand. Be this as it may, Johann Daniel
remained at Dresden, a keyed-instrument
maker and constructor of ingenious barrel-
organs. A composition of his is preserved in
Marpurg's ' Raccolta ' (1757). (6) JOHANN
HEINRICH, the youngest son of Andreas (b. Sept.
24, 1727 ; d. Strassburg, Jan. 15, 1799). His
pianofortes were well known in Paris ; he
made them with organ pedals, and constructed a harpsichord of which the longest
strings were of what may be called the natural
length, 16 feet !

But the greatest of the Silbermann family
was (2) GOTTFRIED (b. Kleinbobritzsch, near
Frauenstein, Jan. 14,[5] 1683 ; d. Dresden,
Aug. 4, 1753). He was at first placed with a
bookbinder, but soon quitted him and went to
(1) ANDREAS at Strassburg. Having got into
trouble by the attempted abduction of a nun,
he had to quit that city in 1707 and go back to
Frauenstein, where he built his first organ
(afterwards destroyed by fire, the fate of
several of his instruments). He appears to
have settled at Freiberg in 1709, and remained
there for some years. He built the cathedral

1 These and other dates from Riemann.
2 Some authorities have described them as uncle and nephew.
3 The Organ, its History and Construction, London, 1870.
4 Gottfried Silbermann.  Langensalza. 1857.
5 According to Mooser.

organ there in 1714. He built, in all, forty-seven organs in Saxony.[1] He never married, and died while engaged upon his finest work, the Dresden court organ. Although receiving what we should call very low prices for his organs, by living a frugal life he became comparatively rich, and his talent and exceptional force of character enabled him to achieve an eminent position.

His clavichords were as celebrated as his organs. Emanuel Bach had one of them for nearly half a century, and the instrument, many years after it was made, when heard under the hands of that gifted and sympathetic player, excited the admiration of Burney.[2] It cannot be doubted that he was the first German who made a pianoforte. He was already settled in Dresden in 1725, when König translated into German Scipione Maffei's account of the invention of the pianoforte at Florence by Cristofori. This fact has been already mentioned (see PIANOFORTE), and we now add some further particulars gained by personal search and inspection at Potsdam in 1881. We know from Agricola, one of J. S. Bach's pupils, that in 1736 Gottfried Silbermann submitted two pianofortes of his make to that great master. Bach finding much fault with them, Gottfried was annoyed, and for some time desisted from further experiments in that direction. It is possible that the intercourse between Dresden and Northern Italy enabled him, either then or later, to see a Florentine pianoforte. It is certain that three grand pianofortes made by him and acquired by Frederick the Great[3] for Potsdam—where they still remain in the music-rooms of the Stadtschloss, Sans Souci and Neues Palais,[4] inhabited by that monarch—are, with unimportant differences, repetitions of the Cristofori pianofortes existing at Florence. Frederick is said to have acquired more than three, but no others are now to be found. Burney's depreciation of the work of Germans in their own country finds no support in the admirable work of Gottfried Silbermann in these pianofortes. If its durability needed other testimony, we might refer to one of his pianofortes which Zelter met with at Weimar in 1804, and praised to Goethe ; and to another spoken of by Mooser in 1857 as having been up to a then recent date used at the meetings of the Freemasons' Lodge at

Freiberg. Gottfried Silbermann invented the CEMBAL D'AMORE, a kind of double clavichord.[5]

A. J. H.

BIBL. — ERNST FLADE, Der Orgelbauer, Gottfried Silbermann. (Leipzig, 1926.)

SILCHER, FRIEDRICH (b. Schnaith, near Schorndorf, Würtemberg, June 27, 1789 ; d. Tübingen, Aug. 26, 1860), composer of Lieder, was taught music by his father, and by Auberlen, organist at Fellbach, near Stuttgart. He was educated for a schoolmaster, and his first post was at Ludwigsburg, where he began to compose. In 1815 he took a conductorship at Stuttgart, and composed a cantata, which procured him, in 1817, the post of conductor to the University of Tübingen. This he held till 1860, when he retired, and died shortly after. His most important publications are—' Sechs vierstimmige Hymnen' (Laupp), ' Dreistimmiges würtemb. Choralbuch ' (ibid.), and ' Swabian, Thuringian, and Franconian Volkslieder,' 12 parts), many of which are his own compositions. Several of Silcher's melodies published in his ' Sammlung deutscher Volkslieder,' etc., have become true songs of the people, such as ' Ännchen von Tharau,' ' Morgen muss ich fort von hier,' ' Ich weiss nicht was soll es bedeuten,' ' Zu Strassburg auf der Schanz,' etc. The Lieder were published simultaneously for one and two voices with PF. and for four men's voices. He edited a Method for harmony and composition in 1851. A biographical sketch of Silcher by Köstlin appeared in 1877. F. G.

BIBL.—A. BOPP, Friedrich Silcher. (Stuttgart, 1916.)

SILOTI, ALEXANDER (b. near Charkow, Southern Russia, Oct. 10, 1863 ; d. 1919), a remarkable pianist, and one of the most eminent of Liszt's pupils. He was born on his father's estate, studied at the Moscow Conservatorium from 1875–81 under Swerew, Nicolas Rubinstein, Tchaikovsky and Hubert, and from 1883–86 with Liszt. After 1883, when he appeared at Leipzig at a concert of the Tonkünstlerversammlung, he was regarded as one of the leading Russian pianists, but he had already appeared with success in Moscow in 1880. From that year till 1890 he was professor at the Moscow Conservatorium ; then he sojourned for several years out of his own country in such places as Frankfort-on-Main, Antwerp and Leipzig, conducted the Moscow Philharmonic concerts in 1901–02, and

[1] Five of 3 manuals, Freiberg, Zittau and Frauenstein ; the Frauenkirche and Katholische Hofkirche at Dresden ; twenty-four of 2 manuals ; fifteen of 1 manual with pedals, and three of 1 manual without pedals. (Mooser, p. 125.)

[2] This clavichord was eventually sold by Emanuel Bach, says Engel, ' because there is among his compositions a Rondo in E minor, written in 1781, headed "Abschied von meinem Silbermann'schen Clavier" (Farewell to my Silbermann Clavichord). See C. Engel, Some Account of Clavichords, with Historical Notices, Mus. T., July 1879. E. J. H[s].

[3] Probably in 1746. The peace of Dresden was signed by Frederick, Christmas Day, 1745 ; he would have time after that event to inspect Silbermann's pianofortes.

[4] The Silbermann piano Burney mentions was that of the Neues Palais. He must have heard the one at Sans Souci, although he does not say so. In all probability the piano J. S. Bach played upon specially, on the occasion of his visit to Frederick the Great, was the one still in the Stadtschloss, the town palace of Potsdam.

[5] In confirmation of this, Mr. E. van der Straeten, in the summer of 1921, in looking through MSS.—in the State and University Library at Hamburg—came across one set that apparently had never been opened since its reception. It contained a very fine-toned pen-and-ink drawing of an instrument called 'Clavier d'Amour' It represents the only authentic illustration of this instrument except one which is said to be in an extremely rare 18th century work by Adlung. It was invented by Silbermann in 1721 ' after untiring thinking and planning.' The idea of an instrument combining the softness of a clavichord with the tone power of a small harpsichord was suggested to him by the wife of the Privy-Secretary Joh. Ulrich Koenig, of Dresden. Her husband, a friend of Silbermann was the first to give an account of the new instrument in the ' Breslauishe gedruckte Sammlungen of 1721.' See illustration and full description, Mus. T., Jan. 1, 1924. E. J. H[s].

after 1903 figured largely as a conductor in St. Petersburg and other great Russian cities.
H. V. H.

He remained in Russia through the Revolution, but escaped in 1919, coming to England where he played, as well as in Germany, and subsequently going to America.

SILVA, ANDREAS DE, was a singer in the Papal Chapel, 1519, and the first to be described as Papal composer.[1] In 1522 he appears to have been in the chapel of the Duke of Mantua. It is natural to identify him with Andreas Sylvanus, from whom Glarean quotes the Kyrie and Osanna of a very peculiar Mass for three voices, ' Malheur me bat,' also with the Andreas Silvanus to whom Sebastian Virdung refers as the intimate friend for whom he wrote his *Musica getutscht*, 1511. But Eitner in *Q.-L.* and *Monatshefte*, xxvi. p. 47, refuses to accept this identification, because he thinks Virdung's friend must have been a German ; and if de Silva had been a German it is unlikely that his works would have found their way into French collections like those of Attaingnant, or Italian collections like those of Gardane and Petrucci. This reasoning, however, is not very convincing, all the less that Eitner himself assumes that the Sylvanus who is the author of the Mass ' Malheur me bat ' is identical with the Silvanus the friend of Virdung. In any case the Sylvanus of the Mass ' Malheur me bat ' is more likely to have been a Netherlander than a German and to be identical with de Silva than with the Silvanus of Virdung. That de Silva was known in Germany appears from the reception of an Italian madrigal by him, ' Che sentisti Madonna,' in Ott's ' Liederbuch,' 1544, attributed to him in all the four part-books. This madrigal has a surprising degree of expressiveness for the time at which it must be supposed to have been written. Besides the works of Silva in the collections of the time, there are two masses and seven motets by him in the Archives of the Papal Chapel. One of the motets, ' Illumina oculos meos, a 6,' deserves notice, as being that on which Palestrina based one of his more important masses a 6, bearing the same title. Among other MS. motets of Silva enumerated in *Q.-L.* there are two mentioned together, ' Virtute magna ' and ' O Regem coeli,' both a 4. Possibly the theme of the two four-part masses of Palestrina in his first book, 1554, may be taken from these motets.    J. R. M.

SILVANA, also called ' Silvana das Waldmädchen,' or ' das stumme Waldmädchen '— the dumb Wood-maiden ; romantic opera in 3 acts ; words by F. K. Hiemer ; music by Weber ; completed Feb. 23, 1810 ; produced Frankfort, Sept. 16, 1810. It is probably founded to some extent on his early opera ' Das Waldmädchen ' (1800), which was afterwards

burnt ; and was to a small extent employed in ' Abu Hassan '. and ' Freischütz.' The overture was used by Weber as the prelude to his music for the wedding of Prince John of Saxony ; and he wrote seven variations for clarinet and PF., for H. Bärmann, on an air from it, ' Warum musst' ich.' It was produced in English (as ' Sylvana '), Surrey Theatre, under Elliston's management, Sept. 2, 1828. It was again revived, with a revised libretto by Herr Pasqué, and with ' musical amplifications,' at Hamburg and Lübeck in the spring of 1885.    G.

SILVANI, GROSEFFO ANTONIO (b. Bologna, late 17th cent. ; d. before 1727), was maestro di cappella at S. Stefano from 1702–25. He inherited the publishing business of Marino Silvani, who may have been his father, and who issued several important collections of motets, etc. His published works are as follows :

Op.
1. Litanie concertate a 4 voci.  1702.
2. Inni sacri per tutto l' anno a voce sola.  1702.
3. Sacri responsorii per . . . la settimana santa a 4 voci.  1704.
4. Inni sacri per tutto l' anno a 4 voci.  1705.
5. Cantate morali e spirituali a 1, 2, 3 voci.  1707.
6. Stabat mater, Benedictus, Miserere, etc., a 8 voci.  1708.
7. Messe brevi concertate a 4 voci.  1711.
8. Motetti a 8 voci.  1711.
9. Motetti con le quatro Antifone a voce sola.  1713.
10. Motetti a 2 e 3 voci.  1716.
11. Messe brevi a 4 voci.  1720.
12. Versi della turba, etc., a 4 voci.  1724.
13. Sacre Lamentazioni a voce sola.  1725.
14. Litanie della B.V. a 4 voci concertate.  1725.

All these have accompaniments (some *ad libitum*) for strings or organ. (*Q.-L.*)    M.

SIMÃO, see PORTUGAL (2).

SIMILAR MOTION is the progression of parts or voices in a similar direction, as—

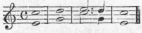

As a matter of contrapuntal effect it is weaker and less effective than CONTRARY MOTION (*q.v.*).
C. H. H. P.

SIMILI, ' like ' ; a word commonly used in a series of passages or figures of similar form, to be performed in exactly the same way. After the first few bars of such passages or figures the word *simili* is used to save trouble of copying the marks of expression and force at every recurrence of the figure. (See ABBREVIATIONS.)
M.

SIMMES (SIMES, SIMS), WILLIAM (late 16th and early 17th cent.), English church music composer. He contributed an anthem to Thomas Myriell's collection ' Tristitia re- medium,' 1616 (B.M. Add. MSS. 29,3′. 2-7). Seven Phantazias for 5 viols by Simmes are at Oxford (Ch. Ch., 716-20.)

ANTHEMS

Arise, a 5.  B.M. Add. MSS. 29,427/33b.  Altus part only.
Away fond thoughts, a 6.  B.M. Add. MSS. 29,366-8.  Cantus, bassus and quintus parts only.  Ch. Ch. 56-60.  Bass part wanting.
Haste Thee, O God, a 5.  B.M. Add. MSS. 29,366-8.  Cantus, bassus and quintus parts only.
Mount up, my soule, a 5.  Ch. C.d 61-66.
Rise, O my soule, a 5.  B.M. Add. MSS. ℠7,402-6.  Incomp.  Ch. Ch. 56-60.  Bass part wanting.  B.M. Add. MSS. 29,366-8.  Cantus bassus and quintus parts only.
J. M˟.

1 Haberl, *Bausteine*, iii. p. 69.

SIMMS, (1) JOHN (b. Stourbridge, Worcs., 1744; d. 1824), organist and violinist, founder of a family of organists. He devoted much time to the construction and improvement of various musical instruments, and was one of the early makers of the 'upright harpsichord.' His eight sons held organistships in Birmingham, Stourbridge and the neighbourhood. The most noted of these were (2) BISHOP, organist of St. Philip's Church (now the Cathedral), 1790–1830, and St. Mary's Chapel, Birmingham. He played at the Commemoration Service held at St. Philip's after the Battle of Waterloo; (3) JAMES, organist of Bromsgrove and Chaddesley; (4) EDWARD, organist of Ashburn and Oakover; (5) JESSE, organist of Handsworth Old Church; (6) SAMUEL, organist of St. Thomas's Church, Stourbridge, for fifty-four years; (7) HENRY, also organist at Stourbridge. (8) HENRY, second son of Jesse (5), succeeded Bishop at St. Philip's and held the post for forty years.

(9) EDWARD (b. 1800; d. 1892), organist, pianist and teacher, eldest son of Jesse (5), was organist at St. Michael's Church, Coventry, for fifty-eight years and conductor of the Coventry Choral Union, studied under Kalkbrenner in London whilst still a boy, and at the age of 13 was appointed organist at Wombourne, near Wolverhampton. George Eliot was one of his pupils.

(10) SAMUEL (b. 1835; d. 1885), son of Samuel (6), succeeded his father as organist at St. Thomas's Church, Stourbridge, remaining there for twenty-six years. He then became organist and choirmaster at St. Cyprian's Church, Hay Mills, Birmingham, until his death five years later. His son, (11) SAMUEL, succeeded him (1885). The Birmingham Glee Union singers were connected with St. Cyprian's; and the choir furnished some of the most noted local singers at the Birmingham Musical Festivals.

(12) FRANCIS HENRY (b. Stourbridge, 1853; d. New Orleans, U.S.A., 1901), grandson of Henry (7), was a pupil of Dr. Arnold. In 1875 he gained in open competition the organistship of All Saints Church, Ryde, I.W. He remained there for fourteen years, and founded and conducted the Ryde Philharmonic Society, which is still (1926) in existence. In 1889 he went to New Orleans to train and introduce the first boy-choir in that city. This was in connexion with St. Paul's Episcopal Church, where he was organist and choirmaster until his death. He was director of music at the H. Sophie Newcomb Memorial College (Tulane University).

SIMON, ANTON YULIEVICH (b. France, 1851), composer, received his musical education at the Paris Conservatoire and migrated to Moscow in 1871, where he became conductor to the Théâtre Bouffe. He was appointed professor of the pianoforte to the school of the Philharmonic Society in 1891, and a year or

two later he was made superintendent of the orchestras of the imperial theatres in Moscow and musical director of the Alexandrovsky Institute. The following is a summary of his principal works :

A. OPERATIC

'Rolla' (op. 40, Moscow, 1892); 'The Song of Love Triumphant' (op. 46, libretto from Tourgeniev by N. Wilde, Moscow, 1899); 'The Fishers' (op. 51, libretto from Victor Hugo by N. Wilde, Moscow, 1900); 'The Stars' (ballet in 5 acts, Moscow, 1902); 'Living Flowers' (op. 58, ballet in 1 act); 'Esmeralda' (mimodrama in 4 acts, Moscow, 1902).

B. ORCHESTRAL

Overture (op. 13); suite (op. 29); 'Danse Bayadère' (op. 34) overture-fantasia on Malo-Russian themes (op. 35); symphonic poems, 'The Midnight Review' and 'La Pécheresse' (opp. 36 and 44); triumphal overture on 3 Russian themes, composed for the unveiling of the monument to Alexander II., Moscow (op. 54).

C. INSTRUMENTAL AND CHAMBER MUSIC

Pianoforte concerto (op. 19); clarinet concerto (op. 30); fantasia for violoncello (op. 42); 2 pianoforte trios (opp. 16 and 25); string quartet (op. 24); quartet for 2 cornets-à-piston and alto and tenor trombones (op. 23); 22 ensemble pieces for wind instruments (op. 26); 4 septets; 4 sextets; 6 quintets; 8 quartets. A considerable number of pieces for one and two pianos; pieces for violin and pianoforte, including the popular 'Berceuse' (op. 28); a Mass (op. 22); three female choruses (op. 33); and upwards of 80 songs.                                              R. N.

SIMONE BOCCANEGRA, opera in 3 acts, with prologue; libretto by Piave, music by Verdi. Produced Fenice Theatre, Venice, Mar. 12, 1857; remodelled and rescored, with a fresh libretto by Boïto, and reproduced La Scala, Milan, Mar. 24, 1881.                    G.

SIMONETTI, ACHILLE (b. Turin, June 12, 1859), violinist and composer. In early youth he studied the violin under Gamba, and composition under Pedrotti, late principal of Rossini's Conservatorio in Pesaro. Later, proceeding to Genoa, he placed himself in the hands of Camillo Sivori, who took great interest in him, and whose clear-cut style and Italian temperament are reflected in his playing. After some successful appearances in Marseilles and Lyons he went to Paris to receive further tuition from Charles Dancla (violin), and Massenet (counterpoint), passed four winters at Nice, and then visited England to fulfil an engagement to tour with the Marie Roze Company and B. Schönberger the pianist. He settled in London and became well known as soloist and member of the LONDON TRIO (q.v.), whilst he occasionally visited Vienna and other continental cities. Besides a series of graceful soli for the violin, which have achieved considerable popularity, he wrote two sonatas for violin and pianoforte and two string quartets.                             W. W. C.

SIMONS-CANDEILLE, see CANDEILLE (2).

SIMOUTRE. NICOLAS EUGÈNE (b. Mirecourt, Apr. 19, 1839), a French violin-maker, the patentee of certain inventions by which he claimed to improve the tone of violins and instruments of that class—either of defective or feeble timbre. The son of a luthier, he was first the pupil of his father, then of Darche in Paris and lastly of Roth in Strassburg. He began work as an independent maker at Basle in 1859, and there published in 1883 his brochure entitled Aux amateurs du violon. In 1886 a second brochure — Un Progrès en *lutherie*—appeared, a German edition being published at the same time entitled *Ein Fortschritt in der Geigenbaukunst* (Rixheim, 1886, 2nd edition, 1887). In 1889 he brought out a small *Supplement* to the above pamphlets. The two last-named works deal mainly with his inventions. The principal of these, called ' Le Support harmonique,' was based upon Savart's scientific discovery that the belly of a violin vibrates unequally. Testing the nodal lines formed by sand distributed upon the belly of a violin when in vibration, Simoutre observed that the fibres of the wood vibrated in alternate sections, *i.e.* one and three vibrated in unison, likewise two and four, and that the vibrations of one and two were as much in opposition to one another as were three and four. Starting from this point, he applied himself to the discovery of a system which should stop the vibrations of alternate fibre sections so as to allow the rest to vibrate in unison, and this he claimed to do with his patent ' support harmonique.' Briefly, this invention consists in glueing two small sections of wood—variable in form and dimensions according to the effect required—upon the centre of the belly and back of the violin transversely. This method, he considered, concentrated the vibrations near the sound-post—where they are most numerous—and by so doing increased the sonority of the instrument so furnished, and at the same time prevented the belly from sinking under the pressure of the bridge. Various experiments for ascertaining the best thickness and forms of the ' support harmonique ' resulted in the discovery that an innovation in the form of the bass bar was necessary where the new system was employed. A semi-detached bar slightly scooped out at the centre, and glued only at each end to the belly of the violin, was patented by Simoutre, that form proving most efficacious where the violin was free from cracks, etc. A third patent applies to the setting of the sound-post in one of the two small circular grooves made for it in the lower ' support harmonique.' In 1890 this maker settled in Paris at 38 Rue de l'Échicquier, where he worked for many years in partnership with his son.

BIBL.—VON LUTGENDORFF, *Die Geigen- und Lautenmacher*, and Simoutre's works already mentioned.                    E. H.-A.

SIMPLIFICATION SYSTEM (organ). This refers to a method formerly in use of planting all the pipes of an organ in semitonal or chromatic order, to simplify the mechanism, but now discontinued for various reasons. (See VOGLER.)                    T. E.

SIMPSON, (SYMPSON) CHRISTOPHER (*d.* 1669), a distinguished 17th-century viola da gamba player famous in his day both as an executant and a theoretic musician. Very little is known of his life, and the exact date of his birth remains problematical, but the few facts that have come to light reveal him to have been the son of a Yorkshire yeoman—a descendant of some Nottinghamshire Simpsons, who spelt their name with a *y* (*vide* Harl. MS. 5800)—a man commended by his fellows for his upright habits, and a staunch upholder of the Cavalier Party against the Parliament. He joined the Royalist army under the command of William Cavendish, Duke of Newcastle, in 1643. He alludes in a passing phrase to the hardships and poverty he endured at this period in his ' Introduction ' to the second edition of his *Division Viol*, 1667, when he thanks his patron —Sir Robert Bolles[1] for the ' Cheerful Maintenance ' he had afforded him. This Sir Robert Bolles and his family were all ardent patrons of music, and at the end of the civil war Christopher Simpson enjoyed their hospitality at their residence, Scampton, Lincolnshire. To him was assigned the musical tuition of Sir Robert's son and heir, John Bolles, and a certain Sir John Barber, and in this congenial musical atmosphere Simpson began to write his valuable book of instructions for the gamba, which he called *The Division Viol*. The excellence of this work is confirmed by Sir Roger L'Estrange, himself a distinguished gamba player, who remarks in the preface to the second edition that ' it is not only the *Best* but the *only Treatise* I find extant upon this argument.' Simpson's pupil, John Bolles, attained a high degree of proficiency as a viola da gamba player, and a laudatory ' Ode ' addressed to him while in Rome is inserted by Simpson, with pardonable pride, in the second edition of his *Division Viol*. On assuming the title at the death of his father, John Bolles showed his regard for his old master by continuing the patronage which had previously been extended him by Sir Robert. This was fortunate ; as was also the fact that Simpson's publications brought him in a good income, for Sir R. Bolles, whose will he witnessed, left him only the sum of £5. Before that event came to pass the eminent gambist had purchased a house and farm—' Hunt-house '—near Pickering, in Yorkshire, and settled this property, by deed, upon his nephew Christopher the son of Stephen Simpson. According to evidence gained from Simpson's will, he died in the year 1669, between the 5th May and the 29th July. Apparently his demise took place at one of Sir John Bolles's residences, for although Hawkins (*History*) states that he died at Turnstile, Holborn, where he had lived for many years, his contemporary Anthony à Wood records ' Anno 1669, Mr. Christopher Sympson, a famous musitian, died at Sir John Bolles house, whether in Lyncolnshire

[1] Davey, *History of English Music* (1921 ed.), p. 274, asserts that ' Bolles had fought on the Parliamentary side in the war.'

or London I know not.' Although nothing is definitely known as to whether Simpson married or not, it may be assumed, from his leaving all his property to his nephew, and all his 'musick-books or whatsoever is of that concernment' to Sir John Bolles, that he did not.

Simpson's skill was greatly respected by his contemporaries, and musicians such as Locke, Salmon, Mace, and Sir Roger L'Estrange have shown their esteem by their various complimentary allusions to him. He lived in an age when the gamba was much cultivated, both by professionals and amateurs; but besides being the best authority on that instrument he was a composer of talent, and Mace (*Musick's Monument*, 1676) ranks him with William Lawes and John Jenkins as a composer of 'Fancies.' The Bodleian (Mus. Sch.) possesses a portrait [1] of Simpson, and there is a miniature of him by T. Flaxman.

### LIST OF PUBLISHED WORKS

1. Annotations on Dr. Campion's *Art of Discant*, 1655. These remarks were introduced into the second edition of Playford's *Brief Introduction*, 1660, and in the other editions until 1684.
2. The Division Violist or an Introduction to the playing upon a ground : Divided into two parts. The first Directing the Hand with other Preparative Instructions. The second, Laying open the Manner and Method of playing Ex-tempore, or Composing division to a ground. To which are Added some Divisions made upon Grounds for the Practice of Learners, London, 1659. W. Godbid, for J. Playford. Fol. (with portrait). Dedicated to Sir Robert Bolles.
Second Edition with title and text in Latin and English thus : Chelys minuritionum artificio exornata : sive Minuritiones ad Basin, etiam Extempore Modulandi Ratio. In tres partes distributa. The Division Viol or the Art of Playing Extempore upon a Ground. Divided into Three Parts. London, 1665. Fol. with portrait. A further supply of this second Edition was published by W. Godbid for Henry Brome at the Gun in Ivy Lane in 1667. Fol. with portrait by Faithorne engraved from a painting by G. Carwarden. Dedicated to Sir John Bolles.
Third edition published by Pearson, with portrait of Simpson engraved by Faithorne, appeared in 1712. With two Sonatas for the gamba.
3. The Principles of Practicle Musick . . . either in singing or playing upon an instrument, London, 1665. Dedicated to Sir John Bache—A compendium of Practicall Musick in five parts teaching by a new and easie method. 1. The rudiments of Song. 2. The principles of composition. 3. The use of discords. 4. The form of Figurate Discant. 5. The contrivance of Canon. W. Godbid for H. Brome, 1667. Dedicated to William Cavendish, Duke of Newcastle. The first part of this, the *Rudiments of Song*, was reprinted in a revised form.
Third Edition. London, W. Godbid for Henry Brome, 1678.
Fourth Edition. W. Pearson for T. Cullen, 1706.
Fifth Edition. London, 1714.
Sixth Edition. London, 1722.
Seventh Edition. 1727.
Eighth Edition. 1732, W. Pearson.
Ninth Edition, with portrait.
In Playford's 'Catch that Catch can,' 1672–73, there is a composition of Simpson's, and Hawkins (*Hist. of Music*) mentions a 'Division on the Ground ' for viola da gamba by Simpson of the year 1665.
In Thomas Campion's *Art of Setting or Composing of Music* there is a composition by Simpson for the viola da gamba.

### MS. COMPOSITIONS

A Series of Suites in Three parts (B M. Add. MSS. 18,940, 18,944).
Months and Seasons, namely Fancies, Airs, Galliards for two Basses and a Treble (*Ib.* 31,436).
Consorts of Parts for two Basses and two Trebles with figured Bass. (Heidelberg, MS. 3193.)
Rules of Theory (B.M. MS. 142).
Fancies for a viola da gamba (Ch. Ch.).
Fancies and Divisions (B.M. MS. 31,436 and Bodl. Lib.).
Musgrave, in his *Obituary*, mentions a MS. (music) under the late 1666, by Christopher Simpson.

BIBL.—HAWKINS, *Hist. Music* ; BURNEY, *Hist. Music* ; MACE, *Musick's Monument* ; LOCKE, *Observations* ; HART, *The Violin and its Music* ; WASIELEWSKI, *Die Violoncell* ; Q.-L. ; FÉTIS, *Biog. des Mus.* ; SIMPSON, *The Division Viol* ; ANTHONY À WOOD, *Life*.

E. H.-A.

SIMPSON, JOHN (*d. circa* 1747), a London music-publisher and instrument-seller of some note. As may be gathered from one of his early engraved labels, he had been employed by Mrs.

[1] See *Mus. Ant.*, Apr. 1913, p. 148.

Hare of Cornhill, the widow of Joseph HARE (*q.v.*), but about 1734 he began business on his own account at the 'Viol and Flute ' in Sweeting's Alley, a street running out of Cornhill, at the back part of the Royal Exchange. In Simpson's early business career this was named 'Swithen's Alley,' but in 1741 references to Simpson give this address indifferently with 'Sweeting's Alley.' He first published sheet songs, which he afterwards gathered into the two volumes as 'Thesaurus musicus' (*c.* 1745–47), and had probably bought the stock and plates of both Mrs. Hare and B. Cooke. He was in business connexion with the proprietors of the 'Printing-house in Bow Church yard,' who were successors to CLUER (*q.v.*).

Simpson's most notable publications are : 'Thesaurus musicus,' in which 'God save the King' probably first appeared; Carey's 'Musical Century,' 1740 ; 'Calliope,' 1746; and much other music now of considerable antiquarian interest. He was succeeded by John Cox, who reissued from Simpson's plates.

At Cox's death, or retirement, Robert Bremner, Thorowgood, and the Thompson family became possessed of many of Simpson's plates, and republished some of his works. In 1770, and thirty years later, Simpson's premises were occupied by John and James Simpson, apparently descendants, who were flute-makers, and, in a small way, music-publishers. Later than this (*c.* 1825) a John Simpson was manufacturer and teacher of the flute and flageolet at 266 Regent Street.          F. K.

SIMPSON, THOMAS, an English musician, who settled in Germany, and in 1610 was viola-player in the Elector Palatine's band ; in 1617–1621 he was in the band of the Prince of Holstein Schaumburg. He was subsequently in the royal band at Copenhagen. He published the following works : ' Opusculum neuer Pauanen, Galliarden, Couranten vnd Volten,' Frankfort, 1610 ; 'Pauanen, Volten und Galliarden,' Frankfort, 1611 ; 'Opus Newer Paduanen, Galliarden, Intraden, . . . mit 5 Stim.,' Hamburg, 1617, and 'Taffel Consort allerhand lustige Lieder von 4 Instrumenten und General-bass,' Hamburg, 1621, containing, besides pieces by Simpson himself, some by Peter Phillips, John Dowland, Robert and Edward Johnson, and others.          W. H. H.

SIMROCK, a famous German music-publishing house, founded in 1790 at Bonn by (1) NIKOLAUS SIMROCK (1752–1834), second waldhorn player in the Elector's band, to which Beethoven and his father belonged. The first of Beethoven's works on which Simrock's name appears as original publisher is the Kreutzer Sonata, op. 47, issued in 1805. But he published for Beethoven an ' Édition très correcte ' of the two sonatas in G and D minor (op. 31, Nos. 1 and 2), which Nägeli had printed so shamefully ; and there is evidence in the letters that Simrock was concerned in others of Beethoven's early works. The next was the sextet for strings and two horns, op. 81*b* (1810) ; then the two sonatas for PF. and violoncello, op. 102 (1817) ; the ten themes with variations for PF. and violin or flute, op. 107 (1820).

He was succeeded in 1834 by (2) PETER JOSEPH (*d.* 1868), and about 1870 his successor, (3) FRITZ AUGUST (*b.* Jan. 2, 1838 ; *d.* Lausanne, Aug. 20, 1901), founded the Berlin house, and there published the principal works of Brahms. (*Q.-L.*) His nephew (4) HANS (*d.* Berlin, June 26, 1910) succeeded, but in 1902 the firm became a company. G.

SÍN, OTAKAR (*b.* Rokytne, Moravia, 1881), Czech composer and pianist. Sín studied at the Prague Conservatoire, became a professor in 1920, and in 1922 was appointed the administrative head of that institution. He has written a symphonic poem, 'Tilottama'; a string quartet; and a considerable number of pianoforte pieces, some admirably adapted for children's use ; two albums of pianoforte pieces (publishers, Chadim and Hudební Matice, Prague). R. N.

SINCLAIR, GEORGE ROBERTSON, Mus.D. (*b.* Croydon, Oct. 28, 1863 ; *d.* Birmingham, Feb. 7, 1917), son of Robert Sharpe Sinclair, LL.D., Director of Public Instruction in India, was educated at St. Michael's College, Tenbury, and at the Royal Irish Academy of Music. He studied successively under Sir Frederick Gore Ouseley, Sir Robert Stewart and Dr. C. H. Lloyd. In 1879 he became assistant organist of Gloucester Cathedral, and organist and choirmaster of St. Mary de Crypt, Gloucester ; in 1880, at the age of 17, he was appointed organist and choirmaster of Truro Cathedral. From 1889 until his death he filled the post of organist of Hereford Cathedral with distinction, and his conducting of the Hereford (Three Choirs) Festivals from 1891 to 1912 brought him into contact with the most eminent English musicians of the time, and ripened his experience as a conductor. In this capacity he exhibited very remarkable powers, being in sympathy with every school of excellence, and being able to impress his own reading of the classical and other works upon all under his command. He was conductor of various Hereford and Herefordshire societies, both choral and orchestral, and of the Birmingham Festival Choral Society (1899–1917). In 1895 he was made an honorary member of the R.A.M., having been L.R.A.M. since 1887, and received the degree of Mus.D. from the Archbishop of Canterbury. In 1904 he was made an honorary fellow of the R.C.O. He was also an ardent Freemason, a Past Grand Organist of England, a Past Master of the Palladian Lodge, No. 120, and Master of the 'Vaga' Lodge, No. 3146. His impetuous character, his skilful pedal-playing, the barking of his dog, and other things, are immortalised in the eleventh variation of Elgar's 'Enigma' set for orchestra. (See *Mus. T.*, 1906, pp. 168 ff.) M.

SINCLAIR, JOHN (*b.* near Edinburgh, Dec. 9, 1791 ; *d.* Margate, Sept. 23, 1857), was instructed in music from childhood, and while still young joined the band of a Scotch regiment as a clarinet-player. He also taught singing in Aberdeen, and acquired sufficient means to purchase his discharge from the regiment. Possessed of a fine tenor voice, he was desirous of trying his fortune upon the stage, came to London and appeared anonymously as Capt. Cheerly in Shield's 'Lock and Key' at the Haymarket, Sept. 7, 1810. His success led to his becoming a pupil of Thomas Welsh. He was engaged at Covent Garden, where he appeared Sept. 30, 1811, as Don Carlos in Sheridan and Linley's 'Duenna.' He remained there for seven seasons, during which he had many original parts. He was the first singer of the long popular recitative and air 'The Pilgrim of Love' in Bishop's 'Noble Outlaw,' produced Apr. 7, 1815. He also sang originally in Bishop's 'Guy Mannering' and 'The Slave,' and Davy's 'Rob Roy,' and acquired great popularity by his performance of Apollo in 'Midas.' In Apr. 1819 he visited Paris and studied under Pellegrini, and thence proceeded to Milan and placed himself under Banderali. In May 1821 he went to Naples, where he received advice and instruction from Rossini. In 1822 he sang, mostly in Rossini's operas, at Pisa and Bologna. In 1823 he was engaged at Venice, where Rossini wrote for him the part of Idreno in 'Semiramide.' After singing at Genoa he returned to England, and reappeared at Covent Garden, Nov. 19, 1823, as Prince Orlando in 'The Cabinet,' his voice and style having greatly improved. He continued at the theatre for a season or two ; in 1828 and 1829 was engaged at the Adelphi, and in 1829–30 at Drury Lane. He then visited America ; and on his return retired from public life. W. H. H.

SINDING, CHRISTIAN (*b.* Kongberg, Norway, Jan. 11, 1856), became a student at Leipzig, at Munich and at Berlin, after which he settled in Christiania and devoted himself to composition.

A very talented pianist, he has written much for his own instrument as well as for stringed instruments. His principal works are the rondo infinito for orchestra, op. 42 ; two violin concertos (in A, op. 45, and D major, op. 60); piano concerto in D flat, op. 6 ; quintet in E minor, op. 5 ; trio in D major, op. 23 ; variations for two pianos, op. 2 ; suite, op. 3 ; studies, op. 7 ; sonatas for violin and piano ; suite for violin and piano, op. 14 ; caprices, op. 44 ; burlesques, op. 48; six pieces, op. 49 ; string quartet, op. 70 ; three symphonies (D minor, op. 21; D major, op. 83; F major, op. 121) ; besides many songs and many arrangements of Folksongs. An opera, 'Det Hellige Bjerg' (The Holy Mount), was produced at Dessau in

1914. Nikisch produced the F major symphony at Leipzig in 1921. Sinding's music is characterised by great facility in construction, tunefulness, variety and elegance. He is always intelligent, and even if not deep is a very pleasing writer, who secures the interest of his auditor.       D. H., with addns.

SINFONIA, see SYMPHONY.

SINGAKADEMIE, see BERLIN.

SINGING is the musical expression of the voice. It is part of our natural condition to possess organs for the production of sound, and perceptions to make them musical, and, being thus equipped, it is but natural that the art of music should be intimately associated with human life.

Like many of the other animals, we express our pain, sorrow, joy, pleasure, hunger, rage, satisfaction and love in sounds which have their vital and instinctive meaning like any of the actions or gestures associated with the elemental functions of human nature. We have no more necessity than they have, however imitative we may be, to look to external phenomena for the origin of this wonderful possession. It is natural to the infant to cry when it is cold or hungry, and crow when it is pleased. So, with the growth of sensibility and perception, a little child knows how to plead with its voice, in tones quite different from those of mere asking, without any vocal training whatever. The same instinct which has enabled the child to appeal to its parents and fellow-creatures has taught man to approach his God with praise and supplication. But the most remarkable indication of the instinctiveness of song is the characteristic growth of the voice organs at the outset of manhood and womanhood. It is as if the full development of the body were crowned with the completion of the instruments of sound, which express with such particular eloquence the passions and emotions attendant upon the great mystery of sex.

Through the growth and refinement of our perceptions, the art of singing becomes the musical expression of every emotion suggested by thought and imagination.

It not infrequently happens that individuals are born to attain by the light of nature to a high degree of accomplishment in this art ; and even when this is not so, the inherent sincerity of imperfect singing can sometimes appeal more powerfully to our feelings than the most efficient training could make it do. While the whole of humanity is probably in some measure acquainted with the feeling of a desire to sing, and the form and condition of the vocal instruments appear to be as a rule normally fitted for the production of musical sound, the wonder is that everybody cannot do it. But there is no doubt that the fault lies more often in defective musical perception than in the condition of the organs of voice.

Music demands a high development of a particular sense, the foundation of which is inborn, though its perfection requires cultivation ; and therefore there are individuals who have all the materials for singing, but are still without the faculty of using them for that purpose. Another important obstacle to the acquirement of the power of singing is that, with the intellectual development of the race has arisen a demand for perfection in speech and diction, which often interferes with the process of vocal training.

It should be remembered that language is a purely artificial acquisition of mankind. We all have to spend years in acquiring habits of speech so that we may understand and explain the ordinary circumstances of life. So local is this, that we grow up speaking the language which prevails around us, by the simple process of imitation, without thinking whether its sounds are musical or not, and this introduces a series of common difficulties which are more linguistic than vocal, and which will be considered more fully later on.

It thus becomes apparent that the art of singing has within it a great deal that is quite outside the province of music. For although the musical expression of the voice is of prime importance, the whole foundations of the instruments involved belong strictly to the province of physiology, like any of the other natural functions of the body, and by far the greater share of its educational side belongs to the study of the speech organs.

The science of phonology (*i.e.* the science of vocal sound) has been specialised from its parent science of physiology, so that it may occupy itself solely with the study of all the problems involved in this important subject, and, by an obligatory knowledge of music and languages, carry out its conclusions in the service of the art.

The first step towards understanding singing is to acquire a knowledge of the forces and instruments which it employs, and their phonological outline should, therefore, be made clear before the fuller details are filled in.

The voice is built upon the same physical principles as a reed-pipe of an organ. There is (1) a wind-chest in which the air is compressed ; (2) a ' reed ' which vibrates and produces the sound ; and (3) a resonator, which gives it certain qualities.

(1) By the act of breathing out, we compress the air which has been taken into the chest. This force in being liberated causes (2) the vocal ' reed ' to vibrate when we bring it into position and the sound thus produced is then modified by (3) the resonator, formed by the hollows in the neck, mouth and nose, which give quality to the sound, and impress upon it the characteristics of language.

Under these headings the components of the

voice can be studied separately, and their more complex combined performances are then more easily understood.

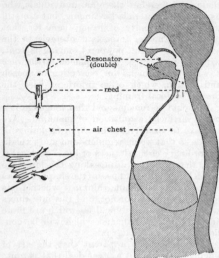

THE BREATH.—The ordinary breathing of everyday life brings oxygen into contact with the blood in the lungs and carries carbonic acid away from it. Elevation of the ribs expands the chest and increases its circumference, and the contraction of the diaphragm lowers its floor and enlarges its capacity in a downward direction. The two actions go on together and draw a sufficient volume of fresh air (30 cubic inches) into the lungs with a slow, easy movement. The used air is more quickly emitted, principally by the elastic recoil of the lungs and chest, and after that there is a slight pause. This occurs about fifteen times a minute.

Breathing for singing is very different. Its whole object is to maintain a long and well-regulated air-pressure for the production of sound. A full breath must often be taken very rapidly, and then kept in a state of controlled compression for as much as 20 seconds. Thus the number of respirations possible in a minute may be reduced to a minimum. This necessitates a much larger volume of breath than is ordinarily needed, not only for the length of time the sound may have to continue, but also for the supply of oxygen to the blood. The first point is, therefore, to secure the power of taking in a large volume of air as quickly as possible. The second point is to give it out with carefully regulated force, for upon this the controlled production of sound entirely depends.

BREATHING IN.—The largest amount of air can be inhaled by the properly combined action of raising the ribs (costal breathing) and of contracting the diaphragm (diaphragmatic breathing). The latter has also been called 'abdominal' breathing, from the fact that the diaphragm is hidden and the evidence of its contraction is the protrusion of the abdominal wall caused by lowering the roof of that cavity. Men make more use of the diaphragm than women, whose upper ribs are more movable, but singers of both sexes have to make good use of both diaphragm and ribs.

There are reasons, especially in women, against the extreme use of the diaphragm on account of the pressure it exerts upon the abdominal organs, besides the difficulty of controlling the breath when so taken. This has caused a great deal of misunderstanding between doctors and singing-masters, and has produced extreme views on either side, neither of which can be supported by phonology.

When the ribs are fully raised, and especially the lower ones (6th-10th) which are the most elastic and movable, and correspond to the thickest part of the lungs, not only is the circumference of the chest increased and its floor widened, but the roof and upper part of the abdomen is also enlarged. Under these circumstances a considerable contraction of the diaphragm will cause no more than a protrusion of the upper part of the abdomen, that is, above the waist and between the margins of the ribs in front, without causing any harmful pressure upon the abdominal organs. The more the lower ribs expand, the more the diaphragm may descend with impunity, and a large in-take of breath can be obtained without danger. It has been called 'central' breathing, because the principal expansion takes place in the centre at the level of the space between the 6th and 7th ribs, and is designed to promote a good proportion of both actions, and to avoid the disproportionate or exclusive use of either the too high costal and clavicular breathing, or the too low purely abdominal breathing, both of which are sometimes advocated by extremists.

BREATHING OUT.—In order to secure an even and continuous air-pressure three forces have to be considered :

1. The elastic recoil of the inflated lungs and expanded chest ;

2. The contraction of abdominal muscles that assist the relaxed diaphragm to return to its place ; and

3. The contraction of muscles that pull down the ribs.

The elastic recoil does most of the work in ordinary breathing out, and is most useful in producing sound, only it is a force that begins with a maximum and rapidly diminishes.

To make the force continuous, it must be augmented by one of the others. These may act together or separately. If they act together they must maintain their proper proportion throughout. If they act separately the diaphragm must be replaced by abdominal contraction first, that is, before the ribs are allowed to descend, for, as has already been stated, the subsidence of the expanded chest while the diaphragm is contracted causes too much abdominal distension.

Those who have developed a good expansion of the lower ribs will be able to maintain that expansion while the diaphragm is supported by the abdominal muscles, and the upper part of the abdomen becomes concave before the ribs are allowed to descend. In this manner very great delicacy in breath-control can be exercised. When the capacity is large enough the ribs can be kept expanded while the diaphragm moves to and fro, opposed by the abdominal muscles, and thus the breathing both in and out becomes entirely diaphragmatic or abdominal. This is the only form in which this is permissible, namely, when the ribs are fully expanded all the time and the movement of the abdominal wall is confined to the region above the waist.

Towards the end of a very long phrase, however, the ribs will have to come down. It is better then that only the lower ribs should be relaxed while the upper ribs remain raised as part of a permanent position.

The permanent expansion of the ribs is partly secured by straightening the upper part of the spine in standing or sitting up straight, and the larger amount of residual air retained in the lungs is of great value in maintaining continuity of air-pressure and tone.

It will be noted that the form of breathing here explained and advocated is practically invisible. It is also designed to add to volume the continuity and control of air-pressure necessary to good phrasing. The permanent expansion of the ribs also assists resonation in the neck, an advantage which will be dealt with later.

The VOCAL REED is formed by two elastic membranes or cords which can be drawn together from their position of rest, so that they meet like curtains, and completely close the air-passage at the upper end of the windpipe, where the larynx begins. Their front ends are fixed close together to the shield cartilage, and behind they are attached to two small triangular cartilages which move very freely upon the thick ring-shaped cartilage supporting them. During breathing in they are wide apart, and during breathing out they approach one another. In the act of whispering, they are definitely drawn, so as to reduce the opening between their edges considerably.

As soon as air-pressure acts upon the elas-

ticity of the edges of the membranes they vibrate, in accordance with the physical laws which govern the action of ' reeds ' in general, This may happen before the whole passage is occluded, and a soft ' breathy' note is produced, but the reed acts most strongly and perfectly when the two cartilages are brought into close contact, so that the whole air-pressure acts upon the vibrating edges of the membranes, and is converted into sound.

Singing is practically confined to the last position. The tremor of the elastic membranes rapidly opens and closes the fine slit between their edges and releases the air-pressure in a quick succession of minute puffs. One group of muscles regulates the movements of the small triangular cartilages, by the action of which the membranes are brought together and drawn aside. Another group is concerned with tightening and loosening the membranes, and thereby regulates the tension upon which the rapidity of their vibration depends.

VOCAL COMPASS.—Every vocal reed may be expected to have a compass of two octaves which can be controlled by this function of tension and relaxation, and it must not be forgotten that this tension is an unconscious act guided solely by sound perception or ' ear,' and cannot be appreciated by any muscular sense as in the case of a voluntary movement.

The general pitch of every voice is determined by the size of the membranes. In men they are both wider and thicker than in women, and their length is generally estimated at about $\frac{7}{12}$ths of an inch, and $\frac{5}{12}$ths of an inch in women.

Roughly speaking, the male voice is about an octave lower than the female, but in either sex all degrees of general pitch exist between certain limits. For convenience three types are usually considered—high, low and middle. The majority of voices are near the middle type in both sexes, while exceptional instances of abnormally high or low are sometimes met with.

The male alto voice has an intermediate position between the two groups, but being an unnatural product it cannot be considered with the others.

Thus every voice has its middle note whence it may be expected to range to the extent of an octave upwards and downwards by performing the same muscular action. In the figure the middle note of each voice is indicated by a double vertical line.

Besides the tension of the membranes there is another physical condition which undergoes variation with every change of pitch, and that is the air-pressure exerted by the breath.

From experiments [1] it is found that the air-pressure varies in about the same ratio as the tension.

Therefore, in a general plan of the vocal compass, the middle note may be regarded as the product of both mean tension and mean air-pressure. The tension is well known to vary in the ratio of the square of the vibrations, and thus both the tension and air-pressure may be represented by the numbers 1, 4, 9, 16, 25, while the vibrations are as 1, 2, 3, 4, 5, in the diagram appended.

| Pressure and Tension. | Vibrations. | Compass. | Working Capacity. |
|---|---|---|---|
| Extreme = 25 | 5 | 3rd + | |
| High = 16 | 4 | 8ve | |
| = 9 | 3 | | |
| Mean = 4 | 2 | Centre | |
| Low = 1 | 1 | 8ve + | |
| Extreme | | 3rd | |

The working capacity of the voice is here represented by a triangle whose apex is opposite the centre of the compass, which signifies that the middle can do the most work when the whole compass is evenly balanced throughout. Then by a common control of tension and pressure the vibrations are varied so that the notes of a two-octave compass can be used at will. With training an extension upwards and downwards of a third more may still be possible, but it is always desirable that the extremes of the voice should be kept for exceptional use only. Composers are accustomed to fix the voices for which they write by the extreme limits only, which is not phonological. It is more important to adapt the principal share of the work to the centre of the voice.

A more or less exact method of estimating the amount of work demanded by a vocal composition has been made use of in the 'song diagram,' of which two examples are here given. Without considering accidentals, the values of the notes are added together and arranged according to pitch. Starting from a vertical line upon which the pitch is indicated, the total values are expressed in horizontal black lines. The diagram so obtained shows upon what notes the principal work lies, and the application to that of the centre of the 'working capacity' reveals at once the type of voice to which the composition is suited.

[1] M'Kendrick, *Schäfer's Physiology.*

The example from 'Tristan and Isolde' shows that Wagner demands for the part of Isolde a high soprano voice of exceptional development, with its centre on *b'*, and a full compass of over two octaves. Mozart's 'Il mio tesoro' only

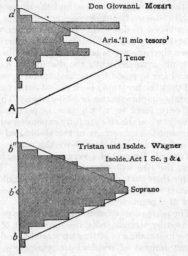

once touches the upper limit of the ordinary tenor compass, and yet it lies so much in the upper part of the voice that it is best suited to a high tenor with a centre above *a*.

The examination of a great number of these diagrams, which are easily made upon paper ruled in squares, will explain a great deal that is interesting to the practical musician, but they do not supply more than a part of what is called the 'tessitura' of vocal music, which includes the length and distribution of phrases and pauses, as well as the declamatory consideration of the question of vocality.

Many voices have been ruined by composers' neglect of vocal considerations, and it is not uncommon to find soprano singers who have lost the middle of the voice entirely. It is not difficult to calculate the great relief to the forces of tension and breath-pressure which even slight transposition will give; and, conversely, the amount of strain which has to be borne by the voice, if the work is pitched too high, cannot fail to wear out and distort the instrument prematurely.

These considerations might with advantage be taken into account by those who are responsible for modern musical PITCH (*q.v.*). It is to be hoped that a wider phonological knowledge may tend to remove some of the bitter struggles that are too often witnessed in the performance of modern music.

ATTACK.—The question of the attack of a note has been much debated among masters. Manuel Garcia, and others who followed him, have insisted upon what he himself described as a ' very slight cough ' before a note in order to secure a distinct attack upon it.

Above the vocal membranes and parallel with them are two muscular folds called the false vocal cords, or ventricular bands. In conjunction with the muscles that bring the membranes together, they form a strong constrictor of the air-passage, to close it firmly when required. This occurs always in swallowing, when the chest has to be held inflated to support a strong muscular action, and also in coughing. The elastic vocal membranes are themselves unable to restrain any air-pressure in the chest, so it was thought necessary to accumulate a little force by constriction with these ventricular bands, and by suddenly relaxing them to allow the force to impinge upon the membranes which were supposed to be held in readiness for the sudden shock. There is no doubt that a crisp attack can be effected in this way, but the sound of the note is always preceded by an explosive noise however lightly it may be done.

The first phonological objection to this 'shock of the glottis' (*coup de glotte*) is that it is quite unnecessary. When the breath is under control and intimately associated as it ought to be with the production of sound, the simultaneous onset of breath force and the proper approximation of the membranes produces a perfectly clear and clean attack, straight upon the note by the ordinary natural action performed with decision.

The introduction of any constriction above the reed cannot be regarded as a natural part of the action of attack. Moreover, the quasi-spasmodic act of constriction produces often an unduly hard attack which is not good for the vocal reed, and its constant repetition produces congestion of the parts around the cartilages, and a troublesome desire to clear the throat.

Phonology insists that the production of sound is always the result of an expiratory act, and that every sound effect, whether it be strong or soft, quick or gradual, must be the outcome of a similar intention in the breath-control. Such control leaves the throat free to its unconscious action, which would be destroyed by any muscular constriction in the larynx.

The ' shock of the glottis ' is part of a time-worn tradition in the teaching of singing, and is often heard in voices that are beautiful as well as in those that are hard and throaty; it is sometimes regarded as essential to the proper pronunciation of German and some other languages of a guttural nature, but artificial fashions of speech cannot be tolerated if they are opposed to the natural uses of the voice organs.

The cessation of a note is brought about by the withdrawal of the membranes. As a rule the membranes spring back elastically to their open position, and some breath-pressure escapes in a puff after the note. The amount of this escape, and consequently the sound it makes,

is a matter of breath-control. A high note is naturally followed by a strong burst, because the pressure is higher than that of a low note. The free release, as this is called, is not objected to in operatic singing, and there is nothing to say against it on phonological grounds. Moreover, it is useful in getting rid of carbonic acid, and in facilitating the quick taking of another breath. It may therefore be left to discretion to make the sound of the release inaudible by breath-control.

Under no circumstances should the note be stopped by constriction of any part of the throat, which is frequently associated with the equally detrimental attack by ' shock ' just referred to. Many singers deceive themselves in the belief that their throats remain open when their notes cease.

One of the difficulties in showing the natural behaviour of the vocal membranes with the laryngoscope is that the power of tolerating a mirror in the back of the throat itself requires a long course of training without which the organs under observation cannot act naturally.

THE RESONATOR.—The second vocal instrument, the resonator, belongs, as such, to a later date in the evolution of the voice as we now hear it. The particular function of the resonator, which warrants its being treated as a separate instrument, is its power of modifying sound by assuming different shapes, which is made use of in the formation of language.

Every hollow space enclosed within walls, but communicating with the outer air, is capable of allowing only certain sound vibrations or waves to continue within it. This is called its resonant note, and its pitch corresponds with the size, and its character with the shape, of the resonant cavity or resonator. The pitch is also affected by the size of its opening. Partly closing it not only changes the character of the note, but also lowers its pitch.

In the case of the voice, in which the reed is strong and the resonator comparatively weak, much of the fullness of the sound must depend upon keeping the openings free. At the same time the cavities should be made as large as possible in order to keep their resonant pitches low, and thereby impart a richer tone to the voice.

The size of the resonator varies a little among men; in women it is about 20 per cent smaller, and in children, smaller still. But all, by the same physiological action, can bring it into similar positions, and thus it is the shape of the resonator that gives characteristic qualities to speech, and language is as intelligible in the mouth of a child as in that of a giant.

The sounds of language are divided into two groups.

1. Vowel sounds, due to open and expanded positions of the resonator suitable for continuous sounds of the best possible quality.

2. Consonants, due to more or less closed positions, and movements of the resonator which give certain characters to the approach to and departure from the vowel positions.

The position of the resonator in forming the vowel sounds is a most important question in the art of singing.

So much latitude is permitted in ordinary speaking that pronunciation in singing has been looked upon as something quite different from it. But when the sound of the voice is at its best, the resonator is in the position most favourable to sound. This principle applies as strongly to speaking as it does to singing, and when singers do not sing as they would speak, it is either because they do not speak properly, or they do not use the resonator naturally.

It cannot be too strongly insisted upon that if the principles of good resonation are carefully adhered to from the first, speech, being solely a matter of education, can always be made beautiful.

This is generally neglected in our schools, where children learn their habits of speech, but it is absolutely essential to singing, and not infrequently it happens that a great part of vocal training is spent upon teaching a singer to use the resonator properly, for the first time.

VOWEL SOUNDS.—In studying the sounds belonging to the five signs U, O, A, E, I, the Italian pronunciation is here adopted—

　　　　　U　　O　　A　　E　　I
English Equivalent　(oo)　(or)　(ah)　(eh)　(ee)

The position A is that in which the whole passage is open and expanded to the fullest extent convenient (natural habits never go to extremes), and from it the others are differentiated by two principal actions.

1. Closure of the opening by the lips, and
2. Raising and advancing the body of the tongue.

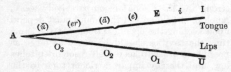

Since A is taken as the basis of our resonation, its position must be closely defined.

The jaw is open at least an inch between the front teeth.

The lips are at rest upon the teeth, and not retracted at the sides.

The tongue lies flat upon the floor of the mouth with its tip and margins touching the backs of the lower teeth.

The base of the tongue is flat enough to make the back of the throat visible from the front.

The palate is held up just enough to prevent breath passing into the nose, but without any conscious effort.

The neck is fully expanded by the combined actions of holding the head erect, the ribs raised, and drawing down the larynx, more by the action of the sterno-thyroid muscles which act upon the larynx from below, than by the sterno-hyoid muscles which bring down the base of the tongue. This position has the form of a double resonator, with two principal resonance chambers uniting in the middle at right angles, where they are joined by a third accessory chamber, the nose.

The back chamber in the neck is shaped like a bag, wide below, where the vocal reed is placed, and narrow above, where it opens into the back of the mouth by an oval opening. The front chamber, in the mouth, is shaped like an irregular hemisphere, with a flat floor and an arched roof and a large round opening in front.

Although the whole resonator acts as one, the back chamber may be said to have most to do with the full resonation of vocal sound ; while to the more variable cavity of the mouth is given the office of forming all the characteristics of language. The accessory cavity of the nose adds to the sound the nasal resonance when required, through the opening controlled by the soft palate. The resonant properties of cavities are demonstrated by blowing a stream of air through or across them, so that their resonant notes can be heard by themselves. This occurs in the whispering voice. The partly closed glottis allows the breath to rush through it without producing any vocal note, and the rushing sound awakens the resonant notes of the air-chambers so distinctly that not only are all the qualities of language distinguishable, but with a little practice the pitch of the resonant notes of the various vowel sounds can be detected. These notes are most distinct, and deeply pitched in the whispering here employed, which requires a fully expanded and open resonator and a reef out-breath with no constriction of the throat whatever.

Following these rules the pitch of the vowel A is commonly found to be $c''$ or $c''\sharp$ among men—and about a minor third higher, $e''\flat$ or $e''$, among women.

The double nature of the resonator can be shown by introducing a tuning-fork of the right pitch into the throat. A strong reinforcement occurs in that position, indicating a ' node ' at the junction of the two chambers, as would be expected. The resonant note may, therefore, be said to belong to both the mouth and the neck cavity acting in unison. This is an important acoustical point, which receives further confirmation in the formation of the other vowels.

The first group of vowels derived from A, by closing the opening with the lips, are three varieties of O, and U which is the most closed. By various degrees of this action, but keeping the jaw still open to the extent of an inch between the front teeth, the positions are obtained for :

|  | A | O³ | O² | O¹ | U |
|---|---|---|---|---|---|
| English Equivalent | ah | not | or | oh | oo. |

By every successive degree of closing, the pitch of the resonant note is lowered, and thus are indicated the several positions which produce the notes of a scale as a simple way of fixing them.

By rounding the lips enough to lower the pitch of A a whole fifth, a good resonant position is found for U (oo), and the deep, middle and shallow forms of O find their proper places upon the three notes intervening.

It will be noticed in practice, as well as in physiological works, that with the closure of the lips there is at the same time a lowering of the larynx and a slight raising of the base of the tongue. Both these actions tend to enlarge and close in the chamber in the neck, and by thus lowering its pitch they maintain the unison of the two chambers, as may be further shown by tapping the cheek and the neck, when both are found to possess the same note.

*Whispered Resonances.*

The second group of vowel sounds owe their character to the position of the tongue. The jaw remains open about an inch as before, then the tongue, with its tip against the back of the front teeth, advances and rises. The lips remain still, the larynx is drawn upwards by the movement of the tongue, but this is restrained to some extent by maintaining the expansion of the neck as in the position of A. This action raises the resonant pitch of the mouth because it becomes gradually encroached upon by the body of the tongue, but while it makes the mouth cavity smaller, it makes the neck cavity larger. When the tongue is so far forward as to touch with its margin the upper molar teeth, the pitch of the mouth resonance may be raised a sixth and the neck resonance lowered a third.

This is the position allotted to the vowel E

neck resonance a fifth, will give a suitable resonance to the vowel I (ee).

The perfect concords of an octave (1 to 2) and a twelfth (1 to 3) established for the relation of the chambers in these two vowel sounds is not a mere accident. It is more probable that

the selection of these sounds as pure vowel sounds in all languages has been due to their particular resonant advantages, for the resonance of a double resonator can only go on perfectly when the component chambers are either in unison or simply related. A further point in the formation of the vowel sounds E and I is that the orifice between the two chambers is made smaller by the approach of the tongue to the hard palate. This lowers the pitch of both, so that the division of the chambers does not take place in linear measurement as upon a monochord.

Intermediate between A and E there are several positions which belong to some of the English vowel sounds in common use. The first movement of the tongue is principally forward, and enlarges the opening of the throat, raising the resonant pitch of both chambers while they remain in unison. This position belongs to the sounds of the unaccented *a* in ' ălone,' the *u* in ' up ' and the *o* in ' love.' But after this the unison can no longer be maintained owing to the disparity of the chambers, and we find their pitches a third apart, which is not very good for the resonation of the sound *er* as in ' earth.' The shallow *ă* as in ' hat ' has resonance chambers a fifth apart, and in the short *ĕ* as in ' get ' they differ by a sixth. Hence all these indefinitely resonated sounds are those which are more frequently varied in pronunciation than any others, and are the most difficult to fix in singing. Between E and I is the short *ĭ* as in ' hit,' in which the chambers are a tenth apart.

The full resonator scale is therefore constructed as follows. The several positions are

*Resonator Scale of Whispered Vowel Sounds.*

| | I. | II. | III. | IV. | V. | VI. | VII. | VIII. | IX. | X. | XI. | XII. |
|---|---|---|---|---|---|---|---|---|---|---|---|---|
| | U | O¹ | O² | O³ | A | . | | ĕ | E | Ĭ | I | |
| | U | oh | or | ŏn | ah | up | her | hăt | get | gate | hit | heat |

(eh) A still further advance of the tongue to its extreme position, when it has raised the mouth resonance an octave, and lowered the

marked by Roman numbers to indicate them for all voices in relation to the pitch of A, which governs that of the others in each individual case. To these must be added in English the more open ' oo ' sound in ' good,' ' would,' etc., which is on I^A between U (oo) and O¹ (oh).

Besides these thirteen simple sounds in English there are several compounds which require a movement from one position to another while the breath continues.

*Whispered Resonances.*

| XI.-I. | VI.-XI. | XI.-VI. | VIII.-VI. | III.-XI. |

i — oo    ă — î    î — ă    â — ă    or — î
English: duke   high   hear   hair   boy

The use of the resonator scale is of similar service in fixing the vowel pronunciation of other languages, and French and German sounds have all their places in relation to the sound of A, slight differences only having to be made to suit national peculiarities.

The same relations will be found to exist, whatever the resonant pitch of A may be. The pitch of U, a fifth lower, and of I (ee), an octave higher, will always be the limits of the scale of twelve notes, although in languages with fewer vowels some of the notes will not be occupied.

It must be remembered that all these sounds have to do solely with *whispered* speech, and are in no way connected with the notes of the vocal reed.

With a little practice the notes of the resonator scale can be heard without difficulty. By tapping with the finger upon the neck, the resonant notes of the back chamber will be heard to rise with the others, up to No. VI., and then fall again as shown in the scale. They can also be heard by the subject himself when the ears are completely stopped.

The CONSONANTS are important to the art of speaking, and therefore also to singing, for they all represent different methods of opening and closing the vowel positions. They are conveniently classified in next column :

It will be noticed that the jaw is only closed when the teeth are obliged to be together to form S.SH, and their sounding companions Z.J (soft), otherwise it must always be kept as wide open as the consonant will allow, in order to have less to do in reaching the vowel positions, which are all open.

What is generally known as 'forward diction' depends upon this condition, and the free use of the tip of the tongue, the lips and the teeth.

The base of the tongue in K and G is brought forward to the hard palate, and not allowed to close up the throat at the back.

This action is easier before A, O and U, when the tongue is either flat or its base somewhat raised ; but before E and I, in which the front of the tongue is high and forward in the mouth, the consonants K and G have been softened by all races who have come under

| | Larynx. | Base of tongue. | Tip of tongue. | Lips. | Lower lip and upper teeth. | Teeth and tip of tongue. | Teeth. |
|---|---|---|---|---|---|---|---|
| **EXPLOSIVES :** | | | | | | | |
| Plain. | .. | K | T | P | .. | .. | .. |
| With Voice. | .. | G | D | B | .. | .. | .. |
| **CONTINUANTS WITH VOICE :** | | | | | | | |
| Nasal. | .. | ÑG | N | M | .. | .. | .. |
| | | | | (soft)(soft) | | | |
| Non-nasal. | .. | .. | L | .. | V | Th | Z.J |
| Roll. | .. | .. | R | .. | .. | .. | .. |
| **ASPIRATES WITHOUT VOICE.** | H | .. | .. | .. | (hard) F | Th | S.Sh |
| | Jaw—open | „ | Very slight closing | Closing lips, not teeth | Lower lip between teeth | Tongue tip „ | Teeth meet |

Latin influence (French, Spanish, Italian and part of English) into an aspirated or partly explosive sound better suited to the position of the tongue.

TONE COLOUR AND REGISTERS. — The importation of language into the art of song has thus involved the careful cultivation of those positions and movements of the resonator which are best calculated to liberate the sound of the vocal reed, and at the same time express with particular distinctness all the various qualities of speech. But the sound of the voice includes yet another quality, namely that of ' tone ' or ' tone colour,' which depends upon whether the maximum of resonation is used or not. This is the especial function of the chamber in the neck.

The formative actions of the front of the mouth may or may not be accompanied by the full expansion of the back chamber of the resonator, and thus the total sound will be full and rich or shallow and light, as the singer thinks fit.

After these considerations it is not difficult to perceive that the question of registers has been confused by the assumption that the different tones of voice were produced by different actions of the vocal reed. The terms ' head register ' and ' chest register ' have, no doubt, been intended to mean conditions in which the singer has felt the sound in the head and in the chest. The former signifies the absence, and the latter the presence, of expansion in the neck.

The chest itself is occupied with the air-pressure and cannot be regarded as a resonator, since it is practically closed, except for the minute slit through which the pressure issues. The 'head register' has been further confounded with the compression of the membranes which also occurs in the upper notes of many voices.

Certain descriptions of the vocal membranes in explanation of the different ' registers ' have been given, and named ' lower thick,' ' upper thick,' ' middle,' ' lower thin,' ' upper thin,' etc. (Lennox Browne), but they have not been confirmed by further observation.

As at present known the membranes behave in the same way throughout the entire compass, and their compression in the high notes must be regarded as a departure from the natural process.

The true high note requires a development of breath power and control, and it would be better for their instrument if singers would refrain from singing by compression, and be satisfied with the compass that their breath power can give them. High notes might become rarer, but their sound would be of better quality.

Other forms of ' register ' due to alternative resonation are used as the singer wishes to express different tone-colour. But by insisting upon the maintenance of the double character of the resonator with all articulation in the front of the mouth, and resonant control in the neck, there are no sudden changes which could produce an obligatory 'register.'

Variety of colour due to control of the resonation of the neck may occur in all parts of the voice. When, however, the base of the tongue is pressed down so as to produce a heavy resonation in the mouth, at the expense of that in the neck, as well as to the detriment of good diction which requires the tongue to be free, it may readily occur that a sudden change has to be made near the middle of the voice, on passing from one note to the next.

Phonology is as much opposed to fictitious tone as to fictitious notes, and prefers to sacrifice the heavy tone of a voice if it is not natural to it, that is, if it is not obtained by the natural actions which are known to govern the sounds of the voice—in this case by expansion of the neck. Therefore the so-called 'registers' cannot be accepted as natural. That they are often acquired is beyond doubt, but it is astonishing how they disappear when singers are relieved of the necessity of thinking about them.

GENERAL PRINCIPLES.—Phonology does not

acknowledge some of the common methods of singing teachers, but it is able to support, on rational grounds, some of the best traditions of the great masters, which are the foundation of the following picture of the use of the singing voice.

The singer stands erect with a broadly expanded chest. He takes a deep breath by expanding both chest and abdomen at the level of the 6th-7th rib. He opens his mouth and throat to the position suitable for the pronunciation of A (ah), and at the same time he thinks of the note he is about to sing. Without allowing the ribs to yield he strikes the note by breathing out with decision, by a contraction at the upper part of the abdomen and a simultaneous approximation of the vocal membranes. If the note is in the middle of his compass, he will sing a succession of notes up to an octave higher and down to an octave lower, and back again, without any movement of his mouth or ribs; being conscious only of the breath force, which produces the notes he hears in his mind. The notes are lifted up and let down upon the breath pressure, controlled by the muscular action felt in the region of the lower ribs.

By changing the position of the resonator other vowel qualities can be given to the whole process, but under all circumstances the production of the notes remains the same. By movements of the resonator before and after the open vowel positions the effects of consonants can be introduced for the formation of words. By expanding the neck from below, a full resonant tone can be given, or withheld, according to the ' colour ' required. The throat is always free, that is, relaxed, open and unconscious.

This is a brief picture of what singing is in the individual, illustrating the action of the two instruments which combine to produce the sound of the voice. The one instrument expresses in music the emotions of the soul, while the other expresses in words the poetic thoughts of the mind. It is the office of the musical composer to bring these two together into the form of song.

Just as it is essential to the writer of vocal music to understand thoroughly the technique of the living instrument for which he writes, so is it also a necessary part of singing to be acquainted with the manner in which the dual expression is conceived in the song. Phonology has supplied the singer with an absolutely material estimate of work to be done by the voice, in the ' song diagrams ' already referred to, but in order to show how the vocal instruments are to be used in the service of art its analysis of song must be carried further.

As presented upon the page, a song consists of a line of music written upon a stave, and a line of words below it, in ordinary character. It is evident therefore from the first that the vocal reed or instrument of music has to perform a musical composition; while the resonator or instrument of speech has to perform a com-position in verse. All that can be said about the performance of music by an instrument, or about the recitation of verse, is applicable to the vocal reed and the resonator, each by itself. The vocal reed, however, has two offices to perform. It is either behaving as a true instru-ment of music, giving utterance to feelings in the direct manner belonging to its nature, or it is lending itself as an instrument of sound to assist, by emphasis and inflexion, the sense of words. In the former case its action is melodic; in the latter, declamatory.

The line of music may be intended by the composer to be interpreted in either of these senses, or it may happen that the feeling suggested by the words is so perfectly treated in the application to it of a form of melody, that both are satisfied, and the song is both melodic and declamatory. Examples of this are rare, and it more often happens that either one or the other element predominates. Not infrequently, however, it occurs that they clash, so that neither is satisfactory.

The rhythm of music, with its division into time measures, and the rhythm of words, with their arrangement into metrical verse, only indicate motion, and when these are applied to one another only the rhythm in which they may move together is emphasised, and nothing more. This cannot be regarded as song composition.

It is the sense of words and not the sound that stimulates the musical sense. The music thus evolved may have no melodic form of its own, in which case it is declamatory, or it may add to the words the power of its own form of expression and become melodic.

Periodicity in poetic expression is as neces-sary to verse as it is to music, and the study of the works of Heine gives a striking illustration of its force. The period of two lines, in which he usually expressed his thoughts, presented to the musician the simplest foundation for melodic form, and how that appealed to the melodic genius of Schubert is seen distinctly in such a masterpiece as 'Am Meer.'

The suiting of music to words may appear to be a subject belonging to the art of composi-tion, but it is necessary to consider it from the point of view of singing, since it forms the foundation of the singer's attitude of mind. The singer must know how to direct his techni-cal ability, and must have some distinct mental intention in singing, or the performance will be nothing more than the mechanical recitation of words and notes.

The sense of the words is always to be con-sidered first, since that is generally the most obvious. With a little analysis the poet's scheme of conveying a succession of ideas may next be detected. It will not then be difficult to see at once whether the composer has adapted

these ideas to a corresponding scheme of melo-dic form, or whether he has been content to use his music as a means of supporting the words only ; and the value of the music as depicting the poetic intention can be readily estimated.

It is not within the scope of this article to carry such analysis into the extensive field of existing examples of song-writing. Modern music is full of examples of declamatory song distorted and exaggerated by the musical exigencies of the pianoforte and orchestral accompaniment.

The melodic form is regarded as a survival of the past which does not really belong to present methods of musical expression. In fact, the sound as well as the sense of the voice has been almost swamped by the wealth of instrumentation which is considered necessary for modern ears. How far this can be carried it is impossible to say, but it is quite possible that singing will soon be regarded as a separate form of art, and composers will either write for the voice or for the orchestra, but not for both together.

In estimating the general character of modern and ancient music the singer can thus realise what part it is that his voice has to take. Throughout the works of the old Italian, English and German masters, up to the end of the 18th century, he will find abundant opportunity for the full exercise of the natural instrument of song. A more highly cultured and intellectually restrained form was the out-come of the literary period which we owe to the German lyric poets, and perfection of diction, with a refined use of musical expression, char-acterises the ' Lied ' and those songs of other nations which are conceived upon that model.

Of the vocal necessities of modern music no more need be said than that the singer must be able to realise the situation. The voice is a living thing, and can be ruined by the strain of singing too loud and too high, as only too many modern singers have discovered, but its powers of endurance, if properly treated, are remark-able, and every singer who understands his work ought to know where to stop.

Besides an excellent technique and an intelli-gent sense for music and poetry, the singer only requires the sincerity which brings to his art the charm of his own personality. If any technique could possibly be learned in order to obtain that inestimable quality, phonology would certainly point to the exercise of the most truly vital of all human functions, and recommend the free and unhindered service of the breath.

The following books will be useful to English readers :

H. PLUNKET GREENE, Interpretation in Song ; W. S. DREW, Voice Training ; H. GREGORY HART, The Singer's Art ; WILLIAM SHAKE-SPEARE, The Art of Singing ; HERMAN KLEIN, The Art of Bel Canto ; Sir F. W. MOTT, Brain and Voice; W. SHAKESPEARE, Plain Words on Singing.
                                           W. A. A.

SINGSPIEL. This term has been in use in Germany for the last 300 years to denote a dramatic representation with music ; not any one particular kind—singing being capable of being employed in such various ways—but any entertainment in which spoken dialogue and singing alternate. In time speech gave way at intervals not only to singing, but to singing by several voices at once. Later, when the spoken dialogue had been brought into entire subjection to music, as was the case in Italy after the revolution effected in the whole nature of dramatic representation by the rise of opera, not only concerted vocal pieces were introduced into the German Singspiel, but instrumental music and its protégé monody as well.

We find the earliest traces of the Singspiel in the German miracle-plays, which were gradually developed outside the churches from the Passions given inside them. The Passions were sung throughout, while in the miracle-plays spoken words in German were introduced, the singing still being in Latin, as for example in the ' Ludus paschalis de passione Domini ' MS. of the 13th century. In course of time the Latin text and consequently the music were thrust into the background. In a 14th-century MS. called ' Marienklage,' preserved in the convent of Lichtenthal near Baden, Mary sings in German. Indeed we already find the typical German miracle-play in the ' Spiel von den zehn Jungfrauen ' performed at Eisenach in 1322, in which all the words sung are German. These plays were generally performed on the eves of the great festivals, such as Whitsunday, Epiphany, etc. Gradually the ecclesiastical element disappeared, leaving only the secular, and thus originated the Shrove Tuesday plays, in which the characteristics of whole classes of society, priests, doctors, travelling scholars, etc., were held up to ridicule. Nuremberg and Augsburg were specially celebrated for these plays, written for the most part by Hans Rosenblut (about 1405), Hans Folz of Worms (about 1480), both living in Nuremberg, and Nicolaus Mercator. They gradually, however, degenerated into obscene pieces, until in the 16th century Hans Sachs and Jakob Ayrer (both of whom introduced music into their plays) started the movement which ended in the reformation of the German stage. By Ayrer we still have a ' Schöns neus singets Spiel.' ' Der Münch im Kesskorb,' sung in 1618 by five persons ' entirely on the melody of the English Roland.' This melody is repeated fifty-four times, and one cannot help suspecting that the English stage was to some extent Ayrer's model.

A reaction from these ' people's plays ' (as they might be called) was caused by the ' school plays ' in Latin, annually performed by the pupils of the Jesuits. Between the acts German interludes with music were introduced, and these were virtually Singspiele in the modern sense. The first Singspiel in imitation of the Italian opera without any spoken dialogue was the lost ' Dafne,' written by Martin Opitz and composed by Heinrich Schütz in 1627. The earliest instance of an independent German Singspiel with singing and spoken dialogue was ' Seelewig,' a sacred Waldgedicht or Freudenspiel. In a spoken play by Harsdörffer (1644) were introduced arias after the Italian manner, composed [1] by Sigmund Gottlieb STADEN (q.v.). The piece is intended for private performance, and written for three trebles, two altos, two tenors, one bass, three violins, three flutes, three reeds and one large horn, the bass being taken throughout by a theorbo. No two voices ever sing at the same time, and the instruments have short symphonies to themselves. The only regular stage at that time was the Italian opera-house of each capital (that of Vienna being built in 1651, and that of Dresden in 1667) and of Nuremberg and other imperial cities. The German Singspiel found a home in Hamburg in the theatre built in 1678, but soon encountered a formidable rival in German opera, founded by Reinhard Keiser. After this, half a century went by before the Singspiel was heard of again.

In 1743 the Döbbelin company in Berlin produced without success a German Liederspiel, ' Der Teufel ist los,' founded on the English piece ' The Devil to pay,' followed by Schürer's ' Doris ' (1747) and Scheibe's ' Thusnelda ' (1749), both very successful. Thus encouraged, Koch's company began to play Singspiele in Leipzig, Weimar, and Berlin, their first piece being ' Die verwandelten Weiber,' another version of ' The Devil to pay,' written by C. F. Weisse, composed by J. A. Hiller, and produced at Leipzig in 1764 with great success. The same authors produced a succession of similar pieces, ' Der lustige Schuster ' (1765), ' Lottchen am Hofe,' and ' Die Liebe auf dem Lande ' (1767), ' Die Jagd ' (1771), ' Ärndtekranz ' and ' Der Dorfbarbier ' (1772). Neefe, Reichardt, Stegemann, Schweitzer, and others, brought to perfection this new species, now called operetta.

Independently of all this going on in North Germany, the German Singspiel had sprung up in Vienna, starting, curiously enough, with ' Die doppelte Verwandlung ' (1767), an adaptation from the French ' Le Diable à quatre,' Sedaine's version of ' The Devil to pay.' Werner, Haydn's predecessor at Eisenstadt, had already produced at the court (German) theatre a Tafelstück (i.e. piece intended for private performance) called ' Der Wienerische Tändelmarkt ' (1760). The marionette plays, of which Haydn was so fond, were Singspiele, and he supplied the court of Esterház with ' Philemon

[1] See M.f.M., 1881, Nos. 4, 5, 6.

und Baucis' (1773), 'Genoveva' (1777), 'Dido,' a parody on a grand opera (1778), and 'Die erfüllte Rache' (1780). 'Der krumme Teufel,' to words by Kurz, was a real Singspiel. Dittersdorf's ' Doktor und Apotheker,' ' Liebe im Narrenhause,' ' Hieronymus Knicker,' ' Rothe Käppchen,' etc., produced at the imperial Nationaltheater, were brilliant successes. Kauer (1751–1831) composed no fewer than 200 Singspiele, and Schenk was almost equally prolific. The classic Singspiel was founded by Mozart with his 'Entführung' (July 12, 1782), which, according to Goethe, threw everything else of the kind into the shade. ' Die Zauberflöte' (1791), too, was styled a Singspiel on the title-page of the PF. score. From this point the Singspiel proper becomes continually rarer, though Wenzel Müller's ' Schwester von Prag,' ' Das neue Sonntagskind,' and a few more deserve mention. Lortzing's works are a mixture of opera and Singspiel, certain numbers in the ' Czaar und Zimmermann,' ' Waffenschmied,' and ' Undine ' being quite in the Lied-style, and the music consequently of secondary importance, while in others the music undoubtedly assists in developing the characters, and raises these portions to the dignity of opera. We are here brought face to face with the main distinction between opera and Singspiel ; the latter by no means excludes occasional recitative in place of the spoken dialogue, but the moment the music helps to develop the dramatic *dénouement* we have to do with opera and not with Singspiel. (See OPERA, Vol. III. p. 701.)

BIBL.—H. M. SCHLETTERER, *Das deutsche Singspiel* (1863, 2nd ed. 1879) ; ROBERT LACH, *Sebastian Saileri ' Schöpfung ' in der Musik. Ein Beitrag zur Geschichte des deutschen Singspiel um die Mitte und in der zweiten Hälfte des 18. Jahrhunderts.* Vienna, 1917. See review Z.M.W., June 1919, pp. 540-42 ; RUDOLFINE KROTT, *Die Singspiele Schuberts.* Vienna Dissertation, 1921; VLADIMIR HELFERT, *Zur Geschichte des Wiener Singspiels.* Z.M.W., Jan./Feb. 1923, pp. 194-209.
                                                    F. G.

SINIGAGLIA, LEONE (*b.* Turin, Aug. 14, 1868), was a pupil of the Conservatorio of his native city, and subsequently studied with Mandyczewski in Vienna, where he enjoyed the friendship and advice of Dvořák, Goldmark, and other musicians. His early works include a number of violin and violoncello pieces, songs, female choruses, etc., and one of these, op. 5, a ' concert étude ' for string quartet, was often played by the Bohemian Quartet. His op. 19 is a set of variations on Schubert's ' Haidenröslein ' for oboe and piano ; op. 20 is a brilliant and very successful violin concerto in A ; op. 22 is a set of variations on a theme by Brahms, for quartet ; op. 26 is a ' Rapsodia piemontese ' for violin and orchestra ; and op. 27 is a string quartet in D, which has won great favour from many of the continental organisations. Two pieces for horn and piano, op. 28, and a romance in A for violin and orchestra, are among his more recent works ; and two ' Danze piemontesi ' for orchestra, op. 31, are arrangements of genuine popular themes. These have been arranged in a variety of ways, and are very successful.        M.

Several of Sinigaglia's orchestral works have been repeatedly played in England, and have been appreciated for their light handling and the distinctive flavour given to his ideas by the Piedmontese folk-song of which he is a student. These include, beside the Rapsodia mentioned above, a ' Danza piemontese ' for orchestra, op. 31, and a suite ' Piemonte,' also for orchestra. His overture to Goldini's comedy, *Le Baruffe Chiozzote*, op. 32, has also become popular. Sinigaglia has edited as his op. 40 a series of Piedmontese folk-melodies in 2 volumes. A list of his works was published in the periodical *Il Pianoforte*, anno 2, No. 12.        C.

SINK-A-PACE—also written CINQUE-PACE, CINQUA-PACE, CINQUE PASS, CINQUE PAS, SINQUA-PACE, SINQUE-PACE, ZINCK-PASS and SINCOPAS—a name by which the original Galliard was known.

Praetorius [1] says that a Galliard has five steps and is therefore called a Cinque Pas. These five steps, or rather combinations of steps, are well described in Arbeau's *Orchésographie* (Langres, 1588). In later times the Galliard became so altered by the addition of new steps, that the original form of the dance seems to have been distinguished by the name Cinq Pas. It is frequently mentioned by the Elizabethan writers, well - known examples being the allusions in Shakespeare's ' Much Ado about Nothing ' (Act ii. Sc. 1), ' Twelfth Night ' (Act i. Sc. 3), Marston's ' Satiromastix ' (Act i.), and Sir John Davies's ' Orchestra ' (stanza 67). The following less-known quotation is from the ' Histriomastix ' (Part 1) of Prynne (who was especially bitter against this dance) :

' Alas there are but few who finde that narrow way, . . . and those few what are they ? Not dancers, but mourners : not laughers, but weepers ; whose tune is Lachrymæ, whose musicke, sighes for sinne ; who know no other Cinqua-pace but this to Heaven, to goe mourning all the day long for their iniquities ; to mourne in secret like Doves, to chatter like cranes for their owne and others sinnes.'

The following example of a Cinque-pace is given by Wolfang Caspar Printz, in his *Phrynis Mitilenaeus, oder Satyrischer Componist* (Dresden, 1696), as a specimen of ' Trichonum iambicum.' A longer example will be found in Dauney's edition of the 17th century Skene MS. (Edinburgh, 1838).

                                        W. B. S.

SIREN. This, though not strictly a musical instrument, has rendered such good service to

1 *Syntagma Mus.* vol. iii. chap. ii. p. 24.

acoustical science that it deserves brief notice ; for fuller details the works referred to below must be consulted. Lord Rayleigh [1] describes it as

'A stiff disc, capable of revolving about its centre, and pierced with one or more sets of holes arranged at equal intervals round the circumference of circles concentric with the disc. A windpipe in connection with bellows is presented perpendicularly to the disc, its open end being opposite to one of the circles, which contains a set of holes. When the bellows are worked, the stream of air escapes freely if a hole is opposite to the end of the pipe ; but otherwise it is obstructed. As the disc turns, puffs of air in succession escape through it, until when the velocity is sufficient, these blend into a note the pitch of which rises continually with the rapid sequence of the puffs. One of the most important facts in the whole science of Acoustics is exemplified by the siren—namely, that the pitch of a note depends upon the period of its vibration. The size and shape of the holes, the force of the wind, and other elements of the problem may be varied ; but if the number of puffs in a given time, such as one second, remains unchanged, so does the pitch. We may even dispense with wind altogether, and produce a note by allowing a card to tap against the edges of the holes as they revolve ; the pitch will still be the same.'

The Siren may be defined as a wind instrument, in which the successive air-waves are produced not at random or by consonance, but by circular rotatory motion, which is susceptible of accurate adjustment as well as measurement. It was originally invented by Cagniard de la Tour, who made it needlessly complicated by using the force of the wind to drive the rotating disc as well as to produce the required note. For this purpose the speaking holes in the top of the small wind-chest were pierced in an oblique direction ; those in the disc sloping in an opposite diagonal. There was also a counting apparatus attached to the upper part of the main axis, with two dials for registering the number of rotations in a given time. This form has been faithfully reproduced in every manual of Physics.[2] The name is said to have been somewhat fancifully, and indeed incorrectly, given it from Homer's sirens, on account of its property of singing under water. It is true that if water be forced through it after the fashion of the turbine, a buzzing or humming sound is produced. Seebeck and others effected material improvements, but the only two which need special notice are the instruments constructed by Helmholtz and Rudolph Kœnig respectively. The former is figured and described in that author's Tonempfindungen,[3] and consists essentially of two sirens united on a single axis, each disc of which possesses four rows of holes susceptible of being separately opened, thus giving means for producing a large variety of intervals.

The upper wind-chest, which looks downwards, can be rotated on its feeding-tube so as to bring about varying changes of phase between the two discs. With this instrument Helmholtz succeeded in producing excellent results, using a small electromotor for driving it at a uniform rate.

The siren of Rudolph Kœnig of Paris is a far more imposing instrument. It was made for W. Spottiswoode, P.R.S., was exhibited by the writer at the British Association meeting at York in 1881, and is now in the physical laboratory of the College of Science at Bristol. It is furnished with more than a dozen rotating discs of different kinds, which fit on to a vertical spindle, above a wind-chest of large size fitted with a keyboard of eight notes. A strong clockwork actuated by heavy weights forms the motive power, and an ingenious counting apparatus is made not only to record the number of rotations, but also to set going automatically a watch movement, and thus obtain by one motion of the observer's hand the speed of the disc, and the time of the observation. By properly computing the rings of perforations, the harmonic series is given by one disc, and the enharmonic scale by another. Indeed there is hardly any law of musical acoustics which it cannot be made to illustrate.[4] For purposes of demonstration the siren is excellent, and also for the illustration of perfect musical intervals ; but for the accurate determination of absolute pitch it is far inferior to Lissajous's optical method ; and still more so to the tuning-fork method, described under SCHEIBLER, and to Prof. M'Leod's Cycloscope.     W. H. S.

SIRÈNE, LA, opéra-comique in 3 acts ; words by Scribe, music by Auber. Produced Opéra-Comique, Mar. 26, 1844 ; as ' The Syren,' Princess's Theatre, Oct. 14, 1844.   G.

SIRMEN (SYRMEN), MADDALENA LOMBARDINI (b. Venice, 1735 ?), a distinguished 18th-century violinist and composer for her instrument, who later, for some unknown reason, discarded her first profession for that of singer.

According to Dr. Burney, Maddalena Lombardini received her musical education at the Venetian ' Conservatorio dei Mendicanti,' and ten or more years before Tartini's death in 1770, she was profiting by his tuition. At this time she probably lived in Padua, so as to be near her master, but in 1760 she had apparently returned to Venice, where she received several letters from him, testifying to the keen interest he took in her career. The carefully written instructions as to bowing and fingering which he sent her in a letter [5] dated Padua, Mar. 5, 1760, constitute a valuable treatise on the art of violin-playing. Dr. Burney's excellent English version appeared in 1779, with the original text and the translation on opposite pages. It was printed in London ' for R. Bremner, opposite Somerset House in the Strand ; by George Bigg, successor to Mr. Dryden Leach.' Although a copy of this work is rarely met with

---

[1] Theory of Sound, vol. i. p. 5.
[2] Deschanel, Nat. Philos. iv. p. 822 ; Everitt's translation. Ganot's Physics, p. 189 ; Atkinson's translation.
[3] Helmholtz, Sensations of Tone, Ellis's translation p. 243 et seq.

[4] A description of this instrument is to be found in Poggendorf'. Annalen, and in the Philosophical Magazine for 1876.
[5] This letter—the autograph of which is preserved at Venice—has been translated into German by J. A. Hiller, and inserted in his Lebensbeschreibungen berühmter Musikgelehrten.

now, the substance of the pamphlet has been frequently quoted and reprinted in full in modern works on the violin. Between 1760 and 1768 Maddalena Lombardini toured in Italy, where she is said to have proved a worthy rival of Tartini's greatest pupil — Nardini. During her travels the young *virtuosa* met Ludovico Sirmen, violinist and conductor at Sta. Maria Maddalena in Bergamo. The acquaintance eventually ended in marriage, and a visit to Paris, where the couple were heard at a Concert Spirituel on Monday, Aug. 15, 1768. The *Mercure de France* speaks in glowing terms of M. and Madame Sirmen's execution of a double violin concerto of their own composition. In 1771, Signora Sirmen came to London, where her début took place at the King's Theatre, on Thursday, Jan. 9. J. C. Bach's oratorio, ' Gioas Rè di Giuda,' was the *pièce de résistance* of the evening. Duport (cadet) played a violoncello solo after the first act, and in the second act, after the duettino, there was a ' Concerto on the Violin by the celebrated Mrs. Lombardini Sirmen.' Her success in the Metropolis was apparently instantaneous, and was repeated on the 10th, 16th, 17th, 23rd and 24th of the same month. During the following February she played frequently at the highest class concerts in London. On Feb. 15 she performed a violin concerto between the first and second parts of Handel's ' Judas Maccabæus' at Covent Garden, and on the 20th between the first and second parts of the ' Messiah.' Her Benefit Concert, under the direction of Bach and Abel, took place at Almack's on Apr. 15 ; Guadagni, Wendling, Fischer, and other celebrated artists of the day assisted her ; but Madame Sirmen, either for a whim, or by request, abandoned for this occasion the instrument on which she excelled, and, according to the advertisement in the *Public Advertiser* of that date, played 'A Concerto on the Harpsichord.' In the month of May her services as violinist were in constant requisition. She repeated her triumphs at the King's Theatre, and, besides playing her violin concertos, contributed some violin *obbligati* to the songs of the principal vocalists. The *Public Advertiser* of May 28, 1771, announces ' The celebrated Signora Sirmen on the violin, being her last performance this season.' The following year she returned to London, and took up her abode in Half Moon Street, Piccadilly. Her services were more than ever sought after. She appeared at nearly all the Lenten Oratorio Concerts at Covent Garden, playing violin concertos between the parts. On Mar. 26, 1772, she had another benefit concert, and on Apr. 1 she introduced a new violin concerto by the eminent violoncellist Cirri, after the second part of Handel's ' Messiah ' at Covent Garden. Her final appearance in England is so announced in the *Public Advertiser* of Apr. 10, at the newly organised Concert Spirituel held in the same

building. Apparently this was not only Signora Sirmen's last performance in England, but it was the end of her brilliant career as a violinist. Whether she was unable to sustain the high reputation she had achieved, or whether she was drawn away from her original bent by the dazzling example of Miss Schmeling (afterwards Madame Mara), can only be surmised. In any case she came to London again in 1774, and according to Dr. Burney [1] her last visit to the metropolis was in the capacity of a singer, in which her success was questionable.

' In " Sofonisba " and " The Cid " '—runs the note—' Madame Syrmen, the scholar of Tartini who was justly admired for her polished and expressive manner of playing the violin, appeared as a singer in the second woman, but having been first woman so long upon her instrument, she degraded herself by assuming a character in which, though not destitute of voice and taste, she laid no claim to superiority.'

After this unfortunate attempt the erstwhile distinguished violinist drifted to the Continent again, and in 1782 she was singing secondary parts at the court theatre in Dresden. In May 1785 she made her last recorded appearance as a violinist at a Concert Spirituel in Paris, but without success, by reason, according to the *Mercure de France*, of the old-fashioned and worn-out music that she played. The fulfilment of the brilliant promise of Signora Sirmen's early career appears to have been arrested after her two brief seasons in London, and for this reason she is chiefly remembered, not so much as a violinist, but as the recipient of Tartini's notable letter.

Her compositions comprise :

1. Six trios à deux violons et violoncelle obligé. Œuvre premier (Welcker and Genaud, Soho). 2. Six Quartettes à deux violons, alto et basse (written in conjunction with her husband). Berault, Paris (1769), also Longman & Broderip, London. 3. Six duets for two violins (dedicated to the Duke of Gloucester). William Napier, London. 4. Six concertos for violin with an accompaniment for two violins, alto, bass, hautboy, and two horns. Hummel, Amsterdam. 5. Six Sonates à deux violons. Hummel, Amsterdam. In the Berlin Bibliothek a copy of these sonatas is embellished with a picture of Maddalena Sirmen. 6. Six concertos adapted for the harpsichord by Signor Giordani. London, 1789, Longman & Broderip, Cheapside, and No. 3 Haymarket. J. A. Hiller mentions a concerto which was published in Venice.

Bibl.—Burney, *History of Music, The Present State of Music in Italy* ; Castil-Blaze, *L'Opéra italien* ; Choron and Fayolle, *Dictionnaire historique des musiciens* ; *Mercure de France*, Sept. 1768 ; *Public Advertiser*, 1771, 1772 ; Fétis, *Biog. des mus., Q.-L.* ; Ch. Bouvet, *Une Leçon de Giuseppe Tartini et une femme violiniste au XVIIIe siècle* (Paris, 1918).      O. R. and E. H.-A.

**SIR ROGER DE COVERLY,**[2] the only one of the numerous old English dances which has retained its popularity until the present day, is probably a tune of north-country origin. Chappell (*Popular Music*, vol. ii.) says that he possesses a MS. version of it called ' Old Roger or Coverlay for evermore, a Lancashire Hornpipe,' and in ' The First and Second Division Violin ' (in the B.M. Catalogue attributed to John Eccles, and dated 1705) another version of it is entitled ' Roger of Coverly the true Cheisere way.' Moreover, the Calverley family, from one of whose ancestors the tune is said to derive its name,[3] have been from time immemorial inhabitants of the Yorkshire village which bears

1 *Hist. Mus.* vol. iii. p. 500.
2 Or more correctly ' Roger of Coverly.' The prefix ' Sir ' is not found until after Steele and Addison had used the name in the *Spectator*.
3 See *Notes and Queries*, vol. i. No. 23, p. 368.

their name. The editor of the Skene MS., on the strength of a MS. version dated 1706, claims the tune as Scottish, and says that it is well known north of the Tweed as ' The Maltman comes on Monday.' According to Dr. Rimbault,[1] the earliest printed version of it occurs in Playford's ' Division Violin ' (1685). In ' The Dancing Master ' it is first found at page 167 of the 9th edition, published in 1695, where the tune and directions for the dance are given exactly as follows :

*Roger of Coverly.*
Longways for as many as will.

The 1. man go below the 2. wo. then round, and so below the 2. man into his own place ; then the 1. wo. go below the 2. man, then round him, and so below the 2. wo. into her own place. The 1. cu. [first couple] cross over below the 2. cu. and take hands and turn round twice, then lead up through and cast off into the 2. cu. place.    W. B. S.

The Scots song, ' The Maltman comes on Monday,' is not, as erroneously asserted by Chappell, by Allan Ramsay, although it is inserted in the first volume of his *Tea-Table Miscellany*, 1724. The English title is not so easily disposed of.

The *Spectator*, 2nd number, 1711, speaks of Sir Roger de Coverley as a gentleman of Worcestershire, and that ' His great grandfather was the inventor of the famous country dance which is called after him.'

Fanciful as this is, it shows that the dance, at that time, was considered an old one. Another origin for the name of the tune is based on a MS. in the writer's possession, inscribed ' For the violin, Patrick Cumming, his Book : Edinburgh, 1723.' At the end the name is repeated, and the date 1724 given. The tune stands as follows, although the Scottish SCORDATURA (*q.v.*) is likely to puzzle the casual reader, since the first notes which appear as G, A, B, C sound A, B, C, D.

Scor-  *The Maltman, or Roger the Cavalier.*
datura (not given in the MS.).

[1] *Notes and Queries*, i. No. 8.

It is well known that the name ' Roger ' was bestowed upon the Royalists during the Civil War, and it is suggested that ' Coverly ' is really a corruption of ' Cavalier.'

As the dance, later, was almost invariably used at the conclusion of a ball, it was frequently called ' The Finishing Dance.' See Wilson's *Companion to the Ball-Room*, circa 1816, and Chappell's *Popular Music* for the modern figure. According to an early correspondent of *Notes and Queries*, the tune was known in Virginia, U.S.A., as ' My Aunt Margery.'    F. K.

SISTINE CHOIR [2] (Ital. *Il Collegio dei Cappellani Cantori della Cappella Pontificia*), a collegiate body, consisting of thirty-two choral chaplains, domiciled—though not in any special buildings of their own—at Rome, where for many centuries they have enjoyed the exclusive privilege of singing at all those solemn services and ecclesiastical functions in which the Pope officiates in person.

The genealogy of the Papal Choir may be traced back to a period of very remote antiquity. It is said—and the tradition is worthy of credit—that a school for the education of choristers was founded in Rome early in the 4th century by S. Sylvester, whose pontificate lasted from the year 314-35. That S. Hilarius (461-468) established one, not much more than a century later, is certain. These institutions, after the lapse of another hundred years, were supplemented by new ones on a larger scale. On the destruction of the monastery of Monte Cassino by the Lombards, in the year 580, the Benedictine Fathers fled to Rome ; and, under the protection of Pope Pelagius II. (577-90), established themselves in a new home near the Lateran Basilica, where they opened schools for the preparation of candidates for holy orders. S. Gregory the Great (590-604) took advantage of this circumstance while working out his system of reform, and turned the seminaries to account as schools of singing. (See SONG SCHOOL.) Under his care they prospered exceedingly, and in process of time attained proportions which enabled him to supply the

[2] The popular name of the Papal Choir is derived from the Cappella Sixtina, built by Pope Sixtus IV. (1471-84).

various Basilicas with singers, who assembled on the greater festivals, and attended the Pope wherever he officiated. And thus arose the practice to which the Church was eventually indebted for the magnificent services of the Sistine Chapel.

These early Scholae Cantorum—sometimes called Orphanotropia, in allusion to the number of fatherless children which they sheltered—were governed by an ecclesiastic of high rank, called the Primicerius, who, assisted by a Secundicerius destined afterwards to succeed him in his office, exercised absolute control over the youths and children committed to his care. Boys were admitted into the preparatory school (*Parvisium*) at a very early age; and if of gentle birth, became at the same time members of the papal household, holding a status like that of the pages at a secular court. After passing through the necessary preparation, the choristers were permitted to take part in the most solemn services of the Church : and when their voices changed, were either prepared for the priesthood or provided for as Cubicularii. The older members of the Scholae were called Subdeacons; but the title was only an honorary one. By their help Rome was so liberally supplied with singers that on more than one occasion the Pope was able to send out skilled instructors for the purpose of encouraging the purest style of ecclesiastical singing in other countries [1]; and, as we hear of no important modification of the system before the beginning of the 14th century, we are justified in believing that it fulfilled its purpose perfectly.

A great change, however, took place during the pontificate of Clement V. (1305–14), who in the year 1305 transferred the Chair of S. Peter to Avignon, leaving his Primicerius and Schola Cantorum behind him in Rome. Too much oppressed by political and ecclesiastical troubles to devote his time to the regulation of details, Pope Clement naturally left the management of his chapel to underlings, who suffered the music to degenerate to a very unsatisfactory level. His successor, John XXII. (1316–34), issued in 1323 the well-known Bull, ' Docta sanctorum,' for the purpose of restraining his singers from corrupting the simplicity of plain-song, either by subjecting it to the laws of measured music, or by overloading it with ornamentation. It is doubtful whether the provisions of this Bull were fully carried out after the decease of its author, whose immediate successor, Benedict XII. (1334–42), was too fond of splendid ceremonial to raise any strong objection on the score of its elaborateness

to the music sung by the twelve choral chaplains who officiated in his private chapel. Indeed, the management of the choir employed by Benedict and his successors at Avignon differed altogether from that of the Roman Schola, which was still carried on under the Primicerius. In Rome, the choristers were taught on the old traditional system, almost from their infancy. At Avignon, the most welcome recruits were French and Flemish singers, who had already earned a brilliant reputation. Now, in those days the best singers were, for the most part, the best composers also ; and in the Low Countries the art of composition was rapidly advancing towards a state of perfection elsewhere unknown. It followed, therefore, that the choir at Avignon contained some of the greatest musicians in Europe, and was indebted to them for faux-bourdons and other polyphonic music, scarcely ever heard at that period except in the Netherlands.

In 1377 Pope Gregory XI. (1370–78) returned to Rome, and carried his choir with him. The contrast between the rival schools now became more apparent than ever ; yet by some means they amalgamated completely. The probability is that Gregory himself united them, forming the two choirs into one body, which was no longer called the Schola Cantorum, nor governed by a Primicerius, but was henceforth known as the Collegio dei Cappellani Cantori, and placed under the command of an ecclesiastic who held the appointment for life, and bore the title of ' Maestro della Cappella Pontificia.' The precise year in which this change took place cannot be ascertained ; though it is certain that the new title was borne by Angelo, Abbot of S. Maria de Rivaldis, in 1397—twenty years after the return from Avignon. After this, we hear of no other maestro till 1464, when the appointment was conferred upon Niccola Fabri, Governor of Rome, who held it for two years. From 1469 onwards the list includes the names of fourteen ecclesiastics, of whom all, except the last, were Bishops. The most celebrated of them was Elziario GENET, of Carpentras, ' Vescovo in partibus ' (1515–26 ?), and the last of the series was Monsignor Antonio Boccapadule (1574–86). Pope Sixtus V. (1585–90) issued Sept. 1, 1586, a Bull (' In suprema '), by virtue of which he conferred upon the college the right of electing, from among their own body, an officer, to whom was committed the duty of governing the choir, for three, six, or twelve months, or in perpetuity, according to the pleasure of the electors.[2] It was clear that the maestri so elected must necessarily be deprived of many of the privileges enjoyed by the ecclesiastical dignitaries who had preceded them ; but, by way of compensation, they were invested with all which were not inseparable

---

[1] For this purpose, John the præcentor was sent to England during the Primacy of Theodore, Archbishop of Canterbury (669–690). At the request of King Pepin (750–68), Simeon, the Secundicerius of the Roman Schola, was sent, in like manner, to France, but recalled by Pope Paul I. in 763, that he might succeed to the office of the then lately deceased Primicerius, Georgius ; while towards the close of the same century two celebrated singers, Theodorus and Benedictus, were sent by Hadrian I. (772–95) to Charlemagne.

[2] Baini, i. p. 272, Note 375.

from the status of a Bishop; and these were still further increased by Pope Clement XIII. in the Bull 'Cum retinendi,' August 31, 1762. It was ultimately arranged that the election should take place annually, and this custom has ever since been strictly observed. The first maestro so chosen was Giovanni Antonio Merlo, who served during the year 1587. Since his time the election has always been fixed for Dec. 28; and for very many years it has been the invariable custom to elect the principal bass.

The Flemish singers, having once obtained a recognised position in the choir, soon began to exercise an irresistible influence over it, and, through it, over every other choir in Christendom. Among the first of whom we have any certain account was Guglielmo DUFAY (q.v.).

The number of singers, which at Avignon had been limited to twelve, was in the 16th century increased to twenty-four, and not very long afterwards raised to thirty-two, which figure still represents the normal strength of the choir, though the assistance of additional *ripieni* is sometimes permitted on extraordinary occasions. After the formal admission of the Netherlanders the compositions sung in the Papal Chapel were almost entirely supplied by the cappellani cantori themselves. The custom was, when any member of the college had produced a mass or other great work, to have it roughly written out, and rehearsed by the entire body of singers, who afterwards decided whether or not it was worthy of their acceptance. If the votes were in its favour, the original autograph was placed in the hands of the *Scrittori* —of whom four were usually kept in full employment—and by them copied, in stencilled notes large enough to be read by the entire choir at once, into huge partbooks,[1] formed of entire sheets of parchment, of which a large collection, richly illuminated and magnificently bound, is still preserved among the Archives of the Sistine Chapel, though a vast number were destroyed in the conflagration which ensued on the invasion of Rome by Charles V. in 1527.

It was Pope Sixtus V. who, at the time of his reform in the government of the choir, mentioned above, conferred upon Palestrina[2] the title of Composer to the Pontifical Chapel. The office was renewed, after Palestrina's death, in favour of Felice Anerio, but was never conferred on any other member of the college. The most famous musicians who sang in the choir[3] after Palestrina were Giov. Maria Nanini, admitted in 1577, Luca Marenzio (1594), Rug-

giero Giovanelli (1599), and Gregorio Allegri (1629-52). Adami also mentions Victoria, whose name, however, is not to be found in any official register. Among more modern maestri the three most notable were, Tommaso Bai, who held the office of maestro in 1714; the Cavaliere Giuseppe Santarelli—Dr. Burney's friend—who entered the choir as an artificial soprano singer in 1749, and died in 1790; and the Abbate BAINI (q.v.), who was received into the college in 1795, became maestro in 1817, and died in 1844. By special favour of Pope Gregory XVI., Baini retained his office for life, but no later maestro has enjoyed the same privilege.

The two settings of the Miserere by Bai and Baini, which for many years past have been used alternately with that of Allegri, are the only works added to the repertory of the chapel since the death of the last-named maestro. Indeed, neither the constitution nor the habits of the college have, since Palestrina, undergone any important change—except, perhaps, in one particular, to be mentioned presently; and hence it is its performances are so infinitely valuable, as traditional indices of the style of singing cultivated at the period which produced the 'Missa Papae Marcelli,' the 'Improperia,' and the 'Lamentations.'

The one point in which a change has taken place is the selection of voices; and it is necessary to remark that, as the change did not take place until seven years after Palestrina's death, the idea that we cannot sing his music in England as he intended it to be sung, for lack of the necessary voices, is altogether untenable. In early times, as we have already seen, the chapel was supplied with soprani, and in all probability with contralti also, by means of the Orphanotropia or Scholae Cantorum, exactly as English cathedrals are now supplied by means of the Choristers' Schools. That this plan was continued until quite late in the 16th century is sufficiently proved by the fact that, between 1561 and 1571, Palestrina held the joint offices of maestro di cappella and maestro dei fanciulli di coro at the Church of Sta. Maria Maggiore, while, between 1539 and 1553 the post of 'Maestro de' Putti,' at the Cappella Giulia, was successively filled by Arcadelt, Rubino, Basso, Ferrabosco, and Roselli. During the latter half of the 16th century, however, these youthful treble voices were gradually supplanted by a new kind of adult male soprano, called the soprano falsetto, imported, in the first instance, from Spain, in which country it was extensively cultivated by means of some peculiar system of training, the secret of which has never publicly transpired.[4] At the close of the 16th century,

---

[1] Mendelssohn, in one of his letters, gives an amusing description of one of these enormous books, which he saw carried in front of Baini, as he walked, in procession, up the nave of S. Peter's.

[2] On the whole of Palestrina's relations with the Papal Choir, which research had proved to be very different from those described by Baini, Rockstro's principal authority, see the article PALESTRINA.

[3] A catalogue of the singers of the Cappella Pontificia was published in *R.M.I.*, 1907.

[4] Nevertheless, this secret does not seem to be altogether lost. A lady traveller in Spain and Portugal, amusingly expressed her surprise, on discovering that certain high flute-like notes, which she believed to have been produced by some beautiful young girl, really emanated from the throat of a burly individual *with a huge black beard and whiskers* !

Spanish soprani were in very great request; and were, indeed, preferred to all others, until the year 1601, when a far more momentous change was introduced.

During nearly the whole of the 17th and the greater part of the 18th centuries the theatres of Europe were supplied with adult male soprano and contralto voices, preserved by a process so barbarous, that at one time it was forbidden in Italy on pain of death. Yet notwithstanding this penalty the system prospered, and enriched the stage with many of its most accomplished ornaments, such as Nicolini Grimaldi, Senesino, Carestini, Pacchierotti, Farinelli and others. It has been said that Farinelli's wonderful voice was accidentally preserved, and the story is probably true; for it is certain that very fine voices are sometimes preserved by accident, and quite reasonable to suppose that such accidents may very frequently happen, though should the sufferers possess no musical talent one is not likely to hear of them. In these purely accidental cases no singer with a good voice has even been refused admission into the pontifical choir; but the transgression of the law, which was formerly punishable with death, now renders the offender *de facto* excommunicate, and therefore effectually prevents his reception into the Collegio. One of the most learned and accomplished musicians in Rome, in command of one of its most celebrated choirs, remembered the admission of three artificial voices, accidentally produced, while he was studying under Baini. Two of them proved too weak to be used, except as *ripieni*; but the third developed into a magnificent soprano. The trained soprano falsetto, which needs no accident to produce it, is not yet extinct.[1]

Italian choirmasters draw a careful distinction between the different voices they employ. The *Voce bianca* or *naturale* is by no means uncommon, but produces only contralto singers. The true adult soprano, *arte fatta* (made by method [2]), is an excessively rare voice, produced 'rather in the head than in the chest or throat,' and lasting, generally, to extreme old age, to the astonishment of the uninitiated hearer, who cannot understand its co-existence with a long white beard.[3] The occurrence of such phenomena is, however, so exceptional, that Pope Pius IX. founded the Scuola di S. Salvatore, near St. Peter's, for the express purpose of supplying the choirs of Rome with boys, subject, as in England, to be discharged on the breaking of their voices.

It remains only to say a few words concerning the style of singing practised by this matchless choir, and the lessons to be learned from it.

For the last three centuries at least there have been preserved certain traditional ornaments and forms of expression which are profound mysteries to the uninitiated (see ALLEGRI; IMPROPERIA). For instance, the Second and Third Lamentations on the three last days in Holy Week are sung, as is generally supposed, by a high voice; but when that voice is too weak for the task it is assisted by another, which, even in the most difficult *abbellimenti*, keeps so exactly with it that the two voices are invariably mistaken for one. Again, there has long been a traditional way of making crescendi and diminuendi which has astonished even the most experienced choirmasters. The secret of this wonderful effect is that not only the amount of tone produced by each individual voice, but the actual number of voices employed, is gradually increased in the one case and diminished in the other. Such effects would no doubt be condemned by English choirmasters as 'tricks,' but they are not tricks. No means can be so condemned, with justice, provided the effect they produce be artistic and legitimate.

BIBL.—F. X. HABERL, *Die römische Schola Cantorum und die päpstlichen Kapellsänger bis zur Mitte 16. Jahrh.* (1887); E. CELANI, *I cantori della Cappella Pontificia* (*R.M.I.*, 1907); KARL WEINMANN, *Die päpstliche Kapelle unter Paul IV.*, 18 pp. (*A.M.*, Jan. 1920); ALBERTO DE ANGELIS, *Domenico Mustafà e la Cappella Sistina* (*R.M.I.*, Anno 29, 1922, pp. 583-607); R. R. TERRY, *Some Sistine Choir Traditions* (*Mus. Ant.*, Oct. 1911); J. W. HENDERSON, *Early History of Singing* (1921).

W. S. R., rev.

**SISTRUM**, an ancient form of rattle used more especially in the worship of Isis: it consisted of a metal frame upon a handle; through the sides of the frame loose metal bars were fitted.

F. W. G.

**SIVORI**, ERNESTO CAMILLO (*b.* Genoa, Oct. 25, 1815; *d.* Via Giulia, Genoa, Feb. 19, 1894), a great violinist. He began the violin at 5, under Restano, and continued it under Costa until about the year 1823, when Paganini met with him, and was so much struck with his talent, as not only to give him lessons, but to compose six sonatas and a concertino for violin, guitar, tenor and violoncello, which they were accustomed to play together, Paganini taking the guitar. This was sufficient to launch the lad into Paganini's style. After a stay of six months in his native city, Paganini left for a tour in Germany in 1824, but before his departure he demonstrated the interest he took in young Sivori by desiring that he should accompany him on his travels. Owing to the child's tender years, however, his parents refused to abandon him to the care of the great violinist. This being the case, Paganini recommended the elder Sivori to place his son with his own former master, Giacomo Costa, and for three years this teacher guided the child's studies so adroitly that when Paganini returned to Genoa in 1827 he found him well equipped as a classical player. Though perfectly satisfied with the progress of his *protégé*, he at the same time considered him lacking in virtuosity, and there-

[1] These statements are founded on information supplied to us by gentlemen resident in Rome, whose high position and long experience render their evidence more than ordinarily trustworthy.
[2] *I.e.* not by operation.
[3] In Adami da Bolsena's *Osservazioni* (Roma, 1711) will be found numerous portraits of soprani and contralti with long beards— many of them priests.

fore suggested a change from Costa's scholastic method to the more volatile system of his intimate friend Dellepiane. Again the boy's progress was astonishing, and at length his father, conquering his objections to a musical career for his son, became desirous that he should make some public appearances outside his own country.

Accordingly, accompanied by his master Dellepiane, Camillo Sivori travelled first to Turin, where he played at a concert on May 3, 1827. He next appeared at Susa on the 5th, Saint Michel 6th, Chambéry 7th, Lyons 16th, Paris 18th, and made his début in London on the 25th. Two days later he was again in Paris, where the Duchesse de Noailles, the Duc de Berri and most of the *dilettanti* of the town interested themselves in him, as did likewise Rossini, Cherubini, Baillot and other eminent musicians of the day. He gave a very successful concert in Paris on Dec. 4. In 1828 Sivori repeated his first triumphs in Paris and London. The autumn of the same year was spent by him in touring in the French provinces. After an absence of eighteen months he at length returned to Genoa in Jan. 1829, and devoted himself earnestly to studying composition with Giovanni Serra, a profound theorist of the classical school, then occupying the post of musical director at the Teatro Carlo Felice in Genoa. During the year 1829 Sivori did little else but study, only acting at intervals as Dellepiane's substitute at the Teatro Carlo Felice, and also at the Conservatorio when the latter was taken ill. He generously gave the entire benefit of these services to his old master, and after Dellepiane's death extended the same charity to his impoverished widow and child for the space of a year. Feb. 1834 found Sivori again in England making his début as a quartet-player in the Queen's Square 'Select Society' meetings at Alsager's house, and on Mar. 28 he played in the first performance of Cherubini's Requiem.

He next traversed Italy, beginning with Florence, in 1839 ; then in 1841 and 1842 visited Prague, Vienna, Leipzig, Berlin, Frankfort, Brussels, St. Petersburg and Moscow. On Jan. 29, 1843, he made his *rentrée* to Paris with a movement from a concerto of his own, his performance of which carried away his audience and procured him a special medal. He also made a vast impression in chamber-music. The brilliantly successful appearance of Jan. 29—when he played his own concerto in E flat, Paganini's concerto in B minor, and the same composer's 'Moïse,' for the G string —took place at the Conservatoire, and that institution presented him with its gold medal of honour. From Paris he went to London, where he made his first appearance at the Philharmonic in May, playing his concerto in A at the same concerts on June 5, 1843, and

repeating it on the 19th (Spohr was in London at the same time) ; returned in 1844, when Mendelssohn, Joachim, Hallé, Piatti and Ernst were here also, and in 1845, when he assisted in the famous performances of Beethoven's Quartets at Alsager's house (see ALSAGER), played at the Musical Union on June 24, etc. etc. Tours in Great Britain and Ireland, and in Holland followed, and in the ensuing year he gave a concert at Brussels (on Mar. 12), returning from thence to Paris and playing *en route* at Liège, Antwerp, Ghent, etc. The season of 1844 was again successfully occupied in London with his own concert at Her Majesty's Theatre, an appearance at a Philharmonic concert under Mendelssohn : a farewell concert at Hanover Square Rooms, where he played the 'Kreutzer Sonata ' with Julius Benedict—a performance which was repeated at the Melodists' Club—and numerous private engagements. In August, Sivori in company with Dohler, Piatti, Henry Russell and Lablache, jun., made a tour of Great Britain. After playing at Hamburg he came to London again during the season of 1845. In 1846 he was again there; on June 27, played Mendelssohn's concerto at a Philharmonic Concert, and was solo violin at Jullien's 'Concerts d'Été.'

He then left for America, in which he remained till 1850, travelling from the Northern States, by Mexico and Panama, to Valparaiso, Rio, Buenos Ayres and Montevideo, and narrowly escaping death by yellow fever. In 1850 he returned to Genoa, and shortly after lost nearly all the money he had made in the new world by an imprudent speculation. In 1851 he was again in Great Britain, touring throughout the whole country. In London he played at Professor Ella's Musical Union concert with Golinelli (pianist) and Piatti. In 1852 he played in Beethoven's triple concerto in C—with Piatti as violoncellist—at the New Philharmonic Society at Exeter Hall under Berlioz's baton. A tour in Scotland in 1853 was followed by a tour in Switzerland, where he broke his wrist in an unfortunate carriage accident at Geneva. On Dec. 15 Sivori played at La Pergola, Florence, returning to Genoa in time for the opening of the Teatro Apollonio. In 1854 he toured in France, and the following year, he married the actress Ortensia Damain, after which he toured in Spain, where the Queen made him Knight of the Order of Carlos III. From Spain he went to Portugal, where the King made him Knight of the Order of Christ the King, and in the spring of 1856 he made appearances in Belgium, Holland and Germany. In 1857 Sivori toured in England with Piatti, and the fourteen-year-old pianist, Arthur Napoleon. In 1862 he scored one more success in Paris in the B minor concerto of Paganini. In 1864 he revisited London, and appeared at the Musical Union and elsewhere. In 1869 Sivori appeared at some of the Monday Popular Concerts in London, and in 1870 toured in France, after which he returned to Genoa and there led a quiet life until his death.

As a man he was always liked—'little, good-tempered, warm-hearted, intelligent Camillo Sivori' is the description of him by an English journalist. He was the only direct pupil of Paganini, and his playing was that of a virtuoso of the Paganini school, with a prodigious command of difficulties, especially of double-stopping, second only to his master. His tone was silvery and clear, but rather thin. His style—judged by a classical standard—was cold and affected, and had little real feeling.

His compositions include :

Two concertos for violin in E flat and A ; cappriccio, La Génoise ; op. 12, Tarantelle napolitaine, violin and orchestra, or piano ; Deux duos concertants for pianoforte and violin ; duet for violin and double bass, written with Bottesini ; Fantaisie Caprice in E ; Fantaisie Étude, op. 10 ; Fantaisie, Fleurs de Naples ; Souvenir de Norma ; Carnaval de Chili ; Carnaval de Cuba ; Carnaval américain ; Tempest Music (Milan, 1860) ; Folies espagnoles ; Variations on ' Nel cor non più mi sento ' and ' Le Pirate ' ; Three Fantasias upon airs from ' La sonnambula,' ' I Puritani,' ' Zapateado ' ; Fantasia on airs from ' Un ballo in maschera,' ' Il Trovatore,' ' Lucia di Lammermoor ' ; Andante Spianato ; ' Trois Romances sans paroles,' with pianoforte accompaniment.

BIBL.—HERON-ALLEN, Camillo Sivori, The Violin Times, Mar. 15, 1894, No. 5, vol. i. ; E. JAMES (Ph. and Lit.D.), Camillo Sivori, a Sketch of his Life, etc. ; G. BENEDIT, C. Sivori (reprinted from the Sémaphore, Marseilles, Mar. 7, 1854) ; ADÈLE PIERROTTET, Camillo Sivori (with pictures) ; G. DA FINO, C. Sivori and F. Romani ; T. L. PHIPSON, Sketches and Anecdotes of Celebrated Violinists ; H. C. LAHEE, Famous Violinists, Musical Standard, Feb. 24, 1894 ; Figaro, Paris, Apr. 1, 1894 ; Journal des Débats, Feb. 28, 1828 ; Siècle, Paris, Feb. 6, 1843 ; Moniteur universel, Paris, Feb. 13, 1843 ; British Minstrel, vol. ii. pp. 165-6 ; FÉTIS, Biog. des mus.

G. ; addns. by E. H.-A.

SIXTH, the interval which embraces six degrees of the scale. There are three forms—the major, the minor and the augmented. (1) The major sixth, as CA, contains 9 mean semitones, and the ratio of its limiting sounds in the true scale is 5 : 3. It is a concord, and in harmony is regarded as the first inversion of the minor common chord. (2) The minor sixth, as CA♭ or EC, contains 8 semitones, and the ratio of its limiting sounds is 8 : 5. It is also a concord, and in harmony regarded as the first inversion of the major common chord. (3) The augmented sixth, which is arrived at by flattening the lower or sharpening the upper extreme sound of a major sixth, as D♭ B, or A♭ F♯, contains 10 semitones, and the ratio of the limiting sounds is 125 : 72. The augmented sixth is a discord, and is usually resolved by moving each note a semitone outwards to the octave, the sharpening or flattening of one of the extreme sounds already implying a straining in that direction. Three forms of the augmented sixth are distinguished by special names : when it is accompanied by the major third it is called ' Italian ' (see a) ; when to this is added the augmented fourth, it is called ' French ' (see b) ; and when the major third and fifth are present (c) it is called ' German.'

(a)    (b)    (c)    (d)

The Neapolitan Sixth is the name by which a chord consisting of a minor sixth and minor third on the subdominant has long been known ; as (d) in the key of C minor. (See INTERVALS ; HARMONY.)    C. H. H. P.

SJÖGREN, EMIL (b. Stockholm, June 6, 1853 ; d. there, Mar. 1918), studied first at the Conservatoire there, and afterwards at Berlin under Kiel for composition and Haupt for the organ. In 1884–85 he made tours through Europe, visiting Vienna, Munich, Venice and Paris. During a stay at Meran he was for six months under the influence of Lange Müller, which affected his work very deeply. From 1891 Sjögren was organist at the Yohanneskyrka at Stockholm, where he was employed in teaching and in composition of all kinds ; chiefly for piano solo, violin and piano, and songs. He was a composer whose works do not display the almost exclusively Scandinavian character of Grieg, but who shows an infusion of German ideas. Among his best-known works are ' Der Contrabandista,' op. 9, for bass voice ; ' Erotikon,' op. 10, for piano ; Novelettes, op. 14, for piano ; the three sonatas, op. 19, op. 24, op. 32, in G minor, E minor and G minor, for violin and piano ; the two sonatas, op. 35 and op. 44, in E minor and A major for piano. Besides these Sjögren wrote a great number of melodies, and detached pieces for the piano. He also wrote much for the voice, as well as many pieces for the organ. His music showed a certain amount of Scandinavian style, coupled with a warm emotionalism which was derived from more southern countries.    D. H.

BIBL.—EMIL SJÖGREN, In memoriam. Med bidrag av Sigrid Elmblad, Gunnar Norlén, W. Peterson-Berger, Helena Nyblom, Berta Sjögren och N. Söderblom, pp. 90 (Stockholm, 1918) ; NILS BRODÉN, Verzeichnis der gedruckten Kompositionen E. Sjögrens (1919).

SKENE MS., see SCOTTISH NATIONAL MUSIC; DAUNEY, William.

SKETCH (Fr. esquisse ; Ger. Skizze ; Ital. schizzo). (1) This name is strictly applied to the preliminary jotting down of a musical idea, or to memoranda of special points of development or orchestration, used by composers in the process of bringing their works to perfection. To analyse the various books of extant sketches by great masters would lie outside the scope of this Dictionary ; we may point out that various sketch-books of Beethoven have been published, which are essential to a knowledge of his methods of working.

(2) A short movement, usually written for the pianoforte, and deriving its name, in some cases, from its descriptive character, in others, from the slightness of its construction.

ŠKROUP, FRANTIŠEK JAN (b. Vosice, near Pardubice, Bohemia, 1801 ; d. Rotterdam, Feb. 7, 1862). Composer of the first Czech opera and of the Czech national anthem, 'Kde domov můj' ('There, where our home is'). He was by profession a lawyer, but gained some experience as a singer and amateur conductor. In 1823 a German opera by Weigl, based on ' The Swiss Family,' was given in Czech, a unique event at that period. Its success was so great that the promoters of the scheme determined to go a step further and produce an opera composed by a Czech to a Czech libretto. Škroup undertook the work, and, having secured the literary services of Chmelenský, he started upon an opera entitled 'Dráteník' ('The Tinker'). The opera was produced at the festival of Candle-mas, 1826. Its reception was extraordinarily enthusiastic, for it had the prestige of being the first native opera ever staged in Bohemia. The music was bright, fluent and uninspired. The brisk overture, in the early Mozartian style, is the best part of the work. There is not much attempt at dramatic characterisation, and the reflection of the folk element is superficial. The national hymn of the Czechs, taken from one of Škroup's later works (' Fidlovačka '), was sub-sequently interpolated at the close of 'Dráteník.' A facsimile reprint of the work, with its original, semi-German, typography, was published by the Umělěcká Beseda (Society of Arts) in 1913 (Prague). Škroup attempted a more ambitious task in ' The Marriage of Libuša ' (1834), but he had not the depth and imagination necessary for epic opera. He was conductor of the State theatre, Prague, from 1827–57, and was the first Czech to occupy this position, which only a few years before had been filled by Carl Maria Weber. Honour is due to Škroup for the industry with which he worked to raise himself from the status of an amateur to such a high position. His last successes as a conductor in Prague were in Wagnerian opera: 'Tannhäuser' (1854), ' Lohengrin ' (1856) and ' The Flying Dutchman ' (1856). He moved to Rotterdam in 1860. His other operas include ' Oldřich and Božena' (Czech) ; ' Der Geisterbraut,' ' Dra-homíra,' 'Der Meergense' (German); incidental music to Tyl's farce ' Fidlovačka ' (1883). Škroup did not found a school of national opera. Between the production of ' Dráteník ' and Smetana's first opera, 'The Brandenburgers in Bohemia '—an interval of thirty years—there was no further progress in this direction.

R. N.

SKUHERSKÝ, František, Z. (b. Opočno, July 31, 1830; d. Budějovice, Aug. 19, 1892, Czech teacher, theorist and composer. He began life as a medical student, but his in-clination to music was so strong that he abandoned this career and studied musical theory under Kittl (q.v.), director of the Prague Conservatoire, and Pítsch (q.v.), director of the Organ School. From 1854–65 Skuherský was director of the Musical Union of Innsbruck, when he was appointed principal of the Organ School in Prague. Other posts came his way : that of court pianist to the Emperor Ferdinand, and director of the court orchestra

(1869) ; lecturer of musical theory at the Czech University, Prague (1882–87). He made a journey to Rome and Regensburg in order to study old church music, especially the Gregorian. He was an hon. member of the Society for the Reform of Church Music in Bohemia (1884). As a teacher he exercised a considerable influence in a progressive direction. His literary work, which must take precedence of his compositions, includes: *Theory of Musical Composition* (1881) ; *Musical Form* (1879) ; *Theory of Harmony* (1885); *The Organ, its management and preservation ; Theoretical and Practical Organ School*. Compositions— operas : ' Samo ' (1854) ; ' Vladimír, bohův zvolenec ' (Vladimir, God's chosen), 1863 ; ' Lova ' (1868) ; ' Rector and General ' (comic opera) ; symphonic poem, ' May ' ; three fugues for orchestra ; pianoforte trio, string quartet and pianoforte quintet.                      R. N.

SLEZAK, Leo (b. Schönberg, Moravia, Aug. 18, 1873), operatic tenor. He was working at a technical institute to become an engineer when his voice developed, and after a brief period of study he made a promising début at Brünn, Mar. 17, 1896, as Lohengrin. He was then engaged for some years at the Berlin Royal Opera, during which he appeared at Covent Garden in 1900, singing Lohengrin to the Elsa of Milka Ternina. Although his vocal method was then rather severely criticised, he accepted an offer to transfer from Berlin to Vienna, where he sang at the Imperial Opera (1901–11). At last, however, in 1908, he decided to go to Paris to study under Jean de Reszke, and both voice and method underwent a marked improvement, the quality and resonance of the head notes gaining especially. This was made manifest at Covent Garden, when he reappeared (June 2, 1909) in a notable revival of Verdi's ' Otello,' singing his exacting music with robust power and beauty of tone. He was at once engaged to undertake the same part at the Metropolitan Opera House, New York, and made his American début therein in Nov. 1909. He remained for three seasons and gave song recitals in several cities. He afterwards won increased fame at the leading European opera houses in the dramatic rôles of Wagner and Meyerbeer.

Bibl.—*International Who's Who in Music* ; Northcott. *Covent Garden and the Royal Opera.*                      H. K.

SLIDE. (1) (Fr. *coulé* ; Ger. *Schleifer*.) (See Ornaments, Vol. III. pp. 769–70.)

(2) (Fr. *glissade* or *port de voix* ; Ital. *portamento*.) To violinists the ' slide ' is one of the principal vehicles of expression, at the same time affording a means of passing from one note to another at a distance. The rules governing the ' slide ' are not restricted, as its use and effect entirely depend upon the judgment of the player, but the following directions are generally observed : (1) A ' slide ' is effected

by allowing the finger already upon the string to move up or down to within a fourth or third of the new note. Care should be taken to keep the fingers strictly within the range of each new position. Another kind of ' slide ' is made by moving the finger over two or more adjoining semitones, without interruption.

In imitation of the matchless *legato* which the human voice alone can attain, violinists frequently employ a ' slide ' limited to adjoining notes. A third ' slide ' is entirely of a brilliant type, and belongs to the *virtuoso, par excellence*, having originated with Paganini. It consists in executing chromatic passages, singly or in thirds, octaves or other combinations, entirely with the same fingers. Paganini's music abounds in this species of ' slide,' as also do the compositions of the masters of the Belgian and French school, who adopted his methods. This ' slide ' did not come into general use until the end of the 18th century or beginning of the 19th. Yet its sister acquirements, the tremolo and shift, were known to violinists a century earlier. Mersenne (*Harm. universelle*, 1636) speaks with delight of such professional violinists as ' les Sieurs Bocan, Lazarin ' and others, who employed a certain ' tremblement qui ravisient l'esprit,' and the same author mentions the violinists who could mount to the octave on every string. Notwithstanding the lack of any direct mention of the ' slide ' previous to the 18th century, the following remark by Jean Rousseau in his *Traité de la viole* (1687) might indicate that the eminent viola da gamba player, Hottman, was acquainted with it :

' It was he [Hottman] who in France first composed melodies (*pièces d'harmonie*) regulated for the viol, so as to make the effect of beautiful singing (*beaux chants*) in imitation of the voice.'

Corelli in the first half of the 17th century founded the correct position and independence of the left hand, but it is doubtful whether he, or his immediate successors, knew the use of the ' slide.' Even at the beginning of the 18th century the generality of violinists relied mostly upon every species of turn and flourish to give expression to their playing. To the ' Beat,' ' Back Fall,' ' Double Backfall,' ' Springer,' etc., writers of violin methods devoted elaborate attention, and, curiously enough, as though foreshadowing the coming of the ' slide,' these very turns were in France called by the name now employed in that country for its English equivalent, *i.e. porte de voix*. Neither Leopold Mozart nor Geminani in the middle of the 18th century mentions the ' slide,' but like their predecessors they consider good taste entirely dependent on the judicious employment of turns. But with Viotti's advent, and his establishment of the French School, the old methods began to give way to a truer mode of expression which found its medium in the change of position on the same string. Viotti's most gifted pupil, Rode, was particularly devoted to this method of playing tender phrases, and no violinist cultivated it more carefully than Rode's imitator and admirer Spohr. The compositions of the latter are full of examples of the ' slide ' in its most classical form, and his *Violin School* contains some of the best instructions and examples of the art to be found.

BIBL.—FELIX HUET, *Études sur les différentes écoles de violon* ; F. GEMINIANI, *The Art of Playing the Violin* ; P.BAILLIOT, *L'Art du violon* ; J. B. CARTIER, *L'Art du violon* ; MERSENNE, *Harmonie universelle* ; JEAN ROUSSEAU, *Traité de la viole*, *La Chronique musicale*, Aug. 1873, *Un Virtuoso en* 1682 ; P. SCUDO, *La Musique ancienne et moderne* ; SPOHR, *Violin School* ; JOHN PLAYFORD, *An Introduction to the Skill of Musick*.                O. R.

(3) A contrivance fitted in some form or other to nearly all wind instruments for the purpose of adjusting the pitch by altering the length of the vibrating air-column. It is also applied in a special form to trombones and to some trumpets for the purpose of filling up those notes of the chromatic scale which lie between the various harmonics or ' open ' notes. For this particular use of the slide principle see TROMBONE and TRUMPET.

For the attainment of the first object the slide may be simple, as on the flute, or U-shaped, as is usual on brass instruments. As the slide is used only for the general adjustment of pitch, it should not move too freely, in case the setting should be accidentally altered. In addition to this main or ' tuning ' slide, brass valve instruments are fitted with slides to the valves for slight adjustments of pitch and for the easy removal of condensed moisture. In instruments such as the flute and clarinet, the speaking length of which varies with the opening of the different side-holes, any permissible alteration of pitch by means of the tuning-slide, or its equivalent in the form of socketed joints, is necessarily small. The reason for this is that the length added by the extension of the slide cannot bear a uniform proportion to the virtually different lengths of the instrument as determined by the different side-holes ; therefore, no considerable alteration of pitch can be obtained on such an instrument without throwing it out of tune within itself. This apparently trifling matter is practically important, and the want of apprehension of it has led many to under-estimate the difficulty and cost of carrying out such a change of pitch as was determined on by the Philharmonic Society of London in 1896, when the present (low) PITCH (*q.v.*) was introduced. The slow progress of the change is largely due to the limitation of the efficiency of the slide, and the consequent need of new instruments constructed to the required pitch.

Attempts have been made to adapt the shifting slide as used on the trombone to the French horn, but the particular proportions of this instrument and others of the horn type do not admit of a successful application of the slide in this way.                                     D. J. B.

SLIVINSKI, JOSEPH VON (*b.* Warsaw, Dec. 15, 1865), studied at Warsaw Conservatorium under Strobl; at Vienna with Leschetizky for four years; and finally with Rubinstein at St. Petersburg. His first appearance in public was in 1890, and he was not long in finding his way to England, where he first appeared at a recital of his own in St. James's Hall, May 17, 1892. In Jan. 1893 he played at one of Henschel's London Symphony Concerts; at the Crystal Palace, Mar. 4; and at the Philharmonic, Mar. 9 of the same year. In the following November he made his first appearance in New York. His playing is remarkable for poetical feeling, as well as for surprising brilliance of touch (*Baker*).                    M.

SLOW MOVEMENT, a generic term for all pieces in slow time, whether separate or forming part of a larger work. It is specially applied to such pieces when they occur in a work in sonata-form. The right of any movement to this title must depend rather on its character than its time indication, for many movements marked Allegretto are strictly slow movements.                                   M.

SLUR (Fr. *légature*, Ger. *Bindungszeichen*, Ital. *legatura*). A curved line drawn over or under a group of notes indicating that the notes included within its limits are to be performed with smoothness, if on a stringed instrument, by a single stroke of the bow, or in singing, in a single breath. (See LEGATO and PHRASING.) In vocal music the slur is employed to indicate the use of PORTAMENTO (*q.v.*), and it is also very generally placed over two or more notes which are sung to a single syllable. In this case, however, the sign is superfluous, since if the passage consists of quavers or shorter notes, the connexion can be shown by writing them in groups instead of separately, while even if the notes are crotchets, the fact of there being but a single syllable sufficiently indicates the *legato*. Moreover, an effect analogous to the slur in instrumental music, whereby the second of two notes is curtailed and weakened, is perfectly possible in singing, and may very probably have been intended by the earlier composers where the sign of the slur is employed. This view is insisted upon by Mendelssohn, who in a letter to G. A. Macfarren [1] strongly objects to the engravers of his edition of 'Israel in Egypt' placing the slur over two quavers or semiquavers which are to be sung to one word.

When the slur is used in combination with a series of dots, thus ♩♩♩♩, it indicates the effect called *mezzo staccato*. (See STACCATO.)
                                      F. T., rev.

SMAREGLIA, ANTONIO (*b.* Pola, Istria,

[1] *Goethe and Mendelssohn*, 2nd ed. p. 77.

May 5, 1854), Italian composer. His parents had decided that he should study engineering, but while attending classes at the Polytechnic in Vienna he happened to hear performances of Beethoven, Mozart and Wagner, which aroused in him such enthusiasm that he left Vienna and entered the Conservatorium at Milan (1872), where he applied himself to the study of composition for some years under Franco Faccio.

His first opera, 'Preziosa,' was given at the Dal Verme Theatre, Milan, in 1879, with considerable success, in spite of the obvious Wagnerian influence it betrays. Equally successful was the next venture, 'Bianca da Cervia,' performed at La Scala in 1882. 'Rè Nala' (Venice, 1887) was the first opera which made Smareglia known in Germany, where 'The Vassal of Szigeth,' produced at Weimar (1889) under Richter, made a very favourable impression, confirmed later by Vienna, Gratz, Munich and Prague. Hanslick defined Smareglia's music on this occasion as 'Italian soul and melody wedded to German science and precision.' 'Cornelius Schutt' was given for the first time at Prague (1893), and soon after, on Brahms's urgent recommendation, at Vienna under Richter. 'Nozze Istriane' (Trieste, 1895), 'La Falena' (Venice, 1896), 'Oceàna' (La Scala, 1902) and 'Abisso' (La Scala, 1914) complete the list of Smareglia's work for the theatre.

Smareglia occupies a singular position amongst modern Italian composers. The Wagnerian influence is unmistakable in his music, and perhaps stands in the way of the rapid and popular appreciation of his more personal qualities. Hanslick was perfectly correct in stating that Smareglia combines the skill of the German with the lyrical impetus of the Italian. In his masterly use of the orchestra, his command of harmony and counterpoint, he stands above his Italian contemporaries. But such music must inevitably show the defects of its qualities. The aristocratic taste of his lyricism has not aroused audiences as more commonplace and less distinguished gifts of others have done. Thus, in spite of the success of his works, he never aroused public curiosity and never won the freedom from material considerations which is the reward of popularity. Smareglia's life was embittered by the loss of his eyesight in 1900. Fortunately he was gifted with a marvellous memory. It was his habit in composing to memorise a whole scene of the libretto, improvise the music on the piano, and then write note for note what he had played. Thus when he became blind he was still able to dictate the whole score of the opera 'Oceàna' from memory.                                F. B.

SMART, a family prominent in English musical life through three generations.

(1) GEORGE, a London music-publisher who had some skill as a performer on the double bass. He was one of a musical family, and the father of Sir George Smart (3). Before entering business, he was an assistant to Robert BREMNER, and had been possibly also employed by William NAPIER. He began in the music trade about 1770, his shop being at the corner of Argyll Street, and numbered 331 Oxford Street. He issued many minor publications, such as country dances and sheet music, and remained at 331 Oxford Street until one of the earliest years of the 19th century, the period of his death. George Smart was one of the founders of a benevolent society for musicians.

(2) THOMAS (d. Aug. 3, 1826 [1]), probably brother to the elder George Smart, was an organist at St. Clement's Danes in 1783. He composed many songs and pieces for the pianoforte and harpsichord. He set to music the well-known song on the death of General Wolfe by Tom Paine, beginning ' In a mouldering cave where the wretched retreat.'        F. K.

(3) SIR GEORGE THOMAS, Knight (b. May 10, 1776; d. London, Feb. 23, 1867), son of George (1), received his early musical education as a chorister of the Chapel Royal under Dr. Ayrton. He learned organ-playing from Dr. Dupuis and composition from Dr. Arnold. On quitting the choir in 1791 he obtained the appointment of organist of St. James's Chapel, Hampstead Road, and was also engaged as a violinist at Salomon's concerts. At a rehearsal of a symphony of Haydn's for one of those concerts the drummer was absent, and Haydn, who was at the harpsichord, inquired if any one present could play the drums. Smart volunteered, but from inexperience was not very successful, whereupon the great composer, ascending the orchestra, gave him a practical lesson in the art of drumming. About the same time he practised as a teacher of the harpsichord and singing. He soon showed an aptitude for conducting musical performances. In 1811, having successfully conducted some concerts in Dublin, he was knighted by the Lord-Lieutenant. In 1813 he was chosen one of the original members of the Philharmonic Society, and between that date and 1844 conducted forty-nine of its concerts. From 1813–1825 he conducted the Lenten oratorios at one or other of the patent theatres, at one of which in 1814 he introduced Beethoven's ' Mount of Olives ' to the English public. In 1818 he directed the City concerts established by Baron Heath. On Apr. 1, 1822, he was appointed one of the organists of the Chapel Royal in the room of Charles Knyvett, deceased. In 1825 he accompanied Charles Kemble to Germany to engage Weber to compose an opera for Covent

Garden, and when Weber came to England in 1826 to bring out his ' Oberon ' he was the guest of Sir George Smart, in whose house he died on June 5.[2] It was mainly by the exertions of Sir George Smart and Sir Julius Benedict that the statue of Weber at Dresden was erected, the greater part of the subscriptions having been collected in England. In 1836 Sir George introduced Mendelssohn's ' St. Paul ' to England at the Liverpool Festival. (On his duties in connexion with the coronation of Queen Victoria, see *Mus. T.*, 1902, p. 18.) On the death of Attwood in 1838 he was appointed one of the composers to the Chapel Royal.

To careful musicianship he added an administrative ability which eminently qualified him for the conductorship of musical festivals and other performances on a large scale, and his services were for many years in request on such occasions all over the country. He conducted festivals at Liverpool in 1823, 1827, 1830, 1833 and 1836; Norwich, 1824, 1827, 1830 and 1833; Bath, 1824; Newcastle-upon-Tyne, 1824 and 1842; Edinburgh, 1824; Bury St. Edmund's, 1828; Dublin and Derby, 1831; Cambridge, 1833 and 1835; Westminster Abbey, 1834; Hull, 1834 and 1840; and Exeter Hall and Manchester, 1836. He was long resorted to by singers desirous of acquiring the traditional manner of singing Handel's songs, which he had been taught by his father, who had seen Handel conduct his oratorios : among the many he so instructed were Sontag and Jenny Lind. He gave lessons in singing until he was past eighty. He edited Orlando Gibbons's Madrigals for the Musical Antiquarian Society, and the Dettingen Te Deum for the Handel Society. He took an active part in procuring the foundation of the Mendelssohn Scholarship. His compositions consist of anthems, chants, Kyries, psalm tunes and glees. In 1863 he published a collection of his anthems and another of his glees and canons. Two of his glees, ' The Squirrel ' and ' The Butterfly's Ball,' were very popular. He died at his house in Bedford Square. A volume entitled *Leaves from the Journal of Sir George Smart*, by H. B. Cox and C. L. E. Cox, was published in 1907.

A younger son of George Smart (1) was (4) CHARLES FREDERICK, who was a chorister of the Chapel Royal, and afterwards a double-bass player in the principal orchestras. Older than Charles, but younger than George, was another brother,

(5) HENRY (b. London, 1778; d. Dublin, Nov. 27, 1823), for a time in his father's business, and subsequently (about 1803) in that of a brewer. This latter trade being unsuccessful, he returned to the musical profession. He had begun his musical education at an early age, and studied the violin under Wilhelm Cramer,

---

[1] W. H. G. F. gives this as the date when Thomas Smart committed suicide.

[2] See *Mus. T.*, 1902, p. 533.

in which he made such progress that when only 14 he was engaged at the Opera, the Concert of Ancient Music, and the Academy of Ancient Music. He was engaged as leader of the band at the Lyceum on its being opened as an English Opera-House in 1809, and continued so for several seasons. He was leader at Drury Lane Theatre from its opening in 1812 until 1821. On June 12, 1819, the band presented him with a silver cup as a token of their regard. He was leader of the Lenten oratorios from the time they came under the management of his brother, Sir George, in 1813, and a member of the Philharmonic Society's orchestra, which he occasionally led. In 1820 he established a manufactory of pianofortes, of a peculiar construction, and on July 22, 1823, obtained a patent for improvements in the construction of pianofortes. He went to Dublin to superintend the début of his pupil, Miss Goward (afterwards Mrs. Keeley), where he was attacked by typhus fever, and died. His son,

(6) HENRY THOMAS (b. London, Oct. 26, 1813; d. July 6, 1879) (known as Henry Smart), was a prominent organist and composer. After declining a commission in the Indian army, he was articled to a solicitor, but quitted law for music, for which he had extraordinary natural faculties, and which he studied principally under W. H. Kearns, though he was to a great extent self-taught. In 1831 he became organist of the parish church of Blackburn, Lancashire, which he resigned in 1836. While at Blackburn he composed his first important work, an anthem for the tercentenary of the Reformation, in 1835. In 1836 he settled in London as organist to St. Philip's Church, Regent Street. In Mar. 1844 he was appointed to the organ of St. Luke's, Old Street, where he remained until 1864, when he was chosen organist of St. Pancras. He was an excellent organ-player, specially happy as an accompanist in the service, a splendid extemporiser, and a voluminous and admirable composer for the instrument. But his compositions were by no means confined to the organ. On May 26, 1855, an opera from his pen, 'Berta, or, The Gnome of the Hartzberg,' was successfully produced at the Haymarket. In 1864 he composed his cantata, 'The Bride of Dunkerron' (his best work), expressly for the Birmingham Festival. He produced two cantatas, 'King René's Daughter,' 1871, and 'The Fishermaidens,' both for female voices. An opera on the subject of 'The Surrender of Calais,' the libretto by Planché, originally intended for Mendelssohn, was put into his hands by Chappell, about 1852, but though considerable progress was made with it, it was never completed. A sacred cantata, 'Jacob,' was written for the Glasgow Festival, produced Nov. 10, 1873, and two large anthems for soli, chorus and organ were written for the Festivals of the London

Choral Choirs Association at St. Paul's in 1876 and 1878—'Sing to the Lord' and 'Lord, thou hast been our refuge.' For many years past his sight had been failing, and soon after 1864 he became too blind to write. All his compositions after that date therefore were committed to paper through dictation.

It is as a composer of partsongs and a writer for the organ that Henry Smart is remembered. His earlier partsongs, 'The Shepherd's Farewell,' 'The Waves' Reproof' and Ave Maria, are lovely; and his organ pieces are full of charming melody and effective combinations. He edited Handel's thirteen Italian duets and two trios for the Handel Society.

In June 1879 the Government granted him a pension of £100 a year in acknowledgment of his services in the cause of music, but he did not live to enjoy it. He was buried in Hampstead Cemetery. His last composition was a Postlude in E♭ for the organ, finished very shortly before the end. His life was written by his friend Dr. Spark (Reeves, 1881). (See the *Mus. T.* for May 1902.)          w. h. h.

SMEGERGILL, WM., see CÆSAR.

SMERT, RICHARD (15th or early 16th cent.), early English composer, described in B.M. Add. MSS. 5665/7b-58 as 'de Plymtree, Co. Devon.' This MS. contains some 23 carols, possibly all by Smert and John Truelove ('Troulouffe'); 9 are unsigned, but the 8 following are by Smert:

'Nowelle . . . tydynges gode y thing to telle,' 'Nowelle . . . who ys there that syngith so,' 'Man be joyfull,' 'Have mercy of me, kyng of blisse,' 'O clavis David,' 'Jhesu fili virginis,' 'Nascitur ex virgine,' 'Blessed mote thou be, swete ihesus.'

They are all for 2 solo voices with 3-part chorus, and the first 'Nowelle' in the above list was printed by Ritson in his 'Ancient Songs' and later by Stafford Smith in 'Musica Antiqua' (1812). Three others, 'Soli Deo sit laudum gloria,' 'O David thow nobelle key,' 'Nesciens mater virgo virum peperit,' are the joint work of Smert and Truelove, and the three remaining are apparently by Truelove alone, although Smert's name is also given at the end of the third, 'Jhesu fili Dei.'          J. Mᴷ.

SMETANA, BEDŘICH (FREDERICK) (b. Litomyšl, S.E. Bohemia, Mar. 2, 1824; d. Prague, May 12, 1884), Czech composer, founder of the National School of modern Czech music.

Smetana's father, manager of the brewery on the estate of Count Waldstein, was something of an amateur musician, and played the violin. The boy seems to have rivalled Mozart as a youthful prodigy. At 5 he took part in a Haydn quartet; at 6 he made a public début as a pianist, playing the overture to Auber's 'La Muette de Portici,' and at 8 he had composed a few dance tunes. He received no systematic tuition, but managed to acquire a good execution, and while at school at Plzen (Pilsen) from 1840-43, he was much sought after in provincial society for his

brilliant performances of Liszt, Thalberg and
Henselt. These facile achievements did not
stifle his wider ambitions. At this time he
wrote in his diary : ' I wish to become a
Mozart in composition and a Liszt in technique.'
In Plzen he associated frequently with the
Kolař family whom he had known since 1831,
when his father had migrated from Litomyšl to
Jindřich-Hradec, and as a child he had played
duets with the musically gifted daughter
Kateřina Ottilie with whom he now—at the
age of 19—fell seriously in love. Kateřina was
then studying in Prague with Josef Proksch,
the most esteemed pianoforte teacher in the
capital. Thanks to her intercessions, the
master interested himself also in Bedřich and
offered to give him lessons on credit. This
was the more helpful because, when after
leaving school the youth determined to follow
the musical profession, his father, whose
fortunes had declined, regarded his choice with
disfavour, and, finally, giving him 20 golden
florins—his entire patrimony—saw him depart
for Prague with many misgivings. Smetana
was actually faced with extreme hardship when
J. KITTL (q.v.)—then Director of the Conservatoire—recommended him as resident music
master in the family of Count Leopold Thun.
The post had several advantages. While the
family was living in Prague, Smetana was able
to associate with musicians more experienced
than himself, and in the holidays, spent at the
Count's summer seats at Ronsperg, or Mon
Repos, in N.E. Bohemia, he saw new aspects
of scenery. His familiarity with the varied
landscape and the rural customs of his native
land is reflected in all his mature works. It
was probably during these long quiet periods
in the country, brooding on the vicissitudes of
first love, that Smetana's ambitions turned
from virtuosity to composition. His first truly
personal avowal in music was the cycle of
piano pieces ' Bagatelles and Impromptus '
(1844), with their rather naïve sub-titles which
reveal his preoccupations : Innocence, Idylle,
Longing, Love, Discord, etc. The pieces have
the lasting charm of sincerity and contain the
germ of much that Smetana—the auto-
biographer, the individualist, the disciple of
Liszt and Berlioz—expressed later on with
greater power and depth in the operas, symphonic poems and string quartets.

In 1848, the year of the abortive revolution
which only ended in the closer oppression of all
Czech patriots, Smetana left the service of the
Thuns. His views were openly on the side of
national freedom, and during these stormy
days he composed a march for the Students'
Legion and a ' Solemn Overture,' op. 4 ; works
which sufficed to make his name suspect.
Thanks to Liszt's encouragement, he opened a
private music school in Prague and married
in 1849, Kateřina Kolař, who had succeeded

him as teacher in the Thun family. The chief
consolation of the difficult years which followed
were his sympathetic relations with Liszt,
Clara Schumann and other distinguished
visitors to Prague. But success seemed impossible in the atmosphere of prejudice and
suspicion which enveloped Bohemian patriots
in the early 'fifties of last century. Smetana,
like other gifted Czechs, accepted a post
abroad—the conductorship of the Harmoniska
Sallskapet at Gothenburg—which promised a
livelihood and freer musical activity. Here he
remained for five years (1856–61). During
this period his nationalism, at least as regards
music, was in abeyance. The group of
symphonic poems which he composed in
Northern Europe is inspired by other histories
and literatures than those of Bohemia, and
strongly influenced by Liszt. ' In the art of
Weimar,' says Prof. Z. NEJEDLÝ (q.v.),
' Smetana found the answer to many questions
which had previously exercised his mind. Liszt's
symphonic poems appeared to him a bold solution,
showing that music might also be brought into touch
with the intellectual movements of the time ; removed
from its intellectual isolation and enabled to play its
part in the fight for the progressive ideas which would
give a better, freer impulse to the life of Europe.'

From Smetana's correspondence with Liszt
and J. Srb we learn something of the origin
of these early symphonic poems. They are
frank programme music. Of ' Richard III.,
op. 12, the composer writes :
' From the first bar I have presented my own
personification of Richard in musical form. This
leading theme dominates the entire work in various
guises. . . . Before the end, I have endeavoured to
depict his dreadful dream in the tent. . . . The close
tells of his fall. The middle section of the poem
describes Richard the victorious king ; from this
point decadence gradually creeps in.'

' Wallenstein's Camp,' op. 14, followed in
1858. The score bears indications for cuts in
the event of its being played in the form of an
overture to Schiller's play. It is interesting to
note that in this work Smetana completely
ignores the opportunities which occur for the
introduction of Bohemian folk melodies. The
third of this group of works, ' Hakon Jarl,'
op. 16, is based on a forgotten tragedy by the
Danish poet Œlenschlager which offers some
picturesque contrast between the vigorous
pagan usurper, Hakon, and the weak King
Olaf, with his rather colourless retinue of
Christian priests and nobles. The three
symphonic poems were all written during
Smetana's Gothenburg period, but their
first performances were reserved for Prague.
Possibly Smetana's modesty caused him to
withhold his own compositions from the
programmes he conducted in Gothenburg,
where he presented not merely the music of
Wagner and Liszt—the most modern of that
day—but also the classical masterpieces of
Mozart, Beethoven and Mendelssohn.

We hear very little of Smetana's domestic
life during this time, but there is every reason

to believe that his early romance with Kateřína turned out happily and that he sincerely mourned her premature death at Dresden, in April 1857, while on her way back to Bohemia, having suffered much from the rigours of the northern winters. That he married again a year later does not prove him callous. He must have needed a companion in exile, although that exile was tempered by much sympathetic appreciation on the part of his Swedish friends. His second wife, a fellow-countrywoman, Barbara Fernandini by name, soon grew homesick in Scandinavia, and Smetana had already foreseen the need to resign his post in Gothenburg when the march of events in his own country hastened his decision to return to Prague. It was due to Italy's victories over Austria, in 1859, that the iron-handed régime under which the Czechs had long suffered was somewhat relaxed, and the whole race began to awaken to fresh hopes and aspirations. The improvement in the political situation brought a responsive vibration into the intellectual and artistic life. The long cherished dream of possessing a theatre of their own in which plays and operas could be given in the Czech language now seemed realisable. With money raised by public subscription a modest Provisional Theatre (*Prozatímní Divadlo*) was opened in November 1862. In this enterprise, in the institution of subscription concerts given by a permanent orchestra, which eventually blossomed into the institution now known as the Czech Philharmonic Society, and in many subsequent musical activities, Smetana led the way (see PRAGUE). He became conductor of the distinguished choral society Hlahol, helped to found the Society of Artists (*Umělecká Beseda*), and generally speaking, fought the battle of modern music as opposed to Italian opera and a pernicious 'star' system. But his work went beyond mere organisation. All his creative faculties were soon concentrated on endowing his people with a series of musical works typically Czech in spirit and treatment. Smetana's aim reached above folk-song opera. In his opinion no national style could be built up on a mere imitation of the folk melodies. 'The essence of his Czech spirit was thought; not playing with tones.' Hence his Czech spirit in no way hindered his feeling of unity with the great world-masters, for, thus conceived, it was not 'national, but of a universal character' (Nejedlý). It was precisely this universalism and insight into all that pertained to musical progress that shortly drew upon Smetana the reproach of Wagnerism from a narrow-minded section of his own people.

The Provisional Opera House being an accomplished fact, the creation of a genuine Czech Opera became a question of national honour. The first of Smetana's eight patriotic operas, 'The Brandenburgers in Bohemia' (*Braniboři u Čechách*), was completed in 1863, but its production was delayed until January 1866, when the composer conducted it in person. The literary material of 'The Brandenburgers' has several points of resemblance to Moussorgsky's historical opera 'Boris Godounov.' It deals with the fortunes of a prince in his minority, a ruthless guardian, a host of avaricious Teutons swarming into Bohemia, as the Polish invaders strive to overrun Russia in 'Boris,' while a whole people rising in rebellion forms the chief protagonist of both dramas. But the librettist, Sabina, had no inspired basis, such as Poushkin's great tragedy, on which to build. The libretto has many faults. Nor had Smetana as yet found a unified and intensely personal musical style, although the work contains the germ of his maturer art in its moments of dramatic emotion, its lyrical flow and national tendency. 'The Brandenburgers,' received with enthusiasm, was subsequently eclipsed by the immense popularity of 'The Bartered Bride' (*Prodana Nevěsta*), but it has recently been revived and is now in the regular repertory of the National Theatre.

While waiting for the production of 'The Brandenburgers,' Smetana composed a comic opera of unrivalled freshness and gaiety of spirit. Throughout his life, which was darkened by much physical and mental suffering, the composer preserved a share of the unconquerable optimism which was his birthright as a Czech. Nejedlý tells us that whereas life in the Bohemian towns was at that time still overshadowed by German oppression, rural Bohemia was—at least in Smetana's eyes—bright with mirth, a place of sunshine and hearty good humour. The libretto of 'Prodana Nevěsta' is also by Sabina, who shows himself much better able to deal with a tale of rustic life than with historical drama. He has given Smetana suggestions which the musician has filled out into a vivid and truthful picture of the national life. Although Smetana turns away from anything sordid or harrowing in peasant life, and sets his figures in a warm and happy atmosphere, there is a realism in the work which is too often ignored in a performance by foreign artists. The sparkling gaiety of the opera should never degenerate into caricature or broad farce. To the Czechs, the opera has a deeper meaning than it can ever convey to the outer world; for at the time when life was at its darkest they found stimulation in its racy humour. To quote Nejedlý again :

'Since Mozart's time there has not been a composer who, with such refined art, and such alluring freshness, could delight the world with such warm, frank and genial humour as the author of "The Bartered Bride." '

From the moment this work was produced at the Provisional Theatre, in September 1870, the Czechs were enraptured by it. The serious operas which followed were often misunderstood by the public for which they were written. Each one consciously embodies some special idea—one might almost say lesson—which Smetana desired to impress upon his people. It took the critical acumen of Hostinský, Procházka and Nejedlý, as well as the devoted services of the conductor KOVAŘOVIC, to set Smetana's operas in a clear light before his fellow-countrymen.

'Dalibor,' which was first heard on the occasion of the laying of the foundation of the permanent National Theatre (*Národni Divadlo*) in Prague, on May 16, 1868, is based on a legend symbolical both of the temperament and national destiny of the Czechs. The tragic, semi-legendary hero Dalibor is the typical liberator, leader and loyal friend, 'the model of what the Czech ought to be.' He personifies the invincible national soul, just as his friend Zdeněk the minstrel, whose wraith visits the hero in the darkest hour of affliction, is typical of the spirit of hope speaking through the medium of music a message of confidence in a happier future. Musically, the opera is a remarkable example of monothematism, being built on one definite subject which generates a wealth of variants used for psychological suggestion. The work disappointed a public still intoxicated by the joyousness of 'The Bartered Bride.' Again accusations of 'Wagnerism' and 'Teutonism' were hurled at Smetana's head, and 'Dalibor,' revered to-day as a kind of fulfilled gospel to the Czechs, met with a cold reception. Nevertheless, as Nejedlý points out, Smetana had now successfully created a pair of contrasting works, grave and gay, basic types of Czech national opera, and had reached the years which mark the zenith of his powers (1868–74).

Smetana's fourth opera, 'Libuša,' was the outcome of the strong current of political and social aspiration which stirred Bohemia at the close of the 'sixties, and coincided with the founding of the National Opera House. The style of the work was conditioned by the events of the time. Smetana described it not as an opera or music drama, but as a 'solemn festival picture' (*Slavné Tableau*), and desired that it should only be presented 'on festivals which touch the whole Czech nation.'[1] The plot is based on a national legend: Libuša, foundress of Prague, finding the need of a consort to help her in ruling the country, takes the unusual and democratic course of choosing Přemysl, a wise and noble-hearted peasant, to be her husband. Libuša has the gift of prophecy, and in the final scene she evokes a vision of the splendid future of her

country. Thus 'Libuša' is the apotheosis of the Czech people and justifies Smetana's sub-title. The work opens with a fine prelude based on the two chief themes—the motives of Libuša and Přemysl, preceded by a brilliant fanfare which recurs in the course of the opera, proclaiming the twofold affirmation of Bohemia's glorious past and future freedom. The work was first performed in the new National Theatre, on June 11, 1881. Smetana's deafness was then so great a hindrance to his conducting that he turned over the task to Adolf Čech.

'The Two Widows' (*Dvě vdovy*), 1874, offers a complete contrast to 'Libuša.' It is a drawing-room comedy opera taken from a little French play by Malleville and adapted to Czech surroundings. The music is lively and romantic, but it has not the spirit nor the bewitching gaiety of 'The Bartered Bride.'

There is as yet no sign of the disordered hearing and nerve trouble which were threatening Smetana in the music of the charming opera 'The Kiss' (*Hubička*), although in reality it was his first triumph over his terrible physical disability. It was written in the house of his son-in-law, the head forester at Jabkenice, in Northern Bohemia. Smetana calls this small masterpiece a comic opera, but its humour has a quality different from the rollicking fun of 'The Bartered Bride.' The quarrel over the kiss refused by the heroine to the too-impetuous lover, paltry as it seems at first, leads on to issues which border on tragedy. Sun and shadow alternate in the music. It was produced at the Provisional Theatre in November 1876, and is one of the most popular repertory operas in Czechoslovakia. It might possibly prove one of the most transplantable of Smetana's works.

'The Secret' (*Tajemství*), completed between 1876–78, is another opera of rustic life, but less touching and less sure in musical treatment than 'The Kiss.' Smetana's last completed opera, 'The Devil's Wall' (*Čertova Stěna*),[2] was begun in March 1881 and finished in April 1882. The score contains a pathetic note to the second act: 'Achieved in spite of terrible and constant hindrances.' The hindrances were ceaseless noises in the head and hours of deep depression and restlessness. Nevertheless, the music of the opera is coherent and melodious, although the freshness and ease of the earlier operas begins to fail. Moreover, the libretto is, to modern ideas, ultra-romantic and confused. The opera was cruelly assailed by Smetana's detractors on its first production in 1878; but on subsequent revival at the National Theatre, under the careful direction of Kovařovic, the public took it into favour and it has remained in the repertory. In 1883 Smetana began to

---

[1] From a letter by Smetana to J. Srb, 1881.

[2] 'The Devil's Wall' is a vast rock which blocks the course of Vltava some distance above Prague.

work on ' Viola,' a libretto founded on Shake-speare's ' Twelfth Night ' by Eliška KRÁSNO-HORSKÁ (*q.v.*), but his powers of concentration had now gone for ever. The work did not progress beyond the first act.

On Mar. 2, 1884, a concert was organised in Prague in honour of the composer's sixtieth birthday, but he was too ill to be present. A few weeks later his friend Srb persuaded him to enter an asylum, where he died on May 12, 1884. Smetana is buried in the cemetery on the Vyšehrad (Prague), the legendary site of Libuša's court.

Side by side with the operas enumerated, Smetana composed a cycle of symphonic poems under the general title of ' Má Vlast ' (My Country) which, although they are all founded on national subjects, have served to carry his fame further afield than any other examples of his art, always excepting the popular overture to ' The Bartered Bride.' There are six of these works : 1. ' Vyšehrad,' an evocation of Bohemia's past, composed after ' Dalibor ' and ' Libuša,' and reflecting some-thing of the tragedy of the first and the splendour of the latter opera ; 2. ' Vltava,' [1] the epic of the river which, rising in the forest of Šumava, flows through Prague, past its ancient monuments, and is lost to view in the shining distance ; 3. ' Šarka,' illustrating the story of the Czech Amazon, Šarka, beloved of the chieftain Ctirad—a drama of love and revenge ; 4. ' From the Fields and Groves of Bohemia ' (*Z Českych Luhuv a Hajuv*), a pastoral containing a rural merrymaking ; 5. ' Tábor,' named after the city most closely associated with Bohemia's struggles for religious and political freedom ; the music largely based on the grand old Hussite Chorale ' All ye who are warriors of God ' ; 6. ' Blaník ': legend tells how the Hussite heroes slumber within the mountain Blaník, ready at any moment to seize their arms and rise to the defence of their country. Smetana has attached clear programmes to each of these symphonic poems. The entire cycle is frequently given in Czechoslovakia in one programme. In 1909 Sir Henry J. Wood played the whole series in London in the course of the Promenade Concerts.

Smetana was never attracted to purely abstract music. Even in his chamber music he works on a definite and almost realistic programme. His two string quartets which he entitled ' From my Life,' are truly auto-biographical. The first, in E minor, describes his youth ; its yearning aspirations and ebullitions, his happy social life and innately Czech love of the dance, his passion for Kateřina, his mature development, and the suggestion of his future misfortune in the long-drawn screeching note from the violins

in the finale. The subject of the quartet has created the form of the work which is clear and organic ; while the quality of the music reflects more happiness than melancholy. Smetana enjoyed the inestimable advantage of a happy childhood, and his later sufferings never overshadowed his memories of it. The second quartet, in C minor, takes up the tale of Smetana's life after the catastrophe of deafness had befallen him. It was written in 1882, amid doubts and hopes as to its destiny, as he confides to his friend Srb in his corre-spondence. It has not the balance or clarity of the earlier work, but, played by the Bohemian (Czech) String Quartet, it never fails to awaken interest and emotion. Another chamber work of Smetana's, very little known in this country, is the sincere elegiac pianoforte trio in G minor, composed as early as 1855, in memory of his eldest daughter Frederica, who died at 5 years of age, having already given evidence of remarkable musical talent.

Smetana's pianoforte music shows in its brilliant virtuosity the influence of Liszt, and in its national tendency the influence of Chopin. It is not, however, in the least imitative. In several collections of polkas, he did for this purely Bohemian dance-form what the Polish musician achieved for the mazurka. The ' Czech Dances ' (1878) are particularly exhilarating in their rhythmic variety and make great demands on the pianist. 'The Three Horsemen ' (*Tři jezdci*), ' The Farmer's Song ' (*Rolnická*) and the ' Sea Song ' (all for male voice choir) are fine examples of his choral style. ' Czech Song,' for mixed chorus and orchestra, embodies ' the charm, variety, joyousness and strength of Czech song, given with all the ecstasy of the Czech musician.

Smetana's position in his own country is unique among musicians. Neither Chopin nor Grieg have quite the same powerful national significance. By his determined optimism and far-sightedness he made his art a wonderful stimulus to the national rebirth. His works are so permeated with the spirit of Czech history and nature ; with the spirit of the national life in its widest sense ; that they are ' the best medium for a Czech to become conscious of his national character.' We have seen by the centenary festival of his birth, celebrated in Czechoslovakia in March 1924, that he is loved, and his music known, through-out the land. Not a provincial town, not a remote village, which did not take some active part in this commemoration. As regards the world in general he has also claims to recogni-tion, and the greatest of these is the joyousness which is the essence of his art. Nejedlý claims that

' this happy gift which has been bestowed not only upon the Czechs, but also upon Europeans in general, will be discovered more and more in proportion as it is noticed that it was not a strong feature in other

---

[1] The German name is Moldau ;  the old Latin form Multava.

musicians of the nineteenth century. . . . Art can never live merely by pessimism, scepticism and sadness. This is why mankind has always considered its special benefactors to be the artists who have been able to infuse gladness into human souls, and therefore joy in life for its own sake. In this respect the nineteenth century never saw a greater genius than Smetana.'

### LIST OF SMETANA'S CHIEF WORKS

* Operas: 'The Brandenburgers in Bohemia' (*Branibofi u Čechách*), 1863 ; 'The Bartered Bride' (*Prodana Nevěsta*), 1866 ; 'Dalibor' (1868) ; 'Libuša' (1872) ; 'Two Widows' (*Dvě vdovy*), 1874 ; 'The Kiss' (*Hubička*), 1876 ; 'The Secret' (*Tajemstvi*), 1878; 'The Devil's Wall' (*Čertova Stěna*), 1882 ; 'Viola' (unfinished), 1883.

Symphonic Works: 'Richard III.' (1858) ; 'Wallenstein's Camp' (1858) ; 'Hakon Jarl' (1861) ; 'My Country' (*Má Vlast*), 1874–79—1. 'Vyšehrad'; 2. 'Vitava'; 3. 'Šarka'; 4. 'From the Fields and Groves of Bohemia' (*Z Českých Luhuv a Hajuv*); 5. 'Tábor'; 6. 'Blaník.' 'The Prague Carnival' (1883).

Pianoforte Works: Six Characteristic Pieces (1848), 2 volumes ; 'Listky do památnika' (Album Leaves), 1851 ; Three drawing-room Polkas (1855) ; Three Poetical Polkas (1855) ; Sketches (1858), 2 vols. ; Memories of Bohemia (1861), 2 vols. of Polkas ; 'On the Sea Shore,' Concert Study (1862) ; Dreams (1875), six characteristic pieces ; Czech Dances (1878), ten pieces.

Vocal and Choral: 'Odrodilec' (The Renegade), 1863, male voice duet ; 'Tři jezdci' (The Three Horsemen), 1863, male choir ; 'Rolnická' (The Farmer), 1868, male choir ; Czech Song, 1868, mixed choir and orchestra ; 'Piseň na moři' (Sea Song), 1877, male choir ; Three Choruses for female voices (1878) ; 'Věno' (The Dower) and 'Modlitba' (Prayer), 1880, both for male choir ; 'Naše piseň' (Our Song), 1883 ; 'Večerni pisni' (Evening Songs), 1879, a cycle of five lyrics.

Chamber Music: Pianoforte trio in G minor (1855) ; 'Z mého života' (From out my Life), string quartet in E minor, 1876 ; string quartet in C minor, 1882.

Besides the above, Smetana left a good many early works—Exercises and Studies, impromptus, transcriptions for piano, etc., and all that remains of them is being published in the fine edition of his Collected Works, edited by Dr. Zdeněk Nejedlý and published by the State (2 volumes have appeared so far).

### BIBLIOGRAPHY

In Czech.—K. Teige, *Skladby Smetanovy* (Prague, Fr. Urbánek, 1893), a valuable commentated catalogue of the composer's works ; C. Hostinský, *Bedřich Smetana a jeho boj o moderni Českou hudbu* (Smetana and his fight for modern Czech music), Prague, Laichter, 1901 ; E. Krasnohorska, *Bedřich Smetana*, Prague, Fr. Urbánek, 1885 ; E. Chvala, *Čtvrstoleti České Hudby Bedřich Smetana* ; *Four Centuries of Czech Music*, Prague, Fr. Urbánek, 1888 ; V. V. Zeleny, *O Bedřichu Smetanovi*, Prague, F. Šimacek, 1894 ; Borecky (*q.v.*) in his *Brief Summary of the History of Czech Music*, gives important information ; a vast number of articles in Czech reviews and newspapers especially, since the centenary of 1924. The most important work, however, is the great biography of Smetana by Dr. Z. Nejedlý which is now appearing simultaneously with the Collected Works and will run into several volumes. *Bedřich Smetana*, a shorter biography by Z. Nejedlý, in the series *Zlatoroh*, 4 vols., Prague. In English.—Zdeněk Nejedlý, *Frederick Smetana*, a useful study which appeared in 1924 (London, Geoffrey Bles). In French.—William Ritter. *Smetana* ('Maîtres de la Musique'). Paris, Félix Alcan, 1907 ; Tiersot, *Smetana* (Paris, Laurens, 1926). In German.—Richard Batka, *Die Musik in Böhmen* ('Die Musik'), Berlin ; Bronislav Wellek, *Friedrich Smetana's Leben und Werken*, Prague, Fr. Urbánek, 1900.   R. N.

**SMETHERGELL**, William, a pianist in London, was author of *A Treatise on Thorough Bass*, 1794, and *Rules for Thorough Bass*, with three sonatas for harpsichord and violin (1795) ; he composed also six concertos for harpsichord or pianoforte with two violins and violoncello (1785), six duets for two violins, op. 17 (1880), six easy soli for violin (1790), six lessons for harpsichord, six overtures in eight parts, and a second set, op. 8. He also adapted compositions from Jommelli and other composers, and wrote songs. (*Brit. Mus. Biog.*) He was organist of St. Margaret on the Hill, Southwark, and Allhallows, Barking.   w. h. h.

**SMITH**, Alice Mary (Mrs. Meadows White) (*b.* May 19, 1839 ; *d.* Dec. 4, 1884), a distinguished English composer. She was a pupil of Sir W. Sterndale Bennett and Sir G. A. Macfarren ; married Frederick Meadows White, Q.C. (afterwards a Judge for the County of Middlesex), Jan. 2, 1867, was elected Female Professional Associate of the Philharmonic Society in Nov. 1867, and Hon. Member of the R.A.M. in 1884.

She was a prolific composer of works of all dimensions. The list embraces :

Two symphonies, in C minor (1863), and G ; overtures to 'Endymion' (1864, rewritten 1871),' Lalla Rookh' (1865), 'Masque of Pandora,' with two intermezzi (1878), and 'Jason' (1879) ; a concerto for clarinet and orchestra (1872) ; an introduction and allegro for PF. and orchestra (1865) ; four PF. quartets, in Bb (1861), D (1864), E, and G minor ; a PF. trio in G (1862) ; three string quartets, in D (1862), A (1870), and G ; also five cantatas for soli, chorus and orchestral accompaniment—' Rüdesheim or Gisela' (Cambridge, 1865), Kingsley's 'Ode to the North-East Wind' (Hackney Choral Association, 1880), Collins's 'Ode to the Passions' (Hereford Festival, 1882), Kingsley's 'Song of the Little Baltung' (1883), Kingsley's 'Red King' (1884) ; partsong, 'The Dream' (1863) ; duet (S.T.) 'Maying' ; many solo-songs, duets, etc.

'Her music,' says the *Athenæum* of Dec. 13, 1884,

'is marked by elegance and grace rather than by any great individuality . . . that she was not deficient in power and energy is proved by portions of the "Ode to the North-East Wind," and "The Passions." Her forms were always clear and her ideas free from eccentricity ; her sympathies were evidently with the classic rather than with the romantic school.'   G.

**SMITH**, Charles (*b.* London, 1786 ; *d.* Crediton, Devon, Nov. 22, 1856), was in 1796 admitted a chorister of the Chapel Royal under Dr. Ayrton, but was withdrawn from the choir in 1798 and became a pupil of John Ashley. In 1800 he sang at the Oratorios, Ranelagh, etc. Upon the breaking of his voice in 1803 he acted as deputy organist for Knyvett and Stafford Smith at the Chapel Royal, and soon afterwards became organist of Croydon Church. In 1807 he was appointed organist of Welbeck Chapel. He composed the music for the following dramatic pieces :

'Yes or No,' 1809 ; 'The Tourist Friend,' and 'Hit or Miss,' 1810 ; 'Anything New,' 1811 ; 'How to die for Love' ; 'Knapschou, or the Forest Fiend,' Lyceum, 1830.

In 1815 he appeared, with success, at the Oratorios as a baritone singer. In the next year he settled in Liverpool, where he resided for many years. He composed many songs and ballads, the best of which is 'The Battle ot Hohenlinden.' He published in 1844 a work called 'Ancient Psalmody,' consisting of adaptations from music of Ravenscroft, Morley, etc. He ultimately retired to Crediton, Devon.   w. h. h.

**SMITH**, David Stanley (*b.* Toledo, Ohio, U.S.A., July 6, 1877), American composer and teacher, studied composition with Parker at Yale, from which university he graduated in 1900, when his 'Ode for Commencement Day,' op. 4, was given. Later he studied in London, Munich and Paris, and in 1903 received his Mus.B. from Yale ; North-western University made him Mus.D. in 1918. In 1903 he became an instructor in the Yale School of Music, subsequently becoming assistant and then full professor, and in 1920 succeeding Parker as Dean of the School. Since 1918 he has been conductor of the Horatio Parker Choir (formerly the Choral Art Club) of New Haven (Conn.), and since 1919 he has conducted the New Haven Symphony Orchestra.

His more important works include :

Symphony No. 1, F minor, op. 28.
Symphony No. 2, D, op. 42.
' A Poem of Youth,' orchestra, op. 47.
' Fête galante,' orchestra, with flute obbligato, op. 48.
' Impressions,' orchestral suite, op. 40.
Overture, ' Prince Hal,' op. 31.
' Five Melodies for Orchestra,' op. 50.
' The Fallen Star,' chorus and orchestra, op. 26.
' Rhapsody of St. Bernard,' soli, chorus and orchestra, op. 38.
String quartets ; sonatas for oboe and pianoforte, and violin and pianoforte ; other chamber music ; many anthems and part-songs.                                       W. S. S.

SMITH, EDWARD SYDNEY (b. Dorchester, July 14, 1839 ; d. London, Mar. 3, 1889), received his first musical instruction from his parents, and at the age of 16 went to Leipzig, where he studied the piano under Moscheles and Plaidy ; the violoncello under Grützmacher ; harmony and counterpoint under Hauptmann, Richter and Papperitz ; and composition under Rietz. He returned to England in 1858, and in the following year he settled in London, where he long enjoyed considerable reputation as a teacher. His compositions, which are confined to PF. pieces, were extremely popular with the numerous class of performers whose tastes are satisfied by a maximum of brilliance combined with a minimum of difficulty. The most successful of his many pieces were ' La Harpe éolienne,' ' Le Jet d'eau,' ' The Spinning Wheel,' and a ' Tarantella ' in E minor, which (like most of his compositions) have been published, and met with the same popularity on the Continent as in England. He is buried in Kensal Green Cemetery.                                   W. B. S.

SMITH, ELIAS (late 16th and early 17th cent.), English organist and composer. He was organist of Gloucester Cathedral in 1620, and had possibly held this post for some time before this date (West's Cath. Org.). An anthem by him, ' How is the gould become dimme,' and described as ' for King Charles the Martyr,' is in some partbooks at Durham Cathedral. The tenor cantoris book belonging to this set is in B.M. Add. MSS. 30,478-9.       J. Mᴷ.

SMITH, ' FATHER,' the usual appellation of BERNARD SCHMIDT (b. Germany, c. 1630 ; d. 1708), a celebrated organ-builder who came to England in 1660 with two nephews, Gerard and Bernard,¹ his assistants. These are very little known, although they built several fine instruments. To distinguish him from his nephews and express the reverence due to his abilities, he was called Father Smith.

His first organ in this country was that of the Royal Chapel at Whitehall, but this cannot have been, as formerly stated, that which Pepys heard and mentions in his Diary on July 8, 1660. Subsequently he built another for the Banqueting Hall of Whitehall (1699). (See ORGAN.) There is considerable

¹ According to Hawkins and Burney, but Horace Walpole alters Bernard's name to Christian.

uncertainty about the many organs in London and the provinces ascribed to him. It does not appear that he built for Westminster Abbey, but he built one for St. Margaret's, Westminster (1675), of which in the following year he was elected organist at a salary of £20 a year. He was now rapidly acquiring fame and was ultimately appointed Organ-maker in Ordinary to the King, apartments in Whitehall being allotted to him, called in the old plan ' The Organ-builder's Workhouse.'

In 1682 the treasurers of the Societies of the Temple had some conversation with Smith respecting the erection of an organ in their church. Subsequently Renatus Harris, who had warm supporters amongst the Benchers of the Inner Temple, was introduced to their notice. It was ultimately agreed that each artist should set up an organ in the church, and in 1684 both instruments were ready for competition. In 1685 the Benchers of the Middle Temple made choice of Smith's organ, which was played by Henry Purcell, but those of the Inner Temple dissented, and it was not until 1688 that Smith received payment for his instrument, namely, £1000.

In 1683 he contracted for the organ of Durham Cathedral. In consequence of the reputation he had acquired by these instruments, he was made choice of to build an organ for St. Paul's Cathedral then in course of erection. This instrument was opened on Dec. 2, 1697. Smith became court organ-builder to Queen Anne. His portrait is in the Examination Schools at Oxford.

In 1755 a Gerard Smith was organ-repairer to Chelsea Hospital. This was probably a grand-nephew of Father Smith, since from the date he could hardly have been his nephew.

                                   V. DE P. ; rev. C.

BIBL.—ANDREW FREEMAN, Father Smith (published by Musical Opinion, 1926), contains the fullest examination of the evidence as to what organs Smith built and what remains of his work.

SMITH, (1) GEORGE TOWNSHEND (b. Horse-shoe Cloisters, Windsor, Nov. 14, 1813 ; d. Aug. 3, 1877), son of Edward Woodley Smith (b. May 23, 1775), a chorister of St. Paul's Cathedral, afterwards lay-vicar of St. George's Chapel, Windsor, from 1795 until his death, June 17, 1849.

George Townshend received his early musical education as a chorister of St. George's, Windsor. On quitting the choir he became a pupil of Highmore Skeats, the chapel organist, and afterwards came to London and studied under Samuel Wesley. He next obtained an appointment as organist at Eastbourne, whence he removed to King's Lynn on being chosen organist there. On Jan. 5, 1843, he was appointed organist of Hereford Cathedral. As such he became, ex officio, conductor of the Meeting of the Three Choirs at Hereford, besides discharging the duties of which post he voluntarily undertook the laborious office of honorary secretary to the festival, and by his untiring and energetic exertions, in the course of the twelve triennial festivals which he directed, raised it musically, from a low to a very high condition, and financially, from a heavy loss to a gain. He composed an 8-voice anthem and a Jubilate for the festivals, and other church music, as well as piano pieces of a popular kind.

His brother, (2) ALFRED MONTEM (b. Windsor, May 13, 1828; d. London, May 2, 1891), was also educated in the choir of St. George's. On quitting it he became a tenor singer, and after belonging to the choir of St. Andrew's, Wells Street, succeeded J. W. Hobbs as lay-vicar of Westminster Abbey; he was also a gentleman of the Chapel Royal (1858). He was distinguished as a ballad singer, and for his skill in recitative. He was a professor of singing at the R.A.M. and the Guildhall School.

Another brother, (3) SAMUEL (b. Eton, Aug. 29, 1821; d. Windsor, Jan. 1, 1917), was admitted in 1831 as one of the children of the Chapel Royal under William Hawes. Shortly after leaving the choir he obtained the appointment of organist at Hayes Church, Middlesex, and was subsequently organist at Eton and Egham. In 1857 he became organist at Trinity Church, Windsor, and in 1861 organist of the Parish Church. He issued some compilations of tunes and chants.    W. H. H.

SMITH, JOHN, Mus.D. (b. Cambridge, 1797; d. Nov. 12, 1861). On Nov. 23, 1815, he was admitted to a situation in the choir of Christ Church Cathedral, Dublin, but failed to secure the appointment of vicar-choral owing to his having quarrelled and gone to law with the Dean in 1824. On Feb. 5, 1819, he was appointed a vicar-choral of St. Patrick's Cathedral. On July 7, 1827, the degree of Mus.D. was conferred upon him by the University of Dublin. He afterwards obtained the appointments of Chief Composer of the State Music, Master of the King's Band of State Musicians in Ireland, and Composer to the Chapel Royal, Dublin; and in 1845 was chosen professor of music in Dublin University. He composed 'The Revelation,' an oratorio, some church music, and several prize glees and other compositions. In 1837 he published a volume of Cathedral Music containing services and chants, and a 'Veni, Creator.'    W. H. H.

SMITH, JOHN CHRISTOPHER (b. 1712; d. Oct. 3, 1795), was son of John Christopher Schmidt, of Anspach, who, a few years later, came to England and became Handel's treasurer. He was agent for the sale of Handel's music. While John Cluer engraved the several works published by Handel on his own behalf, Meares sold them in St. Paul's Churchyard, and Smith at the sign of 'The Hand and Musick-Book' in Coventry Street.

The younger Smith showing a fondness for music, Handel began teaching him when he was 13 years old. He afterwards studied composition under Dr. Pepusch and Thomas Roseingrave, and on Nov. 20, 1732, produced his English opera, 'Teraminta,' and in 1733 another opera, 'Ulysses.' In 1738 he composed an oratorio, 'David's Lamentation over Saul and Jonathan.' About 1745 he travelled on the Continent, remaining absent about three years. In 1754 he was appointed the first organist of the Foundling Hospital Chapel.[1]

When Handel became blind Smith was employed as his amanuensis, and Handel's latest compositions were dictated to him. He also played the organ at Handel's oratorio performances. In 1754 he composed the opera of 'The Fairies,' altered from Shakespeare's 'Midsummer Night's Dream,' which met with great success; in 1756 the opera of 'The Tempest,' adapted from Shakespeare's play, two songs in which, 'Full fathom five' and 'The owl is abroad,' long continued favourites; and in 1760 'The Enchanter,' a musical entertainment. Handel bequeathed to him all his original MS. scores, his harpsichord, his bust by Roubilliac and his portrait by Denner. After Handel's death Smith carried on the oratorios, in conjunction with Stanley, until 1774, when he retired and went to reside at Bath. Besides the before-mentioned works he composed 'Paradise Lost' (Covent Garden, 1760), 'Rebecca,' 'Judith,' 'Jehoshaphat' and 'Redemption,' oratorios (besides compiling two oratorios from Handel's works, 'Nabal' and 'Gideon'); 'Dario,' 'Issipile' and 'Il Ciro riconosciuto,' Italian operas; a Burial Service; and several miscellaneous vocal and instrumental pieces. (See Anecdotes of G. F. Handel and J. C. Smith.) George III. having continued to Smith a pension which had been granted by his mother, the Princess Dowager of Wales, Smith evinced his gratitude by presenting to the King all Handel's MS. scores—now in Roy. Lib., B.M.—the harpsichord and the bust by Roubilliac, retaining only the portrait by Denner. Three large collections of Handel's works exist in Smith's MS.: one belonged to H. B. Lennard, Hampstead, and is now in the Fitzwilliam Museum, Cambridge; another to Dr. Chrysander, now in the Hamburg Library; and a third to the Granville family of Wellesbourne Hall, Warwickshire.    W. H. H., addns.

SMITH, JOHN STAFFORD (b. Gloucester, 1750; d. London, Sept. 21, 1836), son of Martin Smith, organist of Gloucester Cathedral from 1743–82, obtained his earliest musical instruction from his father, and was soon afterwards sent to London to study under Dr. Boyce, and also became a chorister of the Chapel Royal under James Nares. On quitting the choir he became an able organist, an efficient

[1] See *Mus. T.*, 1902, p. 377.

tenor singer, an excellent composer and an accomplished musical antiquary.

In 1773 he was awarded two prizes by the Catch Club, one for a catch, ' Here flat,' and the other for a canon, ' O remember not the sins.' In the next four years he gained prizes for the following compositions : ' Let happy lovers fly,' glee, 1774 ; ' Since Phillis has bubbled,' catch, and ' Blest pair of syrens,' glee (five voices), 1775 ; ' While fools their time,' glee, 1776 ; and ' Return, blest days,' glee, 1777. The tune of his song ' Anacreon in Heaven ' has attained posthumous fame as the STAR-SPANGLED BANNER (*q.v.*). He rendered great assistance to Sir John Hawkins in the production of his *History*, not only by reducing ancient compositions into modern notation, but also by the loan of some valuable early MSS. from his extensive and curious library, from which Sir John culled several pieces to enrich his Appendix. In 1779 he published

' A Collection of English Songs, in score, for three and four voices, composed about the year 1500. Taken from MSS. of the same age ';

among which is the Agincourt song, ' Our king went forth to Normandy.' In 1780 he won another prize from the Catch Club by his ode, ' When to the Muses' haunted hill.' He published at various times five collections of glees, containing compositions which place him in the foremost rank of English glee composers. Besides his prize glees they include ' As on a summer's day,' ' What shall he have that killed the deer ? ' ' Hark, the hollow woods resounding,' and the madrigal ' Flora now calleth forth each flower.' Fourteen glees, fourteen catches, four canons, two rounds, an ode, a madrigal and a motet by him are given in Warren's collections. He also published a collection of songs (1785), and ' Twelve Chants composed for the use of the Choirs of the Church of England.' On Dec. 16, 1784, after having for many years officiated as a deputy, he was appointed a gentleman of the Chapel Royal, and on Feb. 22, 1785, a lay-vicar of Westminster Abbey, being installed, after his year of probation, Apr. 18, 1786. In 1790 he was engaged as organist at Gloucester Festival. In 1793 he published a volume of ' Anthems, composed for the Choir Service of the Church of England.' In 1802, upon the death of Dr. Arnold, he was appointed one of the organists of the Chapel Royal, and on May 14, 1805, upon the resignation of Dr. Ayrton, succeeded him as master of the children. In 1812 he produced his interesting work MUSICA ANTIQUA (*q.v.*). In June 1817 he resigned the mastership of the children of the Chapel Royal. Besides the before-named compositions he produced ' An Ode on the First of April,' for voices and instruments, which was never published. A MS. *Introduction to the Art of composing Music,*

by him, is in the library of the Sacred Harmonic Society, now at the R.C.M., which also contains his Musical Commonplace Book. By his will, dated Jan. 21, 1834, he bequeathed all his property to his only surviving daughter, Gertrude Stafford Smith, and appointed her sole executrix. A few years afterwards she became insane, and in 1844 the Commissioner in Lunacy ordered that her property should be realised and the proceeds invested for her benefit. Through ignorance or carelessness the contents of her house (which included her father's valuable library, remarkably rich in ancient English musical manuscripts) were entrusted for sale to an incompetent auctioneer. The library was sold Apr. 24, 1844, such books as were described at all being catalogued from the backs and heaped together in lots, each containing a dozen or more works ; 2191 volumes were thrown into lots described as ' Fifty books, various,' etc. The printed music was similarly dealt with ; the MSS. were not even described as such, but were lumped in lots of twenties and fifties, and called so many ' volumes of music.' 578 volumes were so disposed of, and there were besides five lots each containing ' a quantity of music.' The sale took place in Gray's Inn Road ; Smith's name did not appear on the catalogue ; nothing was done to attract the attention of the musical world, and two dealers, who had obtained information of the sale, purchased many of the lots at very low prices. These after a time were brought into the market, but it is feared the greater part of the MSS. is altogether lost.

W. H. H.

SMITH, ROBERT (*b. circa* 1648 ; *d.* Nov. 22, 1675), English composer, chiefly of instrumental music and incidental music to plays. When Captain Cooke undertook the reorganisation of the Chapel Royal after the Restoration, Smith, with Humfrey (*b.* 1647) and Blow (*b.* 1649), was one of his first set of choir-boys. He was probably one of those ' who were composers while they were still children of His Majesties Chappell.' Clifford's ' Collection ' (2nd edition, 1664) contains the words of 5 anthems by Humfrey, 3 by Blow and 6 by Smith. On leaving the Chapel Royal, Smith seems to have devoted himself to secular composition. In 1672 he composed the music for Shadwell's ' Epsom Wells,' and two years later (Aug. 3), a warrant was issued

' to swear and admit Robert Smyth musician in ordinary to his Majesty in place of Pelham Humphryes, deceased ' [1]

Like Humfrey and Purcell, Smith died young, and only a year afterwards a similar warrant was issued

' to admit Richard Hart musician in ordinary to his Majesty for the lute, in the place of Robert Smyth, deceased.'

1 H. C. Lafontaine, *The King's Musick.*

Tcm D'Urfey, in a passage from his ' Fool turn'd Critick ' (1678), refers to

' . . . Bob Smith . . . late Composer to the King's Play-House . . . a very Excellent Fellow . . . and one the Town misses very much.'

The following collections contain music by Smith :

1673. Matthew Locke, ' Melothesia ' (3 pieces for harpsichord).
1673. Playford, ' Choice Songs and Ayres ' (21 songs and dialogues).
1676. Playford, ' Choice Ayres, Songs and Dialogues ' (all Smith's songs in the 1673 edn., with others added).
1682. Thomas Greeting, ' The Pleasant Companion ' (a flageolet lesson called ' The Earle of Sandwich Farewell ').

Many of these are in MS. in the British Museum and elsewhere, but the following appear to be unprinted :

' O Time, thy wings ' (dialogue between Philander, Time and Death). Ch. Ch. 23.  Score.
' No, no, 'tis vain.'  B.M. Add. MSS. 29,396.

Ch. Ch. also contains a piece for harpsichord and over 100 compositions for various string combinations by him. (See *Mus. Ant.* Apr. 1911, from which most of the above details are taken.)

See *Mus. Ant.* ii. 171 and iv. 120.            J. M<sup>K</sup>.

SMITH, ROBERT (*b.* Cambridge, 1689 ; *d.* there, 1768), Plumian professor of astronomy, master of Trinity College, Cambridge, from 1742.  He wrote *Harmonics or the Philosophy of Musical Sounds* (Cambridge, 1749, 2nd enlarged edition, London, 1759, with *Postscript upon the changeable Harpsichord*, 1762).

E. v. d. S.

SMITH, ROBERT ARCHIBALD (*b.* Reading, Nov. 16, 1780 ; *d.* Jan. 3, 1829).  His father, a Paisley silk-weaver, finding his trade declining in Reading, removed back to Paisley in 1800.  Robert soon showed a great aptitude for music, and at ten could play the violin.  In 1807 he was appointed precentor at the Abbey Church, Paisley, a situation which he filled for many years.  While there he made the acquaintance of Robert Tannahill the poet, many of whose fine lyrics he set to music.  One of these, ' Jessie, the Flow'r o' Dunblane,' published in 1808, at once made its mark, and was universally admired.

Smith possessed a fine vein of melody, and in vocal composition had at that time perhaps no equal in Scotland.  In 1820 he began to publish (edited by Lady Nairne and other ladies) ' The Scottish Minstrel ' (6 vols. 8vo, 1820–24), containing several hundreds of the best Scottish songs, not a few of them his own, frequently without indication.  It is still considered a good compilation.  In Aug. 1823 he obtained the leadership of the psalmody at St. George's Church, Edinburgh.  Besides anthems and other pieces (published in 1810 and 1819, most of the former written for the boys of George Heriot's Hospital), Smith now found time to publish his ' Irish Minstrel,' which was suppressed owing to an infringement of Moore's copyright, followed in 1826 by an *Introduction to Singing*, and in 1827 by ' Select Melodies of all Nations,' in one volume, one of his best works.

In 1828 he brought out his ' Sacred Harmony of the Church of Scotland,' by which he is now best known.  His health was at no time robust, and he suffered from dyspepsia, from which he died.  He was buried in St. Cuthbert's churchyard.

The late George Hogarth says :

' Smith was a musician of sterling talent. . . . His compositions are tender, and tinged with melancholy; simple and unpretending, and always graceful and unaffectedly elegant. . . . He had the admirable good sense to know how far he could safely penetrate into the depths of counterpoint and modulation without losing his way ; and accordingly his music is entirely free from scientific pedantry.'

His most popular pieces are the songs, ' Jessie the Flow'r o' Dunblane ' and ' Bonnie Mary Hay ' ; the duet, ' Row weel, my boatie ' ; the trio ' Ave Sanctissima ' ; and the anthems, ' Sing unto God,' and ' How beautiful upon the mountains ' ; although many more might be named which are yet frequently sung.  An excellent memoir of Smith is attached to an edition of Tannahill's poems edited by Philip Ramsay, Edinburgh, 1851.

D. B. ; addns. F. K.

SMITH, THEODORE, an 18th-19th century excellent pianist and prolific composer, born at Hanover, according to *Fétis*, who gives no authority.  Probably he lived in Germany for some time, as some of his compositions were published by Hummel in Berlin and by Bossler at Speyer.  The greater part of his life was evidently spent in London, where he enjoyed great popularity, especially as a vocal and instrumental composer, whose works appeared between 1770 and 1810, and a song, ' Over the sunny hills,' was republished in 1856.  He composed church music, an opera, ' Alfred,' vocal duets, songs, concertos and sonatas for harpsichord or PF., with and without accompaniment, duets for harp and PF., etc.  Some of his songs were favourites at the public gardens.  Some of his compositions are given in *Q.-L.*

E. v. d. S.

SMOLENSKY, STEPHEN VASSILIEVICH (*b.* Kazan, 1848 ; *d.* there, Aug. 6, 1909), a leading authority on Russian church music. Having had unusual opportunities of gaining an insight into the customs and peculiarities of the sect known as ' Old Believers,' who have preserved the church music in its primitive forms, Smolensky was led to make a special study of the old manuscripts of the Solovetsky library, preserved in the Clerical Academy at Kazan.  In 1889 he became director of the Synodal School and Choir in Moscow, and in the same year was appointed successor to the ecclesiastic Razoumovsky, as professor of the history of church music at the Moscow Conservatorium.  While working at the Synodal School, Smolensky formed a unique collection of manuscripts from the 15th to the 19th century, including many rare chants and other examples of sacred music.  In 1901–03 he directed the Imperial court chapels. Among his numerous contributions to the abstruse and complicated subject on which he was an authority the principal are : *A Course of Church-Chant Singing* (Moscow, 1900, 5th edition) ; *Old Choral Manuscripts in the Synodal School, Moscow* (St. Petersburg, 1899) ; *Ancient Notation of the Russian Church-Chants* (1901).

R. N.

SMORZANDO (Ital., ' fading away '). A term with the same meaning as MORENDO (*q.v.*), but used indiscriminately in the course of a piece.

SMYTH, DAME ETHEL MARY (*b.* London, Apr. 23, 1858), composer, daughter of General J. H. Smyth, late of the Royal Artillery.

For a short time in 1877 she studied at the Leipzig Conservatorium, and under Heinrich von Herzogenberg after leaving that institution. At Leipzig a quintet for strings was performed with success in 1884, and a sonata for piano and violin in 1887. This latter is numbered op. 7, opp. 3 and 4 being books of songs, op. 5 a sonata [1] in A minor for violoncello and piano. After her student days she does not appear to have used opus numbers. A serenade for orchestra in four movements, in D, was given at the Crystal Palace, Apr. 26, 1890 ; and an overture, ' Antony and Cleopatra,' on Oct. 18 of the same year, the latter being repeated at one of Henschel's London Symphony Concerts in 1892. A far more important work, a Mass in D, was performed at the Albert Hall, under Barnby's direction, Jan. 18, 1893. This work definitely placed the composer among the most eminent composers of her time, and easily at the head of all those of her own sex. The most striking thing about it was the entire absence of the qualities that are usually associated with feminine productions ; throughout, it was virile, masterly in construction and workmanship, and particularly remarkable for the excellence and rich colouring of the orchestration. The Mass in D, however, was not again performed until 1924, when it was given under the direction of Adrian Boult, first at Birmingham, then at Queen's Hall, London, with the Birmingham choir. By that time the composer's fame had been established in opera, she had taken a share in the successful campaign for women's suffrage, and had received the title Dame of the British Empire.

Her ' Fantasio ' (libretto founded by herself on De Musset) was produced at Weimar in 1898 in unfortunate conditions, and it was not until its revival at Carlsruhe in Feb. 1901 that it could be properly judged. The one-act ' Der Wald ' was given at Dresden in Sept. 1901 ; it was produced at Covent Garden, July 18, 1902, with very great success, given again at the Metropolitan Opera-House, New York, in Mar.

1903, and again at Covent Garden on June 26, 1903. It was evident that here was a work of highly romantic character (the treatment of the spirits of the wood as the primary agents in the drama is full of suggestive beauty), by one who had mastered not only all the secrets of stage effect, but who understood how to make her climaxes impressive, and how to differentiate her characters. The German libretto of this, like that of her former work, was written by the composer herself.

Her crowning achievement was the three-act opera ' Les Naufrageurs ' (' The Wreckers '), produced at Leipzig as ' Strandrecht ' on Nov. 11, 1906. The libretto, by H. B. Leforestier, bears some slight traces of being originally intended to suit the conventions of the Paris Opéra-Comique rather than the German stage ; but in any language the wonderful power of the conception, musical and dramatic, must make itself felt. In spite of a performance which was so far from ideal that the composer refused to allow it to be repeated at the same theatre, the work created a profound impression. It was given with far more care and success at Prague on Dec. 22 of the same year. In England ' The Wreckers ' was heard first at the ' Afternoon Theatre ' (His Majesty's) under Thomas Beecham, June 22, 1909, then at Covent Garden, Mar. 1, 1910. The fine treatment of the choruses in the first act, the orchestral introduction to the second act, and, in the same section, the great love-duet which rises in intensity of emotion with the rising of the beacon-flame lit by the lovers to warn ships from the dangers of the coast ; and, in the third act, the whole treatment of the final situation, in which the lovers are left by the people to be drowned by the advancing tide, all these points are among the most remarkable things in modern opera, and it is difficult to point to a work of any nationality since Wagner that has a more direct appeal to the emotions, or that is more skilfully planned and carried out. M., addns.

### LATER YEARS

During her earlier years Ethel Smyth had lived largely on the Continent. From about the time of the production of ' The Wreckers ' she began to be better known in her own country ; for while the operatic field remained as limited as ever, British music was becoming a fashion in the concert-room, and moreover feminism was receiving notoriety from the campaign of the militant suffragists. A number of compositions, including the early violin and piano sonata (A minor), the string quartet (E minor), songs (' La Danse,' ' Chrysilla,' ' Anacreontic ode '), with accompaniment for flute, harp, strings, triangle and tambourine, were given with some frequency in chamber music programmes, and two short choral pieces (' Sleepless Dreams ' and ' Hey Nonny No ! ')

---

[1] First performed in London, Nov. 8, 1926, by May Fussell and Kathleen Long.

were brought out at Queen's Hall by the London Choral Society in 1910. In this year she received the degree of Doctor of Music *honoris causâ* from Durham University.

Ethel Smyth's labours in the cause of women's suffrage bore musical fruit in several vocal pieces performed at a concert of her own compositions which she gave at Queen's Hall, Apr. 1, 1911. Among these was a 'March of the Women,' which was much heard in the streets of London as an accompaniment to the processions of the Women's Social and Political Union at about this time. Eventually she introduced the tune into the overture of her next opera, 'The Boatswain's Mate,' produced by Beecham at the Shaftesbury Theatre, Jan. 28, 1916.

'The Boatswain's Mate' bears the stamp of having been written for the English stage by one whose stage technique was acquired in Germany. Ethel Smyth wrote her own libretto on a story by W. W. Jacobs in *Captains All.* That it is one in which the efficiency of the woman is more than a match for the craft of the men no doubt made its theme congenial to the composer. She took pains to underline this leading motive by making the landlady of the 'Beehive' deal competently not only with the sham burglary of the sailor and the soldier, but with a policeman and a chorus of drunken haymakers in turn. Apart from such moral as this idea may contain, 'The Boatswain's Mate' is conceived in the spirit of light comedy, and the first act is carried out in the manner of English ballad opera, with songs (including a few folktunes used incidentally) and concerted numbers interspersed between spoken dialogue. The music of the second act, however, is continuous, and the influence of the German tradition is felt in its general texture, and particularly in the final monologue of the heroine. The whole work is full of brilliant points of humorous characterisation, amongst which nothing is better done than the chorus of haymakers above alluded to. It has passed into the regular repertory of the 'Old Vic,' for which theatre the composer prepared (1921) a version of the score for small orchestra.

Ethel Smyth's later compositions for the stage consist of two one-act operas; 'Fête Galante' (Birmingham Repertory Theatre, June 3, 1923, and subsequently at Covent Garden by the B.N.O.C. and elsewhere) and 'Entente Cordiale' (R.C.M., July 22, 1925); first public performance, Theatre Royal, Bristol, Oct. 20, 1926. The former, called 'a dance dream in one act,' after a romance of Maurice Baring, is a delicate fantasy ending in tragedy; the latter is a ballad opera on the lines of 'The Boatswain's Mate,' but relieved of any suggestion of purpose behind the farcical situation produced from the British soldier's ignorance of the French language. Both these works were produced under the

composer's direction, and of late years she has frequently conducted her own works, including part of the Mass at Gloucester in 1925. Wood produced her new concerto for violin, horn and orchestra at Queen's Hall, Mar. 5, 1927. She has also written two books of autobiography, the first of which, *Impressions that Remained* (1919, 2 vols.), was hailed as a work of literary genius apart from the intrinsic interest of its matter. It was followed by *Streaks of Life* (1921).　　　　　　　　　　　　　　　　　　　C.

SMYTH (SMITH), (1) WILLIAM was organist of Durham Cathedral from 1588–98, and in 1589 petitioned the Vice-Dean and Chapter for remuneration for mending the organs, and received the sum of 30s. He was a minor canon of the same cathedral from 1594–99. Some of his Preces and Responses were printed in Jebb's 'Responses' (1846), and are still sung at Durham.

Preces and Psalms for Christmas Day, morning. PH.; Durh. E. 4-11.
　Do.　　　　Christmas Day, evening.　do.　do.
　Do.　　　　Easter Day, morning.　　do.　do.
　Do.　　　　Whitsunday, morning.　　do.　do.
　Do.　　　　Easter Day, evening.　　Durh. O.B. A1/21.
　　　　　　　　　　　　　　　　　PH. 38/38 ; Bassus
　　　　　　　　　　　　　　　　　decani part only.

Preces and Responses. PH.
1st K. and C.　Durh. C13/8,13 (incomp.).
2nd　do.　　Durh. C13/88 (incomp.).
10 K.　Durh. O.B. A6/243.

The following anthems by him are in the Durham partbooks made when Cosin was bishop there in 1664. The tenor cantoris partbook of this set is in Brit. Mus. Add. MSS. 30,478-9.

'Almighty and everlasting God.' 'Grant, we beseech Thee.' 'I will preach Thy lawe.' 'I will wash my hands.' 'My heart is set.' 'O God, who through.' 'God who hast taught' (with 2nd part). 'O God, who by the preaching.' 'O Lord, which for our sake.'

His son (2) EDWARD (*d.* 1611), was organist of Durham Cathedral, 1609–11 (West's *Cath. Org.*). As in his father's case, some of his Preces and Psalms were printed in Jebb's 'Responses' (1846), and are still sung at Durham Cathedral.

Preces and Psalms for All Saints Day, Morn. PH. ; Durh. E 4-11.
　Do.　　　Ascension Day, Morn. PH. Incomp. Durh.
　　　　　　E. 4-11.
If ye Lord himself, 'for Gunpowder Treason.' Durh. ; PH. ; B.M. Add. MSS. 30,478-9. Tenor cantoris part only.
O Lord, consider. Verse anthem. Durh. ; B.M. Add. MSS. 30,478-9. Tenor cantoris part only.
O Lord my God. Durh. O.B. A2/272, A5/116.
O praise God in his Holiness. Durh. ; PH. ; B.M. Add. MSS. 30,478-9. Tenor cantoris part only.　　　　J. Mᴿ.

SNARE, a piece of catgut rather loosely stretched across the head of a certain type of drum, which, jarring against the vellum when the drum is struck, produces a peculiar effect. (See DRUM 3.) A group of from four to ten snares is employed. (See also PIPE AND TABOR.)

SNETZLER, JOHN (*b.* Passau, Germany, *c.* 1710; *d.* London, end of 18th or beginning of 19th cent.). This truly eminent organbuilder, after acquiring some fame in his own country, was induced to settle in England in 1740. His first organ was that built for Handel in 1741, and used at the first performance of 'Messiah' in Dublin (Apr. 13, 1742). He built the organ for Chesterfield Church in 1741 and opened a factory in London in 1775. He built the noble instrument at Lynn Regis (1754) ; a very fine one at St. Martin's, Leicester (1774) ; that of the German Lutheran Chapel in the Savoy, which was the first in this country provided with a pedal clavier ; and many others, including chamber organs of high quality. Two stories are current of his imperfect way of speaking English and his quaint expressions. At the competition for the place of organist to his new organ at Halifax (1766), he was so annoyed by the rapid playing of Dr. Robert Wainwright, that he paced the church, exclaiming, ' He do run over de keys like one cat, and do not give my pipes time to shpeak.' And at Lynn he told the churchwardens, upon their asking him what their old organ would be worth if repaired, ' If they would lay out £100 upon it, perhaps it would be worth fifty.'

Snetzler lived to an advanced age. He was the friend and executor of SHUDI (q.v.) who left him his ring containing ' Frederick's picture.' Having saved sufficient money, he returned to his native country ; but after being so long accustomed to London porter and English fare, he found in his old age that he could not do without them, so he returned to London. His successor was Ohrmann. (See HILL, W., & SON.)

v. de P. ; addns. W. H. G. F., etc.

SNODHAM, THOMAS, an early London music printer. He was the son-in-law of Thomas EAST (Este), and succeeded to the latter's business in 1609.

He published a great number of the madrigal books of his period, as Byrd's ' Psalms, Songs, and Sonnets,' 1611 ; Maynard's ' The XII. Wonders of the World set and composed for the Viol de Gamba,' 1611 ; Robert Tailour's ' Sacred Hymns,' 1615 ; a second edition of ' Pammelia,' and other works. By reason of some of his imprints reading ' Thomas Este alias Snodham,' it has been considered that East changed his name. This, however, is a mistake, the fact being that Snodham (who had married into the family and obtained the business) merely desired to be associated with the better-known name.      F. K.

SNOW, VALENTINE (d. Dec. 1770), was possibly son of Moses Snow, gentleman of the Chapel Royal from 1689 until his death, Dec. 20, 1702, and also lay-vicar of Westminster Abbey (Mus.B. Cambridge, 1606), and a minor composer. Valentine Snow became the finest performer upon the trumpet of his day ; was a member of Handel's oratorio orchestra ; and it was for him that the latter wrote the obbligato trumpet parts in ' Messiah,' ' Samson,' ' Dettingen Te Deum,' ' Judas Maccabæus,' etc. No better evidence of his ability can be required. In Jan. 1753 he was appointed (in succession to John Shore, deceased) Sergeant Trumpeter to the King, which office he held until his death.      W. H. H.

SNUFF-BOX, MUSICAL, see MECHANICAL APPLIANCES (4).

SOCIETA ARMONICA (1827–50), founded about 1827 for the purpose of giving subscription concerts in which symphonies, overtures, and occasionally instrumental chamber works were intermingled with vocal numbers usually drawn from the Italian operas. H. Forbes was the conductor, and Tolbecque and the younger Mori were the leaders of the band. Beethoven's overture in C major, Berlioz's overture to ' Les Francs Juges,' Reissiger's overture in F minor, and the overture to ' Les Huguenots,' were among the works which gained a first hearing in England at the Society's concerts ; and Weber's Mass in G was also produced. Among the vocalists who assisted in the concerts were Mmes. Grisi, Persiani, Albertazzi, Bishop, Alfred Shaw, Miss Clara Novello and Miss Birch ; Phillips, Rubini, Tamburini and Lablache, Mario and Ivanoff. The band included Spagnoletti, A. Griesbach, Willy, Wagstaff, Dando, Patey, Jay, Alsept, Lindley, Hatton, Brookes, Dragonetti, Howell, Card, Ribas, Barrett, Harper, etc. Henri Herz, the pianist and composer, and Hausmann the violinist, made their first appearance in this country at the Societa Armonica. The concerts were successively held at the Crown and Anchor Tavern in the Strand, Freemasons' Tavern, and the Opera Concert room in the Haymarket.

     C. M.

SOCIÉTÉ DE MUSIQUE DE CHAMBRE, see PARIS.

SOCIÉTÉ DES CONCERTS DU CONSERVATOIRE, see PARIS.

SOCIETY OF BRITISH COMPOSERS (1905–18). This Society was founded in 1905 with the primary object of promoting the publication of works by British composers. Two years after the Society's formation the number of members (composers) and associates (others interested in the movement) was 254, while 44 works of various kinds, principally chamber-music and songs, had been published. The publication of music was undertaken by the Society, either by defraying the whole or part of the cost, or at the sole expense of the composer concerned (see AVISON EDITION). The Society also gave concerts of British music. With the increasing interest on the part of the general musical public in native work and the development in opportunities for obtaining a hearing in one way or another, the immediate need for the Society's activities diminished and it was dissolved in 1918. The balance of the Society's funds was handed over to the Manns Memorial Fund, a small charity administered by the R.A.M., R.C.M. and G.S.M. on behalf of indigent and deserving students. Frederick Corder was one of the chief promoters of the Society, and he acted as chairman throughout its existence.      N. C. G.

SOCIETY OF BRITISH MUSICIANS, THE (1834 – 65), was founded in 1834 with the object of advancing native talent in composition and performance. In the original prospectus of the Society attention was called to the contrast between the encouragement offered to British painting, sculpture, and the tributary arts at the Royal Academy, and the comparative neglect of English music and English musicians, the overwhelming preponderance of foreign compositions in all musical performances being cited as 'calculated to impress the public with the idea that musical genius is an alien to this country,' and as tending also ' to repress those energies and to extinguish that emulation in the breast of the youthful aspirant, which alone can lead to pre-eminence.' One of the rules adopted was to exclude all foreign music from the programmes of the Society's concerts and to admit none but natives of Great Britain among its members ; but this was set aside in 1841, when the Committee reported in favour of ' introducing a limited proportion of music by composers not members of the Society either British or foreign,' and the suggestion was adopted, though not without strong opposition, in which the editor of the *Musical World*[1] joined.

In its earlier days the Society achieved a complete success, numbering in 1836 as many as 350 members, while its finances were also in a prosperous state. It not only gave concerts of works of established merit, but adopted a system of trial performances at which many new compositions were heard. The programmes included the names of all the leading English writers of the day, who as a rule conducted their own works, among them :

Cipriani Potter, G. A. Macfarren, W. H. Holmes, W. L. Phillips, Sterndale Bennett, J. Hullah, J. H. Griesbach, T. German Reed, W. M. Rooke, H. Westrop, Joseph Barnett, H. C. Litolff, C. Lucas, T M. Mudie, James Calkin, and John Goss.

The music included orchestral and chamber compositions, varied by vocal soli and part-music, to which nearly all the above-named composers contributed, and the members in turn directed the performances. After 1837 the Society began to decline, and even when the introduction of music by foreign composers was resolved upon, in the hope of creating more general interest in the concerts, it failed to restore the Society to prosperity, and after another period of far from successful management a special appeal for support was put forth at the close of 1854. At that date the members included :

H. C. Banister, W. S. Bennett, H. Blagrove, J. B. Calkin, C. Coote, J. T. Cooper, W. H. Holmes, C. E. Horsley, H Lazarus, E. J. Loder, Kate Loder (Lady Thompson) C. Neate, W. S. Rockstro, C. Severn, C. Steggall, C. E. Stephens, J. W. Thirlwall, H. J. Trust, F. Westlake, H. Westrop, J. Zerbini, and Sir George Smart.

This effort was ridiculed in the *Musical World*

[1] See *Musical World* of Oct. 14, 1841.

of Dec. 16, 1854, on the ground that the Society had no true claim to its title, as many composers and artists of note held aloof from it. The movement served, however, to draw some new friends to the ranks, and as a means of fulfilling its objects prizes were offered for chamber compositions, which were gained in 1861 by Ebenezer Prout and Edward Perry for string quintets ; in 1863 by J. Lea Summers and W. Gibbons, also for string quintets; and in 1864 by Ebenezer Prout and J. Lea Summers, for quartets for piano and strings. The umpires on these occasions included Joachim, Molique, Piatti, Cipriani Potter, G. A. Macfarren, A. Mellon, T. M. Mudie and H. Leslie. In 1865 the Society was dissolved, its library was sold by Puttick & Simpson, and C. E. Stephens was appointed custodian of the minute-books, etc. The secretaries of the Society were J. R. Tutton (its founder), 1834–35 ; G. J. Baker, 1835 until his death in 1851 ; J. Rackham, 1851–54 ; W. W. Grice, 1854–55. The honorary treasurers were the three brothers Erat, in succession to each other, in 1834–58 ; and Cipriani Potter held the post in 1858–65. The Society and its library were housed gratuitously at 23 Berners Street, by Erat, from 1834 until 1858, when they gave up the premises ; 1858–59 in Wornum's Music Hall, Store Street ; 1860 in St. Martin's Hall until its destruction by fire on Aug. 26, 1860 (when the Society's property was saved) ; 1860–62 at 44 Charlotte Street, Fitzroy Square, by permission of H. Webb ; and 1862–65 at Collard's, Grosvenor Street, free of all expense. For the first five years the concerts were given at the Hanover Square Rooms, and the trials of orchestral and chamber works were subsequently held at those rooms or at the above-named buildings. On July 20, 1843, the Society gave a complimentary concert to Spohr at Erat's, and on June 15, 1844, at the same place, a complimentary concert to Mendelssohn.    c. m.

SOCIETY OF WOMEN MUSICIANS. This society was founded in 1911 by Gertrude Eaton and Marion M. Scott, with offices at the Women's Institute, Victoria Street, moving to 74 Grosvenor Street, W.1, in 1920. By its organisation of lectures and debates on musical subjects, performances of the music of composer-members, meetings for the practice and study of chamber-music, etc., it has done much to consolidate the musical activities and fellowship of women musicians. It possesses two libraries, a general one of music and books, and a collection of British chamber music formed by W. W. COBBETT (*q.v.*) and presented to the Society in 1924 ; the latter is available to the general public. The first president of the Society was Liza Lehmann, among others who have filled that post being Cécile C. Chaminade, Katharine Eggar, Marie Brema, Kathleen Schlesinger and Fanny Davies.    N. C. G.

SÖDERMAN, August Johan (b. Stockholm, July 17, 1732 ; d. there, Feb. 10, 1876), a prominent Swedish composer.

His father was director of the orchestra at a minor theatre. At an early age he displayed traces of musical genius, and when 18 years of age was selected by Stjernström, the director of the orchestra at the Royal theatre in Stockholm, as instructor to a company of musicians, then on a tour to Finland. On his return Söderman wrote his first operetta, with the fantastic title, ' The Devil's first Rudiments of Learning,' which was performed at the Mindre theatre at Stockholm, Sept. 14, 1856. During the following two years he stayed in Leipzig, studying under Richter and Hauptmann ; in the year 1860 he was appointed chorus-master at the Royal Opera in Stockholm; and from that date until his election as a member of the Swedish Academy of Music, his life was occupied in minor offices in the musical world. About 1865 the generosity of Jenny Lind enabled him to continue his studies in Germany.

His works are about sixty in number—operettas, songs, ballads, partsongs, funeral marches, and cantatas ; of which, however, only half have been printed, and these at the expense of the Swedish Government after his death. Of the printed works we can only mention a few, besides the above-mentioned, namely, two operettas, 'The Wedding at Ulfåsa' and ' Regina von Emmeritz ' ; overture and incidental music to ' The Maid of Orleans ' ; songs ; trios for male voices, containing the Finnish national air ' Suomi sång ' ; a quartet for female voices, ' Bröllop,' very popular in Germany, a Circassian dance, and a concert-overture ; also 'Sacred songs for organ,' containing a number of hymns of great beauty and purity, of which the best known are a Benedictus and an Agnus Dei. Though a Protestant, his chef-d'œuvre is a Mass for soli, chorus and orchestra, which has only been rarely performed in Stockholm, but is considered by his countrymen as equal to any by the great composers, and which is animated by such sincere devotion, and stamped by such a high degree of originality and masterly finish, as to rank among the choicest gems of Swedish music.

Another of his works worth mention is his music to the poetry of Bellman. This poet, whose genius is akin to that of Marlowe, has written a number of rhapsodies, depicting the gay, jovial and careless nature of the Swede, with a force of animal spirit and genuine originality which few other poets have equalled ; and to these productions, which every Swede knows by heart, Söderman set music.

The foreign composers who seem to have influenced his more elaborate productions are Beethoven, Schubert and, in particular, Schumanr. His compositions, though thoroughly

Swedish, are not national ; they bear the impress of the vigorous and energetic nature of the Northerner, which makes Scandinavian compositions so charming. On Söderman's death, a national subscription was at once raised in Sweden for the benefit of his widow and children. It was a token of the gratitude and respect of a musical nation for a great composer.                              c. s⁸.

SOGGETTO (Ital.), subject or theme. The true subject of an orthodox Fugue as opposed to the Andamento, which is a subject of abnormal length ; and the Attacco, which is a mere Point of Imitation.

In its most regular form, the Soggetto consists of a single homogeneous section ; as in No. 1 of ' Das wohltemperirte Clavier.' Occasionally, however, its division into two sections is very clearly marked ; as in No. 7 of the same. Subjects of this last-named class frequently make a very near approach to the Andamento, from which they sometimes differ only in their less extended dimensions. (See Andamento ; Attacco ; Fugue.)  w. s. r.

SOKALSKY, (1) Peter Petrovich (b. Kharkov, Sept. 26, 1832 ; d. Odessa, Mar. 1887), was educated at the University of Kharkov, and while acting as under-master in one of the public schools in the town began to collect the folk-songs of the district. Later in life (1857–1860) he was Secretary to the Russian Consulate in New York, and on his return to Russia became editor of the Odessa News. Sokalsky composed several operas: ' Maria ' ('Mazeppa'), ' A Night in May ' and ' The Siege of Doubno ' (from Gogol's Tarass Boulba). His articles on the Chinese Scale in Russian National Music, and Russian National Music (Kharkov, 1888), are valuable to students of this subject.

(2) Vladimir Ivanovich (b. Heidelberg, May 6, 1863), his nephew, studied law at the university of Kharkov. His unpublished compositions include a symphony in G minor (Kharkov, 1894), a dramatic fantasia, an Eastern march and an 'Andante elegiaco' for violoncello and orchestra. His pianoforte pieces, ' Impressions musicales' op. 1, the pianoforte suite ' In the Meadows,' and some songs have been published.                        R. N.

SOKOLOV, Nicholas Alexandrovich (b. St. Petersburg, 1859 ; d. 1922), composer, studied at the Conservatorium, St. Petersburg, from 1877–85 and was a pupil of Rimsky-Korsakov. His chief compositions are : ' Elegy ' (op. 4), and incidental music to Shakespeare's ' Winter's Tale,' for orchestra ; three string quartets, opp. 7, 14 and 20 ; eight pieces for violin and pianoforte ; six for violoncello and pianoforte ; seven choruses a cappella ; four choruses for female voices ; about eighty songs, and a ballet entitled ' The Wild Swans.'
                                      R. N.

SOL, the fifth note of the major scale according to the nomenclature of France and Italy : =G. See HEXACHORD ; SOLMISATION.

SOLDAT, MARIE (Madame SOLDAT-RÖGER) (b. Graz, Mar. 25, 1864), violinist. In her eighth year she took up the violin, under Pleiner, and appeared in public when 10 years of age, performing the 'Fantaisie-Caprice' of Vieuxtemps. Coming under the influence of Joachim and Brahms she resumed study in the Berlin Hochschule in 1879, remaining there till 1882 and gaining the Mendelssohn prize. She subsequently took private lessons from Joachim, whose repertory both of solo and chamber music she adopted, making a special study of the Brahms concerto, which she introduced for the first time to a Viennese audience under Richter. In 1889 she was married to Röger, a lawyer by profession, but continued her public career. She travelled a great deal as a soloist, visiting England occasionally (playing for the first time at a concert of the Bach Choir, Mar. 1, 1888), and had a following among those who admire solid before brilliant acquirements.    w. w. c.

SOLEÁ, see SONG, subsection SPAIN (4).

SOLER, FR. ANTONIO (b. Olot, Catalonia ; d. Escurial, 1783), Spanish composer. A pupil of the Escolanía at Montserrat, he became maestro de capilla at Lérida and then a monk in the Escurial, where he played the organ and performed and wrote chamber music for the Infante D. Gabriel de Bourbon. His quartets (org. and str.) remain in MS. (Escurial and Bibl. Nac., Madrid). His interesting collection of harpsichord music, showing the influence of Domenico Scarlatti and popular Spanish rhythms, was printed in London.

XXVII. Sonatas para Clave, Por el padre Fray Antonio Soler. London: Robert Birchall. (B.M.; Cambridge: Univ. Lib., Fitz-william Collection ; Hamburg.)

Soler also composed music for plays and interludes by Calderón and other Spanish dramatists of the 17th century (MSS. Escurial, Archivo de Música), which were performed in the following century by monks and seminarists. He published a theoretical text-book, *Llave de modulacion y antiguedades de la musica*, Madrid, 1762, and wrote a quantity of church music, both *a cappella* and with organ and strings. A Requiem (8 v. and continuo) was printed by Eslava.    J. B. T.

SOLESMES, a village near Le Mans, whose Benedictine monastery has become famous through the labours of its monks in the restoration of liturgical music, for which they established a printing press, with special type.

The order of the 'Congregation of France,' better known in England as the 'Benedictines of Solesmes,' was founded in 1833 by Dom Prosper Guéranger, who became the first Abbot. Under Guéranger and his successors, Solesmes became a centre for the study and execution of

plain-song, and was visited by many students from all parts of Europe. In 1901, however, owing to their non-compliance with the new Law of Associations, the monks were expelled from Solesmes, and moved in a body to Appuldurcombe, in the Isle of Wight. In 1909 they settled at Quarr Abbey, near Ryde.[1] Their printing-press having been confiscated by the French Government, the publication of their works was transferred to the firm of Desclée et Cie, Tournai, Belgium. Their choir in the Isle of Wight became the practical exponent of their method.

The work of reform began under Dom Guéranger, who, wishing to restore Gregorian music to its earliest known form,[2] engaged his colleagues Dom Pothier (d. 1923) and Dom Jausions (d. 1870) to examine and compare manuscripts, laying down as a principle that ' where the manuscripts of different periods and different countries agree in their version of a melody, it may be affirmed that the true Gregorian text has been discovered.'

But it was of little use to discover the true text unless the proper method of its performance could also be found. At that time Gregorian music, following the traditions of Zarlino and others, was sung in a slow, heavy, unaccented and unrhythmical style, and accompanied on the organ by a separate chord to each note. This style was afterwards alluded to by the Solesmes monks as the ' hammered,' ' martelé,' style. Guéranger and Pothier, on studying the theoretical works of the 9th and 10th centuries, found that plain-song had anciently a rhythm peculiar to itself, differing in important particulars from that of measured music. The first result of this discovery was that Dom Guéranger ' was able to give the singing at Solesmes a rhythm that no one had yet dreamed of,'[3] and from henceforth the chief aim of the musicians of Solesmes was to perfect the rhythmical theory as well as the musical readings.

In 1881 the first edition appeared of ' Les Mélodies grégoriennes, d'après la tradition,' by Dom Pothier, treating the whole theory of plain-song from an entirely new point of view. This important work has formed the basis of all subsequent studies.

The investigations now went on more earnestly than ever. Photography was called in to aid, monks were sent to the principal libraries of Europe to photograph codices, and the year 1883 saw the publication by Dom Pothier of the ' Liber gradualis a Gregorio Magno olim ordinatus, cum notis musicis . . . restitutis in usum congregationis Benedictinae Galliarum.' This was followed in 1891 by the ' Liber antiphonarius pro vesperis et completorio,' also by Pothier, and in 1896 by the

1 The greater number of the monks has now returned to Solesmes in France (1926).
2 For the reason why the earliest form is preferable to that of the time of Palestrina, see PLAIN-SONG.
3 *Plain-Chant and Solesmes.* Cagin and Mocquereau.

'Liber usualis missae et officii,' by Mocquereau.

But others besides the monks of Solesmes were now in the field, endeavouring to reform the liturgical music. Chief among them was Frederic Pustet of Ratisbon, who obtained from Pius IX. a decree under which he was given, by the Congregation of Sacred Rites, the sole right for thirty years of republishing the celebrated 'Medicean' edition authorised by Paul V. in 1614. The same authority recognised Pustet's publication as the official version of plain-song, and recommended it for use in the whole of the Roman Church. The privileges thus given were confirmed by the next Pope, Leo XIII.

This version (known as the 'Ratisbon' edition), which also claims to be the true music of Gregory, is founded on an entirely different principle from that of Solesmes. It is explained thus in the *Magister choralis* of Haberl (Ratisbon, 1893):

'Since the 13th century a principle has existed of improving the melodies by cutting down their enormous length, which arose, partly through a bad method of execution, and partly through the *manieren* of singers. . . . The revision undertaken by the Congregation of Sacred Rites by order of Pius IX. put the foundation of the Roman Chant on the system followed since the Council of Trent.'

The Solesmes view is that at the time the Medicean edition was authorised, plain-song had reached, not its highest development, but its most decadent stage: that in the time of Palestrina, who is supposed to have had a hand in preparing the edition (see PALESTRINA, p. 24) the traditions of its proper performance had been forgotten for centuries; and that its real apogee was immediately after the time of Gregory the Great, when it was collected and written down, and its method of performance described by the theoretical writers.

To support the truth of these views Dom André Mocquereau (later Prior of the Abbey), who brought exceptional musical training to bear on the work, began in 1889 a quarterly publication, entitled *Paléographie musicale*, consisting of photographic facsimiles of Gregorian, Ambrosian, Mozarabic and Gallican manuscripts, together with exhaustive discussions of the various questions involved. The melodies obtained through the comparative study of many manuscripts on the principle laid down by Guéranger, when sung by the Solesmes choir according to the method explained in the *Paléographie*, proved to be of greater artistic and æsthetic excellence than any other form of plain-song.

Owing to the support given to the Ratisbon edition, the monks did not at first obtain recognition beyond their monastery and a few similar establishments. Their labours were, however, rewarded when in 1904 the new Pope, Pius X., who was well versed in music, established a Papal Commission to prepare a new

Official Edition, and at the same time wrote to Dom Paul Delatte, the Abbot, appointing the monks of Solesmes to be the editors. This edition, known as the 'Vatican edition,' is primarily based on the 'Liber gradualis'; but in the preparation of that work the learned editor had not the abundant means of research at his disposal which have since been available; hence certain deficiencies became apparent when the 'Liber gradualis' came into use. These were removed in the Vatican edition, while the monks issued for their own use a special Vatican edition containing the marks of expression as performed by them.

The practical application of the laws of rhythm to the chant is described in the various 'Methods of Plain-Chant' that have issued from the Solesmes and other presses. The theory underlying what is known to modern students of plain-song as 'Free Rhythm' may be briefly described as follows. Free rhythm arose from the setting of the words of Scripture to music at a time when the idea that melody could have a rhythm of its own, to which the words sung must conform in respect of time-duration, had not yet been thought of. Free rhythm practically obeys all the laws of modern musical rhythm except that of definitely fixed time-relationship. Writing in the 11th century, when its laws were still understood, and when what we call 'Free' was called by musicians 'Prose Rhythm,' Aribo says:

'Good Prose Rhythm requires that there should be a rough balance in the groups of syllables, and, naturally, also in the groups of accents and in the members of sentences: but they are not to be subjected to the rigorous laws of metre.'

In 'Syllabic Plain-song,' in which each syllable has a single note (or at most two or three notes very occasionally), the accentuation of the melody is ruled by that of the words. For rhythmical purposes, as well as for the understanding of the ideas to be expressed by them, words are divided into accented and unaccented syllables, and are also grouped into sentences and 'members of sentences.' This is a law of all language, and syllabic plain-song is simply prose language uttered in melody instead of being spoken. The technical plain-song names for sentences and members of sentences are *distinctiones major* and *minor*, and the *distinctiones* are separated by caesuras. At each caesura there is a *mora ultimae vocis* (*ritardando*) which obeys certain rules.

In 'Melismatic Plain-song,' of which the short passage quoted below is an example, the same laws of 'distinctions' caesuras and 'morae' are applied, the syllables and words of prose being represented in the melody by the groups of neumes, which may not only occur in connexion with the single verbal syllables, but may form long 'Melismata,' apart from the words. The technical name for the melisma is 'Pneuma,' *i.e.* 'Breathing,' which must not be confounded with 'Neuma,' a note, or group of notes. The intimate relation as to rhythm between the neume in melody and the syllable in words is shown by the fact that groups of notes are often called 'Syllabae' by the ancient writers. The chant is now executed more rapidly than in the days of the 'hammered' style; and the notes have no relative time-value, but take their duration from the syllables in syllabic, and from certain rules in melismatic melody.

The opening phrase of the Gradual 'Justus ut palma,' as found in the Ratisbon and Solesmes books respectively, will serve to show the difference between the two versions. The

(When using modern notation the Solesmes editors place dots over accented notes: the dots are not to be read as staccato signs.)

difference in method of performance can only be observed by a visit to one of the many churches in which Solesmes plain-song is now cultivated. Below it is appended the Solesmes example in modern notation, as nearly as its rhythm can be expressed, free rhythm not admitting the exact relation implied by crotchets and quavers. The official organ of the Solesmes Abbey is the *Revue grégorienne*, a bi-monthly periodical, edited by Canon Norbert Rousseau of the Grand Séminaire du Mano, in conjunction with the Benedictines of Solesmes.

The following is a list of the more important works connected with plain-song published by the monks of Solesmes. The dates are those of the latest editions.

1881. Les Mélodies grégoriennes d'après la tradition. Pothier.
1883. Liber gradualis. Pothier.
1889. The Paléographie musicale was begun by Dom Mocquereau, who has acted as editor and chief contributor:
    Vol. I. Antiphonale missarum Sancti Gregorii. 10th century. St. Gall Library, Codex 339.
    Vol. II. and III. The Gradual 'Justus ut palma,' reproduced from over 200 MSS.
    Vol. IV. Antiphonale missarum Sancti Gregorii. 10th-11th century. Library of Einsiedeln, Codex 121.
    Vol. V. and VI. The earliest known Ambrosian Antiphonary. 12th century. British Museum, Codex Add. MSS. 34, 209.
    Vol. VII. and VIII. Antiphonarium tonale missarum. 11th century. Library of the School of Medicine, Montpellier, Codex H. 159. This MS. has alphabetical notation above the neumes.
    Vol. IX. Monastic Antiphonary. 12th century. Capitular Library of Lucca, Codex 601.
    Vol. X. Antiphonale missarum Sancti Gregorii. 9th-10th century. Library of Laon, Codex 239.
    Vol. XI. Antiphonale missarum Sancti Gregorii. 10th century. Library of Chartres, Codex 47.
    Vol. XII. Antiphonaire monastique. 13th century. Library of Worcester Cathedral, Codex F. 160.
In addition to the above, there is a second series of the Paléographie musicale, not published at definite intervals. The first volume contains the Monastic Antiphonary of Hartker. 10th century. Cantorium. 9th century. Library of Saint-Gall, Codex 359.
1889. Origine et développement de la notation neumatique. Mocquereau.
1893. Questions grégoriennes. Mocquereau.
1897. Liber antiphonarius pro Vesperis et Completorio. Pothier. Libri antiphonarii pro diurnis horis. Pothier.
1900. Chants des offices. Mocquereau.
1902. Manual de la Messe. French and Latin. Mocquereau.
1903. Liber usualis missae et officiis. Mocquereau.
1906. Liber usualis missae et officiis. Mocquereau.
1907. Kyriale, seu Ordinarium missae cum cantu gregoriano, ad exemplar editionis Vaticanae, concinnatum et rhythmicis signis a Solsmensibus monachis diligenter ornatum.
1907. Méthode complète de chant grégorien. Mocquereau.
Le Nombre musical grégorien, ou Rhythmique grégorienne. Mocquereau.
Monographies grégoriennes. Simples Notes théorétiques et pratiques sur l'édition vaticane. Mocquereau.

BIBL.—N. ROUSSEAU, L'École grégorienne de Solesmes, 1833-1910 (Desclée, Tournai); C. BELLAIGUE, 'A l'Abbaye de Solesmes' (Revue des deux mondes). (Nov. 15, 1898.)

C. F. A. W.

**SOL-FA.** To 'sol-fa' is to sing a passage or a piece of vocal music, giving to the notes, not the words, but the syllables, Do (C), Re (D), Mi (E), Fa (F), Sol (G), La (A), Si (B), Do (C). Why the two syllables Sol and Fa should have been chosen to designate this process in preference to Do Re, or Re Mi, does not appear. (See TONIC SOL-FA and SOL-MISATION.)

In a hymn written by Arrigo Boïto and composed by Mancinelli, for the opening of the monument of Guido d'Arezzo at Rome, the seven syllables are thus employed:

'*Ut*il di Guido *re*gola superna
*Mi*suratrice *fa*cile de' suoni
*Sol*enne or tu *la*ude a te stessa intuoni,
          *Si*llaba eterna.'

The roll or stick with which the conductors of church choirs in Italy beat the time is called the Sólfa.

                            G.

**SOLFEGGIO** (Fr. *solfège*), an exercise for the voice, to be executed either upon vocal sounds only or upon the syllables of the 'sol-fa' notation. At one period the two methods were known by different names, the former being called a *vocalizzo* (Fr. *vocalise*) and the latter a *solfeggio*. Now both are known as *solfeggi*, although the term *vocalizzo* is still applied occasionally to melodies sung without consonants. There is no need to point out here the antique origin of the sol-fa or the purposes to which it came in course of time to be adapted (see SOLMISATION). It cannot be doubted, however, that the use of the syllabic form, alike for the identification of the notes of the diatonic scale and the value of its aid for correctly uniting vowels and consonants in the study of singing, constituted the root idea of the term *Solfeggio*. Its strict application goes back to the days of Tosi and even more remote authorities. It was employed in the same literal sense by Crescentini, the great interpreter of Cimarosa and Cherubini (after he had left the stage and taken up teaching at Naples), in his celebrated collection of vocal exercises. We find the distinction between the two terms first relaxed in the ' Solfèges d'Italie' published in Paris in 1786. The exercises in this volume were by Scarlatti, Porpora, Caffaro and other eminent Italian musicians, and could be treated either as *solfeggi* or *vocalizzi*. The same freedom of choice was allowed in the case of the later and still more remarkable collection entitled ' Solfèges du Conservatoire,' published by Heugel and edited by Édouard Batiste. It was so entitled because the exercises were all composed by professors (*inspecteurs*) of the Conservatoire, headed by its director, Cherubini, who in that capacity wrote a large quantity of *solfeggi*. Some of the examples here given are extraordinarily difficult, and they throw an interesting light upon the nature of the talent and the capacity for prolonged study that were expected from young singers of the French school in those days. Canons and fugues abound ; a fugue by Catel is in 5–4 time ; and there is an exercise by Cherubini in 5 parts, written in strict counterpoint. Clearly *solfeggi* of this calibre could only have been intended for and mastered by students whose course of instruction extended over a period of several years.

The plan of the above collections was essentially progressive—presenting a gradual crescendo of difficulty ; and that plan has been imitated in all later volumes of the kind, being never departed from, nor, indeed, improved upon. On the other hand, their general level of technical difficulty has shown an almost continuous tendency to descend to a lower plane, in order presumably to meet the requirements of a less exacting age. The result has been to lessen the value of this form of study and to affect the standard of the art of vocalisation. Again, the earlier imitators of the ' Solfèges,' although they worked singly and not in groups, were still most of them, despite their Italian birth, attached to the Paris Conservatoire, and they possessed the merit of developing the *solfeggio* along the lines of contemporary musical progress. The volumes separately produced by celebrated teachers such as Bordogni, Panseron, Panofka and

Vaccaj were followed by the less difficult exercises of Concone, Lamperti and Nava, which were, however, somewhat inferior to the later ones of J. Faure, Lablache and the Marchesis. (It may be noted that, so far as the present writer is aware, Manuel Garcia never taught his pupils *solfeggi* of any kind, but made use only of the exercises included in his famous *Traité de l'art du chant*.) Among the still more recent collections that have flooded the music-stores of Western Europe and America one at least deserves mention, both for the originality and skill shown in the illustration of modern intervals and rhythms, and for the fact that it marks a return to the old system of employing various prominent composers upon a single volume. The ' Répertoire moderne de vocalises-études,' as it is called, consists so far of three books, and the names of the writers include those of Fauré, Hué, Florent Schmitt, Dukas, Hahn, Vincent d'Indy, Laparra, Ravel, Leroux, Bourgault-Ducoudray, Rabaud, Vidal and Widor.

Subjoined is a list of the best-known collections of *solfeggi* or *vocalises* extant at the present time, given under the names of the publishing houses in London at which they are still procurable :

| AUGENER | |
|---|---|
| Solfèges du Conservatoire (Heugel). | Stockhausen, Gesangstechnik (Peters ed.). |
| G. Aprile, Exercices pour la vocalisation (Peters ed.). | Tartaglione, Solfèges. |
| Jane Arger, Exercices du chant. | Pauline Viardot, Une Heure d'étude. |
| Félix Aerts, Solfège gradué. | |
| C. Van den Berghe, Douze Exercices journaliers. | **ENOCH** |
| Bertalotti, Solfeggien (Peters ed.). | F. Abt, Solfeggi et vocalises (and Augener). |
| M. W. Balfe, Solfeggi. | F. Paolo Tosti, Petits Solfèges (and Ricordi). |
| A. G. Benvenuti, 12 Vocalizzi for contralto (Schott). | M. Marchesi, 16 Vocalises. |
| Bonoldi, Études de vocalisation (Schott). | **NOVELLO** |
| Brambilla, Exercices et vocalises. | Geo. Henschel, Progressive Studies. |
| Crescentini, Vocalisen (Peters ed.). | Florence A. Marshall, 70 Solfeggi for Class Singing. |
| Danhauser and Lemoine, Solfèges des solfèges (34 vols.). | Sabilla Novello, Exercises for a Contralto Voice. |
| J. Michael Diack, Vocal Exercises (Paterson ed.). | Panseron, 40 Vocal Exercises. |
| Ettore Gelli, Vocalises (Ascherberg ed.). | „ 42 Vocal Exercises. |
| Etelka Gerster, Stimmführer. | |
| A. L. Hettich, Rep. mod. de vocalises-études. | **RICORDI** |
| Lütgen, Kehlfertigkeit (Peters ed.). | Bona, Vocalizzi (7 parts). |
| Lablache, Exercices (Peters ed. or Ricordi). | „ Solfeggi (various). |
| Massimino, Solfèges. | Bordogni, 36 Vocalises, etc. (and Augener or Novello). |
| Mathilde Marchesi, Vocalises. | Carelli, 24 Solfeggi, etc. |
| S. C. de Marchesi, Vocalises. | Concone, 50 Singing Lessons (and other publications). |
| Panofka, 24 Vocalises, op. 81. | Crescentini, complete Solfeggi. |
| „ 24 Vocalises, op. 85. | A. Guercia, Solfeggi. |
| „ 12 Vocalises pour artistes (and Peters, also Ricordi). | F. Lamperti, Lezioni. |
| | G. B. Lamperti, Solfeggi. |
| Panseron, 12 Vocalises (Peters ed.). | G. Nava, Complete Solfeggi (or Augener). |
| Rodolphe, Célèbres Solfèges. | Panseron, Complete Solfeggi (and other publications). |
| Ricci, Solfeggios (J. Williams ed.). | Righini, Solfeggi. |
| Rossini, Gorgheggi e solfeggi. | Rossini, Gorgheggi e Solfeggi. |
| St. Yves-Bax, Agilité de la voix. | Savinelli, Vocalizzi. |
| Sieber, Solfeggi and Vocalises. | Vaccaj, Metodo pratico (and Augener or Peters). |
| Arnold Spoel, 25 Solfèges. | Varisco, Solfeggi. |
| | H. K. |

**SOLIÉ** (SOULIER), (1) JEAN PIERRE (b. Nîmes, 1755 ; d. Paris, Aug. 6, 1812), was both singer and composer at the Opéra-Comique in its early days. The son of a violoncellist he learnt that instrument, and had a good musical education at the Nîmes *maîtrise*, after which he played in the orchestra and taught singing till his début as a tenor in 1778. His success in the provinces tempted him to go to Paris, but he failed at first, in 1782, and remained away till after three years' success in the largest theatre of Lyons. He was engaged in 1787 for the Opéra-Comique, where he remained, gradually making his way upwards to the first place in the company, especially after relinquishing the part of *tenor de goût* for that of baritone. The baritone was then a novelty, and Méhul wrote for Solié several parts which have since become identified with his name. He next tried his hand at composition, and with equal success, for his opéras-comiques number 33 in all, 'Jean et Geneviève' (1792) being the first, and 'Les Ménestrels,' three acts (1811), the last. 'Le Jockey' (Jan. 6), 'Le Secret' (Apr. 20, 1796), 'Le Chapitre second' (June 17, 1799) in one act; and 'Le Diable à quatre' (Nov. 30, 1809), and 'Mademoiselle de Guise' in three (Mar. 17, 1808), were published. Many of the airs became favourites with the vaudeville writers, and were set to a variety of words. Several may be found in the 'Clé du caveau.'

Solié had several sons; the eldest drowned himself in 1802; but (2) ÉMILE (*b.* Paris, 1801) published in 1847 two pamphlets on the Opéra-Comique and Opéra; also some short biographies of French musicians. He left a son, (3) CHARLES, a conductor, who produced at Nice, in 1879, an opéra-comique, 'Scheinn Baba, ou l'intrigue du harem,' three acts.

G. C.

SOLMISATION (Lat. *solmisatio*). The method of illustrating the construction of the musical scale by means of certain syllables, so associated with the sounds of which it is composed as to exemplify both their relative proportions, and the functions they discharge as individual members of a system based upon fixed mathematical principles.

The laws of solmisation first appear among the Greeks, and after making the necessary allowance for differences of tonality, the principle in those earlier times was precisely the principle by which we are guided now. Its essence consisted in the adaptation to the tetrachord of such syllables as should ensure the recognition of the hemitone, wherever it occurred. Now, the hemitone of the Greeks, though not absolutely identical with our diatonic semitone, was its undoubted homologue; [1] and throughout their system this hemitone occurred between the first and second sounds of every tetrachord; just as, in our major scale, the semitones occur between the third and fourth degrees of the two disjunct tetrachords by which the complete octave is represented. Therefore they ordained that the four sounds of the tetrachord should

be represented by the four syllables, $\tau a$, $\tau \epsilon$, $\tau \eta$, $\tau \omega$; and that, in passing from one tetrachord to another, the position of these syllables should be so modified as in every case to place the hemitone between $\tau a$ and $\tau \epsilon$, and the two following tones between $\tau \epsilon$ and $\tau \eta$, and $\tau \eta$ and $\tau \omega$ respectively.

When, early in the 11th century, Guido d'Arezzo substituted his hexachords for the tetrachords of the Greek system, he was so fully alive to the value of this principle that he adapted it to another set of syllables, sufficiently extended to embrace six sounds instead of four. It is said that in the choice of these he was guided by a singular coincidence. Observing that the melody of a hymn, written about the year 770 by Paulus Diaconus, for the festival of St. John the Baptist, was so constructed that its successive phrases began with the six sounds of the hexachord, taken in their regular order, he adopted the syllables sung to these notes as the basis of his new system of Solmisation, changing them from hexachord to hexachord, on principles to be hereafter described, exactly as the Greeks had formerly changed their four syllables from tetrachord to tetrachord.

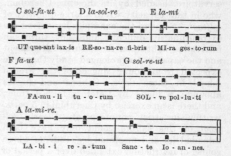

It will be seen from this example that the syllables, *Ut, Re, Mi, Fa, Sol, La,* [2] were originally sung to the notes C, D, E, F, G, A; that is to say, to the six sounds of the natural hexachord; and that the semitone fell between the third and fourth syllables, *Mi* and *Fa*, and these only. (See HEXACHORD.) But, when applied to the hard hexachord, these same six syllables represented the notes G, A, B, C, D, E; while, in the soft hexachord, they were sung to F, G, A, B♭, C, D. The note C therefore was sometimes represented by *Ut*, sometimes by *Fa* and sometimes by *Sol*, according to the hexachord in which it occurred; and was consequently called, in general terms, C *sol-fa-ut*. In like manner A was represented either by *La, Mi* or *Re*; and was hence called A *la-mi-re*, as indicated in our example by the syllables printed

---

[1] The Diatonic Semitone is represented by the fraction $\frac{16}{15}$; the Greek Hemitone by $\frac{256}{243}$, that is to say, by a Perfect Fourth, minus two Greater Tones.

[2] Gerard Vossius in his tract *De quatuor artibus popularibus* (Amsterdam, 1650), mentions the following distich as having been written, shortly after the time of Guido, for the purpose of impressing the six syllables upon the learner's memory—
'Cur adhibes tristi numeros cantumque labori?
UT RElevet (MIserum FAtum SOLitosque LABores.'

above the stave. But under no possible circumstances could the semitone occur between any other syllables than *Mi* and *Fa* ; and herein, as we shall presently see, lay the true value of the system.

So long as the compass of the melody under treatment did not exceed that of a single hexachord, the application of this principle was simple enough ; but, for the solmisation of melodies embracing a more extended range, it was found necessary to introduce certain changes, called mutations, based upon a system corresponding exactly with the practice of the Greeks. (See MUTATION.) Whenever a given melody extended (or modulated) from one hexachord into another, the syllables pertaining to the new series were substituted for those belonging to the old one, at some convenient point, and continued in regular succession until it became convenient to change them back again ; by which means the compass of the scale could be enlarged to any required extent.

For instance, in the following example the passage begins at (*a*), in the natural hexachord of C, but extends upwards three notes beyond its compass, and borrows a B♭ from the soft hexachord of F. As it is not considered desirable to defer the change until the extreme limits of the first hexachord have been reached, it may here be most conveniently made at the note G. Now, in the natural hexachord, G is represented by the syllable *Sol* ; in the soft hexachord, by *Re*. In this case, therefore, we have only to substitute *Re* for *Sol* at this point ; and to continue the solmisation proper to the soft hexachord to the end of the passage, taking no notice of the syllable printed in italics.

The first of these mutations is called *Sol-re*, in allusion to its peculiar interchange of syllables ; the second is called *Re-la*. As a general rule, *Re* is found to be the most convenient syllable for ascending mutations, and *La* for those which extend downwards, in accordance with the recommendation contained in the following distich.

'Vocibus utaris solum mutando duabus
Per *re* quidem sursum mutatur, per *la* deorsum.'

This rule, however, does not exclude the occasional use of the forms contained in the subjoined table, though the direct change from the hard to the soft hexachord, and *vice versâ*, is not recommended.

### Descending Mutations.

1. *Fa-sol.*   From the Hard to the Soft Hexachord, changing on C.
2. *Mi-la.*   Nat. to Hard Hex. changing on E.   Soft to Nat. Hex. changing on A.
3. *Re-la.*   Hard to Nat. Hex. changing on A.   Nat. to Soft Hex. changing on D.
4. *Re-mi.*   Hard to Soft Hex. changing on A.
5. *Re-sol.*   Nat. to Hard Hex. changing on D.   Soft to Nat. Hex. changing on G.
6. *Sol-la.*   Hard to Soft Hex. changing on D.
7. *Ut-fa.*   Nat. to Hard Hex. changing on C.   Soft to Nat. Hex. changing on F.
8. *Ut-re.*   Hard to Soft Hex. changing on G.

### Ascending Mutations.

9. *Fa-ut.*   Hard to Nat. Hexachord, changing on C. Nat. to Soft Hex. changing on F.
10. *La-mi.*   Hard to Nat. Hex. changing on E.
11. *La-re.*   Nat. to Hard Hex. changing on A.   Soft to Nat. Hex. changing on D.
12. *La-sol.*   Soft to Hard Hex. changing on D.
13. *Mi-re.*   Do.     do.    A.
14. *Re-ut.*   Do.     do.    G.
15. *Sol-fa.*   Do.     do.    C.
16. *Sol-re.*   Hard to Nat. Hex. changing on D.   Nat. to Soft Hex. changing on G.
17. *Sol-ut.*   Nat. to Hard Hex. changing on G.   Soft to Nat. Hex. changing on C.

The principle upon which this ancient system was based is that of ' the Movable Ut '—or, as we should now call it, ' the Movable Do ' ; an arrangement which assists the learner very materially, by the recognition of a governing syllable, which, changing with the key, regulates the position of every other syllable in the series, calls attention to the relative proportions existing between the root of the scale and its attendant sounds, and, in pointing out the peculiar characteristics of each subordinate member of the system, lays emphatic stress upon its connexion with its fellow degrees, and thus teaches the ear, as well as the understanding.

So long as the ecclesiastical modes continued in use Guido's system answered its purpose so thoroughly that any attempt to improve upon it would certainly have ended in failure. But when the functions of the leading-note were brought more prominently into notice, the demand for a change became daily more and more urgent. The completion of the octave rendered it not only desirable, but imperatively necessary that the sounds should no longer be arranged in hexachords, but in heptachords or septenaries, for which purpose an extended syllabic arrangement was needed. We have been unable to trace back the definite use of a seventh syllable to an earlier date than the year 1599, when the subject was broached by Erich van der Putten

At (*b*), on the other hand, the passage extends downwards, from the hexachord of G, into that of C. Here, the change may be most conveniently effected by substituting the *La* of the last-named hexachord for the *Re* of the first, at the note A.

(Erycius Puteanus) of Dordrecht, who, at pages 54, 55 of his *Pallas modulata*,[1] proposed the use of *BI*, deriving the idea from the second syllable of la*bii*. No long time, however, elapsed before an overwhelming majority of theorists decided upon the adoption of SI, the two letters of which were suggested by the initials of ' Sancte Ioannes '—the Adonic verse which follows the three Sapphics in the Hymn already quoted.[2] The use of this syllable was strongly advocated by Sethus Calvisius in his *Exercitatio musicae tertia*, printed in 1611. Since then, various attempts have been made to supplant it in favour of *Sa, Za, Ci, Be, Te* and other open syllables; but the suggested changes have rarely survived their originators, though another one, of little less importance—the substitution of *Do* for *Ut* on account of its greater resonance—has, for more than two hundred years, been almost universally accepted. (See Do.) Lorenzo Penna,[3] writing in 1672, speaks of *Do* as then in general use in Italy; and Gerolamo Cantone[4] alludes to it, in nearly similar terms, in 1678, since which period the use of *Ut* has been discontinued, not only in Italy, but in every country in Europe except France.

In Germany and the Netherlands far more sweeping changes than these have been proposed from time to time, and even temporarily accepted. Huberto Waelrant (1517–95) introduced, at Antwerp, a system called ' Bocedisation ' or ' Bobisation,' founded on seven syllables—*Bo, Ce, Di, Ga, Lo, Ma, Ni*—which have since been called the 'Voces Belgicae.' At Stuttgart Daniel Hitzler (1576–1635) based a system of ' Bebisation ' upon *La, Be, Ce, De, Me, Fe, Ge.* A century later Graun (1701–59) invented a method of ' Damenisation,' founded upon the particles *Da, Me, Ni, Po, Tu, La, Be.* But none of these methods have survived.

In England the use of the syllables *Ut* and *Re* died out completely before the middle of the 17th century; and recurring changes of *Mi, Fa, Sol, La*, were used, alone, for the solmisation of all kinds of melodies. Butler mentions this method as being in general use in 1636[5]; and Playford calls attention to the same fact in 1655.[6]

In France the original syllables, with the added *Si*, took firmer root than in Italy; for it had long been the custom, in the Neapolitan schools, to use the series beginning with *Do* for those keys only in which the third is Major. For Minor keys the Neapolitans begin with *Re*, using *Fa* for an accidental flat and *Mi* for a

1 *Pallas modulata, sive Septem discrimina vocum* (Milan, 1599), afterwards reprinted, under the title of *Musathena* (Hanover, 1602).
2 It has been said that in certain versions of the Melody the first syllable of the Adonic verse is actually sung to the note B; but we have never met with such a version, and do not believe in the possibility of its existence.
3 *Albori musicali* (Bologna, 1672).
4 *Armonia Gregoriana* (Turin, 1678).
5 *Principles of Musick*, by C. Butler (London, 1636).
6 *Introductio to the Skill of Musick* (London, 1655).

sharp. (For further modifications in methods of solmisation, see the *Sammelbände* of the Int. Mus. Ges. i. 535, and TONIC SOL-FA.)

w. s. r. ; rev. s. t. w.

SOLO (*Ital.*), ' alone,' a piece or passage executed by one voice or performer. Airs are soli; a pianoforte piece for two hands is a pianoforte solo. A violin solo, strictly speaking, is a piece for the violin alone, like Bach's unaccompanied sonatas ; but the term is often used loosely for a concerto or other piece in which the solo instrument is accompanied by the band, the pianoforte, etc.

In an orchestral piece where one instrument has a passage which is intended to sound out prominently, it is marked ' solo,' as in the second subject of the Adagio in Beethoven's symphony No. 4, which is for the 1st clarinet, and marked *solo* ; in the flute solo near the end of the working-out in the Leonora overture (where, however, the bassoon, equally solo, is merely marked ' 1 '); and in a thousand other instances. In arrangements of pianoforte concertos for two hands, the entry of the solo instrument is marked *solo*, to distinguish it from the compressed accompaniment. (See TASTO SOLO.)　　　G.

SOLOMON. (1) A serenata by William Boyce to words by Edward Moore, produced 1743. The song ' Softly rise, O southern breeze ' was popular for many years.

(2) An oratorio of Handel ; composed between ' Alexander Balus ' and ' Theodora.' It was begun on May 5, 1748, and the memorandum at the end of the work is ' G. F. Handel, Juin 13, 1748, ætatis 63. Völlig geendiget.' The words of the oratorio are supposed to be by Dr. Morell ; but this is not certain. It was produced at Covent Garden Theatre, Mar. 17, 1749, ' with a Concerto,' and was revived by Sir G. Smart at Exeter Hall, Apr. 14, 1836. The Sacred Harmonic Society followed, Dec. 3, 1838 ; and with Costa's additional accompaniments, Apr. 8, 1870.　　　G.

SOLO ORGAN, a manual or clavier of an organ having stops associated with it which for the most part are intended for use *solo*, that is, in single notes as opposed to chords. The solo organ is generally a fourth manual placed above that of the swell ; but it occasionally supersedes the choir organ, and is then placed below the ' Great ' manual. The stops of the solo organ (with the exception of reeds on a high wind pressure) are usually enclosed in a swell-box. (See ORGAN ; ORGAN-PLAYING.)

SOLO STOP. (1) A stop or register of a solo organ or fourth manual. (2) Any stop which can be used as a *solo*—that is, in single notes, *e.g.* a clarinet on the choir organ; a cornopean, hautboy or other reed on the swell organ ; a clarabella or flute on either of the three manuals great, swell or choir. (See ORGAN: Vocabulary of Stops.)　　　J. S.

SOLOVIEV, Nicholas Theopemptovich (*b.* Petrozavodsk, May 9—Apr. 27, O.S.—1846), was intended for the medical profession, but entered the St. Petersburg Conservatorium in 1868, eventually passing into Zaremba's class for composition. In 1871 Serov, being then upon his deathbed, entrusted the orches*ration of his music-drama, 'The Power of Evil,' to Soloviev. About this time his symphonic picture, 'Russians and Mongols,' was given at one of the concerts of the Russian Musical Society. In 1874 Soloviev became a professor at the St. Petersburg Conservatorium. Of his three operas 'Cordelia' (1885) is the best known, having been widely performed in Russia, and also at Prague in 1890. Other compositions comprise a cantata for the bi-centenary of the birth of Peter the Great; an orchestral fantasia on a folk-song; and a number of songs and pieces for pianoforte. As a critic, Soloviev wrote for the *Novoe Vremya, Novosti, Rossia,* etc. He was also well known as a collector of folk-songs.                              R. N.

SOMBRÉE. *Voix sombrée* is the French term for the Veiled Voice (*q.v.*) or *voce velata,* in contradistinction to the *voix claire.*  G.

SOMERVELL, Arthur (*b.* Wintermere, June 5, 1863), Principal Inspector of Music to the Board of Education and Scottish Education Department (Whitehall), has devoted mainly to the interests of education a career which began with conspicuous promise as a composer. Somervell was educated at Uppingham School (from 1877) and King's College, Cambridge (B.A. 1883, Mus.D. 1903). At the University he studied music with Stanford, then went to Berlin to study at the Hochschule with Kiel and Bargiel. In 1885 he entered the R.C.M., and after two years there became a private pupil of Parry. In 1894 he joined the teaching staff of the R.C.M., and in 1901 began his work as an inspector which led to his present important appointment. Apart from songs, which from the first were his most spontaneous form of expression in music, he made his mark in composition with several large works, a Mass in C minor (Bach Choir, 1891), an orchestral ballad, 'Helen of Kirkconnell' (Philharmonic, 1893), and a cantata, 'The Forsaken Merman' (Leeds Festival, 1895). He also wrote 'A Song of Praise' (1891) and 'The Power of Sound' (1895) for the popular festival at Kendal in which he was personally interested, and which has played an important part in the development of the Competition Festivals (*q.v.*). Among later works for the older type of festival were 'Ode to the Sea' (Birmingham, 1897) and 'Intimations of Immortality' (Leeds, 1907).

In later years Somervell has turned more to instrumental composition. His symphonic variations for piano and orchestra, 'Normandy,' a symphony in D minor ('Thalassa') and a

'Concertstück' for violin and orchestra all appeared at about the same time (1912–13). The symphony was first heard under Nikisch at Queen's Hall (Feb. 17, 1913). A quintet for clarinet and strings (London, 1919) and a piano concerto (Guildford, 1921) belong to the same period of composition though their public performance was delayed. The symphony aroused considerable interest on its first appearance because of its complete detachment from all the more sensational acquisitions of contemporary orchestral technique. It was recognised as a sincere and undeniably beautiful piece of writing in a style which would have been perfectly familiar to audiences of 1850 or thereabout. Somervell's art has remained true to the saying that a man's life 'consisteth not in the abundance of the things which he possesseth.' It is always economical of means, direct and unaffected. These qualities give eloquence to his numerous songs, settings of many lyrics of the English poets from Shakespeare to those of the 19th century. They include four cycles : 'Maud' (Tennyson), 'The Shropshire Lad' (Housman), 'James Lee's Wife' (Browning) and 'Love in Springtime.' Of these the 'Maud' cycle takes a place among the classics of English song for the complete unity of feeling existing between poetry and music. The following is a summary of his major compositions. (For a fuller list see *B.M.S. Ann.,* 1920.)

CHORUS AND ORCHESTRA

Mass in C minor. (1891.)
'A Song of Praise.' (1891.)
'The Power of Sound.' (1895.)
'The Charge of the Light Brigade.' (1896.)
Elegy. (Hovingham, 1896.)
'Ode to the Sea,' with sop. solo. (1897.)
'Ode on the Intimations of Immortality.' (1907.)
'The Passion of Christ. An Oratorio for Church Use.' (1914.)
Mass in D minor (men's voices).

ORCHESTRA

Suite, 'Thomas the Rhymer.' (MS.)
Ballad, 'Helen of Kirkconnell.' (See above.)
Suite, 'In Arcady.' Small orch. (Brighton, 1897.)
Symphonic variations, 'Normandy.' PF. and orch. (See above.)
Concertstück. Vln. and orch. (Aachen, 1913.)
Symphony in D minor, 'Thalassa.' (See above.)

CHAMBER MUSIC, ETC.

Quintet. Clar. and strings. (See above.)
'Variations on an Original Theme.' Two pianos.
Pieces for PF. solo, vln. and PF., etc.
Numerous partsongs and solo songs, including the four cycles named above.
'Songs of the Four Nations,' a valuable collection of folk-song.
Various educational works, including 'Rhythmic Gradus' for the PF., sight-reading exercises and technical 'charts.'

c.; incorporating material from M.

SOMIS, (1) Giovanni Battista (*b.* Piedmont, 1676 ; *d.* Turin, Aug. 14, 1763), violinist, studied first under Corelli at Rome, and afterwards under Vivaldi at Venice. Hubert Le Blanc, quoted in Baillot's Violin Tutor, praises the majesty of his style and command over his bow. After his return to Turin he was appointed solo violinist to the King, and leader of the royal band, a position he retained until his death. After having once settled at Turin he appears scarcely ever to have left it ; and so few of his compositions were published that there is little opportunity of directly forming an estimate of him as a player ; but judging from the style of his numerous and well-known pupils, Somis did not merely hand on the traditions of the great Italian masters, but formed a style of his own, more brilliant and more emotional, marking technically, and also, in a sense, musically, a decided forward step in the art of playing the violin. As the head and founder of the Piedmontese School, and the teacher of Leclair, Giardini, Chiabran and Pugnani—the latter again the teacher of Viotti —he occupies a prominent place in the history of violin-playing, and forms the connecting-link between the classical schools of Italy and France. Fétis names as his only published work ' Opera prima di sonate a violino e violoncello o cembalo. Roma 1722 '; but a set of sonatas, op. 4, was published in Paris in 1726, and twelve sonatas, op. 6, in 1734. Besides these, an edition of some of his works appeared at Amsterdam, and a concerto is in MS. in the State collection at Dresden (*Q.-L.*).

P. D., with addns.

(2) LORENZO, apparently a younger brother of Giov. Battista, who also lived at Turin, later residing in Paris, where his second book of 8 chamber sonatas for violin and basso continuo was published in 1740. They show a great advance technically, as well as in respect of their musical conception, and this is noticeable also in two MS. concertos for violin by Lorenzo, one apparently autograph, now in the possession of Newman Flower (see also the sonata op. 2 no. 6 arranged by Alfred Moffat). It appears doubtful whether some of the great violinists who are simply called ' pupils of Somis ' are not pupils of Lorenzo instead of Giovanni Battista, to whom they were attributed by biographers ignorant even of Lorenzo's existence. A portrait of the two brothers, painted in 1765 by a third brother, Ignazio, is in the Liceo Musicale, Bologna.    E. v. d. s.

SOMMACAMPAGNA, GIDINO DA, c. 1350, author of a *Trattato de li rithimi volgari*, which sheds important light upon the song-forms of the 14th century (*Riemann*).

SOMMER, HANS (HANS FRIEDRICH AUGUST ZINCKEN, the last name occasionally transformed into 'NECKNIZ ') (*b.* Brunswick, July 20, 1837 ; *d.* there, Apr. 28, 1922), composer, was educated at Göttingen, where he became professor of Physics ; subsequently he was appointed director of the technical High School of his native place, a post he gave up in 1884. In 1885 he settled in Berlin, in 1888 in Weimar, and in 1898 returned to Brunswick. He won success on the operatic stage with his later dramatic works in a fantastic form : ' Der Nachtwächter ' and ' Loreley ' were both given in Brunswick—the first in 1865, the second in 1891 ; in 1894 a one-act piece, ' Saint Foix,' was given at Munich , two other one-act operas deserve mention, ' Der Meermann,' at Weimar in 1896, and ' Augustin ' ; ' Münchhausen,' in

three acts, and ' Rübezahl ' were given in Brunswick in 1904 ; ' Riquet à la houppe ' at the same theatre on Apr. 14, 1907, and ' Der Waldschratt ' in 1912.

It is by his songs that Sommer's name is best known in England : his op. 3, ' Mädchenlieder,' from Julius Wolff's *Wilde Jäger* ; his op. 4, three sets of songs from the same poet's *Hunold Singuf* ; his op. 5, a set from Wolff's *Tannhäuser* ; his op. 6, to words from Carmen Sylva's *Sappho*, and his songs to words of different authors, opp. 8, 9, 10, 11, 12 and 16, contain many things that are effective for the voice, well expressed, original, and full of a sort of ingenuity that delights all cultivated amateurs. In particular his ' Stell dich ein ' from op. 4, a vocal obbligato to a brilliant pianoforte waltz, and ' Am Waldteiche,' in which the alternate Latin and German words of the poem are cleverly set to music in different styles, are in their way little triumphs of art. He made several contributions to musical literature, such as his *Über die Wertschätzung der Musik* (1898).    M.

SOMMEROPHONE, an instrument of the saxhorn or bombardon class, named after its inventor. It was largely played in the Exhibition of 1851. ' The Euphonic horn of Herr Sommer ' is honourably mentioned in the Reports of the Juries (pp. 331, 335) as ' an instrument of great power as well as sweetness of tone.'    W. H. S.

SON AND STRANGER, see HEIMKEHR AUS DER FREMDE.

SONATA (Fr. and Ger. *Sonate*). The history of the sonata is the history of an attempt to cope with one of the most singular problems ever presented to the mind of man, and its solution is one of the most successful achievements of his artistic instincts. A sonata is, as its name implies, a sound-piece, and a sound-piece alone ; in its purest and most perfect examples it is unexplained by title or text, and unassisted by voices ; it is nothing but an unlimited concatenation of musical notes. Such notes have individually no significance ; and even the simplest principles of their relative definition and juxtaposition, such as are necessary to make the most elementary music, had to be drawn from the inner self and the consciousness of things which belong to man's nature only, without the possibility of finding guidance or more than the crudest suggestion from the observation of things external. Yet the structural principles by which such unpromising materials become intelligible have been so ordered and developed by the unaided musical instinct of many successive generations of composers, as to render possible long works which not only penetrate and stir us in detail, but are in their entire mass direct, consistent and convincing. Such works, in their completest and most severely abstract forms, are sonatas.

The name seems to have been first adopted purely as the antithesis to CANTATA (*q.v.*), the musical piece that was sung. It begins to come into notice about the same time as that form of composition, soon after the era of the most marked revolution in music, which began at the end of the 16th century; when a band of enthusiasts, led by visionary ideals, unconsciously sowed the seed of modern music in an attempt to wrest the monopoly of the art in its highest forms from the predominant influence of the Church, and to make it serve for the expression of human feelings of more comprehensive range. At this time the possibilities of polyphony in its ecclesiastical forms may well have seemed almost exhausted, and men turned about to find new fields which should give scope for a greater number of workers. The nature of their speculations and the associations of the old order of things alike conspired to direct their attention first to opera and cantata, and here they had something to guide them; but for abstract instrumental music of the sonata kind they had for a long time no clue. The first suggestion was clearly accidental. It appears probable that the excessive elaboration of the madrigal led to the practice of accompanying the voice parts with viols; and from this the step is but short to leaving the viols by themselves and making a vague kind of chamber music without the voices. This appears to have been the source of the instrumental canzonas which were written in tolerable numbers till some way into the 18th century. It does not appear that any distinct rules for their construction were recognised, but the examination of a large number, written at different periods from Frescobaldi to J. S. Bach, proves the uniform object of the composers to have been a lax kind of fugue, such as might have served in its main outlines for the vocal madrigals. Burney says the earliest examples of 'Sonatas' he had been able to discover in his devoted inquiries were by Turini, published at Venice in 1624. His description of those he examined answers perfectly to the character of the canzonas, for, he says, they consist of one movement, in fugue and imitation throughout. Sonatas did not, however, rest long at this point of simplicity, but were destined very early to absorb material from other sources; and though the canzona kind of movement maintained its distinct position through many changes in its environment, and is still found in the violin sonatas of J. S. Bach, Handel and Porpora, the madrigal, which was its source, soon ceased to have direct influence upon three parts of the more complete structure. The suggestion for these came from the dance and the newly invented opera or dramatic cantata. The former had existed and made the chief staple of instrumental music for generations, but it requires to be well understood that its

direct connexion with dancing puts it out of the category of abstract music of the kind which was now obscurely germinating. The dances were understood through their relation with one order of dance motions. There would be the order of rhythmic motions which, taken together, was called a branle, another that was called a pavan, another a gigue; and each dance-tune maintained the distinctive rhythm and style throughout. On the other hand, the radical principle of the sonata, developed in the course of generations, is the compounding of a limitless variety of rhythms; and though isolated passages may be justly interpreted as representing gestures of an ideal dance kind, like that of the ancients, it is not through this association that the group of movements taken as a whole is understood, but by the disposition of such elements and others in relation to one another. This conception took time to develop, though it is curious how early composers began to perceive the radical difference between the suite and the sonata. Occasionally a doubt seems to be implied by confusing the names together or by actually calling a collection of dance-tunes a sonata; but it can hardly be questioned that from almost the earliest times, as is proved by a strong majority of cases, there was a sort of undefined presentiment that their developments lay along totally different paths. In the first attempts to form an aggregate of distinct movements, the composers had to take their forms where they could find them; and among these were the familiar dance-tunes, which for a long while held a prominent position in the heterogeneous group of movements, and were only in late times transmuted into the scherzo which supplanted the minuet and trio in one case, and the finale or rondo, which ultimately took the place of the gigue, or chaconne, or other similar dance-forms as the last member of the group.

The third source, as above mentioned, was the drama, and from this two general ideas were derivable: one from the short passages of instrumental prelude or interlude, and the other from the vocal portions. Of these, the first was intelligible in the drama through its relation to some point in the story, but it also early attained to a crude condition of form which was equally available apart from the drama. The other produced at first the vaguest and most rhapsodical of all the movements, as the type taken was the irregular declamatory recitative which appears to have abounded in the early operas.

EMERGENCE (17TH CENTURY).—It is hardly likely that it will ever be ascertained who first experimented in sonatas of several distinct movements. Many composers are mentioned in different places as having contributed works of the kind, such as Farina, Cesti, Graziani, among Italians, Rosenmüller among Germans, and John Jenkins among Englishmen. Burney also mentions a Michael Angelo Rossi,[1] whose date is given as from about 1620 to 1660. The actual structure of large numbers of sonatas composed in different parts of Europe soon after this time, proves a tolerably clear consent as to the arrangement and quality of the movements. A fine vigorous example is a sonata in C minor for violin and figured bass, by H. J. F. Biber, a German, said to have been first published in 1681. This consists of five movements in alternate slow and quick time. The first is an introductory largo of contrapuntal character, with clear and consistent treatment in the fugally imitative manner ; the second is a passacaglia, which answers roughly to a continuous string of variations on a short well-marked period ; the third is a rhapsodical movement consisting of interspersed portions of poco lento, presto and adagio, leading into a gavotte ; and the last is a further rhapsodical movement alternating adagio and allegro. In this group the influence of the madrigal or canzona happens to be absent ; the derivation of the movement being—in the first, the contrapuntalism of the music of the Church, in the second and fourth, dances, and in the third and fifth, probably operatic or dramatic declamation. The work is essentially a violin sonata with accompaniment, and the violin-part points to the extraordinarily rapid advance to mastery which was made in the few years after its being accepted as an instrument fit for high-class music. The writing for the instrument is decidedly elaborate and difficult, especially in the double stops and contrapuntal passages which were much in vogue with almost all composers from this time till J. S. Bach. In the structure of the movements the fugal influences are most apparent, and there are very few signs of the systematic repetition of subjects in connexion with well-marked distribution of keys, which in later times became indispensable.

Similar features and qualities are shown in the curious set of seven sonatas for clavier by Johann Kuhnau, called ' Frische Clavier Früchte,' etc., of a little later date ; but there are also in some parts indications of an awakening sense of the relation and balance of keys. The grouping of the movements is similar to those of Biber, though not identical ; thus the first three have five movements or divisions, and the remainder four. There are examples of the same kind of rhapsodical slow movements, as may be seen in the sonata (No. 2 of the set) which is given in Pauer's ' Alte Meister ' ; there are several fugal movements, some of them clearly and musically written ;

1 An andantino and allegro given in Pauer's 'Alte Meister' as by ROSSI (q.v.) are now known to be spurious (see p. 438), but genuine specimens of Rossi's works are in Torchi's L' arte musicale in Italia, vol. iii. See also Oskar B.e, The Pianoforte, Engl. transl. p. 82.

and there are some good illustrations of dance types, as in the last movement of No. 3, and the ciaccona of No. 6. But more important for the thread of continuous development are the peculiar attempts to balance tolerably defined and distinct subjects, and to distribute key and subject in large expanses, of which there are at least two clear examples. In a considerable proportion of the movements the most noticeable method of treatment is to alternate two characteristic groups of figures- or subjects almost throughout, in different positions of the scale and at irregular intervals of time. This is illustrated in the first movement of the sonata No. 2, in the first movement of No. 1, and in the third movement of No. 5. The subjects in the last of these are as follows :

The point most worth notice is that the device lies half-way between fugue and true sonata-form. The alternation is like the recurrence of subject and counter-subject in the former, wandering hazily in and out, and forwards and backwards, between nearly allied keys, as would be the case in a fugue. But the subjects are not presented in single parts or fugally answered. They enter and re-enter for the most part as concrete lumps of harmony, the harmonic accompaniment of the melody being taken as part of the idea; and this is essentially a quality of sonata-form (see FORM). So the movements appear to hang midway between the two radially distinct domains of form ; and while deriving most of their disposition from the older manners, they look forward, though obscurely, in the direction of modern practices. How obscure the ideas of the time on the subject must have been, appears from the other point which has been mentioned above ; which is, that in a few cases Kuhnau has hit upon clear outlines of tonal form. In the second sonata, for instance, there are two arias, as they are called. They do not correspond in the least with modern notions of an aria any more than do the rare examples in Bach's and Handel's suites. The first is a little complete piece of sixteen bars, divided exactly into halves by a double bar, with repeats after the familiar manner. The first half begins in F and ends in C, the second half goes as far as D minor and back, to conclude in F again. The subject-matter is irregularly distributed in the parts, and does not make any pretence of coinciding with the tonal divisions. The second aria is on a different plan, and is one of the extremely rare examples in this early period of clear coincidence between subject and key. It is in the form which is often perversely misnamed 'Lied-form,' which will in this place be called 'primary form' to avoid circumlocution and waste of space. It consists of twenty bars in D minor representing one distinct idea, complete with close : then sixteen bars devoted to a different subject, beginning in B♭ and passing back ultimately to D minor, recapitulating the whole of the first twenty bars in that key, and emphasising the close by repeating the last four bars. Such decisiveness, when compared with the unregulated and unbalanced wandering of longer movements, either points to the conclusion that composers did not realise the desirableness of balance in coincident ranges of subject and key on a large scale ; or that they were only capable of feeling it in short and easily grasped movements. It seems highly probable that their minds, being projected towards the kind of distribution of subject which obtained in fugal movements, were not on the look-out for effects of the sonata order which to moderns appear so obvious. So that, even if they had been capable of realising them more systematically, they would not yet have thought it worth while to apply their knowledge. In following the development of the sonata, it ought never to be forgotten that composers had no idea whither they were tending, and had to use what they did know as stepping-stones to the unknown. In art, each step that is gained opens a fresh vista ; but often, till the new position is mastered, what lies beyond is completely hidden and undreamed of. In fact, each step is not so much a conquest of new land, as the creation of a new mental or emotional position in the human organism. The achievements of art are the unravellings of hidden possibilities of abstract law, through the constant and cumulative extension of instincts. They do not actually exist till man has made them ; they are the counterpart of his internal conditions, and change and develop with the changes of his mental powers and sensitive qualities, and apart from him have no validity. There is no such thing as leaping across a chasm on to a new continent, neither is there any gulf fixed anywhere, but continuity and inevitable antecedents to every consequent ; the roots of the greatest masterpieces of modern times lie obscurely hidden in the wild dances and barbarous howlings of the remotest ancestors of the race, who began to take pleasure in rhythm and sound, and every step was into the unknown, or it may be better said not only unknown but non-existent till made by mental effort.

The period from about 1600 to about 1725 contains the very difficult steps which led from the style appropriate to a high order of vocal music—of which the manner of speech is polyphonic, and the ideal type of form, the fugue—to the style appropriate to abstract instrumental music, of which the best manner is contrapuntally expressed harmony, and the ideal type of form, the sonata. These works of Kuhnau happen to illustrate very curiously the transition in which a true though crude idea of abstract music seems to have been present in the composer's mind, at the same time that his distribution of subjects and keys was almost invariably governed by fugal habits of thinking, even where the statement of subjects is in a harmonic manner. In some of these respects he is nearer to, and in some further back from, the true solution of the problem than his famous contemporary Corelli ; but his labours do not extend over so much space, nor had they so much direct and widespread influence. In manner and distribution of movements they are nearer to his predecessor and compatriot Biber ; and for that reason, and also to maintain the continuity of the historic development after Corelli, the consideration of his works has been taken a little before their actual place in point of time.

CORELLI'S STYLE.—The works of Corelli form one of the most familiar landmarks in the history of music, and as they are exclusively instrumental it is clear that careful consideration ought to elicit a great deal of interesting matter, such as must throw valuable light on the state of thought of his time. He published no less than sixty sonatas of different kinds, which are divisible into distinct groups in accordance with purpose or construction. The first main division is that suggested by their titles. There are twenty-four 'Sonate da chiesa' for strings, lute, and organ, twenty-four 'Sonate da camera' for the same instruments, and twelve solos or sonatas for violin and violoncello, or cembalo. In these the first and simplest matter for observation is the distribution of the movements. The average, in church and chamber sonatas alike, is strongly in favour of four, beginning with a slow movement, and alternating the rest. There is also an attempt at balance in the alternation of character between the movements. The first is commonly in 4-time, of dignified and solid character, and generally aiming less at musical expression than the later movements. The second movement in the church sonata is freely fugal, in fact the exact type above described as a canzona ; the style is commonly rather dry, and the general effect chiefly a complacent kind of easy swing such as is familiar in most of Handel's fugues. In the chamber sonatas the character of the second movement is rather more variable ; in some it is an allemande, which, being dignified and solid, is a fair counterpart to the canzona in the other sonatas : sometimes it is a courante, which is of lighter character. The third movement is the only one which is ever in a different key from the first and last. It is generally a characteristic one, in which other early composers of instrumental music, as well as Corelli, clearly endeavoured to infuse a certain amount of vague and tender sentiment. The most common time is 3–2. The extent of the movement is always limited, and the style, though simply contrapuntal in fact, seems to be ordered with a view to obtain smooth harmonious full-chord effects, as a contrast to the brusqueness of the preceding fugal movement. There is generally a certain amount of imitation between the parts, irregularly and fancifully disposed, but almost always avoiding the sounding of a single part alone. In the chamber sonatas, as might be anticipated, the third movement is frequently a sarabande, though by no means always; for the same kind of slow movement as that in the church sonatas is sometimes adopted, as in the third sonata of the Opera Seconda, which is as good an example of that class as could be taken. The last movement is almost invariably of a lively character in church and chamber sonatas alike. In the latter, gigas and gavottes predominate, the character of which is so familiar that they need no description. The last movements in the church sonatas are of a similar vivacity and sprightliness, and sometimes so alike in character and rhythm as to be hardly distinguishable from dance-tunes, except by the absence of the defining name, the double bar in the middle, and the repeats which are almost inevitable in the dance movements. This general scheme is occasionally varied without material difference of principle by the interpolation of an extra quick movement, as in the first six sonatas of the Opera Quinta; in which it is a sort of show movement for the violin in a 'Moto continuo' style, added before or after the central slow movement. In a few cases the number is reduced to three by dropping the slow prelude, and in a few others the order cannot be systematised.

In accordance with the principles of classification above defined, the church sonatas appear to be much more strictly abstract than those for chamber. The latter are, in many cases, not distinguishable from suites. The sonatas of Opera Quinta are variable. Thus the attractive sonata in E minor, No. 8, is quite in the recognised suite-manner. Some are like the 'Sonate da Chiesa,' and some are types of the mixed order more universally accepted later, having several undefined movements, together with one dance. The actual structure of the individual movements is most uncertain. Corelli clearly felt that something outside the domain of the fugal tribe was to be attained, but he had no notion of strict outlines of procedure.

One thing which hampered him and other composers of the early times of instrumental music was their unwillingness to accept formal tunes as an element in their order of art. They had existed in popular song and dance music for certainly a century, and probably much more; but the idea of adopting them in high-class music was not yet in favour. Corelli occasionally produces one, but the fact that they generally occur with him in gigas, which are the freest and least responsible portion of the sonata, supports the inference that they were not yet regarded as worthy of general acceptance even if realised as an admissible element, but could only be smuggled-in in the least respectable movement with an implied smile to disarm criticism. Whether this was decisively so or not, the fact remains that till long after Corelli's time the conventional tune element was conspicuously absent from instrumental compositions. Hence the structural principles which to a modern seem almost inevitable were very nearly impracticable, or at all events unsuitable to the general principles of the music of that date. A modern expects the opening bars of a movement to present its most important subject, and he anticipates its repetition in the latter portion of the movement as a really vital part of form of any kind. But association and common sense were alike against such a usage being universal in Corelli's time. The associations of ecclesiastical and other serious vocal music, which were then preponderant to a supreme degree, were against strongly salient points, or strongly marked interest in short portions of a movement in contrast to parts of comparative unimportance. Consequently the opening bars of a movement would not be expected to stand out in sufficiently strong relief to be remembered unless they were repeated at once, as they would be in fugue. Human nature is against it. For not only does the mind take time to be wrought up to a fully receptive condition, unless the beginning is most exceptionally striking, but what comes after is likely to obliterate the impression made by it. As a matter of fact, if all things were equal, the portion most likely to remain in the mind of an average listener, is that immediately preceding the strongest cadences or conclusions of the paragraphs of the movement. It is true, composers do not argue in this manner, but they feel such things vaguely or instinctively, and generally with more sureness and justice than the cold-blooded argumentation of a theorist could attain to. Many examples in other early composers besides Corelli, emphasise this point effectively. The earliest attempts at structural form must inevitably present some simply explicable principle of this sort, which is only not trivial because it is a very significant as well as indispensable starting-point. Corelli's commonest devices of form are the most unsophisticated applications of such simple reasoning. In the first place, in many movements which are not fugal, the opening bars are immediately repeated in another position in the scale, simply and without periphrasis, as if to give the listener assurance of an idea of balance at the very outset. That he did this to a certain extent consciously, is obvious from his having employed the device in at least the following sonatas—2, 3, 8, 9, 10, 11, of Opera 1$^{ma}$; 2, 4, 7, 8, of Opera 3$^{za}$; and 2, 4, 5, and 11, of Opera 4$^{ta}$; and Tartini and other composers of the same school followed his lead. This device is not, however, either so conspicuous or so common as that of repeating the concluding passage of the first half at the end of the whole, or of the concluding passages of one half or both consecutively. This, however, was not restricted to Corelli, but is found in the works of most composers from his time to Scarlatti, J. S. Bach and his sons; and it is no extravagant hypothesis that its gradual extension was the direct origin of the characteristic second section and second subject of modern sonata movements. In many cases it is the only element of form, in the modern sense, in Corelli's movements. In a few cases he hit upon more complicated principles. The corrente in sonata 5 of Opera 4$^{ta}$, is nearly a miniature of modern binary form. The well-known giga in A in the fifth sonata of Opera 5$^{ta}$, has balance of key in the first half of the movement, modulation, and something like consistency to subject-matter at the beginning of the second half, and due recapitulation of principal subject-matter at the end. The last movement of the eighth sonata of the Opera Terza, is within reasonable distance of rondo-form, though this form is generally as conspicuous for its absence in early sonatas as tunes are, and probably the one follows as a natural consequence of the other. Of the simple primary form, consisting of corresponding beginning and end, and contrast of some sort in the middle, there is singularly little. The clearest example is probably the 'Tempo di gavotta,' which concludes the ninth sonata of Opera Quinta. He also supplies suggestions of the earliest types of sonata form, in which both the beginnings and endings of each half of the movement correspond; as this became an accepted principle of structure with later composers, it will have to be considered more fully in relation to their works.

Of devices of form which belong to the great polyphonic tribe, Corelli uses many, but with more musical feeling than learning. His fugues are not remarkable as fugues, and he uses contrapuntal imitation rather as a subordinate means of carrying on the interest, than of expounding any wonderful device of pedantic wisdom, as was too common in those days. He makes good use of the chaconne-form, which was a great favourite with the early composers, and also uses the kindred device of carrying the repetition of a short figure through the greater part of a movement in different phases and positions of the scale. In some cases he merely rambles on without any perceptible aim whatever, only keeping up an equable flow of sound with pleasant interlacings of easy counterpoint, led on from moment to moment by suspensions and occasional imitation, and here and there a helpful sequence. Corelli's position as a composer is inseparably mixed up with his position as one of the earliest masters of his instrument. His style of writing for it does not appear to be so elaborate as that of other contemporaries, both older and younger, but he grasped a just way of expressing things with it, and for the most part the fit things to say. The impression he made upon musical people in all parts of the musical world was strong, and he was long regarded as the most delightful of composers in his particular line; and though the professors of his day did not always hold him in so high estimation, his influence upon many of his most distinguished successors was unquestionably powerful.

THE VIOLIN SCHOOLS.—It is possible, however, that appearances are deceptive, and that influences of which he was only the most familiar exponent, are mistaken for his peculiar achievement. Thus knowing his position at the head of a great school of violinists, which continued through several generations down to Haydn's time, it is difficult to disunite him from the honour of having fixed the type of sonata which they almost uniformly adopted. And not only this noble and vigorous school, comprising such men as Tartini, Vivaldi, Locatelli, Nardini, Veracini, and outlying members like Leclair and Rust, but men who were not specially attached to their violins, such as Albinoni and Purcell, and later, Bach, Handel and Porpora, equally adopted the type. Of Albinoni not much seems to be distinctly known, except that he was Corelli's contemporary and probably junior. He wrote operas and instrumental music. Of the latter, several sonatas are still to be seen, but they are, of course, not familiar, though at one time they enjoyed a wide popularity. The chief point about them is that in many for violin and figured bass he follows not only the same general outlines, but even the style of Corelli. He adopts the four-movement plan, with a decided canzona in the second place, a slow movement first and third, and a quick movement to end with, such as in one case a corrente. Purcell's having followed Corelli's lead is repudiated by enthusiasts[1]; but at all events

[1] Purcell's 'Sonnatas of three Parts,' admittedly composed in the Italian manner, were published in London in 1683, the year of the publication of Corelli's Opera Prima. The so-called 'Golden Sonata' is No. IX. of the 'Ten Sonatas of Four parts' published after the composer's death. See under PURCELL, CHARACTERISTICS OF PURCELL'S ART. Q.

the lines of his 'Golden Sonata' in F are wonderfully similar. There are three slow movements, which come first, second and fourth; the third movement is actually called a canzona; and the last is a quick movement in 3–8 time, similar in style to corresponding portions of Corelli's sonatas. The second movement, an adagio, is the most expressive, being happily devised on the principle above referred to, of repeating a short figure in different positions throughout the movement. In respect of sonata-form the work is about on a par with the average of Corelli or Biber.

The domain of the sonata was for a long while almost monopolised by violinists and writers for the violin. Some of these, such as Geminiani and Locatelli, were actually Corelli's pupils. They clearly followed him both in style and structural outlines, but they also began to extend and build upon them with remarkable speed. The second movement continued for long the most stationary and conventional, maintaining the canzona type in a loose fugal manner, by the side of remarkable changes in the other movements. Of these the first began to grow into larger dimensions and clearer proportions even in Corelli's own later works, attaining to the dignity of double bars and repeats, and with his successors to a consistent and self-sufficing form. An example of this is the admirable 'Larghetto affettuoso' with which Tartini's celebrated 'Trillo del Diavolo' begins. No one who has heard it could fail to be struck with the force of the simple device above described of making the ends of each half correspond, as the passage is made to stand out from all the rest more characteristically than usual. A similar and very good example is the introductory largo to the sonata in G minor, for violin and figured bass, by Locatelli.[1] The subject-matter in both examples is exceedingly well handled, so that a sense of perfect consistency is maintained without concrete repetition of subjects, except, as already noticed, the closing bars of each half, which in Locatelli's sonata are rendered less obvious through the addition of a short coda starting from a happy interrupted cadence. It is out of the question to follow the variety of aspects presented by the introductory slow movement; a fair proportion are on similar lines to the above examples, others are isolated. Their character is almost uniformly solid and large; they are often expressive, but generally in a way distinct from the character of the second slow movement, which from the first was chosen as the fittest to admit a vein of tenderer sentiment.

The most important matter in the history of the sonata at this period is the rapidity with which advance was made towards the realisation of harmonic and tonal principles of structure, or, in other words, the perception of the effect and significance of relations between chords and distinct keys, and consequent appearance of regularity of purpose in the distribution of both, and increased freedom of modulation. Even Corelli's own pupils show consistent form of the sonata kind with remarkable clearness. The last movement of a sonata in C minor, by Geminiani, has a clear and emphatic subject to start with; modulation to the relative major, E♭, and special features to characterise the second section; and conclusion of the first half in that key, with repeat after the supposed orthodox manner. The second half begins with a long section corresponding to the working out or 'free fantasia' portion of a classical sonata movement, and concludes with recapitulation of the first subject and chief features of the second section in C minor; this latter part admitting a certain amount of discursiveness, which is characteristic of most of the early experiments in this form. Similar to this is the last movement of Locatelli's sonata in G minor, the last movement of Veracini's sonata in E minor, published at Vienna in 1714, the last movements of Tartini's sonatas in E minor and D minor, and not a few others. It is rather curious that most of the early examples of what is sometimes called first-movement form are last movements. Most of these movements, however, in the early times, are distinguished by a peculiarity which is of some importance. It has been before referred to, but is so characteristic of the process of growth that it will not be amiss to describe it in this place (cf. FORM). The simple and almost homely means of producing the effect of structural balance by making the beginning and ending of each half of a movement correspond, is not so conspicuously common in its entirety as the correspondence of endings or repetition of cadence bars only; but it nevertheless is found tolerably often, and that in times before the virtue of a balance of keys in the first half of the movement had been decisively realised. When, however, this point was gained, it is clear that such a process would give, on as minute a scale as possible, the very next thing to complete binary form. It only needed to expand the opening passage into a first subject, and the figures of the cadence into a second subject, to attain that type which became almost universal in sonatas till Haydn's time, and with some second-rate composers, like Reichardt, later. The movements which are described as binary must be therefore divided into two distinct classes: that in which the first subject reappears in the complementary key at the beginning of the second half, which is the almost universal type of earlier times; and that in which it appears in the latter part of the movement, after the working-out portion, which is the later type. The experiments in Corelli and Tartini, and others who are close to these types, are endless. Sometimes there are tentative strokes near to the later form; sometimes there is an inverted order reproducing the second portion of the movement first. Sometimes the first subject makes its appearance at both points, but then, may be, there is no balance of keys in the first half, and so forth. The variety is extraordinary, and it is most interesting to watch the manner in which some types by degrees preponderate, sometimes by combining with one another, sometimes by gradual transformation, some nearer and more decisively like the types which are generally adopted in modern times as fittest. The later type was not decisively fixed on at any particular point, for many early composers touched it once or twice at the same period that they were writing movements in more elementary forms. The point of actual achievement of a step in art is not marked by an isolated instance, but by decisive preponderance, and by the systematic adoption which shows at least an instinctive realisation of its value and importance.

These writers of violin sonatas were just touching on the clear realisation of harmonic form as subsequently accepted, and they sometimes adopted the later type, though rarely, and that obscurely; they mastered the earlier type, and used it freely; and they also used the intermediate type which combines the two, in which the principal or first subject makes its appearance both at the beginning of the first half and near the end. As a sort of embryonic suggestion of this, the 'Tempo di gavotta,' in the eighth sonata of Corelli's Opera Seconda, is significant. Complete examples are—the last movement of Tartini's fourth sonata of opus 1, and the last movement of that in D minor above referred to; the last movement of Geminiani's sonata in C minor; the main portion, excluding the coda, of the corrente in Vivaldi's sonata in A major; the last movement of a sonata of Nardini's, in D major; and two capriccios in Bb and C, by Franz Benda, quoted in F. David's 'Hohe Schule,' etc.

The four-movement type of violin sonata was not invariably adopted, though it preponderates so conspicuously. There is a set of twelve sonatas by Locatelli, for instance, not so fine as that in F. David's collection, which are nearly all on an original three-movement plan, concluding with an 'aria' and variations on a ground-bass. Some of Tartini's are also in three movements, and a set of six by Nardini are also in three, but always beginning with a slow movement, and therefore, though almost of the same date, not really approaching the distribution commonly adopted by Haydn for clavier sonatas. In fact the old violin sonata is in many respects a distinct genus, which maintained its individuality alongside the gradually stereotyped clavier sonata, and only ceased when that type obtained possession of the field, and the violin was reintroduced, at first as it were furtively, as an accompaniment to the pianoforte. The general characteristics of this school of writers for the violin, were nobility of style and richness of feeling, an astonishing mastery of the instrument, and a rapidly-growing facility in dealing with structure in respect of subject, key, modulation, and development; and what is most vital, though less obvious, a perceptible growth in the art of expression and a progress towards the definition of ideas. As a set-off there are occasional traces of pedantic manners, and occasional crudities both of structure and expression, derived probably from the associations of the old music which they had so lately left behind them. At the crown of the edifice are the sonatas of J. S. Bach. Of sonatas in general he appears not to have held to any decisive opinion. He wrote many for various instruments, and for various combinations of instruments. For clavier, for violin alone, for flute, violin and clavier, for viola da gamba and clavier, and so on; but in most of these the outlines are not decisively distinct from suites. In some cases the works are described as 'Sonatas or Suites,' and in at least one case the introduction to a church cantata is called a sonata. Some instrumental works which are called sonatas only, might quite as well be called suites, as they consist of a prelude and a set of dance-tunes. Others are heterogeneous. From this it appears that he had not satisfied himself on what lines to attack the sonata in any sense approaching the modern idea. With the violin sonatas it was otherwise; and in the group of six for violin and clavier he follows almost invariably the main outlines which are characteristic of the Italian school descended from Corelli, and all but one are on the four-movement plan, having slow movements first and third, and quick movements second and fourth. The sixth sonata only differs from the rest by having an additional quick movement at the beginning. Not only this but the second movements keep decisively the formal lineaments of the ancient type of free fugue, illustrated with more strictness of manner by the canzonas. Only in calibre and quality of ideas, and in some peculiar idiosyncrasies of structure do they differ materially from the works of the Italian masters. Even the first, third and fifth sonatas in the other set of six, for violin alone, conform accurately to the old four-movement plan, including the fugue in the second place; the remaining three being on the general lines of the suite. In most of the sonatas for violin and clavier the slow movement is a tower of strength, and strikes a point of rich and complex emotional expression which music reached for the first time in Bach's imagination. His favourite way of formulating a movement of this sort was to develop the whole accompaniment consistently on a concise and strongly marked figure, which by repetition in different conditions formed a bond of connexion throughout the whole ; and on this he built a passionate kind of recitative, a free and unconstrained outpouring of the deepest and noblest instrumental song. This was a sort of apotheosis of that form of rhapsody which has been noticed in the early sonatas, such as Biber's and Kuhnau's, and was occasionally attempted by the Italians. The six sonatas present diversities of types, all of the loftiest order; some of them combining together with unfailing expressiveness perfect specimens of old forms of contrapuntal ingenuity. Of this, the second movement of the second sonata is a perfect example. It appears to be a pathetic colloquy between the violin and the treble of the clavier part, to which the bass-keeps up the slow constant motion of staccato semiquavers : the colloquy at the same time is in strict canon throughout, and, as a specimen of expressive treatment of that time-honoured form, is almost unrivalled.

In all these movements the kinship is rather with the contrapuntal writers of the past, than with the types of Beethoven's adoption. Even Bach, immense as his genius and power of divination was, could not leap over that period of formation which it seems to have been indispensable for mankind to pass through, before equally noble and deeply felt things could be expressed in the characteristically modern manner. Though he looked further into the future in matters of expression and harmonic combination than any composer till the 19th century, he still had to use forms of the contrapuntal and fugal order for the expression of his highest thoughts. He did occasionally make use of binary form, though not in these sonatas. But he more commonly adopted, and combined with more or less fugal treatment, an expansion of simple primary form to attain structural effect. Thus, in the second movements of the first and second sonatas, in the last of the third and sixth, and the first of the sixth, he marks first a long complete section in his principal key, then takes his way into modulations and development, and discussion of themes and various kinds of contrapuntal enjoyment, and concludes with simple complete recapitulation of the first section in the principal key. Bach thus stands singularly aside, from the direct line of the development of the sonata as far as the structural elements are concerned. His contributions to the art of expression, to the development of resource, and to the definition and treatment of ideas, had great effect, and are of the very highest importance to instrumental music ; but his almost invariable choice of either the suite-form, or the accepted outlines of the violin sonata, in works of this class, caused him to diverge into a course which with him found its final and supreme limit. In order to continue the work in veins which were yet unexhausted, the path had to be turned a little, and joined to courses which were coming up from other directions. The violin sonata continued to make its appearance here and there as has already been mentioned, but in the course of a generation it was entirely supplanted by the distinct type of clavier sonata.

THE CLAVIER SONATA.—Meanwhile there was another composer of this time who appears to stand just as singularly apart from the direct high road as Bach, and who, though he does not occupy a pedestal so high in the history of art, still has a niche by no means low or inconspicuous, and one which he shares with no one. Domenico SCARLATTI was born in the same year as J. S. Bach. His most valuable contributions are in the immense number of sonatas and studies which he wrote for the harpsichord. The two names are used as synonyms, for each of the thirty ' Esercizii per gravicembalo ' is separately entitled ' Sonata.' But whatever they are called they do not correspond in appearance to any form which is commonly supposed to be essential to the sonata. Neither can they be taken as pure-bred members of the fugal family, nor do they trace their origins to the suite. They are, in fact, in a fair proportion of cases, an attempt to deal with direct ideas in a modern sense, without appealing to the glamour of conscious association, the dignity of science, or the familiarity of established dance rhythms. The connexion with what goes before and with what comes after is alike obscure, because of the daring originality with which existing materials are worked upon; but it is not the less inevitably present, as an outline of his structural principles will show.

His utterance is at its best sharp and incisive; the form in which he loves to express himself is epigrammatic ; and some of his most effective sonatas are like strings of short propositions bound together by an indefinable sense of consistency and consequence, rather than by actual development. These ideas are commonly brought home to the hearer by the singular practice of repeating them consecutively as they stand, often several times over ; in respect of which it is worth remembering that his position in relation to his audience was not unlike that of an orator addressing an uncultivated mob. The capacity for appreciating grand developments of structure was as undeveloped in them as the power of following widely spread argument and conclusion would be in the mob. And just as the mob-orator makes his most powerful impressions by short direct statements, and by hammering them in while still hot from his lips, so Scarlatti drove his points home by frequent and generally identical reiterations ; and then when the time came round to refer to them again, the force of the connexion between distant parts of the same story was more easily grasped. The feeling that he did this with his eyes open is strengthened by the fact that even in the grouping of the reiterations there is commonly a perceptible method. For instance, it can hardly be by accident that at a certain point of the movement, after several simple repetitions, he should frequently resort to the complication of repeating several small groups within the repetition of large ones. The following example is a happy illustration of his style, and of his way of elaborating such repetitions :

It must not be supposed that he makes a law of this procedure, but the remarkably frequent occurrence of so curious a device is certainly suggestive of conscious purpose [1] in structural treatment. The result of this mode is that the movements often appear to be crowded with ideas. Commonly the features of the opening bars, which in later times would be held of almost supreme importance, serve for very little except to determine the character of the movement, and do not make their appearance again.

On the other hand, he carries the practice before referred to, of making the latter part of each half of the movement correspond, to an extraordinary pitch, and with perfect success ; for he almost invariably adopts the key distribution of binary form in its main outlines ; and though it would not be accurate to speak of such a thing as a ' second subject ' in his sonatas, the impression produced by his distribution of repetition and the clearness of his ideas is sufficient, in his best movements, to give a general structural effect very similar to complete binary form on a small scale. In order to realise to what extent the process of recapitulation is carried by him, it will be as well to consider the outline of a fairly characteristic sonata. That which stands fifteenth in the edition of Breitkopf & Härtel [2] begins with eight bars only in E minor ; the next forty-six, barring merely a slight and unimportant digression, are in G major. This concludes the first half. The second half begins with reference to the opening figures of the whole and a little key digression, and then a characteristic portion of the second section of the first half is resumed, and the last thirty-four bars of the movement are a recapitulation in E minor of the last thirty-five of the first half, the three concluding bars being condensed into two.

In many respects his principles of structure and treatment are altogether in the direction of modern ways, and alien to fugal principles. That vital principle of the fugue—the persistence of one principal idea, and the interweaving of it into every part of the structure—appears completely alien to Scarlatti's disposition. He very rarely wrote a fugue ; and when he did, if it was successful that was less because it was a good fugue than because it was Scarlatti's. The fact that he often starts with imitation between two parts is unimportant, and the merest accident of association. He generally treats his ideas as concrete lumps, and disposes them in distinct portions of the movement, which is essentially an unfugal proceeding ; but the most important matter is that he was probably the first to attain to clear conception and treatment of a self-sufficing effective idea, and to use it, if without science, yet with management which is often convincingly successful. He was not a great master of the art of composition, but he was one of the rarest masters of his instrument ; and his divination of the way to treat it, and the perfect adaptation of his ideas to its requirements, more than counterbalance any shortcoming in his science. He was blessed with ideas, and with a style so essentially his own that even when his music is transported to another instrument the characteristic effects of tone often remain unmistakable. Vivacity, humour, genuine fun, are

---

[1] It is only right to point out the recognised custom of repeating phrases on the harpsichord with a change of registration, which may account in some measure for the habit here referred to.

[2] It is also the fifteenth in the ' Esercizii ' ; in Pauer's edition it is No. 18 ; in the ' Trésor des pianistes,' No. 19 ; and occurs on p. 22 of Roseingrave's second volume.

his most familiar traits. At his best his music sparkles with life and freshness, and its vitality is apparently quite unimpaired by age. He rarely approaches tenderness or sadness, and in the whole mass of his works there are hardly any slow movements. He is not a little 'bohemian,' and seems positively to revel in curious effects of consecutive fifths and consecutive octaves. The characteristic daring of which such things are the most superficial manifestations, joined with the clearness of his foresight, made him of closer kinship to Beethoven and Weber, and even Brahms, than to the typical contrapuntists of his day. His works are genuine 'sonatas' in the most radical sense of the term—self-dependent and self-sufficing *sound-pieces*, without programme. To this the distribution of movements is at least of secondary importance, and his confining himself to one alone does not vitiate his title to be a foremost contributor to that very important branch of the musical art. No successor was strong enough to wield his bow. His pupil Durante wrote some sonatas, consisting of a 'Studio' and a 'Divertimento' apiece, which have touches of his manner, but without sufficient of the nervous elasticity to make them important.

The contemporary writers for clavier of second rank do not offer much which is of high musical interest, and they certainly do not arrive at anything like the richness of thought and expression which is shown by their fellows of the violin. There appears, however, amongst them a tendency to drop the introductory slow movement characteristic of the violin sonata, and by that means to draw nearer to the type of later clavier or pianoforte sonatas. Thus a sonata of Wagenseil's in F major presents almost exactly the general outlines to be met with in Haydn's works—an allegro assai in binary form of the old type, a short andantino grazioso, and a 'Tempo di minuetto.' A sonata of Hasse in D minor has a similar arrangement of three movements ending with a Gigue; but the first movement is utterly vague and indefinite in form. There is also an allegro of Hasse in B♭, quoted in Pauer's 'Alte Meister,' which deserves consideration for the light it throws on a matter which is sometimes said to be a crucial distinction between the early attempts at form and the perfect achievement. In many of the early examples of sonata-form, the second section of the first part is characterised by groups of figures which are quite definite enough for all reasonable purposes, but do not come up to the ideas commonly entertained of the nature of a subject; and on this ground the settlement of sonata-form was deferred some fifty years. Hasse was not a daring originator, neither was he likely to strike upon a crucial test of perfection, yet in this movement he sets out with a distinct and complete subject in B♭ of a robust Handelian character:

and after the usual extension proceeds to F, and announces by definite emphasis on the Dominant the well-contrasted second subject, which is suggestive of the polite reaction looming in the future:

The movement as a whole is in the binary type of the earlier kind.

The period now approaching is characterised by uncertainty in the distribution of the movements, but increasing regularity and definition in their internal structure. Some writers follow the four-movement type of violin sonata in writing for the clavier; some strike upon the grouping of three movements; and a good many fall back upon two. A sonata of Galuppi in D illustrates the first of these, and throws light upon the transitional process. The first movement is a beautiful adagio of the arioso type, with the endings of each half corresponding, after the manner traced from Corelli; the second is an allegro, not of the fugal or canzona order, but clear binary of the older kind. A violin sonata of Locatelli, of probably earlier date, has an Allemande of excellent form in this position, but this is not sufficiently definite in the inference it affords to throw much light on any transition or assimilation of violin sonata-form to clavier sonata-form. Galuppi's adoption of a movement of clear sonata-qualities in this place supplies exactly the link that was needed; and the fugal or canzona type of movement being so supplanted, nothing further was necessary but expansion, and the omission of the introductory adagio (which probably was not so well adapted to the earlier keyed instruments as to the violin), to arrive at the principle of distribution adopted in the palmiest days of formalism. Later, with a more powerful instrument, the introductory slow movement was often reintroduced. Galuppi's third movement is in a solid march style, and the last is a Giga. All of them are harmonically constructed, and the whole work is solid and of sterling musical worth.

Dr. Arne was born only four years after Galuppi, and was amenable to the same general influences. The structure of his sonatas emphasises the fact above mentioned, that though the order of movements was passing through a phase of uncertainty their internal structure was growing more and more distinct and uniform. His first sonata, in F, has two movements, andante and allegro, both of which follow harmonically the lines of binary form. The second, in E minor, has three movements, andante, adagio, allegrissimo. The first and last are on the binary lines, and the middle one in simple primary form. The third sonata consists of a long vague introduction of arpeggios, elaborated in a manner characteristic of the time, an allegro which has only one subject but is on the binary lines, and a minuet and two variations. The fourth sonata is in some respects the most interesting. It consists of an andante, siciliano, fuga and allegro. The first is of continuous character but nevertheless in binary form, without the strong emphasis on the points of division between the sections. It deserves notice for its expressiveness and clearness of thought. The second movement is very short, but pretty and expressive, of a character similar to examples of Handel's tenderer moods. The last movement is particularly to be noticed, not only for being decisively in binary form, but for the ingenuity with which that form is manipulated. The first section is represented by the main subject in the treble, the second (which is clearly marked in the dominant key) has the same subject in the bass, a device adopted also more elaborately by W. Friedemann Bach. The second half begins with consistent development and modulation, and the recapitulation is happily managed by making the main subject represent both sections at once in a short passage of canon. Others of Arne's sonatas afford similar though less clear examples, which it is superfluous to consider in detail; for neither the matter nor the handling is so good in them as in those above described, most of which, though not rich in thought or treatment, nor impressive in character, have genuine traits of musical expression and clearness of workmanship.

In the same year with Dr. Arne was born Wilhelm Friedemann Bach, the eldest son of Johann Sebastian. He was probably the most gifted, the most independent, and unfortunately the wildest and most unmanageable of that remarkable family. Few of his compositions are known, and it is said that he would not take the trouble to write unless he was driven to it. Two sonatas exist, which are of different type, and probably represent different periods of his chequered career. One in D major, for its richness, elaborateness, expressiveness, is well worthy of the scion of so great a stock; the other is rather cheap, and though masterly in handling and disposition of structural elements, has more traces of the elegance which was creeping over the world of music than of the grave and earnest nobleness of his father and similar representatives of the grand period. The first, in D, is probably the most remarkable example, before Beethoven, of original ingenuity manipulating sonata-form under the influence of fugal associations and by means of contrapuntal devices. The whole is worked out with careful and intelligible reasoning, but to such an elaborate extent that it is quite out of the question to give even a complete outline of its contents. The movements are three— Un poco allegro, adagio, vivace. The first and last are speculative experiments in binary form. The first half in each represents the balance of expository sections in tonic and complementary keys. The main subject of the first reappears in the bass in the second section, with a new phase of the original accompaniment in the upper parts. The development portion is in its usual place, but the recapitulation is tonally reversed. The first subject and section is given in a relative key to balance the complementary key of the second section, and the second section is given in the original key or tonic of the movement; so that instead of repeating one section and transposing the other in recapitulation, they are both transposed analogously. In each of the three movements the ends of the halves correspond, and not only this but the graceful little figure appended to the cadence is the same in all the movements, establishing thereby a very delicate but sensible connexion between them. This figure is as follows :

The formal pauses on familiar points of harmony characteristic of later times are conspicuously few, the main divisions being generally marked by more subtle means. The whole sonata is so uncompromisingly full of expressive figures, and would require to be so elaborately phrased and ' sung ' to be intelligible, that an adequate performance would be a matter of considerable difficulty. The second sonata, in C, has quite a different appearance. It is also in three movements—allegro, grave and vivace. The first is a masterly, clear and concise example of binary form of the type which is more familiar in the works of Haydn and Mozart. The second is an unimportant intermezzo leading directly into the finale, which is also in binary form of the composite type. The treatment is ·the very reverse of the previous sonata. It is not contrapuntal, nor fugal. Little pains are taken to make the details expressive ; and the only result of using a bigger and less careful brush is to reduce the interest to a minimum, and to make the genuineness of the utterances seem doubtful, because the writer appears not to have taken the trouble to express his best thoughts.

Wilhelm Friedemann's brother, Carl Philipp Emanuel, his junior by a few years, was the member of the younger family who attained the highest reputation as a representative composer of instrumental music and a writer on that subject. His celebrity is more particularly based on the development of sonata-form, of which he is often spoken of as the inventor. True, his sonatas and writings obtained considerable celebrity, and familiarity induced people to remark things they had overlooked in the works of other composers. But in fact he is neither the inventor nor the establisher of sonata-form. It was understood before his day, both in details and in general distribution of movements. One type obtained the reputation of supreme fitness later, but it was not nearly always adopted by Haydn, nor invariably by Mozart, and was consistently departed from by Beethoven ; and Emanuel did not restrict himself to it ; yet his predecessors used it often. It is evident therefore that his claims to a foremost place rest upon other grounds. Among these, most prominent is his comprehension and employment of the art of playing and expressing things on the clavier. He understood it, not in a new sense, but in one which was nearer to public comprehension than the treatment of his father. He grasped the phase to which it had arrived, by constant development in all quarters ; he added a little of his own, and having a clear and ready-working brain, he brought it home to the musical public in a way they had not felt before. His influence was paramount to give a decided direction to clavier-playing, and it is possible that the style of which he was the foster-father passed on continuously to the masterly treatment of the pianoforte by Clementi, and through him to the culminating achievements of Beethoven.

In respect of structure, most of his important sonatas are in three movements, of which the first and last are quick and the middle one slow ; and this is a point by no means insignificant in the history of the sonata, as it represents a definite and characteristic balance between the principal divisions, in respect of style and expression as well as in the external traits of form. Many of these are in clear binary form, like those of his elder brother and his admirable predecessor, yet to be noted, P. Domenico Paradies. He adopts sometimes the old type, dividing the recapitulation in the second half of the movement ; sometimes the later, and sometimes the composite type. For the most part he is contented with the opportunities for variety which this form supplies, and casts a greater proportion of movements in it than most other composers, even to the extent of having all movements in a work in different phases of the same form, which in later times was rare. On the other hand, he occasionally experiments in structures as original as could well be devised. There is a sonata in F minor which has three main divisions corresponding to movements. The first, an allegro, approaches vaguely to binary form ; the second, an adagio, is in rough outline like simple primary form, concluding with a curious barless cadenza ; the last is a fantasia of the most elaborate and adventurous description, full of experiments in modulation, enharmonic and otherwise, changes of time, abrupt surprises and long passages entirely divested of bar lines. There is no definite subject, and no method in the distribution of keys. It is more like a rhapsodical improvisation of a most inconsequent and unconstrained description than the product of concentrated purpose, such as is generally expected in a sonata movement. It was, however, not unfamiliar in those days, and superb examples in the same spirit were provided by Johann Sebastian, such as the ' Fantasia cromatica ' and parts of some of the toccatas. Johann Ernst Bach also left something more after the manner of the present instance as the prelude to a fugue. Emanuel Bach's position is particularly emphasised as the most prominent composer of sonatas of his time, who clearly shows the tendency of the new counter-current away from the vigour and honest comprehensiveness of the great school of which his father was the last and greatest representative, towards the elegance, polite ease and artificiality which became the almost indispensable conditions of the art in the latter part of the 18th century. Fortunately the process of propping up a tune upon a dummy accompaniment was not yet accepted universally as a desirable phenomenon of high-class instrumental music ;

n fact such a stride downward in one generation would have been too cataclysmic; so he was spared the temptation of shirking honest concentration, and padding his works, instead of making them thoroughly complete; and the result is a curious combination, sometimes savouring strongly of his father's style:

etc.

and sometimes coldly predicting the style of the future:

etc.

In general, his building up of movements is full of expressive detail, and he does not spare himself trouble in enriching his work with such things as ingenuity, genuine musical perception and vivacity of thought can suggest. He occasionally reaches a point of tenderness and poetic sensibility which is not unworthy of his descent, but there is also sometimes an uncomfortable premonition in his slow movements of the posturing and posing which were soon to be almost inevitable in well-bred adagios. The spirit is indeed not greatly deep and earnest, but in outward things the attainment of a rare degree of point and emphasis, and of clearness and certainty in construction without emptiness, sufficed to give Philipp Emanuel a foremost place among the craftsmen of the art.

P. Domenico Paradies was Emanuel Bach's senior by a few years. Two of his sonatas, at least, are deservedly well known to musicians. The structural qualities shown by the whole set of twelve emphasise the opinion that binary form was familiar to composers of this period. They differ from Philipp Emanuel's chiefly in consisting uniformly of two movements only. Of these, the first movements are almost invariably in binary form. That of the first sonata is perfectly complete and of the later type; many of the others are of the early type. Some details in the distribution of the movements are worth noticing. Thus the last movement of No. 4 is a very graceful and pretty minuet, which had hitherto not been so common an ingredient in sonatas as it afterwards became. The last movement [1] of No. 3 is called an aria; the arrangement of parts of which, as well as

[1] In some modern reprints of this sonata the order of the movements has been reversed.

that of the last movement of No. 9, happens to produce a rondo, hitherto an extremely rare feature. His formulation and arrangement of subjects is extremely clear and masterly, and thoroughly in the sonata manner—that is, essentially harmonical. In character he leans towards the style of the latter part of the 18th century, but has a grace and sincerity which are thoroughly his own. In a few cases, as in the last movements of the sonatas in A and D, Nos. 6 and 10, which are probably best known of all, the character assumed is rather of the bustling and hearty type which is suggestive of the influence of Scarlatti. In detail they are not so rich as the best specimens of Emanuel's, or of Friedemann Bach's workmanship; but they are thoroughly honest and genuine all through, and thoroughly musical, and show no sign of shuffling or laziness.

The two-movement form of clavier sonata, of which Paradies's are probably the best examples, seems to have been commonly adopted by a number of composers of second and lower rank, from his time till far on in the century. Those of Durante have been already mentioned. All the set of eight by Domenico Alberti are also in this form, and so are many by such forgotten contributors as Roeser and Barthélemon, and some by the once popular Schobert. Alberti is credited with the doubtful honour of having invented a formula of accompaniment which became a little too familiar in the course of the century, and is sometimes known as the AL-BERTI BASS (q.v.). He may not have invented it, but he certainly called as much attention to it as he could, since not one of his eight sonatas is without it, and in some movements it continues almost throughout. The movements approach occasionally to binary form, but are not clearly defined; the matter is for the most part dull in spirit and poor in sound; and the strongest characteristic is the unfortunate one of hitting upon a cheap device, which was much in vogue with later composers of mark, without having arrived at that mastery and definition of form and subject which alone made it endurable. The times were not quite ripe for such usages, and it is fortunate for Paradies, who was slightly Alberti's junior, that he should have attained to a far better definition of structure without resorting to such cheapening.

There are two other composers of this period who deserve notice for maintaining, even later, some of the dignity and nobility of style which were now falling into neglect, together with clearness of structure and expressiveness of detail. These are Rolle and George Benda. A sonata of the former in Eb shows a less certain hand in the treatment of form, but at times extraordinary gleams of musically poetic feeling. Points in the adagio are not unworthy of kinship with Beethoven. It contains broad and daring effects of modulation, and noble richness of sentiment and expression, which, by the side of the obvious tendencies of music in these days, is really astonishing. The first and last movements are in binary form of the old type, and contain some happy and musical strokes, though not so remarkable as the contents of the slow movement. George Benda was a younger and greater brother of the Franz who has been mentioned in connexion with violin sonatas. He was one of the last writers who, using the now familiar forms, still retained some of the richness of the earlier manner. There is in his work much in the same tone and style as that of Emanuel Bach, but also an earnestness and evident willingness to get the best out of himself and to deal with things in an original manner, such as was by this time becoming rare. After him, composers of anything short of first rank offer little to arrest attention either for individuality in treatment or earnestness of expression. The serious influences which had raised so many of the earlier composers to a point of memorable musical achievement were replaced by associations of far less genuine character, and the ease with which something could be constructed in the now familiar forms of sonata, seduced men into indolent uniformity of structure and commonplace prettiness in matter. Some attained to evident proficiency in the use of instrumental resource, such as Turini ; and some to a touch of genuine though small expressiveness, as Haessler and Grazioli ; for the rest the achievements of Sarti, Sacchini, Schobert, Méhul and the otherwise great Cherubini, in the line of sonata, do not offer much that requires notice. They add nothing to the process of development, and some of them are remarkably behindhand in relation to their time, and both what they say and the manner of it is equally unimportant.

JOSEF HAYDN'S CONTRIBUTION.—Midway in the crowd comes the conspicuous form of Haydn, who raised upon the increasingly familiar structural basis not only some fresh and notable work of the accepted sonata character, but the great and enduring monument of his symphonies and quartets. The latter do not fall within the limits of the present subject, though they are in reality but the great instrumental expansion of this kind of music for solo instruments. An arbitrary restriction has been put upon the meaning of the word sonata, and it is necessary here to abide by it. With Haydn it is rather sonata-form which is important, than the works which fall under the conventional acceptation of the name. His sonatas are many, but they are of exceedingly diverse value, and very few of really great importance. As is the case with his quartets, some, which internal evidence would be sufficient to mark as early attempts, are curiously innocent and elementary; and even throughout, with a few exceptions,

their proportionate value is not equal to that of other classes of his numerous works. But the great span of his musical activity, reaching from the times of the Bach family till fairly on in Beethoven's mature years, the changes in the nature of keyed instruments, and the development of their resources which took place during his lifetime, make it inevitable that there should be a marked difference in the appearance and limits of different members of the collection. However, he is always himself, and though the later works are wider and more richly expressed, they represent the same mental qualities as the earliest. At all times his natural bent is in favour of simplification, as against the old contrapuntal modes of expression. His easy good-humour speaks best in simple but often ingeniously balanced tunes and subjects, and it is but rare that he has recourse to polyphonic expression or to the kind of idea which calls for it. Partly on this account and partly on account of narrowness of capacity in the instrument to which in solo sonatas he gave most attention, his range of technical resource is not extensive, and he makes but little demand upon his performers. His use of tunes[1] and decisively outlined subjects is one of the most important points in relation to structure at this period. Tunes had existed in connexion with words for centuries, and it is to their association with verses balanced by distinct rhythmic grouping of lines that the sectional tune of instrumental music must ultimately be traced. It appears not to be a genuine instrumental product, but an importation ; and the fact that almost all the most distinguished composers were connected with opera establishments, just at the time that the tune-element became most marked in instrumental works, supports the inference that the opera was the means through which a popular element ultimately passed into the great domain of abstract music. In preceding times the definition of subject by hard outlines and systematic conformity to a few normal successions of harmony was not universal ; and the adoption of tunes was rare. In Haydn and Mozart the culmination of regularity in the building of subjects is reached. The virtue of this process is that it simplifies the conditions of structure in the whole movement. When a correct system of centralisation is found by which the subject is restrained within the limits which strictly illustrate but one single tonality, the feelings which this suggests to the hearer are such as will be satisfied with equally simple order in all other parts of the complete structure. If the creative power is not sufficiently concentrated and disciplined to restrain the direction of its activity within comprehensible bounds, the result can only be to make perfect balance and proportion impossible. Thus if the first section of a movement is so decentralised

[1] See under HAYDN for a discussion of the composer's importation of folk-song into works of the sonata type.

that its connexion with any particular key cannot possibly be followed by the hearer, one of the primary conditions of abstract music has been violated, and the balance of parts rendered undistinguishable. Yet the subject or section may range broadly in its course, and touch upon many alien tonalities without violating these conditions ; but then the horizon is broadened so as to necessitate an equal relative extension in every part of the movement. If a poet sets out with a passage expanded to the full with imagery and implication, in which almost every word is suggestive of wide horizons of thought, and carries inference behind it as complicated as those which lie in simple external manifestations of nature, it is useless for him to go back afterwards to a more limited and statuesque mode of expression. Even a person of little cultivation would feel at once the violation of artistic proportion. A relative degree of heat and intensity must be maintained at the risk of the work being as a whole unendurable. But if a more restricted field of imagination be appealed to at the outset, the work may be the more easily and perfectly carried out in simpler and narrower limits. In abstract music, balance, proportion, equality in the range of emotional and structural elements are some of the most important conditions. Not that there is to be equal intensity all through, but that the salient and subordinate parts shall be fairly proportionate ; and this cannot be tested or stated by formulas of science, but only by cultivated artistic instinct. In music the art of expressing an idea within the limits and after the manner necessary for abstract music had to be discovered. The process of selection from experimental types had brought this to the closest point consistent with completeness in the latter half of the 18th century. At that time the disposition of the musical mind was specially set upon obviously intelligible order and certainty in the structural aspect of works. It was a necessary condition for art to go through ; and though not by any means the sole or supreme condition of excellence, it is not strange that the satisfaction derived from the sense of its achievement should cause people, in social circumstances which were peculiarly favourable, to put disproportionate stress upon it ; and that later writers who have not been able to keep pace with the inevitable march and change in the conditions of musical utterance should still insist on it as if it were the ultimate aim of art ; whereas in fact its prominence in that epoch was a passing phase having considerable dependence upon unique social conditions, and its existence in art at any time is only one of numberless constituent elements.

The condition of art of that time enabled the greatest composers to express the utmost of their ideas, and to satisfy their audiences, within the limits of a very simple group of harmonies. And this simplified the whole process of building their works to the utmost. Haydn manipulates the resources which lie within such limits to admiration. Hardly any composer so successfully made uniformity out of compounded diversity on a small scale. He delights in making the separate limbs of a subject of different lengths, and yet, out of their total sum, attaining a perfect and convincing symmetry. The harmonic progression of the subjects is uniformly obedient to the principles of a form which is on a preconceived plan, and without some such device the monotony of well-balanced phrases must soon have become wearisome. With regard to the actual distribution of the movements, Haydn does not depart from that already familiar in the works of earlier composers. Out of forty sonatas, comprising works for pianoforte alone, for pianoforte with accompaniment, and some adaptations, ten have only two movements, twenty-nine have three, and only one has four, this last comprising the only scherzando in the whole collection of one hundred and eleven movements. Nearly all the first movements are in binary form with an occasional rondo ; the last is often a rondo, more often in binary form, and occasionally a theme and variations. In the sonatas which have more than two movements, at least twice as many retain the old adagio as those which have the characteristic minuet and trio ; but as a set-off, several of the sonatas either conclude with a dance form, or a rondo, or set of variations in the ' Tempo di minuetto.'

The actual structure of the movements presents occasional peculiarities. In a few cases the pure old binary type, with repeat of first subject at the beginning of the second half, reappears. A considerable number are in the composite form, in which the first subject makes two distinct reappearances in full in the second half, as before described. The two halves of the movement are generally, but not invariably, repeated—the first half almost invariably ; in fact, the absence of the double bar in the middle of the sonata in D major (No. 32 in Breitkopf & Härtel's edition) appears to be the only exception. The distribution of subjects in balancing keys appears to be absolutely without exception, as tonic and dominant, or tonic minor and relative major. Each movement has usually two distinct subjects, but occasionally, as is observable in Haydn's predecessors, the second is not strongly marked. In a few cases the same subject serves for both sections. There are a few examples of his anticipating Beethoven's usage of introducing clear accessory subjects to carry on the sections. Haydn illustrates forcibly the usefulness of defining the main division of the movement, not only by emphasising the harmonic formula of the cadence, but by appending to it a characteristic phrase or figure, the position of which, immediately before the full stop, renders it particularly easy to recognise. The purpose and fitness of this has been already discussed. Haydn's cadence-figures are generally peculiarly attractive, and seem to be made so of set purpose.

As a rule the outlines of his binary movements are more persistently regular than those of his rondos. Haydn was the first composer of mark to adopt the rondo with frequency in sonatas. It had existed in isolation and in suites for a long while, and examples there are in plenty by Couperin and other early Frenchmen, who were much given to it ; and also by various members of the Bach family, including the great Johann Sebastian. But hundreds of sonatas, from the highest to the lowest grade, may be taken at random with a fair probability of not finding a single example. The influence of the opera may probably be here traced again, in the set tunes and dance types as significantly as in the general structure. However, though Haydn's kind of rondo is peculiarly familiar and characteristic, he does not make use of the form in his sonatas nearly so proportionately often as later composers do. The proportion in comparison with Mozart is almost as one to two. The value and appropriateness of this form is a matter of opinion. The greatest masters have used it frequently, and Beethoven with the profoundest effect. The usage of some other composers may be fairly described as obtrusively obvious, and it lends itself with greater readiness than any other plan of its scope to frivolity and commonplace. Haydn's subjects are often singularly slight, but his development of the form is almost always ingenious. Thus he varies his disposition of the episodes, so that sometimes the main subject and a single episodical subject alternate in different circumstances throughout ; at other times they are disposed so as to resemble the recapitulation in binary form. In the returns of the main theme he always exercises some consideration. In hardly any case does he simply repeat the theme as it stands throughout ; commonly each reappearance is a fresh variation. Occasionally the middle repeats are variations, and the first and last statements simple and identical; and sometimes variations of theme and episode alternate. In all such points his readiness and energy are apparent, and make his treatment of the form a model in its particular line.

The slow movements of all the composers of sonatas till Beethoven's time are rather artificial and inclined to pose, owing partly to the weakness and want of sustaining power in their instruments. They contain too little of the deep and liberal feeling which is necessary to make the highest impression, and too much decorative finger-play, corresponding no doubt to the roulades and vocal gymnastics for which

operatic singers found such admirable opportunities in the slow beats of adagios. Haydn's management of such things is artistic, and he occasionally strikes upon an interesting subject, but hardly any of the movements approach to the qualities expected in the ideal slow movement of modern times.

His distribution of the keys of the movements is simple. In some of the earlier sonatas all three are in the same, or major and minor of the same key. In more mature examples he adopts the familiar antithesis of subdominant, which in later works preponderates so strongly. In one case he adopts a very unusual antithesis. This is in the largest and most elaborate of all the sonatas, of which the first and last movements are in E♭, and the middle movement in E♮.

One point requires notice in connexion with his violin sonatas, viz. that they are the very reverse of those of the great school of half a century earlier ; for inasmuch as with them the violin was everything, with Haydn it was next to nothing. Except in obviously late sonatas it does little more than timidly accompany the pianoforte. It was in this manner that the violin, having departed grandly by the front door in the old style, crept back again into modern instrumental music by the back. But small as such beginnings were, Haydn's later and fuller examples are the ostensible starting-point of a class of music which in the 19th century has extended the domain of the solo sonata, by enlarging its effective scope, and obtaining a new province for experiment in the combination of other instruments with the pianoforte upon equal terms, and with equal respect to their several idiosyncrasies.

Johann Christian Bach, the youngest son of Johann Sebastian, was Haydn's contemporary and junior by three years. In his day he was considered an important composer for the pianoforte, and his style is held to have had some influence upon Mozart. (See MOZART, Vol. III. p. 539.) A sonata of his, in B♭, op. 17, is fluent and easily written, but not particularly interesting, and thoroughly in the style of the latter part of the 18th century. It consists of three movements, all in binary form of the older type. Another sonata, in C minor, is, for the date, in very singular form ; beginning with a slow movement, having a fugue in the middle, and ending with a ' Tempo di gavotta.' Its style is not strikingly massive, but there are many traits in it which show that his parentage was not entirely without influence. The fugue, though ably written, has too much of the hybrid effect common in such works, after the harmonic structural ideas had laid strong hold of men's minds, to be worthy of comparison with the genuine achievements of his father. The style of the work is broad, however, and some ideas and turns of expression may not unreasonably be taken to justify the influence attributed to him.

COMPARISON OF HAYDN AND MOZART.—The difference of age between Haydn and Mozart was twenty-four years, but in this interval there was less change in the form of the sonata than 'might be expected. It was, in fact, an almost stationary period, when the attainment of satisfactory structural principles by the labours of a century and more of composers left men time to pause and contemplate what appeared to them to be perfection ; the rhythmic wave of progress poised almost balanced for a short time before the rush which brought about an unexpected culmination in Beethoven.

The difference between Haydn and Mozart is plainly neither in structure nor altogether in style of thought and expression, but in advantages of temporal position. Haydn began nearer to the time of struggle and uncertainty. He found much ready to his hand, and he tested it and applied it and improved it ; and when Mozart came there was little to do but adapt his supreme gifts of fluency, clearness and beauty of melody to glorify the edifice.

The progression of artistic instinct is at present an unexplained phenomenon ; it can only be judged from observation that the children of a later generation are born with a predisposed facility to realise in perfect clearness the forms which preceding generations have been wanderingly and dimly striving after. It is possible that the affinity between genuine music and the mental conditions of the race is so close that the progress of the latter carries the former with it as part of the same organic development. At all events, Mozart was gifted with an extraordinary and hitherto unsurpassed instinct for formal perfection, and his highest achievements lie not more in the tunes which have so captivated the world, than in the perfect symmetry of his best works. Like Haydn's his ideas are naturally restricted within limits which simplify to the utmost the development of the form which follows from them. They move in such perfect obedience to the limits and outlines of the harmonic progressions which most certainly characterise the key, that the structural system becomes architecturally patent and recognisable to all listeners that have any understanding. In his time these formal outlines were fresh enough to bear a great deal of use without losing their sweetness; and Mozart used them with remarkable regularity. Out of thirty-six of his best-known sonatas, twenty-nine are in the now familiar order of three movements, and no less than thirty-three have the first movement in binary form. That binary form is moreover so regular, that the same pauses and the same successions of harmony, and the same occurrences of various kinds, may often be safely anticipated

at the same point in the progress of the movements. He makes some use, often conspicuously, of the device of repeating short phrases consecutively, which has already been described in connexion with Scarlatti's work. Thus in a sonata in D major for violin and pianoforte, the first section of the first movement may be divided into seven distinct passages, each of which is severally repeated in some form or other consecutively. There are some peculiarities, such as the introduction of a new subject in the working-out portion of the work, instead of keeping consistently to development of the principal ideas ; and the filling of the episodes of a rondo with a variety of different ideas, severally distinct ; but as these points are not the precursors of further development, they are hardly worth discussing. It only requires to be pointed out that occasionally in pianoforte and other sonatas he makes experiments in novel distribution and entirely original manipulation of the structural elements of binary and other forms ; which is sufficient to prove not only that he recognised the fitness of other outlines besides those that he generally adopted, but that he was capable of adapting himself to novel situations, if there had been any call for effort in that direction. As it happened, the circumstances both of musical and social life were unique, and he was enabled to satisfy the highest critical taste of his day without the effort of finding a new point of departure.

His treatment of rondo-form is different, and less elementary than Haydn's. Haydn most commonly used a very decisively sectional system, in which every characteristic portion, especially the theme, was marked off distinct and complete. This accorded with the primitive idea of rondos as exemplified, often very happily, in the works of early French composers, and in certain forms of vocal music. The root-idea appears in the most elementary stages of musical intelligence as a distinct verse or tune which forms the staple of the whole matter, and is, for the sake of contrast, interspersed with digressions of subordinate interest. It is so obvious a means of arriving at something like structural balance, that it probably existed in times even before the earliest of which evidence remains. In the earliest specimens to be found in sonatas, the traces of their kinship can be clearly followed. Reference has been already made to the two examples in the sonatas by Paradies, which consist of an aria, a contrasting passage, and then the aria pure and simple again, and so forth. Haydn adopted the general outline. He frequently begins with a complete theme systematically set out with double bars and repeats, and a full conclusion. He then begins something entirely different either in a new related key, or in the minor of the principal key, and makes a complete whole of that also, and so on right through, alternating his main tune with one or more others all equally complete. Under such circumstances his principle of giving variations at each return of the theme or repetition of an episode is almost indispensable to avoid monotony. Mozart rarely makes any point of this plan of adopting variations in his sonata-rondos, because it is not required. He does not often cast his theme in such extremely distinct outlines. In structure it is more what an ordinary binary subject would be ; that is, complete and distinct in itself as an idea, without being so carried out as to make its connexion with the rest of the movement a matter of secondary rather than intrinsic consequence. Haydn's conception is perfectly just and rational, but Mozart's is more mature. The theme and its episodes are more closely interwoven, and the development of the whole has a more consistent and uniform texture. Mozart does not avoid varying his theme ; on the contrary, he constantly puts in the most delicate strokes of detail and of graceful adornment, and sometimes resorts to delightfully ready development of its resources ; but with him it is not so indispensable, because his conception of the form gives it so much more freedom and elasticity.

The central movement of his three-movement sonatas is almost invariably a slow one, commonly in the key of the subdominant. The style of these is characteristic of the time ; that is, rather artificial and full of graces,[1] which require to be given with a somewhat conscious elegance of manner, not altogether consonant with the spirit of later times. They rarely touch the point of feeling expected in modern movements of the kind, because the conception formed of the proper function of the slow movement in his time was clearly alien to that of the 19th century. As specimens of elegance and taste, however, Mozart's examples probably attain the highest point possible in their particular genus.

The technique of his sonatas, from the point of view of instrumental resource, is richer and fuller than Haydn's, but still thin and rather empty in sound to ears that are accustomed to the wonderful development of the resources of the modern pianoforte ; but the refinement and self-containment of his style make him particularly acceptable to artists who idealise finish and elegance in solo performance, and nicety of *ensemble* in works for combined instruments, as the highest and most indispensable condition of art. His instinct for adapting his thoughts to instrumental idiosyncrasies was of a very high order when the instruments

were familiar and properly developed. This with the pianoforte was not yet achieved, and consequently some of his forms of expression are hardly adapted to its nature, and seem in these days to be rather compromises than perfectly suitable utterances.

INFLUENCE OF PIANO TECHNIQUE ON FORM. —With regard to the technical matter of the development of the resources of the pianoforte, Mozart's contemporary, Muzio Clementi, occupies a most important position. Clementi, in his early days, according to his own admission, applied himself rather to the development of the resources of playing than to the matter to be played, and attained a degree and a kind of mastery of which no one before his time had heard the like. When he began to apply himself more to the matter, this study served him in good stead ; and his divination of the treatment most appropriate to the instrument, expanded by this means in practical application, marks his sonatas as among the very first in which the genuine qualities of modern pianoforte music on a large scale are shown. They begin to approach to that broad and almost orchestral style which is sometimes said to be characteristic of Beethoven ; and the use of octaves and fuller combinations of sounds, and the occasional irruption of passages which bring into play stronger muscles than those of the fingers, are all in the direction of modern usage. In respect of structure, it is not necessary to consider more than that he commonly accepted the three-movement type of sonata, beginning with a movement in binary form and ending with a rondo, and having a slow movement in the middle. His handling is free and at the same time thoroughly under control. One of his characteristics is the love of importing little touches of learning or scientific ingenuity into the treatment ; as in the sonata in G (of four movements) in which two canons in direct and contrary motion take the place of the minuet and trio. In another sonata, in F, one figure is woven through the whole substance of the first movement, appearing in the different sections diminished and inverted, and in various phases of expression which quite alter its aspect. His slow movements are sometimes equally simple and expressive, but also frequently of that ornamental order which has been sufficiently commented on.

In one celebrated case he anticipated the modern taste for programme by calling one of his longest and most pretentious sonatas ' Didone abbandonata. Scena tragica.' But appearance of dramatic purpose does not turn him aside from regularity of form any more than in other sonatas. His style is not exempt from the family likeness which is observable in all composers of the latter part of the century. His ideas are large and broad, and not unworthy to have exerted some influence upon both Mozart

---

[1] These graces are of two kinds : (1) Those which survive in early pianoforte music from the habits of the harpsichord-player who gave both accent and sustaining power to his instrument by the use of graces ; (2) Those which imitate the vocal *coloratura* of the operatic singer. (See ORNAMENTS.)

and Beethoven. A certain dryness and reticence makes him unlikely to be greatly in favour in modern times, but his place as an important figure in the development of the sonata in its relation with the pianoforte is assured.

One further composer who deserves some consideration in connexion with the sonata before Beethoven's time is J. L. Dussek, who was born ten years after Clementi, and soon after Mozart. His most noteworthy characteristics are an individual, though not incisive style, and an instinct of a high order for the qualities and requirements of the pianofo.te. There is some diversity in point of value between his early and his later sonatas. The former are rather narrow in idea and structure, whereas the latter, such as op. 70 in A♭, are quite remarkable for freedom and elaboration of form and subject. Both in this sonata and in the op. 77 he makes use of the hitherto almost unknown device of extending the effect of the first sections by subordinate transitions as well as by accessory subjects. In the first movement of op. 70 there is the unusual feature of a happy modulation out and back again in the actual substance of the second subject—a characteristic which is common enough in the works of Schumann and Brahms, but was exceedingly rare in Dussek's time. Another characteristic which Dussek has in common with more modern writers is the infusion of a certain amount of sense and sentiment even into his passages and flourishes, which with his immediate predecessors had been too commonly barren. He also takes thought to enliven his recapitulations by variation or ingeniously diversified transposition of order in the ideas (as in op. 77). His writing for the instrument is brilliant and sparkling, and has certain premonitions of Weber in it. The ideas are sometimes, even in his best works, trite and vapid, but more often delicate and attractive. The slow movements have a sustained and serious manner, also unusual in his time, and said to be derived from his having studied the organ considerably in his younger days. He stands historically with giants on either hand, and this has contributed to make him appear somewhat of a parenthesis in the direct course of sonata development. Their vastness of artistic proportion did not, however, suppress his personality, or extinguish his individuality, which is still clear in his own line, and has exerted some influence both upon the modern style of playing and also upon the style of musical thought of a few modern composers for the pianoforte to whom the giants did not strongly appeal.

BEETHOVEN AND THE 'IDEA.'—The direct line of development after Haydn, Mozart and Clementi is obviously continued in Beethoven. As we have pointed out, the changes which took place after Emanuel Bach's labours were less rapid and remarkable than in times preceding. The finishing touches had been put to the structural system, and men were so delighted with its perfection as structure, that they were content to hear it repeated over and over again without calling for variety or individuality in the treatment, and very often without caring much about the quality of the thing said. The other side of development was technical. The pianoforte being a new instrument, the manner of musical speech best adapted to it had to be discovered. With the earlier composers forms of expression better suited to other instruments were adopted; but by degrees experiments in effect and assiduous attention to the capabilities of the hand, such as Clementi gave in his early years, had brought the mechanism of expression to a tolerably consistent and complete state; so that when Beethoven appeared he was spared the waste of force incident to having to overcome elementary problems of instrumental technique, and the waste of effect incidental to compromises, and was enabled to concentrate all his powers upon the musical material.

Beethoven's works introduce a new element into the problem, and one that complicates matters immeasurably. With his predecessors structural simplicity had been a paramount consideration, and often straitened somewhat the freedom of the idea. The actual subjects seem drilled into a regular shape, admitting of very little variation, in order that the development of the movement might march direct and undeviating in its familiar course. Musicians had arrived at that artificial state of mind which deliberately chose to be conscious of formal elements. Their misconception was a natural one. The existing conditions of art might lead a man to notice that uncultivated people delighted in simple and single tunes, and that cultivated people enjoyed the combination of several, when disposed according to certain laws, and to conclude from this that the disposition was of more importance than the matter. But, in fact, the mind is led from point to point by feelings which follow the ideas, and of these and their interdependence and development it is necessarily conscious; but of the form it is not actively conscious unless the ideas have not sufficient force to possess it, or the necessities of logical consequence are outrageously violated. It is only under peculiar social and intellectual conditions that structural qualities can be so excessively emphasised. The production of a genuine master must be ultimately reducible to logical analysis, but not on the spot or at once; and to insist upon art being so immediately verifiable is not only to set the conclusion to be drawn from its historical development upside down, but to refer the enjoyment of its highest achievements to the contemplation of dry bones. The imagination and the reason must both be satisfied, but before all things the imagination.

In the middle years of the 18th century the imaginative side had not a fair chance. Music was too much dependent upon the narrow limits of the taste of polite circles, and the field of appeal to emotion was not free. But when at last the natural man threw off the incubus that had so long oppressed him, the spiritual uprising and the broadening of life brought a new kind of vigour into art and literature. Beethoven was the first great composer to whom the limitless field of unconventionalised human emotion was opened, and his disposition was ready for the opportunity. Even in the ordinary trifles of life he sometimes showed by an apparently superfluous rebellion against polite usages his antipathy to artificiality, and conversely the bent of his sympathy towards unmistakable realities of human feeling. He thus became the prototype of genuine modern music, and the first exponent of its essential qualities; and the sonata form being ready in its main outlines for his use, and artistic instinct having achieved the most perfect spontaneity in its employment, he took possession of it as an appropriate mode of formulating some of the richest and most impressive of his thoughts. With him the idea asserted its rights. This is not to say that structure is ignored, but that the utmost expansion and liberty is admitted in the expression of the vital parts which can be made consistent with perfect balance in the unfolding of the whole; and this obviously depends upon the powers of the composer. Under such circumstances he can only be guided by the highest development of instinct, for the process of balance and distribution becomes so complicated that it is almost out of the reach of conscious analysis, much more of the dictation of science.

The evolution of this vital ingredient, the idea, is so obscure and difficult that it is out of the question to enter upon it in this place. It is an unhappy fact that the scientists who have endeavoured to elucidate music, with a few great and honourable exceptions, foreseeing that the analysis of ideas was quite beyond their reach, at all events until immense advances are made in the sciences which have direct reference to the human organism, have set their faces to the structural elements, as if music consisted of nothing but lines and surfaces. The existence of idea is so habitually ignored that it necessarily appears to be nonexistent in their estimate of art. On the other hand, the philosophers who have said anything about it appear on the surface not to be in accord; though in reality their views are both compatible and necessary, but require a more detailed experience of the art and of its historical development to explain their inter-

action. But meanwhile the external method of the scientists gains disproportionate preeminence, and conscientious people feel uneasily that there may be no such things as ideas at all, and that they will be doing better to apply themselves to mathematics. And yet the idea is everything, and without it music is absolutely null and void; and though a great and comprehensive mathematician may make an analysis after the event, a synthesis which is merely the fruit of his calculations will be nothing more than a sham and an imposture. In fact, the formulation of the idea is a most vital matter in musical history, and its progress can be traced from the earliest times, proceeding simultaneously with the development of the general structure of the sonata. The expressive raw material was drawn from various sources. The style of expression developed under the influences of religion in the ages preceding the beginnings of instrumental music supplied something; dance music of all orders, mimetic and merely rhythmic, supplied much; the pseudo-realism of the drama, in respect of vocal inflexion and imitations of natural circumstances, also something; and the instincts surviving in the race from countless past ages, the actual cries arising from spontaneous nervous reaction, and many other similar causes, had a share in suggestion, and in actual, though unrealised, motive power. And all these, compounded and inseparably intermingled, supplied the basis of the expressive element in music. Through all the time from Monteverdi to Beethoven this expressive element was being more and more clearly drawn into compact and definite proportions; floating at first vaguely on the surface, springing out in flashes of exceptional brightness here and there, and at times presenting almost perfect maturity by fits of individual good fortune; but hardly ever so free but that some of the matrix is felt to be clinging to the ore. It obtained complete but restricted symmetry with the composers immediately preceding Beethoven, but arrived only at last with him at that expansion which made it at once perfect and intelligible, and yet boundless in range within the limits of the art-material at the composer's command.

Before Beethoven, the development of a long work was based upon antitheses of distinct tunes and concrete lumps of subject representing separate organisms, either merely in juxtaposition, or loosely connected by more or less empty passages. There were ideas indeed, but ideas limited and confined by the supposed necessities of the structure of which they formed a part. But what Beethoven seems to have aimed at was the expansion of the term 'idea' from the isolated subject to the complete whole; so that instead of the subjects being separate, though compatible items, the whole movement, or even the whole work, should be the complete and uniform organism which represented in its entirety a new meaning of the word 'idea,' of which the subjects, in their close connexion and inseparable affinities, were subordinate limbs. This principle is traceable in works before his time, but not on the scale to which he carried it, nor with his conclusive force. In fact, the condition of art had not been sufficiently mature to admit the terms of his procedure, and it was barely mature enough till he made it so.

His early works were in conformity with the style and structural principles of his predecessors; but he began, at least in pianoforte works, to build at once upon the topmost stone of their edifice. His earliest sonatas (op. 2) are on the scale of their symphonies. He began with the four-movement plan which they had almost entirely reserved for the orchestra. In the second sonata he already produces an example of his own peculiar kind of slow movement, full, rich, decisive in form, unaffected in idea, and completely divested of the elaborate graces which had been before its most conspicuous feature. In the same sonata also he produces a scherzo, short in this instance, and following the lines of the minuet, but of the genuine characteristic quality. Soon, in obedience to the spread of his idea, the capacity of the instrument seems to expand, and to attain an altogether new richness of sound, and a fullness it never showed before, as in many parts of the fourth sonata (op. 7), especially the largo, which shows the unmistakable qualities which ultimately expanded into the unsurpassed slow movement of the opus 106. As early as the second sonata he puts a new aspect upon the limits of the first sections; he not only makes his second subject in the first movement modulate, but he develops the cadence-figure into a very noticeable subject. It is fortunately unnecessary to follow in detail the various ways in which he expanded the structural elements of the sonata, as it has already been described in the article BEETHOVEN, and other details are given in the article FORM. In respect of the subject and its treatment, a fortunate opportunity is offered by a coincidence between a subordinate subject in a sonata of Haydn in C and a similar accessory in Beethoven's sonata for violoncello and pianoforte in A major (op. 69), which serves to illustrate pregnantly the difference of scope which characterises their respective treatment. Haydn's is as follows:

etc.

and Beethoven's:

etc.

As has been already explained, an expansion of this kind makes inevitable a similar expansion in the whole structure of the movement, and a much wider choice of relative keys than simple tonic and dominant in the expository sections; or else a much freer movement in every part of the sections, and emphasis upon unexpected relations of harmony. Even without this, the new warmth and intensity of the subject precludes mere reiteration of the accustomed usages, and necessitates a greater proportionate vitality in the subordinate parts of the work. The relative heat must be maintained, and to fall back upon familiar formulas would clearly be a jarring anomaly. In this manner the idea begins to dictate the form.

But in order to carry out in equal measure the development of the idea, every resource that the range of music can supply must be admissible to him that can wield it with relevance. Hence Beethoven, as early as op. 31, No. 2, reintroduces instrumental recitative with extraordinary effect. Later, he resumes the rhapsodical movement which Bach and earlier composers had employed in a different sense, as in the sonata in Eb, op. 81, and in the third division of that in A, op. 101, and in the most romantic of romantic movements, the first in E major of op. 109. And lastly, he brings back the fugue as the closest means of expressing a certain kind of idea. In these cases the fugue is not a retrogression, nor a hybrid, but a new adaptation of an old and invaluable form under the influence of perfectly assimilated harmonic principles. The great fugue in the sonata in Bb, op. 106, for instance, is not only extraordinary as a fugue but is distributed in a perfectly ideal balance of long contrasting periods in different states of feeling, culminating duly with a supreme rush of elaborate force, as complex and as inexorable as some mighty action of nature. In these sonatas Beethoven touches all moods, and all in the absolute manner, free from formality or crude artifice, which is the essential characteristic of genuine modern music. In a few of the earlier sonatas he reverts to manners and structural effects which are suggestive of the principles of his predecessors. But these occasional incursions of external influence are with rare exceptions inferior to the works in which his own original force of will speaks with genuine and characteristic freedom. The more difficult the problem suggested by the thought which is embodied in the subject, the greater is the result. The full richness of his nature is not called out to the strongest point till there is something preternaturally formidable to be mastered. The very statement of the opening bars of such sonatas as that in D minor, op. 31, No. 2 ; C major, op. 53 ; F minor, op. 57 ; B♭, op. 106 ; C minor, op. 111, is at such a level of daring breadth and comprehensive power that it becomes obvious in a moment that the work cannot be carried out on equal proportionate terms without almost superhuman concentration, and unlimited command of technical resources, both in respect of the instrument and the art of expression. In such cases, Beethoven rises to a height which has only been attained by two or three composers in the whole history of music, in that sublimity which is almost his peculiar monopoly.

But, fortunately for average beings and average moods of people who have not always a taste for the sublime, he shows elsewhere, on a less exalted scale, the highest ideals of delicate beauty and all shades of the humours of mankind, even to simple exuberant playfulness. The beauty and the merriment often exist side by side, as in the exquisite little sonata in G, op. 14, No. 2, and in that in F♯ major, op. 78 ; and in a loftier and stronger spirit, in company with more comprehensive ranges of feeling, in the sonata in A, op. 101. In all these and many more there is an ideal continuity and oneness which is musically felt even where there is no direct external sign of the connexion. In a few, however, there are signs of more than this. In the B♭ sonata, op. 106, for instance, the similar disposition of intervals in the subjects of the various movements has led to the inference that he meant to connect them by transformations of one principal subject or germ. The same occurs with as much prominence in the sonata in A♭, op. 110, which is in any case a specimen where the oneness and continuity are peculiarly felt. It is possible that the apparent transformations are not so much conscious as the result of the conditions of mind which were necessary to produce the oneness of effect, since concentration upon any subject is liable to exert influence upon closely succeeding action, whether of the mind or body, and to assimilate the fruit unconsciously to the form of the subject contemplated. This, however, would not lessen the interest of the fact, but would possibly rather enhance it. It only affects the question whether or no Beethoven consciously reasoned about possible ways of extending and enhancing the opportunities of sonata-form—too large a subject to be entered upon here. As a rule, great masters appear to hit upon such germinal principles in the process of composition, without exactly formulating them in so many equivalent terms ; and those who come after note the facts and apply them as useful resources or sometimes as invaluable starting-points of fresh lines of development.

It is a noticeable fact that Beethoven only seldom indicated a programme, and it is extremely rare in him to find even the dimmest suggestions of realism. In fact, as must be true of all the highest music, a work of his is not representative of a story, but of a mental process. Even if it deals with a story it does not represent the circumstances, but the condition of mind which results from its contemplation ; or, in other words, the musical counterpart of the emotion to which it gives rise ; and it is the coherency and consistent sequence of the emotions represented which produce the effect of oneness on the colossal scale of his greatest works which is Beethoven's crowning achievement. With him the long process of development appears to find its utmost and complete culmination ; and what comes after, can in sight of his work, can be little more than commentary. It may be seen, without much effort, that mankind does not achieve more than one supreme triumph on the same lines of art. When the conditions of development are fulfilled the climax is reached, but there is not more than one climax to each crescendo. The conditions of human life change ceaselessly, and with them the phenomena of art, which are their counterpart. The characteristics of the art of any age are the fruit of the immediate past as much as are the emotional and intellectual conditions of that age. They are its signs, and it is impossible to produce in a succeeding age a perfect work of art in the same terms as those which are the direct fruit of a different and earlier group of causes ; and it is partly for this reason that attempts to return to earlier conditions of art which leave out the essential characteristics of contemporary feeling invariably ring false.

BEETHOVEN'S CONTEMPORARIES.—The time produced other real men besides Beethoven, though not of his stamp. Weber and Schubert were both of the genuine modern type, genuinely musical through and through, though neither of them was a born writer of sonatas as

Beethoven was. Beethoven possessed, together with the supremest gift of ideas, a power of prolonged concentration and the certainty of self-mastery. This neither Weber nor Schubert possessed. Beethoven could direct his thought with infallible certainty; in Weber and Schubert the thought was often too much their master, and they both required, to keep them perfectly certain in the direction of their original musical matter, the guiding principle of a consciously realised dramatic or lyrical conception, which was generally supplied to them from without.

As should be obvious from the above survey of the process of sonata development, the absolute mastery of the structural outlines, the sureness of foot of the strong man moving, unaided but direct in his path, amidst the conflicting suggestions of his inspiration, is indispensable to the achievement of great and genuine sonatas. The more elaborate the art of expression becomes, the more difficult the success. Beethoven probably stood just at the point where the extremest elaboration and the most perfect mastery of combination on a large scale were possible. He himself supplied suggestion for yet further elaboration, and the result is that the works of his successors are neither so concentrated nor so well in hand as his. Weber was nearest in point of time, but his actual mastery of the art of composition was never very certain nor thoroughly regulated, though his musical instincts were almost marvellous. He had one great advantage, which was that he was a great pianist, and had the gift to extend the resources of the instrument by the invention of new and characteristic effects; and he was tolerably successful in avoiding the common trap of letting effect stand for substance. Another advantage was his supreme gift of melody. His tunes are for the most part of the old order, but infused with new life and heat by a breath from the genius of the people. His two best sonatas, in A♭ and D minor, are rich in thought, forcible, and genuinely full of expression. He always adopts the plan of four movements, and disposes them in the same order as Beethoven did. His treatment of form is also full and free, and he often imports some individuality into it. As simple instances may be taken—the use of the introductory phrase in the first movement of the sonata in C, in the body of the movement; the rondo structure of the slow movements, especially in the sonata in D minor, which has a short introduction, and elaborate variations in the place of exact returns of the subject; and the interspersion of subjects in the first movement of the sonata in E minor, op. 70, so as to knit the two sections of the first half doubly together. An essentially modern trait is his love of completing the cycle of the movement by bringing in a last allusion to the opening features of the whole movement at the end,

generally with some new element of expression or vivacity. Specially noticeable in this respect are the first and last (the 'Moto perpetuo') of the C major, the last of the A♭, and the first and last in both the D minor and E minor sonatas. Weber had an exceptional instinct for dance-rhythms, and this comes out very remarkably in some of the minuets and trios, and in the last movement of the E minor.

As a whole the Weber group is a decidedly important item in pianoforte literature, instinct with romantic qualities, and aiming at elaborate expressiveness, as is illustrated by the numerous directions in the A♭ sonata, such as 'con anima,' 'con duolo,' 'con passione,' 'con molt' affetto,' and so forth. These savour to a certain extent of the opera, and require a good deal of art and musical sense in the variation of time and the phrasing to give them due effect; and in this they show some kinship to the ornamental adagios of the times previous to Beethoven, though dictated by more genuinely musical feelings.

Schubert's sonatas do not show any operatic traits of the old manner, but there is plenty in them which may be called dramatic in a modern sense. His instincts were of a preeminently modern type, and the fertility of his ideas in their superabundance clearly made the self-restraint necessary for sonata-writing a matter of some difficulty. He was tempted to give liberty to the rush of thought which possessed him, and the result is sometimes delightful, but sometimes also bewildering. There are movements and even groups of them which are of the supremest beauty, but hardly any one sonata which is completely satisfactory throughout. His treatment of form is often daring, even to rashness, and yet from the point of view of principle offers but little to remark, though in detail some perfectly magical feats of harmonic progression and strokes of modulation have had a good deal of influence upon great composers of later times. The point which he serves to illustrate peculiarly in the history of music is the transition from the use of the idea, as shown in Beethoven's sonatas, on a grand and richly developed scale to the close and intensely emotional treatment of ideas in a lyrical manner which has since found its highest exponent in Schumann. In this process Schubert seems to stand midway—still endeavouring to conform to sonata ways, and yet frequently overborne by the invincible potency of the powers his own imagination has called up. The tendency is further illustrated by the exquisite beauty of some of the smaller and more condensed movements, which lose nothing by being taken out of the sonatas; being, like many of Schumann's specimens of intense concentration in short space, the fruit of a single flash of deep emotion. Among the longer movements, the one which is most closely unified is the first of the A minor, op. 143, in which a feature of the first subject is made to preponderate conspicuously all through, manifestly representing the persistence of a special quality of feeling through the varying phases of a long train of thought. Like many other movements, it has a strong dramatic element, but more under appropriate control than usual.

As a whole, though illustrating richly many of the tendencies of modern music, the sonatas cannot be taken as representing Schubert's powers as a composer of instrumental music so satisfactorily as his quartets, his string quintet, and his finest symphonies. In these he often rose almost to the highest point of musical possibility. And this serves further to illustrate the fact that since Beethoven the tendency has been to treat the sonata-form with the fresh opportunities afforded by combinations of instruments, rather than on the old lines of the solo sonata.

Two other composers of sonatas of Beethoven's time require notice. These are Woelfl and Hummel. The former chiefly on account of his once celebrated sonata called ' Ne plus ultra,' in which he showed some of the devices of technique which he was considered to have invented—such as passages in thirds and sixths, and ingenious applications of the shake. The matter is poor and vapid, and as throwing light upon anything except his powers as a player, is worthless. Its very title condemns it, for Woelfl had the advantage of being Beethoven's junior ; and it is astonishing how, by the side of the genuine difficulty of Beethoven's masterpieces, such a collection of tricks could ever have been dignified even by the supposition of being particularly difficult. It seems impossible that such work would have had any influence upon genuinely musical people ; but the sonata has all the signs of a useful piece for second-rate popular occasions ; for which the variations on ' Life let us cherish ' would doubtless be particularly effective.

Hummel in comparison with Woelfl was a giant, and certainly had pre-eminent gifts as a pianoforte-player. Like Weber he had an aptitude for inventing effects and passages, but he applied them in a different manner. He was of that nature which cultivates the whole technical art of speech till able to treat it with a certainty which has all the effect of mastery, and then, instead of using it to say something, makes it chiefly serviceable to show off the contents of his finger repertory. However, his technique is large and broad, full of sound and brilliancy, and when the works were first produced and played by himself they must have been extremely astonishing. His facility of speech is also wonderful, but his ideas were for the most part old-fashioned even when he produced them —for it must not be forgotten that he was eight years younger than Beethoven and twenty-six younger than Clementi. The spirit which seems to rule him is the consciousness of a pianist before an audience, guided by the chances of display. His modulations are free and bold, but they are often superfluous, because the ideas are not on the level of intensity or broad freedom which necessitates or even justifies them. He probably saw that modulation was a means of effect, but did not realise that there is a ratio between the qualities of subject and the development of the movement that springs from it. From this it will be obvious that his sonatas are not written in the mood to produce works that are musically important. He had the very finest possible opportunities through living in Mozart's house during his most impressionable days, and the fruit is sufficiently noticeable in the clearness with which he distributes his structural elements and in much of his manner of expressing himself ; but he had not the inventive gift for musical ideas, which contact and even familiar intercourse with great masters seems inadequate to supply. The survival of traits characteristic of earlier times is illustrated by some of his slow movements, in which he brought the most elaborate forces of his finished technique to serve in the old style of artificial adagio, where there is a hyper-elaborated grace at every corner and a shake upon every note that is long enough ; and if a chord be suitable to rest upon for a little, it is adorned with quite a collection of ingenious finger exercises, artificially manipulated scales and arpeggios, and the like contrivances ; which do not serve to decorate anything worthy of the honour, but stand of their own merits. There are occasional traits of expression and strokes of force in the sonatas, but the technique of the pianist preponderates excessively over the invention of the composer. At the same time the right and masterly use of the resources of an instrument is not by any means a matter of small moment in art, and Hummel's is right and masterly in a very remarkable degree.

CHOPIN'S CHARACTERISTICS.—After the early years of the 19th century, the sonata, in its conventional sense of instrumental work for a solo or at most for two instruments, occupies a smaller and decreasing space in the domain of music. Great composers have paid it proportionately very little attention, and the few examples they afford have rather an effect of being out of the direct line of their natural mode of expression. In Chopin, for instance, the characteristic qualities of modern music, in the treatment of ideas in short and malleable forms specially adapted to their expression, are found abundantly, and in these his genuine qualities are most clearly displayed. His sonatas are less successful, because, though quite master enough to deal with structure clearly and definitely, it was almost impossible for him to force the ideas within the limits which should make that structure relevant and convincing. They are children of a fervid and impetuous genius, and the classical dress and manners do not sit easily upon them. Moreover, the luxuriant fancy, the richness and high colour of expression, the sensuous qualities of the harmony, all tend to emphasise detail in a new and peculiar manner, and to make the sonata-principle of the old order appear irrelevant. The most successful are the sonatas in B♭ minor for pianoforte, op. 35, and that for pianoforte and violoncello in G minor, op. 65. In both these cases the first movements, which are generally a sure test of a capacity for sonata writing, are clearly disposed, and free from superfluous wandering and from tautology. There are certain idiosyncrasies in the treatment of the form, as for instance in the recapitulation, which in both cases is almost limited to the materials of the second section, the opening features of the movement being only hinted at in conclusion. The subjects themselves are fairly appropriate to the style of movement, and are kept well in hand, so that on the whole, in these two cases, the impression conveyed is consistent with the sonata-character. In scherzos Chopin was thoroughly at home, and, moreover, they represent a province in which far more abandonment is admissible. In both sonatas they are successful, but that in the pianoforte sonata is especially fascinating and characteristic, and though the modulations are sometimes rather reckless the main divisions are well proportioned, and consequently the general effect of the outlines is sufficiently clear. The slow movements of both are very well known; that of the pianoforte sonata being the Funeral March, and the other being a kind of romance in Chopin's own free manner, which is familiar to players on the violoncello. The last movement of the pianoforte sonata is a short but characteristic outbreak of whirling notes, in general character not unlike some of his preludes, and equally free and original in point of form, but in that respect not without precedent among the last movements of early masters. In the mind of the composer it possibly had a poetical connexion with the Funeral March. The other last movement is a free kind of rondo, and therefore more consonant with the ordinary principles of form, and is appropriate, without being so interesting as the other movements. The total effect of these sonatas is naturally of an entirely different order from that of the earlier types, and not so convincing in oneness as the works of great masters of this kind of form; they are nevertheless plausible as wholes and in details most effective; the balance and appropriate treatment of the two instruments in the op. 65 being especially noteworthy. The other sonatas for pianoforte, in C minor and B minor, are more unequal. The first appears to be an early work, and contains some

remarkable experiments, one of which at least has value, others probably not. As examples may be mentioned the use of 5-4 time throughout the slow movement, and the experiment of beginning the recapitulation of the first movement in B♭ minor, when the principal key is C minor. In this sonata he seems not to move with sufficient ease, and in the B minor, op. 58, with something too much to have the general aspect of a successful work of the kind. The technical devices in the latter as in the others are extremely elaborate and effective, without being offensively obtrusive, and the ideas are often clear and fascinating; but as a complete and convincing work it is hardly successful.

Sonatas which followed implicitly the old lines without doing more than formulate subjects according to supposed laws do not require any notice. The mere artificial reproduction of forms that have been consciously realised from observation of great works of the past without importing anything original into the treatment, is often the most hopeless kind of plagiarism, and far more deliberate than the accidents of coincidence in ideas which are obvious to superficial observers.

MENDELSSOHN'S ORGAN SONATAS.—As examples of independent thought working in a comparatively untried field, Mendelssohn's six sonatas for the organ have some importance. They have very little connexion with the pianoforte sonata, or the history of its development; for Mendelssohn seems to have divined that the binary and similar instrumental forms of large scope were unsuitable to the genius of the instrument, and returned to structural principles of a date before those forms had become prominent or definite. Their chief connexion with the modern sonata type lies in the distribution of the keys in which the several movements stand, and the broad contrasts in time and character which subsist between one division or movement and another. Different members of the group represent different methods of dealing with the problem. In the large movements fugal and contrapuntal principles predominate, sometimes alternating with passages of a decidedly harmonic character. In movements which are not absolute fugues the broad outlines of form are commonly similar to those already described as exemplified in Bach's sonatas, and in the first and last movements of his Italian concerto. This form in its broadest significance amounts to a correspondence of well-defined sections at the beginning and end, with a long passage of 'free fantasia,' sometimes fugally developed, in the middle. The clearest example in these sonatas is the first movement of the third sonata, in A major, in which the corresponding divisions at either end are long, and strongly contrasted, in the modern quality and more simultaneous motion of the parts, with the elaborate fugal structure of the middle division. In the last movement of the sonata in B♭ the corresponding sections are very short, but the effect is structurally satisfying and clear. In no case is the structural system of keys used with anything approaching the clearness of a pianoforte sonata. Material is contrasted with material, sometimes simply as subjects or figures, sometimes even in respect of style ; as a Choral with recitative, Choral with fugal passages, or harmonic passages with contrapuntal passages. Sometimes these are kept distinct, and sometimes, as in the first movement of the sonata in B♭, they are combined together at the end. The general laying out of the complete works, though based on the same broadest radical principles, is in actual order and manner quite distinct from that of pianoforte sonatas. The longer movements alternate with very short ones, which commonly resemble romances, Lieder ohne Worte, or such expressive lyrical types ; and occasionally the whole sonata concludes with a little movement of this sort, as No. 3 in A and No. 6 in D. They are generally in the simplest kind of primary form with a proportionately important coda. In point of actual style and treatment of the instrument there is a great diversity in different sonatas. In some the solid old contrapuntal style predominates in similar proportion to that in the organ preludes, sonatas, etc., of Bach ; but this rarely occurs without some intermixture of modern traits. The most completely and consistently modern in style is the sonata in D major, No. 5, which is practically in three divisions. The first is a Choral, the second a kind of ' song without words ' in B minor, and the third a species of fantasia, in which the sections are balanced by distinct figures, without more tonal structure than emphasis upon the principal key at the beginning and end, and variety of modulation with some thematic development in the middle. In other sonatas different modes of writing for the instrument are used as a means of enforcing the contrast between one movement and another. Thus in the second sonata the first division is a kind of prelude in a modern manner, chiefly homophonic and orchestral ; the second corresponds to a distinct romance or ' song without words ' with clearly defined melody and graceful and constantly flowing independent accompaniment. In the third movement, which though in 3–4 time has something of a march quality, the modern harmonic character is very prominent, and the last movement is a fugue. Similar distribution of styles and modes of writing are as clearly used in the first and fourth sonatas ; in the former more elaborately.

The Later Romanticists. — Among attempts to add something genuine to the literature of the pianoforte sonata, that in F♯

minor, op. 11, by Schumann, first published under the pseudonym of Florestan and Eusebius, is most interesting. This was clearly an attempt to adapt to the sonata-form the so-called romantic ideas of which Schumann was so prominent and successful a representative.

The outward aspect of the matter is twofold. First, the absolute subordination of the sectional distribution to the ideas contained, and, secondly, the interchange of the subject-matter so as to connect the movements absolutely as well as intrinsically. The first point is illustrated by the continuity of the allegro vivace and the constant shifting and swaying of modulation and changing of tempo ; also by the variety of the subjects and the apparently irregular manner of their introduction, if judged from the point of view of the older sonatas. Thus the part which corresponds to the first section comprises a first subject, containing a figure which may be called the text of the movement, and many subsidiary features and transitions. The second section follows continuously, with new matter and allusions to the first subject, all in a constant sway of transition, till at the end of the first half of the movement a long continuous subject in A is reached, which in its sustained and earnest calmness seems to supply the point of rest after the long preceding period of activity. This same subject is the only one which is given with complete fullness at the end of the whole movement, the rest of the subject-matter, though all represented in the recapitulation, being considerably condensed and curtailed.

The second point is illustrated by the connexion between the introduction and the two following movements. The introduction itself is in an elaborate kind of primary form. Its impressive principal subject is reintroduced in the middle of the succeeding allegro ; and the subject of the middle portion serves as the main staple of the beautiful aria which is the central movement of the whole sonata. The success of such things certainly depends on the way in which they are done, and mere description of them gives very little impress of their effectiveness in this case. There can hardly be a doubt that in these devices Schumann hit upon a true means of applying original thought to the development of the structural outlines, following the suggestion which is really contained in Beethoven's work, that the structure is perceptible through the disposition of the ideas, and not only by emphasising the harmonic sections. The actual distribution of the structure which is hidden under the multiplicity of ideas is remarkably careful and systematic. Even in the development portion there is method and balance, and the same is true of large expanses in the last movement.

The freedom with which Schumann uses subordinate transitions makes the balance of keys a matter requiring great concentration; but it is remarkable in his work, as contrasted with similar modern examples by other composers, that he rarely makes random and unrestrained flights, but keeps within the bounds which make proportionate balance possible.

Schumann's second sonata, in G minor, op. 22, though written during almost the same period, seems to be a retrogression from the position taken up by that in F♯ minor. It is possibly a more effective work, and from the pianist's point of view more capable of being made to sound convincing. And yet in detail it is not so interesting, nor is it technically so rich, nor so full and noble in sound. He seems to aim at orthodoxy with deliberate purpose, and the result is that, though vehement and vigorous in motion, it is not, for Schumann, particularly warm or poetical. The second subjects of the first and last movements are characteristic, and so is a great part of the peculiarly sectional and epigrammatic scherzo. The andantino also has remarkable points about it, but is not so fascinating as the slow movement of the F♯ minor sonata.

The principles indicated in the sonata opus 11 reappear later with better results, as far as the total impression is concerned, in larger forms of instrumental music, and also in the D minor sonata for violin and pianoforte. In this there is a close connexion between the introduction and the most marked feature of the succeeding quick movement, and similar linking of scherzo and slow movement by means of a reference to the subject of the former in the progress of the latter, with a distinctly poetic purpose. The sonata in A minor for the same combination of instruments is not on such an elaborate scale, nor has it as many external marks to indicate a decided purpose; but it is none the less poetical in effect, which arises in the first movement from the continuity of structure and the mysterious sadness of spirit which it expresses, and in the slow movement from its characteristic tenderness and sweetness.

Liszt, in his remarkable sonata in B minor dedicated to Schumann, undoubtedly adopts the same principles of procedure, and works them out with more uncompromising thoroughness. He knits the whole sonata into an unbroken unity, with distinct portions passing into one another, representing the usual separate movements. The interest is concentrated upon one principal idea, to which the usual second subjects and accessories serve as so many commentaries and antitheses, and express the influences which react upon its course. This is further illustrated by the process sometimes defined as 'transformation of themes,' already referred to in connexion with Beet-

hoven's sonatas in B♭ and A♭; which is really no more than a fresh way of applying that art of variation which had been used from almost the earliest times of sonata-writing, in recapitulating subjects in the progress of a movement, as well as in regular set themes and variations; though it had not been adopted before to serve a poetical or ideal conception pervading and unifying the whole work. In the actual treatment of the subject-matter, Liszt adopts, as Beethoven had done, the various opportunities afforded not only by harmonic structural principles, but by the earlier fugal and contrapuntal devices, and by recitative, adapting them with admirable breadth and freedom to a thoroughly modern style of thought. It seems almost superfluous to add that the purpose is carried out with absolute mastery of technical resource, in respect both of the instrument and of the disposition of the parts of the movement.

The pianoforte sonatas of Brahms are as astounding specimens of youthful power and breadth and dignity of style as exist in the whole range of the art. All three appear to have been written before he arrived at the age of 20; and it is certain that he was then more influenced by the romantic theories which Schumann represented than he was in his later works. His adoption of shorter and more individual forms, such as cappricci, intermezzi, rhapsodies, in his mature age, lends at least indirect countenance to the view that the tendency of music is to subordinate form to idea; and that, if the classical form of the sonata is not expansible enough, other forms must be accepted which will admit of more freedom of development.

This implies a question as to the proper meaning of the word 'sonata,' and a doubt as to its being legitimately assimilable to the tendency to centralise the interest upon the idea, as a contrast to the old practice of making an equal balance between two main subjects as a means of structural effect. If the word is to be so restricted, it will only be another conventional limitation, and, it may be added, must before long put an end to further enrichment of the literature of so-called sonatas.

In the finest of Brahms's three early sonatas, that in F minor, op. 5, the first slow movement is headed by a quotation from a poem of Sternau, and another movement is called 'Rückblick.' These are clearly external marks of a poetical intention. In the actual treatment of the subjects there is no attempt to connect the movements; but the freedom of transition, even in the actual progress of a subject (see the second subject of the first movement), is eminently characteristic of the composer, and of a liberal view of sonata development. In the last movement—a rondo—the most noticeable external mark of continuity is the elaborately ingenious treatment of the subject of the second episode in the latter part of the movement. Brahms added no more to the list of solo pianoforte sonatas, but he illustrated the tendency to look for fresh opportunities in combinations of solo instruments, as in his pianoforte quartets and quintet, which are really just as much sonatas as those usually so designated; in fact, one of the versions of the quintet, which stands as a duet for two pianofortes, is in that form published as a 'sonata.' The three for pianoforte and violin require notice as the work of a great master, but throw very little light on any sort of extension of the possibilities of sonata-form. There seems to be a sort of poetic design in the complicated arrangement of the first half of the first movement in the sonata, op. 78, in which the characteristic figures of the first subject reappear, as if to connect each section with the centre of interest; and the half concludes with a complete restatement of the first subject simply and clearly in the original key, as is the case also in the same composer's Serenade in A for small orchestra. It may be observed in passing that this device curiously recalls the early composite form, in which the first subject reappears at the beginning of the second half (see pp. 814-15). There is one other slightly suggestive point—namely, the reappearance of the introductory phrase of the slow movement in one of the episodes of the final Rondo.[1]

Certain traits in his treatment of form, such as the bold digressions of key at the very outset of a movement, and the novel effects of transition in the subjects themselves, have already been described in the article FORM. It is only necessary here to point out that Brahms seems most characteristically to illustrate the tendency in modern music which has been styled 'intellectualism'; which is definable as elaborate development of all the opportunities and suggestions offered by figures, harmonic successions, or other essential features of subjects or accessories, so as to make various portions of the work appear to grow progressively out of one another. This sometimes takes the form of thematic development, and sometimes that of reviving the figures of one subject in the material or accompaniment of another, the object being to obtain new aspects of close and direct logical coherence and consistency. Beethoven is the prototype of this phase of modern music, and the examples of it in his later instrumental works are of the finest description. There are several examples which illustrate this tendency in Brahms's F minor quintet. One of the most obvious is the case in which the cadence concluding a paragraph is formulated, as in the following example at

(a), the phrase being immediately taken up by a different instrument and embodied as a most significant feature in the accessory subject which follows, as at (b).

(a) Pianoforte.

(b) Violin.

Under the same head of intellectualism is sometimes erroneously included that broad and liberal range of harmony which characterises the best composers of the day. This may doubtless call for intellectual effort in those who are unfamiliar with the progress of art, or of inexpansive powers of appreciation, but in the composer it does not imply intellectual purpose, but only the natural step onwards from the progressions of harmony which are familiar to those which are original. With composers of second rank such freedom is often experimental, and destructive to the general balance and proportion of the structure, but with Brahms it appears to be a special study to bring everything into perfect and sure proportion, so that the classical idea of instrumental music may be still maintained in pure severity, notwithstanding the greater extension and greater variety of range in the harmonic motion of the various portions of the movement. In fact Brahms appears to take his stand on the possibility of producing new instrumental works of real artistic value on the classical principles of abstract music, without either condescending to the popular device of a programme, or accepting the admissibility of a modification of the sonata-form to suit the impulse or apparent requirements of a poetical or dramatic principle.

### GENERAL SUMMARY

The whole process of the development of the sonata as an art-form, from its crudest beginnings to its highest culmination, took nearly two hundred years; and the progress was almost throughout steady, continuous and uniform in direction. The earlier history is chiefly occupied by its gradual differentiation from the suite-form, with which for a time it was occasionally confounded. But there always was a perceptible difference in the general tendency of the two. The suite gravitated towards dance-forms, and movements which similarly had one principal idea or form of motion pervading them, so that the balance of contrasts

[1] In the second sonata notice the fusion of the scherzo and slow movement into one.

lay between one movement and another, and not conspicuously between parts of the same movement. The sonata gravitated towards more complicated conditions and away from pure dance-forms. Diversity of character between subjects and figures was admitted early into single movements, and contrasts of key were much more strongly emphasised; and while in the suite, except in extremely rare cases, all the movements were in one key, amongst the very earliest sonatas there are examples of a central movement being cast in a different key from the rest.

In a yet more important manner the capacity of the sonata was made deeper and broader by the quality and style of its music. In the suite, as we have said, the contrasts between one movement and another were between forms of the same order and character—that is, between dance-forms and their analogues; but in the sonata the different movements very soon came to represent different origins and types of music. Thus in the early violin sonatas the slow introductory first movement generally shows traces of ecclesiastical influence; the second, which is the solid kind of allegro corresponding to the first movement of modern sonatas, was clearly derived from the secular vocal madrigals, or part music for voices, through the instrumental canzonas, which were their closest relations. The third, which was the characteristic slow movement, frequently showed traces of its descent from solo vocal music of various kinds, as found in operas, cantatas or other similar situations; and the last movement earliest and latest showed traces of dance elements pure and simple. A further point of much importance was the early tendency towards systematic and distinct structure, which appears most frequently in the last movement. The reason for the apparent anomaly is not hard to find. The only movement in the group on a scale corresponding to the last was the second, and this was most frequently of a fugal disposition. The fugue was a form which was comparatively well understood when the modern harmonic forms were still in embryo; and not only did it suffice for the construction of movements of almost any length, but it did not in itself suggest advance in the direction of the sonata kinds of form, though it was shown to be capable of amalgamation with them when they in their turn had been definitely brought to perfection. In the dance movements, on the other hand, when the fugal forms were not used, all that was supplied as basis to work upon was the type of motion or rhythm, and the outlines of structure had to be found. As long as the movements were on a small scale the structure which obtained oftenest was the equal balance of repeated halves without contrasting subjects, of which the finest examples are to be found in Bach's suites. The last movement was in fact so long a pure suite movement. But when it began to take larger dimensions, emphasis began to be laid upon that part of the first half of the movement which was in the dominant key; then the process of characterising it by distinct figures or subjects became prominent; and by degrees it developed into the definite second section. Meanwhile the opening bars of the movement gradually assumed more distinct and salient features, making the passage stand out more clearly from its immediate context; and in this form it was repeated at the beginning of the second half of the movement, the second section being reserved to make a complete balance by concluding the whole in a manner analogous to the conclusion of the first half. So far the change from the suite type of movement rests chiefly on the clearer definition of parts, and more positive exactness in the recapitulation of the subjects; but this is quite sufficient to mark the character as distinct, for in the movements of the suite (excluding the prelude) balance of subject and key was never systematically recognised. The further development of binary form, in which the recapitulation of the distinct subjects was reserved for the conclusion, took some time to arrive at, but even at this early stage the essential qualities of sonata-form are clearly recognisable.

The violin sonata was naturally the kind which first attained to perfection, since that instrument had so great an advantage in point of time over the keyed instruments used for similar purposes; and its qualities and requirements so reacted upon the character of the music as to make it appear almost a distinct species from the clavier sonata. But in fact the two kinds represent no more than divergence from a similar source, owing to the dissimilar natures of the instruments. Thus the introductory slow movement was most appropriate to the broad and noble character of the violin, and would appeal at once by its means to an audience of any susceptibility; whereas to the weak character of the early keyed instruments, so deficient in sustaining power, it was in general inappropriate, and hence was dropped very early. For the same reason, in a considerable proportion of the early clavier sonatas the third or principal slow movement was also dropped, so that the average type of sonatas for clavier was for a time a group of two movements, both generally in a more or less quick time. In these the canzona movement was early supplanted by one more in accordance with the modern idea, such as is typified in the clavier sonata of Galuppi in four movements (see p. 818), and by occasional allemandes in the earlier sonatas. As keyed instruments improved in volume and sustaining power the central slow movement was resumed;

but it was necessary for some time to make up for deficiencies in the latter respect by filling in the slow beats with elaborate graces and trills, and such ornaments as the example of opera-singers made rather too inviting. The course of the violin solo-sonata was meanwhile distinctly maintained till its climax, and came to an abrupt end in J. S. Bach, just as the clavier sonata was expanding into definite importance.

In fact the earliest landmarks of importance are found in the next generation, when a fair proportion of works of this class show the lineaments of clavier sonatas familiar to a modern. Such are the disposition of the three movements with the solid and dignified allegro at the beginning, the expressive slow movement in the middle, and the bright and gay quick movement at the end ; which last continued in many cases to show its dance origin. From this group the fugal element was generally absent, for all the instinct of composers was temporarily enlisted in the work of perfecting the harmonic structure in the modern manner, and the tendency was for a time to direct special attention to this, with the object of attaining clear and distinct symmetry. In the latter part of the 18th century this was achieved ; the several movements were then generally cast on nearly identical lines, with undeviating distribution of subjects, pauses, modulations, cadences and double bars. The style of thought conformed for a while sufficiently well to this discipline, and the most successful achievements of instrumental music up to that time were accomplished in this manner. Extrinsically the artistic product appeared perfect ; but art could not stand still at this point, and composers soon felt themselves precluded from putting the best and most genuine of their thoughts into trammels produced by such regular procedure. Moreover, the sudden and violent changes in social arrangements which took place at the end of the century, and the transformation in the ways of regarding life and its interests and opportunities which resulted therefrom, opened a new point of public emotion, and introduced a new quality of cosmopolitan human interest in poetry and art. The appeal of music in its higher manifestations became more direct and immediate ; and the progression of the idea became necessarily less amenable to the control of artificialities of structure, and more powerful in its turn of reacting upon the form. This is what lies at the root of much which, for want of a more exact word, is frequently described as the poetic element, which has become so prominent and indispensable a quality in modern music. By this change of position the necessities of structural balance and proportion are not supplanted, but made legitimate use of in a different manner from what they previously were ; and the sonata-form, while still satisfying the in-dispensable conditions which make abstract music possible, expanded to a fuller and more co-ordinate pitch of emotional material.

Partly under these influences, and partly, no doubt, owing to the improvements in keyed instruments, the clavier sonata again attained to the group of four movements, but in a different arrangement from that of the violin sonata. The slow introduction was sometimes resumed, but without representing an ingredient in the average scheme. The first movement was usually the massive and dignified allegro. The two central portions, consisting of a highly expressive slow movement and the scherzo which was the legitimate descendant of the dance movement, were ruled in their order of succession by the qualities of the first and last movements, and the work ended with a movement which still generally maintained the qualities to be found in a last movement of Corelli or Tartini. The tendency to unify the whole group increased, and in so far as the influence of intrinsic character or of the idea became powerful it modified the order and quality of the movements. For particular purposes which approve themselves to musical feeling the number of movements varied considerably, some exceedingly fine and perfect sonatas having only two, and others extending to five. Again, it is natural that in certain moods composers should almost resent the call to end with the conventional light and gay movement ; and consequently in later works, even where the usual form seems to be accepted, the spirit is rather ironical than gay, and rather vehement or even fierce than light-hearted. The same working of the spirit of the age had powerful effect on the intrinsic qualities of the scherzo ; in which there came to be found, along with or under the veil of ideal dance motions, sadness and tenderness, bitterness, humour, and many more phases of strong feeling ; for which the ideal dance rhythms, when present, are made to serve as a vehicle : but in some cases also are supplanted by different though kindred forms of expression. In other respects the last movement moved farther away from the conventional type, as by the adoption of the fugal form, or by new use of the variation-form in a more continuous and consistent sense than in early examples. In many cases the movements are made to pass into one another, just as in the earlier stages the strong lines which marked off the different sections in the movements were gradually toned down ; and by this means they came to have less of the appearance of separate items than limbs or divisions of a complete organism. This is illustrated most clearly by the examples of slow movements which are so modified as to be little more than intermezzi, or introductory divisions appended to the last movement ; and more strongly by a few cases where the distinct lines of separation are quite done away with, and the entire work becomes a chain of long divisions representing broadly the old plan of four distinct movements with kindred subjects continuing throughout.

Since Beethoven the impetus to concentrate and individualise the character of musical works has driven many genuine composers to the adoption of forms which are less hampered by any suspicion of conventionality; and even with sonatas they seemed to have grasped the object in view with less steadiness and consistency than in previous times. Some have accepted the artifice of a programme, others admit some doubtful traits of theatrical origin; others develop poetic and æsthetic devices as their chief end and object, and others still follow up the classical lines, contenting themselves with the opportunities afforded by new and more elaborately perfect treatment of details, especially in music for combinations of solo instruments. In the latter case it is clear that the field is more open than in sonatas for single instruments, since the combination of such instruments as the pianoforte and violin or pianoforte and violoncello in large works has not been dealt with by the great masters so thoroughly and exhaustively as the solo sonata. But in any case it is apparent that fresh works of high value on the classical lines can hardly be produced without increasing intellectualism. The origin and reason of existence of abstract music are, at least on one side, intellectual; and though up to a certain point the process of development tended to reduce the intellectual effort by making the structural outlines as clear and certain as possible, when these were decisively settled the current naturally set in the direction of complication. The inevitable process of accumulating one device of art upon another is shown in the free range of modulation and harmony, and in the increasing variety and richness of detail both in the subjects and in the subordinate parts of works. In such cases the formal outlines may cease to be strictly amenable to a definite external theory; but if they accord with broad general principles, such as may be traced in the history of abstract music so far, and if the total effect is extrinsically as well as intrinsically complete and convincing, it appears inevitable to admit the works to the rank of 'sonatas.' The exact meaning of the term has in fact been enforced with remarkable uniformity during the whole period under survey, and decisively in favour of what is called abstract music. Fair examples of the successful disregard of form in favour of programme or a dramatic conception can hardly be found; in fact, in the best examples extant, programme is no more than the addition of a name or a story to an otherwise regular formal sonata; but on the other hand there is plenty of justification of the finest kind for abstract works in free and more original forms, and it rests with composers to justify themselves by their works, rather than for reasoning to decide finally where the limit shall be.  c. h. h. p.

There is little to add to and nothing to retract from the above statement[1] of principles, but later history has illustrated several aspects of them.

In his discussion of current developments of the sonata Sir Hubert Parry, in a couple of paragraphs not here reproduced, laid stress on Sterndale Bennett's piano sonata 'The Maid of Orleans' and the sonatas of Raff and Rubinstein as examples of poetic treatment of the form. These no longer appear to be salient. Sterndale Bennett's use of literary quotations to explain the purpose of his several movements may show poetic intention, but poetic expression has been often more surely attained in works without these clues. The romanticism of the later 19th century was illustrated in the sonatas of Grieg (one for PF. alone in E minor, three for violin and PF., one for violoncello and PF.), and more consciously in the several sonatas for PF. with descriptive titles by Edward MacDowall, the American composer, and a pupil of both Raff and Liszt. The general trend of taste in the direction of orchestral colouring served to keep the output of solo sonatas rather a small one. Most of the masters of the late 19th century either avoided the piano sonata or attempted it with varying success merely as an occasional stylistic essay.

Its progress in Russia is of some interest. Tchaikovsky left a solitary and not very interesting example, but Glazounov concerned himself more seriously in manipulating the form and Scriabin in his series of ten sonatas for the piano produced a development which must be regarded as of considerable historic importance. Little as at first sight there seems to be in common between the later sonatas of Scriabin and the classical type described above, a perusal of the series in order shows that they represent a personal evolution of idea, and that beginning from conventional standards of structure Scriabin proceeded steadily to that final manner which to some musicians of his generation appeared to possess the force of an apocalyptic revelation and by others was rejected as the rhodomontade of excessive egoism. But here attention may be recalled to that paragraph in Sir Hubert Parry's article above in which, amidst his discussion of Brahms (p. 835), he raises the question of the proper meaning of the word 'sonata,' and with prophetic prescience foreshadows just such developments as have in fact come about in the 'subordination of form to idea' of which Scriabin's work is but one example among many.

A similar process, though a saner one, may be traced in the French school from César

[1] Written for the first edition of this Dictionary, 1883.

Franck to Debussy. Franck himself left no PF. sonata, and indeed only one work, the famous one for violin and PF., which bears the name. But in his whole output as a composer he was much concerned with questions of FORM (see the introduction to that article), and he laid the impress of his views on the school which he founded (see DUKAS; D'INDY; LEKEU). Franck, like Brahms, can be regarded as a neo-classic. His work is capable of analysis along the traditional lines, and only the late appearance of his major works prevented the consideration of them in conjunction with those of Brahms and Liszt. But a wide gap yawns between him and his school and the series of works called ' sonatas ' which were the outcome of the last years of Debussy's career. The viewpoint has changed. The latter no longer takes a standard pattern as normal, to be varied, expanded or condensed. The name has returned to its first connotation of ' a piece of sound,' it does not denote a form independent of the idea.

A few examples of the PF. solo sonata deserve attention among the works of English composers of to-day, notably J. B. DALE, Arnold BAX, John IRELAND and Frank BRIDGE, but the cultivation of the sonata for more than one instrument has been very much wider. The duet sonata for violin or other melodic instrument with PF. has never flagged; the output of works of this kind in all countries is one of the most richly varied departments of the chamber music repertory, and ranges from the gentle clarity of Elgar's sonata in E minor to the desperate deeds of Béla Bartók. Amongst the laborious products of Germany in the generation after Brahms the name of Max REGER (q.v.) stands forward for many ingenious manipulations of the sonata type, and especially for his revival of the sonata for violin alone, which had been dormant since Bach. Reger's activity in this direction has recalled to some minds the saying as to the wisdom of letting sleeping dogs lie. Whatever may be the individual importance of these several manifestations, and this summary can make no attempt at an exhaustive record, the chief fact which emerges is that for the time being the name ' sonata ' has lost the definition gained in three centuries of development. It still implies a work of serious intention and large scope, but the bestowal of the name is largely a matter of chance, and many rhapsodies, fantasies and the like would merit the title as fully as the works which receive it.　　　　C.

BIBLIOGRAPHY

J. S. SHEDLOCK : The Pianoforte Sonata. (1895.)
O. KLAUWELL : Geschichte der Sonate. (1899.)
B. STUDENY : Beiträge zur Geschichte der Violinsonate im 18. Jahrh. (1911.)
BLANCHE SELVA : La Sonate. Étude de son évolution, etc. (1913.) Quelques mots sur la sonate. (1914.)
ROBERT REFOUTÉ : La Sonate de piano. (1922.)

SONATINA (Fr. sonatine). This is a work in the same form and of the same general character as a sonata, but shorter, simpler and slenderer.

The sonatina form has proved peculiarly convenient for the making of pieces intended to be used in teaching. The familiar outlines and the systematic distribution of the principal harmonies afford the most favourable opportunities for simple but useful finger-passages, for which the great masters have supplied plentiful formulas ; and they furnish at the same time excellent means of giving the student a dignified and conscientious style, and a clear insight into the art of phrasing and into the simpler rules of classical form. The most famous and most classical examples of this kind are Clementi's sonatinas, of opp. 36, 37 and 38. And much of the same character are several by F. Kuhlau, which are excellently constructed and pure in style. Of later works of a similar kind there are examples by L. Koehler. Those by Carl Reinecke and Hermann Goetz are equally adapted for teaching purposes, and have also in general not a little agreeable musical sentiment and really attractive qualities. Some of Beethoven's works which are not definitely described as such are sufficiently concise and slight to be called sonatinas : as for instance those in G and G minor, op. 49, which were first announced for publication as ' Sonates faciles ' in 1805. That in G major, op. 79, was published as a ' Sonatine ' in 1810, though it is rather larger in most respects than the other little examples.

C. H. H. P.

Ravel's ' Sonatine ' for PF. is a conspicuous example of the successful treatment of the diminutive form, and Busoni left six specimens, written during the later years of his career, as follows: two in 1910; No. 3, 'Ad usum infantis.' 1915 ; No. 4, 'In signo Joanni Sebastiani Magni,' 1917 ; 'In diem Nativitatis Christi,' 1918 ; 'Sonatina super Carmen,' 1921.　　　C.